The American
Book of Days

The
American
Book of Days
THIRD EDITION

Compiled and Edited by

JANE M. HATCH

THE H. W. WILSON COMPANY

NEW YORK

1978

Library of Congress Cataloging in Publication Data
Hatch, Jane M.
    The American book of days.

    Based on the earlier editions by G. W. Douglas.
    Includes index.
    1. Holidays—United States. 2. Fasts and feasts—United
States. 3. Festivals—United States. I. Douglas, George William,
1863–1945. The American book of days. II. Title.
GT4803.D6   1978   394.2′6973   78–16239
ISBN 0–8242–0593–6

Preface

TO THE THIRD EDITION

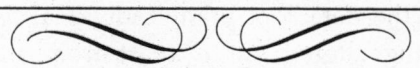

THE THIRD EDITION of *The American Book of Days* continues the work by George W. Douglas first published in 1937. His daughter, Helen Douglas Compton, revised and updated the book in a second edition, published in 1948. Like its predecessors, this new edition profiles the lives of many of the United States' distinguished citizens, explores the richness of its religious traditions, describes the variety of its holidays, customs and festivities, samples its folklore, and reports its ways — both solemn and fanciful — of marking anniversaries and commemorating achievements. The new, expanded edition builds upon the foundation George Douglas laid earlier, working within his concept of a "book of days" to tell what happens or did happen on every day of the year and how, where, and by whom these events are (and have been) observed in this country.

In revising *The American Book of Days* we have removed outdated material and information made inaccurate by the passage of time, discovering in the process that time has wrought far more changes than we might have expected since 1907, when George Douglas began collecting facts for eventual use in the first edition. Since that time, Americans have nearly tripled in number, shifted from a primarily rural to a primarily urban society, and had their lives revolutionized by a multitude of technological innovations.

Many of the ways in which Americans note holidays and anniversaries have also changed, with some special days and observances receiving more attention than before, as evidence of a renewed interest in the nation's history and cultural heritage — a trend intensified by the innumerable observances that took place during the years when the bicentennial of US independence was being celebrated. Conversely, some occasions are now so given over to casual enjoyment that the formal observances that once were common are largely ignored or sometimes omitted, with the original meaning of the days all but forgotten by many people.

Not even the tradition-filled religious observances have remained constant in all respects. Again, there are two opposite trends — on the one hand toward a greater emphasis on form and tradition, both newly appreciated in recent years, and on the other hand toward the greater flexibility and informality that are also hallmarks of the present age. Many of the changes are in response to the trend to ecumenism that has swept through religious groups in recent years — with the result that some of the groups that were most formal in their liturgy have become a little less so, while some of the groups that were least formal in their religious observances have become more so.

As for secular events, the details of many individual festivals and commemorations are constantly being altered, quite apart from any over-all trends (even though other events are carefully kept the same, with their traditions painstakingly preserved from year to year).

Since the last edition of this book appeared in 1948, the dates of many observances have changed as well. "Movable events" — Jewish holy days (which fall on fixed dates of the Hebrew calendar), Christian holy days whose dates depend on the movable feast of Easter, and the many festivals and other observances that are scheduled for such shifting times as the first Monday in September (Labor Day) or the fourth Thursday in November (Thanksgiving) — have changed dates, as they do each year. (See A Note on Movable Events, p. xxvi.) A significant number of other date alterations have taken place as a result of the major revision of the Roman Catholic calendar that became fully effective in the United States in 1972 and the similar calendar revisions now under consideration by certain Protestant denominations. And, of course, some events have simply ceased to take place.

In the process of deciding what new articles should be added, and which earlier ones should be retained, we came to see the book as a whole and to perceive certain large themes running throughout. Accordingly, we added articles to complete the story of discovery and exploration, and of the westward migration, settlement, boundary disputes, and land purchases by which the United States grew to the shape and dimensions it now has. We expanded the amount of space devoted to the establishment of this country as a nation and the creation and ratification of its basic documents. We saw to it that all amendments to the Constitution, rather than only certain ones, are included. We made certain that this new edition of the book includes the early history — up to the point of statehood — of every state in the Union, rather than of only some states. We added articles to complete the coverage of wars in which the United States has been involved. We increased the notice accorded to the history and culture of Native Americans (often within individual articles about Presidents or events in US history). We expanded the book's coverage of the movement for women's rights, with emphasis on its beginnings and early history. We also added a number of articles on the civil rights drive and resulting legislation and court rulings of the 1960s. In addition, we devoted more space to Christian and Jewish holy days. In regard to the former, we tried to achieve a greater balance than before in writing about the forms of observance of the three main divisions of Christianity — Roman Catholic, Eastern Orthodox, and Protestant. In regard to the Jewish holy days, we tried to distinguish between practices of the major groups.

We also added 56 new biographies — after a selection process in which we considered more than 400 names. In the process, we carried forward George Douglas's policy of including all Presidents and chief justices of the United States. We also expanded virtually all biographies in the second edition of the book. In addition, we prepared separate accounts of the assassinations of four Presidents and of one other biographee, civil rights leader Martin Luther King Jr. We also added accounts of recent canonizations of American saints.

We next considered festivals, celebrations, and other current observances — the number of those that take place annually in the United States runs into the thousands — by studying books, periodicals, and other printed sources; perusing countless calendars of events; and canvassing the governors and tourist information officers of each of the 50 states. Drawing on all of this information, we inserted descriptions of hundreds of festivals and events within existing articles about holidays and other observances to which they pertain. In addition we added 33 individual articles on other festivals and events that are now described in the book for the first time; and we updated the innumerable descriptions of festivals and events that appeared in earlier editions of the book. In deciding which events to include in the third edition, we considered especially those that have historical significance, reflect the nation's diverse ethnic and cultural heritage, or illustrate unusual or unique local customs — though our coverage, of course, is representative rather than exhaustive and our choices are purely arbitrary.

We also devoted ourselves to the task of rechecking, as far as humanly possible, every single fact in previous editions of the book. This, too, resulted in our adding new information.

In the course of preparing all the additions noted above, we consulted hundreds of reference works, using the facilities of public and university libraries in several cities and also using our own collection of reference books assembled specifically for the purposes of this book. To check old facts and acquire new ones, we also sent out literally thousands of letters and in this way drew upon the information treasuries of public, university, and special libraries; local history collections; newspaper morgues; archives; museums; historical societies; government offices and agencies; associations; and sponsoring organizations across the nation. To all of these and their representatives we owe an enormous debt of gratitude for their generosity in providing information, as we do to the many religious authorities whom we also consulted.

The research connected with the preparation of the third edition of *The American Book of Days* has taken many years. With the expansion of the first- and second-edition articles and the addition of some 240 new articles and a number of brief notes, we have added perhaps three-quarters of a million words to the book.

Throughout our work we were concerned with the concept of the year as a whole, which is basic to a book of days such as this, and with the balance and symmetry provided by those days and other measures of time that serve as milestones in the calendar year and neatly divide it for us all. Thus, we added new articles under the first day of each of the four seasons, on Leap Year, and on Midsummer's Eve; and we revised such articles as those on New Year's Day, Midsummer Day, Halloween, and New Year's Eve; those on the individual months; and those in the Appendix — including The Days of the Week and The Signs of the Zodiac. A particular contribution to the concept of the year as a whole and the measurement of time in general was made by Hilah F. Thomas, who devoted an enormous amount of scholarship to her new article, The Era, and to her major revision of The Calendar, which brings together important information that, as far as we can discover, has never appeared all in one place before.

The index for the third edition has been significantly expanded, qualitatively as well as quantitatively. Included, in this edition, are entries for holidays and events — whether featured as main articles or mentioned within other articles — and diverse subject headings under which relevant articles are listed.

A word about dates: New Style (Gregorian calendar) dates are used, except where noted. In some cases, however, it has not been possible to ascertain whether a date is New Style or Old Style.

I am deeply indebted to all of the contributors to this edition listed below. But to those who have devoted the most time to this lengthy undertaking — Marilyn Lavin, Catherine L. Mastny, M. Virginia Namee, Marjorie Rose Brown, and Hilah F. Thomas — I must express my particular gratitude, not only for their sustained dedication, but also for the caliber of their writing and of their painstaking and resourceful research, and for making our joint endeavors a pleasure. Thanks also are due to people in the editorial offices of the publisher: to John Jamieson, the Editor of General Publications who was concerned with this book during most of the years of preparation; and to Bruce R. Carrick, his successor. I am also indebted to Ruth Ulman, the Associate Editor of General Publications; to Kim Sinclair for the fresh eye with which she undertook the task of copy editing this volume; to Judith Garodnick, her predecessor; and to a number of others for invaluable editorial help.

Finally, there are not enough words to express my gratitude to two persons not listed below: my husband, Peter Hatch, who has offered unfailing encouragement and served as adviser and editorial consultant throughout the entire project; and his brother, Christopher Hatch, who has been kind enough to read the entire manuscript and lend to this venture the considerable benefit of his editorial comments.

May 1978   Jane Maddox Hatch

CONTRIBUTORS TO THE THIRD EDITION

Barbara J. Bennett

Marjorie Rose Brown

Betty Bytheway

Caroline Goetzel Dudley

Jane Maddox Hatch

Daria Hoydysh

Jane Humphrey

Ruth Kaplan

Marilyn Lavin

Catherine L. Mastny

Deborah Dash Moore

M. Virginia Namee

Hilah F. Thomas

Contents

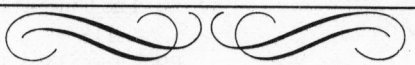

PREFACE TO THE THIRD EDITION v
CONTRIBUTORS TO THE THIRD EDITION ix
IMPORTANT PUBLIC AND LEGAL HOLIDAYS xxiii
A NOTE ON MOVABLE EVENTS xxvi

JANUARY

DATE

January, 1
1 New Year's Day, 2
  The American Lutheran Church Merger
    Becomes Effective, 8
  Feast of the Circumcision, 8
  The Emancipation Proclamation, 9
  First National Flag, 12
  The New Year in Mobile, 13
  The Philadelphia Mummers' Parade, 14
  Pasadena Rose Bowl Football Game, 16
  Pasadena Tournament of Roses, 17
  Paul Revere's Birthday, 19
  Solemnity of Mary, 20
2 Georgia Ratifies the Constitution, 20
3 Alaska Admitted to the Union, 22
  Battle of Princeton, 22
4 Feast of St. Elizabeth Ann Seton, 23
  Utah Admitted to the Union, 27
5 Twelfth Night, or Epiphany Eve, 29
  George Washington Carver's Death, 31
  Feast of St. John Nepomucene Neumann, 33
6 The Epiphany, or Twelfth Day, or Three
    Kings' Day; Old Christmas, 34

DATE

  The Epiphany, or Greek Cross Day; Blessing
    of the Sponge Divers, Tarpon Springs,
    Florida, 38
  The "Four Freedoms" Enunciated, 39
  Sherlock Holmes's Birthday, 40
  New Mexico Admitted to the Union, 40
  Twelfth Night Revels, 43
7 Millard Fillmore's Birthday, 45
  Panama Canal Traversed, 46
  "Russian Christmas," 49
8 Battle of New Orleans Day, 49
  Eleventh Amendment Declared Ratified, 51
9 First Successful Balloon Flight in the
    United States, 52
  Connecticut Ratifies the Constitution, 54
  Richard M. Nixon's Birthday, 55
10 League of Nations Established, 63
11 Feast of the Baptism of the Lord, 65
  Alexander Hamilton's Birthday, 65
12 John Winthrop's Birthday, 71
13 Salmon P. Chase's Birthday, 72
  Stephen Foster Memorial Day, 74
14 Ratification Day, 76

JANUARY — *Continued*

DATE

15 Martin Luther King Jr.'s Birthday, 77
   Vermont Declares Independence, 80
16 Eighteenth Amendment Ratified, 82
17 Feast of St. Anthony the Great, 84
   Benjamin Franklin's Birthday, 85
18 Daniel Webster's Birthday, 88
19 The Epiphany, or Greek Cross Day
   (Old Calendar), 89
   Robert E. Lee's Birthday, 89
   Edgar Allan Poe's Birthday, 93
20 Inauguration Day, 96
   Eve of St. Agnes, 97
21 Feast of St. Agnes, 98
   Stonewall Jackson's Birthday, 101

DATE

22 Frederick Moore Vinson's Birthday, 103
23 Twenty-fourth Amendment Ratified, 105
24 California Gold Rush, 106
25 Robert Burns's Birthday, 109
   Feast of the Conversion of St. Paul, 110
26 Douglas MacArthur's Birthday, 111
   Michigan Admitted to the Union, 113
27 Samuel Gompers' Birthday, 114
28 The United States Withdraws from Cuba,
   116
29 Kansas Day, 117
   William McKinley's Birthday, 119
   Thomas Paine's Birthday, 121
30 Franklin D. Roosevelt's Birthday, 122
31 James G. Blaine's Birthday, 130

FEBRUARY

DATE

February, 132
1 Victor Herbert's Birthday, 133
   Lincoln Abolishes Slavery: National
   Freedom Day, 134
   Lutheran Free Church Joins American
   Lutheran Church, 135
2 Candlemas, or The Feast of the Presentation
   of the Lord, 135
   Dartmouth College Case Decided, 136
   Groundhog Day, 138
   Mexican War Ends: Treaty of Guadalupe
   Hidalgo, 139
3 Illinois Becomes a Territory, 139
4 Mark Hopkins's Birthday, 140
5 Charro Days Fiesta: Brownsville, Texas, and
   Matamoros, Mexico, 141
   Dwight L. Moody's Birthday, 142
   Roger Williams Arrives in America, 143
6 Aaron Burr's Birthday, 145
   Chinese New Year, 146
   France Recognizes the United States, 148
   Massachusetts Ratifies the Constitution, 150
   Spanish-American War Ends, 151
   Twentieth Amendment Proclaimed Ratified,
   151
7 Baltimore Fire, 151
   Eleventh Amendment Ratified, 152
8 Boy Scouts of America Founded, 152
9 Gasparilla Pirate Invasion: Tampa, Florida,
   154

DATE

   William Henry Harrison's Birthday, 155
10 Mardi Gras, or Shrove Tuesday, 156
   Treaty of Paris (1898) Becomes Effective,
   161
   Twenty-fifth Amendment Ratified, 161
11 Ash Wednesday, 162
   Thomas Alva Edison's Birthday, 163
   Melville W. Fuller's Birthday, 166
12 Abraham Lincoln's Birthday, 168
   Georgia Day, 174
13 Anchorage Fur Rendezvous, 176
   First American Magazine, 177
14 St. Valentine's Day, 177
   Arizona Admission Day, 180
   Frederick Douglass's Birthday: Black
   History Week, 181
   Oregon Admitted to the Union, 182
15 Susan B. Anthony Day, 184
   Russell H. Conwell's Birthday, 184
   Cyrus H. McCormick's Birthday, 186
   Maine Memorial Day, 187
16 Cushing Eells's Birthday, 189
   Republic of Lithuania Day, 190
17 Frances E. Willard Memorial Day, 191
18 Jefferson Davis Inaugurated, 193
19 Initiative and Referendum Declared Valid,
   193
   Ohio Statehood Approved, 194
20 John Glenn Orbits the Earth, 194
   Joseph Jefferson's Birthday, 196

FEBRUARY

DATE

21 Washington Monument Dedicated, 196
22 George Washington's Birthday, 197
   Adams-Onís Treaty Signed, 204
   James Russell Lowell's Birthday, 204
23 The Battle of Buena Vista, 207
   Emma Willard's Birthday, 207
24 Arizona Territory Established, 208
   Feast of St. Matthias, 208
   Chester William Nimitz's Birthday, 209

DATE

25 National Bank Act, 211
   Sixteenth Amendment Proclaimed Ratified, 212
26 William F. Cody's Birthday, 212
27 Henry Wadsworth Longfellow's Birthday, 214
   Twenty-second Amendment Ratified, 215
28 Explosion of the "Peacemaker," 216
29 Leap Year, 217
   Ann Lee's Birthday, 218

MARCH

DATE

   March, 222
 1 Articles of Confederation Ratified, 223
   St. David's Day, 223
   Nebraska State Day, 224
   Ohio Admitted to the Union, 225
   Texas Annexed by the United States, 227
 2 Texas Independence Day, 227
 3 Alexander Graham Bell's Birthday, 230
   Florida Admitted to the Union, 231
   Missouri Compromise Finalized, 233
 4 Pennsylvania Granted to Penn, 233
   Vermont Admitted to the Union, 233
 5 The Boston Massacre, 235
 6 Alamo Day, 237
 7 Luther Burbank's Birthday, 240
 8 Simon Cameron's Birthday, 240
   Oliver Wendell Holmes Jr.'s Birthday, 241
 9 Edwin Forrest's Birthday, 243
10 Albany Becomes the Capital of New York, 243
   Treaty of Guadalupe Hidalgo Ratified, 244
11 The Blizzard of 1888, 244
12 Girl Scouts Founded, 245
13 Clarence Darrow's Death, 247
14 Albert Einstein's Birthday, 249
   Eli Whitney Patents the Cotton Gin, 250
15 De Soto Celebration, Bradenton, Florida, 251
   Andrew Jackson's Birthday, 252
   Maine Admitted to the Union, 257
16 James Madison's Birthday, 258
   United States Military Academy Founded, 261

DATE

17 St. Patrick's Day, 262
   Evacuation Day in Boston, 264
   Roger Brooke Taney's Birthday, 265
18 John C. Calhoun's Birthday, 268
   Grover Cleveland's Birthday, 269
19 William Jennings Bryan's Birthday, 271
   Earl Warren's Birthday, 272
20 Neal Dow's Birthday, 275
21 Spring Begins, 276
22 The First Indian Treaty, 277
   Palm Sunday, 278
   Purim (Feast of Lots), 281
   Stamp Act Signed, 282
23 Patrick Henry's Speech for Liberty, 282
24 John Wesley Powell's Birthday, 283
25 The Feast of the Annunciation, 284
   Greek Independence Day, 285
   Maryland Day, 287
26 Robert Frost's Birthday, 287
   Holy or Maundy Thursday, 291
   Prince Kuhio Day, 293
27 The Alaska Earthquake, 294
   Good Friday, 294
28 Holy Saturday, 297
29 Easter, 299
   Delaware Swedish Colonial Day, 304
   Twenty-third Amendment Ratified, 305
   John Tyler's Birthday, 306
30 Easter Monday, 307
   Fifteenth Amendment Proclaimed Ratified, 309
   Seward's Day in Alaska, 309
31 Virgin Islands Transfer Day, 310

APRIL

DATE

April, 313
1 April Fools' Day, 314
2 Pascua Florida Day, 316
  United States Mint Established, 316
3 Washington Irving's Birthday, 318
4 Flag Act of 1818, 319
  Martin Luther King Jr. Assassinated, 319
  Puyallup Valley Daffodil Festival, 322
5 Booker T. Washington's Birthday, 323
  Elihu Yale's Birthday, 325
6 Church of Jesus Christ of Latter-Day Saints
    Organized, 326
  North Pole Discovered, 327
  The United States Enters World War I, 328
7 The *Alabama* Claims, 330
  National Cherry Blossom Festival,
    Washington, D.C., 330
8 Juan Ponce de León Claims Florida for
    Spain, 331
9 Appomattox Day, 333
  La Salle Reaches Mouth of the Mississippi,
    335
10 Salvation Army Founder's Day, 337
11 Civil Rights Act of 1968, 339
  Charles Evans Hughes's Birthday, 340
12 The Civil War Begins, 341
  Henry Clay's Birthday, 346
  Halifax Resolves Day, 347
13 Thomas Jefferson's Birthday, 348
14 Abraham Lincoln Assassinated, 351
  Pan American Day, 353
15 Federal Income Tax Deadline, 354
16 Washington Departs for His Inauguration,
    355

DATE

17 American Academy of Arts and Letters
    Chartered, 358
18 The San Francisco Fire, 359
19 Patriots' Day, 359
20 Gift of The Hague Peace Palace, 362
21 Passover (Pesach), 362
  San Jacinto Day, 364
  Spanish-American War Begins, 365
22 American Lutheran Church Organized, 366
  Arbor Day, 366
  Oklahoma Day, 369
23 James Buchanan's Birthday, 371
  St. George's Day, 373
  William Shakespeare's Birthday, 375
  United Methodist Church Formed, 377
24 Library of Congress Created, 378
25 Feast of St. Mark, 379
26 John James Audubon's Birthday, 380
  Cape Henry Day, 383
  Confederate Memorial Day, 383
  Frederick Law Olmsted's Birthday, 385
  Virgin Islands Carnival, 387
27 Fast Day in New Hampshire, 388
  Ulysses S. Grant's Birthday, 389
28 Maryland Ratifies the Constitution, 393
  James Monroe's Birthday, 395
  Washington State Apple Blossom Festival,
    396
29 Feast of St. Catherine of Siena, 398
  Oliver Ellsworth's Birthday, 399
30 Louisiana Admitted to the Union, 401
  Shenandoah Apple Blossom Festival,
    Winchester, Virginia, 403
  Walpurgis Night or Spring Festival, 404

MAY

DATE

May, 406
1 May Day, 407
  Labor Observances, 410
  Loyalty Day, 411
  Law Day, 411
  Americanism Day in Pennsylvania, 412
  Lei Day in Hawaii, 412
  American Heritage Week in Rhode
    Island, 412

DATE

  Old Dover Days in Delaware, 412
  Battle of Manila Bay, 413
  Feast of SS. Philip and James, 414
2 Kentucky Derby, 414
3 First Medical School in the United States,
    416
  Feast of SS. Philip and James, 416
  Rural Life Sunday or Soil Stewardship
    Sunday, 417
4 Horace Mann's Birthday, 418

MAY

DATE

Rhode Island Independence Day, 419
5 Cinco de Mayo, 420
6 Civil Rights Act of 1960, 421
7 Ascension Day, 422
  Sinking of the *Lusitania*, 423
8 V-E Day, 423
  Harry S. Truman's Birthday, 424
9 John Brown's Birthday, 433
  Feast of St. Christopher, 434
  The Memphis Cotton Carnival, 434
10 The Methodist Church Merger Becomes
   Effective, 437
   Mother's Day, 439
   Fort Ticonderoga Falls, 440
   The First Transcontinental Railroad, 441
11 Connecticut and New Haven United, 442
   Minnesota Admitted to the Union, 442
12 National Hospital Week; Florence
   Nightingale's Birthday, 445
13 Jamestown Day, 447
   Mexican War Begins, 448
   Tulip Time Festival, Holland, Michigan, 449
14 Antioch College Chartered, 450
   Lewis and Clark Depart, 452
   Feast of St. Matthias, 452
15 Congress Resolves to Put Colonies in State
   of Defense, 452
16 Armed Forces Day, 454
   Maifest, Hermann, Missouri, 455
17 Supreme Court Orders School
   Desegregation, 456
   Pentecost, 461
   Norwegian Constitution Day, 464

DATE

18 Rhode Island Prohibits Perpetual Slavery,
   467
19 William Bradford's Death, 468
   The New England Confederation, 469
20 Lafayette's Death, 470
   Dolley Madison's Birthday, 471
   Mecklenburg Independence Day, 472
21 Lindbergh Lands in Paris, 473
22 National Maritime Day, 475
23 Captain Kidd Hanged, 476
   South Carolina Ratifies the Constitution, 478
24 Samuel F. B. Morse Opens First US
   Telegraph Line, 479
25 Feast of St. Bede the Venerable, 480
   Constitutional Convention Opens, 481
   Ralph Waldo Emerson's Birthday, 481
26 Feast of St. Augustine of Canterbury, 484
   Montana Becomes a Territory, 484
27 Feast of St. Augustine of Canterbury, 486
   Cornelius Vanderbilt's Birthday, 487
28 Louis Agassiz's Birthday, 488
   United Presbyterian Church Formed, 491
29 June Week, US Naval Academy, Annapolis,
   Maryland, 492
   John F. Kennedy's Birthday, 493
   Rhode Island Ratifies the Constitution, 498
   The Virginia Resolutions; Patrick Henry's
   Birthday, 500
   Wisconsin Admitted to the Union, 500
30 Memorial Day, 501
31 Seventeenth Amendment Proclaimed
   Ratified, 505
   Walt Whitman's Birthday, 505

JUNE

DATE

June, 509
1 Kentucky Admitted to the Union, 510
  Père Marquette's Birthday, 512
  Royal Poinciana Festival in Miami, 515
  Statehood Day in Tennessee, 516
2 Birthday of John Randolph of Roanoke, 519
3 Jefferson Davis's Birthday, 519
4 Jack Jouett's Ride, 522
5 Gold Clause Repealed, 524

DATE

  Portland Rose Festival, 525
6 D Day, World War II, 527
  Confederate Memorial Day in Winchester,
  Virginia, 530
  YMCA Founded, 531
  Fiesta of Five Flags, Pensacola, Florida, 534
7 Boone Day, 536
8 Frank Lloyd Wright's Birthday, 540

JUNE — *Continued*

DATE

9 Confederate Memorial Day in Petersburg, Virginia, 542
10 Shavuot (Feast of Weeks), 544
11 Kamehameha Day, 545
12 Philippine Independence Day, 547
13 Feast of St. Anthony of Padua, 549
14 Flag Day, 551
    Army Established, 555
    Children's Day, 555
    Harriet Beecher Stowe's Birthday, 556
15 Arkansas Admitted to the Union, 558
    Oregon Treaty Ratified, 560
16 Franklin D. Roosevelt's First Hundred Days End, 561
17 Bunker Hill Day, 563
    Supreme Court Fair Housing Decision, 566
18 Susan B. Anthony Fined for Voting, 566
    War of 1812 Begins, 567
19 Albany Congress Convenes, 568
20 West Virginia Admission Day, 570
21 Summer Begins, 573
    Father's Day, 574
    The Constitution Ratified, 576

DATE

    New Hampshire Ratifies the Constitution, 578
22 The *Leopard* Fires on the *Chesapeake*, 579
23 Midsummer, or St. John's, Eve, 582
    Unto These Hills, Cherokee, North Carolina, 584
24 Midsummer Day, 585
    Feast of the Nativity of St. John the Baptist, 587
    Henry Ward Beecher's Birthday, 590
25 Custer's Last Stand, 591
    Korean War Begins, 594
    United Church of Christ Formed, 595
    Virginia Ratifies the Constitution, 595
26 American Troops Land in France: World War I, 597
27 Helen Keller's Birthday, 598
    Pennsylvania Dutch Folk Festival, Kutztown, Pennsylvania, 600
28 Assassination Precipitates World War I; Treaty of Versailles Signed, 601
    Lutheran Church in America Organized, 603
29 Feast of SS. Peter and Paul, 603
30 Twenty-sixth Amendment Ratified, 606

JULY

DATE

    July, 608
1 Battle of Gettysburg Begins, 609
2 Civil Rights Act of 1964, 611
    President James A. Garfield Shot, 613
    Hussey's Reaper First Exhibited, 615
3 John Singleton Copley's Birthday, 616
    Idaho Admitted to the Union, 616
    Feast of St. Thomas the Apostle, 619
4 Independence Day, 619
    Calvin Coolidge's Birthday, 628
    Stephen Foster's Birthday, 630
    Nathaniel Hawthorne's Birthday, 630
5 P. T. Barnum's Birthday, 631
    David Farragut's Birthday, 633
6 The National Cherry Festival, 635
    Republican Party Founded, 636
7 California Proclaimed Part of the United States, 637
8 John D. Rockefeller Sr.'s Birthday, 641

DATE

9 Braddock's Defeat: The Battle of the Monongahela, 644
10 Allied Troops Land in Sicily, 646
    James Abbott McNeill Whistler's Birthday, 647
    Wyoming Admitted to the Union, 650
11 John Quincy Adams's Birthday, 651
    Grandfather Mountain Highland Games, Linville, North Carolina, 653
12 Henry David Thoreau's Birthday, 654
13 Northwest Ordinance Enacted, 655
14 Bastille Day, 657
    Gerald R. Ford's Birthday, 660
15 Feast of St. Swithin, 665
16 Mary Baker Eddy's Birthday, 665
    Oregon Trail Days, Gering, Nebraska, 668
    Feast of Our Lady of Mount Carmel, 669
17 John Jacob Astor's Birthday, 671
    Columbia University Opens, 674

JULY

DATE

Florida Ceded to the United States, 674
18 John Paul Jones's Death, 676
John Rutledge's Death, 677
19 First Woman's Rights Convention, Seneca
Falls, New York, 678
20 Men Land on the Moon, 680
21 Cheyenne Frontier Days, 682
22 Feast of St. Mary Magdalene, 684
23 James Cardinal Gibbons's Birthday, 685
24 Mormon Pioneer Day, 686
Pioneer Day in Utah, 686
Pioneer Day in Other Western States, 690
25 Feast of St. Christopher, 692
Feast of St. James the Greater, 693

DATE

Puerto Rico's Constitution Day, 694
26 Feast of SS. Joachim and Anne, 695
New York Ratifies the Constitution, 696
27 First Permanent Transatlantic Cable
Completed, 698
28 Fourteenth Amendment Proclaimed
Ratified, 701
29 Feast of St. Martha, 702
Pony Penning on Chincoteague Island, 703
30 The Battle of the Crater, 705
Henry Ford's Birthday, 705
31 All American Indian Days, Sheridan,
Wyoming, 707
Days of '76, Deadwood, South Dakota, 708
Feast of St. Ignatius Loyola, 709

AUGUST

DATE

August, 712
1 John Alden Day, 713
Colorado Admitted to the Union, 714
Francis Scott Key's Birthday, 715
Herman Melville's Birthday, 716
2 The Pecos Bull, Jemez, New Mexico, 718
3 Columbus Sets Sail, 718
Nautilus Cruises Under North Pole, 719
4 John Peter Zenger Acquitted, 719
5 First Use of the Atomic Bomb, 722
John Eliot Baptized, 724
6 Scandinavian Festival, Junction City,
Oregon, 725
Feast of the Transfiguration, 726
Voting Rights Act of 1965, 727
7 Gulf of Tonkin Resolution Approved, 728
8 Charles A. Dana's Birthday, 736
Feast of St. Dominic, 737
9 Free-Soil Party Organized, 738
Feast of St. Matthias, 739
Webster-Ashburton Treaty Signed, 739
10 Herbert Hoover's Birthday, 741
Missouri Admitted to the Union, 744
11 Feast of St. Clare of Assisi, 747
Tishah B'Av, 748
12 Hawaii Annexed to the United States, 749
Old Spanish Days, Santa Barbara,
California, 750

DATE

13 Lucy Stone's Birthday, 752
14 The Atlantic Charter, 753
V-J Day, 754
15 Feast of the Assumption, 755
Natural Chimneys Jousting Tournament,
756
Panama Canal Opens Officially, 758
16 Bennington Battle Day, 758
17 American Indian Exposition, Anadarko,
Oklahoma, 759
Davy Crockett's Birthday, 760
Fulton's Steamboat Sails, 762
18 First United States Government Maritime
Expedition Sets Sail, 763
19 The Constitution's Great Victory, 765
National Aviation Day, 766
20 Benjamin Harrison's Birthday, 767
21 Hawaii Admitted to the Union, 768
Feast of St. Pius X, 769
22 First America's Cup Race, 771
23 Oliver Hazard Perry's Birthday, 773
24 Feast of St. Bartholomew, 774
25 Feast of St. Louis, 775
Pennsylvania Dutch Days, Hershey,
Pennsylvania, 776
26 Nineteenth Amendment Proclaimed
Ratified, 777
Women's Equality Day, 779

AUGUST—*Continued*

DATE

27 Lyndon B. Johnson's Birthday, 783
28 Feast of St. Augustine of Hippo, 787
29 Oliver Wendell Holmes's Birthday, 788

DATE

The Death of St. John the Baptist, 790
30 Huey P. Long Day in Louisiana, 790
31 The Charleston Earthquake, 791

SEPTEMBER

DATE

September, 793
1 World War II Begins, 794
World War II Ends, 794
2 Eugene Field's Birthday, 795
World War II Ends: Japanese Surrender, 796
3 Britain and France Declare War on Germany: World War II, 796
Henry Hudson Enters New York Harbor, 797
Treaty of Paris Signed, 799
4 Los Angeles Birthday Celebration, 799
The Sante Fe Fiesta, 800
5 The First Continental Congress, 803
Nauvoo, Illinois, Grape Festival, 805
Wilhelm Tell Festival, 806
6 Jane Addams's Birthday, 807
Labor Sunday, 809
Lafayette's Birthday, 810
William McKinley Assassinated, 814
7 Labor Day, 817
The Miss America Pageant, Atlantic City, New Jersey, 821
8 Feast of the Birth of Mary, 822
The Galveston Hurricane of 1900, 823
St. Augustine, Nation's Oldest City, Founded, 825
9 California Admission Day, 827
Civil Rights Act of 1957, 829
10 John Smith Assumes Jamestown Council Presidency, 830
11 Battle of Brandywine, 831
The Navajo Nation Fair, Window Rock, Arizona, 832
12 Maryland Defenders' Day, 833
13 John Barry Day, 836

DATE

Feast of St. John Chrysostom, 837
14 National Anthem Day, 838
US Forces Capture Mexico City, 838
15 James Fenimore Cooper's Birthday, 840
William Howard Taft's Birthday, 843
16 Cherokee Strip Day, 844
The Pendleton Round-Up, 846
17 Warren E. Burger's Birthday, 848
Citizenship Day, 850
Baron von Steuben's Birthday, 851
18 Capitol Cornerstone Laid, 854
19 First Battle of Saratoga, 855
Feast of St. Januarius, 855
20 Panic of 1873, 856
21 Autumn Begins (Traditional Date), 857
Delaware Organized as a State, 857
Feast of St. Matthew, 858
22 Nathan Hale Hanged, 858
Preliminary Emancipation Proclamation, 859
23 Autumn Begins, 859
Lewis and Clark Expedition Completed, 860
24 John Marshall's Birthday, 862
25 American Indian Day, 863
Balboa Discovers the Pacific Ocean, 865
Twelfth Amendment Proclaimed Ratified, 866
26 Johnny Appleseed's Birthday, 868
George Gershwin's Birthday, 869
27 Samuel Adams's Birthday, 872
28 Cabrillo Day in California, 873
Frances E. Willard's Birthday, 876
29 Michaelmas Day or the Feast of St. Michael and All Angels, 876
30 Feast of St. Jerome, 879
Mountain State Forest Festival, 881

OCTOBER

DATE

October, 884
1 Rosh Hashanah, 884
  Jimmy Carter's Birthday, 885
  Treaty of San Ildefonso, 888
2 Major John André Hanged as a Spy, 888
  First Pan American Conference Convenes, 890
3 George Bancroft's Birthday, 890
4 Feast of St. Francis of Assisi, 892
  Rutherford B. Hayes's Birthday, 895
5 Chester A. Arthur's Birthday, 898
  Tecumseh's Death, 900
6 Daniel Boone Festival, Barbourville, Kentucky, 901
  British Capture Forts Clinton and Montgomery, 902
  Feast of St. Thomas the Apostle, 904
7 James Whitcomb Riley's Birthday, 904
  Second Battle of Saratoga, 907
8 John Clarke's Birthday, 907
9 The Chicago Fire, 908
  Leif Erikson Day, 909
10 Yom Kippur, 910
  Geauga County Apple Butter Festival, Burton, Ohio, 911
  Oklahoma Historical Day, 911
11 Pulaski Day, 913
  Eleanor Roosevelt's Birthday, 914
  Harlan Fiske Stone's Birthday, 917
12 Columbus Day, 918
  University of North Carolina Day, 921
13 White House Cornerstone Laid, 921

DATE

14 Dwight David Eisenhower's Birthday, 922
15 Sukkot, 928
  Feast of St. Teresa of Ávila, 929
16 Noah Webster's Birthday, 931
17 British Surrender at Saratoga, 932
18 Alaska Day, 935
  Feast of St. Luke the Evangelist, 937
19 Feast of St. Isaac Jogues and Companions, 938
  Peggy Stewart Day, 942
  Yorktown Day, 943
20 Convention of 1818 Signed, 944
  MacArthur Returns to the Philippines, 944
21 Electric Light Bulb Perfected, 947
22 Cuban Missile Crisis, 949
  Shemini Atzeret, 950
23 Francis Hopkinson Smith's Birthday, 950
  Simhat Torah, 951
24 Pennsylvania Day, 951
  United Nations Day, 953
25 Richard E. Byrd's Birthday, 955
26 Erie Canal Opens, 956
27 Theodore Roosevelt's Birthday; Navy Day, 959
28 Czechoslovak Independence Day, 963
  Statue of Liberty Dedicated, 964
29 The Panic of 1929, 965
30 John Adams's Birthday, 966
31 Halloween, 968
  Nevada Day, 972
  Protestant Reformation Day, 974

NOVEMBER

DATE

November, 978
1 All Saints' Day, 978
2 All Souls' Day, 980
  Warren G. Harding's Birthday, 982
  North Dakota Admitted to the Union, 984
  James K. Polk's Birthday, 986
  South Dakota Admitted to the Union, 989
3 General Election Day, 991
  Edward Douglass White's Birthday, 991
4 Feast of St. Charles Borromeo, 993
  Will Rogers Day in Oklahoma, 994

DATE

5 John Dickinson Writes First of the "Farmer's Letters," 995
6 John Carroll Appointed First Roman Catholic Bishop in the United States, 997
7 Harvard Established, 998
  Battle of Tippecanoe, 1001
8 Montana Admitted to the Union, 1002
  Mount Holyoke College Founder's Day, 1003
  United States Troops Land in North Africa, 1005

NOVEMBER — *Continued*

DATE

9 The Great Northeast Power Failure, 1008
10 Marine Corps Birthday, 1010
11 Veterans Day, 1011
  Martinmas, 1013
  Washington Admission Day, 1015
12 Elizabeth Cady Stanton Day, 1016
13 Edwin Booth's Birthday, 1017
  Feast of St. Frances Cabrini, 1019
14 First US Bishop Consecrated, 1022
15 Articles of Confederation Adopted, 1024
16 Oklahoma Becomes a State, 1025
17 Congress Finds a Permanent Home, 1028
  Anne Hutchinson Banished, 1031
18 Asa Gray's Birthday, 1031
19 James A. Garfield's Birthday, 1033
  Lincoln's Gettysburg Address, 1035

DATE

20 Holiday Folk Fair, Milwaukee, Wisconsin, 1037
21 North Carolina Ratifies the Constitution, 1038
22 John F. Kennedy Assassinated, 1040
23 Franklin Pierce's Birthday, 1043
  Stamp Act Repudiated, 1045
24 Zachary Taylor's Birthday, 1046
25 Andrew Carnegie's Birthday, 1049
  Evacuation Day, 1051
26 Thanksgiving Day, 1053
27 Robert R. Livingston's Birthday, 1057
28 The Teheran Conference, 1058
29 Advent Begins, 1059
  Morrison Remick Waite's Birthday, 1060
  Marcus Whitman's Death, 1061
30 Feast of St. Andrew, 1063
  Mark Twain's Birthday, 1065

DECEMBER

DATE

December, 1069
1 Montgomery Bus Boycott Starts, 1070
  Presidential Election of 1824 Deadlocked, 1070
2 The Monroe Doctrine Promulgated, 1072
3 Illinois Admitted to the Union, 1072
  Gilbert Stuart's Birthday, 1073
4 George Washington Takes Leave of His Officers, 1075
5 Twenty-first Amendment Proclaimed Ratified, 1076
  Martin Van Buren's Birthday, 1077
6 Feast of St. Nicholas, 1079
7 Delaware Day, 1080
  Pearl Harbor Day, 1082
8 Feast of the Immaculate Conception of Mary, 1084
  United States Enters World War II, 1085
9 Battle of Great Bridge, 1085
10 Emily Dickinson's Birthday, 1087
  Thomas H. Gallaudet's Birthday, 1089
  Human Rights Day and Week, 1089
  Mississippi Admitted to the Union, 1091
  Treaty of Paris of 1898 Signed, 1093
  Wyoming Day, 1093
11 Indiana Day, 1094

DATE

12 John Jay's Birthday, 1096
  Feast of Our Lady of Guadalupe, 1097
  Pennsylvania Ratifies the Constitution, 1098
13 Feast of Santa Lucia, 1100
14 Alabama Admitted to the Union, 1102
  George Washington's Death, 1104
15 Bill of Rights Day, 1105
16 Boston Tea Party, 1106
  The New Madrid, Missouri, Earthquake, 1108
17 John Greenleaf Whittier's Birthday, 1109
  Wright Brothers Day, 1111
18 Lyman Abbott's Birthday, 1115
  New Jersey Ratifies the Constitution, 1116
  Thirteenth Amendment Proclaimed Ratified, 1117
19 Washington Encamps at Valley Forge, 1117
20 Louisiana Purchased, 1119
21 Winter Begins (Traditional Date), 1120
  Forefathers' Day, 1121
  Feast of St. Thomas the Apostle, 1123
  Veiled Prophet Ball and Parade in St. Louis, 1124
22 Winter Begins, 1127
  James Oglethorpe's Birthday, 1128

DECEMBER

DATE

23 Federal Reserve System Established, 1130
   Hanukkah, 1131
   Joseph Smith Jr.'s Birthday, 1132
24 Christmas Eve, 1135
   War of 1812 Ends: Treaty of Ghent, 1141
25 Christmas Day: Feast of the Nativity of
   Our Lord, 1141
   Clara Barton's Birthday, 1149
26 Feast of St. Stephen, 1151
   Battle of Trenton, 1152

DATE

27 Feast of St. John, Apostle and Evangelist,
   1154
28 Feast of the Holy Innocents (Childermas),
   1155
   Iowa Admitted to the Union, 1157
29 Andrew Johnson's Birthday, 1158
   Texas Admitted to the Union, 1163
   Woodrow Wilson's Birthday, 1163
30 The Gadsden Purchase, 1166
31 New Year's Eve, 1166
   George Marshall's Birthday, 1168

APPENDIX

The Calendar, 1171
The Era, 1177

The Days of the Week, 1181
Signs of the Zodiac, 1184

INDEX 1191

IMPORTANT PUBLIC AND LEGAL HOLIDAYS

THIS LIST contains the names of most legal and public holidays currently designated by the various states or by the federal government. The nine federal holidays (asterisked below) are designated by the President and the Congress and apply only to federal employees and to residents of the District of Columbia. Thus, technically, there are no *national* holidays, although most states, by their own legislative enactment or executive proclamation, observe some or all of the federal dates. In recent years, all states, the District of Columbia, and the Commonwealth of Puerto Rico have observed as legal holidays New Year's Day, Washington's Birthday, Independence Day, Labor Day, Veterans Day, Thanksgiving, and Christmas. Many states have also observed Lincoln's Birthday, Memorial Day, Election Day, and Columbus Day. The balance of the holidays listed below are observed in a few states or, in many cases, just one state or territory. The terms *legal* and *public*, as they apply to holidays, are synonymous..

Since the list of holidays designated by each state and by the federal government may vary from year to year, it is advisable to consult almanacs and such annual publications as *Chases' Calendar of Annual Events* for current observances.

Alaska Day	*Columbus Day
All Saints' Day	Confederate Memorial Day
American Indian Day	Jefferson Davis' Birthday
Arbor Day	Decoration Day (Memorial Day)
Arizona Admission Day	Easter Monday
Armistice Day (Veterans Day)	Evacuation Day
Battle of New Orleans Day	Fast Day
Bennington Battle Day	Father's Day
Bunker Hill Day	Flag Day
California Admission Day	Gasparilla Day
Cherokee Strip Day	General Election Day
*Christmas Day	Good Friday
Colorado Day	Halifax Resolves Day

Hawaii Admission Day
Holy Thursday
Inauguration Day
*Independence Day
Andrew Jackson's Birthday
Thomas Jefferson's Birthday
Lyndon B. Johnson's Birthday
Kamehameha Day
Martin Luther King Day
*Labor Day
Landing Day (Columbus Day)
Robert E. Lee's Birthday
Lee-Jackson Day
Lincoln's Birthday
Huey P. Long Day
Mardi Gras (Shrove Tuesday)
Maryland Day
Maryland Defenders' Day
Mecklenburg Independence Day
*Memorial Day
Mormon Pioneer Day
Mother's Day
Nevada Day

*New Year's Day
Oklahoma Day
Oklahoma Historical Day
Patriots' Day
Presidents' Day
Prince Kuhio Day
Puerto Rico's Constitution Day
Rhode Island Independence Day
Will Rogers Day
Franklin D. Roosevelt's Birthday
San Jacinto Day
Seward's Day
Texas Independence Day
*Thanksgiving
Three Kings' Day (Epiphany)
Harry S. Truman's Birthday
Vermont Town Meeting Day
*Veterans Day
Virgin Islands Transfer Day
VJ Day
*Washington's Birthday
Washington-Lincoln Day
West Virginia Day

The American Book of Days

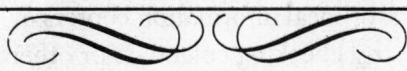

A NOTE ON MOVABLE EVENTS

The dates of certain festivals, holidays, observances, and events change from·year to year. These movable events, as they are called, include all Christian holy days whose dates depend on the movable feast of Easter; Jewish holy days, which fall on fixed days of the Hebrew calendar; and the festivals and observances that are scheduled for such shifting times as the first Monday in September (Labor Day) or the fourth Thursday in November (Thanksgiving).

Each movable event described in *The American Book of Days* is so designated at the beginning of the article; for the sake of consistency, each is listed under the date on which it took place in 1970. Before making plans to attend an event or observe an occasion that is movable, the reader should determine the correct date by consulting almanacs, guidebooks, or local information centers or, in the case of religious observances, by checking calendars or other religious sources.

The reader should also note that certain occasions — while not movable — may in some years be scheduled on other, more convenient, dates close to the actual dates. Such occasions include Lincoln's Birthday, Washington's Birthday, Patriots' Day, Memorial Day, and the Federal Income Tax Deadline. These shifts are designed either to extend or to avoid weekends. Other events have varying dates designated annually by sponsoring organizations.

January

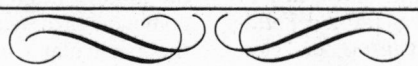

January is the first month in the modern calendar and consists of 31 days. The name (*Januarius* in Latin) is derived from the two-faced Roman god Janus. Some scholars have claimed that the derivation of the name *Janus* is from the Latin *ianua*, meaning "door"; others have explained the name as the masculine form of Diana, which would be Dianus or Ianus.

There are many conflicting theories about Janus and his role in the Roman religion. He apparently figured prominently as the god of all beginnings. As the god of spatial beginnings, he watched over gates and doorways, which were generally under his protection; as the god of temporal beginnings, he presided over the first hour of the day. The first day of the month and the first month of the year were also sacred to him. Of all the gods, including Jupiter, his name was invoked first at the start of important undertakings, perhaps with the idea that his intervention as the "janitor" of all avenues would speed prayers directly to the immortals. As the deity of all beginnings, Janus was also entitled *Consivius* or "sower," in reference to his role as the "beginner" or originator of agriculture.

The worship of Janus existed as a local cult on the Janiculan hill (variously interpreted as "door hill" or "city of Janus") west of Rome, on the bank of the Tiber River. Traditionally, this cult went back to Romulus and the period even before the actual founding of Rome in 753 B.C. In addition, a festival in honor of Janus, called the *Agonalia*, was celebrated on January 9. The officiating priest — in this case the *rex sacrorum* who represented the ancient king in his role as head of the state religion — sacrificed a ram on the occasion. Later Romans, intrigued by the lofty character of this ceremony, proposed various additional interpretations about the possible nature of Janus: perhaps he was a cosmic deity, sky god, or god of water crossings. Discovering in the name Janus the same Latin root as in the name of Diana, the moon goddess, they even imagined him to be a moon deity.

As the animistic spirit of doorways (*ianuae*) and arches (*iani*), Janus guarded the numerous ceremonial gateways in Rome. These freestanding structures were used especially for noteworthy entrances and exits on state occasions. Numa Pompilius, the legendary second king of Rome (about 715–672 B.C.) probably dedicated the famous *Ianus geminus*, the arcade or covered passage facing east and west, which was located at the northeast end of the Roman Forum. A simple, rectangular, bronze edifice, it had double doors at each end that were traditionally opened in time of war and closed in peace. This highly symbolic arcade, sometimes described simply as an arch, was undoubtedly connected with a type of war magic, a superstitious belief that passage through it brought luck to outgoing and incoming armies. The Romans were so often at war, however, that it is said the doors of the structure were closed only twice during the seven centuries between the reigns of Numa and Augustus. Janus was also honored by a less well-known archway, located near the theater of Marcellus in the *forum holitorium* (where vegetables were sold). It was probably erected by the Roman general and consul Gaius Duilius, about 260 B.C., following his victory over the Carthaginian fleet off Mylae.

Janus was closely connected with early Roman coinage. He was represented as a deity with two faces on the ancient *as*, which often had on its reverse side a representation of a ship's prow. An ancient source says that Roman boys liked to toss these coins and bet *capita aut navia* ("heads or ships"), in much the same way that today's youngsters play "heads or tails."

Although Janus was usually depicted with two bearded faces looking in opposite directions — the future and the past — the number of faces represented gradually increased to four. Emperor Domitian (A.D. 81–96), for example, dedicated a temple to *Janus Quadrifrons* or "four-faced Janus." In his role as porter or doorkeeper, the god was sometimes pictured as holding a staff in his right hand and a key or keys in his left. As such, he was termed *Patulcius,* meaning "opener," and *Clusius,* or "closer." In the late Roman Empire, he was portrayed as both a bearded and unbearded figure; in place of the staff and keys, the fingers of his right hand sometimes showed the number CCC, or 300, and those of his left LXV, or 65, for the total 365 days of the year.

The earliest calendars, such as the Egyptian, Jewish, and Greek, did not place the beginning of the year in January. The early Romans originally began the calendar year with *Martius* (see March), and January did not even appear among their 10 months. Numa Pompilius supposedly decreed that 2 new months should be added at the end of the 10 previous ones. He called the first of these additions *Januarius* in honor of Janus, the cult god of the doorways. In 153 B.C., the Roman state proclaimed January 1 to be New Year's Day (see January 1) thus turning the 11th month, *Januarius,* into the first month of the year. For a long time, however, older traditions prevailed and most Romans still considered the year to start in March. Moreover, by the end of the Roman republic, the entire calendar had become highly inaccurate and confused, since state officials were constantly making changes in it for political purposes. In 46 B.C., Julius Caesar instituted a much-needed calendar reform (see Appendix, The Calendar). The resulting Julian calendar — now also known as the Old Style calendar — which became effective in 45 B.C., reinstated January as the first month and January 1 as the first day of the year. In later centuries, however, from the Fall of the Roman Empire through the Middle Ages, there was widespread diversity as to the date on which the year began in different areas. Contributing to the diversity were political fragmentation, meager communications, and the hostility of the Catholic church to pagan traditions. Experimentation with a return to the January 1 new year of ancient Roman times was attempted as early as the 13th century in present Germany. But only in the middle decades of the 16th

century did some European states effectively reestablish this ancient date for starting the civil calendar year. The Gregorian or New Style calendar instituted by Pope Gregory XIII in 1582 also employed this innovation, decreeing January 1 as the beginning of the new year for all Catholic countries. By degrees Protestant countries fell into line as they adopted the new calendar over the next 170 years. Thus, at the brink of the modern era, January 1 reassumed its former place as the start of the new year.

Among non-Roman peoples, the names of the months often stemmed from a natural phenomenon or a seasonal occupation peculiar to the particular month. Such series of month-names have been found in all parts of the world with the exception of South America and Australia. In western Europe, for example, the Anglo-Saxons called January *Wulf-monath* in allusion to the hunger of the wolves, which made them bold enough at that time of year to leave the forests and enter the villages in search of food. The name *Aefter-Yule* was also used to designate the month after the great feast of Christmas. Charlemagne, the early medieval Frankish emperor, appropriately called January *Wintarmanoth,* or "Wintermonth."

In ancient and modern times, particular stones have been connected with the various months. The lucky gem or birthstone often associated with January is the garnet.

JANUARY 1

New Year's Day

So fundamental to everyday life are ways of marking the passage of time that most people feel their own calendar customs have been virtually ordained by nature (see Appendix, The Calendar). In keeping with this feeling, the reflex of Europeans and Americans is likely to be that January 1 is the natural day for beginning the year — what other? In fact, however, many different days have been designated for this celebration at different times and places over the centuries.

The Gregorian, or New Style, calendar now used throughout most of the world starts the year on January 1. Although that date has been recognized as New Year's Day in more and more countries since the "new" calendar was first introduced in 1582, it is actually a rather unnatural day for beginning the year, since it has no special place in the sun's cycle. It is connected neither with the winter or summer solstice nor with the spring or autumn equinox — four dates that do relate to the change of the seasons, and so have prompted many people to observe them as New Year's Day with joyous festivities and often with religious rites. The ancient Egyptians, Phoenicians, and Persians, for example, began their year with the autumn equinox (on or about September 21 in the Gregorian calendar), and the Greeks for many centuries used the winter solstice (December 21 or 22 in the Gregorian calendar); however, other time-honored New Year's celebrations such as the Chinese (see February 6) have been calculated by lunar cycles.

How Europeans, and from them Americans, came to take January 1 as the beginning of the new year is a complicated story embracing nearly two millennia. The ancient Romans, under a very old and quite inaccurate calendar, had originally taken March (*Martius*) (see March) as the first month of the year. But in 153 B.C., the Roman state declared January 1 thenceforth to be New Year's Day, turning the 11th month, *Januarius* (see January), into a new first month. In a pattern that would often be repeated, however, the common people remembered their old traditions and for a long time still considered the year to end with the celebration of the *Terminalia* on February 23, after which intercalation — the insertion of a varying number of days — was made to offset errors in the calendar and so complete the year.

By the end of the Roman republic, the calendar was once more highly confused, since officials had tampered with it to cut short or extend magistrates' terms of office. In 46 B.C., Julius Caesar, as *pontifex maximus* and dictator, instituted necessary reforms. Under his new calendar, subsequently named the Julian calendar (see Appendix, The Calendar), January 1 was reinstituted as New Year's Day. The new calendar became effective the following year (45 B.C.).

The Romans traditionally celebrated the Feast of Janus — the god of doorways and of beginnings, who is depicted as looking both forward to the future and backward to the past — on the first of January. This deity was certainly suitable to the New Year, and to begin the year auspiciously, the Romans offered sacrifices to him. They also exchanged greetings with kin and acquaintances and gave New Year's gifts, called *strenae*, after Strenia, the goddess of strength. According to tradition, the custom of giving *strenae* originated in the eighth century B.C., when the Romans presented the king of the Sabines with branches from the trees consecrated to Strenia, as tokens of good omen. *Strenae* also means "omens" in Latin, and this semantic link captures the superstition and expectancy with which most

peoples have greeted the New Year. As with the Romans and Sabines, New Year's festivities throughout the world still tend to be occasions for smoothing over quarrels and reaffirming human ties.

In time, the Romans replaced with more elaborate gifts the branches of bay and palm traditionally gathered on the first day of the year. During the Roman Empire, courtiers and others gave the emperor New Year's presents of great value, which enriched his personal coffers and became a source of political corruption. Aware of the burden that these traditional gifts placed on the people, the Emperor Claudius issued a decree limiting the amounts to be given. In addition, the New Year's Feast of Janus also was marked by masquerades and public entertainments, which in imperial times degenerated into public orgies.

After their conversion to Christianity in the fourth century, the Roman emperors continued for some time the pagan traditions of New Year's. The young Church, however, increasingly condemned these observances as scandalous and forbade Christians to participate. Much of the struggle between the growing faith and the old pagan culture centered around such public observances. As it gained strength, the Church purposely planned Christian festivals in competition with pagan ones. It established Christmas on December 25 (then the winter solstice) in counterpoint to the Mithraic rites and the Roman *Saturnalia*, for example. Following the biblical account, the Feast of the Circumcision of the infant Jesus then fell eight days later, on January 1 — competing conveniently with the Feast of Janus and New Year's Day. Saint Ambrose declared, "We fast on this day [Circumcision] that the heathen may know we condemn their pleasures." Today, more than a thousand years later, some of the more liturgical communions of the Christian Church — Lutherans, Episcopalians, and those Eastern Orthodox who follow the Gregorian calendar — still celebrate the Feast of the Circumcision on January 1, making New Year's a day when many Christians attend simple church services. Roman Catholics, who now observe January 1 as the Solemnity of Mary, also are among the churchgoers on this day.

The Church remained strongly hostile to the old pagan New Year throughout the Middle Ages. As a result, January 1 was weakened and its observance as New Year's Day may have disappeared for some centuries in parts of Western Europe. Certainly, political fragmentation and poor communications after the collapse of Roman power encouraged diversity to spring up concerning the beginning of the calendar

3

year. Between the 9th and the late 11th centuries, Christmas, celebrating the birth of Jesus, gained wide acceptance as the date for changing the year. Gradually, December 25 thus replaced such earlier New Year dates as January 1, the Franks' March 1, and the late Roman Empire's September 1 (which also continued in use in the Byzantine Empire for many centuries). From Anglo-Saxon times until the reign of Henry II in the mid-12th century, the new year began on Christmas in England, although William the Conqueror briefly tried to institute January 1.

In the High Middle Ages, growing veneration of the Virgin Mary made March 25, the Feast of the Annunciation, or Lady Day — the supposed date of Jesus' conception (see March 25) — an increasingly great Church festival; and in some lands attention focused on this day as an appropriate beginning for the year. The practice of starting the new calendar year from the Feast of the Annunciation spread from the early 11th century on. In England, March 25 became established as the beginning of the calendar year from the late 12th century, and this was also the practice in most domains of the French king and in Florence and Pisa. December 25, however, continued to begin the year in much of the Holy Roman Empire and in Scandinavia. Only on the Iberian Peninsula did January 1 begin the year through the Middle Ages, and even there the dating was changed to December 25 in the 14th century.

By contrast, from the reign of Philip II, king of France, in the early 13th century, the French court began the new year on the movable feast of Easter. With all its inconveniences, this usage spread to districts bordering France on the north and east. However, in folk tradition throughout these areas, the New Year usually continued to be Lady Day or Christmas.

Although scattered attempts to revive the practice of starting the year on January 1 were made as early as the mid-13th century, little came of such efforts until the 16th century. Then, at the threshold of the modern period, a really significant movement developed to restore the ancient civil New Year of January 1. The interest of humanists and their patrons in the literature of antiquity during this period undoubtedly encouraged rulers to imitate the ancient Roman New Year. The increasing administration of government by laymen instead of by priests may also have encouraged detachment of the civil New Year's from the great festivals of the Church. As early as 1532, the Estates of Holland declared January 1 New Year's Day. In 1556, the king of Spain issued a similar decree for his lands; in 1558, the Holy

Roman Emperor did the same for the empire; and in 1563, King Charles IX of France followed suit, though the reform did not take effect until it was registered by the Parlement of Paris in 1567 (see April 1, April Fools' Day). In 1575, Protestant Geneva also declared January 1 as the beginning of the New Year.

By this time, however, the whole Julian calendar was seen to be badly in need of reform. The most pressing of the difficulties was that over the approximately 1,600 years that the Julian calendar had been in use, a small discrepancy between the actual length of the solar year and the length of the year by the Julian calendar had added up to approximately 10 days. With the advice of astronomers, Pope Gregory XIII promulgated the needed changes in 1582, rectifying the above discrepancy by ordering 10 calendar days to be dropped. Among other things, his New Style, or Gregorian, calendar also caused the year to begin on January 1 wherever the new calendar was adopted (except in a few Italian cities).

Although the calendar reformers made this change on ecclesiastical grounds related to the Church's reckoning of Easter, its effect was to strengthen the revival of the ancient pagan date of January 1 for the New Year. Where January 1 had already become New Year's Day — as in Holland, Spain, Portugal, France, and the Holy Roman Empire — adoption of the Gregorian calendar simply caused the year to begin 10 days earlier, on January 1, New Style, instead of on January 1, Old Style. General acceptance of the Gregorian calendar was complicated, however, by the fact that by 1582, many European governments no longer acknowledged papal authority. In predominantly Roman Catholic states and provinces, and in the Protestant provinces of Holland and Zealand as well, the new calendar was instituted rapidly between 1582 and 1584, but most Protestant states would not comply. In 1599, the king of Scotland ordered that thenceforth January 1 should begin the year in his realm, but the Scots celebrated New Year's Day on January 1, Old Style, through 1752, in which year the Gregorian calendar was instituted for all Great Britain by act of Parliament. Denmark and Norway, the Protestant states of Germany, the provinces of the United Netherlands, and the Protestant cantons of Switzerland all introduced the new calendar in 1700 or 1701, and presumably thereafter celebrated New Year's Day on January 1, New Style, although there are indications that the Swiss may not have used that date to begin their calendar year before 1740.

England, Ireland, and the American colonies began the calendar year on March 25, Old

Style, up through 1751, a period extending nearly a century and a half beyond the first permanent English settlement in the New World. By act of Parliament, however, the year 1751 was shortened to 282 days, and the year 1752 was ordered to begin on January 1, Old Style. (Thus the date January 1, 1751, was nonexistent in England and the colonies.) To complete the Gregorian reform for Great Britain, the by then requisite 11 days were dropped from the calendar between September 2 and 14, 1752, so that New Year's Day in 1753 was January 1, New Style. Sweden's first January 1 New Year, New Style, came in 1754, the reformed calendar having been introduced there in 1753. The maverick cities of Florence and Pisa adopted January 1 as the beginning of the year after 1749, but the Republic of Venice held out for its unique date of March 1 until its demise in 1797. Peter the Great, in a *ukase* of 1699, ordered that in Russia the new year begin thenceforth on January 1, Old Style, but the Gregorian calendar was not introduced into Russia until 1918, after the Russian Revolution. Thus the USSR's first January 1 New Year to be observed under the New Style calendar was in 1919. Greece and Greek Orthodox communities made the change to the Gregorian, New Style, calendar in 1924. However, some of the Eastern Orthodox national churches resisted the change much longer, with the result that their New Year observances, on what the old Julian calendar said was January 1, fell on what the Gregorian calendar — and, by the 20th century, most of the world — regarded as January 14.

Tenacious adherence to the Julian calendar was particularly notable among Russian Orthodox churches. Not until the beginning of the 1970s, for instance, did the change to the new calendar become really widespread among Russian Orthodox churches in the United States; and some Orthodox churches have continued to schedule their observances by the Julian calendar even to the present day.

This involved history of the beginnings of the year suggests the relative unimportance of coordinated timing for medieval and early modern European societies. Political rivalries also contributed to the variations, for styling the year in a particular way was an indication of political independence.

Back during the centuries when Christmas began the calendar year, the old Roman New Year of January 1 may have been retained in some manner in the Christmas festivities, which lasted at least for the following week through January 1, and often through Twelfth Night (see January 6). Scattered evidence indeed suggests that for many centuries when it did

not begin the calendar year, January 1 was nonetheless referred to as "New Year's Day" by the English. The Roman custom of lavish New Year's gifts to rulers would seem to have given kings a particular stake in keeping January 1 alive as "New Year's Day," even when they styled their calendars otherwise. Queen Elizabeth I was able to obtain almost her entire wardrobe and jewels from such gifts, and British rulers before and after her benefited from the custom of New Year's gifts until about the end of the 18th century.

Gift-giving among the people at New Year's rather than at Christmas has varied with the centuries. The custom in England is thought to have originated in earliest British history, with the Celtic druids' distribution of branches of the sacred mistletoe as New Year's gifts to the people.

The invading Saxons are also believed to have exchanged gifts at New Year's. Certainly under the Tudor and Stuart monarchs it was the custom for all classes to give New Year's presents to friends and relatives. Among ordinary folk, favorite gifts were multicolored eggs, nuts, apples or oranges studded with cloves, special cakes of mincemeat, and plain or gilded nutmegs. Tenants often presented their landlords with chickens. And women in the wealthier classes were given books, ornamented gloves, or brooches. From the practice of sometimes giving a monetary equivalent of the article came the terms "glove money" and "pin money" — for the little bit of cash that women were allowed to spend as they pleased during the centuries when they lacked economic rights. By the mid-19th century, however, the New Year's gift-giving had died out in England.

As today, New Year's festivities in the past often lasted from late on New Year's Eve (see December 31) to the early hours of New Year's Day, with celebrators bidding the old year farewell and welcoming the new at midnight in one combined set of gestures. One of the most dramatic Old World customs, which was carried to the Americas, was to toll the passing of the year with muffled bells just before midnight. With the tenor bell alone tolling, or amid brief silence, the bells were quickly unmuffled, and just at midnight they then joyously pealed forth the new year's arrival.

In previous centuries, New Year's was a great national festival in Scotland, celebrated more heartily than Christmas. At midnight the people would throng the streets, filled with excitement. Even the most dour Scots relaxed and enjoyed themselves in noisy celebrations. In time, however, pickpockets ruined the street gatherings. Gradually New Year's has become quieter, but it remains a major Scottish holiday.

Many New Year's traditions were followed, with local variations, all over the British Isles. The custom of first-footing is an example. In some districts first-footing meant callers' competing to be the first to place a foot across their friends' thresholds on January 1; suitors especially tried to be the first to call on women they wished to "win." But in many regions people were strongly superstitious about the kind of luck that the first-footer brought in. Householders would invite a person of the desired description to come, sometimes at a price. As "first-footers," men with physical defects and all women were considered ominous, while dark-haired or dark-complexioned men were thought to be a good sign in many places. If the "first-footer" and other callers brought food, coals, or something green — signs of plenty — it meant good luck for the coming year; but it was supposed to be bad luck if they came empty-handed. The poor, especially, performed New Year's rituals to ward off want in the coming year; and country people particularly favored rites to foretell the weather. To take a light out of the house on New Year's Day was very bad luck, portending the death of someone in the family.

A popular custom for many centuries was to prepare a large wassail bowl from which to drink to the health of everyone present just after midnight. (*Wassail* is derived from the Middle English *waes haeil*, "be thou well" — "to your health.") The contents of the wassail bowl were called "lamb's wool" and included ale, sugar, nutmeg and roasted apples. At the toasting, as today, those gathered often sang "Auld Lang Syne." A similar northern practice was to take a "hot pint" of sweetened ale to neighbors just after midnight to toast the new year.

"Wassailing," on the other hand, was an ancient custom of going from house to house with a bowl to beg for one's New Year's gifts. This was done by the poor, and also by children, who were given fruit and nuts. Traditionally, the wassailers would come to the door with sprays of evergreen hung with apples, oranges, and ribbons, and perhaps singing the old wassailers' carol:

> Here we come a-wassailing
> Among the leaves so green;
> Here we come a-wassailing
> So far to be seen.
>
> Love and joy come to you
> And to your wassail too,
> And God bless you
> And send you a happy new year,
> And God send you a happy new year.

In some British villages, the wassail bowl and wassailing were associated not with New Year's but with Twelfth Night, a tremendous celebration in many districts prior to the calendar change, which slowly lost its hold thereafter. The practice of wassailing has become infrequent in the 20th century, though the term remains familiar on both sides of the Atlantic, chiefly from the still-sung carol quoted above.

On New Year's Day itself in former times, many social calls were paid and the entire family gathered for dinner at the home of the head of the family. Such dinners are still common in France. Once it also was customary to send complimentary verses at New Year's. Today, however, New Year's greetings are usually included with wishes for the Christmas season, extended personally and also on the holiday cards that have become a major industry, particularly in the United States.

In the New World, the Spanish, Portuguese, and French colonies began to celebrate New Year's Day on January 1, New Style, soon after 1582, when their mother countries adopted the Gregorian calendar. But the situation was different in the North American colonies of Great Britain. There the year continued to begin on March 25 until 1752, as in England. But despite some unclarity about the question (just as for the mother country), it appears that January 1, Old Style, was celebrated as New Year's Day by the English in the New World, and that they, too, gave gifts on January 1 instead of at Christmas. Certainly Scottish colonists would have felt January 1 to be the correct date for New Year's Day. But one group of English settlers had had strong feelings against observing New Year's Day: the Pilgrims at Plymouth shared the sentiment of Puritans in England that to celebrate January 1 as New Year's Day amounted to blasphemous reverence for the pagan god Janus. The English Puritans referred to January as First Month to avoid all impious associations.

Although they were Calvinists, like the Puritans, the Dutch settlers of the 17th century colony of New Netherland kept the festivities that the New England Puritans shunned. In New Netherland, New Year's Day was the major holiday — a stately occasion of paying calls and giving gifts, for which elaborate preparations were made. In wealthy homes, large punch bowls were filled and foods set out for streams of callers who came to toast each other and their hosts. After the English defeated the Dutch and made New Netherland New York in 1664, British settlers fully adopted the New Year's customs of the Dutch, adding a turkey shoot to the day's activities. In 1773, on the eve of the American Revolution, New Year's festivities were so riotous in New York that the following March the legislature outlawed explosives and the firing of guns at New Year's.

Scottish and English customs blended with those of the Dutch. On New Year's Day in Scotland it had been an ancient practice for boys to go from house to house singing this ditty and asking for money or food:

I wish you a Merry Christmas
And a Happy New Year
A pocketful of money
And a cellar full of beer,
And a good fat pig
To serve you all the year.
Ladies and gentlemen sitting by the fire,
Pity us poor boys out in the mire.

The first four lines, at least, were taken up by boys in rural New York and elsewhere as a jocular holiday greeting.

From colonial Dutch practice, the Presidents of the United States derived a long-observed custom of welcoming the new year by holding open house on January 1. The first capital of the United States after the ratification of the Constitution was New York City. Assuming his presidency in 1789, George Washington was pleasantly surprised the following January by the customs of Dutch origin surrounding the New Year, especially New Year's calling. He decided to hold a presidential reception for the public on next New Year's Day, January 1, 1791. The Washingtons continued the tradition at Philadelphia, and John and Abigail Adams carried it to the new capital of Washington, D.C. Their first reception was held when the White House was still unfinished. Thomas Jefferson, the first President of the opposing party, later continued the custom. A newspaper account of his reception in 1804 reported:

About 12 o'clock the President was waited upon by the heads of departments and other officers, civil and military, foreign diplomatic characters, strangers of distinction, the Cherokee chiefs at present on a mission to the seat of government, and most of the respectable citizens of Washington and Georgetown. . . . Colonel Burrows, at the head of the Marine Corps, saluted the President while the band of music played the President's march [and] went through the usual evolutions in a masterly manner. . . . After partaking of the abundant refreshments . . . and enjoying pleasure which may be truly said to have been without alloy, the company separated about 2 o'clock, and betook themselves to the various places of entertainment provided for the celebration of the day.

In contrast with this brief report, the account of the first New Year's reception held — in 1910 — by President William Howard Taft filled

more than eight columns of the Washington *Star*. The presidential New Year's reception remained a major social event in the capital through January 1, 1933, under President Herbert Hoover. But in 1934, because his lameness made it difficult to stand in a long receiving line, President Franklin Delano Roosevelt discontinued the custom. It has never been revived, doubtless in part because modern transportation now allows Presidents to spend the holiday away from the White House.

The custom of paying New Year's calls has generally declined in the United States during the 20th century. This practice reached perhaps its greatest height in the latter decades of the 19th century. Those who intended to receive their friends and acquaintances sent their names to the newspapers with the hours when they would be "at home," so that callers might know which homes would welcome them. These lists filled many columns and included the names of famous socialites and ordinary citizens alike. However, the tradition was eventually undermined by bad manners, drunkenness, and gate-crashing, and the custom was abandoned.

In the United States today, the gayest parties tend to be held on New Year's Eve, and New Year's Day then is usually spent quietly. But open houses held for friends in the late afternoon of New Year's Day have become increasingly common since the cocktail party has grown in popularity as a way of extending cordiality and repaying social obligations. In reality an updated version of an old custom, these open houses are less lavish than they once were, and are not publicly announced.

It has been remarked that the people of the United States have become event-oriented rather than tradition-oriented about New Year's Day. While gift-giving and important family gatherings still prevail in other lands, many Americans devote at least part of New Year's Day to watching, in person or on television, a choice of spectacles. These include Philadelphia's famous Mummers' parade (see January 1), the climactic "bowl" football games played between the country's leading collegiate teams on or around New Year's Day, and the lavish parades associated with them. The Rose Bowl football game and Rose Bowl parade (see January 1, Pasadena Rose Bowl Football Game) are prototypes. Named for the great stadiums or "bowls" where the championship contests take place, the sports portions of these events engage the attention of much of the country's population throughout January 1.

One of the most purely American ways of celebrating the New Year is certain American Indians' performance, on January 1 and the three succeeding days, of dances traditionally associated with the New Year. Most famous are the corn, turtle, buffalo, and deer dances, variously scheduled at New Mexican Indian pueblos such as Taos and Sandia. Certain Crow Indians in Montana also perform New Year's dances. In Sitka, Alaska, Eskimo games are traditional on January 1.

The first of January is a legal holiday in every state of the Union — though it was not until after 1918 that the day was made a legal holiday in Massachusetts — and in the District of Columbia and all US territories and possessions. It begins the fiscal year for most US taxpayers and is the civil New Year for all US citizens. But certain groups celebrate additional versions of the New Year, in keeping with their ancestral and religious traditions. The Chinese New Year (see February 6) falls in either January or February; the Jewish New Year, Rosh Hashanah (see October 1), in either September or October; and the Moslem New Year on the first day of the month of Muharram — all according to lunar reckonings. Among the declining number of Eastern Orthodox churches in the United States that still follow the old Julian calendar, New Year's Day, falling on January 1, Old Style, is celebrated on January 14 of the Gregorian calendar, since the constantly growing difference between the two calendars now amounts to 13 days.

The American Lutheran Church Merger Becomes Effective

The merger of the American Lutheran Church, the Evangelical Lutheran Church, and the United Evangelical Lutheran Church took place during a constituting convention at Minneapolis, Minnesota, on April 22–24, 1960. The combined bodies took the name of the American Lutheran Church (ALC). Their unification reflected a new ecumenical spirit that has been spreading through the Christian world. The newly combined body became constitutionally operative on January 1, 1961.

Combining the 1,059,195 baptized members of the original American Lutheran Church with the 1,174,494 members of the Evangelical Lutheran Church and the 73,091 members of the United Evangelical Lutheran Church, the new denomination brought together Lutherans of Danish, German, and Norwegian heritage. A fourth group, the 88,396-member Lutheran Free Church, joined with the American Lutheran Church on February 1, 1963.

As of the mid-1970s, the baptized membership of the ALC totaled over three million. With headquarters at 422 South 5th Street, Minneapolis, the ALC is composed of more than 6,000 congregations. Of these, the vast majority are

in the United States; more than 300 others are in Canada, one is in Denmark, and one is in Norway. The North American congregations are divided geographically into 18 districts, which are served by more than 5,000 pastors. Regional offices of the church are in Chicago, Dallas, San Francisco, Washington, D.C., and Saskatoon, Canada. The publishing activities of the unified churches have been merged as the Augsburg Publishing House, and their unified foreign mission program is now active in Asia, Africa, and South America.

A *United Testimony on Faith and Life*, adopted by the uniting churches approximately nine years before the initial merger became effective, sets forth the thinking that led to the union. Having "walked and worked together for . . . more than twenty years," the *Testimony* said, the concerned churches

have learned to know one another both as to doctrine and as to manner of life. . . . Coming out of varying backgrounds . . . they have learned to cherish one another's contributions to the fulness of the Church's life in Christ. Through closer acquaintance and deepening fellowship they have found that the common roots of their faith, in the Holy Scriptures and in the Lutheran Confessions, have given them a common life in communion with the one Lord and Savior.

Their loyalty to the Gospel of Jesus Christ, their Lutheran heritage, and the desperate need of the world seem to call for further exploration of the possibilities of closer fellowship, greater understanding, and closer organizational cooperation or union.

Feast of the Circumcision

The Feast of the Circumcision commemorates the circumcision of Jesus Christ, believed by Christians to be the Messiah whose coming was prophesied in the Old Testament. The biblical account in the Gospel of Luke (2:21) relates that "When eight days were accomplished for the circumcising of the child, his name was called Jesus, which was so named of the angel before he was conceived." As set forth in the Old Testament Book of Genesis (17:9–11), the rite of circumcision was given to Abraham as a token of the covenant that Jehovah had made with him and his descendants, the Hebrew people.

It was after the date of Christmas, commemorating the birth of Jesus, was fixed for the last month of the year (see December 25) that the Christian church began to observe January 1, the supposed anniversary of his circumcision, as a feast day. First observed by the Roman church in the sixth century or earlier, the celebration was adopted in England by the Anglican church in 1549, after it had broken with Rome.

In the United States today, Christ's circumcision is commemorated by the January 1 feast, observed by the Protestant Episcopal, Lutheran, and Eastern Orthodox churches. It is known under various designations. Until implementation of the calendar reform approved in 1969, Roman Catholics similarly observed this day, ranked as a Class I feast, as the Octave of the Birth of Our Lord, Circumcision of Jesus. According to the revised Roman Catholic calendar, now in effect, however, Roman Catholics presently mark the day as the Solemnity of Mary, the Mother of God (see January 1, Solemnity of Mary), thereby emphasizing – in line with the Eastern traditions of the church – the Marian aspect of this commemoration on the octave day of Christmas. Ranked as a "solemnity," the feast is still a holy day of obligation for all Catholics. Episcopalians know the occasion as the Feast of the Circumcision of Christ or as the Feast of the Holy Name of Our Lord Jesus Christ. Lutherans commemorate January 1 as the Feast of the Circumcision and the Name of Jesus.

Many Eastern Orthodox churches observe the day, which they call the Feast of the Circumcision of Our Lord, on January 1 in accordance with the Gregorian calendar, which now is generally followed by the Greek and many other Orthodox churches. Some Eastern Orthodox churches, however – among them some Russian churches outside Russia – observe the Feast of the Circumcision 13 days later in accordance with the Julian or Old Style calendar. For Eastern Orthodox Christians (and for those Byzantine rite Catholics in unity with the Roman Catholic church), January 1 is also the Feast of St. Basil the Great, the fourth century Greek Father of the Church who died at Caesarea in Cappadocia on January 1 in the year 379. In the West, Roman Catholics used to celebrate the Feast of St. Basil on June 14 (a date that the mid-ninth century Martyrology of Odo had erroneously held to be the day of his ordination); according to the newly revised Roman Catholic calendar, however, they now commemorate St. Basil together with another Greek Father of the Church, Gregory Nazianzen, on January 2.

The commemoration of the circumcision of Jesus, of course, differs from church to church. Scripture readings, however, customarily include the passage from Luke cited above. The collect (brief prayer) specified for this day in *The Book of Common Prayer* of the Protestant Episcopal church is as follows:

Almighty God, who madest thy blessed Son to be circumcised, and obedient to the law for man; Grant us the true circumcision of the Spirit; that, our hearts, and all our members, being mortified from all worldly and carnal lusts, we may in all things obey thy blessed will; through the same thy Son Jesus Christ our Lord. *Amen.*

The former Roman Catholic Feast of the Circumcision placed emphasis on the fact that the individual Christian enters into God's new alliance with man through baptism in the name of Jesus, just as Jesus entered into God's covenant with Abraham in submitting to the Jewish ritual of circumcision.

The Emancipation Proclamation

It was during the Civil War that President Abraham Lincoln issued his historic Emancipation Proclamation on January 1, 1863. In it the President declared that all slaves within those states and parts of states then in rebellion against the authority of the federal government "are, and henceforward shall be, free." The President had announced his intention to issue such a proclamation the previous fall (see September 22), in the ill-founded hope that some of the slaveholding Confederate states would have laid down their arms before the January 1 deadline.

Since the Emancipation Proclamation applied only to areas not controlled by the federal government, it had little immediate practical effect. Its long-range effects, however, were major. It broadened the purpose of the war, which the federal government previously saw purely as a struggle to preserve the federal Union. Now the fighting was viewed as not only for union, but also for human freedom. The broadened goal enlisted the ardor of those who opposed slavery and won friends abroad for the Union cause. Britain and France, both wavering earlier, were deterred from recognizing the Confederacy.

Any lingering doubts about the constitutionality of the Emancipation Proclamation, which had been put forward by the President as a war measure, were removed in 1865, when the 13th Amendment to the Constitution, abolishing slavery throughout the United States, was declared effective (see December 18). The text of the proclamation that preceded it on January 1, 1863 (with the introductory section omitted), is as follows:

Now, therefore, I, Abraham Lincoln, President of the United States, by virtue of the power in me vested as Commander-in-Chief of the Army and Navy of the United States in time of actual armed rebellion against the authority and government of the United States, and as a fit and necessary war measure for suppressing said rebellion, do, on this first day of January, A.D. 1863, and in accordance with my purpose so to do, publicly proclaim for the full period of one hundred days from [September 22, 1862] . . . order and designate as the States and parts of States wherein the people thereof, respectively, are this day in rebellion against the United States the following, to wit:

Arkansas, Texas, Louisiana (except the parishes of St. Bernard, Plaquemines, Jefferson, St. John, St.

Charles, St. James, Ascension, Assumption, Terrebonne, Lafourche, St. Mary, St. Martin and Orleans, including the city of New Orleans), Mississippi, Alabama, Florida, Georgia, South Carolina, North Carolina and Virginia (except the forty-eight counties designated as West Virginia and also the counties of Berkeley, Accomac, Northhampton, Elizabeth City, York, Princess Anne and Norfolk, including the cities of Norfolk and Portsmouth) and which excepted parts are for the present left precisely as if this proclamation were not issued.

And by virtue of the power and for the purpose aforesaid, I do order and declare that all persons held as slaves within said designated States and parts of States are, and henceforward shall be, free; and that the Executive Government of the United States, including the military and naval authorities thereof, will recognize and maintain the freedom of said persons.

And I hereby enjoin upon the people so declared to be free to abstain from all violence, unless in necessary self-defense; and I recommend to them that, in all cases when allowed, they labor faithfully for reasonable wages.

And I further declare and make known that such persons of suitable condition will be received into the armed service of the United States to garrison forts, positions, stations, and other places, and to man vessels of all sorts in said service.

And upon this act, sincerely believed to be an act of justice, warranted by the Constitution upon military necessity, I invoke the considerate judgment of mankind and the gracious favor of Almighty God.

January 1, the anniversary of Lincoln's final Emancipation Proclamation, is the date that generally has been regarded as Emancipation Day. Sometimes September 22, the anniversary of Lincoln's preliminary Emancipation Proclamation, is marked instead. In various parts of the country certain other days have been observed as Emancipation Day. Black citizens in Texas, for example, celebrate June 19, the date in 1865 when General Robert S. Granger, in command of the military district of Texas, issued a proclamation notifying the slaves that they were free. Emancipation Day has been noted in some states on the anniversary of their adoption of the 13th Amendment to the Constitution; in others, on the date when they abolished slavery. Thus the anniversary of emancipation has been marked, from time to time, on such varying dates as May 22, May 29, May 30, June 19, August 2, August 4, August 8, September 12, September 22, and October 15, as well as on January 1.

In ordinary years, commemoration of emancipation, on whatever date, is apt to be sporadic, depending on local initiative. However, the centennial of Lincoln's historic document in 1963 was the occasion for major widespread celebration. Many activities were specifically designed to mark the 100th anniversary year of the Emancipation Proclamation.

In January, representatives of the country's three major faiths, Protestant, Roman Catholic, and Jewish, met in Chicago at the National Conference on Religion and Race, which was instrumental in enlisting many of the nation's religious leaders for active roles in the still-unfinished business of achieving equality for all.

Many prominent black Americans were among the guests of President John F. Kennedy at a White House reception timed to coincide with Lincoln's birthday. The reception was highlighted by the presentation of a report by the US Commission on Civil Rights, which detailed progress toward equality in the century since Lincoln's proclamation.

The Century of Negro Progress Exposition, produced by the American Negro Emancipation Centennial Authority, was held in Chicago from August 16 to September 2. With support from various federal departments, a number of states, several foreign governments, and more than 100 business firms, the exposition traced the history of black Americans and stressed fields in which they had made particularly notable contributions. An opening-day event was the issuing of a special US postage stamp commemorating the Emancipation Proclamation. It showed broken chains, in black, silhouetted against a bright blue background.

If the chains were broken, however, they were not completely shed. Some other events of the 1963 centennial year emphasized the fact that in 100 years of freedom, the black citizen had yet to achieve full equality.

In an effort to achieve for everyone those "certain unalienable Rights" of which the Declaration of Independence had spoken, advocates of civil rights began in the mid-1950s to utilize picketing, sit-ins, "freedom" bus rides, mass meetings, boycotts, prayer demonstrations, protest marches, and other forms of nonviolent demonstration to fight discrimination and hasten desegregation. The chief (though far from only) spokesman for the movement in this early phase was the Reverend Martin Luther King Jr. (see January 15). Dr. King, later a winner of the Nobel Peace Prize, borrowed heavily from the precepts of civil disobedience enunciated by Thoreau and perfected by India's Mahatma Gandhi.

Starting in December of 1955 with the successful, year-long boycott launched by Dr. King to desegregate the buses of Montgomery, Alabama (see December 1), the demonstrations came in the wake of the delays in compliance that followed the 1954 Supreme Court decision ordering the desegregation of schools and, by extension, other public facilities (see May 17). As the protests brought a measure of success, including the desegregation of a number of public facilities, the demonstrations were focused on one carefully chosen community after another — including Birmingham, Alabama. There what began as a modest demonstration in the spring of 1963 swelled to massive proportions after police took harsh measures to repress the demonstrators. These methods included the use of attack dogs, high-powered fire hoses, and mass arrests. The situation in Birmingham set off a chain reaction across the nation, with demonstrations taking place in literally hundreds of cities. In the 10 weeks after an uneasy truce was established in Birmingham on May 8, the Department of Justice reported a coast-to-coast total of 758 demonstrations; and nearly 200 instances of desegregation in public accommodations were reported in one six-week period.

The summer of protest, which marked the 100th anniversary year of the Emancipation Proclamation, came to a climax on August 28, 1963, when 200,000 persons joined in a biracial March on Washington for Jobs and Freedom — by far the largest demonstration that had ever been seen in the nation's capital. With the rallying cry of "Freedom Now!" and the theme song "We Shall Overcome," the march had the support of civil rights, religious, labor, and other groups. One of its aims was to garner support for what became the 1964 Civil Rights Act (see July 2), then under consideration by Congress.

The marchers' destination was the Lincoln Memorial. There before the likeness of the man who had penned the Emancipation Proclamation 100 years before, Martin Luther King Jr. capped the day's other addresses with what is remembered as his "I Have a Dream" speech, telling how much remained to be done before emancipation was complete and ending with a dramatic peroration:

Five score years ago, a great American, in whose symbolic shadow we stand, signed the Emancipation Proclamation. This momentous decree came as a great beacon light of hope to millions of Negro slaves who had been seared in the flames of withering injustice. It came as a joyous daybreak to end the long night of captivity.

But one hundred years later, we must face the tragic fact that the Negro is still not free. One hundred years later, the life of the Negro is still sadly crippled by the manacles of segregation and the chains of discrimination. One hundred years later, the Negro lives on a lonely island of poverty in the midst of a vast ocean of material prosperity. One hundred years later, the Negro is still languished in the corners of American society and finds himself an exile in his own land. So we have come here today to dramatize an appalling condition.

In a sense we have come to our nation's Capitol to cash a check. When the architects of our republic wrote the magnificent words of the Constitution and the Declaration of Independence, they were signing a promissory note to which every American was to fall heir. This note was a promise that all men would be guaranteed the unalienable rights of life, liberty, and the pursuit of happiness.

It is obvious today that America has defaulted on this promissory note insofar as her citizens of color are concerned. Instead of honoring this sacred obligation, America has given the Negro people a bad check; a check which has come back marked "insufficient funds." But we refuse to believe that the bank of justice is bankrupt. We refuse to believe that there are insufficient funds in the great vaults of opportunity of this nation. So we have come to cash this check — a check that will give us upon demand the riches of freedom and the security of justice. We have also come to this hallowed spot to remind America of the fierce urgency of *now*. . . . *Now* is the time to rise from the dark and desolate valley of segregation to the sunlit path of racial justice. *Now* is the time to open the doors of opportunity to all of God's children. *Now* is the time to lift our nation from the quicksands of racial injustice to the solid rock of brotherhood. . . . 1963 is not an end, but a beginning. . . .

But . . . we must forever conduct our struggle on the high plane of dignity and discipline. We must not allow our creative protest to degenerate into physical violence. Again and again we must rise to the majestic heights of meeting physical force with soul force. . . . We cannot turn back. . . . I say to you today, my friends, that in spite of the difficulties and frustrations of the moment I still have a dream. It is a dream deeply rooted in the American dream.

I have a dream that one day this nation will rise up and live out the true meaning of its creed: "We hold these truths to be self-evident; that all men are created equal."

I have a dream that one day on the red hills of Georgia the sons of former slaves and the sons of former slaveowners will be able to sit down together at the table of brotherhood.

I have a dream that one day even the state of Mississippi . . . will be transformed into an oasis of freedom and justice.

I have a dream that my four little children will one day live in a nation where they will not be judged by the color of their skin but by the content of their character.

I have a dream today.

I have a dream that one day the state of Alabama, whose governor's lips are presently dripping with the words of interposition and nullification, will be transformed into a situation where little black boys and black girls will be able to join hands with little white boys and white girls and walk together as sisters and brothers.

I have a dream today.

I have a dream that one day every valley shall be exalted, every hill and mountain shall be made low, the rough places will be made plains, and the crooked places will be made straight, and the glory of the Lord shall be revealed, and all flesh shall see it together.

This is our hope. . . . With this faith we will be able to hew out of the mountain of despair a stone of hope. With this faith we will be able to transform the jangling discords of our nation into a beautiful symphony of brotherhood. With this faith we will be able to work together, to pray together, to struggle together, to go to jail together, to stand up for freedom together, knowing that we will be free one day.

This will be the day when all of God's children will be able to sing with new meaning

> My country 'tis of thee,
> Sweet land of liberty,
> Of thee I sing:
> Land where my fathers died,
> Land of the Pilgrims' pride,
> From every mountainside,
> Let freedom ring.

And if America is to be a great nation this must become true. So let freedom ring from the prodigious hilltops of New Hampshire. Let freedom ring from the mighty mountains of New York. Let freedom ring from the heightening Alleghenies of Pennsylvania!

Let freedom ring from the snowcapped Rockies of Colorado!

Let freedom ring from the curvaceous peaks of California!

But not only that; let freedom ring from Stone Mountain of Georgia!

Let freedom ring from Lookout Mountain of Tennessee!

Let freedom ring from every hill and molehill of Mississippi. From every mountainside, let freedom ring.

When we let freedom ring, when we let it ring from every village and every hamlet, from every state and every city, we will be able to speed up that day when all of God's children, black men and white men, Jews and Gentiles, Protestants and Catholics, will be able to join hands and sing in the words of the old Negro spiritual, "Free at last! free at last! thank God almighty, we are free at last!"

First National Flag

In an act crucial to the cause of American independence, the Second Continental Congress on June 15, 1775, chose George Washington (see February 22) as general and commander in chief of the Continental army. Although the actual nomination of Washington was made by Thomas Johnson of Maryland, the idea originated with an earlier speech by John Adams. The delegate from Massachusetts urged the Congress to accept as an army the colonial forces then besieging the British at Boston, and to name without further delay a general who might preserve the colonists' precarious hope of obtaining redress for their grievances against the British motherland.

For that high command, as Adams recalled in his autobiography, he hinted unmistakably to the Congress that he

. . . had but one gentleman in . . . mind . . . a gentleman from Virginia . . . well known to all of us, a gentleman whose skill and experience as an officer, whose

. . . great talents, and excellent universal character would command the approbation of all America, and unite the cordial exertions of all the Colonies better than any other person in the Union.

The suggestion was direct enough to send the always modest Washington, who was attending the Congress as a delegate from Virginia, scurrying from the room while the matter was discussed. After the Congress had voted to adopt the besieging army and unanimously approved Washington as general and commander in chief, the Virginian accepted "the momentous duty" with thanks, but he added characteristically: ". . . lest some unlucky event should happen . . . I beg it may be remembered . . . that I this day declare with the utmost sincerity, I do not think myself equal to the Command I am honoured with."

Declining any pay except reimbursement for expenses, Washington left Philadelphia, where the Congress was meeting, on June 23. Arriving at Cambridge, Massachusetts, just across the Charles River from Boston, he officially took command of his untrained, ill-equipped, ragamuffin force of some 16,000 men on July 3, 1775. In the ensuing months, most of his energies were devoted to equipping and training this raw force, strengthening discipline, and securing longer enlistments than the initial brief commitments, which had found recruits departing inopportunely.

As the months went by, Washington acquired weapons and ammunition, and shaped his unseasoned militiamen into something that resembled a coordinated fighting force. Finally, on January 1, 1776, he was ready to officially proclaim the formation of the Continental army, issuing this announcement from his headquarters at Cambridge. The occasion called for a flag that would serve as the Continental colors, and one of Washington's choosing — which he referred to as the Union Flag — accordingly was hoisted, "in compliment to the United Colonies," as he expressed it. The historic flag-raising took place at Washington's direction, but not in front of his Cambridge headquarters, as has been stated erroneously. Rather, the ensign was raised at a nearby location, atop Prospect Hill in what is now Somerville, Massachusetts, but was then part of Charlestown. The flagstaff, which had served as a liberty pole and flown a red flag, was a 76-foot schooner mast. The site is marked today with a granite memorial tower and observatory, and an inscription pointing out that "from this eminence on January 1, 1776, the flag of the United Colonies . . . first waved defiance to a foe."

The flag had 13 horizontal stripes of alternating red and white, representing the 13 colonies, with the corner (now occupied by 50 stars) bearing a blue canton with the crosses of St. George and St. Andrew. The canton is thus a small version of the British flag then in use. Although Washington had called his army's ensign the Union Flag, others would refer to it by other names — the Great (or Grand) Union Flag, the Continental Flag, the Congress Flag, and, misleadingly, the Cambridge Flag, among others. But the most widely used and best remembered of this early standard's names was the Grand Union Flag.

It is possible that this first flag of the Continental army was not new at the time of the historic flag-raising of January 1, 1776. The same design may have been in use — first, possibly, aboard ship — in the fall of 1775. There is uncertainty as to its exact origins. And there is no evidence to prove that it was, as sometimes alleged, the design of a congressional committee that had met with Washington at Cambridge in October 1775 to consider problems related to organizing an army.

In any event, though Revolutionary soldiers would march under a variety of colonial, regimental, and company flags, the Grand Union flag, which served as the first ensign of Washington's army — the Continental colors — flew over forts and at sea and was a national banner of important symbolism. Gaining rapidly in popularity, it appeared throughout the colonies during 1776 and 1777. It was, in effect, the first national American flag, even though there is no record that the Congress ever designated it so officially.

The first appearance of the Grand Union flag caused some confusion because of the appearance of the British colors in its canton. Indeed, the British in Boston at first mistook it for a signal of colonial compliance with the British monarch's most recent speech calling on the colonists to lay down their arms and submit to British authority. From the colonists' point of view, however, inclusion of the British standard was appropriate enough, especially as it was offset by the 13 red and white stripes of the United Colonies. Although the battles of Lexington and Concord, and of Bunker Hill, had taken place the previous spring (see April 19, Patriots' Day; June 17, Bunker Hill Day), the Declaration of Independence still was six months away (see July 4). As the canton containing the British ensign reflected the colonies' loyalty, however strained, to the motherland, so the 13 stripes reflected their determination that their grievances be redressed. It was not yet conclusively known that what had already begun was the American Revolution.

It was under the flag hoisted at what is now Somerville, Massachusetts, on January 1, 1776, that the Continental army and the colonies would go forward toward freedom. Not until nearly a year after the Declaration of Independence was this first national flag replaced by another — the Stars and Stripes — which had the distinction of being officially designated as the national flag by Congress in June 1777 (see June 14, Flag Day).

The New Year in Mobile

There was a spontaneous and impromptu celebration of the new year in Mobile, Alabama, in 1831, out of which developed many of the Carnival customs of Mobile and other southern cities. On New Year's Eve, Michael Kraft and a few other festive citizens of Mobile dined at a famous Creole restaurant where the wine flowed freely. On their way home in the early morning of New Year's Day, they passed a hardware store belonging to one of their group. Rakes, scythes, gongs and cowbells were hanging outside to indicate what was for sale within. These were seized and the merrymakers visited the houses of numerous sleeping citizens, where they made all the racket possible with the gongs and rakes and other implements. As the man of each house appeared to beseech them to stop the din, he was forcibly impressed into the ranks of the serenaders and compelled to assist in the noisy sport. The last house to be visited was that of the mayor. He recognized the men and invited them in for breakfast.

The next year a large group of revelers — who meanwhile had organized themselves into a mock society called the Cowbellion de Rakin — dined at the same Creole restaurant and again in the early morning serenaded the town with every device that could be used for noisemaking. The third year, the celebration was organized in advance and those taking part were masked.

The annual hilarity grew more elaborate as time went on. The "Cows," as they were called, marched on foot until 1840. That year, however, they departed from mere marching to produce their first complete pageant, Heathen Gods and Goddesses. Two years later, some of the younger "Cows" formed a second mystic society, which they called the Strikers Independent Society. It was followed by a third group, the TDS, organized in 1846. From then until the Civil War, and subsequently, the three mystic societies annually brightened Mobile on New Year's Eve with a parade followed by a tableau and dance for members and guests. The celebration as such came to an end in 1880, when the Cowbellions and the TDS were absorbed by the Strikers — who dropped the parade, though they still hold a gala ball on New Year's Eve.

In the meantime, however, Mobile's New Year festivities had given rise to the elaborate parades that today are a principal part of the Mardi Gras observances in New Orleans and Mobile and, to a lesser extent, elsewhere (see February 10, Shrove Tuesday). Although New Orleans had been the scene of flamboyant Mardi Gras celebrations during the years when the Mobile societies were being formed, there was no established series of parades on Mardi Gras Day itself. It was in 1857 that a group of Mobile Cowbellions went to New Orleans and collaborated with several of that city's residents in forming the Mystic Krewe of Comus, which put on the first of New Orleans' now-famous, float-filled Mardi Gras street pageants that year.

The Philadelphia Mummers' Parade

For sheer sustained gaiety, no annual event in the nation surpasses the New Year's Day perennial known officially as the Philadelphia New Year Shooters' and Mummers' Parade. The flamboyant procession, with its fantastic costumes of silk, satin, and plumes, its cavorting clowns, and the lilting, foot-tapping banjo melodies that are its hallmark, continues from early morning through most of the day, and is known not only to Philadelphia residents and the thousands of foreign or out-of-state visitors who journey to Philadelphia for the occasion, but also to the millions of television viewers throughout the country who also hear the assembly's contagious tunes and watch the strutting, merrymaking marchers in all their festive finery.

According to its historians, the Mummers' parade in Philadelphia had dual origins, deriving both from the traditional Swedish way of welcoming the New Year and from the old English mummers' play of the holiday season. The Swedes, who had settled in what is now Delaware in 1638 (see March 29), expanded their colony up the Delaware River, and in 1643 established the first permanent European settlement in present Pennsylvania — on Tinicum Island at what is now Essington, just below Philadelphia. The Swedish settlers remained as a nucleus even when Swedish control of the colony was displaced, in 1655, by the Dutch — who in turn were dislodged by the English in 1664. The formal founding of Philadelphia took place at the behest of William Penn (see October 24), who arrived in the colony in 1682.

From the beginning, the Swedish settlers and their descendants had an influence disproportionate to their small numbers. Apart from the log cabin, which is perhaps their best-known gift to the New World, the Swedes bequeathed to Philadelphians a holiday celebration that began on Christmas Eve and extended through the week until the New Year. Roaming bands of masqueraders and merrymakers marched about the countryside making sport for everyone.

The English families, who arrived later, brought with them the traditions of the Mummers' play with St. George killing the dragon — and all the concomitant attention to costumes. After the American Revolution, Philadelphians substituted President George Washington for St. George. Along with him, in the company of players, was a character known as Cooney Cracker. Few details of this mummery have been preserved, but it is known that the first two lines of Washington's speech were:

> Here am I, great Washington!
> On my shoulders I carry a gun.

As soon as the character representing Washington had said this, Cooney Cracker interrupted with:

> Here comes I, old Cooney Cracker!
> I swear to God my wife chews terbacker!
> A pipe is good; cigars are better;
> When I get married, I'll send you a letter.

And there was a character representing the devil who performed various antics.

Apart from appearing in this Americanized version of the Mummers' play, Mummers — their ranks swelled by a growing number of costumed persons — marched informally about the city, as the Swedish and English traditions of holiday gaiety merged. Mostly, the bands of Mummers were not organized and consisted of small groups of masqueraders parading within the neighborhood of their homes. An account of the way they were treated appeared in the records of an old Quaker family, as quoted in J. Thomas Scharf and Thompson Westcott's three-volume *History of Philadelphia, 1609–1884:*

It was considered the proper thing in those days to give the leading mummer a few pence as dole, which, in the language of the present time, they would "pool" and buy cakes and beer. It was also regarded as the right thing to do to invite them into the house and regale them with mulled cider or small beer, and homemade cakes. It was considered a great breech [sic] of . . . etiquette to address or [otherwise] recognize the mummer by any other name than the name of the character he was assuming. I remember a little girl who, . . . all . . . curiosity . . . , had discovered a neighbor's boy in the party; and with childish impetuosity she broke out with, "Oh, I know thee, Isaac Simmons! Thee is not George Washington!" This departure from the proprieties of the occasion was made the subject of comment on many returning holidays.

Meanwhile, still another custom was developing — that of "shooting" in the New Year. Particularly in the southern part of the city, bands of men and boys went about making all the din possible, by shouting and by shooting off guns. The favored ammunition varied, but it included blank cartridges and, at least during one period, powdered bottle glass, which was supposed to produce an especially loud report. In due time, the "shooters," as they were called, donned fancy costumes like the other masqueraders.

Philadelphia's more ebullient citizens reportedly celebrated the New Year with shooting and parading for many years before the beginning of the 19th century. A local resident's diary entry took note of the custom: "1781 — January 1 — Firing guns in the night, before day sundry kinds of music . . . paraded the Streets, as they came our way."

The commotion was not always popular, particularly with the city's more proper residents, and there were arrests of celebrating citizens from time to time. Indeed, from 1808 to 1859, masquerades and, by association, the custom of mumming, were technically illegal. The law was more successful, however, in suppressing the masquerade balls which had become popular at the beginning of the 1800s than in quashing the informal processions of mummers through the streets. Indeed, there is little evidence that the law was enforced in the latter regard, although it may have served as a temporary damper. While the law was in effect newspapers gave no specific descriptions of mumming, but they did refer to "great turnouts" and the air of "a festival" pervading the city on New Year's Day. Military parades were not unusual, and the day was further enlivened by the Dutch-originated custom of "visiting," the antecedent of today's common open house, on New Year's Day.

It seems clear that city officials also ignored the New Year "shooting" during the same period. The *United States Gazette* for January 2, 1839, reported that the New Year had been greeted ". . . with the usual demonstration of respect for the parting and coming year. Little men and great boys burnt powder, and kept up a regular 'popping' out of doors. . . ." As far as "shooting" was concerned, only one pertinent entry appeared in the Daily Occurrences Docket of the Walnut Street Prison between 1808 and

1859: "Firing off the Old Year — Two individuals were fined . . . by the Mayor. . . ."

Like fire in a peat bog, the custom of holiday mumming, however it may have been dampened temporarily, seems always to have persisted to some degree and eventually to have resumed in full. Certainly, the custom was alive and well in the years following the Civil War. As for the "shooters," their name is perpetuated in the name of the organization that officially sponsors today's annual gala New Year's Day procession: the Philadelphia New Year Shooters' and Mummers' Association.

The beginning of the parade in its present form was on January 1, 1876, the centennial year of the adoption, in Philadelphia, of the Declaration of Independence. The Silver Crown New Year's Association had been organized a short time before and was the first of the large societies that later participated in the celebration. The report of the 1876 parade appeared in the *Public Ledger*, among other paragraphs, under the heading "Local Affairs":

On New Year's Day the weather was as uncomfortable as usual lately, but it seemed to have little or no effect on the spirits of our citizens who crowded the streets and made the city very lively during the entire day and evening. The Fantasticals or "Shooters" were out in force during the whole day and caused much boisterous amusement. Indians and squaws, princes and princesses, clowns, columbines and harlequins. . . . Minstrel hall [figures in blackface] . . . , Chinese and burlesque Dutchmen, bears, apes and other animals promenaded the streets to the music of the calethumpian cowbell or the more dignified brass bands, and kept up the racket until late at night. Independence Hall was the grand objective for them all, and the old building received many a cheer and serenade, both burlesque and serious. In the middle of the day several of these parties united in one grand parade and made quite a striking display.

But the parade was not yet organized, as is evident from a description of the Mummers in an article in *Scribner's Magazine* for July 1881 by Maurice F. Egan, a Philadelphian, later US minister to Denmark, who wrote:

On New Year's Eve crowds of men and boys dress themselves in fantastic costumes and roam through the Neck [a name given to a district in . . . South . . . Philadelphia] and lower part of the city all night. This custom, doubtless a remnant of the old English Christmas "mumming," grows year by year in Philadelphia, and the mummers, becoming bolder, penetrate as far north as Chestnut Street.

As the system of individual parades went on from year to year, the number of clubs formed to participate in the annual merriment grew.

Fancy capes for captains are said to have made their first appearance in 1889. Reportedly, the same year also saw the introduction of what today is the parade's most popular feature — the string bands whose strutting members march, dance, cavort, drill, and cakewalk up Broad Street to their own inimitably infectious music.

The mummers were not formally recognized by the city government until the parade of 1901. They then received permits for their parade and 42 clubs, multiplied to that number since the formation of the Silver Crown twenty-five years earlier, combined their forces and paraded together on Broad Street, where the mummers still march. The newspapers, however, did not regard the parade of enough importance to describe it on the front pages. A report did appear, though, on the inside pages of one paper:

For two hours yesterday, almost to a minute, the official section of Philadelphia, represented by the public buildings, was given over to mummery so fantastic that the shades of the staid Quakers, who gave it its sobriquet, must have cloaked themselves in their winding sheets and stalked to bournes more sedate. Beneath the eyes of William Penn, at the very knees of Stephen Girard, about the Reynolds statue, three thousand men and boys in outlandish garb frolicked, cavorted, grimaced and whooped, while the Mayor and members of Councils, Judges and other officials, State and municipal, looked on, laughed and applauded. How many thousands of ordinary citizens did the same no one can compute. The grand plaza about the City Hall and the streets converging were choked with people — a healthy, clean and orderly congregation. The city had put its official seal upon mummery, the lawmakers were there as sponsors and directors and from the windows of the courts of justice wives and daughters of the Judges viewed and enjoyed the scene.

Prizes of money were given by the city for the best costumes, comic and otherwise, and for the best bands and most amusing antics. It was agreed that "Philadelphia saw on the first day of the 20th century a procession that Momus himself could not have devised." The parade was led by the Silver Crown New Year's Association. Its members were dressed in elaborate costumes, and in this fancy dress division were also the Golden Crown Association, the George A. Furnival Association, the Elkton Association, and the John F. Slater Association. The comic division included other associations known as the Hardly Ables, the Early Risers, the Mixed Pickles, the White Turnips, the Katzenjammer Band, the White Caps, the Energetic Hoboes, the Red Onions, the Ivy Leaf, the Corinthians, the Half and Half, and the Cucumbers.

By 1930, the parade had become a big-time affair, elaborate in costume and widened in appeal. That year there were 12,000 marchers, an estimated 300,000 spectators, and prizes amounting to $30,000 (a figure later more than doubled). By the 1960s, the parade had grown to such proportions that it took between five and eight hours to wind through the city. By January 1, 1964, when portions were nationally televised for the first time, spectators numbered in the millions. Except in years when bad weather has caused postponement of the parade — usually until the following Saturday — the televising of excerpts, announced by TV celebrities, has continued to be an annual event. In 1975, some 16,000 marchers participated in the parade's customary three divisions — comic, fancy, and string band.

The costumes worn by members of the clubs in the fancy dress division, and especially those of the club presidents, remain the fantastic and elaborate affairs they had become by the 1930s — boasting extravagantly decorative headdresses of ostrich or marabou feathers, and embroidered capes of satin, silk, brocade, or lamé that extend, in some cases, as much as 20 or 30 feet behind the wearers and are supported, when necessary, by scores of pages; indeed, the costumes worn by some participants compete for attention even with the floats which also are part of today's parades. In the comic division, current events and men and women in the public eye are burlesqued. However, one long-traditional part of the merrymaking, the appearance of minstrel clowns in blackface make-up, was protested by civil rights groups in 1964 and no longer has had a prominent place since then. The Mummers' splendor of dress extends to the clubs in the string band division, whose members, like those in other divisions, choose a different theme each year and often invest thousands of dollars in their costumes.

In 1975 a total of 24 clubs took part in the three divisions of what is probably the most joyful of all the nation's better-known New Year observances. Performances of an annual Show of Shows Mummers' String Bands concert by groups that have taken part in the parade customarily follow in February at Philadelphia's Civic Center.

Pasadena Rose Bowl Football Game

One of the foremost collegiate sports events of the year is the football game that was initially arranged as an attraction to supplement the annual New Year's Day Tournament of Roses at Pasadena, California (see January 1, Pasadena Tournament of Roses). Frequently imitated since, what now is known as the Rose Bowl game has been played in Pasadena's Rose Bowl since that huge structure was completed in 1922. Until then, the games took place at Tournament Park in Pasadena.

The first game was played in 1902, when the University of Michigan football team, on a barnstorming tour in the West, was invited to play Stanford University. The score was 49 to 0 in favor of the University of Michigan. (This score was matched in 1948 when Michigan beat Southern California 49 to 0, the highest score ever made in the Rose Bowl.) A chariot race was substituted for the football game in 1903 and continued as the afternoon attraction until January 1, 1916, when the games became an annual event. In 1923 the Rose Bowl, a great stadium now enlarged to seat 104,700 (and on occasion more) persons, was dedicated at the game between Southern California and Pennsylvania State College. After the Rose Bowl was completely paid for, it was deeded to the city of Pasadena.

Originally the championship team of the Pacific Coast Conference, the western contender in the game, simply invited the eastern contender from among the teams that had made the best records during the season. Things became somewhat more specific in 1946, when it was decreed that the winning team in the Big 10 Conference would be the one to confront the Pacific Coast Conference champion in the annual Rose Bowl classic. Since then, there have been other changes, so that today's contenders are: the Big 10 champion and the Pacific 8 Conference champion.

The Rose Bowl, which was the first of the big collegiate "bowl" games, became the prototype for many others. The most important of these — the Orange Bowl in Miami, the Cotton Bowl in Dallas, and the Sugar Bowl in New Orleans, all instituted during the 1930s — are, like the Rose Bowl, televised nationally on New Year's Day (or Eve).

Pasadena Tournament of Roses

The Pasadena, California, Tournament of Roses has been called the world's greatest parade and the description may be merited. Certainly, it is the most widely viewed. Since the late 1960s, curbside viewers have totaled approximately 1.5 million each year. But this is as nothing compared with the more than 125 million in the United States and abroad who watch the proceedings on television (live or taped).

Today's Tournament of Roses procession is perhaps most famous for its approximately 60 floats, of the most intricate design, which are completely covered with fresh flowers and bear an assortment of celebrities and beauty queens and princesses from many places. The floats are interspersed with more than 20 marching bands, which have been invited to participate, and with a notable array of about 200 prize-winning horses and their richly costumed riders. The championship horses are decked with lavish silver trappings, which have been valued at close to $3 million.

The elaborate floats, blanketed with roses, orchids, carnations, chrysanthemums, and dozens of other blooms, are keyed each year to the parade's central theme. In keeping with the Bicentennial of the American Revolution, for example, the themes in 1976 and 1975 were America, Let's Celebrate! and Heritage of America, respectively. In 1975 the individual floats represented everything from symbols of liberty — the US flag, the Declaration of Independence, the Liberty Bell — to noted historic figures — Washington, Lincoln, the Pilgrims — to historically significant events and places — the first Thanksgiving, the Lewis and Clark expedition, the California gold rush, the Oregon Trail and the pioneers who traversed it. There have been innumerable parade themes over the years. Poems, dreams, fairy tales, legends, history, romance, fantasies, books, familiar sayings, famous firsts, headlines, motion pictures, festivals and holidays have all had their moments in the limelight as parade themes. Certain subjects have recurred more often than others. One is music. In a recent parade, when the tournament theme was The Joy of Music, many of the floats depicted individual songs, from "Rhapsody in Blue" and "Parade of the Wooden Soldiers" to "Bridge Over Troubled Waters" and "Stairway to the Stars" — the last made out of a star-studded, floral piano keyboard. Still more ambitious was the floral portrayal of "Winter Wonderland," which showed two children building a snowman, and a romantic couple in a horse-drawn sleigh, crossing a picturesque stone bridge that spanned a frozen stream — all against a background of falling snow and trees graced with giant snowflakes. Even more intricate was the float providing a floral representation of the song "Meet Me in St. Louis," which showed buildings of the city and a trolley car pulled by eight Clydesdale horses.

Children, too, appear repeatedly in parade themes. In one recent year the theme, titled officially Thru the Eyes of a Child, provided the parade with scope for great variety, with floats depicting fairy-tale and other characters from children's literature, various fanciful creatures, children's playthings, or simply things children like to look at, eat, or do. Activities such as blowing bubbles and flying kites over rooftops were given floral portrayals, as were (to sample at random) Punch and Judy, a sweet shop, animal crackers, a dragon, Raggedy Ann and Andy, an apple for the teacher, and Cinderella in her coach, drawn by six white ponies.

In earlier years, travel and related subjects provided the parade theme in several different years, as when the themes were officially designated as Holidays Around the World, Travel Tales in Flowers, and Around the World with Flowers. With the subject matter of the parade varying each year, adventure, Western lore, space, and the home attractions of participating states and cities all have proved to be rich lodes for topics at one time or another.

Whatever the theme of a particular year, its execution is never less than lavish. All told, today's Tournament of Roses parade — which keeps the floatmakers busy working, and blanket-wrapped spectators busy waiting, all the night before — is five and a half miles in length.

It is a far cry from the first Tournament of Roses, held in Pasadena by the Valley Hunt Club on January 1, 1890, at the suggestion of Charles Frederick Holder, a naturalist and author of many books on natural history. Holder was born in Lynn, Massachusetts, in 1851. He served for five years as associate curator of zoology at the American Museum of Natural History in New York and in 1885 went to Pasadena to become a teacher of zoology. Among other things, he was a traveler and lecturer. In 1886, Holder's travels included southern France, where he saw the renowned Battle of Flowers, one of the French Riviera's extravagant celebrations, and well calculated to remind a newcomer that the southern California climate also produced flowers in midwinter. After his return to Pasadena, he suggested to the members of the Valley Hunt Club that on January 1 they decorate their carriages with flowers and drive them over a prearranged route, and that this parade be followed by athletic events. In a letter, Holder wrote that the first parade ". . . consisted of a long line of carriages beautifully decorated with natural flowers, and . . . I am told, [it] was the finest thing of the kind ever seen . . . in this country or in Europe. . . ."

The Valley Hunt Club had charge of the tournament for several years and bore the cost of it, but when it became so elaborate that the cost was burdensome to the members, the Tournament of Roses Association was formed to take charge of the celebration. Holder's original intention was to arrange "an artistic celebration of the ripening of the oranges" at about the beginning of the year, and New Year's Day was chosen as a date when people were free to celebrate.

The tournament passed through several stages in the course of its development. At first it was merely a parade of decorated private carriages, followed by athletic events. Then floral floats were entered for a parade in the morning, with a chariot race or football game in the afternoon, and a ball in the evening. Prizes for floats and for chariot race winners were presented at the ball, over which a queen of the tournament presided. In 1902, the afternoon program consisted of a football game between the University of Michigan and Stanford University.

The following year the first amateur chariot races were run. The winner was awarded $750, while several others in the race received smaller prizes. After four or five years, professional drivers were employed and the prizes were made larger. Burlesque races between burros were added. But interest in the professional chariot races gradually died out and they were abandoned. In 1916, the afternoon football game (see January 1, Pasadena Rose Bowl) took the place of the races.

With the increase in population of the city, the annual parade grew larger from year to year. In 1920 it was two and a half miles long, and it was estimated that more than 1.5 million blossoms were used to decorate the floats. On January 1, 1935, the floats stretched over more than four miles of streets and no one tried to estimate how many millions of blossoms were used, but the Russian Firebird — the float of the Tournament of Roses Association, on which the queen of the tournament rode — was said to contain 250,000 blossoms. The Firebird was fashioned from thousands of yellow chrysanthemums and lavender sweet peas. Behind this bird were three Russian churches made of pink, white, and lavender stocks and sweet peas. The domes were made of yellow pompon chrysanthemums. This float led the procession, the grand marshal of which was Harold Lloyd, the silent film star. (More recent grand marshals have included former President Dwight D. Eisenhower in 1964; Chief Justice Earl Warren in 1955; Vice President Richard M. Nixon in 1953 and 1960; the Apollo 12 astronauts in 1970; and baseball great Henry "Hank" Aaron in 1975, to cite at random.) The Russian Firebird was followed by flower-bedecked automobiles containing the city officials of Pasadena, Los Angeles, Long Beach, and Glendale. A float representing the "bird of paradise," entered by Los Angeles, led the second division. Borne on the float was the city's queen, sitting between two birds of paradise made of blossoms representing their natural colors. In front of the queen were three white floral cranes, standing among talisman roses and maidenhair ferns. Portland, Oregon, was represented by a float showing Cinderella on a coach made of heather, sweet peas, and white carnations surrounded by pink roses. A scene from the opera *Martha* was the subject of the float entered by Los Angeles County. Glendale had a float representing the mythical roc, with a 25-foot wingspread of blue delphiniums. Its beak was of yellow pompons and its crest of poinsettias. The San Diego Metropolitan Water Commission's float, called the River of Destiny, showed Boulder Dam and the Colorado River in blue delphiniums surrounded by mountains of heather and colored pompons. Notable floats in the other divisions represented the legend of King Arthur; a scene from *A Midsummer Night's Dream*; the Hawaiian legend of the sacrifice to Pele, with the volcano Kilauea belching forth poinsettia flames; a 60-foot floral sea serpent and a 25-foot floral pelican. There were 64 floats in all, representing various cities, business corporations, schools and universities. In their wide range of subjects, ambitious depictions, meticulous detail, and exclusive use of fresh flowers, the floats of 1935 were similar to today's, except for a certain amount of streamlining and the increased use of mechanical animation in recent years.

In addition to the afternoon Rose Bowl football game, today's Tournament of Roses parade is followed by a two-day postparade show at Pasadena's Victory Park, where nearly 800,000 persons customarily view the parade floats before the fragile blossoms fade and all is dismantled.

The letdown does not last long, however, because the designing of new floats begins in mid-April — right after announcement of the theme for the next year's Tournament of Roses.

Paul Revere's Birthday

Paul Revere, craftsman, industrialist, patriot of the American Revolution, was born in Boston on January 1, 1735, son of the French Huguenot refugee Apollos De Revoire (or Rivoire). From his father, who anglicized the family name so that "the Bumpkins should pronounce it easier," young Revere learned the silversmith's craft. He read the books on metallurgy of his time, turned out superior work, and was regarded by at least one visiting authority as the only American then knowledgeable in his field. His silver, including the famous Revere bowl, which is widely copied today, is still admired as art. But Revere, a man of apparently prodigious energies, also manufactured surgical instruments and false teeth, sold spectacles, and carved frames for the portraits of John Singleton Copley.

Revere was a member of the politically influential North End Caucus Club, and the acknowledged leader of Boston's mechanic class, from which he was able to supply enthusiastic

volunteers in the colonies' budding efforts to shake off British rule. His emphatic patriotism also was revealed in his work as an engraver, including the cartoons and drawings that made him a leading anti-British propagandist. One of these, his inaccurate but politically effective drawing of the Boston Massacre of 1770 (see March 5), has been described as probably the most famous print in America. In 1773 Revere was one of a committee of three chosen to suggest what form the protest against local sale of British tea should take. The result, a spectacular rebuff to the British, in which Revere participated with 50 other workingmen disguised as Indians, went down in history as the Boston Tea Party (see December 16).

These and other political activities brought him into close contact with such pre-Revolutionary leaders as Samuel Adams (see September 27) and John Hancock. Revere played an important role as the Boston Committee of Safety's main express rider and as official courier for the defiant Massachusetts Provincial Assembly. Soon after the Boston Tea Party he was in New York, apprising local Sons of Liberty of the event. In the spring of 1774, he went by horseback to New York and Philadelphia with an appeal for help in protesting the Boston Port Bill, which threatened ruin for North America's second-largest port. He also carried to the Continental Congress, meeting in Philadelphia, the Suffolk Resolves, a stirring declaration on American rights, subsequently endorsed by the Congress, which outlined measures for defiance of the "Intolerable Acts" of 1774. In December of the same year, he rode off for New Hampshire, where he warned local patriots of British plans for removing a valuable store of munitions from Portsmouth's Fort William and Mary. His message precipitated the colonists' first aggressive act, a raid in which John Sullivan and his men captured the fort's arms and gunpowder. As things turned out, the captured munitions were used — six months later — against the British at the battle of Bunker Hill (see June 17).

During the years of agitation that preceded the American Revolution, Revere's stocky figure was seen galloping across the countryside so frequently that his name even began to appear in London newspapers. This was before his most famous ride of all, however, on April 18, 1775, to warn of an impending British march on Lexington, Massachusetts (where John Hancock and Sam Adams were staying) and Concord, Massachusetts (where the colonists had stored military supplies). A famous poem by Longfellow memorializes the ride, as well as Revere's arrangement with confederates to signal the British approach by hanging lanterns in Boston's North Church steeple — "One if by land, and two if by sea; / And I on the opposite shore will be, / Ready to ride and spread the alarm / Through every Middlesex village and farm." Revere was 40 when he mounted a stout workhorse for the mission. With this forewarning, the colonists were not surprised by the arrival of British troops the next day. The resulting incident marked the beginning of the American Revolution (see April 19, Patriots' Day).

Revere served the Revolution by building a powder mill that helped supply colonial troops with ammunition. More actively, he also served as a lieutenant colonel, but his military career — most notably the command of strategic Castle William in Boston Harbor — was pale beside some of his other endeavors. After hostilities had concluded with independence for the colonies, he became an importer and an increasingly prosperous industrialist. With his sons, he cast hundreds of church bells, some of them notable for their beauty. After long experimenting, he established at Canton, Massachusetts, what became an important mill for the manufacture of sheet copper. It produced the sheathing for the dome of the Massachusetts State House in Boston, and for many US ships, among them the *Constitution*. He also worked with inventor Robert Fulton in making copper boilers for steamboats.

Revere was portrayed by John Singleton Copley as a shirt-sleeved young man with dark reddish-brown hair, strong face and hands, and a look of thoughtful determination; and by Gilbert Stuart as a still-energetic old man. Both portraits are in Boston's Museum of Fine Arts, which also houses the finest collection of Revere's silver. For many years before his death, on May 10, 1818, Revere and his family lived in Boston's North Square, in a two-story frame house originally built in the 1670s. Boston's oldest frame house, containing many of Revere's tools and personal possessions, it has been restored and is open to the public today. The square is the heart of Boston's North End, a section known in Revere's day for the turbulence and independence of its politically active residents. In 1964, the city spent $20,000 restoring the square's 18th century aura with old paving blocks, brick sidewalks, and gas lamps. Also on view in Boston is Cyrus Dallin's bronze statue of Revere astride his galloping horse — in Paul Revere Mall, next to the historic Old North Church, where the lanterns were hung on the night of his most famous ride.

Solemnity of Mary

According to the recently revised Roman Catholic calendar, January 1, which used to be observed by Roman Catholics as the Octave of the Birth of Our Lord, Circumcision of Jesus (see January 1, Feast of the Circumcision), is now listed as Solemnity of Mary, the Mother of God. It is classed as a "solemnity" (equivalent to the former Class I feast) and is a holy day of obligation for all Catholics. The change was made in order to reemphasize the Marian aspect of the commemoration of the octave day of Christmas, which had long been a tradition, especially in the Eastern church. An eighth century manuscript refers to January 1 as the Birthday of St. Mary, while the church office for this day contains antiphons, responses, and prayers honoring Mary's divine maternity. The new feast supersedes the former feast of the Maternity of Mary, which had been listed for October 11. However, among Eastern Catholic churches united with the Roman Catholic church, the Byzantine and Syrian rites honor the Blessed Virgin's motherhood on December 26, whereas the Coptic rite commemorates it on January 16.

JANUARY 2

Georgia Ratifies the Constitution

On January 2, 1788, Georgia became the fourth state to ratify the US Constitution. Like Delaware and New Jersey before it, Georgia sanctioned the new frame of government by the unanimous vote of a specially elected convention. Georgia, founded in 1733, was the youngest of the colonies, and its action was not so crucial to the Constitution's viability as the approbation of such states as Pennsylvania (which had been second to ratify) or Massachusetts (which would be sixth); but it did mark another important step along the path to stronger national government.

When the Continental Congress called for a Constitutional Convention to meet in May 1787, the Georgia legislature appointed six delegates to represent its interests at the Philadelphia meeting. Former Governor George Walton and Nathaniel Pendleton either declined to serve or failed to attend the Philadelphia caucus, and their absence reduced to four the size of the contingent. These men had commissions that authorized them to take whatever steps appeared necessary to render the Articles of Confederation adequate to meet the requirements of the Union.

Abraham Baldwin was the son of a Connecticut blacksmith who went heavily into debt in order to educate his children. The young Baldwin graduated from Yale in 1772, studied theology, and taught divinity at his alma mater until 1779. He then entered the army and served as a chaplain until the conclusion of the War for Independence. Baldwin, who studied law during his military service, moved to Augusta, Georgia, in 1784, won a seat in the state legislature, and served two terms in the Continental Congress. Baldwin sponsored a bill to establish Franklin College, now the University of Georgia, and became the first president of that institution.

William Few was the son of a poor Maryland farmer who moved to North Carolina during the boy's early years. Debts eventually destroyed the family farm, and William Few moved to Georgia in 1776. After the American Revolution Few began educating himself in the study of the law and he won a seat in the state legislature as well as election to two terms in the Continental Congress. A self-made man, Few was still a farmer of modest means in 1787.

William Houstoun was a young member of Georgia's emerging planter aristocracy. Some of his relatives had been high royal officials during Georgia's colonial period, and William Houstoun attended the Inner Temple in London to study law. At the outbreak of the American Revolution, Houstoun returned to Georgia and became a staunch patriot. Houstoun, who combined the practice of law with the ownership of a plantation, was the wealthiest member of the Georgia delegation, but he lacked liquid capital and had heavy debts. William Pierce, another Georgia delegate, said of Houstoun, "Nature seems to have done more for his corporeal than mental powers. His person is striking, but his mind very little improved with useful or elegant knowledge."

William Pierce was the fourth member of the Georgia delegation. Born, probably in Georgia, about 1740, he served with distinction in the Revolution and emerged from the army in 1783 as a major with special citations and a sword from Congress. After the war Pierce became a merchant engaged in the import-export business. Pierce, who was a member of the Continental Congress, created a series of witty and perceptive character sketches of the members of the convention, but declined to describe himself. Instead he left evaluation of his personality to "those who may choose to speculate on it,

to consider it in any light their fancy or imagination may depict." Pierce left the convention in mid-July to go to New York in a futile attempt to save his sagging business fortunes; he went bankrupt in 1788 and died in debt in 1789.

Georgia was a prosperous state during the 1780s. Its population doubled during the decade, as did the volume of exports from its port at Savannah. Georgia owned a large expanse of western territory, and in the convention usually aligned itself with the larger states. Not surprisingly, Georgia — a state in which black slaves formed an important element of the labor force and of the population — voted against any constitutional interference with the slave trade and suggested in vain that blacks be counted equally with whites for purposes of allotting representatives.

Abraham Baldwin, the most able member of the Georgia delegation, perhaps saved the convention from collapse during the heated debate over the nature of representation in the upper and lower houses of the national legislature. On July 2, the delegates voted on a proposal to give each state equal representation in the upper house. Initially five states voted in the affirmative, and six states, including Georgia, voted in the negative. Baldwin, who feared that the small states might leave the convention in protest, decided to change his ballot to produce a tie vote with five states in favor of the proposal, five states opposed to it, and the Georgia delegation equally divided. Faced with this situation, the convention named a committee, which eventually worked out a compromise suitable to both large and small states.

The Constitutional Convention ended on September 17, 1787. In October, a copy of the proposed frame of government reached Georgia for its consideration. The legislature, in emergency session to prepare the state for imminent attack by the Creek Indians, called for a ratifying convention to meet in Augusta on Christmas Day. In the elections for delegates to the convention, which took place in the first week of December, friends of the Constitution won a sweeping victory. Georgians looked upon the proposed new government as their best hope of assistance in their continuing frontier Indian wars, which threatened the very existence of the state.

Georgia's ratifying convention met as scheduled on December 25, 1787. The delegates, who included 2 physicians, 2 lawyers, 3 merchants, 10 planters, 3 small farmers, 3 frontiersmen, 1 full-time public officeholder, and 2 other delegates about whom little is known, spent approximately one week in formal proceedings. Then on January 2, 1788, the convention voted unanimously to adopt the Constitution. To celebrate the occasion, the Georgians fired a cannon salute of 13 shots, 1 for each of the 13 states.

Georgia, like the other colonies that separated from Great Britain, became a unit of the United States in 1776 with the issuance of the Declaration of Independence. As a matter of convenience, however, historians have established the chronology in which states entered the Union in terms of the order of their ratification of the Constitution. They accordingly describe Georgia as the fourth state to join the Union.

JANUARY 3

Alaska Admitted to the Union

Alaska — the region once known as Russian America (see October 18, Alaska Day) and then derisively tagged as "Seward's icebox" before its riches were glimpsed (see March 30, Seward's Day) — became a state on January 3, 1959. More than twice the size of Texas, which had long enjoyed its rank as the nation's largest state, the country's new giant and northernmost outpost was the 49th state to be admitted to the Union.

The region, long a stepchild of absentee governments — first of Russia and then of the United States, which purchased it in 1867 — was hampered in its development by the remoteness of those who controlled it even after it achieved territorial status in 1912. It was difficult for the Congress in Washington to keep in the forefront of its collective mind the day-to-day realities of survival in Nome.

Beginning in 1916, when the first bill for statehood was introduced; in the 27 succeeding years when emphasis shifted to attempts to strengthen Alaska's territorial government; and after 1943, when a bill for statehood was again presented to Congress, there were attempts to form a government more responsive to local needs. The idea of statehood, which Congress debated exhaustively in 1950, was kept alive throughout the decade.

In 1956, a constitutional convention was called by Alaska's territorial legislature. The resulting draft constitution was approved by a vote of the populace in April 1956.

Statehood followed after another period of long discussion between proponents of statehood, who favored local control, and opponents, who thought that higher taxes or loss of federal subsidies might result. Finally, after the US

Senate on June 30, 1958, gave an overwhelming 64 to 20 vote in favor of admission, President Dwight D. Eisenhower on July 7 signed the Alaskan statehood bill and it was declared that he would release a formal proclamation announcing Alaska's admission sometime during the next year. The official recognition of Alaskan statehood came with Eisenhower's declaration of January 3, 1959.

This was immediately followed by an executive order directing the addition of a 49th star to a new US flag that was to become official on Independence Day, July 4, 1959. But the new, 49-star flag had already become obsolete by July 4, 1960, for by then Hawaii had been admitted as the nation's 50th state.

Battle of Princeton

After the defeat of the British at Trenton, New Jersey, in December 1776 (see December 26), Washington returned to the Pennsylvania side of the Delaware River. On the night of December 30–31, however, he moved his men back to the New Jersey side of the river, determined to strike the enemy again. Meanwhile Lord Charles Cornwallis, the British commander in New Jersey, had his own ideas for smashing *his* enemy. Blessed with a superior force of almost 8,000 men and with more expected from Princeton, he took up a position confronting Washington. The American commander, with a smaller force of some 5,000 patriots, stood with his back to the river, prevented from retreating across it both by a lack of sufficient boats and by ice in the river.

To both the British and the American officers, the situation of Washington's Continentals on the night of January 2 looked desperate. Cornwallis, convinced that the American rebels were cut off from escape, delayed action until morning. Washington and his fellow officers looked for a way out of their trap. At an emergency council of war, they made a daring decision. Instead of attempting to retreat, and instead of waiting for Cornwallis's impending attack, they would move forward, slipping north of the enemy lines to attack the British strongholds of Princeton and, they hoped, New Brunswick.

Leaving their campfires burning, with a few brave men to stoke them and keep up a clangor of activity during the night, the main American force, with gun wheels muffled, silently set forth on its desperate trek at 1:00 A.M. on January 3, 1777. In the darkness, it was as much a stumble as a march, over a barely cleared, stump-studded, newly opened back road, but it led them, undetected, around and behind the British left. After they reached a point not far from the Stony Brook bridge on the outskirts of Princeton at about sunrise on January 3, Washington sent General Hugh Mercer with about 400 men to destroy the bridge, a vital link on the main road from Princeton to Trenton. Near their goal, Mercer and his men were sighted by two British regiments under Lieutenant Colonel Charles Mawhood, en route from Princeton to Trenton, where they were to join Cornwallis's main force. In the ensuing bloody melee, the Americans relied on their slow-loading rifles and the British on a devastating bayonet charge. General Mercer was fatally wounded and his men thrown into panic, fleeing in all directions with the British in hot pursuit.

However, Washington, mounted on a white horse and careless of his own safety, dashed from group to frightened group, encouraging, bolstering, urging. Thus rallied, his force of regulars and militia, supplemented now by new arrivals, routed the British. Some of the enemy survivors fled by a roundabout way to Trenton, although most made for the British supply headquarters at New Brunswick. Entering Princeton, the Americans quickly subdued a small British detachment occupying Princeton University's Nassau Hall.

There was no time to tarry, however, especially since Cornwallis, with his main force at Trenton, undoubtedly realized what had happened and could be expected to arrive in Princeton at any moment. Casting a regretful eye in the direction of the tempting British stores at New Brunswick, Washington abandoned his hopes of taking that center and withdrew abruptly, out of the probable British path. When Cornwallis did arrive — "in a most infernal sweat — running, puffing and blowing and swearing at being so outwitted," as the American Brigadier General Henry Knox later gloated — it was too late for pursuit of the vanished Americans.

The battle of Princeton is regarded as being of strategic importance. Together with the patriot success at Trenton a week earlier, it had a galvanizing effect on American Revolutionary morale. Restoring hope in a cause that had seemed almost lost, it stimulated enlistments and, as the British pulled back their farthest outposts, left New Jersey largely free of British troops. Washington, for his part, moved inland to a position of strength on the high ground of Morristown, where his ragged army rested and was replenished over the rest of the winter.

Today the scene of the heaviest fighting of the battle of Princeton is the site of a 40-acre state park. A memorial arch on its western border marks the burial place of unknown American soldiers of the Revolution. The conflict is further commemorated, almost too graphically, by the Princeton Battle Monument, where Nassau, Mercer, and Stockton streets converge. By means of Frederick MacMonnies' bas-relief, it freezes in limestone the moment of General Mercer's bayoneting.

Nearby on Stockton Street is Morven, the official residence of the governor of New Jersey, which served as Cornwallis's headquarters for a time in 1776 and later was host to such distinguished guests as Washington, Lafayette, and Rochambeau.

JANUARY 4

Feast of St. Elizabeth Ann Seton

Elizabeth Ann Seton, a 19th century pioneer in providing parochial education and charity for the sick and poor, was the first native-born American declared a saint. She was canonized during 1975, which was being observed as a Holy Year by the Roman Catholic church, according to the Catholic tradition of marking such a year once each quarter century. Canonization of the new saint, whose feast day is January 4, coincided with the UN-designated observance of 1975 as International Women's Year, and with the Vatican's designation of September 14 — the day she was declared a saint — as Woman's Day. Although not by official design, the canonization of the first American-born saint also coincided with the 1975–1976 celebration of the bicentennial of the American Revolution.

So great was the number of persons wishing to attend the canonization ceremony that it was held in the great square in front of St. Peter's Basilica in Rome. For the occasion, between 100,000 and 120,000 persons — among them 16,000 Americans, including US prelates and representatives of Mother Seton's Sisters of Charity — crowded the vast plaza between the twin arms of Bernini's curved colonnade on September 14, 1975. Paul VI presided over the open-air ceremony, which was part of a two-hour mass. After the formal proclamation of her sainthood, the pope gave his homily in English: "Yes, venerable brothers and beloved sons and daughters," he stated in part, "Elizabeth Ann Seton is a saint!"

The elevation of Mother Seton to sainthood was the culmination of a long process, including acceptance by church authorities of claims of miraculous cures. The effort originated in the order of nuns she founded and was taken up by James Cardinal Gibbons (see July 23). He lent his advocacy to her cause in 1882, marking the beginning of an organized effort on behalf of her sainthood. Following decades of biographical and other investigation by church authorities, Pope Pius XII in 1940 formally requested that the Vatican pursue her cause. After further preliminary actions she was beatified, that is, declared blessed – the step preceding canonization – by Pope John XXIII on St. Patrick's Day, March 17, 1963. Since a vote of the National Conference of Catholic Bishops in November 1971, her feast day has been included in the liturgical calendar for all Roman Catholic dioceses in the United States, to be celebrated as a "memorial" on January 4, the date of her death in 1821.

In her lifetime, "the mother of the American Church," as she sometimes was called, founded the first native religious community for women in the United States; laid the foundation of the American Catholic parochial school system; and opened orphan asylums, which were the forerunners of hundreds of modern foundling homes and child-care centers. Although Mother Seton died before she could start the hospital she had long dreamed of establishing, her order of nuns accomplished her dream a few years after her death. Today there are hundreds of such hospitals, many of them – as well as schools and foundling homes – run by her Sisters of Charity. The order specializes in teaching as well as in nursing and orphan care. Among its institutions are the New York Foundling Hospital in New York City, one of the largest of its type in the world, which celebrated its 100th anniversary in 1969, and the well-known St. Vincent's Hospital, also in New York City.

Elizabeth Ann Bayley was born in New York City to Episcopalian parents on August 28, 1774 – two years before the beginning of the American Revolution. Her father, Dr. Richard Bayley, was a respected physician who became the first professor of anatomy at Columbia University (then King's College) and the first health officer of New York City. Her mother was Catherine Charlton Bayley, daughter of the rector of St. Andrew's Episcopal Church on Staten Island. Related by birth and marriage to socially prominent New York families, Elizabeth Bayley was to meet many important and famous people in the course of her lifetime, among them George Washington, Alexander Hamilton, and John Jay. But New York City at the time had a population of only about 20,000, and the social circle in which her family moved was small and tightly knit. Her parents' second daughter, she was not yet three when her mother died. After the traditional year of mourning, her father married Charlotte Amelia Barclay,

daughter of Andrew Barclay and the former Helena Roosevelt – whose father had established the Roosevelt dynasty in America. The second Mrs. Bayley bore her husband seven children and indulged them to the neglect of his two older daughters. From the time she was eight, Elizabeth Bayley and her sister Mary accordingly lived often with relatives and friends, especially when their father was studying or working abroad, as he sometimes did for years at a time.

From her earliest years, Elizabeth Bayley showed unusually religious inclinations, which deepened and grew stronger as she grew older. People who knew her passed along anecdotes of her youthful piety. Her spiritual awareness and deep faith in God are apparent in the journals and letters she wrote throughout her life.

In 1794, Betty Bayley, as she was then known, was married to William Magee Seton. Her husband was the son of William Seton, an extremely successful businessman who, in 1784, had been appointed to the influential position of cashier of the Bank of New York. At his father's behest, young Seton, when he was only 18, had also joined the bank, which played an important role in the finances of the state and of the young American nation.

On trips to Europe before his marriage, William Magee Seton had traveled to many cities, meeting bankers, importers, and exporters with whom his father had dealings. Acquainted with members of the devout Roman Catholic Filicchi family of Leghorn (Livorno), Italy, he became fast friends with Filippo Filicchi and his brother Antonio, who later were to play a vital part in the life of Elizabeth Seton. From time to time, the Filicchis traveled on business to America, where they, too, knew most of the important politicians, bankers, and merchants of the eastern seaboard. One acquaintance, President Washington, appointed Filippo Filicchi – who had married Mary Cowper of Boston – American consul general at Leghorn, a post he held for four years, until 1798. Apart from such notables as Thomas Jefferson, James Madison, and John Adams, the Filicchis boasted at least one acquaintance not known to the Setons. This was Bishop John Carroll (see November 6), the first Roman Catholic bishop in the United States. Bishop Carroll was also to prove influential in Elizabeth Seton's later life.

The marriage of Elizabeth and William Magee Seton was an extremely happy and affectionate union, although William Seton was afflicted, from the beginning, by tuberculosis. They had many good friends, a lovely house, five children, and a glittering social life. Elizabeth Seton flowered amid the affection and security she had lacked as a child. Even in this happy period, her dedication to the poor was a force in her life and she helped a devout Protestant Scotswoman to organize the Widows' Society of New York to help needy widows and orphans. For her tireless work with the sick and poor, Elizabeth Seton, still in her early twenties, became known as the Protestant Sister of Charity.

The death of her father-in-law in June 1798 was to change the Seton family's whole way of life. As the oldest son, her husband, William, now became head of the family and of the family business — at a time when misfortunes seemed to pile one on top of the other. Because they now were responsible not only for themselves, but also for the seven younger children of the father-in-law's second marriage, they had to move from their small home to a larger one. Illness added to their woes. William Seton contracted yellow fever during an epidemic; and Elizabeth Seton and her second son, born July 20, 1798, were both sickly. Her father, with whom she had been especially close, died in 1801. As tragedies multiplied, Seton ships were seized by pirates and the firm's business interests in Germany and England failed.

During this dismal period, Elizabeth Seton drew daily strength from her religion and eagerly anticipated Sunday worship services, which she attended at Trinity Episcopal Church. There she met one of the most influential people in her life — the Episcopalian minister John Henry Hobart, who arrived at Trinity in 1801 as a 25-year-old curate. Struck by her religious fervor, he gave her religious instruction and support.

By 1803, William Seton's already poor health had been so much worsened by calamitous business losses, and then bankruptcy, that a sea voyage was planned — more as a way to delay death than as a cure. Leaving their four smallest children to the care of relatives and friends, the Setons and their oldest daughter, Anna, sailed from New York on October 2, 1803, bound for Italy and a visit with their friends the Filicchis.

On their arrival in Leghorn on November 18, 1803, they heard more grim news. Word of the yellow fever epidemics in New York had reached Italy and, as a protective measure, the Setons were not allowed to join their waiting hosts but had to remain in the Lazzaretto — a windswept place of detention for sick persons. For the next month, Elizabeth Seton nursed her dying husband in virtual isolation. The Filicchis brought food and as much comfort as they could without passing through the iron gates. When the Setons were released on December 19, William Seton had to be carried out. He died on

December 27, 1803, in Pisa and was buried in Leghorn.

Before he died, William Seton had arranged with their ship's captain to take his wife and daughter back to New York. But the captain himself postponed the late January sailing date. When it got under way a few weeks later, the ship, caught by a storm and damaged while still in the harbor, was forced to return to Leghorn for repairs. When it finally was ready to sail, the child, Anna, was seriously ill with scarlet fever and the captain could not risk the delays of quarantine for his ship by taking her aboard.

All this time, the Setons had been the welcomed guests of the Filicchis, and were impressed with the kindness and religious fervor of the whole family. Antonio and his brother Filippo both discussed the Roman Catholic faith with Elizabeth Seton, and Antonio's wife, Amabilia Filicchi, took her to visit churches and attend religious services.

Finally, in April 1804, the Filicchis were able to get passage for the Setons, and it was decided that Antonio Filicchi should accompany them on the 56-day voyage back to New York. Family and friends were there to welcome them home when they arrived on June 4. The homecoming was a day of great joy, even though the widowed Elizabeth Seton knew she was facing a completely different life — one dependent on charity — to bring up her family of five children. With the Seton fortune long gone, she had fallen from social eminence; and with her announcement that she might become a Roman Catholic, she found she was not even socially acceptable. Anti-Catholic bigotry was rampant in the predominantly Protestant New York City of that day, with the "right" people going to the "right" (non-Catholic) church. Accordingly her friends and relatives turned away, some immediately, some after trying to dissuade her from taking this step. Perhaps the hardest loss was the friendship of her former minister, John Hobart.

However, a few people did offer her financial assistance in spite of their antipathy toward her religious leanings. John Wilkes, one of her benefactors, arranged for her to take in as lodgers 20 boys enrolled in a new school. In this way, it was thought that she could support her family and keep it together.

The arrangement was not to last long, however. Elizabeth Seton was received into the Catholic church on March 14, 1805, at St. Peter's Church on New York's Barclay Street. News of this and fear that she would convert their sons to Catholicism made most parents withdraw their sons from her influence.

Once again the Filicchi family came to her

aid, giving her money and moral support in visits and letters. They also wrote their Catholic friends — laymen and priests — in other American cities, explaining her plight. In moments of religious crisis, her correspondence with these unmet friends sustained her.

Antonio Filicchi, still traveling in the United States on business, looked into schools for Elizabeth Seton's two boys, William and Richard. She had considered going to Montreal, where she would have more religious freedom than in New York. However, thoughts of Canada faded in 1806, when the boys finally were placed in a Catholic school — Georgetown, now Georgetown University, which Bishop John Carroll, the Filicchis' friend, had founded in Washington, D.C.

By 1808 Elizabeth Seton's situation in New York City had worsened and she was literally desperate. Providentially she was then invited to open a school for girls in Baltimore, where more than half of all US Catholics then lived. This meant she would have a means of livelihood and could be with her three daughters and near her sons. In addition, it was a step closer to the religious life that she had been contemplating for some time.

The invitation had come from Father William Dubourg, a Sulpician priest who had founded St. Mary's Seminary in Baltimore in 1791. The oldest Catholic seminary in the United States, St. Mary's of Paca Street was closed in 1969, but two of its buildings are preserved: the Mother Seton House, where St. Elizabeth Ann Seton began her first school; and the chapel, dedicated by Bishop Carroll in 1808 and renovated in 1968.

When Elizabeth Seton started her school, she had a total of seven students — her own three daughters and four other girls. Soon, however, other students came and young women volunteered to assist in the school duties. On June 2, 1809, four of these women joined her in dedicating themselves to the service of God. Although only Mrs. Seton was bound by religious vows at that time, they all wore the cape and cap that, until recent years, were universally worn as the religious habit of the American Sisters of Charity. The costume, which some of the sisters still wear, was, in fact, the standard attire once worn by widows in Italy — which Mrs. Seton had worn since her husband's death there. Bishop Carroll had approved of her desire to live in a religious community and had permitted her to remain the legal guardian of her children at the same time. Otherwise, the American Sisters of Charity might never have come into being.

In June 1809 Elizabeth Ann Seton was appointed Mother of the community and school she had founded. Living according to a religious rule given her by Bishop Carroll, she moved with her own three daughters as well as other followers to Emmitsburg, a village in northwestern Maryland about 50 miles from Baltimore. There, in 1812, the women adapted and adopted the religious rule which had been given to the first Sisters of Charity by St. Vincent de Paul in France in the 17th century. The motto that guided those first Sisters of Charity — The Charity of Christ Urges Us On — is engraved in Latin on Mother Seton's rosary, which is preserved at Emmitsburg today. Mother Seton and 16 sisters took their vows on July 19, the Feast of St. Vincent de Paul, in 1813, and became the first native religious community of women founded in the United States.

Once settled in Emmitsburg, Mother Seton trained her band of nun-teachers, and she herself prepared textbooks for use in her schools — the original private school and other free schools that she opened for children of the poor in the area. Her plans and accomplishments laid the foundation for the American parochial school system. Also in 1809, she founded St. Joseph's College for women in Emmitsburg, which is still administered by the Sisters of Charity.

The number of girls in her community grew and for their religious guidance and training Mother Seton translated religious books from the French and wrote several spiritual treatises. Retaining her dedication to the sick and poor, which had prompted her earlier nickname, the Protestant Sister of Charity, she visited the needy and afflicted in the area and converted many, principally blacks, to Catholicism.

She sent her Sisters of Charity to open an orphanage in Philadelphia in 1814 and one in New York City in 1817. Today, many hundreds of Mother Seton's Sisters of Charity under separate provinces or motherhouses serve in both North and South America and in foreign missions.

After a long illness, Mother Seton died on January 4, 1821, at the age of 47. She was buried in Emmitsburg, near the 15 sisters and novices who had died during the early years of her young community. She was survived by more than 50 sister-members of the community and by her two sons and one daughter. (The oldest and youngest of her three daughters had died before her in 1812 and 1816 respectively.)

Beatified on March 17, 1963, by Pope John XXIII, who referred to her as the "flower of American piety," Mother Seton became Blessed Elizabeth Ann Seton. With the canonization ceremonies held in Rome on September 14, 1975, she became known as Saint Elizabeth

Ann Seton. The first church named in her honor is in Shrub Oaks, Westchester County, New York.

In 1965, Robert Gaspari's seven-foot-high white marble statue of Mother Seton was installed above the portal of the Mother Seton Shrine in the new Our Lady of the Rosary Church at 12 State Street in Manhattan. From its place at the shrine — next door to what was once William and Elizabeth Ann Seton's last home in New York City — the statue looks out over New York Harbor. The 150th anniversary of Mother Seton's death was marked on January 3 and 4, 1971, with special commemorative services at the Chapel of St. Joseph's Provincial House of the Daughters of Charity in Emmitsburg, Maryland, and at an ecumenical service at Trinity Episcopal Church in New York City (to which she had belonged before her conversion to Catholicism). She was further honored 200 years after her birth, when Governor Marvin Mandel of Maryland issued a proclamation declaring 1974 as Seton Bicentennial Year and stating that "the first native-born citizen of the United States to be proclaimed Blessed . . . has brought honor to her country and to this state by her exemplary practice of the virtues proper to her many roles as daughter, wife, mother, religious, educator and ecumenist." When Mother Seton was canonized on September 14, 1975, some 35,000 pilgrims flocked to the Emmitsburg headquarters of her order, where six masses honoring the new saint were said that day.

Utah Admitted to the Union

On January 4, 1896, Utah became the 45th state to enter the Union. Its settlement by members of the Church of Jesus Christ of Latter-Day Saints, unofficially known as the Mormons — who to a large extent still dominate the state — contributed greatly to the uniqueness of Utah's history.

Archeological evidence unearthed in Utah's caves and cliff dwellings sheds some light on the area's early habitation by prehistoric people and such Indian tribes as the Ute, Paiute, and Shoshone; but on the whole, knowledge is sparse. For a considerable period before the 19th century, the area of present-day Utah, like much of the southwestern United States, was claimed by Spain. The incomplete and often vague records left by Spanish explorers indicate that a few men from Francisco Vásquez de Coronado's expedition may have crossed southern Utah in 1540. It was only in 1776, however, that the Spanish missionaries Silvestre Vélez de Escalante and Francisco Atanasio Dominguez made the first large-scale explora-

tions. Having crossed southwestern Colorado, they penetrated eastern Utah near the Grand — now Colorado — River, followed an Indian path over the Wasatch Range, and descended to Utah Lake. A section of their route later became part of the Old Spanish Trail, which stretched from Santa Fe in present New Mexico to Monterey in Alta California.

Since Meriwether Lewis and William Clark passed north of Utah during their famous expedition of 1804–1806, the first Americans to enter Utah probably were four members of the 1811–1812 overland expedition sponsored by John Jacob Astor. By the early 1820s, fur traders, lured by reports of rich beaver streams, had found their way over the rugged terrain and they rapidly depleted the fur supply between 1824 and 1830. Starting in the 1840s, California-bound emigrant trains made their way across the great salt desert. In 1846, for example, the Donner party struggled through the mountains east of the Great Salt Lake and plodded across the desert only to fall victim to heavy snows and starvation farther west. Shortly before 1847, Miles Goodyear set up the first trading post, Fort Buenaventura, at the site of present-day Ogden, thus becoming Utah's first settler.

Farther east, meanwhile, the Mormons were suffering the persecution that had already driven them from New York State to the Midwest. After the murder of their founder and prophet, Joseph Smith (see December 23), at Nauvoo, Illinois, on June 27, 1844, the Mormons turned to Brigham Young and under his leadership sought refuge far beyond the country's western frontier. In 1847, after a harrowing overland trek, they arrived in the parched and barren basin of the Great Salt Lake, where they laid out their new city (see July 24, Mormon Pioneer Day in Utah). As the Latter-Day Saints assembled, and emigrants from this country and abroad swelled their ranks, Mormon communities, settled by small congregations, spread along the western slopes of the Wasatch Range, where irrigation techniques helped to support the rapid growth in population. Although there were sporadic uprisings of local Indians until 1868, the Mormons were generally successful in warding off attacks — in line with Brigham Young's policy: "It is better to feed the Indians than to fight them."

Utah was ceded to the United States in the Treaty of Guadalupe Hidalgo of 1848, which ended the Mexican War. As spokesman for the approximately 11,000 Mormons who had settled in and near Salt Lake City by 1849, Brigham Young held a convention to organize the Latter-Day Saints' aggressive theocracy into a state under the name of Deseret, meaning "honeybee," a word found in the *Book of Mormon*. He claimed a far-flung empire, including the present states of Utah and Nevada, and parts of Arizona, New Mexico, Colorado, Wyoming, Idaho, Oregon, and California. Petitioning Congress for statehood, Young established a provisional government on March 10, 1849, and became governor in the first election.

The petition for statehood failed, however, and Deseret as originally conceived was short-lived; Congress even refused to accept its name. The bill setting up the geographically smaller Territory of Utah — the name was derived from that of the local Ute Indians and meant "people of the mountains" — was signed by President Millard Fillmore on September 9, 1850. The newly established territory consisted of what is now Utah, western Colorado, most of Nevada, and a slice of Wyoming. Brigham Young was appointed territorial governor. The first official census, in 1850, listed 11,380 persons; a decade later the population had reached 40,273.

For the Mormons, the creation of the Territory of Utah triggered innumerable conflicts, not only with the appointive officials sent by the federal government, but also with the ever-increasing influx of non-Mormons, dubbed "gentiles" by the Latter-Day Saints. The "outsiders" soon accused the Mormons of instigating Indian massacres of California-bound emigrants and spread false reports that Brigham Young had authorized the destruction of Utah's supreme court records. In the summer of 1857, President James Buchanan ordered US Army troops, commanded by Colonel Albert Sidney Johnston, to proceed to Utah territory to crush a "state of substantial rebellion." Despite preparations for active hostility, the Utah War, or Mormon Campaign, was terminated peacefully. But bad feelings and friction remained until 1890, when the polygamy issue was finally settled.

Brigham Young's final years before his death on August 29, 1877, had been marked by two struggles: the attempt to preserve Mormon polygamy and the attempt to achieve statehood for Utah. The two were closely connected, for much of the outside opposition to the Mormons came as a consequence of polygamy; and it was this very vocal opposition that prevented the government from admitting Utah to the Union, although petitions for statehood had been regularly presented to Congress since 1849.

Mormon practice of polygamy derived from a divine revelation sanctioning the practice that the prophet Joseph Smith claimed to have received on July 12, 1843. Although there was little concealment of the practice either in Nauvoo, Illinois, or later on in Utah, Smith's controversial revelation was not officially proclaimed until August 1852, when Brigham Young, as his successor, judged the community strong enough and sufficiently isolated to prevent serious consequences. But reformers such as Harriet Beecher Stowe soon linked polygamy with slavery as those "twin relics of barbarism" that must be swept from the face of the earth. After Young's death in 1877, the Reverend De Witt Talmage of Brooklyn, New York, even paused in the midst of a church service to offer a suggestion to the national government: "Now, my friends, now at the death of the Mormon chieftain, is the time for the United States government to strike. . . . Give Phil Sheridan enough troops, and he will teach all Utah that forty wives is thirty-nine too many."

But the existence of polygamy raised difficult legal problems for those legislators who desired its prohibition. The US Constitution did not prevent a man from having as many wives as he wanted. Moreover, legislation against polygamy might conceivably be interpreted as an infringement upon the constitutional guarantees of religious liberty. Antipolygamy laws were nevertheless passed: the first, in 1862, was later supplemented in 1882 and 1887. Under these statutes not only was polygamy forbidden, but the Mormon church was also disincorporated and much of its property temporarily confiscated. Vigorous prosecution was carried on in Utah, where "cohabs" (cohabiters) caught in surprise raids were heavily fined and given prison sentences. Many frustrated the investigators by seeking refuge in the winding foothills of the territory or by making "two-family houses" out of single dwellings by means of camouflage twin-entrance doors. The elderly John Taylor, who had succeeded Brigham Young as president of the church, went into hiding in 1884 and directed the church affairs from seclusion until his death in 1887.

On September 25, 1890, following the Supreme Court decision affirming the constitutionality of the antipolygamy laws, the president of the Church of Jesus Christ of Latter-Day Saints, Wilford Woodruff, issued a statement known as The Manifesto. It was not a revelation, or even an explicit retraction of the Mormons' belief in plural marriage, but merely a declaration of expediency, which read in part:

To Whom It May Concern: Inasmuch as laws have been enacted by Congress forbidding plural marriages, which laws have been pronounced constitutional by the court of last resort, I hereby declare my intention to submit to those laws, and to use my influence with the members of the Church over which I preside, to have them do likewise.

A general church conference held in October supported this move and laid the ban of excommunication on persons continuing to practice polygamy. President Benjamin Harrison granted amnesty to husbands who repudiated their extra wives.

The renunciation of polygamy cleared the way for Utah's statehood, although by the 1890s the once-vast Territory of Utah had been whittled down by the establishment of the territories of Nevada and Colorado in 1861 and Wyoming in 1868. Congress passed the enabling act in 1893; the state constitution was framed and approved in 1895; and Utah entered the Union on January 4, 1896.

JANUARY 5

Twelfth Night, or Epiphany Eve

Twelfth Night, the last evening of the traditional Twelve Days of Christmas, has been observed with festive celebration ever since the Middle Ages. Although the festivities on this occasion — feasting, revelry, pantomimes and dramas, music and dancing — gradually became customary, the date of Twelfth Night, surprisingly enough, remains ambiguous even today. According to some people, Twelfth Night means the evening before the 12th day; according to others, it means the evening of the 12th day itself. Thus both January 5, the eve or vigil of the Feast of the Epiphany, and the evening of January 6, the Epiphany (or Three Kings' Day) itself, have been and are referred to as "Twelfth Night." The one-day discrepancy in date depends upon whether one counts Christmas (see December 25) or the day following Christmas as the first of the 12 days of Christmas.

To add to the confusion, January 5 is also referred to as Old Christmas Eve. According to the Old Style or Julian calendar, Christmas, celebrating Christ's Nativity, fell on what is now January 6 — according to the New Style or Gregorian calendar in common use today. However, the inhabitants of some remote areas of the United States and Great Britain continue to believe that Jesus Christ was really born on Old Christmas Day and therefore on January 5 carry on ancient customs associated with Old Christmas Eve.

The Christian observance of the Twelve Days of Christmas, culminating with Twelfth Night, may have developed from the pagan custom of marking the natural phenomenon of the winter solstice for a number of days. The tradition was firmly embedded in Europe, especially in England, from the 11th century onwards, but reached its height during the reign of the Tudor monarchs Henry VIII (1509–1547) and Elizabeth I (1558–1603). Elaborate pageants, processions, and songfests, combined with

feasting and dancing, were planned for the pleasure of the nobility and royalty under the direction of a mock official known as the Lord of Misrule, who was assisted by his "fool" and "jester." In 1516, Henry VIII's Twelfth Night festival included a masque ball, which was described by a court historian as follows: ". . . at night, the King with XI others, wer disguised after the maner of Italie, called a maske. . . ." After a sumptuous banquet, "maskers came in with six gentlemen disguised in silke, bearing staffe torches, and desired the ladies to daunce."

The Elizabethan period saw the introduction of magnificent Twelfth Night dramatic productions. For a number of centuries miracle plays about the Three Kings had traditionally been performed at this time of year. Staged at first in church sanctuaries to illustrate the religious meaning of the coming of the Wise Men, the dramas later became so secular in tone that they were eventually banned in churches. However, not only did the custom of presenting religious dramas continue to flourish outside church confines, but the staging of secular tragedies, comedies, and historical chronicles also became a Twelfth Night feature, notably in court circles. William Shakespeare's *Twelfth Night* was probably first presented as a command performance for Queen Elizabeth I at Whitehall Palace on January 6, 1601; her successor, James I (1603–1625), had seven of Shakespeare's plays and two of Ben Jonson's performed to celebrate his second Christmas season (1604/1605) as king of England. Especially popular in the early 17th century were the Twelfth Night masques, a new form of courtly theater, which combined music and masquerade. Ben Jonson's masque *Hymen*, for example, was first performed on January 6, 1606, in a splendid court production staged by the distinguished architect Inigo Jones.

Another festive tradition that came to be associated with Twelfth Night was the *gâteau des rois*, "cake of Kings." A special cake — inside of which was usually a bean (sometimes an almond or a coin) — was baked and divided among the guests. Whoever got the piece with the bean became "king of the bean." As ruler of the merry occasion he selected a consort and commanded his "court" to feast and dance. The game was enjoyed by rich and poor alike. In jest, King Francis I of France (1494–1547) once challenged the authority of a newly chosen "bean king" by attacking his temporarily "royal" castle. The "bean king" defended his stronghold with snowballs, eggs, and apples, but in the boisterous excitement a burning chunk of wood from a fireplace was hurled and struck King Francis on the head, wounding him seriously, even though he good-naturedly declared that if he indulged in such tomfoolery as Twelfth Night, he deserved his fate. In 1563, Mary Queen of Scots participated in the selection of the "king of the bean" at Holyrood Palace in Edinburgh. Robert Herrick, the 17th century English poet, vividly described another version of the cake in which a "pea queen" was also chosen. In a poem entitled "Twelfe Night, or King and Queene" (1648), he wrote:

Now, now the mirth comes
With the cake full of plums,
Where Beane's the *King* of the sport here;
Beside we must know
The Pea also
Must revell, as *Queene*, in the Court here.

The late 17th century English diarist Samuel Pepys recorded that, having seen the "bean king" selected, he preferred to retire "leaving my wife and people at their sports, which they continued till morning, not coming to bed at all."

In the 18th century, the lavish celebration of Twelfth Night began to lose its appeal, especially in the more elevated social circles. By the 19th century, extensive observance of the occasion had practically died out even in ordinary households, although scattered remnants of the ancient festivities survived. The "cake of the Kings," for example, continued to enjoy popularity. It outlasted even a temporary change of name during the French Revolution, when, appropriately enough, it was called the "cake of equality." Today the "king of the bean" is chosen in a number of European countries, including Belgium, Portugal, England, France, Germany, and the Netherlands. At the Drury Lane Theatre in London, the cutting of the Twelfth Night cake is an annual ceremony complete with attendants in 18th century dress and wigs.

In some remote rural districts of England, the Twelfth Night merriment includes, as it did in previous centuries, bonfires, masques, and the quaint custom of wassailing the fruit trees. The local inhabitants of the cider-producing regions of the West Country, for example, carry jugs of cider to the orchards and offer toasts to the apple trees to ensure a good yield in the future. In other sections of Europe, particularly in France, Germany, and the Low Countries, young boys dress in exotic clothes and gold paper crowns to represent the Three Kings. Carrying paper star lanterns on long poles, they go begging from house to house on January 5 singing verses such as:

We are the Three Kings.
We sing and we dance,
Carrying the star

Which leads us from afar.
Kind Master and Mistress,
Please give us cakes
For this is Three Kings' Eve.

In Italy, January 5 is known as *La vigilia dell' Epifania* or the Vigil of the Epiphany. Children receive gifts, reminders of those the Magi gave to the infant Jesus. In contrast to Spain — where the gift-giving custom also prevails as part of the festivities on the eve of Three Kings' Day — the presents are not brought by the Wise Men but by the *befana*, a little old woman whose name is probably a corruption of the word Epiphany. The legend is related that when the Three Wise Men from the East were on their way to Bethlehem from Jerusalem, they passed an old woman cleaning her house. She is said to have asked them where they were going and, when they told her, to have asked them to wait until she finished her work, saying she would then go with them. The Wise Men reportedly replied that they could not wait and advised her to follow them. After the old woman had finished her work, she supposedly started out, but the Wise Men were already out of sight by then. Ever since that day, the legend continues, she has been wandering about the world seeking the child Jesus. According to the folklore of Italy, she goes down the chimneys of houses leaving gifts for the children in imitation of the gifts of the Wise Men, in the hope that at last she may find the child whom she is seeking. The same custom was once popular in Russia, where the old woman was known as *Babushka*.

The observance of January 5 as Old Christmas Eve is still part of local tradition in some areas of the West Country in England. On this evening, at midnight, the bees supposedly buzz and the animals drop to their knees to mark the birth of Jesus Christ. Also on January 5, sightseers and pilgrims journey to Glastonbury in Somerset to see what is commonly thought to be the miraculous blooming of a thorn bush. Legend holds that it is the offshoot of a staff planted there in the first century A.D. by Joseph of Arimathaea, the wealthy Israelite reported in Gospel accounts to have provided Christ with a decent burial by securing custody of his body from Pilate and placing it in his own new tomb.

Several of the Twelfth Night customs were introduced into the American colonies. The feasting and revelry flourished especially in the South, where the Christmas season was a time for joy and merriment. In 1759, for example, George Washington regarded Twelfth Night as an appropriate date for his wedding to Martha Custis. The event was marked with a yule log, firecrackers, greenery, and a sumptuous banquet. In the 19th and early 20th centuries, many secular organizations throughout the United States held Twelfth Night festivities, but the custom has rapidly dwindled. The Lotos Club of New York is one of the few places that still stages an annual Twelfth Night banquet (see January 6, Twelfth Night Revels).

Twelfth Night traditionally marks the start of the Carnival season, which ends at Mardi Gras (see February 10), the day before the beginning of Lent on Ash Wednesday (see February 11). In New Orleans, one of the few other places in the United States where Twelfth Night is still the occasion for elaborate festivities, the carnival organization known as the Twelfth Night Revelers officially opens the city's Carnival season on January 6 each year with a splendid private ball and pageant. Since the Lord of Misrule is "king" of this celebration, a "bean queen" is chosen to reign by his side. Although with these and a few other exceptions the elaborate Twelfth Night festivities of yesteryear have faded away in the United States, the eve is still considered the traditional time for removing Christmas trees and other decorative greens. In numerous communities scattered over the country, the discarded greenery is piled high and set afire as a farewell to the holiday season. Indeed, the custom of Twelfth Night bonfires, unlike the balls, banquets and pageantry, seems to have been growing in recent years.

The inhabitants of isolated sections of the Ozarks and the Atlantic coastline continue to regard January 6, Old Christmas Day, as the true Christmas and January 5 as Old Christmas Eve. Like the English West Country people, some of them take stock in the ancient legends that the bees buzz and cattle kneel at midnight on January 5.

George Washington Carver's Death

George Washington Carver, the agricultural chemist whose penchant for practical experimentation was to improve the quality of life for millions of southern farmers and others, was born, probably in 1864, of slave parents, on the Moses Carver plantation near Diamond Grove, Missouri. In devoting his life to bettering the living conditions of others, he proved himself both as a scientist and as a concerned Christian. His life became a source of inspiration for countless numbers of people.

Purchase of the site of his birth — which was established as the George Washington Carver National Monument in 1951 and formally dedicated in 1953 — was authorized by Congress in 1943. Visitors can follow a wooded trail there, passing Robert Amendola's statue of Carver as a boy, amidst the rural haunts of his youth. At the visitor center exhibits and a diorama tell of his life and work, and a demonstration garden features some of the same crops he used in his experiments. A replica of the cabin in which he was born can be seen at Greenfield Village, the museum of Americana that Henry Ford established at Dearborn, Michigan.

Carver's life began near the end of the Civil War with being kidnapped, with his mother, by a band of marauders. Tiny, suffering from exposure and ill with whooping cough, he alone was retrieved by a posse sent out by his master, Moses Carver, with a $300 racehorse as ransom. He remained frail through childhood and was at first brought up by Moses Carver and his wife, from whom he received his name, encouragement to study, and an acquaintance with spelling and the Bible. Even as a child, he showed a talent for growing things, which caused him to be called a "plant doctor." He was 10 when he struck out on his own, working at odd jobs to support himself while he went to school for two years in nearby Neosho, Missouri. He went on to Fort Scott, Kansas, and eventually to Minneapolis, Kansas, where he put himself through high school and began to earn money for college by cooking, laundering, doing odd jobs, and developing the skills of knitting, tatting, and embroidery.

In 1890 he was accepted by Simpson College in Indianola, Iowa, after he had been refused by another college. He subsisted during his first week there on the 10 cents he had left after paying his tuition: 5 cents purchased cornmeal and 5 cents suet, his diet for the week. Subsequently, he supported himself by laundering the clothes of fellow students, meanwhile living in a woodshed, and in a loft, and covering the walls of both with his own paintings.

Apart from other courses, he studied voice and piano with a Simpson art instructor, Etta Budd, whose father was head of the Department of Horticulture at Iowa State College of Agriculture and Mechanic Arts (now Iowa State University) in Ames. She encouraged him to abandon the idea of an art career in favor of scientific agriculture. When the idea took hold, Carver became a student at Iowa State, where he arrived with no material possessions. He lived there in a college office that he paid for by janitoring; earned his board by waiting on tables; covered other expenses with additional jobs; and still managed a full extracurricular program, which included YMCA membership, art, music, and study of the Bible. In his lapel he wore the flower — or sprig of ever-

31

green — that was to be a trademark for the rest of his life. After he had received his B. S. degree in 1894, he was made head of the college greenhouse and placed in charge of bacteriological laboratory work in systematic botany while he earned his master's degree in agriculture, which he received in 1896.

Soon afterwards, Tuskegee Institute's founder, Booker T. Washington (see April 5), invited him to become the first director of Tuskegee's Department of Agricultural Research. It was there that Carver, a deeply religious man who always credited his accomplishments to the inspiration of God, embarked on the projects that helped shift the South away from a single-crop economy, expanded the region's agriculture and prosperity, bettered conditions for its people, and won him international renown. Traveling through the countryside, he urged farmers to diversify their crops by planting peanuts and sweet potatoes, which would enrich the soil, instead of concentrating exclusively on cotton, which exhausted it. He then set out to find uses for the new crops.

The results of his work were astonishing. From peanuts he developed over 300 products, including milk, cheese, coffee, flour, soap, lard, cooking oils, dyes, stains, paper, plastic, insulating board, linoleum, and oils that proved effective in treating the aftereffects of infantile paralysis. From sweet potatoes he developed more than 100 products, among them starch, tapioca, molasses, breakfast foods, vinegar, ink, synthetic rubber, shoe blacking, library paste and the mucilage used on postage stamps. He derived scores of useful products from pecan nuts, and many others from soybeans. From the clays of Alabama he extracted face powder and pigments for paints. From wood shavings he manufactured synthetic marble; from cotton he made paving blocks, paper, fiber for rope; from waste and local materials — rugs, table mats, briquettes, basketry, millinery feathers, and vegetable dyes. Consistently he demonstrated to poor farmers how they could use the things around them — local clays to whitewash their cabins; garden vegetables for more nutritious diets; compost and cowpeas to nourish soil.

In 1935, Carver, who remained at Tuskegee for the rest of his life, was appointed a collaborator in the Division of Mycology and Disease Survey of the US Department of Agriculture's Bureau of Plant Industry. In 1940, he donated his life savings of $33,000 to establish at Tuskegee the George Washington Carver Foundation to continue and expand his research and experiments.

His life story, meanwhile, was recounted in books and magazines, on radio and film, and he became a well-known lecturer. Before his death in 1943 he had become one of the nation's most influential agronomists. He was widely honored — by election as a fellow of the Royal Society of Arts in London; by honorary degrees from Simpson College, the University of Rochester and Selma University; by the Thomas A. Edison Foundation Award; by the Roosevelt medal for distinguished service in the field of science; and by the Spingarn medal awarded annually by the National Association for the Advancement of Colored People, among other honors he received. Carver's first laboratory and hundreds of the products he discovered are among the exhibits housed today in the George Washington Carver Museum at Tuskegee, which also contains a collection of his paintings and needlework. Also at Tuskegee is sculptor Steffen Thomas's bronze bust of Carver, presented to the institute — largely through one-dollar subscriptions from Carver admirers — during the year-long observance that marked the 40th anniversary of Carver's arrival there.

The humanitarian scientist died at Tuskegee Institute on January 5, 1943. In the early years after his death, the week embracing that date was widely marked as Carver Week in various parts of the nation. In 1946, a joint resolution of the 79th Congress designated January 5 as George Washington Carver Day and a proclamation noting his achievements was issued by President Harry S. Truman. The next year a Carver commemorative postage stamp was authorized by the US Post Office Department and the first day of sale was held at Tuskegee Institute on January 5, 1948. A number of states have honored Carver by designating January 5 as George Washington Carver Day in the years since his death. At one time or another these states have included Connecticut, Florida, Idaho, Illinois, Indiana, Michigan, New Jersey, New York, Pennsylvania, Rhode Island, Tennessee, Vermont, and West Virginia. Indicative of the nature of these honors was the proclamation issued in 1975 by New Jersey's Governor Brendan Byrne. Citing Carver as scientist, teacher, and benefactor of mankind, the governor commented that Carver's rise from slavery to prominence "despite all adversity . . . has provided the inspiration for other persons of all circumstances and conditions to strive to overcome difficulties and achieve excellence. . . ."

The anniversary of Carver's death is also marked, on the Sunday nearest January 5, at Tuskegee Institute. Phi Beta Sigma, the fraternity that in 1938 elected Carver to membership in its Distinguished Service Chapter and presented its distinguished service key to him in a special ceremony at Tuskegee, is instrumental in planning the annual program, which includes an address by a distinguished guest speaker. In 1964, which was observed as the 100th anniversary of Carver's birth, the annual remembrance of him in January was followed, in March, by a three-day commemoration. In the course of this gathering, faculty and trustees of the institute and members of the Carver Research Foundation participated in memorial services at his grave.

Students of Carver's life and work take interest in the fact that more than 10,000 pieces of Carver papers (including correspondence, pamphlets, and photographs) are to be found in the Tuskegee archives. Also of interest are the files of the library of Iowa State University, the repository of many of the letters written by Carver to his friend and professor L. H. Pammel over a period of approximately 30 years.

Probably no account of the agricultural chemist's impact would be complete without reference to the National Peanut Festival, now a six-day-long event encompassing parades, a carnival, a fair, and other events, along with attendant celebrities and pageantry, held annually in late October at Dothan, Alabama. Directly or indirectly, the festival recognizes the genius of Dr. Carver, who appeared at the first Peanut Festival, in 1938, to give an illustrated lecture about the peanut and its possible uses.

Feast of
St. John Nepomucene Neumann

On June 19, 1977, a century after his death, John Nepomucene Neumann, "The Little Bishop of Philadelphia," was canonized in Rome by Pope Paul VI, becoming the first American male saint. Tens of thousands gathered for the outdoor ceremony in St. Peter's Square to pay homage to a man who had spent his life in quiet dedication to the church and who had, above all, shunned worldly recognition. The steps toward canonization, which were initiated in the 1880s by Bishop Neumann's supporters in Philadelphia, were climaxed by a 15-minute ceremony in which Pope Paul concluded, ". . . we inscribe his name in the calendar of the saints and establish that he should be devoutly honored among the saints in the Universal Church."

Born in Prachatitz, Bohemia (now Czechoslovakia), on March 28, 1811, John Neumann was one of six children of Philip and Agnes (Lebisch) Neumann. From early childhood he displayed an avid interest in religion and the priesthood, and despite his parents' later urgings that he go into the medical profession, Neumann entered the seminary of Budweis in 1831. An intense student, he eagerly absorbed knowledge of canon law and the scriptures. After completing his courses at Budweis, he went on to the University of Prague. Although he was fluent in many Slavic dialects and at least eight modern languages, he studied English at Prague with the hope of going on to become an American missionary. After graduating with honors from the seminary in Prague in August 1835, he returned to Budweis for ordination. However, because of an overabundance of priests, he was unable to be ordained in his native diocese.

Undismayed, he decided to sail to America in April 1836. Arriving in New York City on June 2, he was received by Bishop John DuBois and was ordained on June 25 in St. Patrick's Cathedral on Mott Street. Because of Father Neumann's fluency in German, DuBois assigned him to Williamsville, New York, where he was to attend a number of frontier missions. During the next four years he journeyed on foot and by wagon, ministering to the poor German immigrant congregations scattered throughout the upstate area. Being of small stature (5 feet 4 inches tall), he began to be fondly called "little priest" by his charges.

In 1840 his self-sacrificing work was brought to the attention of the Redemptorist Fathers, who were establishing a monastery in Pittsburgh. Esteeming their rigorous rule, he joined the congregation. After a period of probation, he made his profession of vows in St. James's Church in Baltimore on January 16, 1842, becoming the first person to be received into the Redemptorist order in the United States.

While a Redemptorist, he continued to preach and minister to the impoverished and sick throughout the Northeast. But after two years, in 1844, he was called upon to head the Redemptorist missions at Pittsburgh. His appointment as superior of the community was a heavy burden for Neumann to bear. Not only did he continue to visit missionary territory in addition to his parish work, but he became instrumental in the building of the elaborate Gothic church of St. Philomena.

His labors were received with gratitude by the Redemptorist order, and in 1846, at the age of 35, he was made vice provincial of the Redemptorists in America and left Pittsburgh for their headquarters in Baltimore. For the next five years Neumann worked as diligently as he had in the past, establishing many parishes and schools and encouraging religious vocations.

In 1851 he was appointed pastor of the unfinished church of St. Alphonsus in Baltimore. This position was much more to his liking because it allowed him to step out of the limelight and afforded him the seclusion he desired. However, this respite from worldly influence was brief, for in 1852 he was selected to succeed Francis P. Kenrick as bishop of Philadelphia. Self-effacing by nature, he strongly opposed the appointment. To forestall his elevation, Neumann went so far as to ask his superiors in the Redemptorist order in Rome to intercede with Pope Pius XI, but the pope remained firm. Although reluctant to accept the post, once consecrated under the rule of obedience, Bishop Neumann applied the same energy and dedication to his new duties that he had to his earlier ones.

During his tenure as Philadelphia's fourth bishop, he was responsible for the establishment of 80 new parishes and the building of hundreds of parochial schools. The schools were staffed by various teaching sisterhoods, some of which he helped bring from Europe. Among those were the Sisters of Notre Dame of Munich and the Sisters of the Holy Cross from France. When Neumann was consecrated as bishop there were only 500 children in Philadelphia parochial schools, and within three years enrollment had increased to 9,000. Because of his work in the Catholic school system he has been referred to by many as the Father of the American Parochial School System.

After serving faithfully for eight years as bishop, Neumann collapsed and died on a Philadelphia street on January 5, 1869, at the age of 48. The cause of his sudden death is uncertain. The sad news was announced at all masses in the diocese the following day.

In 1866, six years after his death, the question of beatification arose. Certain miracles were said to have occurred at his tomb in St. Peter the Apostle Church in Philadelphia. A commission was formed to inquire into his life and give testimony to the Vatican. In 1921 the church pronounced Neumann Venerable, and in 1963 he was proclaimed Blessed. This level of sanctity was one step away from sainthood, for which there would have to be proof that three miracles had taken place through Neumann's intercession. Accounts of three miraculous cures of hopelessly ill young people were accepted by the church: one in Italy in 1923, one in Villanova, Pennsylvania, in 1949, and the third in West Philadelphia in 1963. All three who were cured were present in Rome at the canonization ceremony in 1977.

The canonization was observed in the United States in Philadelphia at St. Peter's, where the bishop's body is on display behind glass in the altar, and at Aston, Pennsylvania, where mass was conducted by Delegate Jean Jadot.

Traditional gifts representing Bishop Neumann's life were presented to Pope Paul during the Vatican rites and included a porcelain bowl containing rice to symbolize his concern for the poor, various medicines representing his care of the sick, a scale model of Bishop Neumann High School in Philadelphia, and bouquets of state flowers of Pennsylvania, New Jersey, and Delaware, three of the states the young immigrant priest served in his first years in this country.

JANUARY 6

The Epiphany, or Twelfth Day, or Three Kings' Day; Old Christmas

The Feast of the Epiphany, a festival of the highest rank, and older than Christmas, is observed in varying degrees by all branches of the Christian church on January 6. The term, from the Greek word *epiphaneia,* refers to the manifestation(s) of the divinity of Jesus Christ.

According to biblical accounts, this occurred when the Three Wise Men from the East (variously known as the Magi or as the Three Kings) came to worship Jesus at the manger in Bethlehem; during his baptism in the River Jordan by John the Baptist, when the Holy Spirit descended upon Jesus in the form of a dove and a voice proclaimed him the Son of God; and when he performed his first miracle by changing water into wine during the wedding feast at Cana. Historically, observances of this threefold anniversary have emphasized the baptism in Eastern Orthodox churches and the visit of the Three Wise Men in Western churches, both Roman Catholic and Protestant.

The existence of a feast on January 6 was first mentioned by the early church father Clement of Alexandria, at the end of the second century. He wrote in the *Stromata* (I, 21) that the Basilidians, followers of Basilides, who founded a heretical sect of Gnostics in Alexandria, kept an all-night vigil on either January 6 or January 10 to commemorate the baptism of Jesus.

The more widely based Christian Feast of the Epiphany, which had the approval of church authorities, probably also originated in Egypt and it undoubtedly flourished in the East in the very early Christian period. It was probably celebrated on January 6 to coincide with, and therefore combat, a pagan feast on that date. The ancient Egyptians, for example, observed the winter solstice and a ritual in honor of the sun god on January 6; and on the previous night, January 5, Alexandrian pagans marked the birth of their god Aeon (Aion) from the virgin Kore, called "the Maiden." In the fourth century, St. Epiphanius described a temple ritual on this occasion:

... on the eve of that day it was the custom to spend the night in singing and attending to the images of the gods. At dawn a descent was made to a crypt, and a wooden image was brought up, which had the sign of a cross and a star of gold marked on the hands, knees and head. This was carried around in procession, and then taken back to the crypt; and it was said that this was done because "the Maiden" had given birth to "the Aion."

Such a belief probably gave rise to the substitution of the seemingly similar Feast of the Nativity of Christ, which was first commemorated on January 6.

Pagans also held that the waters of rivers, particularly the Nile, were endowed with miraculous powers and even changed into wine on this night. Again, the heathen belief could have prompted the transformation of the pagan event into a Christian observance honoring the miracle at Cana. St. John Chrysostom (c. 347–407), one of the four Greek doctors of the church, wrote that the water drawn from the rivers on the Epiphany was holy and could be preserved much longer than water drawn on other days — a literal acceptance of the pagan belief about the Nile waters.

By the fourth century, Christians throughout most of the East celebrated the Feast of the Epiphany in a multiple sense as the anniversary of the physical birth of Jesus Christ; of the adoration of the Magi; of Christ's baptism; and of the miracle at Cana. From the East, the feast entered Europe sometime in the fourth century. It was kept in particular in Gaul, Spain, and northern Italy, primarily as the commemoration of Christ's birth. However, the Feast of Christmas, established at Rome for December 25 (see December 25) by the mid-fourth century, soon became accepted universally throughout Western Christendom as the occasion for celebrating the birth of Christ. Between 380 and 430, the Eastern church also embraced December 25 as the date for the Feast of the Nativity.

As a result, the Epiphany underwent a major transformation liturgically, although it continued to be numbered among the great feasts of the Christian calendar. In the West, its significance centered about the visit of the Magi, and the event came to be regarded as the manifestation of the divine purpose to extend the benefits of the Gospel to the Gentiles, as exemplified by the Magi, as well as to the Jews. In the East, where the Adoration of the Magi was celebrated together with Christmas, Christians placed stress on the Epiphany as the feast of Christ's baptism.

The only Gospel reference to the coming of the Magi is found in Matthew 2:1–2, part of which reads as follows:

Now when Jesus was born in Bethlehem of Judea in the days of Herod the king, behold, there came wise men from the east to Jerusalem, Saying, Where is he that is born King of the Jews? for we have seen his star in the east, and are come to worship him.

The word *magi* stems from the Old Persian *magu*, which refers to a hereditary class of priest-scholars. The term was adopted in neighboring Eastern countries, and it is therefore open to debate from which land the Magi came. There grew up a body of legends concerning these "wise men from the east," revealed in mosaics, manuscripts, and art of the early Christian and medieval periods. The Bible furnishes neither their number nor their names. Various theories have claimed that there were as many as 12 or as few as 2; but throughout the ages 3 has been the most commonly accepted figure, probably because Matthew enumerates three gifts and it was assumed that each had been presented to the Christ Child by a different man. By the sixth century, the three were commonly called "kings" and by the ninth, their names were generally held to be Caspar (Gaspar) or Jaspar, king of Tarsus; Melchior, king of Arabia; and Balthasar, king of Saba or Sheba. The gifts reputedly symbolized royalty (gold), divinity (frankincense) and death (myrrh — used in embalming), given to Christ as king and God, and prefiguring his sacrificial death. The biblical episode had allegedly been foretold by the prophet Isaiah (60:1–6), who referred to Christ's coming, the gifts of gold and incense, and the camels.

When the Wise Men beheld the wondrous star — said by some astronomers to have been what is now known as Halley's comet — they reportedly mounted their dromedaries and set out on their journey. They followed the star until it took them to Jerusalem, where it disappeared. According to the account in Matthew, Herod, the ruler of Palestine, learned that the Three Kings were asking about a child whom they called the king of the Jews. He sent for the learned men among the Jews and asked them where their Messiah was to be born. They told him in Bethlehem. Thereupon, Herod sent for the Three Kings and told them to go there, instructing them to report to him when they found the new king. As they were leaving Jerusalem, according to one form of the tradition, they met an old woman — known in Italy as the *befana* — who unsuccessfully tried to follow them, though not until she had finished cleaning her house. As legend has it, she has been wandering the earth ever since, seeking the child Jesus (see January 5, Twelfth Night).

The star reportedly reappeared to guide the Three Kings to Bethlehem as soon as they were outside the walls of Jerusalem. When Mary heard the approaching dromedaries, she took Jesus in her arms lest he should be taken from her, and it was in this attitude that the seekers found the mother and child. They knelt and adored Jesus as God and Savior of the world and presented their gifts of gold and frankincense and myrrh. Then the Three Kings, warned in a dream, returned to their homes without going back to Herod.

According to tradition, when they reached their own countries they resigned their high offices, distributed their goods to the poor and went about preaching the Gospel of Jesus, the Prince of Peace. It is said that some 40 years later, St. Thomas, meeting the trio of former rulers during his supposed travels in India, baptized them and ordained them as priests. The Three Kings reportedly suffered martyrdom for their faith and were buried together. In the fourth century, Empress Helena, the mother of the Roman Emperor Constantine the Great, found what she was convinced were their bones and carried them to Constantinople, where she placed them in the church of St. Sophia. At the time of the First Crusade the supposed bones of the Three Kings were taken to Milan, and Emperor Frederick Barbarossa, when he captured Milan during his Italian expedition of June 1158, took possession of the bones and is said to have laid them in the cathedral at Cologne in 1164. When the old cathedral was burned in 1248, the relics were saved and deposited in the new one — which was begun that year, completed in 1880, and reopened in 1956 after World War II bomb damage. The relics now rest on the high altar in a gem-adorned, golden shrine, said to be one of the finest examples of the art of medieval goldsmiths.

In Western Europe, the Feast of the Epiphany was from the first an occasion of great religious solemnity. In the year 400, the Roman Emperor of the West, Honorius, forbade attendance at horse races and the circus on January 6 lest Christians be diverted from church services; in 565, Emperor Justinian proclaimed the feast a civil holy day. During the Middle Ages, the Epiphany, like all the major ancient feasts, had its own vigil with strict fast and abstinence regulations and a solemn octave, which became part of the Roman liturgy in the

eighth century. (The octave and vigil were suppressed only in the 1950s.) In the Middle Ages, it was customary to bless homes with newly blessed Epiphany water and incense; later, it became common to write the names of the Three Wise Men with blessed chalk over the doorways to ask their protection.

January 6 also became an occasion of great pageantry. European rulers often represented the Wise Men. In 1378, for example, three monarchs, including King Charles V of France, donned splendid "biblical" attire to hear mass on the Epiphany. In England, where the feast was traditionally considered the end of the Christmas season, it was customary to give dramatic productions on this day to highlight the concluding festivities. As was true elsewhere in Europe, miracle plays were staged, first within churches, later outside, to teach the common people the significance of the event. Tragedies, comedies, and historical plays were performed in the Elizabethan and Stuart periods. It was, for example, on January 6, 1601, that William Shakespeare's *Twelfth Night* was probably first presented in a command court performance at Whitehall Palace for Queen Elizabeth I. In France, the Epiphany was considered a special day for frolicking. Certain members of the clergy — in a ceremony similar to that of the English Boy Bishop (see December 6, Feast of St. Nicholas) — chose a Bishop of Fools, who then offered a mock mass. Church censure ended this custom in the 15th century.

Although much of the pageantry attached to the Feast of the Epiphany in the past has long since disappeared, January 6 is still an important religious commemoration for all Christians. Among Roman Catholics, the feast (classed as a "solemnity") is celebrated in the general calendar on January 6 and is a holy day of obligation in many countries. In those countries where it is no longer mandatory to attend mass — as in the United States — the observance has been assigned to the Sunday between January 2 and January 8 in the recently revised Roman Catholic calendar. Protestant churches mark the Epiphany on January 6 or the nearest Sunday. In Catholic and Protestant churches alike throughout the West, the other manifestations of Jesus' divinity — the miracle at Cana and his baptism — play a role secondary to the Adoration of the Magi, Kings, or Wise Men in Epiphany observances. Roman Catholics, however, now mark the baptism of Jesus Christ as a separate feast in its own right — on the Sunday after January 6, except in years when the date would coincide with the Epiphany, in places where that feast has been transferred to a Sunday (see January 11, Feast of the Baptism of the Lord).

Protestant churches observe the Epiphany with services that may follow a prescribed form — as in the more "liturgical" churches, such as the Lutheran and Episcopalian — or that in any event usually are marked by sermons, hymns, and scripture readings centering upon the theme A Manifestation of the Light to All the World. The most frequent Gospel reading on this day is the story of the Adoration of the Magi, as related in the second chapter of Matthew. In addition, church congregations also often hear the famous prophetic passage from Isaiah 60:1–6, containing the exhortation:

Arise, shine; for thy light is come, and the glory of the Lord is risen upon thee. . . . And the Gentiles shall come to thy light, and kings to the brightness of thy rising. . . . The multitude of camels shall cover thee . . . ; all they from Sheba shall come: they shall bring gold and incense; and they shall show forth the praises of the Lord.

Episcopalians and sometimes other Protestants also are read the passage from Ephesians (3:1–12), in which Paul writes movingly of his mission to extend the riches of the Gospel to the Gentiles by preaching to them. In addition to conventional services of worship, some churches mark the Epiphany by pageants emphasizing the star and the Magi, or by special performances of sacred music that stress the theme of Jesus Christ as the true light, and hope, for every person. Some congregations choose this time for adding figures that represent the Three Kings or Wise Men to a Christmas crèche, which may have been standing since the beginning of Advent, the pre-Christmas season; and they may select this day to sing the hymn "We Three Kings of Orient Are" for the first time during the holiday season.

In the Eastern Orthodox churches, where there is no tradition built around the Wise Men, the day is called the *Theophany*, or the Appearance of God; and is sometimes also referred to as the Feast of the Jordan or the Feast of Lights, referring to the tradition that preternatural lights appeared on the river at the time of Jesus Christ's baptism. The name Feast of Lights also recalls the passage from Isaiah quoted earlier. Although the Eastern Orthodox churches maintain the original threefold commemoration, their stress is placed on the baptism of Jesus Christ as recorded in John 1:29–34; Mark 1:9–11; Matthew 3:16–17; and Luke 3:21–23. In the East, the Epiphany was always the official time for baptisms, whereas in the West Easter (see March 29) and Pentecost (see May 17) were set aside for this purpose in medieval and early Christian times. Persons to be baptized in the East were not called *catechumens* ("those who had been instructed") as in the West, but *illuminandi* ("those who were to be enlightened").

To commemorate the baptism of Jesus Christ, the January 6 feast among the Eastern Orthodox has been long associated with the "blessing of waters." For example, before the czar was dethroned in Russia, the ceremony of blessing the Neva, in commemoration of the blessing of the Jordan by the baptism of Jesus Christ, was observed with great pomp in St. Petersburg (now Leningrad). A pavilion was built on the frozen river, opposite the Winter Palace, and the czar and his court went there. A hole was chopped in the ice large enough to admit a cross, and the metropolitan and his clergy blessed the waters with prayers so that the waters might fertilize the earth and benefit humanity during the ensuing year. At one time, devout peasants broke holes in the ice and threw themselves into the water in the belief that they would be cured of their diseases and remain immune to illness for the next year. Not only was the Neva blessed, but the local clergy blessed the Don, the Volga, and other rivers, and the people, following the example of those in St. Petersburg, bathed in the streams, regardless of the temperature.

Eastern Orthodox churches still commemorate the baptism of Jesus Christ in the blessing of lakes, rivers, and seas by dipping a crucifix into their waters — as in the ceremonies that take place in the United States at Tarpon Springs, Florida (see January 6, The Epiphany, or Greek Cross Day), in New York City (see January 19), and in Long Beach, California. The consecration and blessing of the churches' holy water on the eve of the Epiphany and again on the day of the Epiphany also is traditional in the Eastern Orthodox churches. It should be noted that although the Epiphany is observed on January 6 by those Eastern Orthodox churches that follow the Gregorian calendar, some Eastern Orthodox churches that still adhere to the old Julian calendar observe the Epiphany 13 days later.

Many of the traditional customs connected with the Epiphany are still practiced. In most of the countries of Europe, for example, the Kings' cake is served on Epiphany Eve or Epiphany Day in honor of the Magi, and the person who receives the slice with the hidden bean or coin becomes king for the occasion. January 6 is a day of gifts in numerous lands, and the typical toys, oranges, and candy are brought by various personages. In Italy, the *befana*, a little old woman, leaves presents in imitation of the gifts of the Wise Men (see January 5). In Spain on Three Kings' Day — as January 6 is known in Spanish-speaking countries and Puerto Rico — the Magi, en route to Bethlehem, leaves sweets and toys. There, as in Puerto Rico, the children place grass or straw for the Three Kings' horses beneath their beds or in their shoes and awake the next morning to find that the grateful Wise Men have left gifts in its place. In Germany, where the Epiphany is known as the Festival of the Three Holy Kings, January 6 marks the close of the Yuletide season; folk songs, parties, and the lighting of the Christmas tree for the last time characterize the day, while on Epiphany Eve young boys dressed as the Magi go from door to door to beg for alms.

Puerto Rico celebrates Three Kings' Day, one of the island's major religious holidays, with parades and parties. The Epiphany also is known as Three Kings' Day in the neighboring US Virgin Islands, a reflection of Spanish influence there. The most notable celebration is by Virgin Islanders on St. Croix, where the explosive last day of that island's annual, two-week-long Christmas Festival is on Three Kings' Day. Culmination of the day's festivities is the carnival-like Three Kings' Day parade.

Interestingly, Epiphany also is observed as Three Kings' Day in most of New Mexico's American Indian pueblos, where the Spanish, and Roman Catholic, missionaries' influence persists, side by side with the Indians' own traditions. Apart from the observances of the churches, the Pueblo Indians mark the day with the election of new governors and the performance of the traditional deer and buffalo or eagle and elk dances. Elsewhere in the American Southwest, the dances of the Matachines — patriotic and religious dances which had their origins in Mexico — may be seen in many church plazas on special days, including the Epiphany.

The day of the Epiphany also sometimes is known as Twelfth tide, or as Twelfth Day. The night of January 6 is also termed Twelfth Night on occasion; it also vies with the evening of January 5 for this title and with January 6, Twelfth Night Revels. Epiphany day is referred to as Old Christmas as well. According to the Old Style or Julian calendar, Christmas fell on what is January 6 in the New Style or Gregorian calendar now in common use. In some isolated areas of the United States (sections of the Ozarks and of the Atlantic coastline) and Great Britain (particularly the West Country), the inhabitants still believe that Jesus Christ was born on Old Christmas Day; they therefore continue ancient customs once associated with Christmas on the evening of January 5 (Old Christmas Eve) or at midnight and during the early hours of January 6 (see January 5). One other name for the Epiphany, today used rarely, is Little Christmas, a term that distinguished it from the commemoration of the birth of Jesus after December 25, Christmas, was adopted for the celebration of that event.

The Epiphany, or Greek Cross Day; Blessing of the Sponge Divers, Tarpon Springs, Florida

One of the most beautiful and interesting observances of the Epiphany, the Christian holy day described in more detail elsewhere under January 6, takes place each year under the auspices of St. Nicholas Greek Orthodox Church in the predominantly Greek community of Tarpon Springs, Florida. In common with other Eastern Orthodox churches, St. Nicholas' marks the Epiphany in commemoration of the baptism of Jesus and stresses ceremonies related to the blessing of the waters, which is traditional among Eastern Orthodox churches on this day. The observance at Tarpon Springs, however, which is similar to those held in Greece, is duplicated by only a few other churches in the United States, and then usually on a lesser scale.

The serious ceremonies begin with the blessing of the Tarpon Springs sponge fleet, an annual rite that takes place on the day preceding the Epiphany. The following morning, on January 6, observance of the Epiphany, or Greek Cross Day as it is sometimes popularly called, begins with early prayers, followed by a 10:00 A.M. mass. The Divine Liturgy is celebrated by the ranking guest dignitary — generally a bishop or archbishop important in the Greek Orthodox hierarchy, who has journeyed to Tarpon Springs expressly for the occasion — assisted by other honored clergy and by the pastor of St. Nicholas Church. The Liturgy is followed by the Epiphany sermon at 11:30 A.M. and by the traditional blessing of the waters, at a marble kiosk in the churchyard. Usually, it is the chief visiting dignitary who dips a gold cross and sweet basil three times in the font and asks for divine blessings. Later, parishioners fill small bottles with the holy water to take with them for the sanctification of their homes.

After the Liturgy and blessing of the waters, a procession of ecclesiastical dignitaries in magnificent robes, led by the parade marshal, proceeds to Spring Bayou on the Gulf of Mexico. Apart from the prelates, impressive figures of patriarchal dignity in the dramatic miters of the Eastern church, the procession includes acolytes; the black-robed, chanting, Byzantine choir (which has rehearsed for weeks for this day); flag bearers; Boy and Girl Scouts; bands of local schools; members of patriotic organizations; representatives of various civic groups and schools; and state and local authorities. Many young people of Greek heritage in Tarpon Springs dress in the colorful costumes of their ancestral regions of Greece for the procession. One of the most admired costumes is that of the *evzones* or Greek soldiers who now serve as members of an elite guard: pleated, starched, white skirt, black velvet tunic, and red-tasseled slippers.

When the procession reaches the banks of Spring Bayou, shortly after noon, the chief celebrant of Epiphany Day dips the cross into the waters, praying for divine blessings as he does so. He then throws the cross into the bayou. A member of the church's Byzantine choir, specially chosen for the honor, simultaneously releases a dove — in commemoration of the form in which the Holy Spirit is said to have descended upon Jesus during his baptism in the River Jordan — and the 12 to 40 Greek-American youths who have been waiting for this moment leap into the water to retrieve the cross. A year of good fortune is said to await the young man who grasps the cross and hurries with it to receive a special blessing from the visiting prelate.

Once the solemnities are over, the holy day atmosphere is replaced by a holiday mood. First are the *Glendi* festivities at the waterfront Sponge Exchange. Permeated by the insistent, hypnotic rhythm of *bouzouki* music, the feasting and merrymaking continue through the afternoon. Included on the menu may be such items as *kavourma* (cubed beef cooked Greek style), feta cheese, Greek salad, honey-soaked pastries, and coffee. Capping the celebration is the annual Epiphany dance, usually beginning at mid-evening. Often, it is held in nearby Clearwater.

In recent years, as many as 10,000 or 15,000 persons have been on hand at Tarpon Springs for Greek Cross Day, which was observed for the 73rd time in 1976. Festivals along somewhat similar lines take place under the auspices of Greek Orthodox churches in New York City (see January 19, The Epiphany, or Greek Cross Day, Old Calendar), and, since 1952, at Long Beach, California, on the shores of the Pacific Ocean.

The origin of the sponge divers at Tarpon Springs goes back to 1905, when they were recruited directly from Greece at the instigation of John Corcoris, the first Greek diver to join the growing industry. Prior to this, sponges had been found at Key West as early as 1849, but sponge fishing on a commercial basis was not started in the gulf waters until 1890 when John K. Cheynes, one of the early settlers, sent out the first "hooker" boat and later established the first packing house.

During the Spanish-American War the Greek-manned Key West sponge fleet, fearing Spanish warships, disposed of its cargo at Tarpon Springs. From these small beginnings there developed the Tarpon Springs Sponge Exchange, which was the largest sponge market in the world at its height in 1943. Tarpon Springs' sponge fleet then comprised well over 100 boats and some 600 men who made trips that lasted weeks or even months and went as far as 50 to 80 miles from land, in craft only 25 to 45 feet in length. What seemed like the death knell for the natural sponge industry came in 1944, when the overworked sponge fields were blighted by disease — an affliction compounded by competition from the synthetic sponges developed during World War II. By the mid-1950s, however, the depleted sponge beds began to show new life. During the next decade and a half, demand and sales grew until Tarpon Springs again became one of the world's major suppliers, even though its fleet and volume were only a fraction of their former size.

The "Four Freedoms" Enunciated

World War II, between the Allied powers and the totalitarian Axis nations that sought world dominance under the leadership of Nazi Germany, had been under way in Europe for 16 months (see September 1) when President Franklin D. Roosevelt made his memorable "Four Freedoms" speech to the United States Congress on January 6, 1941. Although the United States, still technically neutral, did not enter the war on the side of the Allies until after the Japanese attack on Pearl Harbor, Hawaii, late in the year (see December 7), it was soon to increase its supply-and-assistance role, which would win it the title "arsenal of democracy."

The President's address of January 6, 1941, presented as his annual message to Congress, was widely quoted as summarizing the goals Americans stood ready to defend. His listing of the "four essential human freedoms" subsequently was used to epitomize the ideology of the Allied democracies as opposed to that of their Nazi and Fascist opponents. In the portion of his speech most frequently cited, the Chief Executive said:

In the future days, which we seek to make secure, we look forward to a world founded upon four essential human freedoms.

The first is freedom of speech and expression — everywhere in the world.

The second is freedom of every person to worship God in his own way — everywhere in the world.

The third is freedom from want — which, translated into world terms, means economic understandings which will secure to every nation a healthy peacetime life for its inhabitants — everywhere in the world.

The fourth is freedom from fear — which, translated into world terms, means a worldwide reduction of armaments to such a point and in such a thorough fashion that no nation will be in a position to commit an act of physical aggression against any neighbor — anywhere in the world.

The "Four Freedoms" address was followed, in March 1941, by congressional enactment of the Lend-Lease Act, permitting the lending, leasing, sale or transfer of arms, equipment and supplies to any country whose defense the President deemed vital to that of the United States. The lend-lease legislation, which Roosevelt had recommended in his "Four Freedoms" speech, contributed significantly to the overwhelming material superiority of the Allies over the Axis powers and to the ultimate defeat of the latter (see May 8, V-E Day; August 14, V-J Day).

The statement of goals contained in the presidential message of January 6, 1941, later was amplified by the declaration known as the Atlantic Charter (see August 14), issued jointly by President Roosevelt and Great Britain's heroic wartime leader, Prime Minister Winston Churchill.

Sherlock Holmes's Birthday

The reputed birthday of Sherlock Holmes, the fictional detective created either by Sir Arthur Conan Doyle, or — as some admirers insist — by Holmes's equally fictitious companion, Dr. Watson, is observed by dinners of the Baker Street Irregulars in New York and of the Sherlock Holmes Society in London. The New York dinners are held faithfully each year on the Friday nearest January 6; those in London on an early January date.

The master sleuth is also commemorated, either on a date close to his supposed birthday or at other times of the year, by many of the approximately 50 Holmes-related "scion" societies which gird the globe. Among the older and more active of these groups are The Five Orange Pips of Westchester County, New York; The Speckled Band of Boston; The Scowrers and Molly Maguires of San Francisco; The Hounds of the Baskerville [sic] of Chicago; The Sons of the Copper Beeches of Philadelphia; The Six Napoleons of Baltimore; and The Red Circle of Washington.

In New York City, the day of the annual birthday dinner is also the date of the Sherlock Holmes Birthday Breakfast, sponsored by still another "scion" society — The Old Soldiers of Baker Street, headquartered at Sault Ste. Marie, Michigan. Later the same day, New York City is the site of the annual William Gillette Memorial Luncheon, named for the playwright and actor best known for his dramatization *Sherlock Holmes,* which he adapted from the A. Conan Doyle stories, and for his appearances in the play's title role.

New Mexico Admitted to the Union

On January 6, 1912, New Mexico entered the Union as the 47th state. In the years since its admission, the state has greatly prospered. The clear, dry air and warm climate have made New Mexico a popular winter resort and retirement center. Its spectacular scenery, combining lofty peaks and vast deserts, and the colorful pageantry of Indian, Spanish-American, and Anglo-American traditions have stimulated all-season tourism. Moreover, the discovery of petroleum and natural gas, in addition to the rich mineral resources and farming and grazing lands already in use, has contributed to the area's rapid development within the last half century.

New Mexico has a long and varied history extending back to the pre-Columbian era. Ancient southwestern Indian civilizations antedated the flourishing culture of the Pueblo Indians found by the early 16th century Spanish explorers along the Rio Grande basin. Spanish interest in the area that was to become New Mexico began in 1528, when Nuño de Guzmán, the governor of New Spain, heard from an Indian named Tejo about the hoards of gold and silver in "seven towns so large that they could be compared in size to Mexico." Determined to reach these settlements, vaguely described as being "northward between the two seas" and "across a grassy desert for 40 days," Guzmán assembled an army of friendly Indians and 400 Spaniards. He set out in December 1529 to find what became known as the fabled Seven Cities of Cíbola, but lost his way. The expedition did establish Culiacán, an important base in northern Mexico for future exploratory parties, before disbanding in 1531.

Curiosity about the reputedly rich territory north of Mexico flared up again five years later. In April 1536, four bedraggled survivors of Pánfilo de Narváez's expedition to Florida, including Narváez's treasurer, Álvar Núñez Cabeza de Vaca, and the Moorish black guide and interpreter Estevanico, turned up near Culiacán after nearly eight years of wandering across the Southwest from Texas possibly as far as to the Gulf of California. Their experiences provided the first solid account of the area which became known as New Mexico (*Nuevo Méjico*) about 1581.

Spurred on by their adventures, Antonio de Mendoza, the viceroy of New Spain, outfitted an exploration party under the direction of the Franciscan missionary Fray Marcos de Niza in 1539. A full-scale expedition headed by Captain General Francisco Vásquez de Coronado followed in 1540–1542 (see September 4, Santa Fe Fiesta). Since neither group had discovered the legendary golden cities or even gold deposits, further Spanish government-sponsored expeditions north of Mexico were suspended by royal ordinance.

However, the Southwest remained an attractive field for missionary activity. Three Franciscans from Coronado's expedition, Juan de Padilla, Juan de la Cruz, and Luis de Escalona, had remained among the Pueblo Indians and in 1544 became the first martyrs of the region. Another friar, Agustín Rodríguez, organized the next attempt to convert the Indians in the summer of 1581. Together with Fray Francisco López, Fray Juan de Santa María, and a military escort, he reached Puaray, one of the pueblos where Coronado had set up his headquarters. Once the soldiers had returned to Mexico, however, the Franciscans were killed as their predecessors had been.

In 1582–1583, Antonio de Espejo led an expedition to ascertain the fate of these friars. His reports about the great mineral wealth and good grazing lands in much of the Pueblo Indian country led in 1598 to Don Juan de Oñate's founding of the first permanent colony in New Mexico at San Juan de los Caballeros, 30 miles north of present-day Santa Fe. It was the second oldest permanent settlement in what is now the United States, the first having been made at St. Augustine, Florida (see September 8) in 1565. In the winter of 1609–1610, Santa Fe, the new capital of the Province of New Mexico, was founded (see September 4).

Colonization in the 17th century proceeded at a slow pace. Having failed as a source of easy gold, New Mexico was of interest to the Spanish authorities only as a frontier buffer for northern Mexico and as a mission field. By 1617, there had been 11 mission churches erected there; 43 had been built by the mid-1620s. Until 1680, however, Santa Fe was the sole Spanish *villa,* or incorporated town, although sparsely populated Spanish settlements had spread along the Rio Grande from Taos in the north to Isleta south of the capital.

Friction between Spanish civil and religious authorities and the differences between Indian customs and the Spanish way of life further hindered the development of Spanish New Mexico. The exploitation of the Indians through forced labor and the exaction of tribute, as well as the suppression of their religion, led to a series of sporadic uprisings beginning as early as 1640. The unrest culminated in the Apache revolt of 1676 and the Great Pueblo Revolt of 1680, which forced the Spaniards to abandon their holdings in New Mexico and seek refuge in Mexico for 13 years. The relentless campaign of Captain General Don Diego de Vargas Zapata Luján Ponce de León restored Spanish rule beginning in 1692.

The 18th century saw the steady development of ranching and mining, as well as the spread of Spanish culture, which has remained to the present. Although intrepid French-Canadian traders penetrated the region as early as the mid-18th century and spread tales of its wealth in minerals and furs, the Spanish strictly limited their trading contacts to other Spanish settlements.

Later, Spanish officials became alarmed at the westward expansion of the Anglo-Americans, which increased after the United States acquired the huge Louisiana region in the Louisiana Purchase of 1803 (see December 20). The Spanish undertook measures, which ultimately proved unsuccessful, to prevent American penetration of Spanish-held Texas and New Mexico. Trade with the new US settlements in the Missouri Valley was discouraged until Mexico achieved independence from Spain in 1821. The independent Mexican republic, which promptly assumed control of New Mexico, legalized economic contacts with the United States. As early as 1822, the Missourian William Becknell took the first wagon loads of merchandise across the plains from Missouri to New Mexico and gained the title Father of the Santa Fe Trail. This important caravan route, operating from Westport (now part of Kansas City) and Independence, Missouri, grew by leaps and bounds. The spring wagon train in 1824, for example, carried $30,000 in goods to Santa Fe and returned with $180,000 in precious metals and $10,000 in furs. In 1860, the route was used by 3,033 wagons, 9,084 men, 6,147 mules, and 27,920 oxen. Only the laying of the Atchison, Topeka and Santa Fe Railroad to Santa Fe in 1880 sounded the death knell for the famous trail.

In 1841, after the independent Republic of Texas had been established (see March 2), a group of Texans attempted to claim for Texas all of New Mexico east of the Rio Grande. Irate Mexican officials shot several of the Texas expansionists caught on New Mexican soil and imprisoned others. The reports circulated later about the mistreatment the jailed Texans were said to have received in Mexico City helped to arouse American resentment against Mexico.

These accounts contributed to the growing strain between the United States and Mexico, which culminated in a declaration of war between the two countries in 1846 (see May 13).

At the outbreak of the Mexican War, the Army of the West, commanded by Brigadier General Stephen Watts Kearny, crossed into New Mexican territory and occupied Las Vegas on August 15 and Santa Fe three days later. On August 23, the erection of Fort Marcy, the first US military fort in New Mexico, was started northeast of Santa Fe. On September 22, Kearny set up a civil government for New Mexico, appointing Charles Bent, a partner in the largest southwestern fur-trading company, as governor. The American takeover, however, triggered local rebellions, Indian insurrections, and political assassinations; and a US military government assumed tighter control of political affairs. At the end of the Mexican War in 1848, the Treaty of Guadalupe Hidalgo (see February 2, Mexican War Ends) ceded New Mexico, which encompassed present-day Arizona and other territory, to the United States.

Delegates meeting at Santa Fe on October 10, 1848, petitioned Congress for a civil territorial government and for an end to Texan claims to New Mexican land. By May 1850 the mood had shifted, and a Constitutional Convention framed a constitution for the "state" of New Mexico, which was subsequently ratified by the inhabitants and submitted to Congress. However, the bid for statehood failed. Instead, a provision of the Compromise of 1850 — the Organic Act of the Territory of New Mexico — made New Mexico a territory and granted her a civil territorial government. Texas, by then a state, relinquished all claims to the area.

The newly established Territory of New Mexico extended from 103° west longitude all the way to California. It was enlarged in 1853 by the purchase from Mexico of 45,535 square miles, west of the Rio Grande and south of the Gila River, known as the Gadsden Purchase (see December 30). The region was deemed vital for the construction of a southern railroad to the Pacific. New Mexico's present boundaries were fixed in the early 1860s. The creation of the Territory of Colorado on February 28, 1861, took away the northeastern section of New Mexico territory, while the Territory of Arizona was fashioned out of New Mexico's western half on February 24, 1863.

The burning issues of the Civil War did not vitally affect New Mexico. In 1861, only 22 black slaves lived in the territory. Yet as a recently conquered Mexican province, the area was understandably not ardently pro-Union. Moreover, the withdrawal of US troops, felt to be more essential elsewhere on the military front, meant that large sections of New Mexico lay open to devastating Apache and Navajo raids.

The US Indian policy for the region, developed in the early 1860s, included the confinement of tribes from all parts of the territory at the Bosque Redondo reservation near the Pecos River. There, sickness, starvation, and hostility among the various tribes added to the Indians' discontent. The Mescalero Apaches fled the reservation in 1866, an action that forced policy changes in Washington. A peace commission negotiated a treaty with the Navajos in 1868, permitting them to transfer to reservations set up on their home ground of northwestern New Mexico and northeastern Arizona. Indian reservations in other sections of the territory also were established — as for the Mescalero Apache in the south in 1873 and for the Jicarilla Apache in the north in 1880. Nevertheless, Geronimo, one of the last prominent Apache leaders, went on the warpath as late as 1885–1886, before his final capture and deportation as a war prisoner to Florida, Alabama, and, finally, Oklahoma.

Great economic strides marked the late 19th century in New Mexico. The construction of the Santa Fe Railroad, especially, opened up a new era of progress as eastern markets became accessible by rail and led to the cattle and mining booms of the 1880s. Another bid for statehood was blocked in 1906, when the people of Arizona rejected a bill proposing Arizona's joint statehood with New Mexico. New Mexico's half-century struggle to obtain statehood ended on June 20, 1910, when Congress passed the enabling act providing for the admission of New Mexico and Arizona as separate states, once each had adopted a suitable state constitution. On January 6, 1912, New Mexico, having fulfilled the requirement, formally entered the Union.

The 60th anniversary of that event was the occasion of special observances throughout the state on January 6, 1972. Santa Fe, the oldest capital in the United States, took on the flavor of the year 1912 for the commemoration. Members of the Sociedad Folklórica dressed in the fashions of that era and received guests at a reception held on the afternoon of January 6 at Santa Fe's historic Palace of Governors. That much-restored adobe structure, originally built in 1610, is regarded as an excellent example of Spanish-Indian architecture. Today it houses the Museum of New Mexico with its outstanding historical and archeological, as well as modern, collections related to the surrounding region and its culture. Earlier, however, the palace served successively as the residence of

Spanish captains general (until 1821), Mexican governors (until 1846), and American territorial governors (until 1909).

Twelfth Night Revels

To most people today Twelfth Night, coming at the end of the traditional Twelve Days of Christmas, falls on January 6, the day of the Epiphany. However, Twelfth Night is also marked sometimes on January 5, the evening before Twelfth Day, with the date depending upon whether one counts Christmas (see December 25) or the day after Christmas as the first day (see January 5, Twelfth Night or Epiphany Eve).

On whichever date it occurs, Twelfth Night always has been a time for festive celebration, since it traditionally marked the beginning of Carnival, the season of boisterous merrymaking which preceded the soul-searching, self-discipline, and abstinence of Lent (see February 11, Ash Wednesday). Twelfth Night celebrations reached riotous heights in Europe during the Middle Ages. Traditionally, the Carnival season, with its balls, masked processions, flamboyant costumes, feasting, and other revelry, extended through the entire period from Twelfth Night until Mardi Gras (see February 10), the day before Lent. The climax of the Carnival season was always on the last few days before Lent, with Mardi Gras the peak of the hilarity.

Today, Carnival is principally observed in Europe and Latin America, and only sparsely in the United States. In recent years the celebration has been confined in most places to the one day of Mardi Gras, or to Mardi Gras and the three or four days preceding it. This is true even of such world-famous carnivals as the ones in Rio de Janeiro, Brazil, and Binche, Belgium. Remnants of the longer celebrations remain, however. Nice, in southern France, and Viareggio, in Italy, have notable carnivals lasting about two weeks. Uruguay, particularly its capital city of Montevideo, celebrates for about a month. Austria goes still further, with a Carnival season that still begins on the traditional Twelfth Night, the festivities continuing through the entire period until Mardi Gras. During that time, Vienna and such other Austrian cities as Salzburg are filled with music, costumes, and special celebrations, including the several hundred balls that take place in Vienna alone. In Germany, the hilarity reaches gargantuan proportions, particularly in Munich's *Fasching* and the *Karneval* of Rhine River communities, most notably Cologne and Mainz. Germany's Carnival season lasts the longest of all — beginning officially on November 11 or, to be more spe-

cific, at 11 minutes after the 11th hour of the 11th day of the 11th month. The Christmas and New Year holidays intervene, however, after the initial burst of gaiety and ceremonies on November 11, so that, in Germany too, it is Twelfth Night or nearly so before Carnival resumes in a sustained way.

The United States's most notable Carnival observance is in New Orleans, where the Carnival or social season officially begins on January 6, under the aegis of the carnival organization known as the Twelfth Night Revelers. Beginning then or earlier, the season's debutantes and other invited guests appear at the 60 to 75 private balls that are interspersed throughout the entire Carnival season between Twelfth Night and Mardi Gras. The balls, like the several dozen parades during the same period, are sponsored by the city's 60 or more secret "krewes," as New Orleans' carnival organizations are known. The season's gaiety reaches its highpoint in the Mardi Gras festivities of the two weeks before Lent. The culmination of the celebration is on the day of Mardi Gras or Shrove Tuesday itself, when the whole city explodes in wild festivity.

As for Twelfth Night, when the New Orleans Carnival season begins, the Twelfth Night Revelers, headed by that traditional Twelfth Night figure, the Lord of Misrule, have marked the occasion with a gala ball annually since 1870 (except for the years of World Wars I and II, and a few omissions in the 1870s and 1880s). The 1970 centenary event was an occasion for special festivity and more than usual ceremony. Since the burning of the original French Opera House in 1919, the Twelfth Night Revelers ball has been held in the New Orleans Municipal Auditorium. It incorporates two features prominent in Twelfth Night observances since medieval times.

One is an elaborate tableau centered around a specific theme. In recent decades the themes have included: Jazz; The Twelve Days of Christmas; Second Childhood; Salute to New Orleans; School Daze; Birds of a Feather; and Moonlight and Roses. The other recurring feature is the awarding of royalty for the evening — to the person who finds a bean in his piece of the traditional Twelfth Night cake. In medieval days (and later), a "king" was named in this way. But at New Orleans Twelfth Night ball, where the Lord of Misrule is king, the bean — a gold one — is employed to find a queen. The recipients of silver beans become members of her court.

Tradition always has figured heavily in Twelfth Night festivities. This probably accounts for the fact that a description of the

Twelfth Night Revelers 1910 ball and tableau gives, with allowances for the passage of time, a fair idea of today's celebrations:

The first scene of the tableau showed a corner of a garden on the shores of a lake with swans swimming in it. Then, startled, the swans swiftly swam away while from the other side of the lake several of the classical gods appeared, rowing. As they floated idly about, the scene changed to another part of the garden, where other gods strolled along flower-bordered walks. As they approached the plants, the buds opened and the garden became a mass of blooms. The third scene showed the Lord of Misrule on a golden throne between fountains that poured forth crystal streams of changing colors. Eight fire-breathing golden lions with flashing eyes stood on high pedestals. Statuary and vases with flowers adorned a terrace on which were assembled all the carnival gods: Venus, the goddess of love; Selene, personifying the moon; Aurora, the dawn; Vulcan, the god of fire; Neptune, god of the sea; Momus, the god of ridicule; Comus, the leader of the revelry — and all the others, as well as Old Sol and his retinue.

The queen of the previous year's ball was escorted to the throne beside the Lord of Misrule, along with her maids of honor. Then the gods formed into platoons and executed an intricate march about the stage. At the end of the march, each took a dancing partner and they assembled at the front of the stage. Thereupon, the cook brought in the king's Twelfth Night cake, after the fashion of the old custom in England and France.

The New Orleans cake was filled with small boxes, one containing a golden bean and the others silver beans. The ladies drew the boxes from the cake. The one drawing the golden bean, who became the queen, was escorted to the throne, took her seat beside the king, and was crowned by the queen of the previous year. After these ceremonies were concluded the ball began.

In other parts of the United States, and elsewhere, it was once customary for many secular organizations to have Twelfth Night celebrations. The custom, which has diminished, is still carried on by the Lotos Club of New York and some other groups. Although the festivities today are on a slightly less elaborate scale, the Lotos Club's annual Twelfth Night banquet still follows in outline a celebration — once typical of many — that it held years ago. It began when a company of trumpeters marched through the corridors and rooms of the clubhouse, sounding the call for dinner in the banquet room. When the guests gathered, the lights were turned down and a spotlight was focused on the choirboys from Christ Church, who sang "While by My Sheep I Watch at Night," "Lo, How a Rose ere Blooming," and "The First Noel." When the lights were turned on, the president of the club was seen sitting on a throne beneath a Christmas canopy. He raised the wassail cup and commanded everyone to forget his cares, and rejoice. During the first course of the dinner, four waits — itinerant serenaders — standing under a street lamp that had been set up in the room, sang of the sorrows of Solomon over his many wives and other merry songs. The room was darkened again and chimes from the galley played Tom Moore's ballad "Believe Me If All Those Endearing Young Charms."

After a time the musicians, clad in Elizabethan costume, were seen to make their way to the kitchen. In a few moments they returned, blowing their oboes and French horns at the head of a procession led by the chef. This functionary wore a sprig of holly in his cap and a cleaver and carver hung from a belt about his waist. Behind him came two under cooks, bearing on their shoulders a litter decorated with greens and holly berries and containing great barons of beef. A third cook marched behind these two, holding high over his head a trencher containing a boar's head. The scullions followed, carrying ladles and gravy boats. The procession marched about the room and through the aisles between the tables and then returned to the kitchen, where the beef was carved.

While the waiters were bringing in the beef, the diners sang "The Roast Beef of Old England," keeping time by pounding the table with their knives. When the beef was served, four cellarmen brought in a great brass bowl filled with flaming Jack Ketch punch. The bowl was put in its place, the lights were lowered again, and the orchestra played the fire music from *Die Walküre*. Then the lights were turned on and the choirboys sang more carols. A well-known comedian of the time, acting as the king's jester, told some merry stories, and there were more songs and music from the orchestra. The feast ended with plum pudding, and was followed by the songs of two soloists.

Although the opening tableau and the bowl of flaming punch have disappeared from the Lotos Club's celebrations of today and filet mignon has supplanted the barons of beef as the main course, the Twelfth Night banquet is still an abundant repast. It is preceded by a preliminary cocktail hour and by a choir concert of carols, after which guests are "chimed" to their tables. The banquet begins with a procession of beefeaters, costumed to resemble London's famous "beefeaters," just after the diners are seated and continues with the music of carolers who stroll through the dining rooms. The highpoint of the festivities still is the procession of members of the kitchen staff, carrying the appurtenances of their occupations. The crowning feature of the procession is the boar's head, decked with spectacles, surrounded by fruit, and carried by two men. The meal is enlivened further with music by a Welsh chorale and by an accordionist or guitarist. Today, as earlier, the traditional plum pudding caps the feast. Afterwards, there is dancing to an orchestra until midnight or so. The merrymaking concludes with the taking down of Christmas decorations, in keeping with the old superstition that it is good luck to remove these on Twelfth Night.

The traditional taking down of decorations, incidentally, has given rise to a custom that has become increasingly popular in the United States in recent years. This is the burning of wreaths, holly, evergreen branches, and Christmas trees in great bonfires on Twelfth Night, or Twelfth Night Eve. The ceremony often takes place in city parks or other central places and there is apt to be a final carol-sing around the bonfire. Sometimes the cutting of a traditional, bean-encompassing, Twelfth Night cake is part of the fun, with the recipient of the bean ruling over the merriment around the fire. Not surprisingly, the modern bonfires derive from ancient custom, as do all Twelfth Night frolicking and merrymaking.

JANUARY 7

Millard Fillmore's Birthday

Millard Fillmore, the 13th President of the United States, was born at Locke — now Summerhill — in Cayuga County, New York, on January 7, 1800. He was the oldest son and second child of Nathaniel Fillmore, who had moved to Locke from Bennington, Vermont, in 1798. He took his first name from his mother, the former Phoebe Millard. The family name of Fillmore originally had been spelled Phillmore, and was so noted when its first known American member bought an estate at Beverly, Massachusetts, in 1704.

Young Fillmore worked on his father's farm and served as an apprentice to a wool carder and cloth dresser. When not working, he spent sporadic short periods in a local one-room school. They were supplemented by one longer, six-month period when he was 18. However, the meagerness of his formal education was more than compensated for by the assiduous

tutoring of his schoolteacher, Abigail Powers, with whom he fell in love. They were married in 1826 and had two children. She died in 1853.

So well had Fillmore been tutored that he was able to support himself by teaching while he learned the law — a study he began at the age of 18 by reading law in the office of a Cayuga County judge. When his family moved to East Aurora, New York, Fillmore continued his legal studies there. He was admitted to the bar of Erie County in 1823, and opened an office in East Aurora. He practiced his profession there until 1830, when he moved to Buffalo, where he made his home for the rest of his life.

Having interested himself in politics, Fillmore became a protégé of the journalist and Whig leader Thurlow Weed, through whose influence he came before the public as a candidate. He was elected to the New York state assembly on the Anti-Masonic ticket in 1828. After serving three terms in the state legislature, Fillmore was elected in 1832 to the national House of Representatives. He declined to stand for reelection at the end of his term but in 1836 was sent again to Congress from his district. He subsequently was twice reelected.

An anti-Jacksonian, Fillmore in Congress was a follower of Henry Clay (see April 12), even though he refused to go along with Clay's fight for reestablishment of the United States Bank. When the Whigs obtained a majority in the House in the election of 1840, Fillmore was made chairman of the powerful Ways and Means Committee and took an active part in framing the protective tariff law of 1842. Two years later, an unsuccessful attempt was made to nominate Fillmore for Vice President. He was, however, nominated that year to be the Whig candidate for governor of New York. Running against Silas Wright, the Democratic candidate, he was narrowly defeated. In 1847, Fillmore was elected as comptroller of New York state. The following year, with strong support from Clay and his followers, Fillmore did receive the Whig nomination for Vice President. Running on the winning ticket with Zachary Taylor (see November 24), he resigned his state office on February 20, 1849, to take up his duties in Washington.

Fillmore could hardly have guessed that with the death of President Taylor on July 9, 1850, he would himself become President in a little more than a year. His unexpected accession to the office of Chief Executive came at a time of grave national crisis. Debate over the issue of extension or nonextension of slavery to new territories had been raging for a decade, raising sectional passions as had no issue before it.

Things reached a fever pitch after the end of the Mexican War (see May 13), when Congress was confronted with the question of what to do with the territory the United States had acquired from Mexico. Particularly, debate focused on California's proposed admission to the Union, and the question of whether it would be a slave or a free state. Partisans of both views hardened their stands, with the antislavery contingent, centered in the North, vowing every effort to prevent the further extension of slavery; and the proponents of slavery, largely in the cotton-growing South, threatening secession if their view was not adopted.

Although Fillmore privately deplored slavery, he considered the threat to national unity an even graver danger. As long as he presided over the Senate as Vice President, he carefully refrained from taking sides. Meanwhile, a historic debate raged for eight months in the Senate over what is known as the Compromise of 1850, the set of measures devised by the conciliatory Henry Clay to ease tensions between the North and South. Among other things, Clay's formula provided for the admission of California as a free state; the organization of New Mexico as a territory with no restriction regarding slavery; adjustment of the disputed border between Texas and New Mexico; abolition of the slave trade in the District of Columbia; and the enactment of a more stringent Fugitive Slave Act.

Although President Taylor opposed the Clay compromise, Fillmore intimated to his chief a few days before the latter's death that in the event of a Senate tie, he would vote in favor of the measures. As President, Fillmore exerted the full weight of his influence in favor of the compromise, at a time when it faltered on the verge of defeat. Indeed, as it turned out, his support was decisive in ensuring passage. He thus stood with Clay in postponing for a decade the confrontation that would nearly tear the nation asunder in civil war. In his anxiety to preserve the Union, Fillmore even signed the much-abhorred Fugitive Slave Act, exposing himself to bitter denunciation by Northern abolitionists and helping to terminate his tenure in the presidency.

His supporters, chiefly Southern Whigs, sought to bring about his renomination in 1852, but failed. Not even General Winfield Scott, who did receive the nomination, could win. In fact, the election marked the final disintegration of the already hopelessly divided Whig party; Fillmore was to be the last Whig President.

He was, however, nominated by the American or Know-Nothing party in 1856, while the new Republican party nominated John C. Frémont. Fillmore, running a poor third in that election, received 874,534 votes; Frémont could claim 1,341,264; and James C. Buchanan, the successful Democratic candidate, ran up a total of 1,838,169, some 377,000 fewer votes than were polled by the combined opposition. Opposing Lincoln's conduct of the Civil War, Fillmore supported General George McClellan for President in the campaign of 1864, and during the Reconstruction period, which followed, he joined President Andrew Johnson in opposing the radical Reconstruction policies of the Republican-dominated Congress.

Fillmore was not idle in retirement. In 1846, he had become the first chancellor of the University of Buffalo. In addition, he was among the founders of a number of other civic or cultural institutions in Buffalo, among them the Buffalo Historical Society and the Buffalo General Hospital. In 1855, Oxford University offered him the degree of doctor of civil laws, but he declined the honor on the ground that he had no literary or scientific attainments that would justify his accepting it.

Five years after the death of his first wife, Fillmore was married again — to the widowed Caroline C. McIntosh, in 1858. The retired President lived another 16 years after his second marriage — until his death on March 8, 1874, in Buffalo. He is buried there, in the Forest Lawn Cemetery.

A replica of the log cabin where Fillmore was born in the then-frontier community now known as Summerhill, in New York, planned under the direction of the Cayuga County historian, has been erected in Fillmore Glen State Park near Moravia, New York.

Panama Canal Traversed

On January 7, 1914, the self-propelled crane boat *Alex. La Valley* made the first passage through the Panama Canal. The first ocean steamer, the SS *Ancon*, passed through on August 3, and the canal was officially opened August 15, 1914.

This opening solved a problem of international commerce that had originally presented itself to the Western world in 1453, when Constantinople fell to the Turks and the great land routes to India and the Orient were closed to Christian Europe. Within half a century, Christopher Columbus set forth in search of a westward water route to the Far East; subsequent explorers soon discovered that the North and South American continents blocked the way. From the 16th century onward, the creation of an interoceanic waterway was considered. Vasco Núñez de Balboa, the discoverer of the Pacific Ocean (see September 25), having explored the Isthmus of Panama in vain for a legendary strait, proposed that the Atlantic and Pacific be joined by a water route through present-day Panama. Hernando Cortes, the conqueror of Mexico, made a similar suggestion. Charles V, the 16th century emperor of the Holy Roman Empire and king of Spain (as Charles I), went so far as to have survey routes of the area mapped out in detail in preparation for the construction of a canal.

Explorations and plans continued to multiply. They reached a height in the 19th century, after the United States had been established as a nation and was expanding rapidly from coast to coast. The westward thrust of settlement emphasized the need for such a waterway, and several times during the 1800s creation of a canal under at least partial American control seemed assured. Then, however, the focus of canal-building efforts centered upon Nicaragua rather than Panama. During the 1840s, conflicting interests of the United States and Great Britain over control of the proposed waterway caused friction until the Anglo-American Clayton-Bulwer Treaty of 1850 provided that neither country would seek exclusive control of the isthmus or of any ship canal across it.

The topography of the Central American isthmus remained unknown or at best vague until the California gold rush of 1848–1849. Would-be prospectors seeking to travel from east to west then developed an alternate water route to the long Cape Horn voyage. Instead of traveling around the Cape, they sailed from eastern US ports, crossed the isthmus by foot, muleback, or boat, and, on the Pacific coast, finally boarded a ship bound for California. But as for construction of the much-discussed canal, which could have made all this much easier, political difficulties invariably arose to stand in the way.

There were other difficulties, too. While the United States was struggling to recover from the Civil War, the French undertook to engineer and finance the canal project. In 1876, an association was formed in Paris to draw up surveys, but only in 1879 was the Panama Canal Company organized with Vicomte Ferdinand de Lesseps, the engineer of the Suez Canal, as president. Excavations for a sea-level canal from Colón on the Atlantic to Panama on the Pacific started in 1881; however, the project proved impractical from an engineering standpoint. In 1887, the French company changed to a lock canal, but, plagued by heat, disease, costly mistakes, and financial difficulties, including misuse of funds, it was finally declared bankrupt in 1889. Over $260 million

had been spent. The French firm was reorganized as the New Panama Canal Company in 1894, primarily with the intention of profitably selling its holdings.

The Spanish-American War of 1898 served to renew interest in the United States in a canal project. Some groups advocated the purchase of the French Panama Canal Company concession; others backed an American business syndicate that had obtained a concession from Nicaragua. A congressional commission, formed to assess the two routes, recommended the one across Nicaragua, since the French were demanding $109 million for their dubious assets. However, the eruption of a volcano on Nicaraguan soil, as well as the reduction of the French concession price to $40 million, caused a reversal. After the way had been cleared with Great Britain in the Hay-Pauncefote Treaty of 1901, which gave the United States the sole right to operate a canal, Congress passed the Spooner Act on June 28, 1902. It authorized President Theodore Roosevelt to acquire the rights and property of the New Panama Canal Company from the French, provided that Colombia (of which the area of the Isthmus of Panama was at that time a province) agree to grant perpetual control of the required strip of land. On January 22, 1903, Secretary of State John Hay and Colombian representative Tomás Herrán signed the necessary treaty, leasing to the United States a 10-mile-wide zone for 100 years.

However, when the Colombian government procrastinated, failing to ratify of the treaty, the inhabitants of what is now Panama — encouraged by supporters of the canal project — revolted, but not until a day after the US warship *Nashville*, capable of preventing action by Colombia, had arrived in the area. Panama then declared its independence from Colombia on November 3, 1903. The new Republic of Panama was recognized by the United States three days later. On November 18, less than two weeks afterwards, Panama signed the Hay-Bunau-Varilla Treaty, giving the United States the right to build a canal in return for payment of $10 million, a $250,000 annuity beginning in 1913, and the guarantee of Panama's independence. Even though many of the rights provided were later relinquished, the hastily negotiated treaty earned the lasting ill will of Panamanians by granting the United States in perpetuity all rights as "if it were . . . sovereign" to the 10-by-50-mile strip of land that was to serve as the site of the canal.

On May 4, 1904, the United States took formal possession of the property, and in 1906, under the eminently qualified John F. Stevens, work was started on a canal with three intricate sets of high-level locks. It was brought to completion by chief engineer George W. Goethals, a US Army officer who, with his associates, overcame monumental technical, personnel, and health problems. Lieutenant Colonel William C. Gorgas of the US Army Medical Department capably supervised an extensive sanitation program, thus enabling long-term construction in what had been one of the world's great pestholes. The canal was opened to international sea commerce on August 15, 1914.

The 1903 treaty with Panama was revised twice after its adoption; the chief changes concerned payment to Panama. In 1936, it was agreed that the sum would be raised to $430,000 a year, and the United States — at Panama's request — withdrew the guarantee of Panamanian independence. In 1955, the annuity rose to $1.93 million. (Subsequently this grew to somewhat over $2 million.) Moreover, the United States gave Panama $28 million worth of property that the Canal Zone administration no longer needed and undertook the construction of a high-level bridge over the Pacific entrance to the canal. (It was officially opened seven years later as part of the Inter-American Highway.) In the early 1920s, the United States paid Colombia $25 million in return for that country's relinquishment of all claims to the canal.

Then, as now, the Panama Canal was regarded as one of the engineering marvels of the world. It has proved to be especially valuable as a strategic link in the defense of the Western Hemisphere, having facilitated the movement of war materials and servicemen to fighting fronts during World War II, the Korean War, and the Vietnam conflict. By its 50th birthday, however, the "Big Ditch" already had become controversial. For one thing, there were many ships — oil tankers and aircraft carriers — too large to use it because of the narrowness of the locks; and it did not have the capacity for the 50 to 60 vessels a day wishing to pass through. Experts, branding it inadequate and obsolete, advocated the construction of a new canal at sea level, eliminating the need for locks, cutting passage time and construction costs, and making the system less vulnerable to attack.

The need for change was also emphasized by the bloody anti-American riots — born of long-standing resentment in the area of "Yankee imperialism" — that erupted in January 1964 with a loss of 24 lives and a suspension of diplomatic relations for three months. Differences between Panama and the United States seemingly were settled when, after months of investigation and negotiation, President Lyndon B. Johnson announced on December 18, 1964, that the United States would proceed with plans for construction of a new canal and would propose to Panama "the negotiation of an entirely new treaty on the existing Panama Canal."

In 1967, the United States and Panama jointly announced that preliminary agreement on new treaties had been reached. The treaties stipulated that the United States would relinquish its exclusive sovereignty over the Canal Zone; integrate the area with the rest of Panama; provide for joint operation and a sharing of benefits of the canal; and safeguard the rights of workers regardless of nationality. There was also an important provision whereby Panama granted the United States an option to construct a new sea-level canal in her territory.

The draft treaties encountered political setbacks in both the United States and Panama, however, and their ratification was delayed. The decisive blow came in 1968, when internal upheavals in Panama resulted in the ouster of newly elected President Arnulfo Arias by a military junta headed by Panamanian strong man General Omar Torrijos Herrera. Torrijos and many of his compatriots claimed that the Canal Zone was being "occupied arbitrarily as a result of a unilateral application and interpretation of the 1903 treaty which is annoying to national dignity." On September 3, 1970, the US State Department announced that the Central American regime had rejected the proposed treaties. Objections centered on the provision creating a governing board composed of five Americans and only four Panamanians to jointly operate the canal until 1999 (at which time it would be handed over to Panama). Dissatisfaction was also voiced about the continuation of the Canal Zone's separate court system, legal code, police force, and stores and other commercial ventures. In early 1972, the United States indicated its willingness to make further concessions, including the return to Panamanian jurisdiction of some additional 30,000 acres of land in the zone and Panamanian control of the zone's stores, postal system, and — under certain conditions — courts and police force. But negotiations on a new canal treaty nonetheless lingered at a standstill. This was true even in spite of a special meeting of the 15-member UN Security Council, which — at Panama's request — met at Panama City in March 1973 to debate the issue: a US veto killed a resolution calling for a new treaty between the two countries involved. No significant hint of future progress was to come until early in 1974.

In the meantime, discussion about the possibility of building a larger, modern, and less vulnerable sea-level canal continued, with a presidential study commission reporting on its six-year study of the subject in 1970.

Early in February 1974 there was a signal of possible future progress toward a new canal accord when the Panamanian head of government, General Torrijos, and the US Secretary of State Henry Kissinger met in Panama for the signing of a Joint Statement of Principles under which a new canal treaty was to be negotiated. The joint declaration provided that Panamanians would, for the first time, take part in the defense of the canal. It also provided for a twelvefold increase — to $25,000,000 — in the United States' annual payments to Panama, though that projected figure fell short of Panamanian wishes. On the most emotional issue of all, the statement of principles indicated that the United States would gradually give up its permanent sovereignty over the Canal and Canal Zone.

Negotiations on this and other matters later resumed, with Ambassador Ellsworth Bunker as the chief US negotiator, but there was a hiatus from March to September 1975 while members of President Gerald Ford's administration, some of whom had hardened their views in the wake of the US debacle in Vietnam (see August 7), reexamined the US position. After they reached a compromise among themselves, negotiations resumed in Panama with the US representatives expressing a willingness to turn full ownership and operation of the canal over to Panama after 25 years, but insisting, however, that the United States be permitted to maintain a strong military presence in the Canal Zone for another 25 years.

This was unacceptable to General Torrijos, who had won wide support among his people for his stand that the US presence must be completely withdrawn from the Canal Zone by the year 2000. Ambassador Bunker and his team returned to the United States in late September. At this juncture, feelings among Panamanians grew more intense on the potentially explosive canal issue.

On September 7, 1977, President Jimmy Carter and General Torrijos signed the Panama Canal treaties, calling for the transfer of the Panama Canal and the Canal Zone by 2000. The signing, which took place in the Pan American Building in Washington, D.C., was witnessed by diplomats representing 26 other American nations. US ratification faced strong opposition, but the Senate voted on March 16, 1978, to ratify the pact guaranteeing neutrality of the canal and on April 18 to ratify the treaty governing operations and defense and the eventual transfer of the canal to Panama on December 31, 1999.

"Russian Christmas"

January 7 is observed as Christmas by those Eastern Orthodox churches, including some in the United States, that still use the Julian calendar introduced by Julius Caesar in the year 46 B.C. Much more common, however, is the observance of Christmas on December 25, according to the now generally used Gregorian calendar instituted by Pope Gregory XIII in 1582.

JANUARY 8

Battle of New Orleans Day

The anniversary of the battle of New Orleans is a legal holiday in Louisiana. Now officially designated as Battle of New Orleans Day, it was formerly known as Jackson Day, or Old Hickory's Day, in honor of Andrew Jackson, who commanded the victorious American forces in the battle. The encounter, remembered as a brilliant victory for American arms, was the last battle in the War of 1812.

Ironically, it was fought after the treaty of peace had been signed. American representatives, including John Quincy Adams, James A. Bayard, and Henry Clay, had been sent to Europe to negotiate a peace. They met the British representatives at Ghent and after long negotiations signed a treaty ending the war on December 24, 1814. Methods of communication, however, were so slow that news of the signing of the treaty did not reach this country for several weeks.

The New Orleans adventure had been undertaken by the British against the advice of the duke of Wellington. Nevertheless, his brother-in-law, Major General Sir Edward Pakenham, was put in command of the expedition. He arrived off the coast of Louisiana with a fleet of some 50 ships and 7,500 soldiers on December 10. On December 23 he reached a point about eight miles from New Orleans with a detachment of troops. He was attacked by General Jackson but successfully resisted the assault, although his advance was checked.

The next morning, General Jackson fell back behind a disused millrace at Chalmette, near New Orleans, and ordered his troops to fortify themselves by throwing up earthworks. Cotton bales were used in the embrasures of some of the batteries and around the magazines. On January 1 the British tried to break the American lines by cannonading them, but they were unsuccessful.

On January 8, 1815, they attempted to take

the American position by frontal assault, but were met by such vigorous resistance that within half an hour some 2,000 of their men were dead or wounded, in contrast to no more than 13 Americans dead and 58 wounded. General Pakenham himself was killed, along with two other generals. The British retreated to their ships 10 days later.

The victory made General Jackson a national hero and laid the foundation for the political strength that later made him President (see March 15). In New Orleans, people danced in the streets for joy. The battle was brilliantly concluded. And the War of 1812, sometimes referred to as the second war of independence, was over (see December 24, Treaty of Ghent). The new American nation was established in the eyes of the world.

The victory is marked annually on January 8 with speeches, wreath-layings, patriotic ceremonies, martial music, and the salute of guns. The commemorative exercises customarily take place at several New Orleans locations — among them Jackson Square, where a statue by Clark Mills shows the general astride his horse. The historic square is the site of an observance sponsored each year by the Chalmette Chapter of the United States Daughters of 1812. Six miles outside the city other ceremonies, held each year by the Society of the War of 1812, take place at the scene of the battle, now known as Chalmette National Historical Park. The day also is marked annually by commemorative masses at several churches, including the Ursuline Convent, where the nuns in 1815 prayed for divine assistance at Jackson's request. Today, their successors attend a Mass of Thanksgiving to Our Lady of Prompt Succor, which is offered annually in fulfillment of a vow made on the eve of the battle.

The sesquicentennial of the battle in 1965, a week-long celebration planned with the cooperation of Congress and federal authorities, was more elaborate than anniversary observances before or since. It began with halftime ceremonies during New Orleans' annual Sugar Bowl football game on New Year's Day and came to a climax at the end of the week. Thursday, January 7, was marked by a multiservice, international military parade that included, among others, a color guard of US, British, and Canadian troops; units from the British HMS *Whirlwind* and the American USS *Newport News*; the Pipes and Drums of the Black Watch, Royal Highland Regiment of Canada; a Loyola University rifle drill team; and bands of the US Air Force and Navy and the New Orleans Police Department. In the evening, official representatives of the United States and Great Britain, descendants of Generals Jackson and Pakenham, Governor John J. McKeithen, Senator Russell B. Long and Representative Hale Boggs of Louisiana, and a long list of other dignitaries attended a sesquicentennial banquet that stressed the theme of amity between the United States and Great Britain.

The next morning, Postmaster General John A. Gronouski officiated at the dedication of a stamp issued in honor of the battle sesquicentennial. The 9 A.M. ceremonies, at the Presbytère in Jackson Square, were followed immediately by a pontifical high mass in historic St. Louis Basilica and by military memorial ceremonies conducted by the Society of the War of 1812. They included the playing of the American and British national anthems, the display of colors, the firing of artillery salutes and sounding of taps, and the placing of wreaths at the Jackson monument. Afterwards, the United States Daughters of the War of 1812 conducted their customary wreath-laying and flag-burning ceremonies in the square. The latter rite, respectfully performed by Boy Scouts, involves the ceremonial raising of a new flag over the statue of Jackson.

The climax of the sesquicentennial week came at 1:30 in the afternoon of January 8, with the rededication of Chalmette National Historical Park, on which the National Park Service had lavished $365,000 in restoration work, road building, explanatory markers, and provision for a new memorial to the men who fell in battle there. Secretary of the Interior Stewart L. Udall was the principal speaker at the battlefield rededication, which was also marked by addresses by Governor McKeithen and others. British, American, and Canadian military units took part in the ceremonies, along with National Guard units from the several states whose men had participated in the long-ago battle. Supersonic jets of the Louisiana Air National Guard meanwhile flew overhead, dipping in salute over the 100-foot Chalmette Monument. At the behest of Secretary Udall, descendants of the warring generals symbolically clasped hands across a cannon, epitomizing the sesquicentennial theme of friendship between the United States and Britain. A sesquicentennial message was sent by President Lyndon B. Johnson, who remarked with poignant reassurance that "the brave men who fought and died 150 years ago in New Orleans had no way of knowing that they were to be the last American and British citizens ever to bear arms against each other."

One of the most notable early celebrations of the anniversary of the battle of New Orleans occurred on January 8, 1828, when Jackson went to that city during his campaign for the presidency and was guest of honor at a large Democratic party gathering.

Another memorable Jackson Day dinner was held in Baltimore in 1911, after the Democratic victory at the congressional elections in the preceding November. Distinguished party leaders were present to outline what they regarded as the proper policy for the party. There were 1,000 guests present, and public interest in the amount of food needed to feed them ran so high that the Baltimore newspapers reported the details: 7,000 oysters, 75 gallons of terrapin, 1,500 pounds of capon, 500 canvasback ducks, 45 Smithfield hams, 3,000 cigars, and 500 bottles of champagne were provided for the occasion.

Prior to 1936, Jackson Day dinners were held in various states and in Washington, D.C., but apparently they never were scheduled regularly and, until that year, were not sponsored by the national committee of the Democratic party. From 1936 on, however, official party dinners have been held throughout the country. They were variously known as Jackson Day dinners, Democratic Victory dinners, Washington dinners, and Jefferson Day dinners until 1948.

Since that year, when a dinner was held in Washington to celebrate the Democratic National Committee's 100th anniversary, the celebrations have been known officially as Jefferson-Jackson Day dinners. They are now held annually throughout the country and perhaps most frequently still take place on January 8, although the dates may vary widely. High-level Democrats customarily address the dinners, which honor Andrew Jackson and Thomas Jefferson as founders of the Democratic party, review accomplishments and basic principles, and raise funds for the party.

Not all commemorations of the anniversary of the battle of New Orleans are political in tone. Massachusetts annually designates January 8 as New Orleans Day. And veterans', hereditary, and patriotic organizations with historic interests sometimes also mark the occasion. One that does is the Veteran Corps of Artillery, State of New York, Constituting the Military Society of the War of 1812. The organization dates from the founding, on November 25, 1790 — the anniversary of Evacuation Day in New York (see November 25) — of the Veteran Corps of Artillery. Its founders were veterans of the American Revolution who were alarmed by the threat to the new US republic of wealthy Tories still remaining in New York and British naval vessels still hovering off the Atlantic coast. With members equipped at their own expense (as they still are today), the corps was the first New York City militia organization to volunteer service in the War of 1812. It subsequently merged — in 1848 — with the Society of the War of 1812, which had been formed in New York on January 3, 1826. Today's membership of the combined organization is composed of descendants of those who fought in the American Revolution and the War of 1812, and veterans of more recent wars, including World War II and the Korean and Vietnamese conflicts. By statute, the organization's annual meeting and banquet are held on the anniversary of the battle of New Orleans. After the presentation of colors, singing of the national anthem, and the invocation, followed by the presentation of honored guests, "artillery punch" is customarily served and toasts are proposed to the nation's armed forces, the President of the United States, the governor of New York, and the heroes of the battle of New Orleans.

Eleventh Amendment Declared Ratified

Under the federal system that the Constitution of 1787 established in the United States, certain powers are vested in the national government; the remainder are retained by the individual states. The framers of the Constitution outlined in detail the areas over which the central government was to exercise jurisdiction, but as early as 1793 the states resented as an encroachment on their sovereignty the constitutional clause permitting lawsuits "between a State, or the citizens thereof, and foreign States, citizens or subjects." To curtail the federal government's authority over such judicial matters, Congress in March 1794 sent the 11th Amendment to the states for their approval. The amendment was declared ratified on January 8, 1798.

The demand for the 11th Amendment stemmed from the Supreme Court's 1793 ruling in the case of *Chisholm* v. *Georgia*. In 1793 two South Carolinians representing a British creditor initiated suit in the US Supreme Court against the state of Georgia — to gain restitution for goods provided the state during the American Revolution. Georgia argued that the nation's highest tribunal had no jurisdiction in the matter since a sovereign state could not be sued without its consent. The Supreme Court ruled otherwise. By a four-to-one decision, the Court accepted the case, ruled against the state of Georgia, and ordered it to pay the debt under consideration.

Reaction to the *Chisholm* decision was immediate. The lower house of the Georgia legislature approved a bill making any federal marshal who tried to collect the debt in question a felon. The legislatures of the other states protested the Supreme Court's ruling only slightly less vehemently. And, more important, the states instructed their representatives in Congress to take action to prevent a repetition of what they believed to be a violation of their sovereign rights.

On March 5, 1794, Congress recommended the 11th Amendment to the states, and on January 8, 1798, after the requisite three-fourths of the states had approved the measure, it was declared in a presidential message to Congress to have been ratified. Later research has shown, however, that the amendment actually had been part of the Constitution since February 7, 1795 (see February 7).

The amendment was a strong affirmation of the states' sovereignty in legal cases in which they might be involved. It denied the jurisdiction of the "Judicial power of the United States" in "any suit in law or equity, commenced or prosecuted against one of the United States by Citizens of another State, or by Citizens or Subjects of any Foreign State."

JANUARY 9

First Successful Balloon Flight in the United States

Through the ages men have dreamed of flying. In legends, the ancients recounted tales of intrepid individuals who dared to ascend into the sky, and throughout the course of history many persons — including the multifaceted genius Leonardo da Vinci — tried to design machines that would allow human beings to defy the force of gravity. Efforts to imitate the birds of the air progressed slowly, but finally in 1783 the first successful manned balloon flight took place in France; 10 years later on January 9, 1793, a hydrogen-filled balloon carried a man above the territory of the United States.

A French citizen, Jean Pierre Blanchard, also known as François Blanchard, was the first man to demonstrate the feasibility of balloon flight in the United States. The idea of flying had fascinated Blanchard from an early age. He studied birds in flight and even constructed an ingenious, albeit unsuccessful, flying machine before his fellow countrymen Joseph and Jacques Etienne Montgolfier in 1783 produced the first hot-air balloon capable of carrying a man. The Montgolfier invention turned Blanchard's attention to lighter-than-air craft. Between 1783 and 1792 he used Montgolfier balloons to make more than 40 flights that delighted and thrilled audiences in such European

cities as Berlin, Warsaw, and Vienna. He also accompanied Dr. John Jeffries of Boston, by balloon, on the first air flight across the English Channel in 1785, a fact that at the time was hailed as "the eighth wonder of the world."

The American public, too, enthusiastically received news of the balloon ascensions that took place in Europe, and many wanted an opportunity to witness such an aerial spectacle. As early as 1784 Peter Carnes tried to duplicate the European achievement. At Baltimore, Maryland, in June 1784 Carnes was able to raise a captive balloon carrying a 13-year-old boy, but when Carnes attempted a second ascension at Philadelphia one month later, his balloon burst into flames. In the years that followed 1784 other Americans made efforts to ascend into the sky, but none were successful.

Believing that many Americans were eager to see a balloon ascension and would pay for the privilege, 39-year-old Blanchard set sail from Hamburg on September 30, 1792. He landed in Philadelphia on December 9 and immediately concluded arrangements for his historic flight. Local newspapers carried advertisements advising of Blanchard's planned flight and inviting interested persons to subscribe five dollars so they might see the spectacle. Meanwhile, a general feeling of excitement swept through Philadelphia — then the temporary capital of the United States — as January 9, 1793, the day of the ascent, approached.

Blanchard chose the courtyard of Philadelphia's Walnut Street Prison as the starting point of his historic flight. The brick walls of the jail yard protected Blanchard's balloon from the curious who might be tempted to tamper with it. Equally important, the enclosure prevented those who did not subscribe five dollars — or the later reduced rate of two dollars — from seeing the preparations for the flight or the sight of the craft ascending from the ground.

Beginning at dawn on January 9 and continuing until 10:00 A.M., the scheduled time of Blanchard's ascent, cannons were fired at regular intervals in Philadelphia to honor the French aeronaut. At 9:00 A.M. inflation of the massive balloon started, and many of the spectators who paid to see the ascent arrived at the courtyard early so that they might watch this procedure. A band provided musical background as the huge yellow silk balloon was filled with hydrogen and, according to one newspaper account, "when it [the balloon] began to rise, the majestical sight was truly awful and interesting."

Promptly at 10:00 A.M. Blanchard, wearing a plain blue suit and a cocked hat with white feathers, took leave of the throng of spectators, who included President George Washington and the minister plenipotentiary of France.

Washington presented Blanchard, who spoke no English, with a letter explaining the Frenchman's mission to any person he might encounter after his descent. This first presidential message to be airborne read:

The bearer hereof, Mr. Blanchard, a citizen of France, proposing to ascend in a balloon from the city of Philadelphia, at 10 o'clock, A.M. this day, to pass in such direction and to descend in such places as circumstances may render most convenient — These are therefore to recommend to all citizens of the United States, and others, that in his passage, descent, return or journeying elsewhere, they oppose no hindrance or molestation to the said Mr. Blanchard; And, that on the contrary, they receive and aid him with that humanity and good will, which may render honor to their country, and justice to an individual so distinguished by his efforts to establish and advance an art, in order to make it useful to mankind in general.

After Blanchard accepted the "passport" from Washington, the artillery fired one last time. Then the intrepid Frenchman entered the blue, spangled boat under the massive balloon. At 10:16 A.M. he tossed out some of the ballast, and slowly the balloon carried him skyward. As Blanchard ascended, he waved a flag, which bore the colors of the United States on one side and those of France on the other, and he doffed his feathered hat to the amazed and delighted throng below.

The spectators in the Walnut Street Prison yard were only a small fraction of the crowd that witnessed Blanchard's ascent. Reflecting on his reactions as he rose above the walls of the jail yard, the Frenchman reported:

. . . I could not help being surprised and astonished, when, elevated at a certain height over the city, I turned my eyes towards the immense number of people, which covered the open places, the roofs of the houses, the steeples, the streets and the roads, over which my flight carried me in the free space of air. What a sight! How delicious for me to enjoy it.

Accompanied only by a small black dog, Blanchard soared far above Philadelphia. Then air currents caught his craft and propelled it east toward Delaware. As the balloon coursed along, Blanchard encountered a flock of wild pigeons. In his *Journal* of the flight he remarked of the incident: "Alas! it was never my intention in traversing the ethereal regions, to disturb the feathered inhabitants thereof: they separated into two different parties and left a passage open for me."

Continuing his journey eastward, Blanchard performed a number of experiments that American scientists had requested. When he reached his maximum altitude he took his pulse and discovered that it was eight beats faster than it had been on the ground. By means of a barometer he also calculated that the balloon had ascended to a height of 5,812 feet and he found that a loadstone that could lift five and one half ounces on the ground could raise only four ounces at that altitude.

After completing his scientific observations, Blanchard snacked on a biscuit and a glass of wine. Then he began preparations for his descent. He placed all breakable objects in a box and secured his canine companion in such a way that he would not be injured when the aircraft returned to earth.

By alternately letting air escape from the balloon and throwing out ballast, Blanchard was able to take advantage of various air currents, and thereby regulate the direction of his descent. His first two efforts to land were frustrated when he encountered a dense forest and then a swamp, but on his third try he found a suitable area situated in a thick wood. The descent was easily accomplished, and at 10:56 A.M. — only 46 minutes after leaving the Walnut Street Prison yard — Blanchard set foot on the ground just outside Woodbury in Gloucester County, New Jersey.

As Blanchard began to consult his compass so that he could calculate his exact location, a local townsman approached the balloon. The sight of the Frenchman's strange craft astonished and frightened the man, but Blanchard, who could speak no English, reassured him by offering the man some of his wine. Within minutes a second townsman appeared, and then still others. They read Washington's missive, and proceeded to help Blanchard pack up his equipment.

At a nearby house, Blanchard was treated to a light meal. Then his flying apparatus was placed on a cart and he mounted a horse for the return trip. Arriving in Philadelphia at 7:00 P.M., he paid his respects to Washington and presented the President with the flag that he had waved during his balloon ascent that morning.

Blanchard's January 1793 flight thrilled and excited many Philadelphians. Unfortunately, however, most of the city's residents chose to watch the spectacle from outside the Walnut Street Prison walls, so that Blanchard did not raise enough money by subscription to meet the expenses of his aerial ascent. Thus, in the months following, he undertook a number of projects to earn additional funds. He wrote an account of his flight, which was sold at five and one half cents per copy, and he gave a number of exhibitions of aeronautic apparatus. These ventures were only moderately successful and Blanchard returned to France at the end of the year.

Since Blanchard's historic flight, especially during the years of World War II and the decades since, advances never dreamed of by the Frenchman have become everyday occurrences in the field of aviation. Yet, as the first to make a successful balloon flight in the United States, Blanchard has earned a place of honor. Even in today's supersonic era, he is remembered in most of the books, exhibits, films, and observances that document progress in aviation. One specific example is in the Penn Mutual Life Insurance Company, whose building now stands on the site of the Walnut Street Prison. The company has made a special effort to recognize the aerial pioneer. It has erected a plaque in the corridor of its building to mark the site of Blanchard's ascent, and to commemorate the 150th anniversary of his balloon flight the company in 1943 reprinted the Frenchman's *Journal of My Forty-fifth Ascension, Being the First in America.*

Connecticut Ratifies the Constitution

Connecticut, on January 9, 1788, became the fifth state to adopt the US Constitution. The margin of victory in the ratifying convention, 128 to 40, suggests the strength of Federalist sentiment in the Nutmeg State. After Connecticut's action, supporters of the new government needed to win approval in only four more states in order to make the Constitution the law of the land.

Three eminent statesmen, Oliver Ellsworth, William Samuel Johnson, and Roger Sherman represented Connecticut at the Constitutional Convention in Philadelphia in 1787. Oliver Ellsworth was a state superior court judge and an accomplished orator. Only 42 years of age, he was greatly "respected for his integrity and venerated for his abilities." William Samuel Johnson was one of America's leading intellectuals. The 60-year-old scholar had been a lawyer and judge and had recently been designated president of Columbia College. Roger Sherman, mayor of New Haven, had been a shoemaker, almanac maker, lawyer, and judge during his 66 years. Despite his almost uncouth appearance, he had a keen mind and was an extraordinarily shrewd politician. Roger Sherman had been a signer of the Declaration of Independence and a member of the Continental Congress.

Connecticut was at a disadvantage under the Articles of Confederation. In colonial days, the state had traded livestock, especially to the West Indies, but the British had closed the market after the Revolution. Designed for carrying animals, Connecticut's fleet was unsuited for shipping other commodities, and the state's businessmen did not have the money to build new vessels. Unable to compete for transatlantic trade, Connecticut became dependent on New York for its European imports. Money, which Connecticut needed to pay its war debts and to invest in various manufacturing and mercantile enterprises, went instead to Manhattan merchants and to the coffers of the New York state government, which levied heavy import duties.

Deprived by the Articles of Confederation of control of its fortunes, Connecticut hoped that a new constitution would spread prosperity more equitably among the states. The Connecticut legislature authorized the state's representatives to the Constitutional Convention at Philadelphia to "discuss upon such Alterations and Provisions agreeable to the general principles of Republican Government as they shall think proper to render the federal Constitution adequate to the exigencies of Government and the preservation of the Union." Oliver Ellsworth, William Samuel Johnson, and Roger Sherman took these directions seriously and worked vigorously to create a document that would foster the interests both of their state and of the nation.

Connecticut's goal was the difficult one of strengthening the Union without undermining the sovereignty of the states. Along with the other smaller states, Connecticut opposed the Virginia Plan, which would have allotted representation in the Congress on the basis of population, and preferred the New Jersey Plan, which would have provided each state with a single vote in the national legislature. Fortunately, however, Connecticut was not doctrinaire in this matter, and its delegates were instrumental in the adoption of a solution acceptable to both large and small states. Historians have sometimes dubbed this "Great Compromise," which authorized representation by population in the lower house and an equal vote for each state in the upper house, the Connecticut Compromise, in recognition of the efforts of Ellsworth, Johnson, and Sherman on behalf of its adoption.

The Constitutional Convention ended its work on September 17, 1787, and in November of that year the Connecticut legislature issued a call for the election of delegates to a ratifying convention, which was to meet in Hartford. In the weeks before the elections Federalists continued a newspaper campaign, which they had been conducting for several months, in favor of the new Constitution. The elections took place in early December at town meetings throughout the state, but the meaning of the outcome was not immediately clear, because the communities did not instruct their representatives either to ratify or reject the new frame of government.

When the ratifying convention opened at Hartford on January 4, 1788, the Federalists immediately took control of the proceedings. Matthew Griswold of Lyme was president of the gathering and Jedediah Strong of Litchfield its secretary. Oliver Ellsworth began the debates with a speech on behalf of ratification. A strong Union was necessary, Ellsworth argued, for purposes of defense, economy, internal harmony, and Connecticut's survival in the midst of powerful neighboring states. Ellsworth's fellow delegates found his arguments persuasive, and on January 9, 1788, voted 128 to 40 to accept the Constitution.

Connecticut and the other 12 mainland colonies became states in 1776, when they declared their independence from Great Britain (see July 4). For purposes of establishing a chronology of the admission of these states into the Union, historians use the dates of their ratification of the US Constitution. Thus Connecticut is considered to be the fifth state to join the Union.

Richard M. Nixon's Birthday

Richard Milhous Nixon, the nation's 37th Chief Executive, experienced extremes of glory and humiliation during his career in public life. When he first ran as the Republican candidate for President in 1960, he suffered a narrow defeat at the hands of Democrat John F. Kennedy. And two years later he experienced a more embarrassing loss to Edmund Brown in the gubernatorial election of his home state of California. Yet in 1968 Nixon made one of the most remarkable political comebacks in American history to win the presidency from the Democrats.

After his first term, Nixon experienced an even more impressive victory on November 7, 1972, when he won reelection to the nation's highest office by a landslide vote that carried 49 of the 50 states and gave him the second highest percentage of the popular vote in the nation's history. In his years as President he was responsible for a number of notable achievements, including diplomatic negotiations with both the Soviet Union and the People's Republic of China that marked a turning away from the cold war era. On August 9, 1974, however, his public career was cut short when he resigned in the face of threatened impeachment. This step was precipitated by the so-called Watergate and related scandals in which not only members of the Nixon administration were eventually implicated, but also the President himself was linked by seemingly overwhelming evidence to the attempted cover-up of wrongdoing within the administration.

Richard M. Nixon was born in Yorba Linda, California, on January 9, 1913. The second of the five sons of Francis and Hannah Milhous Nixon, he spent his first years on his father's lemon farm and then at the age of nine moved with his family to Whittier, California. Young Nixon attended local public schools and in 1930 entered Whittier College.

During his college years, he was active in debate and student politics. He served as class president in his freshman year and, as a senior, won election as president of the Whittier student body. Ranking second in his 1934 graduating class, Nixon won a scholarship for further study at the Duke University Law School.

Like many other students during the Great Depression, Nixon had to work hard to remain in school. To supplement his scholarship at Duke he held a number of jobs, which included working in the law school library and for individual professors. But his outside work did not detract from his academic achievements. He was elected to the Order of the Coif, the honorary legal fraternity, and graduated third in his class in 1937, receiving his LL.B. degree with honors.

The same year, he returned to Whittier. In the fall he was admitted to the California Bar Association and joined the law firm of Wingert and Bewley (later Wingert, Bewley and Nixon). The young attorney remained with the southern California firm for five years. During that time he worked on corporation and tax cases, and in addition acted as town attorney in La Habra, a small town near Whittier.

Shortly after the United States' entry into World War II, Nixon went to Washington, D.C., where he worked for about six months as an attorney in the tire-rationing section of the Office of Price Administration — an experience that made him disillusioned with governmental bureaucracy. In June 1942, he accepted appointment as a lieutenant, junior grade, in the Naval Reserve. After training, he served in the South Pacific as officer in charge of the South Pacific Combat Air Transport Command (SCAT) at Guadalcanal and Green Island. He later carried out various stateside assignments for the navy's Bureau of Aeronautics. By the time of his discharge in early 1946 he had advanced to the rank of lieutenant commander.

In 1946, Nixon sought his first elective office. Even before his release from the Navy, a group of California Republicans endorsed his candidacy for the United States House of Representatives from the state's 12th Congressional District. Nixon did not disappoint these initial supporters. Early in 1946 he captured his party's nomination for Congress, and in the November elections he unseated the Democratic incumbent H. Jerry Voorhis in a campaign that foreshadowed those of his later political career. Displaying a deep understanding of the temper of his constituents and an adroit sense of politics, he took a strong stand against communism; indeed, he alleged that his opponent, Voorhis, had the backing of a communist-dominated organization and he argued that a vote for Voorhis would be a vote for pro-Communist forces. In the early postwar years such a campaign had widespread appeal, and Nixon gained a reputation as a fighter against communism that eventually brought him to national prominence.

Nixon served two terms in the House of Representatives, and during that time he worked on some of its most influential committees. As a member of the House Committee on Education and Labor he aided in drafting the Labor-Management Act of 1947, or the Taft-Hartley Act, as it is more popularly known. Nixon was also a member of the Select Committee on Foreign Aid, which was sent to Europe to examine the war-ravaged economies of that continent, and whose recommendations helped cement bipartisan support for the Marshall Plan.

But the activity that most advanced Nixon's career prior to 1950 was his membership on the controversial House Un-American Activities Committee. The young congressman worked on the bill requiring alleged communist-front organizations in the United States to register with the attorney general, and he also helped with the committee's investigations into alleged communist infiltration of government, schools, and other organizations. When in 1948 Whittaker Chambers, an editor of *Time* magazine, accused Alger Hiss, the president of the Carnegie Endowment for International Peace and a former member of the State Department, of having belonged to the Communist party, Nixon played a leading role in the ensuing investigation, and it was largely because of his persistent efforts that Hiss was indicted and ultimately convicted of perjury.

Nixon's conduct of the Hiss case alienated some portions of the populace. Nixon himself later wrote that it "left a residue of hatred and hostility toward me . . . among substantial segments of the press and intellectual community." But the vast majority of the American people, uneasy with the political frustrations of the cold war, approved of his dogged investigations of Hiss. Nixon became an increasingly prominent figure in national politics.

In 1950, Nixon ran for the United States Senate. His campaign against the Democratic candidate, Representative Helen Gahagan Douglas, was hard fought and feelings on both sides were extremely heated. Nixon accused Mrs. Douglas of being soft on communism; she, in turn, bestowed upon him the uncomplimentary nickname Tricky Dick. Nixon nonetheless won the November contest, and entered the Senate in December 1950, shortly after the resignation of incumbent Senator Sheridan Downey.

During his years in the Senate, Nixon served on the Labor and Public Welfare Committee and on the Expenditures in Executive Departments Committee. In addition to his official duties in Washington, Nixon, in 1951 and 1952, spoke before numerous Republican groups across the country, and these speaking engagements worked to enhance his reputation among the most influential members of the party.

When he addressed a New York State fund-raising dinner in May 1952, he very favorably impressed Thomas E. Dewey, the Republican presidential candidate in 1944 and 1948 and a trusted adviser of General Dwight D. Eisenhower (see October 14). Two months later, when Eisenhower captured the Republican presidential nomination, Dewey and others suggested Nixon as a possible running mate. Eisenhower agreed to their proposal, and at the age of 39 Richard Nixon became a candidate for the second-highest elective office in the nation.

Senator Karl Mundt identified the three issues on which the Republican campaign focused as $K_1 C_2$ — Korea, Communism, and Corruption. The bloody war in Korea (see June 25), the Democrats' alleged softness on communism, and several scandals involving instances of corruption among some administration officials were obvious targets for Republican politicians seeking to oust Democratic incumbents. Smarting under the brickbats, the Democrats temporarily turned one element of the Republican attack back against the GOP. Midway through the 1952 campaign, vice presidential candidate Nixon was accused of having for two years accepted contributions from California businessmen to a private expense fund designed to offset political expenses.

Temporarily unnerved by the disclosures, some Republican leaders called for the candidate to withdraw from the race. Perturbed by these circumstances, Nixon secured prime television time, paid for by the Republican National Committee, and in an emotion-filled extemporaneous speech proclaimed his innocence of any wrongdoing and denied that any part of the fund had ever been devoted to personal use. In an oblique reference to allegations that the wives of some administration officials had received improper gifts of furs, Nixon noted that his wife, Pat, wore a "respectable Republican cloth coat." In the course of the speech he also mentioned the family cocker spaniel, Checkers, which he claimed was the only personal gift he had received while in office. The candidate then asked viewers to determine his future by writing their opinions of his candidacy to the Republican National Committee. The audience response was overwhelmingly favorable, and, thanks to the so-called Checkers speech, Nixon remained on the ticket. General Eisenhower, assured once more of his running mate's probity, embraced the young man publicly and exclaimed "That's my boy."

On November 4, 1952, Eisenhower and Nixon scored an overwhelming victory over their Democratic opponents, former governor Adlai E. Stevenson of Illinois and Senator John J. Sparkman of Alabama. The Republicans captured approximately 33,936,000 ballots and the Democrats approximately 27,315,000, and in the electoral college they gained 442 votes and their rivals 89. On January 20, 1953, Dwight D. Eisenhower took the oath of office as President of the United States and Richard M. Nixon, who had recently celebrated his 40th birthday, became the second youngest Vice President in the nation's history.

Under Eisenhower, the powers and responsibilities of the vice presidency were broadened to an unprecendented degree. The President kept Nixon well informed on his domestic and foreign policies and delegated to him important duties that previous Presidents had reserved for themselves. During Eisenhower's first term Nixon performed the critical political task of keeping dissident factions of the Republican party from disaffection, and on the occasions of Eisenhower's illnesses in 1955, 1956, and 1957, he even presided over several meetings of the cabinet and the National Security Council.

In 1956, the Eisenhower-Nixon ticket easily defeated Democratic hopefuls Adlai Stevenson and Senator Estes Kefauver of Tennessee. During his second term in office Nixon continued to be in the public eye as Vice President. In the spring of 1958, Nixon and his wife Pat made a goodwill tour of South America. Unfriendly mobs of Communist sympathizers assaulted the Nixons in Lima, Peru and Caracas, Venezuela, but the Vice President retained his composure throughout the incidents. The following year, Nixon visited Moscow, where he opened the American National Exhibition. At a display of kitchen appliances, Soviet Premier Nikita S. Khrushchev engaged the American Vice President in a heated discussion of issues on which the United States and the Soviet Union differed. Nixon handled the awkward situation well and his conduct during the so-called kitchen debate was widely applauded in the United States. In all he visited 56 countries during his vice presidency.

Nixon won the Republican presidential nomination in 1960 and Henry Cabot Lodge of Massachusetts was chosen as his running mate. The Democrats selected Senator John F. Kennedy, also of Massachusetts (see May 29) and Senate Majority Leader Lyndon B. Johnson (see August 27) to be their standard-bearers. During the course of the 1960 campaign, Nixon and Kennedy met in a series of four debates, which were shown on television screens across the nation. Nixon, fatigued and suffering from a knee injury, fared poorly in the first of these confrontations, while Kennedy, projecting an image of youth and vigor, conveyed a favorable impression. Reactions to the other three television appearances were more evenly balanced, but some political analysts felt that the first debate was an important factor in the outcome of the November election, in which Kennedy defeated Nixon by the narrow margin of some 118,000 popular votes.

After 14 years of public service in the nation's capital, Nixon returned to California in 1961. He joined a Los Angeles law firm and in 1962 published his political memoir *Six Crises*. The same year he again sought elective office – this time running for governor of California against the Democratic incumbent, Edmund "Pat" Brown. On election day, Brown defeated Nixon by almost 300,000 votes. Nixon contended that unfair treatment by the press had been largely responsible for both this defeat and his failure to win the 1960 presidential race, and the day after the election he revealed his bitterness when he told a group of newsmen: "You won't have Nixon to kick around any more because, gentlemen, this is my last press conference."

In 1963 Nixon moved to New York City, where he became a partner in one of the city's largest law firms. In 1964, it became known as Nixon, Mudge, Rose, Guthrie and Alexander – to which the name Mitchell was later added. Most observers believed that Nixon's political career had ended, but the former Vice President continued to be active in the Republican party and, unlike many prominent Republicans, he endorsed and worked for the election of Arizona Senator Barry Goldwater, the party's presidential nominee in 1964. However, nomination of the conservative Goldwater alienated many moderate and liberal Republicans, badly dividing the party, and on election day Lyndon B. Johnson defeated Goldwater by the largest majority of votes in the nation's history. In the wake of the 1964 Republican disaster, Nixon's political career revived: his faithfulness to the GOP had gained him support among many sections of the party, and he increasingly appeared to be a likely presidential candidate in 1968. But before he could achieve this goal, he had to overcome his reputation as a "loser," acquired from his defeats in 1960 and 1962. To do this, he entered state primary elections and scored impressive victories in the spring of 1968. In July, delegates to the Republican National Convention in Miami Beach, Florida, chose Nixon as their nominee for President on the first ballot.

In the November election, division within the Democratic party and the presence on the ballot of third-party candidate George C. Wallace of Alabama helped Nixon and his running mate, Governor Spiro T. Agnew of Maryland, to achieve victory over the Democratic candidates, Vice President Hubert H. Humphrey and Senator Edmund Muskie of Maine. The popular vote was close: the Republican ticket won 31,785,480 ballots; the Democrats took 31,275-165; and Wallace gained the remaining 9,906,-473. But in the electoral college the margin was greater: Nixon had the votes of 32 states, Humphrey had 13 and the District of Columbia, while Wallace carried only 5 Deep South states.

On January 20, 1969, Nixon took the oath of office and became the 37th President of the United States. His inaugural address strongly emphasized his hope to reunite the American people. When he assumed the presidency, the issue which most divided them was the unpopular war in South Vietnam (see August 7). As critics of the war grew more strident in their demand that the United States end its involvement on behalf of South Vietnam, Nixon responded by accelerating the plan by which South Vietnamese troops were trained to defend their country, thereby permitting the gradual withdrawal of American servicemen. Vietnamization, as the plan was known, did not satisfy all opponents of the war, but enabled Nixon to reduce the number of American troops in Vietnam from about 542,500 in February 1969 to 368,000 in late 1970, with the promise of further reductions to come.

While the American people generally approved Nixon's "winding down" of the Vietnam war, their confidence in his commitment to end US involvement was several times shaken. In April 1970, he approved a joint South Vietnamese-American foray against Communist sanctuaries in Cambodia, precipitating numerous antiwar demonstrations within the United States, including one at Kent State University in Ohio, where National Guardsmen shot and killed four university students. Responding to this tragedy, which outraged large portions of the populace, many colleges and universities closed for the remainder of the 1970 spring semester. Then, in February 1971, the United States supported with air power and matériel a 45-day campaign by South Vietnamese soldiers, who moved across the border into Laos to attack the North Vietnamese supply network known as the Ho Chi Minh Trail. In reply to North Vietnam's subsequent escalation of action against South Vietnam, President Nixon in May 1972 ordered the closing of land and sea supply routes to the North by US military action — the mining of major North Vietnamese harbors and greatly increased US bombing.

Meanwhile, other aspects of foreign policy went on. In an astonishing shift from previous US cold war positions, Nixon announced in July 1971 that he would personally visit the People's Republic of China, whose existence the United States had never officially recognized since 1949, when the current Communist regime took over the Chinese mainland from the Nationalist Chinese forces of Generalissimo Chiang Kai-shek. Nixon's startling pronouncement was only one of a series of steps, including an easing of trade and travel restrictions, that were taken during his administration, to come, in his words, "urgently to grips with the reality of China." Only a few months after Nixon moved to open relations with China the Peking government gained admission to the United Nations, replacing the Nationalist Chinese, headquartered on the island of Taiwan, who were expelled from the world organization.

The President's visit to Communist China, which took place in February 1972, was followed in May by one to the USSR. One result of the Russian trip was an attempt on the part of the two superpowers to retard the nuclear arms race by means of agreements to limit their respective missile systems. Other easing of tensions, including an increase in trade between the two nations, followed.

In Vietnam, however, the war continued, although by May 1972 Nixon had reduced to 69,000 the number of American troops scheduled to remain there. By the fall of the same year, the number had been lowered to less than 33,000. Hopes of eventual total US withdrawal meanwhile persisted, as formal peace talks between participants in the war dragged on in Paris and as secret proposals and counterproposals for ending the conflict were exchanged behind the scenes across the globe.

The peace pact that was eventually signed in Paris on January 27, 1973, provided for an in-place ceasefire, the release of all military prisoners of war and foreign civilians, the withdrawal within 60 days of the 23,000-man US force then in South Vietnam, and the creation of an international force composed of Canadians, Hungarians, Indonesians, and Poles to supervise the truce. North Vietnamese troops already in the South were allowed to remain, but according to the agreement they were not to be replaced; and both the United States and North Vietnam agreed to respect "the South Vietnamese people's right to self-determination."

This cease-fire extricated the United States from the bloody war, but it did not end the fighting. For more than two years following the signing of the truce, conflict continued until the Saigon government unconditionally surrendered on April 30, 1975.

Although foreign policy was a major concern of Nixon's administration, several domestic issues also presented the Chief Executive with serious problems. One of the most critical of these was economic. In the first years of Nixon's presidency, the United States' economy suffered badly; unemployment and interest rates soared, inflation mounted, and the balance of payments in foreign trade tipped to the disadvantage of the United States for the first time in this century. Nixon's initial reaction to the worsening economic picture was to ask for voluntary wage, price, and trade restraints; repeatedly, he refused to impose mandatory controls.

Then, in August 1971, the President announced a drastic reversal in his fiscal policy. He ordered a 90-day wage-price freeze, promised a number of substantial tax cuts, imposed a temporary 10 percent surcharge on imports, and allowed the US dollar to float in the international exchange markets. Later, the controls were extended in a further effort to slow inflation; and the dollar was devalued in conjunction with a global realignment of currencies. It was expected that the latter changes would improve the competitive position of US manufactures abroad and contribute importantly to offsetting the nation's balance of payments deficit. In the fall of 1972, analysts believed that the wage-price controls had been reasonably successful in slowing the rate of inflation without dampening the economy. Indeed, the economy was expanding strongly at the time. The Dow Jones industrial average of stocks closed above the long-aimed-at 1,000 level for the first time in history on November 14, 1972. But the Nixon administration was unable to resolve the basic question of how to substantially lower the high rate of unemployment without fueling a fresh burst of inflation. In seeking a solution to this dilemma, the President again reversed his economic policy in the opening days of 1973

and ended most mandatory price and wage controls, even though the economy suffered from a mounting rate of inflation.

In the course of his presidency, Nixon, by early 1972, had appointed four justices to the Supreme Court, an opportunity enjoyed by few Presidents. All of the President's appointees to the Supreme Court — Chief Justice Warren Burger (see September 17) and Associate Justices Harry A. Blackmun, Lewis F. Powell Jr., and William H. Rehnquist — were conservatives, and their selection reflected the determination of the Chief Executive, an avowed strict constructionist, to reverse the Warren court's trend toward liberal interpretations of the Constitution. Particularly, the President felt that court rulings in some areas had weakened the tools of law enforcement "as against the crime forces in this country."

With 60.8 percent of the popular vote — a majority in a presidential contest exceeded only by that amassed by Lyndon B. Johnson in 1964 — Nixon won reelection as Chief Executive on November 7, 1972, against the Democratic challenger Senator George McGovern of South Dakota. Such an overwhelming endorsement seemed to mean that he would be able to consolidate and expand the foreign and domestic policies begun in his first four years in office. But the dark cloud of Watergate overshadowed Nixon's second term.

Shortly after 2:00 A.M. on June 17, 1972, five men, including James W. McCord Jr., security adviser for the Committee for the Reelection of the President (CRP), were arrested in the act of burglarizing the Democratic National Committee's headquarters at Washington's Watergate complex, where they were discovered with cameras and illegal electronic surveillance equipment. Two confederates monitoring their operation from a nearby location were later apprehended as well. Although it subsequently was asserted that the illicit undertaking had been funded with the approval of CRP officials, President Nixon disavowed any prior knowledge of the escapade. On August 29 he stated that "no one in the White House staff, no one in this administration, presently employed, was involved. . . ." Most people believed him, and the prediction by Senator McGovern that the Watergate scandal would become a major campaign issue never materialized.

By the end of January 1973, the five burglars and two accomplices had pleaded guilty to felonies or had been convicted of them. But US District Court Judge John J. Sirica, who presided at the trials, doubted that the whole truth had been revealed, a suspicion strengthened by a letter he received from McCord, which he made public at the March 23 sentencing hearing. McCord claimed that the defendants had been under pressure to plead guilty and to suppress facts in order to protect higher ranking officials. On March 24 McCord reportedly testified before the Senate Select Committee on Presidential Campaign Activities, which had been established on February 7, that White House counsel John Wesley Dean III and CRP official Jeb Stuart Magruder had prior knowledge of the Watergate break-in.

After these allegations, Nixon reversed his former noncooperative attitude toward the Senate Select Committee. On April 17 he promised that his staff would testify when called, rather than stand behind the shield of executive privilege as before. In a televised address on April 30, he took general responsibility for (while denying knowledge of) any wrongdoing during the 1972 presidential campaign. He also announced the resignations of Dean; H. R. Haldeman, White House chief of staff; John D. Ehrlichman, his chief counselor for domestic affairs; and Attorney General Richard G. Kleindienst. At the same time the President announced his nomination of Elliot Richardson to become the new attorney general, stating that Richardson would have authority to appoint a special prosecutor with full powers to investigate the Watergate affair. The man Richardson chose for that position was Archibald Cox, a Harvard Law School professor and former US solicitor general.

The Senate Select Committee (later known as the Watergate Committee), under chairman Sam J. Ervin Jr. of North Carolina, began televised public hearings on the Watergate scandal on May 17, 1973. Dean testified from June 25 to 29 that Nixon had encouraged efforts to cover up Watergate and had discussed with him the possibility of executive clemency for the conspirators and the payment of hush money. Dean also reported that the White House had engaged in illegal efforts to suppress political opposition and to harass persons noted on an "enemies list." Several officials implicated by Dean, including Haldeman, Ehrlichman, and former Attorney General John Mitchell, who had served as CRP chairman from March 1 to July 1, 1972, denied Dean's allegations in subsequent testimony before the Ervin committee.

Hopes for discovering the truth rose when former White House aide Alexander P. Butterfield told the senators on July 16 that since early 1970 — the White House afterward said it was a year later — the President had tape-recorded all conversations in his offices at the White House and at the Executive Office Building. Both Senator Ervin and Watergate special prosecutor Cox immediately asked Nixon to hand over the tapes relevant to their investigations. Nixon refused the Senate Watergate Committee's request on the grounds that compliance would violate executive privilege and the constitutional doctrine of the separation of powers of the three branches of government. Cox was similarly refused access to the tapes. Both Cox and Ervin then subpoenaed the documents, and the matter went to Judge Sirica for decision. The judge stated that he lacked authority to enforce the Senate committee's order. Regarding Cox's subpoena, Sirica informed the President on August 29 that he himself would have to examine the tapes before deciding whether executive privilege had been properly invoked. Rather than comply, the President appealed the judge's ruling.

On October 12 the US Court of Appeals for the District of Columbia affirmed Sirica's decision, asserting that the President was "not above the law's commands" and that "the Constitution mentions no executive privileges. . . ." Rather than take the case to the Supreme Court, as many had assumed he would, Nixon put forward a "compromise" plan by which he would personally summarize the requested tapes, have the summary's accuracy verified by Senator John C. Stennis of Mississippi after permitting him to hear the tapes, and provide the verified summary to the Watergate investigators. When Cox rejected this compromise, the President ordered him, as "an employee of the executive branch," to cease further efforts to acquire the tapes and related materials through the courts.

Refusing to follow this instruction, Cox explained his reasons at a televised news conference on October 20. That evening, at presidential instruction, Attorney General Elliot Richardson was ordered to dismiss Cox. Richardson resigned rather than participate in what came to be known as the Saturday Night Masaacre. His second-in-command, Deputy Attorney General William D. Ruckelshaus, also refused to carry out the President's order and was promptly fired. Solicitor General Robert H. Bork finally executed the discharge order.

However, public reaction to the firing of Cox was so widespread and so hostile that Nixon finally was forced to release the tapes. The announcement that the President would comply was made by a Nixon lawyer in Sirica's court on October 23. Later, however, another member of Nixon's defense team stated that two crucially important conversations had not been recorded. Still later, he reported that an 18.5-minute gap existed in the tape of a conference between Nixon and Haldeman three days after the Watergate break-in. It developed that there were gaps in some other tapes as well. Judge Sirica turned most of the tapes over to Leon Jaworski, the new special prosecutor whom Nixon, under the pressure of public opinion, had named on November 1 to replace Cox.

Scandals beyond Watergate also plagued the President during these months. On October 10 Vice President Spiro T. Agnew resigned and pleaded no contest to a charge of having evaded federal income taxes in 1967. In return for this virtual admission of guilt, the Department of Justice dropped other charges alleging that Agnew had accepted illicit payoffs during, and since, his tenure as governor of Maryland. Nixon, meanwhile, was embarrassed by revelations of illegal corporate financial contribution to his 1972 presidential campaign; of major public expenditures on his private residences in San Clemente, California, and Key Biscayne, Florida; and of a questionable income tax deduction of $576,000 for turning over his vice presidential papers to the National Archives. In April 1974, the President agreed to pay $432,787 in back taxes, plus interest, to the government.

Meanwhile, on March 1, 1974, a federal grand jury handed up to Judge Sirica indictments of Mitchell, Haldeman, Ehrlichman, and four other former White House or presidential campaign aides on charges of conspiracy in the Watergate cover-up. Doubting that an incumbent President would be liable to indictment, the panel did not indict Nixon. Instead, it took the unusual step of giving to Sirica a sealed report outlining its findings about the Chief Executive's involvement that designated him as an unindicted co-conspirator.

Other inquiries were going forward at the same time. On February 6, 1974, the House of Representatives voted 410 to 4 to grant to its Judiciary Committee, under chairman Peter Rodino of New Jersey, the power to pursue an inquiry as to whether grounds existed for the impeachment of the President. In March the committee received White House tapes and documents that earlier had been provided to the Watergate grand jury. However, the President refused a request for 42 additional tapes and the committee issued a subpoena for them on April 11. Seven days later another subpoena, issued by Judge Sirica at the request of special prosecutor Jaworski, demanded that the President provide tape recordings of 64 conversations and related material.

Unwilling to give up the tapes, yet hoping to reverse the tide that was increasingly running against him, Nixon on April 30 instead released more than 1,250 pages of edited transcripts from the tapes. Of the 42 tapes that the Judiciary Committee had subpoenaed, 11 were declared to be nonexistent or missing. Those transcripts that were published only further tarnished the President's reputation. Not only did they reveal a profane and cynical side of the publicly upright Nixon, but they also belied his professed concern for reaching the truth about Watergate.

On July 9, the House Judiciary Committee issued its own transcripts of eight tapes it possessed. Comparison with the White House transcripts showed important discrepancies, unfavorable to the President. During the remaining days of its investigation, the committee (composed of 21 Democrats and 17 Republicans) closely examined and debated the available evidence. Beginning on July 24, most of its deliberations were nationally televised. On July 27, after exhaustive debate of the issues involved, the committee, by a bipartisan 27-11 vote, passed an article of impeachment that it planned to present for vote of the whole House, accusing Nixon of obstruction of justice. On July 29 a second article of impeachment, passed by a vote of 28 to 10, charged him with abuse of power, failing in his "constitutional duty to take care that the laws be faithfully executed," and engaging "in conduct violating the constitutional rights of citizens." This conduct, said the article, in part, included one or more of the following:

(1) He has, . . . personally and through . . . subordinates and agents, endeavored to obtain from the Internal Revenue Service . . . confidential information contained in income tax returns for purposes not authorized by law, and to cause, in violation of the constitutional rights of citizens, income tax audits or other . . . investigations to be . . . conducted in a discriminatory manner.

(2) He misused the Federal Bureau of Investigation, the Secret Service, and other executive personnel, in violation or disregard of the constitutional right of citizens, by directing, or authorizing such agencies or personnel to conduct . . . electronic surveillance or other investigations for purposes unrelated to national security, the enforcement of laws, or any other lawful function of his office. . . .

(3) He has . . . personally and through . . . subordinates and agents . . . authorized . . . a secret investigative unit within the office of the President . . . which unlawfully utilized the resources of the Central Intelligence Agency [and] engaged in covert and unlawful activities. . . .

On July 30, by a vote of 21 to 17, the committee passed a third article of impeachment accusing the President of contempt of Congress for failure to obey the committee's subpoenas for Watergate tapes and related materials.

As for the 64 additional tapes ordered by Judge Sirica on behalf of special prosecutor Jaworski, after the White House moved to appeal the order, Jaworski, on May 24, asked the Supreme Court to intervene and rule on the matter directly in the interest of speed. The high court's decision, issued on July 24, the same day the Judiciary Committee's televised hearings began, proved ultimately even more disastrous for Nixon than the Judiciary Committee's action. With Associate Justice William Rehnquist, who had served in the Justice Department under Mitchell, withdrawing from the case, the remaining eight members unanimously sustained an order by Judge Sirica that the President must turn over the tapes. They rejected the contention that either "executive privilege" or the doctrine of the separation of powers was reason to withhold evidence from a criminal prosecution.

Nixon's closest aides were appalled when they learned the contents of the subpoenaed tapes. The transcripts, especially those of three conversations between Nixon and Haldeman on June 23, 1972, six days after the Watergate break-in, showed clearly that the President had tried to impede the FBI's investigation of the Watergate affair and that he was concerned with politics, rather than with national security. Showing, as they did, that the President had known of and approved key parts of the Watergate cover-up almost from the beginning, the transcripts, which contradicted his numerous public statements, were like bombshells (though neither they nor other evidence ever proved that Nixon had knowledge of the Watergate break-in prior to its occurrence).

Support for the President had collapsed by now, with even his staunchest defenders on the House Judiciary Committee convinced that the conversations of June 23, 1972, constituted the "smoking pistol" of presidential complicity. On Wednesday, August 7, Republican Representative John Rhodes and Republican Senators Hugh Scott and Barry Goldwater met with Nixon to tell him his supporters in Congress had diminished to a handful and that impeachment and conviction were inevitable.

The President appeared on national television at 9:00 P.M. the following evening and announced that he would resign at noon the next day. In a brief and dignified speech he summed up the achievements of his presidency and stated that he was leaving because his political base in the Congress had eroded. On the morning of August 9, 1974, he bade farewell to members of his administration with an extemporaneous and highly emotional televised address. Escorted by Vice President Gerald Ford, who

in a few hours was to be sworn in as the new President, Nixon, his wife Pat, their daughter Tricia, and her husband Edward Cox left the White House by helicopter on the first leg of the long flight to San Clemente. Left to wind up loose ends for them in Washington were daughter Julie Nixon Eisenhower and her husband David, grandson of the late President Eisenhower.

Scarcely a month later, on September 8, President Ford sought to heal past divisions by granting Nixon a pardon for "all offenses against the United States which he . . . has committed or may have committed or taken part in" during his presidency. Nixon accepted the pardon and expressed sorrow for his handling of Watergate, but he did not confess to any criminal wrongdoing. The pardon was controversial, pleasing those who did not wish to see a former President face trial or imprisonment, but outraging others who thought it a travesty of the concept of equal justice under law. Some of Nixon's closest associates did not fare as well as their chief: on January 1, 1975, Mitchell, Haldeman, and Ehrlichman were found guilty of conspiracy, obstruction of justice, and perjury. Numerous other former Nixon associates also were implicated. Adding the number of corporations that tangled with the law for having made illegal contributions to the 1972 campaign, the total of indicted or convicted persons was several score. The list of misdeeds collectively known as Watergate included illicit wiretapping, illegal opening of mail, "dirty tricks" and other political sabotage, burglary, harassment, payment of hush money, misuse of the government's executive departments, spying on dissidents, and other violations of the rights of individual citizens under the Constitution.

The widespread pattern of illegal behavior on the part of members of the Nixon administration appeared to have been motivated mainly by an acute anxiety over the activities of the antiwar movement; a strong fear that the movement and other dissident groups were somehow under the influence of foreign powers; an excessive concern with unauthorized news leaks to the media; and an anything-to-win-the-election attitude largely inspired by the President's own political philosophy. Because of the importance of the constitutional issues involved, and the violation of freedoms guaranteed citizens in the Bill of Rights, Watergate, as it eventually unfolded, was the nation's worst political scandal and gravest constitutional crisis. What was decided when it was over was that the nation is still a nation ruled by laws, not men.

As for the former President, serious illness, stemming from prolonged phlebitis in his left leg, struck Nixon in autumn of 1974. He almost died after surgery designed to prevent blood clots from traveling from his leg to his heart, and he spent over a month in the hospital in California before returning to San Clemente for further lengthy recuperation. Thereafter, he lived for a long period in virtual seclusion, working on the memoirs that presumably would reveal his own version of his presidential accomplishments and of Watergate. By late 1975 he had begun to emerge slowly from isolation, was reported as thinking ahead to possible future foreign travel, and had decided to break his long silence by agreeing to taped television interviews which were to be released after both the publication of his book and the 1976 presidential elections had taken place.

JANUARY 10

League of Nations Established

One of the most far-reaching results of World War I was the establishment of the League of Nations on January 10, 1920. As the war pursued its relentless course, the public in both Europe and the United States, shocked by the appalling losses, pressed increasingly for establishment of an international peace organization that might prevent such destruction and suffering in the future.

Plans for such a league had long been proposed by unofficial societies in Great Britain, France, and especially in the United States; they had won the support of many influential leaders in public and private life, including former President William H. Taft and the British statesmen Sir Edward Grey and Lord Robert Cecil. By the spring of 1915, the name League of Nations already was commonly used among small interested groups. Both parties in the presidential campaign of 1916 backed US membership in such an organization in their political platforms. The incumbent President, Woodrow Wilson, the Democratic victor, was an ardent advocate of the movement. His famous Fourteen Points, which he proclaimed in January 1918 as essential for the peace settlement, called for the establishment of "a general association of nations . . . affording mutual guarantees of political independence and territorial integrity to great and small States alike."

At the end of World War I, President Wilson urged strongly that provisions for such an association be inserted in the treaty between the victorious Allies — Britain, France, Russia, and the United States — and Germany. The proposal was at first received coldly by some na-

tions, but it nevertheless was generally agreed that one of the tasks of the Paris peace conference, which opened in January 1919, should be the formation of a League of Nations. Finally a commission was appointed, composed of two delegates each from the United States, France, Great Britain, Italy, and Japan, with representatives of five smaller powers subsequently added, to study the different forms of covenant that had been submitted. The work — contrary to either the military or territorial settlements — proceeded quickly. Not only had the topic been studied carefully before and during the war, but also, several 19th century developments in international cooperation provided valuable precedents to guide the plan makers. These included, for example, the growth of such international agencies and bureaus as the Universal Postal Union (UPU), founded in 1874; the creation of the Permanent Court of Arbitration at the Hague Peace Conference of 1907; and the proliferation of international treaties, some bilateral, some multilateral, to — for example — respect the neutrality of certain states or to guarantee the rights of businesses or individuals in the signatory countries (e.g., the International Copyright Convention of 1870).

After several sittings, the commission agreed upon a final draft, entitled the "Covenant of the League of Nations," and inserted it into the Treaty of Versailles. The covenant was submitted for approval on February 14, 1919; the final amended text was unanimously adopted by the conference on April 28, 1919. The concise document of 26 articles set up the central organs of the League of Nations — assembly, council, and secretariat — as well as a broad network of auxiliary institutions of a primarily legal and political, or economic and social, nature. Geneva, Switzerland, was designated as the organization's headquarters. The league formally came into existence only on January 10, 1920, the date of the deposit of the ratification of the Treaty of Versailles by Germany.

The establishment of the league was a decisive step in the history of international relations. It was the first permanent international body of general purpose to encompass much of the world community. The 32 Allied states that had signed the peace treaties, as well as 13 neutral states, were asked to join. Moreover, other self-governing states, dominions, and colonies could become members provided two-thirds of the league assembly approved. On its formal inauguration, there were only 23 members, but the total had risen to 42 by November 1920. Egypt became the 63rd and last league member in 1937, although by that time several leading countries had withdrawn from the organization.

In fact, halfhearted intermittent participation by large and small nations alike contributed greatly to the eventual failure of the league. Of the major powers, only Great Britain and France belonged during the entire span of the league's existence. Japan withdrew in 1933, and Italy withdrew in 1937. Germany, mistrusted as a former Central Power, was allowed to enter only in 1926 and withdrew in 1933 after Adolf Hitler had become chancellor. Russia became a member in 1934, only to be excluded when Soviet troops attacked Finland in 1939.

The greatest blow to the league's prospects — and a major reason for its decline — was the failure of the United States to become a member. President Wilson sought to induce the Senate to ratify the league covenant. The advocates of international cooperation in the interest of peace supported his bid for ratification, but many serious reservations were proposed by senators who opposed Wilson's involvement in European politics and favored a return to isolationism. The President objected to these reservations and when the question of ratification with the reservations came to a vote in March 1920, his supporters in the Senate voted in the negative and the treaty was rejected. The issue of joining the league entered the presidential campaign of 1920, with the Democratic candidate, James M. Cox, favoring it and the Republican candidate, Warren G. Harding, taking an equivocal position. The Republicans won by a large majority. As a result, the United States never joined the league, although it cooperated to a limited extent in peace-enforcement efforts in the 1930s.

The league, although ultimately hampered by the great powers' failure to submit to international will on important issues, nonetheless functioned with a certain effectiveness for nearly two decades, serving in vital instances to prevent war and contributing to the alleviation of human suffering. During this period it faced high odds, for World War I had bequeathed a vast complex of festering grievances, disillusionments, and resentments, which the economic upheavals of the late 1920s and 1930s merely served to aggravate. The league handled to the best of its ability the burdensome responsibilities left it by the 1919 peace treaties, such as the supervision of the Baltic seaport of Danzig, the Saar territory, and Germany's former colonial dependencies in Africa and the Pacific. It was closely associated with the International Labor Organization, founded in 1919 to improve labor conditions in all parts of the world, and with the Permanent Court of International Justice formed at The Hague in 1921. It furthered international cooperation in the fields of economics, communications, and transport, augmenting medical services and intellectual exchanges and suppressing traffic in drugs and enforced prostitution.

But its primary purpose — and the one on which it has been most critically judged — centered upon the basic idea of collective security, the belief that it is the right and obligation of all states to band together to prevent aggressive war as a crime against the entire human community. On this ground, the league — particularly in its early days — actively intervened both in major disputes that seemed to endanger peace and in small but threatening problems of frontier adjustment and minority rights. It settled, for example, the question of the disputed Polish-German frontier in Upper Silesia in 1921, and, as late as January 1935, dispatched genuinely international forces to oversee the Saar plebiscite. Its last major act — the expulsion of the USSR from league membership after the attack on Finland — was in 1939.

By then, however, the league's prestige had been severely damaged by its inability to deal effectively with acts of aggression committed earlier in the 1930s by Italy, Germany, and Japan. When the Japanese army attacked Chinese authorities in Manchuria in 1931, the league was helpless to protect China. In October 1935, the Italian dictator, Benito Mussolini, invaded Ethiopia and occupied and annexed it despite extensive economic sanctions in which 52 league member states participated. Adolf Hitler remilitarized the Rhineland in 1934 and denounced the Treaty of Versailles two years later.

A swift series of crises in the late 1930s — the Spanish Civil War and the German annexations of Austria and part of Czechoslovakia — marked the doom of the league as an agency for the preservation of peace. Small states realized that the organization could not protect them against superior enemy forces. When World War II broke out in September 1939 with the German invasion of Poland (see September 1), no nation seriously suggested that the matter be submitted to the league for judgment. The Finnish appeal for help against the Soviet aggression in 1939 was a mere formality.

Thus weakened, the League of Nations reduced its Geneva secretariat to a skeleton staff in 1940. No further meetings were held during World War II, but economic and social work on a limited scale was carried on in the United States and Canada. In the last years of the war, the Allies, although rejecting any idea of reviving the covenant, which was still nominally in force, began to plan for a future international organization. And, as it turned out, the League of Nations' greatest lasting achievement was its importance as a model for such a new international body. It was on these precedents — aims, principles, institutions, and methods — that the United Nations, founded in 1945 (see October 24), was to a large degree patterned. The League of Nations officially dissolved itself in April 1946. Its services and property, most notably the Palace of Nations in Geneva, were turned over to the United Nations.

JANUARY 11

Feast of the Baptism of the Lord

This is a movable event. See note on page xxvi.

The baptism of Jesus in the River Jordan by John the Baptist was significant as the occasion of a divine sign manifesting Jesus' divinity, and it marked the beginning of his public mission. For many centuries, Jesus Christ's baptism has been stressed by churches of the East in their observance of the Epiphany (see January 6). Western churches, however, place more emphasis at Epiphany on the Adoration of the Magi (or Three Kings) during their visit to the infant Jesus. Since 1961, however, the Baptism of the Lord has been marked by Roman Catholics as a separate feast in its own right. The fixed date of January 13 was at first designated for the new observance. With the Roman Catholic calendar reform of 1969, however, the Feast of the Baptism of the Lord was moved to the Sunday following the Epiphany or January 6. (The observance is omitted in years when it would coincide with the observance of the Epiphany, in places where the Epiphany had been transferred from the traditional January 6 date to the Sunday between January 2 and 8 — as in the United States.) Episcopalians have considered joining Catholics in marking the Feast of the Baptism of the Lord on the first Sunday after the Epiphany, although no decision on proposed changes or additions to the Episcopalian calendar could go into effect before 1977.

The biblical account of the baptism of Jesus is familiar to Christians of all denominations, including those that do not commemorate the event with a special feast day. It appears in all four of the New Testament Gospels, Matthew (3:13–17), Mark (1:9–11), Luke (3:21–23), and John (1:29–34). Perhaps the best-known version is the one in Matthew, which comes soon after the passage quoting John the Baptist's declaration, "I baptize . . . with water for repentance, but he who is coming after me is mightier than I, whose sandals I am not worthy to carry; he will baptize you with the Holy Spirit and with fire":

Then Jesus came from Galilee to the Jordan to John, to be baptized by him. John would have prevented him, saying, "I need to be baptized by you, and do you come to me?" But Jesus answered him, "Let it be so now; for thus it is fitting for us to fulfil all righteousness." Then he consented. And when Jesus was baptized, he went up immediately from the water, and behold, the heavens were opened and he saw the Spirit of God descending like a dove, and alighting on him; and lo, a voice from heaven, saying, "This is my beloved Son with whom I am well pleased."

Alexander Hamilton's Birthday

Alexander Hamilton was one of the most brilliant and influential figures of the American Revolutionary era. He occupied a focal point in the struggle for liberty and in the formation of the fledgling country from the very onset of armed hostilities with Great Britain to the close of President John Adams's term in office more than a quarter of a century later.

Alexander Hamilton was born on January 11 at Charlestown on the island of Nevis in the Leeward group of the British West Indies. His birth year is controversial. Until recently the year conventionally accepted was 1757. It was primarily deduced from a letter that Hamilton had written in 1797 to a Scottish relative, stating "Myself at about sixteen came to this country . . . at nineteen, I entered into the American army as captain of artillery." Since it was known that Hamilton had joined the army in 1776, scholars — especially his son and biographer, John Church Hamilton — concluded that he had been born in 1757. Modern scholars tended to view 1757 skeptically, chiefly because of the extraordinary precocity it implied Hamilton had displayed in his early activities. Recent research, especially in the court records of the Danish colonial archives, suggests that January 11, 1755, rather than 1757, is the more likely birth date.

Alexander Hamilton's birthday on January 11 is frequently noted at institutions and historic spots connected with his name. Columbia University in New York City, for example — which Hamilton attended when it was known as King's College and where both a hall and statue commemorate the distinguished alumnus — occasionally marks the event. The Alexander Hamilton and Wall Street posts of the American Legion generally place a wreath on Hamilton's grave in the south churchyard (near Rector Street) of Trinity Protestant Episcopal Church located at Broadway and Wall Street in lower Manhattan.

Elaborate festivities were staged throughout the United States in honor of the 200th anniversary of Hamilton's birth. An act of Congress dated August 20, 1954, established the Alexander Hamilton Bicentennial Commission. Appointed by President Dwight D. Eisenhower, its eight members included George M. Humphrey, secretary of the treasury, and John A. Krout, vice president and dean of the graduate faculty of Columbia University. After considerable debate, the commission adhered to the traditional date of Hamilton's birth, 1757, and held the celebration on what now appears — in the light of evidence — to have been the 202nd anniversary. On September 16, 1956, President Eisenhower designated January 11, 1957, as Alexander Hamilton Bicentennial Day and called upon the governors of all states to set aside the entire subsequent year "to do honor to his memory with appropriate activities and ceremonies commemorative of his inspiring role in our national life."

On January 11, 1957, major observances were held in Washington, D.C., Chicago, Illinois, and New York City; at US Army posts throughout the world; and at Hamilton's birthplace on the island of Nevis, British West Indies. In New York City, which boasts many close associations with the famous patriot, noontime ceremonies, including patriotic airs and an invocation by Hamilton's great-great grandson, were staged at Federal Hall National Memorial at Wall and Nassau streets, in front of a statue of Hamilton, just a short distance from the sites of separate offices he had occupied while serving as a US cabinet member and as a lawyer. In the afternoon, a eulogy was delivered and wreaths laid on Hamilton's tomb in Trinity churchyard.

Another major celebration took place on the island of Nevis; neighboring St. Kitts, which is separated from Nevis only by a two-mile-wide strait and which was the scene of the courtship of Hamilton's parents, also participated. The extensive festivities got under way on January 10, with the arrival of several of Hamilton's descendants as guests of honor of the Nevis government. Highlights of the following day were the unveiling of a commemorative plaque on the ruins of the Hamilton town house near the center of present-day Charlestown, an English-style garden party, a pageant depicting Hamilton's island life, and an 18th century costume ball. Included in the remainder of the week-long festivities were parades featuring West Indian steel bands; a water carnival and other aquatic events; cricket matches; local art exhibits; plays and concerts.

Throughout the bicentennial year various other tributes were paid to the national hero, among them memorial lectures, exhibits, and the naming of a new bridge over New York City's Harlem River. An exhibition which contained the finest and largest collection of Hamiltonia ever assembled was set up in the Treasury Department Exhibit Rooms in Washington, D.C. (Hamilton's statue stands near the south entrance of the Treasury Building, which is immediately east of the White House.) One of the chief aims of the Alexander Hamilton Bicentennial Commission was to stimulate and publish new books on Hamilton. Not only did several biographies appear during the bicentennial year, but also Columbia University announced plans for the publication of a new multivolume edition of Hamilton papers. During a nationwide search, over 14,000 photostatic copies of his papers were collected.

Alexander Hamilton was the natural son of James Hamilton, fourth son of Alexander Hamilton, Laird of Cambuskeith in the parish of Stevenston, Ayrshire, Scotland; his mother, Rachel Faucitt (Fawcett) Lavien, was the daughter of a French Huguenot physician and wife of John Michael Lavien, a planter of either north German or Danish extraction. She left Lavien in 1750, according to the divorce petition the latter filed after she had failed to stay with him "like a true wife" and had gone to live with James Hamilton. Lavien secured the divorce in the late 1750s on charges of desertion and the out-of-wedlock birth of two children: James in 1753 and Alexander in 1755. Rachel Lavien, being the guilty party, could not under Danish law remarry. James Hamilton proved to be nothing but a drifting trader, and as Alexander Hamilton later commented, his father's fortunes soon "went to wreck." Rachel Lavien, eventually abandoned by James Hamilton, supported the Hamilton household by running a small store and seeking aid from her relatives. She died on February 26, 1768.

Little about Alexander Hamilton's childhood can be documented. The greater part of his youth must have been unsettled and at about 11 he already had to help earn his living as an apprentice clerk in the trading establishment of Nicholas Cruger and David Beekman, New York businessmen who had settled on the Danish-owned island of St. Croix. The young boy, a virtual orphan thrown upon the charity of relatives (although his father lived until 1799), was determined to do well at the rambling white-painted counting house in Christiansted.

Although "delicate and frail," he was highly intelligent and his ambition, industry, and superior mental powers soon brought him rapid advancement. When ill health forced Cruger to leave for the North American mainland for a while, he named his capable assistant manager-in-charge.

In early September 1772, Alexander Hamilton wrote a description of a devastating hurricane that had swept St. Croix the preceding month. The composition, derivative and strained, was written with what one recent Hamilton biographer has termed "the flamboyance of a Gothic novelist."

Good God! what horror and destruction . . . it seemed as if a total dissolution of nature was taking place. The roaring of the sea and wind — fiery meteors flying about in the air — the prodigious glare of almost perpetual lightning — the crash of the falling houses — and the earpiercing shrieks of the distressed, were sufficient to strike astonishment into Angels.

Nevertheless it was accepted for publication in the *Royal Danish-American Gazette*, the leading English newspaper of the Danish islands, and printed on October 3. The account was hailed as a brilliant achievement and ranks as an important milestone in Hamilton's life. It provided the major impetus in the decision to send the gifted islander to the American colonies to continue his education. Backed by his aunts, employer, and special mentor — Dr. Hugh Knox, a Presbyterian clergyman, schoolmaster, and physician — Alexander Hamilton sailed from Nevis for Boston, arriving there in what was traditionally held to be October 1772. Recent evidence, however, indicates that his departure from the West Indies probably took place only in the early summer of 1773.

Once in the American colonies, Alexander Hamilton first attended the grammar school of Frances Barber at Elizabethtown, New Jersey, in order to master Latin, Greek, and mathematics. The serious and diligent student then entered King's College in New York City. His advanced studies were soon disrupted by the mounting colonial insurrection against Great Britain. On July 6, 1774, the young college student attended an open-air mass meeting in "the Fields" (now City Hall Park) in New York City, called to consider a congress of the colonies. There he made an extemporaneous patriotic speech, which was so well reasoned as to attract general attention. Soon afterwards Hamilton contributed a number of letters and broadsides to John Holt's New York *Journal*. He also published, anonymously, two powerful pamphlets: *A Full Vindication of the Measures of Congress from the Calumnies of Their Enemies* (December 15, 1774) and *The Farmer Refuted* (February 5, 1775). Their superb logic and brilliant legalisms were even attributed to John Jay (see December 12), and when it was known that young Hamilton had written them the reputation won by his oratory was increased.

The ardent patriot enlisted in a volunteer band known as the Corsicans — later as the Hearts of Oak — and on August 23, 1775, participated in a raid to rescue cannons from the Battery. He left his college days behind forever when on March 14, 1776, through pressure exerted by influential friends in the New York legislature, the Provincial Congress of New York "Ordered: That the said Alexander Hamilton be, and he is hereby appointed Captain of the Provincial Company of the Artillery of this Colony."

The young captain reputedly received his baptism of fire at the battle of Long Island on August 27, 1776; he was present at the battles of White Plains (October 28), and Trenton (see December 26) in 1776, and the battle of Princeton (see January 3) in 1777. On March 1, 1777, he was made an aide-de-camp on the staff of General George Washington, commander in chief of the American forces, with the rank of lieutenant colonel, and also acted as confidential secretary. The new position was ideal for the talented and ambitious young man — dubbed Little Lion by his fellow aides — who, because of his origins, was determined to prove himself and attain success in Washington's official family.

Hamilton spent most of his time drafting reports and communications and commented upon the difficulty of having "the mind always upon the stretch, scarce ever unbent, and no hours for recreation." But he also acted as liaison officer, notably to French officers because of his fluency in their language; and he was occasionally dispatched to seize much-needed clothing and supplies "with as much delicacy and discretion as the nature of the business demands." As far as the social obligations attached to Hamilton's status were concerned, a visitor to Washington's camp observed:

. . . for the first time, I had the pleasure of knowing Colonel Hamilton. He presided at the General's table, where we dined . . . he acquitted himself with an ease, propriety, and vivacity, which gave me the most favorable impression of his talents and accomplishments.

Hamilton, restive after four years of largely behind-the-lines staff duties, yearning for a chance to win military glory before the conflict ended, discontent for several personal reasons, and resentful at having been denied a long-sought command, finally broke with his commander, resigning irately in February 1781. Fortunately for the impetuous young man, Washington overlooked the quarrel and even ignored the slurs that Hamilton had privately voiced against him. In July 1781 he placed Hamilton in command of a battalion of the Second Brigade Light Infantry in a division commanded by the Marquis de Lafayette (see September 6). During the decisive Yorktown, Virginia, campaign of September and October 1781 — which virtually ended the war in the colonists' favor — Hamilton finally fulfilled his ambition with a spectacular attack on one of the principal British redoubts.

In 1779, Hamilton, eager with his small salary and lack of family inheritance to marry into wealth and power, had outlined for a friend the following guidelines for an ideal wife: she must be young, handsome, sensible, well bred, chaste and tender. "In politics I am indifferent what side she may be of. I think I have argument that will easily convert her to mine. As to religion, a moderate stock will satisfy me. She must believe in God and hate a saint. But as to fortune, the larger stock of that the better. . . ." Hamilton first encountered the young woman who fulfilled all these requirements in November 1777 and married her in December 1780. Elizabeth Schuyler was the second daughter of General Philip Schuyler, a well-known New York property owner and political personage. The young aide's brilliant marriage was not merely a marriage of convenience: Hamilton was deeply devoted to his wife and the eight children she bore. After the American Revolution and his entrance into the practice of law in July 1782, he wrote: "You cannot imagine how entirely domestic I am growing. I lose all my taste for the pursuits of ambition. I sigh for nothing but the company of my wife and baby."

Hamilton's desire to "retire a simple citizen and good paterfamilias" was, so he thought, hindered only by one last duty to his country. The same year he was admitted to the New York bar, he was elected one of New York's delegates to the Continental Congress, where he served in 1782 and 1783. Here he had an opportunity to utilize the knowledge of military and political affairs that he had gained as Washington's aide and secretary — an opportunity that catapulted him into the midst of the political debates of the day.

Publicly and privately, the lawyer voiced his alarm over the instability of the confederation period and the necessity of revising the Articles of Confederation. His genius for constructive political theorizing made Hamilton not merely an articulate observer of the mounting confusion but also a leading advocate for calling the Annapolis Convention in September 1786. As a general commercial assemblage, the convention failed to be effective, attended as it was by delegates from only five states. But two of the youngest representatives, James Madison and Alexander Hamilton, convinced the others present that commercial accord would continue to be out of the question without political unity; the group endorsed a report drafted by Hamilton, which underlined the shaky foundations of the confederation and urged all 13 states to send delegates to a convention "to devise such further provisions as shall appear to them necessary to render the Constitution of the Federal Government adequate to the exigencies of the Union."

Hamilton's role as one of three New York delegates to the Constitutional Convention held in Philadelphia starting in May 1787 was not so significant as his advocacy of the new Constitution formulated at the momentous meeting. He ranks as one of the most renowned Federalists, as the staunch backers of the strong new federal government called themselves — as opposed to the Antifederalists, who favored a less centralized government and supported the axiom that the best government is that which governs least. The Federalists, anxious to obtain ratification of the Constitution by all states, issued a flurry of newspaper articles and pamphlets. Most brilliant among this literature of persuasion was the series of essays written in New York under the name Publius. The first letter was printed in the New York *Independent Journal* of October 27, 1787. By mid-August 1788, a total of 85 letters had appeared in various New York newspapers. Although known to be the joint output of Hamilton, Madison, and John Jay, the papers still pose questions concerning the exact number prepared by each man, especially since some of the essays were collaborations. Hamilton, having composed at least three-fifths or an estimated 51 letters, was the chief author; Madison contributed as many as 26; Hamilton and Madison together wrote at least 3; and Jay 5. The remarkable series, soon published in book form as *The Federalist* and reprinted several times during Hamilton's lifetime, is now regarded as the fundamental historic treatise on the Constitution of the United States. The fight over ratification in predominantly Antifederalist New York state was extremely difficult but, thanks to Hamilton's masterly ordering of persuasive argument, his overwhelming skill in oratory, and the adept support of other Federalists, the state convention finally ratified the Constitution on July 26, 1788.

The inauguration of George Washington as first President of the United States in 1789 (see April 16) was the advent of a period of close collaboration between Washington and Hamilton. The aging Chief Executive needed a younger right-hand man to provide a stimulus in legislation, and Hamilton was "eager to play the political schoolmaster." When Congress created the Treasury Department, the President appointed his former aide as its first secretary on September 11, 1789.

The new cabinet officer had no illusions about the complex task ahead. The confederation had left as a legacy a few clerks, massive debt, and an empty treasury. He had to create a totally new department. Moreover, since the primary troubles facing the first administration were fiscal, the fate and future of the federal Union hung upon the success or failure of Hamilton's remedies. The Organic Act of 1789, which set up the Treasury Department, stipulated that it "digest and prepare plans for the improvement and management of the revenue and for the support of the public credit; receive, keep and disperse the monies of the United States;" collect custom duties and excise taxes; run lighthouses; create aids to navigation; inaugurate a land survey of the country; and run the post office. (Only in 1792 was a separate Post Office Department established.)

Fortunately for the nation Alexander Hamilton was "the right man in the right office." Through bold planning and influential reports, the secretary of the treasury pushed through what has become known as the "Hamiltonian system." He firmly established the groundwork for the nation's financial integrity by creating the national Bank of the United States, establishing the national mint, attracting foreign capital, and paying the domestic debt in full.

Many measures, however, designed as they were to strengthen the central government at the expense of the states, aroused fierce opposition. Funding of the national debt at full value and federal assumption of state debts materialized only because Thomas Jefferson (see April 13) influenced southern voters in their favor, while Hamilton in return swung northern votes to assure the location of the national capital in the South. The levying of excise taxes to raise revenue caused a virtual uprising in western Pennsylvania, forcing the secretary himself in 1794 to accompany troops into the field to oversee the collection of a whiskey excise. Hamilton's *Report on Manufactures*, presented to Congress in the winter of 1791–1792 and often regarded as the capstone of his cabinet career, failed entirely to capture either congressional or popular approval. In it he suggested protective laws to bolster the economy by supporting new industries with import duties or bounties. He argued for the establishment of factories so that a market might be found among industrial workers for the produce of the farms, of which it appeared there otherwise would be a large surplus.

Yet despite setbacks, the value of Hamilton's financial policies was clearly recognized. George Washington noted: "Our public credit stands on that ground which three years ago it would have been considered as a species of madness to have foretold." Even Jefferson, Hamilton's adamant opponent in most fiscal matters, conceded upon becoming President in 1801: "We can pay off his debts in 15 years, but we can never get rid of his financial system." Several decades later the statesman and orator Daniel Webster aptly eulogized: "He smote the rock of national resources and abundant streams of revenue gushed forth; he touched the dead corpse of public credit and it sprang upon its feet."

The political division caused by congressional contests over Hamilton's financial proposals gradually laid the foundation for the two-party system. Advocates of the secretary's measures grouped into the Federalist faction (not to be mistaken for those Federalists who had backed the ratification of the US Constitution), while their opponents, headed by Thomas Jefferson and James Madison, established the Democratic-Republican faction. Differing at first about concentration of power in the central government, and on such domestic issues as the national Bank, tax policy, and public credit, the two factions became irreconcilably split into two national parties over foreign affairs. With the outbreak of the French Revolution in 1789 and war between France and England soon afterwards, Jefferson favored close ties with France. Hamilton, on the other hand, urged neutrality despite France's claims on the United States, stemming from the French-American alliance of 1778. He wished the nation to remain free of entangling pacts, and not to become an instrument of "European greatness." Self-interest, he contended, was the sole possible guide: moral principle, gratitude, and benevolence were irrelevant.

The bitter dissension between the two cabinet members, openly displayed by 1792, led to Jefferson's resignation as secretary of state at the end of 1793. Motivated both by lashing criticism of his conduct of office and by financial pressure — his cabinet position paid only

$3,500 a year — Hamilton finally resigned as secretary of the treasury on January 31, 1795, and resumed law practice in New York City. As the French statesman Talleyrand observed, on seeing the lawyer toiling by candlelight late one evening, "I have just come from viewing a man who had made the fortune of his country, but now is working all night in order to support his family."

Alexander Hamilton retired from the public limelight to the pleasures of family life and his country estate, the Grange, overlooking the Hudson River. The house, presently located on Convent Avenue at West 142nd Street, near its original site, is now known as the Hamilton Grange National Memorial. Hamilton had by no means completely broken his ties with the federal administration. Though his status was unofficial, his advice was still sought on practically all aspects of domestic and foreign policy; he drafted many state papers, including a version of Washington's famous Farewell Address in 1796, on which the retiring President relied heavily (see December 4). Until the decline of the Federalist party in the first decade of the 19th century, the New York lawyer played an influential role as party leader. When danger of war with France arose in 1798, President John Adams appointed Hamilton second in command to George Washington as the virtual head of the army with the rank of major general and duties of inspector general. Hamilton held the position from July 1798 until June 2, 1800, perfecting plans for the defense of the country.

In the presidential election of 1800, Aaron Burr (see February 6) tied with Thomas Jefferson in votes, although the latter was clearly the people's choice. Under the election procedure provided by the Constitution, electors chosen by the various state legislatures voted for two candidates, without specifying which one was to be the Chief Executive. The man with the greatest number of votes — assuming that number constituted a majority of all the electors — was to be President and the one with the second highest number was to be Vice President — an inherently ambiguous situation in case of a tie and one that was clarified in 1804 by ratification of the 12th Amendment, requiring electors to cast votes specifically for President and Vice President (see September 25). After the election of 1800, however, the final, tie-breaking decision reverted to the still strongly Federalist House of Representatives. Although Hamilton and Jefferson differed on many issues, they agreed in mistrusting Burr, whom the former secretary of state described "as a crooked gun, or other perverted machine,

whose aim or shot you could never be sure of." Hamilton wrote: "If there be a man in the world I ought to hate, it is Jefferson. With Burr I have always been personally well. But the public good must be paramount to every private consideration." He counseled his political followers to choose Jefferson. In February 1801 the House of Representatives finally chose Jefferson over Burr, the latter becoming Vice President.

In 1804, Jefferson dropped Burr from the presidential ticket. Burr then unsuccessfully sought the Republican nomination for the governorship of New York state. However, the Republicans turned instead to Morgan Lewis as their candidate. Thus thwarted, Burr succeeded in running on an Independent and Federalist ticket, probably having assured his supporters that if he was successful, he would join New York with those New England areas that wished to secede from the Union to form a Northern Confederacy. The defeat of Burr's bid for the governorship may have resulted from Hamilton's persuasive denunciations. At any rate, the vindictive office-seeker, having left the Republicans and failed the Federalists, attributed his ruination to Hamilton — who had referred to Burr as a "man of irregular and unsatiable ambition . . . who ought not to be trusted with the reins of government." Burr claimed that he had been insulted by Hamilton. Asked to render "a prompt and unqualified acknowledgment or denial" of the defamation, Hamilton refused to retract, replying: "I trust on more reflection you will see the matter in the same light with me. If not, I can only regret the circumstances and must abide the consequences."

The heated exchange led Burr to challenge the Federalist leader to a duel. Although opposed to dueling for moral, religious, and personal reasons — his son Philip had been killed in a duel in November 1801 — Hamilton felt he could not refuse lest he be thought a coward. On the sunny summer morning of July 11, the two opponents faced each other at the Weehawken, New Jersey, dueling ground across the Hudson River from New York City. Burr aimed directly, mortally wounding Hamilton. Hamilton did not intend to shoot his challenger, and apparently only the involuntary movement of his fingers as he was hit caused his pistol to fire wildly into the air. He reportedly remarked shortly afterwards: "Take care of that pistol; it is undischarged and still cocked; it may go off and do harm." After 32 hours of excruciating pain, Hamilton died on July 12.

The immediate repercussions of the most renowned political duel in US history were varied. Alexander Hamilton, previously esteemed as a successful lawyer and head of an almost moribund party, was suddenly an object of national adulation, a hero mourned throughout the country. His funeral, full of pomp, took place on July 14 in New York City. He was buried in Trinity churchyard. Aaron Burr lived for 32 years after the duel, not as a hero but in lasting disrepute as a murderer who had been indicted in New York and New Jersey and was forced to flee to the South.

Alexander Hamilton, a slight man, 5'7" in height, with light hair and complexion, was one of a number of gifted and resourceful personalities who fashioned the American nation in the late 18th century. Although ambitious and highly dedicated, like such contemporaries as Benjamin Franklin and Thomas Jefferson, Hamilton was not a typical cosmopolitan of the era. He preferred to operate in a restricted sphere rather than display broad interest in a variety of scientific and cultural fields. Politics was his forte and it was here that his administrative genius and unfailing belief in the destiny of the United States enabled him to push through measures giving the federal government powers essential to its needs and opportunities.

Both his contemporaries and modern critics have condemned the statesman as a "High Tory" who sought to establish a Leviathan state, a reactionary committed to "aristocratic principles or authoritarian ideas," a foe of democracy and popular government. Indeed, Hamilton's program in support of business enterprise and powerful central government had little appeal for farmers, shopowners, artisans, and states' rights advocates, who were attracted to Jefferson's party rather than to the Federalists. And the "Hamiltonian system," although invaluable in the long run, did impose a strain on the new government and stimulated political emotions to a dangerous degree. On the other hand, Hamilton's conception of the United States as a flourishing industrial nation rather than one of small farmers, as a strong political force controlled by an efficient system of checks and balances and by a clear separation of powers — rather than as a weak entity of limited coercive ability — was more realistic than Jefferson's, even though needing modification by Jefferson's ideas of democracy. Both men were vital in building up the new American nation.

Hamilton, who has been termed one of the first great nationalists, was imbued with the prospect of the country's glorious future. As early as 1782, he wrote: "There is something noble and magnificent in the perspective of a great Federal Republic, closely linked in the pursuit of a common interest, tranquil and prosperous at home, respectable abroad." Sixteen years later he predicted: "I anticipate . . . that this country will, ere long, assume an attitude correspondent with its great destinies — majestic, efficient, and operative of great things. A noble career lies before it."

JANUARY 12

John Winthrop's Birthday

John Winthrop, the devout governor of the Massachusetts Bay Colony and historian of the Puritans, was born at Edwardstone in the English county of Suffolk on January 12, 1588, by the Julian or Old Style calendar in use in England at the time. (His birthdate by the Gregorian or New Style calendar now in use would be January 22.) An earnest Puritan and a natural leader, Winthrop enrolled at Cambridge University's Trinity College at the age of 14, but left without graduating. At 17 he was married, and at 18 he became a justice of the peace. In his own county, where he was lord of the manor of Groton, he became a person of reputation, and property. He subsequently trained for the law at Gray's Inn and practiced in London with considerable success, eventually being admitted to the Inner Temple.

In 1616, he meanwhile had begun a record of his own spiritual life, which told of his efforts, after the death of his second wife, to tame his "rebellious flesh . . . by prayer, reading, meditation. . . ." The diary revealed some heights of mystical experience — as well as a a degree of longing for the world, an appealing human frailty in a man whose life was governed by a code of stern righteousness. The diary ended in 1618, the year of his third marriage. A few years later, in 1623, Winthrop received a lucrative appointment as attorney in the Court of Wards and Chanceries. He also was engaged in drafting parliamentary bills. His sudden loss of the court appointment in 1629, at a time when Puritans were increasingly subject to persecution in the England of Charles I, may have been related to his religious beliefs.

Following this development, Winthrop, already widely acquainted with Puritan leaders, joined those who had become dominant in the newly chartered Massachusetts Bay Company in signing the so-called Cambridge Agreement. They committed themselves to settle in New England if the company and the charter should be moved there — as indeed they were. Winthrop, a wise and just man who was, according to all accounts, ideally suited to govern, was chosen governor of the new undertaking in October 1629. Although it was merely a joint stock company at the time, it soon enough became a colony. Bearing in hand their charter — a document of probably deliberate vagueness which permitted a convenient lack of control from the homeland — Winthrop and the other signatories left England the following March, with a large company, aboard the *Arbella*. It was part of a fleet of four ships that landed some 700 to 900 settlers at what is now Salem, Massachusetts, on June 22, 1630 (N.S.). Winthrop moved his flock rapidly on to Charlestown, where they sojourned briefly until an insufficient supply of fresh water prompted a second move in the fall of 1630 — to the nearby Shawmut peninsula, which the colonists called Boston.

Thus began the "Bible Commonwealth," the colony intended by its Puritan leaders as an example to others — one that they hoped would bring no dishonor to the name of God. The early history of the colony is inseparable from that of Winthrop, the stern and tender man of conscience who was 12 times elected its governor (1629–1634, 1637–1640, 1642–1644, 1646–1649), served virtually all the intervening years as deputy or assistant governor, and spent unstintingly of his strength and fortune on its behalf. After an unfortunate first winter, in which perhaps a fifth of the settlers died of starvation or disease, and the remainder subsisted unenthusiastically on such fare as clams, mussels, and acorns, the colonists found their means of survival in the sea. What was to be a substantial business in fishing, trading, and shipbuilding began with the launching in 1631 of the first Massachusetts-built ship, rapidly followed by others. Such pursuits as farming also were instituted.

With subsistence feasible in the new land, and with the old land subject to hard times and ruled by a High Church king who had dismissed Parliament autocratically, the great Puritan migration, which was to leave an indelible imprint on American history and character, began. In little more than a decade, the population of the colony was close to 15,000. The influx was in no way slowed by the enthusiasm of Governor Winthrop, who had described the country of New England as "exceeding good and the climate very like our own. . . ." More privately, he had written to his wife, "I thank God, I like so well to be here, as I do not repent my coming, and if I were to come again, I would not have altered my course. . . ."

It was consistent with Winthrop's way of thinking that he should regard government as an agent of religion. He opposed unlimited democracy. The colony he led — whose Puritan legacy of probity, duty, conscience was of crucial importance in later US history — was governed by the learned, and religious, few. It was a Puritan theocracy in which the authority of the clergy extended far beyond the pulpit, and dissenters like Roger Williams (see February 5) and Anne Hutchinson (see November 17) were banished. Although the government of the Massachusetts Bay Colony was intolerant of dissent, Winthrop himself was a man of moderation. It was to his clear judgment that the colony was largely indebted for its prosperity and other success. As governor, he consistently defended the colony against possible coercion from England. He also advocated, as early as 1637, an alliance of New England colonies, and when the New England Confederation came into being in 1643, he was its first president. A portrait of Winthrop, presumably done by a contemporary, shows him as a spare, contemplative man with dark hair and beard; tight-lipped, with a long, thin nose and perfectly arched brows echoed by the perfectly arched wrinkles of a lean forehead. He died in office in 1649.

He was survived by his son, John, who became governor of Connecticut (see May 11). He also is survived, to this day, by an important historical work. This is his journal of the Massachusetts Bay Colony, which he began on shipboard in 1630. If it is a shade less interesting than William Bradford's history of the colony at Plymouth (see May 19), it is nonetheless major, and not only as a record of the individual Puritan's constant personal bout with sin. The Puritan strength of character, which had much to do with the survival of the colonies in the early years, and later helped bind together a vast nation, is here revealed. It was not until 1825–1826 that Winthrop's journal — "Puritan in a liberal sense," as it has been described — was published in full, as *The History of New England from 1630 to 1649*.

JANUARY 13

Salmon P. Chase's Birthday

Salmon Portland Chase, the sixth chief justice of the United States, was born on January 13, 1808, at Cornish, New Hampshire. He was the 8th of 11 children of a family whose forebears came from England to Newbury, Massachusetts, in 1640. Chase's father, Ithamar Chase, was a farmer and tavern keeper who, as a member of the Federalist party, held a variety of state and local offices. His mother, the former Janette Ralston, was a descendant of Scottish settlers.

When his father died around 1817, Salmon Chase went to live with his uncle, Philander Chase, the Protestant Episcopal bishop of Ohio. He studied at the minister's church school at Worthington, near Columbus, and in 1821 entered Cincinnati College, where his uncle had just accepted the presidency. Young Chase left the institution after less than a year, and with some months of study was able to enter Dartmouth College as a junior.

After graduating from college in 1826, he went to Washington, D.C., to administer a boys' school. He soon became a friend of William Wirt, the attorney general of the United States under Presidents James Monroe and John Quincy Adams. Chase undertook the study of law with Wirt as his mentor, and on December 14, 1829, gained admittance to the bar.

Chase moved to Cincinnati in 1830 and began his practice of law. He also undertook a variety of intellectual, literary, and scholarly activities. He helped establish the Cincinnati Lyceum and became an author and lecturer. In the years from 1833 to 1835 he published a highly useful three-volume compilation entitled the *Statutes of Ohio*.

Opposition to slavery became a cornerstone of Chase's philosophy in the 1830s. He served as attorney for a number of runaway black slaves and also defended James G. Birney, an early abolitionist leader, before the Ohio Supreme Court against charges of harboring fugitive slaves. In a case before the US Supreme Court concerning those who aided slaves to escape, Chase joined forces with William H. Seward, who later became secretary of state under Abraham Lincoln. They argued, although unsuccessfully, that the federal Fugitive Slave Law of 1793 violated the Constitution, which in no way authorized human bondage.

Originally a Whig, Chase in 1840 joined the antislavery Liberty party, which had nominated James G. Birney for President. In 1848, Chase presided at the Buffalo convention of the Free-Soil party, which opposed the extension of slavery into the territories. Martin Van Buren, the Free-Soil nominee, failed to win the election, but he drew enough votes to deprive Lewis Cass, the Democratic candidate, of the presidency. Chase himself, with the support of Free-Soilers and antislavery Democrats, became a US senator from Ohio in 1849.

Doubtful of the chances for ultimate success of a party based solely on opposition to slavery, Chase entertained thoughts of winning the more broadly appealing Democratic party to the cause. Events of the early 1850s dissipated Chase's hopes, however, and he turned increasingly away from the Democrats. He bitterly fought the Compromise of 1850 and the Kansas-Nebraska Act of Stephen A. Douglas, the Democratic senator from Illinois, since he felt both legislative measures temporized on the issue of human bondage. Indeed, in the "Appeal of the Independent Democrats," Chase and others denounced the Douglas bill, which would have opened the Nebraska Territory to slavery, as a "criminal betrayal of sacred rights."

At odds with both the Whigs and Democrats, Chase soon allied himself with the new Republican party (see July 6). In 1855 he was a successful Republican gubernatorial candidate in Ohio. Chase sought the Republican presidential nomination in 1856 but lost it to Colonel John C. Frémont. He won reelection as Ohio governor in 1857 and remained in that post until the outbreak of the Civil War.

Governor Chase vied for the Republican presidential nomination in 1860, but the delegates at the Chicago convention made Abraham Lincoln their choice. Chase vigorously supported the successful candidacy of Lincoln, and himself won a second term in the US Senate. The new Chief Executive rewarded Chase's loyalty by offering him the post of secretary of the Treasury, and he resigned from the Senate to join the cabinet in this capacity.

As secretary of the Treasury, Chase directed the country's finances during the turbulent years of the Civil War. With the invaluable aid of the financier Jay Cooke, he successfully sold the bonds necessary to raise money for the Union's military machine. Perhaps Chase made his most important contribution by fostering the adoption of the National Banking System (see February 25) in 1863, which served the nation until the establishment of the Federal Reserve System under President Woodrow Wilson.

Salmon Chase engaged in a variety of political disputes during his tenure at the Treasury Department. Firmly believing in the righteousness of the war with the South, Chase thought that Lincoln did not act with enough vigor, and blamed the influence of the less ardent Secretary of State William Seward for what he considered to be the President's laxity. In 1862 the Seward-Chase conflict reached a peak and both men offered to resign from the cabinet, but Lincoln was able to persuade them to remain in their posts.

Unionists dissatisfied with Lincoln's performance as President, such as Horace Greeley and William Cullen Bryant, called for Chase as the Republican nominee in 1864. A congressional committee led by Senator Clarke Pomeroy of Kansas echoed the call and, in a letter that reached the newspapers as the "Pomeroy Circular," cast doubts on Lincoln's ability to win the election. Chase did not actively support these movements, but they naturally hurt his relationship with the President, who captured the nomination and later won reelection. In 1864, Lincoln accepted Chase's proffered resignation, stating that the two men had "reached a point of mutual embarrassment in our official relations which it seems cannot be overcome or longer sustained consistently with the public service."

Despite this rupture in their relationship, Lincoln chose Chase to fill the vacancy in the Supreme Court caused by the death of Chief Justice Roger Brooke Taney on October 12, 1864. Chase accepted and remained as chief justice until his death in 1873. During his tenure he presided over a variety of cases that evolved from the aftermath of the Civil War.

In his capacity as a circuit judge, Chief Justice Chase reorganized and reopened the federal courts in the South. He opposed the prosecution of Jefferson Davis for treason and helped delay the trial until President Andrew Johnson's declaration of universal amnesty freed the former leader of the Confederacy. Despite his mercy for individual rebels, Chase, in cases such as *Mississippi* v. *Johnson* and *Georgia* v. *Stanton*, struck down Southern attempts to prevent enforcement of the Radical Republicans' Reconstruction program.

As chief justice, Chase presided over the 1868 Senate trial of Andrew Johnson, the impeached President. The Radical Republicans, intent on ousting Johnson from office, sought to downgrade Chase's role as judge in the Senate and attempted to bypass traditional legal procedures concerning evidence and testimony. However, he successfully defended the Senate's function as a court of law and defeated efforts to deprive himself of the right to cast tie-breaking votes. The chief justice's integrity helped preserve the decorum of the proceedings and gave Johnson, who narrowly won acquittal, some chance for a fair trial.

Chief Justice Chase still longed to be President and in 1868, unimpressed by Ulysses S. Grant, the Republican candidate, made himself available for the Democratic nomination. His platform of universal amnesty for Southerners and universal suffrage to protect the freed blacks disenchanted some delegates, and the convention instead chose Horatio Seymour of New York. In 1872 Chase might have sought the presidential designation of the Liberal Republicans, who opposed the corruption of the

Grant administration, but ill health as well as other factors removed him from the running.

Salmon Chase married three times and was the father of six daughters. He wed Katherine Jane Garniss on March 4, 1834, but she died on December 1 of the following year. He was married again on September 26, 1839, to Eliza Ann Smith, who remained his wife until her death on September 29, 1845. Finally, Chase wed Sarah Bella Dunlop Ludlow on November 6, 1846; she died on January 13, 1852. It was more than two decades later when the chief justice himself died, on May 7, 1873, after a paralytic stroke.

Stephen Foster Memorial Day

The anniversary of the death of the great song and ballad writer, on January 13, 1864, is marked annually, by proclamation of the President, as national Stephen Foster Memorial Day. The measure authorizing proclamation of the day for "appropriate ceremonies, pilgrimages to his shrines, and musical programs featuring his compositions" was approved by the US Congress in 1951. In Florida, January 13 also marks the beginning of Stephen Foster Memorial Week, established by the state legislature in 1935.

Foster's memory also is commemorated on a year-round basis at several shrines, most notably in Pennsylvania, Kentucky, and Florida. The Stephen Collins Foster Memorial of the University of Pittsburgh, on Forbes Street facing Schenley Park, contains a 700-seat auditorium and related rooms (including offices of Pittsburgh's Tuesday Musical Club, which was instrumental in establishing the memorial) and a 12-sided room dedicated as a Foster shrine and lighted by stained glass windows depicting Foster themes. It also contains the comprehensive Foster Hall Collection, established by Josiah K. Lilly of Indianapolis, of more than 10,000 items related to Foster's life and works — among them manuscripts, letters, personal possessions, books, clippings, first and other editions of his music, portraits, records, and broadsides.

My Old Kentucky Home State Park at Bardstown, Kentucky — the plantation and house once owned by a cousin of Foster's and presented to the state of Kentucky in 1922 — has become the state's most popular tourist attraction. It is the scene of annual presentations of dramatist Paul Green's "The Stephen Foster Story," which had its 17th season in 1975. The musical play, produced with the help of financial support from local citizens, features some 50 Foster songs and is presented nightly throughout the summer, except Mondays, in a state-built amphitheater; performances are given in a nearby indoor theater Sunday afternoons and in bad weather.

What is probably the best-known observance of Stephen Foster Memorial Week takes place annually, beginning on January 13, at the Stephen Foster Center in White Springs, Florida. The special memorial events include Foster-filled musical programs by groups from clubs, universities, and schools throughout Florida and daily concerts from the 200-foot, 97-bell carillon tower. The 1964 program marked the 100th anniversary of Foster's death. It included a eulogy by Dr. Caleb J. King, editor-emeritus of the *Florida Times-Union* of Jacksonville, and a concert of Foster tunes and spirituals, some of them sung by "Jeanie 1962" — Rebecca Ann Jenkins of Orlando, winner of a $1,000 music scholarship in one of the annual contests for 18-to-21-year-old Florida female singers. A "Jeanie" still is chosen each year during the annual Jeanie Auditions and Ball, named for Foster's wife, "Jeanie with the Light Brown Hair," and jointly sponsored by the Stephen Foster Center and the Florida Federation of Music Clubs. Formerly scheduled for the weekend nearest St. Valentine's Day, the auditions and ball now take place on a weekend late in October, at the Stephen Foster Center.

The center, which is open all year, is set in a 250-acre state park on US Highway 41. It includes the Foster Museum, housing historical documents, musical scores and instruments, paintings, animated dioramas depicting his most popular songs, and other Fosteriana. Among other features is a passenger-carrying reproduction of an old riverboat — and there also are facsimiles of the Conestoga wagons used by the settlers who made Foster's "Oh! Susanna" the virtual theme song of their westward migration a century and more ago. Appropriately enough, the center is located on the banks of the Suwannee, or, as Foster's song called it, "Swanee River." The song, also known as "The Old Folks at Home," became the official song of Florida by action of the state legislature in 1935.

Stephen Collins Foster, whose unaffected songs have outlasted the more ambitious, European-inspired music that appeared in this country during the same period, was born on July 4, 1826, in what is now Pittsburgh, Pennsylvania. The 10th of 11 children of a prosperous family, he was 6 when he first gave indications of what his father called his "strange talent" for music. He learned to play the piano at home and as a teenager busily picked out a number of original tunes on it.

The minstrel shows in which blackface performers naively caricatured American blacks —

with songs written in what their composers imagined to be a southern black dialect — were finding wide popularity at the time. As the star of a boyish "Thespian Society," young Foster himself performed some of the minstrel tunes — which were known in the music trade as "Ethiopian." Apart from minstrel shows, his acquaintance with the people and region on which he was to draw for so much of his music probably was limited to a black choir he heard in a Pittsburgh church, and to a single trip to the South, during the 1850s.

This was to visit a cousin, Judge John Rowan, at his plantation near Bardstown, Kentucky. Judge Rowan's Georgian colonial mansion, then called Federal Hill, now is part of the My Old Kentucky Home State Park — named for the song that it inspired Foster to write. Restored with state funds, furnished as nearly as possible in the period of Foster's visit, and staffed with attendants in period costumes, the house is now open to visitors.

Since Foster had no inclination to obtain formal training in music and his family did not urge him to pursue such study, his technical background was always slight. He attended Jefferson College briefly and later went to work as a bookkeeper for a brother in Cincinnati. It was while he was there that several of his songs were published locally (in 1848) and one of them, "Oh! Susanna," swept the country shortly after, prompting his decision to devote full time to songwriting and become the best "Ethiopian composer."

Although some of his compositions were the sentimental ballads of the day, he found his best outlet in minstrel shows, selling many of his Ethiopian numbers to E. P. Christy, who headed a famous troupe. Usually, Foster wrote both the words and music for his compositions. Despite the phenomenal growth of his popularity between 1850 and 1854, however, he was a poor businessman and never reaped proportionate financial returns. His songs — which ultimately numbered more than 200 — included such still-remembered tunes as "Camptown Races," "Massa's in the Cold, Cold Ground," "Old Black Joe," and many others. Along with the already-mentioned "Jeanie with the Light Brown Hair" (which he wrote for his wife Jane), "Beautiful Dreamer," set in slow waltz time, was one of his few non-Ethiopian tunes to find a lasting place in American music.

Eventually, the intemperate habits of the gentle and warmhearted Foster reduced him to real poverty and he was glad to sell his compositions for immediate cash at the sacrifice of future royalties. The quality of his work deteriorated under the pressure for quick composition, complicated by the alcoholism and (according to at least one source) tuberculosis with which he was afflicted after 1860. He spent his last years alone, in New York City's cheap Bowery rooming houses, in one of which he suffered a fall that proved to be fatal. He died, at 37, in the charity ward of Bellevue Hospital.

Tragic as his short life was, the composer who had made such lasting contributions to American music was not forgotten. In 1940, he was the first musician elected to the Hall of Fame for Great Americans. His birthplace, designated the Stephen Foster Memorial House, is among the 100-odd buildings of Greenfield Village, Henry Ford's outdoor museum of Americana at Dearborn, Michigan.

JANUARY 14

Ratification Day

Each year on January 14, Maryland's historic State House at Annapolis is the setting for ceremonies marking the anniversary of an event that took place in its Old Senate Chamber in 1784: the official ending of the American Revolution.

Frequently, it has been assumed that the Revolution ended earlier. Fighting virtually had terminated with the surrender of Lord Cornwallis at Yorktown, Virginia, in 1781 (see October 19). After a delay of nearly two years, the Treaty of Paris by which "His Britannic Majesty [acknowledged] the . . . United States . . . to be free Sovereign & independent . . ." finally had been signed on September 3, 1783. But not until the Continental Congress, meeting in Annapolis, had ratified the treaty did the United States legally "assume among the Powers of the earth, the separate and equal station" of which the Declaration of Independence had spoken.

Ratification did not come easily. Indeed, it was uncertain for a time whether one of the key provisions of the Treaty of Paris — that it be ratified and returned to England within six months — could be met at all. The six-month period was due to expire in March of 1784, and two months had to be allowed for the ocean crossing. As Representative Thomas Jefferson of Virginia repeatedly pointed out, the need for action was urgent. However, the mood of the states was leisurely.

It was not until late November that representatives to the Congress were scheduled to arrive at Annapolis. Once assembled, they found themselves without a quorum. As Maryland's Governor J. Millard Tawes put it in his 1963 Ratification Day address, even when ". . . the

year 1783 drew to a close, only seven of the Thirteen States had sent legal delegations to Annapolis. And to transact major business, such as the ratification of a treaty, nine states had to be represented. . . . So, there they were at the end of December, and nothing could be done because of the absence of Delegates from two states."

Finally, after the insistent prodding of Jefferson, a quorum was assembled. The delegates from Connecticut arrived on January 13. South Carolina Congressman Richard Beresford, until then ill in a Philadelphia hotel, arrived the next day. From that moment, not a second was lost. Meeting in the Maryland State House, which then was serving as the temporary Capitol of the nation, the Continental Congress ratified the Treaty of Paris on the very day of Beresford's arrival.

So it was that on January 14, 1784, the United States of America officially took its place as a sovereign, free, and independent nation among nations. As the Revolution had had its official beginning with the adoption of the Declaration of Independence in Independence Hall, Philadelphia, on July 4, 1776 — even though that occasion postdated by more than a year the historic encounters at Lexington, Concord, and Bunker Hill — so it had its official conclusion in the Maryland State House at Annapolis.

The State House stands today as a registered national historic landmark. The Old Senate Chamber, in which the actual ratification took place, has been preserved exactly as it was at the time and today's visitors (who number more than 100,000 annually) can see the spot where Jefferson stood to read the treaty.

Oddly enough, in view of its importance, modern observances of the anniversary of ratification date only from 1962. It was in that year that Governor Tawes, feeling that the "Act of Ratification should be honored by Americans as highly as Independence Day," began the custom whereby the chief executive of Maryland has proclaimed Ratification Day each year since.

On that day, the 13-star flag in its special Maryland version — containing 12 stars in a circle and the 13th in the center — which was in use at the time of the ratification, flies over the State House and over many of the business establishments of Annapolis. In addition, 13 old-style flags, one representing each of the original states, are displayed on the State House lawn. Often, the governor of Maryland, as well as other state or federal officials, gives an address.

The ceremonies that take place inside the

State House vary from year to year. The observance in one recent year, for example, paid tribute to the Continental army with a performance of the Old Guard Fife and Drum Corps, the oldest active infantry unit in the US Army. Corpsmen, dressed in the uniform of the Revolution, played 18th century instruments and presented 18th century bugle calls and marching pieces. In 1972, the original Treaty of Paris, on loan from the National Archives in Washington, D.C., was put on display in the rotunda of the State House. Other documents relating to the period were also exhibited. At the 1973 program, attended by over 2,000 persons, the recreated First Maryland Regiment, representing the Maryland Line of 1776, marched first to the City Dock to present a military exercise and receive a certificate from the Maryland Bicentennial Commission designating the unit as the official honor guard of the commission. The regiment then marched to the State House, where it fired a flintlock musket salute in honor of Ratification Day.

JANUARY 15

Martin Luther King Jr.'s Birthday

Martin Luther King Jr. had a simple dream — "that one day this nation will live out the true meaning of its creed: 'We hold these truths to be self-evident, that all men are created equal.'" Born on January 15, 1929, King devoted his life to trying to transform this dream into reality. A personification of hope and justice to some, and an object of scorn and vilification to others, Dr. King, in practice as well as preachment, refused "to wallow in the valley of despair" and pursued his dream "with the faith that unearned suffering is redemptive," until an assassin struck him down in Memphis, Tennessee, on April 4, 1968.

The son of Martin Luther King Sr., the pastor of the Ebenezer Baptist Church in Atlanta, Georgia, young King attended public schools in that city, and then went to Atlanta's Morehouse College. It was during his junior year there that he determined on a career in the ministry. He was ordained in his father's church in 1947.

Following his graduation from Morehouse in 1948, King continued his studies at the racially integrated Crozer Theological Seminary in Chester, Pennsylvania. He was an outstanding student, and the first black in the school's history to be elected class president. He received the B.D. degree and won a fellowship for further graduate study.

In 1951, King began his doctoral studies in theology at Boston University. There he met Coretta Scott, a graduate student in music, and in 1953 they were married. King eventually completed his doctoral dissertation and in 1958 he was awarded a Ph.D. degree, but in the meantime his work in the civil rights movement had brought him national prominence.

In 1954, King had returned to the South to become pastor of the Dexter Avenue Baptist Church in Montgomery, Alabama. For a year, the young minister performed routine duties for his black congregation. Then, on December 1, 1955, Rosa Parks, a black seamstress in Montgomery, refused to obey a bus driver's order to give up her seat to a white male passenger.

Mrs. Parks's defiance of the segregationist practice of forcing blacks to sit in the rear of southern buses and to surrender their seats to white passengers resulted in her being fined $14 for refusing to obey the order of a bus driver. More importantly, however, it marked the beginning of a citywide bus boycott by Montgomery's 50,000 black residents. Montgomery's established black leaders initiated the boycott, but they chose King, who was a relatively recent arrival in the city and who had not yet identified himself with any local black faction, to lead the campaign. The bus boycott aroused national attention and gave King an opportunity to dramatize his belief in the efficacy of peaceful civil disobedience.

When, in the course of the boycott, he was arrested, the 27-year-old minister exhorted his followers, "If we are arrested every day, if we are exploited every day, . . . don't ever let anyone pull you so low as to hate them. . . ." Even when his home was bombed, King cautioned more militant blacks against seeking violent revenge. And, in the end, his belief in peaceful protest seemed justified. After the Supreme Court ruled on November 13, 1956, that segregation on buses was unconstitutional, city authorities announced compliance. Integrated bus service was begun in Montgomery on December 21, 1956.

The Montgomery bus boycott made Dr. King an undisputed leader in the civil rights movement. In 1959 he moved his family to Atlanta, where he became copastor with his father of the Ebenezer Baptist Church, but his participation in the drive for equal rights did not diminish. In 1957, meanwhile, King had helped found and was chosen to head the Southern Christian Leadership Conference, and in 1960 he was instrumental in establishing the Student Nonviolent Coordinating Committee.

The Southern Christian Leadership Conference, composed of black ministers and professionals, gave King an organizational base upon which he extended his civil rights campaign throughout the South. During 1961, the conference sponsored freedom rides. On these rides, teams composed of black and white volunteers tested southern compliance with the 1956 Supreme Court decision banning segregation on buses and other transport facilities.

In April 1963, King launched a massive civil rights campaign in Birmingham, Alabama. For five weeks, black citizens participated in protest marches and "sit-ins" at lunch counters where they traditionally had been refused service, and they picketed stores that condoned segregationist practices. These peaceful activities elicited a violent response from many of Birmingham's white citizens. The police turned dogs and firehoses on the demonstrators, and white supremacists were even responsible for the bombing of a black church, which caused the deaths of four young black girls.

Dr. King was arrested during the Birmingham campaign and spent five days in jail. During his confinement, he issued a 9,000-word letter in which he recorded his feeling that "... the Negro's great stumbling block in the stride toward freedom is not the White Citizens Counciler or the Ku Klux Klanner, but the white moderate who is more devoted to order than to justice. . . ."

After Birmingham the cry of "Freedom Now" resounded throughout the United States. Protest marches, picketing, and sit-ins took place in many localities during the summer of 1963, but the culmination of the campaign for civil rights was the march on Washington that took place on August 28, 1963. More than 200,000 blacks and whites gathered in the nation's capital on that day to demand racial equality and, in the shadow of the Lincoln Memorial, this great throng heard Martin Luther King Jr. exclaim:

I say to you today, my friends, that in spite of the difficulties and frustrations of the moment, I still have a dream. It is a dream deeply rooted in the American dream.

I have a dream that one day this nation will rise up and live out the true meaning of its creed: "We hold these truths to be self-evident; that all men are created equal."

I have a dream that one day on the red hills of Georgia the sons of former slaves and the sons of former slaveowners will be able to sit down together at the table of brotherhood.

I have a dream that one day even the state of Mississippi, a desert sweltering with the heat of injustice and oppression, will be transformed into an oasis of freedom and justice.

I have a dream that my four little children will one day live in a nation where they will not be judged by the color of their skin but by the content of their character.

I have a dream today.... I have a dream that one day every valley shall be exalted, every hill and mountain shall be made low. The rough places will be made plains, and the crooked places will be made straight, and the glory of the Lord shall be revealed, and all flesh shall see it together.

This is our hope. This is the faith with which I return to the South. With this faith we will be able to hew out of the mountain of despair a stone of hope....

So let freedom ring. . . .

When we let freedom ring...from every...hamlet, from every state and every city, we will be able to speed up that day when all of God's children, black men and white men, Jews and Gentiles, Protestants and Catholics, will be able to join hands and sing in the words of the old Negro spiritual, "Free at last! free at last! thank God Almighty, we are free at last!"

In 1965, civil rights activists turned their attention to the registration of black voters. In March of that year the Southern Christian Leadership Conference organized and Dr. King led demonstrations against unfair and unreasonable voting requirements in Selma, Alabama. As had been the case the year before in Birmingham, white racists in Selma reacted violently to the campaign to insure blacks their right to the ballot. Police treated the demonstrators harshly, and hundreds of blacks were arrested. King himself was beaten and kicked, but after the drive ended 25,000 persons marched from Selma to Montgomery and there, from the steps of the state capitol, he addressed the assembled crowd.

In 1966, Dr. King took his civil rights campaign north. For several months, he worked in a rented tenement on Chicago's West Side and attempted to initiate efforts to improve the city's slum housing. He led a march on the city hall to demand housing, welfare, education and job reforms, and he also headed several protest marches into all-white neighborhoods, where he encountered unprecedented hostility.

Dr. King had only limited success in Chicago, but city officials and real estate brokers agreed to try to decrease housing segregation. However, in the wake of several northern race riots in 1965 and 1966, black militants began to challenge his moderate, nonviolent methods. King never repudiated those who marched to the rallying cry of "black power," but he remained true to his belief in nonviolence, saying: "The Negro needs the white man to free him from his fears. The white man needs the Negro to free him from his guilt. A doctrine of black supremacy is as evil as a doctrine of white supremacy."

Before 1966, the main thrust of Dr. King's efforts had been to assure black citizens such legal rights as voting and using public facilities; after that date, he devoted his energies to improving the quality of life of black Americans. He was an outspoken critic of US involvement in Vietnam, arguing that the war effort consumed resources that might otherwise have benefited the nation's poor. And he sought to dramatize the plight of the underprivileged with a Poor People's Campaign that was scheduled to begin in Washington, D.C., on April 22, 1968.

As planned, thousands of black Americans encamped in the nation's capital in the summer of 1968 to demonstrate to Congress the need for legislation that would provide better economic opportunities for the nation's poor. But their leader was not with them. On April 3, 1968, Dr. King had gone to Memphis, Tennessee, to help organize a strike of the city's predominantly black sanitation workers. There, on April 4, 1968, James Earl Ray fired a shot that killed him on the balcony of the motel where he had been staying (see April 4). The shot ended the life of a man commonly acknowledged as one of history's greatest leaders in the still unending struggle to achieve full equality for the nation's black citizens.

During his lifetime, Martin Luther King Jr. was honored by many nations and was a recipient of the Nobel Peace Prize. In the United States, his efforts on behalf of blacks were not always so well received: He was often the object of scorn and on several occasions was jailed. But in the years since his death, the nation has endeavored to pay tribute to his memory. In 1968, Senator Edward W. Brooke of Massachusetts, the first black to sit in the US Senate since Reconstruction days, introduced a resolution to have January 15, King's birthday, set aside as a federal holiday. This effort died when the 91st Congress adjourned without acting on Brooke's resolution; however, efforts to have King honored with a federal holiday have continued since that time. In one year, 1971, the Reverend Ralph Abernathy, King's successor as head of the Southern Christian Leadership Conference, led a number of mule-drawn wagons to Washington, D.C.; according to his report, they contained petitions with 3 million signatures urging the creation of the new holiday.

Even as the campaign to have King's birthday declared a federal holiday goes on, many organizations and local and state governments have taken steps to pay tribute to his memory. Connecticut, Illinois, Kentucky, Maryland, Massachusetts, Michigan and Ohio have designated January 15, or a Sunday or Monday near that date, a legal holiday. In addition, in recent years the governors of New York and New Jersey have proclaimed King's birthday a holiday in their states. Special proclamations calling for the observance of January 15 as Martin Luther King Day also have been issued by the mayors of many cities, including the major ones. Even Montgomery, Alabama, where King had been jailed for his earliest activity as a civil rights leader, in 1975 proclaimed his birthday Martin Luther King Day.

Schools have often been closed on the anniversary of his birth. In some communities the day has been observed by having the schools remain open while presenting lessons and assembly programs on King's life and work. Even where schools close, the day itself commonly is anticipated by programs and special studies on King's life during the preceding week.

Many churches and synagogues throughout the country hold special memorial services on King's birthday, and other observances are sponsored by a wide variety of organizations across the nation. One commemoration that usually is the object of particular attention is the interfaith memorial service sponsored in New York City's Harlem by the Baptist Ministers Conference of New York, with the participation of political and civil-rights leaders. The site of this service has been, in recent years, the Convent Avenue Baptist Church at 145th Street.

This and other religious services in New York City, including one at the Cathedral Church of St. John the Divine, are generally surrounded by other events to mark the day. In 1970, for example, Mayor John Lindsay and 200 others marched three miles from the Canaan Baptist Church, where the interfaith service was held that year, to a rally at Central Park Mall, where an additional 300 persons heard demands that January 15 become a legal holiday. Later that day, another rally, arranged by District 65, National Council of Distributive Workers of America, was held at New York's Manhattan Center. There, Mayor Lindsay, Congresswoman Shirley Chisholm, Senator Charles Goodell, and others paid tribute to King. Similar observances have been held at various locations in New York City in succeeding years. A memorial breakfast at the Roosevelt Hotel in 1973 included several moving features that have become standard at birthday and memorial observances honoring Dr. King wherever in the nation they take place: a rendition of the "Battle Hymn of the Republic"; a recitation of portions of King's "I Have a Dream" speech; and the singing of what has become the virtual theme song of the civil rights movement, "We Shall Overcome."

In other communities as well, observances on January 15 are likely to include memorial church services, rallies, and musical and film tributes. Washington, D.C., was the scene in 1975 of a large rally led by an associate of King's, the Reverend Jesse Jackson. Over 3,000 demonstrators demanding more jobs for poor people marched for two hours in the vicinity of the White House.

The observance of King's birthday receives special emphasis in Atlanta, Georgia, where he is buried and where he long shared the pastorate of the Ebenezer Baptist Church with his father. In 1970, King's body was disinterred from its temporary resting place in Southview Cemetery and moved to a crypt near the church. The church, the crypt, and his restored childhood home are to be part of what was dedicated on January 15, 1970, as the Martin Luther King Jr., Memorial Center. Groundbreaking ceremonies, in which King's widow, Coretta Scott King, participated, took place five years later, on January 15, 1975. With the planned addition of a public park, a peace chapel, and a headquarters building, the complex is to be known as the Martin Luther King Jr. Center for Social Change. Envisioned as a living memorial, it is seen as a center for research and action where studies, some of them funded by foundations, can be carried out; where information and personnel of various civil rights organizations can be coordinated; where voter education and registration can be emphasized; and where the economic boycott can be furthered as an instrument of King's brand of "militant nonviolence" for constructive change.

In Atlanta, where King's family is always joined by throngs of others who commemorate the day, a wreath is customarily placed on his grave, and an overflow crowd fills the Ebenezer Baptist Church, where a memorial service is held, with distinguished guest speakers.

Throughout the nation, various schools, parks, housing projects, and other civic developments have been named in King's honor. A portrait of King was hung in the capitol in Atlanta, Georgia, in 1974; he is the first black to be so honored. One of the outstanding tributes to the fallen civil rights leader is the film *King: A Filmed Record . . . Montgomery to Memphis,* which has been viewed in theaters across the country since 1970. The documentary, which traces King's career from 1955 to 1968, won critical acclaim, and the proceeds from its showings have been given to the Martin Luther King Jr. Special Fund to further his work. But those who were closest to King attest that the finest tribute would be not the film, the buildings that bear his name, or the countless observances of his birthday, but the fulfillment

of his dream that blacks and whites would one day live together in true friendship and good will.

Vermont Declares Independence

Vermont did not exist as a separate entity before 1776. In the colonial period both New Hampshire and New York claimed the Green Mountain region, and speculators from both these provinces invested in Vermont lands. In 1764 the British royal government granted the disputed area to New York, but this action did little to resolve the question. The coming of the American Revolution, however, allowed Vermonters to settle their own fate; the people of the Green Mountains took advantage of the chaos created by the dissolution of the British Empire in America and on January 15, 1777, declared their independence.

Vermont's difficulties in the mid-18th century arose from the problems of settling the area. The first European to explore the region was the Frenchman Samuel de Champlain, who arrived in 1609. As a result of his discovery, France controlled the Green Mountains region for the next 150 years. During that time the French established several forts in present-day Vermont to protect French Canada from invasion by the hostile Iroquois Indians, and Roman Catholic missionaries ventured into the rugged Green Mountains to attempt to Christianize the natives. But the French were not interested in actually settling the area, and they built only a few small towns along the eastern shore of Lake Champlain.

Although the French had little intention of colonizing Vermont, they soon realized that the geographical position of the Green Mountain area provided them with an easy access to the English settlements in northern Massachusetts. Repeatedly during the first half of the 18th century, the French or their Indian allies in Canada passed through Vermont and without warning fell upon the vulnerable English towns along the Massachusetts frontier. These unexpected raids terrorized the inhabitants of the remote settlements: During the 1704 attack on Deerfield, Massachusetts, alone, almost 50 English colonists were killed and more than 100 taken captive.

To protect the colonists in northern Massachusetts, the British launched a number of retaliatory raids against the French and Indians in the area of present-day Vermont. They also constructed a series of forts just north of the settlements that were in danger of enemy attack. Fort Dummer, begun in 1724, just north of the

Massachusetts border near what is now Brattle-boro, is significant because it was the first permanent English settlement in the Green Mountains region; but Fort Number Four, built at Charlestown, New Hampshire, in 1740 afforded the greatest protection to the English settlements in the Connecticut River valley.

The English victory during the French and Indian War of 1754 to 1763 ended the threat of enemy attack on the remote Massachusetts settlements and assured the British control of the Vermont area. But even before 1763 the royal governors of New Hampshire and New York had involved themselves in the affairs of the Green Mountain region. As early as 1750 Governor Benning Wentworth of New Hampshire realized that great profits could be made by making grants of land in the Vermont area to speculators. Wentworth's authority to dispose of the Green Mountain region was questionable, for New Hampshire's western boundary had never been established. Wentworth merely assumed that New Hampshire's jurisdiction, like that of neighboring Connecticut and Massachusetts, extended to a line 20 miles east of the Hudson River, and proceeded to grant substantial areas in present-day Vermont to New Hampshire investors.

Between 1750 and 1764 Wentworth made grants of land for 138 towns in the Vermont area to New Hampshire speculators. The governors of New York believed that their own colony rightfully controlled the Green Mountain region, and repeatedly protested to the Crown about Wentworth's "New Hampshire Grants."

In 1764 the king in council acknowledged New York's claim to Vermont by declaring the western bank of the Connecticut River "to be the boundary between the said two provinces of New Hampshire and New York." Unfortunately, his proclamation made no reference to jurisdiction over the Vermont area prior to 1764. Thus, controversy continued: New Hampshirites argued that political authority over Vermont had shifted to New York in 1764 but that the land titles previously given by Wentworth were still valid, while New Yorkers insisted that they had always controlled the Vermont area, and the governor of New York proceeded to make his own land grants to speculators.

For more than a decade the dispute over Vermont raged. The governor of New York was willing to confirm the land titles of those persons who had actually settled in the Vermont areas granted by New Hampshire, but he would not validate the much larger claims held by that colony's absentee speculators. The New Hampshire speculators looked for assistance to John Wentworth, who had succeeded his uncle as governor of New Hampshire. Both as governor and as "Surveyor General of the King's Woods," Wentworth befriended the land investors, but his contribution in the fight against New York authorities could not match that of the most famous of the speculators, Ethan Allen.

A native of Connecticut, Ethan Allen first emerged as a leader of the New Hampshire grantees in 1770. After an unsuccessful attempt to defend the validity of New Hampshire land titles before a New York court in that year, Allen rather ambiguously announced that "the gods of the hills are not the gods of the valleys." Then he returned to Vermont, where he worked to align the actual settlers of the Green Mountain area with the absentee speculators who held New Hampshire grants.

Allen argued that the lands of the settlers would be safe only if all New Hampshire titles were confirmed. He also urged those who lived in what is now Vermont to oppose New York authorities, with force if necessary. The efficacy of this strategy was demonstrated in the fall of 1770 when a group of about 100 Vermonters successfully turned back a New York posse that had come to the Green Mountains to oust a settler. Within a short time, 11 towns in the western part of the Green Mountains raised military companies and Allen was appointed to be their "Colonel-Commandant."

In the early years of their existence, the Green Mountain Boys, as the band led by Allen was known, counted among their membership only a small portion of the residents of what is today western Vermont. Nevertheless, the organization, whose primary interest was the safety of the New Hampshire speculators' land grants, was able to block New York efforts to extend its authority over the Vermont area. Their resistance was so successful that in 1774 the New York assembly ordered the leaders of the Green Mountain Boys to be tried, convicted, and executed if apprehended. This so-called Bloody Act did nothing to curtail the activities of Allen and his followers; indeed, it served only to gain them additional popular support.

Deteriorating relations between England and the American colonies in the 1770s added a new dimension to the politics of the struggle of the Green Mountain Boys. Allen and his cohorts quickly reevaluated the situation and made England the primary target of their wrath. The mother country was the authority to which both New York and New Hampshire looked for support in their claims on Vermont. England's departure from the American scene would deprive New York of the king's 1764 decision as a cudgel to use against the Green Mountain Boys, and would also destroy any pretensions that New Hampshire would have to control of Vermont. Allen began to dream of a completely independent Vermont, which — if England lost Canada, too — might even enjoy access to the Atlantic Ocean through the St. Lawrence River.

Shortly after the first skirmishes of the American Revolution at Lexington and Concord in April 1775, Allen proposed a campaign against the British Fort Ticonderoga at the head of Lake Champlain. The plan was well received and troops from Massachusetts and Connecticut joined Allen and 100 Green Mountain Boys for an attack on Ticonderoga. The British fort fell to the patriots on May 10, 1775. (Its capture was reenacted by descendants of the original Green Mountain Boys 200 years later to the day, as part of the celebration of the bicentennial of the American Revolution.) Two days after the fall of Ticonderoga in 1775, the redcoats at nearby Crown Point likewise surrendered to the Green Mountain Boys under Seth Warner.

After the capture of Ticonderoga, Allen urged pressing the northern campaign, for, as he wrote to the Continental Congress, "Advancing an army into Canada will be agreeable to our friends, and it is bad policy to fear the resentment of an army." The Congress approved the expedition against the province of Quebec, and Allen served without a commission in the campaign. Allen was captured outside Montreal, but the patriots, assisted by a regiment of Green Mountain Boys, captured Montreal in November 1775. Their success in Canada was short-lived, however. Near the city of Quebec, British forces repulsed the colonists' subsequent attack of December 31, 1775, and forced them to retreat to the safety of Fort Ticonderoga.

While British forces in Canada prepared to launch a counterinvasion southward, the inhabitants of present Vermont struggled with the difficulties of their political status. In January 1776, forty-nine leading citizens, still angered by what they considered to be New York's "land-jobbing," issued a declaration in which they refused to join with New York "in such a manner as might in the future be detrimental to our private property." Eight months later, after New York and the other 12 colonies had declared their independence from Britain, the same group decided to poll the residents of the New Hampshire Grants, as Vermont was then known, about the feasibility of forming a "separate district." In time, the decisive step of declaring independence from New York was taken.

On January 15, 1777, at a meeting at Westminster, the Green Mountain Boys and others disenchanted with both New York and New Hampshire announced the formation of the state of New Connecticut. A district in Pennsylvania had already taken the name New Connecticut, however, and so by June 1777 the rebels in the "Grants" decided to call their lands Vermont — from the French words *vert* and *mont*, meaning "green" and "mountain."

Changing its name was the least of Vermont's worries, however. By the time a convention met at Windsor in July 1777 to formulate a constitution, British forces had overwhelmed the patriot defenders at Ticonderoga and threatened to invade the new state. But the patriot victory over British General Burgoyne's forces at the battle of Bennington late in the summer of 1777 (see August 16) saved the fledgling state. Vermont would face other crises before it ratified the US Constitution in 1791 and became the 14th state (see March 4), but the Green Mountain men had survived their first trials.

JANUARY 16

Eighteenth Amendment Ratified

For more than a century, temperance advocates worked to rid the United States of the scourge of alcohol abuse. Motivated by a nexus of complex socioeconomic and religious considerations, the active supporters of Prohibition were never more than a minority of the nation's population. Yet, as a result of their determined efforts, the 18th Amendment to the Constitution, which forbade the import and export of intoxicating liquors and outlawed their "manufacture, sale, or transportation . . . within . . . the United States and all territory subject to the jurisdiction thereof for beverage purposes," gained the approval of the requisite three-fourths (or 36) of the states by January 16, 1919. Thirteen days later, on January 29, 1919, it was declared by proclamation of the acting secretary of state to have been ratified by the required number of states. By its own terms, the 18th Amendment went into effect one year from the date of its ratification, on January 16, 1920.

Over the years, the temperance crusade had drawn support from a number of sources. Early in the 19th century, clergymen and other persons with strong religious affiliations formed the core of the temperance movement, while in the decades that followed, women's organizations — most notably the Women's Christian Temperance Union (see February 17, Frances E. Willard Memorial Day) — became the chief protagonists in the fight against intoxicants. In 1872, Prohibitionists even formed their own political party and ran a candidate for President. When this attempt at direct political action failed to attract sufficient voters to their cause, temperance advocates organized the Anti-Saloon League in 1893 to persuade members of the Republican and Democratic parties to support antiliquor laws.

Temperance workers of the 19th century enjoyed considerable success — at various times a number of states passed antiliquor legislation and hundreds of thousands of persons signed pledges promising to abstain from alcohol — but it was not until the early 1900s that the Prohibition movement gained widespread support. Much credit for the increasing acceptance of abstinence from alcohol belongs to the Anti-Saloon League. After 1893 the league launched a massive campaign to outlaw liquor. By 1914, about a quarter of the states had enacted antiliquor laws. But the growing success of the Prohibition movement may also be seen as a manifestation of the general spirit of reform that swept the United States at the turn of the century.

The Progressive era, as the first decade and a half of the 20th century was known, was a time of major reforms in the United States. Convinced of the possibility of effecting social improvement through law, the Progressives worked for a number of reforms including women's suffrage, government regulation of business, direct election of senators, and the elimination of child labor. Many Progressives believed that a close connection existed between saloon and liquor interests and decadent urban machine politics, and they saw Prohibition as a way to better city life.

Most prohibition and temperance advocates were primarily concerned with the well-being of their fellow human beings and felt that abstinence from alcohol would improve the quality of the commonweal. For these reformers, the all-too-visible toll alcohol abuse had exacted in poverty, ill health, crime, broken homes, and wrecked lives was cause abundant for their zeal. The outlook of some others, including many inhabitants of Protestant rural areas of the nation, reportedly was colored by their perception of alcohol as a symbol of the growing cities and their predominantly Catholic immigrant populations. They felt as threatened by the drinker as by the drink, and their espousal of temperance was to some extent a reflection of the deep tensions which existed between the country and the city in the early 1900s.

Prohibitionists failed to win sufficient congressional support for an amendment outlawing alcoholic beverages in 1913, but the movement against liquor continued to gain supporters in the second decade of the 20th century. The United States' involvement in World War I somewhat strengthened the movement's momentum. Again, mixed reasons were evident. The Lever Act of 1917, passed to insure adequate food supplies for prosecution of the war, forbade the use of grain for the distillation of alcoholic beverages, and by temporarily eliminating a major portion of the country's liquor supply proved the feasibility of nationwide abstinence. On a less admirable plane, war fever created a widespread distaste for beer among certain sectors of the American populace, simply because that beverage had long been associated with the German nation.

By 1917, the United States was ready for what Herbert Hoover called the "noble experiment." On December 18, 1917, Congress passed and proposed to the states the 18th Amendment, which outlawed the sale, import and export of alcoholic beverages beginning one year after the amendment's ratification. The amendment also gave both the national and state legislatures power to enforce Prohibition. On January 16, 1919, the amendment received the approval of the requisite three-fourths of the states and on January 16, 1920, it went into effect.

Even before the 18th Amendment became effective, Congress, on October 28, 1919, passed the National Prohibition Enforcement Act, more commonly known as the Volstead Act. This act vested administration of Prohibition in the Bureau of Internal Revenue and created the post of commissioner of prohibition. But the Bureau's force had at its peak only 3,000 agents, a number wholly inadequate for the mammoth task of controlling the illegal liquor traffic. Throughout the 1920s and the early 1930s, Prohibition legislation was openly flouted. In Rhode Island, a state which (like Connecticut) refused to ratify the 18th Amendment, alcoholic beverages were openly sold in grocery stores; elsewhere many persons distilled their own spirits, frequented speakeasies, or patronized bootleggers.

For 13 years the 18th Amendment remained in force, and it undoubtedly curtailed the consumption of alcohol in the United States. But open defiance of Prohibition created its own social problems — in ill effects from drinking alcohol intended for other purposes; in the rise of gangsterism and racketeering associated with illegal distribution of liquor; in corruption, which spread to enforcement agencies; and in the tendency of widespread flouting of the Prohibition law to encourage disrespect for law in general. In February 1933, Congress recommended repeal of the 18th Amendment. Only 10 months later, on December 5, 1933, three-fourths of the states approved the 21st Amendment (see December 5), and Prohibition came to an end in the United States.

JANUARY 17

Feast of St. Anthony the Great

St. Anthony the Great, also known as Anthony of Egypt, Anthony the Abbot, and Anthony of the Desert, is one of the most widely venerated saints. His feast, formerly ranked Class III and now considered a "memorial" in the Roman Catholic calendar, was observed on January 17 at Jerusalem as early as the 5th century and was introduced in Rome in the 12th century. It is still celebrated on this day by Roman Catholic and most Eastern Orthodox churches, although those Eastern churches still adhering to the Old Style Julian calendar mark the feast 13 days later on January 30.

Anthony was born in Egypt about the year 250 or 251. The exact date is unknown, as is his precise birthplace. One major tradition holds that he came from Koma near Hieracleus, another that he came from Qeman, south of Memphis. His parents were wealthy Christians and gave him a religious education. They died when he was 20 years old, leaving him their property — a fertile farm of more than 200 acres. Anthony was religiously inclined, and one day after he had heard read in church the Gospel containing the words, "If thou wilt be perfect, go and sell all thou hast," he took the injunction to himself and sold most of his property and distributed the proceeds to the needy. He stayed only to see that his sister's education was completed, sending her to a religious house after providing for her with part of his estate.

Anthony then withdrew from the world and adopted various ascetic practices, at first remaining in the neighborhood of his native town. He spent his time in prayer, study, and whatever manual labor was necessary to earn his living. Later, he went farther away to live in an empty tomb. An obliging friend shut him into the empty vault and interrupted his solitude only to bring bread from time to time.

The recluse underwent violent temptations, spiritual and physical. According to the *Life of Anthony* (written by St. Athanasius, one of the saint's disciples and admirers), Satan tried to frighten him from his retreat by assailing him with many tribulations. Once, he and a number of attendant fiends were alleged to have attacked Anthony during the night, and to have beaten him so severely that he was found almost dead in his cell in the morning. Later, the evil spirits reportedly transformed themselves into wild beasts and reptiles, which roared and hissed furiously at him and mangled his body,

but the holy man is said to have taunted them until the roof of his cell opened and a ray of light shot through, silencing the tempters. A voice from heaven declared: "I was here, Anthony, but I waited to see thy resistance." Anthony's wounds were healed, and the roof closed again.

Anthony had led an ascetic life for 15 years when, at the age of 35, he decided to retire into utter seclusion. He took up his abode in an abandoned fort on the mountain Pispir (now called Der el Memun), located across the Nile River from the ancient town of Arsinoë (now El Faiyûm) on Lake Moeris. Here he lived for 20 years without looking at another being. Food was thrown to him over the wall. Pilgrims visited the place, and those who wished to be his disciples lived in caves and huts in the neighborhood. They begged him to come forth and be their spiritual leader. Anthony at length yielded to their insistent importunities, and in the early years of the fourth century, probably about 305, left the solitude of the fort to be their guide on the basis of his own personal religious experiences. For several years, he devoted himself to the instruction of the colony of hermits that continuously grew up around him. He composed no rule for the ascetics' observance, being content simply to organize them into communities of isolated cells and loosely oversee their activities.

Anthony, however, eventually tired of human companionship. He withdrew to a distant retreat on Mount Kolzim, located on the South Qalala desert plateau about 100 miles southeast of Cairo and 20 miles west of the Red Sea. At this spot there now stands the monastery that bears his name: Der Mar Antonios. Here he spent the remaining decades of his long life. The saint received those who, out of curiosity or for advice, went to visit him. Athanasius paid him many visits, thus gathering material for his biography of Anthony. The recluse was so greatly venerated that the Roman Emperor Constantine the Great wrote him, asking to be remembered in his prayers. Anthony voiced his sentiments about the honor in this fashion: "Do not admire if a king writes to us, for he is a man; but admire rather that God has written the law for men and has spoken to us by his own Son."

The holy hermit made occasional trips to the scene of his previous retreat at Pispir to visit his followers in their hermitages. He even ventured at least twice to Alexandria. On one occasion, he preached against Arianism, the heresy that denied Jesus Christ was the Eternal Son of God. On another occasion, he went to console

Christians under threat of martyrdom during the severe early fourth century persecution initiated by Maximin Daia, the Roman official in charge of Syria, Palestine, and Egypt. Anthony supposedly longed for martyrdom himself and returned, disappointed in this aspiration, to his isolated cell to be a "daily martyr to his conscience, ever fighting the battles of the faith." To those who implored him to remain in Alexandria, he replied: "As fish die if they are taken from the waters, so does a monk wither away if he forsake his solitude." He apparently lived to be over 100, dying peacefully on Mount Kolzim. Anthony's grave was discovered in the mid-sixth century, and his bones were taken to Alexandria. When the Moslems conquered Egypt 100 years later, his relics were taken for safekeeping to Constantinople, whence they eventually were taken to France.

Anthony of Egypt is regarded as the founder of Christian monasticism and is often called the first monk. There had, of course, been ascetics before Anthony. A number of "desert fathers" had dwelt in more or less isolated cells to honor God through mental and bodily self-discipline. Paul of Thebes, for example, had faced the hardships of the desert alone for some 50 years before St. Anthony's withdrawal from the world. Anthony, in contrast to these predecessors, is generally credited with having been the first organizer of monasticism as a particular way of life in its own right. Although he passed the majority of his years in solitude, his brief emergence from self-imposed exile at Pispir had been a decisive influence. By the end of the fourth century, Egypt had thousands of aspiring monks. Anthony is also recognized as the patron saint of herdsmen.

Anthony of Egypt did not write the Rule of St. Anthony, which was ascribed to him during the Middle Ages but which was in reality compiled from writings and discourses attributed to him in his biography and in the collection entitled *Apophthegmata patrum* or "Sayings of the Fathers." The rule is still kept by some monks of the Syrian, Coptic, and Armenian churches.

In the late 11th century, a plague of erysipelas — an acute inflammation of the skin accompanied by high fever — swept through France and, according to tradition, St. Anthony's alleged relics, which had been transferred to France from Constantinople, cured some of the afflicted. Stricken persons throughout France prayed to the saint for relief. Because of this the disease came to be known as St. Anthony's Fire. During the High Middle Ages the Order of the Canons Regular of St. Anthony, which survived in France until the French Revolution, was founded for the relief of those suffering from the ailment.

Benjamin Franklin's Birthday

An incredibly versatile and universally admired man, Benjamin Franklin, born in Boston on January 17, 1706, was noted as a printer, writer, scientist, inventor, statesman, philanthropist, public servant, moralist, and diplomat. Today, he is encountered most directly through his posthumously published *Autobiography*. That somewhat guarded account, written long after the events it recalls and marred by inaccuracy of detail, nonetheless remains a classic.

Franklin was this country's best-known representative abroad in its days as an increasingly restless colony and as a new nation. As statesman and diplomat, he helped draft and signed the Declaration of Independence, was instrumental in securing French support for the new republic (see February 6), laid the groundwork for the treaty which brought a successful conclusion to the American Revolution, and was author of the principal compromise that led to adoption of the US Constitution. As if with his left hand, he meanwhile served Philadelphia in many ways and represented Pennsylvania in almost every imaginable official capacity (for years as a member of the Pennsylvania Assembly, for example, and toward the end of his life as president of the Pennsylvania executive council).

As a scientist, he experimented tirelessly, identifying lightning with electricity by means of his famous investigation with a kite during a storm. This experiment and others brought him scientific renown in Europe and America.

As an inventor, Franklin conceived such varied items as a harmonica (mechanized musical glasses), the fuel-saving Franklin stove, bifocal lenses, the lightning rod, and a library chair that doubled as a ladder.

As a printer and editor, he was first known as owner of the *Pennsylvania Gazette*. His practical nature as well as the wit, wisdom, well-turned phrases, and commonsense philosophy that became his hallmarks, were expressed in essays, and in aphorisms — often borrowed — which are well remembered today. Many of them concerned such virtues as thrift, industry, honesty, and moderation. His maxims, attention-holding style, and what has been called an uncanny flair for attracting public attention to his own products brought success to the *Gazette* and other ventures—particularly his *Poor Richard's Almanack*, which was published annually from 1732 to 1757. Modern printing, advertising, and periodicals all owe a debt to him.

Franklin's wide-ranging interests involved him in many other activities, associating his name with a list of accomplishments that few biographies can equal for length or significance. Among other things, he was instrumental in founding the country's first hospital — Pennsylvania Hospital in Philadelphia; its first subscription library — the Library Company of Philadelphia; and its first insurance company — the Philadelphia Contributionship for the Insurance of Houses from Loss by Fire. Having earlier reorganized the postal system of the colonies, he served as the country's first postmaster general. He organized Philadelphia's first fire company, suggested a police force, drew up a plan for paving the streets, and was responsible for better lighting and other civic improvements.

Never at a loss for ideas, Franklin in 1743 proposed formation of a society of "Virtuosi residing in the several Colonies . . . to maintain a constant Correspondence." The result was the American Philosophical Society, today still located in Philadelphia, "for Promoting Useful Knowledge." His proposals also resulted in the formation of an academy, which later became the University of Pennsylvania.

One of the most notable observances associated with Franklin is International Printing Week, which originated in 1928. It is scheduled annually for the week of his birthday (generally the third full week in January) in more than 200 cities in the United States and 26 other nations throughout the world. Observed especially in English-speaking countries, the week is sponsored by the International Association of Printing House Craftsmen. Together with cooperating associations, the craftsmen's 102 clubs in the United States celebrate Franklin's birthday week with addresses by leaders in printing, publishing, and the graphic arts, and with printing competitions, shows of printing machinery, and printing exhibits in stores, libraries, and other locations, as well as with printing demonstrations in shopping centers and elsewhere.

One of the biggest observances of Printing Week takes place in New York City under the auspices of the Printing Industries of Metropolitan New York, with the participation of 83 cooperating organizations in the fields of graphic arts, advertising, communications, and business. Highlights include a Printing Week dinner in observance of Franklin's birthday, when the Franklin Award for Distinguished Service is presented to an outstanding person. Recipients of the award have included Secretary-General of the United Nations U Thant (in 1972) and Presidents Richard M. Nixon, Harry S. Truman, and Dwight D. Eisenhower (in 1971, 1958, and 1956 respectively). Another perennial of New York's Printing Week observance is an exhibit of outstanding examples of printing. In one recent typical year, the exhibit, held in Manhattan's Union Carbide Building, lasted a month and featured some 750 of the 1,000 printing pieces selected for special commendation from 3,000 entries. Also part of the exhibit, which attracted an estimated 25,000 visitors, were demonstrations of ink making, presswork, paper cutting, and platemaking. Mayor John V. Lindsay signed a Printing Week proclamation and there was a wreath-laying ceremony at the Benjamin Franklin statue in New York's Printing House Square, near City Hall. In addition, New York's Printing Week events generally include a variety of educational programs, films, printing plant tours, and store window displays. Similar observances, although usually less extensive, are held in printing centers such as Chicago, Philadelphia, Nashville, Atlanta, Miami, Omaha, Dallas, Seattle, San Francisco, and Los Angeles. Boston — the birthplace of Franklin and a major publishing and printing center — was the scene of one of the earliest celebrations of Franklin's birthday, in 1826. (Consisting of a meeting in Concert Hall followed by a dinner, it was arranged by the Franklin Typographical Society, an organization that had been formed for the relief of needy printers.)

One of the most notable commemorations of Franklin's birth takes place in Philadelphia, where he lived for so long. Philadelphia's Poor Richard Club — an organization of professionals in the fields of advertising, journalism, and public relations, named for Franklin's almanac — observes the day with a breakfast, followed by a motorcade to Franklin's grave at Christ Church Burial Ground at 5th and Arch Streets. After the placing of wreaths from the President of the United States and some 25 organizations, including a number founded by Franklin, the motorcade proceeds to Old Christ Church, at 2nd Street above Market, for a memorial service. Descendants of Franklin who attend the service usually occupy the pew in which he sat. Afterwards, the motorcade proceeds to the Liberty Bell in Independence Hall for a brief observance. Usually, there also is a flag-raising ceremony at Independence Hall. The birthday commemoration continues at the Franklin Institute, founded in 1824, where a deserving national figure is presented with the institute's gold medal and gives an address.

Scientists of the Franklin Institute commemorated the 261st anniversary of Franklin's birthday in 1967, by employing light from the star

Gamma Andromeda — 261 light years from earth — to light candles on a giant birthday cake. The events took place in front of James Earle Fraser's heroic-size statue of Franklin. The main Franklin Institute building — it was completed in 1934 at a cost of some $3 million and contains a museum of the physical sciences — and the new Franklin Institute Research Laboratories adjacent probably constitute the country's most notable physical memorial in Franklin's honor.

The Poor Richard Club's Franklin birthday observance is concluded by a luncheon at the club and a formal dinner that evening at Philadelphia's Bellevue Stratford Hotel.

Elsewhere in Philadelphia, the University of Pennsylvania traditionally marks Franklin's birthday with Founder's Day ceremonies on the Saturday closest to January 17. These include an alumni luncheon, Alumni Awards of Merit for distinguished service to Pennsylvania, and either a special convocation or the ceremonial laying of wreaths at one of the two Franklin statues on campus.

Many other organizations honor Franklin, including The Library Company of Philadelphia ("almost continually"), and the American Philosophical Society, which takes particular note of special Franklin anniversaries. In 1906, for example, it celebrated the 200th anniversary of his birth with four days of meetings attended by a committee of senators and representatives designated by Congress, and by delegates from leading scientific societies of the United States and Europe. With the state of Pennsylvania appropriating $20,000 toward its cost, the observance featured among other things a military parade; a salute from the battleship *Pennsylvania*, anchored in the Delaware River; memorial addresses; and Secretary of State Elihu Root's presentation to the representative of France of a medal voted by Congress. In 1956, the American Philosophical Society marked the 250th anniversary of Franklin's birth by publication of new Franklin studies; by exhibitions of Franklin portraits and other materials; and by an unusual program of "Music Enjoyed by Franklin." Joining libraries and learned societies throughout the world in commemorating the 250th anniversary, the Library of Congress — whose collection of Franklin papers is second only to that of the American Philosophical Society — also opened a major Franklin exhibit on January 17, 1956.

Two annual observances long scheduled to coincide with Franklin's birthday were discontinued in the late 1960s. One was National Thrift Week, inaugurated by the YMCA in 1917. Later, it was sponsored by the National Thrift Committee, a group supported by various savings institutions, which was incorporated

in New York State in 1934 and had headquarters in Chicago. The second was the annual dinner meeting, sponsored by the International Benjamin Franklin Society, which was organized in 1923 and had its headquarters in New York.

These omissions notwithstanding, interest in Franklin seems, if anything, to grow with the years — possibly because he was the most modern of the Founding Fathers and the one who, it has been said, would feel most at home in the 20th century. In recent years, for example, kite enthusiasts have noted his birthday. In 1969, the city of Philadelphia inaugurated the Benjamin Franklin kite flying contest, scheduled annually for the Saturday preceding (or falling on) January 17 on the Mall of Independence Hall. Prizes are awarded for the highest flyer and the most original and best-decorated kites. Since 1968, the International Kitefliers Association has held an annual World Championship Kite Flyoff in Sarasota, Florida, on the Saturday nearest January 17.

Some of the specific details of Franklin's early life include the fact that he was the 15th of Josiah Franklin's 17 children, and the 10th son. As a boy, he worked for a year in his father's tallow chandler's shop and then was apprenticed, at 12, to his brother James, a printer and founder of one of the earliest American newspapers. This was the *New England Courant*, which carried Benjamin Franklin's earliest (although anonymously) published work. Although the terms of Franklin's apprenticeship required him to serve until he was 20 years old, he quarreled with his brother when he was 17 and ran away to New York. Unable to find work there, he continued to Philadelphia. Although he arrived almost penniless, he soon found friends and employment, landing on his feet in characteristic Franklin fashion.

En route, he reflected that he was glad that man was a reasoning creature, as "he could find a reason for anything he wanted to do." Franklin reached this typically practical conclusion when he abandoned his vegetarian practices and ate some of the fish that the cook of the ship on which he was sailing had caught and fried. Having seen the cook clean the fish and find a smaller fish inside it, he reflected that if it was right for the big fish, acting according to natural instinct, to eat the little one, it could not be wrong for him to eat the big one.

In 1725, when Franklin was 19, Sir William Keith, governor of the colony of Pennsylvania, encouraged him to go to London, promising letters of credit and introduction so that Franklin could buy equipment for a printing office, return to Philadelphia, and set up a business. When the governor's promises failed to materialize, Franklin found himself alone, friendless, and jobless in London. With his customary resourcefulness, however, he quickly found employment as a printer. He remained in London a year and a half and then returned to Philadelphia.

There, he soon had a printing establishment of his own and in 1729 he purchased an interest in a dull weekly named the *Pennsylvania Gazette*. Within a year he was sole owner of the *Gazette*, which he rapidly enlivened and edited with distinction until he "retired," if that is the word, at the age of 42 in 1748. The acquisition of the *Gazette*, and the financial security that followed, marked the real beginning of Franklin's illustrious career.

JANUARY 18

Daniel Webster's Birthday

Daniel Webster, who won fame as an orator, statesman, and constitutional lawyer, was born in Salisbury (now part of Franklin), New Hampshire, on January 18, 1782. His father was a New England farmer who had served as a soldier in the American Revolution. Daniel Webster received a preliminary education in neighborhood schools. Since the boy demonstrated precocious intellectual abilities, his father at the cost of considerable financial hardship managed to enroll him in 1796 at Phillips Exeter Academy in Exeter, New Hampshire, and then at Dartmouth College in Hanover. Daniel Webster graduated from Dartmouth in 1801 at the age of 19, having developed into an orator of at least local fame.

Webster vacillated between a career as a schoolteacher and one as a lawyer, finally settling on the latter. After serving in Boston as a clerk in the firm of the noted lawyer Christopher Gore, Webster was admitted to the bar in March 1805. He first practiced law in Boscawen, New Hampshire, and in 1807 continued his profession in Portsmouth, New Hampshire. Also drawn into politics, he was elected to the US House of Representatives from the Portsmouth district in 1812, and was reelected two years later.

In 1816 Webster moved to Boston and devoted himself to law practice. His rapid success in that field has been attributed to his commanding presence, created by his dramatic voice and dark, penetrating eyes, and to his persuasive arguments and quick grasp of the key issues at stake. He came to national attention in 1818–1819 while successfully defending his alma mater in the famous *Dartmouth College* case (see February 2), which eventually was brought before the US Supreme Court. Within the next half dozen years, he also took part in several other cases of national importance, including *McCulloch* v. *Maryland, Gibbons* v. *Ogden,* and *Osborn* v. *the Bank of the United States.*

In the meantime, Webster gained a nationwide reputation as a public orator, speaking, for example, at the Plymouth (Massachusetts) Bicentennial in 1820 and at the 50th anniversary of the battle of Bunker Hill in 1825.

In 1822, Webster had again been elected to the House of Representatives, this time from a Boston district, and he was twice reelected by an overwhelming vote. In the election of 1827, he was chosen to represent Massachusetts in the US Senate, where he served without interruption until 1841 and became a leading political figure. As a champion of New England economic interests, he supported the protective tariff of 1828. He denounced the theory of nullification and states' rights in the famous January 1830 debate with Robert Hayne of South Carolina. His thunderous defense of the Union included the famous words "Liberty *and* Union, now and forever, one and inseparable!" In 1832–1833, Webster backed President Andrew Jackson in arguing against nullification with another South Carolinian, John C. Calhoun. On many other issues, however, especially fiscal matters pertaining to the Bank of the United States, Webster, a Whig of the old school, opposed the aggressive Democratic Chief Executive.

In 1836 Webster received the electoral vote of Massachusetts as the presidential candidate of the New England Whigs, and in 1840 he declined the nomination for Vice President. President William Henry Harrison made him secretary of state in his cabinet, a post he retained under President John Tyler after Harrison's sudden death in 1841. When Tyler broke with his Whig cabinet in September 1841, Webster was the only cabinet member who did not hand in his resignation, thereby gaining the enmity of some of his fellow Whigs. He first completed the negotiations for the Webster-Ashburton Treaty of 1842, which settled with England the boundary of Maine. Webster then resigned as secretary of state in May 1843 and resumed law practice in Boston.

Daniel Webster entered the Senate a second time in 1845 as the successor of Rufus Choate. As senator, he followed the Whig policy of opposing the War with Mexico (see May 13) and the annexation of Texas. He aspired to the nomination for President in 1848, and denounced bitterly the Whig selection of the Mexican War hero General Zachary Taylor. The defeat of Mexico and the subsequent vast acquisition of territory stirred up a great debate over slavery, which threatened to split the Union. Although Webster condemned slavery as an evil, he regarded the preservation of the Union as an even more desirable goal than the abolition of slavery. Risking his own popularity among New Englanders, especially the abolitionists, he actively supported Henry Clay's Compromise of 1850, which he believed to be the only course to avert civil strife. In his last notable speech in the Senate, known as the Seventh of March [1850] speech, he therefore advocated compromise on the issue of the extension of slavery. He was roundly denounced for it in the North.

From 1850 until his health broke in 1852, Daniel Webster served as secretary of state under President Millard Fillmore. When he died at his home in Marshfield, Massachusetts, on October 24, 1852, there was widespread mourning at the passing of one of the most brilliant men the United States had produced. On July 4, 1970, the building at Marshfield that had once served as Daniel Webster's study and law office — the only structure of his vast estate still standing — was opened to the public as a historical monument.

JANUARY 19

The Epiphany, or Greek Cross Day (Old Calendar)

Those Greek Orthodox churches that have not adopted the Gregorian or New Style calendar for their feasts observe the Epiphany — which is more commonly marked earlier (see January 6, The Epiphany, or Twelfth Day) — on January 19, with ancient ceremonies. Among Greek (as well as other Eastern Orthodox) churches, the emphasis of Epiphany observances is on the baptism of Jesus in the River Jordan and the attendant manifestation of his divinity when the Holy Spirit descended upon him in the form of a dove.

In Greece, it is the custom on this day (and the previous evening) not only to bless the baptismal water that will be used within the churches, but also to bless neighboring waters outside the churches, whether they be rivers, springs, lakes, fountains, or the edge of oceans. In Greek Orthodox churches the officiating prelate blesses the waters by dipping a gold cross into them with prescribed ceremony. Waters so blessed are traditionally believed to possess purifying and health-giving powers. Ceremonies similar to those performed in Greece are celebrated by certain Greek Orthodox churches in the United States, among them the one at

Tarpon Springs, Florida (see January 6, Epiphany, or Greek Cross Day; Blessing of the Sponge Divers).

The same kind of ceremony is also performed, on or close to the Sunday nearest January 19, under the auspices of the Greek Orthodox Church of St. Nicholas at 155 Cedar Street, New York City. On that day, it is customary for a procession headed by local prelates and, perhaps, by a bishop or other visiting ecclesiastical dignitary to march from the lower Manhattan church to Battery Park, at the edge of Upper New York Bay. Included in the procession are musicians; a company of priests, deacons, archdeacons, and white-robed acolytes chanting hymns; and several hundred members of the city's Greek community. On the procession's arrival at Battery Park, the officiating church dignitaries board a New York City police launch (which in recent years has supplanted the raft once used) and the chief celebrant throws a gilded wooden cross into the water, simultaneously releasing two white doves. Several men who have volunteered for the honor then dive into the icy water to rescue the crucifix and struggle for its possession. The man who succeeds in the rescue has the reward of carrying the cross back to the church and, according to popular tradition, also is rewarded with a year of good luck.

Robert E. Lee's Birthday

Robert E. Lee's birthday was made a legal holiday in the state of Georgia in 1889. Virginia — where the anniversary is observed as Lee-Jackson Day (now marked on the third Monday in January) — followed Georgia's example in 1890. Other states that also note the Confederate general's birthday as a legal holiday, either on January 19 or on the third Monday of the month, are Alabama, Arkansas, Florida, Kentucky, Louisiana, Mississippi, North Carolina, South Carolina, Tennessee, and Texas.

Lee, who is regarded by many military authorities as the ablest strategist of the Civil War, was born at Stratford, his family's estate in Westmoreland County, Virginia, on January 19, 1807. He was the son of Henry Lee, known as Light-Horse Harry Lee, a distinguished soldier of the American Revolution. His mother — his father's second wife — was the former Anne Hill Carter, a daughter of Charles Carter, belonging to a Virginia family as famous as the Lees.

Henry Lee was forced to leave Stratford in 1811 because of unfortunate investments and complicated ownership rights. (The property was inherited by the children of his first marriage.) Young Robert E. Lee and his family therefore moved to Alexandria, Virginia, where they soon occupied a handsome Georgian mansion. The Stonewall Jackson Memorial, Inc., announced the acquisition of this red brick house on January 19, 1967, the 160th anniversary of the birth of Lee, and opened it to the public.

Robert E. Lee went to school in Alexandria, and as he grew up, looked after his invalid mother. His father was seldom at home and had little contact in general with his family before his death on Cumberland Island on March 25, 1818. Nonetheless inspired by his father's military career, young Lee sought admission to the United States Military Academy at West Point, which he entered in 1825. He was graduated second in his class and was the first cadet to complete the course without receiving a single demerit. Entering the army as a brevet second lieutenant of engineers, Lee served as assistant engineer at Fort Monroe, Virginia, from May 1831 to November 1834.

While there, he was married — on June 30, 1831 — to Mary Ann Randolph Custis, the only daughter of George Washington Parke Custis (grandson of Martha Washington), who lived on the estate originally known as Arlington, across the Potomac from Washington. Arlington House, where Lee and his bride settled and raised their family, has since become known as the Custis-Lee Mansion. Visited by thousands annually, it stands within what is now Arlington National Cemetery, directly overlooking the grave of President John F. Kennedy and a panoramic view of Washington. The mansion, administered by the National Park Service, was named a permanent memorial to Lee by act of Congress in 1955.

After his marriage, young Lee was assigned to various engineering duties until 1846, when war broke out between the United States and Mexico. Lee, then a captain, first reported for service as assistant engineer to Brigadier General John E. Wool, the commander of a secondary force stationed at San Antonio, Texas, Transferred to the Vera Cruz expedition, he won the esteem and admiration of General Winfield Scott, its commander, and performed valuable service in planning for the capture of Mexico City. Lee returned from the Mexican War with his military reputation established at the age of 42 and was promoted for gallantry to the rank of brevet colonel. He was then put in charge of the construction of Fort Carroll in Baltimore Harbor.

After serving there from September 1848 to April 1852, Lee was appointed to fill the post of superintendent at West Point. He remained in this position until March 1855, when Secretary of War Jefferson Davis obtained his transfer to the line and his assignment as lieutenant colonel of the Second Cavalry Regiment. Lee's orders to leave for western Texas to take his first field command came the next month. Later, in 1857, Colonel Lee obtained an extended leave of absence to supervise the running of Arlington, the lovely but sadly neglected estate that his wife had inherited from her father. While there, he was called upon to put down the uprising at Harpers Ferry that had been led by John Brown (see May 9) on December 2, 1859.

From this duty, Lee returned to the Texas border, only to be summoned to Washington in February 1861 to meet the crisis of his life. In December 1860 South Carolina, soon to be followed by other Southern states, had already declared its secession over the issues of slavery and state sovereignty. General Scott, with whom Lee was a great favorite, placed the capable colonel on standing order, with the purpose of promoting him immediately if civil war should erupt.

Although Lee was no politician, he was an intelligent observer and had watched with concern and sadness the mounting strife that would lead to the Civil War. Considering slavery an evil, he, like many of his fellow Virginia landowners, had freed his slaves; but he was equally convinced that any effort to wipe out slavery by force would be a grave mistake. When the secession movement began to gain momentum, Lee hoped that the issue might be settled peacefully. Loyal to the federal government and to the US Army, he was convinced of the advantages of the Union on the one hand, while on the other, he adamantly insisted upon the right of each state to secede from that union at will. It was in keeping with the tradition in which he had been raised that if Virginia seceded he would go with it as a matter of course. Shortly before the crisis, he wrote:

I can anticipate no greater calamity for the country than the dissolution of the Union. . . . Still, a union that can only be maintained by swords and bayonets, and in which strife and civil war are to take the place of brotherly love and kindness, has no charms for me. If the Union is dissolved and the Government dispersed I shall return to my native State and share the miseries of my people and, save in defense, will draw my sword no more.

Events moved more rapidly and radically than Lee had wished. On April 12, 1861, the firing on Fort Sumter touched off the Civil War (see April 12). Lee's military reputation was so distinguished that General Scott advised

President Lincoln to offer his protégé the field command of the US Army. On April 18, Francis P. Blair, a top presidential adviser, informed Lee that the President had authorized such an offer.

Declining the honor with heavy heart, Lee discussed the situation with General Scott, who advised him that he should either resign from the army or accept whatever duty was assigned to him. On April 19, while at Arlington, Lee learned that a Virginia convention had voted in favor of secession and would submit the issue to the people for ratification. Persuaded that secession would not wait for referendum, he resigned from the army on April 20. His wife wrote to a friend shortly afterwards: "My husband has wept tears of blood over this terrible war, but as a man of honor and as a Virginian, he must follow the destiny of his State."

Having already refused the command of what soon would be the Union forces in the great Civil War, Robert E. Lee — ironically enough — now began his rise to leadership of the forces that would oppose them. On April 23 he assumed command of the military and naval forces of Virginia, reorganizing them thoroughly. (At that time he had never commanded more troops in the field than four squadrons of cavalry, and that briefly.) Lee was soon made military adviser, with the rank of general, to Jefferson Davis, who had become president of the Confederacy.

After Lee's efforts to coordinate the movements of the Confederate troops in western Virginia, from July through October 1861, had failed, he set up the South Atlantic coast defenses. In March 1862, President Davis again summoned him to Richmond in the capacity of military adviser. Lee devised the strategy to divert the massive federal reinforcements intended to bolster the Union attack on Richmond, the capital of the Confederacy — plans brilliantly executed by Thomas J. "Stonewall" Jackson. After Confederate General Joseph E. Johnston was wounded during the Peninsular campaign in May 1862, Lee assumed command of the Army of Northern Virginia on June 1. General Lee's brilliant leadership of that army during the next three years was to earn him a place among the world's renowned commanders, and his varied campaigns were to lead him from Virginia to Pennsylvania.

Assuming the offensive upon taking command, Lee ended the threat to Richmond in the Seven Days battles in late June and early July 1862. Resoundingly defeating Union General John Pope at the second battle of Bull Run at the end of August, Lee was himself checked in his first Northern invasion at Antietam, Maryland, in September. The Southern general skillfully repulsed federal advances under Generals A. E. Burnside and Joseph Hooker at the battles of Fredericksburg, Virginia, on December 13, and Chancellorsville, Virginia, in May of the following year.

Lee's defeat at Gettysburg (see July 1) in the summer of 1863 came after the death of General "Stonewall" Jackson, his ablest supporter, had forced the reorganizing of the command of his army with less experienced men. The Gettysburg campaign forced Lee to reshape his military strategy. Hitherto, he had hoped that a stunning victory in the North would force the enemy to sue for peace. Afterwards, aware that increasingly limited manpower and material resources could no longer sustain such a policy, Lee attempted, with dilatory tactics, to wear down the patience of the North by preventing a major showdown.

Pitted against Lee, however, was the equally persistent and stubborn Ulysses S. Grant, the hero of Vicksburg, whom Abraham Lincoln appointed commander of the federal armies in March 1864. Grant, acutely assessing the situation, realized that Lee's Army of Northern Virginia was the chief obstacle to Union victory and he was determined to force Lee to fight. Lee was able to repulse Grant's direct attacks in the Wilderness campaign during May and June. Nevertheless, the Union general managed to trap Lee in the grueling siege of Petersburg, the crucial support center south of Richmond, which lasted during the winter of 1864 and into spring of 1865 (see June 9, Petersburg Memorial Day). This move confined the Southern general to the immediate defense of the Richmond area, thus depriving him of the opportunity for rapid maneuvers that had thus far helped to offset the numerically superior Union forces.

Lee's appointment as general-in-chief of all the Confederate armies on February 6, 1865, was an empty gesture, intended primarily to remove from Jefferson Davis the onerous burden of military defeat, which seemed imminent. Lee showed no intention of exercising his new command and to the end continued to sign himself "Commander of the Army of Northern Virginia." In early April, Grant broke through the Petersburg defenses. His opponent abandoned the lines around Richmond and unsuccessfully attempted to reunite with General Joseph Johnston in North Carolina. Robert E. Lee's subsequent surrender to Ulysses S. Grant at Appomattox Court House in the spring of 1865 (see April 9) brought the war virtually to an end.

Lee returned as a paroled prisoner of war to

Richmond. He could not return to Arlington. That lovely estate, situated on the line of defenses protecting Washington, was occupied by federal troops and became a Union army camp shortly after the Lees departed for Richmond, where the Confederate leader took up his command after Virginia's secession. The federal government subsequently refused to accept payment of taxes from an agent sent by Mrs. Lee and confiscated the Lees' land: technically, she was required by law to appear in person, which she was unable to do. Long afterwards — in 1883, when the Confederate general and his wife were both dead — the government made belated restitution by paying $150,000 for the land to the Lees' son, George Washington Custis Lee, but only after he had pursued the matter all the way to the Supreme Court. Parts of the former Lee holdings were first used as a national cemetery in 1864, when 210 acres were set aside for that purpose. Subsequent additions increased the size of Arlington National Cemetery to 420 acres, before its expansion, which began in 1965 with the use of an additional 190-acre tract of land. Begun as a burial place for Civil War dead, Arlington today contains graves of dead from all wars in which the United States has participated, and is the largest and most famous of the national cemeteries.

After the Civil War, Lee resolutely avoided participation in the many war-kindled controversies that still rankled. Choosing from the positions offered him, in September 1865 he accepted the presidency of Washington College at Lexington, Virginia, and devoted the remaining years of his life to raising its standards of scholarship and increasing the number of its students. He died on October 12, 1870, at Lexington. His wife died three years later.

Shortly after the end of the war, Lee had requested a pardon and restoration of his citizenship from President Andrew Johnson. A required oath of allegiance, which he swore on the same day he assumed the presidency of Washington College, apparently never reached the proper federal authorities. It was discovered 100 years after his death, in 1970, in the National Archives. Five years later, with the overwhelming approval of both houses of Congress, citizenship was belatedly restored to one of the country's most noted sons.

Perceptive of his enemy's weak points, quick to grasp the potentialities of a military situation, and intuitively anticipating his opponents' moves, Robert E. Lee possessed many assets as a commander. Most outstanding, perhaps, was his skillful use of field defenses to implement his military designs, a method not generally applied on a large scale until the early 20th century. Both as a general and as a person, Lee commanded the respect and devotion of his men, who would march anywhere for him and take on any odds. Some of his biographers, however, say that his habit of surrendering his views to those who disagreed with him in planning a battle or campaign was a decided weakness, one that became especially evident after the loss of Stonewall Jackson, his right-hand man.

A handsome man with superb carriage and charming manner, Lee was known for his love of family life, loyalty to kin, and love of animals, especially his famous horse Traveller, on whom he was so often pictured. He was almost universally regarded as the epitome of the word gentleman. Even in the early days of his cadetship at West Point, many of these qualities in his character were apparent. Joseph Johnston, a fellow Virginian and fellow officer during the Civil War, later aptly conveyed the impression that cadet Lee had made on his classmates:

We had the same intimate associates, who thought as I did, that no other youth or man so united the qualities that win warm friendship and command high respect. For he was full of sympathy and kindness, genial and fond of gay conversation, even fun, while his correctness of demeanor and attention to all duties, personal and official, and a dignity as much a part of himself as the elegance of his person, gave him a superiority that every one acknowledged in his heart.

Most impressive was Lee's unfailing response to duty, revealed best, perhaps, in the fateful hour before he met General Grant at Appomattox Court House. Replying simply to queries about his momentous decision to surrender, General Lee replied: "The question is, is it right to surrender this army? If it is right, then I will take all the responsibility."

In memory of this American hero and Southern ideal, the trustees of Washington College changed its name to Washington and Lee. The university's Lee Chapel, which Lee himself designed, contains his grave — in a crypt beneath E. V. Valentine's famous recumbent statue of him. The chapel, which also contains the graves of other famous Lees and today serves as a museum, was restored as part of the four-year Civil War centennial observed throughout the United States in the early 1960s.

Lee has been honored in many ways. Virginia placed a statue of him in Statuary Hall at the national Capitol in Washington, D.C.; another statue adorns the rotunda of the state capitol in Richmond. With Jefferson Davis and Stonewall Jackson, Lee also is depicted in the enormous cliffside carvings that memorialize the Confederacy at Georgia's Stone Mountain state park, east of Atlanta. In the North as well as the South, he is regarded as a great American.

The celebration of the anniversary of Lee's birth is more elaborate in his native Virginia than in any of the other 11 states that observe the day. At his Stratford Hall birthplace (which schoolchildren of the 1930s helped purchase as a memorial) his memory is annually honored by a gala birthday party to which the public is invited. As many as 500 persons attend the event, which generally is held in the evening. For the occasion, the austere old mansion is lighted, inside and out, by 220 flickering candles — a sight that dazzles when there is snow on the ground to reflect the sparkle. Inside, guests are served punch and cake, and aides in each of the 18 rooms answer questions about the Lees or recount the stories of their lives.

Washington and Lee University, of which Lee was president, does not let the anniversary of his birth pass without appropriate ceremonies and eulogistic addresses. Especially noteworthy was the centennial of his birth on January 19, 1907, when the program included a memorable address by Charles Francis Adams, president of the Massachusetts Historical Society, descendant of an illustrious American family, and himself a Northern veteran of the Civil War. In Richmond, there traditionally is a gathering in honor of Lee's memory in the Hall of Delegates of the state capitol, under the sponsorship of the Robert E. Lee Memorial Foundation of Stratford.

The Virginia Historical Society, with headquarters in Richmond's Battle Abbey, honors Lee by holding its annual meeting on his birthday. Varied tribute — the laying of wreaths at Lee statues, for example, or the presentation of special historical programs in schools or on radio and television — is accorded Lee on his birthday by many of the United Daughters of the Confederacy's 900-odd chapters in 34 states and Paris. The UDC's General Organization annually marks the day by placing a wreath at the Lee statue in Statuary Hall in the Capitol at Washington, and District of Columbia chapters of the UDC put on a special program each year. The Sons of Confederate Veterans, headquartered in Hattiesburg, Mississippi, participate in commemorations of Lee's birthday in various cities.

Richmond's Confederate Museum, in "the White House of the Confederacy" — the house occupied by Jefferson Davis as president of the Confederate States of America — is opened to the public without admission fee on the anniversary of Lee's birth and also celebrates the occasion with a reception on the Sunday nearest January 19 that is held either at the museum itself or at the much-visited Robert E. Lee House at 707 East Franklin Street in Richmond. The house, now owned by the museum-affiliated Confederate Memorial Literary Society, was used by Lee's family during the Civil War. In addition, Lee's birthday has often been marked by a memorial service at St. Paul's Episcopal Church in Richmond, which Lee attended and where a stained-glass window has been placed in his honor.

Edgar Allan Poe's Birthday

Critical attention paid to Edgar Allan Poe, who ranks among the geniuses of American literature, increases with the passing years. A number of observances still honor him on January 19, his birthday; on or near October 7, the anniversary of his death; or in April, commemorating the publication by *Graham's Magazine* in April 1841 of his "The Murders in the Rue Morgue," generally recognized as the first example of the detective story, a form Poe is credited with inventing. In New York, for example, the Edgar Allan Poe Awards Dinner is held annually in April by the Mystery Writers of America, with the presentation of Edgars to authors of the outstanding mysteries of the year, and other special awards — Edgars or Ravens — for achievement in associated fields. Apart from the Mystery Writers, schools, and Poe societies or other literary clubs in various American cities — or in France, where Poe has received at least as much attention as in his native land — are most apt to take note of Poe anniversaries, sometimes on an annual basis and sometimes with a quarter or half century intervening between important celebrations.

The Edgar Allan Poe Society of Baltimore is particularly faithful in its commemoration, which has been an annual event since 1923. The observance, held with the participation of students from several Baltimore high schools, includes the laying of wreaths on Poe's grave, followed by a memorial lecture. Over the years, the lecturers have included distinguished European and American authorities on Poe — among them Dr. John Ostrom, editor of *The Complete Letters of Poe* in 1967, Professor Burton E. Pollin, editor of *Poe, Creator of Words* in 1973, and Professor John E. Reilly, author of "Images of Poe: The Picture That Poets Have Given of Poe," a work in progress, in 1975. Originally held on January 19, the Baltimore commemoration has in the last quarter century taken place on the Sunday nearest the anniversary of Poe's death.

Poe observances also take place periodically at Richmond's Edgar Allan Poe Museum, often referred to as the Poe Shrine, at 1914 East Main Street. The museum, founded in 1922, occupies four quaint buildings including Richmond's oldest home.— the Old Stone House. The buildings of the Poe museum open on what is called the Enchanted Garden, which was the setting on several May evenings of 1965 and 1966 — and from time to time since — for a program entitled "None Sing So Wildly Well." A dramatic presentation in which a dozen or so of Poe's poems were linked by a continuity-giving series of fictional letters, the program revolved around the known facts of Poe's life in Richmond.

The museum contains various Poe mementos. Poe exhibitions also are held from time to time at such notable repositories of Poe materials as the Virginia State Library in Richmond; the Enoch Pratt Free Library in Baltimore; and Poe's Philadelphia residence at 530 North Seventh Street — which Richard Gimbel, a collector of Poe manuscripts and first editions, purchased in 1933. The Philadelphia house, which Gimbel restored and opened as a museum, has been refurbished and its garden relandscaped.

The object of this continuing attention, Edgar Allan Poe was born in Boston on January 19, 1809. Both his father, David Poe Jr., the son of a patriot in the American Revolution, and his mother, the British-born Elizabeth (Arnold) Poe, were actors, and Poe was carried about the country with them in his infancy. Both parents died in 1811, however, and the Poe children were distributed among foster parents.

Young Edgar Poe was taken into the home of a successful Richmond merchant, John Allan, and his wife. Allan's wife, who was childless, became Poe's foster mother. In 1815, the Allans took the boy with them to Scotland and England, where he studied at several schools, including the Manor House School near London. He received additional schooling after the family's return to Richmond five years later. But he developed a strained relationship with his guardian because of the latter's lack of consideration for his wife.

In 1826, Poe entered Thomas Jefferson's new University of Virginia at Charlottesville, where he read widely in contemporary literature and showed great proficiency in the study of Latin, Greek, French, Spanish, and Italian. Being pressed for funds, however, he meanwhile accumulated a gambling debt in a vain attempt to meet his expenses. He also demonstrated that alcohol, even in small amounts, had a disastrous effect upon him, signaling the beginning of his struggle with a weakness that he was to battle the rest of his life — albeit with greater success than is often indicated.

Neither circumstance was pleasing to Allan, who refused to pay Poe's debt, took him out of college, and put him to work in his own counting room. Poe did not stay there long, however, but ran away to Boston, where his first published work, *Tamerlane and Other Poems*, was brought out in paper covers in 1827. In desperate need, he enlisted in the US Army in the same year. He served for two years under the assumed name of Edgar A. Perry and was promoted to sergeant major before securing an honorable discharge. His guardian, with whom he was reconciled for a time, then helped with his application for an appointment to the US Military Academy at West Point — assistance rendered at least partly in response to the last wishes of Mrs. Allan, who had died in the meantime.

Allan having remarried, Poe awaited the West Point appointment in Baltimore, where he first met his relatives — a grandmother, Mrs. David Poe; an aunt, Mrs. Maria Clemm; and her daughter Virginia, whom he would later marry. He also published *Al Aaraaf*, his second volume of verse, in 1829. When the West Point appointment came in July of 1830, it was after Poe had had further misunderstandings with Allan. Their differences were subsequently compounded. Permanently cut off from his guardian's financial aid, Poe set about securing his release from the academy by a deliberate neglect of military duties. He was duly dismissed at the end of six months.

Beginning his attempt to support himself by writing, he went to New York, where his third volume of poems was published in 1831. Not long afterwards, he moved to Baltimore, where he lived with Mrs. Clemm and her family in what the public can now visit as the Edgar Allan Poe House at 203 North Amity Street. The house, which has been restored, is administered as the city's chief literary memorial by the Edgar Allan Poe Society.

It was while he was living there that Poe, whose work had gone largely unnoticed until then, turned from verse to prose fiction. Drawing upon his own peculiar and often macabre genius, he showed himself the master of a unique form of short story. His writing — mysterious, full of suspense, rhythmic, at once controlled and passionate — has been often copied but never duplicated.

Poe's earliest real recognition came in 1833, when he won a prize offered by the Baltimore *Saturday Visitor* for his tale "A MS. Found in a Bottle." (Baltimore's Latrobe House on Mulberry Street, where the perspicacious judges decided on the award, today is embellished by an appropriate marker.) Publication of the story led indirectly to Poe's becoming a contributor to, and from 1835 to 1837 editor of, the *Southern Literary Messenger* in Richmond, whose circulation increased sevenfold as a result of his editing and brilliant literary criticism.

He was meanwhile married to his 13-year-old cousin, Virginia Clemm, and in 1837 moved to New York with her and Mrs. Clemm. Unable to support his family there, he went the next year to Philadelphia, where he worked as a free-lance writer and as an editor, first of *Burton's Gentleman's Magazine* and then of *Graham's Magazine*. The latter was distinguished during his tenure by the appearance of his pioneering detective story "The Murders in the Rue Morgue."

Poe's talent increased the circulation of *Graham's* tenfold, making it the leading literary magazine in the United States before he left its employment in 1842. The next year, he won a prize of $100 for his story "The Gold Bug," which was printed in Philadelphia's *Dollar Newspaper* and became the best-known example of the detective story.

The publication of this and other tales notwithstanding, it was a time of extreme hardship. Poe, with no resources, was often in need of the necessities of life, and his wife, whom he would later memorialize as his "beautiful Annabel Lee," had already been ill with tuberculosis since 1841.

They moved to New York in 1844 and Poe became subeditor of the New York *Evening Mirror*, which gave to "The Raven," his most famous poem, its first airing. The next year he became, for some months, editor of the *Broadway Journal*.

In the spring of 1846, Poe rented a small cottage at Fordham, now part of New York City's borough of the Bronx. It was in this house, now a museum (in Poe Park on Grand Concourse at East 193rd Street), that his wife died in January 1847, leaving him overcome with grief. It was here, too, that he composed some of his best-known lyrics, including his haunting poem *The Bells:* "Oh, the bells, bells, bells! . . . the sobbing of the bells. . . ." His other works had appeared in various periodicals or in the series of slim volumes that had been published over the years in spite of job changes and harassing personal emergencies. Included among them were such unforgettable tales as *The Fall of the House of Usher, The Pit and the Pendulum, The Tell-Tale Heart* and *A Cask of Amontillado*.

Poe, who had a weak heart, outlived his young wife by less than three years. In the summer of 1849 he went to Richmond, where he was received with kindness by old friends and recovered his spirits. In late September he started for New York, but on October 3 he was found in desperate condition near a Baltimore polling place and taken to a hospital. When he died four days later, on October 7, 1849, he was buried in an unmarked grave in the churchyard of Baltimore's Westminster Presbyterian Church, at Fayette and Greene streets. The grave was not marked until 1875, when Baltimore schoolteachers, aided by schoolchildren's collected pennies (which were supplemented by a local philanthropist), erected a modest headstone over it.

Although sporadic attempts to celebrate the anniversary of Poe's birth followed, it was not until the end of the first quarter of the 20th century that the Baltimore commemoration, now scheduled to mark the anniversary of his death, became somewhat regular. Meanwhile, an actors' memorial to Poe was erected in New York in 1885, and in 1891 a bust of him was unveiled at the University of Virginia and a tablet placed in the room he had occupied there. In 1902, as the centennial of his birth approached, interest in his career intensified. In 1910, just after the centennial year, a bust of him was erected in the Hall of Fame for Great Americans in New York City.

His cottage in Fordham was restored and moved at about this time to the small park which now bears his name. Even the Military Academy at West Point chose to honor the man it had expelled by placing a Poe Memorial Door in its library. In Baltimore, a tablet was placed in the hospital room in which he had died. Richmond dedicated its Enchanted Garden and Poe Shrine early in the 1920s; and on January 19, 1924, the Authors' Club of Boston erected a tablet announcing that Poe was born in that city. Ten years later the Poe Society of Philadelphia — founded by the same Richard Gimbel who had opened Poe's Philadelphia residence as a museum — held a memorable dinner, complete with an exhibition of Poe first editions and addresses by distinguished men and women of letters, on the 125th anniversary of Poe's birth. In 1949, note of the centennial of his death included the issuing of a commemorative US stamp in his honor.

If Poe-related observances have decreased in number in more recent decades, the serious interest in Poe on the part of students of American literature continues to grow. The lyric beauty of his poems, his mastery of the macabre, and the chilling, nearly unbearable suspense of his tales remain intact.

JANUARY 20

Inauguration Day

The term of the President of the United States started on March 4 until the adoption of the 20th Amendment to the Constitution in 1933 (see February 6). Presidents elected since then have taken office on January 20, Franklin Delano Roosevelt having been the first Chief Executive to do so — at the time of his second inauguration in 1937. When Inauguration Day falls on a Sunday, the oath of office is administered privately, on or ahead of schedule, but the public ceremonies are generally transferred to the following day. This was the case in 1821, 1849, 1877, and 1917, when the ceremonies took place on March 5, and in 1957, when they were staged on January 21. During the next century, Inauguration Day will have to be postponed a day only in the years 1985, 2013, and 2041. In the course of time, March 4 had been a quadrennial holiday in the District of Columbia by act of Congress, and the holiday was automatically changed to January 20 when the date of Inauguration Day was changed.

It was more or less by accident that the nation's first President, George Washington, was not inaugurated until April 30, 1789. Part of the cause was delay in assembling a quorum of the legislators who were needed to count the presidential votes. Although they were due in New York City, then the nation's capital, on March 4, it was not until April 6 that a quorum was achieved and the votes counted. Washington was informed of his unanimous election on April 14 and left his home at Mt. Vernon, Virginia, for the capital two days later (see April 16). After finally arriving in New York, he took the oath of office on the steps of the old Federal Hall (formerly New York's City Hall) at the corner of Wall and Nassau streets. (The building was replaced in 1842 by another, which served various purposes before it was designated as Federal Hall National Memorial in 1955. A well-known statue of Washington stands on its steps, near the spot where he took his oath of office.)

At the beginning of his second term in 1793, Washington took the oath in front of Independence Hall in Philadelphia, then serving as the capital. John Adams was also inaugurated in Philadelphia, in 1797, but by the time Thomas Jefferson was elected, the seat of government had been removed to Washington, D.C., and it was there that his inauguration took place in 1801. Escorted by a body of militia and a procession of citizens, Jefferson walked to the Capitol from a nearby boardinghouse and took the oath of office in the Senate Chamber. In 1809, James Madison was the first President to take the oath in the hall of the House of Representatives, which was used for the ceremony again in 1813, 1821, 1825, and 1833. In 1817, James Monroe became the first to be sworn in at the east portico of the Capitol. Starting in the late 1830s, this became the customary location for the presidential oath-taking. This tradition was broken only in 1909 (when bad weather forced William Howard Taft to use the Senate Chamber) and in 1945 (when Franklin Delano Roosevelt used the south portico for his fourth inauguration).

Over the years, the inauguration ceremonies have slowly developed into a set pattern. At noon, or shortly thereafter, the chief justice of the United States administers the 35-word oath to the President, who customarily rests his left hand on the Bible as he declares: "I do solemnly swear that I will faithfully execute the office of President of the United States, and will, to the best of my ability, preserve, protect and defend the Constitution of the United States." After taking the oath, which is prescribed in the Constitution, the Chief Executive delivers an inaugural address. In 1841, William Henry Harrison gave the longest address (a one-hour-forty-five-minute speech of some 8,500 words); George Washington delivered the shortest (approximately 135 words) at his second inauguration in 1793. Since Monroe's time, it has been customary for the inaugural address, as well as the oath, to be given from the east portico of the Capitol, in the presence of a large crowd assembled on the plaza.

Inauguration Day has attracted to Washington, D.C., an increasing number of spectators, sometimes with disastrous results, as in 1829, when Andrew Jackson's inauguration drew thousands of war veterans and admirers from the West and the South. Some 20,000 of them boisterously crowded the White House at the reception following the inaugural address, damaging furniture, glasses, rugs, and other objects.

The first inaugural ball in Washington was held in honor of James Madison on March 4, 1809, at Long's Hotel on Capitol Hill. This ball became, in the course of time, one of the established features of Inauguration Day. In 1841, William Henry Harrison was the first to dance at his own inaugural ball (actually, there were three, held at separate locations). However, the exertion only compounded the effects of the President's earlier exposure to the cold during his lengthy address and inaugural parade. Coatless and hatless despite the stormy weather, he developed pneumonia and died a month later.

The inaugural ball subsequently grew to such tremendous proportions that it had to be divided among four locations by the time of Dwight D. Eisenhower's second inauguration in 1957; among five locations by the time of John F. Kennedy's inauguration in 1961 and Lyndon B. Johnson's in 1965; and among six locations at Richard M. Nixon's first inauguration in 1969. The attendance jumped from the 400 guests at Madison's ball to the 34,000 who appeared at the inaugural balls marking Nixon's second inauguration in 1973.

Today, most onlookers flock to watch the colorful inauguration parade, the development of which was relatively slow. At first, the new President was simply escorted to the Capitol. Later, because of the many organizations that wished to march, the parade followed the inauguration and was reviewed by the President from a stand erected in front of the White House. The inauguration of Ulysses S. Grant in 1869 was the occasion for probably the most imposing parade up to that time. Large groups of soldiers and members of political organizations from various parts of the country were in the line.

Since then, the size of the parade has varied greatly, depending upon such factors as world and national conditions, the President's personal inclination — and weather. For if Washington's weather is uncertain in March (as it is), it is intimidating in January, and a fair share of inaugural celebrations have been modified by blizzard or downpour. Even when weather is not an overriding consideration, however, inaugural festivities usually are more modest when a President succeeds himself, or when a change in the presidency does not involve a change in political party. When a Republican President succeeds a Democrat, however, or a Democratic President succeeds a Republican, his partisans flock to Washington for the inauguration with organizations marching and waving banners and rejoicing on a grand scale.

This was true, for example, when Republican Dwight D. Eisenhower took over the presidency from Democrat Harry S. Truman in 1953 and when Democrat John F. Kennedy succeeded Republican President Eisenhower in 1961. Apart from television viewers, it was estimated that 1 million persons witnessed the two-and-a-half-hour parade of the Eisenhower inauguration, which included some 27,000 marchers, 65 musical units, 50 floats, 350 horses, 3 elephants, and an Alaskan sleddog team. A governors' reception and two festivals were among other inaugural events, and some 40 stage, motion picture, and television personalities participated in the celebration. The stylish proceedings surrounding the inauguration of President Kennedy lasted for three days and also included a gala Hollywood show, in addition to receptions, a symphony concert, and a parade with more than 32,000 marchers. Approximately 1.2 million persons witnessed Lyndon B. Johnson's parade in 1965.

Richard M. Nixon's second inaugural parade, in 1973 — centered around the theme The Spirit of '76, since it was anticipated that the United States would be celebrating its 200th birthday at the end of his second term in office — included 35 floats, 15 equestrian units, and 50 marching bands. Nixon's four-day gala, staged at a cost of over $4 million, began on Thursday, January 18, with a reception at the Smithsonian Institution and closed on Sunday, January 21, with a special White House religious service. When Gerald R. Ford (see July 14) succeeded unexpectedly to the vice presidency by appointment and then to the presidency when Nixon resigned that office on August 9, 1974, the nation's preoccupation was with the sudden transition of leadership and there were few festivities.

Eve of St. Agnes

The eve of the Feast of St. Agnes (see January 21) is one of those occasions when charms and incantations are supposed to have peculiar virtues. Especially in the British Isles, it has long been regarded as an auspicious time for young women to employ charms reputedly effective in revealing the names and faces of their future husbands. St. Agnes, the Roman virgin who suffered martyrdom under the Roman Emperor Diocletian in the early fourth century, not only had no desire to marry but, according to at least one version of her life, was even prepared to die for the sake of her faith and her virginity as "the bride of Christ," rather than become the wife of the son of a Roman prefect. It is therefore exceedingly strange that this type of custom should have developed about her memory. Although no longer taken seriously, except by the extremely credulous, the various prescribed rituals remain today as reminiscence or as lightheartedly indulged superstition.

According to tradition, one of the charms propitious for foretelling the identity of one's future husband is for a young woman to take a row of pins, pull them out one by one, and stick them in her sleeve, while singing a Pater Noster. Another custom was for the unmarried woman to go into a different district from that in which she lived and spend the night. Before going to bed, she was to take her stocking from her right leg and knit it to the garter from the stocking on her left leg, singing as she did so:

> I knit this knot, this knot I knit
> To know the thing I know not yet,
> That I may see
> The man that shall my husband be,
> Not in his best or worst array,
> But what he weareth every day;
> That I to-morrow may him ken
> From among all other men.

Then she was to lie on her back in bed with her hands under her head. If she observed the formalities with precision, she was assured that her future husband would appear to her in a dream and press a warm kiss upon her lips. If a maid went supperless to bed or, according to another version, fasted all day and ate only a salt-filled egg at night, the charm was supposed to work with greater certainty: the young woman would certainly dream of her lover, who might even appear and quench her thirst with water.

One who could not get away from home for the night was advised to take a sprig of rosemary and a sprig of thyme, sprinkle each thrice with water, and put one in each shoe. Then a shoe with its sprig was put on either side of her bed, while she repeated:

> St. Agnes, that's to lovers kind,
> Come, ease the trouble of my mind.

She then was certain to dream of her husband, seeing his face so clearly as to be able to identify him without difficulty.

The poet John Keats founded his romantic poem The Eve of St. Agnes upon some of these superstitions. His young heroine, Madeline, tested the following advice to discover the longed-for information about her husband-to-be:

> They told her how, upon St. Agnes' Eve,
> Young virgins might have visions of delight,
> And soft adorings from their loves receive
> Upon the honey'd middle of the night,
> If ceremonies due they did aright;
> As, supperless to bed they must retire,
> And couch supine their beauties, lily white;
> Nor look behind, nor sideways, but require
> Of Heaven with upward eyes for all that they desire.

Madeline carefully fulfilled the prescription, and instead of merely dreaming of her lover, Porphyro, awoke to find him present in her bedchamber — and escaped with him from the castle in which she dwelt.

In northern Scotland, young men as well as women used to scatter grain into the cornfields, reciting:

> Agnes sweet, and Agnes fair,
> Hither, hither, now repair;
> Bonny Agnes, let me see
> The lad (or lass) who is to marry me.

As with those who followed the appropriate steps on Halloween (see October 31), the image of the future bride or bridegroom was supposed to appear in a mirror on that very night.

JANUARY 21

Feast of St. Agnes

The Feast of St. Agnes, on January 21, is primarily observed by the Roman Catholic church. Formerly ranked as a class III feast, the day is now classed as an "obligatory memorial" in the revised Roman Catholic calendar. Some Episcopalians also mark the Feast of St. Agnes on January 21, as do some Eastern Orthodox churches. Among the latter, however, those Orthodox churches that still adhere to the Old Style Julian calendar celebrate the feast 13 days later on what, by the Gregorian calendar, is February 3.

Agnes, a young Christian convert, is honored as one of the four great virgin martyrs of the Christian Church. She died for her faith in the early fourth century during the reign of Diocletian (284–305), the Roman emperor who ordered the last great persecution of Christians, starting in early 303. It is generally held that Agnes must have suffered martyrdom in Rome in either 304 or 305. Her cult developed there shortly after her death. By the middle of the fourth century her name was included in the list of Christian martyrs, having been entered in the Depositio martyrum of 354, as well as in other early Eastern and Western martyrologies. St. Jerome, the renowned doctor of the Christian Church who lived in the late fourth and early fifth century (see September 30), commented in his Letter to Demetria: "All nations unite in singing the praises of Agnes, and paying religious honor to her."

One of the most popular of Christian saints, Agnes is regarded as the patron saint of young women (see January 20, Eve of St. Agnes) and the special protectress of bodily purity. Although for over 16 centuries she has been highly venerated and her name has been invoked in prayer and bestowed in baptism, almost nothing is known about her except that she was a virgin who was martyred in Rome. Even the year of her death and the method of execution are matters of debate. As one eminent Church historian aptly observed: "Agnes is one of those saints whose importance and greatness are chiefly revealed by the halo that appears around them."

The many accounts of Agnes's life, written especially during the two centuries after her martyrdom, are both incomplete and contradictory, agreeing only on her extreme youth. (She was probably about 12 or 13 when she met her martyrdom.) Modern authorities have little confidence in their accuracy. Confusion about the facts of the saint's life apparently developed as early as the end of the fourth century, as seen in the variations already expounded by Agnes's two chief early protagonists, Pope Damasus I (who reigned from 366 to 384) and Ambrose, bishop of Milan (340? to 397).

Damasus I composed an epitaph for Agnes, which he had placed on her tomb and which is still preserved in the staircase of the Basilica of Saint Agnes Outside the Walls in Rome. According to this brief statement, Agnes, the daughter of wealthy and devout Christian parents, eluded her nurse's surveillance at the time of Diocletian's persecution to profess the Christian faith of her own free will. "The holy heroine of chastity" then "defied the threats and ragings of the cruel tyrant [presumably the local governor or prefect] who wished to have her noble body burnt in flames."

Damasus' contemporary, the famous fourth century bishop of Milan, Ambrose, wrote a sermon at the request of his sister, Marcellina, a nun in Rome, which he delivered on January 21, probably in the year 377, on the occasion of the feast of St. Agnes. In it, he extolled the young martyr and urged all Christians to follow her saintly example:

Today is the feast of a virgin; let us once more seek purity. It is the feast of a martyr. . . . Let men admire; let children not be discouraged; let wives be astonished; let virgins imitate Agnes; they cannot say her name without honoring her.

This panegyric was later combined with two other sermons about virginity to become part of Ambrose's well-known work on the ideal of a nun, *De virginibus*.

Like Damasus, the bishop of Milan failed to include explicit details about Agnes's family or character, aside from emphasizing the courage she displayed despite her youth: "At that age,

an angry look from her mother was enough to make her tremble . . . [but] unafraid with the executioner's bloodstained hands upon her, Agnes stood motionless amid the noise of the heavy chains that crushed her." As far as the circumstances of her execution are concerned, the bishop commented that she "went to the place of execution more cheerfully than others go to their wedding" and implied that Agnes was beheaded. Yet on another occasion — in the beautiful hymn "Agnes beatae virginis," written in the last quarter of the fourth century — Ambrose suggested that the heroine was stabbed in the throat or breast.

Later accounts of Agnes's life attempted to harmonize and embellish all the discordant material included in the then-surviving traditions and stressed the supernatural and miraculous. Especially influential was the 14th hymn, entitled "Passio Agnetis," of the *Peristephanon*, a collection of stories of martyrs' sufferings. The author was the Latin poet Aurelius Clemens Prudentius, who composed the work about 405, shortly after a visit to Rome in 401–403. The hymns contain first-hand "data," which Prudentius apparently gathered while on pilgrimage to various saintly tombs in the Holy City.

Unlike Damasus and Ambrose, who claimed that Agnes "broke out of her seclusion, for her faith could not be held captive," Prudentius — and the numerous medieval writers who embroidered his version — recorded that Agnes had been the victim of denunciation. Young, attractive, and wealthy, she reportedly was thought most desirable as a wife, and young men from the leading families of Rome allegedly vied for her hand. She was said, however, to have refused to consider marriage in order to become "the bride of Christ" and consecrate her virginity to her heavenly husband. According to one account, the frustrated suitors then denounced Agnes as a Christian to a local official. According to another, the son of a prefect who had fallen madly in love with her became ill because of her rejection of his suit; his father tried all sorts of persuasion to induce the young girl to change her mind, even threatening her with death, and he finally denounced her as a Christian.

Even upon her arrest, Agnes remained true to her vow. When mild promises and seductive allurements proved ineffective, stronger measures were applied. The brave child, anxious to die for her religion, remained unflinching, even when she was threatened with torture. In a final attempt to overcome her resistance, the official (or by another account the young man's father) is said to have sent her to a brothel.

The house of prostitution was located in "the corner of a great square," in one of the vaulted chambers along the arcade of the circus or stadium that had been erected by the Roman Emperor Domitian (who ruled from 81 to 96).

According to tradition, the soldiers who dragged Agnes to the place stripped her of her garments. When she saw herself thus exposed she bent her head in prayer and immediately her hair spread itself about her, covering her body like a garment. The licentious youth of Rome who looked on were, for the most part, struck with awe and cast their eyes downward. But one who gazed at her lustfully was struck blind. With her prayers, Agnes restored his sight. She then was locked in a chamber, where an angel appeared to her with a white robe, which she put on.

These later traditions disagree — as do the earlier accounts — as to whether Agnes was burned to death or was killed by a sword. According to some, it was finally ordered that she be burned. But when she was put on the pyre and the fire lighted, the flames did not touch her, although the two soldiers who guarded her were burned to death. She was then said to have been put to the sword.

Although by the second half of the fourth century the exact circumstances of Agnes's martyrdom had already been forgotten, it was known with certainty that the young saint had been buried in her parents' household cemetery. It was located a short distance from the city limits of Rome — less than 2 miles from the 12-mile city wall that the Roman Emperor Aurelian (270–275) had had erected — along the Via Nomentana, leading out of the Roman capital in a northeasterly direction. Like many of the roads connecting Rome with more distant points, the Nomentana road had become an avenue of tombs and funerary monuments of every size.

At first a modest chapel was placed over the saint's grave. Its entrance was carefully hidden until, with the ascendancy of Constantine the Great and the issuance in 313 of the Edict of Milan, Christianity became one of the lawful religions of the Roman Empire, although not yet the official state religion. Sometime around 324, Agnes's shrine was enlarged and transformed. According to legend, Constantina, Constantine's eldest daughter by his first wife, Fausta, was afflicted with leprosy. She was reputedly cured of the disease after she had prayed as a pilgrim at Agnes's tomb. It is said to have been at her request that Constantine ordered the erection of a basilica over the holy spot, resplendent with a double colonnade of white Phrygian marble, silver lamps, gold and

silver vases, and an archway dedication honoring the martyr. Numerous early medieval popes, notably Popes Symmachus (498–514) and Honorius I (625–638), carried on the task of renovation, expansion, and rebuilding. The shrine, now known as the Basilica of St. Agnes Outside the Walls, is still famous for its mosaics and galleried nave, and for housing in large part the relics of St. Agnes, in an ornate silver sarcophagus solidly encased beneath the altar.

Formerly as many as four churches dedicated to St. Agnes existed in Rome. One of these, Santa Agnese al Circo Agone — better known as St. Agnes in Piazza Navona — still stands on the Piazza Navona, the spot where, according to Prudentius, "the virgin triumphed. . . . Exposed to the dangers of sacrilegious dishonor, her all-conquering virginity had found even the brothel chaste and free of insult." The brothel had been transformed into the crypt of a primitive church as early as the seventh century. A 17th century marble and gold baroque church designed by Francesco Borromini now covers the site and contains the remainder of the saint's relics.

Agnes has played a prominent role in Christian art. As early as the fourth century, she was depicted as an orant, her arms extended in prayer. From the sixth century onwards, Agnes usually has been represented as a young woman bearing a palm leaf or sword and accompanied by, or holding, a lamb. The symbolism of the lamb was undoubtedly suggested both by her innocence and purity and by the resemblance of the Latin word for "lamb," *agnus*, to her name. One of the famous sixth century mosaics in the Basilica of Sant'Apollinare Nuovo in Ravenna, Italy, portrays Agnes going in procession with other female saints — and a capering lamb — to present a crown to the Virgin Mary.

The Feast of St. Agnes on January 21 is marked every year in Rome with a custom rich in symbolism and tradition. Two very young lambs from the sheepfold belonging to the Trappist fathers of the monastery of Tre Fontane near St. Paul's Basilica are crowned and placed in straw baskets, which have been colorfully decorated with red and white flowers and streamers: red standing for Agnes's martyrdom, and white for her purity. They are then taken to the Basilica of St. Agnes Outside the Walls. There, at the end of the solemn feast day mass, just before the Last Gospel, a procession composed of young girls in white dresses and veils, as well as *carabinieri* in red and blue uniforms and cockaded hats, who bear the lambs on their shoulders, proceeds down the center aisle. While the choir chants the special antiphon "Stans a dextris ejus agnus nive candidior" ("On her right hand a lamb whiter than snow"), the lambs are ceremoniously incensed and blessed. They are then shown to the pope at the Vatican and finally placed in the care of the Benedictine nuns of Santa Cecilia in Trastevere, who rear them until Maundy Thursday, when they are sheared (see March 26).

From the lambs' wool are woven approximately 12 pallia a year. The pallium is an article of ecclesiastical apparel consisting of a narrow band of white wool embroidered with crosses and weighted at both ends by means of silk-encased lead. On solemn occasions, archbishops of the Roman Catholic church wear the pallium around the neck, over the chasuble — one end falling in front, one in back. Each archbishop receives the pallium directly from the pope as the special insignia signifying the dignity and jurisdiction of his lofty position and his communion with the Holy See. On June 28, the Vigil of the Feast of SS. Peter and Paul, the pallia are placed in St. Peter's Basilica. There, beneath the basilica's dome and high altar, they repose overnight on an altar in the confessional surrounding the crypt that contains the tomb of St. Peter. Thus are combined, according to an eminent church historian, "the twofold consciousness of the strength of the Prince of the Apostles and the virginal meekness of Agnes." The pallia are then kept, ready for future use, encased in a chest of precious metal in the confessional's niche of the pallia.

Stonewall Jackson's Birthday

Thomas Jonathan Jackson, better known as "Stonewall," was born on January 21, 1824, in Clarksburg, Virginia (now West Virginia). The state of Virginia — regarding Jackson as a Virginian who won most of his fame within its borders — considers him to be one of its heroes. Virginia observes the anniversary of his birth in conjunction with that of Robert E. Lee (see January 19). The third Monday in January is therefore a state holiday known as Lee-Jackson Day (formerly observed on January 19). To mark the occasion, many of the 900-odd chapters of the United Daughters of the Confederacy hold a luncheon or dinner, at which the speaker usually links the names of Lee and Jackson.

Thomas Jackson was the son of Jonathan Jackson, a lawyer who died when his son was a small boy, leaving the family almost destitute. Young Jackson later added Jonathan as a middle name in memory of his father. After his widowed mother had remarried (only to die soon afterwards), Thomas Jackson was reared by a devoted uncle, Cummins Jackson. Through hard work and self-discipline, since he had little opportunity for education beyond attendance at a small country school, Jackson obtained in 1842 an appointment to the US Military Academy at West Point, New York. Although handicapped by inadequate preparation, he graduated in the upper third of his class and received a commission as second lieutenant of artillery in 1846.

The young officer was sent almost immediately to serve in the Mexican War. In Mexico, he distinguished himself at Veracruz, Cerro Gordo, and Chapultepec. He was brevetted a major within 18 months of his graduation. From 1848 to 1851, Jackson was stationed at Fort Columbus and Fort Hamilton, both in New York Harbor. Ordered to Florida in the latter year, he soon accepted an appointment as professor of artillery tactics and natural philosophy at the Virginia Military Institute in Lexington. He accordingly resigned from the army in February 1852.

Jackson returned from a trip to Europe in 1856 to find that the threat of war, which he considered "the sum of all evils," was growing between the North and the South. He remained at the Virginia Military Institute until the sectional differences erupted in the Civil War in April 1861 (see April 12). He then offered his services to the seceding state of Virginia and was ordered to Richmond with part of the VMI cadet corps. Aged 37, he had as yet played no role in public affairs beyond commanding the cadet corps at the hanging of John Brown on December 2, 1859.

When Jackson received a commission as colonel of infantry in the military forces of Virginia and was assigned to command strategic Harpers Ferry, one member of the Virginia Convention — which had to approve the appointment — asked: "Who is this Major Jackson?" Samuel McDowell Moore, the representative for Rockbridge County, in which Lexington was located, replied: "He is one who, if you order him to hold a post, will never leave it alive to be occupied by the enemy."

On June 17, 1861, Jackson was promoted to the rank of brigadier general. He was soon called upon to help defeat the strong Union assault in the first battle of Bull Run on July 21. The impetuosity of the first federal attack caused confusion in the Confederate ranks, with 2,000 men "shouting each some suggestion to his neighbor, their voices mingling with the noise of the shells hurtling through the trees overhead. . . ." As the outcome of the battle hung in suspense, there occurred one of the dramatic episodes of the war. Confederate Brigadier General Barnard E. Bee, trying desperately to rally his panic-stricken troops, glanced toward nearby Henry Hill, where he saw Jackson and his men standing bold and steadfast. Grasping inspiration from the moment, Bee achieved immortality by shouting: "Look, there is Jackson standing like a stone wall. Rally behind the Virginians!" The Southern forces rallied; the Union assault was repulsed; and the sobriquet Stonewall was forever attached to Jackson's name.

Stonewall Jackson's subsequent career as a soldier was brilliant. Promoted to major general on October 7, 1861, he was given command of the Confederate forces in the Shenandoah Valley on November 5. His Valley campaign from March to June 1862 is sometimes considered the most remarkable display of strategy and tactics in American history. It is regarded as a classic example of what a meager force can accomplish when commanded by a leader who realizes the importance of determination, mobility, and secrecy in warfare. With incredible speed, Jackson's army marched and countermarched a total of 630 miles to defeat four Union armies in 39 days. His dashing campaign staved off massive federal attacks on beleaguered Richmond and kept Washington, braced for a Southern invasion, on the brink of nervous prostration for weeks on end. With audacity tempered by skill, Jackson, with fewer than 20,000 men, neutralized the action of over 175,000 enemy troops.

A Confederate soldier tersely summarized Jackson's style of action: "All Old Jackson gave us was a musket, a hundred rounds, and a . . . blanket, and he druv us like hell." Despite Jackson's strictness, his mangy appearance (he was once described as "a particularly seedy, sleepy-looking old fellow, whose uniform and cap were very dirty"), and his personal predilections (devout and sternly religious, he hated to fight on Sundays and preferred to delay a battle rather than miss a prayer meeting), his grim and hungry men idolized their painfully shy and taciturn commander. They fondly called him "Old Jack" or, noting how his blue eyes flashed in the midst of battle, "Old Blue Light." His trusted lieutenant, Richard S. Ewell, however, once fumed: "Dammit, Jackson is driving us mad. He don't say a word . . . no order, no hint of where we're going"; and he was at times convinced that Jackson was insane.

Once Robert E. Lee had succeeded to the command of the Army of Northern Virginia on June 1, 1862, he summoned Jackson to take part in the Seven Days battles on the Yorktown Peninsula late in the month. Despite unspectacular actions at places such as White Oak Swamp

and Beaver Creek Dam, Jackson showed his mettle in August by executing one of his renowned marches. In its course he destroyed the federal base at Manassas Junction on August 27, and, a few days later, participated in the offensive against General John Pope at the second battle of Bull Run, which permitted Lee to carry the war out of Virginia and into enemy territory.

Leading Lee's drive into Maryland, Jackson seized Harpers Ferry on September 15, 1862, and distinguished himself both at Antietam two days later and at Fredericksburg on December 13. At the close of 1862, owing to the military genius of Lee and Jackson, Union forces were as far from Richmond as they had been at the beginning of the year.

Jackson, having been promoted to lieutenant general on October 10, 1862, was henceforth recognized as Lee's right-hand man and was given command over one of the two corps into which the Army of Northern Virginia had been divided. After resumption of the Union offensive in the spring of 1863, Jackson and Lee planned to attack General Joseph Hooker's troops, camped near Chancellorsville, Virginia, in a thick, dismal forest almost 15 miles square, termed the Wilderness. During the night of May 1–2, the two Southern commanders devised one of the most daring strokes in the course of the war. Although Hooker had about 100,000 men and the Confederates had fewer than half that number, Lee and Jackson boldly agreed to split their force. Lee, with fewer than 20,000 men, would hold ground, while Jackson would lead the remaining men through the dense undergrowth to launch a surprise attack on the enemy flank. At 5:15 P.M. on May 2, Jackson's soldiers, having accomplished the move undetected, stormed out — red battle flags waving in the dusk — in a battle formation more than a mile wide and three divisions deep. Within minutes the Union flank had crumbled, its broken remnants dispersing in confusion, while Lee pounded in front.

Upon learning the news of the Union defeat, President Abraham Lincoln exclaimed: "My God! My God! What will the country say?" But Chancellorsville was the costliest victory the South ever won. Not only were the casualties near 13,000, but at the moment of victory, Jackson, out surveying his position at about 9:00 P.M., was wounded by the fire of his own patrols. A North Carolina regiment had mistaken Jackson and his staff for Yankee cavalry. Reeling in the saddle, the general sustained three wounds, with bullets penetrating his right hand and smashing his left arm from elbow to shoulder. After his left arm had been amputated in a field hospital behind the lines, Jackson was moved under hazardous conditions to safer quarters at Chandler's cottage near Guiney's Station, Virginia.

Hearing about Jackson's injury, General Lee wrote on May 3, 1863:

General: I have just received your note, informing me that you were wounded. I cannot express my regret at the occurrence. Could I have directed events, I should have chosen for the good of the country to be disabled in your stead. I congratulate you upon the victory, which is due to your skill and energy.

As the patient continued to improve, Lee dispatched another message: "Give him my affectionate regards, tell him to make haste and get well, and come back to me as soon as he can. He has lost his left arm, but I have lost my right."

On May 7, however, Jackson developed pneumonia, following a fall from the litter on which he was carried from the battlefield. Three days later he died at the age of 39, murmuring, "Let us cross over the river and rest under the shade of the trees."

The death of Stonewall Jackson was disastrous for the Confederate cause. Never again would Lee have at his side a fellow commander who could so swiftly grasp his strategy and brilliantly execute it. Never again would the Southern army carry out those bold thrusts that had enabled it to wrest victory from numerically superior forces. Although his career in high field command lasted only a little over two years, Jackson is regarded as one of the most brilliant military geniuses of the Civil War.

In accordance with Jackson's last wishes, Lexington, Virginia, was his final resting place. A fine bronze statue marks his grave in the Jackson Memorial Cemetery, and a statue by Sir Moses Ezekiel overlooks the parade grounds of the Virginia Military Institute, where Jackson once taught. The museum in the institute's Preston Library displays many interesting items from his life. The only residence Jackson ever owned, at 8 East Washington Street, Lexington, now known as the Stonewall Jackson Memorial, has been opened to the public as a museum by the Stonewall Jackson Memorial Foundation. This nonprofit organization maintains several other historic properties in Virginia, including the military headquarters at North Braddock Street in Winchester, where Jackson and his staff stayed during the winter of 1861–1862.

In Clarksburg, West Virginia, a bronze tablet on West Main Street marks the site of the small brick house where Jackson was born in 1824. An equestrian statue of the general stands in the square across from the hotel named in his honor. At Jackson's Mill, about 20 miles south of Clarksburg, the gristmill at his boyhood home was restored and opened as a museum in 1969, after a half century of neglect.

Memorials to Stonewall Jackson may be found in numerous cities, including Richmond and Charlottesville, Virginia, and New York City (Jackson was elected to the Hall of Fame for Great Americans in 1955). With General Robert E. Lee and Jefferson Davis, the president of the Confederacy, Jackson has been immortalized on the massive Stone Mountain memorial, located in a 3,800-acre state park 16 miles east of Atlanta, Georgia. Carved on a sheer granite mountain face, the huge relief was finally completed after years of halting progress, and dedicated by Vice President Spiro Agnew in 1970.

Two Civil War battlefields recall memorable episodes in the general's career. In 1940, the state of Virginia erected an equestrian statue of Jackson on Henry Hill in the Manassas National Battlefield Park, reputedly on the spot where he received his famous sobriquet. The National Park Service has commemorated Stonewall Jackson's last daring operation in the sunless forest around Chancellorsville, Virginia: an ominously winding road traces his route; a tablet marks the site of his final war council with Lee during the night of May 1–2, 1863; a stone slab near the battlefield indicates the place where his left arm was buried; and the Chandler house, where he died, has been restored.

JANUARY 22

Frederick Moore Vinson's Birthday

Frederick Moore Vinson, the 13th chief justice of the United States, was born in Louisa, Kentucky, on January 22, 1890. Vinson, who during his long political career served in the legislative and executive branches of government, as well as the judicial branch, came from a family of modest means. James Vinson, the jailkeeper in Louisa, died shortly after the birth of his son, Frederick, and responsibility for the upbringing of the baby fell upon his widow, Virginia Ferguson Vinson. Determined that her son should receive a good education, she took in boarders to earn money. Young Frederick Vinson himself contributed to the family funds by running errands and working in local stores.

Vinson prepared at Kentucky Normal School to be a teacher, but by the time of his graduation, in 1908, he had decided not to pursue a career in education. Instead, he enrolled at Centre College of Kentucky, in Danville. There he excelled in his studies, graduated first in his class in 1909, and then remained at Centre to work for a degree in law.

During his years in law school, Vinson taught mathematics in a local preparatory school to help support himself. This extracurricular work did not prevent him from achieving an outstanding academic record. He received his law degree in 1911 and was awarded both the junior and senior law prizes.

Vinson returned the same year to Louisa, where he opened his own law office. Two years later he became Louisa's city attorney, a post he held until 1917, when he joined the US Army. Vinson remained in the military throughout the period of US involvement in World War I, but when the war ended he resumed his law practice and his career in public service. The young veteran became commonwealth attorney for Kentucky's 32nd judicial district in 1921. Three years later, he was a successful Democratic candidate for the national House of Representatives.

With the exception of 1928, when a large number of Democrats lost in the face of a Republican landslide headed by presidential candidate Herbert Hoover, Vinson was returned to Congress in every election from 1926 to 1938. As a member of the House he supported most New Deal legislation and he was an especially ardent proponent of measures benefiting labor. In particular, he advocated the Guffey-Snyder Bituminous Coal Stabilization Act of 1935, which sought to regulate the soft coal industry according to the provisions of the National Recovery Act soft coal code. When the Supreme Court found this act unconstitutional in 1936, he cosponsored the Guffey-Vinson Bituminous Coal Act of 1937. This measure promulgated a code of fair competition in the soft coal industry, provided federal regulation of bituminous coal output, imposed a revenue tax on soft coal, and penalized those producers who did not adhere to the code with a heavy tax.

During his last years in Congress, Vinson served as the chairman of the influential tax subcommittee of the House Ways and Means Committee. Shortly after assuming that post in 1936, he worked for and won congressional approval of a tax on undistributed profits. He was also largely responsible for congressional passage of the Revenue Act of 1938, which made several important modifications in the federal tax structure.

In 1938 President Franklin D. Roosevelt appointed Vinson an associate justice of the US Court of Appeals for the District of Columbia, and in 1942 named him the chief judge of the three-member Emergency Court of Appeals, which was set up to handle disputes arising from World War II price controls. Vinson remained on the bench until May 1943; he then moved to the executive branch of the government, where he became the director of the Office of Economic Stabilization. In this post he grappled with the difficult task of curbing inflation in the wartime economy, and although he alienated many during his two-year tenure, his efforts were moderately successful.

Appointed as administrator of the Federal Loan Agency on March 5, 1945, Vinson became the director of the Office of War Mobilization and Reconversion the following month. He held the latter position until President Harry S. Truman appointed him secretary of the treasury three months later, on July 23, 1945. Vinson's knowledge of tax problems and his experience as a member of Congress made him an excellent choice to head the Treasury Department during the difficult transition from a wartime to a peacetime economy. He served in the post for less than one year, and in that short time he was able to recommend and secure congressional approval for a bill that provided for the first reduction in federal tax rates in 14 years and that exempted almost 12 million persons from the tax rolls.

In 1946, President Truman nominated Vinson to be chief justice of the United States, and in June of that year the Senate confirmed the appointment. Truman's selection of Vinson to replace the late Chief Justice Harlan F. Stone was no doubt prompted as much by Vinson's reputation as a mediator as by his legal expertise. In 1946 the associate justices of the Supreme Court were divided into two factions. The two groups — one led by Justice Hugo Black of Alabama, the other by Justice Robert Jackson of New York — differed on personal as well as constitutional issues, and reports of feuds among the Supreme Court membership had caused a serious loss of prestige to the high tribunal.

Truman's faith in Vinson's abilities as a peacemaker were not unfounded. Within a year of his confirmation as chief justice, overt hostility among the associate justices had come to an end. The tribunal's membership maintained, at least superficially, cordial relations, and, more important, the Court itself regained much public confidence and respect.

During Vinson's seven years as chief justice

the Supreme Court ruled on far fewer cases than it had in the years prior to World War II. But the 758 decisions that were handed down during his tenure involved some of the most pressing issues of the postwar era — most notably in the areas of labor relations and civil rights.

In one of the first cases to come before the Court after his confirmation, Chief Justice Vinson concurred in the verdict upholding fines against the United Mine Workers and the union's chief, John L. Lewis, for contempt of court in continuing a 1946 coal strike after the federal government had seized the mines. The chief justice also wrote the majority opinion in the 1950 case of the *American Communications Association, CIO, et al* v. *Douds*, which found the provision of the controversial Taft-Hartley Act of 1947 requiring labor union officers to sign a non-Communist affidavit to be constitutional. But Vinson was not always on the side of the majority in labor decisions. When the Court, by a six to three vote, in 1952, invalidated President Truman's seizure of the strikebound steel plants in that same year, Vinson defended the President's action, saying in a dissenting opinion that the Founding Fathers "created a government subject to law but not left subject to inertia when vigor and initiative are required."

Between 1948 and 1950 the Supreme Court heard and ruled on a number of important cases dealing with racial segregation in state universities. In the 1948 decision in the case of *Sipuel* v. *Board of Regents*, the Court ruled that Oklahoma could not refuse to admit a qualified black to the state's law school unless it made equivalent legal training available to him within the state. As a result of this opinion, Texas set up a separate law school for the blacks of that state. But in 1950, in the case of *Sweatt* v. *Painter*, the Court ruled that this law school was inferior to that of the University of Texas. In reaching this verdict the Court took into account such qualitative factors as the prestige of faculty members and opportunities for contact with distinguished lawyers and judges. The *Sweatt* opinion had broad implications. It was interpreted to mean that black graduate schools were by their very nature inferior and unequal, and that for this reason states could not refuse to open all their publicly supported schools of higher learning to blacks.

In the case of *McLaurin* v. *Oklahoma State Regents*, the Vinson court took yet another step toward ending the "separate but equal" doctrine that had prevailed since the *Plessy* v.

Ferguson decision of 1896. The *McLaurin* case involved the rights of black students in state universities. In 1950 the Court ruled in this case that black students who had gained admission to state schools of higher learning could not be segregated within these schools or in any other way be treated in a different or discriminatory manner.

Vinson, who had been mentioned as a possible Democratic presidential candidate in 1952, died unexpectedly of a heart attack on September 8, 1953. His widow, Roberta Dixon Vinson, and his two sons, Frederick Jr. and James Robert Vinson, survived him.

JANUARY 23

Twenty-fourth Amendment Ratified

The 24th Amendment to the Constitution, forbidding collection of a poll tax as a requirement for voting in national elections, became effective on January 23, 1964, when it was ratified by the South Dakota legislature. As the 38th state to take such action, South Dakota completed the three-fourths of the nation's states necessary to ratify an amendment before it can become law. The measure was formalized in Washington, D.C., on February 4, when Bernard L. Boutin, head of the General Services Administration, after receiving notification of South Dakota's action, issued a document certifying that the ratification process had been completed by three-fourths of the 50 states. President Lyndon B. Johnson, who signed the document as a witness, declared, "Today, the people of this land have abolished the poll tax as a condition for voting. By this act they have reaffirmed the simple but unbreakable theme of this Republic: Nothing is so valuable as liberty and nothing is so necessary to liberty as the freedom to vote without bans or barriers." The Chief Executive noted that with enactment of the 24th Amendment, "there can be no one too poor to vote. . . . The only enemy to voting that we face today is indifference. Too many of our citizens treat casually what other people in other lands are ready to die for." It was reportedly the first time that an amendment to the Constitution had been certified in the presence of a President.

Specifically affected by the new amendment were the poll taxes that had existed until then in the five southern states of Alabama, Mississippi, Arkansas, Texas, and Virginia. Some of these states elected to continue the taxes in state and local elections; national elections, however, were a different matter. With passage of the 24th Amendment, the presidential election of November 1964 accordingly became the first in which no state exacted a poll tax.

The road to enactment of the amendment was a long one — beginning some 20 years earlier with congressional attempts to outlaw poll taxes by statute. Three different anti-poll-tax bills passed by the House of Representatives were defeated in the Senate by filibusters conducted by southern senators.

In 1949, a southerner of a different mind — Spessard L. Holland of Florida — introduced a proposal for abolishing poll taxes by means of a constitutional amendment. Each year until 1962, when the Senate finally voted its approval by 77 to 16, Senator Holland reintroduced his proposal with a larger number of cosponsors. (Initially numbered at 8 or 10, they totaled 67 by the time of passage.)

Senate approval of the 24th Amendment resolution on March 27 was followed by House approval by a vote of 294 to 86 on August 27. The measure was submitted to the states on September 14, 1962. Illinois was the first to concur officially (on November 14) in the long process of ratification. The measure officially became a part of the US Constitution on February 4, 1964. As finally approved, the 24th Amendment to the Constitution reads as follows:

SECTION 1. The right of citizens of the United States to vote in any primary or other election for President or Vice President, for electors for President or Vice President, or for Senator or Representative in Congress, shall not be denied or abridged by the United States or any State by reason of failure to pay any poll tax or other tax.

SECTION 2. The Congress shall have the power to enforce this article by appropriate legislation.

JANUARY 24

California Gold Rush

On the morning of January 24, 1848, a skilled carpenter named James W. Marshall made a chance discovery of gold, which touched off the California gold rush. Hired by the wealthy landowner and entrepreneur John A. Sutter, Marshall was overseeing the construction of a sawmill on the south fork of the American River in the northern California valley called Coloma or "beautiful vale" by the Indians. He was inspecting work on the tailrace, when the gleam of metal in the streambed attracted his attention. Reaching down into the water, he brought up golden flakes, placed them in his hat, and dashed into the mill, shouting, "Boys, I believe I've found a gold mine." The carpenter conducted a series of inconclusive tests to discover whether he really had found gold; he then took three ounces of the dust to his employer at Sutter's Fort, some 40 miles down river. Sutter later vividly recalled Marshall's visit.

. . . Marshall pulled out of his trousers pocket a white cotton rag which contained something rolled up in it. . . . Opening the cloth, he held it before me in his hand. . . . "I believe this is gold," said Marshall, "but the people at the mill laughed at me and called me crazy." I carefully examined it and said to him, "Well, it looks like gold. Let us test it."

The two men did, and proved that the sample was indeed gold.

John A. Sutter realized that the discovery, if highly publicized, might very well destroy his vast enterprises in California. Born of Swiss parents, Johann Augustus Suter — as he had been baptized — had emigrated to America in his early thirties and amassed a fortune. Possessed of an adventurous spirit, he gradually moved westward. He gained experience trading in the northwest Oregon country before settling in Mexican-owned California in 1839. Sutter induced the Mexican authorities to grant him approximately 49,000 acres in the lower Sacramento Valley; in return, he agreed to create a fortified outpost as a deterrent to the ever-increasing numbers of Anglo-Americans who were encroaching on Mexican territory in the western part of the present United States. The enterprising proprietor constructed not only a fort, but also a colony of houses, warehouses, and stores, as well as a distillery, a mill, a tannery, and a blanket factory at the confluence of the Sacramento and American rivers. John Sutter rapidly expanded his holdings to 146,000 acres, a little empire, which he dubbed New Helvetia. The short, stubby "feudal baron of the Sacramento Valley" later boasted that "I was everything, patriarch, priest, father, and judge."

Sutter's Fort, strategically located where several central and northern overland routes to the West Coast joined, after winding through the high Sierra Nevadas, became a mecca for weary immigrants, a busy trading post, a rendezvous for frontiersmen, and a convenient open door to California for American settlers. In fact, Sutter's unconcealed sympathy for Anglo-Americans, as well as his wealth, power, and independence, made him an object of suspicion in the eyes of the Mexican officials. In 1846, the outbreak of hostilities between Americans and Mexicans in California (see September 9, Admission Day in California) merged with the larger question of the war between the United States and Mexico (see May 13, Mexican War Begins). Sutter at first maintained at least an appearance of loyalty to Mexico; it soon became evident, though, that he was more than willing to condone American dominance. American control of the region did not become official, however, until early in 1848, when California was ceded to the United States by the Treaty of Guadalupe Hildago (see February 2). Just 10 days before, unbeknownst to the Mexican government, James Marshall had discovered the fabulous riches of the "Mother Lode" country.

It was not the first time that gold had been unearthed in California, confirming three centuries of tales about Golden California. In the early 1840s, Mexicans had mined scattered deposits in the Placerita Canyon near Los Angeles. But the discovery of 1848 was soon seen to be a mammoth lode of gold-bearing quartz extending some 150 miles along the western foothills of the Sierra Nevada. Erosion and weathering had freed particles of ore from gold-bearing veins; rapid mountain waters had swept them away and finally deposited them, when the current slackened, in easily accessible rock crevices and streambeds.

Sutter and Marshall tried hard to squelch reports of the rich "strike," and for a while managed to keep them contained, if not absolutely suppressed. But in mid-May, a Mormon, Sam Brannan, ran up and down the streets of San Francisco, displaying gold dust and shouting, "Gold! Gold! Gold! from the American River!" By June, San Francisco had been transformed into a ghost town with three-fourths of its population "gone to the diggings." One city newspaper editor commented that the entire area resounded "with the sordid cry of 'Gold, Gold, GOLD!' while the field is left half-planted, the house half-built, and everything neglected but the manufacture of shovels and pick axes." Initially, the gold fever probably gripped about a thousand persons from San Francisco and such other California settlements as Santa Barbara, San Diego, and Monterey.

The first prospectors (some of whom even went on crutches or on a litter) rushed to the goldfields in the late spring and early summer of 1848, and seemed to stumble upon gold everywhere in the scenic hills. Drought had dried up the mountain streams, revealing gold-bearing gravel. One group took 273 pounds of gold washings from the Feather River in seven weeks, while the first gold seekers to tap the Yuba River resources earned $75,000 in three months. The majority of gold hunters in the initial rush averaged $25 to $30 a day. Life for those prospecting in the long narrow mineral strip was relatively comfortable except for meager food supplies.

The situation changed drastically, however, as reports of the gold strikes spread throughout the Pacific region. Newcomers from Hawaii, Oregon, and northern Mexico poured into California via ships, wagon caravans, muleback, and crude *carretas* in the summer and fall of 1848. Mining camps, erected haphazardly from juniper posts, faded shirts, potato sacks, mud, and stone, mushroomed furiously and fell apart just as rapidly when the gold deposits petered out. Food prices mounted: eggs sold for as high as $3 apiece and flour at $800 a barrel. By the end of the year, between 5,000 and 10,000 persons were working the diggings along the western slopes of the Sierra Nevada.

The news of Marshall's discovery and the subsequent lucky strikes took months to reach the eastern part of the United States. California newspaper accounts, carried across the continent by couriers such as Kit Carson, and others, did not arrive in the East until August 1848. The manifold stories related by both successful and disappointed prospectors were discounted as tall tales. But by the close of 1848, easterners were aware that something extraordinary had occurred in California.

The American military governor of California at Monterey, Colonel Richard Mason, had visited the mineral belt in June to straighten out the confused reports flooding his office. At several of the sites, his aide, William T. Sherman, had sketched maps, which, together with a letter and gold sample, were rushed to Washington, D.C. In his annual message to Congress, on December 5, 1848, President James K. Polk exuberantly reported: "The accounts of the abundance of gold in that territory are of such extraordinary character as would scarcely command belief were they not corroborated by the authentic reports of officers in the public service." As if to back his first official confirmation of the discovery, two days later a courier reached Washington with a tea caddy containing 230 ounces of gold. The last doubts vanished, and the invasion of '49 got under way.

It is impossible to determine accurately the number of persons who participated in the gold rush of 1849. Estimates range from 60,000 to 100,000, more than three-fourths of whom were Americans, with the remainder coming from Western Europe, Australia, South America, and Asia. The Americans used four major routes to California: easterners generally took one of two possible sea routes; southerners and midwesterners followed one of several overland trails.

Within a month of President Polk's message, would-be gold prospectors jammed shipping offices and chartered some 60 vessels regardless of their age or seaworthiness. By February 8, 1849, a total of 136 ships had embarked from Atlantic ports. The New York *Herald* reported:

In every Atlantic seaport, vessels are being filled up, societies are being formed, husbands are preparing to leave their wives, sons are parting with their mothers, and bachelors are abandoning their comforts; all are rushing head over heels toward the El Dorado on the Pacific.

Some 15,000 persons rounded Cape Horn in 1849, making the 18,000-mile trip in six to eight months, with the average being 199 days. Conditions were abominable in the confined quarters, but they were still deemed preferable to the alternative land hardships on the Isthmus of Panama.

Some forty-niners, fearful that the gold would vanish before their arrival, shortened the sea voyage by cutting across the jungles of the isthmus with the aid of native guides, pack animals, and canoes. They then waited in wretched, disease-infested camps in Panama City on the Pacific coast for the infrequent ships that succeeded in returning from San Francisco with their crews still intact. (By July 1850, some 500 vessels were rotting in San Francisco Harbor, their sailors having taken off for the diggings.) The "six-week" shortcut to California lasted considerably longer than advertised and was so exorbitantly expensive that it drew only about half as many persons as rounded Cape Horn in 1849.

The preferred routes were the central and southern overland trails. An estimated 45,000 forty-niners followed the central route; they set out from midwestern towns such as Independence or Saint Joseph, Missouri, and others, traced the Platte River to South Pass, branched out across the grim deserts of the Great Basin, and climbed the high passes of the Sierra Nevada to the Pacific foothills. About 10,000 persons chose the southern route, which was less mountainous and had a more pleasant climate. They usually trekked along the Santa Fe Trail or western Texas trails and later followed either the Gila River or the Old Spanish Trail into southern California.

What is remarkable, despite the high death toll, is the survival rate among the forty-niners, ignorant as they generally were of geography and local conditions, as well as of the privations that awaited them after the seemingly endless journey. Thanks to the continent's breadth, the inhabitants of the Far West had had a year's breathing space after the discovery of gold to prepare for the chaotic inpouring of greenhorns, and become able to offer them some guidance. Far westerners for example, had developed some limited practical mining techniques: they had mastered the gold pan, rocker, Long Tom, and other crude mechanisms needed to supplement the backbreaking work done waist-high in usually freezing waters.

Social development, however, remained embryonic at best, and life was unstable in the string of roaring camps depicted by such writers as Bret Harte and Mark Twain. The very names are indicative of living conditions within the camps: Hangtown, Whisky Diggings, Poverty Hill, Poker Flat, Bedbug. As one disillusioned miner commented: "There's nothing to do but hang around the saloons, get drunk and fight, to lie out in the snow and die." Crime flourished among the newcomers, whose ranks included an increasing number of undesirable drifters who found it easier to gain gold by robbery, murder, and claim-jumping than by toiling for it themselves. More than 1,000 murders were committed in San Francisco during the first eight years of the gold rush, and the situation was worse at the diggings. A favorite tune ran:

Oh, what was your name in the States?
Was it Thompson or Johnson or Bates?
Did you murder your wife and fly for your life?
Say, what was your name in the States?

Home life was practically nonexistent. In 1850, women composed only eight percent of California's population, and even this low figure fell to two percent in the mining belt.

Most forty-niners hardly made ends meet, and hundreds, although disillusioned early, settled in California only because they were too destitute to afford the trip home. Rich strikes came to only a few gold seekers. Interestingly enough, the rare fortunes amassed often resulted indirectly from the mining bonanza. Leland Stanford sold the registered claims he had staked out for more than a half million dollars. Mark Hopkins used the money from his one strike to purchase hardware to resell at exorbitant prices in the camps. Charles Crocker and Collis P. Huntington ran prosperous dry goods and hardware businesses. All four invested $15,000 apiece in the Central Pacific Railroad Company in 1861 and were catapulted into the multimillionaire bracket.

John A. Sutter, however, was not among the fortune makers. As he had feared, the discovery of gold was his ruination. Squatters trespassed on his land and his workers deserted him. Silent mills, decaying hides, unharvested fields, and plundered warehouses were all that remained of his once-mighty empire. The little capital left Sutter was depleted when the US Supreme Court ruled his land title invalid and he was forced to reimburse persons to whom he had granted subtitles. Annually, from 1871 to his death in 1880, the bankrupt ex-magnate unsuccessfully petitioned Congress for reimbursement for his property and services.

Five years after Sutter's death, James W. Marshall also died embittered, broken, and forgotten. Like Sutter, he was an unwitting victim of the gold rush. Prospectors had pursued his every footstep and confiscated his claims in the belief that he had been marked by fate a lucky man. As good luck continued to escape him, Marshall sought consolation in the farfetched claim that he was the lawful owner of all gold found in California. After his irascibility had caused his expulsion from numerous mining camps, the solitary old man spent his final years in a crude cabin located, ironically enough, at Coloma, a stone's throw from the scene of his January 24, 1848, discovery.

In 1849, $10 million came from the California mines. In 1852, they produced a high of $81 million. But soon the surface deposits dwindled and large companies, financed with eastern funds, transformed the unsystematic rush into an efficient industry. In 1853 and 1854, extractions were valued at some $68 million; and from 1865 through 1885, at about $15 million to $20 million yearly. But many an indefatigable prospector had long since wandered off to "strike it rich" in Colorado, South Dakota, or elsewhere.

Today, only memories and ruins mark the gold rush trail. Coloma, the settlement that sprang up around Sutter's mill, is the center of the Marshall Gold Discovery State Historical Park and the scene of an annual Gold Discovery celebration on the weekend nearest January 24. The park contains the cabin in which James Marshall lived at the end of his life; the bronze James W. Marshall Historical Monument showing him pointing to the place of his discovery; and the original sawmill site, marked with a cairn on the bank of the American River. In 1947, archeologists determined the plan of the mill, and later the mill was restored near the original site.

South of Coloma, engulfed in modern-day Sacramento, is Sutter's Fort. Allowed to fall apart after 1850, when it passed out of Sutter's hands, it was restored to its original form at the end of the 19th century. Sutter's adobe home, built about 1839, as well as his stores, warehouses, and barracks, forms a museum and park.

The Mother Lode Highway, otherwise known as California Route 49, meanders through the Sierra Nevada foothills past deserted mine shafts, mounds of rocky debris, rusty machinery, and sun-bleached shacks. The once-flourishing camps, such as Placerville, Volcano, Carson Hill, Downieville, Sierra City, Grass Valley, and Rough and Ready, are now tourist attractions. The best preserved is Columbia, four miles northwest of Sonora, which has been declared both a state and national historic site. This charming town, once a busy center for 15,000 gold seekers, now has a population of 200. Its nearby mines yielded some $87 million until 1860, when the supply ended, but Columbia has nevertheless been continuously inhabited since its heyday. A number of original structures, including the Wells Fargo office, saloons, school, and firehouse, contribute to its authentic atmosphere.

JANUARY 25

Robert Burns's Birthday

Scots the world over gather on January 25, the anniversary of the birth of Robert Burns, to glorify the poet and the country that produced him. Burns and Scottish societies, of which there are many, are the chief celebrators. Observances in the United States usually take the form of dinners during which Scottish songs are sung and after which speeches are made by distinguished persons of Scottish ancestry.

Burns was born in 1759 in a cottage at Alloway, about two miles from Ayr. He was the eldest son of William Burns, a man of integrity, who was oppressed by poverty. Young Robert Burns worked on his father's farm as a plowboy until he was 15. The family moved from one farm to another. The boy was eager to learn and he read the *Spectator*, Locke's *Essays*, and Pope's translation of the *Iliad*. He went to school for a time and learned a little Latin and French. In 1781 he was apprenticed to a flax dresser, but before he began to work, the shop burned and he was left without work or money.

Burns was 25 when his father died and he wrote for him an epitaph, the last line of which declared that "even his failings leaned to virtue's side." Now the head of his family, Robert Burns, with his brother Gilbert, rented the farm of Mossgiel, near Mauchline. He toiled there for four years, earning a bare living and becoming involved in several romances, which immensely complicated his life. In 1786, discouraged by his lot, he decided to emigrate. He accepted a place as bookkeeper on an estate in Jamaica, bought his ticket for the West Indies, and arranged for his first small volume of poems to be published at Kilmarnock. Entitled *Poems, Chiefly in the Scottish Dialect*, it received so hearty a welcome that he gave up his plan to emigrate.

The financial return from the book was only £20, but the social returns were much greater. Because of it he was invited to Edinburgh and welcomed by the literary society of the city. Sir Walter Scott, then a boy of 15, saw Burns and described him this way: "His countenance was more massive than it looks in any of his portraits. There was a strong expression of shrewdness in his lineaments; the eye indicated the poetic character and temperament. It was large and of a dark cast, and literally glowed when he spoke with feeling or interest. I never saw such another eye in a human head."

The second edition of the volume of poems, which appeared in 1787, yielded Burns £600, and with the proceeds he took a walking tour throughout the border towns of England and the eastern Highlands of Scotland and returned to Ayrshire. There he took a farm, and in 1788 married Jean Armour, with whom he had had an affair earlier.

The next year, he received an appointment as excise officer of the district at £50 a year and two years later he was promoted to a similar post at Dumfries at a salary of £70. At about this time, he was asked to help find, and to write or rewrite words for, the traditional Scottish airs collected by George Thomson. This and a similar project begun earlier for James Johnson, in addition to his duties as excise officer, kept him busy most of the rest of his life. The bulk of Burns's songs, building on folk tradition and lovingly portraying the life of rural Scotland, were contained in Johnson's multivolume *Scots Musical Museum* and the several volumes of Thomson's *Select Collection of Original Scottish Airs*. Despite his family's financial need, Burns refused payment, except honorariums, for the songs, which constitute his best-known work and which he himself regarded as a service to Scotland.

Burns died on July 21, 1796, at the early age of 37. His death was caused not, as was long alleged, by excessive drinking, but by rheumatic heart disease brought on by overexertion in his teens, when he performed a man's hard farm labor on an inadequate diet.

Before his death, however, he had done more than any person before or since to recreate the entire body of Scottish song, which he came upon in fragmentary and disorganized form and left a thing of lyric beauty. His fame throughout the world has grown with the years.

Feast of the Conversion of St. Paul

The Feast of the Conversion of St. Paul, on January 25, celebrates the transformation of Saul of Tarsus, scourge of Christians, into St. Paul, Apostle, missionary, leader of Christians and martyr for Jesus' sake. It is not known with certainty just when this feast was first observed, but it is mentioned in the Church calendars and missals of the eighth and ninth centuries, and Pope Innocent III (1198–1216) urged that it be celebrated with great solemnity. Listed as a solemn festival in the records of the Council of Oxford in 1222, held during the reign of England's King Henry III, the feast has continued to be observed by the Anglican church since its separation from Rome. It is also marked by Lutherans. The feast is not celebrated in the Eastern churches.

Saul of Tarsus was a well-educated and fiercely dedicated Jew, a Pharisee and member of the tribe of Benjamin. He was named after Saul, the first king of Israel, who was also a Benjamite, and became known as Paul after his conversion to Christianity (see June 29).

Although he had been educated "at the feet of Gamaliel" — who was greatly respected for his learning and who himself was a tolerant and liberal man (Acts 5:34–40) — Saul of Tarsus had a fiery nature and became an anti-Christian extremist because he thought Christians blasphemed and felt that Christianity was a threat to his religion. He scoured Jerusalem for Christians and when he found them he had them bound and delivered to prison, or to death. He was a witness to the stoning of St. Stephen, the first Christian martyr (see December 26), as the New Testament notes in Acts 8:1 — "And Saul was consenting to his death." What is reported as Paul's own version of this event appears in Acts 22:20.

After considerable success in rooting out Christians in Jerusalem, Saul, "breathing threats and murder against the disciples of the Lord," decided to journey to Damascus and continue what he felt was his holy and righteous work in that city. Securing authority from the chief priest to bind "any belonging to the [Christian] Way" and take them back to Jerusalem, Saul set forth for Damascus. It was on the road there that his dramatic conversion took place, perhaps a few years after Jesus Christ's death.

Many years later — between 60 and 62 — Paul gave to King Agrippa his own account of his conversion, as recorded in the 26th (and also the 9th and 22nd) chapter of Acts. The events leading to Paul's appearance before Agrippa began in Jerusalem when some Jewish pilgrims from Asia, who had seen him in the Temple, erroneously thought he had violated its sanctity by taking Gentiles into the Temple with him. Seeing him again later (according to the report in Acts 21), they accused him of this, and of teaching against their law. In the process, they stirred up members of a Jerusalem mob, who beat Paul and sought to kill him. Roman soldiers arrested him, in effect rescuing him, and placed him in protective custody. While incarcerated, Paul, learning of a plot against his life, demanded his rights as a Roman citizen and asked to be sent to Rome for trial. The procurator (or governor) of Judea, Porcius Festus, agreed. But it seemed to him unreasonable, in sending a prisoner, not to indicate the charges against him. Since he himself could find nothing against Paul, Festus discussed the case with the visiting King Agrippa.

Summoned before Agrippa, Paul brought to bear all his education in law and theology to show that, contrary to the charges against him, he had not turned away from Judaism when he embraced Christianity, but that Christianity was the fulfillment, the promise, of Judaism (Acts 26).

At the end of Paul's defense, the account goes on, the king and the governor and those listening withdrew and "said to one another, 'This man is doing nothing to deserve death or imprisonment.' And Agrippa said to Festus, 'This man could have been set free if he had not appealed to Caesar.'" As it was, Paul was sent to Rome where, a few years later, he was beheaded during Nero's persecution of Christians. Between the time of his conversion and his death, Paul had done more than any single man in history to evangelize the people of many nations and to make the Church universal and catholic.

Paul, like the Church since his time, regarded his encounter on the road to Damascus as the most momentous occurrence of his life. Certainly, the event had a decisive influence on the entire subsequent history of the Christian faith.

Protestants and Catholics alike observe the eight days ending on January 25, the designated anniversary of his conversion, as the Week of Prayer for Christian Unity. Catholics once called the week the Chair of Unity Octave. It was originated in 1908 by an Episcopal presbyter named James F. Watson (who in 1909 became the Roman Catholic Father Paul) and a small Anglican community known as the Society of the Atonement (which also became Catholic in 1909). Today, the week is cosponsored by the National Council of the Churches of

Christ in the USA (Protestant and Eastern Orthodox) and the Graymoor (New York) Ecumenical Institute of the Catholic Society of the Atonement Fathers. In keeping with the modern ecumenical movement, which began among Protestants early in this century, the week traditionally is a time for interdenominational prayer and worship. Since the swell of ecumenical feeling which swept the Christian world in the 1960s — intensified by the hopes for unity and new ecumenical interest of Roman Catholics expressed during the Second Vatican Council (1962–1965) — the eight-day period increasingly has been a time for interdenominational religious services in which Protestants, Anglicans, Roman Catholics, and Eastern Orthodox Christians participate jointly.

The eve of the Feast of the Conversion of St. Paul is marked by an interesting annual recurrence at historic St. Paul's Chapel (Broadway and Fulton Street, New York), the oldest church in Manhattan. Since hordes of people daily pass through its iron-fenced graveyard, using its paths as a shortcut between streets, church authorities are mindful of the legal technicality whereby loss of control of their property could result from its uninterrupted use as a public right-of-way. Each year, they therefore block the cemetery shortcut by closing the churchyard gates for a 48-hour period. The gates are reopened annually on the eve of the Feast of the Conversion of St. Paul, and there is a service in the chapel appropriate to the day, preceding the special service on the day of the feast.

JANUARY 26

Douglas MacArthur's Birthday

General of the Army Douglas MacArthur, supreme commander of Allied forces in the Southwest Pacific during World War II, came from a celebrated army family. Born in Little Rock, Arkansas, on January 26, 1880, he was the son of the former Mary P. Hardy and Lieutenant General Arthur MacArthur — who served for a time as military governor of the Philippines and eventually became the army's senior ranking officer. Arkansas annually honors its native son on the anniversary of his birth, when the governor proclaims January 26 as General Douglas MacArthur Day.

Young Douglas MacArthur attended the US Military Academy at West Point, New York, and was graduated in 1903, the first in his class of 93. Commissioned a second lieutenant and assigned to the Corps of Engineers, he was sent by his own choice to the Philippines and subsequently served in California; as aide to his father in Japan; and as aide to Theodore Roosevelt in Washington. In 1908, after graduating from the Engineering School of Application, MacArthur joined Company K, Third Battalion of Engineers, at Fort Leavenworth, Kansas. In the next four years he served there, at San Antonio, and in the Panama Canal Zone, and acquired the rank of captain. Ordered to Washington, he was appointed to the General Staff Corps and, from April to September 1914, served with the Engineering Corps in the Vera Cruz Expedition to Mexico.

In September 1917, after the United States' entry into World War I, MacArthur was appointed chief of staff of the 42nd (Rainbow) Division with the rank of colonel. (He himself conceived the idea of and named the famous division, which was composed of National Guard units from 27 states, and he directed its organization and training.)

During the war, MacArthur participated in the Champagne-Marne and Aisne-Marne defensives. Given the temporary rank of brigadier general in June 1918, he was placed in command of the 84th Infantry Brigade and led it in the St. Mihiel, Essey, Pannes, Woevre, Meuse-Argonne, and Sedan offensives. He created a sensation by insisting on going into battle with his men. Twice wounded in action, he was decorated 13 times and cited an additional 7 times.

The armistice of 1918 found MacArthur temporarily commanding the 42nd Division once more before serving with the Army of Occupation in Germany until April of the following year. Returning to the United States, he became superintendent of the US Military Academy at West Point in June of 1919. In the three years that he held the post he revitalized the academy by modernizing military training, broadening the curriculum, and instituting compulsory intramural athletics. He was made a brigadier general in the regular army in January 1920.

In 1922, MacArthur again left for the Philippines, where he served in several command posts before being promoted to major general in January 1925. After intervals in command of the Fourth Corps Area in Atlanta and the Third Corps Area in Baltimore, he returned to the Pacific for two years as commanding general of the Philippines Department.

When President Hoover named MacArthur chief of staff of the US Army in November 1930 he was the youngest man ever to hold the position. He was made a four-star general at the same time, the youngest since Ulysses S. Grant. In his new post MacArthur worked to modernize the army, directing its mechanization and motorization. He also urged recognition of the airplane's coming military importance and prepared some of the basic manpower and industrial mobilization plans later used during World War II. In the pacifist climate of the 1930s, however, he was unpopular for his belief that Germany and Japan, then arming, posed a military threat.

With Japan ominously embarked on its program of territorial expansion, President Franklin D. Roosevelt appointed MacArthur (who was due to retire as chief of staff) head of the American military mission to the newly created Commonwealth Government of the Philippines in 1935. In that capacity, he directed organization of the islands' defenses. After President Quezon of the Philippines had commissioned him a field marshal of the Philippine army in 1936, MacArthur — on December 31, 1937 — retired from the US Army at his own request, while continuing to serve the Philippines as field marshal.

Against a background of increasingly strained relations between the United States and Japan, MacArthur was recalled to active duty by the US Army on July 26, 1941. Designated commanding general of US Army forces in the Far East, he was put in command of United States and Philippine troops. A few months later, Japan attacked the US naval installation at Pearl Harbor, Hawaii (see December 7) — precipitating the United States' entry into World War II.

Japan attacked Malaya and the Philippine Islands the same day as Pearl Harbor. Earlier defensive preparations notwithstanding, the attackers quickly overran most of the Philippines. MacArthur's outnumbered men were forced by the enemy to withdraw (December 26–31) from Manila to the Bataan peninsula and the island of Corregidor, where they put up their heroic, and now legendary, defense before being forced to capitulate in April and May of 1942. Ordered out for the defense of Australia by President Roosevelt, MacArthur left the Philippines in March before the capitulation. His arrival in Australia, after a 3,000-mile dash over Japanese-controlled waters, prompted his subsequently famous declaration: "I came through and I shall return."

In April, MacArthur was made supreme commander of Allied forces in the Southwest Pacific Area. His command complemented that of Admiral Chester W. Nimitz (see February 24) in the North Pacific, Central Pacific, and South Pacific areas. Both men operated under the overall strategic direction of the US Joint Chiefs of Staff.

After the battles of the Coral Sea and Midway had raged in other Pacific areas, and while the Guadalcanal campaign proceeded to the east, MacArthur launched a counterattack to secure Papua, the southeastern section of New Guinea, in September 1942. The end of enemy resistance in this region, which he announced on January 23, 1943, was succeeded by actions under his command to secure New Britain and neighboring straits before his main New Guinea campaign — the brilliant "leapfrog" operation along the northern coast toward the Philippine Islands — could proceed from January to September 1944.

True to his promise, MacArthur returned to the Philippines, wading ashore on the east coast of Leyte on October 20, 1944, and calling on the Filipinos to rise and strike (see October 20). The land battle for Leyte was accompanied by one of the great naval battles of modern times (October 23–26). It dissipated the Japanese naval threat and allowed the Allied forces under MacArthur to continue their advances. Heavy land fighting continued on Leyte until Christmas Day, when MacArthur declared the island secure, and into the following year. On Luzon, which the Allies invaded on January 9, 1945, and in some other parts of the islands, hostilities lasted until July and even later, although Manila and Corregidor were liberated by early March.

Confronted by the Allies' advances on land and sea, and by the atomic bomb, which had laid waste two of its home cities, Japan indicated its willingness to surrender on August 14, 1945. World War II came to a close with the official surrender ceremonies held on September 2 aboard the battleship *Missouri* in Tokyo Bay. MacArthur — who had been made a five-star general late in 1944 — was appointed supreme allied commander to accept the surrender and command Allied occupation forces in Japan. He spent the next five years there, supervising reconstruction and the establishment of a democratic form of government.

In 1950, after Communist North Korean troops crossed the 38th parallel to invade South Korea, MacArthur was appointed commander of United Nations forces sent to oppose the action. He was able to stop the North Korean advance at Pusan and to conceive and brilliantly execute a surprise landing far to the invaders' rear, at Inchon. As the UN forces around Pusan moved north to meet the Inchon

forces, the North Korean army was routed, and nearly destroyed. UN forces subsequently crossed above the 38th parallel and proceeded as far as North Korea's Yalu River boundary with Communist China, but were turned back to below the 38th parallel by the sudden intervention of Red Chinese troops. MacArthur's outspoken views at the time — that Communist bases in Manchuria should be bombed and the Chinese coast blockaded to bring an end to hostilities — conflicted with those of President Truman and led to MacArthur's dismissal from his command on April 11, 1951.

The triumphal aspects of his return to the US mainland, complete with a ticker tape parade up New York's Broadway and a memorable address to a joint session of Congress, were in no way diminished by the dismissal. A born leader who inspired extremes of devotion and criticism, MacArthur was seriously considered as the Republican nominee for President in both 1948 and 1952, and was the recipient within his lifetime of many other honors. In retirement he served as chairman of the board of the Remington Rand Corporation.

He died in New York City on April 5, 1964, and is buried in the General Douglas MacArthur Memorial — a restored former courthouse with exhibits pertaining to his life — at City Hall Avenue and Bank Street in Norfolk, Virginia. In 1971, Norfolk was the city of first day issue for a commemorative stamp bearing MacArthur's likeness and released on his January 26 birthday.

Michigan Admitted to the Union

Michigan, the 26th state, was admitted to the Union on January 26, 1837. The Michigan area was probably first visited by Europeans when the Frenchman Étienne Brulé reached the Sault Ste. Marie narrows, strategically located between Lakes Superior and Huron, in 1618. He was followed by other Frenchmen — explorers, fur traders, and missionaries — including Jean Nicolet, who reached Sault Ste. Marie in 1634. Sault Ste. Marie also was the site of Michigan's first permanent non-Indian settlement, founded in 1668 by Père Jacques Marquette (see June 1) as a Jesuit mission. Detroit — as strategic in its way as Sault Ste. Marie, since it effectively controls the entrance to Lakes Huron and Erie — was founded in 1701 by the French under Antoine de la Mothe Cadillac.

The lands now within the boundaries of the state of Michigan passed to the English in 1760 and 1761 and to the United States in 1783, with the signing of the Treaty of Paris after the conclusion of the American Revolution (though it was 1796 before the British actually surrendered Detroit and Mackinac). At first part of the Northwest Territory (from 1787), then part of the new Indiana Territory (from 1803), Michigan was organized as a separate territory in 1805. Although the region was again occupied by Great Britain during the War of 1812, it was virtually all recovered within the next year.

Becoming a permanent part of the United States, Michigan was enlarged by the cession of Indian lands between 1814 and 1836. It set up a state government without federal sanction and applied for statehood in 1835, although its actual admission was delayed until January 26, 1837, by a boundary dispute with Ohio and by debate in Congress over maintaining the balance between free and slave states. With the admission of Arkansas, a slave state, in 1836 (see June 15), Michigan's statehood was assured. Under both the Missouri Compromise of 1820 (see March 3) and the earlier Northwest Ordinance of 1787 (see July 13), slavery was prohibited in the region occupied by Michigan; it could thus enter the Union as a free state, offsetting Arkansas to maintain the nation's uneasy balance between free and slave states. January 26, the anniversary of Michigan's actual admission in 1837, which was formally observed as Michigan Day in earlier years, now is simply noted in passing as the anniversary of statehood.

With a coastline on four of the Great Lakes, including Lake Michigan, the Wolverine State, as it is called, has excellent transportation facilities, which have furthered industrial development. Its principal industry, in which Michigan is the world leader, is the manufacture of automobiles and other motor vehicles, centered chiefly in the Detroit area. In the peak year of 1973, before the full impact of recession and the energy crisis was felt, the world output of passenger cars was approximately 30 million. The United States, with Michigan in the forefront, accounted for the manufacture of 9.66 million of these vehicles. The state's tourist industry, with revenues that have been estimated at more than $1.6 billion a year, rivals automobile production and other manufacturing in importance. Michigan is also a heavily agricultural state and produces mineral ore in important quantities. Particularly since the 1959 opening of the St. Lawrence Seaway, which made the Great Lakes cities into international ports, Michigan has been an important shipping center as well.

Michigan's present constitution was adopted in 1963 and became effective the following year. The state's capital is Lansing.

JANUARY 27

Samuel Gompers' Birthday

Samuel Gompers, the first president of the American Federation of Labor and the man who guided the course of organized labor in the United States for more than four decades, was born on January 27, 1850, in London. After attending school for four years, he was apprenticed in his father's trade of cigar making. When he was 13, his family moved to the United States and settled in New York City.

Within a year, young Gompers had joined the New York Cigarmakers' Union, and he became active in the social clubs and fraternal orders of New York's East Side. Although he attended lectures at Cooper Union, most of his education came from the reading materials that were purchased from common funds for the shops of master cigar makers, where workers took turns reading to one another. He was also exposed to various theories of socialism and to the revolutionary tradition of some of the European immigrants with whom he came in contact, but Gompers preferred the democratic mainstream of American life. He became a naturalized citizen in 1872.

To better the lot of all working people, he looked for inspiration to the British trade unions and their Trade Union Congress. After the Panic of 1873, with its attendant hardships, and a long strike in 1877, which nearly wrecked the Cigarmakers' Union, he and Adolph Strasser reorganized the Cigarmakers along British lines. Strasser became the union's international president, Gompers became president of the New York local, and their thinking became known as the "new unionism." Central to it was their belief that labor should concentrate on immediate economic goals and avoid the kind of political schemes and utopian social experiments on which some earlier reformers had dissipated their energies. They also sought to remedy two previous handicaps to union activity: lack of strike funds and the absence of central control. They raised membership dues, gave national officers jurisdiction over funds, and prepared to establish sickness, accident, and unemployment benefits for workers.

In the process, the Cigarmakers became a model for other unions. But Gompers and Strasser, seeing the need for a national federation of trade unions, which could lobby for favorable legislation and act defensively against employer opposition, regarded their reorganization of the Cigarmakers as merely a first step. In 1881, they were among the main organizers of the Federation of Organized Trades and Labor Unions.

The federation was reorganized as the American Federation of Labor at a convention in Columbus, Ohio, on December 8, 1886. Gompers was elected president of the new AFL and, except for one year (1895), held the position for the rest of his life. A moderate influence, he persisted in his avoidance of political schemes and radical theory, focusing instead on what he considered to be the just goals of labor: higher wages, shorter hours, and greater freedom. A man of stocky build, stern visage, and great personal integrity, Gompers sought to make his federation of autonomous craft unions respected as a defense against radicalism and irresponsible strikes.

To this end, he favored binding written trade agreements and held that the national federation should have authority over local unions, although the authority was to be by moral force — organized consent to collective action, as he put it — rather than by arbitrary rule. Thus the national organization exercised only the powers delegated to it by the organization's constitution, or by annual conventions of members.

Since the AFL was composed of craft unions, the membership — which increased from under 200,000 in 1886 to over 1,750,000 by 1904 — consisted largely of skilled workers. Under Gompers' leadership, it based its efforts to achieve better living on collective bargaining, and on such weapons as the strike, the boycott, and picketing. Its attempts to influence legislation were in line with Gompers' view that — apart from the individual's privilege of "rewarding our friends and punishing our enemies" at the polls — labor should limit its political role to working for laws that would permit it to engage in collective bargaining without interference.

During the 1890s, there was much that labor regarded as interference. Strikes, and the violence that sometimes accompanied them, were quelled by the use of strikebreakers, court injunctions, and state or federal troops. Then came the "honeymoon of capital and labor," from 1898 to 1904, when union membership increased substantially and the AFL received wide recognition from employers. But these labor successes were followed by a period of reaction, including an anti-union, open-shop drive by employers and a Supreme Court ruling that boycotts were in violation of the Sherman Antitrust Act.

In the face of such pressures, Gompers abandoned his political neutrality in the presidential election of 1908, lending his unofficial support to the Democrat, William Jennings Bryan, who ran, without success, on an anti-injunction platform. Meanwhile, Gompers was successfully meeting not only the new hostility toward labor,

but also a challenge from labor forces on the Socialist left. Favoring more extreme tactics, they also objected to the AFL's organization by crafts (and the exclusion of unskilled workers) and sought to organize labor along more militant lines in the Industrial Workers of the World. Although the IWW's effectiveness as a labor federation did not endure, the demand for the industrial organization of labor, in which the IWW was not alone, haunted the AFL until 1935, when disgruntled members broke off from the AFL to form a separate Congress of Industrial Organization under John L. Lewis. Not until 1955 did the two federations reunite as the AFL-CIO, providing for organization both by crafts and by industries.

In 1912 the climate for labor improved with the election of Woodrow Wilson as President of the United States. Wilson had received the unofficial support of the AFL during his campaign, and after his election he succeeded in getting a progressive program of legislation passed through Congress. Two examples of legislation enacted while he was President were the Adamson Act and the Clayton Antitrust Act, which supplemented the Sherman Antitrust Act. The Adamson Act provided an eight-hour day for workers on interstate railroads, while the Clayton Antitrust Act recognized strikes, boycotts, and peaceful picketing as labor's legal rights; drastically limited use of the injunction in labor disputes; and held that labor organizations were not illegal combinations in restraint of trade, as had been argued earlier. Although the Clayton Antitrust Act, at first hailed by Gompers as "labor's Magna Carta," was much weakened by judicial interpretation, the act's general provisions today are regarded as basic rights. The first two decades of the 20th century also saw many states enact new legislation that protected wages and limited hours for women and children, set standards for safety and sanitation, and initiated compensation for workers injured on the job.

Gompers, who was recognized as an important public figure as the strength of labor grew, served as Wilson's official and unofficial adviser on labor and organized the War Committee on Labor during World War I. As head of this group and as a member of the Advisory Commission to the Council of National Defense, he led the AFL in active support of the war effort. The war years were a period of substantial gains and vastly increased membership for the labor movement. They were followed by a resurgence of antilabor feeling in the twenties, prompting the AFL to consider once more its policy of aloofness from politics. In the presidential election of 1924, the organization gave its support, this time officially, to Robert M.

LaFollette, who ran unsuccessfully on the Progressive party ticket.

Gompers died in the same year — in San Antonio, Texas, on December 13 — but his influence on the labor movement lived on. His authoritative account of the rise and growth of American trade unionism, *Seventy Years of Life and Labor*, was published the next year. Today's visitors to Washington, D.C., can see the Gompers Memorial, which stands at 10th Street and Massachusetts Avenue, N.W., within a mile of the AFL-CIO's headquarters building on 16th Street. A film, *The Liquid Fire*, based on the life of Gompers, was produced in 1966 by the George Meany Foundation and the National Broadcasting Company. Released by the AFL-CIO to some 125 television stations in connection with the 1967 celebration of Labor Day (see September 7), it has been seen by millions in the years since then.

JANUARY 28

The United States Withdraws from Cuba

Termination, on January 28, 1909, of the provisional government that had marked the United States' second intervention in Cuban affairs also marked the establishment for the second time of the independent Cuban republic. That republic had come into being after the war with Spain — the Spanish-American War of 1898, in which the United States intervened on behalf of Cuban insurgents who opposed Spanish rule of their island. The Treaty of Paris (1898), which concluded the hostilities, saw the virtual dissolution of the Spanish empire. Puerto Rico and Guam were ceded to the United States — as were the Philippine Islands (in return for $20 million). Spain also relinquished all authority over Cuba, which became an independent republic under US protection.

For three and a half years after this, Cuban affairs were administered by the US War Department, briefly through General John R. Brooke and then through General Leonard Wood. Their terms as governors general were characterized by reforms in public administration; advances in education, construction, and sanitation (including the remarkable conquest of yellow fever based on the work of Walter Reed, Carlos J. Finlay, and others); and preparation for the island's independence.

Steps toward this goal included election of delegates to a convention which, in February 1901, completed work on a constitution for a Cuban republic. As a condition for the end of military occupation, the convention — reluctantly and under US pressure — agreed to attach to the constitution what was known as the Platt Amendment. Designed to preserve Cuba's independence and safeguard the reforms of the occupation, this controversial document also provided for US naval bases in Cuba, and permitted US intervention, if necessary, to maintain the island's independence or preserve order. After the amendment was accepted, Cubans were allowed to elect a president and a congress, which they did on December 31, 1901. With the inauguration of Tomás Estrada Palma, a leading anti-Spanish revolutionary, as the Cuban republic's first president, the United States formally withdrew from Cuba on May 20, 1902.

After new elections, which followed in late 1905 and early 1906, Tomás Estrada Palma became president for the second time, with the support of Cuban conservatives. Although he attempted to lead Cuba to economic prosperity, his administration, plagued by corruption and veterans' pension requests, failed to bring about demanded reforms. Claiming fraud in the elections (which they had lost), supporters of the Cuban Liberal party under José Miguel Gómez revolted against the Palma administration in August 1906.

President Palma, invoking the Platt Amendment, declared that he was unable to maintain order and asked the United States to intervene. At first reluctant to interfere, the United States did send mediators, headed by Secretary of War (later President) William Howard Taft, who attempted to effect a compromise. When this attempt failed, President Palma and his cabinet resigned, leaving the island without a government.

To restore order the United States proclaimed a provisional government on September 29 under Taft. He was succeeeded as provisional governor by Charles E. Magoon the next month.

After order had been restored and new laws had been drafted by a US-headed advisory committee, a new election was held in November 1908. With the inauguration of José Miguel Gómez — leader of the 1906 rebellion — as president on January 28, 1909, US administration of the island officially ceased for the second time.

During the recurring political turmoil of the next several decades there were several other instances of requested, threatened, or actual US intervention in Cuba. In 1934, however, the hated Platt Amendment was abrogated during the administration of US President Franklin D. Roosevelt, who had inaugurated the "good neighbor" era of improved US relations with Latin America. United States commercial interests in Cuba, always a bone of contention, nonetheless remained strong until the confiscation of such properties in late 1960 by the revolutionary regime of Fidel Castro, who had supplanted the long-entrenched dictator Fulgencio Batista y Zaldívar as Cuban chief of state after prolonged and bloody guerrilla warfare.

JANUARY 29

Kansas Day

The admission of Kansas to the Union as the 34th state on January 29, 1861, brought to a close one of the important chapters of US history. That chapter began seven years earlier when Kansas was organized as a territory under the controversial Kansas-Nebraska Act passed by Congress on May 30, 1854.

Repercussions of the Kansas-Nebraska Act, which opened the way for the extension of slavery to the West, were widespread. Debate over the act intensified pro- and antislavery sentiments across the country, making slavery the most inflammatory issue in the land. Passage of the measure inaugurated an era of bloodshed in Kansas which in some ways foreshadowed the Civil War. Politically there were repercussions too, for opposition to the Kansas-Nebraska Act cut across party lines and led to formation of the new Republican party by antislavery Whigs and Democrats and members of some other groups, like the Free-Soil party, which opposed the extension of slavery.

The bearing of the Kansas issue on the birth of the Republican party, and Kansans' historic habit (less pronounced since World War II) of voting Republican probably account for the fact that the anniversary of statehood, officially known as Kansas Day, is an occasion of Republican celebration. It has been so since 1892.

Commemoration of the anniversary began considerably earlier than that, however. It was, in fact, about 1877 when Kansas Day observances originated with a program planned by Paola, Kansas, schoolchildren with the encouragement of an imaginative teacher, L. G. A. Copley. The well-received program was accorded statewide publicity and the observance of Kansas Day became an annual event. Today, hundreds of school classes throughout the state mark the day with brief programs on Kansas. The day also is noted, at least in passing, by various clubs and organizations throughout the state.

Most notable, however, is the flood of Republican organization members who make their

way to Topeka, the state capital, on Kansas Day to hold annual meetings; elect officers; attend assorted breakfasts, luncheons, receptions, and annual banquets; and listen to partisan speeches. Participating groups include the Kansas Day Club, Kansas Republican Veterans Club, and Kansas Federation of Republican Women, as well as the Republican central committees and various party clubs from Shawnee and Sedgwick counties — where Topeka and Wichita, the state's largest city, are respectively located. So many of the political organizations meet that Kansas Day events now are scheduled over a two-day period beginning on January 28. Certain nonpartisan organizations also plan special events in Topeka for Kansas Day or the day before.

An outline of Topeka events in one recent year is representative of the Kansas Day observances which customarily take place: The nonpartisan Woman's Kansas Day Club marked Kansas Day by holding its annual meeting, electing officers, and hearing a luncheon speech about "Old Cars and People." This was followed by a history of "Horseless Carriages Made in Kansas," with presentation to the Kansas State Historical Society of photographs and other related materials. The night before, the Woman's Kansas Day Club held its annual reception at Cedar Crest, the official residence of the governor of the state.

The Kansas Day Club, which also held a number of events on Kansas Day, had the day's largest event. This was its annual banquet, attended by more than 1,000 persons and addressed by then Representative Gerald R. Ford of Michigan, later President, who was minority leader of the national House of Representatives at the time. His talk, in the tradition of such gatherings, promised a bright future for the Republican party and castigated Democratic policies. Earlier the same day, US Senator Frank Carlson of Kansas addressed the Kansas Republican Veterans Club at its annual luncheon.

The previous day, members of the Kansas Federation of Republican Women attended a breakfast and luncheon, and heard a panel discussion by members of the Kansas congressional delegation and addresses by the governor of Kansas and the president of the National Federation of Republican Women. At a banquet that night William L. White, the editor, like his famous father, of the Emporia *Gazette*, spoke to the nonpartisan Native Sons and Daughters — who also chose the occasion for presentation of their Kansan of the Year award.

Some other pre-Kansas Day gatherings — such as the Buccaneer Club's conversation hour, the reception held by four Shawnee County Republican organizations, and the "mixer" put on by the Kansas Young Republican Federation — placed more emphasis on fun than on either politics or history. Generally speaking, however, Kansas Day is a time when Kansans are more than usually conscious of their state's history.

That history began when most of what is now Kansas came into United States possession through the Louisiana Purchase in 1803. The southwestern part of present Kansas was claimed by Spain until 1822 and Mexico until 1848. Parts of the region meanwhile were designated as Indian territory by the US government. For a time — from 1835 to 1850 — part of Kansas also was claimed by Texas. After the Texas claim was reduced, the southwest corner of Kansas still was earmarked as Indian territory until Kansas was organized as a state in 1861.

The prelude to statehood had begun in 1804 and 1806, when Lewis and Clark passed through part of the "Kansas" region. The vast prairies subsequently were crossed and recrossed by such explorers as Zebulon M. Pike, John C. Frémont, and Stephen H. Long — who dismissed the whole area, now known as the nation's wheat basket, as "uninhabitable by a people depending on agriculture." Beginning in 1821, the Santa Fe Trail stretched across the entire length of Kansas. Westward migration through the region continued in the 1830s; and in the 1840s the Oregon Trail carried thousands of Pacific-bound emigrants across the northeastern corner.

But these were all people with destinations farther west. Actual settlement in the Kansas area began when Presbyterians (with representatives of other denominations) founded the first Kansas mission in 1824. Defenses against Indians and marauders followed shortly with the establishment of Fort Leavenworth in 1827, Fort Scott in 1842, and Fort Riley in 1853. Large numbers of permanent settlers did not pour in, however, until Kansas was officially designated a territory by the Kansas-Nebraska Act, signed into law by President Franklin Pierce on May 30, 1854.

It was that act's provision that the residents of the Kansas Territory were to decide whether it should, or should not, permit slavery that sowed the seeds of violent dissension. This was particularly true because the act, which was passed only after months of bitter debate, repealed the Missouri Compromise of 1820 (see March 3). Except in Missouri itself, the hardwon Missouri Compromise had expressly forbidden the extension of slavery to any of the Louisiana Purchase north of latitude 36°30'.

With passage of the Kansas-Nebraska Act, however, the whole inflammatory question of slavery in the territories was again thrown open to question. Looking ahead toward statehood, slaveholders and abolitionists each bent their efforts to securing a majority for their point of view. Determined that Kansas would become a slave — or a free — state, immigrants from Missouri, the South, and northern states flooded in, precipitating the era of "bleeding Kansas" as the contestants sought to determine the issue.

Antislavery men settled in Lawrence, Topeka, and Osawatomie. Advocates of slavery founded Leavenworth, Atchison, and Lecompton. On March 30, 1855, an election of a territorial legislature was held and 5,427 proslavery votes were cast out of a total of 6,307 — amazingly enough, since there were only 2,905 legal voters in the territory. The discrepancy was accounted for by proslavery Missourians who had crossed the border to stuff the ballot boxes and intimidate voters. Territorial Governor A. H. Reeder set aside the election in six of the districts and ordered a new election that resulted in the victory of the antislavery candidates.

When the first territorial legislature met at Pawnee on July 2, 1855, it nonetheless was controlled by a proslavery majority. This majority expelled the members chosen at the second election ordered by the governor. It passed acts making it a capital offense to assist slaves in escaping either to or from the territory and a felony to circulate antislavery publications or to deny the right to hold slaves. Not content with this, it also required all voters to swear to support the Fugitive Slave Law — and secured Governor Reeder's removal.

Antislavery men refused to recognize the legality of the territorial government and in a convention held at Topeka between October 23 and November 11, 1855, they adopted a constitution prohibiting slavery after July 4, 1857, and excluding blacks from Kansas. After their constitution was adopted at a December election (in which the proslavery men took no part), the Free-Soil, or abolitionist, contingent went on to choose state officers and a legislature and set up a rival government in January 1856.

Although the abolitionists wished to avoid armed conflict, violence came when a sheriff of the proslavery territorial government was shot at Lawrence while trying to seize a prisoner. Antislavery leaders were indicted for treason and imprisoned; and on May 21 a mob of proslavery men sacked Lawrence. Three days later, the fiery abolitionist John Brown and his sons retaliated by killing five proslavery men on Pottawatomie creek. Civil war between the two factions began, and continued throughout the month of June until US troops intervened and restored order.

The Free-Soil legislature met at Topeka on July 4, 1856. Dispersed by federal troops, it made another attempt to meet on January 6, 1857, but its members were arrested. Robert J. Walker, who by then had become governor of the territory — the sixth in a rapidly changing series of chief executives — succeeded in arranging a compromise with the Free-Soilers, who agreed to take part in an election for a territorial legislature in October 1857.

Although the abolitionists won the election, the proslavery party meanwhile had called a convention to meet in Lecompton, where they adopted the proslavery Lecompton Constitution on November 7. Declaring that the right of slaveholders in Kansas to their slaves was inviolable, this constitution prohibited the legislature from passing any act of emancipation or preventing the importation of slaves. Then, on December 21, the people of the territory were called upon to decide whether they would have a constitution with slavery (i.e., with the Lecompton provisions) or without.

The proslavery vote was 6,226 — more than half of which was polled along the Missouri border where there were not more than 1,000 qualified voters. Since the great body of antislavery partisans regarded the election as farcical and refrained from voting, the opposition vote was only 569.

Following this, the entire Lecompton Constitution was submitted to the voters by the territorial legislature on January 4, 1858, with 10,226 votes cast against the measure and less than 200 for it. The issue was then taken to Congress, where the Senate ignored the verdict of territory residents and voted to admit Kansas as a state *with* the Lecompton Constitution. The House of Representatives rejected this bill, however, instead passing the English Bill, which usually is referred to as a compromise measure even though it was not much of a compromise: it would have predicated the usual cession of land to a new state upon Kansas voters' acceptance of the Lecompton Constitution by a referendum.

In a ringing defeat for the proslavery forces, Kansas voters rejected this proposition by nearly 10,000 votes, finally ending the struggle to establish slavery in Kansas. The antislavery Wyandotte Constitution subsequently was adopted by Kansans on October 4, 1859. And Kansas was admitted to the Union as a free state on January 29, 1861 — not long before the outbreak of the Civil War, which the Kansas trouble had in part anticipated.

William McKinley's Birthday

William McKinley, the 25th President of the United States, was born in Niles, Ohio, on January 29, 1843. Of Scotch-Irish ancestry, he was the seventh of the nine children of William and Nancy (Allison) McKinley. His great-grandfather, David McKinley, was a soldier in the American Revolution. His father and grandfather were engaged in the iron industry, and he worked with his father as a boy.

After the family moved to Poland, Ohio, McKinley prepared for college at Poland Academy and subsequently entered Allegheny College at Meadville, Pennsylvania. Unable to complete his work toward a degree because of lack of money, he returned to Poland and obtained employment as a teacher nearby. He was teaching when the Civil War broke out.

Not long afterwards, on June 11, 1861, he enlisted in the 23rd Regiment, Ohio Volunteer Infantry, which Brigadier General William S. Rosecrans commanded. Rutherford B. Hayes, a Republican later elected President, succeeded Rosecrans as commander — and on September 24, 1862, commissioned McKinley a second lieutenant for gallantry in the field. McKinley continued with the regiment throughout the war, reaching the rank of captain. On March 13, 1865, he was brevetted major, a title by which he was known in later life.

When he was mustered out, McKinley began the study of law in the office of an Ohio judge and completed his preparation at the Albany (New York) Law School. He was admitted to the bar in 1867 and opened an office in Canton, Ohio. Immediately becoming active as a Republican, he worked on behalf of Ulysses S. Grant's successful candidacy in the presidential campaign of 1868.

McKinley's own political career began the next year, when he was elected prosecuting attorney for Ohio's Stark County — an unusual achievement for a Republican since the county was normally Democratic. McKinley loyally supported the candidacy of his former commander, Rutherford B. Hayes, for the governorship of Ohio in 1875 and attracted national attention with his speeches in favor of the resumption of specie payments.

Elected to the US House of Representatives in 1876, McKinley served there for seven terms, which were interrupted by only a single defeat — in 1882. In time, he became the Republican leader in the House and rose to the chairmanship of the Ways and Means Committee. A highly protective tariff act drawn up by that committee was known by his name.

McKinley lost the election of 1890 as a result

of a reapportionment of Ohio's congressional districts, when Democrats in control of the state legislature gerrymandered his district to give their party a majority. However, the defeat represented hardly a pause in his upward career. He was elected governor of Ohio on the Republican ticket in 1891 and was easily reelected in 1893. With this triumph behind him, he was nominated by the Republicans for the presidency in 1896 and elected over William Jennings Bryan, the Democratic-Populist candidate, by an electoral vote of 271 to 176.

The chief event during McKinley's presidency was the Spanish-American War of 1898 (see April 21), which he carried to what was regarded as a successful end. The treaty of peace that concluded the war provided that Spain withdraw from Cuba and cede Puerto Rico, the island of Guam, and the Philippine Islands (upon payment of an indemnity of $20 million) to the United States.

With Bryan as the Democratic candidate, McKinley was reelected President in 1900. But his tenure was short. In 1901, he was fatally shot while holding a public reception at the Pan American Exposition in Buffalo, New York (see September 6). He died on September 14.

Although the observance is now less widespread than formerly, the anniversary of McKinley's birth for years was observed as Carnation Day in many parts of the country. The celebration was proposed by Lewis G. Reynolds of Dayton, Ohio. In a letter to the editor of the New York *Tribune*, published on January 22, 1903, he said:

It is proper that some annual observance be held in memory of William McKinley. The same loyal impulse that prompted the stoppage of almost all the wheels of industry for those few moments on the day of his burial may find annual expression in this tribute suggested by the Carnation League. The plan of the movement is a simple, inexpensive and attractive one and can be taken part in by the old and the young of either sex. A beautiful, fragrant flower worn in the lapel of the coat or at the throat or in the hair in silent memory of a public servant whose life was forfeited because he was our servant is what is contemplated. The fact that the carnation was President McKinley's favorite flower and was always found in his buttonhole is the reason for its choice as a league symbol. On all other days of the year it will be what it is today—the common people's flower—but on September 14 [it was first proposed to observe the day of McKinley's death] it becomes especially the President's flower and will be worn in silent tribute to his memory. . . . If the Carnation League of America serves the purpose of a perennial memorial to a faithful public servant and at the same time fosters a national brotherhood of patriotism it will be worthy of our people.

The Carnation League was formally organized on January 29, 1903, with a dozen distinguished active trustees, President Theodore Roosevelt, the governor of Ohio, and the Ohio senators as honorary trustees.

Although it was in 1903 that McKinley's birthday became known as Carnation Day, a notable anniversary observance already had taken place in 1902. That year, a memorial association organized to raise money for a monument to McKinley's memory persuaded the governors of many states to issue proclamations calling upon the people to gather in public places to honor the memory of the dead President, and suggesting that special services be held in the schools. Such public meetings and memorial services were widely held and many who attended them wore carnations in the buttonholes of their coats.

At one noteworthy later observance of McKinley's birthday, held by the now defunct Tippecanoe Club of Cleveland in 1908, the principal speaker was William Howard Taft, then secretary of war, later President, who reflected upon "that which I think will be ever remembered as [among] the great and distinguishing characteristics of McKinley's administration – the expansion of the United States into a world power." For in the opinion of Taft, which was not shared by everyone, "That which really [distinguished] the administration of McKinley [was] the war with Spain and the expansion which followed it."

McKinley's association with the red carnation dated from 1876, when nursery owner Levi L. Lamborn of Alliance, Ohio, who publicly debated McKinley in that year's congressional contest, made certain before each debate that his opponent was provided with a carnation boutonniere. The carnation became McKinley's favorite flower and during his presidency he had several fresh blossoms sent to him every day from the White House conservatories. Callers frequently asked him for the flower he was wearing as a souvenir of their visit. The red carnation became the official state flower of Ohio in 1904, upon action of the state legislature.

In 1959, the legislature officially designated Alliance as the home of the state flower. Every other year, when the Ohio General Assembly is in session, its Republican members observe January 29 as Carnation Day. At the suggestion of Republican Frank T. Bow, the Representative in Washington of what once was McKinley's 16th Ohio District, congressional Republicans from Ohio began in 1963 to hold similar anniversary celebrations.

Residents of Alliance – which has adopted

for itself the nickname Carnation City — have been growing red carnations ever since McKinley was presented with one during the 1876 campaign speech at Alliance. Although there is no connection with his birthday, McKinley is indirectly called to mind by the week-long Carnation Festival, which Alliance holds annually, usually during the second week in August. The festival includes a parade, the selection of a carnation queen, and a dance.

Canton, Ohio, McKinley's long-time home, honors him more directly. The imposing McKinley State Memorial, set in Monument Park and housing McKinley's tomb, was built with the contributions of more than a million Americans. The Stark County Historical Society Museum, next to it, includes McKinley memorabilia. There is also a handsome memorial building at Niles, where McKinley was born, dedicated in his honor on October 5, 1917.

Thomas Paine's Birthday

Thomas Paine, the propagandist and humanitarian whose writings on independence inflamed colonial minds by clarifying the issues for which the American Revolution would be fought, was born at Thetford, Norfolk, England, on January 29, 1737. Forced by poverty to leave school at the age of 13, he joined his Quaker father in the trade of corset making. He followed this trade intermittently in various parts of England and also worked at one time or another as a sailor, excise officer, tobacconist, grocer, and schoolteacher — meanwhile educating himself by wide reading of political, social, and scientific works.

In England, however, Paine was oppressed by want; by the death of his first wife and an unhappy second marriage; and by his frustration at the seemingly wide gap between what he was and what he felt capable of becoming. Armed with letters of introduction from Benjamin Franklin, whom he had met in London, he emigrated to Philadelphia in the fall of 1774.

There, he became editor of the *Pennsylvania Magazine*, attached himself to the patriot cause, and soon showed himself the master of a pen that could set men on fire. His pamphlet *Common Sense*, arguing that the American colonies owed no allegiance to the British crown and "should forthwith be independent," was published in January 1776 and had a decisive effect in the colonies, where public opinion hovered irresolutely between the alternatives of limited revolt and an attempt to gain independence. Though it did nothing to alter the apathy of some, the pamphlet, in the under-

stated words of George Washington, "worked a powerful change in the minds of many men." Six months after the publication of *Common Sense*, the Declaration of Independence was adopted by the Second Continental Congress, meeting in Philadelphia, on July 4, 1776. The clashes later recognized as the beginning of the American Revolution already had taken place in 1775 at Lexington and Concord (see April 19, Patriots' Day) and at Bunker Hill (see June 17). After the Declaration, however, the course of the former colonists was set for nothing short of total independence.

Paine served briefly in Washington's army in 1776, and on a November night during the New Jersey retreat demonstrated the truth of a comment Franklin had made: that while some could rule and many could fight, "only Paine can write for us." Huddled over a drum, Paine poured his fervor into what became the first of *The Crisis* papers — starting with the memorable words "These are the times that try men's souls." Widely read and influential, *The Crisis* essays were issued in 11 additional and 4 supplementary numbers during the Revolution, and gave substantial encouragement to the new nation's first patriots.

During the late 1770s, Paine served as secretary of the congressional committee on foreign affairs and then as clerk of the Pennsylvania assembly. In 1781 he went with John Laurens to France, successfully seeking financial aid for the former colonies. At the suggestion of Washington, Congress voted Paine $800 for his services to the nation. He was subsequently presented by the state of New York with a 300-acre farm at New Rochelle; by Pennsylvania with £500; and by Congress with an additional $3,000 in 1785.

After the Revolution, Paine spent the years 1787 to 1802 in England and France. Although his original purpose was to enlist interest in an iron bridge of his invention, he attracted more attention as a propagandist bent on turning both England and France into republics — initially with his *Rights of Man* (1791 and 1792), defending the actions of the French Revolution, which had begun in 1789. The publication gave a spirited defense of the republican form of government with a written constitution, universal male suffrage, and no artificial distinctions of birth and rank — which, said Paine, was the only way that man's "natural rights" could be guaranteed. The sentiments did not win Paine the friendship of the British government, which indicted him for treason and suppressed the pamphlet, fearing that it would lead (as Paine hoped) to revolution. Before he could be brought to trial, however, he escaped to France and rapidly became involved in revolutionary politics there. Named a French citizen, he was elected a delegate to the revolutionary National Convention, which discussed the deposition of King Louis XVI. Paine, who played a significant role in French revolutionary affairs, served a year in the convention. He was attached to the moderate Girondist party and counseled exile, rather than execution, for the king, arousing the suspicion of Robespierre and the increasingly radical Jacobins. After the Jacobins had crushed the Girondists and instituted the Reign of Terror, Paine was arrested and imprisoned for about 10 months, beginning on December 28, 1793. Late the next year, after the fall of Robespierre, he was reinstated in the convention.

Paine's controversial *Age of Reason*, which appeared in two parts in 1794 and 1796, was a defense of deism, the doctrine that reason and nature, as seen in the logical design of the cosmos, are in themselves, and without benefit of supernatural revelation, sufficient proof of the existence of God. Although *The Age of Reason* attacked a strictly literal interpretation of the Bible, it was, in Paine's words, written "lest in the general wreck of superstition . . . we lose sight of morality . . . humanity, and . . . the theology that is true."

Thomas Jefferson's favorable comment upon the work put Paine squarely in the line of fire between Jefferson and the Federalists who were trying to undermine Jefferson. Toward that end, they falsely accused Paine of being an atheist, a charge that long persisted. It can also be said that Paine's own tactlessness, and such works as his vitriolic *Letter to Washington* (1796) did not increase his popularity.

When Paine returned to the United States in 1802 he discovered that although his services to the cause of freedom had not been wholly forgotten, he was nonetheless almost completely ostracized. He spent his last seven years in poverty and deteriorating health. After his death in New York City on June 8, 1809, he was buried in a corner of his farm at New Rochelle, where a monument was erected to him in 1839. His body, however, was removed to England in 1819 at the direction of the British journalist and reformer William Cobbett.

It was not long after the death of Paine, whose religious beliefs found partial expression in Unitarianism, that religious freethinkers began to observe the anniversary of his birth on January 29. In Boston, for example, it was for some years their custom to decorate their houses and places of business with flags on that date.

A dinner in New York on the 1910 anniversary of his birth was marked by the unveiling of a wax statue of Paine. The statue was later placed in the Thomas Paine Memorial Building at 983 North Avenue, New Rochelle, New York, on Paine's former farmland. The building, open five afternoons a week as a museum, was constructed in 1925 (with inventor Thomas Edison turning the first shovelful of dirt) for the express purpose of honoring Paine and housing some of his letters and personal effects — among them the Franklin stove presented to Paine by Benjamin Franklin. It also contains the Hufeland Collection of New York State and Westchester County materials from the revolutionary period. The cottage in which Paine lived, a two-minute walk from the Memorial Building and on the same 300-acre site, also can be visited by the public. The buildings and grounds are owned by the Huguenot-Thomas Paine Historical Association, a merger of the Huguenot and Historical Association and the Thomas Paine National Historical Association.

Despite the controversy that marked his seldom placid life, Paine is respected as a patriot and leading figure of the American Revolution. A bust of Paine was added to the Hall of Fame for Great Americans in New York City in 1945. Some of his original writings are housed in Philadelphia's Independence Hall.

The Huguenot-Thomas Paine National Historical Association honors him by meeting annually on the Sunday nearest his birthday at the museum in New Rochelle and from time to time a wreath is laid at the Paine monument there.

JANUARY 30

Franklin D. Roosevelt's Birthday

One of the United States' most influential Presidents, Franklin Delano Roosevelt, the 32nd to hold the office, was born on January 30, 1882, on his family's Hudson Valley estate at Hyde Park, New York. Roosevelt began his presidency during the darkest days of the Great Depression, giving decisive leadership to an apprehensive nation on the brink of despair. He was still at the helm eight years later when the Japanese attack on Pearl Harbor precipitated the United States' entry into World War II, and he guided the country's course until almost the end of that global conflict. In all, he served as President a little more than 12 years, longer than any other person, and they were 12 of the most crucial years in the history of the nation.

January 30, the anniversary of Roosevelt's

birth, is a legal holiday in Kentucky and in the US Virgin Islands. He is honored on that day or others by citizens from many parts of the world. Not the least of the honors is the resurgence of interest in his life in recent years. One evidence of this is the steady flow of visitors — some 300,000 each year — to his home at Hyde Park, which is now known as the Home of Franklin D. Roosevelt National Historic Site, administered by the National Park Service and comprising more than 93 acres. Also a magnet for visitors is the Franklin D. Roosevelt Library at the same site, which is administered by the National Archives and Records Service. Throngs — up to a quarter of a million annually — visit the museum section of the library, which is open to the public. Scholars and writers who have made advance written application use the book collection and presidential papers in the library. In 1973 J. C. James, director of the library, reported that it had become the third busiest research center in the field of American history, ranking after the Library of Congress and the National Archives in Washington, D.C.

Roosevelt's birthday is now customarily marked annually at his grave at Hyde Park by family members, friends, and representatives of various organizations. The 11:00 A.M. ceremony begins when members of a color guard of cadets from the US Military Academy at West Point march into the quarter-acre rose garden where the President is buried and take their places in front of his grave. Wreaths are laid by a representative of the Roosevelt Home Club of Hyde Park, by the director of the Franklin D. Roosevelt Library, and by representatives of the local March of Dimes organization and of the Lafayette post of the American Legion. A family member then places cut flowers — traditionally yellow and white chrysanthemums — on his grave. Following this the superintendent of the military academy presents the "President's wreath," and a prayer is offered at the graveside. The ceremony concludes with three volleys by a ceremonial firing squad from the academy, followed by the playing of taps.

On a personal level, the story of Roosevelt's presidency is the story of a physical handicap overcome; and for years, many of the observances of his birthday were related to this fact. He was 39 and already involved in an active political life when he was stricken in August 1921 with poliomyelitis, or infantile paralysis, at his summer home on Campobello Island, off the Maine-New Brunswick coast — a retreat that the First Ladies of the United States and Canada dedicated as Roosevelt Campobello International Park in August 1964.

Roosevelt was severely afflicted with polio and for a time doctors despaired of his life. He survived, however, but with both legs and his lower abdomen paralyzed. In the course of years he gained the ability to walk with crutches and then with a cane while his legs were supported by iron braces. Three years after he was stricken, Roosevelt went to Warm Springs, Georgia, and found so much help from swimming in the warm pool there that he acquired the springs, a nearby hotel and cottages, and some 1,200 acres of land. After the American Orthopedic Association had confirmed his findings by experiments with other paralytics, Roosevelt, in January 1927, established the nonprofit Georgia Warm Springs Foundation for the benefit of other polio sufferers. In 1938, the National Foundation for Infantile Paralysis was incorporated with Roosevelt as founder. With support from the foundation's annual March of Dimes, new vaccines were developed that have almost obliterated the threat of polio.

Franklin Delano Roosevelt was descended on his father's side from Claes Martenszan van Rosenvelt, who arrived in New Amsterdam about 1649 from the Netherlands. The New World ancestors of his mother, the former Sara Delano, dated back to Philippe de la Noye, of French-Dutch lineage, who arrived in Plymouth colony in the 1620s. James Roosevelt, the father of FDR (as he came to be called), was vice president of the Delaware & Hudson Railroad and lived on the estate at Hyde Park that his family had owned for a hundred years. His only child grew up there, educated by governesses and tutors, and spent summer vacations on Campobello Island, where he developed a lifetime interest in ships and sailing.

At 14, Franklin Roosevelt, a reserved boy, was sent to the strict Groton School in Groton, Massachusetts, where he sometimes "felt left out" and was an intelligent but not outstanding student. He entered Harvard in 1900, and it was during his freshman year there that his father died. While studying at the university, Roosevelt was a member of, among others, the Fly and Hasty Pudding clubs, both of which he served as librarian; and he did well scholastically. Indeed, he finished the requirements for his A.B. degree in three years, but stayed on for a fourth in order to serve as editor-in-chief of the *Harvard Crimson*.

By then, two important developments had taken place. First, Roosevelt's interest in politics had been intensified by the career of his fifth cousin, Republican Theodore Roosevelt (see October 27). As William McKinley's Vice President, "Teddy" Roosevelt, as he was affectionately known, succeeded to the presidency on September 14, 1901, after McKinley had been shot by an assassin (see September 6). TR won election to the presidency in his own right in 1904 and one of the votes contributing to his substantial victory was that of his cousin Franklin Roosevelt, afterward a lifelong Democrat.

The second important development was marriage. During his years at Harvard, FDR had fallen in love with his shy fifth-cousin-once-removed, Anna Eleanor Roosevelt, self-described as the "ugly duckling" of her socially prominent family. Eleanor Roosevelt, who was to win such admiration in the course of her lifetime that she would ultimately be referred to as the First Lady of the World (see October 11), was the niece of Theodore Roosevelt, and it was he who gave her away when she married Franklin Roosevelt on March 17, 1905.

FDR meanwhile had entered Columbia Law School in the fall of 1904. Following a delayed honeymoon in Europe, the young couple lived in a house on East 36th Street in New York City. The first of their six children (one of whom died in infancy) was born in 1906. After Roosevelt passed the New York bar examination in 1907, he began to practice law in New York City with the firm of Carter, Ledyard and Milburn, an association that lasted about three years. One of his fellow law clerks later recalled his having explained during this period that he wanted, at the first chance, to run for public office and that he would, in fact, like to be President.

While practicing law — in which he had only limited interest, though he felt zest for trying cases in court — Roosevelt also spent a good deal of time at Hyde Park managing the family property and participating in community affairs in Hyde Park and the surrounding Dutchess County area. The opportunity to run for office was not long in coming. As the son of a leading local family, he was offered his district's Democratic nomination for the state Senate in 1910. He was elected after an energetic campaign, even though the district usually voted Republican, and he was reelected in 1912. In Albany, he attracted notice as the leader of a band of insurgents who rebelled against the dominance of Tammany Hall in New York City Democratic politics. In 1911 and 1912 he was prominent in the effort to secure the Democratic presidential nomination for Woodrow Wilson, organizing independent Democrats for Wilson and leading an unofficial delegation to the Democratic convention in Baltimore. After Wilson's election Roosevelt was offered several posts in the new administration. He accepted with enthusiasm the one that meshed with his longtime interest in the sea, serving in Washington as assistant secretary of the navy from 1913 to 1920. Commenting on the appointment, Theodore Roosevelt wrote FDR, "It is interesting to see that you are in another place which I myself once held."

However, although Franklin Roosevelt served creditably in the post, his upward political mobility slowed at this point. His run for the US Senate in 1914 was unsuccessful and although he was nominated as Vice President in 1920 on a ticket headed by James M. Cox, the Democrats lost the presidency that year to Republican Warren G. Harding, whose running mate was Calvin Coolidge. Then came the crippling attack of polio of August 1921, which imperiled not only Roosevelt's political career, but even his life.

Roosevelt's optimism and refusal to accept defeat in the face of this adversity are by now legendary. They shed light on a similar attitude he was to exhibit in a much wider sphere, and with effects on the entire nation, just over a decade later. Determined to regain his health, he ignored his mother's exhortations to retire to a life of leisure (and semi-invalidism) at Hyde Park, and set up for himself a strenuous program of exercise — particularly swimming, which he found most helpful. The effort occupied a large part of his time for the next several years. Through it all, however, his fundamental preoccupation with politics never waned and he kept up an extensive correspondence that kept him in touch with political figures across the nation.

By 1924, his vitality had returned and he resumed work. Dissolving his association with Emmet, Marvin and Roosevelt, the law partnership he had begun with Langdon Marvin in 1910 and reentered in 1920, he entered into a new law partnership with Basil O'Connor. He also resumed his work with the New York office of a surety bonding firm, the Fidelity and Deposit Company of Maryland, of which he had become a vice president after his campaign for the vice presidency of the United States in 1920.

The year 1924 also marked Roosevelt's return to national politics, when he proceeded by wheelchair and then on crutches to the platform at the Democratic National Convention in New York and electrified the gathering with his speech proposing Governor Alfred E. Smith of New York as the party's nominee for President. Although the nomination went to another, Smith was forever after known by Roosevelt's characterization of him as the Happy Warrior.

On the suggestion of an old friend who had written about the restorative potential of the warm, natural springs he owned in western Georgia, Roosevelt proceeded to that spot as soon as the convention was over and found so much help there that he returned the following spring. It was not until 1927 that he purchased this property, vesting title in the Warm Springs Foundation. In the meantime, other polio victims, reading of Roosevelt's "swimming himself back to health," began to flock to the place. Since it was not yet staffed with medical personnel, it was Roosevelt himself who inspired his fellow paralytics with his optimism and supervised their exercises. Ultimately he ventured perhaps as much as two-thirds of his none-too-ample inheritance on the acquisition and upkeep of the Warm Springs center.

In 1928 Roosevelt, then able to walk with braces and canes, again nominated Smith, who became the Democratic candidate for President but who was substantially defeated by the Republican candidate, Herbert Hoover. The same year, Smith persuaded Roosevelt — who had intended for health reasons to spend another two years in private life — to run as the Democratic candidate for governor of New York State. After a vigorous campaign, and in the face of the Republican sweep of most of the nation, Roosevelt was successful in his bid, and he was reelected governor in 1930. His term in that office was one more in a series of similarities between his career in politics and that of his older cousin Theodore Roosevelt.

The Great Depression meanwhile had begun, following the stock market crash of 1929 (see October 29), and it was against this background that the Democrats met at Chicago in 1932 to choose a candidate for President. On the fourth ballot the delegates chose Roosevelt. Characteristically breaking precedent, he flew to Chicago to accept the nomination in person, and pledged in his acceptance speech "a new deal for the American people." His energetic election campaign emphasized the plight of the "forgotten man at the bottom of the economic pyramid." With his vice presidential running mate, John Nance Garner, Roosevelt won overwhelmingly in November over the ticket headed by President Hoover, gaining over 22 million popular votes to the Republicans' 15 million; and 472 electoral college votes to the Republicans' 59.

The nation's economic crisis deepened in the period between election day and Roosevelt's inauguration on March 4, 1933. By the time he had taken office, the nation's unemployed numbered between 12 and 15 million; one-seventh of the population was subsisting on public or private relief; industrial production was down to about half that of 1929; factory gates by the hundreds had closed; ships and locomotives stood idle; and some 5,504 banks had failed. A mood bordering on panic pervaded the nation. Roosevelt, however, was prepared for action. In the interim between election and inauguration, he had gathered around him a group of advisers later referred to as his Brain Trust. They and other experts set their minds to devising programs to meet the crisis.

On Inauguration Day, a Saturday, the new President set the tone for what was to come. Jaunty, confident, and optimistic, he declared in his inaugural address that "the only thing we have to fear is fear itself." On Sunday, March 5, he issued two proclamations. One called the 73rd Congress to meet in special session on Thursday, March 9. The other declared a four-day bank holiday beginning on Monday, March 6, which closed all the nation's banks. Those of demonstrated soundness, a large majority, were permitted to reopen soon afterward under new, stricter controls.

Roosevelt's New Deal began with a series of messages to Congress, interspersed with specific legislation proposed to implement them, which he fired off in rapid order. The country and its legislators were ready for strong leadership. During Roosevelt's famous first "Hundred Days" in office, the special session of Congress acted with breathtaking speed to pass more legislation of consequence than had ever been enacted in any comparable peacetime period, jolting a desperate nation out of its paralysis and starting it on the road to recovery.

Aimed at supplying relief, bringing economic recovery, and avoiding crises of such serious dimensions in the future, the measures were designed to, among other things, stabilize the banking system, create jobs, give financial assistance to the needy, insure better farm income, protect home owners and investors, begin a vast program of public works, and reform dealings in investments and securities. The titles of some of the measures are indicative of their scope: the Emergency Banking Act (March 9); the Emergency Farm Mortgage Act (May 12); the Federal Securities Act (May 27), requiring full information on new issues and in other ways protecting investors; the National Employment System Act (June 6); the Home Owners Refinancing Act (June 13); the Glass-Steagall Banking Act, creating the Federal Deposit Insurance Corporation (June 16); the Farm Credit Act (June 16).

Numerous government agencies were established — among them such "alphabet" agencies as the Civilian Conservation Corps (CCC, created on March 31), which provided work in reforestation, road construction, flood control, soil protection and national park projects for up to a quarter million 18-to-25-year-olds; the Agricultural Adjustment Administration (AAA, May 12), which undertook to raise agricultural purchasing power by subsidizing farmers to curtail basic crops in an effort to eliminate surpluses and raise prices; the Federal Emergency Relief Administration (FERA, May 12); and the Tennessee Valley Authority (TVA, May 18), which involved the government in a precedent-setting effort at regional planning and development designed to benefit residents in a seven-state area. The TVA eventually created a series of 16 dams, provided electrical power and fertilizers, among other things, and contributed to navigation, flood control, land cultivation, and reforestation in the region. Also born in the hundred-day period were the National Recovery Administration (NRA), created under the National Industrial Recovery Act (NIRA, June 16), which provided for industrial self-regulation under federal supervision and included among its goals increased production and employment, prevention of ruinous competition, extension to labor of the right to organize and bargain collectively, and the realization of higher wages and a shorter work week. Also established under the NIRA was the Public Works Administration (PWA), which sought to "prime the pump" of consumer power by adding to employment and business activity by means of a substantial public works program for the construction of roads, public buildings, military airports, and other facilities. The Works Progress (or Projects) Administration (WPA), a huge federal work program consolidating earlier relief efforts (other than the CCC and PWA, which continued separately) was added to the list of alphabet agencies in May 1935. Before its official termination in the early 1940s, the WPA had expended more than $11 million, providing jobs for some 8 million persons. Its more than 250,000 projects emphasized various kinds of construction work and improvements, and also included special writing, art, theater, and music projects whose influence long outlasted the WPA. Supplementing the WPA was the National Youth Administration (NYA), which provided part-time work, usually in schools, colleges, and universities, for 16-to-25-year-olds.

There were other key measures during Roosevelt's first administration. An act was passed creating the Securities and Exchange Commission, with power to regulate stock exchanges and dealings in securities. Congress approved the National Labor Relations (or Wagner-Connery) Act (July 5, 1935), which reasserted labor's right to bargain collectively, strengthened guarantees against coercion by employers, and established the National Labor Relations Board (NLRB) with power to supervise elections (when so requested) to determine employees' choice of a bargaining unit to represent them. The NLRB also was authorized to certify the duly selected union. The Social Security Act was passed (August 14, 1935) to provide old-age insurance and unemployment compensation. Particularly controversial was Roosevelt's program to redistribute the burden of taxes according to ability to pay. Legislation was passed to move toward this goal via inheritance levies, income surtaxes, corporation taxes, and other measures — which his critics labeled as a "soak the rich" approach. During Roosevelt's first term in office, the United States also went off the gold standard. In foreign affairs the nation embarked on the President's Good Neighbor policy in its relations with Latin America and also extended diplomatic recognition to the USSR.

Roosevelt was renominated by acclamation at the Democratic National Convention held in Philadelphia in June 1936. He won reelection in November by a precedent-shattering margin: with a plurality of more than 11 million in the popular vote and all but eight of the electoral votes, he carried every state except Maine and Vermont against the Republican ticket headed by Governor Alfred M. Landon of Kansas. In early 1937 Roosevelt became the first President inaugurated under the terms of the 20th Amendment to the US Constitution, which set January 20 as the date on which presidential terms begin.

His second inaugural address stressed the fact that, despite past accomplishments, a great deal remained to be done; that still, as he phrased it, "I see one-third of a nation ill-housed, ill-clad, ill-nourished." Reforms strengthening or extending the earlier New Deal legislation were enacted during his second term as President, as were acts to replace some New Deal measures that had been declared unconstitutional by a Supreme Court that was increasingly hostile to his program. Among the new enactments were the Bituminous Coal Act; the Farm Tenancy Act; and the Wagner-Steagall Housing Act of 1937, which established the US Housing Authority to assist in the provision of low-income housing. Also passed — in 1938 — were the second Agricultural Adjustment Act; the Food, Drug, and Cosmetic Act, containing important provisions for consumer protection and providing for their enforcement by the

Food and Drug Administration and Federal Trade Commission; and the Fair Labor Standards Act establishing minimum wages and providing for the 40-hour work week.

But the passage of Roosevelt-proposed measures in Congress was increasingly an uphill battle. The New Deal had won ardent admirers. It had pulled the country back from the verge of despair and had established the concept that government, through appropriate regulation of a free society, had a responsibility for maintaining the economic well-being of citizens. But it also had inspired impassioned opposition. Included among the dissenters were not only bankers and businessmen who deplored the deficit financing that helped pay for costly New Deal programs and resented what they saw as too much government regulation, but also other citizens who feared that New Deal concepts would destroy private enterprise and impair such traditional American qualities as frugality, initiative, self-reliance, and the "rugged individualism" that had been prized since pioneer days.

The recession of 1937, which political opponents were quick to call the "Roosevelt recession," did nothing to ease the way of additional New Deal legislation through Congress. Neither did the industrial strife that characterized the late 1930s as labor, with the encouragement of earlier New Deal measures, moved rapidly to organize. Roosevelt's controversial attempt to enlarge — critics said "pack" — the nine-member Supreme Court brought additional antagonism. His proposal, bitterly opposed, died in committee in the Senate, even though he eventually achieved his goal of having a more liberal Supreme Court, especially as a succession of retirements gave him the unusual opportunity to appoint seven new justices, by 1941.

Across the Atlantic, meanwhile, dictatorship and aggression had begun to appear. Most Americans, exhausted by the depression and wary of foreign entanglements, were content, for a time, to look the other way. The tide of isolationism ran strong. Roosevelt was quicker than most of his compatriots to recognize the danger to democracies and all Western civilization in such events as Italy's conquest of Ethiopia in 1935 under the Fascist dictator Benito Mussolini; dictator Francisco Franco's accession to power in the Spanish Civil War of 1936–1939; militaristic Japan's policy of aggression toward China; and especially the actions of Adolf Hitler, the Nazi dictator, who had come to power in Germany in 1933. Under Hitler Germany had remilitarized the Rhineland in 1936; adopted a policy of increasingly oppressive anti-Semitism; annexed Austria in 1938; swallowed up Czechoslovakia in 1938 and 1939; and invaded Poland on September 1, 1939. The last act, which precipitated declarations of war against Germany by Britain and France two days later, marked the beginning of World War II in Europe (see September 1).

Though their prime concern at first was to stay out of the war, most Americans were sympathetic toward Britain, France, and the other Allies and opposed to Germany and its Axis partners, particularly as world domination, brutality, oppression, and the extermination of Jews came to be seen with growing clarity as the deliberate policy of the Nazi-led Axis. As the true nature of the threat became ever more clear — especially after Hitler's blitzkrieging legions swept Norway, Denmark, the Low Countries, and France in 1940, leaving a heroically defiant Britain alone against the advancing tide — the US public's desire to stay out of war began to be increasingly outweighed by its concern for the survival of the free world.

During the country's slow transition away from isolationism, Roosevelt took what actions he could to strengthen the United States and increase its preparedness in the face of the growing menace. He secured congressional appropriations for expansion of a two-ocean US Navy and, after the fighting had begun in Europe in September 1939, he persuaded a special session of Congress to repeal the arms embargo provision of the Neutrality Act of 1937 so that Britain and France could buy arms from the United States on a cash-and-carry basis. As the disasters of 1940 unfolded in Europe, and particularly after the fall of France, his requests for defense appropriations increased. Directly or through intermediaries the US government released for British use mounting stores of "old" or surplus arms, munitions, and aircraft. Then, as the battle of Britain raged, with German bombers blasting that island fortress in preparation for an expected invasion, Roosevelt acted in September to transfer 50 overage US destroyers to the British in exchange for 99-year leases on eight naval and air bases in the Western Hemisphere. The action, by executive order and without the approval of Congress, was controversial, provoking protests from noninterventionists. Later the same month the President signed the Selective Training and Service Act, the nation's first peacetime draft, which Congress had passed after months of debate. A scant 11 days later, Japan officially joined the Axis.

Against this backdrop, Roosevelt meanwhile had been nominated as the Democratic contender for the presidency in the 1940 election and had chosen Secretary of Agriculture Henry A. Wallace as his vice presidential running mate. The Republicans had nominated for President the affable internationalist Wendell L. Willkie, who ran with Senator Charles L. McNary of Oregon. During the campaign both Roosevelt and Willkie went on record as opposing US entry into the war, but as supporting hemispheric defense and aid to embattled Britain. Roosevelt won the November election — becoming the first person ever to hold the presidency for three terms — but with a plurality under 5 million, smaller than his previous margins.

On December 29 the President, in one of his famous radio "fireside chats," emphasized the global nature of the Axis threat and urged a huge effort to increase production and turn the still technically neutral United States into the "arsenal of democracy." Recognizing that Britain soon would exhaust its ability to buy arms on a cash basis, Roosevelt, in his annual message to Congress on January 6, 1941, urged adoption of what became the Lend-Lease Act. This legislation, signed into law on March 11, provided that any nation whose defense the President judged essential to that of the United States could be loaned arms and supplies on the understanding that they could be returned or replaced — either in kind, or by goods, services, or other benefits — after the end of hostilities. Initially intended primarily for Britain and Nationalist China, Lend-Lease assistance was later extended to other countries, eventually reaching a total of more than $50 billion. Britain's Prime Minister Winston Churchill referred to the legislation as the "most unsordid act in the history of any nation."

Such a policy, the President had hoped in his January message to Congress, would make possible a "world founded upon four essential human freedoms" — freedom of speech and expression, freedom of worship, freedom from want, and freedom from fear (see January 6, The "Four Freedoms" Enunciated). Anglo-US goals were defined further in the Atlantic Charter (see August 14). This declaration of common principles, formulated during Roosevelt and Churchill's August 1941 meetings off the coast of Newfoundland, came to serve as a statement of the war aims of the Allies.

With passage of the Lend-Lease Act in March 1941, the United States, still technically neutral, had all but abandoned its claim to that status. Events moved rapidly during the remainder of 1941. Adding to their earlier conquests, the Axis powers were moving relentlessly across Eastern Europe and the war had spread to North Africa (see November 8). In April the United States agreed to defend Greenland against invasion, declaring it vital to the security of the Western Hemisphere. As the international situation worsened, President Roosevelt, on May 27, proclaimed an unlimited national emergency. In June he ordered the freezing of all German and Italian assets in the United States and directed German and Italian consulates to be closed. In July he announced that, by agreement with Iceland, US forces would take over the defense of that country for the duration of the war, and would keep ship convoy lines open as far as Iceland.

As summer turned to fall, German submarines operating in the Atlantic increasingly took their toll of ships carrying goods to Britain. American ships in the Iceland area were among those the Nazi raiders attacked, triggering several reactions. After an attack on the US destroyer *Greer* in early September, ships of the US Navy, theretofore forbidden to shoot unless fired upon, were given new orders on September 11: in Roosevelt's words, "American naval vessels and American planes will no longer wait until Axis submarines . . . strike [the first blow]." Early the next month he asked Congress to repeal the most restrictive parts of the Neutrality Act of 1939, a request Congress granted in mid-November. Thereafter, previously defenseless US merchant ships were armed. For the first time, they also were allowed to go to Allied ports with military supplies, meaning that they could travel all the way to England.

As US friendship was demonstrated in increasingly specific ways, Britain meanwhile had gained another powerful ally in an unexpected quarter. In an incredible gamble, Hitler, who had had a mutual nonaggression pact with the Soviet Union since August 1939, suddenly invaded his supposed ally on June 22, 1941. Roosevelt pledged US aid to the attacked Russians two days later, and on July 12 Britain and the Soviet Union signed a pact of mutual assistance, which precluded the signing of a separate peace treaty with Germany by either power.

Any remaining ambiguity in the United States' increasingly unneutral stance was removed forever when Japan, the Far Eastern member of the Axis, suddenly attacked the US naval installation at Pearl Harbor, Hawaii, on December 7, 1941, "a date which," the President declared, "shall live in infamy." The next day he asked a suddenly united Congress to declare that "since [that] unprovoked and dastardly attack . . . a state of war has existed between the United States and the Japanese

Empire." Within four hours both houses of Congress had approved the declaration of war with only a single dissenting vote. On December 11 Japan's Axis partners, Germany and Italy, declared war against the United States — which reciprocated by declaring war on them the same day.

Although dismal years were ahead, the dreaded invasion of Britain and the feared Axis conquest of the entire free world were averted after the Allies took the offensive — first in North Africa; then in Sicily (see July 10) and on the Italian mainland; and ultimately with the long-awaited second front, beginning with the Allied invasion of France (see June 6, D Day) in 1944.

Roosevelt's role in the war was, of course, immense. He authorized a mammoth effort by scientists to develop an atomic bomb after fellow scientists had persuaded Albert Einstein (see March 15) to warn the President in 1939 about the potential of such a weapon — and the danger that German scientists, already on the track, would develop it first. As one of the major leaders of the free world, Roosevelt also was the author of, or participant in, the major decisions on how the war was to be conducted — where and when offensives were to be launched, in what order, and under whose command. His was an influential presence at the series of wartime conferences with Churchill and with the Soviet Russian Premier Joseph Stalin, the Nationalist Chinese leader Chiang Kai-shek, and others; and he cast his weight strongly in favor of the creation of a postwar organization designed to maintain peace.

In 1944, with the war still raging, Roosevelt was nominated by the Democrats for an unprecedented fourth term. With his vice presidential running mate, Harry S. Truman, he defeated the Republican candidates Governor Thomas E. Dewey of New York and John W. Bricker of Ohio in November, with a plurality of 3.59 million. Before the election Roosevelt had contributed substantially to the conferences held at Bretton Woods, New Hampshire, to plan for international monetary and financial cooperation in the postwar years, and at Dumbarton Oaks, near Washington, D.C., where a framework was drawn up for what later became the United Nations Organization. Soon after his fourth inauguration a plainly exhausted President Roosevelt left to meet with Churchill and Stalin in the February 1945 conference at Yalta in the Russian Crimea. There the leaders concerned themselves with specific measures for the final defeat of the Axis, including Russia's commitment to fight against Japan after Germany was defeated; with details of postwar occupation and boundaries; and with the "earliest possible establishment . . . of a general international organization to maintain peace and security."

To the immense relief of the free world, Germany surrendered in May 1945 (see May 8, V-E Day). The war in Asia (see December 7, Pearl Harbor Day; January 26, Douglas MacArthur's Birthday; February 24, Chester William Nimitz's Birthday) ended after the atomic bomb was dropped on two Japanese cities (see August 5) with effects so devastating that the world still lives in terror of the weapon. The Japanese capitulation followed shortly (see August 14, V-J Day, and September 2, World War II Ends).

President Roosevelt, however, did not live to see the final Allied victory. On April 12, 1945, he had been stricken with a massive cerebral hemorrhage at the Little White House, the modest home he had built at Warm Springs, Georgia, in 1932.

To the present time, everything in the house, which can now be visited by the public, remains as it was when he died, even to the unfinished portrait for which he was sitting at the time. The nearby Franklin D. Roosevelt Museum and Auditorium, situated in a 4,000-acre park, contains Roosevelt mementos and regularly exhibits a 12-minute film depicting his life at the springs. Flags and native stones from the 50 states line the walk that leads from the museum to a memorial fountain at the park's entrance. The entire property was deeded to the state of Georgia in 1947.

Roosevelt's body was taken from Warm Springs to Washington. The flag-draped coffin remained briefly in the East Room of the White House, while on the Capitol the flag flew at half-staff for the seventh President to die in office. Later, Roosevelt's body was taken to his family estate at Hyde Park, New York, and buried in the rose garden, the grave marked — as the President had requested — by a plain white marble tombstone bearing his name and the dates of his birth and death and, below that, the name and date of birth of his wife, Anna Eleanor Roosevelt. (She was buried beside him in 1962.) Apart from the customary wreath-laying ceremony on the President's birthday, the anniversary of his death is marked annually by a memorial service at the grave. In addition a major memorial observance takes place in the rose garden on Memorial Day, usually with a person of national prominence delivering the main address.

In contrast to the elaborate monuments to some other Presidents, the memorial to Roosevelt in Washington, D.C., is, as he had requested, no bigger than his desktop and "plain, without any ornamentation." It is located in the center of what he had referred to as "that green plot in front of the Archives Building." It was dedicated on April 12, 1965, the 20th anniversary of his death. Proposals for a more elaborate memorial have been made from time to time, but agreement has not been reached on the form it should take. In New York City, Welfare Island was renamed Roosevelt Island in 1973 and a memorial to the late President was designed for its southern tip.

One innovation of President Roosevelt's has been of special importance to writers and scholars. He was the first Chief Executive to give his presidential and other papers to the government – which also received his extensive book collection and personal mementos, as well as 16 acres of his Hyde Park land as the site for a building to house them. Presidential papers previously had been considered the personal property of the various Presidents, with the result that from the time of George Washington, many items of historical interest had been treated in disparate and sometimes haphazard ways. Some were simply discarded; others, which fell into the hands of individuals or private institutions, were widely scattered; some were placed in the Library of Congress.

Accepting Roosevelt's gift, Congress, by a joint resolution approved on July 18, 1939, established the Franklin D. Roosevelt Library as a federal agency. The library, erected entirely from funds donated by the President's admirers, was accepted by the government on July 4, 1940. Its establishment created a precedent for the maintenance of presidential libraries by the government, which, by a 1955 act, was empowered to accept and maintain not only the historical materials of any President, but also buildings in which to preserve them.

The Roosevelt Library was substantially enlarged by addition of the Eleanor Roosevelt wings, dedicated on May 3, 1972. Virtually all of Franklin D. Roosevelt's papers, many of them previously subject to restriction, had become available for study by 1972.

JANUARY 31

James G. Blaine's Birthday

James G. Blaine, who at the height of his career was the most popular political leader in the country, was born in West Brownsville, Pennsylvania, on January 31, 1830. He was graduated from Washington (now Washington

and Jefferson) College in Washington, Pennsylvania, at the age of 17. After spending the next half dozen years as a teacher and student of law in Kentucky and Pennsylvania, he moved to Augusta, Maine, and became part-owner and editor of the Kennebec *Journal* in 1854.

Attending the first national convention of the newly organized Republican party in 1856, he played an active role in the formation of the party in Maine. As a journalist he was instrumental in making the name Republican widely known in the East. In 1857 he became editor of the *Advertiser* in Portland, Maine, a position that he held for three years.

At the age of 28, Blaine was elected to the larger house of the state legislature in 1858, and rose to the post of speaker two years later. In the meantime, he had been made chairman of the Republican state committee. He was elected to the national House of Representatives in 1862 and served there until 1876 – as its Speaker from 1869 to 1875.

Blaine was an aspirant for the Republican presidential nomination in 1876, but the publication of what are known as the Mulligan letters, suggesting that he had used his political influence for his personal profit, weakened his support and he lost the nomination. Immediately after that year's election, however, he was appointed by the state of Maine to fill a vacancy in the US Senate. Soon afterwards he was elected to a full Senate term. Blaine was again a candidate for his party's presidential nomination in 1880, but failed for a second time to receive it.

Four years later, however, he finally did win the nomination and ran against Grover Cleveland (see March 18), whom the Democrats had named as their nominee. With the independent Republicans, or mugwumps, bolting the party ticket and opposing Blaine's election, Cleveland was successful. His success was by a narrow margin, however – so narrow that some observers laid the blame for Blaine's defeat on a single issue – his failure to repudiate promptly the speech of a supporter who called the Democrats the party of "Rum, Romanism, and Rebellion." The offending speech, by the Reverend Samuel D. Burchard at New York City's Fifth Avenue Hotel on October 29, 1884, may have cost Blaine the support of Catholic voters in New York City; Blaine, who was present when the remark was made, may or may not have heard it. It is certain, in any event, that he lost the crucial state of New York; that he also lost the presidential election; and that it may, as often alleged, have been for this reason.

President James Garfield, elected in 1880,

had made Blaine secretary of state, but after the assassination of Garfield in 1881 (see July 2) Blaine resigned — although not before he had sought modification of the Clayton-Bulwer Treaty of 1850 between the United States and Great Britain. Modification of its terms was not accomplished until after Blaine's death, but when it did take place, with the Hay-Pauncefote Treaty of 1901, it laid the groundwork for the Panama Canal (see January 7) by making it possible for a canal entirely under US auspices to be constructed across the Isthmus of Panama.

Blaine became secretary of state a second time, under President Benjamin Harrison in 1889. It was through his interest in building a constructive foreign policy that Blaine made his most lasting contribution to history. With an international concern that was well ahead of his time, he was particularly noted for his consistent Pan-Americanism. Long the champion of an inter-American system that would provide for arbitration to offset tensions and prevent conflicts, and that also would facilitate planning of cooperative measures for the mutual advantage of the United States and Latin America, Blaine presided over the first Pan-American Conference (see October 2) during his second term as secretary of state. Also favoring increased trade within the hemisphere, he urged adoption of reciprocity treaties with Latin American nations that might contribute toward that end.

Blaine was the author of *Twenty Years of Congress,* an autobiographical work, and he also published a volume of political addresses. After his resignation from his State Department post in June of 1892, his health went rapidly downhill. He died in Washington, D.C., on January 27, 1893.

February

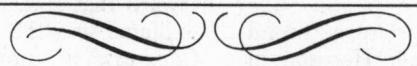

February (*Februarius,* derived from the Latin *februa,* feast of purification) is the second month in the Gregorian or New Style calendar in use today. It usually has 28 days, although in leap years (see February 29) it consists of 29. Like January, February was originally omitted from the early Roman calendar, which was composed of only 10 months, March through December. To complete the calendar year, the Romans inserted a blank number of days or an occasional intercalary month in the "dead" season of midwinter, between the last month of the year — December — and the first month of the next year — March. According to tradition, Numa Pompilius, the legendary second Roman king (about 715–672 B.C.), created the months of *Januarius* and *Februarius* out of this previously unnamed period. He is said to have inaugurated a complicated calendar, operating on a four-year cycle, in which the number of days allotted to February varied from 23 to 29, depending upon the year.

Julius Caesar revised the lengths of the months in his calendar reform, which was adopted in 45 B.C. (see Appendix, The Calendar). His calendar, which is now known as the Julian or Old Style calendar, made February 28 days long, but in every fourth year contained an extra day between February 23 and 24. The Romans, counting back from March 1 — the Kalends or first day of the month — called "both" February 24ths the sixth of the Kalends of March, hence the term *bissextile,* literally meaning "sixth twice," for a leap year. Another explanation, although no longer credited, has been given to account for the changes in the lengths of the months. This holds that Emperor Augustus, after it was proposed that a month be named for him, insisted out of vanity that the month contain 31 days — as many as the

longer months. Specifically, he supposedly did not wish "his" month to have fewer days than July, named after Julius Caesar. Augustus, so the story goes, therefore "stole" time from February to add to August, which had previously had fewer than 31 days.

The name *Februarius* arose from the Roman ceremonies of religious purification and expiation, which took place during that month in anticipation of the new year, which originally began on March 1. Among the most important festivals was the *Lupercalia,* the ancient feast of fruitfulness, or fertility, on February 15. This celebration had originated in early Roman times, when the small settlement on the Palatine Hill earned its livelihood by cultivating the soil and keeping flocks and herds. The rites were under the supervision of a corporation of priests called the *Luperci,* divided into two colleges called *Quinctillani* and *Fabiani,* and each headed by a master (*magister*). In 44 B.C. a third college, the *Luperci Iulii,* was instituted in honor of Julius Caesar; and on February 15 of that year, Mark Antony, as its master, offered to make Caesar king, just a month before the latter's assassination. Shakespeare alludes to the *Lupercalia* in Mark Antony's famous oration in *Julius Caesar:* "You all did see that on the Lupercal / I thrice presented him a kingly crown, / Which he did thrice refuse. . . .

It is not known if the ritual honored some particular deity, such as the god "Lupercus," now recognized as a mere invention of past speculators. Some scholars, however, claim that the *Lupercalia* honored a pastoral deity, probably Faunus. Whatever the case, the *Lupercalian* rites began as the priests assembled in the cave of Lupercal on the southwestern part of the Palatine Hill, where Romulus and Remus, the legendary founders of Rome, were supposed to have been nourished by a she-wolf. There the priests sacrificed goats and a young dog, after which the foreheads of two youthful *Luperci* of high rank were smeared with the blood of the victims. After the blood had been wiped off with wool dipped in milk, ritual required that the two youths laugh. Following a sacrificial feast, they stripped themselves naked to don only a loincloth fashioned from the skins of the slain goats. Holding strips of the hides, they ran around the walls of the old Palatine community, striking all those whom they encountered, but especially women, a process that was believed to ensure fertility and safe delivery in childbirth. The feast probably also served as a rustic purification rite to protect animals and crops.

The *Lupercalia* continued to be observed well into the Christian era. Several scholars contend that Pope Gelasius I introduced the Feast of the Purification of the Virgin Mary, commonly called Candlemas (see February 2), in A.D. 494, to counteract the excesses of the pagan *Lupercalia.*

The Saxons called the month of February *Sprout-kale,* from the fact that kale sprouted at that season. They later changed the name to *Sol-monath* in recognition of the returning strength of the sun. Charlemagne used the designation *Hornung,* referring to the shedding of horns by stags. The lucky birthstone often associated with February is the amethyst.

FEBRUARY 1

Victor Herbert's Birthday

Victor Herbert, the composer, conductor, and cellist who is especially known for the operettas with which he brightened the American stage, was born in Dublin, Ireland, on February 1, 1859. He was the son of Edward Herbert, an attorney, and Fanny Lover Herbert. After the death of his father when young Herbert was three, he and his mother went to live for five years near London, in the home of his maternal grandfather, the Irish novelist, actor, painter, and musician Samuel Lover.

After his grandfather introduced him to music, his mother, an accomplished pianist, began giving him piano lessons. So obvious were his musical gifts that his grandfather urged that he be taken to Germany for further training. In 1867, accordingly, he went with his mother to a village on Lake Constance. After his mother met and married a German physician, Carl Schmid, the family moved to Stuttgart, where Victor Herbert received academic training at the gymnasium and studied music at the Stutt-gart Conservatory, where he specialized in playing the cello. In addition he studied under Bernhard Cossmann, one of the virtuoso cellists of the century, in Baden-Baden. An eager pupil, Herbert recalled years later, "I had exceptional advantages. . . . My lessons were no fifteen-minute affairs, and then away at something else. I was under the constant eye of my master, and I could not help making rapid progress."

Launched upon a successful musical career, Herbert spent some four years touring Europe, giving solo performances and playing in both small-town and important symphony orchestras, principally in Germany and Austria, and also in France and Italy. Some of the orchestras were conducted by world-renowned musicians, Brahms, Liszt, and Saint-Saëns among them, and the experience provided rigorous training. At one point during this period – in 1882 – he became first cellist with the Eduard Strauss orchestra in Vienna. In 1883 he returned to Stuttgart, where he was engaged by the conductor of the Stuttgart Royal Orchestra, the violinist and composer Max Seifritz. Recognizing young Herbert's abilities in the field of composition, Seifritz gave him lessons in composition and orchestration and encouraged him to begin composing seriously. Herbert's first two works of consequence, a suite and a concerto, were introduced by the Stuttgart orchestra with himself as soloist.

By this time the tall, good-looking, Irish musician reportedly had become typically Teutonic in his mannerisms. He won the heart of Theresa Foerster, prima donna of the Vienna Court Opera, who was appearing in Stuttgart. When she was offered a contract with the Metropolitan Opera Company in New York City, she agreed to accept only on condition that Herbert, by then her fiancé, be employed as cellist with the Metropolitan Opera House orchestra. The young couple was married on August 14, 1886, and sailed for the United States soon afterwards.

From the moment he set foot on American soil until his death almost four decades later, Victor Herbert wholeheartedly embraced his adopted land and influenced and was influenced by its musical heritage. For a number of years, he won fame primarily as a leading cellist with such renowned orchestras as the Theodore Thomas Orchestra and the New York Philharmonic. However, from the late 1880s on, he also attracted increasing notice as a conductor. He served as associate conductor of the Worcester, Massachusetts, Festival, where his oratorio *The Captive* was performed in 1891. In 1893 he became bandmaster of the famous 22nd Regiment Band of the New York

National Guard; in 1898, principal conductor of the Pittsburgh Symphony Orchestra; and after 1904, director of his own concert assemblage — the immensely popular Victor Herbert's New York Orchestra.

Although eminently successful as an instrumentalist and conductor, Victor Herbert is now best known as a composer. The music he wrote for the concert and operatic stage is scarcely remembered; but the more than 35 works that he created for the light operatic theater teem with stirring marches, lively drinking songs, lilting waltzes, and tender love duets, and the melodies remain popular to the present. In 1893 a Boston light opera company commissioned him to compose what was to be the first in a vast repertory of Herbert operettas: *Prince Ananias*, first performed in New York City on November 20, 1894.

There soon followed *The Wizard of the Nile* (1895), *The Serenade* (1897), and *The Fortune Teller* (1898), which launched Herbert on a brilliant career as a Broadway composer. Until the end of the first decade of the 20th century, he poured forth captivating operettas, among them *Babes in Toyland* (1903), *Mlle. Modiste* (1905), *The Red Mill* (1906), and *Naughty Marietta* (1910). All America sang and danced to the catchy and superbly orchestrated tunes from these and other Herbert scores. They included the "March of the Toys," "Toyland," "Gypsy Love Song," "Kiss Me Again," "Every Day Is Ladies' Day with Me," "Ah, Sweet Mystery of Life," "I'm Falling in Love with Someone," and "Italian Street Song." Many listeners shared the view of Andrew Carnegie, the American industrialist and philanthropist, who once commented: "My idea of heaven is to be able to sit and listen to the music of Victor Herbert all I want to."

Unfortunately, the carefree waltz era, into which Herbert had injected his magnetic music, drew to a close with the outbreak of World War I, when public attention turned to more sober aspects of life. Although he continued his musical productivity, the majority of the operettas of his remaining years failed dismally, except for the operetta *Sweethearts* (1913), and a few songs, such as "Thine Alone" (from *Eileen*, 1917) and "A Kiss in the Dark" (*Orange Blossoms*, 1922). He did compose an outstanding score for the motion picture *The Fall of a Nation* (1916) — the first original symphonic work intended for a feature film and thus a milestone in its own right — and several well-received numbers for Broadway's renowned Ziegfeld *Follies* (1918–1924).

In 1913, while dining at Shanley's, a well-known New York restaurant, on Broadway, Herbert happened to hear the orchestra there perform several of his melodies. Convinced that living composers should receive recompense for the use of their copyrighted music, he initiated a suit against Shanley's, which was waged in the courts for four years. Finally, in 1917, the US Supreme Court decided — in Herbert's favor — that copyright owners should be paid royalties for public performances of their works staged for profit. Preceding this legal victory, the composer had already taken, as early as 1914, a decisive step to combat such abuse. He was one of the nine founders (and later director and vice president) of a voluntary, nonprofit organization intended to safeguard and further the interests of lyricists, composers, and publishers — an organization that eventually developed into the powerful American Society of Composers, Authors, and Publishers (ASCAP). A plaque in Lüchow's Restaurant in New York, dedicated on June 27, 1951, commemorates the dinner there at which Herbert and his associates drafted plans for the society.

The genial Irish-American bon vivant and epicure, who attracted a wide circle of friends, suffered a fatal heart attack in the office of his doctor in New York on May 26, 1924. At the time of his death, in the age of jazz and ragtime of the 1920s, he considered himself part of a bygone era. He had once lamented: "My day is over. They are forgetting poor old Herbert." But his passing marked the demise not of a "has-been" but of a composer whose works merited a place as classics of the American musical theater. As the music critic Deems Taylor wrote in the New York *World* on June 1, 1924, he had "raised light opera music to a degree of harmonic sophistication that it had never before reached."

In memory of Victor Herbert, a bronze bust by sculptor Edmund Thomas Quinn was unveiled in the Mall of New York's Central Park in 1927. The US Post Office issued a commemorative 3-cent stamp with his likeness on May 13, 1940, and the Liberty ship *Victor Herbert* was launched on August 22, 1943. His life was depicted in the Hollywood motion picture *The Great Victor Herbert* (1939), and several of his operettas were filmed. But the greatest and most lasting indication of his impression on American music is the appeal that his operettas have retained to the present day, as evidenced both by new recordings and by revivals of Herbert works on stage and television.

Lincoln Abolishes Slavery: National Freedom Day

February 1, the anniversary of the day in 1865 when Abraham Lincoln signed the document abolishing slavery, is observed by presidential proclamation as National Freedom Day. The measure (not to be confused with the Emancipation Proclamation issued on January 1, 1863) was passed by Congress on January 31, 1865, and subsequently was ratified by three-fourths of the states to become the 13th Amendment to the Constitution (see December 18). The designation of February 1 as National Freedom Day was authorized by Congress in 1949.

Lutheran Free Church Joins American Lutheran Church

On February 1, 1963, the Lutheran Free Church combined forces with the American Lutheran Church, which was itself the result of a merger of several other groups. For details of both mergers, see January 1, American Lutheran Church Merger Becomes Effective.

FEBRUARY 2

Candlemas, or
The Feast of the Presentation of the Lord

Candlemas, or the Feast of the Presentation of the Lord, sometimes also referred to as the Feast of the Purification of Mary, is observed on February 2 by the Roman Catholic, Episcopalian, Lutheran, and most Eastern Orthodox churches. Those Eastern Orthodox churches that still adhere to the Old Style or Julian calendar, however, celebrate the feast 13 days later on February 15. The feast is in celebration of the occasion when Mary, as required by Jewish law, went to the temple in Jerusalem — both to be purified 40 days after giving birth to a son and to present that son, Jesus, to God. The event is described in the second chapter of Luke.

At the time, Simeon, a holy man living in Jerusalem, had been longing for the appearance of the Messiah and, as the King James version of the Bible relates (Luke 2:26–34):

. . . it was revealed unto him by the Holy [Spirit], that he should not see death, before he had seen the Lord's Christ. And he came by the Spirit into the temple: and when the parents brought in the child Jesus, to do for him after the custom of the law, then took he him up in his arms, and blessed God, and said, Lord, now lettest thou thy servant depart in peace according to thy word: For mine eyes have seen thy salvation, which thou hast prepared before the face of all people; a light to lighten the Gentiles, and the glory of thy people Israel. And Joseph and . . . [Mary] marveled at those things which were spoken of him; And Simeon blessed them. . . .

The biblical account goes on to relate that Anna, a prophetess living in the Temple, "coming in that instant gave thanks likewise unto the Lord, and spake of him to all them that looked for redemption in Jerusalem."

For Roman Catholics, February 2 is a feast rich in ceremony. The candles and tapers that will be used in the churches during the year are customarily blessed by the clergy, an act, symbolic of Simeon's reference to the "light to lighten the Gentiles." After the blessing, the clergy and congregation (or a smaller representative group) march with lighted candles through the church in solemn procession, to the accompaniment of organ and choir music. The procession represents the entry of Christ, the Light of the World, into the Temple in Jerusalem. In Rome, the pope, after officiating at the traditional candle-blessing ceremony, is himself carried in procession with like symbolism.

Episcopalians generally celebrate February 2, unless the feast falls on a Sunday, in which case its observance is transferred to either the following day or any open day during the following week. Only some Episcopalian churches still practice the pre-Reformation ceremonies of the blessing of the candles and the procession, whereas all use the propers — the set lessons, Collect, and psalms — found in the Book of Common Prayer. The Collect for the day, for example, aptly expresses the spirit of the Feast of the Presentation of the Lord:

Almighty and everliving God, we humbly beseech thy Majesty, that, as thy only-begotten Son was this day presented in the temple in substance of our flesh, so we may be presented unto thee with pure and clean hearts, by the same thy Son Jesus Christ our Lord. Amen.

Lutherans note the day as a feast of the Lord in their church calendar and generally observe it when it falls on a Sunday, rarely when it falls on a weekday. The feast is seldom marked by any special ceremonials, although a few individual congregations may at least march in procession with candles. Most churches use the lessons and Collect, specified in Lutheran hymn books, that reflect the emphasis of the day.

Church historians are of the opinion that the feast was celebrated in very early times — the fourth century or earlier — by Christians in the East. Some scholars contend that it was deliberately introduced to counteract and provide a substitute for the excesses of the Roman *Lupercalia* celebrated in mid-February. For many years the celebration was on February 14: since Jesus originally was supposed to have been born on the day of the Epiphany, this occasion, set for 40 days later, was appropriately called *Quadragesima de Epiphania*.

But after December 25 was designated as the anniversary of the Nativity, or Christmas (Christ's mass), late in the fourth century, the Feast of the Presentation of the Lord was celebrated on February 2 — 40 days after Christmas. It appears to have been introduced into the Western church and adopted at Rome in the 7th century under the name *Hypapante*, or "the meeting" between Jesus and Simeon. Although, as in the Eastern church, the occasion was first noted in the West as a significant episode in the life of Jesus Christ, from the 10th century onwards, the Western liturgy began to list the feast as the Purification of the Blessed Virgin Mary, thereby primarily stressing its importance as a Marian feast, rather than as a major feast of the Lord. Roman Catholics continued to emphasize this Marian aspect until the calendar reform of 1969, when the new Roman Catholic Code of Rubrics declared that February 2 should be observed as a feast of the Lord in line with the ancient traditions of the Eastern church. The Protestant churches that note the day have always emphasized the day as a feast day of Christ.

The procession in connection with the observance apparently was introduced in the late 7th century by Pope Sergius I. The blessing of candles became commonplace about the 11th century, especially in England, where it was a major ceremony, thus giving the day its secondary name of Candlemas (Candle mass). Authorities differ on how the day came to be connected with lighted candles. The candle-carrying ceremonies seem to have been derived from ancient Roman customs. One plausible theory holds that Candlemas grew out of the Roman Feast of Purification, when Romans paraded about the city with lighted candles early in February. They patterned their action after the goddess Ceres, who, according to legend, sought her daughter Proserpine by candlelight after Pluto, the god of the underworld, had carried her away to the nether realm of darkness. According to this theory, the church fathers simply modified the pagan Roman custom, which they found difficult to root out, so that it honored Christ the Light of the World and Mary, his mother.

In Puerto Rico, where Candlemas is observed as the feast of La Virgen de la Candelaria, the occasion is marked by huge bonfires that dot the countryside and also traditionally mark the beginning of the sugar harvest. In New Mexico, various Indian pueblos — usually including San Felipe, Cochiti, and Santo Domingo — observe the day with ceremonial Indian dances in addition to the customary masses at pueblo mission churches.

Various superstitions and traditions have been associated with Candlemas over the centuries. One is that the blessed candles, preserved in the homes of the people, would ward off evil. It was supposed, for example, that lighting such a candle during a thunderstorm would preserve a person from harm during the storm.

For many years, February 2 was regarded as the close of the Christmas season, when Yuletide decorations had to be removed to prevent bad luck. Later on, this custom was for the most part transferred to Twelfth Night.

Candlemas also has long been regarded as a particularly favorable day for weather prognostications. The traditions associated with Groundhog Day derive from this fact.

Dartmouth College Case Decided

The Supreme Court, as guardian and interpreter of the Constitution, has exerted a tremendous influence on all aspects of American life. Throughout its history, the high tribunal has stood in judgment on social, political, and economic problems; its decisions, from which there can be no appeal short of constitutional amendment, have helped the nation shape its response to its most pressing issues.

The first two decades of the 19th century witnessed a period of financial chaos in the United States. To force Great Britain to act more favorably toward the United States, Presidents Thomas Jefferson and James Madison instituted a series of nonexportation and nonimportation acts, which lasted from 1806 to 1811. These trade restrictions and the British blockade of American seaports during the War of 1812 severely injured this country's commerce. As a consequence the national economy, which had been based on the export of agricultural produce and various other raw materials to foreign markets, stagnated and then declined.

Deprived of their opportunities to trade, American entrepreneurs turned to domestic manufacturing. From 1812, private industry — particularly textiles in New England — attracted an increasingly high percentage of available capital. In most cases both the amount of money required to begin the manufacturing enterprise and the risk of its failure were so large that no one person could afford to finance such a venture single-handedly. For these reasons, many of the new industries were corporately owned. The corporation had two major advantages over both private ownership and partnership: it allowed a large number of individuals to pool their resources and thereby to accumulate sufficient funds to start their industry, and it did not require stockholders to assume responsibility for the liabilities of the resulting enterprise beyond the extent of their initial investments.

Unfortunately it also had one substantial drawback. Corporations operated under charters granted by their respective state legislatures, and until the 1819 Supreme Court decision in the case of the *Trustees of Dartmouth College* v. *Woodward*, the inviolability of these charter rights against future legislative tampering had not been determined.

The controversy that led to the historic 1819 ruling stemmed from the New Hampshire legislature's attempt to alter the 50-year-old charter of Dartmouth College. In 1754 the Reverend Eleazar Wheelock, a Congregational minister, had established Moore's Indian Charity School in the part of Lebanon, Connecticut, that is now Columbia. Although Wheelock's institution failed in 1768, his hopes of bringing both secular and religious education to the wilds of upper New England soon revived. In 1769 King George III granted a charter for the establishment of a college in New Hampshire, and shortly afterward the colony's governor offered a substantial land grant to encourage Wheelock to found the institution authorized by the English monarch.

Wheelock quickly accepted the challenge. Accompanied by about 30 students and some other settlers, he organized a township — today, Hanover — on the eastern bank of the Connecticut River in 1770. There, in the same year, he opened Dartmouth College, named in honor of the second earl of Dartmouth.

Dartmouth College operated under its original charter and remained under Congregational administration for the next 46 years. Then, in 1816, the school became entangled in a political-religious feud that for several years had pitted New Hampshire's Jeffersonian Republicans, who were predominantly Presbyterian, against the state's largely Congregationalist Federalists. The Republicans won control of the legislature in 1816 and at once initiated measures designed to undermine the opposition party's influence on the college. They increased the number of trustees from 12 to 21, transferred the privilege of appointment from the trustees to the state legislature, and created a board of overseers to supervise the actions of the trustees. All of these innovations were clear violations of Dartmouth's 1769 charter — a fact the school's original trustees were quick to note. Claiming that the New Hampshire lawmakers had ignored the terms of the college charter, the trustees brought suit against the legislature on the grounds that its action violated the obligation-of-contract clause of the federal Constitution.

Although New Hampshire's highest court upheld the legislature, the Dartmouth trustees appealed this decision to the US Supreme Court. When the case came before the Court in 1819, the college's chief advocate was an alumnus, Daniel Webster. Webster served his alma mater well. Indeed, his impassioned concluding plea in its defense is one of the best-known arguments in American legal annals:

... Sir, you may destroy this little institution. It is weak. It is in your hands! I know it is one of the lesser lights on the literary horizon of the country. You may put it out. But if you do so, you must carry through your work. You must extinguish, one after another, all those great lights of science, which, for more than a century, have thrown their radiance over our land.

It is, Sir, as I have said, a small college and yet, there are those who love it. . . .

Sir, I care not how others feel, but, for myself, when I see my Alma Mater surrounded, like Caesar in the senate house, by those who are reiterating stab on stab, I would not, for this right hand, have her turn to me, and say, *et tu quoque, mi fili* [and you also, my son].

Despite the eloquence of Webster's words, the Court had to rule on two very unemotional issues: Was a corporate charter a contract? And, if so, was the contract protected by the Constitution?

On February 2, 1819, Chief Justice John Marshall handed down the Court's decision. On both counts the opinion favored Dartmouth College. In Marshall's own words, the charter was "plainly a contract to which the donors, the trustees, and the crown (to whose rights and obligations New Hampshire succeeds) were the original parties. . . . It is a contract for the security and disposition of property. . . . It is, then, a contract within the letter of the constitution."

The importance of this decision cannot be overestimated. It safeguarded Dartmouth College against legislative encroachments. But, more important, it insured the security of all corporate enterprises operating under the authority of legislative charters and thereby substantially encouraged the growth of business investments during a critical period in the history of manufacturing in the United States.

Not until the case of *Charles River Bridge* v. *Warren Bridge* in 1837 — when the Supreme Court ruled that "while the rights of private property are sacredly guarded we must not forget that the community also have rights" — did the judiciary modify the Dartmouth College decision by recognizing the police power of the states over corporations to protect the public interest from private infringement.

A US postage stamp commemorating the Dartmouth College case was issued in September 1969, during Dartmouth College's 200th anniversary celebration.

Groundhog Day

In the United States, Candlemas is also known as Groundhog Day, a time for forecasting the weather for the next six weeks. The custom of observing the weather on this day to discover what the future weather would be was brought to America by immigrants from Great Britain and Germany. The theory is that if the groundhog, or woodchuck, comes out of his winter quarters on this day and sees his shadow there will be six more weeks of winter, but if the day is cloudy he will not return to his winter quarters for a long sleep, as the winter weather will soon give way to a balmy spring.

In Germany, it was the badger that supposedly broke its hibernation to observe the skies; in the United States, the belief was transferred to the woodchuck. The English and the Scots have many rhymes in which the belief is embodied, among them the following:

If Candlemas Day be dry and fair,
The half o' winter's to come and mair;
If Candlemas Day be wet and foul,
The half o' winter's gone at Yule.

If Candlemas Day be fair and bright,
Winter will have another flight;
But if it be dark with clouds and rain,
Winter is gone, and will not come again.

When Candlemas Day is fine and clear,
A shepherd would rather see his wife on the bier.

The last rhyme is the English variation of a German saying that "the shepherd would rather see the wolf enter his stable on Candlemas Day than the sun." The belief that the weather on February 2 foreshadows by contraries the weather of the succeeding weeks has no connection with any religious festival or saint. In this respect it differs from the belief in the relationship between the weather on St. Swithin's Day and that to follow.

In the past century, the groundhog and his sunrise activities on the morning of February 2 have become the focal point of several US observances in the East and Midwest. Members of the Groundhog Club in Sun Prairie, Wisconsin, for example, have watched their special groundhog's behavior on this day since 1948. They have then traditionally breakfasted on moose milk, coffee, and sweet rolls at the Erich Lenz farm, where the "weather expert" is cared for by the Prairie Groundhogs 4-H Club and the Sun Prairie Chamber of Commerce.

Nowhere in the United States is as much attention paid to Groundhog Day, or as much fun derived from it, as in Pennsylvania, which was largely settled by Germans. Punxsutawney, in the western part of the state, calls itself the "original home of the great 'weather prognosticator,' His Majesty, the Punxsutawney Groundhog." Since 1887, members of the Punxsutawney Groundhog Club have trekked to nearby Gobblers Knob early on the morning of February 2 to note the first appearance of the groundhog. The day's activities include a Groundhog Breakfast and a Groundhog Banquet at the Punxsutawney Country Club. One recent menu for the latter event featured such delicacies as Woodchuck Jello Salad, Soothsayer gravy, Swiss Steak à la Seer of Seers, whipped potatoes à la Gobblers Knob, and Forecaster green beans, and attracted a capacity crowd of 350 persons. The Groundhog King and Queen, selected by vote of their classmates at the Punxsutawney Area High School, preside annually over the Groundhog Hop, which features a well-known musical group. The community actually focuses its attention on the groundhog "Seer of Seers" during much of the year. Punxsutawney holds a Groundhog Festival during the week of July 4 and a Groundhog outing and hunt during the second week in August.

There are a number of observances in the Pennsylvania Dutch region of southeastern Pennsylvania, where large numbers of Germans — or *Deutsch*, which sounded like "Dutch" to English-speaking colonists — settled in the 18th century. The best-known of these events centers on Quarryville in Pennsylvania's Lancaster County, where a group of high-spirited citizens — including the late columnist George W. Hensel Jr., author of the Philadelphia *Inquirer*'s "Down Lancaster Way" — decided in 1907 to organize the Slumbering Groundhog Lodge of Quarryville.

The lodge's first Groundhog Day observance took place on February 2, 1908. On the morning of each February 2 since, members have donned the prescribed regalia — nightshirts, top hats, and golden keys suspended from their necks by heavy chains — and gone into the fields to seek the burrow of a woodchuck. When one finds a burrow he calls to the others and all assemble to attend the awakening of the animal from its hibernation and its emergence into the outer air.

After watching the groundhog, the observers return to town and report his actions to the lodge's chief executive officer — the chairman of the Board of Hibernating Governors, who then announces to the world that the groundhog has seen, or not seen, his shadow. Following the weather prognostication, proceedings are enlivened by some lighthearted pageantry for the benefit of the assembled press and others, and by the dancing of jigs and "stomps" to the music of drums and cymbals, banjos and guitars, fiddles and piano. Favorite musical selections run to humorous, specially composed items about the groundhog and to popular standards of such particular appropriateness as "Me and My Shadow" and "Baby, It's Cold Outside."

In recent years a house in Colerain township purchased by the Slumbering Groundhog Lodge of Quarryville has served as headquarters for the festivities. The structure has been enlarged to accommodate up to 300 persons and is used for social events throughout the year.

Membership in the Slumbering Groundhog Lodge is limited to 80. A few new members are initiated and an honorary membership is accorded to some person of national prominence each year on Groundhog Day. Although meteorologists and other scientists may scoff at the groundhog's weather-predicting ability — as in a survey of one 60-year period that alleged the groundhog had been right only 28 percent of the time — the confidence of lodge members remains unshaken. There exists no better proof of this than the lodge's Creed of Groundhog Faith, which reads in part as follows:

We believe in the wisdom of the groundhog.
We declare his intelligence to be of a higher order than that of any other animal. . . .
We rejoice that he can, and does, foretell with absolute accuracy the weather conditions for the six weeks following each second day of February. . . .
To defend him, his family and his reputation, we pledge ourselves. . . .

In light of these views, the reply of the chairman of the Board of Hibernating Governors to a recent inquiry about the groundhog's accuracy is not surprising. "Your question," said the governor, "confounds me. Our records show that the groundhog has [always] forecast the weather with absolute, 100 percent accuracy."

Mexican War Ends:
Treaty of Guadalupe Hidalgo

On February 2, 1848, the Treaty of Guadalupe Hidalgo, signed in the village near Mexico City, ended the war between Mexico and the United States (see May 13), which had begun in 1846. It provided for Mexico's cession to the United States of what are now the states of California, Nevada, and Utah, most of Arizona, and parts of New Mexico, Colorado, and Wyoming, in exchange for the payment of $15 million by the United States. By the terms of the treaty, Mexico relinquished all rights to Texas north of the Rio Grande, thus setting to rest the border dispute, which had been one of the prime causes of the war. With the annexation of Texas, which had taken place in 1845 (see March 1), and the Gadsden Purchase of southern Arizona and a sliver of southern New Mexico, which took place in 1853 (see December 30), the United States completed its westward expansion across the continent of North America. The treaty was ratified by the US Senate on March 10, 1848.

FEBRUARY 3

Illinois Becomes a Territory

On February 3, 1809, President Thomas Jefferson approved the congressional act that organized the western part of the Indiana Territory as the territory of Illinois. The new entity — west of Vincennes, which remained in Indiana — extended all the way from the Ohio River to the Canadian border and included all of what is now Illinois, most of what is now Wisconsin, and areas in what are today Minnesota and Michigan.

In 1809 Illinois was for the most part an unsettled wilderness. As early as 1673 the French Jesuit Jacques Marquette and his compatriot Louis Joliet explored part of the region. Returning to Canada after an expedition down the Mississippi River, Marquette and Joliet, on the advice of Indians who inhabited the area, set out on the Illinois River. The Frenchmen followed the Illinois on its northwestern course until they reached the Des Plaines River. Then they proceeded up the Des Plaines to a creek that ran east to a low ridge separating the Mississippi basin from the Great Lakes. A portage across the ridge brought the explorers to the south fork of the Chicago River, and from there they continued eastward to Lake Michigan.

Marquette and Joliet were probably the first white men to explore Illinois, and several areas in the state commemorate their visit. A portion of the portage that they discovered in 1673 has been preserved as the Chicago Portage National Historic Site. The wooded 91.2-acre site is administered by the National Park Service and is open to the public. Marquette and Joliet also recorded seeing the Kaskaskia Indian village on their 1673 journey, and Marquette established a mission at the village in 1675. Located near what is now Ottawa, Illinois, the Old Kaskaskia Village is now a National Historic Landmark, but unlike the Chicago Portage, it is closed to visitors.

Although Marquette and Joliet were the first Europeans to visit Illinois, credit for establishing the first white settlements in the area belongs to another French explorer, René Robert

Cavelier, Sieur de La Salle. In 1679 La Salle set out to discover the mouth of the Mississippi River. In the course of his explorations, La Salle spent considerable time in Illinois, and he came to realize the strategic importance of the Illinois River, which provides a water route from Canada to the Mississippi River. To guarantee French control of this vital waterway, he built two forts on the river: Fort St. Louis near Ottawa, Illinois; and Fort Crèvecoeur near Lake Peoria. Today, the site of Fort St. Louis is the 1,451-acre Starved Rock State Park and it has also been designated as a National Historic Landmark; the site of Fort Crèvecoeur is the 86-acre Fort Creve Coeur State Park.

Settlement of Illinois proceeded very slowly. In Illinois — as well as in other places in the New World — the French devoted their efforts to establishing missions and trading posts rather than towns. However, some of the larger missions and posts eventually attracted permanent settlers. For example, the town of Kaskaskia was established near the mouth of the Kaskaskia River around 1703, and Cahokia was founded a little below the mouth of the Missouri River several years earlier. In 1737 one settler, Jean Baptiste Saucier, built a home in Cahokia; that house has withstood the passing of two centuries and is today the oldest house in Illinois.

Illinois remained under French control for a century. In 1712, when Antoine Crozat was granted temporary possession of Louisiana, the Illinois River was made its northern boundary; and in 1721 more than half the area of what is now the state of Illinois, as well as other territory, was included in the seventh civil and military district of Louisiana, which was named Illinois. But the French concentrated their energies on developing the lower Mississippi valley and never tapped the rich resources of Illinois.

With the Treaty of Paris of 1763, France ceded the territory between the Ohio and Mississippi rivers, including Illinois, to Great Britain. Beginning in 1769, Britain allowed settlers from Virginia and its other seaboard colonies to migrate to the newly acquired lands, and as a result of this policy the population of Illinois slowly grew between 1769 and 1774. Then, in 1774, Parliament passed the Quebec Act. The act, which annexed all the territory north of the Ohio River and east of the Mississippi River to the Province of Quebec, and recognized the validity of French civil law in Quebec, deeply antagonized the English colonists; as a result, migration to Illinois and the other areas of the Northwest came to a halt.

During the American Revolution the predominantly French population of Illinois supported the Loyalist cause; nonetheless the patriots were able to score a number of notable victories in the area. In January 1778 Governor Patrick Henry of Virginia gave George Rogers Clark command of an army of 175 men. Clark and his army surprised and defeated the British at Kaskaskia and Cahokia in the summer of 1778, and by the fall of that year won control of the entire Illinois country. Clark's victories in Illinois and at Vincennes, Indiana, in 1779 were especially important since they helped establish the American claim to the Northwest in the peace negotiations with the British that concluded the American Revolution in 1783.

As a result of the Treaty of Paris of 1783 (see January 14, Ratification Day), Illinois came under the jurisdiction of the new American nation. The status of Illinois and the other areas in the Northwest caused a considerable problem. Several states claimed the Northwest Territory because their colonial charters set their western boundaries at either the Mississippi River or the Pacific Ocean. The dispute over land claims even threatened the ratification of the Articles of Confederation, but in 1781 Virginia agreed to cede its western territories to the national government (the action was formalized in 1784) and by 1786 the other states with western claims had followed Virginia's lead. The following year Congress approved the Northwest Ordinance, which established a territorial government for the area north of the Ohio River.

In 1800 Indiana Territory was organized and the Illinois country was included in this new jurisdiction. Illinois remained a part of Indiana Territory until February 3, 1809, when the Territory of Illinois was established. Gaining territorial status was a watershed in Illinois history: before 1809 only a few thousand persons had settled in the area; but between 1810 and 1820 the population of Illinois multiplied fivefold. With congressional approval, a territorial legislature was chosen in 1812, and a constitution was adopted by the people of the area the same year. In 1818 Illinois was admitted as the 21st state (see December 3).

FEBRUARY 4

Mark Hopkins's Birthday

Mark Hopkins, one of the most distinguished educators of his generation and president of Williams College (Williamstown, Massachusetts) from 1836 to 1872, was born at Stockbridge, Massachusetts, on February 4, 1802, the son of a farmer. He entered Williams College as a sophomore and was graduated in 1824 and began the study of medicine, but was recalled to Williams as a tutor in 1825, and taught for two years. He then entered the Berkshire Medical School at Pittsfield, Massachusetts, from which he was graduated in 1829. He opened an office in New York City and soon moved to Binghamton, New York, but Williams College called him back in 1830 as professor of moral philosophy and rhetoric.

Hopkins was ordained as a Congregational minister in 1836. When he resigned as president of the college in 1872 he retained the professorship of moral philosophy and continued as pastor of the college church. He died at Williamstown on June 17, 1887.

Although Hopkins was not a profound scholar, he excelled at arousing the interest and enthusiasm of students. President James A. Garfield, a graduate of Williams, is credited with saying at a dinner of Williams alumni in New York that a log in the woods with Mark Hopkins on one end and a student on the other would be a university. What Garfield actually said was that a log cabin with such a teacher as Mark Hopkins would be a university.

It is said of Hopkins that when a student in his moral philosophy class asked him who would go to heaven he replied that he did not know, but that he was sure that no one would go there who would not feel at home. Hopkins was elected to the Hall of Fame for Great Americans in 1915.

FEBRUARY 5

Charro Days Fiesta:
Brownsville, Texas, and
Matamoros, Mexico

This is a movable event. See note on page xxvi.

A Texas-Mexican border fiesta known as Charro Days, held each year in Brownsville, Texas, and spilling across the border into Matamoros, Mexico, begins each year on Thursday of the weekend before Lent. The celebration, elaborate and colorful as it is, in a region steeped in Spanish-Mexican heritage, has been known to attract as many as 400,000 visitors.

Brownsville is situated on the Rio Grande, opposite Matamoros on the Mexican side of the river. Together they constitute a major border-crossing point. The proximity of the two cities originally suggested the idea of a fiesta recreating the color and romance of the old border area, where Latin-American and Anglo-American met against a background of turbulent his-

tory. Initially Charro Days, which originated in Brownsville in 1938, was purely local; but its fame as a pre-Lenten festival spread until it drew tourists from all over the United States and from Mexico as well. Visitors to the Charro Days Fiesta frequently don costumes and participate in the festivities instead of remaining mere spectators. The fiesta has been officially proclaimed in Matamoros, as well as Brownsville, ever since 1961, although it had the cooperation of Mexican authorities for many years before that. Today, fiesta events take place in both cities.

Charro at one time was the name of a costume worn by the Spanish dons who once ruled Mexico. The term later was extended by popular usage to include the Mexican equestrian outfit, because of its similarity, and the traditionally dashing Mexican horseman as well. During Charro Days, male residents of Brownsville and Matamoros wear variations of the charro costume. It consists of tight-fitting riding breeches trimmed with white suede or silver, a heavily embroidered short jacket, a colorful flowing tie, a serape draped over one shoulder, and a huge sombrero. The men of the region also grow beards for the occasion, and other facial adornments, such as mustaches and long sideburns, are emphasized as well.

The charro's female counterpart during the fiesta is the *china poblana*. The term also refers to her costume, the most popular Charro Days attire for women. According to legend the costume, which is the regional dress of Puebla, Mexico, was worn by a little Chinese girl who was befriended by the Mexican people and became a kind of fairy princess to them. The most striking characteristic of the china poblana is a full skirt of brilliant red and green, richly embroidered in glittering sequins. A white blouse embroidered with red roses vies with the skirt in vividness. A silk *rebozo*, or shawl, completes the outfit.

Other costumes seen during the four-day border fiesta may be typical of any part of Latin America. Among the most striking are those native to states in the southern part of Mexico, such as the *Tehuana*, the lavishly embroidered dress of the women of Tehuantepec.

The children of Brownsville also take part in the fiesta, wearing small replicas of their elders' costumes for the children's parade. This annual event, with some 1,000 children participating, is probably the most famous of all Charro Days features. It is only one of the fiesta's several parades, however. Others include the Grand International Parade, a daytime march through Brownsville and Matamoros, and the Grand Illuminated Parade, held at night with bright lights enhancing the extraordinary brilliance of the charro, china poblana, and other costumes. After the parade there are costume dances in the streets, entertainment by well-known performers from both sides of the border, and one of the several balls that are high points of the fiesta.

In fact, balls, costumed street dancing, and entertainment are nightly features of Charro Days. The entertainment includes variety shows, folk dancing, and pageantry, all of them with Latin themes or performers. Among the most popular attractions are the nighttime festivities that center around the main plaza of Matamoros.

Charro Days are also punctuated by band concerts, the music of marimbas, and the sound of strolling mariachi bands. There are sports events on land and water. Often there is a rodeo and usually there are bull fights in Matamoros. A carnival midway in downtown Brownsville contributes to the gaiety. There are also special window displays and an art show, as well as various Mexican and Latin American exhibits and cultural presentations, some of them staged as preliminary events before the official beginning of Charro Days.

Dwight L. Moody's Birthday

February 5, the birthday of lay preacher Dwight L. Moody, who was the late 19th century's foremost spokesman for the Christian Gospel, is marked as Founder's Day at the Northfield Mount Hermon School, East Northfield, Massachusetts, a coeducational preparatory school with an enrollment of about 1,100 students divided between two campuses. The actual observance takes place on the Sunday nearest February 5, when faculty members and students assemble to participate in a service of worship and to hear Moody's life and Christian message recalled by guest and faculty speakers. This annual Founder's Day Service is followed by a banquet, with present and former faculty, staff, and alumni attending as guests, and with a traditional birthday cake in honor of the occasion. There is also recollection of the founder's one-time remark — that he expected students to be able to do the impossible, "even to eating soup with a one-tine fork." Accordingly the commemoration includes the presentation of a one-tine fork by the president of the senior class to the president of the junior class.

Northfield Mount Hermon was founded by Moody as two separate schools — Northfield, in 1879, for girls and Mount Hermon, in 1881, for boys. The schools were located five miles apart on opposite sides of the Connecticut River. Since their merger in 1971, the two have functioned as one school. It maintains a high college preparatory standing, a nondenominational religious program — in keeping with Moody's feelings about the divisiveness of sectarian doctrines — and a distinctive student work plan.

One of seven children, Dwight Lyman Moody was born in East Northfield in 1837. His first memory was the sudden death of his father, four years later. His mother, who exerted a great influence upon him, was left in impoverished circumstances, but managed to keep her family together. Young Dwight Moody was schooled locally, did chores, and "hired out" to neighboring farmers in the summer. His first public speech, at age 16, before a town lyceum meeting, ended in failure when he forgot what he had intended to say.

He went to Boston when he was 17 and, after a dismal period of job hunting, applied to two uncles in the boot and shoe business there. They agreed that he might perform odd jobs in their store on the condition that he board at a place of their selection, refrain from drinking and gambling, and attend Mount Vernon Church and the young men's Sabbath school.

In view of Moody's lack of enthusiasm for the last requirement, his conversion — through conversation with the Sabbath-school teacher — was surprising. The teacher himself later confessed that he had "seen few persons . . . who seemed more unlikely ever to become Christians of clear, decided view." For Moody, however, the encounter with Christ's message was permanently transforming.

A year later, in 1856, he moved to Chicago, where he continued in the boot and shoe business. While showing great business ability and prospering rapidly, during his nonworking hours he spent all his spare energies as a Sunday-school teacher and superintendent. In 1860 he completely withdrew from business to become an independent city missionary. As an outgrowth of his Sunday-school and slum mission work, he founded what later came to be known as the Moody Memorial Church. From 1861 to 1873 the lay pastor was a member of the Christian commission of the Young Men's Christian Association. He also became president of the Chicago YMCA and encouraged formation of YMCA chapters on college campuses.

In 1870 Moody, then 33, met the organist and singer Ira D. Sankey, who became his associate in the dozens of evangelistic campaigns he led in the years that followed. They began their first meetings in Great Britain in 1873. In the next quarter century Moody preached to millions throughout metropolitan Britain and America, converting thousands. A person of intense and contagious conviction, Moody was a rotund and bearded figure who never managed to suppress the prankish, fun-loving boy within him. With a great flair for the dramatic, he possessed a disarming audacity. His preaching was simple, colorful, and forceful, revealing a dynamic faith. It stressed, above all, the love and mercy of God. Layman that he was — for Moody never became an ordained minister — he nevertheless commanded the cooperation of ministers of many denominations, the enthusiasm of businessmen, and the admiration of university people.

In addition to establishing Northfield and Mount Hermon schools, Moody also founded what now is called the Moody Bible Institute, in Chicago, in 1889. At the Northfield School he instituted annual summer religious conferences, held under various auspices. The Homestead, which Moody purchased as his home in 1875, and where he died on December 22, 1899, still stands adjacent to the East Northfield campus. The house in which he was born, on the Moody Street edge of the East Northfield campus, was the home of his mother until her death. It is now open to visitors at certain times. The old carriage shed attached to it has been converted into the Moody Museum, open only during the summer months. The graves of Moody and his wife are within sight of both buildings, on the hill called Round Top, overlooking the Connecticut valley and the hills of Massachusetts, New Hampshire, and Vermont. On the Mount Hermon campus, Schauffler Memorial Library contains memorabilia associated with Moody and his partner Sankey — letters and hymn books, Moody Bibles, and portraits and a death mask of Moody, as well as porcelain statues and a Currier and Ives engraving of both men.

Roger Williams Arrives in America

Roger Williams, one of the most famous defenders of religious liberty in America, was born in England, probably in London, the son of James and Alice (Pemberton) Williams. Although the exact date of his birth is not known, scholars agree that it was between 1603 and 1607.

As a youth Williams attracted the attention of Sir Edward Coke by his shorthand notes of sermons and speeches, and Sir Edward sent him to Sutton's Hospital, now the Charterhouse

School, in 1621. After several years there, Williams entered Pembroke College, Cambridge University, from which he was graduated with the bachelor of arts degree in 1627.

Interested early in theology, Williams took orders in the Church of England and became chaplain to the household of Sir William Masham at Otes, Essex. Both at Otes and at Cambridge, however, Williams was surrounded by politically active Puritans who accepted the theology of Calvin and sought to bring an end to episcopacy in the Church of England. Increasingly rebellious against what he regarded as the errors of the church and the lack of religious freedom under the autocratic King Charles I, he became a Puritan and then a Separatist — one of those Christians who advocated a complete and overt break from (rather than reform within) the Church of England.

Williams and his wife left England to join the Puritan-dominated Massachusetts Bay Colony, arriving in Boston on February 5, 1631. He declined an invitation to serve as teacher of the church there because he found its members "an unseparated people," refusing to sever completely their ties with the Church of England, even while avoiding what they considered to be the church's errors. Instead he went as teacher to the church at Salem — where he got into trouble for denying the right of civil magistrates to punish persons for religious offenses. As the theocratic Massachusetts Bay government insisted on this right, Williams removed to the avowedly Separatist Plymouth Colony, where he preached and began his missionary work with the Indians, to whom he was always a friend. Indeed he came into direct conflict with the authorities at Plymouth over his insistence that only purchase from the Indians gave a fair title to land — and that the king's patent to the colony therefore was null.

In 1633 Williams returned as assistant, and then pastor, of the church at Salem, where he argued that the power of the civil magistrates extended only to the bodies and goods of men and not to their consciences, and preached other "dangerously liberal ideas." One of these was his denial of the validity of the Massachusetts Bay Colony charter, under which — as Williams pointed out — the king violated Indian rights by giving away land that was not his to give. Such convictions, and his stand for absolute freedom of conscience, led to his banishment from the Massachusetts Bay Colony by the General Court late in 1635.

Plans were made to deport him to England, but Williams, learning of his impending arrest, fled south to the shores of Narragansett Bay with a few followers in January 1636. After suffering the deprivations of a New England winter he crossed to the west bank of the adjacent Seekonk River. There, on land he had bought from the Indians, he founded the city of Providence, the earliest Rhode Island settlement, in June 1636. Establishing a government founded on complete religious toleration, he made the colony a refuge from religious persecution and drew settlers from England and Massachusetts, among them Quakers, with whom he expressed disagreement, Jews, and Anabaptists.

Williams himself was for a brief period a Baptist, after coming to believe in the baptism of believers only. After his own baptism by Ezekiel Holliman, a layman, Williams proceeded to baptize 10 others and, with them, to found the Baptist Church of Christ in Providence in 1638. This was the first Baptist church in America and the first church of any denomination in Rhode Island. By 1639, however, Williams, an incorrigible nonconformist, had withdrawn from the church and declared himself a Seeker — one who espoused the basic Christian beliefs but recognized no one church as the true one.

In addition to the separation of church and state, which was a basic tenet of the colony he founded at Providence, Williams consistently championed the cause of democratic government. He was, in fact, its earliest advocate in what became the United States of America.

Three other communities — Portsmouth, Newport, and Warwick — had sprung up around Narragansett Bay by 1643, when Williams went to England to secure from Parliament a charter that would give legal sanction to these settlements and Providence, and protect them from rival land claims by the Massachusetts Bay and Plymouth colonies. Under the desired patent, which was issued in March 1644 (and which Williams had reconfirmed on a second trip to England in 1651–1654), the entire colony was referred to as Providence Plantations. The four communities were actually consolidated in 1647. Although boundary disputes with Massachusetts, and also with Connecticut, continued into the 1700s, the new colony's survival as a separate entity was assured and the principle of religious freedom reconfirmed by a new charter granted by Charles II in 1663. In that document, which John Clarke, a founder of Newport, was largely instrumental in securing (see October 8), the name of the colony appeared as Rhode Island and Providence Plantations, which remains the official designation of the state today.

In 1654 Williams was elected the first president of the colony under its charter. He held the position for three years and from then until his death in 1683 always held some office. He meanwhile wrote much on religion and on the languages of the Indians. In Indian relations he long served both his own and neighboring colonies as a peacemaker, although he was unable to prevent King Philip's War, which broke out in 1675 (see March 22, The First Indian Treaty).

Although there is no statewide annual observance to honor the founder of Rhode Island, on the Sunday nearest Rhode Island Independence Day (see May 4) the historic First Baptist Meeting House in Providence, whose congregation Williams founded, holds its annual Forefathers Service. Each year visitors — who customarily include a delegation from the Roger Williams Family Association — are invited to this service, which often uses the 18th century order of worship. In 1963 the church also took note of the 325th anniversary of its founding. Hymns for the service were selected from those in use when Williams established the church, and his beliefs were the subject of the sermon. A special exhibit in the vestry was related to the early days of Providence Plantations and the founding of the church.

As part of the church's observance of the US Bicentennial, "God's Providence," an original musical production honoring Roger Williams, was presented at the meeting house on March 2, 1975. The Forefathers Service in May of that year was based on the form of worship in use in the 17th century. In 1976 Forefathers Sunday was advanced to May 16 to permit a special Rhode Island State Bicentennial Ecumenical Service of Religious Freedom on Sunday, May 4.

The founder of Rhode Island is also memorialized by the 453-acre Roger Williams Park in Providence, which is the site of two Williams monuments and the restored home of one of his descendants. Providence is dotted with other evidence of the Williams legacy, which is reflected by memorial tablets, including the one on "Slate Rock," where he first landed in Rhode Island; by markers at such historic points as Roger Williams Spring, site of the first Providence settlement; and by sculpture, including the statue of the state's founder at the Roger Williams Memorial on Prospect Terrace, overlooking a panoramic view of the city.

In addition, a statue of Williams stands in Statuary Hall of the Capitol in Washington, D.C., and a bust of him is included in the Hall of Fame for Great Americans in New York City.

Another well-known statue, in Geneva, Switzerland, is part of a group celebrating outstanding figures of the Protestant Reformation. During the 1936 observances of the 300th anniversary of Williams' founding of Providence, a commemorative 50-cent coin and a 3-cent postage stamp were issued.

FEBRUARY 6

Aaron Burr's Birthday

Aaron Burr, whose popularity and political skill almost made him President of the United States, but who died friendless and alone at the age of 80, was born in Newark, New Jersey, on February 6, 1756. His father was the Reverend Aaron Burr, the second president of the College of New Jersey, which later became Princeton University; and his maternal grandfather was Jonathan Edwards, the New England Calvinist theologian.

Young Burr, whose parents died when he was an infant, was raised in the home of a relative, where he was tutored for a time by the jurist Tapping Reeve, who later married Burr's sister. Burr showed his brilliance early, entering the sophomore class at the College of New Jersey when he was 13 and graduating with distinction at 16. He studied theology for a while and toyed with the idea of following his father's profession, but in 1774 he gave this up to begin the study of law — in Litchfield, Connecticut, where his brother-in-law Tapping Reeve, who was then teaching informally, soon established what became famous as the nation's first law school. (Restored in 1930, the school is maintained today by the Litchfield Historical Society.)

Burr had favored the cause of colonial patriots from early youth. With the outbreak of the Revolution, he interrupted his studies to enlist in the Continental army. He served as captain on the staff of Benedict Arnold during Arnold's unsuccessful campaign against the British at Quebec. After assignment to General Washington's staff for a few weeks, Burr was then transferred to the command of General Israel Putnam. Promoted to the rank of lieutenant colonel in 1777, Burr remained in the army until March 1779, when he resigned because of ill health.

The next year he resumed the study of law. Admitted to the bar in 1782, he opened an office in Albany. He was married the same year to Theodosia Prevost, 10 years his senior and the widow of a British officer. Their daughter,

Theodosia Burr, born in 1783, was to be known for her intellectual accomplishments and later for her loyalty to her father during the dark days of his later life.

In 1783 Burr moved his family to New York City, where he devoted himself to his profession for six years, presided extravagantly over the social events at his Richmond Hill mansion, and entered politics. After serving as a member of the New York legislature in 1784–1785, he was made attorney general of the state by Governor George Clinton in 1789.

In 1791 Burr was elected to the US Senate, defeating candidate Philip Schuyler — the father-in-law of Burr's long-time rival Secretary of the Treasury Alexander Hamilton. Although Burr, a Jeffersonian Republican, who opposed Hamilton's financial and Federalist policies, failed to be reelected to the Senate in 1797, he was chosen a member of the New York state assembly in that year and served there until 1799.

Burr's star meanwhile was rising on the national horizon. In the presidential election of 1796 he received 30 electoral votes. In 1800 he was an active candidate, running with Thomas Jefferson as a Jeffersonian Republican against the Federalist candidates, John Adams and Charles C. Pinckney. Jefferson and Burr triumphed over their opponents but tied with each other, at 73 votes each, in the electoral college. The presidential electors at that time each voted for two candidates with the one receiving the highest number of votes to be President (provided he had a clear majority) and the one receiving the next highest number of votes to be Vice President. In the case of a tie, however, it was up to the House of Representatives to decide the issue. The election of a President in 1800 thus went to the Hamilton-dominated House, which was controlled by the Federalists. For a time they thought of supporting Burr, but after six days of balloting — and Hamilton's clear indications that he regarded Jefferson as the lesser of two evils — they elected Jefferson President on the 36th ballot. Burr automatically became Vice President (1801–1805). The 12th Amendment, ratified in 1804 (see September 25), provided for the separate election of President and Vice President to prevent such deadlocks in the future.

As the Senate's presiding officer, Burr won respect from both friends and opponents. His last act as Vice President was to preside over the impeachment trial of Supreme Court Justice Samuel Chase. Jefferson wanted Justice Chase removed and the friends of his administration sought to influence Burr by offering appointments to office for members of his family. Burr, however, presided "with the dignity and impartiality of an angel and with the rigor of a devil," and the justice was acquitted.

Burr meanwhile had fallen into disfavor with the Jeffersonian Republicans and had been replaced as the vice presidential candidate by Governor George Clinton in the election of 1804. It was also in 1804 that Burr, nominated for the governorship of New York, had again had his ambitions thwarted by Hamilton, whose opposition contributed to his defeat.

After the election the 48-year-old Burr, who for years had ignored his rival's denunciations, challenged Hamilton, then 49, to a duel on the basis of a hearsay insult. The duel, one of history's most famous, between two brilliant and capable men, took place at Weehawken, New Jersey, on July 11, 1804. It brought to an end not only the life of Hamilton, who was shot fatally, but also the political career of Burr, who fled southward in the face of arrest warrants issued by the states of New York and New Jersey.

From this point the record becomes clouded. Burr visited New Orleans, purchased land in the newly acquired Louisiana Territory, and engaged in vague conspiracies — whether to invade Mexico if war broke out over boundary disputes between the United States and Spain, as then expected; whether to engineer the secession of western regions from the Union; or whether a combination of the two, with the aim of establishing an independent republic, never became entirely clear. Betrayed by a co-conspirator, he was arrested and tried for treason in the US Circuit Court at Richmond, Virginia. Found not guilty of an "overt act" of treason, he was acquitted on September 1, 1807. Despite this fact, and his later acquittal of the additional charge of misdemeanor, he remained guilty in the public mind.

Burr went to England in 1808 and sought help in his plans to drive the Spanish from Mexico. When he failed to get it he took his plans to France, but was equally unsuccessful there. He returned, impoverished, to the United States in 1812 and sadly resumed the practice of law in New York: his daughter Theodosia, whose entreaties had prompted his return, had been lost at sea while en route from South Carolina to meet him.

In July 1833 the 77-year-old Burr, whose first wife had died many years before, was married to the wealthy and notoriously flamboyant widow Eliza Brown Jumel of New York, a woman some years younger than he. With the always spendthrift Burr threatening to squander her fortune, they separated after four months. The setting for their far from idyllic marriage was the handsome Morris-Jumel Mansion, once used as Washington's headquarters, which the public can visit today at West 160th Street and Edgecombe Avenue in New York's Washington Heights section.

After colorful proceedings, a divorce decree officially ending the Burr-Jumel union was issued on September 14, 1836 — the day of Burr's death, in a hotel on Staten Island, New York.

Chinese New Year

This is a movable event. See note on page xxvi.

Although the Gregorian calendar was adopted in China in 1912, the Chinese people both on the mainland and on the island of Taiwan, as well as those abroad, continue to regard the date given in the old Chinese lunar calendar as the beginning of the new year. According to that calendar, the year has 354 days and 12 lunar months, about half of them with 30 days and the other half with 29. In order to make the months correspond with the movements of the earth around the sun, a 13th month is inserted every two or three years. The new year begins on the new moon and may occur at any time from January 21 to February 19, inclusive. The years are named for the animals of the Chinese zodiac — as the year of the rat, the year of the ox, the year of the tiger, the year of the hare, the year of the dragon, and so on through the years named for the snake, horse, sheep, monkey, rooster, dog, and pig before the next 12-year cycle begins with another year of the rat. For Americans of Chinese descent 1976, the US Bicentennial year, was a year of the dragon — the most auspicious sign in the Chinese zodiac, according to ancient almanacs. The arrival of the new year is celebrated with festivities that may continue anywhere from a week to a month, although 10 days to two weeks is a common period for the public celebrations.

The Chinese New Year is energetically marked by Chinese in the United States. There are likely to be celebrations in the Chinese communities of Los Angeles, Boston, Chicago, and Philadelphia, for example; and in New York, Honolulu, and San Francisco Chinese New Year is a major event.

In New York festivities customarily begin shortly before midnight on Chinese New Year's Eve, with the first appearance of the huge-headed, silken lions that play such a prominent part in Chinese New Year celebrations; and with the popping of firecrackers and shouts of "gung hay fat choy" or "gung ho sun hee," which translate roughly as "happy new year" or, "may you prosper." The lions (whose heads are three-dimensional, but whose bodies are simply long lengths of cloth) put in a second, and longer, appearance around noontime on New Year's Day. As the lions, approaching from different directions, converge, the dancers concealed beneath them madly outprance one another in a kind of dancing duel. And all the time there is the accompaniment — drums, and the clash of cymbals and the earsplitting staccato of exploding firecrackers. According to traditional beliefs, the combined din drives away evil spirits.

The dancing procession is accompanied by bearers of banners, small characters who tease the lions, musicians, and others. Together they wind through the narrow streets, pausing at each shop while its proprietor emerges with the customary coin-filled red envelope as a good-luck token for the band, and with a bundle of firecrackers, which are ignited on the spot. Often the procession is followed by a program of varied performers — acrobats; unicorn or other dancers; and perhaps a color corps.

New Year's night and the succeeding days are the time for varied celebration — parades with lions and the traditional Chinese dragon — and for other gaiety. The streets resound with the explosion of firecrackers and, often, with the music of youthful drum and bugle corps, and there are appearances of a locally elected Miss Chinatown, and such additional features as Chinese dance, music, and variety shows, as well as such other features as a shadow play and kung fu demonstrations.

In Honolulu, Chinese New Year festivities take place in exuberant form as part of the three-to-four-week Narcissus Festival sponsored by the Chinese Chamber of Commerce. The festival embraces a wide variety of events, among them flower, art, and fashion shows, a Chinese dance presentation, a queen contest and coronation ball, a "Night in Chinatown" with dancing in the streets and a fireworks display, in addition to a dragon parade, and other traditional events associated with the Chinese New Year.

Everywhere, children play prominent roles throughout the celebrations. In one New Year's parade in Philadelphia, for example, a dozen children were dressed as the animals of the Chinese zodiac and an additional 10 served as cloud girls, carrying "clouds," a "sun," and a "moon." In a Los Angeles parade, children carried lighted lanterns and walked behind a gaily cavorting, 100-legged dragon.

Dragons, in fact, are prominent wherever the Chinese New Year is observed. Their long frames supported by 60 or more men (fewer for a small dragon), they are particularly in evidence during the grand finale celebrations that take place at the end of the festivities. That final day the emphasis is often on mummery and fun, with a park or other open space serving as the center of activity. The dragon, a magnificent and undulating creature, makes his way there and so do assorted other merrymakers. Typically they may include stilt-walkers with painted faces; a masked clown in vivid costume; a thoroughly Americanized drum and bugle corps of neighborhood children; Chinese musicians who draw their viols and lutes from a gaily painted music wagon and execute plaintive Oriental airs on them. This day, especially, children are the special audience, before all is put away for another year.

Typical of Chinese New Year's festivities, but on a particularly lavish scale, is the extravaganza staged in San Francisco, the largest Oriental community outside of Asia. Here in "Gum San Dai Fow" — the "great city of the golden hill" — Chinese-Americans, some 90,000 of whom live in the San Francisco Bay Area, have preserved their ancient customs for over 150 years. A New Year's celebration of at least semipublic nature, described as a "great feast," was noted as early as February 21, 1851. Nine years later a Chinese dragon first cavorted on San Francisco streets. The observance was largely confined to the Chinese community for more than 90 years; only in the 1950s did it develop into a major event attracting the attention of the general public as well.

In 1953 the Chinese Chamber of Commerce staged a local Miss Chinatown contest, which grew in scope until in 1958 the competition expanded into the Miss Chinatown USA beauty and talent pageant. In 1963 the San Francisco Convention and Visitors Bureau became a festival cosponsor with the Chinese Chamber of Commerce and began adding additional spectator events and eye-catching pageantry to the celebration, especially by importing dazzling parade regalia from Hong Kong.

By the mid-1970s the artifacts, many of them representing fabulous creatures from Chinese legend, were numbered in the hundreds. Included are towering deities, the 12 symbolic animals of the lunar cycle, Pekingese- and Cantonese-style ceremonial lions, a young (60-foot) dragon, and mythical fish and birds, as well as ornamental lanterns, silken banners, and elaborate costumes.

In one recent year the new year arrived officially on a Saturday and San Francisco had its foretaste of outdoor celebration on the next two days, with teams of ceremonial lion dancers performing afternoons in the streets of Chinatown and evenings at Ghirardelli Square. The city's Chinese residents, meanwhile, also marked the new year privately, holding family gatherings and observing the traditional holiday customs. It was not until after the period of largely private celebration that the Chinese New Year Festival, with its nine days of public festivities, began, a week later. The outdoor opening day program at Union Square featured, as usual, lion dancers, the Miss Chinatown USA contestants, a young dragon, a ceremonial animal representing the year's zodiac sign, classical and folk dancers, and addresses by civic leaders.

That evening the Miss Chinatown USA contest was staged at Nob Hill's Masonic Auditorium at 8:00 P.M.; the coronation ceremony took place at 8:00 P.M. on the following Thursday, at the same location. It was succeeded, the next evening, by the coronation ball, which was held in the Fairmont Hotel's grand ballroom.

During the week of February 10–18, other festival events included lion dances in the streets, programs of Chinese opera, folk dancing, music, and films; cultural and art exhibits such as the display of 13th- to- 19th century Chinese animal figures at the de Young Museum in Golden Gate Park; Chinese cooking demonstrations by leading Chinatown chefs; a fashion show–luncheon featuring the Miss Chinatown USA contestants modeling ancient and modern Chinese styles; a carnival with fun rides at Portsmouth Square; and walking tours of Chinatown featuring, for example, a Buddhist-Taoist temple, rice noodle and fortune cookie factories, a sewing shop, an herb store, a grocery, and a library.

The elaborate festivities reached a climax on Saturday, with the festival's spectacular night parade, which attracted an estimated 400,000 spectators. Its star is traditionally the 120-foot Golden Dragon, "Gum Lung," fashioned out of silk, velvet, papier-mâché, bangles, and bamboo. Its massive head, writhing body, and lashing tail were manipulated by three 22-man student relay teams that had been trained in the classical movements of the dragon dance. Gum Lung twisted its way along an 18-block parade route through Chinatown and was joined in procession by a dragon teaser, drum and cymbal players, a smaller dragon, magnificent floats, Miss Chinatown USA and her court, lantern-bearers, celestial lions, and immense representations of oriental deities and mythological beasts and birds.

Meanwhile, celebrations in San Francisco and in Chinese communities throughout the United States had been going on in individual households for days. Although the traditional New Year's Eve visit to a shrine or temple and the ritualistic vegetarian meal are apparently no longer widespread among westernized Chinese in the United States, Chinese-Americans still regard New Year's as an important family occasion. Blossoming plants, ancestral portraits, seasonal delicacies, candles, and the ritual of honoring and appeasing the Kitchen God are all integral features of the occasion when families gather for the annual reunion dinner; they also exchange gifts, especially the traditional red paper *li shee* envelopes containing money and symbolizing good luck. For the Chinese, the New Year remains a time of philosophical reflection, as well as of relaxation, a time imbued with a sense of privacy in addition to the exuberant public celebration.

With some modifications wrought by time and distance, New Year customs observed by Chinese in this country still reflect the heritage of the homeland. On the Chinese mainland, with the advent of the Communist cultural revolution, many of the old patterns have disappeared, though New Year is still observed there in some of the traditional ways. In the Republic of China on Taiwan the ancient customs are still observed.

France Recognizes the United States

On February 6, 1778, a formal treaty of alliance between France and the United States was signed in Paris. It was the result of intricate negotiations that had been conducted secretly since 1775 and that reflected each country's strong desire to achieve certain specific goals.

Ever since its defeat at the hands of Great Britain in the Seven Years' War (1756–1763), the French government had awaited an opportune moment for revenge. Its goal was to recapture its previous predominance in international affairs. The American Revolution presented an ideal opportunity to undermine British leadership and redress the balance of power in French favor. The calculating French minister of foreign affairs, Charles Gravier, Comte de Vergennes, fully realized the possibilities offered by the colonial revolt. He wrote in 1778: "Providence has marked this era for the humiliation of a proud and greedy power ... glory and inestimable advantages will result. ..."

French manufacturers hoped for profitable business transactions in the United States, which up to then had been cut off from them by the restrictive British Acts of Trade. In fact after the Revolution had ended, Vergennes commented to his minister of finance: "Always keep in mind that in separating the United States from Great Britain it was above all their commerce which we wanted." Sentimental as well as sound practical reasons influenced the French to sympathize with the American cause. French intellectuals, including Voltaire, tended to idealize Americans as a simple unpretentious people with all the virtues of self-made "natural men." To them, America represented a utopia, which would eventually guide the Old World towards an improved way of life.

The American colonists, in turn, realized the advisability of seeking aid from Britain's age-old enemy. Soon after the outbreak of the American Revolution in April 1775, they began wooing France. In November 1775 the Continental Congress appointed a committee on foreign relations. Less than half a year later it dispatched Silas Deane, an American lawyer and merchant, to Paris. Although ostensibly a business agent, Deane had in reality been entrusted with the task of securing arms, supplies, and clothing for the American troops. With the knowledge and protection of King Louis XVI and the French government, a bogus company, Roderigue Hortalez et Cie., was set up by Pierre Augustin Caron de Beaumarchais, the French dramatist, who was also a secret agent of the monarchy. It provided vital military assistance to the hard-pressed revolutionaries. In addition to this unneutral help, American ships, including privateers preying on British vessels, were welcomed at French seaports.

Once the Declaration of Independence had been adopted on July 4, 1776, the Continental Congress decided that other European states, including Spain, Prussia, and Austria, should be asked for aid and that ties with France should be tightened. Benjamin Franklin (see January 17) and Arthur Lee were appointed commissioners to France in addition to Silas Deane. In December 1776 the two newcomers arrived in Paris with proposals for a treaty of friendship and commerce. When the American military outlook reached a nadir during the winter of 1776–1777, Congress, eager to persuade France to become an ally, authorized Franklin to draw up a military alliance. The American agents were able to elicit increased supplies of war materials, but were unsuccessful in persuading the most absolute monarchical regime in Europe to intervene openly in the Revolution. Vergennes refused even to recognize the separate existence of the United States.

The French government abandoned its policy of all aid "short of war" in the late fall of 1777 upon learning of the defeat of the British army and General John Burgoyne's subsequent surrender at Saratoga (see October 17). Vergennes was fearful lest the British government offer the American colonists such sweeping concessions as to settle the conflict — thereby thwarting his ambitions to undermine British supremacy. Indeed, upon receiving news of the British disaster at Saratoga, Frederick Lord North, the British prime minister, advocated an immediate effort to end an unwise war. George III, although ready to concede almost complete autonomy to the colonists, still demanded that they acknowledge his sovereignty — something they were no longer willing to do. In mid-December, a British agent, Paul Wentworth, took an offer of reconciliation to the American commissioners in Paris, who held out adamantly for independence.

In the meantime, the wily Vergennes, who had his sources of information on the activities of Franklin and his fellow commissioners, learned with dismay of the peace feelers that were being extended by Great Britain. In late December and January, the French government moved hastily to recognize US independence and initiated preparations for formal alliance. Two treaties were signed on February 6, 1778. The treaty of amity and commerce provided that France and the independent United States grant each other "most-favored-nation" status; the treaty of alliance — in which France promised "to maintain effectually the liberty, Sovereignty, and independence of the United States," and the United States pledged to defend French territories in the West Indies — was to become effective if actual fighting erupted between France and Great Britain. In addition both parties agreed to obtain each other's consent before concluding a peace or truce with their mutual enemy.

Eleven days later, the British Parliament considered a conciliatory bill authorizing a special peace commission to offer the colonists extensive concessions to be guaranteed by treaty, and the bill was passed. Lord North hoped that the new measures would prevent the Continental Congress from ratifying the French alliance. The peace commission, headed by the Earl of Carlisle, did not reach Philadelphia until June 6. On March 20, meanwhile, King Louis XVI of France already had formally received the American commissioners and shortly thereafter had named Conrad Gérard as the first French minister to the United States. Congress, learning of the Franco-American alliance on May 2, unanimously ratified the two treaties two days later. On September 11 it resolved to appoint a minister to France and three days later named Franklin to the post.

A June 17 naval engagement between French and British vessels meanwhile had activated the February 6 alliance. In July the first direct French aid — a fleet commanded by Admiral d'Estaing — materialized. French reinforcements at first proved disappointing. Only in the fall of 1781 did the French naval forces under Admiral de Grasse and troops under Rochambeau contribute greatly to American success, especially in the decisive Yorktown campaign (see October 19). In April 1779 the French government persuaded Spain to become a French ally. The Spanish, who hoped to win Gibraltar from Great Britain, allowed American privateers to use New Orleans as a base and seized British outposts in West Florida. French espousal of the American cause in the alliance of February 6, 1778, thus became the first major step in turning the American Revolution into a war with important implications for Europe.

Massachusetts Ratifies the Constitution

Massachusetts, on February 6, 1788, became the sixth state to ratify the federal constitution. Of the earlier five, only Pennsylvania was a major state, and so the addition of Massachusetts to the list of affirmative votes was an important victory for the supporters of the new frame of government. The debate over the Constitution in the Bay State was intense, and the Federalists had to use all their powers of persuasiveness and sense of political compromise to achieve their goal.

In the years immediately after the American War for Independence, Massachusetts found the Articles of Confederation increasingly inadequate. As early as 1785, Governor James Bowdoin in his inaugural address called for a convention to amend the Articles. Shipowners suffered inconveniences and loss of revenues because the Articles left regulation of both internal and foreign commerce to the states. Domestic matters, such as the passage of inflationary paper money legislation and an insurrection of poor farmers led by Captain Daniel Shays in the western part of the state, also produced calls for a stronger government.

When the Continental Congress on February 21, 1787, asked the states to appoint delegates to a convention to revise the Articles, Massachusetts quickly dispatched Francis Dana, Elbridge Gerry, Nathaniel Gorham, Rufus King, and Caleb Strong. Dana never attended the gathering and Strong returned home in August, but Gerry, Gorham, and King remained in Philadelphia until the conclusion of the Constitutional Convention on September 17, 1787. Gerry served as chairman of the Grand Committee of the convention, composed of one delegate from each state, which worked out several important compromises between the large and small states. King was a member of the Committee of Style and Arrangement, which prepared the final draft of the proposed Constitution.

Gorham and King applauded the nationalist bias, which was obvious among the Convention delegates; but Gerry, on the other hand, became increasingly dissatisfied. On September 15 Gerry explained his displeasure to the meeting, and he, along with Virginia representatives George Mason and Edmund Randolph, refused to sign the new Constitution. Gerry protested against the powers of Congress "to make what laws they may please to call necessary and proper," "to raise armies and money without limit," and "to establish a tribunal without juries." He spoke in favor of calling a second Constitutional Convention to remove these defects. In a later letter to the Massachusetts legislature, Gerry deplored the absence of a bill of rights from the new frame of government, but admitted that the proposed Constitution had merit and might, by amendments, be rendered a worthwhile document.

Having completed its task, the Continental Congress referred its handiwork to the states. On October 18, 1787, the Massachusetts General Court issued a call for a ratifying convention to meet in January 1788. On the appointed day 364 delegates from 318 towns met; 46 communities, mostly in the Maine district, which was then part of Massachusetts, sent no representatives.

Gorham, King, and Caleb Strong, three of Massachusetts' delegates to the Constitutional Convention in Philadelphia, won election to the ratification meeting. They eagerly supported the proposed Constitution, as did such other notables as former governor James Bowdoin, Theophilus Parsons, Theodore Sedgwick, and Fisher Ames. The Antifederalist opposition lacked such an elite leadership group, but initially may have had the allegiance of a majority of the delegates.

Supporters of the Constitution worked vigorously to persuade the doubtful. During the Philadelphia convention they published in Boston newspapers and in pamphlets masses of propaganda designed to sway the country delegates. Federalists persuaded the convention to discuss each article of the Constitution separately, a procedure that allowed their highly capable spokesmen additional opportunities to present their position.

Outside the meeting hall, Federalists actively sought to gain the support of Massachusetts' most prominent nondelegates for the Constitution. To win over the Revolutionary firebrand

Samuel Adams, who was a friend and political ally of Elbridge Gerry and who had been silent on the new frame of government, the Federalists, two days before the convention opened, staged a mass meeting of 400 Boston mechanics and tradesmen at the Green Dragon Inn. The participants at the rally adopted a set of strong resolutions in favor of ratification, and this outburst by his constituents prompted Adams to announce his approval of the Constitution. The Federalists won the politically powerful governor John Hancock to their side by promising him their backing for the office of Vice President, and even of President, in the event that Virginia ratified too late to allow the selection of its favorite son, George Washington, for the honor.

On January 31, 1788, Hancock announced his support for a Federalist plan to ratify the Constitution and subsequently to amend the document at the earliest opportunity. Proposed revisions included reservation to the states of all powers not specifically delegated to the federal Congress, safeguards for the rights of jury trial in civil suits, and grand jury indictment in criminal cases. After some additional debate, the convention adopted Hancock's motion by the close vote of 187 to 168 and declared the Constitution ratified on February 6, 1788.

Counties near the coast, including the commercial seats in Suffolk and Essex counties, gave the strongest support to ratification. Agrarian interior areas, such as Worcester, provided the bulk of Antifederalist votes. Nevertheless, once the issue was decided almost all acquiesced in the result, and for years afterward Hancock and Adams, with the support of the Federalists and former Antifederalists, held the chief offices in the Bay State.

In compilations that list the 50 states in order of their admission to the Union, Massachusetts is usually ranked sixth, since it was the sixth state to ratify the Constitution. For the 13 original states, the former British colonies, their existence as states really dates from the creation of the nation. They *were* the United States; and their statehood from the beginning obviated for them the procedure followed by most later states, which usually passed through a territorial period before achieving statehood.

Spanish-American War Ends

On February 6, 1899, the US Senate ratified the Treaty of Paris, signed December 10, 1898, ending the Spanish-American War (see April 21). It was signed on February 10, 1899, by President William McKinley.

Twentieth Amendment Proclaimed Ratified

The 20th Amendment to the Constitution of the United States, known as the "lame duck" amendment, provides that the terms of the President and Vice President shall begin on January 20 and those of senators and representatives on January 3 instead of on March 4; and that Congress shall convene on January 3 of each year instead of the first Monday in December. The amendment as a whole, proposed to the state legislatures by the 72nd Congress in March 1932, was proclaimed in effect on February 6, 1933, with 36 of the then 48 states having ratified it. By October 15, 1933 — when the specific provisions outlined above became effective — the amendment had been ratified by all the states.

Other sections of the amendment, effective immediately upon ratification, provided for succession in case of the death or failure to qualify of a President-elect. (The remaining vagueness concerning succession and the continuity of executive power in the event of presidential disability was removed by the 25th Amendment to the Constitution, ratified in 1967 [see February 10]).

When the Constitution was originally adopted, the date of March 4 was selected for the President's inauguration in order to provide time for election returns to be assembled and for newly elected candidates to reach the capital. By the time the 20th Amendment was proposed, however, improved methods of transportation and communication had made this long delay after the November elections unnecessary. The customary short session of Congress, beginning in December and attended by members who had been defeated the month before — popularly called "lame ducks" — had been similarly outdated.

FEBRUARY 7

Baltimore Fire

The fire that swept some 150 acres of downtown Baltimore on February 7, 1904, is usually referred to as "disastrous" or "devastating." Fortunately, the fire took place on a Sunday, when most offices and factories were closed, or it might have been even more destructive.

As it was, the great fire destroyed most of the city's business center, with a loss that has been variously estimated between $70 million and $150 million, the evidence weighing toward the higher figure. The Baltimore blaze, which raged for about 30 hours, was the biggest fire since the Chicago conflagration of 1871. When it was over, 80 business blocks and some 2,600 buildings had been demolished.

During the next three years particularly, buildings sprang up at a rapid rate, old ones were modernized, streets were widened, and new docks installed. Much of the work was under the watchful eye of the Burnt District Commission. Before all the activity was over, Baltimore's business district had been almost entirely rebuilt and what had not been rebuilt had been renovated.

Skyscrapers made their first appearance in Baltimore during this period. Other improvements coincided with the new construction. Cesspools gave way to sewers, for example, and cobblestones to smooth pavements. A modern system for purifying the city's water supply was installed. Although Maryland's chief metropolis found itself no exception to the burgeoning of highways and new buildings that swept most of urban America during the 1960s, the beginnings of modern Baltimore date from the conflagration of 1904.

Eleventh Amendment Ratified

Article V of the US Constitution stipulates that amendments to that document will be valid "when ratified by the Legislatures of three-fourths of the several states, or by conventions in three-fourths thereof. . . ." On March 5, 1794, Congress submitted to the states the 11th Amendment to the Constitution, which denies "the Judicial power of the United States" in "any suit . . . commenced or prosecuted against one of the United States by Citizens of another State, or by Citizens or Subjects of any Foreign State." This amendment was not declared ratified until early in 1798 (see January 8), but by February 7, 1795, 12 of the 15 states that then comprised the federal Union — or more than the necessary three-fourths majority — had approved the measure. Thus, almost three years before it gained official recognition, the 11th Amendment had in fact become a part of the Constitution.

FEBRUARY 8

Boy Scouts of America Founded

The anniversary of the founding of the Boy Scouts of America (BSA), on February 8, 1910, is observed every year by that multimillion-member organization as a feature of Boy Scout Month, an annual anniversary celebration extending throughout February. The month-long observance, which was inaugurated in 1970, succeeded the earlier annual celebration of Boy Scout Week from February 7 to 13. The change was designed to provide greater leeway in scheduling the numerous anniversary activities connected with the nation's largest youth organization.

Among the February events generally staged on a local basis in a council, pack, troop, or post, are the customary unit activities: Cub Scout blue and gold dinners, Scout troop parents' nights, and presentation of advancement awards. Special flag ceremonies, shopping center demonstrations, and window displays, as well as reports by youths and adult volunteers describing the past year's achievements, are also traditional features throughout the country. Attendance at religious services, especially on Scout Sabbath (which is scheduled on a Saturday and Sunday close to the date of the organization's founding) also is encouraged.

Some annual anniversary activities — above all the national public speaking contest sponsored jointly by the Reader's Digest Association and the Boy Scouts of America — are built around the theme of the year. Get Involved For Them (GIFT), aimed at furthering community progress through "awareness and involvement in service opportunities," was the theme from September 1973 through August 1974, for example; and the theme Be Prepared For Life was chosen for 1974–1975 to encourage fitness and safety in order to conserve human resources. From September 1975 through August 1977, a two-year Spirit of '76 program was keyed to the nation's commemoration of the bicentennial of the American Revolution. The Boy Scouts' birthday observance includes the annual Report to the Nation, required under terms of the Scouts' federal charter and given to the President of the United States, who is the honorary president of the Boy Scouts of America. Every President since William Howard Taft has accepted this position. In 1972, for example, 15 Scouts and Explorers — 3 chosen on the basis of such criteria as community service and scouting records and 12 who were winners of the regional public speaking contests — presented Richard M. Nixon with his official membership card and with the specially bound report on the year's accomplishments. With Nixon's resignation from the presidency, on August 9, 1974, his successor, Gerald R. Ford, became the first Eagle Scout ever to serve as Chief Executive.

In 1960 the golden anniversary of the founding of BSA was celebrated throughout the year with many observances, but especially during Boy Scout Week and during the week-long

Fifth National Jamboree attended by 56,377 boys and leaders who camped at Colorado Springs, Colorado. President Dwight D. Eisenhower spent a day with the Scouts there.

Boy scouting began around the turn of the century with the publication of a military pamphlet, "Aids to Scouting," by a British cavalry officer, Robert S. S. Baden-Powell, who had scouted extensively on the Indian and African frontiers. He came to world renown and national acclaim as the Defender of Mafeking during the Boer War. He was returned to England and found himself well known as the author of the pamphlet, which had fascinated boys and educators alike with its emphasis on the need for building a strong character to cope with the rigors of service on the frontiers of the British Empire.

Challenged to lend his prestige and talents as a writer and illustrator to promote scouting as an activity for existing youth groups, Baden-Powell conducted an experimental camp for boys of varied backgrounds and confidently developed his new concept. His book *Scouting for Boys* was an immediate success on its publication in 1908, and the young general resigned from the army to devote the rest of his life to the Boy Scouts. For this work he was knighted, and later made Lord Baden-Powell of Gilwell. As chief Scout of the World, he saw millions of boys pass through the ranks of scouting in nearly every country of the world before he died, in Kenya in 1941, at the age of 84.

In 1909 a Chicago newspaper publisher, William D. Boyce, was lost in a London fog when a boy came up and saluted, saying, "May I be of service to you, sir?" Boyce told him the address he was seeking and the boy took him there. The publisher offered the boy a shilling, but he refused it, saluting again. "Sir, I am a Scout," he said. "Scouts do not accept tips for courtesies." Startled, Boyce asked for an explanation and the boy told him of the British Boy Scout Association and offered to take him to its headquarters. At the Scout office, Boyce learned of the work of Sir Robert Baden-Powell and the organization.

He returned to the United States and early in 1909 started the organization of the Boy Scouts of America — which in some ways was similar to then current efforts by others to work with boys. (Among other organizations intended to interest boys in wholesome activities were Ernest Thompson Seton's Woodcraft Indians and Dan C. Beard's Sons of Daniel Boone, which ultimately merged with the Boy Scouts of America.)

After a permanent organization had been formed, the Boy Scouts of America was incorporated by a number of prominent men at the behest of William Boyce under the laws of the District of Columbia on February 8, 1910. It was chartered by the US Congress in 1916. Since 1910 more than 52 million boys have received Scout training. As of the mid-1970's there were some 6 million members of the Boy Scouts of America.

The Scout program is open to boys aged 8 to 18. Those in the 8-to-10 year bracket join as Cub Scouts. Boys 11 to 18 may be Boy Scouts. The more independent Explorer program, co-educational in recent years, is intended for young men and women between the ages of 15 and 21.

The aim of the Boy Scouts of America is to develop the character and personal fitness of boys and train them for the duties of adult life and participating citizenship through influence brought to bear on their work and recreation. The organization's charter and bylaws declare the intention to ". . . promote, through organization, and cooperation with other agencies, the ability of boys to do things for themselves and others, to train them in Scoutcraft, and to teach them patriotism, courage, self-reliance, and kindred virtues. . . ." The purpose is stated in the Scout Oath or Promise, which is as follows: "On my honor I will do my best to do my duty to God and my country and to obey the Scout Law; to help other people at all times; to keep myself physically strong, mentally awake, and morally straight." There are 12 points of the Scout Law: "A Scout is trustworthy, loyal, helpful, friendly, courteous, kind, obedient, cheerful, thrifty, brave, clean, and reverent."

The scouting movement, which is nonsectarian and without military or political connection, promotes energetic outdoor activities, including camping, which is a regular feature of the Scout program, and such activities as nature conservation and forestry. Scouts play a prominent role in many community services as well, including such undertakings as emergency traffic control, disaster aid, and safety campaigns. Swimming, cooking, lifesaving, first aid, and woodcraft are among the skills that Scouts develop. There are standards of achievement for advancing from rank to rank within the several phases of the program. Most of the Scout activities employ the skills required for advancement.

In 1972 the Boy Scouts of America published a new handbook and launched a major effort to make the Scouting program more relevant to today's youth by advocating a more flexible advancement program and the development of modern skills such as communications, space exploration, and personal management. In 1969 it inaugurated an eight-year-long plan called Boypower '76, which has as its goal the involvement in Scouting of a greater number of boys in disadvantaged rural communities and in inner city areas, where scouting has gained in popularity in recent years. Project SOAR (Save Our American Resources) is an ecology program that stresses national conservation and an understanding of humanity's interdependence with the environment. (In one recent year SOAR participants gathered one million tons of trash and cleared 400,000 acres of parks and 200,000 miles of highways and streams.) Another project, Operation Reach, is aimed at preventing drug abuse.

Scouts wear prescribed uniforms when on scouting duty, although there is more informality about this than previously, and new red berets have been introduced, and the traditional neckerchief has been made optional. They also wear a badge which resembles a fleur-de-lys, but is really the North sign of the mariner's compass and was used by Baden-Powell for his military scouts. It means "Follow me — I know the way."

Cub Scouts are organized into neighborhood dens and packs; Boy Scouts join patrols and troops; and Explorers have posts as their unit. An executive board, composed of adult volunteers who are leaders in their professions, directs the national organization. All local scouting is governed by local councils; there are over 400 councils within the United States, served by six national regions. Headquarters of the Boy Scouts of America is in New Brunswick, New Jersey.

FEBRUARY 9

Gasparilla Pirate Invasion
Tampa, Florida

This is a movable event. See note on page xxvi.

Tampa, Florida, began in 1904 to hold a Gasparilla festival based on the exploits of José Gaspar, a Spanish pirate of the late 18th century who referred to himself by the diminutive term Gasparilla, or "little Gaspar." In that year a company of business and social leaders organized a club that they called Ye Mystic Krewe of Gasparilla. In the years since, members of the krewe, who now number about 500, have built the pirate festival into one of the nation's largest and best attended celebrations. In recent years some 700,000 persons have jammed the city's piers, bridges, rooftops, and sidewalks each year in February for what now

is officially named the Gasparilla Pirate Invasion and Parade of the Pirates. The day of the pirate invasion has been declared a legal holiday in Florida's Hillsborough County (in which Tampa is located), and "all city, county, and state offices, and banking institutions may remain closed," according to Florida statute.

The idea for the original festival originated with George W. Hardee, a New Orleans man who in 1904 was working in Tampa for the federal government. Seeking a way to add color to a May festival that was being planned in Tampa, he seized upon the legends about Gasparilla, who had plied the area's Gulf coast waters. A few weeks after Hardee presented his idea to several city leaders, Ye Mystic Krewe of Gasparilla was formed. Plans were then made to secure costumes, "capture the city," and crown a king at a huge coronation ball during the anticipated May festival.

That year's first appearance of the krewe was in marked contrast to today's flamboyant, cannon-booming invasions. Krewe members, some 40 or 50 strong and mounted on horseback, simply headed a parade from the waterfront through the downtown streets. At the coronation ball several nights later, E. R. Gunby was crowned as King Gasparilla I. The festival continued in similar vein in 1905 and 1906. Although it was then dropped for the next three years, it was revived in 1910.

The next year, 1911, saw an important change, for it was then that the invasion by sea was added to the festival. The krewe of 1911 sailed up Tampa Bay in a three-masted schooner named the *Samuel T. Beacham*, disembarked at the Alhambra-like Tampa Bay Hotel (now part of the University of Tampa), and were welcomed with enthusiasm by Tampa residents.

Since then the seaborne invasion has become the most colorful part of the Gasparilla festival. Today's "pirates," however, arrive aboard the three-masted, fully rigged *José Gasparilla*, a 164-foot craft which is on year-round display in Tampa's harbor. Built specially for the festival in 1953–1954, it is an exact replica of a West Indiaman used by pirates in the 18th century. Among its unusual features are special holds for the thousands of balloons released at the climax of the invasion each February. Decked with over 300 flags and pennants, manned by 500 costumed pirates, and accompanied by several hundred pleasure craft, the *José Gasparilla* sails up the bay and into Tampa's Hillsborough River with its cannons firing salutes. After the ship has landed at the docks behind the Curtis Hixon Convention Center, its krewe of buccaneers goes over

154

the side and "captures" Tampa and its mayor, raising the pirate flag above the city hall.

The invasion, which takes place at noon on the Monday following the first Tuesday in February, marks the beginning of six days of carnival, timed to coincide with the second week of the Florida State Fair, which is also held in Tampa. The swashbuckling invasion is followed by a three-hour-long victory parade with members of the Mystic Krewe, some 50 to 60 elaborate floats, 25 or 30 bands, and dozens of marching units. The floats, which may cost as much as $15,000 apiece, are sponsored by commercial enterprises, civic organizations, neighboring cities, and the managements of other festivals; and trophies are awarded for the outstanding entries in various categories. The customary highlight of Tuesday's festivities is the coronation ball (not open to the public) where, amid much pomp, the Gasparilla king and queen for the previous year step down from their year-long reign over Ye Mystic Krewe of Gasparilla and a new king and queen are crowned.

Tampa's Latin Quarter, Ybor City — the Spanish-Cuban-Italian section, which still retains some of the atmosphere created by its original Cuban settlers — meanwhile has its own celebration, beginning on Sunday with the Ybor City Navy's traditional "conquest" of a federal ship, which lies peacefully waiting at anchor until it is boarded by "attackers" (armed with loaves of Cuban bread and followed by smiling señoritas), who quickly accept the ship's "surrender." Ybor City's celebration comes to a climax with Pirate Fiesta Day, usually on Thursday of Gasparilla week. There is day-long gaiety on this occasion, with street dances, costume contests, entertainment by Spanish musicians and dancers, and the dispensing of a famous local specialty — Spanish bean soup or *sopa de garbanzo*, of which each visitor receives a hearty portion, along with a slab of crisp Cuban bread, and coffee. Indeed, the occasion is known as the *Fiesta Sopa de Garbanzo*. Festivities reach a crescendo shortly after nightfall, when the pirates of Gasparilla appear in Ybor City for Pirate Fiesta Night, highlighted by a spectacular torchlight parade in which pirate garb is seen amidst the authentic Spanish costumes.

On Saturday night the pirate ship sails away amid a blaze of fireworks as both the festival and the fair come to an end.

It is said that Spanish-born José Gaspar, the villain-hero of the Gasparilla pirate invasion, was the last of the pirates to sail the Spanish Main. Although facts are few and some scholars doubt that there ever was such a person, evidence points to the probability that the bloodthirsty Gaspar actually existed. Reportedly he was a lieutenant in the Royal Spanish Navy and began his career as a pirate by leading a mutiny aboard a Spanish sloop-of-war in 1783. From then (or earlier — there are contradictions about dates) until his death in 1821, he terrorized Florida's Gulf Coast — often from an island 100 miles south of Tampa which he made his headquarters and which today bears his name. According to what is believed to be Gaspar's own diary, he captured and burned 36 ships in his first dozen years of piracy, and an unknown number thereafter.

He met his end by launching one attack too many — on a US Navy warship, the USS *Enterprise*, which he had mistaken for a helpless merchantman. The *Enterprise* let loose with a stunning volley. Minutes later, with his men falling around him, the masts of his ship down, a gaping hole in its hull, and a boarding party approaching, Gaspar ended it all by wrapping a length of anchor chain around his waist and leaping into the sea as he brandished his sword in a final defiant gesture.

Wishful thinkers still search the Florida coast for the treasure they feel sure he must have buried somewhere.

William Henry Harrison's Birthday

William Henry Harrison, the ninth President of the United States, was born at the plantation of Berkeley in Charles County, Virginia, on February 9, 1773. He was the third son of Benjamin Harrison, whose ancestors came to America from England in 1633.

Benjamin Harrison was governor of Virginia and one of the signers of the Declaration of Independence. His son William Henry entered Hampden-Sidney College in 1787. In 1790 he went to Richmond to study medicine and a few months later went to Philadelphia, where he studied under Dr. Benjamin Rush. After his father's death in 1791, young William Harrison decided to enter the army and was commissioned as an ensign in the First Infantry Regiment. He served in the Northwest Territory, rose to the rank of lieutenant, and was acting aide-de-camp to General Anthony Wayne.

After further promotion, to the rank of captain, Harrison resigned from the army in 1798 and was appointed secretary of the Northwest Territory. The next year he was elected as its first delegate to Congress. He was influential in obtaining passage of the act that divided the Northwest Territory into the territories of Ohio and Indiana, and in 1800 was appointed governor of the new Indiana Territory.

As governor, he was presented with two utterly irreconcilable assignments: to see that the Indians were treated justly by the settlers, and to secure the cession of as much Indian land as possible for the US government. Harrison succeeded in obtaining grants of millions of acres of land in Indiana and in what became the territory of Illinois in 1809. Not surprisingly, however, the Indians resented the influx of white settlers, and the brilliant Shawnee chief Tecumseh (see October 5) set about forming a confederation of Indian tribes to prevent the occupation of their lands. In November 1811 Harrison led a force of about 1,000 men against the Indians in the battle of Tippecanoe, defeated them, and took possession of their settlement there. The site of the encounter is now designated as the Tippecanoe Battlefield State Memorial; it is not far from Lafayette, Indiana.

After the War of 1812 began between the United States and Great Britain, Harrison was named a brigadier general and given command of all US Army troops in the Northwest. He saw active service in battles against the British forces and their Indian allies. His victory at the battle of the Thames (near Chatham, Ontario), which resulted in the death of Tecumseh on October 5, 1813, virtually ended British activities in the Northwest and was followed by the pacification of most of the Indians of the region.

Harrison was succeeded as governor of Indiana in March 1813 by Thomas Posey and was raised to the rank of major general. In May of the next year he resigned from the army for the second time and took up residence on his farm at North Bend, Ohio, near Cincinnati. He was elected to the national House of Representatives in 1816 and served there until 1819. He then was a member of the Ohio Senate from 1819 to 1821 and subsequently was elected to the US Senate, where he served beginning in 1825 and was chiefly notable for chairmanship of the Committee on Military Affairs.

Through the influence of Henry Clay, whose supporter he had been, Harrison was appointed, after three years in the Senate, as the first US minister to the young nation of Colombia. Arriving in Bogotá in February 1829, at a time when the enemies of President Simón Bolívar, who had liberated the region from Spain, were actively revolting against him, Harrison was accused of sympathizing with the revolutionists. He was recalled the following summer by President Andrew Jackson, who had assumed office in March.

Back in the United States, Harrison was an unsuccessful anti-Democratic candidate for President in 1836, running as a Whig and receiving only 73 electoral votes against Van Buren's 170. Undiscouraged, Harrison's supporters immediately began to organize a movement to bring about his nomination in 1840. The three leading Whig contenders for the presidential nomination were Harrison, Daniel Webster, and Clay. Webster withdrew in December 1839 and his influence, along with that of political leader Thurlow Weed of New York, was strong enough to win the nomination for Harrison. John Tyler (see March 29) was nominated as the Whig candidate for Vice President.

The campaign is remembered for its slogans — like the still recalled cry of "Tippecanoe and Tyler too!!" — and for its campaign literature, which emphasized pictures of Harrison seated in front of a log cabin. Harrison was elected with 234 electoral votes against 60 for the Democrats' badly defeated Van Buren.

Inaugurated on March 4, 1841, Harrison, refusing both hat and coat despite inclement weather, marked the occasion by riding a white horse to the Capitol. There he delivered a lengthy inaugural address before leading the inaugural parade to the White House. One month later to the day he died of pneumonia.

Forty-eight years after that tragedy, Harrison's grandson Benjamin followed him into the presidency. The William Henry Harrison State Memorial, consisting of Harrison's tomb and a monument on 14 acres overlooking the Ohio River, can be visited today at North Bend, Ohio. Also open to visitors is Grouseland, the mansion at Vincennes, Indiana, in which Harrison lived while he was governor of the Indiana Territory. Berkeley Plantation (Harrison's Landing), the handsomely restored ancestral home of William Henry and Benjamin Harrison, located on the James River between Richmond and Williamsburg in Virginia, and open daily, is also a magnet for travelers.

FEBRUARY 10

Mardi Gras, or Shrove Tuesday

This is a movable event. See note on page xxvi.

Shrove Tuesday, or Mardi Gras, is the day immediately preceding the beginning of Lent on Ash Wednesday. Like the dates of Lent, a period of fasting and penitence in which Christians prepare for Easter, Shrove Tuesday is a movable observance whose date depends on the date of Easter. Ash Wednesday is 40 days before Easter, not counting Sundays, and Shrove Tuesday is 41.

As observed in New Orleans, Shrove Tuesday is probably the United States' most elaborate celebration. By proclamation of the governor, the day is a legal holiday in several parishes and many municipalities of Louisiana. In addition it is a legal holiday throughout the state of Alabama and in some counties of Florida. It is also marked in parts of Mississippi and to some extent elsewhere in the United States.

Shrove Tuesday is the concluding day of the carnival festivities that for centuries have preceded the austere Lenten season, especially in the predominantly Roman Catholic countries of Europe. But although the church by the Middle Ages had put its imprint upon the celebrations, or at least allowed dispensation for what could not be easily suppressed, the idea of carnival probably originated with pre-Christian pagan rites. These rituals, particularly including fertility rites, marked the approach of spring, with its attendant rebirth of nature, and sought to ensure good crops. Not only the early Egyptians, but also the ancient Greeks and Romans, celebrated at about this time of year.

Carnival as it survives today spread from Rome, where masked and costumed revelers took part in annual processions and pelted one another with confetti. During the Middle Ages, Florence and Venice became famous for their carnival pageantry, replete with floats, splendid costumes and masks, and, in the case of Venice, flower-decked gondolas. Major Spanish cities staged sumptuous carnivals and lavish balls, and the Portuguese held floral balls and mock battles with confetti.

Beginning in the 1400s the French — whose term *mardi gras* translates literally as "fat Tuesday" — also had costume balls. Their celebrations came to include long, float-filled parades, flower battles and, in some places, a Shrove Tuesday procession led by a fat ox. The ox was traditionally followed by a triumphal car bearing a child known as the "king of the butchers." To Germans, the night before Lent became known as *Fastnacht,* meaning the night before the fast.

In English-speaking lands, Shrove Tuesday is the preferred term. The verb "to shrive" means to hear or make confession and to grant absolution or impose penance. The Anglo-Saxon *Ecclesiastical Institutes* refers to the custom of going to confess one's sins in order to approach Lent with appropriate penitence: "In the week immediately before Lent everyone shall go to his confessor and confess his deeds

and the confessor shrive him." Accordingly, the last three days before Lent — Shrove Sunday, Shrove Monday, and Shrove Tuesday — are collectively known as Shrovetide.

Particularly in England, Shrove Tuesday also is sometimes called Pancake Tuesday, in allusion to the old custom of making pancakes on this day. As no meat was to be eaten in Lent, all the fats in the house were used in making the pancakes. An account of this custom is contained in a 17th century English book protesting against the excesses once practiced on the day:

There is a thing called wheaten flower, which the sulphury necromantic cooks do mingle with water, eggs, spice and other tragical, magical enchantments, and then they put it little by little into a frying pan of boiling suet, where it makes a confused dismal hissing — like the Lernean snakes in the reeds of Acheron, Styx or Phlegeton — until at last by the skill of the cook it is transformed into the form of a flip-jack, which in our translation is called a pancake, which ominous incantation the ignorant people do devour very greedily — having for the most part well dined before — but they have no sooner swallowed that sweet, candied bait, but straight their wits forsake them and they run stark mad, assembling in routs and throngs of ungovernable numbers, with uncivil civil commotions.

It was customary for cakes to be fried in each household, and when one side of a pancake was cooked for it to be tossed into the air so that it turned over and fell back into the frying pan with the uncooked side down. The name *flapjacks* survives to this day in the United States, where the cakes are made of buckwheat flour, cornmeal, or rice as well as of wheat flour.

In England and Scotland it long was customary to play a boisterous game of football, accompanied by much horseplay, on Shrove Tuesday. There was a custom, too, of beating fighting cocks to death — perhaps as a vicarious punishment of the cock whose crowing recalled to the apostle Peter that he had denied his Lord, Jesus — though there are other theories as to the origin of the brutal custom.

From Europe the idea of pre-Lenten carnivals in general, and a climactic Shrove Tuesday celebration in particular, spread to the Western Hemisphere. Some notable celebrations developed in Latin America, where boisterous pre-Lenten festivities take place in such cities as Montevideo, Uruguay; Buenos Aires, Argentina; and — most spectacularly — Rio de Janeiro, Brazil, where the annual hilarity approaches madness. In Puerto Rico, much but not all of what used to be an elaborate pre-Lenten carnival in San Juan is now combined with celebrations surrounding the feast day of that capital's patron saint in June. However, San Juan residents still celebrate to some extent, and Arecibo and some other Puerto Rican communities place heavy emphasis on parades and other pre-Lenten festivities, which reach a climax on Shrove Tuesday.

At one time the carnival period generally extended from Epiphany through Shrove Tuesday. Today, however, it is usually limited to the three days — or sometimes the four or five days — just before Lent.

At Mobile, Alabama, where one of the best-known observances takes place, festivities last for 10 days or longer. And at New Orleans, the site of North America's most flamboyant, and one of the world's most famous, celebrations, the carnival season begins on Twelfth Night or the Epiphany and reaches its zenith during the last 11 to 14 days before Lent. These are collectively known as Mardi Gras, even though that term applies literally only to Shrove Tuesday, when the hysteria that has been mounting detonates in a final, city-wide burst of noise, parades, masquerading, pageantry and frenzied jubilance.

Elsewhere in the United States, Mardi Gras is celebrated from one to three days in such places as Biloxi, Pascagoula, and Pass Christian, Mississippi; in Lafayette, Franklin, and some other communities of Louisiana; by Louisianans living in other cities, among them Washington, D.C.; and in parts of Florida. There are other celebrations from time to time. Generally speaking, Mardi Gras observances are most prevalent in parts of the South with a French or Spanish heritage. However, Mardi Gras is also sometimes celebrated by citizens of French descent in such northern Maine border towns as Fort Kent, Madawaska, and Van Buren.

The English custom of observing Shrove Tuesday as Pancake Tuesday is carried on in parts of the United States — notably in Liberal, Kansas, where the day is marked as International Pancake Day. The women of Liberal race along a 415-yard, S-shaped course, flipping pancakes as they go, and then compare their speed with that of the women who compete in a similar and much older race in Olney, England. The German tradition of eating fried crullers — Fastnacht Kuchen — on Shrove Tuesday is preserved by the so-called "Pennsylvania Dutch" people, of German descent, in Pennsylvania's Lancaster County.

Some American Mardi Gras celebrations, however, have been discontinued. This is true, for example, of the elaborate celebration which

Memphis, Tennessee, held for some years during the 19th century — and in 1931 revived in a different manner as the famous Cotton Carnival held annually in May (see May 9).

Just when these celebrations began in what is now the United States is uncertain. Louisianans point out that when French colonizers under Pierre Charles le Moyne, Sieur d'Iberville, camped near the mouth of the Mississippi River on Shrove Tuesday in 1699 they named their site Point du Mardi Gras — and may, perhaps, have celebrated approximately at the same time. D'Iberville also founded Biloxi, Mississippi, slightly east of its present location, in 1699, and Biloxians would like to think that Mardi Gras festivities began there almost immediately. In 1702 d'Iberville's younger brother, Jean Baptiste Lemoyne, Sieur de Bienville, founded Fort Louis de La Mobile — the colony that moved to the present site of Mobile, Alabama, eight years later — and some Alabamans hold to a tradition that his soldiers began celebrating Mardi Gras the very year the fort was founded. It is generally agreed, however, that the Mobile festivities in their present exuberant form did not get under way until 1830.

New Orleans is relatively modest in its claim that Mardi Gras observances began there in 1827. The celebration was introduced by a company of young men of French descent who had been sent to Paris to be educated. They had enjoyed the Mardi Gras festivities in that city and when they returned home in 1827 they organized a procession of street maskers who marched about the city on the day before Ash Wednesday. In the course of time this developed into a parade of boys, armed with bags of flour and cudgels, who marched about the streets indulging in horseplay with other marchers.

The wearing of masks, which is still customary on Shrove Tuesday, dates back at least to medieval times and the Mardi Gras celebrations of France and Italy. The first recorded instance of processions of masqueraders in New Orleans is dated 1838. However, it was nearly two decades later when New Orleans began its custom of celebrating the day with a parade of floats carrying symbolic figures — an idea borrowed from Mobile's 19th century New Year frolic (see January 1). It was in 1857 that the Mystick Krewe of Comus, a secret organization formed in New Orleans that year, put on the first of the now-famous street pageants. Setting the precedent for today's spectacular parades, it was a torchlit scenic procession held at night. The subjects illustrated in that first street pageant were the demon characters of Milton's *Par-*

adise Lost. After the parade, members of the organization went to the old Gaiety Theatre and there presented a series of tableaux.

The Mystick Krewe of Comus gave an annual parade until 1861, when the celebration was interrupted by the Civil War. It was resumed from 1866 until 1884, when it was suspended until 1910 and then again resumed. Other temporary suspensions were occasioned by bad weather in 1933 and by World Wars I and II and the Korean War.

In 1870 another society, the still active Twelfth Night Revelers, was organized to celebrate the beginning of the carnival season in New Orleans. It gave a street parade for a while, preceding a ball in the once famous French Opera House. Although the parade has been abandoned, the Twelfth Night Revelers still initiate the official carnival season with an elaborate ball and tableau on January 6 (see Twelfth Night Revels). The opera house having been destroyed by fire in 1919, these festivities and many other carnival balls now take place in New Orleans' big Municipal Auditorium, which frequently houses two balls on a single evening during the carnival season.

The organization known as Rex was formed during the visit of the Russian Grand Duke Alexis Alexandrovich Romanoff to New Orleans in 1872. For his entertainment, it was proposed that the different units of maskers should be consolidated into a single group and parade in his honor. The resulting organization became permanent, and its king, Rex, was — and still is — recognized as the King of the Carnival, the Sovereign Lord of Misrule.

The Krewe of Proteus, organized in 1882, still gives a spectacular annual street pageant followed by an elaborate ball and tableaux on Monday, the night before Shrove Tuesday. The Knights of Momus, founded in 1872, parade and give a ball on Thursday of the preceding week, and other carnival societies, including the Krewe of Nereus, the High Priests of Mithras, the Atlanteans, the Elves of Oberon, the Knights of Babylon, and the Krewe of Alpheus celebrate with splendid private balls replete with elaborate pageantry and prescribed, almost ritualistic, formalities. Between January 6 and Shrove Tuesday, when New Orleans' carnival season comes to a riotous finish, there are more than 60 such balls. Invitations, which are issued only by krewe members, are highly prized, hard to acquire, and not transferable — which means that the general public and visitors from out of town are virtually excluded.

The pageant-balls are not the only features of the New Orleans social season, however. It is during the last 11 days of carnival that festivities reach a climax with the public (as distinct from private) celebrations for which the city is famous. During this time some 25 lavishly costumed parades, by day or brilliantly torchlit by night, wind their way through New Orleans streets. The streets and the famous wrought-iron balconies of houses along the line of march are crowded with people. (Other, less elaborate parades also take place in the suburbs of New Orleans.)

Two krewes established in recent years, Bacchus and Argus, represent a departure from tradition. A national celebrity, rather than a local one, is invited to preside over their festivities as king, and he does not present a court. These krewes adhere to tradition in staging elaborate parades but do not hold tableau balls.

The parades and related activities are sponsored by the krewes and by various marching societies and smaller carnival organizations. Along with the marching bands, they reach a crescendo during the last six days before Lent. Each of the processions is made up of as many as 15 or 20 sumptuous floats, all centered around a common theme and interspersed with bands, drill teams, and civilian and military marching units. The ways in which the theme is carried out may be elaborate indeed, and the average parade lasts two or three hours.

The krewe's captain and his aides, mounted, masked, and costumed, are prominent in each parade. Then come the king's float (each krewe has its carnival royalty), the theme or title float, and others, which interpret the theme. The widely ranging themes have included The Odyssey, Take Me Out to the Ball Game, Great Treasures of Literature, Old King Cole and His Jolly Subjects, There's No Business Like Show Business, and Lost Cities in Fact and Fancy.

It is customary for each street pageant to pause several times en route while the king raises a champagne toast to honored figures along the line of march — members of his family; his queen, traditionally a current debutante who watches the cavalcade from the balcony of one of the city's more exclusive clubs; and the mayor, city council members, and other dignitaries stationed in the reviewing stand at Gallier Hall. Also customary is the tossing from passing floats of colorful baubles and, in recent years, special doubloons minted by the various krewes. These treasured trinkets, the famous carnival "throws," precipitate mad scrambles on the part of spectators, whose gaiety mounts steadily with their cries of "Hey, throw me something, mister."

Each krewe has its own traditionally distinguishing features. The Krewes of Iris and Venus, for instance, are among several all-women krewes. As a god of the sea, Proteus, who has one of the most elaborate street pageants, is habitually enthroned on a giant, scalloped seashell. Zulu krewe members are noted for their madcap antics, their much-treasured carnival "throws" (gilded and decorated coconuts), and the unpredictability of their parade route. The Elks Krewe has the longest parade — between 125 and 175 floats — and the parade of Rex is the most elaborate.

The climax of the carnival comes on Shrove Tuesday, when New Orleans business comes to a standstill amidst the general hilarity. Residents and thousands of visitors join in the merrymaking. Open houses, street dancing, and the blare of Dixieland bands are the order of the day.

Men, women, and children don masks and fancy dress and wander about town with boisterous abandon. The costumes are varied and spectacular. Persons prominent in the news are impersonated and sometimes burlesqued. The streets swarm with pirates, princesses, dancing girls, Roman soldiers, African warriors, monks, devils, angels, medieval knights and ladies, clowns, dragons, monsters, spacemen, cartoon characters, Spanish dons, French cavaliers, Oriental potentates, ancient Egyptians, Greek gods, Vikings, toreadors, cannibals, Tarzans, "flappers" of the 1920s, animals, birds, and flowers, and scores of figures from history, legend, and fantasy.

In one recent typical year, the fun-filled, six-float parade of the Krewe of Zulu began early on Shrove Tuesday morning. As the only unmasked Mardi Gras principal, Rex, the king of carnival, came next.

Rex, who is customarily a New Orleans businessman and civic leader, reigned over a regal procession of 23 floats centered around the theme To the Ladies — Bless Them All. First came two special bandwagons, the traditional throne float of Rex, and the *Boeuf Gras,* or fat ox, of French custom. Behind this was the theme float, featuring goblets, and a giant champagne bottle. The women honored on succeeding floats were a varied group — Eve, Helen of Troy, Cleopatra, Delilah, Joan of Arc, Brunnhilde, Lady Godiva, Queen Isabella, Pocahontas, Catherine the Great, Marie Antoinette, the goddess Shaktri, Calamity Jane, the Dowager Empress of China, Victoria Regina, Lillian Russell, Madame Butterfly, and the Statue of Liberty, among others. A mammoth parade and gala procession followed.

According to custom, New Orleans' carnival street pageants ended that evening with the elaborate, flambeaux-lit parade of the Mystick Krewe of Comus, which is not only the oldest but also the most exclusive of all the carnival organizations. Later the same evening, the magnificent private balls of Rex and Comus took place, with all their traditional ritual, in different halls of the Municipal Auditorium. Just before midnight, Rex and his court, according to long custom, visited the Comus ball. As they entered, the orchestra sounded Rex's familiar theme song, "If Ever I Cease to Love." After the two monarchs, their queens, and courts participated in a ceremonial grand march around the ballroom, Rex and Comus took their places on a double throne, which they occupied until the official close of carnival. This came, as always, at midnight.

In Mobile, Alabama, Mardi Gras celebrations take place as part of a two-month period in February and March known as the Mobile Azalea Trail Festival, which includes America's Junior Miss Pageant and many other events, and highlights local blooms along a 35-mile floral route. It also includes some 15 or so Mardi Gras parades and numerous Mardi Gras balls. For the most part, the latter begin right after the New Year and continue until Shrove Tuesday, although three of Mobile's oldest mystic societies hold their dances before January 1. The Strikers society, formed in 1842, has a gala on New Year's Eve. The Santa Claus Society, which was 88 years old in 1975, usually has its ball the Friday night before Christmas. And the oldest women's mystic society, the Follies, celebrates during the first part of December.

But it is not until 10 to 14 days before Shrove Tuesday that the tempo of Mobile's pre-Lenten celebrations really accelerates. As elsewhere, events multiply as the actual day of Mardi Gras approaches.

While Mardi Gras celebrations in New Orleans and Mobile stem from the same traditions and have many similarities, they also have differences. In Mobile, the King of Carnival is known not as Rex, but as Felix. He arrives at the city on his royal yacht and selects his own queen. He is accompanied by a retinue of courtiers and is formally welcomed by his subjects. Mobile's 15 or 16 pre-Lenten parades are as colorful as those in New Orleans, although not necessarily as long. One or two Mobile parades preserve a tradition of many decades — having the floats drawn by costumed mules — unlike New Orleans, which saw its last mules in the celebration of 1951. Another contrast is

Mobile's custom of having all guests at Mardi Gras balls take part in the dancing — rather than limiting the dancing to krewe members and those women specially "called out," as in New Orleans. Mobile's Mardi Gras parades take place both at day and at night. On Shrove Tuesday there is general masking and the parading lasts all day long, with most agencies of local government and almost all private business closed for the festivities.

Biloxi, Mississippi, which also puts on a series of fancy-dress balls throughout a long carnival season, similarly devotes itself to masking and frolic on Shrove Tuesday. That day there are two, float-filled daytime parades, sponsored by the Gulf Coast Carnival Association, and a grand feature parade, which tops off the celebration at night.

Treaty of Paris (1898) Becomes Effective

At the conclusion of the Spanish-American War (see April 21) in 1898, a commission was appointed to negotiate a treaty of peace. American and Spanish commissioners met in Paris, and a treaty was written under which Spain ceded to the United States the Philippine Islands (for $20 million to offset Spanish expenditures there); the island of Guam; and Puerto Rico. Spain also agreed to withdraw from Cuba and leave the settlement of affairs on that island to the United States, which then administered Cuban affairs on a temporary basis until May 1902 and again from late 1906 until early 1909 (see January 28).

The treaty was submitted to the US Senate by President William McKinley on January 4, 1899, for ratification. A memorable debate on it was conducted in open session, with opponents of the measure leveling charges of imperialism, particularly in regard to the projected US acquisition of the Philippine Islands. Departing from the position of much of his party, Republican Senator George F. Hoar of Massachusetts opposed ratification on the ground that the United States had no constitutional power to hold the Philippine Islands. However, Senator John C. Spooner of Wisconsin, another Republican, said that the islands constituted "the bitter fruits of the war" and insisted that the United States had the right to acquire territory, although he did not think it expedient for the country to hold "permanent dominion over far distant lands and people."

While the debate was in progress William Jennings Bryan, who had been the Democratic candidate for President in 1896, went to Washington and advised Democratic senators to vote for ratification of the treaty, even though he opposed permanent US acquisition of the Philippines. His support turned out to be decisive. As the Republicans did not have the two-thirds majority necessary for ratification, Democratic votes were needed if the treaty was to become effective. After several weeks of debate, the vote was taken on February 6 and the treaty was ratified with only one vote to spare. Of those voting for the measure, 10 were Democrats. Three Republicans voted against ratification.

The treaty was returned to President McKinley, who signed it on February 10, 1899, completing ratification. The act marked the formal conclusion of the Spanish-American War.

Twenty-fifth Amendment Ratified

On February 10, 1967, the Twenty-fifth Amendment, establishing clear lines of succession in case of presidential disability, became part of the US Constitution with ratification by the 38th state. In a parliamentary photo finish, the legislatures of North Dakota, Minnesota, and Nevada competed for the honor of being the 38th body to ratify the amendment, which became law automatically when three-fourths of the nation's 50 states thus signified their approval.

The amendment, which empowers the Vice President to act as President when the President is physically or mentally unable to perform the duties of his office, also enables the President to nominate a Vice President if that post should become vacant. Under previous provisions of the Constitution it was clear that the Vice President would take up the duties of the presidency in case of the President's death, removal, resignation, or inability to discharge his responsibilities. But the Constitution offered only silence on the question of how such presidential disability was to be determined.

This ambiguity led to a situation in which the Vice President was not clearly empowered to take over either in the case of President James A. Garfield, who was incapacitated for 10 weeks prior to his death in 1881, or of President Woodrow Wilson, who was bedridden and unable to transact official business for most of the 18 months before his second term expired in 1921. When Vice President Lyndon B. Johnson was elevated to the presidency after the assassination of President John F. Kennedy in November 1963, the office of Vice President was left vacant for almost 14 months and legislators were again reminded of the constitutional gap that had existed for nearly two centuries.

On July 6, 1965, Congress proposed the 25th Amendment, designed to encure the continuity of presidential power. In slightly abbreviated form, its text is as follows:

SECTION I

In case of the removal of the President from office or his death or resignation, the Vice President shall become President.

SECTION II

Whenever there is a vacancy in the office of Vice President, the President shall nominate a Vice President who shall take the office upon confirmation by a majority vote of both houses of Congress.

SECTION III

Whenever the President transmits to the President pro tempore of the Senate and the Speaker of the House of Representatives his written declaration that he is unable to discharge the powers and duties of his office, and until he transmits to them a written declaration to the contrary, such powers and duties shall be discharged by the Vice President as Acting President.

SECTION IV

Whenever the Vice President and a majority of either the principal officers of the executive departments or of such other body as Congress may by law provide, transmit to the President pro tempore of the Senate and the Speaker of the House of Representatives their written declaration that the President is unable to discharge the powers and duties of his office, the Vice President shall immediately assume [these] powers and duties ... as Acting President.

Thereafter, when the President transmits to the President ... of the Senate and the Speaker of the House ... his written declaration that no inability exists, he shall resume ... his office unless the Vice President and a majority of either the principal officers of the executive department or of such other body as Congress may ... provide, transmit within four days ... their written declaration that the President is unable to discharge ... his office. Thereupon Congress shall decide the issue.... If the Congress ... determines by two-thirds vote of both houses that the President is unable to discharge ... his office, the Vice President shall continue to discharge the same as Acting President; otherwise, the President shall resume the powers and duties of his office.

Section II of the 25th Amendment was first applied in 1973, following the resignation of Vice President Spiro T. Agnew. President Richard M. Nixon nominated Gerald R. Ford, who was sworn in as Vice President on December 6.

A year later the same provision was again exercised. Upon Nixon's resignation from the presidency — the first such resignation in US history — Ford assumed the office on August 9, 1974, and subsequently nominated former New York governor Nelson A. Rockefeller for the vice presidency. Rockefeller took the oath of office on December 19, 1974.

FEBRUARY 11

Ash Wednesday

This is a movable event. See note on page xxvi.

Ash Wednesday is observed by the Western church, both Roman Catholic and Protestant, as the first day of Lent. In the Eastern Byzantine rite, the first day of Lent is marked on the Monday before Ash Wednesday of the Roman rite. The date of Ash Wednesday is movable, occurring between February 4 and March 11, depending upon the date of Easter (see March 29).

The origin of the Lenten penitential season before Easter dates back to early Christian times, perhaps as early as the fourth century. Pope Gregory I the Great (590–604) established Ash Wednesday as the beginning day of this period of preparation (or the first day of Lent), when he extended the formerly brief pre-Easter penitential observance to a total of 40 weekdays (*Quadragesima*), ending with Holy Week with its climactic last three days: Holy Thursday (see March 26), Good Friday (see March 27), and Holy Saturday (see March 28). Biblical precedent undoubtedly determined the number of days considered appropriate for Christians to prepare for the great feast of the Resurrection: Christ had fasted 40 days in the desert; God's Chosen People had stayed 40 years in the desert; Moses had spent 40 days on Mount Sinai; the giant Goliath had threatened Israel for 40 days, until he was slain by David; the prophet Elijah, subsisting only on a little cake and water, had traveled 40 days to Mount Horeb; and Jonah had preached 40 days to the Ninevites.

Pope Gregory I urged disciplinary practices in a spirit of self-examination and penitence not only on Ash Wednesday but throughout Lent. He wrote:

From this day unto the joys of the Paschal solemnity there are six weeks coming ... that we, who through the past year have lived too much for ourselves, should mortify ourselves to our Creator in the tenth of the year through abstinence. Whence, most dear brethren, as ye are bid by the law to offer the tenths of your substance, so contend to offer to him also the tenth of your days.

The name Ash Wednesday (*Dies cinerum* in Latin) probably dates from at least the eighth century. The use of ashes symbolizing penance derives from an ancient and venerable custom, the roots of which can be traced to the Bible. Christ referred to ashes (Matthew 11:21), in condemning the unbelieving towns in which he had worked miracles: "Woe unto thee, Chorazin! woe unto thee, Bethsaida! for if the mighty works, which were done in you, had been done in Tyre and Sidon, they would have repented long ago in sackcloth and ashes."

In the early church, ashes and sackcloth were also used as signs of repentence for grave sins. In a public display of penance, offenders, such as criminals and adulterers, were compelled to walk barefooted and in sackcloth into church to receive holy water and ashes. It is not known when the practice of distributing ashes not only to public penitents but to all members of the congregation became widespread; it was probably sometime in the ninth century. A passage from Aelfric's *Lives of the Saints,* written in Anglo-Saxon in 996–997, seems to indicate that the custom was already commonly observed:

We read in the books both in the Old Law and the New that the men who repented of their sins bestrewed themselves with ashes and clothed their bodies with sack cloth. Now let us do this little at the beginning of our Lent that we strew ashes upon our heads to signify that we ought to repent of our sins during the Lenten fast.

Like holy water, candles, and blessed palm, ashes gradually came to be considered in the Roman Catholic church as sacramentals or sacred signs resembling the sacraments, which signify spiritual effects obtained through the church's intercession.

As the first day of Lent, Ash Wednesday was the beginning of a period of strict fasting and abstinence. Since the consumption of dairy products and meat was forbidden, breads, pastry, soups, vegetables, and fish (especially herring) became the staple Lenten diet. Several of the common foods of today, such as pretzels and hot cross buns, originated as special Lenten features in medieval times.

Roman Catholics still observe the custom of receiving ashes on Ash Wednesday. Communicants are exhorted to approach the altar to receive ashes. The priest dips his thumb into previously blessed ashes and marks the sign of the cross on the recipient's forehead, repeating, "Remember, man, that you are dust, and unto dust you shall return," or "Repent, and believe the Good News." The ashes used are still made by burning the remains of the palms blessed on Palm Sunday of the previous year. For Roman Catholics, the Apostolic constitution entitled *Paenitemini,* effective since February 23, 1966, allowed other penitential works to be substituted for the usual observance of fast and abstinence during Lent. In the United States, Ash Wednesday and Good Friday remain the only days of the church calendar on which strict fast and abstinence must still be observed; however, all Fridays in Lent are days of abstinence.

The custom of imposing ashes on Ash Wednesday has largely disappeared in Protestant churches, although, particularly in recent years, some Lutherans and many Episcopalians do receive them. For Protestants, the historic emphasis on penitence and contrition remains, with stress on self-denial and spiritual self-examination in the days of Lent to follow. The Episcopalian *Book of Common Prayer* aptly expresses this thought in the collect for Ash Wednesday (which is repeated daily throughout Lent, until Palm Sunday).

Almighty and everlasting God, who hatest nothing that thou hast made, and dost forgive the sins of all those who are penitent; Create and make in us new and contrite hearts, that we, worthily lamenting our sins and acknowledging our wretchedness, may obtain of thee, the God of all mercy, perfect remission and forgiveness; through Jesus Christ our Lord. Amen.

Special religious services are held on Ash Wednesday by the Church of England, and in the United States by Episcopal, Lutheran, and some other Protestant churches. The Episcopal Church prescribes no rules concerning fasting on Ash Wednesday, which is carried out according to members' personal wishes; however, it recommends a measure of fasting and abstinence as a suitable means of marking the day with proper devotion. Among Lutherans as well, there are no set rules for fasting, although some local congregations may advocate this form of penitence in varying degrees. In many churches, both Protestant and Roman Catholic, the special midweek services or programs of religious study that will continue throughout Lent are announced or begun on Ash Wednesday.

Thomas Alva Edison's Birthday

It was on February 11, 1847, that Thomas Alva Edison, who was to invent the phonograph, make the incandescent light commercially feasible, and contribute importantly to the motion picture industry, was born at Milan, Ohio — in the two-story, red brick house that visitors can still see on Edison Drive. The anniversary of Edison's birth, for years observed simply as Edison Day in schools and elsewhere, is now commemorated in several ways.

The Thomas Alva Edison Foundation, headquartered in Southfield, Michigan, annually sponsors a massive program of cooperation between industry and education, known as Edison Science and Engineering Youth Day, in which corporations, research centers, professional societies, and other groups participate as sponsoring organizations. The day, which is observed in 22 nations, usually results in more than 200 programs in the United States alone. In 1975 the governors of 40 states proclaimed Edison Science and Engineering Youth Day.

Seventy percent of the US programs take place on or about February 11, although their duration may be anywhere from the usual one or two days to as long as a month. School assembly programs by industry spokespersons, industrial and laboratory tours, seminars, discussion groups, scientific demonstrations, special luncheons or dinners, essay contests, science project competitions, industrial training for science teachers, and the distribution of specially prepared publications are some of the exchanges that go on. These have the purpose of disseminating information about and encouraging careers in the technical, engineering, and scientific fields of Edison's interest and strengthening science education at the secondary school level. Local chambers of commerce and such agencies as the federal Energy Research and Development Administration are also among organizations that may sponsor Edison Science and Engineering Youth Day observances. A highlight event held annually on February 10, 11, and 12 to call attention to the many local programs is the International Edison Birthday Celebration. Each year it is held in one of the world's major cities.

A different kind of festival is the Edison Pageant of Light at Fort Myers, Florida, where Edison spent nearly a half century of winters after first going there in ill health in 1885. Timed to include his birthday, the pageant is a 10-day-long celebration crowded with events. Features include coronation of the King and Queen of Edisonia; a mammoth children's parade followed by a gala birthday party; a competition among various North American high school bands; and a spectacular finale, the Grand Parade of Light, a nighttime procession of over 100 bands, floats and marching units, annually witnessed by as many as 80,000 persons. Other events scheduled as part of the Edison Pageant of Light included, in one recent and fairly typical year, golf, tennis, and shuffleboard tournaments, sailing races, a square dance, a flower show, a variety show, a colorful turtle race, and exhibitions of art, ceramics, and the region's famous seashells. Beginning in 1975, the Thomas Edison Great American Award has been conferred annually in recognition of outstanding achievement in a field that began with an Edison invention. The recipient also must demonstrate high standards of Americanism and moral character.

During the Edison Pageant of Light, and at other times of the year, too, the public can visit the 14-acre estate Edison's widow gave to the city of Fort Myers to be preserved as a memorial to her husband. It includes the winter home that Edison designed and brought by ship from Maine; the tropical botanical gardens with which he surrounded it; his laboratory; and the Edison Science Museum, completed in 1967, which houses inventions and mementos. Except for the World War II years of 1942–1945, the Edison Pageant of Light has been an annual tribute since it began as a three-day event in 1938.

Thomas Edison was of Dutch ancestry on his father's side and Scottish on his mother's. He spent his first seven years in Milan, Ohio. Later the family was in Port Huron, Michigan, where Edison had his only formal schooling — for three months in 1854. He was, however, an eager reader and had developed a strong interest in chemistry by the time he was 10.

Two years later Edison became a newsboy for the Grand Trunk Railway. At 15 he began to earn his living as a telegraph operator. He subsequently pursued this occupation in a number of cities, while devoting most of his free time to study and scientific experiments.

Edison's first patent was for an electrical vote recorder in 1868. The achievement hardly caused a pause in his labors. Within the next decade he had improved a stock ticker; devised duplex, quadruplex, and automatic telegraph systems; discovered the phenomenon of "etheric force," which became the foundation of wireless telegraphy; and invented the "electric pen." The last item developed into the mimeograph machine, which produces multiple copies from stencils.

By selling various telegraphic appliances, Edison realized some $40,000. With this money he established his own laboratory at Menlo Park, New Jersey, in 1876 — the famous "invention factory" where Edison and his team of scientifically skilled staff members achieved their greatest successes. The laboratory and many of the buildings that surrounded it can be seen today at Greenfield Village, the museum of Americana that Edison's friend and admirer

Henry Ford established at Dearborn, Michigan, in 1929. On view at the laboratory's original site in Menlo Park is the Edison Memorial Tower, erected in 1938 and topped with a replica of the incandescent light bulb that first shone there.

Edison's invention in 1877–1878 of the carbon transmitter, which utilized compressed lamp-black buttons to change sound into a varying electrical signal and back again, marked an important advance. In making commercial telephones practical, Edison's carbon telephone transmitter helped substantially to bring Alexander Graham Bell's newly invented telephone into general use. It also led to development of another taken-for-granted commonplace of 20th century life, the microphone.

Because so many modern inventions have come about as a synthesis of the contributions of many, the task of establishing priority has often been difficult. But when Edison in 1877 applied for a patent on the "phonograph or speaking machine" now regarded as one of the outstanding examples of his inventive imagination, the US Patent Office could find no precedent for the invention. Edison's initial model, which cost $18, was a primitive device consisting of a tinfoil-covered cylinder cranked by hand. When he perfected a motor-driven model a decade afterwards, he utilized cylindrical records made of wax. The improved version rapidly came into widespread use. Subsequently he introduced a new form of phonograph, which substituted a flat disk for the cylinder and employed a diamond needle to reproduce music. He also originated a dictating machine, the Ediphone.

On October 21, 1879, Edison succeeded not, as so often stated, in *inventing* the electric light, but in producing the first incandescent lamp of practical value — a lamp suitable for inexpensive production and wide distribution (see October 21). It contained a loop of carbonized cotton thread, enclosed in a vacuum, which shone for more than 13½ hours before it sputtered out. Edison subsequently introduced the improvements essential to its common use.

His interest in lighting by electricity meanwhile had led him to incorporate the Edison Electric Light Company in 1878. To go with his new light bulb, he developed whole systems to generate and distribute (as well as to regulate and measure) electricity for light, heat, and power. As the systems evolved it became necessary for him to fabricate such totally new devices as switches, safety fuses, insulated wire, and light sockets with the so-called Edison base. He developed motors, junction boxes, and underground conductors, among innumerable

other contrivances, and made vast improvements in generators. His persistent and tireless efforts resulted in the construction, in 1881 and 1882, of the world's first central electric-light power plants. One of these was in London. The other was the Pearl Street plant in New York City, a prodigious feat of engineering.

In the course of all this, he made his sole important discovery in the realm of pure, as opposed to applied, science in 1883. This was what came to be called the Edison effect, by which he showed that an incandescent lamp could be made to function as a valve that would admit negative, but not positive, electricity. Although Edison himself failed to see any practical use for the discovery, it was the foundation for later development of the electron tube. As if with the other hand — though he actually had many other hands in the persons of his assistants — Edison meanwhile built and demonstrated the nation's first electric railroad (in 1880). In 1885 he patented a method for transmitting telegraphic signals from ship to ship (or from ship to shore) and from moving trains to railroad stations.

The next year Edison moved into Glenmont, the many-gabled mansion in Llewellyn Park, West Orange, New Jersey, which was to be his home for the rest of his life. A year later he also moved his laboratory to West Orange. Interestingly enough, this laboratory with its emphasis on team, rather than individual, research, may have been Edison's most important invention of all, since it served as the prototype for the team concept so widespread in industrial and in foundation- and government-sponsored research today. The laboratory buildings and the mansion have been officially designated the Edison National Historic Site, administered by the National Park Service, since 1962 and can be visited by the public.

A large number of the items at the laboratory have to do with the early history of the motion picture, an art form that eventually drew on the contributions of many. The role Edison played was an important one, for it was on October 6, 1889, when he demonstrated the Kinetoscope on which he had been working for two years (and on which he applied for a patent in 1891), that the motion picture became a reality. A peephole device in which photographs of a moving object, taken in rapid succession, could be viewed on a new type of film just introduced by George Eastman, the Kinetoscope was displayed publicly for the first time on April 14, 1894, in New York City. The pictures it showed were taken with Edison's Kinetograph, a camera specially developed for the purpose.

Later the same year, several of Edison's machines were exported to England and France, where they inspired others to individual solutions of the problems of presenting motion pictures to larger audiences than a peep show could accommodate. Edison's own device, which contained no means of projecting the pictures on a screen, was improved to provide for this after he acquired the patent for a projector that Thomas Armat invented in 1895. The resulting combination was known as the Vitascope. Edison's company immediately busied itself with turning out films — over 1,700 in all, including the historic *Great Train Robbery*, the first motion picture to tell (however silently) a story. It was shot by Edwin S. Porter, an Edison cameraman, in 1903. By synchronizing the Kinetoscope with his phonograph, Edison in 1913 also introduced the Kinetophone — the first talking movie. The talking pictures, produced by others, which transformed the industry in the late 1920s, drew on his groundwork.

In his laboratories at Fort Myers and West Orange, Edison meanwhile was busy with other projects: work on a magnetic method for concentrating iron ores; development of a superior storage battery, utilizing nickel and iron and an alkaline electrolyte; invention of the fluoroscope after experiments with the X rays that W. C. Roentgen had discovered and named in 1895; work on more than 40 vital devices for the military as head of the Naval Consulting Board during World War I; and efforts, supported by Henry Ford and Harvey S. Firestone, to find a plant that would provide a substitute for rubber.

In all, Edison was granted well over 1,000 patents. The firms that made and marketed his and his staff's inventions were in time consolidated into the Edison General Electric Company, which eventually was absorbed by the General Electric Company.

The darling of the press, Edison was the recipient, during his lifetime, of almost every conceivable honor. He died at West Orange on October 18, 1931. If it was true that the inventions he left behind him had favorably altered the daily lives of people the world over, it was also true, as Leo Rosten pointed out, that Edison's influence was greater than his inventions.

Melville W. Fuller's Birthday

Melville Weston Fuller, eighth chief justice of the United States, was born in Augusta, Maine, on February 11, 1833. He was the son of

Frederick A. Fuller and Catherine M. Weston, both of whom belonged to prominent New England families. Melville Fuller's ancestors included Edward Fuller (whose name appeared on the Mayflower Compact of 1620), distinguished educators and churchmen, and especially men eminent in law. His father, both his grandfathers, and six uncles were either judges or lawyers. His maternal grandfather, Nathan Weston, sat on the Supreme Court bench of Maine from 1820 to 1841 and for the last seven years was chief justice there.

In September 1849 Melville Fuller, then 16, entered Bowdoin College in Brunswick, Maine, which at that time offered primarily a classical and theological curriculum. He was graduated with honors in the class of 1853. He began the study of law in the offices of two uncles, Nathan Weston and George Melville Weston, in Bangor, Maine. Starting in the fall of 1854, he attended Harvard Law School for six months. On his admission to the bar in Maine in 1855, the young lawyer first began the practice of law in the office of his uncle Nathan Weston in Bangor. In the summer of 1855, he went to Augusta, Maine, where he assumed — in partnership with another uncle, Benjamin A. G. Fuller — the editorship of the *Age*, a well-known Democratic newspaper in the state. He served as president of the Common Council of the city and as city solicitor in 1856.

Just as his life was becoming established in Augusta, Fuller left for the West, probably out of disappointment over a broken engagement. He moved to Chicago in May 1856. A few days after his arrival, he wrote a series of letters for the Augusta *Age*, in which he set down his favorable impressions of that then young city. He added: "In the midst of the whirling, active, busy life of this great city, it is difficult to know where to commence." By September 1856 he had become a partner in the firm of Pearson and Dow, having been admitted to the Illinois bar on June 15. His practice and his reputation grew with the growth of the city.

Although Fuller's cases involved practically every field of law, real property and commercial law were his specialties. One of the best-known cases was his defense in 1869 of the Reverend Charles Edward Cheney, the rector of the Episcopalian Christ Church in Chicago. Cheney, a Low Churchman of evangelical leanings, had gotten into difficulty with his High Church sacerdotal bishop. The issue concerned Cheney's omission of the word "regenerate" as stated in the infant baptismal liturgy (the accepted prayer book holding that the child after baptism was "regenerate"). Cheney's omission was regarded as an offense against the law of the church. The rector, charged with canonical disobedience and called before an ecclesiastical tribunal, was deposed despite Fuller's spirited and erudite defense. Cheney then proceeded to organize the Reformed Protestant Episcopal Church, taking most of his congregation with him. The case therefore led to years of litigation in the civil courts over conflicting claims to the church property. The US Supreme Court — in a decision favoring Fuller — finally ruled that the property rightly belonged to the trustees of Christ Church and was in no way subject to the bishop's control.

Equally famous because of the intricacy of the issues involved was the Lake Front case concerning Chicago's ownership of the shores of Lake Michigan. In 1883 the state of Illinois initiated a suit to reclaim the lake front, which was then being occupied under certain statutes and ordinances by several railroads, including the Illinois Central. Fuller devised arguments under which Chicago held that it, rather than the state, owned this property. In his opinion the grants to the railroads either were void or else had been repealed by later acts and the city could claim the land legally in line with its riparian rights as owner of Michigan Avenue, which bordered the lake front. Fuller's theories were eventually upheld in substance by the US Supreme Court.

In November 1861 Melville W. Fuller was elected one of four delegates to represent Chicago at a convention to be held at Springfield, Illinois, the following January to revise the constitution of the state of Illinois. In 1862 he was elected a member of the Illinois House of Representatives. He took office in January 1863, and by the session's end was all but the leader of the house. As a delegate from Illinois to the Democratic National conventions of 1864, 1872, 1876, and 1880, Fuller acquired a national reputation in Democratic politics. Sound money, free trade, states' rights, governmental economy, and preservation of civil rights were the pillars of his political thinking. In 1876 he made a speech proposing the nomination of Governor Thomas A. Hendricks of Indiana as presidential candidate. Hendricks, however, was chosen vice presidential running mate of Samuel J. Tilden of New York. Melville Fuller took no active part in politics after the convention of 1880. He instead became involved in the fledgling Chicago Literary Club, while developing his law practice into one of the largest and most successful in Chicago.

After Grover Cleveland had become President of the United States in 1885, he asked Melville Fuller, with whom he was on friendly terms, to assume several government positions. Eight months after his inauguration, Cleveland suggested that Fuller become chairman of the Civil Service Commission; he later asked him to become solicitor general and one of three Pacific Railway commissioners. Fuller refused all offers on the grounds that they would be detrimental to his family life.

Fuller was married twice. On June 28, 1858, he married Calista O. Reynolds, daughter of a leading Chicago butcher and packer; she died on November 13, 1864, leaving him with two small daughters. On May 30, 1866, he married Mary Ellen Coolbaugh, daughter of the president of Chicago's largest bank. She and Fuller had six additional children. Fuller's quiet home life in Chicago was ideal, and the formal society of Washington, D.C., did not attract him.

When the office of chief justice became vacant by the death of Morrison R. Waite on March 23, 1888, President Cleveland had to consider various factors — age, location, professional eminence, reputation for integrity, and political philosophy — in selecting his nominee for the post. It was especially important, for example, that — given the sectional issues that frequently came before the Court — the justices be from different parts of the country. Although Illinois provided more litigation in the Supreme Court than any other state except New York, it had no representatives on the Court. Moreover, the Democrats of Illinois, who had strongly supported Cleveland's bid for election, were unrepresented in his cabinet. The Illinois politicians stated their case so convincingly that Cleveland, who was seriously considering the nomination of Senator George Gray of Delaware to the chief justiceship, yielded and named Fuller on April 30, 1888.

When rumors about his possible nomination spread, Fuller anxiously wrote his wife: "It is quite clear . . . [that] I am one of the persons [Cleveland] is seriously considering. I can not contemplate such a thing without serious misgiving. It would be an entire change of life and at my age not to be contemplated as a matter of course. . . . I hope he will not tender the appointment to me." At the moment of decision, however, the Chicago lawyer accepted the appointment, although with hesitation, "trusting," as he wrote to the President on May 5, 1888, "that the country will never have cause to regret your calling me to it, and earnestly hoping that God will give me strength equal to the exalted responsibilities imposed." The appointment was confirmed and the commission issued to him on July 20.

Of striking appearance, with silver hair and mustache, the chief justice had a sensitive, scholarly face and courtly manners. He performed the functions of his office ably and with versatility. As *Harper's Weekly* stated on his appointment, he had had wider experience in all branches of law than any other member of the Court. His opinions, numbering more than 850, were characterized by directness, clarity, common sense, and exhaustive research. In his 22 years as chief justice, Fuller leaned toward strict construction of the Constitution. Under his guidance, the Court settled countless new problems stemming from increased immigration, colonial expansion overseas, and unparalleled industrial growth.

As presiding officer, Melville Fuller won the affection and respect of both his colleagues and the American bar. Reportedly his success was due in part to his rare mixture of gentleness and courage, sympathy and impartiality, and humor and determined independence. He diplomatically avoided acrimony in the conference room, conciliating highly individualistic men who had great pride of opinion. It was for his unusual ability as an administrator, however — a skill that elevated the Court in the esteem of professionals and public alike — that Fuller was chiefly known. Probably none of his predecessors had rivaled him as business manager of the Court. When he first assumed the chief justiceship, the Court was more than four years behind in its case workload; in a few years' time, Fuller had brought the calendar almost up to date, and he struggled to keep it so during the remainder of his life. Supreme Court Justice Oliver Wendell Holmes aptly summarized Fuller's executive abilities:

He had the business of the Court at his fingers' ends, he was perfectly courageous, prompt, decided. He turned off the matters that daily called for action easily, swiftly, with the least possible friction . . . and with a humor that relieved any tension with a laugh.

On December 11, 1889, a little more than a year after taking his seat on the bench, Chief Justice Fuller was selected to deliver the address commemorating the 100th anniversary of the inauguration of George Washington as first President of the United States, before both houses of Congress. In 1897 he accepted appointment to the commission established to deal with the longstanding boundary dispute between Venezuela and British Guiana; in 1899 he was a member of the arbitration commission that sat in Paris to settle the dispute.

From 1900 to 1910 he served as a member of the Permanent Court of Arbitration at The Hague, in the Netherlands. Despite his declining health, particularly after the death of his second wife in the summer of 1904, Chief Justice Fuller served with distinction in all his functions until his own death at Sorrento, Maine, on July 4, 1910.

FEBRUARY 12

Abraham Lincoln's Birthday

President Abraham Lincoln, the Great Emancipator, who would champion "government of the people, by the people, for the people" and preserve the Union through four years of civil war, was born in Hardin County, Kentucky, on February 12, 1809. Lincoln, who became the Chief Executive on March 4, 1861, is universally regarded as one of the nation's great Presidents. Contributing to his wide appeal were his uncommon skill at suiting words to purpose, his unfailing respect for human worth, his determination in the face of sometimes almost devastating odds, and his remarkable lack of malice. A reflection of the high esteem in which he is held is the fact that his birthday is observed in so many parts of the world. The story of his rise from humble beginnings to the nation's highest office and of his subsequent martyrdom by an assassin's bullet has subtracted nothing from the admiration accorded him by people around the world.

In the United States his birthday is widely observed — in many states as a legal holiday, generally on February 12, although a few states commemorate the anniversary on the first Monday in February. This is not to mention such states as Massachusetts, where February 12 is celebrated as Lincoln Day by annual proclamation of the governor even if it is not technically a legal holiday. In short, Lincoln's Birthday is a day for commemoration in much of the country, particularly by patriotic organizations and in schools. The school observances, which are mandatory in some states, may include assembly programs, commemorative exercises, special displays, and study.

Also keyed to Lincoln's birthday is the timing of Race Relations Sunday on the Sunday nearest February 12. This observance, sometimes known as Brotherhood Sunday, was officially sponsored by the National Council of Churches, a federation of 34 Protestant and Eastern Orthodox bodies, for 41 years until 1965. Since then sponsorship of the observance, which continues on a nationwide basis, has been taken over by individual denominations within the National Council. The day is also marked as Race Relations Sunday by several Roman Catholic groups and — on the Jewish Sabbath, the preceding day — by several Jewish organizations. In the forefront of those marking the day as Brotherhood or Race Relations Sunday are branches of the National Association for the Advancement of Colored People across the nation, which tie the observance in with both Lincoln's Birthday and the founding of the NAACP on the same day in 1909, and also with the birthday of the black abolitionist Frederick Douglass close to the same time. Black, or Afro-American, History Week, sponsored annually since 1926 by the Association for the Study of Afro-American Life and History, generally includes both Lincoln's and Douglass's birthdays.

The close proximity of these anniversaries — plus Brotherhood Week, which follows shortly, — have concentrated emphasis on February as the month for observances related to the goal of brotherhood. In a few states the celebration of Lincoln's and Washington's birthdays has been combined, on the third Monday in February, under the name Presidents' Day or Washington-Lincoln Day. The entire month of February also is observed in a number of states as American History Month.

Among specific commemorations of Lincoln's Birthday, one of the best known takes place at the Lincoln Memorial in Washington, D.C., where government officials and foreign diplomats, led by the President of the United States or his representative, gather at noontime to place wreaths before Daniel Chester French's massive statue of Lincoln, which dominates the memorial building's splendidly simple interior. Also participating in this commemoration are a US armed forces band, an all-services honor guard, and members of the Military Order of the Loyal Legion of the United States. The last-named (male descendants of Union officers in the Civil War) are instrumental in sponsoring the observance. Either at the Lincoln Memorial or in a message released from the White House, the President customarily issues a Lincoln's Birthday address. Usually it calls attention to the nation's accomplishments and shortcomings in the area of civil rights and race relations.

At Lincoln's long-time home city of Springfield, Illinois, his birthday is marked by an annual pilgrimage to his tomb by members of the American Legion, the Veterans of Foreign Wars, and other patriotic groups, and in 1975 and 1976 a Lincoln symposium was held at the Old State Capitol. At Vandalia, briefly the capital of Illinois and site of what is now known as the Vandalia State House State Memorial, where Lincoln served in the House of Representatives, the anniversary of his birth is also the occasion for appropriate celebration. Lincoln's Birthday observances take place sporadically in other Illinois communities. Other cities also mark the day in special ways. One of them is Philadelphia, where commemorative ceremonies are held in Independence Square, and the Union League customarily celebrates with a black-tie evening highlighted by a Lincoln Day address by a noted scholar.

All across the nation, meanwhile, local Republican organizations continue to mark the birthday of the first Republican President with the Lincoln Day dinners that have become as customary for Republicans as the annual Jefferson-Jackson Day dinners are for Democrats. Republican notables customarily address the banquets, reflecting on partisan glories of the past and hopes for the future, and news stories the next day are filled with quotations from their talks.

Thoroughly as Lincoln's Birthday is commemorated in ordinary years, such perennial events are as nothing compared with important anniversaries of his birth like the Lincoln Sesquicentennial in 1959. Probably the outstanding observance of that memorable year was an address by the poet and Lincoln biographer Carl Sandburg before a joint session of both houses of the US Congress. Specially convened for the sesquicentennial, the session was also attended by members of the cabinet and diplomatic corps and the assembled justices of the Supreme Court — as well as viewed by a vast television audience. The principal speech was preceded by a medley of Civil War songs presented by "The Idlers," a choral group from the US Coast Guard Academy; and by actor Fredric March's reading of that high point of Lincoln's eloquence, the "Gettysburg Address" (see November 19). Then came the main address. According to eyewitness accounts, seldom have the halls of Congress been so hushed as before the spell of Sandburg's commemoration of "a man ... both steel and velvet ... hard as rock and soft as drifting fog. ..."

More or less simultaneously, others were finding other words to describe Lincoln. One of them was Mayor Willy Brandt of West Berlin, who took part, with diplomats of 21 nations, in the big sesquicentennial tribute to Lincoln in Springfield, Illinois. Brandt and Governor William G. Stratton of Illinois were among speakers at a banquet for 1,500 persons, held in the Illinois State Armory to cap Springfield's daylong observance.

The events in Washington and Springfield, however, were only two of literally thousands that marked the 150th anniversary of Lincoln's birth. Including ceremonial exercises, speeches, patriotic music, broadcasts, and film showings, they ranged from elaborate banquets to simple ceremonies in small villages. Indeed, sesquicentennial observances took place in most of the capitals of the free world. In the United States, commemorations extended throughout the sesquicentennial year. They included innumerable exhibits, a number of noteworthy publishing events, the issue of three commemorative postage stamps, and erection of an enormous statue of Lincoln at the highest point along the coast-to-coast Lincoln Highway — 12 miles east of Laramie, Wyoming.

The sesquicentennial year was preceded by a good many earlier Lincoln events of note. The first formal commemoration of his birth took place at the Capitol in Washington, D.C., on February 12, 1866, when both houses of Congress assembled to note the anniversary of his birth and express their grief over his death the previous April. President Andrew Johnson and his cabinet, diplomats, the Supreme Court justices, the governors of the states, military and naval officers named in resolutions of thanks by Congress, and a large number of citizens crowding the galleries were present for the memorial joint session. Flags on all public buildings were displayed at half-mast and the whole city of Washington was pervaded by a funereal atmosphere. The officers of the government and the invited guests gathered in the hall of the House of Representatives silently and reverently and waited for the proceedings to begin as though they were at a religious service.

The exercises began at noon with the playing of a selection from *Il Trovatore* by the Marine Band. Then the Reverend Charles E. Boynton, chaplain of the House of Representatives, offered a prayer, after which Lafayette S. Foster, president pro tempore of the Senate, who presided, made a brief speech, referring to the assassination of Lincoln and its effect upon the country, and concluding as follows:

The Senate and House of Representatives thought proper to commemorate this tragic event by appropriate exercises. This day, the birthday of him we mourn, has properly been selected. An eminent citizen, distinguished by his labors and services in high and responsible positions at home and abroad, whose pen has instructed the present age in the history of his country and done much to transmit the fame and renown of that country to future ages, the Honorable George Bancroft, will now deliver a discourse.

Bancroft, the historian, who had been selected on brief notice after Edwin M. Stanton, Lincoln's secretary of war, had declined to serve, delivered his famous review of the career of the Great Emancipator. The New York *Tribune* of the next day commented that Bancroft's address

. . . deals with him [Lincoln] as one who was molded by events and acted as their agent rather than as one whose force of character made the times take shape in accordance with his will. It is well known that Mr. Lincoln had the same view of his own relation to affairs. He thought himself put at the head of the Republic in order to execute the will of the people as from time to time indicated — not to take the lead in public business, not to announce a policy, not in a single instance to transcend popular expectation, not to show himself guided and uplifted by prophetic inspiration.

In Jersey City, New Jersey, on the same day as Washington's official tribute, the Lincoln Association — formed the previous autumn by several residents of the city's old Third Ward who had been meeting periodically in a small club room — held the first of many Lincoln observances that would take place there and in other parts of the country. Deciding that something should be done in memory of the President, the members had agreed to change the name of their club to the Lincoln Association and to observe the anniversary of Lincoln's birth with a dinner each year.

The first president of the reorganized club was William B. Dunning. He was succeeded by James Gopsill, elected at the first dinner on February 12, 1866. Under his leadership the club grew until its annual Lincoln dinners were attended by 300 or more persons and addressed by some of the nation's most noted men. William Walter Phelps, the legislator and diplomat, said at the association's 23rd annual Lincoln gathering that it was "the one association in this broad land that has never failed to celebrate his birthday since his death."

The name of Lincoln was used by the newly organized Republican Club of New York City in 1887 to attract attention to itself when it announced that its first dinner was to be in celebration of Lincoln's birthday. This dinner was described by the press as "the most notable celebration of the day ever held in the city." "With such a start," said the *Tribune* prophetically, "it seems most likely that the celebration may become an established custom."

At this first dinner, held at Delmonico's Restaurant, 280 persons were present, including many of the most prominent Republicans of the country. Among others, addresses were made by Governor Joseph B. Foraker of Ohio; Senator Benjamin Harrison of Indiana, soon to become President; Chauncey M. Depew, later a Senator from New York; Governor Richard J. Oglesby of Illinois; and Henry Cabot Lodge of Massachusetts, then serving his first term in the House of Representatives. James G. Blaine of Maine, who had been the Republican candidate for the presidency in 1884, wrote a letter of regret, which referred to the widening interest in Lincoln and the tendency of all to honor him. He said in part:

The Republican party makes no attempt to narrow the possession of a fame that is recognized on all continents, that will last through the centuries, that belongs to humanity. But the political organization which supported Mr. Lincoln has the right to claim the prestige of his name as it continues to labor in the great field where he wrought until all the harvests of his plantings are gathered and garnered.

By the time of the 100th anniversary of Lincoln's birth, in 1909, his memory had become a precious heritage to the people of the nation, regardless of geographical section or political belief. Private and unofficial celebration of the day had become widespread earlier. At the dinner of the Lincoln Club of New York in 1891, Hannibal Hamlin of Maine, who had been Vice President during Lincoln's first term as President, made the journey to New York, undeterred by his 81 years, to make an address. In it he urged that the anniversary be made a national holiday, a suggestion that was greeted with enthusiastic applause.

The next year, 1892, the legislature of Illinois, the state in which Lincoln spent his mature years, made the anniversary a legal holiday. Four years later the legislatures of New Jersey, New York, Minnesota, and Washington followed suit, as many other states have since. Massachusetts, however, instead of creating a legal holiday, authorized the governor, by law in 1905, to call upon the people by proclamation to observe the day with appropriate exercises. One of the early proclamations issued under this authority bore the signature of Curtis Guild Jr. and appeared on February 1, 1908. It contained a long eulogy of Lincoln and ended in this way:

Let cannon and bell at high noon call the people from sport or study or toil, to reflection on that great life so nobly lived. Let the universal display from tenement to State House of the flag of the United States of America remind the people that our country is the United States because of Abraham Lincoln.

Elaborate preparations were made for observing the 100th anniversary of Lincoln's birth in 1909. A memorial association had been organized to buy the 116-acre Lincoln farm three miles south of Hodgenville, Kentucky, including the log cabin in which Lincoln was born. The farm was established as a national park in 1916 and has been officially known as the Abraham Lincoln Birthplace National Historic Site since 1959. (Ten miles to the northeast, today's traveling public can also see another log cabin associated with Lincoln. This is the reconstructed version of Knobb Creek Farm, to which his family moved in 1811, and from which he said his earliest recollections dated.) Hodgenville also marked the 100th anniversary of Lincoln's birth by placing in its public square the Lincoln statue that still stands there. Congress, meanwhile, had declared the centenary-year birthday a holiday in the District of Columbia and the territories, and the US Post Office Department issued a two-cent commemorative postage stamp in honor of Lincoln. Theodore Roosevelt, then President of the United States, went to Hodgenville as the guest of the memorial association to lay the cornerstone of a marble and granite structure to enclose the famous log cabin and delivered an eloquent tribute to Lincoln.

While centenary exercises were in progress at the place of Lincoln's birth they also were going on at Springfield, Illinois. A mass meeting there was addressed by French Ambassador Jean Jules Jusserand, British Ambassador James Bryce, and three-time presidential candidate William Jennings Bryan. Memorial tablets were placed on the building in which Lincoln had his law office and on the First Presbyterian Church, which he attended, and an elm was planted in his honor on the grounds of the state supreme court, in which he tried some 200 cases. The Springfield Chapter of the Daughters of the American Revolution marked the 1909 anniversary of Lincoln's birth by holding a reception in the only home Lincoln ever owned — at the corner of Springfield's 8th and Jackson streets. Faithfully restored, even to its original tan color of "Quaker brown," the house, where Lincoln lived from 1844 to 1861, is a National Historic Site, open to the public.

The centenary of Lincoln's birth was also widely noted elsewhere. In New York City, it was estimated that a million persons took part in the various events. The official celebration of the city was held at Cooper Union, where Lincoln made his famous speech of February 27, 1860, which displayed his breadth of vision and marked him for the presidency. Mayor George B. McClellan presided. Addresses were made by various notables and a memorial tablet was placed on the center column at the back of the stage, recording the fact of the historic appearance of Lincoln in the hall. The celebration in the city's Republican Club was addressed by Booker T. Washington, the black founder and president of Tuskegee Institute, who was born a slave and freed by Lincoln's Emancipation Proclamation.

In Chicago 50 public meetings were held by as many different organizations. The city was "fairly buried beneath flags," according to a newspaper account. Store display windows were filled with Civil War relics and portraits of Lincoln, and the streets were crowded with marching paraders. The principal exercises were held in the municipal auditorium, with Woodrow Wilson, president of Princeton University and later President of the United States, making the chief address.

In Boston official celebrations included a meeting under the auspices of the city, addressed by former governor John D. Long of Massachusetts, at which Julia Ward Howe, author of "The Battle Hymn of the Republic," read a poem. There was also a meeting of the Government of the Commonwealth in the State House, addressed by US Senator Henry Cabot Lodge. At one o'clock a company of cornetists mounted the belfry of nearby Park Street Congregational Church and played "The Battle Hymn of the Republic" and "America," while members of a crowd that filled the streets and the corner of neighboring Boston Common stood with uncovered heads.

In Pennsylvania the Lincoln centenary was observed on the battlefield at Gettysburg with ceremonies held on Seminary Ridge, where some of the fiercest fighting of the Civil War had occurred. The famous address made by Lincoln in 1863, on the occasion of the dedication of the Gettysburg National Cemetery was read.

Vice President Charles Fairbanks spoke at a celebration in Pittsburgh and Vice President-elect James Sherman was the chief speaker at the observance in Harrisburg, the Pennsylvania capital. President-elect William Howard Taft was guest of honor at a dinner in New Orleans, a city not officially celebrating Lincoln Day, but Taft made appropriate reference to the anniversary. In some other Southern cities, the centenary was officially observed. In Birmingham, Alabama, Lincoln exercises were held in the public schools for the first time and, in Texas, for the first time in the history of the state, many cities celebrated the day. In Arkansas it was observed as a semiholiday, and a dinner was given in Little Rock at which prominent Confederate soldiers responded to Lincoln toasts. Ordinarily, however, these states are among those that do not officially mark Lincoln's birthday as a holiday.

Considerable notice of the centenary was taken abroad. The mayor of Lincoln, England, cabled greetings to President Theodore Roosevelt: "The Lincoln City flag waves over the Guild Hall to-day in sympathetic commemoration of the event." An address on Lincoln was delivered at the University of Berlin by German-born Professor Felix Adler of New York, and he unveiled a bust of Lincoln by sculptor Leonard Wells Volk, which had been presented to the university. In Paris Americans held a celebration with an address by Professor Henry van Dyke of Princeton University. There was a similar celebration in Rome with Lloyd Griscom, the American ambassador, as the speaker. And the Brazilian government paid tribute to Lincoln by displaying the national flag on all the public buildings in Rio de Janeiro and by firing a salute of 21 guns from warships in the harbor.

The Lincoln Memorial, the great monument in classic Greek style in Washington's West Potomac Park, enshrining a heroic statue of Lincoln, grew out of the interest aroused by the celebration of the 100th anniversary of his birth. Senator Shelby Moore Cullom of Illinois introduced in Congress in 1910 a bill providing for the erection of a memorial in the national capital. It was passed in 1911, creating a commission to have charge of the work. Former President Taft became chairman of the commission, which approved a design for the building by New York architect Henry Bacon and commissioned the sculptor Daniel Chester French to execute the now famous statue of Lincoln seated in a chair. Workmen broke ground for the Lincoln Memorial on Lincoln's Birthday in 1914 and the cornerstone was laid a year later to the day. Among articles placed within the cornerstone was a sketch of the life of his father by Robert Todd Lincoln, who later presented to the Library of Congress a collection of his father's letters, manuscripts, and papers, which became accessible to scholars in 1947. In the completed Lincoln Memorial, Lincoln's Gettysburg Address and second inaugural address are engraved on the walls of the chamber containing the statue. Also in the building are mural decorations by Jules Gurin, showing in allegory the principal events in Lincoln's life.

The building was dedicated on Memorial Day, May 30, 1922, at exercises over which former President Taft, by then chief justice of the United States, presided as chairman of the Memorial Commission. Robert R. Moton, successor to Booker T. Washington as the head of

Tuskegee Institute, was the first speaker. He paid tribute to Lincoln as the emancipator of blacks. Edwin Markham, the poet, read a poem, and Chief Justice Taft presented the memorial to President Warren G. Harding, who received it as the representative of the nation.

Abraham Lincoln was the son of Thomas and Nancy Hanks Lincoln. Samuel Lincoln, his first American ancestor, came from the town of Hingham, near Norwich, England, where a 14th century church now containing a bust of Abraham Lincoln is the site of a service honoring him annually on his birthday. The son of a disinherited father, Samuel Lincoln emigrated in 1637 to the namesake town of Hingham, Massachusetts, where he settled the next year.

Descendants of Samuel Lincoln migrated west and southward to Pennsylvania and Virginia. The President's grandfather went to Jefferson County, Kentucky.

Abraham Lincoln's father, Thomas, an unschooled frontiersman frequently on the move, lived in various places in Kentucky, the state where Lincoln was born. The family moved to Spencer County, Indiana, in 1816. There the President's mother, Nancy Hanks Lincoln, died of a fever in 1818, on the farm where he later grew to manhood. The site, south of Lincoln City, was established in 1963 as the Lincoln Boyhood National Memorial, adjacent to Lincoln State Park. Other Lincoln attractions are nearby, on the 325-mile Lincoln Heritage Trail, which retraces for visitors Lincoln's path through Kentucky, Indiana, and Illinois.

When Lincoln was 21 his family — including his much-loved stepmother, the former Sarah Bush Johnston — moved to Illinois. They settled 10 miles west of Decatur, at a site now known as Lincoln Trail Homestead State Park. Young Lincoln worked as a farm laborer and then struck out on his own, working at a variety of occupations. Among other things, he served as a store clerk in New Salem. He must have impressed his neighbors with his ability, for in 1832 he was chosen captain of a company of volunteers for service in the Black Hawk War. When he returned from the campaign he settled in New Salem and became a partner in the general store there. He was also postmaster and a deputy surveyor. Meanwhile he devoted himself to the study of law. Lincoln's New Salem, now a state park two miles south of Petersburg, has been painstakingly restored as it was when he lived there. A 19th century frontier settlement reincarnated, it is an attraction of unusual historical interest.

At 25 Lincoln was elected to the state legislature. Repeatedly reelected, he served there for four terms, 1834–1841. In the meantime,

he was admitted to the bar in 1836. He moved to Springfield, which had just become the state capital, the next year and opened a law office there. Married to Mary Todd in 1842, Lincoln was elected a representative to the US Congress in 1846 and began serving the following year — just as Stephen A. Douglas, later his rival, began his service in the Senate.

Lincoln did not choose to stand for reelection when his two-year term expired. Oddly enough, however, he rose to greater prominence in his supposed retirement to private life. Returning to law, he practiced in Springfield and on a wide circuit throughout much of Illinois — so wide a circuit that hardly a community in the state is without its Lincoln associations today. An example is the first place in the country to be named for him, the town of Lincoln, which came into being with the help of his legal services. As a lawyer Lincoln was noted for lucidity, thorough preparation, a knack of quickly grasping the central issue, a clear and colorful turn of phrase, and an honesty that became legendary.

During the 1960s the Old State Capitol in Springfield, which had been remodeled at the end of the 19th century, was torn down and reconstructed as it had been in Lincoln's time. The chambers of the Illinois Supreme Court, where Lincoln argued cases, and the House of Representatives, where he served for eight years (and where his body lay in state), can be seen — along with the oil lamps, quill pens, vests hanging on pegs, and eyeglasses left on a ledger to create the illusion of stepping back in time.

When the issue of the extension of slavery into free territory arose — particularly in regard to the Kansas-Nebraska Act, which Douglas had largely formulated, reopening the whole question — Lincoln opposed such extension. Meanwhile, like thousands of other former Whigs, he found himself drawn to the new Republican party, which antislavery Whigs and Democrats, together with Free-Soilers, had begun forming in Michigan in 1854.

At the state convention in Bloomington, when the Republican party in Illinois was formed in 1856, Lincoln made a strong antislavery speech, although he was himself no abolitionist. He did, however, object to the extension of slavery and regarded the institution as unjust. He supported the Republican candidate, John C. Frémont, for President and was one of the presidential electors in the state. (Previously, Lincoln had been an elector for the Whigs' William H. Harrison in 1840 and Henry Clay in 1844.)

In 1858 Lincoln was nominated for the US Senate by the Republicans to run against Douglas, the Democratic candidate. During the campaign he and Douglas debated the issues in a series of seven public meetings — the famous Lincoln-Douglas debates — which lifted Lincoln into the national consciousness even though he did not win the election.

The next year his friends began to talk of him for the presidency. On February 27, 1860, Lincoln gave an address at Cooper Union, in New York City. A statesmanlike discussion of the problems before the country, it was highly praised in the East. Among other things it clearly stated the issues on which the Republicans could wage their forthcoming election campaign.

Lincoln was nominated for the presidency at the convention in Chicago in May 1860 and was elected over two Democratic candidates and one candidate of the Constitutional Union party.

Before he took office on March 4, 1861, determined to preserve the Union, seven Southern states had already seceded. The Civil War broke out a little more than a month later with the firing on Fort Sumter (see April 12). It was fought and won under his direction. Although Lincoln's primary concern had been to quell hostilities and keep the nation whole, he realized before long that the issue could not be successfully concluded so long as the institution of slavery remained in force. Accordingly, in September 1862, he issued a proclamation declaring his intention of freeing all slaves in the rebelling states January 1, 1863 (see January 1, The Emancipation Proclamation). The proclamation was consistent with his address at Gettysburg the next year which declared in part: "Four score and seven years ago our fathers brought forth upon this continent a new nation, conceived in liberty and dedicated to the proposition that all men are created equal." The astute Lincoln probably was never more wrong than in remarking at Gettysburg that "the world will little note, nor long remember, what we say here . . . ," for the address came to be regarded as an example of eloquence seldom excelled in the nation's history.

Lincoln was reelected to the presidency in November 1864. There was no time, however, to carry out the promise of his second inaugural address. Made as victory drew near for the Union forces, it urged on the nation a policy of reconciliation toward the secessionist South: "With malice toward none, with charity for all . . . let us strive to finish the work we are in; to bind up the nation's wounds. . . ."

So said Lincoln. But Lincoln was shot in Ford's Theatre in Washington, D.C., by John Wilkes Booth, an actor, on April 14, 1865 (see April 14). The President died the following morning, and charity was not the outstanding feature of the postwar Reconstruction period that followed his passing from the scene.

Georgia Day

On February 12, 1733, James Oglethorpe (see December 22), together with 120 other Englishmen disembarked at Yamacraw Bluff in what is now Savannah, Georgia, to start a new colony. An unlikely combination of altruistic and imperialistic desires motivated Oglethorpe and the other trustees to establish the Georgia settlement: they wanted to provide a refuge for England's oppressed and often imprisoned debtor class, and at the same time they realized the importance of creating a colony that would serve as a buffer between Britain's southern colonies and the Spaniards who occupied Florida. To accomplish their dual purpose, Oglethorpe and his colleagues devised an intricate scheme of regulations for setting up and governing their American colony. Unfortunately most of their elaborate project failed, largely because of unrealistic planning. But despite many early disappointments and crises, Georgia gradually grew and eventually prospered: today the citizens of the state look back to the arrival of the first colonists and celebrate the anniversary of their February 12 landing as Georgia Day.

In the centuries since Oglethorpe and his followers arrived at Savannah, Georgians have observed February 12 in many ways. The earliest settlers of Georgia marked the occasion by firing salutes and giving toasts in honor of Oglethorpe and the other trustees. The custom of saluting the trustees on February 12 seems to have been an annual occurrence in the colony, at least until control of Georgia reverted to the British Crown in 1752. But not all Georgians were always satisfied that appropriate honor was given the trustees on these occasions. Indeed, in 1740 when the colony was engaged in fighting the Spaniards in Florida during the War of Jenkins' Ear, one resident was so disappointed by the February 12 ceremonies of that year that he confided to his journal the hope "that ages to come will celebrate this day annually here in a better manner."

The observances that have marked the major anniversaries of Georgia's founding since then would have pleased the 1740 writer. Large-scale celebrations took place in the state on February 12, 1833, the centennial of the landing of the Oglethorpe party, and newspapers on that day even suspended publication so that their employees might attend the festivities. In

1908 a river pageant was held in Savannah to commemorate the 175th anniversary of the 1733 landing, and still more elaborate events took place during the bicentennial celebration in 1933.

To mark the 200th anniversary of the founding of Georgia, the federal government issued a special commemorative stamp bearing the likeness of James Oglethorpe, and cities and towns throughout the state held observances on February 12, 1933. But quite appropriately, the largest bicentennial celebration took place in Savannah. Several of the city's churches, including the Episcopal Christ Church and Trinity Methodist Church, noted the state's bicentennial of its founding. Some congregations held special services on February 12, and distinguished clergymen delivered patriotic addresses on the occasion. In addition a historical pageant was held in Savannah's municipal auditorium, and many of the city's most distinguished residents helped re-create some of the significant events of Georgia's past.

Although, until very recent times, only the major anniversaries of the founding of Georgia occasioned large civic celebrations, the initial steps toward making February 12 a day of special annual observance in Georgia took place at the beginning of the 20th century. In her book *Georgia Land and People,* published in 1900, Frances L. Mitchell of Athens, Georgia, first suggested that each year the state's citizens celebrate the date of the Oglethorpe party's arrival in Savannah. The Joseph Habersham Chapter, Georgia Society, Daughters of the American Revolution, enthusiastically embraced Frances Mitchell's idea, and in the years that followed encouraged the state's legislators to designate February 12 as Georgia Day. Joseph M. Terrell, the state's chief executive from 1902 to 1907, also urged that the day be set apart and in 1909, John M. Slaton, the president of the state senate, introduced in the legislature the first bill obliging the schools of Georgia to hold exercises on February 12, Georgia Day. The bill was approved on August 13, 1909. Later legislative action followed with the 1933 amendment to the Code of Georgia, which states that it is "the duty of the State Superintendent of Schools to arrange programs for the proper observance of these occasions, and of the Superintendent and teachers to direct the attention of the pupils to these dates and topics by practical exercises." This legislation, which makes Georgia Day a "special day" of observance rather than a legal holiday, was confirmed in Georgia Laws of 1941.

Since 1909 schools throughout Georgia have scheduled special events to mark the anniversary of Georgia's founding. In Atlanta, where practice is typical of most of the rest of the state, elementary school pupils may participate in plays and pageants depicting Georgia history, while high school students often attend patriotic films or see other exhibits of materials related to Georgia's past. Other academic exercises on Georgia Day frequently include the writing of compositions on Georgia's history and the lives of its distinguished citizens, and readings and recitations on these same topics. In 1976 there was a Georgia Day commemoration at Atlanta's Archives and Records Building, presented as part of the nation's observance of the Bicentennial.

For many years a number of Georgia organizations held more or less private observances to mark the anniversary of the founding of the state. But not until the 1960s did the idea of making February 12 the occasion of a major annual public celebration gain popularity. At that time a group of civic-minded Savannah residents — most notably Robertine McClendon and Mrs. Leopold Adler II — put forth a plan to make Georgia Day a commemoration of the state's early history that would educate and entertain the residents of the city and visitors from other areas. The Historic Savannah Foundation, a nonprofit corporation that was founded in 1955 to preserve and restore areas of the city of particular historic or architectural interest, lent its aid to the project. February 12, 1965, the 232nd anniversary of Georgia's founding, was officially proclaimed Georgia Day and was celebrated by a day-long commemoration in Savannah.

From a day-long event sponsored by 31 organizations, Savannah's Georgia Day celebration has expanded into a week of festivities sponsored by more than 80 groups. On the first Sunday of Georgia Week — which actually numbers eight days — church services generally take place at the Old Salzburger Church in Ebenezer, Georgia. The services at Ebenezer, a small town outside Savannah, are of particular note since they follow the 1734 order of service.

During the week of events that follow, Savannah residents and visitors have many opportunities to become acquainted with the unique heritage of Savannah, its dignified homes, and the charm of its squares, gardens, and tree-lined, cobblestone streets. The Historic Savannah Foundation plays an especially important role in this aspect of the celebration. In some years the foundation has sponsored a Landmarks in Use walking tour, and also a tour by candlelight. During these tours many of the restored buildings in the Savannah Historic District, the two-and-a-half square mile area in downtown Savannah that has been designated a Registered National Historic Landmark, are open to visitors. The foundation also conducts tours at the Colonial Cemetery, Savannah's burial ground from about 1750 to 1853. Many distinguished residents are interred in this cemetery, which was converted to a city park in 1896 and later fell into neglect. The Trustees Garden Club of the Historic Savannah Foundation undertook a relandscaping project to make the park a showplace of the city.

Many of the city's museums have special exhibits during the Savannah celebration and a considerable number of events, including lectures on historical and architectural subjects, recall various aspects of Georgia's past. At the restored Juliette Gordon Low Birthplace, the Regency structure where the founder of the Girl Scouts was born, there are exhibits and events of interest, including one day devoted to a demonstration of the rolling of sweet wafers and their tasting. The Maritime Museum housed in historic Fort Jackson, on the Savannah River just east of the city, is among museums with exhibits pertinent to Georgia's past, and a number of others offer special attractions. Receptions and meetings are also scheduled during Savannah's Georgia Week observance, including one at the Cunningham Golden Age Center, which holds an open house with members in costume serving refreshments made from colonial recipes. In addition efforts are made to involve children in the Georgia Week program, and activities, such as a special art exhibit and a puppet show, are designed to stimulate young people's interest in the state's history.

February 12, the actual anniversary of Georgia's founding, is the day of greatest festivity in Savannah. At 11:00 A.M. on February 12 (or a preceding or following weekend day), a procession forms at Oglethorpe's Bench, west of Savannah's city hall. Participants in the march generally include the governor of the state, the mayor of the city, members of patriotic organizations, and schoolchildren. At the start of the procession the paraders hear a special greeting from Savannah's mayor; then they proceed along Bull Street. The procession pauses at Johnson Square, where the Society of the Cincinnati lays a wreath at the monument marking the grave of Nathanael Greene, the quartermaster general of the Continental army who settled near Savannah after the American Revolution. Elsewhere in the square, members of the Bonaventure Chapter of the Daughters of the American Revolution place a wreath at Christ Church. Farther along the line of march, the Daughters of the American Revolution, Savannah Chapter Junior Members, lay wreaths in Wright Square at the monument honoring the friendly Tomochichi of the Yamacraw tribe, who signed a treaty with Oglethorpe, and in Chippewa Square at the Oglethorpe Monument designed by Daniel Chester French.

Since 1966 a governor's luncheon and Georgia Day program have followed the Georgia Day procession. With few exceptions the chief executive of the state has been present at this function. Later in the day the Savannah Historical Research Association sponsors the Oglethorpe dinner, an annual event once held on the birthday of Georgia's founder, but which in recent years has become part of the February 12 commemoration.

On the second Sunday morning of Georgia Week, services in Savannah's various historic downtown churches take note of the anniversary of the founding of Georgia. At noon the Savannah Fire Department and the downtown churches ring out their bells, heralding "the arrival of General Oglethorpe." From then until midafternoon a country fair atmosphere prevails at Emmet Park and along the Strand, with entertainment, lunch, music, and Georgia Day booths featuring historic memorabilia, handmade items, baked goods, and other fare.

Meanwhile, usually beginning at 2:00 P.M., Savannah's celebration reaches its culmination with a pageant that climaxes the eight-day Georgia Week. Since its inception in 1966 the reenactment of the landing of the Oglethorpe party has become one of the most popular attractions of the city's celebration. Citizens of Savannah, arrayed in authentic costumes, take the parts of Georgia's first European settlers and of the Indians who inhabited the area before they arrived. State and local dignitaries join Savannah residents and visitors to witness the colorful presentation.

FEBRUARY 13

Anchorage Fur Rendezvous

This is a movable event. See note on page xxvi.

The Anchorage Fur Rendezvous, a 10-day, community wide celebration held each February in the mountain-rimmed largest city of the 49th state, has snowballed from small beginnings four decades ago to become Alaska's biggest event. Climax of the Rendezvous, or "Rondy," which is sponsored by a nonprofit civic group called Greater Anchorage, Inc., continues to be the annual World's Championship Sled Dog Races, run in three 25-mile heats on the last three days of festivities. But there are other attractions of note — including a 30-block-long parade; a Miners and Trappers Ball with particular emphasis on costumes from the Gay Nineties–Gold Rush era; coronation of the Fur Rendezvous Queen; judging of what may be the world's most impressive beard-growing contest, and crowning of "Mr. Fur Face"; selection of a King and Queen Regent from the ranks of long-time Alaskan residents; the performance of Eskimo dances and the famous Eskimo blanket toss; and vaudeville and melodrama performances.

The World's Championship Sled Dog Races, with prize money that during the mid-1970s totaled over $13,000, draws mushers and their teams of huskies, malamutes, and occasionally other breeds from all over Alaska, many parts of Canada, and as far away as New England — which numbers among its residents the Wayland, Massachusetts, veterinarian, Dr. Roland Lombard, who scored upset victories over local mushers to become the world champion sled dog racer in 1963, 1964, 1965, 1967, 1969, 1970, 1971, and 1974. The championship races are sponsored by Greater Anchorage, Inc., which raises prize money by the sale of sweepstake tickets, Rondy buttons, and other items. They are preceded by a number of preliminary sled dog races, among them the women's championship races. Junior championship races also take place.

While sled racing holds the spotlight, it is far from being the only athletic undertaking among the more than 70 events that make up the Anchorage Fur Rendezvous. The roster customarily includes the All-Alaska Basketball Classic; the All-Alaska Judo Tournament; the Curling Bonspiel; the Alaska Table Tennis Championships; the World's Championship Cross-Country Snowmobile Race; the State I.S.U. Indoor Rifle Championship; a cross-country ski trek; snowshoe racing; auto racing — on ice, at speeds of 80 to 90 miles per hour; as well as hockey and weight lifting — not to mention such less athletic events as the chess and bridge tournaments and the mosaic arts and photography contests. Residents and visitors, some of them sporting the fur hats, specially grown beards, and fur-lined parkas, that are particularly in evidence at Rendezvous time, can also enjoy the art shows; Alaskan movies; rock, mineral, and stamp exhibits; trade fair; dance festivals; concerts; variety acts; and the carnival midway.

Often referred to as the Mardi Gras of the North, the Anchorage Fur Rendezvous had its inception in 1936. Originally billed as a winter sports carnival, in 1937 it acquired its present name — from the trappers' custom of bringing fur pelts to town for sale. Fur and fur products, much emphasized in the first years of the Rendezvous, receive less attention today, although they still appear in the fur hat contest, Rondy Fur Style Show, and outdoor fur auctions. Variously managed in its early years by civic groups, fraternal and service organizations, special committees, and the Anchorage Chamber of Commerce, the Fur Rendezvous came under the sponsorship of Greater Anchorage, Inc., when GAI was founded in 1955 with express responsibility for directing it.

Under the aegis of GAI, the originally modest Rendezvous has expanded from 3 to 10 days in length, arrived at its present crowded agenda, and reached an annual budget of close to $250,000. Anchorage itself has had an even more phenomenal expansion. Population of the greater Anchorage area increased from 3,700 before World War II to over 150,000, including US Army and Air Force personnel, in 1975.

First American Magazine

February 13, 1741, marked the appearance of America's first magazine — Andrew Bradford's *American Magazine, or A Monthly View of the Political State of the British Colonies,* published in Philadelphia. Like its closest successor, Benjamin Franklin's *General Magazine, and Historical Chronicle, for All the British Plantations in America,* which appeared in print in the same city three days later, it bore the date of January 1741.

Both magazines were short-lived. Bradford's publication met its demise in three months. Franklin's survived it by only three months. Both were forerunners, however, of the approximately 100 magazines — most also of brief duration — that were eventually founded in the American colonies; and of the numberless periodical publications that have succeeded them since.

FEBRUARY 14

St. Valentine's Day

The story of what has become the year's most romantic day, February 14, begins in a decidedly unromantic way, with the early martyrologies. These histories of early Christian martyrs mention at least two saints named Valentine associated with February 14. One of them is described as a priest of Rome and another as bishop of Interamna, now Terni. Both men suffered martyrdom in the second half of the third century and were buried in the Flaminian Way. (What was known to the ancient Romans as the Flaminian Gate was later called the Gate of St. Valentine from a church in the immediate neighborhood dedicated to one of the St. Valentines. It is now known as the Porta del Popolo, or Gate of the People.)

Little is known of either of the most commonly mentioned Valentines. (Claims as to the number who existed run as high as seven or eight.) The few known facts of their lives are so interwoven with undocumented traditions that it is impossible to separate fact from legend.

The theories about how the name of Valentine came to be connected with the day on which lovers send tokens to one another also are varied. One is based on the belief throughout rural Europe during the Middle Ages that the birds began to mate on February 14. Chaucer, in his *Parliament of Foules,* refers to the belief in this way:

For this was Seynt Valentyne's day.
When every foul cometh ther to choose his mate.

English literature, following Chaucer, contains frequent references to February 14 as sacred to lovers. Shakespeare, Drayton, and Gay are among those who mention it in this connection, and the diarist Samuel Pepys several times discusses the day and its related customs. The *Paston Letters,* covering the period from 1422 to 1509, contain a letter by Dame Elizabeth Brews to John Paston, with whom she hoped to arrange a match for her daughter, which runs this way:

And cousin mine, upon Monday is St. Valentine's day and every bird chooseth himself a mate, and if it like you to come on Thursday night and make provision that you may abide till then, I trust God that ye shall speak to my husband and I shall pray that we may bring the matter to a conclusion.

The affair must have been managed to her satisfaction, for among the letters is one addressed by the young woman herself "Unto my right-well beloved Valentine, John Paston, Esquire."

Those who do not think that the old opinion about the mating of the birds on February 14 is sufficient to explain the connection between St. Valentine and lovers suggest that the association grew out of the similarity between the Norman word *galantin,* meaning a lover of women, and the name of the saint. They think that Galantin's Day, with the initial g frequently pronounced as *v* led to confusion in the popular mind.

Another theory is that the association with lovers is a survival in Christianized form, of a practice that occurred on February 14, the day before the ancient Roman feast of the *Lupercalia.* At that time the names of young women were put in a box from which they were drawn by chance, an arrangement under which a young man became the gallant of a young woman for the next year, or at least became her partner for the festival.

It is said that the early Christian clergy objected to this custom and substituted the names of saints for the names of young women. Each young man was to try to emulate the saint whose name was drawn for him during the next 12 months, though — as Richard Le Gallienne, writing in 1892, was to comment 13 or more centuries later — "To expect a woman and to draw a saint is ever a disappointment to mortal man!"

Since the drawing occurred on February 14, the day of the saint, in both its original and amended form, the association with St. Valentine was clearly established. This still did not explain the association with lovers, however. For that, the theory connecting the day with the mating season of the birds seems the most plausible. The drawing of the names of young women from a box on Valentine's Day continued for centuries. The young man and woman who were paired by this method were once in the habit of giving presents to each other. Later only the man gave a gift.

In England, where common observance of Valentine's Day dates from the 1400s, many customs grew up in connection with the day — that the first person of the opposite sex whom one met on the morning of Valentine's Day would become his or her true love; that one could discover the identity of the latter via a dream induced by sleeping on a pillow with five bay leaves pinned to it — or by any of a number of other quaint and inconvenient procedures.

Then, by the 17th century the custom of sending valentines to one's favorite developed. At first, these were simple, homemade items. Not until about 1800 did the first commercial valentines appear. After post offices had been established and postal rates reduced to within common reach, the mail was crowded with sweet messages every year. Stores offered valentines in various designs and at various prices. In some cases prices soared — $10 is one reported high — as certain individual designs achieved pinnacles of lavishness.

In the United States the observance of Valentine's Day and exchanging of valentines reached what was probably an all-time high in popularity at about the time of the Civil War. An 1863 periodical published in Boston remarked that "with the exception of Christmas there is no festival throughout the year which is invested with half the interest belonging to this cherished anniversary."

In the late 19th century comic valentines, some of them coarse, could be purchased for a cent – in the early part of the present century the Chicago post office rejected some 25,000 on the ground that they were not fit to be carried through the mail. However, also during this period there were many fine valentines being sold, including "real lace" ones.

By the first third of the 20th century the custom of sending valentines was observed especially by and for children. Their parents sent affectionate messages to them and they sent similar messages to their playmates and parents. Children in kindergartens and the lower primary grades were taught how to make valentines. Then, as now, a valentine box with a slit top, in which children could "mail" their valentines, was a common classroom feature. At home, children made their own valentines, with parental help, by drawing on the stock of gilt cupids, red hearts, and colored papers that stores supplied for the purpose. Outside the classroom today, however, handmade valentines have been largely supplanted by commercially printed versions.

People of all ages send valentines, serious and comic – to their own true loves, but also to family members and friends. Since the identity of the sender of a valentine is traditionally a mystery, valentines are frequently unsigned and often are playfully addressed in disguised handwriting.

The present widespread distribution of valentines brings gladness not only to senders and recipients, but also to members of the greeting card industry, which in recent decades has grown to mammoth proportions. Soon after Christmas and New Year greetings have been exchanged, stores are stocked for this next major card-sending occasion. As the day approaches, candy stores are filled with red, heart-shaped boxes of chocolates; and florists augment their supplies of red roses – long a symbol of romance – which will be given on Valentine's Day.

Hearts, cupids, bows and arrows appear everywhere, not only in stores and mailboxes but also on dinner tables and on valentine gifts. In the form of confections, they are incorporated into fancy desserts. Many modest family celebrations take place on this day. So, for that matter, do romantic dinners à deux, and a good many dances and parties, sponsored privately or by organizations and clubs.

A few gala costume balls still take place as well. However, not many of today's events are so elaborate as one held early in the present century in Symphony Hall, Boston, by the Boston Conservatory of Music. It was attended by more than 1,900 dancers, splendidly attired in the costumes of various periods – from those worn by knights of the Middle Ages to those associated with pirates of the Spanish Main. Butterflies, gypsies, operatic and Shakespearean characters were all represented, and prizes were awarded for the most beautiful costumes. A contemporary account of the grand march described the scene:

As they passed slowly, eight abreast, down the sides and across the center of the floor they appeared to be some ancient manuscript, wonderfully illuminated, come to life. Juliet smiled up at Weary Willie; a white robed nun of the 14th century paced demurely at the side of Charles II; Faust bent over the hand of a cowgirl; Hamlet joked with Carmen; the Arabian princess drew aside her veil to dimple at a plaided Scotchman.

Like the festivities, the valentines of today are less elaborate than the artifacts of yesteryear with their lavish arrays of lace, ribbons, hearts, flowers, clasped hands, cupids, bows and arrows, and pairs of turtledoves. In keeping with the current trend for nostalgia, however, the early valentines can be seen increasingly in the exhibits of romantic memorabilia that are likely to be scheduled around Valentine's Day.

The period before February 14 is a busy one for the post offices in such communities as Love, Mississippi; Darling, Pennsylvania; Romance, Arkansas; Eros, Louisiana; and Kissimmee, Florida, whose names inspire people from afar to send their valentines there to be postmarked and forwarded. In the early 1970s the Loveland, Colorado, post office alone annually remailed some 300,000 valentines from all over the country, after postmarking the envelopes in red with its own distinguishing cachet.

Largely missing from today's messages are both the excessive sentimentality of Gay Nineties valentines and the cruelty of the earliest, so-called comic, valentines. Apart from the serious, rhyming declarations of love that still abound, the contemporary emphasis is on the light touch.

Valentine's Day remains, as ever, a day to express love. Few who observe it go as far as

TV personality Garry Moore, who once hired four skywriting airplanes to produce for his wife's delight a three-mile-wide heart, pierced by a six-mile-long arrow and ornamented with their names.

Not even Moore's spectacular gesture, however, has caused one of the oldest and simplest valentine messages to become outdated:

> Roses are red, violets are blue,
> Sugar is sweet, and so are you.

The verse is, of course, customarily signed "Guess Who?"

Arizona Admission Day

In Arizona February 14 is observed as Admission Day, a legal holiday. The observance commemorates the date on which President William Howard Taft signed the proclamation admitting Arizona as a state in 1912. By historical coincidence, the February 14 admission date lacked only 10 days of being the anniversary of Arizona's creation as a territory 49 years earlier – by an act of Congress in 1863 (see February 24).

Apart from the fact that state offices close, Arizona business goes on much as usual on Admission Day. There are no regularly recurring statewide ceremonies. However some schools and patriotic groups have programs that mark the day and recall the early history of the area.

The history of Arizona is unbelievably long. Archeological finds indicate that human beings have lived in what is now Arizona for at least 10,000 years, perhaps for 20,000 years, and possibly longer. Some of the notable remnants of early Indian cultures that can be seen today – cliff dwellings, fortifications, and ruins, preserved in national monuments or otherwise – date from the years between 800 and 1500.

Written records of the region's history began about four centuries ago. The first European to go to Arizona was probably Fray Marcos de Niza, in 1539. He returned to Spanish Mexico with tall tales, spun by Indians to please him, of the "Seven Cities of Cibola," where "gold and silver were the only metals" and in common use by the natives. The fabled Seven Cities of Cibola, which Marcos de Niza claimed to have sighted but apparently did not visit, were, in fact, the impoverished villages of the Zuñi Indians in what is now northwestern New Mexico, close to the Arizona border.

Unfounded as they were, the reports set in motion the great expedition of 1540–1542 headed by Francisco Vásquez de Coronado, who set forth from Mexico to secure the rumored riches and conquer the region for Spain. Crossing Arizona to Cibola, he dispatched several subsidiary parties to different areas of Arizona. García López de Cárdenas thus became the first European to see the Grand Canyon. Pedro de Tovar explored the Hopi Indian villages. An allied group under Hernando de Alarcón meanwhile investigated the mouth of the Colorado River, far to the south. However, Coronado's main force continued east across New Mexico and explored parts of the Great Plains in what are now Texas and Kansas before returning to Mexico.

White settlement was slow. The soil was arid, and no riches were found. The Indians fiercely defended their land – there was bloodshed intermittently for nearly 300 years. Those who went were mostly missionaries from Spanish Mexico, who pursued their proselytizing goals for a half-century or more before their expulsion as a result of the great Indian revolt of 1680. Perhaps the most notable of the missionaries who began penetrating the region, undeterred, a dozen years later, was the tireless Father Eusebio Francisco Kino, a Jesuit, who established a number of missions in southern Arizona in the two decades before his death in 1711. Missionary efforts by Jesuits continued until 1767, when they fell from favor in Spain and were replaced by Franciscans in the dominions of Spain.

During the Mexican rule, which replaced Spanish domination after the successful conclusion of the Mexican Revolution in 1821, the only important non-Indian settlements in the south of Arizona were those at Tubac and Tucson, Apache raids having prompted the desertion of most others. But as early as 1826 Anglo-American fur trappers began coming in by way of the Gila River valley. After 1840 soldiers, adventurers, and a few pioneer settlers filtered into Arizona. So did prospectors, particularly after the beginning of the California gold rush in 1848 and Henry Wickenburg's gold strike northwest of Phoenix in 1863. (The town of Wickenburg today annually recreates its Gold Rush Days with a parade, related events, and gold panning during the second weekend of February.)

Most of Arizona – everything, that is, north of the Gila River – was ceded to the United States by Mexico at the end of the Mexican War in 1848. It became part of the territory of New Mexico, created in 1850. That part of Arizona between the Gila and the present Mexican boundary was added to the territory in 1853 by the Gadsden Purchase. Under its terms certain boundary vaguenesses were clarified and the United States acquired — for an eventual price of $10 million — land that explorations had indicated was desirable for a proposed southern railroad route to the Pacific Ocean.

In 1856 a convention at Tucson petitioned Congress for the right to create a separate Arizona territory, but Congress, divided over the question of slavery in the territories, put the matter aside. Early in the Civil War the Confederate States did recognize Arizona as a separate territory. Texas Confederate troops occupied southern Arizona for a few months of 1862 before Union troops from California reoccupied the area for the federal government. It was not until February 24, 1863, however, that a separate territory of Arizona was officially established by Congress.

A movement for Arizona statehood, already the subject of years of agitation, began to assume more definite shape in 1891 when residents ratified a constitution framed by the legislature at the new territorial capital of Phoenix (later the capital of the state). Congress, however, declined to approve the constitution and also rejected later bills providing for statehood. The people of Arizona in turn disapproved of proposed congressional legislation that would have admitted Arizona and New Mexico as a single state.

Finally a new state constitution submitted in 1910 was approved by Congress and President William Howard Taft, on condition that a clause providing for the recall of judges be eliminated. After that condition was accepted by the territorial electorate, Arizona was formally admitted as the 48th state, on February 14, 1912. The last word on judges, however, came from the people of Arizona, who restored the controversial provision for recall to the state constitution before their first year of statehood had ended.

Frederick Douglass's Birthday: Black History Week

February 14 — the date on which (according to his calculation) the abolitionist orator and journalist Frederick Douglass was born in 1817 — is commemorated as a focal point of Black, or Afro-American, History Week (originally called Negro History Week). (This is a movable event. See note on p. 2.) The nationally observed week, which has been sponsored since 1926 by the Association for the Study of Afro-American (formerly Negro) Life and History, generally begins on the second Sunday in February, always includes Douglass's birthday, and, whenever the calendar permits, embraces the birthday of Abraham Lincoln. Widely marked by schools, churches, libraries, clubs, and other groups, the week emphasizes the special contributions of blacks to civilization. In observance of the US Bicentennial, a special, broader program was adopted for Black History Week in 1976. Its theme, America for All, included an examination of the history of blacks, American Indians, Asians, and Spanish-speaking people in the United States.

Born in Tuckahoe, Maryland, Frederick Augustus Washington Bailey, as Douglass was originally known, was the son of Harriet Bailey, a black slave of part-Indian blood, and an unknown white father. His only recollections of his mother were "a few hasty visits in the night on foot," Douglass said later, adding that he had "hardly become a thinking thing" when he "first learned to hate slavery." He was eight years old when he left the care of his grandmother to spend a year working on the plantation managed by his master, Captain Aaron Anthony. His next duties, in service of the family of Hugh Auld in Baltimore, marked a turning point in his life. Mrs. Auld helped point him in a new direction by secretly teaching him to read and write — knowledge he soon employed in writing free passes for runaway slaves.

He was 16 when he was returned to the plantation on the death of his master. In due time he was hired out to, and brutally flogged by, a man named Covey, whose scars he bore on his back for the rest of his life. In 1836, during subsequent service to William Freeland of St. Michael's, Maryland, Douglass attempted, unsuccessfully, to escape. Instead he was returned to the Aulds in Baltimore. He was 19 by then, and Hugh Auld had him apprenticed to a ship caulker — an acquaintance with things of the sea that may have provided the idea for Douglass's second, and successful, escape attempt, on September 3, 1838. Having learned his trade, he posed as a sailor and managed to escape by rail — first to New York City, where he married a young, free black woman, and then to the greater safety of New Bedford, Massachusetts. There he protected his identity by assuming the name of Douglass (borrowed from the hero of Sir Walter Scott's *Lady of the Lake*) and found employment as a day laborer for three years.

In the summer of 1841 he attended a meeting of the Massachusetts Anti-Slavery Society on Nantucket Island, and found himself delivering an extemporaneous address. So effective was his passionate oratory that he was made an agent of the society and spent the next four years, at some danger to himself, lecturing throughout New England and the middle states in favor of abolition. His words were so eloquent that some listeners, persuading themselves that a man of his capabilities could never have been a slave, accused him of being a fraud. To set the record straight, he published an autobiography, *Narrative of the Life of Frederick Douglass,* in 1845.

The possibility of recapture as a fugitive slave was a continuing problem. To avoid the danger, Douglass spent the years 1845–1847 in England and Ireland, where his lectures did much to sway British public opinion in favor of abolition. He did not return to the United States until his freedom had been purchased with the help of English friends, who raised £150 for the cause.

On his return he settled in Rochester, New York, where he founded the weekly antislavery newspaper *North Star,* which he edited (later as *Frederick Douglass's Paper*) until 1860. His reputation as an orator continued to grow as he added pleas for woman suffrage to his addresses on abolition. He played a role in politics and worked with Harriet Beecher Stowe in an effort to set up an industrial school for young blacks. At first a follower of the abolitionist editor William Lloyd Garrison, after 1851 he supported the more conservative James G. Birney, who favored abolition by constitutional political methods. Although he was consulted by John Brown he refused to have any part in Brown's attack upon Harpers Ferry. But once the bloodletting of the Civil War had become inevitable, Douglass was among the first to urge that the Union army use black troops, and he helped to form two regiments from Massachusetts. He was called into consultation by Lincoln and preceded him to the realization that the nation must address itself to the problems of blacks before the war could be concluded. After the Emancipation Proclamation in 1863 (see January 1), Douglass turned to demanding land and ballots for the freedman, so that he who had become "in law, free" would not remain "in fact, a slave."

Appointed to the Santo Domingo Commission in 1871, Douglass was marshal of the District of Columbia from 1877 to 1881, and then became recorder of deeds for the district. His second marriage, in 1884, to Helen Pitts, a white woman, caused a controversy, which he dismissed lightly, remarking that, as his first wife had been the color of his mother, his second was the color of his father. Douglass, who was the US minister and consul general in Haiti from 1889 to 1891, continued his active support of civil rights for blacks and other social reforms until the very end of his life. On the day of his death, February 20, 1895, he had attended a woman suffrage convention. His 14-room home, Cedar Hill, on an eight-acre hilltop site in Washington, D.C.'s, Anacostia Heights (1411 W Street, S.E.), is now a national memorial, a gift of the Frederick Douglass Memorial and Historical Association. It is open to the public.

The first home in which Douglass lived in Washington, a 19th century town house located behind the Supreme Court building (at 316-318 A Street, N.E.), now houses the Museum of African Art and the Frederick Douglass Institute. At the time of its opening in 1964, the museum was the first in the country devoted solely to African art. Afro-American art was added to the collection when the institute came into existence two years later. One room is a re-creation of Douglass's study, with his desk and typewriter and various memorabilia warmly evoking the spirit of the man.

Oregon Admitted to the Union

On February 14, 1859, Oregon joined the federal Union. Although Oregon's admission to statehood was considerably complicated by the dispute over slavery, the 33rd member of the Union managed to overcome these difficulties and gain statehood just months before slavery divided the United States into two armed camps.

The first government in Oregon had come into existence during the period when both the United States and Great Britain claimed the area between the 42nd parallel on the south and parallel 54'40° on the north and jointly occupied this Oregon Country — including the present state of Washington — under the Convention of 1818. Beginning in 1841, some residents of the region that is now Oregon tried to institute a provisional government modeled after that set up in the Old Northwest by the Ordinance of 1787 (see July 13). Their efforts to establish such a government met with difficulty in Oregon, where the populace was divided on such critical issues as national allegiance and religion. But the need for order eventually overcame objections to the projected government, and within a few years a provisional government, independent of both the United States and Britain, was in operation in Oregon. The year 1843, meanwhile, was marked by the arrival of the first really large group of American settlers to reach the area over the Oregon Trail, the vanguard of a tide of travelers that would swell to a flood (see July 16, Oregon Trail Days, Gering, Nebraska). By 1844 the expansionist demand "Fifty-four forty or fight!" had become a Democratic campaign slogan.

When the inhabitants of Oregon received word in 1846 that the United States and Great Britain had reached a compromise on the 49th parallel as the boundary between the United States and Canada, they rejoiced in the expectation that the US Congress would quickly provide a territorial government for their region. President James K. Polk recommended territorial status for Oregon, and a bill was introduced in Congress that would have brought such a government into existence. However, southern congressmen feared the creation of a northern territory in which slavery would almost certainly be outlawed, particularly since the area was neither dependent upon a slave economy nor suited to slavery by climate. They therefore prevented passage in 1847 of the legislation necessary to bring the Oregon Territory into being.

In November 1847 hostile Cayuse Indians killed the Protestant missionaries Marcus and Narcissa Whitman and other members of the mission they had established at Waiilatpu, near the site of present Walla Walla, Washington (see November 29). This incident precipitated clashes between the Cayuse and the Oregon settlers, and the emergency situation forced Congress in 1848 to reconsider territorial government for that portion of the Pacific Northwest lying below the 49th parallel. In 1848 southern congressmen again attempted to block the creation of a territory where slavery would be outlawed, but this time they did not succeed. The bill organizing without slavery the area bounded by the 42nd and 49th parallels, the Rocky Mountains and the Pacific Ocean passed both houses of Congress on August 14, 1848, and the measure was signed by President Polk.

Polk immediately appointed a governor and other officials for the new territory. They arrived in Oregon City on March 2, 1849, and the following day the territorial government replaced Oregon's provisional government. Oregon retained territorial status for 10 years, but in 1853 Congress reduced the size of Oregon by separating the region north of the Columbia River to form the Territory of Washington. Oregon assumed its present dimensions, south of the Columbia and the 46th parallel.

For more than a year after Oregon's acquisition of territorial status, Congress took no action to confirm the land titles of settlers in the Pacific Northwest. Then, in September 1850, Congress approved the Donation Land Act. This legislation guaranteed 640 acres to each married couple that settled in the territory before December 1, 1850, and stipulated that half this acreage belonged outright to the wife; the law also provided 160 acres to each husband and an additional 160 to each wife who took up residence in Oregon after December 1, 1850, but before December 1, 1853.

The Donation Land Act and the discovery in 1848 of gold in nearby California spurred the growth of Oregon, but the decade of the 1850s was not without troubles. In 1853 Indian uprisings began in southern Oregon, where recently arrived white settlers had displaced the Indians from their lands. Hostilities between the two groups continued for several years and caused considerable hardships and difficulties. But by 1858 the Indians were pacified and confined to several reservations located along Oregon's northern coast and in the relatively barren eastern portion of the territory.

Oregonians soon grew tired of their dependent territorial status. The settlers believed that the regular US Army, which had sought to protect the Indians, had not been stern enough with them. They wanted Congress to assume the debt that they had incurred in fighting the Indians and securing the region. The pioneers, moreover, were thoroughly dissatisfied with the postal service and with the process of distributing lands and guaranteeing claims.

To many Oregonians, statehood seemed to offer a solution to their problems. The settlers would receive more direct control over their own affairs and they would have better representation in Congress. Unfortunately, several obstacles, most notably the slavery issue, lay between them and their goal.

Congress took up the subject of statehood for Oregon in 1856. The House of Representatives passed an enabling bill that authorized the territory to call a convention to draw up a state constitution, but the Senate defeated the measure. It was a time of volatile tempers, and many politicians, especially southerners, did not want to admit to the Union a state whose constitution was expected to forbid slavery. Even antislavery Republicans were wary of admitting Oregon, which had a reputation for favoring the Democratic party.

Undaunted by their opponents, the residents of Oregon in 1857 (as they had in 1854, 1855, and 1856), voted overwhelmingly to form a state government. In accordance with the popular will the territorial legislature convoked a constitutional convention, which opened on August 17, 1857, at the Salem courthouse. Even within the convention, however, the slavery controversy was a hindrance to unity, and the question of whether Oregon would or would not permit slavery was left for decision of the populace in the same election that would decide the fate of the proposed constitution.

When Oregonians went to the polls on November 9, 1857, to vote on the new frame of government, its supporters were victorious by a majority of 3,980 votes. An even larger majority, of 5,082, voted against allowing slavery. The largest majority of all, of 7,559, went further, approving a provision by which noncitizens — a category in which that year's Dred Scott decision had placed blacks — would be denied the right even to enter Oregon.

Confronted with Oregon's unilateral formation of a state constitution, Congress was still bitterly divided on whether to admit Oregon to the Union. Southern Democrats were angered at the prospect of another free state, and northern Republicans worried about the likelihood of another Democratic state. Nevertheless, on February 14, 1859, Congress voted, by an extremely narrow margin, to admit Oregon; and the 33rd state became part of the Union.

Oregon is one of the many states that have chosen to commemorate the date of their admission to the federal Union. Although February 14 is not a legal holiday, it is an official "day of commemoration," and schools throughout the state schedule special observances to mark the occasion.

FEBRUARY 15

Susan B. Anthony Day

February 15, the anniversary of the birth in 1820 of the woman suffrage leader Susan B. Anthony, is observed as Susan B. Anthony Day.

Memorial tributes to the suffrage leader on her birthday take place in various parts of the United States. Verbal tributes are often presented in Congress and floral tributes are placed at the statue of the suffrage pioneers — Anthony, Elizabeth Cady Stanton, and Lucretia Mott — in the crypt of the Capitol in Washington, D.C. A memorial ceremony has frequently been held in the crypt. Ceremonies honoring Susan B. Anthony sometimes also are held at her grave in Rochester, New York. Special school programs around the time of her birthday often

emphasize the contributions of women, as well as the forms of discrimination against them.

Women's organizations play a large role in sponsoring memorial observances. For many years the National Woman's Party planned the ceremonies, which were open to the public, in the crypt of the Capitol; in recent years, the organization has sometimes chosen other ways to mark the day. Among observances of the 150th anniversary, in 1970, of Susan B. Anthony's birth was a fund-raising party in New York City for the National Organization for Women (NOW).

A number of states honor Susan Anthony on her birthday. For example, Susan B. Anthony Day in New York is designated by gubernatorial proclamation, and in Connecticut February 15 is celebrated as a "special day." By statute, the anniversary is observed by the public schools of California and Minnesota; and Michigan's governor designates a week in early February as Susan B. Anthony Week. Legislation was introduced in Congress to make Anthony's birthday a federal public holiday. Some states honor the woman suffrage leader on August 26, the date the 19th, or so-called Anthony, Amendment was proclaimed ratified. (See also June 18, Susan B. Anthony Fined for Voting, and August 26.)

Russell H. Conwell's Birthday

Russell H. Conwell, clergyman, lawyer, and college president who for years toured the nation as one of its most noted lecturers, was born in the Berkshire hills at South Worthington, Massachusetts, on February 15, 1843. The son of a poor abolitionist family, he was born in a two-room farmhouse that served as a way station of the Underground Railroad. He attended the district school four miles away, and before he was 10 years old he had committed to memory the first three books of Milton's *Paradise Lost.* Later he attended Wilbraham Academy, a boys' preparatory school near Springfield, Massachusetts, and during the same time taught at a district school. The additional work, however, did not detract from his schoolwork. He was made captain of the debating team and drillmaster of the military corps and was graduated, in 1859, at the age of 16.

In 1860 Conwell entered Yale, but did not stay to complete his law studies there. In 1862, responding to President Abraham Lincoln's call for men to serve in the Union forces in the Civil War, Conwell left school and enlisted for military duty. He organized a company of men from his home county, was unanimously elected their captain and, at the age of 19, received his commission from Massachusetts Governor John Albion Andrew.

Among the boys in the county was one named John Ring, who was too small to be admitted to the company but who was so anxious to go with the soldiers that Conwell took him along as his servant. It was because of his acquaintanceship with John Ring, in addition to other experiences, that Conwell, who had thought himself an atheist, became seriously religious. One of Ring's duties was shining Conwell's decorative sword, which hung in his tent. One day, during the battle of New Bern, North Carolina, at the junction of the Neuse and Trent rivers, Conwell's men were forced to retreat at the onslaught of Confederate forces. They fled across the river, setting the bridge behind them afire. Just as the bridge was burning, young John Ring remembered the sword in his captain's tent. Rushing through the flames, he retrieved it, and began making his way back across the flaming bridge. When he was halfway over, the Confederate officer saw him and, impressed by his heroic attempt, ordered his men to cease firing. The Union and Confederate men then watched in silence while the youngster struggled on. He reached the other side with the sword but was so badly burned that he died a short time later. The incident so deeply impressed Conwell that he thereafter kept the sword hanging at the head of his bed as a constant reminder of the boy's unselfish heroism. From that time on, he vowed to devote 16 hours each day to useful work — 8 for himself and 8 for John Ring.

Having attained the rank of lieutenant colonel, Conwell was finally sent home after being seriously wounded in the battle of Kenesaw Mountain in northwest Georgia. At the close of the war he entered the law school at Union University in Albany, and upon graduating in 1865 was admitted to the bar. He then went to Minnesota, where he opened a law office in Minneapolis. To add to his income, he became the Minneapolis correspondent of the St. Paul *Press* and shortly thereafter, with the aid of some businessmen, founded the Minneapolis *Daily Chronicle*. Even with his journalistic venture, Conwell continued to attend to his growing law practice, and taught music and elocution in his spare time.

When his health began to fail, Conwell left Minneapolis and spent a year in Europe. Finally, a bullet that had lodged in his lung during the battle of Kenesaw Mountain was extracted, and he recovered. He moved to Boston, where he opened two law offices, wrote for the Boston *Traveler* and the New York *Tribune,* and published the Somerville (Massachusetts) *Journal.* In spite of his busy schedule, he managed to keep one of his offices open at night to give free legal advice to the poor who could not see him during the day. At times he would be visited by 50 or more persons in a single evening.

In 1874 Conwell took up residence in Newton Center, a Boston suburb and the seat of the Baptist Newton Theological Seminary. It was there that he decided to become a minister. He closed his law office in 1878 and offered his services to a struggling Baptist church in Lexington, Massachusetts, where he was ordained in 1879. There were only 18 persons in his first congregation, but the next Sunday the church was crowded with people trying to get in. On the third Sunday the services were held in the town hall, where they continued to be held until a new and larger church was built.

Conwell remained in Lexington for 18 months before he was asked to become pastor of a church formed by members of the Tenth Baptist Church in Philadelphia. Responding to the call of the small and debt-ridden congregation, Conwell assumed duties as pastor of the Grace Baptist Church in Philadelphia on Thanksgiving Day, 1882. As his congregation grew, he saw the need for a new church building. Touched by the death of a little girl who had saved 57 cents for a new church, he related her story to friends of the church who, in their turn, were inspired to buy a lot for the new building. In 1891 Dr. Conwell organized the new Baptist Temple, which eventually grew into one of the largest institutional churches in the United States, numbering among its offspring three hospitals and Philadelphia's Temple University.

In 1923, in recognition of his work, Conwell was given the Philadelphia Award, which is presented annually to a deserving citizen of the city. The award consisted of a gold medal and a cash prize of $10,000, drawn from a trust fund established by Edward Bok, the longtime editor of the *Ladies' Home Journal.* Conwell used the money for philanthropic purposes, as he had used all other money that came into his possession. A lecturer in frequent demand, he earned, it is estimated, over $10 million on the lecture platform, all of which (save money for traveling expenses) he gave away. His most famous lecture was "Acres of Diamonds," which he delivered more than 6,000 times and for which it is said he received some $8 million. This lecture was never twice the same, but it always began with a tale told to him by an Arab guide he had hired in Baghdad, while traveling down the Euphrates River.

The story related how a prosperous and contented Persian named Ali Hafed was one day visited by a Buddhist priest who told him how the world was made; how granite, copper, silver, gold, and diamonds were made from the molten mass in the earth's interior; and how, if he had a diamond mine, Ali Hafed could place his children on thrones. Hearing this, Ali Hafed quickly became discontented and asked the priest where diamonds could be found. Learning that they supposedly came from a river that ran over white sands between high mountains, Ali Hafed sold his farm and went to search for the gems. He traveled the world over, spent all his money, and died in poverty.

One day, the story continued, the man who had bought Ali Hafed's farm took his camel to drink in the brook in the garden and saw a flash of light coming from the sands. He picked up a stone with a bright spot in it that reflected all the colors of the rainbow. He took the stone into his house, not knowing what it was. But the same priest that had visited Ali Hafed also happened to visit the later owner of his farm and identified the precious gem. Rushing to the little stream, they found other diamonds, and out of this mine, so the story went, came the Kohinoor and Orloff diamonds and the crown jewels of England.

The moral of the lecture reflected the prevalent view of the time that one could find wealth and opportunity in one's own backyard and that, indeed, one should work to achieve riches in order to be able to help others. Russell H. Conwell died in Philadelphia on December 6, 1925, having lived according to his own teachings.

After his death, Conwell's birth date was designated by Temple University, of which he was the founder and first president, as Founder's Day. In 1934, when the university was 50 years old, Founder's Day exercises extended over a whole week and were attended by distinguished educators from across the country. More recently Founder's Day at Temple University usually has been observed with a dinner celebration on or around February 15. A particularly memorable celebration took place in May 1963, with a jubilee climaxing the 75th anniversary of the granting of the university's charter on May 12, 1888.

One of the notable achievements of Conwell's busy life, Temple University had its beginnings in 1884. Conwell, then pastor of Philadelphia's Grace Baptist Church, was visited by a workingman who wanted to prepare himself for the Christian ministry but had no money to study and was compelled to work during the daytime to support himself. After some discussion Dr. Conwell offered to devote one evening a week to teaching the man himself. The man thereupon asked if he might bring a friend with him and was told to bring as many as he wished. On the appointed evening, Dr. Conwell began teaching his first seven students the rudiments of Latin. By the third evening there were some 40 young men in the class, and a room was hired in which to teach them. Within two years there were so many students that it became necessary to hire a separate building. By May 12, 1888, when the school obtained a college charter, it already had 590 students; and when the right to grant degrees was obtained in 1891, instruction, which previously had been given only at night, began to be offered during the day. In 1907 the school became a university and adopted its present name. Since its founding in 1884 it has grown from a single building to a modern complex of five campuses, the largest of which are the 76-acre urban campus at Broad Street and Montgomery Avenue, Philadelphia, and the 186-acre Ambler Campus in nearby Montgomery County's Upper Dublin township. In its early days, the institution's expenses were paid almost entirely by Dr. Conwell from the proceeds of his lectures. In 1965, however, Temple University became a state-related Commonwealth University by act of the Pennsylvania legislature, along with the Pennsylvania State University and the University of Pittsburgh, and began receiving state financial support.

Cyrus H. McCormick's Birthday

Cyrus Hall McCormick, whose reaper is said to have been second only to the railroad in its importance to the development of the United States, was born on February 15, 1809, in Virginia's Rockbridge County. His father, Robert McCormick, was a farmer and inventor who had spent two decades trying, unsuccessfully, to develop a grain-cutting machine when his 22-year-old son took up the task. With careful study and using different principles from his father's, young McCormick managed to construct a horse-operated reaper which received its first public demonstration in a Virginia wheat field late in July 1831. Viewers, who saw that it could cut as much grain as six men with scythes, were astonished.

Almost certainly, McCormick's reaper was invented before that of Obed Hussey, although Hussey was first to obtain a patent. With the two men's inventions, which followed centuries of abortive efforts by others, harvesting machinery became practical for the first time. Unlike Hussey's machine, which lacked the essential reel, McCormick's employed all seven of the mechanical principles that have since been found necessary to machine harvesting.

Apprised that an April 1834 magazine gave notice of a reaper invented by Hussey in 1833, McCormick warned Hussey of the priority of his own invention and took out a patent on June 21, 1834. During the rest of the decade, McCormick, a man of seemingly limitless energy, kept adding improvements to his machine. But it was not until after the panic of 1837, which contributed to the demise of the iron-manufacturing business in which he and his father had been engaged, that McCormick concentrated on his reaper in earnest.

The machine was an early success. At first it was manufactured in small lots in Virginia. By 1845 it was in use on most of the larger western farms. McCormick, a rarity among inventors in also possessing a good business sense, soon became convinced that he should supervise all manufacture himself, in his own factory, and that it should be located near the Midwest's expanding wheat fields.

He opened his factory in Chicago in 1847. Although he was faced with widespread competition after his original patent expired in 1848, he had by then established the usefulness of his product.

He continued to prosper despite two decades of almost constant litigation. By 1850 he had managed to establish a nationwide business. His reaper was the chief attraction of the 1851 London world's fair at the Crystal Palace. He became world-famous overnight and repeated his success by prize-winning demonstrations at subsequent expositions and fairs at home and abroad.

By 1856 McCormick reapers were selling at the rate of some 4,000 a year and McCormick had long since become a millionaire. His machine, which he continued to improve until his death, played an important role in helping the North win the Civil War, by enabling the Union to feed both soldiers and civilians while also securing funds from Europe by means of a lucrative export trade in grain.

As for the longer-range implications of McCormick's reaper, its importance can hardly be overestimated: it revolutionized agriculture, changing the way of life of large segments of the population, vitally affecting the nation's economy, and giving important impetus to the settlement of the country's vacant lands. Armed with labor-saving machines that made it possible to farm more land, with fewer hands, than ever before, farmers were encouraged to mi-grate westward, clearing and cultivating new territories as they went. With the advent of the reaper, farming became mass production — agriculture for sale as well as merely for use. The success of the reaper fostered development of other labor-saving farm machinery and helped spread the agricultural revolution, which — apart from increasing farm output — also freed large numbers of farmers to settle in the country's swelling cities and contribute to the growth of the nation's new industries.

McCormick, though he is known primarily as an inventor, also contributed to modern business methods. In some ways foreshadowing Henry Ford, he stressed the invention of labor-saving machinery that made mass production possible in his factory. He also pioneered in advertising citing testimonials, guarantees, and field trials, and in the use of cash and deferred payments for merchandise.

In 1902–1903, some years after McCormick's death on May 13, 1884, his McCormick Harvesting Machine Company was consolidated with other firms to become the International Harvester Company, one of the world's largest manufacturers of agricultural equipment.

Maine Memorial Day

The American battleship *Maine*, under command of Captain Charles D. Sigsbee, was sent to dissension-torn, Spanish-ruled Cuba in January 1898 as an ostensibly friendly (but iron-fisted) gesture toward Spain. Actually, the ship was sent to be ready to rescue any Americans whose safety might be imperiled by the unrest surrounding Cubans' efforts to free themselves from the Spanish yoke. The Spanish government had been charged with intolerable cruelties, and the sympathy of the people of the United States was all on the side of the revolting Cubans. Indeed, expeditions for their relief were frequently organized within the United States and, although American authorities tried to prevent such activities in the name of neutrality, they were not always successful.

The government in Washington, interested in the peace of the island, meanwhile was in correspondence with the government in Madrid in an attempt to settle the Cuban troubles to the satisfaction of all concerned. There was resentment in certain Spanish circles in Havana, however, over the presence of the *Maine* in the harbor.

On February 15 — the day that some states, among them Connecticut and Massachusetts, now designate as *Maine* Memorial Day — the Spanish warship *Alfonso XII* and the American Ward Line steamer *City of Washington* were anchored not far from the *Maine* in Havana harbor. The day had been unusually warm for the season. The evening heat was so oppressive that the officers and men on the two battleships and the passengers on the merchant ship were relaxing, trying to keep cool. At 9:00 P.M. Captain Sigsbee had just finished writing a report to Theodore Roosevelt, then assistant secretary of the US Navy, on the advisability of continuing the practice of placing torpedo tubes on cruisers and battleships; and he was about to begin a letter to his wife. At 9:10 the bugler began to blow taps.

At 9:40 P.M. everything was quiet on the ship and the captain was folding the letter which he had written to his wife. In an instant, as the captain explained afterward, "there came a bursting, rending and crashing sound or roar of immense volume, followed by a succession of heavy, ominous metallic sounds and reverberations." The explosion had occurred under the sleeping quarters of the crew and had wrecked the vessel so completely that it sank within a very short time. It had a complement of 26 officers and 328 men. Two of the officers and 250 of the men were killed outright and 8 died later in Havana hospitals. Captain Sigsbee was the last man to leave the ship. He took refuge on the *City of Washington* and sent the following dispatch to the Department of the Navy:

Maine blown up in Havana harbor . . . tonight and destroyed. Wounded and others on board Spanish man-of-war and Ward Line steamer. Send lighthouse tenders from Key West for crew and the few pieces of equipment above water. No one has clothing other than that upon him. Public opinion should be suspended until further report. All officers believed to be saved. Jenkins and Merritt not yet accounted for. Many Spanish officers, including representatives of General Blanco [the island's Spanish captain-general] now with me to express sympathy.

Charles W. Newton, a captain in the National Guard, was in Havana at the time of the explosion. He had gone there with General Arthur L. Goodrich, the owner of the Hartford (Connecticut) *Courant,* to see if conditions were as bad as reported. He and General Goodrich were seated in a park overlooking the harbor when the explosion occurred. His description of what he found and what he saw indicates the critical nature of the situation. He said:

Thousands of natives, driven into the city by the Spaniards, were starving. Every morning the authorities would line up men suspected of inciting to revolt and shoot them down. There were street riots all the time. Nevertheless the Spanish officers had a gay time and there were bull fights all the time.

That night (February 15) we left the Hotel Inglaterra and went to sit in the park. There was plenty of high feeling and we thought maybe the hotel would be blown up. However, nothing serious had happened and I said to Arthur: "We'll be leaving for home tomorrow and nothing much has happened. I wouldn't mind seeing some excitement, even if we had to swim out to the *Maine* for protection." Just as I said these words there was a great flash out on the water and a few seconds later a big boom. We could barely see the *Maine* in the darkness. It began sinking slowly by the stern. Its powder magazines let go, just like a fireworks blast. It was awful. The ship continued to burn for hours, just that portion that remained out of water. Goodrich and I were afraid that would be a signal for a general fight, so we ran to a warehouse and took shelter until three o'clock in the morning. Then we got aboard the *City of Washington* to which Admiral Sigsbee was taken after every living man had been removed from the *Maine*. Two days later we returned to the states.

The immediate impression in the United States was that the Spanish authorities were responsible for the destruction of the ship. This feeling and the indignation aroused by Spanish cruelties, with other contributing causes, led to the Spanish-American War, which began in April 1898 (see April 21). The war resulted in expulsion of Spain from the island and independence for Cuba under US protection.

As far as the destruction of the *Maine* was concerned, however, a naval court of inquiry that sat in the case found that although the explosion was, in its opinion, caused externally by an underwater mine, it was impossible to "obtain evidence fixing the responsibility . . . upon any person or persons." This finding, as indicated above, did not stop a large number of Americans, incited by the "yellow press" of the day, from blaming Spanish agents for the incident. Subordinate Spanish officers stationed in Havana were particular objects of suspicion by some. Others blamed Cuban insurgents who, they claimed, had discovered an explosive device planted by the Spanish and sought to employ it to their own ends. The insurgents' intention, according to these unsubstantiated allegations, was to explode the device near, but not under, the *Maine* in hopes of precipitating US action on behalf of Cuban independence. An independent Spanish investigation had an entirely different conclusion from that of the American board of inquiry — that the *Maine* was wrecked by an interior explosion. Proponents of each theory cited supposedly impeccable sources and the various views have their partisans. No additional evidence. has ever been unearthed to settle the matter conclusively. Some authorities believe the disaster was accidental, even if the explosion was external. In any event, the exact circumstances surrounding the catastrophe are likely to remain a mystery forever.

For some years the anniversary of the destruction of the *Maine* was observed regularly by the US Navy and by Spanish-American War veterans' associations in Havana and the United States. Currently the navy has no regulations requiring observance of the day, although naval units may participate in local observances. Some states observe the day officially. For example, Connecticut observes February 15 as *Maine* Memorial Day, and Massachusetts observes it as Spanish War Memorial Day and *Maine* Memorial Day.

The wreck of the *Maine* was allowed to remain in Havana harbor for 14 years. On February 15, 1909, the Havana Camp of the Spanish War Veterans was organized and its first act was to adopt a resolution calling on Congress to lift the wreck, recover the bodies of the dead that were still in it, and tow the ruined hull out to sea and sink it. Similar resolutions were adopted by the Spanish War Veterans and by other organizations in the United States and on May 9, 1910, Congress authorized the work to be done. It was completed on March 16, 1912, and memorial services were held in Havana over the bodies of an estimated 64 sailors taken from the wreck. The recovered bodies were accorded burial in Arlington (Virginia) National Cemetery, near the mainmast of the sunken ship, which today stands as one of Arlington's most eloquent memorials.

On February 15, 1912, the cornerstone was laid for the monument to the *Maine* dead that now stands at the Columbus Circle entrance to New York City's Central Park. Another notable *Maine* monument, erected by the government of Cuba in Havana, was dedicated on February 15, 1926. Memorial exercises were held annually at its base for many years. In 1960, however, a year after his accession to power, Cuban Premier Fidel Castro ordered removal of the eagle that topped the memorial, an anti-United States gesture that resulted in damage to the monument's main shaft.

There are other memorials of the *Maine*: the ship's foremast stands at the US Naval Academy at Annapolis, Maryland, where it is used to display storm-warning flags. And the base of the *Maine*'s conning tower can be seen at Canton, Ohio — the longtime home of President William McKinley, who would have preferred peace but bowed to public opinion in asking Congress for a declaration of war against Spain a little more than two months after the sinking of the *Maine*.

FEBRUARY 16

Cushing Eells's Birthday

Cushing Eells, founder of Whitman College in Walla Walla, Washington, was a Congregationalist missionary to the Indians of the Pacific Northwest during that region's early settlement in the 1800s. The college, which was founded in 1859, is Washington's oldest institution of higher learning and a lasting memorial to Dr. Marcus Whitman and his wife, Narcissa, friends and fellow missionaries of Cushing Eells, who were killed at their Waiilatpu (Washington) mission in 1847 (see November 29, Marcus Whitman's Death).

A coeducational, liberal arts institution with an enrollment of about 1,100, Whitman College also preserves the memory of other notable pioneers of the Pacific Northwest in the names of several of its buildings and in such positions as the Cushing Eells Professorship of Philosophy, established in 1896. The college campus houses the Whitman Museum, one section of which is devoted to material illustrating the history of the Northwest from the time of Marcus Whitman to the present.

For years the anniversary of Dr. Eells's birth was observed as Founder's Day at Whitman College — a custom that originated with the college's celebration of the centennial of Eells's birth in 1910. For the next 38 years February 16 was observed at the school with a Founder's Day convocation service. Alumni groups throughout the country would likewise mark that day, or a nearby date, with banquets and representative speakers from the college. While this practice has been discontinued, annual alumni meetings traditionally still are held during the month of February.

Cushing Eells, familiarly known during the later years of his life as Father Eells, was born in Massachusetts on February 16, 1810. According to a memorial pamphlet entitled *Father Eells*, written at the time of Eells's death by Dr. Stephen B. L. Penrose (president of Whitman College from 1894 to 1934). Cushing Eells became a serious, practicing Christian at the age of 15, and decided to devote himself to missionary work. In 1834 he was graduated from Williams College in Williamstown, Massachusetts, and in 1837 from Hartford (Connecticut) Theological Seminary, known at that time as the East Windsor Theological Institute. Choosing South Africa as his field of work, Eells was commissioned as a missionary to the Zulus by the American Board of Commissioners for Foreign Missions. A war among the Zulus, however, prevented him from going to Africa.

Instead he remained in this country, where he became important in pioneering missionary efforts in the area of the Pacific Northwest. Protestant missionaries' interest in that region had been awakened in 1831, when four Northwest Indians arrived in St. Louis, Missouri, with a party of fur trappers, and reports quickly spread that they had come to seek religious instruction for their tribes. Churches in the East soon became interested in carrying their Christian teachings to the Indians of the new area and, before long, missionaries were making their way west to the Oregon country, then a vast Pacific coast region held jointly by Great Britain and the United States.

On July 27, 1834, Jason Lee, a young Methodist minister from New England, preached the first Protestant sermon west of the Rockies at Fort Hall, near what is now Pocatello, Idaho. In the carousing that followed Lee's stern instruction, a man was killed, whereupon Lee also performed the first Protestant funeral service in Idaho. Later that year he started a Methodist mission in the Willamette Valley in Oregon, near the site of what is now Salem.

Other missionaries followed Lee in rapid succession. In 1835 Samuel Parker, a Presbyterian minister, traveled with Dr. Marcus Whitman to explore the Northwest region for future missionary work. A year later Whitman and his wife, together with another missionary couple, crossed the continent and began their work with the Indians.

Cushing Eells and his wife were sent to the Oregon country by the American Board in 1838. It took them a year to reach what is now eastern Washington, where, in the spring of 1839, they began their work with the Spokane Indians. Eells built a log cabin with pine boughs for a roof and lived there for nine years, preaching to and instructing the Indians.

The killing of Dr. Whitman, his wife, and 12 others on November 29, 1847, sparked a widespread Indian uprising, which forced Eells and his family to flee south and take refuge in the Willamette Valley. He did not return until the Indian wars had ended in 1858 and the "upper country" was reopened for non-Indian settlement. Coming to Waiilatpu in 1859, he found only the ruins of the Whitman mission and the unmarked common grave of the missionary victims. When he stood over the grave of his friend, Eells had a vision of a school, in honor of Whitman, for the Christian education of the young people of the region.

Eells, who had begun as a foreign missionary among the Spokane Indians, became a home missionary without salary and devoted himself to the white settlers who were moving into the Walla Walla Valley. He earned his living by farming on the old mission claim so that he might preach on Sundays. On December 20, 1859, his vision of a school became a reality when the territorial legislature of Washington granted a charter for Whitman Seminary. It had been intended to build the school at the Whitman mission at Waiilatpu, but as the community of Walla Walla was growing rapidly, it was established there. The first building was dedicated in October 1866, and Dr. Eells assumed charge of the school soon after it was opened. In 1883 an amended charter was granted to Whitman College, and in 1907 the school was released by the Congregational Education Society of Massachusetts from any legal denominational connection.

Meanwhile, Cushing Eells had been elected school superintendent of the county, but he still devoted five days of the week to teaching, attending to his official duties as superintendent on the sixth. He also continued to preach and traveled about Washington founding churches. He helped organize churches in Oregon at The Dalles and in Washington at Cheney, Chewelah, Colfax, Medical Lake, Skokomish, Spokane, Sprague, and Walla Walla. As part of its centennial in November 1964, the Congregational Church in Walla Walla honored Cushing Eells as its cofounder. Dr. Eells served as pastor of six of these churches and helped them by means of various gifts — he donated bells to nine and, out of his meager earnings, gave the churches some $12,000. When he died in 1893, he left $5,000, about all that he possessed, to Whitman College. Upon his death Lyman Abbott, the Congregationalist clergyman, author, and editor, described Cushing Eells as a "man of quiet and beautiful character, of unsurpassed consecration, and one to whom the republic of the United States owes a far greater debt than to many who have occupied a more conspicuous place in its history."

Republic of Lithuania Day

On February 16, 1918 — earlier Russian control of Lithuania having been displaced by the German occupation of World War I — the Lithuanian National Council, composed of 20 prominent leaders of varying political views, proclaimed restoration (with German sanction) of the Independent Democratic Republic of Lithuania. The concept of independence was, however, hardly new, for Lithuania earlier had been an independent state for more than five centuries (1251 to 1795).

Formal recognition was extended to the Republic of Lithuania by the major western powers between 1918 and 1922. United States recognition, for example, came on July 22, 1922. Considerably before that, however, World War I had concluded with the capitulation of Germany and its allies in November 1918. And the Constituent Assembly of the Republic of Lithuania had been elected in April 1920. The constitution of the new republic was promulgated on August 1, 1922.

Friction with its larger neighbors — Poland, Germany, and Russia — has seemed to be the fate of Lithuania during most of the 20th century. Except for a period of occupation (1941–1944) by Nazi Germany during World War II, Lithuania has been under the control of Soviet Russia since June 15, 1940. Expatriates of the Independent Democratic Republic of Lithuania, now scattered throughout the free world, still protest as illegal the technical incorporation into the USSR on August 3, 1940.

The anniversary of the proclamation in 1918 of the restoration of Lithuania's independence is celebrated on February 16 wherever persons of Lithuanian descent have settled. In the United States, Maryland came early to the list of celebrants. The day has been observed there ever since 1935, when a joint resolution of the General Assembly of Maryland directed the governor to proclaim February 16 annually a time for the commemoration of the republic's founding. It further directed the governor to call upon state officials to display the US flag on all government buildings and invite citizens to observe the day in schools and churches with appropriate ceremonies. In Baltimore a banquet, accompanied by a musical program, is usually held at Lithuanian Hall, 851 Hollins Street, and there are special commemorative services at the church of St. Alphonsus, the Lithuanian Roman Catholic church. Guests and speakers at the banquet usually include Maryland's present and/or former governors, an assemblage of judges and Washington notables, and distinguished members of various Lithuanian communities in the United States.

Elsewhere in the United States, other governors — who have included the chief executives of Illinois, Massachusetts, Michigan, Nebraska, New Jersey, New York, Rhode Island, and Texas — also proclaim February 16 as Republic of Lithuania Day and mayors of many US cities and towns follow suit. A number of US senators and representatives also are likely to take note of the day on Capitol Hill.

Those gatherings that do not take place exactly on Republic of Lithuania Day are frequently held on the preceding or following Sunday. Usually there are special religious services and mass rallies that include artistic performances, as well as speeches by prominent Lithuanian leaders, representatives of local governments, and members of Congress. Those attending the rallies often adopt resolutions protesting the incorporation of Lithuania into the USSR, seeking US support for Lithuanian freedom, or calling the attention of the United Nations to the question of Soviet colonialism. In many communities the rallies are accompanied by banquets in which distinguished guests participate.

FEBRUARY 17

Frances E. Willard Memorial Day

Frances Elizabeth Willard, a reformer in several fields best known for her successful promotion of the Woman's Christian Temperance Union, died on February 17, 1898. At its national convention that year in St. Paul, Minnesota, the WCTU voted to observe annually the date of her death and establish in her honor a memorial fund to be used in organizing new branches, strengthening weak ones, and promoting the work of the Temperance Union in other ways. The money was to be raised by public meetings held by each local union in the United States on or near February 17, with the fund thus acquired to be administered (as it still is) by the union's national corresponding secretary. The fund has been used toward the work of the WCTU organizations that exist throughout the United States. In addition local unions mark February 17 as Frances E. Willard Memorial Day by placing flowers in the churches of some communities.

"Frances Willard — brave and fearless, Frances Willard, regal, peerless," as she was described in a poem by Ray Nance Smethers, was born on September 28, 1839, at Churchville, New York. She was graduated from the Northwestern Female College at Evanston, Illinois, in 1859 — just six years after the lakeside community was first settled as the site of Northwestern University. Evanston, which grew up around the university, was to become known as a religious and educational center and the headquarters of a number of national organizations, including the WCTU. It became Frances Willard's permanent home.

However, nearly a dozen years intervened between her graduation from college and her status as a permanent resident of Evanston.

Among other things, the interval included a period as preceptress of Pittsburgh Female College; service as principal of the Genesee Wesleyan Seminary at Lima, New York, in 1866 and 1867; and two and a half years of European travel and study.

In 1871, after her return to the United States, she was named president of the newly formed Evanston College for Ladies. In this capacity, she is said to have been the first woman college president to confer degrees upon women. In 1873 Evanston College for Ladies merged with Northwestern University, where Frances Willard promptly became professor of aesthetics and dean of women.

She resigned from this position in 1874 on her election as corresponding secretary of the new National Woman's Christian Temperance Union. This reform-minded society had been organized that year at a meeting in Cleveland, Ohio, assembled in response to a call issued from Chautauqua, New York, and signed by Martha McClellan Brown, Jennie Fowler Willing, and others. Attended by women from 16 states, the gathering at Cleveland was the first of a continuing series of conventions held annually by the WCTU.

Like some abortive earlier temperance efforts, the WCTU sprang into being as a reaction to the increased liquor traffic, and political influence of liquor interests, that developed in the United States during and after the Civil War. With the more or less concurrent campaign for woman suffrage, the temperance movement was a harbinger of the nationwide wave of social, political, and economic reform that was to crest in the first two decades of the 20th century.

Annie Wittenmyer, WCTU's first president, was succeeded in 1879 by Frances Willard, who served as president until her death and was, in fact, its guiding light. It was she who wrote the declaration of principles adopted by the WCTU on its founding in 1874. Besides containing a pledge of total abstinence from all intoxicants, the declaration stated:

We believe in the golden rule and that each man's habits of life should be an example safe and beneficent for every other man to follow; we believe that God created man and woman in His own image, and therefore we believe in one standard of purity for both men and women, and in the equal right of all to hold opinions and to express the same with equal freedom; we believe in a living wage; in an eight hour day, in courts of conciliation and arbitration, in justice as opposed to greed of gain, and in "Peace on earth and good will to men."

In 1883 the WCTU president completed a 30,000-mile organizing tour to every state in the Union and set up a local organization in each of them. With her on the trip, which included visits to every community of more than 10,000 people, was her lifelong friend Anna Gordon, later herself a president of WCTU. Not surprisingly, the year 1883 marked the Temperance Union's greatest expansion in the United States. Frances Willard also carried the WCTU program abroad, founding the World Woman's Christian Temperance Union in 1883 and becoming its president in 1891. Today the world organization has branches in more than 40 countries.

In 1888 the temperance leader had joined the suffragists May Wright Sewall and Susan B. Anthony in founding the National Council of Women. Frances Willard, whose powers of leadership Susan Anthony recognized in describing her as "a bunch of magnetism," became the national group's first president.

In the course of her life Frances Willard, who was an excellent public speaker, skilled as a lobbyist and molder of public opinion, became one of the most famous women of her time. She was especially influential in the temperance movement, but also in the effort to achieve woman suffrage and in the fields of politics (among other things, she helped found the Prohibition party) and education. In many respects, as her declaration for the WCTU indicates, her thinking was ahead of her time. It was she who introduced the now widespread honor system in student government. Her creed, "No sectarianism in religion, no sectionalism in politics, no sex in citizenship," has a contemporary ring.

During her lifetime Frances Willard was widely honored for her work. Schools, dormitories, a settlement house, a church, and other buildings, hospital rooms, scholarships, fountains, and trees have been named after her. Stained-glass windows have been dedicated in her name and her likeness appears in plaques, busts, and statues. Perhaps most notably, Illinois chose a statue of her to represent the state in Statuary Hall in the Capitol at Washington, D.C., where it can be seen today. At the time she was the only woman so honored, although she has been joined by others since.

Frances Willard is also honored in Indiana's impressive state capitol building at Indianapolis, where a tablet in tribute to her was unveiled in 1929. She was elected to the Hall of Fame for Great Americans in 1910.

Her home in Evanston, Illinois, built in 1865,

was designated as a National Historic Landmark in 1965. Authentically preserved, it houses memorabilia of her career and is open to the public. Behind it stands the three-story brick building that serves as national headquarters of the WCTU. The organization has approximately 250,000 members in the United States.

FEBRUARY 18

Jefferson Davis Inaugurated

By the time Jefferson Davis — who had served as United States senator from Mississippi from 1847 to 1851 — returned to the Senate in 1857 after a stint as secretary of war, he had become the acknowledged leader of the Southern bloc. A strong champion of states' rights, Davis favored the extension of slavery into the territories and economic development of the South as a counterbalance to Northern power. (See June 3, Jefferson Davis's Birthday.)

He had little to do with the movement for secession until Mississippi on January 9, 1861, became part of the Southern Confederacy, which would oppose the North through four long years of Civil War (1861–1865). After Mississippi's act Davis, a reluctant secessionist, maintained in a Senate speech that the states had the constitutional right to secede from the Union and that Congress had no right to interfere with the domestic institutions of any state. Withdrawing from the Senate on January 21, 1861, he cast his lot with his state.

Although he would have rather been offered the command of Southern military forces, members of a Confederate congress meeting in Montgomery, Alabama, unanimously chose Davis as president of the Confederacy's provisional government on February 9. He was inaugurated at Montgomery on February 18, 1861, and began to organize the new government. The domed and colonnaded building where that government was formed functions as Alabama's state capitol today. Opposite it, at Washington and Union streets, is the handsome and much visited First White House of the Confederacy, where Davis and his family lived for a few months in 1861.

Some time after Jefferson Davis's inauguration at Montgomery he was elected to the office for a six-year term by popular vote. He was inaugurated for the second time on February 22, 1862, at Richmond, Virginia, which became the Confederate capital. During the war the Confederate congress met there in the state capitol building, still in use, which Thomas Jefferson designed. Davis's Richmond residence, still standing at 1201 East Clay Street, is now a Confederate museum containing personal effects of Davis and others.

FEBRUARY 19

Initiative and Referendum Declared Valid

Two cornerstones of the reform movement that swept the nation at the start of the 20th century were the initiative and the referendum, forms of direct legislation designed to ensure the triumph of popular will over any obstructionism by recalcitrant legislatures. Under the initiative a specified number of a state's voters — it varies from 5 to 15 percent depending upon the law of the state in question — can initiate legislation by means of a popular petition. If by state law the proposal then goes directly before the people in a popular election, the method is known as the direct initiative. However, if the requirement is that the proposal instead go to the legislature for approval before it can become law — and to the people only if the legislature fails to enact it — the procedure is known as the indirect initiative. In either case, the effect is to force consideration of the proposal and ensure that it is put to a vote.

The referendum is applied to measures approved by a legislative body. Under terms of the referendum a requisite number of citizens can force a legislature to submit a measure it has passed to a vote of the people before it becomes law. In the United States the kind of referendum most commonly employed is the so-called optional type, instituted by petition of the people in connection with ordinary acts of legislatures. There is also, however, what is known as the mandatory referendum, by which some state constitutions and city charters require that certain kinds of laws be submitted to the electorate for approval. Almost everywhere this includes state constitutions and amendments to them. (Both the optional and the mandatory referendum are to be distinguished from the kind of referendum in which a legislature of its own volition submits a particular matter to popular vote, either merely to secure advice or to determine the question.)

In the United States the initiative and optional referendum were first adopted by South

Dakota in 1898 and then by Oregon in 1902. In due course, however, the validity of these methods of direct legislation was disputed and a test case was taken to the US Supreme Court for final decision. The Court decided on February 19, 1912, that adoption of such political devices as the initiative and referendum lies within the discretion of the people of the states and that when these devices are adopted the courts must accept them.

However, the initiative and referendum as applied to state and local proposals are a different matter from amending the federal Constitution — as Ohio discovered when it attempted to submit the question of the ratification of an amendment to its voters. The validity of such ratification was disputed and this case, too, was taken to the Supreme Court. It was the decision of that body that a state had no power to change the method of amending the US Constitution laid down in that document itself. The constitutional provision therefore remains as it was — that amendments shall be submitted to the legislatures of the states or to conventions in the states called for the purpose of considering them. (An amendment to the federal Constitution becomes effective only after three-fourths of the state legislatures or specially called conventions have ratified it.)

As commonly used in the United States today, the initiative and optional referendum are patterned on the forms of direct legislation that came into wide use in Switzerland after 1830. Actually, however, the device of the initiative was recognized on this side of the Atlantic as early as 1777 — in Georgia's first constitution, which gave voters the exclusive right to propose amendments to it. The automatic referendum on state constitutions and amendments to them, which has been called a purely American invention, was first used in adopting the constitution of Massachusetts in 1780. Connecticut adopted the obligatory referendum — for amendments to the state constitution proposed by the legislature — in 1818. But the initiative and referendum in any form were known long before that, in Greek city-states and other early democracies.

Bulwarked by the Supreme Court's landmark decision of February 19, 1912, the initiative and referendum are in use in almost half of the states. Although used in Maine, Maryland, Massachusetts, Michigan and Ohio, the initiative and referendum are most commonly employed west of the Mississippi. Perhaps the most notable use over the years has been in Oregon and California.

Ohio Statehood Approved

On February 19, 1803, Ohio, which earlier had been part of the Northwest Territory, was admitted to the Union by an act of Congress. That is, federal laws were extended over Ohio on February 19. For some reason, however, Congress never formally ratified Ohio's admission, and the date on which its statehood became official was therefore never designated.

When the oversight came to attention during the 1953 sesquicentennial celebration of Ohio's statehood, Congress belatedly settled the matter by ratifying the admission retroactively — and fixing the date. By joint resolution of the House and Senate, Congress declared that Ohio had officially become a state on March 1, 1803, when the Ohio state legislature convened for the first time (see March 1).

FEBRUARY 20

John Glenn Orbits the Earth

On February 20, 1962, boosted aloft by an Atlas-D rocket, the *Friendship* 7 space capsule, carrying astronaut John H. Glenn Jr., soared into space from a launching pad at Cape Canaveral, Florida. Under the aegis of the National Aeronautics and Space Administrations's Project Mercury, Glenn was the first American and the third man to attempt to orbit the earth.

An estimated 135 million people followed television coverage of his flight at some time during the day, while millions more kept pace by radio. The launching took place at 9:47 A.M. (Eastern Standard Time). At 9:48, Colonel Glenn was reported experiencing the space-travel phenomenon of weightlessness. At 9:59 it was confirmed that he was in orbit. At 10:09 a tracking station in Nigeria made radio contact with him; 19 minutes later he was over the Indian Ocean; 12 minutes after that, he had seen the lights of Perth, Australia, turned on for him in a special gesture of greeting. In another 29 minutes, he was in radio contact with a tracking station in Mexico. At 11:24, an hour and 37 minutes after lift-off, he had completed his first orbit.

Meanwhile, as NASA's Mercury Control Center at Cape Canaveral broadcast a tape recording, waiting millions heard his ebullient voice, speaking from space: "Flight turning out real fine. . . . Capsule is in good shape. . . . All systems are Go. . . . Zero G [gravity] and I feel fine. . . . Oh! that view is tremendous."

In the next few hours Glenn repeated the process twice, and reports were transmitted back to a waiting world from tracking stations around the globe. The flight's three orbits were completed despite erratic behavior of the automatic system controlling the attitude of his capsule – a problem he solved by manual control – and despite the alarm caused by a malfunctioning signal. Fortunately the signal was wrong in indicating that the heat shield, which was to prevent his capsule from incinerating in the heat of reentering the earth's atmosphere, had become unlatched.

It remained intact during the scheduled firing of three retro- (braking) rockets to slow the capsule and bring it out of orbit. As expected, radio contact was lost momentarily during the torrid heat of reentry – a phenomenon on which Glenn commented when relieved listeners heard his voice again at 2:35: "Boy, that was a real fireball."

His capsule splashed into the Atlantic Ocean, off the Bahamas, at 2:43. The pickup, 18 minutes later, by the destroyer *Noa*, signaled the release by post offices across the country of a special commemorative stamp. Shortly after emerging from his capsule, Glenn received the telephoned congratulations of President John F. Kennedy, who declared in a statement that space "is the new ocean, and I believe the United States must sail on it and be in a position second to none."

Counting technical personnel and the 15,000 people, mostly aboard ships, who stood by for recovery, search, and rescue operations, some 30,000 persons played a part, directly or indirectly, in Glenn's feat. During his 4 hours and 56 minutes of flight, the astronaut had passed through 3 days and traveled a distance of about 81,000 miles. Traveling at altitudes that varied from 99 to 162 miles, he achieved the astonishing speed of 17,545 miles per hour. His history-making trip through space, which succeeded those of the Russians Yuri Gagarin (1 orbit) and Gherman Titov (17 orbits) in 1961, was followed by other efforts, including the flights of Scott Carpenter and Walter Schirra (3 and 6 orbits respectively in 1962) and Gordon Cooper (22 orbits in 1963); and both countries' efforts to place men on the moon, a goal achieved by the United States on July 20, 1969.

Glenn returned to a hero's welcome and honors too numerous to list. After two days of debriefing on Grand Turk Island, he was flown to Florida for a reunion with his family. His wife and two children were escorted to Florida

by President Kennedy, who presented NASA's Distinguished Service Medal to Glenn in a ceremony at Cape Canaveral. Other celebrations followed in quick succession: a February 26 parade in Washington, D.C., where Glenn addressed a joint session of Congress and testified in support of the administration's space program; a March 1 ticker-tape parade and luncheon in New York, where Glenn and his six fellow US astronauts were honored by Mayor Robert F. Wagner and other dignitaries; and a March 3 welcome by 50,000 people in Glenn's home town of New Concord, Ohio (population 2,127).

John Glenn, who was born in nearby Cambridge on July 18, 1921, grew up in New Concord. At high school he won letters in football, tennis, and basketball, and was elected president of the junior class. He enrolled at New Concord's Muskingum College (which has granted him an honorary degree since), but left in his third year to train as a naval aviation cadet. He was commissioned a second lieutenant in the US Marine Corps in March 1943 and promoted in the ensuing years.

During World War II, he flew 59 fighter-bomber missions in the Pacific. Later he spent two years as a pilot on the North China patrol and in Guam, became a flight instructor, and attended amphibious warfare school. After a jet refresher course, he was assigned to duty in the Korean conflict, in the course of which he flew another 90 missions. He subsequently became a test pilot and served with the Fighter Design Branch of the navy's Bureau of Aeronautics in Washington, D.C. He made headlines on July 16, 1957, when he made the first transcontinental flight at supersonic speed, from Los Angeles to New York. For this feat, and his service in World War II and Korea, he was 5 times awarded the Distinguished Flying Cross and 19 times the Air Medal.

Glenn became a lieutenant colonel on April 1, 1959. Eight days later, he was among the 7 chosen from 110 military test pilots who had volunteered to become the country's first astronauts. The long preparation for space flight that followed included intensive study – of such subjects as desert and water survival, geography, meteorology, aviation biology, astronomy, astronautics, and astrophysics – and exposure to simulated phenomena of space, including weightlessness, high heat, and strong gravitational forces.

In May and July of 1961, respectively, Glenn served as backup pilot for astronauts Alan B. Shepard and Virgil I. Grissom, who made the first US suborbital flights. Glenn was chosen on November 29, 1961, to make the United States' first manned orbital flight. He has said: "People are afraid of the future, of the unknown. If a man faces up to it and takes the dare of the future, he can have some control over his destiny. That's an exciting idea to me."

In January 1964 Glenn announced he would retire from the Marine Corps and become a candidate for Ohio's Democratic nomination for the US Senate. His projected candidacy was abandoned, however, by a fall in his own household. The accident, which injured his inner ear and affected his sense of balance, delayed his return to civilian life. In October 1964, after a long period of recuperation, he was promoted (over his own objections) to full colonel, with President Lyndon B. Johnson officiating in a White House ceremony. After Glenn's retirement from the Marine Corps, which followed, he became a director of a firm manufacturing soft drinks, with responsibilities relating to its international operations. He also continued an active association with NASA's space program.

After an unsuccessful bid for the spot in 1970, Glenn gained the Democratic nomination to represent Ohio in the US Senate in 1974 despite the opposition, in the primary battle, of the state Democratic party. He was also victorious in the November election, defeating his Republican opponent by a margin of more than two to one and going on to take his seat in the Senate in Washington.

On the first anniversary of his historic flight, Glenn was on hand for presentation of his *Friendship 7* space capsule, space suit, and associated items to the Smithsonian Institution in Washington, D.C., where they were exhibited in a temporary building pending construction of the new National Air and Space Museum.

Joseph Jefferson's Birthday

Joseph Jefferson, one of the most distinguished American actors of the 19th century, was born in Philadelphia on February 20, 1829. His birthplace, at the corner of Sixth and Spruce streets in that city, is marked by a wooden sign, and a bronze tablet rests on the boulder marking his grave near his home on Buzzards Bay in Massachusetts.

The fourth actor in a family of actors and managers, and the third of the same name, Joseph Jefferson made his stage debut at the age of three as Cora's child in Kotzebue's *Pizzaro* and at four appeared in Washington, D.C., in one of Thomas Dartmouth Rice's popular "Jim Crow" minstrel shows. His father, who began to play in western and southern cities in

1838, died of yellow fever in Mobile, Alabama, on November 24, 1842, and was buried in that city's Magnolia Cemetery. His grave there is marked by a stone erected by his son in 1867.

After his father's death, Jefferson spent many years as a strolling player and for a brief time in 1856 studied in Europe. In November of that year, he joined actress Laura Keene's company in New York and, in 1857, scored a success in the role of Dr. Pangloss in George Colman's *The Heir at Law*. A year later he won fame with his portrayal of Asa Trenchard, opposite the English actor E. A. Sothern, in Tom Taylor's *Our American Cousin*.

While gaining prominence as an actor, Jefferson began to search for a character, both humorous and pathetic, around whom a play could be written. He finally settled on Rip Van Winkle and wrote a short play about him. His 1859 dramatization of the Washington Irving story, however, was only moderately successful and, while in England in 1865, he commissioned the Irish-American playwright Dion Boucicault to revise the play. The Boucicault version, with Jefferson in the leading role, opened in London at the Adelphi Theatre in 1865. An immediate success, Jefferson's Rip Van Winkle delighted London audiences for 170 successive nights. Returning to the United States the following year, he re-created the part in performances throughout the country, winning for himself both wealth and acclaim.

During his long career Joseph Jefferson was a friend of many leading figures of the day. His summer home on Buzzards Bay adjoined that occupied by President Grover Cleveland, and the two frequently went fishing together. When not working, Jefferson spent his winters at his large plantation in Louisiana. A distinguished actor, Joseph Jefferson was also a landscape painter and the author of an autobiography, originally published in *Century Magazine* (1889–1890). He was a member of the American Academy of Arts and Letters and, in 1893, succeeded Edwin Booth as lifetime president of the club, mainly for actors, known as The Players'. Professionally active even late in life, "Jo" Jefferson died on Easter Sunday, April 23, 1905, in Palm Beach, Florida, only a year after his last stage appearance on May 7, 1904, in Paterson, New Jersey.

FEBRUARY 21

Washington Monument Dedicated

By the time the stark white obelisk called the Washington Monument was finally dedicated in Washington, D.C., on Saturday, February

21, 1885, nearly 100 years had gone into the planning and execution of a fitting memorial to the first President in the nation's capital. The monument's unparalleled location was suggested by the extraordinary and long unappreciated Major Pierre Charles L'Enfant when he submitted his master plan for the city in 1791. L'Enfant died a broken and disappointed man without realizing that the basic features of his plan for a spacious city adorned by long, unbroken views would one day be adopted; or that a Washington memorial more glorious than the one he envisioned would stand almost where he said it should — at the intersection of two of the city's most magnificent long views. Set on a knoll, mirrored in a reflecting pool and ringed by 50 American flags — one for each state, a total neither Washington nor L'Enfant could have anticipated — the Washington Monument is the centerpiece of a north-south view that stretches from the White House to the Jefferson Memorial; and of an even more compelling east-west vista, extending from the domed Capitol to the Lincoln Memorial. Washington himself had selected the same site for a monument but he had seen it as a memorial to an unknown soldier of the American Revolution, not to himself.

Others thought differently, however. The idea of a monument in honor of the first President was proposed to Congress within a week of Washington's death in 1799. The generally sympathetic legislators looked at designs but took no action for about a half century. Finally a speech by Henry Clay helped spur action, and a private organization, the Washington National Monument Society, was established in 1832 with the purpose of raising funds for the project. In 15 years the society obtained some $87,000 and selected Robert Mills as architect of the proposed monument.

Remembered today as the United States' first native-born professional architect and creator of such Washington landmarks as the Post Office, Treasury building, and former Patent Office (now the Fine Arts and Portrait Galleries), Mills planned a granite shaft faced with white marble. Although the finished monument was slightly lower than in Mills's original plan (it stands 555 feet, 5⅛ inches instead of 600 feet), its other dimensions — 55 feet square at the base and 34 feet square at the top — are close to his original specifications. However, an ornate base also envisioned by Mills is missing, some say fortunately, from the austerely handsome final result.

Building the Washington Monument took almost as long as thinking about it. The site admired by L'Enfant and Washington having been selected, the cornerstone was laid on July 4, 1848. Robert C. Winthrop, Speaker of the House of Representatives, delivered an appropriate oration. During the first stage of construction the monument rose to a little more than 150 feet of its proposed height — a so-called "high-water mark" of initial effort clearly visible today. Work had to be abandoned in 1854, as the funds of the Monument Society had been exhausted and an appeal for more had met with no response. The Civil War and political, and even religious, dissension further delayed the undertaking.

Finally Congress in 1876 appropriated funds and set the Army Corps of Engineers to work to complete the project in not quite matching marble. Construction was finished on December 6, 1884, when a capstone of pure aluminum was put in place. Arrangements were made by Congress for the dedication of the memorial obelisk and on Saturday, February 21, 1885, ceremonies were held at its base and in the House of Representatives. The orator for the occasion was the same Robert C. Winthrop who had spoken at the laying of the cornerstone 37 years earlier. Total cost of the undertaking has been variously reported at between $1.2 million and $1.3 million.

Today the Washington Monument is visited annually by more than a million persons, who can enjoy a panoramic view of Washington from the observation room near the top. Those with patience to wait in line reach that lofty lookout by elevator. However, persons whose energy exceeds their patience can arrive, breathlessly, at the same destination by means of a flight of 898 steps.

FEBRUARY 22

George Washington's Birthday

"First in war, first in peace, and first in the hearts of his countrymen," George Washington was not only the father of his nation; he was also its foundation. As befits the nation's first President, the American people have honored Washington in many ways. Monuments throughout the country testify to his greatness (see February 21, Washington Monument Dedicated), and the nation's capital, one state, and more than 20 cities and towns bear his name. But perhaps the celebrations of his birthday that occur each year best keep alive his memory and ideals.

Public attention was first paid to Washington's birthday on February 11, the date of his birth under the Old Style or Julian calendar in use in England and the American colonies at the time, rather than on February 22, the date under the New Style or Gregorian calendar adopted by England during Washington's lifetime. There are also two different years given for Washington's birth date, depending on which calendar is followed. Under the Julian calendar, Washington was born on February 11, 1731, but under the Gregorian calendar, on February 22, 1732. This is because the Gregorian calendar, among other things, shifted the beginning of England's calendar year to January 1 from March 25. This involved omitting the dates in January, February, and most of March for one year, 1751. To indicate both reckonings, sources sometimes give Washington's year of birth as 1731/32.

The addition of 11 days to his birth date is explained as follows: under the Julian calendar, by the 18th century, inaccuracies in reckoning the length of the year had accumulated to such a point that the solar equinox was occurring 11 days in advance of its calendar reckoning. In adopting the new, Gregorian calendar in 1751, Parliament decreed that 11 days were to be legally omitted from the month of September in 1752 to correct this error. The day after September 2 thus became September 14.

Technically this change required the addition of 11 days to the birth dates of British and American persons born between 1700 and 1752. The people so affected were slow to make the change, however, since they were accustomed to the old dates. George Washington, for example, long celebrated his birthday on February 11. Thus at Valley Forge the band of the Fourth Continental Artillery serenaded the general on the occasion of his 46th birthday on February 11, 1778. Three years later, Count de Rochambeau, commander of the French allies then stationed in Newport, Rhode Island, honored Washington by declaring February 11 a holiday. To celebrate the day, the French troops paraded through the city, and the French and American officers dined together.

Richmond, Virginia, claims the honor of being the first locality to sponsor a public celebration of Washington's birthday. As was the case at Valley Forge and in Rhode Island, Richmond in 1782 held its special festivities on February 11, and according to one report "demonstrations of joy" filled the city on that day. But by the following year the Gregorian calendar introduced in 1752 had gained sufficient acceptance to affect the celebration of the Commander in Chief's birthday.

In 1783 Talbot Courthouse in Maryland, and Cambridge, Massachusetts, and New York City commemorated the 51st anniversary of Washington's birth. While the first two communities honored Washington on February 11,

the third paid its tribute 11 days later. On the morning of February 22, 1783, guns in New York harbor sounded a salute, and in the evening a number of men dined together, heard speeches praising Washington, and exchanged 13 toasts — 1 for each of the original 13 colonies. These exercises were simple when compared with observances that occurred in later years, yet New York's 1783 ceremonies are generally recognized as the first public acknowledgment of Washington's birth to take place on February 22.

During Washington's first terms as President, celebrations of his birthday — by this time widely accepted as February 22 — increased. On the Chief Executive's birthday in 1790 Congress, then meeting in New York City, adjourned and extended him congratulations. That same day the Tammany Society of New York, a benevolent fraternity that had been founded in 1789, praised Washington at ceremonies that included the drinking of the traditional 13 toasts. When in the following year Philadelphia became the nation's capital, the new seat of government continued the custom of honoring the President on his birthday. On February 22, 1791, artillery and light infantry paraded through the city, a salute was fired at noon, and members of Congress and other dignitaries offered Washington their congratulations. A banquet in Philadelphia was the high point of festivities, marking the President's 60th birthday in 1792, and militia companies marched in the city to note the anniversary in 1793.

The development of two political parties, the Federalists and the Antifederalists or Jeffersonian Republicans, affected celebrations of Washington's birthday during his second term in office. Although the President had tried to avoid party ties, his policies reflected unmistakable Federalist leanings. The Jeffersonian Republicans realized the strength Washington's prestige lent to the Federalist cause and, unwilling to give their opponents the slightest advantage, they objected to even the seemingly innocent observances of the President's birthday. In 1793, when Philadelphians decided to hold their annual Assembly Ball on February 22 to honor Washington, the Antifederalists denounced the affair as idolatrous, and three years later they defeated a resolution calling for Congress to adjourn on his birthday.

Even after Washington retired from the presidency, the Jeffersonian Republicans believed that celebrations of his birthday would serve the Federalist cause. Only the universal grief elicited by his death in 1799 (see December 14) temporarily obscured such partisan feelings. Before adjourning later in December 1799, Congress, with bipartisan support, passed a resolution calling on the nation to observe February 22, 1800, with appropriate exercises.

Many localities acted upon the suggestion. They included Philadelphia, where the Freemasons and the Society of the Cincinnati, an organization of officers who had served in the American Revolution, arranged special ceremonies. The day's events included a military parade and services at Zion, St. Mary's, and German Reformed churches. President John Adams and Vice President Thomas Jefferson were among those who attended these tributes to the late President.

Observances of February 22 were few and attracted little public notice during the first three decades of the 19th century. But by 1832, the centennial of Washington's birth, the Federalist party had dissolved and feelings that the occasion served political purposes had similarly disappeared. By that time the nation's first President stood as a national hero above party politics, and many localities eagerly sponsored celebrations of the 100th anniversary of his birth. Some, including Boston, recognized the anniversary for the first time; others that had previously noted the occasion planned festivities of unprecedented scope. The centennial-year birthday celebration in New York City — on February 22 — was particularly interesting. Cannons resounded and church bells pealed throughout the city; General Morgan Lewis, a hero of the Revolution, read an oration praising his former commander; militia officers and other citizens gave a grand ball; and Washington's sword, pistols, and other memorabilia were placed on display.

After 1832, celebrations of Washington's birthday were firmly established. The University of Pennsylvania, for example, continued a tradition begun in 1794 of holding special ceremonies on February 22. Although this observance at first received only local attention, it grew in importance so that by the end of the 19th century such dignitaries as Presidents William McKinley, Theodore Roosevelt, and William Howard Taft accepted invitations to speak.

Tributes to the first President were not confined to eastern cities: the new states in the West also observed February 22, most with celebrations far more reserved than the one held at Los Angeles in 1850. That town's leading citizens had planned a ball to mark the occasion, but failed to include the community's rougher members in the festivities. The latter group resented their exclusion and retaliated by firing a cannon into the ballroom while the

dance was in progress. A gun fight followed, and several men were killed and others wounded. Though of dubious distinction, it was a Washington's birthday celebration not soon forgotten.

The many and varied observances of February 22 that were held in the 18th and 19th centuries pale in comparison with the celebration that occurred in 1932, the bicentenary of Washington's birth. On February 2, 1932, President Herbert Hoover called upon "every community and every association to do honor to the memory of Washington during the period from February 22 to Thanksgiving Day." The President himself led the country in paying tribute on February 22. He addressed a joint session of Congress at the Capitol, reviewed a military parade in Alexandria, Virginia, and laid a wreath on Washington's tomb at his Mount Vernon home overlooking the Potomac. But the ceremonies on Washington's birthday were just the beginning of the bicentennial festivities. During the eight months that followed, countless observances — including the planting of memorial trees in parks and on school grounds — took place in almost every American community. To mark the anniversary the Post Office Department issued a series of 12 memorial stamps bearing portraits of Washington taken from the works of well-known painters and sculptors. And before official observances ended on November 24, the first President of the United States was accorded worldwide recognition. Forty countries in Europe, Asia, and South America held special celebrations to honor Washington on the Fourth of July, the anniversary of US independence, and many foreign cities renamed streets and squares for him.

In recent years Americans have continued the custom of commemorating Washington's birthday — though another date change has occurred. Public Law 90-363, changing the federal observance of certain holidays to Mondays, was enacted by the US Congress in 1968 and became effective in 1971. According to its provisions, Washington's Birthday is observed as a legal public holiday on the third Monday in February. Although the federal law technically applies only to federal employees and the District of Columbia, almost all of the 50 states have taken individual action to make their observances of Washington's Birthday, which is a legal holiday throughout the nation, coincide with the federal date. In a few states the occasion is officially known as Presidents' Day, or as Washington-Lincoln Day, but most states retain the direct traditional title, Washington's Birthday. Apart from whatever observances may be sponsored by state or local authorities, patriotic groups, and local chapters of veterans' organizations, most of the nation's schools hold special exercises to honor the first President. In Washington, D.C., a wreath-laying ceremony at the Washington Monument is attended by the President, or his designated representative, and a host of other dignitaries. Members of the House of Representatives and the Senate traditionally take time from their schedules to hear a reading of Washington's Farewell Address (see December 4).

The ideals of the father of this nation also have led the National Conference of Christians and Jews to choose the week in which February 22 occurs for its annual observance of Brotherhood Week. The programs the organization sponsors throughout this week promote mutual understanding among people of varied racial, religious, and national backgrounds.

Other observances of Washington's birthday are countless. In Virginia a wreath is laid on his grave at Mount Vernon. In New York City Boy Scouts place a wreath at the statue of Washington in front of the Federal Hall National Memorial at Wall and Nassau streets, a few feet from where Washington took his first oath of office as President; and members of the Knights of Columbus, accompanied by fifers and drummers, parade up Fifth Avenue to St. Patrick's Cathedral, at which a memorial mass is celebrated. Valley Forge State Park, Pennsylvania, is the site of Cherries Jubilee, a Washington's Birthday celebration lasting several days and including historical reenactments, military presentations, and entertainment. Ever since 1913 Valley Forge has also been the scene of a Boy Scout pilgrimage on Washington's Birthday.

One of the most interesting Washington's birthday celebrations takes place in the border-crossing communities of Laredo, Texas, and Nuevo Laredo, Mexico, which for more than 75 years have celebrated the anniversary of Washington's birth with an exuberant international fiesta lasting several days. Pageants, parades, speeches, bullfights, dances, and stock shows are only a few of the many activities scheduled.

Also in a light-hearted vein, residents of Saco and Biddeford, Maine, have continued a 200-year tradition of burning "tar-tub" fires on February 22, although in recent years barrels have replaced the "tar-tubs." Other colorful events include the Washington's Birthday Foxhunt in Long Beach, North Carolina; the famous donkey races at St. Croix in the Virgin Islands; the National George Washington Birthday Cele-

bration in Alexandria, Virginia; and the Washington's Birthday Holiday Review in the restored colonial town of Williamsburg, Virginia. Stores in most areas now hold special Washington's Birthday sales, and many businesses serve cherry pie to their customers.

The New York chapter of the Sons of the American Revolution holds a Colonial Ball each year on the Friday preceding the legally designated Washington's Birthday holiday. Color guards and fife and drum corps participate, all in uniforms of the American Revolution, and debutantes who are descendants of patriots who fought in the conflict are presented during the gala affair.

George Washington was born at Bridges Creek, Westmoreland County, Virginia. His parents were Augustine Washington and his second wife, Mary Ball Washington. When Augustine Washington died in 1743, George Washington's older half brother Lawrence inherited the main family lands and named them Mount Vernon. The brothers lived together on this property for several years before George Washington moved to a farm near Fredericksburg, which was his patrimony.

Washington was a member of an influential family, but in other respects his youth was ordinary. He cut short his education at the age of 15; he had acquired some proficiency in mathematics, but his grasp of other subjects was limited. Stories of Washington's precocious adolescence, like the widely repeated cherry-tree episode, were the fabrications of his early biographers, especially Parson Mason Weems, who wrote the book entitled *The Life and Memorable Actions of George Washington*.

Washington benefited by the marriage of his half brother to Anne Fairfax, a member of one of the leading families of Virginia. In 1748 the Fairfaxes allowed young Washington to assist James Genn in his survey of their properties in the Shenandoah Valley. Washington found this experience most rewarding and perfected his techniques so well that in 1749 he became public surveyor for Culpeper County.

George Washington maintained close contact with his half brother Lawrence, who became almost a second father to him after their own father's death. In 1751 the two half brothers journeyed together to Barbados, where it was hoped that Lawrence, suffering from tuberculosis, would recover his health. Unfortunately the trip was unsuccessful. Lawrence died in 1752, after his return to Virginia. George, then scarcely out of his teens, became executor of Lawrence's estate and received title to the family home of Mount Vernon.

In 1753 Governor Robert Dinwiddie of Virginia chose George Washington, despite his youthful 21 years, as his emissary to the French forces attempting to fortify territory claimed by Virginia northwest of the colony. Washington had to travel almost as far north as Lake Erie in order to deliver to the proper commander the ultimatum demanding French withdrawal. Not unexpectedly his adversaries politely refused, and Washington returned to Virginia without satisfaction.

Virginia decided that a more aggressive policy would be necessary to curb the French threat, and in 1754 Washington led two companies north to build a fort at the confluence of the Allegheny and Monongahela rivers, where the Ohio River is formed (now Pittsburgh, Pennsylvania). Washington discovered that the French had already established a post, Fort Duquesne, on the site, but he was able to inflict some damage by defeating a party of French and Indians at Great Meadows on May 27. The French counterattacked and captured Washington, together with his men, in a battle on July 3 at Fort Necessity, the Virginians' aptly-named entrenched camp. Released by the French, the British colonists were returned to the Old Dominion within a short time.

British troops under General Edward Braddock arrived in 1755 and undertook an expedition with the Virginia militia against the French. Braddock chose Washington, who knew the terrain to be covered, as his aide-de-camp. The joint effort met defeat on July 9 at the battle of Monongahela (see July 9): Braddock fell mortally wounded, and Washington's appointment expired with the general's death.

Governor Dinwiddie, in the autumn of 1755, commissioned Washington as a colonel in command of the provincial militia. Given the responsibility of defending 350 miles of frontier with 700 irregular troops, Washington must have learned many hard lessons that later served him well. In 1758 Washington cooperated in another Anglo-Virginian venture against the French at Fort Duquesne; the troops, under General John Forbes, managed to force the French to abandon the stronghold. Finally assured that Virginia was safe, Washington resigned his commission.

Almost immediately afterwards, on January 6, 1759, he married Martha Dandridge Custis, the widow of Daniel Parke Custis. By this marriage he added approximately $100,000 worth of property to his sizable patrimony, thereby becoming one of the wealthiest men on the continent. Although the union failed to produce children, Washington took his wife's off-spring as his own and proved to be a devoted father.

Washington won election in 1758 to the Virginia House of Burgesses and served in that body for most of the years prior to the American Revolution. As troubles with the British increased, he found himself on the side of the patriot radicals. He denounced the Stamp Act of 1765 (see November 23, Stamp Act Repudiated), commenting to an associate that the Parliament "hath no more right to put their hands in my pocket, without my consent, than I have to put my hands in yours for money."

In 1770 Washington supported strong agreements not to import British goods, as a means of putting pressure on the London government. He did not approve the violence of the Boston Tea Party of 1773, but he sympathized with Massachusetts' determination to stand up to the British government. When the governor of Virginia dissolved the House of Burgesses in 1774, Washington remained resolute and participated in the extralegal meetings of the assemblymen in the Raleigh Tavern in Williamsburg.

Virginia sent Washington as a representative to the First Continental Congress, which met in Philadelphia in 1774, to petition King George III for the redress of colonial grievances. He also appeared as a delegate at the Second Continental Congress, which met also in Philadelphia, in May 1775. Consistently dressed in the blue and buff uniform of the Fairfax militia company, he served on committees that drafted military regulations and prepared the defense of New York City.

New Englanders, who had already clashed with British soldiers in April 1775 at Lexington and Concord, Massachusetts, were eager to win southern support in their crisis. To insure this cooperation, John Adams, a leader of the Massachusetts patriots encouraged the Congress to select Washington as commander of the American armies. The Virginian accepted the post and received his commission on June 17, 1775. He refused all monetary compensation except for his expenses.

Washington personally directed the siege that wrested control of Boston from the British during the winter of 1775 and 1776 (see March 17, Evacuation Day in Boston), and led the unsuccessful defense of New York City in the fall of the latter year. His troops defeated the English in daring attacks on Trenton, New Jersey, in 1776 (see December 26), and Princeton, New Jersey, in early 1777 (see January 3); but they were less successful during the following summer, when the Americans lost the city of Philadelphia. Washington led the final Middle Atlantic operations in New Jersey in 1778, and was present at the defeat of Lord Cornwallis at Yorktown in October 1781 (see October 19).

General Washington's chief value to the Revolutionary War effort was not as a strategist or tactician, but as an inspiring leader of men under the most stressful conditions. Almost single-handedly, he was able to keep his tattered army together during the harsh winter of 1777 and 1778 at Valley Forge, Pennsylvania (see December 19). Repeatedly, as at the Newburgh, New York, encampment in 1783, he managed to preserve the integrity of the army and prevent rash actions by the hotheaded. When he took leave of his men at Fraunces Tavern in New York City on December 4, 1783 (see December 4), the shedding of tears was understandable.

After the Revolution Washington retired to Mount Vernon, where he hoped to resume a normal private life, but the needs of the fledgling nation, weakly allied under the Articles of the Confederation, again drew him into public affairs. Delegates from Virginia and Maryland met at his estate to resolve their mutual problems, and the success of these discussions led to the larger convention at Annapolis in 1786, at which five states were represented. The Annapolis participants issued a call for a Constitutional Convention to meet in Philadelphia in May 1787.

Delegates from 12 states attended the Philadelphia assemblage and they chose Washington, who represented Virginia, to preside at the conference. Washington, as usual, remained taciturn, but let all know that he favored the creation of a strong national government equipped to meet the needs of the United States. The general was the logical popular choice to fill the office of Chief Executive, to which he was elected under the terms of the new Constitution.

After an arduous journey (see April 16, Washington Departs for His Inauguration), he took the oath of office on April 30, 1789, as the first President of the United States, on the balcony of the Federal Hall in New York City (see January 20, Inauguration Day). He spent a good part of his first months in office choosing men to assist him in exercising the functions of the executive branch of the government. Washington selected his fellow Virginian Thomas Jefferson to be secretary of state, and the New Yorker Alexander Hamilton to be secretary of the Treasury.

Jefferson and Hamilton had opposing views

of the future of the United States, and Washington suffered great strains trying to keep peace between his two associates. The secretary of state favored an alliance with France and maintenance of federal powers at the minimum level, whereas the secretary of the Treasury was more sympathetic to England and thought a powerful central government essential to the growth of the United States. In the end the President found himself leaning more toward the position of Hamilton's Federalist faction, and Jefferson, the chief spirit of the emerging Republican party, resigned his post in 1793.

Washington won unanimous reelection as President in the autumn of 1792. He devoted much of his second term to keeping the United States out of the European war then raging between England and France. On April 22, 1793, the Chief Executive issued his "Neutrality Proclamation" — in which, however, he did not actually use the word *neutrality*. The President warned Americans not to engage in hostile actions against England or France because the United States was at peace with both of them. And again in his "Farewell Address" of September 17, 1796, Washington warned the nation to stay clear of permanent alliances with foreign powers and to rely on temporary ones for emergency situations. The Chief Executive never delivered the message orally, but it appeared in the press, first in the pages of the Philadelphia *American Daily Advertiser*.

George Washington retired from public office at the end of his second term as President, and returned to his beloved Mount Vernon. When war with France appeared imminent in 1798, he assumed the burdens of commander of the provisional American Army, but fortunately the crisis soon passed without conflict. In December 1799 he contracted a severe throat infection after a long ride in a snowstorm. The 18th century medical technique of bloodletting only sapped his strength, and he died after one day of illness (see December 14).

Many places connected with Washington's life attract thousands of tourists each year. One of the most popular is the George Washington Birthplace National Monument, which is located on the Potomac River 38 miles from Fredericksburg, Virginia. Fire destroyed the house in which Washington was born, on the estate later known as Wakefield, but the Wakefield National Memorial Association has constructed a memorial mansion patterned after surviving buildings of the period. The homestead contains numerous 18th century household goods and farm tools, and on February 22 visitors are treated to cider and gingerbread made from the recipe of Mary Washington, the mother of the first President.

Across the Rappahannock River from Fredericksburg is Ferry Farm, where Washington spent his early childhood and part of his later youth. Ferry Farm was supposedly the scene of the fabled incident concerning Washington and the cherry tree, and it was there that he threw a Spanish silver dollar across the river. Of the original complex of buildings, only Washington's surveying office and an icehouse remain.

In Fredericksburg itself there are several interesting structures associated with Washington's life. The Rising Sun Tavern, where Washington and his officers celebrated the British defeat at Yorktown, stands at 1306 Caroline Street. The white clapboard building has been restored and contains a collection of English and American pewter. At the local Masonic lodge there is a Gilbert Stuart portrait of the first President and visitors may see the 17th century Bible on which Washington was sworn to membership. On Charles Street is the house Washington bought for his mother, who lived there until her death in 1789. It is open to the public. The most magnificent home in the city is Kenmore, on Washington Avenue. The beautiful red-brick mansion, which was once owned by Washington's brother-in-law, Colonel Fielding Lewis, has been restored and is furnished with antiques. And at the edge of Kenmore's grounds, next to Meditation Rock, where Washington's mother frequently went to be alone, towers the Mary Washington Monument obelisk.

As a young man Washington spent a considerable amount of time in western Virginia. In the town of Winchester, the building Washington used as his surveying office in 1748, and as his headquarters during the construction of Fort Loudon in 1756 and 1757, still stands. In the eastern part of Virginia, the town of Alexandria, which Washington later inhabited, is the site of still other reminders of his residence. The George Washington Masonic National Memorial is particularly noteworthy. Built between 1922 and 1933 at a cost of more than $7 million, this 333-foot-high structure is modeled after the ancient lighthouse at Alexandria, Egypt. It contains such memorabilia as the chair in which Washington sat while presiding as first Worshipful Master of the Alexandria No. 22 Lodge and the trowel he used when he laid the cornerstone of the Capitol (see September 18).

Mount Vernon is, of course, the most famous of Washington's residences. In 1674 John Washington, the great-grandfather of the first President, purchased 5,000 acres seven miles south of Alexandria, Virginia. Before 1735 Augustine Washington, George Washington's father, constructed the nucleus of the present mansion on this site, and in 1752 the future President inherited the property, which by then covered 8,000 acres. Washington spent many happy years on the plantation and he worked hard to improve its operation. He was greatly interested in scientific farming techniques, and as early as 1766 he introduced a system of crop rotation.

In 1858 the Mount Vernon Ladies' Association of the Union acquired the mansion and 500 acres surrounding it. The association carefully restored the house, grounds, and outbuildings as they were during Washington's occupancy. Many of the furnishings were Washington's own possessions; others are typical of the period. A sound and light show, donated by the French government, was first presented at Mount Vernon in 1976, the year of the US Bicentennial.

To insure that the view from the estate would never be marred by unsightly structures, the US Congress during the 1960s created the 1,000-acre Piscataway Park across the Potomac River from Mount Vernon. Many of the more than a million visitors who each year visit Mount Vernon also ferry across the Potomac to the park, where picnic facilities are available and a 30-acre model farm and museum recreate 18th century agricultural techniques.

Thousands of tourists each year visit the many places where Washington and the troops under his command fought so bravely to win American independence. Valley Forge State Park and Washington Crossing State Park, both in Pennsylvania, are only two of the many areas connected with Washington's military career. Still another is the New Windsor, New York, encampment where the Commander in Chief stayed with his soldiers during the winter of 1782 and 1783. The state-owned cantonment is located about 60 miles north of New York City, and the officers' hut on its grounds is the only building that has survived from any of Washington's winter encampments. The focal point of the area, however, is the reconstructed 110-foot by 30-foot log Temple of Virtue, where Washington on March 15, 1783, quieted rumors of a possible army rebellion.

Nearby is yet another Revolutionary War site. The Jonathan Hasbrouck House in Newburgh, New York, was Washington's headquarters between April 1782 and August 1783, and it was there that he originated the military decoration of the Order of Merit, today known as the Purple Heart. The state of New York owns the house and operates a small museum in it.

Memorials to Washington abound throughout the land. Perhaps the best known is the Washington Monument in the nation's capital, dedicated in 1885 (see February 21). Also in the capital is Herbert Haseltine's gilt equestrian statue at Washington Cathedral. Washington's likeness is also seen on the steps of New York's Federal Hall National Memorial, where J. Q. A. Ward's statue of him stands almost on the spot where he was inaugurated as President; and in the rotunda of the capitol of Virginia at Richmond, which houses the only statue for which Washington ever posed — the celebrated work of French sculptor Jean Antoine Houdon. The likeness of the Father of His Country, many times magnified, is also seen looking out over the hills of South Dakota, in the enormous stone portrait carved by Gutzon Borglum on the face of Mount Rushmore. Elsewhere Washington is fittingly remembered at Washington Square in New York, where Fifth Avenue begins at the triumphal Washington Arch, fashioned after the Arch of Triumph in Paris to commemorate the centenary of Washington's inauguration as President; and Washington Square, Philadelphia, where a statue of Washington stands at the Tomb of the Unknown Soldier of the American Revolution, before a white slab bearing the chiseled words "Freedom is a light for which many men have died in darkness."

The first major public monument to Washington was erected in Baltimore. It was designed by Robert Mills, architect of the Washington Monument, and its cornerstone was laid on July 4, 1815, though it was not completed until 1829. Located on Mount Vernon Place, it gave to Baltimore the title of Monument City. On July 4, 1827, before the Baltimore monument was completed, the people of Boonsboro, Maryland, erected in honor of Washington a cairn of stones 54 feet in circumference and 15 feet high.

Adams-Onís Treaty Signed

The Adams-Onís Treaty, signed in Washington, D.C., on February 22, 1819, by US Secretary of State John Quincy Adams and the Spanish minister Luis de Onís, concluded the first period of the westward expansion that would eventually extend the territory of the young United States all the way to the Pacific Ocean. The US boundaries that the treaty established were not to change in any important respect for a quarter of a century. According to the agreement, which is also known as the Florida Purchase Treaty, the Treaty of 1819, and the "transcontinental" treaty, Spain abandoned its claim to West Florida and ceded East Florida (see July 17) to the United States in return for $5 million, which the United States agreed to pay toward claims of its citizens against Spain.

At the same time, the United States gave up its claim to Texas. This was a move it later regretted (see April 21, San Jacinto Day), even though the agreement at last specified the southern boundary of the Louisiana Purchase. The western boundary of that huge region had never been a question, since the area was commonly held to extend to the Rocky Mountains. But the vagueness of the southern boundary had caused endless confusion ever since the United States acquired the vast Louisiana territory in 1803.

Specifically the Adams-Onís Treaty established the Louisiana Purchase boundary from the mouth of the Sabine River on what is now the Louisiana-Texas border, northward along the Sabine to the 32nd Parallel, thence north to the Red River, west along the Red to 100° longitude, north to the Arkansas River, west and north along that waterway to its source, thence to the 42nd Parallel, and west along that line to the Pacific Ocean. Thus was established the boundary between Spanish Mexico (which would soon be independent) and the United States.

By acceding to the 42nd Parallel line — which eventually became the northern border of California, Nevada, and Utah — Spain in effect abandoned its claim to the Oregon country. That sizable area north of the 42nd Parallel and west of the Rocky Mountains was left to two contenders — Britain and the United States, which would jointly occupy the region until 1846, when the Oregon Treaty divided the territory between the two claimants along the 49th Parallel, establishing the United States' northern boundary in the Northwest.

The Adams-Onís Treaty received final ratification by the US Senate on February 19, 1821.

James Russell Lowell's Birthday

James Russell Lowell, a prominent 19th century American writer and critic, had a rich and varied career as poet, essayist, crusader, editor, professor, and finally diplomat. During the first part of the 20th century his prestige remained such that his birthday was celebrated in some public schools. By mid-century, however, this fame dwindled. The 20th century brought the American people an abundance of divergent literary talent and saw a revision of critical values away from the "genteel tradition," which Lowell embodied with his wit, refinement, and good sense. But if the renown of Lowell's own writings has faded, his significance as a major critic, commentator, and educator to his own generation and the next endures. He was a dominant figure in the opening of New England culture, so long under the strictures of Puritanism, to the riches of experience in modern European literature and especially to Romanticism.

Lowell was born in Cambridge, Massachusetts, on February 22, 1819, in Elmwood, the same house in which he would die in 1891. His father was the Reverend Charles Lowell, minister of the West Church (Unitarian) of Boston. His mother was Harriet Brackett Spence of New Hampshire, a sensitive, mystical woman who loved old ballads and deeply influenced her son. Stately and spacious in its 18th century architecture, Elmwood still stands today at 33 Elmwood Avenue in Cambridge, on what was nicknamed Tory Row after the many wealthy supporters of the British crown who lived there before the American Revolution. Today Elmwood is owned by Harvard University.

James Russell Lowell was reared in comfort, studied at the classical school of William Wells in Cambridge, and entered Harvard College. When he graduated in 1838 he was the class poet and already knew and loved literature. But his next years were filled with painful uncertainty about his life's course. Hesitantly he entered the Harvard Law School, taking his degree in 1840; but he never practiced. Perhaps influenced by reading Romantic writers, Lowell evinced the strong if vague enthusiasms, the attachment to sensibility, and the instability of temperament that typifies the Romantic movement.

His engagement to the beautiful, talented Maria White of Watertown, Massachusetts, no doubt helped him make sense of his future. She greatly encouraged Lowell in his literary work, although this delayed their marriage more than four years because of his scant earnings. Early in 1843 he coedited *The Pioneer: A Literary and Critical Magazine*. During its short life, Edgar Allan Poe, Nathaniel Hawthorne, John Greenleaf Whittier, and Elizabeth Barrett (later the wife of Robert Browning) contributed to the magazine, suggesting Lowell's discrimination as an editor. At the time of his marriage in December 1844, he had also launched himself as poet and critic, in his own volumes and in magazines.

Maria Lowell was a committed abolitionist as well as poet. Through her and her husband's friends, James Russell Lowell enlisted in the antislavery cause. Turning his Romantic sentiments, his ideal of the poet as seer, and his quest for the good life to the aggressive work of reform, he went to Philadelphia for several months, just after his marriage, as an editorial writer for the *Pennsylvania Freeman*. Later he was a corresponding editor of the *National Anti-Slavery Standard* in New York. In 1845, at the time of the annexation of Texas as a slave state, Lowell composed "The Present Crisis," an often quoted poem, which became famous as a hymn in some Protestant churches in the 20th century:

> Once to every man and nation
> Comes the moment to decide,
> In the strife of truth with falsehood,
> For the good or evil side. . . .

His longer poems of this period, such as "The Vision of Sir Launfal" (1848), were characteristically Romantic in their faith in human nature, their search for the good life, and their sympathy with common people and situations.

Also in 1848, a work appeared that clearly indicated Lowell's capacity to become a more serious and less sentimental writer. Written in Yankee dialect, *The Bigelow Papers*, first series, satirized the participation of the US government in the Mexican War. With many other New Englanders, Lowell opposed this war on the grounds that it would extend slavery and increase the influence of the southern states in the Union. In the *Papers* he deftly caricatured the ideal of military glory, ridiculed jingoistic journalism, and denounced volunteering. Shrewd, critical, realistic, and sagacious, *The Bigelow Papers* stand in a rich tradition of American humor including works of Washington Irving and Mark Twain. They gained Lowell a considerable political and patriotic, as well as literary, following.

Lowell's growth from sentimental idealism into mature criticism was hastened by personal events during his late twenties and early thirties. The Lowells' adored first child died at the age of 15 months, early in 1847. This death inspired Lowell's "She Came and Went," "The Changeling," and "The First Snow-fall" — some of his best-known short poems. Later in that year a second daughter, who would survive Lowell, was born. But afterwards the couple lost two other children in infancy. In 1851–1852 they spent 15 months in Europe, far from the antislavery struggle, while he studied art and literature. It was in Rome that their infant son died. In Massachusetts a year and a half later, deeply grieved by her children's deaths, Maria Lowell herself died on October 27, 1853.

The loss of his beloved wife was a tragic blow to Lowell. He sustained himself with friends and his writing, though the surest source of his inspiration was removed. While the year 1848 had seen the publication of four of his major books, including a humorous rhyming estimate of contemporary literary figures called *A Fable for Critics*, in the period from 1849 to 1864 no additional books appeared. Yet this decade and a half was formative and productive for Lowell.

In 1855 he gave a series of public lectures at the Lowell Institute in Boston. Soon afterwards Harvard College appointed him Smith Professor of French, Spanish, and belles lettres to succeed Henry Wadsworth Longfellow on his resignation. This chair was the first established in modern languages and literature in the United States, in 1819. The scholarly studies he had pursued as an amateur became Lowell's professional work, and he applied himself seriously to his teaching. To prepare himself for the post, in 1855 he went abroad alone to study for more than a year, mostly in Germany and Italy. A year after his return he married Frances Dunlap, who had been his daughter's governess during his absence.

In 1857 Lowell became the first editor of the newly founded *Atlantic Monthly*. Under his skillful editorship the magazine became an important vehicle of liberal thought on politics, religion, and letters, gathering a group of the nation's finest writers of that period. Lowell continued as editor and as a regular contributor until 1862. In 1864 he became joint editor of the *North American Review* with Charles Eliot Norton.

Access to these journals encouraged Lowell to publish his literary studies as professor, as well as his reflections on contemporary letters. He also continued to write poetry, which became more reflective and less lyrical. Literary and political criticism predominated in his later writings, and most of his books after 1863 were collected essays.

Placed at the literary center of things, James Russell Lowell developed into one of the most perceptive critics of the period. Despite grave weaknesses of organization and exuberant verboseness, Lowell's criticism revealed a keenly receptive mind, deeply nurtured in the classics of European literature — which he perceived with greater historical sensitivity than most of his contemporaries. Above all Lowell possessed a sure sense for literary values and merit. With the significant exceptions of Walt Whitman and Henry David Thoreau, Lowell discovered and appreciated the outstanding American writers of the 19th century. As critic he was guided by a defined set of literary criteria. His Romanticism appeared especially in his attention to imagination, which he explored on three levels; "spiritual," "plastic," and "expressive." Norman Foerster in his *American Criticism* asserted that Lowell arrived at "the sanest and most comprehensive conception of literature formed in America prior to the 20th century."

The Civil War rekindled Lowell's earlier passion for freedom and for social change. He composed a second series of *The Bigelow Papers*, graver in tone, emphasizing repeatedly to Northerners that their cause was just and that they would win, under God. He urged them to go forward with a steady purpose in unity. He conceived the task in large terms: the North had not only to liberate blacks from slavery but also to liberate whites from the idea of slavery. Lowell called upon his readers to construct the Union to endure, with slavery stamped out forever. In 1865 he wrote his fervent "Ode Recited at the Commemoration of the Living and Dead Soldiers of Harvard University, July 21, 1865," achieving grandeur in the difficult form of the recitative ode and producing what is probably his best poem.

In 1876, at the age of 57, Lowell had a brief direct role in politics as a delegate to the Republican National Convention, where he helped select Rutherford B. Hayes as the nominee for President over James G. Blaine. Afterwards Lowell was a member of the electoral college, where he supported his pledge to Hayes against Samuel J. Tilden, the Democratic candidate, in a contest of unprecedented closeness. For this service to the barely victorious Republican party, Lowell was asked to become minister to Spain.

He served in Madrid as a highly decorous and popular ambassador from 1877 to 1880, using the time in part to improve his knowledge of Spanish and Spanish literature. On the basis of his diplomatic success, Lowell was made minister to Great Britain in 1880. In England he was much in demand for his grace in public speaking and his witty, urbane conversation. In these years he not only healed the personal rancor he had felt toward England during the Civil War; through his speeches he also interpreted Americanism and defended democracy, heightening respect abroad for American institutions and letters.

In February 1885 Frances Lowell died after a long illness, and in June of that year Lowell returned to private life. He died on August 12, 1891 at the age of 73.

James Russell Lowell was buried in the

Mount Auburn Cemetery in Cambridge, Massachusetts. In 1905 he was elected to the Hall of Fame for Great Americans.

FEBRUARY 23

The Battle of Buena Vista

One of the crucial battles of the war between Mexico and the United States was fought in February 1847 at Buena Vista, a small settlement south of Saltillo in the Mexican state of Coahuila. The battle marked the successful end of the American military campaign in northern Mexico and made the reputation of the already popular General Zachary Taylor, who shortly afterwards became a national hero, and subsequently was elected President.

Commanding a force of about 4,800, the advancing Taylor had occupied a strong position near Buena Vista on February 21. There he had waited for attack by General Antonio López de Santa Anna, who had arrived from the south with a force of about 20,000 Mexicans. The attack began with a skirmish on the afternoon of February 22 and ended, after a great deal of seesawing, with what amounted to a decisive victory for the vastly outnumbered Americans. Jefferson Davis, then a captain, distinguished himself for gallantry during the bloody battle. After the fighting ended in more or less of a draw late on February 23, the Americans held a distinct advantage and Mexican morale was low. Santa Anna accordingly retreated southward during the night. The victory weakened the Mexican forces and thus contributed to the success of General Winfield Scott's campaign to the south, which resulted in the fall of Mexico City in September and the subsequent conclusion of the Mexican War.

Emma Willard's Birthday

The great efforts made in the 19th century toward the improvement of female education in the United States owed much of their early success to the work of Emma Hart Willard, a distinguished educator and pioneer in the movement for educational equality for women. Descended from Thomas Hooker and other leaders of the Connecticut colony, Emma Willard was born on February 23, 1787, in Berlin, Connecticut, where she spent her early years and received her schooling. Finding her vocation early in life, she began teaching at the age of 16, and only four years later (in 1807) became head of the Middlebury (Vermont) Female Academy. She held that post until 1809, when she married a prominent Middlebury physician, Dr. John Willard.

In 1814, still motivated by an unceasing desire to raise the level of female education in the United States, Emma Willard opened her home in Middlebury as a boarding school for girls, where she put her revolutionary theories into practice. She made innovative additions to the limited curriculum then usually offered to women by offering such subjects as mathematics and philosophy, previously taught only to men. Although advanced for its time, the school, known as the Middlebury Female Seminary, was successful and marked the beginning of advanced education for American women.

An advocate of publicly financed education, as well as of better female education, Emma Willard in 1819 addressed to the New York State legislature her *Plan for Improving Female Education,* in which she proposed state aid in the founding of girls' schools and equality of educational opportunity for women. The plan was rejected by the legislature, but found favor with New York Governor DeWitt Clinton, who invited the educator to move her Middlebury school to Waterford, New York. The same year (1819), the New York legislature chartered the school as the Waterford Academy, but still provided no financial assistance. In 1821, on the invitation of local citizens and with the aid of private loans, Emma Willard moved her school to Troy, New York, where it became known as the Troy Female Seminary, the first school in the country to offer college-level education to women. Under her direction, the seminary won fame not only nationally but also abroad, becoming the model for later institutions of higher learning for women.

Retiring from active management of the seminary in 1838, Emma Willard traveled, wrote, and lectured extensively on behalf of public and female education. She wrote several widely used textbooks and, in 1831, published a volume of verse entitled *The Fulfillment of a Promise,* of which the best-known poem is "Rocked in the Cradle of the Deep." She died in Troy on April 15, 1870. In recognition of the importance of her lifework, Emma Hart Willard was elected to the Hall of Fame for Great Americans in 1905, one of the first three women so honored.

In 1892 the Troy Female Seminary was renamed, in honor of its founder, the Emma Willard School and, as emerging women's colleges gradually replaced female seminaries, it was reorganized as a secondary-level school. In recent years the school has provided secondary education for some 350 girls from all parts of the United States and from foreign countries. In 1910 the Emma Willard School was moved to the Mount Ida section of Troy, and its old campus in downtown Troy became the site of Russell Sage College. A statue of Emma Willard still stands on the college grounds.

The Emma Willard School annually observes its founder's birthday on or around February 23, usually with an assembly program or a special speaker. For a time, Emma Willard alumnae groups also celebrated an annual Emma Willard Day, but this observance was discontinued after 1964. The practice was begun in 1959, when the Emma Willard Alumnae Association designated October as the month during which the various alumnae groups could set aside a day commemorating their school's founder. Each year the number of groups participating in Emma Willard Day celebrations increased and, in 1962, alumnae groups in 34 United States communities and one at The Hague, in the Netherlands, observed the day with luncheons, book fairs, theater benefits and social gatherings. The school's 150th anniversary occurred in 1964, and various events were held throughout the entire academic year (1964-1965). For example, October 28 was set aside by the school as National Emma Willard Day, while New York Governor Nelson A. Rockefeller proclaimed May 8, 1964, as the day honoring the famed educator.

FEBRUARY 24

Arizona Territory Established

Arizona, which earlier had been part of the Territory of New Mexico, was organized as a separate territory by an act of Congress on February 24, 1863 (see also February 14, Arizona Admitted to the Union).

The centennial of Arizona's creation as a territory was marked in various parts of the state in 1963 and 1964. In Phoenix, a two-and-one-half hour historical pageant was presented nightly from April 19 to 28, 1963, at the state fairgrounds. Called The Arizona Story, the pageant involved a cast of about 1,000 (not to mention cattle, horses, and covered wagons) and traced the region's history from the time of Spanish conquerors to the present day. Phoenix, the present state capital, became the permanent capital in 1889, while Arizona was still a territory.

In Prescott, which became the territory's headquarters in 1864, not long after the territorial government was organized at Navajo

Springs on December 29, 1863, centennial events took place in 1964. They began on or near May 17, the 100th anniversary of Fort Whipple, the frontier army post at Prescott. Initially they included a Centennial Shoot program on May 16 and May 17 and Recollections of 1864 on May 22, featuring territorial costumes and old-time entertainment. On September 26 the centennial of the first legislature to meet in Arizona was marked by a commemorative session at Prescott. Other centennial-year events at Prescott included a house and garden tour, square-dance festival, ice-cream social, chuck-wagon dinner, mining day, county fair, horse show, and performances of the Arizona Road Show.

Feast of St. Matthias

The Feast of St. Matthias is observed on February 24, and in leap years on February 25, by the Protestant Episcopal and the Lutheran churches. The Roman Catholic church used to observe the feast on February 24; the early Christian Martyrology of Jerome recorded this date and Matthias was honored at Rome from the 11th century onwards on this occasion. However, according to the recent Roman calendar revision, the commemoration has been transferred to May 14, so that the saint — whose feast previously often had fallen in Lent — might be honored in Eastertide, near Ascension Day. Eastern Christian churches, however, both Catholic and Orthodox, continue to honor St. Matthias on August 9.

St. Matthias was one of the original group of disciples during the ministry of Jesus Christ and, after the crucifixion, was chosen as the Apostle to take the place of Judas Iscariot, who had betrayed Jesus and later took his own life. According to the Acts of the Apostles (1:15–26), Matthias' selection took place after the Ascension of Jesus, when some 120 of his disciples were gathered in Jerusalem for common prayer. At that time, the Apostle Peter explained the inevitability of the betrayal as a fulfillment of the prophecy of David and proposed that a successor to Judas be chosen. Two candidates for the apostleship were named — Joseph, called Barsabas, who was surnamed Justus, and Matthias. The selection was by lots, which fell in favor of Matthias, and he was appointed the twelfth Apostle.

Beyond this account of his selection, nothing authentic is known about St. Matthias. According to one ancient tradition, he preached in Judea and then in the ancient country of Colchis on the eastern shore of the Black Sea, where he suffered a martyr's death. According to another, he was stoned at Jerusalem and then beheaded. Still a third tradition holds that he was crucified and that his body, kept for a long time in Jerusalem, was later translated to Rome by St. Helen.

Chester William Nimitz's Birthday

Chester William Nimitz, who became commander in chief of the US Pacific Fleet in World War II and led the American naval forces to final victory in the Pacific, was born on February 24, 1885, in Fredericksburg, Texas. The town is located near Austin in the Texas Hill Country. Originally settled by German pioneers, the Hill Country still reflects its German heritage in its architecture and traditions. The town of Fredericksburg itself recalls its origins in such customs as its weekly ringing of the *Abendglocken,* or vesper bells, signaling the beginning of Sabbath each Saturday evening. Yearly events, such as the Easter Fires Pageant held on the eve before Easter, and the Night in Old Fredericksburg, held in July, recreate scenes from the town's early pioneer life.

Prominent among the community's frontier landmarks is the Nimitz Hotel, founded by Charles Nimitz, a retired sea captain and grandfather of the admiral. Built in the shape of a steamship, complete with a pilothouse and ship's bridge, the hotel, in its active years, offered shelter to such historical figures as Robert E. Lee and Rutherford B. Hayes. It now forms part of the Admiral Nimitz Center, which depicts the career of the famed admiral, with particular emphasis on his role in the Pacific Theater during World War II. On the grounds of the one-square-block area are planes, landing craft, tanks, and artillery. Restored 19th century buildings and a stagecoach that carries visitors to and from the parking area recreate the flavor of old Fredericksburg.

Although his parents — Chester Bernhard and Anna (Henke) Nimitz — had moved from Fredericksburg to Kerrville, Texas, when he was very young, Chester Nimitz occasionally returned to Fredericksburg to visit with his grandfather at the Nimitz Hotel. There the future admiral heard many tales of the sea. His youthful ambitions, however, lay elsewhere. While still in high school, Nimitz hoped to become a soldier and applied for entrance to the US Military Academy at West Point. Lack of vacancies there, however, led him to take a qualifying examination for entrance into the US Naval Academy at Annapolis. He came through the examination and in 1901, at the age of 15 — before he had completed high school — Nimitz was appointed to the academy. He did not receive his high school diploma until October 1945, a month after he signed the Japanese surrender papers at the end of World War II. On that occasion, the 60-year-old Nimitz, dressed in his fleet admiral's uniform and escorted by cowboys on horseback, rode on a horse-drawn buckboard from his nearby boyhood home to receive his long-awaited diploma at a ceremony at the Tivy High School in Kerrville.

At Annapolis, Nimitz excelled in mathematics and physical education and, in January 1905, graduated seventh in his class, with the rank of "'passed midshipman." After two years of service on the *Ohio* and other ships — including the *Panay,* his first command — Nimitz received his commission and in 1909 asked for additional duty on a battleship. Instead he was given a submarine assignment, and assumed command of the *Plunger* at the age of 24. From May 1912 to March 1913, while commanding the submarine *Skipjack,* Nimitz was also commander of the Atlantic Submarine Flotilla. During this time he was awarded a Silver Life Saving Medal for bravery in saving one of his crewmen from drowning. The medal was the first of the many honors to be awarded Nimitz through the years. During his lifetime he was to receive five Distinguished Service Medals, as well as other decorations.

Shortly after his marriage to Catherine Vance Freeman in 1913, Nimitz spent a brief time in Germany and Belgium studying Diesel engines. Returning to the United States that same year, he applied his new knowledge to the building of the navy's first Diesel engine for the oil tanker *Maumee,* and in 1916, already a lieutenant commander, he served as that vessel's executive officer and chief engineer. During World War I, from August 1917 to February 1918, Nimitz was again assigned to submarines, as aide and later as chief of staff to Rear Admiral Samuel B. Robison, commander of the US Atlantic Submarine Fleet. For his services during the war, the Navy Department awarded Nimitz a special Letter of Commendation for "meritorious service."

In the following years, Chester Nimitz held numerous posts on shore and at sea. In 1920 he received the Victory Medal with Escort Clasp for his services as commander of the cruiser *Chicago.* In 1926, already a commander, Nimitz was sent to establish a Naval Reserve Officers' Training Corps unit at the University of California. He subsequently commanded two different submarine divisions and various surface vessels. Then, from 1935 to 1938, he served as assistant chief of the Bureau of Navigation, assuming duty as chief of that bureau in 1939.

By 1938 Chester Nimitz had reached the rank of rear admiral and in 1940 was one of the two candidates for the post of commander in chief of the Pacific Fleet. Although the assignment was given to the other candidate, Husband E. Kimmel, the latter's service in that capacity was short-lived. The Japanese surprise attack on Pearl Harbor on December 7, 1941, precipitating US entry into World War II, changed the course of events for individuals as well as nations: Pending an investigation of the Pearl Harbor disaster, Admiral Kimmel was relieved of his post and on December 31, 1941, Rear Admiral Chester W. Nimitz became the new commander in chief of the US Pacific Fleet.

Not long afterwards — in April 1942 — he assumed the additional title of commander in chief, Pacific Ocean Areas. With conduct of the war in the entire Pacific area under the strategic direction of the US Joint Chiefs of Staff, the vast reaches of the Pacific Ocean were, for organizational purposes, divided into three areas under Nimitz's authority. These were the North Pacific Area (above the 42nd parallel); the Central Pacific Area (including the Hawaiian, Marshall, Mariana, Caroline, Palau, and Ryukyu islands, as well as Midway, Tarawa, and Iwo Jima); and the South Pacific Area (south of the equator). As the war progressed, Nimitz retained direct command of the first two areas, while delegating direction of forces in the third area, at first to Vice Admiral Robert L. Ghormley and later to Admiral William F. Halsey. The overall command of Nimitz — whose subordinates also included Admirals Thomas C. Kinkaid, Marc A. Mitscher, Richmond K. Turner, and Raymond A. Spruance — complemented that of General Douglas MacArthur, supreme commander of Allied Forces in the Southwest Pacific Area.

Strategically and materially, Nimitz set out to chart the course of victory almost immediately after assuming his new command. While new ships were being built to replace those lying at the bottom of Pearl Harbor, he strengthened his combat teams and established repair stations and maintenance squadrons to support his new fleet. Under his direction the nearly destroyed Pacific Fleet was rebuilt to an eventual strength of some 2 million men and 1,000 ships. As fast as men, ships, and weapons became available, he switched from purely defensive to offensive operations.

Nimitz's strategy for war on the Pacific front, however, was not made public. To the question "What is the Pacific Fleet doing?" his reply was only "hoomana wa nui," a Hawaiian phrase meaning "be patient."

Allied patience was first rewarded in May 1942, when the Japanese suffered heavy aircraft losses in the battle of the Coral Sea, and later when they were turned back, with substantial naval losses, at Midway. Indeed the battle of Midway marked a turning point in the Pacific war. By late 1942 Admiral Nimitz's announcement earlier that year that a "momentous victory . . . is in the making" was well on the way to realization. A later series of successful battles included action at Tarawa in the Gilbert Islands in late 1943; a great naval victory in the battle of the Philippine Sea (also known as the first battle of the Philippines) in June 1944; and the occupation of the adjacent Mariana Islands, including Saipan, Guam, and Tinian, in June and July of the same year. Occupation of the Palau Islands — Peleliu, Angaur, Ulithi, and others — southwest of the Marianas, followed. Perhaps the best brief summary of the role played by Nimitz, and the sea, land, and air forces under his command, during these latter days of the war was contained in the presidential citation accompanying a decoration later presented to Admiral Nimitz:

Initiating the final phase in the battle for victory in the Pacific, [he] attacked the Marianas, invading Saipan, inflicting a decisive defeat on the Japanese Fleet in the First Battle of the Philippines and capturing Guam and Tinian. In vital continuing operations, his Fleet Forces isolated the enemy-held bastions of the Central and Eastern Carolines and secured in quick succession Peleliu, Angaur and Ulithi.

With the landings in the Palaus in mid-September 1944, forces under Nimitz had advanced more than 4,500 miles across the Pacific from Hawaii since US entry into the war. After difficult early campaigns in southeastern New Guinea and New Britain, forces under General MacArthur meanwhile had traversed nearly 1,500 miles from the Admiralty Islands by way of northwestern New Guinea to the island of Morotai. The twin drives under Nimitz and MacArthur brought the Allies to the threshold of the Japanese-held Philippine Islands. The presidential citation to Nimitz quoted above continued with a description of the climactic joint operations to reoccupy the beleaguered Philippines: "With reconnaissance of the main beaches on [the island of] Leyte effected, approach channels cleared and opposition neutralized . . . the challenge by powerful task forces of the Japanese Fleet resulted in a historic victory in the three-phased Battle for Leyte Gulf" in late October 1944. One of the great naval battles of modern times, this action dissipated the Japanese naval threat and allowed Allied land forces to continue their advances until Luzon, the chief Philippine island, was finally declared secure in July 1945.

"Fleet Admiral Nimitz," as the citation put

it, meanwhile "culminated long-range strategy by successful amphibious assault" on Iwo Jima, and also on Okinawa in the Ryukyu Islands. Marine, army, and naval forces cooperated against bitter Japanese opposition in various stages of these two bloody campaigns. While the battles raged, Japanese suicide planes inflicted heavy damage in an attempt to drive Allied naval power from the western Pacific. The attempt, however, was unsuccessful and the two hard-fought actions took the Allied Pacific forces to the doorstep of Japan.

Even when their situation became desperate, however, the Japanese authorities at first refused to heed an ultimatum to surrender issued in late July 1945 during the conference of Allied leaders at Potsdam, Germany. The Potsdam Conference of US President Truman, British Prime Minister Churchill, and Russian Premier Stalin followed the surrender of Nazi Germany, Japan's World War II ally, in early May. Final capitulation of the Japanese followed the use of a new weapon — the atomic bomb — which US planes dropped on the Japanese cities of Hiroshima and Nagasaki in early August with terrible destruction and paralyzing effect. The result was total demoralization of the enemy war effort. Japan on August 10, 1945, announced its acceptance of the Potsdam ultimatum with certain provisos, to which the Allies responded with reservations that were finally accepted by Japan on August 14 — the day celebrated in the United States as V-J Day (see August 14).

But the naval war had already been won before that date under the command of Chester Nimitz — who, on December 19, 1944, had been appointed to the newly created top naval rank of Admiral of the Fleet. The appointment made him a five-star admiral. On September 2, 1945, aboard the USS *Missouri*, which lay anchored in Tokyo Bay, Nimitz participated in the signing of the Japanese surrender papers, which formally brought World War II to a close.

Before and after the war's end, Admiral Nimitz was the recipient of scores of honors, both in the United States and abroad. They included at least 19 honorary degrees. More than a dozen foreign nations awarded Nimitz their major decorations, while the United States paid tribute to him by designating October 5, 1945, as Nimitz Day in Washington, D.C. The occasion was observed with a ceremony at the White House, during which President Harry S. Truman presented Admiral Nimitz with a medal for his wartime service as commander in chief of the Pacific Fleet and Pacific Ocean Areas. After World War II Nimitz remained on continuous active duty in the navy, serving in various capacities. From December 1945 to December 1947 he was chief of naval operations and in 1948, in San Francisco, he served as special assistant to the secretary of the navy on the Western Sea Frontier. After 1947 he made his home at the Naval Quarters on Yerba Buena Island in San Francisco, where he lived the rest of his life.

Nimitz died in San Francisco on February 20, 1966, only four days before his 81st birthday. Learning of his death, Secretary of Defense Robert S. McNamara said: "The world has lost a distinguished citizen whose energies and vision were devoted without stint to a long lifetime of service. In the death of Admiral Nimitz the nation has lost one of our greatest naval leaders."

FEBRUARY 25

National Bank Act

Apart from Alexander Hamilton's first national bank — the first Bank of the United States, whose charter had expired after 20 years of life in 1811 — and the subsequent second Bank of the United States, which existed from 1816 to 1836, it was the widespread system of state banks that comprised the nation's entire banking system in the years preceding the Civil War. As the hostilities of that conflict proceeded, however, the government found it necessary to borrow large amounts of money to finance the war. These needs, coupled with the losses and confusion resulting from uncertain banking conditions in much of the country — under the free banking system then popular anyone who complied with a number of minimal requirements could organize a bank — prompted plans to create a more satisfactory banking system.

Soon after the start of the Civil War, it was proposed that banks be permitted to organize under a new federal law and issue circulating notes based on US government bonds. These bonds, purchased from the government by the banks, were to serve as security for their notes. It was some time, however, before Congress was able to agree on the plan. Finally, in February 1863, the legislation usually referred to as the National Bank Act was passed. It was signed by President Abraham Lincoln on February 25.

This act, with the amendments adopted later, authorized banks to be incorporated throughout the country under federal law and to operate in a strictly controlled way, thus supplying the nation with a safe, uniform bank-note currency. The act established minimums for cash reserves and provided that part of the reserves could be deposited in certain central reserve cities. In addition it regulated the capital of the banks according to population, with a minimum of $50,000 in communities with populations under 6,000. An amount equal to at least one-third of its paid-up capital was to be invested by each bank in the government bonds, upon which the banks could issue circulation notes up to 90 percent of the par value of the bonds, redeemable in lawful money on demand.

It was hoped that a market for the government bonds would thus be created, but the plan did not work as well as expected at first. However, when an act was passed by Congress in March 1865, imposing a prohibitive 10 percent tax on the circulating notes of state banks, more than 1,000 of them converted themselves into national banks by taking out federal charters. (However, some others, particularly those that had not been in the business of circulating notes, simply remained as they were. By continuing to function under their state charters, they gave rise to the United States' unique dual banking system.) One of the purposes of the 10 percent tax was to force out of circulation the notes of the state banks, many of which had abused their power of circulation to the sorrow and heavy loss of noteholders. In this, it was effective.

The power to issue bank notes that circulate as money, now a function of the federal reserve banks, was retained by the national banks until March 11, 1935, when the only government bonds carrying the circulation privilege were called for redemption by the US Treasury. In actual practice, however, the note-issuing function had been gradually taken over by the federal reserve banks since creation of the Federal Reserve System as the central bank of the United States in 1913 (see December 23). Comprised of 12 regional banks, the Federal Reserve System is coordinated by a central board in Washington, D.C.

Sixteenth Amendment Proclaimed Ratified

The 16th Amendment to the Constitution was proposed to the state legislatures by the 61st Congress in 1909, and was declared ratified by the secretary of state on February 25, 1913. This amendment provided for a federal income tax, stating in its entirety that "the Congress shall have power to lay and collect taxes on incomes, from whatever sources derived, without apportionment among the several States, and without regard to any census or enumeration."

It was the first constitutional amendment adopted in the 20th century. The 15th Amendment had been adopted in 1870.

FEBRUARY 26

William F. Cody's Birthday

The famed scout, Indian fighter, and showman William Frederick Cody, popularly known as Buffalo Bill, was born on a farm near Le Claire in Scott County, Iowa, on February 26, 1846. His boyhood home there has been disassembled and reconstructed in his hometown of later years, Cody, Wyoming, where it is now part of the Buffalo Bill Museum. The town of Cody, located in the Big Horn Basin of Wyoming, was founded in 1901 by Buffalo Bill, who chose its site, founded its first newspaper, and built its leading hotel.

William Cody first went to the Big Horn Basin in 1882 and was greatly impressed by the beauty and potential wealth of the land. He returned there in 1894, making his permanent home on the TE Ranch near what became Cody. Determined to develop the surrounding country, he invested in an extensive irrigation system for the entire Cody area. The project, however, grew so immense that he persuaded state and federal agencies to undertake further development of the area. The result was a complex irrigation system that included the Buffalo Bill Dam, completed in 1910. To help further the growth of the Cody country, Buffalo Bill encouraged the building of the Chicago, Burlington and Quincy Railroad into Cody and the establishment of a stage line to Yellowstone National Park. Visitors to Cody can reach Yellowstone by way of the scenic 53-mile-long Buffalo Bill Highway, which leads past several sites that recall the frontiersman. Located just outside Cody, in the Buffalo Bill State Park, are the Buffalo Bill Dam and Reservoir. Some miles on are Wapiti and, farther west, Pahaska, both established by William Cody as resting points for travelers to Yellowstone Park. Pahaska is also the site of Buffalo Bill's old hunting lodge, built in 1902 — Pahaska Tepee, where he entertained visitors from the East and Europe.

The town of Cody provides a home for the Buffalo Bill Historical Center, operated by the Buffalo Bill Memorial Association and comprising three museums under one roof. The Buffalo Bill Museum, dedicated on July 4, 1927, is a replica of William Cody's TE Ranch and includes, along with his Iowa farmhouse, his guns, saddles, trophies, and personal effects. A notable collection of paintings and sculpture by such famous depicters of Western lore as Charles M. Russell and Frederic Remington is housed in the Whitney Gallery of Western Art. The Plains Indian Museum contains a vast collection of Indian materials such as war shirts, cradles, tomahawks, pipes, bead and quill work, jewelry and shields, plus personal belongings of many famous Indian leaders. In the mid-1970s the center acquired a comprehensive collection of firearms from the Winchester Gun Museum in New Haven, Connecticut. The more than 5,000 specimens in the museum span a period of 2,000 years, up to the time "the West was won." The center is open daily from May to September.

In Buffalo Bill tradition, Cody, Wyoming, each summer is the scene of almost-nightly rodeos and an annual, two-day July 4 Cody Stampede. Buffalo Bill's birthday celebration each year on February 26 is an elaborate community affair. A commemorative program is usually held at the base of the heroic-size bronze equestrian statue of Buffalo Bill created and given by Gertrude Vanderbilt Whitney.

Although he was born in Iowa, William Cody spent much of his boyhood in Kansas; his father, Isaac Cody, had moved to Salt Creek Valley, near Fort Leavenworth, Kansas, in 1854. Left to his own resources after his father's death in 1857, and having received little schooling, Cody began work at the age of 11 as a mounted messenger for the freighting firm of Russell, Majors and Waddell. In 1860, when the same firm initiated the Pony Express, Cody, at the age of 14, was among its first riders. His scouting career began early in the Civil War. In 1863 he served as a Union scout with the Ninth Kansas Cavalry in its operations against the Kiowa and Comanche Indians, and in 1864 he enlisted in the regular US army and again served as a scout in military campaigns in Tennessee and Missouri.

From 1867 to 1868 William Cody was employed by the firm of Goddard Brothers to provide buffalo meat for the builders of the Kansas Pacific Railroad. His exceptional hunting skills soon earned him the nickname of Buffalo Bill; he himself estimated that he killed 4,280 buffalo within 17 months. He returned to scouting in 1868, serving as chief scout for the Fifth US Cavalry for four years. In 1872 he was persuaded by Colonel E. Z. C. Judson, who wrote under the name of Ned Buntline, to appear in his play based on Cody's scouting adventures, *Scouts of the Prairies.* Cody played the leading role for four years. Then, in 1876, he rejoined the US Army in the Sioux War. That year, during one of the campaigns of the war, Cody killed the Cheyenne Chief Yellow Hand in a duel. The story of that feat quickly spread, through the popular dime novels of the day, making Buffalo Bill a favorite hero of the wild West.

In 1872 Cody had been elected to the Nebraska legislature but declined to serve. With a partner, he established a cattle ranch north of North Platte, Nebraska, which later served as rehearsal grounds for his Wild West Show. The ranch, called the Scout's Rest Ranch, was designed in the form of the state of Nebraska and has now been restored as a museum. The town of North Platte still honors Buffalo Bill during its annual Nebraskaland Days Celebration, which is held in the third week in June, and observed with street dancing, a frontier revue, trail rides and parades. A rodeo commemorates the first rodeo of 1882, arranged by William Cody, on the request of North Platte citizens, as a Fourth of July celebration. On that occasion, Buffalo Bill presented a three-day "western" show, complete with cowboys and Indians, buffalo and bronco riding. Its success led to the organization, in 1883, of the traveling Wild West Show, which played to enthusiastic audiences throughout America and in Europe. In 1887 it played in London for Queen Victoria's Jubilee and in 1893 scored a great success at Chicago's World's Fair. It featured such personalities as sharpshooter Annie Oakley and, for one season, Chief Sitting Bull. In the last Sioux resurgence of 1890-1891, William Cody and the Indians who toured with his show proved helpful in negotiating for peace. Today, a reenactment of Buffalo Bill's Wild West Show is staged nightly during July and August at a site two miles west of North Platte, on US Route 30.

After 1894 Colonel Cody made his home on the TE Ranch in Wyoming. He continued to tour with his show, and at the same time devoted much energy to the development of the surrounding country. Fond of the home of his last 20 years, William Cody wanted to be buried on Cedar Mountain overlooking the Buffalo Bill Dam and the town of Cody. However, he fell ill en route to his home and died in Denver, Colorado, on January 10, 1917. He was buried atop Colorado's Lookout Mountain, some 16 miles west of Denver, within sight of the Continental Divide and a magnificent panorama of the Rocky Mountains. His burial ground is the site of a museum containing his guns, clothing, and other mementos.

The hero of numerous western tales, Buffalo Bill was himself the author of several books describing his frontier adventures. Among them was an autobiography entitled *The Life of Hon. William F. Cody Known as Buffalo Bill.*

FEBRUARY 27

Henry Wadsworth Longfellow's Birthday

Henry Wadsworth Longfellow, one of the most popular American poets of the 19th century, was born February 27, 1807, in Portland, Maine. The most widely read poems in the English language until recent times, his works also were translated into a score of diverse tongues, including Russian and Portuguese. During Longfellow's lifetime his popularity in England rivaled that of Alfred Lord Tennyson, the British poet laureate. The Poet's Corner of Westminster Abbey displays a memorial bust of Longfellow — the first American to be so honored.

His father, Stephen Longfellow, was a well-to-do lawyer and trustee of Bowdoin College in Brunswick, Maine. His mother, born Zilpah Wadsworth, was descended from the *Mayflower* Pilgrims John Alden and Priscilla Mullens Alden. In highly fictionalized form, Longfellow told the story of these two famous forebears in his long narrative poem *The Courtship of Miles Standish*.

Longfellow entered Bowdoin College as a a sophomore and graduated in 1825 in the same class as Nathaniel Hawthorne and one class behind Franklin Pierce, who later became the 14th President of the United States. Although his father wanted him to be a lawyer, Longfellow had decided to pursue a literary career. Bowdoin provided an acceptable solution to both father and son by offering Longfellow a newly created professorship in modern languages and sending him to Europe for three years of preparation for the new post.

By the time he returned to the United States to take up his teaching duties at Bowdoin late in 1829, Longfellow had a knowledge of French, Spanish, German, and Italian. He remained at Bowdoin until 1835, when he resigned. After another year of study in Europe, he became professor of modern languages and belles lettres at Harvard. During that year of study abroad, Longfellow's first wife, the former Mary Potter, died in childbirth.

It is said that when the young widower went to Harvard as a professor he applied for lodgings in Cambridge's famous Craigie House at 105 Brattle Street, which had been used as George Washington's headquarters in 1775–1776. The house, built in 1759, was then owned by a family that had fallen on hard times. The landlady reportedly mistook the youthful looking Longfellow for a student and was about to turn him away when he revealed his identity. An admirer of his travel book, *Outre-Mer: A Pilgrimage Beyond the Sea* (1833–1834), she thereupon gave him the best room in the house. In 1843, when Longfellow married his second wife, Frances Appleton, his father-in-law, Nathan Appleton, a wealthy Boston merchant, bought this Georgian Colonial house and gave it to the couple as a wedding present. Their six children were born in this two-story, yellow clapboard house with white pilasters, now designated the Longfellow National Historic Site and open to the public.

Visitors to Boston's Beacon Hill may also view' the Appleton mansion at 39 Beacon Street, where Longfellow and Francis Appleton were married. Frances Longfellow's father had built the red-brick Federal town house with pillared portico and wrought-iron balcony in 1818. With the building that is its twin, next door, the house is now maintained by the Women's City Club of Boston and is open to the public one day a week.

Longfellow's long and distinguished career at Harvard and his many contributions to the teaching of modern languages and literature have been overshadowed by his own writings. He was at Harvard for 18 years (1836–1854), during which he introduced thousands of young American men to the literary treasures of Europe — some of which he himself had translated. He resigned from his Harvard professorship when he was 47 years old, to devote himself to writing.

The year after his resignation he brought out *The Song of Hiawatha*, one of his most famous poems, and three years later *The Courtship of Miles Standish*. His *Tales of a Wayside Inn* was nearly completed when tragedy shook his life: his wife, Frances, was burned to death when she accidentally set her dress on fire in 1861.

To cope with his personal sorrow, to which were added the harsh realities of the Civil War, and his responsibility for the upbringing of six children, Longfellow immersed himself in work, translating Dante's *Divine Comedy* (1864–1867), and writing sonnets and longer poems. He made one more trip abroad and was given honorary degrees by Oxford and Cambridge universities and received in private audience by Queen Victoria.

Longfellow died on March 24, 1882, having achieved fame, wealth, and success. His influence on his generation of Americans was great, and it continued for several more generations. Well into the 20th century, a list of favorite American poems would surely contain several of Longfellow's works: "The Psalm of Life," "The Wreck of the Hesperus," "The Village Blacksmith," and "Excelsior." His longer poems, too — *Evangeline, The Song of Hiawatha,* and *The Courtship of Miles Standish* — remained popular for decades among ordinary Americans, if not with critics. When the Hall of Fame for Great Americans was opened in New York City in 1900, Longfellow was among the first to be elected for inclusion.

The Song of Hiawatha, Longfellow's Indian legend published in 1855, has often been commemorated in succeeding years. The fruit of Longfellow's deep interest in Indian lore, the character of Hiawatha was actually a combination of many Indians of many tribes. (The legendary Onondaga chief Hiawatha is thought to have founded the Iroquois Confederacy in the 16th century.) Many regions, especially in the Great Lakes area, honor all tribes in annual Hiawatha pageants and parades.

Perhaps the first known performance of Longfellow's poem about Hiawatha was held by Ojibways on Lake Huron in 1900, a few years after Longfellow died. The Ojibways sent an invitation on birchbark to Longfellow's daughters, saying in part: "Ladies: We loved your father. The memory of our people will never die as long as your father's song lives and that will live forever."

One of the largest annual pageants is sponsored by the Hiawatha Club in Pipestone, Minnesota. There, each year since 1949, The Song of Hiawatha Pageant, with a cast of 200, has been presented during the last two weekends in July and the first weekend in August in a three-acre natural amphitheater. Glacial boulders thousands of years old form a background for the 1,500-foot stage, near the spring-fed lake that now fills one of the area's oldest and deepest quarries. Long ago the Indians named the boulders The Three Maidens and, since they seemed to be standing guard over the quarry, the Indians customarily left a sacrifice before they quarried the stone there, which they carved into ceremonial pipes. Nearby, as a monument to the American Indian, the Pipestone National Monument, annually visited by thousands, has been established to preserve the Pipestone quarries and the surrounding area, considered sacred by many Indian tribes.

Longfellow's *Evangeline* has also been immortalized in another region never seen by the poet. Just north of St. Martinsville, Louisiana, tourists can visit the Acadian House Museum in the Longfellow-Evangeline State Park and see a statue of Emmeline Labiche, an Acadian thought to be the real-life Evangeline.

In Portland, Maine, Longfellow's boyhood home, the Wadsworth-Longfellow House at 487 Congress Street, can be visited during summer months. The city's first brick house, it was built in 1785 by the poet's grandfather Major General Peleg Wadsworth and is maintained today by the Maine Historical Society. The Longfellow Garden Club maintains its garden.

In Portland's Longfellow Square, at the intersection of State and Congress streets, stands a statue of Longfellow by the sculptor Franklin Simmons. Schoolchildren donated their pennies to pay for this memorial, which was unveiled on September 29, 1888. Portland also honored the poet in 1957 by observing the 150th anniversary of his birth. The Congressional Record of February 27, 1957, carries in its appendix an article entitled "The One-Hundred-Fiftieth Anniversary of the Birth of Henry Wadsworth Longfellow," presented by Maine Senator Frederick G. Paine in the US Senate.

In Brunswick, Maine, visitors can see the house where Longfellow and Hawthorne lived while they were students at Bowdoin, at 25 Federal Street. Bowdoin has an endowed chair, the Longfellow Professorship of Modern Languages, and each year awards a Longfellow scholarship for the study of belles lettres. The Hawthorne-Longfellow Library on Bowdoin's campus displays letters, manuscripts, portraits, and memorabilia of the two most famous members of Bowdoin's Class of 1825. In 1975, in honor of that class the library mounted an extensive exhibition entitled "150 Years Ago: The Class of 1825."

Also of interest to Longfellow devotees is the Wayside Inn in Sudbury, Massachusetts, which Longfellow made famous with his *Tales of a Wayside Inn.* A handsome, red clapboard building, filled with period furniture and still operating as an inn and restaurant, it originally was restored by Henry Ford. Damaged by fire in 1955, it was again returned to its former appearance through a Ford Foundation grant. In keeping with Ford's original purpose, it is operated on a nonprofit basis as a historical and literary shrine, maintained by revenues from the inn.

Twenty-second Amendment Ratified

When the Founding Fathers drew up the US Constitution in 1787, they devoted considerable attention to the office of the President. They specified who would be eligible to hold the office, outlined the manner in which the Chief Executive was to be elected, detailed his powers and duties, and even provided for his removal if convicted of "Treason, Bribery, or other high Crimes and Misdemeanors." Yet nowhere in the original frame of government did the founders of the nation set a limit upon the number of four-year terms that an individual could hold the highest office in the land. Not until 164 years after the adoption of the Constitution, when ratification of the 22nd Amendment was completed on February 27, 1951, was a restriction placed on the number of terms a President could serve.

Even though the federal Constitution had not specifically limited the time any individual could serve as Chief Executive, George Washington, the first President, had begun the tradition of stepping down from the office after two terms. From 1796 until 1940, all Presidents followed Washington's example, and none sought a third term. Then, in 1940, Franklin D. Roosevelt broke the tradition. Roosevelt, a Democrat, ran for and won a third term as President in 1940, and then, four years later, was again elected.

Roosevelt's long tenure as President dismayed many persons. Some Republicans felt that his personal popularity and charisma denied a perhaps equally qualified member of their party from being elected President; other individuals, for less partisan reasons, argued that such monopolization of so powerful an office might one day lead to authoritarian rule. During Roosevelt's lifetime, Congress took no official action on the matter of presidential tenure; two years after his death, however, the federal legislature, in March 1947, submitted the 22nd Amendment to the states for approval.

It took almost four years for the amendment to be approved by the requisite three-fourths of the states: ratification was completed when the 36th state, Minnesota, approved the amendment on February 27, 1951. Administrator of General Services Jess Larson certified on March 1, 1951, that the new addition to the Constitution had been adopted by the required number of states.

The amendment established two terms as the maximum length of time any one person could hold the nation's highest office and set a limit of one additional term for any person who served more than two years of a term to which another individual had been elected. However, the amendment did "not apply to any person holding the office of President, when this Article was proposed by the Congress." Thus, Harry S. Truman — who had become President upon Roosevelt's death in April 1945, served the three remaining years of his predecessor's term, and then was elected to his own four-year term in 1948 — could have sought another term as President. His decision, however, announced on March 29, 1952, was not to run again.

It has been difficult to assess the impact of the amendment. Some political observers have argued that the amendment creates for Presidents in their second term a lame duck situation because their reelection is impossible.

FEBRUARY 28

Explosion of the "Peacemaker"

The US Steam Sloop *Princeton* lay in the Potomac River in February 1844 waiting to be shown off. Captain Robert F. Stockton, the commander, had invited President John Tyler, his cabinet, many members of Congress, the President's fiancée, Julia Gardiner, and other distinguished guests — about 300 in all — to take an excursion aboard the *Princeton* on February 28. They would be able to inspect the first warship to be driven by a screw propeller. The ship had a steam power plant and an iron hull that made it virtually invulnerable to enemy shot and shell.

The *Princeton* had been designed by John Ericsson (whose most famous design, the ironclad *Monitor*, was to make history in the Civil War). A naturalized American citizen of Swedish origin, Ericsson was to contribute greatly to the US Navy and Army by many marine designs and ordnance inventions.

One of his earliest interests was artillery. Because of limitations of technology and knowledge, the forging and casting of cannons was a tremendous challenge. By trying a new approach, Ericsson had forged a huge cannon named the "Oregon." Perhaps the most enormous gun in any navy of the time, it had a 12-inch bore, was 13 feet long (carefully designed with iron reinforcing bands), weighed 16,000 pounds, and fired 225-pound cannonballs.

Ericsson tested his masterwork hundreds of times at a naval testing ground at Sandy Hook, New Jersey. The gun's breech developed a crack during the test firing but, after reinforcement, the cannon was as strong as ever, and was mounted on the *Princeton's* foredeck.

Captain Stockton was pleased with the wondrous Oregon, but not satisfied. He had also grown inordinately resentful of the talented Ericsson. The vainglorious captain decided he should have two great guns instead of one, and he set about the job of providing the second one himself, ignoring Ericsson's cautions about the difficulties — and dangers — inherent in iron forging and cannon casting.

At the Hamersley Foundry in Philadelphia, far from Ericsson's interference, Stockton produced what he considered his masterpiece. The "Peacemaker," bigger than the Oregon except for the equal bore, was 14 feet long, weighed 25,000 pounds, and was a foot thicker at the breech than the Oregon. But it was without reinforcing bands. And it had not been carefully tested before it was mounted alongside the Oregon.

On the day of the great excursion, the *Princeton* steamed down the Potomac, and the guests gathered around for the firing of the Peacemaker. (The Oregon was ignored — as was the absent Ericsson, who was never invited to set foot aboard the ship he had designed.)

Loaded with 40 pounds of powder for each 225-pound cannonball, the Peacemaker impressed the guests, as was intended. After three or four balls had been shot, Captain Stockton — an excellent host — invited the guests to move to the dining saloon below where they would enjoy libations, music, and a "sumptuous collation."

During the postprandial festivities, a ship's officer informed the captain that a guest was above and requested another firing of the Peacemaker. The captain refused, until he learned that the request came from Secretary of the Navy Thomas W. Gilmer. Then Stockton, a career naval officer, went up on deck to do the actual firing himself.

A number of guests had gathered around the gun to note the effect of the shot. The Peacemaker was loaded with 25 pounds of powder — a smaller charge than had been used a few hours earlier when the full assemblage was gathered at the gun. Yet when it was fired, a tremendous explosion shook the whole ship. The left side of the Peacemaker had burst and several thousand pounds of iron fragments went hurtling into the crowd gathered to the left of the gun.

Among those killed were Secretary of State Abel P. Upshur; Secretary of the Navy Gilmer; Virgil Maxcy, former *chargé d'affaires* in Belgium; Commodore Beverly Kennon, chief of the navy's Bureau of Construction; David Gardiner, father of the President's fiancée; President Tyler's personal servant of many years; and two members of the gun crew. Among those stunned by the explosion but not seriously injured were Captain Stockton himself and nine sailors. Senator Thomas Hart Benton of Missouri suffered a burst eardrum, and Mrs. Gilmer, remarkably, was unhurt.

The *Princeton* made for Alexandria at full speed, and anchored at about 4:30 P.M. Passengers were taken back to Washington by the steamer *I. Johnson.* The next day the bodies of the dead were moved to the White House, where they lay in state in the East Room until the funeral, which took place at the Capitol on Saturday, March 2. A committee appointed to investigate the tragedy exonerated Captain Stockton.

FEBRUARY 29

Leap Year

Leap Year occurs every four years and has 366 days instead of 365, the extra day always falling on February 29. The origin of Leap Year can be traced back to the calendar reform initiated by the Roman ruler Julius Caesar and adopted in 45 B.C. (see reference to the Julian, or Old Style, calendar in the article on the calendar in the Appendix). Caesar — with the help of his astronomers, especially Sosigenes, a Greek mathematician from Alexandria, Egypt — fixed the solar year at 365 days, six hours (or 365¼ days). At the end of four years, the extra six hours per year made an additional day. Caesar therefore decreed that following three years of 365 days each, there should be a fourth year of 366 days. He added the extra day to February, which, having only 28 days, was the shortest month of his new Roman calendar. It was inserted between February 23 and 24. The Romans, counting back from March 1 — the Kalends or first day of the month — considered both February 24 and the extra day the sixth of the Kalends of March. Therefore the extra or intercalary day was called *bis-sexto calendas,* and the year with the extra day a "bissextile" year, literally meaning "twice sixth."

But not even Julius Caesar's sweeping reform had quite made the calendar year correspond with the astronomical year. Since the earth actually takes 365 days, five hours, 48 minutes, and a little over 45 seconds to revolve around the sun, Caesar's move to fix the mean length of the year at 365¼ days caused an ever-widening discrepancy between the Julian calendar and the seasons of the year. In March 1582 Pope Gregory XIII therefore abolished the use of the Julian or Old Style calendar and substituted what became known as the Gregorian or New Style calendar. In so doing, he not only canceled 10 days, but also acted to correct the inaccuracy of the Julian intercalation, which amounted to three days every 400 years. After some calculation, he ordered that Leap Year be omitted in all centenary years from then on, except those that are divisible by 400. Thus, the year 1600 was a Leap Year, but

1700, 1800, and 1900 were not, although February 29 continued to be listed for those years in the unreformed calendars issued by countries that had not yet adopted Gregory XIII's reform. The year 2000 will be a Leap Year, since it can be divided by 400. The Gregorian calendar brought the calendar year in line with the astronomical year, except for a gain of 26 seconds a year, which will add up to a full day only after 3,323 years have passed.

The reason the English term *Leap Year* is used for Julius Caesar's bissextile year is unknown, but a number of explanations have been proposed. According to the most widely held hypothesis, the extra day every four years and the day preceding it were once regarded as one in the eyes of the law. The regular day, however, was deemed the "legal" day, while the additional day was judged not to be legally a day. Lacking legal status in the English courts, February 29 was therefore missed or "leaped over" in the records, since whatever happened on February 29 was dated February 28.

Uncertainty also surrounds the origin of the right traditionally accorded to single women to propose to unmarried men on February 29 and throughout Leap Year. According to popular belief, the association of marriage with Leap Year can be traced to an ancient Irish legend concerning St. Patrick and St. Bridget, and set in 5th century Ireland. Bridget complained to Patrick that her charges in the nunnery were unhappy because they were denied the chance ever to propose marriage. (Celibacy in religious orders was then based on private vows, not church requirements.) Patrick suggested that women be given the privilege of proposing every seven years. Bridget begged that the right be allowed every four years, and Patrick obliged by granting Leap Year — "the longest of the lot." Bridget then proposed to Patrick, who declined, promising instead a kiss and a silk gown.

This legend may not be a satisfactory explanation of why women were permitted to woo during Leap Year, contrary to the long-prevailing tradition that accorded the initiative to men exclusively. By the Middle Ages, however, an unwritten law prevailed in the British Isles that a single man bold enough to decline a woman's proposal during Leap Year was required to pay a forfeit of a kiss and either a silk dress or a pair of gloves. Any woman intending to exercise her right of proposing marriage was expected to let a scarlet petticoat show beneath her dress. In 1288 the Scottish Parliament enacted the following law:

. . . it is statut and ordaint that during the rein of hir maist blissit Megeste, for ilk yeare known as lepe yeare, ilk mayden ladye of bothe highe and lowe estait shall hae liberte to bespeke ye man she likes, albeit he refuses to taik hir to be his lawful wyfe, he shall be mulcted in ye sum ane pundis or less, as his estait may be; except and awis gif he can make it appeare that he is bethrothit ane ither woman he then shall be free.

Similar laws giving women the prerogative to propose during Leap Year were soon introduced on the Continent as well. The custom was legalized throughout France and, by the 15th century in parts of Italy, such as Genoa and Florence. It eventually spread to the United States, where it is a well-known tradition, but one that apparently is no longer taken seriously and has little influence in boosting marriage statistics in Leap Years.

Ann Lee's Birthday

Ann Lee was the founder of Shakerism in America. Her birthday is not celebrated, but events commemorating the history of the movement take place every summer at sites and museums devoted to the Shaker heritage.

Born the daughter of a blacksmith on February 29, 1736, in Manchester, England, Ann Lee was sent to work early with her five brothers and two sisters, and she remained illiterate. She worked first as a cotton mill hand, then as a cook in the Manchester Infirmary, and eventually as a cutter of fur for hats.

In 1758 she joined a society called the Shaking Quakers, or Shakers, which had been formed during the Quaker revival of 1747 under Jane and James Wardley. The arrival in England of some exiled radical French Calvinists known as Camisards had set off the revival; and the name "Shaking Quakers" — and soon "Shakers" — attached itself to those English Quakers who began to follow Camisard worship, meditating, then trembling, shaking, shouting, marching and singing. Public confession of sins was a focus of Shaker worship, and the group actively expected the Second Coming of Christ.

Four years after becoming a Shaker, Ann Lee married Abraham Standerin (Stanley or Standley in Shaker history), who was a blacksmith in Manchester. Her health seriously declined, and the four children she bore died in infancy. She later became obsessed with the idea that sexual relations were sinful and began to preach celibacy. During a jail term in 1770 for "profaning the Sabbath," she had a powerful vision of Jesus Christ, which confirmed her faith. After her release from prison she continued to preach publicly, and the English Shakers soon acknowledged her as the Wardleys' successor and as their leader. Thereafter she was called Ann the Word or Mother Ann, and her position on sex and marriage was incorporated into Shaker belief. Marriage was not prohibited but it was held to be imperfect beside celibacy, which was intended to make followers less self-seeking and to purify them for the expected Second Coming.

Ann Lee had a vision that she was Jesus Christ in a second appearance, and her followers also made this one of their tenets. The Shakers maintained that God was equally male and female, and that Adam — created in God's image — had the nature of both sexes, as did angels and spirits. Christ was one of the higher spirits, who representing the male principle, had revealed himself in Jesus, the son of a Jewish carpenter. In Mother Ann, daughter of an English blacksmith, the female principle of Christ shone forth. For the full revelation of the Father-Mother God, both of Christ's appearances were held necessary. With the second revelation in Mother Ann and the founding of the Shakers, it was believed that Christ's kingdom on earth had begun; notwithstanding, the Shakers were millennialists — that is, they looked to the future fulfillment of the kingdom of God.

In 1774, at the age of 38, Ann Lee felt herself directed in a vision to leave England for the American colonies, then on the verge of rebellion against Great Britain. Her band of eight arrived in New York City on August 6, 1774, and marched up "Broad Way." Two members of the group purchased land near Albany, where the village of Watervliet would later be, and Mother Ann and her husband stayed in New York to work. When he became ill, they lived in poverty, as her wages from washing and ironing were meager. On his recovery Standerin rejected his Shaker principles and went to live with another woman.

Mother Ann rejoined the group near Albany in the summer of 1776, and for three and a half years they lived communally, constructed their buildings, and conducted religious meetings. Their development was shaped by visions that came to her regarding the ordering of the "Church." Her disciples referred to themselves as "the first witnesses of the Gospel of Christ's Second Appearing." After her death in 1784

they organized themselves into The United Society of Believers in Christ's Second Appearing, or The Millenial (sic) Church. (In this way, the first Shaker society in the United States is said to have been founded in 1787 at New Lebanon, New York, and the society at Watervliet organized immediately thereafter; that is, the societies came into existence formally only after Mother Ann's death.)

After Ann Lee left England, the Shakers died out there, but in America the movement grew rapidly. Her conversions were greatly helped by the Baptist and Congregational revivalism that swept eastern New York and western Massachusetts in the 1780s. She gained followers among the converts at a revival held in New Lebanon in 1780. Knowledge of the group spread as Mother Ann preached throughout the region and became celebrated for the gift of tongues and an ability to work miracles. The Shakers were accused of blasphemy for their claims of power over physical disease. They refused to bear arms or take oaths, in keeping with their Quaker origins, and thus were suspected of British sympathies during the American Revolution. In July 1780 the authorities in Albany arrested "Ann Standerren" and the Shaker elders on the charge of high treason and imprisoned her until December.

During the next year religious revivals enlarged the number of Shaker disciples. Mother Ann and certain elders set out to tour New England in May 1781. They met with nascent groups of Shakers, called many public meetings, and encountered considerable persecution. On this trip the practical aspects of Mother Ann's teachings clearly emerged. Her saying became famous: "Put your hands to work and your hearts to God. . . . Do all your work as though you had a thousand years to live, and as you would if you knew you must die tomorrow." She urged cleanliness, honesty, frugality, and simplicity on her listeners. The Shakers' later achievements were based on this reverent, disciplined attitude toward the material tasks of life.

Mother Ann returned exhausted to the community at Watervliet in July 1783. She died on September 8, 1784, at the age of 48. After her death her followers wove from her reminiscences and what was known of her life a hagiography in which much was said of her persecutions and miraculous escapes.

Under Mother Ann's successors the Shaker sect flourished. Hearing of the revival of 1800–1802 in Kentucky, the society at New Lebanon sent three members to bear witness there. Despite bitter opposition, these Shaker preachers were able to found five societies – in Ohio, Kentucky, and Indiana. In 1894 a society was founded as far south as Narcoosee, Florida, but it closed in 1910. In all, 18 Shaker societies have existed in the United States.

These communities were among the most successful of the perhaps 200 American utopian experiments in the late 18th and 19th centuries. As Professor David Potter has written,

The Shakers . . . developed a fully articulated and homogeneous culture, with a value-system and a way of life which was expressed not only in their religion, but was reflected in their unique social organization, their economic system, and their educational pattern. Their writings, their music, their pictorial art, their crafts, their household furnishings, and their architecture all display facets of a closely integrated culture. . . . This culture represented a deliberate alternative to the prevailing American culture, and therefore it offers a perspective upon American culture at large.

Shakerism reached its greatest numerical strength in the 1830s, when there were perhaps 6,000 members in various communities. Each society was organized under principles of common possession of property, self-sustenance apart from the "world's people" (non-Shakers), and a celibacy in which the sexes were separated but equal. Essential to the Shaker vision was an affirmation of human interdependence and mutual help. "We believed we were debtors to God in relation to Each other, and all men, to improve our time and Talents in this Life, in that manner in which we might be most useful," read a Shaker covenant of 1795.

A Shaker community was organized in "families" of 30 to 90 men and women. In these a tension was maintained between separation of, and cooperation between, the sexes. Shaker men and women worked, ate, and slept separately, but their lives were joined in a "family" governed by a council of elders, and their separate quarters were together in a single building. The Shaker societies cared for thousands of homeless children and orphans over the years, educating and teaching them trades. At 21 an individual could leave the community or stay to become a Shaker, as he or she preferred. When whole families wished to join, they tested Shaker life for a trial period. If they liked it, husband and wife thereafter lived apart, entrusting the care of their children to the community.

Posterity imagines the Shakers as prim and subdued, but this is a distortion. They were devout, plain in dress, and quiet in conduct. But their essential joyfulness is unmistakable in their spirited music and the strong decorative colors of their cloth, furniture, and buildings – red-purple, yellow ochre, deep blue. Their worship ritual of marching and dancing, with songs and rhythmic, symbolic gestures was also striking. One of their leaders in the late 19th century, Frederick W. Evans, explained the rites of the sect:

We move our hands in a gathering form, expressive of one's desire to obtain the treasures of the spiritual realm. Sometimes we are led to go forth in the dance which seems to quicken the body and soul and kindle anew the fire of truth. We use some stronger means to banish the elements of worldly bondage by shaking, as an expression of our hatred of all evil; are bold in denouncing idolatry, pride, deceit, dishonesty and lust.

The Shakers were friendly and charitable towards the "world's people" from whom they had withdrawn and during crises shared their produce with outsiders. They were ahead of their time in their careful use of their resources, and non-Shaker neighbors recognized them as highly gifted artisans, farmers, mechanics, and businesspeople. They pioneered in scientific stock breeding and adopted crop rotation ahead of many contemporaries, introducing it on the Kentucky frontier. The Shakers also pioneered in certain phases of mass production in the United States, particularly in the canning industry. In the communal kitchens, they preserved foods for sale as far away as New Orleans, and they packaged seeds from their extensive herb gardens. They also made patent medicines and ointments from the herbs, for sale throughout the country. The name Shaker became synonymous with dependable quality.

The Shakers' vitality is clear also in their invention of labor-saving devices to increase production. Among their inventions were the circular saw, a revolving oven for even baking, the flat broom (soon to replace all others), the wooden clothespin, the first pea sheller, and a system of gravity-flow water power using the streams on their lands. They also developed a low-vacuum vessel of such worth that Gail Borden, founder of the Borden Milk company, spent four months in the New Lebanon community studying it in order to improve his process for condensing milk.

From the 1860s on, the sect decreased in number as fewer conversions were made. In 1975, almost 200 years after Ann Lee's death, two dwindling communities of Shakers remained – in Canterbury, New Hampshire, and Sabbathday Lake, Maine. The advanced ages of the remaining Shakers pointed, however, to the complete extinction of the sect in a few years.

Yet in the late twilight of the society, certain Americans sensitive to the past have developed a strong interest in the Shaker heritage and achievement. Social and art historians have commented upon the contrast between Shaker functionalism in household furniture and decoration and the dominant 19th century mode of ornamentation and embellishment; in the 20th century, Shaker antiques and reproductions look strikingly "modern." Individuals in several localities joined together in the 1950s and 1960s to restore local Shaker sites, hoping to conserve for future generations illustrations of the Shaker spirit of simplicity, devotion, and craft.

One such impressive restoration, Hancock Shaker Village, located on some 1,000 acres, five miles west of Pittsfield, Massachusetts, can be visited in summer and early fall. It is a Massachusetts Historic Landmark and a National Historic Landmark. Organized in 1790–1791, the Hancock Shaker Society persisted until 1960, when a nonprofit group, Shaker Community, Inc., took it over for development as an educational center and museum devoted to Shakerism and to other communitarian experiments in American history. Nineteen buildings remain, including the famous Round Stone Barn, which was widely copied in the later 19th century. To raise money for further restoration, an annual Kitchen Festival is held in mid-August with food products made from old Shaker recipes and tastings. A series of "World's Peoples" breakfasts and dinners, for which reservations are needed, is also held in the summer and early fall.

Hancock Shaker Village is not to be confused with the New Lebanon Shaker Village (sometimes called Mount Lebanon), which is nearby and under different management. Two miles east of Lebanon, New York, on US Route 20, the New Lebanon Shaker Village is on the site of the first official Shaker society (1787) and is itself a National Historic Landmark. Visitors are welcome.

Not far away, one mile west of Old Chatham, New York, off State Route 66 is another Shaker museum. Open from May to October, this is a private institution not situated on former Shaker land, but its six buildings house a large collection of Shaker items. A festival is held each August.

In Kentucky the little town of Auburn on US Route 68 has a large Shaker museum open from May through September, and the rest of the year by appointment. Auburn was founded by the Shakers, and since 1962 has held a Shaker Festival annually in mid-July, with a tour of its historic buildings and an art show. A pageant called Shakertown Revisited is performed nightly during the festival, with townspeople taking leading roles.

Also in Kentucky extensive restoration has been done on the 21 buildings of Shakertown at Pleasant Hill, seven miles northeast of Harrodsburg on US Route 68. Beautiful unsupported twin staircases spiral up in the Trustees House, where visitors from the "outside world" once stayed and where overnight guests are accommodated now. Fine cabinetmaking is carried on; reproductions of Shaker articles are created by traditional Shaker methods in the Village Crafts Shop. Shakertown at Pleasant Hill is open all year.

Sabbathday Lake, Maine, has a small indoor-outdoor Shaker museum today, including the great communal kitchen built in 1830. And at Canterbury, New Hampshire, on State Route 106 northeast of Concord, visitors can see the white meetinghouse built in 1782 and around it the sparely furnished houses of the Shakers, with a museum of inventions and handicrafts. The museums in the two communities are open during the summer.

A Shaker museum may be found in Shaker Heights, near Cleveland, Ohio. This suburb was named for the North Union Shaker Society, which was once situated there with its communal grist and woolen mills.

March

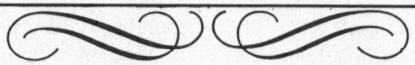

March, named after the Roman god Mars, is the third month of the modern calendar and has 31 days. The early Romans, following a precedent attributed to Romulus, the legendary founder of Rome, started their calendar year with March (*Martius*). They originally designated only 10 months, March through December (seen in the derivation of December from the Latin word for 10, *decem*). It was reputedly the second Roman king, Numa Pompilius (about 715–672 B.C.), who divided the previously unnamed "dead" season of midwinter into January and February and added these 2 months to the end of the other 10. Thus March retained its position as the first month and also continued to be the beginning of the yearly cycle of Roman religious festivals.

In 153 B.C. the Roman state designated January 1 as New Year's Day, thereby turning the 11th month, *Januarius*, into the first month of the year. This order was kept under the calendar reform that Julius Caesar instituted in 46 B.C., creating the Julian, or Old Style, Calendar (see Appendix, The Calendar). For a long time, however, older traditions prevailed and most Romans still considered March as the first month. Even after the fall of the Roman Empire and throughout the Middle Ages, local diversity prevailed, although March 25 was generally accepted as the beginning of the calendar year in Western Europe. Only with the pope's introduction of the Gregorian, or New Style, calendar in 1582 (see Appendix, The Calendar) did January 1 assume predominance as New Year's Day in Roman Catholic countries. In most Protestant countries, however, there was a delay before the new calendar, with its January 1 new year, was adopted. Scotland adopted the January 1 new year, but not the new calendar, in 1600. In England and its colonies the change to the new calendar, decreed by act of Parliament in 1751, became effective in 1752. In early colonial days in the New World, the year therefore began in March. Thus a transaction that began on February 27, 1720, and ended on April 2, 1721, lasted only a little more than a month, not 13 months, as might have been thought.

According to Roman belief, the god for whom the month of March was named was the father of Romulus. The second-ranking god after Jupiter, Mars was considered from earliest times one of the most important Roman deities.

Ultimately, he became known as the god of war and guardian of the Roman state. In this capacity, he was served by a warrior-priesthood — the *Salii* or Leapers — who were responsible for conducting elaborate festivities in his honor. Numbering 24 and divided into two groups located on the Palatine and Collini hills, the *Salii* were arrayed in ancient warrior dress: a short military cloak; helmet; breastplate; sword, spear, or staff; and sacred shields (*ancilia*), said to have been the gift of Jupiter. Thus clad in the symbolic armor of the Roman state, the priests marched about Rome on several occasions during the month of March to herald the coming military campaigns in the spring fighting season. In the course of these processions, they danced, displayed their weapons, chanted to the gods, and offered sacrifices of horses, bulls, and rams. Most important of these festivities dedicated wholly or partially to Mars were March 1, *Feriae Martius*, New Year's Day in the old Roman calendar; March 14, the second *Equirria*, when horse races were held on the Field of Mars (*Campus Martius*) in preparation for the opening of the season of arms; March 19, *Quinquatrus*, originally the feast of Mars, later changed into a feast of Minerva; and March 23, *Tubilustrium*, the purification of the war trumpets.

Although the *Tubilustrium* marked the end of

the March rites, the god of war was also honored in October, when both the sacred shields and the weapons of the army were purified and retired for winter. The worship of Mars then seems to have been at a standstill, until the advent of spring warfare was announced by the *Quirinalia* on February 17 (Quirinus closely resembled the war god) and the first *Equirria* on February 27 (when the cavalry horses were ceremonially purified, or lustrated).

Since spring was the season for renewed activity not only in war but also in agriculture, Mars seems to have appropriately served both as god of war and as god of vegetation. From earliest times, he was invoked to avert storms, disease, and famine and to promote prosperity of crops, animals, and farms. Certain characteristics of the Mars cult at Rome bear out his dual role. His festival months of March and October are periods of growth, ripening, and harvesting, while the leaping of his priests also could have been intended to encourage fertility of the soil, especially the growth of grain. Moreover, sacred to Mars were not only the spear and shield but also the wolf, woodpecker, and fig tree. It is therefore evident that Mars, although of unknown origin, became prominent as a chief deity of the Italic peoples early in their settlement of the Italian peninsula, and the Mars cult reflected their daily activities of clearing forests and cultivating crops, as well as of waging war.

The old Saxon name for the month the Romans had named March was *Hlyd-monath*, meaning the boisterous month; it was occasionally called *Lencten-monath*, meaning lengthening month, as the days are then perceptibly longer. The Dutch called it *Lent-maand*, which refers to the same change in the length of the days. In North America, the Sioux, counting their year as starting with the vernal equinox in March, referred to March as the "month of bad eyes." According to an old saying in England and Scotland, possibly based on weather conditions, March borrowed from April the last three days in the month, which are termed the borrowed days. The lucky birthstone often associated with March is the bloodstone.

MARCH 1

Articles of Confederation Ratified

Formal ratification of the Articles of Confederation, often referred to as the nation's first constitution, took place on March 1, 1781, after the delegates of Maryland finally signed the document, thus making it effective.

Although the articles had been formally adopted by the Second Continental Congress, meeting at Philadelphia in 1777 (see November

15), ratification was delayed because of Maryland's refusal to sign until Virginia had agreed to relinquish its vast western territorial claims.

St. David's Day

March 1 is the day St. David, patron saint of Wales, is honored — not only in Wales but by Welsh groups all over the world. The Welsh in America, for example, have observed this celebration from very early times. There was a large migration of Welsh to Pennsylvania at the end of the 17th century, and they gave Welsh names to many settlements near Philadelphia: Bala Cynwyd, Bryn Mawr, St. David's, and Berwyn. Nearby farming areas settled by Welsh were named Gwynedd Valley, Pennlyn, and North Wales.

According to the Welsh Society of Philadelphia, a group of Welsh purchased a tract of 30,000 acres adjacent to Philadelphia in 1681. It was thereafter known as the Welsh Barony, which was paid for in part by a quitrent of one shilling for every 100 acres, payable to the proprietor every St. David's Day. By the terms of the purchase, the "barony" was to be a separate realm, wherein all causes, crimes, and disputes were to be heard and determined by Welsh officers and tribunals, using the Welsh language.

These settlers belonged to several different churches, but they were one in all things Welsh. They maintained the Welsh language and customs and evinced a zeal to preserve interest in Welsh history and traditions. The origins of what is now called the St. David's Society in some places, and the Welsh Society in others, can be traced through old journals and periodicals. In the February 25, 1729, issue of the *Pennsylvania Gazette*, the notice of the settlers' intention to form a society appeared:

We are informed that several Gentlemen and other Persons of Reputation, of the honorable Stock of Ancient Bretons, design to erect themselves into a Society, to meet annually on the first day of March, or St. David's Day, so-called. In order thereto, on the first of next Month, there will be a Sermon preached in the ancient British language by Dr. Wayman in this City, and a Psalm set to the Organ; from thence the Society are to go and partake of a handsome Collation at the House of Robert Davis, at the Queen's Head, in King Street.

The next issue of the *Pennsylvania Gazette* described the occasion of that first meeting on March 1, 1729:

Last Seventh Day, many Gentlemen and others of the ancient Bretons met and walk'd in regular order, with Leeks in their Hats, to the Church, where was preach'd, in the old British language, (as it is said), an excellent Sermon on the Five first Verses of the

3rd Chapter of the 2nd Book of Timothy. From thence they return'd, in the like order, to the Queen's Head, where was a handsome Dinner prepared, after which the following Healths were drank [sic], under discharge of Cannon, viz: The King and Church; Queen Caroline; the Prince and Royal Family; Prosperity to the ancient Bretons and this Province; the Proprietor's health, and his Honour, Governor Gordon's and many other healths. . . . This, it is said, is designed to promote Love and Friendship, being a Yearly Custom, not only in several parts of England, but likewise in several of his Majesty's Colonies in America, and other parts of the World.

The *American Weekly Mercury* dated March 7, 1732, gave an account of the society's annual dinner that year:

Wednesday last being St. David's Day, and the Birthday of her Majesty, Queen Caroline, the society of ancient Bretons met at the house of Owen Owens, at the sign of the Indian King in Market Street, from whence they proceeded to Church, where there was Divine Service suitable to the Day. After Church, they waited on his Honour, our Governor, who was pleased to dine with them. After Dinner, all the Loyal Healths were drank [sic], under the Discharge of Cannon, and the Day concluded with Musick, Mirth and Friendship.

Besides the "Musick, Mirth and Friendship" enjoyed at the annual St. David's Day dinner, the Society of Ancient Bretons (Britons) regularly maintained its practice of dispensing financial aid to destitute Welsh immigrants.

On March 1, 1798, the society adopted a resolution to incorporate and appointed a committee to prepare a constitution. The Philadelphia group was formally incorporated under its present name of the Welsh Society on March 30, 1802. The doors of the Welsh Society are open to all males of Welsh descent.

Joseph Sill, a prominent Philadelphia merchant, made the following entry in his diary for March 1, 1836:

St. David's Day. The Welsh Society gave their annual dinner which I was invited to address as an officer of the St. George's [Society]. The dinner was numerously attended and consisted of all the luxuries of the season. The toasts were heartily responded to and much good humor prevailed. After the cloth was removed we had some glees and excellent songs by amateur and professional singers and the night passed pleasantly away.

The Welsh are noted for fine choral singing; and celebrations of St. David's Day, wherever Welsh people gather, are enlivened by singing. Welsh communities in many areas of the United States — for example, Pennsylvania, Ohio, Wisconsin, and Florida — observe March 1 as St. David's Day. The St. David's Society of New York has held an annual banquet on March 1 since 1835. On March 1, 1968, the Philadelphia Welsh Society placed a bronze tablet at Philadelphia's City Hall commemorating the Welsh contribution to the establishment of the city and the nation. A city band played Welsh tunes and hundreds of people gathered to witness the ceremony.

St. David left no writings confirming significant dates and events of his life. However, it is known that he was a monk, an ascetic, and a bishop who founded or restored many monasteries and greatly influenced religious life in Wales. He may have been born about 460; the date of his death is given variously as the year 500 (most probable) or 589. According to tradition, his birthplace was Henfynw in Cardiganshire, Wales. He became the first bishop of Mynyw (now called St. David's) in Pembrokeshire, Wales, where he founded his first monastery and where he later died on March 1. In 1120 the cult of St. David was approved by Pope Calixtus II. Special indulgences were granted to those who made a pilgrimage to St. David's shrine in the cathedral in Pembrokeshire.

In celebrations of St. David's Day, it was the custom for Welshmen to wear on their helmets or hats a leek, the floral emblem of Wales. (In some places, including the United States, the daffodil now replaces the leek.) In Shakespeare's *King Henry V* (Act IV, scene i), King Henry responds to the questions of Pistol by saying that he is a Welshman and knows Fluellen. Pistol replies: "Tell him I'll knock his leek about his pate upon Saint Davy's day."

Nebraska State Day

In Nebraska, March 1 is State Day, the anniversary of the state's 1867 admission into the Union. The governor, as the law requires, annually issues a proclamation commemorating the event and requests the state's citizens to celebrate this part of their heritage. (When March 1 falls on a Saturday or Sunday, the governor may designate the preceding Friday or following Monday State Day.) Schools may hold programs devoted to Nebraska's natural resources, pioneer days, or admission to the United States.

Popular history reports that Francisco Vásquez de Coronado entered Nebraska in 1541 during his unsuccessful search for the mythical kingdom of Quivira and the Seven Cities of Cibola. Many scholars doubt that he visited the region, however, and think that the first European to see the area must have arrived later. In any event, few followed in Coronado's alleged footsteps during the next two centuries. Fur traders occasionally passed through, though, and in 1714 Étienne Veniard, Sieur de Bourgmont, the French explorer, first called the land "Nebraska." The word probably comes from the Oto Indian word *Nebrathka* or *Nibthaska*, meaning "flat water," a reference to the shallow Platte River, a tributary of the Missouri.

The United States acquired title to Nebraska in 1803 as part of the Louisiana Purchase. After that time a number of men investigated the territory, including Lewis and Clark, who passed through in the course of their expedition (see September 23). Major Stephen H. Long called the area a "great desert," which succinctly reported the impression of most early observers.

Beginning in the 1820s the Platte Valley, Nebraska's most important topographic feature, became a significant part of the road to the Far West. Fur traders were the first Europeans to use the thoroughfare, and the pioneers soon followed. In 1841 the first group of settlers heading for the vast Oregon region passed through the Platte Valley along the south bank of the river. Their path became the Oregon Trail. In 1847 Brigham Young led the Mormons to Utah along the opposite bank.

Nebraska's political history began with Illinois Senator Stephen A. Douglas's dream of a transcontinental railroad with Chicago as its eastern terminus. Congress would not authorize construction of the line until there was a civil government established in the sprawling Nebraska region through which the line would have to pass. Southerners were hesitant to organize the territory as it lay above the 36°30′ line, which the Missouri Compromise had designated as the northern boundary of slave territories. Douglas overcame their objections with his Kansas-Nebraska Act, which nullified the Missouri Compromise by dividing the region into two territories, with the inhabitants of each having the right to permit or prohibit slavery. Northern reaction to the act was emphatically adverse — and led directly to the creation of the Republican party (see July 6).

During its territorial period, Nebraska grew slowly and steadily. Omaha was the capital, and Brownville, Nebraska City, Plattsmouth, and Florence became important towns. The chief business of the region was overland transportation, including wagons, stagecoaches, and, in 1860–1861, the Pony Express. The Homestead Act of 1862 (awarding 160 acres to each pioneer who settled the land) and the development of the railroads greatly encouraged immigration. The former made it economically feasible for farmers to obtain land, and the latter made possible settlement in the interior, away from the territory's eastern boundary, the Missouri River.

Nebraskans rejected opportunities to join the Union in 1860 and 1864, but in 1866 they finally approved a constitution drafted by the territorial legislature. Nebraska became the 37th state on March 1, 1867. The representatives of the populous South Platte region controlled the first state legislature and moved the capital from Omaha to the village of Lancaster, which they renamed Lincoln.

Nebraska is a conservative state, proud of its reputation for economy in government. The people normally vote Republican, but turned to the Populists in the 1890s and the Democrats in the 1930s when faced with depressions. In 1937 Nebraska inaugurated a unicameral legislature, which is unique among American state governments.

Today, residents of the once sparsely settled Plains state number more than 1.5 million. Agriculture provides the primary source of income. Among the states, Nebraska ranks high in total value of livestock and poultry on farms and ranches and in commercial livestock slaughter. Wheat, corn, oats, and beans are staple crops, and new ones such as safflower and sesame are being developed.

In 1967 State Day marked the beginning of a nine-month celebration of Nebraska's admission centennial. Local festivities such as pageants, fairs, rodeos, and exhibits formed the core of the observance. Among the events were Nebraskaland Days at Lincoln in June, which recalled the frontier period with rodeos and a parade, and shooting and roping competitions. Late in July the Ash Hollow pageant in Lewellen featured an outdoor historical play. Another centennial special was a rerunning of the Pony Express from St. Joseph, Missouri, to Fort Laramie, Wyoming — a breathless dash punctuated by a celebration at the Gothenburg (Nebraska) station on August 16. In June there was a rodeo at North Platte, the home of William F. ("Buffalo Bill") Cody, the originator of the Wild West show. The Centennial State Fair took place in Lincoln in September.

Ohio Admitted to the Union

In 1803 Ohio, the first state to be created from the area of the Northwest Territory, became the 17th member of the Union. The date of Ohio's admission was not definitely designated in 1803. But during the state's sesquicentennial year of 1953 a joint resolution of Congress declared that Ohio officially had joined the federal Union on March 1, 1803, the date when its state legislature convened for the first time.

Even before 1803, many citizens of Ohio had desired admission to the Union, but Arthur St. Clair, the governor of the Northwest Territory and an ardent Federalist, resisted the formation of the new state. St. Clair believed that Ohio was too far removed from the seat of the central government to participate actively in the affairs of the nation. In addition he feared that sympathies for the rival Jeffersonian Republicans, later known as Democratic-Republicans, were so strong in Ohio that its admission to statehood would be a source of substantial support for these opponents of the Federalists. Further, he was convinced that the people under his jurisdiction did not have adequate knowledge to take part in forming governmental policies.

To prevent the creation of a state from a portion of the Northwest Territory, St. Clair tried to use the very means by which the Northwest Ordinance, in 1787, had provided for areas of the territory to gain admission to the Union (see July 13). The document of 1787 stipulated that a region had to have 60,000 residents before it could apply for statehood. Realizing that subdividing the Northwest Territory would make it difficult, if not impossible, for any given area to amass the required number of inhabitants, St. Clair as early as 1790 put forth a plan to create three separate territories from the region under his jurisdiction. No action was taken on this initial suggestion, but the idea was not forgotten.

An important step toward the eventual creation of the first state in the Old Northwest region was taken in 1798, when a census showed that the territory had more than the 5,000 adult male residents required for the territory to advance to the second, or representative, stage of government. In December of that year Governor St. Clair issued a proclamation ordering the election of a territorial legislature, which was to meet in Cincinnati. The call to select representatives evoked a mixed response. The inhabitants of what is now Ohio were eager to choose delegates to the proposed legislative gathering, but the residents of the more westerly regions of the territory were reluctant to assume the financial burden of sending representatives to distant Cincinnati.

The western counties' disinclination to send delegates to Cincinnati made apparent the difficulty of governing the large Northwest Territory and revived interest in plans for subdividing the area. St. Clair seized the opportunity to put forth again his suggestion for the creation of three separate territories with seats of government at Marietta, Cincinnati, and Vincennes. The Jeffersonian Republicans objected to his proposal, however, since they realized it would divide the strongly Republican Scioto Valley and thereby indefinitely delay Ohio's admission to statehood. Instead they advocated that the

Old Northwest be split into only two territories and that the dividing line extend from the mouth of the Kentucky River (west of Cincinnati) to Fort Recovery in what is now eastern Indiana, and from that point directly north to the Canadian border. According to this proposal, the western part of the region, to be known as Indiana Territory with its capital at Vincennes, would have included most of what are now Indiana, Illinois, and Wisconsin, part of Minnesota, and the western half of Michigan. The diminished remainder of the Northwest Territory, with its seat of government at Chillicothe, was to include all of Ohio and the eastern part of Michigan. The plan of the Jeffersonian Republicans gained the approval of the US Congress on May 7, 1800.

The Division Act of 1800 did not end St. Clair's effort to block Ohio's admission to the Union — or, failing that, to diminish the influence of the Republican Scioto Valley on the area's future politics. With the support of Cincinnati and Marietta, two towns that resented the establishment of the territorial capital at the Scioto Valley town of Chillicothe, the governor urged an alteration of the 1800 division along lines he had previously suggested. For a time, he enjoyed considerable success. The territorial legislature passed a redivision bill, which — if approved by Congress — would have changed the boundaries of the territory; it also passed an act that would have returned the seat of government to Cincinnati.

As soon as the redivision bill was passed, the Scioto Valley Republicans launched an intensive campaign in the nation's capital to prevent congressional approval of the measure. They submitted numerous petitions, bearing thousands of signatures, in opposition to the proposed change of boundaries, and they enlisted the aid of a noted Virginia Republican, Representative William B. Giles, in their fight against redivision. Their efforts were successful, for Congress rejected the territorial legislature's bill by an overwhelming margin of 81 to 5.

After defeating the redivision measure, the advocates of statehood pressed for Ohio's immediate acceptance into the Union. Congress and President Thomas Jefferson were sympathetic to this desire, and on April 30, 1802, Jefferson signed an enabling act, which the national legislature had previously endorsed. The act authorized the election of delegates to a convention, which would meet on the first Monday in November 1802 to consider the feasibility of statehood and to draw up a constitution for the proposed new state; it also set as Ohio's western boundary the meridian from the mouth of the Great Miami (now Miami) River northward to a line drawn eastward from the southern bend of Lake Michigan.

Ohioans enthusiastically responded to news of the enabling act, and the 35 delegates to the November convention reflected the citizenry's desire for immediate statehood. One observer counted 26 Jeffersonian Republicans, 7 Federalists, and 2 persons of unknown political affiliation among the representatives to the convention. The forces favoring statehood were so strong that by the time the delegates met on November 1, 1802, the few emissaries who opposed Ohio's admission to the Union realized that further resistance was futile, and when the vote on statehood was taken only one delegate dissented.

Shortly after the opening of the November meeting, Governor St. Clair received permission to address the gathering in an unofficial capacity. He could not reconcile himself to the inevitability of Ohio's statehood and he denounced the enabling act as "in truth a nullity," which, he said, had divested the people of the territory "of the rights they were in possession of without a hearing — bartered away like sheep in a market." The speech infuriated the Republicans; President Jefferson removed St. Clair from office, and the former governor, who never again held a public position, retired to Pennsylvania where, broken and impoverished, he died in 1818.

Ignoring St. Clair's protestations, the convention drew up the constitution for the new state in only 25 days. Reflecting the difficulties its framers had had with St. Clair, the document severely restricted the powers of the governor. The constitution also provided for a supreme court of three — later four — justices, but it vested the greatest authority in the new state in a bicameral legislature.

The people of Ohio were not called upon to ratify this 1802 constitution. Instead the convention merely called upon them to elect the new state's legislature and scheduled that body to meet on the first Tuesday in March 1803. In the meantime, Thomas Worthington carried to Washington Ohio's acceptance of statehood and a copy of the new constitution, signed by all the members of the November 1802 convention. Federal laws were extended over Ohio on February 19. However, Congress did not mark Ohio's admission to the Union with any official ceremonies or statements; thus in 1953 the day of the first meeting of the Ohio legislature, March 1, 1803, was selected as the date when Ohio had become a state.

Chillicothe served as Ohio's state capital until 1810, when the seat of government was moved to Zanesville. In 1812 the government returned temporarily to Chillicothe while public buildings were under construction in Columbus. The latter city became Ohio's permanent capital in 1816.

Texas Annexed by the United States

On March 1, 1845, President John Tyler signed into effect the joint congressional resolution providing for the annexation of Texas by the United States. The measure, which had the wholehearted support of US settlers in Texas, had been passed by the Senate on February 27 and by the House of Representatives on February 28.

No one asked the opinion of Mexico, which, before the historic battle of San Jacinto on April 21, 1836, considered itself to be in possession of Texas (see March 2, Texas Independence Day, and April 21, San Jacinto Day). The annexation of Texas was a prime cause of the war between the United States and Mexico, which began in 1846 (see May 13, Mexican War Begins). Texas meanwhile had become the 28th state of the United States late in 1845 (see December 29).

MARCH 2

Texas Independence Day

March 2, Texas Independence Day, is a legal holiday in Texas, commemorating one of the most important events in Texas history: the Texas declaration of independence from Mexico in 1836. In addition it has been designated Texas Flag Day and Sam Houston Day by the Texas legislature. The latter are "special observance days," rather than legal holidays, although in reality the distinction is of slight significance since they fall on Texas Independence Day.

The first steps toward Texan independence began as early as 1810, when the region was still a Spanish possession. Once Mexico — in a successful revolt against Spain — had gained control over Texas in 1821, American settlements grew rapidly. Individuals and *empresarios*, like Stephen Austin, were, according to a contemporary observer, "spreading out like oil upon a cloth." The number of US settlers, which had exceeded 7,000 early in the 1820s, tripled within the next decade, and continued to swell rapidly thereafter. Colonies were established at such places as Brazoria, Washington-on-the-Brazos, San Felipe de Austin, Anahuac, and Gonzales. Mexico, beset by revolution and a rapid succession of administrations, was itself experiencing a confused period of politics after the birth of the Republic of Mexico in 1824. Its harried government thus was in no position to handle the Texans, alienated by linguistic, cultural, and religious differences, as well as by their own political aspirations. Mexico, fearing an Anglo-American seizure of Texas, made sporadic attempts to tighten control over the area by restricting foreign immigration, encouraging Mexican colonization, abolishing slavery, levying high duties, and establishing military garrisons.

As tension mounted and grievances remained unredressed, there occurred the first in a series of political moves that would eventually lead to open revolt. Representatives from every important community in Texas, except San Antonio, gathered at San Felipe de Austin in October 1832. In their attempt to seek greater liberties under Mexican law, they appointed committees to draft memorials asking for repeal of the ban on immigration and for tariff reductions, efficient and just local government, permission to organize their own militia, and removal of confusion in issuing land titles.

Most of all, the Texan colonists desired the separation of Texas from the Mexican state of Coahuila, to which it was joined politically, and the admission of Texas to Mexican statehood "on an equal footing with any of the states of the [Mexican] Union." The proposals were reconsidered and reaffirmed at a second convention in San Felipe de Austin in April 1833. The additional step was taken of drafting and adopting a constitution for the proposed new state of Texas. Stephen Austin was sent to Mexico with the proposals to plead for civil rights. He subsequently was imprisoned there for almost two years, a move that served only to aggravate the already strained relations between the province and the Mexican national government.

As long as the hope of similar resistance from liberal elements in other parts of the Mexican republic existed, the Texans' position was tenable; but in 1834, Antonio López de Santa Anna established himself as a reactionary dictator in Mexico. His centralist forces crushed liberal opposition in one Mexican state after another, until only the Texans remained. A "consultation" of Texans met at San Felipe de Austin from October 16 to November 14, 1835, and issued a "declaration of the causes of taking up arms." It stated that Texas would continue to be loyal to Mexico as long as that nation was governed by the constitution and laws "that were framed for the political association" — referring to the constitution of 1824, which Santa Anna had virtually overthrown. The Texans were not yet engaged in actual revolt against Mexico, however, and the conference by a large majority voted down a motion to secede.

It soon became increasingly evident that the struggle for a Mexican federal constitution was hopeless, and, as Santa Anna's army marched toward the border, the Texans found themselves face to face with the dilemma of choosing between total submission to the new regime or adoption of a new framework for the continuation of their struggle. As early as December 20, 1835, the citizens of Goliad boldly proclaimed a declaration of independence from Mexico. By mid-January 1836 the lingering hopes of conservatives were dispelled when Austin, released from prison in Mexico a few months before, encouraged open rebellion and complete separation as goals.

The "declaration of the causes of taking up arms" had included a statement in which the Texans reserved the right "to withdraw from the union, to establish an independent government, or to adopt such measures as [may seem] best calculated to protect . . . rights and liberties." In this spirit, delegates from nearly all sections of Texas were elected on February 1 and were asked to convene in a month's time at Washington-on-the Brazos.

Washington-on-the-Brazos, the first settlement in Stephen Austin's land grant of 1821, sprawled over the bluff above the muddy waters of the Río de los Brazos de Dios (River of the Arms of God). The town was still very backward in 1836, judging from this description made on February 13 by William Fairfax Gray, a lieutenant colonel in the Virginia militia:

Left Washington at 10 o'clock. Glad to get out of so disgusting a place. It is laid out in the woods; about a dozen wretched cabins or shanties constitute the city; not one decent house in it, and only one well defined street, which consists of an opening cut out of the woods. The stumps still standing. A rare place to hold a national convention in. They will have to leave it promptly to avoid starvation.

Nevertheless, 58 delegates assembled there on March 2, 1836. Many had come hundreds of miles on horseback and had left their families exposed to the dangers of conflicts with Indians — and the added threat of the Mexican army.

The delegates could not have foreseen, when they were elected the previous month, that their meetings would coincide with military disaster on the Texas frontier. Even as they convened, Santa Anna's assault on the Alamo, begun on February 23, was nearing its tragic end (see March 6). The entire border defenses lay exposed, and the Mexican troops were preparing, with executions, expulsions, and confiscations, to mark their advance into the heart of Texas.

Although their decision making came at a

moment when the Texan cause for independence seemed most hopeless, the delegates at Washington-on-the Brazos were able and courageous, and they efficiently embarked upon the business for which they had been summoned. Their first act was to appoint a five-man committee to draft a declaration of independence. The committee, probably headed by George C. Childress, drew up a document enumerating 14 specific grievances against Mexico and declaring Texan independence:

The necessity of self-preservation, therefore, now decrees our eternal political separation.

We therefore, the delegates, with plenary powers, of the people of Texas, in solemn convention assembled, appealing to a candid world for the necessities of our condition, do hereby resolve and declare that our political connection with the Mexican nation has forever ended; and that the people of Texas do now constitute a free, sovereign and independent republic. . . . Conscious of the rectitude of our intentions, we fearlessly and confidently commit the issue to the decision of the Supreme Arbiter of the destinies of nations.

The now historic declaration was unanimously adopted on March 2, 1836, and was signed the following day.

The convention at Washington-on-the-Brazos labored 17 days in an unfinished one-story wooden structure. "In lieu of glass," read one account, "cotton cloth was stretched across the windows, which partially excluded the cold wind." Meeting almost constantly in two, sometimes three, sessions daily, the convention's members worked to prepare for the separation of Texas from Mexico. They drew up and adopted a constitution, provided for military forces to defend the new Texan republic by appointing Samuel Houston commander in chief of all land forces of Texas, and formed an interim government with David G. Burnet as provisional president. On March 17 the government of the republic, together with most of the inhabitants of Washington-on-the-Brazos, fled before the invading Mexican army.

However, the Republic of Texas forced Mexico to recognize its independence the next month at the battle of San Jacinto (see April 21). It remained an independent nation under its Lone Star flag for 10 years. The United States, among other countries, recognized Texan independence on March 3, 1837.

Texas was annexed by the United States on March 1, 1845 (see March 1), in an action that was a principal cause of the Mexican War (see May 13). It subsequently became part of the United States when it entered the Union as the 28th state in December 1845 (see December 29).

For Texans, March 2 also commemorates Sam Houston, who was born of Scotch-Irish descent near Lexington, Virginia, on that date in 1793. After his father died in 1806, his mother resettled in the Tennessee frontier country. Rather than submit to working as a clerk in a trader's store, Houston ran away from home at 15 to live with Cherokees for nearly three years. He then fought in the Creek campaign under Andrew Jackson in 1814, and was seriously wounded in the Battle of Horseshoe Bend. Tall, vigorous, and handsome, a forceful speaker, Samuel Houston was admitted to the bar in 1818 and practiced in Lebanon, Tennessee. He also did well in state and national politics. From 1823 to 1827, he represented the 9th district of Tennessee in Congress; and in 1827 the Jacksonian Democrats swept him to victory as governor of the state and marked him for a bright political future.

Following a disastrous marriage, however, Houston resigned the governorship in 1829 and once more lived with Cherokees, by whom he was adopted with the name Co-lon-neh (the raven). In 1830 and 1832 he visited Washington, where he exposed the frauds practiced by government agents against Indians. President Jackson commissioned him in December 1832 to work out treaties with the Indians in Texas, lest American traders in the area be attacked. Determined to become a permanent Texas settler himself, Houston settled at Nacogdoches and for a short time quietly practiced law. He was quickly recognized, however, as the type of leader needed by the aggressive, adventurous, land-greedy pioneers who opposed Mexican oppression.

Houston was elected a delegate to the meeting at San Felipe in April 1833 and was a member of the Washington-on-the-Brazos convention that declared Texas independence. Appointed commander in chief of the revolutionary forces, General Houston was at first severely criticized in the dark days after the loss of the Alamo for his retreat before Santa Anna's superior forces. He brilliantly redeemed himself at the battle of San Jacinto.

The war hero was elected president of the new Republic of Texas on September 1, 1836, and the new capital was named in his honor. He held office until December 1838, and then again from 1841 to 1844. After Texas had been admitted to the United States, he was one of the first US senators from Texas. A dedicated Union Democrat, he served for 14 years until his inflexible Unionism caused his defeat, just prior to the Civil War. Elected governor of Texas for the third time in 1859, Houston adamantly opposed secession and refused to join the Confederacy. Because of this, he was deposed from the governorship in March 1861. He died at Huntsville, Texas, two years later.

To commemorate the significant period in Texas history that started with the opening of the Washington-on-the-Brazos convention on March 2, 1836, and ended with Sam Houston's victory at San Jacinto and the birth of the Republic of Texas, the calendar week in which March 2 falls is set apart each year by the Texas legislature as Texas Week. It was so designated by a resolution written on November 1, 1931, and passed and approved the following September. The week, beginning on Sunday and ending on the following Saturday, is usually observed by schools and sometimes by local, professional, and civic organizations, with such events as historic pageants, assembly programs, plays, and park beautification projects. In 1970 a Texas Independence Day celebration was staged on March 2 at Washington-on-the-Brazos State Park. Washington itself, despite its place in Texas history, never attracted more than a few hundred residents, but the nearby state park contains a reproduction of the early one-story frame capital of the Republic of Texas and the granite Texas Declaration of Independence Monument. Sam Houston has been memorialized in the naming of Houston, Texas, and by that city's Sam Houston Park, a project of the Harris County Heritage Society with restored buildings reflecting Houston as it existed in the early 1800s.

MARCH 3

Alexander Graham Bell's Birthday

Alexander Graham Bell, the inventor of the telephone, was born in Edinburgh, Scotland, on March 3, 1847. He was the son of Alexander Melville Bell, a teacher of the deaf, who developed a physiological alphabet called Visible Speech, which showed the position of the vocal organs as they formed sounds. The younger Bell, also interested in the problems of the deaf, used the alphabet to teach the deaf to speak.

Bell was educated at the University of Edinburgh and at University College, London. While still at school and immediately afterwards he worked with his father in teaching the deaf. In 1870 the family migrated to Canada, and both father and son began lecturing in Canada and the United States. Beginning in 1871, Alexander Graham Bell lectured on speech training in US cities, including Boston, where he did pioneering work with the deaf and in 1872 opened a school to train teachers of the deaf. He was appointed professor of vocal physiology and the mechanics of speech at Boston University the following year. His teaching methods have been of lasting value.

When first in Boston, Bell was employed by Gardiner Greene Hubbard, an attorney, to teach his deaf daughter, Mabel, whom Bell later married. While teaching in Boston, Bell was also conducting experiments with electricity. A man of many talents and skills, he had become interested in mechanics and electricity early in life.

When Hubbard learned of Bell's experiments, he became interested in the work, and in 1873 he and Thomas Sanders — a Salem leather merchant whose deaf son was also a Bell pupil — offered to finance a project. Bell was trying to transmit many signals over one wire. He finally succeeded with an invention called the harmonic telegraph. It was the solving of this problem — plus his acute musical ear and knowledge of the mechanics of human speech and hearing — that enabled Bell to invent the telephone, an instrument that transmits and receives alternating pitches over a wire, duplicating the human voice electrically.

The first words successfully transmitted on the telephone were the famous ones Bell spoke to his assistant, waiting in another room: "Mr. Watson, come here, I want you." Bell was issued his first patent on the process on March 7, 1876. The most significant demonstration of the telephone occurred that summer at Philadelphia's Centennial Exhibition, where Bell introduced his invention during the Independence Day celebration. Since then, his creation has revolutionized communications all over the world. To mark the 100th anniversary of the invention, the first telephone conversation, between Bell and Watson, was reenacted in Boston on March 10, 1976, by teenage descendants of the two men, using a replica of the original equipment. A commemorative 13-cent US postage stamp was issued the same month.

The Bell Telephone Company was formed by Bell and his two backers, Hubbard and Sanders, in July 1877. Bell took little interest in the company after 1881, although he testified frequently in lawsuits to defend his patent. However, since Hubbard, then his father-in-law, promoted the company, Bell was able, unlike many inventors, to reap rich profits from his early labors. Most of the telephone service in the United States today is provided by the Bell System, which grew out of the original invention. The Bell System comprises separate corporations under a parent organization, the American Telegraph and Telephone Company.

In 1880 the French government awarded Bell the Volta prize for his invention of the telephone, and he used this money and profits from his patent to establish the Volta Laboratory in Washington, D.C. A division of this laboratory, the Volta Bureau for the Deaf, was established by Bell for the increase and diffusion of knowledge relating to the deaf. Under the name Alexander Graham Bell Association for the Deaf, it continues his work today.

Bell became an American citizen in 1882. He lived in Washington, D.C., for most of the rest of his life, devoting himself to research in many fields. It was at the Volta Laboratory that the first successful phonograph record was produced. With associates, Bell also patented several improvements on Edison's phonograph. He invented the photophone, a device that transmits sound by light rays, and the audiometer, an instrument that measures the intensity of sounds. Continuing in his research on deafness, Bell also explored the nature and causes of deafness and made an in-depth study of the relationship of heredity to deafness. He founded the American Association to Promote the Teaching of Speech to the Deaf.

While serving as president of the National Geographic Society (1896–1904) Bell did much to promote popular membership in the society and helped develop its technical journal into today's widely known *National Geographic Magazine*. Bell was also appointed by Congress as a regent of the Smithsonian Institution.

After 1895 Bell's principal interest was aviation. He invented the tetrahedral kite, which carried a man aloft, and encouraged Samuel Pierpont Langley's experiments with heavier-than-air craft. In 1907, with Glenn H. Curtiss and others, Bell founded the Aerial Experiment Association, which contributed substantially to early aviation. It developed and built flying machines that were demonstrated in three successful public flights in 1908. In contrast to the earlier flights of the Wright brothers, which took place in a remote location and received little attention, these demonstrations aroused widespread interest in aviation progress. Bell and his associates also developed the tricycle landing gear and the aileron, a hinged, movable section of an airplane wing still in use to control roll.

Another of Bell's interests was marine engineering — his hydrofoil speedboat, developed with F. W. Baldwin, set a world record (70.86 mph) in 1919; and in genetics — he bred a flock of twin-bearing sheep.

While in his Canadian summer home near Baddeck on Cape Breton Island, Nova Scotia, Bell died on August 2, 1922. He is buried atop a nearby mountain. Many of his inventions and mementos are displayed at the tetrahedron-shaped Bell Museum, in Baddeck, the Canadian government's memorial to Bell.

Florida Admitted to the Union

Florida was the last of the Atlantic seaboard states to gain admission to the Union — on March 3, 1845. Twenty-four tumultuous years passed from the time the United States acquired possession of the territory from Spain before statehood could be granted — during the administration of President John Tyler—to the country's southernmost mainland area.

With the US Senate's second ratification, on February 19, 1821, of the Adams-Onís Treaty (known also as the Florida Purchase Treaty) between Spain and the United States, and the exchange of ratifications three days later by representatives of the two governments, the last foreign holding east of what is now Texas was eliminated (see February 22, Adams-Onís Treaty Signed, and July 17, Florida Ceded to the United States). Formal transfer of the territory to the United States was made on July 17, 1821. The only sizable settlements were at Pensacola, on an arm of the Gulf of Mexico in the extreme northwestern part of the territory; St. Augustine, on the eastern (Atlantic) coast at almost the same latitude; and Fernandina, on the Atlantic coast close to the northern border. Fewer than 5,000 people lived in Florida.

The man chosen to be the first American governor — Andrew Jackson, military hero and, later, President of the United States — was no stranger to the area. With his troops, Jackson had twice captured Spanish-held Pensacola, once during the War of 1812, just prior to his victory in the battle of New Orleans, and again in 1818 (see March 15, Andrew Jackson's Birthday). As administrator of Florida, however, Jackson ruffled feathers both there and in Washington, D.C., and after eight months he resigned the post.

Florida was organized as a territory with its present boundaries in 1822. Settlers, many of them from nearby states, rushed in, especially to the northern part of the territory. So greedy for land were the newcomers that they brought great pressure to bear on the US Congress to remove the Seminole Indians from the territory and to make the entire area available for settlement. The Seminoles, who had been allowed their freedom by the Spaniards, protested vigorously but finally, in 1823, agreed to live within certain specified areas. As the number of settlers increased and pushed steadily southward, sometimes coming into conflict with the Seminoles, pressure was again exerted on the federal government to expel the Seminoles.

In 1832 and 1833 the Indians signed treaties agreeing to surrender their land in Florida in return for an equal amount of land in the western United States. However, the Seminoles had second thoughts about these agreements and decided to resist federal attempts to enforce the treaties and to remove them from the territory. In the fierce warfare that followed from 1835 to 1842, a conflict known as the Second Seminole War, the Indians were doomed to defeat. Most of them were killed or relocated in the Indian Territory, now Oklahoma (see June 23, Unto These Hills, Cherokee, North Carolina). A group of about 100 Seminoles under Osceola evaded attempts to relocate them, however, by retreating into southern Florida's swamp wilderness. They were the nucleus of the tribe now living on reservations northwest of Lake Okeechobee and in the southern Everglades. Osceola himself was seized during a period of truce and died in prison in Charleston, South Carolina.

Tallahassee was selected as the capital of the new territory in 1824. Located in the northwest, it lies about 20 miles north of the Gulf of Mexico and slightly closer than that to Florida's northern border with Georgia. It was an important Indian town at least as early as 1539, when the Spanish explorer Hernando de Soto and his party visited it; its name, of Indian origin, means "old town."

Development was quickly spurred by construction of a road linking Pensacola with St. Augustine. Pensacola, with its excellent harbor, had been of major importance during the period of Spanish sovereignty. St. Augustine, the oldest city in the United States, dated its existence as a permanent settlement from 1565, when Pedro Menéndez de Avilés claimed the site for Spain (see September 8). In the area between these two historic cities, many large plantations were founded immediately after American sovereignty was established. New towns came into existence, and a substantial number of northerners settled in those along the eastern coast. Jacksonville, near the mouth of the St. Johns River, about 35 miles north northwest of St. Augustine, was laid out as a town in 1822; it is today the most populous city in Florida. (The Fort Caroline National Monument commemorates a settlement made in Jacksonville by French Huguenots in 1564 but wiped out by Spaniards from St. Augustine the following year.) A few cattlemen migrated to the southern part of Florida.

The influx of settlers, which had begun so quickly and continued so steadily, decreased greatly in the latter part of the 1830s. Warfare with the Seminoles and failure of territorial banks during the financial panic of 1837 combined to dissuade prospective newcomers.

Floridians had gained the right to elect their territorial legislative council in 1826. The council was superseded in 1838 by a house of representatives and a senate. In December 1838 and January 1839 a convention meeting in the boom town of St. Joseph drafted a proposed state constitution. Situated on a bay of the Gulf of Mexico, in the northwestern part of Florida, St. Joseph had been founded a scant three years earlier and was destined to disappear during the 1840s, following destructive hurricanes and an epidemic of yellow fever. Port St. Joe, which has a Constitutional Convention Museum, subsequently grew up just to the west. The selection of St. Joseph as the site for the convention was due to the strenuous efforts of the town's promoters. Although the location of the building or buildings in which the meetings were held is not known, a monument "to commemorate the birth of Florida, and the assembly of the first Constitutional Convention, of this State" was dedicated on the site of the ruined town in 1923.

The citizens of Florida, however, held varying opinions as to the desirability of gaining statehood. Ratification of the proposed constitution was by a slim margin of about 100 votes. Petition was immediately made to the US Congress to grant statehood, but the divided minds of the Floridians prompted diverse requests to Congress during ensuing years — the division of the area into two territories, postponement of the whole matter, and a repetition of the original request. Controversy and delay also went hand in hand with the congressional desire not to admit a slave state, as Florida would be, without admitting a free state at the same time, a practice known as "pairing." Finally, when Iowa was also ready for admission — as a free state — Florida was admitted to the Union on March 3, 1845, as the 27th state, with its capital at Tallahassee.

Only 16 years later — after considerable growth, including a start of the tourist business that was to become one of the state's principal industries — Florida declared itself seceded from the Union on January 10, 1861. As a "'sovereign and independent nation," Florida joined with other Southern states to form the Confederate States of America.

During the ensuing Civil War, Union forces captured Florida's chief ports and blockaded its coast, but the area's many inlets provided both refuge and bases of operation for blockade runners. The interior of the state remained in Southern hands, and, apart from a major battle at Olustee in 1864 and another engagement outside Tallahassee in 1865 (both resulting in Confederate victories), there was little actual fighting in Florida. Throughout the war Florida was an important source of supplies, foodstuffs, and manpower for the rest of the Confederacy.

At the close of the war, in 1865, a new state government was organized and a new state constitution framed. However, neither met with federal approval, for Florida's proposed constitution withheld the vote from blacks and the new legislature in 1866 refused to ratify the 14th Amendment to the US Constitution, which included a provision granting citizenship to former slaves. In accordance with the federal Reconstruction policies in effect in the South, therefore, a quasi-military government was instituted in Florida, which became part of the Third Military District. During this period of federal rule, blacks were registered as voters.

In early 1868 a revised state constitution — known as the Carpetbag Constitution — was drafted and ratified by Floridians. This constitution was found acceptable, and, with Florida's acceptance of a stipulation that universal manhood suffrage would never be repealed, the US Congress voted to restore the full rights of statehood, including representation in Congress, to Florida on June 25, 1868.

Celebration of the state's centennial year, 1945, was severely limited by the United States' involvement in World War II. During the year, however, the anniversary was marked by school exercises and projects, local observances and exhibits, various publications, and broadcast presentations. Commemorations placed their stress on looking to the future as well as to the past. A three-cent Florida centennial stamp depicting the state seal, the historic city gate of St. Augustine, and the state capitol was issued by the federal government. Further national recognition of the occasion was accorded by the Library of Congress in Washington, D.C., which held a Florida centennial exhibition from March 3 through May 31.

Missouri Compromise Finalized

On March 3, 1820, the first Missouri Compromise became final. According to this agreement, Maine was admitted to the Union as a free state, Missouri was allowed to set up a state government with no restrictions against slavery, and slavery was prohibited in the remainder of the Louisiana Purchase north of latitude 36°30'. The March 1820 legislation did not, however, end the dispute over Missouri, and still further compromise was necessary before Missouri gained statehood in August 1821 (see August 10).

MARCH 4

Pennsylvania Granted to Penn

On March 4, 1681, William Penn secured a grant to what is now the state of Pennsylvania, in payment of a debt owed his father by the British crown (see October 24, Pennsylvania Day; William Penn's Birthday).

Vermont Admitted to the Union

On March 4, 1791, Vermont gained statehood. Vermont was not one of the 13 original states. Indeed, the inhabitants of the Green Mountains in 1777 took advantage of the chaos of the American Revolution to declare themselves independent of their neighboring states as well as of Great Britain. But in the years that followed Vermont's 1777 declaration of independence (see January 15), Vermont repeatedly tried to become a member of the federal Union. For more than a decade Vermont's status remained controversial, but finally the disputes over the region were resolved, and in 1791 the area won acceptance as the 14th state. In commemoration of their state's admission to the Union, Vermonters today celebrate the first Tuesday in March as Town Meeting Day and on that day they conduct important town meetings throughout the state.

The convention that met at Westminster declared Vermont's independence on January 15, 1777, but this action did not bring a unified state into existence. The southwestern area around Bennington strongly supported an independent status for Vermont, but the remainder of what is now the state was less enthusiastic. Most of the region east of the Green Mountains in the Connecticut Valley considered joining the New Hampshire towns east of the Connecticut River in a separate "Valley state," and the southeastern portion of Vermont, which was heavily populated by settlers from New York, retained strong ties with that state. In addition, British forces occupied most of the northern region, including all the territory along Lake Champlain, so that area had no opportunity to align itself with the new Vermont government.

Despite the lack of unified support for a separate Vermont, a convention met at Windsor in July 1777 to draw up a state constitution. The

Vermont frame of government drew heavily from that adopted by Pennsylvania in 1776 but included several additions. Vermont's constitution was the first specifically to prohibit slavery and to provide for universal manhood suffrage. The 1777 document was never submitted to Vermont's inhabitants for ratification; nevertheless, it became and substantially remains their basic frame of government.

The framers of the Vermont Constitution hoped that after they had drawn up that document, the Continental Congress would approve their application for statehood. Their aspirations were ill founded, however. The Congress upheld New York's contention that it had jurisdiction over the Green Mountain area and denounced Vermont's claims to independence.

In May 1778 Ethan Allen, who nearly three years earlier had been taken prisoner by the British during the American patriots' unsuccessful campaign against Quebec, was exchanged and returned to Vermont. A land speculator whose financial interests would be best served if Vermont were independent of New York, Allen used his considerable talents in the years that followed to strengthen the state. And since his influence was greatest in the Bennington area, he worked particularly hard to insure the dominance of that region in the politics of the new state.

At the first meeting of the Vermont legislature in the spring of 1778, the representatives from the Connecticut Valley put forth a plan to include New Hampshire areas located east of the Connecticut River within the jurisdiction of Vermont. A number of towns on the western frontier of New Hampshire were dissatisfied with what they believed to be inadequate representation in that state's legislature and were willing to transfer their loyalties to the new state of Vermont. Allen, however, could not tolerate the admission of these towns because they would shift the balance of political control from western Vermont to the Connecticut Valley, and he quickly acted against this "Eastern Union."

Allen wrote to the governors of Vermont and New Hampshire protesting the former state's admission of the New Hampshire towns, and he traveled to Philadelphia, where he promised the New Hampshire delegate to the Continental Congress that the towns on the eastern bank of the Connecticut River would be returned to his state if New Hampshire supported Vermont's application for statehood. When he returned to Vermont, Allen gave the state legislature — which was meeting in Windsor in eastern Vermont — an extremely negative report on the reaction of Congress to Vermont's taking over the New Hampshire towns. He warned that "the whole power of the United States of America will join to annihilate the State of Vermont, to vindicate the right of New Hampshire, and to maintain inviolate the articles of confederation. . . ." Allen's dire words had their intended result. In the fall of 1778 the Vermont legislature decided not to recognize the inclusion of the New Hampshire towns in the eastern Vermont counties, and when the representatives reconvened in the western Vermont town of Bennington in February 1779 the western delegates, who this time outnumbered their eastern counterparts 29 to 21, were able to end the New Hampshire towns' association with Vermont.

As a result of the legislature's ejection of the New Hampshire towns, most of the area west of the Connecticut River declined further connection with Vermont. The fledgling Green Mountain State thus was reduced to a small number of western towns and a few isolated eastern towns. Allen realized this situation could not be tolerated and he began to intimidate the inhabitants of southeastern Cumberland County (today Windham County) to persuade them to join with Vermont.

Since the inhabitants of Cumberland County refused to acknowledge Vermont's draft law, Allen used this excuse to lead 100 of his Vermont followers into its precincts. There, he arrested 36 persons who sympathized with New York. As a show of force Allen persuaded a Vermont court to fine these "Yorkers." Vermont's governor, Thomas Chittenden, eventually pardoned the Yorkers, but the incident had considerable impact. The Yorkers wrote to New York's Governor George Clinton that Allen was "more to be dreaded than death with all its terrors," and Clinton, in turn, made a protest to the Continental Congress.

Although the war against Britain occupied the full attention of the Continental Congress, that body in 1779 realized it could no longer ignore the Vermont question. Congress asked the bordering states — New York, New Hampshire, and Massachusetts — to allow the national government to establish their respective boundaries. Vermont, however, was not asked to participate in these negotiations. Exclusion from the deliberations greatly antagonized the Vermont legislature that met in October 1779, and that body reaffirmed its independent status.

The war emergency delayed the Continental Congress's consideration of the problem. Meanwhile some Vermont leaders, perhaps acting on the belief that the Congress would never recognize an independent Vermont, began to explore the practicality of an alliance with the British. Ethan Allen and his brother, Ira Allen, realized that an enlarged Vermont would improve their bargaining power with the British. Thus with the help of the loyalists who inhabited the Connecticut Valley, Ira Allen persuaded a large number of the towns on both sides of that river to rejoin Vermont in April 1781. Then, at the urging of Ethan Allen, a number of towns located between the Hudson River and the area claimed by Vermont also voted to join Vermont.

News of Vermont's interest in negotiating with the British, and its absorption of New York and New Hampshire towns, quickly came to the attention of the Continental Congress. Ethan Allen even admitted to the president of the Congress that he had corresponded with the British colonel Beverly Robinson. But Allen showed no remorse over his activities, for he also stated: "I am as resolutely determined to defend the independence of Vermont as Congress that of the United States...."

The bold actions of Vermont's leaders impressed the Congress, and for a time it seemed that the Green Mountain State might gain admission to the Union in 1781. Congress could not acquiesce in Vermont's absorption of the New York and New Hampshire towns, but it resolved that Vermont be granted statehood if the towns in question were returned to the respective states. Unwilling to give up the towns, the Allens and some of their political allies continued to explore a possible rapprochement with British Canada. But the patriot victory at Yorktown in the fall of 1781 helped end the interest of most members of the Vermont legislature in a reunion with Britain; and the Vermont lawmakers, eager to be included in the United States, brought Vermont's association with the New York and New Hampshire towns to an end.

Despite Vermont's expulsion of the towns in question, it did not immediately gain the much-desired admission to the federal Union. Southern members of Congress were reluctant to increase the number of New England members in the Union, while those who represented states with western claims balked at establishing a state in an area claimed by one of the original states. Congress's failure to accept Vermont as a state disappointed many inhabitants of that region and revived the Allens' hope for a reunion with the British.

For a number of years the Allens urged upon the British their plan to cement a union between Vermont and Canada. But the British showed little enthusiasm for a commercial network extending along the waterways of Lake Champlain and the St. Lawrence River. By the Treaty of Paris of 1783 they recognized the northern boundary of the United States in the affected area to be the 45th parallel and thus they tacitly acknowledged the jurisdiction of the new American nation over the area of Vermont.

In the years following the end of the American Revolution, Vermont remained a center of controversy. The Cumberland (now Windham) County towns of Brattleboro, Guilford, and Halifax tried to restore their ties with the government of New York, but Ethan Allen brought them into submission. At Guilford he threatened: "I, Ethan Allen, do declare that I will give no quarter to any man, woman or child who shall oppose me, and unless the inhabitants of Guilford peacefully submit to the authority of Vermont, I swear I will lay it as desolate as Gomorrah, by God." Not all of Vermont's problems were so easily solved, however. Vermont suffered from some of the difficulties that beset the 13 original states during the "critical period" of the Articles of Confederation government. Inflation of currency was particularly serious. In fact, the fiscal situation deteriorated to such a point that debtors rioted in Rutland and Windsor in 1786, and the Vermont legislature was forced to pass a bill recognizing produce as legal tender for debt.

During the years after 1783 Vermont ceased its petitions for admission to the United States. Then, shortly after the adoption of the Constitution of 1787, Alexander Hamilton of New York persuaded Congress to reconsider Vermont statehood. In 1789, New York, which had previously blocked efforts to create a new state from the area that it claimed, agreed to consider a compromise. Settlement of the decades-old controversy followed in 1790. New York received $30,000 from Vermont in settlement of all land claims, and, in turn, agreed to Vermont's admission. The way was thus cleared for Vermont statehood, and the inhabitants of the area acted swiftly to join the Union. On January 6, 1791, Vermont ratified the US Constitution by a vote of 105 to four; and on March 4, 1791, Congress voted unanimously for Vermont to become the 14th member of the Union.

MARCH 5

The Boston Massacre

When British troops were quartered in Boston in 1768 the people of the city, especially the radicals favoring independence, resented it. There were frequent minor clashes between the civilians and the soldiers. One such clash occurred on March 5, 1770, when seven soldiers under the command of Captain Thomas Preston were pelted with stones and snowballs in King

Street (now State Street) by a crowd of 50 or 60 people. Under the tension of the moment, one of the soldiers fired his gun and the others followed him. Three of the crowd were killed outright and two others were mortally wounded.

One of the men killed immediately was one of the crowd's leaders, Crispus Attucks, who is often referred to as the first martyr of the American Revolution. Attucks was born in slavery about 1723 in the area of Framingham, Massachusetts, and is believed to have been of black, white, and Indian blood. In 1738 his master, Colonel Buckminster, sold him to William Brown. At the age of 27 Attucks took his first step toward liberty by running away from Brown. Brown advertised for him unsuccessfully in the Boston *Gazette*. By the time Attucks led members of the crowd from Dock Square to King Street, where they confronted the British soldiers, he had worked as a sailor for 20 years on whaling ships. John Adams described Attucks, who was six feet two inches tall, as "almost a giant in stature."

Champions of American independence — including Paul Revere, whose engraving of what became known as the Boston Massacre became a propaganda classic — lost no time in exploiting Attucks' death. Attucks and three other men killed were buried together, after an impressive funeral march, in the now-historic Granary Burying Ground, on Tremont Street, where they were later joined by other early patriots, including Revere and Samuel Adams. On the day following the Boston Massacre a mass meeting was held in an overflowing Faneuil Hall, where speeches were made denouncing the outrage and demanding that the troops be removed from the city at once. Faneuil Hall is today called the Cradle of Liberty because of mass meetings like this one, which were held in the famous assembly place during pre-Revolutionary days.

A week after the Boston Massacre, the British troops were transferred to Castle Island in Boston Harbor. In November, the soldiers and their commander were tried for murder and were defended by John Adams and Josiah Quincy. Two were found guilty of manslaughter and received light sentences, and the others were acquitted. Although Adams, as a lawyer, defended the soldiers, as a patriot he wrote in 1816: "Not the Battle of Lexington, not the surrender of Burgoyne or Cornwallis, were more important events in American history than the battle of King Street on March 5, 1770."

The next year the people of Boston, including many distinguished citizens, held a meeting in Old South Meeting House to commemorate the event. This custom of observing the anniversary of the Boston Massacre on March 5 was encouraged, especially by the Sons of Liberty, who staged a procession and oration to keep up resentment against the British. The observance was intended to show "the fatal effects of the policy of standing armies, and . . . of quartering regular troops in populous cities in time of peace." After the adoption of the Declaration of Independence in 1776 and the colonists' successful conclusion of the American Revolution in 1783, it was decided that the observance of the anniversary of the massacre should be combined with the observance of the day on which the Declaration of Independence had been adopted (see July 4, Independence Day).

This fact notwithstanding, March 5 is still the occasion for celebration. As required by law, the governor of Massachusetts annually issues a proclamation designating the day as the Anniversary of the Boston Massacre. The city of Boston, in cooperation with various black and civil rights groups, stages an observance that usually includes patriotic songs, recitation of the Pledge of Allegiance to the Flag, and speeches recalling the sacrifice of Attucks, whose blood, it is often said, was "the first . . . spilled for American liberty." These ceremonies customarily take place at the site of the Massacre in what is now State Street, beneath the east balcony of the city's Old State House, where the Declaration of Independence had its first reading in Boston in 1776.

Apart from the usual daytime observance, in 1970 — the 200th anniversary of the massacre — and in 1975 — the 200th anniversary of the beginning of the American Revolution — the same site also was the setting for an evening reenactment of the Boston Massacre, staged by the Charlestown Militia Company with the participation of neighboring militia units.

In 1888 a monument in memory of Crispus Attucks and the other four victims of the massacre was erected on Boston Common. The spot where the men fell, near the Old State House, was marked with a circle of paving stones, which can be seen today. Attucks was honored more specifically in the naming of American Legion post number 151 in Philadelphia, which still bears his name.

In New Jersey, March 5 is marked as Crispus Attucks Day. Newark, in 1968, became the first city in the nation to honor Attucks formally by proclaiming March 5 a school holiday and holding a special program. Presented by the Newark Human Rights Commission and the Crispus Attucks Society, the program featured historian John Williams as the principal speaker. The commemoration continued with Newark Mayor Hugh J. Addonizio's proclamation of March 17-

24 as Crispus Attucks Week, as well as with a parade conducted by the Crispus Attucks Society on Sunday, March 24. In subsequent years the annual parade has honored both Attucks and civil rights leader Martin Luther King Jr. (see January 15); it has been held in some years on or near the date of the Boston Massacre and in others on a date in April close to the anniversary of King's 1968 assassination (see April 4). Attucks has received increased attention in recent years, both in other New Jersey cities and elsewhere in the nation, where local school systems often mark March 5 with special programs and displays.

MARCH 6

Alamo Day

The anniversary of the fall of the Alamo, on March 6, 1836, in San Antonio, Texas, has great significance for Texans. Originally, the Alamo – today a national historic landmark – was known as Mission San Antonio de Valero, in honor of a Spanish viceroy. Its history extends back to the early days of Spanish settlement in Texas.

A Spanish expedition discovered an Indian village called Yanaguana in 1691 and christened the spot San Antonio de Padua. Though a cross and chapel were erected immediately in the new Spanish settlement, it was not until the second decade of the 18th century that the construction of a mission was begun by friars and artisans led by the Spanish Franciscan Fray Antonio de San Buenaventura Olivares. After a severe hurricane destroyed the primitive structure in 1724, the mission was moved to a nearby location, which became its permanent site – the present-day Alamo Plaza in the heart of downtown San Antonio.

The predecessor of four other missions along an eight-mile stretch of the tree-lined San Antonio River, Mission San Antonio de Valero originally consisted of a chapel, a two-story adobe convent and hospital building, a convent yard, and a plaza some two and a half acres in extent. The first stone of the chapel, which was to become a cherished relic of the Texan Revolution of 1835–1836, was laid on May 8, 1744. The finished structure, with its walls of hewn stone 4 feet thick and 22½ feet high, was formally dedicated only in the next decade. Surrounding the mission complex was a strong wall, 8 feet in height and varying in thickness from 2½ to 3½ feet.

With the disappearance of the Indians from the vicinity, Mission San Antonio de Valero

ceased to operate as a church institution in 1793. Unoccupied for several years, the abandoned and partially collapsed mission was secularized and fortified. It was used irregularly as barracks by Spanish troops in the early 19th century. A record of an 1803 baptism held in the former mission chapel already referred to the location as the Alamo.

According to some historians, the name Alamo is derived from the name of one of the military companies that occupied the mission, the Flying Company of San Carlos de Parras, from the Pueblo de San José y Santiago del Álamo in Mexico. Early records of these troops referred to their home in abbreviated fashion as the "pueblo del Álamo." Other scholars claim that the name came from the fact that the grounds around the mission were once covered with a grove of cottonwood trees – or, in Spanish, *álamos*.

Falling progressively into decay, the Alamo was a forgotten ruin, more than 100 years old and filled with debris, when the historic siege and massacre that took place there in 1836 made its name a rallying cry in Texas' struggle for independence from Mexico.

Beginning in the early 1820s, American colonists under *empresarios* like Stephen Austin had rushed to Texas (see April 21, San Jacinto Day). While at first generously allotting land grants to these foreign settlers, the Mexican government gradually grew distrustful of their increasing political ambitions and overwhelming numbers. Fearing an Anglo-American seizure of Texas, the Mexicans enacted a series of stringent measures aimed at tightening political control over the Texan area and restricting American immigration.

The main body of colonists, having accepted Mexican citizenship in good faith, at first tried moderate measures to secure greater liberties while remaining part of the Mexican union. They held meetings at San Felipe de Austin in October 1832 and again in April 1833 to protest Mexican oppression. The chief bone of contention was the colonists' desire that Texas – until then joined to the Mexican state of Coahuila – be separated from it and admitted to Mexican statehood "on an equal footing with any of the states," under a new, liberal constitution (see March 2, Texas Independence Day).

The situation, however, deteriorated once General Antonio López de Santa Anna firmly established himself as the reactionary dictator-president of Mexico. Affairs came to a climax in 1835, when Santa Anna, having dissolved the legislature of Coahuila and Texas, ordered Mexican troops northward to bring the Texans to heel. The first serious clash occurred at Gonzales on October 2, when a volunteer Texan army, armed with squirrel guns and hunting knives, defeated a Mexican force. Most of the Texan combatants, however, still had ambiguous feelings about what political goals they hoped to achieve from resistance. As one soldier wrote:

I cannot remember that there was any distinct understanding as to the position we were to assume toward Mexico. Some were for independence, some for the Constitution of 1824 [virtually voided by Santa Anna's arbitrary takeover], and some for anything, just so it was a row. But we were all ready to fight.

A week later, a force of about 50 Texans stormed the fort at Goliad to capture $10,000 worth of military supplies. A "consultation" of Texans, meeting at San Felipe de Austin from October 16 to November 14, 1835, issued a "declaration of the causes of taking up arms," but no attempt was made to secede from Mexico.

After seizing the Goliad arsenal, the Texans besieged San Antonio, where Santa Anna had sent his brother-in-law, General Martín Perfecto de Cos, to command the northern Mexican forces. On December 5 the Texans inched their way house by house into the town. By the night of December 8 they had forced a Mexican surrender in the partially ruined Alamo. It was humiliating for the Mexicans to be forced to relinquish a stronghold that they had held for more than 100 years, especially since it was their last foothold in Texas suitable as a base for military operations.

By the close of 1835 all Mexican troops had withdrawn from Texas, and many Texans thought the fighting was over. Others, however, realizing that their case for a new, liberal constitution was hopeless, began to lay plans for continuing the struggle against Mexican rule on a new basis. On December 20, 1835, the inhabitants of Goliad had already issued a declaration of independence. By mid-January of the following year, even the moderate Austin was encouraging complete separation from Mexico as the most desirable goal. A general convention to enact wide-ranging political changes was set by Texans for March 1 at Washington-on-the-Brazos.

At the start of February, as delegates were being elected for this convention, Santa Anna was assembling in Saltillo a large army under his personal command. He reportedly boasted: "If the Americans do not beware, I shall march through their own country and plant the Mexican flag in Washington." To ensure the success of his undertaking, the general burned candles at the pilgrimage shrine of the Virgin of Guadalupe near Mexico City — while at the same time he robbed the church to hire soldiers.

During this uncertain period before the Texan political goals had been clarified, confusion, apathy, and bickering among insurgents throughout Texas prevented the orderly supervision of military affairs. Some Texan leaders were convinced, however, that the Alamo in San Antonio should be held to bar Santa Anna's expected march into the interior. Colonel William Barret Travis, a young South Carolina lawyer who had earned a reputation as a firebrand for driving out the Mexican garrison at Anahuac, Texas, in June 1835, lightly garrisoned the Alamo with about 150 volunteers. Among them was James Bowie, an American land speculator and prospector in Texas, as well as a noted frontiersman whose epic-making deeds were already legend and after whom the bowie knife — which he wielded with deadly skill — was probably named. David ("Davy") Crockett, another famed hunter and scout, who had reputedly shot 105 bears in one year and who had served in Congress for three terms, was also present. James Butler Bonham, after borrowing funds to journey to Texas to fight for freedom, joined his lifelong friend Travis. In addition, some 20 to 30 noncombatants sought refuge within the walls of the mission compound.

Once Santa Anna and about 1,000 Mexicans had laid siege to the Alamo on February 23, they hoisted a blood-red flag signifying no quarter. The outnumbered and outgunned Texans responded to the demand for unconditional surrender with a cannon blast. Their position deteriorated steadily during the first days of the siege, when the arrival of reinforcements swelled Mexican forces to an estimated 4,000 to 5,000. Travis, fully aware of the perilous situation, pleaded for aid from other Texan outposts in a heroic message dated February 24, 1836, and addressed "To the People of Texas and all Americans in the World":

...I call on you in the name of Liberty, of patriotism and everything dear to the American character to come to our aid with all dispatch. The enemy is receiving reinforcements daily and will no doubt increase to three or four thousand in four or five days. If this call is neglected, I am determined to sustain myself as long as possible and die like a soldier who never forgets what is due to his honor and that of his country. VICTORY OR DEATH.

The appeal was answered by only 32 courageous men from Gonzales who slipped through the lines at 3:00 A.M. on March 1, even though defeat seemed inevitable. They raised the number of beleaguered Texans to about 187 (some scholars have estimated the total at about 200). While Santa Anna fired upon the mission walls for many days without making a breach, the delegates at Washington-on-the-Brazos drew up a declaration of independence on March 2 and continued to prepare for the separation of Texas from Mexico. Their action thus fulfilled one of Colonel Travis's last wishes, made in a letter to a friend:

Let the Convention go on and make a Declaration of Independence. . . . Let the Government declare [the Mexicans] public enemies, otherwise she is acting a suicidal part. . . . I shall treat them as such, unless I have superior orders to the contrary. . . . My respects to all friends, and confusion to all enemies. God bless you.

At daybreak on March 6, the 13th day of the Alamo siege, the Mexicans assaulted in force. The exhausted Texans awoke to the chilling sound of the Mexicans' *degüello* bugle call, meaning no quarter, and sprang to their posts. An eyewitness of the battle described the steady fire of cannons and small arms as a "constant thunder." Twice repulsed, the Mexicans breached the walls on the third attempt. Travis fell as they penetrated the mission. "The Texans defended desperately every inch of the fort," reported a Mexican soldier, "muzzle to muzzle, hand to hand, musket and rifle, bayonet and bowie knife." But finally the overwhelming Mexican numbers prevailed. The last survivors withdrew to the stone barracks and former chapel and fought until they were either riddled with grape and musket shot or impaled by bayonets. James Bowie, confined to bed with a raging fever, fired from his cot in the chapel building until slain. Most authorities agree that Davy Crockett died at his post, although some maintain he was one of five prisoners killed in cold blood after the battle upon order of Santa Anna. No male defender survived; some male servants and slaves, however, were among the 15 or more persons — mostly women and children — who were spared. The Texans' bodies were piled on layers of brush and wood and burned. The estimates of Mexican losses during the battle vary all the way from 600 to 1,600.

The brutality of Santa Anna aroused the Texans to fury, and they went into the battle of San Jacinto on April 21 with the cry "Remember the Alamo." They defeated Santa Anna, took him prisoner, and forced him to sign a treaty pledging the use of his influence to bring about a recognition of their independence.

An April 14, 1838, account described the Alamo as follows:

An outer wall inclosed the fort in front and reached out into the plaza, where was an entrance through two large gates. The walls had been partly demolished by cannon shots and the gates had been torn and twisted around and piles of rocks had been thrown up here and there. The ashes were still to be seen where the slain Texans were burned.

In 1849 Major E. B. Babbitt of the US Army repaired the chapel to serve as a quartermaster depot. He restored the walls to support a new roof, leaving the carved entranceway as originally constructed. In 1883 the chapel-fort was bought by the state for preservation as a monument. The surrounding property was added in 1905. In 1913 the city of San Antonio began restoration work, which was completed by 1939. As part of the 1936 Texas Centennial program, the state appropriated $250,000 to complete purchase of the block and convert the area into a park.

All that actually remains of the "cradle of Texas liberty" besides ivy-covered, crumbling walls is the little low chapel, dwarfed by a modern skyscraper. It remains as built, in the form of a cross with small rooms on each side of the large central part. Left of the chapel is the Alamo Museum in Spanish colonial style, opened to the public on October 11, 1937, and dedicated on October 14, 1938. It contains relics of the battle and of the Republic of Texas era.

The Heroes of the Alamo Cenotaph dominates Alamo Plaza, near the center of the former fortress grounds. Erected in 1939 and dedicated within a year, the cenotaph's blunt shaft displays on the south a heroic male figure, the Spirit of Sacrifice, rising from the sarcophagus of the slain heroes. On the north, the female Spirit of Truth bears under her arms shields of Texas and the United States. Representations of Travis, Crockett, Bonham, and Bowie provide focal points of interest among the groups of defenders on either side, while the names of the known heroes are engraved on the rim.

The celebration of March 6, Alamo Day, as Texas Heroes Day, began in 1897. Alamo memorial services have usually been held since then under the auspices of the Daughters of the Republic of Texas, who, since January 26, 1905, have been the official custodians of the historic building. Commemoration of the Alamo defenders is traditionally part of the Fiesta San Antonio (see April 21, San Jacinto Day), held annually in San Antonio during the last part of April. State, county, and municipal officials, military personnel, schoolchildren, and members of patriotic, civic, and professional organizations go in solemn pilgrimage to hear the names of the heroes recited and to place flowers in front of the former mission chapel.

MARCH 7

Luther Burbank's Birthday

California observes Arbor Day on the anniversary of the birth of Luther Burbank. Since 1886, Arbor Day had been celebrated with the planting of trees on various dates, but in 1909 the state legislature passed a bill providing that March 7 of each year, "being the anniversary of the birthday of Luther Burbank . . . [be] set apart and designated Bird and Arbor Day." And since 1915 the day has been known as Conservation, Bird, and Arbor Day. According to the statute that designated it as such, the day is observed "not as a holiday, but by including in the school work of the day suitable exercises having for their object instruction as to the economic value of birds and trees, and the promotion of a spirit of protection toward them, and as to the . . . value of natural resources, and the desirability of their conservation."

Luther Burbank was still alive when he was thus honored. He is also honored in California by the Luther Burbank Rose Festival in Santa Rosa. This three-day celebration, full of art and flower shows, music, sports, dances, and various special events, is highlighted by a Rose Festival parade. Occurring annually in mid-May, it succeeds an earlier Rose Carnival at which Burbank himself was a frequent honored guest. Today's reinstituted festivities have been held annually since 1950 under the auspices of the Santa Rosa Junior Chamber of Commerce. (The predecessor celebration took place intermittently in the years between 1894 and 1926, when it was abandoned because of Burbank's death that year. It was held once afterwards, in 1932.)

Burbank was born on a farm in Lancaster, Massachusetts, on March 7, 1849. He was educated until he reached the age of 15 in public schools and then at the Lancaster Academy — as well as by his own reading in the local library, including the works of Charles Darwin. He began market gardening in a small way as a youth and then, at 21, bought land near Lunenburg, Massachusetts, and began his life work of plant breeding. Within three years he had developed a new variety of potato now known as the Burbank potato. Shortly after that, in 1875, he migrated to Santa Rosa, California, where he established his nursery and greenhouse.

For the rest of his life he lived and worked there, experimenting with the production of new varieties of flowers, fruits, and vegetables. Their improvement through plant breeding, which utilized the methods of selection and hybridization, as well as grafting, has helped farmers use their land more productively and contributed greatly to the economy of the state and nation. Burbank produced new forms of tomatoes, corn, squash, beans, peas, artichokes, asparagus, corn, chives and rhubarb, among other innovations. He worked intensively with plums, prunes, and berries and introduced, for example, the famous Shasta daisy, a number of new strains of roses, and various lilies. In all, during more than 50 years of work Burbank developed over 800 new strains and varieties of fruits, flowers, and forage plants — including a spineless cactus — through experimentation with countless numbers of seedlings. Since his purpose was a practical rather than a theoretical one, he did not keep systematic records of his experiments, and many details of his work have not been available to scientists interested in heredity. His work, however, stimulated worldwide interest in the field of plant breeding.

Burbank's birthplace and garden office buildings can be seen in Greenfield Village in Dearborn, Michigan, Henry Ford's collection of historic buildings and museum of Americana. Burbank's grave and California home, now the Luther Burbank Memorial House and Gardens, are today owned and maintained by the Santa Rosa Junior College. The gardens are open to the public.

The plant breeder's work is described in his writings, which include *New Creations* (1893–1901), a series of catalogs describing new plant varieties; the 12-volume *Luther Burbank: His Methods and Discoveries;* the eight-volume *How Plants Are Trained to Work for Man;* and, with Wilbur Hall, *The Harvest of the Years* and *Partner of Nature.* The tireless Burbank died on April 11, 1926. At the time, he was working on more than 3,000 experiments, and he was growing thousands of botanical species, many of them native to other countries.

MARCH 8

Simon Cameron's Birthday

Simon Cameron, the first powerful state "boss" in American politics, was born March 8, 1799, in Lancaster County, Pennsylvania, the state he later controlled. Orphaned at the age of nine and receiving little schooling, he was thrown on his own resources early in life.

His early years were spent in newspaper publishing, a trade that brought him into contact with the worlds of both business and politics. Becoming an apprentice in a printing office in Harrisburg, he worked there until he was 22, when he went to Doylestown to edit a Democratic newspaper. A year later he returned to Harrisburg as a partner in the ownership of a newspaper, worked a short while in Washington, D.C., also in the newspaper business, and then returned again to Harrisburg as owner of the Harrisburg *Republican.*

Thus, by the age of 25, Cameron was well established in business and he was by this time also beginning to be influential in the state Democratic party. Ownership of the newspaper gave him influence in state and national politics, and he became an associate of James Buchanan, later to be elected President. In 1826 Cameron was appointed state printer, a profitable post that provided the means for branching out into the many business interests that together with shrewd investments later brought him a great fortune.

As soon as he had accumulated enough capital, he pursued his fortune in banking, canal and railroad construction, iron and steel manufacturing, and eventually ownership of railroads. He began buying small local railroads and later united them into a network known as the Northern Central line.

Meanwhile, Cameron's political strength and ambitions increased. He promoted the nomination of Andrew Jackson for the presidency in 1828 and the election of James Buchanan to the Senate in 1834. In 1845 Cameron himself was elected to replace Buchanan in the Senate when Buchanan left to enter President James Polk's cabinet. Originally a regular Democrat, Cameron was by this time well on his way to becoming one of the most powerful political bosses in the country, a status he retained thenceforth. However, he had maneuvered his election to the Senate through means that brought him the enmity of Buchanan (who had had another candidate in mind) and the regular Democratic party members. Cameron was supported in that election by a coalition of Whigs, Native Americans, and Protectionist Democrats. His next two attempts at reelection to the Senate were unsuccessful, but he succeeded on his third try, in 1857, as the candidate of the new Republican party.

In 1860 Cameron was unsuccessful as a Republican presidential candidate and gave his support to Lincoln in return for a promise made by Lincoln's managers for a cabinet post. Lincoln kept the promise, appointing Cameron as secretary of war, but with considerable reluctance. The President's misgivings proved justified when corruption in the awarding of army contracts and appointments aroused the nation. Cameron had run the war office with the same favoritism that characterized his tactics in Pennsylvania.

Largely to ease him out of the cabinet, Lincoln sent him to Russia as the American minister. While there, Cameron succeeded in getting Russia's support for the Union side during the US Civil War. Within a year, though, he resigned and returned to the United States to campaign, unsuccessfully, for a seat in the Senate — in the same year that the House of Representatives passed a resolution of censure against him. Still undaunted, he tried again in 1867 and won a seat, which he held until he resigned 10 years later — so that he could relinquish his seat to his son, James Donald ("Don") Cameron.

Don Cameron kept the seat in the Senate for many years and was secretary of war under Ulysses S. Grant. He also assumed control of the Republican machine in Pennsylvania, which he ran for two decades in succession to his father. Following the younger Cameron, the state political dynasty was controlled successively by Matthew Stanley Quay, Boies Penrose, William S. Vare, and Joseph R. Grundy, each selected by his predecessor. This Republican machine was so powerful that it dominated Pennsylvania politics until 1936, when Franklin D. Roosevelt carried the state in a presidential election.

Simon Cameron spent the latter period of his life in retirement. He died at 90, on June 26, 1889. Attributed to him is a famous cynical definition of an honest politician as "one who, when he is bought, will stay bought."

Oliver Wendell Holmes Jr.'s Birthday

Oliver Wendell Holmes Jr., the celebrated American jurist and son of the distinguished American writer and physician of the same name (see August 29), was born in Boston on March 8, 1841. A member of a very well-known family of clergymen, lawyers, and judges, he inherited their Puritan sense of responsibility along with his father's wit and charm. His father's friends were such men as Ralph Waldo Emerson, James Russell Lowell, and Henry Wadsworth Longfellow. The son, growing up among these Boston Brahmins while his father became famous as a poet and as author of *The Autocrat of the Breakfast Table,* early showed a critical and independent spirit as well as an interest in philosophy and art; among his friends were Charles Francis,

Henry and Brooks Adams, Henry and William James, and Charles Sanders Peirce.

Holmes received the best education available, at a dame school, Public Latin School in Boston (directed by his future father-in-law), and at Harvard College. Just after his graduation from Harvard in 1861 he was commissioned in the Massachusetts 20th Volunteers, one of the most heroic divisions fighting for the Union in the Civil War. On the staff of General H. G. Wright, Holmes fought in some of the bloodiest battles of the war — Ball's Bluff, Antietam, and Fredericksburg — and was wounded three times.

He was the subject of his father's essay "The Captain." Much influenced by having such great responsibility early in life, Holmes met the challenge with a characteristic realism. Upon returning to Boston a hero, he shocked social sentimentalists who talked of warfare in glorious terms by calling war an "organized bore."

After completing studies at the Harvard Law School in 1866, Holmes made the first of many trips to England, where he developed lifelong friendships. Though a primary interest in these years was philosophy, he decided on law as his career, and, after being admitted to the bar in 1867, he began practicing in Boston. Within the next few years he became a master of his profession. In addition to his association with a Boston law firm, he began lecturing as an instructor on constitutional law at Harvard Law School and contributed to, and from 1870 to 1873 edited, the *American Law Review*. He also edited the 12th edition of Kent's *Commentaries,* then the most comprehensive work on law, which appeared in 1873. Meanwhile, in 1872, Holmes was married to Fanny Bowditch Dixwell, a Bostonian of great charm.

In 1880 Holmes delivered a series of lectures at Boston's Lowell Institute, which were published the following year in the book that made him famous: *The Common Law.* This book has become a classic in its field, for it so reoriented legal inquiry that its ideas have become part of basic juristic thought. Holmes's approach to this study of the law is the essence of the book; it is summarized in the opening sentence — "The life of the law has not been logic; it has been experience." Holmes was examining the very foundations of the law, and in so doing he substituted a critical attitude for one of unquestioning reverence. The orthodox view of the common law, that body of American law inherited from the (unwritten) English common law, was that it embodied a perfect legal system and that legal opinions were to be achieved through a series of logical deductions based on hallowed precedent.

But Holmes the philosopher was not orthodox. He questioned the sources and sanctions of the law. He considered what is appropriate lawmaking by courts and what should be left to legislation. He recognized the unconscious ingredients of adjudication and sought to distinguish between these and conscious considerations. He saw the law as a response to historic needs and distinguished between the immediate impetus for the formation of individual laws and the later application of the structure of those laws. The law as a whole, he held, was comprehensible only in terms of the needs of the society it regulated. It could not be understood simply as a collection of rules erected on a foundation of logic.

As a result of the international acclaim for this book, Holmes was offered the newly created Weld Chair at the Harvard Law School in 1882. Within another year he was appointed an associate justice of the supreme judicial court of Massachusetts. He accepted this appointment, preferring the service and conflict of the court to the ivory tower of the scholar, even though he distinguished himself as a scholar and philosopher. He was associated with the Massachusetts court for 20 years, serving for the last 3 as its chief justice. His work there left almost 1,300 opinions, which, if considered as a whole would make up the most comprehensive and philosophic body of law for any period of American history.

In 1902 Justice Holmes was appointed an associate justice of the US Supreme Court by President Theodore Roosevelt. Holmes held the post for 30 years, earning his place in judicial history as one of the Court's greatest members, unsurpassed in the depth of his perception and the originality of its exposition. It is the work of the Supreme Court to interpret the Constitution, and when the decision of the nine members of the Court is not unanimous, both the dissenting and majority opinions are studied. During his years with the Court, Justice Holmes delivered so many dissenting opinions that he came to be known as the Great Dissenter, but his dissents have been highly influential, serving as precedents for many of today's legal decisions.

Holmes joined the Court at a time when vigorous legislative activity reflected a drastically changing society that was becoming increasingly powerful through technological development. He studied the claims of contesting structures of power with detachment, unaffected by personal prejudice or political interest. He viewed the law as an expression of overlapping social policies and thought the judicial function was that of accommodating conflicting needs.

He was considered the leader of the liberal wing of the Court because he usually ruled to permit social legislation (although he was not sympathetic to all views considered liberal in his day). A strong advocate of judicial restraint, he firmly believed that the will of the electorate, or its elected representatives, should not be thwarted lightly.

Many of Holmes's opinions are important because the issues contained a germ of a wider theory that had a bearing on the interpretation of the Constitution. He criticized the Sherman Antitrust Act, for example, in the *Northern Securities* case (1904), but his conception of the nature of commerce paved the way for an increasingly broad interpretation of the commerce clause. In the case of *Schenck* v. *US* (1919), a case governing interpretation of the First Amendment's language on freedom of speech, he ruled that "the question in every case is whether . . . words are used in such circumstances and are of such a nature as to create a clear and present danger"—a now famous declaration. In the same year he made an eloquent plea, in the *Abrams* case, for "free trade in ideas."

Many of Holmes's most important opinions were written in the last years of his life. He resigned from the Supreme Court in 1932 at the age of 90 and died three years later, on March 6, 1935. Buried at Arlington National Cemetery, he left the bulk of his estate to the nation. In addition to *The Common Law*, his published works include *Speeches* (1891, revised in 1913 and 1938), *Collected Legal Papers* (1920), *Dissenting Opinions of Mr. Justice Holmes* (1929), *Representative Opinions of Mr. Justice Holmes* (1931), *Justice Oliver Wendell Holmes: His Book Notices and Uncollected Letters and Papers* (1936), and two volumes of letters (1941 and 1953).

MARCH 9

Edwin Forrest's Birthday

Edwin Forrest was the first American actor to win international acclaim. Born in Philadelphia on March 9, 1806, of Scottish and German parentage, Forrest made his debut in Philadelphia when he was only 14, playing in *Douglas* by John Home. He gained subsequent experience by touring the frontier circuit for several years, and then playing supporting roles with the English actor Edmund Kean. When Forrest was 20 he scored a brilliant success while making his New York debut in Shakespeare's *Othello*. The performance established him as one of the great tragedians of his century.

In the next decade he became the leading American actor, playing various Shakespearean

tragic roles and commissioning tragedies by American playwrights to provide vehicles for his vigorous style of acting. In 1836, he appeared at the Drury Lane Theatre in London in a specially written play, *The Gladiator,* by Robert M. Bird, which won for its author a cash prize offered by Forrest, and provided the actor with one of his most successful roles — that of Spartacus.

Forrest's success in England and in the United States was so great that he amassed a large fortune. He built a castle, which he called Fonthill, on the Hudson River. Later, however, he sold the castle and bought an estate in the northern part of Philadelphia, which he called Spring Brook and to which he transferred his large library and art collection.

It was when he was in London in 1845 that a long-running feud began between Forrest and the English Shakespearean actor William Charles Macready. The feud aroused the anti-British feelings that years later caused the Astor Place riot of 1849 while Macready was appearing in New York City; in that riot 22 people were killed and 36 were injured. However, neither this disaster, nor a sensational divorce suit Forrest brought against his wife, the former Catherine Sinclair, diminished the actor's popularity. He continued to play to large audiences until his final performance, as Richelieu in Bulwer-Lytton's *Richelieu, or The Conspiracy*, in 1871.

It was only a year after his retirement that Forrest died, at his Philadelphia mansion, on December 12, 1872, of a stroke. He left the greater part of his estate to found the Edwin Forrest Home for Retired Actors in Philadelphia. Members of the home commemorate their benefactor's birth by laying a wreath at his crypt annually on March 9. Forrest is buried at St. Paul's Protestant Episcopal church, which is preserved as a historic site in Philadelphia. He is also honored by the annual Shakespearean performances held at the home on April 23, Shakespeare's birthday. In 1976, the 200th anniversary year of American independence, a special bicentennial birthday salute was staged in Philadelphia's Independence Square at noon on Forrest's March 9 birthday.

MARCH 10

Albany Becomes the Capital of New York

Following the defeat of British General John Burgoyne at Saratoga in 1777 (see October 17), Albany was the seat of government of New York at intervals for the next 20 years. It was not until March 10, 1797, however, that it was definitely selected as the capital of the state and plans were made for the erection of a State House.

An important inland seaport and transportation crossroad, the Albany site had been the object of several early colonization efforts. In 1540 the French established a short-lived trading post thereabouts. Later the region reverted to wilderness, until in 1609 Henry Hudson, a sea captain in the employ of the Estates General of Holland, sailed the *Half Moon* 142 miles up the river that today bears his name. He claimed the territory, and within five years the Dutch established a trading post, Fort Nassau, in the area, but they abandoned it in 1619. The first actual settlers were 18 Walloon families sent out by the Dutch West India Company, who arrived in 1624.

Disembarking on the banks of the Hudson 17 years after the English settlement at Jamestown, Virginia, and three years after the Pilgrims had established their colony at Plymouth, Massachusetts, these settlers built Fort Orange — the third oldest permanent settlement within the limits of the 13 original colonies. To populate this area further, the Dutch West India Company originated a system of patroonships. The only successful patroon was Kiliaen Van Rensselaer, who in 1630 received an extensive tract of land surrounding Fort Orange. He in turn rented the land to settlers recruited in Holland. This colony, originally called Rensselaerwyck, became Beverwyck in the 1650s. After the transfer of New Netherland from the Dutch to the English in 1664, the name of the village was changed to Albany in honor of the Duke of York and Albany, who later became King James II of England.

For several decades after the English conquest of New Netherland, the Van Rensselaer family petitioned the British crown to obtain recognition of the patroonship. These efforts failed, and in 1686 Thomas Dongan, governor of the colony of New York, granted Albany a city charter — under which it still operates. The document, the oldest city charter in the United States, gave complete control of all vacant lands within the city limits to the mayor, aldermen, and commonality. Pieter Schuyler was the first mayor.

Perhaps the most significant event to occur in the city was the famous intercolonial conference of 1754, known as the Albany Congress. At this meeting delegates from the New England colonies, New York, Pennsylvania, and Maryland considered Benjamin Franklin's plan for a federation of colonies. Many historians consider this to have been the first attempt at intercolonial cooperation prior to the American Revolution.

Among the many historic and governmental places of interest in Albany that are open to visitors are the Schuyler Mansion and other early homes, the State Education Building (which houses the state museum and the state library), the French chateau-style Capitol, and the massive new governmental and cultural complex known as South Mall.

Treaty of Guadalupe Hidalgo Ratified

On March 10, 1848, the Treaty of Guadalupe Hidalgo was ratified by the US Senate, ending the war between Mexico and the United States, which had begun on May 13, 1846 (see May 13). The treaty was signed at the village of Guadalupe Hidalgo, near Mexico City, on February 2, 1848 (see February 2).

MARCH 11

The Blizzard of 1888

The legendary blizzard of 1888, certainly the most famous snowstorm in US history, hit the northeastern states on March 11 of that year. The blizzard conditions — high winds, low temperatures, and heavy snowfall — continued for 36 hours. Blustery winds whipped the snowfall into impassable drifts, and people lost all sense of direction in the driving, swirling snow. The result was 400 deaths due to exposure to the cold temperatures and merciless winds. One victim was Roscoe Conkling in New York City, the leader of the Republican party in New York and US senator from 1867 to 1881. Conkling, at the time in private law practice, walked from his office in Wall Street to his house on 14th Street during the blizzard. He died about a month later from the effects of exposure.

In New York City the 20.9-inch snowfall was blown into 12-foot-high drifts — in Herald Square the snow measured 30 feet deep. All transportation was brought to a standstill, except for sleighs. The stock exchanges closed. Communications were cut off, and telegraph messages from New York City to Boston had to be transmitted by way of England.

New York City was isolated from the rest of the country and virtually the world, and New Yorkers were marooned in their homes, threatened by a food panic in addition to their other woes. Because of the snowdrifts, fire-fighting equipment could not reach fires, which caused an estimated property loss of $25 million.

Not long after the storm, an organization called the Blizzard Men of 1888 was formed in New York City. For years, members of the group met each year to mark the anniversary of the storm by recalling their experiences. Although the stories they exchanged seemed like tall tales, there was probably little need for exaggeration. One member, who had been a boy in Philadelphia at the time of the storm, recalled that the snowdrifts reached the second-story windows of his house and that 28 horses were hitched to the snowplow on the streetcar tracks. Another member noted that the wind velocity was 84 miles per hour and that the thermometer registered four degrees below zero Fahrenheit. A salesman in a shoe store reported that he sold 1,200 pairs of men's rubber boots that week.

Although there have since been heavier snowfalls — at least one heavier one in New York City alone: on December 26, 1947, a paralyzing 25.8 inches of snow fell in less than 16 hours — no storm has equaled the Great Blizzard of 1888 in the unfortunate combination of severe cold, strong winds, heavy snowfall, number of human casualties, and extent of property damage. Even to the present time, newspapers continue to note the anniversary of the legendary Blizzard of '88.

MARCH 12

Girl Scouts Founded

The Girl Scout Birthday, on March 12, is the anniversary of Juliette Low's 1912 founding of the Girl Scouts of the United States of America in Savannah, Georgia. It is the focal point of Girl Scout Week, observed each year by the organization's more than 3 million members. The week, which always begins on the Sunday of the week containing March 12, is marked with special birthday ceremonies and other observances by troops of 6- through 17-year-old Girl Scouts in the United States and Troops on Foreign Soil (composed of American girls who are living abroad) in countries around the world. Traditionally, each of the seven days of Girl Scout Week highlights one of the program areas — such as service, citizenship, international friendship, the out-of-doors, health, and safety — that are stressed in the Girl Scouts' program of helping girls to "develop as happy, resourceful individuals willing to share their abilities as citizens in their homes, their communities, their country and the world." The United States, as represented by the Girl Scouts of the USA, is one of the approximately 100 member nations of the World Association of Girl Guides and Girl Scouts.

The 50th, 60th, and 64th birthdays of girl scouting in the United States were observed with particular ceremony. In the golden anniversary year of 1962, Vice President of the United States Lyndon B. Johnson was co-host of a March 12 congressional luncheon held in Washington, D.C., with 80 members of Congress and their Girl Scout daughters or granddaughters among the 181 persons in attendance. The US Post Office issued a four-cent commemorative stamp, and Girl Scout Week became Girl Scout Month in that milestone year. To mark the organization's 60th birthday, in 1972, a facsimile edition of the first Girl Scout handbook, *How Girls Can Help Their Country,* was published.

In 1976 Girl Scouts held a twofold celebration, marking US Girl Scouting's 64th birthday and the nation's bicentennial. Around the world, Girl Scouts lit candles, symbolic "flames of freedom," at 5:00 PM on March 12. The lighting of "flames of freedom" symbolized gifts of service by Girl Scouts to communities across the nation. A national pledge of service had been made at the opening ceremony of the Girl Scout national council meeting in Washington, D.C., on October 26, 1975, when First Lady Betty Ford, honorary Girl Scout president, lit the first symbolic flame.

The existence of a US organization devoted to citizenship, service, health, and character-building in girls was foreshadowed early in the life of Juliette ("Daisy") Gordon, born on October 31, 1860. (The house in Savannah in which she was born, now called the Juliette Gordon Low Girl Scout National Center, is both a Girl Scout shrine and a national historic landmark.) One of the six children of Eleanor Kinzie Gordon and Captain William Washington Gordon, she grew up as an adventurous child with a penchant for pets, games, drawing, writing, and an early flair for organization, as evidenced in the Helpful Hands club she formed to make clothes for needy children. At 14 she was sent to boarding school in Virginia, and she later attended a French school in New York City and traveled extensively in the United States and abroad. On November 21, 1886, she was married to a wealthy Englishman, William Mackay Low, whose family owned a house on Savannah's Lafayette Square. The young couple took up residence in London, where Juliette Low, undaunted by the progressive deafness that had begun to afflict her, became a famous hostess. She returned to the United States during the Spanish-American War of 1898, helping her mother organize a hospital for soldiers in Florida, where her father, by then a general, was stationed. At war's end, she rejoined her husband in England.

After the death of her husband in 1905, Juliette Low filled the next six years' uncertainty about the purpose of her life with art studies and travel. In the spring of 1911, however, her interest in the scouting movement was aroused through a chance meeting with Sir Robert S. S. Baden-Powell, who had founded the Boy Scouts in England three years earlier (see February 8). The enthusiasm of Baden-Powell and his sister Agnes — who in 1910 had joined him to form the Girl Guides as a sister organization to the Boy Scouts — proved to be contagious. In a short time, Low became a Girl Guide leader, starting her first troop of guides in a lonely valley of Scotland during the summer of 1911. On her return to London in the fall, she founded two more troops.

It was in 1912 that she transported the Girl Guides idea to Savannah, where she organized 18 girls from a friend's school into the first US troop on March 12. The first name in the register that the girls signed was that of a younger Daisy Gordon, Juliette Low's niece and namesake (who, as Daisy Gordon Lawrence, has since been frequently honored as the first Girl Scout). For a time, Low herself led the pioneer US troop, teaching fire building, simple outdoor cookery, knot tying, and other skills that were novelties to the girls of 1912. Meanwhile, she also trained new leaders to carry on the work. After her return to England, she sent back innumerable letters to push the work ahead — including advice to the Savannah troops, instructions to adults who were organizing new troops elsewhere, information about the movement to others she wanted to interest. On subsequent US visits, she traveled the Eastern seaboard, charming, persuading, and impelling workers into effort on behalf of the movement.

In 1913, the year that the name of the US organization was changed from Girl Guides to Girl Scouts, she opened a national headquarters in Washington, D.C., and put it in the charge of the first paid Girl Scout worker, Edith D. Johnston of Savannah. As a result of Low's energetic promotional activities, inquiries poured into the new national office from all parts of the country, and membership increased rapidly. Headquarters of the organization were moved in 1916 to New York City. Within the next three years, the membership roll reached 41,225.

Juliette Low retired from the presidency of the organization in 1920, receiving the title of founder. She devoted her remaining years to the development of international guiding, acting as liaison between the Girl Scouts of the United States and the Girl Guide organizations of European countries during her constant travels. She attended the first three international conferences of Girl Guides and Girl Scouts, held in England in 1920, 1922, and 1924; and she saw a dream realized when the fourth international conference was held in the United States in 1926. One of her successors as president of the Girl Scouts of the USA, Lou Henry Hoover, who held the post in 1922–1925 and 1935–1937, was the wife of the 31st President. Honorary presidents have included all the nation's First Ladies since Edith Wilson.

At the time of Juliette Low's death, on January 17, 1927, there were more than 140,000 Girl Scouts, with troops in every state of the Union. Membership in the organization she had founded, financed, promoted, and directed during its early years continued to grow under new leadership after her death. By the time of the Silver Anniversary Convention in Savannah in 1937, members numbered more than 400,000. On July 3, 1948, President Harry S. Truman signed a bill authorizing a three-cent Juliette Gordon Low commemorative postage stamp. During World War II a liberty ship was named in her honor, and in 1954 the city of Savannah, where she had been laid to rest in her Girl Scout uniform, named a new school for her. Low's October 31 birthday meanwhile had been designated as Girl Scouts' Founder's Day in 1920. It is the occasion of annual observances by Girl Scout troops across the nation.

Requirements for membership in the organization, which was chartered by the US Congress on March 16, 1950, are that girls be 6 through 17 years old, actively participate in the Girl Scout program, pay annual national membership dues, and adhere to the Girl Scout Promise and Law. New wording of the Promise and Law was adopted in 1972. The Promise now states, "On my honor, I will try: to serve God, my country and mankind, and to live by the Girl Scout Law." The Law stipulates that a girl do her best to be honest, fair, helpful, cheerful, friendly and considerate, a sister to every Girl Scout; respect authority, use resources wisely, protect and improve the world around her; and show respect for herself and others through her words and actions.

The Girl Scouts have adapted their program to changing needs and social patterns over the years. As one scout herself put it, "They don't think of us anymore as little girls in green selling cookies or playing games." The emphasis today is on relevance — to the problems of the world, nation, and individual community, and on programs that will help to provide real answers. Girl Scouts today are concerned with combating racism; encouraging ecological conservation; helping the elderly, disadvantaged, and handicapped; and providing community services.

Within this broad outlook, the program, in general terms, is as follows: Members are divided into groups called Brownie Girl Scouts (ages 6 to 8 or grades 1, 2, and 3); Junior Girl Scouts (ages 9 to 11 or grades 4, 5, and 6); Cadette Girl Scouts (12 to 14 or grades 7, 8, and 9); and Senior Girl Scouts (14 to 17 or grades 10, 11, and 12).

The variety of program materials available to

all Girl Scouts is designed to help develop the individual and to provide sufficient choices to meet different needs and situations. The four program emphases — deepening self-awareness, relating to others, contributing to the community, and developing values — permeate activities. These are carried out in troops and in camps. Some of the specific activities, which cover a wide range, fall under such headings as being useful (community service, career exploration, homemaking, first aid); developing responsibility (citizenship, preserving the environment); being creative (arts and crafts, music, dance, dramatic arts, storytelling); and having fun (hikes, games, organized excursions, sports, outdoor living).

Brownie Scouts learn to make friends and develop simple skills. Juniors broaden talents and develop new skills, working toward any of 47 proficiency badges, each with its own set of requirements, in fields that interest them. In addition, Juniors may earn the Sign of the Arrow and the Sign of the Star. Each is a symbol that a girl has participated in activities related to the basics of Scouting. Cadette Girl Scouts, who concentrate on 12 "challenges," can strive for their choices among more than 60 more advanced, proficiency badges. One goal many Cadettes work toward is First Class, the highest award in Cadette Girl Scouting. The more independent Senior Scouts may form troops concentrating on the arts, the diversity of cultures, the natural world, or their own special interests. In addition, Senior Scouts may become involved in Senior Service Aide projects arranged with libraries, hospitals, museums, and other institutions and organizations to provide opportunities for both community service and career exploration, and to give the girls the training, skills, and experience necessary for such service.

Girl Scouts who are at least 13 years old may attend events with nationwide participation sponsored by the national organization or by councils. International opportunities for Seniors include attendance at gatherings in one of the centers of the World Association of Girl Guides and Girl Scouts (in Switzerland, England, Mexico, and India); visits to Girl Scout and Girl Guide camps abroad; and living with families in other countries.

The Girl Scouts' organization is guided by volunteer leadership with the support of administrative staff at the national and council levels. The councils, which are established, developed, maintained, and financed by local volunteers, make scouting available to girls in communities across the nation, often with the cooperation of clubs, schools, church or synagogue groups, and other organizations. The national organization, which charters the councils, is financed principally by nominal annual membership dues. The organization's governing body is the National Council, consisting of delegates elected by Girl Scout councils throughout the United States. Adult membership accounted for 511,000 of the more than 3 million members reported by the organization in 1975.

MARCH 13

Clarence Darrow's Death

Clarence Seward Darrow, one of the most famous criminal lawyers in the history of the United States, died on March 13, 1938. In his relentless lifelong campaign against hatred, ignorance, prejudice, and bigotry, Darrow invariably chose to represent the underdog, attempting to secure for his clients equal rights, equal protection, and a fair trial. During the 1903 anthracite coal strike, for example, he reminded the arbitration commission selected by President Theodore Roosevelt that the operators, not the workers, possessed every asset in the hearings: "Their social advantages are better, their religious privileges are better, they speak the English language better. . . . They can hire . . . expert accountants, and they have got the advantage of us in almost every particular, and we will admit all that — " " at which point, the chairman interjected, "All except the lawyers."

Darrow followed in the footsteps of the 18th century Italian criminologist Cesare Beccaria in adamantly opposing capital punishment. He used persuasive oratory to plead for more than 100 persons accused of murder. Only one of them was ever given the death sentence. Darrow's brilliantly argued cases, based on the principle of justice tempered with kindness and understanding, made him a legend years before his death. In his obituary, the Chicago *Daily News* came to the conclusion that "in the pure sense of the word, Darrow was not a criminal lawyer. He was rather a practicing philosopher, a student of society, of crime, its causes and cures."

Born near Kinsman, Ohio, on April 18, 1857, Clarence Darrow had completed only one year of law school when he was admitted to the bar of Ohio in 1878. After practicing law in Ashtabula, Ohio, he settled in 1887 in Chicago, where he soon made an impact as a public speaker and lawyer. He won the respect and friendship of a powerful supporter, John Peter Altgeld, an established attorney and political leader who was to be elected governor of Illinois in 1892. Through Altgeld's influence, Darrow was appointed assistant corporation counsel, then acting corporation counsel, of Chicago. Darrow and Altgeld shared a deep concern for the so-called Haymarket anarchists, a common bond which helped to draw them even closer together.

Not long before Darrow went to Chicago, the city had been violently disrupted by the Haymarket Square riot. During a mass rally condemning police brutality in the McCormick Works strike, a bomb had been hurled, killing seven policemen and wounding 67 other persons. Eight anarchists had been arrested as perpetrators. Although conclusive evidence of their guilt had been lacking, four of the men were executed; one committed suicide on the eve of his execution; one received a 15-year prison sentence; and the remaining two were condemned to life imprisonment. Convinced that their trial had been a travesty, Darrow became involved in the amnesty movement for the three jailed anarchists, and in 1893 he was instrumental in persuading Governor Altgeld not only to pardon the imprisoned men, but also to exonerate their fellow anarchists who had been executed.

After serving a few years as Chicago's legal adviser, Clarence Darrow accepted the position of general attorney for the Chicago & North Western Railway. In 1894 the American Railway Union, under the presidency of Eugene Victor Debs, boycotted the servicing of pullman cars in support of striking workers of the Pullman Car Company of Pullman, Illinois, whose wages had been cut. Darrow found himself siding with the strikers and hard pressed to reconcile his own sympathies with the position he had to uphold as representative of the railroad corporation. When the railroads were granted an injunction against the strikers and Debs was indicted for conspiracy and imprisoned, the highly regarded corporation lawyer gave up his lucrative career. He became the champion of labor before the union was recognized as a lawful organization entitled to wield the weapons of the strike and boycott to improve wages and working conditions. Darrow's celebrated defense of Eugene Debs brought him nationwide recognition in labor and criminal affairs. From then on until he eventually "retired" at an advanced age, Darrow exerted his courtroom skill in a series of notable trials embracing a variety of controversial causes.

The William D. Haywood, Charles H. Moyer, George Pettibone, and Steve Adams cases revolved around the bombing murder of Frank Steunenberg, former governor of Idaho, on December 20, 1905. The 1920 Communist labor case, involving the 1919 Illinois Sedition Act, centered upon 20 Communists who had been accused of advocating a forceful overthrow of the government. In the Scopes trial of 1925, Darrow served as defense counsel — in this case unsuccessfully — for a Tennessee schoolteacher who had violated a state law that prohibited the teaching in public schools of Darwin's theory of human evolution from lower forms of life. In this so-called monkey trial, one of Darrow's targets was the fundamentalist political leader and orator William Jennings Bryan, a member of the prosecution staff. The 1926 *Sweet* case concerned racial violence arising from housing segregation in Detroit, while the 1932 Thomas H. Massie trial in Honolulu focused on the revenge slaying of an alleged rapist.

One of the most famous of Darrow's defenses was in the 1924 Chicago "thrill" murder trial of two youths, Nathan Leopold and Richard Loeb, both sons of prominent, respected, and wealthy Chicago businessmen. Wanting to commit the perfect crime "for the sake of a thrill," the two kidnapped and murdered 14-year-old Bobby Franks. Darrow, having been begged to defend the youths despite their confessions, accepted the difficult assignment not, as was rumored at the time, because of the fee expected from the millionaire parents, but because of the opportunity the case offered for expressing his ideas on capital punishment. The 67-year-old veteran attorney delivered a moving, 12-hour-long plea, by which he saved his clients from execution on the grounds of temporary insanity. A contemporary newspaper reporter commented that the lines in Darrow's face were "deeper, the eyes haggard. But there was no sign of physical weariness in the speech, only a spiritual weariness with the cruelties of the world." Nathan Leopold, whose parole in 1958 and later death triggered a revival of public interest in Clarence Darrow, once remarked that Darrow was "the kindest man I have ever known. To me, at least, Mr. Darrow's fundamental characteristic was his deep-seated all-embracing kindness. . . . He hated superficiality and refused to conform for conformity's sake."

Indeed, Clarence Darrow remained steadfast in his convictions to the end of his life. In 1934, he was asked by President Franklin D. Roosevelt to serve as chairman of a board reviewing charges that the National Recovery Administration was siding with big business. The Darrow review board investigated some 3,000 complaints and 34 NRA industrial codes during 47 public hearings spread over a four-month period. Although admitting that the NRA had accomplished much in eradicating child labor and shortening working hours, Darrow was still convinced that "not in many years have monopolistic tendencies in industry been so forwarded and strengthened as they have been through the perversion of an act excellently intended to restore prosperity and promote general welfare." As *Newsweek* noted: "Clarence Darrow is on one of his peculiarly cool and deadly rampages again. As a foreman of a kind of governmental grand jury to tell the administration how the NRA is working, he has brought in a report saying it's doing perfectly terrible." In the following year, the Supreme Court declared the compulsory code system of the NRA unconstitutional.

The public image of Darrow, whom Lincoln Steffens called "the attorney for the damned," was that of an uncommonly learned and moving orator, whose speeches were filled with historical examples, quotations, and analogies drawn from wide reading. The true magnetism of the often disheveled figure who paced back and forth in court with his hands in his pockets, shoulders hunched and head bowed — and the key to his success — was his keen intuition about human nature. Sometimes angry, scathing, and pitiless, sometimes witty and jovial, sometimes tearful, he used emotions as well as logistics and rhetoric to achieve his goal: mercy toward fellow human beings. As the eulogy delivered at his funeral stressed:

In his heart was infinite pity and mercy for the poor, the oppressed, the weak and erring — all races, all colors, all creeds, and all human kind. Clarence Darrow made the way easier for man. He preached not doctrine but love and pity, the only virtues that can make this world any better.

MARCH 14

Albert Einstein's Birthday

Scientific inquiry, said Albert Einstein, one of the greatest physicists the world has known, is prompted by "the cosmic religious experience" — the attempt to experience all existence "as a unity full of significance." Einstein, whose thinking laid the foundation of the atomic age and paved the road to the exploration of space, was born at Ulm, Germany, on March 14, 1879. After study in mathematics and physics, he was graduated from the Federal Institute of Technology in Zurich in 1900. In 1902 he was appointed examiner of patents at the Swiss Patent Office in Berne, a position that gave him modest financial security, as well as time for contemplation and the pursuit of some spare-time projects.

One of these was work toward a Ph.D. degree, which he received from the University of Zurich in 1905. The other was publication, the same year, of a series of papers of incalculable importance. One of them changed the concept of the basic building blocks of matter and energy by proving and enlarging upon Max Planck's quantum theory that radiant energy is given out not in a steady wave, but in tiny particles, or quanta. The paper, which, among other things, explained the photoelectric effect (the basis of electronics), came to have far-reaching practical applications, including television and automation, and won for Einstein the 1921 Nobel Prize in physics.

Another of the 1905 papers explained the Brownian movement of small particles suspended in liquids, giving the world its first visible proof that matter is made up of molecules. Two others, dealing with the inertia of energy and the characteristics of electricity in motion, had their bearing on his historic 1905 publication, *The Special Theory of Relativity*.

Together with his later *General Theory of Relativity*, the Special Theory altered the concept of the entire universe. For one thing, it obliterated the age-old distinction between matter and energy. As Einstein showed with his now-famous equation $E=mc^2$, matter and energy are interchangeable, a truth resoundingly demonstrated by the explosion of the first atomic bomb at Alamogordo, New Mexico, on July 16, 1945.

Einstein's Special Theory also showed that the supposed absolutes of space, time, and mass, by which people were accustomed to making measurements, do not apply beyond earth's own neighborhood to the universe at large. Since space is constantly in motion (not stationary as had been thought) it is constantly changing and cannot provide an absolute frame of reference. And since heavenly bodies are geared to widely different systems (the earth, geared to the solar system, is only one example), their motions have meaning only in relation to each other.

The scientist who hopes his calculations will prove true for all systems in the universe therefore must allow for variations in both time and space — as Einstein proceeded to do, by use of the equations of the Lorentz transformation. He went on to demonstrate that mass, another supposed absolute, is no more constant than time or space. For the mass of a moving body increases with its speed in relation to a stationary observer. The differences, imperceptible at ordinary speeds, assume vast practical importance as the body approaches the speed of light. Indeed, a body would have infinite mass if it could actually attain the speed of light — which it cannot, Einstein reasoned, because a body of infinite mass also would have infinite resistance to motion. Thus, the velocity of light, traveling at 186,284 miles per second, emerges as the top limiting speed, and one of the few absolutes, of an otherwise variable universe.

Einstein's Theory of Relativity, presented at an Austrian scientific congress in 1908, was greeted with acclaim, and a deluge of teaching offers. A series of prestigious academic posts followed in Zurich, Prague, and Leiden. In 1913 a position was created for him, the directorship of Berlin's Kaiser Wilhelm Institute. A year later, his election to the Prussian Academy of Sciences brought him a stipend that allowed him to devote full time to research.

Einstein's *General Theory of Relativity* (1916) grew out of this period of freedom. In it he pointed out that, in terms of the universe at large, it is useless to speak of (three-dimensional) space without taking time into account. His theory forever changed the idea of space and time as two separate entities; instead the universe is perceived as a four-dimensional "space-time continuum" — something, that is, in which space and time can be considered only as continuous and inseparable. With the aid of mathematical symbols and equations, he showed that it is possible, if not to visualize, at least to begin to deal with this universe, in which time is the fourth dimension.

The General Theory is also remarkable for Einstein's ideas of gravity, which is not, he said, a "force," as commonly thought. Thus moons and stars and other heavenly bodies do not exert a force upon each other across space, as had been believed. Instead, each creates certain conditions — gravitational fields — in the space around it, and it is the structure of these fields, not some mysterious "pull," that determines the course of moving bodies — somewhat as rocks, hills, and valleys determine the path of a stream. With his laws describing the routes moving bodies follow, Einstein demonstrated that motion, like almost everything else in the universe, is relative: it can be judged only in connection with a system of reference.

He went on to reveal some other unexpected characteristics of gravity: it can affect time, for time intervals vary according to the gravitational field in question, and it can affect light, causing it to pass through a gravitational field in a curve instead of in the expected straight line.

In short, Einstein explained that the universe is not at all like a great, precisely conditioned machine, as had been thought since the time of Newton. Everything in it is in constant motion, fluctuating, always changing, the parts interacting to alter one another's behavior and characteristics. It is, however, an orderly universe, and Einstein sought to define the laws of nature that govern that order. In this attempt, he perceived "the illimitable superior spirit who reveals himself in the slight details we are able to perceive with our frail and feeble minds."

Einstein was married to his cousin, Elsa Einstein, a widow, in 1917, after his first marriage ended in divorce. In the years that followed, he received most of the Western world's important honors, wrote a number of books on scientific and other subjects, and was active in humanitarian causes. In 1933, after the rise of Hitler in Germany, Einstein, an anti-Fascist, a pacifist, and a Jew, moved to Princeton, New Jersey. There he was associated with the Institute for Advanced Study for the rest of his life, continuing to work there even after his "retirement" in 1945.

He became a US citizen in 1940. A year earlier, aware of Nazi nuclear research, he had written President Roosevelt about the possibility of atomic war. The letter resulted in the establishment of the Manhattan Project and US development of the atomic bomb, hastening the end of World War II.

In 1952 Einstein, who devoted much of his energy after the war to urging disarmament and some form of world government, was offered the presidency of Israel. He declined, feeling himself unsuited for the post. Instead he continued his frustrating lifelong search for an ultimate synthesis whereby atoms and stars would be shown to be governed by the same fundamental laws — a bridge, in short, between the Quantum Theory and relativity, whose seemingly unrelated theoretic bases had always annoyed his orderly intellect. In March 1953 he was at last able to announce his Unified Field Theory, which unified under one set of laws the two principal forces of the universe — electromagnetism and gravitation. Later work by other scientists went further toward unifying the two concepts and suggested that Einstein, without realizing it, had already come close to his goal of ultimate synthesis. The key, as announced by Princeton University scientists with the Already Unified Field Theory of 1957, lay rather in the reinterpretation of what was already known, with Einstein's theories of relativity as a tool, than in any search for new scientific theories.

Unfortunately, Einstein did not live to realize the extent of his achievement. On April 18, 1955, he died of a ruptured aorta. He left as legacy new vistas of scientific knowledge so vast that their eventual implications have as yet been only glimpsed.

Eli Whitney Patents the Cotton Gin

Eli Whitney, a native of Massachusetts, was born in rural Westboro on December 8, 1765. As a boy, he showed little enthusiasm for study, but he excelled in the ingenious use of his hands as he learned craftsmanship in his father's metalworking shop. Belatedly deciding (at 18) that he would like to go on to college, he taught school for five years or more to earn the money for this purpose. At the age of 26 he was graduated from Yale College.

After graduation he went to Georgia as a tutor. He taught and lived at Mulberry Grove near Savannah, the plantation belonging to the widow of the Revolutionary War general Nathanael Greene. While he was there, some of Mrs. Greene's planter friends complained about the problems of cotton production and asked Whitney if he could invent a machine for separating the seed from the fiber of the cotton. Relatively little cotton was then grown in the South because of the tedious process of freeing the seed from the fiber by hand. It is said that it took one person two years to turn out an average bale of cotton.

Whitney, a mechanical genius, soon conceived of a device that could separate seeds from the fibers of the short-staple cotton. In 1793 he produced the first cotton gin, for which he obtained a patent on March 14, 1794. The gin is a cylinder, covered with many teeth, which revolves against a grate of closely spaced parallel bars holding the cotton full of seeds. The teeth of the cylinder pull the cotton fibers through the bars, leaving the seeds behind. This process made possible a 50-fold increase in the average daily output of cotton. Modern ginning technology has evolved from Whitney's system.

Following the invention of the gin, the cultivation of cotton in the South expanded rapidly and slave labor became more profitable. The great increase in the production of cotton benefited mill owners as well as planters, since it led to the wide use of cotton fabrics, which were made still less expensive by the subsequent general adoption of the power loom in the cotton mills.

South Carolina voted Whitney an award of $50,000 in recognition of the importance of his invention, but since Congress refused to renew Whitney's patent in 1812, he received relatively little profit for the machine that revolutionized the economy of the South and had a profound effect throughout the world. Whitney later devoted himself to the personally more profitable business of munitions manufacture, and he introduced an important innovation with his concept of interchangeable parts. He died in New Haven, Connecticut, on January 8, 1825.

MARCH 15

De Soto Celebration
Bradenton, Florida

This is a movable event. See note on page xxvi.

The week-long De Soto Celebration held each year in mid-March at Bradenton, Florida, commemorates the landing in Florida on May 30, 1539, of Hernando de Soto, the young Spanish explorer, with his band of several hundred conquistadores. Though there is disagreement as to their exact landing place, authorities agree it was on the west coast of Florida, probably be-

tween Tampa and Estero bays. More specifically, according to a commission appointed by Congress, the explorers probably disembarked at what is now known as Shaw's Point, just west of Bradenton on Tampa Bay. The locale, at the mouth of the Manatee River, is now the site of the De Soto National Memorial, 30 landscaped acres administered by the National Park Service.

As de Soto's men stepped off their ship, plumed, brightly armored, and exuberant in their hope for gold, silver, and gems, they could not have guessed the hardships that awaited them. Under the leadership of the brave, determined, and ruthless de Soto, they set out in May 1539 on what was to be a 4,000-mile wilderness trek — the first important exploration by Europeans of the North American interior. Along the way, they pressed Native Americans into service and slaughtered those who stood in their way.

The expedition went as far north as the Carolinas and Tennessee and as far west as Oklahoma. Its members found heat, cold, hunger, swamps, hostility, and disease, but no gold or jewels. De Soto himself died in Louisiana on May 21, 1542, of a fever of unknown origin, and was buried in the Mississippi River.

The Bradenton celebration that today bears his name began in 1939, when a group of business and professional men combined to produce the first de Soto pageant. It has grown ever since and now is produced by an organization known as the Conquistadores, which was formed for the purpose in 1948. The event now lasts a week and, with the preliminary events, somewhat longer. Officially, the celebration is sponsored by the Hernando De Soto Historical Society of Bradenton.

It begins in earnest when 35 authentically costumed conquistadores, who have been elected for the occasion, reenact the original landing at the De Soto National Memorial under the sponsorship of the Hernando De Soto Historical Society. Included in the crew is the new de Soto (whose identity has been a closely guarded secret until this moment). Disembarking from a replica of de Soto's *San Cristobal*, the conquistadores come ashore in longboats. Their arrival occasions a skirmish with "Indians" (representing the original Timucua), whom the Spaniards overcome. Unlike the original event, the skirmish (as well as a reconstruction of the Indians' village) is in full view of a grandstand full of spectators, usually including the governor of Florida and members of the Spanish embassy.

The next day, de Soto and his men follow up their successful landing by penetrating the wooded areas of Shaw's Point. They press forward five miles on foot until they reach a clearing and find themselves, not entirely unexpectedly, in Bradenton. They immediately lay siege to the town and neighboring communities, raiding the county court house with a good deal of pageantry, and arresting county officials. (They also are likely to arrest adult males foolhardy enough not to have grown the beards that are customary during the week of festivities.)

There are slight variations in the week-long program from one year to the next. The conquest customarily goes off like clockwork. In one typical year, the capture of the courthouse in downtown Bradenton took place at 4:00 P.M. on Monday; outlying Cortez Plaza fell to the invaders at 5:30. The conquest continued on Tuesday and Wednesday, with the afternoon capture of shopping centers in the Westgate and Bayshore sections of Bradenton. The week's various triumphs were followed by a masquerade ball on Monday at Beall Auditorium, a square dance on Tuesday at the Palmetto Trailer Park, and a fashion show and selection of the queen's court at the Bradenton Municipal Auditorium on Wednesday.

On Wednesday there were tours of local points of interest, and on Thursday an out-of-state bands national competition was held at Manatee High School's Hawkins Stadium. The highpoint of Friday morning was the children's parade in neighboring Palmetto and the capture of Palmetto by conquistadores in the afternoon; while the evening was climaxed by the coronation ball at Bradenton Municipal Auditorium, where conquistadores appeared in costume, the reigning queen was saluted, and the identity of the new queen, chosen from 10 finalists, was made known. With the new de Soto and his captain and crew, the queen, the runner-up de Soto princess, and the queen's court then began a one-year reign, including public appearances locally and elsewhere in the nation.

Saturday's and Sunday's events also included grand parade, beginning at 7:30 in the evening, from Hawkins Stadium through downtown Bradenton. The parade, featuring floats, bands, conquistadores, and the queen and her court, was preceded by a special show at the stadium.

Saturday and Sunday's events also included an orchid show, and, on Sunday, open house at Gamble Mansion, the Confederate shrine in nearby Ellenton. Scattered throughout the week, meanwhile, had been band concerts; an art show; an antique show; competitive events in lawn bowling, sailing, tennis, shuffleboard, horseshoes, bridge, pistol shooting, bicycle riding, and fishing; yacht races; motorcycle and drag races; and three preseason games of the Pittsburgh Pirates. There was also a beard contest and the ensuing "shave-off" against time.

Andrew Jackson's Birthday

Andrew Jackson, the seventh President of the United States, was born at the Waxhaw settlement on the border line then disputed by North and South Carolina, on March 15, 1767. Both states have since claimed him as their native son, although most sources agree with Jackson, who in later years said that he had been born in South Carolina. His birthday is observed as a legal holiday in Tennessee, where he lived most of his adult life and which he served as a leader during its early years of statehood.

Of Scotch-Irish descent, he was born to parents who had emigrated from Ireland to the American frontier. Perhaps it was the rigor of Jackson's early life that instilled in him the grit, determination, and sheer stubbornness that later earned him the nickname Old Hickory. His father, Andrew Jackson, a farmer, died a few days before the birth of his son and namesake. His mother, Elizabeth Hutchinson Jackson, died in 1780; and his two older brothers also died during the closing years of the American Revolution, leaving him alone in the world at an early age.

Jackson, meanwhile, had begun his own long military career at the age of 14 by taking part in a local skirmish after the British invasion of the Carolinas. Briefly a prisoner of the British, he declined to polish a captor's boots with the announcement that he was "a prisoner of war, not a servant."

Jackson was 17 and the revolution was over when he began to study law, at Salisbury, North Carolina, in 1784. He was admitted to the bar in 1787. The next year, at 21, he was appointed prosecuting attorney for the region of North Carolina that would become the state of Tennessee on June 1, 1796. Having settled in what was then the stockaded frontier community of Nashville, he developed a thriving law practice, engaged in land speculation, and earned the loyalty of the landowners and creditors who became his political allies for the next three decades. He also became acquainted with Rachel Donelson Robards, daughter of Mrs. John Donelson, in whose home he lodged. In the mistaken belief that she was legally divorced from the absent Captain Lewis Robards, Rachel Robards and Jackson, both 24, were married in August 1791. The divorce was not actually granted until two years later, however, and a second wedding ceremony was performed for Jackson and Rachel Robards on January 17, 1794; but Jackson's political enemies capitalized on the misunderstanding for years afterwards.

In January 1796 Jackson became a delegate to the convention that framed a constitution for Tennessee. Later that year he was elected as the new state's first representative to the House of Representatives in Washington — where the beginning of his tenure coincided with the closing months of the administration of President George Washington. Jackson — resenting Washington's support of the controversial Jay Treaty, which he thought too favorable to Britain — was one of 12 congressmen who opposed the adoption of a cordial reply to Washington's Farewell Address near the close of the President's second term.

Jackson was elected to the US Senate in 1797 but resigned after serving about a year. He returned to Tennessee, where he served with great popularity as a judge of the state's superior court from 1798 until 1804. He returned to private life in the latter year, living as a planter and engaging in a variety of trading and mercantile enterprises. He meanwhile had become major general of the Tennessee militia in 1802, a post he still held when war with Britain seemed imminent a decade later, prompting his call for Tennessee volunteers to be prepared for duty. After the War of 1812 was officially declared by Congress in mid-1812, Jackson offered his services and those of the militia he commanded to the federal government.

He and his men were sent to fight the Red Sticks faction of the Creek Indians, who were allied with the British and a threat to the southern frontier. A months-long campaign culminated in Jackson's final triumph in March 1814 at the battle of Horseshoe Bend in east central Alabama. The victory, which so crushed the Creeks that they were never again a threat, wrung from them the cession by treaty of millions of acres of land in present Alabama and Georgia, opening a wide new region to settlement.

Jackson, who was now a hero in the eyes of land-hungry westerners, next moved south. On his own initiative he invaded Florida, which was then a Spanish possession, and in November he drove a British fleet from the harbor at Pensacola, where it was berthed with the consent of the Spanish.

Learning that the next move in the War of 1812 was to be a British attack upon New Orleans, Jackson, who had been commissioned a major general in the US Army, hastened to that city's defense. By the time he arrived there, he was wracked by what has been variously described as malaria and dysentery. On January 8, 1815, barely able to stand without assistance,

he nonetheless arose from his sickbed to lead his men in overwhelming the British.

This victory (see January 8), one of history's most stirring military triumphs, in effect opened the vast West to American settlement. As part of the War of 1812, which sometimes has been called the United States' second war of independence, the victory — though won, ironically, after the treaty of peace had been signed in Europe — helped establish the prestige of the new nation in the eyes of the world. It made Jackson a national hero and set him firmly on the road to the White House.

Although offered the post of secretary of war by President James Monroe, Jackson preferred to remain in the army. In 1818 he received orders to quell the Seminole Indians and runaway slaves who had been crossing the border from Spanish Florida into Georgia on raiding parties. The Seminoles earlier had been unwillingly displaced from territory the Creeks had ceded under duress in 1814. After easily subduing the Indians, Jackson decided (without official authority) to extend his campaign. He led his troops all the way to Pensacola, where they captured the Spanish fort. On the way he hanged two British subjects whom he had accused of inciting the Indians. His exploits in foreign territory — particularly the hangings — were very embarrassing to the US government, but at the same time they helped its position in the negotiations then under way for the purchase of Florida, for Jackson's feats demonstrated Spain's weakness in the area.

The Adams-Onís Treaty, by which the United States purchased Florida from Spain, was signed in 1819 (see February 22), but was not ratified by Spain until 1821. In the latter year Jackson was appointed provisional governor of the territory. He immediately antagonized the inhabitants by imprisoning one of the two Spanish governors on charges of failing to abide by terms of the treaty. His relations with officials in Washington were also poor. After only eight months, Jackson resigned.

Previously hesitant to agree with those who considered him presidential timber, Jackson in 1822 accepted a nomination for the presidency from the Tennessee legislature. In order to increase his political power and thereby his chances of election in 1824, he campaigned, successfully, for the US Senate and took his seat in 1823.

Including Jackson, there were four contenders for the presidency in the election of 1824, each of them representing a different faction of the disintegrating Democratic-Republican party. The electoral college gave the largest number of votes, 99, to Jackson. Secretary of State John Quincy Adams received 84; Secretary of the Treasury William Harris Crawford, 41; and Henry Clay, Speaker of the House of Representatives, 37. Because no candidate received a majority of the vote, in accordance with provisions of the Constitution the election devolved upon the House of Representatives, with each state having one vote. At this point Clay gave his support to Adams, virtually ensuring the election of the latter. Jackson's supporters were outraged, claiming that the popular will had been disregarded — Jackson had received 43.1 percent of the popular vote as well as a plurality of the electoral vote. They were quick to hurl the accusation of "corrupt bargain" when Adams appointed Clay secretary of state.

Jackson served in the Senate from March 1823 to October 1825, when he resigned. He and his numerous enthusiastic supporters began a lengthy campaign for the presidential election of 1828. They opposed Adams's policies, which were based on the philosophy of a strong central government, and depicted Jackson as an advocate of states' rights and of placing political power in the hands of the people. Even though Jackson was no uneducated backwoodsman, his supporters built up a homespun image of the man that had particular appeal in the western and southern regions then being settled. They pictured Adams as one of an "aristocratic" minority that was controlling the government.

In 1828 the Democratic-Republican party split into two factions. Adams was chosen to be the presidential candidate of the faction that called itself the National Republican party. His only opponent was Jackson, the candidate of the faction that retained the Democratic-Republican label. The campaign, on both sides, is considered one of the most bitter in history. Unjustified attacks by Adams's supporters, but not by Adams himself, concerning what they termed the "adulterous" relationship between Jackson and his wife Rachel during the period between their first and second marriages upset Rachel Jackson so much that they are believed to have contributed to her death on December 22, 1828.

The election was a milestone in American history. Jackson was widely looked upon as a symbol and champion of the democratic spirit sweeping large parts of the country, particularly the more newly settled areas. Hundreds of thousands voted for the first time; more than three times as many ballots were cast as had been in the previous presidential election. Jackson was victorious. The popular vote was 647,286 for Jackson and 508,864 for Adams; Jackson received 178 electoral votes to Adams's 83.

At the time of his inauguration Jackson was in mourning for his wife, so there were no official ceremonies of celebration. However, in the evening of Inauguration Day, the President held a reception for the public at the White House. It was a joyous, noisy, boisterous affair attended by about 20,000 persons, who did thousands of dollars' worth of damage. Washington had never seen anything like it.

Upon assuming office, Jackson began rewarding his supporters with government positions, even when to do so involved removing capable officeholders. One reason for his adoption of this policy was his determination to break the control over the federal government held by northern financial interests and southern plantation owners. This controversial spoils system immediately became of major importance in American political life and remained so until the latter part of the 19th century. More controversy was aroused by Jackson's formation of the Kitchen Cabinet, a group of intimates whose counsel he valued above that of his official cabinet members. Both the Kitchen Cabinet and the spoils system figured importantly in Jackson's success in building the Democratic party into a major political machine. (Jackson's supporters tended increasingly to call themselves Democrats, rather than Democratic-Republicans, in order to distinguish themselves from the opposing National Republican faction.)

Self-confident, determined, hot-tempered Old Hickory exerted strong leadership in the presidency. His administration was even termed by some "the reign of King Andrew I." Controversy surrounded him, including a heated rivalry between Vice President John C. Calhoun and Secretary of State Martin Van Buren for a dominant position of influence. Jackson's veto of a bill to renew the charter of the Second Bank of the United States evoked a tremendous amount of criticism and was the principal issue of the 1832 presidential campaign.

The system of nominating political candidates at party conventions, which gave the people a greater voice in the selection of candidates, was instituted in 1832. Jackson was nominated unanimously by the Democratic (or Democratic-Republican) party convention. His principal opponent was Senator Henry Clay of Kentucky, who had been instrumental in preventing him from gaining the presidency in 1824 and who now headed the National Republican party ticket. Clay was chiefly responsible for bringing the bank rechartering issue before the Congress in 1832, despite the fact that the charter did not expire until 1836.

Since its founding in 1816, the Second Bank of the United States had served as the fiscal agent of the government, receiving its revenues and paying them out on the order of the proper official. Jackson believed that the Congress had acted outside of its constitutional powers in chartering the Bank and, furthermore, that such a central bank was not needed. Many considered the Bank too powerful. By refusing to accept notes issued by local banks that were not payable in specie (gold or silver), it acted to restrict, on a nationwide basis, the amount of credit that could be extended. Many banks and individuals, particularly in the less developed areas of the West and South, favored the granting of easy credit in order to make more money available for the purchase of land and for other forms of economic expansion. It was also felt that, because of the large amount of currency it controlled and the loans it could grant, the Bank was in a position to wield, if it so desired, far too much political influence.

Another sore point, stressed by anti-Bank partisans, was the fact that the successful operation of the Bank had given its stockholders a good return on their investment. The Bank was accused of being a monopoly controlled by eastern financiers. Thus, at a time when there was widespread sentiment in the country for equality, foes of the Bank claimed that it was making the rich richer and the poor poorer. Furthermore, because a quarter of the Bank's stock was held by foreigners, some of the Bank's enemies succeeded in raising the feared, though unfounded, specter of a possible takeover of the US economy by a foreign power.

In February 1831 a resolution introduced in the Congress to prevent the rechartering of the Second Bank failed to pass. Jackson, who had begun his attack on the Bank in his first annual message to the Congress, in 1829, resumed it in December 1831. Pro-Bank partisans, including, notably, Senator Henry Clay of Kentucky (see April 12) and Senator Daniel Webster of Massachusetts (see January 18), thereupon decided to press the issue to a decision before the presidential election of 1832. Their strategy was to push through the Congress a bill to recharter the Second Bank. They believed Jackson would veto such a bill, and that his veto would arouse the nation against him so that he would be defeated at the polls. Then, with a new President who was friendly to the Bank, the rechartering could be accomplished in fact.

The projected rechartering act was easily passed by the Congress and was roundly denounced by Jackson when he vetoed it in July 1832. However, Clay and Webster had misjudged the mood of the country — if not actually in terms of public support for the Bank, at least in terms of Jackson's personal popularity. With Clay his only real opponent for the presidency in the 1832 election, and the rechartering of the Bank the principal issue, Jackson was swept back into office with 56.6 percent of the popular vote and 219 electoral votes, while Clay garnered only 49 electoral votes. Jackson was now free to move against the Bank.

Asserting that federal deposits were not safe in the Second Bank of the United States, Jackson instructed Secretary of the Treasury William J. Duane to withdraw them. When Duane refused, Jackson removed him from office and replaced him with Roger B. Taney of Virginia, who had been serving as attorney general and was later to become chief justice of the United States (see March 17). Taney ceased making deposits in the Bank and used the money already there to pay bills. The state banks that were selected to receive federal deposits immediately became known as "pet banks."

Some economic dislocation was inevitable as a result of such a major change in the world of finance. The opponents of the President and the friends of the Bank denounced Jackson in bitter terms and charged him with producing a financial panic. The President's friends charged the still functioning Bank with causing the panic by reducing its circulation and restricting its loans.

Shortly before the depression of 1833–1834 ended, Clay introduced in the Senate a resolution condemning the President as having, in his actions concerning the Bank, "assumed upon himself authority and power not conferred by the constitution and laws, but in derogation of both." Senator Thomas Hart Benton of Missouri led the defenders of the President during the many weeks of debate before the resolution was passed on March 28, 1834. It was the first presidential censure. On April 15 Jackson responded with an official protest against the resolution. Three years later the censure resolution was expunged by the Senate.

Another major issue during Jackson's administration was the question of the right of a state to nullify a federal law. The exponents of the doctrine of nullification, including Calhoun, who resigned the vice presidency in December 1832 to become a senator from South Carolina and a leader of those advocating states' rights, contended that the individual states could nullify any federal law they deemed to be unconstitutional. Jackson contended that the states had no such power. The issue was joined when Calhoun and others declared the protective tariff act of 1832 to be unconstitutional, claiming it to be discriminatory because it aided the industrial North and hurt the agricultural South. When

South Carolina threatened to secede from the Union if any federal action was taken to force its citizens to pay the higher import duties, Jackson stood firm and made preparations for possible military action. A compromise was reached, however, involving a new tariff bill that provided for a gradual reduction in duties.

Jackson still enjoyed great popularity at the end of his second term, so great that he probably could have been elected for a third term. But because no President before him had served more than two terms, Jackson declined to be considered for renomination. As head of the Democratic party, however, he virtually dictated the choice of its next candidate, Martin Van Buren. His endorsement ensured the latter's election to the presidency in 1836.

After leaving office in 1837, Jackson lived quietly at his Tennessee home, the Hermitage. In 1804 he had bought 1,200 acres near Nashville, and for 15 years he and his wife had lived in a log cabin that was standing on the grounds at the time of his purchase. When he returned from the Seminole wars, Jackson determined to build a new house for his wife. (He himself was so ill that he did not expect to live long.) The beautiful colonial brick mansion was completed in 1819. Jackson had it enlarged in 1831 and rebuilt after a disastrous fire in 1834. It is still completely furnished with original pieces, including some in late Federal and early Empire styles. Upon his death at the Hermitage on June 8, 1845, Jackson was buried beside his wife in the garden. (The couple had no children.) The "early" Hermitage, the log cabin in which the Jacksons lived, also still stands on the 700-acre grounds of the landmark, which is administered by the Ladies' Hermitage Association. The entrance to the grounds, which are open to the public, is located on US Route 70N, about 12 miles east of Nashville. On the highway opposite the Hermitage stands a small church in which Rachel and Andrew Jackson worshiped. Jackson donated the land on which the red-brick building was constructed in 1823, and, although it was built for the community, the structure came to be known as "Rachel's church." The interior of the church has been restored, and original pieces, including the communion table used by the President, are preserved there.

In 1910 Andrew Jackson was elected to the Hall of Fame for Great Americans. He has been and continues to be honored in many other ways as well. Each year on the anniversary of his birth, March 15, which is observed as a legal holiday in Tennessee, a wreath brought or sent by the President of the United States is placed on Jackson's grave in the garden of the Hermitage. Usually the President himself attends the birthday observance at Jackson's home once during his four-year term of office, and he frequently uses the occasion to make an important address to the nation. When the President does not attend the ceremonies, a dignitary representing him places the presidential wreath and makes an address. Pageantry provided by the color guard of the Tennessee National Guard and a fireworks display add to the celebration on the Hermitage grounds, which are open without charge on that day.

During the week of Jackson's birthday, tribute is paid him in various ways throughout Tennessee. Radio speeches and newspaper editorials honor him. Students compete in writing essays about him, and often a number of the contest winners are invited to a ceremony in the governor's office in Nashville on March 15. A number of Jackson Day dinners, sponsored by the Democratic party, are held. Both Jackson and President Thomas Jefferson are honored as founders of the Democratic party, and since 1948 joint Jefferson-Jackson Day dinners have been held annually throughout the nation, under the sponsorship of the national committee of the Democratic party. Many of these celebrations are held on January 8, the anniversary of the battle of New Orleans, from which Jackson emerged a national hero, but they also are held on other, widely varying, dates. In addition to honoring the founders of the party, all of these dinners — including those in Tennessee, where they still are simply called Jackson Day dinners — provide an occasion for high-level Democrats to review accomplishments and outline objectives of the party. They are also important fund-raising events.

Jackson and Confederate army commander Robert E. Lee are jointly honored in Virginia, where the third Monday in January is observed as Lee-Jackson Day.

In another form of tribute, various places have been named in Jackson's honor. Among them are the cities of Jackson, capital of Mississippi; Jacksonville, Florida; and Jackson, Tennessee. A famous equestrian statue of Jackson by the American sculptor Clark Mills stands in Lafayette Square, in front of the White House, in Washington, D.C. A copy of the statue stands in Jackson Square in New Orleans; another copy is in Nashville. North Carolina, which still considers Jackson one of its sons, honors him in its capital city of Raleigh. The landscaped six-acre square on which the capitol faces is the site of an equestrian monument to Jackson and two other Presidents born in the state, Andrew Johnson and James K. Polk.

Maine Admitted to the Union

Maine, the largest of the New England states, was admitted to the Union on March 15, 1820, as the 23rd state. It was given its nickname, the Pine Tree State, from the early abundance of white pine trees, which still comprise one of Maine's foremost natural resources.

Archaeological evidence indicates human habitation of the area as early as prehistoric times. The earliest inhabitants are called the Red Paint People because their graves customarily contained various quantities of a bright red pigment (powdered hematite). Later tribes of Newfoundland and New England used this red pigment or paint not only to color their huts, canoes, and weapons, but also to decorate their own bodies.

European exploration of the area began, some believe, with Leif Ericson, son of Eric the Red, in the first decade of the 11th century. Five hundred years passed without exploration, until Columbus's voyage awakened interest. During the years 1497–1499, John Cabot and his sons, Lewis, Sebastian, and Santius, made several voyages to the Western Hemisphere at the bidding of England's King Henry VII. England was later to base its claim to the New World on Cabot's voyages, although for many years thereafter it more or less ignored the new land.

Giovanni da Verrazano (or Verrazzano), an Italian navigator in the service of France, sighted Maine in 1524, a year before the Spanish explorer Estevan Gómez. The subsequent years brought many Europeans but most of them, seeking a route to the Indies, merely sailed past Maine.

In the first decade of the 17th century, the kings of England and France each granted charters for that area of the New World that included Maine. There ensued over a century of bitter competition, filled with raids, claims and counterclaims. Under charter from France's King Henry IV in 1604, Pierre du Guast, Sieur de Monts, accompanied by adventurers including Samuel de Champlain, established the first Maine colony on St. Croix Island at the mouth of the St. Croix River, near what is now Calais.

After a hard winter the French colonists left St. Croix and moved across the Bay of Fundy to Port Royal (now Annapolis Royal), Nova Scotia. Champlain, however, continued to explore Maine, discovering many of its rivers, providing the first detailed maps of the islands off the mainland and, more important, mapping the jagged coastline of Maine with its many natural harbors. The French, including many missionaries who later followed the Sieur de Monts to the New World, were more successful in establishing friendly relations with the Native Americans than were the English explorers who soon arrived.

The first British newcomer, Captain George Weymouth (or Waymouth), landed at Monhegan Island in 1605. He obtained valuable information that helped future English colonists, but also assured those colonists a hostile reception by kidnapping five Indians to take back to England. That infamous act, plus subsequent years of continual incursions by the white men and constant breaking of treaties, insured long years of Indian wars in Maine.

When he returned to England with his five captives, Weymouth's adventures caught the imagination of many of his countrymen, including Sir Ferdinando Gorges, military governor of Plymouth, England. In 1606, when King James I granted a charter to the Plymouth Company, Sir Ferdinando and Sir John Popham underwrote an expedition to the New World to be led by Sir John's nephew, George Popham. Arriving at Allen's Island, one of the present Georges Islands, on Sunday, August 9, 1607, the colonists gathered for prayers of thanksgiving, the first English religious service on New England soil. The Popham colony was established near the mouth of the Kennebec River on the Sagadahoc Peninsula.

The colonists, however, had not brought sufficient supplies, and more than half of them returned to England in December, promising to send supplies as soon as possible. George Popham stayed, but, like several of the other settlers, he did not survive the cruel winter. In the spring, the ship bringing supplies from England arrived with news of the death of Sir John Popham. Rather than face another Maine winter, the disheartened colonists returned home in September 1608 aboard the first ship to be built in the New World, the *Virginia of Sagadahoc*.

The Dutch flag sailed into Maine's Casco Bay in 1609 with Henry Hudson's storm-damaged ship, the *Half Moon*. Hudson, looking for a route to the Indies, put in to repair his ship, was greeted with hospitality by the Indians, and reciprocated by stealing their supplies.

The name New England apparently was given to the area by Captain John Smith, who in 1614 put in briefly at Monhegan Island and the abandoned Popham colony site and charted the coast from Rhode Island to Nova Scotia. He returned to England with a rich cargo of furs and fish from the New World and reported the land agreeable for colonization and settlement. However, the hardships suffered by the Popham colony were not put aside easily. To prove that Europeans could endure the climate, Captain

Richard Vines and his 16-man crew spent the winter of 1616–1617 at a site at the mouth of the Saco River. A few years later, Vines returned and established the first successful settlement at Saco, and this was followed by other coastal settlements west of Penobscot Bay.

In 1635 Sir Ferdinando Gorges, appointed governor general of all New England, sent William Gorges, his nephew, to act as his deputy in the New World. The latter set about organizing the government, and in 1639 Maine's first legislative and judicial court was held at Saco. In 1639 Sir Ferdinando received the charter for "The Province and Countie of Maine" from Charles I of England. The name Maine was probably taken from the region of Maine in northwest France as a salute to Charles's queen consort, Henrietta Maria, daughter of King Henry IV of France.

After Sir Ferdinando's death in 1647, Parliament invalidated his grant, but his heirs, disregarding Parliament's action, sent a deputy governor to Maine. With the confusion of grants and leadership, Maine settlers tried to form their own body politic. Their effort met with no great success, and the province of Maine came under the rule of the Massachusetts Bay Colony in 1652, despite the protests of the Maine settlers.

King Charles II restored the charter for the province of Maine to Ferdinando Gorges, grandson of the earlier Sir Ferdinando, in 1664. Massachusetts judges were ordered out of Maine, and royal commissioners went in to establish an independent government. There followed a long period of political upheaval, international squabbling about rights, and Indian warfare, which reduced the number of Maine settlements to three or four. In 1677, during this period, Gorges sold to Massachusetts all rights to Maine for £1,250 (roughly $6,000).

The British sovereigns William and Mary gave Massachusetts its second charter in 1691, and the province of Maine became the district of Maine, governed by Massachusetts. By 1732 the white population of Maine had been either wiped out or driven out by the long years of Indian wars. To stimulate resettlement, Massachusetts offered free land in Maine. Within a decade Maine's population grew to 12,000, but again the settlers were dispersed by Indian wars.

Still chafing under Massachusetts rule, Maine fought well and hard during the American Revolution and the War of 1812. The people of the District of Maine began to agitate for separation from Massachusetts at the close of the Revolution. They did not succeed, however, until 1820, when Maine was admitted to the Union as a free state through the Missouri Compromise (see August 10, Missouri Admitted to the Union). Its population at that time was 298,335. Its capital, first at Portland, was moved to Augusta in 1832.

MARCH 16

James Madison's Birthday

The eldest of 12 children, James Madison, fourth President of the United States and a major architect of the Constitution, was born at the home of his maternal grandparents in Port Conway, Virginia, on March 16, 1751. Soon afterward, his mother returned with her son to her husband's home, Montpelier, a plantation in Orange County, Virginia. It was at Montpelier, just a few miles northeast of the home of Thomas Jefferson, Madison's lifetime associate, that Madison spent his youth and his retirement years.

A Scottish tutor began Madison's formal schooling when he was 12; he studied the classics, French, and Spanish. Later, after further tutoring, he entered the College of New Jersey (now Princeton University). While there, he excelled in the study of history and government and was one of the founders of the American Whig Society, a debating club that became celebrated in the history of the college. Completing a four-year course in three years, he was graduated in 1771, but he remained at the college for part of another year to study Hebrew, ethics, theology, and law. He continued his studies in law and theology after his return to Virginia, and it was eventually remarked of him that "he knew more of theology than most ministers."

The first political issue he concerned himself with was the controversy raging in Virginia over religious toleration. Madison, who felt that free exercise of religion was a matter of right — and not of mere toleration — argued in favor of religious freedom and against the principle of an established church, as in Virginia, where the Church of England held sway. In 1776 he became a delegate to the Virginia constitutional convention. As a member of the committee that drafted the Virginia constitution, including that portion of the document known as the declaration of rights, he was influential in formulating the article on religious freedom whose adoption eventually had significance far beyond Virginia's borders.

He was elected to the Governor's Council in 1778 and served there until late the next year. He was sent as a delegate to the Continental Congress during the later stages of the American

Revolution and served there from March 1780 until December 1783, when he returned home because of illness in his father's family.

During the next few years away from Congress Madison resumed his study of the law — in order, as he wrote Edmund Randolph, the Virginia statesman, to have a profession in which he could "depend as little as possible on the labour of slaves." He also began studies of confederacies throughout history, studies that gave him an understanding of the national government as it then existed under the Articles of Confederation. He wrote Jefferson, then in France, asking him to buy books, especially "whatever may throw light on the general constitution and *droit public* [public law] of the several confederacies which have existed."

Madison was not away from public service long, however, for he was elected by his county to the Virginia House of Delegates in 1784. He served there until 1786, playing a major part in securing passage of the article on religious freedom that disestablished the Anglican church. In so doing, he and Thomas Jefferson fought and defeated a project supported by Patrick Henry and others to impose a general tax for the support of religion. During those years, Madison also countered proposals for the issue of paper money, since the states issuing the money were not supplying the federal Treasury with the funds needed to back that money.

In these years, Madison was also influential in bringing about a series of interstate conferences dealing with commercial problems, which ultimately led to the calling of the Constitutional Convention in Philadelphia in 1787. He was elected a member of the Continental Congress for a second time in 1786. In May 1787 he took his seat in the Constitutional Convention as a delegate from Virginia.

In preparation for this important responsibility, Madison in April 1787 prepared a paper based on his studies of confederacies, in which he declared that a confederacy could not survive long if it acted exclusively upon states and failed to act directly on individuals as well. He fashioned an outline for reorganizing the government, and his proposals for a new system of government contributed in great measure to the formulation of the Virginia Plan (see June 21). Madison's proposals so influenced the work of the Constitutional Convention that he is known today as the Father of the Constitution.

In his recommendations of April 1787 Madison set forth his views on various provisions that he felt should be embodied in the proposed constitution. He wrote that the large states should

have more representatives in the national legislature than the small states; that the national government should have "positive and complete authority in all cases which require uniformity"; that the national supremacy should extend to the judiciary departments; that the national legislature should be composed of two houses with differing terms of office; that there should be a national executive; and that the national government should guarantee the tranquility of the states against internal as well as external dangers.

He immediately took a prominent part in the deliberations of the Constitutional Convention, attending every session and taking copious notes on the debates. These notes were eventually published (in 1840) as his *Journal of the Federal Convention* and are the most complete record of the proceedings. He also contributed to a brilliant series of essays written by himself, John Jay, and Alexander Hamilton and published in New York newspapers under the signature of "Publius." Defending the new Constitution and urging its ratification, these papers, now classics, were published in book form as *The Federalist* in 1788 — after the Constitution had been officially adopted by the Constitutional Convention at Philadelphia on September 17, 1787. After transmittal to the Continental Congress, the Constitution was submitted to the state legislatures for submission in turn to the delegates of the states' specially chosen ratifying conventions.

Madison was active in securing the approval of the Virginia ratifying convention. With allies including John Marshall, later chief justice of the United States, he opposed the Antifederalist faction led by Patrick Henry, George Mason, and others, winning Virginia's approval for the new Constitution by a majority of 10 votes. However, this effort cost Madison valuable political support in Virginia, and he was not elected to a seat in the first Senate under the new Constitution. He was elected a member of the House of Representatives, however, in spite of Patrick Henry's opposition, and served in this capacity from 1789 to 1797.

Madison soon became a leader of the House and was active in framing the legislation necessary for the organization of the new government, including proposals for the establishment of three of the first executive departments — Foreign Affairs (now State), the Treasury, and War (now Defense). He also proposed 9 amendments to the new Constitution that became the basis of the 10 now known as the Bill of Rights (see December 15). In addition, he was active in these years in the formation of the Antifederalist, or

Jeffersonian Republican party (later known as the Democratic-Republican party). When the Federalists – led by Hamilton, whose financial policies Madison opposed – came into control of the government, he voluntarily retired from Congress at the expiration of his term on March 3, 1797.

During this period of his life, Madison, a bachelor until he was in his forties, married the vivacious Dorothea ("Dolley") Payne Todd (see May 20), a young Quaker widow from Philadelphia. Dolley Madison, famous as a charming and tactful hostess, was a great asset to the scholarly Madison, first at Montpelier and later at the White House. She was hostess at the White House not only during her eight years as First Lady, but also in the previous eight years, when she was unofficial hostess for the widowed Thomas Jefferson.

Following his service as a member of Congress, Madison remained in retirement less than a year, for in 1798 he began working with Jefferson to oppose the repressive Federalist legislation known as the Alien and Sedition Acts. Madison drew up the states' rights resolutions adopted by the Virginia legislature, condemning the acts as unconstitutional and declaring that

in case of deliberate, palpable and dangerous exercise of other powers not granted by the said compact [the Constitution], the states, who are parties thereto, have the right and are duty bound to interpose for arresting the progress of the evil, and for maintaining within their respective limits the authorities, rights and liberties appertaining to them.

When this declaration was later cited as justification for the South Carolina nullification resolutions, Madison explained that he did not mean that a state could by its own action nullify an act of Congress, but that if the states regarded such an act as unconstitutional they should either work for its repeal or for an amendment to the Constitution that would invalidate it. Jefferson drafted similar resolutions adopted by Kentucky.

Disapproval of the Alien and Sedition Acts, thus aroused, contributed to the defeat of the Federalist party in the next election. Jefferson was elected the third President of the United States in 1800, and he appointed Madison his secretary of state. In this office, Madison was Jefferson's chief adviser during his two terms of office. Madison himself was elected to the presidency in 1808 and took office the following March.

During these years the major problem confronting the administration was dealing with issues arising out of the Napoleonic wars in Europe. Jefferson, and later Madison, tried to maintain neutrality, but neither France nor England respected this position; it was impossible to resolve the problems of conflicting interests. These problems continued through Jefferson's administrations and into Madison's. Ultimately, Britain's impressment of American sailors and seizure of cargoes, together with suspected British instigation of Indian border hostilities, brought about the demand for declaring war. Congress was dominated by the "War Hawks" of the South and West and, although the country was not prepared to fight, Madison acceded to their demands by advising a congressional declaration of war against Great Britain on June 1, 1812. On June 18 he signed the document produced by Congress. The war, now known as the War of 1812, then was called "Mr. Madison's War" by those who opposed it, principally northeasterners.

Congress did not take adequate economic measures to provide for the war, and for this and other reasons, the conflict initially was filled with disasters for the United States. A low point came in August 1814, when the British took Washington, briefly, and set fire to the White House and other buildings. However, the tide began to turn – perhaps at Baltimore, where Francis Scott Key penned the "Star-Spangled Banner" during the unsuccessful British bombardment of September 1814 (see September 12). Thereafter, the United States achieved some notable victories. With the increasing war successes, the careworn Madison regained much of his popularity. (Even with the handicap of a war many opposed he had meanwhile managed election to a second term of office in 1812.) The war was concluded with the Treaty of Ghent on December 24, 1814. Although the rest of Madison's presidency was relatively uneventful, the pride and national self-awareness that swept across the country following its wartime success had lasting import in welding together, reinforcing, and thoroughly establishing the new nation – in the world's eyes as well as its own. Some people called it the second war for independence. Unsurprisingly enough, the remaining events of Madison's "uneventful'" second term were other statements of national self-assertion, including a protective tariff act, steps to bolster the US Army and Navy, and a charter for a new (the Second) Bank of the United States.

After the end of his second term, on March 4, 1817, Madison returned to private life. His last years were spent at Montpelier. He supported Jefferson in founding the University of Virginia in 1819, and he became its rector following Jefferson's death in 1826.

Madison died at Montpelier at the age of 84,

on June 28, 1836. He and his wife, who outlived him by more than a decade, are buried on the lawn of his estate. Today, Montpelier is a privately owned, racehorse-breeding farm not open to the public, although the graves of the Madisons may be visited.

United States Military Academy Founded

March 16 marks the anniversary of the founding of the US Military Academy by act of Congress dated March 16, 1802. Each year, on or about this date, graduates and friends of the academy throughout the world take note of the anniversary as Founders Day.

The original act authorized a Corps of Engineers, setting its strength at five officers and 10 cadets, and provided that it be stationed at West Point, New York, and constitute a military academy. Today the faculty numbers approximately 450 and the Corps of Cadets (student body) has an authorized strength of 4,417. The authorization was raised from 2,529 in an act of Congress signed by President Lyndon B. Johnson on March 3, 1964.

In October 1975 Congress approved and President Gerald R. Ford signed into law legislation directing that women be admitted to West Point and the other US service academies. The admission of women to West Point in July 1976 broke a 174-year-old tradition yet preserved the total integrity of the Corps of Cadets. Each cadet, male or female, is subject to the same requirements for graduation and commissioning and the same standards of admission and training, except for those minimum essential adjustments required because of physiological differences.

West Point, situated on the west bank of the Hudson River, about 50 miles north of New York City, was an important military post during the American Revolution and has been occupied continuously by Regular Army troops since January 20, 1778. The experience of the American Revolution called attention to the need of a national military academy for the training of the country's armed forces.

In May 1776 General Henry Knox, the American Revolutionary officer and adviser to General Washington, had urged the establishment of a military academy. With Washington's approval, Congress, on October 1 of the same year adopted a resolution appointing a committee to prepare plans for such an academy. On June 20, 1777, it was ordered that a corps organized as "a military school for young gentlemen previous to their being appointed to marching regiments," be created. This was done at once, and

in 1781, at the request of General Washington, the resulting corps was marched from Philadelphia to join the garrison at West Point, where an engineering school, a laboratory, and a library had already been opened. But this was not regarded as adequate, and two years later Washington discussed with his officers at nearby Newburgh, New York, the plans for a military academy.

In his message to Congress on December 3, 1793, President Washington called attention to the need for such an institution. On May 9, 1794, Congress authorized the organization of a Corps of Artillerists and Engineers, with a school of instruction for them at West Point. Originally the grounds of what is now the academy consisted of 1,795 acres purchased in 1790 from Stephen Moore; today the post proper and the nearby summer training site at Camp Buckner comprise about 16,000 acres. The buildings used for the school were burned in 1796 and the work of the academy was suspended until 1801.

The military academy as it is now known was formally organized on March 16, 1802. Its original purpose was to train technicians for all branches of the military service, as well as to encourage the study of military art nationally, thus raising the level of training of the militia and encouraging the practical study of various fields of knowledge.

The War of 1812 focused attention on the need for trained officers, and President James Madison urged upon Congress the importance of making the academy a scientific as well as a military college. Congress, by the act of April 29, 1812, increased the strength of the Corps of Cadets to 250, enlarged the academic staff, and placed the cadets under the discipline of published regulations.

The act of 1812 also required that the cadets be taught "all the duties of a private, a noncommissioned officer, and an officer," a requirement that, according to Emory Upton in *The Military Policy of the United States* (1904), was the "key to the character for efficiency and discipline which the graduates have since maintained." Rules requiring mental and physical examinations for cadets being promoted to the corps were approved by President James Monroe in 1818.

A year earlier, Colonel Sylvanus Thayer, called the Father of the Military Academy, had become its fifth superintendent. He served in the position for 16 years, instituting principles of academic and military training designed to develop habits of mental discipline and high standards of scholarship in the cadets.

The four-year, college-level course at the United States Military Academy leads to the bachelor of science degree and a commission as second lieutenant in the US Army. The academy produces officer-graduates who are trained leaders, with academic and military knowledge enabling them to discharge their duties in a wide range of specialized fields. Training in both the standard academic and advanced studies programs is designed to provide cadets with a foundation in the basic sciences, applied sciences and engineering, language and literature, and national security and public affairs. Elective courses taken during the upper-class years permit cadets to concentrate in any of these areas that are of particular interest to them.

West Point's impressive physical plant, in a scenic setting overlooking the Hudson River, has been substantially augmented in response to 1964 legislation that authorized the near-doubling of the Corps of Cadets. The ambitious expansion program included both new construction and the modernization and enlarging of existing facilities. One addition, provided not by federally appropriated funds but by a grant from the Richard King Mellon Trust, includes improvements to the natural amphitheater below Battle Monument and the construction there of a lookout up the Hudson. The location is seen as the site of band concerts and other good-weather activities for cadets and for the millions who visit West Point as a national historic landmark.

The list of famous West Point graduates is a long one, including such names as President Ulysses S. Grant; General Robert E. Lee; General John J. Pershing, commander in chief of the American Expeditionary Forces in World War I; President Dwight D. Eisenhower; General George S. Patton Jr.; and General of the Army Douglas MacArthur. On the academy's grounds stand a number of monuments memorializing noted graduates. Those of varying rank who have carried out the West Point motto, Duty, Honor, Country, include many who have died while serving their country. Captain Colin P. Kelly Jr., Class of 1937, the first casualty among USMA graduates in World War II, was among this number. The Military Academy also contributed heavily to leadership among the American forces committed to the defense of South Korea during the Korean conflict of 1950–1953 and to those who participated in the long-continuing Vietnam conflict that ended in the mid-1970s.

MARCH 17

St. Patrick's Day

The Feast of St. Patrick, bishop and confessor, is celebrated on March 17 by Roman Catholics and some Episcopalians. St. Patrick is called the Apostle of Ireland and is that country's patron saint.

Many of the facts about Patrick have been buried under centuries of Irish legend, and there is a great deal of controversy and speculation about the chronology of events in his life and especially about the date of his death.

Patrick was born about 385 or 389, possibly in Bannavem Taberniae, a village near the mouth of the Severn River, in what is now Wales, when the region was part of the Roman Empire; hence he is described as a Romano-Briton. His father, Calpurnius, or Calpornius, was a Roman *decurio* (*decurio* has been variously defined as alderman, magistrate, deacon, or member of the village government). Although his parents were Christian and Patrick was baptized, he was a worldly youth who gave little thought to religion. However, when he was about 16, a group of Irish marauders or pirates raided the area of Bannavem Taberniae and carried off Patrick and hundreds of other young men and women to be sold as slaves in Ireland. For six years, possibly in Slemish in County Antrim, Patrick worked as a herdsman, and during this time of slavery and frequent solitude, he felt an increasing awareness of God. Patrick's *Confession*, which he wrote when he was older, opens with this passage:

I, Patrick, a sinner, the most rustic and the least of all the faithful, and in the estimation of very many deemed contemptible, had for my father Calpornius, a deacon, the son of Potitus, a presbyter, who belonged to the village of Bannavem Taberniae; for close thereto he had a small villa, where I was made a captive.

At the time I was barely 16 years of age, I knew not the true God; and I was led to Ireland in captivity with many thousand persons according to our deserts, for we turned away from God and kept not His commandments, and we were not obedient to our priests who used to admonish us about our salvation. And the Lord brought us the indignation of His wrath, and scattered us amongst many nations even to the utmost part of the earth, where now my littleness may be seen amongst strangers.

And there the Lord opened the understanding of my unbelief so that at length I might recall to mind my sins and be converted with all my heart to the Lord, my God, who hath regarded my humility and taken pity on my youth and my ignorance, and kept watch over me before I knew Him, and before I had discretion, and could distinguish between good and evil; and He protected me and consoled me as a father does his son.

During his sixth year of slavery, Patrick had a dream in which he was told to escape. Following the instructions given him in the dream, he made his way to the harbor and boarded a ship, which carried him out of captivity. He returned to his home, less worldly and more religious than when he had left it. While he was enjoying his reunion with his family and the warmth and comforts of home, however, he heard "the voice of the Irish" calling him to go back to Ireland, and he determined that he must return to the land where he had truly found his faith to share that faith with the Irish pagans.

In preparation for this he went to the Continent, traveling to Gaul (France), Italy, and some of the Tyrrhenian islands, visiting monasteries and living the life of a religious. For perhaps a dozen years he stayed in Gaul under the tutelage of St. Germanus (or Germain), the bishop of Auxerre, who was much involved with fighting the Pelagian heresy in Britain.

Patrick had from the first made known his desire to return to Ireland but, perhaps because his education had been so long ignored and was considered inadequate, his religious superiors had not acceded to his request. St. Palladius was chosen over Patrick as the first bishop of Ireland. After a year or two in Ireland, however, Palladius went to Scotland, and Patrick took his place, probably in 431 or 432. He had first been made a bishop and given the name of Patrick in place of his original name, Succat.

Patrick's arrival in Ireland was greatly opposed by the druid priests, who wielded great political and religious authority in pagan Ireland. They captured Patrick many times, and as many times he escaped. He had an imposing presence and an immensely winning personality, by which he obtained the support of the kings and local chieftains. He traveled in all parts of Ireland, making converts to Christianity, founding monasteries, schools, and churches, which would in time turn pagan Ireland into the "Isle of Saints."

Not all of the opposition came from the druids. Some clergymen objected to Patrick's mission and methods. There was, for instance, much dispute over such things as the great bonfires that were secular or pagan spring rites. As various peoples became Christians, the bonfires were often prohibited on the grounds that they constituted a pagan ritual. St. Patrick, however, caused much consternation among the druids by "christening" their spring fires, making them a symbol of Christ, the Light of the World. Traditionally, Patrick started his bonfire at Easter on the Hill of Slane (Slaine) in County Meath. Through the centuries, opposition to the Christianized fire rite diminished, and the blessing of the fire is now part of the Roman Catholic liturgy of the Easter Vigil.

Patrick, who is referred to as the Father and the Founder of the Church in Ireland, established his see at Armagh, and after approximately 30 years of what was one of the most successful missionary lives on record, he retired to Saul in Downpatrick, where he died on March 17, in or about the year 461. He was buried in Downpatrick in County Down, and many pilgrims each year visit the stone there carved with a "P," which supposedly marks his grave.

Many of the legends about Patrick are portrayed in pictures and statues of the saint. The most famous emblem associated with him is the shamrock, which he supposedly showed to a king to convey the idea of the Holy Trinity. Others include the cross, harp, baptismal font (signifying his many converts), and demons and serpents (Patrick is said to have driven all the snakes out of Ireland).

St. Patrick's Day provides the occasion for the biggest annual parade held in New York City. The parade was probably first held in New York City in 1762, although perhaps even as early as 1684, when the city was still confined to the lower tip of the island of Manhattan. When the city spread uptown, the parade was held on what is now lower Fifth Avenue. The early St. Patrick's Day parades in New York City were sponsored by the city's Friendly Sons of St. Patrick, which was organized by Irish Catholics and Presbyterians. Later, in 1838, the parade came under the auspices of the Ancient Order of Hibernians, the organization that is still its sponsor. In 1879, the year St. Patrick's Cathedral was completed, the parade was extended farther up Fifth Avenue in order to be reviewed by the archbishop and clergy standing in front of the cathedral. At one time the parade route up Fifth Avenue stretched all the way from 44th Street to 110th Street. The resulting traffic jams became intolerable, however, since the longer route took more hours to cover. The route was finally shortened to end at 86th Street, where the procession now turns right and disbands a few blocks to the east. Even so, today's mammoth parade lasts from noon until 5:00 or 6:00 P.M., creating a huge traffic problem. The necessity of avoiding even larger problems is one reason why many out-of-town and out-of-state bands that seek to march in the parade must be turned down each year.

As many as 125,000 marchers annually march up the two-and-a-half-mile parade route, still passing St. Patrick's Cathedral at 50th Street, and the reviewing stand at 64th Street, where government officials, guests, and local politicians gather to watch the spectacular event. Honored guests usually include the Irish consul in New York City and, frequently, Dublin's lord mayor in the eye-catching blue robes and tricorn hat of his office.

A mounted police escort unit precedes the parade's lead formation, the band of New York's famous regiment, the Fighting 69th, now the

165th Infantry Regiment of the New York National Guard. The band, marching behind its two mascots, shaggy Irish wolfhounds named Pat and Mike, has been the traditional military escort for the parade since 1851. The number of participants varies each year, but in one more recent year there were a reported 345 marching units, including 120 bands, fife-and-drum corps, and bugle-and-drum corps. The skirl of bagpipes played by colorfully kilted pipers is heard frequently during the parade, perhaps the largest such unit being the Emerald Society's Pipe and Drum Band of the City of New York Police Department. Throughout the line of march, the air is filled with the strains of such melodies as "McNamara's Band," "Dear Old Donegal," "Great Day for the Irish," "When Irish Eyes Are Smiling," and "My Wild Irish Rose."

Bands and high-stepping marching units in bright uniforms, led by baton-twirlers, come from many different states to take part in the parade. Marching units made up of students, police officers, firefighters, members of the armed forces, fraternal groups, and other organizations make an impressive sight. Representatives of all 32 counties of Ireland also march. Beautiful banners identify the various organizations and recall such Irish heroes as Brian Boru, Hugh O'Neill and Owen Roe O'Neill, Napper Tandy, Robert Emmet, and Daniel O'Connell.

Among the many other American cities where St. Patrick's Day parades are staged are Chicago, Atlanta, Baton Rouge, Boston, and Philadelphia, all with large Irish-American populations. Another is Savannah, which has one of the oldest annual St. Patrick's Day parades in the South, dating from 1812. In Boston a St. Patrick's Day parade was first held even earlier — on March 17, 1737. It was under the auspices of the Charitable Irish Society, organized by Irish Protestants. The celebration was evidently well known, because when the British evacuated Boston on March 17, 1776, General George Washington selected "Boston" as the password for the day and "St. Patrick" as the proper response.

Whatever the celebrating city, a touch of green is seen everywhere on St. Patrick's Day — in derbies, ties, boutonnieres, pennants, buttons, kerchiefs, and other apparel. Even food and drink are colored for the occasion, a touch that transforms such commodities as beer and bagels. A few tint their hair green for the day. Others dip their white dogs into emerald-colored baths. For St. Patrick's Day, 1965, the mayor of Chicago ordered 100 pounds of emerald green dye poured into the Chicago River. Irish airline flight attendants take part in St. Patrick's Day parades in American cities from coast to coast and present another touch of green — shamrocks flown in from Ireland — to city officials.

Ireland's St. Patrick's Day parades traditionally have been more restrained than those in most American cities. Even the largest one, in Dublin, for many years could in no way compare with the enormous New York City celebration. However, since 1968, Dublin's annual celebration has grown tremendously. The St. Patrick's Day festivities in Dublin — where they are billed as the Irish Mardi Gras — have attracted large numbers of North American tourists.

Evacuation Day in Boston

The evacuation of Boston by British troops took place on March 17, 1776, and Bostonians have been celebrating the anniversary of the day in one way or another ever since. Particular attention is, of course, devoted to important anniversaries, such as the 125th in 1901, when there was an elaborate celebration with parades, public meetings, and dinners with much oratory; and the 175th in 1951, when the Dorchester Heights site of the British debacle was designated a national historic site. The 200th anniversary was observed in 1976, during the nationwide celebration of the US Bicentennial.

In ordinary years the celebration generally is arranged by residents of the southern part of the city (which includes Dorchester Heights), although city and state officials usually participate. The 1908 celebration, which began with a dinner at Bethesda Hall on March 16, has retrospective interest because of the remarks there of the chairman of the committee in charge: "We will never rest content until the tramping of our local parades shall be heard in Washington and legislative enactment shall make March 17 a national holiday."

Although this hope was never realized, Evacuation Day has since 1938 been designated by proclamation of the governor as a legal holiday in Massachusetts' Suffolk County. That historic county, in which government offices are closed for the occasion and public schools are likely to hold special exercises in honor of the day, includes Revere, Chelsea, and Winthrop, as well as Boston.

At the outbreak of the American Revolution the peninsula of Boston was highly vulnerable to attack either from Charlestown, located on an arm of land to the north, which the British had secured at staggering cost in the battle of Bunker Hill (see June 17); or from Dorchester Heights, on another arm of land to the south.

Because of miscalculation or exhaustion after their Bunker Hill engagement with stubborn colonials, the British failed to immediately follow up their victory at Bunker Hill with what would have been the logical next step: an assault on Dorchester Heights.

George Washington, who took command of the Continental army two and a half weeks after Bunker Hill, was quick to take advantage of the British oversight. Training and equipping his ill-prepared force, he proceeded with what history recalls as the Siege of Boston. As soon as he had collected sufficient ammunition and guns, notably the British cannon hauled at his instance from the captured Fort Ticonderoga (see October 17), Washington was able to take Dorchester Heights without opposition.

On the evening of March 4 — while American forces kept up a distracting fire on British lines to obscure what was going on to the rear — the American General John Thomas with 2,000 handpicked men took possession of the Heights. Since fortifications were an immediate necessity and the frozen ground made it impossible for the men to dig in, they carried with them prefabricated entrenchments — timber frames filled with hay, fascines, and barrels to fill with dirt and stones, all loaded on a train of 350 wagons and carts, which moved with the army in the dark. Having arrived on the Heights, the men erected a timber wall, fronted it with an additional fortification made of felled trees, and placed the barrels filled with stones before that. It was, in the words of one observer, "a most astonishing night's work." When day broke on the morning of March 5 the British saw two redoubts on the Heights, armed with cannons and commanding the city.

General Sir William Howe, the British commander, was astounded, and Vice Admiral Molyneux Shuldham, whose ships were now vulnerable to bombardment, admitted that if the Americans could not be driven from their position he could not keep a single vessel in Boston Harbor. Accordingly, a picked company of 2,400 soldiers under the command of Sir Hugh Percy was dispatched in boats, under cover of darkness, to dislodge the Americans. But the New England weather was clearly on the side of the Americans. A sudden storm drove some of the boats ashore, and it rained so hard in the morning that none of the British troops could move. Even with good weather, the attack would have been launched against almost impossible odds from the British point of view. With bad weather, it was delayed — long enough for the Americans to make their position impervious to assault.

Realizing that all was over, General Howe bowed to the inevitable, calling a council of war, which decided that the city the British had occupied so long should be evacuated. Hoping that the step would save the British fleet, Howe agreed to take his forces from the city if they were allowed to go without molestation.

Assent to this plan was tacit, with Washington maintaining a watchful attitude, ready to attack if the British made a hostile move. The actual evacuation was delayed until March 17, when the British troops were taken aboard the ships along with some 1,000 Loyalists. After pausing off Nantasket for 10 days, the fleet sailed for Nova Scotia, bearing about 11,000 soldiers, sailors, and British sympathizers.

After the evacuation was completed the Continental Congress thanked Washington for the delivery of the city from the British and voted him a gold medal. Except for skirmishes, the American Revolution, whose historic early clashes had been in New England at Lexington and Concord (see April 19) and Bunker Hill, thenceforth was fought on other grounds.

Roger Brooke Taney's Birthday

The life of Roger Brooke Taney spanned the historic years from the American Revolution to the Civil War. A member of a wealthy, slave-owning family, he was born on March 17, 1777, in Calvert County, Maryland; by the time of his death in Washington, D.C., on October 12, 1864, he was chief justice of the United States. During his 28 years on the bench of the Supreme Court, he helped formulate several momentous decisions that affected the course of the nation.

After graduating from Dickinson College in Carlisle, Pennsylvania, in 1795, Taney read law and gained admission to the bar of Calvert County, Maryland, in 1799. He was elected a delegate to the General Assembly of the state and in 1801 moved to Frederick. Taney served in the state senate from 1816 to 1821. In 1823 he took up residence in Baltimore and from 1827 to 1831 was attorney general of Maryland.

Originally a Federalist, the young politician broke with the party in 1812. During the following years the nation experienced a period of one-party politics in which various factions among the Jeffersonian Republicans, later known as the Democratic-Republicans, vied for dominance. By 1824 Taney had allied himself with the group led by Andrew Jackson of Tennessee.

In the 1824 election Jackson received more popular votes than any of the other three candidates, John Quincy Adams of Massachusetts, Henry Clay of Kentucky, and William H. Crawford of Georgia, but failed to secure the necessary majority of electoral votes. The selection of the president fell to the House of Representatives, which chose Adams. Jackson's supporters felt cheated and immediately began preparations for the next election.

A number of electioneering innovations, such as public rallies and street demonstrations, helped make the presidential campaign of 1828 unusually memorable. In Baltimore, Roger B. Taney and his associates staged a Jackson gala in conjunction with ceremonies commemorating the city's successful resistance to the British in the War of 1812. The festivities commenced with the firing of a cannon and a parade of 700 marshals. Orators described the exploits of Old Hickory, as Jackson was called, against the British and Indians, and the crowd responded with cheers for their idol.

Jackson's second bid for the White House, in 1828, was successful, and he did not forget those who had supported him. In 1831 the President took Taney into his cabinet as attorney general. The Maryland lawyer entered his post during a period of crisis, the struggle over the fate of the Second Bank of the United States.

Incorporated in 1816 for a period of 20 years, the Bank had an ambivalent character as a private enterprise and as a public servant holding the deposits of the US Treasury. Under the leadership of Nicholas Biddle of Philadelphia, the institution served as a strong central bank that regulated the money supply and thereby kept a check on the expansion of credit. Unfortunately, its very effectiveness gained it enemies.

Many state bankers resented the advantage that federal patronage gave their giant competitor. Others felt that the Bank's conservative policies unduly hampered their activities, which sometimes far exceeded the bounds of sound financial judgment. Finally, some strict-constructionist Democratic-Republicans like Andrew Jackson believed that the government had exceeded its constitutional powers in establishing the institution.

President Jackson wanted a simple deposit bank associated with the Treasury and enjoying no power to make loans or acquire property. In his annual message delivered in December 1829, he questioned the constitutionality and even the expediency of the Bank, which, he claimed, had failed to establish a sound currency. Senator Thomas Hart Benton of Missouri, Jackson's close friend, renewed the attack in 1831 and put particular emphasis on what he regarded as the institution's overbearing role in the national economy.

Although the Bank's charter was not due to expire until 1836, Biddle, alarmed at the Ben-

ton attack, decided to force the issue by requesting early renewal. Congress passed the bill extending the Bank's existence, but the President vetoed it on July 10, 1832. Jackson's message was weak in economic theory, but it was strong in democratic philosophy and included a denunciation of all laws granting special privileges to the powerful. Taney played a part in drafting the executive statement and was responsible for the section in which Jackson argued that the President was not bound by the interpretation of the Constitution enunciated by the Supreme Court.

Some historians have suggested that Taney's interests in the Union Bank of Maryland, for which he was counsel, helped invigorate his opposition to the Philadelphia institution. Whatever the reason, Taney remained a foe of Biddle. In 1833 Jackson decided to cripple the Bank of the United States by removing all federal money from its vaults. When Secretary of the Treasury William J. Duane (from Pennsylvania) opposed this course, the President secured for Taney a temporary appointment to the Treasury post, and the compliant Marylander carried out Jackson's wishes.

In 1835 Jackson appointed Taney an associate justice of the US Supreme Court, but the Senate refrained from acting on the appointment. The death of Chief Justice John Marshall (see September 24) on July 6, 1835, gave the President another opportunity to reward his friend, and he nominated Taney to become the nation's new chief justice. This time the Senate granted its consent, and Roger Brooke Taney took his seat on the Supreme Court. He was the fifth chief justice in American history and the first Roman Catholic to hold that high honor.

On the bench, Taney acted in opposition to some of the trends set by Marshall. Taney curbed monopolies and weakened his illustrious predecessor's defense of the sanctity of contracts (see February 2, Dartmouth College Case Decided), as can be seen in his decision in the *Charles River Bridge* v. *Warren Bridge* case. This found Taney arguing that Massachusetts, which had authorized the building of a toll bridge by the Charles River Bridge Company in 1785, did not impair its original contract by authorizing the construction of the nearby Warren Bridge in 1828.

Taney's most important decision came in 1857, over the volatile slavery issue. The *Dred Scott* case involved questions concerning the legal rights of blacks; the extent of Congress's power over slavery; and the extraneous matter of whether the Missouri Compromise was constitutional. The chief justice's conservative, pro-Southern interpretations inflamed Northern opinion and aggravated the feelings of distrust and anger then tearing the nation apart. The case, among the most famous in the history of the Supreme Court, provided a key issue in the critical period preceding the Civil War.

In 1832 or 1833, Dr. John Emerson of St. Louis had purchased the slave Dred Scott. Emerson became an army surgeon and took Scott with him on assignment to Rock Island, in Illinois, a free state that had no slavery. He later moved with Scott to Fort Snelling, located in federal territory (now Minnesota) above 36°30' north latitude. Except in Missouri, the Missouri Compromise, passed by Congress in 1820, had outlawed slavery north of that line in all the vast, trans-Mississippi area earlier acquired through the Louisiana Purchase. Dr. Emerson returned to slave-holding Missouri in 1838 and Dred Scott accompanied him.

Emerson died several years later, and in 1846 Scott attempted to buy his freedom (and that of his wife, whom he had married while at Fort Snelling) from the doctor's widow. When the latter refused his request, Scott, with the assistance of an army officer and a lawyer, took his case to court in St. Louis. This lower court ruled in his favor, accepting the argument that Scott's earlier residence in a free state and territory had ended his servitude. The Missouri supreme court, however, reversed the decision, justifying its stand on the basis of a Missouri law that declared that any slave who voluntarily returned from a free state automatically resumed his bonds.

Mrs. Emerson's remarriage to Dr. Calvin C. Chaffee, a Massachusetts politician with antislavery leanings, further complicated matters. Under Missouri law she lost jurisdiction over Dr. Emerson's estate, including slaves, which had been left in trust for her daughter. John F. A. Sanford of New York, Mrs. Chaffee's brother, became administrator of the Emerson property. Scott's lawyers immediately renewed the litigation, but this time brought their case before the federal courts because the plaintiff and defendant were no longer residents of the same state.

Before a US circuit court, Sanford argued that Scott, as a slave, was not a citizen of Missouri and had no right to bring suit. Judge R. W. Wells rejected this contention but found that the law supported the Emerson estate's right to retain Scott. At that point, Scott's lawyers determined to appeal to the Supreme Court.

The justices heard the case argued in 1856 and deliberated on February 15, 1857. Justice Samuel Nelson of New York held that, by Missouri law, Scott remained a slave despite his temporary residence on free soil. Nelson's moderate opinion would have limited the Court's involvement in the slavery controversy, but his fellow judges thought it inadequate. The proslavery majority, particularly James Wayne of Georgia, wanted a strong pronouncement to counteract the long dissenting statements promised by antislavery justices Benjamin Curtis of Massachusetts and John McLean of Ohio.

Each of the nine judges issued an opinion, but the majority agreed that blacks could not be citizens and that the Missouri Compromise was unconstitutional. Chief Justice Taney's statement was particularly inflammatory. He argued that at the time of the signing of the Declaration of Independence and drafting of the Constitution black slaves "were considered as a subordinate and inferior class of beings . . . and whether emancipated or not . . . had no rights or privileges but such as those who held the power and the government might choose to grant them." Thus, Dred Scott could not be a citizen and had no right to sue in the circuit court of Missouri.

Taney then proceeded to consider the legality of the Missouri Compromise. The chief justice stated that the 1820 agreement was invalid because it violated the constitutional provision (the 5th Amendment) that forbids the deprivation of property without due process of law. He thus held, in effect, that Congress could not enact legislation that limited slaveholders' property rights.

Roger Brooke Taney remained chief justice until his death in 1864. He was buried in Frederick, Maryland, which has erected a monument in memory of him. His house, built in 1815, and open from May to October or by appointment, is at 123 South Bentz Street. In the drawing room is a painting showing the chief justice administering the oath of office to President Abraham Lincoln in 1861. Portraits of the other six Presidents — Martin Van Buren, Benjamin Harrison, James Polk, Zachary Taylor, Franklin Pierce, and James Buchanan — at whose inaugurations Justice Taney officiated are in this room, as is a bust of the chief justice. The dining room contains a collection of likenesses of Taney. A miniature, which is the earliest of his portraits, was a gift to his future wife, Anne Key — the sister of Francis Scott Key, who wrote the "Star-Spangled Banner." One of the rooms in the house is dedicated to Key. It contains a collection of portraits and papers of the Key family, along with a magazine, dated 1814, containing the first printing of the "Star-Spangled Banner."

Interestingly enough, Taney himself freed his own slaves. In the living room of the slave quarters is preserved the record of their freedom.

MARCH 18

John C. Calhoun's Birthday

John Caldwell Calhoun, the pre–Civil War champion of states' rights, whose views remain controversial issues today, was born on March 18, 1782, in the Abbeville District of South Carolina. His father, an Irish immigrant named "Pat" Calhoun, was a farmer and political leader in South Carolina's up-country. Young Calhoun was largely self-taught until, at 18, he entered the famous "log college," where he was schooled by his brother-in-law, the Reverend Moses Waddel, later president of the University of Georgia. Thus prepared, Calhoun was able to enter the junior class at Yale College, from which he was graduated in 1804. He subsequently studied at the Litchfield, Connecticut, Law School.

In 1807 Calhoun was admitted to the bar in his native South Carolina and shortly thereafter was elected a member of the South Carolina legislature. He served there in the sessions of 1808 and 1809 during debate over a constitutional amendment that adjusted legislative apportionment of the state's two distinct regions — the wealthy low-country of the planters and the poorer up-country of the farmers. Calhoun, who always considered himself an up-countryman, became associated with low-country interests as well, and he gained entrance into South Carolina plantation society when he married his aristocratic cousin, Floride Bonneau Calhoun of Charleston in 1811.

His nearly four decades on the national political scene began the same year, when he was elected to the US House of Representatives — just as Henry Clay was becoming Speaker of the House. The two men quickly became leaders of the young "War Hawks," who urged President James Madison into the War of 1812 with Britain. Calhoun also followed a nationalistic course in other respects, voting for the protective tariff of 1816 and, like Clay, promoting what was called the "American system" to bring improvements and prosperity to all sections of the country.

For a time, Calhoun joined with the nationalists who favored use of federal funds to build new national roads and canals. Named chairman of a committee to consider setting up a permanent fund for this purpose, he urged passage of his so-called bonus bill with arguments that were curious in view of his later philosophy: the very size of the United States, he said, was a threat to its unity, and new roads and canals would help to overcome this difficulty. Congress passed the bill, which would have made large revenues available for con-

struction, had it not been killed by the veto of President Madison.

Calhoun served in the House of Representatives until 1817, when he became secretary of war, a post he held during President Monroe's two terms of office. During the election of 1824, Calhoun was an unsuccessful presidential contender along with Andrew Jackson, William H. Crawford, and Clay. But he was elected to the vice presidency under the successful candidate, John Quincy Adams. Four years later, Calhoun was reelected Vice President under Jackson, whose victory he had helped make possible.

Calhoun's thinking had meanwhile changed since the days when he favored protective tariffs and federal funds for highways. For one thing, Calhoun himself had become a farmer and the cotton- and slave-based Southern economy had begun its drastic decline. For another, Calhoun had been impressed, during debate over the 1820 Missouri Compromise, with the thinking of John Randolph of Roanoke, who had called attention to a fundamental point: if the South admitted the right of the Northern congressional majority to prohibit slavery in the new US territories, it would in the process be recognizing simple majority rule. Calhoun's changed views on tariffs were evident in 1827, when he used his vote as Vice President to defeat in the Senate a bill that would have increased protection for New England woolen manufacturers and sheep raisers.

But the crucial point in the formation of Calhoun's thinking came in discussion of the so-called tariff of abominations of 1828, which he opposed on the grounds that it was unconstitutional and benefited the North at the expense of the South. He set forth his arguments in his famous South Carolina Exposition, the first systematized presentation of the doctrine of nullification and states' rights. Briefly, he held that the states, which had created the Union, were the final authority as to whether acts of the federal government were constitutional; and that it was the duty and privilege of each state to nullify a law it deemed unconstitutional, so that the law had no force within its boundaries unless three-fourths of the states could agree on a constitutional amendment to uphold it.

The doctrine, which translated what might have been mere opinion into a plan of action, had long-lasting implications. Segregationists were still quoting it well over a century later, during the intensified drive for black civil rights that characterized the 1960s. But its first application came much earlier: South Carolina voted to nullify the tariff of 1832 (and 1828).

In so doing, it added fuel to a controversy between Calhoun and President Jackson that had been fomented, or at least fanned, by political enemies bent on ruining Calhoun's chances at the presidency. Calhoun contributed his share to the ill feeling by objecting to Jackson's spoils system of political reward. So did Calhoun's wife, the aristocratic Floride, who — to Jackson's outrage — led cabinet wives in snubbing Peggy Eaton, the charming and controversial wife of his secretary of war. When South Carolina, armed with Calhoun's "Exposition," voted for nullification, Jackson viewed the action as close to anarchy and threatened to arrest Calhoun. Calhoun resigned as Vice President in 1832 and was succeeded by Martin Van Buren, a politically skillful widower whose courtesy to Peggy Eaton had won him Jackson's regard.

Within a year of his resignation, however, Calhoun had returned to Washington in the new role of US senator, which he filled (except for a brief interlude as President Tyler's secretary of state in 1844–1845) until the end of his life. As senator, he opposed both big business and big government, while seeking to unite the Democratic party and devote it to states' rights and agricultural interests. He secured the annexation of Texas (as secretary of state) and opposed the war with Mexico in 1846–1848. The nullification crisis, meanwhile, had been averted under the compromise tariff of 1833 sponsored by Henry Clay. But the questions of slavery and states' rights remained unanswered. In 1833 they were the subjects of a historic debate between Calhoun and Daniel Webster (see January 18), defining the concepts of government held by the supporters and opponents of slavery.

By the time of the debate over Clay's Compromise of 1850, Calhoun was thinking most specifically of the need for legislation that would safeguard economic interests on a regional basis, restoring the vanished balance between the economically slowed South and the rapidly developing North. The debate over the compromise, which Calhoun opposed, partly because it provided for the admission of California as a free state, marked the last appearance of the Senate's "great triumvirate" — Clay, Webster, and Calhoun, with Calhoun defending Southern interests, insisting that the North recognize the South's equal rights in all new territory, and calling for an end to Northern agitation against slavery. His arguments made it evident that he clearly understood the threat to the Southern economy inherent in proposals for abolition.

But by the time he was scheduled to present these views, on March 4, 1850, Calhoun, ill and anxious, was too weak to make a speech, although he dragged himself to the Senate to hear

his argument read by Senator Mason of Virginia. Calhoun died on March 31. Events of the next decade gave tragic emphasis to the warning he had issued a few weeks before his death: the South, he had said, "cannot remain, as things now are, consistently with honor and safety, in the Union."

The white-pillared home of Calhoun can be visited today on the campus of Clemson College in Clemson, South Carolina. The state of South Carolina chose to be represented in the Capitol's Statuary Hall, in Washington, D.C., by a statue of Calhoun. In early 1976 the statue was moved to the floor below and included there, in the east front lobby of the Capitol, in a group comprising representatives of the 13 original states.

Grover Cleveland's Birthday

(Stephen) Grover Cleveland, President of the United States from 1885 to 1889 and again from 1893 to 1897, is known as the 22nd and 24th President because of the interval between his terms. He was born in the Old Manse of the First Presbyterian Church of Caldwell, New Jersey, on March 18, 1837 — the fifth of nine children of Anne Neal Cleveland and the Reverend Richard Falley Cleveland, a descendant of an early colonial family. Named for his father's predecessor in the pastorate, young Cleveland dropped the name Stephen in childhood.

When he was very small, the family moved from Caldwell to Fayetteville, New York. He attended school there until family financial troubles forced him to work in a village store, and both teachers and students liked his frank nature and admired his studiousness. In 1850, when his family moved to Clinton, New York, Cleveland entered the Clinton academy to prepare for Hamilton College. However, his father's death in 1853 caused him to give up his college plans in order to help support his mother and the younger children.

After a year as a bookkeeper and teacher in the New York Institution for the Blind in New York City, Cleveland moved west in search of better opportunities. In Buffalo, New York, he stopped to work on an uncle's book for stock farmers. Soon he became a clerk and law student there in the firm of Rogers, Bowen and Rogers. Through great effort and self-denial he was admitted to the bar in 1859, at the age of 22.

At the outbreak of the Civil War, Cleveland chose not to follow two brothers into the Union army. When drafted in 1863, he hired a substitute as provided for in the conscription law of the time. Political opponents later suggested that Cleveland's decision indicated Southern sympathies, but during the war he was supporting his mother and two sisters.

In Buffalo, Cleveland joined the Democratic party with his law associates and became very active locally. He entered public life first in 1863 when he was appointed assistant district attorney for Erie County. While participating in politics in the 1860s and 1870s, Cleveland was building a flourishing law practice, to which he would later return calmly whenever defeated for public office.

The first electoral defeat came immediately, in 1865, in the election for county district attorney. Nonetheless, in 1870 he was elected sheriff of Erie County. In this office Cleveland at once demonstrated to the voters his exceptional energy and honesty. A decade later, in 1881, the Democrats nominated the 44-year-old bachelor for reform mayor of Buffalo and won. Cleveland was so successful in his broad attack on political and social corruption in Buffalo that before he had served a full year Democrats in the state nominated him for governor of New York. Because he was not a part of the inner circle of state politicians, Cleveland drew many independent and reform Republican votes in 1882 to win the governorship by a large plurality. As governor, he attracted the attention of the country by his courage in putting the general interest before the demands of party leaders and in freely exercising his veto power.

Cleveland's burgeoning reputation led the national Democratic party to nominate him for the presidency before his term as governor had ended — despite objections from the Tammany bosses of the Democratic organization in New York City. In 1884 the Democratic party had been without national power for 23 years. Party leaders saw their opportunity to defeat a divided and demoralized Republican party by running Cleveland on a reform platform. After a bitter mudslinging campaign, Cleveland defeated James G. Blaine by a narrow popular majority but with clear victory in the electoral college.

Grover Cleveland's first four years as President were considerably smoother than his second term. In the 1880s and 1890s the United States was experiencing far-reaching changes in its economic life and in the composition of its population. But the turbulence that accompanied these changes was to hit Cleveland's second administration hard. The dedication of the Statue of Liberty in New York harbor on October 28, 1886, a ceremony in which he participated during his first term (see October 28), reflects the forces of social change and the problems he faced as President.

During his first administration Cleveland demonstrated characteristic political independence, firmness, and zeal for reform. He strongly supported the creation of a federal civil service based on competitive examinations to replace the spoils system of political patronage. He vetoed many private pension bills designed to reward congressmen's friends. And he drew down the wrath of the politicians and risked the voters' displeasure when he vetoed a major bill that would have depleted the Treasury to recompense veterans for nonmilitary disabilities. In addition, President Cleveland attacked high US tariffs as inflationary, stating that they unduly rewarded protected industries at the expense of consumers. The election campaign of 1888 opened amid public furor over an administration-favored bill to lower tariffs.

On June 2, 1886, Cleveland, then 49, married his former ward, the beautiful 21-year-old Frances Folsom, in the Blue Room of the White House. He is the only President whose wedding ceremony took place in the White House.

In 1888 the Democrats renominated Grover Cleveland despite opposition within the party. Although he won the popular vote by a slender plurality, Cleveland lost to Benjamin Harrison, the Republican candidate, by 168 to 233 electoral votes. He returned to law practice in New York City for the next four years.

In 1892, however, Cleveland was renominated for President by the Democrats in the face of fierce opposition from Tammany Hall. In this election, he defeated Benjamin Harrison and James B. Weaver, the Populist candidate, by a sound margin in the electoral college, though with only a small plurality of the popular vote.

The United States was rent by economic strife as Cleveland's second administration opened. A financial panic soon after he took office touched off one of the most severe depressions in American history. The public blamed Cleveland and the Democrats for events whose long-range causes were little understood, and the Democratic party itself split into factions with conflicting views on monetary policies. Cleveland fought to limit the silver currency in circulation, in an attempt to avert inflation. The "pro-silver" congressmen bitterly opposed him. The pro-silver forces spoke for agrarian sections of the country, which were suffering severe hardship and looking to the free coinage of silver for economic relief. President Cleveland achieved the repeal of the Sherman Silver Purchase Act of 1890 with the help of the Republican minority in Congress. But this action failed to reverse the depression. While business continued to grapple with failures and uncertainty, unemployment rose and wages dropped.

Also during Cleveland's second term, the Pullman Palace Car works in Chicago were the scene of a fierce labor war, which spread into a major rail strike, with riots and bloodshed in a number of places. Over the protests of the governor of Illinois, the President sent federal troops to Chicago to put down the strike, in the name of moving the mails and assuring interstate commerce. The business world applauded the President's action, but organized labor was embittered.

With the exception of his strong intervention in a boundary quarrel between Great Britain and Venezuela, President Cleveland was stanchly antiimperialist in his foreign policy, unlike his Republican successor, William McKinley.

Grover Cleveland left the presidency extremely unpopular. In 1896 antiadministration forces gained control of the Democratic national convention and refused to endorse Cleveland's record, instead nominating William Jennings Bryan (see March 19) on a free-silver platform. Cleveland joined the "sound money" Democrats in bolting the convention to nominate a different candidate — John M. Palmer — who lost, as did Bryan.

Cleveland retired to Princeton, New Jersey, where he was soon elected a trustee of Princeton University and named Stafford Little lecturer on public affairs. In 1905 he agreed to serve on a three-man board of trustees to reorganize the Equitable Life Assurance Society. In retirement his views on business were often sought, and he had leisure to write two books and numerous articles.

In the last years of his life, Cleveland's unpopularity with the electorate faded and he came more and more to be regarded as one of the political sages of the country. At his death on June 24, 1908, expressions of esteem poured forth, no doubt in part to allay earlier bitterness, but also because he had come to symbolize to Americans certain cherished ideals and virtues. President William Howard Taft wrote for the 75th anniversary of Cleveland's birth:

Grover Cleveland earned the sincere gratitude of his countrymen. . . . He was a great President . . . because he was a patriot with the highest sense of public duty, because he was a statesman of clear perceptions, of the utmost courage of his convictions and of great plainness of speech, because he was a man of high character . . . and because throughout his political life he showed these rugged virtues of the public servant and citizen.

In Cleveland's honor the Grover Cleveland Memorial Tower was erected at the graduate college of Princeton University. The First Presbyterian church in Caldwell, New Jersey, agreed to sell the manse in which he had been born to a memorial association a few years after his death. Located at 207 Bloomfield Avenue, the Grover Cleveland Birthplace was dedicated in 1913 and was restored completely in 1937 under a Works Progress Administration project. Since 1945 it has been maintained by the State

of New Jersey as a memorial and a museum open to the public. Many local celebrations honoring Cleveland were established when he died but have ceased with the passage of years. He is buried in the Princeton Cemetery at Witherspoon and Wiggins streets.

MARCH 19

William Jennings Bryan's Birthday

William Jennings Bryan, who was the most popular leader of the Democratic party for many years, was born in Salem, Illinois, on March 19, 1860. He was graduated from Illinois College in 1881. A college oratory prize foreshadowed his later career. He was graduated from the Union College of Law in Chicago in 1883 and began law practice in Jacksonville, Illinois. In 1887 he moved to Lincoln, Nebraska, where in 1890 he was elected to the US House of Representatives. He served there for two terms.

In Congress, Bryan made full use of his gift of oratory and he was much in demand as a public speaker. The Democrats of the time attributed the panic of 1893 to the gold standard and felt that bimetallism was the panacea for the depression that followed the panic. Bryan became the party's leading proponent of the free coinage of silver at the ratio of 16 ounces of silver to one of gold.

While still in the House, he unsuccessfully sought election to the Senate. He became editor of the Omaha *World-Herald* in 1894, resigning in 1896 after he was nominated for the presidency by the Democratic National Convention.

The nomination was a signal honor for Bryan — then only 36 — and a tribute to his persuasiveness as a speaker. As a delegate to the convention, he had mounted the platform on the third day and delivered his famous "Cross of Gold" speech in denunciation of the gold standard. It ended with a resounding declaration that is still included in collections of famous quotations: "You shall not press down upon the brow of labor this crown of thorns, you shall not crucify mankind upon a cross of gold." Enthusiastically applauded, Bryan was nominated for President on the fifth roll call the next day. The National Silver party and the Populists also nominated him, but he was defeated by William McKinley, the Republican candidate.

Again nominated by his party's convention in 1900, Bryan was once more defeated by McKinley. He then returned to Lincoln, Nebraska, where he established and edited *The Commoner*, a weekly newspaper that kept his name and views before the people for many years. Called the Great Commoner, he dedicated himself to speaking for "the toiling masses," who fanatically idolized their champion — a man of imposing looks and great personal charm, with a voice that made him the greatest orator of his day.

He was nominated for the presidency for the third time in 1908 but was once again defeated — this time by the Republican William Howard Taft. Bryan's influence in his party nonetheless continued, and it was largely because of his efforts that Woodrow Wilson was nominated in 1912.

Wilson, successful in his campaign, took Bryan into his cabinet as secretary of state, an office Bryan resigned in June 1915 because of his opposition to the war policy of the President. As secretary of state, Bryan had negotiated a large number of arbitration treaties, which he had hoped would prevent war.

He was a popular lecturer, and on his retirement from the cabinet (and even while he was still secretary of state) he lectured in many parts of the country. In the course of his career, he was influential on behalf of a number of important measures that eventually were adopted. Woman suffrage, the popular election of senators, prohibition, the income tax, and requirements for public disclosure of newspaper ownership were among them.

Over the years, Bryan became one of the country's best-known advocates of Fundamentalism. As a Fundamentalist, he believed the Bible should be interpreted literally in every instance, even when it dealt — allegorically, others held — with natural history. He accordingly regarded Darwin's theory of evolution as the root of many of the theological errors of the day and was instrumental in drafting state legislation forbidding the teaching of evolution in public schools. This prohibition became law in Oklahoma, Mississippi, and Tennessee.

After Bryan had retired from politics, he divided his time between selling real estate in Florida (where he moved in 1921) and propounding Fundamentalism. Thus in 1925, when John T. Scopes, a biology teacher in the high school at Dayton, Tennessee, was charged with teaching evolution in the public schools in violation of Tennessee's state law, Bryan volunteered to act as an attorney for the prosecution. Scopes was convicted but never sentenced.

Bryan himself never left Dayton. Five days after the trial, weakened by his exertions in the heat of a southern summer, he died suddenly, on July 26, 1925.

A college named for Bryan was founded in Dayton in 1930. He is further memorialized in Salem, Illinois, his birthplace, where a statue of him by Gutzon Borglum stands in Bryan Memorial Park.

In Lincoln, Nebraska, Bryan's home from 1902 to 1917, Fairview, is open to the public in the spring and summer months and may be visited by appointment at other times of the year. It is located on the grounds of Bryan Hospital at Sumner Street near 48th Street. Fairview's first floor and part of the second have been restored and filled with original furnishings and memorabilia.

Earl Warren's Birthday

Earl Warren, the 14th chief justice of the United States, was born on March 19, 1891, in Los Angeles. His father, Methias Warren, who changed the family's surname from Varren, had come in his infancy to the United States from Stavanger, Norway. Warren's mother, Crystal Hernlund Warren, emigrated from Sweden when she was young and spent her formative years in Minnesota.

Methias Warren, an employee of the Southern Pacific Railroad, was an early member of Eugene V. Debs's American Railway Union and in 1895 lost his job when he joined a strike against the line. He later prospered as a master railroad car repairman and as a dabbler in real estate. The elder Warren met a tragic death in 1938, when an unidentified robber murdered him.

Earl Warren worked at a variety of odd jobs after school and during summer vacations; he delivered newspapers, drove an ice wagon, sold books, and acted as a railroad callboy rounding up train crews. He also worked as a cub reporter for a newspaper, the Bakersfield *Californian*.

Warren prepared for his later career by studying political science for three years at the University of California at Berkeley and then entering the institution's school of law. He received a B.L. degree in 1912 and a J.D. in 1914; on May 14, 1914, he won admission to the state bar. He joined the legal department of the Associated Oil Company in San Francisco but then moved across the Bay to become a law clerk in the firm of Robinson and Robinson in Oakland.

When the United States entered World War I in 1917, Warren applied for the Army Officer Training Corps, but minor surgery made it impossible for him to be available before the quotas were filled. Undaunted, he enlisted as an infantryman and took basic training at Camp Lewis, Washington. The young lawyer managed to advance from private to first sergeant in four weeks and became an officer candidate in January 1918. Commissioned a second lieutenant in May of that year, he instructed recruits at Camp Lee, Virginia, and officer trainees at

Fort MacArthur, Texas. He left active duty as a first lieutenant on December 11, 1918, but retained a captaincy in the reserves until 1935.

Assemblyman Leon Gray, a onetime member of Robinson and Robinson, helped Warren to secure in 1919 the post of clerk of the judiciary committee of the lower house of the California legislature. After the legislative session ended, Warren joined Gray's law office in Oakland, but he quickly moved on to become deputy attorney for that city (1919–1920).

In May 1920 Ezra Decoto, the district attorney of Alameda County, appointed Warren as one of his assistants, and by 1923 the rising public servant had become chief deputy district attorney. Warren, who also served as legal adviser to the Alameda Board of Supervisors, succeeded Decoto as district attorney when his mentor resigned in 1925, and he persuaded the voters to grant him a full term in the 1926 campaign. Reelected in 1930 and 1934, he earned a reputation as a crime fighter and "racket buster."

Warren was a successful public prosecutor for 13 years but found the role a distressing one. "I never heard a jury bring in a verdict of guilty," he once commented, "but that I felt sick at the pit of my stomach." Much to his credit, as district attorney he never had a conviction reversed by a higher court.

A Republican who served as a national committeeman for the party from 1936 through 1938, Warren nonetheless won the nomination of the Democrats and Progressives as well as of the Republicans when he successfully sought election as attorney general of California in 1938. He immediately made good his pledge of nonpartisanship by urging a jury to convict the secretary of the outgoing Republican governor for selling pardons to prisoners. As attorney general, Warren closed the flourishing illegal dog-racing tracks in the state and harassed gambling ships operating just beyond the three-mile limit of Long Beach.

At the outbreak of World War II, Warren focused his attention on national security and shaped the Uniform Sabotage Prevention, or Warren, Act. In the uneasy days after the Japanese attack on the US installation at Pearl Harbor on December 7, 1941, he actively supported the forced removal of 110,000 Japanese aliens and Nisei (Japanese-Americans) from strategic spots along the West Coast to inland detention camps. In retrospect, he shared with many others feelings of guilt and preferred not to speak of it.

Warren ran for the office of governor of California in 1942, easily defeating the Democratic incumbent, Culbert Olson, by 342,000 votes.

Characteristically, he promised a bipartisan administration and vowed: "I am a Republican, but ... I shall seek the support of people of both parties. I can do this honorably because I am independent, and therefore in a position to serve the people fairly, regardless of their politics or mine." He won the nomination of both major parties in 1946, one of only three governors in the history of the state to win reelection. In 1950 he became California's first three-term chief executive when he decisively defeated James Roosevelt, son of President Franklin D. Roosevelt.

As governor, Warren appointed both Democrats and Republicans to important political positions and increased the responsiveness and efficiency of several agencies, including the Public Works and Industrial Relations departments. He advocated a variety of programs directed at easing the burdens on the less affluent: he supported a reduction in the sales tax, raised old age pensions, expanded unemployment insurance coverage, and encouraged the appropriation of funds for child-care centers. He won wide recognition for his programs and became an aspirant for national office.

Warren gave the keynote speech at the Republican National Convention in 1944 and led the California delegation into the camp of Thomas E. Dewey, the governor of New York. In November 1947 Warren announced that he wanted to be the party's candidate for President in the following year, but he lost the designation to Dewey. Although he had declined the vice presidential nod in 1944, he accepted it in 1948. To the surprise of almost everyone, the Dewey-Warren combination, heavily favored by the pollsters to win the November election, failed to oust Harry S. Truman from the White House. Warren again sought the presidential nomination in 1952, but Dwight D. Eisenhower became the Republican standard-bearer instead.

Although Warren had no experience as a member of the judiciary, President Eisenhower in 1953 appointed him to succeed the deceased Fred M. Vinson as chief justice of the United States. Eisenhower noted that Warren's "reputation for integrity, honesty, middle-of-the-road philosophy, experience in government, experience in the law," showed him to be a man who had "no ends to serve except the United States." On October 5, 1953, Associate Justice Hugo L. Black administered the oath of office to Warren as the new leader of the Supreme Court.

In his earliest days on the high bench, Warren seemed to follow the lead of Associate Justice Felix Frankfurter, the Court's most eloquent spokesman for traditional jurisprudence. Frankfurter thought the Court should thwart the will of the Congress only in those rare instances when a law clearly contradicted the Constitution. The venerable jurist was also particularly circumspect about curbing the powers of the state to protect itself against malefactors.

Warren was neither a deep theoretician nor a virtuoso legal technician. His major desire, he told the editors of *Fortune* magazine, was to be fair. "A legal system," he said, "is simply a mature and sophisticated attempt, never perfected, to institutionalize this sense of justice and to free men from the terror and unpredictability of arbitrary force."

As Warren gained experience on the bench, he aligned himself less frequently with Frankfurter and agreed almost consistently with Black. The latter was an ardent civil libertarian and defender of the Bill of Rights. With Warren and Black in the lead, the Court after 1954 worked vigorously to enforce individual rights where they were denied and to protect them where they were threatened. Warren's earnest desire was that the Supreme Court be a "people's court."

The justices in 1954 reversed a decision, which their predecessors had made in the 1896 case of *Plessy* v. *Ferguson*, that restricting blacks to separate but equal public facilities did not constitute illegal discrimination. Relying heavily on psychological and sociological arguments, the Court in the historic case of *Brown* v. *Board of Education of Topeka* (see May 17) unanimously stated that racially segregated elementary schools were inherently unequal and that their existence denied equal protection of the law to black citizens. The Court quickly ordered the states to place public schools on a racially nondiscriminatory basis "with all deliberate speed." Some localities complied quickly, but many others have devised means to circumvent the ruling.

From 1960 to 1966 the Warren Court made it clear that civil authorities could not deprive individuals suspected of crimes of basic rights guaranteed under the Constitution. In *Mapp* v. *Ohio* (1961) the justices forbade states from introducing at trials evidence obtained through unreasonable search or seizure. In the landmark case of *Gideon* v. *Wainwright* (1963) the Court affirmed the right of indigent persons to court-appointed counsel at state felony trials. In the cases of *Escobedo* v. *Illinois* (1964) and *Miranda* v. *Arizona* (1966), the Court declared that police at the time of arrest must inform prisoners of their right to see a lawyer and stated that suspects had the right to have counsel present during interrogations.

Many of the Supreme Court decisions during Warren's tenure as chief justice were contro-

versial, and some conservative groups even demanded that Congress remove him from the bench. Many citizens were particularly distressed by the Court's ruling in the case of *Engel* v. *Vitale* (1962) that the New York State Board of Regents could not draw up a prayer for use in public school classrooms. In keeping with the doctrine of the separation of church and state, the justices, divided six to one, argued that, even if pupils retained the right not to participate, "it is no part of the business of government to compose official prayers to be recited as a part of a religious program carried on by government." In the case of the *School District of Abington Township* v. *Schempp* (1963), the Court banned Bible reading and recitation of the Lord's Prayer in public schools.

Politically, the Warren Court's most significant decisions may have been those that dealt with apportionment of seats in state legislatures. Traditionally, a disproportionately large number of delegates from rural areas held seats in many state assemblies and senates and in the US House of Representatives, thus wielding the power to prevent legislation designed to alleviate urban distress. In *Baker* v. *Carr* (1962) the Court agreed to hear cases related to the problem, and in *Reynolds* v. *Sims* (1964) it determined that the states must apportion both chambers of their legislatures by population in such a way as to treat all their citizens as equally as possible. In the case of *Westberry* v. *Saunders* (1964) the justices declared that all congressional districts should include approximately the same number of inhabitants.

After the assassination of President John F. Kennedy in 1963 (see November 22), President Lyndon B. Johnson placed on Warren's shoulders the heavy responsibility of conducting the government's inquiry into that tragedy. The chief justice and six other noted Americans worked for almost a full year on the case. On September 27, 1964, the Warren Commission issued its 888-page report, which concluded that Lee Harvey Oswald, acting independently, fatally shot Kennedy in Dallas, Texas. The commission's findings have been challenged by many who are convinced that not all the facts have been disclosed.

In mid-June 1968 Warren informed President Johnson that he wished to retire from the Court. He stepped down at the end of the next Court year in June 1969. At a press conference Warren expressed satisfaction with his 16 years on the bench and listed *Baker* v. *Carr* (reapportionment), *Brown* v. *Board of Education* (segregation), and *Gideon* v. *Wainwright* (rights of accused persons) as his three most significant decisions. President Richard M. Nixon appointed

Warren F. Burger to replace Warren as chief justice.

On October 14, 1925, Warren married Nina Palmquist Meyer, a Swedish-born widow, and adopted her son, James. The Warrens became the parents of five more children, Earl Jr., Robert, Virginia, Dorothy, and Nina. Warren, a Baptist and a Mason, made a habit of starting and concluding each day by reading from the Bible. For recreation, he favored deer and duck hunting and was an avid baseball and football fan.

The man who, it has frequently been said, as chief justice exerted the most profound influence on his country's law and way of life since the time of Chief Justice John Marshall a century and a half earlier, died on July 9, 1974, at the age of 83. Following a US Army honor funeral, which was attended by people from all walks of life, the noted jurist was buried in Arlington National Cemetery.

MARCH 20

Neal Dow's Birthday

An early leader in the temperance movement, which assumed prominence in the United States in the 19th and early 20th centuries, Neal Dow became world famous as the Father of Prohibition in Maine, the first state to prohibit the sale of liquor. Born in Portland on March 20, 1804, Dow was trained by his Quaker parents in the principles of peace, industry, thrift, and temperance. Although he espoused these principles throughout his long life, Dow was eventually dismissed from the Society of Friends because he came to disagree with it on the propriety of using arms.

Educated at the Friends Academy in New Bedford, Massachusetts, Dow then joined his father in the tanning business and accumulated a large fortune. His first temperance speech was made in opposition to serving liquor at a dinner of the Deluge Engine Company of Portland. His plea was successful. No liquor was served to the firemen at the dinner.

Dow was a delegate to the first temperance convention in Maine when the State Temperance Society was organized in 1834. Four years later he helped found the Maine Temperance Union, whose members were pledged to total abstinence from liquor. It was not until 1845, · however, that he persuaded this organization to favor legislation forbidding the sale of intoxicants in the state. The Maine legislature passed the first state prohibitory law the next year, though it was too weak to be fully effective.

Dow, elected mayor of Portland in 1851, was immediately made chairman of a committee to urge more stringent antiliquor legislation. He drafted a bill that was passed by large majorities in both houses of the state legislature and then signed into law by Governor John Hubbard on June 2, 1851, which is generally regarded as the date when Prohibition began in Maine. The statute became widely known as the Maine Law. In the next 10 years it served as the model for Prohibition laws in more than a dozen other states, most of them later repealed or made invalid by court decisions. Dow, who maintained a lifelong dedication to the cause of temperance, continued to lecture widely on the subject after passage of the law. He was reelected mayor of Portland in 1855 – in which year the Maine Law was temporarily repealed as a result of Portland's "June riot," led by anti-Prohibitionists. It was reenacted in response to popular sentiment in 1858.

Dow was 57 years old when the Civil War erupted. Nearly as intense in his opposition to slavery as to alcohol, he volunteered his services on behalf of the Union and became colonel of the 13th Regiment of Maine volunteers. During the conflict he rose to the rank of brigadier general. Twice wounded, he was taken prisoner while recuperating. Eventually exchanged for a Confederate major general, Fitzhugh Lee, Dow returned home in temporarily broken health.

After the war, he continued to speak and write on behalf of Prohibition, traveling extensively in the process. He was the candidate of the Prohibition party for President in the election of 1880, winning a total of 10,305 votes. Four years later, owing to his efforts, the constitution of Maine was amended to prohibit the sale of intoxicants in the state, as the Maine law already did.

By the time Dow died – in Portland on October 2, 1897 – the temperance movement, which had waned during the years of the Civil War and the following decade, had seen a resurgence under the leadership of Frances E. Willard of the Woman's Christian Temperance Union (see February 17 and September 28) and others. Members of temperance groups, which again flourished, triumphed in 1919 with passage of the 18th Amendment, legislating Prohibition on a nationwide scale (see January 16).

Few of those who had worked hardest for the measure lived to see their labors undone with passage of the 21st Amendment, repealing the 18th, in 1933 (see December 5) after a stormy period of attempted enforcement and all but universal violation of the law. Since then the question of abstaining from alcohol has generally been regarded as a matter for personal decision, although there are still a number of counties and municipalities, in various parts of the country, where availability of alcoholic beverages is determined by local option.

Repeal, as enacted by the 21st Amendment, remains, however, the general order of the day. Notwithstanding this fact, the era of the totally unregulated pre-Prohibition saloon and the flagrant abuses associated with the manufacture and distribution of liquor is gone. Broad federal regulations apply to many facets of manufacturing, bottling, and distributing alcoholic beverages. And all states today exercise some form of liquor control — either by licensing, with its attendant standards, or by a state monopoly in which alcoholic beverages are sold through state-owned stores, as in Maine and a number of other states.

MARCH 21

Spring Begins

In the United States, and the north temperate zones generally, the season of fresh growth and new life known as spring begins, as most sources put it, on "about March 21." In actual fact, the three-month period begins on either the 21st or a day earlier. The exact moment when the sun is at the vernal equinox, officially signaling the change of season, varies slightly from year to year because of the gamut of oscillations and wobbling motions that Earth manifests both in its rotation on its axis and in its elliptical course around the sun.

Spring is the first season of the astronomical year, coming between winter and summer. Its start can be precisely defined astronomically. The ecliptic, the plane in which the sun seems to revolve around the earth and in which the earth really revolves around the sun, is divided into four 90° sections, each beginning with a definite point: two solstices and two equinoxes. The amount of time taken by the sun to cover each of these divisions is termed a season. The season of spring begins at the vernal equinox when the sun, as seen from the earth, passes through the intersection of the ecliptic and the celestial equator, having then a longitude of exactly 0°. Its rays extend from the North to the South Pole, and day and night are an equal 12 hours throughout the world.

In antiquity the start of the year was often reckoned from the vernal equinox, which was also chosen as the point from which to calculate — in an eastward direction — the 12 zodiacal constellations, starting with Aries (see The Zodiac at end of book). The vernal equinox has since been known as the first point of Aries, and spring is therefore said to begin when the sun enters the zodiac sign of Aries. Hipparchus, the second century B.C. Greek astronomer whose calculations form the groundwork of the present zodiacal system, correctly estimated that because of the precession of the equinoxes — the retrograde motion of the equinoctial points — the vernal equinox moves slightly west each year. Therefore, the first point of Aries, which during Hipparchus's time was found in the constellation Aries, is now in Pisces, the next constellation to the west.

During the spring season, the sun leaves the celestial equator and progresses along the ecliptic north of the equator. At the summer solstice (see June 21) the sun enters the zodiac sign of Cancer, having reached a longitude of 90° and its maximum declination of +23° 27'. (The latter figure represents the sun's distance from the celestial equator, the term "declination" being used by astronomers to correspond with terrestrial latitude). The season then ends. In the Northern Hemisphere, spring is the second longest season after summer. The discrepancy in the length of the seasons is attributable to the earth's varying velocity in its yearly orbit; this in turn is caused by the elliptical shape of its orbit and by the laws of motion. The earth moves most quickly at the beginning of the year (in early January) and most slowly at midyear (in early July).

In terms of earthly weather, the four seasons do not invariably coincide with the astronomical seasons. In many parts of North America, where spring is popularly considered to comprise the months of March, April and May, the climate of March may still be that of winter; and May can sometimes seem like summer. In Great Britain, spring is popularly thought to include February, March, and April.

The difference in the seasons, notably the consistent variation in weather, is caused by the tilt of the earth's axis (23½°), as well as by its elliptical course around the sun. When the North Pole inclines away from the sun around December 21, the time of the winter solstice (see December 21), the sun's rays are slanted, solar heat is less concentrated, and temperatures consequently are low. By the end of spring the North Pole points directly toward the sun and the opposite conditions prevail. In the Southern Hemisphere, since the movement of the South Pole is opposite to that of the North Pole, the seasons are reversed. Astronomical spring starts there about September 23 and ends about December 21.

Spring, a transitional period between the extreme temperature cycles of winter and summer, is the chief season of planting and germination, when life, light, and apparent order in the universe once more prevail over what the ancients regarded as the chaos of the dark, barren winter season. Spring profoundly influenced the ancients and played an important role in mythology, folklore, and art. Ancient painters and sculptors often depicted spring as a female figure carrying flowers. The early Christians regarded the seasons as symbolic of the course of human life, seeing spring as rebirth or resurrection after the death that winter seemed to symbolize. The practice of adorning basilicas with symbolic representations of the seasons continued into the Middle Ages, culminating in the 13th century with the beautifully carved depictions of the seasons and the individual months in the French cathedrals of Paris, Chartres, and Reims. These spring scenes reveal the harsh realities of the laborer's everyday tasks in preparing the fields for cultivation and dressing the vineyards. Renaissance artists tended to view spring more lightheartedly: Botticelli's famous painting *Primavera* is a prime example of the glorification of the joys of awakening nature.

Pleasure at the annual greening and blossoming of the landscape is still much in evidence today, particularly as reflected in the numerous flower festivals and house and garden tours that take place across the nation each year. The season is marked by all kinds of beginnings: seed planting, graduations, weddings. It embraces such characteristically springlike observances as Arbor Day, Bird Day, May Day, and Walpurgis Night, the celebration known to Americans of Scandinavian descent as "spring festival." Even the season's major religious holidays epitomize the arrival of spring, at least indirectly. The Jewish Passover refers to renaissance; or, more exactly, release from physical and spiritual bondage and from the labors of winter. The Christian Easter — which may have borrowed its name from Eostre, Teutonic goddess of spring and fertility — is a joyful celebration of resurrection and eternal life, with the hymn words, "Christ the Lord is risen today, alleluia!" ringing out across the land. In spring, too, the always religiously meaningful dances of the American Indian, as performed at the pueblos of New Mexico and elsewhere, also have a seasonal significance — as prayers for fruitfulness of fields and animals and people, or for fructifying rain.

MARCH 22

The First Indian Treaty

On March 22, 1621, Governor John Carver of the Plymouth colony made a treaty with Massasoit, sachem of the Wampanoags, pledging friendship and alliance between the Indians and the colonists. This was the first treaty between the Indians and the European settlers made within the 13 colonies. It remained in effect for 54 years, during which time it was respected by both parties.

The territory over which Massasoit ruled embraced nearly all of southeastern Massachusetts. By the time the Plymouth colonists arrived in 1620, however, the Wampanoags, though still powerful, had been reduced in number by a mysterious pestilence, variously described as smallpox, yellow fever, and plague, which had struck them down several years earlier.

The epidemic had a devastating effect, killing off perhaps a third of all Indians in southern New England, upsetting the balance of power between the various tribes, and perhaps contributing to the willingness of the Wampanoags to make friends with the colonists. Those involved in the preliminary conversations that led to the treaty included Edward Winslow (who later became governor of Plymouth colony) and two English-speaking Indians living in the area — Squanto, a Pawtuxet, whose helpfulness to the Plymouth Pilgrims knew no bounds, and Samoset, a Pemaquid, who introduced him to them.

Whatever his motivation, Chief Massasoit — whose bronze likeness (by Cyrus Dallin) today overlooks Plymouth Harbor — was friendly to the colonists and true to his word. He took 60 warriors with him to Plymouth and there signed the historic agreement.

The treaty of peace and alliance signed by Massasoit and Governor Carver appears in slightly differing forms in William Bradford's work known as *The History of Plymouth Plantation*, in Nathaniel Morton's *New-Englands Memoriall*, and in *Mourt's Relation*, named for the author of its preface. *Mourt's Relation*, appearing in London in 1622 and comprising a journal by Bradford and letters to England from various colonists including Bradford and Winslow, was the earliest account of the Plymouth Pilgrims. As edited by Dwight B. Heath under the title *A Journal of the Pilgrims at Plymouth* (New York, 1963), *Mourt's Relation* contained this version of the treaty:

1. That neither he [Massasoit] nor any of his should injure or do hurt to any of our people.

2. And if any of his did hurt to any of ours, he should send the offender, that we might punish him.

3. That if any of our tools were taken away when our people were at work, he should cause them to be restored, and if ours did any harm to any of his, we would do the like to them.

4. If any did unjustly war against him, we would aid him; if any did war against us, he should aid us.

5. He should send to his neighbor confederates, to certify them of this, that they might not wrong us, but might be likewise comprised in the conditions of peace.

6. That when their men came to us, they should leave their bows and arrows behind them, as we should do our pieces when we came to them.

Lastly, that doing thus, King James would esteem of him as his friend and ally.

The treaty worked well. A contributor to *Mourt's Relation* wrote: "We have found the Indians very faithful in their covenant of peace with us, very loving and ready to pleasure us. . . . So that there is now great peace amongst the Indians . . . and we, for our part, walk as peaceably and safely in the wood as in the highways in England."

Peace between the colonists and Indians lasted throughout the life of the Wampanoag chief. After Massasoit's death in 1661 his son Wamsutta (Alexander) succeeded him. In 1662 Wamsutta died (murdered by the English, the Wampanoags suspected) and his brother Metacomet — whom the colonists called King Philip — became chief. Encroachment by the colonists on Indian territory and the settlers' execution in 1675 of three Indian warriors accused of murdering a prosettler informer led directly to what is known as King Philip's War. Directed against colonists throughout New England, the war involved not only the Wampanoags but all the tribes with which Metacomet in the previous decade had been making treaties in anticipation of a stand against the growing colonial tide.

In the course of the war, the most devastating ever fought on New England soil, 52 of the region's 90 towns were attacked by Indians. Twelve or 13 of them were completely destroyed, others were deserted, all suffered damage. Perhaps 1,000 colonists, including 600 men of military age, and eventually 3,000 Indians lost their lives. One of the two Indian raids that laid Deerfield, Massachusetts, low was part of King Philip's War. The Great Swamp Fight of December 19, 1675, also part of the war, took the lives of Metacomet's Narragansett allies in a night full of terror. The site is marked by the Great Swamp Fight Monument, off Rhode Island Route 2, three miles northeast of Kenyon, Rhode Island. The event is commemorated with the Great Swamp Memorial Pilgrimage, in which Indians participate to this day — annually in late September.

Eleven days after his wife and son were captured on August 1, 1676, Metacomet was himself killed and his head taken off to be exhibited on top of a pole at Plymouth for the next quarter century. The war — which resulted in the virtual destruction of the Wampanoags and an end to Indian resistance throughout southern New England — did not terminate with the death of Metacomet. On frontiers as far north as the Penobscot River in Maine, it dragged on until 1678, involving numerous tribes.

Not until more than a century later did the Indians of the Northeast again seek in such a concerted way to stem the relentless advance of white settlement. But this was many miles to the west, under the leadership of the towering, and doomed, Tecumseh (see October 5).

Palm Sunday

This is a movable event. See note on page xxvi.

For Christians the world over, Palm Sunday, commemorating Jesus Christ's triumphal entry into Jerusalem, ushers in the most important and solemn week of the church year. A movable feast, Palm Sunday is always celebrated a week before Easter, and its date each year depends on the date set for Easter (see March 29). The days between the two Sundays comprise Holy Week, a period especially devoted to the commemoration of the events of the last week of Jesus' life on earth. According to Christian belief, it was during Holy Week (sometimes called Great Week) that Jesus performed the essential work of the Redemption — that is, redeeming human beings from the bondage of sin and effecting a reconciliation between them and God, making it possible for them to attain eternal communion with their Creator.

Christian theologians hold that the Redemption is one unified event encompassing Christ's Passion (that is, suffering), death, and Resurrection. From earliest times, Holy Week was considered the Christian Passover, signaling Jesus' passing over from this life to life with his heavenly Father. Christians believe that in their celebration of the rites of Holy Week, they reenact the drama of the Redemption, themselves dying to the world in the death of Jesus on Good Friday (see March 27) and experiencing new life in God through Christ's Resurrection on Easter Sunday. The purpose of Holy Week services, then, is not only to commemorate these events, but to relive the mystery of Christ in each Christian life.

The events and circumstances of the Redemption had been foretold in the Old Testament, and the New Testament records that Jesus alluded several times to his Passion, death, and Resurrection. The drama of the Redemption, the core of Christianity, began to unfold on Palm Sunday with Jesus Christ's entry into Jerusalem.

Knowing full well what awaited him in Jerusalem, Jesus went to that Holy City for the Feast of the Passover, according to Jewish custom. He was greeted as a triumphant king by the people, who had heard about or witnessed his miracles and looked to him as the temporal ruler sent in answer to their prayers for a leader who would deliver them from the domination of the Roman Empire. All four Evangelists record Jesus' entry into Jerusalem in the New Testament, where the specific accounts are found in Matthew 21:1–11, Mark 11:1–10, Luke 19:28–40, and John 12:12–16. On Palm Sunday, Christian worshipers customarily hear the story of the first Palm Sunday read to them from one of these sources in their churches. Roman Catholics, some Episcopalians and Lutherans, and others also hear the account of Jesus' subsequent suffering during the first Holy Week on this day.

Among biblical reports of the first Palm Sunday, the briefest is the summary found in the Gospel of John:

The next day a great crowd who had come to the feast [the Passover] heard that Jesus was coming to Jerusalem. So they took branches of palm trees and went out to meet him, crying, "Hosanna! Blessed be he who comes in the name of the Lord, even the King of Israel!" And Jesus found a young ass and sat upon it; as it is written, "Fear not, daughter of Zion; behold thy king is coming, sitting on an ass's colt!"

His disciples did not understand this at first; but when Jesus was glorified [that is, after his Resurrection and Ascension], then they remembered that this had been written of him and had been done to him.

It is often pointed out that the animal Jesus chose to ride symbolized humility and was the antithesis of violence, war, or domination by force; and that the image of a horse, by contrast, would have been one of arrogance, as of a temporal ruler returning victorious from battle. In keeping with this, many worshipers, notably Lutherans and Episcopalians, also hear on Palm Sunday a reading from Philippians (2:5–11): "Let this mind be in you, which was also in Christ Jesus: Who . . . made himself of no reputation, and took upon him the form of a servant, and was made in the likeness of men: And . . . humbled himself, and became obedient unto death, even the death of the cross."

The Palm Sunday account in the Gospel of John also explains the crowd's exuberant expectations concerning Jesus, and the Pharisees' antagonism, which would lead to his arrest, trial, and death: "The crowd that had been with him when he called Lazarus out of the tomb and raised him from the dead bore witness. The reason why the crowd went to meet him was that they heard he had done this sign. The Pharisees then said to one another, 'You see that you can do nothing; look, the world has gone after him.'" With this, the drama of Holy Week begins to unfold.

To this day, Palm Sunday celebrations in Christian churches commemorate Jesus' triumphal entry into Jerusalem. Even in those Protestant churches that do not specifically reenact the original Palm Sunday procession, it is recalled indirectly by the regular processional entrance of the choir at the beginning of the service. This is particularly true when the choir members carry palms, as they sometimes do, or when they sing one of the hymns traditionally associated with Palm Sunday. Perhaps the best known of these, familiar throughout Christendom and dating from the ninth century, is the one that begins with these words:

> All glory, laud, and honor
> To Thee, Redeemer, King,
> To whom the lips of children
> Made sweet hosannas ring.

Members of the congregation, standing in their pews, join in the singing.

In many churches, however, there is a conscious effort to reenact the specific events of the first Palm Sunday with a procession in which both clergy and congregation participate. The procession now is usually within the church, although it sometimes starts outside the church, with the priest or minister representing Jesus and the congregation representing the people who welcomed Christ so joyfully. In Roman Catholic churches, the people hold palm branches throughout the procession and the reading of the New Testament account of the day. The blessing of the palms, before the procession, is an integral part of the service. The priest invites the congregation to participate in the celebration fully, with words recorded in the revised Roman Missal:

> Dear friends in Christ, for five weeks of Lent we have been preparing, by works of charity and self-sacrifice, for the celebration of our Lord's paschal mystery. Today we come together to begin this solemn celebration in union with the whole Church throughout the world. Christ entered in triumph

into his own city, to complete his work as our Messiah: to suffer, to die, and to rise again. Let us remember with devotion this entry which began his saving work and follow him with a lively faith. United with him in his suffering on the cross, may we share his resurrection and new life.

A prayer, the blessing and distribution of the palms, the Gospel account, and often a brief homily follow before the priest says, "Let us go forth in peace, praising Jesus our Messiah, as did the crowds who welcomed him to Jerusalem." The procession (or entrance) follows before the celebration of the Mass.

In Episcopalian and many other churches, the palms are distributed at the end of the service as the congregations leave the churches. Sometimes a palm, made into a small cross, is worn tucked into a hatband or pinned on a lapel. Some people use the palm, often made into a cross, as a bookmark.

As is true today, the distribution of palms among Western Christians had earlier been familiar chiefly in the liturgical churches, most notably the Roman Catholic and Protestant Episcopal. Today, however, the custom is also becoming familiar to some other congregations of Christians, even some not usually thought of as liturgical churches. This is only one of many changes in Western churches that have brought Christian congregations, Catholic and Protestant, closer together in liturgical observances, including those of Holy Week.

For Roman Catholics, changes in the observance of Palm Sunday involve the colors of vestments, points of ritual, and selection of prayers for the procession and mass. In the Catholic, Episcopal, and some other Protestant church calendars, Palm Sunday — the sixth Sunday of Lent — is designated also as Passion Sunday.

Celebration of Palm Sunday by Eastern Orthodox churches sometimes coincides with and sometimes follows the date set in the Western Christian churches. Throughout Holy Week, solemn worship services are scheduled in the Albanian, Bulgarian, Carpatho-Russian, Greek, Russian, Serbian, Syrian, Ukrainian, and other Orthodox churches. Palms are distributed in some of the Eastern churches, but in others, branches of pussy willow are used in lieu of palms. This custom is particularly prevalent among those whose origins are in northern regions where palms are not available. Palm Sunday is also known as Willow Sunday in many European countries for this reason. In some countries, it is called Branch Sunday or Blossom Sunday, and in place of the unobtainable palms the people carry branches from other trees or plants: olive, box, yew, spruce, and willow. The names of the trees or plants used in place of palms often include the word "palm," as in the English "palm willow."

In Italy, people may give blessed palms as a peace offering or sign of reconciliation to those with whom they have quarreled. In Austria, the Bavarian region of Germany, and some Slavic countries, farm families gather in the afternoon of Palm Sunday and walk over their farms, singing hymns and placing sprigs of blessed palm in pastures or fields, and also in barns and stables, to avert misfortune and ask God's blessing on their crops and animals. In many American homes the palms are kept throughout the year, hung on a wall or fastened to a door or religious picture as a reminder of the historic journey of Jesus Christ into Jerusalem.

The solemn observances commemorating those occurrences in Jesus Christ's life that began on the original Palm Sunday make up the most important week of the Christian year. Despite ethnic variations and the liturgical changes of recent years, the celebration of Palm Sunday today is basically the same as that carried out by the earliest Christians.

After the persecutions of Christians abated in the fourth century, people from many countries made Holy Week pilgrimages to Jerusalem to visit the Christian holy places. One such pilgrim, a Spanish woman named Eutheria (Etheria), or Silvia, kept a journal that provides one of the earliest accounts of the Palm Sunday celebration in Jerusalem, dating from about 390. It describes how the crowds of pilgrims gathered on the Mount of Olives and listened to the account of Jesus' entry into Jerusalem. Then, singing and waving palm and olive branches, the pilgrims marched toward the city as the bishop, representing Jesus, rode on a donkey. At the end of each hymn, the pilgrims sang "Hosannah to the Son of David. Blessed is He that cometh in the name of the Lord."

In many American communities, Palm Sunday is also the occasion for the performance of programs of sacred music. These programs may continue throughout Holy Week and may begin earlier than Palm Sunday. The concerts may be church-sponsored and held on church premises, or they may be scheduled under secular auspices as special events or part of the musical community's regular concert series.

Choral, orchestral, or instrumental (usually organ) concerts most frequently offer classical sacred music, such as Johann Sebastian Bach's *St. John Passion* or *St. Matthew Passion;* George Frideric Handel's *Messiah*, including the famous "Hallelujah Chorus" (for which the audience traditionally stands); Charles Gounod's *La Rédemption;* César Franck's similarly titled work; A. R. Gaul's *The Holy City;* Franz Joseph

Haydn's *Seven Last Words*; Ludwig van Bee-thoven's *Christus am Oelberg* (Christ on the Mount of Olives); Théodore Dubois' *Les Sept Paroles du Christ* (The Seven Last Words); Gounod's similarly named composition; John Henry Maunder's *Olivet to Calvary;* and Sir John Stainer's *Crucifixion*. Some Holy Week musical programs now combine modern offer-ings with the classical. In a number of cases, the break with tradition is complete, with only con-temporary music, sometimes with a rock beat, performed.

Concerts of sacred music are also performed on some college campuses during Holy Week. For example, the Messiah Festival has been held during Holy Week since 1892 at Bethany College, Lindsborg, Kansas.

College drama groups and professional the-ater companies also put on plays or pageants in keeping with the theme of Holy Week. One of the best-known professional groups produces the Black Hills Passion Play, so named because the permanent home of the theatrical group is in the Black Hills of South Dakota. During Holy Week, however, the performance is seen in an amphitheater near Lake Wales, Florida, where the group performs for two or three months a year. During the summer months, this same pro-duction takes place in an amphitheater at Spear-fish, South Dakota.

In some areas, Palm Sunday celebrations ac-knowledge the coming of spring with a splash of local color. For example, in St. Augustine, Flor-ida, Palm Sunday is the day set aside for the Blessing of the Fishing and Shrimp Fleet, one of the oldest festivities in the country's oldest city. The event draws thousands of spectators and participants to the town's sea wall and Bridge of Lions overlooking Matanzas Bay. A priest stands on the City Yacht Pier and blesses the shrimp trawlers and other fishing craft, as well as privately owned vessels. Freshly painted and decorated with colorful pennants for the occasion, the varied craft circle past the pier in single file to receive their blessing.

Not quite so colorful but certainly as spec-tacular in its own way is the tradition in New York City, where some skyscrapers keep win-dows lighted in the form of a cross each night during Holy Week.

Purim
(Feast of Lots)

This is a movable event. See note on page xxvi.

Purim, the Feast of Lots, is celebrated by Jews on the 14th day of the month of Adar, a date that falls in either February or March. A day of great rejoicing, it commemorates the deliv-erance of the Jews in Shushan, the capital of Persia, from a plot to destroy them. The story is told in the Book of Esther, one of the five small Megillot, or Scrolls, of the Bible that are read on five different Jewish holidays.

The story is probably a historical romance. The book begins as King Ahasuerus, commonly identified with Xerxes, decides to depose his queen, Vashti, because she refuses to obey him. During his search for a successor to Vashti, many beautiful maidens are presented to him. Finally the king selects Esther, an orphan (orig-inally named Hadassah) brought up by her cousin Mordecai. The fact that both are Jews is not known by Ahasuerus.

At this time the king's prime minister, Ha-man, holds a parade through the streets of Shu-shan. Everyone who sees the vain Haman is re-quired to bow down before him and all obey except for Mordecai, who refuses, saying that as a Jew he must bow only before God. This refusal enrages Haman, who thereupon convinces king Ahasuerus that the Jews are a useless and dis-loyal people and should be exterminated. Ha-man draws lots, or *purim*, to fix the date for the slaughter of the Jews and for the confiscation of all Jewish property.

When Mordecai hears of the cruel proclama-tion, he persuades Queen Esther to undertake the deliverance of her people. She directs a fast of three days by all Jews, including herself, after which she is to go before the king, although the queen is not expected to appear before him un-less summoned. (Today, in commemoration of the Fast of Esther [Taanit Esther], Orthodox and Conservative Jews fast from sunrise to sun-set on the 13th day of Adar — unless the 13th occurs on the Sabbath, in which case the fast is observed the preceding Thursday.)

Esther's appearance delights the king, who receives her graciously and promises to dine with her and Haman on two successive nights. On the night after the first banquet the king, sleepless, orders the national records read aloud to him. The part that is read tells of the revela-tion, by Mordecai, of a plot against the king's life, a service for which Mordecai has never been rewarded. Upon hearing this, the king calls his prime minister and asks him, "What shall be done to the man whom the King de-lighteth to honor?"

Haman, thinking that the king means to honor him, suggests a pageant through the streets of Shushan at which a great noble shall attend the honored man. Thereupon the king orders a pageant in honor of Mordecai and com-mands Haman — who is appalled at this turn of events — to attend Mordecai.

The next night, at the second banquet, Esther reveals to the king that she is a Jew and begs him to rescind the order for the destruction of her and her people. The king, realizing the extent of Haman's evil plot, revokes his decree and orders that Haman and all his sons be hanged on the gallows that Haman had prepared for Mordecai. In addition, Ahasuerus appoints Mordecai his prime minister and issues an order permitting the Jews to slay their enemies on the day that the Jews themselves were to have been killed. Then, as the Book of Esther records (9:20–28):

Mordecai . . . sent letters unto all the Jews that were in all the provinces of the King Ahasuerus . . . to enjoin them that they should keep the fourteenth day of the month Adar . . . yearly, [the day] wherein the Jews had rest from their enemies, and the month which was turned unto them from sorrow to gladness, and from mourning into a good day; that they should make them days of feasting and gladness, and of sending portions one to another, and gifts to the poor. And the Jews took upon them to do as . . . Mordecai had written unto them; because Haman . . . the enemy of all the Jews, had devised against the Jews to destroy them, and had cast Pur, that is, the lot, to . . . destroy them; but when [Esther] came before the king, he commanded by letters that [Haman's] wicked device, which he had devised against the Jews, should return upon his own head; and that he and his sons should be hanged on the gallows. Wherefore they called these days Purim after the name of Pur. . . . The Jews ordained, and took upon them . . . that [this day] should be remembered and kept throughout every generation.

Today, Jews celebrate Purim as prescribed in the Book of Esther. It is a day of feasting and rejoicing. The festival meal, which begins in late afternoon on the 14th of Adar, may extend until late in the evening. Gifts are exchanged between relatives and friends on Purim and gifts are also given to the poor. Special three-cornered pastries — called *Hamantashen,* or Haman's hats — filled with poppy seeds or prunes are eaten. Children dress up in costumes impersonating Esther or Mordecai or Haman. Often, plays specially written for Purim are presented, or else a Purim party or a carnival may be held. Since Purim is only a semiholiday, there is no religious prohibition against working.

Unlike most of the other Jewish holidays, Purim has no marked religious features, other than the portrayal of Esther's loyalty to her people, and her courage. The Book of Esther itself contains no mention of God. The main content of the services held in synagogues on Purim is the reading of the Megillah or scroll of the Book of Esther. Whenever Haman's name is mentioned during the reading, both children and adults shake rattles (called *gregers*), stamp their feet, and generally make noise to drown out the sound of Haman's name.

The custom also developed during the Middle Ages that Jewish communities commemorate the anniversary of their deliverance from a special peril, and thus different communities often celebrated several special Purims in addition to the one observed on the 14th day of Adar. However, owing to Jewish migrations during the past century, most of the special Purims are no longer observed.

Jews today celebrate Purim to express their hope and confidence that they will survive every future Haman as they have survived those in the past. Exuberant joy is the keynote of the holiday.

Stamp Act Signed

On March 22, 1765, King George III approved the Stamp Act, the first direct tax ever levied upon the American colonies by Parliament, little realizing the vehemence of the protest the act would provoke. George Grenville, chancellor of the exchequer, estimated that this act, which required tax stamps to be affixed to various colonial legal documents and commercial papers, would yield revenues of £60,000 a year. This sum, together with impost receipts, would have paid approximately a third of the yearly cost of maintaining the 10,000 British troops defending American borders against French invasion, thereby substantially alleviating the burden borne by the sorely pressed English taxpayers.

The American colonists, however, refused to accept the Stamp Act as a justifiable means of contributing to their own defense. Instead, shouts of "No taxation without representation" echoed up and down the American seaboard, and the following year Parliament was forced to repeal the act (see November 23).

MARCH 23

Patrick Henry's Speech for Liberty

When a provincial convention assembled in Virginia in March 1775, Patrick Henry, regarding war as inevitable, introduced a resolution providing for the organization of the militia in order to put the colony in shape for defense. It was bitterly opposed by the Loyalists. On March 23 Henry defended his resolution in one of his most famous speeches. It reportedly concluded with the ringing words:

There is no retreat but in submission to slavery. Our chains are already forged. Their clanking may be heard on the plains of Boston. The next gale that

sweeps from the North will bring the clash of resounding arms. Our brethren are already in the field.
Why stand we here idle? What is it that the gentlemen wish? What would they have? Is life so dear or
peace so sweet as to be purchased at the price of
chains and slavery? Forbid it, Almighty God! I know
not what course others may take, but as for me, give
me liberty, or give me death!

His prophecy of the "clash of arms" from the
North was fulfilled within less than a month, for
on April 19 the battles of Lexington and Concord were fought.

Henry's speech, which fanned the flames of
the American Revolution and which still stands
as a masterpiece of patriotic oratory, was made
by a man who had little formal education but
who could draw, in the course of his career, not
only on his own studies and ambition but also
on his background as member of a family generously endowed with material and educational
advantage. In the course of his lifetime, Henry
contributed mightily to the foundation of the
United States of America.

He was born on May 29, 1736, in Studley,
Hanover County, Virginia. After failing twice as
a storekeeper and once as a farmer, Henry was
admitted to the bar in 1760. His courtroom oratory as a trial lawyer soon won him a wide reputation and an impressive practice in Virginia.

In 1765, at the age of 29, he was elected to
the Virginia legislature, the House of Burgesses.
That same year he wrote the Virginia Resolutions, which included not only a denunciation of
the Stamp Act (see March 22) but also an assertion of the right of the colonies to legislate for
themselves, independently of the British Parliament.

After 1774 and 1775, when he went to Philadelphia as a delegate to the First Continental
Congress and part of the Second, most of Henry's
public life was divided between serving as governor of Virginia and serving in the Virginia legislature. Chosen the first governor of Virginia
in May 1776, he was reelected in 1777 and 1778,
serving the maximum continuous time allowable
under Virginia's new constitution. Later, however, he was Virginia's governor again (1784–
1786) between terms in the Virginia legislature
(1780–1784 and 1787–1790).

Frustrated in his own military ambitions, Henry, as governor, effectively supported George
Washington in many ways. In 1778 he sent
George Rogers Clark on a military expedition to
the Illinois country, which led to the expulsion
of the British from the Northwest.

In the last decade or so of his life, Henry was
offered but declined some of the most prestigious national offices, including those of secretary of state in Washington's cabinet (1795),

chief justice of the Supreme Court (1795), envoy
to France (1799), governor of Virginia 1796),
and US senator (1794). He agreed to serve again
in the Virginia legislature, to which he was
elected in 1799, but died before he could take
his seat.

His death took place on June 6, 1799, at Red
Hill, the home of his last years, five miles east of
Brookneal, Virginia. Today's visitors to Red Hill
can see Henry's grave and the reconstructed
main house, as well as the cook's cabin, smokehouse, stables, and Henry's law office, all maintained by the Patrick Henry Memorial Foundation.

Travelers through Virginia's Hanover County
can see a stone marker at the site of Patrick Henry's birthplace in Studley. Not far away, in Hanover, is another landmark associated with Henry
— the Hanover Courthouse, where he first won
fame as an orator during litigation known as the
"Parson's Cause." The courthouse, dating from
about 1733, stands on the main thoroughfare,
dominating the village green. Henry's stirring
"Give me liberty, or give me death" speech was
delivered at Virginia's second provincial convention, meeting in Richmond at St. John's Episcopal Church, a serene white clapboard structure
built in 1741 and open to the public today.
About nine miles northwest of Ashland is Scotchtown, the architecturally notable home where
Henry lived from 1771 to 1777, the years when
he made his deepest imprint on American history. The restored house — later the childhood
home of Dolley Payne Madison — is a national
historic landmark administered by the Association for the Preservation of Virginia Antiquities
and is open several days a week from April to
October and by appointment.

MARCH 24

John Wesley Powell's Birthday

John Wesley Powell, born on March 24, 1834,
in Mount Morris, New York, was the first white
man to explore the treacherous canyons of the
Green and Colorado rivers by boat. His daring
trip began on May 24, 1869, and was successfully completed on August 29 of the same year.
The journey took Powell and his group of 11
men through nearly 900 miles of uncharted
waterways and was the last major exploration in
the continental United States.

John Wesley Powell was the son of Joseph
and Mary (Dean) Powell, who had emigrated
from England. His father was a Methodist Episcopal preacher who spent most of his life bringing the Gospel to western frontier towns. It was

not until young Powell was in his late teens that his father finally settled the family in Wheaton, Illinois. Because of this nomadic early life, Powell's formal schooling was constantly interrupted and most of his education was received at home. Early in life he showed an interest in natural history and botany, but after settling in Wheaton he chose to prepare to follow his father's profession and studied at the Illinois Institute (now Wheaton College), Oberlin College, and Illinois College. However, in 1854 he enrolled in the State Natural History Society and during the following years became absorbed in trips and collections. He traveled alone down the Mississippi, Illinois, and Ohio rivers. His collections brought him some recognition, and in 1858 he was made secretary of the Illinois Society of Natural History.

Powell's career was interrupted by the outbreak of the Civil War, in which he enlisted as a Union soldier. He soon became an officer and a member of General Ulysses S. Grant's staff. In 1862 he was wounded at the battle of Shiloh and lost his right arm at the elbow. Nevertheless, he returned to active duty, and by the time he was honorably discharged on January 14, 1865, he had risen to the rank of brevet lieutenant colonel. While in the army, he had married his cousin Emma Dean.

After Powell's discharge he was appointed professor of geology at Illinois Wesleyan University, and a year later he became lecturer and curator of the museum of Illinois Normal University. In 1868, while still serving as curator, he formulated a plan to lead a boat expedition down the unexplored canyons of the Green and Colorado rivers. The following year he received grants from the federal government and the Smithsonian Institution to help finance an 11-man exploration party with 4 boats. Although this daring trip made Powell something of a national hero, it was not until his second trip, in 1871–1872, that he made substantial geological findings. On this later expedition he was accompanied by such famous geologists as Grove Karl Gilbert, Clarence E. Dutton, and W. H. Holmes. Together they formulated some of the basic principles of structural, or geotectonic, geology. Powell later described his findings in two publications: *The Exploration of the Colorado River of the West* (1875) and *The Geology of the Eastern Portion of the Uinta Mountains* (1876).

Powell continued his explorations of the area until 1875, when he was named director of the second division of the US Geological and Geographical Survey of the Territories (known after 1877 as the Survey of the Rocky Mountain Region). This post enabled Powell to gather extensive information on the plateau country and peoples of Utah, western Colorado, and northern Arizona. He became alarmed at the ruinous consequences of dry land homesteading and unscrupulous land speculation and in 1879 issued the prophetic *Report of the Lands of the Arid Region of the United States*. In this report Powell expressed a fear that poor land policies might cause irreparable damage to the soil resources of the West. His concern, as well as his recommendations for new land management programs, went unheeded until the tragic Dust Bowl years of the 1930s, when the report's guidelines became the foundation of a reformed national land policy.

In 1879, when all western Survey divisions were consolidated as the US Geological Survey under Clarence King's directorship, Powell was chosen to oversee the new Bureau of Ethnology of the Smithsonian Institution, studying Indian tribes. Upon King's resignation in 1880, Powell was named director of the Geological Survey as well. Under his guidance, the Survey became the largest and most powerful bureau of its kind in the world, and a model scientific organization. Powell initiated an innovative series of detailed geologic and topographic maps, which is still being continued. However, his attempts to improve land management in the West were opposed by speculators and undermined by congressional budget cuts. In 1894 he resigned from the Geological Survey but continued to serve as head of the Bureau of American Ethnology. He also wrote several philosophical treatises, among them *Truth and Error, or the Science of Intellection*, published in 1898. He died on September 23, 1902.

MARCH 25

The Feast of the Annunciation

This Christian feast celebrates the announcement made by the angel Gabriel to Mary that she was chosen to become the Mother of Jesus. Most Christians believe that at the instant of her humble consent, Jesus was miraculously conceived. Therefore, the date is set at nine months before Christmas, the feast celebrating Jesus' birth. However, if March 25 falls during Holy Week or Easter Week, the Feast of the Annunciation is transferred to the Monday after Low Sunday (which is the first Sunday after Easter). The feast was instituted in the East in about A.D. 430. Roman, and subsequently universal, observance dates from the seventh century. The New Testament account of the Annunciation, as it appears in the King James Version of the Bible in Luke 1:26–38, follows:

The angel Gabriel was sent from God unto a city of Galilee, named Nazareth, to a virgin espoused to a man whose name was Joseph, of the house of David; and the virgin's name was Mary. And the angel came in unto her, and said, "Hail, thou that art highly favored, the Lord is with thee; blessed art thou among women." And when she saw him, she was troubled at his saying, and cast in her mind what manner of salutation this should be. And the angel said unto her: "Fear not, Mary: for thou hast found favor with God. And, behold, thou shalt conceive in thy womb, and bring forth a son, and shalt call his name Jesus. He shall be great, and shall be called the Son of the Highest; and the Lord God shall give unto him the throne of his father David: And he shall reign over the house of Jacob forever; and of his kingdom there shall be no end." Then said Mary unto the angel, "How shall this be, seeing I know not a man?" And the angel answered and said unto her, "The Holy Ghost shall come upon thee, and the power of the Highest shall overshadow thee: therefore also that holy thing which shall be born of thee shall be called the Son of God. And, behold, thy cousin Elisabeth, she hath also conceived a son in her old age; and this is the sixth month with her, who was called barren. For with God nothing shall be impossible."

And Mary said, "Behold the handmaid of the Lord; be it unto me according to thy word." And the angel departed from her.

The Angelus, a prayer recited three times daily (morning, noon, and night) at many religious institutions, repeats the angel's salutation to Mary and her gentle reply.

The Feast of the Annunciation is observed by the Roman Catholic church; by many Protestant bodies, including the Protestant Episcopal and Lutheran; and by Eastern Orthodox churches. In the new Roman Catholic calendar the day, formerly called the Annunciation of Mary, is now known as the Annunciation of the Lord. Those Eastern Orthodox churches that use the Gregorian calendar celebrate the feast on March 25; those using the Julian calendar celebrate it on April 7.

Greek Independence Day

Greek Independence Day — commemorating March 25, 1821, the day the Greeks began their long struggle for independence from the Ottoman Empire (Turkey), which had ruled Greece for almost 400 years — is marked in various communities on this side of the Atlantic by friends of Greece and by many of the almost 3 million Greek-Americans living in the United States.

Greek freedom from the subjugation of the Ottoman Turks had been dreamed of for many generations before Alexander Ypsilanti (1792–1828) proclaimed Greece independent in 1821, thus beginning the wars which stretched over almost a decade before freedom was at last obtained. Ypsilanti was a Phanariot, that is, a member of an educated class of Greeks who lived in Constantinople in the Greek quarter, which was called the Phanar. Since the Moslem Turks generally would not condescend to learn foreign languages, the sultan customarily chose from among the educated Greeks of Constantinople when he sought a governor for one of the Ottoman Empire's many provinces. In these positions, the Phanariots earned a reputation as greedy and unjust rulers, often more despised by their subjects than the Moslem conquerors.

Control of many of these provinces passed, at times, from Ottoman to other Asian or European powers. Often the same provinces were ruled alternately by Turkey and Russia. Two such provinces were Moldavia and Walachia, now regions in modern Rumania, which at that time had sizable Greek populations.

The Ypsilanti family had been high officials in both Moldavia and Walachia since at least as far back as the grandfather of Alexander Ypsilanti, who was also named Alexander (c. 1725–1807). He had served as governor of each of the two provinces and was ultimately executed by the sultan for alleged conspiracy.

His son, Constantine (1760–1816), also was appointed the sultan's governor, first of Moldavia and then of Walachia. Although the Greeks — many of whom had scattered throughout Europe after the Turkish conquest of Greece in the 15th century — preferred independence, lacking that they preferred the rule of Christian Russians to that of Moslem Turks. Because of his suspected pro-Russian inclinations, Constantine, then governor of Walachia, was deposed by the Turkish sultan but was reinstated shortly thereafter when Russia occupied the province during one of its wars with Turkey.

Constantine had supported the Serbian insurrection against the Turks in 1804 and hoped himself to gather an army to fight for Greek independence. His plans, however, were foiled by the Treaty of Tilsit between Russia and France in 1807, and he instead found himself a political exile, seeking refuge in Russia. His hopes, dashed by the complex international relations and agreements of the times, were carried to completion by his two sons, Alexander and Demetrios (1793–1832).

The brothers had gone with their exiled father to Russia and there both served in the Russian army. Alexander, who became a general, had been made leader of the Philike Hetairia, a secret organization formed to work for Greek independence.

Ypsilanti was a revered name to Greeks in Moldavia and Walachia. Along with the governor of Moldavia, they rallied to Alexander when, in 1821, with strong Russian support, he staged a revolt at Jassy, Moldavia's capital, and boldly proclaimed Greek independence from Ottoman rule. Unfortunately, however, the Rumanians of the region, who had endured cruel and unjust treatment by the Phanariots for many generations, turned on the Greeks, helping the Turks to victory and winning Rumanian rule for themselves.

Meanwhile, under international political pressure, Russia withdrew its support of Ypsilanti, who was overwhelmingly defeated by the Turks. However, the Turkish forces had been diverted to quell the Moldavian revolt, and thus the revolt, unsuccessful in itself, contributed to the success of the simultaneous rebellion in the Peloponnesus, the southernmost region of continental Greece, which culminated in Greek independence after many years of war. After his defeat at Jassy, Alexander Ypsilanti fled to Austria, seeking refuge, and was instead imprisoned there.

His younger brother, Demetrios, who had been at his side during the revolt at Jassy, later went to the Peloponnesus and entered the battle there of Greeks against Turks. He was commander of the Greek forces in eastern Greece from 1828 until his resignation in 1830.

The Greeks fought bravely, and their degree of success from 1821 through 1824 surprised and confounded the Ottoman army. To turn the tide of the war, the sultan sought and received the intervention of Egyptian forces. From 1825 to 1827 the Greeks fought what was almost inevitably a losing battle against Egyptian and Turkish armies. Finally Britain, France, and Russia stepped in and, lending support to the Greeks from 1827 to 1829, they not only routed the Egyptian and Turkish forces but also demanded and received the sultan's recognition of Greece's independence.

Demetrios Ypsilanti, who, following the defeat at Jassy, had participated in the capture of the chief Turkish fortress in the Peloponnesus in 1821, and in 1825 had courageously resisted the armies of Ibrahim Pasha, has been honored by the naming of an American city. Ypsilanti, a city of about 30,000 population situated between Detroit and Ann Arbor in southeastern Michigan, began as an Indian village and French trading post in about 1809 and was settled in 1823, when the Greek struggle for independence captured worldwide admiration. Ypsilanti appropriately boasts many fine examples of Greek Revival architecture, and a bust of Demetrios Ypsilanti rests on a marble column at Cross and Washtenaw streets.

The courageous Greek fighters stirred the imaginations of many poets and writers of the time, including England's adventurous Lord Byron, who immortalized their brave stand in the third canto of his famous *Don Juan*. Not content with words, Byron, then 36, outfitted a ship and himself journeyed to Greece to take part in the struggle for independence. He died at Missolonghi on April 19, 1824, a few months after his arrival in Greece.

Perhaps the most notable US celebration of Greek independence is the one that takes place each spring in New York City, where the main event is a colorful and lively parade up Fifth Avenue. Because of the rain and wind that are common to New York in March, however, the parade does not take place on the anniversary itself but is postponed to a later date in the hope of more pleasant marching weather.

The actual date of New York's parade in honor of Greek independence is the third Sunday in May. In 1976 an estimated 25,000 marchers — including members of many Hellenic organizations, and school and church groups from New York and nearby states — participated in the parade and about 250,000 spectators watched the floats, bands, drum majorettes, and uniformed marchers celebrate the 155th anniversary of the start of Greece's wars for independence.

Musicians, dancers, and marchers in colorful costumes representing various regions of Greece stepped along the parade route from 62d Street to 79th Street. At 79th Street the parade turned east to march past the executive office of the Greek Orthodox Archdiocese of North and South America and the Greek Consulate building.

One of the highlights of the parade was a group of evzones, the elite palace guard, flown in from Greece for the parade. They wore the striking evzone uniform: a voluminous-sleeved white tunic, its skirt shorter than a kilt; white leggings; red slippers with enormous black pompoms on the toes; and a tasseled red cap.

After leading the parade to the reviewing stand at 68th Street and Fifth Avenue, the evzones formed an honor guard for the dignitaries and special guests stationed there, while the parade passed. Chief among the dignitaries present was Archbishop Iakovos, primate of the Greek Orthodox Church of North and South America. Later in the week, Archbishop Iakovos attended the Greek Independence Day parade in Chicago, where residents of Greek descent inaugurated an annual parade in 1968.

Following the parade in New York City — which in some years was greeted by demonstrations against the dictatorship of the military junta that seized power in Greece in 1967 and ruled for seven years — some 1,000 members and friends of the Greek-American community attended a banquet at the Waldorf-Astoria Hotel. Guest of honor was General James Van Fleet, Retired, who earned the Greeks' gratitude and warm esteem when he headed the successful American military mission to Greece from 1948 to 1950, as part of the program of economic and military aid outlined in the Truman Doctrine. Other dignitaries attending the $50-a-plate dinner included Archbishop Iakovos and the Greek consul. Proceeds of the banquet went to the Hellenic College in Boston.

Maryland Day

March 25 is Maryland Day, or Founder's Day, a legal holiday in that state commemorating the arrival there of the first colonists in 1634. Maryland, the first proprietary colony on the American mainland, was named after Henrietta Maria, the consort of King Charles I of England. In 1632 Charles appointed George Calvert, Lord Baltimore, the proprietor of 10 million acres of land between 40° north latitude and the south bank of the Potomac River; a line drawn east from the mouth of the Potomac constituted the southern boundary on the Eastern Shore. The king, in return for one-fifth of any gold or silver found there and for the symbolic payment of two arrowheads a year, granted the proprietor almost absolute control over the colony. Lord Baltimore could make laws with the consent of the freeholders, establish courts, levy taxes, control commerce, and grant lands. Maryland was a feudal barony in the wilderness.

Lord Baltimore, who had been a member of the London Company and the Council for New England, was an early leader in the colonization of America. In 1622 he received a grant of part of Newfoundland and established the colony of Avalon there. He visited Newfoundland in 1625 and Virginia in 1629, and, finding the southern climate more to his liking, he decided to undertake another settlement in the latter vicinity. As proprietor, Baltimore could garner great profits by renting some lands while retaining the rest until the growth of the colony increased their value. Moreover, religion, as well as economics, interested him in the venture. A convert to Catholicism in 1624, Baltimore envisioned Maryland as a refuge for his coreligionists, who suffered much in Anglican England.

Cecilius Calvert, the second Lord Baltimore, received Maryland's charter in June 1632, shortly after his father's death. He spent much of his fortune in recruiting some 200 men and women who set sail for the colony from England on November 22, 1633, on board the *Ark* and the *Dove*. The two ships sailed the West Indian route across the Atlantic, stopping at Barbados and arriving at Chesapeake Bay on February 27, 1634. Led by the 28-year-old governor, Leonard Calvert, the brother of the second Lord Baltimore, the colonists on March 25 erected a cross on St. Clements Island (also known as Blakiston Island) and held a thanksgiving service. A few days later they established St. Mary's, a few miles north of the Potomac River, as the capital.

The population had a mixed composition from the very beginning. Most of the original immigrants were Anglicans, but two Jesuits and 17 Catholic couples were among the group. The Protestant preponderance increased when disaffected Puritans left Anglican Virginia and established Providence (later Annapolis), Maryland. Increasing danger to the colony's religious peace and its character as a haven for Catholics prompted Lord Baltimore to instruct Governor William Stone, a Protestant, to have the legislature pass an "act concerning Religion." This toleration act, which granted religious liberty to all who affirmed a belief in the divinity of Jesus Christ, marked a limited but significant step forward in 1649.

A number of monuments are reminiscent of Maryland's early history. A tablet at Cowes on the Isle of Wight commemorates the departure from Britain of the *Ark* and the *Dove* for the voyage across the ocean. A bench on the St. Mary's River marks the spot where the colonists purportedly first touched shore after leaving St. Clements Island. In St. Mary's, the Leonard Calvert monument in Trinity Churchyard guards the place where the government was established, and the Hans Schuler Freedom of Conscience statue symbolizes the colony's pioneering efforts for religious toleration. The public can also visit in St. Mary's a replica of the building that served as the capitol of the colony from 1676 until 1695, when the Protestant town of Annapolis became the seat of government.

MARCH 26

Robert Frost's Birthday

A man who is identified with New England perhaps more closely than anyone else has been, Robert Lee Frost, was born not there but the whole width of the continent away, in San Francisco, on March 26, 1874. He was the son of William Prescott Frost Jr. and Isabelle Moodie Frost. During his 88 years, Robert Frost became the United States' unofficial poet laureate, one of the few poets of his time whose work was widely read and loved by the public in addition to being acclaimed by critics.

Many years passed, however, before Frost's

poetry was recognized and accepted, years when he drifted from one kind of work to another and in and out of school. He spent his first 11 years in the hurly-burly of young San Francisco, where he participated in campaigns with his politically active father, marching in torchlight processions and plastering saloons with literature. (A Southern sympathizer during the Civil War, Frost's father named his son for the Confederate general Robert E. Lee.) Upon his father's death, Robert Frost and his mother and younger sister returned to his father's home territory of New England for the burial. Without funds to return West, they settled in Lawrence, Massachusetts.

To support her family, Robert Frost's mother went to work as a teacher. Although she helped her son, he was a poor student throughout elementary school, so poor indeed that she developed the habit of reading to him — which may account for the fact that he did not read a book for himself until he was 13 years old. But in high school his interest was fired so strongly that he graduated as covaledictorian of his class, sharing the honor with a girl named Elinor White, who later became his wife. His enthusiasm for poetry developed in high school, too, and poems of his were published in the school paper.

With the financial help of his paternal grandfather, who hoped he would become a lawyer, Frost enrolled at Dartmouth College in 1892, but he was unhappy in the college atmosphere and left after only a few months. From the age of 12 he had worked summers in a shoe shop or on a farm, and then after finishing high school he was employed for a while in a textile mill in Lawrence, where his grandfather held a responsible position. He subsequently turned his hand to teaching, farming, and newspaper reporting, all the while continuing to write poetry. Elinor White had been determined to complete her college education before marriage; but as soon as she graduated from St. Lawrence University in 1895, she and Frost were wed.

Having decided to qualify himself to teach Latin and Greek, Frost in 1897 entered Harvard College (again with the financial aid of his grandfather). He did well and was granted a scholarship, but after two years he withdrew again from academic life, perhaps for reasons of health. By then he had two children.

Not understanding Frost's preoccupation with poetry and disappointed by his failure to continue his formal education, Frost's grandfather nevertheless bought a farm in Derry, New Hampshire, and gave him the use of it in 1900. It was a rather poor farm, and, as Frost himself admitted, he never worked too hard at farming. He therefore soon went back to teaching as well, to augment his income. So great did his academic reputation grow that the New Hampshire

superintendent of schools called him the best teacher in the state. Frost was even offered a one-year post to teach psychology at the New Hampshire State Normal School in Plymouth. He accepted with relish.

At about this time, under the terms of his grandfather's will, the ownership of the Derry farm was transferred to Frost. Although his poem "My Butterfly, an Elegy," had been published in the New York *Independent* when he was only 20, Frost had generally been unsuccessful in gaining any real acceptance of his poetry. In hopes that the literary climate in England might be more favorable, he sold the farm and in 1912 sailed for England with his wife and four children. There he became acquainted with various poets, including Ezra Pound, Edward Thomas, Lascelles Abercrombie, and W. W. Gibson; the two last-named were members of a group of English poets known as Georgians because of their inclusion in Edward Marsh's series of anthologies entitled *Georgian Poetry*.

Frost soon set to work compiling a collection of poems he had written over the years. It was accepted by the first publisher to whom he submitted it and came out in 1913 under the title *A Boy's Will*. The volume won the 39-year-old poet immediate recognition. A second collection, which was published the following year as *North of Boston*, won not only critical acclaim for Frost but also, for the first time, financial success.

American publishers then quickly became interested in him. He and his family arrived back in the United States in 1915 just after the American publication of *North of Boston*, when his fame was spreading. Frost was delighted with what he considered his well-deserved rewards after all the years of rejection of his work.

Frost returned to New England and bought a farm near Franconia, New Hampshire. Five years later he bought another farm near South Shaftsbury (now known as Shaftsbury), Vermont. He continued writing and was much sought after to lecture and to read his poetry, which he did very effectively. This demand increased constantly throughout his remaining 50 years. Though he had never earned a college degree, he was associated during the rest of his life as a faculty member with such outstanding institutions as Amherst College, the University of Michigan, Harvard University, and Dartmouth College ("the first college I ran away from"). More than 40 honorary degrees were conferred upon him by colleges and universities in the United States and Great Britain. Frost also was one of the earliest poets-in-residence; he held his first such post at the University of Michigan from 1921 to 1923.

Teaching by the book was not Frost's style.

He felt that students could get that sort of learning either on their own or from other teachers. He was concerned with challenging them to be real, and not to look for "different" things to write about but to discover their own ways of expressing their thoughts and feelings about common situations and experiences.

Once, Frost asked his students whether there was anything in the papers they had just handed in to him that any of them would like to keep. When there were no affirmative answers, he tossed the papers all into the wastebasket, remarking that evidently the students considered their themes to be of little value and that he "wasn't going to be a perfunctory corrector of perfunctory writing."

The private life of the poet was not serene. His sister became mentally ill. Of his four children who survived childhood, a daughter died following childbirth and his son committed suicide. Frost felt both losses deeply. The death of his wife in 1938 was a blow from which he had great difficulty recovering.

His public attitude was one of steadfastness, affirmation, humor; but his was a complex personality. Reported to be both enormously sensitive and egotistical, he was also rebellious and determined. Those who knew him well found him to be sometimes gloomy, cantankerous, petty, and mean, but never defeated.

Frost's beloved New England — its natural beauty, its traditions, the character and speech of its people — is central to his poetry. He was a listener, "minding [other people's] business," anxious to know how contemporary people went about the business of living, and recording in pithy, colloquial language what he saw and learned and felt. By definition, he said, "all poetry is a reproduction of the tones of actual speech." Frost wrote in classical forms with great ingenuity as well as eloquence, wit, and humor; he set himself the challenge of making the forms his own through the use of "dramatic tones of meaning" and the rhythm of language.

A philosophic poet, he was a master at illustrating universal truths through the depiction of particular, common incidents. Hope is an ingredient in much of his poetry, but there is also a good portion of darker, more somber work (Frost used the word "cruel"). His work shows his religious faith and his stoical refusal to be defeated by pain or difficulty.

Among the best known of Frost's lyric poems are "Mowing," "Revelation," "The Tuft of Flowers" (all contained in the volume titled A Boy's Will); "The Road Not Taken," "Birches," "A Time to Talk" (all in Mountain Interval); "Fire and Ice," "Stopping by Woods on a Snowy Evening" (both in New Hampshire); "Acquainted with the Night" (in West-Running Brook); "Di-

rective" (in Steeple Bush); and "Take Something Like a Star" (in An Afterword).

His well-known narrative poems and essayistic poetic reflections include "Mending Wall," "The Death of the Hired Man," "Home Burial," "The Wood-Pile" (all in North of Boston); "New Hampshire," "Paul's Wife," "Two Witches" (all in New Hampshire); and the title poem of West-Running Brook.

Frost wrote also two plays in blank verse, A Masque of Reason and A Masque of Mercy. Both deal with biblical characters. They were less well received than his other work.

Having survived a lengthy period of nonsuccess before publication of his first volume, Frost subsequently received the recognition he so greatly needed as reassurance that he was a good poet. On his 80th birthday, in musing about what honor he most desired, Frost said he would like to leave behind "a few poems it would be hard to get rid of." In fact, he had the highly unusual experience of seeing his work become classic while he was still living. His poems were published in 22 languages, and American editions set publishing records for poetry.

He had the unique distinction of being awarded the Pulitzer Prize in poetry four times. Elected a member of the National Institute of Arts and Letters and of its prestigious inner body, the American Academy of Arts and Letters, he received the institute's gold medal. In 1958 he held the post of consultant in poetry at the Library of Congress, and in 1962 the Congressional Gold Medal was conferred upon him.

Three times Frost traveled abroad at the request of the State Department as a good-will ambassador for the United States. His first such trip was to South America in 1954. In 1961 he went to Israel and Greece. Then in 1962, the year before his death, he traveled to the Soviet Union and realized his hope of having a face-to-face meeting with Premier Nikita Khrushchev, in which he put forth his personal appeal for a rivalry for excellence between the two great powers, rather than a rivalry of ideology.

One of Frost's most gratifying honors was President-elect John F. Kennedy's invitation to read a poem at his inaugural ceremonies. Frost and Kennedy greatly admired each other, and the two had become good friends. It was the first time a poet participated in a presidential inauguration.

Frost died on January 29, 1963, in a hospital in Boston, after cancer surgery. He was mourned the world over. Among the many tributes were those of President Kennedy and Premier Khrushchev. A poetic tribute was printed in the Soviet government newspaper Izvestia. A few months later an anthology of Frost's poetry was published in the Soviet Union for the first time; although over 10,000 copies were printed, bookstores' supplies were exhausted a few days after publication.

The celebrated poet was buried on a hillside in the Old Bennington Cemetery in Old Bennington, Vermont, not far from Shaftsbury, where he had made his home for many years. Frost's grave and those of his wife and four of his children are marked by an elaborately carved seven-foot slab of blue granite. "I had a lover's quarrel with the world" is the epitaph Frost chose for himself; it is a line from his poem "The Lesson for Today."

Frost's farm on Buck Hill Road in Shaftsbury is now a national historic site. Known as The Gully, it is a quarter of a mile east of US Route 7.

The farm home in Derry, New Hampshire, which was given to Frost by his grandfather has also been named a national historic site. The Robert Frost Homestead, as it is officially designated, is located on New Hampshire Route 28, about two miles southeast of the town of Derry. In this vicinity Frost wrote many of his earlier poems, among which are a good number of those best known and loved.

Before his death, plans had been made for the new general library of Amherst College (to which the poet had very close ties) to be named for him. It became the first general library in the United States — and the second in the world — to be named for a poet. At the ground breaking for the Robert Frost Library on October 26, 1963, President Kennedy and the poet Archibald MacLeish paid eloquent tribute to Frost. Of Frost's method and purpose, the President remarked, "He brought an unsparing instinct for reality to bear on the platitudes and pieties of society" and he "saw poetry as the means of saving power from itself." The library, which was opened in September 1965, contains the major existing collection of Frostiana. Included are hundreds of books (some containing inscriptions) by or about Frost, photographs, three boxes of manuscripts, and other items pertaining to the poet and his work.

Dartmouth College marks its association with the poet with the Robert Frost Room in its Baker Library. At the dedication of the room in 1962, Frost presented the manuscript of his last volume of poetry, *In the Clearing*, to the collection. In addition, it contains first editions of each of Frost's books and memorabilia of his relationship with the school.

In late 1963 Frost's daughter, Lesley Frost Ballantine, whose husband was a professor at New York University, gave most of her father's library to that school. Containing a total of about 3,200 volumes, including many on archeology, exploration, history, and travel, it constitutes the Robert Frost Library within the university's Division of Special Collections. Almost 1,000 of the volumes are first editions of works presented to Frost by their authors, William Butler Yeats, Ezra Pound, John Masefield, Walter de la Mare, and other writers. Such mementos of the poet as photographs and press clippings are also included in the collection.

Among other noteworthy repositories of Frostiana are Harvard University and the Library of Congress. Of interest in the latter's collections are letters (most notably his correspondence with the author and editor Louis Untermeyer), manuscript poems, limited editions, autographed volumes, and Frost's reading copy of the poem "Dedication," which he wrote for President Kennedy's inauguration. (He actually recited another poem in its place, from memory, when glaring sunlight and a stiff breeze made it impossible for him to read the work he had composed for the occasion.)

At Middlebury College, in Middlebury and Ripton, Vermont, memories of Frost abound. For 43 years he was associated with the college's Bread Loaf School of English in Ripton, and he was a founder of the Bread Loaf Writers' Conference, which is held there every August. At the time of his birthday in the year following his death (1964), the college held a week-long observance, which featured numerous exhibits of his work. He was honored also in a series of lectures at the Bread Loaf School of English.

In 1966 "Robert Frost: A Re-evaluation" was the theme of the fall meeting of the Northeastern College English Association at the Bread Loaf campus. Frost was honored through lectures, panel discussions, tours, a film, and a performance of his plays, *A Masque of Reason* and *A Masque of Mercy*.

Vermont issued a commemorative bronze medal honoring the poet in March 1964. It can be seen in the Robert Frost Room of Starr Library on the Middlebury campus. The room houses a complete collection of Frostiana that includes about 250 books by or about Frost and some 1,500 other items, such as pamphlets and periodicals containing his work, book reviews, news items, photographs, college bulletins, sheet music for his poetry, tape and disc recordings, and original manuscripts. A film, *Robert Frost: A Lover's Quarrel with the World*, which was researched at the library, won a Motion Picture Academy Award in 1963.

Frost's farm in Ripton, where he was living at the time of his death, is also a national historic site, bought by Middlebury College in December 1966. The 150-acre farm, which includes the farmhouse and the cabin in which he lived and wrote, is maintained by the college as a memorial to the poet. With the exception of some books that have been removed, the cabin is furnished just as Frost left it. It is not generally open to the public, but may occasionally be visited by arrangement with Middlebury College. The cabin is located on a small dirt road leading off Vermont Route 125, which in 1972 was dedicated as the Robert Frost Memorial Drive, a mile north of Ripton. The road winds through exceptionally scenic countryside.

In August 1964 Middlebury College and residents of the Ripton area joined to dedicate a Vermont Historic Sites marker on Route 125 just a half mile from the Frost cabin in the woods. The marker cites Frost's distinction as a poet and recalls his warm, close ties with Vermont and, in particular, with Ripton and Middlebury College. It also contains the following inscription:

Breathes there a bard who isn't moved
When he finds his verse understood
And, not entirely disapproved
By his Country and his neighborhood?
— Robert Frost, 1961

Around and near the marker, Vermont and the US Forest Service developed the Robert Frost Memorial Wayside Area. It includes, in a lovely pine grove, a picnic area with running water, tables, and fireplaces. Within the area is a plaque inscribed with some of Frost's best-known poems.

To help familiarize people with the poet's life and work and the countryside he loved, area residents have organized A Day with Robert Frost, which is held annually in the late summer. A visit to the Bread Loaf School of English campus, viewing of films of and about Frost, a visit to the Frost cabin, and a picnic lunch at the Wayside Area or the Bread Loaf campus are typical highlights of the program.

In the centennial year of his birth, Frost was honored with the issuance of a commemorative US postage stamp.

Holy or Maundy Thursday

This is a movable event. See note on page xxvi.

On Holy Thursday, the Thursday before Easter (see March 29), Christians commemorate the major events that occurred on this day in the earthly life of Jesus Christ. Three of these events are best known as the Last Supper — the ceremonial Passover feast or seder (see April 21); the Agony in the Garden (detailed in Matthew 26: 36–46, Mark 14:32–42, and Luke 22:39–46); and Judas's betrayal of Jesus with a kiss. After this betrayal, Jesus was immediately seized and led off for questioning by the Pharisees and el-

ders, who then bound him over to the guards to be brought the next day before Pontius Pilate, the Roman procurator of Judea, who, the high priests insisted, should condemn him to death (see March 27, Good Friday).

On Holy Thursday, Protestant, Roman Catholic, and Eastern Orthodox churches celebrate Christ's institution, during the Last Supper, of the Eucharist — also known as Communion or the Lord's Supper. Some of the more liturgical churches also celebrate the institution of the priesthood. Note also is taken on this day of Jesus' reminder to his disciples of the commandment of brotherly love, which is central to Christian belief. In Western churches the main service on Holy Thursday is held in the evening, a time appropriate to the events being commemorated, and also a time when the largest congregations can attend. In Eastern Orthodox churches, the Divine Liturgy is celebrated in the morning, and the Service of the Holy Passion is held in the evening.

Among the Eastern Orthodox the ritual of the washing of the feet may be performed before the latter service, perhaps in the afternoon. In Roman Catholic churches a similar ritual may be performed just before the evening mass. In either case, the ceremony of the washing of the feet is a direct imitation of Jesus and his example of humility and service as recorded in the 13th chapter of the Gospel of John. There it is noted that during the last Passover supper he would eat with his disciples, Jesus, knowing the hour was near for his betrayal by Judas,

rose from supper . . . and girded himself with a towel. Then he poured water into a basin, and began to wash the disciples' feet, and to wipe them with the towel with which he was girded. . . . When he had washed their feet . . . and resumed his place, he said to them, "Do you know what I have done to you? You call me Teacher and Lord; and you are right, for so I am. If I then, your Lord and Teacher, have washed your feet, you also ought to wash one another's feet. For I have given you an example, that you also should do as I have done to you."

It is in remembrance of Jesus' demonstration of humility that the ritual of the washing of the feet continues to be carried out on Holy Thursday in some churches today. The minister, be he priest or bishop, does the ceremonial washing of the feet, usually of 12 men chosen from the clergy or from the lay congregation. The number 12 represents the number of the Apostles whose feet Jesus washed. Centuries ago, kings and other rulers often washed the feet of the poor, choosing as many poor people as the number of years the ruler had lived.

In most churches the main ritual of Holy

Thursday is the Service of the Lord's Supper, commemorating the Passover meal Jesus shared with his Apostles and his institution of the Eucharist during that event, remembered with joy and sorrow. The Gospel of Matthew 26:26–29) recounts the occasion:

Now as they were eating, Jesus took bread, and blessed, and broke it, and gave it to the disciples and said, "Take, eat; this is my body." And he took a cup, and when he had given thanks he gave it to them, saying, "Drink of it, all of you; for this is my blood of the covenant, which is poured out for many for the forgiveness of sins. I tell you I shall not drink again of this fruit of the vine until that day when I drink it new with you in my Father's kingdom."

Holy Thursday is also called Great Thursday, especially in Slavic countries, because of the important events it marks. Less obvious is the derivation of the name "Maundy Thursday," which comes from the Latin word for commandment, *mandatum*, the first word in an antiphon sung during the ritual of the washing of the feet. The words of the antiphon come from the Gospel of John (13:34–35), which quotes Jesus' statement to his disciples on the first Holy Thursday: "A new commandment I give to you, that you love one another. . . . By this all men will know that you are my disciples, if you have love for one another."

In Roman Catholic churches, the tabernacle, the sacred receptacle that usually houses consecrated hosts (the bread or wafers used in Communion) on the main altar, is empty and stands open at the beginning of Holy Thursday services as a reminder that it is the giving of the gift of Communion that is celebrated on this day and that before the Last Supper there was no Eucharist. During this mass, enough hosts are consecrated to distribute to the faithful who wish to receive Communion on Good Friday, the one day of the year when consecration is not permitted. After the Holy Thursday mass, the communion hosts for the next day's service are placed in a ciborium (an altar vessel similar to a chalice). Hymns of adoration are sung, clouds of incense are sent heavenward, and after a joyful but reverent procession around the church the hosts are placed in a special repository at a side altar or in a small chapel where the Catholic faithful can venerate Jesus Christ's Eucharistic presence among them. The main altar is quietly stripped, and all crucifixes are removed or covered in preparation for the Good Friday services.

The mass on Holy Thursday begins what Roman Catholics refer to as the sacred triduum, the three days before Easter Sunday, which are considered together as the Lord's Passover. During the Gloria Patri of the Holy Thursday mass, the bells or chimes ring out in Roman Catholic churches for the last time until the Easter Mass of the Resurrection. The solemn joy of Holy Thursday gives way to the somber tone of Good Friday.

In the United States, Roman Catholic bishops also celebrate a Chrism Mass in their cathedrals on the morning of Holy Thursday, blessing the holy oils that will be used throughout the year for church rituals such as baptism, ordination, confirmation, and last rites. Clerical representatives of churches within each diocese attend the Chrism Mass in the cathedral and take a supply of the holy oils back to their parishes.

Among liturgical Protestant churches, Holy Thursday worship services may bear some resemblance, great or small, to the Roman Catholic forms. In nonliturgical churches — a category embracing many Prostestant denominations — Holy Thursday worship services tend to be comparatively simple. Usually there are no processions or sounding of bells, and reenactment of Jesus' washing of the disciples' feet is rare. However, the Gospel accounts of this and the other important occurrences of the original Holy Thursday are read aloud to the congregations during the services. What is most emphasized, in music, prayers, and the minister's meditation from the pulpit, is Jesus' institution of Communion; and it is the reenactment of that central event of Christianity that Protestant ministers and worshipers principally concern themselves with on this day. Church members or "those who love the Lord" are invited to partake. Joining in Communion, worshipers are reminded of the injunction of Jesus, "this do in remembrance of me" (1 Corinthians 11:24). The attitude is one of worshipful gratitude, in a solemn, almost austere, context. For although there is stress on the ultimate triumph of Jesus' sacrifice, in every mind is the knowledge that Good Friday, commemorating that sacrifice, is just ahead — as the hymns sung on Holy Thursday usually reiterate.

Eastern Orthodox Christians mark Holy Thursday by celebrating their Divine Liturgy (equivalent to the Roman Catholic mass) in the morning. They then gather again in the evening for the mournful Service of the Holy Passion. This service includes readings from 12 Gospel lessons on the Passion (suffering) of Christ, the chanting of a litany, and hymns of the Crucifixion. In Greek Orthodox churches and some others, after the fifth reading, a large crucifix is carried in procession around the church by the priest, preceded by acolytes and chanters, and by other clergy, and then erected in the center of the church.

The Greek Orthodox patriarch in Istanbul

blesses the Holy Light (Fire) on Holy Thursday and this light is carried to all parts of the world to be used to light the candles of the faithful during their Easter Resurrection services — a dramatic sign of Greek Orthodox unity.

Holy Thursday is observed as a legal holiday in the US Virgin Islands.

Prince Kuhio Day

The Prince Kuhio Festival, held every year since 1970 on the island of Kauai, pays tribute to a man who represented the Hawaiian people during their struggle to maintain their old traditions while emerging as a modern republic.

A full-blooded Hawaiian, Prince Jonah Kuhio Kalanianaole was born of royal ancestry on March 26, 1871, on the island of Kauai. His mother and father, High Chief David Kahalepouli Piikoi and Princess Kinoiki Kekaulike, died when he and his two older brothers were very young. Their maternal aunt, Kapiolani, consort of King Kalakaua, the last reigning monarch of what was then the Kingdom of Hawaii, adopted the children. The king and queen began their reign in 1874, and the children were made princes by royal proclamation 10 years later.

As a possible successor to the throne, Prince Kuhio was sent to colleges and private schools in Honolulu, California, and England to receive the best education possible. But in 1893 the course of his future was suddenly altered. The Hawaiian monarchy was overthrown, and the Republic of Hawaii was established. A steadfast royalist, Kuhio joined a group of revolutionaries engaged in acts to overthrow the new republic and restore the monarchy. Their acts of treason against the republic quickly led to their arrest, and Prince Kuhio was sentenced to serve one year as a political prisoner. While in prison he was visited frequently by Elizabeth Kahanu Kaauwai, daughter of a chief of Maui, whom he later married upon his release and pardon in 1895.

The following years were filled with inner struggle for Prince Kuhio. The abolishment of the monarchy and, with it, many of the old traditions, was something the young prince had great difficulty coping with. For several years he traveled abroad and even contemplated taking up permanent residence in a foreign country. But in 1901 he decided to return to his native land and serve his people within the new framework of government.

While Prince Kuhio had been abroad, Hawaii had become a territory of the United States, and, upon his return, he found many political parties vying for power. In 1902 he decided to join the Republican party and was nominated as candidate for election as the first delegate to represent the Territory of Hawaii in Congress. He was elected to his first term in 1903 and was reelected for the next 10 consecutive terms until his death in 1921.

During his political career he worked tirelessly for the good of the Hawaiian people. His concern for the diminishing numbers of his race prompted him to urge the passage of the Hawaiian Homes Commission Act. This act, which was passed in 1921, provided homesteads for Hawaiians at nominal rents and for government loans to the settlers. Some of his other accomplishments were the development of Pearl Harbor as a strategic military base, the establishment in 1917 of the Hawaiian Civic Club to help preserve Hawaiian culture, and the designation of Kilauea volcano as a national park.

He died on January 7, 1921, and his remains are entombed at the Royal Mausoleum in Nuuanu Valley on the island of Oahu. His casket bears the inscription "Ke Alii Makaainaana" — "Prince of the Citizens." Memorial services honoring Prince Kuhio are held at the mausoleum.

The Prince Kuhio Festival is a week-long celebration on the island of Kauai during the latter part of March, including March 26, the date of Prince Kuhio's birth. The festival pays tribute to him by featuring many of the old Hawaiian customs and traditions he strove to preserve, three of which are the exciting outrigger canoe races, the ancient hula dances, and the songs of the islands.

The canoe races are usually held on the opening day of the festival and again on the date of his birth. The early Hawaiians designed the outrigger by taking the sturdy Polynesian *kaukahis* (single canoes) and adding to them the protective outrigger section to keep the boat from capsizing in heavy seas. For those islanders the outrigger was one of the most important aspects of their way of life. The canoe builders were maintained at the court of the chiefs, and the actual construction was attended by special religious ceremonies. To become oarsmen it was necessary for young men to undergo a strict regime of training, and once qualified, they were looked upon as perfect examples of island manhood. This tradition is still maintained, for the most part, with the young oarsmen of today undergoing the same rigorous training as their ancestors.

Another ancient art a visitor can enjoy at the festival is the performance of the hula. Originally danced by men only, it was eventually danced primarily by women. To be chosen as a dancer was a high honor, and acquiring sufficient skill required a lifetime of dedication and practice. Girls began their apprenticeship at the age of three or four by entering the temple and seldom emerged until their mid-teens, when they had become accomplished dancers. Although the hula seems simple to the casual observer, it involves intricate steps as well as graceful hand motions, which tell the story of the dance.

The Prince Kuhio Festival features many other colorful attractions — cultural exhibits; parades with flower-decorated floats and marching units; sporting events, including a women's outrigger canoe race; and performances of Hawaiian music. In addition, visitors can see many of the memoirs of Prince Kuhio on display at the Kauai Museum in Lihue.

The festival culminates in a spectacular Holoku parade and the elegant Prince Kuhio Ball, which evokes memories of Hawaii's royal past.

MARCH 27

The Alaska Earthquake

The severest earthquake ever to strike North America, and the second strongest ever recorded anywhere in the world, gripped Alaska on March 27, 1964. Registering at least 8.4 on the Richter Magnitude Scale, it exceeded even the 8.25 fury of the San Francisco quake of 1906. Damage was worst in Anchorage, the 49th state's largest city, where the entire downtown business section was leveled, whole streets dropped as much as 20 feet, and cars and shattered buildings piled up on top of one another. The trouble was compounded by quake-caused landslides, made worse by the fact that much of the Anchorage area rested on an unstable layer of "bootlegger clay" — clay already soupy in some places from moisture that it had absorbed earlier. In the most spectacular of many landslide disasters, 77 suburban Anchorage homes, borne on a slippery carpet of moving earth, tumbled over a bluff into Cook Inlet.

Landslides, rockslides, and snow avalanches also occurred elsewhere in southern Alaska, especially in the coastal regions, as did the phenomenon popularly known as tidal waves and scientifically termed by seismologists as tsunamis, or seismic sea waves. Such Alaskan ports as Kodiak, Kenai, Seward, Cordova, and Valdez suffered major — in some cases almost overwhelming — damage. (The old town of Valdez, where every building was damaged, had to be totally rebuilt — on a safer, rock-firm site four miles away from the old one. The ice-free port is the southern terminus of the Trans-Alaska oil pipeline.) Giant waves also wrecked coastal regions in Canada, Oregon, and California. The communities of Depoe Bay and Seaside, Oregon, and Crescent City, California, were among those affected. Even as far away as Siberia, Japan, and Hawaii, coastline havoc was wrought by quake-triggered tidal waves. In Houston, Texas, sections of earth moved up or downward nearly five inches. The waters of the Gulf of Mexico peaked to "in-resonance" waves six feet high. One report would have been ludicrous had it not been frightening: the Alaskan quake spilled water over the edges of swimming pools in faraway Texas and Louisiana.

In all, 114 lives were lost on the North American borders of the Pacific Ocean, a toll that would have been higher had the quake not taken place at 5:36 p.m., just after the business areas that were to suffer heavily had partly emptied. Property damage from the earthquake soared to an estimated $750 million, some $200 million of it in Greater Anchorage alone.

Less than two years later, however, that determined community had recovered and was bigger and shinier than ever, with the debris barely visible to remind one that it could all happen again. (One site, known as Earthquake Park, has been left unreconstructed. This fenced area looks exactly as it did after the disaster.) Anchorage is in one of the world's two most active earthquake areas, one being the shorelines on both sides of the Pacific, the other path running through the Mediterranean Sea, Asia Minor, the Himalaya Mountains, and the East Indies.

Though the major destruction of the Alaska earthquake took place during the catastrophic first five minutes, after-quakes went on for weeks. As late as October 1, the earth still trembled.

Good Friday

This is a movable event. See note on page xxvi.

Good Friday, the Friday before Easter Sunday, is the most somber day of the Church calendar, contrasting sharply with the Sundays that precede and follow it (see March 22, Palm Sunday; March 29, Easter). On this day Christians commemorate the Passion (suffering) and death of Jesus Christ on the cross.

To the early Christians, who regarded Jesus as the Son of God and long-hoped-for Messiah, the original Good Friday seemed to mark the end of all they had hoped and believed. Particularly did their despair deepen when Jesus did not miraculously descend from the cross and triumph over the temporal powers in the manner of an earthly king or conqueror. Almost all his followers had scattered and vanished after his arrest on what is now commemorated as Holy Thursday (see

March 26). Not until Easter Sunday, with the Resurrection of Jesus, did their faith and hope revive. And not until Pentecost, the 50th day after Easter (see May 17), when they received the gift of the Holy Spirit in accordance with Jesus' earlier promises, were they transformed from frightened, ineffectual beings to the eloquent disciples portrayed in the New Testament as they went forth boldly, in the face of great danger, to proclaim Jesus' teachings of love and eternal life.

In view of the grief associated with the Crucifixion, many have questioned why the day observed as its anniversary is known in English as Good Friday. One theory is that the term is a corruption of the earlier "God's Friday." Another theory holds that the "Good" refers to the good that came to humankind through the life and death of Jesus. In various periods and places, the day has also been known as Long Friday, and as Holy, or Great, Friday.

Christians today still relive the sorrow of the first Good Friday. The sorrowful mood extends from Good Friday until Holy Saturday evening, which in many churches is marked by an Easter Vigil service beginning after sundown or, often, near midnight and extending into the beginning of the new day of Easter. Then the mood goes from sadness to joy, and the church literally goes from darkness to light (see March 28, Holy Saturday).

While many Christian churches in the United States still hold, from noon to 3:00 P.M., the traditional *Tre Ore* (three-hour) services on Good Friday long popular among both Catholics and Protestants, the time and length of Good Friday services are decided increasingly by individual churches, and the long *Tre Ore* services are less common than formerly. Both the three-hour services, commemorating the hours Jesus hung on the cross, and briefer forms of Good Friday worship concentrate mostly on the Seven Last Words, the seven separate utterances Christ made from the cross, drawn from the four Gospel accounts of the Crucifixion. These are interspersed with sermons, prayers, traditional Good Friday hymns, and intervals for silent prayer and meditation. In some communities, ministers from different churches share the responsibility for conducting a service held jointly for all their members. For Roman Catholics and some others, the Stations of the Cross (meditations on the sufferings of Christ) frequently are a part of Good Friday devotions.

Whatever the exact form of their worship, Christians of all denominations also associate with Good Friday the prophetic words from the 53rd chapter of Isaiah commonly read as part of Good Friday services:

He was despised and rejected by men; a man of sorrows, and acquainted with grief; . . . Surely he has borne our griefs and carried our sorrows; . . . he was wounded for our transgressions, he was bruised for our iniquities; upon him was the chastisement that made us whole. . . . the Lord has laid on him the iniquity of us all.

The words reflect not only the remorse felt by individual Christians on this day, but also basic Christian belief as to its meaning.

Among Protestant denominations, Lutheran and Episcopalian churches are most likely to follow set liturgical forms on Good Friday, with prayers and biblical readings specifically prescribed for the day. Even within these two liturgical denominations, however, there is considerable variety from one church to another as to the exact form — and time (which may vary from noon to evening) — of Good Friday worship services. In addition to *Tre Ore* services, both groups may hold services of Holy Communion or vesper services with litany. A few Lutheran and other Protestant churches have revived a custom dating from the fourth century and long practiced by Roman Catholics, holding the service of *Tenebrae* in the evening. Traditionally taking place on Wednesday, Thursday, and Friday of Holy Week, this service consists of a series of psalms and responses, accompanied by the symbolic extinguishing of a set of candles, indicating the darkness associated with Jesus' death but also foreshadowing the Resurrection in that one candle remains lighted at the end of the service, after being temporarily removed from view.

Among the nonliturgical Protestant denominations, there is even more variety in the services held on Good Friday. The *Tre Ore* devotions are gradually being outnumbered by briefer services. Traditional prayers may be interspersed with others that individual ministers compose afresh for Good Friday each year. There also is more latitude in the choice of Scripture readings and the general form of the service. Commemoration of the Crucifixion, however, is always the theme of the day, and a Gospel reading of the Crucifixion account is standard. Generally speaking, the historic preference of the nonliturgical Protestant churches for the simpler forms of worship is evident on Good Friday, as throughout the rest of the year, although their services are no less solemn than those of churches that place heavier emphasis on formal ritual. Much as Protestant practice permits individual variations, however, innovations are usually intermingled with traditional forms, with the emphasis most often on the latter. This is particularly true of many Protestant churches that have developed an increased appreciation for traditional liturgy.

Some of the more liturgical churches, conversely, have shown increased flexibility and an interest in new forms. Roman Catholics have officially adopted a revised form of worship for Good Friday. Usually held in the afternoon or early evening, this revised rite has replaced the *Tre Ore* devotion in most Catholic churches. Episcopalians and some others are considering a new form of Good Friday service very similar to that of Roman Catholics. This is in keeping with the ecumenism of the present age, which has led several major denominations to undertake studies of the entire church year in view of their interest in steps toward common expression of the Christian faith.

In the new liturgy used by Roman Catholics, the Good Friday worship service is divided into three parts. During the first part, the Liturgy of the Word, readings from the book of Isaiah (52:13–53:12) and St. Paul's epistle to the Hebrews (4:14–16; 5:7–9) precede the main reading, which is the account according to John (18:1–19:42) of Jesus' betrayal, arrest, trial, Crucifixion, and burial (with Pilate's permission) by Joseph of Arimathea and Nicodemus in a new tomb in a garden near the place of the Crucifixion. After this reading a brief sermon may be given, and the first part of the liturgy is concluded with prayers of general intercession for a wide variety of groups, including public officeholders and those in special need. The prayers are for believers and nonbelievers alike, in keeping with the Christian belief that Christ died for everyone.

In the Veneration of the Cross, the second part of the Roman Catholic liturgy for Good Friday, the cross is brought to the altar and elevated while the priest intones, "This is the wood of the cross." The people respond, "Come let us worship." While the choir or congregation sings appropriate antiphons or hymns, the people approach the cross individually and reverence it, by genuflecting before it or by kissing it.

The Holy Communion service, the third segment of the Good Friday Liturgy, follows. The altar, which was stripped on Holy Thursday, is now covered with a cloth, and other altar appointments are brought out. The hosts — Eucharistic bread or wafers that have been blessed on Holy Thursday and placed in a repository — are now carried to the main altar. Good Friday is the one day of the year when the Mass is not celebrated in the Roman Catholic church. After prayers and hymns, the priest receives Communion and distributes the Blessed Sacrament to the people who approach the altar. Post-Communion prayers are said, the congregation departs in silence, and the altar is again stripped. For the worshiper, the emptiness of the church — its ornaments removed, its ritual minimized — be-

speaks the emptiness of a life without Jesus Christ. For Roman Catholics and some other Christians, Good Friday and Ash Wednesday remain the only two days of the year when strict rules of fast and abstinence are observed; that is, a minimum of food is eaten (fasting) and meat and poultry are not eaten (abstinence).

Most Eastern Orthodox Christians maintain a much stricter fast and abstinence throughout Lent, and their Holy Week ritual is elaborate. As in Roman Catholic churches, where it is called Holy Mass, the Divine Liturgy of the Orthodox is not celebrated on Good Friday. Instead, the Service of the Royal Hours is held on Good Friday morning, with psalms, Old Testament prophecies, and New Testament readings, culminating in the account of the Passion and Crucifixion.

In the Greek Orthodox and some other Eastern churches, during the afternoon of Good Friday there is a vesper service of the Descent from the Cross of the Body of Christ. The large cross taken in procession around the church on Holy Thursday now stands in the front of the church. On Good Friday afternoon, the *epitaphion* — a cloth icon depicting the body of Christ — is carried around the church in preparation for the ceremonial burial and then placed in or on a bier. Flower petals are strewn on the icon, and masses of flowers adorn the bier, the flowers symbolizing the entombment of Jesus, who was, as noted in Scripture, given the customary Jewish burial using spices, myrrh, and aloes. The flowers are later given to members of the congregation to take home as reverently cherished mementos.

On the evening of Good Friday, Eastern Orthodox churches hold the *Epitaphios* (or Lamentation) service, which represents the burial of Jesus. During this service, members of the congregation hold lighted candles as they join with the clergy and choir in singing the sorrowful lamentations over Jesus' death. The service reaches its climax with a procession in which the *epitaphion* is carried around the church, often on the outside of the edifice, and the blessing of Jesus is invoked. The bier and image of Jesus remain in the front (or center) of the church until after the Saturday morning liturgy, when they are moved to one side. Unlike Roman Catholics, who omit the celebration of Mass on the morning of Holy Saturday, Eastern Orthodox Christians celebrate the Divine Liturgy then.

Having the bier in the church, as the Eastern Orthodox do, recalls the early days of the Christian church, when the faithful observed the 40 hours between Jesus' death and Resurrection in strict fasting and prayer. This was a widespread custom as early as the second century. Many early Christians made a pilgrimage to Jerusalem and kept their 40-hour vigil (or "wake") at the Holy Sepulchre, where Christ is said to have been buried. In other cities shrines of the Sepulchre were reproduced in a number of churches, and the faithful would often visit more than one of these shrines during Good Friday and Holy Saturday.

In Latin countries, Holy Week is traditionally the occasion for pageants and processions. The most famous of these observances takes place in Seville, Spain. The Spanish customs found their way to the Latin countries of the New World, where the observances are still maintained in many of the larger cities and even more often in the small towns and villages where the old traditions are most likely to be cherished and preserved. Here, as in some other parts of the world, Jesus is given the funeral procession he did not actually have. In Mexican observances, the climax of the funeral procession comes when Mary, represented by a statue, meets the lifeless body of her son. The statue of Mary, draped in black, is carried into the church and placed on the altar, while the cross is placed in front of the altar. The mood of the worshipers is that of persons making condolence calls to bereaved members of a family.

Like most events of Holy Week, Good Friday has inspired artists in every field for centuries. Michelangelo's *Pietà*, the sculpture of Mary holding the body of her crucified son, is perhaps the best known example. Richard Wagner's *Parsifal*, the opera based on the search for the Holy Grail, is frequently heard during Holy Week and includes a passage known as the "Good Friday Spell."

Observed throughout the United States, Good Friday is a legal full or partial holiday in more than 10 states and a full legal holiday in Puerto Rico and the US Virgin Islands.

MARCH 28

Holy Saturday

This is a movable event. See note on page xxvi.

The day before Easter is called Holy Saturday or the Vigil of Easter. In the words of the revised Roman Missal, "On Holy Saturday, the Church waits at the Lord's tomb, meditating on His suffering and death." Until recent years, in most Western Christian churches, no services were held on Holy Saturday for many centuries. It was as if all activity had been suspended in a state of limbo, the same state Jesus' followers were in on the day after the Crucifixion: Jesus had died but he had not yet risen. Even today, most churches are empty and seemingly forlorn until after nightfall, when the Easter Vigil service — restored in the mid-1950s (and since) by some liturgical churches — begins.

Dating from the early centuries of the Christian church, the Easter Vigil services are the most dramatic of the Church Year. In the Roman Catholic church the restoration of the Easter Vigil, or, as it is sometimes called, the Night Watch of the Resurrection, was accomplished under Pope Pius XII and was more or less universal throughout the church by 1955. Some Episcopal and numerous Lutheran churches have restored very similar rituals on a provisional basis in recent years. Permanent adoption of the Easter Vigil will be considered by general conventions of both denominations, probably before the end of the 1970s.

All Easter Vigil services have pronounced similarities, since they stem from a common origin far predating any divisions within the Christian church. However, since the use and form of the Roman Catholic and Eastern Orthodox vigils are established, and not subject to ratification or early revision, they are the ones detailed below.

The Roman Catholic version is set forth in the revised Roman Missal. According to this, the solemn beginning of the Roman Catholic Easter Vigil is called the Service of Light, and the opening words explain the night's ceremony and the reasons for it:

Dear Friends in Christ, on this most holy night, when our Lord Jesus Christ passed from death to life, the Church invites her children throughout the world to come together in vigil and prayer. This is the passover of the Lord: if we honor the memory of his death and resurrection by hearing his word and celebrating his mysteries, then we may be confident that we shall share in his victory over death and live with him for ever in God.

As observed by Roman Catholics, the Easter Vigil service begins after nightfall and consists of four parts. It opens with the Service of Light, which takes place in a darkened church or area outside the church. The dark symbolizes the death of Jesus, the Light of the World. The congregation gathers around the priests, ministers, deacons, and acolytes as the celebrant lights a new fire, symbolizing Jesus' passing from death to life. The blessing of the new fire is followed by the blessing of the new paschal (Easter) candle, which during the Vigil service will be placed on the main altar of the church, where it will remain until Ascension Day, a period symbolizing the 40 days Jesus remained with his disciples between his Resurrection and his Ascension into heaven (see May 7).

In blessing the new paschal candle, the chief

celebrant presses five large grains of incense into the candle in the form of a cross. The grains of incense represent Jesus' five wounds, suffered on Good Friday. With a stylus, the celebrant traces the first and last letters of the Greek alphabet at either end of the vertical shaft of the cross, the alpha above, the omega below, symbolizing that God is the beginning and the end of all things. The four numerals of the current year are then inscribed, one in each quadrant formed by the cross.

The paschal candle is then lit with the new fire, and the tapers held by members of the congregation are ignited from it, while the refrain "Christ our Light" and the response, "Thanks be to God," are intoned three times. The lights of the church go on as the procession of celebrant, ministers, and assistants approaches the main altar. The Easter Proclamation, or "Exsultet," is sung at this point. The service then continues with Part II of the Easter Vigil — the Liturgy of the Word. This consists of a series of readings from the Old Testament, always including the account from Exodus of the Israelites' safe passage through the Red Sea, followed by the New Testament readings of the Epistle and the Gospel.

The third part of the Vigil service is the Liturgy of Baptism, which includes the blessing of water and the baptismal font. Centuries ago, new members of the church were baptized during this Easter Vigil ceremony; today, if there are new members to be baptized, the ceremony takes place during this part of the service. In any event, all members of the congregation renew their baptismal vows at this time. The fourth and final part of the Vigil Service is the Mass, or Liturgy of the Eucharist, wherein the faithful participate in communion.

Throughout Lent, the "Gloria" (the hymn "Glory to God") has not been sung nor have bells been rung in Catholic churches. On Holy Saturday night, the altar candles have been lit, and during the Easter Vigil mass the "Gloria" is sung, the worshipers hear the "Alleluia," and church bells are rung, all emphasizing the joyousness of the celebration.

Although for Western Christian churches the restoration of the Easter Vigil service is fairly recent, the Eastern Orthodox churches had never broken the tradition of holding an Easter vigil. At about 11:00 P.M. on Holy Saturday the Orthodox gather in cathedrals and churches. A service with the choir chanting laments recalling the Crucifixion of Jesus and his descent into Hades (or Limbo) is followed by the Glorious Resurrection Service at 11:45 P.M., when the lights of the church are extinguished and Pre-Resurrection hymns are sung. With the church

in total darkness, the choir sings the hymn "Behold the dawn and rise of day," recalling the women who went to Christ's tomb on the first Easter Sunday and discovered that the tomb was empty (Matthew 28, Mark 16, Luke 24, and John 20).

At midnight the Royal Gates of the Altar are opened and the Orthodox celebrant comes forth, carrying lighted candles and proclaiming to the congregation, "Come Ye, take light from the light that never wanes. Come Glorify Christ risen from the dead." The Orthodox faithful take their "new light" home with them, shielding the taper from the elements to preserve the flame, and use it to light candles in front of their favorite icons at home throughout the year.

In the Orthodox midnight service, after the worshipers have received the light they follow the celebrant and his ecclesiastical retinue in a procession outdoors, as all chant: "Thy Resurrection, O Saviour, Angels sing in the heavens." Outside, the celebrant mounts a platform, reads from the Gospel of John, and joyously intones the triumphant "Christos Anesti" — "Christ is risen from the dead, in death trampling upon death; and upon those in tombs hath he bestowed life." The congregation and choir repeat this traditional refrain many times and other Resurrection hymns are sung. After the proclamation, "Christ is risen!" and the joyously shouted response, "He is risen indeed!" the doors of the church are flung open and the church is revealed as fully illuminated. (Orthodox Christians will greet friends with an embrace and this same refrain and response for the next 40 days.) All then reenter the church to hear the Divine Liturgy.

After the Easter sermon, the celebrant gives absolution alike "to those who have kept the fast and to those who have fasted not," in the words of St. John Chrysostom. (The Orthodox Lenten fast has always been more austere and demanding than the Lenten fasts of Western Christians.) Members of the congregation then receive the Holy Eucharist, partaking of both the bread and the wine, symbolizing the Body and Blood of Christ in Holy Communion.

It is a spectacular, warm, and dramatic culmination of the six weeks of Lent, a time for joy after the time for penance and prayer. Easter has come: "Christ is risen." It is cause for the candles to be lighted, the bells to be rung, and the "Alleluia" to be sung — terminating the dark, somber period of preparation for this event. The white vestments worn by the clargy of every rank also betoken the joyousness of the feast, and the spirit of joy overflows into the following period of 50 days.

Members of some Eastern churches in the

United States still maintain cherished ethnic traditions. On Holy Saturday many Russian Orthodox Christians, and others of Slavic origin, prepare to end their Lenten fast by taking baskets of their food to their churches for the ancient custom of the Blessing of the Pascha (Easter) Baskets. The baskets contain foods they will eat in celebration of Easter. Filled for the most part with foods from which people have abstained during the Lenten season, the baskets typically contain bread, lamb, butter, cheese, salt, colored eggs, and other foods symbolic of the season. After the priest blesses the pascha baskets, the food is taken home to be eaten.

Since the Easter season is for all Christians a good time to celebrate things held dear, special festivities take place in many localities. In the Mexican community of Los Angeles, for example, the Blessing of the Animals takes place annually on Holy Saturday in the city's old Spanish Plaza. The colorful ceremony, in which residents acknowledge the service and loyal affection of animals of all sorts, is held at the old Plaza Church.

Participants gather beforehand in tiny Olvera Street, just off the plaza, which has been restored as a Mexican street market. The animals may range from oxen and other farm animals to canaries, puppies, cats, and turtles. Beribboned and flower-trimmed bird cages, fishbowls containing plain or exotic creatures, cages, cases, leashes — and sometimes just small arms — hold ordinary or unusual pets. The larger animals, often garlanded with flowers, are driven or led by their owners, many of them in Mexican costumes.

Early in the afternoon, Sunset Boulevard, on the north side of the plaza, is closed to traffic as owners and pets begin their procession from the north end of Olvera Street into the plaza. The parade approaches a platform adorned with flowers in Plaza Park. There a priest surrounded by altar boys blesses each animal as it passes.

Another well-loved local ethnic tradition is the annual Easter Fires Pageant, in Fredericksburg, Texas, which was founded by a group of German colonists in 1846. The pageant, enacted by schoolchildren in Fair Park, is said to have had its origin in a tense episode from the town's early history. According to the story, it was Easter eve when a party of Comanches, ordered by their chief to keep the settlers under surveillance, built watch fires. When the alarmed children of a newly arrived family asked why the fires were burning, their inventive mother quickly replied that Easter rabbits were at work, boiling the traditional Easter eggs — or, according to a slightly different version, burning wildflowers to make dyes with which to color the eggs. In due time, peace was established between the settlers and the Indians, and the tension receded. Today, however, the hillside Easter fires are rekindled annually and the pageant is repeated each year to retell the story.

MARCH 29

Easter

This is a movable event. See note on page xxvi.

Easter Sunday, commemorating the Resurrection of Jesus Christ, is the most important feast of the Christian ecclesiastical year, since Christ's Resurrection is the central pillar on which the Christian faith is built. Christians, who believe in the divinity of Jesus, base this belief in part on the miracles he performed while he was on earth and particularly on the culminating miracle of his resurrection from the dead on the third day after he was crucified. Jesus himself had foretold his resurrection, to which there are many references in the New Testament, as well as in the prophecies of the Old Testament. Christians believe that the Resurrection was the fulfillment of those prophecies. Without the first Good Friday — the day of the Crucifixion (see March 27) — there would have been no Easter Sunday. Without the Resurrection, there would be no Christian church.

The story of the Resurrection is told by each of the four Evangelists in the New Testament: Matthew 27:57–28:10; Mark 15:42–16:12; Luke 23:50–24:50; and John 19:38–20:30. According to the Gospel of Matthew, after Jesus died on the cross, Joseph of Arimathea, a wealthy man who was a secret disciple of Jesus, obtained permission to bury him from Pontius Pilate, the Roman procurator of Judea:

And Joseph took the body, and wrapped it in a clean linen shroud, and laid it in his own new tomb, which he had hewn in the rock; and he rolled a great stone to the door of the tomb, and departed. . . . Now after the sabbath, toward the dawn of [Sunday,] the first day of the week, Mary Magdalene and the other Mary went to see the sepulchre. And behold, there was a great earthquake; for an angel of the Lord descended from heaven and came and rolled back the stone, and sat upon it. His appearance was like lightning, and his raiment white as snow. And for fear of him the guards trembled and became like dead men. But the angel said to the women, "Do not be afraid; for I know that you seek Jesus who was crucified. He is not here; for he has risen, as he said. Come, see the place where he lay. Then go quickly and tell his disciples that he has risen from the dead, and behold, he is going before you to Galilee; there you will see him. . . ." So they departed quickly from the tomb with fear and great joy, and ran to tell his disciples. And behold Jesus met them and said, "Hail!" And they came up and took hold of his feet and worshiped him. Then Jesus said to them, "Do not be afraid; go and tell my brethren to go to Galilee, and there they will see me."

Easter is the culmination of Holy Week, which has been called "the week that changed the world." For the estimated 1 billion Christians throughout the world, the Feast of Easter, celebrating the risen Christ's victory over death, is the foundation of their faith: during the preceding Holy Week, Jesus suffered and died for humankind, thus offering all people hope of redemption. In his Resurrection from the dead on the first Easter Sunday, Christians find reaffirmation of his divinity and hope for their own resurrection, their own victory over death.

The joyousness of the occasion is manifested not only in the prayers and sermons in the various Christian churches, but in such outward signs as flowers, music, and the donning of white vestments by clergy in some churches. In a more secular vein, citizens mark the glad tidings with new spring finery and Easter bonnets. There are special foods associated with Easter, as well as folk customs and games.

Other secular and religious traditions have grown up around the celebration of Easter. For example, while the Bermuda lily, frequently called the Easter lily, is most commonly associated with this holiday, many other flowers also are used to decorate churches, town squares, parks and other public places, signifying the joy and promise of Easter and also incorporating the celebration of spring, which dates from pre-Christian times. There is a vast variety of joyous Easter music, frequently including the word "Alleluia" (or "Hallelujah"), derived through the Latin and Greek from Hebrew, which means "Praise ye Jehovah." This is a joyful exclamation used by most Christian churches in their Easter worship services, as well as in music — such as the familiar hymn, sung as the choir enters in procession at the beginning of Easter services in many Protestant churches and some others:

Christ the Lord is ris'n today, Alleluia!
Sons of men and angels say; Alleluia!
Raise your joys and triumphs high, Alleluia!
Sing, ye heav'ns, and earth reply. Alleluia!

Lives again our glorious King: Alleluia!
Where, O death, is now thy sting? Alleluia!
Dying once, he all doth save: Alleluia!
Where thy victory, O grave? Alleluia!

The Roman Catholic Easter Mass also has joy, hope, and love for its keynotes. Prayers emphasize redemption and resurrection. Almost every church has its version of this sentence, which appears in the new Roman Catholic Missal for Holy Week: "On this day, O God, you overcame death through your only-begotten Son, and opened to us the gate of everlasting life." Catholics continue with the words "Help us continually to carry out by our actions the desires that you put into our hearts...." — a petition also set forth, with only slight differences, in the hymnal long used by Missouri Synod Lutherans. Many other Lutherans and Episcopalians add these or very similar words: "Grant us so to die daily unto sin, that we may evermore live with him who died and rose again for us...." One of the traditional Easter prayers in the *Pilgrim Hymnal* long familiar to Congregationalists and many other Protestants says in part: "Almighty God, who hast brought again from the dead our Lord Jesus, ... giving him victory over death and the grave: Grant us power, we beseech thee, to rise with him to newness of life; that we may ... share in ... eternal joy ... through the grace of that risen Saviour, who liveth and reigneth with thee, world without end."

Eastern Orthodox Christians usually celebrate Easter later than Western Christians. However, the main themes of Easter — joy, hope, love, and redemption — are the same in their services and music and in their traditional Easter customs and rituals. Having attended the celebration of the Divine Liturgy beginning the previous midnight, Eastern Orthodox Greeks, for example, return to church on Easter Day to hold their Vesper Service of Love, known by the Greek word *agape*. During this service the paschal hymns of the Orthodox proclaim, "Today is the Day of Resurrection! Let us shine with the Feast! Let us embrace one another. Let us say to our brethren that because of the Resurrection, we forgive all things to those who hate us, and in this wise, exclaim Christ is risen from the dead." During the *agape* service, to proclaim the belief that Jesus' teachings are for all nations, the Gospel is read in the different national languages of the various Orthodox groups. At the end of the service, it is customary for members of the congregation to embrace one another as a manifestation of Jesus' abiding love for all humankind.

Eastern Orthodox Russians, like their Greek counterparts, also are more demonstrative than Western Christians in their celebration of Easter. After church services, members of Russian Orthodox congregations gather to crack the colored shells of hard-boiled eggs for good luck and then, according to ritual, to kiss one another three times. The egg-cracking custom is simple and has been adopted by many non-Orthodox persons purely for the fun of it. While one person holds an Easter egg with his fingers wrapped around it, leaving only the top unprotected, another taps his or her egg against it. The person whose egg does not crack is the one who wins good luck. During this ritual, one participant traditionally says, "Christ is risen," and the other responds, "He is risen indeed!" The colored eggs and other special Easter foods, including ham, lamb, cheesecake (*paskha*), and the cylindrical dough cake (*kulitch*), are frequently taken to church to be blessed beforehand by the priest or archbishop.

The subject of the timing of Easter has been controversial from the early centuries of the Church. Indeed, setting the date of Easter — and determining when it should fall in each future year — was an extremely complicated matter. Since the Passion, Death, and Resurrection took place during the Jewish feast of Passover, any effort to establish the date of Easter was bound to be influenced to some extent by the Jewish calendar and also by the lunar cycles on which the months of the Jewish calendar depend. However, the Julian calendar then in use by most Christians was a solar calendar (like today's Gregorian calendar, which succeeded it). In view of the natural incommensurability of the lunar and solar cycles, both of which thus were involved in calculating the date of Easter, there was a built-in difficulty in establishing the date to begin with (see Appendix, The Calendar).

The week-long Passover festival begins after sundown on the 14th day of the month of Nisan. Since the Resurrection took place during Passover, some early Christians, known as Quartodecimans, chose to observe Easter on the 14th of Nisan. In the Jewish lunisolar calendar, this is a fixed date. As translated into terms of the Julian (and later the Gregorian) calendar, however, it appears as a movable feast whose date can vary widely from year to year. And in both calendars, the 14th of Nisan (or its Julian equivalent) could fall on any day of the week. Although this did not trouble the Quartodecimans, other early Christians felt strongly that Easter should always be celebrated on a Sunday, since according to the Bible that was the day of the actual Resurrection. Much of what came to be known as the Easter Controversy centered around this difference of opinion, with the Quartodecimans ultimately overruled.

Other considerations also accounted for a lack of uniformity as to the date on which Christians observed Easter in the early centuries of the Church. One complicating factor was that astronomers in different centers of the Mediterranean world possessed differing degrees of astronomical knowledge or used different methods of calculation, and in consequence they achieved different results when attempting to compute the correct date for the observance of Easter.

Finally the question of the date of Easter was taken up by the Ecumenical Council of Nicaea, presided over by Emperor Constantine, in A.D. 325, which sought to establish a uniform date to be observed by all churches throughout Christendom. Although the exact wording of the "Nicene" ruling on Easter is uncertain, and some specifics remained to be agreed upon in later centuries, the council apparently did decide important elements of the rule that eventually predominated. The council's synodical letter, together with a letter of Emperor Constantine, indicates two decisions: that all Christians should thenceforth celebrate Easter together, after the fashion of the Roman and Alexandrian Churches (whose reckonings were not fully identical at the time, however); and that the celebration of Easter should not coincide with the beginning of the Jewish Passover.

Both Western and Eastern Orthodox Christians have since cited the authority of the Nicene Council for their Easter rule, even though the dates on which they celebrate Easter usually differ, according to their somewhat different interpretations. This rule, as it came to be formulated, was that Easter should be celebrated on the first Sunday after the first full moon on or after the vernal equinox. This formula is accepted by both Western and Eastern Orthodox churches to this day. Some scholars assert that the Easter rule contained the additional stipulation that Easter must be observed *after* the beginning of Passover, in order to follow the biblical sequence of events. Western Christians, whose Easter can fall on any Sunday from March 22 to April 25, do not adhere to this additional requirement. Eastern Orthodox churches, however, hold firmly to the precept that Easter must always follow the start of Passover. The result is that, while the Eastern Orthodox Easter may coincide with the Western celebration in some years, it more frequently occurs from one to five weeks later than the Western feast. In either case, Easter is a "movable" feast, whose date changes each year, in both West and East. It should be noted, however, that even though the date of Passover is not a factor in determining the date of Easter among Western Christians, it is generally agreed that there is more than a chronological link between the two feasts. Indeed, Easter is often referred to as "the Christian Passover."

The dates of numerous Christian observances are determined by the date of Easter each year. The events leading up to the death and Resurrection of Jesus are described in connection with those observances — Holy Thursday (see March

26), Good Friday (see March 27), and Holy Saturday (see March 28). Other related days whose dates are dependent upon the date of Easter include Ascension Day (see May 7) and Pentecost (see May 17).

As for the difference in Easter date between West and East, for many years there have been renewed attempts by some Church leaders to set an Easter date that would be acceptable to all Christians — Protestants and Roman Catholics in the West, and Orthodox Christians in the East — so that they could emphasize their unity of belief by celebrating the central feast of Christianity on the same day. One result of the Second Vatican Council, held under Roman Catholic auspices between 1962 and 1965, was the "Constitution on the Sacred Liturgy," indicating openness to such an idea.

For Eastern Orthodox Christians, Easter marks the beginning of the ecclesiastical year, whereas Western Christians start their ecclesiastical year with the first day of Advent, the season preceding Christmas. The name Easter does not appear in the Bible, and the origin of the English word is uncertain. The Venerable Bede, the eighth century English monk and scholar, suggested that the word may have derived from the Anglo-Saxon name of a Teutonic goddess of spring and fertility, Eostre, or Eastre, whose symbol was the hare. However, other possible derivations have been suggested as well. Certainly, people celebrated spring rites long before the time of Jesus, rejoicing that winter was dead and that spring had been reborn. To the Christian, Easter signified a new kind of rebirth.

In the United States, Easter is the day when more people go to church than at any other time — even those who do not usually attend church during the rest of the year. For most people, Easter is a celebration with both sacred and secular traditions, whose origins have often been forgotten. The colored Easter eggs, used not only by Eastern Orthodox groups but almost universally, derive from the fact that the egg was an ancient symbol of life and hence was deemed suitable for celebrating the Resurrection. In many countries, futhermore, eggs were among the foods not permitted during Lent in the days when Lenten fasts were more rigid than now, and thus they were relished on Easter along with many other special foods forbidden during Lent.

If some children grow up with the strange idea of Easter bunnies laying Easter eggs, including both the large chocolate-covered ones and those of jelly-bean size, it is only because the fertility of the rabbit makes that animal a symbol of life also. The new clothes — "Easter finery" — worn on Easter Sunday probably had their origins in the fact that early Christians who were baptized during the Easter Vigil services wore new white robes for the occasion. Throughout the centuries, new Easter attire has been associated with the concept of newness and a fresh beginning.

In the United States, the new clothes became an excuse for the Easter parade which, in New York City at least, is not really a parade in the usual sense but more of a fashion promenade. More than a dozen blocks of fashionable Fifth Avenue are closed to vehicular traffic to allow pedestrians — who frequently exceed 50,000 — to walk in the street. In earlier, less populated times, the well-dressed people coming out of churches on or near Fifth Avenue enjoyed a stroll on a mild Easter Sunday. Friends would greet each other and admire one another's attire. In recent years, people have flocked to New York for the Easter parade from many cities and frequently see other visitors with cameras who, like themselves, are waiting for the "parade" to start. But there are no marching bands, no baton twirlers, no banners held high by organized groups. The onlookers themselves constitute the Easter parade, which is simply made up of the large numbers of people who come to see and be seen.

One of the nation's oldest Easter parades originated in Atlantic City, New Jersey, in 1876. Up to that time, Atlantic City's famous oceanside boardwalk was stored away, protected from the sea and harsh winter weather, from early September to late spring. But in 1876 the city fathers, hoping to attract tourists from Philadelphia's Centennial Exhibition, had the boardwalk brought out earlier than usual and thus began the resort city's traditional Easter parade. In more recent years, prizes have been awarded for attractive or unusual hats worn in the parade, still held on the five-mile-long boardwalk, now open all year. Easter parades are held in other places also, most notably in St. Augustine and Miami in Florida; along Michigan Boulevard in Chicago; and in Asbury Park, New Jersey. Many Easter parades have special features, often springing from tradition or regional flavor. In St. Augustine, the background of the city as the oldest permanent settlement in the United States plays a large part in the celebration of Easter. The Easter parade there — the Parada de los Caballos y Coches — is a colorful afternoon event incorporating antique, horse-drawn Spanish carriages, decorated floats, a color guard, drill teams, beauty queens, men on horseback wearing Spanish armor, women in centuries-old Spanish costumes, the city's "royal family" — descendants of St. Augustine's earliest settlers — and an entourage of about 100 costumed attendants. Perhaps the most famous feature of

St. Augustine's Easter parade is the elaborate headgear worn by the carriage horses — flower-decked, beribboned hats loaned for the occasion by nationally prominent women. St. Augustine's Easter parade is part of the old city's annual Easter Week Festival, begun in 1958.

Most of the Easter parades and other holiday festivities take place after late Sunday morning worship services. Often these are preceded by earlier "sunrise services," which take place at dawn. Most typically, these programs of worship are interdenominational or nonsectarian and set in outdoor locales of particular beauty or significance — on mountaintops, in parks, in cemeteries, at the shores of rivers or oceans, at national monuments, overlooking such natural wonders as Arizona's Grand Canyon — or simply on whatever open land is convenient.

Probably the first Easter sunrise service in the United States was the one held in 1743 by the devout Moravians who had settled in Bethlehem, Pennsylvania. The simple dawn service of praise and prayer continues today, and it begins with the famous Moravian Trombone Choir playing paschal hymns from the steeple of Bethlehem's Central Moravian Church. The pattern of the Moravians' dawn service was set in 1732 in what is now East Germany, when a group of young Moravian men in Herrnhut, Saxony, conceived the idea of going at sunrise to God's Acre, as they called their graveyard, for worship and praise — as the women had gone to the empty tomb of Jesus at dawn on the first Easter Sunday.

A similar service, still maintained, was instituted in 1771 by the Moravians who in 1766 had founded the village of Salem, North Carolina (now restored as Old Salem and part of the city of Winston-Salem). Preparation for this event begins as early as 1:30 A.M., when units of the 500-member Moravian band start roaming the city's streets, playing instrumental chorales to awaken townspeople for the sunrise service. Before dawn, crowds gather on Salem Square in front of Old Salem's Home Moravian Church. The service, in which 12 churches cooperate, begins when the minister steps out of the church, mounts a podium, and gives the traditional salutation, "The Lord is risen" — to which the congregation responds, "The Lord is risen indeed." Joyful hymns are sung until daybreak, when the people quietly walk in long lines to the God's Acre cemetery, where they reaffirm their belief in a resurrected Lord.

Easter sunrise services are often also held in other parts of North Carolina, including Asheville, Bald Mountain, and Boone, and in hundreds of other locations throughout the United States. On a hillside at Holy City, 22 miles northwest of Lawton, Oklahoma, in the Wichita

Mountains Wildlife Refuge, thousands of people begin to assemble several hours before midnight the preceding evening. They are dressed warmly and carry blankets, food, and hot coffee because they are prepared to watch the six-hour Easter pageant, The Oklahoma Oberammergau (based on the German Passion play), which has been presented on a mammoth natural stage annually since 1926. The area is said to bear an extraordinary resemblance to the Holy Land and features full-size reproductions of various biblical landmarks. The pageant begins at midnight, the beginning of Easter day, and is timed so that its stirring climax — the Resurrection scene — occurs at sunrise.

In Colorado, the Garden of the Gods, near Colorado Springs, has been the scenic location for Easter sunrise services annually attended by thousands since 1921. The site, with Pike's Peak as a towering backdrop, evidently was given its name because of its spectacular natural formations of red sandstone in the shapes of pillars and spires. Also renowned is the Easter sunrise service held annually at the dramatic Park of the Red Rocks, southwest of Denver.

Although there is no accurate count, California may have more sunrise services than any other state and perhaps the widest variety of settings, ranging from navy vessels at anchor off San Diego Bay to mountain sites, such as Mount Davidson near San Francisco, or locations such as the Hollywood Bowl, where huge crowds start arriving the previous midnight to attend what has been called "the most elaborate sunrise service of all," inaugurated in 1921.

In Riverside, California, southeast of Los Angeles, as many as 20,000 people make the annual Easter sunrise pilgrimage to Mount Rubidoux Memorial Park on the west edge of the city, where what is said to have been the first nonsectarian sunrise service took place in 1909. The World Peace Tower stands on the side of the mountain — which legend claims was once the site of sun worship — and on the mountain's crest is a cross erected in memory of Father Junípero Serra, the Spanish Franciscan who founded nine of the early California missions. Dawn services are also held at a number of sites in and around San Diego, some of them notably scenic. Among them are the Outdoor Organ Pavilion in the city's famous Balboa Park, the foot of Serra Cross in historic Presidio Park, Cabrillo National Monument at the tip of Point Loma, the summit of cross-topped Mount Helix in suburban La Mesa, and the crest of La Jolla's Mount Soledad with its towering cross and superb view.

Halfway across the continent to the east, the oldest Easter sunrise service in Arkansas is held amid towering pine trees and huge boulders on the summit of Hot Springs Mountain in Hot Springs National Park. The service, instituted in 1935, traditionally begins as the sun comes over nearby Indian Mountain and casts its rays on an enormous cross hewn from native timber.

Other well-known sunrise services are those traditionally held at the National Memorial Cemetery of the Pacific, set in Punchbowl Crater, high above the center of Honolulu, Hawaii; at scenic Natural Bridge and at Arlington National Cemetery and a number of other historic sites in Virginia; in the natural pine grove at Rindge, New Hampshire, which has been dedicated as a war memorial; and in a number of Florida locations. These include the Stephen Foster Memorial overlooking the Suwannee River at White Springs; the Mountain Lake Sanctuary and Bok Singing Tower atop Iron Mountain near Lake Wales; Cypress Gardens' Lake Eloise; and St. Augustine's Castillo de San Marcos, where worshipers gather atop the old fortress's thick walls.

Not all Easter sunrise events are held outdoors. One of the most remarkable has been held in the Memorial Coliseum at Marion, Indiana, since 1937 (with a five-year hiatus during World War II). This is a one-hour-long pageant without dialogue, portraying events in the last week of Jesus' life from Palm Sunday to Easter. The 2,000 costumed actors, both children and adults, are all members of the community, as are the accompanying chorus of more than 500 voices, the 62-piece orchestra, the behind-the-scenes corps of 72 make-up artists, and the costume, prop, and scenery crews. As one resident of Marion put it, "There are no stars, no 'personalities,' and no individual merits glory for the event," which is reverently staged with the support of more than 60 churches and many community organizations.

In and around New York City, sunrise services take place at scores of places — in natural settings such as city parks of all sizes and at Bear Mountain State Park, 45 miles north of the city, and in such indoor settings as Manhattan's Radio City Music Hall. The famous motion picture theater is transformed into a huge worship setting for the dawn service sponsored by the Protestant Council of the City of New York.

In Native American villages of the American Southwest, the observance of Easter is likely to have a dual nature. In most of New Mexico's pueblos, for example, Easter is marked in a Christian way by masses in the pueblos' generally Roman Catholic churches. It is also marked in a traditionally Indian way with green corn dances and ceremonial foot races. Customarily, Easter Day is also the time for the opening of the irrigation ditches in most pueblos — a different kind of new beginning.

In their village just north of Tucson, Arizona, Yaquis observe the days of Holy Week with their own dances and pageantry. While these performances have much to do with Jesus (and portray other biblical figures, such as the Virgin Mary, Judas, and Pilate), they also contain much that is of specifically Yaqui heritage, sometimes overlaid with a Spanish flavor brought from their original home in Mexico. The Yaquis' acted-out version of the events of Holy Thursday, Good Friday, Holy Saturday, and Easter is quite unlike anything found elsewhere; indeed, the events portrayed may not be entirely recognizable to the non-Indian Christian who is untutored in the complicated symbolism involved and unfamiliar with the significance of the spectacular masks and costumes. Recognizable to all, however, are the white cross and the representations of Mary and Christ. In the most significant symbolism of the week-long pageantry, Jesus, whom the Yaquis have earlier portrayed as an old man, is represented as a newborn baby after the Resurrection.

For Christians the message is the same at all sunrise services: Easter, the celebration of the Resurrection, means for them a new dawn, a new beginning, a new era.

Delaware Swedish Colonial Day

On March 29, 1638, Swedish settlers under the command of a Dutchman, Peter Minuit, sailed up the Delaware River and founded the colony of New Sweden, erecting Fort Christina where Wilmington now stands. Fort Christina Monument, at the foot of East 7th Street, in the little Fort Christina State Park, now marks the actual landing place at a point called The Rocks. The landing marked the start of the first permanent settlement in what was later to become the state of Delaware. In commemoration of the event, the governor of Delaware annually proclaims March 29 as Delaware Swedish Colonial Day.

Thus, in 1965 Governor Charles L. Terry Jr. issued a document reminding citizens of the historic significance of the anniversary and requesting "that on this day, and in the days following . . . schools, churches, patriotic and historical societies, and other institutions and organizations commemorate this historic occasion with appropriate ceremonies." He also asked that the federal and state flags be displayed on such occasions by state, county, city, and town governments and called for the flags of the United States and Sweden to be flown at Fort Christina Monument.

The first real observance of Delaware Swedish Colonial Day took place in 1938, the 300th anniversary of the Swedes' historic landing. The Delaware Swedish Colonial Society was founded as plans for the tercentenary began, with the purpose of commemorating the landing annually and preserving materials related to Swedish settlements in America. It was during the 1938 observance that Fort Christina Monument, by the Swedish sculptor Carl Milles, was presented as a gift from the schoolchildren of Sweden. President Franklin D. Roosevelt and Prince Bertil of Sweden both took part in the dedication ceremonies.

During another big commemorative year — 1963, when the 325th anniversary took place — a plaque was unveiled identifying Fort Christina Park and nearby Old Swedes Church as national historic landmarks. Also on view in the park is a log house, reminding visitors that log houses, which dotted the early American landscape, were a form of dwelling contributed to the new frontier by Swedish settlers.

Apart from the exercises, which are held irregularly by individual schools, churches, and organizations, the principal annual observance of Delaware Swedish Colonial Day is conducted under the auspices of the Delaware Swedish Colonial Society. There are ceremonies each year at The Rocks and (on the Saturday nearest March 29) at Old Swedes' Church, which was built in 1698 and now is known officially as Holy Trinity [Episcopal] Church. Other ceremonies take place at society headquarters in the venerable Hendrickson House, a Swedish colonial farmhouse erected in 1690 and later moved to its present location at 606 Church Street, on the church grounds. It now serves as a museum and library of the Swedish colonial period. Commemorative events include a wreath-laying ceremony at the Milles monument and an annual dinner attended by local dignitaries and guests from Washington, D.C., and from Sweden. A representative from the Swedish embassy generally attends, and members of the Swedish royal family have also frequently been guests.

The history of the original Swedish colony, which spread through the Delaware Valley, including what is now Philadelphia, is short but colorful. Although its population never exceeded 300 or 400 people, they and their ancestors bequeathed a considerable Swedish heritage to the region. Reminders of that heritage can be seen today in various parts of Delaware, at the American-Swedish Historical Foundation and Museum in South Philadelphia, and in several of Philadelphia's early Swedish churches — most notably the Gloria Dei (Old Swedes') Church at Delaware Avenue near Christian Street.

Minuit was succeeded as governor of New Sweden by others, the most important of whom was a severe but well-qualified man of profane tongue and mammoth proportions, the 400-pound Johan Björnsson Printz. He governed the colony from 1643 to 1653, making Tinicum "Island," at what is now Essington, just southwest of Philadelphia, the capital of New Sweden. Although only the foundation of his residence, the Printzhof, remains, visitors to Essington's Governor Printz Park can still see several Swedish log houses nearby. The most noteworthy — perhaps the oldest building of its kind in the country — is the John Morton House, about a mile away on Route 420 at Darby Creek. The oldest part of the house was built in 1654.

Governor Printz was succeeded by another Swede, Johan Rising, who arrived in 1654 and immediately seized Fort Casimir, which the Dutch — who all along had regarded the Swedish settlements as encroachments — had built between Fort Christina and the sea (where New Castle now stands). The Swedish triumph over the Dutch was short-lived, however, for in 1655 the entire colony of New Sweden was taken over by the Dutch under the autocratic Peter Stuyvesant, the governor of New Netherland, to the north (which had as its principal settlement New Amsterdam — later New York City).

But the tenure of the Dutch was also short. In 1664 the entire Delaware country, along with New Netherland, was seized by the English (who were at war with the Dutch in Europe) and came under the sway of the duke of York, later James II.

Even though his own title to the Delaware region did not actually become legal until later, the duke of York, on August 24, 1682, transferred the area to William Penn, the Quaker colonist, who sought unimpeded water access for his new colony of Pennsylvania. What would later be Delaware thus became the Three Lower Counties of Pennsylvania.

It remained so until 1776, when Delaware became a separate state with the adoption of a state constitution on September 21 — after struggling for separate political power during most of its 94 years as part of Pennsylvania. The same year, Delaware joined other colonies in signing the Declaration of Independence. Later, on December 7, 1787, it became the first state to adopt the Constitution of the United States.

Twenty-third Amendment Ratified

With the ratification on March 29, 1961, of the 23rd Amendment to the Constitution, the theretofore disfranchised residents of the District of Columbia — the seat of national government whose boundaries are coterminous with the city of Washington — were empowered for the first time to have a voice in the selection of the President and Vice President of the United States. (Though the amendment enabled Washingtonians to vote in presidential elections, they still had no representation in Congress and no role in selecting their own municipal government. The District was still governed by Congress through three commissioners appointed by the President with Senate approval; and the commissioners remained subordinate to House and Senate District committees.)

In accordance with the provisions of the 23rd Amendment, the District of Columbia was accorded three electoral votes, the minimum number. In its essential portions, the amendment read as follows:

SECTION 1. The District constituting the seat of Government of the United States shall appoint . . . a number of electors of President and Vice President equal to the . . . number of Senators and Representatives in Congress to which the District would be entitled if it were a State . . . ; they shall be . . . considered, for the purposes of the election of President and Vice President, to be electors appointed by a State. . . .

SECTION 2. The Congress shall have power to enforce this article by appropriate legislation.

Ratification of the 23rd Amendment was completed on March 29, 1961, when Kansas became the 38th state to ratify the measure — making up the necessary three-fourths of the states. Approval by the Ohio legislature followed 42 minutes after that of Kansas. In the final count, Arkansas was the only state to refuse its approval. The amendment was formally declared a part of the Constitution on April 3, 1961.

John Tyler's Birthday

John Tyler, the 10th President of the United States, is often skimmed over quickly by historians, yet he achieved a number of firsts. He was the first Vice President to succeed to the nation's highest office through the death of an elected President. He was the first President married in the White House. And he was the first President against whom an impeachment resolution was introduced in the House of Representatives. (It failed.)

Tyler was born March 29, 1790, at Greenway, his family's home, near Williamsburg in Charles City County, Virginia. His father, the Honorable John Tyler, had an illustrious career of public service — as governor of Virginia, Speaker of the Virginia House of Delegates and as a US district judge.

Young John Tyler was graduated from William and Mary College in Williamsburg in 1807 and was admitted to the Virginia bar in 1809. At the age of 21 he was elected to the Virginia legislature (the House of Delegates) as a member of

the Jeffersonian Republicans, forerunners of the Democratic-Republicans and the present Democratic party. He served five consecutive terms in the state legislature before being elected in 1816 to the national House of Representatives, consistently acting with the states' rights wing of his party.

Prompted by ill health and business considerations, Tyler resigned from Congress in 1821. He returned home, bought Greenway (which had gone to his older brother on their father's death) and lived there quietly as a private citizen until 1823, when he was again elected to the state legislature.

In 1825 Tyler was elected governor of Virginia. During his two years in that post, he gave priority to the development of roads and schools, as his father had done before him.

Tyler resigned from the governorship on his election to the US Senate in 1827, taking his Senate seat on March 4 of that year. Elected for a second Senate term, Tyler continued to alienate his fellow Democratic-Republicans by his opposition to President Andrew Jackson — an opposition that was sharpened by the President's refusal in 1833 to continue the deposit of federal funds in the Bank of the United States. When Henry Clay introduced a resolution to censure the President for this action, Tyler voted for it.

A man of great integrity, Tyler resigned his Senate seat in February 1836 when the Virginia legislature adopted a resolution requiring the two Virginia senators to vote to expunge the resolution of censure from the record. Rather than vote as instructed and go against his conscience in the matter, Tyler left the Senate and the Democratic party. Later in 1836 Tyler — now a member of the Whig party, which had been formed by Andrew Jackson's adversaries — was defeated for Vice President on a states' rights Whig ticket. He subsequently returned, once again, to the Virginia legislature in 1838.

In 1840 General William Henry Harrison, who had been lauded as the hero of the battle of Tippecanoe, was elected President and Tyler Vice President on the Whig ticket. Their campaign slogan, Tippecanoe and Tyler Too, is one of the most famous in American electoral history.

One month after his inauguration, Harrison became the first American President to die in office. With no precedent for guidance, there was much discussion about whether the Vice President should succeed as President or should simply serve as Acting President until new elections could be held. Tyler, however, was successful in maintaining his claim to both the title and the undiminished powers of the presidency.

Almost immediately, though, his independent stands alienated the Whigs as thoroughly as they had earlier alienated the Democrats; for most of his three years and 11 months in office he was, as he has been called by historians, a "President without a party."

Notwithstanding his lack of party support, Tyler made an outstanding record as an efficient, economical administrator and as a foresighted negotiator in both domestic and foreign relations. During his administration a treaty was negotiated with China, permitting increased American trade with that country; the Seminole War was terminated; Dorr's Rebellion in Rhode Island was quelled without the introduction of federal troops; the Monroe Doctrine was enforced and strengthened; and the Webster-Ashburton treaty with Great Britain negotiated the northeastern boundaries of the United States — long a source of discord beween Canada and the US.

Perhaps Tyler's most notable achievement was the annexation of Texas after many frustrations. It was just two days before the end of his presidency that he signed the joint congressional resolution for the annexation of the Lone Star State, on March 1, 1845 — marking the first time that a joint resolution was employed in foreign relations instead of a treaty.

Also to Tyler's credit was the reform and reorganization of the navy and the encouragement of its scientific work. For example, he called for the establishment of a depot for nautical charts and instruments, which developed into the US Naval Observatory. He also signed an act testing the feasibility of setting up a national system of magnetic telegraphs, which has had wide-ranging effects, especially in the US Weather Bureau.

The Whigs, who had made Tyler Vice President, found it hard to support him as President. Controlling both houses of Congress, they sought the rechartering of the Bank of the United States, an action to which Tyler was as much opposed as Andrew Jackson had been. Twice the Whigs passed a bill to recharter the Bank, and twice President Tyler vetoed it. His cabinet members — all appointed by Harrison — responded by resigning en masse, with the single exception of Secretary of State Daniel Webster, who stayed only long enough to complete negotiation of the Canadian border treaty.

In 1844 the Whigs selected Henry Clay as their presidential candidate. Tyler, who returned to the Democratic party that year, threw his support to James K. Polk, the Democratic candidate, who was inaugurated as President on March 4, 1845.

After the rigors of political office, Tyler retired to Sherwood Forest, a 1,200-acre plantation a few miles from his Greenway birthplace, and lived the life of a Virginia gentleman. With him

was his second wife, Julia Gardiner Tyler of Gardiner's Island, New York, whom he had married on June 26, 1844. (His first wife, Letitia Christian, an invalid when the Tylers moved into the White House, had died in 1842.)

Though he consistently supported Southern positions during the years of his retirement (even while hoping the institution of slavery would die a natural death), Tyler initially stood firmly against secession. Shortly before the outbreak of the Civil War, he suggested that the border states meet to discuss compromises that might save the Union. The resulting convention was called by the Virginia Assembly and met in Washington in February 1861 with Tyler acting as chairman. It was only after the peace effort had proved futile that he voted for secession in the Virginia secession convention and served in the Provisional Confederate Congress. Later elected to the Confederate House of Representatives, he died on January 18, 1862, in Richmond, before he could take his seat.

Descendants of President Tyler still live at the Sherwood Forest plantation, which he bought in 1842. After his purchase, Tyler kept adding to the original house, built in 1780, until its dimensions must have broken a record of some sort — being 300 feet long and a single room deep. The privately owned house, which is open to the public, has been designated as a national historic landmark. It displays some original furniture, unusual woodwork, Italian marble mantels, and 18th century outbuildings. It is on state Route 5, a few miles east of Charles City, Virginia. A monument erected to Tyler by Congress in 1915 can be seen at the site of his burial in Richmond's Hollywood Cemetery.

MARCH 30

Easter Monday

This is a movable event. See note on page xxvi.

The day after Easter Sunday is called Easter Monday, or Pasch Monday, a word derived through the Greek, Latin, and Old French from the Hebrew word for Passover: *Pesah* or *Pesach*. In any language, it is an occasion for joy and sometimes merrymaking.

Easter Sunday, in addition to being the greatest of Christian religious observances, also marks the end of Lent. In years past, Lent was truly "the penitential season," and devout Christians practiced great austerities, fasting, abstaining entirely from certain types of food (including eggs in some instances) and avoiding most forms of public entertainment for the six weeks preceding Easter. Therefore, when the great day finally dawned, people celebrated. It was the time for feasting, games, and fun, as well as joyous worship.

Folk customs vary somewhat from country to country, but in most European countries the celebrations extended beyond Easter Sunday and continued into, or throughout, the following Easter Week. Even today, some European countries observe either Easter Monday or Easter Tuesday, or both, as national holidays.

Before Christianity, people of ancient cultures held spring celebrations following the limitations and restrictions of winter. Since the egg has traditionally symbolized life, it often figured prominently in the celebrations of spring. Near and Far Eastern mythologies abound with stories centering on eggs and their symbolism. The various Easter Week games and contests using eggs, still common in many countries, probably had their inception in Egypt and other parts of the ancient world.

Fittingly, it was through a young White House resident that the ancient customs reached the United States to provide a now long-cherished American custom, the Easter Egg Roll on the White House lawn on Easter Monday.

The custom originated during the administration of President James Madison (1809–1817). Madison had married the widowed Dorothea (Dolley) Payne Todd, who had a son, John Payne Todd. One day the boy told his mother of a game that children had played in ancient Egypt. The game consisted of rolling hard-boiled eggs, with shells specially decorated for the occasion, against the bases of the pyramids. This account evidently appealed to the fun-loving Dolley Madison, who believed that American children would also enjoy the game, and that the hilly sweep of the Capitol grounds would be a fine locale for egg rolling. Actually, egg-rolling contests had been a custom in England and other European countries for centuries. In these contests, children would roll hard-boiled eggs down a hill, and the child who rolled the greatest number of eggs without cracking the shells was the winner. This was to be the game rule for Dolley Madison's egg rolling too. A contemporary description of the children gathered on the Capitol's terraced grounds on the occasion of Washington's first Easter Monday egg-rolling contest indicates that the event was a success:

At first the children sit sedately in long rows; each has brought a basket of gay-colored hard-boiled eggs, and those on the upper terrace send them rolling to the line next below, and those pass on the

ribbon-like streams to other hundreds at the foot, who scramble for the hopping eggs and hurry panting to the top to start them down again. And as the sport warms, those on top who have rolled all the eggs they brought finally roll themselves, shrieking with laughter. Now comes a swirl of curls, ribbons and furbelows, somebody's dainty maid indifferent to bumps and grass stains. A set of boys who started in a line of six with joined hands are trying to come down in somersaults without breaking the chain. On all sides the older folks stand by to watch the games of this infant carnival.

From the beginning, adults were not admitted unless accompanied by a child, a stipulation put to profitable use by enterprising young Americans who, for a fee, would escort adults past the gates and then return for others who wished to get a closer look at the chaotic proceedings.

Except for an interruption during the Civil War, the Easter Monday Egg Roll took place on the Capitol grounds from its inauguration by Dolley Madison until 1877, when the locale was changed during the administration of President Rutherford B. Hayes. After Capitol officials complained that the grass was being ruined by the thousands of pairs of small feet, the tradition of the Easter Monday Egg Roll was saved by the President's wife, Lucy Webb Hayes, who invited the children to use the White House lawn. At the time, the First Family numbered five children among its members, two of whom — Fanny, 9, and Scott, 6 — were young enough to enjoy the event themselves. From that time, April 2, 1877, to the present, the Easter Monday Egg Roll has been held on the most famous lawn in the land, and it is customary for a member of the First Family to make an appearance for the occasion.

After the egg-rolling fun, the gates to the White House lawn are open to the adults for a concert by the US Marine Band, a tradition begun by Benjamin Harrison during his presidential administration (1889–1893). Members of the First Family often add their own touches to the celebration.

The White House Egg Roll, suspended during World War I, was revived in 1921 by President Warren G. Harding. Discontinued again during World War II, and for some time thereafter because worldwide food shortages made it inappropriate, the custom was again revived on April 6, 1953, by President Dwight D. Eisenhower and Mamie Eisenhower.

Egg-rolling events are also held in other towns and cities, sometimes on the grounds of a public building or a mansion, sometimes in a churchyard. These festivities may be sponsored by the municipality or by specific groups within a community, such as members of a church. In New York City, the municipal parks department sponsors an Easter Egg Roll on the Great Lawn in Central Park — sometimes on the day before Easter rather than on Easter Monday.

While rolling colored eggs on Easter Monday is still a lively event in parts of England, many European countries have other egg games or contests on Easter Monday and Tuesday. In parts of France, Switzerland, and Luxembourg, for example, there are races in which each contestant must balance an egg on a spoon or carry large numbers of eggs while carefully running — sometimes as far as a neighboring village. Egg "duels," in which two participants try to crack each other's eggs, are popular in a number of countries.

In northern England, a once-favorite game for Easter Monday and Easter Tuesday was called "heaving" or "lifting." On Easter Monday, groups of women would surround any man they met in the street and "heave" him over their heads three times (or lift him as he sat on a seat made by two women grasping each other's wrists). After this they would sprinkle him with water and each give him a kiss. In turn, the man would make an offering of money, which would help fund the festivities. The next day it was the men's turn to "heave" the women they met on the street in the same fashion. Some forms of this game are still played today. On Easter Monday in some places, friends who meet switch each other playfully or lightly tap each other. A Polish version of this jollity, called the *dyngus*, is still observed by some residents of South Bend, Indiana, with the men "switching" the women on Easter Monday.

In once-Dutch New York City, the St. Nicholas Society — founded by Washington Irving to preserve the early history of New York — has retained the tradition of the Paas Festival, which members have celebrated for more than 125 years. In one year, for example, the Paas Festival was an integral part of the society's annual ball, held at the Waldorf-Astoria Hotel, where members gathered and, among other forms of entertainment, cracked hard-boiled eggs.

Fifteenth Amendment Proclaimed Ratified

The 15th Amendment to the Constitution — one of three early post–Civil War amendments intended to secure the rights of blacks as persons and as citizens — was proclaimed ratified on March 30, 1870, thirteen months after it had been proposed in Congress. As ratified by the states, the amendment read as follows:

SECTION 1. The right of citizens of the United States to vote shall not be denied or abridged by the United States or by any State on account of race, color, or previous condition of servitude.
SECTION 2. The Congress shall have power to enforce this article by appropriate legislation.

However plain the amendment's language, the struggle to secure full implementation of its provisions and those of the 13th and 14th amendments (see December 18; July 28) had not ended a century later (see Civil Rights acts, April 11, May 6, July 2, September 9).

Seward's Day in Alaska

This is a movable event. See note on page xxvi.

Seward's Day celebrates the signing, on March 30, 1867, of the treaty purchasing Alaska from Czarist Russia for $7 million. It is a legal holiday in Alaska, and since 1971 it has been observed on the last Monday in March. The treaty negotiated by William Henry Seward, then secretary of state under President Andrew Johnson, was not highly regarded in his time, however. Alaska was called "Seward's folly," "Seward's icebox," and "Johnson's polar bear garden" until the discovery of gold in the region changed public opinion.

Seward, an expansionist, had acted quickly and quietly. With the Russian minister Baron Edoard de Stoeckl, he worked out details in an all-night meeting. The treaty was signed by the two men at 4:00 A.M. on March 30 and on the same day was presented to the US Senate for ratification. The senators, annoyed with the speed and secrecy of Seward's actions, debated for a week and finally ratified the treaty by a one-vote margin on April 9, 1867.

The Russian flag had flown in Alaska since the middle of the 18th century. Czar Peter the Great had in 1725 commissioned the Danish navigator Vitus Jonassen Bering to determine whether Asia was separated from America or whether it was one continuous land mass. Preparations were necessarily lengthy, and Bering finally sailed in 1728. On that first voyage, he discovered that the two continents were indeed divided by what is now called the Bering Strait. Actually, at one point only about 50 miles of water separate the two continents.

Bering found some islands but, perhaps because of fog, did not see the Alaskan mainland until 1741, during his second voyage. Returning home, he was shipwrecked and died on what is now called Bering Island in the Bering Sea. His men, however, built a new ship out of the wreckage of the old one and finally reached Russian soil with tales of a wealth of furs to be had from the herds of seals they had seen.

For several decades thereafter, Russian adventurers and seal hunters from other nations plundered the seas and shores of Alaska. During these decades, Russians set up trading posts and settlements scattered along Alaska's coast.

By the mid-1800s, with the seal herds decimated by wanton slaughter, Russia viewed Alaska as an economic and political liability and therefore considered selling its North American colony. Arrangements to sell it for $5 million began with President James Buchanan but proceeded slowly. The negotiations, interrupted by the American Civil War, were resumed with Seward, who had been secretary of state in Lincoln's cabinet and continued in that post when Andrew Johnson assumed the presidency after Lincoln's assassination.

Seward had expected to pay $5 million for Alaska, and Russia apparently would have been glad to sell at that price. But Baron de Stoeckl, acting for Czar Alexander II, had been told to use his own judgment. Through clever strategy, he got Seward to offer $7 million and to add $200,000 for the costs of the exchange.

More than a year later, Baron de Stoeckl showed how wily he was when he smoothly got an appropriations bill through a balking, stalling Congress by employing skillful lobbyists and also by allegedly paying substantial sums to at least two influential and supposedly incorruptible members of congress. Although the formal transfer ceremonies had taken place in Sitka on October 18, 1867 (see October 18, Alaska Day), Congress did not actually pass the appropriations bill to pay Russia for Alaska until July 14, 1868.

Seward's price for Alaska no longer seems high. Each year Alaska's natural resources return many times the original investment — even though only a small fraction of the state's land mass has been adequately surveyed for minerals. Natural gas, coal, oil — much of it offshore — have proved far more valuable than Alaska's widely heralded gold resources, as have its seafood and lumber. Its minerals, at least 20 in number, include silver, copper, lead, platinum, uranium, tungsten, and molybdenum.

The town of Seward (founded in 1903), with its gulf port and railroad and airport facilities, was a major port of entry for US troops during World War II. A peninsula on the western coast is also named for Seward. Today the purchase of Alaska is regarded as the crowning international achievement in the careers of both William Seward and President Andrew Johnson.

Seward was 71 when he died on October 10, 1872, in Auburn, New York. During the 1967 centennial observance of Alaska's purchase, a likeness of Seward appeared on the antique bronze Alaska Purchase Centennial medal designed by Robert D. Vodica. The Centennial Exposition in Fairbanks also honored Seward by naming for him one of the major exhibit buildings on its 40-acre grounds.

MARCH 31

Virgin Islands Transfer Day

March 31 is a legal holiday of great significance in the US Virgin Islands. It marks the date on which the formal transfer ceremonies from Danish to US control took place in 1917.

The Virgin Islands — now divided politically into the Virgin Islands of the United States and the British Virgin Islands — are a group of about 100 small islands, islets, and cays in the West Indies. Covering a total area of about 200 square miles, they are located about 34 miles east of Puerto Rico and extend for approximately 60 miles. They dominate the Anegada passage between the Atlantic Ocean and the Caribbean Sea. St. Croix, St. Thomas, St. John, and Tortola are among the nine major islands in the group.

Christopher Columbus discovered the Virgin Islands on his second voyage to the New World in 1493. He named them Las Virgines in honor of St. Ursula and her companions. The islands had previously been called Ay Ay by their inhabitants, the Caribs and Arawaks. Since King Ferdinand and Queen Isabella of Spain were given in 1494 a papal grant to all lands west of the 46th meridian of longitude — the famous line of demarcation — the Virgin Islands became Spanish territory. Their subsequent history was that of colonial expansion and exploitation by European powers: in the 16th century by Spain and during the 17th century by the English, Dutch, French, and Danes, who contested Spain's supremacy. In the 1650s the French gained possession of St. Croix. In 1666 the British occupied Tortola, which had been controlled by the Dutch since 1648. The Danish West Indian Company settled St. Thomas in the early 1670s, giving the name Taphus to the first community — which later became known as Charlotte Amalie. The company claimed St. John a decade later, and purchased St. Croix from France in 1733. The Danish West Indian Company's control lasted until the Danish ruler King Frederick V purchased the islands in 1754.

They remained a royal colony, known as the Danish West Indies, until 1917. Only twice during this long period did a foreign power, Great Britain, occupy the islands — once in 1801 and again from 1807 to 1815.

The Danes introduced slave labor to work the profitable sugar plantations. Even after the bottom had dropped out of the sugar market, the Danish West Indies continued throughout the 19th century to enjoy a commercial boom as a free port and as a coaling station in the days of sailing vessels and paddle steamers. But longhaul steamships and the opening of the Panama Canal (see August 15) robbed the islands, especially St. Thomas with its fine harbor of Charlotte Amalie, of much of their economic value.

After the sugar boom ended, Denmark expressed interest in selling the colony. As early as 1865, the United States reacted favorably, but the US Senate opposed the negotiations. Rising support for the Panama Canal project resulted in renewed American interest in the Virgin Islands in 1902, but this time the Danish legislature rejected the treaty of transfer. In the early stages of World War I, when Denmark expected a German invasion at any moment, the US government grew increasingly apprehensive that the Germans would seize the strategic Danish colony, which lay so close to one of the approaches to the Panama Canal. American officials assailed the Danes with a combination of pleas and soft threats — voiced in diplomatic language and implying that "certain circumstances" involving "another European power" could result in US occupation of the Danish West Indies. Moreover, the argument went, the sale of the islands would remove one of the chief incentives for a German invasion of Denmark. As part of the agreement, the United States would recognize Danish rule over Greenland.

Denmark finally agreed to sell its possessions in the Virgin Islands — the three large islands of St. Thomas, St. Croix, and St. John, together with about 50 small islets and cays with a total area of 132 square miles — provided that the United States submit terms that would "not lead to haggling" and that the islands would retain their free-port status forever. In 1917 the US government offered $25 million ($295 per acre), then regarded as an exorbitant sum for land that amounted to hardly more than a tenth the size of Rhode Island, the smallest state. (By the end of the 1960s sellers were receiving as much as $30,000 an acre for land in desirable residential areas on St. Thomas and St. Croix.)

Once the terms were mutually acceptable, the formal transfer ceremony took place, on March 31, 1917. In Washington, D.C., the Danish minister, Constantine Brun, accepted payment. The news was immediately telegraphed to New York, then cabled to San Juan, Puerto Rico, flashed by wireless to the cruiser *Hancock* in the harbor at Charlotte Amalie, and carried ashore to St. Thomas via rowboat. There, both Danish and American honor guards in white uniforms stood in formation on opposite sides of the parade ground before red-walled Fort Christian. Once the message had been delivered, at 4:48 P.M., the Danish honor guard presented arms; the Danish national anthem was played; and a cannon boomed 21 times as the red and white Danish flag was slowly lowered for the final time after 251 years of Danish rule. At 4:53 P.M. the American honor guard presented arms; a band played the "Star-Spangled Banner"; and, to the roar of the cannon, the Stars and Stripes was raised. As a last gesture, the Danish representative, Admiral Henri Konow, and Admiral Edwin T. Pollock of the US Navy drew their ceremonial swords.

After 1918, when the German threat subsided with the defeat of Germany in World War I, the Virgin Islands dropped into obscurity. Aside from the fact that the American flag flew over government buildings, the transfer of sovereignty resulted in little change. The islands retained their Danish flavor — Danish architectural features, street names, and businesses — and even the currency remained Danish until 1934. Originally under the supervision of the US Department of the Navy, the Virgin Islands were transferred to the Department of the Interior in 1931.

The United States had purchased the islands primarily for their strategic importance, and, together with Culebra Island and Vieques (or Crab) Island, administered by Puerto Rico, they are still considered one of the most vital keys to defense of the Panama Canal Zone and the Caribbean. A more unexpected result, however, was the transformation of this poverty-stricken territory into a vacationers' paradise. Although Prohibition and the declining sugar trade had left the islands so destitute that Congress had had to appropriate over $400,000 in 1930 for relief work, 30 years later the Virgin Islands had become a major tourist center of the Western Hemisphere. Post–World War II economic prosperity in the United States, expanding airline networks, the islands' free-port status as well as their scenic and climatic assets, combined to spur tourism. The number of visitors increased from under 50,000 per year in the early 1950s to more than 1 million in the mid-1970s. Resort developers, real estate agents, and home-site buyers rushed to snatch up once "worthless" land.

The US Virgin Islands, with a 1970 population of 63,200, have the status of an organized but unincorporated territory, still under the administration of the US Department of the Interior. The territory's government, divided into three branches — executive, legislative, and judicial — is organized under the Revised Organic Act of the Virgin Islands, enacted by the US Congress in 1954. Previously, the islands' governor was appointed by the American President, with the advice and consent of the US Senate. On August 23, 1968, however, President Lyndon B. Johnson approved a bill granting the islanders the right to elect their own governor; in 1970 Melvin E. Evans was popularly elected governor for a four-year term. The islands' legislature is a unicameral house of 15 senators, popularly elected for two-year terms. Judicial power is vested in a court of record, designated the District Court of the Virgin Islands, together with two lower courts serving the two main legislative districts. The judge of the District Court is appointed for an eight-year term by the President of the United States, with the consent of the Senate. The US Constitution is the basic law of the land, and all local legislative acts must conform to it.

Native Virgin Islanders, about 80 percent of whom are blacks, received US citizenship in 1927, and in 1936 universal suffrage was granted to all eligible persons who could read and write English. Citizens of the United States who have lived one year in the Virgin Islands and are 21 or over have the right to vote in local elections. They have no vote in presidential elections, nor are they represented in Congress. The first legislative representative from the Virgin Islands to Washington, however, was elected in November 1968.

Transfer Day, normally observed with a parade and other gaiety, was the occasion for a major celebration in 1967, when the governor of the Virgin Islands proclaimed Semi-Centennial Year in honor of the 50th anniversary of the islands' transfer to US control. Washington commemorated the event by issuing an airmail postcard. The series of festivities officially started on March 31, the traditional holiday, which this time was extended through April 2.

Concurrent with the three-day Semi-Centennial Celebration was American-Danish Festival Week from March 29 through April 4, with a number of pre-festival events also scheduled, especially at Christiansted on St. Croix, the former seat of the islands' government under the Danes. Stressing Danish-American friendship, the week featured not only speeches and exhibits, but also a visit by the full-rigged, three-masted training ship *Danmark*, crewed by young officers and 80 Danes from 15 to 20 years of age. On March 27 Torben Ronne, the Danish ambassador to the United States, and Frederick Harhoff, the consul general in New York City, placed wreaths in the old Lutheran cemetery on St. Croix and presented a gift of furniture to Government House, the former capitol — which is now part of the Christiansted National Historic Site, administered by the National Park Service. On March 28, following the display of the cornerstone for the privately financed St. Croix Cultural Center, the Danish ambassador gave a luncheon for officials of the US Department of the Interior and the Friends of Denmark Society. That afternoon two exhibits, "Denmark Today" and "The Danish West Indies through 250 Years," were unveiled on St. Croix and St. Thomas respectively.

The 50th anniversary of Transfer Day, on March 31, was also a gala occasion in the capital of Charlotte Amalie on St. Thomas, as the main thoroughfare, Dronnigens Gade — the scene of a colorful parade — resounded with the music of steel and brass bands. The formal transfer ceremony of 1917 was reenacted that day on St. Thomas, on St. Croix on April 1, and on St. John on April 2. Danish-American Week closed with a luncheon given on St. Thomas by Ambassador Ronne for US and Virgin Island notables, followed by afternoon tours of the library, museum, and Danish shop displays.

The climax of the yearlong Semi-Centennial Celebration came in October, when the governors of all 50 states, Guam, Samoa, and Puerto Rico, having boarded the American liner *Independence* in New York City, landed in the Virgin Islands for the 59th National Governors' Conference.

April

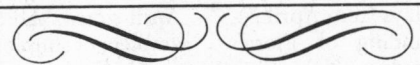

April is the fourth month of the Gregorian calendar and has 30 days. It was formerly the second month in the ancient Roman year, when March began the calendar. The origin of its name has been lost. The most commonly accepted theory is that *Aprilis*, the Roman name for the month, is derived from the Latin verb *aperire*, meaning "to open," in allusion to the opening, or blossoming, of buds of trees and flowers in this season. On the other hand, the Romans sometimes named months for divinities. April was sacred to Venus, the Roman goddess of love, and her festival was held on the first day of the month. Some scholars have therefore conjectured that the month *Aprilis* had originally been called *Aphrilis*, a Latin name derived from Aphrodite, the Greek goddess of love, whom the Romans equated with Venus.

A number of important Roman festivals took place in April. On April 4, the *Megalesia*, or *Megalensia*, honored Cybele (the Magna Mater or Great Mother), a goddess whose cult was native to Phrygia in Asia Minor (now central Turkey). The cult had been established at Rome on April 4, 204 B.C., in the Temple of Victory on Palatine Hill. In 191 B.C. a special temple was erected in her honor on the hill. The festival of Cybele was marked by a procession and banquet, as well as by combined games and scenic performances known as the *ludi megalenses*.

April 15 was the *Fordicidia*, the Feast of the Cows, when ancient rites were conducted to ensure the prosperity of the crops. A cow in calf (*forda*) was sacrificed, and attendants of the vestal virgins then took the calf from its mother to burn it. Its ashes, gathered up by the vestals, were used a few days later at the *Parilia*.

This was the annual Roman festival of flocks and herds, staged on April 21 in honor of Pales, the pastoral deity (god or goddess) and special protector of cattle. The lustral rite, which was celebrated in early spring to purify the animals, stalls, and herdsmen, consisted of several stages. After the sheep and shepherds had been sprinkled with water, the cattle stalls were cleansed with laurel-twig brooms and decorated with leaves and wreaths. Sulphur, laurel, and rosemary, together with olive wood, were then burned, their smoke wafting through the barns to purify the flocks and herds. Gifts of milk, meat, cakes, and millet were offered to Pales. The senior vestal virgin handed the celebrants the ashes of the calf that had been slain on April 15 at the *Fordicidia*. By then, the ashes had been mixed with the blood of the horse that had been sacrificed to Mars, the god of war, the previous October. Finally — in a procedure that anticipates the customs and superstitions still associated with Midsummer's Eve bonfires — the sheep and cattle were forced to leap across bonfires of hay and straw; the herdsmen imitated them, as, facing east, they jumped three times over the flames to conclude the lustration and guarantee prosperity and propagation.

The *Parilia*, a basically pastoral rite reflecting a rural environment, undoubtedly originated long before the founding of the city of Rome, which, according to one tradition, occurred in 753 B.C. It is said that Romulus, the founder of Rome, had himself played a significant role in conducting the cleansing and renewal rituals of the *Parilia*. The rite was therefore accorded a conspicuously important place in the Roman state calendar: April 21 was set aside to commemorate not only Pales, but also the founding of Rome. A public holiday known as the *Natalis urbis Romae* (birthday of the city of Rome), the day was marked by music, street dancing, and general revelry.

On April 25, the *Robigalia*, special ceremonies honored Robigus, the spirit of mildew, who was invoked to ward off any threat of red mildew from the wheat and corn crops. The ceremonies were performed in a sacred grove north of Rome.

Starting on April 28 the Romans celebrated the boisterous *Floralia*, the festival honoring Flora, the goddess of flowers. Instituted in 238 B.C., the *Floralia* was originally a movable feast whose dates were determined by the progress of crops and plants. In 173 B.C.., after violent storms had severely harmed the corn crop and vineyards, the Roman senate decreed it an annual festival extending six days from April 28, the anniversary of the founding of Flora's temple, through May 3. The riotous celebrations included licentious dramatic productions and games and were usually accompanied by excessive drinking.

April was called *Ostermonath* or *Eosturmonath* by the Anglo-Saxons after Ostra or Eostre or Eastre, the goddess of spring, from whom the Christian festival of Easter may also derive its name.

APRIL 1

April Fools' Day

April Fools' Day, or All Fools' Day, takes its name from a centuries-old tradition among the English, Scots, and French of playing practical jokes on April 1. The day has persisted in American folkways and affections since colonial times, although it has naturally not received official recognition or encouragement from schools or government and is only occasionally mentioned in print. It has been well called "a holiday of the mind, not of the state." In the United States as the 20th century has progressed, April Fools' Day appears to have been observed somewhat less widely and enthusiastically. In England some observers noted a decline in the custom as early as the 1870s.

Perhaps one reason for the persistence of April Fools' Day is that children in the United States are often introduced to it within the family — either by having jokes played on them that underscore their gullibility in an unforgettable manner, or by one parent's playing a joke on the other, giving a glimpse of the childlike spirit in adults and an occasion for shared laughter at grown-ups. The aim of April fooling has always been to put over some prank or impossible request on an unwary person who has not yet noticed what day it is. When the fooled person

grows confused or realizes that he has been taken in, the joker calls out "April fool!" — an exclamation of triumph that also explains that it is jest. "For successful April fooling," the antiquarian Robert Chambers wrote a century ago, "it is necessary to have some considerable degree of coolness and face." One of the charms of the day is the chance it gives to try out the poker face.

In some places if April fooling is not carried out before noon, it is traditional to call the prankster the "April fool" for having tried his tricks too late. An April fool in Scotland is called an April *gowk*, the Scottish word for cuckoo, the emblem of simpletons. In England related names for the fool are an April *gob, gawby, or gobby*. Or he may be called an April *noddie*.

The most popular form of April fooling has customarily been the "fool's errand" in which an unsuspecting person is sent on an absurd mission — for example, to buy some pigeon's milk or a copy of the *History of Adam's Grandfather*. In France the fool may be sent for some sweet vinegar or for a stick with one end. Of course everyone the fooled person approaches for help at once perceives the joke. "Thus by contrivers' inadvertent jest, / One fool exposed makes pastime for the rest," runs an old rhyme.

Many different explanations have been offered for the origins of April Fools' Day. Some may be as fanciful as April Fools' jokes themselves. In 1760 the dilemma was set in verse in *Poor Robin's Almanac*:

> The first of April, some do say,
> Is set apart for All Fools' Day.
> But why the people call it so,
> Nor I, nor they themselves do know.
> But on this day are people sent
> On purpose for pure merriment.

One rather unlikely explanation is that the day arose from an ancient farcical representation of the sending of Jesus from Annas to Caiaphas, from Caiaphas to Pilate, from Pilate to Herod, and from Herod back to Pilate at the time of Jesus' trial and crucifixion. In the Christian calendar these events are commemorated in late March or April during Holy Week. Another debatable theory is that April Fools' Day is a relic of the festival of *Cerealia*, held at the beginning of April in Roman times. This festival recalled the legend in which the goddess Ceres, hearing the echo of the screams of her daughter Proserpina as she is being carried off to the lower world from the Elysian meadows by Pluto, goes in search of Proserpina's voice. But Ceres' search is a fool's errand, for it is impossible to find the echo. It is also sometimes asserted that April Fools' Day is a remnant of an ancient Celtic custom concerning the beginning of spring.

The impression prevails, however, that the custom of April fooling had something to do with the observance of the spring equinox (usually March 21 in the Gregorian calendar). It is striking that at this time of year, although not precisely on April 1, customs of fooling people are found in lands as far apart as Sweden, Portugal, and India. For the European countries, at least, part of the connection may be that at the vernal equinox nature seems to play with human beings, sending them sunshine or rain according to whim.

The similarity of April fooling to one aspect of the Hindu festival of Holi (or Huli) has especially fascinated folklorists. Originating in an ancient fertility rite at the beginning of spring, Holi is a five-day Hindu fire festival celebrated in high spirits with bonfires and outdoor dancing. For numberless centuries unsuspecting persons have been sent on fool's errands on the final day of Holi, March 31, just as they are on April Fools' Day. This practice once brought mirth to high and low castes in Indian society; today, however, Holi seems to be losing its appeal for city dwellers.

Certain students have argued that the strong resemblance between April Fools' Day and the last day of Holi indicates a prehistoric common origin, attesting to the great antiquity of April Fools' Day. It seems just as likely, however, that the European and Hindu celebrations arose quite separately, and in different eras, to incarnate a common human fascination with themes of imposture and gullibility, wisdom and foolishness, and "loss of face." Virtually all peoples have woven fool's errands into their folk tales. That fact still leaves open the interesting question of why customs of fooling so often coincide with the beginning of spring.

Whatever its global affinities, the tradition of April Fools' Day was brought early to the American colonies by English, Scottish, and perhaps French, settlers. (Later the first two nationalities introduced it to Australia.) But its beginnings in Britain are unclear. The first allusion to April, or All Fools', Day in English literature dates from the end of the 17th century (Dawks's *Newsletter*, April 2, 1698). Literary allusions become more frequent from the time of Addison and Steele's *Spectator* (1711–1712; 1714), but April fooling existed before it was mentioned in print — no doubt long before. Antiquarians are cautious, but many believe that the custom was prevalent in France earlier than in Britain and,

if so, may have been imported from across the Channel.

April fooling may have first become customary in France after the adoption of a calendar reform by young Charles IX in 1564, making the year begin on January 1. The influential King Philip II of Spain had recently decreed January 1 New Year's for his realm, and this also had been the practice in ancient Rome for a number of centuries, beginning before the time of Jesus Christ. Through much of France in the Middle Ages, however, New Year's Day had been observed on March 25 at the time of Lady Day, or the Feast of the Annunciation. This plan had been favored by the medieval Church because the bacchanalian flavor of the old pagan celebration of the new year on January 1 was thus avoided. Furthermore, with March 25 as its beginning, the year commenced on the traditional anniversary of the angel's announcement to Mary that she would bear a son, that is, on the anniversary of the conception of Jesus.

Like most medieval festivals, New Year's had been celebrated throughout the week following the festival day. This period of seven days after March 25 was called the octave of New Year's, because with the festival day it lasted eight days. Under the old (Julian) calendar arrangement, most French people had exchanged calls and given gifts (*étrennes*) on April 1, the final day of the New Year's octave. Charles IX's proclamation of 1564, changing New Year's Day to January 1, took several years to be recognized because of slow communications and popular attachment to tradition. Conservatives especially objected to the change. In time, jokers began to ridicule the conservatives' attachment to the old New Year's by making calls of pretended ceremony and sending them mock gifts on April 1. It is thought that the widespread French tradition of April fooling arose from this.

In France the hoax is called a *poisson d'avril*, an "April fish." Whether this is because April fish tend to be easily caught or because the sun was leaving the zodiacal sign of Pisces (the Fishes) on April 1 under the Julian calendar — which was used in France until 1582 — no one knows. Today in France confectioners display chocolate fish in their windows on April 1, and as a joke friends send each other unsigned humorous postcards with pictures of fish.

In England and the British colonies, March 25 remained the New Year until 1751–1752, in Scotland until 1600. Regardless of whether April fooling came to the British Isles from France or originated from celebrations on April 1 as the last day of the New Year's octave, a familiar repertory of jokes played on the day has built up in the English-speaking world. Outside the home, the custom of playing pranks is celebrated chiefly by schoolchildren. They may write "kick me" on a piece of paper and pin it surreptitiously on the back of a friend, waiting for the result with barely suppressed glee. Or they may tie a string to a purse, drop the purse on the sidewalk, and then conceal themselves with the end of the string in their hands. When someone stoops to pick up the purse, they pull it out of his reach. Sometimes they may put a brick under an old hat and wait for someone to try to kick it out of his way. Balls of cotton covered with chocolate to look like candies may also be prepared, or balls of salt and pepper. Some children find delight in telling an adult that there is a hole in his sock, a thread on her coat, or a spot on his cheek — and then laughing uproariously and shouting "April fool!" as the victim looks for it.

Nor are adults above playing pranks. A mother may mischievously put circles of cloth inside her family's pancakes so that they cannot be cut. And in cities that have an aquarium or zoo, it has been common for one person to tell another in his office to call a certain telephone number because "Mr. Fish" or "Miss Fox" or "Mrs. Lyon" wants to speak to him. The caller realizes that he is an April fool when the number proves to be that of the local zoo or aquarium! "Mr. Gardiner" may be called at the botanical garden or florist's, or the butcher's telephone number may be given and the prospective victim told that "Mr. Lamb" or "Miss Wiener" has a message for him.

April Fools' Day has generally resisted the commercialization that has made many long-loved celebrations more tawdry and less genuinely communal than they once were. However, in recent years at least two promotional events in the United States have taken April Fools' Day as their starting point. Since 1945 the Humor Societies of America has sponsored National Laugh Week during the first 10 days of April to honor and draw public attention to aspiring and well-known comedians — the 20th century's "court jesters." Publicity Stunt Week has also been sponsored by a public relations firm during the first week of April since 1960 to increase commercial and popular awareness of the effectiveness of publicity stunts in bringing persons or products into the news dramatically. Unusual and intriguing stunts are encouraged and an award is given for the top stunt of the year.

That a genuinely folk feeling continues to surround April 1 can be seen in the fact that people often hesitate to commit important acts, such as marrying or launching a new business enterprise, on April 1. Thus the day's traditional association with unreality and imposture has its effect. Some are able to ignore this, however. The most famous case was Napoleon I of France, who married his second wife, Marie-Louise of Austria, on April 1, 1810. For this his subjects called him an "April fish."

APRIL 2

Pascua Florida Day

This is a movable event. See note on page xxvi.

The date the Spanish adventurer and explorer Juan Ponce de León discovered Florida in 1513 is uncertain. He sighted an extensive unknown coastline (of what is now Florida) around March 27 and followed the coast northwards. He probably stepped ashore somewhere between St. Augustine and the mouth of the St. Johns River early in April, perhaps, as some historians claim, on April 2. The only pertinent date known with absolute certainty is April 8, when the explorer and some of his party disembarked to plant a cross and claim the newly discovered land for Spain (see April 8). Ponce de León named the land Pascua Florida because of its discovery at Eastertime, "in the time of the Feast of Flowers."

In 1953 the Florida legislature designated April 2 Florida State Day, to be known as Pascua Florida Day because Ponce de León had first sighted Florida about that date. When April 2 falls on a Saturday or Sunday, the governor of Florida may proclaim either the preceding Friday or the following Monday as State Day. The idea was originally suggested by a social studies teacher in Jacksonville, Mary A. Harrell. The legislature also empowered the governor to annually proclaim March 27 through April 2 as Pascua Florida Week, to honor, as the 1973 proclamation stated, "the rich lore of that early discovery that molded the destiny of Florida's future and subsequent nickname, 'The Flower State.' " On April 2 and during Pascua Florida Week, schoolchildren and adults are urged to observe the period with commemorative exercises and special programs.

United States Mint Established

As Article I, section 8, of the US Constitution conferred on Congress the exclusive power to coin money and to regulate its value, it became necessary to make some provision to exercise this power. In January 1791 Alexander Hamilton, the first secretary of the treasury, dealt with the coinage problem in his report to Congress. Hamilton's recommendations, which were strongly influenced by the thinking of Thomas Jefferson and the financier Robert Morris, called for three major provisions: (1) a decimal system of coinage; (2) the dollar as the basic unit of money; and (3) bimetallism, with both silver and gold as legal tender in a ratio of 15 to 1. According to Hamilton's recommendation, the gold dollar would contain 24.75 grains of pure gold and the silver dollar would contain 371.25 grains of pure silver.

On April 2, 1792, Congress ratified this plan and passed an act establishing a mint for the coinage of money. (The word *mint* is derived from a Latin term meaning money.) The first coins, copper cents and half cents, came from the mint in 1793. Silver dollars were first coined in 1794. Gold eagles ($10) and half eagles ($5) appeared in 1795 and soon afterward half dollars, quarters, ten-cent and five-cent pieces were also produced on a large scale.

Only Massachusetts, which between 1652 and 1683 minted the famous pine-tree shilling, successfully coined money during the colonial period. Instead, the colonies relied generally on English money, the Spanish dollar, ordinary barter, tobacco and other warehouse receipts, emergency issues of paper currency, and other expedients. Such an inadequate supply of money was a major grievance against the parent country up to the time of the American Revolution.

After the colonies united to resist Great Britain, the Second Continental Congress authorized an issue of paper money. Provision was made for its redemption within three years, and each colony was held responsible for its proper proportion of the issue. Because the first issue of $3 million was inadequate, there were many subsequent issues, and all pretense of redemption was abandoned. The currency's value depreciated until in 1782 it took 500 Continental dollars to buy one Spanish silver dollar. (George Washington once said that it took a wagonload of money to buy a wagonload of provisions.) The depreciation in value of this Continental currency was so great that people got in the habit of saying of a useless thing that it was "not worth a Continental."

Despite attempts to stabilize finances during the Confederation period, currency continued to be one of the major problems plaguing the new nation. Seen in this perspective, Hamilton's plan was viewed by many as a panacea that would place American finances on a sound footing. However, the system, which undervalued gold, proved to be a complete failure, and not until after the Civil War was there a really satisfactory national coinage.

The first mint, provided for in the act of 1792, was opened in Philadelphia. In the course of time other mints were established in San Francisco, California; New Orleans, Louisiana; Carson City, Nevada; Dahlonega, Georgia; Charlotte, North Carolina; and Denver, Colorado. Of these, only the Philadelphia and Denver mints are currently operating. Both are open to the public.

The US Mint in Denver is located at 320 West Colfax Avenue, near Denver's Civic Center complex. Half-hour tours are conducted through the clatter and bustle of Denver's huge money-making operation.

The mint at Philadelphia, where dies of coins are made as well as designs of medals conferred by Congress, is the more important. With its removal from its previous quarters, built in 1900 at 16th and Spring Garden streets, to a new building on Independence Mall, it also became the world's largest and most modern mint, with a capacity of producing anywhere from 2 billion to 8 billion coins a year (depending on the number of shifts worked). At half its maximum capacity, the mint turns out 4 billion coins a year. This works out to 1 million coins an hour, or nearly 399 a second. Appropriately enough, the mint is a mere few hundred feet from the site of the original mint, which, in 1792, was the first public building erected by the government of the young United States. Up to 2,500 visitors an hour can now view the entire coin-making process from a glass-enclosed balcony that runs the full, two-block length of the mint. The tour includes a visit to a numismatic museum housing historic coins and medals.

There have been many changes in the laws governing coinage and in the denominations of coins in use since the US Mint first began coining money in Philadelphia in 1793. In the first place, the mints no longer make gold coins at all. Some other coins no longer in use are the half-cent, 2-cent, 3-cent, and 20-cent pieces, and the silver half dime.

Though there have been innovations as well as discontinuations — the nickel, for instance, which was introduced in 1866 — there have also been long periods of little change. The Coinage Act of 1965, which President Lyndon B. Johnson signed on July 23, 1965, provided for the first major change in US coinage in approximately a century. Prompted by a world shortage of silver and the need to conserve that metal for industrial and military uses, it authorized departure from the silver alloy that had long been used. According to the act's provisions, silver was entirely eliminated from quarters and dimes, and it was substantially reduced in the half dollar.

APRIL 3

Washington Irving's Birthday

Washington Irving, the first American writer to gain international fame, was born in New York City on April 3, 1783. The youngest of 11 children of a prosperous merchant, he was showered with affection, pampered, and indulged, especially by his brothers.

This family warmth molded the warm, generous character of Washington Irving and helped make possible his whimsical, polished, sophisticated style as a writer. The "baby of the family" grew up to be the literary idol of America and the toast of European capitals as well. During a period when cultivated Europeans still considered Americans a band of unwashed barbarians, they nevertheless fell under the spell of the witty, urbane Irving, who had a true zest for living and an unerring instinct for elegance and good taste.

From early boyhood, Irving was in frail health — which turned out be somewhat advantageous. Because of his poor health, he was exempt from the rigors of formal education to which all of his brothers had been subjected. And, to regain his health, he often traveled in the United States, Canada, and Europe. These travels brought him improved health, a cosmopolitan attitude, and a store of material for future writing.

Starting in his teens, he frequently traveled up the Hudson — "this glorious river," he called it — to stay with married sisters who lived in the country. It was there that young Irving became absorbed in the legends and folklore of the early Dutch settlers that appear in so much of his later work.

Given more leisure than his older brothers, who were working in the family business or practicing their own professions, he was free to pursue his own interests in theatrical, literary, and social circles. He did not have a college education, but since it was considered necessary for every young gentleman to be trained in a profession, he studied law, intermittently, in the offices of Josiah Ogden Hoffman, an affable man with a teenage daughter, Matilda. If Irving was lukewarm about the law, he was ardent about Matilda, and the two became engaged.

While supposedly studying law, he wrote a series of whimsical essays, which were published (1802–1803) in the *Morning Chronicle*, his brother Peter's paper, under the pen name of Jonathan Oldstyle, Gent. — the first of many pseudonyms Irving was to use. At 21 he went to Europe for his health and remained for two years. Returning to New York in improved health, he resumed the social whirl and, less fervently, the study of law. After passing the bar examination late in 1806, he ostensibly set up shop as a lawyer in his brother John's office. Meanwhile, with his brother William, J. K. Paulding, and other friends, he was collaborating on a series of essays entitled *Salmagundi; or, The Whim-Whams and Opinions of Launcelot Langstaff, and Others* (1807–1808).

In 1809 he published *Diedrich Knickerbocker's History of New York*, which amused readers in New York and Europe and made its author internationally famous. But Irving, now 26, had a personal grief to deal with. His beloved fiancee, Matilda Hoffman, had died suddenly. Stunned with shock and sorrow, Irving became aimless and restless. There followed a 10-year moratorium on his whimsical writing.

His brothers tried to interest him in several projects that they hoped would occupy his mind. Finally, in 1811, he took up residence in Washington, D.C., as a lobbyist for the Irving brothers' importing firm — an essentially social job for which he was eminently suited. He was warmly welcomed into diplomatic and political circles as one of the country's most famous writers. During the War of 1812, after the British had burned the capital, Irving served briefly in 1814 as aide-de-camp to Governor Daniel D. Tompkins, acquiring the rank of staff colonel with the Iron Grays of the New York State militia.

In 1815 the brothers' business began to falter, and Irving set out for England to attend to the firm's interests in Liverpool. He could do little to save the business, but he made important literary contacts in London, most notably with Sir Walter Scott and Lord Byron, both of whom had admired his work.

Scott's encouragement, and perhaps the family's business reverses, formed the turning point in Irving's long-neglected literary career. He began to write again. *The Sketch Book of Geoffrey Crayon, Gent.* (1819–1820), a collection that included "Rip Van Winkle" and "The Legend of Sleepy Hollow," was a great success in England and the United States.

For the next several years, Irving continued to travel, often in quest of health, and to write about the places he visited — Germany, Austria, France, Spain, and England, and their history or legends. Early in 1826 he was invited to the American legation in Spain to translate Martín Fernández de Navarrete's book on Columbus. He became fascinated with the subject and wrote his own *Life and Voyages of Christopher Columbus* (1828) and *The Companions of Columbus* (1831).

Completely absorbed in Spain and its Moorish heritage, Irving lived for a while in the Alhambra, the Moorish citadel in Granada, and later wrote *The Conquest of Granada* (1829) and *The Alhambra* (1832). Even today, Americans who visit the Alhambra can hear the Spanish tour guides report that "Washington Irving slept here," and they can stay at the nearby Hotel Washington Irving.

From Spain Irving went to London, where he served as secretary of the US legation, from 1829 to 1832. By the time he returned to New York in 1832, he had been away from home for 17 years, yet he was tumultuously received. The public had followed his career with interest and pride, and his *Knickerbocker's History* had grown, instead of fading, in popularity. The United States had its first literary idol.

These were years of great excitement in America's wild west, and Irving traveled to the western frontiers and wrote *A Tour of the Prairies* (1835). *The Adventures of Captain Bonneville* was published in 1837, and *Astoria*, written with a nephew, came out in 1836.

In 1835 Washington Irving moved into Sunnyside, which he described as "a little, old-fashioned stone mansion, all made up of gable ends and as full of angles and corners as an old cocked hat." He lived in the lovely house, located in Tarrytown, New York, on the Hudson River, for the rest of his life, except from 1842 to 1846, when he was US minister to Spain.

Although his home was a busy place, with visits from friends, dignitaries, and relatives — several of whom lived with him in Sunnyside — Irving continued to write, then concentrating mostly on biographies. His last published work was a five-volume biography, *George Washington* (1855–1859).

Washington Irving died at Sunnyside on November 28, 1859, and is buried in the churchyard of the Old Dutch Church of Sleepy Hollow in North Tarrytown. Sunnyside, his home from 1835 to 1859, can be visited year round.

Irving is memorialized in the city of his birth, New York, by the naming of Irving Place and Washington Irving High School.

The enduring importance of Irving's work is indicated by two honors conferred in the mid-1970s. A 10-cent postage stamp depicting "The Legend of Sleepy Hollow" was issued in 1974. In the same year the New York Public Library mounted a major exhibit entitled "Irving: Man of Many Worlds." It marked the 125th anniversary of the founding of the city's first free public library, the Astor Library, of which Irving was president. The 300 items on display included memorabilia associated with his work for his family's importing business as well as literary treasures such as rare books, diaries, notebooks, and segments of manuscripts.

APRIL 4

Flag Act of 1818

On June 14, 1777, the Continental Congress approved a flag for the United States consisting of 13 alternate red and white stripes and a union of 13 white stars on a blue field. The anniversary of that action is observed as Flag Day (see June 14).

Congress evidently intended to continue to represent each state with a star and a stripe because, following the admission of Vermont and Kentucky to the Union, it voted on January 13, 1794, to add two stars and two stripes to the national banner. This act became effective on May 1, 1795, and the flag remained unchanged for 23 years.

When Congress met to consider the flag in 1818, however, five more states had joined the Union, and several territories were also petitioning for statehood. No longer was it feasible to continue the old plan for the flag. For this reason, on April 4, 1818, President James Monroe signed a congressional bill providing that the flag be redesigned, that the number of stripes be reduced to the original 13, and that there should be 20 stars. The act further ordered that "on the admission of every new state into the Union one star be added to the union of the flag and that such addition shall take effect on the Fourth of July next succeeding such admission."

The flag has been made in accordance with this design since that date. It was last redesigned in 1959, when it underwent two revisions. At the admission of Alaska to the Union on January 3 President Dwight D. Eisenhower ordered that, effective on July 4 of that year, the flag would consist of 49 stars arranged in 7 rows of 7 stars each, with alternate rows indented. After Hawaii became a state on August 21, 1959, the flag was again altered, and the present 50-star flag with 5 rows of 6 stars each and 4 rows of 5 stars each became the nation's official banner on July 4, 1960.

Martin Luther King Jr. Assassinated

Dr. Martin Luther King Jr. arrived in Memphis, Tennessee, on April 3, 1968, to organize support for the city's predominantly black sanitation workers, who had been on strike since February

12. Speaking before a gathering of 2,000 people that evening, King spoke of the inevitable dangers faced by those who fought for civil rights. He concluded:

Like anybody, I would like to live a long life; longevity has its grace, but I'm not concerned about that now. I just want to do God's will. And He's allowed me to go up to the mountain. And I've looked over, and I've seen the promised land. I may not get there with you, but I want you to know tonight that we as a people will get to the promised land. So I'm happy tonight. I'm not worried about anything. I'm not fearing any man. Mine eyes have seen the glory of the coming of the Lord.

King's eloquence was prophetic; the next day, April 4, 1968, an assassin's bullet struck him down.

That day, he and his aides had worked in his room at the Lorraine Motel, which they had chosen because of its black ownership. Toward evening their meeting ended, and the participants prepared to go to dinner. King stepped onto the balcony outside his room and chatted with a member of his staff, the Reverend Jesse Jackson, who was standing below in a parking lot. Jackson introduced the musician Ben Branch, who was scheduled to play at that evenings's church rally. The civil rights leader, leaning over the railing, greeted Branch and asked him to play the spiritual "Precious Lord" at the gathering. As King straightened up, he was shot by a .30-06 bullet, which pierced his face and neck. The impact of the bullet lifted him off his feet and dropped him on his back on the concrete balcony floor.

Jesse Jackson, Ralph Abernathy, Andrew Young, and other associates rushed to the fallen leader. They tried, unsuccessfully, to stop the bleeding. A fire department ambulance carried King to St. Joseph's Hospital, but surgery performed there failed to revive him, and doctors pronounced him dead.

King's assassin had fired the fatal bullet from a dingy boardinghouse across the street from the Lorraine Motel. The suspect, later identified as James Earl Ray, an escaped convict, immediately fled the site, but local, state, and federal law enforcement officers were soon tracking him. The authorities finally captured Ray at a London airport. Back in the United States a jury convicted him of murder and sentenced him to 99 years in the penitentiary.

On hearing of King's assassination, national leaders expressed a sense of horror. Vice President Hubert Humphrey, attending a congressional dinner, stated:

Martin Luther King stands with our other American martyrs in the cause of freedom and justice. . . .

The apostle of nonviolence has been the victim of violence. . . . An America of full freedom, full and equal opportunity, is the living memorial he deserves, and it shall be his living memorial.

President Lyndon B. Johnson asked every citizen to reject the blind violence that struck down the nonviolent King, but not all Americans responded to his plea.

Nights and days of rioting, looting, and burning plagued many cities, as some blacks angrily reacted to the news of the murder. Youths rampaged through the streets of ghettos, burning to the ground large sections of their own communities and despoiling the stores of black as well as white merchants. Police officials, anxious not to make martyrs and to keep bloodshed to a minimum, risked the criticism of property-conscious citizens by their restrained response to the rioters, most of whom were young teenagers.

Washington, D.C., which had escaped serious urban riots in the earlier 1960s, suffered the worst damage. The plundering began on the Thursday evening when King was shot and continued for several days. Looters struck stores only two blocks from the White House, and arsonists set blazes whose smoke hung over government buildings. On Friday President Johnson called for 6,500 army and National Guard troops to aid the city's 2,900 police officers, and he soon sent for another 6,000 regulars. By late Saturday, the soldiers and police were able to restore some order.

Chicago, the site of King's unsuccessful campaigns for open housing in 1966, also felt the wrath of rioters. Looters, arsonists, and a few snipers carried on their destructive work, and police bullets cut down at least nine blacks. Mayor Richard J. Daley pleaded for calm, but Chicago officials finally had to use 12,500 federal soldiers and Illinois guardsmen to restore order.

New York City escaped relatively unscathed. Although window-breakers and looters were active in some black areas, police restraint, the cooperation of community leaders in Harlem, and the presence there of Mayor John Lindsay on the nights following the assassination helped to calm the anger.

Coretta Scott King, the wife of the slain leader, immediately stepped forward to continue her husband's work. On April 8, the day before King was buried, she led between 20,000 and 40,000 marchers through the streets of Memphis in a demonstration in support of the sanitation workers her husband had wanted to help. Walter P. Reuther, president of the United Automobile Workers; Dr. Benjamin Spock, pediatrician and Vietnam war opponent; Charles S. Cogen, president of the American Federation of

Teachers; Harry Van Arsdale, president of the New York City Labor Council; John deLury, president of the Uniformed Sanitation Men's Association of New York; actors Ossie Davis and Godfrey Cambridge; singer Harry Belafonte; and Representatives John Conyers and William Fitts Ryan were among the dignitaries who marched in the front ranks with Coretta King. At the Memphis city hall, she addressed the crowd, challenging all to carry on her husband's work. She reminded the throng of what King had often said: An unearned suffering is redemptive.

If you give your life to a cause in which you believe, and which is right and just — and it is — and if your life comes to an end as a result of this then your life could not have been lived in a more redemptive way.

"I think," she declared, "that this is what my husband has done."

In anticipation of the funeral, many communities held special commemorative services. President Johnson declared April 7 Martin Luther King Memorial Day. In New York City, thousands of people gathered at lunchtime on April 8 in a Manhattan garment center meeting sponsored by District 65 of the Retail, Wholesale, and Department Store Union. At approximately the same time, 500 persons who had marched downtown from Harlem held a memorial service at United Nations Plaza. Lindsay attended both events.

On April 8 some 200 diplomats and UN staff members attended a memorial service for King at the Church Center for the United Nations. Arthur Goldberg, the US ambassador to the world body, led the American delegation. Philip A. Johnson, associate general secretary of the World Council of Churches in the United States, reminded the worshipers that commemorations were only the beginning and that "the world now awaits the only eloquence that will make any difference — the eloquence of deed."

On April 9 people from all stations in life gathered in Atlanta, Georgia, to attend King's funeral. Among them were members of Congress, many governors, and leading representatives of major religions.

Funeral services began at 10:43 A.M. at the Ebenezer Baptist Church, of which King and his father, the Reverend Martin Luther King Sr., had been copastors. At the request of Coretta King, the ceremony included a taped excerpt from the last sermon preached by King at the church. In the talk, King described what he hoped would be his eulogy.

If any of you are around when I have to meet my day, I don't want a long funeral. And if you get somebody to deliver the eulogy, tell him not to talk too long. . . . Tell him not to mention that I have a Nobel Peace Prize — that isn't important.

Tell him not to mention that I have 300 or 400 other awards — that's not important.

Tell him not to mention where I went to school.

I'd like somebody to mention that day that Martin Luther King Jr. tried to give his life serving others.

I'd like for somebody to say that day that Martin Luther King Jr. tried to love somebody. . . .

I want you to be able to say that day that I did try to feed the hungry. I want you to be able to say that day that I did try in my life to clothe the naked. I want you to say on that day that I did try in my life to visit those who were in prison. And I want you to say that I tried to love and serve humanity.

Yes, if you want to, say that I was a drum major. Say that I was a drum major for justice. Say that I was a drum major for peace. I was a drum major for righteousness.

And all of the other shallow things will not matter.

When the services ended after noon, the pallbearers carried the coffin from the church, and, to symbolize King's identification with the poor, placed it upon a faded green wooden wagon drawn by two mules. Then about 50,000 mourners began the three-and-one-half-mile march through the streets of Atlanta to Morehouse College, where King had been an undergraduate, for an open-air service. At Morehouse Dr. Benjamin H. Mays, president emeritus of the college, gave a eulogy as part of the 90-minute program:

I make bold to assert that it took more courage for King to practice non-violence than it took his assassin to fire the fatal shot. The assassin is a coward: he committed his foul act and fled. When Martin Luther King disobeyed an unjust law, he accepted the consequences of his actions. He never ran away and he never begged for mercy. . . . He was supra-race, supra-nation, supra-denomination, supra-class, and supra-culture. He belonged to the world and to mankind. Now he belongs to posterity.

King's body was carried in a hearse from the college to South View Cemetery, a burial area established by black citizens after the Civil War. There, at approximately 5:30 P.M., he was buried beside his grandparents. The epitaph on his tombstone catches the irony of his life and death: "Free at last, free at last; thank God Almighty I'm free at last."

Americans across the nation commemorated the first anniversary of King's death on April 4,

1969. Coretta King and their four children visited his grave, to which many individuals and groups had sent floral wreaths. Almost all major cities held memorial services. In New Orleans some 400 black marchers, headed by a mule-drawn wagon with a coffin draped in black crepe, paraded through the downtown area to City Hall, where the leaders read a list of grievances and called for reform in the city's government, schools, and police force.

King's remains were moved on January 13, 1970, from Southview Cemetery to a crypt near the Ebenezer Baptist Church. Two days later, on January 15, his birthday, the church, the crypt, and his childhood home were officially dedicated as part of a memorial to be known as the Martin Luther King Jr. Center for Social Change in Atlanta. Other commemorations throughout the nation also marked Dr. King's birthday (see January 15), and many persons urged that the federal government declare January 15 a legal holiday in his honor.

Puyallup Valley Daffodil Festival

This is a movable event. See note on page xxvi.

Washington's Puyallup Valley Daffodil Festival takes place early each spring. The 18-mile-long Puyallup Valley is located east of Tacoma, Washington, between Puget Sound and snow-capped Mount Rainier. To draw attention to the golden carpet of some 30 million daffodils that covers the valley in spring, civic leaders in Tacoma and the valley communities of Puyallup, Sumner, Orting, Fife, and Spanaway sponsor the festival each year. It customarily begins in late March or early April, when the blooms are at their best. Besides the magnificent fields of daffodils, some 50-odd events contribute to the success of the nine-day-long festivities. They include the daffodil queen's coronation and ball, the grand floral parade, an Arabian horse show, the marine regatta, and track, field, and other sports competitions.

The state of Washington is considered the "nation's bulb basket," since it produces 20 percent of the country's narcissus, 20 percent of its bulb irises, and 80 percent of its tulips. Ideal soil, moisture, mild winters, and other growing conditions, together with innovations in the use of machinery in the fields, have combined to foster the development of the industry. Not only are the Northwest bulbs 10 to 20 percent larger than imported ones, but the blooms appear two to three weeks ahead of those raised in Europe.

A large portion of the state's acreage in bulb production is found in the Puyallup Valley. The bulb industry there started as early as 1910, when George Lawler made the first, albeit small-scale, commercial plantings. The US Department of Agriculture examined the valley in 1923 to seek a substitute crop for the area's hop production, which was hard hit with the advent of Prohibition. Acting upon the department's recommendation that the region would be an excellent place for extensive bulb production, W. H. Paulhams of Sumner summoned a meeting of all persons eager to implement the suggestion.

The year 1925 is generally given as the start of Puyallup Valley's fame as a bulb center. By 1971 over 1,000 acres were devoted to the industry. In addition to the sale of bulbs, there is a large market for forcers (bulbs placed in hot-houses and forced into early spring bloom) and for cut flowers (used for spring and Easter promotions, especially in department stores). For example, about 18 million daffodil blooms are shipped every year from the Puyallup Valley. Extensive air shipments of cut flowers, however, mean that the flowers are picked before the buds open. But "mother blocks" remain in the valley for display purposes and provide a spectacular attraction for visitors to the festival.

The first Puyallup Valley Daffodil Festival was held on April 6, 1926, at the estate of Charles Orton, near Sumner, under the auspices of the Sumner Garden Club. Civic leaders from 15 nearby towns attended the garden party, held amidst many varieties of blooming daffodils. The following year the Sumner chamber of commerce sponsored a bulb banquet and, with help from the Tacoma and Puyallup chambers of commerce, chose a daffodil queen from one of the valley communities. As visitors from Tacoma and Seattle enthusiastically flocked to visit the blooming fields on weekends in late March and early April, the modest festivities became well known. Representatives from the participating communities met in 1934, creating a steering committee to form a more ambitious program of events. One proposal was that the masses of blooms be utilized for a parade of flower-bedecked floats through Tacoma and the valley towns.

From these small beginnings the present elaborate festival was born in 1934. The activities of the noncommercial, nonprofit festival corporation are supported mostly by local contributions. A festival board of directors is composed of members of the chambers of commerce of Tacoma, Sumner, and Puyallup; the Lions Clubs of Fife, Orting, and Spanaway; the Tacoma Yacht Club; and the Northwest Bulb Growers Association.

Typical of the present, 9- or 10-day, event-filled celebration was the 37th annual festival in 1970. Together with surrounding events, the program stretched from March 1, when booster buttons went on sale, through May 30, with the chief attractions crowded into the official Puyallup Valley Daffodil Festival Week from April 4 through 12. Throughout March and early April a number of sports competitions were scheduled, including handball, basketball, volleyball, and badminton tournaments, wrestling matches, and the Daffodil Classic intercollegiate ski meet at nearby Crystal Mountain. Daffodil Week proper started on Saturday morning, April 4, with the first major event, the 9th annual Junior Daffodil parade in Tacoma. Thousands of youngsters in colorful outfits drew or rode on miniature floats, wagons, bicycles, and tricycles — all bedecked with daffodils — or showed off pets wearing daffodil collars. In the early afternoon, the traditional hanging of the baskets ceremony took place, as daffodil baskets were put on display along the main streets of Sumner, Puyallup, and Orting.

On Sunday morning, April 5, an old-fashioned rail excursion aboard the Daffodil Special Train, a feature inaugurated in 1965, took visitors from Tacoma past the spectacular daffodil fields to Orting. There hundreds of persons enjoyed an afternoon-long, open-air, chicken barbecue, sponsored by the Orting Lions Club, in the city park. An Orting preschool smorgasbord was also featured in the high school gym.

The daffodil queen's coronation took place at Pacific Lutheran University in Tacoma the evening of April 6. As the high point of an evening of stage entertainment, the nine daffodil princesses, chosen from the high schools of the area, competed for the title of daffodil queen.

The "most magnificent mutt show" took place for the first time three evenings later. Prizes were awarded to the outstanding dogs of unknown pedigree: the funniest looking, shaggiest, best dressed, smallest, and biggest. Top honors went to the "most magnificent mutt of all." On April 10, 11, and 12, the Arabian horse show drew entries from Washington and neighboring states, as well as from Canada. In all, 522 horses were shown in 65 classes. The three-day flower show, scheduled over the same period, attracted participants from the area's garden clubs. The amateur and professional exhibitors displayed specimens of the several hundred varieties of locally grown bulbs.

One of the most eye-catching events, and probably the best attended, was the annual grand floral parade of decorated floats, drill teams, and mounted units on Saturday, April 11. The parade is unusual since it travels through several communities, beginning in Tacoma at 10:00 A.M. and continuing, after a lunch break, through Puyallup and Sumner for a total distance of 15 miles. Some floats and bands go through a fourth community, Orting. The 1970 parade theme, The Greatest Show on Earth, saluted the world of the circus. The 30 floats used more than 1.25 million freshly cut daffodils. The daffodil queen, for example, appeared in the gaping mouth of an enormous tiger created from 45,000 white and yellow daffodils. This particular float later represented the festival in 11 other parades from Portland, Oregon, to Vancouver, British Columbia.

Marine events on nearby Puget Sound round out the daffodil festival. Each year on the final Sunday of the festival, a marine parade and regatta are staged along the picturesque waterfront of Tacoma's Commencement Bay (part of Puget Sound). The regatta is one of the few seagoing floral parades of its type in the country. In 1970, as usual, yachts, fishing craft, powerboats, outboards, and cruisers, ingeniously covered with daffodils, were reviewed from the official reviewing stand at Tacoma's Old Town Dock.

The first annual daffodil festival dragboat championships on Spanaway Lake near Parkland, south of Tacoma, thrilled the public on Sunday afternoon. Some 40 boats roared at speeds up to 165 knots in the American Powerboat Association's officially sanctioned competitions to provide an exciting close to the major events of the 37th annual Puyallup Valley Daffodil Festival.

The festival's events remained basically the same in the following years. However, by 1975 two junior parades signaled the opening of festival week: the traditional junior daffodil parade in Tacoma in the morning, and the Sumner Day parade in Sumner in the afternoon. A lively finale to the week was provided that year on Sunday afternoon by the daffodil festival musical vaudeville, presented at Pacific Lutheran University.

Appropriately, in the US bicentennial year, 1976, the theme of the 43rd annual Puyallup Valley Daffodil Festival was America's 200 Years.

APRIL 5

Booker T. Washington's Birthday

Booker Taliaferro Washington was born on April 5, 1856, in the cramped slave quarters of James Burroughs's plantation near Halesford in Franklin County, Virginia. The son of a mulatto slave mother and a white father, Booker T. Washington lived the first seven years of his life as a slave. In 1865, after emancipation, his mother moved with her family to Malden, West

Virginia, where young Washington soon found work in a salt furnace and then in a coal mine. In spite of the exhausting work in the mines, he also managed to go to public school for a few months.

Determining in 1872 to pursue his ambition for learning, he set off with only $1.50 in his pocket to walk the 500 miles to Hampton Institute in Virginia. There, he earned the esteem of General Samuel C. Armstrong, the director of the school. Washington studied at Hampton Institute for three years, working as a janitor at the school to pay his expenses. Upon graduation he returned to Malden, where he taught for two years at a school for blacks. There he instructed children during the daytime and adults at night. In 1878 he left Malden to attend Wayland Seminary in Washington, D.C., and eight months later he returned to Hampton Institute to take charge of its night school. While at Hampton he also helped to start a unique educational program for 75 American Indians.

In 1881 General Armstrong recommended Washington to be principal of the just-established Tuskegee Normal and Industrial Institute — later known as Tuskegee Institute — Alabama's first normal school to train black teachers. In accepting the position, Washington began his life's work at Tuskegee.

The start was inauspicious. Arriving there to open the school on July 4, he found only a miserable house, $2,000 in teaching salaries provided by the state, and a handful of pupils. By the time of his death in 1915 Washington had built Tuskegee into a school with a national reputation, an endowment of some $2 million, and a plant of more than 100 well-equipped buildings, where over 1,500 students studied 38 trades and professions under nearly 200 faculty members.

The physical expansion of the institute testified to Washington's success as an educator, since he had made Tuskegee the proving ground for his theories on industrial education. Washington felt that, for the American black, "the opportunity to earn a dollar in a factory just now is worth infinitely more than the opportunity to spend a dollar in an opera house." While emphasizing the dignity of manual labor and the importance of cleanliness, proper diet, and other good habits, he also stressed the necessity of knowing a trade. At Tuskegee he tried to provide students with a useful education. He felt that the best interests of black Americans were more likely to be served by providing them with education and the opportunity for material advancement than through political agitation for civil and voting rights, which some less audible voices urged in his lifetime.

In 1895 Washington spoke at the Cotton States Exposition in Atlanta. In his speech he referred to black and white relations, saying: "In all things that are purely social we can be as separate as the five fingers, yet one as the hand in all things essential to mutual progress." This speech, which some regarded as a tacit acceptance of segregation and others saw as an attempt to conciliate the races, brought Washington instant national recognition. Especially in the white world, he came to be regarded as *the* spokesman for blacks, and he was increasingly in demand, both in the United States and in Europe, as a public speaker. Those who wished to establish or contribute to black educational institutions sought his advice before allocating their funds. Most black job- or office-holders who owed their positions to federal appointment were indebted to a recommendation from Tuskegee's director, whose counsel was regularly heeded by Washington, D.C., officials. In 1905 President Theodore Roosevelt, like President William McKinley before him, visited Tuskegee, paying its founder a great honor. Other influential admirers were President William Howard Taft and industrialists Andrew Carnegie and John D. Rockefeller.

The emphasis placed by Washington on the potential rather than the grievances of blacks, as well as his ability and willingness to compromise, contributed to his acceptance by whites. However, this acceptance led to opposition, mainly from black intellectuals such as W.E.B. DuBois. They feared that Washington's stress on industrial education might keep blacks in virtual bondage and regarded his attitude toward the white establishment as excessively conciliatory. Those who opposed his views stressed the importance of fighting for political and civil rights — something Washington thought unwise and sought to avoid. Many historians feel that Washington adopted the only approach that could have been effective during the turn-of-the-century era in which he came to prominence, though others contest that assertion.

Washington's lifelong concerns were broad, including not only Tuskegee Institute and the immediate community around it, but also the well-being of all blacks in the United States. In 1892 he founded the Tuskegee Conference, which dealt with rural problems encountered by Alabama blacks and encouraged self-improvement. The National Negro Business League, which Washington started in 1900, reached black businessmen all over the country. His ideas also found expression in his public-speaking tours and in the many books he wrote, among them his best-selling autobiography, *Up from Slavery* (1901), which has been widely translated. Among his other books are *The Future of the American Negro* (1899); *Life of Frederick Douglass*, about the influential black abolitionist (1907); and a second autobiography, *My Larger Education* (1911).

Washington's strenuous work hastened his death, and he died on November 14, 1915. He was buried near the chapel at Tuskegee Institute.

In 1922 the school unveiled an eight-foot-high bronze monument that represents Washington as lifting a veil of ignorance from the head of a freed black slave. Every year, as close as possible to his birthday, the students and faculty of Tuskegee Institute honor him with their observance of Founder's Day. Approximately 3,500 students attend Tuskegee, a coeducational, nonsectarian school with an endowment (including certain reserve funds) of over $14 million and more than 160 buildings on a campus of 5,189 acres.

In 1945 Washington was elected to the Hall of Fame for Great Americans, in New York City. Tennessee has honored him by the naming of Booker T. Washington State Park, near Chattanooga. The federal government in 1957 established the site of his birthplace and childhood home in Virginia's Franklin County as the Booker T. Washington National Monument. The 217-acre site includes a replica of the slave cabin in which Washington was born, and a self-guiding trail that tells of his life on the plantation. The visitor center shows a film about his career.

That career was important and fruitful. Mild as his way may seem in retrospect, most observers agree that Washington's journey from a slave childhood to a position of preeminence was remarkable, that Tuskegee Institute was an extraordinary achievement, and that his work in vocational and industrial training and in rural extension was influential in education for blacks and whites alike. Since 1881, the year of Washington's arrival, the lives of more than 60,000 Tuskegee students have been touched directly by his contributions in the direction of economic emancipation and self-realization.

Elihu Yale's Birthday

Elihu Yale, one of the earliest benefactors of what is now Yale University, was born in or near Boston on April 5, 1649. His father, David Yale, who had emigrated from Wales in 1638, was one of the early settlers of New Haven, Connecticut, now the home of Yale University — although the man for whom the university is named never saw New Haven: his parents moved to Massachusetts before he was born and returned to Great Britain when he was about three years old.

Elihu Yale was educated in London and, when he was about 21, joined the British East India Company. He was sent to Madras, India, and worked his way up in the organization. In 1687 he was made governor of Fort St. George in Madras, a post he held until 1692. He stayed in India as a private merchant-trader and returned to London a wealthy man in 1699.

Two years later, in 1701, a group of Connecticut clergymen started the Collegiate School, later to become Yale University. Most of the students lived in the homes of the founding clergymen-teachers, who were scattered in many towns in the colony of Connecticut. In 1716 the founders began to build in New Haven but soon realized they needed more money than could be raised locally. Jeremiah Dummer, the colony's agent in England, was interested in the school and asked Yale, who was already known as a philanthropist, for assistance. So, it is said, did Cotton Mather, one of the teachers at the school.

One of them evidently suggested that the grateful trustees might name the school after the benefactor they so desperately needed: "If what is forming at New Haven might wear the name of Yale College, it would be better than a name of sons and daughters." Thus persuaded, Elihu Yale, then close to 70, dispatched nine bales of goods, including books, rich fabrics from India, and a portrait of King George I. Sold on arrival in Boston, the goods brought £ 562 12s — the largest gift the school would receive for more than 100 years. The trustees of the school heard the good news just before commencement in 1718 and immediately voted to name the new building Yale College.

Elihu Yale died in London on July 8, 1721, and was buried on July 22 in the churchyard of St. Giles in Wrexham, North Wales (near Liverpool, England).

In July 1968 a group of Yale men, aged 18 to 84, marked the 250th anniversary of the naming of Yale College by visiting the tomb of their first great benefactor. A ceremony took place at the Wrexham parish church, whose tower has been duplicated in Yale University's Memorial Quadrangle. Yale's President Kingman Brewster Jr. laid a wreath at Elihu Yale's tomb. Later, the chairman of the Yale Club of London placed a plaque on the site of Plas Gronow, the family home of Elihu Yale outside Wrexham.

Yale College became Yale University in 1887. At present, Yale has more than 9,000 students, almost equally divided between graduate and undergraduate, and a student-faculty ratio of about seven to one. The campus covers 175 acres plus 500 acres of playing fields. In addition to Yale College, the university consists of a number of professional or graduate divisions, including those devoted to medicine (founded in 1813), divinity (1822), law (1824), art and architecture (1865), music (1894), forestry (1900), and drama (1955). Also in this sizable complex are the Institute of Far Eastern Languages, the Peabody Museum of Natural History, an art gallery, a computer center, and one of the four largest library collections in the United States, comprising more than 6 million volumes.

APRIL 6

Church of Jesus Christ of Latter-Day Saints Organized

The Church of Jesus Christ of Latter-Day Saints, unofficially known as the Mormon Church, was organized formally on April 6, 1830. The anniversary is still observed annually during the Church's General Conference in Salt Lake City, Utah, which is regularly scheduled to include this date.

However, the religious body had its actual inception in visions reportedly experienced by the prophet Joseph Smith Jr. (see December 23) in 1820 and 1823. The first of these, by Smith's account, took place when he acted on the biblical promise of James 1:5 — "If any of you lack wisdom, let him ask of God, that giveth to all men liberally . . . and it shall be given him" — and inquired which of the many contending Christian sects was right. He reportedly was informed that he must join none of them, for they were all in error.

It was in 1823, according to Smith, that he learned from the angel Moroni of the existence of secret records, written upon gold plates, which told of the ancient inhabitants of North America and set forth "the fulness of the everlasting Gospel" as Christ had delivered it to them after his Resurrection. Later, Smith would deduce from the mysterious, pictographic script on the plates that these ancient inhabitants — American Indians — were descended from Israelites via the tribe of Joseph, whose members had reached the continent of North America by migration.

In the visions of 1823, Smith recounted, he learned of the plates' location — hidden in a hill named Cumorah in ancient times. The hill was located between Palmyra and Manchester, New York. But, he related, although he visited the place annually as instructed, nearly four years passed before the heavenly messenger Moroni granted him permission to remove the plates and begin their translation with the aid of marvelous stones provided with them. Moroni, in Mormon belief, was the son of Mormon, a fourth century prophet. According to Latter-Day Saints tradition, it was primarily Mormon's abridgment of earlier records that was preserved on the gold plates revealed to Smith.

The translation of the plates, which would appear as *The Book of Mormon* (published in 1830), was performed by Smith with the aid of the schoolteacher Oliver Cowdery and others, who transcribed the records from his dictation. It was in the course of the deciphering, according to Smith, that John the Baptist appeared to Cowdery and him on May 15, 1829, and ordained them into the Priesthood of Aaron. The priestly order, one of two recognized by Mormons, bears the name of Aaron, the brother of Moses, generally regarded as the first high priest of Israel. Less than a year later, according to the testimony of Smith, the Apostles Peter, James, and John also appeared to the two men and bestowed upon them the Melchizedek Priesthood, named for the biblical "priest of the most high God," who was king of the variously identified Salem — probably Jerusalem, in the view of modern scholarship.

It was while *The Book of Mormon* was in the hands of the printer that Joseph Smith Jr., Oliver Cowdery, Hyrum Smith, Samuel H. Smith, Peter Whitmer Jr., and David Whitmer gathered at Fayette, New York, and organized the Church of Jesus Christ of Latter-Day Saints under New York state laws. The Mormons, with their hotly contested views and sometimes controversial customs, were hounded by prejudice, hostility, and the repeated threat of mob violence throughout their early years. It was the antagonism or suspicion of their non-Mormon neighbors — "Gentiles," as the Mormons called them — that lay at the root of each of their increasingly arduous migrations.

The first move — in 1831 — was to Kirtland, Ohio, where the Latter-Day Saints fashioned a temple, which is still visible. Subsequent removals found the Mormons successively establishing residence in western Missouri; in the place they named Nauvoo, Illinois; and ultimately in the Great Salt Lake Valley in Utah, where they founded Salt Lake City in 1847 (see July 24). Their arrival there, under the leadership of Brigham Young, signaled the end of a heroic trek. It included a disastrous encampment near the site of Omaha, Nebraska, where 600 died during the winter of 1846–1847. Most of them now rest in Omaha's Mormon Cemetery. The journey also included passage over the incredibly difficult terrain of the Rocky Mountains. Indeed, the story of Mormon migration is one of the epics of the settlement of the West.

It was true from their beginning that no difficulty deterred the Latter-Day Saints from those objectives perceived as the will of God, particularly the restoration of what they believed to be the true church and Gospel of Christ, in keeping with their founder's original calling. Within a month of the formal organization of the church on April 6, 1830, the Mormons sent out missionaries to the surrounding states. Missionaries were sent to Canada in 1833 and to Great Britain in 1837. Five years later, eight ships were chartered to carry Mormon converts from Britain to the United States. These steps were the beginning of the Mormon missionary work that by 1976 encompassed 156 missions in some 46 countries, including 52 missions in the United States.

Today, the Mormons' missionary efforts continue as strong as, or stronger than, ever. Indeed, the high point of the Latter-Day Saints' history in recent decades is the large number of converts to Mormonism. By 1976, membership in the Church within the United States had risen to about 2.9 million, up from 1,965,786 in December 1962. Worldwide, the membership figure was over 3.7 million by 1976. The Mormons also point with pride to an extensive and continuous building program. In recent decades, this has accounted for many new buildings of worship, among them chapels in many of the mission fields. In addition, the number of Mormon temples, worldwide, has been brought to 20, including 12 in the United States.

To Mormons and non-Mormons alike, the principal sight of mountain-rimmed Salt Lake City is Temple Square. It includes a visitors' center at South Temple and Main streets; the domed and acoustically superb Tabernacle, where organ recitals are given and the world-famous Mormon Tabernacle Choir can be heard rehearsing or broadcasting at certain specified hours, and where a worship service is open to visitors on Sundays; the imposing, six-spired, gray granite Temple, topped by a gilded statue of Moroni, used for the church's most sacred rites and closed to non-Mormons; the assembly hall, which seats 2,000, is open to the public, and is sometimes used for worship; the monument to the gulls who miraculously saved the pioneers' crops from a plague of crickets the year after their arrival; and several monuments to Mormon pioneer leaders. Also of interest nearby are the Lion House and Beehive House, which served as Brigham Young's office and as residences for his numerous wives and still more numerous children. The Mormon practice of polygamy, begun in 1843 with what the Mormons believed to be divine sanction, has been discontinued since the formal disavowal of the

practice by Mormon officials in 1890. Disavowal of polygamy preceded (and was a prerequisite to) Utah's admission to statehood.

North Pole Discovered

The discovery of the North Pole by men of three races on April 6, 1909, was the culmination of nearly a quarter century of effort. Those who reached the pole on that date were Robert E. Peary, a white man who originated and led the effort; Matthew A. Henson, a black man who had served as ship's cook, carpenter and blacksmith, and then as Peary's servant before becoming his coexplorer and most valuable assistant; and four Eskimo guides — Coqueeh, Ootah, Eginwah, and Seegloo.

Peary, who was born at Cresson, Pennsylvania, on May 6, 1856, was graduated from Bowdoin College in 1877. After graduation he served as a cartographic draftsman in the US Coast and Geodetic Survey for two years before becoming an engineer in the US Navy in 1881. As part of the navy's corps of civil engineers — to which he remained attached until his retirement, with leaves for his explorations — he served as assistant engineer in chief of the Nicaragua Canal survey.

Having meanwhile become interested in Arctic exploration, Peary made his first trip to the Far North in 1886. His association with Henson, whom he had met when the latter was a clerk in a Washington clothing store, dates from this first expedition, in which Henson, then about 19, served as a member of the crew. In Greenland, Peary and a Danish friend journeyed inland from Disko Bay, and over the Greenland ice sheet a distance of 100 miles. They reached a height of 7,500 feet above sea level.

Seven companions accompanied Peary on his second exploration of Greenland, in 1891. They included his wife and Henson, who was to accompany him on all of his Arctic explorations and twice save his life, as Peary once saved his. On this tour, Peary made several contributions to scientific knowledge, the most important of which was the verification of Greenland's island formation. He also proved that the polar ice cap extended beyond 82° north latitude and discovered the Melville meteorite on Melville Bay. Peary also encountered the "Arctic highlanders," an isolated Eskimo tribe; he befriended them, and they assisted with his later surveys. Henson, meanwhile, was learning the Eskimo language and becoming a master sled dog driver and an expert in the numerous other skills necessary for Arctic survival.

Peary continued his work with further expeditions in 1893–1895 and voyages during the summers of 1896 and 1897. In 1898 he announced his intention to travel to the North Pole. During the next four years, he sought possible routes from camps at Etah on the northwest coast of Greenland and Fort Conger on neighboring Ellesmere Island. Despite all his efforts, however, he fell short of reaching the North Pole on several attempts, including those of 1902, when he reached 84°17' north latitude, and 1905, when he reached 87°6'.

Undaunted by previous failures, Peary and his party set sail on July 17, 1908, on the ship *Roosevelt* on still another expedition to the Pole. They spent the Arctic winter in a base camp on Ellesmere Island and on March 1, 1909, began the final trek north from Cape Columbia.

On April 6 Peary and his party, which included only Henson and four Eskimo guides, reached the top of the world. This was after days of exhausting effort during which they had traveled 18 to 20 hours a day, menaced by the dwindling food supplies and cold. Henson reached the Pole first with two of the Eskimos. Peary, exhausted and barely able to walk, arrived 45 minutes later and took a reading, which confirmed Henson's calculation of their location. Henson then proudly planted the US flag at the Pole, 90° North. Not only the achievement but also its interracial nature seemed to please both Peary and Henson, who later reflected that "from the beginning, wherever the world's work was done by a white man, he [was] accompanied by a colored man."

The men built an igloo and camped for more than 30 hours at the Pole, making astronomical observations. On both the first and second days they traveled several miles in each direction, crossing and recrossing the Pole, to make sure they had technically achieved their goal. Finally, at 4:00 P.M. on April 7, they headed south and, with favorable conditions, made the return trip to Cape Columbia in 16 days. The entire effort cost Henson, who was 10 years Peary's junior, a loss of 35 pounds and left him exhausted for weeks. It cost the life of one Eskimo, who was drowned during the return trip.

When Peary and his party returned to Newfoundland they found that they were not the only ones claiming to have reached the North Pole. Dr. Frederick A. Cook, who had served as surgeon on Peary's 1891 expedition, said that he was the first to perform the feat, but his report failed to withstand scrutiny by the University of Copenhagen. The National Geographic Society accepted the discovery of the Peary expedition as the authentic one, and Congress voted its thanks and promoted Peary to rear admiral. This was in 1911, the year of Peary's retirement from the US Navy. He received numer-

ous other awards as well, including the rank of grand officer of the French Legion of Honor, before his death on February 20, 1920. Peary's tomb can be visited today at Arlington (Virginia) National Cemetery, just outside Washington, D.C.

Henson received some of his recognition rather belatedly. In 1945 Congress awarded him a medal for "outstanding service to the Government of the United States in the field of science," and, near the end of his life, President Dwight D. Eisenhower honored him at the White House. Henson, born August 8, 1866, in Charles County, Maryland, died at the age of 88 in New York City on March 9, 1955 — two months before the death of Ootah, the last survivor of the trip to the Pole, who died near Thule, Greenland, at the age of 80 in May 1955.

Explorers Hall of the National Geographic Society's Washington headquarters at 17th and M streets, N.W., houses a number of mementos of the Peary expedition. They include one of his sleds, a camera, and the flag carried to the North Pole. There are also a book of photographs by Peary and a taped transcript of an address he made shortly after his return from the 1909 expedition. The hall is open to the public.

The United States Enters World War I

In the summer of 1914 the major European powers went to war (see June 28). When the fighting ended more than four years later, 28 nations on five continents had become involved in the conflict. Alliance commitments and immediate threats to their national and economic security forced many countries to lose no time in placing their armies on the battlefield. Others, including the United States, attempted to maintain a neutral position and waited several years before making the momentous decision to declare war.

At the outset of hostilities in Europe, President Woodrow Wilson appealed to the people of the United States to be "impartial in thought as well as action." For many of the country's 32 million foreign-born or children of immigrant parents, such disinterest in the outcome of the war was difficult. But even among those who openly sympathized with one side or the other, there were few in 1914 who wanted the nation to intervene in the war.

For almost three years, the United States clung to its neutral status despite numerous provocations both by the Allies (chiefly Britain, France, and Russia) and by the Central Powers (Germany, Austria-Hungary, and nations that sided with them). As a neutral, this country had the theoretical right to trade with any belligerent. But in practice, the British blockade of the North Atlantic severely limited US commerce with Germany and Austria. The British redefined contraband to include even foodstuffs, and they forced neutral merchant vessels to put in at Allied ports, where they were searched for contraband goods. In addition, they established import quotas for neutral nations located near Germany and blacklisted a number of American firms suspected of dealing with the enemy. The Wilson administration strongly protested all of these measures, but to no avail.

Although the British prevented the United States from reaping maximum profits from wartime commerce, the Germans violated, in Wilson's words, "the fundamental rights of humanity." The Germans planned to break the Allied blockade with the submarine. A new weapon, which could be easily destroyed when on the water's surface, the submarine or U-boat (from the German *Unterseeboot*), as it was also called, relied on surprise attack. It could not, as the ordinary rules of war required, search an enemy merchant ship for contraband and make provision for the safety of passengers and crew before sinking a vessel.

In February 1915, the Germans announced their intention to launch submarine torpedoes without warning against all enemy merchant ships encountered in the waters surrounding the British Isles. Realizing the danger inherent in this policy for Americans traveling aboard belligerent vessels, Wilson notified the Germans that he would hold them to "strict accountability" if any US citizens lost their lives or property because of Germany's submarine operations. On May 7, 1915, a German torpedo struck the British Cunard liner *Lusitania*, and 128 Americans died as the great ship sank (see May 7). Wilson strongly protested this action, and the German government finally assured him that it would modify its submarine activities.

Despite this promise, little change was made in U-boat operations. On March 24, 1916, several Americans were injured when the French ship *Sussex* was torpedoed. Wilson could not passively accept this incident. In April he threatened to break diplomatic relations with Germany unless that government immediately abandoned its "present methods of submarine warfare against passenger and freight-carrying vessels." The Germans did not want to risk American intervention in the war. For that reason, on May 4 they promised to discontinue sinking merchant ships without warning on the condition that the United States compel Britain also to account for its violations of neutral rights.

The *Sussex* pledge, as it was called, allowed the United States to remain neutral for a while

longer, but in Europe the fighting continued. In December 1916 Wilson attempted to mediate a settlement of the war. This effort, like similar ones in January 1915 and January 1916, proved unsuccessful. Neither the Allies nor the Central Powers were interested in beginning negotiations to end the war, and Wilson's plea for a "peace without victory" went unheeded.

Until 1917 the United States was able to maintain its uneasy neutral position in the war. Then, on January 31 of that year, the German government announced that it was about to renew total submarine warfare against merchant shipping in the waters off the British Isles and in the Mediterranean. The Germans realized that this action would bring the United States into the war on the side of the Allies, but they believed that they would be able to subdue England before American forces could be mobilized. Their strategy was almost successful.

On February 3 Wilson severed diplomatic relations with Germany, but the United States was still reluctant to enter the war. Congress even denied the President power to arm the nation's merchant vessels. However, Wilson was able to override what he considered to be the decision of "a little group of willful men representing no opinion but their own." His advisers uncovered a 1797 statute authorizing the President to arm the merchant fleet, and by relying on this law Wilson was able to order US merchant vessels armed on March 12.

By March 1917 it was becoming increasingly apparent that US interests were being jeopardized by the European war and that this country would eventually be forced to intervene in the conflict. On March 1 Wilson made public the Zimmermann note. This message from German foreign secretary Arthur Zimmermann to the German ambassador to Mexico had been intercepted by British intelligence. It proposed that the ambassador induce the Mexican government to ally itself with Germany if the United States went to war against the Central Powers; in return, Germany would help Mexico regain its "lost territory in New Mexico, Texas, and Arizona." The message also suggested that Mexico press Japan to ally itself with Germany.

The Zimmermann note and Germany's sinking of five American ships in March eliminated the last remnants of American tolerance for the German effort. Meanwhile, the czarist regime in Russia was overthrown and replaced by a provisional republican government. With the seeming end of tyrannical rule in Russia, the Allied cause appeared to be truly a war against autocracy. Public opinion in the United States now strongly favored participation in the fight against Germany. Wilson delayed no longer. He called Congress into special session on April 2, 1917. Announcing that "the world must be made safe for democracy," Wilson asked Congress to declare war. On April 4 the House of Representatives approved the war resolution, and two days later, on April 6, 1917, the Senate also agreed. The United States had entered World War I.

APRIL 7

The *Alabama* Claims

On April 7, 1865, the United States and Great Britain began correspondence on the matter of damages arising from the Civil War. The Americans were the more aggrieved party, seeking compensation for the multimillion dollar losses inflicted on their commerce by English-built Confederate warships. Captain Raphael Semmes's *Alabama*, the most notorious of these raiders, captured 62 merchant vessels in two years before the Union cruiser *Kearsarge* sent it to the bottom of Cherbourg harbor in June 1864. The *Alabama*'s career was so remarkable that the whole controversy over war reparations was dubbed the *Alabama* Claims Dispute.

The United States charged that the British government had contravened its own foreign enlistment law of 1819, which prohibited British subjects from outfitting ships to engage in wars in which their country was neutral. The British only belatedly responded to the complaints of the American minister, Charles Francis Adams, thus allowing the *Alabama* to escape unmolested from its Liverpool shipyard. The Americans also charged that the British had not excercised adequate care to prevent other ships from operating out of their West Indian ports.

In their defense the British pointed to their seizures in 1863 of the raider *Alexandra* and of two ironclad "Laird rams," all of which had been intended for Confederate use. The British government was, however, willing to negotiate, and eventually the new American minister, Reverdy Johnson, and Prime Minister Gladstone's foreign secretary, Lord Clarendon, agreed to submit the question to an arbitrator. They concurred further that the arbitrator was to be selected by four commissioners, with two each to be chosen by the United States and Great Britain.

Unfortunately, however, the road to compromise was not to be that smooth. Prodded by the bellicose Charles Sumner, who thought that the cession of Canada to the United States would provide a more proper solution, the Sen-

ate rejected this Johnson-Clarendon Convention by a vote of 54 to 1.

Only when Sumner lost his position as chairman of the Foreign Relations Committee was President Grant's secretary of state, Hamilton Fish, able to obtain a settlement. In the resulting Treaty of Washington of 1871 the British government expressed regret and agreed to make remunerations, the amount of which a tribunal of arbitration would determine. The President of the United States, the queen of England, the king of Italy, the president of the Swiss Confederation, and the emperor of Brazil each appointed one member to this board, which met at Geneva, Switzerland, from December 1871 to September 1872. The tribunal awarded the United States $15.5 million in gold for losses caused by the raiders but rejected an American request for additional money to compensate for such "indirect" damages as the transfer of a number of ships to foreign registry.

This marked the first time that two major nations used an international arbitration commission to settle a dispute amicably. Congress on June 23, 1874, created a court of claims to which American business interests could submit proof of their losses and collect their proper share of the compensation. But many years were still to pass before all the cases were settled.

National Cherry Blossom Festival Washington, D.C.

This is a movable event. See note on page xxvi.

The National Cherry Blossom Festival, held annually in April or late March, had its origin with a friendly gesture of the city of Tokyo — the gift of 3,000 cherry trees to the city of Washington, D.C., in 1912. The first of the trees, which today surround Washington's graceful Tidal Basin, were planted by Helen Herron Taft, wife of President William Howard Taft, and Viscountess Chinda, wife of Yasuya Uchida, the Japanese ambassador to the United States.

The festival was discontinued during World War II. Several patriotic groups wished to have the trees destroyed as "alien," but equally determined conservationists were able to save the renamed "Oriental" cherry trees.

Today the trees, which can also be seen in Washington's East Potomac Park and at Kenwood, Maryland, are the focal point of a six-day festival emphasizing the friendship between the two countries, which attracts thousands of visitors annually. The dates of the festival are timed to coincide with the blossoming of the cherry trees, which usually takes place between March 20 and April 15 and lasts for about 10 or 12 days.

The dates, set a year in advance, are also scheduled so that festival events do not coincide with observances of Easter and Holy Week. The timing of the festival is thus related to that of the movable feast of Easter.

The first ceremony connected with the trees took place in 1927, when some Washington schoolchildren reenacted the original planting — a pageant repeated annually until 1934, when the District of Columbia government put on a more ambitious, three-day program including the crowning of the first Cherry Blossom Festival queen.

The Washington Convention and Visitors Bureau became sole sponsor of the postwar festival in 1948 and expanded the program to a week. Under the aegis of the Convention and Visitors Bureau, which continued as sponsor until 1973, the fame of the National Cherry Blossom Festival — and particularly the fame of the blossoms themselves — has grown. In 1974 the National Conference of State Societies took over as sponsor of the festival, with the Downtown Jaycees sponsoring a related parade.

The schedule for the festival in one typical year included, on Monday, an orientation program and tea at the Decatur House attended by the festival princesses. There were 50 princesses that year, representing 48 states, the District of Columbia, and the territory of Guam.

The second day, Tuesday, the princesses attended a breakfast at a department store, lunched at the National Zoo, and then made their initial public appearance at the official opening ceremony beside the Tidal Basin. American and Japanese dignitaries were on hand for this event, at which the previous year's queen and the daughter of the first minister of Japan followed festival tradition by lighting a 300-year-old Japanese stone lantern. The ceremony included music by the US Air Force Ceremonial Band, posting of the colors by the Color Guard of the District of Columbia National Guard, the playing of the national anthems of the United States and Japan, and the introduction of participating notables.

That evening there was a congressional reception in the Dirksen Senate Office Building. After the welcome by the president of the National Conference of State Societies, presentation of the colors by a joint armed forces color guard, and the reciting of the Pledge of Allegiance to the Flag, presentation of the princesses by members of their state Congressional delegations followed. Entertainment was provided by the Madrigal Singers of the Wilton (Connecticut) High School.

On Wednesday a beauty clinic was held for the princesses, who then participated in the festival's traditional fashion show and luncheon. Honorary chairman of the event was Mrs. Fumihiko Togo, wife of the Japanese ambassador. Each princess was presented by the president of her state society or a representative of that officer. The kind of Japanese touch that recurred intermittently throughout the festival was provided by the table decorations, which were examples of *origami*, the ancient Japanese art of paper folding. Featured was a particular kind of bird — the *orizuru*, or crane, symbolizing long life. Later in the day the princesses were invited to the White House to meet President and Mrs. Gerald R. Ford, and in the evening the princesses and their parents attended a theater party.

On Thursday, after witnessing the changing of the guard at Arlington National Cemetery's Tomb of the Unknowns and touring the National Gallery of Art, the princesses were luncheon guests at a Japanese restaurant in Bethesda, Maryland. That evening many of the state societies hosted receptions at which the individual princesses were officially crowned.

The next morning the ambassador from Japan hosted a reception for the princesses at the Embassy of Japan. Luncheon and a tour of the US Capitol followed — as did the past Cherry Blossom princesses' Pi Alpha Kappa Sorority dinner for the new princesses, and a rehearsal for the next evening's ball.

On Saturday afternoon the three-hour Cherry Blossom parade, sponsored by the Downtown Jaycees, drew an enthusiastic audience. The parade featured over 100 units, including bands, drill teams, floats, special marching units, and clowns. That evening, at the Cherry Blossom ball, the princesses, accompanied by escorts, were presented in the order of their states' admission to the Union. Each was preceded by a US Marine bearing the flag of the state she represented. The climax of the evening came when the District of Columbia's mayor spun the "wheel of states" to select the new queen from among the princesses. She was ceremoniously crowned by the Japanese ambassador.

APRIL 8

Juan Ponce de León
Claims Florida for Spain

Although the peninsula of Florida was sighted by earlier navigators (it was shown on the 1502 Cantino map of the New World), its first known European visitor was the Spanish adventurer and explorer Juan Ponce de León. On April 8, 1513, scarcely more than 20 years after Christopher Columbus's discovery of America, Ponce de León claimed Florida for Spain.

Juan Ponce de León, believed to be the first European (the Vikings possibly excepted) to touch the shores of what is now the United States, was born in San Servos, León, Spain, about 1460. After fighting against the Moors of Granada, he accompanied Columbus on the latter's second voyage to America, in 1493. From 1502 to 1504 he assisted in the conquest of Higuey, the eastern region of Hispaniola, and was appointed *adelantado*, or governor, of that province. On August 12, 1508, he found a rich port (*un puerto rico*) on the island of San Juan Bautista (later to be renamed Puerto Rico), which had been discovered by Columbus in November 1493. Engaged in exploring the island in 1508, Ponce de León became its temporary governor the following year. He and his companions established a colony at Caparra near what is now San Juan. Having apparently amassed a fortune in gold, land, and slaves, the explorer was ready for new adventures.

Ponce de León lived in an age in which adventurers were drawn to the Gulf of Mexico region in the hope of finding a passage to the Pacific or in quest of mythical wonders. One prevalent myth was the persistent legend told by the inhabitants of the Caribbean area about the Fountain of Youth, a spring whose health-restoring waters granted the mental and physical powers of youth to the aged. Peter Martyr, Ponce de León's contemporary and author of *The Decades of the New World or West India*, addressed to Pope Leo X, wrote one of the few contemporary literary accounts of it:

Among the islands on the North side of Hispaniola there is one about 325 leagues distant, as they say which have searched the same, in which there is a continual spring of running water, of such marvellous virtue, that the water thereof being drunk, perhaps with some diet, maketh older men young again. And I here must make protestation to your holiness not to think this to be said lightly or rashly, for they have so spread this rumor for a truth throughout all the court, that not only all the people, but also many of them whom wisdom or fortune hath divided from the common sort, think it to be true. But if you should ask my opinion herein, I will answer that I will not attribute so great power to nature, but God hath no less reserved this prerogative to himself. . . .

Ponce de León, having lived some time in the West Indies, undoubtedly knew of this tradition, although it is not known what his opinion of it may have been. In any event, the fabled spring did not figure prominently among the inducements that attracted him toward new adventure. The patent authorizing him to search for and conquer the unknown "Bimini Islands" north of Cuba — the supposed location of this spring — granted by Ferdinand V, the Spanish king, and signed on February 23, 1512, dealt with more prosaic matters: the crown's share in any gold deposits and the subjugation of the natives as slaves in the mines. Clear-cut in tone, it did not give the remotest impression of romance. Although many scholars have now completely dismissed the tale about a fabulous fountain as motivation for Ponce de León's voyage, it is nevertheless possible that the Spanish adventurer (then aged 53) was not averse to including this quest among other tantalizing goals.

In any case, he sailed from Puerto Rico with three vessels on March 3, 1513, on a northwestern course. After landing briefly at San Salvador in the Bahamas, he threaded his way through uncharted islands. On March 27 he probably sighted one of the Abaco Islands (the most northerly of the Bahamas) and soon afterwards an extensive unknown coastline. Having no grounds for suspecting that the land mass was anything more than just another island (he certainly never dreamed it was a peninsula jutting out from the immense North American continent), Ponce de León followed the coast northward. He probably sailed from near Palm Beach to a spot somewhere between what is now St. Augustine and the mouth of the St. Johns River. There, near the 30th Parallel, his expedition landed early in April and remained for a short time. On April 8, in the name of the Spanish king, Ponce de León took possession of the "island," which he named La Florida. The great Spanish historian Antonio de Herrera (1559–1625), who is thought to have had access to Ponce de León's original notes or logbook (now lost), wrote an account of the voyage. According to this, the area was named La Florida "because it had a very pretty view of many cool woodlands, and it was level and uniform: and because, moreover, they discovered it in the time of the Feast of Flowers (*Pascua Florida*)" — the season of Easter.

Determined to be the first to circumnavigate the large "island," Ponce de León continued northward; then, reversing his course, he traced the eastern coastline to its tip. He passed through the treacherous waters of the Florida Keys and sailed up the western coast of Florida, probably to the area around Charlotte Harbor and as far north as at least 27°30'. The inhabitants of La Florida — then consisting of four tribes, the Calusa, Tegesta, Timucua, and Apalachee, totaling about 10,000 — resisted conquest; there was no sign of gold, or of the rejuvenating waters of the Fountain of Youth; moreover, after seven weeks of sailing, Ponce de León still had not circumnavigated the "island." Disillusioned, he turned back on May 23 and arrived in Puerto Rico, empty-handed, on September 21. In tracing much of the coastline of Florida, however, he had contributed a noteworthy geographical service.

After helping to quell a revolt that had flared up in Puerto Rico during his absence, the discoverer of Florida returned to Spain in 1514. He seems to have given a highly favorable account of his exploits since, on September 27, he obtained a royal grant to colonize "the island of Bimini and the island of Florida," of which he was appointed civil and military governor. Other adventures — such as an expedition against the fiercely resisting Caribs who inhabited the lesser Antilles — as well as lack of finances, prevented Ponce de León from immediately embarking for Florida. Only in 1521 did he finally decide to take possession of the area under the authority of his patent. Gathering together two vessels and 200 men,

as a good colonist, he took mares and heifers and swine and sheep and goats, and all kinds of domestic animals useful in the service of mankind: and also for the cultivation and tillage of the field he was supplied with all [kinds of] seed, as if the business of colonization consisted of nothing more than to arrive, and cultivate the land and pasture his livestock.

Sailing from Puerto Rico on February 20, Ponce de León and his companions probably landed near Charlotte Harbor on the west coast of Florida. Indian resistance and the outbreak of disease demoralized the Spaniards and hindered the growth of their colony, which persisted for five months. Once its leader himself had been severely wounded in a skirmish with Indians, the entire Spanish expedition abandoned the venture and sailed to Havana. Juan Ponce de León — the "valiant Lion," according to his epitaph — died soon afterwards, in June 1521.

Expeditions by subsequent Spanish explorers, especially Pánfilo de Narváez and Hernando de Soto, established the fact that Florida was not an island and bolstered Spain's claim to an immense area covering much of the present southeastern United States. Alarmed at the encroachments of French adventurers in the early 1560s, King Philip II of Spain commissioned Pedro Menéndez de Avilés to drive out the French and firmly implant Spanish colonies in Florida. The founding of St. Augustine, the oldest city in the United States, in 1565, was therefore the first permanent result of the claim Juan Ponce de León had made more than a half century before.

The nature of the legend about the Fountain of Youth kept it alive during the credulous age of the 16th century, but it attracted little notice thereafter until modern writers, seeking a romantic theme, revived it and focused it around Ponce de León. Whether or not he actually searched for the fountain, St. Augustine commemorates the legend at the Fountain of Youth Memorial Park. The spacious, oak-shaded grounds are reputedly Ponce de León's first landing place and the spot where he and his men refilled their water casks. In developing the area as a commercial attraction and memorial to the Spanish explorer, St. Augustinians have housed the spring, misnamed the Fountain of Youth, in a mission-type building of Spanish design surrounded by a coquina wall. The luxuriant subtropical gardens contain a statue of Ponce de León, and a historical museum. An Indian burial ground, unearthed by Smithsonian Institution archeologists on the site of an ancient Indian village, is protected by a massive reproduction of a Timucuan communal house.

It was not until many centuries after Ponce de León's discovery of Florida that entrepreneurs became aware of the restorative value not of the Fountain of Youth, but of the balmy air and sunny climate of the state of Florida. At the end of the 19th century, the ornate Ponce de Léon Hotel was built in St. Augustine to attract the luxury tourist trade.

The short-lived colony founded by Ponce de León in Florida is commemorated by the Ponce de León Historical Park and Shrine on Charlotte Harbor, three-and-one-half miles west of Punta Gorda. The park's unspoiled natural setting features a nature trail and several sandy beaches, as well as historical markers telling the story of the explorer's activities in Florida.

APRIL 9

Appomattox Day

On April 9, 1865, in the quiet town of Appomattox Court House, Virginia, Lieutenant General Ulysses S. Grant of the Union army accepted the surrender of General Robert E. Lee of the Confederacy. Thus ended the American Civil War after four blood-stained years and the expenditure of more than 600,000 lives.

Time ran out for the Confederate States of America in the spring of 1865. General Grant was in Virginia, close to Richmond, the Confederate capital, and even closer to Petersburg, which supplied it, and which Grant had had under siege for nearly 10 months (see June 9). On March 25 Lee unsuccessfully tried to smash through the besieging Union forces at Petersburg's Fort Stedman. After his defeat convinced him that the capital could not be held much longer, Lee made contingency plans, in case of a forced withdrawal, to extricate his men and go south to North Carolina. There, he hoped, they could join forces with General Joseph E. Johnston's troops.

The Union army, at this juncture, had 115,000 men and the Confederate army 54,000. Grant used his numerical power to envelop the enemy. From March 30 to April 1 at Five Forks, detachments from the two armies fought for possession of the Southside Railroad, Lee's best hope for escape should Richmond and Petersburg fall. General Philip H. Sheridan's horsemen defeated Southern troops under General George E. Pickett and captured 5,200 of them.

Back at Petersburg, General Grant probed relentlessly at the Confederate lines. When Lee had to dispatch three brigades to cover the defeated Pickett's reorganization, the Union's VI Corps made a decisive breakthrough opposite Fort Fisher on April 2. The Confederates under General James Longstreet held Petersburg until nightfall, when the Southern troops evacuated that town and Richmond. General Godfrey Weitzel of the Union army entered the Confederate capital on April 3 and accepted its surrender.

From Petersburg, Richmond, and Bermuda Hundred the men of Lee's army headed for Amelia Court House, where they hoped to get desperately needed rations and take the Richmond and Danville Railroad south to join Johnston. Sheridan pursued the Confederates south of the Appomattox River, where one of General George A. Custer's Union cavalry brigades defeated an element of General Fitzhugh Lee's horse troops at Namozine Church on April 3. The rest of Robert E. Lee's men retreated north of the James River.

When the Confederates converged at Amelia Court House, they found no food and learned that Sheridan had reached Jetersville, thus cutting off the Richmond and Danville Railroad escape route. Lee had no choice but to lead his men to the west. On April 5 Sheridan sent General Henry E. Davies's cavalry brigade northwest from Jetersville to search for the enemy. At nearby Paineville, the First Pennsylvania Cavalry fell upon the Southerners' wagon train and burned 200 vehicles. The next day the Union forces destroyed the rear guard of General Richard S. Ewells at Sayler's Creek. On April 6 the Southerners sustained between 7,000 and 8,000 casualties.

The remnants of the Confederate army reached Farmville on April 7. They received rations at last and were able to repulse Union at-

tacks. Lee renewed the withdrawal that night. On the morning of April 8, Custer found another Confederate supply train at Appomattox Station and captured it along with 30 artillery pieces. He then proceeded a few miles northeast and discovered the Southern line of defense drawn up southwest of Appomattox Court House.

Hungry and exhausted, Lee's men could run no farther. The Southern commander knew that April 9 would be decisive. At 5:00 A.M. he sent Fitzhugh Lee's cavalry against the hastily constructed earthworks along the Bent Creek Road. The Confederates were momentarily successful, but the Union infantry soon enveloped their position. When the II and VI Corps attacked Longstreet's rear guard, Lee knew the end had come. His opponent had written to him on April 7, inviting him to surrender, and now the Virginian said to his aides: "There is nothing left for me to do but to go and see General Grant, and I would rather die a thousand deaths."

General Lee put on a fresh dress uniform and rode to the farmhouse of Wilbur McLean in Appomattox Court House. At 1:30 P.M. General Grant arrived in his mud-spattered fatigues. The two men tried to ease the tension by conversing about the Mexican War, during which they had briefly met as comrades. They then quickly came to terms that were quite conciliatory. The Confederate officers and men were released upon giving their paroles not to take up arms against the United States again. Arms, artillery, and public property were surrendered. Officers were allowed to keep their side arms and horses. When Lee pointed out that some of his enlisted men also had their own horses and mules, Grant allowed those to be retained as well.

Joseph E. Johnston's army was still in the field, but he surrendered to General William T. Sherman at Durham Station, North Carolina, on April 18. President Andrew Johnson, who succeeded the assassinated Abraham Lincoln, rejected the originally proffered terms, which included concessions of a political nature, and so Sherman obtained a simple military surrender on April 26. The area where the agreement was made is now the Bennett Place State Historic Site, a 30-acre park in Durham dedicated in the 1920s.

Today the Appomattox Court House National Historical Park encompasses the grounds where the last scenes of the Civil War took place. Visitors can see the Confederate cemetery and the sites of the headquarters of the opposing generals. Woodson's Law Office and Meek's house and store contain furnishings from the period. The McLean House, where the surrender was signed, was dismantled in 1892 and reconstructed in 1949. One of every 13 bricks in the present building is from the original. Surrender Triangle, located along Stage Road, marks the spot where the defeated Confederates stacked their arms.

Thousands of people attended Civil War Centennial celebrations in 1965 at the park. Major General Ulysses S. Grant III, grandson of the Union leader, and Robert E. Lee IV, great-grandson of the Confederate leader, participated in the ceremonies. Additional thousands, including Vice President Hubert Humphrey, flocked to North Carolina's Bennett Place Historic Site for day-long ceremonies commemorating the surrender there. Indeed, the centennial marking the conclusion of the war between North and South was a yearlong affair with countless special observances, frequently timed to coincide with the anniversaries of specific events, in countless localities across the United States, particularly throughout the South. Martial music was often heard; eloquence abounded; Confederate and Union uniforms were seen; pageants recreating important events were staged; and books, magazine articles, and newspaper stories reflected the intensity of continuing public interest in the nation's most heartbreaking war. The Civil War Centennial stamp, which was issued in honor of the 100th anniversary of national peace, bore the name Appomattox, with President Lincoln's famous words, "With malice toward none. . . ."

La Salle Reaches Mouth of the Mississippi

Many explorers during the 16th and 17th centuries directed their efforts toward finding a water route leading west across the continent of North America to the Orient. The quests for a passage to the treasures of the East were futile. But the early adventurers in the interior regions of what is now the United States did come upon a mighty north-south waterway. Early in 1682 René Robert Cavelier, Sieur de La Salle, led the first party of Europeans to navigate the Mississippi from its juncture with the Illinois River to the Gulf of Mexico. On April 9, 1682, the expedition reached the river's mouth, and on that day La Salle claimed the vast territory lying on either side of the "Father of Waters," as well as on the borders of all its tributaries, for France.

La Salle was born in 1643 in Rouen, France. The son of a wealthy burgher, young La Salle received an excellent education. He attended the Jesuit college in his native city, and then at the urging of his father entered the Society of Jesus.

The regimented life of the Jesuits held little appeal for La Salle, and shortly after his father's death in 1665 he left the order. The following year, at the age of 23, he went to Montreal, where Jean Cavelier, his elder brother and a member of the Sulpician order, had emigrated. The Sulpicians held the seigneury of Montreal, and they assisted La Salle by granting him land along the St. Lawrence River.

For two years, La Salle worked to develop his lands. But during that time, stories of the West so attracted him that in 1669 he abandoned his agricultural efforts. In July of that year he set out from Montreal with a group of Sulpicians who intended to start missions in the West. Traveling up the St. Lawrence River to Lake Ontario, the party made its way west along the lake's southern shore. At a village on the far side of the lake, the expedition encountered the great French explorer Louis Joliet, who persuaded the missionaries to push on to the Northwest. La Salle, however, decided to continue on his own to explore the region south of Lakes Erie and Ontario.

The exact location of La Salle's adventures between 1669 and 1673 is unknown. He later claimed to have discovered the Ohio River and to have descended that waterway as far as the site of Louisville, Kentucky, during this period. But modern historians have rejected these assertions.

La Salle's explorations made him a favorite of the Comte de Frontenac, the governor of New France, who shared his interest in the interior of the American continent. Shortly after becoming governor in 1672, Frontenac subdued the Iroquois and built a fortification on the northern shore of Lake Ontario (today the site of Kingston, Ontario), which he named after himself. Frontenac wanted official sanction for the fort, which he had erected on his own initiative, and a monopoly of the fur trade in the region. To accomplish these ends, the governor sent La Salle to France in 1674 to plead his case before the court. La Salle's mission was successful. The explorer gained Fort Frontenac as a seigneury and exclusive rights to trade in the area.

After his return to America in 1674, La Salle used Fort Frontenac as a base of operations for his fur-trading ventures and probably for expeditions through the region of the upper Great Lakes. He went back to France in 1677 to seek additional favors from the king, and again he succeeded. He gained a title of nobility and permission to explore the West and trade in all furs excepting beaver.

The Jesuit priest Jacques Marquette and the explorer Louis Joliet came upon the Mississippi River and navigated its waters as far south as its junction with the Arkansas River in 1673 (see June 1, Père Marquette's Birthday). But they had little interest in the waterway since it flowed in a north-south direction, rather than westward across the continent. La Salle, however, realized the importance of the river, and he determined to claim the bordering lands for France. La Salle harbored great animosity toward the Jesuits — perhaps dating from his earlier association with them. Fearing they might gain control of the Mississippi valley, he also strongly desired to set up a government for the area that would have no connection with the powerful order.

La Salle embarked on his first attempt to go down the Mississippi in 1679. On his journey to the river he paused at Detroit, and then at Green Bay, Wisconsin, to collect pelts gathered by an advance party. These furs he ordered loaded aboard the *Griffon*, the boat he had had specially built to carry the skins back to Montreal. The *Griffon* mysteriously disappeared during its return trip, but La Salle, who had no knowledge of its fate, proceeded with his expedition.

Traveling by canoe, La Salle and his companions went along the west shore of Lake Michigan from Green Bay to the mouth of the St. Joseph River, in Michigan. There the party met and joined with La Salle's chief lieutenant, Henri de Tonti, and the men under his command. The 34-member expedition then went up the St. Joseph, crossed overland to the Kankakee, and descended that river to the Illinois. Continuing their journey westward, they went down the Illinois and in January 1680 they reached Lake Peoria, where they built Fort Crèvecoeur.

Late in February 1680 La Salle sent the Recollect friar Louis Hennepin, together with Michel Accault (or Accou) and Antoine Auguella, to investigate the area of the upper Mississippi. Captured by Sioux in April 1680, the three men were taken as prisoners to the region of Minnesota. The Sioux allowed their captives considerable freedom. Hennepin and his companions acquired knowledge of Minnesota and discovered the Falls of St. Anthony, at the site of Minneapolis, before another renowned French explorer, Daniel Greysolon, Sieur Duluth, effected their rescue in the summer of 1680.

Meanwhile, La Salle and four others returned to Fort Frontenac to settle outstanding debts and to obtain additional supplies. Starting early in the spring, they took 65 days to reach their destination. Business affairs detained La Salle at Frontenac for several months, and not until late autumn did he and his companions return to Fort Crèvecoeur.

While he was away, La Salle put Tonti in charge of Fort Crèvecoeur, and he had such confidence in his lieutenant that he expected upon his return to be able to continue his expedition to the Mississippi. This was not to be, however. During his absence, La Salle sent a messenger instructing Tonti to occupy a natural

fortification, now known as Starved Rock, which he had noticed en route up the Illinois River, against Indians. Tonti went north to this site, but later was forced to vacate it in the face of an imminent Iroquois attack. With Tonti occupied by this errand and La Salle at Frontenac, most of the adventurers with the expedition deserted from Fort Crèvecoeur; and an impending attack by the Iroquois caused the missionaries at Crèvecoeur to flee also.

As La Salle was making his way back to Crèvecoeur, he received word that the fort had been abandoned. Deeply concerned about the safety of Tonti, he journeyed as far as the Mississippi to search for him. La Salle finally returned east to Frontenac without finding any trace of his lieutenant. But Tonti, who had been captured, managed to gain his freedom, and in June 1681 he and La Salle were reunited at Mackinac.

Undaunted by the failure of his first venture to the Mississippi, La Salle again set out early in 1682, accompanied by Tonti and more than 50 Frenchmen and Indians. Traveling by way of the portage at Chicago that had been discovered by Marquette and Joliet in 1673, the party reached the Mississippi on February 6, 1682. La Salle's expedition proceeded down the mighty river without difficulty, passing the site of New Orleans on April 6, 1682, and three days later arriving at the Gulf of Mexico. There La Salle unfurled the white Bourbon banner and claimed the lands watered by the Mississippi and all its tributaries "in the name of the most high, mighty, invincible and victorious Louis the Great, by Grace of God King of France."

To hold the area he had claimed, La Salle planned to establish forts and colonies in the Illinois region and at the mouth of the Mississippi. In December 1682 he started work on Fort St. Louis along the Illinois River. He sent two men to the site of Chicago to build another outpost at the important portage there, which provided a connecting link between the Great Lakes and the Mississippi. But just as La Salle seemed about to cement his vast empire, Joseph Antoine Lefebvres, Sieur de La Barre, replaced Frontenac as governor of New France.

Unlike his predecessor, La Barre did not favor La Salle; indeed, the new governor was closely allied with the Jesuits and was easily influenced by the explorer's rivals, who wanted to end his trade monopoly in the Mississippi region. Thus, shortly after becoming governor, La Barre took drastic measures against La Salle. He ordered the explorer to surrender command of his fort on the Illinois River and recalled him to Quebec to question him regarding alleged misdemeanors.

Realizing the difficulty of obtaining fair treatment from La Barre, La Salle decided to take his case to the French monarch. Louis XIV had originally believed the explorer's expedition along the Mississippi to be "wholly useless." But by the time La Salle arrived in France, that nation was at war with Spain, and the king recognized the strategic value of holding the Mississippi against an enemy that was also interested in the area.

After naming La Salle governor of Louisiana and restoring to him all of his former commands and privileges, Louis equipped the explorer with four ships so that he might establish a colony at the mouth of the Mississippi. The expedition left France in July 1684, but the mission was ill fated. The Spanish captured the main supply vessel; and La Salle became ill in the West Indies, where the expedition became disorganized during his long recuperation. When he continued on his way with less than half his original company, his ships overshot the mouth of the Mississippi, landing instead at Matagorda Bay in Texas, where La Salle was disappointed in his initial hope that the bay would turn out to be the great river's western outlet.

The party built a fort near the Garcitas River and subsisted on the buffalo that inhabited the region. But the situation of La Salle and his men became desperate. Repeated attempts to find a land route to the Mississippi were unsuccessful. Two of their remaining three ships meanwhile had been wrecked and the third had returned to France.

Finally, La Salle and some others in the party made an effort in 1686 to find their way to Canada to seek help. They again set off in search of the Mississippi, which they knew could lead them there. Their search, however, was again unsuccessful.

In January 1687 La Salle and about half of the 45 remaining members of the expedition once again went forth to try to obtain assistance. But they were no more successful this time in finding the long-sought Mississippi. La Salle himself was not to survive the accumulated frustrations of his expedition. After traveling overland for several months, his men mutinied on March 18, 1687, near what is now Navasota, Texas. They killed La Salle and left the body of the man who had gained such a vast territory for France to be devoured by animals.

APRIL 10

Salvation Army Founder's Day

When the Salvation Army celebrates Founder's Day, it marks the birthday of William Booth, the remarkable Englishman who began the or-

ganization, which has gained international respect for its good works over the past 100 and more years.

William Booth was born on April 10, 1829, in Nottingham, England. His father, not very successful in his own trade as a builder, wanted a secure and financially rewarding future for his son and therefore apprenticed him to a pawnbroker to learn what was a lucrative profession in 19th century England. Behind the pawnbroker's counter, young William Booth was barraged by situations of human misery and economic suffering; it was an experience that made a lifelong impression on him and influenced his whole life's work. Another factor, equally important, helped mold the man and his career. When he was about 15, Booth experienced religious conversion in a Wesleyan Methodist chapel. He felt particularly drawn to preaching, and while he was a pawnbroker's apprentice he served locally as a Methodist lay preacher.

At age 19, his apprenticeship over, he sought work in the pawnshops of Nottingham. Failing to find a position, he finally moved in 1849 to London, where he found employment with a pawnbroker in Walworth. There, too, he dedicated his hours after work to preaching. However, he wanted to be involved in more evangelical work than was possible in his duties as an official lay preacher, and so he began holding open-air meetings, a move that did not sit well with his local minister. Booth subsequently joined the Methodist New Connexion, the first group to secede from the Wesleyan Methodist Church, and after completing studies he was ordained as a minister in 1858.

Catherine Mumford (1829–1890) had been one of the group that left the original Methodism, and she and Booth were married in 1855. Catherine Mumford Booth was as remarkable as her husband. Brought up by religious parents — her father was a carriage builder by trade and a sometime Methodist lay preacher — she was schooled in the theology of the day. Because of poor health in adolescence, she received most of her education at home. The invalid youngster grew into a strong-minded woman, an untiring social worker who spent her time and energies for and among the poor, and she championed social causes ranging from women's rights to a campaign that led to passage of the Criminal Law Amendment Act. Her belief that women had the right to preach the Gospel was outlined in the cogent pamphlet *Female Ministry* (1859), and she set an example by beginning to preach in her husband's church at Gateshead, in the north of England, in 1860. Her talent for oratory, combined with her religious convictions and her dedication to social causes, later made her a well-known speaker at meeting halls in London's West End. It was because of her urging and support that William Booth gave up his secure life as a Methodist minister to embark in 1861 on a career of itinerant evangelism, which he felt was his true vocation.

After four years of traveling and preaching throughout England, Booth — whose plan for taking the Gospel message to city slum dwellers was too radical for his church to accept — severed all connections with formal religion. He became an independent evangelist and settled with his family in London in 1865. Invited to speak at open-air and tent meetings in London's East End, a slum district notorious for its crime rate, human degradation, and misery, Booth made his first appearance there on July 2, 1865. (The Salvation Army consequently regards that day as its founding date.) Before long, Booth was regularly leading these outdoor meetings in the East End and getting a tremendous response. His religious zeal and genius for organization instilled in the people he reached the desire to reach out and help others in turn. His movement, first called the East London Revival Society, soon became known as the Christian Mission. In 1878, it was renamed the Salvation Army and carefully organized with military ranks, uniforms, flags, bands, and books of orders and regulations, with Booth as its first commander.

It was Booth's initial intention simply to bring the Gospel to the millions of people who had never attended any church. Most of all, he wanted to reach those people who, he thought, might not be welcomed by "respectable" church congregations. Soon, however, he realized that his preaching could not be optimally effective while people lacked the basic essentials of food, shelter, and warm clothing. He felt it was necessary to save not only souls, but minds and bodies too. Therefore the work was expanded from street preaching to the organization of social reforms and the establishment of food and shelter depots, children's homes, and agencies for helping discharged criminals. Soon people began to refer to members of Booth's Army as the purveyors of "soup, soap and salvation." Booth really did reach for "lost souls." Before he was scheduled to speak at a rally, he would send out word to the far reaches of the slum areas, "Come, drunk or sober." And recipients of the message did come, drunk or sober.

Booth's organization by then had become, in his own words, a "volunteer army of converted working people." He himself is said to have crossed out the word "volunteer" in this descriptive phrase and substituted the word "Salvation" — giving the organization its present name. Converts-become-helpers donned the Army's uniforms and groups would go to street corners, as they still do, and there play drums, cornets, and tambourines to attract audiences. As crowds gathered, the Salvationists would preach the Gospel and offer hope to the people in the audiences.

For many years, the Salvation Army was greeted with a great deal of hostility, which came from the more conventional forms of organized religion, and also from established society and government. Some of the opposition even came from the poor whom Booth was trying to help. The Army's street preachers, who were kicked, beaten, and showered with eggs, became unintentionally the cause of riots. The very Salvationists who bore the brunt of these attacks sometimes were placed in jail for disturbing the peace. Not only did the attackers assault the Salvationists; they also wrecked the properties in which the Salvation Army carried on its spiritual and social work on a neighborhood basis.

Despite all obstacles, however, the organization persevered and finally prevailed. Its numbers grew vastly, as did the variety of work in which members engaged, endeavoring to meet human need in any form.

Soon the Salvation Army was carried to many nations. In 1880 George Scott Railton and seven women were sent from England to organize the Salvation Army in the United States. Their efforts were received by Americans very much as the efforts of William Booth had first been received in London. But in the course of time the value of their work was appreciated, and Railton and his successors received valuable support from persons interested in helping the unfortunate and destitute. In addition the Salvation Army established outposts in 18 other countries around the world during the 1880s.

In 1890 Booth, in collaboration with W. T. Stead, published his most influential book, *In Darkest England and the Way Out,* in which he explained his efforts and gave concrete proposals for relieving poverty and loneliness, dealing with vice and moral danger, and salvaging wasted lives. In explaining the endeavors of the Salvation Army, the book made the organization's obvious good work less suspect in the eyes of those who had been hostile. Slowly Booth was given recognition — by the city of London, which made him a freeman; by Oxford University, which conferred an honorary doctorate upon him; and by the British government, which invited him to the coronation of King Edward VII in 1902. That same year, Booth accepted an invitation to open a session of the US Senate with a prayer.

Catherine Mumford Booth lived to see only

some of the honors and recognition conferred upon her husband and the organization that she had so effectively helped to build. She was "promoted to glory," in the Salvationists' phrase, in 1890 in Clacton, England. The Booths' eight children also had played roles in building the Salvation Army. After their mother's death, however, two sons and a daughter left the Army because of disagreements and dissension. (One of these was Ballington Booth, who later formed the Volunteers of America, an organization in some respects similar to the one he had left.)

The Salvation Army's Evangeline residences for businesswomen are named for Evangeline Booth, the founders' seventh child, who spent her life working for the Salvation Army. She began evangelistic preaching when she was 17; worked as a field commissioner in London for five years; became commander of the Canadian Salvation Army in 1895; came to the United States in 1904, where she served as commander for 30 years; and became the first woman elected a general of the International Salvation Army. She died in Hartsdale, New York, in 1950.

William Booth himself, in spite of increasing loss of sight and ultimate blindness, continued his evangelical and humanitarian works until he was past 80. He made his last public appearance in London's Royal Albert Hall on his 83rd birthday. Four months later, on August 20, 1912, he died in London. The work he started was continuing in the mid-1970s in more than 80 countries of the world, under the guidance of approximately 16,800 officers, in more than 16,000 corps and outposts. Using over 140 languages, the Army administers almost 4,000 social institutions and services.

Although he lived in the Victorian age, when such issues were avoided, William Booth did not shrink from discussion of poverty, prostitution, illegitimacy, homelessness, hunger, alcoholism, drug addiction, and crime — or from confronting these problems. He dealt with them by providing homes, training schools, soup kitchens, hospitals, and other needed services. Counseling, help in adjustment for released prisoners, work rehabilitation programs, a missing persons bureau, camps, residences, family service agencies, rehabilitation programs for alcoholics and drug addicts, day-care centers, and publications are some of the services that the Salvation Army now provides. The Army also works in times of disaster — wars, earthquakes, floods, and fires — when it provides food, shelter, clothing, and comfort to victims.

In 1965 the Salvation Army celebrated its centennial with observances in all parts of the world. In the United States there were special events throughout the year in keeping with the Army's centennial theme of A Century of Service to God and Man. The observance included a yearlong evangelistic crusade, "Christ for the world." In addition, open houses at Salvation Army institutions, special commemorative religious services, and other anniversary events were scheduled to mark the actual July 2 anniversary of the organization's founding. Salvationists from around the world participated in a centennial congress at the Royal Albert Hall in London, held from June 24 through July 2.

The Salvation Army maintains flexibility in order to meet contemporary problems. The organization notes, however, that its goals never change. Those goals are summed up in the inscription on the cornerstone of the Salvation Army's US national headquarters at 120 West 14th Street in New York City: "This building is erected to the glory of God and the welfare of mankind."

APRIL 11

Civil Rights Act of 1968

On April 11, 1968, President Lyndon B. Johnson signed the Civil Rights Act of 1968 into law. The legislation made it a federal crime to engage in such activities as harming civil rights workers, crossing state borders to incite riot, and manufacturing, selling, or demonstrating firearms and certain kinds of explosives for use in riots. In addition, it extended broad rights to Native Americans in their dealings with the courts, with their tribal governments, and with authorities on the local, state, and federal levels. But perhaps the most important part of the act banned racial discrimination in the sale and rental of approximately 80 percent of the homes and apartments of the United States.

Before 1968, a number of states passed "open housing laws," barring racial discrimination in the selling and renting of real estate. Many observers believed these statutes were important steps toward eventually ending the racial polarization of American society and urged Congress to adopt similar federal legislation against segregated housing. As early as 1966 President Johnson proposed an open housing bill to Congress, but despite strong support from some members, the majority were reluctant to approve such a measure.

In both 1966 and 1967 Congress refused to pass an open housing bill, and opponents of the legislation were hopeful of again defeating a fair housing statute in 1968. Then, early in April 1968, the civil rights leader Dr. Martin Luther King Jr. was killed by an assassin's bullet (see

April 4). King's murder outraged the nation and precipitated riots in the black ghettos of cities across the country.

A few weeks before King's death, the National Advisory Commission on Civil Disorders, which President Johnson had established after the Detroit and Newark riots of 1967, made public its findings. In its report the commission warned of the prevalence of white racism and noted that "our nation is moving toward two societies, one black, one white — separate and unequal." The wave of violence that swept the nation in April 1968 dramatized the commission's grimly prophetic findings. The combined circumstances of King's death, the riots that followed, and the commission's call for "common opportunities for all within a single society" helped spur Congress to act affirmatively on the Civil Rights Act of 1968.

By April 10, 1968, both the Senate and the House of Representatives had approved the Civil Rights Bill of 1968, and on April 11, 1968 — exactly one week after the assassination of King — President Johnson signed it into law. Recalling the long and arduous battle to gain enactment of the bill, Johnson said:

We did not get it in 1966. We pleaded for it again in 1967, but the Congress took no action that year. We asked for it again this year, and now at long last this afternoon its day has come.

I do not exaggerate when I say that the proudest moments of my Presidency have been times such as this when I have signed into law the promises of a century.

As President Johnson stated after signing the new legislation, "In the Civil Rights Act of 1968 America does move forward and the bell of freedom rings out a little louder." Somewhat limited in its effectiveness in the years since its passage, the 1968 act was but one step in the ongoing quest for equality of opportunity.

Charles Evans Hughes's Birthday

Charles Evans Hughes, the 11th chief justice of the United States, was born in Glens Falls, New York, on April 11, 1862. The only son of Mary Catherine Connelly Hughes and the Reverend David Charles Hughes, a Baptist preacher who had emigrated from Wales in 1855, he was a precocious youth. He completed high school at the age of 13, and after a year of independent study he enrolled at Madison (now Colgate) University. Young Hughes remained at the school for two years, but when his father accepted the pastorate of a Baptist church in Providence, Rhode Island, in 1878, he transferred to Brown University so that he might continue to live near his parents. His academic record at Brown was outstanding: he was elected to Phi Beta Kappa and graduated third in his class in 1881.

After teaching for a year in Delhi, New York, Hughes entered Columbia University Law School. Again he excelled in his studies; at his graduation in 1884 he received his LL.B. degree with highest honors and was presented with a three-year fellowship. That same year he was also admitted to the bar and began practicing law with the distinguished New York City firm of Chamberlain, Carter and Hornblower.

By 1891 Hughes's relentless attention to his work had severely impaired his health. To regain his strength, he temporarily gave up private practice and accepted a teaching position at the Cornell University Law School in Ithaca, New York. In 1893 he returned to New York City, where he became associated with the firm of Carter, Hughes, and Dwight and at the same time served as a special lecturer at both the Cornell University Law School and the New York Law School.

Hughes's public career began in 1905. He first served as counsel to a New York state legislative commission investigating gas costs, and he then directed a probe into the practices of the state's insurance companies. His efforts in both investigations met with great success. His disclosures drastically curtailed the corrupt practices of the state's utility companies, and he won nationwide recognition for changing New York's insurance business "from a public swindle into a public trust."

Running on the Republican ticket in 1906, Hughes defeated his Democratic rival, the publisher William Randolph Hearst, to win election as governor of New York. His two terms in this office—he was reelected in 1908—were notable for several major reforms. New York became one of the first states in the nation to establish a Public Service Commission to regulate utility rates, and in addition the governor secured legislative approval for labor and welfare bills, changes in the operation of the state government, and laws designed to reduce illegal racetrack gambling.

In 1910 President William Howard Taft named Hughes associate justice of the US Supreme Court. Hughes's appointment occurred just as the Court began to hear cases testing the constitutionality of new so-called Progressive legislation. It was a critical period in the history of American reform: if the Court upheld the Progressives' laws, it would open the way to more extensive federal and state involvement in matters such as regulation of industry and railroads, limitation of working hours, and prohibition of child labor. If the Court found this legislation unconstitutional, the reform movement would be severely set back. Hughes well understood the significance of these cases, and the majority of his opinions during his six-year tenure reflected his support for most of the Progressive reform efforts.

In 1916 Hughes resigned from the Court to accept the Republican nomination for President. During the months before the election he toured the country, making countless speeches in order to defeat his Democratic rival, the incumbent President Woodrow Wilson. Wilson, however, already had widespread support because of his domestic policies and efforts to maintain American neutrality in World War I. Wilson won the election, and Hughes left public life to resume his private law practice.

He returned to government service in 1921, when Republican President Warren G. Harding selected him to be secretary of state. As the head of the State Department, Hughes negotiated a separate peace with Germany after the Senate rejected the Treaty of Versailles; even more important, he did his utmost to insure US participation in world affairs in spite of the country's policy of isolationism after World War I. In the latter area, Hughes enjoyed limited success: he won worldwide acceptance for his scheme of naval arms limitations; he was largely responsible for the adoption of several treaties designed to stabilize the politics of the Far East; he assisted several Latin American countries in settling their boundary disputes; and he gained approval for the Dawes Plan to reduce German reparations payments and thereby restore the European economy. However, despite his repeated efforts, the Senate refused to approve US membership in the League of Nations.

In 1925 Hughes resigned as secretary of state in order to devote himself to private legal practice. The firm of Hughes, Rounds, Schurman and Dwight represented some of the largest corporations in the country, and at times Hughes's efforts on their behalf seemed contrary to the public interest — a fact that would shortly cause him considerable difficulty. Less controversial were his efforts in the cause of international cooperation. Between 1926 and 1930 he served at various times as a member of the Permanent Court of Arbitration at the Hague, as chairman of the US delegation to the Pan American Conference, and as a judge of the Permanent Court of International Justice.

The nomination of Hughes as chief justice of the United States in 1930 by President Herbert Hoover elicited an adverse reaction from the liberals in the Senate. During the 1920s the conservative members of the Supreme Court had declared unconstitutional many laws designed to effect social and economic change. Hughes's activities as a corporation lawyer made him a perfect symbol of all the liberals found objectionable in the Court. They agreed with Senator George Norris of Nebraska when he said of Hughes, "No man in public life so exemplified the influence of powerful combinations in the financial and political world"; and they worked hard to block his nomination. The Senate's heated debate over Hughes lasted four days, but on February 14, 1930, he was confirmed as chief justice by a vote of 52 to 26.

During the 1930s, cases testing the constitutionality of the highly controversial and innovative New Deal measures came before the Court. Since the four conservative justices—George Sutherland, Willis Van Devanter, James McReynolds, and Pierce Butler — consistently rejected this legislation and the liberal coalition of Louis Brandeis, Benjamin Cardozo, and Harlan Stone as frequently upheld it, the votes of the unaligned Hughes and his colleague Owen Roberts were critical in determining the fate of many New Deal laws. Hughes agreed with the majority of the Court when it struck down the National Recovery Administration and the Agricultural Adjustment Act in 1935 and 1936, and his votes helped sustain such other important legislation as the Tennessee Valley Authority, the Wagner Act, and social security laws.

Hughes served as chief justice until 1941, when he wrote to President Franklin D. Roosevelt that "considerations of age and health make it necessary that I be relieved of the duties which I have been discharging with increasing difficulty." He died in Osterville, on Cape Cod, Massachusetts, at the age of 86, on August 27, 1948.

APRIL 12

The Civil War Begins

The sectional conflict that led to the firing on Fort Sumter on April 12, 1861, had a long history. The institution of slavery had plagued the United States from the nation's earliest existence. At the time of the American Revolution, critics of the patriots' opposition to Great Britain asked how the colonists could decry tyranny while holding half a million persons in bondage. Some Southerners, indeed, withheld support of the Declaration of Independence until Thomas Jefferson agreed to delete from it his denunciation of slavery. At the Constitutional Convention in 1787, the Founding Fathers spent days arguing about slavery, the slave trade, and the effect of the presence of a host of unfree blacks in the

South on proposals concerning taxation and representation.

In the first half of the 19th century, the North grew rapidly and began to industrialize. To preserve its relative economic strength and an equal political voice at least in the Senate, the South advocated the expansion of slavery into the western territories, a movement that was anathema to the North. Major political battles ensued as Northerners became increasingly angered by the expansionist appetite of the "slavocracy" and Southerners developed an intense fear of the national government as a threat to their slave society.

Only grudging accommodations prevented even greater troubles. The Compromise of 1820 admitted Missouri to the Union as a slave state in return for the entrance of Maine as a free state, thus preserving the South's equal voice in the Senate. More important, the Missouri Compromise forbade the extension of slavery into the Louisiana Territory above 36°30' north latitude.

Many Americans condemned the War with Mexico from 1846 to 1848 (see May 13) as an attempt by supporters of the South to extend the area available for slavery. Twice during the conflict David Wilmot, a Pennsylvania Democrat, won strong Northern support by proposing a ban on the introduction of slavery into any territory taken from Mexico, but Congress rejected this Wilmot Proviso. The Compromise of 1850 partially calmed the North by establishing California as a free state and by ending the slave trade in the nation's capital of Washington, D.C.; on the other hand, the South received a strong law requiring the return of fugitive slaves.

After 1850, hopes of compromise faded as slavery became a moral issue beyond political solution. *Uncle Tom's Cabin* by Harriet Beecher Stowe (see June 14) appeared in book form in 1852 and filled many Northerners with repulsion for the treatment of human beings as mere chattels. The decision of the US Supreme Court in the *Dred Scott* case of 1857 — that the Missouri Compromise's 36°30' doctrine represented an unconstitutional limitation on the property rights of slave owners — alienated even more residents of the free states.

Southerners also found the situation intolerable. Denounced as immoral, they countered with a description of slavery as a positive good, "civilizing" the slave. Angered by the cries of abolitionists for an end to slavery in the South, slaveholders saw little reason why they should not have opportunity to extend the institution to the western territories.

Political parties, the vehicles of compromise, found themselves unable to overcome the new spirit of discord. Reflecting the inflexibility of their constituents, the Democratic party broke into factions, and the Whigs totally disbanded. Gradually dissidents from all camps formed the Republican party (see July 6), based on opposition to the extension of slavery. Both Republicans and Democrats recognized that the 1860 election would be crucial.

Senator Stephen A. Douglas of Illinois, the leading contender for the Democratic nomination, advocated that the residents of the territories, prior to admission to the Union, have the power to accept or outlaw slavery within their own areas. Antislavery Northerners distrusted Douglas because he had formulated the Kansas-Nebraska Act of 1854 (see January 29, Kansas Day), which applied this policy of "popular sovereignty" to two territories above 36°30' north latitude. Southerners disliked Douglas because he argued that people could keep slave owners out of their territories by simply not passing the police regulations necessary to maintain the system.

Douglas remained the strongest candidate when the Democratic convention opened in Charleston, South Carolina, on April 23, 1860, but he did not have enough strength to control the gathering. When a majority of the delegates accepted popular sovereignty as part of the platform, the representatives of eight Southern states walked out, thus making it impossible for Douglas to garner the two-thirds vote necessary for nomination. The Democrats adjourned and reconvened in Baltimore on June 8, but the Southerners again bolted rather than accept Douglas. The remaining delegates thereupon nominated Douglas.

Dissident Southern Democrats held their own convention in Baltimore on June 28 and drew up a platform demanding that their section enjoy an equal opportunity to take part in the settlement of the territories. They then nominated John C. Breckenridge of Kentucky for President, thus placing a third candidate in the field. In May the newly formed Constitutional Union party, a coalition of conservatives from several defunct political organizations, meanwhile had met in Baltimore and chosen John Bell of Tennessee to run on a platform denouncing sectionalism and encouraging support of the Constitution.

The Republicans had convened in Chicago on May 16, jubilant over the chaotic state of the Democrats. Unwilling to forfeit their advantageous position, the Republicans turned away from their foremost contenders, William H. Seward of New York and Salmon P. Chase of Ohio, both of whom were noted for their radical opposition to slavery. Instead, they nominated Abraham Lincoln of Illinois, Douglas's unsuccessful opponent in the 1858 senatorial election and a foe of the extension of slavery into the territories.

Lincoln received 1,866,452 votes in the November 6 election, only a plurality of those cast, but he won the necessary majority in the electoral college with 180 votes, not one of which came from a slave state. Douglas obtained 1,375,157 votes, but his strength was so dispersed that he garnered only 12 electoral ballots. Breckenridge won 847,953 votes and 72 electoral votes, all from slave states. Bell won 590,631 votes and 39 electoral votes from slave-owning border states.

Many Southerners were unable to reconcile themselves to Lincoln's election. Although he claimed not to be an abolitionist, he was the candidate of the North's antislavery party. Furthermore, Lincoln's victory confirmed the increasing political and economic dominance of the Northeast and West.

Unable to maintain their relative sectional strength, Southerners looked away from the Union toward a world of their own. On December 20, 1860, South Carolina, the most defiant of the Dixie commonwealths, repealed its ratification of the Constitution and announced its secession from the United States. Mississippi on January 9, 1861, Florida on January 10, and Alabama on January 11 followed South Carolina's example. The similar actions of Georgia on January 19, Louisiana on January 26, and Texas on February 1 brought to seven the number of rebellious states. On February 4 the first six met in Montgomery, Alabama, to form the Confederate States of America, and Texas soon joined the new federation.

Not all Southerners were in accord with the secessionists. Some, known as cooperationists, wanted to give Lincoln time to show his intentions: if he proved to be an abolitionist, then the slave states could leave with a demonstration of unity rather than in a piecemeal manner. Georgia cooperationists conducted a vigorous but futile campaign against secession. In Texas, Governor Sam Houston, an ardent Unionist, held out until the secessionists forced him to call a special convention. That gathering, however, decided that Texas should withdraw from the Union, and it won the approval of a plebiscite for its decision.

James Buchanan remained in the White House during the opening months of the secession crisis. A lame-duck President with Southern sympathies, Buchanan was politically and psychologically unable to act effectively against the rebellious states. Other leaders took up the slack and attempted to engineer a compromise satisfactory to the contending sections. Senator John J. Crittenden of Kentucky put forward the most important proposal, which offered federal protection for slavery in the states where it already existed and permission for the institution to expand to the territories south of 36°30′ north latitude.

Lincoln had no authority to act prior to his inauguration, but he exerted a powerful behind-the-scenes influence. Through his friends, the President-elect made it clear that he would not accept any proposal that authorized the extension of slavery into the territories and thus doomed the hopes of Crittenden and others who wished to conciliate the South. The nation could only wait for the March 4 ceremony at which the new President would take office and announce his plans.

In his first inaugural address Lincoln outlined his obligations and intentions, but he avoided a call to action. He declared the constitutional separation of the states to be as impossible as a physical one, and he affirmed that he had an "oath in Heaven . . . to 'preserve, protect, and defend'" the government. Yet Lincoln offered to support a constitutional amendment designed to guarantee the domestic institutions of the states, including slavery, and promised that the federal government would not resort to violence unless attacked. The new President ended his speech with the hope that

the mystic chords of memory, stretching from every battlefield and patriot grave to every living heart and hearthstone all over this broad land, will yet swell the chorus of the Union when again touched, as surely they will be, by the better angels of our nature.

Once in office, Lincoln had to deal with the gravest threat to the national government, the demand of the Confederate States of America for the surrender of the four remaining federal forts in the South. Forts Jefferson and Taylor in Florida appeared secure, but to assure the safety of Fort Pickens, Florida, Lincoln ordered troops waiting in Pensacola harbor to join the forces already at that outpost. In January, however, the *Star of the West,* a merchant steamer bearing reinforcements and provisions for Fort Sumter, had been driven away from Charleston harbor by South Carolinians. By the time of Lincoln's inauguration, Major Robert Anderson's garrison at Fort Sumter had supplies for only six additional weeks.

On March 5, 1861, the day after Lincoln assumed office, Secretary of State William H. Seward brought the President letters from Anderson, reporting that his situation was virtually hopeless. In light of the commander's pessimism, Seward and the aged General Winfield Scott advised the President to surrender Fort Sumter. During the following weeks, Seward and Scott continued to bring Lincoln messages from Southern Unionists and Northern conservatives, urging him not to provoke South Carolina lest the remaining slave states also declare secession. On March 15 the cabinet advised the President to withdraw Union forces from the fort.

Many Americans strenuously opposed any concession on Sumter, however. Some Republicans advised the President that surrender to the Confederates on this point would destroy both the party and the government. Postmaster General Montgomery Blair and his father, Francis P. Blair, formerly a trusted adviser of Andrew Jackson, warned Lincoln that to evacuate the fort would be an ignominious "surrender of the Union." Blair's brother-in-law, Gustavus Vasa Fox, a retired naval officer, presented a plan to relieve Sumter with troops and supplies.

The President kept his silence for several weeks. While sending Fox to inspect Fort Sumter, Lincoln also dispatched his friend Stephen A. Hurlbut, an Illinoisan with relatives in Charleston, to visit the South Carolina capital. On March 27 Hurlbut reported that even the moderate men in the state would fire on any ship that attempted to bring provisions, let alone troops, to Sumter.

After a state dinner on March 28, Lincoln informed his cabinet that Scott now advocated abandoning both Pickens and Sumter as a means of guaranteeing the support of the remaining slave states for the Union. The proposal did not sit well with the cabinet. The next day the cabinet reversed its former position, and all the members save Seward argued that Lincoln should hold both Pickens and Sumter. The President then issued orders for expeditions to both outposts.

On April 1 Secretary Seward, dismayed by the failure of his policy to win acceptance, offered a desperate alternative solution. He advocated that the President conciliate the South by yielding Sumter while holding Pickens and unify the nation through the creation and exploitation of a crisis with a foreign nation. Lincoln rejected the proposal and stated that his policy would be to maintain all federal positions.

On April 4 Lincoln told Fox to carry out his plans for an expedition including a chartered steamboat with 200 soldiers and one year's provisions, a gunboat, three tugs, and three warships, one of which was later diverted to the Pickens convoy. The President advised Major Anderson of the mission and, on April 6, dispatched a message to Governor Francis W. Pickens of South Carolina to inform him of the shipment of provisions to Fort Sumter.

The South Carolina authorities dared not allow the reinforcement of Sumter, lest the fort indefinitely threaten the activity of one of the Confederacy's leading ports. Governor Pickens ordered General Pierre G. T. Beauregard on April 11 to demand Anderson's surrender. The Union major asked for permission to delay evacuation until his supplies ran out, but the Confederates, aware that the relief ships were approaching, refused his request.

The Confederates gave Anderson until 4:00 A.M. on April 12, 1861, to surrender Fort Sumter. When the major held firm past the deadline, Beauregard ordered the Charleston shore batteries to fire on the fort. It is often alleged that it was Edmund B. Ruffin, the South Carolina radical, who pulled the lanyard that set off the first shot. At 2:30 P.M. on April 13, after 34 hours of intense but bloodless bombardment, the Union troops, their ammunition expended, surrendered their burnt-out post. In the interim, Fox's ships arrived and, with the permission of the Southerners, took the defenders off their island fort.

Jefferson Davis, the president of the Confederate States, condemned Lincoln's Sumter policy as a maneuver designed to make the South appear to be the aggressor. Some historians, particularly Charles W. Ramsdell, have supported Davis's interpretation and blamed Lincoln for starting the Civil War. Most students of the issue, including David Potter and Kenneth Stampp, deny the President's guilt and assert that the Southern view bestows on Lincoln too great a control of events.

In the attempt to provision Sumter, Lincoln followed a strategy of calculated risk to preserve the Union. The President believed that the government would gain nothing by the surrender of Sumter, but he also recognized that any expedition to provision the fort would be fraught with risks. The North might suffer a psychological defeat if the mission failed; worse, the federal government might well seem the aggressor if in the course of the operation the Confederates managed to draw the first fire from the fort.

It was acts of secession that made the crisis inevitable. Lincoln could have kept the peace only by the surrender of the Union, a price that he could not constitutionally pay. As the historian Richard N. Current stated: "In preserving the Union, Lincoln would have been glad to preserve the peace also, but he was ready to risk a war."

President Lincoln on April 15 issued a proclamation asking the states to provide 75,000 militiamen to put down the insurrection in the South. On April 19 he ordered the navy to blockade the ports of the Confederacy. Lincoln's April 15 declaration sealed the fate of the nation for the four following years.

The state of Virginia, previously divided on the question, declared its secession from the Union on April 17, two days after Lincoln's proclamation. A number of Virginians who were leaders in the US Army, most notably Robert E. Lee, followed their state into secession. Arkansas on May 6, Tennessee on May 7, and North Carolina on May 20 also joined the Confederacy.

The slave states of Delaware, Maryland, Kentucky, and Missouri remained loyal to the Union. The Delaware legislature raised troops in response to Lincoln's call, and pro-Northern elements in Maryland, with the aid of the federal government, arrested officials with Confederate sympathies. Kentucky at first announced its neutrality but called for federal troops when it was invaded by the Southern army. Missouri underwent an intrastate conflict to determine its allegiance, with the pro-Union forces gaining victory by March 1862.

Confederate armies enjoyed early successes, especially on July 21, 1861, at the first battle of Bull Run in Virginia, near Washington, D.C. There General Joseph E. Johnston repulsed an attack by Union forces under Brigadier General Irvin McDowell, and, with the aid of reinforcements under General Thomas J. ("Stonewall") Jackson, drove them in a disorderly retreat toward Washington. Northerners were shocked by the Southern effort, and Lincoln replaced McDowell with Major General George B. McClellan.

Northern armies were more successful in 1862, although the Confederates scored a repeat victory near Bull Run on August 29–30, 1862. Earlier in the year, however, Union forces under General Ulysses Simpson Grant defeated the Confederates in Tennessee at Fort Henry on February 6 and at Fort Donelson on February 16. Grant's men turned what was almost a defeat into a victory at Shiloh in Tennessee on April 6–7. On September 17 McClellan won a technical victory in one of the bloodiest battles of the war, defeating the Southerners in a near standoff at Antietam, Maryland. The killed and wounded totaled close to 24,000, more or less evenly divided between the two sides. McClellan's victory gave President Lincoln enough political leverage to issue on New Year's Day, 1863, the Emancipation Proclamation, ordering the freeing of slaves in areas controlled by the rebels (see January 1).

The turning point of the Civil War came in 1863 with the Union victory at Gettysburg, Pennsylvania, between July 1 and 3 (see July 1), which ended the Southern penetration of Northern territory. On July 4 Grant accepted the surrender of Vicksburg, Mississippi, thus assuring Northern control of the Mississippi River and dividing the South in half. These twin successes ended all Southern hopes of obtaining aid from foreign nations.

Union forces continued the attack in 1864. General William T. Sherman set out from Chattanooga, Tennessee, on May 7 on his March through Georgia and captured Atlanta on September 2. On November 14 Sherman began his March to the Sea, during which his men cut a wide path of destruction between Atlanta and Savannah, which fell on December 22. In the spring of 1864 Grant began a siege of nearly 10 months outside Petersburg, Virginia, near the Confederate capital of Richmond (see June 9, Confederate Memorial Day in Petersburg). The costly operation eventually brought final victory.

By the spring of 1865 the Southerners were no longer able to hold off their opponents. On April 2 the Confederate commander, General Robert E. Lee, evacuated both Petersburg and Richmond. Grant requested Lee's surrender on April 7, and two days later he received it at Appomattox Court House, Virginia. The act virtually ended the war (see April 9). Northerners rejoiced at the restoration of the Union, but the assassination of President Lincoln by John Wilkes Booth on April 14 brought a time of mourning rather than celebration.

In terms of the relative number of casualties, the Civil War ranks as the costliest American war: between 33 and 40 percent of the Union and Confederate soldiers involved became casualties. The North lost 359,528 dead and 275,175 wounded, while the South suffered 258,000 killed and at least 100,000 wounded. The social, economic, and psychological devastation cannot be calculated.

The Fort Sumter National Monument, authorized by Congress on April 28, 1948, includes both Fort Sumter, located in the bay approximately three miles southeast of Charleston, and Fort Moultrie, the less formidable fortification on Sullivan's Island, nine miles to the east, where Major Anderson and his troops had been garrisoned until December 1860. Both outposts display not only their Civil War aspects but also the numerous changes made between 1865 and 1900, particularly during the Spanish-American War. The National Park Service, which administers the site, has made historical excavations and established a museum at Fort Sumter and is doing the same at Fort Moultrie. Dominated by its central gun battery, Sumter has numerous markers and interpretative exhibits that indicate features of interest. The national monument is accessible by private boat or by the Fort Sumter boat leaving from the Charleston municipal yacht basin at the foot of Calhoun Street.

The National Park Service also preserves many other monuments connected with American Civil War history. The Manassas National

Battlefield Park in Virginia contains over 3,000 acres, including the site of the first and second battles of Bull Run. The Fort Donelson National Military Park in Tennessee commemorates the first major Union victory of the conflict. The Shiloh National Military Park in Tennessee and the Antietam National Battlefield site in Maryland honor those who fell in two exceptionally bloody battles of 1862.

The 3,671 acres of the Gettysburg National Military Park in Pennsylvania constitute one of America's greatest historical treasures. Grant's victory on the Mississippi River and the siege that preceded it are commemorated by the Vicksburg National Military Park in Mississippi. The Appomattox Court House National Historical Park in Virginia marks the location of Lee's surrender to Grant in 1865.

Henry Clay's Birthday

Henry Clay, the Great Compromiser and legislative leader of the pre–Civil War period, thrice candidate for the presidency, was born in Virginia's Hanover County on April 12, 1777. He was the seventh of nine children of prosperous parents, John Clay and Elizabeth Hudson Clay. High-spirited, impulsive, intelligent, and above all ambitious, he was far from handicapped by his lack of formal schooling. As a young man, he studied under two of Virginia's most noted lawyers, after being named secretary to one of them, and was admitted to the bar at the age of 20. Somewhere along the line, he earned the nickname of Handsome Harry.

Preceded by his mother, Clay soon moved to that land of opportunity for young lawyers, Kentucky, then the scene of frequent land-claim litigation. In 1797 he settled in Lexington, then the cultural center of the frontier, and there, two years later, he married Lucretia Hart, the daughter of a wealthy local businessman. His early career reads like a present-day success story. Shrewd, skillful in debate and with a flair for oratory, he had become one of Kentucky's leading lawyers by the time he was 23.

He had meanwhile begun political activity, as a Jeffersonian Republican, soon after his arrival in Lexington. He served from 1803 to 1806 as a member, and from 1807 to 1809 as Speaker, of the Kentucky legislature. In 1806 and again in 1809 the state of Kentucky sent him to Washington to fill unexpired terms in the US Senate.

After that, the hot-tempered Clay was seldom absent from the national capital. Elected to the House of Representatives, he served there, usually as Speaker, from 1811 until 1825 (except

for a period devoted to personal affairs in 1821–1823). An ardent nationalist who favored US expansion and championed the economic interests of western pioneers, he joined them in their demands that the British (long suspected of instigating Indian violence) be forced out of Canada and compelled to recognize American rights on the high seas. With John C. Calhoun (see March 18), he headed the young congressional War Hawks who pushed President James Madison into the War of 1812 with Britain. Two years later, Clay was one of the commissioners who negotiated the peace Treaty of Ghent.

Back in Congress, Clay popularized, although he did not invent, the "American system" associated with his name – a program designed to bring prosperity to the United States, which was now free for the first time in its history to work out its own future without foreign interference. The program called for the development and interdependence of the country's three major regions and their products – the East (manufactures), South (cotton), and West (food). Clay accordingly advocated passage of the tariff acts of 1816 and 1824 to protect manufacturers, and he backed legislation for internal improvements at government expense, including new roads and canals. Reversing his earlier position on another big issue of the day, he also favored creation of the Second Bank of the United States as guarantee of a stable currency and proposed that revenues from the sale of public lands be distributed to state governments. He became the great champion of recognition for the new Latin-American republics and futilely nurtured hopes of being named secretary of state by President James Monroe. In 1819 he incurred the enmity of Andrew Jackson by urging that he be censured for his invasion of Florida (see March 15).

Outspoken though he was, Clay was also congenial and could be conciliatory. He performed what may have been his greatest services as a compromiser. In 1820 he became known as the "Great Pacificator" for his tact in dealing with the controversy over Missouri's admission to the Union as a slave state. To ease the furor, he helped frame the famous Missouri Compromise, designed to preserve the balance between free and slave states and, it was briefly hoped, to settle similar questions in the future. By its provisions, Missouri was admitted as a slave state, and Maine as a free state; and slavery was forever prohibited in the Louisiana Purchase north of 36° 30′ latitude (except in Missouri).

It was during Monroe's second term as President that the Jeffersonian Republican organization broke into factions, one of which later became the Democratic party, headed by supporters of Jackson. In the election of 1824 not only did Jackson run, but John Quincy Adams and William H. Crawford were also presidential candidates, along with Clay, who, as Speaker of the House, was the most popular man in Congress. Although Clay as fourth runner was automatically ruled out when the many-sided contest had to go to the House of Representatives for decision, he controlled enough votes to decide the election. To the everlasting resentment of Jackson, Clay swung his support to Adams, who became President and named Clay secretary of state (1825–1829). Jackson supporters for years raised cries that the appointment was the result of corrupt political bargaining – an accusation that never was substantiated, although it plagued Clay until the end of his life.

When Jackson defeated Adams for the presidency in the election of 1828, Clay retired temporarily to the 600 stately acres of Ashland, his estate in Lexington, from which he fired off criticisms of Jackson's administration and maintained contact wtih national political leaders. In 1831, Clay was elected to the Senate. Late the same year, he became a presidential nominee on the National Republican ticket. He was roundly defeated by Jackson in the ensuing election, largely because of his support of the national Bank.

In the Senate (where he served from 1831 to 1842 and from 1849 to 1852) Clay helped to conciliate South Carolina, eliminating the threat of secession during the so-called nullification crisis, by sponsoring the compromise tariff of 1833. The next year, the Senate adopted Clay's resolution censuring President Jackson for having removed government deposits from the national Bank. (The resolution was expunged in 1837). Jackson's successor, Van Buren, skirted the troublesome Bank issue by establishing an independent federal treasury – over Clay's opposition.

In 1840, the ever-aspiring Clay was denied the Whig nomination for President: William Henry Harrison, a man less prominently identified with the Bank issue, ran successfully against Van Buren, but died after a month in office. The fact that Harrison's successor, Vice President John Tyler, was a supposed Clay supporter did not save Clay from a period of frustration during which most of his legislative proposals were defeated, or vetoed by the President.

Clay, discouraged, resigned from the Senate in 1842. But when Tyler's unsuitability for the

Whig leadership became apparent, the party, in search of a candidate for 1844, turned to Clay. He ran against the ardent expansionist James K. Polk, a Democrat, and went bitterly down to his third defeat in a presidential election. He hoped in vain for renomination in 1848. By then, however, he had reached the age of 71 and the Whigs passed him by in favor of a military hero, General Zachary Taylor, who became the nation's 12th President.

When Clay returned to the Senate in 1849, it was just in time to serve his nation once more as the Great Compromiser. His Compromise of 1850 was designed to quell the growing controversy between North and South over the extension of slavery into new territories. The Compromise provided, among other things, that California would be admitted as a free state, and that the large territory acquired as a result of the Mexican War (see May 13 and February 2) would be organized without regard to slavery. With its passage, sectional tensions eased and the Civil War – which might have come out differently had it begun earlier, when the North and South were of more nearly equal strength – was postponed for a decade.

Clay, whose health had already begun to fail in the year of his last great triumph, declined steadily thereafter, an 1851 vacation in Cuba notwithstanding. On June 29, 1852, he died of tuberculosis in Washington's National Hotel. Four of his 11 children survived him.

Clay, who had been one of the pioneers of the horse breeding for which Kentucky is now famous, was buried in the heart of the state's white-fenced, rolling, bluegrass country. His grave is at Lexington Cemetery, which comprises 170 handsomely landscaped acres and also contains the graves of 500 Confederate and 1,110 Union veterans of the war he helped delay. His estate, Ashland, occupied by four generations of the Clay family, is two miles southeast of Lexington at East Main Street and Sycamore Road. Probably designed by the architect Benjamin Latrobe, and with a garden devised by Pierre L'Enfant, the city planner of Washington, D.C., Ashland – complete with its silver doorknobs and hinges – has been designated as a national historical landmark.

Halifax Resolves Day

April 12 is a legal holiday in North Carolina commemorating that date in 1776, when the provincial congress authorized the colony's delegates to the Second Continental Congress to join with representatives from any other colonies

347

in a declaration of independence. Several factors precipitated this first official sanction of separation from Great Britain: the increasing realization that the mother country would never agree to American demands; the growing belief in the possibility of a colonial military victory; and, perhaps most decisive, the failure of the British to reestablish royal rule in North Carolina during the early spring of 1776.

On the eve of the American Revolution, political sentiment in North Carolina was fairly evenly divided: the Lowland Scots and Scotch-Irish, who had come to the colony early in the 18th century and controlled North Carolina's government, provided the impetus for the patriot movement; the Highland Scots, who had recently settled in the Piedmont region and resented exclusion from public office by the earlier arrivals, formed the core of Loyalist support. In August 1775 the royal governor, Josiah Martin, had been forced to flee to the safety of a British ship anchored in the Cape Fear River; but, recognizing the strength of the Loyalists, he represented to the home government that if they were supported by a body of British troops the colony might be kept under imperial control.

In the winter of 1775–1776 a force under Sir Henry Clinton was sent south with instructions to act first in North Carolina. Commissions were issued to influential men in the colony. These men, under the direction of Governor Martin, enlisted about 1,500 Loyalists. The patriots, aware of what was going on, called out the militia and took the field under Colonel James Moore. When Sir Henry Clinton was expected at Cape Fear, 80-year-old General Donald Mc-Donald, in command of the Loyalist force, moved to join him. Colonel Moore ordered parties of militia to post themselves at Moore's Creek Bridge, over which McDonald would have to pass. The patriots fought a decisive battle at this bridge on February 27, 1776, defeating the Loyalists, taking 850 prisoners, and capturing a large store of military supplies. Inspired by this victory, delegates elected to a provincial congress that met at Halifax on April 4 were ready to declare themselves. On April 12 they unanimously adopted a resolution allowing their representatives to the Second Continental Congress "to concur with the delegates of the other Colonies in declaring Independency."

In the 1970s the Halifax Historic District was established to preserve and display Revolutionary relics. However, only five buildings of the period remain. During the celebration on April 12, 1976, marking the 200th anniversary of the Halifax Resolves, residents of Halifax wore colonial dress, and exhibits dealt with the life of the area over the preceding two centuries.

APRIL 13

Thomas Jefferson's Birthday

Unique in the wide range of his interests and talents, the third President of the United States was undoubtedly one of the most gifted of Americans. A Revolutionary leader and spokesman, statesman, diplomat, scholar, linguist, writer, philosopher, political theorist, architect, engineer, scientist, farmer, and agriculturalist, Thomas Jefferson was honored at home and in Europe esteemed as the foremost American thinker of his time.

On April 13, 1743, Thomas Jefferson was born at Shadwell, his family's farm in Goochland (now Albemarle) County, Virginia. His father, Peter Jefferson, had married Jane Randolph, a member of one of the most prominent families in Virginia, and become a successful planter, surveyor, and member of the House of Burgesses. Young Thomas enjoyed the advantages of a scion of a leading Virginia family. He received his early training in small private schools and then went to the College of William and Mary in Williamsburg, from which he was graduated in 1762. Jefferson completed his education by reading law with Judge George Wythe, the outstanding legal teacher of the era, and was admitted to the bar in 1767.

The eldest son, Jefferson at the age of 14 had inherited the 2,500-acre Shadwell estate and its 30 slaves from his father. During the decade preceding the American Revolution, he supplemented the income from Shadwell with that of his thriving law practice. Jefferson entered the colony's House of Burgesses in 1769, and at the age of 27 he became a county lieutenant. On January 1, 1772, he began the new year by marrying Martha Wayles Skelton, a widow and the daughter of John Wayles, a prominent lawyer. They lived at Shadwell, where Jefferson was in the process of building Monticello, the home he had designed.

Jefferson was one of a number of young men, including Patrick Henry and Richard Henry Lee, who took the lead in opposing England's colonial policy in the 1770s. In 1773 these 3 were among the 11 men appointed by the House of Burgesses to an intercolonial committee of correspondence to voice grievances. In 1774 Jefferson wrote A Summary View of the Rights of British America, his most important contribution to pre-Revolutionary thought. Grounding his position on a philosophy of natural rights, he argued that Parliament had authority over neither internal nor external colonial affairs. He then went on to claim that only through the king were the provinces bound to England.

On June 21, 1775, two months after the beginning of the Revolution, Virginia sent Jefferson to the Continental Congress. His first major act was the writing, with John Dickinson, of the "Declaration of the Causes and Necessities of Taking Up Arms." The document, adopted on July 6 by Congress, stated that colonists would die before they were enslaved by Britain and implied that America might possibly accept a foreign ally. He soon after drafted a letter to the British prime minister, Lord North, rejecting his proposal that the American colonies tax themselves for their own defense rather than be taxed by Britain.

By the spring of 1776 American sentiment was strongly in favor of independence from Britain. In June Congress appointed a committee consisting of Jefferson, Benjamin Franklin, John Adams, Robert Livingston, and Roger Sherman to draw up a declaration of independence. The committee decided that Jefferson should draft the document and accepted it with few changes. Perhaps his most enduring monument, the Declaration of Independence eloquently reflects his belief in a political theory based upon natural rights and the influence of the English philosopher John Locke and of French theorists. It is also evidence of the increasing radicalism of Jefferson and many of his contemporaries: in 1774 he had accepted the king as the tie to Britain; in 1776 he rejected even this connection, supporting the Revolutionary position with a listing of "abuses and usurpations" on the part of King George III.

Jefferson returned to Virginia during the Revolution. In September 1776 he left the Continental Congress and again took a seat in the House of Burgesses. There he worked hard to implement the theories underlying the Declaration of Independence in Virginia, most of which was then controlled by a small number of rich slave owners. He was instrumental in obtaining the abolition of the feudal vestiges of primogeniture and entail; he drafted an ordinance (later used as a model for the First Amendment) for religious freedom, which, when passed, disestablished the Anglican church; and he initiated a public school system. All these measures worked to undermine social stratification based on artificial privileges. However, his efforts to curtail the major abuse of Virginia society met with failure, for he was not able to win acceptance for his proposals to end the slave trade and to gradually emancipate blacks.

Jefferson became governor of Virginia in 1779. The British invaded the state during his administration, which ended in 1781. Some critics claimed that Jefferson's handling of Virginia's defense was inept, but a legislative investigation later cleared his name. Jefferson remained out of office for two years and used the respite from controversy to write *Notes on the State of Virginia*, which was published in Paris in 1785. The death of his wife on September 6, 1782, left Jefferson disconsolate; in 1783 he was elected to Congress and decided to accept the office to help overcome his depression.

During his one-year term he devised and was responsible for the adoption of the nation's decimal system of currency. He also drew up the Ordinance of 1784, which never went into effect but which served as the basis of the Northwest Ordinance three years later. In addition he worked on the Land Ordinance of 1785, the provisions of which are still used today in determining township boundaries. Jefferson left Congress in 1784 to go to France to negotiate a commercial treaty. There he succeeded Benjamin Franklin as minister to France and served in the post until 1789.

The Constitutional Convention took place in 1787 while Jefferson was absent from the United States, and, at first, he worried about the instrument of government the convention had produced. He was sent a draft of the constitution by James Madison and approved it but was disturbed by the omission of a bill of rights to preserve individual freedom. His qualms were removed, however, when a bill of rights was promised, and he accepted the position of secretary of state in the new US government under President George Washington.

In his new office Jefferson found himself frequently at odds with Alexander Hamilton, the secretary of the treasury. Domestically, Jefferson opposed Hamilton's attempt to strengthen the national government at the expense of the state powers. In foreign affairs Jefferson sympathized with the French revolution against despotism and wished to support France in its struggle against external enemies, including England. Hamilton, on the other hand, wanted the United States to be allied with Great Britain. Despite Jefferson's efforts, Hamilton's policies gained favor with President Washington, and on December 31, 1793, Jefferson resigned in protest.

Jefferson returned to private life for three years, but even in his absence those who were disenchanted with the administration looked to him as their leader. These dissidents had formed an Antifederalist faction strong enough to attempt to win control of the government in the national election. (The Antifederalists, then called Republicans, came to be known as Jeffersonian Republicans or Democratic-Republicans; by the 1830s they were officially known as Democrats.) In 1796 they fell short of their goal as the Federalist John Adams won the presidency, and Jefferson became Vice President. Jefferson opposed a number of Federalist measures. The Alien and Sedition Acts, which restricted individual liberties, including freedom of speech and of the press, especially irritated him, and in response he drafted resolutions passed by the legislature of Kentucky, which declared that the states had the right to judge when the national government overstepped its constitutional limitations.

When Adams and Jefferson again met in the presidential election of 1800, the latter was victorious. In the electoral college both he and Aaron Burr, also a Democratic-Republican, received 73 votes, but the House of Representatives declared Jefferson President and Burr his Vice President. Ironically, Hamilton, his former archrival, was one of his stronger supporters, since Hamilton distrusted Burr even more than he disapproved of Jefferson.

Jefferson's accession to the presidency gave a more liberal image to the government but did not bring radical change. His administration supported repeal of unpopular Federalist excise taxes, reduced the country's military expenditures, and relieved the national debt. Jefferson's greatest achievements as President, however, probably were the 1803 purchase from France of the 828,000-square-mile Louisiana Territory for $15 million, virtually doubling the nation's size, and his dispatching of Lewis and Clark to explore the newly acquired land.

In 1804 Jefferson and George Clinton, his running mate, were unanimously elected President and Vice President. One of Jefferson's major concerns during his second administration was preventing American involvement in the Napoleonic wars between Great Britain and France, while safeguarding the rights of Americans as citizens of a neutral nation. Repeated futile efforts — including the passage of the Non-Importation Act of 1806 and diplomatic negotiations — were made to halt the increasing British seizures of American vessels and the impressment of their seamen. In June 1807 the British frigate *Leopard* fired upon the American frigate *Chesapeake* when its captain refused to let the vessel be searched for British deserters. In an attempt to salvage American neutrality, Jefferson signed the Embargo Act, which virtually forbade all trade with foreign nations. This measure was so unpopular and economically injurious that in 1809, just before he left office, Jefferson was obliged to sign the Non-Intercourse Act, which replaced the Embargo Act and permitted trade with all nations except England and France.

After 60 years of government service, Jeffer-son retired to Virginia, where he remained for the rest of his life. There he assumed his major task of founding the University of Virginia, at Charlottesville. He led the legislative campaign for establishment of the university; was the architect of the buildings and the curriculum; procured the faculty, books, and scientific equipment in England and on the Continent; and served as chairman of the governing board. The university opened in 1825 with an enrollment of 40 students.

Living at Monticello, near Charlottesville, Jefferson spent time renovating his home, experimenting with farming methods, and designing mechanical devices. He served as adviser to Presidents James Madison and James Monroe and renewed his friendship with John Adams, with whom he carried on an extensive correspondence.

Jefferson died on July 4, 1826, the 50th anniversary of the approval of the Declaration of Independence. His death preceded by a few hours that of John Adams.

The anniversary of Jefferson's birth is now a legal holiday in the states of Alabama, Missouri, Nebraska, Oklahoma, and his native Virginia. Indeed, Americans have long celebrated the April 13 anniversary.

A dinner party held by Democrats in 1830 remains one of the more noteworthy commemorations. On that occasion, President Andrew Jackson silenced the supporters of Vice President John C. Calhoun, who had hoped to use the event to propound their states rights' philosophy, by offering the stirring toast, "Our Federal Union: It must and shall be preserved."

Jefferson has continued to be honored with more or less regularity by Democrats in different parts of the country, at first often on an informal basis. Since 1936, however, the Democratic National Committee has officially sponsored annual dinners throughout the nation to honor both Jefferson and Jackson as founders of the Democratic party. An occasion on which the party's achievements are praised, hopes expressed, and funds raised, the dinners were for a time variously known as Jefferson Day dinners, Jackson Day dinners, Democratic Victory dinners, or Washington dinners. Since 1948 the gatherings have been officially designated as Jefferson-Jackson Day dinners. They are held on widely differing dates, sometimes as late as April, but often on January 8, the anniversary of the battle of New Orleans, in which Jackson played a key role.

The University of Virginia for years celebrated Jefferson's birthday as Founder's Day, although the date was shifted to early fall in 1975. The observance, jointly sponsored by the university and the nonprofit Thomas Jefferson Memorial Foundation (which owns and administers Monticello), commences with an academic procession from the university's Rotunda to Cabell Hall, where a nationally known figure in academia or national affairs customarily gives the main address. The celebration is the occasion for presentation of awards for academic achievement and for announcing the recipient of the Thomas Jefferson Award, made annually to a leading member of the university community. Generally, there is special music for the Founder's Day ceremonies, which are preceded a day or two earlier by a foundation-sponsored dinner at Monticello for university and foundation representatives and which are followed by a wreath-laying ceremony and the playing of taps at Jefferson's grave at Monticello.

A number of impressive monuments honor Jefferson. A 60-foot-high head of Jefferson, along with heads of George Washington, Abraham Lincoln, and Theodore Roosevelt, was designed and carved by Gutzon Borglum on the cliff of Mount Rushmore National Park, 25 miles south of Rapid City, in the Black Hills of South Dakota. Washington, D.C. is the site of the Jefferson Memorial, which was dedicated on April 13, 1943. Rudulph Evans's 19-foot-tall statue of the third President stands on a black granite pedestal in the center of the domed, white marble memorial beside the cherry-tree-rimmed Tidal Basin. Jefferson's own words adorn the memorial's inner walls, one of which bears what must be his most famous utterance, from the Declaration of Independence:

We hold these truths to be self-evident, that all men are created equal, that they are endowed by their Creator with certain unalienable Rights, that among these are Life, Liberty, and the pursuit of Happiness. That to secure these rights, Governments are instituted among Men. . . . We . . . solemnly Publish and Declare, That these . . . Colonies are, and of Right ought to be Free and Independent States. . . . And for the support of this Declaration, with a firm reliance on the Protection of Divine Providence, we mutually pledge . . . our Lives, our Fortunes and our sacred Honor.

Jefferson's pledge "I have sworn upon the altar of God eternal hostility against every form of tyranny over the mind of man" is inscribed around the base of the dome.

Perhaps the greatest monument to Jefferson is his home, Monticello, on the plateau atop an 857-foot mountain. The major construction began after 1768 but was not completed until 1809. Jefferson made the smaller outbuildings, such as the dairy and stable, inconspicuous by building them into the slope of the hill. The house, a national historic landmark, has 35 rooms in its three stories. Jefferson's possessions were sold after his death to pay his debts, but many have been recovered in more recent years and now adorn the house. The mansion and its 700 acres are open to the public. In St. Louis, Missouri, the 91-acre Jefferson National Expansion Memorial was established in 1935 to commemorate the part Jefferson played in westward expansion and settlement. The site's most striking feature is the huge stainless steel Gateway Arch, designed by Eero Saarinen and dedicated in 1968.

Publication of a 60-volume edition of Jefferson's papers was begun in 1950 by Princeton University Press.

APRIL 14

Abraham Lincoln Assassinated

It was on April 14, 1865, at about 10:30 P.M., that President Abraham Lincoln was fatally shot in the back of the head as he sat in a box at Ford's Theatre in Washington, D.C., while viewing a performance of *Our American Cousin*, by Tom Taylor. The assassin, John Wilkes Booth, an actor, felt his action would somehow help the devastated South, which had just surrendered to Federal forces. Booth was apprehended 12 days later at a farm near Bowling Green, Virginia, where he too was fatally shot — either by himself or by a pursuing soldier, Boston Corbett. President Lincoln, who never regained consciousness, was taken across the street to a boardinghouse owned by William Petersen, a tailor, and died there at 7:21 on the morning of April 15.

In life, Lincoln had had his political foes. In death he had almost none. The nation — wide segments of which had discerned greatness in his insight, courage and resolution, high moral principle, and eloquent insistence on preserving the Union during the exhausting years of the Civil War — now embarked on a demonstration of grief that was as remarkable for its depth as for its unanimity. The poet and biographer Carl Sandburg described the country's shock at the death of Lincoln:

Thousands on thousands would remember as long as they lived the exact place where they had been standing or seated or lying down when the news came to them, recalling precisely in details and particulars where they were and what they were doing when the dread news arrived.

Lincoln, who had dreamed of the event beforehand, was the first US President assassinated. He was also the first President to lie in state in the rotunda of the US Capitol, where his body was on view on April 19 and 20, after lying in state at the White House. The next day his bier was conveyed to the railroad station, where it commenced a long journey back to Springfield, Illinois, his home for 24 years before he became President. The funeral procession, which reversed the route Lincoln had followed to his first inauguration, took 12 days. The train, draped in dark bunting, made stops en route while people in Baltimore, Harrisburg, Philadelphia, New York, Albany, Utica, Syracuse, Cleveland, Columbus, Indianapolis, and Chicago paid their respects.

It was Lincoln himself who had unknowingly pointed to the appropriateness of Springfield as his place of burial. Departing from there on February 11, 1861, to assume the presidency, he had expressed himself, characteristically, with a candor all could comprehend:

My friends, no one, not in my situation, can appreciate my feelings of sadness at this parting. To this place, and the kindness of these people, I owe everything. Here I have lived for a quarter of a century, and have passed from a young man to an old man. Here my children have been born, and one is buried. I now leave, not knowing when or whether ever I may return, and with a task before me greater than that which rested upon Washington. Without the assistance of that Divine Being who ever attended him, I cannot succeed. With that assistance, I cannot fail.

Lincoln's feeling for his Springfield neighbors was not unrequited. The National Lincoln Monument Association, organized by the citizens of Springfield, came into being — with the purpose of raising funds for a tomb and memorial — on the very day of his death. From May 4, 1865, the day of his funeral in Springfield, until December of the same year, Lincoln's body remained in a receiving vault and then was removed to another temporary vault northeast of the present Lincoln Tomb State Memorial in Springfield's Oak Ridge Cemetery. Construction of the tomb was begun in 1869. Lincoln's body was transferred to a crypt in the partially completed monument in 1871. Control of the tomb, which was dedicated in 1874, was turned over to the state of Illinois in 1895. Reconstructions of the tomb took place in 1901, the year the President's body (which earlier had been the subject of a kidnapping attempt) was placed in the present cement vault 10 feet below the floor of the tomb, and again in 1931.

On the cenotaph inside the monument are simply the name and dates, "Abraham Lincoln, 1809–1865." Inscribed on the wall are the words spoken by Secretary of War Edwin M. Stanton as he looked on the lifeless face of Lincoln: "Now he belongs to the ages."

The stature of Lincoln, who was respected in life, grew in death. Memorials multiplied beyond easy numbering. Notable among them is the Lincoln Memorial Garden in Springfield, 80 acres of native trees, shrubs, and flowers on the shore of Lake Springfield, just south of the city. Probably the two most famous memorials to Lincoln are the superbly simple Lincoln Memorial — with its inspiring seated figure by Daniel Chester French — in Washington's Potomac Park, facing the Washington Monument and the US Capitol across a long vista; and the 60-foot-high head of Lincoln, along with heads of Presidents George Washington, Thomas Jefferson, and Theodore Roosevelt, designed and carved by Gutzon Borglum on the towering cliff of Mount Rushmore National Memorial, 25 miles south of Rapid City in the Black Hills of South Dakota. Also noteworthy are two statues by Augustus Saint-Gaudens in Chicago's Lincoln and Grant parks.

Ford's Theatre, housing the Lincoln Museum and a Lincoln library, was reopened to the public on January 21, 1968, upon completion of a $2.7 million National Park Service project, which took more than two years to restore the building to its exact appearance on the night of the assassination. The reopening ceremonies, presided over by Secretary of the Interior Stewart L. Udall, were keynoted by Vice President Hubert Humphrey, who quoted Lincoln's second inaugural address in dedicating the restored theater. Others who participated included North Dakota's Senator Milton R. Young, who 22 years earlier had initiated congressional efforts to have the theater restored; and Senator Charles H. Percy of Illinois, who read excerpts from Lincoln's writings. A subsequent program of folk music, opera, and dramatic excerpts — all keyed to Lincoln or his lifetime — was introduced by actress Helen Hayes and narrated by actors Henry Fonda, Fredric March, and Robert Ryan.

A little more than a week later, the theater was the setting for what was called an Inaugural Evening, attended by members of the cabinet of President Lyndon B. Johnson and guests. Included was a dramatic presentation of Stephen Vincent Benét's *John Brown's Body* — the first offering of the new National Repertory Theater. In addition to repertory productions at Ford's Theatre during the winter, a sound and light program was presented during spring and summer months. Across the street from the theater, at 516 10th Street, N.W., the building known as the House Where Lincoln Died is also open to the public.

The anniversary of the assassination has been marked from time to time in various ways. Perhaps most notable was the dedication of the

Emancipation Statue, in Washington's Lincoln Park, on April 14, 1876. The statue was sculpted in bronze by Thomas Ball and paid for by the donations of emancipated slaves. And as part of the Civil War Centennial, a four-year-long nationwide event that embraced scores of observances, the US Marine Band, the US Army Chorus, and a combined color guard representing the nation's military services participated on April 16, 1965, in commemorative ceremonies at Washington's New York Avenue Presbyterian Church, the church Lincoln had attended as President.

Pan American Day

Throughout the Western Hemisphere April 14 is observed as Pan American Day, a time for emphasis on the culture, contributions, and harmonious interrelation of Latin and North American nations. The first celebration itself took place in 1931, but its origins go back much further.

They date, in fact, to what is frequently called the first Pan American Conference (see October 2) — even though there had been inter-American conferences on a more limited scale before it. This gathering, called and presided over by President Benjamin Harrison's Secretary of State, James G. Blaine, opened in Washington, D.C., on October 2, 1889, and remained in session until April 21, 1890. Officially, it was titled the First International Conference of American States.

On April 14, the date still celebrated, the conference adopted a resolution forming what has since grown in scope to become the Organization of American States (OAS), the world's oldest international organization and today a powerful force for preserving hemispheric peace and cooperation. Initially, however, the organization was more immediately concerned with the collection and distribution of commercial information, and its name was the International Union of American Republics. Composed of nations of North, Central, and South America, the union was to operate through a permanent bureau in Washington, D.C. (Canada has never been a participating member of the inter-American organizations but in 1974 became an OAS observer.)

Subsequently designated the Pan American Union, this bureau today serves as the OAS's permanent General Secretariat. Housed in a handsome marble structure erected through the generosity of the American industrialist and philanthropist Andrew Carnegie, the Pan American Union is situated on 17th Street at the corner of Constitution Avenue, N.W. The building, known as the House of the Americas, is one of the most interesting in Washington. Visitors,

who flock to it, particularly admire its fountain-centered courtyard, located at the center of the building. Filled with tropical trees and plants, it is covered with a sliding glass roof in winter and is open to the sky in fair weather. Also worthy of remark are the building's Permanent Council Chamber, equipped for simultaneous interpretation in the four official OAS languages, Spanish, English, Portuguese, and French; its bust-lined Hall of Heroes, overlooking the courtyard, which displays the flags of member nations; the magnificent chandelier-hung Hall of the Americas, reserved for inter-American receptions, concerts by American artists, and state banquets; and the Aztec Garden behind the building.

The celebrations that fall on and around April 14 were initiated by the predecessor organization. It was on May 7, 1930, that the governing board of the International Union of American Republics adopted a resolution setting forth the desirability of observing a day to be known as Pan American Day in all the American republics. The proposal went on to suggest April 14, the date of the resolution that had created the Union of American Republics, as an appropriate date. According to the recommendation, each government represented in the union was to designate that day as Pan American Day and provide for the display within its borders of the flags of the various American nations.

The governments acted on the recommendation, each in its own way. In the United States, President Herbert Hoover issued a proclamation on March 7, 1931, ordering that the flag be displayed on all government buildings on April 14 and inviting schools, civic associations, and the people of the United States generally to observe the day with appropriate ceremonies, "thereby giving expression to the spirit of continental solidarity and to the sentiments of cordiality and friendly feeling which the government and people of the United States entertain toward the peoples and governments of the other republics of the American continent."

Pan American Day was thus observed for the first time in 1931. The ceremonies in Washington were held in the Pan American Building, attended by the President of the United States and the members of his cabinet and by the diplomatic representatives of the other American republics. Addresses were made by the President and the secretary of state, as well as by the Mexican and Cuban ambassadors. Ceremonies at the OAS always constitute one of the hemisphere's keystone observances of Pan American Day. They are attended by OAS diplomats and other officials of member countries.

The President of the United States and a number of governors and mayors traditionally issue proclamations in honor of Pan American Day. Ceremonies initiating the day often take place at the seats of state or local governments. Schools, colleges, civic organizations, public libraries, art galleries, organizations with an international orientation, Spanish language clubs, and Romance language departments are prominent among sponsors of special observances. Pan American institutes (or societies, clubs, or associations), Hispanic institutes, Latin American clubs or studies groups, Hispanic-American alliances, Latin American citizen groups, Inter-American centers — such groups, as well as their Spanish-named counterparts — are frequently moving forces behind Pan American Day celebrations, as are clubs devoted to any single Latin American country. Miami and other cities with large Latin populations are likely to be the scenes of particularly enthusiastic commemoration.

Celebrations, which can last as long as a month, although they are usually limited to Pan American Day or Pan American Week, take place in numerous US cities. Programs vary tremendously in kind as well as in location. Pan American Day banquets (or luncheons, buffets, or receptions), often followed by dances, and invariably garnished with speeches and interlaced with Latin melody, are perhaps the most frequent kind of celebration. There are also special concerts, film festivals, gallery showings, and other exhibits, all with a special emphasis on Latin American culture and development.

Dedications with inter-American overtones are often scheduled for Pan American Day. This was true, for instance, in 1963, when the Plaza of the Americas on Michigan Avenue was dedicated in Chicago. It was true, too, in 1965, when St. Augustine, Florida, then celebrating its 400th anniversary year, chose April 14 for the dedication of its new Pan American Center. And it has been true at many times and a number of places since. Throughout the hemisphere, wherever there is a statue of the South American liberator Simón Bolívar, who first conceived the ideal of continental unity, it is frequently the custom to place a wreath on the monument on Pan American Day. In the United States, two Bolívar sculptures so decorated are in New York City — at Central Park South and the Avenue of the Americas — and in Washington — in the triangular park behind the Pan American Union building and opposite its administrative annex.

It was in 1948 that representatives of 21 American republics, meeting in Bogotá, Colombia, at the Ninth International Conference of American States, chartered the new Organization of American States. In so doing, they replaced the Union of American Republics and gave the inter-American system its first compre-

hensive constitution. It was this charter that designated the Pan American Union — a name that had been popularly used for the whole organization for some years — as the central permanent agency and general secretariat of the OAS.

The charter also created three representative bodies. One of these, which was to meet every five years, was the organization's supreme authority: the Inter-American Conference (succeeding the International Conference of American States). The others were the Meeting of Consultation of Ministers of Foreign Affairs, which was to consider matters of urgent common interest whenever they arose; and the Council, which was to supervise the secretariat (Pan American Union) and perform other functions. Under the provisions of the amendment to the OAS charter that took effect on February 27, 1970, the General Assembly replaced the Inter-American Conference as the supreme organ.

The purposes of the Organization of American States — purposes that in some ways resemble those of the earlier Union of American Republics, but in other ways are broader — are the consideration of mutual concerns in economic, technical, cultural, political, and legal matters; the preservation of hemispheric peace; and the maintenance of collective security. The Treaty of Reciprocal Assistance, signed by member states at Rio de Janeiro in 1947, stated that an attack upon one American state should be considered as an attack upon all. It was in light of hemispheric provisions for mutual defense that the OAS voted approval of the action of President John F. Kennedy on October 22, 1962, announcing an embargo on Soviet shipping of offensive weapons to Communist Cuba, where launching sites for Soviet missiles had been discovered.

Under the OAS, the periodic conferences of hemisphere nations that characterized the earlier Union of American Republics continue. Though an independent regional association, the OAS maintains close cooperation with the United Nations in accordance with terms of the OAS charter.

APRIL 15

Federal Income Tax Deadline

Each year millions of frenzied Americans spend countless hours poring over seemingly unending columns of figures and pages of instructions in order to meet the deadline for filing their federal income tax returns. (The deadline is always extended when April 15 occurs on a Saturday or Sunday.) Many attempt to untangle their own fiscal affairs; others, dismayed by the intricacies of the process, seek the counsel of accountants or lawyers. But whatever the means chosen for the preparation of the return, the income tax has become a fact of 20th century life.

This was not always the case. The United States had no experience with this form of taxation until the Civil War. Then, faced with the extraordinary costs of the conflict, both the North and the South decided to tax personal incomes as a means of raising much needed revenues. But these first levies were only emergency measures; the end of the war brought immediate repeal of the tax legislation.

The process of industrialization that swept the United States after the Civil War made the ownership of corporate stocks and bonds, rather than landholding, the principal source of national wealth. As the inequity of financing the government through property taxation became evident, certain groups began to urge the replacement of this means of raising revenue with a permanent, graduated tax based on personal income. Agrarian organizations especially pressed this demand. Suffering during the depression of the 1870s, the farmers blamed their plight on unfair tax burdens and increasingly high tariffs on imports of essential manufactured goods. They saw a readjustment of the tax and tariff laws as the means of relieving their economic ills.

The return of prosperity in the 1880s sidetracked tax and tariff reform, but when hard times reappeared in the early 1890s, the farmers renewed their demands. In 1892 the platform of the Populists, a new third party with widespread appeal in the agrarian South and West, called for a graduated income tax. James B. Weaver, the party's candidate in the ensuing presidential contest, garnered over 1 million votes, and his success indicated to the Democrats and Republicans that they could no longer ignore the issue. Within two years Congress had passed the Wilson-Gorman Tariff, which slightly reduced import duties and imposed a two percent tax on annual incomes exceeding $4,000.

Opponents of the tax did not passively accept the new legislation; instead they initiated procedures designed to test its constitutionality. The test case, *Pollock* v. *Farmers' Loan and Trust Company*, came before the Supreme Court in 1895. The Court heard arguments for two days and then handed down its decision. By a five-to-four vote it found the tax provision of the Wilson-Gorman Tariff to be a direct tax and therefore a violation of Article I of the Constitution, which stipulates that such taxes must be apportioned among the states on the basis of population.

This historic decision made a new constitutional amendment the absolute prerequisite for any further income tax legislation. Several years elapsed before the proponents of the tax could acquire sufficient support for such an amendment, but the rise of the Progressive reform movement of the early 20th century insured their ultimate success. Finally, on July 12, 1909, Congress agreed to the 16th Amendment (see February 25) and submitted it to the states for ratification. Just over three and a half years later, on February 25, 1913, the amendment — which allows Congress to tax incomes "without apportionment among the several States, and without regard to any census or enumeration" — gained the approval of the necessary three-fourths of the states and became part of the law of the land.

Income-tax rates have increased considerably since 1913, when the Underwood-Simmons Tariff Act provided for the first constitutional levy — of one percent on incomes over $4,000. During World War I and World War II the income tax not only provided needed revenues but also served as a curb on those who sought to amass large fortunes from the conflicts. Even before World War II, tax rates had risen to such a degree as to make the initial one percent seem ludicrous by contrast. Since the administration of Franklin D. Roosevelt the tax has been a major source of government revenue. Critics have pointed out that some corporations and wealthy individuals have managed, through tax loopholes, to avoid paying their just share of the tax. Consequently, Congress has tightened some loopholes, but tax reform remains a perennial issue.

APRIL 16

Washington Departs for His Inauguration

On April 16, 1789, George Washington set out from his estate at Mount Vernon in Virginia. His destination was New York City, where he was to be inaugurated as the first President of the United States.

Washington's inauguration was the culmination of more than seven years of debate about the form of government best suited for the fledgling nation. The Treaty of Paris of 1783, which ended the Revolutionary War, ushered in a period of constructiveness and creativity in political affairs. However, the shortcomings of the Articles of Confederation under which the original 13 states were joined — especially the national government's complete dependence upon the good will of the individual states — became increasingly apparent. Washington, pessimistic about the country's future, wrote on May 18, 1786, that "something must be done, or the fabric must fall, for it is certainly tottering." At first he advocated amending the Articles of Confederation, but later, following the outbreak of Shays' Rebellion and virtual civil war in Massachusetts in 1786, he urged more radical reforms towards the formation of "an indissoluble union."

The practical needs of the young nation inevitably drew Washington back into public affairs although he had hoped to enjoy a private life at Mount Vernon after leading the Revolutionary forces to victory. As early as the spring of 1785 he opened his estate to delegates from Virginia and Maryland, whose discussions there resolved common problems concerning the navigation of the Potomac River. The meetings led to the larger Annapolis Convention in 1786, attended by delegates from five states. The report of these participants included a call for a convention "to render the Constitution of the Federal Government adequate to the exigencies of the Union."

George Washington was chosen one of Virginia's five delegates to the Constitutional Convention, which met in Philadelphia in May 1787. After a quorum had been obtained, he was unanimously elected its president by the delegates from the 12 states represented. (Rhode Island did not participate.) In the four months during which he presided, Washington remained silent in the debate, but on the side he made it known that he desired the formation of a strong national government. Although he again expressed his wish to retire quietly from the public eye, he was obviously the leader to serve as the nation's Chief Executive under the new constitution, which was ratified by the states in 1788. Members of the electoral college, meeting on February 4, 1789, were unanimous in voting for him for President. The election, however, was not yet official. The Constitution required that Congress convene and that the president of the Senate open the ballots in the presence of both the Senate and the House.

The Continental Congress had intended that the newly established government should convene on "the first Wednesday in March next" (March 4, 1789) at Federal Hall in New York City, then the nation's capital. By March 5 a mere handful of the legislators needed to count the presidential vote had assembled. The quorum had still not been reached by March 30. Washington, awaiting the official decision, was in the meantime making careful preparations for his probable departure from Mount Vernon. Ironically enough, although he was one of the wealthiest men of his day (his estate was valued at more than half a million dollars), he consid-

ered himself obligated "to do what I never expected to be reduced to the necessity of doing": to borrow money at interest to clear his debts in Virginia. Forced to appeal to personal acquaintances since his credit was not judged good enough, Washington contacted "the most monied man I was acquainted with," Charles Carroll of Carrollton, Maryland, who declined the request because of his own financial difficulties. At last Richard Conway, a wealthy resident of Alexandria, Virginia, responded favorably to the following letter sent by Washington on March 4, 1789:

Never till within these two years have I experienced the want of money. Short crops, and other causes not entirely within my control, make me feel it now very sensibly. To collect money without the invention of Suits seems impractical . . . and Land, which I have offered for sale, will not command cash at an undervalue, if at all. Under this statement, I am inclined to . . . borrow Money on Interest.

Conway at first lent Washington £500 at 6 percent interest, then extended a further loan of £100 to cover his expenses on his trip to New York City.

On April 6, 1789, the necessary quorum was obtained and the electoral votes tallied. Charles Thomson, who had served as secretary of the Continental Congress, informed Washington of his unanimous election about noon on April 14, made a brief speech, and extended a letter from the president pro tempore of the Senate, which said in part: "Suffer me, Sir, to indulge the hope, that so auspicious a mark of public confidence will meet your approbation." Washington accepted the appointment, stating "I shall therefore be in readiness to set out the day after tomorrow." However, his personal sentiments about his decision were better reflected in the letter that he had written Henry Knox shortly beforehand:

My movements to the chair of Government will be accompanied by feelings not unlike those of a culprit who is going to the place of his execution: so unwilling am I, in the evening of a life nearly consumed in public cares, to quit a peaceful abode for an Ocean of difficulties, without that competency of political skill, abilities and inclination which is necessary to manage the helm. . . . Integrity and firmness is all I can promise.

On April 16 Washington left his home. His progress from Virginia to New York was a triumphal procession far different from the "quiet entry devoid of ceremony" he had requested. Speeches, toasts, cannon shots, militia parades, banners, and archways decorated with laurel marked each step of the long and somewhat taxing journey. At Trenton, New Jersey, there were ovations and orations, and 13 young girls in white strewed flowers. This celebration made an especially vivid impact, offering as it did such a marked contrast with the icy crossing of the Delaware River that Washington's ragged troops had made at that very spot in 1776 during the darkest days of the Revolution.

On April 23 Washington embarked from Elizabeth Town, New Jersey, for New York City on an elaborate barge rowed by 13 pilots dressed in white smocks and black-fringed hats. It had been constructed for the event with funds donated by 46 prominent citizens. The 15-mile boat trip took the President-elect past Staten Island, through the Upper Bay and inner harbor to Murray's Wharf at the foot of Wall Street in Lower Manhattan. Washington later commented in his diary:

The display of boats which attended and joined us on this occasion, some with vocal and some with instrumental music on board; the decorations of the ships; the roar of cannon and the loud acclamations of the people, which rent the skies as I passed along the wharves, filled my mind with sensations as painful (considering the reverse of this scene, which may be the case after all my labors to do good) as they were pleasing.

At the landing, richly carpeted steps and crimson upholstered railings added to the effect. One spectator observed that "the General was obliged to wipe his eyes several times." Once Washington had reached his new quarters at Cherry Street, dignitaries and former officers pressed forward to greet him; later that evening, Governor George Clinton of New York gave a banquet in his honor.

The inauguration itself did not take place for another week. During the following days, members of Congress heatedly argued issues of etiquette and nomenclature, Finally the Senate, which had favored designating the Chief Executive as "His Highness the President of the United States of America and Protector of the Rights of the Same," agreed to follow the House's simpler title of "The President of the United States." In the meantime Washington reworked and polished his inaugural address, discarding a prepared 64-page speech and substituting instead a short text that, when read, lasted less than 20 minutes.

On the morning of April 30, Inaugural Day, Washington awoke at dawn to the thunder of 13 cannon shots and the ringing of church bells. At noon he donned a suit of brown broadcloth with silver buttons decorated with spread eagles, silver-buttoned shoes, and his dress sword. He deliberately chose this suit, spun in Connecticut, to encourage native textile manufacturers. Reportedly "the cloth was of a fine fabric, and as handsomely finished, as any European superfine clothing."

Washington proceeded to Federal Hall at Wall and Nassau streets. A crimson canopy, a dais with an armchair, a small table, and a large Bible on a red pillow had been placed on the balcony of the Senate Chamber there. Robert R. Livingston, the chancellor of the State of New York, administered the presidential oath and then exclaimed: "Long live George Washington, President of the United States!" President Washington retired inside the Senate Chamber to read to Congress his inaugural address in a voice described as "deep, a little tremulous." After the ceremony, he attended a service at St. Paul's Chapel on Broadway and was then escorted to his place of residence to rest before the evening receptions and fireworks.

The President resided at Cherry Street until February 23, 1790. The US government changed the location of the capital to Philadelphia in 1790, and Washington took the oath of office for his second term in that city on March 4, 1793.

Federal Hall in New York City, where Washington took his first presidential oath, is no longer standing. In 1812 it brought $425 when it was sold for salvage. Thirty years later it was replaced by the present Federal Hall, a Greek Revival structure with massive Doric columns, which served primarily as a customs house. This building is on a site occupying only about half of the area of the razed hall. Designated a memorial national historic site in May 1939, it became in August 1955 a national memorial administered by the National Park Service of the Department of the Interior for "the inspiration and benefit of the people of the United States commemorating the founding of the Federal Government and related historic events." On its steps is the well-known bronze statue of Washington by John Quincy Adams Ward. In the rotunda inside Federal Hall is a rust-colored piece of sandstone from the balcony of the original hall. Known as the Washington Stone, it is supposedly the one on which the President stood while taking the presidential oath. The Bible on which Washington swore is owned by St. John's Masonic Lodge. Documentation and exhibits concerning the opening months of his presidency to August 30, 1790, are displayed in the Washington Room.

Every year on April 30 a commemorative program is staged at Federal Hall. At noon on Friday, April 30, 1971, the 182nd anniversary program took place at the historic site, which is now overshadowed by the glass and steel skyscrapers of New York City's financial district. Instead of the sea of friendly faces that greeted Washington's eyes, there was only a hurried crowd of a few hundred persons who paused briefly during their lunch hour to listen and watch. The traditional exercises included patriotic band music and speeches, a display of Revolutionary War flags, and a recitation of Washington's prayer by Henry DuBois. Attired as General George Washington, commander in chief of the Continental Armed Forces, the 85-year-old DuBois had been portraying this role for 29 years. The program was sponsored by a number of groups, including the New York City Shrines Associates, the New York City American Revolution Bicentennial Committee, the New York State American Revolution Bicentennial Commission, and the National Park Service.

APRIL 17

American Academy of Arts and Letters Chartered

The American Academy of Arts and Letters and its parent body, the National Institute of Arts and Letters, are considered the United States' two most prestigious societies honoring accomplishments in the fields of music, literature, and art. The 250 members of the institute are among the most honored of this country's artists, writers and musicians; the elite of their number are the 50 members of the institute who are elected to the American Academy of Arts and Letters on the basis of special distinction.

The institute was founded in 1898 for the purpose of furthering literature and the fine arts in the United States and was incorporated in 1913 by an act of Congress signed by President William Howard Taft. The academy was created as a section or inner body of the institute in 1904 and was incorporated (chartered) by an act of Congress signed by President Woodrow Wilson on April 17, 1916. It is more than likely that the institute and its academy were inspired by and patterned after the Institut de France and the renowned Académie Française, whose members are often called the Forty Immortals.

The original members of this country's institute, chosen by a committee of the American Social Science Association "as representing the highest artistic achievements of their time," included such eminent individuals as authors Henry Adams, George Washington Cable, William Dean Howells (who was to serve as president of the academy from 1908 to 1920), and Mark Twain; naturalist John Burroughs; painter John LaFarge; composer Edward MacDowell;

sculptor Augustus Saint-Gaudens; and two future Presidents of the United States, Theodore Roosevelt and Woodrow Wilson (both chosen for membership on the basis of their literary works). The memberships of the National Institute of Arts and Letters and the American Academy of Arts and Letters are maintained at 250 and 50, respectively, by annual elections to fill any vacancies caused by death.

The main function of the two honor societies — to stimulate and encourage the arts — is carried out by conferring honors and awards for work of distinction brought to the attention of the selection committees by individual members of the institute and academy. No application may be submitted for any of the grants and awards, which total approximately $110,000 each year.

The awards and honors are conferred at the annual ceremonial held at the institute and academy in May, and new members are formally inducted on this occasion, which has come to be a spring festival of the arts for many Americans. Exhibitions of works of art, books, manuscripts, musical scores, and recordings by newly elected members are held every spring, and the works of recipients of art and literary awards and honors are also included. Other regularly scheduled art exhibitions are held during the year. While the exhibitions are in progress, the art gallery and museum are open to the public from 1:00 to 4:00 P.M. daily except Mondays and holidays.

The American Academy and the National Institute of Arts and Letters occupy two buildings, each designed by a member of the academy, on Audubon Terrace on Manhattan's upper West Side. One building houses the art gallery, where regular exhibitions are held, and the 760-seat auditorium where the annual ceremonial takes place. The other building, called the Administration Building, contains the executive offices, the members' room, the museum, the library, and the Hassam room.

The members' room, reserved for meetings of the academy, contains 50 numbered chairs, each bearing a plaque inscribed with the names of previous and present occupants. Art, books, and manuscript exhibitions are held in the museum, which houses a collection of manuscripts including many original manuscripts of poems, essays, and stories by past and present members, and a collection of correspondence between members and officers of the institute and academy. Because most of this correspondence deals with cultural matters, the letters are of historical significance. The library, limited to books by and about members, includes more than 15,000 volumes, most of which are first editions, many of them inscribed. The Hassam room contains a permanent exhibition of the work of Childe Hassam, American painter and etcher (1859–1935), as well as an art reference library.

The Administration Building is at 633 West 155th Street, between Broadway and Riverside Drive. The art gallery and museum are on Audubon Terrace, on the west side of Broadway, between 155th and 156th streets. The entrance to the auditorium is at 632 West 156th Street.

The art book and manuscript collections are available for study or reference by accredited scholars by appointment with the librarian. Borrowing privileges are restricted to members.

APRIL 18

The San Francisco Fire

At 5:12 A.M. on April 18, 1906, the ground began to quake under San Francisco, California, to the sound of jangling church bells. The tremor signaled the displacement of land surfaces along the San Andreas fault from Upper Mattole in Humboldt County to San Juan in Benito County, a distance of 270 miles. The earthquake was the worst to that date in the United States: the tremor lasted 60 to 75 seconds and reached 8.25 points on the Richter scale. Shock waves traveled from Los Angeles in the south to Coos Bay, Oregon, 750 miles to the north. Residents of Winnemuca, Nevada, 300 miles east, also felt the ground tremble. Displacement was mostly horizontal, reaching an apex of 21 feet at Tomales Bay. There was little vertical shifting.

The earthquake was felt most intensely in San Francisco, where the effect reminded one writer of a "terrier shaking a rat." It took lives throughout the city, with the greatest number of the dead concentrated in the produce district and the area south of Market Street. The tremor subsided within minutes, but it set off more than 50 blazes, which quickly became the main danger. The worst, which razed the Hayes Valley section, began when a woman attempted to cook on a stove the quake had damaged. It immediately became known as the Ham and Eggs Fire. Within 20 hours flames consumed most of the business district, all of the area south of Market Street, Chinatown, and Hayes Valley. Public transportation and the telegraph were inoperative, and 100,000 were homeless. The fire burned for two and a half days more.

San Francisco's mains broke early in the disaster, but the fire fighters drew water from the bay to save most of the wharves and a number of buildings. Experts used dynamite to raze structures and create a firebreak to control westward advance of the flames along Van Ness Avenue.

However, less capable use of explosives in other areas served only to start more blazes. Finally, after the water mains were repaired, San Franciscans were able to end the holocaust.

The conflagration was the worst in American history. It consumed an area six times as large as that destroyed in the London fire of 1666. The earthquake and its aftermath leveled 490 city blocks containing 2,831 acres, and did an estimated $500 million worth of damage. The business district and three-fifths of the city's homes and lodgings were in ruins. Worst of all, 450 died in the disaster.

Bleak as the disaster was, San Francisco had brighter days ahead. The rest of the United States and Europe provided thousands of dollars in financial aid, which was efficiently employed. Insurance payments of $300 million were also forthcoming, although only six companies paid in full without delay and without demanding a cash discount. Rebuilding in earthquake-proof and fire-resistant materials began immediately. San Franciscans completed the task quickly, and in 1915 their beautiful new city was the host of the Panama Pacific International Exposition.

APRIL 19

Patriots' Day

The American Revolution began on April 19, 1775, with the battles of Lexington and Concord. Through the years the state of Massachusetts has continued to celebrate the anniversary of the "shot heard round the world" as Patriots' Day, a legal holiday. In 1968, however, the Massachusetts legislature changed the date of the actual observance to the third Monday in April. (In 1970, under the new system, the celebration was on April 20.)

Massachusetts was tense in the spring of 1775. Since the previous year the province had languished under the so-called Intolerable Acts, which were imposed by the British Parliament in retribution for the Boston Tea Party of December 16, 1773 (see December 16). England ordered the port of Boston closed until the colonists paid for the shipment of tea, which had been destroyed to protest taxation by Parliament. The governor's powers were increased to the detriment of local autonomy, and royal officials were put beyond the jurisdiction of provincial courts in capital cases.

The royal government's harassment provoked a portentous response in the Bay Colony. In October 1774 Massachusetts set up a Provincial Congress, an extralegal legislative body of revolutionary tendencies. Committees of Correspondence communicated the incendiary message of Massachusetts' experience to other mainland colonies. Militia units drilled with special intensity, and the patriots seized British military stores in Boston and Charlestown and accumulated their own in Concord and Worcester.

General Thomas Gage, the British commander in chief in America, who had taken over the governorship of the unruly province in 1774, received authorization on April 14, 1775, to take decisive action to regain control of events. Determined to seize the colonists' supplies in Concord, he kept the mission a secret, waiting until the last minute to inform Lieutenant Colonel Francis Smith, the commander of the expedition, of his objective. Despite all of Gage's precautions, the watchful and suspicious Americans became aware of the plans. Brigadier General Hugh Percy learned that the colonists were expecting trouble and told the governor, but Gage thought it too late to turn back.

At about 10 P.M. on April 18, the patriot leader Dr. Joseph Warren dispatched William Dawes to warn their comrades at Concord. As Dawes was going by way of Boston Neck, Warren shortly afterward sent Paul Revere by another route across Charlestown Neck. The two riders reached Lexington and then set out for Concord. Between 1 and 2 A.M. they ran into a British patrol assigned by Gage to intercept messengers. Dawes escaped, but the soldiers seized Revere, whom they released shortly. The poet Henry Wadsworth Longfellow made Revere and his ride known to the world; Dawes is remembered only by historians.

Lieutenant Colonel Smith and his second-in-command, Marine Major John Pitcairn, had an elite British force of approximately 700 men, making up eight infantry and eight grenadier companies, at their disposal for the mission. At dusk on April 18 they assembled their men on Boston Common, and in the darkness they made their way to a spot near what is now Park Square, where the men boarded boats. The oars were muffled as they silently rowed to Phips Farm, now East Cambridge. Wet and uncomfortable, the redcoats landed before midnight and wasted two hours awaiting unnecessary extra provisions. The column then began its march, crossing a waist-deep ford to avoid using a noisy wooden bridge.

Pitcairn led the advance guard of six light companies. His men encountered the patrol that had captured Revere. These men passed on the false report, which Revere had invented for their benefit, that 500 militiamen were waiting at Lexington. Pitcairn proceeded slowly, allowing Smith's men to catch up in case he needed reinforcement, and it was about 5 A.M. when the British were able to see Lexington.

At sunrise on April 19 Captain John Parker and only about 70 armed men were assembled on Lexington green. The other minutemen were getting gunpowder from the meetinghouse where they had hidden it. Pitcairn formed his numerically superior force in a battle line and ordered the colonists to lay down their arms. Tradition relates that Captain Parker had instructed his men: "Don't fire unless fired upon! But if they want a war, let it begin here." Actually, the captain was more prudent. Recognizing that resistance would be futile, Parker ordered his men to disperse. Suddenly, however, gunfire crackled and a quick fight ensued, leaving 8 Americans dead and 10 wounded; only one British soldier was injured.

Who really fired "the shot heard round the world?" Nineteenth century American historians, such as George Bancroft, blamed the British; John Fiske went so far as to claim that Major Pitcairn personally pulled the first trigger. Twentieth century scholars are less sure. It seems that the militiamen on the green did not fire and that Pitcairn did not give the order to shoot. Most likely the culprit was an American spectator or an impetuous British soldier.

Smith and Pitcairn proceeded from Lexington to Concord, six miles away. The British searched the town and Barrett's Farm for provisions, but they found little, since the patriots had removed most of the supplies. The delay, however, permitted about 400 militiamen under Major John Buttrick to close in on the British companies stationed at Concord's North Bridge. A battle between the Americans and British ensued. Each side suffered several casualties as the colonists drove the regulars back in disorder.

Smith regrouped his men and left Concord about noon. The retreat was bloody. Americans hidden behind fences, bushes, and buildings sniped at and ambushed the British column. The unorthodox tactics exacted a high number of British casualties. Some 1,400 reinforcements under General Percy joined the disheartened column at Lexington, and both contingents set out for Boston. The return was ugly as the patriots continued their sniping, and the British, in retaliation, looted and burned houses along the road and killed all male inhabitants. By dusk the British had reached Charlestown Neck and the protection of their naval guns. Nineteen officers and 250 enlisted men had been killed or wounded that day.

The battle aroused the people of the colonies. Those in New England resolved to confine the British army to Boston. New Hampshire voted to raise 2,000 men; Connecticut, 6,000; Rhode Island, 1,500; and Massachusetts, 13,600. The city was soon encircled by patriot troops (see June 17, Bunker Hill Day). The news spread from colony to colony. Arms and ammunition were seized, provincial congresses were formed, and before the end of the summer the power of the royal governors had been completely destroyed.

Massachusetts abounds in memorials to the first battle of the Revolution. Lexington Green, the scene of the initial skirmish, is administered by the town government; it contains several tributes of interest. The Revolutionary Monument of 1799, located in the southwest corner of the green, commemorates the eight Americans who fell there on April 19, 1775. In 1835 their bodies were removed from the old burying ground and placed in a tomb behind the memorial. Henry H. Kitson's statue of a minuteman, erected in 1899, dominates the east side of the common. The militia leader's famous words, quoted earlier, are inscribed on a marker in the northwest corner of the green.

The Lexington Historical Society administers the Buckman Tavern, which is depicted in the background of nearly every illustration of the battle scene. Its walls still pockmarked by the British musket balls, the building now serves as headquarters for Lexington Minute Men, an organization devoted to perpetuating the traditions of Captain Parker's company. The society also administers the Hancock-Clarke House, from which patriot leaders Samuel Adams and John Hancock were evacuated before the battle in order to avoid capture by the British. In 1876 the building was moved from its original site to its present location across the road.

Over 600 acres of roadside and landscape along the more than four-mile route between Lexington and Concord that the British troops followed constitute another point of interest. These grounds are part of the 750-acre Minuteman National Historic Park, opened in 1959 and operated by the National Park Service. The site, which has been restored to its 1775 condition, contains original stone walls, boulders, and other features.

One hundred fifty acres of the park lie on either side of the Concord River, where it is spanned by a replica of the gently arched North Bridge. Daniel C. French's bronze statue of a minuteman stands guard 150 feet beyond the western end of the bridge. Inscribed on its base are words from Ralph Waldo Emerson's "Concord Hymn":

By the rude bridge that arched the flood,
  Their flag to April's breeze unfurled,
Here once the embattled farmers stood
And fired the shot heard round the world.

The Concord area features other points of interest, including Nathaniel Hawthorne's residence, The Wayside. The park has acquired the

building because it served during the Revolution as the home of Samuel Whitney, the mustermaster of the Concord militia. The Society of the First Parish owns and operates Wright's Tavern in Concord. There the minutemen assembled when the courthouse bell signaled that the British were coming.

Massachusetts residents have celebrated Patriots' Day almost every year since the 18th century. Festivities in Concord generally are prefaced by Patriots' Eve balls, at which many guests appear in period gowns and uniforms. Then, just after the stroke of midnight, a leading citizen reenacts the ride of Dr. Samuel Prescott. The 20th century impersonator of Prescott, who carried Revere's message from Lexington to Concord, gallops along Route 2A to Wright's Tavern, where a large crowd awaits the rider and pealing church bells herald his arrival. A reading of Longfellow's version of the midnight ride of 1775 and concerts by fife and drum corps conclude the preparatory activities.

Cannon booms, church bells, fire alarms, and drummers beating a staccato "1-7-7-5" awaken the towns of Lexington and Concord at dawn on April 19. Before the numerous ceremonies begin, however, the traditional pancake breakfasts sponsored by local civic organizations provide sustenance for both participants and spectators.

In one typical year, festivities commenced at 5:30 A.M. in Concord with flag-raising exercises held at Bullrick Hillside, which overlooks the Old North Bridge and the battleground. By 7:30 A.M. selectmen from the surrounding towns that responded to the call for assistance in 1775 had gathered at Concord's Monument Hall, many of them wearing the traditional tricornes of the minutemen and carrying muskets.

Next a parade of 10,000 minutemen, armed forces groups, horsemen, bands, and scouting organizations made its way from the center of town to the battlefield. There ceremonies included an invocation by a local clergyman, the reading of the governor's proclamation by the president of the junior class at Concord-Carlisle Regional High School, and a greeting from the governor. Following a drill by minutemen units, the annual surprise award was presented to a leading citizen of Concord. Then representatives of British military and naval veterans decorated the graves of the British soldiers, and US Army officials similarly decorated the Minuteman Monument. The exercises closed with the playing of "Taps," "God Save the Queen," and "The Star-Spangled Banner."

The center of attention then moved to Lexington. At 1:00 P.M. reenactments of the rides of Paul Revere and William Dawes ended with the impersonators' arrival at the Minuteman Statue. However, the highlight of the occasion was

Lexington's parade. This event and the pleasant spring weather attracted more than 75,000 spectators. Bands and military groups participated, and youth, civic, and commercial organizations entered patriotic floats in the hope of winning one of the awards presented by the chamber of commerce. Following the parade, visitors could witness the Sixth Massachusetts Continentals' demonstration of musket and cannon firing or tour the historic houses of the area.

Other Massachusetts towns and cities hold similar celebrations. In Boston, for example, the Revere and Dawes rides are reenacted, and the impersonators usually carry proclamations from the city's mayor to the officials of the towns along their routes. A ceremony in which the mayor or other high city official lays a wreath at the foot of the statue of Paul Revere in front of historic Old North Church is among the high points of Boston's celebration, which is climaxed by an armed forces parade. Roxbury, Brookline, Cambridge, Somerville, and Medford are among other Massachusetts communities that annually recall the original Patriots' Day with their own versions of patriotic fervor and historical pageantry.

Probably the most famous of all Patriots' Day festivities, however, is the Boston Marathon, which has been an annual feature since 1896. Sponsored by the Boston Athletic Association, the 26-mile race is run from the town of Hopkinton to Boston.

APRIL 20

Gift of The Hague Peace Palace

During the last quarter of the 19th century all of the European powers except Great Britain introduced the principle of compulsory military training for every able-bodied male citizen. The growth of vast national armies resulting from this policy convinced many that the specter of war was at hand. But there were some who would not passively accept the possibility of such disaster. Innumerable peace societies sprang up in Europe and the United States, and their members argued that if the major national governments would agree to limit armaments and arbitrate international disputes war might be avoided.

Hopes for world peace were encouraged when Czar Nicholas II of Russia suggested that an international conference meet at The Hague in 1899 to consider a general disarmament. Although the participating nations could not agree to a limitation on arms, the meeting did result in the establishment of the first permanent court of international arbitration. The court had one glaring defect — there was no mechanism by which nations could be forced to submit their claims to arbitration — but in the euphoric months immediately following the first Hague Peace Conference this was overlooked. Attention centered instead on providing a suitable peace palace at The Hague.

Shortly after the conference had adjourned, Lyudvig von Martins, the Russian minister in Berlin, approached Andrew White, the American ambassador at The Hague, with the suggestion that one of the latter's compatriots might be able to contribute the funds needed for the construction of the peace palace. White immediately thought of Andrew Carnegie (see November 25). In the years following the Civil War, Carnegie had ruthlessly built his fortune in the steel industry, but by 1899 he had embarked upon an extraordinary philanthropic career. White wrote to Carnegie concerning the palace and after several months of desultory correspondence received an invitation to Carnegie's castle in Scotland. Carnegie said nothing of the palace until the final day of White's visit, when he agreed to supply the necessary funds if such an agreement proved acceptable to the government of the Netherlands.

An accord with the Dutch was reached, and on April 20, 1903, Carnegie donated $1.5 million for the peace palace. Construction of the building on land contributed by the Dutch government was begun in 1907 and completed in 1913. Since then it has served as the seat of the Permanent Court of Arbitration. The Permanent Court of International Justice, established in 1922, and its successor, the International Court of Justice, created in 1946 as an organ of the United Nations, have also been housed in The Hague Peace Palace.

APRIL 21

Passover (Pesach)

This is a movable event. See note on page xxvi.

Passover (in Hebrew, *Pesach*), or the Feast of Unleavened Bread, is one of the most important and elaborate celebrations of the Jewish year. As it began more than 3,000 years ago and continues to the present day, it is also one of the oldest festivals known to history. Beginning at sundown on the 14th day of the month of Nisan (March–April), the Passover is observed by Orthodox and Conservative Jews for the next eight days, and by Reform Jews, and in Israel, for the next seven. Its high point is the seder, a ceremonial meal served in all Jewish homes on the first night; and by Conservative, Orthodox, and some Reform Jews on the second night as well. Many Reform synagogues observe a home seder one night and on the other have a community seder in the synagogue for members and their guests. The seder is also served in hotels or central meeting halls for those away from home.

Passover is a celebration of the Exodus, the deliverance of the Jews under Moses after their many generations of captivity in Egypt. Thus it is a festival of freedom from bondage, marking the real beginning of the Jewish nation.

The entire story of the Jews' deliverance, including their safe passage across the Red Sea, is recounted in the Old Testament in the Book of Exodus. According to this account, the Jews, obeying the injunction of Moses, remained in their houses on the fateful night before their exodus from Egypt, dressed ready for their journey, and ate unleavened bread and the sacrificial (or paschal) lamb. Fulfilling Moses' prediction, the firstborn of the Egyptians were slain, both humans and animals, so that no Egyptian household remained without its dead.

The term "Passover" refers to the way in which God, when he smote the firstborn of the Egyptians, passed over the houses of the Jews in Egypt, as their lintels and doorposts had been marked with the blood of sacrificial lambs in accordance with God's instructions to Moses. Fulfillment of the prediction caused the Pharaoh to summon Moses in the night and urge him to depart in haste from the land with his people. Later, reconsidering the loss of their servants, the Jews, the Egyptians pursued them and were swallowed by the waters of the sea, which, according to the biblical account, parted to allow the Jews to pass dry-shod but closed upon the Egyptians.

After the Jews reached the Promised Land some 40 years later, they continued Passover as Moses had originally instructed them. Except for the now discontinued offering of sacrificial lambs on the eve of Passover — an annual ritual from the Jews' entry into Israel until the destruction of the Second Temple in Jerusalem — the Passover rites of biblical times have been observed to this day. Essentially the observance is a reliving, on an individual basis, of the original Passover experience and an expression of gratitude for it. It also serves to preserve the history of the people and to instruct the young. Passover customs are deliberately arranged for the delight of children and for their participation.

In preparation for the Passover celebration, houses are cleaned, traditional foods are prepared, and special dishes and cooking utensils,

unused during the rest of the year, are placed in readiness. During the seven or eight days of the actual Passover observance only unleavened bread, the traditional matzos or bread of affliction, commemorating the Jews' hasty departure from Egypt before the leaven or yeast in their bread had time to rise, is eaten. On the night before Passover eve, Orthodox Jews make certain that there is no yeast or leavened bread in their homes. The head of each household conducts a ritualized search by candlelight. The leaven is then burned.

The seder finds the head of the family in the place of honor, provided (like other males) with cushions in memory of the ancient manner of freemen who reclined at table, and with his family, guests, and servants all seated at table with him in recognition of the equality of all before God. In the center of the table are the symbolic Passover foods, including unleavened bread; bitter herbs in remembrance of the hardships of slavery; a roasted egg, as a free-will or voluntary offering; salt water, signifying tears; *haroset*, a mixture of apples, nuts, cinnamon, and wine, representing the bricks and mortar used in Egypt; and a roasted shank bone of lamb, symbolizing the sacrificial lamb of tradition. There is wine on the table, and four cups or glasses are drunk by each participant, each cup at a fixed point in the ceremonial meal, with a fifth cup placed on the table for the prophet Elijah, who, it is believed, will pave the way for the coming of the Messiah.

The focal point of the seder is the reading aloud of the story of the Exodus. The account, as related in the *Haggadah*, is in response to four questions, asked by the youngest child of the family, as to the meaning of the evening and its customs, beginning with the traditional "Why is this night different from other nights?" Commencing his answers, the head of the household responds: "We were slaves in Egypt, but the Lord our God brought us out with a mighty hand and an outstretched arm." In addition to the Exodus account, the seder includes benedictions, psalms, and prayers of thanksgiving. The family service ends on a note of gaiety with children and adults joining to sing various folk songs. Midway through the service the meal proper is served.

Among Orthodox and Conservative Jews, the first two and last two days of Passover are regarded as holy days. Reform Jews and Jews in Israel regard the first and the seventh days as holy. The seventh or eighth day, like the last day of each of the major Jewish festivals, includes a memorial service for the dead. Special Passover services are held in synagogues throughout the Passover season.

San Jacinto Day

One of the most important days of the year for Texans is April 21, the anniversary of the battle of San Jacinto. A legal state holiday, San Jacinto Day marks the victory, in 1836, by which Mexico was forced to recognize the independence of Texas.

Mexico itself had been independent from Spain for only 15 years at the time of the battle, and, like Spain before, Mexico considered the area of Texas to be within its boundaries. Since the United States also claimed the area, the question of ownership was complicated.

The conflicting claims, which led, at least indirectly, to the battle of San Jacinto, went back to the long-standing confusion over exactly what lands constituted the Louisiana territory. That vast region had been controlled by France (beginning in 1682), by Spain (from 1762 to 1800), and again (briefly) by France. When the United States acquired Louisiana from France by the Louisiana Purchase in 1803 (see December 20), the region was vaguely understood to extend from the Mississippi River to the Rocky Mountains and from the Gulf of Mexico to what is now Canada. But although the French probably considered Texas part of Louisiana, the wily Napoleon declined to define Louisiana's boundaries precisely, remarking that "if an obscurity did not already exist, it would perhaps be good policy to put one there." The Adams-Onís Treaty of 1819, by which the United States acquired Florida from Spain while renouncing its claim to Texas (see July 17) did nothing to clarify matters, since the United States regretted the renunciation soon afterwards. The situation was soon complicated further by Mexican inducements for US pioneers to help settle the vast open spaces of Texas.

The first direct step toward Texas' independence had come in 1810, at the beginning of the revolution by which Mexico expelled the Spaniards who had ruled it so long. The Texans, assisted by forces from the United States, chose that moment to set up a government of their own, with Nacogdoches as their capital. Texas' independence at that time was brief, however, since the forces of Spain — which remained in power until 1821 — soon broke up the new government.

In 1820, meanwhile, Moses Austin had petitioned the Spanish governor of Texas for a grant of land big enough to provide farms for 300 families of American settlers. He learned in 1821 that his request had been granted, but he died before he could carry out his plan for settlement. Instead, the idea was implemented by his son, Stephen Austin, who secured confirmation of his father's grant from later Mexican regimes and learned that he could have as much land as

he wished, at no cost, and at a location of his own choice.

Later Mexico continued to offer large gifts of land, either to individual settlers or to the *empresarios* who, like Austin, contracted to bring them. The result of the official generosity was a flood of US settlers. The number exceeded 7,000 early in the 1820s, tripled within the next decade, and continued to swell thereafter.

Mexican authorities, unprepared for the size of the response, became alarmed lest the region become a US province. The alarm was not lessened by the nature of the settlers, who considered themselves subject to no one and who were totally unaccustomed to the Spanish-Mexican style of arbitrary rule.

By 1826 the settlers, resenting Mexican misrule — as the Mexicans resented some violations of the provisions for land settlement — proclaimed the eastern part of Texas an independent republic. As such it survived for only a short time. It was after this act of insurrection that the Mexican authorities ordered a stop to further American immigration in 1827, although they did not enforce the order until 1830. Then they dispatched troops to carry out their decrees, ejecting recent arrivals.

Two years later there was another revolt, followed by the calling of a convention, which elected Stephen Austin president. The authority of Mexico over Texas nonetheless continued, and Austin was sent to Mexico to demand reforms. Instead of getting a hearing, he was made a prisoner.

After his release in July 1835 Austin — who previously had favored neither annexation nor revolt — became involved in the Texas Revolution. The first battle of that revolution was fought on October 2, 1835, at Gonzales. After this victory, the Texans captured San Antonio, where they fortified themselves in the Alamo. Santa Anna, the Mexican general and dictator, began his long siege of that bastion on February 23, 1836.

While the siege was going on, another conference of Texans, meeting on March 2, formally declared Texas independent of Mexico (see March 2). It was just four days later, on March 6, 1836, that the outnumbered defenders of the Alamo were massacred by Santa Anna's men (see March 6).

The provisional government of Texas, meeting on the day of the tragedy, appointed Sam Houston "commander in chief of all land forces of the Texian Army, regulars, volunteers and militia," supplementing his earlier appointment as commander only of regulars. Directly after the new appointment, Houston went to Gonzales and there learned of the Alamo tragedy. Gathering an army as he went, Houston retreated east toward the Brazos River, followed closely by Santa Anna. Arriving at the point where Buffalo Bayou joins the San Jacinto River, Houston made camp — and waited for the enemy to make a mistake.

The mistake came on the afternoon of April 21, when Santa Anna's men failed to post lookouts. Nearly 1,600 strong, they were taken by surprise by Houston's force of some 900 Texans, who had crossed a mile of prairie to reach them, screened only by sparse trees and rising ground and inspired by the slogan "Remember the Alamo." The battle lasted 18 minutes. In that time 630 Mexicans were killed and 730 taken prisoner, at a cost of 9 Texan lives. Santa Anna was made a prisoner the next day and was forced to sign a treaty by which he pledged to do what he could to secure recognition of Texas as an independent republic, with boundaries extending as far south as the Rio Grande. The battle of San Jacinto, one of the most decisive in American history, confirmed the independence of Texas and also paved the way for its annexation by the United States on March 1, 1845. The site of the battle, 22 miles east of Houston and now a state park, has been designated a national historic landmark. The scene of the battle is marked by a 570-foot stone shaft topped with a lone star and housing a museum in its base.

Five months after the battle, a new Texan constitution was ratified, and General Houston became the first president of the new republic, after defeating Stephen Austin in an election. Austin served as the republic's secretary of state until his death a few months later.

The first of a long series of celebrations of the victory of San Jacinto took place in Houston in 1837. The program included the erection of a liberty pole upon which was placed the lone-star flag of the republic. In the afternoon, after prayer, a speech was delivered at the same hour that the battle was fought. Two evening dances were held — including one for the heroes of San Jacinto.

Since then the anniversary celebrations have spread across Texas, which became a state on December 29, 1845. Today, there are special San Jacinto Day exercises in the public schools of the state and other observances in various cities.

One of the most notable celebrations, the Fiesta San Antonio, is held annually in San Antonio and always scheduled to include the anniversary of the battle. A focal point of the observance, which was first staged to welcome President Benjamin Harrison to the city in 1891, is the Alamo, where coronation ceremonies for King Antonio customarily take place on the first Saturday evening of the fiesta. Two days later, on Monday, the Alamo is always the destination of a solemn pilgrimage. Thousands gather there

to hear the names of the Alamo's 187 defenders intoned and to bank the former citadel with flowers. State, county, municipal, and military leaders take part in the ceremonies, along with schoolchildren and members of patriotic and other organizations.

San Antonio's fiesta, which became a yearly event in 1896, originally was patterned in part on the flower carnivals of Nice in southern France, with a battle of flowers commemorating the battle of San Jacinto. Like the Alamo pilgrimage, the huge Battle of Flowers parade remains a high point of the celebration, winding through miles of San Antonio's downtown streets before more than half a million spectators. In one typical year, the parade took place on the seventh day of the festival and lasted all afternoon.

Fiesta San Antonio, which had grown into a three-day celebration by the mid-1930s, had expanded to a 10-day event by 1970. One of the events still held is the arrival and crowning of King Antonio, held on Saturday. The Fiesta River parade, on Monday, is sponsored by the Texas Cavaliers. It is a water parade with elaborate floats, many of them carrying musical units, winding their way along the San Antonio River to the reviewing stand at Arneson River Theater.

Another outstanding event, held on Wednesday, is the coronation of the fiesta queen — Her Gracious Majesty, Queen of the Court, sponsored by the Order of the Alamo — and the honoring of her attending princesses and duchesses. The coronation is followed by a reception and ball.

A popular addition to Fiesta San Antonio is Night in Old San Antonio, four evenings of gaiety in the 300-year-old restored La Villita section. The fiesta also includes fireworks, a carnival midway, street dancing, a band festival, a children's dance fete, military reviews, a flower and fashion show, and evening entertainment with a Spanish or Mexican flavor. The celebration concludes on the final weekend with the Fiesta Flambeau, a torchlit parade on Saturday evening with scores of glittering floats, followed on Sunday by a *Charreada*, or Mexican horse show.

Spanish-American War Begins

Replying to a declaration of war by Spain on April 24, 1898, the United States declared that a state of war had been in effect between the two countries since April 21 — the day when the main squadron of the US Atlantic fleet had been ordered to Cuban waters. The United States' intervention, on behalf of Cuban insurgents who for decades had been trying to free Cuba from Spanish rule, came about against a background of pro-Cuban sympathies that had been mounting gradually in the United States for some time.

The conflict had its origins in Spain's attempt to maintain its position as a power in the New World. The pride and remembered glory of a once vast empire played an important role in Spanish determination to retain control of Cuba. Spanish voyages of exploration and settlement had created an empire that included large areas within what is now the United States; Mexico and Central America; all of South America except Brazil; small colonies in Africa and the Far East; and various islands around the globe. Spain remained a great imperial power until the time of the Napoleonic Wars. Then, in 1808, the French emperor Napoleon I put his brother Joseph on the throne of occupied Spain. The result was a series of upheavals in Spain and in the Spanish colonies. By 1819 all but Cuba, the Philippine Islands, and some holdings in the Caribbean, Africa, and the Far East, had gained their independence.

After a Cuban patriots' revolt in 1895, Spain introduced the *reconcentrado* system, under which peasant families were relocated in fortified cities while the countryside was ravaged to destroy insurgents' sources of supply. This policy, like the earlier unsuccessful Ten Years' War for independence (1868–1878), brought great suffering to Cuba's rural population and increased sympathy in the United States. Pro-insurgent feelings also were inflamed by sensational coverage of Cuban events in the so-called "yellow press," notably William Randolph Hearst's New York *Journal* and Joseph Pulitzer's New York *World*. The rivalry of the two newspapers perhaps reached its apex with inflammatory accounts of the sinking of the US battleship *Maine*, with a loss of 260 lives, in Havana harbor on February 15, 1898 (see February 15).

The *Maine* had been sent to Havana for the protection of American citizens and American property in Cuba. Our involvement had grown significantly. Americans had a huge stake in the island's economy, with substantial sugar and mining investments and enormous trading and shipping interests. Another factor was the US hope of building an Atlantic-to-Pacific canal across the Central American isthmus and Cuba's strategic location in any such project.

Although most Americans, including President William McKinley, had hoped for a peaceful settlement of the Cuban situation, war sentiment was fed by the exaggerated Hearst and Pulitzer reports; by a Spanish diplomat's contemptuous reference to President McKinley, in a stolen letter that was widely publicized by Hearst; and by the sinking of the *Maine*, in which Spanish complicity was readily suspected but never proved.

On April 11 McKinley asked Congress for authority to intervene in Cuba. Congress responded with resolutions that demanded Spain's withdrawal from Cuba and defined terms for US intervention and on April 22 passed an act authorizing the enlistment of volunteer troops. The Spanish declaration of war, which came two days later, was followed by the United States' retroactive declaration, placing the beginning of hostilities on April 21.

The war itself was a brief and one-sided contest, with some of the major engagements fought halfway around the world, in the Philippine Islands (see May 1, Battle of Manila Bay). Action in Cuba included encounters at Santiago, where much of the Spanish fleet was destroyed; at Las Guásimas and El Caney; and at San Juan Hill, where the volunteer Rough Riders of Theodore Roosevelt and Leonard Wood won fame.

An armistice supposedly stopping the fighting (though an attack on Manila took place the following day) was signed on August 12, 1898. Details of the peace (see January 28, United States Withdraws from Cuba) were set forth in the Treaty of Paris of 1898, signed on December 10. The treaty was ratified by the US Senate on February 6, 1899, and signed by the President four days later (see February 10). Spain emerged from the conflict with all but the last remnants of its colonial empire gone and its long influence in the New World at an end. Cuba became an independent republic under US protection. At the end of the war, the United States had become a world power of greater magnitude, with new interest in the Pacific and an increased stake in the affairs of the Caribbean.

APRIL 22

American Lutheran Church Organized

At a constituting convention held in Minneapolis, Minnesota, on April 22–24, 1960, the American Lutheran Church, the Evangelical Lutheran Church, and the United Evangelical Lutheran Church merged as the American Lutheran Church, effective as of January 1, 1961 (see January 1, American Lutheran Church Merger Becomes Effective).

Arbor Day

"Other holidays repose upon the past; Arbor Day proposes for the future." The words of the originator of Arbor Day, Julius Sterling Morton, pinpoint the significance of this day, which focuses on the value of trees. Today conservation of the natural environment is universally acknowledged to be of major importance; however, Morton was one of the earliest conservationists — at a time when even the term was unknown. In honor of the Nebraska City newspaper editor, who in 1872 proposed the first Arbor Day as an occasion for tree planting, Nebraska now celebrates Arbor Day as a legal holiday on April 22, the anniversary of Morton's birth. (In Nebraska City, Morton's home town, there is a particularly enthusiastic celebration.)

The day, which takes note of the beauty of trees as well as of their practical uses, is observed not only throughout the United States but, in their own manner, by many other countries. In the United States, Arbor Day is observed on a number of different dates in addition to April 22, the date marked by Nebraska, the first state to note such an occasion. The most commonly observed date in the United States is the last Friday in April, the day widely proposed for the uniform observance of a National Arbor Day.

One of the first Americans to concern himself seriously with the need for more trees was the pioneering John Chapman, who became known as Johnny Appleseed (see September 26). A few years after the American Revolution, Chapman set out from his native Massachusetts with a pouch of apple seeds and little else. Fruit trees were scarce in the developing western areas, so he wandered through present-day Pennsylvania, Ohio, Illinois, and Indiana, planting apple trees.

Several decades later Julius Sterling Morton, who became known as the Father of Arbor Day, also went west, when he was only a child. At the age of two Morton, who had been born in Adams, Jefferson County, New York, on April 22, 1832, moved with his family to Michigan, where he received his elementary education at the Methodist Episcopal Academy in Albion. Entering the University of Michigan, he transferred to Union College in Schenectady, New York, from which he was graduated with a B.A. degree in the class of 1854. Morton married in October 1854, and the following year he and his wife settled on the treeless plains of Nebraska, where he edited the Nebraska City *News* and also became active in politics. In the course of his career he served as a member of the Nebraska territorial legislature, as secretary of the territory, and for a time as acting territorial governor. After Nebraska gained statehood in 1867, he ran unsuccessfully as a Democratic candidate for the governorship and for a seat in the US Senate.

He also developed new agricultural methods and fervently advocated improved agricultural methods through his newspaper writings and in other ways. He was a member of the state board of agriculture and was appointed secretary of agriculture by President Grover Cleveland, serving in that capacity from 1893 to 1897. At the same time (1893–1896) he was president of the American Forestry Association. He died in 1902.

Believing that the Nebraska prairie area in which he homesteaded would benefit from trees — which could serve as windbreaks, hold moisture in the soil, and provide lumber needed for shelter — Morton began planting trees and urging his neighbors to do the same. He felt, however, that his idea was not catching on rapidly enough, and when he joined the state board of agriculture he seized the opportunity to propose that a specific day be set aside for the planting of trees. His resolution included a provision for prizes to be awarded to the county agricultural society and to the individual who properly planted the largest number of trees on the first Arbor Day, and he proposed April 10, 1872, for that designation. The idea proved unexpectedly popular: a million trees were planted in Nebraska on that one day alone.

So successful was the day that it was made an annual event in 1884, and in 1885 the state legislature passed an act specifying April 22, the anniversary of Morton's birth, as the date on which Arbor Day would thenceforth be celebrated as a legal holiday. About 350 million trees — an astounding total — were planted in Nebraska within 16 years after that first Arbor Day in 1872. Interest in tree planting continued, and today the state has a national forest planted by Nebraskans that covers more than 200,000 acres and from which seedlings are provided to other countries that have seriously depleted forests. In 1895 Nebraska proudly adopted the nickname the Tree Planter's State, by which it was known for years, although today it is more commonly referred to as the Cornhusker State or the Beef State.

A number of years after his death Morton's 52-room mansion, Arbor Lodge, near Nebraska City, was given to the state by his heirs. The house, which contains relics of early Nebraska, and the surrounding 65-acre woodland, which boasts more than 150 varieties of trees and shrubs, constitute the Arbor Lodge State Historical Park. Open to the public from spring until fall, the park attracts many visitors. The Arbor Day Memorial Association of the state erected a monument in honor of Morton on the grounds. A life-size statue of him was presented by the state of Nebraska for the Statuary Hall collection of the United States Capitol in Washington, D.C. In addition, a memorial tree, the J. Sterling Morton Elm, was planted on the Capitol grounds in 1932, the 100th anniversary of his birth.

Another outstanding proponent of tree planting in the United States, and one of the earliest advocates of the establishment of Arbor Day as a holiday, was the 19th century educator Birdsey Grant Northrup, born in Kent, Connecticut. He organized village-improvement associations and urged the removal of fences from front lawns and the planting of trees. Northrup traveled in the United States, Europe, and Asia, advocating the beautification of the landscape with trees. Credit for the attractiveness of such towns as Litchfield, New Milford, and Norfolk, Connecticut; Geneseo, New York; and Barre, Great Barrington and Lenox, Massachusetts, is largely his.

Agricultural organizations and town authorities promoted the observance of Arbor Day, and three years after its inception in Nebraska two other states, Kansas and Tennessee, also observed an Arbor Day, as did Minnesota the following year. Much greater stimulus was provided, however, by Ohio's first observance in April 1882. It was timed to coincide with the meeting in Cincinnati of the American Forestry Association and the American Forestry Congress. John B. Peaslee, the superintendent of schools in Cincinnati, was one of the earliest supporters of the Arbor Day movement. Cincinnati's public schools were closed for the occasion, and thousands of children took part in the festivities — complete with parade, banners, brass bands, 13-gun salute, speeches, poetry recitations, and refreshments — in Eden Park. What was called Authors' Grove was planted, each tree being named for a distinguished author, statesman, or soldier and marked with his name.

Taking account of the great interest of the Cincinnati children in Arbor Day and the benefits to be reaped by children from its observance, the American Forestry Congress in 1883 adopted a resolution calling for the annual observance of the day in all schools throughout the country. Two years later a similar resolution was adopted by the National Education Association. The movement spread rapidly across the nation with the result that all 50 states now observe an annual Arbor Day, and Puerto Rico and some US territories also do. To encourage planting, state governments and the federal government have at various times offered such incentives as free seeds or plants to landowners or payment of a cash bounty for trees planted. Since the free distribution of seeds and plants has sometimes been considered unfair to the nursery industry, however, it has largely been abandoned, although nurseries themselves sometimes provide such free bounty.

Part of the early growth of the Arbor Day movement was adoption of the concept by other countries, including Canada, Great Britain, France, Spain, Russia, Norway, China, and Japan. However, although peoples in other parts of the world had never before set aside a particular day for tree planting, they long had treasured trees and had used them widely for ornamental purposes and as the focal point of various customs. For example, the Aztecs planted a tree at the birth of each child. This custom spread to other groups, and some Indians in Mexico still practice it. Tradition holds that in colonial times a bride in America would bring to her new home a tree from her father's land and would nurture it carefully.

The most widespread observance of Arbor Day in the United States is in the public schools. Various state laws provide for exercises to be held in the schools to promote the planting and protection of trees and shrubs and an appreciation of their value. The exercises may include pageants, music, poetry, special projects, bulletin-board displays, and talks on the value of trees, in addition to the planting of trees. Many other individuals and groups, among them officials of state and local governments, civic organizations, conservation groups, service clubs, Boy and Girl Scouts, farmers, and sports organizations, also plant trees on Arbor Day, usually in cooperation with county and state conservation or forestry officials.

Trees are planted on the grounds of state capitols and of school buildings, in school forests, in community forests, along roads and highways, in parks, on all types of public and private property for both ornamental and practical purposes. Sometimes a class in school, or a local Scout troop, takes the responsibility of caring for the young trees during the coming year. Trees are also often planted as memorials; the Capitol grounds and other areas in Washington, D.C., are the site of many trees planted in honor of outstanding Americans. It was a schoolyard tree planting that furnished inspiration for the painting *Arbor Day* by the artist Grant Wood.

A few states celebrate the day under the name Arbor and Bird Day and put emphasis on planting trees and shrubs that are attractive to birds. With present-day knowledge of ecological interdependency, the observance of Arbor Day is often tied in with broader conservation programs on such topics as the soil, recreation areas, and wildlife. A central point of these programs is that wise conservation practices are the responsibility of every citizen.

Every year on Arbor Day, the President, the First Lady, or a presidential designate plants a special tree on the White House grounds. On the occasion of the 100th anniversary of Arbor Day in 1972, a fern leaf beech was planted on the grounds of the presidential residence. Among the Nebraskans present for the planting of the living monument, and for the White House reception that followed, was Mrs. Frederic Lattner, granddaughter of J. Sterling Morton.

Arbor Day is now celebrated in every state, but since it has never been made a federal holiday, diversity persists. Each state designates its own date for the celebration, and such considerations as local climatic conditions often outweigh the desire for a uniform date of observance.

Legislation to establish the last Friday in April as National Arbor Day — an idea originated in 1939 by Edward H. Scanlon, editor and publisher of *Trees* magazine, and later promoted by the National Arbor Day Committee with Harry J. Banker of West Orange, New Jersey, as executive secretary — has been introduced repeatedly in Congress, with actual passage in 1970 and again in 1972. In both cases, however, amendment made the measure effective for only one year. Under the terms of the 1970 measure, which was enacted as a joint resolution of Congress, President Nixon issued a proclamation designating April 24, the last Friday in April 1970, "as National Arbor Day, and calling upon the people of the United States to observe such day with appropriate ceremonies and activities." Again responding to congressional request, he issued a similar proclamation designating the last Friday in April as National Arbor Day in 1972.

By that time, 22 states had passed legislation making the last Friday in April Arbor Day in their respective states, and an additional seven states had Arbor Day legislation pending that would specify the same day if enacted. Since the presidential proclamations of 1970 and 1972, efforts to have the last Friday in April permanently declared as National Arbor Day by Congress have continued. Such legislation, like that relating to other federal holidays, would be binding only upon the District of Columbia and on federal employees throughout the United States. In practice, however, the states have usually passed legislation to make their observances conform to the dates chosen for federal holidays. Many environmentalists, feeling that Arbor Day would receive more attention and that its objectives would be strengthened by such uniformity of observance, hope that such will ultimately be the case for Arbor Day.

Oklahoma Day

On April 22, 1889, a frantic land "run" opened up the first section of what is now Oklahoma to white settlement. Known as the Unassigned Lands, the area consisted of approximately 2 million choice acres in the center of the vast region then called the Indian Territory. The 1889 run was instrumental in paving the way for the organization of Oklahoma Territory in 1890 and eventual statehood in 1907. April 22, an official holiday proclaimed as Oklahoma Day or Oklahoma 89ers Day, is observed each year throughout the state with parades, rodeos, and patriotic speeches. In 1949 the Oklahoma legislature passed a law designating Guthrie in Logan County — the territorial and later the first state capital — the city for the official celebration. The elaborate ceremonies staged there on the anniversary of the opening of Oklahoma for settlement are known as 89ers Days.

The land rush of April 22, 1889, was a major innovation in the history of the hitherto entirely Native American-populated area. Apart from the Plains tribes who had roamed there earlier, most of the Indians had arrived in the region as a result of the US government's policy by which Indians of the Southeast were transplanted from their ancestral homes to locations west of the Mississippi River in the 1820s, 1830s, and 1840s. The removal effort reached massive proportions after Andrew Jackson had become President in 1829. On May 28, 1830, Congress had passed the Indian Removal Act, empowering the President to "negotiate" with tribes to give up their eastern holdings in exchange for land beyond the Mississippi, which was to be theirs "as long as the grass grows, or water runs," in the words of Jackson. When the Indians resisted removal, the US military supervised a vast, involuntary, and tragedy-filled migration to the West.

The large, vaguely defined trans-Mississippi region that had become popularly known as the Indian territory meanwhile gained a more official status in 1834, when Congress set aside an area including all of what is now Oklahoma, except the Panhandle, as the Indian Territory. The unsettled region, regarded as a barren wilderness fit only for Indians, was divided among what were called the Five Civilized Tribes — Chickasaw, Creek, Seminole, Choctaw, and Cherokee — who had been driven from the Southeast (see June 25, Unto These Hills). After these tribes had, for the most part, sided with the Confederacy during the Civil War, the US government, partly in retaliation, split the Indian Territory from north to south in 1866; it forced the five Indian groups to relinquish the western part of their lands. From 1866 to 1883, the federal government made numerous small grants from this vast new territory at its disposal to other tribes, among them the Cheyennes, Apaches, Arapahoes, Comanches, Kiowas, and Pottawatomies. By the mid-1880s, the only major land block that had not yet been assigned was the fertile central region known as the Unassigned Lands, and later as Old Oklahoma, or the Oklahoma District.

When the spirit of "Go West, young man"

was renewed after the hiatus of the Civil War, the Indian Territory, once thought of little or no value, grew more and more attractive to white settlers. Cattle drovers, traveling from northern Texas across the Indian Territory to the railroad depots in Kansas, quickly discovered that the herds grew fat on the lush grasslands. The region's most famous longhorn trail was reputedly named after Jesse Chisholm, a mixed-blood Cherokee who used the route after the Civil War to get supplies to his trading post at Anadarko. Passing through the sites of several modern-day Oklahoma towns, such as Waurika, Duncan, Marlow, El Reno, and Enid, the trail reached the busy stockyards of Abilene, Kansas. In 1871 some 700,000 cattle were driven over the Chisholm Trail, while in the peak period of 1867 to 1871, an estimated 40,000 boxcars carted 1.5 million longhorns to slaughterhouses in Chicago and Kansas City. The rapidly developing range cattle industry so enhanced the worth of the Indian Territory that whites vied to rent pastures on Indian land and ran prosperous ranches nominally under Indian ownership.

Soon not only cattlemen but land-hungry homesteaders coveted the Indian Territory. Even before the railroad had reached the area of Oklahoma in the early 1870s, white settlers had illegally squatted on Indian land, ignoring all treaties. In the late 1870s newspaper articles urged settlement of what was referred to erroneously as "public land" open to homestead entry. Spurred on by these accounts, several groups of homesteaders drew up elaborate colonization schemes and to a limited extent implemented them until ejected by US soldiers. President Rutherford B. Hayes was finally forced to reiterate officially the ban on settlement in 1879 and again the following year. Nevertheless, pressure to open the Indian Territory, especially the central Unassigned Lands, increased steadily until the "boomers" – persons "booming" or pushing for settlement of the region – succeeded in transferring the issue to Washington, D.C.

Agitation by railroad companies, land sharks, and impatient frontier farmers eventually caused Congress to modify its Indian policy and open at least part of the Indian Territory to white settlement. In 1885 Congress empowered the President to conduct negotiations with the Creeks and Seminoles to extinguish all possible tribal claims to the central Unassigned Lands. By 1889 the government had managed to obtain a clear title to the unoccupied land. Soon afterwards President Benjamin Harrison announced that the Oklahoma District – as the Unassigned Lands were then termed – would be opened to entry under the Homestead Act of 1862, precisely at high noon on April 22, 1889.

Each successful homesteader would be permitted to claim one 160-acre plot free of charge.

The actual land run was a scene of picturesque confusion, making a fascinating page in American history. Estimates of the number of persons who milled along the "district" border on the morning of the historic event range all the way from 20,000 to 100,000. The US Army did its utmost to keep the excited settlers restrained behind the starting line. But some wily opportunists, known as *Sooners* (thus accounting for Oklahoma's nickname, the Sooner State), managed to evade the guards and sneak into the district before the official opening. The few Sooners who were later caught lost their claims, but many succeeded in carrying off the gamble.

At noon on April 22 the federally appointed timekeepers at the border signaled a cavalry trumpeter stationed on high ground. He in turn sounded "dinner-call" on his bugle, thus setting in motion one of the wildest and most extensive land runs in history. The whooping settlers, mainly midwesterners and southerners, tore across the line by various means of transportation: spirited thoroughbred horses, plodding nags, buckboards, covered wagons, and even bicycles. The prospect of free land had been so alluring that by nightfall nearly all of the almost 2 million acres were occupied, some claims having as many as six contenders. What at dawn had been a barren prairie was by dusk staked-out homesteads and bustling tent-and-shack communities boasting populations as high as 15,000. Among the towns that sprang into existence were Oklahoma City, Guthrie, Kingfisher, Edmond, and Norman.

The land rush of 1889 triggered a series of additional runs in 1891, 1892, and 1893, as the federal government attempted to regulate migration by allowing homesteaders to settle only one new section at a time. Especially prominent was the opening of the Cherokee Outlet on September 16, 1893. The homesteading procedure was completed by lottery and allotment in the opening years of the 20th century.

In 1890 Oklahoma Territory was created around a nucleus consisting primarily of the panhandle and the now booming Oklahoma District. Other western sections of Oklahoma were gradually added to Oklahoma Territory. The eastern area still owned by the Five Civilized Tribes became known as Indian Territory (not to be confused with the original Indian Territory set aside by Congress in 1834). The two territories combined to enter the Union as the state of Oklahoma on November 16, 1907.

Guthrie, where the April 22 anniversary is commemorated always with the greatest acclaim, had been a small depot on the Santa Fe railroad line when the land rush of 1889 transformed it in half a day into a prairie metropolis. Situated some 80 miles from the starting border, the conveniently located site, which had a federal land office, had attracted some 15,000 persons from 32 states, three US territories, and six foreign countries by the evening of the first day. Four months later, the expanding town boasted three newspapers, waterworks, schools, hospitals, and even electrically lighted streets. A year later it was the obvious choice for the capital of Oklahoma Territory.

Guthrie celebrated the anniversary of the 1889 run as early as 1890. The exercises, featuring music and patriotic addresses, drew 5,000 spectators. In the following years various programs were scheduled, as old pioneers — especially the 89ers who had made the original run — gathered for annual picnics and banquets. In 1915 the 89ers participated in a reenactment of the land rush, which was filmed for motion pictures. In the late 1920s the large-scale celebrations of the April 22 anniversary, which had been customary in the early days after the run, were reintroduced by the local American Legion post, the majority of whose members were descendants of the first settlers. Since then Guthrie has marked its birthday with a full-scale 89er festival. The celebration has grown each year in size and attendance, becoming the official state observance in 1949. It usually features a chuckwagon feed, street carnival, rodeo, and grand parade.

Characteristic of the 89ers Days at Guthrie was the four-day celebration held in 1970. Some 40,000 persons crowded into the town, which normally has a population of about 10,000, to enjoy the 41st annual event. The tribute to the pioneers who had rushed into Oklahoma 81 years before swung into action on April 22. Approximately 1,200 persons attended a chuckwagon dinner at the Logan County Fairgrounds. Prizes were awarded for the most outstanding pre-statehood costume, as well as for the most impressive beards. The local Jaycees staged a street carnival in downtown Guthrie on April 23 and April 24, and the International Rodeo Association sponsored a rodeo, which thrilled spectators at the fairgrounds during the last three days of the celebration.

The highlight of the festival was the colorful pioneer parade staged on the morning of April 25. This climactic event was preceded by a breakfast in honor of the 89ers Queen. Western gunslingers then presented a mock bank robbery and gunfight along Guthrie's Main Street, while numerous children watched in wide-eyed suspense. The three-hour parade, one of the largest attractions of its kind in the state, was headed by state officials and dignitaries and featured 123 marching and riding units. Western dances concluded the festivities.

Other Oklahoma communities, such as Midwest City, Lexington, and Norman, also stage celebrations commemorating the anniversary of the land rush. In Norman (founded on the same day and in the same manner as Guthrie), the chamber of commerce, Senior Citizens Center, and Round-Up Clubs jointly sponsor a four-day program to recognize the 89ers and perpetuate the state's traditions. It generally includes a barbecue, rodeo, square dance, arts-and-crafts exhibit, and luncheon with singing and fiddling. The climax is reached on the Saturday following April 22 with a pioneer parade featuring bands, floats, riding club groups, and the few surviving pioneers of the area.

The US Naval Station on the Aleutian island of Adak, Alaska, stages probably the most remote Oklahoma Day celebration in the world. The annual program is held usually in early fall rather than in April, when spring snows still blanket the island. It attracts an audience of about 2,000 members of the armed forces and their families, civil servants, and native islanders. While the royal blue state flag of Oklahoma waves beneath the American flag on the station flagpole, the festivities generally get under way with what is known as the Boomer-Sooner land rush. Oklahomans assigned to the classified installation dash across a huge map of their state drawn on the floor of an airplane hangar to claim "homesteads," this time their own hometowns. Sports events, square dancing, pie-eating competitions, talent shows, and greased-pig contests frequently are among the many activities scheduled for Adak's Oklahoma Day.

APRIL 23

James Buchanan's Birthday

James Buchanan, 15th President of the United States and Chief Executive just before the outbreak of the Civil War, was born near Mercersburg, Pennsylvania, on April 23, 1791, to James and Elizabeth Speer Buchanan. His father was a Scotch-Irish Presbyterian who had gone in 1783 to south-central Pennsylvania, where he became a successful storekeeper. Young James Buchanan attended a school in Mercersburg and was graduated in 1809 from Dickinson College in Carlisle, Pennsylvania. He read law diligently for three years in Lancaster, Pennsylvania, and at the age of 21 was admitted to the bar.

Buchanan proved an exceptionally able lawyer. Within three years his earnings were more than $11,000, a very large income at that time. The legal learning and oratorical skill that made him a fine lawyer also recommended him for politics. He entered the Pennsylvania House of Representatives in 1814 as a Federalist and served two terms. Buchanan then expected to retire from politics, but personal calamity intervened. His fiancee died suddenly, before he was able to heal a quarrel that had caused her to break their engagement. Buchanan put aside thoughts of marriage and turned fully to politics and its associations. He never married. Later, his orphaned niece, Harriet Lane, acted as his hostess, surrounding him with the most charming society of the time.

Buchanan was elected to Congress in 1820 and served for a decade in the House of Representatives, eventually becoming chairman of the judiciary committee. The disbanding of the Federalist party in the 1820s forced him, as a moderate, to choose between the Whig party and the Democratic-Republican party (soon after to be called the Democratic party). He chose the Democrats, unlike many Federalists, and soon established cordial relations with Andrew Jackson, whom he actively supported for President in 1828.

In 1830, after again attempting to retire from politics, Buchanan accepted the ambassadorship to Russia. His stay in St. Petersburg was marked by minor successes that won him popularity at home, such as negotiating an important commercial treaty between Russia and the United States. The experience directed his interests to international affairs.

On his return to the United States in 1833, Buchanan was elected from Pennsylvania to fill an unfinished term in the US Senate and was twice reelected. He became an important "party man," supporting the programs of Presidents Jackson and Martin Van Buren.

Agitation over slavery now began to divide the parties. As senator, Buchanan shared the common opinion of Pennsylvanians that slavery was morally evil, and he upheld the constitutional right to petition for abolition. At the same time he emphasized that under the Constitution Congress had no control over slavery in the states and held that the national government had a duty to protect slavery where it existed. Buchanan also publicly sympathized with southern whites' fears that abolitionism would set off slave revolts, endangering white homes. He declaimed against abolitionist "fanaticism." His positions avoided the question of the extension of slavery into the territories.

The Democrats nominated James K. Polk in the election of 1844, passing over the favorite-son candidacy of Buchanan. When Buchanan delivered Pennsylvania's uncertain electoral votes to Polk, he gained a claim to high office. Polk named him his secretary of state. Though the initiative in foreign affairs was as often the President's as his own, Buchanan served in the post with distinction from 1845 to 1849 and greatly enhanced his public popularity with his tact and high patriotism. An expansionist, Buchanan employed his diplomatic skill in resolving the dispute with Britain over Oregon and in the question of the annexation of Texas. In settling the Mexican War, he was subordinate to Polk. But Buchanan was largely responsible for the President's reiterations of the Monroe Doctrine to deter further British involvement in the Western Hemisphere. As secretary of state, Buchanan was strongly interested in Central America, and he personally opened the dormant question of Cuba with an unsuccessful attempt to purchase the island from Spain.

When the Whigs won the presidency in 1848 with Zachary Taylor, Buchanan retired to Wheatland, a country estate near Lancaster. In 1852 friends made a great effort to win the Democratic nomination for Buchanan, but the party's convention eventually chose the unknown Franklin Pierce of New Hampshire. Buchanan campaigned vigorously for Pierce and must have been severely disappointed to be offered the ministry to Great Britain, rather than an influential position at home, after Pierce's victory.

Although Buchanan's opportunities for action as ambassador were curtailed by Washington, his two years in Great Britain were socially agreeable, and they shielded Buchanan from controversies over the extension of slavery under Pierce. Buchanan's popularity with white Southerners and many Democrats was heightened by the Ostend Manifesto, which he secretly drew up at Ostend, Belgium, with the US ministers to Spain and France in October 1854.

The Ostend Manifesto contained a historical discussion of the Cuban question followed by the recommendation that the United States purchase Cuba from Spain, or, if Spain refused to sell, that Cuba be seized. The authors were anxious to prevent European interference, especially the possible emancipation of slaves in Cuba, or a slave revolution. The manifesto read in part: "We should . . . be recreant to our duty . . . should we permit Cuba to be Africanized and become a second St. Domingo, with all its attendant horrors to the white race, and suffer the flames to extend to our neighboring shores, seriously to endanger or actually to consume the fair fabric of our Union." The document argued that "self-preservation is the first law of nature, with States as with individuals." In the event that Cuba became necessary to US safety, then "by every law, human and divine, we shall be justified in wresting it from Spain if we possess the power." Secretary of State William L. Marcy, speaking for the US government, repudiated the manifesto.

In 1856 Buchanan became the Democratic nominee for President, on a platform stating that the Compromise of 1850 (including the Fugitive Slave Act) was final and reiterating that Congress should not interfere with slavery in the territories. When he spoke (infrequently) during the campaign, he denounced the abolitionists. He was elected by popular plurality over John C. Frémont, the first nominee of the newly organized Republican Party, and Millard Fillmore, the candidate of the Whig and American (Know-Nothing) parties.

James Buchanan hoped to easily heal the increasingly bitter sectionalism of the country. The warnings given by the realignment of political parties (the destruction of the Whigs and the growth of the Republicans hostile to the South and slavery) seem not to have alarmed him. The new President genuinely relied on "strict construction" of the Constitution and judicial decision to fashion a compromise between pro-slavery and antislavery forces and to avert internal warfare. Thus, in his inaugural address, Buchanan referred to slavery in the territories as "happily a matter of but little practical importance" because the Supreme Court would shortly settle the question "speedily and finally." Buchanan's allusion was to the Dred Scott decision, which would soon infuriate the North. By dividing his cabinet equally between Northerners and Southerners, Buchanan sought to maintain a delicately balanced peace. He was a man divided in roles and interests — close in politics and friendship to many wealthy white Southerners and clearly a white supremacist, but deeply opposed to secession and morally opposed to slavery. Under the circumstances, he lashed out most at the group pushing the conflict to total crisis — the abolitionists.

Buchanan's hoped-for successes in foreign policy were wholly overshadowed by the financial panic of 1857 and the struggle over slavery in Kansas. In 1858 Buchanan favored granting Kansas statehood under the proslavery Lecompton Constitution. This decision identified the administration with the Southern Democrats and precipitated revolt among the supporters of Stephen A. Douglas, opening the way to Abraham Lincoln's election in November 1860. Meanwhile a religious revival and John Brown's raid further stirred emotions.

There are grounds for the view that Buchanan pursued a pro-Southern policy, although in the end he sought to preserve the Union, embittering old Southern allies. However, Buchanan has also been charged with fostering secession by his argument that although the states had no right to secede the federal government had no power to prevent them, since it could employ force in a state only at the demand of the lawful authorities. While his reluctance to act after South Carolina announced its secession on December 20, 1860, threw almost the entire burden of reversing secession on Lincoln, Buchanan almost certainly could not have prevented secession by a tougher stand and might have provoked it sooner.

Early in 1861 Buchanan moved slowly to oppose South Carolina: he refused to remove federal troops from Charleston harbor and tried to reinforce the garrison there; he announced his intention to protect federal property if it was attacked. Not finding constitutional authority to act beyond this, he simply held on until Lincoln's inauguration in March 1861 and then retired to Wheatland.

During the Civil War James Buchanan backed the federal government as a Union Democrat and wrote a careful defense of his administration. He died on June 1, 1868, at the age of 77.

Wheatland, built in 1828 and purchased by Buchanan in 1848, is now a national shrine, elegantly furnished with his belongings and those of his niece. The handsome Federal home is located on Pennsylvania Route 23, a mile and a half west of Lancaster, at 1120 Marietta Avenue. It is open to the public from mid-March through November.

St. George's Day

The feast of St. George, patron saint of England since the Middle Ages, is celebrated by Roman Catholics and many Protestants on April 23. However, long before the Middle Ages, St. George was greatly venerated in the East. (Those Eastern Orthodox churches that still use the Old Style, or Julian, calendar mark May 6 as St. George's Day.)

Russians in pre-Revolutionary times would not plow or work in the fields before St. George's Day, when the fields customarily were blessed and put under the care and protection of the saint. In Russia, St. George's Day was then the occasion for conferring the Order of St. George and other military distinctions.

Although there are many traditions about St. George, little is definitely known about him except that he was martyred in the year 303 in Diospolis (now Lydda, or Lod), in Palestine, where there is a church dedicated to him. A decree attributed to Pope Gelasius I at the end of the fifth century includes St. George among those saints "whose names are reverenced among men, but whose actions are known only to God."

According to one tradition, George was born in Asia Minor, then a province of the Roman Empire. He joined the Roman army and rose to the rank of captain. When the Roman emperor Diocletian began to persecute Christians, George rebuked the emperor. He was immediately imprisoned and subjected to such cruel torture that the Eastern churches call him the Great Martyr.

The most popular legend — the slaying of the dragon — did not appear until the 12th century. According to the story (possibly based on ancient Greek myth), an enormous dragon satisfied its hunger with human victims. The terrorized populace drew lots to determine who should be offered to the dragon, and one day the lot fell to the king's young daughter. The princess, dressed as a bride, was sent off to the marshy lair of the dragon. George happened to be riding by and asked her where she was going. When he heard her story, he insisted on fighting the dragon. After a fierce struggle he transfixed the monster with his spear. Then he asked the princess for her cincture, of which he made a leash that he tied about the neck of the dragon. The princess led the monster like a lamb back to the city, and George told the people not to be afraid, but only to be baptized and accept Christianity. The people were all converted and George then cut off the dragon's head. To this day the emblem of St. George is a dragon.

St. George was the patron of soldiers and a great hero in the East for many centuries before his name spread to England in the eighth century. English churches were dedicated to St. George before the Norman Conquest in 1066. By the time of the Middle Ages, when knighthood flourished, George — in oft-repeated stories — was given all the attributes of a knight and became more and more identified with England.

G. K. Chesterton discusses the adoption of St. George as England's patron saint in *A Short History of England*. Chesterton begins his chapter on the Crusades "with the name of St. George. His first appearance, it is said, as a patron of our people, occurred at the instance of Richard Coeur de Lion during his campaign in Palestine. . . . In nothing were the medievals more free . . . than in their acceptance of names and emblems from outside their most beloved limits . . . a passionately patriotic community more often than not had a foreigner for a patron saint. . . . Thus as the English gradually became a nation, they left the numberless Saxon saints . . . behind them . . . and invoked a half mythical hero, striving in an eastern desert against an impossible monster."

It is not difficult to imagine that during the fighting of the Crusades in Eastern lands, where Eastern Christians routinely called upon St. George for strength in battle, King Richard I (the Lion-Hearted) would invoke the aid of the soldier-saint for his own men: "St. George, St. George for England." In Shakespeare's *Henry V* (1598), the king proposes a battle cry before the battle of Agincourt: "God for Harry! England and Saint George!" In Edmund Spenser's *Faerie Queene* (1589), the Red Cross Knight is St. George, symbolizing holiness and the Church of England.

As early as 1222 St. George's Day was set apart as a special holiday, and in 1415 it was ordered that the day be celebrated as a feast of the highest rank. It remained a holy day of obligation for Roman Catholics in England until 1778. Pope Benedict XIV declared St. George Protector of the Kingdom of England in the middle of the 18th century, after centuries of English devotion to the saint.

An emblem of St. George has from earliest times been part of the uniform of the Knights of the Garter. When, in 1347 or 1348, King Edward III founded the Order of the Garter, England's highest order of knighthood, he placed it under the patronage of St. George. St. George's Chapel in Windsor Castle is considered the spiritual home of the Order of the Garter.

The cross of St. George — a red cross on a white field — was worn by English soldiers and sailors as early as the 13th century, and it remains the ensign of the British navy and is also flown from English parish churches on high holy days. Today the cross of St. George, patron saint of England, is incorporated in the British Union Jack along with the cross of St. Andrew, patron saint of Scotland, and the cross of St. Patrick, patron saint of Ireland.

It is not only in wartime that English people look to St. George for sustenance and deliverance. In many parts of the world, including Canada and the United States, English natives or nationals (or their sons and daughters) turn to a St. George Society in time of need.

The first St. George Society in America was probably the one organized by Englishmen in Philadelphia, where they held their first meeting at the Tun Tavern on April 23, 1729. For many years thereafter, members held an annual dinner to celebrate St. George's Day. This society was succeeded in 1772 by an organization that described itself as the "Society of the Sons of St. George established at Philadelphia for the advice and assistance of Englishmen in distress." Among its early members were William Penn, founder of Pennsylvania; the merchant Robert Morris, a signer of the Declaration of Independence, who has been called the "financier of the American Revolution"; and Benjamin Franklin. Meetings of the society were suspended during the American Revolution but were resumed in the latter part of the 18th century. The Society of the Sons of St. George is still operating in Philadelphia today.

There are also St. George societies in Charleston, South Carolina, and Baltimore, Maryland. The St. George Society in New York City, probably the largest and most active in the United States, celebrated its 200th anniversary in 1970 with a dinner and dance held at the Plaza Hotel. Supported by donations from its 800 members, it supplies financial assistance, maintains a number of hospital beds in St. Luke's Hospital, provides necessities or mere human concern for people in city hospitals, gives out clothing, administers two cemeteries, and arranges funerals and burials.

A completely different organization honoring the saint is the St. George Association of the United States of America, which was established to fulfill the "profound desire on the part of Protestants everywhere to unite under the banner of Unity, and to dedicate themselves to the betterment of their fellow men, through a concerted demonstration of their Faith in Protestantism under Christ Jesus." The first chapter of the St. George Association was founded in 1937 by members of the New York Police Department. The national roster now includes approximately 30,000 members in more than 80 chapters. They consider St. George "the emblem of Christian progressiveness." The association's seal shows St. George slaying the dragon.

William Shakespeare's Birthday

The accepted date of the birth of William Shakespeare is April 23, 1564. The only available records show that he was baptized on April 26, and since it was the custom to have the baptism three days after birth, the date is probably correct. Although the poet and dramatist was regarded with affection and respect by his contemporaries, and although he himself had predicted that "not marble, nor the gilded monument of princes shall outlive this powerful rhyme," he could have hardly envisaged the pinnacle of fame on which he stands today. As Ben Jonson, his fellow playwright and friend, wrote a few years after his death, William Shakespeare "was not of an age but for all time."

It is not surprising, therefore, that more than 400 years after Shakespeare's birth, actors, theatergoers, scholars, and Shakespeare lovers in many countries, including the United States, regard the conjectural date of his birth as an occasion for remembering the most celebrated author in the English language. April 23 is most widely observed in Shakespeare's birthplace, the Warwickshire town of Stratford-upon-Avon, England. Annually on the Sunday nearest April 23, a sermon is preached in Holy Trinity Church, where Shakespeare is buried. The mayor of Stratford holds a civic reception at the town hall. English folk dancing, a formal luncheon with commemorative speeches, a procession to the parish church to lay wreaths and flowers on Shakespeare's grave, and a Shakespearean theatrical production at the Shakespeare Memorial Theatre add to the festivities there.

In the United States Shakespeare's popularity — surpassing that of any other playwright — dates back to the early 19th century. James Russell Lowell, Ralph Waldo Emerson, and Edgar Allan Poe are among the American men of letters who wrote knowledgeably about Shakespeare. The Shakespearean tradition in the American theater was fostered by Edwin Forrest, who portrayed the great Shakespearean characters as early as 1826; Junius Brutus Booth, who played a western frontier circuit before miners and pioneers; and Edwin Booth, who was not only an excellent actor but a competent manager who organized touring companies to present Shakespeare's plays across the country in the mid-19th century.

The celebration of Shakespeare's birthday in the United States started at least as early as 1851, when admirers founded the Shakspere (sic) Society of Philadelphia. They usually gathered for a sumptuous dinner on April 23. Little is done today to observe the occasion officially on a nationwide scale. Local groups, however, sponsor lectures, dances, concerts of Elizabethan music, theatrical performances, or Shakespeare festivals. The numerous American Shakespeare societies, such as the Shakespeare Society of New York and that of Washington, D.C., hold annual dinners on this date and occasionally confer awards on actors and scholars. It is also customary to lay wreaths at the bases of statues of Shakespeare in various parks and squares.

One of the most interesting annual celebrations is held in the Edwin Forrest Home for Retired Actors in Philadelphia. Forrest, one of the first American actors to win international acclaim, was famed for his playing of various Shakespearean tragic roles. When he died in 1872 he left his home, Spring Brook, in the northern part of Philadelphia, as a home for actors. But it was 1876 before the complications in the settlement of the estate could be unraveled and the home opened to actors. In the course of years the 106-acre property increased in value so that it was thought advisable to sell it. It was sold in 1925 for $600,000. About one-fourth of this sum was used to build a new home, in Tudor style, facing Fairmount Park on a 2-acre plot. Edwin Forrest's will provided that there should be a celebration each year of the anniversary of Shakespeare's birth, a provision that is still faithfully carried out. The celebration is held in the large hall of the home, and distinguished actors and others interested in Shakespeare pay tribute to the dramatist.

The women's committee of the Great Lakes Shakespeare Festival in Lakewood, Ohio — a suburb of Cleveland — annually marks the anniversary. In 1970 the program was appropriately held in a member's Tudor-style mansion. A trio of musicians from the Cleveland Institute of Music offered a program of Elizabethan music. There was also a lecture on the England of Shakespeare's day.

The Oregon Shakespeare Festival, staged at Ashland, a small town in the scenic Rogue River Valley, ranks as the oldest of the country's annual Shakespeare festivals. In 1935 Angus L. Bowmer, a drama professor at Southern Oregon College, first produced Shakespeare's plays on a crude Elizabethan-style stage. The inaugural season was presented over the three-day July 4 weekend as part of an Independence Day celebration. Local skeptics, scoffing at the idea that Shakespeare would attract a crowd, scheduled some boxing matches as a drawing card over the same weekend. Not only were the plays' production expenses covered, but the boxers' deficits as well. After an interval during World War II, the Ashland Festival resumed in 1947 and has steadily expanded since. The authentic 55-foot Elizabethan stage, completed for the 1959 season, was built to the dimensions given in the contract for the erection of the Fortune Theatre in London in 1599. Ashland is the only Shakespeare festival in America that performs Shakespeare's works as they were originally meant to be presented — without interruptions or intermissions, on a curtainless platform, and with multiple playing areas at different levels.

The San Diego National Shakespeare Festival annually presents plays by Shakespeare in Balboa Park in downtown San Diego from early June until mid-September. Established in 1949, the group performs in a replica of Shakespeare's Globe Playhouse (the original stood on the south bank of the Thames in London), which was designed for the California Pacific International Exposition of 1935–1936. The intimate house, with only 420 seats, exudes an Elizabethan atmosphere with its triple balconies and wood-beamed interior. Before each play, authentically costumed madrigal singers and Elizabethan dancers, including a much-bedecked "Queen Bess," perform on the theater green.

The American Shakespeare Festival is located in Stratford, Connecticut, in a bucolic setting along the Housatonic River. Founded in 1955, it is the newest of the three Stratford theaters, the others being in England and Canada. In June 1975 the centenary of the English theater was celebrated with a weekend-long Elizabethan fair and medieval jousting tournament. The playhouse (built in 1932 to replace the 19th century structure burned in 1926) is the oldest Shakespearean stage in continuous use. Canada's theater, at Stratford, Ontario, was founded in 1953 as offshoot of the one in England. The Connecticut repertory company performs in a striking teakwood playhouse, embellished with British shields and flying pennants, which is a modern adaptation of the Old Globe Playhouse.

During the 1950s and 1960s, Shakespeare festivals featuring professional, collegiate, and local talent were organized throughout the nation, in states including Colorado, Georgia, Florida, Michigan, Ohio, Utah, and Vermont.

The New York Shakespeare Festival, first organized in 1954, received a permanent center when the Delacorte Theater, a 2,300-seat amphitheater in Manhattan's Central Park, opened in 1962. Free performances are given there throughout each summer. Since 1961 the Shakespeare Festival in Washington, D.C., has presented free performances at the outdoor Sylvan Theater on the sloping lawn of the Washington Monument.

The Folger Shakespeare Memorial Library, located two blocks from the Capitol in Washington, D.C., is a world-famous research library and museum devoted to Shakespeareana and the literature and history of Shakespeare's age. It derives its name from its benefactor, Henry Clay Folger, the first president of the Standard Oil Company of New York, who amassed one of the most extensive Shakespeare collections in the world. To house the material Folger commissioned the construction of the library. It was dedicated by President Herbert Hoover on April 23, 1932, the 368th anniversary of Shakespeare's birth. The dignified classical building, ornamented with quotations from Shakespeare and reliefs of his characters, is administered, in accordance with Folger's will, by the trustees of Amherst College, Folger's alma mater. It contains a theater modeled on an Elizabethan playhouse, a reading room resembling the large hall of a Tudor college, and a 129-foot-long hall with a 30-foot ceiling reproduced from a 16th century manor house.

In 1964, the quatercentenary of Shakespeare's birth, Great Britain, beginning on April 23, was the scene of eight months of festivals, pageants, exhibitions, play readings, and scholarly debates, all centered on Shakespeare. Stratford-upon-Avon continued to be the mecca for Shakespeare admirers. The half-million-dollar Shakespeare Center, which houses an outstanding collection of Shakespeare memorabilia and works, is termed an "international birthday present," since funds for its construction were contributed from all over the world. It was ceremoniously opened by Eugene R. Black, former president of the International Bank for Reconstruction and Development and chairman of the American 1964 Shakespeare Committee. A huge pavilion exhibition depicted the playwright's life.

The quadricentennial tribute was as fervent on the American side of the Atlantic as on the British. The US government took official note of the anniversary with the formation of the 1964 Shakespeare Anniversary Committee, appointed by President John F. Kennedy and continued by President Lyndon B. Johnson. Scholars, educators, directors, producers, actors, writers, critics, and civic leaders from the 50 states helped to formulate and execute the committee's program "to reawaken interest in the vitality of the English language through the works of William Shakespeare." Art exhibits based on Shakespearean themes, musical selections (some with only remote connections with Shakespeare or his works), television and radio programs, revivals of film versions of the plays, and even a 6-by-9-foot plaster-of-paris birthday cake sent on tour around Connecticut — all marked the quadricentennial.

The Shakespeare Association of America staged a glittering banquet featuring an address, play readings, and Elizabethan music at the Pierpont Morgan Library in New York City. The association produced a special 1964 anniversary issue of its journal, the *Shakespeare Quarterly*, comprising essays by outstanding American Shakespeare scholars. At the Folger Library's anniversary feast of Elizabethan delicacies, guests raised their tankards to drink a noble toast and sang "Happy Birthday to William."

The 1964 summer theater season provided the high point of the American homage to Shakespeare. Twenty professional festivals and some 80 university-sponsored programs were scheduled. Among the most ambitious was Stanford University's Summer Festival of the Arts in Palo Alto, California, which featured as its inaugural season a seven-week tribute; besides concerts, exhibitions, and lectures on the campus, the nation's two oldest Shakespeare festivals — the Oregon Shakespeare Festival Company and the San Diego National Shakespeare Festival Company — presented their repertories. In the East the New York Shakespeare Festival's mobile theater group performed during a nine-week tour of New York City. At least 18 of Shakespeare's plays were also offered in such widely scattered places as Tucson, Arizona; Dallas, Texas; Seattle, Washington; and Minneapolis, Minnesota.

Little information has been unearthed about the recipient of all this homage. A number of scholars — and their adherents — have questioned the authorship of the plays, ascribing the works to one or another of Shakespeare's contemporaries, but such theories and conjectures have not had wide support in recent years.

William Shakespeare was the third of eight children and the eldest son born to John and Mary Shakespeare at Stratford-upon-Avon. His father was prominent in municipal affairs, rising to become high bailiff and justice of the peace in the town. His mother was a member of the prosperous, landed Arden family. Young Shakespeare undoubtedly received a fairly sound education. At 18 he married Anne Hathaway; they had three children before he set out for London, some time between 1584 and 1590. There Shakespeare probably served first as a stage apprentice, performing minor parts and menial tasks; but by 1592 he had become an established actor and a rising dramatist.

In 1594 or 1595 Shakespeare joined the dramatic company known as the Lord Chamberlain's Men (later the King's Men), where he enjoyed the dual function of playwright and performer. Hardworking, with an eye for business, he became part-owner of the new Globe Playhouse in London in 1599 and, in 1609, of the Blackfriars Theatre.

Having amassed a moderate fortune, he retired to his family and property in Stratford in about 1610. There he died on his 53rd birthday, April 23, 1616. During his lifetime he had produced an incomparable body of work: a sequence of 154 sonnets, several long poems, and 37 plays.

United Methodist Church Formed

On April 23, 1968, the 10,289,214-member Methodist Church and the 746,099-member Evangelical United Brethren Church merged to form the United Methodist Church. The uniting conference, which settled the administrative and legal technicalities arising from such a merger, was attended by 400 accredited Evangelical United Brethren delegates and 800 Methodist representatives. They officially inaugurated the United Methodist Church by participating in a joint service and procession in the Dallas Memorial Auditorium.

In uniting, the two churches followed a well-established ecumenical tradition, for each one had resulted from a previous merger. The Methodist Church, which traces its origins back to the beliefs and preaching of the Anglican clergyman John Wesley in the early 18th century, was the product of the merger of the Methodist Episcopal Church, the Methodist Episcopal Church, South, and the Methodist Protestant Church, on May 10, 1939 (see May 10). The Evangelical United Brethren Church, with its membership mostly in Pennsylvania and Ohio, was formed in 1946 when two denominations, the Evangelical Church and the Church of the United Brethren in Christ, agreed to unite; they both originated among the German-speaking population in Pennsylvania as part of the evangelistic movements of the late 18th and early 19th centuries. Jacob Albright (1759–1808), a Lutheran who converted to Methodism, founded what became the Evangelical Church, and Philip William Otterbein (1726–1813), a minister of the German Reformed Church, was a founder of the Church of the United Brethren in Christ.

The two merging Protestant churches — whose general conferences adopted the plan of union in November 1966 — shared a common religious and historical background; they held the same basic doctrines of faith with emphasis upon a life devoted to Christ and prayer; even their ecclesiastical organizations, both episcopal with bishops as heads, were similar. In fact, had it not been for the fact that the Methodist church initially was directed to English-speaking persons and the Evangelical Church and the Church of the United Brethren in Christ to German-speaking persons, the separate bodies might have formed one church from the very beginning of their spiritual activities in America.

As of 1976 the United Methodist Church had over 39,000 churches and 10,063,046 members — by far the largest of the 19 Methodist bodies in the United States which have a total membership of more than 12.5 million.

A distinctive feature of the church is the conference system, whereby each Methodist preacher has membership in an annual conference and every four years delegates are sent to a general conference, the top lawmaking body in the church. The principal agencies of the United Methodist Church are located in New York City; Evanston, Illinois; Nashville, Tennessee; Washington, D.C.; Dayton, Ohio; and Lake Junaluska, North Carolina.

APRIL 24

Library of Congress Created

On April 24, 1800, the Congress of the United States created the Library of Congress by approving an act providing "for the purchase of such books as may be necessary for the use of Congress at the said city of Washington, and for fitting up a suitable apartment for containing them." Although originally intended specifically as a parliamentary collection to aid the legislative branch of the government, the Library of Congress — in more than a century and a half of existence — has expanded its services until, despite its name, it has become the national library of the United States. Besides serving members of Congress and other government officials, the reference library meets the needs of the general public, scholars, and libraries both in this country and abroad.

Ranking as one of the largest libraries — if not the largest library — in the world, LC — as the institution is often familiarly called — possesses outstanding collections of manuscripts, prints, maps, motion pictures, records, and books, as well as tapes, microcards, and reels and strips of microfilms. It also offers such added benefits as lecture and concert series, traveling exhibits, a special division for the blind and physically handicapped, bibliographical and duplication facilities, printed catalog cards, and cataloging information on machine-readable magnetic tapes. The library is maintained chiefly by congressional appropriations but also derives funds from private donations, which are administered by the Library of Congress Trust Fund Board. The $137,895,200 appropriated by Congress for the library's operations in fiscal 1977 was a far cry from the $5,000 Congress set aside for book purchases at the institution's founding in 1800.

The original nucleus of 3,000 volumes, amassed from 1800 to 1814 and housed in the Capitol, was burned on August 24, 1814, in the British attack on Washington during the War of 1812. The loss was mitigated by the purchase in January 1815 of former President Thomas Jefferson's private library, comprising more than 6,000 volumes. This splendid collection, considered remarkable in its day, formed the basis around which the library built up its holdings in diverse fields. But it too suffered a Capitol blaze, on December 24, 1851, and was reduced by half.

Despite setbacks, the Library of Congress continued to augment its collection substantially during the course of the 19th century through annual congressional appropriations; special purchases, such as the Peter Force collection of primary materials relating to American history (1867) and the Rochambeau collection pertaining to the American Revolution (1883); bequests; foreign exchanges; and items transferred from other government agencies, including the Smithsonian collection of almost 40,000 volumes (1866). Moreover, in 1870 a congressional act made the Library of Congress the official depository of copyrighted and official publications. In

1897 a copyright department was set up on the library premises. The national legislature also approved the purchase for LC of the presidential papers of George Washington, James Monroe, Thomas Jefferson, and James Madison — a project that has since grown to encompass about 1.8 million items in 23 presidential collections. The personal papers of other famous men and women have been gradually acquired as well.

By the end of the 19th century, the Library of Congress housed an extensive national reference collection comprising some 740,000 volumes, 250,000 prints, 40,000 maps, 200,000 pieces of music, and 18,000 bound newspaper volumes. The cramped Capitol "apartment" stipulated by the congressional act of 1800 had long been inadequate, and in 1897 the library transferred its holdings to its own $7 million Italian-Renaissance-style building and grounds on Capitol Hill. As the institution added personnel, services, and material in the first half of the 20th century, however, even these quarters proved insufficient. On April 5, 1939, the library's five-story annex was opened, making available a total floor space of some 36 acres and 270 miles of shelves. In 1976 the structure was formally named the Thomas Jefferson Building.

Space shortage nonetheless remains a chronic problem for the library, whose total holdings in June 1977 included more than 73 million items. Among them were some 18.4 million volumes and pamphlets, 3.5 million maps, 3.6 million volumes and pieces of music, 875,000 reels and strips of microfilm, and 247,000 motion picture reels. In the fiscal year 1969 the US Copyright Office transferred its quarters to Arlington, Virginia, while the Geography and Map Division was forced to move to nearby Alexandria, Virginia, the following year. In 1965 Congress approved the planning and erection of a greatly needed third building on a site located just south of LC's main building. The structure, named the James Madison Memorial Building, was begun in 1973 with a 1980 target date for completion.

To organize its tremendous network effectively, the Library of Congress is divided into seven departments, administered by directors and ultimately headed by the Librarian of Congress. There are the Processing, Research, and Administrative departments; the Congressional Research Service — established in 1914 to serve as the principal research and information body for Congress; the Reader Services Department; the US Copyright Office; and the Law Library, with possibly the most complete legal holdings in the world. This comprised 1,373,600 volumes in 1976 not counting the thousands of related volumes in the Library of Congress's general collection.

Statistics for the 1976 fiscal year testify to the widespread use of the various services the library divisions provide. More than 1.2 million visitors used the library's services; and over 1.5 million reference requests, made in person, by telephone, or by letter, were filled. The interlibrary loan service lent about 114,000 volumes. The Congressional Research Service furnished members of Congress and congressional committees with more than 349,000 reference and research replies. The US Copyright Office processed over 468,000 copyright claims, transferring some 384,000 of the deposits that accompanied the registered claims to LC's Processing Department for inclusion in the library's own holdings or for other uses.

APRIL 25

Feast of St. Mark

The feast of St. Mark, one of the four Evangelists, is observed on April 25 by Roman Catholic, Greek Orthodox, and some Protestant churches.

Mark, whose full name was John Mark, was not one of the 12 Apostles but was one of the larger number of disciples, the band of men who were closely associated with the Apostles. He was especially close to Peter and at least some of the time to Paul.

Mark's mother was a widow of Jerusalem who owned a house spacious enough for large gatherings of Christians. Peter evidently considered Mark's mother a friend, for it is related that it was to her house he went in A.D. 43 after he had been led out of prison by an angel. It is in the New Testament account of this event that Mark is first mentioned.

According to the Acts of the Apostles, Peter went to the house of Mary, "the mother of John who was surnamed Mark," where many Christians had gathered to pray — possibly for the safety of their imprisoned leader. Mark knew Peter well for many years and it was from Peter that Mark drew most of the information recorded in his Gospel.

In 45 Mark and Barnabas, his uncle or cousin, accompanied Paul on his first missionary journey. Mark went only as far as Perga in Pamphylia and then returned to Jerusalem. Paul was angered by this, and five years later he refused Barnabas's request to take Mark on Paul's second missionary journey. Instead, Mark accompanied Barnabas to Cyprus.

In 61 Mark was in Rome, reconciled with Paul, who in an Epistle asked the Colossians to welcome Mark "if he comes to you." Whether Mark spent the years before and after this traveling in Asia Minor is not recorded. But he was in Rome with Peter in the year 64 — the year Peter was martyred. In an Epistle written at that time, Peter affectionately refers to "my son Mark."

Sometime between Peter's death in 64 and about the year 70, Mark wrote his Gospel, mostly summarizing the things that Peter had told him during their long, close friendship, which endured at least for the last 20 years of Peter's life.

Mark was evidently working in or near Ephesus in 67, according to an Epistle from Paul to Timothy, who was in charge of the Church at Ephesus. In the letter Paul, having premonitions of his own death, asked Timothy to come to Paul in Rome and to bring Mark, "for he is useful to me for the ministry."

According to tradition, Mark became the first bishop of Alexandria and was martyred there about 74 or 75. His followers reportedly obtained possession of his body and put it in a sepulcher, which became a shrine visited by the faithful. Early in the ninth century Venetian merchants trading in Alexandria are said to have acquired the relics and carried them to Venice, where a church was built over them. This original church was destroyed by fire in 967. The present Basilica of St. Mark in Venice, graced with delicate masonry and studded with mosaics, is one of the most famous churches in the world. Its main structure, designed by Byzantine architects, was completed in 1071. In following centuries, embellishments were added, so that the basilica today is a mixture of Byzantine and Gothic architecture, richly adorned with sculpture and rare forms of marble. What are said to be the remains of St. Mark, the patron saint of Venice since the ninth century, lie under the main altar.

An English superstition holds that on the eve of St. Mark apparitions of those who will die within the ensuing year can be seen in the churchyard. In Maxwell Anderson's 1942 play *The Eve of St. Mark*, a young American soldier, who will not return from the war, appears in spirit to his mother and his sweetheart.

APRIL 26

John James Audubon's Birthday

It was supposed for many years that John James Audubon, the artist and naturalist whose drawings from life of the birds of North America broke new ground in the field of ornithology, was born near New Orleans about 1780, the exact day and year being unknown. Audubon himself, in fact, created this impression. F. H. Herrick, Audubon's biographer, however, finally stated with seeming authority that Audubon had been born on April 26, 1785, the son of a Creole woman who died not many years later. The place of his birth has been said to be Les Cayes, Haiti. (Notwithstanding the seeming authenticity of this statement, a few sources still intimate that Audubon may have been descended from members of the French nobility who changed their names or in other ways sought to disguise their identities during the French Revolution.)

Regarded by most authorities as the natural son of Captain Jean Audubon, a trader, planter, and officer in the French navy, and his Creole mistress, young Audubon was taken to France in 1789, where he was formally adopted several years later by Captain Audubon and his wife. Educated in France — though he had scant enthusiasm for formal studies — Audubon lived there in relative luxury.

No one knows how he first came to draw birds. However, the interest that began as an apparently spontaneous pastime never waned. Sent to study drawing in Paris under the French painter Jacques Louis David, Audubon found himself impatient with the dull plaster casts that he was expected to draw, and he felt too restricted with only black chalk on white paper. On his own he experimented in watercolors with the bright hues that would later characterize his work. Even working independently, however, he found that neither carefully constructed wooden birds nor ordinary stuffed birds could serve as adequate models for the impression of life he hoped to capture on paper; and when he roamed the woods and fields near his parents' country home, his drawings of the live birds he saw there still were, at first, only stiff profiles of what appeared to be cardboard creatures — though they often exhibited an Audubon innovation that would persist in his later work. This was the depiction of sprays of leaves or berries as perches for his birds, or the inclusion of some other hint of natural habitat.

His chance for concentrated study of birds in their natural surroundings came in 1803, when he was sent to America, supposedly to enter business, and settled at Mill Grove, an estate northwest of Philadelphia that was owned by his father. There, on Perkiomen Creek and in the surrounding countryside, young Audubon began in earnest to paint the birds of North America, which were to become better known through his than through any other brush. He studied and sketched the birds in motion outdoors. And, hunting them, he learned to place them in lifelike attitudes indoors, where he could paint them carefully.

It was while Audubon was living at Mill Grove that he met Lucy Blakewell, whom he married in 1808 and whose love and admiration sustained him when others thought his work impractical. It was during their courtship that Audubon, painting a portrait of her, accidentally discovered the technique of softening his watercolor tones with an overlay of pastel crayons, a process that was to give a special quality to his later bird drawings.

Today, Mill Grove and the 120 acres surrounding it can be visited as the Audubon Shrine and Wildlife Sanctuary, near the village of Audubon in Pennsylvania's Montgomery County, near Valley Forge State Park. The house, built in 1762, and now restored, contains period furnishings and a collection of Audubon's paintings and prints. Some 159 species of birds have been sighted in the sanctuary.

Important as it was, Audubon's time at Mill Grove was actually rather brief and interrupted by a yearlong stay in France during which he saw his father and stepmother for the last time. Audubon returned to the United States in 1806 and opened a general store in Louisville, Kentucky. In 1810 the store, never a success and neglected by Audubon in favor of his other interests, was moved to a more westerly Ohio River location in Henderson, Kentucky — a site chosen by him because it was on the route of a great American bird migration. The John James Audubon State Park, including densely wooded tracts and two lakes that still serve as a magnet for migratory birds, is two miles north of Henderson on US Route 41. Within the park's borders is the Audubon Museum, housing mementos of Audubon's days in Henderson and a collection of his celebrated paintings and first edition prints.

When Audubon lived in Henderson, however, it seemed unlikely that he would ever be famous. Plagued by a series of unsuccessful business ventures, he was bankrupt by 1819. Forced to sell all he owned, he moved his family for a brief time to Shippingport (near Louisville), where he sought unsuccessfully to gain a living by turning out portraits and giving drawing lessons. He also played his flute or violin at local balls and taught young people the dance steps he had learned long before in France. The family also lived briefly in Cincinnati, where Audubon was employed to stuff and mount birds and fishes for the city's new Western Museum.

Wherever Audubon went during these difficult early years — and there were more difficult years to come — he followed the same pattern, employing every talent he possessed to eke out a precarious living by means that would still permit him to move toward his main goal — discovering, studying, and laboriously painting the birds of North America. If these were years of

slow accomplishment (his chosen subject was vast), they were also years of exasperating frustration, the joy of discovery mixed with the hardships of poverty and long separations from his family. His wife, meanwhile, supplemented the family income as a teacher and governess.

Past discouragements notwithstanding, Audubon in 1820 took a major step. Encouraged by his wife, he determined to complete his studies of North American birds and embarked by flatboat on a painting and drawing excursion that was to take him all the way down the Mississippi and allow him to explore its banks, always tirelessly in search of new varieties of birds to paint.

Coming to rest in New Orleans, an ideal setting from which to embark on bird-searching excursions, he earned a meager livelihood by painting portraits and giving drawing lessons, although clients were scarce. Often penniless, he was engaged at last for a summer of tutoring at Oakley plantation, four miles east of St. Francisville, in Louisiana's West Feliciana Parish. Audubon came to love the area, which he had time to explore thoroughly, producing 32 of his most famous bird paintings in the process. From then on he always thought of the region as home. The white, two-story Oakley House and its 100 surrounding acres, today a wildlife sanctuary, have been known as Audubon Memorial State Park since their purchase by the state of Louisiana in 1949. Both are open to the public.

Audubon's summer at Oakley brought him sufficient funds to send for his wife, who joined him in New Orleans. When her position as a governess there ended abruptly, she was engaged as a governess at Weyanoke, the home of a family named Percy, at Little Bayou Sara. Audubon himself soon was also hired by the Percy family, to give music, drawing, and dancing lessons to local children, again with the understanding that he also would have time for his own work.

By October 1822 he had accumulated over 200 bird paintings that pleased him and set off for Philadelphia in search of a publisher. After a winter-long pause in Shippingport, where he earned money for the trip by turning out newly popular paintings of American scenery, he arrived in the spring of 1823 in Philadelphia, where he found encouragement but no publisher. In New York, which he visited in the summer, he found neither, though in both places he was advised that his best chance of publication lay in Europe.

First, however, he returned to see his family at Bayou Sara, after a long trip with work stops whenever he ran out of money. Four seasons and more passed happily at Bayou Sara before Audubon — with sufficient funds at last and over

400 of his bird portraits – sailed from New Orleans to Liverpool, in the spring of 1826.

In Europe his work began to receive attention. Exhibitions of his paintings in Liverpool, Manchester, and Edinburgh attracted wide interest and brought a flurry of invitations, introductions to influential persons, recognition in art and scientific circles, and demands for the shy Franco-American to appear at dinners and meetings of learned societies. As always, money was a pressing problem, and he worked furiously, occupied not only with the paintings that paid his expenses, but also with socializing and public appearances, which were important in an effort that would absorb him for several years – securing subscriptions for a published version of his bird paintings.

In London Audubon became acquainted with a skillful engraver, Robert Havell Jr., beginning what was to be a long association. Audubon's best-known work, the generously proportioned *Birds of America*, with engravings by Havell, was published in elephant folio size, allowing for the life-size portrayal of birds on which Audubon had always insisted. It appeared in parts between 1827 and 1838.

After a trip to America in 1829 (he was dissatisfied with some of his bird paintings, which he wanted to replace, and found omissions of certain other species, which he sought to fill), Audubon returned to Britain with his wife, who relinquished the security of her Feliciana Parish teaching position in order to accompany her husband and assist in his grand project.

This project soon expanded with Audubon's determination to supplement the splendid *Birds of America*, which would ultimately boast 435 hand-colored plates, with a text. This *Ornithological Biography*, describing the birds and containing numerous vignettes of life on the American frontier, eventually ran to five volumes, published from 1831 to 1839, and was supplemented by a catalog, or systematic index, *A Synopsis of the Birds of North America* (1839). In these works Audubon had the assistance and collaboration of a young Scottish naturalist, William MacGillivray, who was responsible for much of the scientific information.

From 1826 until 1839, when the vast undertaking on which he had labored for so many years with alternating delight and despair was finally completed, Audubon divided his time between Europe and America. In 1831–1832 he managed an excursion of which he had long dreamed – to the Florida Keys. The Key West home of Captain John H. Geiger at 205 Whitehead Street, where Audubon stayed, is now open to visitors. Restored by the Mitchell Wolfson Foundation and filled with furnishings of the

period, it contains many Audubon prints and one of the world's few complete sets of the original elephant folio *Birds of America*. In 1833 he ventured, still in search of birds, as far as Labrador, and in 1837 he went to Texas.

His sons, Victor and John, assisted in his work, as they were to continue to do after Audubon's final return to the United States in 1839. Settling, typically, where he could overlook one of the nation's great waterways, he purchased a small estate above the Hudson River at what is now Manhattan's West 155th Street – after the income from a work that was at last to bring some prosperity, a miniature (or octavo) edition of the *Birds*, seemed assured. (The elephant folio edition had brought much acclaim, but less money.) There, aided by his sons and by John Bachman, who worked on the text, Audubon undertook an ambitious new work, *Viviparous Quadrupeds of North America*. Two volumes of plates for the new enterprise came out in parts in 1845 and 1846, and the three-volume text was issued between 1846 and 1854.

Before the text was completed, however, Audubon himself had died – on January 27, 1851. He was buried at a site on his own land that is now Trinity Cemetery, extending from Riverside Drive to Amsterdam Avenue between 153rd and 155th streets. Audubon Terrace, a harmonious Classical Revival complex housing five small museums at Broadway between West 155th and 156th streets, also stands on what was once his property.

Not without artistic or scientific flaws, Audubon's paintings are nevertheless unsurpassed of their kind. Treasured by art collectors and lovers of nature, they have also achieved lasting popular esteem.

Lucy Audubon, who survived her husband by many years, returned to teaching to support herself. One of her pupils, George Bird Grinnell, became editor of *Forest and Stream* and in 1886 organized a society for the study and protection of birds, which he named the Audubon Society. Many branches were soon formed, and in 1905 the National Association of Audubon Societies was organized. Today, this organization – its name now simplified to the National Audubon Society – is one of the largest groups devoted to the conservation of wildlife, scenic beauty, and other natural resources. Because the society believes that people will want to protect wildlife and natural beauty if they know something about the world of nature, conservation education – through its magazine and other publications, through lecture series, and through camps and nature centers – is a major part of its program. Many of its activities and publications are designed to interest children and guide them toward an understanding of the natural world around them. The society has its headquarters in New York City.

Cape Henry Day

Virginians, mindful of their state's role in the early history of the nation, take pride in remembering Virginia's primacy among the 13 original English colonies on the North American mainland. The establishment of Jamestown, the first capital of the province and earliest permanent settlement, on May 13, 1607, antedated by more than a decade the better known landing of the Pilgrims at Plymouth Rock in 1620. Each year on April 26 Virginians commemorate this aspect of their past by celebrating the anniversary of the arrival of Captain Christopher Newport and his band of adventurers at Cape Henry.

Located on the south side of Chesapeake Bay, 10 miles east of present-day Norfolk, the Cape Henry promontory must have been a welcome sight to the weary English voyagers. Its appearance on the horizon signaled the conclusion of an arduous four-month journey across the Atlantic Ocean. Captain Newport, Edward Wingfield, Bartholomew Gosnold, and 30 others disembarked on April 26. They were impressed by the beauty of the country and, after a skirmish with some Indians, returned to their vessels for the night. The expedition of 110 men and four boys had made the voyage in three vessels, of which the longest, the *Susan Constant*, measured 75 feet. A group of men went ashore on the second day and spent some time in exploration. On April 29 the men set up a wooden cross and named the area Cape Henry in honor of the Prince of Wales, the eldest son of James I. They then renewed their trek inland to the site that became Jamestown.

The Association for the Preservation of Virginia Antiquities in 1896 commemorated the landing by placing a plaque on the nearby Old Cape Henry Lighthouse, the first lighthouse erected by the federal government. Since 1920 there has been an annual pilgrimage to the Cape Henry site, inspired by the leadership of Mrs. Frantz Naylor. The Cape Henry Memorial, consisting of a quarter acre of ground and a cross erected in 1935 by the Daughters of the American Colonists, marks the location of the landing. These words by James Branch Cabell are inscribed on the base of the cross: "Here, at Cape Henry, first landed in America, upon 26 April 1607, those English colonists, who, upon 13 May 1607, established at Jamestown, Virginia, the first permanent English settlement in America." Each year, usually on the Sunday closest to April 26, the Order of Cape Henry 1607, holds a service at the memorial. The latter part of this patriotic and religious ceremony is based upon the Anglican service held in 1607. A proclamation by the governor of Virginia and a message from the President of the United States customarily highlight the observance.

The US War Department originally administered the Cape Henry Memorial, but on January 19, 1939, pursuant to an act of Congress, Cape Henry became part of the Colonial National Historic Park, which also includes Jamestown and Yorktown. The National Park Service of the Department of the Interior controls the memorial, but there are no facilities or special services available. The Fort Story Military Reservation surrounds the site, and the US Army allows visitors at the area throughout the year.

Confederate Memorial Day

Although the idea of a memorial day, and of decorating the graves of the dead, is ancient, the institution of a purely American memorial day grew out of the desolation and heartbreak of the Civil War. There are contradictory claims as to where the first memorial day observance took place. Claimants include Vicksburg, Mississippi; Boalsburg, Pennsylvania; Petersburg, Virginia; Columbus, Mississippi; Waterloo, New York; Richmond, Virginia; and Charleston, South Carolina. It is certain, however, that all of the early observances grew out of spontaneous individual acts toward the end of, or just after, the Civil War.

Confederate Memorial Day, widely observed in southern states, which were largely members of the Confederacy, is marked on a number of different dates — among them the fourth Monday in April (Alabama and Mississippi); May 10, the anniversary of the 1865 apprehension of Jefferson Davis by Federal cavalry (North Carolina and South Carolina); and June 3, Jefferson Davis's birthday (Kentucky and Louisiana).

April 26 is a legal holiday in Florida and Georgia. On this date in 1865 two notable events took place. One was the final surrender of Confederate General Joseph E. Johnston to the Union army's General William T. Sherman at what is now known as Bennett Place State Historic Site, near Durham, North Carolina. That historic encounter took place 17 days after the war's near-conclusion with the surrender of General Robert E. Lee, commander in chief of Confederate forces, to General Ulysses S. Grant at Appomattox Court House, Virginia (see April 9).

On the same day that Johnston and Sherman were meeting near Durham, some women in Vicksburg, Mississippi, were performing a gesture of private grief and salutation by decorating the graves of soldiers who had fallen in the course of the conflict. In so doing, Sue Landon Vaughan and her companions paid tribute to those killed before the end of the 47-day siege of strategically located Vicksburg on July 4, two years earlier. What is now known as Vicksburg National Cemetery is situated two miles north of the bluff-top city that dominated the Mississippi valley in the crucial early days of the Civil War. Interred within the cemetery's borders are more than 18,000 war dead, nearly 13,000 of them unidentified. They include not only those who lost their lives at Vicksburg, but also many who died within a 150-mile radius of that center. Vicksburg — partially surrounded by a crescent-shaped, 1,740-acre National Military Park on the site of the remarkably preserved defenses and siege lines — brings the saga, heroism, and tragedy of the war alive for today's visitors as much as any city in the nation.

Another of the important early observances of Confederate Memorial Day took place on April 25, 1866, in Columbus, Mississippi, where Friendship Cemetery houses the remains of men killed during the battle of Shiloh in 1862 and of others who died in the Columbus Military Hospital. Included in their number were between 1,400 and 1,500 Confederate soldiers and between 40 and 100 Union soldiers who died as prisoners of war.

Like other early observances, the one at Columbus was spontaneous. During the early spring of 1866, several local women had busied themselves with tending the graves of the Confederate dead. Inspired by their example, other women joined them in a public memorial on April 25. All who participated carried with them spring flowers with which to decorate the graves. They arrived at the cemetery in a procession led by young girls in white dresses. These were followed by wives and widows dressed in black, and by carriages bearing elderly participants. At the graves, members of the procession formed themselves into a square while they listened to a prayer and a commemorative speech before placing their flowers on the graves of their dead. As if with a single spontaneous impulse they then remembered the Union dead who also lay nearby and turned to lay magnolia blossoms upon the graves of their former enemies.

Word of the generous gesture spread rapidly, evoking an appreciative response in the North. Horace Greeley's New York *Tribune* commented:

The women of Columbus, Mississippi, have shown themselves impartial in their offerings to the memory of the dead. They strewed flowers alike on the graves of the Confederate and of the National soldiers.

Francis Miles Finch, a young attorney in Ithaca,

New York, reacted with a poem called "The Blue and the Gray." Reprinted in newspapers, memorized by students, and widely discussed throughout the nation, it appeared originally in the September 1867 issue of the *Atlantic Monthly* and read in part as follows:

By the flow of the inland river,
Whence the fleets of iron have fled,
Where the blades of the grave grass quiver,
Asleep are the ranks of the dead;
Under the sod and the dew,
Waiting the judgment day;
Under the one, the Blue;
Under the other, the Gray. . . .

From the silence of sorrowful hours
The desolate mourners go,
Lovingly laden with flowers
Alike for the friend and the foe;
Under the sod and the dew,
Waiting the judgment day;
Under the roses, the Blue;
Under the lilies, the Gray. . . .

Sadly, but not with upbraiding,
The generous deed was done;
In the storm of the years that are fading
No braver battle was won;
Under the sod and the dew,
Waiting the judgment day;
Under the blossoms, the Blue;
Under the garlands, the Gray.

Apart from the more widespread observances on April 26, May 10, or June 3, some individual communities have settled upon their own dates for marking Confederate Memorial Day. The choice of date is often tied to an event of local historical importance. Winchester, Virginia, for example, observes it on the anniversary of the death of General Turner Ashby, and Petersburg, Virginia, commemorates the anniversary of its own hours of defensive glory (see June 9). The rest of the state of Virginia observes Confederate Memorial Day on a date coinciding with that of the national Memorial Day. (A number of southern states join officially in the national observance on May 30, observing an additional and separate Confederate Memorial Day. This is true of Florida, North Carolina, Kentucky, Louisiana, and Tennessee.)

Whatever its date, Confederate Memorial Day is marked with solemnity and similar rites throughout the South. Services include addresses, the decoration of graves, and the playing or singing of appropriate musical selections. Frequent choices include "Dixie," which became the unofficial anthem of the South after it was played at Jefferson Davis's inauguration as president of the Confederacy and adopted as a marching song by Confederate troops. Another selection often heard on Confederate Memorial Day is "How Firm a Foundation," said to have been the favorite hymn of both Davis and General Lee. Drum and bugle corps often are in attendance at the ceremonies. A military honors squad customarily fires a salute, and a bugler blows Taps. Local chapters of the United Daughters of the Confederacy sponsor many of the memorial observances throughout the South and occasionally in other states as well; in fact, the UDC plays a preeminent role in the commemorative ceremonies that take place on Confederate Memorial Day, often with the cooperation of the Sons of Confederate Veterans, the Children of the Confederacy, and, at times, other organizations. In addition to the ceremonies outlined above, wreaths are laid at Confederate monuments wherever they exist on Confederate Memorial Day. One of these is sculptor Sir Moses Ezekiel's Confederate monument at Jackson Circle in Arlington (Virginia) National Cemetery.

Frederick Law Olmsted's Birthday

Frederick Law Olmsted, the father of American urban landscape architecture, was born in Hartford, Connecticut, on April 26, 1822. A man of varied accomplishments, he devoted his talents primarily to the improvement of life in the greatest cities of the United States through the development of public parks. Olmsted's imagination and expertise created Manhattan's Central and Morningside parks, Brooklyn's Prospect Park, Boston's Franklin Park, and Philadelphia's Fairmount Park.

Frederick Law Olmsted was the son of John Olmsted, a successful merchant whose forebears arrived in Boston from England in 1632, and Charlotte Law Hull Olmsted. The boy's mother died when he was four years old, and his father then married Mary Ann Bull, a deeply religious woman. Olmsted's father and stepmother shared a love for nature, which they communicated to Frederick and his younger brother John.

Aware of the shortcomings of his own education, Olmsted's father decided not to take responsibility for his son's instruction and instead delegated it to a series of country parsons. Ironically these clergymen apparently were fundamentalist and anti-intellectual, the antithesis of what the elder Olmsted intended. Frederick Olmsted reacted quite negatively to the narrow ways of these teachers, and his experiences left him hostile to organized religion.

In 1837 Olmsted planned to attend Yale College, but sumac poisoning so weakened his eyesight that he could not continue his education. Instead he became an apprentice to Frederick A. Barton, a civil engineer, in Andover, Massa-chusetts, and, subsequently, Collinsville, Connecticut. During his two and one-half years with Barton, Olmsted acquired many of the skills that he would later put to use.

In August 1840 Olmsted began to pursue a career in commerce, as a clerk with Benkard and Hutton, French dry-goods importers in New York. He left this employment in March 1842 and spent the next year attending lectures at Yale. In April 1843 he signed on as an apprentice seaman on the bark *Ronaldson*. Olmsted spent a year on the *Ronaldson*, and during that time he sailed to China, but he gave up the sea on the completion of the voyage.

Upon returning to the United States, Olmsted decided to devote himself to scientific farming. He received his first training at the farm of David Brooks, his uncle, in Cheshire, Connecticut. He also attended lectures at Yale on geology and scientific farming given by professors Benjamin Silliman and John T. Norton. He then spent from April to October 1846 at the prize-winning farm of George Geddes near Owego, New York.

In 1847 John Olmsted bought his son a small farm at Sachem Head, Connecticut. This venture did not prosper, and in January 1848 the elder Olmsted purchased another farm for him — the richer Akerly farm on Staten Island, New York. Frederick Olmsted made his new holding into a beautiful homestead as well as a model of scientific agricultural management, but again the undertaking was not a financial success.

In 1850 Olmsted sailed for Europe with his brother and a friend, Charles Loring Brace. They spent four weeks on the Continent and then made a walking tour of rural Britain. In 1852 Olmsted published the product of his journey, *Walks and Talks of an American Farmer in England*.

Critics acclaimed Olmsted's first book, and Henry J. Raymond, who only a short time before had founded the New York *Times,* was favorably impressed by the author. Raymond, who had established the *Times* in part to counter the intemperate journalism of the day, had noted that Olmsted shared his view that the radical abolitionists were presenting a distorted image of the United States abroad. Raymond accordingly commissioned Olmsted, who like him was a Free-Soil Whig, to travel through the South and make reports on life and manners there.

In 1856 Olmsted published his reports as *A Journey in the Seaboard Slave States*. Shortly thereafter he traveled to Texas with his brother and then returned to the North alone via New Orleans and Richmond. After this second visit Olmsted published *A Journey through Texas* in 1857 and *A Journey in the Back Country* in 1860. The three books, condensed into two volumes that appeared as *The Cotton Kingdom* in 1861, form perhaps the most accurate description of the antebellum South.

Olmsted's appraisal of the South was harsh. He concluded that the South had rejected democracy in favor of protecting the interests of a small, self-styled aristocracy and was appalled by the brutalities of slavery. He also argued that only six Southern communities — Charleston, Louisville, Mobile, New Orleans, Richmond, and St. Louis — deserved to be called cities. Noting that frontierlike conditions had ill effects, he found the almost total neglect of the general welfare not surprising.

Olmsted's travels convinced him of the superiority of the North's urban-commercial complexity, which held the promise of a better life for vast numbers of people. He was not blind to the deficiencies of municipalities like New York, Boston, and Philadelphia, but he blamed the overwhelming pursuit of profit rather than urban life for these flaws. The erstwhile farmer envisioned the city as the ultimate hope as well as the apparent destiny of 19th century America but recognized that improving the quality of urban life was imperative.

Two tendencies in city life particularly disturbed Olmsted. He believed that the density of population of the great centers was hazardous to health and created an atmosphere in which the inhabitants, unable to develop stable relationships with their neighbors, became apprehensive, hard, and selfish. Olmsted noted with dismay that such conditions led businessmen and merchants, the leaders of urban America, to make their residences away from the cities that had produced their wealth.

Reacting positively to the challenge, Olmsted decided to devote the rest of his life to an attempt to rehabilitate American cities. His principal goal was the creation of environments that would entice the social elite to remain in the urban areas and that would offer public recreation areas. Eventually Olmsted came to see the ideal city as a unit with a core devoted to business and administrative activities, and with contiguous suburban areas, thus combining the best features of the countryside with the amenities of urban life.

In 1857 influential New Yorkers urged Olmsted, who had been a friend of the early landscaper Andrew Jackson Downing, to apply for the superintendency of Central Park, which the city (then consisting only of Manhattan Island) was to construct according to the plan of Captain Egbert L. Viele. Olmsted, who received endorsements from such notables as Peter Cooper and Washington Irving, received the post on September 11, 1857. He associated himself with the English architect Calvert Vaux, and the two men submitted a plan called Greensward, which in 1858 won a competition for a new design for the park.

Olmsted became architect-in-chief of Central Park on May 17, 1858. He and Vaux struggled against politicians who sought to make the enterprise a reservoir of patronage. Years passed before the project was completed, but by 1860 Olmsted and Vaux had achieved some successes, and the park became popular with residents. Olmsted had transformed a wasteland of rocks, swamps, and pastures into an artful arrangement of wooded hills, artificial lakes, and gentle fields.

The Civil War interrupted Olmsted's new career. He took a leave of absence to serve as general secretary of the US Sanitary Commission, the privately supported, volunteer organization whose functions were later taken over by the American Red Cross. Olmsted's duties included the establishment of field hospitals and supervision of the care of the wounded and dying. In 1863 Olmsted resigned from the commission, physically and emotionally exhausted, but he then helped found the Union League, which was established in part to aid in soldier relief.

Political pressures prompted Olmsted and Vaux to resign from their Central Park assignment. In August 1863 Olmsted, in the hope of restoring his health, accepted the position of superintendent of the Frémont Mariposa mining estates in California. During two years in the West Olmsted helped set up the Yosemite Park state reservation, now Yosemite National Park, and served as the area's first commissioner. He also designed Golden Gate Park in San Francisco, the Oakland Cemetery, and the grounds and residential village of the University of California at Berkeley.

Olmsted returned to New York in 1865 and made the city his center of operations for the next 13 years. In the summer of 1865 Olmsted and Vaux were reappointed as landscape architects of Central Park. Olmsted continued his efforts until 1878, when political complications finally ended his association with the project. In the intervening years between 1865 and 1878, Olmsted and Vaux, who in 1860 had been named "landscape architects and designers to the Commissioners north of 155th Street," had also laid out Riverside Park and the upper reaches of Manhattan Island. In addition they had drawn up comprehensive plans for the development of Brooklyn (which was an independent city until 1898) and had created Brooklyn's Prospect Park. Olmsted also made plans for improvements on Staten Island, New York, and for land subdivisions in Irvington and Tarrytown in Westchester County.

Other communities also gained the benefits of Olmsted's talents between 1865 and 1878. He designed several municipal parks, including South Park in Chicago and the Mount Royal Park in Montreal, and he created the beautiful residential suburb of Riverside, near Chicago. In 1874, in recognition of his achievements, Olmsted received the assignment of landscaping the grounds of the Capitol in Washington, D.C.

The pioneer American landscape architect — who helped introduce that new term — took a European holiday early in 1878, and after his return to the United States he set up his base of operations in Boston. He devoted his efforts to the design of the park system of Boston, including Franklin Park in the West Roxbury section. In cooperation with professors Asa Gray and Charles Sprague Sargent, he planned the notable Arnold Arboretum, also in the West Roxbury area. In addition, Olmsted was engaged in a number of projects outside the Boston region. He collaborated with Leopold Eidlitz and H. H. Richardson in the design of the state capitol at Albany, New York; took part in the site selection and development of plans for Stanford University in Palo Alto, California; and was occupied with devising a program for the protection of Niagara Falls. Olmsted continued to create and make suggestions for urban parks, including Belle Isle Park in Detroit and Morningside Park in New York City.

Two projects drew most of Olmsted's attention during his final active years. He took special interest in the creation of Biltmore, George W. Vanderbilt's estate in Asheville, North Carolina, and designed other retreats for Vanderbilt and for Rockefeller. Fittingly, it was Olmsted who laid out the grounds for the great White City of the World's Columbian Exposition in Chicago in 1893. This remarkable collaboration of architects and artists was intended to give inspiration for the design of future urban communities, and it gave rise to the American "City Beautiful" movement. The grounds for the exposition later became Chicago's Jackson Park.

Frederick Law Olmsted retired from practice in 1895 and died on August 28, 1903. With Olmsted's passing, America lost, in the words of the 19th century architect Daniel H. Burnham, a man "who paints with lakes and wooded slopes; with lawns and banks and forest-covered hills; with mountainsides and ocean views."

Recent concern with ecology and urban environment has brought Frederick Law Olmsted again to the public's attention. In 1972, to celebrate his 150th birthday, a national Olmsted Sesquicentennial Commission was established with urban authority Frederick Gutheim as chairman. The cities of Atlanta, Boston, and Chicago commemorated Olmsted's birth, and in New York City the Department of Parks sponsored a gala celebration in Central Park. An actor dressed to impersonate Olmsted spoke appropriate words, and the participants feasted on a giant green cheesecake made in the shape of the park, which despite many problems remains a favorite place of recreation. In the autumn New York City's Whitney Museum held a major Olmsted exhibition under the direction of William Alex.

Virgin Islands Carnival

This is a movable event. See note on page xxvi.

For sheer exuberance, few events surpass the carnival that explodes annually in the capital city of Charlotte Amalie, on the island of St. Thomas in the US Virgin Islands. Unlike the Carnival in New Orleans and many other parts of the world, which is a specifically pre-Lenten celebration before the period of denial and self-examination in which Christians prepare for Easter, the Virgin Islands carnival is held *after* Easter, usually in the last week of April. Although carnival is generally preceded by a week (and more) of preliminary events, its official dates run from Sunday until midnight the following Saturday.

The Virgin Islands carnival has its roots in a custom dating from slave days, when Danish plantation owners allowed workers to celebrate after the weeks of toil that went into the sugarcane harvest, with antics, masquerading, and dancing in the streets to the beat of bamboula drums. In its modern form, the carnival began abortively with a one-day gala held on February 14, 1912. That year's festivities, which began at 4:00 A.M., included the procession of "King" Valdemar Miller, his flag bearer, and 60 costumed men on "spirited steeds" from a gaily decorated launch to the market place, where "Queen" Casilda Duurloo and two pages —including Ralph M. Paiewonsky, later the governor of the islands — awaited them. A royal parade followed, headed by a brass band, through Charlotte Amalie's narrow streets. Subsequent events included a boat race; greased-pole climb; donkey, bicycle, and carriage parades; union laborers' procession; confetti battle; and torchlight parade "with combined bands" — followed by "illuminations" and general amusements, which lasted until 4:00 the next morning.

When the celebration was over, everyone agreed it had been a tremendous success and the matter was dropped. Both carnival and the spirit to make it possible were absent during the next 40 years. That four-decade period witnessed the outbreak of World War I, the depression of the 1930s, the impoverishment of the island, widespread emigration to the US mainland (the United States purchased the Danish-owned islands in 1917), and World War II.

It was 1952, in fact, before the carnival reappeared. When it did, it did so with gusto and on an expanded basis. It has been an annual event ever since.

Nowadays the entire community, and thousands of visitors from the mainland and neighboring islands, get swept up in the fever as the streets swarm with processions, buildings reverberate with melody, and revelers oscillate to the pulsating beat of bands and to calypso and steel-drum rhythms.

Preliminary events begin a week or more before the carnival opens officially. Among the most important are the coronation of the queen of the carnival and the coronation ball, held in various locations. The carnival queen is selected on the basis of talent, poise, and personality during a fashion and talent show generally held several weeks beforehand. Runners-up become her court. There also is a competition in which two children are selected to be the carnival's prince and princess.

For six days a calypso tent, featuring nightly the exertions of calypso singers from throughout the Caribbean, holds forth in Lionel Roberts Stadium. Performers, whose lyrics — often improvised — may deal with current events or satirize someone in the audience, battle it out for the title of Calypso King. Among the stars who have participated in the calypso tent's show are such West Indians as the Mighty Sparrow, Lord Melody, King Fighter, Canary, Bitter Bush, Mighty Terror, and Calypso Rose.

The week-long carnival proper, which begins on Sunday, is officially set aside as Carnival Week by proclamation of the governor, who also proclaims the last two days of the week as public holidays. Opening day is marked by the lighting of the carnival lights, which are strung in zigzag fashion from one end of town to the other.

Carnival Village, the conglomeration of booths that has been set up in the center of town and that will serve as the hub of carnival activities all week, is a major attraction. The Children's Village opens officially on Sunday afternoon, and the Adult Village opens the following afternoon. The village, decorated with bunting and flags of the five nations that have governed the Virgin Islands, is a center of carnival night life, selling local products and all kinds of West Indian food and drink. Local bands meanwhile provide marathon entertainment, and steel

bands emerge from the village nightly, followed by hundreds of revelers who shuffle and sway through the streets. The undulating processions — road marches and tramps, as they are called locally — are known also by such names as Bamboushay, Roas-a-Tramp, and Carnival Jump-Up.

Various other events — a produce fair, water sports, athletic events, contests, and special "days" — meanwhile go on throughout carnival week. But the real climax comes at the end of the week, with the children's parade (on Friday) and the grand carnival parade (on Saturday). The latter is a particularly colorful event, with bands, mummery, floats, troupes, and floupes (which combine elements of both floats and troupes). The traditional "big heads," mystery men cavorting behind giant masks, are still part of the parade today. So are the "war parties" of Carib Indians who battle fierce-looking "Zulus" in traditional stick fights. So, too, are the graceful Bamboula and Quadrille dancers; the limbo dancers; and the astonishing Mocko Jumbi, who dance on 10-foot stilts. Perhaps most characteristically of all, that famous and recent development in West Indian music, the steel band, is represented by troupe after troupe of marchers. Other participants may masquerade in any costume they fancy — for example, as Hawaiians, Roman charioteers, clowns, or Spanish conquistadores.

The grand carnival parade culminates at the stadium, where special demonstrations are repeated for the judges and prizes are awarded for the best entries in various categories. Afterwards, the parade and carnival are topped off with music at Carnival Village, a display of fireworks, and one final, ebullient, hip-shaking tramp from Village to market place. Then, at midnight, all is over until the next year's carnival.

APRIL 27

Fast Day in New Hampshire

This is a movable event. See note on page xxvi.

New Hampshire is the only state in which there is still a legal holiday known as Fast Day. Although it was for years marked on the last Thursday of April, the state legislature in 1949 shifted the observance to the fourth Monday in April. In so doing, it anticipated the trend toward Monday holidays of more recent years. Although the date of Fast Day is set by statute, it is customary for the governor to issue a proclamation officially designating the day each year.

So far as the general public is concerned, the original purpose of the day as an occasion of spiritual significance marked by prayer and fasting seems to have been overlooked throughout most of the 20th century; and the prayer services and special exercises that were once customary have much diminished in number. As one resident recently summarized it, Fast Day today is much more commonly used as "an opportunity for recreation, opening up summer camps, the performance of spring chores, and out-of-town shopping."

Governor H. Styles Bridges took note of this fact as early as 1935, in explaining New Hampshire's custom of observing Fast Day:

The fact that the season of outdoor sport is then opening in this latitude tends to secure a general observance of the day so far as ceasing from labor is concerned. . . . I do not know personally of any instance of its observance by fasting. Some church services are held and the official proclamation usually recalls the original reason for establishing Fast Day, and the existing need for a continuance of the thought that inspired the first observance.

That reverent and hope-filled thought pervaded New England in the days of its early settlement. Days of "public humiliation, fasting and prayer" were commonly proclaimed by the royal governors, usually about the middle of April. For generations, prayers for a bountiful harvest characterized New England's spring Fast Days, which corresponded to Thanksgiving. The earliest official record of a Fast Day proclamation issued in New Hampshire appeared in the provincial papers of 1679. That proclamation designated February 26 for the commemoration. Later acts of the New Hampshire legislature confirmed the Fast Day observance in 1861 and 1899, with the last Thursday of April traditionally set aside for the purpose, until the 1949 change.

Long before that, however, there had been changes elsewhere. In most places, the custom of observing Fast Day had faded out, both in statute and in practice, after the American Revolution. Massachusetts formally abolished its Fast Day in 1895 and substituted Patriots' Day on the grounds that the former occasion no longer retained the austere religious character it had once had. A few years later, Maine repealed the law establishing its Fast Day, for similar reasons.

In New Hampshire too there were thoughts of dropping the observance. The earliest known effort to abolish Fast Day occurred in 1897, when Governor Ramsdell, in a message to the legislature, urged it to follow the example of Massachusetts. His recommendation was not adopted.

Similar later proposals were also defeated and a concerted anti-Fast Day effort in 1917 came to naught. To this day, New Hampshire retains its now unique observance. But if the day has been secularized in modern times, the memory of its historical reason for being has not entirely disappeared.

Ulysses S. Grant's Birthday

Ulysses Simpson Grant, the 18th President of the United States, was born April 27, 1822, in Point Pleasant, Ohio. He was baptized Hiram Ulysses Grant by his parents, Hannah Simpson Grant and Jesse Root Grant. Jesse Grant, a tanner by trade, moved with his family to Georgetown, Ohio, in 1823. Though without formal education himself, he insisted that his children be educated. With true public schools lacking, Ulysses Grant attended subscription schools until he was 17. Hating his father's tannery, he preferred to work in the fields and developed a kindly mastery over animals.

Jesse Grant won his son an appointment to the US Military Academy at West Point in 1839. Though not enthusiastic about the prospect of a military career, young Grant set off for the East. The congressman who recommended Grant to West Point had erroneously presented his name as Ulysses Simpson Grant, and Grant accepted the change.

His career at the Military Academy was generally undistinguished. Although he was the best horseman there, he was only an average student, except in mathematics, in which he excelled. He was quiet, courted no one's favor, and counted the days until he could escape from military life.

His graduation in 1843 — 21st in a class of 39 cadets — entailed a period of service as an army officer. Grant hoped to serve in the cavalry, but instead he was commissioned a brevet second lieutenant in the infantry.

In 1845 he joined the army of General Zachary Taylor in Texas. Though he opposed the Mexican War on principle, Grant fought with great personal bravery throughout the conflict. He distinguished himself at Monterrey by a daring ride through enemy lines in search of ammunition.

After the war, Grant married Julia Dent on August 22, 1848. He was stationed at Sackett's Harbor, New York, until 1852, when he and his regiment were ordered to the Pacific coast via Panama. Because of the danger of the assignment, Julia Grant did not follow.

The trip was a senseless nightmare. Cholera struck, and Grant buried most of his men en route. He spent the next two years in the wilds of the Pacific Northwest, lonely for his wife and child, Frederick. His promotion to the rank of captain in 1853 was small consolation. Grant took to drink and resigned from the army after being censured for intoxication.

Dispirited and without money, he rejoined his family in St. Louis in August 1854. After he had unsuccessfully tried to earn a living as farmer, real estate agent, and customhouse clerk, he went to work in a leather goods store owned by his father and run by two of his brothers in Galena, Illinois. However, their condescending attitude made his stay uncomfortable.

In April 1861 the Federal installation at Fort Sumter was bombarded by Confederate guns, and President Abraham Lincoln called for volunteers. Responding to the call, Grant volunteered for military service. Once back in the army, however, he was shuttled from one menial job to another. He was drillmaster, then military clerk, then mustering officer. He asked to lead a regiment, but his letter making the request never was answered. After six weeks of uncertainty he was appointed colonel of the 21st Illinois Volunteers Infantry Regiment. He had drilled his men scarcely a month when they were ordered to Missouri.

Then Grant, to his own surprise, was promoted to brigadier general. Within two months, he was commanding 20,000 green troops. In January 1862 Grant was ordered to move up the Tennessee River in a plan to drive out the Confederates holding West Tennessee by attacking their weak center at Fort Henry on the Tennessee River and nearby Fort Donelson on the Cumberland River. Fort Henry quickly succumbed on February 6 to cannon fire from gunboats. Fort Donelson's batteries, however, repulsed the Federal gunboats, and on February 15 the garrison attempted to fight its way free of the Union forces. Grant came upon the scene of battle late in the day to see his center and right flank about to collapse. In a cool maneuver, he attacked with his left and carried the day. The following morning he won unconditional surrender. This victory gave his initials U.S.G. a new meaning — Unconditional Surrender Grant—and provided the discouraged North, which had not won a battle since the war had begun, with renewed spirit.

Grant wished to pursue the fleeing enemy farther up the Tennessee but was hampered by a lack of will to pursue that proved habitual on the part of many of the Union's senior officers. Instead of allowing him to follow up his advantage, General Henry W. Halleck diverted some of Grant's troops for another operation and slowed his main force, allowing Confederate troops to regroup 40,000 strong at Corinth, near Tennessee's southern border.

Grant's army lay at Pittsburgh Landing waiting for reinforcements before engaging the enemy. However, the Confederates did not wait, but attacked Grant frontally in a surprise attack on April 6, 1862. The ensuing battle of Shiloh was extremely bloody and poorly led on both sides. Having made little preparation for defense or security on April 6, the Union forces were driven back in confusion, until their backs were at the Tennessee River. Grant had badly injured his foot, but chose to spend the night with his men on muddy ground under torrential rains. The next morning, the arrival of fresh troops gave Grant the confidence to counterattack. His attack, when he was expected to retreat across the river, finally turned the battle into a victory of sorts. The Confederate troops were driven off. Yet 13,000 of 63,000 Union troops were wounded, killed, or missing in the encounter, as were nearly 11,000 of 40,000 Confederates.

Grant was widely criticized for his leadership and tactics at Shiloh. Not expecting an attack, he had chosen to drill his new recruits rather than dig them into trenches. Grant responded to his critics with silence. Lincoln, however, announced, "I can't spare this man; he fights."

The eastern theater of war gave the cause for Lincoln's concern. There the Union's formidable Army of the Potomac was so timidly and unimaginatively led that even Confederate mistakes did not result in Union gains. Even so, the battles of Antietam in September 1862 and Gettysburg in July 1863 finally blunted the offensive capability of the South.

In the West the Confederates still held one stronghold: Vicksburg, Mississippi, on the Mississippi River. Grant had spent the latter part of 1862 trying fruitlessly to reach through he muddy woods north of Vicksburg. Meanwhile the national press was vituperative, calling him an inept drunkard, and the Confederates expected him to retreat to Memphis in disgrace. Grant persisted, however, and in January 1863 sent his army of 36,000 down the Mississippi by steamer to a point opposite Vicksburg. Twenty-five miles south of that point, he crossed the river, then cut loose from his supply line and marched 35 miles northeast until he was directly east of Vicksburg. Meanwhile General John C. Pemberton, commanding the Confederates at Vicksburg, was completely fooled by a raucous diversionary attack known as Grierson's Raid.

The Union forces in the area then joined together. Skirmishing as they went, Grant's 36,000 troops won the day through brilliant maneuvering across impossible terrain, heavily wooded and cut by deep ravines. Initially outnumbered (though they were later reinforced), the Union troops were caught between Confederate troops to their east and the strong force defending Vicksburg to the west. Grant drove off the eastern forces, made an about-face and proceeded to outflank and outfight the Confederates outside Vicksburg. A siege was established, and the city surrendered on July 4, the day after the Confederates had been stopped at Gettysburg. After Port Hudson, Louisiana, surrendered four days later, the Mississippi was in Union hands, and the Confederacy was cut in two.

Lincoln promoted Grant to major general in the regular army after the fall of Vicksburg. His direction of the bloody Chattanooga campaign in the fall opened the way for a Union drive toward Atlanta. Then on March 9, 1864, Grant (with the rank of lieutenant general) was given command of all the Federal armies and went to Virginia to direct the Union's most important military force, General Meade's Army of the Potomac.

Grant impressed no one but President Lincoln. The nation's highest general refused to deck himself out in ornamental clothing so dear to other generals. Short, stocky, and a bit stooped, Grant had a seedy, unkempt look. He was usually unshaven, occasionally pretending that his stubble was a beard. He slouched around camp with his hands stuck deep into baggy pockets, a cigar clamped in his resolute mouth. In his public aspect, he was taciturn. Only occasional witticisms revealed an active mind behind his impassive countenance.

Grant was a deeply compassionate general, but he refused to play-act for his men. This was due partly to his lack of political ambition, an attitude Lincoln valued, since many Union generals fancied themselves presidential material. Grant scorned the professional military life and was in turn scorned by professional soldiers. He was the first of Lincoln's generals to agree wholly with Lincoln's war aims: to press in simultaneously upon the South from three directions. By maintaining this simultaneous offensive, the Union armies would nullify the South's advantage of interior defense lines. The South's smaller armies would be denied mobility; the Confederacy would be cut into pieces. This was Grant's strategy. It proved costly, but it worked.

In May 1864 Grant marched the Army of the Potomac south and met Lee's army in the wilderness near Chancellorsville, Virginia. The fighting through the dense underbrush resulted in many casualties but was indecisive. Then in a series of bloody battles that included Spotsylvania, North Anna River, and Cold Harbor, the indomitable Grant drove the brilliant Lee slowly southward, past Richmond. At Petersburg came a new stage in warfare, forecasting the grimness of World War I. Both armies settled into opposing lines of trenches, occasionally making costly forays over open ground.

Lincoln narrowly weathered the election of 1864, emerging the victor. Shortly afterwards, in mid-November 1864, General Sherman left the Atlanta area and began his march to the sea.

While Sherman's army moved across the South, Grant's strength continued to grow. On April 2, 1865, Lee finally broke contact with Grant's forces in front of Petersburg after the long siege and set out toward the west, with Grant in pursuit. Union cavalry raced ahead, and Lee's army was surrendered at the little town of Appomattox Court House, where Lee surrendered to Grant's magnanimous terms on April 9, 1865 (see April 9), effectively ending the war.

After Lincoln's assassination on April 14, 1865, Vice President Andrew Johnson became President. Congress was not in session at this time, and Johnson, using his presidential powers, began to enact his own reconstruction program. He also granted pardons to many white Southerners, who were quickly reestablished in positions of power. Southern legislatures, newly assembled under the Johnson program, passed "black codes" for the regulation of the newly freed black population. Many Northerners thought that these codes came close to returning blacks to a condition of servitude and felt that they virtually nullified the recently passed 13th Amendment, then in the process of ratification by the states.

When Congress returned to session in December, it was with considerable alarm. The extent of presidential power exercised by Lincoln during the war had annoyed the legislators. Now, with peace established, they intended to reassert congressional authority and they were in no mood to give power or privilege back to people whom they regarded as rebels and traitors to the Union.

After it became clear that Congress would have to override Johnson's veto in order to enact its own program of reconstruction, the congressional elections of 1866, offering Radical Republicans a chance to gain strength, grew in importance. Even Johnson became involved in the electioneering. In a step unprecedented for a President, he set out on a national speechmaking tour, dragging along the pliant Grant, now a great popular hero, and other dignitaries to help his public image. However, by his abusive and repetitive speeches and by his too-heated response to baiting by mobs and to libel in the press, Johnson embarrassed even his friends. The net effect of his trip was actually to help the cause of his Radical Republican opponents, who triumphed. Grant came away from the experience convinced that the President lacked popular support.

In 1867 members of an overwhelmingly Republican Congress took their seats and, over Johnson's vetoes, began to enact a program of political reconstruction for the South that included military government of the entire region.

Grant angered Johnson by supporting the right of Secretary of War Edwin Stanton, a Radical Republican, to hold office after Johnson had sought to remove him. The fight, however, endeared Grant to the Radical Republicans and paved the way for his nomination for President on the Republican ticket in 1868.

In that year's election, Grant was elected President by a large electoral vote, though he had only a slight edge in the popular tally. For a time, he enjoyed life in the White House. He tried to run the administrative branch of government like an army staff but had some difficulties on that account. In the conduct of foreign affairs, he gave his very competent secretary of state, Hamilton Fish, a free hand. Fish's skill contributed to the amicable settlement by international arbitration of the *Alabama* Claims dispute over damage done by British-built Confederate warships during the Civil War.

Questions of finance were central to Grant's domestic policy. During the War, greenbacks had been issued to raise money for the government. Many greenbacks had been bought by speculators. With the rise in value of this paper currency, a dispute arose over whether it should be redeemed at original rates or at current value. Generally speaking, Eastern business interests wanted a deflationary policy, while debtors and speculators hoped for an inflationary policy. With inside information on administration policy, two stock speculators, Jay Gould and James Fisk, organized a corner on gold, thus precipitating a disastrous day on Wall Street, known as "Black Friday," on September 24, 1869. By dumping gold onto the open market, the Treasury foiled the scheme. But the machinations of Gould and Fisk were the beginning of a whole series of scandals that were to besmirch both the first and second administrations of Grant.

Grant was an uncomplicated, patriotic man who expected others to attend to the business of government in the same spirit. Some others, however, did not hold this attitude but went into government to get rich. Although Grant himself introduced some reforms, he suspected no one and refused to listen to cries for the kind of thoroughgoing civil service reform that was obviously needed. Thus a split arose within Republican ranks. Members of one section of the party dubbed themselves Reform, or Liberal, Republicans. Their interest was to rid the Republican party of the spoils system, political corruption, and vindictiveness toward the former Confederate states. In May 1872 this Liberal Republican faction met and nominated the brilliant but erratic Horace Greeley for President. His nomination was also endorsed by the Democrats. The regular, or Radical, Republicans were still interested in preserving the right of blacks to vote, whereas this concern had faded from the minds of Liberal Republicans. Nominated on a superpatriotic Radical Republican platform, Grant was reelected by a wide margin, carrying all but six states.

Grant's second term was marked by a wave of corruption at all levels of government. Although the President was incorruptible himself, his trust was betrayed by the venality of high appointees and others and by the friendship of influential persons within his administration with unscrupulous financial interests. The effort to build a railroad to the Pacific became infested with speculators and unprincipled legislators scheming to line their pockets. In St. Louis and elsewhere, a Whiskey Ring defrauded the government of several million dollars in taxes with the aid of Treasury officials and Grant's private secretary. The War, Interior, and postal departments were all scenes of scandals. Grant, himself honest, left the White House a poor man; yet his judgment had been bad, and many of his closest associates were tainted.

With a few thousand dollars saved from his salary, Grant set out in May 1877 to see Europe. He traveled for two years, returning home in the autumn of 1879. In 1880 a small "Grant for President" boom quickly died.

Grant retired to an apartment on New York City's upper East Side in 1881. He lived on the income from gifts of admirers totaling $250,000, which he invested. These investments eventually went bad, however, and in 1884 Grant entered an unsuccessful business partnership in which he was badly exploited.

Perhaps as a result of his lifelong addiction to cigars, Grant had meanwhile contracted throat cancer. Knowing that he had not long to live, he agreed to write a book of personal memoirs to provide his family with an income. For the quiet to do this work, Grant was moved to what is now known as the Grant Cottage, still maintained as he left it, at Mount McGregor, New York. In severe pain, he worked stoically. He completed the manuscript on July 19, 1885, and died four days later. The memoirs, remarkable for their straightforwardness and eloquence, were published by Mark Twain. They sold well and eventually brought Grant's family almost $500,000.

Spontaneously, the nation grieved the passing

of this simple, patriotic man. He had expressed the wish that he be buried in New York City; accordingly, funeral preparations were begun there. Grant's body lay in state for two days at City Hall as many thousands of mourners came to pay their last respects. The funeral was an elaborate affair of state, and President Grover Cleveland declared a national day of mourning. Over 500 celebrities, including the President, and hundreds of thousands of others watched as the casket was drawn by 24 black horses to the burial place overlooking the Hudson River.

The Grant Memorial Association was soon formed to erect a suitable monument over his grave. John Duncan designed a massive structure whose interior is reminiscent of Napoleon's Tomb. Over 90,000 people contributed to build the memorial, which is at Riverside Drive and West 122nd Street. It was opened to the public in 1897, and since that time has been visited by millions. Inside are mural maps of battles and busts of other Civil War heroes. The site was declared General Grant National Memorial on May 1, 1959.

Observances of the anniversary of Grant's birth were begun in the years immediately following his death and continued annually for years afterward. Marked by dinners, meetings, and speeches, the observances soon became widespread. They included those organized in 1887 and 1888 by the now-defunct Americus Club of Pittsburgh; the Army and Navy Club of Hartford; the Metropolitan Methodist Episcopal Church of Washington, D.C., which Grant had attended during his presidency; and the Grant Birthday Association in New York City, in which Generals William T. Sherman and Charles H. T. Corliss were active. There were even proposals, which never came to fruition, that Grant's birthday be made a legal holiday. One such proposal came in 1888 from former Vice President Hannibal Hamlin of Maine as he addressed the Massachusetts Club of Boston at its first celebration of the April 27 anniversary. An idea of the scope of the observances, now largely discontinued, comes from accounts of the dinner held the same year at Delmonico's restaurant by the Grant Birthday Association in New York. Responding to a toast by General Sherman, the orator and businessman Chauncey Depew remarked:

The one hundred years of our national existence are crowded with an unusual number of men eminent in arms and statesmanship, but of all the illustrious list only one has his birthday a legal holiday—George Washington. Of the heroes and patriots who filled the niches in the temple of fame for the first century the birthdays of only two are of such wide significance that they receive wide celebrations — Lincoln's and Grant's.

Today Grant is principally recalled by monuments and by places with which he was associated. In Washington, D.C., for instance, a large equestrian statue at the east end of the Mall, near the Capitol, depicts Grant surrounded by charging cavalrymen and artillery caissons. Many of the battlefields where Grant served are today war memorials. Among them are Fort Donelson National Military Park and Cemetery, Tennessee; Chickamauga and Chattanooga National Military Park on the Georgia-Tennessee border; Pea Ridge National Military Park, Arkansas; Petersburg National Battlefield, Virginia; Shiloh National Military Park and Cemetery, Tennessee; Vicksburg National Military Park and Cemetery, Mississippi; and Appomattox Court House National Historical Park, Virginia. Grant's headquarters at Appomattox is one of several buildings there restored to their 1865 appearance.

Grant's birthplace at Point Pleasant, Ohio, has been reconstructed and is open to the public. Memorial services are occasionally held there on the Sunday nearest the anniversary of Grant's birth.

In Galena, Illinois, where Grant lived for periods before and after his presidency, a home purchased for him by grateful townspeople in 1865 has been restored by the Illinois Division of Parks and Memorials. The broad-eaved, two-story brick structure — for years the object of an annual Boy Scout pilgrimage — draws an increasing number of visitors. Grant's horsehair furniture, White House china and silver, and Brussels rugs are maintained as they were during his lifetime; even a selection of the cigars he liked is seen. The house is the chief magnet among other attractions of Galena, which was an 1850 frontier town. The community is the site of several historical home tours and festivals held periodically on weekends during warm-weather months. In 1974 these included the U. S. Grant Civil War Canton — a Civil War pageant and battle reenactments — on May 17–19.

APRIL 28

Maryland Ratifies the Constitution

Maryland, on April 28, 1788, officially became the seventh state to ratify the proposed US Constitution. In actuality, the delegates performed the act of ratification on Saturday, April 26. After the signing, the document was taken to a print shop. The shop was closed until Monday, however, and the paper was redated April 28.

As in Delaware, New Jersey, Georgia, and Connecticut, supporters of the new government faced little opposition in Maryland. Thus ratification was accomplished quickly and without much bitter argument or sharp political maneuvering.

Citizens of Maryland had been among the earlier proponents of strengthening the Articles of Confederation. In March 1785 four commissioners from Maryland met with four counterparts from Virginia at George Washington's Mount Vernon residence to discuss problems relating to the navigation of Chesapeake Bay and the Potomac River. The negotiators reached agreement swiftly on jurisdiction over the Potomac and on the apportionment of the expenses for marking the Chesapeake channel. In their report the representatives suggested that their respective legislatures adopt uniform currency, commercial regulations, and customs duties. The Maryland legislature approved the plan and suggested that Delaware and Pennsylvania be included in future discussions of matters of mutual interest.

After Congress called on February 21, 1787, for the assembling of a Constitutional Convention, Maryland agreed to send a five-man delegation. The legislature initially appointed Charles Carroll of Carrollton, Gabriel Duvall, Robert Hanson Harrison, Thomas Sim Lee, and Thomas Stone, but all of them declined to serve. Apparently, domestic political considerations, including opposition to plans to issue large amounts of paper money, seemed more important than the Constitutional Convention to these noted leaders. Two weeks after the date set for the opening of the Philadelphia gathering, the Maryland legislature named another, much less distinguished, five-man contingent.

Luther Martin, then in his early forties, was the most capable member of the delegation. A lawyer and former schoolteacher, Martin had been a member of the Confederation Congress and state attorney general. At the convention he became a prominent foe of plans to strengthen the federal government.

James McHenry, an Irish-born surgeon, served as secretary to George Washington during the War for Independence and became his trusted friend. Only 33, he had served in the Maryland senate and in the Confederation Congress. He made little impression at the convention.

Daniel Jenifer of St. Thomas, 64, was the senior member of the Maryland contingent. A man of means, respected in his home state, he had served in Congress and was one of Maryland's commissioners at the Mount Vernon Conference. Amiable, but aware of his shortcomings as a politician, Jenifer was not outspoken in Philadelphia.

Daniel Carroll and John Francis Mercer both had had experience in the Confederation Congress. Affluent and well-connected, these two men were rising Maryland politicians in 1787. Carroll was 56, and Mercer, at 28, was the youngest member of the delegation.

Maryland's contribution to the Constitutional Convention was not noteworthy. Predictably, this small state supported resolutions granting each state an equal vote in the Senate, but the delegation was not able to reach a decision on the preferred system of voting in the House. Eventually, however, Maryland gave its assent to the great compromise, which provided for equal representation of states in the Senate and proportional representation by population in the House.

Contentious Luther Martin gained notoriety with his oration against the aggrandizement of power by the central government. On June 27 and June 28 Martin presented a two-day speech to the weary delegates, arguing against representation proportional to population in Congress. Although Martin's position that the national government should be formed for the states rather than for individuals was plausible, his rambling harangue only antagonized his fellow convention members.

In September the Constitutional Convention concluded its business in Philadelphia. Maryland's delegates joined those of the other states in signing the proposed federal Constitution, which they sent to Congress for referral to the states for approval. The framers then returned to their home states to prepare to take part in the process of ratification.

After the October 1787 state elections, the Maryland legislature began its consideration of the new Constitution. The delegates to the Convention gave their accounts of the Philadelphia proceedings, and their impressions varied. Luther Martin presented an indictment of the new frame of government, which later appeared in print as *The Genuine Information*, while James McHenry ably refuted Martin's contentions and spoke in favor of the proposed Constitution.

Maryland's Senate called for a ratifying convention and proposed that the election of convention delegates — in which only candidates with at least £ 500 of property could compete — take place in January and that the convention assemble early in March. In the Maryland House, Samuel Chase and other Antifederalist leaders persuaded the members to postpone the election and convention until April, remove the property qualifications for candidates, and omit the statements in favor of ratification from the call for the convention. The Senate, for the sake of quick ratification, agreed to the House's terms.

Voters appeared at the polls in unusually

large numbers on election day. Approximately 10,000 Marylanders cast ballots, and a large majority of them chose candidates favoring the Constitution; the Federalists elected 65 delegates and the Antifederalists 12. When the convention met, the Federalists simply allowed opposition speakers such as Chase and Martin to express their views and then called for an immediate vote on ratification. Late on Saturday, April 26, 1788, the Maryland convention approved the new Constitution by a vote of 63 to 11.

Various factors led Maryland to strongly favor the new Constitution. A small state, Maryland looked forward to the protection that a powerful national government could provide. Baltimore merchants and manufacturers also found advantages in certain provisions of the new Constitution. And most important drew much support from the tobacco-planting aristocracy, which hoped that the new government would be able to curb democratic programs, suggested by such men as Samuel Chase, that would undermine their political and economic dominance.

Maryland and the 12 other colonies that separated from England became states at the time of the Declaration of Independence. For purposes of establishing a chronological order of the entry of these 13 states into the Union, however, historians have used the dates of their ratification of the Constitution. Thus Maryland is listed as the seventh state.

James Monroe's Birthday

James Monroe, the fifth President of the United States and promulgator of the Monroe Doctrine, was born in Westmoreland County, Virginia, on April 28, 1758. Of Scottish and Welsh ancestry, he was the eldest of five children of Spence Monroe, a farmer and circuit judge, and Elizabeth Jones Monroe.

Monroe was tutored at home until he was 12 and then attended a parson's school. A member of the gentry, he entered the College of William and Mary at 16 but after only two years left to join the Continental army. Rising from the rank of lieutenant to lieutenant-colonel in four years, he fought in many of the most famous battles of the American Revolution, including those at Harlem Heights, White Plains, Trenton, Brandywine, Germantown, and Monmouth.

By 1780 Monroe's military career was at an end, and he returned to his native state, where he studied law with Thomas Jefferson. In 1782 Monroe was elected to the Virginia legislature, and the next year he was sent to the Continental Congress, where he remained for three years. In 1786 he was admitted to the bar and began to practice law in Fredericksburg. That same year he returned to politics, elected to the Virginia Assembly. As a member of the Virginia ratifying convention of 1788, Monroe worked with such Antifederalists as Patrick Henry to defeat the proposed national constitution. Their efforts, however, were doomed to failure, and Monroe came to accept the new frame of government.

A member of the US Senate from 1790 to 1794, Monroe was active in the party of the Jeffersonian Republicans (later known as Democratic-Republicans and ultimately as Democrats), which opposed many policies of the Washington administration. President Washington appointed Monroe as minister to France in 1794, but his failure to assuage the French hostility aroused by the Jay Treaty between the United States and England led to his recall two years later.

Monroe served later as governor of Virginia from 1799 to 1802. Meanwhile, the election of the Republican candidate, Thomas Jefferson, to the presidency in 1800 assured Monroe of a place of importance in the national government. In 1802 and 1803 he and Robert R. Livingston — with instructions only to purchase New Orleans and West Florida from France — exceeded their authority and doubled the area of the United States by acquiring the entire Louisiana Territory. After completing these spectacularly successful negotiations, Monroe served as minister to England in 1804 and then went to Madrid, where he failed to settle a boundary dispute between the United States and Spain. Nevertheless, Jefferson dispatched him in 1806 to England to negotiate a treaty along with William Pinkney. The mission, whose purpose was to effect a cessation of British interference with American commerce and to receive indemnity for seizure of vessels, resulted in the Monroe-Pinkney Treaty. Its terms were so weak, however, that Jefferson did not even submit it to the Senate.

Monroe was elected governor of Virginia a second time in 1810, but he resigned after several months to become secretary of state in the cabinet of President James Madison in April 1811. In 1814 he was appointed secretary of war to replace John Armstrong, who resigned under public pressure after the British burning of Washington, D.C. He also continued serving as secretary of state until the conclusion of the War of 1812.

In 1816 Monroe was elected President, receiving almost 85 percent of the electoral votes. By the time Monroe ran for reelection in 1820, the Federalist party, which had supported such unpopular causes as the War of 1812 and had not won the presidency in 20 years, had completely disintegrated. For this reason Monroe captured all but one electoral vote, and the absence of party bickering and dispute during his administration has led historians to characterize his time in office as the "era of good feeling."

Perhaps Monroe's best-known action as President was the issuance, on December 2, 1823, of the doctrine that bears his name. The Monroe Doctrine, a declaration that was directed against European attempts to restore the power of Spain in Latin America and against Russian encroachments in western North America, clearly rejected any further European interference in the Americas and established the United States as the protector of the Western Hemisphere.

The pertinent part of the message follows:

We owe it, therefore, to candor and to the amicable relations existing between the United States and [the European] Powers to declare that we should consider any attempt on their part to extend their system to any portion of this hemisphere as dangerous to our peace and safety.

With the existing colonies and dependencies of any European Power we have not interfered and we shall not interfere. But with the Governments who have declared their independence, and maintained it, and whose independence we have, on great consideration, and just principles, acknowledged, we could not view any interposition for the purpose of oppressing them, or controlling, in any manner, their destiny, by any European Power in any other light than as the manifestation of an unfriendly disposition towards the United States.

His presidency completed, Monroe retired in 1825 to his handsome Oak Hill in Loudon County, Virginia. He remained active, becoming a regent of the University of Virginia in 1826 and serving in the 1829 Virginia Constitutional Convention, which amended the state constitution. Congress awarded him $30,000 in 1826 to ease the monetary problems caused by expenditures in public service, but in 1830 he was forced to move to New York City, with his daughter, because of financial difficulties.

Monroe's death, like that of John Adams and Thomas Jefferson, who died within a few hours of each other in 1826, came on the anniversary of the nation's independence. While in New York, Monroe died on July 4, 1831. His remains were reinterred in 1858, the centennial year of his birth, with great ceremony at Hollywood Cemetery in Richmond, Virginia.

Monroe's privately owned home, Oak Hill, a national historic landmark located near Leesburg, is open to the public during Virginia's statewide Historic Garden Week at the end of April each year. The public may also visit Monroe's "cabin castle," Ash Lawn, which, like his residence at Oak Hill, was designed by Thomas Jefferson. The boxwood-framed Ash Lawn is outside Charlottesville, near Jefferson's Monticello. James Monroe's law office, museum, and memorial library located in Fredericksburg, Virginia, is the principal depository for his books and papers. His desk and other furniture, reproductions of which are in the White House, are found here. The University of Virginia operates the law office, which is open to the public.

Washington State Apple Blossom Festival

This is a movable event. See note on page xxvi.

The Washington State Apple Blossom Festival is held annually in Wenatchee, the largest municipality in central Washington. The city is nestled between the majestic Columbia River, near its junction with the Wenatchee, and the snow-capped Cascade Mountains. Wenatchee is often referred to as the Apple Capital of the World; thousands of carloads of apples are shipped to all parts of the United States from the railroad center dubbed the "appleyard."

Beginning in 1970, the festival, which is timed to include the first weekend in May, was extended to a full 6 days from Tuesday through Sunday. In 1972 the celebration was expanded to 9 days, and in the years since, the festival events have generally lasted for 11 days each year. At this time of year, the fragrant orchards of the Wenatchee Valley are in full bloom. The gala event in Wenatchee draws up to 100,000 visitors each spring.

The Washington State Apple Blossom Festival has the distinction of being the oldest blossom festival in the United States, as well as the state's oldest major civic fete. Its origins extend back to 1920, when Mrs. E. Wagner, a native of New Zealand, recalled the blossom festival in her former home and suggested to the Ladies' Musical Club that a similar celebration be held in Wenatchee. The first of the Blossom Days, as the festival was initially entitled, was conceived as a modest musical tribute to the chief industry of the developing community. A simple program held in Memorial Park consisted of speeches and songs. In 1921 the first festival queen was chosen from the student body of the local high school to "rule over" the Wenatchee Valley, and a parade was staged. By 1923 the one-day event had grown to include not only a queen but a King Apple and four lesser queens. Only the selection of the Apple Blossom Queen survived as an annual feature, but during the first 10 years a pageant, show, fireworks display, and other events were added, and neighboring communities were invited to participate.

Community effort grew more extensive, and Blossom Days became known as the Wenatchee Apple Blossom Festival, or the North-Central Wenatchee Apple Blossom Festival. It was held annually with the exception of 1932 and the years during World War II. By 1946 the first day of a then two-day celebration included a schoolchildren's costume parade, a royal banquet, and a queen's ball attended by the governor and other dignitaries. The second day featured the festival parade — even then the numerous elaborately decorated floats took two hours to pass the line of march — followed by the coronation of the Apple Blossom Festival Queen and a pageant, Year's at the Spring, presented by high school students. Evening entertainment consisted of a baseball game and a fireworks display.

Although financed and produced by Wenatchee, the festival was designated the Washington State Apple Blossom Festival in 1947. The change of title was made in view of the festival's importance as one of the nation's largest civic celebrations and in recognition of the widespread participation of people throughout the state and the Pacific Northwest.

Dances, horse shows, stage presentations, carnival rides, and hydroplane races on Lake Entiat 15 miles north of Wenatchee were gradually added, and by 1965 the festival was extended to four days. In 1967 the festival formed a sister relationship with the Aomori Apple Blossom Festival of Japan, and the Washington State Apple Blossom Queen traveled to Japan as guest of the Aomori Broadcasting Company, which sponsors the Japanese event. One of the highlights of the Washington State Apple Blossom Festival's golden anniversary in 1969 was the visit of the queen of the Aomori festival and the governor of the Aomori prefecture.

The Washington State Apple Blossom Festival is sponsored, financed, and planned by citizens and businesses of Wenatchee. A semi-autonomous division of the Wenatchee Chamber of Commerce, which supplies staff and quarters for the production, the Festival has its own 21-member board of directors appointed by the president and board of directors of the chamber.

Every year a director general heads the festival and is assisted by two assistant director generals of finance and program. Funds are raised through button and program sales, festival and festival-sponsored presentations, sponsorships by local businesses, and concession arrangements. Various committees with members from all parts

of the local population coordinate the activities. Very noticeable at festival time are the Wenatchee Applarians. Founded in 1959 and modeled on the successful Portland Rosarians, the pink-and-white-uniformed men serve as the official festival hosts and booster group.

Beginning its second half-century of festivities in 1970, the Washington State Apple Blossom Festival was preceded by the pre-festival selection of the royalty of Applaria in February. Seniors from the two local high schools were eligible for the competition. Ten finalists, who were evaluated on the basis of beauty, personality, and academic excellence, were selected by high school students. For two weeks they were presented to the public and were the guests of numerous service clubs and businesses. In February the queen and two princesses were chosen. The 1970 Apple Blossom Festival Queen was robed in crimson velvet and received the festival's jeweled crown.

Among the attractions open daily during the 1970 festival were the famous Ohme Gardens, located high above the Wenatchee Valley on rocks hewn by the Columbia River. Also drawing visitors was the 12th annual Washington State Art Exhibition at Wenatchee Valley College, which featured works from the western United States and Canada. Moon rocks gathered during the Apollo XII landing were on display at the Rocky Reach Dam, one of the biggest hydroelectric projects on the Columbia River. Other attractions were the North Central Washington Museum's exhibition of arts, crafts, antiques, and photographs of past festival queens, as well as a carnival offering rides and games.

The Music Theatre of Wenatchee's production of *My Fair Lady* opened on Wednesday. One of the festival's most popular attractions, the yearly show utilizes the talents of 200 to 300 local people. The theater's offerings have included *The King and I, The Sound of Music, South Pacific,* and *Kiss Me, Kate.*

On Friday the Gingko gem and mineral show, featuring every phase of lapidary art, with gem and mineral displays, as well as handcrafted jewelry, was added to the regular daily attractions. What was perhaps the high point of the day, however, began at 10:30 A.M., when over 3,500 area schoolchildren, dressed in humorous and imaginative costumes and riding an assortment of gaily decorated vehicles, participated in the festival school parade to the accompaniment of junior high school bands. Visitors could afterwards choose among the YMCA handball tournament, the Appleatchee drill team competition, and the antique sale and collectors' market. At 2:00 P.M., the Appleatchee horse show, for years a top festival drawing card, offered spectators one of the best equestrian exhibitions in the Pacific Northwest. The show, with state and national association sanction, drew 350 entries from California to Alberta, Canada. Youngsters flocked to the 2:30 P.M. YWCA Youth Theatre musical presentation of *Sleeping Beauty*. Other productions for children have included *Tom Sawyer*, *Babes in Toyland*, and *Aladdin*.

A full schedule of events continued on Friday evening. There were the 5:30 P.M. Apple Relays, a 7:00 P.M. Appleatchee Horse Show, an 8:15 P.M. performance of *My Fair Lady*, and teenage dancing and the queen's ball at 9:00 P.M. A joint effort of the student bodies of both local high schools, the ball is the occasion on which admiring subjects meet the royal court and the 40-odd visiting festival and community queens.

The festivities on Saturday began at dawn with the traditional Kiwanis outdoor pancake breakfast. Scheduled from 4:00 to 9:00 A.M., the "foodfest" assures onlookers and out-of-town bands and marching units a substantial feast before the start of the 10:00 A.M. grand parade. Early risers also had an opportunity to attend a horse show, a pre-parade pageant, and a drill team competition, as well as the daily festival features. The 51st grand parade, rated in the top 10 of the nation, featured 60 community floats, 60 high school bands, mounted units, drill teams, and celebrities, including the grand marshal, Navy Captain Richard F. Gordon Jr., an Apollo XII astronaut and native of Washington. Spectators three- and four-deep lined the 20-block parade route through central Wenatchee. The three-hour parade could also be viewed on television throughout eastern Washington.

Also on Saturday, a host of events provided entertainment for all ages: an 11:00 A.M. YMCA handball tournament, a 12:30 P.M. antique sale, 1:30 P.M. stock car races, and a 2:00 P.M. horse show. An old festival favorite was the Bandorama competition at 2:00 P.M., when the musical talent and precision marching of 10 top high school bands from the Pacific Northwest were judged. Festival crowds had an opportunity to view the University of Washington football team in a full intrasquad scrimmage in the Apple Bowl at 2:30 P.M., while other sports fans watched the 6:00 P.M. Lucky Drafters softball game or the 7:00 P.M. Appleatchee horse show. A wide variety of evening entertainment was offered — a performance of *My Fair Lady* at 8:15 P.M., a teen dance and a country and western show at 9:00 P.M., and the Apple Blossom Festival ball at 9:30 P.M.

The last day of the festival, Sunday, got off to an early start with both a horse show and the Apple Blossom Festival Autocross (auto racing for all classes of cars on a challenging course) at

8:30 A.M. At 9:00 A.M. the antique sale continued, and an hour later the Daroga Park motorcycle races started. Early afternoon stock car races and a horse show brought the 51st Washington Apple Blossom Festival to a close.

APRIL 29

Feast of St. Catherine of Siena

In her 33 years of life, St. Catherine of Siena became one of the brightest lights of the Roman Catholic Church and one of the most colorful figures of the Middle Ages. Born in Siena, Italy, on March 25, 1347, she died in Rome on April 29, 1380, and was canonized by Pope Pius II in 1461. Although April 30 had for several centuries been designated as her feast day (except in Siena, where it was marked on April 29), the date was moved to April 29 when the Roman Catholic calendar was revised. With St. Teresa of Avila, St. Catherine in 1970 became one of the first two women named a doctor of the church.

Catherine was the youngest of a very large family. Her father, Giacomo di Benincasa, was a prosperous wool dyer. Catherine was evidently a happy child: her biographers record her "excessive gaiety." From her earliest childhood she was religiously inclined. She is said to have had her first vision at the age of six, and at the age of seven she took a vow of virginity. Vows taken at such a young age were not considered binding, and Catherine's mother, the practical and realistic Monna Lapa, did not let it deter her from badgering Catherine to marry. Catherine steadfastly refused and — to her mother's absolute frustration — with equal firmness refused to enter a convent.

In her 16th year Catherine entered the Third Order of St. Dominic, whose members are lay people who live by a religious rule, though not in convents or monasteries. As a Dominican tertiary, Catherine was entitled to wear the black and white habit of the Dominicans, and for three years she lived as an anchorite in a small room in her father's house, conditioning herself to live on a ration of a spoonful of herbs each day and with a few hours' sleep.

After this austere period of prayer and fasting, Catherine came out of seclusion and at 19 devoted herself to caring for the sick and poor of her neighborhood, which was called Fontebranda. From her first contacts with people, her special insight and understanding were apparent. People from many walks of life clustered around her — artists, politicians, merchants, soldiers, priests, lawyers, and members of prominent Sienese families.

The ordinary citizens of Siena were puzzled

by her way of life. What were they to make of this young woman who wore nun's garb yet lived at home and — worse still — went about freely with numbers of young men, who were seen entering and leaving the large Benincasa house at all hours? Scorning what they did not understand, the townspeople nicknamed Catherine the Queen of Fontebranda and her companions the *Caterinati*, which might be loosely translated as "Catherine's crowd" or the "fans of Catherine."

The jeers failed to deter Catherine's devoted followers, who called themselves the *bella brigata* — the happy band of friends. They were attracted by her natural gaiety, asceticism, spiritual insight, common sense, and serenity. Church historians were later to designate them more formally as the School of Mystics.

The Italian cities of the period were far from peaceful. Always at odds with one another, these autonomous communes engaged in interminable rivalry. The one thing on which they seemed to agree was that the pope belonged in Rome — not in Avignon, where Clement V, the first of a long line of French popes, had established the papal residence in 1309.

Catherine and her loyal band traveled in Italy, trying to restore peace and order among neighboring communes. When she was 23 or 24, she wrote to the French-born Pope Gregory XI, begging him to leave Avignon and to return to Rome, the traditional home of popes.

At the request of the Florentine commune, Catherine traveled to Avignon to intercede with Gregory. With 23 members of her *bella brigata*, including four priests, she arrived in Avignon in May 1376 and stayed for three months. According to some, they were the most fateful months in the history of the church, at least to that time.

Against great odds, including the opposition of the French king, Charles V, and French prelates and politicians, Catherine persuaded Gregory XI to return to Rome. Before he left France, Catherine had returned to Italy and devoted herself to reviving the religious life of the people in the rural regions of the city-state of Siena.

On Gregory's death in Rome on March 26, 1378, an Italian was elected to the papacy. The situation within the church was still seething, however, with resentment persisting between French and Roman partisans, and rival communes backing one faction or another in the struggle to control the papacy. Discontented cardinals responded to the elevation of the Italian pope, Urban VI, by choosing another, and eventually a third. Their action marked the beginning of the Great Western Schism, which lasted from 1378 until 1417, and ushered the church into an era of chaos.

Catherine supported Urban, who had been

duly elected, and he summoned her to Rome in 1378. She spent the remainder of her life there, helping the destitute and sending letters to influential people urging active support on Urban's behalf. Before her death, she succeeded in reconciling Pope Urban and the Roman Republic.

Although Catherine herself never learned to write well, she dictated letters — sometimes to several scribes at once. Some 400 of these letters, dealing with duty to God, are extant. Again dictating to a number of scribes, Catherine wrote the book *Dialogo della Divina Provvidenza* (Dialogue of Divine Providence) in the five days of October 9 through 13, 1378. Her works are considered classics of the Italian language of the 14th century.

Catherine was buried under the high altar of the Dominican Church of Santa Maria sopra Minerva in Rome. Her head was later removed and enshrined in the Dominican Church in Siena.

Oliver Ellsworth's Birthday

Oliver Ellsworth was the third chief justice of the United States, serving from 1796 to 1800, following John Jay and John Rutledge. Though the chief justiceship crowned his career, Ellsworth made his deepest contributions to American government in his earlier political roles, most strikingly in the US Senate. He was also a framer of the Constitution.

Ellsworth was born on April 29, 1745, in Windsor, Connecticut, the second son of Captain David Ellsworth and Jemima Leavitt Ellsworth. His father wanted him to become a clergyman, and so he was educated by the Reverend Joseph Bellamy of Bethlehem, Connecticut, and then sent to Yale College in 1762. He remained at Yale for two years, then transferred to the College of New Jersey (now Princeton University). He was graduated from college in 1766 and returned home to study theology with the Reverend John Smalley of New Britain, Connecticut. Within less than a year Ellsworth decided to abandon theology and study law. He worked at it for four years, teaching part of the time.

In 1771 he was admitted to the bar. He tried to practice law at Windsor but had so few clients that he had to support himself by farming and chopping wood. The next year he married Abigail Wolcott of East Windsor. He later said that his law earnings during the first three years had amounted to £3 a year in Connecticut currency. Not possessing a horse, he had to walk to Hartford when court was in session — a round trip of 20 miles. In 1775 Ellsworth moved to Hartford, where his practice improved rapidly. Four years later Noah Webster, who began the study of law in his office, said that Ellsworth had from 1,000 to 1,500 cases on his lists and that there was hardly a suit tried in the city in which Ellsworth did not appear on one side or the other. By shrewd management he built his income into a fortune.

Ellsworth entered politics as a representative of Hartford in the Connecticut General Assembly. In 1777, at the age of 32, he was appointed state's attorney for Hartford County. In 1780 he became a member of the Governor's Council, serving until 1785, when he was made a judge of the state Superior Court. He served in that capacity for four years until he became US senator from Connecticut.

From 1777 to 1783, during the American Revolution, Ellsworth divided his energies between service to Connecticut and to the struggling central government of the 13 former colonies. While state's attorney, he also became one of Connecticut's delegates to the Continental Congress. There he was active on important committees and was reelected five times, until in 1783 he declined to serve further. He had served simultaneously on Connecticut's Council of Safety and as one of five on its Committee of the Pay Table.

The Revolution won, and the Articles of Confederation providing an ineffective system of government in the eyes of many, the Constitutional Convention was called at Philadelphia in 1787 to draft a new federal constitution. Ellsworth, along with Roger Sherman and William Samuel Johnson, represented Connecticut. He became a member of the important committee on detail that wrote the first and decisive draft of the Constitution. With Sherman he proposed the crucial "Connecticut compromise," providing for a federal legislature of two houses: in the upper house each state was to be equally represented; in the lower house representation was to be on the basis of population. This arrangement ended the quarrel between the large and small states at the convention, and it continues to be an essential feature of the federal system in the United States. Ellsworth is also credited with the insertion of the term "United States" in the Constitution, although this phrase had been adopted 11 years earlier by the Continental Congress to replace the name "United Colonies" and therefore was not Ellsworth's own invention. Among his other positions at the convention, Ellsworth backed the continuance of the international slave trade, arguing that moral responsibility should remain with the people of those states that legally sanctioned it.

It is said that Ellsworth did not wait for the convention to conclude but rushed home to work for Connecticut's ratification of the Constitution.

During the ratification debates his "Letters to a Landholder," appearing in the *Connecticut Courant* and the *American Mercury* (1787–1788), were widely circulated and had an influence somewhat like that of the *Federalist* papers by Alexander Hamilton, James Madison, and John Jay in New York.

At the age of 44, tall, dignified, and commanding, Ellsworth was chosen one of the first two senators from Connecticut under the Constitution. He seems to have been especially suited to the work necessitated by the newness of the government, and his great familiarity with organizational and administrative matters gave him a predominant place among his Senate colleagues during the next seven years. A century afterwards, the memory of his prestige and authority continued in the traditions of the Senate. The first rules of the Senate were reported by Ellsworth. He put forward a plan for printing its journal; shaped the report from conference on the first 12 amendments to the Constitution (which became the 10-amendment Bill of Rights); wrote the measure that admitted North Carolina to the Union; and designed the act that forced Rhode Island to join. He helped draw up the government of the territory south of the Ohio; framed the first bill regulating the consular service; and energetically supported Hamilton's scheme for funding the national debt and for incorporating the Bank of the United States. Ellsworth's most weighty single contribution was the organization of the federal judiciary. He was the chief author of the Federal Judiciary Act of 1789, which remains the foundation of the US court system.

In 1796 Ellsworth resigned from the Senate to accept appointment by President Washington as chief justice, after John Rutledge had failed to receive Senate confirmation, and William Cushing, the senior associate justice, had declined. (It is accepted usage to call Rutledge the second chief justice — and therefore Ellsworth the third — even though Rutledge's appointment was never confirmed. In fact Rutledge was acting chief justice from his presidential appointment on July 1, 1795, until his rejection by the Senate on December 15, 1795. Ellsworth was named by Washington on March 4, 1796.) Historians have found Ellsworth an unremarkable jurist whose opinions reveal common sense but no outstanding knowledge of the law. The position of justice gave little scope for the forensic talents that had given Ellsworth his skill at the bar, in the Constitutional Convention, and in the Senate.

In 1799 Ellsworth very reluctantly accepted President John Adams's call to go to France with William Vans Murray and William R. Davie in a commission to negotiate a settlement of grievances — particularly the restrictions placed on American vessels. Adams was anxious to avert a war, which many in his own Federalist party wanted, and Ellsworth agreed that negotiation was the lesser evil. The disappointing terms offered by Napoleon did not fulfill the commissioners' instructions or hopes, but a compromise was arranged providing for freedom of commerce between France and the United States. The Treaty of Morfontaine (September 30, 1800), commonly known as the Convention of 1800, was ratified by the Senate when Napoleon agreed that it should supersede and abrogate the treaties of 1778, thus formally releasing the United States from its defensive alliance with France.

The hardships of the winter journey to France, which took four months because of storms, ruined Ellsworth's health. He resigned the chief justiceship while still in France and did not return with the other commissioners but remained in England for a time in an effort to recover his health. He returned to America in the spring of 1801, still ill, and took up his residence in his native Windsor. He was appointed chief justice of the Connecticut Supreme Court but was unable to serve. For the next six years, after he had "begun to die," as he wrote a friend, he occupied himself with agriculture and reading theology and wrote a weekly column on agricultural topics for the *Connecticut Courant*. He died on November 26, 1807, at the age of 62 at the stately frame house in which he lived in Windsor.

His father had built this home in 1740, and it came into Oliver Ellsworth's possession, probably in 1782. It remained in the family until 1903, when 116 of his descendants deeded it to the Connecticut Daughters of the American Revolution as a museum and chapter house. The Ellsworth Homestead, at 778 Palisado Avenue, is located just north of Windsor. It is open to the public from May through October and is owned by the Ellsworth Memorial Association of the Daughters of the American Revolution.

APRIL 30

Louisiana Admitted to the Union

On April 30, 1812, Louisiana became the 18th member of the Union. It was the first state to be created from the vast area of the Louisiana Purchase (see December 20, Louisiana Purchased). Thus it was quite appropriate that Louisiana formally gained statehood on the ninth anniversary of the official date of cession.

The nine-year period from the beginning of US jurisdiction over Louisiana in 1803 to statehood in 1812 was a time of considerable difficulty and frustration for the inhabitants of that region. The vast area of Louisiana had come under the control of France in 1682, when René Robert Cavelier, Sieur de La Salle, reached the mouth of the Mississippi River and claimed the lands bordering the river and its tributaries for King Louis XIV. The first French settlers came to what is now Louisiana in 1699, and they, and those who followed, firmly established the customs, government, and language of their homeland in the area at the mouth of the Mississippi.

For more than 70 years following La Salle's explorations, the Mississippi valley, including what is now Louisiana, remained under French control. Then, in 1762, France ceded its claim to the area west of the Mississippi to Spain. Spanish rule over the vast territory lasted until 1800 when Spain returned the area to France. But even during the time of Spanish jurisdiction, the settlers clung to their French language and traditions.

The US purchase from France of the vast, ill-defined area west of the Mississippi in 1803 disrupted the lives of the inhabitants of New Orleans and the surrounding countryside to a much greater extent than had the previous period of Spanish rule. On March 26, 1804, the US Congress passed an act dividing the Louisiana Purchase into two parts: the Territory of Orleans, comprising that "portion south of the Mississippi Territory and on an east and west line, to commence on the Mississippi River at the thirty-third degree of north latitude and extend west to the western boundary of the cession"; and the District of Louisiana, composed of the remainder of the area purchased. The act provided that the District of Louisiana, or upper Louisiana, as it was also known, be placed under the jurisdiction of the government of the Indiana Territory, but it established a separate government for the Territory of Orleans.

The government that Congress set up for the Territory of Orleans was unlike any other then existing in the United States or its territories. It consisted of a governor vested with full executive powers, to be appointed by the President; a 13-member legislative council, to be named by the President; a superior court of three judges, also to be presidential appointees; "and such inferior courts and justices of the peace as the Legislature of the Territory might establish." English was made the official language of the territory, and "the importation of slaves from foreign countries was forbidden, and that of those from the United States was allowed only to citizens, bona fide owners, removing to the Territory."

The congressional debate preceding the passage of the 1804 act was heated. One Massachusetts representative claimed that the inhabitants of the new territory were not ready for full citizenship and should be treated "as if they were a conquered country." Others disagreed. Indeed some members of Congress felt the government established for the Territory of Orleans was too harsh and even contrary to the treaty of cession, which guaranteed that "the inhabitants of the ceded territory [the Louisiana Purchase] shall be incorporated in the union of the United States and admitted as soon as possible according to the principles of the federal Constitution to the enjoyment of all the rights, advantages and immunities of citizens of the United States."

The government that Congress established for the Territory of Orleans greatly dissatisfied the residents of what is now Louisiana. They had expected immediate admission to statehood and resented the territorial status that Congress imposed. Furthermore, they disliked the introduction of jury trials — a phenomenon that previously had had no place in their legal system — and they were unhappy that English had been made the territory's official language, since few could read or speak it.

To protest the Act of 1804, the mayor of New Orleans resigned, and on June 1, 1804, a group of planters and merchants met in New Orleans to initiate more practical measures. They drew up petitions asking Congress to repeal the March legislation relating to the division of the Louisiana Purchase and to the prohibitions against the importation of slaves. They also decided to request immediate statehood for Louisiana. In the weeks following, they circulated these memorials among the populace, and late in the summer they sent a committee of three to Washington, D.C., to place their demands before Congress.

In November 1804 President Thomas Jefferson suggested to Congress that improvements be made in the government of the Louisiana Purchase territory, and in December 1804 Pierre Darbigny, Pierre Sauvé, and Jean Noel Destréhan presented to the House of Representatives the petition that had been circulated through the Orleans territory during the previous summer. Congress acted quickly in 1805 to correct the harsher aspects of the government it had established the previous year. On March 2 it passed an act setting up a separate territorial government for upper Louisiana and created a government for the Orleans territory that was similar to that established for the Northwest Territory in 1787. The New Orleans government consisted of a house of representatives to be elected by the inhabitants of the territory; a leg-

islative council whose five members were to be chosen by the President from among 10 nominees presented by the elected house; and a governor, secretary, and judges of the Superior Court, who would be named by the President with the consent of the Senate. The 1805 act also provided that the territory be admitted to statehood as soon as its free population numbered 60,000.

The new government did not entirely please the inhabitants of the Orleans territory, and one official remarked that "the people of Louisiana complained that in this form, as in the preceding, their lives and property were in some degree at the disposal of a single individual." In addtion the territory was plagued by external difficulties. In 1806 Spanish troops attempted to establish a post near Natchitoches in an area claimed by the United States. About the same time Aaron Burr, the former Vice President of the United States, became involved in a plot whose end was never fully ascertained, but which may have included a plan to detach an area of the Louisiana Purchase from the United States.

Fortunately neither the Spanish raids nor the alleged Burr conspiracy developed into a major threat to the Orleans territory. Instead the area continued to prosper, and by 1809 the territorial legislature petitioned Congress for statehood. William C. C. Claiborne, the territorial governor, forwarded the petition to Washington with a letter listing a number of reasons for denying the legislature's request. Nevertheless, the Senate approved the petition in March 1810. The House of Representatives, however, sent it to a committee, and Congress adjourned before the House had voted on the question.

In December 1810 Louisiana's request for admission to the Union again came before Congress. Opponents of the statehood bill cited the difficulties posed by the ill-defined boundaries between the territory and the possessions claimed by Spain in the Southwest, and the French culture of almost all the inhabitants. But Congress had promised that the Territory of Orleans would be admitted to the Union when its population reached 60,000 free inhabitants, and the 1810 federal census showed the area to have 76,550 free residents. On February 11, 1811, Congress authorized the Orleans territory to draw up a state constitution. A convention meeting from November 1811 to January 1812 formulated the necessary frame of government for Louisiana and on April 8, 1812, Congress gave its approval to this work.

The new state of Louisiana was originally to have encompassed the area of the present state west of the Mississippi and the Isle of Orleans. But only four days after Congress had approved

Louisiana's constitution, that body passed an act that added the area of West Florida between the Mississippi and Pearl rivers (the so-called Florida Parishes) to the new state. Thus it was a substantially enlarged area that ended its territorial status and officially became the state of Louisiana on April 30, 1812.

Like other Southern states, Louisiana declared its secession from the Union shortly before the beginning of the Civil War. Its full rights of statehood were restored in July 1868, after the drafting of a new constitution that enfranchised black citizens.

The constitution of 1868 was succeeded by the far more restrictive one of 1898, and that in turn was succeeded by a number of others. The state's 10th frame of government, the much-amended constitution of 1921, was in force until January 1, 1975, when a new constitution adopted the previous year became effective.

Shenandoah Apple Blossom Festival, Winchester, Virginia

This is a movable event. See note on page xxvi.

Each year on the Thursday, Friday, and Saturday closest to May 1, Winchester, the seat of Frederick County in Virginia's historic Shenandoah Valley, receives 200,000 to 250,000 visitors to the Shenandoah Apple Blossom Festival. Winchester, Virginia's apple center, is a busy city of 16,000. Its three-day fete provides a jubilant welcome to spring against a colorful backdrop of extensive apple orchards in full bloom — Frederick County and adjoining Clarke County produce 2 million bushels of apples each year.

The festival has been celebrated annually, with the exception of the World War II years, since 1924. Early in that year Frank L. Sublett was elected the first president of Shenandoah Valley, Inc., a regional chamber of commerce for the 140-mile-long valley between the Blue Ridge and Allegheny mountains. He proposed that the city of Winchester stage an Apple Blossom Festival as its contribution toward the organization's campaign "to publicize the historic, scenic, and industrial assets of this already far-famed section of Virginia and West Virginia."

The undertaking was approved at a large meeting held in Winchester on April 22. A phrase from the benediction pronounced at the close of the meeting was adopted as a motto: "The bounties of nature are the gift of God."

On May 3, 1924, some 30,000 persons jammed the streets of Winchester to view the first festival parade, which included several bands, fire fighting equipment, and makeshift floats. US Assistant Secretary of War J. W. Weeks crowned Elizabeth Steck as Apple Blossom Queen at an official coronation on the steps of Winchester's Handley High School.

The purpose of the Apple Blossom Festival is still "to welcome spring, celebrate the blossoming of the apple trees, and call attention to the apple industry of the area," but from its modest beginnings the event has grown significantly. As early as 1934, the two-day fete was drawing 120,000 visitors. At that year's elaborate May 3 coronation ceremony, young women from about 30 schools and colleges formed the court of the queen, which included a crown bearer, train bearers, and maids of honor. The chief event of the second day was a parade described as the Trail of the Pink Petals. The parade's historical section, over a mile in length, reviewed the history of the Shenandoah Valley by representing figures such as Joist Hite and his companions, who were the first settlers in 1732; George Washington, who drafted plans for Fort Loudon in 1756; and Robert E. Lee and Thomas Jonathan ("Stonewall") Jackson, who commanded Confederate troops in the area during the Civil War.

Year by year the program has expanded until it is now replete with a float parade, a firefighters' parade, an antique auto show, an apple pie baking contest, a country music jubilee, an ambitious "pageant of springtime," and an impressive coronation ceremony. There are college princesses from the four-state Appalachian fruit-growing region, a Miss Apple Blossom, various notables, and well-known entertainers. Young women from various parts of the world have been crowned as the festival's queen by an assortment of dignitaries, including governors, senators, military figures, and members of nobility; daughters of prominent American families who have been selected include Kathryn Eisenhower, Laura MacArthur, Neva Goodwin Rockefeller, and Luci Baines Johnson.

Over 2,000 volunteer festival workers lend their talents to this community and regional endeavor, working through numerous committees and a headquarters staff to prepare for the three days of pageantry, parties, and parades (and a pre-festival day for local residents). They plan the historic-scenic tours, exhibits, concerts, baton-twirling events, and numerous other activities.

In 1970 the 43rd annual Shenandoah Apple Blossom Festival began with pre-festival events on Wednesday, April 29. The queen-designate, Merie-Ellen Fong, daughter of US Senator Hiram Fong from Hawaii, ceremoniously sliced an apple pie for the presidents of Winchester civic organizations and was officially introduced to the public at a joint civic club luncheon. A late afternoon reception in her honor, with press and radio representatives in attendance, was followed that evening by a firemen's reception in honor of country singer Del Reeves, who was to be the marshal of the firemen's parade.

The festival proper started the next day with an 8:30 A.M. apple pie baking contest, in which Virginia, West Virginia, Maryland, and Pennsylvania high school students competed. An hour later the queen-designate and her court toured the blossom-filled orchards, as did thousands of tourists throughout the festival. At 10:00 A.M. the amusement rides and exhibits opened on Frederick County Court House Square. At noon the Woman's Auxiliary of the Virginia State Horticultural Society sponsored the Ladies' Apple Blossom Luncheon.

Focal point of the afternoon was the coronation ceremony at Handley High School, crowning Queen Shenandoah XLIII. After a musical program at 2:00 P.M., a bugle fanfare by a naval ROTC honor guard from the University of Virginia, and the appearance of a color guard from Randolph-Macon Academy announced the grand entrance of the queen-designate and her court. Among the latter were princesses, representing the horticultural groups and schools of the Appalachian apple-growing region, and various dignitaries, including Virginia's governor, who acted as officials to the court.

A Pageant of Springtime, following the coronation, presented about 1,000 talented volunteers, most of them from the four-state area. The pageant, titled Love Makes the World Go 'Round, offered song and dance numbers such as "Fiesta in Mexico," "Aloha Hawaii," "Egyptian Intrigue," "Manhattan Moods," and "Winter Carnival in St. Moritz."

Thursday's events continued with an honorary fire chief beauty contest in the afternoon and the annual firemen's night parade featuring volunteer firemen, fire-fighting apparatus, fire engines, scores of bands and marching units, and color guards from eight states. The rest of the evening was devoted to dancing, with a special teen-age dance (repeated the following night), a young couple's dance, and, by invitation, the formal queen's ball.

Friday began with the sixth annual sports breakfast. The event customarily features leading sports figures. Special 1970 guests were quarterback Len Dawson of the Kansas City Chiefs and track and field star Jesse Owens, winner of four gold medals in the 1936 Olympics.

Following a 10:30 A.M. repeat performance of the Pageant of Springtime and the presentation to the assembled crowd of the queen and her court, the great attraction of Friday, and perhaps of the entire festival, was the 1:30 P.M.

Grand Feature parade. Known throughout the country, the four-hour-long spectacle featured 50 intricate floats and nearly 90 bands from 14 states, as well as precision drill teams, drum and bugle corps, majorettes, and celebrity guests in individual cars. One of these, the astronaut Captain Walter M. (Wally) Schirra Jr., served as grand marshal of the parade.

Beginning at 7:30 P.M., the 12th annual Apple Blossom Spring Fling, held by private western dance clubs of the area, with the Blue Ridge Twirlers as hosts, took place at the Frederick County Junior High School. The 10th annual Shenandoah Apple Blossom Country Music Jubilee meanwhile opened at the Winchester Armory, with a country music show. A country music dance followed.

On the last day of the festival, there was an all-day Apple Blossom Twirling Meet, the largest ever held in the region, and the selection of Miss Majorette of the Blossoms. At 10:30 A.M. the Antique Automobile Club of America held a spring meet, which was officially opened by the festival queen. Three additional events marked the day as the Big Country Music Jubilee Day. A country music contest from 10:00 A.M. to 6:00 P.M. matched amateurs and professionals in competition for prizes. A country music show was performed from 7:00 to 9:00 P.M. And at 10:00 P.M. a country music dance served as the grand finale of the year's Shenandoah Apple Blossom Festival.

Walpurgis Night or Spring Festival

The spring festival known as Walpurgis Night takes place on April 30, the eve of one of the feast days of St. Walpurgis. Though not universally marked in the United States, it is observed by many Scandinavian clubs and associations, especially in centers that have a large population of Scandinavian descent. This is particularly true in some East Coast metropolitan areas, in the Midwest, and in sections of the West Coast; elsewhere, festivities are scattered and sometimes sporadic.

Walpurgis Night is generally celebrated in parks with the bonfires that customarily mark the observance in the Old World and with speeches, songs, and other music. Information about local events is available from Scandinavian-language newspapers or such institutions as Philadelphia's American Swedish Historical Museum, which itself sponsors a Walpurgis Night celebration. This is usually held on the last Saturday in April, with a program that consists of singing, folk dancing, the traditional bonfire, and Swedish-style refreshments.

Walpurgis Night, often simply called "spring festival," takes its name from St. Walpurgis — or Walpurga or Walburga — an English missionary and abbess in Germany who died about 780. It is not known why the festival, which has come down through Nordic and Teutonic tradition, was named for her, but the observance took the place of a pagan festival that earlier had marked the beginning of summer. The occasion is popularly celebrated in some Scandinavian countries today. In Sweden, for example, people build fires, sing traditional spring songs, and make speeches welcoming the spring. There is an impressive observance at Stockholm's open-air folk museum at Skansen, but the celebration is especially a student festivity, marked at the Swedish universities of Uppsala, Lund, Göteborg, and Umea, with the donning of white caps traditional to the occasion and the cheering of spring.

Afterwards there is singing and, later on, there are the characteristic bonfires.

In the long history of superstitions connected with Walpurgis Night, the fires have had the purpose of frightening away witches, who, according to popular lore, ride broomsticks, he-goats, and other conveyances to an appointed rendezvous on this date. The meeting is said to take place on a high mountain. Traditionally the site preferred is the Brocken, the tallest peak of Germany's Harz Mountains and scene of the witches' sabbath in Goethe's *Faust*.

One of the various forms of St. Walpurgis's name is Valborg (or Vaubourg), and in Swedish the eve of her feast day is sometimes called *Valborgsmässoafton*, referring to the mass with which her day, May 1, once was customarily marked. February 25 is another of the feast days of St. Walpurgis.

May

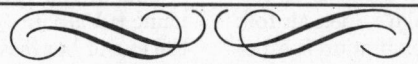

May, originally the third month, *Maius,* of the ancient Roman calendar, is the fifth month of the Gregorian, or New Style, calendar used today. It has 31 days. The origin of the name is uncertain. Some scholars derive the word from the Latin *maiores,* meaning "elders," contending that the month was intended to honor the senior members of the population just as the following month, *Junius,* from *iuniores,* meaning "juniors," commemorated the younger generation. A more widely accepted theory holds that May is derived from *Maia,* a name bestowed on two different goddesses in ancient mythology. The more important of the two goddesses was the Greek Maia, the eldest of the Pleiades, who were the seven daughters of Atlas, the god who bore the world on his shoulders, and the Oceanid nymph, Pleione. In a cave on Cyllene — a mountain in northeastern Arcadia, Greece — Maia became by Zeus, the chief of the gods, the mother of Hermes. Hermes, who corresponds to the Roman god Mercury, was known especially as the swift messenger of the gods and as the god of commerce and trade.

The Romans tended to identify the Greek Maia with a more obscure Roman goddess of spring known as Maia Maiesta, to whom the priests of Vulcan, the god of fire, offered sacrifices on the first day of May. To add to the confusion, Maia Maiesta was in turn sometimes identified with Bona Dea, the "good goddess" of fertility in both the earth and in women; this undoubtedly occurred because Bona Dea's festival also fell on May 1, the dedication date of her temple on the Aventine Hill. Bona Dea was variously described as the sister, daughter, or wife of Faunus, the ancient rustic Roman god worshiped as the bestower of fertility in men. Accordingly she was occasionally called Fauna. As befitted a prophetic goddess who revealed her oracles only to females, Bona Dea's temple was taken care of and her rites attended solely by women, all males being strictly excluded. Even her name was never uttered before a man. At the festival of Bona Dea on May 1, a vestal virgin performed the required rituals at night in the house of the current consul or praetor.

On May 1, May Day, which fell in the midst of the *Floralia* (see April) the Romans customarily went in procession to the grove of the Camenae on the outskirts of Rome just beyond the Porta Capena. Located there was the grotto of Egeria, the spirit of the local stream who, legend claimed, had been the spouse and adviser of the legendary ancient Roman king, Numa Pompilius. The grief and tears Egeria displayed at her husband's death supposedly caused her to be changed into a stream, under which guise she was worshiped by pregnant women in particular.

The Romans regarded May as unlucky for marriages since the festival of the unhappy dead, the *Lemuria,* took place that month. Held on May 9, 11, and 13, the *Lemuria* was a private domestic ritual to honor the *lemures* or *larvae,* the ghosts of dead persons. In its original form the *Lemuria* had probably been a sort of expulsion ritual to frighten away evil spirits in spring, when demons were traditionally very active. Especially bothersome were those spirits who either lacked kinsmen or wandered about unappeased, threatening to revenge various oversights, such as the failure to provide fitting burial rites for them. In the course of time, the ceremony was transformed into a private appeasement of family ghosts, conducted in individual households. To quiet these spirits and prevent them from returning to scare the living, the head of the family arose at midnight. Having washed his hands, he went through the house barefooted, tossing black beans over his shoulder without glancing back and exclaiming: "With these beans, I redeem myself and my family." He carried out this procedure nine times. It was believed that the ghosts followed in his footsteps and gathered up the beans. The family head then repeated the hand washing and banged brass vessels together loudly. In the final stage of the ritual, he commanded nine times, "Ghosts of my fathers, depart," and at last was permitted to look behind himself. The Roman belief that May was an inauspicious month for marriages supposedly helps to account for the popularity of June as the month for weddings.

The Anglo-Saxons called May *Thrimilce* because the cows could then be milked three times daily. The lucky birthstones associated with May are the agate and the emerald.

MAY 1

May Day

May Day ranks as one of the oldest holidays. Since antiquity the first of May has been celebrated with a variety of festivities. Many primitive pre-Christian agricultural civilizations voiced their gladness and thankfulness to the gods for the arrival of spring and the rebirth of nature. The Romans, especially, held a joyous feast in honor of the flower goddess, Flora, and the coming of May. With variations, the ancient Roman celebration became imbedded in the Western European tradition, especially in the British Isles, where a significant Celtic religious festival had been held on May 1 and its eve. In Elizabethan England, May Day — with its maypole and general merriment — was one of the merriest holidays of the year. To a limited extent the May Day observances were carried to the New World.

Today in parts of England and the United States, young children still go "a-maying" and dance on greens and school lawns. May queens are occasionally chosen to reign over American college campuses and English village fetes. In Hawaii, May Day is known as Lei Day, a festive occasion for donning colorful garlands of flowers as a sign of friendship and goodwill. But in the 20th century, May 1 observances are no longer confined to the joyous springtime revels that traditionally characterized the advent of May. By the late 19th century the day had already taken on a new connotation as Labor Day in many sections of the world. In the United States, although the official Labor Day is far removed from May Day, Socialists, Communists, and other leftists have traditionally held rallies and demonstrations on May 1. In Communist nations, May Day, which was once a festival of spring rejoicing, ironically has been transformed into an occasion for exhibiting military might and deifying the state. In reaction to these grim Communist May Day displays, Americans instituted Loyalty Day after World War II to reaffirm the heritage of American freedom. More recently, Law Day was proclaimed on May 1 as a day of national dedication to the concept of government under law. In the 1960s and 1970s, political demonstrations by leftists, and also by pacifists, on May 1 have made many contemporary May Day events seem even more removed from the carefree celebrations of previous centuries.

Some scholars claim that the May Day festivities can be traced to the spring festivals of India and Egypt, when the renewal of the fertility of nature was celebrated. In ancient Greece, the revelers expressed gratitude to Demeter, the goddess of agriculture and vegetation, who had once again rejuvenated nature and instilled new fruitfulness in the world. Of all the ancient festivities, the Roman *Floralia* bears the greatest similarity to the later May Day celebrations of Western Europe. It was held in honor of Flora, the goddess of flowers and springtime. Although tradition gives credit for originating the festival to Romulus, the legendary founder of Rome in 753 B.C., the festival is actually believed to have been instituted in Rome in 238 B.C. The *Floralia* was first a movable feast whose annual date depended upon the progress of crops and flowers. In 173 B.C., however, when unseasonable weather had seriously delayed the blossoming of flowers, the Roman senate made definite arrangements for its celebration and made it an annual festival extending from April 28 to May 3.

The festivities, which sometimes involved licentious dramatic productions and games, were most important at the Temple of Flora in Rome. Traditionally, the first person to lay a wreath or garland on the statue of Flora was guaranteed good fortune in the coming months. Chains formed of entwined blossoms were wound around the temple columns, while white-robed women and girls, adorned with flowers, scattered petals along the streets nearby. Children fashioned small statues of Flora, which they decorated with blossoms. With the advent of Christianity, these "May-dolls" became crude images of the Virgin Mary.

The beginning of May, in particular May 1 and its eve, was also a sacred time elsewhere in Europe. The priestly druids, in the Celtic communities of pre-Christian northern and western Europe, celebrated the feast of Beltane on May

407

1. Although originally common to all Celtic peoples, the rites were observed especially in Ireland and Scotland. The most noteworthy ceremony was the kindling of sacred bonfires termed beltane fires. The origin of the word *beltane* is unknown, although it appears to be the name of a god, Bel, combined with the Celtic word for fire, *teome,* thus "Bel's fires." Possibly Bel was connected with the Celtic god Belenos, whose cult was well known in Gaul. Although it is uncertain whether Bel was a solar deity, the timing of the festivities around May 1 suggests that they were intended to honor and stimulate the sun as a life-giving force at the beginning of the warm weather.

Cormac, the early 10th century archbishop of Cashel, Ireland, provided the first recorded reference to the age-old Celtic custom of lighting bonfires on the hills on May Day Eve. Various ancient rites were performed about them. The participants leapt over the flames to ensure diverse blessings: to win husbands, to guarantee safe childbirth, to ward off illness. Even cattle were driven between two fires to protect them from disease. The embers were scattered on the fields to assure a good growing season and harvest. The fire rites were also considered a precaution against evil spirits and other sinister powers, which supposedly roamed the earth on May Eve. Sometimes a large circular oatmeal cake, regarded as a solar symbol, was pushed down the hillside. This Beltane cake was divided among those present at the rituals. The unfortunate person (or persons) who received a piece blackened with charcoal from the fire was termed *cailleach-bealteine,* the beltane carline (or churl), a name of great reproach. Generally the victim had to submit to mock quartering (reminiscent of the human sacrifices made by the early Celts) and bombardment with eggshells.

The ancient Celtic custom of lighting bonfires on hilltops continued throughout the Middle Ages in the British Isles and lingered on as a vestige of the druidical Beltane rite until the late 18th century. However, May Day celebrations, as practiced in England especially, owed far more to Roman than Celtic influences. Undoubtedly the Romans who occupied Britain from the first century to the early fifth century introduced there the revels connected with the festival of Flora. In medieval and Tudor England, May Day was a universally celebrated public holiday, a true festival of nature following the interminable winter months. All classes of people, even royalty and nobility, rose at dawn to go "a-maying." Women rose before sunrise to wash their faces with the dew, a custom believed to beautify the skin. The 17th century English diarist Samuel Pepys alludes to such an excursion in his famous diary, stating that his wife got up about 3:00 A.M. to "go with her coach abroad, to gather May-dew. . . ." As late as 1791, a London newspaper reported that "yesterday, being the first of May, a number of persons went to the fields and bathed their faces with the dew on the grass with the idea that it would render them beautiful."

The entire population of the medieval English village hurried out into the fields and woods to collect flowers and tree boughs, which they brought back in triumph. The focal point of the procession was the maypole, usually of birch, which was pulled by flower-bedecked oxen. The inhabitants then passed the rest of the day merrymaking. The local May Queen, surrounded by attendants, sat in a bower of blossoms and foliage, while various sports events, pageants, and dances were performed before her. Gaily outfitted jesters on hobby horses, Morris dancers in exotic dress and jingling bells, chimney sweeps in sooty clothes, "Robin Hood," "Maid Marian," and the merry band, and "Jack-in-the-Green" concealed in a light wooden frame covered with flowers and foliage traditionally provided entertainment. The maypole, erected for the day on the village green, presented a colorful sight with its decorations of garlands and streamers, the loose ends of which were grasped by dancers who wove intricate patterns as they encircled the pole. The entwined ribbons became unplaited when the dancers changed direction. In larger towns, especially in London, maypoles were made of durable wood and erected permanently.

With the ascendancy of the Puritans in the mid-17th century, the frivolous May Day festivities, which were often accompanied by excesses, were found offensive. Maypoles were found particularly objectionable. The *Anatomie of Abuses,* written in 1583, referred to them as "stinckyng idols," about which the people "leape and daunce, as the heathen did." The Parliament of 1644 prohibited their erection, declaring on April 6:

> The Lords and Commons do further order and ordain, that all and singular Maypoles that are, or shall be erected, shall be taken down, and removed by the constables, tithing men, petty constables, and churchwardens of the parishes, where the same be, and that no Maypole be hereafter set up, erected, or suffered to be set up within this Kingdom of England . . . the said officers to be fined 5 shillings weekly until the said Maypoles be taken down.

May Day was observed only surreptitiously until the Restoration of the Stuarts in 1660 removed the Puritan restrictions. When Charles

II returned to London in 1661, a 134-foot cedar maypole — the tallest ever seen in the city — was "reared with great ceremony and rejoicing in the Strand." When the great pole rotted at the base in 1717, it was bought by Sir Isaac Newton and removed to Essex, where it was set up in a park as a support for his 124-foot telescope.

Although May Day was never so whole-heartedly celebrated after the Puritan ban as it had been in the rural communities of medieval England, the May Day customs were practiced to a large extent during the 18th and 19th centuries in England. The American writer Washington Irving (1783–1859) described the May Day festivities he witnessed during a visit to England:

I shall never forget the delight I felt on first seeing a Maypole. It was on the banks of the Dee, close to the picturesque old bridge that stretches across the river from the quaint little city of Chester. . . . The mere sight of this Maypole gave a glow to my feelings and spread a charm over the country for the rest of the day.

Some of the May Day traditions are still being kept alive in certain areas of England. Morris dancers perform on village greens and an occasional maypole is raised. One of the most attractive ceremonies to welcome May is the annual service of praise and thanksgiving sung from the tower of Magdalen College, Oxford.

Although May Day seems to be a part of England's tradition more than of any other country's, it is observed in various ways throughout Western Europe. In France, for example, some people rise early May Day morning to find the first lilies of the valley in the woods. They press the flowers to send as tokens of love and affection to friends. In some cantons of Switzerland, village bachelors chop down small pines *(maitannli)* on May Day Eve and decorate them with blossoms and streamers. They then plant the trees before the houses of their sweethearts or of women they respect; for those whom they do not admire, they leave ugly straw puppets.

May Day Eve is a popular holiday full of folk traditions in Scandinavia. Many of the customs date back to the Middle Ages when April 30, popularly known as Walpurgis Night (see April 30), was believed to be the night when evil spirits, especially witches, mounted their broomsticks to fly to a rendezvous with Satan. This famous witches' sabbath supposedly took place at the Brocken Peak in Germany's Harz Mountains. According to an ancient tradition, lighted fires would frighten away the wicked spirits and deter them from injuring people or animals. Today, in Sweden especially, great bonfires are burned and the merrymakers, mostly university students, sing songs and make speeches in honor of returning spring. The students don their white velvet caps and tuck sprigs of May flowers in their lapels. Two sturdy young men personifying winter and summer stage a mock contest; the outcome is inevitable and winter is defeated.

In the United States, May 1 has never enjoyed the same kind of tradition and ceremony that it has enjoyed abroad. The Puritans, objecting to all secular celebrations, carried with them to America their dislike of May Day. The inhabitants of the Plymouth colony in New England were naturally scandalized when, on May 1, 1627, an Anglican named Thomas Morton dared to erect an 80-foot pine maypole, decorated with flowers, ribbons, and antlers, at his nearby plantation, Merry Mount. Moreover it was rumored that Morton and his cohorts had even danced with Indian women. The stern Puritan leader John Endecott had the pole chopped down and all antics halted. He renamed Merry Mount, calling it Mount Dagon after the Philistine idol that fell before the ark. Morton, charged with having traded arms with the Indians, was sent back to England.

Because of this inauspicious beginning, the May Day traditions that did take root in the New World were those introduced by English settlers of different religious denominations and by immigrants of various nationalities who came to America in later years. Today in some parts of the United States, children perform the almost-forgotten ritual of the maypole dance; sometimes they pick spring flowers and fill "May baskets," which they hang on the doorknobs of friends' and neighbors' homes. Morris dances are occasionally performed at special exhibitions. On American college campuses, especially at women's colleges, it was customary to select and crown May Queens, carry flower chains, dance around maypoles, and present musical spring pageants. The celebrations took place on May 1, or on a more convenient date in May.

May Day festivities are no longer so widely observed by colleges, except for small spontaneous gestures such as festooning a large May Day sign with crepe paper. But Smith College in Northampton, Massachusetts, for example, carries on the May basket tradition started by the class of 1912. Every year a May festival is held at Bryn Mawr College in Bryn Mawr, Pennsylvania. Very early May Day morning the seniors are awakened by the sophomores, who sing songs and present a May basket to each senior. After breakfast the classes, led by a local band, march in procession to the five maypoles, one for each undergraduate class and one for the graduate school. The May Queen, traditionally the president of the senior class, receives a gift from the president of the college. Various activities fill the day, including an Elizabethan pageant, Morris dancing, class singing, and senior hoop races — the winner of which supposedly will be the first to be married. In the evening, dancing, madrigals, and a May Day play conclude Bryn Mawr's exuberant welcome to May.

Some of the other customs connected with May Day have been brought to the United States by peoples of backgrounds other than English. In Seattle, for example, where there is a large population of Swedish descent, the Swedish Club holds an annual Spring Festival on the last day of April. Besides songs and speeches, bonfires characteristic of Walpurgis Night are kindled. Interestingly enough, the maypole ceremony typical of the English festivities is a highlight in Seattle not of May Day but of Midsummer (see June 23 and June 24).

Labor Observances

For many workers around the world, May Day is not a time for reviving old customs and merrymaking, but a day dedicated to the interests of the laborer. It is observed in practically every advanced industrial country except the United States and Canada, and is a public holiday in several countries of Western Europe, such as France, Germany, and Italy. The first tenuous connection between labor and the ancient May Day was made in 1833, when Robert Owen, the British social reformer, chose May 1 as the date for the start of the millennium. Oddly enough, although the United States observes Labor Day officially in early September, the first strong link between May 1 and labor was formed in this country. In 1884 a number of American trade unions chose May 1 as the day "from which eight hours shall constitute a day's labor." The decision to launch an intensive campaign for an eight-hour working day resulted in widespread strikes, including one set for May 1, 1886. During a demonstration that ensued on May 4, 1886, at Chicago's Haymarket Square, a bomb exploded, killing 11 persons and wounding over 100 others.

In the late 1880s several states named May 1 as Labor Day, although the American Knights of Labor had instituted Labor Day on the first Monday in September as far back as 1882. In 1889 the first Paris congress of the Second International, acting on the suggestion of a German Socialist, resolved:

There shall be organized a great international demonstration at a fixed date, so that on the agreed day, in every country, and in every town, the workers shall call upon the state for legal reduction of the working day to eight hours. . . . In view of the fact that a similar demonstration has been decided upon by the American Federation of Labor for the First of May 1890 . . . this date is adopted for the international demonstration.

On May 1, 1890, there were large militant demonstrations in European capitals and industrial cities, as well as numerous May Day meetings in the United States. In 1894 the US Congress made the official date of Labor Day the first Monday in September, a designation that remains in force today. The International Labor Day, however, remained May 1.

Labor's struggle, against opposition, to enforce its right to an annual May Day holiday abroad led to frequent and bloody battles. Police were often called in as bombs were hurled and buildings burned in many European cities. In the end, the workers gained their way. May 1 soon became an occasion not only for demonstrations on behalf of the cause of labor, but also for rallies by extreme radicals, by Communists, and by Socialists to show opposition to the government. At the third congress of the Second International at Zurich in 1893, speakers urged the socialist objective that May Day also

. . . must serve as a demonstration of the determined will of the working class to destroy class distinctions through social change and thus enter on the road, the only road, leading to peace for all peoples, to international peace.

The European observance has been reechoed in the United States in the 20th century. Radicals in America have imitated the example of their counterparts abroad and staged sometimes bitter demonstrations on May Day, especially in large cities. In New York City's Union Square, for example, May Day rallies have been held since 1924.

On May 1, 1896, May Day spread to Russia, when a May Day leaflet written in prison by Lenin was distributed to the workers of 40 factories in St. Petersburg (now Leningrad). By May 1, 1914, one million Russian workers were participating in the May Day strikes. Following World War I and the successful Russian Revolution of 1917, the ancient and tradition-rich May Day was the date the Russian Communists selected for even more forceful "May festivities." Making May Day one of their great holidays, they used it as an occasion to laud their doctrines and rededicate themselves to the cause of the international proletariat, exhorting the workers of the world to unite and cast off their chains. As early as the 1920s and 1930s, the Communist May Day had become a time for massive military reviews in Moscow's Red Square. As Communist rule expanded, similar demonstrations of armed power were staged in satellite countries. Fidel Castro fittingly selected May Day 1961 for his public announcement that Cuba had turned to communism and would henceforth abolish elections. Recently, however, the stress on weapons has diminished somewhat, and sports as well as missiles are being emphasized.

Loyalty Day

In 1947 the US Veterans of Foreign Wars designated May Day as Loyalty Day, a day to reaffirm loyalty to the United States. It was intended to be a "direct positive weapon" against communism, especially the American Communist Party, which was disseminating its doctrines at US May Day rallies. The Veterans of Foreign Wars received such hearty support from civic organizations, schools, churches, and the armed forces that a joint resolution of the US Congress officially designated May 1 of each year as Loyalty Day. All persons were urged to "fly the U.S. flag and observe Loyalty Day in schools and other suitable places with appropriate ceremonies."

Recognition of Loyalty Day spread rapidly as governors and mayors throughout the country proclaimed the day. School programs, flag presentations, sermons on loyalty, patriotic exercises, and parades marked the occasion. In Delaware, for example, Loyalty Day ceremonies were held at such historic places as the Cooch's Bridge site, where on September 3, 1777, the Stars and Stripes was supposedly first unfurled in battle.

Of the thousands of Loyalty Day observances across the land, the New York City parade is traditionally one of the biggest. It is usually held the last Saturday of April and is sponsored by the New York County Council of the Veterans of Foreign Wars. The parade originated as a means both of counteracting the May Day rallies at Union Square and offsetting the Communist May Day march along Eighth Avenue. In 1948 New York's Mayor William O'Dwyer led the first Loyalty Day parade down Fifth Avenue. The marchers, estimated at 30,000 to 40,000 (with onlookers numbering about 750,000) represented religious, fraternal, civic, social, ethnic, and government organizations. Boy Scouts, color guards, drill teams, drum and bugle corps, high school bands of the metropolitan area, and brightly costumed groups symbolizing the heritage of nations now under Communist rule provided a fervent answer to the Communist May Day celebrations. In the following years the Loyalty Day parades were staged on a large scale in both Manhattan and Brooklyn, attracting, for example, more than 80,000 marchers in 1955.

By the late 1960s, however, the political ramifications of the unpopular Vietnam War (see August 7) had seriously affected the Loyalty Day parades. Billed as demonstrations in support of American soldiers in Vietnam, the parades were openly criticized by pacifists and others who denounced American intervention in Vietnam. In 1968, while a few thousand marchers turned out for the traditional Loyalty Day parades in Manhattan and Brooklyn, some 87,000 persons participated in the Vietnam peace parade down both sides of Central Park and rallied in the park's 12-acre Sheep Meadow. In the 1970s, May 1 rallies sponsored by pacifist, antiestablishment, leftist, and war-protest groups proliferated. In contrast the Loyalty Day marchers paraded before sparsely scattered onlookers and a half-empty reviewing stand. Loyalty Day in other sections of the country prompted similar reactions.

Law Day

In recent years another new way of observing May Day was inaugurated through the efforts of the American Bar Association. In 1958, upon its urging, President Dwight D. Eisenhower instituted Law Day on May 1. It was not a coincidence that Law Day also fell on May Day. Like Loyalty Day, it was conceived as another attempt to emphasize the fact that the United States is a nation dedicated to the principle of democratic government under law, and not ruled according to the caprice of one person or a small clique. Law Day is therefore not a "lawyers' day," but rather an opportunity to commemorate the role of law in the United States. Its avowed educational and patriotic purposes are: "to foster respect for law; to increase public understanding of the place of law in American life; to point up the contrast between freedom under law in the United States and governmental tyranny under Communism."

Law Day did not become official nationwide until 1961, when a joint resolution of Congress designated May 1 as Law Day. In his proclamation, President John F. Kennedy asked all Americans to display the flag and observe the occasion "with suitable ceremonies." Law Day is also proclaimed annually by governors and mayors across the nation. In the years since 1961, as many as 100,000 Law Day exercises of various kinds have been staged annually. They have been sponsored by the American Bar Association, in cooperation with more than 1,400 state and local bar associations and with the backing of many major national organizations in the public service, educational, patriotic, and business fields. Typical programs, held in schoolrooms, civic and service clubs, churches, and courtrooms include sermons, addresses, mock trials, courthouse tours, films, radio and television shows, dramatic skits, library exhibits, special naturalization hearings, window displays, and essay contests.

Americanism Day in Pennsylvania

In Pennsylvania May 1 is also proclaimed as Americanism Day. Since Communists had chosen this date for their political and military demonstrations, the Pennsylvania legislature in 1939 adopted a resolution urging the governor to issue a proclamation inviting the people to join in a "real celebration of Americanism Day." Various groups and organizations joined in observing the day with parades and patriotic speeches. Uniontown, Pennsylvania, puts on one of the chief annual celebrations of Americanism Day. Sponsored by the American Legion, the program generally includes appropriate activities in all schools in the county; an evening banquet; and a night parade, which is usually the largest staged in the area during the year.

Lei Day in Hawaii

Quite apart from political connotations, May Day, a day associated with flowers since antiquity, has added significance in Hawaii. It is dedicated to the lei, the handsome garland of flowers, which is Hawaii's traditional sign of friendship and aloha spirit. The wearing of the lei is, of course, a much-practiced modern-day Hawaiian custom. Visitors to the island are frequently welcomed with necklaces of carnations, jasmines, or orchids. But, although leis are presented and worn many times during the year, a special effort is made on May 1 to have everyone wear a lei.

It was in 1928 that the poet Don Blanding voiced the idea of having a special day on which to honor the lei, proposing that the custom be carried out each year. In response, Mrs. John T. Warren, a writer, suggested that the day be May Day, not only a time traditionally connected with flowers, but also one when blossoms were especially lovely in Hawaii. And her slogan, "Lei Day is May Day," caught the popular imagination. The Lei Day festivities have remained very much the same since they were started on May 1, 1928. The occasion is still a one-day celebration, staged by individual communities on Oahu and the neighboring islands of Hawaii. Schoolchildren in homemade costumes present programs of Polynesian songs and dances before a school queen and her court.

The major Lei Day celebration, however, takes place in Honolulu. The exercises are held along the sea at the Waikiki Shell in Queen Kapiolani Park. Tourists, as well as residents, are asked to dress in gaily colored island clothes — *muumuus, holokas,* and aloha shirts — complete with *leis,* naturally. On the morning of May 1 entries are received for the statewide lei contest. The garlands, fashioned out of blossoms, seeds, leaves, ferns, and pods, combine floral brilliance and skillful arrangement. They are judged in numerous categories and over 50 prizes are awarded. Afterwards the hundreds of leis remain on display in the official state lei exhibition. Early afternoon entertainment features Hawaiian music and singing, but the highpoint is reached in the colorful program staged at sunset. In a festive show of island pageantry, authentic native chanting and the blowing of the conch shell, as well as bearers with *kahilis* and tabu sticks, herald the arrival of "royalty" — the Lei Queen and her court. Popular entertainers then present an evening of songs and hulas.

American Heritage Week in Rhode Island

In Rhode Island and Delaware, May 1 is also a time for recalling the rich heritage of the colonial past. Rhode Island annually proclaims American Heritage Week early in May, not only to bring attention to its attributes, but also to commemorate its 1776 severance of ties with England two months before the signing of the Declaration of Independence. The week's festivities include May Day breakfasts, which have been sponsored by the Grange and local churches since 1867. The breakfasts, given in private homes, clubs, Grange halls, and churches, are offered on several days.

Old Dover Days in Delaware

Since 1933 Dover, the capital of Delaware, has celebrated Old Dover Days on the first weekend in May. Several "colonial-flavored" events and crafts exhibits are staged in this town created by William Penn in 1683. In some years the festivities have included dancing around a maypole on the town green. Many of Dover's old homes, boxwood gardens, and historic public buildings are open to the public for the occasion.

Battle of Manila Bay

When the Spanish-American War broke out on April 21, 1898 (see April 21), Commodore George Dewey was in Hong Kong with four cruisers, his flagship *Olympia*, the *Baltimore*, the *Boston*, and the *Raleigh*, as well as two gunboats, the *Concord* and the *Petrel*. He received orders on April 24 from Secretary of the Navy John Davis Long "to proceed to the Philippine Islands; commence operations at once against the Spanish fleet; capture vessels or destroy."

Dewey's Asian Squadron sailed immediately, and arrived at the entrance to Manila Bay on the evening of April 30. The Spanish fleet, under the command of Admiral Patricio Montojo and consisting of four cruisers, three gunboats, and three vessels in poor repair, lay off Cavite naval point. At 5:40 A.M. on May 1, when the American ships were about 5,000 yards from the Spanish fleet, Dewey quietly ordered Captain C. V. Gridley, the commander of his flagship: "You may fire when you are ready, Gridley."

The US fleet then raked the Spanish line, swinging in an oval pattern past the Spanish ships at a range of between 5,000 and 2,000 yards. Upon receiving an erroneous report that there was a shortage of ammunition, Dewey ordered a temporary ceasefire at 7:35 A.M., but at 11:16 he renewed action. An hour and a quarter later, the battle was over.

The Spanish fleet, with not one-third of the American firing power, had been completely disabled or destroyed; Spanish losses were 381 men killed and wounded. None of the American ships was damaged; 8 men were wounded. Within 10 days of the battle, Dewey had been promoted to the rank of rear admiral. Congress authorized bronze medals to be struck and awarded to the officers and men who had taken part in the battle, and on March 3, 1899, Dewey was named Admiral of the Navy. The title was especially created for him by Congress the previous day.

Since Dewey did not have enough men to occupy Manila he blockaded the bay. Finally, on August 13, the day after an armistice was signed between the United States and Spain, American troops under Major General Wesley Merritt, supported by Dewey's fleet, occupied the city. On February 10, 1899, the Treaty of Paris formally ending the Spanish-American War was signed by President William McKinley. Under its terms the United States took possession of the Philippine Islands in consideration of payment of $20 million.

For many years the anniversary of the battle of Manila Bay was celebrated annually by the Dewey Congressional Medal Men's Association, composed of the officers and men who took part in the battle. Other organizations of war veterans usually participated in the celebration. The exercises were held for a number of years in the Philadelphia Navy Yard, where the *Olympia* was tied up after it was put out of commission in 1922. It was customary to hold a parade of war veterans in one of the streets leading to the navy yard in advance of the formal exercises on board the *Olympia*. At the celebration in 1934, Admiral Dewey's flag, which was shot down during the battle of May 1, was restored to the ship and hoisted to its proper place. It had been bought by a patriotic citizen at an auction of some of the household effects of the admiral. The exercises on board the ship consisted of patriotic speeches by officials of veterans' organizations.

Today there are no formal celebrations of the battle of Manila Bay. However, the *Olympia*, the last survivor of the Spanish-American War fleets, is part of a naval exhibit of historic vessels in Philadelphia and is berthed at the north side of Pier 11, on the Delaware River at Race Street. Visitors can see bronze footprints at the spot where Dewey stood while commanding the battle of Manila Bay.

The *Olympia* was launched in 1892 and is named after the capital of the state of Washington. After the Spanish-American War it was made the flagship of the US North Atlantic Squadron. Later it was used as a training ship for midshipmen at the US Naval Academy. When World War I broke out, it was named the flagship of the US Patrol Force and served on patrol and escort duty off Norfolk and Nova Scotia. Late in 1918 it began service as the flagship of the US Naval Forces Eastern Mediterranean, and in October 1921 it carried the body of the American Unknown Soldier, killed during World War I, home from Le Havre, France. In 1922 the *Olympia* was put out of commission and tied up in the Philadelpia Navy Yard.

Congress ordered the cruiser scrapped in 1954, but interested citizens sent in contributions to save it and it was taken to Pier 4 in Philadelphia and opened to tours. In August 1963 the Cruiser Olympia Association took over the ship from the US Navy and restored it to its original condition. It was maintained as a national shrine and a navy museum by a group of volunteer navy veterans. The ship was located at Pier 4 South on the Delaware River, at the foot of Chestnut Street in Philadelphia until it was moved to Pier 11.

Dewey was honored in many cities by the naming of streets and squares for him. In New York there is Dewey Place in Brooklyn, and

Dewey Avenue in the Bronx. Dewey Square, in Manhattan, was so named on May 3, 1922 but was later renamed A. Philip Randolph Square.

Feast of SS. Philip and James

The relics of SS. Philip and James repose in the Church of the Holy Apostles in Rome, which is dedicated to them. The church was consecrated on May 1, which was at one time the universal date for this feast in Western churches. However, Roman Catholics now celebrate May 3 as the feast day, whereas the Episcopal and some other communions still observe May 1. Eastern Orthodox churches also honor these two saints, but on various days.

Philip, like Peter and Andrew, came from Bethsaida in Galilee and, also like them, died on the cross. It was Philip, after he was called to be an Apostle, who brought Nathanael, called Bartholomew, to Jesus (John 1:45–49). Other references in the New Testament mention specific conversations between Philip and Jesus — before the miracle of the loaves and fishes and at the Last Supper, to name two instances. After Jesus' death and the first Pentecost, Philip may have preached in Asia Minor and died there in Hierapolis of Phrygia.

James was called James the Younger, the Less, or the Little, to distinguish him from James the Greater, the Apostle who, with Peter and John, held a certain precedence among the Apostles.

Beyond the fact that James the Younger was an Apostle and the son of Alphaeus, almost nothing is known of him with certainty. He is often identified with one of the several other Jameses prominent in the New Testament, and particularly with James, the brother — or cousin — of Jesus, who became the first bishop of Jerusalem. Some sources identify the two, and the story of James's death in about A.D. 62 — by stoning, or being thrown from the pinnacle of the Temple after refusing to recant his faith in Jesus —has been told of both. There is a strong trend in modern biblical scholarship, however, to distinguish between the two men. There has been similar confusion about the authorship of the Epistle of James in the New Testament, which is commonly attributed to James, the kinsman of Jesus.

MAY 2

Kentucky Derby

This is a movable event. See note on page xxvi.

The Kentucky Derby, first run in 1875, is held every year on the first Saturday of May at Churchill Downs in Louisville, Kentucky. It derives its name from another well-known horse race, instituted in 1780 by the 12th earl of Derby and still held annually at Epsom Downs near London. The Derby ranks as one of the top sporting events in the United States. With the Belmont Stakes (run in June at Belmont Park, near New York City), and the Preakness (run in late May at the Pimlico Race Course, near Baltimore, Maryland) the Kentucky Derby is one of the Triple Crown races. Only a horse that has won all three races in one year — like Secretariat in 1973 — can qualify as a Triple Crown winner. In 1976 the 102nd Run for the Roses — as the Kentucky Derby is called because of the garland of red roses placed on the winning horse's neck at the winner's circle — took place before the eyes of over 115,000 cheering spectators at the track and several million television viewers at home.

Kentuckians have long been interested in horse racing and breeding. The first horse races in Lexington were staged in 1787, and the first jockey club was organized 10 years later. Almost two centuries of tradition and experience, therefore, as well as ideal natural conditions, have made the Lexington and Louisville area of Kentucky the leading US center for the raising of thoroughbred horses. Within a radius of 20 miles of Lexington, bluegrass combines with the unusually rich vegetation to produce lush blue-green meadows. Graceful thoroughbreds, frolicking on the more than 200 horse farms in the heart of the bluegrass country, have become the very symbols of the Blue Grass State.

Although Louisville produces bourbon whiskey, tobacco, and baseball bats, the world knows it primarily as the "Derby town" and home of the renowned Churchill Downs racetrack, named after the family that owned the land on which the track stands.

The inspiration behind the Kentucky Derby came from Colonel Meriwether Lewis Clark Jr., the man who developed most of the rules governing the sport of horse racing in the United States. In 1875 Colonel Clark organized Churchill Downs as the Louisville Jockey Club, and he served as president of the track from 1875 to 1894. As part of the Churchill Downs program, he offered the Kentucky Derby. The race was to be for three-year-olds, carrying weight not in excess of 126 pounds. (Guides at Churchill Downs like to point out enigmatically that no "horse" can ever win, or even enter, the Derby — a true statement, for in racing parlance only a thoroughbred over five years of age is termed a "horse."

The first Derby race, on May 17, 1875, was a deliberate attempt by the Louisville aristocracy to transplant the social ambiance of the English Derby. The day after the race the local press dwelt upon the stylish crowd and 10,000 carriages present at the 80-acre track and lawn of Churchill Downs before mentioning that a horse named Aristides had won the race.

The first running was a memorable one. Aristides — owned by H. Price McGrath, a Kentucky horse breeder and gambler — had been entered as a pacemaker for Chesapeake, also owned by McGrath. Aristides ran so well, however, that when the time came for Chesapeake to pass him, Chesapeake was too far behind to overtake his pacemaker. Seeing what had happened, McGrath signaled Aristides' jockey to go for the finish line. Aristides reached the wire a winner in what was regarded as the remarkable speed of 2:37 3/4 minutes, then the fastest on record for a three-year-old at the mile and one-half distance. (In 1896 the course was shortened to a mile and one-quarter.)

Over the next few years, the Kentucky Derby continued to gain in popularity. A visitor to Derby Day in 1877 described the setting and influx of spectators as follows:

Green fields and woodlands lay on the left, a cottage dotted here and there over the plain. Behind, the Nashville railroad winding its way like a snake through the woodlands. In front there was a vast cloud of dust that indicated the road over which the vast throng was approaching.

In 1878 the Short Line Railroad added a special 19-car train to accommodate Derby fans. For the 1882 running, the seating capacity at Churchill Downs was doubled.

Following the death of Colonel Clark in 1899, however, interest in racing at Churchill Downs declined for several seasons. In an attempt to recapture its lost prestige, Colonel Matt J. Winn agreed to become general manager of the track in 1902. He scheduled the race for Saturday rather than a weekday, and he turned the Kentucky Derby from an inbred Louisville social occasion into a nationwide attraction. With his knack for showmanship and promotion, Winn set the race well on the way to ranking as one of the best-known sporting events in the world.

In 1895 the first unit of the present clubhouse and grandstand at Churchill Downs was constructed. Although much of the original structure is no longer visible because of additional construction, the Edwardian twin towers still predominate and have become the trademark of the track.

Churchill Downs is now an immense, 145-acre complex, boasting the longest stands and greatest number of reserved seats of any racing course in the world. Its elaborate facilities include luxurious jockey quarters; a special glassed-in section of the clubhouse, seating over 1,275; and a press box accommodating 500. The stable section alone houses 1,200 horses during the spring and fall racing meets. Some 75,000 plants are grown in its five greenhouses each winter for display in the track gardens in the spring. A museum contains souvenirs of Churchill Downs and photographs, programs, and other mementos of past Kentucky Derbies.

The Kentucky Derby purse, which in 1875 amounted to less than $3,000, reached approximately $50,000 in 1922; it remained at that amount until 1934, when it was reduced to about $30,000. In 1937 the purse again totaled about $50,000. In 1971 the winner received $145,500, out of a gross purse of $188,000. In 1976 the Derby gross purse was $217,700, of which $165,200 went to the winning owner.

Before 1975, when a limit of 20 mounts was imposed, the largest field to start in the Derby was 23, in 1974; the smallest fields — 3 starters in each race — were in 1892 and 1905. The fastest time for the mile-and-one-half course — 2:34 1/2 minutes — was made by Spokane, in 1889; on the mile-and-one-quarter course Secretariat clocked 1:59 2/5 in 1973. The slowest winner for the mile and one-half was Kingman, in 1891, at 2:52 1/2; on the mile-and-one-quarter course, Stone Street's time was 2:15 1/5, in 1908.

Just minutes after every Kentucky Derby, the winning owner is invited to a private party given by the president of Churchill Downs. There, since 1951, the lucky horseowner traditionally sips a mint julep from a special sterling silver cup; it is decorated with a wreath of roses at the bottom, in imitation of the garland placed over the champion's neck, and a replica of a thoroughbred horse's shoe, authentic even in such details as correct size and nail holes. Each cup later becomes part of the cup collection displayed at the Downs.

The Kentucky Derby is still the climax of Louisville's social season, despite the fact that it has become a national institution, but it is not the only attraction offered visitors to Louisville at Derby time. A 10-day Kentucky Derby Festival, featuring a steamboat race, a golf tournament, stage entertainment, bicycle races, a parade, and coronation ball, runs from late April through Derby weekend, ending the Sunday after the Derby itself. Begun in its current form in 1956, the festival has expanded to become one of the nation's better-known festivals.

Among the highlights of the 15th Kentucky Derby Festival in 1970 were the annual coronation ball, at which the Queen of Pegasus is traditionally selected from among five Kentucky students; a live music show featuring country and western bands; and the Pegasus parade, watched by an estimated 250,000 people lining the parade route through downtown Louisville and, for the first time, televised nationwide.

Perhaps the most colorful event of the entire festival was the race between the *Belle of Louisville* and the *Delta Queen,* two sternwheelers that annually pit their reputations in a contest of speed on the Ohio River. Belching pitch-black smoke, the steamboats raced upstream to Six Mile Island and back — a course of 12 miles — to determine which one would sport the traditional prize of "gilded antlers" in its pilothouse. Thousands of spectators crowded the river banks for the Battle of the Great Sternwheelers, thus bearing out Mark Twain's comment:

I think that much the most enjoyable of all races is a steamboat race. . . . Two red-hot steamboats . . . neck and neck, straining every nerve . . . quaking . . . and groaning from stem to stern, spouting white steam from the pipes, pouring black smoke from the chimneys . . . parting the river into long streaks of hissing foam — this is sport that makes a body's very liver curl with enjoyment.

He added: "A horse-race is pretty tame and colorless in comparison," but obviously was not referring to the Kentucky Derby.

Finally the strains of "My Old Kentucky Home" at 5:30 P.M. on May 2 heralded the running of the 96th Kentucky Derby at Churchill Downs, as 17 of the finest three-year-olds moved out onto the track for the post parade. A short 2:03 2/5 minute-run later, Dust Commander, a Kentucky-bred colt, was proclaimed winner of the mile and one-quarter event by five lengths over the favorite, My Dad George. The year 1970 was the first in which a female jockey rode in the Kentucky Derby.

At 11:00 A.M. on Sunday, May 3, the Kentucky Colonels and their guests went to The Forest, the Anchorage home of a fellow colonel, to enjoy a barbecue replete with ham, fried chicken, burgoo, and all the trimmings, before they departed for home.

MAY 3

First Medical School in the United States

On May 3, 1765, Dr. John Morgan presented, at a special meeting of the board of trustees of the College of Philadelphia (now the University of Pennsylvania) a proposal for the establishment of a "professorship . . . of Physick and Surgery, as well as the several occupations attending upon these necessary and useful arts." On the same day, he was chosen to be the college's "professor of the Theory and Practice of Physick." At commencement exercises, on May 30 and 31 of that year, Morgan outlined his philosophy of medical education and the manner in which it would be taught. Dr. William Shippen Jr. was appointed professor of anatomy and surgery at a subsequent meeting of the trustees in September 1765. In establishing a medical department with the appointment of Drs. Morgan and Shippen, the College of Philadelphia founded the country's first medical school. The first classes began in November of the same year. The University of Pennsylvania's School of Medicine, into which the new school evolved, observed the bicentennial of medical education in the United States in 1965.

Morgan, a graduate of the College of Philadelphia, had studied medicine with a Philadelphia physician and served for three years as surgeon in the French and Indian War. He then went abroad and continued his studies in Paris, London, and Edinburgh. He graduated from the University of Edinburgh with the degree of M.D. in 1763. While abroad he conceived the idea of establishing a medical school in the United States. It was on his return that he suggested the plan to the trustees of the college in Philadelphia. (Later, from 1775 to 1777, he was director-general of hospitals and physician-in-chief of the Continental army. He subsequently undertook what became a substantial medical practice, corresponded with learned persons, and was the author of several publications. He died in Philadelphia on October 15, 1789.)

Dr. Shippen, who had been lecturing on anatomy and operating the nation's first maternity hospital, in Philadelphia, since 1762, was a pioneer in making obstetrics a recognized branch of medicine. From the appointment of Drs. Morgan and Shippen as its first professors developed one of the great medical colleges of the country — the first of the professional schools now maintained by the University of Pennsylvania, and the first school for postgraduate professional training established in the United States. Shippen, who served from 1777 to 1781 as chief of the Continental army's medical department, became a founder and president, from 1805 to 1808, of the College of Physicians of Philadelphia. He died in 1808.

Feast of SS. Philip and James

The Episcopal and some other Western churches celebrate the feast of SS. Philip and James on May 1, the traditional date (see May 1). The Roman Catholic church, which from the sixth century also marked May 1 as the feast day of the two saints, transferred its observance to May 11 in 1955, and to May 3 — the first free day after the original observance — in its calendar reform of 1969.

Rural Life Sunday
Or Soil Stewardship Sunday

This is a movable event. See note on page xxvi.

In an era of increasing concern about the abuse of the environment, the emphasis of Rural Life Sunday is on the concept that the Earth belongs to God, who has merely granted humanity the use of it, along with the responsibility of caring wisely for it. The day is observed in the United States in both rural and urban areas on the fifth Sunday after Easter. Known also as Rogation Sunday — a term deriving from the Latin *rogare*, to ask — it had its origin in France in the second half of the fifth century, when Mamertus, bishop of Vienne, designated Rogation Sunday and the following Monday, Tuesday, and Wednesday (Rogation Days) as a time of penitance, and of praying, for God's beneficence and protection from evil. As was natural in view of the spring season, the prayers said on these days came to stress agricultural concerns, with entreaties for God's blessing upon the soil, the seed, and the cultivators of the earth. (These days immediately precede Ascension Day, which falls on Thursday of the same week.)

The day was first observed as Rural Life Sunday in 1929, at the suggestion of the International Association of Agricultural Missions, and according to plans adopted by the Home Missions Council of North America and the Federal Council of Churches. All Christian churches were invited to observe the day with a special service prescribed by the Federal Council, which included prayers and hymns.

In 1950 the Federal Council, the Home Missions Council, and the International Association of Agricultural Missions combined with eight other independent religious bodies to form the National Council of the Churches of Christ in the United States of America, a cooperative federation now representing about 30 Protestant and Eastern Orthodox denominations. Rural Life Sunday is sponsored in the United States by the National Council of Churches and the National Catholic Rural Life Conference — the latter formed in 1923 at the behest of Bishop Edwin V. O'Hara and now numbering some 5,000 rural pastors, teachers, farmers, economists, sociologists, agricultural agents, and officials among its membership. Sponsorship of

Rural Life Sunday by the two organizations is through the National Association of Soil and Water Conservation Districts (NACD), a nongovernmental organization.

Rural Life Sunday has been observed annually by churches of many Christian denominations throughout the United States ever since its inception in 1929. The forms of the observance are left largely to the discretion of the individual churches. The National Council no longer prescribes an order of worship for the day, but several denominations and some state councils of churches prepare such an order. The National Council prepares a litany, and it cooperates in making hymn and Scripture suggestions, which are published in the Soil Stewardship booklet issued annually by the NACD and distributed nationwide to churches of all faiths. Many churches sponsor group discussions based on the material in the booklet, which identifies areas of concern and stresses the need for initiative to be exercised by church members as well as nonmembers. The seeds and the soil are still blessed in many localities, but there is also considerable stress on the unity of all of life and the interdependence of all segments of society. Plays and pageants deal both with the importance of the values of rural living and with the interdependence theme.

Under the sponsorship of the NACD, the week beginning with Rural Life Sunday is now widely observed as Soil Stewardship Week, and the Sunday itself is alternatively termed Soil Stewardship Sunday. As a result of the broadening of emphasis in recent years, observances now include a call for individual action on problems connected with air, and water, and noise pollution, with congestion, with conservation of open spaces and recreational areas, and with provision of sufficient food and fuel supplies. In metropolitan areas education is considered mandatory to avert what the 1968 Soil Stewardship booklet saw as the danger that "oncoming urban generations will be so dissociated from the resources which support them, and from a genuine understanding of environmental functions, that present lessons will be forgotten and past mistakes made again."

Pulpits are still exchanged by city and country pastors on Rural Life, or Soil Stewardship, Sunday, and congregants participate in the observances, indicating their business, professional, and personal concerns. Members of local agricultural organizations, such as 4-H Clubs, Future Farmers of America, the American Farm Bureau Federation, the National Grange, and the Farmers' Educational and Co-Operative Un-

417

ion of America, are encouraged to attend and share in the observances. In certain states the 4-H Clubs are the special sponsors of Rural Life Sunday, and in some churches 4-H Sunday is observed on the same day.

MAY 4

Horace Mann's Birthday

The life of Horace Mann, coinciding as it did with the great reform movements of the first half of the 19th century, prompts the familiar question as to whether the times created the man, the man the times, or both. It was on May 4, 1796, in Franklin, Massachusetts, that Mann, who was to become known as the Father of American Public Education, was born — into an atmosphere of poverty and self-denial. His early formal education was sporadic, totalling 8 or 10 weeks a year at the hands of poor teachers. But he received a continuous informal education — self-administered in the Franklin town library. With the help of an itinerant schoolmaster's occasional tutoring, Mann managed to enter Brown University as a sophomore at the age of 20. After brilliant work, including a demonstrated interest in education, social reform, and politics, he was graduated with high honors in 1819. His valedictory address, which has been described as a model of humanitarian optimism, gave promise of things to come.

Mann returned to Brown briefly to tutor (1819–1821) in Latin and Greek. Meanwhile, however, he had read law with an attorney from Wrentham, Massachusetts, and it was not long before he turned his full attention to that field. He attended the Litchfield (Connecticut) Law School and was admitted to the Massachusetts bar in 1823. He practiced law at Dedham (where he first settled) and Boston (where he moved later) until 1837.

In the meantime he had espoused a number of humanitarian and reform causes and shown that legal training and skill in public speaking are valuable assets for the public servant. Equipped with both he was elected in 1827 to the Massachusetts house of representatives. He served there until 1833, when he became, for four years, a member of the state senate. As a representative he had been instrumental in establishing in Worcester a state hospital for the mentally ill. As senator — more specifically as president of the senate during his last two years in the state legislature — he signed the bill that made history in 1837 by establishing a state board of education.

Ignoring the advice of friends, Mann, to whom the cause of education had long been dear, put aside law and politics and became secretary of the new board. Thanks to his moral leadership and driving energy, the board's influence extended far beyond what its limited powers would have led anyone to expect. He labored tirelessly to arouse public opinion in favor of increased appropriations for schools and better facilities and teacher training. He helped secure a new state law that required children under 12 to spend at least six months of the year in school. Finding that there were not enough well-trained teachers, he established the nation's first state normal school, at Lexington in 1839. During his 12 years in office, Massachusetts' appropriations for public education were more than doubled. Fifty new public high schools were opened. Under his leadership many of the ills of Massachusetts' decentralized educational system, which had placed control of schools with economy-bent local districts, were overcome by the reassertion of a centralized state influence. Teaching methods and curricula were revised and teachers' salaries raised. During his tenure Mann also found time to establish and edit a biweekly, *Common School Journal*, for teachers.

He also lectured extensively and issued 12 annual reports to the board of education. These reports, covering a wide range of topics and illuminating many problems, substantially influenced the course of education in the United States. The reports, which declared that a republic cannot for long be both ignorant and free, set forth the argument for the public school, championing universal education. They called for nonsectarian schools, open to children from all social, ethnic, and religious backgrounds, to be financed and controlled by a concerned citizenry. In 1843 Mann made a five-month tour of Europe. He devoted his annual report that year to a survey of European educational conditions and methods. Among other things, he recommended the abandonment of corporal punishment.

The suggestion aroused the opposition of those who feared that it would undermine classroom discipline, just as the idea of nonsectarian schools had brought opposition from the clergy, and the establishment of a state board of education had prompted charges that local authority was being violated. With public opinion marshaled behind them, however, most of Mann's views ultimately triumphed. It is not too much to say that their effect upon the American educational system was revolutionary.

In 1848 Mann resigned from the school board to fill the seat made vacant in the US House of Representatives by the death of former President John Quincy Adams. As was the case with a number of other reformers, Mann's humanitarian zeal extended to more than one cause. During his five far from peaceful years in Congress, he made no secret of his strong abolitionist sentiments. In 1852 he was defeated as the Free-Soil party's candidate for governor of Massachusetts.

But although his remaining years were few, his strong idealism, ability to contribute, and willingness to serve were still substantial. He was in his fifties in 1853, when he became the first president of a new nonsectarian college, which was committed to equal opportunities for blacks and women, and which would, like Mann, also pioneer in education. This was Antioch College, founded a year earlier in Yellow Springs, Ohio, and some of its pioneering was in its now widely known cooperative work-study program.

In June of 1859 Mann counseled one of Antioch's graduating classes with words that might have served as his own epitaph: "Be ashamed to die until you have won some victory for humanity." When he himself died on August 2 of the same year, he had no cause for shame. He was survived by his wife, the former Mary Peabody. She was one of Massachusetts' famous Peabody sisters; the others were Elizabeth, the noted educator and transcendentalist, and Sophia, the wife of Nathaniel Hawthorne.

Rhode Island Independence Day

Each year the state of Rhode Island celebrates two Independence Days — July 4 and May 4. The latter is the anniversary of Rhode Island's own renunciation of allegiance to Britain, two months before the national Declaration of Independence.

Britain's post-1765 imperial policy had devastated the economy of the tiny Rhode Island colony. The inhabitants were traders, and the basis of their commerce was the sugar and molasses that for decades they had obtained from the French and Spanish West Indies. The Sugar Act of 1764, however, prohibited such exchange. The American colonists were forced to trade only with the British islands, where sugar and molasses were much more expensive and much less abundant.

To enforce the new mercantile regulations, British revenue cutters plied the coastal waters in search of smugglers. One of the most efficient, and therefore despised, of these vessels was the Gaspée, which patrolled Narragansett Bay off Rhode Island. On June 9, 1772, the cutter went aground on a sandspit near Providence, and the colonists seized the opportunity to end its career.

That night a party of patriots boarded the Gaspée, terrorized the crew, and then set the vessel aflame.

This action was a serious offense. The British government sent a special commission to Rhode Island to investigate the incident, and empowered its members to transfer the scene of the suspects' trial to England. The commission never made any arrests, but the provincial press widely publicized Britain's theoretical violation of an accused individual's right to trial by a jury composed of members of his community.

The Gaspée experience made Rhode Islanders particularly sensitive to every British infraction of colonial rights thereafter. Following the Boston Tea Party, Rhode Island led the outcry against the harsh retaliatory measures imposed by the British. The General Assembly enthusiastically sent delegates to the First Continental Congress and authorized charters for several new military companies. Throughout the colony, arms manufacturers and ammunition stores steadily increased. The fighting at Lexington and Concord on April 19, 1775, likewise roused Rhode Island, and within a month a 1,500-man army of observation was sent to Boston to act "for the safety and preservation of any of the colonies."

Relations between Great Britain and its American colonies worsened during the remainder of 1775, and by the time the General Assembly met in May 1776 desire for independence was strong in Rhode Island. Traditionally each elected officer in the colony had sworn allegiance to the king before assuming his duties. This practice ended on May 4, 1776, when both houses of the General Assembly approved an act repealing the "Act for the more effectually securing to His Majesty, the allegiance of his subjects, in this his Colony and Dominion of Rhode Island and Providence Plantations."

The preamble to the act related that protection and allegiance were reciprocal and asserted that the king, in violation of the compact, had introduced fleets and armies into the colony to force upon the people a detestable tyranny. It further asserted that under such circumstances it became the right and duty of a people to make use of the means at hand for their preservation, and, therefore, that the act of allegiance was repealed. The new act directed that in all writs and processes of law, wherever the name and authority of the king had been employed, there should be substituted "the Governor and Company of the English Colony of Rhode Island and Providence Plantations." It was also declared that the courts were no longer to be the king's courts and that written instruments should no longer bear the year of the king's reign.

The bold deed of Rhode Island was an important step toward independence, and rebellion spread quickly after May 4. On May 15 a Virginia convention instructed its delegates to the Second Continental Congress to "declare the United Colonies free and independent states." Less than a month later, on June 11, the Congress appointed a committee consisting of Thomas Jefferson, John Adams, Benjamin Franklin, Roger Sherman, and Robert R. Livingston. The product of their work was the Declaration of Independence of July 1776.

Rhode Island, the only state to have declared its independence singlehandedly, commemorates the event during May, Rhode Island Heritage Month. The Newport Artillery Company, which was chartered in 1741 and is the oldest active military organization in the United States, recently revived the practice of firing cannonsalutes on May 4. The company generally marches from its armory on Clark Street to Newport's Washington Square at 6 P.M. The 15-minute ceremony that follows includes the raising of a liberty cap atop the flagpole there, the raising of the American flag, the firing of salutes from a 1750 cannon (believed to be the oldest in the world), and the lowering of the cap and flag.

At the homestead of the Revolutionary General Nathanael Greene in Anthony, Rhode Island, an Independence Day celebration also is traditionally held on or near May 4. The program features a procession of members of the Kentish Guards, which were chartered in 1774, accompanied by units from other patriotic, veterans', and scouting organizations. Local dignitaries give brief orations, but the most colorful event is the minuet that is danced by schoolchildren from nearby towns. The two-and-a-half-story gabled homestead — Mount Vernon of the North, as it is known — has been restored and contains 18th century furnishings. It is owned by the Nathanael Greene Homestead Association and is open to the public.

On the Sunday that precedes May 4, the First Baptist Church in Providence annually holds its Forefathers' Service. The church was organized in 1638 by the colony's founder, Roger Williams, and the present building dates from 1775. A grant from John D. Rockefeller financed a complete restoration of its interior. The Forefathers' Service is particularly significant since it features such 18th century forms of worship as Scriptural readings with comment and psalm-singing without instrumental accompaniment.

Elsewhere in the state the anniversary of Rhode Island's declaration of independence is marked during Rhode Island Heritage Month by events that vary from year to year and from one community to another. However, they are likely to include programs and exhibits with historical themes; tours of historic homes, gardens and public buildings; and concerts — band concerts, presentations of 18th century music, and, in several places, concerts of church chimes. From time to time a Rhode Island Heritage or Independence Day ball is held. Individual events are generally related to a statewide Rhode Island Heritage Month theme, which changes each year.

MAY 5

Cinco de Mayo

One of the great days in Mexican history is known as the *Cinco de Mayo,* or the Fifth of May. It is the anniversary of the 1862 battle of Puebla, in which Mexican forces against overwhelming odds defeated French invaders. The battle itself was not of great military importance since the victory represented only a temporary setback for the French troops; it nevertheless appealed to the imagination of the Mexicans and gave them the moral confidence they needed to win victory in the long run. May 5, a national holiday in Mexico, is therefore celebrated with festivities by Mexicans both at home and in foreign countries. In the United States the anniversary is observed especially in the southwestern states of Texas, Arizona, and California.

The following events led to the much celebrated battle: Mexico had defaulted payments on bonds to France, Spain, and England. An arrangement was made by the three European countries at a conference held in London on October 30, 1861, to make a joint naval demonstration against Mexico in order to compel payment to the bondholders. Fleets of the three powers sailed for Veracruz, arriving there near the end of the year. It was announced that there was no intention of conquering Mexico and that nothing was desired but a settlement of just claims. A conference was arranged with Mexican representatives, and a preliminary agreement was reached. Thereupon the British and Spanish fleets sailed for home in April 1862. The French — whose Emperor Napoleon III was eager to establish a centralized monarchy under French control in Mexico as a means of achieving hegemony in Spanish America — started a war of conquest.

On May 4, 1862, the commander of the French forces communicated this message to France's minister of war:

We have over the Mexicans such superiority of race, of discipline, and organization that I beg Your Excellency inform the Emperor that tomorrow, at the head of 6,000 of my choice troops, I will attack, and I consider that Mexico is mine.

When he attacked the forts of Loreto and Guadalupe on May 5, however, 2,000 Mexican soldiers under General Ignacio Zaragoza drove the men back with serious losses and finally won the day. The French ultimately conquered the country, and put Archduke Maximilian of Austria, the brother of Emperor Francis Joseph, on the throne on June 12, 1864, only to have him deposed and shot by the Mexicans on June 19, 1867, after a troubled reign.

The city of Puebla, Mexico, which had been known as Puebla de los Angeles, changed its name to Puebla de Zaragoza as a tribute to the general who had defended it from the French. The body of the general lies in the Panteón de San Fernando in the capital, Mexico City. In Puebla the grave of some of the French and Mexican soldiers who lost their lives in the battle is marked by a striking monument. It is topped by a white marble group representing an Angel of Peace, and Mexican and French soldiers shaking hands as a symbol of friendship between the two countries. Puebla is the scene of a fiesta and a reenactment of the famous battle annually on May 5. The city's celebration includes a military parade, usually attended by the president of the republic, and a *combate de flores* (battle of flowers) in the evening. Elaborate displays and sham battles are also staged in Zacapoaxtla, Peñón, and Mexico City, where, as in numerous other Mexican cities, a street is named for the day.

In the southwestern United States, especially in the border area, people of Mexican extraction hold festivities on and around May 5. Mexican social clubs and organizations generally sponsor a variety of events, such as parades, patriotic speeches, bullfights, and beauty contests. In San Antonio, Texas, for example, there are festive gatherings in two of the city's parks, with such features as a chicken barbecue and Mexican dances and music. There also is an official, early morning flag-raising ceremony at the Mexican Consulate at 127 Navarro Street, after which consular officials and members of the San Antonio Centro Cultural Infantil and the Sociedad Ignacio Zaragoza, together with representatives of similar groups from Corpus Christi, Beeville, and Goliad, meet at Goliad on an annual pilgrimage to General Zaragoza's birthplace. The hero of the 1862 battle was born in Goliad, then part of Mexico and known as Bahía del Espíritu Santo, on March 24, 1829. The birthplace site was designated a state park in 1960 and was dedicated on May 5, 1967.

The annual program in Goliad generally includes a recitation of the battle events, a display of standards and flags, an honor guard composed of several little girls, and the singing of the Mexican and US national anthems. The highlight is the laying of floral wreaths at the foot of the stone monument marking the birthplace site. A bust of Zaragoza (which ordinarily stands on a pedestal in the state park museum) is placed at the site for the May 5 ceremonies. The bust was presented to Goliad by the people of Puebla de Zaragoza, Mexico, in 1962, the 100th anniversary year of the battle. Other elaborate ceremonies during that commemorative year included a relay race — with Americans running from the Goliad birthplace to the Mexican border, and Mexicans from the border to Puebla. The runners carried a metallic urn partially filled with earth from the birthplace to Puebla, where the president of Mexico deposited it at the battle monument.

In numerous places throughout Arizona, residents of Mexican descent stage local celebrations each May 5. Among the most impressive have been those given in the twin border cities of Nogales, Arizona, and Nogales, Sonora, Mexico. Here, for example, the 100th anniversary celebration extended for several days and included two sessions of the Grand International Fiesta parade with bands, floats, and marching units from both sides of the border, as well as fireworks, the coronation of the Fiesta Queen, Indian dances, bull and cock fights, barbecues, balls, street dancing, and strolling *mariachis*.

Festivities including parades, dances, music, and speeches — or at least modest music and dance programs — are staged in several southern California communities, among them Calexico (across the border from Mexicali, Mexico). San Diego has had celebrations from time to time. In Los Angeles, an official observance, complete with orchestras and bands, banners and flags, visiting dignitaries, speeches, and Mexican dances, takes place at City Hall. On a more informal scale, Mexican organizations in the city usually mark the day with special fiestas featuring picnics, sports events, instrumental music, singing, and dancing in an atmosphere of spontaneous celebration.

MAY 6

Civil Rights Act of 1960

After passage by a vote of 311 to 109 in the House of Representatives and by 71 to 18 in the Senate, the civil rights bill of 1960 became law on May 6, 1960. The new act made it a crime to obstruct integration in public schools, and it provided for federal referees in voter-registration disputes, carrying forward the intent of the Civil Rights Act of 1957 (see September 9).

MAY 7

Ascension Day

This is a movable event. See note on page xxvi.

The Feast of the Ascension celebrates Jesus Christ's departure from the midst of his Apostles and his ascension into heaven, as described in the New Testament, 40 days after his Resurrection (see March 29, Easter Sunday). During those 40 days, Jesus was reported to have met with the Apostles on many occasions, telling them what he expected of them — "you shall be my witnesses . . . to the end of the earth" — and what they could expect from him — the gift of the Holy Spirit (see May 17, Pentecost). Then, on the first Ascension Day, when the Apostles were gathered together, Jesus led them out to the Mount of Olives. There he departed from them and, as they watched awestruck, ascended into heaven.

Ascension Day is a principal feast and ranks with Christmas, Easter, and Pentecost in the universality of its observance among Christians. It is designated as one of the 12 major feasts of Eastern Orthodox churches, as a major holy day by Episcopalians, and as a feast of the first class — that is, of prime importance — by Roman Catholics, for whom it is a holy day of obligation.

In the church calendar the Feast of the Ascension marks the close of Eastertide, climaxing the events of the Passion, Death, and Resurrection of Jesus Christ. Services are held on Ascension Day in many churches, including the Episcopalian, Lutheran, Eastern Orthodox, and Roman Catholic.

In Roman Catholic churches, a symbolically important part of Ascension Day services is the extinguishing of the paschal candle — lit during the Easter vigil services — signifying Jesus Christ's departure from earth. The date of the Eastern Orthodox observance of Ascension Day, though it falls on the traditional 40th day after Easter, customarily differs from that in Western churches because the rules by which the Eastern Orthodox calculate the date of Easter differ from those followed by the churches of the West.

In most churches Ascension Day services include readings chosen from those portions of the New Testament that describe the last acts of Jesus during his human life on earth. The Gospel of St. Luke, for example, closes with a brief account of the events of that original Ascension Day:

And he led them out as far as to Bethany and he lifted up his hands, and blessed them. And it came to pass, while he blessed them, he was parted from them, and carried up to heaven. And they worshipped him, and returned to Jerusalem with great joy: And were continually in the temple, praising and blessing God. Amen.

In many versions of the Bible, the Gospel of St. Mark also concludes with a brief reference to the Ascension.

In his prelude to the Acts of the Apostles, St. Luke gives a more thorough account:

The former treatise have I made, O Theophilus, of all that Jesus began both to do and teach, until the day on which he was taken up, after that he through the Holy Ghost had given commandments unto the apostles whom he had chosen: to whom also he showed himself alive after his passion by many infallible proofs, being seen of them forty days, and speaking of the things pertaining to the kingdom of God: and, being assembled together with them, commanded them that they should not depart from Jerusalem, but wait for the promise of the Father, which, saith he, ye have heard of me. For John truly baptized with water; but ye shall be baptized with the Holy Ghost not many days hence. When they therefore were come together, they asked of him, saying, Lord, wilt thou at this time restore again the kingdom to Israel? And he said unto them, It is not for you to know the times or the seasons, which the Father hath put in his own power. But ye shall receive power, after that the Holy Ghost is come upon you: and ye shall be witnesses unto me both in Jerusalem, and in all Judea, and in Samaria, and unto the uttermost part of the earth. And when he had spoken these things, while they beheld, he was taken up; and a cloud received him out of their sight. And while they looked steadfastly toward heaven as he went up, behold, two men stood by them in white apparel; which also said, Ye men of Galilee, why stand ye gazing up into heaven? This same Jesus, which is taken up from you into heaven, shall so come in like manner as ye have seen him go into heaven. Then returned they unto Jerusalem from the mount called Olivet, which is from Jerusalem a sabbath day's journey.

From earliest times, the celebration of the Ascension — a time of joy in the final triumph of the risen Jesus Christ — has stressed its theological significance rather than simply commemorating a historical event. Part of the preface of the mass celebrated in Roman Catholic churches on Ascension Day reads: "Christ was lifted up to Heaven to make us sharers in His divinity." St. John Chrysostom, writing in the fourth century, said: "Through the mystery of the Ascension we, who seemed unworthy of God's earth, are taken up into heaven. . . ." The same thought is carried forward in the collect prescribed for Ascension Day in *The Book of Common Prayer* of the Protestant Episcopal Church:

Grant, we beseech thee, Almighty God, that like as we do believe the only-begotten Son our Lord Jesus Christ to have ascended into the heavens; so we may also in heart and mind thither ascend, and with him continually dwell, who liveth and reigneth with thee and the Holy Ghost one God, world without end. *Amen.*

According to tradition, the Feast of the Ascension is one of the earliest festivals of the Christian church, dating from the year 68. No written record of its celebration as a liturgical feast, however, occurs before the fourth century.

In both the Roman Catholic and the Episcopal church, the Feast of the Ascension is marked by a vigil and an octave — that is, by devotions on the eve of the feast and by a period of eight days dedicated to the observance itself. Over the centuries many customs grew up around the celebration of the feast. For example, during the Middle Ages it was traditional for people to dine on pheasant, partridge, or some other bird on Ascension Day in commemoration of the fact that Jesus had "flown" to heaven. During church services from about the 13th to the 17th centuries, it was quite common for celebrants to re-enact the Ascension by raising a crucifix or a statue of the resurrected Jesus, suspended from a rope, until it disappeared through an opening in the church roof.

Sinking of the *Lusitania*

On May 7, 1915, the British Cunard liner *Lusitania* was torpedoed without warning by a German submarine. The liner was en route from New York to Liverpool and was off the coast of Ireland when it was struck. Though hit by only one torpedo, the ship quickly sank, with the loss of 1,198 passengers, of whom 128 were American. Among those drowned were Charles Frohman, the theatrical manager; Elbert Hubbard, the popular author and lecturer; and Alfred G. Vanderbilt, a son of the railroad magnate Cornelius Vanderbilt.

At the time of the *Lusitania* disaster, World War I, which had begun in July 1914, had bogged down in prolonged and bloody trench combat. Thus both Germany and the major Allies — Britain, France, and Russia — looked to the sea war to break the deadlock. With submarine warfare, Germany tried to wrest from Britain control of the high seas and in February 1915 announced that merchant vessels in British waters would be sunk without warning.

The United States, while officially neutral, had become the source of munitions for Britain and cotton for Germany. It was common knowledge that British passenger ships also carried munitions, and the *Lusitania* was no exception. Among other items, it carried 4,200 cases of small arms.

Britain had protested the German position on unarmed ships, and the American government supported the British view. Germany, meanwhile, had asserted that passengers on transatlantic ships were serving merely as a screen for military shipping. Just before the *Lusitania* sailed, the German embassy in Washington had posted a newspaper notice to prospective passengers on British ships, warning that they might be sunk. Since no one believed that Germany would dare attack the *Lusitania,* the warning was ignored. The timing of the advertisement, however, later made it difficult for Germany to sustain the claim that the sinking was unpremeditated.

Although Americans were shocked at what they considered to be the deliberate killing of civilians, public opinion was not generally in favor of military retaliation. President Woodrow Wilson acted cautiously. At no time did he consider action stronger than a diplomatic break with Germany. However, he acted with enough firmness to prompt the resignation of his isolationist secretary of state, William Jennings Bryan. Southern sentiment was rabidly against Britain because of German purchases of American cotton. The German-American and Irish-American communities were also upset when Wilson pressed the German government for diplomatic concessions. Yet when negotiations dragged, and when German spy scandals came to light, public support for the Allies increased. Thus the *Lusitania* affair was the first of many incidents that eventually prepared American public opinion for war against Germany.

MAY 8

V-E Day

World War II ended in Europe — while continuing to rage in Asia — on May 7, 1945, when Germany surrendered unconditionally to the Western Allies and the Soviet Union at Reims, France. It was 2:41 A.M. (8:41 P.M. of the previous day on the east coast of the United States) when the act of military surrender was signed in a large schoolhouse, the advance headquarters of General Dwight D. Eisenhower, supreme commander of the Allied Expeditionary Forces. However, the surrender did not become effective until approximately midnight of May 8, the date officially celebrated in the United States as V-E Day. From Washington, D.C., President Harry S. Truman announced on radio the end of World War II in Europe and issued a proclamation:

The Allied Armies, through sacrifice and devotion and with God's help, have won from Germany a final and unconditional surrender. The Western World has been freed of the evil forces which for five years and longer have imprisoned the bodies and broken the lives of millions upon millions of free-born men. They have violated their churches, destroyed their homes, corrupted their children and murdered their loved ones. Our armies of liberation have restored freedom to these suffering peoples, whose spirit and will the oppressors could never enslave.

Much remains to be done. The victory in the West must now be won in the East. The whole world must be cleansed of the evil from which half the world has been freed. United, the peace-loving nations have demonstrated in the West that their arms are stronger by far than the might of dictators or the tyranny of military cliques that once called us soft and weak. The power of our peoples to defend themselves against all enemies will be proved in the Pacific as it has been proved in Europe.

For the triumph of spirit and of arms we have won, and for its promise to peoples everywhere who join us in love of freedom, it is fitting that we, as a nation, give thanks to Almighty God, who has strengthened us and given us this victory.

Now, therefore, I, Harry S. Truman, President of the United States of America, do hereby appoint Sunday, May 13, 1945, to be a day of prayer. I call upon the people of the United States, whatever their faith, to unite in offering joyful thanks to God for the victory we have won and to pray that He will support us to the end of our present struggle and guide us into the way of peace. I also call upon my countrymen to dedicate this day of prayer to the memory of those who have given their lives to make possible our victory.

There was rejoicing throughout the United States on V-E Day, but awareness of the war in the Pacific still to be won tempered the general relief, as did the national grief over the death of President Franklin D. Roosevelt. Public demonstrations were moderate compared to the triumphant victory mood that was to sweep the nation on V-J Day the following August.

In New York and other large cities crowds resembling those of New Year's Eve gathered to express their jubilation by tooting horns and staging impromptu parades. On the other hand, business as usual was the rule in most offices, factories, and defense plants, where employees reported for their shifts and went quietly about their work. Perhaps the most significant indication of a prevailing spirit of intense but sober interest in the event was the fact, revealed by a radio poll, that 64 percent of all adult listeners, then the largest radio audience in history, tuned in on President Truman's address officially confirming the surrender.

Today, although V-E Day is not widely celebrated, it is a day of historic interest with vivid personal memories for many Americans. The anniversary is customarily noted in the communications media, often with special programs.

One such program took place on May 8, 1965.

Television, by that time, had long since come of age during the postwar era; and early electronics achievements in the field had been succeeded by such developments as communications satellites that could make possible live intercontinental television broadcasts. One such satellite, *Early Bird,* was responsible for a historic transatlantic confrontation between General Eisenhower (who by then had also served his country as President) and another hero of World War II, Field Marshal Viscount Montgomery of Great Britain. The program highlighted films of the warfare in Europe, with recollections by the two leaders. General Eisenhower was interviewed in New York by the Columbia Broadcasting System; and Viscount Montgomery was interviewed by the British Broadcasting Corporation in London, where he was seated in what had served during the war as Prime Minister Winston Churchill's subterranean war room.

General Eisenhower's reflection that the promises of Allied victory, "the bright hopes we had then," had not been fulfilled, since war still existed in some parts of the world, led Viscount Montgomery to question "where we're going to finish up." Eisenhower, referring to the importance of controlling modern weapons, warned that if nuclear war ever broke out "it would be just Armageddon." Adding that "we are still striving" for peace, he asserted that "the free nations . . . must get themselves together to say: 'Listen. Freedom is the big thing we're talking about, liberty — not the petty little differences we have between ourselves.' "

There was particular note of the May 8 anniversary in 1970, the 25th anniversary of the return of peace to Europe — or "VE Day 25," as one newspaper headline called it. Veterans and civilians old enough to remember in the various Allied nations recalled the joyous occasion with enthusiasm; some visited the sites of wartime encounters, and there were special programs and acts of remembrance in various places. In the United States, publication of the first volumes of General Eisenhower's private papers by the Johns Hopkins University Press was timed to coincide with the anniversary.

Harry S. Truman's Birthday

The man who was thrust unexpectedly, while World War II still raged, into the presidency of the United States and leadership of the free world was born in Lamar, Missouri, on May 8, 1884. Just under 61 years later, he was catapulted into office by the sudden death of President Franklin D. Roosevelt on April 12, 1945.

Harry Truman was the first of three children born to John Anderson Truman and his wife, the former Martha Ellen Young. His grandparents, of English and Scottish descent, had come to Missouri from Kentucky four decades earlier. By giving him a middle initial only, his parents avoided the choice of naming him for grandfather Anderson Shippe Truman or grandfather Solomon Young. The initial — "S" — was frequently used without a period, often by Truman himself in signing his name with a continuous stroke. In his autobiographical books, however, he used "S." and he indicated that he had no preference between the two forms.

During Harry Truman's earliest years the family moved several times, living for five years on Missouri farms. In 1890 they settled in Independence, a suburb of Kansas City, in Missouri's Jackson County. The glasses worn by the shy Harry Truman prevented him from participating in most of the usual boyhood sports, and instead he became a voracious reader. His grandfather Young's tales of leading wagon trains and driving cattle across the unsettled West to California and Utah helped stimulate in him a tremendous appetite for historical information. Another source of later pleasure, though it inspired other boys' taunts at the time, was piano instruction, which his mother had insisted upon.

After a family financial setback ruled out college, and his poor eyesight kept him out of the US Military Academy at West Point, Harry Truman held several jobs. He was a bank clerk in Kansas City in 1906 when his father asked him to help manage the 600-acre Young farm near Grandview, Missouri. Although he accepted this responsibility, and managed the farm alone after his father's death in 1914, a farmer's life did not satisfy him completely, and he engaged in some business ventures on the side.

While he was in Kansas City his military ambitions had prompted him to join the National Guard. He served until 1911, and when his unit was called up in 1917, during World War I, he reenlisted. After attending the Fort Still (Oklahoma) Artillery School, Truman was shipped to France where, as a captain, he commanded Battery D of the 129th Field Artillery, 35th Division, American Expeditionary Force. He saw action at St. Mihiel, in the Meuse-Argonne offensive, and at Verdun. A skillful leader, he revealed an ability to win the respect and affection of even the most hard-bitten men. After the war he remained in the Army Reserve and was promoted through the ranks to colonel.

When he returned to Independence in 1919, he married Elizabeth (Bess) Wallace, whom he claimed to have loved since the day they met at a Sunday School picnic when she was five and he was six. In 1924 their only child, Mary Margaret, was born.

After his marriage, Truman had opened a men's clothing store in Kansas City with an army companion. The venture, successful at first, failed in the economic recession of 1921. Although his partner went through bankruptcy proceedings, Truman refused to do so, and over the next fifteen years he paid his creditors in full, a total of about $28,000.

John Truman had long been active in Democratic politics, and his son Harry became involved, as a matter of course, at an early age. While he was managing the Young farm, he was appointed to a local post as overseer of highways and later to the office of postmaster. The self-confidence he had gained from his wartime leadership increased his readiness for political office and in 1922 he announced his candidacy for the post of judge of the Jackson County Court, an administrative board of supervisors, despite its name. After several months of impressive campaigning he won the support of Thomas J. Pendergast, the boss of the Democratic machine that controlled politics in Kansas City and later in much of Missouri. Truman had been introduced to Tom Pendergast by the political leader's nephew, whom he had known in the army. Thus began a long political association — one for which Truman would later often be criticized, as allegations of the machine's corruption mounted. While Truman, a person of strong party and personal allegiance, maintained his loyalty to the Pendergasts through the years, he disclaimed any subservience to them and avoided any involvement in graft or corruption. Through his unquestioned personal integrity and his own vote-getting ability, he managed to maintain an independent position in relation to the organization.

Truman's attractiveness as a candidate was enhanced not only by his genial personality and reputation for honesty, but by his excellent war record and his wide contacts through active membership in the American Legion, the Army Reserve, the Baptist Church, and the Masons. These factors combined to give him wide support and he won the election for judge of the Jackson County Court.

The post was administrative, not judicial, but Truman felt that some knowledge of the law would be helpful to his career and so he began two years of evening study at the Kansas City School of Law. Although he was defeated for reelection in 1924, when he had strong opposition from the Ku Klux Klan as well as from a rival Democratic faction, he was a successful candidate in 1926, and again in 1930, for presiding judge of the county court (which included Kansas City in its jurisdiction). His years of service in these county court posts, which involved the supervision of all county roads and public buildings, demonstrated his flair for efficiency and his honesty in handling the large budget.

Having developed a solid political base by 1934, Truman asked support for a higher position from Tom Pendergast — who proposed him for nomination to the US Senate. After a hard fight in the Democratic primary, Truman won election easily, despite predictions that he would be a puppet of the machine. In his campaign, he had endorsed the New Deal policies of President Franklin Delano Roosevelt.

During his first term as senator, Truman worked quietly and hard. He became knowledgeable in the field of transportation and was instrumental in the drafting of the Civil Aeronautics Act of 1938 and the Transportation Act of 1940. Montana's Burton K. Wheeler, chairman of the Senate's Interstate Commerce Committee, of which Truman was a member, taught him how to conduct an investigation. When the names of Missouri politicians surfaced during the probe into railroad financing that preceded formulation of the transportation act, Pendergast was among those who put pressure upon subcommittee chairman Truman. Truman responded by instructing committee investigators to treat the investigation like all others. However, he fought strenuously — though unsuccessfully — in the Senate to prevent reappointment of a US district attorney for western Missouri who had won election-fraud convictions against 35 ward leaders of the Pendergast organization.

As Truman's Senate term neared its end in 1940, Pendergast was in jail, his machine had collapsed, and some 47,000 names fraudulently included on Missouri voting lists had been removed. Truman was criticized for his association with the machine; and he had not attracted favorable notice from President Roosevelt, whose New Deal program he had staunchly supported. These handicaps notwithstanding, Truman characteristically decided to make every effort to win renomination. When two anti-Pendergast candidates joined the race, they succeeded in canceling each other out and Truman again walked off with the Democratic nomination. He won election again, but by a considerably slimmer margin than in 1934.

After personally investigating reports that graft and waste were rampant in the growing national defense program — including allegations of favoritism in the awarding of defense contracts in his home state — an outraged Truman, early in his second term, introduced a bill to establish a Senate watchdog committee. The Special Committee to Investigate Contracts under the national defense program was created in March 1941 with Truman as chairman. The wide-ranging Truman committee, noted for its courage and impartiality, exposed many forms and areas of corruption and waste, propelling its chairman into national prominence. It was credited with saving the government hundreds of millions of dollars during World War II.

When President Roosevelt decided to run for a fourth term in 1944, his Vice President, Henry A. Wallace, had lost considerable support from Democrats who thought him too liberal. Roosevelt, anxious to replace him with a candidate who was backed by all factions of the party, turned to the well-liked and respected Truman — who would rather have continued the Senate work he found so satisfying. In addition to chairing that body's Truman committee, he also was serving on six others, including the important Appropriations, Military Affairs, and Interstate Commerce committees.

The electorate returned Roosevelt to office, and he and Truman were installed the following January. Roosevelt did not confide in the new Vice President, however, or prepare him in any way for the presidency.

Less than three months later, both Truman and the nation were stunned by Roosevelt's sudden death from a cerebral hemorrhage on April 12, 1945. Harry S. Truman thus became the 33rd President of the United States and the first ever to accede to the office in wartime. His sense of awe of the presidency, and his feeling of unpreparedness, found expression when he said to a group of reporters, "Boys, if you ever pray, pray for me now."

Following in the footsteps of a strong and popular Chief Executive, Truman immediately indicated that he would adhere to Roosevelt's policies and that he wanted to retain his cabinet and advisers (whose knowledge of secret wartime undertakings he would particularly need). He made it equally clear, however, that he would make his own decisions.

Even before Roosevelt's death the wartime alliance among Britain, the Soviet Union, and the United States was suffering strain, as the Russians evidenced a determination to dominate Eastern Europe, despite agreements guaranteeing people in formerly Axis-occupied lands the freedom to choose their own governments. President Truman, attending the United Nations' founding conference in San Francisco on April 25, bluntly reproached Soviet Foreign Minister Vyacheslav Molotov on this matter.

The war was waged according to plans put into effect before Roosevelt's death, and on May 8 Germany surrendered to the Allies, effectively ending the war in Europe. In the Far East, however, the war continued and Truman was called upon to make a decision of surpassing importance. On April 25 he had learned for the first time, from Secretary of War Henry L. Stimson, that the United States was developing the atomic bomb, a weapon judged capable of causing unprecedented devastation. The question was whether this weapon should be used against Japan; Truman made the critical decision that it should, believing that its use would shorten the war and save as many as a million lives.

Truman met at Potsdam, Germany, with British Prime Minister Winston Churchill (and his successor, Clement Attlee) and Soviet Premier Joseph Stalin during the last half of July. Most of the agreements at the Potsdam Conference concerned Europe, the postwar occupation, and control of Germany. Machinery was set up for the formulation of peace treaties, and Japan was given an unconditional surrender ultimatum.

The first atomic bomb was dropped on August 6 (local time) on the Japanese city of Hiroshima (see August 5), and three days later Nagasaki was bombed. The death toll from the two strikes was more than 100,000; damage was catastrophic, and casualties from radiation poisoning continued for years afterward. On August 8, meanwhile, the Soviet Union had joined the war against the badly shaken Japanese. On August 14, 1945, Japan surrendered. The peace treaty formally ending World War II in the Pacific was signed early the next month (see September 2.)

Rather than return to its earlier isolationist stance, the United States after World War II determined to work toward the prevention of any future holocausts. The new awareness of the awful potentialities of atomic warfare and worldwide evidence of other war-wrought suffering were reason enough for the nation's major postwar emphasis on foreign policy. But additional impetus came from the Soviet Union's increasing attempts to extend its influence in Europe and the Middle East, and a growing US resolve to frustrate them. The era of the cold war had begun.

At first, Truman's response to Soviet aggression seemed confined to ineffective verbal weapons. However, on learning in early 1947 that Great Britain could no longer afford to provide economic and military aid to Greece and Turkey — both struggling to remain free of Communist domination — he seized the opportunity to propose American aid, not only for those two countries but for use anywhere "to support free peoples who are resisting attempted subjugation by armed minorities or by outside pressures." This new policy designed to contain Soviet expansion and halt the spread of communism became known as the Truman Doctrine.

The highly successful Marshall Plan, suggested by Secretary of State George C. Marshall in June 1947, was an outgrowth of this policy. Officially known as the European Recovery Program, it dispensed some $12.5 billion during its nearly four years of existence (1948–1951), contributing importantly toward rebuilding warshattered economies in Western Europe, where it also was credited with preventing Communist takeovers. Participation in the plan had also been offered to, but rejected by, the Soviet Union and its Eastern European satellites. Distrustfully the Soviets had also rejected, in 1946, an American plan to turn over control of atomic energy to the United Nations.

The diplomatic and political cold war between the Soviet Union and its satellites on the one hand, and the Western nations on the other, had many fronts. In Germany the lack of agreement among the former Allies prevented progress toward a peace settlement. The Western occupying powers — the United States, Great Britain, and France — therefore began making plans, with German approval, to unite the sectors under their control. In hopes of thwarting their plans, the Soviet Union in June 1948 blockaded all land routes to West Berlin, which was also under the control of the three Western powers but completely surrounded by the Soviet occupation zone of Germany. President Truman, who long before had concluded that the Russians respected only force, would not consider abandoning the city to them. He immediately instituted an airlift that, with British participation, brought in needed provisions for almost a year — until the Soviets withdrew the blockade.

During his first term as President, Truman led the United States into a relationship with Europe that went far beyond any previous peacetime involvement. In this he had bipartisan backing. In domestic affairs, however, he fared less well, despite the fact that the Democrats controlled Congress during most of his first two years in office. What later became known as his Fair Deal policies, begun in 1945, encountered opposition from a bloc of Republicans and southern Democrats similar to that which had defeated much of President Roosevelt's New Deal legislation, of which the Truman program was a continuation and extension.

Truman was not a hard-to-reach President. His relations with the press were very good. He enjoyed warm camaraderie and occasionally indulged his penchant for playing practical jokes on his family and friends. His well-known bluntness could have a sharp tone, however, as Dean Acheson, secretary of state in Truman's second term, indicated in commenting on the frequent need to issue "clarifications" after some of the President's press conference remarks.

Although Truman had initially asked Roosevelt's cabinet to remain, he soon began to surround himself with people of his own choosing. Within his first few months in office, he named six new cabinet members.

One notable cabinet replacement was that of Henry A. Wallace, in September 1946. Wallace, who had been appointed secretary of commerce by Roosevelt, opposed the United States' postwar hard-line policy toward the Soviet Union. When he publicly stated his opposition, the President asked for his resignation — a move that alienated liberals.

Trying to steer the country on a course that would avoid both inflation and recession as the booming wartime economy underwent reconversion to peacetime activities was one of Truman's major concerns. In this connection he urged continuation of price controls, a higher minimum wage, increased unemployment benefits, expanded Social Security coverage, national health insurance, large-scale federal subsidies for housing, and a full-employment plan. He also advocated civil rights guarantees and job rights for blacks, a federal antilynching law, abolition of the poll tax, and universal military training. Unification of the three branches of the armed forces was one of many recommendations by a commission, headed by former President Herbert Hoover, that Truman had appointed to study the organization of the executive branch of the federal government. In 1947 Congress approved the plan and the forces were subsequently integrated under a Department of Defense. Beyond that, the legislature turned an almost completely deaf ear to the President's proposals. Health and civil rights legislation of the type he recommended was not enacted until almost two decades later. He succeeded, however, in bringing about the desegregation of the armed forces by executive order in 1948, and he directed that steps be taken to end discrimination in the federal civil service.

Considered friendly to labor when he assumed office, Truman nevertheless acted vigorously when he thought union demands were excessive. Strikes were numerous in the postwar period, interfering considerably with economic reconversion. In response, Truman took over struck industries if he deemed their shutdown a threat to the public interest. He took such action when a serious rail strike loomed in the spring of 1946 and also called on Congress to authorize the drafting of anyone who refused to work in

an industry that had been seized. Although Congress denied his request, the strike did not materialize. The same year, Truman also took over the coal mines, in a battle with the powerful union leader John L. Lewis of the United Mine Workers, and prevailed again. Lewis and the union were fined heavily for ignoring a court injunction forbidding a strike. Truman vetoed the Taft-Hartley Act of 1947, which banned the closed shop and placed other restraints on labor unions, but Congress overrode his veto.

By the next election year, 1948, not only labor but many other segments of the public were unhappy either with the postwar inflation or with one or another of Truman's domestic policies. Convinced that the President could not be reelected, Democratic party leaders tried to persuade General Dwight D. Eisenhower to let his name be placed in nomination for the candidacy. When Eisenhower refused, the party felt it had no other choice but Truman.

During the campaign that followed, almost every politician and pollster, Republican and Democrat, believed Truman to be a sure loser. The strong civil rights plank in the party platform had alienated the traditionally Democratic South, and Governor J. Strom Thurmond of South Carolina drew considerable support there as presidential nominee of the new States' Rights ("Dixiecrat") Party. Democratic strength was lost also in the large northern and western cities to Henry A. Wallace on the ticket of the Progressive Party, which had been newly formed by discontented liberals.

Almost alone, Truman believed he could get through to the people with his message. He campaigned by riding trains nearly 32,000 miles across the nation, addressing friendly crowds from back platforms at whistle-stops. In his extemporaneous, hard-hitting talks, which became known as his "give 'em hell" speeches, he presented himself as the defender of Roosevelt's New Deal policies and disclaimed responsibility for the legislative failures of what he called the "do-nothing" Republican-controlled 80th Congress.

In contrast with Truman, whose efforts were unsparing and vigorous, the Republican candidate, New York's Governor Thomas E. Dewey, appeared overconfident and unwilling to discuss the issues. Election night was unforgettable. Accepting Dewey's victory as a foregone conclusion, an early edition of the next day's Chicago *Tribune* proclaimed in a banner headline, "Dewey Defeats Truman." Truman relished that headline for years to come, for morning showed him to be unquestionably the winner with more than 24.1 million votes to fewer than 22 million for Dewey. The electoral college vote was 303 to 189. Thurmond and Wallace had received somewhat over a million votes each.

The President immediately renewed his efforts to secure adoption of his Fair Deal programs. In this he was no more successful than he had been during his first term. Although returned to Democratic control, Congress in reality was again dominated by an unsympathetic coalition of Republicans and southern Democrats. In 1950 involvement in the Korean conflict — a state of undeclared war — brought about financial strains and economic controls that were to be additional obstacles in the path of Truman's domestic goals.

Meanwhile, Russia's increasing influence in Eastern Europe greatly concerned the West. A major accomplishment during Truman's second term was the signing in 1949 of the North Atlantic Treaty and the creation of the North Atlantic Treaty Organization (NATO) to carry out the treaty's objectives of cooperation and collective self-defense among the United States, Canada, and Western European signatories. This was the first military pact ever entered into by the United States in peacetime. Continuing to support Truman's foreign policy, Congress passed the Mutual Defense Assistance Act of 1949 to provide large amounts of military aid to NATO members and other friendly nations.

Also in 1949, much angry criticism was directed against Truman administration policy when the Nationalist Chinese, under Generalissimo Chiang Kai-shek, lost control of the mainland to Communists after years of conflict. In a step debated long afterwards, most US aid to the Chinese Nationalists had been withdrawn earlier in the year, after a Truman-appointed commission had failed in its efforts to reconcile the two sides and reported that a Communist victory over the corruption-plagued Nationalist regime was inevitable.

Elsewhere on the international scene, Truman carried the ideas exemplified by the Marshall Plan a step further by proposing (as one recommendation in his 1949 inaugural address) that the United States provide economic assistance for underdeveloped countries. This Point Four program was carried out on a large scale in Latin America, Africa, and Asia.

A source of considerable national unrest, and one of Truman's most vexing concerns, was the issue of "Communists in government," which reached a head in 1950. In a case that the President had described as a "red herring," a federal court ruled that the former State Department official Alger Hiss had committed perjury when he denied that he had conducted espionage for the Soviet Union in the 1930s. Further, after the Soviet Union surprised the West by detonating

its first atomic bomb in late 1949, it was learned that Soviet spies had acquired US atomic secrets during World War II. And it was alleged — in unsubstantiated charges by Republican Senator Joseph R. McCarthy of Wisconsin, who headed a Senate investigative committee — that the government was currently riddled with subversives. The issues became even more sensitive when the North Korean Communists invaded South Korea in June 1950 (see June 25), involving the United Nations and the United States in conflict there. The widespread unease weakened public confidence in Truman. He had consented to various security measures, but he refused to sign the McCarran Internal Security bill, which he felt could be used against the innocent as well as the guilty. He cited his belief that in a free country the law is designed to "punish men for the crimes they commit, but never for the opinions they have." The bill became law despite his veto, but the Supreme Court subsequently ruled many of its provisions unconstitutional.

When Communist North Korean forces equipped by the Soviet Union crossed the 38th Parallel to invade South Korea on June 25, Truman promptly called for a special session of the United Nations Security Council (which, as it happened, the Soviet Union was boycotting at the time). The Security Council branded the action unprovoked aggression and requested that UN members aid South Korea, and Truman ordered US forces into action under General Douglas MacArthur — a decision he later called the most difficult of his presidency. One reason for his decision was his fear that the fledgling United Nations, whose strongest free-world member was the United States, would be severely weakened if it was unable to repel this flagrant aggression. Another consideration was the belief that the Communists were testing, in Korea, the willingness of the United States to fulfill the promises it had made through the Truman Doctrine and various collective-security treaties. Failure to act, the President believed, would encourage future Communist encroachment in the Middle East and Western Europe, and weaken the confidence of free-world nations that the United States could be relied upon to honor its commitments to them.

The US involvement in Korea, never formalized by a congressional declaration of war, was viewed as a "police action," with the President committing military forces to action on his authority as Commander in Chief. To provide sufficient troops, Congress later authorized the first peacetime military draft. Other countries also sent forces, which were unified with those of the United States under General MacArthur.

After being pushed to the southern tip of

the country, UN forces made a daring landing at Inchon, in the northernmost part of South Korea, near the capital city of Seoul, in September. Maintaining their powerful offensive, by late 1950 they had driven the invaders far back into North Korea, advancing — despite warnings from Communist China — almost to the Chinese border. On November 26 the Chinese Communists entered the battle in strength and, joining the North Koreans, pushed the UN forces back, driving into South Korea and recapturing Seoul.

With the Chinese intervention, President Truman was more concerned than ever about the possibility that the hostilities would precipitate a third world war and he directed his policy toward containing the conflict but pursuing the goal of restoring freedom to South Korea. However, General MacArthur, though aware of the official US stand, continued to urge publicly that UN forces bomb air bases in China. Because of his insubordination, and in order to ensure that US policy be clearly understood, Truman took the controversial step of removing the venerated MacArthur from his command in April 1951 and replacing him with General Matthew B. Ridgway.

Meanwhile, the UN and South Korean forces had battled their way back to retake Seoul and by late spring the battlefront had stabilized in the area around the 38th Parallel. In an atmosphere of stalemate, truce negotiations began in July 1951, but were not completed until two years later, after Truman's term of office had ended.

Claiming wartime emergency authority, Truman in 1952 seized the steel mills to forestall a strike when the steel companies refused to comply with a Wage Mediation Board wage increase without a price increase. The seizure was declared unconstitutional, however, and the strike that followed was ended only when the President reluctantly agreed to a price increase.

Meanwhile, congressional charges of maladministration and corruption had been made against officials in several government agencies and against some White House aides. Truman, with his characteristic loyalty, disbelieved or ignored the charges, some involving old friends, for a considerable time before finally dismissing a number of persons and ordering his attorney general to take proper additional steps. Instead, the latter, who evidently feared political repercussions for the Democrats, acted to hinder any investigation, and was dismissed by the President in April 1952. The whole affair was damaging to Truman.

A brazen but unsuccessful attempt to assassinate the President had been made on November 1, 1950, by two Puerto Rican nationalists who tried to storm the presidential residence in broad daylight. The President was not injured, but one terrorist and a Secret Service man were killed and several others wounded in the assault.

The Trumans had been living in Blair House, across the street from the White House, since discovering in 1948 that the White House needed immediate structural renovation. (One early indication had come when a piano belonging to the President's daughter, Margaret, went through the floor of her sitting room.) The Trumans were a close family, with the President's great affection for his wife and daughter unconcealed. As First Lady, Bess Truman stayed in the background, but he discussed public affairs with her and sought her opinions. Margaret Truman pursued a career as a singer, and when a critic was uncomplimentary, the President lashed out at him in a famous angry letter.

The 22nd Amendment to the Constitution, ratified in 1951 (see February 27), limited presidential terms to two, but specifically exempted Truman. Nevertheless, he announced in March 1952 his decision not to seek another term. At the time, the country's continuing domestic problems, and widespread unhappiness with the stalemate in Korea, had reduced his popularity to a low level.

Never having had "the complex of being a big shot," as he put it, Truman found the transition from major world figure to private citizen of Independence, Missouri, relatively easy. With his zest for living, his consuming interest in politics, and his fund of historical knowledge, he followed domestic and world affairs closely. Even former critics of some of his policies held him in high regard, and there was wide interest in his views on current happenings — as evidenced by the familiar scene of reporters in search of a quote, trying to keep up with him on his habitual 6:30 A.M. walks. He also spoke out in other ways, writing occasional newspaper columns; discussing the decisions of his presidential years in a series of 26 television documentaries; speaking at Democratic rallies; and campaigning for Democratic candidates. On his travels, he was quickly recognized, even when he attempted to remain incognito.

Offered lucrative positions after he left office, Truman declined, saying he would do nothing to commercialize the prestige and dignity of the presidency. Instead he set a goal for the rest of his life: "teaching young people the meaning of democracy as exemplified in the Republic of the United States." To this end he addressed college and university audiences, held discussions with students, and worked energetically at arranging his presidential papers so that they would be readily available to scholars.

When the city of Independence offered to provide land for a library to house these and other materials pertaining to the presidency, Truman embarked on a lecture tour to help raise, from private subscriptions, the $1,750,000 needed for its construction. After the library was completed in 1957, Truman turned it over to the National Archives and Records Service of the federal government, which administers it. He himself worked there on five or more days a week and took particular pleasure in the many groups of schoolchildren who visited the library and were enthralled by the talks he gave and his eagerness to answer their questions. In addition he wrote two volumes of memoirs, *Year of Decisions* (1955) and *Years of Trial and Hope* (1956); later he wrote a book about his post presidential activities, *Mr. Citizen* (1960).

Truman's 80th birthday, in 1964, was the occasion for much celebration. The public festivities began in Independence, where the nation's leaders gathered to give him a luncheon and thank him for the Point Four program and for his aid to agriculture. A large birthday party in Kansas City followed, as did a trip to Washington, D.C. There he spoke to the National Press Club and attended a luncheon given for him by the Supreme Court and a dinner for 300 by his Senate colleagues. On his birthday he was invited to the Senate, where 27 Democrats and Republicans rose to pay tribute to him.

Shortly before his birthday, he had represented the United States at the funeral of King Paul of Greece — a country whose citizens had unveiled a statue of Truman in Athens the previous year. Other honors accorded the former President for his contributions to peace and freedom included the Freedom House award in 1965 and the naming of the Harry S. Truman Center for the Advancement of Peace, which was opened at Hebrew University in Jerusalem in 1966.

Truman was quoted as saying he expected to live to be 90, and he almost did. Death came to the spirited former President in a Kansas City hospital on December 26, 1972, at the age of 88. By then the political differences of the past had dimmed with time. He was remembered for his integrity, courage, decisiveness, vigor, warmth, and fairness — and also for his willingness to accept responsibility without trying to shift blame to others, as reflected in the famous sign on his White House desk: "The buck stops here." Truman's forthrightness had made him believable and he was seen as having been both self-confident enough and unpretentious enough not to care unduly how others regarded him. "I did what had to be done," he had said. "I don't care a hoot what history says about me."

In a survey made public in 1962, seventy-five leading American historians ranked Truman ninth in "greatness" among Presidents of the United States, an appraisal bestowed primarily for his conduct of foreign affairs. On his death, tributes poured in from the leaders and people of the world. Winston Churchill had told Truman directly, "I must confess, sir . . . [that since the death of Roosevelt] you, more than any other man, have saved Western civilization."

The funeral plans drawn up by the military (which is responsible for the funerals of former Presidents) were revised at Truman's death by his family in order to put less strain on his 87-year-old-widow. Truman himself had rejected any idea of lying in state in Washington. Instead of a full state funeral, which encompasses four or five days, a modified state funeral was held in Independence. On December 27 Truman's body was accorded military honors as it was taken by motorcade along a one-and-a-half-mile route from the funeral parlor to the Truman Library, where the coffin, attended by an honor guard, was placed in the main lobby. President and Mrs. Richard M. Nixon and former President and Mrs. Lyndon B. Johnson paid their respects at the bier, and then the library was opened for 20 hours of public viewing. During this period, which ran through the night, an estimated 75,000 persons passed the coffin.

A short funeral service was conducted the following day in the auditorium of the library. As Truman had requested, there were no eulogies. Both the service and the burial were private. The approximately 250 invited guests included mostly hometown friends, and some close political friends. The former President was buried in the spot he had chosen, near his office window at the rear of the library. A single slab covers the grave and the adjacent area, which is reserved for his wife's grave. In accordance with Truman's instructions, the inscription consists only of a listing of important dates in his life, including the terms of the public offices he held. December 28 was declared a day of national mourning by President Nixon, and many memorial services were held, in houses of worship and in government buildings across the country. On January 5 a memorial service held in the National Cathedral in Washington, D.C., was attended by dignitaries of the United States and foreign nations.

The following week the city council of Independence established the Harry S. Truman Public Service Award to be conferred on the local, state, or national public servant deemed to best exhibit the qualities that distinguished Truman in his years of public service. The award is presented annually on December 26, the anniversary of his death.

In May 1973, at the first Kansas City birthday party in Truman's honor (given annually), the first Harry S. Truman Good Neighbor Award was conferred on former Chief Justice of the United States Earl Warren. Another ceremony on May 8, 1973, at the Truman Library, initiated the sale of an eight-cent postal stamp bearing the President's likeness. The Truman Library is also the scene of a birthday celebration still held each year.

There are several buildings that are associated with the former Chief Executive. Truman's favorite spot during his presidential years was Key West, Florida; and the house in which he stayed (the Little White House), now the residence of the commander of the Key West Naval Base, has on occasion been open to the public as part of a tour of historic homes and gardens.

In Lamar, Missouri, the small white frame house in which Truman was born in 1884 has been historically restored by the Missouri State Park Board. Dedicated on April 19, 1959, as the Harry S. Truman Birthplace State Historic Site, it attracts more than 30,000 visitors each year. It is located at the junction of US 71 and 160 (1009 Truman Avenue, at 11th Street), 125 miles south of Kansas City.

A large part of the family farm near Grandview, Missouri (immediately south of Kansas City), which Truman worked before World War I, is now occupied by a shopping center named Truman Corners (just off US 71). On its promenade is a plaque detailing the history of the farm. The farmhouse, which is privately owned, has been only slightly altered.

From the time of Truman's marriage in 1919 to Bess Wallace, their home was a 14-room white Victorian house at 219 North Delaware Street in Independence, which had belonged to the Wallace family. Mrs. Truman continued to live there after her husband's death. The house is not open to the public. After Truman's presidency, the road that runs beside the house (and on into Kansas City) was renamed Truman Road, and a number of local businesses began to use the former President's first or last name — a practice Truman discouraged. However, toward the end of his life he did permit his name to be used for the new Harry S. Truman Sports Complex in Kansas City, comprising the Royals (baseball) Stadium and Arrowhead (football) Stadium.

Near the courthouse in Independence stands an equestrian statue of President Andrew Jackson, Truman's idol and the man for whom Jackson County was named, commissioned by Truman when he was a county judge. Visitors also can enjoy the well-planned county park system, which took shape under Truman's supervision.

But the pride and joy of Truman's post presidential years, and of his hometown still, is the Harry S. Truman Library. Located at Route 24 and Delaware Street, eight blocks from the Truman home, it is visited by more than 300,000 persons annually. A boomerang-shaped, one-story structure of white stone and glass, overlooking a park, the library was visualized by Truman as not only housing his own papers and mementos, but placing primary emphasis on the presidency in general, so that citizens might become better informed about the role of the President in the United States system of government.

Entering the main lobby, visitors see Thomas Hart Benton's notable mural of westward-bound pioneers striking out from Independence along the Santa Fe and Oregon trails. The Truman Library has three sections: the library proper, the museum, and the area used by Truman for his offices and storerooms. Truman's private office, visible through a window from the courtyard, is being kept just as it was while he was alive. Scholars and researchers have access, by special arrangement, to the library's more than 10 million pages of documents, 40,000 books, 60,000 photographs, and audio-visual materials, including microfilms of almost all the presidential papers of all the Presidents contained in the Library of Congress.

One of the exhibits in the museum, which is open to the public, is a replica of Truman's White House office. In a recording that visitors can play, Truman describes the various items and furnishings in the room. The building's small auditorium was the scene of President Johnson's 1965 signing of the Medicare bill (in the presence of Truman, whom he called its father), and of what were among Truman's most enjoyable hours, his question-and-answer sessions with schoolchildren. Children can still hear his answers to questions about the government and be inspired to take an active interest in politics by viewing a film he made for that purpose.

The Presidential Room, containing the large round table used at the United Nations founding conference in 1945, displays original documents relating to each of the Presidents. Other rooms and galleries contain a wide variety of memorabilia and exhibits, among them the Japanese surrender document that officially concluded World War II; cartoons satirizing Truman and his administration; a map showing all the stops on his 1948 whistle-stop campaign; gifts from foreign governments; and a rare numismatic collection.

To provide financial assistance to scholars who are researching the presidency or his administration, Truman established the Harry S. Truman Library Institute for National and International Affairs. He turned over most of his lecture fees to the institute, and at the time of his death many memorial contributions were received.

Also of interest are the Truman Library grounds. Situated there are a replica of the Liberty Bell, given by France; an eternal flame presented by the American Legion; and a sapling from a magnolia tree said to have been planted on the White House grounds by President Andrew Jackson.

A memorial service honoring President Truman is held annually on May 8, the anniversary of his birth, at his gravesite in the library's courtyard. And each year on July 4 the city of Independence officially celebrates the nation's independence on the grounds of the Truman Library.

In order to preserve the older part of Independence as Truman knew it during his lifetime, the Harry S. Truman Historic District has been established. It takes in roughly the area from his home on North Delaware Street to the Truman Library.

MAY 9

John Brown's Birthday

John Brown, a radical advocate of the abolition of slavery in the United States, was born at Torrington, Connecticut, on May 9, 1800. His father, Owen Brown, was an abolitionist and helped black slaves escape to freedom in the North or in Canada by means of the Underground Railroad. John Brown's mother, Ruth Mills Brown, died when he was eight years old. Brown spent his boyhood in Hudson, Ohio. He had little formal education — later in life he said that to him school meant confinement and restraint — but he liked to read, though he loved roaming in the wilderness even more.

Brown took up both his father's migratory habits and his trade as a tanner. When he was 20 Brown married Dianthe Lusk; they had seven children. In 1825 the family settled in Richmond, Pennsylvania, setting up a tannery and an Underground Railroad station. This was the first of ten migrations, which took Brown through Connecticut, New York, and Ohio before he finally went to Kansas. En route, he engaged in many different kinds of businesses — working in tanneries, land speculating, sheep raising, and farming — but he was unsuccessful in all of them. In 1831 his wife died and shortly afterwards Brown remarried. His second wife, the former Mary Anne Day, bore him 13 more children. Brown's continued economic failures, coupled with the problems of supporting an enormous family, led him in 1849 to go to North Elba, near what is now Lake Placid, New York.

There, on land donated by a wealthy New York abolitionist, a free black farming community had been established. Brown stayed for two years, trying to help the community.

In 1855 five of Brown's sons went to Kansas to establish a homestead and to help win the territory for freedom. A few months after his sons' arrival in Kansas, Brown responded to their plea for help in fighting the proslavery forces from neighboring Missouri, and joined them at the Osawatomie colony. He soon became the leader of the antislavery men, as well as the captain of the local militia. The sack of the town of Lawrence on May 24, 1856, by proslavery men helped turn the cause of "free soil" into a crusade and stimulated Brown, who believed he was following the will of God, to retaliate. Three days later he led a small group of men on a raid to Pottawatomie, where they killed five proslavery men. In revenge, a large group of proslavery men from Missouri sacked and burned Osawatomie on August 30. The border warfare continued until it was finally suppressed by federal troops in mid-September. (See also Kansas Day, January 29.)

The reputation "Old Osawatomie" Brown acquired in Kansas made him a terror to all proslavery men and a hero to many abolitionists. Ralph Waldo Emerson called him "a pure idealist of artless goodness." When Brown returned to the North from Kansas in 1856, he met the abolitionists of the Massachusetts State Kansas Committee who had been supplying him and other Free-Soilers with arms, supplies, and money. Brown by this time had become obsessed with the cause of abolition and the need to free the slaves. In 1858 he returned to Kansas and made a daring raid on a Missouri plantation, liberating 11 slaves. Eluding his pursuers, he guided the slaves safely to Canada.

That year, with the financial and moral encouragement of many abolitionists, including Frederick Douglass, Brown held a convention in Canada — in Chatham, Ontario — disclosing his plans to liberate the slaves by setting up a free state in the mountains of Virginia to which the slaves could flee. The convention adopted a provisional constitution for the state and named Brown commander in chief.

Brown proceeded to put his plan into effect by renting a farm across the river from Harpers Ferry, Virginia (now West Virginia). There he gathered a small group of men, black and white, and on the night of October 16, 1859, he crossed the river and seized the federal armory and rifle works. A small group of his men went to nearby Charlestown, Virginia (now Charles Town, West Virginia), to seize hostages and recruit slaves. Then Brown and his followers retreated into the brick fire-engine house in the armory compound. By morning the news of the raid had spread and 17 militia companies were blocking the roads to any escape.

Brown and his men managed to fight off the militia. However, when 90 marines under the command of Robert E. Lee attacked the engine house, the abolitionists were overcome. Brown was captured fighting next to the bodies of his two dead sons.

He was tried in a Virginia court at Charlestown and convicted of "treason and of conspiring and advising with slaves and others to rebel, and of murder in the first degree." Despite 17 affidavits attesting that Brown was insane (as his mother had been), Governor Henry A. Wise decided not to have Brown examined, and the question of Brown's sanity remains a matter of historical debate. He was sentenced to death and hanged at Charlestown on December 2, 1859.

Although the expected slave uprising never occurred after the signal at Harpers Ferry, Brown's behavior during his trial enhanced his stature among abolitionists. He consistently maintained that he was an instrument in God's hands and he refused to be held accountable to anyone but his Maker for his mission to free the slaves. Brown accepted his death sentence with a confident declaration: "I cannot now better serve the cause I love . . . than to die for it."

The passions aroused by Brown's raid and his death even more sharply divided antislavery and proslavery antagonists. The former glorified him as a martyr to the cause of human freedom, while the latter vilified him as a common assassin. When the Civil War broke out, the memory of John Brown was kept alive by Northern troops who marched into battle singing: "John Brown's body lies a-mouldering in the grave but his soul goes marching on."

In 1906, almost 50 years after the well-remembered raid, the spirit of "Old John Brown" was evoked by 100 men and women who gathered at Harpers Ferry at the birth of the civil rights movement. Led by W. E. B. Du Bois, the black scholar and writer, the movement had begun a year before at a secret meeting at Niagara Falls. Abandoning secrecy, the group met at Harpers Ferry and, in an "Address to the Nation," written by Du Bois, clearly enunciated its demands. The address was both a declaration of independence from Booker T. Washington and his policies of compromise and a program for the future: "We claim for ourselves every single right that belongs to a freeborn American . . . and until we get these rights we will never cease to protest and assail the ears of America. . . ." Three years later the Niagara mili-

tants joined with a larger group of men and women to found the National Association for the Advancement of Colored People (NAACP), which has worked vigorously since its inception on behalf of equality.

John Brown has always been regarded by black Americans as a great national hero. In 1935, on the anniversary of his death, a group dedicated a monument to him at what is now known as John Brown's Farm (where he is buried), at North Elba, New York. (North Elba is three miles south of Lake Placid, off New York Route 73.) The monument is of heroic size and represents Brown with his arms about the shoulders of a black youth. In 1965 Malcolm X, the militant Black Muslim leader, told white Americans that "if you are for . . . our people — then you have got to be willing to do as Old John Brown did."

Today Harpers Ferry National Historical Park stands as a monument to the memory of John Brown. White flagstones mark the spot where the arsenal stood. The brick engine house in which Brown and his followers held out has been rebuilt. It is located, appropriately, on the grounds of what was formerly Storer College, one of the first black colleges in the United States. (It is now the Mather Training Center, operated by the National Park Service.)

In the John Brown Memorial Park at Osawatomie, Kansas, the cabin Brown occupied, which served as an Underground Railroad station during the Civil War, is still standing, as is a life-size statue of Brown dedicated in 1910 by Theodore Roosevelt. It is inscribed: "John Brown of Kansas, he dared begin; he lost, but losing won."

Feast of St. Christopher

The Feast of St. Christopher is celebrated on May 9 by Eastern Orthodox churches using the Gregorian (New Style) calendar. However, in those Eastern Orthodox churches that still adhere to the Julian (Old Style) calendar, the observance is 13 days later, on May 22. The legends and the few known facts of the life of the saint are set forth in the article listed under July 25, the date on which St. Christopher is commemorated by some members of Roman Catholic churches in the West.

The Memphis Cotton Carnival

This is a movable event. See note on page xxvi.

The Cotton Carnival, held annually during the second week of May, is the biggest event of the year in Memphis, Tennessee, and one of the more colorful celebrations in the country. Hundreds of thousands of people attend the carnival, mostly from Tennessee, Mississippi, and Arkansas, but also from numerous other states and countries. They come to be dazzled by the spectacular fireworks displays, the pomp, pageantry, and parades, and they listen to the music, watch or join contests, tour the city, and enter into the citywide fair, which has one of the world's largest midways.

With all its frivolity and gaiety, the Cotton Carnival has a specific purpose: to promote cotton and the land of cotton. More than one-third of the nation's cotton crop is bought or sold in Memphis. The days of revelry are sponsored by the Memphis Cotton Carnival Association, a nonprofit civic organization, with the cooperation of state, county, and city departments, and of fraternal and other clubs in Memphis. One of these is the Crown and Sceptre Society, an organization of sponsors and contributors founded to help finance the lavish carnival. Other local societies – the Memphi, the Osiris, Ra-Met, Sphinx, and Shelbi – also stand ready to provide financial aid for the carnival.

Each year a completely different theme is used for the Memphis Cotton Carnival. The schedule of events varies from time to time, but in recent years – when the carnival has extended over eight or nine days, in contrast to the earlier five – the pattern has been more or less as follows:

A month before the actual carnival dates, precarnival events get under way with the coronation of King Cotton and the queen, who act as king and queen of the carnival. The royal pair is chosen by a special committee and their names are kept secret until just before their coronation. Their royal court includes princesses, ladies-in-waiting, and ladies of the realm – each representing a town in the mid-South, although some have come from as far away as Texas and Florida. Together with their escorts, the royal guardsmen and young pages, they comprise a court of 200. Precarnival happenings build up the spirit of carnival for a full month.

Carnival week itself begins on a Saturday. The Carnival Sports Classic events, among which are a hot-air balloon race, softball and tennis tournaments, a sailing regatta, sports-car and powerboat (including hydroplane) races, pistol matches, and bicycling and jogging competitions, get off to a good start on the weekend. Some of the sporting events run straight through the week. Saturday is also the occasion for the first of carnival week's popular horse shows, both amateur and professional.

What might be called the official ceremonial opening of the carnival is the Great River Pageant, three hours of entertainment and spectacle on Saturday evening. The highlight is a waterborne, regal procession that begins at dusk and lasts for perhaps 45 minutes. It consists of a flotilla of gaily decorated and brilliantly illuminated barges carrying the king, queen, and royal court, gliding across the Mississippi River into the port of Memphis. A crowd of approximately 250,000 spectators stands on the bluffs overlooking the Mississippi and lines the levee for miles along the waterfront. While the river spectacle progresses along the Mississippi, the crowds are entertained by an elaborate display of fireworks and music from several bands. The royal barge, anchored in the river, remains on display all week.

As the king and queen leave their barge and go ashore, they are greeted with ceremony by municipal officials, the president of the Memphis Cotton Exchange, and the year's Maid of Cotton – an attractive and talented young woman selected from representatives of the various cotton-growing states.

For several months before the carnival, the Maid of Cotton, cosponsored by the Cotton Carnival, the National Cotton Council, and the Memphis *Press-Scimitar,* travels widely throughout the United States and Canada and also visits countries in Europe, Asia, and South America with a wardrobe of cotton fashions that she wears on her appearances. In the course of her travels she invites mayors, governors, and other dignitaries to attend the Cotton Carnival in Memphis. Many of them go to enjoy the merrymaking; others go to get ideas for their own local celebrations.

Such carnival celebrities as King Cotton and the queen, and the Maid of Cotton, are supplemented by other carnival royalty. There is, for instance, the queen of the Crown and Sceptre Society. She is selected by a ceremonial drawing of lots from some 20 or 25 candidates, each of whom represents a business concern in the Memphis area. The ceremony takes place at some time during carnival week – perhaps during the Great River Pageant on the opening Saturday, or in some years in the course of a special luncheon held early in the week. Each of the Memphis secret societies (as well as other groups) also chooses its own king and queen, who reign during the special entertainments held in the various club rooms throughout carnival week. These include the traditional gala parties, formal dances, and dinners for the different societies' royalty, members, and guests.

Monday and Tuesday, the third and fourth days of the Cotton Carnival, are marked by the public's first visits to the sidewalk café art exhibit, set up on Court Square, in downtown

Memphis, especially for the big annual celebration. The week-long art show, which opens on Monday morning, brings with it the musical entertainment — rock and jazz performances alternating with several band concerts per day — that is an almost continuous feature throughout the daylight hours of carnival week.

Wednesday is usually the occasion of the Maid of Cotton fasion show and luncheon, honoring the Maid of Cotton and featuring many of the original designs worn on her earlier travels. Late in the afternoon comes one of the parades for which the Cotton Carnival is famous — the Jubilee coronation parade, presided over by the king and queen of the Jubilee organization.

One of the carnival's always popular features, tours of homes and gardens in Memphis and the surrounding area, is generally scheduled for Thursday and Friday. Usually these pilgrimages are arranged to include modern houses on one of the two days and pre–Civil War mansions on the other. The tour of antebellum homes, some as much as 200 years old, includes some of the handsome structures across the border in Holly Springs, Mississippi. The trip gives tourists the opportunity to visit large cotton plantations and see different types of plantation homes, where they are greeted by hostesses dressed in the fashions of a long-past era of the Deep South.

Other carnival events go on in the meantime. Thursday noon, for example, is usually the time for the mayors' luncheon, sponsored annually by the Memphis *Press-Scimitar* and attended by perhaps 85 mayors from communities in surrounding states. Thursday night, at least in recent years, has been the time for the Battle of the Bands. Local amateur and semiprofessional rock groups compete in this event, introduced in 1969, which is sponsored by a soft-drink manufacturer.

A highlight of Friday — Children's Day — is the children's parade, beginning late in the forenoon, with 10,000 to 15,000 costumed children from all the local schools participating, many of them dancing and singing along the line of march. Bigger boys pull the 35 to 40 floats that elementary school children throughout the city have designed, built, and decorated under the direction of the recreation department of the City Parks Commission. One of the week's most successful events, the children's parade is presided over by the carnival's junior king and queen, two children of 12 or younger selected by the youngsters themselves and officially crowned by the carnival king and queen.

Friday noon is likely to be the scheduled time for the Dixie Belle Luncheon and Fashion Show

honoring Miss Dixie Belle, the winner of a contest sponsored each year by the Memphis Cotton Carnival Association. She is chosen from the 50 finalists selected customarily from several hundred local entrants in the 16-to-20-year-old age bracket.

One of the events always timed to coincide with the carnival begins early Friday evening. This is the Cotton Makers' Jubilee Parade, which proceeds down Main and Beale streets. The latter is the famous Beale Street immortalized in the song "Beale Street Blues" (1917) by W. C. Handy.

The Cotton Carnival reaches its climax on Saturday with the Grand Parade, changed in recent years from an illuminated nighttime spectacle to a daytime extravaganza commencing in the late forenoon. A gigantic procession, it contains between 30 and 35 floats. A dozen or more of them are theme floats, colorfully depicting one aspect or another of the year's theme and carrying the 50 finalists of the Miss Dixie Belle contest. The 20 or so remaining floats bear the king and queen of the Cotton Carnival, the royal court, the Maid of Cotton, the queen of the Crown and Sceptre Society, Miss Dixie Belle, the king and queen of each of the secret societies, and other carnival royalty, including the navy princess, who represents the US Naval Training Center in suburban Millington, Tennessee. Also part of the Grand Parade are visiting dignitaries, numerous marching and equestrian units, and some 50 to 75 bands — part of the perhaps 100 high school and college bands from all over the nation that appear in the course of carnival week, replete with dazzling uniforms and lively drum majors and majorettes.

Numerous other events — some perennials with schedules that change from year to year, and some unique happenings — are also officially part of the Memphis Cotton Carnival; a number of others, while not official carnival events, are customarily scheduled to take place during carnival week. These cover a wide range, including cultural events — such as performances by the Metropolitan Opera Company, which have embraced the carnival period in recent years — and parties timed for this period by private hosts and hostesses.

Though Cotton Carnival events technically come to a close on Saturday, they blend so imperceptibly into the related semiofficial, actually postcarnival, events that continue on Sunday (or perhaps longer) that Memphis's latter-day Mardi Gras is to all intents and purposes a nine-day affair, rather than the officially programmed eight-day festival. Between scheduled events, carnival visitors can also tour Front Street, the heart of the world's largest cotton market; visit sampling rooms of some of the leading cotton firms; and go to the Cotton Exchange, where they can see exhibits featuring cotton from seed to finished product. They can also visit free exhibits at the Brooks Memorial Art Gallery in Overton Park; or the Museum of Natural History and Industrial Arts, in what is popularly called the Pink Palace, in Chickasaw Gardens; or the Memphis Academy of Arts. Or they can take the children to the Children's Pet Show in Overton Park, one of the largest free zoos in the nation. Visitors are also welcome to tour the Cotton Carnival's headquarters and float factory at 547 North Main Street throughout the year.

The spirit of the Cotton Carnival is contagious. It begins with the more than 100 committees and thousands of citizens who give their time to the planning and preparation, spreads to the art students who join the professional staff in building and decorating the elaborate floats and displays, radiates pride of community to all the citizens of Memphis, and comes to include the guests who also feel a part of the celebration.

The all-pervasiveness of the present-day fete was a long time building. The idea of a cotton carnival goes back to the old Memphis Mardi Gras, which originated in 1872 during the difficult times of the post–Civil War period. At that time, members of the Mystic Society of Memphi directed and personally financed an annual celebration to help Memphis forget the unpleasant memories of the war and the subsequent yellow fever epidemics that had devastated the city and surrounding area. The old one-day Mardi Gras was discontinued in 1881, taken over in 1891 as a commercial project, and abandoned in 1901.

The modern Memphis Cotton Carnival, which grows more lavish each year, originated in 1931 when a theater manager called in representatives of local cotton firms to discuss a tie-in between the local product — "white gold," as cotton was then called — and the promotion of a movie entitled *Cabin in the Cotton*. There and then, this small group of Memphis citizens decided to raise the drooping spirits of the Depression era by sponsoring an annual celebration in honor of King Cotton. Thus the Memphis Cotton Carnival Association was born. Under its aegis, the Memphis Cotton Carnival has successfully raised spirits ever since. It has grown steadily as time has passed. The carnival, a minimum of five days in length during the decade of the 1960s, expanded to seven days in 1967. It reached its present duration in 1969,

and would have done so a year earlier, had not the 1968 Cotton Carnival been canceled because of the death of Martin Luther King Jr., who was assassinated in Memphis a month before the carnival was scheduled to open.

MAY 10

The Methodist Church Merger Becomes Effective

An early example of the ecumenical spirit that has characterized 20th century Christianity was the merger of the Methodist Episcopal Church, the Methodist Episcopal Church, South, and the Methodist Protestant Church to form the Methodist Church. The unification, which became effective on May 10, 1939, was achieved during a uniting conference at Kansas City, Missouri, held from April 26 through May 10. Nine hundred delegates and 50 bishops attended. On the final evening 14,000 persons, mostly Methodists, from all parts of the country packed the auditorium to witness the closing events. After a solemn procession of delegates, bishops, and the three chairmen of the Joint Commission for church union — Bishops John M. Moore, Edwin H. Hughes, and James H. Straughn — the "Declaration of Union" was read; it was then adopted without dissent by the assembled bishops. The Greater Kansas City Messiah Chorus marked the triumphant moment with the "Hallelujah Chorus" from George Frideric Handel's *Messiah*.

As the Episcopal address, read by Bishop John M. Moore on the first day of the conference, had stressed, the movement toward union was a logical one. The merging church organizations, having split in the past over issues of church government, had never diverged in doctrine:

On the larger matters we are already in agreement. Since we have never separated in faith, we will have no theological discussions. . . . This Methodism is no fabrication of ambitious, selfish ecclesiastics. It is rather the flowing together of great streams going out to the same seas.

The merger, Bishop James H. Straughn later commented, therefore gave all members the supreme satisfaction that "we are together again in one family, one home, witnessing to earnest yearning for an obedience to that ancient prayer for the unity of Christ's people." His thought was similar in spirit to the congratulatory message that President Franklin Delano Roosevelt had sent the conference from his Warm Springs, Georgia, retreat:

To a world distracted by malice, envy, and ill will, the Kansas City assembly is a harbinger of better things. . . . The Methodists have pointed the way to union. May God prosper the work and hasten the day when Christians of all confessions shall present a united front to combat the forces of strife that threaten our heritage of religion.

The Methodist movement started in the early 18th century with the evangelistic preaching of John Wesley (1703–1791), an Anglican clergyman and a fellow of Lincoln College, Oxford, who was assisted by his brother, Charles, and George Whitefield. Small numbers of Oxford students who gathered about these men to share their personal Christian experience were soon dubbed Methodists in reference to the methodical manner in which they strictly observed what they saw to be their religious duties. Members of the Holy Club, as the group was called, were punctilious in their daily worship and study, set themselves a schedule for visiting the sick and those in prison, and conducted schools among the poor.

The emphasis of Methodism was on personal salvation through faith, fellowship in Christian service, and love for others. The stress of the movement was on religion as an inner experience, on conversion, and on testimony, and it was characterized by the strong social conscience of its adherents. It was brought to the American colonies in the mid-18th century. Without Wesley's knowledge, local preachers, especially Irish immigrants, began to spread his beliefs in Maryland in about 1764 and in New York two years later. By 1768, groups of Methodists in Maryland, Pennsylvania, New York, and New Jersey had modeled themselves upon Wesley's English "societies." American independence from England following the Revolution necessitated the establishment of an independent Methodist ecclesiastical body in the United States. The Methodist Episcopal Church, which adopted the order of worship and religious precepts set down by Wesley, came into being at the "Christmas Conference" held in Baltimore, Maryland, on December 24, 1784. The first General Conference, the supreme policy-making body of the church, met in 1792.

Several schisms occurred in the church, although none was caused by doctrinal differences. The first serious split was in 1830. The dispute centered about the issue of lay representation in the church governing body, and reflected the general desire of the reformers to establish a broader base in church administra-

tion by limiting episcopal power. The controversy resulted in the formation of the Methodist Protestant Church in Baltimore. This was a nonepiscopal church with equal lay and clerical representation in its conferences that spread rapidly in Maryland, Pennsylvania, and neighboring states. Four years after its founding, it had a membership of 26,587.

The separation of the Methodist Episcopal Church, South, took place in May 1845 at a meeting in Louisville, Kentucky, called by southern church leaders. The division materialized in general over the increasingly bitter issue of slavery and specifically over the suspension of a slaveholding bishop who was not acceptable to northern Methodists. Despite its organization as an independent body, the 460,000-member Methodist Episcopal Church, South, retained the same doctrines and discipline as the parent Methodist Episcopal Church; however, at its first General Conference following the Civil War, it adopted the position of the Methodist Protestant Church in allowing both lay and clerical representation at its general and annual conferences.

Since the two major schisms had not been caused by doctrinal divergences, the reconciliation of the three Methodist churches was broached as early as the 1870s. In fact in 1868 the Methodist Episcopal Church had already moved toward clerical and lay representation at its conferences, a trend that eventually resolved the chief issue that had caused the formation of the Methodist Protestant Church in 1830. In 1870 the way was paved for healing the Methodist division between north and south when the General Conference of southern delegates welcomed northern representatives. In 1905 the two Methodist Episcopal bodies agreed on a joint hymnal and order of worship.

The movement for unification of the three major Methodist churches gained momentum in the 20th century. The first plan for union between the northern and southern Methodist Episcopal churches, voted upon in the mid-1920s, was adopted by the Methodist Episcopal Church but rejected by the Methodist Episcopal Church, South. In the 1930s a new plan of union, this time including the Methodist Protestant Church as well, won the support necessary for adoption. The great reunion of May 10, 1939, brought together the largest number of Protestants — approximately 8 million — that had as yet been merged.

The Methodist Church, long active in publishing, education, and nursing, sent out its first foreign missionary in 1833. In 1939 the three merging churches had a total of 1,454 missionaries in the foreign field: 1,065 in Asia, 225 in

South America, 152 in Africa, and 12 in Europe. The number of Methodists, full-fledged members and probationers alike, in these foreign areas was 679,320.

On April 23, 1968, the Methodist Church united with the Evangelical United Brethren Church to form the United Methodist Church (see April 23). As of 1975, the new church had over 39,195 churches and over 10,063,046 members.

Mother's Day

This is a movable event. See note on page xxvi.

Each year Americans set aside the second Sunday in May to pay tribute to their mothers. Across the land, children of all ages use the occasion to honor their mothers with tokens of appreciation such as flowers and candy, or with more personal expressions of affection, such as letters, telephone calls, and visits. The day, which provides an excellent opportunity for remembering mothers and expressing gratitude to them, is one of the most widely celebrated holidays of the year.

Americans are not alone in honoring their mothers on a special day; nor did they originate the idea. Both the ancient Greeks and Romans held festivals to pay tribute to mothers, and Christians during the Middle Ages honored Mary, the mother of Jesus, with appropriate observances each year. In England the fourth Sunday in Lent was celebrated as Mothering Sunday, and in Yugoslavia a similar event was traditionally held shortly before Christmas season; on their respective holidays Britons and Slavs visited their mothers and brought them small gifts.

In comparison with these early European observances, the establishment of a similar holiday in the United States is of relatively recent origin. During the Civil War Julia Ward Howe, the author of "The Battle Hymn of the Republic," suggested that July 4 be renamed Mother's Day and urged that the occasion be used for promoting peace. Mrs. Howe's idea was never put into effect, but shortly after the end of the Civil War, Anna Reeves Jarvis of Grafton, West Virginia, began to work for a similar holiday. In 1868 Mrs. Jarvis organized a committee in her home town to sponsor a Mother's Friendship Day. The object of this observance was to reunite families that had been divided during the Civil War. Mother's Friendship Day allegedly brought together a number of brothers who had formerly fought against one another, but Mrs. Jarvis's dream of an annual "memorial mother's day, commemorating [each mother] for the service she renders to humanity in every field" did not gain widespread acceptance during her lifetime.

Others also showed an early interest in establishing Mother's Day. In 1887 Mary Towles Sasseen, a teacher in Henderson, Kentucky, organized a special musical affair to honor her pupils' mothers. This tribute became an annual event in her classes, but she did not content herself with the success of this celebration. Until her death, in 1916, Miss Sasseen worked unceasingly to popularize such recognition of mothers: in 1893 she published a pamphlet describing her classroom ceremonies and for years she traveled across the nation urging other educators to adopt similar observances in their schools.

While Miss Sasseen was promoting her plan, Frank E. Herring of South Bend, Indiana, also took up the cause of establishing Mother's Day. In an address to his fellow members of the Fraternal Order of Eagles in 1904, Herring suggested that mothers be honored throughout the nation on a special day each year.

Although the above-mentioned persons have justly been given credit for their contributions to the establishment of Mother's Day, Anna M. Jarvis, daughter of Anna Reeves Jarvis, was most directly responsible for organizing the observance in the United States. On May 9, 1907, the second anniversary of her mother's death, she invited friends to her home in Philadelphia. At this gathering, she outlined her plan for making her mother's dream of a nationwide day in honor of mothers, living and deceased, a reality. The following year Miss Jarvis carried out her hope. On May 10, 1908, the second Sunday of the month, church services in which mothers were honored were held in both Grafton, West Virginia, and in Philadelphia. The Andrews Methodist Episcopal Church — later Andrews Methodist Church — in Grafton was the scene of a particularly impressive observance. Its minister, Dr. H. C. Howard, preached a sermon inspired by the biblical quotation "Woman, behold thy Son; Son, behold thy mother," and Miss Jarvis provided hundreds of carnations, her mother's favorite flower, for each mother and child in attendance.

The 1908 observance was only the beginning of Miss Jarvis's efforts. For years, she worked diligently to popularize her idea; she wrote hundreds of letters to church and business leaders, to newspaper editors and members of Congress, and she even brought the need for a Mother's Day observance to the attention of the President of the United States. Miss Jarvis's single-minded labors were rewarded. In 1910 the governor of West Virginia issued the first Mother's Day proclamation, and by 1911 Mother's Day services were held in all the states of the Union. In 1914

President Woodrow Wilson, responding to a joint resolution of Congress, issued a proclamation setting aside the second Sunday in May "for displaying the American Flag, and as a public expression of our love and reverence for the mothers of our country."

Mother's Day quickly won popular acceptance both at home and abroad. In the United States and in many foreign nations, church services patterned after those held in 1908, as well as personal expressions of appreciation to mothers, became customary on the second Sunday in May. Many persons also continued the custom of wearing carnations on the occasion, although after a time the practice was modified so that white carnations were worn to honor deceased mothers, and red ones were worn by those whose mothers were living. In 1934 the US Post Office Department further commemorated Mother's Day by issuing a three-cent stamp depicting the famed portrait of James Whistler's mother.

Meanwhile Miss Jarvis continued her efforts to make Mother's Day truly an occasion on which children would show their appreciation to their mothers. In return for her work, she won numerous honors. She was a delegate to the World Sunday School Convention in Zurich, Switzerland, in 1913; she spoke before many noteworthy groups; and Japan acclaimed her Mother's Day idea "a great American gift."

Unfortunately the course of Miss Jarvis's personal life was not so happy as the story of the development of Mother's Day. As commercialization began to encroach upon the observance of the day, she became embittered. She initiated lawsuits against those seeking profits from Mother's Day, and when these failed she turned away from the world. Within a short time she lost her property, and her blind sister, Elsinore, to whom she had devoted her life, died. In the face of such misfortune, Miss Jarvis's own health failed, and in November 1944 she was forced to ask for public assistance. Realizing her desperate plight, some friends came to her aid and provided funds so that she might spend her final years in a private sanatarium — in West Chester, Pennsylvania. Deaf and nearly blind, childless herself, the woman whose efforts had brought happiness to countless mothers died in 1948.

Today Mother's Day is celebrated throughout the world. In the United States the President and the governors of many states issue proclamations declaring the second Sunday in May Mother's Day. Observances of the day of course center around the family. Many churches hold special services on Mother's Day, and sermons generally are based on themes indicating the unique bond between mother and child. A number of Protestant churches designate the day as the Festival of the Christian Home.

Many areas also sponsor special events to mark Mother's Day. For example the Fruit Growers Association of Rhode Island each year holds festivities near Greenville in the heart of the state's apple region. The blossoming orchards are themselves a breath-taking sight, but Mother's Day is further enlivened by ceremonies that include the crowning of a queen chosen from the teenage members of the Rhode Island State Granges. Many mothers go to see the blossoms and coronation as part of the celebration.

A number of organizations have, at various times, promoted various aspects of Mother's Day celebrations. The earliest of these was the Mother's Day International Association, which was incorporated in 1912 to encourage a greater observance of the day. As the holiday gained widespread acceptance, this association faded from existence and was replaced by others. In 1933 the American Mother's Committee was founded "to develop and strengthen the moral and spiritual foundations of the American home and to give the observance of Mother's Day a spiritual quality representative of ideal motherhood." This organization is still active and one of its best-known functions is its annual selection of the American Mother of the Year. Still another organization — the nonprofit National Committee on the Observance of Mother's Day, founded in 1941 — promotes the commercial aspects of the day, which in recent years have amounted to more than $1 billion annually.

The Andrews Methodist Church in Grafton, West Virginia, host to the first Mother's Day observance in 1908 and of services each Mother's Day since, has become the International Mother's Day Shrine. Its governing body, the International Mother's Day Shrine Inc., organized in March 1962, purchased the two-story brick building where Anna Jarvis's 1908 services took place, and has worked diligently to make the shrine attractive. Buildings originally neighboring the church structure — which is now surrounded by a park — were demolished in connection with an urban renewal project. The shrine, located on East Main Street in downtown Grafton, is open to the public.

Fort Ticonderoga Falls

Emerging from the 4:00 A.M. darkness on May 10, 1775, Ethan Allen and his Green Mountain Boys caught the British by surprise and captured strategic Fort Ticonderoga, at the junction of Lake Champlain and Lake George, in the first offensive action of the American Revolution. Benedict Arnold, later best known as a traitor to the American cause, helped conceive the action and was among those who crossed with Allen from the Vermont to the New York side of Lake

Champlain to participate in the daring exploit. This first American victory in the War of Independence not only yielded control of vital waterways leading to Canada and to New York City; it also provided the colonists with badly needed cannons, which were dragged the following winter all the way to Boston. There they were crucial in the action of Dorchester Heights that resulted in expulsion of the British (see March 17, Evacuation Day in Boston).

Two hundred years to the hour after the Green Mountain Boys' lightninglike takeover of Fort Ticonderoga, their costumed descendants reenacted the event — beginning at 4:00 A.M. on May 10, 1975 — at the original site. The reenactment of the capture was repeated several times during the day, with the dramatics punctuated by firing demonstrations (of cannons and muskets), an ox roast and chicken barbecue, a fife-and-drum corps muster, the opening of 18th century Revolutionary encampments, demonstrations of crafts, and military drills. It was the first major event in New York State's celebration of the US Bicentennial.

The First Transcontinental Railroad

The vision of connecting the east and west coasts of the North American continent with railroad tracks originated among those interested in trade with the Orient, and even before the Mexican War the New York merchant Asa Whitney had advocated this enterprise. US acquisition of California and the discovery of gold in that state provided the final impetus that prompted Congress in March 1853 to authorize a survey of the possible routes westward from the Mississippi River.

However, bitter sectional rivalries prevented the selection of an eastern terminus and route, and the depression following the Panic of 1857 ended hopes that the proposal would quickly become a reality. Only when the Civil War had brought an end to support for a southern route were the Republicans able to fulfill their 1860 platform pledge to rescue the transcontinental railroad from its planning-board limbo.

On July 1, 1862, President Abraham Lincoln signed the first Pacific Railroad Act, which authorized two companies — the Central Pacific and the new Union Pacific — to construct the transcontinental line. The former railroad was to build eastward from California and the latter westward from the Missouri River. The government gave the companies alternate sections of public lands in a checkerboard pattern contiguous to both sides of the right-of-way. A 30-year loan in US bonds provided a per-mile-of-track subsidy of $16,000 over the Plains, $32,000 on

the plateau between the Rocky Mountains and Sierra Nevada, and $48,000 across the mountains.

The Central Pacific Railroad, directed by Collis P. Huntington and Leland Stanford, broke ground on January 8, 1863, at Sacramento, California. The Union Pacific began its construction at Omaha, Nebraska, on December 2, 1862, with a ceremony highlighted by a speech by George F. Train, the appropriately named merchant-author. Progress came slowly, only with the solution of various problems. In 1864 a more generous second Pacific Railroad Act doubled the land grants and gave the government a second instead of a first mortgage on railroad property. Labor shortages were more persistent, but General Grenville M. Dodge, the chief engineer of the Union Pacific, managed well with crews of ex-soldiers and rugged Irish immigrants brought from New York City. Charles Crocker, Dodge's Central Pacific counterpart, found his work force by importing more than 6,000 Chinese laborers. The US Army protected the Union's employees from raids by the Sioux, and the Central placated the less warlike western Indians by giving the chiefs free rides.

The railroaders drove relentlessly through summers and winters in a race for government mileage subsidies. This quest for speed proved to be quite expensive. Experts have estimated that working through the winter snows of the high Sierras, and other daring exploits, increased construction costs by 70 percent.

Both companies reached Utah early in 1869 and their forward crews passed each other with parallel lines. The Congress named Promontory, Utah, as a compromise nexus for the railroads. At final tally, the Union Pacific had built 1,086 miles of track and the Central 689 miles, but the latter had had to deal with the mountains.

Officials from both companies met at Promontory on May 10, 1869, for ceremonies joining the two lines. President Leland Stanford of the Central Pacific and Vice President Thomas C. Durant of the Union Pacific used a hammer of Nevada silver to drive the final spike, a golden one, into a tie of polished California laurel. Each took turns delivering the blows until Stanford completed the job. Telegraph operators reported each strike of the mallet and the completion of the project set off wild celebrations throughout the nation.

The federal government has established a Golden Spike National Historic Site to mark the spot where the Union and Pacific met, and each year railroading history buffs reenact in costume the famous May 10 ceremony. The Railroad Village Museum, 25 miles west of the site at Corrine, Utah, contains exhibits commemorating the driving of the golden spike.

441

MAY 11

Connecticut and New Haven United

The first general court of Connecticut to include representatives from the towns that had comprised New Haven Colony met on May 11, 1665. This was more than three years after John Winthrop Jr. had obtained a royal charter granting Connecticut jurisdiction over the area previously controlled by New Haven.

Prior to 1662, neither Connecticut nor New Haven had a royal charter; colonization of both areas took place without the legal sanction of the king. It was the natural migration of Massachusetts inhabitants that accounted for the settlement of Connecticut. In 1635, the attraction of the colony's rich farmlands caused an exodus from Dorchester and Watertown to the area around Hartford. The following year the Reverend Thomas Hooker arrived, and under his guidance a compact of government was drawn up. The Fundamental Orders of Connecticut closely followed the system of the government then operative in Massachusetts. The only major deviation from the Bay Colony model was the provision for citizenship: in Massachusetts, membership in the Puritan Congregational church was a prerequisite for admission to political privileges; in Connecticut, the only requirement for freemanship was acceptance by the majority of householders in the township. Since the original settlers were staunch Puritans, however, only those with similar religious beliefs proved "acceptable," and in practice Congregational church members also controlled Connecticut. The Fundamental Orders remained the sole basis of the colony's government for more than 20 years. Not until 1660 was any effort made to obtain royal recognition.

The colony at New Haven was likewise established without a royal charter. Under the leadership of the Reverend John Davenport and Theophilus Eaton, a merchant, Puritans fleeing religious persecution in England arrived in New England in 1637. They stopped briefly at Boston, but the religious controversies then raging in that town made them unwilling to stay. Instead the followers of Davenport and Eaton determined to found a new settlement. In the spring of 1638, without royal knowledge of their activity, they established New Haven on the shore of Long Island Sound. Other towns quickly sprang up around the original settlement, and in 1643 the common need for protection caused Stamford, Guilford, and Milford to join with New Haven. The new colony adopted the Mosaic law as its judicial frame and limited citizenship to church members. Many of New Haven's leading citizens were merchants, and under their influence the colony quickly expanded. By 1662 it controlled a number of new settlements on the Sound, several towns on Long Island, and a struggling colony in Delaware.

The English civil war afforded the Connecticut and New Haven colonies protection for two decades. The parliamentary government had executed King Charles I in 1649, and Oliver Cromwell and his Puritans held the reins of power until 1660. Royal authority was reestablished with the restoration of Charles II to the throne in that year, and any colonial government that ignored the crown thenceforth risked its own existence.

Connecticut was quick to curry favor with the king. In 1662 the colony sent John Winthrop Jr. to England to negotiate for a charter. New Haven failed to take similar action. It could not afford the luxury of sending an emissary to the king, and its reputation as a refuge for Charles I's regicides made it unlikely that Charles II would have turned a favorable ear even if such a delegate had appeared at court.

The charter Winthrop received in 1662 incorporated New Haven into the Connecticut Colony. New Haven, however, refused to accept this action and for nearly two years struggled to maintain its independent existence. It petitioned the New England Confederation (see May 19) to redress its grievances against Connecticut, and at first that body upheld New Haven. But the English conquest of New Netherland in 1664 ended any hope of continued independence. The Roman Catholic Duke of York controlled New Netherland, and his charter could be interpreted so as to include the New Haven area within his jurisdiction. Fearing the expansion of the adjoining Catholic domain, the confederation quickly reversed itself and in September 1664 agreed to Connecticut's control of the New Haven region. The following November royal commissioners — disregarding the Duke of York's claim — established Long Island Sound as Connecticut's southern boundary.

New Haven reluctantly agreed to these terms on December 15, 1664. A formal act of submission was passed on January 5, 1665, and on May 11 the first General Court of the combined colonies was held.

Minnesota Admitted to the Union

On May 11, 1858, Minnesota became the 32nd member of the federal Union. Before admission to statehood, the region had had a rich history as the home of several Indian tribes, the scene of European explorers' and fur trappers' adventures, and an area that had attracted thousands of hopeful pioneers. As a state, Minnesota, located in the heart of America's "breadbasket," continued to make important contributions to the history and strength of the nation.

Apart from the 14th century Norsemen who, some have alleged, may have reached the area, Frenchmen, seeking fur pelts and a western passage through the North American continent, were the first white men to go to what is now called Minnesota. Pierre Esprit Radisson and Médart Chouart, Sieur des Groseilliers, may have visited the region, possibly even as early as 1654 or 1655. Daniel Greysolon, Sieur Duluth (Dulhut), led a party to Minnesota in 1679 for the purpose of improving relations between the Chippewa and Sioux Indians who inhabited the region. On the western shore of Lake Superior, near the site of the city that today bears his name, Duluth held a council with the Sioux; then he and his men continued inland to the Mille Lacs Sioux village, where he recorded that "on the second of July, 1679, I had the honor to set up the arms of His Majesty in the great village of Nadouecioux called Izatys, where no Frenchman had ever been, nor to the Songakitons and Quetbatons, distant 26 leagues from the first, where I also set up the arms of His Majesty in the same year 1679." Duluth sent members of his expedition to probe the wilderness west of Mille Lacs, and they reported seeing a "great lake whose water is not good to drink." But the exact area they explored is unknown; perhaps they reached the Pacific Ocean or came upon the Great Salt Lake.

In 1680 Louis Hennepin, a Flemish priest sent by René Robert Cavelier, Sieur de La Salle, to explore the area of the upper Mississippi, discovered the Falls of St. Anthony. The adventures surrounding Hennepin's coming upon this great power source, which centuries later helped make Minneapolis the milling center of the United States, were recounted in the *Description de la Louisiane*, which was published in Paris in 1683. Whether Hennepin himself actually wrote this book is questionable, but there is no doubt that its tales about the Minnesota wilderness aroused great interest in Europe.

Meanwhile, French explorers and trappers continued to venture into the region of Minnesota. In 1700 Pierre Charles Le Sueur led a party up the Minnesota River to the Blue Earth River. There he built Fort L'Huillier, a small trading post that for two years was a lucrative fur-trading center.

Between 1701 and 1714, the War of the Spanish Succession occupied the energies of the French in both the Old and New Worlds. On the North American continent, the hostilities with England put a temporary end to explorations in the Northwest, and not until 1727 did the French again sponsor an expedition to that re-

gion. In that year, however, René Boucher, Sieur de La Perrière, led a party into the area of the upper Mississippi. In September the expedition landed at the upper end of Minnesota's Lake Pepin, where Fort Beauharnois was built. The fortification, which included a number of buildings and a small chapel, might have served as a base for French explorations farther west. But La Perrière returned to Montreal in 1728, and shortly after his departure the soldiers at Beauharnois became involved in attacks and counterattacks against the Fox, and later the Sioux, Indians.

In 1731 Pierre Gaultier de Varennes, Sieur de la Vérendrye led an expedition into Minnesota. The men in the Vérendrye party established Fort St. Pierre at the western end of Rainy Lake in 1731 and built the larger Fort St. Charles at Lake of the Woods in 1732. The latter fortification served as a base of operations for extensive French explorations in the Midwest during the decades that followed.

Between 1756 and 1763 French and English forces again clashed, and the English victory in the French and Indian War cost France its empire in the New World. By a secret treaty, France in 1762 ceded the area west of the Mississippi to Spain, and by the Treaty of Paris of 1763 it surrendered Canada and its claims east of the Mississippi to England. These treaties technically divided control of Minnesota between Spain and England, but in practice the latter nation controlled the entire Minnesota region for the next 50 years — even though by the Treaty of Paris of 1783 England officially turned over its claim to eastern Minnesota to the new American nation, which made it part of its newly created Northwest Territory four years later (see July 13).

During England's half-century of dominance of Minnesota, a thriving fur trade developed in the area. Independent traders were active in the Minnesota wilds at this time, but the North West Company, an organization of Montreal businessmen, conducted by far the most extensive operations in the area. Each year during the last decades of the 18th century, pelts worth tens of thousands of dollars were collected at Grand Portage, and from there sent to Montreal, where they were reshipped to Europe. As the center of the British fur trade, Grand Portage, located on the western shore of Lake Superior in northeastern Minnesota, has a place of great importance in the state's history. Accordingly, Grand Portage was declared a national monument in 1958. A trading post, similar to the one that originally occupied the site, has been built and is open to the public.

Although the United States formally gained

control of eastern Minnesota by the Treaty of Paris of 1783, and of western Minnesota by the Louisiana Purchase of 1803, the nation did not make any substantial efforts to exert its authority in the area until after the War of 1812. Then, realizing that American claims to the Midwest would be recognized only if the nation actually occupied the area, the United States built a series of frontier forts that would serve as defenses against foreign enemies and hostile Indians. In 1819, a US Army expedition, which was taken over by Colonel Josiah Snelling the following year, set out to build the first American fortification in Minnesota. Located at the juncture of the Minnesota and Mississippi rivers, on land that explorer Zebulon M. Pike had purchased in 1805 from the Sioux, the fort was virtually completed by 1822. Originally known as Fort St. Anthony, it was renamed Fort Snelling in 1825.

As an "isle of safety" in the wilderness and as a center from which expeditions to explore, survey, and eventually settle the surrounding region went forth, Fort Snelling played a critical role in the growth of Minnesota. In 1960 its importance was recognized when the fort was declared a national historic landmark. Four of its original buildings are still standing and the public is welcome to visit these and the other attractions at the fort and the surrounding Fort Snelling State Park, six miles southwest of what is now St. Paul.

Although the United States effectively removed the British presence from the upper Mississippi region in the years following the war of 1812, Minnesota did not attract American settlers for several decades. Instead, as had been the case during the periods of French and British dominance, most white men who visited Minnesota in the early 19th century were either explorers or fur trappers. And like their predecessors these hardy adventurers played an important part in Minnesota's history. The explorers conducted numerous expeditions into the Minnesota wilderness and eventually discovered Lake Itasca, the source of the Mississippi River, while the traders, most of whom were associated with John Jacob Astor's American Fur Company, reaped great profits from the pelts of the region.

Changes in fashion, which curtailed the demand for furs in the 1830s and 1840s, brought an end to the dominance of the trapper and explorer in Minnesota. In 1837, meanwhile, the US government negotiated treaties with the Sioux and Chippewa Indians that extinguished the Indians' title to the triangle of land between the Mississippi and lower St. Croix rivers. This

opened the first wedge to permanent settlement, and within a few years the influx of migrants (which neighboring areas had already experienced) began to reach Minnesota. Lumberers followed the fur traders into the region. Minnesota became not only a major lumbering area, but also an important transportation center, first as the northern terminus of the growing traffic on the Mississippi River, and later as the western terminus of the inland waterway extending through the Great Lakes to points east. (Ultimately, after the opening of the St. Lawrence Seaway in the 20th century, the inland water route would stretch all the way to the Atlantic Ocean, paralleling the path of the early fur traders.)

With new interest in the region, the population of what would soon be the State of Minnesota mounted. By 1849, about 4,000 white persons inhabited the area, and the towns of St. Paul and Stillwater counted 910 and 609 residents respectively.

During the 19th century much of the area of present Minnesota was successively included in the jurisdictions of the Indiana, Illinois, Michigan, Wisconsin, and Iowa territories. Michigan gained statehood in 1837 and Iowa in 1846. When Wisconsin was admitted to the Union in 1846, Minnesota's legal status was temporarily ambiguous. Faced with this situation, a convention that met at Stillwater on August 26, 1848, decided to send Henry Hastings Sibley as a delegate to the national Congress. Sibley asked Congress to form a new territory of "Minnesota" to serve the needs of the area's residents, and that body complied on March 3, 1849.

In 1851, 1854, and 1855 the US government concluded treaties with the Sioux and Chippewa that opened to settlement most of the area in Minnesota west of the Mississippi and about half the northern region of the territory. The opening of these rich lands resulted in a population boom of almost unprecedented dimensions. Between 1850 and 1857 Minnesota's population grew from 6,077 to 150,037 and countless farms and towns appeared across the expanse of the territory. (The advent of the railroads after the Civil War would account for further large gains.)

Minnesota did not remain a territory for long. Its rapid growth quickly made it eligible for statehood and on February 26, 1857, Congress approved an enabling act that empowered Minnesota officials to call a constitutional convention. The convention met on July 13, and by August 28, 1857, it had drawn up a state constitution. This document was approved in a popular referendum on October 13, 1857, and it was submitted to President James Buchanan on January 6, 1858. In the nation's capital, Minnesota's application for admission to the Union became entangled with the more controversial issue of Kansas' statehood (see January 29), so that several months passed before Congress finally approved the application on May 11, 1858, and Minnesota was admitted to the Union as the 32nd state.

MAY 12

National Hospital Week

Florence Nightingale's Birthday

National Hospital Week is an annual observance "to focus attention on the work that hospitals are performing in providing high-quality year-round care in the community." Its dates always include May 12, the anniversary of the birth of Florence Nightingale, whose pioneer endeavors in nursing inspired progress in the hospital systems of both England and the United States.

The origins of National Hospital Week can be traced to 1920, the 100th anniversary of Florence Nightingale's birth, when Matthew O. Foley, the editor of a hospital magazine in Chicago, decided that something should be done by the hospitals to honor her memory. He began to urge an annual observance of the date of her birth and promoted the idea so successfully that, in 1921, leaders in the health field, aware of the need for informing the public about the human side of hospitals, as well as the contributions of Florence Nightingale, initiated National Hospital Day on May 12. Only a few hospitals, however, took note of the anniversary in that year.

After growing in recognition and popularity throughout the 1920s, 1930s, and 1940s, National Hospital Day was extended to a week-long observance in 1953 to give hospitals more time and greater flexibility in planning and implementing public information efforts and meaningful programs within individual communities. It is sponsored by the American Hospital Association, the nationwide professional, educational, and research organization that speaks for approximately 7,000 hospitals and health care centers in the United States. Most of these member institutions commemorate National Hospital Week, as do several hospitals in Canada and other foreign countries.

Since no detailed calendar of specific events or mandatory activities is issued, diverse local programs may include, for example, exhibits of informational material, recognition of employee achievements, and community orientation projects regarding the services of hospitals, where on any given day 1.5 million Americans are patients. Hospital administrators and personnel are frequently invited to serve as guest speakers at local business luncheons and school assemblies and to give radio and newspaper interviews. In general, emphasis is placed on each of the significant functions of hospitals: patient care, education, research, and community health. An effort is made to keep members of the public up to date about progress in the hospital field and to make them better informed about the costs a hospital incurs: for instance, to be prepared for all emergencies, a modern hospital must fill a shopping list of more than 10,000 items — from antibiotics to X-ray films. It is customary for hospitals during this week to open their doors to the public by holding receptions and conducted tours.

In recent years the American Hospital Association has chosen and promoted an annual theme designed to make hospitals better understood, better financed, and better appreciated not only during National Hospital Week but throughout the year. Months in advance of the week, the theme is promoted on a nationwide scale through the use of posters, lapel buttons, bumper stickers, and other advertising devices. Broad enough in scope to fit the existing needs of every category and size of hospital, the theme usually focuses on further clarifying an aspect of hospital operation. In 1962, for example, under the banner of Your Hospital . . . Uniting Science and Patient Care, National Hospital Week concentrated on explaining how hospitals combine the most modern scientific services with dedicated patient care, carried out by trained and skilled personnel and adapted to suit individual requirements. The 1963 program, Today's Hospitals . . . Career Center for America's Youth, was created to inform parents, teachers, guidance counselors, and students about the more than 200 job classifications, from therapist to stenographer, that make hospitals the third largest employer in the United States.

In 1970 the American Hospital Association changed its format by adopting a primary theme as a base — Your Hospital Cares! — and adding a secondary theme — Our First Concern Is Your Health. To implement this slogan hospitals throughout the country used various means to tell the public that they do indeed care and are prepared to fulfill today's demands for health service, while working hard to meet the escalating demands of the future. In Oak Lawn, Illinois, art students were asked to design uniforms that nurses might wear in the year 2000, and the best entries were modeled by guides at a local health fair. In Chicago a community-wide health program concentrated on instruction about summertime emergencies, such as insect bites, sunburn, shock, and sunstroke. A Cleveland hospital invited its 1,500 employees on tours through 12 specialized departments to demonstrate how their jobs and those of their fellow workers enable the hospital to function efficiently. Twenty AHA member institutions in northeastern New York pooled resources to sponsor an exhibit and demonstration of hospital equipment at the area's largest shopping plaza. The display, manned by technicians and nurses, included a working model of an artificial kidney and attracted an estimated 150,000 persons.

The 1971 National Hospital Week, held May 9 through 15, celebrated both the 50th anniversary of the National Hospital event and the 150th anniversary of Florence Nightingale's birth. Its theme, Your Hospital Cares — But Who Loves a Hospital? implied that although people do not enjoy being sick, many persons, both patients and employees, have reason to "love a hospital."

A new commitment by hospitals — to provide a framework for keeping all people healthy, not just for bringing sick people back to health — was reflected in the theme of one recent year, We Want You . . . in the Picture of Health. Another recent National Hospital Week theme was Your Hospital . . . a Caring Community, Your Health . . . Our Common Concern. Observances focused on the role of the nation's 3 million hospital employees, stressing their concern with the quality, availability, and cost of health care both inside and outside hospital walls.

Florence Nightingale was born in Florence, Italy, on May 12, 1820, the second daughter of well-to-do and cultured British parents. Vivacious and intelligent, she was an intensely emotional child, who at a young age developed an extraordinary capacity for self-criticism and introspection. In 1837 she heard the voice of God summoning her to service; by 1844 her uncertainties about the form this service should take had been resolved, and nursing became her obsession. At that time hospitals were popularly regarded as little better than almshouses, patients were neglected, and nursing was considered a disreputable calling. Indeed most nurses themselves considered their occupation as meaningless or, at most, menial. Almost all were un-

trained as nurses, and alcoholics and prostitutes were among their ranks.

Although her socially ambitious mother was determined to arrange a brilliant marriage for her, Florence Nightingale was steadfast in rejecting even the proposal of Richard Monckton Milnes, whom she described as "the man I adore," for the sake of her objective. After years of misery and frustration caused by family opposition to her chosen career, she was finally allowed to gain her first nursing experience with the Protestant deaconesses at Kaiserswerth, Germany, in 1851. She also trained briefly with the Sisters of St. Vincent de Paul in Paris. Firmly committed to the goal of lifting nursing into an honorable occupation for women, she became, in 1853, the superintendent of a small hospital, the Institution for the Care of Sick Gentlewomen in Distressed Circumstances, on Harley Street, London.

Through study and tireless attention to detail, Florence Nightingale made herself an expert in hospital administration. Her brilliant reorganization at Harley Street soon became widely admired, and she herself gained a reputation of some note.

The Crimean War, meanwhile, was under way, with Britain and France having declared war against Russia, in support of Turkey, in March 1854. By October of that year England reverberated with reports about the appalling neglect of British soldiers wounded in the conflict.

The work that Florence Nightingale had conducted at Harley Street with such success prompted a request by British Secretary at War Sidney Herbert that she take charge of an official plan for introducing female nurses into British Army hospitals in the Crimean Peninsula. He made clear to her that if the nursing project succeeded, "an enormous amount of good will have been done now . . . a prejudice [against women in military nursing] will have been broken through and a precedent established which will multiply the good to all time."

It was a challenge that the woman who would become known as the founder of modern nursing could not refuse. She went to the front with 38 nurses and established a new type of war hospital at Scutari and Balaklava. By superhuman effort, she triumphed over official jealousy, resentment, and intrigue, and managed to secure necessary supplies, enforce discipline, and introduce sanitary reforms into "hospital" buildings that were vast, dilapidated, filthy, and rat-infested, with inadequate sewerage and a contaminated water supply. Unsparing of herself, she frequently worked 20 hours at a time, making nightly inspections of the vast wards with a lamp in her hand. Within months of her arrival the mortality rate among patients had been slashed. Her efforts to ease the sufferings of wounded soldiers stirred the imagination of people in all parts of the world — including poet Henry Wadsworth Longfellow, who was inspired to write "Santa Filomena" (1857), with its famous verse:

> A Lady with a Lamp shall stand
> In the great history of the land,
> A noble type of good,
> Heroic womanhood.

Upon her return to England, Florence Nightingale deliberately sought to escape the fame that surrounded her. She intended to devote the rest of her life to the British Army and eagerly studied food, housing, and sanitary conditions in military establishments at home and in India. Her years of experience and study and her administrative gifts were so striking, however, that she was gradually forced to turn to civil as well as military nursing. In July 1860, with a testimonial fund of £45,000 raised for her benefit after the war, she opened the Nightingale School and Home for training nurses at St. Thomas's Hospital, London. Professional nursing as it is known today is said to date from this time.

Florence Nightingale was highly critical of the low repute in which nursing was held by contemporary opinion. She wrote, scathingly: "No man, not even a doctor, ever gives any other definition of what a nurse should be than this — 'devoted and obedient.' This definition would do just as well for a porter. It might even do for a horse." She also said, succinctly: "It seems a commonly received idea among men, and even among women themselves, that it requires nothing but a disappointment in love, or incapacity in other things, to turn a woman into a good nurse." She insisted that the training and education of a nurse consist of two aspects of equal weight: acquisition of formal knowledge, involving a rigorous routine, and character development. So as not to perpetuate the criticism to which their calling was already subjected, her nurses were required to be beyond reproach in their personal lives as well as in their profession.

Although her health was broken from years of deprivation and overwork, Florence Nightingale's advice was constantly sought for on matters of sanitation and nursing throughout her long life. A busy, but tranquil old age was marred only by her gradually approaching blindness. In 1907 she became the first woman to receive the British Order of Merit. By 1910, the jubilee of the founding of the Nightingale training school, and the year of her death at the age of 90, over 1,000 training schools for nurses had opened in the United States alone.

MAY 13

Jamestown Day

On May 13, 1607, a colonizing expedition sponsored by the London Company disembarked 50 miles from the mouth of the James River and established the first permanent English settlement in America. Jamestown was not an immediate success. Expectations of a lucrative trade with the Indians and dreams of vast gold and silver discoveries had prompted the 105 colonists — mostly disbanded soldiers and fortune hunters — to come to the New World. They were ill-prepared to cope with the malarial swamps of the region and saw little potential in the rich soil, which constituted the true treasure of Virginia.

Seventy-three settlers fell victim to famine and disease during the first seven months of Jamestown's existence. Despite this dismal beginning, the London Company (sometimes called the Virginia Company) continued to send men and supplies to the colony and these, combined with Captain John Smith's compulsory work program (see September 10) saved Jamestown. The "starving time" ended in 1610. But the introduction of tobacco by John Rolfe in 1612 was the most significant factor in improving the colony's fortunes. By 1614 the colonists were exporting their tobacco to England and the profits gained from this single product allowed Virginia to become economically self-sufficient.

To attract more settlers to Virginia, the London Company in 1619 repealed the harsh code of martial law that had been instituted in 1612. In its place the company instructed the colony's governor to call a general assembly. Twenty-two burgesses (each town, plantation, or hundred people selected two representatives) gathered in Jamestown from August 9 to 14, 1619. This first colonial legislature marked the beginning of representative government in America. Although ravaged by fire during Bacon's Rebellion in 1676, Jamestown continued to be the meeting place of the House of Burgesses and thus the capital of the "Old Dominion" until 1700, when the seat of government was moved to Williamsburg.

Today Jamestown is a historical site maintained by the Association for the Preservation of Virginian Antiquities and the National Park Service. The former organization owns the west end of the town site, which contains such objects of interest as the Memorial Cross marking the earliest cemetery of the town, the Pocahontas Monument, the statue of Captain John Smith, and the Old Church Tower — the only surviving ruin from 17th century Jamestown. The association is also responsible for a commemorative service that annually takes place on the Sunday nearest May 13, Jamestown Day. Included in the program of this event are speeches, readings, and choral selections. The College of William and Mary generally participates in these ceremonies, and addresses by British and American public figures provide pertinent thoughts on the occasion. A procession to the Memorial Cross and a wreath-laying ceremony highlight the formal observance, which concludes with a memorial prayer, the singing of the national anthem, and the pronouncement of a benediction.

Since 1934 the remaining areas of the town site and island have been part of the Colonial National Historical Park. Several archaeological excavations in these sections have revealed the foundations of many of the original buildings, and streets and fences have been restored to enable visitors to comprehend more fully the size of the first permanent settlement. The National Park Service also administers a Visitor Center and museum, which provide invaluable information on the history of Jamestown.

Adjoining the Colonial National Historical Park is the Jamestown Festival Park, built by the Commonwealth of Virginia in 1957 to commemorate the 350th anniversary of the founding of Jamestown. There the public can explore replicas of such buildings as the James Fort of 1607 and Powhatan's Lodge, which was the scene of John Smith's trial. Moored on the river front of the park are reproductions of the three ships that brought the first settlers to Jamestown and these are also open to visitors.

Mexican War Begins

The congressional declaration of war on Mexico, on May 12, 1846, was the culmination of a long series of events. Some of the irritants in relations between the two countries — which went back originally to confusion over the boundaries of the Louisiana Purchase and over the rights of American settlers — continued during the period from 1803 to 1836 (see March 2, Texas Independence Day, and April 21, San Jacinto Day).

It was the 1845 annexation of Texas — by then a free republic whose officials sought the annexation — and controversy over what constituted its southern border that set off the war more directly. Texas, according to Texans, extended all the way south to the Rio Grande. Mexico claimed, however, that Texas extended only as far as the Nueces River.

Even in the United States the measure for annexation was controversial. Unable to secure the two-thirds vote necessary for Senate ratification of the measure, proponents presented it as a joint congressional resolution instead. Providing that Texas was to be admitted directly to statehood, the measure passed both houses by a simple majority and was signed by President John Tyler on March 1, 1845 (see March 1), just before he left office. Texas became a state on December 29 of the same year (see December 29).

Other factors contributing to the Mexican War included a dispute over claims against the Mexican government by American settlers who had suffered property or personal damage during the changes of government that followed Mexico's successful revolution against Spain. In the background, there was also the desire of the United States — by then gripped with its vision of a "manifest destiny to overspread the continent" and suspicious of the territorial designs of other powers — to gain possession of the Mexican provinces of California and New Mexico.

Accordingly, President James K. Polk, who had been elected on a platform favoring the "re-annexation" of Texas, dispatched John Slidell on a diplomatic mission to Mexico in November of 1845. Slidell's assignment was to secure Mexico's agreement on the Rio Grande as Texas' southern boundary. If feasible, he also was to arrange the purchase of California and New Mexico, for which the United States was prepared to offer up to $30 million or $40 million and assumption of its citizens' claims against Mexico.

Slidell's stay in Mexico dragged on for months while the Mexican government, under the pressure of local politics, declined to receive him. The final refusal came on March 12, 1846.

Four days earlier an American army under General Zachary Taylor had begun advancing from the Nueces River, where it had been since the previous summer, to the mouth of the Rio Grande, where it arrived on March 24. Elements of Taylor's force followed the river inland to a point opposite Matamoros, where the Mexicans had assembled between 5,000 and 6,000 men. In the weeks that followed, both armies devoted themselves to building fortifications — the Americans undeterred by the Mexicans' April 12 warning to withdraw beyond the Nueces or face the prospect that "arms and arms alone must decide the question."

The spark was not long in coming. On April 24 the Mexican commander sent word that, in his view, hostilities were already under way. Taylor countered that the "responsibility must rest with them who actually commence them."

That very day 1,600 Mexicans crossed the Rio Grande, killed or wounded 16 members of an American reconnaissance party, and captured most of the rest. Advised of the news, President Polk delivered, with the approval of his cabinet, a war message in which he asserted that "Mexico has . . . shed American blood upon . . . American soil." Although some Americans still questioned whether hostilities had begun on American or on Mexican soil, a declaration of war was passed by the House of Representatives the same day, May 11, and by the Senate the following day.

Even before war had been declared officially, "Old Rough and Ready" Taylor, who became a national hero during the hostilities, had driven the Mexicans back across the Rio Grande, with victories at Palo Alto and Resaca de la Palma, in the vicinity of Matamoros. He occupied Matamoros itself on May 18 and took Monterrey on September 24. The resistance in northern Mexico ended before the winter was over, with Taylor's defeat of the scourge of the Alamo, General Antonio López de Santa Anna, in the hotly contested battle of Buena Vista, on February 22 and 23, 1847.

In the meantime two other aspects of the war went forward. These were the United States' blockade of Mexico's east- and west-coast ports and the occupation of New Mexico — a vast region embracing most of what is now the US southwest — by Colonel Stephen Kearny.

From New Mexico, Kearny's instructions took him with part of his force to California. On the way he learned of the "bear flag revolt" of a handful of American settlers in the Sacramento Valley. The settlers had declared California independent in June 1845 and prepared to challenge Mexico as the Texas settlers had done earlier. The adventurer Kit Carson and Captain John C. Frémont of the US Army, who was in California at the time, joined forces with the revolutionists. On the California coast, where the names of Commodores Sloat and Stockton are still well remembered in this connection, US Navy personnel took possession of Monterey, San Francisco, and Los Angeles. In the north of California other points were occupied with little resistance. When Kearny arrived in San Diego in December of 1846, he was able to proceed with setting up a provisional California government.

Back on the Mexican front, General Winfield Scott meanwhile proposed, and Polk approved, an expedition to Veracruz. When that city fell to Scott on March 29, 1847, the way was opened to victories at Cerro Gordo, Contreras, Churu-busco, Molino del Rey, and the hill of Chapultepec, which dominated the capital, Mexico City. Chapultepec won, the American forces entered Mexico City on September 13 and 14, 1847. To all intents and purposes, the war ended several days later.

Technically, however, it was concluded on February 2, 1848, with the signing of the Treaty of Guadalupe Hidalgo (see February 2). In accordance with the terms of this agreement, Mexico gave up all claim to Texas and recognized the Rio Grande as its own northern boundary. Mexico also ceded both California and New Mexico to the United States. In return the United States paid Mexico $15 million and assumed the claims of its nationals against the Mexican government.

Tulip Time Festival
Holland, Michigan

This is a movable event. See note on page xxvi.

One of the nation's most popular flower festivals is the annual four-day Tulip Time Festival, which begins on the Wednesday nearest May 15 in Holland, Michigan. The city, founded by Dutch immigrants in 1846, is the nation's largest center of Dutch culture. The idea that tulips should be planted as a civic undertaking to beautify the city of Holland originated as the suggestion of Lida Rogers, a local high school biology teacher, in 1927. A hundred thousand bulbs were put in the next fall — to such public acclaim that more were planted for the next year. The phrase "Tulip Time in Holland," coined for news releases describing the project, encouraged an already mounting public interest. Before long, residents found themselves searching for added festival atmosphere to go with the tulips.

The first official Tulip Time Festival followed, in 1929. It has been an annual event ever since, attracting visitors by the hundreds of thousands. Highlight of the opening Wednesday is the early afternoon street scrubbing ceremony in which the mayor and town council examine the streets, discover that they are dirty, and order them scrubbed. Several hundred local residents in authentic Dutch costumes, some of them carrying pails of water hung from the traditional Dutch shoulder yokes, do the job with brushes and willow brooms. Sometimes the laborers include visiting dignitaries, as in 1965, when Governor George Romney and his wife, also in Dutch costumes, lent a helping hand.

The scrubbing is closely followed by the Volks Parade, with bands and floats, and colorful Dutch dresses, baggy pants, and starched hats by the hundred. It is followed by one of the highlights of the festival, a performance by the famous Klompen Dancers — more than 600 girls from Holland and nearby West Ottawa who have practiced their Dutch folk dances all spring under the tutelage of their high school gym instructors. The girls, wearing wooden shoes, and outfits carefully copied from those worn in various regions of the old Netherlands, perform several times each day during the festival. The street, or sidewalk, scrubbing is also repeated each day.

Thursday's big additional festival feature is the Children's Parade, with more than 3,000 local schoolchildren marching through the business section in Dutch costumes and carrying facsimiles of products and objects associated with Holland. Another festival high point takes place on Saturday morning, when top baton twirlers from all parts of the country take part in the Tulip Time Baton Twirling Contest to select a national champion. The contest, which has been a part of the festival since 1958, is open to competitors from every state. It is followed, later on Saturday, by an invitational band festival in which outstanding bands from Michigan high schools are judged, during a two-and-a-half-hour performance, on the basis of their music, marching, special maneuvers, and showmanship. Shortly afterwards comes the third big parade of the Tulip Time Festival. This one, the Parade of Bands, features more than 50 bands drawn from many states and accompanied by floats and costumed marching units.

Other festival events have been added over the years — some to become traditional events and others to change from year to year. The program of recent years has generally included on Wednesday evening the Festival Musicale, presented by the 60 mixed voices of the combined Magnachords Male Chorus and the Bel Canto Singers of Holland and, late Wednesday afternoon, a program portraying life in the old Netherlands, called Dutch Heritage, which features authentic costumes from various provinces. This is repeated daily during the festival. On Thursday evening there is usually a concert by the Hope College Symphony Orchestra and a band concert put on by Saladin Temple's Million Dollar Shrine Band of Grand Rapids, Michigan. One of the big features of Friday evening is the Parade of Barbershop Quartets presented by the Holland chapter of the Society for the Preservation and Encouragement of Barbershop Quartet Singing in America. There are also two square dances, on Friday and Saturday evenings, art exhibits, organ recitals at Hope College, and an antique show; and the big Saturday evening windup features music and entertainment prepared for the occasion by the music and fine arts departments of local high schools.

Flowers, which were the beginning and reason for the Tulip Time Festival, can be seen in brilliant array in the Tulip Lanes, which today stretch for eight miles along Holland's streets. Visitors who wish to see the tulips can do so by starting at 12th Street and River Avenue and following the posted arrows. The Tulip Lanes' burst of color is supplemented by other displays: there are special plantings in the park at Eighth and Lincoln streets and at local nurseries; and a flower show sponsored by the Holland Garden club is held annually at festival time.

In addition there are elaborate plantings at one of the attractions of which townspeople are proudest — the 200-year-old, grain-grinding windmill "De Zwaan," which was dismantled in its native Vinkel, Holland, and reassembled in the city of Holland, in time for the 1965 festival. Prince Bernhard of the Netherlands was on hand for the dedication. Said to be the only authentic Dutch windmill in the United States, the 125-foot-tall "Swan" is set on Windmill Island, a $500,000 park project that includes its own canal, dikes, drawbridge, and post office and remains open to visitors throughout the summer and into the fall. Its attractions include the *draaimolen* (merry-go-round) and Little Netherlands, a miniature Dutch village.

Netherlandish flavor also permeates such other points of interest as the Netherlands Museum, with collections portraying Dutch background and folklore and the heritage of the city of Holland; two wooden shoe factories; and the Tulip Time Dutch market, open from 9:00 A.M. to 9:00 P.M. at festival time. There such foods as Dutch *saucijzenbroodjes* ("pigs-in-the-blanket") can be sampled; visitors can watch a Dutch glassblower, wooden-shoe maker, candlemaker, and other artisans at work; see frequent performances by Klompen dancers; and view a 30-foot model of a reclamation project that includes dikes, canals, and locks. A mile north of Holland on the US Route 31 bypass, those interested can visit the Dutch Village with its canals, windmills, tulips, Dutch farmhouse and barn, street organ concerts, folk dances, arts and crafts demonstrations, films of the Netherlands, and varied exhibits and amusements.

MAY 14

Antioch College Chartered

On May 14, 1852, Antioch College, located in Yellow Springs, 18 miles east of Dayton in southwestern Ohio, was chartered. It was the earliest American educational institution of first-class standing that was both nonsectarian and fully coeducational.

The idea for such a college had been broached

as early as 1837 by members of the Christian Connexion, a religious body that had arisen in various eastern states at the beginning of the century. The movement to establish an innovative college began to gather momentum in 1849 under the impetus of Alpheus Marshall Merrifield, a building contractor of Worcester, Massachusetts. On May 8 and 9, 1850, an informally chosen committee on education gathered in New York to draw up a plan for a college to be submitted to delegates from widely scattered Christian Connexion congregations in the United States and Canada at a national convention in October 1850 at Marion, Orange County, New York. There it was resolved that "our responsibility to the community, and the advancement of our interests . . . demand of us the establishment of a College" and that "this College shall afford equal privileges to both sexes."

In recognition of the financial support of Ohio members, who contributed six times as much money as members in all the other states combined, it was decided to locate the college in that state. Yellow Springs was selected as the site, and construction of campus buildings began early in 1852. Upon its completion, Antioch Hall, designed to accommodate 1,000 students, was one of the largest buildings in Ohio. By January 26, 1852, the decision had been made to close the proposed curriculum to theological study, a step that was significant for the institution's pioneering role in nonsectarian education on the college level.

The Committee on Faculty then approached Horace Mann (see May 4) to ask whether he would accept the presidency of the new college that would admit students without regard to sex, color, or religious affiliation. The 56-year-old Mann, who for twelve years had been secretary of the Massachusetts Board of Education, was a well-known educator and social reformer noted for furthering common-school education and teacher training. He was attracted by the idea of having a free hand in developing Antioch College and commented: "It involves considerations of vast importance — not to myself merely — these I could easily dispose of — but considerations of vast importance to the rising generations of the country in whom I feel so deep an interest."

Mann was elected president of Antioch on September 17, 1852. Dedication and inauguration ceremonies took place on October 5, 1853, and a permanent board of trustees was elected on September 4 of the following year.

The new college was the object of much attention. When it opened its doors in the fall of 1853, it had attracted over 1,000 applicants, most of whom were unprepared. Of the 150 students who took the required written entrance examinations, only 8 passed; others were enrolled in a related preparatory school. During Horace Mann's six-year presidency, 40 students — 9 women and 31 men — were graduated from the college, while 325 other college students and over 1,500 preparatory students were directly influenced by his educational methods.

Mann was imbued with an "enthusiasm for humanity." He aimed at the individual's highest possible development and stressed that a combination of scholarship and character development would result in intellectual and spiritual freedom. To attain this end, Mann planned a curriculum modeled on the highest academic standards of the period, as practiced in the top eastern colleges. Courses in science, history, composition, literature, and modern languages — with less emphasis than was then usual on classical languages — were supplemented by electives in drawing, design, and music. And, as the president stated with pride: "In all this Great West, ours is the only institution, of a first-class character, which is not, directly or indirectly, under the influence of the old-school theology." Great stress was also placed upon hygiene, general conduct, and moral habits.

Elected president of Antioch College three times, Mann devoted the last years before his death on August 2, 1859, to fulfilling these goals and experienced perhaps greater satisfaction in his achievements than in his previous accomplishments as a lawyer, politician, and state official. As his wife, Mary Peabody Mann, wrote in a letter to her sister Sophia Peabody Hawthorne (the wife of Nathaniel Hawthorne) in 1858: "What Mr. Mann has done in these five years for five hundred or more young people is worth all the toils and labors of his life." One of his students later summarized Mann's achievements: he established high literary and moral standards; he raised educational requirements on all levels; he demonstrated the practicality of coeducation; and he imparted the mastery of knowledge while promoting both self-reliance and improved health among students.

After the first few decades of its existence, Antioch College — although retaining its tradition of well-known names and accomplishments — experienced a decline that was not arrested until the 1920s. Then Arthur E. Morgan, an educator and noted civil engineer, was selected president of Antioch. In 1921 he began to revitalize the college by revamping the curriculum around the goal of "learning what life means and how to make the most of it." Firmly committed to the merits of the small community, he implemented the "co-operative" work-study program as a means of providing practical experience, as well as of training managers for business and industry. The program, as he envisaged it, should commonly require at least five years to earn a

B.A. or B.S. degree; the student should spend the first year on campus and the remaining four in alternate periods of work and study. Morgan was convinced that such a program would enable students to acquire assets not readily obtainable in a classroom situation: self-reliance, initiative, courage, adaptability, responsibility, and practical adjustment to life. Some 200 colleges and universities offer cooperative programs now.

Antioch College, which celebrated its centennial in 1953–1954, still has a reputation for widely divergent learning environments, cultural pluralism, individualized attention, openness to educational experimentation, and extensive training outside the classroom. In line with Horace Mann's last words to his students, "Be ashamed to die until you have won some victory for humanity," the college stresses the application of knowledge to civic action.

The 100-acre, park-like campus at Yellow Springs now includes over 40 buildings. Students, usually with half on campus at one time, complete an undergraduate program for a B.A. or B.S. degree in four to five years. By graduation, most of them have held four to six different "co-op" jobs in business, industry, government, school systems, social agencies, or research laboratories under some 700 employers in 30 states and several foreign countries.

In recent years Antioch College has moved away from its Yellow Springs nucleus, establishing a network of centers in various parts of the country and an international education program with centers in Canada and Europe.

Lewis and Clark Depart

The Treaty of Paris of 1783, which established the independence of the United States, gave the fledgling nation title to all lands east of the Mississippi River. In the colonial period, settlement had extended inland only to the Allegheny Mountains, and observers thought that generations would pass before American cities and farms would border the Mississippi. Still, the citizens of the adventurous young nation not only sought to reach the river, but also dreamed of laying claim to the vast expanse between it and the Pacific Ocean. Early in 1803 President Thomas Jefferson persuaded Congress to appropriate $2,500 for an exploration of the uncharted trans-Mississippi region, and by the Louisiana Purchase of 1803, he bought from France the vast territory between the Mississippi and the Rocky Mountains.

Jefferson named Meriwether Lewis and William Clark, military men who had spent considerable time in wilderness areas, to lead the exploring party that probed the newly acquired territory and the region beyond the Rocky Mountains. Lewis and Clark and the more than 40 soldiers and civilians with them spent the winter of 1803–1804 near what is now St. Louis, Missouri, preparing for their mission. Then, on May 14, 1804, the expedition set out on the adventure, which lasted two years and took the explorers through areas of the Northwest that hitherto had not been visited by whites. Their historic overland journey (see September 23, Lewis and Clark Expedition Completed) ended in 1806 with their triumphant return to St. Louis — and a world that had thought them lost forever.

Feast of St. Matthias

The feast of St. Matthias (see February 24), the disciple who was selected by lots to be the 12th Apostle and the replacement for Judas Iscariot, Jesus' betrayer, is observed on May 14 by the Roman Catholic church. Commemorated on February 24 until recently, it is now listed for May 14 in the revised Roman calendar to avoid having it fall during Lent and to place it in Eastertide close to Ascension Day. The original date is kept by the Protestant Episcopal and Lutheran churches.

MAY 15

Congress Resolves to Put Colonies in State of Defense

On May 10, 1775, the Second Continental Congress met in Philadelphia to coordinate the actions of the American colonies in the continuing crisis with Great Britain. News from Massachusetts of the battles of April 19 at Lexington and Concord, and allegations of atrocities committed by British troops retreating from the engagements to Boston had angered moderate delegates and driven even conservatives like John Dickinson of Pennsylvania to despair of the possibilities of reconciliation. Five days later, on May 15, the Congress took an important step toward a total military rebellion against Great Britain, resolving that "these colonies be immediately put in a state of defence."

Congress advised the colonies to prepare their militia units, in which all able-bodied men between the ages of 16 and 50 were supposed to serve. The Philadelphia delegates offered a general plan for the most efficient organization of militia companies, the combination of these smaller groups into battalions and regiments, and the proper allocation of officers throughout the structure. The congressional directive granted company-size elements the power to select their own leaders, and authorized political patriot groups to appoint regimental officers on the provincial level.

In a decision of even greater importance, the Philadelphia assembly took steps to establish an intercolonial "American" army. John Adams of Massachusetts offered the forces besieging the British troops in Boston as the nucleus of a Continental army, and the Congress on June 14 resolved to raise six additional companies in Pennsylvania, Maryland, and Virginia to assist in the New England operations. The delegates requested the colonies to raise specified numbers of troops and authorized them to appoint officers up to the rank of colonel.

Congress reserved for itself the power to choose generals in the Continental army and decided immediately to name a commander in chief. George Washington was the leading candidate for the post. Forty-three years of age, the Virginian had gained military experience in the French and Indian War, serving for a time as an American aide-de-camp to the ill-fated General Edward Braddock. The fact that Washington was one of the wealthiest men in America made him attractive to conservatives. In politics he was a moderate acceptable to both radicals and conservatives. On June 15 Thomas Johnson of Maryland nominated Washington as commander in chief; John Adams, New England's radical spokesman, seconded the selection in the hope of enlisting Southern support for beleaguered Massachusetts; and the delegates gave their unanimous consent.

Washington, who attended the session in his Virginia militia uniform, accepted the honor. He made a modest speech to the Congress, and offered to serve without salary. The new commander then prepared to depart for Massachusetts to join the patriot soldiers who were encircling Boston, where the British troops had taken refuge.

On June 17 Congress named a number of other general officers, including Artemas Ward, Charles Lee, Philip Schuyler, and Israel Putnam as major generals. The delegates also designated Horatio Gates as adjutant general, James Warren of Massachusetts as paymaster general of the main army, and Jonathan Trumbull Jr. as paymaster of the forces in New York. The Congress then deferred to Washington for the selection of officers for the posts of quartermaster general, and commissary of artillery.

Aware of the vulnerability of the provincial legislatures to the powers of the royal governors, the Congress on July 18 advised the colonies to appoint extralegal committees of safety to supervise matters relating to defense during the recesses of the colonial assemblies. The provinces quickly responded, and the committees of safety became strong bodies, which sometimes operated in arbitrary ways to win the cooperation of the reluctant. At the same time, the Continental Congress reminded the colonies to ensure the safety of their harbors and seacoasts.

Congress next faced the problem of raising money for the defenses. Gouverneur Morris of New York was most active in developing a plan to issue paper money, which the delegates adopted on June 22. According to the proposal, Congress was to issue not more than $2 million in bills of credit backed by Spanish milled dollars. The confederated colonies then pledged to redeem them within seven years, with each colony paying a share of the debt proportionate to the size of its population.

As subsidiary measures to secure the American military position, Congress took action to improve relations with the colonies' Canadian and Indian neighbors, to establish a post office, and to set up a military hospital. The Congress on May 29 requested the "oppressed inhabitants of Canada" to extend cooperation to American efforts to preserve liberty. On July 13 the delegates appointed commissioners to secure treaties of neutrality with the Indians in the northern and middle colonies, and on July 19 designated other negotiators to deal with the tribes in the South. On July 26 the Congress named Benjamin Franklin postmaster general and authorized the erection of a string of stations from New England to Georgia that would offer the ways and means "for the speedy and secure conveyance of Intelligence from one end of the Continent to the other." Finally, on July 27, the assembly made provisions for a hospital establishment, including a director general and chief physician, 4 surgeons, 1 apothecary, 20 surgeons' mates, 2 storekeepers, 1 nurse to every 10 sick, and occasional laborers. Dr. Benjamin Church of Boston, who later proved to be an informer for the British, became the director general and chief physician.

Before adjourning on August 2, the delegates issued two important declarations. Much to the distress of the radicals, Congress on July 5 adopted the Olive Branch Petition, designed by John Dickinson of Pennsylvania as a final plea for reconciliation between England and its colonies. The petition, which King George III eventually refused to receive, restated the Americans' grievances, professed the colonists' attachment to the crown and begged that the monarch prevent further hostile action until a peaceable solution could be achieved. On July 6 the assemblage endorsed a "Declaration of the Causes and Necessity of Taking Up Arms," a statement drafted by John Dickinson and Thomas Jefferson, which rejected independence as a goal but presented the colonial point of view in the most forceful manner:

We are reduced to the alternative of chusing an unconditional submission to the tyranny of irritated ministers, or resistance by force. — The latter is our choice. — We have counted the cost of this contest, and find nothing so dreadful as voluntary slavery. . . . Our cause is just. Our union is perfect. Our internal resources are great, and, if necessary, foreign assistance is undoubtedly attainable. . . . With hearts fortified with these animating reflections, we most solemnly, before God and the world, declare, that, exerting the utmost energy of those powers which our beneficent Creator hath graciously bestowed upon us, the arms we have been compelled by our enemies to assume, we will, in defiance of every hazard, with unabating firmness and perseverance, employ for the preservation of our liberties; being with one mind resolved to die freemen rather than to live slaves. . . .

The words of this declaration were to be more prophetic than those of the Olive Branch Petition. Lexington and Concord became not isolated incidents but the first battles of the American Revolution, a protracted war between the united colonies and Great Britain. Fortunately for the Americans, the actions taken by the Second Continental Congress proved a solid foundation on which they were able to construct a lasting triumph and a new nation.

MAY 16

Armed Forces Day

This is a movable event. See note on page xxvi.

To increase military efficiency and encourage interservice cooperation, Congress on July 26, 1947, approved the National Security Act. This legislation coordinated the US Army, Navy, and Air Force into a single National Military Establishment, created the new cabinet post of secretary of defense, and consolidated the executive departments of War and of the Navy into a single Department of Defense — by which name the National Military Establishment came to be known. In keeping with this emphasis on the unity and common purposes of the various branches of the US military, a new day of observance, Armed Forces Day, came into existence in 1949, when it was designated as the third Saturday in May.

Prior to 1949, the three largest branches of the armed services had held elaborate observances on three separate days of the year: the army on April 6, the anniversary of US entry into World War I; the navy on the October 27 birth date of Theodore Roosevelt, its champion; and the air force on the second Saturday in September — close to the date when it was first established as a separate service on September 18, 1947. President Harry S. Truman's proclamation of 1949, initiating the third Saturday in May as Armed Forces Day, did not totally eliminate these individual celebrations. But it did more or less reduce them to intraservice or private commemorations designed to promote the particular traditions and achievements of each of the branches of the armed forces. Perhaps most indicative of this shift in emphasis is the fact that the army has totally abandoned its former observance of April 6 and now internally celebrates only the anniversary of its founding on June 14.

Commemorations of each service unit's days of importance are generally confined to military installations, but celebrations of Armed Forces Day reach a much wider audience. Each year the President of the United States, the governors of Alabama, Montana, Rhode Island, and Vermont, and the mayor of New York City are among those who issue official proclamations declaring the third Saturday in May as Armed Forces Day. In Tennessee the governor proclaims the entire week including this day as Armed Forces Week. Throughout the country both civilians and the military participate in the day's events. Citizens express their gratitude to the nation's more than 3 million service members with parades, special church services, military balls, and other events. The armed forces, for their part, take the opportunity to acquaint the public with the latest military advances: many army posts hold open house featuring tactical and weapons displays; the navy often permits civilians to tour vessels in port; and numerous air force bases present demonstrations of precision flying.

Often the President and highly placed members of the defense establishment are witnesses to special exhibitions of the nation's defense readiness, as in 1969 when President Richard M. Nixon watched elaborate naval exercises from the aircraft carrier USS *Saratoga* off Norfolk, Virginia. Together with Admiral Thomas H. Moorer, chief of Naval Operations, and Henry A. Kissinger, his assistant for national security affairs, the President had flown by helicopter from the White House to the carrier for the Armed Forces Day observance. Earlier in the day, he had marked the occasion by bestowing two Medals of Honor at a White House ceremony.

For the civilian populace probably the most

lavish observance of Armed Forces Day is the mammoth parade held each year in New York City. In recent years US Army, Navy, Air Force, Marine, Coast Guard, Reserve, and National Guard units; the various US service academies; and the American Legion, Veterans of Foreign Wars, and other veterans' organizations have provided as many as 9,000 marchers for this event. The parade, which has as its theme Power for Peace, generally proceeds down Fifth Avenue from about 96th to 62nd streets. Marching bands play martial music, and tanks and other military equipment are interspersed throughout the line of march. Thousands of spectators line the avenue, and city and state officials are usually present to review the proceedings.

Maifest
Hermann, Missouri

This is a movable event. See note on page xxvi.

The *Maifest*, held annually on the third weekend in May in Hermann, Missouri, is designed as a reminder of the town's German heritage.

As such, it has much in common with the purposes of the town's first settlers. For the town of Hermann —named for the hero-prince who drove the Roman legions from Germany in the first century A.D. — was intended as the principal settlement of what was to be a German "state" in the United States, a New World colony where the German language and customs would be kept intact.

The idea for such a state was set forth in a pamphlet published in 1833 by Friedrich Muensch and distributed among the German people of Philadelphia. The notion proved to be a contagious one, for within three years a German Settlement Society had been formed, a constitution adopted, shares in the project sold at $25 apiece, and a committee of three sent out to choose a suitable location.

Of the committee's three suggestions, its description of what is now the site of Hermann was the most enthusiastically received, and a schoolmaster, George F. Bayer, was dispatched to purchase the necessary land. The first settlers were five families who arrived by Missouri River boat on December 6, 1837, and spent a miserable first winter until they were joined by 230 other laborers the next spring, and an additional 200 or so in 1839.

Wine making and grape culture were the chief industries of the town until the advent of Prohibition in 1920, when they were abandoned. Located directly on the Missouri, Hermann also became known as perhaps the most prosperous of the river towns between St. Louis and Kansas City. It was a center for ship building and for boatmen.

During the 19th century the town was known as Little Germany, and Sunday boat and railroad excursions brought pleasure seekers from St. Louis and elsewhere for the several German festivals held at Hermann each year. Among them was a small *Maifest* – a festive occasion with a band leading a parade through town to the picnic grounds.

The local theater, with productions of Goethe and Schiller, also was popular from Hermann's early days, and so were music, dancing, and membership in the *Turnverein* (gymnastic society). There was a German-language newspaper, church services were held in German, and there was an attempt to preserve the German language through the schools — first with a separate German school and later by having public school classes conducted in both German and English. Since World War I, however, German has been simply one of the subjects taught in the otherwise English-language schools.

In other ways, too, Hermann's purely German character inevitably gave way to Americanization during the 20th century, and it became clear that effort must be expended if the town's unusual heritage was to be preserved. One of the first steps was the work of half a dozen citizens to enlarge Hermann's 100-year-old *Maifest*. The first "large" *Maifest*, officially sponsored by the Brush and Palette Club, took place in 1952, with such features as a historical pageant, a tour of old homes and other historic buildings, German meals, and a parade built around a Good Old Days theme.

Since then a larger group of citizens has formed the nonprofit Historic Hermann, Inc., which not only sponsors the annual *Maifest* but has as its overall purpose the preservation of the arts, culture, homes, and historic sites of the early German settlers. The *Maifest*, which now attracts 40,000 to 50,000 visitors annually to the town of about 2,600 people, has an aura of nostalgia and *Gemütlichkeit* (good nature, comfortableness, and geniality). Festivities customarily begin with preliminary entertainment on Friday evening.

In one typical year, the program included all of the features introduced in 1952, as well as some new ones. During the weekend there were six performances of the Musik Halle Show, an hour of nostalgic musical numbers and a comedy called "It Was a Good Time," in the City Park Rotunda. Also held there on Friday and Saturday evenings was the Concert in the Park, a choral presentation featuring Hermann's Hungry Five. Saturday evening there was an Old Time Dance in Eagle Hall. Apart from the big *Alte*

Zeiten (Old Time) parade on Sunday, with prizes in the "most unique" category and in the categories of horse-drawn, "motor-drawn," and antique vehicles, there were a separate children's parade Saturday morning; an antique show and sale; craft demonstrations; old-time movies; a quilt display; and an abundance of food. Included were bratwurst, German potato salad, *Schnitzbrot,* ham, chicken, and other delicacies served by various church groups.

City Park was also the site of the popular farmers' market, which had handwork, foods, and farmers' products for sale and featured demonstrations of such arts and crafts as weaving, spinning, caning, and wood carving. Roving entertainers, who added to the gaiety of the *Maifest* by performing at various times and places during the weekend, included such groups as the McCluer High School Dancers; the Hermann Schuhplattlers; the Hermann Elementary School Folk Dancers; the German Band of Germantown, Illinois; and the Montgomery City Town Band.

MAY 17

Supreme Court Orders School Desegregation

History was made on May 17, 1954, when the US Supreme Court ruled unanimously in the case of *Brown* v. *Board of Education* that racial segregation in public schools was unconstitutional. Specifically, it held that segregation violated both the equal protection clause of the 14th Amendment and the due process clause of the 5th Amendment. No matter how "equal" separate schools for black and white students might be, the decision held, the very quality of being separate was "inherently unequal." The new ruling overturned the Court's 1896 decision (*Plessy* v. *Ferguson*) that segregated facilities, if equal, did not constitute discrimination — the famous "separate but equal" doctrine that for the next 58 years was used to justify the segregation of schools and many other facilities.

With the Court's 1954 decision, any such basis for the prolonging of segregation ceased to exist. The implications of the decision, as later spelled out through directions to lower courts and in a second *Brown* case, extended considerably beyond public schools to include public housing developments, public parks, and tax-supported colleges and universities. As attempts to flout the ruling touched off what was to become a mammoth drive for civil rights in other areas as well, the decision's indirect effects extended still further.

Opposition to the school desegregation order initially was most pronounced in the South, where it was first put into effect. Until the *Brown* case, *de jure* segregation had prevailed throughout the South: public places were segregated by state and local law, and the idea of desegregated public facilities of any kind ran counter to decades of custom. Moderate opinion notwithstanding, most Deep South and border states devised foot-dragging tactics to delay desegregation — if possible forever. In some places, violence was perpetrated by segregationist extremists who also sought, by intimidation, to deprive blacks of their right to vote. Later, however, when implementation of the school desegregation ruling began in other parts of the country, it was realized that antidesegregation sentiment was not merely a regional matter. Vocal opposition to the Supreme Court decision was also encountered in the North, Midwest, and West. There, school segregation, where it existed, was not a matter of law but *de facto*, resulting from widespread segregated housing patterns. Controversy over establishing racial balance in schools — especially if this meant busing students out of their own neighborhoods or across suburban boundary lines — was as vociferous above the Mason-Dixon Line as below.

The Supreme Court underlined its 1954 decision with several others. One, on May 31, 1955, emphasized that the desegregation of schools must proceed "with all deliberate speed." A second, on May 27, 1963, pointedly stressed that the concept of "deliberate speed" did not countenance "indefinite delay in elimination of racial barriers in schools" and called for the prompt vindication of "plain and present constitutional rights."

Meanwhile, in September 1957, Congress had enacted the first Civil Rights Act since 1875 (see September 9). Important as the new act was, it seemed to intensify resistance to school desegregation. The inevitable confrontation between federal and state authority on this issue came that same month at Little Rock, Arkansas, when Governor Orval Faubus called out the state national guard to prevent nine black children from entering the previously all-white Central High School — to avert, as he declared, public disorder. When the governor defied a federal district court order to admit the children, President Dwight D. Eisenhower dispatched federal troops to ensure their enrollment.

Against this background of resistance to legally required desegregation, black Americans — who had been "freed" from slavery in 1863 and waited almost one hundred years for the equality promised them in the 13th, 14th, and 15th amendments — meanwhile had neared the end of their patience. There began a new, widespread, and determined drive to achieve what a century of waiting had failed to provide. Although it was set in motion as an indirect result of the Supreme Court's school desegregation ruling, the goals of this broad civil rights drive extended far beyond schools to include demands for an end to discrimination in many other areas as well, among them voting, employment, and housing.

Part of the effort centered around a long series of court battles, waged initially by the National Association for the Advancement of Colored People and subsequently also by the US Department of Justice and others. More spectacular, however, was the wave of carefully planned nonviolent demonstrations that swept the country in the late 1950s and during the 1960s. They included such tactics as picketing, boycotts, mass meetings, "sit-ins" at segregated lunch counters and restaurants, marches, prayer meetings, voter registration drives, and the "freedom rides" with which interracial groups of travelers eventually forced desegregation of interstate buses, trains, and waiting rooms.

The deviser of much of the movement's strategy and its chief spokesman was the young southern black minister Martin Luther King Jr. (see January 15), who based his concept of love on the teachings of Jesus and his practical strategy on the tactics of nonviolent protest enunciated by Henry David Thoreau and perfected by India's Mahatma Gandhi. Support for the rights movement was interracial. It came from students, religious leaders, individuals of varied backgrounds, and civil rights organizations. The latter included the NAACP, the Urban League, King's own Southern Christian Leadership Conference, and organizations such as the Congress of Racial Equality (CORE) and the Student Nonviolent Coordinating Committee (SNCC) that later moved away from the civil rights moderates to take a more activist position.

As the rights drive progressed, laying bare the issues and bringing attention to them, the various forms of protest shifted their focus, with the name of one community after another taking its place in news headlines across the nation. Among the hundreds of demonstrations that took place, there were scores of key engagements.

A few of the most crucial were the following:

The successful, yearlong boycott, beginning in December 1955, to desegregate the buses of Montgomery, Alabama (see December 1). It was this boycott that first brought King — and the civil rights movement — to worldwide attention;
The confrontations between state and federal power at Little Rock, Arkansas, in 1957; and at Oxford, Mississippi, where James Meredith became the first black student to enter the University of Mississippi, in 1962;

The massive demonstrations at Birmingham, Alabama, in the summer of 1963. Greeted with harsh police measures, the Birmingham protests set off a nationwide chain reaction of demonstrations, including the famous March on Washington of 1963 (see January 1, Emancipation Proclamation), and did much to ensure passage of the Civil Rights Act of 1964 (see July 2);

The Mississippi Freedom Summer in 1964 — a large-scale voter registration drive gruesomely punctuated by the murder of three young civil rights workers;

The demonstrations against restrictive voter registration requirements in Alabama, begun in February 1965 at Selma, where harsh repressive methods by police galvanized nationwide indignation and ensured congressional passage of the Voting Rights Act of 1965 (see August 6). The upheaval at Selma was followed by a triumphant, five-day rights march from Selma to the state capital at Montgomery.

Beginning in 1965, however, an increasing number of issues distracted the attention of the public, government, and press from the civil rights drive. Among these were the Vietnam war, mounting economic difficulties, unemployment, a worldwide oil shortage, and the series of scandals and abuses known as Watergate. There were other concerns as well, including the assassination of Martin Luther King Jr. in 1968 (see April 4). In addition, there was a hardening of positions by extremist minorities of both races. Some whites took part in the "white flight to the suburbs," a population shift away from central cities. Others, prompted by fear that progress in the matter of civil rights would create competition between whites and blacks for jobs and other opportunities, became part of an anti-desegregationist "white backlash" against what they regarded as "too much too soon." Some white segregationists even resorted to nonpeaceful means in their protests against busing to achieve school integration. Blacks, including many moderates, and some white civil rights advocates as well, meanwhile endorsed the slogan of "black power," which different people variously interpreted to mean physical power, economic power, voting power, or, simply, self-respect and economic hope. Some blacks moved toward the idea of separatism, as opposed to the ideal of a mixed society. Some showed impatience with the concept of nonviolent protest that had been so eloquently expressed by King.

The years since the mid-sixties have been periodically disrupted by urban riots, including those of the "long, hot summers" of 1966 and 1967, and those that broke out in ghettos across the nation after the King assassination in 1968, as well as by other violence instigated at one time or another by members of both races. In addition, the presidency of Lyndon B. Johnson, who had urged much of the civil rights legislation of the 1960s upon Congress and achieved the passage of important domestic legislation in his "war against poverty," ended in 1969. Before then, the mounting US involvement in the Vietnamese war not only had cost Johnson political support but also had diverted needed funds from his plan for a "Great Society" that would deal with the problems of the poor, sick, and old by the expenditure of massive federal funds. Although the President's program did much to create jobs, construct low-cost housing, provide better education and health care, and help the elderly, it was the poor, a group including a disproportionately large number of blacks, who were most affected when the program was slowed — and later largely dismantled by the succeeding administration.

In the years since the late 1960s the civil rights drive has continued, but with less visibility: demonstrations have been de-emphasized, and the movement's moderate leaders have concentrated on pushing for programs to meet pressing social and economic needs — needs that increased in urgency as unemployment, already high among blacks, mounted in 1974 and 1975, and continued at unacceptably high levels into the late 1970s. The unemployment of the seventies cut across all racial lines but affected a decidedly higher percentage of black citizens than white. The eradication of poverty, improved employment opportunities, job training, better housing, more and better education, increased voter registration, wider use of the power of the ballot box, the election of more blacks to political office, and efforts to secure from Congress and the administrations the funds needed to finance meaningful programs on a national scale — these became the civil rights objectives of the decade ending in the late 1970s. With the rights legislation of the 1960s having made most forms of overt discrimination illegal, and with many a literal or figurative "white only" sign having fallen, "the crucial issue," as rights theorist Bayard Rustin observed, had become economics.

As for the fate of school desegregation, the original issue that had sparked the larger civil rights drive, it was in the 17 southern and border states that had required segregation by law (and another four that allowed it) that the Supreme Court's *Brown* v. *Board of Education* decision of 1954 first had effect. The Court waited until May 1955 before spelling out the principles it recommended for compliance with its historic ruling. After it did so, the District of Columbia promptly desegregated its schools, and some of the border states moved without delay to set up programs for desegregation in the gradual manner the Court initially envisioned. Elsewhere in the region the early reaction to the desegregation ruling was one of fierce noncompliance. After that, progress toward integration began at a snail-like pace. It was not, however, totally absent. In the 11 southern states, the percentage of black children attending school with whites finally crept slowly upward from no more than 2.5 percent at the beginning of the 1964–1965 school year to approximately 7.7 percent by February of 1966 and to 16 percent in 1967. Such increase as there was came with the encouragement of the Civil Rights Act of 1964 and the prodding of the US Office of Education — backed by a landmark December 1966 decision of the US Court of Appeals for the Fifth Circuit, which upheld the agency's guidelines on integration.

Just before the start of the school year in 1969, federal officials were forecasting that the proportion of blacks going to desegregated schools in the 11 southern states would be close to 40 percent, or double that of the previous year. Still, the pace of integration during the 15 years following *Brown* was sluggish, and in October 1969 the Supreme Court once again underscored the ruling by handing down its emphatic "desegregate now" decision. This ruling stressed that "'all deliberate speed' for desegregation is no longer constitutionally permissible. . . . The obligation of every school district is to terminate dual school systems at once and to operate now and hereafter only unitary schools." The Court showed the following January that it meant what it said when it refused a request by certain southern school districts to postpone temporarily their scheduled desegregation. The US Department of Justice took steps in the summer of 1970 when it undertook widespread action to enforce school desegregation in the South. By the fall of 1970 the schools of the South had achieved a greater degree of desegregation than those in any other part of the country. By the end of the 1972–1973 school year 46 percent of black pupils in the 11 states of the former Confederacy were in predominantly white schools, and fewer than 9 percent remained in all-black schools. Between 1964 and 1974 the percentage of the region's black children attending school with whites had changed from 2 to 90 percent. Contributing to the change was a Supreme Court ruling in April 1971 that cities in the South must bus pupils to schools outside their own neighborhoods, if necessary, to overcome the region's outlawed *de jure* segregation.

There has been less progress toward offsetting the *de facto* school segregation caused by the largely segregated housing patterns of the North, Midwest, and West. Nowhere in these regions was it stated by law that schools must be segregated; but it so happened that they frequently were. As blacks continued to leave the South — a post–World War II migration spurred by hope of economic opportunity elsewhere — they accounted for a majority of the population in more and more northern cities. The resulting numerical imbalance in the inner cities was intensified by the simultaneous exodus of northern whites who moved from these cities to the suburbs as their prosperity permitted or inclination directed. Attempts to integrate city schools thus were complicated by the sheer mathematics of population, which found white schoolchildren vastly outnumbered in inner cities. To achieve any racial balance at all, it became clear, would necessitate the busing of students to unfamiliar neighborhoods over the vociferous outcries of parents who insisted on "neighborhood schools" for their children. Moreover, the Supreme Court's 1971 decision on busing to overcome the *de jure* school segregation of the South specifically did not apply to the *de facto* segregation in other parts of the nation. Later court decisions would bring further confusion over the question of how to achieve full desegregation of northern schools — and the schools of the predominantly white northern suburbs posed mathematical conundrums almost as challenging as those of the predominantly black schools of the inner cities. Also to be taken into account in connection with the rate of northern desegregation was the charge — frequently heard in the early years of implementing the *Brown* decision — that federal authorities enforced school desegregation requirements less stringently in the North than in the South.

Whatever the reasons, it was the fall of 1971 before school desegregation really began on a large scale in the North. That year, integration plans went into effect in a number of cities as a result of court orders, pressure from the federal government or state governments, or voluntary action. Late in the 1960s the federal government had started to act against some northern school districts under provisions of the Civil Rights Act of 1964 or by instituting lawsuits. Civil rights groups also had brought action in the courts, and the result of these undertakings was beginning to be felt. But in this instance again, dealing with the *de facto* segregation of the North was legally a slower and more difficult process than dealing with the *de jure* segregation of the South, where it was clear that school systems had been segregated intentionally.

In the North, as in the South, where segregation existed it was the responsibility of local school boards to prepare plans for desegregation — and the responsibility of federal district courts to see that such plans were implemented. Members of some school boards seemed unwilling to desegregate and others seemed puzzled, or baffled, by the logistics of their particular local situations — although no more so than many parents, legislators, federal officials, and the courts on various levels, which in some cases contradicted each other.

Various plans were put forward to accomplish the goal of desegregation. These included enlarging school districts for a greater racial mix, redrawing district lines, "pairing" schools — and busing. In the North, as in the South earlier, busing was the most controversial, but sometimes the only effective, solution. In some communities it provoked extreme, even violent reactions. Even ardent integrationists were perplexed by the issue of busing.

There was a considerable period of confusion as alternative methods of desegregation were considered in communities across the nation and as legislative, executive, or judicial actions took place on federal, state, or local levels. A few of the more significant developments merit discussion.

In January 1972 a federal district court judge ordered that the school system of Richmond, Virginia, which was 70 percent black, be integrated with the school systems of two Richmond suburbs, which were 91 percent white. Such a desegregation plan had potential for application in other cities across the nation, but the proposed merger was disapproved by a federal appeals court, which held that the district judge lacked constitutional authority to combine school districts across city-suburban lines. In a widely watched case, the matter was taken before the US Supreme Court for what was expected to be a precedent-setting decision. With Associate Justice Lewis F. Powell Jr. abstaining as a former member of the Richmond and Virginia boards of education, the Supreme Court justices split evenly with a 4-to-4 vote on May 21, 1973 — thus letting stand the ban of the appeals court on the projected merger.

The Supreme Court's first ruling in a major northern school district segregation case, and its first affecting a city that had never had a dual school system, came in June 1973, when it turned its attention to Denver and established that segregated northern school districts could be found guilty of *de jure* discrimination even when the racial separation was not required by law — if the segregation had occurred as the result of actions of the school board. This, the Court found in a 7-to-1 ruling, was the situation in Denver and in such a case, it held, remedial action must be taken. In so ruling, the Supreme Court indicated that cities in the North would be treated in the same way as cities in the South and took a big step toward eliminating the distinction between *de jure* and *de facto* segregation. At the beginning of the next school year, Denver proceeded with a court-ordered desegregation plan that relied on busing.

By 1974, school desegregation action in the South had been mainly accomplished and the North had started on its own period of legal and political contention over racial separation in the schools. Those who sought desegregation solutions for their own communities hopefully awaited a decision that would affect Detroit. Contradicting a lower court, an appeals court judge had ordered that Detroit's school district, whose pupils were close to 70 percent black, be merged with 53 school districts in the suburbs of Detroit, whose pupils were 80 percent white. Cross-district busing was to take place in both directions in order to achieve racial balance. In July, when this order was appealed, however, the Supreme Court ruled against the plan in a 5-to-4 vote. Speaking for the majority, Chief Justice Warren Burger held that since the suburban school districts had done nothing to help create the problem of segregation in the inner city, they should not be compelled to contribute to its solution. Only where school district lines had been purposely drawn to separate the races, or where discriminatory actions in one school district had caused segregation in another, would a plan for desegregation that involved more than one district be warranted. This seemingly far-reaching decision came as a blow to civil rights proponents, who feared it would prevent busing across school district lines almost everywhere and severely set back the cause of equality. However, many legal experts took the position that the Detroit case by no means settled the question of metropolitan-area busing across school district lines. In addition to pointing out that much more desegregation could be accomplished even within individual school districts in many parts of the nation, they noted Associate Justice Potter Stewart's comment that in some future case similar to Detroit's he might change his position if it could be shown that a state's housing policy had helped create school segregation. They felt such evidence had already been given in the Detroit case and could be better emphasized in future cases. They also felt it would be possible to prove that zoning decisions and such things as mortgages and the location of public housing projects could contribute to segregation, and they hoped yet to meet the difficult criteria the Supreme Court had set down.

More bad news for rights advocates was soon to follow. Just after the Detroit decision Congress approved legislation to extend and provide funding for the Elementary and Secondary Education Act, including in the measure a provision that a pupil could be bused for racial desegregation no farther than the school next closest to his or her home, unless a court determined that more extensive busing was needed to protect the student's constitutional rights. Nor could a pupil be bused across school district lines unless the lines were discovered to have been purposely drawn to encourage segregation.

Both the legislation and the Detroit schools decision came at what was probably the high point of antibusing sentiment. President Richard M. Nixon had earlier expressed his opinion that busing was an undesirable method for achieving desegregation and exerted the weight of his office against it; and President Gerald R. Ford, who was shortly to succeed him, would soon repeat the attack.

In Boston, meanwhile, federal district judge Arthur Garrity Jr., after finding a pattern of intentional segregation by the Boston School Committee, ordered desegregation of the city's schools in June 1974. Some 18,200 of the city's 94,000 public school students were to be bused in the first year of desegregation and about 26,000 the second year. When the buses rolled and school opened in the fall of 1974, antibusing forces reacted with a fury reminiscent of violent scenes in the South during the early days of desegregation there, staging a boycott of the schools. School opened the next year with less of an uproar, partly because the mayor and other previously ambivalent officials took a tougher stand against disruption, but there still were racial fighting and angry demonstrations surrounding the high schools of the tension-filled Charlestown and South Boston areas. The rebellious school committee offered scant cooperation to the judge and appealed the desegregation ruling to the Supreme Court. But Judge Garrity was not shaken from his earlier finding that the school committee had "intentionally segregated schools at all levels; . . . built new schools for a decade with sizes and locations designed to promote segregation; maintained patterns of overcrowding and underutilization that promoted segregation at 26 schools and expanded the capacity of approximately 40 schools . . . when students could have been assigned to other schools with the effect of reducing racial imbalance." The Supreme Court ruling, in 1975, let stand his earlier ruling that the city's schools were unconstitutionally segregated and that busing was required to integrate the system racially. Repeating a pattern seen in other cities, South and North, Boston's school controversy cooled after the initial stages of desegregation. The opening of the 1976 school year witnessed some incidents, but fewer than the year before. And the start of school in fall 1977 was virtually uneventful.

Meanwhile, in a case showing that the Supreme Court's much-noted decision regarding Detroit's racially unbalanced schools was not the last word, an appellate court concluded in 1974 that Louisville and its suburbs had deliberately segregated pupils, and ordered the busing of 30,000 students between the 50 percent black schools of downtown Louisville and the 90 percent white suburban Jefferson County. One of the arguments put forward by the plaintiffs was that the city had allowed some of its inner-city white students to attend schools in Jefferson. Before reaching its conclusion that there had been official collusion between town and county, the court followed the suggestion of the US Supreme Court — that it study the Detroit case. Ugly violence flared in Louisville with rioting, injuries, and police charges, when the busing program was introduced in September 1975, but National Guard units finally were called out and calm was restored.

While these and similar events were going on in most major and many smaller communities across the nation, a few other things also were taking place. In 1975 the Voting Rights Act of 1965 was extended for seven years. Foes of busing failed to secure enough congressional votes to initiate an amendment that would prevent federal courts from ordering busing plans for local communities. A Gallup poll showed that most white parents did not object to school integration — though it remained clear that busing to make it possible often aroused strong protest during the early stages of integration. The Supreme Court ruled in June 1976 that private nonsectarian schools — including some of the private academies that have sprung up as an alternative to public school desegregation — may not exclude children on the basis of race. Although school desegregation was very far from complete in the North, Midwest, and West and the question of how to achieve it was still being worked out — often painfully — on an almost case-by-case basis, the US Commission on Civil Rights was able to issue a report in August 1976 asserting that "desegregation works." And while it seemed likely that the rights struggle would continue long into the future with its curious, uneven gait — two steps forward and one back — it was not as if nothing had happened in the years since *Brown* v. *Board of Education.*

Pentecost

This is a movable event. See note on page xxvi.

Pentecost — or Whitsunday, as it is commonly called in Britain — is a movable feast, celebrated on the seventh Sunday or 50th day after Easter, counting Easter as the first day. Since antiquity Pentecost has ranked among the principal feasts of the Christian church. Its name, meaning 50th (day), derives from the Greek. Pentecost has a threefold significance — it commemorates the descent of the Holy Spirit upon the Apostles, the assembling of the first Christian community, and the official birthday of the Christian church. Initially Pentecost was so intimately linked with Easter, commemorating the Resurrection of Jesus (see March 29) that the 50 days separating the two celebrations were considered one continuous season of rejoicing. The seventh Sunday after Easter was regarded as the apex of this paschal season and officially closed Eastertide. Its crucial position in the Church Year is evident from the fact that the pre-Reformation Christian churches generally number the Sundays following Pentecost as the First Sunday After Pentecost, the Second Sunday After Pentecost, and so forth.

Pentecost is still observed ceremonially by all Christian denominations, both Eastern and Western. In the newly revised Roman Catholic calendar, the feast, formerly Class I, is ranked as a "solemnity." It is also solemnly observed among both liturgical and nonliturgical Protestant churches. The Collect contained in Lutheran hymnals fittingly expresses the meaning of the feast for all Christians:

O God, who didst teach the hearts of Thy faithful people by sending to them the light of Thy Holy Spirit, grant us by the same Spirit to have a right judgment in all things and evermore to rejoice in His holy comfort: through Jesus Christ, Thy Son, our Lord. . . . Amen.

The story of the first Pentecost is related in detail by Luke in the second chapter of the Acts of the Apostles. Obedient to the command of Jesus, after his Ascension (see May 7), which took place 40 days after the first Easter, the Apostles gathered with Mary and the other disciples in Jerusalem to await the coming of the Holy Spirit. On one occasion at the close of his earthly ministry, Jesus had promised that he would pray to the Father that the "Comforter" might come to abide with them (John 14:16–17). On another occasion, he had declared: "And, behold, I send the promise of my Father upon you: but tarry ye in the city of Jerusalem, until ye be imbued with power from on high" (Luke 24:49). Timid, fearful, and uncertain of what to expect, the Apostles followed their instructions, keeping a prayerful vigil in an upper room.

The 10th day of their vigil was the important Jewish feast of Shavuot (see June 10). It was also known as the Feast of the First Fruits, since it was a celebration of thanksgiving for the first fruits of the wheat and barley harvest after the spring planting. Another designation it had received was the Feast of Weeks, occurring as it did at the close of a "week of weeks" or after the seven-week harvest period, which had started on the second day of Passover (see April 21). Since the Feast of Shavuot fell on the sixth day of the month of Sivan — the 50th day after the first day of Passover — the feast had gained yet an additional name, Pentecost. Finally, according to ancient Jewish tradition, the Feast of Shavuot was also the anniversary of Moses' receiving of the Ten Commandments, centuries before.

As the Apostles were praying in one room on this highly significant Feast of Shavuot, or Pentecost, the Holy Spirit appeared to them with remarkable spiritual gifts:

When the day of Pentecost had come, they [the followers of Jesus] were all together in one place. And suddenly a sound came from heaven like the rush of a mighty wind, and it filled all the house where they were sitting. And there appeared to them tongues as of fire, distributed and resting on each one of them. And they were all filled with the Holy Spirit and began to speak in other tongues, as the Spirit gave them utterance.

In line with Jesus' promise, "But ye shall receive power, after the Holy Spirit is come upon you: and ye shall be witnesses unto me, both in Jerusalem, and in all Judea, and in Samaria, and unto the uttermost part of the earth" (Acts 1:8), the Apostles underwent a complete psychological transformation. The once huddled band of frightened men became a bold and dynamic company that fearlessly bore witness to the Word of Jesus Christ.

Having received the gift of tongues — the ability to speak in diverse languages — the Apostles immediately began to preach the Christian faith to the vast multitude that thronged the streets of Jerusalem. As Luke related (Acts 2:5), "And there were dwelling at Jerusalem, Jews, devout men, out of every nation under heaven." Pious Jews from Jewish communities all over the eastern provinces of the Roman Empire — Mesopotamia, Pontus, Phrygia, Egypt, Libya, Crete, Arabia — had flocked to their religious center for

the Feast of Shavuot, which, together with Sukkot (see October 15) and Passover (see April 21), was one of three occasions during the Jewish religious year for pilgrimages to Jerusalem.

Luke recorded (Acts 2: 7–8; 12–18) that the pilgrims were astonished

. . . and marveled, saying one to another, Behold, are not all these which speak Galileans? And how hear we every man in our own tongue, wherein we were born?. . . . And they were all amazed, and were in doubt, saying one to another, What meaneth this? Others mocking said, These men are full of new wine. But Peter, standing up with the eleven, lifted up his voice, and said unto them, Ye men of Judea, and all ye that dwell at Jerusalem, be this known unto you, and hearken to my words: for these are not drunken, as ye suppose, seeing it is but the third hour of the day. But this is that which was spoken by the prophet Joel; And it shall come to pass in the last days, saith God, I will pour out of my Spirit upon all flesh: and your sons and your daughters shall prophesy, and your young men shall see visions, and your old men shall dream dreams.

Peter continued at length and as a result of his sermon, some 3,000 present professed belief in Jesus Christ and were baptized. Armed with zealous champions and a growing body of converts, the Christian church was fully equipped to embark upon its mission of salvation, passing from the Jewish, or national, phase to the universal.

Pentecost, although replete with Jewish significance, gained a multifold Christian meaning independent of, yet connected with, the Jewish festival. Just as the Feast of Shavuot thanked God for the first fruits of the earth, the Christian Pentecost was a feast of thanks to God for the first fruits of the Holy Spirit, procured for humanity ultimately through Jesus Christ's death on the cross. Just as Shavuot was considered the anniversary of the bestowal of the Ten Commandments, so Pentecost became the birthday of the Christian church. The Old Covenant between God and Israel was now succeeded by the New Covenant established by Jesus as set forth in the New Testament.

Records are lacking to show when Pentecost began to be observed annually by Christians, but it may have been as early as the first century. The celebration certainly existed before the earliest extant documentation from the third century. As far as the term Pentecost is concerned, the early Fathers of the Church frequently referred to the whole 50-day period from Easter to Pentecost as "Pentecost." It soon became a noteworthy occasion for Christian jubilation, marked with special sermons, readings, prayers, and hymns expressing the dominant mood of thanksgiving and praise. In fact the Council of

Nicaea in 325 specifically banned any form of kneeling during the Pentecost season as evidence of a too penitential attitude and for the same reason outlawed fasting.

As a designation solely for the 50th day of the period, the word *Pentecost* in the narrow sense appeared for the first time only in the proceedings of the Council of Elvira at the beginning of the fourth century. The 43rd canon made its observance obligatory, condemning vehemently the trend to observe it together with Ascension Day, 40 days after Easter. Once its importance in the Church calendar had been fully established, Pentecost took precedence over all feasts except Easter and had an octave assigned it. St. Gregory Nazianzen, the Greek Father of the Church, was already singing its praises as the "day of the Spirit" in the fourth century.

As the prominent feast of the Church Militant, intended to display the strength and vitality of the church on Earth, Pentecost — more technically the vigil on the preceding Saturday — became a principal occasion on which baptisms were performed. Baptisms became very common occurrences in Britain on this occasion, probably because rivers and streams, which were often the scenes of early baptism ceremonies, would have been too cold in the northern climate before this late spring feast. The English term *Whitsunday,* or simply *Whitsun,* is supposed to be a contraction of White Sunday, used to refer to the white robes the candidates for baptism wore during the vigil.

Except for the baptismal service on the Vigil of Pentecost, surprisingly few liturgical observances developed about the feast. Vestments for the day were often red to symbolize the blood of martyrs and perhaps the tongues of fire. Elaborate Latin hymns to the Holy Spirit were composed during the course of the Middle Ages. The most renowned were "Veni, Sancte Spiritus" ("Come, Holy Ghost"), the sequence of the Mass, which was written before 1200, and "Veni, Creator Spiritus" ("Come, Creator Spirit"), which is also sung in divine office and at such solemn occasions as papal elections and ordinations. Usually the large paschal candle placed near the altar on Holy Saturday (see March 28), the day before Easter, and taken away on Ascension Day, was returned for a final appearance on Pentecost.

After the 7th century the feast of Pentecost expanded into a week-long festive period when work was prohibited and even law courts shut down. The Christian church limited the observance to three days in the late 11th century. Pope Clement XIV abolished Whit Tuesday as a church holy day in the 18th century. In 1911 Pope Pius X ordered Whit Monday dropped as a day of religious obligation for Roman Catholics. In most Western European countries, Protestant and Catholic alike, however, Whitmonday or Whitsun Monday is still a legal holiday.

In the Middle Ages many curious nonliturgical customs grew up around the Whitsunday services. In Italy and Germany, red rose leaves were scattered from the ceilings of the churches to represent the tongues of fire that had descended upon the Apostles. In France it was once customary to blow trumpets during the services on the day to recall the sound of the mighty wind. Doves were sometimes released from the roofs of churches. In some parts of Europe overzealous churchgoers even dropped burning straw balls from the roof beams to symbolize the tongues of fire, but this custom was soon banned for obvious reasons.

In the British Isles Whitsunday figured prominently in various ways that were not purely religious. In Scotland it was one of the quarter days — days beginning each quarter of the year — on which rents were generally paid and buildings and lands occupied or left. Although Whitsunday is a movable feast, a Scottish act of 1693 set its legal date for May 15 for convenience in such secular matters. In England men were expected to contribute to the church on the feast — the amount usually being predetermined according to the number of fireplaces or chimneys in their houses; the collection was dubbed the "hearth" — or "smoke-money" collection. As was true on May Day, it was commonly believed that any wish made precisely at sunrise on the day of Pentecost would be granted; and church services were invariably followed by merrymaking and feasting. Maypole dancing, courtship games, and excursions to gather greenery were popular. Today some of the medieval customs attached to Whitsuntide still survive in Great Britain. In the English Cotswolds, for example, the Morris dance, performed by six men in white garments who jingle bells and flutter ribbons, is traditionally held at Bampton, in Oxfordshire, on Whitmonday.

In the New World the Dutch settlers who came in the 17th century to the colony of New Netherland (in what is now New York State) celebrated the feast of *Pinkster* with much rejoicing and gaiety. On this day and several thereafter, they visited relatives and neighbors and staged a variety of sports events and festive activities.

In the United States, Pentecost is primarily a religious feast celebrated by the various Christian churches. Of the few nonliturgical observances on Pentecost Sunday, the most noteworthy, perhaps, is the annual festival at Point Loma, California on San Diego Bay, observed by members of San Diego's Portuguese community. The origin and theme of the festival date back to early 14th-century Portugal.

The early 14th century Portuguese Queen Isabel won fame for her work as a peacemaker, a task in which she turned to the Holy Spirit for courage and guidance. Upon her plea, for example, her brother, James II of Aragon, and her son-in-law, Ferdinand IV of Castile, refrained from war and submitted their feud to the arbitration of Isabel's husband, King Diniz (Denis) of Portugal. When Diniz himself and their son, the Infante Alfonso, raised arms against each other in 1323, Isabel galloped into the midst of battle. Braving the glittering swords and the "arrows raining about her," she "joined her hands in supplication, her weakness her only weapon." Her intervention so impressed the belligerents that they made a peaceful compromise. According to contemporary chroniclers, on the night following the striking incident, Queen Isabel received a vision in which the Holy Spirit instructed her to have a church erected as a memorial in his honor.

Queen Isabel not only had the church constructed but out of gratitude and devotion to the Holy Spirit also arranged for charitable works, in particular the distribution of meat and bread to the poor, to be carried out on each Pentecost. Eventually the Portuguese Confraternity of the Holy Ghost was founded to oversee this yearly practice. Queen Isabel was canonized by Pope Urban VIII in 1625.

The special observance inaugurated by Isabel not only spread throughout Portugal, where Pentecost still ranks as an important national feast day and holiday, but was also brought to America by Portuguese immigrants, such as the fishing community that settled in the San Diego area. The Point Loma festival reflects Isabel's twofold purpose of honoring the Holy Spirit and showing charity to the needy. Earlier, on the seventh Sunday before Pentecost, a crown symbolizing the royalty of Saint Isabel is ceremoniously carried to St. Agnes's Church and placed on the high altar during mass. Its care is entrusted to a particular family during the week until the next Sunday, when the same procedure is repeated. On the Sunday before Pentecost, the president of the year's Feast of the Holy Ghost usually receives the crown for display in his home.

On Pentecost a young girl chosen by the president to impersonate Queen Isabel bears the crown in a formal procession (which includes a band and drill team) to the church. While the familiar Pentecost hymn "Veni, Creator Spiritus" is sung at the conclusion of mass, the queen is triumphantly crowned and holds a scepter with the figure of a dove to symbolize the dominance of the Holy Spirit. She is then escorted to the local Portuguese hall, where an elaborately prepared meal is distributed to the needy. The adjective *Pentecostal* — apart from its reference to the feast — is used by various Christian groups that emphasize direct inspiration by the Holy Spirit.

Norwegian Constitution Day

Around the world, Norwegians and persons of Norwegian descent observe May 17 as Norwegian Constitution Day.

The Norwegian Constitution was one of the many results of the political upheaval caused by the Napoleonic Wars. Prior to and during the wars, Norway was joined with Denmark in the Twin Kingdoms of Denmark and Norway. The ruler of the Twin Kingdoms, Frederick VI, resided in Denmark and considered himself the king primarily of that nation. His policies reflected a disregard for Norway. During the wars, Frederick allied himself with Napoleon against Great Britain and Sweden. This alliance caused great hardships for Norway: its shipping was curtailed because of the British blockade of its coast, and Norway's long border with Sweden left it exposed to the constant possibility of invasion. But even more important, Frederick's involvement with Napoleon threatened the very existence of the Twin Kingdoms, for the British, Russians, and Prussians agreed to allow Sweden to annex Norway after the French emperor's final defeat.

In October 1813 Napoleon was crushed at the battle of Leipzig, and within a few weeks the Swedes marched against Denmark to force the cession of Norway. The Swedes defeated the Danes in the region of Holstein, and on January 14, 1814, Frederick agreed to a peace. In accordance with the resulting Treaty of Kiel, Denmark ceded Norway to Sweden.

News of the Treaty of Kiel reached the Norwegian capital of Christiania (now Oslo) on January 24, 1814. The citizenry was outraged by the idea of Norway's union with its longtime enemy Sweden, and Crown Prince Christian Frederick, a cousin of King Frederick, who served as his commander in chief in Norway, was reluctant to abandon his hereditary claim to the Norwegian throne. Thus the Norwegians and the crown prince joined forces to make Norway an independent nation.

Although Christian Frederick initially planned to proclaim himself king of an independent Norway by virtue of his hereditary claim to the Norwegian throne, he met strong resistance to such an action. Many Norwegian leaders argued that after Frederick VI renounced his rule, sovereignty returned to the people of Norway. Christian Frederick wisely accepted this reasoning and called an assembly to write a constitution for the nation. That body came together at Eidsvoll, near the capital, on April 10, 1814.

On May 17, 1814, the assembly completed its work, and on that same day the constitution was signed and Christian Frederick chosen king. The new frame of government established a limited and hereditary monarchy and, like the US Constitution of 1787, it provided for a division of power among the executive, legislative, and judicial branches of government. The king, together with a council of state, or cabinet, was to exercise executive authority; legislative power would rest with the National Assembly, or Storting; and judicial authority was to be the prerogative of the nation's courts of law. The 1814 constitution reflected liberal political thought; not only did it outline the form of the new national government, but it included guarantees of basic human and civil rights.

In theory the Norwegian constitution established a "free, independent, indivisible and inalienable kingdom." In practice, however, the nation did not have adequate strength to guarantee the existence of such a government. Sweden, on the other hand, did have a powerful army, and in July 1814 its troops invaded Norway to enforce the provisions of the Treaty of Kiel. The Swedes easily defeated their weaker neighbors and after only a few weeks of fighting the Norwegians agreed to an armistice.

After months of negotiations Norway and Sweden agreed to the Act of Union in August 1815. The act of 1815 differed from the Treaty of Kiel in several important respects. According to the terms of the earlier treaty, the Danish king ceded control of Norway as payment of war reparations; according to the later act, Norway voluntarily entered into the union with Sweden. Moreover, the act of 1815 recognized Norway's sovereignty over its internal affairs and it did not impair the guarantees of the 1814 constitution. The union of Norway and Sweden under one king lasted until a separation was effected in 1905.

Although altered numerous times during the past 150 years, the constitution of 1814 is still Norway's basic frame of government and is revered as such by her citizens. For many years Norwegians have set aside May 17 to commemorate its adoption. Prior to 1870 the day was observed with speeches and festivities honoring the men who wrote the constitution. But in 1870 the Norwegian poet Bjørnstjerne Bjørnson suggested that the celebration center around a children's parade. Bjørnson's idea won immediate acceptance, and since 1870 young people have marched on May 17. Children throughout Norway take part in these Constitution Day events, but the parade is particularly impressive in Oslo. As many as 40,000 young people, each carrying a Norwegian flag, have marched past the royal palace and paid their respects to the monarch and his family on May 17.

Children are not alone in celebrating the anniversary. On May 17 the entire nation joins in the festivities. Buildings are decorated and fly the national banner, college and university students sponsor colorful parades, wreaths are laid on the graves of the men responsible for Norway's independence, and the reports of fireworks resound throughout the land.

In 1964, the 150th anniversary of the adoption of the constitution, festivities were particularly lavish. Early in the morning of May 17 members of the Norwegian parliament, government, and supreme court attended a jubilee service in the Oslo Cathedral. After this the royal family reviewed the capital's traditional children's parade, and then joined the leaders of government at nearby Eidsvoll to take part in a meeting commemorating the adoption of the constitution. Meanwhile, throughout the nation churches held jubilee services, public schools sponsored special assemblies, and children marched. It was a colorful celebration: flags flew from every mast and many children and adults wore picturesque national costumes. In a more cultural vein, the Oslo University library sponsored an exhibit of original documents associated with the 1814 constitution, and pictures, letters, and uniforms pertaining to the previous 150 years of Norwegian history; a four-volume history of the Norwegian Storting was published; and facsimiles of the handwritten constitution were printed.

Also in 1964 Norwegian-Americans held observances in Minneapolis, Brooklyn, Oakland, San Francisco, Los Angeles, Seattle, Madison, Baltimore, and Washington. Many distinguished Norwegians and Americans, including the bishop of Stavanger, Norway, and Vice President Hubert Humphrey took part in the sesquicentennial events. Norway's King Olav V sent messages to the rallies in New York City, San Francisco, and Minneapolis expressing his "earnest hope that the feeling of kinship which prevails today between Americans of Norwegian ancestry and Norwegians at home will be preserved." To mark the anniversary, the Congress resolved: "That the congratulations and best wishes of the Congress . . . are hereby cordially extended to Norway's Storting, upon the occasion of the 150th anniversary of the adoption of the Norwegian Constitution." President

Lyndon B. Johnson added his personal congratulations, noting that "Norway has been in the forefront of countries committed to the development of human societies based on social justice and individual freedom."

Even in years that are not major anniversaries of the adoption of Norway's 1814 constitution, many cities in the United States are the scenes of celebrations on or near May 17. Norwegian churches and societies generally sponsor these festivities and, depending on the number of Norwegian-Americans in a particular area, the day's events may be large or small. In Boston, for example, Norwegian descendants observe May 17 by decorating the statue of Leif Ericson that stands on Commonwealth Avenue and by holding a ball.

New York City is the scene of one of the largest Norwegian Constitution Day observances in the United States. Each year on the Sunday nearest May 17 Norwegian church groups, social organizations, and athletic societies sponsor a mammoth parade in the Bay Ridge section of Brooklyn. In recent years as many as 100 units, attired in colorful Norwegian garb and accompanied by bands and floats, have marched past the reviewing stand at McKinley Park at 74th Street and Fort Hamilton Parkway. The parade is customarily followed by a program held in McKinley Park. The national anthems of Norway and the United States open these ceremonies, which frequently feature a performance by the Norwegian Singing Society, the crowning of Miss Norway of Greater New York, and an address by a well-known personage. In 1970 the Honorable Edvard Hambro, Norway's ambassador to the United Nations, was the principal speaker at Brooklyn's May 17 festivities, and New York Mayor John Lindsay proclaimed the day as Norway's Independence Day. In addition to the Bay Ridge ceremonies, Norwegian sailors in port generally gather at Brooklyn's Norwegian Seamen's Church to mark the anniversary, and the Norwegian Club holds a banquet on or near May 17.

In San Francisco May 17 observances are a long-standing tradition. As early as 1894, May 17 was proclaimed Norway Day at the San Francisco Exposition in Golden Gate Park. Twenty years later, in 1914, the city marked the centennial of the 1814 constitution with day-long ceremonies and activities, which included sermons and Norwegian songs, as well as games and races. In 1939 Crown Prince Olav and Crown Princess Martha were present for the elaborate San Francisco exercises in honor of the 125th anniversary of the Norwegian constitution, and in 1964 a two-day program of events was the highlight of the city's celebration of the sesquicentennial of the 1814 document. However, San Francisco's observances of Norway's Constitution Day have not been limited to just these years; under the sponsorship of the Norwegian National League of San Francisco, which was organized in 1908, appropriate exercises take place each year on May 17. In 1970 the May 17 observance centered around a program in Golden Gate Park. The traditional children's parade, the playing of the Norwegian and American national anthems, folk dancing, and the reading of greetings from the government of Norway were only a few of the afternoon's many events.

Since many Norwegian-Americans reside in the Midwest, it is only natural that a number of elaborate May 17 observances take place in that region. In Minneapolis the Norwegian Singers have traditionally sponsored a program on the weekend closest to May 17. Prior to 1966 this event was held in Loring Park in front of the statue of the Norwegian violinist Ole Bull, but since 1966 Minnehaha Park has been the scene of the observance. Minneapolis's Norwegian Constitution Day ceremonies generally feature singing by local Norwegian choral groups that are affiliated with the Norwegian Singers' Association of America. Also included in the festivities are folk dancing, band music, greetings from the consul general of Norway and from the mayor of the city, and an address by a well-known person. In addition, the Norwegian Glee Club of Minneapolis usually holds a dinner dance at one of the city's leading hotels; and the Joint Committee of the Twin City Sons of Norway lodges sponsors a dance at the Sons of Norway Center.

May 17 festivities appropriately also take place at Stoughton, Wisconsin, which calls itself the Norse Capital of the United States, with some justification, since 80 percent of its population is of Norwegian descent. Although Stoughton officially celebrates May 17, or *Syttende Mai*, on the Sunday nearest that day, the city's observance actually extends throughout the weekend in which that Sunday occurs. On Saturday the tens of thousands of tourists who go to Stoughton for the event may view store window displays of Norse antiques and artifacts, sample authentic Norwegian foods, watch folk dancing exhibitions, or attend a hootenanny. On Sunday a colorful parade of floats, bands, and marchers in Norwegian costume takes place at 2 P.M. After the parade a folk dance and band concert are held and a smorgasbord is served.

Illinois is another midwestern state in which May 17 celebrations occur. Norwegians in Chicago have observed May 17 for more than 75 years. In 1970 Norwegian Constitution Day events there took place on May 16 and May 17. On the former day, ceremonies were held in the Serbian Orthodox Hall. These featured greetings from the president of the Norwegian National League and also from the Royal Norwegian consul general; singing of the Norwegian and American national anthems; an address by the Norwegian ambassador, H. E. Gunneng; and the performance of choral selections and folk dances. On the latter day, a colorful parade of marchers in Norwegian dress and brightly decorated floats proceeded from Keeler Avenue to Logan Square. There a program similar to that of the previous day was witnessed by several thousand spectators.

Hundreds of miles north and west, the tiny coastal town of Petersburg, Alaska, is the home of so many persons of Norwegian descent that it is known as Little Norway. Since 1958 the town has noted the anniversary of the Norwegian constitution — as well as celebrated the season's championship salmon hauls and the first landings of Pacific coast halibut — with a Little Norway Festival on a weekend close to May 17. In recent years the three-day festival has included smorgasbords, pancake breakfasts, pageants, and special programs featuring patriotic exercises and square dancing, as well as salmon bakes and saltwater fishing excursions.

MAY 18

Rhode Island Prohibits Perpetual Slavery

Before January 1, 1808, when the Slave-Trade Act forbidding the importation of slaves into the United States took effect, aversion to slavery — as reflected in literature and legislation — was based primarily on moral and religious grounds. The Puritans and Quakers especially opposed slavery, but neither of these colonial groups developed an effective plan for abolishing it. Starting on May 18, 1652, however, the General Court of Election held at Warwick, Rhode Island, with Samuel Gorton, the founder of Warwick, as moderator, enacted during its three-day session one of the first colonial laws limiting slavery.

One of several "Acts and Orders" (which were devoted principally to a revision of practice and procedure in trial courts), the statute carefully stipulated the period in which any person, black or white, could be kept in slavery in the colony:

Whereas, there is a common course practised amongst Englishmen to buy negers [sic], to that end that they may have them for service or slaves forever; for the preventinge of such practices among us, let it be ordered, that no blacke mankind or white [may be] forced by covenant bond, or otherwise, to serve any man or his assignes longer than ten years, or until they come to be 24 years of age, if they be taken in under 14, from the time of their coming within the Liberties of the Collonie, and at the end or terme of ten years . . . [are to be set] free, as is the manner with the English servants. And that man that will not let them goe free, or shall sell them away elsewhere, to that end that they may be enslaved to others for a long time, he or they shall forfeit to the Collonie forty pounds.

This law against perpetual slavery is judged to be — with one exception — the first legislative enactment for the suppression of involuntary servitude in the history of the United States. Previously the Massachusetts "Body of Liberties" of 1641, drawn up chiefly by Nathaniel Ward, the lawyer, clergyman, and author, had included the provision that there should "never be any bond slaverie, villinage or captivitie amongst us unles it be lawful captives taken in just warres, and such strangers as willingly selle themselves or are sold to us." In 1646 the Massachusetts General Court enforced this provision by ordering that certain blacks, who had been unlawfully transported from Africa, be returned to their native land, together with a letter expressing the disapproval of the court.

Although the 1652 Rhode Island statute was enforced for some time, it had either been repealed or had fallen into disuse by the beginning of the 18th century. A Rhode Island act of February 1708 recognized perpetual slavery, placing a duty of £3 on all blacks imported. From 1700 onwards, Rhode Island citizens engaged to a greater and greater extent in the flourishing slave-carrying trade. Although they did not import many slaves for their own use — the dangers to slaves of the harsh New England climate and the character and political and religious views of the settlers provided little stimulus for slavery — the Rhode Islanders became the greatest slave traders in the American colonies, operating a sort of clearinghouse for other areas. Only in 1779 did Rhode Island pass an act preventing the sale of slaves out of the state. In 1784, eight years after the Declaration of Independence, Rhode Island's legislature approved a law to abolish slavery gradually in the state. Three years later an act prohibiting participation in the slave trade finally set a fine of £1000 on every vessel caught in such a venture and £100 on each slave transported.

MAY 19

William Bradford's Death

William Bradford, the judicious and faith-strengthened governor of Plymouth colony and historian of the Pilgrims, was born, probably in March 1590, at Austerfield in the English county of Yorkshire. He was only a year old when his father died, leaving the boy's rearing, as a farmer, to his uncles and grandfather. When he was 12, Bradford first read the Scriptures. At Scrooby, in Nottinghamshire, he ignored the counsel of friends in order to attend meetings of a dissident religious sect, the Separatists, in the home of Elder William Brewster. The group, which favored separation from that "pudle of corruption," the established Church of England, was the target of local persecution and also felt the wrath of King James I, who warned the Separatists to conform or be harried out of the land. Under the leadership of Elder Brewster and pastor John Robinson, members of the Scrooby congregation fled to a tolerant Holland in 1608. Bradford, who was not more than 19 at the time, went with them, first to Amsterdam and a year later to Leyden, where he was apprenticed to a silk manufacturer. Despite his relative youthfulness, he became a leader of the group.

Although the congregation's membership tripled in exile, life was economically hard for its members, their children were increasingly "Dutchified," and the group lacked the kind of autonomy best suited to the unhampered carrying out of its religious ideals. By 1617, with the prodding of Bradford and others, a number of members had determined to move to the New World. Lengthy negotiations brought forth the offer of financial backing by London merchants, a charter from the Virginia Company of London, and a proposal that the Separatists form a joint-stock company to set up a trading post in America. Bradford and Brewster were among the 35 who accepted the offer. With 67 Londoners (most of them probably not Separatists), they boarded the *Mayflower* at Plymouth, England, and set sail on September 16, 1620 (by the New Style calendar). Contrary to their plans, they dropped anchor outside Virginia Company jurisdiction — and consequently outside the legal provisions of their patent — in the harbor of what is now Provincetown, Massachusetts, on November 21. Before landing, they drew up, for their own self-government, the Mayflower Compact, which became one of the written landmarks of democracy. It was designed, according to Bradford's account, to prevent the defection of certain restless souls who threatened to strike out on their own when they found themselves in a legal no man's land.

Bradford, who was among the 41 adult males who had signed the compact, also was among those who set out by small boat to find a spot that might prove more "fitt for situation" than Provincetown's barren sand dunes. The die was cast when they sighted Plymouth, across Cape Cod Bay, on December 21 (see December 21, Forefathers' Day) and returned to Provincetown for the rest of the voyagers — who have been referred to as Pilgrims ever since their permanent settlement at Plymouth.

The discovery of what was variously known as Plymouth, New Plymouth, and Plimoth Plantation as a suitable place for habitation was preceded by tragedy. While Bradford was helping choose a permanent site, his wife, Dorothy May, was drowned in Cape Cod Bay on December 17. It was the beginning of the tragedies that filled the Pilgrims' first winter. Their "victuals being much spente" in the course of their ocean voyage, their struggle to build houses and find food at Plymouth was made more difficult by exposure, pneumonia, tuberculosis, and scurvy. Over half the group died during the first year. Bradford himself was seriously ill but recovered — fortunately for the surviving colonists, who unanimously elected him governor after the death of Governor John Carver in 1621.

Although he pressed for rotation of the office, Bradford, who exercised wide governmental and religious authority in the settlement's early years, was reelected governor for all but 5 of the next 35 years. Under his prudent guidance, fortified by the judicious advice of Elder Brewster, the colony became politically and economically sound, if not prosperous. One of the governor's early acts was the signing of a treaty with neighboring Indians — who instructed the colonists in cultivation and partook with them of the first American Thanksgiving feast (see November 26) in the fall of 1621. The colony was put on a sounder legal footing the same year, when it obtained a charter from the New England Council. In 1623, the year of his remarriage — to the former Alice Carpenter, widow of Edward Southworth — Bradford put an end to the communal land system first employed and granted each male colonist an acre as his own. A plentiful harvest followed and the settlers subsequently also found some small profit in the fur trade. By 1627 Bradford and the other Pilgrim fathers were able to buy out the London merchants who had financed their expedition, thus severing their financial connection with England. Although it was his purpose to maintain Plymouth as a separate and independent colony, Bradford cooperated with other colonies in such enterprises as the war against the Pequot Indians and was four times a delegate to, and twice president of, the New England Confederation, a military alliance of Plymouth with the colonies of Massachusetts Bay, Connecticut, and New Haven.

A self-taught man, Bradford was skilled in several languages and possessed a simple and direct prose style, shot through with sincerity of religious faith. The most notable of his several writings, *History of Plymouth Plantation, 1620–1647*, is among the major literary accomplishments of his day. A lucid, unpretentious account, it details the history of a devout people with matter-of-fact eloquence, and remains today the best source of knowledge about the Pilgrims. Although the manuscript was completed in 1651, six years before Bradford's death at Plymouth on May 19, 1657, it was not published in full until 1856, after its discovery in London following a long disappearance. It is housed today in the state archives of Massachusetts.

Although Plymouth colony, which sent out offshoots in the form of neighboring towns, grew to include a sizable area, it eventually was overshadowed by the Massachusetts Bay Colony, by which it was absorbed in 1691. Plymouth nevertheless retains historical significance as the second permanent English settlement in America; and Bradford as its historian and leading statesman.

Plimoth Plantation, a reconstruction of part of the original colony, on view outside the center of present-day Plymouth, contains replicas of a number of the Pilgrims' thatch-roofed houses, including Bradford's. The *Mayflower II*, a replica of the original, is anchored nearby. In the center of town a number of buildings and monuments have Pilgrim associations of interest. The legendary Plymouth Rock can also be seen. Plymouth is the scene, annually on Thanksgiving Day and on Friday afternoons in August (although dates should be checked locally) of a Pilgrim Progress procession, with each marcher representing a survivor of the Pilgrims' first winter, en route to worship.

The New England Confederation

On May 19, 1643, delegates from Massachusetts Bay, Plymouth, New Haven, and Connecticut met at Boston and adopted the 12 articles of the New England Confederation "for mutual safety and welfare." In so doing they reacted to the precariousness of life in the frontier settlements. In 1636–1637, for instance, war with the Pequot Indians of Connecticut had brought tremendous suffering and bloodshed to the colonists — and for that matter had nearly annihilated the Pequots, though other tribes remained. The Indians on whose lands they encroached were not the only problem of the colonists, who were equally threatened by the expansion of the Dutch and French into territory claimed by the English.

The individual colonies could not safely stand alone against such obstacles. Thus the common danger posed by the Dutch, French, and Indians drove them to form the first intercolonial union. Under their written agreement each colony through its general court annually chose two church members to be delegates to the New England Confederation. The confederation had no control over the internal affairs of any colony, but the consent of six of the eight commissioners was sufficient to determine matters of intercolonial concern. Their jurisdiction included declarations of both offensive and defensive wars, apportionment of defense expenses, supervision of relations with the Indians, and approval of foreign treaties.

Despite its seemingly great powers, the confederation could not prevent the New Haven colony from being absorbed by Connecticut when Charles II granted the latter colony its charter in 1662. This failure cost the confederation much prestige, but its fortunes revived during King Philip's War in 1675–1676. In that time of grave danger the confederation successfully coordinated the colonists' efforts against the hostile Wampanoag Indians. Unfortunately, however, Massachusetts' attempts to dominate the organization after the Indian crisis caused bitter feelings, and the confederation was dissolved in 1684.

This was shortly after England had revoked the charter of the Massachusetts Bay Colony, whose theocratic government had always been reluctant to recognize its dependency on the mother country and had often resorted to footdragging and evasion to avoid compliance with British policy. The necessity for replacing the charter with some other form of royal control prompted Britain to try out in New England a long-contemplated plan for improving colonial administration by consolidating the colonies into a few large provinces. With others, the same colonies that had participated in the New England Confederation thus were again united, but in a less voluntary way, under the Dominion of New England, established in 1686.

The Dominion, at first set up on a temporary basis under a New Englander named Joseph Dudley, became a more formal unit with the arrival of Sir Edmund Andros in December of that year. Commissioned by King James II as governor of the Dominion of New England, Andros ruled an extensive area that ultimately included the colonies or regions of Massachusetts Bay, Plymouth, Maine, New Hampshire, Rhode Island, and Connecticut, to which were added New York and New Jersey. A tactless man, strict in enforcement of unwelcome edicts and overzealous (the colonists thought) in his royalist administration, Andros was arrested and sent back to England by Boston Puritans when they learned in April 1689 that James II had been deposed.

Under these circumstances the Dominion of New England came to an abrupt end, and no further plans were put forward for consolidating the colonies.

MAY 20

Lafayette's Death

No other European has been so widely and intensely admired in America as the Marquis de Lafayette, the young French nobleman who was so taken with the cause of freedom that he left his home to participate in the American Revolution. So indebted were Americans for the influence that he exerted on their behalf that they made him an honorary citizen of the United States. Until 1963, when Congress conferred US citizenship upon Winston S. Churchill, the wartime leader of Great Britain, Lafayette was the only foreigner ever to be so honored.

Lafayette received plaudits without parallel during his own lifetime – particularly when he revisited the United States in 1824–1825 – and is still honored by Americans on the anniversary of his death. That event, on May 20, 1834, saddened his adopted nation as much as his own. When President Andrew Jackson received the news a month later, on June 21, he ordered for Lafayette the same military honors that had been accorded to Lafayette's close friend George Washington: 24 guns fired at dawn, flags flown at half-mast, and a cannon discharged every half hour at every army post and on every navy ship; and the wearing of crepe arm bands by army and navy officers for half a year. The Senate and the House of Representatives adopted a joint resolution expressing the sorrow of Congress and the President sent a copy to Lafayette's son, Georges Washington Motier de Lafayette. A letter indicating the grief of the nation was also included. While senators and representatives went into mourning for 30 days, memorial services and eulogies were held all over the country. The few surviving American Revolution veterans of the Order of the Cincinnati held their last parade.

In May 1934 special events highlighted the centenary of Lafayette's death. Major exhibits took place in many countries of the world ranging from Poland to Argentina. In the United States the Maison Française at Rockefeller Center sponsored a Lafayette exhibition from May 4 through 31, and a relic of the battle of Yorktown, the cannon of Gâtinnais, was prominently displayed. On May 3 Congress issued a joint resolution in observance of the anniversary. On May 21 members of the Senate and the House of Representatives, the cabinet, the Supreme Court, top army and navy personnel, and members of leading patriotic societies met in joint session to receive the greetings of the French president and to hear President Franklin Delano Roosevelt deliver a memorial address. The President urged Americans to "cherish [Lafayette's] memory above that of any foreigner."

Although Lafayette's September 6 birthday (see September 6) is not marked with any notable celebrations at present, May 20 is regularly observed. Since 1935 the governor of Massachusetts has annually proclaimed Lafayette Day on this date. Every year May 20 is noted in New York City, where members of French-American societies, usually joined by the French Consul General, lay a wreath on Lafayette's statue at Union Square, with speeches and band music. The memorial ceremony in 1953, the 119th anniversary of Lafayette's death, took place in Washington, D.C., where President Dwight D. Eisenhower and French Ambassador Henri Bonnet placed wreaths at the base of Lafayette's statue in Lafayette Square, across the street from the White House. On May 20, 1958, following the 200th anniversary, the preceding September, of Lafayette's birth, a special medal was bestowed upon A. H. Sulzberger and 24 other Americans who had aided in the bicentennial observance. In May 1966 Mayor John Lindsay of New York City accepted the US flag that had flown over the French general's grave in Paris since July 4, 1964. It was presented by the French Consul General in behalf of Le Comité Français du Souvenir de La Fayette.

Le Comité Français du Souvenir de La Fayette was founded in Paris on May 10, 1924, by Henry Jay Kahn. Its primary purpose is to foster the memory of the Marquis de Lafayette and his deeds in behalf of democracy. During World War II, when the society was temporarily suspended in France, its founder transferred its various activities and ceremonies to the United States. In 1955 the American Division was incorporated in New York City and was granted a New York State charter. Besides conducting the memorial service for Lafayette at Union

Square each year, its members encourage the erection of monuments to the French general and award portraits of Lafayette, executed at the École des Beaux Arts in Paris, in cooperation with schools and organizations named Lafayette. Recipients have included Lafayette High School in Buffalo, New York, Lafayette High School in Brooklyn, and the Lafayette National Bank of Brooklyn. In early spring, members of the organization visit a Revolutionary site connected with Lafayette and Washington.

Two other American organizations are closely associated with the memory of Lafayette, one the Order of Lafayette, and the other the American Friends of Lafayette. Membership in the Order of Lafayette, founded in 1958 by Hamilton Fish, is limited to officers who served in France or French territories in World War I or World War II. Its purpose is to strengthen the traditional friendship between the United States and France. The organization's Freedom Award is presented annually at a dinner-dance. Recipients have included Presidents Herbert Hoover and Eisenhower, and General of the Army Douglas MacArthur.

The second group, the American Friends of Lafayette, founded in 1932, includes private individuals, historical societies, universities, and colleges interested in the study of Lafayette. Besides the general aim of promoting friendship between the United States and France, the purpose of the association is to further historical research through the collection of books and manuscripts concerning Lafayette and the awarding of scholarships and prizes. It maintains a bibliographical archive and a library featuring Lafayette mementos, engravings, and letters, and it also publishes a *Gazette*.

Dolley Madison's Birthday

Dolley (commonly but incorrectly "Dolly") Madison, wife of James Madison, the fourth President of the United States, has become legendary as the outstanding hostess of the early American presidencies and as one of the best loved American First Ladies. She was born Dorothea Dandridge Payne on May 20, 1768, in what is now Guilford County, North Carolina, where her Virginia parents were spending a year with an uncle. She was the eldest daughter of John Payne and Mary Coles Payne, a cousin of Patrick Henry.

The family returned to Virginia while she was still an infant and lived at Scotchtown in Hanover County until she was 15. Probably one of the oldest plantation houses in Virginia, built around 1719, Scotchtown had belonged to Patrick Henry from 1771 to 1778. It is located on Virginia Route 685 and has been restored by the Association for the Preservation of Virginia Antiquities.

Coming conscientiously to abhor slavery, John Payne, a Quaker, freed his slaves in 1783. He moved to Philadelphia, where he engaged unsuccessfully in business. After his death in 1792, his widow supported herself by keeping a boardinghouse for men in Philadelphia.

On January 7, 1790, at the age of 21, Dolley Payne married John Todd Jr., a lawyer of the city and a member of the Quaker Society of Friends, to which her own family also belonged. In 1791 the Todds purchased a house on the corner of Fourth and Walnut streets near Independence Hall in Philadelphia, a house visitors can now see as the restored Todd or Dolley Madison house, as it is variously called.

Dolley Todd and her husband had two sons, but only John Payne Todd, born on February 29, 1792, lived to maturity. His father and brother were less fortunate. The elder John Todd died on October 24, 1793, during a yellow fever epidemic which killed between 4,000 and 5,000 people — about one-tenth the population of Philadelphia. Their second infant son died a few hours afterwards. After her husband's death, young Dolley Todd and her surviving son lived with her mother in Philadelphia.

Dolley Todd was introduced to James Madison by Aaron Burr, then a senator. Madison was in Philadelphia as a representative in Congress from Virginia. On September 15, 1794, the 43-year-old bachelor, famous for his work in drafting the US Constitution and in arguing for its adoption, and Dolley Todd were married at the home of her sister, Mrs. George Steptoe Washington, at Harewood in Jefferson County, Virginia (now part of West Virginia). By a twist of fate years later, this sister, the then widowed Lucy Payne Washington, was to remarry in the Madisons' home at the White House. (At the time it was called simply the President's House.) This was the first White House wedding, held on March 29, 1812, and Dolley Madison was hostess.

It has been said wryly that Dolley Todd accepted Madison's marriage proposal even though he was 17 years older and an inch shorter, and had been rejected by at least one other woman. Blue-eyed, black-haired Mrs. Madison complemented her frail, scholarly husband well, however, and they were apparently very happy together during their 41 years of marriage. Her warmth, charm, and great gifts as a hostess assisted him in politics. Indeed in the next decades she became the toast of Washington, D.C., through her natural friendliness, her keen memory of persons and their interests, and her unfailing tact. White House social events were not again infused with quite the same degree of glamour and vivacity until 1961, when Jacqueline Kennedy, the wife of President John F. Kennedy, became First Lady. Perhaps Dolley Madison's secret lay in her response to a remark by Henry Clay, who once declared to her: "Everybody loves Mrs. Madison." "Mrs. Madison loves everybody," she merrily replied. The point also has been made that she was brilliant in the things she did not say and do.

When President Thomas Jefferson appointed James Madison secretary of state in 1801, Dolley Madison moved into the center of the social life of the capital, and there she continued for the next 16 years. As Jefferson was a widower, he often invited the gracious, capable Dolley Madison to act as his official hostess at the White House. She helped create the Jeffersonian style of hospitality, lacking the earlier pomp of entertainment under George Washington and John Adams but generously drawing together the most interesting people in the capital for conversation with the President. By her own presence and style, Dolley Madison helped to lend social grace to Jefferson's administration.

In 1809, when her husband became President, Dolley Madison followed Jefferson's taste in furnishing the White House and entertaining in a manner more continental than English. But presidential entertaining became more elaborate under the Madisons. She was, for example, hostess at the first inaugural ball, which was held in Long's Hotel on Capitol Hill, on January 20, beginning at 7:00 P.M. (see January 20).

All personal additions that the Madisons made to the White House were destroyed when the British burned the mansion on August 24, 1814. Instructed by her husband to flee the advancing army, Dolley Madison waited stubbornly until the very last minute to leave. She is famous for having saved a carriageful of state papers and for insisting at the last minute that Gilbert Stuart's portrait of George Washington be removed from its frame and rescued. This painting now hangs in the East Room of the White House and is the one object saved from President Adams's time. The Madisons lived out their second term in private residences while the mansion was being reconstructed.

When Madison's term expired in 1817, Mrs. Madison went with him to Montpelier, his estate in Orange County, Virginia, and presided gracefully over his house and his plantation until his death in 1836. Earlier she had helped him enlarge Montpelier following Jefferson's suggestions for a stately portico. Today the estate is

privately owned, but its graveyard, where James and Dolley Madison are buried, is open to the public. It is located six miles from Orange, Virginia, a mile off Virginia Route 20.

Immediately after her husband's death, Dolley Madison devoted herself to preparing his manuscript of the debates in the Constitutional Convention (1787) for publication. This was bought by the US government under President Andrew Jackson. When almost 70, in 1837 she returned to Washington with her niece Anna Payne, whom she adopted, and again became a noted and honored social figure, though privately her last years were troubled by financial difficulties and the waywardness of her son.

In 1844 Dolley Madison's appearance in the visitor's gallery of the House of Representatives evoked a motion, which passed unanimously, to grant her an honorary seat in the House. Her last public appearance was at a reception in the White House in February 1849, when she passed through the rooms on the arm of President James K. Polk. She died on July 12, 1849, at the age of 81.

Some years later, her grandniece, Lucia B. Cutts, published a selection of Dolley Madison's private letters, with biographical introductions, as *Memoirs and Letters of Dolly Madison, Wife of James Madison, President of the United States.* The volume has been mistakenly referred to as Dolley Madison's "diary," in the same genre as *A White House Diary* (1970) by Lady Bird Johnson, wife of President Lyndon B. Johnson. But actually Dolley Madison's letters were written, as her editor says, "without the most remote idea of publication," over a period of 50 years.

Mecklenburg Independence Day

May 20 is a legal holiday in North Carolina commemorating the alleged adoption of the Mecklenburg Declaration of Independence on that date in 1775. A popular tradition holds that Colonel Thomas Polk, commander of the Mecklenburg County militia, after consulting community leaders, ordered each company of citizen soldiers to select two delegates to attend a convention in Charlotte. They reportedly met on May 19 with the intention of setting up a local government, as the British government had declared the colonies to be in a state of rebellion. During the debates, the story continues, a messenger arrived with news that the colonials had fought battles against the redcoats at Lexington and Concord the previous month. Aroused by this news, many delegates reportedly brought before the convention far-reaching resolutions. At 2:00 A.M. on May 20, according to this tradition, the delegates adopted the Mecklenburg Declaration of Independence.

Most historians do not accept this account, however, and the evidence overwhelmingly supports the belief that the declaration is, in the words of Thomas Jefferson, a "spurious document." The actual course of events in North Carolina in May 1775 seems to have been as follows:

On May 31 a convention met in Mecklenburg County and passed a series of resolutions that "annulled and vacated all civil and military commissions granted by the Crown." The delegates further pledged that "until Parliament should resign its arbitrary pretensions" the Provincial Congress would exercise all legislative and executive powers within the colony. These bold resolves were then sent to the North Carolina delegation at the Second Continental Congress then meeting in Philadelphia; but they were never presented to the Philadelphia gathering.

Much to the Mecklenburg patriots' chagrin, the first accounts of the American Revolution passed over the proceedings of May 31, 1775, in silence. Those who had participated in the convention would not be so easily ignored, however, and in the ensuing decades used every means to make certain that they be accorded an honored place. After a fire in 1800 destroyed the records of the Mecklenburg Convention, North Carolina's one-time revolutionaries, who became further and further removed from the facts as time went on, had to rely on their recollections to prove their case. On April 30, 1819, the Raleigh *Register* published what Joseph Graham, one of the delegates, remembered to have been the Mecklenburg Declaration of Independence of May 20, 1775. Events that had taken place over a period of many months, 44 years earlier, blended into a single experience in Graham's fading memory and he embellished the substance of the convention's resolves with the immortal phrases of Thomas Jefferson's Declaration of Independence.

The genuineness of the so-called Mecklenburg Declaration of Independence was widely accepted until the discovery in 1847 of a Charleston newspaper of June 16, 1775, containing the proceedings of the Mecklenburg Convention. The old newspaper challenged the authenticity of the Mecklenburg Declaration of Independence for two serious reasons: It proved that the delegates had met on May 31 rather than May 20; and in setting forth the full text of the resolutions it showed that they contained no mention of "independence."

Even though the North Carolina patriots may not have been the first to call for independence, the action of Mecklenburg County marked an important step on the road to the Revolution. And the Resolves of May 1775, bearing as they do the unmistakable stamp of courage, still merit the attention of students of the period.

MAY 21

Lindbergh Lands in Paris

Setting out on May 20, 1927, Charles Augustus Lindbergh flew nonstop from New York to Paris to win a $25,000 prize offered for the first successful flight of this kind. Taking off from Roosevelt Field on Long Island, he covered 3,610 miles in 33½ hours, landing the next day at Le Bourget airfield, just outside Paris.

Lindbergh, a lanky, handsome, and quiet American then only 25 years old, caught the imagination of millions of people around the world. At Le Bourget, he escaped being mobbed by wildly cheering crowds when they mistakenly carried off someone else. The French government made him a Chevalier of the Legion of Honor. He was also welcomed in Brussels and London before his triumphant return to the United States.

Lindbergh's interest in flying had developed early. Born in Detroit on February 4, 1902, he grew up in Little Falls, Minnesota, and in Washington, D.C., where his father represented Minnesota's sixth district in Congress. Young Lindbergh attended the University of Wisconsin at Madison, but gave up his studies after less than two years there, in order to study flying. He soloed in 1923, and enlisted in the US Air Service Reserve in 1924. In 1926 he became an airmail pilot. When the prize for a nonstop flight to Paris was offered by a French-American philanthropist Raymond Orteig, Lindbergh went to San Diego to supervise the construction of a custom-designed monoplane, with the financial backing of several St. Louis businessmen. The plane was appropriately named *Spirit of St. Louis*. On May 10, 1927, Lindbergh flew the craft from San Diego, via St. Louis, to New York in a record-breaking 21 hours and 20 minutes.

Although it is often remembered as such, Lindbergh's exciting solo trip to Paris was not the first nonstop transatlantic flight. That record is held by the British aviators Captain John Alcock and Lieutenant Arthur Whitten Brown, who flew from Newfoundland to Ireland in June 1919. But Lindbergh's was the first transatlantic solo flight and it is he who is best remembered.

Lindbergh's honors upon returning home began with a Broadway parade and the award of both a congressional Medal of Honor and the first Distinguished Flying Cross ever presented. In 1928 he received the Woodrow Wilson Award for Distinguished Service. His many awards are on display at the Missouri Historical Society on Lindell Boulevard in St. Louis.

Lindbergh actively contributed to the progress of early aviation. Apart from flying the goodwill tours to many countries, which served to intensify interest in the future of flying, he served as a technical adviser to the aeronautics branch of the US Department of Commerce and also to private airlines, personally pioneering many of their routes in the early days of commercial flying. His career also importantly influenced the development of military aviation. Among other things he helped the visionary work of the little-known rocket pioneer Dr. Robert H. Goddard, obtaining financial backing for the man who was mercilessly taunted for his talk of sending men to the moon in giant rockets. In the 1930s, Lindbergh also worked with the surgeon and biologist Dr. Alexis Carrel on the construction of a perfusion pump, or mechanical heart, used experimentally to keep organs alive outside the body.

Lindbergh's personal life was always marked by his modesty and desire for privacy, particularly after he and his wife, Anne Morrow Lindbergh, endured the harrowing press exposure that surrounded the kidnapping and murder of their young son and the ensuing sensational murder trial in the early 1930s. To escape publicity they lived for a time in Europe before returning to the United States in 1939.

Despite a flurry of unpopularity occasioned by his strong support of an isolationist foreign policy during the early days of World War II, Lindbergh quietly threw himself into the Allied effort once the United States entered the war, contributing significantly to the aviation advances of the time. He served as a consultant to US aircraft manufacturers and in this capacity also flew combat missions in the Pacific. He also acted as a civilian consultant to the nation's air forces. In the early postwar period he went to Europe with a US Navy technical mission to look into Germany's wartime aviation advances. Until 1941 and beginning again in 1954, he held reserve commissions in the Army Air Corps and its successor, the US Air Force. His writings include *We*, published in 1929, and *The Spirit of St. Louis*, which won him a Pulitzer Prize after its publication in 1953. Some of Anne Lindbergh's books, such as *North to the Orient* (1935) and *Listen! The Wind* (1938), describe their flights together.

Lindbergh died on August 26, 1974. In his later years he labored energetically for the conservation of rare animal species.

Observances marking Lindbergh's 1927 flight are not frequent, partly because of the aviator's own aversion to the limelight and his preference, as a longtime friend puts it, for concentrating on the present and future. In 1933 St. Louis, which has served as a departure point for explorers and pioneers since the days of Lewis and Clark, unveiled a bronze plaque to commemorate the historic flight. Since then the achievement has been regularly noted in the press, particularly in St. Louis, New York, and Paris; and marked by observances from time to time, with important anniversaries receiving particular attention.

One such anniversary was the 40th, in 1967, when the governors of some states joined North Carolina's Dan Moore in proclaiming May 21 Aviation Day. The anniversary was celebrated by aeronautical bodies and other organizations and received special coverage by publications such as *Aerospace* and *Air Power Magazine*. It was also observed, flamboyantly, by two American doctors, Francis Sommer of Barbourville, Kentucky, and John Rieger of Los Gatos, California, who sought to duplicate Lindbergh's pioneering trip. Employing his flight plan, they took off on May 20 from New York's Kennedy Airport in a single-engine Beechcraft plane. Then 19 hours, 54 minutes, and 32 seconds later they landed — not at Le Bourget as planned, but at a small airport at Cormeilles-en-Parisis, northwest of Paris. That morning Le Bourget was closed to private aircraft because of unusual activity related to the impending opening of the Paris Air Show. The biennial international air show was timed to approximate the date of Lindbergh's flight and in other ways do him honor. The show's US exhibit, for instance, featured a replica of his plane and was the site of a ceremony commemorating his flight. The actual plane is on exhibit at the National Air and Space Museum in Washington, D.C.

Concurrently in New York, a marker noting Lindbergh's achievement was being unveiled at the point from which he had taken off in his $10,000 Ryan monoplane on May 20, 1927. Had he been present, he would not have recognized the spot, for what was once Roosevelt Field had since become the Roosevelt Field Shopping Center. Lindbergh, however, was not present. Characteristically, he had ignored the celebrations.

In 1977 the 50th anniversary of Lindbergh's historic feat was observed on a wide scale in the United States and France; the commemoration, climaxed by a reenactment of the transatlantic flight (with Mrs. Lindbergh at Le Bourget), included air shows, films, and exhibits.

MAY 22

National Maritime Day

National Maritime Day, observed annually on May 22, calls to mind the contribution of commercial shipping to the prosperity of the United States. Seafaring people discovered and settled the nation, and their descendants have maintained a continuing interest in transoceanic trade. From the first steam-driven ship to the first nuclear-powered merchant vessel, Americans have helped lead the way in faster and safer transportation of vital and valuable cargoes.

Appropriately, the celebration of National Maritime Day occurs on May 22, the anniversary of the 1819 sailing of the *Savannah,* the first steam-propelled vessel to attempt a transatlantic crossing. Owned by a Georgia steamboat company, the *Savannah* was constructed at the Corlears Hook shipyard in New York. Nothing was left to chance; the vessel was fitted out with both a steam engine and sails. It left New York on March 8, 1819, and after eight and a half days at sea arrived in its home port of Savannah, Georgia.

In actual fact, the *Savannah* had been built for use in the coastal trade between New York and Georgia, but the Panic of 1819 so depressed the nation's commerce that its owners were forced to abandon their original plan. They decided, instead, to sell their ship abroad and scheduled it to sail on May 20. The accidental drowning of one of the crewmen delayed the *Savannah's* departure until May 22, when it left port laden only with the 1,500 bushels of coal and the 25 cords of wood necessary to power the engine across the Atlantic. Advertisements in a local newspaper announcing the epochal steam voyage had attracted neither passengers nor cargo.

The *Savannah* crossed the Atlantic with ease, but the first use of steam on a transatlantic voyage resulted in one amusing incident. Authorities at the naval station at Cape Clear in Ireland sighted large amounts of smoke billowing from the *Savannah* and, not knowing of its steam engine, they concluded it was on fire. They dispatched a royal cutter, the *Kite,* to her assistance and the English sail craft chased the American ship for almost an entire day before it was realized that a steam engine and not an uncontrolled fire was responsible for the smoke clouds.

After 29 days at sea, the *Savannah* arrived in Liverpool, England, on June 20. Sailing vessels had crossed the Atlantic in less time, and according to her log the *Savannah* had used the steam engine for only about 90 hours of the voyage. Yet the novelty of using steam during a transoceanic passage attracted great attention in Liverpool. People crowded at the waterfront to greet the American craft and during the 25 days that it remained in the English port, many persons went aboard the *Savannah.* At least part of their excitement and curiosity, however, was caused by unfounded rumors that the ship might attempt to win the large reward offered by Jérôme Bonaparte for rescuing his brother, Napoleon, from St. Helena.

From England, the *Savannah* sailed to Stockholm. Despite the eagerness of the Swedish king to purchase the ship, a satisfactory financial agreement could not be reached in Stockholm, and so the *Savannah* set out for St. Petersburg on September 5. The Russian government had previously expressed interest in acquiring a steam vessel, but even though the czar himself may have gone on a short excursion aboard the American ship, no sale was made.

On October 10 the *Savannah* began its trip back to the United States. Since the high cost of coal in Europe made the use of its engine too expensive, it relied entirely upon the sails during the return passage, and not until it reached the mouth of the Savannah River was the engine fired. The arrival home on November 30 attracted little attention.

After sustaining large fire losses in January 1820, the owners of the *Savannah* were forced to sell their ship at auction. Its engine was removed and it was put in service as a coastal sailing packet. It was wrecked during a storm off Long Island in November 1821.

Short as its existence was, the *Savannah* has a just claim to fame as the first vessel to use steam to cross the Atlantic. Its log book and the sterling silver coffee urn that was presented to the captain just after the historic voyage are today on exhibit in the US National Museum, administered by the Smithsonian Institution, in Washington, D.C. Further recognition of the importance of the 1819 voyage in the history of the merchant marine was accorded in 1962 when the world's first nuclear-powered merchant ship — built as a joint project of the US Maritime Commission and the Atomic Energy Commission — was named the NS *Savannah.* The city of Savannah takes pride in and has perpetuated the memory of the vessel that bore its name. In 1919 the city celebrated the centennial of the ship's transatlantic passage with a series of pageants and parades, and today a model of the craft can be seen in the Savannah city hall.

But the greatest acknowledgment of the *Savannah's* accomplishment was the choice of May

22, the date of the beginning of her transoceanic passage, for the observance of National Maritime Day. In accordance with a joint resolution of Congress, President Franklin D. Roosevelt issued the first proclamation designating May 22 National Maritime Day early in May 1933. In honor of the contributions of the merchant marine to America, the President called upon the citizens of the United States to fly the flag on their homes and ordered government officials to display the national banner on all federal buildings. Local authorities had only limited time to prepare for the first observance of May 22, but despite this short notice a number of places did hold special events. For example, in New York City former New York governor Alfred E. Smith addressed a public meeting and urged Americans to patronize this country's shipping, which was then suffering from the effects of the Great Depression. Savannah celebrated National Maritime Day even in 1933, and by 1934 more than 50 cities observed May 22.

In recent years commemorations of National Maritime Day have so grown that the nation now observes Merchant Marine Week during the week of May 22 and approximately 500 localities hold special events on May 22 itself. The President of the United States still issues a proclamation designating the observance each year, and the governors of Alabama, Massachusetts, and North Carolina similarly mark the occasion.

The activities that are held to emphasize the importance of the American Merchant Marine to the commerce and defense of this nation are many and varied. Each year the Maritime Administration, the US Department of Commerce, the US Postal Service, and various maritime industry groups, such as the American Merchant Marine Institute, the Committee of American Steamship Lines, the Lake Carriers' Association, the Pacific American Steamship Association, the Propeller Club of the United States, and the Shipbuilders' Council of America sponsor a National Maritime Day poster contest. High school students across the country compete for the grand prize of $500, and the winning poster, which is designed to illustrate a slogan chosen by the contest committee, is displayed throughout the month of May on all postal trucks in the nation. Many mayors and postmasters join in ceremonies, placing the first poster on the trucks in their respective localities and issuing proclamations designating May 22 as Maritime Day in their areas.

Although National Maritime Day is observed across the nation, festivities are particularly colorful in American port cities. Ships are opened for public inspection; parades and band and glee club concerts are held; and cadets from United States service academies are on hand. Luncheons and special ceremonies are also common activities on May 22, and government officials frequently address these gatherings.

New York City's 1970 observance of National Maritime Day was of particular note since conservationists took the opportunity to call attention to the deteriorated condition of the port. A flotilla of sailing vessels, accompanied by three police launches and a 100-foot catamaran used by the US Army Corps of Engineers to collect debris, toured the offshore waters to demonstrate the advanced pollution in the bay and to visit nautical restoration sites including the South Street Seaport in Manhattan and the Alice Austen House on Staten Island. A speech by Vice Admiral Arthur R. Gralla highlighted the more traditional ceremonies at Castle Clinton in New York's Battery Park.

MAY 23

Captain Kidd Hanged

Captain William Kidd, perhaps the most famous of all pirates, belied the stereotype of a buccaneer. Historians know little of his early life, except that he was born about 1645 in Greenock, Scotland, the son of John Kidd, a Calvinist minister. Neither a hardened felon nor a social outcast, Kidd first appears in the records around 1690 as a respectable New York City shipowner and a staunch supporter of the English government.

Shortly before then, England's Glorious Revolution of 1688 had brought Protestant William III and his wife Mary to the throne in place of the Roman Catholic James II. War with France ensued when that country gave shelter to the deposed monarch and took up his cause. The French government, employing a common wartime tactic, commissioned privateers to prey on English shipping. Kidd, in turn, put his ship to the service of William and Mary and did his best to protect England's commerce in the area of the West Indies.

Financially, Kidd was secure. In 1691 he married Sarah Oort, the widow of John Oort, a sea captain, and of William Cox, a wealthy merchant. On the tax assessment list of 1695 Kidd held a place among the wealthiest 10 percent of the New York City population. Kidd's house, located in Manhattan's East Ward, stood on Queen Street, fronting the strand of the East River. Today its site lies at Pearl Street and Hanover Square.

In the fall of 1695 William Kidd met in London with Robert Livingston, a fellow Scot who was one of the leading men in New York Province. Together with Richard Coote, the earl of Bellomont, they planned an expedition to enrich themselves and to rid the seas of the pirates that plagued the trade of England's East India Company. On October 10 Kidd signed an agreement to command the expedition and to divide one-fifth of the profits with Livingston, who was to help finance the venture. Bellomont, who became governor of New York, New Hampshire, and Massachusetts in 1697, promised to provide four-fifths of the necessary capital in return for a corresponding amount of the gain. The earl managed to raise his share by accepting as partners some of the most powerful men of the realm, including Edmund Harrison; the lord chancellor, John Somers; the first lord of the Admiralty, the earl of Oxford; and the secretaries of state, the earl of Romney, and the duke of Shrewsbury.

On April 23, 1696, Captain Kidd left Plymouth, England, in the *Adventure Galley,* a 287-ton vessel that carried 34 guns. He sailed to New York City, where he added more men to his crew. While in his home port, Kidd lent his runner and tackle to help in the erection of the original Trinity Church, the principal Anglican church in the colony. The *Adventure Galley* hoisted anchor again on September 6, rounded the Cape of Good Hope in December, and proceeded to Madagascar, a pirate haven.

Conditions aboard the *Adventure Galley* were harsh: the ship leaked and one-third of the crew died on the voyage to Madagascar. The men were to receive no pay unless they took prizes, and their early lack of success increased their dissatisfaction. The crew became mutinous and, at some point, the strain proved too much for the captain. Kidd cast off his role as protector for that of predator; the pirate hunter turned to piracy. On January 30, 1698, he took his most valuable prize, the Armenian *Quedagh Merchant,* a 400-to-500-ton vessel worth perhaps as much as £70,000.

Many knowledgeable persons had suspected that Kidd's mission might be perverted. Benjamin Fletcher, the governor of New York colony, for one, was unfavorably impressed by Kidd's crew. In 1697 Fletcher wrote to the Lords of Trade in England:

Many flockt to him from all parts men of desperate fortunes and necessitous in expectation of getting vast treasure. He sailed from hence with 150 men as I am informed great part of them are of this province. It is generally believed here, they will have money *per fas aut nefas,* that if he misse of the design intended for which he has commission, 'twill not be in Kidd's power to govern such a hord of men under no pay.

Having scuttled the *Adventure Galley* and transferred his crew to the *Quedagh Merchant,* Kidd left Madagascar in September 1698. By April 1699 he had arrived at Anguilla in the West Indies, where he learned that the government had declared his crew and him to be pirates. He then set sail for the mainland in a fresh vessel, the *Antonio.* When he reached Oyster Bay, Long Island, he met with his friend James Emmot, the most important attorney in New York City. Emmot served as a negotiator between Kidd and Governor Bellomont and arranged for the captain to surrender himself.

Kidd landed in Boston on July 2, 1699, expecting that the governor would pardon him. The captain attempted to excuse his activities as involuntary deeds forced upon him by a mutinous crew. Bellomont, who had drawn Kidd ashore with the lure of possible pardon, was not satisfied with the explanation and imprisoned him.

Bellomont sent Kidd to England as a prisoner. On April 14, 1700, the Board of Admiralty questioned the captain and committed him to the jail at Newgate. The House of Commons, hoping to be able to implicate some of the peers who had financed Kidd's expedition, ordered him to appear before it prior to standing trial. The captain therefore languished in Newgate until the next session of Parliament, in March 1701. Unable to involve the financiers, the commissioners then sent Kidd to stand trial.

William Kidd went to "Old Bailey" criminal court on May 8. The prosecution charged him with the killing of William Moore, a gunner on the *Adventure Galley.* The captain admitted that he had struck the sailor with a bucket, but claimed he did it in the course of subduing a mutiny. The judge claimed that it was intentional murder and the court convicted Kidd. The government also charged him with piracy against five ships. Kidd defended himself by saying that the vessels carried French passes, but the court again found him guilty.

Most historians agree that the trial of Captain Kidd was conducted questionably. The prisoner had no qualified counsel and the only witnesses against him were two hardly disinterested men from the *Adventure Galley.* The charge of murder in the Moore case seems unduly harsh inasmuch as Kidd could hardly have premeditated it. The captain had taken French passes from two vessels, but the prosecution suppressed this evidence.

On May 9 the judge sentenced Captain William Kidd to be hanged. The prisoner responded "My Lord, it is a very hard sentence. For my part I am innocentest of them all, only I have been sworn against by perjured persons." On May 23, 1701, Kidd was hanged, protesting his innocence to the end.

Years after his death Captain Kidd became the center of legend and controversy. Stories of his buried treasure drove many to fruitless searches for hidden riches. The strange proceedings of his trial won for the captain sympathizers who doubted his guilt. The full story may never be known.

South Carolina Ratifies the Constitution

South Carolina on May 23, 1788, became the eighth state to ratify the federal Constitution. Historians accordingly list South Carolina eighth in the chronology of the admission of the 50 states to the Union. Of course, South Carolina and the other 12 colonies had assumed statehood more than a decade before the meeting of the 1787 Constitutional Convention, when they promulgated the Declaration of Independence in July 1776.

Four delegates represented South Carolina at the Constitutional Convention held in Philadelphia in 1787. Pierce Butler, an English noble by birth, came to America as an officer in the British army. He eventually sold his commission and settled in the New World. Butler, 43 years old in 1787, had served in the South Carolina legislature and had recently won election to the federal Congress. Charles Pinckney, brilliant but annoyingly aggressive, was only 29 years old and one of the convention's youngest members. Charles Cotesworth Pinckney, only in his early forties in 1787, had risen to the rank of brigadier general during the American Revolution. A cousin of Charles Pinckney, he had received his education at Oxford University in England and was a prominent lawyer. John Rutledge, then in his late forties, was the leader of the South Carolina contingent. Rutledge, who served South Carolina as congressman, governor, and chancellor, was a renowned orator and was influential in the drafting of the Constitution.

Charles Pinckney was one of the more active members of the convention. After Edmund Randolph presented Virginia's proposals for an ideal Constitution on May 29, the brash young South Carolinian submitted his own plan of union. The Pinckney plan did not have the breadth of the Randolph resolutions, but it did prove useful on a number of minor points to the Committee of Detail, which made the first full draft of the Constitution.

John Rutledge of South Carolina was the chairman of the Committee of Detail, on which Edmund Randolph of Virginia, Nathaniel Gorham of Massachusetts, Oliver Ellsworth of Connecticut, and James Wilson of Pennsylvania also served. Rutledge and Randolph were influential in the committee's decision to recommend that the Constitution not interfere with the slave trade, allow no tax on exports, and require a two-thirds vote of both houses to impose levies on imports. In later debate the convention accepted the provision concerning taxes on exports but, on the advice of a compromise committee composed of one delegate from each state, forbade interference with the slave trade only until 1808 and authorized the Congress to place duties on imports by a simple majority vote.

The Philadelphia convention completed its work on September 17, 1787, and official copies of the proposed Constitution first appeared in South Carolina on October 4 of that year. Propaganda pieces from Pennsylvania in support of the new government and from New York in opposition to it soon followed in the newspapers. By December, groups of South Carolinians formed on each side and issued their own arguments.

South Carolina's vulnerability to attacks from the sea by foreign enemies or on the frontier from Indians fostered a general appreciation of the proposed Constitution. The state had suffered greatly during the American Revolution and looked for protection in the future from a strong national government. Low-country planters, a number of whom were experiencing financial difficulties, were the chief opponents of the new frame of government; they tended to be parochial in their political outlook and also disliked the provisions of the Constitution that discouraged legislation favorable to debtors.

Convening in January 1788, the South Carolina legislature (despite the objections of former governor Rawling Loundes, who opposed the Constitution) ordered the election of delegates for a ratifying convention and established April 11 and 12 as the dates for the election. The Federalists achieved great success in the contests for delegates and were ready to assume control of the ratification caucus when it convened on May 6. With the conclusion foregone, the delegates spent two weeks in desultory debate and issued a resolution declaring that all powers not expressly delegated by the Constitution to the central government were reserved to the states. Then the South Carolina representatives, by a margin of 149 to 73 votes, ratified the Constitution of the United States on May 23, 1788.

MAY 24

Samuel F. B. Morse Opens First US Telegraph Line

It was on May 24, 1844, that the United States' first telegraph line was formally opened, with the initial message clicked out by the man who had produced the first practical telegraph instrument, Samuel Finley Breese Morse. The historic line stretched from Washington to Baltimore and carried as Morse's first officially telegraphed words the sentence "What hath God wrought!" Actually, however, earlier messages had been sent often during the line's construction. One of them, on May 1 of the same year, had brought to Washington the news that the Whigs, meeting in Baltimore, had nominated Henry Clay as their candidate for the presidency. The telegraphed news, which arrived in Washington an hour before a train carrying the same information, heralded a new era of rapid communications.

Morse's invention followed a century in which Europeans, and some Americans, had experimented with the idea of communicating by electrically transmitted signals. His was not, as he thought for some years, the first electric telegraph to be proposed. There was, for instance, the detailed description of an electromagnetic telegraph published by Joseph Henry in 1831, several years before Morse had completed construction of his first working telegraph, around 1835.

At that time Morse was known mainly as a portrait painter and as the chief founder and first president of the National Academy of Design. Born in Charlestown, Massachusetts, on April 27, 1791, he was the son of the noted clergyman and geographer Jedidiah Morse and had been graduated from Yale in 1810 before studying painting at London's Royal Academy under Washington Allston. In the process of becoming one of the most respected American artists of his time, Morse had put in years of artistic effort, some of them impoverished, in such cities as Boston, Charleston, New York, and Washington.

He had been studying art in Europe and was on his way back to New York, where the institution now known as New York University would soon appoint him professor of painting and sculpture, when his life was altered by a thought-provoking conversation on shipboard. The year was 1832 and the conversation — about the newly developed electromagnet — prompted Morse to wonder "why intelligence may not be transmitted instantaneously by electricity."

He straightway set down his original idea of an electromagnetic telegraph. Subsequently he developed an apparatus involving a sender and receiver, which was improved after much experimentation by the addition of Joseph Henry's magnet. (A university colleague had made Morse aware of Henry's work.) Morse's own most important contribution to the telegraph was a system of electromagnetic renewers or relays that made it possible to send messages long distances and by way of many stations and branch lines.

Politically the inventor had been active in the anti-Catholic nativist movement and was its candidate for mayor of New York City in 1836 and again in 1841. In 1837 he gave up painting to devote his full time to the telegraph, filing a caveat at the patent office in Washington, D.C., and also beginning a vain attempt to secure European patents. Leonard Gale, a scientific colleague at the university, and Alfred Vail, who gave financial and other assistance, became partners in Morse's enterprise in the same year. A third partner, Representative F. O. J. Smith of Maine, was acquired in 1838, while Morse was trying to persuade Congress to construct an experimental telegraph line.

By that year Morse had also worked out the Morse code, an alphabet of dots and dashes, since modified, for use with his machine. In 1843 Congress appropriated $30,000 for construction of the experimental line from Washington to Baltimore, and Vail, who was more persevering than the other early partners, received Morse's official first message at the Baltimore end of the line on May 24, 1844. The same year, the US Patent Office granted Morse his patent. Although Congress in 1847 decided not to continue the government's ownership of the 44-mile experimental line, enthusiasm for Morse's telegraph spread like wildfire. Numerous private companies were organized under his patent privileges.

As new instruments were patented in the 1840s and 1850s, Morse, who had his own characteristic flair for controversy, found himself immersed in litigation. By 1854 matters had progressed as far as the Supreme Court, which upheld his rights.

By the time of the Civil War the telegraph was playing an important communications role, particularly in the North, where the telegraph system proved more mobile than in the South and communications lines could be moved, sometimes even during battle. Like the railroad and the McCormick reaper, the telegraph had great importance in unifying the still relatively new United States. Psychologically, it may have played the most important role of all.

In contrast to Morse's lean early days, his last years were filled with honors and financial rewards. He died in New York City on April 2, 1872.

Until the telephone came into use, his telegraph provided the public with its only means of rapid communication. From the mid-19th century until the 1920s, Morse's was the most universally used code. Although it began to be replaced by printing telegraphs and by the teletype after 1900, it is still in some use today, particularly in its cable form. It is also used on some radiotelegraph circuits and in certain situations where requirements call for easily movable stations with simple equipment.

MAY 25

Feast of St. Bede the Venerable

St. Bede, one of the most learned, most influential, and most respected men of Western Europe, lived almost his entire life within a few square miles, a small area of England circumscribed by monastery walls.

Born in Durham County, England, in 673, Bede was sent to the nearby Benedictine monastery when he was seven and put under the charge of St. Benedict Biscop to be educated.

Biscop, a warrior turned Christian, had founded the monastery of Wearmouth in 674 and its sister house, Jarrow, eight years later. In his own travels, Biscop had become impressed with the learning and culture of other countries. When he founded his monastery he determined to make some of this learning and culture available to the people of northern England. He placed great emphasis on a good library for his students and never passed up the opportunity to obtain a good book — scarce though books were in those days. Biscop's library enabled Bede to become for many centuries the greatest of scholars.

After Bede's early education he stayed at the monastery to study for the priesthood. Ordained at the age of 30, he spent the rest of his days teaching, writing, and performing his monastic duties — all of which he did meticulously. He spent this quiet life completely within the monastery walls except for two trips, one to York to visit Archbishop Egbert and the schools flourishing in that area, and one to the monastery at Lindisfarne, where the well-loved St. Cuthbert had been prior. Bede wrote two biographies of St. Cuthbert, one in prose and one in verse.

A superb teacher, Bede trained an estimated 600 students who, in turn, taught thousands of English boys in succeeding generations. One of Bede's students trained Alcuin, who became known as "the schoolmaster of his age" and who developed a system of elementary education and later a liberal arts curriculum that became the model for medieval Europe. Born about the time Bede died, Alcuin referred to the supreme scholar as "Blessed Bede, our master."

Bede's writings fall into three categories: theological — mainly commentaries on the Bible; scientific — ranging from grammatical works to chronology studies in which he calculated calendar years; and historical — for which he is best known. His *Ecclesiastical History of the English People* is even today the sole source of information about Saxon history from 597 to 731.

In his writing Bede summarized all the knowledge in all fields up to his time. Equally important, he took infinite pains to be objective and to document his statements. His method of writing and the sources he used are recorded in a brief note at the end of his *Ecclesiastical History*. Virtually all that is known about his life is also recorded in that same brief note, written four years before he died. In the note, which follows, he refers to himself as Baeda, using the Old English spelling of Bede:

Thus much concerning the ecclesiastical history of Britain and especially of the race of the English, I, Baeda, a servant of Christ and priest of the monastery of the blessed apostles St. Peter and St. Paul, which is in Wearmouth and at Jarrow, have with the Lord's help composed, so far as I could gather it, from ancient documents, or from the tradition of the elders, or from my own knowledge. I was born in the territory of the said monastery, and at the age of seven I was, by the care of my relations, given to the most reverend Abbot Benedict, and afterwards to Ceolfrid, to be educated. From that time I have spent the whole of my life within that monastery, devoting all my pains to the study of the scriptures; and amid the observance of monastic discipline, and the daily charge of singing in the church, it has ever been my delight to learn or teach or write. In my 19th year I was admitted to the diaconate, in my 30th to the priesthood, both by the hands of the most reverend Bishop John and at the bidding of Abbot Ceolfrid. From the time of my admission to the priesthood to my (present) 59th year, I have endeavoured for my own use and that of my brethren, to make brief notes upon the Holy Scripture, either out of the works of the venerable fathers or in conformity with their meaning and interpretation.

He then gave a list of 34 books that he had written, and concluded: "And I pray Thee, loving Jesus, that as Thou hast graciously given me to drink in with delight the words of Thy knowledge, so Thou wouldst mercifully grant me to attain one day to Thee, the fountain of all wisdom and to appear forever before Thy Face."

St. Bede continued working until literally the moment of his death. He was engaged in a translation of the Gospel of St. John when, two days before the Feast of the Ascension in the year 735, he called each of his fellow monks to his bedside to tell them goodbye, to give them small gifts of pepper and incense, and to beg their prayers. He then continued to work, dictating his translation to a young scribe. On May 27, Ascension Day, when the scribe had written the last sentence, Bede asked to be laid on the floor on his hair cloth, and, singing the antiphon from the Office of the Feast of the Ascension, he died.

He had attained such stature as a scholar that contemporaries spoke of him as "the Venerable Bede" — as he is still usually called. His reputation did not fade with time. More than a thousand years after his death, in November 1899, he was named a Doctor of the Church — the only English Doctor of the Church — by Pope Leo XIII and declared a saint. Bede's feast day, originally May 27, is May 25 in the revised Roman Catholic calendar. Episcopalians revere Bede for his great learning and holy life.

Bede's tomb is in the cathedral of Durham. The cathedral had its origins in 995 as a shrine to St. Cuthbert, whose life Bede had chronicled; begun in 1093 on the same site, the church is one of the finest examples of Norman architecture in England.

Constitutional Convention Opens

The American Revolution made the United States independent, but it did not give the new country national unity. In 1777 the common desire for freedom from Great Britain had bound the 13 original states into a government based on the Articles of Confederation. But in the years following the Peace of Paris of 1783, a number of incidents repeatedly proved the inadequacy of the Confederation government, and by 1787 many shared the feeling of George Washington that "something must be done or the fabric will fall." To revise and strengthen the Articles of Confederation, a convention of representatives of the various states opened in Philadelphia on May 25, 1787. In the months that followed, the delegates to the Philadelphia meeting drew up the US Constitution, which has served as this nation's frame of government ever since its ratification (see June 21).

Ralph Waldo Emerson's Birthday

Ralph Waldo Emerson, the American philosopher, essayist, and poet, lived nearly 80 years. By his death in 1882, a country hurtling into industrialization faced formidable obstacles to heed his call for individual self-reliance — obstacles that Emerson never took into account. In his early and middle years, however, writing out of a significantly different America, Emerson had deeply influenced thinking Americans. Some believe that no writer has more deeply influenced American thought and culture.

Members of Emerson's own generation were highly self-conscious about America's relation to Europe and to the past, and in need of a philosophy that would vindicate a break with tradition and teach people to freely create the new. They heard Emerson out eagerly as he urged them, with humor and keen observation, to seize their own birthright in thought and action, following their God-given intuition. Emerson also had an unusual impact on European letters for an American of his time, impressing such diverse writers of later generations as Friedrich Nietzsche, Maurice Maeterlinck, and Henri Bergson. Radical and optimistic, his peculiarly American philosophy expressed and helped to shape the American conviction that people have the power to change all things and that change itself is good.

Emerson was born on May 25, 1803, in Boston, Massachusetts, to the Reverend William and Ruth (Haskins) Emerson. Ancestry and education would have placed him in the Brahmin class of Boston, but the family was not wealthy. When Emerson was eight years old, his father, the cosmopolitan and literary minister of Boston's oldest church, died, leaving the education of his children to his wife. The boy attended the Boston Latin School, and with the help of various jobs and his mother's economies, was able to attend Harvard College, from which he graduated at the age of 18 — as class poet.

For several years afterwards, Emerson taught at a girls' school run by his brother. After hesitation he decided to prepare for the ministry, following seven direct ancestors in this field. It was to prove an unsatisfactory choice, but not before he had gained important skills and insights. In 1825 he entered Harvard Divinity School, where today his room is marked with a plaque in Divinity Hall. He was "approbated" to preach the next year and earned money by giving sermons while he continued his studies. Slowed by poor health, Emerson wintered in St. Augustine, Florida — still a rough outpost; it was before the defeat of the Seminoles by the US army — hoping that the climate would be salutary.

At divinity school Emerson discovered his oratorical skill and found that his strength lay in the exercise of "moral imagination" more than in the systematic defense of doctrine. Though already disturbed about certain church teachings, he was pushed ahead by ambition, and in 1829 was called to the pulpit of the Second Unitarian Church of Boston and ordained. Soon afterwards he married Ellen Tucker of New Hampshire. Meanwhile his fame as a preacher in Unitarian circles grew; but underneath the fame, he was restless.

Emerson was open to the "new voices" of the times, including those of Thomas Carlyle, Samuel Taylor Coleridge, and the Swedenborgians. Also at this time, his older brother returned from Germany with word of Goethe and of the new biblical criticism with its systematic doubt about the historicity of miracles. Emerson's sermons took on a characteristic idealism, stressing personal "uses of the spirit" rather than traditional Christianity. "Chilly" by nature, Emerson also found the routine of his pastorate taxing — as his parishioners found themselves unconsoled by his calls. After his young wife died of tuberculosis early in 1831, he found it increasingly difficult to continue. He desired a freer and, to him, more vital vocational framework in which to express his intellectual and spiritual powers. In the summer of 1832, at the age of 29, he refused, as a matter of conscience, to administer the symbolic Lord's Supper to his congregation, no longer regarding it as necessary. In this way Emerson provoked the termination of his ministry.

Released from previous restrictions, but in bad health and without a clear alternative for his life, Emerson sailed for the Mediterranean. He traveled in Italy, England, and Scotland, seeking out such distinguished Europeans as Coleridge, Wordsworth, and Carlyle in hopes that the example of these great men would illuminate and fortify him in his search for his own experience of God — for an intuition of "spirit within him" that would allow him to be self-reliant in his judgment and in his vision of the world.

Returning to America in 1833, Emerson began to write his short work *Nature*, which would have great impact on the thought of New England. He continued the journal he had begun as a Harvard undergraduate, which became a mine of ideas for later essays. Above all he launched himself as a lecturer, offering courses in natural history and biography. If a little unusual for a former minister, these subjects derived naturally from Emerson's emerging philosophy. For him the picture of natural history developing in Europe and America through study and classification of animal and plant species confirmed the spiritual connection between man and nature. Biography enabled him to explore models of human greatness and moral self-reliance.

Emerson was now struggling to become an independent literary man — a social and vocational role then almost unknown in America. In his achievement of independence, which helped others to follow, he was aided by the spread of lyceums at this time. The first lyceum had been founded at Millbury, Massachusetts, in 1826, by Josiah Holbrook, a collaborator of the educator Horace Mann. It offered a paid-in-advance series of lectures to satisfy the public's craving for knowledge on a variety of subjects. As the lyceum movement expanded westward in the 1830s, offering townspeople a new form of education and entertainment and a social occasion other than weekly prayer meetings, Emerson became a favorite speaker. Much of his livelihood would come from such lecturing, and often it was money hard earned, for travel from town to town at the time involved many inconveniences, delays, and discomforts. Emerson's prominence on the lecture platform suggests the strong cultural influence that New Englanders gained over the rest of the country in this period, partly through the lyceums.

As early as 1834 Emerson made his home in Concord, Massachusetts. The following year he married Lydia Jackson of Plymouth, Massachusetts, bringing her to live first in the Old Manse, which his grandfather had built about 1765. There, just off Monument Street, Emerson finished his long essay *Nature*, published anonymously in 1836. From 1842 to late 1845, the Old Manse housed another famous man of letters, Nathaniel Hawthorne. Today, furnished as it was in 1845, it is designated a National Historic Landmark and is open to the public daily from Patriot's Day to Veterans Day. The house is next door to a scenic site which now epitomizes tranquillity — Concord battleground and North Bridge of Revolutionary fame. As Emerson wrote in his hymn for the dedication of the battle monument on July 4, 1837:

> Here once the embattled farmers stood
> And fired the shot heard round the world.

In 1836 the Emersons moved to what became known as the Emerson House. In this square frame house, near the junction of Lexington Road (Massachusetts Route 2A) and the Cambridge Turnpike, he lived and worked until his death. Today it is furnished as it was in Emerson's lifetime, except that the study and library are replicas. Rich in Victorian furniture and portraits, it also is designated a National Historic Landmark, and is open to the public, except Mondays, from April 19 to December 1. Emerson's original library is now at the Antiquarian Museum, directly across the turnpike from the house and open daily from April 19 to November 11.

For two years after 1841, young Henry David Thoreau (see July 12) joined the Emerson household and wrote there under Emerson's tutelage, in exchange for performing certain household and editorial duties. Emerson encouraged the young individualist, editing his poems and supporting his writings on nature. His encouragement of Thoreau is just one example of the leadership Emerson gave contemporaries in the intellectual and spiritual renovation that more and more of them found necessary. However, his peaceful married life in Concord, with its daily schedule of writing, walking, and conversation with friends, is deceptive, for it was from this calm haven that Ralph Waldo Emerson launched a philosophic attack upon old religious and scientific beliefs that shook traditional New England.

To liberate himself, Emerson had had to replace the mechanistic, deterministic, and materialist philosophy of man and nature that underlay contemporary Unitarianism (and was founded on Newton's physics and Locke's psychology of sensation) with a philosophy that was new in its bases. He laid down its essentials in the essay *Nature:* Men were not merely passive recipients of sensations from the external world, bound by material causes and effects over which they had no control. In such a world there was no place for passionate spirit and real piety; and men became strangers to themselves. The truth was rather that all nature was a great living organic reality, immanent with spirit, still unfolding, and embracing man — the most active of her creatures — in an intimate bond. Man shared with nature the indwelling of the Over-Soul, which Emerson defined as "that Unity, that Over-Soul, within which every man's particular being is contained and made one with all other." Thanks to his limitless powers of perception, man was capable of understanding nature's laws. Through his ideas he could participate fully in the yet-to-be-formed future and fashion from nature a world suited to human needs. Human free will was thus reclaimed and reemphasized in Emerson's idealistic philosophy, and nature was returned to the moral service of man. It has been well said that Emerson "opened the channel through which the new romantic concept of an organic nature flooded American thought." He was also in tune with the European romantics in his faith in the freedom and creative power of the individual.

Emerson's written style is distinctive. Weak in overall construction but brilliant in aphorism, his essays were for the most part delivered first as lectures and changed little for publication. The effective unit of his thought is the sentence. His prose is poetic, and his essays are intuitive, developing by recurring images and themes.

In 1837, in the Phi Beta Kappa address at Harvard College, Emerson applied his insights directly to the attitudes behind the educational process of his day. Entitled "The American Scholar," his talk was an impassioned plea for Americans to do their own thinking and no longer lean on the cultures of Europe and the ancient world. Emerson's audience, deeply concerned with the New World's presumed inferiority, was electrified. The address made him famous.

The succeeding year Emerson was asked to deliver an address at the Harvard Divinity School. Once again he spoke with a directness and courage born of a philosophy not adopted from others but won for himself and intuitively right-feeling. He unequivocally attacked the Church as dead and the ministry as antiquated; and called on the scholar to free himself from the Church and to seek "a new revelation commensurate to the present age."

The response to this speech was shock rather than delight, as leaders in the Church and university rose to defend their beliefs and institutions against an attack at the roots. Emerson was not welcomed at Harvard for a generation, and for a time he was virtually *persona non grata* on the lecture circuit as well. The experience drove home to him the fact that ideas do not themselves bring reform, at least in any immediate sense. But being unsuited by constitution for public strife, he did not himself become an active reformer in the 1830s and 1840s.

His initiatives up to that time nonetheless made him spokesman for a group of like-minded New England thinkers, known as the Transcendentalists, who included in their number persons very much interested in reform. Among the group were Thoreau; author-philosopher Orestes Brownson; clergyman-abolitionist Theodore Parker; educator and mystic Bronson Alcott; the influential Unitarian minister William Ellery Channing; Unitarian clergyman and reformer James Freeman Clarke; and author, critic, and feminist Margaret Fuller, who was the first editor of the Transcendentalists' magazine, *The Dial.*

Emerson himself took over the editorship of that publication in 1842. As editor, he stressed poetry and metaphysics rather than questions of practical reform, which did not arouse his sympathy any more than did the experiments of some of his friends in utopian communal living. The only reform that seemed to Emerson of lasting value was individual moral regeneration, and he wrote and spoke eloquently on its behalf.

His *Essays, First Series* had appeared in 1841. The collection included one of his finest pieces, "Self-Reliance." "To believe your own thought," Emerson wrote, "to believe that what is true for you in your private heart is true for all men — that is genius. . . . In every work of genius we recognize our own rejected thoughts; they come back to us with a certain alienated majesty. Great works of art . . . teach us to abide by our spontaneous impression with good-humored inflexibility. . . ." He also wrote, more pungently, "Society everywhere is in conspiracy against the manhood of every one of its members. . . . The virtue most in request is conformity. . . . The objection to conforming to usages that have become dead to you is that it scatters your force. It loses your time and blurs the impression of your character. . . . It is easy to see that a greater self-reliance must work a revolution in all the offices and relations of men. . . ."

The *Essays, Second Series,* published in 1844, took up similar themes, but gave greater weight to Emerson's experience of limitations in pursuing his high goal of self-activation. In *Representative Men* (1849), he increasingly balanced the test of action with the test of perception in his judgment of men.

In 1846 Emerson's *Poems* appeared. Over a century later, they are not highly regarded. The next year he lectured in England and found that fame had preceded him. He revisited his friend Carlyle and was warmly received by the literary world. *English Traits* (1856) gathered lectures about his reactions to England and the English.

Emerson's interests shifted as tensions in the nation grew in the 1850s. The great and bitter issues of this period in American politics fill his *Journal.* Always sympathetic to the abolitionist cause, he became outspoken in his criticism of slaveholding. On the eve of the Civil War he established the Saturday Club, a group of distinguished New Englanders who met for monthly discussions. The group included Nathaniel Hawthorne, Henry Wadsworth Longfellow, Louis Agassiz, Oliver Wendell Holmes, and John Lothrop Motley. Along the way Emerson in 1855 became one of the first critics to appreciate the gifts of Walt Whitman.

During the 1860s Emerson showed lessening powers as a writer and thinker, although a second volume of his poems, *May Day and Other Pieces,* appeared in 1867. He had accommodated himself to society, and the form in which he had couched his revolt had been largely assimilated; by then there was a new generation that could little imagine the upheaval that had been caused by his first addresses.

In the 1870s Emerson grew amiably senile. He died on April 27, 1882, at Concord, and was buried there on Author's Ridge in Sleepy Hollow Cemetery. In 1900 he was elected to the Hall of Fame for Great Americans, and in 1903 the 100th anniversary of his birth was celebrated in England and in the United States, especially in Concord and Boston, with speeches by distinguished admirers. The 150th anniversary of his birth was noted in Concord in 1953. The American Unitarian Association and the First Parish Church of Concord sponsored a lecture on Emerson, which was attended by an overflow crowd of 800 persons. Out-of-town delegates toured the sites connected with Emerson. Professor Howard Mumford Jones said, in part: "Emerson realized that the greatest evil of our time is moral cowardice. The serenity of his essays shows his belief in the ultimate triumph of the good and his faith that the individual conscience can deal with evil." In his own time, however, such men as Herman Melville, Nathaniel Hawthorne, and Henry James Sr. had felt that Emerson assigned evil too small a role in human affairs.

MAY 26

Feast of St. Augustine of Canterbury

St. Augustine of Canterbury, an Italian Benedictine monk sent to England at the end of the sixth century, converted thousands of Anglo-Saxons to Christianity and became the first archbishop of Canterbury. He is often called the Apostle of England, and in that country his feast day is celebrated by Anglicans on May 26, the date of his death. His feast day in the revised Roman Catholic calendar is May 27 (see May 27). The Protestant Episcopal Church commemorates St. Augustine on May 26, counting the optional observance among its lesser feasts.

Montana Becomes a Territory

During the dark days of the Civil War while federal troops were fighting to preserve the integrity of the Union, the United States Congress was faced with necessity of establishing a viable government in the area of what is now Montana. In the spring of 1864 the national legislature passed an enabling act creating the territory of Montana in the great Northwest. On May 26, 1864, President Abraham Lincoln affixed his signature to this measure.

An area rich with natural resources and beauty, Montana has yielded slowly to the intrusion of white settlers. In 1742 or 1743 the French fur traders François La Vérendrye and Louis Joseph La Vérendrye, his brother, probably visited eastern Montana. The snowcapped peaks of the American West captivated François, and he reportedly exclaimed: "This is truly the Land of the Shining Mountains." But the

Vérendryes returned to Canada without exploring western Montana, and for the remainder of the 18th century only an occasional fur trader disturbed the tranquil wilderness.

Shortly after he purchased the Louisiana Territory from Napoleon in 1803, President Thomas Jefferson authorized the American explorers Meriwether Lewis and William Clark to undertake an extensive expedition through the newly acquired lands. With the assistance of the Indian guide, Sacagawea, Lewis and Clark proceeded west across Montana on their trek to the Pacific in 1805. Then on their return east in 1806, they undertook the first major explorations of the region by white men: Lewis and several members of the party ventured into northern Montana in the area of the Marias River while, farther south, Clark and his companions surveyed the valley of the Yellowstone River.

Lewis and Clark found many streams rich with beaver in Montana and their reports of excellent trapping opportunities quickly attracted fur traders to the region. In 1807 Manuel Lisa of New Orleans outfitted 42 men and led them to the mouth of the Bighorn River. There they constructed Montana's first trading post.

Lisa was only the first of many fur traders to tap Montana's beaver resources. During the next 70 years, trappers, working on their own or for British or American companies, took thousands of pelts out of the Montana wilds. Vast fortunes were amassed from this beaver trade — the most notable of which was that made by John Jacob Astor and his American Fur Company.

Although some white men were interested only in fur profits, others wanted to take Christianity to the Indians who inhabited Montana. In 1841 the Belgian-born Jesuit priest Pierre Jean DeSmet founded St. Mary's Mission in the Bitterroot Valley. Three years later another Jesuit, Italian-born Anthony Ravalli, joined the western Montana mission. Father Ravalli was a man of many talents: in addition to proselytizing he built a sawmill and a gristmill, and dispensed herbal medicines to the Indians. And after the Jesuits were forced to leave the Bitterroot Valley in 1850, Father Ravalli established the St. Ignatius Mission and a boarding school for Indians in the Mission Valley of northwestern Montana.

Only hardy woodsmen seeking beaver skins and zealous religious eager to make converts braved the Montana wilderness prior to 1860. But in the next decade the discovery of gold brought thousands of prospectors to the region. As early as 1852 François Finlay may have found the yellow metal, and in 1858 James and Granville Stuart definitely uncovered gold. The Stuarts effectively mined their claim in the spring of 1862, but it was not these initial discoveries that brought the population boom to Montana.

The strike that lured so many prospectors occurred in July 1862 when John White and his party discovered gold along Grasshopper Creek. By the fall of 1862 it was apparent that this was a major find, and news of the new goldfield spread quickly. The town of Bannack was immediately laid out near the site of the strike and by the spring of 1863 the area had almost 1,000 inhabitants.

On May 26, 1863, six prospectors found an even more lucrative gold deposit along a small creek in the foothills of Montana's Tobacco Root range. The prospectors named the gold-rich area Alder Gulch because of the large numbers of alder trees on the banks of the creek, and for a time they tried to keep their discovery secret. But their efforts to conceal the location of the deposit were futile; within six months of the strike, perhaps 10,000 gold seekers had flocked to Alder Gulch — which was soon known as Virginia City — and by mid-1864 the population of the area had swelled to some 35,000.

In July 1864 gold was also discovered at Last Chance Gulch north of Virginia City. Again thousands of prospectors swarmed to the new mining fields, and Last Chance Gulch soon became the site of Helena, Montana's third boom town and the present capital.

The gold rush necessitated the establishment of a viable and easily accessible government for Montana. The part of the area east of the Rocky Mountains, which came under United States jurisdiction as a result of the Louisiana Purchase, had, since 1803, been successively a part of the Louisiana country and of Missouri Territory, Nebraska Territory, and Dakota Territory; the mountainous western region of Montana remained under the control of Great Britain until the Oregon Treaty of 1846, under which Britain recognized US authority in the area. In 1848 northwestern Montana was included in the Oregon Territory, and later it was incorporated into the Washington Territory. In March 1863, when the US Congress created the Idaho Territory from the area of what is now Montana and Idaho, and virtually all of Wyoming, the entire eastern and western sections of Montana came under a single government for the first time.

The Montana mining camps and boom towns were breeding grounds of lawlessness and violence, and it soon became apparent that the territorial capital (now Lewiston, Idaho) was too distant and too inaccessible to deal effectively with the problems of the gold fields of present Montana. In the spring of 1864 the US Congress responded to the need for a new territory. And on May 26, 1864, President Abraham Lincoln signed the enabling act creating the Montana Territory.

For 25 years Montana existed as a territory. During that time the territorial capital was moved several times: from Bannack, the original capital, to Virginia City in 1865 and from there to Helena in 1875. Montana prospered during the latter half of the 19th century, and mining continued to be the major source of income, although prospectors gradually turned their attention from gold to silver and finally to copper.

The Montana Territory was also the scene of Custer's Last Stand. In June 1876 Sioux and Cheyenne warriors annihilated the US Army troops commanded by General George Custer. The incident was, of course, the most famous American Indian victory. But the triumph was short-lived, and eventually the tribes of Montana were forced onto small reservations.

Gaining the status of territory was an important step toward Montana's acquisition of statehood in 1889 (see November 8, Montana Becomes a State). In 1964 citizens marked the centennial of Montana's becoming a territory with elaborate festivities throughout the state. Although the hundreds of centennial-related events extended throughout the year, they were particularly plentiful during the spring and summer months on or after May 26. Community after community had its Centennial Day or Days — or Homesteaders Days, or Founders and Pioneers Days, or Frontier Days, or Old Settlers Day, or Old Timers Day, or Territorial Day. There were parades, historical pageants, Indian dances, fairs, balls, musical events, contests, and exhibits, all with a centennial flavor, and there were sports events, including more than 100 rodeos. Fabled Virginia City celebrated on May 24 with a Pony Express race. Helena, Montana's capital, marked the exact anniversary on May 26 with the Governor's Centennial Ball and a reenactment of the signing of the Montana Territory act. One highlight of the centennial summer months was the spectacular historical pageant known as The Montana Story, staged in ten different communities with local casts of nearly 1,000 at each. Another highpoint was a reenactment of Custer's Last Stand near Hardin, on the Crow Indian Reservation — which surrounds the actual site of the battle, now designated as the Custer Battlefield National Monument.

Celebration of the centennial was not restricted to Montana. The feature most visible beyond the state's boundaries was a special train bearing some 300 Montanans — cowboys, Indians, mule-skinners, musicians, state officials, and other representatives; 72 horses; a chuck wagon and a Conestoga wagon; and exhibits reflecting Montana's quintessentially western heritage. Included were paintings and sculpture in which such artists as Frederic Remington and Charles M. Russell preserved their recollections of the Old West; a $1 million collection of gold; and relics relating to episodes in Montana's history like the Custer debacle, to vigilante groups of the once-wild West, and to such legendary figures of its past as the tough-talking, hardriding, softhearted crack shot, "Calamity Jane" Canary, or Burke. Pervading all were aspects of the exhibit reflecting Montana's still unspoiled great outdoors. The centennial train's round trip from Billings, Montana, included stops in Omaha; Kansas City; St. Louis; Louisville; Cincinnati; Charleston, West Virginia; Washington, D.C.; Baltimore; Philadelphia; and New York — where seven cars of exhibits returned later as Montana's exhibit at the 1964–1965 New York World's Fair. En route back to Montana, the centennial train's exhibits were shown to the citizens of Pittsburgh, Cleveland, Chicago, Milwaukee, Moline, and Minneapolis.

Even in years that are not special anniversaries, visitors to Montana can view some of the places that were important in its days as a territory. One of the most interesting is Virginia City, with its several museums and numerous restored buildings, described in at least one source as "a Williamsburg in the West," though it is, of course, in marked contrast to that re-creation of another era, region, and type of community. Designated as a National Historic Landmark, what is now the Virginia City Historic District, centering on Lower Wallace Street, turns the clock back to the 1860s and 1870s, bringing a mining boom town of the West's most colorful period to life in authentic detail. Among other attractions visitors can see the building in which the territorial legislature met, the office of Montana's first newspaper, the Wells Fargo Express Office, an old assay office, livery stable, barber shop, general store, blacksmith shop, the Bale of Hay Saloon, Rank's Drugstore, and other points of interest, including the wooden sidewalks and nearby Boot Hill Cemetery. State Senator and Mrs. Charles A. Bovey were prime movers of extensive restoration both at Virginia City and at nearby Nevada City, once the site of a booming mining camp, and accessible today by narrowgauge railroad in summer months.

MAY 27

Feast of St. Augustine of Canterbury

St. Augustine was one of 40 Benedictine monks chosen from their monastery in Rome and sent by Gregory the Great (pope and saint) as missionaries to England at the end of the sixth century. Their mission was to strengthen the remaining church in Celtic Britain and to convert the Anglo-Saxons who separated the Celtic Christians from the rest of Christendom.

By the time the band of monks got as far as southern Gaul, a crisis occurred, or possibly the monks realized they were bereft of missionary zeal. They sent Augustine back to Rome to ask Pope Gregory to excuse them from the assignment.

However, this particular mission was a dream of long standing for Gregory who, before he became pope, had once set off for England himself but was recalled to duties in Rome. Once elected pope, he had to give up any thought of going himself but he had the authority to see that missionaries did indeed reach England. The time was propitious since Ethelbert, king of Kent, had married a Christian — Bertha, daughter of a Frankish king — and the people of Kent were less hostile to Christians than were other Anglo-Saxon kingdoms. Gregory of course insisted that the monks continue their mission and he made Augustine the abbot, or leader, of the group.

With this new authority, Augustine brought his monks safely to England. They landed in 597 on the Isle of Thanet, in Kent, where Ethelbert received them warmly, promised shelter and protection, and gave them land in Canterbury, the capital of Kent. On their arrival in Canterbury, the missionaries found that the ancient and long-abandoned church of St. Martin had been restored and prepared for their use.

Ethelbert, one of the strongest rulers in southern England, welcomed the opportunity for education and culture that the missionaries could provide for the people of his kingdom. Augustine did not disappoint the king. He had brought many books with him and, perhaps even more important, he inspired a love of learning that soon became characteristic of Anglo-Saxon England and paved the way, certainly, for the greatest Anglo-Saxon scholar of them all, St. Bede the Venerable.

On June 2, 597, Ethelbert himself was baptized, thus becoming the first Christian Anglo-Saxon king. Thereafter the new faith spread rapidly among the Anglo-Saxons. Their acceptance of Christianity and its teachings opened to them the history and literature of the ancient world, and brought them into communication with the Christian nations of Europe. On one Christmas Day, it is said, Augustine baptized more than 10,000 Anglo-Saxons. Soon Augustine had made Ethelbert's capital, Canterbury, a Christian center and a seat of learning.

Augustine was not so successful, however, with the Celtic Christians. They refused to accept his authority, refused to accept the method for reckoning the date of Easter used by other Christians, and were convinced that Augustine was weakening the Church by his less austere Roman ways. Augustine, on his part, was prob-ably not as tactful as he might have been in winning over the Celts.

At any rate, Augustine became archbishop in 601 and made Canterbury his seat. Besides being the first archbishop of Canterbury, he is known as the Apostle of England — although he probably spent less than 10 years there. He died around 604 or 605. He is sometimes called St. Austin in Britain, where his feast is celebrated by Anglicans on May 26, the day of his death. His feast day in the revised Roman Catholic calendar is May 27 (it was formerly May 28).

Canterbury's fame increased greatly after the murder of Thomas à Becket in 1170 and it became a place of pilgrimage. Chaucer's *Canterbury Tales* is a collection of stories told supposedly by pilgrims on their way to Canterbury.

Cornelius Vanderbilt's Birthday

Cornelius Vanderbilt, the American capitalist and industrialist who ranks as one of the great promoters of US steamship and railroad lines, was born at Port Richmond, Staten Island, New York, on May 27, 1794. Although his paternal Dutch ancestors, who settled on Long Island in the late 1600s, wrote their name Van der bilt. His parents were Cornelius Vander Bilt and Phebe Hand Vander Bilt. The industrialist himself preferred the form Van Derbilt. This preference notwithstanding, however, other family members consolidated the name as Vanderbilt within his lifetime, and he is customarily referred to in that way.

The elder Cornelius Vander Bilt was a farmer of modest circumstances with lightering activities around the harbor of New York as a sideline. As a member of a large family with little means, young Cornelius Vanderbilt had to help his father at an early age and consequently received little formal schooling.

At 16 the enterprising youth borrowed enough money from his parents to purchase a modest sailing ship with which to transport passengers and farm produce between Staten Island and Manhattan. Within the next few years he built up his business by provisioning forts in the New York City harbor during the War of 1812, buying sturdy schooners for an eastern seaboard trade between New England and the South, and engaging in shipping up and down the Hudson River.

In 1818 he abandoned his private ventures to serve as captain on Thomas Gibbons's ferry line between New York City and New Brunswick, New Jersey — a vital link for passenger and freight transport between New York and Philadelphia. It was during his 11 years as captain that Cornelius Vanderbilt first displayed the ruthless side of his character in contesting, on Gibbons's behalf, a steam-navigation monopoly in New York waters that the state legislature had previously granted to the rival Robert Fulton. The tenacious Captain Vanderbilt held out against fierce odds until 1824, when the Supreme Court in the famous case of *Gibbons* v. *Ogden (9 Wheaton 1)* invalidated such monopolies as unconstitutional.

In 1829 the ambitious businessman invested his savings to found his own steamboat enterprise on the Hudson River. By cutting rates and engaging in similar cutthroat practices to eliminate or intimidate competitors, he soon was able to extend his concerns to the Long Island Sound region and even to Providence and Boston. By the age of 40 Vanderbilt had amassed probably half a million dollars. In 1840 he had an elaborate mansion built on Staten Island for himself, his wife (the former Sophia Johnson, whom he had married in 1813), and their numerous children. A few years later the social-climbing head of the household transferred his family to a town house on Washington Place in Manhattan.

The 1850s made Vanderbilt, already a millionaire who was dubbed "Commodore," into a business colossus. The discovery of gold in California and the subsequent gold rush offered him a chance to open up his own transportation network to the West Coast, not across the Isthmus of Panama or around South America like other routes, but across the Isthmus of Nicaragua. The investment involved in creating the land-and-sea route — docks, a 12-mile-long macadam road through practically impassable terrain, and the construction of eight steamers to ply between the United States and Nicaragua — was substantial. But the Accessory Transit Company, as the precarious venture had been chartered, was eminently successful. By drastically reducing the New York–San Francisco fare and offering a "shorter" route — by all of two days — the skillful manipulator gained much of the land-sea passenger trade and reportedly netted some $10 million.

Between 1855 and 1861 the multimillionaire operated a freight and passenger service across the Atlantic Ocean between New York City and Le Havre, France. He hoped to reap considerable profits while the Crimean War, which had broken out in 1854, occupied his British competitors. With the outbreak of the American Civil War, however, he abandoned this disappointing venture, and indeed all shipping enterprises, to turn his attention to railroads.

In the early 1860s Cornelius Vanderbilt purchased stock in the New York and Harlem Railroad at a low price. Somewhat later, he bought stock in the Harlem line's main competitor, the Hudson River Railroad. By 1867 the financier and manager had gained control of the New York Central Railroad, which ran between Albany and Buffalo. In each of these takeovers, the Commodore showed himself to be even more domineering and ruthless than his unscrupulous rivals, who did their best to ruin him. Only in the case of the Erie Railway, the stock of which Vanderbilt tried to control in 1868, was he outwitted by opponents who flooded the market with fraudulent shares. Although the railroad magnate lost a small fortune in this abortive effort, he quickly recouped his losses by vastly expanding his railroad network.

Cornelius Vanderbilt first united the New York Central and Hudson River lines in 1869; three years later he leased the Harlem Railroad to it, thereby fashioning an efficiently run and highly lucrative system from three formerly unimpressive enterprises. Then, starting in 1873, he acquired the Lake Shore & Michigan Southern, Michigan Central, and Canada Southern railways, which enabled him to extend his transportation network from New York City to Chicago. As part of this extensive through-service, he built Grand Central Terminal in New York City.

The entrepreneur died in New York on January 4, 1877. He bequeathed the bulk of his wealth, estimated at over $100 million, to his son, William Henry, leaving most of the rest to his second wife, Frank Armstrong Crawford (Sophia Vanderbilt had died in 1868), and his daughters. Tight-fisted with his money, Vanderbilt refused to bestow philanthropic gifts until the last years of his life. In 1873 he made his most memorable contribution to the small Central University of the Methodist Episcopal Church in Nashville, which had been chartered the previous year and which opened in 1875. The Commodore eventually endowed this educational institution, which was renamed Vanderbilt University in his honor, with a million dollars.

MAY 28

Louis Agassiz's Birthday

(Jean) Louis (Rodolphe) Agassiz, charismatic apostle of natural history and one of America's most outstanding teachers of science, belongs to the bright galaxy of immigrants of superior talents and cultivation. His dynamic work as an American educator after 1846, when he was 39 years old, rested on his earlier attainments and training in Europe.

He was born at Môtier-en-Vully in the French-speaking canton of Fribourg, Switzerland, on May 28, 1807, the son of a Protestant pastor. From his mother, Rose Mayor, young Louis Agassiz derived his love of plants and animals and also a personal radiance that drew others to him. At the age of 10 he was sent to the gymnasium (preparatory school) in Bienne, where, he later recalled humorously, he struggled with "the rudiments of many desperate studies." At 15 he went to the academy at Lausanne, and two years later he began medical studies at the University of Zurich.

Itinerant, like most students in German universities, Agassiz enrolled at Heidelberg in 1826. In 1827 he transferred to the larger University of Munich, and became an ardent student of Ignaz von Döllinger, the pioneer embryologist.

In Munich Agassiz labored over a rich collection of Brazilian fishes, brought back in 1821 by two outstanding German naturalists. Agassiz's *Fishes of Brazil* was published in 1829 with many colored plates and hailed as a most important scientific record of a local fish-fauna to that point. Just 22 years old, Agassiz took his Ph.D. at Erlangen in 1829 on the basis of this first book. The next year Agassiz went on to take the degree of doctor of medicine at Munich. Simultaneously he launched investigations of fish fossils that would result in superb works over the next 15 years, particularly his five-volume *Recherches sur les poissons fossiles* (1833–1844). This became a foundation work for research into all forms of extinct life.

On leaving Munich late in 1830, however, Agassiz could only wonder whether he would have to devote himself to the practice of medicine in order to earn a living. Financing his scientific schemes was to be a constant difficulty. Late in 1831 the young naturalist left for Paris — then the center of zoological and medical research. There he spent part of each long day studying the fossil fishes in the Museum of Natural History of the Jardin des Plantes. Soon Georges Cuvier, the renowned comparative anatomist, became interested in Agassiz and assigned to him the entire subject of fossil fishes, giving him his own notes and collections. Working at the Jardin des Plantes to reconstruct the life of the primitive seas, Agassiz was following great scientific traditions.

Despite poverty as a student in the Latin Quarter, Cuvier's protégé was becoming known. Alexander von Humboldt, the celebrated Prussian naturalist and explorer, sought Agassiz out. Humboldt helped Agassiz continue his investigations by advancing him money and assisted Agassiz more permanently in 1832 by arranging a special professorship in natural history at Neu-châtel, sponsored by the king of Prussia, sovereign of the canton until 1846.

This position gave Agassiz an essential base, but little income and insecure tenure. Undaunted, he plunged into teaching and turned the town of Neuchâtel into a center of scientific activity. Always a free spirit, Agassiz prepared lectures on topics interesting to him for his friends and neighbors and like some beneficial Pied Piper encouraged groups of children to troop about the countryside with him learning the elements of nature at firsthand. Likewise Agassiz instructed his adult students on energetic field trips. Agassiz downgraded the use of books except in detailed work. "It is not textbooks we want, but students," he would say. "If you study nature in books, when you go out-of-doors you cannot find her." His students were taught to gather and arrange the necessary facts, not absorb categories of facts organized by others. Agassiz considered natural science excellent training for other fields.

In 1833 Agassiz married Cécile Braun, sister of his dear friend Alexander Braun. A highly gifted artist, she was responsible for some of the finest plates in her husband's works on fossil fishes and fresh-water fish forms. In 1835 their son Alexander was born, and later two daughters, Ida and Pauline. Agassiz also took a number of close friends and colleagues into his household. Simultaneously, he set up a lithographic press to publish his works.

In 1838 his position as professor was made more secure and financially rewarding by a sizable grant of funds for public education in the canton of Neuchâtel — once again provided by the king of Prussia. The improvement was to be a mixed blessing, however, because Agassiz expanded his work far beyond his means.

By his drive and winning enthusiasm, Agassiz was able both to carry old projects forward and initiate new ones before he had irretrievably overextended his resources. Between 1839 and 1845, numerous volumes on ichthyology and mollusks appeared. *Nomenclator Zoologicus* his painstaking work on classification, came out between 1842 and 1846. These publications elicited interest in several countries, including Great Britain and the United States, and brought offers of cooperation.

In addition, in the summer of 1836 Agassiz had entered a new line of research on the action of glaciers in shaping the earth's surface. Accepting the glacial theory of other investigators in the Rhône valley, Agassiz brilliantly perceived that glaciers must have acted on a far larger area of Europe. He began to look for evidence in Switzerland of the hypothesized period of extreme cold. In 1837, in a famous address at Neuchâtel, Agassiz argued that there had been glacial action from the North Pole as far south as the Mediterranean and Caspian seas. While critics scoffed at the audacious novelty of this thinking, Agassiz, with some distinguished colleagues, set up a complicated series of investigations that lasted through the next decade. Late in 1840 his two-volume *Études sur les Glaciers* appeared, followed by two other works on glaciers. Before Agassiz's death the main lines of his theory were widely accepted.

In 1845 his establishment at Neuchâtel succumbed to economic and personal strains. The press was closed down. Several close friends departed. And Cécile Agassiz, frail and careworn, asked to return with the children to her old home in Carlsruhe. Members of Agassiz's family saved him from financial disaster, but his debts were to burden him for years.

Although he had earlier declined positions in several larger European cities, when Agassiz set out in 1846 on a long-planned trip to the United States, everyone sensed that the move would probably be permanent. Acclaimed in Paris and England, he embarked for the New World on the great adventure of the second half of his life.

Agassiz's lucid intellect, picturesque but accurate English, and warm personality won the heart of Boston and New England in the course of the lectures at the Lowell Institute that were the official purpose of his trip. Despite his depression over family and financial problems he threw himself into new work, traveling the eastern seaboard to meet scientific workers and government officials, who as yet were little involved in scientific activities. Agassiz later spoke of his new country as "a land where Nature was rich, but tools and workmen few and traditions none." Amid the dearth he rapidly became the leading figure in American natural history.

Joined by old coworkers from Neuchâtel, Agassiz developed in Cambridge, Massachusetts, a busy center of scientific endeavor. As always, finances were a problem, and after attempting to support his research by lecturing, Agassiz suffered a nervous breakdown. Nevertheless, encouraged by his friendship with the head of the US Coast Survey, by chances to do marine research on the survey steamer, and by political upheaval in Switzerland, Agassiz decided to remain in America. Early in 1848 he accepted the chair of natural history at the new Lawrence Scientific School of Harvard University.

The same year, before they could be reunited, Cécile Agassiz died in Europe of tuberculosis. From this time on Agassiz's ties to America grew stronger (he became a naturalized citizen in 1861). In 1850 he married Elizabeth Cabot Cary of Boston, who assisted him in all later work. Soon he brought his little daughters to the United States. His son, Alexander, who later became a famous naturalist, was already with him. To help finance her husband's work, Elizabeth Agassiz opened a school for girls. The profits from the school also went to pay off the debts Agassiz had contracted before coming to America.

In addition to teaching, writing, and collecting, Agassiz traveled extensively throughout the United States, lecturing to large and interested audiences on scientific subjects. Most significant of his American works were the four volumes of his *Contributions to the Natural History of the United States*. In Part I, a philosophical "Essay on Classification," Agassiz argues against Charles Darwin's theory that the evolutionary process is moved by natural selection among genetic strains. Though scientifically in the forefront of his time, Agassiz apparently partially misconceived the thesis, believing Darwin asserted continual evolutionary progress in absolute terms, instead of the adaptation of species by separation and segregation as the environment changed. Agassiz's hostility to Darwinism also sprang from his philosophical idealism with roots in his strong Reformed Christian heritage. He believed that every species had been separately generated as a "thought of God" and that the structural affinities among species were not proofs of common descent but sprang from "associations of ideas in the Divine Mind." One writer has said that Agassiz "had an intensely religious mind, although he was totally out of sympathy with sects and creeds and the outer shell of Christianity."

Certainly there was a religious fervor, in the best sense, about his work. Two projects bear special mention. In 1859, after strenuous efforts to raise funds and make zoological collections for the project, he presided over the opening of Harvard's remarkable Museum of Comparative Zoology, still functioning today as part of the University Museum. And in the summer of 1873 he opened the Anderson School of Natural History on Penikese Island in Buzzards Bay, Massachusetts, giving actuality to his novel idea of a summer school where he could train teachers of science. In an old barn on the island, he lectured daily on a great range of subjects to the 30 men and 20 women he had selected from the hundreds of applicants. This one-session school was the forerunner of all American marine research stations and summer schools.

Agassiz made journeys to Brazil (1865), to the Rocky Mountains (1868), to Cuban waters (1869); and in late 1871 he set out with his wife on a sea voyage around South America to California. The trip, though exhausting, enabled him to see evidence of glaciation in Chile. Louis Agassiz died in Cambridge on December 14, 1873, and was greatly mourned by his students. "He had been a student all his life long, and when he died he was younger than any of them," one wrote. He was buried in Mount Auburn Cemetery in Cambridge, with a great boulder from the Aar Glacier in Switzerland placed over his grave as a monument.

Louis Agassiz was elected to the Hall of Fame for Great Americans in 1915, the first time foreign-born citizens were admitted.

In 1879, in memory of Agassiz's contributions to the theory of the Ice Age, a great North American glacial lake, now extinct, was named Lake Agassiz. At its fullest, the lake extended 700 by 250 miles over parts of present Minnesota, North Dakota, Manitoba, and Ontario. Some of the largest Canadian lakes are relics of it, and the Manitoba lowland and the Red River system lie in its basin. Also named for Louis Agassiz is the Agassiz Glacier in Glacier National Park, Montana. The mountain-born naturalist has been remembered as well in the names of four mountain peaks: Mount Agassiz on the edge of the White Mountain National Forest in Bethlehem, New Hampshire; Utah's Mount Agassiz in the Uinta Mountains in Duchesne County; California's Mount Agassiz, also called Agassiz Needle, in the Sierra Nevada in eastern Fresno County; and northern Arizona's Agassiz Peak (one of the San Francisco Peaks) in Coconino County, which visitors can view by driving 15 miles north of Flagstaff on US Route 89 to Sunset Crater National Monument and climbing on foot to the crater's rim. In Switzerland, the Agassiz Pass rises 12,631 feet, above the Grindelwald in the Bernese Oberland. Agassiz's name has also been given to a trawl used in collecting marine life for scientific study.

United Presbyterian Church Formed

The way was paved for creation of the new United Presbyterian Church in the USA when two previously separate bodies — the Presbyterian Church in the USA and the United Presbyterian Church of North America — agreed, after years of correspondence, to unite. In doing so, they followed a venerable tradition, for each church had behind it a long history of other mergers. The former Presbyterian Church in the USA can point to important unions in its history in 1758, 1801, and 1870, and to the 1906 union with the Cumberland Presbyterians and the 1920 union with the Welsh Calvinistic Methodist Church. In the case of the former United Presbyterian Church of North America, the history of mergers goes back to 1782, when the Reformed Presbyterians and the Associate Presby-

terians joined, in one of the earliest church unions in America. The resulting body went into the UPCNA union in 1858. Presbyterians thus have a long tradition, predating the 1800s, of participation in the spirit of ecumenism sweeping Christendom in the second half of the 20th century.

The merger of Presbyterian Church in the USA with the United Presbyterian Church of North America came about after "Concurrent Declarations" were distributed throughout both churches as part of a plan of union. The declarations "convenanted and agreed" that each of the uniting bodies would elect, according to its own form of government, "a General Assembly to meet on the twenty-sixth or twenty-seventh day of May, 1958, at Pittsburgh." After each of the general assemblies met separately, commissioners of the two groups were to meet together on May 28, 1958, to "be constituted as one body."

A description of this joint meeting — which served as the opening session of the General Assembly of the new united church — appeared in *The General Assembly News,* published the next day. "USA Presbyterians and United Presbyterians have joined hands," said the account, and "a new chapter in church history has been written. With the . . . symbolic clasp of hands [of moderators Harold R. Martin of the USA Presbyterians and Robert N. Montgomery of the United Presbyterians] a new Church yesterday came into being."

Following the symbolic handshake of the two moderators, and of Stated Clerks Eugene Carson Blake and Samuel W. Shane, the 1,200 participating commissioners and hundreds of onlookers spontaneously joined in singing the doxology, beginning with the familiar words "Praise God from whom all blessings flow." Two lines of commissioners, 850 USA Presbyterians and 350 United Presbyterians, marching from separate churches in a drenching rain, merged to enter Pittsburgh's Syria Mosque. Three banners carried at the head of the procession symbolized the two former churches and the new denomination.

Inside Syria Mosque more than 4,000 persons took part in the sacrament of Holy Communion, while an overflow crowd of 1,200 watched proceedings by closed-circuit television, listened to Dr. Montgomery's sermon, "The Quest for Unity," and heard his reading of the proclamation, which officially declared "that from now henceforth" the two groups "are one united Church, known as The United Presbyterian Church in the United States of America."

Presbyterianism, the founder of which is considered to be John Calvin, made its appearance in the Western Hemisphere with some of this country's earliest colonists. The first Presbyterian church in what was to become the United States was established about 1640 and the first presbytery was organized about 1706.

As of 1974, the United Presbyterian Church in the USA, which is the largest of the nation's Presbyterian denominations, had a membership of approximately 2.7 million. The denomination, which has 8,729 churches in the United States and Puerto Rico, has its headquarters at the Interchurch Center, 475 Riverside Drive, New York City. As a denomination, it has been in the forefront of discussions toward the possibility of future unions between various Protestant churches.

The United Presbyterian Church has complete missions in 38 countries and participates in mission partnerships in 27 others.

MAY 29

June Week, US Naval Academy Annapolis, Maryland

This is a movable event. See note on page xxvi.

Of all the events traditional to the United States Naval Academy at historic Annapolis, capital of Maryland, the most colorful are those associated with June Week, the week preceding the academy's graduation ceremonies, which always fall on the 40th Wednesday after Labor Day. In addition to its much-photographed dress parades, June Week includes such events as the famous Ring Dance and the Farewell Ball and generally attracts some 50,000 persons to the academy.

It culminates with the graduation of approximately 900 midshipmen, witnessed by some 20,000 midshipmen, instructors, and visitors. June Week customarily runs for six days prior to graduation ceremonies.

What probably was the start of June Week came in 1846, a year after the academy's founding, when its first superintendent, Commander Franklin Buchanan, authorized a Great Naval Ball. After the ball 40 midshipmen paraded for the Board of Examiners — whose annual inspection then took place shortly before graduation — presenting a cross section of activities in rifle, artillery, and close-order drill for the visiting dignitaries. Although the two inspections presently made each year by the Board of Examiners (now known as the Board of Visitors) take place at various times, and the Great Naval Ball has become the Farewell Ball, it was the parade and ball of 1846 that set the precedent for today's June Week.

The events of June Week 1975 were indicative of the usual program. The first event, on Friday, May 29, was the dedication parade. Thousands of friends, relatives, and visitors watched this first of June Week's three dress parades, held on historic Worden Field. In the afternoon a concert was given by the Naval Academy Band at the Chapel Walk Bandstand. Afterwards the Plebe Recognition ceremony at Herndon Monument marked the close of the freshman year for the Class of 1978. The plebes then stormed the monument, a well-greased, 20-foot obelisk, to place on its top a midshipman's cap. That evening the midshipmen's popular music committee presented the year's final concert of popular music, in the academy's huge Halsey Field House.

The first of the traditional June Week athletic matches between the Naval Academy and West Point's United States Military Academy were held the next day. The competitions held at Annapolis, which vary somewhat from year to year, were in track and lacrosse in 1975. Additional athletic events were scheduled at West Point.

All of this was merely warm-up, however, for the most important social event of the year at Annapolis — and one of the most romantic of the entire collegiate circuit. This is the famous Ring Dance, marking the close of the junior year, at which each of the academy's second classmen receives his class ring from the young woman of his choice. According to long tradition, she dips it into a binnacle of water collected from the Seven Seas before stepping with her midshipman into a huge replica of a ring, where she places his ring on his finger. The fact that the ceremony, which is sealed with a kiss, bears some resemblance to a betrothal is by no means lost on the Annapolis midshipmen, many of whom seize upon the occasion for the announcement of their own engagements. In such cases they may slip miniatures of their class rings on the fingers of their wives-to-be before proceeding to Dahlgren Hall for the formal hop that follows immediately.

Sunday was the quietest day of June Week in 1975, with morning church services followed in the afternoon by a salute from the Navy's famous Steel Band from San Juan, Puerto Rico, and in the evening by the Superintendent's garden party honoring the First Regiment of the graduating class (the Second Regiment was duly honored the following night). The following morning, Monday, Worden Field was the scene of what is known as the Commendation Parade, with the academy's superintendent presenting commendatory letters to those graduating midshipmen who had exhibited officer-like qualities to an outstanding degree. In the afternoon, the

Blue Angels, the US Navy Flight Demonstration Team, exhibited their great skill in precision flying.

The next day, Tuesday, was a study in the precision, close-drill work, and smart appearance for which the Annapolis midshipmen are famous — beginning with the famous Color parade, on Worden Field, at which the white-gowned, garden-hatted color girl (selected by the midshipman commander of the Color Company) transfers from the current to the new Color Company the flags it will be privileged to carry during the next year. The new Color Company is the winner of competition among the 36 companies of the academy's brigade of midshipmen, who have been graded on the basis of academics, intramural sports, professional drills, and parade performances. (Although the color competition was instituted in 1867, it was only in 1871 that the color girl — the daughter, it so happened, of Superintendent John L. Worden — made her first appearance.) In the afternoon there was the presentation of prizes and awards to outstanding members of the graduating class in Halsey Field House.

Tuesday evening's Farewell Ball was followed by the next morning's graduation exercises, with Vice President Nelson Rockefeller as principal speaker. Since 1966 the graduation ceremonies, at which graduating midshipmen receive bachelor of science degrees and commissions in the navy or marines, have taken place (except in bad weather) in the 28,000-seat Navy-Marine Corps Memorial Stadium. In 1975 as always the graduation ceremonies were followed directly by the graduates' jubilant hat throwing (a custom since 1912).

Although many June Week events are restricted to the academy's faculty and midshipmen and their guests, public requests for tickets to the graduation ceremonies are honored to the extent possible, and such outdoor events as band concerts, some of the athletic events, the Blue Angels' demonstration, and the dress parades are open to visitors who wish to attend.

Originally named the Naval School, the academy opened on October 10, 1845. Its founding was at the insistence of Secretary of the Navy George Bancroft, the historian and educator, who expressed dissatisfaction with the haphazard training young naval officers were receiving and secured the permission of President James K. Polk and Secretary of War W. L. Marcy to use the army's obsolete Fort Severn for the purpose. The institution, which began with a mere 10 acres and fifty midshipmen, now has more than 4,000 midshipmen, occupies 329 acres, and occupies over 200 major buildings. A program of new construction includes the 650,000-volume Nimitz Library, the multimillion-dollar Engineering Studies Complex, a sailing center, and a recreation area. The academy's predominantly French Renaissance style of architecture was established in 1899, when the institution — which received its present name in 1850 — was almost completely rebuilt to the designs of architect Ernest Flagg. In 1959 the Naval Academy's curriculum was extensively revised in answer to the challenges of the nuclear age and advanced ship technology. There are now over 25 possible majors, ranging from aerospace engineering to oceanography, and the curriculum includes some 580 courses. A historic and controversial innovation came in 1976, when the first women were accepted for admission to the academy.

John F. Kennedy's Birthday

For many Americans the election of John Fitzgerald Kennedy as the 35th President of the United States in 1960 marked the beginning of a new era in this country's political history. Kennedy was the first Roman Catholic and the youngest man ever chosen Chief Executive. He was also the first person born in the 20th century to hold the nation's highest office.

Born in Brookline, Massachusetts, on May 29, 1917, Kennedy was descended from two politically conscious, Irish-American families that had emigrated from Ireland to Boston shortly after potato blight and economic upheavals had struck their homeland in the 1840s. Kennedy's grandfathers, Patrick J. Kennedy and John F. ("Honey Fitz") Fitzgerald, became closely associated with the local Democratic party; Kennedy served in the Massachusetts legislature, and Fitzgerald won election as mayor of Boston. In 1914 the marriage of Joseph P. Kennedy and Rose Fitzgerald united the two families. John Fitzgerald Kennedy was the second eldest of Joseph and Rose Kennedy's four sons and five daughters.

Joseph P. Kennedy was an extraordinarily successful businessman. Despite the relatively modest means of his family, Kennedy attended Harvard College, and upon graduation in 1912 began a career in banking. During the 1920s he amassed a substantial fortune from his investments in motion pictures, real estate, and other enterprises, and unlike many magnates of his era he escaped unscathed from the stockmarket crash of 1929. Joseph Kennedy himself was never a candidate for elective office, but he was deeply interested in the Democratic party. He made large contributions to the presidential campaign of Franklin D. Roosevelt in 1932; in return, Roosevelt appointed him chairman of the recently established Securities and Exchange

Commission, where his business expertise proved especially helpful in drafting legislation designed to regulate the stock market. In 1937 Roosevelt named Kennedy US ambassador to Great Britain.

Despite his wealth and political influence, the Democratic Irish-Catholic Joseph Kennedy never won the acceptance of Boston's Protestant elite. He deeply resented this, and determined that his sons' achievements would equal, if not excel, those of their Brahmin counterparts. Toward this end he modeled their lives and educations after those enjoyed by the Yankee upper class.

John Kennedy, like his brothers and sisters, grew up in comfortable homes and attended some of the nation's most prestigious preparatory schools and colleges. He was enrolled at the age of 13 at Canterbury, a Catholic preparatory school staffed by laymen, but transferred after a year to the nonsectarian Choate School, where he completed his secondary education before entering Princeton University. Illness forced him to leave the college before the end of his freshman year, but the following autumn he resumed his studies, at Harvard.

Kennedy's college years coincided with a time of world crisis. The future President had unusual opportunities to combine knowledge gained in the classroom with his own firsthand observations. As a government major at Harvard, he benefited from the teachings of some of the nation's most prominent political scientists and historians, men who in the late 1930s were acutely aware of the growing menace of Nazism. Moreover, in 1938 Kennedy spent six months in London assisting his father, who was then serving as US ambassador. This stay in England gave the young student an excellent opportunity to witness for himself the British response to the Nazi aggression of the 1930s, and he used the insights gained from the experience in writing his senior thesis. This thesis, in which Kennedy attempted to explain England's hesitant reaction to German rearmament, was extremely perceptive, and in 1940 it was published in expanded form in the United States and Great Britain under the title *Why England Slept*.

After receiving his B.S. degree *cum laude* from Harvard in 1940, Kennedy briefly attended the Stanford University Graduate School of Business, and then spent several months traveling through South America. Late in 1941, when the United States' entry into World War II seemed imminent, Kennedy joined the US Navy. As an officer he served in the South Pacific theater, where he commanded one of the small PT or torpedo boats that patrolled off the Solomon Islands.

On April 25, 1943, Kennedy assumed command of PT-109, the vessel on which, only a little more than four months later, his courage and strength were put to their first serious test. On the night of August 2, 1943, the Japanese destroyer *Amagiri* rammed PT-109. The force of the destroyer sliced the American craft in half and plunged its 11-man crew into the waters of Ferguson Passage. Burning gasoline spewed forth from the wrecked torpedo boat, setting the waters of the passage aflame; but Lieutenant Kennedy retained his composure, directed the rescue of his crew, and personally saved the lives of three of the men. Kennedy and the other survivors found refuge on a small unoccupied island, and during the days that followed he swam long distances to obtain food and aid for his men. Finally, on the sixth day of the ordeal the crew was rescued.

Kennedy's bravery did not go unnoticed. For his deeds in August 1943 he subsequently received the Purple Heart and the Navy and Marine Corps Medal. Injuries sustained during his courageous exploits and an attack of malaria ended Kennedy's active military service, however. Later in 1943 he returned to the United States, and in 1945 he was honorably discharged from the navy.

After leaving the navy, Kennedy, like many other young men who had served their country during World War II, had to make a decision about his future career. At Harvard he had become increasingly interested in government, but he did not originally plan to seek public office. Members of the Kennedy family had expected that the eldest son, navy pilot Joseph P. Kennedy Jr., would enter politics – a hope cut short when he was killed in a plane crash during the war. Deeply affected by his older brother's death, John Kennedy in 1945 compiled a memorial volume, *As We Remember Joe*, which was privately printed. Shortly afterwards he determined to pursue the career that had been the choice of his late brother.

Appropriately, Kennedy sought his first elective office in East Boston, the low-income area with a large immigrant population that several decades before had been the scene of both his grandfathers' political activities. Announcing his candidacy for the Democratic nomination for the US House of Representatives in the 11th Congressional District early in 1946, Kennedy, with the assistance of his family and friends, campaigned hard and long against several of the party's veterans and won the primary. Since the district was overwhelmingly Democratic, Kennedy's victory in the primary virtually guaranteed his election in the November contest. As expected, on November 5, 1946, he easily defeated his Republican rival and at the age of 29 began his political career as a member of the House of Representatives.

East Boston voters returned Kennedy to Congress in 1948 and 1950, and for the six years he represented the 11th District he continuously worked to expand federal programs, such as public housing, social security, and minimum wage laws, that benefited his constituents. However, in 1952 the young politician decided against running for another term in the House. Instead he sought the Senate seat held by the Republican Henry Cabot Lodge.

The incumbent Lodge was well known and popular throughout Massachusetts; in contrast, Kennedy had almost no following outside of Boston. But from the moment he announced his candidacy for the Senate, Kennedy, assisted by his family, friends, and thousands of volunteers, conducted a massive and intense grass-roots campaign. This hard work brought results: on November 4, 1952, when the landslide presidential victory of Dwight D. Eisenhower carried hundreds of other Republican candidates into local, state, and federal offices throughout the nation, the Democratic Kennedy defeated Lodge by a narrow margin to become the junior senator from Massachusetts.

On September 12, 1953, Kennedy married the beautiful and socially prominent Jacqueline Lee Bouvier, who was 12 years his junior. Shortly after their marriage, Kennedy became increasingly disabled by an old spinal injury, and in October 1954 and again in February 1955 he underwent serious surgery. A product of the months of convalescence that followed was his *Profiles in Courage,* a study of American statesmen who had risked their political careers for what they believed to be the needs of their nation. Published in 1956, *Profiles in Courage* immediately became a best seller, and in May 1957 it won for its author the Pulitzer Prize for biography.

During his years in the House and for the first half of his Senate term, Kennedy concerned himself primarily with the issues that particularly interested or affected his Massachusetts constituents. However, when he resumed his congressional duties after his prolonged convalescence, national rather than local or state affairs primarily attracted his attention.

His determination to run for higher office became evident at the Democratic National Convention in 1956. Adlai Stevenson, the party's presidential nominee, declined to name a running mate, and instead left the choice of a vice presidential candidate to a vote of the delegates. Seizing this opportunity, Kennedy mounted a strong, if last-minute, campaign for the nomina-

tion – in which he was narrowly defeated by Senator Estes Kefauver of Tennessee. Kennedy's efforts were not entirely unrewarded, however. He proved himself to be a formidable contender and, perhaps more important, he came to the attention of the millions of television viewers across the nation who watched the convention proceedings. He was reelected to the US Senate in 1958.

Shortly after the defeat of Stevenson in 1956, Kennedy launched a nationwide campaign to gain the 1960 Democratic presidential nomination. During the four intervening years, the Massachusetts senator developed the organization that would help him win his goal. Through his personal appearances and writings, he also made himself known to the voters of the United States. Kennedy's tactics were successful. He won all the state primaries he entered in 1960 – including a critical contest in West Virginia, where an overwhelmingly Protestant electorate dispelled the notion that a Catholic candidate could not be victorious – and he also earned the endorsement of a number of state party conventions.

The Democratic National Convention of 1960 selected Kennedy as its presidential candidate on the first ballot. Then, to the surprise of many, Kennedy asked Senator Lyndon B. Johnson of Texas, who had himself aspired to the first place on the ticket, to be his running mate. Johnson agreed, and the Democratic slate was complete. For its ticket, the Republican National Convention in 1960 chose Vice President Richard Milhous Nixon and Kennedy's earlier political rival, Henry Cabot Lodge.

Throughout the fall of 1960, Kennedy and Nixon waged tireless campaigns to win popular support. Kennedy drew strength from the organization he had put together and from the fact that registered Democratic voters outnumbered their Republican counterparts. Nixon's strength stemmed from his close association with the popular President Eisenhower and from his own experience as Vice President, which suggested an ability to hold his own with representatives of the Soviet Union in foreign affairs. The turning point of the 1960 presidential race, however, may have been the series of four televised debates between the candidates, which gave voters an opportunity to assess their positions on important issues, and unintentionally also tested each man's television "presence." Kennedy excelled in the latter area and political experts have since claimed that his ability to exploit the mass media may have been a significant factor in the outcome of the election.

On November 8, 1960, the voters of the United States cast a record 68.8 million ballots, and selected Kennedy over Nixon by the narrow margin of fewer than 120,000 votes in the closest popular vote in the nation's history. In the Electoral College the tally was 303 votes to 219.

John Fitzgerald Kennedy took the oath of office as the 35th President of the United States on January 20, 1961. A number of notable Americans participated in the ceremonies: Richard Cardinal Cushing of Boston offered the invocation, Marian Anderson sang the national anthem, and Robert Frost read one of his poems. Kennedy's inaugural address, urging Americans to "ask not what your country can do for you — ask what you can do for your country," was memorable. The new Chief Executive also asserted, "Now the trumpet summons us again . . . to bear the burden of a long twilight struggle . . . against the common enemies of man: tyranny, poverty, disease and war itself."

Both challenges were in keeping with what observers would later mark as Kennedy's greatest contribution: a quality of leadership that extracted from others their best efforts toward specific goals. Many felt themselves influenced by his later reminder to a group of young people visiting the White House — that "the Greeks defined happiness as the full use of your powers along the lines of excellence."

Whether because of his leadership, the climate of the times, or the conjunction of the two, Kennedy's term as President coincided with a marked transformation in the mood of the nation. Before that, complacent in their peacetime prosperity, most Americans were preoccupied with individual concerns. Now came a widespread awareness of needs not previously recognized. No longer could Americans ignore pressing problems that confronted them both at home and abroad, and increasingly, they showed a willingness to try to effect meaningful changes. The new mood was one of challenge, but also one of hope.

As he had promised in his inaugural address, Kennedy successfully sought the enactment of programs designed to assist the "people in the huts and villages of half the world." The Alliance for Progress, a program — ambitious but ultimately less than successful — for the economic growth and social improvement of Latin America, was launched in August 1961 at an Inter-American Conference at Punta del Este, Uruguay. The Peace Corps, which offered Americans a unique opportunity to spend approximately two years living and working with peoples in underdeveloped countries, was a more successful attempt to aid emerging nations throughout the world.

In the realm of foreign affairs, Kennedy's record was a mixture of notable triumphs and dangerous setbacks. He allowed the Central Intelligence Agency to carry out plans laid before his administration for an invasion of Cuba by anti-Communist refugees from that island. Between 1,400 and 1,500 exiles landed on April 17, 1961, at the Bay of Pigs, but suffered defeat when an anticipated mass insurrection by the Cuban people failed to materialize. Severely embarrassed, the administration nevertheless successfully encouraged the creation of a private committee, which ransomed 1,178 invasion prisoners for $62 million.

Cuban Premier Fidel Castro, after repelling the Bay of Pigs invasion, turned to the Soviet Union for military support and allowed the Russians to install secret missile sites in Cuba. From these locations, 90 miles from US soil, the USSR could launch missiles capable of striking deep into the American heartland. Reconnaissance by US observation planes uncovered the Soviet activities. Taking a decisive stand, President Kennedy, on October 22, 1962, announced that the United States would prevent the delivery of offensive weapons to Cuba. Kennedy demanded that the USSR abandon the bases and threatened that the United States would "regard any nuclear missile launched from Cuba against any nation in the Western Hemisphere as an attack by the Soviet Union on the United States, requiring a full retaliatory response upon the Soviet Union." After a week of intense negotiations, Soviet Premier Nikita S. Khrushchev agreed to dismantle all the installations in return for a US pledge not to invade Cuba.

The divided city of Berlin, meanwhile, had proved to be another Russian-American sore point, with difficulties growing out of World War II. In June 1961 the Soviet Union, still technically in a state of war with a divided Germany, announced that it planned to sign a separate peace treaty with East Germany (formerly the Soviet occupation zone) by the end of the year. The Soviet Union also demanded that West Berlin, still jointly occupied by Allied British, French, and US forces, become a demilitarized "free city" at the same time, asserting that this step would mean an end to Allied access and other Allied rights. Vehemently asserting the legality of the Allied presence, President Kennedy responded in July by doubling the American draft call and recalling certain reserve and National Guard units to active duty in order to add 200,000 men to the armed forces of the United States. On August 13 the East Germans erected a fortified wall, which physically sealed off the eastern sector of Berlin and cut off the substantial flow of East German refugees into West Berlin. After a period of pronounced tension, however, the crisis passed without further conflict, and eventually the Russians and East

Germans eased their harassment of West Berlin. Two years later, in June 1963, the residents of that beleaguered outpost gave Kennedy a hero's welcome when he visited the city. He won even greater affection from them by proclaiming "Ich bin ein Berliner" — "I am a Berliner."

President Kennedy gave wholehearted support to American efforts in space exploration. During his administration the nation increased its expenditures in that area fivefold, and the President promised that an American would land on the moon before the end of the 1960s. (On July 20, 1969, two American astronauts fulfilled the President's pledge by becoming the first human beings to set foot on the lunar surface.)

During his presidential campaign, Kennedy had stressed the necessity of improving the American economy, which was then suffering from a recession. His aim was to follow a fiscally moderate course, and the achievement of a balanced budget was one of his major goals. As President he managed to stimulate the sluggish economy by accelerating federal purchasing and construction programs, by the early release of more than $1 billion in state highway funds, and by putting $1 billion in credit into the home construction industry.

During his administration, however, increasing hostility developed between the White House and the business community. Anxious to prevent inflation, the President gave special attention to the steel industry, whose price-wage structure affected so many other aspects of the economy. After steel manufacturers insisted on raising their prices in April 1962, Kennedy, by applying strong economic pressure, forced the producers to return to the earlier lower price levels. His victory earned him the enmity of many business people, however.

Kennedy sympathized with the aspirations of black Americans, but he included no comprehensive civil rights legislation in his New Frontier program, fearing that the introduction into a conservative Congress of such measures would imperil all his other proposals. The President relied, instead, on his executive powers and on the enforcement of existing voting rights laws. He forbade discrimination in new federally aided housing, appointed a large number of blacks to high offices, and supported Justice Department efforts to secure voting rights and to end segregation in interstate commerce. In 1962 he used regular army troops and federalized National Guard units to force the admission of a black, James Meredith, to the University of Mississippi, and in 1963 he used federal National Guardsmen to watch over the integration of the University of Alabama.

Despite his broad visions of the American future, Kennedy enjoyed limited success in translating his ideas into legislative reality. A coalition of Republicans and conservative southern Democrats in the 87th Congress stymied many of his plans for the introduction of social measures. And even after the Democratic party increased its majority on Capitol Hill in the 1962 elections, Congress was slow to cooperate, although it probably was ready to do so just before his presidency came to an end.

John F. Kennedy presided over the executive branch of the United States government for only a little more than 1,000 days. During that time American involvement in Vietnam and other areas of Southeast Asia increased moderately, but the beginnings of a thaw in the cold war were also noticeable, and in 1963 the Soviet Union and the United States signed the Nuclear Test Ban Treaty. Kennedy's years in the White House were also marked by increased social consciousness by the US government. With the Great Society program of his successor, Lyndon Baines Johnson, Congress eventually enacted a number of Kennedy's proposals, including medical care for the elderly and greater opportunities for black Americans (see July 2, Civil Rights Act of 1964 and August 6, Voting Rights Act of 1965).

In addition to his various governmental programs, Kennedy's presidency was also notable for a new, vital style. John and Jacqueline Kennedy and their two children, Caroline and John Jr., quickly captured the imagination of the nation, and their activities were widely reported by the media. Certainly the Kennedys exuded a youthful vibrance, and their interests seemed unending. Jacqueline Kennedy was responsible for redecorating the public rooms of the White House and inviting a glittering array of cultural and intellectual leaders to the executive mansion.

An assassin's bullet abruptly ended the life of John Fitzgerald Kennedy on November 22, 1963 (see November 22), as he rode in a motorcade through the streets of Dallas, Texas. The entire nation mourned the tragic death of the Chief Executive. Many millions watched on television as the 35th President was buried at Arlington National Cemetery on November 25, 1963.

Every state of the United States and almost every nation in the world has erected memorials to Kennedy. One of the monuments dearest to his family is the house at 83 Beals Street in Brookline, Massachusetts, where the late President's parents lived from 1914 until 1921 and where four of their children — including John — were born. The house was repurchased by the Kennedys in 1966 and was designated a National Historic Site by Congress in 1967. On May 29, 1969, the 52nd anniversary of John F. Kennedy's birth, the family turned over the deed of the house to the National Park Service.

Both of President Kennedy's younger brothers, Robert F. and Edward M. Kennedy, served in the Senate. Many of the former President's compatriots hoped to see his goals and promise carried forward when Robert Kennedy, who had served as his attorney general and closest adviser, announced early in 1968 that he would seek the Democratic nomination for President. In another tragedy that shook the nation to its roots, Robert Kennedy was shot down by an assassin just after claiming victory in the California presidential primary. He died in Los Angeles just over 25 hours later, on June 6, 1968.

Rhode Island Ratifies the Constitution

Rhode Island, on May 29, 1790, became the last of the 13 original states to ratify the US Constitution. In the time intervening since the end of the Constitutional Convention at Philadelphia in September 1787, the Rhode Island legislature seven times refused to call a ratifying convention, and the Antifederalist forces defeated the Constitution once in a plebiscite. Only after the national government, with George Washington as President, had been in operation for more than one year did Rhode Island call a convention whose delegates acquiesced in the new arrangement by the narrow vote of 34 to 32.

Rhode Island did not respond to a congressional summons in 1787 to send delegates to the Constitutional Convention at Philadelphia. The smallest state was faring well under the Articles of Confederation, which gave each state one vote in the Congress regardless of the size of its population and required unanimous approval of any changes in the frame of government. Economically Rhode Island prospered in the years after the American Revolution, and its success was due in part to congressional impotence to regulate foreign trade.

In 1782 Rhode Island's rejection had doomed a proposed amendment that would have given the Confederation Congress power to levy a five percent duty on imports. Rhode Island earned its livelihood in commerce and feared that it would lose control of its destiny under such a provision. Of equal importance, the little state did not want to lose the revenues that accrued from its own schedule of import duties and were used by the state to retire the Revolutionary War debts that it owed to its citizens.

Perhaps as many as three-fourths of the Rhode Island electorate owned state securities, which the government had pledged to honor in full.

Returns from commercial duties serviced most of the debt in the early postwar period, but the state had to resort to sizable direct taxation on property in ensuing years as the burden of interest increased severalfold. Rhode Islanders were in the awkward position of paying heavy taxes to pay interest on money owed to themselves, and in 1786 they resorted to issuing large amounts of paper money in the hope of being able to liquidate the debt in two to seven years.

It is perhaps not surprising that the state's residents initially found little that seemed attractive in either the Philadelphia Convention of 1787 or the Constitution that its delegates produced. To begin with, these New Englanders were the heirs of a strong democratic tradition, and they instinctively distrusted the powerful central government called for by the Constitution. In addition they were in the midst of their paper money plan, which went into operation in September 1787. At such a time Rhode Islanders could have little enthusiasm for the new frame of government and its conservative monetary policies, which would not countenance their state's experiment in debt retirement.

In its October 1787 session, one month after the conclusion of the Philadelphia convention, Rhode Island's legislature met and began its evaluation of the Constitution. To the chagrin of the Federalists, who favored the new scheme of government, the Antifederalists dawdled and put off consideration of proposals to call a ratification convention until the February session. Instead the legislators ordered the printing and distribution of 1,000 copies of the Constitution so that "the freemen may have an opportunity of forming their sentiments" of the new government and communicate these feelings to the assembly.

At the February session William Bradford of Bristol, Henry Marchant and George Champlin of Newport, and Benjamin Arnold and Jabez Bowen of Providence spoke in favor of the convocation of a ratifying convention. The Antifederalists, led by Jonathan J. Hazard of Charlestown and Job Comstock of East Greenwich, countered their arguments and defeated their proposal by a large majority. The opponents of the Constitution adopted by a vote of 43 to 15 a substitute proposal to submit the Constitution directly to the freemen of Rhode Island in their town meetings.

Meeting on March 24, 1788, the Rhode Island freemen defeated the Constitution proposal by a vote of 2,708 to 237. Federalists generally refused to participate in these proceedings and their abstention accounts for the lopsided margin of victory. Rather than cast their ballots, supporters of the Constitution, especially in the cities of Providence and Newport, issued resolutions calling for a ratification convention like those held in the other states.

Also in March, Federalists in the state legislature repeated their proposal for the convocation of a ratifying convention — again in vain, as the opposition won by a 27-vote margin. But despite this defeat the supporters of the new government remained undaunted and they took heart when New Hampshire on June 21 ratified the Constitution. Victory in New Hampshire provided the Federalists with the minimum of nine states necessary to put the new Constitution into effect. In Providence Federalists planned festivities for July 4 to celebrate not only Independence Day but also the ratification of the Constitution; intimidated by possible interference from an Antifederalist mob, however, they restricted their merriment to what was ostensibly a commemoration of the politically safer Independence Day.

Five more times in 1788 and 1789, Antifederalists in the Rhode Island legislature defeated Federalist proposals for the calling of a ratifying convention. The opponents of the Constitution won by a vote of 40 to 14 in October 1788, by 44 to 12 in December 1788, and by similarly one-sided margins in March, June, and late fall 1789. Despite these victories each day of successful operation of the United States under the new Constitution brought increased pressure on Rhode Island to join the Union.

In the summer of 1789 the US Congress decreed that after January 15, 1790, all goods entering the United States through members of the old Confederation that had refused to ratify the Constitution — namely North Carolina and Rhode Island — should be taxed as items entering from foreign countries, unless they actually had been made within the two states' own boundaries. On a more positive note, the Congress in October 1789 sent to the governors of the various states 12 proposed constitutional amendments designed to placate critics who feared that the central government would limit civil liberties. Reacting to these proposals, North Carolina reversed itself and on November 21, 1789, accepted the new federal government. North Carolina's capitulation left Rhode Island isolated in an untenable position as the year 1790 approached.

Reconvening on January 11, 1790, the Rhode Island legislature once again took up the issue of the Constitution. After much debate the Federalist proposal to call a ratifying convention won in the assembly on January 15 by a vote of 34 to 29. The next day, a Saturday, the senate received the measure from the assembly but rejected it by a five-to-four margin, as Lieutenant Governor Daniel Owen aligned himself with the Antifederalists. Unhappy with this outcome, the assembly met in special session on Sunday and repeated its call for a convention. With one Antifederalist who was a preacher absent because he objected to the conduct of governmental affairs on Sunday, the Senate then reconsidered the bill. Lieutenant Governor Owen and three senators again opposed the measure, and the four Federalist senators supported it. Finally, Governor John Collins, although nominally an Antifederalist, cast the deciding ballot in favor of the convocation of a convention.

Winning approval for a ratifying convention was but the beginning of the contest for Rhode Island Federalists. On election day, February 9, 1790, the opponents of the Constitution elected a majority of the delegates chosen for the ratifying convention — which met on March 1 at the old state house in South Kingstown. The Antifederalists elected Lieutenant Governor Owen as chairman of the convention. Owen and Jonathan J. Hazard provided the Antifederalists with leadership, and Jabez Bowen and Henry Marchant led the Federalists.

The Antifederalist leaders were not confident of victory. And indeed there were some grounds for their fears that less determined delegates would be swayed by the Federalists — who suggested that the convention ratify the Constitution in the expectation that beneficial amendments, including a Bill of Rights, would soon be added to the Constitution. Hoping that an Antifederalist victory in the spring legislative elections would impress the weak of spirit, the opponents of the Constitution voted to adjourn the convention until May 24.

As expected, the Antifederalists scored a sweeping victory in the April 21 elections, but other political developments diminished the significance of their victory. By the time the delegates to the ratifying convention had reassembled, they had learned that the Congress was considering punitive legislation against Rhode Island. Many federal legislators wanted to end commercial relations between the Union and the state and to demand from recalcitrant Rhode Island quick repayment of its Revolutionary War debt. Upset by these possibilities, the leaders of Providence made it known that the city was ready, if the convention rejected the Constitution, to secede from Rhode Island and seek accommodation with the United States.

The second Rhode Island ratifying convention lasted less than one week. Confronted by threats from both Congress and the city of Providence, the delegates could not listen only to the popular voice expressed in the spring elections. Late in the afternoon of May 29, 1790, the delegates voted 34 to 32 to accept the US Constitution, and the governor immediately informed President Washington of the news.

A special session of the state legislature quickly chose Rhode Island's first two US senators, and in August the people elected delegates to the House of Representatives.

Rhode Island and the 12 other American colonies became states in 1776 when they declared their independence from England. However, for purposes of establishing the chronological order in which these states entered the Union, historians customarily use the dates on which they ratified the Constitution. According to this computation, Rhode Island is the 13th member of the United States.

The Virginia Resolutions

Patrick Henry's Birthday

On May 29, 1765, nine days after he became a member of Virginia's House of Burgesses, the fiery young orator Patrick Henry introduced in that legislative body what history recalls as the Virginia Resolutions. Seven in number, Henry's militant resolutions were written in opposition to the much-loathed Stamp Act (see March 22); they asserted the colonies' right to legislate for themselves and upheld the principle of no taxation without representation.

Even though they were softened somewhat by subsequent action of the legislature, the resolutions were published by colonial newspapers in their entire original form. Quoted throughout the colonies, they caused turmoil from Boston to Charleston and powerfully encouraged the movement that became the American Revolution.

Young Henry had turned 29 the day he presented his resolutions. The well-remembered speech with which he introduced them called to the attention of King George III the disastrous fate of some earlier rulers. It concluded with the lines: "Caesar had his Brutus, Charles the First his Cromwell, and George the Third —"

At this point Henry's impassioned speech is said to have been punctuated with cries of "Treason." Undaunted, he continued: "— and George the Third may profit by their example! If this be treason, make the most of it."

The words today are only slightly less familiar than the "give me liberty or give me death" with which Henry concluded his most celebrated speech of all. But that was not until 10 years later, on March 23, 1775 (see March 23, Patrick Henry's Speech for Liberty).

Wisconsin Admitted to the Union

Wisconsin, the 30th state, entered the Union on May 29, 1848. The Badger State was the last to be formed in its entirety from the old Northwest Territory, which the Confederation Congress incorporated in 1787. Including the whole area north of the Ohio River and east of the Mississippi River, the territory held within its boundaries the states of Illinois, Indiana, Michigan, Ohio, parts of Minnesota, and Wisconsin.

Jean Nicolet, a Frenchman, was the first known European to visit Wisconsin. Nicolet's sojourn at Green Bay in 1634 began a highly profitable fur trade between his countrymen and the Indians of the region. In 1654 and 1655 Médart Chouart, Sieur de Groseilliers, and Pierre Esprit Radisson explored the Green Bay region of present Wisconsin. In 1659–1660 they investigated the Lake Superior section of Wisconsin. In 1660 seven French traders went to Chequamegon Bay on Lake Superior, and between 1679 and 1689 Daniel Greysolon, Sieur Duluth, investigated the lands west of Lake Superior and some tributaries of the Mississippi River. Nicolas Perrot in the same era built posts, extended French influence among the Indians, and officially claimed the whole upper Mississippi for the king of France in 1689.

Roman Catholic priests were among the earliest Europeans in Wisconsin. The Jesuit René Ménard, who accompanied the Chequamegon Bay exploration in 1660, was the first of the many missionaries who worked in what is now Wisconsin among such tribes as the Winnebago, Chippewa, Menominee, Fox, Sauk, and the Potawatomie. Father Claude Allouez founded a mission at Chequamegon Bay in 1665, and later established a successful mission at De Pere. Father Jacques Marquette (see June 1), forced to abandon the Chequamegon mission in 1671, went on to found the mission of St. Ignace on the north shore of the Straits of Mackinac. There he was joined by Louis Joliet in December 1672. The next spring the two embarked on their expedition of discovery in the upper Mississippi territory.

Early in the 18th century, England emerged as France's primary adversary in the Wisconsin area. Indian allies of the French killed a band of Fox Indians near Detroit in 1712, and a series of wars lasting until 1740 between the French and the area tribes ensued. In the French and Indian War, or the Great War for Empire, from 1754 to 1763, England finally defeated the French and drove them from North America. The English then solidified their control of the region by putting down in 1765 the Indian insurgency led by Chief Pontiac and by taking over operation of the fur trade.

Wisconsin's traders remained loyal to England during the American Revolution. One of them, the mixed-blood Charles Michel de Langlade, who had fought against the English in the French and Indian War, led raids against American settlements west of the Allegheny Mountains in the later conflict. The efforts of the pro-British traders were to no avail, however, and Wisconsin became part of the United States by the Treaty of Paris, which concluded the American Revolution in 1783. British traders from Montreal nevertheless continued to exploit the fur trade in the area until the conclusion of the War of 1812.

United States Army garrisons erected at Fort Howard (Green Bay) and Fort Crawford (Prairie du Chien) in 1816 gave evidence of increased American activity in Wisconsin. The area was part of the Indiana Territory from 1800 until 1809 and of the Illinois Territory from 1809 until 1818. Wisconsin in 1818 became part of the Michigan Territory until 1836, sending representatives to the legislature's sessions in Detroit after 1824. Between 1829 and 1848, 11 treaties extinguished Indian titles to Wisconsin land and increased the acreage available to settlers.

American citizens began to go to Wisconsin after the War of 1812. Members of the American Fur Company capitalized on an 1816 law excluding foreigners from the pelt trade. After 1822 miners poured into the southwestern sector of Wisconsin to search for lead deposits; their numbers reached 2,500 by 1830. Many of the miners returned south each autumn to avoid the harsh winters, and they earned the nickname "suckers" after a Mississippi River fish with similar habits. The more hardy adventurers, who passed the winters in hillside caves in Wisconsin, gained the sobriquet "badgers," and this tenacious creature became the symbol of the state's people.

Pioneers continued to enter Wisconsin, especially after the Black Hawk War of 1832 broke the remaining Indian power. The government opened public land offices at Mineral Point in 1834 and at Green Bay in 1835. By the end of 1836 settlers, many of whom came from eastern states, purchased 878,014 acres. These newcomers gravitated toward the southeast region of Wisconsin and founded Milwaukee and other cities along the Lake Michigan shore.

Wisconsin gained territorial status in 1836, with its territory extending all the way west to the Missouri River. Henry Dodge, a hero in the

Black Hawk War, became governor. The first legislature, which met at Old Belmont in Lafayette County, selected Madison as the permanent capital. Although it shrank in size when the Iowa Territory, extending west from the Mississippi to the Missouri, was carved out of it in 1838, the Wisconsin Territory continued to grow in population, and on August 10, 1846, the Congress authorized the convocation of a constitutional convention, a key step on the road to statehood. The electorate rejected the first proposed constitution, which had unusually liberal provisions concerning women's rights and an elective judicial system. A second convention drew up a frame of government more acceptable to the voters, and Wisconsin entered the Union on May 29, 1848.

MAY 30

Memorial Day

This is a movable event. See note on page xxvi.

Honoring the dead has been a practice of many civilizations. The ancient Druids, Greeks, and Romans decorated the graves of their loved ones with garlands of flowers. Among Chinese, the centuries-old Festival of Tombs, an ancestral remembrance day known as *Ch'ing Ming,* has long been a special occasion for visiting cemeteries and for performing rituals in memory of the dead. So has Japan's ancient Feast of Lanterns, or *Bon,* when Japanese welcome the visiting souls of the departed and light their way back to the hereafter with lanterns sent across the waters in miniature boats. In Christian countries, Roman Catholics and Episcopalians pray for the departed on All Souls' Day (see November 2). It is a day for decorating graves with wreaths, flowers, or candles. Such countries as Rumania, Finland, and Turkey have also set aside special days to pay tribute to deceased loved ones.

In the United States, the dead have been honored on Memorial Day, or Decoration Day as it is also (decreasingly) known, since the time of the Civil War. The location and date of the first ceremony paying tribute to the dead is disputed, but even before the fighting between the North and South had ended, women in many communities of the South — where most of the battles took place — had begun the practice of placing flowers on the graves of fallen Confederate soldiers. Graves of Federal soldiers who died south of the Mason-Dixon line generally were also decorated with flowers.

Spontaneous gestures of remembrance also

took place in the North, as in the village of Waterloo, New York, which honored its war dead on May 5, 1866, by closing its businesses for the day, flying the flag at half-mast, decorating the graves of fallen soldiers, and holding other ceremonies at the three cemeteries in the area. In 1967 a proclamation of President Lyndon B. Johnson and a joint congressional resolution officially recognized Waterloo as "the birthplace of Memorial Day." The community responded on May 30 of that year by dedicating the Waterloo Memorial Day Museum, which contains relics of the 1866 event and Civil War memorabilia.

"Firsts" are difficult to establish, however, particularly for an observance like Memorial Day, which had its origins in numerous, widely separated, individual acts of commemoration. It is not surprising, therefore, that Waterloo's claim to priority is disputed by a number of other communities. One such is Boalsburg in central Pennsylvania, which some years ago erected a sign proclaiming itself "Boalsburg, an American village, birthplace of Memorial Day." The claim dates from the October Sunday in 1864 when Emma Hunter, placing flowers on the grave of her father — Colonel James Hunter, who had commanded the 49th Pennsylvania Regiment in the battle of Gettysburg the previous year — encountered a Mrs. Meyer, paying similar tribute at the grave of her son. The two women agreed to meet the following year to again decorate the burial places, and their idea, gradually adopted by others, was an established custom in Boalsburg by May 30, 1869.

Other observances took place in 1865 — at Vicksburg, Mississippi (see April 26); Petersburg, Virginia (see June 9); and on May 30 in Charleston, South Carolina, where black schoolchildren strewed flowers over the four trenches in which the remains of several hundred Union soldiers had been interred. Additional early precedents for Memorial Day occurred in 1866, when the graves of war dead were decorated in Columbus, Mississippi; in Lynchburg, Virginia; and on Belle Isle, at Richmond, Virginia, on May 30. Women's memorial associations had existed since 1866 throughout the South, two of the earliest being founded almost simultaneously in Columbus, Georgia, and Jackson, Mississippi, where members decorated the graves of both Confederate and Union soldiers. It was a gesture of similar impartial generosity by the women of Columbus that did most, perhaps, to spread the idea of strewing flowers on soldiers' graves; this inclusion of their former enemies in the tribute prompted not only an editorial in Horace Greeley's New York *Tribune,* but also a poem — "The Blue and the Gray" by Francis Miles Finch —

which appeared in the *Atlantic Monthly* in September 1867 and swept the country.

In the years immediately following the end of the Civil War, an increasing number of memorial observances, similar to those held earlier, took place throughout the nation. Delegations of women from the North also visited cemeteries in the South where Union soldiers were buried and decorated their graves with flowers. Adjutant General Norton P. Chipman of the Grand Army of the Republic, the organization of Union veterans, realized that the nation was eager to honor those who had died in the fighting, and he suggested to General John A. Logan, the commander in chief of the G.A.R., that arrangements be made for the organization to decorate the graves of Union soldiers on a uniform date throughout the country. General Logan approved the plan and issued an order to all Grand Army posts:

The thirtieth day of May, 1868, is designated for the purpose of strewing with flowers or otherwise decorating the graves of comrades who died in defense of their country during the late rebellion, and whose bodies now lie in almost every city, village and hamlet churchyard in the land. In this observance no form of ceremony is prescribed, but posts and comrades will in their own way arrange such fitting services and testimonials of respect as circumstances may permit.

It is the purpose of the commander-in-chief to inaugurate this observance with the hope that it will be kept up from year to year while a survivor of the war remains to honor the memory of his departed comrades. He earnestly desires the public press to call attention to this order and lend its friendly aid in bringing it to the notice of comrades in all parts of the country in time for simultaneous compliance therewith.

Department commanders will use every effort to make this order effective.

The first national Memorial Day on May 30, 1868, was the occasion of more than 100 exercises honoring those who had died in the Civil War. The most noteworthy ceremonies of the day were held in the National Cemetery at Arlington, Virginia. General Ulysses S. Grant was present at the services, and General James A. Garfield was the main speaker. Garfield noted, in part:

I am oppressed with a sense of the impropriety of uttering words on this occasion. If silence is ever golden, it must be here beside the graves of fifteen thousand men whose lives were more significant than speech and whose death was a poem the music of which can never be sung. With words we make promises, plight faith, praise virtue. Promises may not be kept; plighted faith may be broken; and vaunted virtue be only the cunning mask of vice. We do not know one promise these men made, one pledge they gave, one word they spoke; but we do know they summed up and perfected, by one supreme act, the highest virtues of men and citizens. For love of country they accepted death, and thus resolved all doubts, and made immortal their patriotism and virtue.

Observances of Memorial Day quickly multiplied in the years following 1868. In 1869 more than 300 exercises marked the day, and in 1873 New York became the first state to designate May 30 a legal holiday. Rhode Island followed New York's lead in 1874, Vermont in 1876, New Hampshire in 1877, Wisconsin in 1879, and Massachusetts and Ohio in 1881. Memorial Day gained such rapid acceptance that by 1890 it was a legal holiday in all the northern states.

With the exception of some of the southern states that annually observe a memorial day on a Confederacy-related anniversary of special significance, Memorial Day is a legal holiday throughout the United States. Moreover, some of the states that observe a separate Confederate Memorial Day also mark the national Memorial Day. The passage of time has brought about a number of changes in the observance, however. Most notable is the fact that Memorial Day has become an occasion for honoring all those who died in the service of the nation — in the Spanish-American War, World War I, World War II, and the Korean and Vietnamese wars, as well as on Civil War battlefields. Indeed, in a development of particular significance to friends and families who have suffered losses, usage has extended the observance still further, making it a time to honor the memory of all deceased persons, civilian as well as military.

Moreover, the date of Memorial Day in most places is no longer fixed on the traditional May 30. On June 28, 1968, President Lyndon B. Johnson signed legislation shifting the dates of certain holidays to provide Americans with an increased number of three-day weekends. One provision of the new statute was that Memorial Day be observed on the last Monday of May each year. Since Congress has power to set holidays only for the District of Columbia and employees of the federal government, the 1968 law technically had only a limited application and in any event did not become effective until 1971. Before then, however, most state legislatures had passed legislation to bring their states into conformity with the practice of the federal government and thus with one another. By 1971 most states of the nation followed the schedule of federal holidays by marking Memorial Day on the last Monday of the month — on May 31 in 1971, for example, and May 29 in 1972.

Each year the President of the United States issues a special Memorial Day proclamation which, by request of a joint resolution of Congress in 1950, includes a call for citizens to observe the occasion as a day of prayer for peace. Governors of numerous states have similarly marked the day with proclamations. For the most part the nation has responded enthusiastically to these calls to honor the country's dead, and particularly those killed in battle or in defense of freedom; but in the late 1960s and early 1970s, Memorial Day in many places was also a time when antiwar sentiments were expressed.

The large national cemeteries, where thousands of war dead are buried, are the scenes of the most extensive ceremonies on Memorial Day. Arlington (Virginia) National Cemetery continues to be the site of one of the nation's most elaborate observances. On Memorial Day in 1958 the bodies of unknown servicemen who had died in World War II and the Korean conflict were interred next to the Unknown Soldier of World War I, and each year on Memorial Day the President or a representative places a wreath at what is now the Tomb of the Unknowns, formerly designated as the Tomb of the Unknown Soldier. Near the austerely simple tomb, on a terrace commanding a dramatic view of the nation's Capitol across the Potomac in Washington, is the Greek-style Arlington Memorial Amphitheatre. It is within this oval, open-air structure of white marble that a high-ranking government official addresses the several thousand onlookers who generally attend the Memorial Day services, which follow the wreath laying at the Tomb of the Unknowns.

Since 1896 Memorial Day exercises have also been held each year at Gettysburg National Military Park in Gettysburg, Pennsylvania, site of the great Civil War battle. Since the inauguration of these annual services, nine Presidents and most, if not all, governors of Pennsylvania have marked the occasion with an address at the Gettysburg National Cemetery. The exercises at Gettysburg are extremely moving. In recent years, a large parade from the Gettysburg High School to the National Cemetery has begun the day's official events. At the cemetery, representatives of the Sons of Union Veterans, Veterans of Foreign Wars, the American Legion, and World War I Veterans customarily place wreaths on the unknown soldiers' graves, and some 1,800 grade-schoolchildren strew flowers on the 3,075 Civil War veterans' graves. Girl Scouts and Boy Scouts also decorate the burial sites of those who died in the Spanish-American War, World War I, World War II, and in Korea and in Vietnam. These ceremonies are followed by a program that includes the recitation of Lincoln's Gettysburg Address, a speech by a distinguished public official, playing of the patriotic hymn "America," and the singing of both "The Battle Hymn of the Republic," popular among Union partisans during the Civil War, and "The Star-Spangled Banner."

Other observances take place at widely scattered locations. At the site of the Civil War battle of Antietam, which raged around Sharpsburg, Maryland, on September 17, 1862, the Memorial Day commemorations began in 1868 and have continued to be held each year since. Exercises at Antietam National Cemetery are preceded by a wreath-laying ceremony and band concert in Sharpsburg. Following a parade, which draws participants from several surrounding states, a second concert introduces the Memorial Day services at the cemetery, on the edge of town. Here are buried many who died in what has been called the bloodiest one-day battle of the Civil War. High-ranking military officers, members of Congress, and state dignitaries usually are present as guest speakers and special guests. The ceremonies include the laying of additional wreaths, and conclude with the firing of volleys and the playing of taps.

Services reflecting local traditions meanwhile take place at the National Memorial Cemetery in the Punchbowl Crater in Honolulu, Hawaii. There, flower leis woven by schoolchildren of the islands are draped on the graves of the 17,000 Americans who died in the Pacific during World War II.

Memorial Day observances are by no means limited to the big national cemeteries. In towns and cities across the land, veterans' groups, civic organizations, family groups, and individuals decorate graves with flowers or with small American flags on and in advance of Memorial Day. On the day itself, flags fly at half-mast, and relatives and friends visit the final resting places of their loved ones. In many communities, large and small, there are parades, usually leading from the business center to the local cemetery. Alternatively, the parade destination may be a park or square where a monument or other special memorial stands. Parade participants include veterans and armed forces personnel, color guards, members of civic organizations, local bands and drum-and-bugle corps, Boy Scouts, Girl Scouts, Camp Fire Girls, and schoolchildren. Exercises following the parade often are sponsored or cosponsored by veterans' groups and traditionally have the participation of community officials. Customarily they include memorial addresses, prayers, the playing of hymns and patriotic airs, and the further decoration of graves.

In some of the larger cities several parades, each followed by memorial exercises, are held. In New York City, for instance, parades take place in each of the boroughs, but the largest of these events is one held in Manhattan. The line of march proceeds up Riverside Drive from 72nd Street to the Soldiers and Sailors Monument at 89th Street. There city officials are on hand and memorial services are conducted.

Perhaps the most colorful Memorial Day exercises are the ones commemorating those who died at sea. From several seaports small boats go out each year and strew flowers on the water. What may be the best known of these services takes place at Depoe, Oregon, where a flotilla from the Coast Guard joins with privately owned fishing vessels. Early in the morning of Memorial Day a program including music and the firing of volleys is held on shore. Then the Fleet of Flowers goes to sea, military planes fly overhead, and passengers on board the boats toss flower bouquets and wreaths into the sea.

Gloucester, Massachusetts, a community of seafarers since its founding in 1623, is the scene, annually on Memorial Day, of a memorial service for people lost at sea during the preceding year. Appropriately it is held at the community's famous bronze statue of the Gloucester Fishermen, which stands at harbor's edge, itself a memorial to fishermen lost at sea.

Perhaps one of the most quietly inspiring settings for Memorial Day services is the Cathedral of the Pines near Rindge, New Hampshire. Established by Dr. and Mrs. Douglas Sloane in 1945 as a memorial to the son they lost in World War II, the open-air "cathedral" is a forest of pine trees situated high on a flat hilltop and containing two National War Memorials. Its focal point is the simple Altar of Nations, built of stones sent by people of all faiths from many parts of the world. Placed on the altar each Memorial Day is a white rose from the governor of each of the 50 states and from each US territory. Although it was recognized by Congress as a memorial to all American war dead, the Cathedral of the Pines, which is "dedicated to Almighty God as a place where all people may worship," is under the authority neither of state or federal government, nor of any individual religious group.

Memorial Day is primarily a time to honor the departed, but it has also become, increasingly in recent years, a time of leisure and relaxation. In Indianapolis, the famous "500" automobile race held each Memorial Day weekend climaxes the month-long "500" Festival, attracting thousands of spectators. Memorial Day has also traditionally marked the beginning of summer activities.

MAY 31

Seventeenth Amendment Proclaimed Ratified

The men who assembled in Philadelphia in 1787 to draw up the US Constitution both respected and feared the citizenry of the new nation. The experience of the American Revolution had taught them that a government cannot remain unresponsive to the will of its constituents. Yet a democratic system had no precedent in modern history, and many argued that the masses could not be trusted to govern themselves responsibly.

Under these circumstances the Constitutional Convention labored to establish a frame of government that would both insure the voice of the people and curb the feared "excess of democracy." The process that the Constitution specified for the selection of the national legislature clearly reflected the dual objective. The document gave the people at large the right to elect their delegates to the House of Representatives, but reserved to the supposedly more learned and experienced state legislatures the power to elect the members of the Senate.

This system proved adequate until the end of the 19th century. But as the era of the robber barons advanced, corporate control and corruption of state legislatures steadily increased. More and more these bodies sent senators to Washington who failed to represent the best interests of their constituencies and instead worked unscrupulously for legislation favorable to the great financial powers within their respective states. During the first decade of the 20th century the reputation of the Senate reached its nadir. Federal courts indicted 3 of its members for accepting bribes, and more than 12 others faced charges of similar corrupt practices.

Americans always prided themselves, however naively, on the pristine qualities of their political institutions and found such blatant abuses profoundly disturbing. Their response was progressivism, a movement aimed at improving the quality of political and social life. Under the leadership of civic-minded members of the established middle class, Progressives sought to make the political process more responsive to popular control.

Convinced that the citizenry was capable of selecting the best people to fill governmental offices, the reformers argued that direct popular election of the Senate would insure the integrity of that body. Such a change in electoral procedure, however, required a constitutional amendment, and the upper house on several occasions had refused to assent to this legislation. Reform was at least temporarily halted on the national level, but this did not deter the Progressives. Instead they rechanneled their efforts toward altering election practices within the individual states.

The chief weapon in the campaign to restore good government was the primary election, the method by which candidates for public office are directly chosen by the people. In the first decade of the 20th century, the primary won wide acceptance throughout the nation, and by 1909 the electorate in 29 states had selected the senatorial nominees. The state legislatures subsequently elected these candidates, but it became increasingly evident that this action was a mere formality.

The voice of the people in determining their representation in the Senate could not be denied. A scandal involving the election of William Lorimer, an Illinois political boss, in 1909 forced the upper house to end its resistance to a constitutional amendment. By May 16, 1912, both houses of Congress had given their approval to the 17th Amendment and proposed its enactment to the legislatures of the states. Just a year later, on May 31, 1913, a proclamation by the secretary of state declared the amendment to have been ratified by the necessary three-fourths of the states, and it became part of the Constitution.

Walt Whitman's Birthday

Walt Whitman, the most original American poet of the 19th century, whose work was the precursor of free verse, shattered traditional patterns of poetry and invented for himself a new prosodic form with which to sing the praises of democracy, the common man, and all existence. His poetry, which was revolutionary both in form and content, met with a mixed reception from the contemporary public. Some readers were offended by its unrhymed, unmetered (but not unrhythmical) lines; its sensuality; its rugged, unprettified phrases. Others praised its freedom, inventiveness, and extraordinary vitality.

Life — abundant, unhampered, procreating; death, "lovely . . . soothing . . . delicate death"; and rebirth were among Whitman's greatest themes. So, too, were the relatively new, exuberantly expanding United States, "themselves . . . essentially the greatest poem." in his opinion. And so, also, was the symbolic "I," often interpreted as egotism, by which he identified himself and all humanity as one with the universe and one another. *Leaves of Grass,* the work by which he is chiefly known, opened with what may be the archetypal Whitman poem, eventually called "Song of Myself," though it was at first untitled. Among its nearly 2,000 lines of quintessential Whitman are these:

I celebrate myself, and sing myself,
And what I assume you shall assume,
For every atom belonging to me as good belongs to you. . . .
And I know that the spirit of God is the brother of my own. . . .
I am the mate and companion of people, all just as immortal and fathomless as myself,
(They do not know how immortal, but I know.) . . .
And I know the amplitude of time.
I am the poet of the Body and I am the poet of the Soul. . . .
I am the poet of the woman the same as the man. . . .
I hear all sounds running together, combined, fused or following,
Sounds of the city and sounds out of the city, sounds of the day and night. . . .
I believe a leaf of grass is no less than the journey-work of the stars. . . .
I have said that the soul is not more than the body,
And I have said that the body is not more than the soul,
And nothing, not God, is greater to one than one's self is,
And whoever walks a furlong without sympathy walks to his own funeral drest in his shroud. . . .

The poet's admirers formed what was probably one of the earliest fan clubs in America: the Walt Whitman Fellowship, founded in 1887 while the Good Gray Poet, as he was so misleadingly called, still lived, met each year to celebrate his birthday. After his own lifetime, Whitman's popularity increased. By 1969, the 150th anniversary of his birth, countless numbers of Walt Whitman scholars and admirers in many countries, including Japan, Russia, Israel, and Canada, were celebrating the sesquicentennial in various ways throughout the year.

Across the United States, the 150th anniversary of Walt Whitman's birth was celebrated by lectures, seminars, films, exhibits, musical programs, readings, and dramatic presentations. At least one Whitman celebration, at the poet's birthplace in Huntington, Long Island, New York, was tape-recorded by the Voice of America. The Poetry Society of America made its 1969 annual dinner meeting at Delmonico's in New York City a tribute to Walt Whitman.

The Library of Congress in Washington, D.C., opened an exhibit of Walt Whitman manuscripts and memorabilia in the spring and held it open to the public until the fall. Other Whitman exhibits were mounted at the University of Kansas in Lawrence, and at Brown University in Providence, Rhode Island.

Publishing houses and university presses brought out a string of publications by or about Whitman; for example, the University of Alabama published a bilingual (Spanish and English) volume of tributes to Whitman by Spanish poets. Southern Illinois University Press issued a collection of essays by Whitman scholars, and the University of Missouri at St. Louis published a special Whitman issue of the journal *American Transcendental Quarterly*.

New York University held a week-long Whitman observance with lectures by Whitman experts, a display of woodcuts and photographs, and a musicale of Whitman's poems sung to music especially composed for the occasion. The Whitman celebration at Hunter College in New York included a film, readings, and lectures.

In addition to publishing several books by Whitman scholars, Wayne State University in Detroit doubled the size of each issue of its quarterly, *The Walt Whitman Review*, during the sesquicentennial year. The International Christian University of Tokyo sponsored a playwriting contest with Walt Whitman as the subject, with the prize-winning play to be produced by Wayne State University Theatre. California State College at Long Beach held a special Whitman seminar during the summer of 1969.

In New York State, the town board of Huntington, Long Island, to honor its most famous native son, proclaimed May 1969 Walt Whitman Month. The Walt Whitman Birthplace Association in Huntington sponsored a month-long celebration of the 150th anniversary of the poet's birth. From May 1 to May 31 Huntington held a Walt Whitman festival. Whitman was the subject of talks given at Huntington service clubs, including the Rotary and Kiwanis; at the shopping center, appropriately named Walt Whitman Mall; at the Huntington Public Library; and at the Huntington Township High Schools.

On May 31 a full day's program brought the Huntington celebration to a climax. Members and guests of the Walt Whitman Association — whose headquarters are at 330 Mickle Street, Camden, New Jersey, in the house where Whitman lived for the last 20 years of his life — took a bus trip to Huntington to join the celebration. The Performing Arts Foundation of Huntington staged a tribute to the poet in the Walt Whitman High School auditorium. Outstanding Whitman authorities tape-recorded commentaries to be preserved in the Walt Whitman Birthplace Archives in Huntington.

During the Huntington celebration, Whitman scholars received awards, read new poems dedicated to Whitman, and participated in seminars. There was an art and poetry competition, complete with exhibit and prizes. The Huntington

Historical Society mounted an exhibit and showed films about Walt Whitman.

Musical portions of the May observance included concerts by the Huntington Symphony Orchestra and the Huntington Philharmonia. With the Symphony Orchestra, a chorus of students from Huntington and Northport high schools performed Whitman's "And Thou America." With the Philharmonia, Whitman's "I Hear America Singing" was the vocal offering. An International Jazz Concert featured readings — excerpts from Whitman's *Leaves of Grass* — with a jazz accompaniment, underlining the thought that Whitman was a modern poet although he lived in the 19th century. His influence on American writers in the 1920s was profound.

Whitman's words have perhaps even more import today than in his own century. One example of his modern flavor comes from his essay *Democratic Vistas,* written in 1871:

I say we had best look our times and lands searchingly in the face, like a physician diagnosing some deep disease. Never was there, perhaps, more hollowness at heart than at present, and here in the United States. Genuine belief seems to have left us. The underlying principles of the States are not honestly believ'd in, (for all this hectic glow, and these melo-dramatic screamings,) nor is humanity itself believ'd in. What penetrating eye does not everywhere see through the mask? The spectacle is appaling. We live in an atmosphere of hypocrisy throughout. . . . It is as if we were somehow being endow'd with a vast and more and more thoroughly-appointed body, and then left with little or no soul.

Whitman — poet, teacher, journalist, printer, and carpenter — was born on May 31, 1819, at West Hills, Huntington, in a house built by his father, Walter Whitman; he was the second of eight children. The family moved on from Long Island, where the senior Whitman tried to make a living as a farmer, to Brooklyn, where he worked as a carpenter, and then back to another town on Long Island.

Walt Whitman's first move to Brooklyn was at the age of 4. He attended school in Brooklyn until he was 11 and then went to work as an errand boy in a law office. The lawyers encouraged him to continue his education, providing him with books, study space, and time to read comfortably between chores. He went on educating himself at newspaper and printing offices, where he worked as a printer's devil and then as an apprentice printer.

When serious fires and economic disasters swept New York and made printing jobs scarce, Whitman returned to Long Island and, at age 17, took the first of a series of teaching jobs. Conveniently for Whitman, who had much else to occupy him, school terms were only three months long at the time. He taught in seven different schools between 1835 and 1841.

On June 16, 1838, the 19-year-old Whitman started his own newspaper, *The Long Islander,* which he ran for a year — writing and printing the paper and even delivering it by horse and buggy to Long Island farm homes, where he talked with the homespun and grass-roots people that were to influence him all his life. *The Long Islander* still publishes a special issue to celebrate Whitman's birthday each year and for the sesquicentennial in 1969 its pages carried tributes to Whitman from many countries.

Whitman's newspaper career overlapped his teaching career. He held many newspaper jobs between 1838 and 1849, becoming the editor of the Brooklyn *Eagle* when he was 27. He quit the newspaper business in 1849 and went to work for his father, building houses in Brooklyn. Thereafter, at various times, he was carpenter, printer, journalist, poet, and proprietor of a bookstore in Brooklyn. He finally gathered a selection of 12 of his poems, which he published in 1855 as *Leaves of Grass*. Whitman had probably begun work on the poems as early as 1847. He was to revise and add to the original *Leaves of Grass* until the last year of his life, bringing out a total of nine editions. Of these the last (1892) version, containing several hundred poems, was by Whitman's own deathbed statement the one definitive edition. It contained, one commentator said, all of Whitman's poems "that are worth reading."

In 1862, during the Civil War, Whitman went to Washington, D.C., to care for his younger brother George, who had been wounded while serving as a lieutenant with the 159th New York Regiment in Virginia. Though his brother's injury was less severe than had been feared, the conditions of other wounded men and the lack of care so appalled Whitman that he stayed on for three years as a volunteer nurse, treating both Northern and Southern soldiers, writing journalistic accounts of what he saw, and gathering notes for poems. A book of his war poems, *Drum-Taps,* was published in 1865. Whitman's two famous Lincoln poems, "O Captain! My Captain!" (untypically, in conventional rhyme and meter) and "When Lilacs Last in the Dooryard Bloom'd," were among those to come out of the war.

To support himself during this time, he worked as a clerk in a government office. He lost that job in 1865 because his superior disapproved of *Leaves of Grass,* which he found indecent. Whitman's friends rallied to his cause, and the same year Whitman obtained a clerkship in the Treasury Department. Out of that fracas came the still-used epithet the Good Gray

Poet, which was the title of a pamphlet written by a friend during the campaign to reinstate Whitman in government employment.

In 1873, Whitman suffered a paralytic stroke, which left him a semi-invalid for the rest of his life. He moved to Camden, New Jersey, where he lived with one of his brothers until his death, on March 26, 1892. Whitman is buried in a tomb of rough-cut stone, which he designed, in Camden's Harleigh Cemetery at Haddon Avenue and Vesper Boulevard. The Walt Whitman Home at 330 Mickle Street, Camden, has been a state museum since 1923 and is the headquarters of the Walt Whitman Association. The house contains original furnishings and mementos and is open to the public.

In Huntington, Long Island, the house where Walt Whitman was born also is open to the public. Sponsored by the Walt Whitman Birthplace Association, the house, at 246 Walt Whitman Road, was officially opened on May 31, 1952, as the highlight of the Walt Whitman birthday celebration that year. Purchase of the house was made possible by the contributions of schoolchildren and by the fund-raising efforts of local newspapers and interested citizens. Long before its purchase, the house had been set apart with an inscription: "To mark the Birthplace of Walt Whitman . . . The Good Gray Poet . . . Erected by the Colonial Society of Huntington, 1905." Thousands of people visit Whitman's birthplace each year.

June

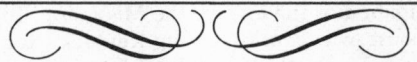

June, the Latin form of which is *Junius,* was formerly the fourth month in the old Roman calendar. It is the sixth month in the Gregorian, or New Style, calendar in use today and has 30 days. There are many theories about the origin of the name. In the *Fasti* — a poetical description of the Roman festivals from January through June commingling superstitions, folklore, history, and religious observances — the Roman poet Ovid states that the name is derived from *juniores,* meaning "youths," for a month dedicated to the young, just as May, derived from *maiores,* meaning "elders," is a month dedicated to the old. In another passage, however, Ovid has Juno, the sister and wife of Jupiter, the chief of the gods, claim that June had been named in her honor.

The Romans regarded Juno primarily as the guardian of all women and protector of their lives in all crucial moments. Her special relationship with women is easily seen in the diverse forms under which she was worshiped. As Juno Unxia and Pronuba, she played a leading role in furthering and protecting marriages; as Juno Caprotina, she was invoked for aid by female slaves; as Juno Lucina, she was turned to as a source of strength in time of childbirth; as Juno Sospita, she was called upon as a rescuer in perilous situations. Finally, as Juno Regina, the queen of the gods, she was worshiped in conjunction with Jupiter on the Capitoline Hill in Rome.

Not only did Ovid himself put forth conflicting theories on the derivation of the name, but other authorities — ancient and modern — have suggested additional hypotheses as well. One is that *June* comes from the Roman gentile, or clan, name *Junius.* Another connects June with an individual member of the Junius clan: Lucius Junius Brutus, a distinguished Roman leader who liberated the Romans from their oppressive Etruscan overlords about 510 B.C. According to tradition, the father and older brother of Lucius Junius Brutus had been killed by the Tarquins, the ruling dynasty of Etruscan kings. He himself had avoided death at the hands of King Tarquin the Proud by pretending to be an idiot. Later, he was instrumental in inciting a widespread revolt against the Etruscans and expelling their dynasty. An early fifth century A.D. Roman writer, Ambrosius Theodosius Macrobius, explained that June had therefore been named after Lucius Junius Brutus since "in this month, that is, on the Kalends of June [the first day of the month], after Tarquin had been driven out, he, bound by his vow, erected a shrine to . . . Carna [the goddess of the internal organs of the body] on the Caelian mount [one of the seven hills of ancient Rome]."

The Roman hero was subsequently elected one of the first praetors — the office of consul did not yet exist — of the newly established Roman republic. When Lucius Junius Brutus's two sons plotted to restore the Etruscan monarchy, he ordered them executed for conspiracy. He was slain in combat with the son of his mortal enemy (Tarquin the Proud), who was attempting to reestablish the Etruscan dynasty.

The tale recounting the naming of June in honor of Lucius Junius Brutus was probably invented many years after the death of that Roman hero, perhaps as late as the first century A.D. It may have been disseminated by Julius Caesar (102 B.C.–44 B.C.) or Augustus Caesar (63 B.C.–A.D. 14), either of whom would have had good reason to find such a precedent useful in justifying and sanctioning his own policy of calling a month after himself.

One of the most important June festivals in Rome was that of Vesta, the goddess of the hearth, which took place from June 7 to 15. It was considered such a sacred occasion that all secular activities were kept to a minimum: even marriages could not be celebrated. During the festival, a number of rituals were performed. On the central day of the *Vestalia*, June 9, three senior vestal virgins prepared a sacred cake of mola (meal), mixing it with salt. This *mola salsa*, or "salt meal," was offered to Vesta in her temple, the oldest in Rome, alleged to have been constructed on the Palatine Hill by the legendary King Numa Pompilius in 716 B.C. The festival of Vesta concluded with the cleansing of the temple storehouse in anticipation of the approaching harvest. The storehouse was considered of great significance, since not only Vesta, as goddess of the hearth, but also the Penates, the deities of the household, dwelt there to protect the food supplies of the city.

Apart from the period of the *Vestalia*, Roman women believed that June was the most favorable month for marrying. It is probable that this view arose in part from the belief that May marriages were considered unlucky and in part from Ovid's theory that June was named for Juno, the protector of women and guardian of marriages. However this may be, the popularity of June as a marriage month has survived through the centuries.

The Anglo-Saxons variously called June "the dry month," "midsummer month," "the earlier mild month" (before July, "the mild month"), and "joy time." June is the month of the summer solstice, the time when the sun has apparently moved to the point farthest north from the equator and seems to stand still before moving south again — hence the word "solstice," of Latin origin, meaning a "standing still of the sun." The lucky birthstones frequently associated with June are the pearl, emerald, and agate.

JUNE 1

Kentucky Admitted to the Union

Kentucky, originally a part of Virginia, was admitted to the Union as the 15th state on June 1, 1792, by an act of Congress that had been approved on February 4 of the same year. Following the passage of the act, a constitutional convention met in Danville on April 2 and completed its work on April 19. The constitution drafted by the convention went into effect on June 1 without being first submitted to the people for ratification. June 1, the anniversary of statehood, is not officially observed on a regular basis in Kentucky, although elaborate celebrations took place on the 100th, 150th, and 175th

anniversaries, and plans for the state's bicentennial were in progress by the 1970s.

The area of what is now called Kentucky attracted the attention of both the French and the English in the 17th and 18th centuries. The first Europeans who touched upon its borders were adventurers looking for an all-water passage west to the Pacific Ocean. In the second half of the 17th century, Robert Cavelier, Sieur de La Salle, the great French explorer, may have followed the course of the Ohio River to the falls near which the city of Louisville is now situated. In 1682 he claimed the vast region drained by the Mississippi River and its tributaries, including Kentucky, for King Louis XIV, and called it Louisiana.

For more than 100 years after La Salle's explorations, only isolated bands of fur traders and hunters penetrated the region and brought back tales of a beautiful but almost deserted land beyond the Appalachian Mountains. However, as one Indian chief predicted, the area was to be a "dark and bloody ground." None of the tribes that roamed the territory — Cherokee, Shawnee, Seneca, or Iroquois — had been successful in securing the rich hunting grounds, full of bears, deer, and buffalo, as its own domain. Thus there were internecine struggles for possession; and further troubles occurred when white settlers arrived in the area.

The first exploration of practical importance was undertaken only in 1750, when British interest in the region, stimulated by rivalry with the French for supremacy not only in the Ohio valley but also in all of North America, mushroomed. In that year Dr. Thomas Walker (1714–1794), a Virginia physician and land agent for the Loyal Land Company of Charlottesville, Virginia, crossed a natural passage (near the point where Virginia, Kentucky, and Tennessee now meet) from Virginia into what is now eastern Kentucky. He named it the Cumberland Gap after William Augustus, duke of Cumberland, the third son of King George II of England. Scouting for a suitable spot for a settlement, he explored the Big Sandy region of Kentucky. (At Barbourville, in southeastern Kentucky, the Thomas Walker state park shrine features a replica of the log cabin he built in 1750.)

Within a few months of Walker's expedition, the Ohio Land Company dispatched the frontiersman Christopher Gist on a similar surveying mission. Gist, tracing an old Indian trail, reached the Falls of the Ohio and returned east via Walker's Cumberland Gap route. Although both Walker and Gist penned vivid accounts of their travels, their ventures into the "dark and bloody ground" were not immediately fruitful in encouraging settlement, because of the fierce frontier warfare between the French and the British. Only after the British victory in the French and Indian Wars, confirmed in the Treaty of Paris of 1763, did settlers from the eastern seaboard area start to trickle into Kentucky. In so doing they blatantly defied the royal proclamation of 1763, which guaranteed the local Indians their hunting grounds west of the Appalachians and prohibited white penetration of the vast western expanse.

The first major white movement into Kentucky was instigated by Colonel Richard Henderson, a North Carolina attorney and land speculator who, with others, founded the Transylvania Company with the express design of throwing open most of Kentucky. In 1769 the renowned backwoodsman Daniel Boone, who soon began to act as an agent for the Transylvania Company, started the arduous task of exploring the Kentucky wilderness and pinpointing suitable spots for settlement (see June 7, Boone Day).

Numerous hunters and surveyors followed in Boone's footsteps. One of the most important was James Harrod, who in 1774 founded Harrodstown (now Harrodsburg), the first permanent settlement within the borders of the present state, eight miles south of the Kentucky River in eastern Kentucky. In March 1775 Richard Henderson and several of his Transylvania Company partners, imbued with somewhat grandiose plans for a 14th colony of Transylvania in the region, met with more than 1,000 Cherokee Indians at Sycamore Shoals on the Watauga River near what is now Elizabethton, Tennessee. They purchased for £2,000 in baubles and supplies a piece of land, reputedly Cherokee-owned, covering most of Kentucky and part of Tennessee. Earlier the same month, even before the treaty was signed, the Transylvania Company had dispatched Daniel Boone and a party of 30 to perform one of Boone's outstanding accomplishments — the clearing of the trail that would become famous as the Wilderness Road, extending some 250 miles from Long Island on the Holston River in northeastern Tennessee west and north through the Cumberland Gap to the Kentucky River, deep in Kentucky.

Actually, however, the Transylvania Company was acting illegally, as it had no right to purchase the immense region which, far from lying exclusively in Cherokee hands, fell partly within the chartered boundaries of Virginia and partly within those of North Carolina. The area was in fact disputed between the two colonies. On December 6, 1776, Virginia affirmed its authority over the region by creating Kentucky County — practically covering the entire extent of today's state — out of this western land.

The well-to-do Virginia plantation owners, who controlled the colony's government, soon found themselves very much occupied with Revolutionary War campaigns on their own soil and failed to provide adequate protection for distant Kentucky County. The self-reliant frontiersmen had to fend for themselves against British-instigated Indian raids. But between 1775 and 1795 thousands of pioneers from Virginia, Maryland, Pennsylvania, and the Carolinas, especially, continued to pour through the Cumberland Gap over the Wilderness Road or float down the Ohio River on barges to Kentucky. As early as 1780 Kentucky County was split into three sections: Fayette, Jefferson, and Lincoln counties, and the 1790 census showed a population of 73,667.

Many Kentuckians, convinced that Virginia could not provide sufficient protection and governmental supervision, came to advocate independent statehood; others favored the creation of a separate nation. A few even contemplated alliance with Spanish Louisiana. A number of conventions, held at Danville starting in 1784, prepared the groundwork for statehood, and Virginia responded favorably to the matter of ceding the title to its western land, provided the US Congress admit the area as a state. Congress passed the preliminary act in February 1791; a state constitution was drafted in April of the following year; and on June 1, 1792, Kentucky became the 15th state of the Union and the first one west of the Appalachian Mountains. The state constitution granted full manhood suffrage, making Kentucky the first state in the nation to extend such a right.

By the start of the 19th century, even Kentucky's age-old Indian difficulties had been alleviated with General Anthony Wayne's decisive victory over British-supported Indians at the Battle of Fallen Timbers near Toledo, Ohio, in August 1794. The question of free navigation down the Mississippi River to the Spanish-held port of New Orleans, a factor indispensable to the state's economic prosperity, was temporarily solved in 1795 by the so-called Pinckney's Treaty with Spain and permanently guaranteed by the Louisiana Purchase, made by the United States in 1803 (see December 20). Between 1800 and 1850 Kentucky grew quickly, strategically located as it was, with developing trade and shipping on the Ohio and Mississippi rivers.

Like the other border states, Kentucky was split by divisive cultural, economic, and geographical interests. Its slaveholding farmers of the central Blue Grass country and poor whites of the mountain regions were torn by the same political and social rivalry that characterized the relationship between the tidewater gentlemen farmers and mountain frontiersmen of Virginia. Slavery and aristocratic social ties, on the one hand, caused many Kentuckians to sympathize with the South just before the outbreak of the Civil War, while northern business connections and pro-Union political traditions inclined others to side with the North. Both the vocal antislavery element and the equally outspoken proslavery faction lost to the conciliatory group, which aimed at compromise and a united nation above all – in the tradition of Kentucky's great statesman Henry Clay, the Great Compromiser.

With passions running high for both North and South in Kentucky, the birthplace of the Union's Abraham Lincoln and the Confederacy's Jefferson Davis, the inhabitants preferred to remain technically neutral. In the course of the Civil War, however, Kentucky's strategic location was to make it a buffer zone and battlefield for invading forces, and its citizens would join the armies of both sides.

Despite Kentucky's official declaration of neutrality, war came forcibly to the area with the invasion of southern Kentucky by Confederate troops early in September 1861. With its neutrality thus ended, the state officially announced its allegiance to the Union, even though the divisions among the populace remained. Union forces under the then little-known Ulysses S. Grant reacted to the Confederate incursion by taking Paducah, Kentucky, which controlled the entrance to both the Tennessee and Cumberland rivers, and by seizing Fort Henry and Fort Donelson, Confederate posts that were respectively located on the two rivers, just over the border in Tennessee.

Both Confederate and Union troops entered Kentucky again before the war was over. The Confederate invasion of central Kentucky in late summer and fall 1862 brought Union forces in hot pursuit. The eventual collision of the two armies, near Perryville on October 8, ended somewhat inconclusively, but with the Confederate forces departing from the state. Thereafter Kentucky was devoid of armed Confederates, except for guerrilla activity, which persisted until the end of the war. The strategically situated Ohio River community of Louisville had been secured by Union forces early in the war, on September 21, 1861. Established as a Union military headquarters, it remained a major supply depot throughout the North-South hostilities, and largely escaped the ravages of war.

Kentucky's particularly deep divisions among friends and kin were reflective of its status as a border state. Typical of the divided households, ironically, was that of Mary Todd Lincoln, the wife of the Union's President: her brother, three half brothers, and three half sisters' husbands went south to serve the Confederacy. Appropriately, in view of the deep divisions, Kentucky was represented by a star on both the Union and Confederate flags.

In spite of Kentucky's formal pro-Union allegiance, the postwar period was one of increasing bitterness toward the federal government, caused primarily by emancipation of slaves without compensation even to loyal Unionists, and by Kentuckians' general disapproval of the congressional Reconstruction policy applied in the South.

The late 19th and 20th centuries saw the growth of industrialization in Kentucky, as well as the development of the state's tourist attractions. Horse breeding and horse racing – epitomized by the famous Kentucky Derby – fox hunting, tobacco raising, and the manufacture of bourbon whiskey have become practically synonymous with the Bluegrass State, officially styled the Commonwealth of Kentucky.

Père Marquette's Birthday

Jacques Marquette, the gentle young French Jesuit who journeyed to the New World in 1666 as a quiet missionary, is celebrated in history as the codiscoverer, with Louis Joliet, of the Mississippi River.

In 1965 the 89th Congress of the United States designated the years 1968 to 1973 as the Père Marquette Tercentenary, a national observance recognizing the priest-explorer's life and work, especially from 1668 – the year he came into what is now the United States by way of Sault Sainte Marie on the Michigan-Ontario border – to 1673, the year he and Joliet explored the Mississippi River.

Appointed National Père Marquette Tercentenary Commission chairman by President Lyndon B. Johnson, James C. Windham, a prominent Milwaukee businessman and a member of the Board of Trustees of Marquette University, pointed out Père Marquette's impact on the nation: "It is indeed fitting that the entire country join in this effort to honor Father Marquette, a gentle and courageous missionary-explorer. He ventured into the uncharted wilderness, and through his journal made known to the world the beauties and vast potential of the Mississippi River and the Great Lakes basin. His discoveries marked a crucial step in opening the door to the West."

Local and statewide tercentenary observances were held in states touched by Marquette's travels – Michigan, Wisconsin, Iowa, Illinois, Minnesota, Missouri, and Tennessee.

The national observance of the tercentenary was launched early in 1968 with the issue of a special six-cent stamp commemorating "Marquette – Explorer," which showed Père Marquette and French *voyageurs* in a birch canoe, their means of transportation on the Mississippi. Another early observance of the tercentenary was a symposium held at Marquette University in April 1968, on "The Contribution of Religion to the Life of Man in Society." The symposium was cosponsored by the National Tercentenary Commission; the Johnson Foundation of Racine, Wisconsin; and Marquette University.

Among the many projects initiated by the National Tercentenary Commission were the first scholarly biography of Jacques Marquette, by the Reverend Joseph P. Donnelly, professor of history at Marquette University, as well as the *Père Marquette Symphony*, written by the composer Roy Harris. The first performance of the symphony took place on November 8, 1969, at Milwaukee's Performing Arts Center, across the street from Père Marquette Park.

At a civic dinner preceding the symphony performance, the world's premier explorers of the moon and its environs, recently returned Apollo XI astronauts Neil Armstrong, Michael Collins, and Edwin Aldrin, became the first recipients of the Père Marquette Discovery Medal. The Père Marquette Discovery awards were inaugurated in 1969 by the Marquette University Père Marquette Tercentenary Committee in cooperation with the National Tercentenary Commission. The awards are presented annually to people whose achievements in the field of exploration and discovery bear the same distinguishing marks as those of Père Marquette — "a questing spirit, a uniqueness in deed, and a consuming dedication to the improvement of mankind and his environment." The bronze medals, which hang about the neck on a ribbon of blue and gold ribbon (Marquette University's colors), were designed by Edmund Lewandowski.

The most dramatic commemoration of Marquette and Joliet's discovery of the upper Mississippi was the tricentennial reenactment of their expedition. The 1973 group, led by Reid Lewis, an Illinois teacher of French, consisted of six historians and environmental scientists and a Jesuit priest from Chicago. The party set off from St. Ignace on May 17 in two fiberglass canoes and followed the 300-mile route of Marquette and Joliet to the mouth of the Arkansas River. The arrival of the canoes at communities along the Mississippi sparked tricentennial celebrations of the original voyage.

The eldest son of a prominent and fairly well-to-do family in Laon, France, Jacques Marquette was born on June 1, 1637. When he was nine he was sent to Reims (Rheims) to be educated by Jesuits. After receiving his college degree at the age of 17, he entered the Society of Jesus at Nancy, France, on October 7, 1654.

During his school days and throughout his Jesuit training period, he heard reports of French Jesuits' adventures in the New World. From the time he was nine years old, he had wanted to become a foreign missionary, and this ambition never deserted him. Five years after he joined the Jesuit religious community, he volunteered to go as a missionary to whatever land his superiors elected, but was encouraged instead to continue his training, while keeping alive his missionary hopes.

In 1665, with a master's degree completed and nearing the end of his long Jesuit training, Marquette again volunteered. The time was ripe for more missionaries to the New World; more specifically, Jesuits were sought to work with the Indians of New France, as Canada was then called. First, however, Marquette was ordained in the cathedral at Toul on March 7, 1666. On September 20 he arrived in Quebec.

Shortly afterwards he again set out, this time for Trois Rivières (Three Rivers), about 70 miles from Quebec on the St. Lawrence River. There, under the direction of Father Gabriel Druillettes, Marquette, like other uninitiated Jesuit missionaries, spent two years in training, which included learning Indian languages and customs, and wilderness survival. Marquette had always had a facility for learning languages, and he became familiar with at least six Indian dialects. More important, perhaps, he grew to know and respect the Indians.

In 1668 Marquette was assigned to work with the Chippewa Indians at Sault Sainte Marie, which had been founded two years earlier by Père Claude Allouez, as the first permanent mission in Michigan. The next year Marquette was sent to work with the Hurons and Ottawas at La Pointe de St. Esprit on Chequamegon Bay in Wisconsin, another mission founded by Père Allouez — who subsequently went on to evangelize the Indians in the Green Bay area.

While at La Pointe, Marquette heard from Indians many tales of the Great River. He became interested mainly because if such a river did exist it would provide a route for missionaries to reach many tribes of Indians living in the hinterland and thought, until then, to be geographically inaccessible.

In 1671 intertribal hostility — caused probably by a single Huron trespasser — broke out, and the Sioux drove the Hurons and other tribes Marquette had befriended out of La Pointe. With his Indian friends Marquette went east, and founded a mission at the site of St. Ignace, on the Straits of Mackinac, in the Upper Peninsula of Michigan. There he built a church and taught and lived with the Indians. He earned their respect and love, which he reciprocated, and he came to think of the mission in St. Ignace as his home.

Toward the end of 1672 Louis Joliet appeared at St. Ignace. Joliet, Canadian born and educated, had been sent to France for a year to be trained in hydrography, the study of bodies of water. He had traveled the Great Lakes area for many years as a trapper and trader and knew the Indians and the geography of that part of Canada and Wisconsin and of Michigan as well as any white man. He, too, had heard stories about the Great River and in 1672 had been commissioned by the French government to locate the river and chart its course. The French, like the Spanish, felt that the Mississippi might flow to the Pacific Ocean, opening new worlds and providing access to the Orient.

Marquette was appointed to accompany Joliet for several reasons. First, it was the custom of French expeditions to take a priest along as chaplain for the explorers. The second reason had to do with the Jesuits' wish to learn more about that uncharted area in order to establish a mission among the Illinois Indians. Marquette, who knew the Illinois dialect and customs, thus was a particularly appropriate choice to accompany Joliet and his five woodsmen-adventurers.

Their preparations made during the winter, the seven men set out in two birch canoes on May 17, 1673, after Marquette said his farewells to the Indian families of St. Ignace, promising to return if he could. Marquette was then 36 years old and Joliet was 28.

The explorers went through the Straits of Mackinac, across Lake Michigan to Green Bay and into the Fox River. They stopped to seek advice and aid from the Mascouten Indians at the Jesuit Mission of St. Francis Xavier, near what is now De Pere, Wisconsin — which was, as Marquette wrote in his journal, "the terminus of previous French explorations. They have gone no further than this place." There were limits beyond which even the Indians would not go, as the voyagers learned when they asked for guides.

Père Marquette's journal reads:

The following day which was June 10 [1673], two Miami who were assigned to us as guides embarked with us in the presence of a throng of Indians who stood dumbfounded by the spectacle of seven Frenchmen in two canoes undertaking what seemed to them such an extraordinarily hazardous expedition. We were led to believe that about nine miles up the river we could cross to a stream which emptied into the Mississippi. Furthermore, we were pretty sure that we had to travel west southwest, but the route was so cluttered with swamps and small lakes that it is easy to go astray, especially since the river is so full of wild rice that it is difficult to determine the channel. That is why we needed the two guides. They served us well, and led us to the portage [now Portage, Wisconsin] which is only two-and-a-half miles long. After the Indians helped us to carry the canoes over

to the river, they left us to the care of Providence, alone in this unexplored land.

A later entry in the journal takes up the narrative: "A hundred-twenty miles of paddling brought us to the mouth of our river at 42½ degrees north latitude. On the 17th day of June, with a joy that I cannot express, we floated out upon the Mississippi River."

Eight days later, following a footpath from the river to a village, the explorers came upon friendly Illinois Indians who warned them that if they continued they would face many dangers from the river itself and from hostile tribes. The explorers decided to go on nonetheless, and the Illinois presented Marquette with a symbolic feathered peace pipe, widely respected by Indians of various tribes. As they continued down the river, the explorers did indeed have arrows shot at them; but Marquette raised the calumet high and the two canoes were given safe passage.

When they approached the mouth of the Arkansas River, they met Akansea Indians who warned them that if they went farther they would meet not only hostile Indians with firearms but also hostile white men. The Akansea told them the mouth of the great river was only five days away. By this time the French explorers knew that the Mississippi emptied into the Gulf of Mexico and not the Gulf of California. They realized that the white men the Indians warned about were the Spanish, who had known about the lower Mississippi for over 100 years — Hernando De Soto had been buried in the river in 1542. Since France and Spain were traditional enemies in the Old World, and rivals in the New, Marquette and Joliet thought it the better part of valor to turn around, rather than risk capture and have their information about the river lost to France. Less than 10 years later, in 1682, another French explorer, Robert La Salle, following much the same route from Mackinac, reached the mouth of the Mississippi and claimed the river, its tributaries, and the land adjacent for France, naming it Louisiana in honor of King Louis XIV.

On July 17 Marquette, Joliet, and their men reversed their course. Having traveled down the west bank of the Mississippi, they made the difficult return upstream along the east bank.

They paddled upriver (up several rivers, in fact — the Mississippi, the Illinois, and the Des Plaines) before they discovered the famous Chicago Portage — today designated as a National Historic Site — which thenceforth would link the waters of the Mississippi with those of the Great Lakes for explorers, traders, and settlers. Beyond the portage, Marquette and Joliet continued on the Chicago River, which led them to Lake Michigan. They became the first Europeans to land on the site of Chicago, where those two bodies of water meet. Four months and 2,000 miles after they had embarked on their historic journey, the explorers arrived back at the Mission of St. Francis Xavier (De Pere, Wisconsin), in September 1673.

The trip had taken its toll of Marquette's health, and he stayed at the mission while Joliet, anxious to get his maps and information back to New France's Governor Frontenac, hastened to depart for Canada. Unfortunately, within sight of Montreal, his canoe overturned in the Lachine Rapids, and Joliet's notes and maps were lost, although he himself survived. Because of this misadventure, Marquette's journal became the official account of the expedition.

Marquette, feeling somewhat stronger by the autumn of 1674, left De Pere to keep his promise of returning to establish a mission among the Illinois Indians. He got as far as Chicago, where a severe winter and his recurring ill health forced him to stay until spring. In April he completed his journey to the Illinois, preaching to the tribe on Holy Thursday and Easter Sunday. By this time he was aware that his health would not be restored, and he explained to the Illinois that he wished to return to his home at the mission in St. Ignace, 300 miles away.

Marquette was so weak by this time that he had to be carried and cared for. Several Illinois Indians accompanied him on his return trip to St. Ignace, which he had left in company with Joliet just two years before. As the Indians paddled the canoe up Lake Michigan, Marquette grew weaker. Finally, he asked them to stop and take him ashore to die.

They took him to a high hill near the mouth of what is now Père Marquette River. There, within a few hours, Marquette died peacefully, on May 18, 1675, and there he was buried. The burial site is marked by a boulder in Père Marquette Park in Ludington, Michigan.

Two years after Marquette's death Indian friends from St. Ignace found his grave and honored the wish of their revered missionary "to return to his little chapel on the Straits." As was their custom, the Indians disinterred the body, excised the bones and carried them to St. Ignace, where they were buried beneath the chapel in which Marquette had preached. The chapel was destroyed by fire in 1706 and the location of the tomb was unknown until it was accidentally discovered in 1877. In 1882 some of the bones were sent to Marquette University, and a marker was erected by the citizens of St. Ignace to show the missionary's second burial place. The site is at the corner of State and Marquette streets in St. Ignace, opposite a statue of Marquette and the Old Mission Church Museum.

Writing Marquette's obituary, the head of the Jesuit missionaries at that time said he was "all things to all men, a Frenchman with the French, a Huron with the Hurons, an Algonquin with the Algonquins." Marquette, who had died two weeks before his 38th birthday, had spent less than nine years in the New World. His name has been given to a river, a lake, several cities and towns, a railroad, a university, many parks throughout the Great Lakes area, and a national forest in Michigan's Upper Peninsula.

A marble statue of Père Marquette, presented by Wisconsin, stands in the Capitol in Washington, D.C. In 1897 the sculptor Gaetano Trentanove, a Florentine, went to Marquette, Michigan, for the unveiling of a bronze replica.

Père Marquette pageants were introduced in various parts of Michigan as early as 1930. The St. Ignace pageant was initiated by the Knights of Columbus in 1949 and sponsored as an annual event. Expanded in 1966 and retitled "The Black Gown Tree," the music-and-drama spectacle became a community project of religious, fraternal, and civic groups under the sponsorship of the nonprofit Father Marquette Historical Production Association. The 1971 pageant marked the 300th anniversary of Marquette's founding of St. Ignace.

The St. Ignace pageant is repeated several times for thousands of spectators during the Labor Day weekend. More than 100 townspeople, many of them Indians, are in the cast of the pageant, which reenacts the landing of Marquette at St. Ignace and recalls his life with the Indians and his explorations. A special Roman Catholic mass takes place outdoors on Sunday. On Labor Day thousands of natives and visitors participate in another local tradition, the Labor Day Mackinac Bridge Walk, a four-and-a-half mile championship race walk. This is followed by a general recreational bridge walk — a stroll taken by more than 15,000 people in some years.

Royal Poinciana Festival in Miami

This is a movable event. See note on page xxvi.

An annual celebration honoring Miami, Florida's Royal Poinciana Fiesta lasts approximately one week and is held during late May or early June to coincide with the blooming of the trees in that area. The high point of the fiesta is the coronation of Queen Poinciana and her Court. The queen is chosen among students at the University of Miami (located at Coral Gables, one of 27 municipalities constituting Greater Miami). Members of the queen's court are chosen among students at local high schools.

The fiesta in 1970 opened on Monday with an official banquet and fashion show for the queen and her court of 13, after which awards were presented for the annual Poinciana art exhibit. The exhibit, which was open to the public throughout the week, featured paintings, ceramics, and sculptures of Florida fauna, with emphasis on the poinciana. Entries in the exhibit, sponsored by the Miami Art League, were judged by a jury and cash prizes were awarded. On Wednesday the coronation ceremony took place during a special public concert held at the city's Bayfront Park bandshell. In the course of a second public concert, given on Friday, awards were presented to the owners of the three handsomest poinciana trees in the metropolitan area. Both band concerts featured vocal and instrumental soloists.

The fiesta is an outgrowth of a project for planting royal poincianas sponsored in 1937 by public-spirited citizens of Coral Gables. With the cooperation of that city's chamber of commerce, 100 of the trees were set out during June of that year. The Miami Chamber of Commerce cooperated in the project, and Mayor E. G. Sewell of Miami proclaimed July 20, 1937, as the first Royal Poinciana Planting Day.

It was in 1940, largely through the efforts of Mrs. Robert G. Lassiter, that the idea of a festival came to fruition. A student queen was chosen by the University of Miami and a coronation ceremony was held in Miami's Bayfront Park. This event was the nucleus of activities sponsored each year thereafter by the Royal Poinciana Committee, a group of public-minded residents.

Although the broad outlines of the fiesta have remained, the schedule of events has varied somewhat from year to year. In 1941, a pageant was part of the festivities. The festival continued as an annual observance in early June throughout World War II. In 1945 there was a typical program in the park on June 7, which included music by a concert band and vocal soloists, exhibition dancing, public addresses, and the coronation of the Royal Poinciana Festival queen, who was attended by six ladies-in-waiting with escorts from the various branches of the armed services. In 1946 a city-sponsored art show, held in the park auditorium, was incorporated into the festival. As has been the case with more recent showings, a large number of canvases portraying poincianas were included in the exhibits. The first prize was awarded for the most realistic painting of the tree. In some years there have also been caravan tours to homes at which spectacular poinciana trees were flowering and ceremonial plantings and distribution of poinciana blooms.

In 1961, after the Royal Poinciana Committee's decision that the fiesta had grown too large for it to handle properly, sponsorship was taken over by the City of Miami Beautification Committee. In 1970 the City of Miami joined that committee as cosponsor.

In 1940 it was estimated that there were approximately 50,000 royal poincianas in the Greater Miami area. Today, as a result of continued plantings, the number has greatly increased. One of the most striking of tropical trees, the royal poinciana is native to Madagascar and is cultivated in warm climates elsewhere. It is common throughout southern Florida and southern California, and is found in Hawaii, the Philippines, the West Indies, India, and Ceylon. It is named for Philippe de Lonvillier de Poinci, governor of the French West Indies in 1635 under Cardinal Richelieu. The slaves on the islands at that time were from Madagascar, and it is possible that the seeds of the flower were taken to the islands and thence to the United States in the straw bedding on the slave ships.

The blooms of the poinciana measure from three to four inches across; each has five widely spread red petals, one of which is dotted and streaked with yellow. Ten long stamens reach from the flower, adding to its beauty. The profuse flame-colored blossoms give the effect of a tree on fire. Remarkable too are the seedpods, which are two feet or more in length and purplish-brown in color. When not in bloom, the royal poincianas, with their soft green leaves, are admired for their lacy, fernlike foliage. Fast-growing, the trees have strong gnarled trunks and spreading branches that can reach 40 feet above the ground.

The history of the flower in Florida began when early settlers in Redlands, a community near Miami, planted the trees around their homes. In 1929 the superintendent of parks in Miami, Gerry Curtis, planted poincianas along South Miami Avenue, thus giving it the name Route of the Poinciana. In 1936 Wade Livingston Street traded a piece of land on a main upstate highway to a friend for 3,000 young royal poinciana trees to be distributed to residents of the Greater Miami area.

The poinciana is sometimes confused with the poinsettia, the familiar red "Christmas flower," but the two flowers are of different species.

Statehood Day in Tennessee

The Tennessee legislature in 1929 passed an act designating June 1, the anniversary of the admission of Tennessee to the Union, as Statehood Day. Tennessee's admission as the 16th state was the climax of a long and complicated struggle for an independent status separate from the previously settled areas of Virginia and North Carolina.

The Spanish, French, and English in turn touched upon, explored, and laid claim to the region that is now Tennessee, setting off a rivalry for its possession that was not settled in favor of the English until the Treaty of Paris in 1763. The Spanish explorer Hernando de Soto was probably the first European to set foot within the boundaries of the present state. He may have crossed the southeastern section as early as 1540 on his march from Florida. About 1541 he and his men, having reached the Mississippi River, stopped hastily to gather supplies and construct crude rafts on a lofty bluff, presumed to be the site of Memphis in southwestern Tennessee. There was, however, no attempt at colonization.

Over 130 years passed before other Europeans visited the area. Starting in the late 17th century, French adventurers, including the intrepid missionary Jacques Marquette and his companion, Louis Joliet, explored the Mississippi River and its tributaries and undoubtedly visited the western portion of Tennessee. Robert Cavelier, Sieur de La Salle considered this western region part of the vast area of French Louisiana and constructed Fort Prud'homme near what is now Memphis about 1682. Subsequent French explorers erected Fort Assumption at the same strategic location.

The Spanish and French explorations of Tennessee were minimal in comparison with the inroads made by English fur traders and "long hunters" in the 18th century. Although Virginians are known to have traded with the local Indians there as early as the 1670s, the 1750 expedition led by the Virginia physician and land agent Thomas Walker, who also penetrated the area of Kentucky, is regarded as the decisive beginning of the steady English probing of the region.

In 1756, during the French and Indian War, British soldiers established Fort Loudoun (named after John Campbell, the 4th earl of Loudoun, then commander in chief of the British military establishment in North America) on the Little Tennessee River some 30 miles south of what is now Knoxville. Four years later Cherokees killed the garrison of this outpost and the scattered frontiersmen it defended. After the British victory in the protracted struggle for supremacy in North America had been achieved in 1763, Native Americans, especially the Cherokees, were partially appeased by a royal proclamation guaranteeing them their hunting grounds west of the Appalachian Mountains and forbidding colonists along the eastern seaboard from settling on these lands.

Lured by tales spun by hunters and speculators, land-hungry Virginians and North Carolinians nevertheless ventured west across the mountains. In 1769 border settlers, primarily from Pittsylvania County, Virginia, built a few log cabins along the Holston and Watauga rivers in what they presumed to be Virginia soil, but which was in reality the northeastern corner of Tennessee. When the western boundary between Virginia and North Carolina was subsequently surveyed, the settlements were discovered to be in what then was North Carolina.

The colony of North Carolina failed to provide either adequate government or protection from Indians for its westernmost inhabitants, whom it referred to as the "off-scourings of the earth." The hardy, self-sufficient residents of the first Watauga River valley settlements therefore met in 1772 to form a "homespun government" for the "preservation of their ideals of liberty." It became known as the Watauga Association. For the first time frontiersmen west of the Alleghenies had joined together in drawing up a written agreement for civil government. The general committee of 13, empowered to act as a legislature, itself elected 5 of its members to wield executive and judicial powers. A clerk, an attorney, and a sheriff were also elected. The laws of the Royal Colony of Virginia served as models "so near as the situation of affairs would admit," and provisions for recording deeds and wills were stipulated. The Watauga Association (commemorated today by a monument on the Carter County Courthouse lawn in Elizabethton, the site of one of the original Watauga settlements, in eastern Tennessee) survived for several years; it soon gained additional support from the Brown Settlement, which had been made on the Nolichucky River in the early 1770s.

Any thought the Wataugans may have had of eventually founding a separate royal colony became obsolete with the outbreak of the Revolutionary War in 1775. Instead they organized their area into the Washington District. In 1777 the district, at the request of its residents, was formally annexed to North Carolina and gave its name — altered to Washington County — to North Carolina's entire territorial claim west of the Alleghenies to the Mississippi River.

The redoubtable frontiersmen, including such renowned fighters as John "Nolichucky Jack" Sevier, participated in several Revolutionary War campaigns, helping to defeat the British in the important battle of Kings Mountain (October 1780) in South Carolina. Meanwhile, exploration and settlement over the mountains continued apace. The war years saw the creation of Nashborough (later Nashville), founded by the ubiquitous explorer James Robertson — sometimes dubbed the Father of Tennessee.

After the Revolution, North Carolina, wishing to avoid the financial burden of defending its westernmost territory, ceded it to the US government in 1784 on condition that the cession be accepted within two years. The Watauga River valley settlers in eastern Tennessee were distressed by an action taken without their approval and dismayed at the prospect of finding themselves without any government protection whatsoever. They met in convention at Jonesboro on August 23, 1784, and declared their intention of forming a new state of Franklin (at first "Frankland," "land of the free"). They deemed the move essential to assure protection against Indian attacks, validity of land titles, and stable government. Delegates were chosen for a later convention, which would organize the new governmental apparatus.

North Carolina soon rued its action, repealed the act of cession, and tried to alleviate grievances, but the separatist movement had become too vigorous for reconciliation. The precarious civil government of Franklin was beset with financial problems, Indian harassment, and a hopeless struggle to wrest recognition from North Carolina and the US Congress. It tottered on for four years under the leadership of the war hero John Sevier, now governor, whose annual salary had to be paid in animal skins. The Franklinites and the Cumberland settlers eventually found it necessary to gain support by intriguing with Spanish Louisiana, whose control of the mouth of the Mississippi River vitally affected the area's economic development.

By the late 1780s the situation of the State of Franklin was confused. North Carolina put an abrupt halt to the possibility of having the territory fall under the control of Spanish Louisiana by reenacting the cession of its western claim. Sevier was arrested on charges of treason. The US Congress accepted the cession and created on May 26, 1790, the "Territory of the United States South of the River Ohio" with, as governor, William Blount, who had served as a member of the Continental Congress and delegate to the federal Constitutional Convention. Finally arrangements were made for its admission to the Union as a state. A constitutional convention met in January 1796 at Knoxville, the first capital, and drafted the constitution, which Thomas Jefferson described as "the least imperfect and most republican" of any state. It went into effect without submission to a popular vote, and on June 1 Tennessee, with substantially its present borders, became the 16th state of the Union. John Sevier, having been pardoned and restored to favor, became the first governor of the state and served several terms.

Settlers flocked into Tennessee by land and water, especially through the Cumberland Gap over the famous Wilderness Road hacked out by Daniel Boone. The state's population numbered over 100,000 by 1800, and prosperous centers such as Memphis, soon a leading town of the cotton-growing delta, sprang into existence during the next half century. The state nurtured many famous fighters, including Andrew Jackson, Samuel Houston, and David Crockett. It gained its nickname, the Volunteer State, from the high number of volunteers who answered the call to service when the Mexican War broke out in 1846.

After the election of Abraham Lincoln as President of the United States in 1860 and the subsequent formation of the Confederacy, the people of Tennessee, in February 1861, voted down a proposal to summon a convention to consider the question of secession. Public opinion shifted rapidly, however, with the firing on Fort Sumter in the spring of 1861, the actual beginning of the Civil War. A second popular referendum, held on June 8, 1861, saw the victory of the pro-Confederate faction as secession was approved by two-thirds of the voters, those against the move being East Tennesseans who owned few slaves and who were loyal Unionists. On June 24 the governor of Tennessee issued a proclamation declaring the state's independence of the federal government, thus making Tennessee the last of the 11 Southern states to leave the Union.

In the meantime, a pro-Union convention of delegates representing all the eastern and some of the middle counties had been held on June 17 and had petitioned the US Congress for admission of their area to the Union as an independent state. The request was denied.

Tennessee's extensive river network provided ideal invasion routes during the conflict, and second only to Virginia, the state was the bloodiest battlefield of the war; according to one historian, over 450 minor skirmishes and major encounters took place within its boundaries.

In February 1865 an amendment to the Tennessee state constitution of 1834 liberated the slaves. In 1866 Tennessee became the first of the former Confederate states to have its privileges of statehood restored, thereby escaping the congressional Reconstruction. Nevertheless, the native radical Republicans in power enforced similar harsh measures in Tennessee, and the postwar era was marked by bitter feelings.

In the late 19th century and in the 20th, Tennessee developed its mining, manufacturing, and other industrial assets. A landmark in American economic history was the creation of the Tennessee Valley Authority (TVA), an independent government corporate agency, by Congress in 1933. The TVA has contributed to the development of the entire Tennessee River basin and has stimulated the state's industrial and tourist potentialities in a variety of ways: furnishing cheap hydroelectric power, improving river navigation, preventing floods, and planning forest and soil conservation projects.

JUNE 2

Birthday of John Randolph of Roanoke

John Randolph of Roanoke was born June 2, 1773, in Cawsons, Virginia, now part of the city of Hopewell. His background was distinguished; the Randolphs were one of the leading families in Virginia, and his maternal relations, the Blands, were equally prominent. Young Randolph was both brilliant and restless. In 1787 he enrolled in the College of New Jersey (now Princeton University). He remained there one year and then studied briefly at Columbia College. Then in 1791 he returned to his native state and completed the last two years of his formal education at the College of William and Mary.

In 1799 the Virginia electorate sent Randolph to the national House of Representatives. The new congressman's political career began during a time of sharp party division: the Federalists advocated a strong central government; the Democratic-Republicans favored state's rights. Randolph was an ardent Democratic-Republican, and the election of Thomas Jefferson, his copartisan, to the presidency in 1880 insured his rapid political advance. At 28 he not only became the chairman of the powerful Ways and Means Committee but also was his party's spokesman in the House of Representatives.

Randolph's break with the Democratic-Republican leadership began in 1804. In that year Jefferson determined to move against the Federalist-dominated judiciary and, in particular, against Associate Justice of the Supreme Court Samuel Chase. Chase had enjoyed a distinguished career. He had been a signer of the Declaration of Independence and a member of the Continental Congress; in 1796 President George Washington had appointed him to the Supreme Court. However, Chase was also a staunch Federalist, and some of his rulings had been prejudiced by his strong partisan feelings. His continued presence on the bench was intolerable to the Democratic-Republicans, but according to the Constitution he could be removed from office only if found guilty of "high crimes and misdemeanors."

Randolph was given the responsibility for securing such a conviction. This task was almost impossible since there was no evidence to substantiate the charges brought against Chase. However, the Democratic-Republican leadership ignored this fact and, when the justice was acquitted, blamed Randolph for mismanaging the impeachment proceedings.

Following the Chase trial, growing philosophical differences widened the gap between him and the leaders of his party. After 1804 Democratic-Republicans such as Jefferson, James Madison, and James Monroe began to espouse nationalist policies similar to those advocated by the Federalists. Randolph viewed such actions as contrary to the original principles of the party. He soon emerged as the leader of the former Democratic-Republicans who contended that the party's leaders were betraying its fundamental states' rights doctrine.

The party of Jefferson remained in power until the election of Andrew Jackson in 1828, and throughout most of this period Randolph, as a member of the House of Representatives, opposed most of the party's important actions. It was his belief that Jefferson's embargo act in 1806, the presidential candidacy of James Madison in 1808, the War of 1812, the chartering of the Second Bank of the United States in 1816, and the Missouri Compromise in 1820 were all violations of the party's states' rights doctrine. Randolph was especially harsh in his treatment of Henry Clay. A brilliant orator, he used his talents to the full in his numerous attacks upon the nationalist President John Quincy Adams and Clay, who was Adams's secretary of state. Randolph's branding of Adams and Clay as "a combination of a Puritan and a blackleg" led to a duel between himself and Clay in which neither was wounded.

In 1831 Randolph was appointed minister to Russia. However, after he had served for only one month, illness forced him to resign. Throughout his life Randolph had been troubled by several chronic illnesses. After 1831 his health failed rapidly. He died in Philadelphia on May 24, 1833. He was buried at Roanoke, the site of his father's homestead. According to tradition, he left instructions that his face be turned to the west so that he might keep his eye on the Kentuckian Henry Clay. In 1879 Randolph's remains were moved to Richmond.

JUNE 3

Jefferson Davis's Birthday

The 10th child of Samuel Davis, a Revolutionary War veteran, Jefferson Davis (named for Thomas Jefferson) was born in a farm cabin in Christian County, Kentucky, on June 3, 1808. His father had lived near Atlanta, Georgia, for a time after the American Revolution, before moving with his family to Christian County in central Kentucky, where he made a living by raising cattle and growing tobacco. Ironically, his youngest son, the future president of the Confederacy, thus was born scarcely a hundred miles from the Kentucky birthplace of Abraham Lincoln, his

Civil War adversary. The Lincoln family moved north from Kentucky, eventually settling in Illinois; the Davis family moved south, to Wilkinson County, Mississippi, shortly after the birth of Jefferson.

When Jefferson was only seven, he rode on ponyback hundreds of miles northward to become a student in the Roman Catholic Seminary in Washington County, Kentucky, which his Baptist parents had permitted him to enter. After two years he returned home to study in the local schools, subsequently entering Transylvania University, at Lexington, Kentucky, in 1821, at 13. When he was 16, his representative in Congress appointed him to the US Military Academy at West Point. Upon his graduation in 1828, he was commissioned a second lieutenant in the US Army. (Robert E. Lee was in the class behind him.) Davis spent seven years in army posts in Wisconsin and Illinois; he served in the Black Hawk War, in which Abraham Lincoln was an officer of volunteers. While stationed at Fort Crawford, Wisconsin, commanded by Colonel Zachary Taylor, Davis met Sarah Knox Taylor, Taylor's daughter, and married her in 1835 against her father's will. Three months after their marriage she died of malaria.

Davis had resigned from the army before the marriage and returned to his home in Mississippi. With a small inheritance from his father and a larger sum from his eldest brother, Joseph, who was very wealthy, he settled a plantation called Brierfield on rough land overlooking the Mississippi River. This land adjoined several of his brother's plantations, and the area, a large peninsula in the Mississippi, was known as Davis Bend.

Jefferson Davis spent the next 10 years overseeing the plantation. He worked his land alongside his slaves and is reputed to have treated them well. One unusual aspect of his plantation was his institution of a black jury system to try slave offenses. He was one of the "enlightened" planters who saw slavery as a school to "civilize" blacks, whom they had no thought of freeing.

In 1845 Davis entered the local aristocracy when he married Varina Howell. Elected as a Democrat to the 29th Congress, he served in the US House of Representatives until June 1846, when he resigned to serve in the Mexican War, organizing a volunteer regiment known as the Mississippi Rifles. Under his former father-in-law, General Taylor, Davis and his regiment fought valiantly. Davis won widespread praise for his bravery at the battle of Buena Vista — and from that moment on thought of himself as a surpassing military commander.

Withdrawing from the army in 1847, Davis was elected to the US Senate from Mississippi.

He was an avid supporter of President James K. Polk and his expansionist policies. Davis's vision was essentially one in which the South would expand into the "empty" areas of the West, thus gaining in national political power. He opposed California's entrance into the Union as a free state in 1850. This California question, and the whole inflammatory issue of free-versus-slave states and territories, contributed to a wave of secessionist sentiment throughout the South.

In 1851 Davis resigned from the Senate to run for governor of Mississippi. The election was a conflict among extreme states' rightists, Southern nationalists, and "cooperationists." Davis's campaign appears to have been designed to allow the Mississippi Democratic party a face-saving retreat from the brink of secession. Losing the election, he returned to his plantation, but in 1853 he was appointed secretary of war by President Franklin Pierce.

Davis's years as secretary of war were among his happiest. His health was robust, and he enjoyed the endless rounds of social events that were a part of Washington governmental life. He was responsible for the acquisition from Mexico of the strip of territory in the Southwest known as the Gadsden Purchase, which he wanted in US hands so that a railroad to the Pacific might be built through the South to the West.

At the close of his service as secretary of war, Davis was again sent to the Senate by Mississippi. Until his state declared secession, he hoped for some plan short of an actual break with the Union, though he never doubted the right of the South to secede. On January 21, 1861, he announced the secession of his state 12 days earlier and withdrew from the Senate himself.

Mississippi immediately appointed Davis to command its state troops, although he himself had hoped to be commander of all the South's armies. Instead, he was chosen as a compromise president by a convention of seceding states, in an effort to attract uncommitted Southern states to the Confederacy. Although he was not anyone's first choice, Davis was widely respected as a moderate Southern nationalist. He was inaugurated provisional president at Montgomery, Alabama, on February 18, 1861 (see February 18). Then, with the choice confirmed by an election in October 1861, he was again inaugurated, formally, at Richmond, Virginia — which by then had become the capital of the Confederacy — on February 22, 1862. Meanwhile, the Civil War, which was to wrack the nation for four years, had begun with the firing upon Fort Sumter on April 12, 1861.

Austere, now in frail health, and often irritable, Davis was plagued by a lack of cooperation among the Confederate states. When he tried to tax the states and to institute a draft, he was bitterly opposed by extreme states' rightists, who called him a dictator. But he was a compassionate man, loyal to friends, and he possessed marked leadership qualities.

Davis himself never once doubted that the South would win the war. As the conflict dragged on, however, the South's manpower reserves were drastically depleted. Increasingly, there were calls for the enlistment of slaves into the army. Robert E. Lee finally lent his support to this plan, even to the extent of offering freedom to those slaves who would fight for the Confederacy. Finally, on March 13, 1865, in the most desperate hours for the South, Davis signed the Negro Soldier Law, authorizing the enlistment of blacks but leaving their emancipation to their masters and to the states. A few regiments were raised, but the war was soon over.

When Richmond fell, Davis fled toward Mexico. Captured at Irwinville, Georgia, on May 10, 1865, he was imprisoned at Fort Monroe for two years but was never brought to trial, partly because the political status of the Confederate states during the war was never definitively settled. Two former enemies of the South, Horace Greeley and Gerritt Smith, came forward, and Davis was released on their bond on May 13, 1867. The war had impoverished him, and he lived at Beauvoir, an estate near Biloxi, Mississippi, on the Gulf coast, owned (and later bequeathed to him) by Sarah Dorsey, a friend of his wife's.

In 1863 his former estate of Brierfield, as well as his brother's and some adjoining property — the whole Davis Bend area — had been taken over by the federal government to be leased free of charge to about 600 freedmen. The Davis Bend community was a highly successful experiment in which the freedmen governed themselves and profitably cultivated extensive cotton fields. However, by 1867 most of the white owners, including Davis's brother Joseph, had repossessed the land and the experiment ended.

Since Jefferson Davis refused to ask the federal government for a pardon, he himself retrieved none of his former privileges or properties. He spent three years writing *The Rise and Fall of the Confederate Government*. At 82 he died in New Orleans, on December 6, 1889.

Jefferson Davis's memory is honored by many white southerners. His birthday (or the first Monday in June) is a legal holiday in Alabama, Florida, Georgia, Mississippi, South Carolina, and Texas. The day is also a legal holiday in Kentucky, Louisiana, and Tennessee, but in those states it is observed as Confederate Memorial (or Decoration) Day (see also April 26, June 6, and June 9), when the graves of Civil War dead are decorated during suitable ceremonies. The United Daughters of the Confederacy, usually in conjunction with the Sons of Confederate Veterans and the Children of the Confederacy, plan, or play a prominent role in, most Confederate Memorial Day observances, including those on Davis's birthday. The exercises customarily include the placing of Confederate flags or flowers — usually red roses — on individual graves, and the placing of wreaths on monuments, as well as memorial addresses, prayers, musical tributes, the firing of salutes, and, often, the recitation of the Pledge of Allegiance to the Flag of the United States of America and the Salute to the Confederate Flag. Processions, pageants, or the presentation of awards may also be part of the proceedings. Frequently, June 3 is also the occasion for luncheons or meetings featuring addresses or films devoted to the life and contributions of Davis.

In Arkansas, Jefferson Davis's Birthday is noted not as a legal holiday but as a special memorial day, one of a half dozen days which that state so designates annually. Mississippi has honored Davis by donating a statue of him to Statuary Hall in the Capitol at Washington, D.C. It is the custom of the United Daughters of the Confederacy to place a wreath there annually, on or near his June 3 birthday.

The Sunday afternoon nearest Jefferson Davis's birthday is the time also for the Confederate Memorial Services held annually at Arlington National Cemetery in Virginia, where the Confederate Monument at Jackson Circle is the site of services conducted by the Confederate Memorial Committee. The committee's members are drawn from the various Confederate patriotic organizations in and around the Washington, D.C., area — notably the United Daughters of the Confederacy, the Sons of Confederate Veterans, and the Southern Relief Society. Before the ceremonies, the Children of the Confederacy decorate the graves of the Confederate soldiers buried around the monument, and there is always a brief prelude concert by the US Marine, Air Force, Army, or Navy band. Central to the ceremonies is the impressive wreath-laying ceremony, with the first wreath laid by the President of the United States or by his designated military aide. Other wreaths are laid in place by the commander in chief of the Sons of Confederate Veterans, the president general of the United Daughters of the Confederacy, and then by the presidents and commanders of Virginia, Maryland, and District of Columbia divisions of the various Confederate organizations.

Also central to the observance at Arlington

are the eulogy and tribute by a distinguished speaker honoring those who died in the service of the Confederacy. Musical selections customarily include the national anthem; "Dixie," which was first played at Jefferson Davis's inauguration as President of the Confederacy; and "How Firm a Foundation," which was the favorite hymn of Davis and of two other pivotal figures of the Confederacy, Robert E. Lee and Thomas Jonathan ("Stonewall") Jackson. The ceremonies begin with an invocation, a presentation of the colors, the Pledge of Allegiance to the Flag of the United States of America and the Salute to the Confederate Flag; they conclude with a benediction, the retiring of the colors, and the firing of three volleys. Afterwards, the assemblage moves to the Tomb of the Unknowns, where a memorial wreath is placed "in tribute to those who have served our country."

Arlington National Cemetery, on land once part of the Custis-Lee estate, was first used as a burial place in 1864, when Union soldiers who had died on the Civil War battlefields of Virginia were interred there. It was after a suggestion made by President William McKinley in 1898 that a plot was set apart for Confederate dead — many of them wounded prisoners who had died in Washington hospitals and had been buried in various parts of the District of Columbia. Following congressional action in keeping with the President's recommendation, they were disinterred and moved to Arlington, where they are today memorialized annually on the Sunday nearest Jefferson Davis's birthday.

Another notable ceremony in which Davis is honored on the anniversary of his birth is the annual Massing of the Flags ceremony, which takes place in Richmond with appropriate addresses and music and the presentation of flags of the various Southern states in the order of their secession declarations. (Several other states that contributed troops to the Confederacy also participate, making a total of 14.) This colorful event, which draws visitors from all over the South and beyond, is held at the Jefferson Davis Monument, one of the statues of Southern heroes that line Monument Avenue. The program is conducted by the United Daughters of the Confederacy with the cooperation of the Sons of the Confederate Veterans and the Children of the Confederacy. The governor of Virginia issues a statement of recognition, calling attention to the Massing of the Flags Ceremony and the UDC designation of June 3 as Jefferson Davis Day.

Also in Richmond, the Confederate Memorial Literary Society entertains members and guests annually on Jefferson Davis's birthday at a formal reception held on the main floor and in the gardens of its headquarters, the Museum of the Confederacy at 1201 East Clay Street. Several hundred persons attend this event in what is known as the White House of the Confederacy (it served as Davis's residence during the Civil War).

There are numerous monuments to Davis throughout the states of the Confederacy. In Jefferson Davis Memorial State Park at Irwinville, Georgia, a bronze bust marks the spot where he was captured by federal troops. Just outside Atlanta stands the 138-foot-high Stone Mountain Memorial to the Confederacy, carved on the face of a granite monolith towering over the 3,800 acres of the Historic Stone Mountain Park. On a scale with the carvings on Mount Rushmore in South Dakota, the relief images of Robert E. Lee, Stonewall Jackson, and Davis attract many visitors to the park each year.

The Jefferson Davis Monument State Shrine, on US 68 in Fairview, Kentucky, is the tallest concrete-cast obelisk in the world, standing 351 feet high. It marks Davis's birthplace and overlooks a 22-acre park. Nearby is a replica of the log home in which Davis was born. Similarly, Biloxi has preserved the estate of Beauvoir, where Davis spent the last 12 years of his life. After serving for 37 years as the Soldiers Home for Mississippi Civil War Veterans, it was turned into the Jefferson Davis Shrine and Memorial Gardens. On the 50 acres of landscaped grounds are the home, a museum with Confederate relics and Davis memorabilia, the library cottage where Davis wrote, a guest cottage, and a Confederate cemetery.

Montgomery, Alabama, has preserved the first White House of the Confederacy, where Jefferson Davis lived for three months, as a Confederate shrine. A bronze star embedded between columns of the portico of Alabama's state capitol at Montgomery marks the spot where Davis was inaugurated president of the Confederacy.

JUNE 4

Jack Jouett's Ride

This is a movable event. See note on page xxvi.

Jack Jouett Day, which commemorates an act of heroism during the American Revolution, is celebrated on the first Saturday in June in Charlottesville, Virginia, but deserves to be known more widely. Through the night of June 3 and into the dawn of June 4, 1781, young John Jouett Jr., always known as Jack, galloped at great peril for some 45 miles along an abandoned road to warn Governor Thomas Jefferson and the Virginia legislature that British dragoons were swooping down on them.

Born on December 7, 1754, in Albemarle

County, Virginia, Jack Jouett became a captain in the Virginia militia. He was the second son of the former Mourning Harris and John Jouett Sr., owner of the Swan Tavern at the county seat of Charlottesville, and a member of the American branch of the De Jouhet family, prominent French Huguenots who had fled to England after the revocation of the Edict of Nantes. Before the outbreak of the American Revolution young Jack Jouett, with 202 other citizens, had signed the Albemarle Declaration, renouncing allegiance to King George III of England. Later he had urged the acceptance of the Declaration of Independence in Virginia.

His father, who helped provision American troops during the Revolution, owned a farm six miles east of Louisa, Virginia, and presumably it was on his business that Jack Jouett Jr. was somewhere in the vicinity of Cuckoo Tavern, Louisa County, at the critical moment. To his amazement the captain saw Lieutenant Colonel Banastre Tarleton (known as the Hunting Leopard) sweep by at the head of 180 British dragoons and 70 mounted infantry. Jouett at once guessed that Tarleton's goal was the capture of Thomas Jefferson, then at his home, Monticello, near Charlottesville, and of the General Assembly of Virginia. As the Revolution progressed, the latter body had moved west — first from Williamsburg to Richmond and then from Richmond to Charlottesville — because a force under General Benedict Arnold was threatening Richmond. Tarleton's raid, ordered by Lieutenant General Lord Charles Cornwallis, was as yet completely unheralded, although Cuckoo Tavern was only a 24 hours' ride from Charlottesville in normal circumstances.

Jouett's alertness and courage, his guerrilla-like knowledge of the countryside, and the swiftness of his thoroughbred mare enabled him to accomplish his self-assigned mission. In the tensest of races, he covered the distance from Cuckoo Tavern to Charlottesville between about 10 o'clock at night and 4:30 the next morning. Since the British were on the main road, he had to use a track nearly impassable in places, and the lashing branches overhead are said to have permanently scarred his face. He narrowly escaped capture several times by the troops he was paralleling, and if it had not been just a day before the full moon, the ride would probably have been impossible.

Jouett arrived before dawn at Jefferson's mountaintop home, after crossing the Rivanna River at the Milton Ford and warning the colonists guarding it. He immediately roused Jefferson and his guests, giving them time to make plans coolly and to secure important papers. Nevertheless Jefferson barely escaped; he relied on his telescope to tell him when the enemy reached Charlottesville, and by that time a detachment was nearly upon him.

After a restorative glass of Madeira, Jouett had meanwhile remounted and dashed across the few miles from Monticello to Charlottesville to awaken the other legislators. They hastily convened and agreed to meet three days later at Staunton, in Virginia's Shenandoah Valley. Seven laggards — among them the renowned pioneer Daniel Boone—were captured by Tarleton's men, but the main group escaped.

By his warning, Jouett saved not only Jefferson, but three others who also had signed the Declaration of Independence — Richard Henry Lee, Thomas Nelson Jr., and Benjamin Harrison, ancestor of two future Presidents. Also saved were the famous orator Patrick Henry and John Tyler Sr., father of the President of that name. Had Jouett not steeled himself for his ride, these prominent rebels, who had given crucial leadership to the Revolution, almost certainly would have been taken into captivity and run the strong risk of trial for treason in Great Britain. At the time of Jouett's ride it was impossible for the colonists to guess that the British surrender at Yorktown was only months away. As of June 1781 fortune seemed to have turned against the colonists; removal of the Virginia leaders would have been a severe blow to American morale.

Safely in Staunton on June 15, 1781, Virginia's General Assembly passed a resolution commending Jouett for his "activity and enterprise" and ordering that he be presented with "an elegant sword and a pair of pistols as a memorial" of their high esteem for his service. The pistols were delivered in 1783, but the sword, ordered by Governor James Monroe from Paris, did not follow until 1804.

Two years after his tumultuous ride Jouett moved across the mountains to the wilderness part of Virginia, which would soon become the state of Kentucky. He settled first in Mercer County, near Harrodsburg. There he married Sallie Robards, sister of Lewis Robards, the husband of Rachel Donelson Robards, who later married Andrew Jackson. Since he sat in the Virginia General Assembly from Mercer County, Jack Jouett became involved in Lewis Robards' embittered efforts to divorce his wife by act of the legislature. However, Jouett was later a warm friend of Andrew Jackson and visited often at the Hermitage, Jackson's home outside Nashville, Tennessee. Jouett was also on close terms with Kentucky's great congressman Henry Clay. After urging the separation of Kentucky from Virginia at the convention in Danville, Jouett sat for several terms in the Kentucky legislature, first from Mercer County and then from Woodford County, to which he moved. He foresaw the importance of the bluegrass country in stock breeding and was a prime mover in importing horses and cattle from England.

Much against the wishes of Jack Jouett, his son Matthew Harris Jouett became a painter. Jack Jouett had hoped this most promising of his many children would become a "gentleman," and protested that Matthew Harris was "nothing but a damned sign painter." The "sign painter," in fact, was a portraitist of such sensitivity and skill that some critics have compared him favorably with Gilbert Stuart, briefly his teacher.

Jack Jouett died in 1822 at the age of 67 in Bath County, Kentucky. His burial place has been located in the family graveyard at Peeled Oak, Bath County. It has been said that "fame hung back from Jack Jouett." Until a resurgence of interest in Revolutionary War history in Charlottesville, the gripping ride of June 3–4, 1781, was largely forgotten. In 1922 the Jack Jouett Chapter of the Daughters of the American Revolution was organized in Charlottesville. Its members have worked to commemorate Jouett's exploit and to further his recognition. As a result of their efforts a Virginia state historical marker was placed at the approximate starting point of Jouett's ride in a highway triangle in the little community of Cuckoo, Virginia, where US routes 522 and 33 cross. To supplement the brief information on the marker, members of the DAR also placed a monument consisting of a boulder with a bronze tablet in Cuckoo. They also placed an engraved brass star at Monticello to commemorate Jouett's heroism. A sesquicentennial celebration of the ride was widely attended in Monticello in 1931. In 1940 the Virginia legislature proclaimed June 4 Jack Jouett Day and called upon the citizens to observe it annually. In 1938 Governor Chandler of Kentucky had proclaimed June 4 Jack Jouett Day for his state, but the proclamation expired after that year. A Kentucky historical highway marker noting Jouett's ride stands today at the old Jouett home in Woodford County, on the McCouns Ferry Road leading to the Kentucky River, south of Versailles. The house, which is privately owned, is not open to the public.

In recent years Jack Jouett Day has been observed chiefly at a meeting by the Jack Jouett Chapter of the DAR in Charlottesville with an address on Jouett's adventure. Guests and members of other DAR chapters are generally invited to these meetings. In 1975 a special Jack Jouett Day program took place at Castle Hill Plantation, 12 miles from Charlottesville. After addresses by the administrator of the Albemarle Bicentennial Commission and the regent of the Jack Jouett Chapter of the DAR, there followed a picnic, folksongs, and two performances of a pageant called Jack Jouett's Ride.

JUNE 5

Gold Clause Repealed

On June 5, 1933, Congress, by joint resolution, revoked the clause in federal and private obligations that stipulated that payment was to be made in gold. Henceforth legal-tender currency would be the accepted medium for fulfilling such contracts. This action, which came close to the end of Franklin Delano Roosevelt's famous first "100 Days" as President, was an attempt to make the government's then-recent abandonment of the gold standard more effective.

Under a gold standard monetary system the basic unit is a fixed weight of gold or is kept at the value of such a fixed weight. The Currency Act of March 14, 1900, had made the gold dollar, which weighed 25.8 grains, nine-tenths fine, the basic unit of value. The system was fiscally conservative in that it did not allow the money supply to keep pace with the world economy's increasing need for currency and because the provision that the holder of any type of American legal tender could exchange it for gold on demand discouraged any moves toward inflation.

Roosevelt, believing that the gold standard only reinforced the deflationary trend present in the Great Depression, which had plagued the nation since 1929, sought to secure greater control over the value of the dollar for the government. The President had plans to achieve recovery through monetary manipulation; he thought that a controlled devaluation of the dollar would encourage exports, raise domestic prices, and lead to an increase in production. A presidential proclamation on March 5, 1933, invalidated the redemption-in-gold provision of the Currency Act of 1900 and forbade the exportation of the metal without Treasury approval. The Emergency Banking Relief Act of March 9 authorized the secretary of the Treasury to call in all gold and gold certificates, and provided a maximum penalty of 10 years' imprisonment and a fine of $10,000 for those who hoarded the metal. On April 19 Roosevelt announced that the United States was no longer on the gold standard. This last measure meant that the government no longer recognized an obligation to meet international payments in the precious metal, and it represented an effort to give the US economy independence from that of the rest of the world.

The abandonment of the gold standard did boost prices temporarily as the exchange value of the dollar declined, but when winter approached, the economy faltered. Following the theories of Professors George Warren and Frank Pearson of Cornell University, the government again resorted to currency inflation and began to buy gold until its per-ounce value rose in December 1933 to $34.06 from the October level of $29.01.

Gold buying inhibited the deflation but afforded no panacea. Devaluation failed to stimulate prices because there was no concomitant increase in the money supply or in bank credit and because European nations quickly adjusted to the American inflation. President Roosevelt finally decided to stabilize the dollar, and, in accordance with the Gold Reserve Act of January 30, 1934, he set the price of the troublesome metal at $35 an ounce (thereby reducing the dollar to 59.06 percent of its pre-1933 gold content) and required the US Treasury to maintain a gold backing of only 25 percent for the Federal Reserve notes it issued. Thus from 1934 to 1970 the nation was on a modified gold standard, sometimes called a gold bullion standard. In 1970, however, the dollar was cut free from virtually any gold standard when the Treasury was no longer required to maintain even a 25 percent gold backing of its notes, and, as of December 31, 1974, the US government allowed private citizens to buy and sell gold as a commodity for the first time since 1933.

Portland Rose Festival

This is a movable event. See note on page xxvi.

Portland is renowned as the City of Roses and is the home of the famous Portland Rose Festival. Located on both banks of the Willamette River, near its confluence with the mighty Columbia, the city, Oregon's largest, is noted for attractive residential sections, parks, and flower gardens, which flourish in excellent growing conditions: clear air (despite extensive industry), fertile soil, and sufficient rainfall.

Portland's association with the rose extends back into the history of Oregon. Probably in the early 19th century, traders of the Hudson's Bay Company, carrying with them seeds of the wild rose from England, introduced the earliest roses into the Pacific Northwest. Finding a congenial home in the rich Oregon soil, the wild rose became known as the Oregon Sweet Briar and still flourishes in the Portland region. From the 1840s on, pioneers arriving by way of the Oregon Trail – the beaten path from Independence, Missouri, to the Willamette Valley — brought rose plants with them. Hastily erected log cabins and crude houses throughout the area were soon bedecked with roses; one variety in particular, which came to be known as the Mission Rose, grew from slips cut from a prolific parent bush located at the Jason Lee Methodist Mission near Salem.

Each June since 1907, with the exception of 1918 and 1926, Portland has staged an elaborate rose festival. Growing from a notable city event to one of America's outstanding civic pageants, the festival is the biggest event in Portland, as well as the world's largest celebration of the rose. It comprises events of a mardi-gras-like diversity, including a rose show, carnivals, sports events, stage entertainment, and a ski tournament on the slopes of Mt. Hood, east of the city. The climactic grand floral parade attracts bands, floats, and marching units from as far as 1,500 miles away.

The rose festival's origins go back to 1888, when Mrs. Henry L. Pittock held a rose show in a tent in her front yard at 10th and Washington streets, now called the Pittock Block, and invited her friends and neighbors to exhibit roses. On May 21, 1889, the Trinity Church Guild sponsored a rose show. During the next few years a rose show was part of either the flower festival held by the local women's club or the floral show held by the state horticultural society.

In 1902 the Portland Rose Society was organized. Mrs. J. C. Card was elected president and Mr. F. V. Holman first vice president. On June 10, 1904, the society, to supplement its annual exhibition, staged the Portland Rose Society Fiesta, highlighted by a floral parade with decorated carriages, bicycles, and automobiles. The fiesta was judged a success and was repeated in the two succeeding years.

As part of its Lewis and Clark Centennial Exposition, Portland presented on June 3, 1905, the greatest amateur rose show that had ever been held in the United States. It was remembered for the introduction of a new red rose named J. B. Clarke and for a speech by Mayor Harry Lane suggesting a Portland "festival of roses."

In 1906 F. V. Holman, who by then had risen to the presidency of the Portland Rose Society, carried forward the mayor's enthusiasm by proposing to some of the leading citizens that a festival be held in conjunction with the annual rose show. A plan was agreed upon, and on June 20 and June 21 twenty illuminated floats on flatcars, driven on the rail of Portland's electric trolley network, were the chief attractions of the first Rose Festival pageant. The festival also included an exhibition of 10,000 roses and other flowers in the Forestry Building and a parade of automobiles and horse-drawn carriages decorated with flowers. It was so brilliantly successful that within the month enthusiastic citizens, mostly businessmen, incorporated the Rose Festival Association with a capital stock of $10,000 and the declared purpose of holding an annual floral fete, which, it was thought, would call favorable attention to both the state of Oregon and the city of Portland.

The second festival, in 1908, lasted for a week, beginning on June 1. It was presided over by a "ruler" called Rex Oregonus, whose identity was kept secret until he removed his bushy beard at the festival's annual ball, and by Queen Flora, portrayed by Carrie Lee (Chamberlain) Wood, daughter of the governor of the state. Two US cruisers and five torpedo boats anchored in the harbor to do honor to the festival. As in the first year, there was an exhibition of flowers and a parade of decorated vehicles. In addition there was a nocturnal parade of allegorical floats depicting The Spirit of the Golden West.

By 1910, when the first moving pictures of the festival were taken, the automobile had so increased in popularity and efficiency that that year's festival had a procession five miles long of decorated cars and trucks. A train of six trolley cars was loaded with roses, and on one day of the week-long festival these flowers were thrown from the cars to the spectators lining the sidewalks. Another highlight was an aerial exhibition demonstrating the Preble dirigible.

In 1915 the rapidly growing festival was widely advertised by the slogan — selected from thousands in a contest — The Whole World Knows the Portland Rose. In subsequent years other promotional events advertised the city as a rose center. The Union Pacific named a crack train the *Portland Rose*. Members of the city's Women's Advertising Club met excursion and convention trains and handed each passenger a rose; they gave an honorary membership in the Mystic Order of the Rose to distinguished visitors, including Franklin Delano Roosevelt, Herbert Hoover, Ernestine Schumann-Heink, and Amelia Earhart, who were initiated with the pledge that they speak or write of Portland as the "city of roses." Rose cuttings were made available for free distribution; in 1946, a supply of 30,000 was exhausted in less than two hours.

Rex Oregonus was deposed in 1914 and since then a queen has ruled over the festival in his stead. From 1914 to 1930 she was chosen annually from among young Portland socialites; since 1930 the queen has been a Portland high school senior, chosen from a court of princesses, each of whom has been elected by the student body of her high school.

In 1911 some delegates of the Portland Commercial Club decided that a new civic organization would be useful to assist in the rose festival. The Royal Rosarians were organized the following year. In their function as official hosts, they handle most of the program pageantry and preside at the coronation of the festival queen. In addition, during the course of the festival, they conduct an impressive knighting ceremony in which honors of the "Realm of Rosaria" are bestowed upon prominent visitors. The members wear elegant white suits, each with an embroidered red rose on the left sleeve, and white hats and shoes.

By 1922 the Portland Rose Festival had become so popular that floats were entered in the parade not only from Portland but from other communities in Oregon, as well as from California, Washington, and British Columbia. As the festival increased in size, events were added or changed each successive year.

In 1970, the 62nd Rose Festival — Fantasy in Flower — attracted more than 500,000 visitors from all parts of the nation and many foreign countries. Now comprising 10 days of varied events, the festival begins annually on the Friday before Portland schools close for the summer. This prevacation scheduling not only coincides with the period when Portland's roses are likely to bloom most profusely; it also tends to guarantee the availability of the princesses of the royal court, who are from Portland high schools; the junior princesses, from grade schools; and the high school marching bands.

Representative of those held since, the 62nd festival began on Friday, June 5, with the official opening of the Rose Festival Center, an entertainment and exhibit headquarters open to the public. Center features generally include such attractions as stage shows, a circus, band concerts, hobby displays, commercial exhibits, ethnic food stands, concessions, and carnival rides. In 1970 sections were devoted to a gardeners' market and displays of foreign gifts, Oregon products, and Oregon arts and crafts.

Saturday and Sunday were marked by the Rose Festival drag races and the Marine Day events at Willamette Park. The two days of water sports and special aquatic exhibits began with an impressive parade of more than 100 festive yachts, which proceeded through the heart of Portland on the Willamette River before tying up at Swan Island. Waterskiing displays and boat races were among the attractions.

In the evening came the unique parade of hilarity known as the Merrykhana. Customarily the first of the festival's three big parades, the Merrykhana is a zany, circus-like event, quite unlike the dignified grand floral parade near the end of the festival.

Monday saw the opening of the Rose Festival tennis tournament at the Irvington Tennis Club, where top tennis players matched skills all week. The selection and coronation of the queen, one of the festival's major events, was staged on Monday evening at the Memorial Coliseum. Thousands of vociferous adherents of the 13 candidates attended. Opening music by the Rose Festival concert orchestra was followed by an introduction and welcome by the master of ceremonies and homage by the Royal Rosarian Honor Guard. After the presentation of the individual princesses, the judges chose the queen to rule the Realm of Rosaria in the coming year. Ceremonially invested with her jewel-studded crown, golden scepter, and robe, the new monarch was given the key to the city, delivered a proclamation to her "subjects," and departed majestically with her court to the strains of the recessional.

The schedule of events for Wednesday included the arrival of several Canadian ships, traditionally part of the "Rose Festival Fleet," which sailed under Portland's bridges and tied up for viewing at the Willamette's West Side Seawall. US naval vessels made their own impressive arrival at the same hour on the following afternoon.

Highlighting Thursday's events and dominating much of the festival's final three days was the opening of the Rose Show, at Portland's Masonic Temple. The oldest and largest rose show in the United States and one of the world's best, this exhibition draws up to 20,000 individual blossoms, an array of entries requiring a space the size of a football field. It includes roses of every variety, brought to Portland from all parts of Oregon and from as far away as Vancouver and Boise. The emphasis on roses continued on Friday, with the Royal Rosarians' "knighting" ceremony for new nobles, and the Junior Rose Festival parade — one of the nation's largest parades of youngsters, with over 10,000 participants. It was followed by the queen's ball in the evening.

The spectacular climax of the Portland Rose Festival is the grand floral parade on the festival's last Saturday. In 1970 the 11 divisions of the parade included 46 floats interspersed with marching bands and colorful foot and mounted units. Each year many outside communities and many organizations and companies participate by entering floats. Whether professional or amateur, the exhibitors work for weeks preparing their models, which must be completely decorated with fresh flowers only.

After the floats have completed the parade route through downtown Portland, they are taken to an area near the heart of the city, where the public is invited to admire the intricate craft.

In addition to the finals of the Rose Cup sports car races at Delta Park on June 14, the closing day of the festival also saw the finals of the Rose Festival tennis tournament at the Irvington Tennis Club. A chief attraction of the day was the Golden Rose ski tournament, held on the slopes of 11,245-foot Mt. Hood. A traditional event, the ski tournament draws national champions and expert collegiate skiers. Timberline Lodge is the site of the closing banquet ceremonies, after the winners have received their cups from the Portland Rose Festival queen.

JUNE 6

D Day, World War II

In the early hours of June 6, 1944, forces of the World War II Allies — American, British, Canadian, and French — set sail from England to launch an invasion of continental Europe. Across the cold waters of the English Channel, the greatest armada ever assembled made its way toward the beaches of Normandy in France. This D day assault, the product of three years of planning, broke the Nazi stranglehold on the Continent and led to the eventual surrender of Germany and its Axis partners.

British strategists had begun planning for an invasion of Europe after Germany's conquest of France in 1940 had driven the Allies from the Continent. At the Atlantic Conference of August 1941 the British outlined their strategy to the Americans. They envisioned the operation as a *coup de grâce* to be administered to the Nazis only after blockade, air bombardment, and internal subversive action had severely weakened Germany. Britain deeply wished to avoid repetition of the bloody infantry contests of World War I.

The attack by Japan, Germany's Far Eastern ally, on the US naval base at Pearl Harbor on December 7, 1941 brought the United States into the war against the Axis powers and introduced a new trend into the military planning; American strategists stressed the need to defeat Germany's ground forces in order to break the will to fight and did not want to delay the invasion of Europe until the Nazis were moribund. German successes on the eastern front against the USSR, which had been brought into the war on the Allied side in the summer of 1941, increased the necessity of striking early.

General Dwight D. Eisenhower, appointed on March 9, 1942, by US Chief of Staff General George C. Marshall to be head of the Operations Division of the War Department, strongly advocated an early cross-Channel invasion of Europe from England. For reasons of communications and logistics, England was best located to serve as the base of operations and it already had airfields from which to bombard Germany. Eisenhower considered the cross-Channel assault so vital that he argued that the United States should shift its focus of operations from the Atlantic to the Pacific theater if the Allies did not agree to the plan.

President Franklin D. Roosevelt approved the plans of the War Department and sent Marshall and presidential assistant Harry Hopkins to England to present arguments in favor of the cross-Channel invasion. The American envoys also impressed upon the British Chiefs of Staff the importance of allowing the American forces time to gain combat experience. The mission was a success: on April 14, 1942, the British endorsed the American plan for an invasion, and the Allies agreed to 1943 as the target date.

Meanwhile, British strategists suggested campaigns in North Africa or the Middle East to divert the Germans' attention from the hard-pressed Russians. Although American military men feared that such Mediterranean adventures might upset the scheduling of the main invasion, they reluctantly accepted the plan for a North African landing. However, execution of the African operation and initiation of the Italian campaign along with increased activity in the Southwest Pacific indeed delayed preparations for the European invasion: planners soon realized that the assault could not come until 1944.

In January 1943 at the Casablanca Conference, the British and American Combined Chiefs of Staff created an office to prepare for the invasion of northern Europe. Lieutenant General Sir Frederick Morgan of Britain became the Chief of Staff to the Supreme Allied Commander, who had not yet been named. COSSAC, as Morgan's office became known, immediately began planning and chose the beaches of Normandy as the landing site for the invasion. The Quadrant Conference of August 1943 approved Morgan's work, and the Teheran Conference in November gave the final approval to a May 1944 cross-Channel assault.

Most observers expected General Marshall to command the European invasion, but in December 1943 General Dwight D. Eisenhower, then the head of ETOUSA, the European Theater of Operations for the United States Army, received the appointment. Eisenhower had been battle-tested in the Mediterranean campaigns and had the personality necessary to keep the Anglo-American military alliance operating smoothly. Marshall continued as chief of staff, a post in which his strategic and organizational abilities were most valuable.

On January 17, 1944, Eisenhower took command of SHAEF, the Supreme Headquarters Allied Expeditionary Forces, which replaced COSSAC. British Air Chief Marshal Sir Arthur William Tedder became deputy supreme commander and American General Walter Bedell Smith became chief of staff. Admiral Sir Bertram

Ramsay and Air Chief Marshal Sir Trafford Leigh-Mallory commanded the naval and air elements of the Expeditionary Forces.

SHAEF devised plans for a Normandy landing to be followed by an advance across a wide front. After driving the Germans back across the Rhine River, the Allies would then envelop the industrialized Ruhr region. The final assault would thrust deep into Germany to destroy the Nazis in their homeland.

May 1944 was the month originally set for the invasion, but Eisenhower rescheduled it for June because this made it possible to increase the strike force from three to five divisions. Allied air forces made use of the delay and the good flying weather to attack Axis transportation centers and coastal defenses throughout the month of May. During the final month the Allied forces practiced their beach landing techniques.

SHAEF established three landing zones for the Allied armies. The British Second Army, composed of English and Canadian troops and commanded by Lieutenant General M. C. Dempsey, was to strike between Bayeux and Caen at beaches designated Sword, Juno, and Gold. Lieutenant General Omar Bradley's US First Army had two landing sites to the right (or west) of the British: the V Corps under Major General Leonard T. Gerow was to invade at Omaha Beach and the VII Corps under Major General J. Lawton Collins had Utah Beach on the right flank as its objective.

German defenses in Normandy were strong, but several factors favored the Allies. Field Marshal Gerd von Rundstedt, the German commander in chief for the west, expected that the Allied invasion would strike at Pas de Calais, near Belgium, where the Channel was narrowest, and not in Normandy. Hitler guessed that Normandy was the target, but his orders to strengthen defenses in that area came too late. Von Rundstedt thought that the enemy should be allowed to land and then be destroyed by well-placed mechanized reserves. Fortunately for the Allies, the Nazis accepted the belief of General Field Marshal Erwin Rommel, commander of German Army Group B in the Netherlands-Loire district, that the Germans must stop the invaders at the coast. Consequently, the Germans spread their defense along the coast and failed to keep a sufficient reserve force to counter penetration of their front lines. Allied air superiority further limited the Nazis' defensive capabilities.

Eisenhower's burden increased as D day approached. Plans called for the 82nd and 101st Airborne Divisions of the US Army to drop behind German lines, but Leigh-Mallory continued to argue that the jumps would bring excessive casualties. Omar Bradley argued that the airborne phase was absolutely necessary to prevent disaster at Utah Beach, and Eisenhower decided to follow his advice.

Factors of the moon, tide, and time of sunrise limited D day to June 5, 6, or 7. Early on the morning of June 4, Group Captain J. M. Stagg, chief Allied meteorologist, informed General Eisenhower that the weather on June 5 would be unfavorable because of 45-mile-per-hour winds expected to hit the Normandy beaches. Although June 4 was a beautiful day, with no visible hint of what the morrow held, Eisenhower took Stagg's advice and postponed the invasion for 24 hours. As Stagg had predicted, June 5 was stormy. But on the morning of the 5th the group captain was able to forecast acceptable weather for June 6. Eisenhower again accepted his word and set the assault for the following morning.

Late on the night of June 5, more than 900 planes and 100 gliders of the US Ninth Air Force took off from British fields with the parachute jumpers of the 82nd and 101st Divisions. Fog and heavy antiaircraft fire awaited them at the coast of France and caused the soldiers to land in groups scattered over a much larger area than planned. Yet Leigh-Mallory's fears proved unfounded, and the paratroopers, fighting in small groups, managed to secure bridges and access roads to Utah Beach. Their efforts contributed greatly to the battle's outcome.

In the early hours of June 6 the huge armada began to move across the Channel: 1,796 vessels carried the three British divisions and 931 ships the two American divisions. About halfway across the Channel, the faster combat vessels moved ahead to their predesignated positions while the transport vessels bearing the troops and equipment moved behind them.

An hour and one half before sunrise, the preliminary naval bombardment began. Ten minutes later, 480 B-24s dropped 1,285 tons of bombs on the mainland; but, unfortunately for the invaders, the projectiles landed behind, rather than on, the beach defenses. As the naval and air attack began, the transports, standing 11 miles offshore out of range of the German batteries, unloaded troops and equipment into smaller Landing Craft Transports (LCTs). The landing craft then undertook the hazardous run to the beaches.

Tanks comprised the first assault wave heading for Omaha Beach. The commander of the LCTs in the western sector of the beach recognized that the seas were too rough for normal procedures and brought even the amphibious tanks to the shoreline. An army captain in the eastern sector was not so prudent and lost 27 of his 32 amphibious tanks when he launched the tracked vehicles 5,000 yards from the beach.

Eight waves of infantrymen and one of artillery followed the tanks onto Omaha Beach. German defenses were even stronger than expected because Allied intelligence had missed the presence of the 352nd Infantry Division in the area. American casualties ran as high as 66 percent in some sectors of the beach, but the troops gradually pushed inland.

Utah Beach, unprotected by cliffs like those overlooking Omaha, posed fewer problems for the attacking Americans. The reservists and foreign volunteers comprising the Nazis' defending 709th Regiment lacked the martial qualities of the units encountered elsewhere. Moreover, poor communications made the Germans' situation worse; General Friedrich Dollman of the Seventh Army did not even learn of the attack until hours after it began.

In other D day landings British, Canadian, and French soldiers meanwhile successfully stormed Gold, Juno, and Sword beaches. Their experiences paralleled those of the Americans at Utah, rather than Omaha, Beach. By the end of the first day the Allies had established bases at each of the five invasion points.

The Normandy struggle continued until July. The American V Corps took Isigny, and on June 12 the VII Corps took the key city of Carentan. Then General Joseph ("Lightning Joe") Lawton Collins began a drive across the Cotentin Peninsula to capture the port city of Cherbourg. Obeying Hitler's orders to fight until the end, the Germans withstood a terrific pounding, but the battle came to a close on June 26 with the capture of the city and a large number of its defenders, including General Karl Wilhelm von Schlieben.

Approximately 130,000 men landed at Normandy during D day; 72,215 were British and Canadian, and 57,300 were American. The British dropped 7,900 paratroopers and the Americans 15,000. British and Canadian forces suffered more than 4,000 casualties, and about 6,000 Americans were killed or wounded.

A free Europe and unending rows of crosses in Normandy cemeteries are D day's most meaningful memorials. Each year simple D day ceremonies at the burial grounds commemorate the men who fell in the invasion. Along the Normandy coast, the hulks of half-submerged craft still protrude from Channel waters in mute witness to the day's losses. Surrounding beaches also provide sporadic reminders of the awesome battle as their sands occasionally surrender rusted rifles and helmets.

Special ceremonies marked the 20th anniversary of D day in 1964. Official representatives of the United States, Britain, Canada, and France laid wreaths and participated in services at cemeteries and seaside towns. From across the seas, survivors of the battle returned to the now peaceful scenes; General Dwight D. Eisenhower, former President of the United States, was perhaps the most famous of these visitors. He reminisced for the Columbia Broadcasting System as he returned to famous battlefield sites, including the column at Pointe du Hoc honoring the American rangers who scaled its sheer cliffs.

Britain's Royal Navy now uses Southwick House, in which Eisenhower made the final decision to launch the invasion, as its school of navigation and aircraft direction. The war map room in the building, located near Portsmouth, England, looks exactly as it did in 1944. Two clocks in the room read 6:25 A.M., the hour and minute of Eisenhower's approval of June 6 as D day.

General Eisenhower in June 1967 dedicated an 8-by-24-foot mural in the World War II Room of the museum at his alma mater, the US Military Academy at West Point. William Linzee Prescott, an army paratrooper with the 82nd Division on D day, created the painting, which West Point's class of 1944 commissioned. General J. Lawton Collins praised the mural, which depicts 7,000 yards of invasion beach, as giving an accurate impression of the confusion of the battle and the gallantry of the soldiers.

Among other ceremonies in 1969 marking the 25th anniversary of the D day invasion was one at the Eisenhower Center in Abilene, Kansas, opening a display of artifacts connected with the landing. Both the library and the nearby museum displayed weapons and other equipment. Among the items exhibited was a map of possible invasion points conceived by General Alfred Jodl, the German commander.

Confederate Memorial Day in Winchester, Virginia

The Civil War divided the nation into two armed camps, but the North and South shared a common grief in the staggering loss of life that both sides suffered during the conflict. No war in the history of the United States ever produced more casualties in proportion to the number of combatants involved; the Confederate army counted approximately 258,000 soldiers killed, while the Union dead numbered more than 359,000. Sorrow was so intense in the last days of the war and in the years that followed that a number of places in both the North and the South held special ceremonies to honor those who had fallen in battle. These services gradually became traditional. Today most of the country observes the national Memorial Day and most southern states take note of special Confederate memorial days. A number of these observances take place on the anniversary of events of special significance to particular localities. Of these, one notable example takes place in Winchester, Virginia, where June 6 has been commemorated each year since 1866.

During the Civil War the Shenandoah Valley, in which Winchester is located, was important to the Confederacy both as a source of provisions and as a possible route for an invasion of the North. Six major battles were fought in the vicinity of Winchester; the town changed hands more than 70 times as Confederate and Union forces alternately exercised control of the region. The extensive fighting that took place in the valley resulted in a large number of casualties: estimates of the number of Northern and Southern soldiers who died in the area of Winchester are generally placed at about 7,500.

Because of the exigencies of war, many of the battle dead were buried in hastily dug graves, and soon after the fighting ended the inappropriateness of these final resting places became apparent. As early as the spring of 1865 — only weeks after Robert E. Lee's surrender at Appomattox — farmers preparing to plant their fields in the area unearthed the bodies of several Confederate soldiers. The likelihood that such desecration would recur greatly disturbed one citizen of Winchester, Mrs. Philip Williams, who had headed the town's women's relief corps during the war, and she determined to secure a proper resting place for the Southern war dead.

Together with her sister-in-law, Mrs. A. H. H. Boyd, Mrs. Williams organized the women who had nursed and otherwise assisted the soldiers who had fought in the vicinity of Winchester into the Ladies Confederate Memorial Association. The avowed purposes of the association were to reinter in one graveyard all those who had died for the Confederate cause within a 12- or-15-mile radius of Winchester; and to encourage people of the region to come to the proposed cemetery each year to decorate the grave sites with flowers and evergreens. To finance the purchase of land for the cemetery, the association and a committee of town representatives appealed to the citizens of the South. The economic plight of the former Confederate states after the war was desperate, but the Winchester appeal received an overwhelmingly favorable response. By the spring of 1866 sufficient funds were accumulated so that the association could buy land for the cemetery and begin the arduous task of reinterment.

The work of removing to a single graveyard the bodies of the 2,494 Confederate dead who were buried in graves scattered in the Winchester area proceeded rapidly. By the fall of 1866 the reinterment was completed, and on October 25 of that year Stonewall Cemetery was officially dedicated. Thousands of persons were on hand for the solemn and impressive October 25 services. Former Virginia governor Henry A. Wise addressed the assembly, and the remains of General Turner Ashby, a wealthy and influential Shenandoah Valley planter and politician who had died on June 6, 1862, during a rearguard action at Harrisonburg, Virginia, were brought from the University of Virginia to their final resting place at Stonewall Cemetery.

According to the plan devised by the Ladies Confederate Memorial Association and the Winchester town committee, each of the Confederate states was assigned a separate lot in Stonewall Cemetery, in which were buried the dead of that state whose remains could be identified. A headboard recording the name, rank, company, and regiment of the deceased originally stood at each gravesite, but most of these wooden markers have since been replaced by marble or granite headstones. In addition the 815 unknown dead in the graveyard have also been remembered. The bodies of the unknown soldiers occupy the center mound of the cemetery, and in 1879 the Ladies Memorial Association erected a marble monument — believed to be the first such tribute to unknown dead — which stands almost 50 feet high and which is inscribed with the words "Who they were, none know, What they were, all know."

Since 1866, June 6, the anniversary of the death of General Ashby, has been observed as a memorial day in Winchester. In recent years ceremonies marking the occasion have taken place on the Sunday afternoon nearest June 6, but despite this change of date, the services remain true to the intention of the founders of the Ladies Memorial Association, who wanted to honor the fallen soldiers of the Confederacy. Under the sponsorship of the Turner Ashby Chapter of the United Daughters of the Confederacy and the Turner Ashby Junior Chapter of the Children of the Confederacy, assisted by the reactivated Company K, 5th Virginia Regiment, each of the state monuments in Stonewall Cemetery is decorated with a large state flag, two Confederate flags are unfurled from the Monument to the Unknown, and a memorial flag is placed on each of the individual graves.

The Winchester memorial services in Stonewall Cemetery attract a considerable audience — particularly from Virginia and West Virginia. Generally included in the day's program are such events as a salute to the flags, recitation of poetry, an address by a noted speaker, and choral presentations. The ceremonies end with the traditional firing of a volley and playing of taps.

Winchester is also the site of a large national cemetery where approximately 4,500 Union soldiers who died in the Shenandoah Valley battles have been buried. In addition General Philip Sheridan's Headquarters at the corner of Piccadilly and Braddock streets and General Stonewall Jackson's Headquarters on North Braddock Street are noteworthy places of interest for many visitors.

YMCA Founded

Although it consisted of only 12 members at its birth in London on June 6, 1844, the Young Men's Christian Association was destined to have a strong worldwide impact before many years had passed. It grew healthily from the first. Within seven years, a YMCA was founded in the United States, in Boston. The movement, which supports all activities (social, physical, educational, religious) that help men, women, boys, and girls realize their full potential as persons, in the late 1970s had over 9 million members and program participants in the United States and many millions more in 86 countries around the globe.

Its sister but unaffiliated organization, the Yonng Women's Christian Association, had its beginnings in England 11 years later than the YMCA. In the late 1970s YWCAs in the United States had nearly 2,500,000 members. The World YWCA, comprising millions of members in 81 national associations, is one of the largest international women's organizations.

George Williams was the young man whose idea sparked the creation of the YMCA. He was born on October 11, 1821. At the age of 15 he left his farm home in Dulverton, Somerset, to work in London. With the advent of the Industrial Revolution, many young men migrated from rural areas to newly developing urban areas, which were ill prepared to cope with the influx. Such communities offered little in the way of diversion or intellectual stimulation, and large numbers of those who were separated from their families were drawn to gambling halls, saloons, and brothels.

Deeply disturbed by what he felt to be a general lack of religion, Williams began to organize prayer meetings for his London coworkers and in some nearby villages. As enthusiasm grew, a Bible class was started, and missionary and literary societies were formed. The owner of the dry-goods firm (George Hitchcock and Company) for which Williams was a clerk became a supporter and made larger quarters in the shop available for meetings. Meanwhile, prayer groups had sprung up among workers in other companies.

On June 6, 1844, Williams proposed to a meeting of members of his and another business house that they form a "Society for Improving the Spiritual Condition of Young Men engaged in the drapery and other trades." The proposal was unanimously approved, and the name Young Men's Christian Association was given to the society thus created. A reading room was established to serve as the center for its activities, which consisted primarily of discussions, lectures, personal counseling, Bible study, and prayer meetings. The society grew rapidly, and branches were formed in various cities. By 1851 there were 24 YMCAs, with a total of 2,700 members, functioning in Great Britain.

The founders' enthusiasm impelled the movement across the English Channel to seek fertile soil in Europe. It took hold so well that 30,360 young men were active in 397 "Y"s in seven European countries by 1854. The international body now known as the World Alliance of Young Men's Christian Associations was formed the following year in Paris, during the first world conference of YMCAs. Williams, who remained very active in the association, was knighted for his work by Queen Victoria in 1894, eleven years before his death.

Among the first YMCAs to be formed outside Great Britain was the one founded in Boston in 1851. Upon reading an article about the London Y, Thomas V. Sullivan, a retired sea captain who had thrown himself into religious work and was making news as a "missionary-at-large" on the Boston waterfront, knew he had come to the end of his search for an instrument through which to broaden his work. He brought together more than 30 young men to discuss his idea, and on December 29, 1851, in the chapel of the historic Old South Meeting House, the Boston YMCA was founded on the same principles as those of the London society.

Within three years 48 other Ys had sprung up across the country, and they continued to multiply. In 1854 the YMCAs of Canada (where a Y had been formed in Montreal a month before the one in Boston) and those of the United States joined in a cooperative International Committee. Not until 1924 did the US associations organize their own separate National Council (though the International Committee also continued to function).

The emphases of American YMCAs broadened considerably beginning in the late 1850s, when classes in language, music, and gymnastics were first offered. Branches were organized to serve special groups, such as railroad workers,

members of the armed forces, college students, and increasingly large numbers of rural young men who were moving to the cities. The maintenance of residences became an important service. The success and influence of the YMCA movement may be seen in the establishment of counterpart Jewish organizations, Young Men's Hebrew Associations, founded in Baltimore in 1854 and in New York City in 1874.

Around 1900, YMCA night schools and classes in industrial education were instituted. Physical and social recreation were stressed. Physical fitness became a byword, and the Y early assumed a position of leadership in offering swimming and water-safety instruction. Both basketball and volleyball were invented by Y staff members during the 1890s.

One of the major YMCA programs involves the Hi-Y (boys), Tri-Hi-Y (girls), and Co-Ed Hi-Y groups for those of high school age. These teenagers are encouraged to develop their resourcefulness and are able to influence Y policy. In the context of citizenship training, they also learn how their state (and sometimes national) governments function, in part through field trips. The junior-high-age groups (Junior Hi-Y and Junior Tri-Hi-Y) and grade-school-age groups (Gra-Y and Tri-Gra-Y) are more largely recreational in nature. Other activities especially popular among youngsters are camping and various parent-child activities, especially the Y-Indian Guide program for fathers and sons.

Cultural activities of all types are sponsored by the YMCA, including orchestral groups and public-affairs forums. The range in classroom instruction is as wide and includes vocational training. Programs are adapted to the needs of the times; in recent years, increasing emphasis has been placed on guidance and education for both youth and adults in the areas of drug abuse and health and fitness, including sex education, and on serving the needs of families and senior citizens.

A new idea took shape in the early 1970s, when the YMCA assisted in setting up Metro Centers in various cities. Never housed in Y buildings, the centers are operated by and for young adults, almost entirely on a voluntary basis. Their activities emcompass whatever the young people decide upon; such diverse projects as a theater, bookshop, food cooperative, and coffee house have been put into operation. Each center has its own individual name.

During the late 1960s, YMCA community-outreach workers began to seek contact with adolescents to help them cope with their special difficulties: alienation, aimlessness, lack of communication, unemployment, drug addiction, and out-of-wedlock pregnancy. Mobile units are often used to provide visibility for the program. In addition, a juvenile-justice program was initiated in urban areas across the country. In the belief that correctional institutions can do more harm than good and that communities can best solve their own problems, the Y works to obtain custody of juvenile offenders. The juveniles then receive counseling while living either at home or in Y facilities in the community and participating as much as possible in normal community life. In this project, the YMCA is working together with other organizations that have similar goals, including the Young Women's Christian Association on a local level.

The Armed Services Department had its origin at the time of the Civil War, when the YMCA became deeply involved in rendering aid to the fighting men of both the Union and the Confederacy, offering social and moral support and helping the wounded and prisoners of war. The department has since provided recreational, spiritual, and welfare services on a large scale during times of war and has worked with prisoners through neutral countries. Beginning with World War II, when the YMCA became a founding member of the United Service Organizations (USO), this work has been done in cooperation with other USO members. Civilian YMCAs offer special services to off-duty members of the armed forces. Also of significance in the history of the American YMCA was its sponsorship of both the Boy Scouts of America and the Camp Fire Girls when they were founded.

The YMCAs of the United States are linked through the National Council of YMCAs, and most are affiliated also with a state or regional body. Each individual Y, however, is autonomous and develops its own program. The organization, Protestant in its origins, is dedicated to Christian ideals and values but has no religious qualification for membership and is affiliated with no church. Membership is open to everyone, with no restrictions.

The various national "Y" bodies are affiliated through the World Alliance of YMCAs, which has its headquarters in Geneva, Switzerland. Substantial contributions have been made by the US Young Men's Christian Associations to the expansion of the movement throughout the world. American leadership and financial assistance are given to developing Ys in many other countries. The goal of these Ys is to become self-sustaining, and the amount of assistance is reduced in stages as it is replaced by local support.

Cultural and industrial exchange programs with countries around the world, including Communist nations, are sponsored by the American YMCA. A principal focus in these exchanges is a concern with the problems of people. There is also contact with Communist youth at international youth conferences, some held under Y auspices, and in a camping exchange program with the Soviet Union under which American youths and camp administrators have spent time in the USSR and Soviet administrators and counselors have come to the United States.

The founding of the Young Women's Christian Association had an impetus similar to that of the founding of the Young Men's Christian Association. In 1855 two organizations dedicated to improving the situation of women were formed by women in England. The General Female Training Institute was founded by Mary Jane Kinnaird (Lady Kinnaird) primarily to house nurses returning from the Crimean War. Concern for the spiritual needs of all women prompted Emma Robarts to form the Prayer Union. In 1859 the two merged as the Young Women's Christian Association.

The plight of young women drawn to the cities as a result of the Industrial Revolution was at least as bad as that of the men. In the United States their need for guidance, housing, and opportunities for recreation soon brought about the founding of the first American YWCA. Its genesis was in the Prayer Union Circle, almost immediately renamed the Ladies' Christian Association, formed by Caroline D. Roberts in 1858 in New York City.

Eight years later a YWCA was established in Boston, and thereafter the movement spread rapidly, as the YMCA had for a number of years. Help in securing jobs was another need that was soon met, through placement service and vocational training. Classes were offered in penmanship, bookkeeping, stenography, sewing-machine operation, practical nursing, and, when it was decided that females were strong enough, typing (or "typewriting," as it was called). Other activities included group singing and classes in astronomy, physiology, and calisthenics. Swimming became a major activity in the 1890s and remains an important part of the extensive health, physical education, and recreation program.

Establishment of its first summer camp, Sea Rest, at Asbury Park, New Jersey, in 1874, made inexpensive vacations possible for working women. Today, the YWCA also maintains many day camps and child-care centers (it pioneered in the field of day nurseries).

The YWCA's development in many ways paralleled that of the YMCA. Residences have been maintained, classes in a broad range of subjects offered, and opportunities for recreation provided. The autonomous local YWCAs belong to the Young Women's Christian Association of the United States of America, in an organizational pattern similar to that of the YMCA. All females over 12 may become members; there are no other qualifications. Males, and girls under 12, may join as associate members, participating in the educational and recreational activities. Family involvement has been stressed in recent years, with hobbies, sports, and camping among the activities enjoyed by parents and children together. Programs for senior citizens have also been organized. The Y-Teen program includes citizenship training and service projects as well as educational, recreational, and social activities. Younger girls may take part in a number of activities. A YWCA goal is to provide for individual development, emphasizing group thinking, working, and acting.

As circumstances and needs have changed, the concerns and activities of the YWCA have changed in emphasis, though not in purpose. In its attempts to improve conditions for working women, the YWCA early pressed for an eight-hour working day, prohibition of night work, and the right of labor to organize. It was an early advocate of unemployment insurance, and later it supported the Equal Rights Amendment. Considering its members to be citizens of the world, the organization has taken stands on international issues; for example, it declared itself in favor of US membership in the League of Nations and the Permanent Court of Justice at The Hague.

A number of independent organizations had their birth in the YWCA, among them the National Travelers' Aid Association, the National Federation of Business and Professional Women's Clubs, and the American Council for Nationalities Service. Like the YMCA, the YWCA also was one of the founding members of the United Service Organizations (USO), through which it continues a program of assistance to armed forces personnel that was begun during World War I.

By 1894 the YWCA movement had become such a significant force that the World Young Women's Christian Association was founded to link the various national bodies, including the YWCA of the USA. Its headquarters are in Geneva, Switzerland. In a program similar to that of the US Young Men's Christian Associations, the US Young Women's Christian Associations cooperate with other national YWCA bodies through the World YWCA to provide personnel and financial assistance for YWCA development in other countries. In addition to its leadership-training work abroad, the American YWCA regularly invites foreign staff and volunteers for study, experience, and observation in the United States.

During National YWCA Week, observed each year during the last full week of April, YWCAs across the United States participate in a concentrated effort to make the organization and its work known to the public and to potential members.

The World YMCA-YWCA Week of Prayer and World Fellowship is observed internationally by members of both organizations during the second week of November each year. (In the United States, it is called the World Mutual Service Week.) The week is dedicated to prayers for peace and better understanding among all peoples and to increasing the sense of belonging among member bodies of these multinational brother-sister organizations.

Fiesta of Five Flags
Pensacola, Florida

This is a movable event. See note on page xxvi.

Not many cities in the United States can claim to have been under the jurisdiction of five different national governments at different periods of their history. Pensacola, Florida, can. It was Spanish (1559–1562, 1696–1719, 1723–1763, and 1781–1821), French (1719–1723), and British (1763–1781). Ceded to the United States in 1821 and made a state in 1845, Florida, including Pensacola, became part of the Confederate States of America during the Civil War. The full privileges of statehood were restored in 1868.

Pensacola has other claims on history as well. Although St. Augustine was the country's first permanent European settlement, Pensacola actually was founded six years earlier, in 1559, with the landing of the Spanish Don Tristán de Luna and a group of Dominican missionaries on what is now known as Pensacola Beach. This is on Santa Rosa Island, across Pensacola Bay from mainland Pensacola, and it was the site of the country's first Christian service of worship. Although a disastrous hurricane and other misfortune forced the abandonment of Pensacola in 1562, it was resettled in 1696 by the Spanish, who — like others later — coveted it as the most valuable natural harbor on the Gulf Coast. The harbor was subsequently contested in battle seven times.

As the harbor attracted early settlers, Pensacola's climate later was a magnet to the US Navy, which established its Naval Air Station there in 1914. More recently the area has been known to tourists for its white beaches and its 400-mile coastline of salt and fresh water.

It was this history and these attributes that

members of Pensacola's Chamber of Commerce contemplated in December of 1949, when they set out to attract visitors to the long-overlooked Florida panhandle region where Pensacola is located. What they hoped to establish was some appropriate event — a successor, perhaps, to the city's Mardi Gras festival, which had been discontinued with the advent of World War II. They planned as their focal point a reenactment of the landing of Don Tristán de Luna and the presentation of an authentically attired queen and court of knights and princesses in a historically accurate pageant. As with King Rex of the New Orleans Mardi Gras, the identity of the person chosen to portray Don Tristán was to be a closely guarded secret each year, with much suspense until the moment of unmasking. The idea for this Fiesta of Five Flags — to which parades, treasure hunts, beauty contests, dances, and an abundance of water sports were added — met with immediate acceptance, although it was decided at the outset that it was too big an undertaking for the chamber of commerce to handle alone.

Within weeks a nonprofit, independent organization was formed to manage the fiesta. The first Fiesta of Five Flags took place in 1950, with 16 events and a budget of $35,000. By 1973 the number of events had grown to 57 and the budget to about $85,000. Annual attendance, which is now likely to exceed 50,000 persons, has grown steadily. Sponsored by contributions from the city of Pensacola, the county of Escambia, the Santa Rosa Island Authority, corporations, industries, local merchants, and individuals, the Fiesta of Five Flags used to be held during the first full week of June (except in those years when June 1 marked the beginning of the first full week, in which case the festivities took place during the second full week of June). In 1972 and 1973 the fiesta took place in April, but in 1974 it was again scheduled for early June.

The main festivities are crowded into what is really nine days, although the highlights are concentrated in the period from de Luna's Wednesday evening landing through the La Fitte Masquerade Ball on Saturday night. Pre- and post-fiesta events extend for several months.

Among the principal fiesta events are the already mentioned de Luna landing and pageant, which generally take place on Wednesday evening. An impressive yacht parade escorts Tristán de Luna to his encounter with Indian Chief Mayoki, in a reenactment of the meeting of their historic counterparts. Indian drums and authentic Indian dances complete the ceremony. The event is followed on Thursday with de Luna's own parade and ball. The highlight of

Friday is the Grand Fiesta parade with over 100 units usually participating. Saturday is Youth Day, starting off with a Youth Day parade and continuing with such events as a children's treasure hunt, and the finals of the Disneyland cartoon costume contest, initiated in 1966. Another big procession — the Krewe of La Fitte illuminated nighttime parade — also generally takes place on Saturday. Named for a privateer who terrorized early shipping, the parade is sponsored by the Krewe, a nonprofit fraternal group founded in 1954. Its members, who toss candy and trinkets instead of plundering, are costumed as masked buccaneers "sailing" on their parade floats. Following the crowning of La Fitte's queen (usually on the balcony-terrace of the San Carlos Hotel), guests attend a gala masquerade ball, at which Krewe members and their partners promenade at the municipal auditorium.

This is one of a number of public and private balls that take place during fiesta week. Among them are the previously mentioned de Luna Ball and Coronation, and the invitational Order of Tristan Ball, usually held on Friday evening. Other noteworthy fiesta events include an air show (the US Navy's Blue Angel flight demonstration team was the featured attraction in 1973), and there are square dancing, band concerts, and sandcastle-building contests. The sporting events that round out the Fiesta of Five Flags are legion. Usually included are archery, golf, bowling, and other tournaments; regattas; a waterski show; a model airplane meet; a spearfishing rodeo; and a surfboard contest. Pre-fiesta events often include special exhibits and antique shows.

In anticipation of the US bicentennial celebration in 1976, the fiesta planning committee decided to commemorate, each year after 1972, one of the five flags that have flown over Pensacola. For example, during the 24th annual Fiesta of Five Flags, held from April 25 through April 29, 1973, the festivities centered about the blue and gold fleur-de-lis of France and had as their theme *Vive la France*. That year the arts and culture of the period of French control were emphasized. In addition to the regular fiesta attractions, the French touch included French cooking lessons; exhibits of French costume dolls, posters and lithographs; a French flea market, puppet show, and sidewalk drawing contest; French flower sellers; an evening of French music and dances, and a "Tour de France of Pensacola" bicycle race. The French consul general in New Orleans, Jean Jacques Peyronnet, was the grand marshal for the de Luna parade.

JUNE 7

Boone Day

The annual Boone Day celebration held by the Kentucky Historical Society each June 7 took on special significance in 1969, the 200th anniversary of the day Daniel Boone, America's most famous frontiersman, reportedly first glimpsed "Kentucke," the virgin woodland that would become the 15th state.

In 1969, as in most other years, the celebration was held in the society's headquarters, the Old State House in Frankfort, the capital of Kentucky. Members of the historical society and guests were addressed by the mayor of Frankfort and the governor of Kentucky. There was also a musical program, and later the cast and audience joined in the singing of "My Old Kentucky Home," Kentucky's state song, before consuming a buffet luncheon.

The June 7 date is taken from the writings of John Filson, a Kentucky pioneer born in Pennsylvania, who went to Kentucky in 1783 and taught school. Filson wrote a book, *The Discovery, Settlement and Present State of Kentucky*, published in 1784, with an appendix titled "The Adventures of Col. Daniel Boon." The information in the appendix, written in the first person, supposedly came from Boone, although Filson was the actual author. The schoolmaster's style apparently pleased the unlettered Boone, who declared that every word of Filson's account was true. Historians, however, do not consider the work completely reliable.

Whatever historical inaccuracies may occur in Filson's book, it served to spread the name of Daniel Boone to people of many countries who were excited by the American adventure and the heroes of the New World. Boone became the prototype of the rugged individualist, courageous, self-sufficient, and highly intelligent. A number of editions of Filson's book were published, including several in London and Paris, and the Boone "autobiography" no doubt inspired the seven stanzas Lord Byron devoted to Boone in the eighth canto of *Don Juan*, published in 1823.

Boone was not the first white man to see Kentucky. Several others had preceded him. However, more than any other man, Boone literally opened Kentucky and the West to American settlers, physically leading them on foot by way of what is now called the Wilderness Road, through the Cumberland Gap.

Daniel Boone was born, probably on November 2, 1734, about 11 miles from Reading, Pennsylvania, of Quaker parents. His grandfather George Boone, a weaver and small farmer, had left his home near Exeter, England, and come to America in 1717, arriving in Philadelphia on October 10 of that year. His son, Squire (a name, not a title), followed his father's vocations and also raised stock and became a blacksmith.

Squire Boone's son Daniel, who had little or no regular schooling, helped in his father's work from early youth. By the time the boy was 12, he was an expert hunter; even before his father had given him his first rifle he had proved his marksmanship and hunting prowess with a spear.

As the spring thaw came to Pennsylvania in 1750, the family started for North Carolina. En route they stopped for about a year in the Shenandoah Valley, arriving at their destination — Buffalo Lick on the north fork of the Yadkin River — in 1751. Four years later, when a contingent of North Carolina militia joined a British military expedition against the French stronghold of Fort Duquesne (now Pittsburgh), Daniel Boone went along as a wagoner and may even have met the British commander's aide-de-camp, the 23-year-old Colonel George Washington.

General Edward Braddock, commander of British forces in North America and leader of the expedition, had been in America only five months. He and his British regulars were unfamiliar with Indian fighting methods and, scornful of the colonials, ignored their warnings and suggestions. On July 9, 1755, while crossing the Monongahela River, Braddock and his men were attacked by a French and Indian force of about half their number, and the battle turned into a bloody rout. Two-thirds of Braddock's troops were killed or wounded. Braddock himself was mortally wounded and died four days later.

Boone escaped on one of his horses, as did John Finley, a Virginia hunter and trader who, like Boone, had joined Braddock as a wagoner. The acquaintance of the two men was to prove significant. Finley had already been to Kentucky and with great excitement described the wilderness to Boone.

Boone returned home to North Carolina where, on August 14, 1756, he married 17-year-old Rebeccah Bryan, a neighbor. She was to bear 10 children, and she may have inspired Boone's famous saying that all a man needed was a good gun, a good horse, and a good wife. In 1759 he moved his young family to Virginia, away from the threat of local Cherokees, who bitterly resented settlements in what had historically been their domain.

Over the next few years Boone probably took part in other battles of the French and Indian War, which continued until its official conclusion with the Treaty of Paris of 1763, which expelled the French from Canada and the Ohio Valley. The British followed up their victory over the French by moving to eliminate several sources of friction in the New World. One such British move, based on the belief that encroachment by settlers lay at the root of Indian unrest, was the issuing of the Proclamation of 1763. The document, which forbade settlement west of the Appalachian Mountains, was widely ignored by frontiersmen and land speculators. (Indeed it was increasingly a source of annoyance to would-be settlers. In the end it was simply one more on the list of colonial grievances against the British crown before the American Revolution.)

Boone, always restless, and eager for new areas to explore, was fascinated by stories about Florida, which the British took from Spain in 1763. After a visit to Florida, Boone returned home in 1765 and declared that he would like to settle in Pensacola. His wife, however, objected and Boone abandoned the project.

Some time later, when John Finley visited Boone, the two men decided to head for Kentucky. Setting out on May 1, 1769, Finley, Boone, and Boone's brother-in-law, John Stuart, took along three other men to act as skinners and camp aides. The party evidently passed through the Cumberland Gap on June 7, and made camp in what is now Estill County in Kentucky.

In the next four or five months the exploring-hunting party accumulated many pelts and hides; and Boone and Stuart were captured by Shawnees. By the time the two were released and returned to their party, the other men, even Finley, had had their fill of Kentucky and were ready to head back to the settlements.

About the time Finley and the skinners left, Boone's brother Squire appeared, accompanied by a man named Neeley. Some time later Stuart set out alone to hunt or explore and never returned to camp. The Boones and Neeley waited anxiously at their winter camp site for Stuart to return. But after a while Neeley, who could stand the wilderness no longer, also set off for the settlements. (It was not until five years later that Boone, while clearing the Wilderness Road, came upon what might have been a clue to John Stuart's fate: a powder horn initialed J. S., not far from a human skeleton.)

When Squire Boone had to go back to civilization in May 1770 to sell the brothers' accumulated pelts and get more ammunition, Daniel was left alone for what turned out to be three delightful months of exploring this virgin land of beautiful hills and trees, and all manner of wild animals. It may have been the happiest three months of Boone's life. At some time during this period another group of hunters, supposing themselves alone in the wilderness, were frightened by what seemed to them the sound of weird howling, unlike anything they had ever heard before. Investigation showed, however, that it was "only [Boone] . . . lying on a deerskin, alone in the wilderness, singing to the sunset out of his joyous heart."

Squire Boone returned to the base camp on July 27, and the Boones continued their long hunt until March 1771, when they gathered up their valuable pelts and furs — including buffalo and bear — and at last started home. On the way Indians attacked them and spared their lives, but robbed them of their furs, so the two brothers arrived home empty-handed, with many stories to tell, but nothing to show for their last eight months of hunting. Even so, Boone had seen Kentucky and knew he would return to live there.

In September 1773, with about 40 others, including his own family, Boone set out for the Kentucky region with packhorses, livestock, and other supplies, and plans to settle. However, his group was driven back by Indians, who killed some of their number, including Boone's oldest son, 16-year-old James.

After the Powell Valley Massacre, as the settlers were to call it, most of the group returned to North Carolina, but Boone and his family spent the winter on the neighboring Clinch River, where they found an abandoned cabin. In May 1774 Boone set off alone to stand once more at the side of his son's grave in Powell Valley. Boone was later to describe the visit as the most melancholy moment of his life.

One of the men interested in land speculation west of the Appalachians was the Scottish peer Lord Dunmore, then British colonial governor of Virginia. He had sent out several parties of surveyors to Kentucky, and some of them were still there when the war between Virginians and Indians, which came to be known as Lord Dunmore's War, broke out. Lord Dunmore assigned Boone to track down the surveyors and warn them of their danger. This Boone did, but before he returned he stopped to visit the new settlement of Harrodsburg, Kentucky, founded in 1774, which was to become Kentucky's first permanent settlement. A competent surveyor himself, he also took the time to lay off some lots and claim land. Then he headed back home to the Clinch, covering in all an 800-mile stretch of wilderness in two months.

Lord Dunmore's War was still raging, and Boone, a lieutenant of the Virginia militia, joined the Indian-fighting forces of Andrew Lewis and may have been one of the 1,100 frontiersmen who fought the Shawnee warriors led by Chief Cornstalk on October 10, 1774. As a result of that battle, which took place at Point Pleasant, in what is now West Virginia, Indian power was diminished in the Ohio Valley, and the way west was opened for additional white settlers.

Revolutionary sentiments meanwhile were already running high on the eastern seaboard. With official British attention concentrating on stifling the spark of revolt, speculators began to eye the rich land of Kentucky. Among them was Colonel Richard Henderson, a North Carolina attorney and a judge in the king's court. Like others he ignored the British prohibition against the westward movement of settlers across the Appalachians. Henderson and a group of men founded the Transylvania Company with the intention of opening to settlers most of present Kentucky, under the name Transylvania, which he hoped would be recognized as the 14th colony.

Boone now became an agent for Henderson's Transylvania Company and took on the assignment of exploring the territory, negotiating with the resident Cherokees, and leading settlers through the wilderness to their new land of Transylvania.

On March 17, 1775, about 1,000 Cherokees gathered at Sycamore Shoals on the Watauga River, near what is now Elizabethton, Tennessee, close to the North Carolina border. There, in exchange for £10,000 worth of trinkets and goods, Cherokee chiefs signed the treaty relinquishing Kentucky and deeding the land bounded by the Ohio and Kentucky rivers, and extending to the south watershed of the Cumberland River to Richard Henderson and his Transylvania Company.

Boone could not wait through the socializing and oratory that preceded the treaty; he was a week into his journey by the day of the actual signing. With the first division of settlers — 30 men wielding axes, and rifles when needed — Boone set out to mark and clear the 250 miles from the Long Island of the Holston River in northeastern Tennessee to the Kentucky River deep in the present state of Kentucky. Boone marked the pioneer trail that would be known as the Wilderness Road following the trace, or path, made by buffalo and Indians, clearing brush, chopping branches, blazing trees or using stone markers along the miles of mountain ridges, through almost impassable valleys and across rushing streams. The men in Boone's trailblazing party knew they were on a great adventure, and some of them kept diaries. One man wrote about a "turrible mountain that tried us all almost to death to git over it and we lodge this night . . . under a grait mountain & Roast a fine fat turkey for our supper."

There were other terrors of the trail. Indians, outraged at the intrusion, took their toll of the trailblazers, killing some and wounding others. Lest his band of men lose courage and bolt, Boone sent a message to Henderson to send down reinforcements to quickly "flusterate" the Indians, who were trying to drive the settlers out, and enable Boone and his men to "keep the country whilst we are in it."

Henderson and another group of settlers quickly set off for Kentucky, following the recently blazed trail. Although Boone and his men had clearly marked the trail, the literal wilderness of the Wilderness Road was still to be reckoned with. (It would be 20 years before wagons could be used on the trail but in those 20 years 100,000 people took themselves and their possessions over the mountainous passes and into Kentucky.)

On April 1, 1775, Boone and his men arrived at their destination and began building a fort. Their settlement, which was to become Boonesboro (or Boonesborough), was southeast of what is now Lexington, Kentucky. Henderson and his group were not too far behind. Once arrived, most of the men would not be kept within the protective walls of the fort, but set about claiming their own parcels of land, and building houses to which they could bring their wives. Under the aegis of Richard Henderson, Daniel and Squire Boone and delegates from other Kentucky settlements gathered on May 23, 1775, to decide the rules by which they would be governed.

During the next two years, while the 13 colonies were becoming increasingly involved in the War of Independence against Britain, Boone was fully occupied by hunting, trapping, surveying, and defending the new Kentucky settlements against Indians, whose raids and attacks were at least partly encouraged by British money. When Kentucky became a county of Virginia in late 1776, Boone was made a captain of the Virginia militia; he was later promoted to major and then lieutenant colonel.

In February 1778 Boone and a group of 30 Boonesboro men went to the Blue Licks on the Licking River to obtain salt for the settlement. Leaving the salt camp one day to check his beaver traps, Boone was captured by a war party. Taken back to the Shawnee camp, he learned from Chief Blackfish that the Indians were on their way to take Boonesboro.

Boone, famous for his speed in running, was also a fast thinker. He convinced Blackfish that the winter was no time to take the women and children of Boonesboro through the deep woods and up to the British commander in Detroit, who would buy the captives from the Indians. Instead, Boone suggested, he would talk the men at Blue Licks into surrendering if Blackfish promised they would not be tortured or humiliated by having to run the gauntlet. Blackfish agreed, the men surrendered, and the Indians made their way with their white captives to Detroit, where the prisoners were delivered into British hands — all except for Boone, whose popularity with the Shawnees was so high that they refused to sell him to the British commander. Instead they adopted him into their tribe as the son of Chief Blackfish and gave him the name Sheltowee, which means "big turtle." For months Boone lived with Shawnees as a captive they respected and made comfortable — but still a captive.

When Boone learned that the Shawnees were planning a full-scale attack on Boonesboro and that he, as the adopted son of the chief, was to go along and persuade the settlers to surrender, he escaped. He traveled so fast that the Indians were unable to catch him; he covered 160 miles in four days (three days on foot). He was a strange but welcome sight when he returned to Boonesboro, his head plucked free of his usually long hair except for the Shawnee-style scalp lock. Having warned the settlers of the imminent attack, Boone led a group of scouts and fighters north into Ohio to strike at the oncoming Indians and then raced back to help in the defense of Boonesboro. He got back to the fort on September 6, just a day before the arrival of Blackfish and 450 Shawnee warriors. Although there were only 50 rifles within Boonesboro's fortified walls, many of them fired by boys, the Indians were driven off.

After spending some time in the East, Boone returned to Kentucky with his family and more settlers in October 1779, and the next year he established Boone's Station near what is now Athens. It was also in 1780 that the county of Kentucky was divided into 3 parts, and Boone was elected to the Virginia legislature.

The Commonwealth of Kentucky was admitted to the Union as the 15th state on June 1, 1792. But Boone, in spite of his enormous service to Kentucky as a pioneer, founder, soldier, and legislator, now found himself bankrupt and in debt. He had laid claim to 100,000 acres of land, but had been careless about filing claims. That, plus the fact that Virginia had never recognized the Transylvania Company's original land claims, and the general confusion and incompetence of early land courts, left him with no defense to protect his property.

One by one a series of ejectment suits wiped out Boone's ownership of his many tracts of land. The first of these suits had begun in 1785. Boone moved in the spring of 1786 to Maysville, in northeastern Kentucky, where he was again elected to represent his community in the legislature. Maysville, which had been settled in about 1782, was a transportation center with a thriving commerce during the two-year period in which Boone and his wife ran a tavern and trading station there.

Late in 1788 Boone is thought to have left Kentucky and moved his family to Point Pleasant in what is now West Virginia. There he was appointed lieutenant colonel of Kanawha County and in 1791 was once again elected as a legislative representative. Learning that the Wilderness Road, which he had blazed almost 20 years before, was to be widened to accommodate wagons, Boone wrote to Isaac Shelby, Kentucky's first governor, whom he had known in the early Boonesboro days: "I think my Self intitled to the ofer of the Bisness as I first Marked out that Rode in March 1775 and Never rec'd anything for my trubel and Sepose I am no Statesman I am a Woodsman and think My Self as Capable of Marking and Cutting that Rode as any other Man."

Boone was unsuccessful, however, and after this disappointment and with his last tract of Kentucky land lost through an ejectment suit, a disgusted Boone put Kentucky behind him forever. In 1799 he set out for what is now Missouri — then part of the vast Spanish province of Louisiana. Boone, then 65, had unusually high physical stamina. He prepared for the trip out of Kentucky by felling a huge tree, which he made into a dugout to transport his wife, children, and household possessions down the Big Sandy River while he and some companions went on foot, herding the livestock all the way.

Once in Missouri, it seemed for a while that Boone had finally received the recognition he deserved. The Spanish officials of the area welcomed him warmly and granted him a large tract of land at the mouth of the Femme Osage Creek, near the Missouri River. On July 11, 1800, he was appointed chief magistrate for the Spanish crown of the Femme Osage District.

But here, again, land ownership became an uncertain thing. First, Spain ceded Louisiana to France in 1800. Then, only three years later, the vast province was sold to the United States in the Louisiana Purchase. Boone's land title, guaranteed by the Spanish governor, was voided by US land commissioners on technicalities.

Finally, after many government delays and many petitions by Boone, his large land holdings in Missouri were in part restored to him by direct intercession of Congress in 1814. Boone sold the land and traveled back to Kentucky to pay his debts — which left him with a great sense of satisfaction and, tradition says, 50 cents.

Boone's wife, Rebeccah, died in 1813 after 56 years of marriage. Boone went to live with his son, Nathan, in what was probably Missouri's first stone residence. He continued to hunt and trap and enjoy life until, at almost 86, he died on September 26, 1820. Missouri's territorial legislature went into mourning for Boone, the prototype of the American frontiersman. Just three years after his death, James Fenimore Cooper published the first of his Leatherstocking Tales — five novels whose central character some allege was based on Boone — dramatizing the clash between the frontier wilderness and encroaching civilization. Indirectly they helped to spread Boone's fame around the globe.

Although Boone and his wife both died in Missouri, their remains were returned to Frankfort, Kentucky, in 1845, where they were reinterred, and a monument was erected in memory of one of the most colorful figures of early America. The grave is in Frankfort Cemetery on East Main Street.

The Daniel Boone Homestead, where Boone was born and lived until he was 16, can be seen by visitors to Pennsylvania. It can be reached by driving seven miles east from Reading to Baumstown and then north for one mile. The homestead is on 600 acres, which provide nature trails and camping and picnicking facilities for the public except on a few holidays.

Boone, North Carolina, where the frontiersman had a cabin, is the site of a Daniel Boone Monument and replica museum, which overlooks the Yadkin River: Each summer Kermit Hunter's outdoor drama *Horn in the West*, staged in the Daniel Boone theater, a mile east of town off US route 421, can be seen nightly except Mondays from late June through late August.

In Missouri the Daniel Boone Home (c. 1803) near Wentzville, northwest of St. Louis, is authentically furnished. The museum, as well as camping and picnicking facilities, is open to the public at certain times of the year.

Visitors to Kentucky can see many places or events that honor Daniel Boone. The Daniel Boone National Forest in eastern Kentucky has 465,000 acres of spectacular scenery, which include the Red River Gorge, sometimes called the Little Grand Canyon of the East; the Natural Arch Scenic Area south of Somerset; and the Yahoo Falls Scenic Area.

At the Cumberland Gap National Historical Park, half a mile south of Middlesboro in the southeastern part of the state, visitors can hike over two miles of the Wilderness Road trail blazed by Boone. Barbourville, not far away, annually offers the Daniel Boone Festival in October to celebrate Boone's Kentucky explorations. Men grow beards for the occasion

and wear coonskin caps. Among other activities, there is a reenactment of the treaty signing by which the Cherokee relinquished the Kentucky area.

Elsewhere in the state, Fort Boonesborough State Park, southeast of Lexington, is eight miles south of Winchester, off US Route 227. On the site of Boonesboro, it offers picnicking, playground, and other recreation facilities, and a few historical reminders.

In Harrodsburg, Kentucky, which the explorer once visited, an outdoor drama, *The Legend of Daniel Boone*, is performed nightly except Mondays throughout the summer months at the Old Fort Harrod State Park Amphitheatre.

JUNE 8

Frank Lloyd Wright's Birthday

One of the most inventive of modern architects and, in the judgment of many, the greatest, was Frank Lloyd Wright. Cantankerous, opinionated, an iconoclast and a genius, he exerted an enormous influence on contemporary architecture in the United States and Europe.

The man who was to design more than 600 completed buildings and foment a revolution in design with his concepts of "organic architecture" — architecture, that is, in which buildings harmonize with their users and surroundings — was born on June 8, 1869, in Richland Center, Wisconsin. His interest in architecture already declared, he entered the University of Wisconsin at the age of 15, even though it had no courses in his subject. For this reason his formal training was in civil engineering, rather than in architecture, a fact that probably had a profound effect on his work: engineering was the tool around which he could wrap his originality, his daring, his willingness to innovate. It made possible his amazing variety as an architect and his fresh, flexible, imaginative approach to each new building.

With characteristic independence, Wright left the university in 1887, before graduating. He went to Chicago, took a job as a draftsman and, in 1888, designed his first executed work — a house for his aunts at Spring Green, Wisconsin. The same year, he went to work in the Chicago office of Louis Sullivan, who shared his aversion to classic form, taught him the basics of architecture, and instilled in him ideas for radical design. Sullivan, sometimes called the Father of Modern Architecture, was the only architect to whom Wright ever admitted a debt (though he later deplored the skyscraper construction in which Sullivan had pioneered). Wright, who at 19 became chief designer under Sullivan and his partner Dankmar Adler, was given a five-year contract, which enabled him to begin building his own house in suburban Oak Park in 1889 and to marry Catherine Lee Clark Tobin in 1890. They had six children.

It fell to Wright to handle most of the firm's residential commissions, while Sullivan and Adler concentrated on commercial buildings. Wright took on outside assignments also, a practice that led to a break with his employers.

Wright set up his own business in 1893 and turned out designs in keeping with his precepts of organic architecture. He held, for instance, that the style of a building should be subordinate to human needs; that it should seem to grow out of its surroundings and harmonize with them in the color and texture of its materials — which he chose with extraordinary respect and imagination; that interior space should be open, free, with a minimum of confining walls; that there should be, in effect, a blending of indoor and outdoor space. Rebelling against the conventional box, he built a series of long, low, ground-hugging houses with sweeping horizontal lines and overhanging eaves. This new form, known as "prairie style," became the basis of modern residential design. Two outstanding examples of this style are the Coonley house (1908) in Riverside, Illinois; and the Robie house (1909, now owned by the University of Chicago), which has been designated a national historical landmark by the US Department of the Interior.

Wright had already erected two nonresidential buildings, which became famous. One of these, the Larkin Company's administration building (1904) in Buffalo, New York, was the first office building to have air conditioning, doors of plate glass, double-glass windows, and all-metal furniture. The other building, the Unity Temple (1906) in Oak Park, Illinois, marked a turning point in the use of poured concrete for a monumental public building.

Wright went to Europe in 1909 in connection with the Berlin publication of a portfolio of his work, which had wide influence in Europe. After his return home he began work in Spring Green, Wisconsin, on Taliesin East, whose Welsh name means "shining brow." Designed to be a studio, farm, and school, as well as "a home where icicles by invitation might beautify the eaves," it was twice destroyed by fire (in 1914 and 1925) and twice rebuilt.

Wright's most notable work of the period, however, was his revolutionary design for the Imperial Hotel in earthquake-prone Tokyo. Completed in 1922, it was placed on a cushion of soft mud and employed a unique arrangement of concrete supports and cantilevered floors. An elastic edifice whose walls and floors had a sliding quality never before achieved, it was the only large structure in Tokyo to survive the disastrous earthquake of 1923.

The architect meanwhile had developed a new method of construction, which utilized precast concrete blocks threaded with steel reinforcing rods. Sometimes, as with the Millard house (1923) in Pasadena, the blocks would be pierced and patterned, giving the appearance of a kind of woven house.

Wright, who had married for a second time in 1922 and a third in 1928, set up his Taliesin Fellowship in 1932. Ultimately between 40 and 65 young architects studied with him each year, spending the April–November term at Taliesin East and the December–March term in Taliesin West, which Wright began constructing near Phoenix in 1938.

Wright wrote many books and frequently took to the lecture platform — as often as not to denounce the "international style" of modern architecture. In his later years he continued to turn out series of remarkable buildings. Perhaps the most outstanding was Fallingwater (1936), the E. J. Kaufmann house, spectacularly cantilevered over a waterfall in Bear Run, Pennsylvania. Along with a $500,000 endowment for its maintenance, the structure was presented in 1963 to the Western Pennsylvania Conservancy for use as a recreation center.

Wright's triumphs include the S. C. Johnson and Son administration building (1939) and research tower (1950) in Racine, Wisconsin; "Usonian" houses — among them the Friedman house near Pleasantville, New York — which he envisioned as ideal democratic American architecture; the V. C. Morris gift shop (1949) in San Francisco; and the Price Tower (1956) in Bartlesville, Oklahoma. One of his largest commissions was his design of 16 buildings planned for construction on the campus of Florida Southern College at Lakeland between 1936 and 1960.

Controversial to the last, Wright died at the age of 89 on April 9, 1959, in Phoenix — just a few months before his circular Guggenheim Museum, shaped in the form of a spiral ramp, opened in New York City amid a storm of comment, pro and con. Among projects of Wright's that have been completed since 1959 by his associates are two other circular buildings, the Greek Orthodox Church (1963) in Milwaukee and the Grady Gammage Auditorium of Arizona State University at Tempe (1964).

JUNE 9

Confederate Memorial Day in Petersburg, Virginia

The city of Petersburg, Virginia, observes June 9 as Confederate Memorial Day in commemoration of the heroic defense of the city on that day in 1864, during the Civil War. A crucial rail and supply center, Petersburg commanded the southern approach to the Confederate capital of Richmond, 22 miles to the north. Union General Ulysses S. Grant, leading General George G. Meade's Army of the Potomac, had tried to reach Richmond from the north, but had been kept at bay by the Army of Northern Virginia under General Robert E. Lee at the bloody battles of the Wilderness and Spotsylvania Court House in May 1864. Although neither of these operations was a Federal victory — together they cost the Union 33,000 men — Grant resumed his advance southward, and Lee was compelled to retreat.

Drawing nearly opposite Richmond at nearby Cold Harbor on June 3, Grant then attempted a major assault on the Confederate forces. He had, however, underestimated the staying power of Lee's army. Grant's force was defeated. Losing 12,000 men on that one day alone, the Union commander abandoned the idea of a direct onslaught on Richmond and sidestepped skillfully, withdrawing to the east. His plan now was to bypass Richmond and focus his attention on Petersburg, the life-sustaining funnel through which food and supplies had to pass to Richmond. If Petersburg could be taken, he reasoned, the Confederacy would surely fall. To accomplish the capture, he planned not merely to withdraw eastward from his own trenches, as his initial moves seemed to indicate, but to turn his withdrawal into a wide-swinging, reverse-"C" movement, which would take his men south across the James River and then abruptly westward toward Petersburg.

While the main armies of both Lee and Grant were still north of the James River, Grant's projected arrival at Petersburg was being preceded by an expedition sent out from the Army of the James for an advance thrust at Petersburg. Its purpose, in keeping with Grant's broad, overall strategy, was to see if the city might not be taken by a sudden onslaught even before Grant — who was detained north of the river while he masterminded complicated logistics and awaited the completion of several important missions — began to move.

As Grant had suspected, in view of the manpower requirements of the just-completed actions to the north, Petersburg was weakly held,

though it was strongly fortified. It was defended at the time by a 2,400-man brigade, under Brigadier General Henry Alexander Wise, which had been hastily reinforced, to some extent, by a contingent from the command of General P. G. T. Beauregard. Beauregard's main force, which would soon move up to Petersburg's defense, was then located at Bermuda Hundred, a short distance northeast, keeping an eye on the principal force of Major General Benjamin F. Butler, commanding officer of the Army of the James. The Confederates had largely bottled up the force of Butler behind his own defense lines, on Bermuda Hundred neck at the junction of the James and Appomattox rivers. Acting on Grant's orders, Butler nonetheless was able to send General Quincy A. Gillmore over the Appomattox River on June 9, at the head of what was to prove an abortive expedition against Petersburg. Had the Federals realized how lightly the city was held, and had General Gillmore not been hampered by the habitual caution he shared with Butler and other high-ranking officers in the Army of the James, Petersburg might have been taken at that time.

The Federal force, which numbered perhaps 4,500 men, approached the city by two routes. Encountering formidable earthworks on the City Point Road and suffering a repulse on the Jerusalem Plank Road, Gillmore concluded that the city was too strongly fortified to take. Thus thwarted, he turned back — and was abruptly relieved of his command by Butler. June 9, the day of this victory, is remembered by Petersburg as one of its hours of glory.

On the night of June 12 Grant began the delicate operation of moving his 100,000-man army east from Cold Harbor, completely misleading Lee, who still thought he meant to attack Richmond. Grant then made his sharp turn to the south, and on the night of June 14 began the carefully planned crossing of the James. It would take two days to complete.

Meanwhile Grant ordered Butler to reinforce Brigadier General William Farrar "Baldy" Smith's force and send it across the Appomattox River on the morning of June 15 to strike at Petersburg, this time with real muscle. The June 15 onslaught was the beginning of four days of repeated attacks and bloodshed. They were marked by valor on the part of soldiers on both sides. The performance of the rival leaders is also worthy of remark. For the Confederates these were days of extraordinary skill and leadership by General Beauregard, who now held the city but could muster no more than 9,000 infantry for his defense. However, for the Federal generals, who had at their disposal some 35,000 hard-fighting men, these were days of blunder, confusion, poor staff work, tangled communications, and missed opportunity — days in which, for one reason or another, the Union troops' initial hard-won advantage was never energetically pursued.

Now apprised of Grant's intentions, Lee, meanwhile, had begun moving south from Richmond. Before the lack of organization of Grant's subordinates, and those on whom they depended for information, had been remedied, Lee's forces began pouring into Petersburg during the afternoon of July 18. By night the city's lines were strongly held by Lee's men. Even General Beauregard afterwards declared that Petersburg had earlier been "clearly at the mercy of the Federal commander, who had all but captured it" on June 15, but failed to grasp the prize he could have had. Now, however, it was too late. The city was so firmly held that the chances for a successful frontal assault by the Federals had diminished to the vanishing point.

Grant reluctantly settled down for a siege, which was to last almost 10 months. Much of the action during that seemingly endless period centered upon the attempts of both sides to control the railroad supply lines that were so vital to the Confederacy.

The most dramatic incident of the siege, however, was the result of a suggestion by members of the 48th Pennsylvania Regiment, many of them former coal miners. Receiving approval for their plan, the men dug a tunnel 511 feet long, extending from the Union lines to a point under a key Confederate fort. The tunnel ended with lateral branches extending 40 feet in either direction. Filled with four tons of powder, these were exploded on the morning of July 30, 1864. Although the resulting blast blew the fort, men, and weapons sky high, creating an opening through which Union soldiers were supposed to rush beyond the Confederate lines, their movement was slowed by a combination of orders that were not carried out, instructions that were never given, and a total lack of leadership on the part of subordinate officers. The Union move had been perfectly planned; but it was totally wrecked in the execution.

Word of exactly what they were supposed to do had never reached the men involved. Lacking this information, they piled into the enormous crater created by the explosion, together with large numbers of half-entombed Confederate wounded, rather than going around the crater and seizing positions beyond, as intended. Mistaking the crater for some sort of sheltered position, like an outsized rifle pit, and with no leadership to the contrary — not one commander of the four divisions involved was in front leading his men — they simply stayed there. A whole precious hour, opportunity to charge forward unopposed, elapsed before Confederates from other sectors of the Petersburg defense were able to make a substantial response. By the end of that hour, however, Confederate guns had been placed in a position to shell the crater, reinforcements had been rushed into place, and artillery activated. The unfortunate, ill-led invaders were mowed down with a deadly fire, and the already stalled Union advance ground to a halt. Grant afterwards referred to the event as a "disaster," the "saddest affair I have witnessed in this war." Confederate General William Mahone, who was instrumental in the repulse, concurred in a scathing postwar comment on the ineptitude involved.

The crater where hundreds of Confederate and 4,000 Union soldiers tragically met their deaths can be seen today, a gaping hole 170 feet wide, 50 feet across, and 30 feet deep. The anniversary of the conflict of July 30, 1864, for years was marked from time to time as Crater Day by organizations of Confederate veterans and sons of veterans, though it has now been many years since the last regular July 30 observance was held. In 1964, however, the citizens of Petersburg marked the centennial of the July 30 Civil War engagement by dedicating a monument at the crater as a centennial memorial.

After the debacle at the crater, the Federals' siege of Petersburg went on for month after wearying month, punctuated by abortive Union thrusts in the direction of Richmond and the dispatch of expeditions to sever crucial rail lines. Thrust and expedition alike were met by Confederate countermoves, but Grant finally took over a portion of the Weldon Railroad and was extending his line around to the left in an effort to surround and isolate Petersburg. At last a decisive moment came on April 1, 1865, when forces under General Philip Sheridan scored a crushing defeat over Confederate troops at Five Forks, southwest of Petersburg.

The victory was pivotal. Grant, who in the evening learned of the success, ordered an immediate general assault on Petersburg. The town bombardment continued throughout April 2. That night Confederates began crossing to the one possible escape route, on the north side of the Appomattox River. When Petersburg fell, Richmond did too. Its evacuation also began after dark on April 2. The next day Major General Godfrey Weitzel entered Richmond, and Grant rode into Petersburg. It was the beginning of the Confederate retreat, which ended with the surrender of Lee to Grant at Appomattox Court House (see April 9).

In 1865 local women of Petersburg marked

the first anniversary of the city's transient triumph by decorating the graves of the city's defenders in the graveyard south of historic Old Blandford Church. In so doing they initiated what was to be an annual custom of long duration. Some 30,000 Confederate soldiers eventually were numbered among the soldiers of six wars who today lie buried in Blandford Cemetery. Although the state of Virginia marks May 30 as Confederate Memorial Day, it is on the anniversary of the brave stand of June 9 that Petersburg still memorializes its Confederate war dead, and decorates the graves in the section of Blandford Cemetery set apart for them.

Petersburg, where the last major engagement of the Civil War took place, is the site of the 1,522-acre Petersburg National Battlefield. Under the administration of the National Park Service, it preserves Confederate and Union fortifications and portions of seven battlefields, including the ominous crater. The National Battlefield, which has a visitor center, is east and south of Petersburg, the site of the longest siege in the history of the United States.

JUNE 10

Shavuot (Feast of Weeks)

This is a movable event. See note on page xxvi.

The Feast of Weeks is one of the three great Jewish pilgrimage festivals, the others being Passover and Sukkot (Deuteronomy 16:16). One of the joyous holidays, Shavuot begins on the sixth of the Hebrew month of Sivan (May or June), 50 days after the first day of Passover — and thus is sometimes called the Jewish Pentecost, from the Greek word meaning "fiftieth." A day of grateful rejoicing, Shavuot celebrates the gifts of the harvest, and, more important, commemorates that great event in Jewish history, God's gift of the Ten Commandments to Moses on Mt. Sinai. In the Bible (Exodus 34:22) Shavuot is also referred to as *Hag HaKatzir*, that is, Feast of the Harvest and as *Yom HaBikhurim*, literally, Day of the First Fruits.

Shavuot is observed at the end of the wheat and barley harvest season. The counting of the weeks begins on the second day of Passover with the offering of an *omer*, or sheaf, of barley (Leviticus 23:10, 15-16; Deuteronomy 16:9-10); the word *sabbath* used in Leviticus ("And ye shall count unto you from the morrow after the sabbath . . .") has been interpreted as meaning in this context the first day of the feast of Passover. When the Temple in Jerusalem was standing, all adult male Jews were expected to bring their first *omer* of barley to the Temple as a thanksgiving offering. In addition they were directed to offer their first fruits of the harvest, which were often two loaves of bread baked from the new wheat. After the Temple was destroyed in A.D. 70, however, Jews simply recited the prayers associated with the offering of the *omer* and the first fruits.

The 49 days (or seven weeks) between the offering of the *omer* and the first day of Shavuot are marked by the custom of "the counting of the *omer*." Every evening in the synagogues Orthodox Jews say a special prayer. On the first evening of Shavuot they stay in the synagogues late into the night reading a compilation of prayers and passages from the Bible. On the following night the Book of Psalms is read.

Meanwhile, however, they have passed through the sad, six-week period, which extends from the last day of Passover until Shavuot. These are called the *Sefirah* days, a time for Orthodox and Conservative Jews of partial mourning when no weddings or celebrations are allowed.

The holiday of *Lag ba-Omer* (literally the 33rd day of counting the *omer*) is an exception to this otherwise sad period. A joyous day given over to the pleasure of children, it is marked by games and frolic and reveling in the joy of the outdoor world — in contrast to the studiousness of ordinary days. Picnic excursions to fields and woods are common on this day, with youngsters traditionally carrying archers' bows and arrows with them for use in pleasant competition in the course of the outings.

Shavuot, like almost all of the other Jewish holidays, has a historical significance as well as an agricultural one. After the destruction of the Second Temple this aspect — the celebration of the giving of the Torah on Mt. Sinai — and the confirmation of a covenant between God and the Jews were emphasized. Shavuot thus is also called *zeman matan toratenu*, "the season of the giving of our law." During the past century the importance of this part of the holiday has been stressed by Reform and Conservative Jews, who instituted the custom of confirmation, or affirmation of Judaism, on Shavuot. Boys and girls, who have usually completed 10 grades in religious school, present a special program in the synagogue on the morning of the first day of Shavuot, which includes the reciting of the Ten Commandments.

In addition to confirmation, the special morning services in the synagogue include the reading of the Book of Ruth, telling of Ruth's acceptance into the fold of Israel.

It is traditional to decorate both synagogues and homes with spring flowers and greenery during Shavuot. Dairy dishes, especially blintzes (thin rolled pancakes filled with cheese) and milk and honey are popular. Orthodox and Conservative Jews celebrate two days of Shavuot as full holidays, whereas Reform Jews together with all Jews living in Israel observe only the first day.

Shavuot is an important holiday for Jews. It commemorates the anniversary of God's Covenant with the Jews. On Shavuot Jews reaffirm this Covenant by reaccepting the Mosaic laws. Whereas Passover celebrates the Exodus from Egypt, the time when the Jews received physical freedom, Shavuot marks the time when the Jews received spiritual freedom. Thus Shavuot marks the consummation of the purpose of the Exodus: There can be no real freedom without moral and spiritual discipline.

JUNE 11

Kamehameha Day

In Hawaii citizens have set aside June 11 as an annual holiday on which to extol the contributions of King Kamehameha. Appropriately they have chosen as an occasion for state-wide gaiety and celebration a day to honor the king who perhaps affected their lives more than any other, for it was Kamehameha I who united the Hawaiian Islands into a single kingdom, giving to these scattered green oases in the Pacific the unity they maintain today.

For centuries the beautiful Hawaiian archipelago with its Polynesian inhabitants remained isolated from the rest of the world. Then, in the last decades of the 18th century, a prosperous trade arose between the American continents and the Orient. In 1778 the English explorer Captain James Cook commanded the first European ships to visit the islands. Cook named his discovery the Sandwich Islands in honor of the first lord of the Admiralty, the earl of Sandwich.

In the years that followed Cook's visit, an ever-increasing number of American and European vessels plied the Pacific, and many visited the Sandwich Islands. For the most part the Polynesians received the foreigners hospitably. They replenished the ships' supplies of food and water, and in return received iron tools and armaments, which had previously been unknown in the islands.

The introduction of European arms contributed to the unification of the islands under a central government. For centuries control of the islands was divided among several chiefs. These leaders engaged in countless bloody battles to extend their jurisdictions, but without iron and steel weapons they won only limited victories.

Kamehameha I, who was to bring the islands under a unified government, was a powerful warrior and the nephew of Kalaniopuu, the king of the island of Hawaii. Shortly after the death of his uncle in 1782, Kamehameha (whose date of birth is uncertain) became the leader of the chiefs of the western part of the island, and with their assistance he defeated his cousin King Kiwalao at the battle of Mokuohai. The victory gave Kamehameha and his allies undisputed control of the northwestern part of the island of Hawaii.

In 1782 and again around 1785 Kamehameha tried to conquer the remainder of Hawaii, and in 1786 he launched an attack against the neighboring island of Maui. These efforts were not successful. Kamehameha returned to western Hawaii and during the next four years accumulated a sizable supply of European arms.

In 1790 Kamehameha resumed battle. This time he subdued Maui, Lanai, and Molokai, but before he could complete his campaign his cousin Keoua, the brother of Kiwalao, attacked his territory on the island of Hawaii. Kamehameha was forced to return to Hawaii to protect his lands.

By the summer of 1791 Kamehameha had defeated Keoua and thereby gained control of the entire island of Hawaii. But while Kamehameha was fighting to secure and expand his holdings on Hawaii, the chiefs of the leeward islands rebelled. Kahekili and Kaeo, the kings of Molokai and Maui respectively, even attempted to invade Kamehameha's territory on Hawaii, but they were defeated and forced to return to Maui.

Peace reigned on the islands for several years. Then in 1794 King Kahekili, who controlled Maui, Lanai, Molokai, and Oahu, and who indirectly ruled Kauai, died. Within a short time after Kahekili's death, his brother Kaeo and his son Kalanikuple were at war. When Kaeo threatened to attack Kalanikuple, the latter king appealed to the commanders of the three British and American ships then at Honolulu for assistance. The commanders gave Kalanikuple ammunition and advice, and with this aid he defeated Kaeo.

Emboldened by his successful victory over Kaeo, Kalanikuple determined to attack Kamehameha on Hawaii. To aid in this venture, Kalanikuple seized the two British ships that had previously assisted him, and on January 12, 1795, the vessels, with the king and his chiefs on board, put to sea. But Kalanikuple's plot was foiled; soon after the ships left the harbor two British mates retook the vessels, put Kalanikuple and his queen adrift in a canoe, and then steered a course for Hawaii.

Kamehameha seized the opportunity afforded by the failure of Kalanikuple's operation. Quickly gaining possession of Maui and Molokai, he pushed northward to Oahu. Kalanikuple's warriors on that island valiantly attempted to resist Kamehameha's forces, but by the summer of 1795 Kamehameha had won control of the island.

After 1795 only the island of Kauai and its dependency Niihau remained outside Kamehameha's jurisdiction. The aggressive king attempted an invasion in 1796, but had to postpone it when he lost many of his canoes in the tempestuous seas between Oahu and Kauai. Later in the year Kamehameha returned to Hawaii to put down a rebellion, and so Kauai was again spared.

Kamehameha remained on Hawaii until 1802, building a fleet of special double canoes and acquiring a stockpile of military equipment to ensure him victory in the next attack on Kauai. Then, in that year, Kamehameha took his army and fleet to Maui, and late in 1803 or early in 1804 he moved to Oahu to launch the invasion. However, fate again intervened to deprive Kamehameha of his prize, as an epidemic decimated his forces before he could assault Kauai.

Kamehameha finally acquired Kauai by peaceful means. As early as 1805, he appealed to King Kaumualii to recognize his sovereignty and to pay him an annual tribute. The Kauaian leader was willing to accept these terms, but, fearing for his life, he refused Kamehameha's demand that he make his submission in person at Oahu. Finally, in 1810, through the mediation efforts of an American trader, Captain Nathan Winship, Kaumualii agreed to go to Oahu, where he recognized Kamehameha as his suzerain.

Having unified the islands under his rule, Kamehameha returned to his native island of Hawaii in 1812. During the last years of his life he lived mainly at Kailua, in the Kona district of the island. The Hawaiian archipelago remained peaceful and stable, and Kamehameha devoted his time to encouraging trade and agriculture, to rebuilding the *heiaus* (temples to the gods) and to pursuing his favorite avocation, fishing.

The kingdom founded by Kamehameha the Great, as he came to be known, lasted almost 100 years. After his death in 1819, his son Kamehameha II succeeded him as ruler of Hawaii. Kamehameha II outlawed the traditional taboo system and welcomed the American missionaries, who introduced Christianity into the islands. Upon the death of Kamehameha II, his brother, Kamehameha III, became king. The liberal Kamehameha III ruled the island for 30 years, and during that time he organized a constitutional government and undertook a program whereby land was more equitably distributed among the archipelago's inhabitants.

The last direct descendants of Kamehameha I to rule the Hawaiian Islands were his grandsons — Kamehameha IV, whose reign lasted from 1854 to 1863, and Kamehameha V, who ruled from 1863 to 1872. Control of the archipelago then passed to Lunalilo, who ruled for only one year and was succeeded by Kalakaua. He died without an heir in 1891, thus allowing his sister Liliuokalani to assume the throne. Ousted by a coup in 1893, she was Hawaii's last royal ruler.

Today Hawaiians recall the creation and early history of the Hawaiian kingdom and Kamehameha I's importance as the unifier of the islands. It was in 1872 that Kamehameha V proclaimed June 11 a day to honor his grandfather. The day is celebrated each year as Kamehameha Day, a legal holiday in Hawaii and an occasion of great festivity.

The day's observance begins at 9 A.M., when representatives of Hawaiian societies conduct a memorial ceremony, singing chants extolling Kamehameha the Great, and draping long leis of yellow *plumeira* and *maile* vines on his statue, opposite Honolulu's Iolani Palace. This is followed by a parade in Honolulu featuring floats, bands, horseback riders, and marching groups. On one float a handsome Hawaiian represents Kamehameha I and wears a replica of the golden mamo-feather cloak and Grecian-styled helmet once worn by Kamehameha I. (The originals are kept in Honolulu's Bishop Museum and are displayed on June 11.) A princess is chosen to represent each of the eight major islands and rides on horseback, accompanied by a float decorated in the color of her island and by musicians and dancers. The Hawaiian fraternal and civic societies march in full regalia, and also enter floats. The Royal Hawaiian Band and the National Guard Band also participate, as do the colorful horseback *pa'u* riders — women wearing the traditional long, full, bright-colored skirts that were the riding dress of 19th century Hawaii.

The parade ends at Iolani Palace, formerly the home of Hawaii's monarchs and now the state capitol of Hawaii. Here a pageant is presented representing the five kings of the Kamehameha dynasty. In the evening a program of Hawaiian dances and music is held at an outdoor theater.

Another traditional part of the celebration is the Holoku Ball, held the evening before the holiday. The women wear *holokus*, the formal dress of old Hawaii, and prizes are awarded for the most authentic and most beautiful gowns. An elaborate Hawaiian pageant also takes place at this time.

Celebrations consisting of parades, canoe races, and balls are also held on the other Hawaiian islands. Luaus are likewise prepared throughout the islands on Kamehameha Day. These traditional feasts give visitors an excellent opportunity to sample such Polynesian delicacies as *poi,* Kalua pig, *haupiu* and *kulolo.*

JUNE 12

Philippine Independence Day

The Philippine Islands were for several centuries under foreign domination before the establishment of independence in 1946. The story of how June 12 came to be observed as Philippine Independence Day dates from the beginning of that domination.

Spain, on the basis of the discoveries made by Ferdinand Magellan, was the first European nation to claim possession of the Philippines. Magellan, a Portuguese by birth, reached the islands in 1521 during his circumnavigation of the world. The Filipinos received the Europeans with hostility and killed Magellan in a struggle. In 1564 another Spanish representative, Miguel López de Legazpi, sailed from Mexico to the Philippines and finally subjugated the island inhabitants.

Other European nations envied Spain's control of the critical Philippine archipelago along the Pacific trade routes. On October 6, 1762, during the Seven Years' War, British soldiers captured Manila, the principal city of the islands, but the Treaty of Paris of February 10, 1763, which ended the conflict, restored the islands to the Spanish. In the 19th century the strength of Spain ebbed, however, and the merchant ships of Great Britain and the United States came to dominate the commerce of the area.

Filipinos, never fully reconciled to Spanish control, began a series of rebellions in 1843. Native priests, especially Father Peláez and Father Opolinario de la Cruz, spearheaded the movements. Although abortive, these uprisings fostered the development of strong nationalistic feelings in the islands, which, with the opening of the Suez Canal in 1869, became even more important in the world economy.

Revolution in Spain ousted Queen Isabella II in 1868 and led to the establishment of a new regime. The new government sent a number of creative administrators to the Philippines, and they allowed the islands greater autonomy, permitted the publication of liberal journals, and encouraged freer political discussions. The collapse of the Spanish regime in 1871, however, ended the experiment, and a reactionary governor general took office in Manila. Responding to a small-scale mutiny of Filipino soldiers at Cavite in January 1871, the restored government executed three priests, sent a number of leaders to penal colonies, and exiled a number of intellectuals.

Despite the Spanish abuses, many Filipino leaders were willing to remain within the Spanish empire. The Propaganda Movement, a publicity campaign started in Madrid by Filipino exiles, sought reform rather than revolution. Dr. José Rizal, the author of the book *Noli Me Tangere* (Touch Me Not), which described the hardships endured by the islanders, became the leader of the group. Rizal returned to Manila in 1892 and founded the Liga Filipino to encourage the political and social advancement of his people. But within a short time Spanish officials exiled him to the island of Mindanao, and both the Propaganda Movement and the Liga Filipino became moribund.

More militant Filipinos abandoned the conciliatory approach of the Propaganda Movement. In Manila in July 1892 Andrés Bonifacio founded a secret society, the Katipunan (Sons of the People), whose avowed goal was to win independence by force. In 1896 Spanish officials sought to arrest the leaders of the Katipunan, but instead set off a wave of violent uprisings throughout the Philippines. The Spaniards retaliated with repressive tactics, including the execution on charges of sedition of José Rizal, who had actually advised the rebels to be more moderate.

In 1897 Emilio Aguinaldo emerged as the foremost rebel leader, and a revolutionary assembly proclaimed a provisional republic and named him president. Aguinaldo proved unable to defeat the Spanish in battle and in December 1897 agreed to the Pact of Biac-na-bato by which the insurgent leaders voluntarily exiled themselves to Hong Kong. In return the Spanish agreed to pay the rebels for surrender of their weapons and to assist families that had been harmed by the war. Unfortunately neither side lived up to the agreement.

In 1898, as a consequence of the Spanish-American War, the United States became involved in the struggles of the Filipinos. On the evening of April 30 Commodore George Dewey's Asiatic Squadron sailed into Manila Bay in search of the Spanish fleet, which it easily overwhelmed in a brief, one-sided operation early the following morning (see May 1, Battle of Manila Bay).

Lacking the necessary manpower to undertake land operations against Manila, Dewey simply blockaded the port. Meanwhile, Emilio Aguinaldo was called back from exile by the Americans to lead a native insurrection against the Spanish. It was on June 12, the day that would ultimately be recalled as Philippine Independence Day, that Aguinaldo declared the islands independent and established a provisional government. By the end of July, reinforcements arrived from the United States; on August 13 General Wesley Merritt, supported by Aguinaldo, attacked Manila and on the following day received the Spanish capitulation.

Negotiations necessarily involved the fate of the Philippines. Resolved to have a ship-coaling station in the Far Pacific, unwilling to allow the Spanish to reassert their colonial control, and fearful that another world power would attempt to seize the area, President William McKinley determined that the United States would take over the islands. A number of Americans, some for altruistic, anti-imperialist reasons and others on account of racist biases, opposed the acquisition of the area. But the Senate, on February 6, 1899, ratified the Treaty of Paris, which ended the Spanish-American War, and, in the process, provided for US acquisition of the Philippines in return for a payment of $20 million.

Aguinaldo and other Filipino leaders, who expected the United States to grant immediate self-government, were disappointed by the American acquisition. Even before the United States approved the Treaty of Paris, the rebel leader on January 5, 1899, had called for the Philippine people to declare their independence; and on February 4 the populace rose in revolt against the foreign newcomers. Guerrilla warfare between the US Army and the Filipinos continued for several years, but, by the end of 1899, about 70,000 American troops had defeated a Filipino army of almost equal size, and in March 1901 Aguinaldo himself was captured.

President McKinley, on January 20, 1899, appointed President Jacob Schurman of Cornell University to lead a fact-finding commission to determine the future of the Philippines. The investigators concluded that the Filipinos desired and deserved independence, but required training and experience before they would be able to assume the responsibilities of autonomy. Schurman advocated an extensive educational program and opportunities in local self-government to equip the islanders for the future.

Federal Circuit Judge William Howard Taft led the second Philippine Commission, established by President McKinley on April 7, 1900, to establish civil government on the islands. American military rule of the archipelago ended on June 12, 1901, and Taft's five-man commission took office on July 4, 1901. Taft proclaimed equal rights for all Filipinos, separated church and state, instituted freedom of assembly and of the press, and began to put Schurman's proposals into effect. The commission later added three Filipino members.

The US Congress, by the passage of the Pacific Organic Act on July 1, 1902, increased the strength of democratic government in the islands. The bill created a popular assembly as the lower house of a bicameral legislature in which the Taft commission became the senior body. A governor general appointed by the United States exercised executive powers. At the inauguration of the assembly chosen in the first general elections in 1909, the United States renewed its promise of eventual independence for the islands.

Passage of the Jones Act on August 29, 1916, marked another step on the way to Philippine independence. The bill reaffirmed US commitment to independence for the islanders and gave them effective control of their domestic affairs. The act provided for male suffrage and a bill of rights, established an elective senate in place of the Philippine Commission, and vested judicial power in the Supreme Court of the Philippines.

In 1934 the US Congress passed the Tydings-McDuffie Act, which called for the creation on July 4, 1936, of a Philippine Commonwealth under a native chief executive. Manuel Quezon became the first president and Sergio Osmeña the first vice president of the commonwealth. The United States retained control of foreign relations and kept troops in the islands, but promised that in 10 years the Philippines would become an independent republic.

World War II unavoidably delayed the planned transfer of sovereignty. Japan invaded and occupied the Philippines in 1942, and set up a puppet republic in the following year. Filipino resistance fighters gallantly opposed the Japanese and shared in the final Allied victory. The United States honored its promise and granted full independence to all Philippines on July 4, 1946.

Manila celebrated on that day with speeches, flag raisings, planes circling overhead, a 21-gun salute, and a parade led by crack troops of the Philippine Army, which the United States had returned to Philippine command on June 30. Paul McNutt, the retiring US Commissioner, whom President Harry S. Truman had appointed as the first American ambassador to the Philippines, read the formal proclamation that transformed the commonwealth into a republic.

Manuel Acuña Roxas, the republic's first president, delivered a public address, as did General Douglas MacArthur, who had liberated the islands from the Japanese.

Profoundly conscious of their ties with the United States, Filipinos for many years set aside July 4 as the occasion for their own national festivities. But in 1962 President Diosdada Macapagal changed the date of the observance to June 12, the anniversary of the declaration of Philippine independence from Spain made by Emilio Aguinaldo in 1898.

Philippine Independence Day is celebrated throughout the islands. Almost every town has a parade with a local Miss Independence Day as a featured participant. At the conclusion of the march, appropriate outdoor ceremonies in plazas — often near a statue of Dr. Rizal, the George Washington of the Philippines — bring to mind the deeper significance of the festivities. Filipinos often recall their ties with America, and in Manila the US ambassador is usually a guest and sometimes the featured speaker at Independence Day ceremonies. The programs end at noon with the pealing of church bells and the sounding of sirens. After the conclusion of the official events, Philippine citizens devote the remainder of the celebration to recreational activities. In many areas games and athletic contests are held in the afternoon and the explosion of firecrackers can be heard throughout the islands. In the evening the larger towns sponsor Independence Day balls and fireworks displays.

Hawaii, which has a large Filipino population, commemorates Philippine independence with a Fiesta Filipina, held in 1970 between May 2 and June 27. The celebration features music, folk dancing, games, and pageantry of the Philippines.

JUNE 13

Feast of St. Anthony of Padua

The Feast of St. Anthony of Padua is celebrated by Roman Catholics on June 13. Statues and pictures of St. Anthony usually show him carrying the child Jesus in his arms and holding a lily. He is one of the best-loved saints, yet much of his popular image bears little likeness to the actual man. Far from resembling that familiar meek and timid plaster figure, Anthony was a rousing preacher with a tongue that blistered prelates, clergy, and laity. He did not spend his life contemplating lilies in a quiet monastery garden. Instead, he burned himself out traveling from southern Italy to northern France, preaching against heresies and against the laxity of church members. His scriptural knowledge was enormous and his speaking effectiveness was unparalleled. His contemporaries called him the Hammer of the Heretics and the Ark of the Testament.

Although his greatest popularity today is among Italian Catholics, Anthony was born in Lisbon, Portugal, probably on August 15, 1195. After 1211 his father, a knight, served Portugal's King Alfonso II. When he was 15, Ferdinand, as he had been christened, entered the religious order called the Canons Regular of St. Augustine in Lisbon. Well-meaning relatives visited him often, and finally, after two years, to avoid these distractions without hurting the feelings of his relatives, Anthony asked to be transferred to the Augustinian monastery at Coimbra, a day's distance away.

At Coimbra the Augustinians had an excellent school of biblical studies, and for eight years Anthony immersed himself in the history, language, and interpretation of Scripture. He was made guest-master of the house at Coimbra, caring for the needs of travelers and guests.

His life was changed abruptly by one group of these guests. They were five Franciscan friars who were en route to Morocco as missionaries. Shortly after they arrived in Morocco, the five Franciscans were murdered and their remains were returned to Coimbra for burial. Although he had known them only briefly, Anthony was deeply shocked by their deaths and could not keep his mind on his studies. He decided that he too would join the Franciscans and go to Morocco, knowing that he risked a martyr's death.

Although Anthony was successful in getting to Morocco as a Franciscan, poor health struck him shortly after he landed there and his superiors ordered him home. The ship that was supposed to carry him back to Portugal, however, was blown off course by a storm, and Anthony landed at Messina in Sicily in about 1220 or 1221. He probably accepted this as God's will inasmuch as Italy was the home of St. Francis of Assisi, who had founded the Franciscan order. (It is, in fact, possible that St. Anthony met St. Francis before the latter's death in 1226.)

Anthony reported to his Franciscan superiors in Italy and was sent to a hospice in Forlì, where he obediently did menial chores. His superiors there were not aware of his great learning or his ability as a preacher and, but for an accident of circumstance, they might never have known.

The discovery took place when a large group of important clergy and laymen was gathered for an ordination ceremony at Forlì and the invited speaker did not appear. None of the Franciscans volunteered to step in, and the superior abruptly called on Anthony to preach. The sophisticated and learned audience was stunned by this unknown friar's mastery of Scripture, his charm, and his preaching talents.

From that time on, Anthony was assigned as preacher to all of Italy. With his Franciscan companions he traveled from town to town and drew crowds so large — as many as 40,000 — that town squares could not hold them. When Anthony was to speak, tradespeople shuttered their shops, courts of law were closed, and the people of the surrounding areas gathered outside the towns, often coming the night before so as to get a better place to hear the remarkable preacher.

Anthony gave his last sermon during Lent in Padua, which was literally invaded for the occasion. Neither food nor accommodations for the crowd could be found but the people kept coming. After this, the weary and ill Anthony was invited to rest at the estate of a friend outside the city. While they were walking on the grounds there, his companions saw a large tree whose branches could be formed into a roof, and they made a rustic shelter there for Anthony, appropriate for the Franciscan way of life.

On June 13, 1231, as he rested under this tree, Anthony had a premonition of his own death and, not wishing to inconvenience his host, he asked his companions to take him back to the monastery at Padua. They put him in an ox cart and began the hot, dusty journey towards the city. Before they reached there, however, Anthony's condition worsened and they stopped instead at a convent in Arcella, where they propped him up in a sitting position to ease his discomfort. Although he was having great trouble breathing, he began to sing a hymn and with the words still on his lips, he died. He was not quite 36 years old. Because he was buried on a Tuesday, that day of the week is sometimes referred to as St. Anthony's Day, and weekly devotions to St. Anthony are held in some churches on every Tuesday of the year.

Anthony was canonized within a year after his death — on May 30, 1232 — by Pope Gregory IX, who also declared him a Teacher of the Church. He also received the title of Confessor, accorded to saints who have lived lives of outstanding sanctity and heroic virtue but who have not been martyred. On January 16, 1946, Pope Pius XII declared Anthony a Doctor of the Church with the title Doctor Evangelicus in honor of his great preaching ability. The title Doctor of the Church is conferred upon ecclesiastical writers of great learning and sanctity, in recognition of the advantage derived by the Church from their teachings.

Today St. Anthony, who was a truly kind man with a great love for the poor, is most popularly venerated as an apostle of charity. His aid is invoked for both spiritual and worldly needs. Many Catholic women pray to St. Anthony for happy marriages and healthy children. In various locales, he is the patron saint of lovers, miners, travelers, and sailors. He is called upon to find lost objects, to aid women during childbirth, and to cure fevers and animal diseases. In Portugal, Italy, France, and Spain, where sailors and fishermen regard him as their patron saint, a shrine containing a statue of St. Anthony is often seen on the masts of ships. The men pray to him for safety in storms or in the face of other dangers, and may even scold him (sometimes turning his face to the mast as punishment) if he does not produce what they regard as a proper response to their prayers.

Many churches in the United States are named for St. Anthony of Padua and these often celebrate his feast day in a special way. One of the most outstanding celebrations is sponsored by the Shrine Church of St. Anthony of Padua in New York City's Greenwich Village. Located at the corner of West Houston and Sullivan streets, St. Anthony's is in one of the original Little Italy sections of New York. The church, which is staffed by Franciscan friars and brothers, is over 100 years old and is the oldest Italian Roman Catholic congregation in New York.

Members of the congregation celebrate the Feast of St. Anthony in spiritual as well as worldly ways. The celebration goes on from the weekend before the actual feast day through the weekend after. Many of the same events take place annually, but the exact schedule differs somewhat from year to year.

The outdoor festival, one of the liveliest street fairs in New York, attracts thousands of people during each of the approximately 10 days of the celebration. Indeed, busloads of people, including former neighborhood residents, come from near and far. Festivities center on Sullivan Street, where several ordinarily drab blocks are transformed into a glittering arcade by row upon row of illuminated arches. Under the bright lights are food and fun for everyone, including a Ferris wheel and other amusements. The streets are lined with stalls, which offer tantalizing fragrances of pizza, hero sandwiches, *calzone*, and other Italian foods to be eaten on the spot or sausages and cheeses to be purchased and taken home. Other booths sell Italian pastries, such as *zeppole;* Italian ices; *spumoni* on a stick; *torrone*, and other candies and sweets. Still other stalls provide games of chance or skill. Balloons, souvenirs, hats, and other novelties as well as religious mementos of the celebration are also much in evidence.

For many who attend the celebration of the

Feast of St. Anthony the most important event may be one or more of the religious services in St. Anthony's Church. To serve the huge crowds, the Franciscans in residence secure the help of fellow friars from other cities to carry the heavy church schedule. For example, there is a solemn novena to St. Anthony, that is, special prayers on nine consecutive days before his actual feast day. Six times daily, from morning until night, the novena prayers and sermon are held in the church, three times in Italian and three times in English.

On one special day, parents take their children to the church for the Blessing of the Children, asking that St. Anthony keep their children healthy. On another day there is the Blessing of the Sick, when young and old are brought into the church, some in wheelchairs or on stretchers, asking St. Anthony to cure their ills or to give them the strength and fortitude to endure their afflictions.

The climax of the spiritual celebrations takes place on the feast day itself, June 13, when many masses are offered in the church. Lilies, which play a part in several miracles associated with St. Anthony, and blessed bread, a reminder of his great charity to the poor, are distributed in the church throughout the day. Early in the evening a solemn procession forms at the church and winds through the city streets. Altar boys, members of church societies, and schoolchildren, some of them dressed as Franciscan Friars, all participate. Other students, some wearing bright red capes, also walk in the procession, as do men and women carrying candles. St. Anthony occupies the place of honor on the main float, and seated in rows behind the statue are small girls in the white dresses and veils of their first communion. Eighth-grade girls walk alongside the float and take the alms offered in honor of St. Anthony. The practice of giving alms to the poor in conjunction with offering prayers of petition or thanksgiving is known as St. Anthony's Bread, so named in the 19th century, when a young Frenchwoman promised loaves of bread for the poor if St. Anthony granted the favor she asked.

A Franciscan bishop is invited to officiate in the solemn procession and he carries the relic of St. Anthony to be venerated by onlookers along the procession route. When the procession returns to St. Anthony's Church, the faithful enter the church for the Solemn Benediction of the Most Blessed Sacrament.

The Feast of St. Anthony is also an occasion for celebration in many Puerto Rican communities, including Barranquitas, Ceiba, Dorado, Guayama, and Isabela. Some of the Indian pueblos of the American Southwest also take special note of the day with Roman Catholic church services in Spanish followed by purely Indian events. In New Mexico, for instance, corn and/or buffalo dances are held in celebration of St. Anthony's Day — or San Antonio's Day, as it is called locally — at Taos, San Juan, Santa Clara, San Ildefonso, Sandia, Cochiti, and sometimes other pueblos.

JUNE 14

Flag Day

Creation of an American nation from the 13 colonies that rebelled against Great Britain in 1776 was not easily accomplished. Prior to their decision to end their connection with the mother country, the colonies had enjoyed separate existences and had established few interprovincial ties. But their common fight against British rule brought the colonies more than independence; gradually the colonies came to the realization of a national identity. As a symbol of this new union the former British provinces adopted a national flag on June 14, 1777.

During the initial battles of the American Revolution, the rebels fought under the banners of the individual colonies or even those of local militia companies. For example, patriots from Massachusetts marched under ensigns depicting a pine tree emblem, while some units of minutemen in Pennsylvania and Virginia gave their allegiance to a flag bearing a coiled rattlesnake and the warning "Don't Tread on Me." Other early revolutionary flags included the banner adopted by the Associators of Hanover, Pennsylvania, showing a rifleman and carrying the words "Liberty or Death"; the flag of two militia units at Charleston, South Carolina, which proclaimed "Liberty" in white letters on a blue field; and the so-called Bunker Hill Flag, a British blue ensign that the colonists modified by the addition of a pine tree to the St. George's Cross in the banner's canton.

Such a great diversity of flags reflected a similar lack of unity in the rebels' efforts against Great Britain. The first "national" flag—the Continental Colors, known also as the Grand Union Flag — became so on a purely unofficial basis. Commander in Chief George Washington designated it to be flown to celebrate the formation of the Continental army, which was announced on New Year's Day in 1776 (see January 1, First National Flag). The flag, with 13 alternating red and white stripes and a canton bearing the crosses of St. George and St. Andrew, may have been in use elsewhere as early as the fall of 1775. This Grand Union flag, as it became known, was an appropriate selection: the colonists had not declared independence, and the presence of the British Union ensign in the canton symbolized many Americans' hope of eventual reconciliation with Britain; but at the same time the pattern of 13 stripes, one for each colony, was tacit recognition of the rebels' increasing unity of purpose.

The Grand Union flag was first raised on January 1, 1776, on Prospect Hill in Somerville, near Washington's headquarters at Cambridge, Massachusetts. In the months that followed, the banner, which bore no symbol associated with a particular colony or locality and which was thus a truly national ensign, won wide acceptance. The flag flew from patriot masts along the entire Atlantic seaboard. But the Continental Congress's declaration of independence in July made the banner, incorporating the British Union Flag in its design, obsolete, and the Congress never officially accepted the flag. However, the Grand Union's significance as this country's first national ensign should not be underestimated. In recognition of its importance, a granite memorial tower and observatory was dedicated on Prospect Hill in 1903. Inscribed on its side are the words:

From this eminence on January 1, 1776, the flag of the United Colonies, bearing thirteen stripes and the crosses of St. George and St. Andrew first waved defiance to a foe.

Concerned with the business of conducting the war against Great Britain, the Continental Congress did not give its attention to the matter of an official national banner until almost a year after the adoption of the Declaration of Independence. Then, on June 14, 1777, Congress resolved:

That the flag of the thirteen United States be thirteen stripes, alternate red and white; that the union [canton] be thirteen stars, white in a blue field, representing a new constellation.

The 1777 legislation provided only the barest specifications for the new flag. It did not limit the number of points in the design of the stars; it did not set forth a particular arrangement for the stars and stripes; nor did it designate a designer for the national banner.

Numerous contradictory and unsubstantiated legends attribute the creation of the first Stars and Stripes flag to such various personages as John Hulbert, a Long Island cordwainer; John Paul Jones, the American naval hero; and Francis Hopkinson, a signer of the Declaration of Independence. But tradition generally credits Betsy Ross with making the original Stars and Stripes banner. The story of the Philadelphia upholsterer dates from 1870, when her grandson, William J. Canby, read a paper before the Historical Society of Pennsylvania.

Canby based his report on conversations with his maternal grandmother, Mrs. Ross, which had taken place shortly before her death in 1836. At the time of these talks, Mrs. Ross was 84 and her grandson was 11. In 1857 Canby wrote down his grandmother's recollections, and in 1870 he published her story, 94 years after the fact. The appealing vignette of General Washington visiting the needlewoman quickly caught the popular imagination, and Betsy Ross's name became linked with the banner of 13 alternate red and white stripes and a blue canton bearing a circle of 13 five-pointed stars. Historians, however, have not been able to corroborate Canby's report; the only provable facts known about Mrs. Ross are that she was a patriot upholsterer living in Philadelphia during the American Revolution, and that some time before May 1777 she made several Pennsylvania naval flags of unknown design.

Just as the identity of the designer and maker of the original Stars and Stripes flag is shrouded in mystery, the exact date of its first raising is also unknown. But authorities do agree that the ensign gained increasing acceptance during the summer of 1777, and most believe that rebel forces first fought under the ensign at the battle of Bennington in August 1777. The Bennington flag is recognized as the oldest Stars and Stripes banner, and is on exhibit at the Bennington Museum in Bennington, Vermont. Its design reflects the latitude the Continental Congress allowed flag makers in its specifications. The blue field is nine stripes in width; 11 of its 13 seven-pointed stars are arranged in an arch over the numerals "76" on the field, while the remaining two occupy the upper corners. Interesting, too, is the fact that the highest and lowest of the ensign's 13 stripes are white rather than red.

Historians do not know if the Continental army regularly fought under the Stars and Stripes following its introduction on the battlefield at Bennington, but there is no doubt that the American navy consistently flew the ensign from the masts of its ships. Indeed, Navy Commander John Paul Jones once wrote:

The Flag and I are twins. . . . So long as we can float, we shall float together. If we must sink, we shall go down as one.

Jones was true to the flag. When the commander sailed his sloop, the *Ranger*, from Portsmouth, New Hampshire, on November 1, 1777, the national banner went to sea for the first time;

and when French men-of-war saluted the ship as it left Quiberon Bay in France on February 14, 1778, foreign vessels acknowledged the Stars and Stripes for the first time.

Although many flag "firsts" are associated with exploits of the American Revolution, it was the winning of independence in 1783 that made the Stars and Stripes the legally recognized banner of the United States. With nationhood, however, some changes were effected in the ensign; for as the young republic matured and expanded, its flag reflected its growth. In January 1794, shortly after the admission of Vermont and Kentucky to the Union, Congress made the first of several alterations in the flag legislation of 1777. Yet, like similar enactments that have followed during the course of US history, the 1794 law — which added two stars and two stripes to the banner to represent the two new states — did not change the flag's basic design of stars and stripes.

The 15-star and 15-stripe flag approved in 1794 served as this country's banner from 1795 to 1818, and is perhaps best remembered as Francis Scott Key's inspiration for the national anthem. The circumstances surrounding Scott's writing were quite dramatic. Harsh fighting took place between British and American forces during the War of 1812, and a particularly bitter battle occurred from September 12 to September 14, 1814, when the British attacked Baltimore, Maryland. Key was aboard a warship in the city's harbor throughout the conflict, and at the break of dawn on September 14 he sought some assurance that the enemy had not penetrated the American defenses. The sight of the national flag flying over Fort McHenry quickly quieted his fears, and his elation upon beholding the flag prompted him to pen the immortal verses of "The Star-Spangled Banner." The flag had had 11 holes shot in it during the battle. In 1912 it was presented to the Smithsonian Institution in Washington, D.C., where it is still preserved. In 1931 Congress officially adopted Key's paean as the national anthem.

Upon the admission of Vermont and Kentucky to the Union, two new stars and two new stripes had been added to the flag. But in 1818 so many new states carved from the Old Northwest Territory were either applying for statehood or about to do so that Congress realized it would be no longer practical to increase the number of stripes on the flag. For this reason, the federal legislature passed a third law affecting the national banner. The measure, which went into operation on July 4, 1818, fixed the number of stripes in the flag at 13 and provided for the automatic addition of a new star for each state entering the Union thereafter.

Following the adoption of the 1818 legislation, Congress approved no significant flag law for almost 100 years. National banners during the remainder of the 19th and the early 20th centuries were made according to the prescribed stars and stripes design, but there were still no official specifications regarding the placement and proportions of the stars and stripes. Then in 1912 President William Howard Taft issued two executive orders that ended the latitude previously allowed flagmakers. Taft's orders established the proportions of the height and width of the flag and its canton, and the proportionate width of each stripe and diameter of each star. Also beginning in 1912, the government began to standardize the arrangement of the stars on the flag's canton.

As the visible symbol of the nation, the Stars and Stripes rapidly won the respect of American citizens. Slower to gain popular acceptance was the establishment of formal ceremonies centering around the banner. In fact the first Flag Day observance did not take place until June 14, 1861, almost a century after the official adoption of the ensign, and it occurred then only because the people of Hartford, Connecticut, wished to express their support for the Union during the opening days of the Civil War. The 1861 Hartford exercises were not repeated in the years that immediately followed. But in 1877, on the 100th anniversary of the adoption of the banner, Congress ordered that the flag be flown over public buildings on June 14.

During the final years of the 19th century, observances of Flag Day on June 14 won only gradual recognition. In 1889 George Bolch, the principal of a free kindergarten for the poor in New York City, decided to hold patriotic exercises on June 14. The ceremonies at Bolch's school attracted considerable attention, and within a short time the New York State legislature passed a law providing that:

It shall be the duty of the State Superintendent of Public Schools to prepare a program making special provision for observance in the public schools of . . . Flag Day.

In accordance with this act the superintendent ordered that the flag be displayed on every public school building beginning at nine o'clock in the morning, and that appropriate patriotic exercises also be held.

Citizens in other areas of the nation also worked to promote Flag Day. William T. Kerr, who resided first in Pittsburgh, Pennsylvania, and later in Philadelphia, is recognized by many as the Father of Flag Day. As a schoolboy, Kerr began to urge the observance of the day, and his enthusiasm never waned. Interest was also shown by Bernard J. Cigrand of Chicago, a navy officer and flag historian. Cigrand had a leading role in persuading the American Flag-Day Association, which had been founded in his home city in 1894, to schedule its observance on June 14 rather than on the third Saturday in June as had been its original intention. Still another person closely associated with establishing Flag Day was Joseph H. Hart, a businessman of Allentown, Pennsylvania. Hart led a campaign to urge that a special flag day be set aside, and as a result of his efforts the Allentown Flag Day Association was formed in 1907.

Because of the work of Kerr and the others, the desire to celebrate Flag Day came to the attention of the American populace and, perhaps even more important, influenced the actions of government leaders. As early as 1893, the mayor of Philadelphia ordered that the banner be displayed on all city buildings on June 14; and four years later the governor of New York similarly commanded that the flag be flown over all public structures on that day. In 1916, President Woodrow Wilson issued a proclamation asking the nation to observe June 14 as Flag Day, and President Calvin Coolidge acted similarly in 1927. But not until August 3, 1949, did Congress agree to a joint resolution and President Harry S. Truman officially designate June 14 as Flag Day.

Even before the federal government acted, the efforts of special Flag Day associations, the Fraternal Order of Elks, and the American Legion prompted many schools and localities to hold special celebrations on June 14. Programs on the day traditionally center around the Pledge of Allegiance to the Flag, which was written by James B. Upham and Francis Bellamy in 1892. But other popular June 14 exercises include flag-raising ceremonies, the singing of the national anthem, and the study of flag etiquette.

Flag Day is observed as a legal holiday in the state of Pennsylvania. In recent years, the President of the United States and the governors of many states have issued special Flag Day proclamations, and the governors of Montana, North Carolina, South Dakota, and Tennessee have designated the week of June 14 as Flag Week. Since 1952, Flag Week has been sponsored by the Star-Spangled Banner Flag House Association, whose headquarters are in the Flag House located at 844 East Pratt Street, Baltimore, where Mary Young Pickersgill sewed the flag that inspired Francis Scott Key. "To maintain in native Americans, and to instill in new citizens, a concept of the ideals of American patriotism, together with the rights and privileges of American citizenship" the Association recommends a special calendar of Flag Week events. Flag Week begins on the Sunday before June 14, and communities are urged to hold special observances on that day. In Baltimore such exercises are held annually at Fort McHenry National Monument, where in one recent year spectators saw the US Marine Flag Pageant and heard the Marine Corps Band. Other days in Flag Week have been designated Industry, Education, Government, Youth Activities, and Defense days, and appropriate ceremonies are outlined for these days. Like the house of Betsy Ross, Fort McHenry and the Star-Spangled Banner Flag House are among the few places in the nation where the United States flag is properly flown night and day. Elsewhere, it customarily is lowered at sunset.

On Flag Day and the days near it, the American flag is displayed at many homes, businesses, and public buildings. Across the nation, schools arrange appropriate exercises, and communities hold special observances designed to instill pride in the national banner. Flag Day celebrations generally include a traditional program of patriotic speeches, small parades, and flag ceremonies. But some areas have developed unique methods to honor the flag: New York City is annually the scene of several large parades; Allentown, Pennsylvania, centers its observances around a naturalization court session believed to be the only open-air naturalization session held in the East; and in Detroit the J. J. Hudson Company department store annually unfurls its 104-foot-by-235-foot banner, one of the largest flags in the world.

In 1977 Flag Day observances throughout the nation focused on the 200th anniversary of the adoption of the 1777 official banner. Participating in the special events and ceremonies were the armed forces, veterans' organizations, schools, and patriotic and civic groups.

Although there is little evidence to substantiate the Betsy Ross legend, her name has been so closely associated with the American flag that it seems only fitting for Flag Day ceremonies to take place, as they do, at the Ross residence, 239 Arch Street in Philadelphia. This patriotic observance attracts large numbers of tourists, who may also tour the historic home.

Perhaps the most colorful, and certainly the most international, Flag Day observance occurs each year at Old Fort Niagara in Fort Niagara State Park, Youngstown, New York. Originally built by the French in 1726, the fort passed into British hands during the French and Indian War, became American property in 1796, and was the scene of bitter fighting between British and American forces during the War of 1812. During its colorful history, the flags of three nations have waved over the fort, and this fact is basic to the site's Flag Day celebration.

Like those at many other places, Fort Niagara's Flag Day observance, which occurs on the Sunday nearest June 14, includes a band concert, a parade, military drill, and the firing of cannons. But unique to the fort are exercises centering around the presentation of the replicas of three historic flags. Representatives of the United States, Canada, and France are generally on hand to address the throng, which has been estimated at as high as 10,000 persons, and to watch the French colors raised to the accompaniment of the "Marseillaise," the British Union Jack to "God Save the Queen," and the American flag to "The Star-Spangled Banner."

Army Established

More than a year before the signing of the Declaration of Independence, the Second Continental Congress established the Continental, or American, army. The patriots who fought in the earliest battles of the American Revolution — at Lexington, Concord, Fort Ticonderoga, and Crown Point — had been members of New England militia companies. These local units had been able to endure the first clashes with the British, but they could not provide sufficient men or arms for extensive campaigns against the enemy. Successful long-term resistance to the redcoats required intercolonial cooperation.

Less than a month after the battles of Lexington and Concord, the Massachusetts Provincial Congress requested the Second Continental Congress, then meeting in Philadelphia, to consider such "matters as may be necessary to the defense of this colony and particularly the state of the army therein." The Bay Colony needed weapons and other supplies from the other colonies. In return it offered to allow the Continental Congress to assume the "regulation and general direction" of the 15,000 New England troops then besieging British-held Boston "for the general defense of the rights of America." The Congress agreed to this arrangement. It sent flour and gunpowder to Boston, and then took steps to unify the military forces of the various colonies.

The most important actions toward the creation of an intercolonial army took place in mid-June 1775. On June 14 Congress ordered the formulation of a "draft of rules and regulations for the government of the army" and recruited 10 rifle companies from Pennsylvania, Maryland, and Virginia for service in Boston. The following day the Philadelphia gathering appointed George Washington of Virginia to be "General and Commander in Chief of the Army of the United Colonies" and began to name generals for Continental commissions.

Although the Continental Congress all but disbanded the army in June 1784, the present-day US Army considers June 14, 1775, to be the date of its establishment. According to a directive of the Department of the Army, observance of the anniversary should neither overshadow June 14 celebrations of Flag Day nor detract from Armed Forces Day commemorations that occur on the third Saturday in May. For this reason, special programs to mark the event are generally confined to army posts. Both the secretary of the army and the chief of staff send letters of congratulation to major command headquarters on June 14, and the army encourages its larger posts to hold open houses, weapons demonstrations, military parades, and other activities appropriate for the occasion.

Children's Day

This is a movable event. See note on page xxvi.

As is true of many American celebrations, Children's Day is a New World adaptation of an Old World custom. A day emphasizing the role of Christianity in the development of the young, it is marked each year by many Protestant churches, most often on the second Sunday in June. The occasion was first observed in the United States in the middle of the 19th century.

Before then, church services had been devoted from time to time to the children of the congregation, sometimes including them as participants. Such services were considered particularly appropriate occasions for the baptism of boys and girls. Frequently an offering was taken to benefit children, perhaps to help some of those in the Sunday school to further their education or for the work of the Sunday school itself. Concerts were sometimes given on that day by young people.

But it was not until the second Sunday of June 1856 that the first of what came to be widespread annual observances centered around children was arranged by the Reverend Charles H. Leonard, pastor of the Universalist Church of the Redeemer in Chelsea, Massachusetts. Dr. Leonard conceived the day as a time for children to be dedicated to Christian living and for their parents to be rededicated to fostering their sons' and daughters' Christian development. Children were baptized during the service, which was devoted especially to their interests. The day was at first called Rose Sunday, then Flower Sunday, but within a few years it came to be known as Children's Day or Children's Sunday. The Methodist Episcopal Church was the first denomination to give formal recognition to the day. A recommendation for such recognition was made in 1865. At its next meeting, in 1868, the General Conference of the Church voted for the second Sunday in June to be thenceforth set aside for observances in honor of children.

In 1867 the Universalist Convention took official action, designating Children's Sunday the day for the baptism of children. Other Protestant sects soon showed interest, and by the early 1880s many of them had included observance of the day in their calendars.

Although the second Sunday in June is the day on which Children's Sunday is most commonly observed, another date may be chosen instead. Some individual churches annually select the date for their observance, with the result that the scheduling may vary from year to year. Usually, however, the celebration is in June.

Observance takes many forms. Traditionally each child has carried a flower or a bouquet or basket of flowers, sometimes marching in procession into the church with the blooms. However, variations have been introduced in that practice. Flowering plants may be given to the children or occasionally they are given brightly colored balloons instead of flowers.

Children's Sunday is often celebrated on the last day of the Sunday-school year. Accordingly, it is frequently an occasion on which children are awarded certificates for having completed the work of their grade; or they may even have made mortarboard caps to wear for their "graduation" from one grade to another. Those who are advancing from one particularly designated grade to the next — those who are entering the second, third, or fourth grade, for example — may be presented with Bibles for their own use. Awards for good attendance may be made on Children's Sunday, and it is a time when exhibits of the children's work are likely to be on view.

The various denominations frequently provide their member churches with ideas and suggestions for programs to help make the day meaningful. Activities may be confined within the Sunday school, climaxed, perhaps, by the coming together of all classes for a songfest. Exercises may be held outdoors, but it has long been common for special recitations and choral singing by boys and girls to be included in the church's regular worship service in the church sanctuary, and the emphasis in recent years has been to encourage greater participation by children in this service.

Today in some churches the entire service is led by boys and girls; the minister's only active part is in giving the benediction. In other churches the minister also gives a short sermon appropriate to the theme of the day. Sometimes each of the Sunday school grades participates, even including the kindergarten, whose members may sing a simple hymn or other song. Young people read the Scripture lessons and lead the congregation in prayer. They also may present a playlet or a responsive reading, or give brief personal talks.

The scope of Children's Sunday observances is sometimes broadened further to include new high school and college graduates, with recognition given to the significance of this time in their lives. Differing patterns of observance are reflected in the fact that the second Sunday in June has been given such names as Youth Sunday and Church School Sunday by some churches. In some instances, stress is placed on bringing the family together in worship and making parents more familiar with what is happening in the Sunday School. The exercises may take place, for example, during a luncheon attended by the church-school members and their families. Increasingly, today, the emphasis of Children's Day is on relevance — on relating religious faith to the problems and circumstances that youngsters encounter in their daily lives.

The Old World roots of Children's Sunday are found in a May Day custom. In former times, May 1 was the day on which children were confirmed in the Roman Catholic and the Lutheran churches. The children carried flowers, usually wildflowers or flowering branches, in procession to their churches. Probably the prominence of flowers in the celebration accounts for the early names of the day in the United States, Rose Sunday and Flower Sunday. A later blooming season for flowers in this country, especially in the northern part where the annual observance began, caused the change of date from May Day to, usually, early June.

Harriet Beecher Stowe's Birthday

Harriet Elizabeth Beecher Stowe, author of the inflammatory *Uncle Tom's Cabin* — probably the most effective piece of antislavery propaganda ever published — was born in Litchfield, Connecticut, on June 14, 1811, daughter of the noted Calvinist clergyman Lyman Beecher. The role of her mother, who died when she was four, was more or less taken over by her oldest sister, Catharine.

Harriet Beecher grew up in a stern Puritan household full of ideas and devotion to causes. Of her father's 13 children by three marriages, she and her brother Henry Ward Beecher earned lasting reputations, and at least five other brothers and sisters (including Catharine) were prominent in their own lifetimes for their work in education, the ministry, abolition, and/or women's rights. She was at first a student in the school that her sister had set up in Hartford, Connecticut, and subsequently taught there.

Harriet Beecher was about 21 when her father gave up the pulpit of Boston's Park Street Church to become president of Cincinnati's new Lane Theological Seminary — which, apart from training ministers, came to be an abolitionist center. In Cincinnati Catharine promptly set up a pioneering, if short-lived, college for women, the Western Female Institute. Harriet served as an assistant in this enterprise, and did some writing for local journals. Henry, meanwhile, studied at the seminary, where his professors included Calvin Ellis Stowe, a scholar versed in Greek, Arabic, and Hebrew, who, on January 6, 1836, married Harriet.

In spite of the want and worry occasioned by her husband's uncertain health, Harriet Beecher Stowe labored constantly over her writing, amid a sea of pots, pans, and small children, in the years that followed. She wrote stories and essays, and a first book, *The Mayflower, or Sketches of Scenes and Characters among the Descendants of the Pilgrims*, which was published in 1843. Her 18 years in Cincinnati gave her opportunity to observe the institution of slavery as practiced in the slave state of Kentucky, just across the Ohio River, and as movingly reported by fugitive slaves passing through Cincinnati.

When her husband was appointed professor of religion at his alma mater, Bowdoin College, the family moved to Brunswick, Maine, in 1850 — as the North reverberated with abolitionist sentiment and agitation against the new Fugitive Slave Law. In Brunswick she received a deluge of letters describing the tragic effects of the law. Burning with sudden incandescence, she sat down — with inspiration which, she said, was not her own, but God's — to write *Uncle Tom's Cabin, or Life Among the Lowly* for the *National Era*, for an antislavery newspaper of Washington, D.C. Her hero became the best-known black character in fiction: Uncle Tom, a pious, elderly slave of sterling character, subjected (after the death of a kind master) to the fatal cruelties imposed by Simon Legree. Eliza, Topsy, and Little Eva were other memorable characters.

As a newspaper serial (June 5, 1851–April 1, 1852), the supposedly true-to-life story caused little stir. But when it was published in book form in 1852, a storm broke loose — not only in the so-called New England conscience, which so influenced American history and literature, not only in the South, where the book precipitated an uproar, but around the world. The first American novel to sell more than a million copies, it was translated into at least 23 languages. In Europe its appearance was a literary event, with Macaulay, Heine, George Sand, and Tolstoy among admirers of its author's power, dramatic flair, ability to hold her reader — and incendiary message. Surprisingly, considering her views, the book did not attempt to place all blame on the slaveholding South — but left it to the Yankee-born Simon Legree to epitomize the worst evils of slavery. Despite the literary faults of *Uncle Tom's Cabin*, which included sentimentality, its influence was enormous in spreading the abolitionist cause. In fact, when she actually met President Lincoln in 1861 or 1862, the legend arose that he greeted her with "So you're the little woman that started the war."

While the book contributed substantially to abolition by making people "see" slavery in terms of "real" people, it also bequeathed to several post-Emancipation generations of Americans the "Uncle Tom" image. Uncle Tom's character, which in the novel included such qualities as devoutness and moral strength, deteriorated in the dramatizations that subsequently flooded the stage, imprinting on the public mind the image of a fawning, spineless and caricatured creature, injurious to black dignity and white understanding. "Uncle Tom" has become a term of derision used to describe a subservient black.

Suggestions that her picture of slavery was overdrawn prompted the author's attempt to document her book with *A Key to Uncle Tom's Cabin*, published in 1853. She journeyed to Europe the same year and again in 1856 and 1859. She was idolized in England until she published a controversial magazine article about Byron in 1869. Meanwhile her second antislavery novel, *Dred; a Tale of the Great Dismal Swamp*, came out in 1856. She subsequently contributed to the new *Atlantic Monthly* and to the *Independent* and the *Christian Union*, publications with which her brother was editorially associated. And she turned from sociological novels to fiction depicting New England life — perhaps most notably in *The Minister's Wooing* (1859), a charming romance that challenged the strict Calvinism long espoused by her family, and *The Pearl of Orr's Island* (1862), set in a Maine fishing village.

In 1852 her husband had become a professor at the Theological Seminary at Andover, Massachusetts, where the family lived until his retirement in 1863, when they moved to Hartford. She remained there in seclusion after her husband's death in 1886, meanwhile having spent many winters at the estate she had purchased in Mandarin, Florida, after the end of the Civil War. She herself died on July 1, 1896, at the age of 85.

Harriet Beecher Stowe is buried with her husband at Andover. Now a national landmark, the house where they lived in Brunswick, Maine, still stands on Federal Street. Nearby is the First Parish Church, where at a communion service she first had her vision of Uncle Tom's death, the germ of her book.

JUNE 15

Arkansas Admitted to the Union

On June 15, 1836, Arkansas was admitted to the federal Union. Arkansas was the third state to be created from the vast area of the Louisiana Purchase. Thus, like its neighboring south-central states, the 25th member of the union was visited and ruled by the Spanish and French before coming under the jurisdiction of the United States.

The first European to visit the region that is today Arkansas was the Spaniard Hernando de Soto. The exact path of de Soto's 1541 explorations is unknown, but it is probable that de Soto's party crossed the Mississippi near present Helena, Arkansas, proceeded northward to the mouth of the St. Francis River, and then went southwest to the Arkansas River. De Soto's search for gold next took him farther west to Hot Springs and Caddo Gap; but after he and his companions failed to find the precious metal they journeyed down the Ouachita River, and after wintering at either Camden or Calion they continued on into the area that is now Louisiana.

De Soto's party did not establish any permanent settlements in Arkansas, and, indeed, no other white men ventured into "The Land of Opportunity" for more than 130 years. Then, in 1673, the French explorers Jacques Marquette and Louis Joliet sailed down the Mississippi as far as the mouth of the Arkansas. Marquette and Joliet remained at the Indian village of Mitchigamea, close to the junction of the Mississippi and Arkansas, for about one month. Having learned that the Mississippi emptied into the Gulf of Mexico, and having been warned of both hostile Indians and hostile white men (Spaniards) to the south, the Frenchmen decided to return north to Canada.

Like de Soto before them, Marquette and Joliet left no permanent reminder of their sojourn in Arkansas. This, however, was not the case with the next Europeans to visit the region. Early in 1682 a party of Frenchmen led by René Robert Cavelier, Sieur de La Salle, journeyed down the Mississippi and on April 9 reached the mouth of the great waterway. La Salle claimed all the territory bordering the Mississippi and its tributaries for King Louis XIV of France and planned to fortify the region from the Great Lakes to the Gulf of Mexico. However, he died in 1687, in the course of a later attempt to establish the first settlement in the vast area he had brought under French control. In June 1686, meanwhile, his most trusted lieutenant, Henri de Tonti, who had set out on an unsuccessful expedition to find his former leader, built a small fort in Arkansas.

This first permanent white settlement in Arkansas was modest. Tonti left only six Frenchmen in 1686 at what became known as Arkansas Post, and within one year four of these men had abandoned the fort. But Tonti, who is known as the Father of Arkansas, continued to assist at the settlement. He granted the Catholic church a large tract of land near the post and arranged for a priest to minister to the white residents of the settlement and to teach the neighboring Arkansas Indians.

Tonti's faith in the Arkansas Post — today known as Arkansas Post National Memorial — was not unfounded. Located about 15 miles west of the Mississippi, near the junction of the White and Arkansas rivers, the post served early settlers, trappers, and hunters. Its significance as a trading center was drastically diminished when New Orleans was established at the mouth of the Mississippi in 1718, but throughout the period of French rule over Louisiana the post served as an important link between French settlements along the Gulf of Mexico and those in the upper Mississippi valley.

Even after the establishment of the Arkansas Post, however, settlement of the surrounding area proceeded very slowly. In 1718 the Scottish financier John Law was given a tract of 80,000 acres on the Arkansas River about seven miles from the post. Law planned to colonize this land with about 1,500 settlers from Germany and France. The first contingent, of about 800 (mostly Alsatians) arrived in Arkansas in 1720. They built cabins on Law's land and with the assistance of friendly Indians managed to survive their first winter in America. But within the year, Law went bankrupt, and without his financial backing the settlement collapsed. The colonists abandoned the Arkansas tract and many resettled a few miles outside New Orleans.

Law's unsuccessful venture was the only major attempt to colonize Arkansas during the period of French rule. Some French trappers and priests entered the area during the first half of the 18th century, and the many rivers, prairies, bayous, and mountains that bear French names are a reminder of these early adventurers. But the number of white men who came to Arkansas during the French period was extremely small, and thus in 1762, when France ceded its lands west of the Mississippi to Spain, only 88 persons inhabited the Arkansas Post.

Under Spanish rule the population of Arkansas continued to grow very slowly. A number of new settlements were made, including those at Montgomery's Landing, Hopefield, Portia, and Dardanelle. But a census in 1785 revealed that the non-Indian residents totaled only 196. In 1800 Spain transferred the entire trans-Mississippi region back to France, and three years later, when the area came under the jurisdiction of the United States as a result of the Louisiana Purchase, Arkansas could still count only about 600 non-Indian inhabitants.

For administrative reasons, the US Congress divided the Louisiana Purchase region into two separate territories in 1804 and included Arkansas in the District of Louisiana, or Upper Louisiana, as it was also known — which was then attached to the Territory of Indiana. In 1805 Congress gave Upper Louisiana separate territorial status and designated the lower part of present Missouri and all of present Arkansas as the District of New Madrid within the new territory. The following year the District of New Madrid was further subdivided when its southern region was recognized as the District of Arkansas.

During the first years of US control, fairly extensive explorations were undertaken in Arkansas. The entire length of the Arkansas River was mapped and the course of the Ouachita River was plotted as far west as Hot Springs. But during this period Arkansas attracted few new permanent residents, and by 1810 its number of white inhabitants had risen to only 1,062.

After Louisiana gained statehood in 1812, Congress changed the name of the territory of Upper Louisiana, which included Arkansas, to the Missouri Territory. Until 1819 Arkansas remained a part of the Missouri Territory and during that time Arkansas attracted a number of settlers from the section of the territory that today comprises southeastern Missouri. These new residents were victims of the New Madrid earthquake of 1811–1812, which was felt over an enormous area and severely rocked an area of the Mississippi valley extending southward 300 miles from the mouth of the Ohio. The disaster so devastated parts of southeastern Missouri that in 1815 the federal government authorized persons who had inhabited that hapless region to select other unorganized lands located elsewhere in the territory.

In 1819 Congress separated the area of Arkansas and most of what is today Oklahoma from the Missouri Territory and created from these regions the new Arkansas Territory. The territorial capital, first at Arkansas Post, was moved to Little Rock in 1821. When Congress considered territorial status for Arkansas, antislavery forces attempted to amend its territorial act so that no more slaves could be brought into the territory and those already there would be freed when they reached 25 years of age. The opponents of slavery won Senate approval for their measures, but the House of Representatives rejected the ban against slavery and thereby allowed the "peculiar institution" to continue to exist in the region.

When Arkansas became a territory in 1819, the total number of white residents was about 14,000. In the years that followed, the population grew steadily. The victims of the New Madrid earthquake and veterans of the War of 1812, who had been promised land bounties at the time of their enlistments, helped account for the increase in Arkansas inhabitants during the two decades after 1819. But even more important was the fact that after the Missouri Compromise of 1820, banning slavery north of latitude 36°30′, Arkansas was the only area under jurisdiction of the United States into which slavery could expand.

In the 1820s and 1830s cotton was by far the most profitable commodity produced in the United States. However, cotton quickly exhausted the soil of the southeastern states where it was first intensively cultivated and planters were forced to seek new lands farther west. Arkansas's climate proved to be ideally suited to the growing of cotton, and since there was no restriction against slaves in the territory, many planters chose to establish themselves in the underpopulated territory.

By 1833 the population of Arkansas had increased to 40,026, and many residents began to think of statehood. This number was almost 20,000 short of the 60,000 inhabitants required for admission to the Union; nevertheless, in December 1833 Arkansas's congressional delegate asked the Committee on Territories to report "as to the expediency of admitting the Territory into the Union as a state." At the same time that Congress was considering Arkansas's statehood, it received a similar request from Michigan. Since Michigan was to be a free state, its admission to the Union would upset the sectional balance of free and slave states, which had been established by the Missouri Compromise of 1820 — unless Arkansas, where slavery was firmly established, also gained statehood.

Southerners regarded the situation as urgent. In 1835 Arkansas's delegate in Congress wrote: "Let Michigan get into the union without us, and we are then completely at the mercy of both houses of Congress." To prevent this from happening, Arkansas lawmakers took an unprecedented step. When a census in 1835 showed that Arkansas had more than the 60,000 residents necessary for statehood, the governor sent a message to the territorial legislature expressing his feeling that "there can be no doubt but that, upon the application of the representatives of the people, Congress will freely grant to the people of Arkansas the requisite powers." But the Arkansas legislature did not wait for the federal Congress to initiate action regarding Arkansas statehood. Instead the legislature, which met in October 1835, passed a bill calling for the election of delegates to a convention that would meet in January 1836 to draw up a state constitution.

By the end of January 1836 Arkansas's constitution was completed and a copy was sent to Congress. The admission bill easily passed in the Senate, but in the House there were extended debates on the propriety of Arkansas's having formed a state constitution before receiving federal authorization to do so and also on the presence in the constitution of clauses permitting slavery in the new state. But the forces opposing Arkansas statehood were not sufficiently strong to permanently block the area's admission to the Union. On June 6 Arkansas's congressional delegate persuaded the House to adopt a resolution that it would "consider until disposed of" the Arkansas and Michigan statehood bills. Seven days later the House passed the Michigan bill, and after 25 hours of further debate also approved Arkansas's statehood application. On June 15, 1836, President Andrew Jackson signed the bill making Arkansas the 25th member of the federal Union.

After the outbreak of the Civil War, Arkansas declared its secession on May 6, 1861. Full privileges of statehood were not restored until June of 1868, after a new constitution enfranchising blacks had been drawn up under Radical Republican auspices and provision had been made for ratification of the 14th Amendment, a prerequisite for restoration to the Union. The Reconstruction period drew to a close in Arkansas with the beginning of the return of home rule and the enactment of a new constitution in 1874. In substantially amended form, that document remains in force in Arkansas today.

Oregon Treaty Ratified

Asserting the "clear and unquestionable" title of the United States to all of the Oregon country — a vast region occupied jointly by the United States and Great Britain — the Democratic platform of 1844 pressed for what it called the "reoccupation" of Oregon. It thus placed the party squarely in favor of what an 1845 magazine article was to call the nation's "manifest destiny to overspread the continent allotted by Providence for the free development of our yearly multiplying millions." The phrase, written in connection with the annexation of Texas, was applied to the Oregon dispute in an influential newspaper editorial and in the halls of Congress. It soon swept the entire nation.

The Oregon country, which stretched from the Rocky Mountains to the Pacific Ocean and from the 42nd Parallel on the south to 54°40′ on the north, included what are now the states of Washington, Oregon, Idaho, and parts of Wyoming and Montana, as well as Vancouver Island and much more of what became the Canadian province of British Columbia. The United States and Britain found themselves in joint possession of this huge tract after Spain and Russia abandoned their own conflicting claims to the area. Spain, which had once claimed the whole Pacific coast, in effect surrendered all rights north of California to the United States in the Florida Purchase Treaty of 1819. Russia, which once claimed the coast as far south as San Francisco, abandoned all rights below the parallel 54°40′ by a treaty concluded with the United States in 1824.

Both of the remaining contenders had substantial claims to the region. Britain based its claim on an agreement with Spain in 1790; on the explorations of Captain James Cook, Captain George Vancouver, and Sir Alexander McKenzie between 1778 and 1793; on the early fur-trading enterprises of the Hudson Bay Company; and on the establishment of Fort McLeod as the first settlement in the Oregon interior in 1805. The United States rested its claims to the Oregon country on the treaties mentioned above, on Captain Robert Gray's discovery of the Columbia River in 1792; on Lewis and Clark's extensive expedition of 1804–1806; on the fur-trading post with which John Jacob Astor founded Astoria, Oregon, in 1811; and on the presence of the thousands of US settlers who streamed over the Oregon Trail beginning in the 1840s.

As joint occupants of the huge area, Britain and the United States found themselves unable to agree on how to divide it. They sidestepped the issue in 1818 with a treaty providing for 10 years' joint occupation. In 1827 they renewed the understanding indefinitely, but agreed that either party could terminate the agreement on one year's notice.

In the meantime, negotiations went on. Beginning in 1826, the United States repeatedly offered to agree to a boundary along the 49th parallel — which already marked the country's border from what is now northern Minnesota to the Rockies. The British preferred the Columbia River (largely *below* the 49th Parallel) as a boundary. They also wanted access to Puget Sound and the Strait of Juan de Fuca between Vancouver Island and what later became the state of Washington.

An event that had a marked effect on the Oregon question took place late in 1841, when Senator Lewis F. Linn of Missouri brought before the US Congress a bill that — had it been enacted — would have provided military protection for the Oregon Trail and a grant of free land to every adult male immigrant who found his way to Oregon. Though the bill failed to pass in the final showdown two years later, the discussion surrounding it did much to encourage American settlement of the Oregon country.

While the matter hung in the air, many a land-hungry settler set out for Oregon in anticipation of the bill's passage. As the Oregon Trail began to swarm with immigrants, British apprehensions rose. So did Americans' interest in the new land. When Oregon became an issue in the presidential campaign of 1844, expansionists welcomed the uncompromising stand of the successful Democratic candidate, James K. Polk, and the campaign slogan of Fifty-four Forty or Fight.

With friction between the two countries intensified by the campaign and the British stand stiffened, Polk asked Congress's permission to give the required one year's notice to end the agreement for joint occupation. Between Polk's request — in his first annual message to Congress, on December 2, 1845 — and the introduction of the appropriate resolution in the House of Representatives on January 5, 1846, Britain asked the United States to renew its earlier offer to settle along the 49th parallel. Polk refused, but he did allow his secretary of state, in late February, to advise the US Minister in London that negotiations would be reopened if Great Britain initiated the step.

While Britain waited for a politically feasible moment to conciliate on this point, debate dragged on in the US Congress. Finally, on April 23, the resolution for ending the joint occupation of Oregon was passed by both houses and transmitted to President Polk. He delivered the required one-year's notice on May 21.

The notice was followed shortly by action from the British, in the form of a draft treaty, which reached Washington on June 6. It suggested that the contested boundary be along the 49th parallel to the Pacific, with Vancouver Island going to Britain. It also sought to guarantee free navigation of waters neighboring the

island for both parties and of the Columbia River below the 49th parallel for Britain.

Polk felt the treaty was reasonable, but in view of his own strong stand on the whole Oregon question, he took the unusual step of asking the advice of the Senate before formally submitting the treaty for that body's ratification. Senate reaction was favorable and formal submission of the treaty followed.

Amid groans from extreme expansionists and the gratification of moderates, Senate ratification of the treaty became a fact on June 15, 1846.

JUNE 16

Franklin D. Roosevelt's First Hundred Days End

When Franklin D. Roosevelt took office as the 32nd President of the United States on March 4, 1933, a massive economic depression was gripping the nation. Between 12 million and 15 million Americans were unemployed, almost all the country's banks were either closed or operating under state-imposed restrictions and, perhaps most dismaying, the majority of the citizenry was convinced that nothing could be done to stem the course of the great financial crisis. The new Chief Executive realized that the most pressing task before him was to dispel the general feeling of helplessness that had fallen on the nation. On March 5 Roosevelt proclaimed a four-day national bank holiday beginning on Monday, March 6, and he summoned the 73rd Congress to convene in special session on Thursday, March 9. The period from March 9 to June 16, 1933, has become famous as Roosevelt's Hundred Days. During that time the President electrified the country by taking a number of vigorous actions designed to alleviate the most pressing problems of the Great Depression; and by so doing he restored to the nation the self-confidence needed for economic recovery.

The banking crisis, which paralyzed the nation's financial operations, was Roosevelt's first concern. The financial emergency of 1933 might even have prompted so drastic a step as nationalization of US banking, but Roosevelt chose a more conservative approach. The Emergency Banking Act, which he sent to Congress on March 9, gave the President broad discretionary powers over gold movements, provided stringent penalties for hoarding, authorized an issue of new federal reserve notes, and permitted the reopening of sound banks and the reorganization of insolvent ones. Shortly after Congress convened, both the House and Senate approved the President's banking bill. Three days later, on

Sunday evening, March 12, Roosevelt broadcast his first "fireside chat" over the radio. The President assured the American people of the safety of their banks, and when the banks began to re-open on Monday, March 13, citizens showed their confidence in the new President by depositing more funds than they withdrew.

Only hours after the banking bill was approved — and days before he knew of its effect — Roosevelt, on March 10, sent a second message to Congress. This time the President asked for power to cut $400 million from veterans' payments and another $100 million from federal employees' salaries. A number of members of Congress opposed Roosevelt's Economy Act, but despite their disapproval the bill passed the House on March 11 and the Senate four days later.

Next, Roosevelt turned his attention to a less serious matter. The 1932 Democratic platform had pledged an end to prohibition, and in February 1933 the 72nd Congress had voted to repeal the 18th (Prohibition) Amendment. But before the 21st (Repeal) Amendment could gain the approval of the requisite three-fourths of states, the new Chief Executive announced at dinner on March 12, "I think this would be a good time for beer." The following day he sent a bill to Congress that modified the Volstead Act in order to legalize beer and light wines, thereby supplying additional revenue. That week Congress approved the measure, and on March 22 Roosevelt signed the Beer-Wine Revenue Act into law.

Encouraged by his initial successes with Congress, Roosevelt determined to use the special session to try to gain approval of additional legislation. On March 16 the President sent his farm bill to Capitol Hill. Roosevelt's proposals for raising the incomes of agricultural workers included a domestic allotment plan that sought to reduce crop surpluses by restricting the acreage under cultivation; institute a tax on the processing of agricultural commodities, which would be used to finance cash subsidies for farmers who agreed to limit their production; and assure those who cooperated that their purchasing power would be equal to that enjoyed in the years before World War I. The Agricultural Adjustment Act easily passed the House, but it met considerable opposition in the Senate. Many senators favored some kind of inflationary amendment to Roosevelt's farm bill, and the President tried to satisfy their demand by accepting an inflationary amendment and announcing on April 19 that the United States had gone off the gold standard. However, even after this concession the Senate delayed action on the farm bill. The Agricultural Adjustment Act and

the Emergency Farm Mortgage Act, which provided for the refinancing of farm mortgages, gained approval on May 12 only after the Farmer's Holiday Association had threatened to begin a nationwide agricultural strike.

During his first weeks in office, Roosevelt also won passage of legislation designed to alleviate the suffering caused by the massive unemployment resulting from the depression. On March 21 the President sent his unemployment relief message to Congress. Roosevelt urged the national legislature to create a Civilian Conservation Corps and to appropriate federal funds for the relief projects being carried out by state and municipal governments. Congress responded by approving the Civilian Conservation Corps Reforestation Relief Act on March 31 and the Federal Emergency Relief Act on May 12. The former measure established the Civilian Conservation Corps, which provided work in the nation's forests and on public projects for male citizens between the ages of 18 and 25; the latter legislation authorized outright grants totaling $500 million for city and state relief.

The unemployed also benefited from other legislation passed during the Hundred Days. When Roosevelt took office, banks were foreclosing on home mortgages at a rate of more than 1,000 per day. To deal with this situation, Congress approved the Home Owners Refinancing Act. The Act, which went into effect on June 13, 1933, created the Home Owners Loan Corporation. Authorized to issue bonds amounting to $2 billion the corporation during its three-year existence helped more than 20 percent of the nation's homeowners retain their dwellings.

While much of the legislation of the spring of 1933 provided short-term assistance to millions of Americans, Roosevelt and the Congress realized that a much broader program was necessary to revive the economy. In mid-May the President sent the National Industrial Recovery Act to Congress. Despite considerable opposition in the Senate, the bill won congressional approval and was signed into law on June 16. The NIRA, as it was popularly known, called for self-regulation of the nation's industries under government supervision. Under the act, industrial and trade organizations were permitted to draw up fair competition codes and the President was authorized to prescribe similar codes for industries that failed to enter into voluntary agreements. The codes, which permitted price agreements and established production quotas, were exempt from antitrust laws, but the National Recovery Administration, a governmental agency, set up under the NIRA, was empowered to insure compliance with and prevent abuses of the codes. The NIRA provided for close cooperation between government and industry, but it also gave a measure of protection to workers. The act sought to establish maximum hours and to assure laborers at least a minimum wage; even more important was Section 7A of the measure, which guaranteed the right of workers "to organize and bargain collectively through representatives of their own choosing." Also a part of the NIRA was the Public Works Administration, set up under Title II of the act with a $3.3 billion appropriation for the construction of roads, buildings, and other facilities whose creation would increase employment.

During the special session, Roosevelt and the Congress also began to make some progress toward curbing the abuses in the exchange of securities and in banking that had contributed to the economic difficulties leading to the depression. The Federal Securities, or "Truth-in-Securities," Act of 1933, which became law on May 27, forced stockbrokers to give complete information to investors about new issues of securities that were being offered publicly or sold through the mail or in interstate commerce, and required most new issues to be registered with the Federal Trade Commission (later with the Securities and Exchange Commission). The Glass-Steagall Banking Act of 1933, which went into effect on June 16, created the Federal Deposit Insurance Corporation. The corporation guaranteed individual bank deposits up to $5,000 (later increased to $10,000), and other provisions of the act enabled the Federal Reserve Board to curb excessive speculation on credit, separated commercial banking from investment banking, and permitted savings and industrial banks to join the federal reserve system.

In addition to approving legislation designed to relieve the misery of the depression and to curtail abuses that helped bring about the economic collapse, the special congressional session also established the Tennessee Valley Authority. Throughout the 1920s a number of members of Congress had urged that the hydroelectric and munitions plants built during World War I at Muscle Shoals, Alabama, be used to manufacture fertilizer and to provide power for Tennessee Valley residents. Twice Congress had approved federal operations at Muscle Shoals, but Presidents Herbert Hoover and Calvin Coolidge both vetoed the bills. Roosevelt, however, envisioned the TVA as more than a power-generating facility; he saw it as an opportunity to experiment in regional development planning and wanted the TVA to engage in such wide-ranging activities as flood control, soil conservation, and the diversification of the area's industries. On April 10 Roosevelt brought the Tennessee Val-

ley Act to the attention of Congress. The legislature quickly approved the bill, and on May 18 the Tennessee Valley Authority became a reality.

In all, 15 bills were enacted into law during the Hundred Days. In addition to the aforementioned legislation, Congress approved and Roosevelt signed into law the Emergency Railroad Transportation Act, which attempted to eliminate duplication of rail services and promptly reorganize faltering rail lines; a bill abrogating the gold clause in public and private contracts; and an act reorganizing agricultural credit operations. The legislation of the spring of 1933 did not eliminate the problems of the depression. When the Hundred Days ended on June 16, 1933, with the adjournment of an exhausted 73rd Congress, the US economy was still in the doldrums. But the national attitude had undergone a radical transformation. The citizenry responded positively to the actions of their energetic President. Gone was the feeling of hopelessness that had frustrated Americans to the point of despair in March; in its place was a restored confidence that they would eventually overcome the financial crisis that gripped the nation.

JUNE 17

Bunker Hill Day

Buoyed by the victories that marked the beginning of the American Revolution at Lexington and Concord (see April 19) in 1775, the Massachusetts patriots established their colony's capital at Boston, where the British redcoats had taken refuge. The Provincial Congress met on April 23 and voted to raise an army of 30,000 New England men. Connecticut, New Hampshire, and Rhode Island were unable to send their full quotas, but by June, 15,000 Americans had gathered in the towns outside Boston.

General Artemas Ward, the commander in chief of the Massachusetts contingent, held the patriot center with 9,000 men at Cambridge. Major General John Thomas commanded the army's right wing, comprising 5,000 men stationed at Dorchester, Jamaica Plains, and Roxbury. The remaining forces, including Colonel John Stark's New Hampshire regiment, covered the colonists' left flank at Charlestown Neck, Chelsea, and Medford.

Thomas Gage, the governor of Massachusetts and the commander in chief of British forces in America, had 6,500 soldiers in the Boston garrison. King George III had ordered him to proclaim martial law in Massachusetts, but the rebels' numerical superiority suggested that he rely on tact as well as terror. General Gage had Major General John Burgoyne exercise his literary gift by writing a proclamation offering amnesty to all colonists who laid down their arms, with the exception of the patriot leaders Samuel Adams and John Hancock. "Gentleman Johnny's" plea to the "infatuated multitude" amused or annoyed the colonists, but had little other effect.

Military preparations then replaced political maneuvering. General Gage had planned to take Dorchester Heights, one of the pieces of unoccupied strategic high ground lying on the periphery of Boston. Learning of the British intention on June 13, the rebels decided to move first and fortify another dominant position, Bunker Hill on Charlestown Neck.

On the evening of June 16, Colonel William Prescott collected a force of about 1,200 men on Cambridge common and began the march to Charlestown Neck. Brigadier General Israel Putnam of Connecticut met them there with entrenching equipment. The troops moved beyond Bunker Hill to what later became known as Breed's Hill. There Prescott revealed to his fellow officers the nature of their mission and requested their advice as to the location of the fortifications. Imprudently the council of officers decided to put their main effort into the defense of the less important and less tenable Breed's Hill: Bunker Hill, adjacent to the north, would be a secondary location.

Work began at midnight under the direction of Colonel Richard Gridley, who had gained engineering experience in the colonial wars against the French and Indians. At 4:00 A.M. dawn revealed the colonial entrenchments to the men aboard the British sloop *Lively*. They turned their guns on the Americans, but their fire was ineffective against the rebel stronghold.

At a council of war, General Gage and his staff decided that they must oust the Americans from their new position as quickly as possible. Unable to see how far the patriot defenses extended, the British commanders chose to land troops at Moulton's Point on Charlestown Neck, a safe spot out of range of the patriot redoubt. According to the plan devised by Major General William Howe, the British soldiers would then launch a two-pronged attack on the Americans — an assault on the front and an enveloping movement around the enemy's left flank.

The necessity of waiting for the high tide, and other preparations, delayed the start of the operation for about six hours. The Americans used the interval to strengthen their position. Colonels John Stark and James Read arrived with their regiments from Medford. Stark shrewdly placed most of his men along the undefended beach between the Mystic River and the eastern end of the patriot line. He detached the remainder to assist Captain Thomas Knowlton, whose soldiers were stationed behind a railed fence barricade to his right.

Fifteen hundred men landed at about 1:00 P.M., but Howe, their commander, decided to wait for reinforcements to assist in the assault on the improved American line. Soon the 47th Regiment, the First Marine Battalion, and six additional companies joined the British troops on the beachhead. Brigadier General Robert Pigot advanced with the 43rd and 38th regiments against the redoubt, but their effort was stopped by the patriot marksmen's musket fire.

Simultaneously with Pigot's movement, Howe led the drive on the American left. Grenadiers and elements of the 5th and 52nd British regiments hit the rail fence frontally, while 11 light infantry companies attempted to turn the left end of the patriot line. The rebels beat back both groups with heavy fire. Stark arranged his men in three ranks, one of which was always firing as the other two reloaded. The British light infantry alone left 96 of its men dead on the field.

Howe quickly regrouped his forces and attempted a second assault. This time the British light infantry executed a secondary attack on the American left, while Howe and Pigot went after the redoubt. The Americans waited until their opponents were as close as 100 feet from them and then drove them back by shooting.

Sir Henry Clinton joined Howe and Pigot on the beachhead after this second failure. The three British generals then prepared for a third assault on the colonial redoubt; this time they wisely advised their troops to drop the 100-to-125 pounds of equipment each had carried on the previous attempts. Reinforced with fresh troops 400 strong, the redcoats again moved forward against the redoubt.

Preparing for a bayonet charge, the British advanced in column until they were within 10 yards of the defenders. Naturally they suffered heavy casualties. The Americans, critically short of ammunition, fought gallantly, even engaging in hand-to-hand combat with stones against the British bayonets. Finally the attackers took the position and the rebels fell back. The British, however, were so exhausted that they pursued the Americans only as far as neighboring Bunker Hill.

One hundred forty Americans, including Dr. Joseph Warren, the president of Massachusetts' Provincial Congress, died in the battle of Bunker Hill; and about 301 patriots of the approximately 2,000 who actually fought in the engagement suffered wounds. British losses were much higher: of the 2,500 redcoats involved in the encounter, 40 percent were casualties. Nineteen officers and 207 men died; and 70 officers and 758 men fell wounded.

The battle of Bunker Hill encouraged the colonists and discouraged any thoughts of reconciliation with the mother country. The Americans had proved to themselves that they could stand up to the redcoats. And the battle had shown the British that the rebels were not to be underestimated. Rather, they were to be regarded as dangerous foes. Never again were British forces quite so aggressive in their military planning. Furthermore, and to their sorrow, the British postponed indefinitely any thoughts of occupying Dorchester Heights. George Washington, who arrived on July 2, 1775, to take command of the forces surrounding Boston, was able to wait until he had sufficient guns and ammunition to seize that vital terrain. In March 1776 he took the Heights without opposition. Rapidly fortifying the position, he thereby rendered the British position in Boston untenable. On March 17, 1776, an occasion still marked annually as Evacuation Day in Boston (see March 17), Howe and his forces departed from the city by ship.

In 1823 Massachusetts citizens organized the Bunker Hill Monument Association to erect a suitable tribute to the deeds of their forebears. By 1825 they had acquired several acres, near the site of the patriot redoubt, on Breed's Hill. On June 17, 1825, exactly 50 years after the battle, several thousand persons paraded from downtown Boston to the hill to see the cornerstone-laying ceremonies. Military units, followed by 200 veterans of the American Revolution — including 40 survivors of the Bunker Hill engagement — led the procession. The grand master of the Freemasons, the president of the Monument Association, and the aged Marquis de Lafayette, who was visiting the United States at the time, laid the cornerstone.

The 221-foot-high plain granite shaft, 31 feet square at the base and 15 feet square at the top, reached completion on June 17, 1843, eighteen years after the cornerstone laying. It stands in a four-acre park in a residential section of Charlestown. Once a separate municipality, Charlestown today is part of the city of Boston. A statue of Colonel William Prescott, the American commander at the battle, stands near the Bunker Hill Monument. The Commonwealth of Massachusetts, which owns and administers the monument, invites the public to visit both the small museum connected with the monument, and the monument's tower — which can be reached via an interior spiral staircase.

Daniel Webster spoke in 1825 and in 1843.

His "Bunker Hill Orations" are famous pieces of American oratory. In them Webster set the tone for the laying of the cornerstone, saying that the people had "assembled to commemorate the establishment of great public principles of liberty, and to do honor to the distinguished dead." He concluded by praying that the "country itself become a vast and splendid monument, not of oppression and terror, but of Wisdom, of Peace, and of Liberty, upon which the world may gaze with admiration forever." It was at the dedication of the completed memorial in 1843 that Webster eulogized George Washington, describing him as "First in war, first in peace, and first in the hearts of his countrymen."

Another reminder of the historic clash of 1775 is Jonathan Trumbull's painting *The Battle of Bunker Hill,* which hangs in the Yale University Art Gallery at New Haven. Executed in 1786, it depicts the death of Dr. Joseph Warren as the British seized the Breed's Hill redoubt. At the far left, General Israel Putnam calls for the patriots to retreat, while at the right center, British Major John Pitcairn dies in the arms of his son, a marine lieutenant. Peter Salem, the black American who fired the shot that struck Pitcairn, also appears in the painting.

Bunker Hill Day is an annual holiday in Boston and throughout Suffolk County, Massachusetts. During the morning, patriotic societies hold commemorative services at the Bunker Hill Monument grounds, where a dignitary customarily delivers an oration. The participants also lay a wreath at the statue of Prescott. State and city officials, often including the governor of Massachusetts and mayor of Boston, are usually in attendance. Distinguished guests also frequently include Massachusetts representatives to Congress, home from Washington for the occasion.

In the afternoon as many as 200,000 persons view a three-hour parade through the streets of Charlestown. The procession generally begins on Vine Street and continues along Bunker Hill Street and in a circuitous four-mile route to Bunker Hill Monument and the parade's termination point beyond. Bands, drum and bugle corps, military units, civic organizations, public officeholders, and candidates for office traditionally appear among the more than 5,000 marchers. In 1975, the 200th anniversary of the battle, the conflict was several times reenacted over a period of several days.

Though it is primarily a solemn commemoration, Bunker Hill Day is not without its air of holiday celebration. In 1969, for instance, an art fair was held at the Monument, and free ice cream was distributed. The previous evening the parade chief marshal's dinner was held in

Post 26 American Legion Hall, and the Majestic Knights of Columbus, with three visiting musical units, staged a drum and bugle exhibition in the Ryan playground at Sullivan Square.

Supreme Court Fair Housing Decision

On April 11, 1968, the Civil Rights Act of 1968, signed by President Lyndon B. Johnson, became effective. It included fair housing provisions, although concern was voiced that they fell short of entirely wiping out racial discrimination in housing. A little more than two months later, on June 17, 1968, the US Supreme Court went beyond the 1968 statute. In a 7 to 2 decision, the Court upheld the validity of a sweeping then 102-year-old law that specifically forbade racial discrimination in selling or renting any kind of property.

The almost forgotten law, dating from 1866 and invoked once in 1903 in the case of the *United States* v. *Morris,* had been promulgated to strengthen the effectiveness of the 13th Amendment, enacted in 1865, which stated that "neither slavery nor involuntary servitude shall exist within the United States, or any place subject to their jurisdiction." The Civil Rights Act of 1866 had explicitly provided "that all . . . citizens of the United States . . . of every race and color, without regard to any previous condition of slavery . . . shall have the same right, in every State and Territory in the United States . . . to inherit, purchase, lease, sell, hold, and convey real and personal property . . . as is enjoyed by white citizens. . . ."

Most of the handful of lawyers aware of the existence of the Reconstruction Era law generally assumed that it had aimed merely at assuring the rights of former slaves to possess property; they failed to realize the full implications of the all-encompassing statement. But in 1966 lawyers for the National Committee Against Discrimination in Housing attempted, by resurrecting the 1866 statute, to get around the longstanding failure of the US Congress to enact fair housing provisions. In the case of *Jones* v. *Mayer,* they represented Joseph Lee Jones, a black bail bondsman in St. Louis and his white wife, Barbara Jo, who had not been allowed to purchase a home in a St. Louis development because Mr. Jones was black. The case, which the interracial couple had inaugurated on September 2, 1965, was dismissed by the Federal District Court and then by the US Court of Appeals for the Eighth Circuit, both of which ruled that neither the 1866 statute nor for that matter the US Constitution forbids racial discrimination in property transactions by private owners.

The Supreme Court's 1968 ruling on the side of Mr. and Mrs. Jones reached beyond the less sweeping fair housing provisions — intended by January 1, 1970, to cover about 80 percent of all housing sold or rented in the country — that had been enacted by Congress in the Civil Rights Act of April 1968. That legislation immediately banned discrimination in the sale or rental of 900,000 federally insured housing units; then by January 1, 1969, in 19.8 million multifamily housing units; and thirdly, by January 1, 1970, in 31.3 million single-family houses where sale or rental was handled by a broker.

According to the 1866 law, racial discrimination is prohibited even in real estate transactions involving single-family homes sold or rented privately by their owners without a broker and also in two- to four-family units. Justice Potter Stewart summed up the majority opinion as follows:

At the very least, the freedom that Congress is empowered to secure under the Thirteenth Amendment includes the freedom to buy whatever a white man can buy, the right to live wherever a white man can live. If Congress cannot say that being a free man means at least this much, then the Thirteenth Amendment made a promise the Nation cannot keep.

JUNE 18

Susan B. Anthony Fined for Voting

Testing for women the citizenship and voting rights extended to male blacks by the 14th and 15th amendments, suffragist Susan B. Anthony led a group of women who registered and voted in a Rochester, New York, election in 1872. Their action set off a celebrated legal case. Anthony was arrested, tried, and, on June 18, 1872, sentenced to pay a fine. Adamant in her refusal to do so, she was allowed to go free, by a judge who feared she might appeal the case to higher courts.

Susan Brownell Anthony was born in Adams, Massachusetts, in 1820 on February 15, which is now observed as Susan B. Anthony Day (see February 15). As Quakers, her parents belonged to a group that had always recognized the equal rights of women — an attitude their daughter inherited. Susan Anthony, a person of remarkable intellect and strong personality, was educated at her father's school and subsequently served as a teacher herself for 15 years.

Her first reform activities were in the field of temperance. When she was prevented — because she was a woman — from addressing a temperance meeting, she joined with others in 1852 to form the Woman's State Temperance Society of New York, the first organization of its kind. She also lectured widely, urging the abolition of slavery. But she came to realize that women could work effectively for social reform only if they obtained the same rights and privileges as men, and she eventually turned her major attention toward that end.

Although the causes of blacks' rights and women's rights were promoted more or less inseparably until after the Civil War, a separate women's rights convention had been held at Seneca Falls, New York, in 1848 by Elizabeth Cady Stanton and others. It had been followed by other women's meetings, including one at Worcester, Massachusetts, in 1850, headed by Lucy Stone. But it was when women found themselves excluded from provisions of the 14th and 15th amendments — uncertain of passage even without being attached to the less popular women's cause — that a separate women's rights movement began in earnest.

Susan B. Anthony, who has been described as the dynamic force that galvanized the new women's movement into effective action, first met the pioneering Stanton at a temperance meeting in 1851. Thus began a friendship that lasted 50 years. With Stanton, Anthony obtained New York State laws granting women rights over their children and control of their own earnings and property as early as 1860. Together the two women brought out the militant women's rights newspaper *The Revolution* from 1868 to 1870, with Anthony as publisher and Stanton as an editor.

It was in 1869 that they organized the National Woman Suffrage Association. Stanton was elected president of the new organization and Anthony became head of its executive committee. The stated purpose of the organization, which held a national convention in each of the next 50 years, was to secure the vote for women by means of a constitutional amendment. The Anthony Woman Suffrage Amendment was introduced before a congressional hearing in 1868, the first of a half-century of unsuccessful annual presentations. Across the nation and in Europe, Anthony meanwhile lectured eloquently on behalf of suffrage and contributed to leading magazines. With Stanton and Matilda Joslyn Gage, she compiled the first three volumes of the *History of Woman Suffrage*, which ultimately embraced the years 1881–1922.

While the National Woman Suffrage Association began its effort on the national level, the American Woman Suffrage Association, founded in 1869 under the leadership of Stone and others, was specifically geared for work in the states. In 1890 the two organizations merged, as the National American Woman Suffrage Association. Anthony served from 1892 to 1900 as president of the new group, which pressed its campaign on both the national and state levels. In 1888 she organized the International Council of Women and in 1904 the International Woman Suffrage Alliance.

Susan B. Anthony died in Rochester, New York, on March 13, 1906. Her advocacy had had its influence in the granting of women's voting privileges by several states; and her work paved the way both for passage of the 19th Amendment, which finally gave all American women the right to vote in 1920 (see August 26), and for the recognition of human rights later expressed in the charter of the United Nations.

Anthony's birthplace, at Bowen's Corners, East Road, Adams, Massachusetts, is now privately owned and not open to the public. The Adams Free Library and the North Adams Public Library have some items — books, a portrait, photographs, momentos — pertaining to her, and the Henry E. Huntington Library and Art Gallery at San Marino, California, maintains the Susan B. Anthony Memorial Collection. A statue of her can be seen in the Capitol at Washington, D.C., and in 1950 she was elected to the Hall of Fame for Great Americans in New York City. The Susan B. Anthony Memorial, Inc., owns and operates the Susan B. Anthony house, built in 1845, at 17 Madison Street, Rochester, New York. The house, which is open to the public several days each week, was Anthony's home from 1866 to 1906.

War of 1812 Begins

The War of 1812 began with a declaration of war on Great Britain by Congress on June 18, 1812. The action, which came after heated debate between congressional "hawks," such as Henry Clay and John C. Calhoun, and "doves," such as John Randolph of Roanoke, was a result of, among other things, Britain's violation of American rights on the high seas. This included such annoyances as searching US vessels and impressing American seamen into the British navy. All this was within the context of Britain's longstanding war with France. That, in turn, was part of the Napoleonic Wars, which had been going on for years, involving most of Europe at one time or another.

France tried to exclude British goods — or goods cleared through Britain — from countries under French control. Britain forbade nonbelligerents' vessels to trade with France or French dependencies without first touching at English ports. And both countries sought to restrict the rights of neutrals. In view of British naval superiority, the French stricture had less effect on American shipping than the British ban, which extended to trade in American ships between Europe and the West Indies — a lucrative traffic that American shippers were more than willing to assume while hostilities raged abroad.

Americans, especially western Americans, chafed at suspected British incitement of Indian warfare on the frontier. Such hostilities served as a barrier to westward expansion by the new United States — and gave Indian settlements the potential of becoming, as the British hoped they would, a permanent buffer state between the United States and British possessions in Canada.

Although these were the obvious causes of conflict, certain less manifest hopes, such as the desire of western and southern Americans to acquire Canada and Florida, helped create a climate for war. But not until after Congress had declared war did President James Madison realize how ill-equipped for such a contest his young nation was — or how baseless were the hopes of hawks who dreamed of taking Canada at one sudden swoop.

Had Britain not also been preoccupied with war in Europe, it is entirely possible the United States would have lost the contest. To begin with, three American expeditions aimed at Montreal in the summer of 1812 came to naught. So, really, did early US successes at sea, like the triumph of the *Constitution* over the *Guerrière* (see August 19) and the *United States* over the *Macedonian.* The principal American achievements of the war were on the Great Lakes. They included such accomplishments as Oliver H. Perry's famous Lake Erie victory over Britain's Great Lakes fleet in September 1813. It was also in 1813 that William Henry Harrison defeated British and Indian forces in the battle of the Thames, in which the Indian chief Tecumseh was killed (see October 5). But after a number of other engagements, which saw successes on both sides, the war in the north was a draw by the late summer of 1814.

Britain meanwhile had reestablished its supremacy on the sea the previous year. After that, most oceangoing American ships either were captured, or confined to port for the rest of the war — victims of the British blockade of the eastern seaboard, which had a devastating effect both on American commerce and on US government revenues.

The British also embarked on a series of hit-and-run attacks along the coast, attacking victoriously at Bladensburg, Maryland, in August 1814 and continuing on to Washington, where they burned the White House and other public buildings. Not very long afterwards, however, British forces were turned back before they reached Baltimore, notwithstanding the ferocity of their September 13–14 bombardment of Fort McHenry. It was that spectacular and useless assault that inspired Francis Scott Key, who witnessed the event, to write "The Star-Spangled Banner."

The setback at Baltimore, coupled with the almost simultaneous American victory in the September 11 battle of Lake Champlain, was important in helping persuade the British to end the war. Negotiations for peace had, in fact, been going on for some time. In the end both sides found it expedient to back down from their strongly stated original demands and to sign, on December 24, 1814, at Ghent in Belgium, a peace treaty. The Treaty of Ghent dealt with none of the issues over which the war had ostensibly been fought, but it ended a serious financial drain on both governments and brought important advantages, directly and indirectly, to the Americans (see December 24).

The British fleet that had been turned back at Baltimore meanwhile retired to Jamaica. From there they launched an attack on New Orleans that became the most devastating British debacle of the war — the battle of New Orleans (see January 8), fought two weeks after the treaty had been signed. Although that battle obviously had no effect on the already concluded terms of peace, it was important in restoring the confidence of the young American nation, which then embarked on a period of continental expansion and withdrew from the European political scene.

JUNE 19

Albany Congress Convenes

Several times during the 17th and 18th centuries the British colonies in North America, while retaining their separate identities and governments, joined together for reasons of mutual defense and assistance. As early as 1643, for example, Massachusetts Bay, Plymouth, Connecticut, and New Haven formed the New England Confederation, an association empowered to declare war and settle intercolonial problems and deal with Indian affairs. Other ventures in intercolonial cooperation were against the backdrop of the worldwide struggle for empire between England and France, whose territory was later recognized to have been a major prize of this power contest, conflicts related to the rivalry extended, off and on, for three-quarters of a century, from 1689 until the Treaty of Paris of 1763.

During King William's War of 1689 to 1697, New York coordinated its defense (in 1690) with that of its neighbors Connecticut and Massachusetts; and Governor Benjamin Fletcher of New

York suggested that provinces as far away as Virginia provide troops to protect his colony's frontiers. At the time of Queen Anne's War of 1702 to 1713, plans for concerted colonial action were put forth, and during King George's War of 1744 to 1748, a combined force of men from the New England colonies directed a campaign against the French stronghold of Louisbourg on Nova Scotia's Cape Breton Island. But perhaps the most notable attempt of the colonies to work together before the difficult years preceding the American Revolution was the Albany Congress that convened on June 19, 1754, on the eve of the French and Indian War — the conflict that would end in 1763 with the ousting of the French from virtually all of North America.

In the early 1750s the possibility of an alliance between the Iroquois Indians and the French posed a great threat to the British colonies in America. Realizing this danger, the British Board of Trade, in the autumn of 1753, sought to strengthen the wavering Iroquois loyalty by asking the representatives of Virginia, Maryland, Pennsylvania, New Jersey, New York, New Hampshire, and Massachusetts to meet together and to try to settle any difficulties that they might have with the Indians. When the intercolonial conference convened in Albany, Virginia was preoccupied with its own dealings with the Ohio Valley Indians and thus did not send a representative to the distant meeting. But the six other colonies, excepting New Jersey, complied with the British request, and Connecticut and Rhode Island also sent delegates.

The representatives to the Albany Congress included some of the most outstanding leaders of the colonies. Among others, Massachusetts sent Thomas Hutchinson, who had served as speaker of the General Court, and who was a member of the provincial council; Rhode Island's delegation included its chief justice, Stephen Hopkins, who in 1755 became the colony's governor and later signed the Declaration of Independence; and New York was represented by its lieutenant governor, James De Lancey. But from Pennsylvania came undoubtedly the most important member, Benjamin Franklin.

A total of 25 colonial delegates met with the 150 Iroquois who attended the Albany Congress, and the Iroquois Nation expressed serious grievances against the British. In particular, they resented the colonists' — and especially the New Yorkers' — abuses of the fur trade and their encroachment on Iroquoian lands. In addition, Chief Hendrick of the Mohawks — one of the Iroquois nations — remarked that from 1751 to 1754 the colonists had neglected the Indians, while during that same time, he noted, "the French are a subtle and vigilant people, ever

using their utmost endeavors to seduce and bring our people over to them." Hendrick then went on to deny the colonists' accusations that the Iroquois were permitting the French to occupy their lands. He took the colonies to task for failing to provide adequate defenses for their own borders. And he concluded by charging that certain Albany merchants were involved in trading munitions with the French in Canada.

The Albany delegates responded to each of the Iroquois grievances. Their explanations of the colonists' past behavior and their promises of improved conduct in the future at least superficially satisfied the Indians, and in the days following July 5, 1754, the Indians seemed willing to renew their friendship with the British. The Iroquois asked for a prohibition on the sale of rum in Indian territory, requested that a church be erected at Canojoharie in the Mohawk Valley "to make us Religious and lead better lives," and warned the British of the dangers of leaving their frontier regions unprotected. Then, on July 9, 1754, the British and Indians concluded their official negotiations, and a few days later the Iroquois returned to their homes with 30 wagonloads of gifts.

Although called for the specific purpose of cementing closer relations with the Iroquois, the Albany Congress also considered a much broader issue. On June 24 the question "whether a Union of all the Colonies is not at present absolutely necessary for their security and defense" came before the assembly. A number of the Albany delegates had no authorization from their respective colonies to discuss the possibility of establishing an intercolonial union, but this did not impede their consideration of the matter. The representatives unanimously agreed that a colonial union could best handle the emergency situation created by the threatened alliance between the French and Indians, and they then proceeded to examine various plans for setting up the proposed union.

Even before the opening of the Albany Congress, Benjamin Franklin had recognized the urgent need for a union of the British colonies. The French had taken possession of the Forks of the Ohio River in May 1754. Writing in his *Pennsylvania Gazette* that month, Franklin noted:

The confidence of the French in this undertaking seems well grounded in the present disunited state of the British colonies, and the extreme difficulty of bringing so many different governments and assemblies to agree to any speedy and effectual measures for our common defence and security, while our enemies have the great advantage of being under one direction, with one council, and one purse.

As early as 1751 Franklin had devised a preliminary plan of union, and he incorporated many of his earlier ideas in the "Short Hints toward a Scheme for Uniting the Northern Colonies," which he presented to the Albany Congress.

Franklin's "Short Hints" provided for a supra-colonial government to be established by an act of Parliament and to consist of a grand council and a president-general. According to the plan the assembly of each colony would select at least one member of the council, and the larger colonies would have additional representation in that body proportioned according to the "sums they pay yearly to the General Treasury"; the president-general would be an appointee of the Crown and have the power to veto all acts of the grand council. The authority Franklin vested in the grand council and the president-general was extensive: they would attend to Indian treaties, control the course of British settlement, erect forts, provide soldiers, and in short do "everything . . . necessary for the defense and support of the Colonies in General, and increasing and extending their settlements, etc."

The Albany Congress also considered plans of union advanced by Richard Peters of Pennsylvania, Thomas Hutchinson of Massachusetts, and Thomas Pownall, the sympathetic freelance observer of colonial defense problems, who held important posts in several colonies before his eventual return to England. But after due deliberation the delegates chose Franklin's outline as the basis for the colonial union they deemed so necessary. On July 10 the Congress prepared the final draft of the "Plan of a Proposed Union." It called for an act of Parliament to form a union of all British colonies in North America, excepting Nova Scotia and Georgia, in which "each Colony may retain its present constitution"; it provided for a president-general, appointed by the Crown and having final veto power, and a grand council, whose members would be elected by the colonial assemblies; and it vested in the president-general and grand council responsibility for Indian affairs and other matters related to the defense of the colonies.

Despite the strong arguments favoring the creation of a colonial union, the plan of a "general Government" of the colonies in America was emphatically rejected by both the colonial assemblies and the British government. In 1754 the Americans believed that a centralized union threatened the individual autonomy of each colony and the British thought that a general government encroached upon the royal prerogative. But the "Albany Plan of Union," which provided for a central government whose member colonies would retain their separate identities, fore-shadowed other governments in America. Less than three decades later, the Articles of Confederation of 1781 embodied the plan's federal ideas, and in 1787 Federalist thinking provided the basis for the US Constitution.

JUNE 20

West Virginia Admission Day

On December 31, 1862, Congress passed an act providing for the admission of West Virginia to the Union as an independent state on condition that certain changes be made in its proposed constitution. Those changes were made, and, on April 20, 1863, President Abraham Lincoln issued a proclamation that admission should take effect 60 days later. Thus West Virginia entered the Union as the 35th state on June 20. West Virginia Admission Day, celebrated on June 20, is a legal holiday in the state, proclaimed by the governor and observed with the display of flags and local parades and festivities. Special note of the day is taken in those public schools that are then in session.

1963, West Virginia's centennial of statehood, was filled with special commemorative activities, held not only on June 20, but throughout the year. An estimated 20,000 persons took part in planning and executing the varied programs and projects. Local county activities included talent contests, sports events, restoration of historic landmarks, house and garden tours, craft exhibits, pageants, and parades.

Stotesbury, for example, a town located south of Beckley in the southern part of the state and the site of the country's first coal-town museum, featured exhibits depicting the history of coal production and mining techniques during the course of the century. The Shepherdstown Fisheries staged the Trout Festival, at which a new type of gold-colored trout, appropriately called the Centennial Golden Trout, was introduced. In honor of the state's 100th birthday, several trout streams were stocked with the golden fish, reputed to be "a fierce fighter in water and a superb delicacy on the table." The *Rhododendron,* the reconstructed centennial showboat named for West Virginia's state flower, wended its way along the shorelines of the Ohio, Monongahela, and Kanawha rivers, recalling the exciting riverboat era of the 19th century. Ballet performances and old-fashioned dramatic productions were staged in the showboat's beautifully decorated interior.

The statewide programs, generally sponsored by the West Virginia Centennial Commission, offered a variety of appealing attractions. In late April the centennial queen, chosen through county competitions to preside at centennial celebrations and represent West Virginia in out-of-state festivities, was crowned at the state capitol in Charleston; a lavish coronation ball followed at the city's civic center. The commission sponsored a series of painting, sculpture, folk drama, folk opera, and poetry contests, centering on such themes as the state's historical traditions, scenic beauty, and industrial progress. Thousands of West Virginians participated and cash prizes were awarded. An eight-car exhibit train containing displays about West Virginia's history, natural resources, and multifold development toured the state during summer 1963. A National Youth Honor Science Camp, set up near the National Radio Astronomy Observatory at Green Bank, West Virginia, enabled 100 top students, selected through nationwide competition, to stay two to three weeks at this world-famous center for discovering, measuring, and identifying radio waves from outer space.

Probably the two most colorful statewide events were those recalling West Virginia's unique path to statehood. On April 20, 1963, Governor William Barron of West Virginia, members of the state legislature, and their spouses dressed in authentic costumes of the 1863 era to reenact the first momentous session of the West Virginia legislature at Wheeling, the first capital. And President Abraham Lincoln's proclamation declaring West Virginia a state was read aloud once again. Other events marking the anniversary in Wheeling included a mock fire, extinguished with the help of an 1863 fire engine, a serenade of Civil War songs by "Union soldiers," special store sales of old-fashioned goods such as calico, and a costume ball.

The climax of the centennial year came on West Virginia Admission Day, June 20. A commemorative stamp and medallion were issued and there were special events in Charleston. After a pioneer birthday breakfast for persons born on June 20 and a horse and wagon parade, official ceremonies were staged on the steps of the massive, yellow-domed state capitol building, on the bank of the Kanawha River. President John F. Kennedy, the featured speaker, delivered a brief address, in which he spoke about West Virginia's birth during the Civil War and the state's progress in recent years. The ceremony ended with a 35-gun salute and the raising of the 50-star US flag, as well as a weatherbeaten 35-star one, over the capitol plaza. Other events featured in Charleston on June 20 included the serving of a giant, 35-layer centennial birthday

cake free to the public, the release of 100 balloons, musical programs, water-skiing exhibitions, a legislative baseball game of "House vs. Senate" (with state supreme court members serving as umpires), a Statehood Day parade, an ox roast, and the 35th Star, a special evening program honoring West Virginia statehood, which was followed by fireworks.

The admission to the Union of the Mountain State, as West Virginia is nicknamed, was unusual since it was born out of the Civil War. The movement for independence from Virginia, in which the area was included, originated long before June 20, 1863, extending back into the early history of this country.

Artifacts, skeletons, and numerous conical-shaped mounds found in West Virginia, especially along the Ohio and Kanawha rivers, indicate that the area was settled by the prehistoric Mound Builder Indians. By the late 17th century, when white settlers began to appear in the region, less sedentary Indian tribes regarded the mountainous territory — traversed by three major Indian trails — primarily as a convenient hunting area.

Permanent white colonization came fairly late and was the result of pressure exerted by English-French rivalry over possession of the Ohio River Valley. The English struggle for control there began in 1671, when Major General Abraham Wood, a seasoned frontiersman, sent an exploratory party from what is now Petersburg, Virginia, to study "the ebbing and flowing of the waters on the other side of the mountains." Captain Thomas Batts crossed the towering Allegheny Mountains and may have traced the course of the New River as far as the falls of the Great Kanawha. About the same time, Robert de La Salle and other French explorers examined the Mississippi River and its tributaries and soon planted colonies near the mouth of the Ohio River.

Both powers were determined to manipulate the nomadic Indian tribes for purposes of trade and strategy. Scores of traders and trappers undoubtedly passed through sections of West Virginia in the late 17th and early 18th centuries. In 1716 Governor Alexander Spotswood of Virginia and 30 cavaliers crossed the Blue Ridge Mountains and may have reached what is now the West Virginia county of Pendleton.

According to tradition, the first permanent white settlement in West Virginia was made in 1731 by a Welshman, Morgan Morgan, on Mill Creek in Berkeley County. Within a few years, ambitious and resourceful Welsh, Scotch-Irish, and German pioneers, trekking from Pennsylvania and Maryland, had occupied the area along the rivers emptying into the Potomac River from the south. Much of this land — surveyed by George Washington, among others — technically belonged to Lord Thomas Fairfax as proprietor of the Northern Neck of Virginia.

After the English victory over the French in the French and Indian War of 1689–1763, the Indians sold an immense area including West Virginia to the British. The large-scale trans-Allegheny migration that followed triggered both vigorous Indian resistance and a royal proclamation barring colonists from settlement west of the Alleghenies. Nevertheless an estimated 25,000 to 30,000 immigrants spilled over the mountains to settle the upper Ohio River Valley before the American Revolution. The first US census, of 1790, showed a population of 55,873 for the region of West Virginia.

As early as 1776 the separatist tendencies of the western Virginians gave rise to thoughts about breaking off from eastern Virginia and establishing a new colony to be called Vandalia. Neither this plan nor subsequent schemes to found a state of Westsylvania in 1783 materialized. The history of western Virginia from the end of the Revolutionary War to the outbreak of the Civil War revolved around the increasingly bitter division between the eastern and western sections of the region. The two areas differed socially, politically, culturally, economically, religiously, and geographically. Rolling hills and vast plantations characterized the Tidewater and Piedmont parts in the east, offering a striking contrast with the mountainous Allegheny and trans-Allegheny sections, where small-scale, diversified farming prevailed. The Anglican and Episcopalian slave-owning gentlemen farmers of primarily English origin who inhabited eastern Virginia tended to look down upon the German, Scotch-Irish, and Welsh frontiersmen of western Virginia, who owned few slaves and belonged to dissenting religious sects. The two groups differed radically on matters of taxation, public improvements, and the basis for political representation.

The long-simmering western resentment of the political ascendancy wielded by the undemocratic eastern Virginians was not quenched by changes made in the Virginia constitution in 1830 and 1851. Bitterness and friction mounted steadily, and the intensified regional controversy over slavery — with eastern Virginians for and western Virginians against the institution — sparked the final crisis.

In response to the firing on Fort Sumter in April 1861, the Virginia Convention, meeting at the capital of Richmond, threw in its lot with the Confederacy and passed an ordinance of secession from the Union. There was much dissatisfaction in the west, with two-thirds of western Virginia's representatives voting against the measure. Meetings of protest were held, and on May 13, 1861, delegates from 26 western counties and what is now Frederick County, Virginia, met at Wheeling and called a convention to meet on June 11. At this Second Wheeling Convention, representatives from 34 counties branded the Virginia secession null and void, and declared the state government offices at Richmond vacant, in effect announcing their independence. Following passage of a resolution that called for organization of the "Restored Government of Virginia" on the basis of loyalty to the Union, they elected Francis H. Pierpont as provisional governor. Waitman T. Willey and John S. Carlile were named as Virginia's two US senators and were admitted to the Senate in Washington, D.C,. replacing Virginia's former US senators, who had followed their state into the Confederacy.

The first official steps toward creation of a new state in West Virginia came between August 6 and 21, when the Second Wheeling Convention gathered in adjourned session. On August 20 the convention voted 48 to 27 to create the new state of Kanawha, as it was at first called, including 39 western counties. The decision was overwhelmingly approved in a popular referendum on October 24. In late November 1861 another convention met at Wheeling to draft a state constitution. One of the convention's acts was to discard the name Kanawha in favor of West Virginia. It also decided the boundaries of the new state. Since it was of great economic and military value to control that area of northern Virginia crossed by the main line of the Baltimore and Ohio Railroad on its route west, it was deemed advisable to add to the western counties an additional parcel of eastern counties, thus accounting for the irregularly shaped "eastern panhandle" of present West Virginia. Other additions subsequently enlarged the state to its present dimensions.

In fulfillment of the federal Constitution's requirement that "no new States shall be formed or erected within the Jurisdiction of any other State . . . without the consent of the Legislatures of the States concerned as well as of the Congress," the legislature of Virginia's "restored government" — that is, its government at Wheeling, which was loyal to the Union, as distinct from Virginia's Confederate regime at Richmond — gave formal assent to the separation of West Virginia from Virginia. Once Congress had voted, at the end of 1862, to admit the new state of West Virginia, the fate of the new political entity rested with President Abraham Lincoln. After careful debate the President justified the action as a war measure and aptly remarked, "It is said that the admission of West Virginia is secession. Well, if we call it by that name, there is still difference enough between secession against the Constitution and secession in favor of the Constitution."

West Virginia's constitution was overwhelmingly ratified by the people of the region on March 26, 1863. Lincoln issued his proclamation of the new entity's impending statehood on April 20, and on June 20, after new state and county officers had been elected, West Virginia entered the Union officially. The Pierpont restored government of Virginia departed from the new state's precincts to Alexandria, Virginia, near the federal capital, and Arthur I. Boreman, inaugurated as West Virginia's first governor, established his government at Wheeling. During the Civil War West Virginia was the scene of countless raids and counterraids and sharp political splits within families. For example, Thomas J. "Stonewall" Jackson, a native of what is now West Virginia, remained loyal to Virginia and played a leading role as a top-ranking Confederate general, while his sister remained a confirmed Unionist.

In the late 19th century, large-scale tapping of West Virginia's extensive mineral resources, especially the huge deposits of bituminous coal, touched off the industrial development of the area. Even after West Virginia's coal mines gave up more than 6.5 billion tons, from 1883 to 1961, the state's reserve still was estimated at more — perhaps substantially more — than 60 billion tons.

Physical geography has been a determining factor in the development of the state. In the 20th century widespread strip mining became a controversial issue, but the Mountain State, with its scenic attractions, remains a popular tourist center.

JUNE 21

Summer Begins

In the United States and the north temperate zones generally, summer — the second and warmest season, coming between spring and fall — begins, according to most sources, "about June 21." Actually, the three-month period starts on either the 21st or a day later. The precise moment at which the sun reaches the summer solstice, officially marking the change of season, differs slightly from one year to the next because of the multitude of oscillations and wobbling motions the earth manifests during its daily rotation on its axis and in its annual elliptical orbit about the sun.

Each of the four seasons has a precise beginning astronomically. The ecliptic, the plane in which the sun appears to revolve around the earth and in which the earth actually revolves around the sun, is divided into four 90° sections, each starting with a definite point: two equinoxes and two solstices. Summer begins at the summer solstice (Latin *solstitium*, from *sol*, meaning "sun," and *sistere*, meaning "to stand still") located halfway between the vernal equinox, the start of spring (see March 21), and the autumnal equinox, the start of fall (see September 23). The time span needed by the sun to cover the 90° section from the summer solstice to the autumnal equinox is termed the season of summer.

Summer is also said, somewhat anachronistically, to begin when the sun enters the zodiac sign of Cancer, the crab (see Appendix, The Zodiac). The second century Greek astronomer Hipparchus, whose calculations form the basis of the zodiacal system, estimated correctly that in his time the summer solstice began when the sun entered this sign. He also noted that owing to precession — the retrograde motion of the equinoctial points — there is a gradual displacement of the constellations in regard to them. After a cycle of slow motion lasting 25,800 years, the constellations will again be in the same zodiacal positions as in Hipparchus's time, when the summer solstice was found in the constellation of Cancer. It is now actually in the sign of Gemini.

About June 21, the sun reaches its greatest northern declination (a term used by astronomers to correspond with terrestrial latitude) of +23° 27' and a longitude of 90°. It then seems to "stand still" for several days, during which period the times of sunrise and sunset vary so imperceptibly that the days appear to be of equal length. The sun's rays extend across and beyond the North Pole as far as 23° 27' and on the other hand fall short of the South Pole 23° 27', reaching only the near side of the Antarctic Circle. During the course of summer the sun's north declination constantly decreases. As observed from the terrestrial equator, the sun crosses closer and closer to the meridian until the autumnal equinox, when it reaches a celestial longitude of 180° and a declination of 0° and is said to enter the sign of Libra. The season of summer then terminates.

In the Northern Hemisphere, summer is the longest season. The earth moves most rapidly in early January and most slowly in early July, the variation in velocity during its annual orbit being caused by the laws of motion and the orbit's elliptical shape. Astronomically speaking, the summer season comprises the months of June, July and August, although in some regions of the North American continent climatic factors cause May also to be a summer month meteorologically. In Great Britain, summer popularly includes May as well as June, July, and August.

At the summer solstice, when the North Pole points directly toward the sun, the sun's rays are vertical and the amount of solar radiation absorbed daily by the earth's surface is high. Consequently temperatures rise, with the hottest weather usually occurring early in August. By the winter solstice (see December 22), opposite conditions prevail. In the Southern Hemisphere the seasons are reversed, since the South Pole moves in the opposite direction from the North Pole. Astronomical summer in the Southern Hemisphere starts about December 22 and ends about March 21.

Because of the extended days of sunshine and the resulting period of high temperatures, summer is the prime growing season for plant life. Like the other seasons, it influenced the development of mythology and folklore. For example, Midsummer (see June 24) with its elaborate solar rites was an especially important festival in ancient and medieval times and continues to be celebrated with bonfires and special traditions even today. There are still many other festivals and events also associated with summer, taking their impetus in whole or in part from the characteristic climate of the season. In ancient and medieval art summer was frequently personified as a woman carrying sheaves of grain and a sickle.

Father's Day

This is a movable event. See note on page xxvi.

The third Sunday of June is generally observed as Father's Day throughout the United States. Although an isolated church service in Fairmont, West Virginia, honored fathers in July 1908 at the suggestion of Jessica ("Babs") Clinton Clayton, it is Sonora Louise Smart Dodd of Spokane, Washington, who is most frequently credited with originating—in 1909—the idea for a Father's Day observance that spread far beyond the confines of her own church.

Her inspiration was her own father, William Smart, a Civil War veteran who had been widowed when his daughter and five sons were very young—one of them, in fact, newborn, since the mother had died in childbirth. Realization of the difficulties he must have had raising his young, motherless family on a farm in eastern Washington and appreciation for his constant devotion to his family sparked Mrs. Dodd's desire to honor all fathers.

Because her idea for the observance of Father's Day centered around special church services—though she also saw it as a day when fathers should receive words of affection and small gifts from their children—Mrs. Dodd discussed her idea with her minister. Through him she put the idea to the Spokane Ministerial Association and the Spokane Ministers Alliance. Members of the clergy warmly approved of the project. With the city's YMCA also joining in sponsorship, the first Father's Day was celebrated in Spokane on the third Sunday of June—the month of her father's birth—in 1910, with local ministers calling the attention of their congregations to the appreciation fathers deserved. June 19 was the actual date of that initial observance. The first Father's Day proclamations were released by the mayor of Spokane and the governor of Washington, M. E. Hay, another early enthusiast, who followed the lead of Spokane in setting the third Sunday in June as the date for the observance. Among the first notables to endorse Mrs. Dodd's idea formally was the orator and political leader William Jennings Bryan, who complimented her on the inspiration for Father's Day and remarked that "too much emphasis cannot be placed upon the relation between parent and child."

Two years after Spokane's initial observance, Vancouver, Washington, across the state to the west, was the site of one of the other celebrations. It took place at the suggestion of the pastor of the Irvington Methodist Church in 1912, and at least one newspaper report later indicated that the people of Vancouver believed theirs to have been the original observance of the day.

The observance of Father's Day did not spread rapidly—not, for instance, as rapidly as Mother's Day, whose celebration in this country predated it only slightly. Indeed, communication was so limited that without knowing that Father's Day was already being observed in at least some western states, several people in various other parts of the country also hit upon the idea independently—though to this day Mrs. Dodd's is the name most often linked with the beginning of the celebration.

When a Father's Day celebration was discussed (but abandoned) in Chicago in 1911, it was as though the idea were entirely new. Jane Addams, the eminent social worker, leader in the peace movement, and suffragist, reportedly indicated her approval by saying, "Poor father has been left out in the cold. He doesn't get much recognition. . . . It would be a good thing if he had a day that would mean recognition of him."

President Woodrow Wilson officially approved the idea for Father's Day in 1916. While Wilson was still President, a Father's Day of a different kind was observed on November 24, 1918, when at the suggestion of *Stars and Stripes,* the official newspaper of the World War I American Expeditionary Force in France, the fathers at home wrote to their sons in the field and the sons in the field wrote home. Arrangements were made for the delivery of the letters without delay and, since the war had ended with the armistice celebrated 13 days earlier, delivery was possible without risk.

When a teenager in Drewry's Bluff, Virginia — Katherine Lawrence, later Katherine Lawrence Burgess of Miami — began efforts to honor fathers with a letter to a newspaper it was nearly a decade after the first Spokane celebration, although she apparently was unaware of the similar efforts that had preceded hers. Subsequently, in 1921, she persuaded the governor of Virginia to proclaim a Father's Day, and in due time registered the name National Father's Day association with the US Patent Office. When she learned of Mrs. Dodd's earlier activities, however, she reportedly withdrew any claims to priority in establishing the day.

Harry C. Meek, president of the Uptown Lions Club of Chicago, meanwhile, was also enthusiastic about establishing a day to honor fathers. His interest began as early as 1915, and he put forward the idea in talks before various Lions clubs. He was able to bring about the observance of a day for fathers in 1920. In honor of his achievement the Lions Clubs of America presented him with a gold watch, erroneously inscribed to him as the "Originator of Father's Day," and bearing the date of his birthday, June 25, 1920. (The Lions had held their observance on the Sunday nearest that date, which happened to be the third Sunday in June.)

Mr. Meek, who devoted more than two decades of effort to promoting the observance of Father's Day, called on both President Warren Harding and President Calvin Coolidge in unsuccessful attempts to have the day marked with issuance of a presidential proclamation. (Both Presidents were apprehensive about possible commercialization of the day.) At least two resolutions introduced in the House of Representatives before observance of Father's Day had become widespread also failed in their objective of having the day officially designated at the behest of Congress. However, President Woodrow Wilson earlier had played a ceremonial part in the 1916 commemoration, pressing from his White House desk a button that unfurled a flag at a celebration in Spokane. And President Coolidge, in a 1924 communication to Mr. Meek, did recommend the widespread observance of Father's Day "to establish more intimate relations between fathers and their children, and also to impress upon fathers the full measure of their obligations."

Although Father's Day is almost universally marked in the United States today, it is not an official holiday in all parts of the nation. However, most state governors each year proclaim that Father's Day will be observed on the third Sunday of June in their states. Many mayors also issue proclamations in connection with their communities' celebrations of Father's Day.

The observance of Father's Day is promoted by the Father's Day Council, Inc., formerly the National Father's Day Committee, founded in 1936, which each year sponsors an annual award banquet in New York City to honor the Father of the Year and fathers in special categories. Those chosen as Fathers of the Year have included Presidents, entertainers, and other notables. Community groups in individual towns and cities also often select Fathers of the Year as part of their own local celebrations. Speakers at religious services usually pay special tribute to fathers, often taking as their text the Old Testament injunction "Honor thy father and thy mother," given to Moses as one of the Ten Commandments (Exodus 20:12 and Deuteronomy 5:16). One originally intended feature of Father's Day, the wearing of a red rose to honor a living father, or a white rose to honor one not living, has been largely discontinued in recent years. The more commercial aspects of Father's Day — deplored by many — have burgeoned; an estimated $1 billion is spent each year for gifts.

In the days preceding the 1970 celebration of Father's Day, Mrs. Dodd, still living in Spokane at the time, appeared on three major television network programs. She stressed the fact that one very important, timely, and practical value attached to the observance of Father's Day was to help bridge the "generation gap," since the day provides an occasion for children to express appreciation of their fathers and for fathers to acknowledge their responsibilities to their children.

These moral and religious responsibilities are summed up in "A Father's Ten Commandments," a statement originated by the National Father's Day Committee, which is often reprinted in local papers or circulated in leaflet. form around the time of Father's Day.

Father's Day is also celebrated in at least 20 foreign countries, although not necessarily on the same day as in this country.

The Constitution Ratified

The War for Independence was but the first phase of the American Revolution. Having established their rights to life, liberty, and the pursuit of happiness, the citizens of the new country had to prove themselves capable of attaining the goals of the Declaration of Independence. It was not certain that success would justify the adventure, for in the years immediately following the Treaty of Paris of 1783, the United States lacked even that basic instrument of a nation, an effective government.

By 1776 most of the colonies that broke away from England had existed over a century. Diverse in economy and social organization, they were bound together by a common danger rather than a common identity. To an extent the rebel states were as reluctant to surrender their independence from each other as they were eager to win it from Great Britain. The Articles of Confederation, under which they united in 1777 to prosecute the war, reflected this desire for autonomy.

The Articles of Confederation, in reality, established the apparatus of an alliance rather than of a government. There was no provision for a national executive, as the states vested power in a Congress in which each of them held one vote. The articles limited the legislature's authority to certain vital matters, and required the assent of nine states to enact legislation even in these spheres. The agreement of all 13 members was necessary to institute any changes in the frame of government.

Postwar difficulties amply illustrated the shortcomings of the Confederation. The government's inability to make the states comply with the terms of the Treaty of Paris, requiring the payment of debts owed to British subjects, gave England an excuse not to evacuate its garrisons in the northwest region of the United States. The American economy suffered as the states failed to give Congress the power to levy duties on imports, a measure that would have enabled the government to extract commercial concessions from foreign countries. By 1787 George Washington warned: "Something must be done or the fabric will fall; it is certainly tottering."

In 1785 Virginia and Maryland took the first steps leading to the revamping of the government. Delegates from these states arranged to confer with Washington at Mount Vernon on the problem of navigation rights in the Potomac River and Chesapeake Bay. Representatives from Pennsylvania and Delaware were present to negotiate related questions. Encouraged by this effort at cooperation James Madison sug-

gested to the Virginia legislature that it invite all the states to a meeting in Annapolis, Maryland, to discuss commercial matters. Only five states sent emissaries to the Annapolis Convention of September 1786, and so the delegates called for a new gathering to meet in Philadelphia in May 1787 "to render the Constitution of the Federal Government adequate to the exigencies of the Union." On February 21, 1787, Congress approved the planned convention, provided it work "for the sole and express purpose of revising the Articles of Confederation."

May 14 was supposed to be the opening day, but the convention did not attain the necessary quorum of 7 states until May 25. In all, however, 55 delegates from 12 states ultimately attended the gathering, as only Rhode Island refused to participate. Some of the most notable leaders of the Revolutionary era were present, including George Washington and the elder statesman of the new nation, Benjamin Franklin, then 81. However, most of the members were young, having an average age of 42 years; only eight had signed the Declaration of Independence. The majority were college graduates and almost all were men of affairs, chiefly lawyers.

The convention unanimously chose George Washington to be its president. He took no part in the discussions, but he put his prestige on the side of those forces advocating a strong central government. Each state had one vote and, provided there was a quorum, the majority vote of the states present would decide issues. The members met from 10:00 A.M. to 3:00 P.M. each day from May 29 to September 17, except for Sundays, a 2-day Fourth of July recess, and the 10 days between July 26 and August 6.

The delegates realized that they could not heed Congress's admonition to restrict themselves to a mere revision of the Articles of Confederation. Even if there had been no other problems, the stipulation requiring unanimous consent to change made it unfeasible to work within the framework of the Articles. So on May 30 the convention members resolved that their task was the establishment of a national government.

The convention's goal was to create a central government strong enough to unify and direct the nation, yet not so strong as to endanger the rights of the citizenry and of the individual states. The new government would necessarily be a federation of the states and, as James Madison later pointed out in the *Federalist* essays, the diversity inherent in this type of structure greatly limited its capacity for power. To protect further against the central authority's power to encroach on liberty, the delegates, following the concepts of the French political theorist Montesquieu, divided the proposed national government into three balanced branches — executive, legislative, and judiciary — each of which would check the power of the other two.

The composition of the new Congress constituted a major problem for the convention. Frustrated by the one-state, one-vote principle of the Articles of Confederation, the larger states wanted greater influence in future national legislatures. On May 29 Edmund Randolph of Virginia suggested a system of government favorable to the larger states. The Virginia Plan provided for a bicameral Congress in which each state's membership would be proportioned to its free population. On June 15 William Paterson of New Jersey offered a counterproposal more to the liking of the smaller states. The New Jersey Plan, as it became known, would have given each state equal representation in a unicameral national legislature with significantly increased powers.

The solution to the conflict between the large and small states, and proportional versus equal representation, eventually was based on a suggestion that had been introduced by Roger Sherman of Connecticut. The Great Compromise, as it was later called, provided for a bicameral legislature in which each state would have an equal voice in the upper house of Congress, but would be represented in proportion to its population in the lower house. In the ensuing discussion the delegates agreed that representatives to the lower house would be elected directly by the citizens, whereas the members of the upper house would be selected by the individual state legislatures. (The latter arrangement has since been superseded by the 17th Amendment, ratified in 1913, which provided for the direct election of senators.)

The Great Compromise removed the largest obstacle to the success of the convention. Further compromises dissolved the remaining difficulties. The delegates decided that taxation, like representation in the lower house of Congress, would be proportioned among the states according to population — and that for both purposes five black slaves would count as three free persons. The southern states, whose economy centered around the sale in the world market of tobacco and other staples produced by slave labor, won an agreement that there would be no taxation of exports and, for at least 20 years, no ban on the importation of slaves.

The manner of electing the President was the final important issue. A committee composed of one delegate from each state devised the electoral college system. According to this each state would choose, in a manner prescribed by its leg-islature, a number of electors equal to its total representation in both houses of Congress. The electors of each state would meet and vote for two persons, at least one of whom was not a resident of their state. The person who attained the majority of the electoral votes was to become President and the person who received the next highest number of votes was to become Vice President. If no candidate gained the necessary majority, then the House of Representatives, with each state having one vote, would choose the President.

Oliver Ellsworth of Connecticut, Nathaniel Gorham of Massachusetts, Edmund Randolph of Virginia, John Rutledge of South Carolina, and James Wilson of Pennsylvania composed the Committee of Detail, which drew up the first draft of the Constitution. On September 8 the convention appointed Alexander Hamilton of New York, Dr. William S. Johnson of Connecticut, Rufus King of Massachusetts, James Madison of Virginia, and Gouverneur Morris of Pennsylvania as a Committee of Style and Arrangement to prepare the final report. The convention delegates met for the final time on Monday, September 17. They were urged to vote favorably on the fruit of their collective labors in a speech written by the ailing Benjamin Franklin and read to them that day by James Wilson. Franklin's persuasive words have often been quoted since:

I confess that there are several parts of this Constitution which I do not at present approve, but I am not sure I shall never approve them. . . .

I doubt too whether any other convention . . . may be able to make a better Constitution. For when you assemble a number of men to have the advantage of their joint wisdom, you inevitably assemble with those men all their prejudices, . . . passions, . . . errors of opinion, . . . local interests, and . . . selfish views. . . . It therefore astonishes me . . . to find this system approaching so near to perfection as it does. . . .

Thus, I consent . . . to this Constitution because I expect no better, and because I am not sure that it is not the best. . . . On the whole, . . . I cannot help expressing a wish that every member of the convention who may still have objections to it would, with me, . . . doubt a little of his own infallibility and, to make manifest our unanimity put his name to this instrument.

Thus encouraged, the delegates approved the Constitution and sent it to the Congress with a recommendation that it be referred to the states for ratification by special conventions.

Thirty-nine of the 42 delegates who had stayed to the end of the proceedings signed the document. As they stepped forward to affix their signatures, the ever-observant Franklin reflected on the half-sun depicted on the back of the chair that Washington had occupied throughout the months of deliberations. James Madison recorded Franklin's words in his journal: "I have often and often in the course of the session, and the vicissitudes of my hopes and fears as to its issue, looked at that [sun] behind the President without being able to tell whether it was rising or setting. But now at length I have the happiness to know that it is a rising and not a setting sun."

Contrary to the requirement of the Articles of Confederation, the Philadelphia convention determined that ratification by nine states would put the new Constitution into effect. Not everyone, however, approved of the new document. The opponents of the new Constitution, known as Antifederalists, worried about the absence of specific protections for individual liberties and feared that the new central authority would seriously undermine the powers of local governments. Promises of future amendments, which would constitute a Bill of Rights (see December 15), won a number of undecided voters to the cause of ratification, as did arguments such as those put forth by Alexander Hamilton, John Jay, and James Madison in *The Federalist*.

The people in each of the 13 states elected representatives for special conventions to discuss ratification. Delaware, Pennsylvania (after some controversy), New Jersey, Georgia, and Connecticut ratified quickly. Federalists then won a narrow victory in Massachusetts and easier ones in Maryland and South Carolina. New Hampshire, on June 21, 1788, became the ninth state to support the new frame of government, thus putting it into operation. Virginia and New York soon followed. North Carolina and Rhode Island were dissatisfied with the proposed Constitution and did not immediately join the Union. However, North Carolina finally accepted the new system in November 1789, and Rhode Island in May 1790.

The Constitution of the United States was formulated in the same building and room as was the Declaration of Independence. Pennsylvania had erected the structure in 1732 to serve as the colony's statehouse; the room that later became so historic was the chamber of the provincial Assembly. Now known as Independence Hall, the building is the heart of Independence National Historical Park in Philadelphia. A gem of handsome landscaping, studded with red-brick architecture of the Colonial and Federal periods, the park is administered by the National Park Service. It contains some 21.84 acres, 15.62 of which are owned by the federal government. Included are numerous structures of historic interest, among them three that played major roles during the period of new nationhood: Con-

gress Hall, which served as the home of the national legislature from 1790 to 1800; the City Hall, where the Supreme Court met; and the building that housed the first Bank of the United States.

The Constitution, product of all the delegates' long-drawn-out labors, as well as related documents, is on public display in the National Archives building in Washington, D.C. The building is located on Pennsylvania Avenue between 7th and 9th streets, N.W.

New Hampshire Ratifies the Constitution

Although the statehood of the 13 original states dates from their declaration of independence from Great Britain in 1776, historians customarily place the first 13 states in chronological order according to the date on which they ratified the federal Constitution of 1787. Since New Hampshire, on June 21, 1788, became the ninth state to ratify the Constitution, it is generally considered the ninth state in the federal Union.

New Hampshire was one of the smaller and less populous of the 13 original states, and its approval of the new frame of government therefore was probably not so essential to the success of the federal experiment as that of some of the larger states. In another respect, however, New Hampshire's approval was pivotal. Article VII of the Constitution specified that the agreement of nine states would suffice to bring the new government into existence. It was thus the affirmation of New Hampshire, the ninth state, that made the Constitution of 1787 legally operative.

To gain New Hampshire's approval of the Constitution, the Federalists, as those who favored the new frame of government were known, had to overcome considerable apathy. The state had, for the most part, fared well under the Articles of Confederation, and many New Hampshirites failed to recognize the urgent need to reform the government. Indeed the state legislature did not even respond to the appeal of the 1786 Annapolis Convention that the states send delegates to a convention the following May to consider revisions of the Articles of Confederation. New Hampshire therefore was not represented when the Constitutional Convention convened in Philadelphia on May 25, 1787.

Since the New Hampshire legislature claimed that the state could not afford to send delegates to the Constitutional Convention, John Langdon, a wealthy citizen, offered to pay the expenses of such representatives. With the financial obstacle removed, the legislature late in June 1787 named four deputies, Langdon, Nicholas Gilman, John Pickering, and Benjamin West, to go to the Philadelphia convention "to discuss and decide upon the most effectual means to remedy the defects of our federal Union." Pickering and West never attended the constitutional meetings, but Langdon and Gilman arrived in Philadelphia at the end of July 1787.

By the time Langdon, who had served as Speaker of the New Hampshire House of Representatives, president of the state, and delegate to Congress, and Gilman, who also had been a member of the Confederation Congress, appeared at the convention most of the major issues before that body had been resolved. The New Hampshire delegates therefore did not engage in public debate on such problems as representation in the national Congress, but their private correspondence indicates that they agreed with the compromises worked out by the other members of the convention. Langdon and Gilman remained in Philadelphia until September 1787, and during the final weeks of meetings on the Constitution they helped decide such important questions as the length of terms for the President, senators, and representatives, and the power of Congress to regulate foreign and interstate commerce.

The Constitutional Convention concluded its labors on September 17, 1787, and then submitted the new frame of government to the states. Supporters of the Constitution in New Hampshire immediately launched a campaign to win their state's approval of the document, and the state president, John Sullivan, called the legislature into special session in December to select a ratifying convention. Since many towns refused to bear the added expense of sending a representative to the special session, there was no quorum in attendance at the December meeting. But despite the absence of more than two-thirds of the legislators, the December session was able to set the time and place for the ratifying convention. And realizing that the voters were hesitant to accept any additional burdens, they scheduled the ratifying convention to run concurrently with the regular session of the legislature, which was to take place at Exeter in mid-February 1788.

Many of the towns that had refused to finance delegates to the special legislative session took advantage of the opportunity to send representatives to the regular legislative session and the ratifying convention. In mid-February 1788, when the first session of the convention met, the vast majority of New Hampshire's towns were represented, and that gathering considered the merits of the Constitution without further delay. For 10 days the convention debated the frame of government, and during that time the Federalists came to realize that a majority of the delegates opposed the document. Fearing that ratification would be defeated if a vote were immediately taken on the Constitution, they requested — and won — a four-month adjournment.

Federalist support was concentrated around Portsmouth, situated at the mouth of the Piscataqua River, since the fishing and shipbuilding industries of that area would greatly profit by the national regulation of commerce proposed by the new Constitution. But the Piscataqua region alone could not bring about ratification, and to gain additional votes the friends of the Constitution waged a spirited campaign during the four-month adjournment. The Federalists aimed their efforts at New Hampshire's northern towns and those situated along the Connecticut River because their representatives seemed most likely to change their negative votes. This tactic was successful. On June 17, 1788, the delegates reconvened. They debated the question of ratification for four days. Then, on June 21, 1788, by a vote of 57 to 47, New Hampshire became the ninth state to ratify the Constitution.

JUNE 22

The *Leopard* Fires on the *Chesapeake*

On June 22, 1807, the British frigate HMS *Leopard* engaged the US frigate *Chesapeake* in the waters off Norfolk, Virginia. Three Americans lost their lives during the encounter, and 18 more were wounded. The incident was one of the most serious in a number of events that gradually led the United States and Great Britain into the War of 1812.

At the conclusion of the War for Independence, the young United States had looked forward to a long era of peace and prosperity. Its erstwhile opponent Great Britain could not be so sanguine. The British government had no reason to believe that its longstanding quarrel with France would not occasionally break into open war. The coming of the French Revolution signaled the renewal of hostilities. During the last decade of the 18th century, England joined the various coalitions that sought to restore the monarchy in France. The French, however, withstood the preliminary attacks, and eventually Napoleon Bonaparte emerged to lead them in a long series of wars against the British.

Economics inevitably drew the Americans into the ongoing British-French struggles. The United States was a commercial nation involved in carrying goods across the Atlantic. When war erupted in Europe, both England and France turned to the United States to supplement their merchant marines. The plight of the European powers offered the Americans great profits, but risks accompanied the increased opportunities.

Britain's naval dominance in the Atlantic made the French especially dependent on the US maritime fleet. In time of peace, France did not allow US vessels to carry goods between its Caribbean colonies and Europe, but during its struggles against Great Britain, France opened the West Indies to the young American nation. The British naturally protested, invoking their "Rule of 1756," which declared that trade prohibited in peace had to remain illegal in war; and they threatened to seize American vessels carrying French products.

American merchants used a tactic known as the "broken voyage" to circumvent British objections to their trade with France. American shippers picked up their cargoes in the French West Indies and first brought them to American ports, where the goods theoretically were unloaded and taxed, thereby "breaking" the voyage. Then merchants reshipped the original items to French ports as American rather than West Indian products.

Britain temporarily accepted the ruse. In a court case involving the *Polly*, an American ship seized by the British navy, the British in 1800 accepted the defense's contention of a "broken voyage." But as the war with France became more intense, and the Americans began only to "touch base" in US ports without actually unloading or paying levies, the British attitude hardened. In the *Essex* case of 1805, the British prize courts, reversing an earlier court decision, outlawed the reexport trade.

The *Essex* decision was only the first of a series of actions that adversely affected American shipping interests. In May 1806 the English instituted a "paper blockade," that is, one not supported by ships stationed off the affected ports, of Europe from the Elbe River to Brest. In November 1806 Napoleon issued the equally unenforceable Berlin Decree, which forbade all commerce with Britain and authorized the seizure of vessels trading with the British. Finally, in January 1807, the British retaliated with an order-in-council barring ships from the coasts of France and its allies.

England controlled the seas and was in a better position than France to enforce its decrees. The Americans thus directed most of their wrath against the British, and by 1807 the relationship between the United States and England had badly deteriorated.

The *Leopard-Chesapeake* affair took place during this tense period. The timing only aggravated the consequences of the incident, which was a serious matter in its own right. The confrontation, which concerned the impressment issue, another dimension of the question of neutral rights, brought Britain and the United States to the brink of war.

Impressment, in the Anglo-American context, was the British practice of stopping and searching American vessels, and of removing sailors born in the British Isles so they might serve in the Royal Navy. The British, desperately in need of sailors to battle the French, justified their actions on the principle of "once an Englishman always an Englishman." Some of the impressed men had been legally naturalized as US citizens, others had obtained naturalization papers illegally, and a number were actually deserters from the British navy. All had found the high wages of the American peacetime fleet more attractive than either the poor pay of England's commercial vessels or the prospects of battle faced by the British navy. But whatever the actual background of these pirated mariners, the highhanded manner in which the British seized them was a continuing source of friction between the United States and England.

Although impressment had long provoked American ill-feeling toward Great Britain, not until 1807 did the issue become so important that the United States considered war. On March 7, 1807, a number of the crew of the British 16-gun sloop *Halifax*, which was cruising in American waters, seized their vessel's jolly boat and used it to escape to Norfolk, Virginia. The commander of the *Halifax* complained to the British consul and to American naval authorities in Norfolk in an effort to regain his sailors, but he received no satisfaction. Instead, when the officer met the deserters on the streets of Norfolk, one of them, Jenkin Ratford, treated him to a fusillade of salty language and declared that in the land of liberty he could do what he pleased.

Angered by their inability to retrieve deserters, some of whom had allegedly signed on the US frigate *Chesapeake*, the commander of the *Halifax* and a number of other officers complained to Admiral George Cranfield Berkeley in Nova Scotia, who commanded all British ships on the North American station. Without waiting for advice from London, Berkeley issued a fateful order. He directed that all captains and commanders of British vessels, in case of meeting the *Chesapeake* outside the territorial waters of the United States, stop the frigate and search it for deserters from the British warships *Bellona, Belleisle, Triumph, Chichester, Halifax,* and *Zenobia*.

Captain S. P. Humphreys, commander of the *Leopard*, carried Berkeley's order, dated June 1, 1807, to Chesapeake Bay. Humphreys arrived at nearby Lynnhaven Bay on June 21, and at 6:00 the next morning anchored a short distance to the east, about three miles north of Cape Henry lighthouse. At 7:15 on June 22 the *Chesapeake* weighed anchor from Hampton Roads and set sail for the Mediterranean Sea. As the *Chesapeake* passed Lynnhaven Bay at 9:00 A.M., the British battleship *Bellona* sighted it and signaled to the *Leopard* to lift anchor and reconnoiter to the southeast by east.

Hours passed before the *Leopard* and *Chesapeake* made contact. At 3:30 P.M. the British vessel hailed the American about 8 to 10 miles southeast by east from Cape Henry. The British announced that they had dispatches for Commodore James Barron, the American commander. Barron, who thought that the English merely wanted him to carry mail to Europe, as a traditional naval courtesy, invited them to send an officer on board the *Chesapeake*.

Lieutenant Meade from the *Leopard* met Commodore Barron shortly before 4:00 P.M. He presented a note from Captain Humphreys explaining Admiral Berkeley's directive and demanding the right to carry it out. Expecting that Humphreys would respect his word, Barron wrote a reply stating that he was not aware of the presence among his crew of any deserters from the ships mentioned in Berkeley's list and that he could not allow his ship to be searched. Meade returned to the *Leopard* with Barron's message. Unfortunately, Humphreys did not believe that Berkeley's orders allowed him to accept the American answer. The English captain brought his vessel nearer to the American and called, "Commodore Barron, you must be aware of the necessity I am under of complying with the order of my commander-in-chief." Barron, knowing that the crew of the *Chesapeake* would require at least half an hour to prepare the frigate for combat, sought to delay. Twice Barron called through his trumpet, "I do not hear what you say." After the second exchange the *Leopard* fired a single shot across the bow of the *Chesapeake*, and a minute later another. At 4:30 P.M. the British ship opened up with all its weaponry against the helpless American frigate. The *Leopard* discharged three full broadsides point blank into the *Chesapeake* at a distance of not more than 200 feet. The Americans managed to fire only a single shot.

Twenty-two shots ripped the *Chesapeake*'s hull, and 10 tore the sails. The firing mutilated the three masts and cut much of the rigging.

Three American sailors died, 8 suffered severe wounds, and 10 less serious injuries. Barron had no choice but to strike his colors.

When the firing ceased, several British officers boarded the *Chesapeake*. They seized three men who they claimed had deserted from the *Melampus*. Berkeley's order had not mentioned that vessel, and the men, two whites and one black, were actually American citizens who had been illegally impressed into service on the *Melampus*. The British also found Jenkin Ratford who, unknown to Barron, had joined the *Chesapeake* under the name Wilson.

Barron, in accord with his situation as a defeated commander, offered to turn the *Chesapeake* over to British control. Humphreys' instructions, however, did not call for capturing the frigate and so he declined to take the vessel. The Americans, degraded and outraged, then turned their battered vessel and headed back to Norfolk.

Americans were chagrined by Britain's cavalier treatment of the *Chesapeake*, and many favored violent retaliation. President Thomas Jefferson, however, sought to avoid war and relied instead on economic measures and other steps. After ordering British warships out of American waters, he called a special session of Congress for October 1807, and secured from the legislators an appropriation of $850,000 with which to strengthen the US fleet. In December Congress, on Jefferson's recommendation, passed an embargo act setting forth the President's further response to affronts to sovereignty. According to its provisions, which Jefferson saw as a form of "peaceful coercion," all US vessels were forbidden to sail for foreign ports, and foreign ships were barred from carrying goods out of American ports; even by overland routes all exports were prohibited. This tactic, together with the earlier measures, was intended to satisfy the popular demand for action and also to reduce the possibilities for future hostile encounters. It was the President's hope and belief that, rather than endure the loss of American exports, the warring powers would decide to reform and to treat US naval and merchant marine vessels with respect. Unfortunately, however, Jefferson's embargo harmed the American economy more than the economies of Britain and France, and in later years the US government resorted to less extreme sanctions against the warring powers.

The question of reparations for damage inflicted on the *Chesapeake* was not laid to rest until November 1811, when the United States accepted a British offer of settlement. Even with reparations paid and with two of the impressed seamen returned — one had meanwhile died and one had been hanged as a deserter — the question of British impressment of American seamen remained an important issue when differences between the United States and Great Britain finally culminated in the War of 1812.

JUNE 23

Midsummer, or St. John's, Eve

Long before the Christian era, Midsummer Eve and Midsummer Day (see June 24) were celebrated throughout Europe near the time of the summer solstice, when the days are longest and the sun appears to be at its highest point in the sky. The practice probably began with early sun worshipers who built fires to symbolize the sun and expressed in their celebration their year-round dependence on the sun's life-giving light and warmth and their joy at the arrival of summer weather. Numerous customs, notably dancing around the fires and leaping over the flames or embers to ensure a variety of blessings, grew up around the belief that the fires had mystical power to cure people of diseases and protect them from various dangers — including the fire-fearing witches or evil spirits who were supposedly at large on Midsummer Eve.

All-night merrymaking became the rule, and as sun worship faded — leaving behind a legacy of bonfires and associated customs — the emphasis on Midsummer Eve turned to young lovers and romantic fancies. Some of the universal hopes nurtured by the celebration are summed up by Puck in Shakespeare's *A Midsummer-Night's Dream*: "Jack shall have Jill; Naught shall go ill; The man shall have his mare again, and all shall be well." In keeping with the belief that Midsummer Eve was a night when supernatural beings roamed the earth, customs developed in some places similar to the "trick-or-treat" of Halloween, with people going from door to door begging sweets or firewood.

When the Feast of the Nativity of St. John the Baptist was instituted on June 24, early in the history of the Christian church, many of the established forms of celebrating Midsummer's Day and Midsummer's Eve were transferred to St. John's Eve and feast day — somewhat paradoxically, since the pagans had celebrated midsummer as an excuse for unbridled license, while the austere John had exhorted people to "repent, for the kingdom of heaven is at hand." However, the retention of many of the Midsummer customs now used in honor of St. John is easy to understand, since they included such natural forms of expression as singing, dancing, building the bonfires, and decorating doorways, windows, or — as in Mexico — wells, with boughs or flowers of the season.

In many areas on or near a body of water, people wade or bathe, some say as a symbol of John baptizing Jesus. This is notably the custom in Puerto Rico, for example, where families pack lunches on Midsummer Eve and go to beaches, where they build bonfires and spend the hours from midnight to dawn eating, singing, and bathing in the Caribbean. Traditionally, this must be done between midnight and dawn in order to have its best effects — which, according to some, may include prosperity and marital bliss. In some parts of the world where bodies of water are not so conveniently located, people walk through the Midsummer morning dew instead of bathing. In either case, great health-giving or protective powers are ascribed to the waters or dew. Medicinal herbs gathered on St. John's Eve or Day also are said to have a special efficacy.

Midsummer, or St. John's, Eve also is supposed to be a time for foretelling the future — particularly for discovering the identity of the person one will marry. Numerous folk rituals are prescribed to this end, and they vary from country to country. One cherished tradition, in Scandinavia and some other parts of Europe, is the belief that the placing of seven varieties (or some other locally specified number) of flowers under one's pillow will surely induce a dream about one's spouse-to-be.

The bonfires, often called St. John's Fire in predominantly Christian countries, are still an almost universal part of Midsummer Eve celebrations. Although smaller fires sometimes are lighted in the streets of towns or cities or in rural valleys, the most popular locations, particularly for the larger blazes, are places from which they are visible for a great distance — high on hills or mountains, beside lakes, and along seacoasts. Some of the old superstitions regarding the fires' special power remain or are playfully reenacted in many parts of the world. Thus, people still practice the custom of jumping over the smaller bonfires, or bonfire embers, in hopes that this will assure such future benefits as good grain harvests, healthy livestock, true love, personal health, and happiness. The ashes of the fires also are believed by some to have beneficial properties.

In certain areas of France, the bonfires are replaced by burning torches, which are tossed high into the air. In other French regions, the custom is to cover wagon wheels with straw, set them ablaze, and roll them down a hillside, creating a spectacle that can be viewed from afar. Breton fishermen are said to have their own version of St. John's Fire, even when they are sailing in distant waters. Crew members place discarded clothing in a barrel, which is hoisted on the mainmast and set afire while the men assemble below to watch, sing, pray, and celebrate. All the ships in the fishing fleet set their fires at the same time so that even though the crews are separated they can share the celebration.

Aside from their relationship to sun worship in pagan days, the bonfires on Midsummer Eve have always also served the practical purpose of warming the revelers and providing light for their all-night merriment. When use of the fires was retained for celebrating the Eve of St. John the Baptist, religious authorities could justify this by citing Jesus' description of John the Baptist, related in the Fourth Gospel (John 5:35): "He was a burning and a shining light: and ye were willing for a season to rejoice in his light."

Most Midsummer observances that have made their way to the United States have been borrowed from Scandinavia, where — with the important exception of Sweden — bonfires are an almost universal part of the celebration. In Finland, bonfires are everywhere that night, sponsored by cities and towns and by virtually every club and society. Purists and traditionalists may wait until exactly midnight to light the blazes, but most people get on with the gaiety earlier by lighting the fires as soon as there is a suggestion of late-evening twilight, or whenever they feel like it. There is, of course, no "night," or at least no full darkness; the sun at this time of year shines a full 24 hours in the northern reaches of Finland, Sweden, and Norway, and the sky is, at most, a deep, midnight blue in the southern parts of Scandinavia.

In Finland it is an evening for traditional regional costumes, and every Finn who owns one (perhaps half the population) gets it out for the occasion. The bonfire site — at a coastal point, usually, perhaps on the edge of one of Finland's 60,000 lakes — and a nearby pier, barn, or pavilion for dancing are the center of each community's activity. Usually there are speeches and a program — including perhaps folk dances and imported "pop" entertainment — before the start of the dancing, which, punctuated by refreshments and other merriment, is likely to last all night.

In Denmark, Midsummer, or St. John's, Eve — *Sankt Hans Aften* — is also a time for gala celebration everywhere, an occasion, in some places, for fetes marked by singing about the romantic midsummer sun, and by short speeches, singing-games and dances, and sometimes fireworks. Elsewhere in Denmark, the gaiety is shared by friends and families rather than entire communities. All who can depart from their year-round homes to the vacation cottages with which the Danes have dotted their coast. Wherever the celebration, food, conviviality, and late hours are customary; and bonfires burning on hills, or on the shores of coastal hamlets, are the climax, with people going out in boats to view them. The Danes add their own touch to the blazing spectacle, often topping their Midsummer Eve bonfires by burning effigies of witches that symbolize all the discomforts of winter.

In Norway the observation of Midsummer, or St. John's, Eve — called *Jonsok* — varies widely. In many places, little or no note is taken of the occasion. In others, the main festivities are gatherings of family or friends for picnics complete with (though sometimes without) Midsummer Eve fires. It is the time of year when school is out and many city dwellers adopt a holiday air, join in a mass exodus to island or coastal cottages, and stay up late, or all night, like some of their rural counterparts. In some places the celebration can encompass bonfires, picnics, fireworks, and dancing. Among the most impressive sights are the huge bonfires that light up certain coastal points and fjords, with boats of all sizes, decorated with flowers and green branches, hovering offshore so that passengers can watch the fires, and perhaps a display of fireworks as well. There are music and dancing (usually modern) and (for the hardy) a swim at sunrise.

Fires are a far less important part of Midsummer Eve celebrations in Sweden, having largely been transferred to Walpurgis Eve (see April 30) in the course of centuries. In their place, the centerpiece of the Swedish celebration is the typically Swedish *majstång*, or maypole, found in virtually every town and village on the eve of what the Swedes call *Midsommar* or *Johannes Döparens dag* (John the Baptist's Day). The pole, which is the hub of activities, usually is made of a peeled spruce trunk wound round with evergreen garlands interspersed with green leaves and fragrant birch branches. The raising of the maypole signals the beginning of the nightlong festivities.

Throughout Sweden, townspeople hurry home from work and dress in their new summer clothes or traditional regional costumes to be in time for the fun. Music continues until dawn, and dancers perform around the pole to the sound of nonstop fiddling until weariness overtakes them. The first part of the evening is devoted to traditional folk steps, a form of ring dancing. More modern dancing may follow in a convenient barn, or on an open-air dance platform or nearby pier. Outdoor refreshments and games are interspersed throughout.

In the United States the Danish "burning of the witches" has been adapted to a celebration in at least one community — Ephraim, Wisconsin, founded in the mid 19th century by a band of Norwegian Moravians along the shore of Green Bay, on Door Peninsula. Even today, most of the community's permanent residents are of Norwegian or Swedish descent. Ephraim, with its white frame houses clustered around Eagle Harbor, has for a number of years held a *Fyr-Bål Fest*, a name referring to the bonfire festivities by which the community marks Midsummer. The two-day celebration, sponsored by the Ephraim Business Council, is usually held on the weekend nearest the first day of summer and is presided over by a "Viking chieftain," a local resident chosen on the basis of his contributions to the community. Although the balloting for the Viking chieftain is held in advance, his identity remains a secret until he is brought by boat to Ephraim's shores on the first evening of the celebration. Children dressed as elves are among the first to receive the Viking chieftain when he lands at Ephraim. After his coronation, the chieftain proclaims the official opening of summer and lights a bonfire in which an effigy of the Winter Witch is burned. The fire signals other groups, gathered at other spots along the Eagle Harbor shoreline, to light their bonfires, rimming the harbor with blazes.

A great Midsummer Eve bonfire also figures importantly in Valdez, Alaska, where Midsummer also is celebrated in the Scandinavian manner on the weekend nearest June 21. This is also the time for Midnight Sun celebrations in certain other parts of Alaska (see June 24, Midsummer Day). Valdez residents borrow from the Danes in calling their celebration the festival of St. Hans — St. John, or John the Baptist. The St. Hans Festival became an annual event in Valdez in 1961, and it provides many activities for both adults and children, so that entire families can enter into the celebration welcoming the summer season. As in many parts of Scandinavia, the people begin several days before the festival to gather wood for the huge bonfire. On the big night, the bonfire is lit and kept burning until dawn, while everyone eats, plays games, or takes a turn at the square or folk dancing.

The midnight sun — that far-northern natural phenomenon in which day does not turn to night but goes from twilight to dawn without the usual darkness between — is, of course, more pronounced in the area of Alaska above the Arctic Circle. There the effect is similar to that in northern Scandinavia. Temporarily, at least, light seems to have conquered darkness — an appropriate remembrance of St. John the Baptist — and summer is launched.

Unto These Hills
Cherokee, North Carolina

This is a movable event. See note on page xxvi.

Something of the heartache, suffering, and heroism of the Cherokee Indians is captured in a historical drama presented each summer in the town of Cherokee, North Carolina, capital of the Eastern Band of Cherokees, who live on the Cherokee reservation at the edge of Great Smoky Mountains National Park. The drama, Kermit Hunter's *Unto These Hills,* records the history of the Cherokees' tragic relations with whites from the time of Hernando de Soto's explorations in 1540 to the Cherokees' forced removal in 1838–1839 from their beloved Smoky Mountains to the so-called Indian Territory (now Oklahoma) by way of the grave-strewn Trail of Tears. The title is taken from Psalm 121:1–2 ("I will lift up mine eyes unto the hills . . .").

Although the Indian Territory was land that the United States government had set aside as a home for the Five Civilized Tribes of the Southeast — the Cherokees, Chickasaws, Choctaws, Creeks, and Seminoles, who were largely removed to it between 1820 and 1845 — it was soon divided with western tribes. Later it was swallowed up entirely by Oklahoma when it became a state in 1907. Apparently forgotten was President Andrew Jackson's promise to the Indians that their land grants would last "as long as the grass grows, or water runs."

The Cherokees who take part in North Carolina's annual drama-spectacle are descendants of the handful of Cherokees who escaped removal to the Indian Territory by hiding in remote regions of the Smoky Mountains. They and their descendants became known as the Eastern Band of Cherokees as distinguished from the larger group — members of the tribe who became unwilling residents of the West under conditions of great hardship.

During the tide of westward expansion that settled this country (while pushing the Indians farther and farther from their original lands), white colonists and settlers exhibited a number of admirable traits — bravery, fierce independence, determination, self-reliance, and a democratic outlook that could (as the British had learned) be overwhelming in its exuberant assertion that all men are created equal. As the westward push developed, however, some other traits grew stronger in the character of pioneers: greed, ruthlessness, brutality, a fever to push on, and a lust for land, no matter how acquired. Frontier fever was at its peak in 1828, when Andrew Jackson, the champion of the frontier, was elected President. By then the so-called spirit of the frontier (which was far from unopposed in Congress and elsewhere) could be loosely translated as "move the Indians out," by any means.

One of the early steps of Jackson's administration was enactment, in 1830, of the Indian Removal Act, authorizing the President to initiate (but not to force) exchanges of real estate by which Indians would be given land beyond the Mississippi in place of their eastern holdings. Although the act made no provision for the forcible removal of Indians, it might as well have. State laws, particularly in Georgia (where many of the Cherokees lived), Mississippi, and Alabama, discriminated against the Indians and blocked their way to legal recourse. The federal government, on the one hand, tried to induce the Indian nations to sign treaties giving up their eastern lands; on the other hand, it declared itself unable to protect the Indians against the abuses and repeated treaty violations made possible under state laws.

Subject to federal blandishments, discriminated against by the states, and terrorized by unscrupulous white settlers and speculators who coveted their land, the Choctaws, Chickasaws, and Creeks more or less agreed to (or were forced into) removal between 1830 and 1836. In Florida, where the Indians resisted the pressure of advancing white settlers, the Seminole Wars took place before all but a remnant of the Seminoles were either killed or transported to Indian Territory.

The Cherokees who, next to the Seminoles, resisted longest probably suffered most. Finally, after a treaty bitterly opposed by most Cherokees was signed by a minority group, US Army troops under General Winfield Scott were ordered to remove the entire tribe. Cherokees in Georgia, North Carolina, and neighboring regions were hunted down and herded into detention camps. Divided into 1,000-member contingents, they were moved to Indian Territory during the harsh winter months of 1838–1839. Some 17,000 Cherokees made the 1,000-mile trip to Oklahoma, most of them on foot since there were only enough wagons for children and the elderly or disabled. The arduousness of the journey and the Cherokees' woe at leaving the homes and farmlands they loved were compounded by the army's lack of experience in moving large numbers of people and by unscrupulous suppliers who reneged on their contracts

to supply the travelers' needs. But the worst enemy was winter. Nearly 1 out of every 4 Cherokees died en route from the cold, of exposure, or of resulting diseases. As one contemporary source reported in the *New York Observer*, "They buried 14 or 15 at every stopping place . . ." and went "ten miles per day only on the average."

Perhaps the most moving part of the drama *Unto These Hills*, which has been staged annually at Cherokee since 1950, concerns those Cherokees who hid in the Smoky Mountains to escape deportation, and the heroism of the Cherokee Tsali, who sacrificed his own life to keep General Scott from hunting his people down to the very last. Although the fate of the Cherokee nation at the hands of the young US republic was not unique, the annual re-creation of this history, which has been termed "America's foremost Indian drama," is one of the best ways for non-Indians to approach an understanding both of their own background and of the sad record of relations between their own forebears and native American Indians. With a cast of approximately 140 actors, the two-part, 14-scene play is presented in a natural amphitheater, Cherokee's Mountainside Theater, nightly (except Sundays), from late June through late August. As of the close of the 1972 season almost 3 million people had attended the drama since its inception in 1950.

Admissions go toward the work of the nonprofit Cherokee Historical Association, producer of the play, which also sponsors Oconaluftee Indian Village — the authentic re-creation of a 200-year-old community — next door to the theater, and the Museum of the Cherokee Indian, also in Cherokee. Through the success of *Unto These Hills* and companion attractions, the association, by mid-1972, was able to expend nearly $3 million in salaries, supplies, and projects as direct benefits for the Cherokee Indians.

JUNE 24

Midsummer Day

The celebration of Midsummer has existed throughout Europe from pre-Christian times. Christian and pagan customs long ago became curiously mingled. The traditional bonfires and revelry of Midsummer Night are remnants of ancient sun-worship (see June 23, Midsummer's Eve); the Feast of the Nativity of St. John the Baptist, whom Jesus called "a burning and a shining light," came to be celebrated on Midsummer Day.

The term *midsummer* is actually a misnomer, since Midsummer Day does not occur in the middle of summer. Rather, it is near the time of the summer solstice, which marks the beginning of summer (see June 21) in the Northern Hemisphere. It is at this time of year that the days are longest: the sun at its noontime elevation appears to stand still for several days (rather than moving according to its usual pattern), and all people are reminded of their year-round dependence on the sun's life-giving light and warmth.

Midsummer is celebrated, with local variations, in Europe and in many Latin American countries. However, the observance is especially enthusiastic in the northern reaches of Scandinavia, which is sun-starved most of the year; and most of the Midsummer observances that have found their way to the United States are borrowed from that region. There, the mood of rejoicing is intensified by the length and severity of the winter behind. With the arrival of warm weather comes freedom to pursue the activities that have been curtailed by the cold.

Midsummer and the eve preceding it thus are a time for visiting friends and relatives, enjoying traditional foods, and, in some places, wearing traditional costumes and performing folk songs and folk dances. Above all, the celebration of Midsummer is a paean to nature, a time to appreciate the world outdoors. Picnics are the order of the day, and to eat inside is almost unthinkable. In some places, processions or pageants recalling national triumphs may be part of the festivities.

For Swedish people, the ancient Midsummer celebration has had a double significance since 1523. It was on Midsummer Day in that year that the Swedes asserted their independence from the Danish crown under a young national leader named Gustavus Vasa, who became King Gustavus I. Ever since, they have looked upon Midsummer Day — an observance they have been marking on the Saturday between June 19 and June 25 since 1953 — in much the way that Americans view the Fourth of July.

Swedes celebrate Midsummer with particular exuberance — beginning with the nightlong merrymaking of Midsummer Eve. Probably the most colorful celebrations are in Sweden's Dalarna region, where costumes are particularly plentiful and the old folk songs and dances have been carefully preserved. Another traditional touch in evidence everywhere in Sweden is the border of newly-cut birch twigs framing doorways. This is part of the customary "green welcome," whereby everything — including verandas, balconies, boats, cars, and fireplaces — is decorated with green leaves and branches as a sign of hospitality.

In Finland, Midsummer Day is a double celebration, too, observed with Finnish Flag Day on the Saturday between June 20 and June 26. As it is elsewhere, Midsummer is a day for visiting. Festivities begin the night before with bonfires everywhere. Traditional regional costumes are much in evidence.

Unlike Sweden and Finland, both Denmark and Norway still celebrate Midsummer Day on its original June 24 date, though in most parts of both countries it is more a time for gatherings of families or friends than an occasion for big community-sponsored festivities. Visiting, feasting on traditional specialties, and enjoying nature are the pastimes of the day, and people travel to vacation cottages. Festivities reach their high point on Midsummer Eve.

In the United States the largest celebrations of Midsummer are held by persons of Scandinavian descent. In Minnesota's Twin Cities area of Minneapolis-St. Paul, for example, an annual Svenskarnas Dag, or Swedes' Day, celebration brings together a greater concentration of Swedes than exists anywhere outside of Sweden. The general public also is invited to this Midsummer celebration, and the attendance sometimes exceeds 50,000, with visitors from many states and Canada.

Modeled on Midsummer Day celebrations in Sweden, the program begins with a Lutheran religious service in Swedish, frequently conducted by a visiting Swedish clergyman. Between the religious service in the forenoon and the afternoon's festivities, a band concert provides entertainment and sets the holiday mood. The afternoon program consists of folk dances and songs, performances by musical groups, and speeches by visiting or local dignitaries. The celebration has been attended by members of the Swedish royal family, virtually every Swedish Ambassador to the United States, and by American senators, governors, Supreme Court justices, and other distinguished persons.

This observance is held in Minneapolis's Minnehaha Park on the Sunday nearest Midsummer Day. It started as an annual picnic or Midsummerfest for the Swedish Good Templar Lodges of Minneapolis and St. Paul. In 1910 the general public was invited to attend, and the program was enlarged to include athletic contests for young and old. In 1915 the outing was officially called Svenskarnas Dag. That same year, the crowning of a Midsummer queen was instituted. Svenskarnas Dag in 1933 was a great success, and it was decided that it could become even bigger if other Swedish organizations were invited to cosponsor the annual event. Since that time, numerous Swedish organizations have jointly undertaken the event under the corporate name of Svenskarnas Dag, Inc., a nonprofit organization.

In the Chicago area, Svenskarnas Dag has been celebrated since 1911 by the International Order of Good Templars. Smaller Midsummer celebrations are observed in some of Chicago's Swedish Lutheran churches and by other Swedish groups, as well as by a few corps of the Salvation Army serving in Swedish-American communities. In Geneva, Illinois, the Geneva Swedish Festival is held in the Good Templars Park each year.

Local Swedish organizations in Rockford, Illinois, as in other places, hold their own private Midsummer celebrations, but since 1951 the Midsummer observance sponsored by the Swedish Historical Society of Rockford has been arranged for the community at large. This festival is held in Sinnissippi Park, usually in late June, and draws about 3,000 people. Each year a *majstång* or maypole is decorated and raised, a queen is crowned, and there are music, dancing, speeches, and food.

At Ephraim, Wisconsin, the *Fyr-Bål Fest* incorporates many Scandinavian customs traditionally seen in old-country Midsummer celebrations, among them the bonfires, authentic folk dancing, and the "green welcome" at doors — in the form of welcome mats of interwoven evergreen boughs. The program also incorporates some of the more familiar events of a typical American shore community, such as a trophy race, held at the Ephraim Yacht Club.

A "fish boil," a holdover from pioneer days that is typical of the region, has become a part of the tradition of Ephraim's Midsummer celebration, featuring great, steaming vats of seafood — usually whitefish and trout — cooked with potatoes and onions in various outdoor locations and served with cole slaw and cherry or apple pie. The celebration (held on the weekend nearest the first day of summer) continues through Sunday and is officially closed with a parade. During this event, dancers from nearby Washington Island, the site of an Icelandic colony, perform native Scandinavian steps, adding to the color and excitement of Ephraim's *Fyr-Bål Fest*.

In Seattle, Washington, the Midsummer celebration is sponsored by the Vasa Order of America, the largest Swedish national organization in the United States. The celebration is held on the weekend nearest Midsummer's Day in Vasa Park, which is owned and operated by the local lodges of the Vasa Order of America. (The organization takes its name from the same Gustavus Vasa who was proclaimed the first king of Sweden in 1523.) The outstanding feature of Seattle's celebration is the erection of the maypole, decorated with leaves and flowers, as in Sweden; usually those preparing the maypole wear Swedish provincial costumes. Once the pole is firmly in place, everyone joins in the lively folkdancing.

Midsummer Day and Eve are celebrated by Scandinavian groups — folk dancers or fraternal organizations, for instance — in some Eastern cities and in a number of other Midwestern and West Coast communities with large populations of Scandinavian descent. San Diego's Balboa Park has in some years been the scene of a Midsummer festival sponsored by the House of Pacific Relations. Like so many of the Midsummer events transplanted to the United States, however, its scheduling has actually been keyed to the first day of summer, June 21, which is literally the longest day of the year.

In northern Alaska, instead of a celebration on Midsummer Day, the weekend nearest June 21 is set aside for celebrations of the midnight sun — that is, the period when the sun can be seen at midnight and there is no real darkness. In Nome, for example, where the sea ice does not melt until mid-June, residents and visitors gather on the weekend nearest the 21st for the Midnight Sun Festival, the first celebration after winter's end. For the occasion, the entire population wears frontier costumes, men grow beards, and there are parades and floats — all recalling the region's gold rush period. One climax of the festivities is a Days of '98 ball. Other high points are assorted competitions — a baby contest, competitions for the best beard and costume, and a raft race, starting at midnight, down the Nome River. Not to be outdone, Fairbanks, Alaska, has its Midnight Sun Baseball Festival, with the Alaska Goldpanners playing at midnight without artificial lights.

Feast of the Nativity of St. John the Baptist

To Christians St. John the Baptist was possessed of nearly unparalleled credentials: in the words of Jesus Christ, as reported in Matthew 11:11, "Truly, I say to you, among those born of women there has risen no one greater than John the Baptist."

Mentioned by all four of the Evangelists at or near the beginning of their Gospels, John was the cousin and precursor of Jesus Christ.

John was indeed unique. His coming was foretold by the prophets Isaiah and Jeremiah. He was born during the reign of Herod, when his parents were advanced in years. When grown, John spent years in the wilderness as a hermit, preparing for his mission; when he began to preach, his popularity was so great that civil and religious authorities thought him a potential source of danger and rebellion. Despite his austerity and outspokenness, people flocked from the city and the countryside to hear him and to be baptized by him.

In those Christian churches that commemorate the lives of saints, St. John the Baptist ranks high — second only to the Virgin Mary — in liturgical importance. While most other saints' feasts are celebrated on the day of their death, St. John is the only saint, other than Mary, whose birth is celebrated. Roman Catholics, Eastern Orthodox Christians, Episcopalians, and Lutherans honor him on what has been designated as the anniversary of this day. The Roman Catholic and Eastern Orthodox churches commemorate his death also (see August 29). Eastern Orthodox Christians celebrate additional feasts of St. John as well, including a feast marking his conception.

The Feast of the Nativity of St. John the Baptist is one of the oldest introduced into the liturgies of the Eastern and Western churches. For many centuries the feast — sometimes called Summer Christmas — was celebrated, like the Nativity of Jesus, with three masses, one said at midnight, the second at dawn, and the third on the morning of the feast. This unusual honor resulted from the tradition, upheld by the Church fathers, that John was sanctified, that is freed from the stain of original sin, in his mother's womb. According to tradition this happened when the Virgin Mary visited Elizabeth, John's mother, three months before his birth.

The story surrounding John's birth is recorded in the opening chapter of the Gospel of Luke. Zechariah, a priest, and his wife, Elizabeth, who were both advanced in age, had prayed for a son for many years. While Zechariah was performing his priestly offices in the temple, the angel Gabriel appeared, announcing that Elizabeth would bear a son who should be called John. Zechariah questioned the angel and for his skepticism was stricken dumb until the prophecy was fulfilled.

Luke relates that when Gabriel announced to Mary that she was to become the mother of Jesus, he told her that her elderly kinswoman Elizabeth had also conceived a child, for with God nothing is impossible. In haste, Mary visited Elizabeth, and when Elizabeth heard her greeting, the child leaped in her womb. Elizabeth, Luke continues, was filled with the Holy Spirit and exclaimed: "Blessed are you among women,

and blessed is the fruit of your womb! And why is this granted me, that the mother of my Lord should come to me? For behold, when the voice of your greeting came to my ears, the babe in my womb leaped for joy." Each woman knew the other was with child though each had guarded her secret.

Elizabeth's child was born and Zechariah regained his speech as had been foretold. Filled with the Holy Spirit, Zechariah prophesied concerning the redemption of Israel by Jesus and also concerning the mission of his own son John: "And you, child, will be called the prophet of the Most High; for you will go before the Lord to prepare his ways."

John grew and then remained in the wilderness as a hermit until the time came for his public ministry. Then, according to Luke 3:1:

Now in the fifteenth year of the reign of Tiberius Caesar, Pontius Pilate being governor of Judea, and Herod being tetrarch of Galilee, . . . the word of God came to John . . . in the wilderness; and he went into all the region about the Jordan, preaching a baptism of repentance for the forgiveness of sins.

The Gospel of Matthew takes up the report in chapter 3:

In those days came John the Baptist, preaching in the wilderness of Judea, "Repent, for the kingdom of heaven is at hand." For this is he who was spoken of by the prophet Isaiah when he said, "The voice of one crying in the wilderness: Prepare the way of the Lord, make his paths straight." Now John wore a garment of camel's hair, and a leather girdle around his waist; and his food was locusts and wild honey. Then went out to him Jerusalem and all Judea and all the region about the Jordan, and they were baptized by him in the river Jordan, confessing their sins.

The Jewish priests and people had been awaiting the Messiah, whose coming had been foretold by the Old Testament prophets, and many of them thought John was he. John, however, clearly denied this, stating that his mission was to prepare the way for the Messiah. Asked why he was baptizing if he was not the Christ, John replied, "I baptize . . . with water for repentance, but he who is coming after me is mightier than I, whose sandals I am not worthy to carry; he will baptize you with the Holy Spirit and with fire."

This took place in Bethany, according to the Gospel of John, which goes on to relate that the next day John the Baptist — who had never met Jesus — saw him approaching. John 1:29–34 tells of the Baptist's instant exclamation:

"Behold, the Lamb of God, who takes away the sin of the world! This is he of whom I said, 'After me comes a man who ranks before me, for he was before me.' . . . For this I came baptizing with water, that he might be revealed to Israel." And John bore witness, "I saw the Spirit descend as a dove from heaven, and it remained on him. I myself did not know him; but he who sent me to baptize with water said to me, 'He on whom you see the Spirit descend and remain, this is he who baptizes with the Holy Spirit.' And I have seen and have borne witness that this is the Son of God."

As related in the sixth chapter of Mark, John continued his ministry of preaching repentance for sins, baptizing the people, and preparing them to receive the Messiah until his great popularity with the people and his outspokenness caused Herod Antipas to imprison him. Herod had put away his own wife and married Herodias, the wife of his half brother Philip. John the Baptist fearlessly denounced this marriage, and Herodias vowed vengeance. Her daughter, Salome, whose dancing pleased Herod, obtained for Herodias the head of the Baptist on a platter.

Although the time-span of his public ministry was short, John's influence was great. Because he had pointed Jesus Christ out as the Lamb of God, some of his own disciples — among them the Apostles Andrew and John, left John to follow Jesus — a step the Baptist approved (John 3:28–30):

You yourselves bear me witness, that I have said, I am not the Christ, but I have been sent before him. . . . He must increase, but I must decrease.

John's influence was still evident 30 years later when the Apostle Paul on his journeys met and baptized people who had not known Jesus but who had been baptized by John (Acts of the Apostles 18:24–27 and 19:1–7).

The Feast of the Nativity of St. John on June 24 occurs near the summer solstice, when the days begin to grow shorter. The Nativity of Christ is celebrated on December 25, near the winter solstice, when the days begin to grow longer — a convenient choice, since the Christian observance then coincided with and had a chance of competing with the old pagan revelries that for centuries had taken place on June 24 and the preceding evening, near the time of the summer solstice. Many scholars recalling John's explanation that Christ must increase and he (John) must decrease point out the appropriateness of the dates of these two important feasts. Apparently, however, the selection of June 24 as the Feast of the Nativity of St. John was based merely on the fact that, according to Scripture, John was six months older than Jesus. Following the Roman custom of calculating dates by counting backwards from the Kalends, or first day of the following month, Church authorities retrospectively fixed the birth of Christ at eight days before the Kalends of January, i.e., on December 25. John's nativity, then, was put at eight days before the Kalends of July, and since June has only 30 days, the feast was assigned to June 24.

For the French in Canada, the Feast of the Nativity of St. John the Baptist is one of the biggest celebrations of the year and is considered a national holiday in the province of Quebec. Some French Canadians prefer the fetes held in the small towns. The more elaborate celebrations in the cities of Montreal and Quebec, which follow masses in parish churches, include games and parades, street dancing, outdoor eating, carnival attractions, bonfires, and fireworks. Sometimes the gaiety lasts for days.

In the United States perhaps the largest celebration of the feast of St. John is the San Juan Fiesta, which takes place in New York City on the Sunday nearest June 24. From its inception in 1953, the San Juan Fiesta has been the year's biggest event for New York's Hispanic-American families. It originated when, aware of the city's rapidly growing Puerto Rican population, Francis Cardinal Spellman, then archbishop of New York, instituted a special observance of St. John the Baptist, the patron saint of Puerto Rico and of its capital city, San Juan. That year a Pontifical High Mass in St. Patrick's Cathedral was attended by a capacity crowd. After two successive years of an overflow attendance, the celebration was moved outdoors in 1956 to the Fordham University campus in the Bronx where 35,000 Spanish-speaking New Yorkers gathered for the occasion.

The 195-acre Randall's Island was chosen as the site in 1957, and that year 50,000 people attended. By 1969, the number had grown to an estimated 250,000. In 1970, instead of the usual San Juan Fiesta, a midnight mass was held in Downing Stadium on Randall's Island and attended by about 10,000 people. A dramatic candlelight procession preceded the mass, which was concelebrated by Terence Cardinal Cooke, archbishop of New York, and some 40 Spanish-speaking priests of the archdiocese.

In 1971 the San Juan Fiesta returned to a daytime celebration incorporating the religious, civic, and cultural aspects of Hispanic life in an afternoon-long program in the Olympic-size stadium. It remained at Randall's Island until 1975, when the event was moved to Central Park. Religious ceremonies officially open the San Juan Fiesta. The cardinal is escorted by a long and colorful procession of local and visiting dignitaries, clergymen of various faiths, altar boys, and members of church organizations with their distinctive parade banners, sashes, and other identification. After mass is said at the altar, which has been erected especially for the occasion, the cardinal presents the San Juan Fiesta Medal to a lay member of the Hispanic community who has distinguished himself in civic or humanitarian endeavors. The coveted medal is a copy of the official seal of the city of San Juan.

After these formalities comes the traditional breaking of the piñata. In this case the piñata, a huge hanging papier-mâché figure containing hundreds of separately wrapped presents, such as candy and toys, is broken by an honored guest. Blindfolded, he is given a baseball bat with which to hit the piñata, releasing the presents within, which the youngsters scramble to gather.

When the excitement of the piñata party is over, the cultural part of the program begins. The air is filled with music from bands, orchestras, and singers. Hispanic folk dancers perform in colorful costumes.

In Puerto Rico, which was the inspiration for the New York fiesta, the celebration of the Nativity of St. John the Baptist — San Juan Bautista — usually goes on for several days, sometimes a week. Since 1960, many aspects of what was once Puerto Rico's pre-Lenten Carnival season have been incorporated into the festivities honoring the patron saint of San Juan in June, notably public parties, street dances, and concerts. Events move toward a climax on St. John's Eve, when families spend a night-long vigil on beaches, with picnic lunches, bonfires, singing, and midnight dips in the Caribbean — an allusion to the baptizing activities of John. At dawn they attend Mass and afterwards they enjoy feasting, dancing, parades, games, and other entertainment. The largest celebrations are concentrated in park areas, especially those with bandshells and paved areas for dancing, seats for spectators, and picnic tables.

The feast is also celebrated in regions of the United States where the influence of early Spanish missionaries is still evident. For example, in San Juan Bautista, California, inland from Monterey Bay, where Spanish Franciscans founded the Mission San Juan Bautista in 1797, the Fiesta de San Juan Bautista is celebrated in conjunction with a weekend rodeo. The celebration, whose date varies, starts on a religious note with mass at the mission church. The rest of the day's events include broncobusting and other rodeo events, a barbecue, a parade, and dancing in the plaza.

In a number of the pueblos of New Mexico, the feast is celebrated by American Indians. San Juan Day corn dances are traditionally held in Taos, Isleta, Cochiti, Santa Ana, Laguna, Acoma, and San Juan.

Various groups regard St. John the Baptist as their patron saint. In some areas, for example, St. John is considered the patron saint of shepherds, perhaps because of his words "Behold the Lamb of God." In other areas he is the patron saint of tailors or furriers because he fashioned his own clothes of animal skins. In other places masons and carpenters take him as their patron because of the scriptural description of his mission to "make ready the way of the Lord, make straight all his paths."

The earliest artistic representation of the Baptist, depicting him baptizing Jesus, dates from the second century and is in the catacombs of St. Callistus in Rome. Also in Rome is the St. John Lateran basilica, which, according to the *Catholic Encyclopedia*, Emperor Constantine had built and dedicated in 324 to St. John the Baptist. Since rebuilt and usually referred to as the Lateran, this basilica is regarded as the church of highest dignity, not only in Rome, but throughout the Latin rite of the Roman Catholic church. The Lateran is the pope's own patriarchal basilica and thus carries the title Cathedral of Rome. Further evidence that John the Baptist was highly venerated throughout the Church from early times is the fact that 15 churches were dedicated to him in the ancient imperial city of Constantinople.

Henry Ward Beecher's Birthday

One of the most famous pulpit orators in America, Henry Ward Beecher, who became a symbol and spokesman for Protestantism in the mid-19th century, was born on June 24, 1813, in Litchfield, Connecticut. The eighth child of a noted Calvinist preacher, Lyman Beecher, he was the brother of novelist Harriet Beecher Stowe (see June 14).

His natural boisterousness and aversion to study notwithstanding, Henry Beecher was educated at Mount Pleasant Collegiate Institute in Amherst, Massachusetts, and at Amherst College, of which he became a graduate in 1834. He was never a noted student, but he achieved popularity as a leader and became an excellent public speaker. He followed his college training with three postgraduate years at Cincinnati's Lane Theological Seminary, of which his father had become president in 1832, and began his preaching as an independent Presbyterian in Cincinnati.

In 1837 he took two important steps. He married Eunice White Bullard, and he accepted his first pastorate — of a Presbyterian church in Lawrenceburg, Indiana, with a membership of 20. Two years later he became minister of a

Presbyterian church in Indianapolis, where he remained for close to eight years.

As a minister he emphasized the love of God and stressed the joy and glory of Christian life. Believing that God "loves a man in his sins for the sake of helping him out of them," Beecher was convinced that preaching effectiveness lay in bringing about a moral change in the listener — an aim to which his sense of drama, extraordinary ability as an orator, and flow of figurative language were well suited. His mounting reputation as a pulpit- and lecture-platform orator was widened with publication in 1844 of his *Seven Lectures to Young Men*, on coping with the perils and vice of frontier settlements — a timely message in view of the great westward migration then in progress in the United States.

In 1847 Beecher accepted a call to the pulpit he was to occupy for the rest of his life, in the newly established Plymouth Congregational Church in Brooklyn, New York. His preaching there drew huge crowds, averaging some 2,500 a week by the early 1850s. His sermons, printed in pamphlet form, were circulated widely and his church came to claim the largest membership of any in the country. Throughout the nation and beyond, Beecher's statements and personal life became the subject of interest and he became a newsworthy, and at times controversial, figure.

In time he became one of the leading champions of the abolition of slavery, favoring disobedience of the Fugitive Slave Law while he opposed armed coercion of the slave states. As a popular speaker, Beecher frequently employed strong rhetoric, particularly on behalf of moral causes like abolition. Once, as the national debate arose over whether the Kansas territory would enter the Union as a free state or a slave state, he went so far as to assert that rifles were greater moral agencies than the Bible. This utterance gave rise to the term "Beecher's Bibles," which northern settlers in Kansas and Nebraska applied to the Sharps repeating rifles with which they intended to make the territory a free state.

Uncle Tom's Cabin, written by his sister Harriet, meanwhile was exciting already inflamed tempers on the subject of slavery. During the Civil War he traveled to England in 1863 and defended the Union position to audiences that were at first hostile to the Northern viewpoint, but warmed to the cause under the Beecher spell. Like many other abolitionists, Beecher was a champion of woman suffrage as well. He also advocated civil service reform. After the Civil War he championed a moderate Reconstruction policy. A modernist in religion, he supported such controversial theories as the doctrine of evolution and accepted scientific biblical criticism, while holding firmly to his belief in miracles. In addition to his addresses and sermons, Beecher expressed his outspoken and often courageous views in the *Independent*, a Congregational publication that he edited for several years beginning in 1861, and in the nondenominational *Christian Union* (later the *Outlook*), which he edited from 1870 to 1881.

His later years were to some extent blighted by a scandal involving him, at least by reputation, with the wife of Theodore Tilton, who had been Beecher's friend and protégé. Even Beecher eventually realized that he had been indiscreet, but whether only indiscretion had been involved was never entirely clarified, either by the adultery suit brought by Tilton in 1874 or by the two ecclesiastical tribunals that exonerated Beecher without entirely managing to restore his reputation.

Through all the scandal, Beecher's Brooklyn congregation was staunch in its loyalty, and he remained active for another decade, continuing to exert an influence on public issues, among them the successful candidacy of Grover Cleveland for the presidency in 1884, which he supported. Over the years Beecher was the author of a number of published works in addition to his sermons. They included *Star Papers* (1855), *New Star Papers* (1859), *American Rebellion: Report of Speeches Delivered in England . . .* (1864), and *Norwood: A Tale of Village Life in New England* (1867). Two of his most important works were *Evolution and Religion* (1885), and the four-volume *Life of Jesus the Christ* (1871–1891).

One of the most widely known ministers the country had ever seen, Beecher died suddenly, of apoplexy, on March 8, 1887. He was survived by his wife and 4 of their 10 children. As pastor of Plymouth Church, he was succeeded by a former editorial associate, Lyman Abbott.

JUNE 25

Custer's Last Stand

George Armstrong Custer was born on December 5, 1839, the son of Emanuel and Maria Ward Fitzpatrick Custer of New Rumley, Harrison County, Ohio. He spent most of his youth in Monroe, Michigan, where he resided with Lydia Reed, his half sister. In 1857 he left the Midwest for the US Military Academy in New York.

At West Point Custer managed to hide his talents. His mischievousness earned him numerous demerits, and he graduated near the bottom of the class of 1861. The new second lieutenant then rushed off to join his unit, the Second US

Cavalry, and arrived in time to participate in the first battle of the Manassas, or Bull Run, an early defeat for the Union forces in the Civil War.

Custer rose through the ranks with amazing speed. At the age of 23 he became the youngest brigadier general in the annals of the US Army, and two years later he won another temporary promotion to the rank of major general. The recipient of many awards, Custer had the honor of accepting the flag of truce of the Confederate Army of Northern Virginia at Appomattox Court House at the end of the Civil War.

Peace brought a reduction in the size of the army, and most officers surrendered their wartime commissions. Custer reverted to a lieutenant colonelcy and took command of the Seventh Cavalry. He spent his remaining years with his wife, the former Elizabeth Bacon, in remote posts on the western frontier.

In 1874 Custer's Seventh Cavalry left Fort Abraham Lincoln in the Dakota Territory to explore the Black Hills. The region was part of the Great Sioux Reservation, set aside by an 1868 treaty signed at Fort Laramie, Wyoming, for the Sioux and Cheyenne tribes. However, prospectors with Custer's 1874 expedition confirmed the existence of gold deposits in the Black Hills, and miners soon invaded the Indian lands.

The army sought to keep the fortune hunters away, but lacked the necessary manpower. The Indian tribes therefore assumed the task of defending their semisacred lands; bands of Sioux and Cheyenne roamed the Black Hills and killed a number of white intruders. Some reservation Indians slipped away to join forces with Crazy Horse and Sitting Bull, determined leaders who had had no part in the 1868 treaty. They rejected a government ultimatum to return to their reserved settlements by January 31, 1876.

In 1876 the army designed a campaign to encircle and capture the militant Sioux and Cheyenne who were in southeastern Montana. General George Crook marched north from Fort Fetterman in Wyoming, Colonel John Gibbon came east from Fort Ellis in Montana, and General Alfred Terry moved west from Fort Abraham Lincoln in the Dakotas. The three were to join forces near the Yellowstone River and conduct their operation.

Terry and Gibbon met in June and camped at the mouth of the Rosebud Creek in Montana. On June 22 Custer's Seventh Cavalry, the largest element in Terry's command, proceeded south down the creek to reconnoiter. By the morning of June 25 the Seventh had reached the crest of the divide separating the Rosebud from the Little Bighorn River, and the scouts spotted

smoke in the valley, indicating that the Indians might be there.

Suspecting that the Sioux had discovered his whereabouts, Custer decided to attack immediately rather than wait until June 26 as Terry had planned. Wanting to take no chance on the Indians' escaping, Custer divided the Seventh into three battalions, the largest of which he led himself. He proceeded west with five companies along the north bank of a stream leading toward the Little Bighorn Valley. This rivulet later became Reno Creek. Major Marcus A. Reno led three companies in a course parallel to Custer's, but on the other side of the water. Captain Frederick A. Benteen proceeded in the same direction with three companies, but farther to the south.

Major Reno crossed the Little Bighorn River at about 2:30 P.M. and encountered a surprisingly large band of Indians. The troopers dismounted and managed to hold off their opponents for half an hour, but they finally had to retreat back across the Little Bighorn. They took up defensive positions and were not a factor in the rest of the battle.

Custer had evidently planned to attack the Cheyenne and Sioux on the right flank and the rear. Unfortunately for Custer's battalion of Seventh cavalrymen, Reno had to fall back before his commander was able to cross the Little Bighorn. The Indians therefore were able to turn their full attention to Custer's men; perhaps as many as 5,000 set out after the approximately 225 troopers. The overwhelmingly outnumbered cavalrymen shot their own horses and used their bodies as shelter from the enemy's bullets and arrows. This gruesome tactic was of no avail: the Indians killed every one of the cavalrymen. Only Comanche, the mount of Captain Myles W. Keogh, remained alive on the battlefield, and he had been shot seven times.

Major Reno, joined by Captain Benteen, maintained his position through the night. The Sioux and Cheyenne attacked again at dawn on June 26 and continued their harassment until late afternoon, when they withdrew. The cavalry-men feared that the Indians might return, however, and continued to act cautiously.

General Terry and Colonel Gibbon left the mouth of Rosebud Creek on June 21 and traveled west along the Yellowstone River. They then turned south and proceeded up the Bighorn River. On June 27 an advance party led by Lieutenant Bradley came upon the Custer battlefield and met the troopers of Reno and Benteen. The following day those remnants of the Seventh Cavalry began burying their more than 200 dead.

The war with the Sioux continued for years. The army repaid the Indians with defeat after defeat. In 1877, after one army victory, Chief Crazy Horse, who had led the Indians at the battle of Little Bighorn, attempted to negotiate with the soldiers at Fort Robinson. He was betrayed and killed with a bayonet. Other diehard warriors fled across the border into Canada. From this vantage they attempted to continue their fight, but their cause was hopeless. Finally, in July 1881, Sitting Bull and his followers returned to the United States and surrendered. Nine years later, on December 29, 1890, the Sioux met their final defeat when the US Army vanquished a group of Sioux — many of them unarmed — at Wounded Knee, South Dakota. At the Wounded Knee Battlefield, located about 16 miles northeast of Pine Ridge, are a monument and a museum and a library containing Indian displays. Wounded Knee was once again the site of violence in 1973, when militant Indians occupying the hamlet clashed with federal officers.

The battle of Little Bighorn brought lasting posthumous fame to Custer and ignominy to Major Marcus Reno. Reno was holding off a Sioux advance five miles from the place where Custer and his men perished, but Custer's wife and friends in the years following the battle persuaded the American public that it was cowardice that kept Reno from assisting the lieutenant colonel. Even after an army hearing had exonerated the major of any misconduct in the affair, the calumny continued. Finally, in 1880, several minor breaches of conduct — which are themselves now in question — led the army to dismiss Reno for "conduct unbecoming an officer." He died in 1896 and was buried in an unmarked grave. For years his case was debated. Then, in 1967 Charles Reno, a great-grandnephew of the major, with the support of the American Legion and two historians, retired Colonels Chester K. Shore and George Walton, appealed to the army to restore his forebear's military rank and honors and to rebury him in the Custer Battlefield National Cemetery. The army granted this request and Reno's body now reposes with the victims of the Little Bighorn tragedy.

More fortunate in his association with Custer's Last Stand was its sole survivor, the horse Comanche. Despite his serious wounds, the clayback charger was nursed back to health. By order of the regimental commander at Fort Lincoln, Colonel S. Sturgis, a special stall was built at the fort and Comanche was never again ridden or worked. His sole function in his final years was to be led on all ceremonial occasions in saddle and bridle with reversed boots. He died at the age of 29 in 1891. The body has been mounted and may be seen displayed in a glass case at the Dyche Museum of the University of Kansas in Lawrence.

The actual scene of Custer's encounter with the Sioux, and of the Reno-Benteen defenses five miles away, is today known as the Custer Battlefield National Monument. The 765.34-acre site, which was designated a National Cemetery in 1879 and reclassified a National Monument in 1946, is located 15 miles south of Hardin, Montana, and is administered by the National Park Service. Hundreds of thousands of tourists each year visit the area. A museum on the grounds contains Custer memorabilia, Indian relics, and displays pertinent to the battle. But the main points of interest are the markers that indicate the positions where the soldiers fell and were first buried and the granite monument that stands only six feet from the place where Custer was slain. The monument is inscribed with the words: "In memory of the officers and soldiers of the 7th United States Cavalry who fell near this place fighting the Sioux Indians on the 25 of June 1876." At its base are buried many of the victims of that fatal day as well as soldiers who died in other battles with Indians. Custer's remains, however, lie elsewhere. He was interred at his alma mater, the US Military Academy at West Point, New York.

Surrounding the Custer Battlefield National Monument is the Crow Indian Reservation. In 1964, the 75th anniversary of Montana's statehood and the centennial of its existence as a territory, the Crow Agency, which administers the 3,600-square-mile Crow Reservation, sponsored a reenactment of Custer's Last Stand. Joe Medicine Crow, an anthropologist and a member of the tribe, collaborated in the writing of the pageant's script. The hour-long drama featured many descendants of participants in the 1876 battle and was performed in the authentically simulated settings — reconstructions of the Fort Laramie Army Post, the Little Bighorn Indian village, and the battlefield. The 1964 reenactment proved so successful that the Crow agency has made it an annual event. The pageant is generally held on a weekend in late June.

The day before the 1976 reenactment, the National Park Service held its own ceremony commemorating the 100th anniversary of the battle. Russell Means, leader of the militant American Indian Movement, told the audience of whites and Indians: "Tomorrow is our day of celebration. In your Bicentennial year, we, the Indian people, have a centennial year — a year that gives us pride and dignity. We bear no ill will." After the ceremony, the Indians performed a victory dance around the spot that marked the "last stand."

Observances of Custer's Last Stand are not limited to Montana: neighboring South Dakota also commemorates the event and pays tribute to the leader of the army's forces. One of the principal reenactments of the battle takes place each year at Custer. In late July the town, which is situated in the area where a prospector with Custer's 1874 expedition found gold, celebrates Gold Discovery Days. The festivities include a parade and Indian dances and rodeos, but the high point of Discovery Days is a pageant. More than 1,000 people, including Indians, participate in this great outdoor spectacle. They bring to life much of the history of the Black Hills, of which Custer's war against the Sioux was such an important part.

Three miles east of Custer is Custer State Park. With a total area of 109 square miles, it is one of the largest state parks in the United States. Animals native to the area — such as bison, Rocky Mountain goats, deer, and bighorn sheep — roam over the grounds, while rarer species are housed in the park's zoo. Camping facilities have been provided and visitors enjoy fishing and swimming in the park's four lakes and numerous streams.

Although Custer's bravery at Little Bighorn is widely commemorated, tribute is also paid to Chief Crazy Horse, the leader of the Sioux during the battle. Atop Thunderhead Mountain, five miles north of Custer, South Dakota, Korczak Ziolkowski has been carving out of the mountain a three-dimensional monument to the chief which, when completed, will be the largest granite statue in the world. The Crazy Horse Memorial, designed to show the chief mounted on a horse, is to be 641 feet long and 563 feet high. The work, in progress for many years, was scheduled for completion in 1980. Plans also include a great Indian center complete with a hospital, museum, and university at the base of Thunderhead Mountain.

Within an hour's journey of the Crazy Horse Memorial is Hot Springs, South Dakota. From the middle of June until the end of August each year, Paha Sapa, an organization that takes its name from the Indian expression meaning black hills and whose members are South Dakotans who have purchased $1-shares in the corporation, sponsors the Chief Crazy Horse pageant. A cast of 212 persons clothed in authentic dress takes part in the extravaganza. The dramatic production draws upon recollections of descendants of the actual warriors at Little Bighorn to insure the historical accuracy of his script. The work has been a great success. Held in a natural amphitheater on the Fall River, the pageant attracts thousands of spectators each summer. The proceeds from the event are divided among numerous local churches and charities.

Korean War Begins

The years following World War II brought not peace but a new kind of conflict. The Western powers and the Communist block vied with each other in a tense diplomatic game with the fate of the world as the stakes. The United States and the Soviet Union, the leaders of the opposing forces, managed to avoid the Armageddon of direct confrontation, but the Communist and free worlds tested each other's strength and determination in Korea.

After World War II, control of Korea had passed from Japan to the Soviet Union and the United States. In 1945 these two powers temporarily divided the country at the 38th Parallel, with the USSR responsible for the northern half and the United States for the southern. In theory a single, independent Korean republic was to be established within a short time, but postwar hostility interfered with this plan. Instead, by 1948 two separate governments existed in Korea: the Democratic People's Republic in the north, recognized by the Soviet Union; and the Republic of Korea in the south, backed by the United Nations and the United States.

Soviet and American troops withdrew from Korea in 1948 and 1949 respectively. The Soviets left behind a well-trained, well-equipped, native army in North Korea; in contrast, the Americans handed over defense of South Korea to a weak and ineffective military. North Korea did not delay in taking advantage of the situation.

On June 25, 1950, North Korean armored divisions crossed the 38th Parallel and within three days captured the South Korean capital of Seoul. This aggressive action immediately spurred the free world to take measures to prevent the complete Communist takeover of South Korea. After its June 25 call for a cease-fire went unheeded, the UN Security Council on June 27 appealed to its members to "furnish such assistance to the Republic of Korea as may be necessary to repel the armed attack and restore international peace and security." The United States responded quickly. That same day President Harry S. Truman commanded United States naval and air forces to proceed to Korea, and on June 30 he ordered American ground troops into the combat zone.

Although 16 nations had military personnel in Korea by the beginning of July 1950, American troops constituted more than 80 percent of the entire UN forces. In the first months of the difficult combat the UN troops and its South Korean allies continuously lost ground to the North Koreans, and at the end of August fighting centered around Pusan, in southeastern Korea. The tide of the battle turned in early September. Under the direction of their commander, General Douglas MacArthur, the UN forces not only held their position at Pusan but began a successful counteroffensive. Seoul was recaptured on September 26, and by October 1 the troops of the Communist North had been driven above the 38th Parallel.

Buoyed by the September victories the UN General Assembly on October 7 authorized Mac-Arthur to take the necessary steps to insure "a unified, independent and democratic Korea." United Nations troops crossed the 38th Parallel on October 9, and by the end of the month they had beaten the Communists back to the Manchurian border. But they did not hold this position for long. Chinese foreign minister Chou En-lai had warned that the people of his country would not "supinely tolerate seeing their neighbors being savagely invaded by imperialists." On November 26 the Chinese launched a massive counterattack.

The Communists pushed the UN troops south to below the 38th Parallel, reoccupying the cities of Pyongyang and Seoul, but by the end of January 1951 the UN forces had rallied. They battled their way back to the 38th Parallel and even won some territory in the eastern sector north of that dividing line. Yet they could not score a major victory against the Communists. In the spring of 1951 a front stabilized, along which fighting continued for the next two years.

Truce negotiations began in July 1951. For almost two years they dragged on, and at times it seemed as though agreement would never be reached. Then finally, on July 27, 1953, an armistice was signed ending the Korean War — which, ironically, no nation had ever officially declared to be a war. In accordance with the terms of the armistice, South Korea acquired approximately 1,500 square miles of territory above the 38th Parallel, which had previously been the border between the north and south. But it was a costly gain; the combined number of US, UN, and South Korean casualties was 498,255 and the forces of North Korea were reported to have suffered approximately 1.6 million killed and wounded.

United Church of Christ Formed

The first union in the United States of churches with differing forms of church government and divergent historical backgrounds took place on June 25, 1957, when the General Council of the Congregational Christian Churches and the Evangelical and Reformed Church came together to form the United Church of Christ. The purpose of the union, in the words of a church representative, was "to express more fully the oneness in Christ of the churches composing it, to make more effective their common witness in Him, and to serve His kingdom in the world."

Since each of the uniting bodies was itself the result of earlier mergers, the combined church had a long record of the kind of ecumenical outlook that was to permeate much of Christendom in the second half of the 20th century. One of the uniting denominations, the Evangelical and Reformed Church, had come into being with the union in 1934 of the Evangelical Synod of North America and the Reformed Church in the United States. Brought to this country by immigrants from Germany and Switzerland, both groups had their roots in the Reformation movement in Europe, tracing their lineage to Calvin, Luther, Melanchthon, and Zwingli. In America the Evangelical Synod had its origins in Missouri in 1840, whereas the Reformed Church had begun in Pennsylvania in 1725.

The other uniting denomination, the General Council of the Congregational Christian Churches, was formed in 1931 when the Congregational and Christian churches, each resulting from several previous unions and each tracing its ancestry largely to Reformation movements in England, came together. Congregationalism had been brought to the New World by the Pilgrims who founded the colony at Plymouth and by the Puritans who settled in the Massachusetts Bay Colony. In this country the Congregationalists were joined by the Congregational Methodists in 1892, by the Evangelical Protestants in 1923, and by the German Congregationalists in 1925. The Christian Church had brought together Methodists from North Carolina, Baptists from Vermont, and Presbyterians from Kentucky in 1820.

Today the United Church of Christ has a total membership of more than 2 million persons, in approximately 7,000 local churches. The aim of its combined Christian fellowship, as officially expressed, is to fulfill the spirit of the beliefs and traditions that "were characteristic and most highly prized" in both the Congregational Christian and the Evangelical and Reformed churches.

Virginia Ratifies the Constitution

Virginia, on June 25, 1788, became the 10th state to ratify the US Constitution. Although the new frame of government officially became the law of the land after adoption by 9 of the 13 states, approval by Virginia, one of the largest and most influential members of the Continental community, was critical to its success. Moreover, Virginia's decision gave Federalists in New York enough leverage to bring that prosperous and centrally located state into the new Union.

During the years after the American Revolution, Virginians ranked among the foremost critics of the Articles of Confederation. In 1785 George Washington served as host at Mount Vernon to delegates from Virginia and Maryland who sought to resolve difficulties involved in navigation of the Potomac River and Chesapeake Bay. In 1786, at Virginia's invitation, representatives from five states met in Annapolis, Maryland, for a convention on commercial affairs. The delegates proposed that the Congress convoke a Continental convention "to render the constitution of the Federal Government adequate to the exigencies of the Union." When the Congress made provision for such a gathering, Virginia was the first state to appoint representatives to the Philadelphia convention.

Seven delegates represented Virginia at the Constitutional Convention held in Philadelphia from May through September 1787. George Washington, the commander in chief of American forces during the Revolution, served as president of the gathering. At 55 years of age, the general was perhaps the most popular man in the new nation. James Madison, 36 years old, was essentially a scholar in politics, whose thorough knowledge of public affairs convinced many of his greatness. George Wythe, 61 years of age, was a signer of the Declaration of Independence, a judge of Virginia's high court of chancery, and a professor of law at the College of William and Mary. George Mason, 62 years of age, was the author of the Virginia Declaration of Rights and supported the wide distribution of governmental power among the states. Edmund Randolph, governor of Virginia, John Blair, a member of the state's judiciary, and Dr. James McClurg, once professor of medicine at William and Mary, completed the delegation. Patrick Henry, a localist who "smelt a rat," declined to serve, and Richard Henry Lee and Thomas Nelson, who also won election to the convention, followed his example.

On May 29 Edmund Randolph, on behalf of the Virginia delegation, suggested a program of action to the convention. Presented in the form of 15 resolutions, the Virginia Plan was essentially a new frame of government designed to replace rather than to revise the Articles of Confederation. The Randolph resolutions, which appeared to be actually the handiwork of James Madison, provided for the separate branches of government — the executive, the judiciary, and a bicameral legislature.

Election by the populace was to be the mode of selection for members of the lower house under the Virginia Plan. These delegates in turn were to choose the members of the upper house from nominations made by the state legislatures. Each state was to receive representation in both chambers in proportion to its population or to the amount of its contribution to the national coffers. The national legislature was to have all the authority of the Confederation Congress and additional powers to meet situations beyond the competence of the separate states and was also to enjoy the right to annul state laws that violated the Articles of Union.

Under the Virginia Plan the legislature was to select an executive, eligible for only one term, and a national judiciary, including supreme and inferior courts. The judiciary was to have jurisdiction over maritime questions, cases involving foreigners, and matters affecting the "national peace and harmony." The executive and a "convenient number of the national judiciary" were to constitute a council of revision, which could veto acts of the national legislature.

The Constitutional Convention on May 30 resolved itself into a committee of the whole and debated the Virginia Plan until June 13, when the delegates received a report embodying Randolph's program in 19 resolutions. Many at the Philadelphia gathering, especially members from the smaller states, were hostile to the Virginia vision of the United States, and William Paterson of New Jersey on June 15 presented a set of revisions of the Articles of Confederation more in accord with their philosophy. On June 19, after three days of debates, the delegates voted to pursue the formation of a new government following the Virginia guidelines.

Virginia's Plan of Union, altered by some significant compromises, became the basis of the Constitution, which the convention devised during July and August. The delegates made representation in the lower house proportional to population, but assigned an equal number of seats in the upper house to each state. Among other important changes the state legislatures received the right to select the members of the upper house, and the President became eligible for reelection. On September 17 the convention gave its final approval to the proposed Constitution and referred it, via the Congress, to the states for ratification.

Convening in October 1787, the Virginia legislature immediately considered the convocation of a ratification convention. The House wanted to schedule the special election of delegates for March 1788 and the convention for May, but acquiesced in the Senate's request to delay these events until April and June respectively. Both supporters and opponents of the proposed Constitution thus had months to try to convince the populace of the correctness of their positions.

Antifederalist propagandists managed to produce much more newsprint than did the friends of the Constitution. Statements against the new frame of government by the Revolutionary firebrand Richard Henry Lee, and by two Virginia delegates to the Philadelphia Convention, George Mason, and Edmund Randolph, who refused to sign the completed Constitution, circulated through the state. Federalist writers were not so prolific, and not even the *Federalist* papers, imported from New York, were so influential as the statements by the Virginia dissidents.

However, Federalists proved more adept than their opponents in oral arguments, the focusing of campaigns on specific contests, and the selection of candidates. The advocates of the new Constitution paid special attention to the area west of the Blue Ridge Mountains, which would elect 46 delegates and where almost no printed matter had circulated. They also put forward as candidates many military heroes in the hope that the voters might associate them with the beloved George Washington, the Federalists' best asset.

April's election of delegates to the Virginia ratifying convention justified the Federalists' tactics. They won 85 seats or fully one-half of 170 contests. The Antifederalists could count 66 of the victors in their ranks and perhaps three others categorized as "doubtful." Little is known about 16 of the delegates, 12 of whom came from what is now Kentucky and 4 of whom came from the Trans-Allegheny region.

Patrick Henry led the Antifederalist forces in the ratifying convention. George Mason — who refused to sign the new Constitution because it allowed the continuation of the slave trade and permitted the imposition of duties on commerce by a simple majority rather than by a two-thirds vote — ably assisted him. Henry managed to convert three of the supposed Federalists by his vivid descriptions of the loss of liberty that he claimed ratification would produce, and won over 10 of the Kentuckians with arguments that the federal authorities would bargain away the rights of navigation of the Mississippi River.

Having no single delegate capable of matching Patrick Henry in prestige and oratorical powers, the Federalists made maximum use of the galaxy of highly capable individuals in their ranks. Edmund Pendleton and George Wythe lent the Federalist cause their prestige, and James Madison and John Marshall provided two keen intellects to counter Henry's arguments. Madison's success in persuading Edmund Randolph to change his mind and support ratification not only embarrassed the Antifederalists

but added a shrewd political strategist to the Federalist side. By their combined efforts the Federalists managed to persuade the four Trans-Allegheny, two of the Kentucky, and one of the "doubtful" delegates to affirm the new Constitution. When the final tally was taken on June 25, the Federalists had won by 89 to 79 votes.

A variety of factors produced a Federalist victory in Virginia. Especially important was the harsh wartime experience of Virginia, which convinced many of the necessity for a strong Union. Doubtless, too, the influence of most of Virginia's greatest statesmen, including the incomparable George Washington, proved decisive.

Virginia's ratification of the Constitution on June 25, 1788, has led historians to rank the state 10th in the chronological list of the admission of states to the Union. Of course, Virginia was a state in the years before 1788. Virginia and the other 12 original members of the United States of America had become states on July 4, 1776, the day on which they adopted the Declaration of Independence — although technically Virginia had declared its own independence even before the Declaration of Independence, and had adopted on June 29, 1776, a constitution that established it as an independent state.

JUNE 26

American Troops Land in France: World War I

The US Congress declared war on Germany on April 6, 1917 (see April 6, The United States enters World War I). Less than three months later, on June 26, 1917, several units of the US First Infantry Division disembarked in France. Several more months elapsed before the country mobilized sufficient military strength to influence the outcome of the war.

The US Army numbered only 200,000 enlisted men and officers in April 1917. But the nation acted quickly to meet the urgent need for additional troops. On May 18, 1917, Congress approved the Selective Service Act, and in less than a month more than 9 million American men between the ages of 21 and 30 had registered for the draft. To train the new recruits and inductees, 32 camps and cantonments were built. By the end of the War these installations had prepared nearly 4 million men, only about half of whom were draftees, for service in the army.

General John J. Pershing, who landed in France on June 14, 1917, commanded the American Expeditionary Force. ("Lafayette, we are here," the statement often attributed to Pershing, was actually made on July 4 at the tomb of Lafayette by Colonel Charles E. Stanton, chief disbursing officer of the AEF.) According to Pershing's orders, US troops were to remain "a distinct and separate component of the combined [Allied] force." The exigencies of war at times necessitated abandoning this plan. But for the most part the US Army did maintain an independent role, subject after April 1918 to the supreme Allied commander, Marshal Ferdinand Foch of France.

By the time the fighting ended on November 11, 1918, more than 2 million American soldiers had landed in France. Of these approximately 1.4 million saw combat. Their presence decisively influenced the outcome of the war. They gave the Allies numerical superiority on the western front and contributed to such significant victories as Belleau Wood, Saint-Mihiel, and Meuse-Argonne.

JUNE 27

Helen Keller's Birthday

Helen Adams Keller, the heroic blind and deaf American who by her courage, indomitable spirit, and remarkable achievements made valuable contributions to the education of other blind and deaf persons, was born a normal child at Tuscumbia, Alabama, on June 27, 1880. Her family on her father's side was connected with the Lees and Spotswoods of Virginia and on her mother's side with the Adamses and Everetts of Massachusetts.

When Helen Keller was about 19 months old, a short but devastating illness, perhaps scarlet fever, robbed her of her sight and her hearing and consequently of articulate speech. Locked in darkness and silence, she became a wild, unruly child full of rages and rarely smiling. Worried about her education, not knowing if indeed she could be taught or whether they could find a teacher, her parents consulted a Baltimore eye specialist who felt their child was educable. The specialist suggested that the Kellers consult Alexander Graham Bell, inventor of the telephone who, like his father, had been deeply involved in educating the deaf to speak.

Bell directed the Kellers to his son-in-law, Michael Anagnos, who was then director of the Perkins Institution in South Boston (now the Perkins School for the Blind in Watertown, Massachusetts). Mrs. Keller had already read about the Perkins Institution in Charles Dickens's *American Notes,* in which he wrote of Laura Bridgman, the first blind and deaf person to be successfully educated, who was trained at Perkins and later worked there as a sewing teacher.

The teacher selected for Helen Keller was Anne Mansfield Sullivan, who at the age of 10 had been put into Tewksbury Almshouse and was later sent to Perkins because of her own partial blindness. At Perkins Annie Sullivan, as she came to be known, learned the hand alphabet used to communicate with the blind deaf. Her own vision improved by treatment, she had graduated from Perkins just the year before the Kellers began their search for someone to teach their daughter. She was 20 years old when she arrived at the Keller house in Tuscumbia.

Helen Keller later wrote, "The most important day I remember in all my life is the one on which my teacher came to me. It was the third of March, 1887, three months before I was seven years old."

That first meeting was stormy. Brought forward to greet her new teacher, Helen grabbed Annie Sullivan's purse and groped about in it for candy. Finding none, she flew into a rage that lasted for days. These events were dramatized in William Gibson's play *The Miracle Worker,* which opened on Broadway in October 1959 and was based on the book *Anne Sullivan Macy: The Story behind Helen Keller* by Nella Braddy, published in 1933. *The Miracle Worker,* a powerful drama that won many awards first as a play and later as a film, was seen by millions of people all over the world.

When Annie Sullivan finally gained Helen's attention, she began to spell words into the child's hand. But this method, so useful with the deaf, had its drawbacks with someone who had been blind from infancy. The various patterns traced on her palm by her teacher signified nothing to the child.

One day as student and teacher were walking outdoors, they passed the pump in the yard near the house. As Helen Keller later told it:

We walked down the path to the well-house, attracted by the fragrance of the honeysuckle with which it was covered. Someone was drawing water and my teacher placed my hand under the spout. As the cool stream gushed over one hand, she spelled into the other the word "water," first slowly, then rapidly. I stood still, my whole attention fixed upon the motions of her fingers. Suddenly I felt a misty consciousness as of something forgotten — a thrill of returning thought; and somehow the mystery of language was revealed to me. I knew then that "w-a-t-e-r" meant the wonderful cool something that was flowing over my hand. That living word awakened my soul, gave it light, hope, joy, set it free. There were barriers still, it is true, but barriers that in time could be swept away.

For the next 50 years Annie Sullivan, whom Helen Keller always called Teacher, was there to help sweep away barriers for her student. Soon the eager child knew many words besides "water" and, with a true zeal for knowledge, she learned whole sentences and then whole stories, all within about three months after Annie Sullivan's arrival. It was at this time that the young teacher wrote to Michael Anagnos at the Perkins Institution: "Something tells me that I am going to succeed beyond all my dreams."

In May 1888 Helen Keller, not quite eight years old, was taken to the Perkins Institution, where she learned to read braille and for the first time met and played with other afflicted children. Eager to learn how to speak, she was taken to the Horace Mann School for the Deaf in Boston in the spring of 1890. There she met her first speech teacher, Sarah Fuller, who taught her to "hear" or lip-read by placing her fingers on the lips and throat of the person speaking. Despite instruction, Helen Keller's speech was never completely clear and, though she was understandable if she used short words and spoke slowly, it was usually necessary for her companion to repeat her words for others, either at social gatherings or when she was lecturing before audiences.

Helen Keller's formal schooling began when she was 14, at the Wright-Humason School for the Deaf in New York City, and was continued in Massachusetts at the Cambridge School for Young Ladies, where she prepared to enter Radcliffe College. She passed the Radcliffe entrance examination, which was the same given to unhandicapped applicants, and entered Radcliffe in 1900.

Her years at Radcliffe were marked by endurance, perseverance, and sheer obstinacy on the part of Helen Keller and of Annie Sullivan, who had to spell into her pupil's hand every word of the textbooks and lectures. Helen Keller could write and also use a typewriter with skill by this time. Her assignments for an English composition course conducted by Harvard's famous "Copey," Professor Charles Townsend Copeland, became chapters in her most widely read book, *The Story of My Life*, which was serialized in the *Ladies' Home Journal* and first published as a book in 1902. It has since been published in at least 50 languages. She was to continue her writing career for most of her life. In 1904 Helen Keller was graduated *cum laude* from Radcliffe, receiving her Bachelor of Arts degree with honors in German and English. The next year Annie Sullivan married John Macy, a social critic, and Helen Keller lived with them. Influenced by Macy's political thought and by her own braille reading of H. G. Wells and, later, of Marx and Engels in German braille, Helen Keller joined the Socialist party in 1909 and was for many years an active member.

After World War I, popular tastes did not run to her inspirational type of writing and, needing an income, she ventured into vaudeville, always with Annie Sullivan at her side. With a 20-minute act, they toured the country between 1920 and 1924. The curtain went up on a drawing room setting, and to the background music of Mendelssohn's "Spring Song" Annie Sullivan made her entrance and told the audience something about Helen Keller's life, and then her pupil came on stage and said a few words for herself. A New York *Times* review of the debut at the Palace Theater in New York City said, "Helen Keller has conquered again, and the Monday afternoon audience at the Palace, one of the most critical and cynical in the world, was hers." For her part, Helen Keller loved the excitement of her new career. She developed a lifelong interest in the theater and formed friendships with such diverse artists as Jascha Heifetz, Harpo Marx, Sophie Tucker, and Charlie Chaplin.

She felt that her real lifework, however, was to help in the education and rehabilitation of handicapped children and adults, especially those with afflictions similar to hers. She had been active to some degree in this type of work since 1915, when the Permanent Blind Relief War Fund (later called the American Braille Press) was founded and she was named a member of its first board of directors.

From 1924 until her death, she was a staff member of the American Foundation for the Blind and traveled extensively in the United States, lecturing and promoting increased help for the blind. In the 1920s Helen Keller, the Macys, and Polly Thomson, who had joined the household in 1914, all moved from Wrentham, Massachusetts, to Forest Hills in Queens, New York. After the death of John Macy, in 1932, and of her beloved Annie Sullivan in 1936, Helen Keller moved with Polly Thomson to Westport, Connecticut, which was within commuting distance of New York City.

When the American Braille Press became the American Foundation for Overseas Blind, working jointly with the American Foundation for the Blind, in 1946, Keller was appointed to its staff also, as counselor on international relations. In this capacity she traveled tirelessly, circling the globe on behalf of the blind. Her own achievements and her warm personality impressed audiences, and her work for the blind was monumentally successful. Between 1946 and 1957 she visited 35 countries on five continents, working to improve the education, vocational training, and living conditions for the blind of all nations. She had amazing stamina even at the age of 75, when she made a 40,000-mile, five-month tour through Asia.

She received decorations and honors from many foreign governments; awards from civic, educational, and welfare organizations, both national and international; and honorary degrees from universities in many countries. Many of these are on public display in the Helen Keller Room of the American Foundation for the Blind at 15 West 16th Street in New York City, where visitors can also see the foundation's Polly Thomson Room.

Helen Keller's Tuscumbia, Alabama, birthplace, Ivy Green, built by her grandfather in 1820, was made a permanent shrine in 1954. Visitors can see the main house; the smaller cottage where Helen Keller was born and which was later used, at Annie Sullivan's insistence, as the isolated living quarters for teacher and pupil; and the pump where Helen Keller learned her first word. Each year during July and August *The Miracle Worker* is performed on Fridays and Saturdays at Ivy Green.

Ivy Green, at 300 West North Common, is open to the public year-round except on certain holidays. The little town of Tuscumbia is in the northeast corner of Alabama, not too far from the state line of Tennessee, which each year proclaims a Helen Keller Day in June.

In 1954, on the 50th anniversary of her graduation, Radcliffe College presented Helen Keller with its Alumnae Achievement Award, dedicated the Helen Keller Garden in her honor, and greatly pleased her by naming a fountain in the garden for Anne Sullivan Macy.

On her 80th birthday, in 1960, the American Foundation for Overseas Blind established the Helen Keller International Award for Distinguished Service to the Blind, to be presented periodically to individuals who have made outstanding contributions to work for the blind on a world level, or in countries other than the United States. The third presentation of this award, a bronze sculpture called *The Spirit of Helen Keller*, was made in April 1970 to John Wilson, director of London's Royal Commonwealth Society for the Blind. The actress Katharine Cornell, who had been a close friend of Helen Keller's, made the presentation in New York City. The first of these awards had gone to a Canadian, the second to a Frenchman.

During her lifetime Keller met some of the most famous people of the 19th and 20th centuries. In addition to Alexander Graham Bell, they included Mark Twain, William James, and every President of the United States from Grover Cleveland to John F. Kennedy. In 1961 she made her last major public appearance in Washington, D.C., where she received the Lions Club Humanitarian Award for her lifetime of service to humanity and for providing the inspiration for the adoption by the Lions International of their sight-conservation and aid-to-the-blind programs.

Helen Keller died in her home in Westport, Connecticut, on June 1, 1968, less than a month before her 88th birthday. After private cremation, a funeral service was held in Washington Cathedral, Washington, D.C. Her ashes were buried in the cathedral's St. Joseph's Chapel, next to her companions in life, Anne Sullivan Macy and Polly Thomson (the latter who had died in 1960).

Helen Keller's writings, articles, and books, spanned a period of 55 years. In addition to her still widely read autobiography, Helen Keller also wrote before World War I (in chronological order) *Optimism, The World I Live In, The Song of the Stone Wall,* and *Out of the Dark.* After the war there was a hiatus of almost 10 years before she resumed writing. In the next 30 years she produced the books *My Religion; Midstream — My Later Life; Helen Keller's Journal, 1936–37; Let Us Have Faith; Teacher* (about Annie Sullivan); and *The Open Door.* Shortly before her death she remarked: "I believe that all through these dark and silent years God has been using my life for a purpose I do not know. But one day I shall understand and then I will be satisfied."

Pennsylvania Dutch Folk Festival
Kutztown, Pennsylvania

This is a movable event. See note on page xxvi.

One of the country's most written-about festivals is the Pennsylvania Dutch Folk Festival held annually in Kutztown. The dates vary but always include July 4. The eight-day celebration, which is generally attended by 140,000 to 150,000 each year, centers on the arts, crafts, farming methods, food and folkways of the so-called Pennsylvania Dutch, both "plain" and "fancy."

The "Dutch," who today inhabit the rich farmlands of southeastern Pennsylvania, are descendants of the Germans — that is, *Deutsch,* which sounded like "Dutch" to English-speaking Americans — of various religious sects who flocked to Pennsylvania in the early and mid-1700s. War-weary and persecuted, they were attracted by the promise of religious freedom in the colony, which the idealistic Quaker William Penn had established in 1681.

Today's "plain Dutch," who shun modern dress and conveniences as distractions from the devout life, are descended from the early Brethren, Dunkard (Baptist), Mennonite, and Amish settlers. "Plainest" of the plain are the "team" (or strict) Mennonites and (particularly) the Amish, who avoid using electricity, telephones, and automobiles or tractors; drive about in horse-drawn carriages; avoid photographs, which they interpret as graven images; refuse to take oaths or perform military service; live in spotless homes, which are devoid of curtains and other decorative luxuries; and dress somberly in the garb of their ancestors. Men wear black coats, broad-brimmed flat hats, and (if they are married) beards; women wear long skirts, aprons, high-button boots and poke bonnets. Patriarchal, austere (but gentle), hard-working, the fundamentalist plain people do not take their self-imposed separatism and discipline lightly.

For them, the opposite of "plain" is "fancy," or worldly. The term is applied to the very people who take part in the Kutztown festival — descendants of Lutheran or Reformed Germans; or "plain" folk gone "fancy." Since the restrictions of the plain Dutch would prevent their participation, or even attendance, most of the 200-odd artisans and about 1,000 volunteers who work at the festival attractions are "worldly Dutch," who understand the philosophy and purpose of their plain neighbors but who, as far as their own lives are concerned, have made their peace with the modern world.

The Pennsylvania Dutch Folk Festival, which is held at the 35-acre fairgrounds on the edge of Kutztown, first took form in 1950, two years after the nonprofit Pennsylvania Folklife Society, which sponsors it, was founded by Professors Alfred L. Shoemaker, Don Yoder, and J. William Frey. Although the festival is open daily from morning to night, with square dancing after an evening stage program, it is primarily a daytime attraction, with craft exhibitors leaving at dusk.

Typically, the festival — without the hucksterism that mars similar events — includes a hundred or so craft, farming, and culinary demonstrations; food in prodigious quantities; entertainment by local performers (who may, for instance, expound on snake or funeral lore or dispense planting advice); a major pageant; and shorter performances throughout each afternoon. All features are designed to set forth for the interested the heritage and ways of the Pennsylvania Dutch.

Among the annual highlights (presented by "worldly" Dutch) are an Amish wedding performed twice daily in the traditional way — without rings, flowers, or other material symbols — and an Amish barn raising. The main daily presentation, beginning at 2:30 and at 7:30 in the evening, is Brad Smoker's panoramic history of the Plain Dutch, "Men of One Master." The pageant depicts the struggle of the plain people to remain apart from the world from the time they came to America in the mid-1700s.

In one typical year, other daily features included a "hanging," a country auction, performances by the Heidelberg Polka Band, a balloon ascension, seminars on Pennsylvania Dutch folk culture, and a witchcraft trial. There were also children's games from noon to 5:00 daily, and hoedown and jigging exhibitions from noon to 5:00 as well.

One of the most popular features, introduced in 1965, is the quilting contest and demonstrations of quilt making. Other crafts exhibited included rug weaving, basket weaving, tinsmithing, butchering, rake manufacture, corn husking, candle making, taffy pulling, home building, hay pitching, butter churning, sausage smoking, soap boiling, water witching, threshing with flails, and cider making. Other exhibitions showed the making of apple butter in huge vats that simmered fragrantly all day, or demonstrated the painting of the traditional bright designs known as hex signs, which can be seen on barns of the Pennsylvania Dutch. Exhibits also included farm and kitchen implements; examples of colorful Pennsylvania Dutch folk art; and livestock.

Among other festival features are lectures and demonstrations on the preparation of Pennsylvania Dutch food specialties. There are à la carte specialties and full meals dispensed at the fairgrounds' dining pavilion or in food tents provisioned by local church groups at moderate prices. The visitor might sample the array of relishes known as the "seven sweets and sours"; continue with pretzel soup and brei or rivvel soup (which is made of chicken broth and fresh corn); and choose among such offerings as hot onion pie, pepper and cabbage, ponhaws (oatmeal scrapple), stuffed pig's stomach, pigs' feet, sausage in thick milk gravy, baked ham, fried chicken, potato filling, pork and sauerkraut. Anyone still able to do so can make a further selection from regional dessert specialties — Amish vanilla pie, chocolate funny cake, and the famous shoofly pie.

JUNE 28

Assassination Precipitates World War I; Treaty of Versailles Signed

On the evening of August 4, 1914, Sir Edward Grey, England's foreign secretary, looked out from his office window into the London twilight. "The lamps are going out all over Europe," he said. "We shall not see them lit again in our lifetime." His country and the Continental powers were entering a night of war; before the dawn 10 million people would die.

The incident that precipitated World War I had occurred only a few weeks before Grey made his prophetic statement. The Balkans had been the scene of several crises involving the independent kingdom of Serbia and the Austro-Hungarian Empire. Serbia envisioned itself as the center of a future pan-Slavic state, but Austria-Hungary frustrated these ambitions by its annexation of Bosnia-Herzegovina in 1908 and its continuing efforts to acquire still more territory in the area. Relations between the two countries deteriorated to such an extent that in 1911 the Serbs formed a secret terrorist organization, Union or Death, popularly known as The Black Hand, to agitate against Austria-Hungary.

On June 28, 1914, the heir to the Austro-Hungarian throne, Archduke Francis Ferdinand, and his wife, Archduchess Sofia, planned to inspect the army at Sarajevo, the capital of Bosnia-Herzegovina. Since June 28 was the date of the Turkish conquest of the old Serbian kingdom in 1389 and also the anniversary of the Serbian victory over Turkey in the Second Balkan War in 1913, Serbian nationalists considered the timing of the archduke's visit to be an intolerable insult to their country. In revenge The Black Hand determined to assassinate him. As Francis Ferdinand toured Sarajevo, he escaped injury from a hand grenade. However, death in the person of Gavrilo Princip awaited him as his motorcade slowed at a river crossing. Princip fired two shots with his automatic pistol. The first hit and killed the archduchess; the second struck the archduke, who uttered the single word "Sofia" and then died.

The assassination of Francis Ferdinand outraged world opinion; more important, it provided a focus for the tensions that had been growing in Europe. For 40 years conflicting national interests, economies, and ambitions had driven the Continental powers to prepare for such a crisis. France, Germany, Italy, Austria, and Russia each possessed huge standing armies, and previously formed alliances further insured each country's military might. Thus by 1914 Europe was ready for war, and throughout the summer of that year the Triple Alliance of Germany, Austria-Hungary, and Italy edged toward combat with the Triple Entente of England, France, and Russia, later to be known as the Allies.

Only a week after the archduke's assassination, Germany signed a diplomatic "blank check." With this guarantee of German support for any action it might take, Austria-Hungary on July 23 issued an ultimatum to Serbia, which it blamed for the assassination. Although the Serbian government agreed to many of the ultimatum's demands, it refused to allow the Austrian police or military to participate in its investigation of the Black Hand plot. Austria-Hungary, however, would accept nothing less than total compliance with the ultimatum, and on July 28 declared war on Serbia.

Austria-Hungary's declaration initiated a chain reaction as the other European powers in turn honored their alliance commitments. On July 29 Russia, responding to its agreement to aid Serbia, started the full mobilization of its armies. Although German efforts to effect an Austrian-Russian settlement temporarily decreased these activities, Russia renewed its total mobilization on August 1.

Events proceeded rapidly after this decision: On August 1 Germany declared war on Russia, while France readied its troops in support of the czar. The following day Germany announced its intentions to violate Belgian neutrality; two days later Great Britain responded to this action by joining forces with France and Russia. When Austria-Hungary went to war against Russia on August 6, only a little more than a week had passed since the Austro-Hungarian declaration against Serbia. Yet in that short time all the members of the Triple Alliance and the Triple Entente — with the exception of Italy, which remained neutral until 1915 and then renounced the former grouping to join the latter — had brought their troops to the battlefield.

World War I began in Europe, but before the fighting ended, at 11:00 A.M. on November 11, 1917, 28 nations on five continents had become involved. Airplanes, tanks, submarines, and poison gas had seen their first wartime use, and these new weapons had contributed to unprecedented war losses. Ten million people had died; 20 million had been wounded, and direct war costs had reached an estimated $180.5 billion.

Peace negotiations began shortly after the November armistice, and on June 28, 1919, the fifth anniversary of Archduke Francis Ferdinand's assassination, the Treaty of Versailles, chief among the five treaties that terminated World War I, was signed by a vanquished Germany and the victorious Allies. (Other treaties dealt respectively with Austria and Hungary, by then separated, and their allies Bulgaria and Turkey.) According to the Treaty of Versailles, Germany accepted full responsibility for the war, made substantial territorial cessions, and agreed to a drastic limitation of its army and navy. The treaty also required Germany to pay for the civilian damage caused by the war and to bear the costs of the occupation armies.

But reparations were not the sole concern of the delegates at Versailles. The peacemakers of 1919 were interested in preventing another world conflict. Toward this end, the Versailles treaty provided for the establishment of the League of Nations (see January 10), an organization designed to arbitrate future international disputes.

The Versailles treaty was ratified by the governments of most of the combatants. However, the Senate of the United States refused to accept the Versailles document. Eventually the United States — which had entered the war on the side of the Allies in 1917 (see April 6) — made a separate peace with Germany; but this nation never became a member of the League of Nations.

Lutheran Church in America Organized

One important example of the trend toward church unity that has characterized the 20th century took place when the Lutheran Church in America was organized at Detroit in 1962. On June 28 of that year the LCA came into being by consolidation of the American Evangelical Lutheran Church (of Danish background, founded in 1874), the Augustana Evangelical Lutheran Church (of Swedish background, founded in 1860), the Finnish Evangelical Lutheran Church (founded in 1890), and the United Lutheran Church in America (of German background, founded in 1918). The merger took place after six and a half years of negotiation by representatives of the four denominations concerned.

The new Lutheran Church in America began functioning formally on January 1, 1963. As of December 31, 1964, its membership was 3 million baptized persons. The largest of the three major Lutheran bodies in the United States and Canada, the LCA now has over 6,000 congregations and almost 8,000 ordained ministers.

The national body, which has its administrative headquarters in New York City, is divided into 32 jurisdictional units, known as synods, all but one of which are organized on a geographical basis. (The one exception, known as the Slovak Zion Synod, is made up of congregations whose members desire to maintain Slovak customs and language.) Three of the synods are located in Canada, the rest in the United States. Throughout the church, services are conducted primarily in the English language, although the church's cosmopolitan character is shown by the fact that 15 other languages are used on occasion.

JUNE 29

Feast of SS. Peter and Paul

The Feast of SS. Peter and Paul has been celebrated by Christians on June 29 since the early centuries of the Christian era. The oldest extant church calendar, one found in a Roman work of the year 354, bears witness to this fact, listing the joint celebration of the two great Apostles on June 29.

Around the year 319 the Emperor Constantine had basilicas built in Rome over the supposed tombs of the two saints. According to tradition St. Peter had been crucified head down on Vatican Hill, and an oratory had been built over his burial place by Anacletus, who was pope from A.D. 76 to 88. The great Basilica of St. Peter, Rome's largest church, stands on the same site. St. Paul had reportedly been beheaded and buried on the Ostian Way, where his basilica, called St. Paul's outside the Walls, now stands. (The walls referred to in the name of Rome's second largest church are the city fortifications built by Emperor Aurelian in the third century.)

By the end of the fourth century great crowds of the faithful flocked to Rome annually for the June 29 feast day, making a pilgrimage from St. Peter's Basilica to St. Paul's, which was located on the other side of the city. The pope would first celebrate a solemn pontifical mass at St. Peter's and then proceed to St. Paul's to celebrate a second solemn pontifical mass on the same morning.

Because of the great distance between the two churches — and the continued growth of the city, which added obstacles — attending services at both churches on the same morning became increasingly difficult. This was especially true for those people from outlying districts who had spent part of the night, or longer, traveling to the city.

Hence in the sixth century the liturgy of the feast was divided. June 29 remained the Feast of SS. Peter and Paul but the principal ceremony took place only in St. Peter's Basilica on that morning. The next day, June 30, became known as the Commemoration of St. Paul, and on that morning the pope said the solemn pontifical mass at St. Paul's basilica. However, with the changes in the liturgical calendar that followed the Second Vatican Council of 1962–1965, the Roman Catholic church reverted to the joint celebration on June 29 and dropped the June 30 Commemoration of St. Paul.

Eastern Orthodox churches, which honor the two saints by observing a special Lenten season named for them, also celebrate the feast of SS. Peter and Paul on June 29. So do some Protestant churches, notably the Lutheran. Others, the Episcopal church in particular, celebrate June 29 as the Feast of St. Peter, omitting St. Paul, whom they (and others) venerate in connection with the anniversary of his conversion (see January 25).

Scripture passages designated for reading on June 29 in these, the more liturgical of the Christian churches, differ from one denomination to another. However, the passage in Matthew 16 containing Peter's famous confession of Christ (detailed below) is customarily read in Roman

Catholic, Eastern Orthodox, and Lutheran churches. Roman Catholics and Lutherans also hear the verses of Acts 12:1–11, recounting Peter's miraculous release from prison. At their morning prayer service Episcopalians customarily hear the account in Acts 11:1–18 of the vision that directed Peter to include Gentiles in his ministry; and at evening prayer they are read the Scripture passage from John 21:15–22, which contains Jesus Christ's admonition to Peter to "feed my sheep." Earlier in the day the same Gospel message is read at matins in Eastern Orthodox churches. Episcopalians attending evening prayer also hear Peter's ringing testimony to the lasting power of the resurrected Jesus Christ, as recounted in Acts 4:8–20. Also included in the Eastern Orthodox liturgy for June 29 is Paul's autobiographical account of his life and trials as an ambassador for Jesus.

Apart from both being devout Jews, SS. Peter and Paul were very different in origin and background; yet they became the two strongest pillars of the infant Church. Each traveled, Paul more than Peter, preaching the message of Jesus Christ to thousands of people and building the foundation of the Church among Jews and Gentiles in many countries and against terrible odds. Both died in Rome, as noted above, almost certainly as martyrs during Nero's persecution of Christians between A.D. 64 and 67.

Peter, the Prince of Apostles, known as Simon bar-Jona (son of Jona) was a simple Galilean fisherman living in Bethsaida when Jesus called him and his brother, Andrew, with the words recorded in Matthew 4:19: "Follow me and I will make you fishers of men." According to the Gospel of John (1:42), it was at their first meeting that Jesus changed Simon's name to Cephas, or Peter, derivatives of the Aramaic and Greek, respectively, for the word "rock." Peter was present at most of the important events of Jesus' earthly ministry and was the first Apostle to whom he appeared after the Resurrection.

Peter, whom Roman Catholics regard as the first pope, was the acknowledged leader of the Apostles from the beginning. According to the account in Matthew 16:13–19, when Jesus questioned his disciples, they reported that he was said by some to be John the Baptist or Elijah or Jeremiah or one of the prophets. But Simon Peter said, "You are the Christ, the Son of the living God." Jesus answered:

Blessed are you, Simon bar-Jona! For flesh and blood has not revealed this to you, but my Father who is in heaven. And I tell you, you are Peter, and on this rock I will build my church, and the powers of death shall not prevail against it. I will give you the keys of the kingdom of heaven, and whatever you bind on earth shall be bound in heaven, and whatever you loose on earth shall be loosed in heaven.

In contrast to the uneducated Peter, who had been with Jesus from the beginning of his public ministry and who effortlessly accepted him as the Son of God, the well-educated Paul had never met Jesus and, in fact, was very likely the foremost anti-Christian of his day. Paul, known as Saul before his conversion, was born probably a year after Jesus, at Tarsus in Cilicia, a region of southeastern Asia Minor. Like his father, Saul, a Jew descended from the tribe of Benjamin, was a Pharisee and a Roman citizen. When he was about 15 years old he was sent to Jerusalem to study at the Temple. There he was a pupil of the famous Rabbi Gamaliel, a leading figure in the Sanhedrin, the Jewish legal and religious institution in Jerusalem that exercised the functions of a court.

While some Jews accepted Jesus as Christ, the long-awaited Messiah, and thus the fulfillment of the Scriptures, others looked upon him as dangerous, believing his teachings to be hostile to the Jewish religion, and regarding his followers as blasphemers. Saul of Tarsus belonged to the second group, and his raging hatred of Christians went far beyond his teachers' and friends' anti-Christian feelings. When he not only had learned the trade of tentmaking, but also had completed his excellent education at the Temple, where he learned Jewish law, theology, and Scripture, Saul began what he felt to be his lifework: he sought out Christians and had them bound and delivered to prison, sometimes to certain death.

Saul was present at the death of St. Stephen, the first Christian martyr, a year or two after the crucifixion of Jesus, and in fact held the coats of the men who were stoning Stephen. Stephen's death signaled the beginning of the severest persecutions of the infant Church, in which Saul played a leading role. So consuming was his desire to root out Christianity that he obtained authority from the high priest in Jerusalem to go to Damascus to continue his search for Christians.

One of the most famous stories from the New Testament, related in the ninth chapter of Acts, concerns Saul's dramatic conversion on the road to Damascus by a blinding light from heaven and the voice of Jesus saying, "Saul, Saul, why do you persecute me?" Saul, who was felled by the experience, remained blind for three days and neither ate nor drank. The men accompanying him were reported to have heard the words but to have seen nothing.

Meanwhile, the scriptural passage continues, Jesus appeared in a vision to a disciple at Damascus named Ananias, instructing him to go to Saul and lay hands upon him so that he might regain his sight. The succeeding verses (13–14) reveal the early Christians' well-founded fear of Saul. But Ananias obeyed and caused Saul to be filled with the Holy Spirit and to have his sight restored. Saul was baptized, and he took food and was strengthened. Soon he was preaching in the synagogues, proclaiming Jesus as the Son of God, to the amazement of all who had heard him before his conversion.

The Jews were enraged by his defection and plotted against him. The Christians were still too afraid of their former persecutor to believe that he had been converted. While the fury of the Jews merely increased, however, the Christians slowly began to accept this Saul of Tarsus, now become the Apostle Paul.

Paul became the most important Christian missionary the world has ever seen. In his three principal missionary journeys he traveled by land and sea, establishing the Church in the hearts of peoples of many regions. As he traveled he wrote letters to the scattered groups of his converts so that, even though he was not always physically present with them, he could advise and teach them and further explain his interpretation of Jesus' words. These letters to groups and to individuals make up most of the second half of the New Testament and include Paul's Epistles to the Romans, Corinthians, Galatians, Ephesians, Philippians, Colossians, Thessalonians, and Hebrews, as well as to Timothy, Titus, and Philemon.

Paul endured many dangers on his travels. He was shipwrecked, flogged, stoned, imprisoned, banished from several cities, and persecuted by Jewish religious leaders who felt he had betrayed their religion. At various times in his career his enemies conspired to kill him but succeeded only in getting him arrested.

Paul was imprisoned in various places. Ultimately he was taken into custody at Jerusalem, after his presence there had touched off a riot. Fearing that his Roman captors planned to have him tried by the Jewish religious authorities at Jerusalem, Paul pointed out that his Roman citizenship gave him the right to appeal to Rome — which was true and indisputable.

On the way to Rome, where he was again held in custody and finally martyred, Paul and his fellow passengers were shipwrecked off the island of Malta. The circumstances that followed, which are recorded in Acts 28:1–6, gave rise to one of the colorful legends that have grown up around SS. Peter and Paul. According to the account, when Paul and his storm-tossed companions had safely reached the shores of Malta, he gathered wood for a fire. Its heat reportedly drove out of the firewood a viper, which bit him. Although the witnesses were sure he would die, he remained unharmed. The story was the basis for a belief, persisting in some parts of the world today, that a person who prays well on the Feast of SS. Peter and Paul will be pro-

tected from snakebites throughout the year.

Many people also attribute to Peter and Paul responsibility for the weather, a chore they inherited from their pagan predecessors Thor and Woden of ancient Germanic mythology.

Less fancifully, Paul is the patron saint of tentmakers, theologians, and ropemakers — the last probably a reference to the rope used to lower him over the city wall after his escape from prison in Damascus.

St. Peter is the patron saint of fishermen and sailors in some areas, as well as of keymakers (according to Matthew 16:19 he was to carry the keys of Christ's kingdom). Since the 10th century he has been referred to in popular tradition as the heavenly gatekeeper, who guards the celestial premises and admits or turns away applicants according to their merits.

In many countries the Feast of St. Peter is most warmly marked in fishing villages and ports. Perhaps the largest American celebration of the event takes place in Gloucester, Massachusetts, once a great shipbuilding area and still an important fishing and fish-processing center. For decades the community's Italian-American fishermen, their families, and friends have held a St. Peter's Fiesta on the weekend closest to the June 29 feast day.

At the turn of the century many Sicilian fishing families came to the United States and settled in the fishing port of Gloucester. From the beginning this group upheld the folk and religious customs of their native land. Chief among these was the special honor paid to St. Peter, their patron saint. In 1926 an Italian-American fishing captain provided a life-sized statue of St. Peter, which was enshrined in the community and which attracted men, women, and children who came to offer their prayers and ask St. Peter's intercession for the safe return of fishing crews and for the success of the catch. On the Feast of St. Peter the saint was honored in the Roman Catholic mass said in church, and also with a procession during which the statue would be carried through the streets of the Italian district. Indeed the whole day was given over to celebration.

By 1931 the women of the community who had initiated the procession decided that still greater festivities were in order and prodded the men into action. The result was the organization of the St. Peter's Fiesta Committee, which annually plans the weekend-long celebration. This has become the traditional highlight of the year for people in the area and beyond.

During St. Peter's Fiesta, flags, bunting, colored lights, and streamers decorate Gloucester's Italian-American section. Some 50 archways hung with colored lights are erected over the streets. A double bandstand is built — several stories high so that everyone can see, as well as hear, the two bands that play nightly during the festival.

A huge block dance held on Thursday evening precedes the fiesta's customary formal opening amid concert band music on Friday night. However, the largest crowds and the biggest events come on Saturday and Sunday of the fiesta weekend. On Saturday morning the mass in honor of St. Peter is celebrated at St. Ann's Church. In the afternoon, on Saturday and Sunday, there are sports events, which include fishing boat races. There is also a greasy-pole contest, in which young men try to retrieve a red flag from the end of a well-greased 50-foot spar extending out over the water — without falling in. On both days the sports events are followed by concert music, and the festivities are brought to a close each night with an hour-long display of fireworks.

The climax of the weekend is reached on Sunday. In the morning the statue of the honored saint is moved from the St. Peter's Club, whose members are mainly Italian-American fishermen, to an outdoor altar erected on the waterfront for the occasion and decorated with hundreds of flower arrangements.

Eight fishermen carry the statue there in a solemn procession of clergy, members of Roman Catholic organizations, several drum and bugle corps, and various bands. Well-rehearsed and beautifully costumed children ride on colorful floats, which usually depict religious themes. When the statue of St. Peter is put into place near the outdoor altar, a solemn pontifical mass is celebrated, usually by the Roman Catholic archbishop of Boston, who also officiates at the blessing of the fleet on Sunday afternoon.

For that event the harbor is filled with the townspeople's fishing boats, almost 100 of them, decked with signal flags for the occasion, and many pleasure craft from the surrounding resort areas. People throng the piers to hear the words of the blessing, which begins, "Bless these boats and those who sail thereon. Stretch forth to them Thy right hand as Thou did to Peter and his fishermen. Keep them safe from every peril."

The reference is to the New Testament incident in which Peter is made a classic example of the importance of faith. It appears in Matthew 14:22–34, which tells how Jesus came walking toward the disciples on the water. The terrified disciples wondered if they were seeing a ghost. When Jesus reassured them, " 'It is I; have no fear' . . . Peter answered . . ., 'Lord, if it is you, bid me come to you on the water.' [Christ] said 'Come.' So Peter got out of the boat and walked on the water [towards Jesus]; but when he saw the wind, he was afraid, and beginning to sink

he cried out, 'Lord, save me.' Jesus immediately reached out his hand and caught him, saying . . . , 'O man of little faith, why did you doubt?' "

As the blessing of the fleet is completed, all the vessels in the harbor blow their foghorns. The blasts can be heard all over Cape Ann and the usually mournful tones of the foghorn become for this one occasion a happy sound.

Apart from its serious side, the St. Peter's Fiesta offers an amusement area with such carnival rides as the Ferris wheel and the whip, and numerous food stalls featuring Italian foods and such typically American viands as hot dogs, popcorn, ice cream, and cotton candy. At about midnight on Sunday, when a giant fireworks display has brought the annual festivities to a close, eight Italian-American fishermen lift the statue of St. Peter on their shoulders, carry it around Gloucester's Fort section, near the piers, and then return it to its place at the St. Peter's Club until the following year's fiesta.

Another colorful blessing of the fleet ceremony is held in Provincetown, Massachusetts, where Portuguese fishermen of the town and pleasure-craft owners from surrounding areas honor St. Peter on the last Sunday in June. The boats, freshly painted for the summer, are festooned with signal flags and sometimes also with flowers. After the blessing the spectators frequently toss flowers into the water in memory of those who have been lost at sea.

St. Peter is honored inland, too. In a number of New Mexican Indian pueblos, for instance — including Laguna, Acoma, Santa Ana, San Felipe, Santo Domingo, Cochiti, and Isleta — San Pedro's Day is generally marked by traditional Indian ceremonial dances, which are quite unrelated to the Christian masses that may precede them in some of the pueblos' Roman Catholic churches. The several villages of Laguna pueblo add an unusual custom on this and several other patron saints' feast days. On June 29 all the residents named Peter climb to the top of their houses and toss food down from the rooftops. The ceremony is repeated on the feasts of St. John, St. James, and St. Lawrence with participants named for those saints.

JUNE 30

Twenty-sixth Amendment Ratified

Eighteen-year-olds gained the right to vote in all elections — local, state, and federal — with the ratification of the 26th Amendment to the US Constitution on June 30, 1971. The amendment was approved by Congress and submitted to the states for ratification on March 23, 1971.

It was ratified in only three months and seven days, far more rapidly than was the previous record holder, the 12th Amendment, which took six months and six days.

The text of the 26th Amendment is as follows:

SECTION 1. The right of citizens of the United States, who are eighteen years of age or older, to vote shall not be denied or abridged by the United States or any state on account of age.

SECTION 2. The Congress shall have the power to enforce this article by appropriate legislation.

When Congress approved an extension of the Voting Rights Act of 1965 in June 1970, it attached to the measure an amendment that would have lowered the voting age to 18 in all elections, effective January 1, 1971. (As of the time of Congress's extension of the act, only four states had given the vote to persons under 21 years of age: Georgia and Kentucky allowed 18-year-olds to vote; Alaska, 19-year-olds; and Hawaii, 20-year-olds.) Although President Richard M. Nixon declared himself in favor of a lowered voting age, he and many constitutional experts believed that such a change could not be applied to local and state elections by congressional legislation. The President therefore pressed for a constitutional amendment to guarantee the vote to 18-year-olds, while at the same time asking for an immediate court test of the constitutionality of the new legislation.

In August the Justice Department filed two suits in the Supreme Court, one against Arizona and Idaho and another against New Hampshire and North Carolina. In these suits the Justice Department asked the court to uphold the provisions of the amendment to the Voting Rights Act. At the same time the court was considering suits filed by Texas and Oregon in which the section of the law dealing with the right of 18-year-olds to vote was challenged. By a vote of five to four, the Supreme Court ruled on December 21, 1970, that the provision of the law empowering 18-year-olds to vote in presidential, vice-presidential, and congressional elections was constitutional. However, it ruled invalid that part of the law that lowered the voting age in state and local elections, stating that Congress does not have authority to legislate in that area.

On the day the court handed down its decision, Senator Edward M. Kennedy, Democrat of Massachusetts, introduced into the US Senate a draft of a constitutional amendment to give 18-year-olds the vote in all elections. As soon as Congress had given final (and overwhelming) approval, the amendment was ratified by the states of Minnesota, Connecticut, Delaware, Tennessee, and Washington (March 23, 1971). Other states acted swiftly, too, and the necessary approval of three-fourths of all the states was obtained on June 30, 1971, when Ohio became the 38th state to ratify the amendment. As of that date, therefore, the United States acquired an additional 11 million eligible voters, aged 18 through 20. A question existed as to how many of them would exercise their right, because a large number of students were expected to have to vote by absentee ballot, a process that many voters had not taken the trouble to use in the past. The new voters had the opportunity, however, to make their voices heard in gubernatorial and large mayoral elections, and in many other state and local contests, within just a few months of gaining the vote. They were also able to vote in the 1972 presidential primaries and election. Thus the cause of the frustration felt in 1968 by many 18- through 20-year-olds who worked zealously in the presidential campaigns but could not cast ballots was eliminated before the 1972 elections.

July

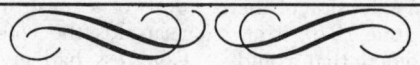

July, originally the fifth month of the Roman year, was accordingly known as *Quintilis*, derived from the Latin word for five, *quinque*. When the ancient calendar was revised, January and February being added to the beginning of the calendar year, July became the seventh month, but still retained its original name. It was renamed July in 44 B.C. in honor of Gaius Julius Caesar (c. 102 B.C.–44 B.C.), the Roman statesman, military leader, and writer. Ambrosius Theodosius Macrobius, a Roman writer of the early fifth century A.D., explained the circumstances behind the change of name:

... the month was called *Julius* in honor of the dictator Julius Caesar in accordance with a law proposed by the consul Marcus Antonius, the son of Marcus. It was so called because Julius had been born in this month on the fourth day before the Ides of Quintilis [the 15th day of July].

Mark Antony (c. 83 B.C.–30 B.C.), a kinsman of Caesar's through his mother, had unsuccessfully tried to persuade the Romans to make Caesar emperor. The best that he could do was to induce the Roman senate to vote to Julius Caesar the tribute of having his natal month called after him. The number of days allotted July, previously only 30, was also raised to 31. Mark Antony played a prominent role later in Roman affairs, being perhaps best known today as the lover of the Egyptian queen Cleopatra and the man who in Shakespeare's *Julius Caesar* delivers a moving oration over the dead body of Caesar following the dictator's assassination at the hands of Marcus Junius Brutus and other conspirators.

The naming of July after Julius Caesar was the first historical example of applying to the Roman calendar the custom, practiced especially in the eastern part of the Mediterranean world, of calling a month after a living ruler. The honorific month seems to be of Athenian origin, the first person known to have received the privilege in the Greek calendar being the ancient king of Macedon and conqueror of Athens, Demetrius Poliorcetes, in 307 B.C. The custom thence spread throughout the East and eventually to Rome.

The honor was a fitting tribute to Julius Caesar, who after the long years of civil strife had undertaken numerous administrative reforms at Rome, including the revision of the inaccurate ancient calendar. The resulting calendar, adopted in 45 B.C. (see The Calendar), remained in effect until Pope Gregory XIII revised it in the 16th century.

July 7 was the festival of Juno Caprotina, in honor of Juno in her role as protector of female slaves. On July 8 the important festival of Castor and Pollux, the twins called the Dioscuri, took place. Castor and Pollux were identified with the zodiacal constellation Gemini ("twins"). The cult of the twins, renowned for athletic and military prowess, was a popular one in Rome, and a temple in their honor was erected in the Forum.

The Anglo-Saxons called the month of July *Litha se oefterra*, meaning "lithe," or "mild"; *Heg-monath*, meaning "hay month"; and *Maed-monath*, because the meadows were in bloom and the cattle were then turned out to feed. Until the end of the 18th century, the name of the month was pronounced with the accent on the first syllable (as noted in Samuel Johnson's dictionary), thus recalling its derivation from *Julius*. For example, the English poets Sir John Suckling and William Wordsworth rhymed it with *newly* and *truly* respectively. The lucky birthstones often associated with July are the ruby and the onyx.

JULY 1

Battle of Gettysburg Begins

Victory and conquest are only occasionally synonymous. In the American Civil War the goal of the South was not to conquer the North but to gain from it recognition of the Confederate States' self-proclaimed independence from the Union. To win meant not to lose, and, in that perspective, the Southern invasion of Northern territory in the summer of 1863 was a tactic of offense in a strategy of defense. The Confederate leaders hoped that a thrust deep into hitherto secure Union states would undermine the enemy's morale and significantly increase the already sizable number of Northerners willing to accommodate the South's demands. Such an attack would also shift the theater of conflict into Union territory and might force the recall of Federal troops that were putting extreme pressure on vital western Confederate installations at Chattanooga, Tennessee, and Vicksburg, Mississippi.

Confederate General Robert E. Lee spent the month of June 1863 maneuvering the three corps of his 89,000-man Army of Northern Virginia north from Fredericksburg, Virginia, toward Pennsylvania. General Joseph Hooker followed Lee's path and kept his Union forces, the 120,000-man Army of the Potomac, interposed between the enemy and the federal capital at Washington. During the month Hooker, angered by interference from the federal general-in-chief, Henry W. Halleck, asked to be relieved of command, and President Abraham Lincoln ordered General George G. Meade to take the assignment in Hooker's stead. Meade's objective was to catch and defeat Lee before he could cross the Susquehanna River and attack the Pennsylvania state capital of Harrisburg.

By the end of June the opposing armies had crossed the Pennsylvania state line and were concentrated near Gettysburg, approximately 36 miles southwest of Harrisburg. On the morning of July 1 elements of the two forces accidentally met, touching off the most memorable battle of the Civil War. Major General John Buford's federal cavalry, scouting ahead of the main units, encountered General James J. Pettigrew's brigade of Lieutenant General Ambrose P. Hill's Confederate III Corps as it moved toward Gettysburg to capture a supply of shoes reported there. Buford recognized the importance of the town as a communications center and undertook a valiant effort to defend it. Although badly outnumbered, his cavalrymen repulsed assaults by rebel divisions commanded by Major Generals Henry Heth and William D.

Pender. The Federal I and XI Corps, under Major Generals John F. Reynolds and Oliver O. Howard respectively, came to Buford's aid.

The fighting, which began at 10:00 A.M., slackened around noon. The Confederates had taken McPherson's Ridge west of Gettysburg and were threatening to overrun Seminary Ridge, their next obstacle. During the afternoon the battle resumed as the Confederate II Corps under Lieutenant General Richard S. Ewell arrived in the battle area. The rebels drove the Federal I and XI Corps from Seminary Ridge back to Cemetery Hill. Although the first day of the battle of Gettysburg thus ended as a Southern victory, Meade resolved that this was the proper time for a showdown with Lee.

During the night of July 1/2, Meade aligned the main body of federal troops along Cemetery Ridge, which ran in a north-south direction. Expecting that Lee would attack his northern flank in an attempt to cut his lines of communication along the nearby Baltimore Pike, Meade placed additional troops in the area of Cemetery and Culp's hills to the northeast of the ridge. He gave little coverage to Round Top and Little Round Top on his southern flank.

Lee dispersed his army along the Union front with Ewell's corps on the north, Hill's in the center, and Lieutenant General James Longstreet's I Corps on the south. The Confederate commander had considered attacking the enemy's northern flank, but Ewell's report that he would not be able to take Cemetery and Culp's hills dissuaded him. Lee's attention then focused on the federal southern flank, which he planned to attack with two of Longstreet's divisions. He ordered Ewell and Hill to make secondary attacks in their sectors to prevent Meade from sending assistance to the exposed flank.

After numerous delays the second day's fighting began about 4:00 P.M. as Major General John Bell Hood's division of Longstreet's I Corps drove forward. Severe fighting ensued in what historians still refer to as the Wheat Field, the Apple Orchard, and the Peach Orchard on the southern flank, and Hood suffered a wound that permanently deprived him of the use of his left arm. Hill and Ewell failed to attack with enough vigor in their sectors, however, and Meade was able to shift his troops and stop the rebel advance.

Both sides held councils of war after the July 2 engagement. The progress of the battle had discouraged Meade, and with hesitation he decided to continue his stand in Gettysburg. Lee, on the other hand, was confident that the next day would bring victory. Morale was high, the Confederates were gaining ground, and Major General George E. Pickett had just arrived with a fresh division. Lee planned to assault the center of the federal line with 10 brigades supported by 159 artillery pieces. Only Longstreet disagreed: he thought that the Southerners should first allow the Northerners to take the offense, and then repulse them with heavy losses as they had done at Bull Run, Antietam, and Fredericksburg.

General Longstreet commanded the rebel force that made the assault on July 3. Historians have called the action Pickett's Charge, but that Virginia general led only 4 of the 10 Southern brigades that engaged the Northerners. The Confederate infantry began its attack about 1:45 P.M. They advanced steadily with Brigadier General James Pettigrew's 4 brigades on the left and Pickett's men on the right. Major General Isaac R. Trimble's 2 brigades followed Pettigrew's troops.

Meade guessed that Lee would strike his center because he had previously attacked both flanks. The federals accordingly worked through the night perfecting their defenses and were ready for the Confederate assault. As the rebels drew close, the Northerners directed heavy fire into the two brigades on Pettigrew's left flank. Trimble's men were badly placed to give assistance, and so the Southern line began to collapse. The battle ended as Longstreet withdrew and reorganized his forces.

Rain on July 4 prevented an expected federal attack, and Lee took advantage of the weather to begin his retreat to the South. The Confederate military effort had reached its crescendo; although few recognized it, the turning point of the Civil War had been reached.

Approximately 88,000 Union and 75,000 Confederate troops participated in the battle of Gettysburg. There is considerable disagreement about the accuracy of the casualty reports, but approximately 3,155 federal and 3,903 Confederate soldiers lost their lives. The total wounded, missing, and dead reached approximately 23,049 for the North and 28,063 for the South.

The scene of the battle annually attracts thousands of visitors. The battlefield was established as Gettysburg National Military Park on February 11, 1895, and the National Park Service, which administers its more than 3,000 acres, has made a visit to the area a highly educative and rewarding experience. Many of the 31 miles of roadway winding through the grounds run along actual battle lines, so that visitors can easily visualize the strategy of the combatants. Farm buildings that dotted the scene in 1863 have also been retained, and farmers who lease the land from the government raise crops similar to those produced at the time of the conflict. Over 1,400 monuments and markers may be seen at the park. Of these, the structures that many states have erected to the memory of native sons who participated in the battle are noteworthy. One of the newest facilities in the park is the visitors' center, where the public may prepare to tour the battlefield by first viewing the numerous exhibits and obtaining informative literature. Paul Philippoteaux's famous *Gettysburg Cyclorama*, a 370-foot painting that was done between 1881 and 1884 from original sketches and photographs, may also be seen there.

The battlefield has been the locale for numerous observances. Between July 1 and 6, 1913, approximately 55,000 Civil War veterans visited Gettysburg. On July 3 of that year, the 50th anniversary of Pickett's Charge, troops of 150 former Confederate and 180 former Union men reenacted the famous assault. Rebel yells and replies of "hurray for the white trefoil" rang through the air as the veterans, who by then ranged in age from 62 to 112, reenacted the charge. The following day President Woodrow Wilson spoke at Gettysburg and urged the former soldiers to "lift your eyes to the great tracts of life yet to be conquered in the interest of righteous peace." The peace he hoped for was soon to be shattered by the outbreak of World War I.

The 75th anniversary of the battle of Gettysburg in 1938 was the final major observance in which actual Civil War veterans participated (the last surviving Union soldier died in 1956, the last Confederate in 1959). The highlight of the 1938 ceremonies was the July 3 dedication of the Eternal Light Peace Memorial. In the presence of President Franklin D. Roosevelt and an audience of 500,000 — including 1,359 Union veterans and 486 Confederate veterans — the 51-foot limestone shaft inscribed with the words "Peace Eternal in a Nation United," and surmounted by an eternal flame, was unveiled by a Union veteran and a Confederate veteran. Except for a brief period during World War II the flame has burned daily since 1938, and until the lighting of the flame at the grave of President John F. Kennedy in Arlington National Cemetery it was the most visited memorial of its kind in the United States.

Numerous events marked the centennial of the battle of Gettysburg in 1963. The three-day commemoration was prefaced by a program sponsored by the Gettysburg Fire Company on June 30. Former President Dwight D. Eisenhower, himself a resident of the area, was the principal speaker, and the US Army Field Band presented a concert.

The official beginning of the 1963 observances took place on July 1 at the Eternal Light Peace

Memorial. The program opened with the governors or other distinguished representatives of the 29 states whose citizens fought at Gettysburg placing large evergreen wreaths at the base of the monument. Following this tribute Governor William W. Scranton of Pennsylvania welcomed the visitors to the battlefield; US Postmaster General J. Edward Day dedicated the Gettysburg commemorative stamp; and the Pennsylvania Commandery of the Military Order of the Loyal Legion and the Gettysburg Battlefield Preservation Association presented deeds to recently acquired battlefield lands to John A. Carver Jr., assistant secretary of the interior. The ceremonies closed with youthful descendants of those who fell during the battle rededicating a new torch of peace while costumed bands played the "Battle Hymn of the Republic" and Confederate war songs.

The following day the scene of the celebration shifted to downtown Gettysburg, where a two-hour pageant-parade with the theme of Strength through Unity was held. More than 5,000 members of the armed forces and more than 1,500 Sons of Union Veterans, members of the Confederate High Command, reactivated Civil War units, and the North-South Skirmishers Association participated, the latter groups wearing the traditional blue and gray uniforms of the Union and the Confederacy respectively, and all marched to music provided by bands from Illinois, New York, Maryland, Virginia, Pennsylvania, and North Carolina. The North Carolina 26th Regiment Band from Tarheelia attracted perhaps the greatest attention, since its members played original Civil War arrangements on period instruments. Just before the parade began, a thunderstorm drenched Gettysburg, but even it failed to dampen the enthusiasm of both paraders and onlookers. A throng of 35,000 spectators — many wearing Civil War dress and displaying beards grown for the occasion — stood along the line of march and seemed especially pleased by the presence of Robert E. Lee 4th, the great-grandson of the Confederate general; and by a tall, solemn impersonator of Abraham Lincoln, who had so unforgettably noted the losses at Gettysburg in dedicating the National Cemetery there on November 19, 1863.

The third day's ceremonies took place at Cemetery Ridge, the site of Pickett's Charge. At 3:00 P.M. on July 3, 1963, some 500 members of the Confederate High Command and reactivated Civil War units, dressed in Confederate uniforms and carrying the Stars and Bars, reenacted the famous charge. After crossing the battlefield to the cluster of trees where the assault had been stopped a century before, the Southern representatives encountered 500 members of the Sons of Union Veterans, reactivated Civil War units, and the North-South Skirmishers Association, clad in the blue garb of the Union forces. This time, however, both sides joined in a pledge of allegiance to the flag of the United States.

Each morning throughout the centennial celebration, Vignettes of History, a series of episodes that sought to depict the actual deeds of the men during the battle, were presented at several areas in the park. In addition, every evening between July 1 and 3 the National Park Service sponsored a campfire program featuring the MGM film *The Battle of Gettysburg.*

Since 1949 the Gettysburg Volunteer Fire Department has sponsored ceremonies in the years that were not major anniversaries of the battle. The annual commemorative program, which occurs on the Sunday prior to July 1, generally includes invocations by the local clergy, speeches by distinguished guests, and an armed forces band concert. Among those who have participated in the celebrations have been Dwight D. Eisenhower, Richard M. Nixon, and General Maxwell Taylor. On Thursday of the anniversary week, a military and civil parade with floats illustrating a historical theme is traditionally held. The Second Army band always leads this parade, and a general officer selected from one of the armed services is parade marshal.

Tourists in Gettysburg find themselves surrounded by interesting sites. Visitors may, for instance, see the Jennie Wade House and Museum. Jennie Wade, the only civilian to die during the battle, was killed by a Confederate musket ball while baking bread. Her house contains furnishings of the Civil War period, as well as period guns and other armaments. Another place of interest is the Hall of Presidents, which boasts a collection of wax representations of all the Presidents of the United States. One of the chief attractions in the area, however, has no direct connection with the famous battle of 1863. This is the farm, adjacent to the battlefield, that was the home of former President Eisenhower during his retirement years until his death in 1969.

JULY 2

Civil Rights Act of 1964

On July 2, 1964, the most sweeping civil rights legislation since the Reconstruction era was signed into law in a nationally televised ceremony by President Lyndon B. Johnson, the man who had pushed it through Congress. As enacted the Civil Rights Act of 1964 was more far-reaching than President John F. Kennedy — who proposed it — had dared to hope. Passage of the measure was within the context both of grief over the assassination of Kennedy and of a stirring in the nation's conscience, which had been pricked by the civil rights revolution then nearly a decade old. Clearly the discrimination that still persisted 100 years after the Emancipation Proclamation was incompatible with the doctrine of the Founding Fathers, who held self-evident the truth that all men are created equal.

As passed by substantial majorities — 289 to 126 in the House and 73 to 27 in the Senate — the Civil Rights Act of 1964 prohibited discrimination on the basis of race in public accommodations, in publicly owned or operated facilities, in employment and union membership, and in the registration of voters. Although generally requiring remedies to be attempted first on a local or state basis, the law authorized the US attorney general to initiate legal suits to end discrimination in jobs, public accommodations, and public facilities; to enter private civil rights suits of general public importance; and to request trial by a three-judge federal court in any voting rights suit.

Among other important provisions was the granting of authority to the attorney general to bring school desegregation suits in cases in which private citizens proved unable to sue effectively; such actions, it was hoped, would hasten school desegregation, which had gone on at a foot-dragging pace since the Supreme Court's historic ruling in 1954 (see May 17). Though it had quickened perceptibly, the pace of desegregation in schools and some other facilities still lagged at the end of the 1960s — despite another lever provided by the 1964 act.

This was Title VI, prohibiting discrimination in all federally aided projects and programs throughout the country, and providing, as a last resort, for the cutoff of federal funds where discrimination persisted. Since federal aid to state and local programs had grown to mammoth proportions in the years since Franklin D. Roosevelt's New Deal, the availability of federal funds was regarded as a potentially powerful inducement to further desegregation. The inducement was, for a time, blunted, however, by the economies in nonmilitary government spending caused by heavy US involvement in the Vietnam war after 1964, and later by economies designed to slow inflation.

The 1964 act, which made a sixth-grade education a (rebuttable) qualification for voting and authorized technical and financial help in the desegregation of school districts, also made other provisions: it established a federal Equal Employment Opportunity Commission to investigate and fight alleged discrimination in employment. It created a Community Relations Service, in the Commerce Department, to help localities conciliate racial disputes. It granted the right of appeal if a federal District Court judge ordered back to a state judge a case that a criminal defendant had tried to remove from the state, on the ground that his civil rights would be denied there. And it ordered the Bureau of the Census to assemble statistics, by race, on registration and voting in areas designated by the Commission on Civil Rights — leaving implicit the possibility that such statistics could be used to enforce a long-overlooked clause of the 14th Amendment providing for a loss of seats in the House of Representatives for states in which voting discrimination existed.

Despite the legal testing of various provisions that awaited it, and the remaining necessity for major efforts at persuasion before complete compliance could be ensured, the Civil Rights Act of 1964 and the amplifying Voting Rights Act of 1965 (see August 6) were powerful aids in the march toward equality.

Many of the provisions of the new acts had appeared earlier in the 14th and 15th amendments to the Constitution; the Reconstruction acts of 1867 and 1868; and the civil rights acts of 1866 and 1875, which were declared unconstitutional by the Supreme Court in 1883 — the last in a ruling that for seven decades virtually halted federal efforts to protect blacks from discrimination by private persons who acted without the aid of state authority. In 1896 the Supreme Court provided a further setback for civil rights in its *Plessy* v. *Ferguson* ruling that segregated facilities did not constitute discrimination so long as accommodations were equal — a decision that stood until May 17, 1954, when the Supreme Court ordered schools desegregated, upsetting the entire "separate but equal" concept.

The obstructionist tactics of those who opposed the 1954 ruling led to the civil-rights acts of 1957 (see September 9) and 1960 (see May 6) — and to the widespread movement for civil rights, which first came to world attention with the bus boycott begun late in 1955 by the Reverend Martin Luther King Jr. in Montgomery, Alabama (see December 1). As the nonviolent civil disobedience espoused by King — and, before him, Thoreau and Gandhi — spread, the name of one American community after another took its place in newspaper headlines across the nation. But it was the huge Birmingham, Alabama, demonstrations in the spring of 1963 — carried out in the face of ruthless measures by police officers who used dogs and high-power fire hoses — that did most to shock the nation and ensure passage of the Civil Rights Act of 1964.

As the mass media presented dramatic photographs of the brutality at Birmingham, setting off demonstrations in hundreds of other communities, the civil-rights proposals that had been the subject of a special message to Congress by President Kennedy on February 28, 1963, awaited congressional action. Kennedy chose the dates of June 11 and 19, respectively, for a nationally televised speech and a second (and stronger) civil-rights address to Congress. In August the urgency of such pleas was underlined for Congress and the nation by the historic March on Washington of 200,000 civil rights advocates. With their significance thus emphasized, many of the measures Kennedy had proposed were encompassed in the Civil Rights Act of 1964 — which had progressed as far as the House Rules Committee when the President was assassinated on November 22, 1963.

Recognizing both a favorable climate for rights legislation and the desire of members of Congress to pay tribute to their fallen leader, Kennedy's successor, President Johnson, chose the occasion of his first address to Congress, a few days later, for an impassioned plea for swift and favorable action on the pending legislation. On July 2, 1964, the bill was signed into law by the new President, just five hours after it received final congressional approval.

President James A. Garfield Shot

At the conclusion of a cabinet meeting on June 30, 1881, President James A. Garfield (see November 19) asked Robert Lincoln, the secretary of war and the son of Abraham Lincoln, about a nightmare the late President had had shortly before his assassination. The secretary told of the dream in which his father had seen a corpse on a catafalque in the East Room. In the dream Lincoln asks, "Who is dead in the White House?" and the sentry guarding the body replies, "The President." Garfield and the other officials listened intently as Lincoln recounted the incident, but they were only momentarily impressed by its prophetic quality. No one present would have believed that only two days later, on July 2, 1881, an assassin's bullet would strike Garfield.

The day of the tragedy was to have been the beginning of a holiday for the 20th President. To escape the hot Washington summer, Garfield had planned to go first to the New Jersey seaside resort of Elberon and then to Williamstown, Massachusetts, where he was to attend his 25th class reunion at Williams College. A special railroad car had been engaged for the President and his accompanying cabinet members, and it had

been added to the train that was scheduled to leave Washington's Baltimore and Potomac Railway depot at 9:30 A.M. on July 2, 1881.

Garfield and his secretary of state, James G. Blaine, arrived at the railroad station at Sixth and B streets at about 9:20 A.M. of the fateful day. After remaining in Blaine's carriage for 10 minutes, the two men made their way to the train. The waiting room of the depot was almost deserted, but as the President and secretary of state passed the empty benches, two gun shots rang out. The bullets found their intended target; Garfield gasped, "My God, what is this?" and sank to the floor.

Garfield's assailant, Charles J. Guiteau, fled from the scene immediately after firing the shots, even though he realized that he would not be able to escape and was ready to accept imprisonment. But he feared that the inflamed emotions of the moment might result in his being lynched on the spot, and as patrolman Patrick Kearney apprehended him, he said, "Keep quiet, my friend. I wish to go to jail."

Guiteau's life, like his actions and words at the Baltimore and Potomac depot, had been a combination of the erratic and the calculating. His father, Luther Guiteau, was the superintendent of schools of Freeport, Illinois, but counted among his friends John H. Noyes, the founder of the polygamous Utopian community at Oneida, New York. Young Charles Guiteau joined the Oneida group in his late adolescence, but soon found agricultural work unappealing. He then went to New York, where he tried to propagate his religious views in a short-lived newspaper, the New York *Theocrat*. Moving to Chicago, he married there and took a position as a clerk in a law firm. Despite his respectable occupation for 11 years Guiteau made his living by swindling and cheating; among his victims were gullible merchants, pawnbrokers, and boardinghouse owners.

He fell upon hard times after 1873. His wife, growing tired of her husband's questionable activities, divorced him; and New York newspapers exposed his improper behavior as a collection lawyer. During the next few years, Guiteau tried to earn his living as a lawyer, but he became increasingly unbalanced and began to entertain the delusion that he would eventually become President of the United States.

James Garfield's candidacy for the White House in 1880 sparked Guiteau's hopes. He offered his services as a public speaker to the Republican party and passed out copies of his prepared speech, "Garfield and Hancock," to all who would accept them. Guiteau even sent a copy to the candidate with the suggestion that he should receive the appointment as US consul in Vienna as his reward. After Garfield's inauguration Guiteau managed to see the President at the White House, where he importuned the Chief Executive for appointment as consul in Paris. When the President gave Guiteau no satisfaction, the ambitious young man futilely sought the assistance of Secretary of State Blaine, who also paid him little heed. Frustrated beyond his limited endurance, Guiteau — in a portentous letter that Garfield probably never saw — warned the President to remove Blaine, or "you and the Republican party will come to grief."

Blaming Garfield personally for his plight, Guiteau came to believe that he was part of a divine plan to remove the President. On June 6, with money borrowed from a cousin, he bought a .44-caliber British Bulldog pistol, a box of cartridges, and a penknife from O'Meara's Gun Shop. He selected a firearm with a white bone handle because — as he later testified at his trial — he believed it would look better in a museum.

For the next four weeks Guiteau divided his time between target practice, at an isolated place along the Potomac, and following Garfield through the streets of the capital. Guiteau let several opportunities to shoot the President pass. But when he heard that Garfield would be leaving Washington on July 2, he decided that that day would give him the best opportunity to carry out his plan.

Early on July 2 Guiteau wrote a letter explaining his intended action. He asserted that he held no ill will toward Garfield but that the "President's tragic death was a sad necessity, [and] . . . it will unite the Republican party and save the Republic." Then Guiteau left for the depot.

The two shots critically wounded Garfield. One bullet lodged in his back; the other grazed his left arm. In a state of deep shock and only partially conscious, the President was moved to the second floor of the depot. Members of his cabinet quickly gathered at his side. The sight of the stricken President was particularly upsetting to Robert Lincoln, and he remarked in dismay: "How many hours of sorrow I have passed in this town."

The first doctors to examine Garfield did not believe that the President would live to the end of the day. But they permitted him to be moved. In a bed hastily mounted on a wagon, he was brought back to the White House only a few hours after he had started out for his intended summer holiday.

For two days Garfield was close to death; then, on July 5, his condition stabilized and for the first time since the shooting he was able to retain food. The numerous doctors attending the President concluded that the bullet that had entered his back had deflected downward through his peritoneal cavity and become embedded in the front wall of his abdomen. But since they were unsure of its exact location — indeed, their belief that it was lodged in the abdomen later proved to be wrong — they hesitated to probe for the bullet. Instead their treatment of the President amounted to little more than intensive nursing care, and blood poisoning posed the greatest threat to Garfield's life in the days that followed.

Room number 18, situated on the south side of the second floor of the White House and commanding a view of the Potomac River became Garfield's sickroom. The doctors attending the President insisted that he have absolute silence, but they allowed his wife, Lucretia, and his children to visit frequently. Several trusted advisers and the wives of cabinet members were also permitted to see him; the latter often helped fan Garfield during the hot Washington summer.

After he survived the initial crisis, many observers believed that Garfield would recover. Then, on July 23, the President took a turn for the worse, and after that date his condition steadily deteriorated. His doctors realized that infection along the track taken by the bullet endangered his life, but, in that era before antibiotics, they were helpless.

Popular concern for the President centered not on the threat of blood poisoning but on the lesser problem of discovering the exact location of the bullet that still was lodged somewhere in Garfield's body. Alexander Graham Bell offered assistance, and by the end of July he perfected an induction-balance electrical device, with which he hoped to pinpoint the miniscule object. On August 1 Bell used his invention on Garfield. His findings were inconclusive, and in any case the President was, by that time, so weak that he probably would not have survived surgical attempts to retrieve the bullet.

Throughout his long ordeal Garfield displayed courage and fortitude. But by the end of August, his physical condition, according to one close friend, was "absolutely critical." The heat of the Washington summer compounded the President's suffering, and he desperately wanted to leave the nation's capital. At first his doctors were reluctant to move their patient, but they finally agreed that a stay at the seashore might prove beneficial. Charles Franklyn offered Garfield the use of his 25-room house in Elberon, New Jersey, and plans to transport the stricken President to that resort were quickly put in motion.

Garfield withstood the railroad trip to Elberon on September 6, 1881, so remarkably well that hopes for his recovery again surged. On September 8 one of his doctors remarked to a reporter: "The man is convalescent." But three days later the weakened President developed pneumonia. On the morning of September 19 he suffered a chill. That afternoon he complained of severe chest pains, and in the evening he lost consciousness. He died at 10:35 P.M. on September 19, 1881.

Garfield's death plunged the nation into mourning. On September 21 his body was returned to Washington and for the next two days the President's casket lay in state in the Rotunda of the Capitol. During that time more than 100,000 persons filed past the bier. On September 23 a special service honoring Garfield took place in the Rotunda, and then his remains were placed aboard a funeral train and carried to their final resting place in Cleveland, Ohio.

As the train passed through the major cities, towns, and villages along its route, bells tolled to express the nation's grief. Thousands of citizens stood along the railroad tracks and paid their final respects to the fallen leader. In downtown Cleveland a public funeral was held for Garfield, and then his remains were entombed at Lakeview Cemetery several miles away. In 1885 a circular tower 180 feet high surrounded by a porch depicting in bas-relief important moments in Garfield's career was erected at the final resting place by the Garfield National Monument Association.

In the months following the services at Lakeview, the world joined the United States in mourning its loss. Commemorative services were held in many faraway places: the Conservative Club in Liverpool, England, was draped in black, and a memorial book entitled *Sorrow of the People of Buenos Aires for the Death of General James A. Garfield, Late President of the United States* was published in Argentina. In the United States public observances honoring Garfield did not conclude until February 27, 1882, when President Chester A. Arthur eulogized his predecessor before a joint session of Congress.

On November 14, 1881, before the official mourning for Garfield ended, the trial of his assassin began. Guiteau based his defense on a plea of insanity, but on January 5, 1882, he was found guilty as charged. He was hanged on June 30 before a crowd of 250 spectators.

Garfield's death produced one salutary result. The bizarre motivation of his assassin emphasized to the nation's citizens the abuses of the spoils system, whereby governmental jobs were distributed as rewards for support during election campaigns. In the months following Garfield's death, an outraged public opinion increasingly came to favor ending such distribution of patronage and helped gain congressional and presidential approval for the Pendleton Act, which established the Civil Service Commission in 1883.

A memorial of a different kind had its impetus many years later, when eight-year-old Bruce Frankel of Asbury Park, New Jersey, decided in 1958 that the site of Garfield's death at nearby Elberon merited a fitting marker. The Franklyn house where the President had spent his last days no longed stood, but young Frankel, determined that its location should be suitably indicated, had collected $60 from his friends and schoolmates when a local monument manufacturer heard of his efforts and offered to donate an appropriate marker. The three-foot monument was unveiled in 1962, and President John F. Kennedy noted the occasion by sending an official message.

Hussey's Reaper First Exhibited

Obed Hussey of Maryland exhibited a reaper in public for the first time on July 2, 1833, on the grounds of the Hamilton County Agricultural Society in New York. Late in December the same year, he obtained a patent on it.

There had been reaping machines long before Hussey's. Pliny, writing in A.D. 23, mentions one used in the lowlands of Gaul. It consisted of a cart carrying a box on the front edge of which were sharp projecting teeth. Pushed through the grain by an ox, it caught the heads of the grain, and a man sitting in the box raked them in. During the latter part of the 18th century and the first part of the 19th century, a number of reapers were invented, but they were not satisfactory. Hussey's machine contained pointed knives, which vibrated through a bar and cut the grain. The grain fell on a platform from which it was raked by a man riding on the machine.

Although Hussey was the first to secure a patent on his reaper, his experiments had been simultaneous with those of Cyrus H. McCormick (see February 15), who first demonstrated his reaper publicly in the late harvest of 1831. McCormick's machine, patented in 1834, was probably first in time of actual invention. It was similar to Hussey's in many respects but employed in addition the vital principle of the reel. Although Hussey manufactured his machine (which was better suited for mowing) in competition with McCormick's (which was better for reaping) from 1834 to 1858, he was eventually overshadowed by his rival. Hussey himself died in 1860. The machine he had invented ultimately became the basis of the modern mower.

JULY 3

John Singleton Copley's Birthday

America's foremost colonial portrait artist, John Singleton Copley, was born July 3, 1738, in Boston, of Irish parents. When he was 10, his widowed mother married Peter Pelham, a painter and engraver, and young John Copley learned much about art from his stepfather and the artists who held workshops in Pelham's studio and were regular visitors in the Pelham house.

By the age of 18, Copley was a professional portrait artist and he had a rapid success. His clarity of style and remarkable characterization became much talked about and his services much sought after. Soon he had commissions to paint the portraits of many of the most important people in New England.

Shortly after his painting *Boy with a Squirrel* was exhibited in London in 1766, Copley was elected fellow of the Society of Artists of Great Britain. The strong interest in this painting brought Copley's name to the attention of Benjamin West, an American painter living in London. West was a likable man who was welcomed into England's highest circles, counting among his patrons King George III and among his friends great men of art, literature, and politics, including Sir Joshua Reynolds, Samuel Johnson, and Edmund Burke. He was a charter member, and later president, of the Royal Academy.

West soon began to urge Copley to go to England but Copley, not yet 30, was much in demand in America and kept busy painting portraits commissioned in Boston, New York, and Philadelphia.

In 1769 Copley married Suzannah Clarke, the daughter of a wealthy Boston merchant. The couple lived on Beacon Hill, where their son, also named John Singleton Copley, was born in 1772.

Motivated by the mounting pressures of the American Revolutionary movement and his lifelong desire to study art in Europe, Copley left Boston with his family in June 1774 and studied on the Continent for a time before finally settling in London. Enormously successful in England, Copley received commissions to paint the portraits of members of the royal family as well as of other notables, English and American. Within a few years after his arrival in London he was elected to membership in the Royal Academy.

His studies in Italy had broadened his style and, in addition to portraits, he began to paint historical subjects. His early American portraits, however, have won higher praise than his later work. Near the end of his life Copley suffered ill health and financial problems but by that time his son, educated in London, had become a successful British lawyer and was able to provide assistance.

The senior John Singleton Copley died in London on September 3, 1815. In 1827 his son was made a baron. As Lord Lyndhurst he was three times lord chancellor of England and led the Tories in the House of Lords.

Many of Copley's finest paintings are preserved in public museums in this country and abroad. Boston has several of his early American paintings, which are treasured not only for their artistic vigor and individuality, but as a graphic record of the times. Boston's Museum of Fine Arts, for instance, has Copley's portraits of Paul Revere and Samuel Adams and the well-known *Brook Watson and the Shark*. Other paintings by Copley are on display at the Boston Public Library. His hometown also has honored its famous son in the naming of Copley Square.

In 1965 the 150th anniversary of Copley's death was commemorated by a traveling loan exhibition of his works — oils, pastels, miniatures, drawings, and engravings — seen in many museums throughout the country, including the Metropolitan Museum of Art in New York City.

Idaho Admitted to the Union

On July 3, 1890, Idaho entered the Union as the 43rd state. Its entrance marked the culmination of the area's rapid political and economic growth, which had been triggered by the discovery of gold within its boundaries in the 1860s. The name of the new state was first used during the 1850s to designate a region in what is now Colorado that is still known as Idaho Springs. The word *Idaho* is derived from the Shoshone term *Ee-Da-How*, referring possibly to the ubiquitous purple columbine flower of the area, but also variously translated as "gem of the mountains" or "behold the sun coming down the mountain."

Before the mid-19th century, Idaho formed part of the vast northwest Oregon, or Columbia River, country claimed by Spain, Russia, Great Britain, and the United States. In 1818 a treaty stipulated joint rule of the area by the United States and Great Britain. At first limited to 10 years, joint rule was later extended. In 1846 the United States gained sole possession of the Oregon country below the 49th Parallel. The strong US claim to this northwestern area stemmed primarily from the explorations by Meriwether Lewis and William Clark, who were probably the first white men to pass through Idaho, in 1805. Pacific-bound, they crossed the Continental Divide at Lemhi Pass, traversed the Bitterroot Mountains, and followed the Clearwater, Snake, and Columbia rivers. They passed through the same part of Idaho again the next year, on their return.

Reports of the numerous fur-bearing animals in the area attracted trappers, the majority of them acting as the agents of large fur companies. In 1809 David Thompson, a noted explorer for the British North West Company, penetrated Idaho from the north and erected the trading post of Kully-spell House on the eastern banks of Lake Pend Oreille. In the spring of 1809–1810 alone, the region's pelt yield totaled almost fifty 90-pound packs. Andrew Henry of the Missouri Fur Company made an unsuccessful attempt in 1810 to establish a trading post near what is now Rexburg, Idaho, and the next year Wilson Price Hunt, representing John Jacob Astor's Pacific Fur Company, explored the Snake River country. Captain B. L. E. Bonneville's expedition entered the region in 1832, and two years later Fort Hall was built by a Bostonian, Nathaniel Wyeth, on the east bank of the upper Snake River.

The Reverend Henry H. Spaulding, chief assistant of the intrepid American missionary Dr. Marcus Whitman, was active in establishing a school, a grist mill and sawmill, and a printing press for Indians at Lapwai (near what is now Lewiston, Idaho), in 1836. Several years later Jesuit priests led by Father P. J. De Smet founded a missionary settlement on the Coeur d'Alene River. Mormon missionaries, extending their horizons northward from their desert-blooming settlement in Salt Lake City, Utah, set up a mission and colony in the valley of the Lemhi River in 1855. Three years later the Mormon settlers, beset by early frosts, plagues of grasshoppers, and hostile Bannock and Shoshone Indians, were recalled by their leader, Brigham Young. None of these early missions — Protestant, Catholic, or Mormon — can be regarded as a permanent establishment in Idaho. On June 15, 1860, however, another pioneering band of Mormons — unaware that they had left Utah — founded a permanent agricultural settlement in Franklin, in the southeastern part of Idaho. June 15, the anniversary of their arrival, was proclaimed Idaho Pioneer Day in 1911. In former years it was a legal holiday throughout the state and an occasion for picnics and pioneer reunions.

Although numerous emigrant parties rolled over the Oregon Trail starting in the 1840s, going through southern Idaho en route to the Far West, the great tide of settlers passed Idaho by. Thus the Idaho area, which had been transferred from the Oregon Territory to the newly formed territory of Washington in 1853, continued to rank among the "unsettled" portions of the Far West. It was only the backwave of the westward movement that finally resulted in widespread settlement: Idaho became the first region to be populated from the west rather than from the east. Captain E. D. Pierce's discovery of gold in 1860 at Orofino Creek, a tributary of the Clearwater River, lured hordes of prospectors from Oregon, Washington, California, and Nevada, as well as smaller numbers from the East, to Idaho. Mining towns mushroomed as the strike was followed by others — on the Salmon River in 1861, in the Boise River basin in 1862, and in the Owyhee River country in 1863.

The competing gold rushes stimulated growth of rival mining centers, one in the north around the supply center of Lewiston, the other in the south around Boise and Idaho City (first named Bannock). Numerous and vocal enough to demand a new government administration separate from that of Washington Territory, the miners were also willing to join forces to assure independent territorial status. The bill setting up the territory of Idaho was signed by President Abraham Lincoln on March 3, 1863, during the troublesome days of the Civil War.

The new territory, comprising the eastern portions of the Washington Territory and the western portions of the Dakota Territory, was the largest ever created in the United States. It included all the area of what are now Idaho, Montana, and Wyoming, as well as a small western portion of North and South Dakota and Nebraska. On March 17, 1863, William H. Wallace was appointed the first territorial governor by Lincoln, who was his close friend. In July of that year, Governor Wallace proclaimed Lewiston the capital, and it was there that the first and second sessions of the territorial legislature were held, starting in December 1863 and November 1864 respectively. Soon afterwards the capital was transferred to Boise, where it has remained. The official count taken in Idaho, in September 1863, revealed a substantial population of 32,342 (though it was to drop to about 15,000 by the Census of 1870).

The Idaho Territory, as set up in 1863, was short-lived. The territorial act itself provided that nothing in it should be so construed as to prevent the government of the United States "from attaching any portion of said territory to any other state or territory." A little over a year later, Montana gold-seekers persuaded Congress to create the Montana Territory out of a large northern section of Idaho Territory. In 1868 Wyoming was also taken away, leaving Idaho — as it is now — reduced to an irregularly shaped area with the northern panhandle practically severed from the southern region by the steep Salmon and Snake River canyons.

By the late 1850s the federal government had confined most of the Indian tribes in the northern part of the region to reservations. Even as late as 1877, however, the Nez Percés' Chief Joseph was traversing Idaho in the masterly, cross-mountain retreat — more than 1,000 miles through nearly impossible terrain — by which he sought to lead his famished and war-weary tribe to refuge in Canada. The "retreat" was one of history's great examples of military genius, coupled with mass fortitude. In its course, the suffering and vastly outnumbered Indians, encumbered with their own refugees, alternately bested, held off, or eluded the pursuing US Army. At last the Indians were defeated — just 30 miles short of the Canadian border. The Nez Percés' feat of skill and endurance has long been remembered, as has the heroic Chief Joseph's eloquent and heartbreaking speech of surrender.

As the Idaho Territory progressed agriculturally and industrially, a movement for statehood gained momentum. A constitution was adopted in 1889, and Idaho entered the Union the following year. Polygamy, practiced by the Mormons, was an issue in Idaho during its early days, as in several neighboring areas. There had been large migrations of Mormons into southern Idaho from the 1860s onwards, and in 1883 Idaho's territorial legislature had passed laws denying polygamists the vote and restricting the Mormons in other ways. The US Congress had earlier declared polygamy unlawful in 1862. After the constitutionality of such restrictive laws was upheld by the US Supreme Court in 1890, the heads of the Mormon church ruled that polygamy was not an essential article of faith, and Idaho removed its anti-Mormon restrictions.

In 1963 Idaho celebrated its Territorial Centennial statewide, with parades, dances, barbecues, and pageants. The focal point of activity was the Greater Boise Centennial Celebration from June 27 to July 6, to which more than 165 Ada County and Greater Boise area organizations contributed their services. Beginning on Thursday, June 27 with Old-Fashioned Bargain Days sponsored by local merchants, the variety of events continued with the centennial ball and coronation of Miss Centennial on Friday evening. Fiesta Day, on Saturday, started with a gigantic centennial parade in the morning and ended with the evening National Appaloosa Horse Show and the finals of the Miss Idaho pageant. Sunday, designated Religious Heritage Day, featured an afternoon centennial picnic.

An old-time rifle shoot, singing, square dancing, street dancing, and a fireworks display were among the events offered on Monday. The first performance of a historical pageant, *The Idaho Story* (which continued each evening thereafter until the conclusion of the celebration) was also staged. Its cast of 1,000 depicted outstanding episodes in the history of the state from the Lewis and Clark expedition to the Atomic Age. On Youth Day, Tuesday, most activities were for the children, with sports events, such as Little League baseball games and the junior tennis tournament, and a children's parade and talent show. On Ladies' Day, Wednesday, women and girls were conducted on a special tour of the Idaho State Museum and competed in a croquet match and a spelling bee. A rodeo highlighted Thursday, and Friday — Industry, Commerce, and Labor Day — included among other events an old-fashioned printing display. The chuck-wagon breakfast and the finals of the beard-growing contest — followed by a beard "shave-off"— provided fun for all on Saturday, July 6.

Throughout the centennial summer, several special events were presented at Boise. Among them were the exhibit Idaho Art — Past and Present and the Centennial Air Show, held at Gowen Field on July 14, featuring the US Air Force acrobatic team, known as the Thunderbirds, and the US Army exhibition parachutists, called the Sky Divers.

Other areas of the state also celebrated the anniversary with centennial activities. Pocatello presented a series of changing displays with such themes as Travel in the Late 1800s and the First Newspaper in Idaho, and dedicated a memorial to the Utah Northern Railroad. The inhabitants of Marsing recaptured the spirit of the early days in Owyhee County with a parade, a whisker-growing contest, and a reconstruction of a typical mining camp. A statewide centennial square dance was held at Treasure Valley, while Twin Falls was the location of the Idaho Centennial Gemorama. In addition to a rodeo, Caldwell residents sponsored a trip to Silver City, one of the best-known western ghost towns, located about 60 miles to the south in the Owyhee Mountains. Kellogg combined its own jubilee — the 75th anniversary of the discovery of the profitable Bunker Hill mine — with the centennial celebration and offered an old-fashioned miners' picnic, as well as sewing and chopping competitions with participants dressed in the fashions of 75 to 100 years ago. One of the concluding events of the 1963 Centennial Year was Poetry Day in Idaho, honoring some 200 contemporary Idaho poets.

Feast of St. Thomas the Apostle

Roman Catholics, who had long venerated St. Thomas — the original "doubting Thomas" and one of the 12 Apostles of Christ — on December 21, have observed the Feast of St. Thomas on July 3 since the recent reform of the Roman Catholic calendar. The change to the reputed date of the transfer of his relics was made in order to make the Advent season more free from interruption by other observances for Catholics.

For other Christians who mark the occasion, notably Episcopalians and Lutherans, the date of the Feast of St. Thomas is still December 21, and it is under that date that the account of the saint's life will be found. Eastern Orthodox Christians venerate St. Thomas on still another date — October 6, or 13 days later where the Julian calendar is still used.

JULY 4

Independence Day

Political independence was not the goal of the American colonists, but rather an alternative accepted only as a last resort. The authorities in England, speaking as much from worry as from knowledge, occasionally whispered that their transatlantic cousins wanted a separate existence, but there is little evidence that many provincial patriots seriously considered severing the ties before 1776. Thomas Jefferson, the author of the Declaration of Independence, could write even in June 1775 that "I am sincerely one of those . . . who would rather be in dependence on Great Britain, properly limited, than on any other nation on earth, or than on no nation."

Early arguments in defense of the American position had stressed the colonists' allegiance to the British king and Parliament and blamed worsening relations on overzealous and unprincipled advisers who unduly influenced the British government. As late as 1773 most provincials still recognized Parliament's right to regulate trade and to make laws affecting them, save in the sensitive area of taxation. They denied principally England's power to raise money from colonies separated from the mother country by 3,000 miles — colonies that could never expect to enjoy adequate representation in the House of Commons.

American grievances against England had ac-cumulated in the years after the conclusion of the French and Indian War in 1763. The British government, in severe financial distress as a result of military expenditures, sought to streamline its colonial administration and make the colonies pay more money into the empire's coffers. In particular, King George III and his ministers wanted the provincials to pay at least part of the enormous costs of defending England's New World settlements. The Americans professed their willingness to help, but objected strenuously to British attempts to levy taxes on them unilaterally. Measures such as the Stamp Act of 1765 (see March 22) drew especially strong opposition. The Stamp Act was repealed in 1766, but the Townshend Acts of 1767 levied new duties. Merchants retaliated by boycotting British imports, and by 1770 all the Townshend duties were repealed except that on tea.

Troops were sent to maintain order, and clashes between patriots and British soldiers broke out. In 1770 the Boston Massacre (see March 5) was the consequence of a struggle between angry citizens and soldiers, who fired into the crowd. Attempts at reconciliation were made, but the revolutionaries continued their agitation. In 1773 resistance to the hated tax on tea — and to the monopoly of the East India Company — led a group of citizens to stage the Boston Tea Party (see December 16). In order to punish the rebelling colonists, Parliament passed the "Coercive" or "Intolerable" Acts of 1774, which authorized the closing of the port of Boston and prohibited town meetings without the governor's consent.

On September 5, 1774, the First Continental Congress convened in Philadelphia. The Congress, representing 12 colonies, condemned the Coercive Acts; denounced Britain's imposition of taxes during the past decade; and adopted a declaration of rights which included the rights of "life, liberty and property."

Gradually the colonists reconsidered their opinion of King George's benevolence. Patriot blood shed at Lexington, Concord, and Bunker Hill, Massachusetts, in 1775 (see April 19 and June 17), and the king's proclamation of August 23, 1775, stating that the Americans were in rebellion, badly weakened the bonds between England and the American colonies. By 1776 the colonists were ready to accept the inflammatory *Common Sense* by Thomas Paine (see January 29), with its description of King George as the "royal brute" and its call for an end to his reign in the New World.

In the spring of 1776 the colonists advanced, step by step, toward independence. On April 12 the North Carolina convention instructed its delegates to the Second Continental Congress, then meeting in Philadelphia, to vote for independence. In turn the Virginia convention, which met in Williamsburg on May 15, directed its delegates to ask the Congress to "declare the United Colonies free and independent states, absolved from all allegiance to, or dependence on the Crown or Parliament of Great Britain." On the same day the Continental Congress, at the suggestion of John Adams, recommended that the various colonies provisionally assume all the powers of government.

Richard Henry Lee, a delegate from Virginia to the Congress, brought the question of independence before that body on June 7. With John Adams's support, Lee advanced the following motion: "Resolved, that these United Colonies are, and of right ought to be, free and independent States, that they are absolved from all allegiance to the British Crown, and that all political connection between them and the State of Great Britain is, and ought to be, totally dissolved." In subsequent debate moderate representatives persuaded their colleagues to delay a final vote for three weeks; but, in the meantime, "that no time be lost, in case the Congress agree thereto," John Adams, Benjamin Franklin, Thomas Jefferson, Robert R. Livingston, and Roger Sherman were appointed as a committee to draft a declaration of independence.

On July 1 the Congress resumed debate on the Lee resolution and approved it the following day, thus officially dissolving the political bonds with England. On July 2 the Congress formally voted for independence. That same day Jefferson brought his committee's proposed declaration of independence before the delegates, and for two days they debated its merits and made revisions. The representatives of 12 colonies ratified the final version on July 4, and John Hancock, the president of the Congress, and Charles Thomson, its secretary, signed the document on that day. On July 9 the Provincial Congress of New York ordered its delegates in Philadelphia, who had abstained from voting on July 4, to endorse the document, and finally the Continental Congress on July 19 resolved to have the "unanimous declaration" engrossed on parchment. Fifty-six names were affixed to the manifesto.

Written primarily by Thomas Jefferson, who was perhaps the most eloquent as well as one of the youngest of the Revolutionary leaders, the Declaration of Independence began with a preamble, which was an assertion of philosophic principles concerning natural rights. "The Unanimous Declaration of the Thirteen United States of America," as the document was titled on parchment, began with these ringing assertions:

When in the Course of human events, it becomes necessary for one people to dissolve the political bands, which have connected them with another, and to assume among the Powers of the earth, the separate and equal station to which the Laws of Nature and of Nature's God entitle them, a decent Respect to the Opinions of Mankind requires that they should declare the causes which impel them to the Separation.

We hold these Truths to be self-evident, that all Men are created equal, that they are endowed by their Creator with certain unalienable Rights, that among these are Life, Liberty, and the Pursuit of Happiness — That to secure these Rights, Governments are instituted among Men, deriving their just Powers from the Consent of the Governed, that whenever any Form of Government becomes destructive of these Ends, it is the Right of the People to alter or to abolish it, and to institute a new Government.

Jefferson did not design the document as a vehicle to express original concepts, but rather to articulate tenets that seemed "self-evident" to most Americans. On May 8, 1825, as an old man, he wrote to Richard Henry Lee that his task had been

not to find out new principles, or new arguments, never before thought of, not merely to say things which had never been said before; but to place before mankind the common sense of the subject, [in] terms so plain and firm as to command their assent, and to justify ourselves in the independent stand we [were] impelled to take. Neither aiming at originality of principle or sentiment, nor yet copied from any particular and previous writing, it was intended to be an expression of the American mind. . . . All its authority rests then on the harmonizing sentiments of the day, whether expressed in conversation, in letters, printed essays, or the elementary books of public right, as Aristotle, Cicero, Locke, Sidney, etc.

A catalog of specific colonial grievances constituted the second section of the Declaration. Significantly, the authors did not mention Parliament, whose authority over the colonies they had denied for the past two years, but rather blamed George III for all wrongs. By declaring the monarch the villain and terminating their allegiance to him, the rebels severed what they alleged to be their sole link with the British Empire.

The third, and final, part of the Declaration was a reiteration of the Lee resolution, asserting the colonies to be independent from England. The document ended with the delegates' statement that "for the support of this Declaration, . . . we mutually pledge to each other our Lives, our Fortunes, and our Sacred Honor."

Philadelphians were the first citizens to hear

the Declaration promulgated, as John Nixon, a member of that city's Committee of Public Safety, read it to them on July 8 in the yard of the Pennsylvania State House — now known as Independence Hall. There was great popular exultation with much cheering and with the continuous ringing of church bells long into the night; the militia even used up some of the precious gunpowder to fire volleys in salutes to independence. Other details in contemporary accounts are interesting. Charles Biddle, in his autobiography, says: "I was in the old State House Yard when the Declaration . . . was read. There were few respectable persons present." And Deborah Logan, who lived in a house facing the square, wrote that "the first audience of the Declaration was neither very numerous nor composed of the most respectable class of citizens."

Residents of New York, including George Washington and several army brigades, heard the Declaration read on July 9. That evening the citizens spiritedly rejoiced and tore down a lead equestrian statue of George III.

Boston received the Declaration of Independence with tumultuous celebration on July 18, when the document was read to the public from the balcony of what now is known as the Old State House, overlooking the site of the 1770 Boston Massacre. A stunned instant of silence was followed by pandemonium. Members of the crowd ripped down the British lion and unicorn that graced the building. These wooden symbols of royalty, soon supplemented by every other Tory sign the long-irritated Bostonian populace could find, were used to start the biggest bonfire the city had ever seen. Dignitaries in the State House quaffed toasts to independence, and the booming of cannons resounded for hours across the city, which the British had unwillingly evacuated four months earlier (see March 17).

Toasts "in grateful deliverance from the British" were also drunk in Providence and in Worcester, Massachusetts, where news of the Declaration was greeted by "a great beating of the drums," the ringing of bells, and "sustained shouts of huzza, firing of musketry and cannon, and bonfires." Things were somewhat more restrained in Amherst, New Hampshire, where residents reacted to the verbal stand for independence by holding a prayer service, followed by a decorous parade. In Delaware the people burned a painting of George III as part of their rejoicing. Georgia, the most remote colony, received the news before the middle of August, and Savannah officials marked the occasion with an outdoor feast.

On July 2, 1777, it occurred to someone in Philadelphia that the first anniversary of independence should be celebrated. The time was short and the country at war, but arrangements for an official dinner were made and Congress adjourned for the day. John Adams, in a letter to his daughter, said that the bells rang all day and that there were bonfires in the streets and fireworks in the evening. Adams's party went on board the *Delaware*, to be greeted by a 13-gun salute. The anniversary dinner was served at 3:00 P.M. with music furnished by "a band of Hessians taken at Trenton." Between toasts a company of soldiers stationed outside fired volleys. After dinner there was a parade of the soldiers in the city. In the evening Adams took a walk for exercise and

was surprised to find the whole city lighting up their candles at the windows. I walked most of the evening and I think it was the most splendid illumination I ever saw; a few surly houses were dark, but the lights were very universal. Considering the lateness of the design and the suddenness of the execution I was amazed at the universal joy and alacrity that was discovered and the brilliancy and splendor of every part of this joyful exhibition.

Like most of his contemporaries, Adams thought that July 2, the anniversary of the adoption of the Lee resolution, would be the date of the festivities. "It ought to be commemorated," Adams wrote, "as the day of deliverance, by solemn acts of devotion to God Almighty. It ought to be solemnized with pomp and parade, with shows, games, sports, guns, bells, bonfires, and illuminations, from one end of this continent to the other, from this time forward, forevermore."

Instead of July 2, however, the United States set aside July 4, the anniversary of the approval of the Declaration of Independence, as the day for the yearly observances. Now a legal holiday in all 50 states and in the territories, July 4 is a day of nationwide festivity. Observances have been in accord with Adams's suggestions. Virtually every locality sponsors special Independence Day celebrations. Parades, band music, speeches, pageantry, and a patriotic show of red, white, and blue are the order of the day in communities across the nation. In some places the ringing of bells — an old tradition revived in recent years — is customary. Athletic and children's programs frequently supplement other activities. Citizens either participate in these events or join with family and friends to mark the occasion privately. The countless beaches and picnic areas across the land are crowded. In the evening the skies are lit with the colorful fireworks displays that have traditionally climaxed the celebration of independence, although setting these off now is generally a carefully supervised community event, rather than the dangerous undertaking of individual amateurs. The traditional bonfires are less in evidence than they once were, although they are still seen where local fire ordinances permit. Observances vary in the different regions of the country, and July 4 programs reflect local customs.

One of the customary celebrations takes place in Washington, D.C., where the nation's capital rejoices with, among other things, a band concert, speeches, and a pyrotechnic display. Appropriately the festivities take place near the Washington Monument.

In addition to the traditional parade, history-conscious Bostonians customarily observe the Fourth of July by reenacting the city's first public reading of the Declaration of Independence from the balcony of the Old State House and decorating the graves of three signers of the Declaration of Independence — John Hancock, Robert Treat Paine, and Samuel Adams. There is also an annual parade. The procession commences at City Hall, where the mayor and other officials are on hand for the official flag raising and playing of the national anthem. It pauses for the honors at the Granary Burial Ground, continues to the Old State House for the reading of the Declaration, and proceeds to the oration exercises at historic Faneuil Hall, the scene of the pre-Revolutionary mass meetings that earned its nickname as the Cradle of Liberty. The Faneuil Hall exercises have been held annually in approximately the same form ever since 1783. Boston's celebration usually also includes fireworks exhibitions in Boston Harbor or on the Charles River. Musical, dance, and other recreational events are scheduled for the two days surrounding the Fourth.

Philadelphia, where the Continental Congress declared this nation's separation from Great Britain, has always been the scene of particular celebration. This is true today, but certainly not more so than on July 4 in 1788, the year the Constitution was adopted by the nine states whose approval was needed to put it into effect. The report on the 1788 celebration, prepared by Francis Hopkinson, the chairman of the committee on arrangements, contained apparent references to Benjamin Franklin's "rising sun" allusion — apropos of the design on the chair from which George Washington had presided over the Constitutional Convention: "I have often and often in the course of the session and the vicissitudes of my hopes and fears as to its issue, looked at that behind the President without being able to tell whether it was rising or setting. But now at length I have the happiness

to know that it is a rising and not a setting sun." Hopkinson described Philadelphia's 1788 celebration in his report:

The rising sun was saluted with a full peal from Christ Church steeple and a discharge of cannon from the ship *Rising Sun, . . .* anchored off Market Street, and superbly decorated with the flags of various nations. Ten vessels in honor of the ten States [that had ratified the Constitution] . . . were dressed and arranged through the whole length of the harbor, each bearing a broad white flag at the masthead, inscribed with the names of the States.

The day's most notable event was a grand procession, more than a mile and half in length, which took three hours to march over a three-mile-long route. Military troops were followed by allegorically garbed figures, political and international dignitaries, and a float bearing a symbolic "federal edifice."

James Wilson of Pennsylvania, a signer of the Declaration of Independence, mounted the float and delivered an oration; soldiers fired volleys; and the company went to dinner. The toasts were announced "by the trumpet," Chairman Hopkinson related, "and answered by a discharge from the ship *Rising Sun,* at her moorings."

Over 80 years later Philadelphia was the natural choice for the chief site of Centennial observances — the United States International Exhibition. In this undertaking, authorized by Congress in 1872, 39 foreign countries, as well as the American states and territories, participated. Opening the Centennial exhibition on May 10, 1876, President Ulysses S. Grant addressed a crowd of 200,000. The President pulled a lever, activating the huge 1,500-horsepower Corliss steam engine that energized all the displays in Machinery Hall and that became itself the most popular presentation of all the industrial and technological equipment shown. (Another device, Alexander Graham Bell's new telephone, drew smaller crowds.) Occupying an enclosure of 236 acres in Fairmont Park, the exposition encompassed a number of large buildings and smaller structures. The main building, then the largest building in the world, covered 20 acres and was devoted principally to manufactures and mining products; other buildings and pavilions featured such themes as agriculture, education, architecture, and women's achievements. Art treasures lent by England, France, Italy, and Spain were shown, as were arts and crafts from Latin America, Europe, Africa, and the Far East.

The exposition closed on November 10, 1876, having registered a remarkable attendance of 9.8 million — one-fifth of the total US population. The success of the project was particularly impressive in view of contemporary depressed economic conditions. Furthermore, though it gratified the American sense of pride and accomplishment in commerce, agriculture, and technology, this 19th century world's fair nonetheless broadened cultural and educational horizons, counteracting a tendency toward provincialism.

Philadelphia's annual celebration has over the years grown into Freedom Week. Independence National Historical Park is the central point of the observance, which takes place during the week preceding July 4. Festivities usually commence on the last Saturday in June in Elfreth's Alley, which Philadelphians claim as the nation's oldest residential street in continuous use. Local guides in colonial garb escort visitors on tours of the area's old houses. On the Wednesday preceding July 4 the Festival of Fountains parade is held on Benjamin Franklin Parkway. Special events occur at the city's numerous historic sites throughout the week, but on July 4 itself activities center upon Independence Hall. A nationally prominent speaker, sometimes the President, gives a keynote address, and the Declaration of Independence is usually read during the patriotic exercises.

In Wyoming, Pennsylvania, near Wilkes-Barre, festivities celebrating Independence are combined with commemorative services for the 300 victims of the British and Indian massacre in Wyoming Valley on July 3, 1778. Many patriotic organizations donate floral wreaths to bedeck the Wyoming monument obelisk, and the day's ceremonies generally include an appropriate address. The borough of Lititz, in Pennsylvania Dutch country, holds one of the most unusual July 4 ceremonies. Since 1818 this tiny community has sponsored a festival of candles. Just after dark on Independence Day, a Queen of Candles is selected during a candlelight ceremony. Then thousands of tapers arranged in the shape of stars, wheels, crescents, and pyramids are lit throughout the Lititz Springs Park. Some of the illuminated candles are floated on the lake. After the "fairyland of candles" burns itself out, spectators are treated to a fireworks display.

An old-fashioned July 4 celebration takes place each year in Bristol, Rhode Island, which began its observance in 1777. Week-long festivities come to a climax on Independence Day with patriotic exercises, a mammoth parade, a greasy-pole climb, a vaudeville show, a fireworks display, and — most famous — an annual Fireman's Muster, in which engine companies from all over New England engage in a water-squirting competition.

Another well-known event, held annually since 1959 by Detroit and neighboring Windsor, Ontario, is the International Freedom Festival staged to commemorate July 1, the date in 1867 on which Canada was granted dominion status, as well as July 4. Canadian and American dignitaries attend the celebration; parades, sports contests, concerts, and numerous other activities attract tens of thousands of spectators.

Also on a lavish scale are the two days of festivities at Birmingham, Alabama. The celebration, which encompasses varied entertainment, concerts, and military demonstrations, among other activities, is said to be one of the largest of its kind in the country.

Traditional observances of another sort highlight Native American celebrations of Independence Day. On and off the big western reservations special powwows are held on or about July 4. One of the biggest and best known of these events is the huge, three-day All Indian Powwow in Flagstaff, Arizona. Thousands of Indians from 20 or more tribes gather to participate, and many more thousands of tourists enjoy the evening ceremonials, dances and games, the encampment and rodeo. In Kotzebue, Alaska, north of the Arctic Circle, July 4 is the occasion of the annual Eskimo games, which include kayak races, and the awarding of prizes to the Eskimo who catches the biggest beluga whale.

Other Indian events scheduled for the Fourth or surrounding days include the Fourth of July Powwow at the Chippewa Red Lake Reservation in Minnesota; the celebration in Owyhee on the Duck Valley Western Shoshone Reservation in Nevada; the ceremonial dances at the Mescalero Apache Reservation in south-central New Mexico; the Nambe ceremonial held at the Nambe Waterfall, with dances performed by residents of Nambe and neighboring pueblos of New Mexico. The Wisconsin legislature has taken special note of the nation's first inhabitants by designating July 4 as Indian Rights Day and recommending that appropriate exercises be held throughout the state.

July 4 rodeos recall another aspect of the American past. Two of the nation's largest and oldest such events are the Frontier Days Rodeo held each year in Prescott, Arizona, and the West of the Pecos Rodeo held annually in Pecos, Texas. Many other rodeos — a fraction of the hundreds that take place each year — are customarily scheduled on or around the Fourth, including the Silver Spurs Rodeo in Kissimmee, Florida; Border Days in Grangeville and the rodeo at Rupert, both in Idaho; the gatherings at Lenapah and Hinton in Oklahoma; South Dakota's Black Hills Roundup in Belle Fourche; the Will Rogers Range Riders Rodeo in Amarillo, Texas; and the Cody Stampede in the Wyoming town founded by William F. ("Buffalo Bill") Cody.

A hallmark of Independence Day is the parade. In hundreds of communities large and small, local organizations arrange and participate in processions with uniformed bands and marching units and patriotic floats. An example of a small-town parade is that in Chatham, on Massachusetts' Cape Cod, which features fire department vehicles and antique automobiles. More elaborate is the one in Bridgeport, Connecticut, once the home of P. T. Barnum; this parade, staged on a grand scale as part of the city's annual Barnum Festival (see July 5), has become a tradition.

Celebrations of Independence Day are countless and as varied as the people who inhabit the nation. Race-car enthusiasts may spend the holiday watching Colorado's annual auto race up the 14,110-foot Pike's Peak or thrill to the excitement of the Medal of Honor–Firecracker 400, a 400-mile stock-car event at the Daytona International Speedway in Florida. A contest of a different kind, over 50 years old, is the six-mile footrace from the center of Seward, Alaska, to the top of Mount Marathon and back.

Two other events that add variety to Independence Day observances take place respectively in Hannibal, Missouri, and Ontario, California. In Hannibal, Mark Twain's home town, youngsters battle it out in the National Fence Painting Contest, staged annually on or near July 4 as part of the town's Tom Sawyer Days. In Ontario the attraction is a two-mile-long picnic table along Euclid Avenue. Guests provide their own lunches and view the parade and entertainment that highlight the community's July 4 Celebration and All-State picnic. Bemidji, Minnesota, holds its four-day Paul Bunyan Water Carnival, an annual event for more than a quarter century, over the Fourth of July weekend.

In a more historical vein, the restored community of Williamsburg, once the capital of Virginia, approaches the Fourth gradually, with its annual Prelude to Independence from late May to July 4. Colonial Williamsburg greets the anniversary of independence itself with the firing of 18th century cannons and the ringing of bells at the nation's second-oldest college, William and Mary, and at the venerable Bruton Parish Church.

Independence Day is celebrated not only in the states and in such outlying areas as the Commonwealth of Puerto Rico, the Panama Canal Zone, the US Virgin Islands, and the territory of Guam, but in some foreign lands as well. Although for years it was also customary for US consulates and embassies throughout the world to hold open houses and garden parties, these gatherings are now less common.

Over the years Independence Day has been selected for the inauguration of many important undertakings in the United States. Governor DeWitt Clinton of New York, for instance, turned the first sod for the digging of the Erie Canal on July 4, 1817. Charles Carroll, the last surviving signer of the Declaration of Independence, performed the same service for the construction of the Baltimore and Ohio Railroad, the country's first commercial rail transport for passengers and freight, on July 4, 1828. The cornerstones for several monuments to Washington – in Baltimore and Boonsboro, Maryland, and in Washington, D.C. – were laid on July 4, in 1815, 1827, and 1848 respectively. The French chose July 4, in 1884 for the formal presentation, in Paris, of the Statue of Liberty, their gift to the American people. The first Pacific cable was inaugurated by President Theodore Roosevelt on July 4, 1903. President Harry S. Truman declared the Philippines independent on July 4, 1946. When Alaska and Hawaii were admitted to the Union in 1959 and 1960, respectively, July 4 was the occasion for the first raising of the new American flags, as it will again be should any new states be admitted.

In years of special significance Independence Day is celebrated with special fervor. The Bicentennial of the American Revolution, commemorating events of the years 1775 through 1783, inspired plans for the most elaborate and widespread observances, especially in the climactic year of 1976 and on the focal day of July 4. But even as early as 1972 anniversary celebrations of the struggle for independence were beginning. On June 11, 1972, off a breakwater at Pawtuxet on Narragansett Bay, Rhode Islanders staged symbolically the June 9, 1772, burning of the British revenue schooner *Gaspee*. The ship had been sent to enforce the Stamp Act, and the episode is regarded by some as the first confrontation in the colonies' rebellion. The event was part of Rhode Island's Gaspee Days (June 3–11) and of the Year of the Gaspee proclaimed in Rhode Island.

Many other local Bicentennial events, programs, and projects were planned, among them the restoration of historic areas and downtown districts, the composition of operas and ballets with patriotic themes, the construction and expansion of civic centers and museums, the presentation of historic festivals and exhibits, and numerous reenactments of Revolutionary actions – including the Boston Tea Party.

Federal funding and coordination of Bicentennial events was provided by the American

Revolution Bicentennial Administration (ARBA), established by act of Congress, December 11, 1973, as the successor organization to the American Revolution Bicentennial Commission. ARBA was created "to stimulate, coordinate, schedule, and facilitate the planning and implementation of . . . activities appropriate to the commemoration of 200 years of our national heritage of individual liberty, representative government, and attainment of equal and inalienable rights." Working with state Bicentennial commissions, other federal agencies, and private and civic organizations, ARBA not only provided historical and informational materials for distribution but established standards for programs and projects; prepared a master calendar of local, state, national, and international events; and provided grants-in-aid for approved projects. ARBA was authorized to administer, in addition to appropriated funds, nonappropriated funds derived from the sale of commemorative medals struck by the US Mint.

Congress adopted three Bicentennial themes around which planners might organize their efforts: Heritage '76, a summons to place the nation's heritage in historical perspective and to focus on the unfolding panorama of American history; Festival USA, an opportunity for Americans to share among themselves and with those of other lands "the traditions, the culture, the hospitality, and the character of the United States and its people"; and Horizons '76, "a challenge to every American . . . to help make America 'the more perfect union' and to improve the quality of life for the third century."

According to one estimate, the "beautiful mosaic of individual efforts" — as ARBA director John Warner characterized the ongoing Bicentennial celebrations — involved more than 25 million Americans in preparation or attendance and cost more than $500 million in government and corporate funds. The calendar of events was crowded with a rich, almost bewildering, variety of historical, military, cultural, theatrical, technological, and ethnic programs. The following list of representative festivities and projects (some of them innovations, some of them annual events with special Bicentennial emphasis) indicates the diversity, color, and geographic range of the birthday party that began long before July 4, 1976, and continued long after: The Freedom Train (a red, white, and blue steam locomotive pulling a string of cars across the country for 21 months with a display of historic, technological, and popular artifacts); an exhibition of documents and artifacts relating to the lives of the Delaware signers of the Declaration of Independence (Wilmington); Paul Revere's Boston (fur-

niture, portraits, and silver at the Boston Museum of Fine Arts); museum exhibits in Washington, D.C. (art and furniture of the Revolutionary period; rare books, prints, and maps; a 200-year record of American women); traveling museum exhibits (Industrial Heritage U.S.A.; U.S.A.: The First 200 Years; the World of Franklin and Jefferson; The Black Presence in the Era of the American Revolution; Frontier America: The Far West); the Bicentennial Barge (a floating display featuring the early history of New York State); *The Common Glory* (a play performed at Williamsburg, Virginia); Festival of the Americas: A Latin American Salute (Miami Beach); the Aquatennial (hydroplane races, a fish fry, and an ethnic festival at Minneapolis); Spirit of America concerts (folk, jazz, rock, and gospel music at Englewood, Colorado); Mid-American Pow-Wow (Wichita, Kansas); National Hot-Air Balloon Races (Indianola, Iowa); Kamehameha Cultural Festival (Kawaihae, Hawaii); Battle of Bennington commemoration (Bennington, Vermont); Paul Bunyan Days (St. Maries, Idaho); Benedict Arnold's March on Quebec (traveling from Massachusetts to Canada); New Jersey Festival of the Ten Crucial Days (reenactments of Washington's marches, battles, and crossing of the Delaware); Yorktown Day (a solemn memorial at Yorktown, Virginia).

The events of the Bicentennial year 1976 began on January 1 with the Tournament of Roses parade in Pasadena, California, and continued with thousands of local and state commemorations — all leading up to the joyous nationwide celebration of Independence Day itself. To describe more than a few of the 23,000 holiday observances across the nation would be impossible; however, the following wide-ranging survey, written by staff reporter John L. Hess and published in the New York *Times* on July 5, 1976, details the variety, the scale, the exuberance of noteworthy activities and spectacles — many old-fashioned and traditional, though more lavish on this special day; some radical or "revolutionary" in the 20th century sense; a few unique and historic in themselves.

A Day of Picnics, Pomp, Pageantry and Protest
© 1976 by The New York Times Company.
Reprinted by permission.

The nation celebrated its 200th birthday yesterday with pageantry and prayer, with games and parades, with picnics and fireworks, with the peal of bells and the chant of protests.

It began with a flag-raising atop Mars Hill Mountain in Maine, where dawn reached the continent, and moved on to Fort McHenry, in Baltimore Harbor, where it was greeted by the rocket's red glare of the national anthem. The activities were to end nearly a day later with an indigenous festival in American Samoa.

At 2 P.M., eastern daylight time, descendants of the Revolutionaries laid hands symbolically on the Liberty Bell in Philadelphia, and bells rang in the 50 states and in American communities overseas. At Independence Hall, President Ford read the day's keynote address. Alluding to the uneasy and self-questioning mood of the country, he said:

"Liberty is a living flame to be fed, not dead ashes to be revered, even in a Bicentennial year. It is fitting that we ask ourselves hard questions, even on a glorious day like today.

"Are 'the institutions under which we live' working the way they should? Are the foundations laid in 1776 and 1789 still strong enough and sound enough to resist the tremors of our times? Are our God-given rights secure, our hard-won liberties protected?

"The very fact that we can ask these questions, that we can freely examine and criticize our society is cause for confidence in itself."

The President said that much needed to be done in the nation's third century to increase the freedom of its citizens and improve the quality of life. He ended, however, on a reiteration of American's modern role as a world standard-bearer.

"The world may or may not follow," he said, "but we lead because our whole history says we must; liberty is for all men and women as a matter of equal and unalienable right. The establishment of justice and peace abroad will in large measure depend upon the peace and justice we create here in our own country, for we still show the way."

This being an American festival, many new records were claimed: the largest cherry pie (60 square feet), at George, Washington; the largest cake (69,000 pounds), at Baltimore; the largest fireworks display, in Washington, D.C.; the largest gathering of sailing ships, in New York Harbor.

Yet many sponsors of celebrations were disappointed at the turnouts. The Philadelphia parade, planned for 70,000 marchers, drew about half that many, according to officials. They attributed this to fear of violence arising from two protest marches. Elsewhere, worry over traffic and crowding was called the reason for low turnouts.

Popular beaches were thronged, automobile races and baseball games drew holiday crowds, and much of the nation spent the day in family gatherings, linked, perhaps, to the Bicentennial by daylong television coverage. . . .

In New York, the parade of the tall ships up the Hudson caught the national spotlight. In Boston and nearby Concord and Lexington, ceremonies were relatively subdued. "Minutemen" fired a 21-musket salute over John Hancock's grave, and the USS *Constitution* fired her cannon for the first time in 95 years. At historic Faneuil Hall, the president of Boston University, John Silber, delivered a gloomy municipal oration under the title "Counterfeits of Democracy."

"Increasingly," he said, "we confuse the pursuit of happiness, guaranteed by the Declaration of Independence, with the pursuit of pleasure."

Bostonians brought the celebration to an uproarious

but peaceable conclusion . . . on the Esplanade along the Charles River. A throng that was larger than any longtime resident could remember ever assembling in the historic city, perhaps nearly half a million, crowded onto the narrow strip of park between the Back Bay and the river. They heard a rousing rendition of Tchaikovsky's "1812 Overture" played by the Boston Pops Orchestra directed by Arthur Fiedler, in his shirtsleeves.

In Washington, hundreds began the Bicentennial with nightlong vigils at the Lincoln and Jefferson Memorials. The People's Bicentennial Commission greeted the dawn at the Jefferson Memorial with a blast from a ram's horn, then led a crowd estimated at 5,000 persons in a march to the Capitol for a demonstration under a banner reading "Independence From Big Business."

Larger crowds watched an official parade, went to churches, toured the Capitol and watched a ceremonial reading of the Declaration of Independence at the National Archives Building, where a birthday cake 7 feet tall was cut and distributed to the first several hundred takers.

In the absence of President Ford, Vice President Rockefeller delivered the Bicentennial Address at the Washington Monument in the evening.

"Like every generation," he said, "we face today what seem like insurmountable problems. But the lesson of our extraordinary past is simply this: that every such challenge is an opportunity; that it has been the creative response to such challenges over these 200 years that has brought America its greatness."

Near the Washington Monument, French specialists set up 22 tons of fireworks for what was billed as the biggest such extravaganza in the country. But Vancouver, Washington, claimed the record for a single fireworks rocket, 165 pounds.

At unusual mass naturalization ceremonies, oaths of citizenship were administered to 7,141 persons, mostly exiles from Cuba, in Miami; 2,300 in Chicago and 1,000 in Detroit.

In Salt Lake City, where the official parade was held on Saturday to avoid disturbing the Sabbath, several hundred persons held a mock parade, including a Bicentennial garbage truck, a George Washington on a motorcycle, and kazoo bands. . . .

The Bicentennial menu at public and private festivals around the world was dominated by hamburgers, hot dogs, munchies and drinks in tab-top cans, but here and there folklore revived clambakes and other early Americana. There were rodeos, sack races and ox roasts.

In some towns, Indians in feathers and buckskins joined Colonials in parades. Many Indians boycotted the festivities, however.

The United States Information Agency sent Bicentennial television programs by satellite to 30 countries, including Poland and Yugoslavia. American embassies and military bases around the world held open house.

Nearly everywhere in the 50 states, the day ended with a bang. At the close of the fireworks in Washington, a battery of laser guns spelled out on the clouds, "1776-1976, Happy Birthday, USA."

Among the most elaborate and stirring spectacles of the day was Operation Sail, the State of New York's official Bicentennial event, staged in the harbor of New York City and on the Hudson River. A parade of 225 sailing ships flying the flags of 31 nations, Operation Sail was the culmination of more than four years of intensive planning. The gathering of ships got under way in May, with a transatlantic race for sail training vessels. On July 1 the assembled fleet started its procession from Newport, Rhode Island, to New York. The tallest ships sailed along the south shore of Long Island, the smaller vessels along the north through Long Island Sound and down New York City's East River.

On July 4, starting at 11:00 A.M. and led by the US Coast Guard's three-masted bark *Eagle*, the ships sailed from lower New York Bay, through the Narrows between Brooklyn and Staten Island, and thence up the Hudson as far as the George Washington Bridge. While an estimated 6 million New Yorkers and visitors jammed the Manhattan shore of the Hudson and hundreds of thousands more watched from the New Jersey side, as many as 10,000 pleasure boats thronged the waters to enjoy the pageant of sail that included a unique collection of 16 tall-masted ships — oceangoing square-rigged vessels of impressive size and with vast expanses of canvas. All day long the tall ships and the smaller craft made their stately way up and down the Hudson. The largest was the USSR's *Kruzenshtern*, a 375-foot, four-masted bark built in Germany in 1926 and used in the Australian grain trade. The last of the Cape Horners still in service, the *Kruzenshtern* was rebuilt by the Soviet Union as a schoolship to train merchant seamen. Also in the fleet were the Japanese bark *Nippon Maru* (318 feet), the Argentine full-rigged *Libertad* (338 feet), the Chilean barkentine *Esmeralda* (370 feet), and the Portuguese bark *Sagres II*, distinguished by the Maltese cross on each sail.

The ships of Operation Sail passed a 13-mile-long international naval review of US and foreign vessels anchored on either shore as part of the Independence Day salute. This flotilla of 53 modern naval ships of 23 nations — most devoted to anti-submarine warfare — included the US missile cruiser *Wainwright* (one of 23 US ships), a Dutch destroyer, 2 British frigates, 2 Israeli missile boats, and a Swedish minelayer. Viewing the sailing and naval vessels were 3,000 guests — national, international, state, and city officials — who were welcomed aboard the 80,000-ton, 1,039-foot aircraft carrier *Forrestal*, anchored near the Verrazano-Narrows Bridge. Among the officials were President Gerald R. Ford, Vice President Nelson A. Rockefeller, and the navy, state, and defense secretaries. President Ford arrived by helicopter and at 2:00 P.M. rang the ship's bells 13 times to honor the 13 colonies that had declared their independence in 1776. This bell ringing was in accordance with the White House Bicentennial Independence Day proclamation signed June 29, 1976:

. . . I, Gerald R. Ford, President of the United States of America, do hereby proclaim that the two hundredth anniversary of the adoption of the Declaration of Independence be observed by the simultaneous ringing of bells throughout the United States at the hour of two o'clock, eastern daylight time, on the afternoon of the Fourth of July, 1976, our Bicentennial Independence Day, for a period of two minutes, signifying our two centuries of independence.

I call upon civic, religious, and other community leaders to encourage public participation in this historic observance. I call upon all Americans, here and abroad, including all United States flag ships at sea, to join in this salute.

As the bells ring in our third century, as millions of free men and women pray, let every American resolve that this nation, under God, will meet the future with the same courage and dedication Americans showed the world two centuries ago. In perpetuation of the joyous ringing of the Liberty Bell in Philadelphia, let us again "proclaim liberty throughout all the land unto all the inhabitants thereof." . . .

Around the country, in small towns and large cities, Americans followed the President's example by ringing bells at 2:00 P.M. eastern daylight time. Perhaps the most extraordinary effort took place in Washington, D.C. in Washington Cathedral, where a team of men and women pulling bell ropes for 3 hours 17 minutes rang a peal of Stedman caters on the cathedral ring of 10 — a feat requiring 5,040 pulls.

In Philadelphia at least one million people were present to observe the day. At Independence Square a crowd of 25,000 heard the President, who had arrived from Valley Forge, Pennsylvania, where he signed a bill making the scene of Washington's 1777–1778 encampment a national site. Thousands more saw the Liberty Bell, which had been temporarily housed outside Independence Hall for maximum viewing and which was sounded with a rubber hammer. Hundreds of other bells in churches throughout the city took up the ringing. Along Market Street throngs watched a mammoth parade of 50,000 marchers and floats representing all 50 states.

In New Orleans traditional observances were augmented by a food festival offering Creole and Cajun dishes. On Jackson Square, near the Mississippi, crowds listened to a jazz concert honoring the great trumpeter Louis Armstrong, who was born in New Orleans on July 4, 1900.

On the Pacific Coast, the city of San Francisco celebrated the bicentennial of its own founding as well as that of the country with another sea spectacle, the Gathering of the Eagles — a regatta of some 4,000 ships from the West Coast of the United States and from other Pacific nations. Several parades were held, too, including one sponsored by the Filipino-American Council of San Francisco commemorating Philippine Independence Day.

The night of July 4 has always been the time to set the sky ablaze, and the Bicentennial provided the occasion for displays more extravagant than those of ordinary years. From the record-breaking pyrotechnics at the Washington Monument to San Francisco's presentations at Candlestick Park and Alcatraz Island in San Francisco Bay, Americans were dazzled by the brilliant effects created for this milestone anniversary. Perhaps the greatest crowds of all, estimated at hundreds of thousands, massed for the half-hour show above New York Harbor — the largest and most impressive in the city's history. A synchronized display keyed to music and commentary broadcast by radio, visible for 15 miles, and punctuated by a 200-gun salute from ships in the harbor, the exhibition was prepared with the cooperation of the US Armed Forces and other federal agencies, police and fire departments, and religious and business organizations. At the end of the spectacle, which was fired from islands and barges in the harbor, the spectators on the shore faced the Statue of Liberty — the torch illuminated in gold — to sing "The Star-Spangled Banner" as a helicopter-towed flag of red, white, and blue lights flew above. During the program those with radios heard, as they watched the fireworks explode, drum rolls, patriotic music, and stirring words, including those of Presidents George Washington, Abraham Lincoln, Ulysses S. Grant, and John F. Kennedy, and those of Julia Ward Howe, Emma Lazarus, and Martin Luther King Jr. Among the selections chosen for their relevance on Independence Day were excerpts from Lincoln's Gettysburg Address, which dedicated the nation to "a new birth of freedom," and from King's exhortation to "Let freedom ring" as his dream envisioned a time when all people might join hands and sing "Free at last! Free at last!"

Calvin Coolidge's Birthday

A prototypical New Englander, Calvin Coolidge, 30th President of the United States, was born in the tiny community of Plymouth Notch, nestled in a valley of the Green Mountains of Vermont, on July 4, 1872. He was named John Calvin for his father, but later dropped the first name.

Coolidge's paternal ancestors had immigrated to the American colonies from England in the 1630s. John Coolidge Sr. was a severe, hard-working, and frugal man who farmed and kept a country store. Books did not interest him, but business and politics did. He served two terms in the Vermont legislature. Calvin Coolidge's mother was less austere, a person who liked poetry and had a leaning toward mysticism. She died when her son was only 12, leaving the home without the benefit of her warmth.

Young Coolidge attended the Plymouth district school until 1885, when he entered the academy at Ludlow, 10 miles from his home. He completed his preparation for college at St. Johnsbury Academy, entering Amherst College in 1891. He was graduated *cum laude* in 1895. His essay "The Causes of the American Revolution" was awarded a gold medal by the American Historical Society as the best college senior essay on history.

In the autumn of 1895 Coolidge began to study law in the office of Hammond & Field in Northampton, Massachusetts, and was admitted to the bar two years later. He began his climb up the ladder of Republican politics immediately. He served on the city council of Northampton in 1899, although he had been a resident there for only four years. He was city solicitor for the next two years, and then clerk of the courts for one year. Elected to the lower house of the Massachusetts legislature, Coolidge served there in 1907 and 1908. He subsequently was mayor of Northampton in 1910 and 1911. A member of the state senate for the following three years, he served as president of that body in 1914–1915. In his address on taking the chair he stated his conception of the nature of law:

Men do not make laws. They do but discover them. Laws must be justified by something more than the will of the majority. They must rest on the eternal foundation of righteousness. That state is the most fortunate which has the aptest instruments for the discovery of laws.

Beginning in 1916 Coolidge served three successive one-year terms as lieutenant governor of Massachusetts. Elected governor in 1918, he then held that office for two terms (1919 and 1920).

The steady success of Coolidge in politics was due partly to the lack of bossism in Massachusetts politics at the time, a situation that enabled men of ability to rise quickly. It was also due to Coolidge's personality, which was well suited to the times. His celebrated (public) taciturnity — as he said, "I have never been hurt by what I have not said" — and his patent integrity would become an increasingly welcome contrast to the flamboyance and political abuses of the Prohibition era. Coolidge personified to a remarkable degree the traits admired in New England — thrift, industry, honesty, common sense, and simple living — a heritage claimed from Puritan forebears and frequently seasoned, as in Coolidge, with terse wit. Throughout his career he worked for a government of low taxes and balanced budgets. Having been a good student, he continued his reading beyond school and applied his academic talents to his political life. He derived much of his success from the fact that he generally knew more than anyone else about any legislative matter under review.

As governor, Coolidge captured the national spotlight in 1919 with his deployment of the state militia to keep order after Boston's police had struck for higher wages and better working conditions. When police authorities refused to reinstate the strikers, the entire police force was dismissed and replaced. Coolidge, replying to the objections of Samuel Gompers, president of the American Federation of Labor, asserted that "there is no right to strike against the public safety by anybody, anywhere, any time." His response to the public concern for law and order was greeted by nationwide approval, and Coolidge rode on a wave of popularity to another term as governor.

While silent himself, Coolidge was happy enough to hear others push his name forward as a possible nominee for national office. This happened at Chicago in 1920, when Warren G. Harding was pressed on the Republican National Convention as the party's candidate for President by a cabal of powerful senators and politicos. When the business of selecting a vice presidential candidate came before the convention, the delegates, rebelling against further dictation by party bosses, began to stamp and shout for Coolidge at the mere mention of his name. He was nominated on the first ballot by 647½ votes. The Republican ticket was elected and Coolidge began his national career on March 4, 1921.

On August 2, 1923, fate thrust the presidency upon Silent Cal, as he was affectionately called, when President Harding died suddenly while returning from a trip to Alaska. The news of Harding's death reached Coolidge while he was visiting his father in Plymouth, Vermont. At 2:47 A.M. on August 3, he took the oath of office by the light of a kerosene lamp in the sitting room of the house. It was administered by his father, who was a justice of the peace. Arriving in Washington, Coolidge took the oath again and officially assumed the responsibilities of the presidency.

Said the laconic Coolidge later, "I thought I could swing it." It was his image of absolute incorruptibility that brought the Republican party safely through the storm of Harding administration scandals, which were revealed shortly after Harding's death. As President, Coolidge quietly effected a reformation in the administration. His opposition to immediate payment of a veterans' bonus brought him further admiration as a man of principle. Thus he entered the 1924 Republican National Convention with increased popularity. He won both the nomination and the election, buoyed by the country's apparent economic boom.

All was not well, however. Farmers in particular had not shared the illusive prospect of endless prosperity. Their skepticism was to prove justified. Coolidge, who was fond of posing for pictures as an old country farmer, actually had little real empathy for either farmers or industrial workers. He was however, full of admiration for such industrial giants as Henry Ford and John D. Rockefeller. The outstanding feature of Coolidge's program, if it could be called a program, was a laissez-faire attitude toward big business and industry, coupled with governmental inaction on emerging economic problems. He stood in favor of high tariffs, low taxes, reduced immigration quotas, economy in government, and noninvolvement in international affairs.

Though it came with a built-in loophole (someone else might choose what he did not), Coolidge's statement in August 1927 that he did "not choose to run" for the presidency in 1928 was taken as a refusal. Even if the impression of nonavailability was mistaken, as some historians now believe, it is possible that Coolidge's reticence prevented clarification. In any event the Republican party looked elsewhere for a candidate and chose Herbert Hoover, who had served ably as secretary of commerce under Harding and Coolidge.

Coolidge retired to Northampton, Massachusetts, where he bought a large house. He had planned to practice law and read, but his health failed. His spirit, too, flagged during the Great Depression, which descended upon the nation in 1929 and which was seen as the result of his economic policies and lack of foresight. The country nonetheless was genuinely grieved at Coolidge's sudden death on January 5, 1933. He was buried in a rural cemetery at Plymouth Notch, Vermont, not far from the little white house where he was born. The Coolidge Birthplace is now restored as part of the Plymouth Historic District, which also includes the general store and post office, which his parents ran, and the Coolidge Homestead, where he grew up. The Homestead is preserved as it was when

Coolidge took the presidential oath there in 1923. Visitors are welcomed at the Birthplace and the Homestead from late May until mid-October and at the store throughout the year. Coolidge's name is also commemorated in the Calvin Coolidge State Forest, in Pinney Hollow off Calvin Coolidge Memorial Highway.

Farther south — in Northampton, Massachusetts, where Coolidge got his start in politics — is the Calvin Coolidge Memorial Room of the Forbes Library, which has on display his papers and mementos. The yellow brick Masonic Building on Northampton's Main Street housed his law office. Coolidge's early home in Northampton can be seen at 21 Massasoit Street, as can The Beeches, the handsome, postpresidential home in which he died, on Hampton Terrace.

Stephen Foster's Birthday

The anniversary of the birth of composer Stephen Foster, on July 4, 1826, is observed in conjunction with Independence Day festivities at the Stephen Foster Memorial in White Springs, Florida. For a biography of Foster and details of other observances related to him, see Stephen Foster Memorial Day, January 13.

Nathaniel Hawthorne's Birthday

Nathaniel Hawthorne, who probed deep into the human soul with his novels and tales to become one of the country's greatest writers of fiction, was born on July 4, 1804, in Salem, Massachusetts. He was greatly concerned with the implications and effects of sin, a preoccupation inherited in large part from his Puritan ancestors. These included William Hathorne — (as the name was originally spelled) — one of the settlers of the Massachusetts Bay Colony under Governor John Winthrop and later a magistrate in Salem. Both William Hathorne, who ordered a Quaker woman whipped in public, and his son, John, who was a judge at the infamous Salem witch trials, seem to have exemplified the stern and intolerant aspect of Puritanism.

Nathaniel Hawthorne's own father, a sea captain, died in a distant port when his son was four. Although young Hawthorne had three sisters, he grew up with books as his chief companions. He gained an intimate knowledge of Puritan history and wondered whether his family's declining fortunes could be punishment for the crimes his ancestors had committed in the name of righteousness.

After his graduation in 1825 from Bowdoin College in Brunswick, Maine, where he knew Longfellow and Franklin Pierce, Hawthorne returned to his mother's home in Salem, where he lived for a dozen years in almost complete solitude. Ostensibly uneventful, they actually were years of intense, crucial effort. With liberal use of a wastebasket, which received much of his output, he trained himself in the art of writing.

His first important work — apart from *Fanshawe*, an undistinguished novel of college life, which he brought out anonymously and at his own expense in 1828 — was a collection of what he called *Twice-Told Tales*, published earlier in various magazines, which appeared in 1837, and in an enlarged edition in 1842. The collection contained many of the tales now regarded as classics, among them moral allegories such as the story called "The Ambitious Guest," in which the narrator relates — in a mountain inn just below the avalanche that is about to destroy him — his hopes for earthly immortality; and the poignant story "The Minister's Black Veil." Among other tales in the collection were historical sketches, such as "Endicott and the Red Cross" and "The Maypole of Merry Mount," in which Hawthorne chose crises in colonial Puritan history as his jumping-off point for attacks against such vices as pride, hypocrisy, self-righteousness, bigotry, and cruelty.

Still lacking sufficient funds to provide a living, Hawthorne in 1839 secured a post in the Boston Custom House with the help of his friend Pierce. By 1841, however, he was back at his literary endeavors, producing several children's books — *Grandfather's Chair, Famous Old People, Liberty Tree, Biographical Stories for Children* — and spending some months at the Transcendentalists' utopian Brook Farm, on a site near West Roxbury, Massachusetts, which can still be visited.

He meanwhile had fallen in love with the lively and artistic Sophia Peabody, one of Boston's famous Peabody sisters. They were married in 1842 and moved to the Old Manse at Concord, Massachusetts. The house, which still stands, was the scene of days full of flowers, books, writing, and loving companionship, as reported in Hawthorne's *Passages from the American Notebooks*, published much later, and in his essay, "The Old Manse." More immediately, it provided the title for a second collection of tales, *Mosses from an Old Manse* (1846), which, like its predecessor, was more of an artistic than a financial success. Unable to pay the rent, Hawthorne and his family moved to his mother's home in Salem late in 1845. By 1846 he had pulled political strings to secure a position in the Custom House at Salem, which he held until a Whig victory over the Democrats caused his dismissal three years later.

His unwelcome leisure made it possible for him to produce his masterpiece *The Scarlet Let-*

ter, published in 1850. One of the greatest of all American novels, the book exemplifies Hawthorne's deftness in dissecting human character, his mastery of symbolism, his skill in creating a pervasive and almost hypnotic mood. With the gentle, deep, relentless probing of conscience and guilt that was his custom, he tenderly, perceptively, and frighteningly detailed the lives of four persons living in the age of stringent Puritan punishments: the relatively fortunate Hester Pyrnne, whose sin of adultery, proclaimed by the scarlet "A" she is forced to wear, is open and confessed; the Puritan minister Arthur Dimmesdale, whose hypocrisy in concealing his role as her partner brings him to the verge of insanity; Pearl, the small flicker of sunshine who is their daughter; and Hester's lost husband, the once-humane Roger Chillingworth, who sacrifices his soul in his determination for revenge. As in other Hawthorne works, the message is an essentially Christian one — that inevitable as sin is in human nature, it is not the irrevocable end. There are always possible those lessons of the human heart — humility, remorse, confession of fault, loss of self-concern, subservience to divine will — that could lead to redemption.

After publication of the book, which made Hawthorne famous, he moved near Lenox, Massachusetts, where he became friendly with Herman Melville, a resident of nearby Pittsfield, and wrote his somber *House of the Seven Gables* (1851), in which the sin of the father is visited upon successive generations. The house of the title can be visited in Salem today. The novel was succeeded by *The Blithedale Romance* (1852), which drew upon Brook Farm as its setting; by a collection of great tales titled *The Snow Image and Other Twice-Told Tales* (1852); and by two of Hawthorne's famous children's books: *A Wonder-Book for Girls and Boys* (1852) and *Tanglewood Tales* (1853).

In the spring of 1852 Hawthorne purchased a large house known as The Wayside, which is still on view in Concord. There he again enjoyed the companionship, without sharing the optimistic philosophy of, some of the Transcendentalist reformers. (True reform, he felt, could only be of the human heart, and all else was useless.) They included Thoreau; Emerson, whose family had owned the Old Manse before the Hawthornes lived there; and the Alcotts, who preceded the Hawthornes as residents of The Wayside. It was in this house that Hawthorne produced a campaign biography of Franklin Pierce, who was elected President in 1852.

Hawthorne was rewarded in 1853 with a lucrative appointment, as US consul in Liverpool, England. He resigned at the end of Pierce's term, in 1857, but remained abroad, traveling with his family for the next two years in Italy — which was the setting of *The Marble Faun,* a novel that reexamined the problem of evil, exploring the possible contribution of sin, and remorse, to spiritual maturity. The book was published in 1860, the year the Hawthornes returned home to Concord and the year in which his health began to fail mysteriously. *Our Old Home* (1863), containing some of the material from his English journals, was the last book published during his lifetime. He died in his sleep the night of May 18/19, 1864, in Plymouth, New Hampshire, where he was on a trip with his friend Pierce.

The centennial of Hawthorne's death was noted in a number of places, among them his alma mater, Bowdoin College, which held a symposium on the American novel. (Bowdoin has long awarded an annual Hawthorne short story prize.) In New York City the Grolier Club mounted an exhibit including a striking collection of Hawthorne first editions, as well as letters and newspaper accounts relating to his life and works.

JULY 5

P. T. Barnum's Birthday

P. T. Barnum, the showman, would rejoice at the show that takes place around the time of his July 5 birthday each year in Bridgeport, Connecticut, where he lived and served as mayor. Known as the Barnum Festival, the celebration began in 1949 and was observed with particular enthusiasm in the Barnum sesquicentennial year of 1960 and in its silver jubilee year of 1973. The 10-day festival was expanded in 1975 to last six weeks, beginning in late May. More than a million people joined the festivities in Bridgeport and the surrounding participating towns.

The festival has a few solemn moments on (or near) Barnum's birthday, when festival officials participate in memorial ceremonies at his statue in Seaside Park and place flowers on his grave in Mountain Grove Cemetery. But before then come a good many events that Barnum himself might have preferred. They begin with the Lions Kickoff dinner, with dancing until dawn, and presentation of a symbolic whip and whistle to the festival's ringmaster — who has earned the honor through yearlong labor as chief executive of the festival.

Other traditional events include a Wing Ding with a children's parade featuring miniature floats, prizes for best entries, clowns, elephants, circus acts, and free lemonade; the Champions on Parade Show, in which five award-winning drum and bugle corps compete for the Barnum Festival trophy; an art show; an antique show; and a carnival midway with rides, sideshows, and nightly entertainment by area bands, novelty acts, tumblers, and singers. Festival events are presided over by a king and queen selected from area high schools on the basis of character, poise, personality, and scholarship. Coronation of the two takes place during an evening of entertainment by headline performers. Winners of other festival-connected contests bring to mind two of Barnum's greatest discoveries: singer Jenny Lind — the winner of a vocal competition becomes her namesake during festival events — and Tom Thumb. The celebrated midget, who in real life was Charles Stratton, was married to the diminutive Lavinia Warren; the two are represented during the festival by winners of a contest for elementary-school children.

The high point of the festival is one of the nation's largest street processions: the annual Fourth of July parade with clowns, floats, marching units, and bands. Sometimes the parade is held on the Sunday nearest July 4, rather than on Independence Day itself. On one of the last evenings, the festival is climaxed by an exhibition of fireworks that has been described, in prose worthy of Barnum himself, as "a sky-shattering display of aerial pyrotechnics." It originates from Seaside Park, the shorefront area that was his gift to the city, but can be seen from other locations as well.

Publicity genius, hoaxer par excellence, and the greatest showman of his day, Phineas Taylor Barnum was born in Bethel, near Danbury, Connecticut, on July 5, 1810. Until he went to New York City at the age of 24, he pursued a variety of unremarkable occupations and edited an antislavery newspaper in Danbury.

No one knows when — or whether — he issued the famous pronouncement "There's a sucker born every minute." But his career in show business indicates that such a thought may have crossed his mind. His rise as impresario began in 1835 with his purchase and exhibition of a black woman named Joice Heth, aged about 80. He claimed she was 161 and said she had been the nurse of George Washington.

He followed this first test of public credulity by purchasing Scudder's American Museum and Peale's Museum in 1841 and using their combined collections for his new American Museum, which he directed in New York City from 1842 until 1865. Apart from the humor, ingenuity, and gall, which were part of all Barnum enterprises, the museum included legitimate curios, a menagerie, and stellar attractions, which he pro-

moted with the extravagant advertising that made him famous. They included the woolly horse; the "original" Siamese twins, Chang and Eng; the Fiji mermaid (constructed from the top half of a monkey and the bottom half of a fish); and — last and least — the "Egress." More than 20 million people viewed the celebrated midget General Tom Thumb in the museum and during his triumphant tour of the Continent, with Barnum, in 1844.

One of Barnum's greatest coups took place in 1850, when he engaged the Swedish singer Jenny Lind for a 95-concert tour of the eastern United States. As a result of his skillful promotion, tickets brought fabulous prices — $650 in one case — when they were auctioned off before concerts. The tour netted $176,675 for Lind, and a still more robust $500,000 for Barnum.

He retired in 1855 to Iranistan, one of several homes he had in Bridgeport. He subsequently became mayor of the city and served in the Connecticut legislature.

When misfortune struck, in the form of bankruptcy brought on by unwise business ventures, it revealed only that Barnum's resourcefulness was as alive as ever. He reopened his American Museum in New York and embarked on his last great speculation — The Greatest Show on Earth, a circus-menagerie that he opened in Brooklyn in 1871. It became a huge enterprise 10 years later, when Barnum joined his foremost competitor to form the Barnum & Bailey Circus. One of its greatest attractions was Jumbo, a six-and-one-half-ton elephant purchased by Barnum from London's Royal Zoological Society. "The only mastodon left on earth," as he termed Jumbo, is preserved at the Barnum Museum of Natural History, founded at Tufts University in honor of Barnum, a university trustee, in 1883. Barnum's other contributions to circus history included addition of a second, and later a third, ring to the circus. The innovation, which delighted spectators and distressed performers, started a trend that still distinguishes the US circus from the European.

Flamboyant though he was, and delighting in his own notoriety, the fun-loving Barnum led a respectable personal life and as a showman drew his own distinct, if personal, line between fraud and what he regarded as harmless hoax. Among other things, the pioneer publicist was author of several books — *The Art of Money Getting, How I Made Millions, The Humbugs of the World,* and an autobiography.

Barnum died on April 7, 1891, in Philadelphia, requesting with his last breath to know the circus's receipts that day. Barnum & Bailey was sold to the Ringling brothers in 1907. As Ringling Brothers and Barnum & Bailey Circus, it is still billed under Barnum's original slogan, The Greatest Show on Earth.

Barnum bequeathed a sum of money, to which his wife added, for the erection of the Barnum Institute of Science and History in Bridgeport. Along with offices, the imposing three-story Victorian structure on the corner of Main and Gilbert streets housed special exhibits and Barnum memorabilia. Since its renovation in 1967 it has been known as the Barnum Museum. It contains materials pertaining to Barnum's childhood and to his political and civic life, as well as to his career as a showman; furniture from his home, a life-size portrait, circus relics, and the stuffed hide of one of his elephants are among the varied exhibits. The displays on one floor depict the history of Bridgeport. Also on view is a 3,000-year-old Egyptian mummy.

Other Barnum memorabilia in Bridgeport are found in the Bridgeport Public Library, at Broad and State streets, and in the circus gallery of the Museum of Art, Science and Industry at 4450 Park Avenue.

David Farragut's Birthday

David Glasgow Farragut, the most famous Union naval officer of the American Civil War, was born on July 5, 1801, in Campbell's Station, Tennessee, a few miles southwest of Knoxville. His father, George, the son of Spanish parents, served with distinction in both the patriot land and sea forces during the American Revolution. After the colonies won independence, George Farragut settled in Tennessee and married Elizabeth Shine, a young woman of Scottish descent.

In 1807 President Thomas Jefferson appointed the senior Farragut sailing master of the US Navy, and the family moved to New Orleans. David's mother died there when he was seven, and after the age of nine, he never saw his father again. Fortunately Commander David Porter, in charge of the New Orleans naval station, adopted the youngster in gratitude for the care that the Farragut family had previously given his own father during his final illness.

On December 17, 1810, the secretary of the navy, at Porter's request, appointed the 9-year-old boy a midshipman, and in 1811 he went on his first voyage on his guardian's frigate, the *Essex*. During the War of 1812 the *Essex* cruised in the Pacific Ocean and made several captures. The young Farragut performed his shipboard duties well, and when Porter decided to take the captured enemy vessels to the Chilean port of Valparaiso, he made his 12-year-old protégé the master of one of the prizes, the *Alexander Barclay*. This trip marked the end of Farragut's service in the War of 1812. The British ships *Phoebe* and *Cherub* trapped and sank the *Essex* in Valparaiso harbor on March 28, 1814. Farragut was captured and remained a prisoner until November 1814.

Farragut spent the years 1815 to 1820 sailing the Mediterranean Sea on the line ships *Independence*, *Washington*, and *Franklin* as an aide, successively, to Commodores Bainbridge and Chauncey and Captain Gallagher. The young man then accompanied his naval schoolmaster, Charles Folsom, to his new post as American consul to Tunis. The young Farragut spent nine months there and undertook studies in French, Italian, English literature, and mathematics.

In 1821 he returned to the United States and in the following year sailed on board the *John Adams*, which was carrying Joel R. Poinsett, the American envoy to Mexico, to Veracruz. Subsequently Farragut was reunited with Porter, when he sailed in the commodore's antipirate Mosquito fleet for two years. During this tour Porter gave the young man command of his first ship, the *Ferret*.

David Farragut married Susan C. Marchant of Norfolk, Virginia, on September 24, 1823. He was devoted to his wife and nursed her through 16 years of illness until her death in 1840. On December 26, 1843, Farragut married Virginia Loyall, the daughter of a prominent Norfolk resident. As both his spouses came from the same city, Farragut felt strong ties with Norfolk and made it his home until 1861.

Meanwhile promoted to lieutenant in 1825, Farragut sailed in the same year on the *Brandywine*, which returned the Marquis de Lafayette to France after his famous American tour. During the next 15 years, a slack period for the US Navy, he gained additional experience sailing in the waters off Mexico and Brazil. In September 1841 he won the rank of commander and took charge of the sloop *Decatur*.

The Mexican War of 1846 to 1848 gave valuable experience to many American military leaders, but Farragut found it a period of excruciating frustration. Not until February 1847 did the navy respond to his request for duty in the Gulf of Mexico and grant him command of the sloop *Saratoga*. But even this assignment failed to satisfy him, for he received only insignificant blockading assignments in the gulf waters.

Commander Farragut held a variety of posts in the 1850s. He served as assistant inspector of ordnance and in 1854 published the results of his research in this field in *Experiments to Ascertain the Strength and Endurance of Navy Guns.* In August 1854 he left for the West to establish a navy yard at Mare Island, California; he received his captaincy there in 1855. He returned East at the end of the decade and spent the crucial winter of 1860-1861, when the Confederate States of America was being formed by secessionist Southern states, in Norfolk.

On April 17, 1861, less than a week after the outbreak of the Civil War, the Virginia Secession Convention passed the ordinance that took Virginia out of the Union. Farragut was unable to accept this decision, and on the following day moved his family north, to the village of Hastings-on-the-Hudson in New York. He remained there until September, when he was made a member of the naval board that had convened at New York.

Farragut's decision to leave his Virginia home in order to remain loyal to the federal government favorably impressed the Northern authorities. On January 9, 1862, he was appointed commander of the Gulf of Mexico Blockading Squadron, and on the 20th he received orders to destroy the defenses guarding New Orleans and to capture the city. Farragut set sail on February 2 from Hampton Roads in the new steamer sloop *Hartford*, which served as his flagship on the mission.

By mid-April the Union task force was ready to begin its operation against a formidable enemy. Fort Jackson on the west side of the Mississippi, Fort St. Philip on the east, and a flotilla supporting them formed the Confederate defense chain interposed between Farragut and New Orleans. On April 18 Union navy commander David D. Porter — the son of Farragut's foster father — opened the battle by bombarding Fort Jackson. His efforts continued for several days without marked effect.

Farragut finally broke the deadlock with the daring decision to run his ships past the forts without completing their destruction. At dawn on April 24 he sailed his 17 vessels past the fortifications. Despite heavy enemy fire, all but three were successful. Next, the Union forces engaged and destroyed the Confederate flotilla. This action stripped New Orleans of its defenses, and on April 25 the port surrendered to Farragut. President Lincoln and the Congress were properly grateful to the audacious sea leader and in July officially conferred on him and his men the thanks of the nation. On July 30 Farragut received a promotion to rear admiral; he was the first man to hold that rank in the US Navy.

Blockade duties, necessary but uninspiring, occupied most of Farragut's time for the next year. In August 1863, however, he was able to

visit New York, where he was greeted with enthusiasm. The city's chamber of commerce officially congratulated him, and the Union League Club presented him with a sword and a gold and silver scabbard.

Admiral Farragut sailed from New York in January 1864 for the Gulf of Mexico to command an assault on Alabama's Mobile Bay at the mouth of the Mobile River. Fort Morgan on the east side and Fort Gaines on the west protected the entrance to the bay, which was blocked by mines or "torpedoes," except for a narrow passage lane. On August 5 Farragut attempted to breech the defenses; four ironclads led his 14 wooden ships.

The Federal ironclad *Tecumseh* struck a mine and sank, carrying down all aboard. Immediately the warning "Torpedoes ahead" went up, and the advance slowed. Farragut was undeterred; "Damn the torpedoes!" he ordered and his ship, the *Hartford*, took the lead. The Union armada soon passed the forts, dispersing the Confederate flotilla, and Mobile Bay fell to Farragut. Fort Gaines surrendered two days later on August 7 and Fort Morgan on August 23, completing the blockade of Mobile, which had been the last important Confederate port on the Gulf coast.

In December 1864 President Lincoln appointed Farragut to the newly created rank of vice admiral, and in July 1866 he received another unprecedented promotion, to admiral. Like the vice admiralcy, the rank was created especially for him. Sixty-five years of life and long service in Southern waters had taken their toll on Farragut by this time, and the government granted the navy's first admiral a leave of absence to recuperate. He again went to New York and, with a gift of $50,000 bestowed on him by the city's foremost citizens, bought a residence there.

Farragut was given command of the navy's European Squadron in April 1867 and he set sail on the *Franklin*. His visit to the Old World turned into a goodwill tour that lasted until his return to New York on November 10, 1869. He then toured various places in the United States. He died during one such trip on August 14, 1870. President Ulysses S. Grant and members of his cabinet went to New York City to attend the funeral service on September 30. He was interred at Woodlawn Cemetery the same day.

Several likenesses of Admiral Farragut may be seen along the East Coast. Augustus Saint-Gaudens's statue, which was commissioned by the Farragut Monument Association and unveiled in 1881, stands in Madison Square in New York City; Vinnie Ream's bronze statue of the admiral, which was done at the request of the federal government and was also completed in

1881, is the focal point of Farragut Square in Washington, D.C.; and H. H. Kitson's statue of Farragut, which was erected in 1893, is an attraction in Boston's Marine Park. Graduates of the US Naval Academy donated the stained glass windows that honor the admiral in the academy's chapel in Annapolis, Maryland.

JULY 6

The National Cherry Festival

This is a movable event. See note on page xxvi.

The National Cherry Festival, honoring one of Michigan's chief crops, is held annually in July in Traverse City, Michigan. Usually lasting the better part of the week, it is scheduled during the first full week after Independence Day. In 1970 the 44th gala, which opened on Monday, July 6, drew approximately 300,000 people to the city of 20,000, which is located on Lake Michigan's Grand Traverse Bay. During the years following 1970, the festival attracted greater and greater numbers of people; in 1975 more than half a million persons attended.

The 1970 festival opened with a two-minute Salute of Noise, followed by an official opening of the festivities by the mayor of Traverse City. Then a procession of cars circled the Old Mission Peninsula, where hundreds of thousands of trees were heavy with cherries. The streets were lined with groups of singers, whose music was broadcast over local radio stations, as was the traditional blessing of the cherries in ceremonies at the orchards. Other Monday events — in addition to the opening of the midway — were frog and turtle races, a pet show, and open houses at the US Coast Guard Air Station and on the Coast Guard cutter *Mackinaw*. Monday afternoon marked the beginning of the cherry orchard tours, which were conducted through Friday. The festival's first day was climaxed by the arrival at Clinch Park Marina of the National Cherry Queen and her court, chosen from among some 20 Michigan contestants during competitions held in late June. The young women (each in her own boat) were brought into the Marina in a formation called a Royal Wedge. On arrival they were greeted by the young princes and princesses, garbed in red velvet and wearing crowns laden with cherries. After dark Grand Traverse Bay was the scene of a colorful Venetian Night boat parade, the first of the week's five festive processions.

Tuesday was designated Children's Day at the midway. The day's events included a cherry pie eating contest, a junior cherry-recipe baking contest, a simulated air-sea rescue, a cherry hunt for children, and a beach party for teenagers. Also on Tuesday was the opening of Cherry Lane, featuring specially built booths where cherry products and festival souvenirs could be purchased and viewed throughout the week. Fresh cherries, cherry ice cream, cherry fudge, baked cherry goods, cherry pizzas, and a host of other cherry specialities, including such gift items as cherry jewelry, were among the items exhibited on Cherry Lane.

Among activities on Wednesday were the second annual bicycle race, covering a 12½-mile course; a repeat of Tuesday's pie-eating contest; and the National Cherry Festival fashion show and luncheon. Additional events included a matinee at the local playhouse — which gave special performances throughout the week — and a second cherry hunt for children. In the evening a Festival of Balloons parade took place, in which floats, a variety of old (and some new) cars, dragsters, and dune buggies used balloons as their primary decorations.

Thursday again provided entertainment for children and a cherry bake-fest, as well as an open house at the US Coast Guard Air Station, and concerts at different locations by half a dozen high school bands. One of the day's highlights was the popular youth parade, held in the afternoon. Storytime in Cherryland, the theme of the 1970 event, called forth a profusion of youthful, costumed figures representing storybook characters of all descriptions. The parade, full of decorated floats and marching, musical, and twirling groups, was followed by another climactic feature, the sixth annual John Minnema Memorial High School Band Competition and Pageant, held at Thirlby Field. Nine high school bands from three states competed for the Governor's Trophy in this contest, which got off to a spectacular and deafening start when the bands marched onto the field for a mass rendition of "The Star-Spangled Banner." The bands then separated and performed the individual routines that have made this event the musical high point of the festival.

Friday was marked by the governor's reception and press conference, which was open to the public; by more high school band concerts; and by the cherry smorgasbord luncheon, which the governor and other dignitaries attended. In the afternoon a Grand Cherry Royale parade was held, and during the evening there was a display of fireworks over Grand Traverse Bay, and the President's Ball.

Saturday afternoon was the time for the equestrians' delight, the eagerly awaited parade of horses stepping along in mounted patrols, matched teams, and special units. Sailing fans too had their day on Saturday, with the afternoon regatta on Grand Traverse Bay. The day's schedule also included matinee and evening rodeo performances; a square dance; and the Cherry Festival concert. Like other concerts scheduled for evenings during the festival week, the last event was held at the National Music Camp at Interlochen Center for the Arts, 15 miles south of Traverse City.

After an informal, nondenominational worship service, the festival was concluded on Sunday with yet another rodeo show and more sailing races.

During the 1970s some changes were made in the festival events. Some were scheduled on a different day. The nature of some events was altered, as in the case of the beach party for teenagers, which in 1972 was incorporated into an Aqua Fun frolic for ages 7 to 17. A few events have been discontinued, among them the President's Ball.

A number of major new events have been added to the already full festival calendar. Most are sporting competitions: a tennis tournament, canoe and foot races, and waterskiing shows. Also of note are a young people's art exhibit, and antique and arts and crafts shows and sales. The festival fashion show and luncheon has been named the Royal Pageant of Fashion and Luncheon since 1971, and beginning in 1972 the youth parade has been known as the Junior Royale.

Since 1971 the three big parades of the week have been Heritage on Parade, the Junior Royale, and the Cherry Royale. Heritage on Parade, the opening parade on Wednesday evening, blends past, present, and future, partly in a serious manner and partly in a spirit of fun and frivolity. The Junior Royale takes place on Thursday afternoon. And the grandest of the parades, the Cherry Royale, is held Friday afternoon with specially selected bands, floats, and marching units.

The festival celebrates one of Michigan's chief agricultural and processing enterprises. The state has over 2 million cherry trees; it ranks first among the states in the production of cherries. Large-scale cherry growing began in the early 1890s, with the rediscovery of what pioneer farmers had learned earlier: that the region's combination of climate and light soils was perfect for the production of cherries.

To growers, who faced the threats of winterkill, spring frosts, and pests, cherry growing was an annual gamble. In 1923 the churches of the Grand Traverse Bay region were asked to pray for the success of the harvest. From this came the Blessing of the Blossoms ceremony, begun the following year and held in the orchards on a Sunday in May when the cherry bloom is at its peak. In 1926 the area held its first celebration of the harvest – in July, when the cherries had reached perfection. Attended by some 3,000 persons, the observance lasted one day and consisted of a parade and the coronation of a queen. Two years later the harvest celebration was designated as the National Cherry Festival by Michigan's state legislature.

In 1935 the managers of the festival recalled the apocryphal story of George Washington and the cherry tree told by Parson Weems in his short biography of the first President. They had a tree dug from a Michigan orchard and transported to the grounds of the boyhood home of Washington, where it was transplanted on February 22 by George Steptoe Washington of Philadelphia, a collateral descendant. He was assisted by Anna May York of Traverse City, the festival queen for 1934.

Over the years the festival has grown from one day to six or seven days beginning in 1968.

Republican Party Founded

The Republican party arose in a period of widespread popular dissatisfaction with existing political organizations. Although there is much controversy surrounding the exact date and place of its beginnings, July 6, the anniversary of the 1854 meeting at Jackson, Michigan, which selected the party's first statewide slate of candidates is considered by many the occasion of the party's founding.

Slavery was the issue around which the party was built. The Missouri Compromise had temporarily forestalled the impending conflict over the future of the institution in 1820. In that year Henry Clay of Kentucky engineered an agreement that allowed Missouri to enter the Union as a slave state, while banning slavery in the rest of the Louisiana Purchase area north of latitude 36°30′. Such a solution was only a temporary expedient: it would maintain sectional peace only as long as there were equal numbers of slave and free states.

In 1850 the admission of California as a free state ended this balance. The South, with nowhere to expand, seemed doomed to remain a minority section. Then in 1854 Senator Stephen A. Douglas of Illinois proposed "popular sovereignty" for the Kansas-Nebraska territories in an effort to gain Southern support for the central transcontinental railroad route he favored. The South quickly rallied to his cause, and on May 30, 1854, Douglas's Kansas-Nebraska Act voided the 1820 settlement and allowed the inhabitants of those regions, both located above the 36°30′ demarcation, to choose whether or not they would allow slavery.

Even before the Kansas-Nebraska Act became law the many Northerners dismayed by its projected violation of the Missouri Compromise realized that they were unable to act effectively against it. This was particularly true in view of the unsatisfactory political alternatives then before them. The Whig party was moribund and the Democratic party was split — between the Southern "slavocracy," supporting Douglas, on the one hand, and those unalterably opposed to the expansion of slavery on the other.

Creation of a new party seemed the only answer. On February 28, 1854, Ripon, Wisconsin, became the site of an important early meeting that led in this direction. The 50 dissident Whigs, Democrats, and Free-Soilers who met there to denounce Douglas's measure, then still before Congress, determined to set up a new party. Allen Bovay, an organizer of this gathering, persuaded Horace Greeley, the editor of the influential New York *Tribune*, to urge dissident factions throughout the North to adopt the name *Republican*.

The new party grew rapidly. Republican candidates ran for state and congressional offices in 1854, and on February 22, 1856, an informal meeting in Pittsburgh called for a national convention in Philadelphia on June 17 to select candidates for President and Vice President. All the Northern states were represented, as well as Maryland, Virginia, and Kentucky; the territories of Minnesota, Nebraska, and Kansas; and the District of Columbia. Robert Emmet of New York, formerly a Democrat, was the temporary chairman and Colonel Henry S. Lane of Indiana the permanent presiding officer.

Colonel John C. Frémont, the explorer and onetime senator from California, won the new party's presidential nomination and William L. Dayton of New Jersey was the choice for Vice President. The platform supported Congress's right and obligation to bar slavery from the territories. James Buchanan of Pennsylvania, the Democratic candidate, won the 1856 election with 174 electoral votes, but Frémont made an impressive showing with 114 electoral votes, comprising those of 11 of the 16 free states. Millard Fillmore, the standard-bearer of the nativist American (Know-Nothing) party, won only Maryland's eight votes.

Republicans won control of the House of Representatives in 1858, and prospects looked good for 1860. That year the national convention met on May 16 at the Chicago Wigwam and selected Abraham Lincoln as the presidential nominee on the third ballot. Hannibal Hamlin of Maine became his running mate.

The 1860 Republican platform emphasized the nonextension of slavery, but there were other planks as well. The party advocated a protective tariff, homestead legislation, and a transcontinental railroad. Such a well-balanced program reflected the diversity of people under the Republican banner. The majority of the new party's faithful were former Whigs, but many of other persuasions also joined; indeed, one-half of the delegates at the 1860 gathering were former Democrats.

Abraham Lincoln received less than 40 percent of the popular vote, but won the four-cornered election. He garnered 180 electoral votes in contrast to 72 for the Southern Democrat John C. Breckinridge of Kentucky and 39 for Constitutional Unionist John Bell of Tennessee. Stephen A. Douglas, the Democratic candidate, finished second in the popular vote, but received only 12 votes in the electoral college.

Lincoln's victory in 1860 inaugurated almost three-quarters of a century of Republican national dominance. Only defeats by Grover Cleveland (in 1884 and 1892) and by Woodrow Wilson (in 1912 and 1916) interrupted Republican control of the White House until 1932. However, the Great Depression broke the Republican grip on national power as the people sent Democrats Franklin D. Roosevelt and Harry S. Truman to the White House for the next 20 years. The returning Republican ascendency under Dwight D. Eisenhower, who was elected President in 1952, was followed by the Democratic administrations of John F. Kennedy, elected in 1960, and Lyndon B. Johnson, who succeeded him in 1963, before the Republicans regained national power with the election of Richard M. Nixon as President in 1968.

JULY 7

California Proclaimed Part of the United States

Citizens of the United States did not appear in large numbers in California, then a province of Mexico, before the colonization of the San Joaquin Valley in 1843. Even by 1846 only about 500 Americans had settled among the 8,000 to 12,000 Mexicans of Spanish descent and 24,000 Indians. But despite the small percentage of US citizens in the area, the interest of the US government in the fertile and strategically located Mexican province was great, and shortly after the Mexican War erupted, an American naval officer on July 7, 1846, raised the Stars and Stripes in California.

Americans throughout the 1840s were eager to add California to the Union. In 1842 Commodore Thomas ap Catesby Jones, incorrectly believing that the United States and Mexico were at war and that a British fleet was ready to seize California, set sail from the coast of Peru. Jones landed at Monterey and raised the American flag there on October 20 before the US consul in Monterey, Thomas O. Larkin, advised him that the two neighboring nations were still at peace. Commodore Jones promptly lowered the flag, President John Tyler apologized to Mexico, and the United States made reparations.

Jones's timing was poor. James K. Polk, who succeeded Tyler in the White House, was much more active in fostering the expansion of the United States to the Pacific Ocean in fulfillment of its "manifest destiny." In October 1845 Polk appointed Thomas Larkin confidential agent with the assignment of encouraging Californians to join the American Union or at least to establish independence under the protection of the United States. Polk's hopes for California soon came to fruition, thanks to the efforts of John Charles Frémont and to the outbreak of war with Mexico over the issue of the location of the southern boundary of the United States.

Undertaking his third important government exploring expedition, Frémont, then a young brevet captain in the US Topographical Corps, reached the California frontier in December 1845 and camped near Sutter's Fort with part of his band of 60 hardy men. (The remainder of his party, traveling a longer and more southerly route to avoid possible snows, rejoined the expedition later.) From Sutter's Fort, Frémont traveled with a single companion to Monterey, more than 100 miles south, which was the headquarters of General José Castro, the military commandant of California. Meeting with Castro the American adopted a conciliatory attitude and received what seemed to be the commandant's tacit approval for members of the Frémont expedition to tarry in the Californian province, reprovisioning themselves and perhaps returning north or exploring southeastward, toward the Colorado River. The spot to which the full expedition repaired, when reunited in mid-February, was about 13 miles southeast of San José, about midway between San Francisco and Monterey. All was quiet until the latter part of the month, when the expedition moved on, not toward the northeast or southeast as might have been expected, but in a southwesterly direction toward the main settlements of the province, including Monterey. Keeping east of that center, Frémont camped some 25 miles away, near present Salinas. The movements of

his well-armed band apparently alarmed the Mexican authorities, with the result that Castro soon reneged on his supposed agreement and ordered the Frémont party out of the area. Angered, Frémont refused, raising the American flag and standing his ground for three days on nearby Hawk's Peak in the Gabilan Mountains. Finally, as Castro prepared for assault with a superior force, Frémont defiantly withdrew to the north, but at a leisurely pace.

Frémont had reached Klamath Lake on the Oregon frontier by May 9, when Lieutenant Archibald H. Gillespie of the marines overtook him with dispatches and correspondence from home. The content of the documents that Gillespie gave Frémont was innocuous, but the lieutenant may also have borne secret oral instructions. In any case Frémont and his expedition returned to California immediately, where they camped on the Sacramento River, not far from Sutter's Fort.

As Frémont approached, the Mexican leaders in California, who had long been feuding, were at odds over the issue of revolution in Mexico. Castro announced his support for General Mariano Paredes, who had deposed José Herrera as president of Mexico. However, the civil governor of Mexican California, Pío Pico, responded by calling for a general council in Santa Barbara. It was widely thought that the purpose of the council would be to proclaim California's independence and place it under the protection of a foreign government, perhaps Britain or France. In response to this internal challenge, Castro diverted his attention from the Americans and dispatched forces against Pico's headquarters at Los Angeles. Castro also ranged up and down northern California in a troop-raising effort designed to meet a threat from any quarter — Pico, the Americans, or Britain.

With the encouragement of Frémont, American settlers in the Sacramento Valley took advantage of Castro's preoccupation, seizing their opportunity against a Castro lieutenant who had collected horses along the north edge of San Francisco Bay and was leading them south, possibly for use against Pico. On June 10 some of the settlers attacked part of the Mexican expedition. On June 14 another American party captured Sonoma, north of present San Francisco. With the consent of all, one of their number, William B. Ide, a New Englander who had been resident in California for about a year, drew up a proclamation declaring the independence of the American settlements. The insurgents claimed that the Mexicans had promised them republican government and lands, but instead had imposed a dictatorship and forbidden them to buy or rent ground.

William L. Todd, a nephew of Mary Todd

Lincoln, designed a flag for the newly proclaimed Republic of California. Made of cotton and decorated by means of a pot of berry juice and a blacking brush, the standard bore on a white field the name of the republic, a rough likeness of a grizzly bear, and a star. Not surprisingly, historians have come to call the uprising the Bear Flag Revolt.

Casting off his supposed neutrality in favor of an open and active role, Frémont himself reached Sonoma on June 25. Along with Gillespie and some others, he subsequently crossed the bay to San Francisco, then known as Yerba Buena. There, during the night of July 1/2, Frémont spiked the guns of Castillo de San Joaquín, the old fort near the presidio. He then returned to Sonoma, where he accepted the proposal of the settlers that he direct the affairs of the Bear Flag Republic.

The life of the California republic was short, however, for the Mexican War quickly brought American military intervention in the area. Commodore John D. Sloat, the commander of the US Navy's Pacific Squadron, anchored off Mazatlán on Mexico's west coast, learned by late May that war had broken out in Texas between the United States and Mexico. Acting on standing instructions for such an eventuality, Sloat set sail for California on June 8 — a day after his earlier impression of hostilities had been emphasized by news that Commodore David Conner had blockaded Veracruz, on Mexico's east coast. Sloat's flagship, the *Savannah*, which raced the British ship *Collingwood* under Rear Admiral Sir George Seymour, to the North, arrived at Monterey on July 2.

On July 7 Commodore Sloat sent Captain William Mervine and 250 marines and seamen ashore to claim California for the United States. Sloat had the American flag raised and issued a proclamation that was read to the populace in Spanish and in English. He guaranteed the civil and religious rights of persons who accepted United States citizenship, and allowed those who chose to refuse it either to remain neutral or to leave. Those who decided to depart would receive time to sell their property. Sloat promised not to interfere with existing real estate titles or the property of the clergy, and announced that the military would take no private property without giving just compensation.

On July 6, meanwhile, Sloat directed Commander John B. Montgomery, stationed on the sloop of war *Portsmouth* in San Francisco Bay, to raise the American flag over that city. Montgomery landed with 70 men and carried out the mission on July 9. Sloat also directed Lieutenant James W. Revere to occupy Sonoma, where the rebels gladly raised another American flag in place of their standard.

Learning of these developments, Frémont spent a few days readying his augmented force, which would be known as the California Battalion, and assuring the security of the Sacramento Valley. With 160 specially selected men, he then hurried south to meet Sloat in Monterey.

The timid Sloat, however, already worried that he might have exceeded his own instructions, was disturbed by the lack of official authorization for the actions Frémont had taken. Fearing that he was in the midst of repeating Thomas ap Catesby Jones's earlier misadventures, Sloat decided to remain in Monterey rather than to pursue the Mexicans. Sloat also refused to take Frémont's Sonoma battalion into his service. His misgivings aggravated by ill health, Sloat was ready to return to the East.

Commodore Robert F. Stockton arrived in Monterey with the frigate *Congress* on July 15 and eight days later took command from the departing Sloat. Stockton suffered none of the uneasiness of his predecessor. On July 24 he commissioned Frémont as major in command of the California Battalion of Mounted Riflemen, which became popularly known as the Navy Battalion. Stockton then sent Frémont and his men, reinforced by 80 marines on the *Cyane* to occupy San Diego. Stockton himself secured Santa Barbara and then set sail himself on the *Congress* for San Pedro.

Stockton landed at San Pedro on August 6 and proceeded with more than 300 men to Los Angeles, where Castro and Pico, who had resolved their differences in the face of the common enemy, were preparing defenses. As the Americans approached, Castro dispatched a courier to warn them that Los Angeles would be their burial ground. Undaunted, Stockton told the messenger to have Castro toll the bells of the town on the following day at 8:00 A.M. to announce the Americans' arrival. Stockton proved more correct in his assessment of the situation than Castro: American combined forces occupied Los Angeles on August 13, after the Mexicans fled without offering resistance.

Coming from San Diego, Frémont reached Los Angeles at nearly the same time as Stockton. Then, on August 17, Stockton announced the annexation of California by the United States. He proclaimed himself governor, and divided California into three military districts. Frémont, who was to command in the north, was sent back to his old stronghold in the Sacramento Valley, where he was to recruit as large a force as possible. Gillespie was placed in charge of the southern region, and Stockton himself took command of the central portion of California. On August 22 he reported to the Navy Department that "peace and harmony" once more reigned in California.

Reports of the enemy's flight proved to be premature, however. Under the leadership of Captain José Maria Flores, Mexican forces regrouped and on September 23 surrounded Los Angeles. On September 30 Captain Gillespie capitulated and withdrew with his men to Monterey. Flores then issued a proclamation that placed blame for earlier defeats on the cowardice of the leaders and called for the expulsion of US forces from California and the reestablishment of the area as part of Mexico. By October 29, when Flores became governor and military commandant, he had restored all of California south of San Luis Obispo to Mexican control.

Stockton set out immediately to reconquer California. The commodore ordered Frémont to hurry south to Santa Barbara to obtain horses, and dispatched Captain Mervine to land at San Pedro. Neither tactic was immediately fruitful. Frémont was in Santa Barbara when he learned that Mervine, after attacking a large number of the enemy near San Pedro, had been repulsed. Learning, in addition, that the enemy had stripped the countryside of the horses and cows that would be needed for transportation and food, Frémont turned north for Monterey, hoping to find the needed animals there. Stockton, meanwhile, arrived at San Pedro on October 23, but found no supplies; he then returned to San Diego just in time to stave off an assault on that city.

Beleaguered, the Americans began to improve their tactics and defenses. As they proceeded with these programs, news arrived on December 3, 1846, that Brigadier General Stephen Watts Kearny was approaching from the east and desired to make contact. Stockton immediately dispatched Captain Gillespie with 35 men to meet the new forces.

General Kearny reached California after a highly successful expedition that had bloodlessly conquered New Mexico for the United States. On July 31, 1846, Kearny had announced to the inhabitants of the Mexican territory that he intended to join it to the United States, and the following day he dispatched a letter to Governor Manuel Armijo warning him against resistance. By August 15 Kearny had reached Las Vegas, New Mexico, and proclaimed it a part of the United States and on August 18 he had occupied Santa Fe. General Kearny then established a temporary territorial government under Charles Bent and on September 25 set out for California.

Kearny led 300 men toward California, but after October 6, when he met the scout Kit Carson — who was bound for Washington with news of the conquest of California — the general sent back 200 of his men. Kearny asked Carson to accompany him, and the two, along with approximately 100 men, crossed the Colorado River on November 25 and entered California. Even with his numbers bolstered by the addition of Gillespie's party, Kearny was bested by a smaller Mexican force at the village of San Pascual on December 6. After moving on some 9 or 10 miles, Kearny's force was still sorely threatened by the enemy until the latter were driven off on December 10 with the help of a relief force sent by Stockton. Kearny then proceeded to San Diego, where he joined Stockton on December 12.

Stockton and Kearny initially established a good working relationship. Stockton, whose naval rank as commodore was the equivalent of the army rank of brigadier general, offered Kearny the command. Kearny tactfully declined and agreed to command under Stockton. The two officers then laid plans for joint operations against the opposing forces.

On December 29, 1846, Stockton and Kearny set out across the 130 miles of sands and mountains that lay between them and Los Angeles. On January 7, 1847, the Americans discovered approximately 1,000 of the enemy drawn up in an excellent position on the bank of the San Gabriel River. The next day Stockton crossed the river with his troops in line. Kearny then charged and displaced the Mexicans from their positions while Stockton repulsed a flanking attack by the enemy. The Americans pursued the retreating Mexicans and clashed with them on several occasions before January 10, when Stockton was able to have Gillespie once again raise the United States flag in Los Angeles.

While Stockton and Kearny carried out operations in the south, Frémont carried on his search for recruits in northern California. With about 400 men organized into nine companies, eight of cavalry and one of artillery, Frémont proceeded south on November 30, 1846, from the area of San Juan Bautista. The advancing Americans captured several of the enemy, including Don Jesús Pico, a distinguished citizen whom Stockton had previously taken prisoner and released on the condition that he would not fight again. A court-martial sentenced Pico to death for violating his parole, but Frémont pardoned the condemned man and won his friendship.

The Americans under Frémont entered Santa Barbara on December 27, 1846. They resumed the march on January 5, 1847, and on January 11 learned that Stockton and Kearny had captured Los Angeles. That same day, as they approached San Fernando, on the outskirts of Los Angeles, the Americans encountered the enemy. Frémont called on them to surrender, but the

Mexicans would agree only to a conference. Assisted by his new friend Pico, Frémont met their leaders and induced them to capitulate. The resulting Treaty of Cahuenga of January 13, 1847, was signed by Frémont, was generous, and its terms included a provision that no Mexican or Californian remaining in the area had to take an oath of allegiance to the United States until a final peace ending the Mexican War was signed. The agreement brought hostilities to an end throughout California.

Victory brought to the fore dissension within the American leadership. Stockton and Kearny had cooperated in the defeat of the adversary, but once peace was restored, the commanders vied with each other for control of California. Stockton claimed the right to organize the government by virtue of his position as military commander and the orders originally given to Sloat; Kearny argued that his orders from Washington authorized him to establish a government in California.

Frémont found himself in a difficult situation. On the one hand, Stockton, who was returning east, had granted him his post as military commandant and offered to make him governor. On the other hand, Kearny, who was going to make himself governor, was Frémont's superior in the army and had promised to make him his successor in California. Frémont decided to support Stockton, and on January 16, 1847, the naval officer named him to be governor.

Angered by Frémont, Kearny warned the young officer that he was guilty of insubordination, and left Los Angeles for San Diego. On February 13, 1847, Kearny received fresh orders from Washington, which confirmed his power to establish a new government. Kearny immediately set up a provisional government at Monterey, but Frémont, remaining in Los Angeles, ignored him. Finally, when Kearny was ready to return east, the general appointed Colonel Richard B. Mason to be governor, and on May 31 Kearny, Stockton, and Frémont set out for Washington to have their differences settled.

Back in the East, Frémont faced a court-martial on charges of mutiny, disobedience, and conduct prejudicial to order. The tribunal found him guilty of all charges and ordered him dismissed from the army. President James K. Polk reviewed the proceedings and took an ambivalent stance, which offended his fellow Democrat Senator Thomas Hart Benton of Missouri, who was Frémont's father-in-law. Polk, who did not believe the evidence substantiated the charge of mutiny, approved the proceedings, but following the court's recommendation for clemency, he remitted Frémont's punishment and restored him to military duty. Frémont re-jected the compensation and resigned from the army. A popular figure, he later emerged as a leader of the fledgling Republican party and in 1856 was its first presidential candidate.

JULY 8

John D. Rockefeller Sr.'s Birthday

John Davison Rockefeller, the redoubtable American industrialist, capitalist, and philanthropist, was born on July 8, 1839, to William Avery and Eliza (Davison) Rockefeller in the hamlet of Richford, New York, where his father, a small trader, had a farm. When John was 12 years old, his family moved to Cleveland, and there he completed two years of high school, the extent of his formal education. At the age of 16 he became a clerk in a Cleveland commission house at low wages, of which he saved a little every week. In this way, at the age of 20 he was able to enter the produce commission business in his own right, with M. B. Clark as his partner. During the Civil War Rockefeller prospered as a wholesaler in grain, hay, and meat in Cleveland, accumulating a small fortune of $50,000 by 1865.

In these years he followed his mother's religious bent in becoming a leading member of the Erie Street Baptist Church and began donating one-tenth of his income to charities. In 1864 he married Laura Celestia Spelman. In time four children, Bessie, Alta, Edith, and John D. Rockefeller Jr. were born.

From such modest beginnings, John D. Rockefeller Sr. was to become one of the wealthiest and most powerful men in post–Civil War America, his life inseparably linked with the production of a new source of energy, petroleum, and with the rapid growth of monopolistic capitalism. While he was still a schoolboy, in the early 1850s, whale oil, the main illuminant until then, had become scarce, and its price rose to such a point that people were eager for a cheaper substitute for their lamps. In western Pennsylvania, S. M. Kier began gathering crude oil from local seepages to refine into kerosene and to sell as a cure-all. Advertisements for kerosene soon prepared a market outdistancing Kier's supplies of crude oil, and other means of extracting oil were sought. When E. L. Drake, drilling for oil near Titusville, Pennsylvania, released a gusher on August 27, 1859, the rush was on to enter the oil business.

Four years later Rockefeller and Clark entered oil refining as a sideline after seeing the business opportunities afforded by a recent railroad link between Cleveland and the oil lands of Pennsylvania. They bought one small Cleveland refinery and brought Samuel Andrews, an experienced oil technologist, into their partnership. By the end of the Civil War, Rockefeller was prepared to concentrate on oil enterprises. He bought out Clark and reorganized the partnership into Rockefeller and Andrews. To build a second, larger refinery at Cleveland called the Standard Works, Rockefeller brought his brother William (1841–1922) into a firm called William Rockefeller and Co. Not long after, to build up the export and eastern trades, an eastern affiliate was established in New York under this brother. By drawing talented men to his enterprises, John D. Rockefeller magnified his own keen abilities many times. In 1867 Henry M. Flagler, who was to become an expert negotiator of lower freight rates for the Rockefeller companies, joined the partnership.

Rockefeller saw that any field so lucrative and so easily entered as oil would be crowded with competitors. To protect his investments and enhance his profits, he learned how to thin the ranks. He first experimented in small ways with "stabilizing," if not dominating, the refining industry of Cleveland. By 1870 he was ready for a larger step. He brought a group of capitalists together in the Standard Oil Company of Ohio, with himself as president. This joint-stock corporation absorbed his earlier companies and employed more than 1,000 workers. It was well capitalized at $1 million; such strong capitalization was an important first step in all Rockefeller's enterprises.

Until this time Rockefeller had concentrated on refining. But since crude oil was worthless to the consumer, refining in fact put him at the strategic center of the entire petroleum business. As Rockefeller clearly saw, any refiner who could monopolize the middle step would be able to name terms to producers and to set prices for wholesalers and consumers. It became his ambition to gain wider and wider control of the various aspects of the oil industry so that he could bring them all under one management, eliminate waste, and maximize profits.

The refining competition was located mainly near Cleveland, Pittsburgh, and New York, and in the Pennsylvania regions. Rockefeller first went after the Cleveland refineries, offering rivals cash or stock in the Standard Oil Company for their properties. Holdouts were run out of the business by Rockefeller's slashing his prices below cost. Afterwards, without fear of competition, he could again raise prices. Within a short time he effectively controlled refining in Cleveland.

Economies in operation were also vital in driving out competition; Rockefeller's genius for efficiency soon put his enterprises ahead. A highly accurate cost-accounting system was one product of his fine sense for detail. Soon his firms were making their own barrels and erecting warehouses. To bring the refineries into more direct touch with wholesalers, he invested in fleets of barges and tankers. He also bought up as much of the pipeline from the oil fields to the railroads as he could, to lessen dependence on outsiders and to gain another point of control.

Crucial to Rockefeller's progress toward monopoly was the obtaining of favorable rates on the rail shipment of his oil. Since rail rates were not standardized at the time and rail lines were highly competitive, a rail customer as large as Standard Oil could demand lower rates than smaller concerns offering less business. Rockefeller saw that discriminatory rates (more flatteringly referred to as "preferential") would keep competitors' prices higher than his and contribute to their failure. Under-the-counter rebates from rail companies to the strongest shippers were a favorite and pernicious form of discriminatory rates. Though not strictly illegal at the time, Rockefeller and Flagler's tactics were coercive and grasping in the extreme. The secrecy surrounding them suggests that the participants knew that their deals offended all sense of fair competition. When word of a proposed rebate scheme with the South Improvement Company leaked out in 1872, there was a public outcry. But the financial panic of 1873 weakened Rockefeller's already overextended rivals, and in the next few years he was able to buy up most of their plants at low cost.

Organizing so vast an empire as Rockefeller put together, on the basis of a company with no rights outside Ohio, was a complex undertaking. In 1882 Rockefeller and his associates created a new business organization, the Standard Oil Trust, capitalized at $70 million, which drew together and centralized their various enterprises — by then some 40 companies. Under the trust form, stockholders placed their stocks in the hands of nine trustees, among them John D. Rockefeller, in exchange for trust certificates of ownership. By 1882 Standard Oil of Ohio already controlled approximately 90 percent of refining in the United States and dominated the world market in petroleum products. Through efficient marketing systems, excessively low prices for a time, and merciless deals against rivals, the trust went on to capture the wholesale trade and finally also the retail trade of the entire United States in petroleum products. Once in control, however, Standard Oil again raised prices to recoup its losses, and thereafter could maintain its prices at a level of its choosing.

Anti-Rockefeller feeling swelled. Many people were not mollified by the quality products and reliable supply offered by the Standard Oil Trust, and demanded that widespread benefits, especially lower prices, flow from the greater efficiency made possible by such a monopoly. Instead gains were passed on to stockholders in annual dividends averaging between 30 percent and 48 percent after 1882. Rockefeller and his chief associates owned a large proportion of this stock. As a result the Standard Oil Trust, together with the other combines like Andrew Carnegie's in steel, came to be synonymous with predatory wealth in America.

A major struggle against the monopolists began, in which two incompatible philosophies of the sources of and the right to industrial wealth were brought into open conflict. Crusading journalists, later derided by their targets as "muckrakers," led the attack against Rockefeller and others. The reformers argued that profits from great industries rested as much on the work of laborers as on the acumen and risk of owners and managers. From this it followed, in the reformers' view, that profits should be broadly distributed through higher wages and lower prices, instead of flowing mainly to a few already wealthy men who had put up the fiscal capital. Wealth, in sum, was not an individual but a social product and should be generally shared.

With religious fervor, the captains of industry held an opposed economic and social creed, which had deep roots in traditional American values. They argued that capitalists and industrialists played a primary role in the creation of wealth; that the men whose executive ability, aggressiveness, and intense application had created profitable businesses and made jobs for thousands had earned the lion's share of the profits. As a matter of justice and as an incentive to further risk taking, they held, the rewards of economic success should remain individual and "private." In effect these industrial leaders did not make a distinction between the public interest and their own. Their view was shared by many who admired them as heroes, and who dreamed of making fortunes themselves, in Horatio Alger style.

Despite widespread public hostility toward Rockefeller and the other rulers of trusts, the battle against them was protracted and in many respects ineffectual. Monopoly capitalism would be modified but not overthrown. The gigantic new combinations went unregulated, in part because corporate law was then a matter for the individual states. Proud of economic development and imbued with doctrines of laissez-faire, American voters were generally opposed to increasing the power of the central government. Not until 1887 did Congress pass the Interstate Commerce Act, designed to regulate abuses in rail rates and practices and to break up trusts.

And because the very idea of federal government regulation was not yet well accepted, the US courts soon rendered this act ineffectual by adverse interpretation. The Sherman Anti-Trust Act of 1890, making unlawful any monopoly or combination of restraint of interstate trade, proved equally weak for nearly a decade. Thus, though the Ohio supreme court in 1892 dissolved the Standard Oil Trust, the companies of the trust continued to maintain their ties and their near monopoly through interlocking directorates. And by 1899 one of the group's enterprises, the Standard Oil Company of New Jersey, had been strengthened to the point where it could manage the whole combination. This was legal under a New Jersey law allowing an incorporated company to buy, hold, and vote stock in any other corporation or corporations in New Jersey or in any other state. Although the Standard Oil combination continued to be known popularly as a trust, because of its power to dictate prices, control was now centralized in a holding company.

Such technicalities did not soften public ire, but they delayed legal action. In 1906 the US government brought suit against Standard Oil of New Jersey under the Sherman Anti-Trust Act. In 1911 the US Supreme Court dissolved the combination (with gross assets at the time of $860 million) on the grounds that it had entered into monopolistic agreements unreasonably restraining interstate commerce.

With this decision of 1911, John D. Rockefeller Sr. formally retired from his enterprises to devote himself to philanthropy. He had wished to withdraw in the 1890s, but his associates would not let him, saying that "cases . . . were pending in the courts; . . . if any of [them] had to go to jail, he would have to go with [them]." However, as public criticism mounted, Rockefeller played only a shadow role in management. After 1895 his role as president of Standard Oil was largely titular. However, the common saying that in later life he devoted himself to giving away his fortune is somewhat misleading, for while he distributed many, many millions, his stock holdings continued to earn many additional millions for him and his children, and the combination of men and companies that he and his brother and son had put together, known informally as the Rockefeller Group, gained a position in the American economy that was challenged only by the powerful combination headed by the financier J. P. Morgan. In the 1970s, the descendants of John D. Rockefeller continued to exercise immense influence in the US economy and in public policy.

Rockefeller brought to philanthropy both his organizational brilliance and his talent for seeking out and employing persons of great ability.

With the guidance of Frederick T. Gates, his first major donation founded the University of Chicago in 1891. Thirty-five million dollars, given over the following years, enabled this university to become a great institution of higher learning. In 1901 he founded the Rockefeller Institute for Medical Research, which in 1954 became Rockefeller University. Its buildings, surrounded by handsome gardens, which are open to the public, are located in New York City, east of York Avenue at 66th Street. In 1902 Rockefeller established the General Education Board to make donations to educational and research agencies, including libraries; and in 1913, the prestigious Rockefeller Foundation was founded to promote "the well-being of mankind throughout the world." In its first years, it supported medical research, education, and public health, making major contributions to the fight against malaria, yellow fever, and hookworm. It also assisted in relief and reconstruction after World War I. In 1918 Rockefeller established the Laura Spelman Rockefeller Memorial Foundation in memory of his wife, to further the social sciences and child welfare; in 1929 this foundation, with its $58 million endowment, was consolidated with the Rockefeller Foundation. Thereafter the latter expanded into new research areas, particularly agriculture, the humanities, and the natural and social sciences. The Baptist Church, the YMCA, and the Anti-Saloon League were also generously supported by John D. Rockefeller. His benefactions exceeded $530 million.

Rockefeller died at his home in Ormond Beach, Florida, on May 23, 1937, at the age of 97.

JULY 9

Braddock's Defeat:
The Battle of the Monongahela

England and France were enemies in the New World as well as in the Old, and by the mid-18th century their ambitions in the former were as irreconcilable as in the latter. The Ohio Valley, the gateway to the American West, became the focus of the conflict in the 1750s. The English expected their colonies to expand into the region, and the province of Virginia, whose charter gave it a claim to the region, granted over 1 million acres to groups of speculators and promoters such as the Ohio Company and the Loyal Land Company. The French, on the other hand, viewed the trans-Allegheny area as the natural connection between their settlements in Canada and those in Louisiana. Canada's governor, the Comte de La Galissonière, promoted his country's claim by sending out an expedition of soldiers that imbedded in the ground at important locations lead plates proclaiming France's right to the territory.

Both countries elaborately justified their respective claims to the Ohio Valley. English colonial charters in several cases granted all land from sea to sea, and by the Treaty of Lancaster of 1744 Britain had purchased the region from the Iroquois Indians, who claimed title by right of conquest. French pretensions arose from the alleged exploration of the area in 1679 by Robert Cavelier, Sieur de La Salle. Galissonière's plaques announced "the renewal of possession which we have taken of the said river Ohio, and of all those which fall into it, and of all the territories on both sides as far as the source of the said rivers, as the preceding kings of France have enjoyed or ought to have enjoyed it, and which they have maintained by arms and by treaties, particularly by those of Ryswick, Utrecht, and Aix-la-Chapelle." In reality, however, La Salle had probably never reached the Ohio, and the treaties mentioned did nothing to substantiate the French position.

Neither England nor France followed up its claims with significant settlements until the Marquis Duquesne, who assumed the Canadian governorship in 1752, built French forts in 1753 at Presque Isle and Fort Le Boeuf (now Erie and Waterford, Pennsylvania, respectively). These wooden forts presented a greater threat than leaden plaques, and Lieutenant Governor Robert Dinwiddie of Virginia answered the challenge by sending a young militia major, the 21-year-old George Washington with a letter warning the French to leave the area. On December 11 Washington delivered the message to Captain Jacques Legardeur de St. Pierre at Fort Le Boeuf; the French commandant rejected the request and the young Virginian returned home.

Backwoods diplomacy degenerated into a wilderness war within a few months. On April 17, 1754, a detachment of over 1,000 Frenchmen surprised, captured, and then released a band of 41 Virginians under Ensign Edward Ward as they were erecting an English fort at the Forks of the Ohio — the confluence of the Allegheny and Monongahela rivers — today the site of Pittsburgh. The French razed the English structure and replaced it with Fort Duquesne (which the English would one day rebuild as Fort Pitt).

As Ward retreated he encountered Washington arriving with 120 soldiers belatedly sent to protect the fort builders. Determined to recapture the Forks, Washington on May 28 attacked and defeated a French advance party at Jumonville Glen, approximately five miles east of Uniontown, Pennsylvania. Washington then returned to the Great Meadows, where he built the modest and appropriately named Fort Necessity. Reinforcements joined him at his encampment, and he received word of his promotion to colonel, but neither additional numbers nor increased rank enabled him to hold off the enemy. The French captured the insubstantial Fort Necessity on July 3 and sent Washington and his men back to Virginia. The scene of Washington's only surrender, in what became the opening battle of the French and Indian War, is today known as Fort Necessity National Battlefield and is administered by the National Park Service.

The Ohio Valley dispute was only one part of a greater Anglo-French conflict in America, and the arrival in America in February, 1755 of Major General Edward Braddock as commander in chief of British forces indicated that a general frontier war was imminent. English campaign plans included attacks on Fort Niagara by the Massachusetts governor, Major General William Shirley, and on Fort St. Frederic at Crown Point, New York, by William Johnson, the colony's Indian agent. Braddock himself intended to drive the French from Fort Duquesne.

Two regular Irish regiments formed the core of the force that Major General Braddock had assembled across the Allegheny Mountains at Fort Cumberland, Maryland. The addition of 3 independent companies and 11 companies of Virginia, North Carolina, and Maryland militia brought the complement to 2,500 men. The expedition left Fort Cumberland on June 7, but difficult terrain and inadequate transportation reduced its speed to two miles a day. At the suggestion of George Washington, who accompanied Braddock as a civilian aide-de-camp, the British commander reduced the size of the force to a lightly supplied contingent of 1,450 men capable of completing the 110-mile journey with speed. The streamlined column renewed the trek on June 20, traversing the Endless Mountains, as the Alleghenies were called.

By July 9 the Anglo-American expedition was near Fort Duquesne, crossing the Monongahela where the town of Braddock is now located. As the vanguard, under Lieutenant Colonel Thomas Gage, advanced toward the location selected for the final encampment, it encountered a party of approximately 290 French regulars and militia, supported by more than 600 Indians. Gage, later famous as the British commander in chief in the colonies at the beginning of the American Revolution, quickly lined up his men and fired on the French, a number of

whom fled. Colonel Gage probably could have broken through the enemy line, but, not knowing its strength, he retreated instead.

Upon hearing the commotion Braddock ordered the main body of his force forward. Tremendous confusion ensued as it ran into Gage's retreating troops. Captain Jean Dumas, who had assumed command of the French force when Captain Daniel de Beaujeu was killed, took advantage of the situation by deploying his men on both sides of the road along which the English and Americans were proceeding. The French brought an intense fire to bear on the Anglo-American column. Braddock had five horses shot from under him and then fell himself, mortally wounded. In the three-hour battle, Braddock's expedition suffered 63 of its 83 officers and almost 1,000 soldiers killed or wounded. The French lost fewer than 60 men.

The survivors of the battle of the Monongahela, as the engagement came to be known, escaped to their campsite east of Uniontown, where Braddock died on July 13. The English had lost the first major battle of the French and Indian War, which they also referred to as the Seven Years' War. Trained British soldiers had proved inadequate in frontier fighting: as Washington commented, they had been "most scandalously beaten by a trifling body of men." Yet better days would come, and by 1763 the Anglo-American troops had driven the French from Canada, ending the French threat to the English colonies.

US Highway 40 follows part of the route used by the Anglo-American force on its march to the Monongahela. Named Braddock's Trail in honor of the general, the section formed part of the famous Cumberland Road connecting Cumberland, Maryland, and Wheeling, West Virginia. Fort Necessity, carefully restored and equipped with a visitors center, is the first point of interest on this sector of US 40. Mount Washington Tavern, erected in 1816 on the hill above the fort, serves as a museum. It houses a number of historical items, including some relics of the fort and of Braddock's expedition.

In 1824 workmen repairing Braddock's Trail uncovered a skeleton and the uniform of a high-ranking British officer. Historians believe that these are the remains of General Braddock, whom Washington buried in the road so that the Indians would not find and desecrate his grave. General Braddock's remains were reinterred about 100 yards away at the Old Orchard Camp. A marker erected in 1913 identifies the site, which also lies along US 40.

Washington's Spring, visited by George Washington in 1753, 1754, and 1755, lies farther along the highway. A tablet describes the site, near Jumonville Glen, where Washington's troops clashed with the French in 1754. Also near the glen are the grounds of Dunbar Camp, where Braddock divided his forces. Named after Colonel Thomas Dunbar, the second in command of the expedition, the site is now a Methodist camp for children.

Braddock's men passed through some magnificent primeval forests on their march and camped at one point in a location so awesome as to be called the Shades of Death.

The battle scene has been depicted by Alonzo Chappel in a painting at the Chicago Historical Society and by Edwin Willard Deming in a painting at the State Historical Society of Wisconsin in Madison.

JULY 10

Allied Troops Land in Sicily

In January 1943, before the Allied conquest of North Africa, US President Franklin D. Roosevelt and British Prime Minister Winston Churchill met at Casablanca to discuss offensives. American military strategists wanted to concentrate on gathering men and materiel in England in preparation for a cross-channel invasion of mainland Europe. The British argued that such an assault would not be possible for another year and convinced their comrades of the necessity of maintaining pressure on the Mediterranean area. As a result of the conference, Roosevelt and Churchill ordered General Dwight D. Eisenhower to set in motion Operation Husky, an invasion of the island of Sicily.

Allied strategists wanted Sicily in order to secure the Mediterranean line of communication. Control of the island in addition to Tunisia would allow the Americans and British to dominate the Mediterranean Sea at one of its most narrow and critical points. The planners also hoped to divert some German attention from the USSR, to make possible Turkey's entrance into the war as an active ally, and to put pressure on Italy. But they did not initially envisage the island as the stepping stone to the Italian mainland that it subsequently became. Attacks on Sardinia and Corsica would have been more logical starting points for a European invasion, because occupation of those islands would have forced a broader dispersal of Axis troops along the western Italian coast. Only at the Trident conference in Washington, D.C., in May did Churchill obtain Roosevelt's consent for Eisenhower to exploit Husky with the objective of eliminating Italy from the war.

Eisenhower's final plan placed General Harold R. L. G. Alexander in command of the Allied ground forces, which received the designation of the Fifteenth Army Group. General George Patton's Seventh Army made up the American element, the first complete US unit of army size to fight in World War II. General Bernard L. Montgomery's Eighth Army, which had distinguished itself in North Africa, was the British component. Patton's and Montgomery's forces were to strike simultaneously at the southeastern corner of Sicily on July 10, 1943.

Patton's Seventh Army, which had responsibility for the western sector of the beach, divided into three groups for the invasion. Major General Lucian Truscott's Joss Force was to land in the Licata area, secure the port and airfield, protect the attackers' western flank, and make contact on the eastern flank with the II Corps. Lieutenant General Omar Bradley's Shark Force was to land in the Gela-Scoglitti area, capture the airfields at Ponte Olivo and Comiso, and make contact with the American Third Division on the left and the British on the right. Major General Hugh J. Gaffey's Kool Force was to act as the reserve.

Montgomery's Eighth Army, which had responsibility for the eastern area of the invasion zone, was to attack at the same hour as the Americans. The British were to establish beachheads between Syracuse on the east and Pozzallo on the west, and coordinate with Bradley's II Corps in the vicinity of Ragusa. The Eighth Army was also supposed to capture the airfields in the region and continue its attack north toward the major port of Catania.

During the month of June and in early July Allied fliers weakened the Axis defenses in the invasion area with severe bombardment. The attacks enabled the Allies to capture the islands of Lampedusa, Linosa, and Pantelleria, located between Tunisia and Sicily, and thus deprive the enemy of advanced air bases. The bombers repeatedly struck bases in Sicily, Sardinia, and Italy, putting many ground installations out of operation and reducing the number of planes available to the defenders to 1,400. These deadly missions culminated in a major raid on the night of July 9 and July 10, just hours before the troops landed on the beaches.

General Patton assembled and trained his men at North African ports from Bizerte all the way west to Algiers, and Montgomery similarly used the island of Malta and towns as far east as Port Said and Alexandria. On the morning of July 9 ships bearing both armies approached Malta and proceeded toward the objective. At 2:30 A.M. on July 10, the troops made their landings against little opposition, a sign that they had achieved tactical surprise.

The American and British elements were both initially successful. On the right flank of Bradley's II Corps, Major General Troy H. Middleton's 45th Infantry Division secured Scoglitti and Vittoria, while on the left flank Major General Terry de la Mesa Allen's First Infantry Division landed near Gela. Men from Joss Force captured Licata by 11:30 A.M. Montgomery's troops took a major highway bridge over the Anapo River near Syracuse, seized Avola and Noto, and advanced toward Pachino.

On July 11 and July 12 the Germans and Italians counterattacked several times in the vicinity of the Gela beachhead. The Americans repulsed the attackers on all occasions, and the invaders continued their operations. The American 45th Division captured airfields at Comiso and Biscari on July 11 and July 14 respectively, and the First Division took the air base at Ponte Olivo on July 12. The British proceeded north from their landing sites, seizing Palazzolo and Vizzini by July 14.

Air reconnaissance revealed that the German and Italian defenders were withdrawing to the northeast, fighting only delaying actions and making only local counterattacks. General Alexander modified his strategy accordingly, and ordered the Seventh Army to attack toward the northwest instead of concentrating on protecting the left flank of the Eighth Army. Montgomery was to continue his advance up the eastern coastline around both sides of Mt. Etna and to make the port of Messina his final objective. Alexander hoped by his plan to split the enemy forces, isolate the western portion of the island, and cut off the main route of escape to the Italian mainland.

Patton established the Provisional Corps under Major General Geoffrey Keyes, deputy commander of the Seventh Army, to assist the II Corps in the American operations in the northwest. Composed basically of the Third Infantry Division, the Second Armored Division, and the 82nd Airborne Division, the Provisional Corps had the city of Palermo as its major objective. Between July 15 and July 23 the Seventh Army made important advances, and on the evening of July 22 the Provisional Corps seized Palermo. On the next day Patton entered the city in triumph with the Second Armored Division. News of Palermo's fall had immediate repercussions in Italy, where on July 24 and July 25 a palace revolt toppled the Mussolini government.

Montgomery's drive toward Catania encountered heavy resistance from German and Italian forces. Recognizing Montgomery's hesitance to continue a frontal attack along the coast, General Alexander modified his battle plan, and ordered Patton to strike eastward from Palermo toward Messina to cut off the enemy's route of retreat. Montgomery decided to refrain from offensive operations south of Catania until Patton had reached a position from which they could launch a coordinated final attack. Unfortunately the week of delay allowed the enemy to develop a system of strong defenses.

General Patton pushed east from Palermo along the only two possible routes in the mountainous regions, sending the 45th Division along the coast and the 1st Division along the Gangi-Nicosia-Randazzo road. On August 2 the Seventh Army reached the San Fratello–Troina area, and Montgomery's Eighth Army pushed north to the Simeto River. The Germans and Italians by that time realized that the loss of Sicily was inevitable. On July 31 General Alfredo Guzzoni decided to evacuate Italian troops and shortly thereafter Field Marshal Albert Kesselring, supreme commander of German forces in Italy, authorized the withdrawal of the Germans.

American and British forces continued to attack the retreating enemy, but were unable to prevent successful evacuation to Italy. Patton attempted three amphibious landings behind the German lines, but even these daring maneuvers failed to disrupt the foe's skillful retreat. The Allies entered Messina on August 17, but by then the Germans had escaped from Sicily, taking with them 100,000 troops, 9,800 vehicles, and 47 tanks, which would prove useful in defending the next Allied objective, the Italian mainland.

James Abbott McNeill Whistler's Birthday

One of the most famous paintings in the world, popularly called "Whistler's Mother," went begging for a buyer for 20 years. The portrait was formally titled *Mrs. George Washington Whistler* and was later referred to by the artist as *Arrangement in Grey and Black No. 1.* The Royal Academy in London refused to show it in 1872. When the portrait was exhibited in America it could not find a purchaser even at a ridiculously low price. Finally, in 1891, the French government bought it for $600. Not until 1926 was it finally given its present place of honor in the Louvre.

James Abbott McNeill Whistler, who lived abroad most of his life, was born in Lowell, Massachusetts, on July 10, 1834. Whistler's grandfather, John Whistler, an Irishman by birth, served in the British army under General John Burgoyne during the American Revolution. After Whistler's discharge he returned to America,

became an officer in the American army, and
was commandant of Fort Wayne when his son,
whose naming leaves no question of loyalty, was
born. George Washington Whistler, father of
the artist, also went into the US Army, distinguishing himself as a draftsman while a student
at the US Military Academy at West Point.
Graduated in 1819 as a second lieutenant, he
had several surveying and teaching assignments
before he and another West Pointer, William
Gibbs McNeill, were assigned to working on
railroads. Whistler helped to plan the location
and supervised the construction of the Baltimore and Ohio and the Baltimore and Susquehanna railroads.

In 1833 Whistler, then a first lieutenant, resigned from the army to become engineer to the
Proprietors of Locks and Canal at Lowell, Massachusetts, where his son James Abbott McNeill
Whistler was born. The elder Whistler continued to supervise railroad construction and also
became consulting engineer for the Western
Railroad of Massachusetts and chief engineer
for the line in 1840. His engineering skills received much notice and acclaim, especially
when he located the section of track between
Springfield and Pittsfield through the Berkshire
Hills in a narrow river valley. A Russian commission inspecting American railroads at the
time reported the engineering feat to the czar
and Whistler was invited to go to Russia as consulting engineer for the proposed railroad between St. Petersburg and Moscow.

Meanwhile the family had moved from
Lowell to Stonington, Connecticut, and then to
Springfield. James (Jimmie) Whistler, one of
five sons born to George Washington Whistler
and his second wife — his friend McNeill's sister,
Anna Matilda McNeill of Wilmington, North
Carolina — had begun to make pencil drawings
at the age of four.

George Washington Whistler went to Russia
in 1842 and began the planning of the railroad.
He also supervised construction of the iron
bridge over the Neva River and fortifications
and docks at Kronstadt, the commercial harbor
of St. Petersburg until the 1880s. For these
works, he was decorated by the emperor with
the Order of St. Anne in 1847. His family joined
him in St. Petersburg in 1843, when James
Whistler was nine years old.

While in Russia, the boy studied at the Academy of Fine Arts. On one of the family's several
trips to England, Sir William Boxall painted a
portrait of young Whistler at 14. The portrait is
in the Freer Gallery of Art, Washington, D.C.,
which houses one of the most important Whistler collections in the world.

Whistler's father died in Russia in 1849. The
family returned to America and settled in Pomfret, Connecticut, where the boy was sent to
school to prepare for entrance to West Point. He
entered the Military Academy in 1851 but remained there only three years. Yet he was immensely proud of his West Point days for the
rest of his life. For about a year afterwards,
Whistler worked as a draftsman and map engraver for the Coast Survey in Washington, D.C.,
learning techniques of etching, which were valuable in his later years.

In 1855, with an annual allowance of $350,
he sailed for Paris to study with the classicist
Swiss painter Charles Gleyre. As it turned out
Whistler never returned to the United States
but spent the rest of his life in Europe, chiefly
in Paris and London.

Largely self-trained, he was variously influenced by the naturalism of Courbet and the
English Pre-Raphaelites, the strong tonalities of
Velásquez, and the concepts of composition and
the serenity of Japanese art. Yet he belonged to
no one school of art. Strongly individualistic in
all things, Whistler imitated no one. Although
his early landscapes, mostly nocturnal urban
subjects, were realistic, he later rejected realism,
saying, "If the man who paints only the tree or
flower or other surface he sees before him were
an artist, the king of artists would be the photographer."

If Whistler can be said to have settled anywhere, it was in the Chelsea district of London,
long favored by artists and writers. During his
stays in London he occupied several residences
a stone's throw from the Thames River on
charming Cheyne Walk — they included numbers 21, 96, and 101 — and numbers 13 and 46
on Tite Street. Whistler's stepsister also was living in London, married to Sir Francis Seymour
Haden, the British surgeon and etcher. Lady
Haden and her daughter are the figures in Whistler's *At the Piano*. His mother went to live in
England in 1863.

Whistler had a special feeling for the Thames.
Even before 1860 Baudelaire praised Whistler's
ability to capture the fog and darkness on the
Thames with a fresh and unusual interpretation
rather than mere factual representation.

Other appreciation of Whistler's work came
more slowly. In 1860 the Royal Academy in
London did show *At the Piano* (now in Boston),
which Whistler had painted in 1859. But for
years before and after, his paintings were rejected by the French academic salon as well as the
Royal Academy in London. Both had turned
down *The Little White Girl*, which caused a
sensation when it was finally shown at the Salon
des Refusés, the gallery founded by Emperor
Napoleon III to exhibit works of art — mostly

impressionistic — which the traditionalists had snubbed as too avant-garde. *The Little White Girl* was shown among paintings by American artists at the Paris Exposition in 1867 and is now in the National Gallery of Art in Washington, D.C. Whistler subtitled it *Symphony in White, No. 1.* It was the first in a series of paintings with musical titles — employing such terms as symphony, nocturne, and arrangement — that were indicative of Whistler's feeling that the composition of paintings and their harmonies of color were more important than their subjects.

Whistler had won a considerable reputation as an etcher, publishing his first group of etchings in Paris in 1858. Four hundred plates reveal that he was a prodigious worker in etchings as well as in lithographs, watercolors, pastels, and oils. Yet he found time for social life, enjoyed playing the eccentric dandy, and became a drawing room idol known for his countless vendettas and caustic wit which, some feel, impeded his recognition as an artist. In his conversation as in his art, Whistler often sacrificed fact for effect. At one social gathering his friend Edgar Degas, the French impressionist, told Whistler, "My friend, you behave as though you had no talent."

The English art critic John Ruskin became one of Whistler's most famous enemies. In 1877 Ruskin visited the Grosvenor Gallery, which was showing eight of Whistler's paintings, including *Nocturne in Black and Gold: The Falling Rocket* (painted in 1874 and now in the Detroit Institute of Arts). Of it Ruskin wrote, "I have seen, and heard, much of Cockney impudence before now, but never expected to hear a coxcomb ask 200 guineas for flinging a pot of paint in the public's face." Whistler sued Ruskin for libel.

At the trial, in 1878, another of Whistler's nocturnal scenes (probably *Old Battersea Bridge*, painted about 1877 and now in the Tate Gallery, London) was shown in court and Whistler was asked if he would say that it was "a correct representation of Battersea Bridge." Whistler answered:

I did not intend it to be a "correct" portrait of the bridge. It is only a moonlight scene and the pier in the center of the picture may not be like the piers at Battersea Bridge as you know them in broad daylight. As to what the picture represents, it depends upon who looks at it. To some persons it may represent all that is intended; to others it may represent nothing. . . . My whole scheme was only to bring about a certain harmony in color.

He won the case but was awarded only one farthing. He wore the coin thereafter as a charm on his watch chain. It was an expensive victory. Legal costs and a sharp decline in the popularity of his paintings — which after all had been be-

littled by a well-known critic — led him into bankruptcy. In September 1879 he went to Venice and for more than a year practiced his first-learned art, etching. By the time he had returned to London, the climate had changed. The strong feelings stirred up by the trial had passed over. His Venetian etchings were well received, and once more his portraits became fashionable. Although he was never elected to the Royal Academy of Arts in London, in 1886 he became president of the Royal Society of British Artists and during his two-year tenure accomplished much to bridge the gap between French and British art and to improve the manner in which pictures were displayed.

Whistler's life achieved a measure of stability when on August 11, 1888, he married Beatrix Godwin, the widow of his friend Edward William Godwin, the architect. Her death on May 10, 1896, was a shattering blow to Whistler. When, in 1897, the International Society of Sculptors, Painters and Engravers was established and asked him to be president, he accepted and immersed himself in the work.

Some 12 years earlier the artist had summed up his thoughts about naturalism in what came to be called Whistler's "ten o'clock" lecture, later published as a book. Another book, *The Gentle Art of Making Enemies*, published in 1890, opens with Whistler's account of the Ruskin affair, goes on to give his philosophy of art ("art for art's sake"), and records brilliant examples of Whistler's conversational wit.

By the turn of the century Whistler's health was failing and voyages to Africa, Corsica, and other places brought no improvement. He returned to London in 1901 and died there on July 17, 1903. He was buried in Chiswick Cemetery on July 22, 1903.

Although he received little recognition as an artist before he was 50, Whistler died a man of many honors. He was an officer of the French Legion of Honor and a member of German, French, Italian, and English societies of artists. A stela honoring Whistler and designed by Augustus Saint-Gaudens was erected at West Point. Soon after Whistler's death a great memorial exhibition of his works was shown in London, in New York City, and in Boston. In 1930 Whistler was further honored by election to the Hall of Fame for Great Americans.

In 1934 the 100th anniversary of Whistler's birth was celebrated by the Lowell (Massachusetts) Art Association in the house at 243 Worthen Street, where he was born. The house was built in 1824 for the chief engineer of the local canal system and was occupied by the Whistler family for four or five years. In the course of time it fell into disrepair and was used as a boardinghouse. The Lowell Art Association bought it in 1908, restored it, and maintains it as a social and art center. Now called the Whistler House and Parker Gallery, it is open to the public during most of the year.

Whistler's famous portrait of his mother was used as the design for a US postage stamp issued in honor of Mother's Day in 1934 — another centennial tribute. Although this painting — his most famous portrait — hangs in the Louvre, the United States has more of his paintings than any other country.

The largest single collection of Whistler's work is in the Freer Gallery of Art, now part of the Smithsonian Institution in Washington, D.C. The donor, Charles Lang Freer (1856–1919), a railway and industrial magnate, had been a collector of Oriental art and Whistler works long before he met and became a friend of Whistler. The Peacock Room of the Leyland House, decorated by Whistler, is part of the Freer collection. The many Whistler paintings to be seen in this collection include *Blue and Gold, Valparaiso Bay* (1866), and *The Thames in Ice* (1859). Also in Washington, D.C., the Library of Congress has an invaluable collection of Whistleriana, donated by the children of Joseph Pennell, his official biographer, who were in possession of the diaries of his mother.

The Metropolitan Museum of Art in New York City has Whistler's *Nocturne in Green and Gold, Cremorne Gardens at Night;* several portraits including those of Sir Henry Irving, Connie Gilchrist, and Theodore Duret; and a Whistler lithograph, *The Thames. Sarasate* (1884) is in the Carnegie Institute in Pittsburgh and *Yellow Buskin* (1878) in the Philadelphia Museum of Art. Whistler's portrait of Miss Cicely Alexander (1873) is in the National Gallery in London. His portrait of Thomas Carlyle (1873) is in Glasgow.

Wyoming Admitted to the Union

On July 10, 1890, Wyoming became a state. The 44th member to join the federal Union was — and remains — sparsely populated. But the Indians, explorers, fur trappers, railroad builders, gold prospectors, cowboys, and other people who have inhabited its regions have given Wyoming a rich and colorful history.

Indians were the sole inhabitants of the rugged and beautiful Wyoming terrain until 1806, when John Colter entered the region. Colter, who is generally recognized as the first non-Indian definitely known to have set foot in what is now Wyoming, had been a member of the Lewis and Clark expedition. But when that party began its return journey east in 1806, Colter de-

cided to remain in the Northwest. Throughout 1806 he trapped in the area south and east of what is now Yellowstone National Park, and in 1807 his search for pelts took him into the park area itself.

During the early decades of the 19th century the Pacific Northwest attracted many fur trappers, and these woodsmen explored much of Wyoming. In 1811 a party of 50 trappers sponsored by John Jacob Astor's Pacific Fur Company and led by Wilson Price Hunt crossed Wyoming on its way from St. Louis to the mouth of the Columbia River, where they built Fort Astoria. This expedition proved the feasibility of a central overland route to the Pacific. The following year members of the 1811 group returning to St. Louis under the leadership of Robert Stuart again traveled through Wyoming. Using a more southerly route than on their outward journey, the expedition came near, if it did not actually discover, South Pass, the important crossing point in the Continental Divide.

Even after the expeditions of Hunt and Stuart, fur trappers confined their activities to eastern Wyoming until 1824, when a party led by Thomas Fitzpatrick crossed the Continental Divide at South Pass. Fitzpatrick — or Broken Hand, Chief of the Mountain Men, as he was known to the Indians — is often credited with the discovery of the pass. But even if he was not actually the first non-Indian to come upon the crossing point, it was because of his efforts that the South Pass was publicized.

The Wyoming wilderness remained the domain of Indians and fur trappers during the 1820s and 1830s. Each year trappers and natives met with representatives of eastern fur companies at the annual "fur trade rendezvous" and exchanged their pelts for supplies and trinkets. The first permanent trading post in Wyoming was established near the junction of the Laramie and North Platte rivers in 1834. Initially known as Fort William, then as Fort John, and finally as Fort Laramie, this settlement quickly became the center of the Wyoming fur trade. In 1849 the federal government purchased the fort, and until 1890 it served as a garrison for army troops. Fort Laramie is now a National Historic Site and is open to the public.

In 1841 settlers started to flock to Oregon and a new era in the history of Wyoming began. One of the most popular routes to the Pacific was the 2,000-mile Oregon Trail, which extended from Independence, Missouri, to Fort Vancouver in the Oregon Country. Much of the trail adhered closely to the route that the trappers Robert Stuart and Thomas Fitzpatrick had blazed decades earlier. It proceeded from Independence to the Platte River and followed that stream's north branch from the western part of what is now Nebraska. After continuing to Fort Laramie in southeastern Wyoming, the trail continued west across the southern part of Wyoming and through the famous South Pass in the Rocky Mountains. After reaching Fort Bridger in the southwestern section of Wyoming, the trail continued northwest to the Snake River Valley, which it followed to Fort Boise. From there the route continued via the Grande Ronde Valley and across the Blue Mountains to the Columbia River, and along that mighty waterway until it eventually ended at Fort Vancouver.

Between 1841 and 1869 more than 300,000 persons went west along the Oregon Trail, and in so doing passed through Wyoming. Some went to the Oregon Country; others, after the discovery of gold in California in 1849, branched southwest in what is now Idaho and found their fortune in the California gold fields; only a handful of this vast number decided to remain in Wyoming. But the westward migration had a lasting effect on the area, for Wyoming became a vital link between the Pacific Northwest and the central and eastern United States. Early in the 1850s stagecoaches provided monthly service across Wyoming. By 1860 the pony express served the area, and in 1861 a telegraph system was established with stations at such places as Fort Laramie, South Pass, and Fort Bridger.

In 1861 the Civil War began, with fighting between the Northern and Southern states. The war effort necessitated the removal of large numbers of federal troops from garrison duty in the Northwest, and as the soldiers left, Indian defiance increased. Indian raids were common in Wyoming in 1862, 1863, and 1864, and hostilities became so serious that 1865 was known as the Bloody Year on the Plains. At the end of the Civil War several US Army expeditions were sent out to quell the troubles. The army established a precarious peace with the Sioux in 1868, but conflicts did not end until 1876, when the army decisively defeated the Indians.

In 1867 a major gold discovery was made in South Pass, and within a short time 15 mining camps had opened in the area. At about the same time the Union Pacific Railroad started to push across southern Wyoming. The town of Cheyenne was established in southeastern Wyoming in 1867 and a number of smaller settlements along the route of the railroad followed in quick succession.

As early as 1865 a proposal had been made to establish a separate government for Wyoming, and the area's substantial population increase following the gold strike of 1867, and the advance of the railroad spurred action on this proposition. On July 25, 1868, the Wyoming Organic Act, which created the Territory of Wyoming out of parts of the territories of Utah, Dakota, and Idaho, gained approval. Cheyenne was selected to be the territorial capital. Wyoming's first legislature convened there on October 12, 1869, and it was during this session that women of the territory were enfranchised (see December 10).

Wyoming prospered as a territory. Shortly after the Civil War, Texas cattlemen began to move their stock north to graze on Wyoming's great open ranges, and by 1884 approximately 800,000 head of cattle had journeyed along the Long Trail from Texas to Wyoming. In the 1880s settlers also began to establish homesteads in the territory. In only two years, more than 3 million acres that had previously been owned by the government or the railroads passed into private hands, and in only 10 years the territory's population increased 300 percent.

On July 10, 1890, Wyoming was admitted to the Union. When news of its statehood reached Wyoming, there was great rejoicing. In Cheyenne most buildings were draped with red, white, and blue bunting, and on July 23 a parade took place. Bands, state officials, and citizens marched, and many of Cheyenne's businessmen provided decorated wagons to commemorate Wyoming's new status. After the parade official ceremonies took place at the capitol building. Theresa A. Jenkins was the principal speaker at these exercises, and Esther Morris, who had been to a large degree responsible for gaining the passage of the woman suffrage bill in 1869, presented a flag to the state government. Morris said:

On behalf of the women of Wyoming, and in grateful recognition of the high privilege of citizenship that has been conferred upon us, I have the honor to present to the State of Wyoming this beautiful flag. May it always remain the emblem of our liberties, and the flag of the Union forever.

The governor then spoke, a special poem written for the occasion was recited, and other appropriate ceremonies took place to mark Wyoming statehood.

JULY 11

John Quincy Adams's Birthday

John Quincy Adams, the eldest son of John and Abigail Smith Adams, was born on July 11, 1767, in the section of Braintree, Massachusetts, that is now part of the city of Quincy. His father (see October 30), who was already decrying British colonial policy in articles for the Boston *Gazette,* was soon to emerge as a leader in the fight for independence and eventually become President of the United States. The younger Adams followed in the paternal footsteps — all the way to the White House.

The peripatetic nature of his father's life provided John Quincy Adams with a varied education both in and out of schools. In 1778, at the age of 10, he accompanied his father on a mission to France. Placed in a school at Passy, he studied French and Latin. In 1780, while his father was on a diplomatic mission in Amsterdam, he attended the Latin School in that city. The next year Francis Dana, the American envoy to Russia, took the youth to St. Petersburg as his secretary. John Quincy Adams performed similar services for his father in 1782–1783 and then returned to the United States. The young man graduated from Harvard in 1787, and after gaining admission to the bar in 1790 began to practice law in Boston.

In 1789 John Adams became Vice President under the country's first President. Washington soon found use for his son. He named Adams, still in his twenties, minister to Holland in 1794, a post he held for two years. In 1797 the elder Adams succeeded Washington as Chief Executive, and John Quincy Adams became minister to Prussia for the period of his father's presidency.

The accession of the Jeffersonian Republicans to national power after the election of 1800 closed the avenues of executive preferment to the sons of Federalist Presidents. John Quincy Adams switched his interests to the legislative branch of government and won a seat in the Massachusetts senate in April 1802. He failed to achieve election to the US House of Representatives in November 1802, but his colleagues in the legislature sent him to the US Senate in the following year. He arrived too late to take part in the ratification of the Louisiana Purchase but voted for the appropriation of funds for the purchase. Always a man of independent judgment, Adams rejected the opposition of his fellow New Englanders to President Jefferson's embargo act. He remained resolute in his support of the measure as the best means of avoiding war and lost so much popularity that he had to resign.

Academic interests temporarily called Adams away from politics as he devoted more time to his post as Boylston professor of rhetoric and oratory at Harvard College, a position he held from 1806 to 1809. He soon returned to the national scene, however, when President James Madison appointed him as minister to Russia, where he served until 1814. In that year he served as chairman with James Bayard, Henry Clay, Albert Gallatin, and Jonathan Russell on the peace commission that negotiated the Treaty of Ghent, ending the War of 1812 with England. Adams then became minister to Great Britain.

President James Monroe appointed John Quincy Adams secretary of state in 1817, an office that he filled with ability and distinction. He obtained the cession of Florida from Spain in 1819 and contributed greatly to the proclamation of the Monroe Doctrine. It was on his advice that the President made the declaration unilaterally, instead of in tandem with Great Britain as the British foreign secretary, George Canning, had suggested. Adams thought "it would be more candid, as well as more dignified, to avow our principles explicity to Russia and France, than to come in as a cock-boat in the wake of the British man-of-war."

John Quincy Adams was ready to make his bid for the White House in 1824. Andrew Jackson defeated him in the popular vote, but none of the four candidates — Jackson (99), Adams (84), William Crawford (41), or Henry Clay (37) — received the necessary electoral majority. On February 8, 1825, the House of Representatives, with each state having one vote, chose Adams President over Jackson by a vote of 13 to 7, with Crawford receiving the remaining 4 votes. In this crucial contest Clay gave his support to Adams, whose secretary of state he later became. Followers of Jackson, however, saw this as evidence of a "corrupt bargain," and the charge gained popular credence.

As President, Adams retained his independence of mind, but was not politically prudent. In his inaugural address he advocated a major program of internal improvements, a national university, and other measures that alienated large numbers of his sectionally minded constitutents. Even worse he failed to build up a personal political machine, and in 1828 the smoothly operating apparatus supporting Andrew Jackson easily wrested the presidency from him.

Adams returned home in defeat, but a year after his retirement he was elected to the House of Representatives by a Massachusetts district and reelected every two years for the remainder of his long life. Becoming prominently identified with the cause of antislavery in these later years, he opposed the annexation of Texas in 1836 and the extension of blacks' servitude. He also fought the adoption of the "gag rule," forbidding discussion of antislavery petitions, from 1836 until its defeat in 1844. A firm believer in the natural rights of man, which constitutions might recognize but could not create, he believed that the US Constitution could be defended only so far as it recognized those rights.

At the age of 80 Adams suffered a stroke in the House of Representatives on February 21, 1848. He was carried to the Speaker's office, where he died two days later.

Quincy, Massachusetts, has absorbed part of the old town of Braintree, but many relics connected with the Adams family remain just as they were. John Quincy Adams was buried beside his father in the First Unitarian Church there. An inscribed tablet surmounted by a bust of him is located near the pulpit, opposite a similar memorial to his father. The houses in which the second and sixth Presidents were born still stand at the junction of Franklin Street and Presidents Avenue. Popularly known as the "little red houses," these 17th century buildings are national historic sites — as is the nearby family mansion, the Old House, located at 135 Adams Street. The National Park Service administers these monuments, which contain a large amount of memorabilia, and are open to the public.

Grandfather Mountain Highland Games
Linville, North Carolina

This is a movable event. See note on page xxvi.

For two days each July, North Carolina's Grandfather Mountain, near Linville, resounds to the skirl of bagpipes and blazes with the color of tartans, as MacGregors, MacDougalls, MacLeods, Morrisons, MacMillans, MacNeils, and others — several thousand members of some 100 clans and thousands of additional onlookers — converge on the area for the Grandfather Mountain Highland Games and Gathering of Scottish Clans. Although there are similar gatherings elsewhere in the United States, particularly in the northeast, the one near Linville reportedly is the largest of its kind on this side of the Atlantic. Indeed a visitor from Scotland was heard to remark at one celebration that she had never seen so many kilts in one place, even in Scotland.

The event is not only a large one (with attendance usually reaching more than 50,000), it is also authentic. Many of the participants are descendants of the Scots who settled in the Carolinas in colonial times, some as a result of the defeat of the Jacobites at the battle of Culloden in 1746, and the ensuing strictures against the gathering of clans, the speaking of Gaelic, or the wearing of tartans. When the Scots emigrated, they took with them the traditional Scottish games and competitions that are seen at Grandfather Mountain now.

The Highland Games were initiated in 1956 by Scots-descended Agnes MacRae Morton of Linville's founding MacRae family, with the assistance of Donald F. MacDonald, who served as the event's first president until he moved to Scotland in 1961. They are held on the second weekend of July each year, under the sponsorship of 50 clans and Scottish societies, including the Burns Society of Charlotte, North Carolina; the Caledonian Society of Cincinnati; the Scottish Historic and Research Society of the Delaware Valley; and the Saint Andrews Societies of Baltimore, Maryland; Charleston and Columbia, South Carolina; Atlanta and Savannah, Georgia; the Middle South; the State of New York; Washington, D.C.; and Williamsburg, Virginia. Most of the events take place in the mountainside MacRae Meadows, a grassy field 4,000 feet above sea level, surrounded by rhododendron, Highland pine, thistle, mountain ash, and myrtle, and not far from the rocky crags that have been reminding transplanted Scots of home ever since they first arrived in the area.

The festivities get under way on Saturday with novice events in piping and dancing, and, an official *ceud mile failte* (100,000 welcomes) for visitors and honored guests. The latter may include clan dignitaries, and state or national officials. Official introductions are followed by the passing in review of the tartan-clad pipe bands.

The competitions begin in the early afternoon. Platform number one has Highland dancing, as organized by the US Highland Dancers' Association. Participants, in full Highland dress and arranged by age groups, perform such intricacies as the sword dance, Highland fling, *seann truibhas*, hornpipe, jig, and Highland reel. Piping and drumming competitions take place simultaneously on platform number two.

On the main field, meanwhile, track-and-field and Scottish events are in full swing with competitors from Virginia, the Carolinas, and other states, and their colleges. Included are such familiar events as the running and standing broad jumps and the running high jump; the pole vault and shot put; dashes of various lengths; a cross-country race; and a tug-of-war. Spectators show a particular fascination, however, with the rigorous, grunt-punctured labors of the bare-chested, kilt-clad Highland wrestlers.

Highland costume is also required for two other favorite events, the tossing of the sheaf and the tossing of the caber. The former consists of picking up a sheaf of gorse, heather, or hay with a pitchfork and tossing it over a crossbar suspended between two upright poles. The crossbar is raised after each round, and contestants are eliminated one by one on successive tries until there is a winner.

Although the sheaf toss is not for weaklings,

even greater brawn is needed to compete in the caber toss, for the caber (*cabar* in Scottish Gaelic), which looks like a small telephone pole, may be between 16 and 20 feet long and may weigh from 90 to 150 pounds. The contestant, who picks the caber up by its small end, staggers off to a running start with the caber held upright, then tosses it — aiming it so that it turns end over end and falls straight forward, touching a chalk mark on the ground.

Saturday's main events are preceded by an informal *Ceilidh*, held on Friday evening in the auditorium of Lees-McRae College in Banner Elk, North Carolina, a short distance from Linville. Singing, piping, and exhibition dancing are presented. The festivities have also been enlivened with Friday evening piping concerts at Sugar Mountain Lodge.

The fun of the *Ceilidh* is repeated on Saturday evening, and there is also a formal tartan ball, which is by invitation only and is usually attended by patrons of the games, celebrities, and heads of sponsoring societies. At the ball, winners of the various Highland dance competitions demonstrate their skills, and the top pipers and drummers play such numbers as "Scotland the Brave" and "Highland Laddie."

Sunday morning is given over to a worship service and "kirking of the tartans," followed by lunch and meetings of the clans. Shortly after noon, meanwhile, the Highland shoot, a tournament of the North Carolina Archery Association, takes place. It is followed by children's special events and a fencing competition. What is perhaps the most stirring highlight of the games comes at 2:00 P.M. with the appearance of the Massed Bands, which pass in review, followed by the Parade of Tartans, with tartan banners of some 50 clans carried by prominent clan members. The day's activities conclude with a final group of competitive events — the sheaf toss, caber toss, piping, Highland wrestling, tug-of-war, and exhibition of champions.

JULY 12

Henry David Thoreau's Birthday

Henry David Thoreau, the essayist, poet, and naturalist who believed in shaping one's life by inner principle, was born on July 12, 1817, in Concord, Massachusetts, where his father manufactured graphite pencils and his mother ran a boardinghouse. As a boy he delighted in the outdoors and enjoyed hunting and fishing. He studied at the Concord Academy and, at a sacrifice to his family, entered Harvard in 1833.

Retiring by nature, he held himself apart from college life and exhibited some of the independent spirit that was to rule his later life. He attended chapel in a green coat "because the rules required black," studied well but had little regard for the rank system, and preferred his own to a charted route through books in the college library. During these years he came into contact with exponents of transcendentalism, who viewed God as immanent in nature, stressed the relationship between the indwelling spirit in nature and the indwelling spirit of human beings, took intuition to be the highest form of knowledge, and glorified individualism.

Their thinking struck a responsive chord in Thoreau, who in 1837 demonstrated his own individuality with a nonconformist commencement piece scorning "the commercial spirit." It was during the same commencement week that America's leading Transcendentalist — Ralph Waldo Emerson (see May 25), who had become a resident of Concord — presented at Harvard his stirring declaration of intellectual independence from Europe, "The American Scholar." Among other things the address advised the seeker of truth (in words Thoreau later would live out) that "the ancient precept 'Know thyself' and the modern precept 'Study nature' [had] become at last one maxim."

After graduation Thoreau returned to Concord, where he taught in the town school, helped with his father's business, wrote in the journal that he would keep faithfully for the rest of his life, and practiced his chosen craft by writing poems and literary essays. In September of 1839 he and his brother John took the voyage that Thoreau was to immortalize in his joyous first book, *A Week on the Concord and Merrimack Rivers*. The book, which was not published until 1849, wove a subsequent decade of spiritual adventure into its fabric and showed Thoreau's relationship to nature as "one and continuous everywhere" and his own thought-filled life as "constantly as fresh as this river."

With his brother, he meanwhile had begun to conduct a private school at Concord in 1838. He had also begun his long association with the Concord Lyceum, as curator and lecturer, and he had had his first poem published in the new Transcendentalist magazine, *The Dial*, which was being edited at Concord under the auspices of, among others, Emerson and Margaret Fuller. After his brother's poor health forced the closing of their school in 1841, Thoreau accepted Emerson's invitation to live in his house and carry on his own work there, in return for services as a handyman-caretaker and as editorial assistant on *The Dial*.

Emerson helped turn Thoreau to nature writing, edited his poems stringently, introduced him to leading literary figures and, in 1843, sent him as tutor to the William Emersons of Staten Island — hoping he might be able to sell his work in New York. But Thoreau failed to find a market, disliked city life, and returned home disappointed and in debt. He summarized the next year with a brief entry in his journal: "Made pencils in 1844."

The great spiritual adventure of his life and the period of his most ecstatic communication with nature began on Independence Day of 1845, when he commenced a two-year stay in a simple cabin that he built in the woods on the shore of Concord's Walden Pond. In the resulting masterpiece, *Walden,* he later explained that he went there "because I wished to live deliberately, to front only the essential facts of life, and see if I could not learn what it had to teach, and not, when I came to die, discover that I had not lived." His experience in choosing this self-reliant and independent course led him to counsel others: "If a man does not keep pace with his companions, perhaps it is because he hears a different drummer. Let him step to the music which he hears, however measured or far away."

In September 1847 Thoreau returned to civilization and — except for an interval managing Emerson's household — spent the rest of his life in his father's home. From there he helped in the family business, worked as a surveyor, participated in an enjoyable social life, and delighted in daily walks about Concord. He brought with him the tangible results of his stay in the woods: the first draft of *A Week on the Concord and Merrimack Rivers* (which he published at considerable loss to himself in 1849), and new journals from which a number of later works would be gleaned.

The most notable of these was *Walden: or Life in the Woods,* which he worked on, corrected, and added to from the time of his return until its publication in 1854. It became a symbol of integrity and inner freedom, affirming Thoreau's belief that individuals have the ability to elevate their own lives "by conscious endeavor." His most famous essay, "Civil Disobedience," which so influenced Gandhi and later practitioners of passive resistance, meanwhile had been published in 1849. It was prompted by Thoreau's brief jailing, several years earlier, for nonpayment of the Massachusetts poll tax in protest against the Mexican War and slavery.

In his later life Thoreau, who said that he had "travelled a good deal in Concord," visited other parts of New England. He went several times to Maine, and also to Cape Cod and to Canada, recording both the literal trips and his spiritual excursions in his journal. Although signs of tuberculosis, which would cut his life short, had appeared as early as 1852, he remained active. He took the last of his three trips to Maine in 1857. He was increasingly vocal in his opposition to slavery following his lecture "Slavery in Massachusetts" (1854), with several impassioned speeches in defense of John Brown in 1859.

Thoreau went to Minnesota in search of health in 1861. He returned home further weakened and spent his last months feverishly editing manuscripts, which he left for his sister Sophia to publish after his death, on May 6, 1862.

They included *Excursions* (1863), *The Maine Woods* (1864), *Cape Cod* (1865), and *A Yankee in Canada* (1866). As published in 1906, the standard edition of his works ran to 20 volumes. His writing consistently championed the individual against materialistic society, and moral imperatives as superior to institutions created by human beings.

Thoreau's admirers may visit the Thoreau room in Concord's Antiquarian Museum; the Emerson house, also in Concord; and the site, marked by a cairn, of Thoreau's cabin at Walden. Also accessible to visitors are the Thoreau Lyceum on Belknap Street and, behind it, a reproduction of his Walden cabin.

A bust of Thoreau was placed in New York's Hall of Fame on the centenary of his death, in 1962. By congressional decision, development of what he had called Cape Cod's Great Beach — 50 miles of outer shore stretching from Chatham to Provincetown — as the Cape Cod National Seashore under supervision of the National Park Service was authorized in 1961. It was dedicated on Memorial Day in 1966 with Massachusetts dignitaries — Governor John A. Volpe, Senators Leverett Saltonstall and Edward M. Kennedy, and Representative Hastings Keith — and US Secretary of the Interior Stewart L. Udall among those participating in the exercises. In 1967, the 150th anniversary of his birth, Thoreau, whose writings and philosophy won greater favor in the 20th century than in his own lifetime, was the object of widespread attention. A commemorative postage stamp bearing his likeness was issued on his birthday and sold first by the post office in Concord.

JULY 13

Northwest Ordinance Enacted

Even as patriot soldiers were fighting the British to gain American independence, the Continental Congress was laying plans for the future of the United States. Legislators with a vision of a large united nation sought to obtain central control of the vast western lands, located west of the

Allegheny Mountains, east of the Mississippi River, and north of the Ohio River, which New York, Connecticut, Virginia, and Massachusetts claimed by virtue of their colonial charters and patents. In 1780 the Congress promised to use any western lands surrendered to the Confederation — the "firm league of friendship" of the states under the Articles of Confederation — for the good of the whole country and eventually create out of the domain several new, equal states. Virginia responded to the pledge by renouncing its claim in 1781, and New York, Massachusetts, and Connecticut followed suit in 1781, 1785, and 1786 respectively.

The Continental Congress quickly established a committee under Thomas Jefferson of Virginia to devise a plan of government for the newly acquired territory, which included 265,878 square miles of land and water. On March 1, 1784, the day that the Congress accepted Virginia's cession of its western claims, Jefferson presented his program. He proposed that the government eventually carve not more than 10 new states from the territory. Believing that democracy fared best in small jurisdictions, Jefferson, who seriously underestimated the size of the area, urged that none of the 10 states be larger than 150 miles square. The Virginian's scheme advocated the abolition of slavery and universal manhood suffrage, and promised a great deal of self-government for the inhabitants. Settlers, upon their petition or by direction from Congress, could set up a government modeled on the constitution and laws of any one of the 13 original states, and, when the population reached 20,000, they could devise a republican constitution of their own choosing. Finally, when the inhabitants of the territory became as numerous as the population of the least populous state, they could apply for admission to the Union. The Continental Congress rejected Jefferson's suggestion banning slavery from the Northwest but accepted the rest of his proposal on April 23, 1784.

Administrative obstacles delayed the implementation of Jefferson's territorial ordinance, and conservatives in the Congress strove to undo his work. Led by Rufus King of Massachusetts, the conservatives persuaded the Congress to empower the appointed territorial governor with an absolute veto, and to limit the right to vote and to hold office to property owners. Under the influence of King and his associates, the Congress also raised the number of inhabitants required for the organization of a territorial legislature from 500 to 5,000, and set the population mandatory for admission to the Union at a figure equal to one-thirteenth of the population of the original states. The last provision would have kept Wisconsin out of the Union until 1900.

Conservative fears of unruly westerners had lessened by 1786, and the Congress decided to revamp its territorial enactments. Working from Jefferson's program as modified by a committee whose spokesman was Nathan Dane, the Continental Congress on July 13, 1787, passed its most famous piece of legislation, the Northwest Ordinance. The statute set what became the unique US procedure for the creation of states — followed throughout the rest of the new lands the nation acquired as it expanded to the Pacific. The new law placed a congressionally appointed governor, secretary, and three judges in charge of the territory initially, and promised the establishment of a bicameral legislature when the free adult white male population reached 5,000. The ordinance provided for the eventual creation from the territory of three to five fully equal states, each of which would have a population of at least 60,000 as a prerequisite for statehood. The Congress guaranteed freedom of worship, trial by jury, and publicly supported education and, in accord with Jefferson's earliest proposal, banned slavery in the Northwest. Additional stipulations, devised by Dane, prohibited any laws impairing the obligation of contracts, and established rules of inheritance that insured the democratic distribution of land.

Arthur St. Clair became the first governor of what was known officially as the Territory Northwest of the River Ohio, and on July 15, 1788, inaugurated the government at the territorial capital of Marietta. His first official act was the founding of Washington County. The first territorial legislature met in 1799 with 22 members from nine counties sitting in the House of Representatives.

In May 1800 Congress divided the Northwest Territory into two governments, separated by a boundary line from the mouth of the Kentucky River north to Canada. The diminished Territory Northwest of the River Ohio, with its capital at Chillicothe, lay east of the line; and Indiana Territory, with its capital at Vincennes, lay to the west. William Henry Harrison, who became the first governor of the Indiana Territory, was later elected President of the United States.

Ohio, admitted to the Union as the 17th member state in 1803, was the first state formed from the Northwest Territory. Congress created the Michigan and the Illinois territories from Indiana Territory in 1805 and 1809 respectively. Illinois gained statehood in 1818 (see December 3) and Michigan in 1837 (see January 26). The remainder of Indiana Territory became the state of Indiana in 1816, and a portion of Michigan Territory organized as Wisconsin Territory in 1836 gained admission to the Union as the state of Wisconsin in 1848. Eventually a small portion of what had been the Northwest Territory became a part of Minnesota, which gained statehood in 1858.

JULY 14

Bastille Day

The storming of the Bastille in Paris, on July 14, 1789, the first serious act of violence of the French Revolution, was widely regarded as a blow for freedom against the tyranny of the Bourbon kings who had so long ruled France. Started about 1369 at the order of Charles V, the prison-fortress, with its eight towers and 100-foot walls, dominated Paris. Beginning in the 17th century, it housed political prisoners primarily, including many persons of fame or influence who had displeased the court or were deemed a threat. "The Man in the Iron Mask," Voltaire, the Marquis de Sade, and Cardinal Louis de Rohan were among the Bastille's famous tenants.

Most prisoners were relatively well treated, despite tales to the contrary. What made the Bastille notorious and a hated symbol of royal absolutism was the fact that critics of the regime were detained within its walls through the use of an arbitrary and secret order of imprisonment known as a *lettre de cachet*. Inaugurated by Louis XV, the letter was nothing less than a commitment paper ordering the Bastille's jailer to confine in a cell a particular person until further notice — which frequently never came.

Therefore, when the Parisians began to revolt in 1789, they launched their first attack on the detested prison, in hopes of capturing ammunition as well. They took it by storm, killing the governor and seven of his men, throwing its archives to the winds, and releasing the prisoners. There were only seven at the time, none of them political prisoners, but they were nevertheless carried through the streets of the city and hailed as victims of oppression. The Bastille was dismantled piece by piece for souvenirs. Very little of the ancient fortress remained when it was officially ordered razed two days later.

The Marquis de Lafayette, who had been named commander of the National Guard the day after the Bastille fell, secured the key to the former fortress. In a March 17, 1790, letter, he explained his reasons for offering it to George Washington:

Give me leave, my dear General, to present you . . . with the main key of the fortress of despotism. It is a tribute which I owe as a son to my adopted father, as an aide de camp to my general, as a missionary of liberty to its patriarch.

Lafayette entrusted the two-toothed, seven-inch piece of iron to Thomas Paine for transmittal to Washington. It still occupies a place of honor among the memorabilia hanging in the central hallway of Washington's home, Mount Vernon.

Predisposed to the cause of liberty and social equality, Americans hailed the destruction of the Bastille with joy. A public celebration was held in Philadelphia on the first anniversary of the event, July 14, 1790. Ships along the river front were decorated with flags and salutes were fired from the several French vessels anchored in the harbor. There was a dinner at Oeller's Hotel, with toasts to both King Louis XVI and the French people. Another dinner was held at Ogden's Hotel on the same day by the officers of Colonel John Shee's Fourth Philadelphia Regiment.

By 1793 the French revolutionaries, having become increasingly radical, had not only abolished the monarchy and set up the First Republic, but had charged Louis XVI with treason and executed him. Passions — for liberty and against the tyranny of the murdered French king — had also risen on this side of the Atlantic, to judge by J. Thomas Scharf and Thompson Westcott's description of a 1793 Bastille Day dinner in their *History of Philadelphia, 1609–1884:*

It was probably at this dinner that the head of a pig was severed from its body and being recognized as an emblem of the head of the murdered King of France, was carried around among the guests. Each one, placing the cap of liberty on his head, pronounced the word "tyrant" and proceeded to mangle with his knife the head of the luckless creature doomed to be served for so unworthy a company.

As Americans grew more and more accustomed to the heady draught of liberty, their observance of Bastille Day as a separate public event gradually diminished. The obvious exception was the 100th anniversary in 1889, which was celebrated in leading American cities.

Later, during the First World War, pro-French sympathies led to a renewed observance. By 1917, the United States had officially entered World War I, joining with France and the other Allies against Germany. Americans at home and abroad marked the first wartime Bastille Day. General John J. Pershing, commander in chief of the American Expeditionary Force, ordered his troops to commemorate the occasion, and at the annual military parade in Paris he was given a place of honor in the reviewing stand beside the French president, Raymond Poincaré. To raise funds for prisoners of war, Parisians sold medals with the profiles of George Washington and the Marquis de Lafayette on one side and the dates July 4, 1776 and July 14, 1789 on the other. The US national anthem was sung during the evening performance at the Opéra Comique.

Elaborate celebrations were staged in New York City and Philadelphia. The demand for the return of Alsace-Lorraine to France dominated the New York events, which included a Fête Nationale de Juillet held by the Association Démocratique des Canadiens et Français de New York at the Harlem Casino.

In Philadelphia the 1917 anniversary of the fall of the Bastille was celebrated, appropriately, at Independence Hall. French flags flew from the front windows, and a facsimile of the key of the Bastille was displayed in the Supreme Court Room. There was a parade in honor of the occasion.

In 1918, with the Allies advancing toward victory, preparations began weeks in advance for an even more sumptuous observance of Bastille Day. The nationwide celebration was arranged by a national committee, of which former President William Howard Taft was the honorary chairman. There were also local committees in different cities. Proclaimed a holiday by the governors of several states, Bastille Day was also officially observed at every US Army and Navy installation. As in the preceding year, President Woodrow Wilson cabled greetings to the French president and people, and the French flag was flown from the White House staff. Ninety cities, including Denver, Kansas City, New Orleans, Chicago, Omaha, Saint Paul, and Boston, asked the national Bastille Day organization for guest speakers.

In New York City, Mayor John Hylan ordered the French flag flown from all public buildings and asked New Yorkers to do the same at home. A large rally, held at Madison Square Garden and presided over by Charles Evans Hughes, attracted a capacity crowd of 12,000 persons. The colorful exercises were highlighted by a military tableau with soldiers, sailors, and marines of every nationality in the Alliance, and speeches by the French ambassador, Jules Jusserand; the British and Italian ambassadors; and Samuel Gompers, president of the American Federation of Labor. The French societies in New York and the vicinity gathered at Manhattan Center at a benefit to raise war funds, while French people and Francophiles conducted special exercises at the Joan of Arc statue on Riverside Drive. A French aviator daringly flew under all of New York City's bridges.

In 1919 American soldiers joined in the Bastille Day victory fetes in Paris. They proved to be very popular dancing partners with the Parisian women, especially in the intricacies of the tango. In the victory parade of Allied soldiers, the Americans were put first in the line of march.

At home American officers who had rendered distinguished service in the war received awards from the Legion of Honor from French ambassador Jusserand at a special Washington, D.C. ceremony. Patriotic societies in New York City sponsored a concert attended by 10,000 people at Lewisohn Stadium, and French organizations celebrated once more at Manhattan Center.

During the 1920s and 1930s Bastille Day continued to be observed in a traditional manner. The American President annually sent greetings to the French head of state. French societies in leading US cities staged special events — bazaars, concerts, field games, balls, and speeches. French and American veterans staged parades. In 1936 the observance coincided with the 50th anniversary of the Statue of Liberty, a gift of the French people to the United States. The Bastille Day exercises were therefore staged partly on board the French liner *Normandie* and partly on Bedloes Island in New York harbor in the shadow of the statue.

On July 14, 1939, festivities marking the 150th anniversary of the fall of the Bastille were held with much fanfare at the flag-bedecked French Pavilion of the New York World's Fair. The numerous visitors little anticipated the striking contrast that the celebration would offer the following year, after World War II had erupted in Europe. By July 1940 France had been ignominiously defeated by Hitler's armies, and Marshal Henri Pétain, who had signed the armistice, became the head of the collaborationist Vichy government, controlling the unoccupied section of France. Soon General Charles de Gaulle was to proclaim from London the continued resistance of the Free French.

In New York City, on the saddest Bastille Day in history, French war veterans joined other French people in a day of mourning, gathering at the French Roman Catholic Church of Saint Vincent de Paul to offer a solemn mass for those French killed in the war. At several other churches the French flag had been draped in black crepe, and the congregation wore both black and tricolor armbands.

The sympathy of the American people for the French plight inspired a renewal of interest in

Bastille Day from coast to coast. In 1941 a special July 14 radio program was broadcast from Beverly Hills by the Fight for Freedom Organization; and the Woodstock, New York, chapter of France Forever arranged a *bal musette* or dance with accordion music. By December the United States had entered World War II on the side of France, England, and the other Allies.

In 1942 two widely divergent groups marked Bastille Day in New York City. On the one hand, the Vichy government representatives attended only a solemn high mass at the Church of Saint Vincent de Paul. The Free French, on the other hand, supporting the resistance movement headed by General de Gaulle, refused to resign themselves to defeat. Instead they staged a week-long observance entitled Free French Week, organized by all the Free French groups, the Central Committee of French Societies, and the Association of French Veterans. Leading up to Bastille Day, each day of Free French Week was designated with a special title and featured special activities; and on July 14 there were elaborately planned ceremonies, including an afternoon reception for the American press, a gathering of 1,600 persons at the French legation, and a diplomatic reception in honor of representatives of the Allied governments. At a mass meeting at Manhattan Center, which was attended by several thousand Americans and Free French, messages were read from, among others, General John J. Pershing and General Douglas MacArthur (then at headquarters in Australia); and an address by General de Gaulle, summoning his compatriots everywhere to stand firmly behind the Allied cause, was transmitted directly from London.

A similar spirit of enthusiasm was evident throughout the rest of the United States. In California July 14 was declared the Day of Fighting France; in San Francisco and Los Angeles the French flag was flown at the city halls and the "Marseillaise" was sung; and feature articles and photographs appeared in newspapers throughout the country.

The 1943 festivities in New York City were highlighted by street dancing, a traditional note of Bastille Day gaiety in Paris that had had to be omitted there during the wartime curfews. A sign marked the area closed off for dancing. "French territory: New Yorkers — Don't believe all you hear — There was a France — There is a France — There will be a France — ALWAYS."

In the years immediately following World War II, a variety of special programs marked Bastille Day. On July 14, 1945, the city-wide celebration in New York centered on the Waldorf-Astoria Hotel, where French people and Americans joined in celebrating the first truly joyous fete since the fall of France in 1940. At a formal gathering at the French Embassy in Washington in 1947, French ambassador Henri Bonnet presented the Médaille Militaire posthumously to Franklin Delano Roosevelt. In 1949, the 160th anniversary of the fall of the Bastille, the festivities in Central Park, New York City, were attended by hundreds of American and French veterans.

Since the 1950s, July 14 has continued to be commemorated in several American cities. In New York, where French influence abounds, the day typically includes morning services at French Protestant and Roman Catholic churches; a reception sponsored by the French Consulate; and a dinner-dance held by Franco-American societies at a leading hotel. On occasion additional events have been included. In 1954, for instance, there was an all-French concert at Lewisohn Stadium, complete with intermission speeches, a color guard of veterans of World Wars I and II, and young women in French provincial costumes. In 1965 some 500 persons were invited to the French consulate to watch the unveiling of a bronze plaque bearing the names of the French ships and regiments that had fought in the American Revolution.

In Louisiana, an area linked with French traditions, Bastille Day is commemorated in widely diverse ways. July 14 is celebrated by French-speaking societies and the French Consulate with pomp and splendor in New Orleans, and with black-tie dinners and toasts in Baton Rouge. In contrast is the informal Gallic rural flavor instilled into the Bastille Day celebration held at Kaplan, Louisiana. As advertised, it is "America's only communitywide celebration of France's national holiday," and has been a traditional event there for more than three generations. The French-speaking, Acadian town of Kaplan is a rice-growing, agricultural community located west of New Iberia, some 30 miles from the Gulf of Mexico. Bastille Day events there range from a "fais do do" (an Acadian folk-flavored street dance) and fireworks to amateur athletics and bicycle riding contests. Bastille Day in Kaplan originated with Eugene Eleazer, an emigrant from France in 1888, who became mayor in 1920. Under his inspiration and guidance, the town held its first July 14 fete in 1906, an event repeated ever since except briefly during World War II.

In France, Bastille Day has continued to be celebrated as the great national holiday. During World War II, even Nazi orders could not suppress patriotic observance. In peacetime, frivolity is the keynote in Paris. On the evening and night of July 14, cafés on the banks of the Seine are crowded; and not even thunder, lightning, or sheets of rain can deter the dancing and outdoor celebrations. There are customarily free performances, for those who manage to squeeze in, at the Comédie Française and the Opéra Comique, as well as additional street dancing and other merriment.

On the morning of July 14, there has traditionally been an impressive military parade down the broad, tree-lined Champs-Élysées, with tanks rumbling down the thoroughfare and sleek Mirage jets soaring overhead. In some years however, the formality and the military aspects of the parade have been deemphasized in favor of color and festivity.

Gerald R. Ford's Birthday

At a time when controversy and concern over the conduct of the federal government seemed to engulf the nation, Gerald Rudolph Ford became the 38th President of the United States — the first to take office under the 25th Amendment. He was elevated to the presidency on August 9, 1974, when his predecessor, Richard M. Nixon (see January 9), resigned the office under threat of impeachment. In the history of the country, no other President had resigned from office.

Ford was the first to fill the presidential office without having been popularly elected either President or Vice President. Just 10 months earlier President Nixon had selected Ford to replace Spiro T. Agnew, the elected Vice President, who had been under criminal investigation and who had resigned October 10, 1973, after pleading no contest to a charge of income tax evasion.

The man who assumed leadership of the country in such difficult circumstances had the advantage of sturdy roots. He was born Leslie Lynch King Jr. on July 14, 1913, in Omaha, Nebraska, the only child of Dorothy Gardner King and Leslie King, a wool trader. His parents were divorced in 1915, and his mother returned with her two-year-old son to her family in Grand Rapids, Michigan.

There she married Gerald R. Ford, a paint salesman, and a strong and fair-minded man who was undisputed head of the house. He demanded truthfulness and hard work of her son, whom he adopted and gave his own name, and of the three sons subsequently born of the marriage. The Fords were active in community and church affairs, which often formed the basis for dinner-table discussion. Gerald Ford Sr.'s example as a doer was copied by all of his sons. The eldest, who became known as Jerry, felt tremendous respect and affection for his adoptive father, who became the dominant influence in his life.

In 1929 Gerald Ford Sr. and a partner went into the paint-manufacturing business. The family moved from its home on Union Avenue in Grand Rapids to the more fashionable East Grand Rapids area. No sooner had they moved, however, than the Great Depression struck, making it necessary for them to relocate to a less expensive house.

Young Gerald Ford strove for good grades in school and during his early years was not particularly outgoing. Having picked up his father's love for athletics, he made a name for himself in high-school football. In his junior and senior years he was chosen All-State center, and his team won the state championship in the latter year.

His football prowess helped gain him a scholarship to the University of Michigan. As he had in high school, he found part-time work waiting on tables and washing dishes. Ford was named the most valuable player in his senior year, and his skill on the field again opened a door for him.

Offered a position as assistant football coach and coach of the boxing team at Yale University, Ford felt it might make possible the realization of a long-held ambition to attend law school. Turning down offers to play professional football, he accepted the Yale offer and spent considerable time that summer taking boxing lessons. Not until his fourth year at Yale, however, was he able to persuade the law school faculty to let him take some courses on a trial basis, to prove he could handle them while continuing to coach. In 1941 he graduated in the top third of a class of which almost 80 per cent were members of Phi Beta Kappa.

Besides athletics and law, another field claimed some of Ford's interest for a time while he was at Yale. A friend who modeled persuaded him not only to put up money to help a friend of hers open a new modeling agency in New York City, but also to do some modeling himself. In a *Look* magazine picture story, for example, Ford and the young woman were depicted as a handsome, outdoorsy pair enjoying a ski weekend.

Returning to Grand Rapids with his LL.B. degree, Ford was admitted to the Michigan Bar and put organized sports behind him. With the intention of specializing in labor law, he opened an office with Philip Buchen, a friend from the University of Michigan. However, his plans were changed less than six months later by the United States' entry into World War II.

Ford enlisted in the US Navy in 1942 and, with his background in sports, was assigned to a physical-training unit (known as the "Tunney fish" program, since former boxing champion

Gene Tunney headed it). For a year he worked unhappily with aviation cadets at the University of North Carolina at Chapel Hill, until his superiors finally agreed to his requests for transfer to active duty.

The USS *Monterey*, a new light aircraft carrier on which Ford subsequently served as both director of physical training and an assistant navigation officer, saw major action in the Pacific as part of the US Third Fleet. He said it was a lucky ship. Though it was repeatedly under attack, its worst enemy turned out to be the great pacific typhoon of December 1944, a severe storm that took 800 lives and capsized three destroyers. Ford was almost one of the 800. Losing his footing, he slid across the flight deck and over the edge, fortunately dropping to a catwalk beneath, rather than into the raging sea.

In 47 months of active duty, Ford accumulated 10 battle stars and an excellent service record. His superiors' critiques contained such evaluations as "excellent leader," "outstanding," "steady, reliable, resourceful," "excellent organizer" and "at his best in situations dealing directly with people because he commanded the respect of all." Upon his release from active duty he became a lieutenant commander in the naval reserve.

"All I was interested in was enjoying life and getting on with my law practice," Ford said with regard to his plans when he returned in late 1945 to live with his parents in East Grand Rapids. He joined a highly respected law firm, with which Philip Buchen was already associated, and began to realize how much the times had changed.

As he became involved in the struggle of young veterans and their wives to find housing, he learned that their difficulties stemmed from the banking, zoning, and real estate interests controlled by the local Republican political boss. He reestablished contact with some local good-government forces that had begun to build a political base shortly before the war, and with them created the Independent Veterans Association, of which he became vice president. It lobbied vigorously, and its considerable degree of success elated Ford and turned his thoughts toward political office.

Actually Ford had had a brief encounter with politics in the summer of 1940, when he eagerly volunteered to work in the presidential campaign of the maverick Republican Wendell Willkie. Although Willkie lost the election decisively, he did very well in the Grand Rapids area and even managed to carry the state.

In the postwar period, Michigan's prestigious Republican senator Arthur H. Vandenberg was among the most influential members of Congress. Previously an isolationist, he had changed dramatically to become a leading internationalist as a result of World War II. Ford had experienced the same change in attitude. So in 1948, when Ford, with the backing of the good-government group, decided to challenge the incumbent isolationist, machine-politician Republican who represented his district in the US House of Representatives, he was encouraged by Vandenberg.

During the primary election campaign Ford moved through his district from early morning until late at night, seeming to appear wherever and whenever people congregated, trying to meet and talk with every voter. Ford volunteered to help busy farmers and struck up conversations while pitching hay or doing other chores. Although his campaign platform was based principally on internationalism, Ford approached individual voters by asking what he could do for the voter if elected. His opponent relied solely on the support of his machine, which did not regard Ford's candidacy as a threat.

Toward the end of the campaign, however, when the incumbent became worried about increased signs of popular support for Ford, he demanded that the party boss secure removal of the Quonset hut Ford had set up in downtown Grand Rapids to serve as his headquarters. Pressure was accordingly applied to Ford's law firm, but the firm supported him, and the hut remained. Ford was victorious in the primary, with 23,632 votes to 14,341 for his opponent.

In addition to the warmth with which voters responded to his campaign style and candor, another factor contributing to his success was the large number of women working for him. It was unusual at the time for women to be asked to help in that way, and they responded enthusiastically.

One of Ford's campaign workers was his fiancée, Elizabeth (Betty) Bloomer Warren, whom Ford had met in Grand Rapids after the war. A talented dancer who had studied with Martha Graham in New York, she had earlier considered pursuing a career as a dancer. She shared Ford's love of sports and had even played on a girls' football team.

Between primary day, September 14, and general election day, November 2, the candidate and his fiancée barely managed to sandwich in their wedding, on October 15, 1948. Their two-day honeymoon included attendance at a political reception. Four children were subsequently born to the Fords: Michael Gerald, John Gardner, Steven Meigs, and Susan Elizabeth.

In November Ford won election to the US House of Representatives with 60.5 percent of the total vote. On the same day Democrat Harry S. Truman was unexpectedly returned to the presidency.

Taking to heart some advice on how to please his constituents, the new member of Congress immediately began to "service" his district. Each visitor to his office was welcomed with open arms and photographed with Ford, or, if he was not there, at his desk. Ford, or his wife, made time to take important personages to lunch or dinner. Every person who wrote to Ford received a reply. Mention in a hometown newspaper of a birth, marriage, death, or an award or the like, elicited an appropriate note from the congressman – who signed all his own mail, often adding a personal note. He did not use the congressional pork-barrel system, but his constituents were never far from his mind. So successful was Ford's staff in working with the district that other lawmakers used similar techniques.

Ford became a member of the Appropriations Committee during his second term, and this position opened many doors for him, particularly after he had gained a reputation as the House member most knowledgeable about defense-spending budgets.

Not long after entering Congress, Ford had recognized that real power resided in the Speaker of the House, and set his sights on winning that job. That ambition and the belief that he was in a strong position in the House were probably mainly responsible for his rejection of Republican backing to run for the Senate or the Michigan governorship in 1952 and later years.

In early 1952 Ford was one of a group of Republican congressmen urging Dwight D. Eisenhower to seek the Republican presidential nomination that year. Eisenhower was nominated and elected, with Richard M. Nixon as his Vice President. Ford and Nixon had been friends from the time they served together in the House, and because Eisenhower left most of the political aspects of the presidency to his Vice President, Ford now had a friend at the top.

Later Nixon had strong backing from Ford on a number of occasions. One was in 1956, when a segment of the party wanted to "dump" Nixon in favor of another vice presidential nominee for Eisenhower's second term. Another instance was in 1960, when Ford felt that Nixon's training and his conduct – for example, during Eisenhower's illnesses – qualified him for the presidency. That year's election went to John F. Kennedy, the Democratic candidate, however.

Meanwhile, Ford's reputation for honesty and candor had put him in great demand for political dinners and rallies, though he was a public speaker of only moderate ability. Being ambi-

tious, he was glad of the opportunity to become familiar with other areas of the country and their concerns. In 1960 he let his name be put forward, unsuccessfully, as a candidate for the vice presidential nomination. He began to climb the ladder three years later, becoming chairman of the House Republican caucus. Then, in a revolt among Republican House members in 1965, Ford was installed as minority leader. He gained considerable public exposure as a result, through the "Ev and Jerry Show," a weekly television program on which he and Senate minority leader Everett Dirksen presented the Republican view on current issues.

Ford was a loyal party man, and he represented a conservative district. As a legislator he usually followed the views of his party. He indicated deep reservations about civil-rights laws, but finally voted for those that seemed sure to pass. His position on social-welfare legislation was strongly conservative. He authored no major piece of legislation. He believed ardently in strong US defenses, and supported spending authorizations to provide them. Anxious for military victory in Vietnam he urged President Lyndon B. Johnson to bomb more heavily and to blockade North Vietnamese ports.

After President Kennedy was killed in 1963, President Johnson named Ford the Republican House member to serve on the Warren commission to investigate the circumstances of the assassination.

One of Ford's more controversial actions as representative came after two of President Nixon's appointees to the Supreme Court were rejected by the Senate in 1969 and 1970. It was the first time in 40 years that the Senate had voted down a President's Supreme Court nominee. At that point, Ford called for a special House investigation to determine whether there were grounds to impeach one of the sitting Supreme Court justices, William O. Douglas. Ford stated some years later that he had moved in order to forestall an actual impeachment resolution that a small group of Republicans and Democrats planned to introduce, and to indicate the need for a single standard for judging all Supreme Court members or prospective members.

Nixon, who had successfully sought the presidency in 1968, was reelected four years later. When Agnew resigned in October 1973, Nixon quickly nominated Ford to fill the vacancy. It was the first exercise of the procedures set forth in the 25th Amendment to the Constitution (see February 10).

Ford, though politically ambitious, nevertheless had to do some hard thinking. He had promised his wife that he would retire from politics, probably to law practice in Grand

Rapids, after his next term. That commitment had been made easier by his weakening hopes of ever becoming Speaker; the Democrats' control of the House of Representatives seemed too secure.

His decision, with his wife's acquiescence, was to accept the nomination. Thereupon every aspect of his life was subjected to an unparalleled, detailed investigation, from which he emerged with the label "Mr. Clean." Confirmation by a majority vote of both houses of the Congress, as required by the 25th Amendment, was easily obtained. As congressman, Ford's openness and friendly manner, and his integrity, modesty, and willingness to listen to the opinions of others, as well as his conscientious work, had won him widespread respect and liking among his peers in both parties. He genuinely liked people, and was proud to be able to say, "I have had lots of adversaries, but no enemies that I can remember."

On December 6, 1973, in the chamber of the House of Representatives, Ford was sworn in as the 40th Vice President of the United States. He brought with him his penchant for hard work and long hours, and spent most of the next eight months traveling around the country — more than 100,000 miles — and giving 500 speeches in 40 states in an effort to improve the image of the Republican party and of President Nixon, while presenting himself in his new role as a party leader. The President, particularly, had suffered substantial loss of support as a result of the Watergate scandals and subsequent cover-up efforts by members of his White House staff. Involved in the Watergate affair were alleged illegal activities by, or at the behest of, various members of the Nixon administration, directed in large part toward ensuring the President's 1972 reelection and raising funds or conducting political espionage for that purpose.

During the long investigation of Watergate-related matters, Ford's information on the subject was only that which was public knowledge. He knew of no impeachable offense committed by the President, as he often stated — and he wished to know of none: since he would succeed to the office if Nixon resigned or was removed through impeachment proceedings, he tried scrupulously to avoid any word or action that could possibly influence the course of events.

By the end of July 1974, disclosures resulting from the investigation led the House Judiciary Committee to adopt Articles of Impeachment charging Nixon with obstruction of justice and other abuses of power. By early August an almost complete defection from the President had occurred among members of the House, who were about to vote on whether to accept the impeachment articles, and the Senate, which would officiate in an impeachment trial if they did. Advised of the probability of his impeachment, Nixon, on August 8, announced his decision to resign. Earlier that morning he spoke privately with Ford, informing him that he would step down the next day.

At noon on August 9, 1974, Gerald R. Ford, who had never aspired to the office of President, took the oath in the East Room of the White House. The 61-year-old Ford was in excellent physical condition to meet the demands of the presidency. He had made a habit of swimming daily in the pool of his home in suburban Alexandria, Virginia, in which the family had lived for 19 years. Golfing and skiing were other frequently indulged forms of recreation.

His ability to remain good-natured under difficult circumstances would stand him in good stead. So would his amicable relations with reporters, whose services he considered vital to a free country. He was determined that his policy of openness be followed by members of his administration, in contrast with White House policy of the most recent past.

He had had, however, little time to prepare for the presidency. Economics and foreign affairs were relatively unfamiliar fields. In the latter area Ford was aided enormously by Nixon's secretary of state, Henry Kissinger, who stayed on in the new administration to keep the nation's foreign policy on the same course. Too, Ford had been a part of the legislative branch for 25 years, and such a rapid transition to responsibility for the executive branch was bound to be difficult. In Congress he had exercised leadership by reconciling differing points of view, and he was more known for this than as an innovator or for broad imagination.

The new President pledged to work closely with Congress, and to refrain from what the legislature considered to be usurpation of its powers by several of his predecessors. He moved slowly in making cabinet and staff changes. His nomination on August 20 of Nelson Rockefeller, former governor of New York, to fill the vice presidency, also under the provisions of the 25th Amendment, was the subject of prolonged congressional hearings before the choice was finally confirmed in December 1974.

Inflation, cited by Ford as the country's number one problem, was accompanied by what was soon seen as a full-scale recession. "Stagflation" was the term concocted for the ominous new combination of inflation with economic stagnation. There were wide differences of opinion as to what constituted the proper prescription for the malady. Some felt that establishment of wage and price controls and other strong measures were of crucial importance. Others, including Ford, who opposed mandatory controls, preferred to rely on voluntary measures. However, despite the President's calls during his early months in office for a nationwide emphasis on frugality and energy conservation, both prices and unemployment continued to rise while industrial production decreased. By December unemployment in the United States had risen to 6.5 percent and the nation's jobless would later swell to a still higher figure. In addition to this, there was serious concern for the economy in many other parts of the world as well. Almost everywhere problems were magnified by a growing world energy shortage, as well as impending shortages of key raw materials. Although such long-threatened shortages had been anticipated by experts, it was only in the 10 months preceding Ford's inauguration as President that an awareness of the true dimensions of these problems had burst upon the consciousness of most people.

In Ford's case, the "honeymoon" period normally enjoyed by a new President with Congress and the people lasted only about a month. It ended abruptly on Sunday, September 8, when he announced his granting of an unconditional pardon to former President Nixon for any federal crimes he "may have committed or taken part in" during his tenure as Chief Executive. The move was taken with almost no consultation and drew criticism on the grounds that a pardon could not be granted when there had been no confession of guilt and that justice was not served by the action. Rather than putting the Watergate affair to rest, as the President had hoped, his action reemphasized the matter as a divisive national issue. On October 17 Ford made what was, for a President, a singular appearance before a congressional panel of inquiry, assuring a subcommittee of the House Judiciary Committee that there had been no "deal" with Nixon concerning the pardon.

One result of the Watergate scandals was passage of legislation — which Ford signed in October — authorizing public financing of future presidential elections and primaries and limiting contributions to and spending by presidential, vice presidential, and congressional candidates.

Earlier the President had effected a plan of conditional amnesty for Vietnam War draft evaders and deserters. Like the Nixon pardon, it was intended to heal some of the divisions of the past, but acceptance of the offer was slow.

As the November 1974 congressional elections approached, President Ford again traversed the nation, seeking to strengthen his party by campaigning vigorously for Republican candidates. His efforts notwithstanding, the electorate gave the Democrats a more than two-thirds majority in the House of Representatives and a nearly two-thirds majority in the Senate. Although Watergate contributed to the poor Republican showing, inflation had become the main concern of voters, only 38 percent of whom took the trouble to vote. It was the lowest turnout in almost 30 years.

The new President's first venture in overseas summitry came soon after the election, when he journeyed to the Far East to meet first with Emperor Hirohito and Premier Kakuei Tanaka in Japan, then with President Park Chung Hee in South Korea, and Soviet Communist party leader Leonid Brezhnev in Vladivostok. The last of the three meetings, apart from reaffirming the steps toward Russian-US detente taken under President Nixon, culminated in the announcement that a preliminary agreement on limitation of nuclear weapons would be signed the following year.

Although he had at first stated that he would not seek election for a full term, in 1976, Ford warmed to the challenges of his office and later announced that he would run. He received the Republican nomination — meeting strong opposition from conservatives supporting Ronald Reagan — and contended vigorously with the Democratic candidate, Jimmy Carter, with whom he participated in three televised debates seen by viewers across the nation. According to public opinion polls, Ford lagged behind Carter, but he campaigned effectively and was only narrowly beaten in the November election. The popular vote was 40.8 million for Carter and 39.1 million for Ford; the electoral vote was 297 for Carter, 240 for Ford, and 1 for Reagan.

In January 1977 Carter was inaugurated as the 39th President and Ford left the White House to pursue a very full schedule of activities. With homes in Palm Springs, California, and Vail, Colorado, Ford and his wife busied themselves with the publication of their respective memoirs and with television and other appearances. Far from retiring from public and political life, Ford has conferred with President Carter at the White House, discussing, among other topics, ratification of the Panama Canal treaties and Middle East peace negotiations; lectured on government and fiscal policy at colleges and before business groups; received briefings on disarmament talks; met foreign leaders; and spoken out critically or sympathetically on problems faced by the Carter administration.

In September 1977 Ford dedicated a park in Omaha, the city of his birth. Gardens in the park surround a gazebo that contains memorabilia donated to Omaha by the former President. Housed in another pavilion is a marble tablet inscribed with words spoken by Ford as he took office: "Our long national nightmare is over. Our Constitution works."

JULY 15

Feast of St. Swithin

Well loved in his native England even before his death more than a thousand years ago, St. Swithin (or Swithun) still has his feast day, July 15, marked on Anglican calendars. The English made him a saint by acclamation two centuries before Rome introduced the process of canonization. Out of this affection and pious devotion grew many folk tales that are more charming than accurate.

By tradition St. Swithin and St. Swithin's Day are associated with the weather. The old rhyme holds:

> St. Swithin's Day, if thou dost rain,
> For forty days it will remain;
> St. Swithin's Day, if thou be fair,
> For forty days twill rain nae mair.

The exact date and place of Swithin's birth are not definitely known, but he was probably born somewhere around A.D. 800 in or near Winchester, which was the capital of the Anglo-Saxon kingdom of Wessex and a famous center of learning especially noted for its religious scholars. Swithin became a monk in the Old Abbey of Winchester and was gradually advanced and became prior of that religious community. Evidence of Swithin's eminence in his own time is provided in a charter granted by Egbert, king of Wessex, in 838, which bore the signatures of "Elmstan, *episcopus*" (bishop) and "Swithunus, *diaconus*" (deacon).

St. Swithin's connection with the royal family was direct and of long standing. King Egbert, recognizing and appreciating the humble monk's many talents and fine qualities, put Swithin in charge of the education of his son Ethelwulf, the heir to the throne, who was to become the father of Alfred the Great. When Bishop Elmstan died, Swithin was chosen to succeed him and was consecrated Bishop of the See of Winchester in 852. In this high office Swithin made many improvements in the city, including construction of several churches and a fine stone bridge to span the local river, the first such bridge to be built in the region. When Ethelwulf assumed the throne of Wessex, he made his former teacher, Swithin, his adviser not only in religious matters but also in the arts.

The legend connecting St. Swithin with the weather is probably based on stories of his burial. It is said that Swithin had asked to be buried in a certain part of the churchyard — one that was superstitiously avoided as a burial place by the townspeople. For one thing, rain from the church eaves poured directly onto the area. For this and perhaps for other, unknown, reasons, local residents, although they constantly walked across the spot, shunned it as a last resting place. Whether Swithin's choice of this particular location, considered a "vile place," for his own grave-site was made because of the humility for which he was famous or in an attempt to fight the townspeople's superstition, or for some other reason is not known. However, after his death in Winchester in 862, he was buried according to his wishes in his chosen location in the churchyard.

Devout people came to visit his grave, and among those pilgrims and others who prayed to St. Swithin there were reports of a great number of healing miracles, as well as affectionate stories of the saint's performing such kindly acts as making whole a basket of eggs that had been broken when the old woman carrying them to market tripped and fell.

St. Swithin's popularity continued to increase, and more than a hundred years after his death, well-meaning clergy decided that his humble grave in the churchyard was not a fit resting place for so distinguished a personage. The legend associating Swithin with the weather is linked to their decision to remove his remains from the churchyard and reinter them in Winchester Cathedral, then being rebuilt. According to one version of the story, the faithful townspeople felt this would be against the saint's wishes. Nevertheless, a great assembly of clergy convened, with much pomp and ceremony, on the appointed day. But before the actual disinterment could begin, a downpour halted the ceremony. The heavy rain continued for forty days, long enough to discourage the plan for all time. The alleged deluge was interpreted as an undeniable reinforcement of what the townspeople had believed all along — that St. Swithin did not wish to be removed.

As a matter of record, however, Swithin's body was indeed moved to Winchester cathedral, on July 15, 971. Moreover, it appears that the weather was clear. Contrary to the legend, townspeople and clergy alike seem to have rejoiced at the due honors that finally were bestowed on their "homemade saint." There was a grand ceremony and a splendid feast to mark the occasion. It is this date, July 15, that is still commemorated as the Feast of St. Swithin.

JULY 16

Mary Baker Eddy's Birthday

Seemingly a failure by the time she was middle-aged, Mary Baker Eddy later became one of the most remarkable women of the 19th century. Her influence extended to all parts of the United States and to many other countries through the religion that she founded, the Church of Christ,

Scientist, whose members are more familiarly known as Christian Scientists. The acceptance of her teachings widened, and the branches of her church increased after her death. According to *Webster's New Collegiate Dictionary* (1973), Christian Science is a religion

that derives its teachings from the Scriptures as understood by its adherents, and that includes a practice of spiritual healing based on the teaching that cause and effect are mental and that sin, sickness, and death will be destroyed by a full understanding of the divine principle of Jesus's teaching and healing.

Mary Baker was born at Bow, near Concord, New Hampshire, on July 16, 1821, the youngest of six children of Mark and Abigail Baker, both devout descendants of old New England families. Too frail to attend school regularly, she received instruction at home from her family, mostly from her brother Albert, a student at Dartmouth College who was later to study law in the office of Franklin Pierce, subsequently the 14th President of the United States. Albert Baker was elected to the US House of Representatives shortly before his death in 1841.

When Mary was 14, the family moved to Sanbornton Bridge (now Tilton), New Hampshire, and, when her health permitted, she attended Sanbornton Academy and also Holmes Academy in Plymouth, some miles away. According to parish records, she joined the Congregational church in Sanbornton when she was 17. Early in life she began writing prose and poetry, some of which was published in local newspapers and periodicals. Later her writing consumed more and more of her time as she continued to formulate her thoughts on the healing powers of religion and on the interpretation of the Scriptures.

In December 1843 Mary Baker married George W. Glover, whose sister had married her oldest brother, Samuel, 10 years earlier. After their wedding the couple went to Charleston, South Carolina, where Glover had a building and contracting business. The following July Glover died. His widow returned to her family in New Hampshire, where, on September 11, 1844, she gave birth to her only child, George Glover.

After her mother's death in 1849 and her father's later remarriage, she left the family home and began what must have been the most difficult stage of her life. For many bleak years she moved between New Hampshire, Maine, and Massachusetts, living with family, with friends, and in rented rooms — destitute and ill, with no home of her own.

She had had a number of suitors and finally married Daniel Patterson, an itinerant dentist who was interested in homeopathic medicine. She herself had also become interested in homeopathy, having for years gone to physicians, spiritualists, and faith healers with no alleviation of her illness — which she described as "spinal inflammation, and its train of sufferings, gastric and bilious."

The undependable Daniel Patterson was a poor provider, and they were separated often and for long periods. Meanwhile, homeopathic remedies had not helped her. She had, however, heard the stories that had spread throughout New England of remarkable cures effected by a mental healer, Phineas Parkhurst Quimby; his book *Questions and Answers*, published in 1862, had added luster to his name.

Her hopes for a cure awakened, she traveled to Portland, Maine, for her first meeting with Quimby, which took place on October 10, 1862. Her health was temporarily improved by his treatment, and for a while she became his disciple, even helping, under his guidance, to treat some of his patients. Her lifelong concern about her own poor health and her great devotion to the Bible made it easy for her to accept Quimby's assertion that he had discovered Jesus' secrets of healing. Quimby further believed that the Bible provided the key to solving all the problems of the world.

The year 1866 was the turning point of her life. She was 44. Her father had died, her illness had recurred, she was estranged from her family, she would soon separate permanently from her husband (from whom she secured a divorce in 1873); and in January 1866 Quimby, her mainstay, died. Then living in Swampscott, near Lynn, Massachusetts, she wrote a poem entitled "On the Death of P. P. Quimby Who Healed with the Truth that Christ Taught," which was published in the Lynn *Advertiser*.

On February 1, 1866, a few weeks after Quimby's death, she slipped on the ice and injured her chronically troublesome back. Three days later, still confined to her bed, she read, according to her own account, the New Testament passage (Matthew 9:2–8) that tells of Jesus' healing a paralytic:

And, behold, they brought to him a man sick of the palsy, lying on a bed: and Jesus seeing their faith said unto the sick of the palsy; Son, be of good cheer; thy sins be forgiven thee. And, behold, certain of the scribes said within themselves, This man blasphemeth. And Jesus knowing their thoughts said, Wherefore think ye evil in your hearts? For whether is easier, to say, Thy sins be forgiven thee; or to say, Arise, and walk? But that ye may know that the Son of man hath power on earth to forgive sins, (then saith he to the sick of the palsy,) Arise, take up thy bed, and go unto thine house. And he arose, and departed to his house. But when the multitudes saw it, they marvelled, and glorified God, which had given such power unto men.

In her *Miscellaneous Writings,* published in 1896, she recalled the importance of the occasion: "As I read, the healing Truth dawned upon my sense; and the result was that I rose, dressed myself, and ever after was in better health than I had before enjoyed." Thus was the discovery of Christian Science made in February 1866, a date officially regarded as the beginning of the church, which now has more than 3,000 branches around the world.

During the years that followed her recovery, Mary Baker Glover — she had resumed her previous married name — began to delve more into the healing ministry of religion. She began to practice healing successfully, with some disputed but many noteworthy results. She also devoted herself to what she regarded as the even more important task of formulating her thoughts on how healing should be practiced and teaching others her philosophy of healing. Residents of the many rooming houses she stayed in during those years gave witness to the fact that she worked long hours over her writings. She let others read her works and soon small groups gathered around her to learn and discuss her thoughts about healing. Many of these people became her pupils and were later established as healers in their own right.

Her fortunes improved by 1875, and she bought a house of her own in Lynn. Never again would she be compelled to live in a rented room. That same year she brought out the first version of *Science and Health* — previously rejected by many commercial publishing houses — which was to become the Chrisian Science textbook. All told, 382 editions of the work were published during her lifetime. Editions of *Science and Health* published after 1883 had appended to them her Bible commentary, *Key to the Scriptures.* She continued revising the book until her last years.

On January 1, 1877, Mary Baker Glover, then 55, married one of her disciples, Asa Gilbert Eddy, and from that time forward she was known as Mary Baker Eddy. Her husband, a sewing machine salesman, became the first of her students to use the title Christian Science Practitioner. Their marriage was short-lived: he died of organic heart disease on June 3, 1882. She later remarked that she could have saved him, had she not been put off by his assurance that he had the situation under control. "I have cured worse cases before," she is reported to have said, "but I took hold of them in time."

When she first formulated her principles of healing, she hoped that established Protestant churches would accept her teachings. She met, however, with strong resistance — even open hostility — from both organized religion and organized medicine. Although she was reluctant to form a separate church, when she saw no other recourse she took over the organizing of her own church. She not only drew up the tenets of the church but chose the directors, the 12 charter members, and the 20 additional persons to be known as First Members of the First Church of Christ, Scientist. She also laid down the administrative bylaws, still in force today, in the *Church Manual,* a publication that she had personally revised through 89 editions by the time of her death. In 1879 the Church of Christ, Scientist, with headquarters in Boston, was chartered under Massachusetts law and Mother Eddy, as her disciples called her, became pastor, being ordained by her followers in a special ceremony.

Although she went to Boston to lecture and to conduct services, she continued to live in Lynn, and in 1881 she organized the Massachusetts Metaphysical College there, first holding classes in her Lynn home. She moved to Boston in 1882, however, and later taught in her Boston headquarters, a rented house at 569 Columbus Avenue. Approximately 4,000 Christian Science practitioners were trained at the college before she closed it in 1889. Her students fanned out across the country, setting up their healing practices for the most part in larger cities.

In 1883 she founded the *Journal of Christian Science,* now called the *Christian Science Journal,* to, in her words, "bring to many household hearths health and happiness, and increased power to be good and to do good." Meanwhile the Christian Science movement was growing, and in January 1886, she suggested that a National Christian Scientists' Association be organized, and the association held its first meetings the following February. A year later, when the association met at Boston's Tremont Temple, Christian Scientists from 14 states attended. Two years later 800 delegates gathered at Chicago, and the highlight of that convention was a personal appearance by the founder at the Central Music Hall, where 4,000 people gave her an ovation. From that time on, she was a national figure, and Christian Science was recognized as a nationwide movement.

In 1888 Mary Baker Eddy moved her residence from Boston to Concord, New Hampshire, to be freed from the details of management of her organization. She nevertheless kept a tight rein on it; but, away from headquarters, she could concentrate on the revisions of her textbook and manual and on other writings. These included *Retrospection and Introspection* (1891), *Messages to the Mother Church* (1900, 1901, and 1902), *Unity of Good* (1908), and *Rudimental Divine Science* (1908). After 10 years in Concord, she moved to a large house in Chestnut Hill, a suburb of Boston. To combat "yellow journalism" she founded *The Christian Science Monitor* in 1908, a daily newspaper still published in Boston that has earned the respect of journalists and editors throughout the country.

Early meetings of Christian Scientists in Lynn had been attended by up to 20 persons in private homes. When attendance in Boston grew, and larger assembly places had to be found, meetings were sometimes held in the Baptist Tabernacle on Shawmut Avenue. In 1880 she rented Hawthorne Hall, familiar to culture-bent Bostonians, who often went there to hear famous authors and lecturers. Eventually the 200-seat capacity Hawthorne Hall proved too small, and the more spacious Chickering Hall was rented for the Christian Science meetings.

More and more, however, the disciples felt that they should have their own building. Finally, in the spring of 1894 the cornerstone was laid for the First Church of Christ, Scientist. The edifice was fully paid for before its dedication on January 6, 1895. In response to the requirements of an enlarged membership, it was succeeded by what became known as the Mother Church, the massive Italian-Renaissance-style structure built next to it in 1904, and still one of the showplaces of Boston. Mary Baker Eddy visited the church, at Massachusetts and Huntington avenues, only twice. She died in Chestnut Hill on December 3, 1910.

The Mother Church (so named in 1909) adjoins the Publishing House, where *The Christian Science Monitor* and other Christian Science publications are produced. Visitors can tour the Publishing House, including its famous, walkthrough "mapparium" — a colored glass globe of the world, which visitors view from the inside.

In Brookline, Massachusetts, visitors are also welcomed at the Mary Baker Eddy Museum at 120 Seaver Street, which houses exhibits concerned with Mary Baker Eddy's life and accomplishments. Evidences of the movement she founded are to be seen in many other places. Christian Science booklets and bulletins, pamphlets, and papers are available in reading racks in depots and waiting rooms all over the country, and free reading rooms in downtown locations of many cities provide Christian Science literature.

About 80 percent of all Christian Scientists live in the United States. According to US statistics compiled in 1936, there were 2,113 Christian Science churches in the United States with a membership of 268,915. Figures for later years are generally not available for publication. Indeed, it is against the policy of the church to number its people or report such statistics.

Oregon Trail Days
Gering, Nebraska

This is a movable event. See note on page xxvi.

Gering, Nebraska, in the broad, flat valley of the North Platte River, is the scene of the big Oregon Trail Days celebration held annually on the Thursday and Friday nearest July 15. Through what is now Gering passed the 2,000-mile Oregon Trail, which led from Independence, Missouri, via the south bank of the river, to various points in the Oregon Territory beyond the Rocky Mountains.

Along the trail's wearisome length, thousands upon thousands of worn travelers tested their endurance during the vast migration that marked the settlement of the West. Some remained on the Oregon Trail all the way. Others, however, turned off in Wyoming or Idaho to join the rush for gold, which had been discovered in California in 1848. Still others — the Mormons, who had been expelled from Illinois in 1846 — took a slightly different route, the more or less parallel Mormon Trail, which ran along the north side of the North Platte River, before they turned south and founded Salt Lake City.

In all, a quarter of a million people — traders, missionaries, settlers, adventurers, government explorers — passed through the valley between 1841 and 1869. Included in the procession were Brigham Young and the Mormons; John C. Frémont, the soldier and explorer who was later to be a Presidential candidate; and Marcus Whitman, the missionary who ministered to the Indians of what afterwards became the state of Washington (see November 29). Among the transients were the riders of the Pony Express, who galloped by regularly on their mail deliveries in 1860 and 1861.

The Pony Express relay riders did not pause. But to other wayfarers, the hulking, 800-foot mass of Scotts Bluff, three miles from Gering and now a national monument, beckoned irresistibly after hundreds of miles of treeless plains. The bluff, which dominates the river valley, became a favorite camping ground.

July 15 — the date Gering's Oregon Trail Days events are timed to approximate — is a few days after the anniversary of the first major wagon train encampment chronicled at Scotts Bluff, in 1843. In 1970, the 49th annual observance took place on Thursday and Friday, July 16 and 17.

Oregon Trail Days activities offer many reminders of the history, human adventure and pioneer spirit associated with the old Oregon Trail. Both the Kiddies Parade, which was introduced in 1954 and in which some 600 or 700 youngsters participate on Thursday, and the major parade, in which perhaps 2,000 people take part on Friday morning, incorporate many floats and costumes depicting the Oregon-bound settlers, the Gold Rush, the Pony Express, the Mormon migration, and the alarmed Indians who tried unsuccessfully to stem the westward thrust. Many of the vehicles — wagons, stagecoaches and simpler rigs — also reflect the drama of the great migration. So do the community's special window displays related to pioneer days. And so may the speeches of visiting dignitaries — who usually include the governor or his wife, or representatives to the state or national legislature.

Oregon Trail Days events also evoke the era of the region's earliest settlers, after the Pony Express had been put out of business by the first transcontinental telegraph line (completed in 1861); after travel on the Oregon Trail had trickled to a halt with completion of the first transcontinental railroad in 1869; after the Indian fighting had ended — after the frontier, in short, had been pushed farther west.

The Homestead Act, providing settlers with free land, meanwhile had been passed by Congress in 1862, and Nebraska had become a state on March 1, 1867 (see March 1). It was almost two decades later that the first homesteaders began to arrive in the North Platte Valley in 1884 and 1885.

Gering itself was founded by homesteaders in 1887. It is the early settlers — and those who came after them up through 1920 — who are privileged to register as Old Settlers during Oregon Trail Days and are, in fact, the honored guests of the event. As of 1972, some 500 to 600 of the 35,000 to 40,000 who witness Trail Days at Gering (population about 6,600) qualified as Old Settlers. Coming from all over western Nebraska and the two adjacent counties of Wyoming, they are feted both days at barbecue luncheons at which old-time fiddlers entertain, and they elect two of their number — who will lead the next year's big parade — as honorary president and vice president of the Old Settlers and Oregon Trail Days. Along with anyone else who wishes, Old Settlers also attend two meetings of Gering's Half Century Club, both with special Old Settlers' programs.

Other activities during the celebration include street sports (races, contests, and "penny scramble") and special entertainment (juggling, tumbling, and other novelty acts) for youngsters;

concerts by the Gering Municipal Band; Sioux dances and powwow; carnival rides; variety shows; square dancing with well-known callers; an Oregon Trail window contest display; barbecues; ice cream social; and a horseshoe-pitching contest. Also featured is the appearance of the Oregon Trail Days queen, crowned at a pageant held a week earlier. She is one of the attractions of the big parade on Friday — along with bands; marching units; animal-drawn carriages; antique cars; and numerous floats, floral and otherwise, in addition to the historical entries.

In special anniversary years the Oregon Trail Days observance has been expanded to three days with additional events, such as the historical pageant with which Gering's diamond jubilee was marked in 1962. Those in the Gering area can visit the Oregon Trail Museum (open daily) at Scotts Bluff National Monument, see the trough of the old Oregon Trail nearby, and climb to the summit of the bluff by foot trail or paved road. Other Oregon Trail landmarks, including Chimney Rock to the east and Laramie Peak (Wyoming) to the west, are visible from the top.

Feast of Our Lady of Mount Carmel

The Feast of Our Lady of Mount Carmel is the principal feast of the Roman Catholic Carmelite order of friars. Carmelites celebrate the occasion when — on July 16, 1251 — the Virgin Mary is said to have appeared to St. Simon Stock, also called Simon Anglus or Simon the Englishman, then prior general of the Carmelites, and to have given him the scapular, an apronlike garment worn about the neck as a symbol of the cross and yoke of Jesus Christ and as a sign of devotion to Mary and a belief in her intercession.

The Carmelite order dates from the 11th century, when a community of hermits was founded in Palestine to live according to the monastic principles of Elijah (Elias), the great Hebrew prophet who worshiped God on Mount Carmel in the 9th century B.C. During the Crusades the Carmelites moved to Cyprus, and to Italy, France, and England. After the scapular was given by the Virgin Mary to St. Simon Stock, many lay people adopted the devotion of the scapular, and more Carmelite monasteries appeared in England, Scandinavia, and other parts of Europe.

The Feast of Our Lady of Mount Carmel, celebrated by the Carmelites since the 14th century, was extended to the whole Catholic church in 1726. In the church's 1960 Code of Rubrics it was reduced to a commemoration, or optional memorial.

In the United States the feast is mainly celebrated in Carmelite institutions and in the churches dedicated to Our Lady of Mount Carmel, of which there are some 130. Many Italian-American communities have special celebrations in honor of Our Lady of Mount Carmel. Perhaps one of the oldest celebrations in the United States is the one associated with St. Joseph's Church in Hammonton, New Jersey. The celebration had its start on July 16, 1875, when a group of Italians, all recent immigrants, gathered in a private home and knelt before a picture of Our Lady of Mount Carmel to give thanks for their safe journey to America. After praying, the group held a small procession outside, like those that have always been a part of such celebrations in Italy and other countries of Europe.

By 1878 the group had grown so that the celebration was moved to a nearby school. Since 1886, when Hammonton's first St. Joseph's Church was built, the celebration has been associated with the church — which is located today at North Third and French streets. The church has a special shrine to Our Lady of Mount Carmel, a focal point for pilgrims who come from many parts of the country to attend part or all of the novena — nine days of special devotion — customarily preceding the feast. Outside the church a festival offers Italian foods, entertainment, and fireworks displays.

On July 16, the end of the novena and day of the feast itself, masses are said in the church throughout the morning. In the afternoon the main street of Hammonton is filled with a mile-long procession, highlighted by a statue of Our Lady of Mount Carmel. The procession, which includes bands, floats, and banners — many honoring saints of special significance to Italians — lasts for five hours or longer. As many as 25,000 people watch or participate in the procession. Blessings, small scapulars, holy cards, and other mementos are distributed and some 5,000 individuals receive Communion at one time. As many as 4,000 candles are lighted at a special temporary outdoor shrine. Many of the pilgrims are Italians or persons of Italian descent who have moved from Hammonton but who return annually for the feast, helping to swell the community's population to more than double its normal size.

Another long-established celebration in honor of Our Lady of Mount Carmel is held in New York City in a once predominantly Italian area now part of East, or Spanish, Harlem and home to large black and Puerto Rican populations, as well as to Italian-Americans and their descendants. The observance in what used to be called Italian Harlem had its beginning in 1882. It was then that recent Italian immigrants who had come to New York gathered in a rented room and gave thanks to Our Lady of Mount Carmel for their safe arrival in America. In 1884 a church was built on East 115th Street and Pleasant Avenue and dedicated to Our Lady of Mount Carmel, and from that time the annual celebration has been connected with the church. Attendance continued to grow until it reached its peak during the 1950s, when as many as 200,000 arrived annually to participate in the novena to Our Lady of Mount Carmel. Although this number has diminished, approximately 100,000 people, from near and far, still visit the church's shrine of Our Lady of Mt. Carmel during the month of July. Many of them are former residents of the neighborhood who return from other cities. For those who cannot attend personally, novena prayers are broadcast by radio in English and Italian.

The novena in New York to Our Lady of Mount Carmel is officially opened with a street procession. A statue of Our Lady of Mount Carmel is placed on a float, which is drawn by 10 men during the procession. Young girls in their First Communion dresses and veils cluster around the statue, and small scapulars and holy cards are given out. On the eve of the feast, 3,000 to 4,000 people participate in an impressive candlelight procession. It is not unusual to hear Italian, English, Spanish, and Haitian French simultaneously used for singing and praying, as these are now the languages of the changing neighborhood.

On the day of the feast, local leaders and members of various community and church groups gather to mark the opening of the day's festivities. At 10:00 A.M. a firecracker is set off, and a flock of white doves, bred by a neighborhood resident, is sent into flight by the signal. The release of the doves is in turn the sign for the procession to begin. It is actually the first of three processions held on the feast day, each covering a different section of the neighborhood. Throughout the nine days of the novena, musicians on an outdoor bandstand provide popular and classical music. The streets around the church are roped off for a great festival and bazaar, complete with food, entertainment, outdoor dancing, and tables where participants eat, rest, and sip *espresso*. The colorfully decorated stalls, which cover a 10-block area, attract as many as 5,000 persons a night.

In Brooklyn, New York, the Church of Our Lady of Mount Carmel, at North Eighth and Havemeyer streets, holds the 17-day celebration in July, honoring its patron and other saints for whom Italians have special affection. The annual parish bazaar, a six-block fair, is held during the same period. An outdoor candlelight procession opens the celebrations, with parishioners, members of parish societies, and pilgrim devotees of Our Lady of Mount Carmel participating. The procession is led by the uniformed Mount Carmel Cadet Corps. One of the most spectacular features of the opening procession is a 75-foot-high steel *giglio* — a papier-maché-covered tower built to resemble a lily — which honors St. Paulinus, a fifth century bishop of Nola, an ancient town that was home to the ancestors of many Brooklyn Italians. The *giglio* used in Brooklyn's festa weighs four tons, includes a platform for a band of musicians, and is carried by 100 strong men.

The next evening the parish bazaar opens for 17 straight nights, providing such foods as ravioli, lasagna, pepper and sausage sandwiches, Italian ices, and pastries. A *mandolinata*, or musical program, is also held on each of the 17 nights. Another great procession takes place, following a different course, on a subsequent Sunday afternoon, with a statue of Our Lady of Mount Carmel carried the length of the procession route by 30 men. As many as 10,000 people have attended this event. Attendance during the week is estimated at about 5,000 a night during the celebration. Novena services in honor of Our Lady of Mount Carmel begin on July 7 and are given twice nightly, once in English and once in Italian. On July 16 the novena closes with a solemn high mass in the morning and another procession at 5:00 P.M., followed by benediction services in the church.

As elsewhere in the Latin world, the Feast of Our Lady of Mount Carmel is widely observed in Puerto Rico, with celebrations lasting a week or more. In some places festivities take place on the beach, as in Cataño, where a statue of the Virgin is carried out to sea on a float on the night of the 16th to assure the good fortune and safety of fishermen in the coming year. On other days water sports figure prominently in the gaiety during the observance at Cataño, which is located across the harbor from San Juan. In Ponce, on the island's south shore, a giant regatta, masquerades, and street parades are held. Other communities in Puerto Rico that hold celebrations in honor of Our Lady of Mount Carmel include Arroyo, Río Grande, Barceloneta, Cidra, Hatillo, Morovis, Villalba, and Culebra.

JULY 17

John Jacob Astor's Birthday

John Jacob Astor, founder of the Anglo-American millionaire Astor family and the richest man in America at his death in 1848, made the bulk of his fortune by shrewd investments in New York City real estate. But he is better known as the commanding force in the American fur trade after the Revolution and as a capitalist connected intimately with the westward expansion of the United States in the early 19th century.

Astor emigrated to the United States from the German duchy of Baden, by way of England. He was born in the village of Waldorf near Heidelberg on July 17, 1763, the third son of a genial, improvident butcher and his hardworking wife. Self-improvement and wanderlust marked the sons of this family: when John Astor decided to leave home at the age of 16, his brother George had already established a musical instrument store in London, and his brother Henry had opened a butcher shop in New York. In 1780 John Astor set out on foot for the Rhine. He worked his way down the river on a timber raft, earning enough for passage to England.

During the last few years of the American Revolution, he worked for his brother in London, learning English (though to the end of his life he spoke with a heavy German accent) and all that he could about America, his cherished goal. In November 1783, after the treaty of Paris was signed following the conclusion of the American Revolution, he embarked for New York with a capital of $25 and seven flutes. His vessel was frozen in the Chesapeake Bay for two months en route to Baltimore, and this delay gave time for conversations with a passenger who was engaged in the fur trade. Astor decided then to enter that business.

On arriving in New York in March 1784, he lived first with his brother Henry, and he soon opened his own music shop on Water Street. In 1785 or 1786 he married Sarah Todd, who, it is said, gave him $300 in cash and a very keen sense for evaluating furs. By 1786 he had launched himself in the fur trade and was making purchasing trips as far west as Mackinaw (in what is now northern Michigan) and to Canada. As a result of tireless effort and sharp business practices, by 1800 Astor had built up a fortune of $250,000 and become the country's leading fur trader.

He also began to purchase New York real estate in large amounts. Shortly before his death a half-century later, Astor — by then a multimillionaire — asserted, "Could I begin life again knowing what I now know, I would buy every foot of land on the island of Manhattan." By that time the growth of American cities had become rapid, and Astor saw how enormous the profits in real estate would continue to be. In 1839 a section of northwest Queens, on Long Island, New York, settled as Hallet's Cove in the 17th century, was renamed Astoria for him and incorporated. This residential, industrial, and commercial community in the New York City borough of Queens today testifies to one aspect of Astor's entrepreneurship.

In the early years of the 19th century, however, Astor was preoccupied with the entire northern half of the North American continent and beyond, through the fur and tea trades. His men were already dominating the fur trade of the Great Lakes region when President Jefferson's acquisition of the huge Louisiana Purchase lands in 1803 sparked his imagination and opened broader trading vistas. Astor followed the reports of Lewis and Clark's expedition of 1804–1806 with keen interest. In 1808 he gathered his holdings into the American Fur Company, chartered in New York state, and established the Pacific Fur Company and the South West Company as subsidiaries.

By this time he was fully engaged in a twin commercial struggle to monopolize the American fur trade and to compete with and eventually push out of business the great Canadian fur interests, particularly the Hudson's Bay Company and the Northwest Company. Astor devised a daring scheme to further both these ends, and but for larger international circumstances his plan might have succeeded. Wishing to circumvent the St. Louis merchants' hold over the western fur trade, he decided to found a Pacific emporium at the mouth of the Columbia River, the farthest point reached by Lewis and Clark. Such a depot, as yet undreamed of by anyone else, would enable his companies to ship precious furs directly to eager Chinese markets. Middlemen would be avoided, and his furs would bring even larger profits in exchange for Chinese tea. (The ever-shrewd Astor was also a prince of the tea trade by this time.) According to his plan, tea would be carried straight from China to Europe to be exchanged once again at high profits for goods to be imported to the United States at still further profit. To complete the global circuit, a ship with goods for trappers would be dispatched from the East Coast to go around South America to the Oregon territory.

Astor's emporium on the Columbia River was the key to an expanded and accelerated world trade. He realized also that his settlement would strengthen the American claim to the Oregon territory vis-à-vis Great Britain, the other active claimant.

In 1810–1811, Astor sent out a land party to lay commercial claim to the area explored five years earlier by Lewis and Clark and to interest Indian tribes in trapping for the Pacific Fur Company. At the same time Astor equipped a sea party for the long trip around Cape Horn, with orders to found and provision Fort Astoria at the mouth of the Columbia and to await the overland party.

By land, harsh competition with the Canadian Northwest Company hindered the venture from an early point, as did Indian hostility and a precipitous terrain. But despite many difficulties, Fort Astoria was established in 1811 on the south bank of the Columbia, some 12 miles from the open sea. If the War of 1812 with Great Britain had not broken out, the settlement might have become permanent. However, after a calamitous expedition by the settlers to trade with a northern Indian tribe, Astor's supply ships were cut off by the British navy in 1813.

Following these reverses, Astor's field partners sold Fort Astoria's trading goods and abandoned the company's posts to its rivals. Astor was enraged at this "betrayal," but his partners did well to salvage anything at all in 1813. Soon after, a British warship took possession of Fort Astoria, fulfilling earlier threats, and the outpost was renamed Fort George. Later, this takeover was considered an act of war and brought the Oregon country into the peace negotiations between Britain and the United States.

If the War of 1812 undercut his western vision, John Jacob Astor made millions from it all the same by lending money at exorbitant rates to a desperate US government in 1814. And in spite of his retreat from the far western fur trade, he shortly achieved a virtual monopoly of the trade within US territory. By 1817 his men wholly controlled the Mississippi valley, often riding roughshod over government officials; and after 1822 they controlled the upper Missouri valley as well. This monopoly continued after his retirement from the fur trade in 1834.

Astor was then 70 years old, and his withdrawal from the fur trade was doubtless prompted in part by weariness. Moreover, despite his vigorous campaign against the Rocky Mountain Fur Company, an American competitor, Astor was disappointed in the profits from furs. By 1834 the great days of the fur trade were behind, as Astor had astutely calculated. After 1838 the market rapidly declined as other products replaced fur in fashionable men's hats. But in all that the fur trade had wrought on the North American continent, John Jacob Astor had had a large role. The trade's "mountain men" had done much to mark out wilderness paths and the most advantageous sites for settlement. At the same time, the fur traders had helped break up Indian communities and culture by systematically passing out liquor as an incentive for "cooperation." Moreover, as they went about manipulating the fur trade, Astor and his partner, William Henry Ashley, did much to forge a fateful partnership between private enterprise and the US government for developing the American West. Astor was highly influential in Washington, D.C., and was a founder of the

Second United States Bank. He successfully lobbied in Congress for legal barriers against Canadian fur competitors. And in 1821–1822 he persuaded Congress to abolish government trading posts for furs — which had been established as early as 1796.

In his book *Astoria* (1836), Washington Irving glorified Astor's role in opening the West, perhaps to an exaggerated degree: the original Fort Astoria was a transient settlement. The place was restored to the Americans in the peace negotiations after the War of 1812, but they made no effort to reoccupy it until the mid-1840s. In the interim it was replaced by Fort Vancouver under a farsighted Canadian, Dr. John McLoughlin. Until 1834 British Canadians controlled the region, and they retained the largest role there until the Oregon Treaty awarded the region to the United States in 1846.

In 1847, after American interest in the Oregon country had revived and large-scale westward migration had begun, the first post office west of the Rocky Mountains was established in Astoria. The city was chartered in 1867 and remains proud of its early history. Visitors today are attracted to the 125-foot-high Astor Column, built in 1926 on Coxcomb Hill. From the tower's observation room and platform, guests enjoy a sweeping view of the Pacific Ocean, the broad Columbia spanned at its mouth by a 4.1-mile bridge, Young's Bay, the high Coast Range, and the surrounding countryside. A pictorial frieze commemorating Oregon's first settlement wraps its way around the entire length of the column. A replica of Fort Astoria may be seen in downtown Astoria; and at the Columbia River Maritime Museum, exhibits covering a century and a half tell the history of the river, its tributaries, and the northwest coast. An annual event is the Astoria regatta and fish festival in late August, featuring a parade, a boating competition, and a public dinner.

With the early dream of Fort Astoria wrecked and the fur trade relinquished, John Jacob Astor devoted his later years to managing his fortune. He died in his New York home on March 29, 1848, at the age of 84. His estate was conservatively estimated at $20 million, and it has been reckoned at over $25 million. He left all but $2 million to his son William Backhouse Astor. (An older son, John Jacob, was mentally handicapped.)

It has been said that "the amassing of wealth was [Astor's] ruling passion, and few devices that could contribute to that end were neglected by him," and that despite his wish to be known as public-spirited, "there is evidence that this ruling passion still possessed him at the close." Nevertheless, one of Astor's bequests boldly contrasted with his own mercenary version of success. Washington Irving and the librarian Joseph Green Cogswell persuaded him to leave $400,-000 to found and endow a great public library for New York City. (He had earlier envisaged a huge monument to George Washington.) Astor's gift established what was to become the first great research library broadly accessible to the public, setting an example in philanthropy soon followed by other wealthy Americans. The original Astor Library building, constructed in three stages in 1853, 1859, and 1881 under the direction of Astor's son and grandson, still stands today at 425 Lafayette Street, just off Astor Place in New York City. Elegant and capacious, the building once influenced style throughout the nation and was toured by visiting celebrities as one of New York's cultural attractions.

The structure has not been used as a library since 1911, when the Astor collection was moved uptown to the New York Public Library building at 42nd Street and Fifth Avenue. From 1920 to 1965, the original Astor Library building served as the headquarters of the Hebrew Immigrant Aid Society. Its designation as a landmark by the Landmarks Preservation Commission narrowly rescued it from wreckers in 1965. Early in 1966 it was purchased by the New York Shakespeare Festival to serve as a year-round home in which contemporary plays would be offered at subsidized prices to complement the festival's free Shakespeare productions in Central Park.

Since 1966 the Astor Library landmark building, renamed the New York Shakespeare Festival Public Theater, has been converted by stages into a flourishing theater center, with administrative offices, workshops, rehearsal halls, and three working theaters: the Anspacher Theater, which occupies what was once the main reading room (1967); the Other Stage, an experimental and children's theater (1968); and the Newman Theater (1970). The Astor Library was the first structure rescued and remodeled for new uses under the New York Landmarks Law, which requires that the exterior of a landmark building be preserved; wherever possible, the interior decor of the 19th century library was also preserved.

On May 23, 1895, the Astor Library and the Lenox Library (incorporated in 1870) merged to become the New York Public Library, which was housed in the Astor Library building and further endowed at the founding with a bequest from the political leader Samuel J. Tilden. One of the world's most renowned libraries, the New York Public Library now occupies the massive edifice fronting Fifth Avenue from 40th to 42nd streets; opened in 1911, the structure was erected by the City of New York and is maintained by municipal funds. Located in the building are the privately endowed reference or research libraries and the headquarters of the coordinate tax-supported branch system (a free circulating library network consolidated in 1901 with a $5.2 million gift from Andrew Carnegie). The research libraries, which grew from the gifts of Astor, Lenox, Tilden, and other donors, hold more than 5 million books, as well as vast general and specialized collections of maps, photographs, prints, periodicals, and pamphlets. Astor's benefaction became a cornerstone not only of a great library, free and accessible to the public, but of a rich resource for scholarship and learning.

Columbia University Opens

King's College — later to become Columbia University — opened on July 17, 1754, in New York City after several years of controversy. The colonial legislature in 1746 made provisions to raise money for the school through public lotteries. The province amassed £17,000 within five years and gave it to the trustees, but disagreements threatened the future of the project. Dissenting Protestants felt uneasy about the role of the Church of England in the administration of the institution: two-thirds of the trustees were Anglicans, and some were even vestrymen of Trinity Church. William Livingston, a lawyer, a Presbyterian, and a member of the leading family in the colony, argued for a liberal, nonsectarian college in a series of articles in the *Independent Reflector,* a weekly newspaper. In reality Livingston merely wanted to prevent the establishment of an Anglican college, but he argued in libertarian terms. He stated that a sectarian institution would intensify animosities in the religiously heterogeneous province and perhaps enable the faction that controlled higher education to dominate the colony. Livingston envisioned a college established by the colonial assembly as the most desirable solution since it would make it possible for all groups to have a voice in educational matters.

The charter of King's College was a conciliatory document designed to resolve the dispute and unify all factions in the support of the school. It authorized the board of governors to include, besides other ex-officio representatives, not only the rector of Trinity Church but also the senior ministers of the dissenting congregations, the Reformed Protestant Dutch, Ancient Lutheran, French, and Presbyterian churches. The result was to make the college almost nonsectarian. Indeed, of all the institutions of higher learning established in the colonies prior to the American Revolution only King's never had a theology faculty associated with it.

Although the college officially dates its existence from October 31, 1754, the day on which its charter from King George II was granted, by that time it had already been in operation for a few months. The Reverend Samuel Johnson of Stratford, Connecticut, assumed the office of president on July 17, 1754, and greeted the first class of eight students in a schoolhouse donated by Trinity Church.

The capture of New York City by the British in 1776 closed the college for the duration of the War for Independence, and its buildings served as a military hospital. The institution reopened after the New York state legislature granted it another charter and a new name — Columbia College — on May 1, 1784. This revised document ended the former requirement that the institution's president be an Episcopalian and that selections from the liturgy of the Church of England be used at the school's religious services. In 1787 title to Columbia was transferred from the state to the trustees.

Trinity Church provided the land for the college from a section of lower New York City known as the King's Farm, on a site now bounded by Barclay, Church, and Murray streets. In 1857, during the presidency of Charles King, Columbia relocated to Madison Avenue and 49th Street, and 40 years later it moved to its present home on Morningside Heights on the upper West Side of Manhattan.

Columbia officially became a university in 1896, the change in terminology reflecting almost a century and a half of growth. The law school opened in 1858, a school of engineering in 1864, and a school of architecture in 1896. The graduate faculties of political science, philosophy, and pure science began operation in 1880, 1890, and 1892 respectively. In 1891 Columbia absorbed the College of Physicians and Surgeons, one of the nation's great medical schools. Not including Teachers College, Barnard (women's) College, or the College of Pharmacy, which are affiliated with it, Columbia University in the late 1970s reported an enrollment of more than 16,000 graduate and undergraduate students and a faculty of approximately 3,700.

Florida Ceded to the United States

Florida was claimed for Spain on Easter Day in 1513 by Juan Ponce de León (see April 8). During the next half century, the peninsula was explored by other Spaniards — Pánfilo de Narváez, who perished by shipwreck in the Gulf of Mexico after he had fled from Indians in northwest Florida; Hernando de Soto (see March 15), who landed on Florida's west coast and explored 4,000 miles to the north and west before he, too, perished; Tristán de Luna, who founded Pensacola on Florida's Gulf coast panhandle (see June

6, Fiesta of Five Flags); and Pedro Menéndez de Avilés, who founded the city of St. Augustine on Florida's east coast (see September 8). Two centuries passed before the rivalries of European powers for North American lands reached their peak. However, a foreshadowing of what was to come took place after a body of French Huguenots established a fort at the mouth of the St. Johns River, above St. Augustine, in 1564. In two notably bloody incidents, the Spaniards under Menéndez drove out the French the following year. With the threat of foreign competition thus removed, Spanish control of Florida remained uninterrupted until 1763.

That year marked the conclusion of the Seven Years' War in Europe, of which the French and Indian War was the American aspect. Peace became official with the 1763 Treaty of Paris between victorious Great Britain on the one hand, and France and Spain on the other. One of the provisions of that document was that Havana, Cuba, which the British had conquered, would be returned to Spain in exchange for Florida, which would go to Britain. That nation also received, from France, additional land, which extended the area of Florida from that state's present border at the Perdido River all the way to the Mississippi, though it did not include strategically located New Orleans.

The treaty marked the start of two decades of British rule in Florida. It was a period of prosperity, during which the British separated the region into East and West Florida, with the Apalachicola River as the dividing line. East Florida was similar to, but somewhat smaller than, the present state of Florida, having a shorter western panhandle.

It was during Britain's 20-year control of the Floridas that the 13 orginal colonies revolted against Britain. The Floridas remained loyal to Britain during the American Revolution and were a haven for Loyalists, who flocked there from the rebelling colonies. When the American Revolution formally ended with the 1783 Treaty of Paris between Britain and the new United States, relations between European powers again influenced the fate of the Florida region. Related treaties that Britain signed respectively with France (ally of the United States) and Spain (ally of France) became effective simultaneously with the Treaty of Paris. In accordance with the Anglo-Spanish agreement, the Floridas were retroceded to Spain in return for the abandonment of Spanish hopes for gaining British-occupied Gibraltar.

Spain was to have — or claim — control of the Floridas until 1821. This time, however, its grasp was not so firm; and it was to become less so as time went on. For years after the United States acquired the vast Louisiana Purchase territory from France in 1803, debate raged as to whether West Florida (or at least that portion between the Perdido and Mississippi rivers) had been included in the transaction, as the United States claimed, or had not been, as Spain claimed. The Louisiana Purchase, meanwhile, served as an impetus for the ever-continuing westward thrust that would eventually carry US settlers all the way to the Pacific coast. They were already moving into West Florida and neighboring areas.

President James Madison in 1810 declared West Florida to be under the jurisdiction of the United States. Two years later, portions of West Florida were lopped off by the US Congress, which annexed the area west of the Pearl River to the new state of Louisiana and incorporated the land between the Pearl and Perdido rivers into the Mississippi Territory. (The latter strip of Gulf coast was subsequently divided between Mississippi, which became a state in 1817, and Alabama, which was admitted to the Union in 1819).

Control of West Florida by the Spanish, who still claimed the disputed region, became even more tenuous after the outbreak of the War of 1812 between the United States and Great Britain. Part of the area — including the Spanish fort at Mobile and the land between Mobile and the Perdido — was occupied by US General James Wilkinson's forces in 1813. Late in 1814 Andrew Jackson captured Spanish Pensacola en route to his triumph in the battle of New Orleans. Jackson, again without authorization, took Pensacola for a second time in 1818, after he had been sent to quell Indian conflicts along the Florida-Georgia border.

Negotiations that the United States hoped would end the Floridas controversy were meanwhile going on between the United States and Spain. They were temporarily interrupted by what the Spanish regarded as the effrontery of Jackson's incursion. Still the Spanish, preoccupied by difficulties at home and revolutions in Latin America, were willing to settle, particularly after Jackson's exploits further demonstrated the weakness of Spanish control in the contested region.

The result was the Adams-Onís Treaty, by which Spain abandoned its claim to West Florida and ceded East Florida to the United States in return for $5 million, which the United States agreed to pay towards claims of its citizens against Spain. The treaty, including its Florida and other important provisions, was signed early in 1819 (see February 22) and ratified by the US Senate two days later. Because of delays by the Spanish government, the Senate again ratified the treaty on February 19, 1821, after Spanish approval of the document. The exchange of ratifications between representatives of the two governments was completed on February 22, 1821, although it was not until July 17, 1821, that the cession of Florida to the United States was actually formalized.

Official US occupation, with Andrew Jackson as the first governor, came the same year. Florida was organized as a territory with its present boundaries in 1822. In 1845 Florida became a state (see March 3).

JULY 18

John Paul Jones's Death

John Paul Jones, the distinguished Revolutionary naval commander, was born John Paul in the parish of Kirkbean, Kirkcudbrightshire, Scotland, on July 6, 1747. His father, also John Paul, was the gardener for William Craik, a member of Parliament. The younger John Paul attended the parish school until the age of 12, when he began his naval career as an apprentice aboard the *Friendship*. His training as a member of this ship's crew was brief: his first voyage took him to Fredericksburg, Virginia, and during the stay in that port the *Friendship*'s owner suffered financial reverses that forced him to terminate his new recruit's apprenticeship. Fortunately, however, John Paul had relatives in America. His elder brother, William, worked in Fredericksburg as a tailor, and John stayed with him and continued his study of navigation.

At the age of 19 John Paul returned to sea. For several years he labored aboard slavers that plied the waters between the North American coast and the West Indies. In 1769 he took command of his first ship, the merchantman *John* of Dumfries, a vessel engaged in the West Indian trade.

Seafaring in the 18th century was not an occupation for the timid. So few were the incentives to attract men to the hard life of a sailor that captains frequently had to fill their crews with criminals and other undesirables. Harsh punishment was necessary to maintain order aboard ship, and it was not unusual for captains to be accused of inhumane treatment of their charges. Captain Paul was no exception. On his second voyage as commander of the *John*, he flogged the ship's carpenter for neglect of duty, and the man died at sea several weeks later. The carpenter's father charged Paul with murder, but he was cleared of this accusation. Shortly afterward, Paul became captain of the *Betsey* of London. In 1773 the crew of this vessel mutinied, and during the ensuing fight the sailors' leader fell victim to John Paul's sword. John Paul insisted that the man had rushed upon the weapon, thereby causing his own death. But in the absence of sympathetic witnesses, he acted upon friendly advice and returned to Fredericksburg incognito. While there he took the name of Jones, and was thereafter known as John Paul Jones.

The American Revolution ended Jones's self-imposed exile from the sea. He offered his services to the Continental Congress and on December 7, 1775, was commissioned a lieutenant. The Congress assigned him first to the *Alfred*, and in 1776 put him in command of the *Providence*. Jones quickly proved of value to the American cause: on one cruise alone the vessel captured 16 prize ships. On June 14, 1777, he took charge of the sloop *Ranger* and sailed for France. After refitting his ship in Brest, France, he set out for the Irish Sea on April 10, 1778. Thirteen days later he entered the English harbor of Whitehaven, where he spiked the guns in the forts and made an unsuccessful attempt to burn the shipping. Then he visited St. Mary's Island in Solway Firth, intending to seize the earl of Selkirk as a hostage. Finding that the earl was not on the island, Jones crossed the sea to the Irish coast and captured the British sloop *Drake*, after an hour's battle. Twenty-eight days after its departure, the *Ranger* returned to Brest with many prisoners and 7 prize ships.

The French, who were about to go to war against the English, were impressed by Jones's raids and in January 1779 gave him command of the ship *Duc de Duras*, an old East Indiaman of 40 guns. Refitted and renamed the *Bonhomme Richard* in honor of Benjamin Franklin, the author of the *Poor Richard* almanacs, the vessel sailed from L'Orient with one American ship and four French ships on August 14. En route to the British coast, this small squadron took 17 ships. Then, on September 23, Jones sighted a fleet of 39 British merchant ships, convoyed by the 44-gun *Serapis* and the 22-gun *Countess of Scarborough*.

Only three of Jones's ships took part in the ensuing battle. Jones attacked the *Serapis* with the *Bonhomme Richard* and by skillful maneuvering brought the two ships together. The early fighting heavily favored the British, but when the commander of the *Serapis* called upon Jones to surrender, he replied, "I have not yet begun to fight." An American grenade set off a powder explosion on the deck of the *Serapis*, and after the British ship's mainmast collapsed, its captain surrendered. Jones transferred his crew from the burning *Bonhomme Richard* to the *Serapis* and took his prize to Texel, Holland.

The *Bonhomme Richard–Serapis* engagement

assured Jones's fame as a naval leader. Among other honors, Jones received the French cross of the Institution of Military Merit. Upon his return to the United States in February 1781, Congress thanked him formally and on June 26 gave him command of the *America,* which was then being built in Portsmouth, New Hampshire, and would be the largest ship in the Continental navy. Jones spent a year supervising its construction, but after its completion the vessel was given to France.

In 1783 the Continental navy was disbanded, and Jones returned to Europe to collect the prize money due this nation as a result of his raids. The mission was successful, and he came back to the United States for the last time in 1787. On October 17 of that year Congress awarded Jones a gold medal for his services to this country. He was the only officer of the Continental navy to be so honored.

In 1788 Jones accepted an offer from Catherine the Great to enter the Russian navy and fight against the Turks. Commissioned as rear admiral, Jones took command of a Russian squadron on the Black Sea on May 26, 1788, but because of the jealousy of the Russian officers he was deprived of his command. Catherine, however, conferred on him the cross of the Order of St. Anne. He returned to Paris in June 1790, where he spent the remainder of his life, dying there on July 18, 1792. He was buried in the old St. Louis Cemetery for foreign Protestants.

An 1845 movement to have Jones's remains brought to the United States was blocked by his relatives in Scotland. In 1899, however, the effort was successfully revived, and after a six-year search remains that are believed to be the commander's were located. In 1905 a naval squadron with a French cruiser as escort carried the body to the United States, where it was interred at the Naval Academy at Annapolis. The academy held memorial services in 1906, and President Theodore Roosevelt and French Ambassador Jules Jusserand gave addresses. In 1913, Jones's remains were transferred to their final resting place, a $75,000 marble sarcophagus in the crypt of the academy's chapel.

Several areas in the United States call Jones to mind. In Washington, D.C., a monument was erected in 1912 in Potomac Park. In Portsmouth, New Hampshire, the public can see the boardinghouse, now a museum, open in spring and summer, at 43 Middle Street, where Jones stayed while he supervised the construction of the *America.* Owned and maintained by the Portsmouth Historical Society, the 18th century building contains a collection of items relevant to the town's history. Jones's home in Fredericksburg, Virginia, privately owned, is located at Caroline Street and Lafayette Boulevard.

John Rutledge's Death

John Rutledge, a founder of the American republic, Revolutionary leader of South Carolina, and second chief justice of the United States, was born in Charleston (then Charlestown), South Carolina, or in nearby Christ Church Parish, in September 1739 on an unknown day. His father, Dr. John Rutledge, had come from England in 1735 and settled in Charleston, marrying Sarah Hext, an heiress. John, the eldest of their seven children, was born soon after his mother turned 15. By birth he belonged to the cultivated planter class of coastal South Carolina, whose wealth from rice and indigo assured their social and political dominance of the colony in the 18th century.

Dr. Rutledge supervised his son's education until his death in 1750, when John was 11. The boy was also taught by the minister of Christ Church and by a classics tutor. He was then sent to London to study law in the Middle Temple. In 1760 Rutledge was called to the English bar, and in 1761 he returned to practice in Charleston, where he won immediate success in his first case. Two years later he married Elizabeth Grimké. They had 10 children.

John Rutledge entered politics in 1762, when he was elected from Christ Church Parish to the Carolina Commons House. He was to hold this seat for 14 years, until he became president or governor of the rebellious province in 1776. It was in this active provincial legislature — dominated by the planters and their allies and accustomed to resisting interference from the crown — that his political philosophy took shape. There he soon revealed the quickness, determination, intensity of conviction, presence, and oratorical brilliance that thereafter marked his leadership. His rise was rapid. At the age of 25 he became attorney general of South Carolina (1764–1765), and in 1765 he was sent as a delegate to the colonial congress called to protest the Stamp Act. There he chaired the committee that wrote the memorial against the act to the House of Lords.

In 1774 Rutledge reappeared in intercolonial politics as a representative to the First Continental Congress in Philadelphia, having gained the confidence of the Carolina merchants as well as of the more bellicose planters in the hot discussions of the previous months. In Philadelphia Rutledge first argued for colonial self-government within the British Empire. This position, together with his successful battle to exempt rice from the boycott list against Britain, put Rutledge in a very strong political position in South Carolina. The next year he was reelected delegate to the Second Continental Congress. He urged that regular governments be set up in the colonies, replacing those directed by royal governors. On November 4, 1775, the Congress advised South Carolina to proceed accordingly if necessary.

Armed with this directive and prepared to break with Great Britain, Rutledge returned to South Carolina, where he gave further service to the American Revolution. His election to the extralegal Council of Safety and service on the committee that wrote the South Carolina constitution of 1776 fulfilled his ambition to play a major role in the reorganization of the province. In March, when the provincial congress adopted the new constitution and was transformed into the general assembly, the 37-year-old Rutledge was elected its president.

As chief executive of the first independent government in the American colonies, John Rutledge led South Carolina well. He defended Charleston successfully against British attack on June 28, 1776, at Fort Moultrie — a site that may be visited today on the lower tip of Sullivan's Island, South Carolina. This victory freed the southern colonies from invasion for nearly three years. In addition, the local Cherokee Indians were subdued and the province prospered economically.

In 1778 Rutledge, who was a foe of democracy, vetoed a more liberal constitution for South Carolina and resigned the presidency. But when invasion was again imminent, in February 1779, he was recalled and elected governor. He took the field, desperately combating the British with inadequate forces, since the central government was reluctant to release forces to the outlying states. In May 1780, after a siege of two months, Charleston surrendered. The provincial assembly vested Rutledge with plenary powers before adjourning. As others despaired, and the state was split between Loyalists and rebels, John Rutledge retired to the North Carolina border towns, implored Washington and Congress for aid, and encouraged local militia officers such as the Swamp Fox, Francis Marion, to undertake what amounted to guerrilla warfare — to wear the enemy down and to enlist the local inhabitants in the struggle. As the fighting went forward in 1781, Rutledge took steps to restore civil government. He issued terms of pardon and called for an election of members to an assembly to meet in January 1782. Soon after, he stepped down as governor, as required by law.

Peace having been restored to the former colonies, in 1782 Rutledge was elected to both the state assembly and the Continental Congress. In 1784 his election to the chancery court of South Carolina launched his judicial career, and from 1784 to 1790 he sat in the South Carolina House of Representatives. But in 1787 his efforts were required on the national stage as well.

With Charles Cotesworth Pinckney, Charles Pinckney, and Pierce Butler, he represented South Carolina at the Constitutional Convention in Philadelphia, where he served as chairman of the committee on detail. In the convention he labored for the interests of the planters of the lower South and of South Carolina, struggling to recover from extensive war damages. Rutledge vigorously opposed restrictions on the slave trade and was influential in the compromise that extended the trade to 1808. He argued that society should be divided into classes for representation and that office holding should be restricted to men of property. Rutledge also championed legislative supremacy rather than an independent executive and urged the assumption of states' debts by the national government.

After an active role in the South Carolina ratifying convention, in 1789 Rutledge was appointed senior associate justice of the Supreme Court by President Washington, but in 1791 he resigned to become chief justice of South Carolina. In 1795, on John Jay's retirement, he indicated his interest in the US chief justiceship to Washington. The President appointed Rutledge in July 1795 during a recess of Congress, and Rutledge presided at the August sitting of the court. But in December the Senate refused to confirm his appointment — whether it was because of his bitter public attack on the Jay treaty earlier in the year, or because of his increasing mental instability, is not wholly clear. Since the death of his wife in 1792 John Rutledge had suffered intermittent attacks of insanity, and after his rejection by the Senate his mind failed completely. He died on July 18, 1800, and was buried in the churchyard of St. Michael's at Charleston — a beautiful church that may be visited today.

John Rutledge strongly embodied the ideas of the ruling group of 18th century South Carolina. He was its most skilled and devoted leader, and his role in freeing the lower South from British rule and in bringing South Carolina into the Union was crucial.

JULY 19

First Woman's Rights Convention
Seneca Falls, New York

The American movement for women's rights, which achieved an intermediate goal — the franchise — with ratification in 1920 of the 19th Amendment to the US Constitution (see August 26) and which had a marked resurgence in the

1960s, had its formal start on July 19, 1848, when the first convention to discuss the rights of women was held at Seneca Falls, New York. It was attended largely by residents of western New York state.

This was the beginning of the organized women's movement. But a few voices had been raised since colonial days. In 1647, Margaret Brent appeared before the Maryland assembly to demand the right to vote in an unprecedented — and unsuccessful — appeal. Thomas Paine, the writer best known for his advocacy of the American Revolution, was also a consistent champion of the vote for women. Other early proponents of equality for women included the Quakers, who historically favored granting women the vote.

Some delegates to the Continental Congress also favored woman suffrage, and the matter was roundly debated while the US Constitution was being drafted. So intense were the feelings pro and con, however, that the Congress was forced to sidestep the issue by leaving it to the individual states to formulate voting regulations, including any rules novel enough to give the franchise to women. Also sidestepped was the subject of slavery, on which the delegates were similarly unable to agree. In order to achieve ratification of a federal Constitution, it was necessary to keep the status of women and slaves unchanged.

Books such as A Vindication of the Rights of Women, issued in 1792 by the English writer Mary Wollstonecraft, had an influence in intellectual circles on this side of the Atlantic. So, too, did such later works as The Equality of the Sexes (1838), by the southern abolitionist Sarah Grimké, and Woman in the 19th Century (1845), by the literary critic and reformer Margaret Fuller. But these were isolated works. At mid-19th century the traditional belief that women were inferior and that their only proper roles were childbearing and housekeeping still held sway. Rare were those who accepted women as adult human beings with fully developed individual attributes and rights equal to those of men. To all intents and purposes, the law regarded women as subject creatures whose property, earnings, and children belonged entirely to their husbands and who possessed no possibility of legal redress for inequities.

That women were regarded as a second- or third-class beings became unmistakably clear to two American women active in the cause of abolition, when they journeyed to London to attend the World Anti-Slavery Convention in 1840. One of these was Lucretia Coffin Mott, a 47-year-old Philadelphian. A devoted reformer, she was, like her husband James Mott, an ardent

Quaker; and she had traveled extensively as a lecturer, speaking at Quaker meetings in various parts of the United States. The other woman was a youthful resident of Seneca Falls, Elizabeth Cady Stanton (see November 12), a recent bride who had traveled with her husband, Henry Brewster Stanton, a journalist and abolitionist, to attend the London meeting.

Because they were female, however, Mott and Stanton were denied official accreditation and could not be seated in the convention. Their attempt to take part touched off a lengthy debate in which noted clergymen put forward the claim that equal status for women was contrary to God's will. Finally — unlike six less fortunate women who also had been excluded — Mott and Stanton were granted the privilege of being seated where they could *hear* the proceedings, but they were hidden from view by a curtain and denied the right to speak.

The rebuff was to have historic consequences, for it convinced Mott — who had previously lectured unstintingly on behalf of abolition, peace, labor rights, and temperance — that emphasis should be placed on women's rights. The subject occupied much of her attention for the rest of her life. In the association that grew from their joint exclusion from the London conference, Stanton, who was to become a dynamic advocate of equality, was much influenced by Mott.

The discussions that they held in London led directly to the Woman's Rights Convention called in 1848 at Seneca Falls. The gathering, held in the chapel of the Wesleyan Methodist Church, approved Stanton's celebrated bill of rights for women. This was the famous Declaration of Sentiments, patterned after the US Declaration of Independence, asserting that women are the equals of men and are entitled to all the rights and privileges of citizenship, including the right to hold property, to control their own wages, and to have a voice in the management of their children — as well as the right to vote. Apart from the abolition of legal inequities, the declaration also demanded wider educational and professional opportunities for women.

A similar convention was held in 1850 in Salem, Ohio, a Quaker center and an important station on the Underground Railroad. It was followed by the first national women's rights convention, which took place in Worcester, Massachusetts, in the autumn of 1850 under the leadership of the charismatic Lucy Stone (see August 13) and a distinguished group of eastern women and men. Present at the Worcester gathering were 250 delegates representing 9 states.

The organized effort to achieve rights for women, begun in 1848, led to some tentative early steps. For example, Kentucky in 1852 passed a law permitting widows with children of school age to vote for school district trustees. Other states enacted remedial legislation permitting married women to own property.

JULY 20

Men Land on the Moon

On July 20, 1969, at 4:17 P.M. eastern daylight time a spacecraft launched by the United States glided in and came to rest in the Sea of Tranquility on the moon. At 10:51 the door of the lunar module *Eagle* opened; astronaut Neil A. Armstrong slowly descended the steps of his craft and five minutes later stepped onto the moon. That step, and his historic words, "That's one small step for a man, one giant leap for mankind," were seen and heard by an estimated 600 million spellbound inhabitants of Earth.

Thus for the first time in human knowledge, life from the planet Earth moved to another body in space. The astronauts would explore, survive, and return to their home planet safely, bringing back vital information for future interplanetary contact — and all within the view and hearing of fellow beings. July 20 would become a day remembered around the world as Moon Day.

Armstrong, a 38-year-old civilian and commander of the Apollo 11 moon mission, was joined on the moon 18 minutes later by Air Force Colonel Edwin E. ("Buzz") Aldrin Jr., 39 years old and pilot of the lunar module. Armstrong's first act after stepping outside the module was to pause on the second rung of the nine-step ladder and pull a lanyard, releasing a television camera that transmitted to the world the sight of his very first steps on the moon. After Aldrin joined him they showed television viewers a plaque, which would remain on the moon, with the words: "Here men from the planet Earth first set foot upon the moon July, 1969, A.D. We came in peace for all mankind." The men then planted an American flag made of metal on the lunar surface, stepped back, and saluted.

The mission was the first attempt ever at a manned moon landing. The flight had been launched from Cape Kennedy, Florida, on July 16 at 9:32 A.M. eastern daylight time atop a 363-foot Saturn 5 launch rocket. Aboard with Armstrong and Aldrin was 38-year-old Air Force Lieutenant Colonel Michael Collins, pilot of the command module *Columbia*, which would circle the moon during the mission and then take the moonwalkers back to Earth.

It was the two crucial space vehicles, *Colum-*

bia and *Eagle*, together with their Saturn rocket launcher, that constituted Apollo 11. After separation from one another, the Apollo 11 components were referred to by their individual names. In describing early phases of the space trip, however, commentators used the collective name Apollo.

Less than 12 minutes following takeoff, after two of the Saturn's three stages had fired in succession, Apollo 11 went into a two-and-one-half-hour orbit around the earth. The orbiting was to assure that the astronauts had a vehicle that checked out as fully capable of the moon trip. Then a firing of the Saturn's third-stage engine boosted Apollo 11 out of its 115-mile-high orbit and into a route to the moon. The astronauts then separated the *Columbia* command ship in which they were riding from the Saturn's third stage, turned the *Columbia* around, and locked its nose into a connecting device on the *Eagle* lunar landing craft — which was still connected to the third stage of the Saturn launch vehicle. The linked command ship and lunar module now pulled free of the remaining rocket stage — which was fired by a radioed command from Houston ground control into a solar orbit, removing it from the path of Apollo 11.

During the three-day coasting journey toward the moon that followed, the astronauts transmitted several color telecasts of their flight. At one point Armstrong radioed: "Out of my window right now I can observe the entire continent of North America, Alaska, over the Pole, down to the Yucatan peninsula, Cuba, the northern part of South America, and then I run out of window."

After a three-day flight, the joined command ship *Columbia* and the lunar module *Eagle* swept into an orbit of the moon. Aldrin and Armstrong then dressed in white pressurized space suits and, leaving Collins behind in the command craft, crawled through a tunnel into the lunar module. Once inside it, they activated the electrical power and checked all the instrument settings on the cockpit panel. The *Eagle's* four legs with yard-wide footpads were extended from the ship, ready to land it on the moon's surface. Then the *Eagle* and *Columbia* were separated. When all the latches had been loosed, Armstrong radioed ground control: "The *Eagle* has wings."

Columbia remained in orbit around the moon while the *Eagle* went about its historic business: after the descent rocket was fired, the craft coasted rapidly toward the target area on the moon under its automatic guidance system. Suddenly, when they were about 400 feet from the moon, the astronauts saw that their ship's navigation and guidance system was taking them into a rocky crater surrounded by huge boulders, and some distance beyond the intended landing site. In addition they received an alarm signal indicating that the onboard computer was being overworked. Taking manual control of the ship, Armstrong quickly accelerated its speed and took it four additional miles to a safe landing spot. The craft touched down with only a few seconds' fuel remaining. Then he radioed: "Houston, Tranquility Base here. The *Eagle* has landed," Houston responded: "Roger, Tranquility, we copy you on the ground. You got a bunch of guys about to turn blue. We're breathing again. Thanks a lot."

The first duty after landing was to check the spacecraft's systems, its supplies of oxygen and fuel, and its ascent engine, to be sure that the men would be able to leave the surface of the moon — at a moment's notice if necessary. Suiting up for the moonwalk took more than three hours.

Once on the moon, the astronauts checked and photographed the *Eagle* from all angles to be certain that no flight or landing damage had occurred. They studied the depressions — only one to two inches deep — that the *Eagle*'s footpads had made in the moon's dust. Then they tested the best way to run and walk on the moon, which has only one-sixth the Earth's gravitation. Their efforts made it seem as if they were frolicking with childlike excitement, trying two-legged kangaroo jumps and then hopping in slow motion with six- to-eight-foot strides.

Scientific work included gathering 48 pounds of rocks and soil samples to take back to Earth. They also took a sample of subsurface soil, and Aldrin found in the process that he could force a core tube only about five inches downward into the soil, but that lunar soil was surprisingly easy to move sideways. The astronauts set up a solar-wind-composition detector, a seismic detector, and a laser reflector. The solar-wind collecting device, which the astronauts took back to Earth with them, showed that the lunar soil was rich in solar-wind particles. The seismic detector was planted on the moon to monitor moonquakes, internal lunar activity, and meteoroid impacts. The laser reflector, also left behind, gave scientists on Earth a more accurate knowledge of the *Eagle*'s landing site. It also provided information on the motions of the Earth and moon, and the distance between them. The men took dozens of photographs during their 2-hour-21-minute walk on the moon.

On July 21 at 1:54 P.M. eastern daylight time, after spending more than 21½ hours on the moon, Armstrong fired the rocket that returned the *Eagle* to lunar orbit. At 5:35, approximately 69 miles from the moon, the craft redocked with the command module, and the two moonwalkers reentered the *Columbia*. They then jettisoned the lunar module, which went off into space.

After an emergency-free return trip, Apollo 11 made a perfect splashdown in the Pacific Ocean at 12:50 P.M. eastern daylight time on July 24. Helicopters took the astronauts and their capsule to the aircraft carrier *Hornet*, where the men were put in quarantine. On August 10 they were released to enjoy the plaudits of an excited nation and world. The information concerning atmospheric conditions on the moon and its soil, terrain, and geological history resulting from the venture has been an immense contribution to knowledge of the universe and to future space exploration.

The moon landing was the result of years of scientific preparation and the expenditure of millions of dollars. Although both the United States and the Soviet Union had been engaged in extensive space research, the Russians on April 12, 1961, were the first to place a man — cosmonaut Yuri Gagarin — in orbit around the Earth. On May 25, 1961, President John F. Kennedy addressed Congress on the difficulties, problems, and challenges of a successful space program for the United States. He said: "I believe we should go to the moon . . . before this decade is out." The decision to send men to the moon came after Gagarin had made one orbit of the Earth, but before the American John H. Glenn Jr.'s successful three-orbit flight on February 20, 1962.

During the International Geophysical Year of 1957–1958, the United States had proposed putting a satellite in orbit to learn more about the Earth. But in October 1957 Russia had become the first nation to achieve such a goal by placing the unmanned Sputnik I in orbit outside the Earth's atmosphere. When the United States launched the Explorer I satellite in January of the following year, the space race was under way.

For the United States, the next important developments in space came with the Mercury program, in which Alan B. Shepard Jr. made a suborbital space flight in May 1961 and John Glenn and Leroy Gordon Cooper orbited the earth in February 1962 and May 1963 respectively. Among other things, Mercury gave information about the experience of weightless flight. Adding to knowledge that would be invaluable later were the flights of Ranger 7, 8, and 9, which followed. The unmanned spacecraft telecast to Earth nearly 18,000 "close-up" photographs of various areas of the moon before each crashed on its surface.

The first United States "soft," i.e., nondestructive, landing on the lunar surface was made in June 1966 by Surveyor I, which sent back over

11,000 television photographs. Further unmanned landings resulted in the photomapping of almost all of both the dark side and the light side of the moon. March 1965, meanwhile, had marked the beginning of the crucial Gemini program. With more earth orbiting and with the additional achievement of "walks" in space, the Gemini flights were directed toward providing information for the series of Apollo flights leading to a manned landing on the moon. The Gemini program developed the ability for orbit-changing and for rendezvous activities for a lunar module and a mother ship, and provided men with the experience of working in the vacuum outside of their spacecraft.

The space program had one tragedy in the years before the first moon landing: in January 1967 three astronauts, Roger B. Chaffee, Virgil I. ("Gus") Grissom, and Edward H. White II, who had been the first American astronaut to walk in space outside his craft, were killed in a ground test inside an Apollo command module. After a redesign of some of the systems in the command module, astronauts Frank Borman, William A. Anders, and James A. Lovell Jr., flying the Apollo 8 mission, became the first men to see the hidden side of the moon, in December 1968.

Neil A. Armstrong, the first man to walk on the moon, was born in Wapakoneta, Ohio, on August 5, 1930. He took flying lessons as a teenager and received his pilot's license on his 16th birthday. He was an aviator in the US Navy from 1949 to 1952, and flew 78 combat missions during the Korean War. After his naval service he completed his studies at Purdue University and in 1955 received a bachelor of science degree in aeronautical engineering. He then became a test pilot at Edwards Air Force Base in California, flying the F-100, F-101, and F-50, as well as the X-1 and X-15 rocket planes, setting records for speed and altitude. After he was named the first civilian astronaut in September 1962, his first assignment was to be backup command pilot to L. Gordon Cooper on the Gemini 5 mission. Armsrong served as command pilot on the Gemini 8 flight in March 1966. In this capacity he performed the first docking of two spacecraft in orbit. Training for the Apollo missions in 1968, he was almost killed when his lunar landing trainer lost power and crashed. He was named commander of the Apollo 11 flight in January 1969.

Edwin E. Aldrin was born in Montclair, New Jersey, on January 20, 1930. He was graduated third in his class of 475 from the US Military Academy in 1951. Following his father, who had been an officer in the US Army Air Corps (piloting biplanes and setting several cross-country speed records), Aldrin transferred to the air force and earned his wings within a year. Like Armstrong, Aldrin also served in the Korean War. A pilot of F-86 jet planes, he completed 66 combat missions. A recipient of the Distinguished Flying Cross, he was awarded a doctor of science degree in aeronautics by the Massachusetts Institute of Technology in 1963; and in October of the same year he became the first holder of a doctoral degree chosen to be a US astronaut. In November 1966, as pilot of the last flight in the Gemini series, he spent slightly over five and a half hours outside his craft in space, where he performed a number of engineering and scientific assignments.

The pilot of the command module *Columbia*, Michael Collins, was born on October 31, 1930, in Rome, where his father was serving as military attaché to the US Embassy. Collins, a graduate of the US Military Academy at West Point, subsequently transferred to the air force and was sent to California, where he became an experimental flight test officer at Edwards Air Force Base. One of 14 astronauts appointed in October 1963 by the National Aeronautics and Space Administration, Collins finished his basic training at the Manned Spacecraft Center in Houston, Texas, and was named backup pilot to James Lovell Jr. on the Gemini 7 flight. His initial space flight mission was in July 1966, when he served as pilot of Gemini 10. Twice during its three-day flight, Collins stepped outside his craft to undertake engineering tasks in space. Also involved was an Agena vehicle with which Gemini 10 had rendezvoused and conducted docking operations. One of Collins's assignments was to recover scientific equipment attached to the other craft. He was named to the crew of Apollo 8, but back surgery precluded his participation in the assignment. The Apollo 11 flight was Collins's last mission as an astronaut. Later in the same year he joined the US State Department as assistant secretary of state for public affairs. A lieutenant colonel during the Apollo 11 flight, Collins was promoted to colonel immediately afterward.

JULY 21

Cheyenne Frontier Days

This is a movable event. See note on page xxvi.

In 1897 Cheyenne, the capital and largest city of Wyoming, arranged a Frontier Day celebration to keep alive the sports and customs of the early days of the state. Since that time it is estimated that well over 2 million visitors have attended the rodeo festivities, which now comprise six days of activity and excitement during the last full week of July. Known as the "daddy of 'em all," Cheyenne Frontier Days is one of the oldest and largest outdoor western events, with an annual attendance of up to 100,000. This gala occasion is an action-packed reenactment of the Old West with colorful historical parades, thrilling night arena shows, Indian dances, and old-time melodramas.

This tribute to the rugged individualism of western America began when Cheyenne, now a modern city, was still considered a cattleman's town. In fact, in the early 1880s Cheyenne ranked as the wealthiest cattle-raising city, per capita, in the world. In August 1897 a group of Cheyenne businessmen who were returning from the annual Potato Day celebration in Greeley, Colorado, decided that their city also should have an annual festival. Colonel E. A. Slack, the owner and editor of the Cheyenne *Daily Sun Leader*, suggested that, since Cheyenne was the center of a highly developed ranching region, an old-time day of some sort — to be named Cheyenne Frontier Day — with "all the old-timers together, cow punchers and wild horses," would be most appropriate. As plans crystalized, Slack publicized the proposal, and on August 30 a meeting attended by the leading citizens considered an exhibition of cowboy and range sports. A committee, headed by Warren Richardson, fixed the date of the first celebration for September 23.

Fifteen thousand persons turned out for the event. The Frontier Day program began with a mock battle between the Sioux and the US Cavalry at what was formerly Fort D. A. Russell. There followed an exciting array of cow pony races, pitching and bucking horses, steer-roping, a demonstration of Pony Express relay riders, and scenes from the Overland Trail, including an ox train, a stagecoach holdup, and most hair-raising of all, the capture and hanging of a man by masked vigilantes.

The next year the performance expanded to two days. Additional features included a pioneer picnic, a dog and hare coursing contest, a cornerstone laying, and a reenactment of the first election in Wyoming. William F. ("Buffalo Bill") Cody was a sort of grand marshal for a colorful parade consisting of his Wild West performers, mounted riders, 20 Sioux brilliantly arrayed in full ceremonial costumes, white-uniformed German uhlans, British lancers, Arabs, and Turks, a squadron of the US 6th Cavalry, the most up-to-date fire engine available, and a cowboy brass band on horseback.

In 1908 Frontier Park, the nucleus of the present arena (now seating over 13,000), was estab-

lished. The rodeo facilities have since expanded to include an Indian village, a carnival midway, horse stables, stock corrals, and a camping ground for the contestants. The celebration itself has grown more elaborate from year to year as unusual events, such as the wild chuck-wagon races, have been added. Since 1931 a queen, Miss Frontier, and her lady-in-waiting have presided over the Cheyenne Frontier Days. Miss Frontier must be not only a gracious and poised hostess and goodwill ambassador for the festival, but also a descendant of one of the region's families and an accomplished horsewoman.

Despite its development into a major international attraction, Cheyenne's western celebration is still managed in every detail by local volunteers, for whom the event is a year-round project. The Frontier Days committee is helped considerably by three groups: the Heels, a men's organization whose members assist in production, timing, and judging duties; the W-Heels, the women's counterpart, whose members maintain the 60 old-time western vehicles that form an important part of the parade regalia and select the 600 women and children who ride in them; and the X-JWC, one of Cheyenne's oldest federated women's clubs, whose members prepare the parade costumes.

In 1970 the 74th annual Frontier Days celebration began with pre-festival weekend events. On Friday early-comers visited the Hell on Wheels Tent Town in Holiday Park. A bit of Old Cheyenne, it re-created the rowdy days when the town drew more than its share of professional gunmen, soldiers, promoters, and gamblers who enjoyed the quick money and cheap liquor in some 60 saloons. Cheyenne had had the reputation of being a "hell on wheels" until eastern journalists, incredulous that a city could thrive on the high western plains, nicknamed it the Magic City on the Plains in 1869. The tent town was open daily during rodeo week, as were the carnival rides and attractions. The Miss Frontier coronation ball started at 6:30 P.M. on Sunday. Following a buffet and the coronation of the queen, the guests, who were dressed in western gear, enjoyed dancing.

The first "go round" calf roping in Frontier Park took place on Monday morning. Visitors who preferred to wait for the main rodeo competitions attended the display of wagons and Clydesdale horses, antique auto show, or Indian family area with Sioux tepees. From 5:00 P.M. to midnight, a lively banjo band played old and new favorites for a sing-along. At 6:30 P.M., Sioux Indians staged a half-hour exhibition of ceremonial dances in downtown Cheyenne. The public then participated in street square-dancing or watched the first of the night arena shows, featuring name entertainment and specialty acts, Indian dances, and chuck-wagon and chariot races. Also offered on Monday evening were three performances by the Cheyenne Summer Players of an old-fashioned melodrama.

The rodeo's official first day is traditionally named Denver Post Day. Annually since 1908 hundreds of rodeo-bound cowboys have piled out of the Denver *Post*'s special train to give a final boost to Frontier Days and to be greeted by Wyoming dignitaries, chanting Indians, and cheering onlookers. In 1970, besides visiting the steer-wrestling "go round" and the various displays, the crowds lined up for the first of three downtown street parades. Cheyenne's parades are famous especially for their large collection of old-time vehicles — family coaches, covered wagons, stagecoaches, even an ambulance and a hearse — drawn by horse, ox, and mule teams. These vehicles, polished relics from the Old West, have rolled grandly down the streets of Cheyenne since the early 1920s, when Mrs. Fred D. Boice Sr. borrowed outstanding specimens from friends to add interest to the parade. Soon other women opened their family trunks to donate elegant 19th century clothing and volunteered their assistance in planning and preparing this costume addition. The parades also feature Oglala Sioux in handmade costumes; western riders carrying the flags of the 50 states; missiles from the nearby Warren Air Force Base; marching bands from the entire Rocky Mountain area; show-business personalities; Miss Frontier and queens from regional rodeos, and colorful floats depicting the history of Cheyenne and Wyoming. Between parades in 1970, the historic vehicles were displayed at Frontier Park.

At 1:30 p.m. Tuesday, the rodeo opened with the stirring grand entry, which heralded each of the six rodeo performances on Tuesday through Saturday. Featured in the grand entry were gaily clad riders, flag bearers, rodeo contestants, Indians, Miss Frontier, and the members of the Frontier Days committee, all marching to the blaring music of a military band. Having grown from a local contest into a world-famous competition, the Cheyenne rodeo attracts stars of the rodeo circuit, who compete for purses totaling over $100,000 and hope to win valuable points toward a world championship.

The first two events were the girls' goat-tying contest and the Shetland pony bucking contest in which winners of children's rodeos competed. Events sanctioned by the Rodeo Cowboys' Association followed: bareback riding, saddle bronc riding, Brahma bull riding, calf and steer roping, and bulldogging or steer wrestling.

Although not a standard event, horse racing has nonetheless grown to be one of the favorite features of the rodeo. Mustang saddle horses, thoroughbreds, and quarterhorses raced mile, half-mile, and 300-yard stretches. Chuck-wagon racing, another recent addition to the program, featured wagons pulled by four-horse stagecoach teams. The wild-horse race was the final and undoubtedly most chaotic daily competition of the 1970 rodeo.

Tuesday evening was also action-packed, with the night arena show, glittering carnival midway, ballroom dancing, and downtown concerts, Indian dances, square-dancing, and presentations of the melodrama. Wednesday got off to an early start with a free chuck-wagon breakfast. A civic project, prepared and cooked by the Kiwanis Club and served by Boy Scouts, it enticed countless festival visitors with free flapjacks, ham, coffee, and entertainment by local high schools and service clubs. Early risers also had an opportunity to visit the slack steer-roping "go round," the displays, or the T-Birds Fly-Over at the Warren Air Force Base. The 1:30 p.m. second rodeo and the evening program remained basically the same as in the preceding day.

On Thursday spectators flocked to the second lavish Western American parade at 10:00 a.m. and to the third 1:30 p.m. rodeo. On Friday highlights were provided by another chuck-wagon breakfast and the fourth afternoon rodeo. The fifth afternoon rodeo, preceded by the third downtown parade, took place on Saturday, Rodeo Cowboy Day. At the 2:00 p.m. rodeo finals on Sunday the top cowboys tested their prowess, strength, and sheer nerve on the slippery backs of bucking steers and horses. The winners of the six events were awarded championship trophies at 4:30 p.m., thus bringing to a close the 74th annual Cheyenne Frontier Days celebration.

JULY 22

Feast of St. Mary Magdalene

In observing the Feast of St. Mary Magdalene, the Roman Catholic church honors a woman closely associated with the ministry of Jesus as recorded in the Gospel accounts. She has been identified as the unnamed sinner in Luke 7:37–50 who, repentant, entered the Pharisee's house where Jesus had been invited to dinner, washed his feet with her tears and dried them with her hair, and anointed them with precious ointment. In Luke 8:1–3 she is Mary, called Magdalene, "out of whom went seven devils" — a woman healed of evil spirits and one of those caring for the needs of Jesus and the Apostles in their travels. John (11:2) identifies Mary of Bethany (sister of Martha and Lazarus, who was raised from the dead by Jesus) as "that Mary which anointeth the Lord with ointment, and wiped his feet with her hair."

Many find it impossible to identify the unnamed penitent or Mary of Bethany with the woman called Mary Magdalene, that is, Mary of Magdala. The Eastern churches honor 3 Marys as separate saints, adhering to the conclusions of Origen, the early Greek theologian and teacher.

According to the Scriptures, Mary Magdalene was present at the Crucifixion. She was one of the women who went to Christ's tomb to perform the rituals for the dead, found the tomb empty, and ran to tell the Apostles Peter and John. She was the first to whom Christ appeared after the Resurrection.

Some legends claim that Mary Magdalene traveled with Martha and Lazarus to France and converted the whole of Provence to Christianity. As there is difference of opinion about her identity, so there is lack of agreement on what became of her after the Ascension. The Eastern churches hold that she retired to Ephesus with Mary, the mother of Jesus, and St. John, the beloved disciple; that she died there; and that her body was transferred to Constantinople in the ninth century and is preserved there.

JULY 23

James Cardinal Gibbons's Birthday

James Gibbons, the Roman Catholic cardinal whom Theodore Roosevelt hailed in 1917 as the most venerated, respected, and useful citizen of the United States, was born in Baltimore, Maryland, on July 23, 1834. The son of Irish immigrants, he spent his childhood in both the United States and Ireland. In 1837 the family returned to Ireland, staying there 10 years before settling down again in America, first in New Orleans and a few years later in Baltimore.

Drawn to the priesthood, James Gibbons prepared for his vocation by attending St. Charles College in Ellicott City, Maryland, near Baltimore. After graduation in 1859, he studied theology at St. Mary's Seminary in his home town of Baltimore. He was ordained a Roman Catholic priest on June 30, 1861. Later that year he was named pastor of St. Bridget's Church in the Baltimore suburb of Canton. During the Civil War, Gibbons served as a volunteer chaplain at nearby Fort McHenry, where he aided captured Confederate as well as Union soldiers.

As a local pastor, he had displayed such administrative skill during the four years following his ordination that in 1865 he was appointed secretary to Archbishop Martin J. Spalding of Baltimore. The following year Gibbons greatly impressed the participants at the Second Plenary Council of Baltimore, which had been called to devise ways and means of governing the Catholic church in the United States. It established important guidelines in matters pertaining to education, clerical conduct, ecclesiastical property, parochial duties, and the organization of dioceses.

In 1868 the promising Gibbons was given the difficult task of organizing and heading the newly established vicarate apostolic of North Carolina. Consecrated bishop of Adramyttium – the youngest bishop in the entire Catholic Church – he participated in the Vatican Council of 1869–1870 in Rome. In 1872 he left North Carolina to become bishop of Richmond, Virginia.

The nine years that Gibbons spent as a missionary in the South were the formative ones of his career, giving him a vast and diverse experience with all types of people of different creeds. It was then that Gibbons conceived of an easily understandable brief summary of the doctrines of the Roman Catholic faith. His famous exposition of Catholic doctrine, *The Faith of Our Fathers*, was the result. The work, which is still in print, proved to be one of the most widely read statements of Catholic apologetics ever written, with some 40 US editions and 70 in England. Throughout his career, despite his tremendous workload as an administrator, Gibbons frequently contributed articles on topics of national concern to leading periodicals. He also wrote several other books, including *Our Christian Heritage*, *The Ambassador of Christ*, and the autobiographical *A Retrospect of Fifty Years*.

In 1877 the highly regarded church administrator was appointed coadjutor to and designated successor of the archbishop of Baltimore, James R. Bayley. Five months later, the archbishop's death caused James Gibbons to be appointed to head the oldest archdiocese in the United States. He became the first native of the city to serve in this position.

In 1883 Pope Leo XIII appointed Archbishop Gibbons apostolic delegate to preside over the Third Plenary Council of Baltimore, attended by 14 archbishops and 60 bishops of the United States. This council, which convened in 1884, formulated norms that have influenced the history of the Catholic church in this country ever since. Among the numerous significant results of actions taken were the introduction of the Baltimore catechisms and the establishment of the Catholic University of America in Washington,

D.C. A dedicated proponent of Catholic higher education, Gibbons served as first chancellor of the university when it opened in 1889 and as president of the board of trustees until his death in 1921.

On June 30, 1886, Pope Leo XIII named Archbishop Gibbons the second American cardinal. (Pope Pius IX had named Archbishop John McCloskey of New York City the first American cardinal in 1875.) On his installation as cardinal on March 25, 1887, Gibbons received the titular church of Santa Maria in Trastevere in Rome. The speech that he delivered in Rome on this occasion revealed the deep faith in and admiration for the American system of government that permeated his entire career. Like Pope Leo XIII, he was persuaded that democracy greatly benefited the Catholic church. He was constantly impressed by the general lack of strain in church-state relations in the United States as compared with the frequent tensions found in Western Europe, and praised the American policy of disestablishment.

Cardinal Gibbons's love of the United States and its institutions showed itself in his far-reaching civic, humanitarian, and religious activities. He was lauded as the champion of labor when he acted vigorously against a Quebec prelate's condemnation of the Canadian branch of the Knights of Labor as a secret society incompatible with the Roman Catholic faith. Although the ban was at first upheld by Rome, Gibbons came to labor's defense and convinced the pope that the organization could not be considered in this light. Owing to his efforts, the ban was raised. Later he is reported to have commented to his biographer, A. S. Will, "Ah, what a struggle it was on both sides of the water! I had so many difficulties that I wonder I got through them. Bishops are so hard to persuade!"

Of immigrant background himself, Cardinal Gibbons was acutely aware of the problems involved in integrating the Catholic church into American society, where suspicion of Catholicism as "un-American" was deeply imbedded. The nativist fears that Roman Catholics would hand the nation over to the pope and his "foreign priestcraft" mounted in the late 19th century, when as many as half a million Catholic immigrants came to the United States in a single year. Gibbons strongly favored early assimilation of foreign newcomers into the general American population. He therefore reacted vehemently against the so-called Cahensly Movement, which advocated the nomination of Catholic bishops in the United States according to the representation of national immigrant groups within a particular diocese; for example, adherents of the movement held that only German bishops should administer dioceses in which German-speaking Catholics formed the overwhelming bulk of the congregation, and German should become the official church language in that area. The cardinal opposed such a trend on the grounds that such "foreign enclaves," if permitted in the United States by the Holy See, would work to the detriment of the Catholic church in America, causing it to be regarded to an even greater extent as an exotic foreign transplant.

The path James Cardinal Gibbons chose often required tenacity and courage, and he was fully aware of the taxing demands that his position entailed. He once remarked to a friend:

I am always anxious about my public utterances. Speak out I must frequently. My position requires it. The public interests of the Church demand it. But I am always afraid of erring by excess or defect, and no one knows better than myself that my judgment is not equal to the demands upon it.

Americans of all professions, Catholics and non-Catholics alike, respected this resolute, far-sighted, and prudent church leader for his patriotism, civic spirit, and interest in progressive social reform. In 1911 many of the nation's most noted citizens, led by President William H. Taft, assembled in Washington, D.C., to pay homage to Cardinal Gibbons on the occasion of his 25th anniversary as cardinal and 50th anniversary as a priest. Ten years later, on March 24, 1921, he died, having devoted almost 60 years of his life to the Catholic church.

JULY 24

Mormon Pioneer Day

Pioneer Day in Utah

The history of Utah as a political community dates from the arrival of Brigham Young and his fellow members of the Church of Jesus Christ of Latter-Day Saints, unofficially known as the Mormons, in the Great Salt Lake Valley, on July 24, 1847. This anniversary, which has been celebrated every year since 1849, was made a legal holiday by the Utah territorial legislature on March 9, 1882. Still a major observance in the state, it is the only widespread Utah celebration other than those of national significance. The festive spirit prevails not only on July 24, but during the preceding week with a continuous round of rodeos, parades, dances, entertainment, and speeches honoring the Utah pioneers.

In 1820 Joseph Smith (see December 23), the Mormon founder and prophet, first aroused enmity by telling his neighbors in the area around Palmyra, New York, that he had received a vision of God and His Son. Acting upon instructions he claimed to have received in subsequent visions, Smith published the *Book of Mormon;* formally organized his church on April 6, 1830; and rapidly gained converts. As early as 1831, the sect, hounded by persecution and hatred, was forced to begin its long exodus. Over the next decade the Mormons moved from New York to Kirtland, Ohio; to several localities in Missouri, including Independence and Far West; and back east to Illinois. Members of the church settled in Commerce, Illinois, which Joseph Smith renamed Nauvoo, meaning "the beautiful plantation." Smith reigned supreme as mayor of Nauvoo, commander of its militia, and head of his religion. But there, too, nonbelievers, termed "Gentiles" by the Mormons, envied the Mormons' prosperity and political influence, and rumors of the practice of polygamy caused a stir even among some believers. When Smith ordered the destruction of a newspaper that was critical of his policies, he provoked the mounting resentment, which took the form of legal action and mob violence. Ultimately his move resulted in his imprisonment at Carthage, Illinois, and his murder in jail on June 27, 1844.

Although disputes about the succession to leadership in the church followed, and there was some splintering into factions, the majority of Mormons chose to follow Brigham Young, a 43-year-old churchman of unusual ability. He was often advised to abandon Nauvoo and resettle in some unwanted territory. Even as early as 1842, Smith had stated that "his people could yet be driven to the Rocky Mountains where they would build a city of their own, free from molestation." Continued hostility in the surrounding Illinois communities after Smith's death convinced Young that the only place where the Mormons could find refuge would be in such an isolated and desolate terrain, far beyond the frontier. Determined that this should be the Mormon's last exile, the grimly resolute leader meant to go so far that the "new Zion" would have time to grow to independent strength before animosity could again menace it. Familiar with the accounts of expeditions under John C. Frémont and other western explorers, Young and his colleagues were drawn to an area known as the Great Salt Lake.

Autumn and winter 1845 were devoted to preparations for the 1,000-mile trek. Instead of one mass exodus, Young organized the faithful into parties, then into companies, hundreds, fifties, and tens. Skilled craftsmen, hunters, and even brass bands were assigned to each party. Scouts were sent ahead to locate suitable way stations, plant crops, build bridges and cabins, dig wells, and establish ferries. Early in 1846, after promising his followers that "the angels of God will go with you, even as they went with the children of Israel when Moses led them from the land of Egypt," Young led the vanguard of 2,000 from Nauvoo across the frozen Mississippi River to Iowa, where they established the Camp of Israel.

As soon as additional companies could be assembled on the Iowa side of the river, they too started on the trail for the land of freedom in the West. Dragging their heavily loaded wagons across Iowa, they halted only long enough to set up temporary settlements for those who followed: Garden Grove, 150 miles from Nauvoo; Mount Pisgah, 100 miles beyond; Council Bluffs on the Missouri River; and finally Winter Quarters near Omaha, Nebraska, where more than 600 sod houses and log cabins were hastily constructed and food was stored for the harsh months ahead. Riding from Council Bluffs, Iowa, to the Mississippi River, a witness declared that 12,000 Mormons were drifting across Iowa in July of 1846. Entering Nauvoo in the fall, an anti-Mormon mob found only a deserted city, where one intruder felt it necessary to tread on tiptoe, "as if walking down the aisle of a country church, to avoid rousing irreverent echoes from the naked floors." Ironically, the Gentiles who had threatened them with confiscations, ultimatums, and bullets had killed barely two score of their number in all. But at Winter Quarters disease slew the faithful by the hundreds. Most of them lie buried in the Mormon cemetery in Omaha.

The following spring, in April, Young and his advance party organized to continue the migration: 143 men with 70-odd wagons, 90-odd horses, 52 mules, 66 oxen, 19 cows, dogs, chickens, seed, implements, and a six-pound cannon. Before the start was made, three women and two boys, Perry Decker and Young's nephew Lorenzo S. Young, were added. For three and a half months, the pioneers plodded across the seemingly infinite prairie grass and sagebrush of the Great Plains and struggled over mountains and through ravines choked with underbrush.

Brigham Young became ill with what was then called mountain fever. For a time it looked as if he, like Moses, would seek the promised land but never enter it. In order to reach the Salt Lake Valley without delay, his party was divided into two groups. One, commanded by Orson Pratt, pushed forward and reached the destination on July 22, 1847. On July 23 Young, riding in a wagon, was driven from the trail to an elevation from which he could see the surrounding country. The Great Basin, in which the Great Salt Lake lies, was spread out before him, and he gazed upon it with content. "Enough," he said. "This is the place. Drive on." On this spot the impressive Emigration Canyon monument, honoring Young and other early figures in Utah's history, was erected in 1947, the centennial of settlement.

At first the followers were not so sure about the new location. As they broke through the Wasatch Range, they viewed "a broad and barren plain hemmed in by mountains, blistering in the burning rays of the midsummer sun," "the paradise of the lizard, the cricket, and the rattlesnake." Accustomed to the fertile green fields of Illinois, they could not view this bleak country with its somber sagebrush, ashen soil, and tall sunflowers as a promised land. But from the beginning, the pioneers were dedicated to the task of transforming their settlement into a place where they could "become a mighty people in the midst of the Rocky Mountains."

The very afternoon the advance riders reached the site, they planted potatoes and turnips and dammed a creek to moisten the sun-baked soil. On July 24, after Young had arrived in the valley, the embryo city, two miles square after the model of Nauvoo and Kirtland, was laid out with solemn ceremonies and consecrated. The land on which the faithful settled was officially Mexican territory, not to be formally ceded to the United States until 1848 in the Treaty of Guadalupe Hildago ending the Mexican War. However, the Mormons were not perturbed about legal possession: the only inhabitants for hundreds of miles were scattered bands of seminomadic Indians. The West was for most Americans "God's country," and literally so for the Mormons, who believed that they had been led westward by divine guidance. The day after his arrival, Young climbed a peak to the north of the encampment and exclaimed: "Give us ten years in this place, and we'll ask no odds of Uncle Sam or the devil."

The original company of Mormons was soon enlarged when word was sent back that the "promised land" had been found. By the end of autumn 1847 about 2,000 Mormons had reached the Salt Lake Valley. The immigrants suffered great hardships for the first year or more, especially when the verdant fields were invaded by hordes of grasshoppers. Fighting back with herculean energy, but nearly despairing of saving their crops, the settlers were saved by white gulls that devoured the insects, known as Mormon crickets.

The westward movement of gold seekers to California from 1849 onwards soon made the Mormons prosperous. Their new city was on one of the routes to the West Coast, and thousands passed through the valley. Although Young thundered that "gold is for the paving of streets [and] the business of a Saint is to stay home and make his fields green," he did not forbid his followers to supply the immigrants with fresh horses and food supplies at high prices.

Converts from the East, and especially from England and Scandinavia, braving the hardships and perils of the overland trek, poured into the Salt Lake Valley. It is estimated that between 1847 and 1869 — when the Union Pacific railroad to the West Coast was completed — some 80,000 followed the trail of the Mormon pioneers, most of them in covered wagons, some pushing their belongings in handcarts. Under the guidance of the older pioneers, these settlers spread out along the western slopes of the Wasatch Mountains, then along fertile valleys with adequate water supplies. Within a few years, more than 400 communities had been founded. On March 10, 1849, the Mormons organized the provisional state of Deseret, a word, taken from the Book of Mormon, meaning "honeybee." On September 9, 1850, the Territory of Utah was set up, thus slowly linking the Mormons' destiny to the mainstream of American life (see January 4, Utah Admitted to the Union).

After the poor harvests of 1847 and 1848, the crops of 1849 were so good that a great celebration was planned for the anniversary of the founding of the city, the first of many July 24 celebrations. At daybreak a cannon salute was fired, and bands marched through the streets arousing the citizens for the great event of the day. A procession soon formed, headed by a mounted marshal in military uniform. It included 12 bishops of the church bearing the banners of their wards, 24 young men dressed in white with white scarfs across their right shoulders and coronets on their heads, 24 young women in white with white scarfs over their right shoulders and wreaths of roses on their heads, church leaders escorting Young, and 24 other Mormons carrying staffs, the upper ends of which were red with white ribbons. When the procession reached the structure called the "bowery," which served as the first church — a building 60 by 100 feet with a canopy 100 feet wide on each side — it was received with shouts of "Hosanna to God and the Lamb" by the people assembled there.

After several inspiring addresses, the procession continued, marching on to the feast prepared for the occasion. This was served on tables that were 1,400 feet long and spread, as Young said, "with all the luxuries of field and garden and with nearly all the vegetables of the world." The seats were filled and refilled by men and women who had been deprived even of some necessities for many months. The transient strangers within their gates were also fed, as well as a large number of Indians who had been attracted to the city by the celebration. Twenty-four formal toasts, and many informal ones, were proposed. In describing the event, a local newspaper said that "everyone was satisfied and not an oath was uttered, not a man intoxicated, not a jar or disturbance to mar the union, peace and harmony of the day."

The 10th anniversary in 1857 was commemorated in various sections of the territory, but the greatest celebration took place on the shore of Silver Lake at the head of Big Cottonwood Canyon. Almost 2,600 Mormons, in about 500 vehicles drawn by 1,500 horses, mules, and oxen, labored up the trail to pitch their tents at a spot about 25 miles southeast of Salt Lake City. Young addressed the group at sunset on July 23 and dancing followed. On July 24 the American flag was flown from the two highest peaks above the encampment, and a holiday spirit prevailed as the participants prayed, played games, sang, and danced to six brass bands.

Both the Jubilee Year of 1880, the 50th anniversary of the Mormon church, and the 1897 Semi-Centennial Jubilee of the Mormons' arrival in the Salt Lake Valley were widely observed. The latter occasion attracted an estimated 60,000 visitors to Salt Lake City, where the celebration closed with a parade featuring a replica of the first pioneer train and the wagon from which Brigham Young uttered the statement "This is the place." (The wagon is now displayed in the Pioneer Memorial Museum in Salt Lake City.)

Since its first settlement, Utah has grown into a populous state and Salt Lake City has expanded from a 40-acre group of log houses protected by a stockade into a great modern city. The manner of celebrating Pioneer Day has changed with the increasing resources of the people. The biggest celebration still takes place in Salt Lake City and is known as Days of '47. Presented annually since 1943, the festivities involve the cooperation of the Church of Jesus Christ of Latter-Day Saints, the Daughters of Utah Pioneers, city and county officials, and local businessmen. Highlights generally include the selection and coronation of a queen, dances, a youth parade, a pops concert, a rodeo, a mounted cavalcade, a pioneer dinner, a reception, an old-fashioned sidewalk sale, and a gala parade.

Typical of the Days of '47 was the 27th celebration staged in 1970, primarily from Monday, July 20, through Saturday, July 25, with other events scattered from May through early July. The selection of the queen and two attendants took place on May 16 at the state capitol. The coronation of the queen was held on June 6.

Special celebrations on July 4, which are also designated as among the Days of '47 activities, included the traditional bell-ringing ceremony at 10:00 A.M. on the steps of Salt Lake City's Pioneer Memorial Museum. The bells are those that the Mormons had hauled with them across the Plains — such as the one from the abandoned Temple in Nauvoo, Illinois — or had made in the early days of their settlement in Utah. An evening patriotic program, with speeches, military music, drills, mounted cavalcade, and fireworks, started at 8:30 P.M. in Derks Field, the ballpark. The popular Days of '47 pops concert, featuring guest artists and the Salt Lake Philharmonic Orchestra, took place at the Highland High School auditorium at 8:00 P.M. on July 14.

Beginning on July 20 and coninuing through July 23 the High-Noon Hilarities — sidewalk variety shows combined with pioneer music and dancing — were staged at various downtown locations two or three times daily. The Youth Parade, in which about 10,000 children participated by preparing floats and decorating bicycles, wagons, and other vehicles, was held July 21. A dance, with many participants in authentic pioneer dress, took place at 8:00 P.M. at Liberty Park, the former home and farm of Brigham Young. July 22 featured a 6:00 P.M. horse parade and also marked the start of the rodeo, staged in the Salt Palace and repeated in three evening and two matinee performances. Late in the afternoon of July 23 there was a reception at the Pioneer Memorial Museum.

On Friday, July 24, Pioneer Day itself, the traditional Sunrise Service was held at Linsay Gardens. The service, with music and a flag ceremony, was attended by 350 persons. The mammoth July 24 parade, watched by thousands of spectators, began promptly at 9:00 A.M. at the Brigham Young Monument on Main Street and proceeded to Liberty Park. Beauty queens, civic leaders, antique automobiles, ox-drawn wagons, and marching bands from all over the state joined in the two-hour march. Although the parade centered upon the arrival of the Mormons, the more than 135 ornamented floats depicted modern themes as well as those from the past.

Since 1901 the Daughters of Utah Pioneers have held a noon luncheon at Hotel Utah after the parade; originally intended to honor living pioneers, the luncheons continued to be held after the last surviving pioneers died. The climax of the 1970 celebration was a brief visit by President Richard M. Nixon, members of his family, and several cabinet members. After delivering a speech from the steps of the Church Office Building at 6:00 P.M., the President proceeded to the Salt Palace for the indoor rodeo, at which he was guest of honor.

Another summer attraction in Salt Lake City, in addition to the Days of '47 events, is *The Promised Valley*, a historical pageant depicting the Mormon trek to the area in 1847. Held annually since 1967, this production is performed nightly, except Sundays, during July and August, in an outdoor theater near Temple Square. Its cast of more than 100 singers, dancers, and musicians from the Salt Lake City region is drawn principally from church organizations and the University of Utah.

Although Salt Lake City has always staged the largest and most elaborate festivities in the state, Pioneer Day has been commemorated in the outlying districts too, since the first years of settlement. Services, games, dancing, and parades, complete with makeshift floats fashioned from hayracks and decorated with sagebrush, sunflowers, and lace curtains, were usual in the early days. An evening ball often followed, the tickets paid for with potatoes, carrots, eggs, homemade soap, or tallow candles. More than two dozen Utah communities, including Brighton, Woodruff, Panguitch, Vernal, Ogden, and Manti, observe July 24 with parades, rodeos, sports events, dances, dramatic productions, community breakfasts, talent shows, and livestock exhibits.

Ogden, laid out by Brigham Young in 1850 and now Utah's second largest city, annually stages its famed Pioneer Days around the July 24 anniversary. The 36th annual celebration in 1970 included a 130-unit parade on July 24 (featuring the US Air Force Band and Miss Rodeo America, Miss Rodeo Utah, and Miss Rodeo Queen Ogden) and a rodeo, held nightly except Sunday, during the week of July 24 at the Old Pioneer Stadium.

Since 1967 the residents of Manti, 80 miles south of Provo, have presented a 90-minute evening pageant, *The Mormon Miracle*, portraying highlights from Mormon history and doctrine such as Joseph Smith's visions, the receiving of the *Book of Mormon*, and the westward trek of the Latter-Day Saints. Staged on the south slope of Temple Hill against the background of the impressive Manti Temple, the drama attracted approximately 35,000 persons during its four-night-run in July 1970, and was expanded to a six-night-production in July 1971.

Pioneer Day in Other Western States

Pioneer Day is celebrated not only in Utah but also in the surrounding states, which have a large Mormon population. At a Pioneer Day celebration in St. Anthony, Idaho, in 1934, US Senator William Borah of Idaho aptly expressed the rea-sons why Mormons, and indeed all Americans, owe a debt of gratitude to the intrepid pioneers who undertook the great trek to the West:

It was one of the great and marvelous treks of history. . . . The Mormon people naturally view the events with a deeper feeling of respect and reverence than others experience. . . . Yet everyone capable of being moved by deeds of great daring, by patient suffering, by a spirit of devotion which never failed, a leadership which never faltered, readily join . . . in paying tribute to those pioneer men and women who . . . faced the perils and privations of the wilderness, and [settled there].

As emigrants from the eastern United States and abroad (especially from England and Scandinavia) swelled the Mormon ranks in and around Salt Lake City, Brigham Young organized his aggressive theocracy into the provisional state of Deseret, meaning "honeybee," a word taken from the *Book of Mormon*. His projected empire embraced what are now Utah and Nevada and parts of Arizona, Colorado, New Mexico, Wyoming, Idaho, Oregon, and California. Young's ambitious plans for Deseret were doomed to failure, for Congress instead set up the much smaller territory of Utah in 1850. Nevertheless, Mormon colonists spread out into the areas once claimed as part of Deseret.

The first Mormon attempt to expand northward beyond Utah was made in May 1855. Brigham Young dispatched 27 men under the command of Thomas Smith to set up a mission and colony in the Lemhi River Valley of Idaho — then a 22-day trip from Salt Lake City. After three years, the settlers, beset by hardships, returned home. In June 1860 a second, more successful band of Mormon home-seekers established a permanent agricultural settlement in Franklin in the accessible southeastern section of the present state of Idaho.

The Mormons who left Utah took with them the custom of celebrating July 24 as Pioneer Day. To mark the anniversary, they held morning religious services and a program of speeches, songs, and recitations, followed by a round of family or community banquets, races and games for all ages, and an evening dance. In 1895 the Mormons who had erected crude log cabins in the Snake River area, 12 miles northeast of what is now St. Anthony, Idaho, were aroused on Pioneer Day by the blast of a cleverly devised "cannon" — in reality a blacksmith's anvil that a powder explosion had hurled into the air.

Although not a legal holiday as in Utah, Pioneer Day in Idaho is still annually commemorated by its considerable Mormon population. Idaho has remained, with the exception of Utah, the state with the highest percentage of Mormons. Such southeastern Idaho communities as Pocatello, Montpelier, Franklin, Rigby, Rexburg, and St. Anthony have a strong church membership, as do such places as Hagerman and Meridian in the more western Twin Falls and Boise areas. The observances on July 24 generally include barbecues, group picnics, relay games, musical entertainment, and occasionally a parade or rodeo.

One of the biggest celebrations is held in Idaho Falls, the chief city of the upper Snake Valley in the southeastern part of the state. First known as Taylor's Ferry and then as Taylor's Bridge and Eagle Rock, Idaho Falls got its start in the 1860s, with the discovery of gold in Idaho. In 1887 the Mormons founded the Eagle Rock Ward there and erected a wooden chapel. The city is now the location of a Mormon temple. The celebration of Pioneer Day, sponsored by the Latter-Day Saints Stakes in the Idaho Falls area, which may run to four days, consists primarily of a rodeo, a musical, and a gala parade. In 1970 the schedule of events included nightly performances of Sigmund Romberg's operetta *The Student Prince*, from July 21 through July 24, at the Idaho Falls Civic Auditorium, and a rodeo staged at Tautphaus Park on the evenings of July 23, 24, and 25. Featured on July 24 itself were a Star-Time Revue in the civic auditorium from 10:00 A.M. to 2:00 P.M.; a variety of daytime activities, such as athletic events, boat rides on the Snake River, and an art exhibit; and a 6:00 P.M. parade.

Although Pioneer Day is not a legal holiday in Arizona, there, too, it is commemorated with special celebrations in Mormon-settled areas throughout the state. As early as the 1860s, a colony of Mormon pioneers founded Fredonia in northwestern Arizona along the Utah border. In the 1870s they settled the northeastern towns of St. Joseph (now Joseph City), Snowflake, and Show Low; the central Arizona towns, such as Pine; and Mesa and Jonesville (now Lehi) in the south central Salt River Valley. The largest Mormon settlements in the state eventually developed along the Upper Gila River in Graham County: Pima, Safford, and Thatcher, among others. Many of these towns still observe July 24, although in some cases the traditional customs and, indeed, general interest in pioneer traditions seem to be dying out. In Mesa, the site of a Mormon temple, Pioneer Day used to be a big community affair, complete with parades, barbecues, field days, and dances; at present the modest program may include a children's costume party or a social gathering.

In other Arizona Mormon communities, however, major events, such as rodeos and parades, are still staged. In St. Johns in eastern Arizona,

the annual Pioneer Day celebration usually lasts two days. In one typical year, a rodeo began at 1:30 P.M., and at 6:00 P.M. hundreds gathered for the campfire circle, where supper was prepared and eaten. This was followed by a Camporama program at 8:00 with songs and dances based on a pioneer theme, and by a dance at 9:00. On July 25 the annual parade got off to a colorful, early morning start; a rodeo in the afternoon was followed by a steak supper and a dance.

Several hundred persons attend the annual Graham County celebration of Pioneer Day, which is held alternately at Pima, Thatcher, and Safford. Highlights, depending upon the locality, can include a frontier-style horse race, a carnival, a rodeo, and games. The annual Pioneer-of-the-Year award, originated in 1959 by Mrs. Harry Felshaw for the traditional Pioneer Day, is presented to noteworthy local individuals or couples, aged 80 or over, who have contributed their services to the development of the county.

The tiny community of Pine, Arizona, usually celebrates the Friday or Saturday closest to July 24 with a parade of floats and costumed pioneers in covered wagons or other mid-19th century means of transportation. A program of songs, pioneer stories, and speeches of historical and religious nature is generally followed by a barbecue, sports contests, and an evening dance.

Nevada, included in Brigham Young's original state of Deseret, remained part of the new Mormon commonwealth even when the federal government set up the Territory of Utah in 1850. Mormon pioneers made what was probably the first permanent settlement in what is now Nevada. In about 1849 they transformed a roofless stockade in the Carson River Valley in the extreme western part of the area into a small settlement named Mormon Station. Renamed Genoa in 1855, it became a stopover on the early route to California. This unincorporated town of fewer than 100 residents observes July 24 with a modest celebration, as do other towns, such as Lund, in the eastern part of the sparsely populated state.

Pioneer Day is celebrated each year throughout Wyoming in many communities, such as Kemmerer, Green River, Fort Bridger, Evanston, and Lyman in the southwest; Lovell, Cowley, Byron, Powell, Burlington, Cody, and Worland in the northwest; and Laramie and Cheyenne in the southeast. The observances include parades, community singing, retelling of pioneer stories, square-dancing in pioneer costumes, and picnics. At the annual Cheyenne Frontier Days (see July 21) it is customary for Mormons to sponsor a float in the traditional parades.

July 24 is celebrated in California in areas

that have substantial Mormon populations. In centers such as Oakland, San Francisco, San Jose, Sacramento, and Long Beach, local church wards sponsor religious services, picnics, excursions, parades, dances, social gatherings, and special exercises devoted to reviewing the trek of 1847. San Diego also pays tribute to the Mormon Battalion, a group of 500 men who enlisted in the US Army in 1846 to fight in the Mexican War and who marched from Fort Leavenworth, Kansas, to San Diego, where they were released from service. Many of these Mormons, having played a significant role in the early settlement of California, subsequently made their way to Utah. The San Diego exercises are usually held in the area of the Mormon Battalion Monument in Presidio Park.

JULY 25

Feast of St. Christopher

The popularity of St. Christopher goes beyond church walls and extends to many people of diverse religious beliefs who like the idea of having the protection of the patron saint of travelers. Statues of St. Christopher accordingly are commonly seen on automobile dashboards, and medals of the saint often appear on car sunvisors, as well as on key chains and charm bracelets. Soldiers are among those who often carry a medal of St. Christopher for protection.

The legends about St. Christopher that have been handed down for centuries are still cherished, and his popularity was not diminished by the announcement in 1969 that the Roman Catholic church had removed his name, along with those of many other saints, from its universal calendar. Veneration of these saints was left as an optional matter to particular churches, religious communities, or individuals. The sanctity or existence of the affected saints was not necessarily questioned. (In some cases, the purpose was merely to replace the names of certain saints with those of more contemporary or better-known saints.) The exclusion of St. Christopher, as of some of the others, was based on a lack of reliable biographical data, on the clouding of facts by centuries of legends, or on confused identity — facts concerning several persons of the same name jumbled into one composite "biography."

Much of the confusion and many of the legends connected with St. Christopher doubtless sprang from his name, which comes from the Greek *Christophoros* and means "Christ-bearer." In the early days of Christianity, this name was frequently bestowed in the rite of baptism, which makes all Christians "Christ-bearers," or Christophers, in a manner of speaking. All that is actually known about St. Christopher is that, according to the Roman Martyrology, a man called Christopher was martyred in Asia Minor in about A.D. 250 during persecutions ordered by Emperor Decius. There is even uncertainty about the name Christopher bore before becoming a Christian.

This lack of biographical facts notwithstanding, the cult of St. Christopher started early, and a church was named after him in Bithynia, Asia Minor, in A.D. 452. By the sixth century, devotion to St. Christopher had grown strong in the East, and by the ninth century had spread to the West.

According to one of the most popular legends, Christopher was a gentle person, of great physical strength and gigantic stature, who vowed to serve the greatest king in the world. He served the greatest king of his region, and happily so, until he realized that the king feared the devil. Interpreting this to mean that the devil was greater than the king, Christopher went into the service of the devil. Soon, however, he learned that the devil feared Jesus Christ, so he decided to serve Jesus if he could find him.

As the legend continues, Christopher wandered about Asia Minor in search of his new master and finally came upon a Christian hermit who told him about Jesus, converted him to Christianity, and baptized him with the name of Christopher. The hermit explained to his eager convert that the best way to serve the heavenly master was to perform well the earthly work for which he was best suited. Christopher then went to a nearby river and became a ferryman, carrying people across on his strong shoulders while using a staff to keep his balance in the swirling waters.

One day, the story goes on, a small child approached and asked Christopher to carry him across the river on his shoulders, a seemingly easy task. As Christopher made his way across the river, however, the weight of the child became so great that he feared neither he nor his small passenger would reach the other side. When they finally did arrive safely, the child is said to have explained the overwhelming burden to the puzzled Christopher. "Marvel not, Christopher, for with me thou has borne the sins of the world."

With this, the child bade Christopher plant his walking staff in the earth. The staff immediately became a tree. Christopher then realized that he had met the Christ for whom he had been searching, and he faithfully continued to serve him by using his great strength to help others across the rushing stream, preaching

Christ, and finally suffering the death of a martyr. In pictures and statues, or on medallions, St. Christopher is usually represented with the Christ child upon his shoulders. He himself is often seen leaning on a staff, and straining his mighty muscles to support the child's tremendous weight.

In the Middle Ages, a widespread belief that whoever looked upon a picture or statue of St. Christopher would be free from harm for the rest of the day led to the practice of putting up an image of the saint opposite church doors. The prevalence of medals and other likenesses of Christopher today is an extension of this custom. Also during the Middle Ages, St. Christopher was listed among the Fourteen Holy Helpers, a group of saints chosen to be invoked for protection against specific dangers or by certain groups of people, such as travelers.

The hermit's message to St. Christopher, that he could best serve Christ by using wisely his natural talents and abilities, is also the foundation for the Christopher movement. Through programs heard or seen over several thousand radio or television stations, and the *Christopher News Notes,* the Christophers reach millions of Americans. Their purpose is summed up in the "Christ-bearer" meaning of the name, and they attempt to encourage everyone to show individual responsibility and initiative in raising the standards of all phases of human endeavor. The Christophers stress that positive action is essential and that little is accomplished by criticizing or complaining. Their motto is "Better to light one candle than to curse the darkness." Although founded by a member of the Roman Catholic Maryknoll order, the Christopher movement, with headquarters in New York City, embraces people of other denominations and creeds.

Eastern Orthodox churches celebrate the feast of St. Christopher on May 9, or 13 days later where the Julian calendar is used.

Feast of St. James the Greater

The Feast of St. James, the first of the Apostles to suffer martydom, is celebrated on July 25 by the Roman Catholic and Episcopalian communions. The Eastern Orthodox churches also honor this saint but on different days.

James and John (Apostle and Evangelist) were the sons of Zebedee, a comparatively prosperous fisherman on the Lake of Galilee. Like the brothers Andrew and Simon Peter — the first two to be chosen — James and John were mending nets when Jesus called them to be Apostles. Because of their fiery tempers and impulsive nature, Christ dubbed them "sons of thunder."

If there was such a thing as an inner circle among the 12 apostles, it was composed of Peter, James, and John. Their particular closeness to Jesus is borne out by scriptural references that list them as present at such important events in the life of Christ as the Transfiguration (Mark 9:2) and the agony in the Garden of Gethsemane (Mark 14:32–33).

St. James is the only Apostle whose martyrdom is explicitly reported in the New Testament. Herod Agrippa I, grandson of Herod the Great, ruled over Judea from A.D. 41 until his death in 44. When he took power, he deemed persecution of the Christians in Jerusalem a political expedient. James was one of the victims. The biblical account relates the event: "Now at this time, Herod the King set hands on certain members of the Church to persecute them. He killed James the brother of John with the sword" (Acts 12:1–2). This was in the year 42 or 44. According to tradition, the man who betrayed James to Herod was so moved by James's defense of his faith that he was converted and was beheaded with the Apostle.

St. James is called "the Greater" to distinguish him from the other Apostle of the same name who was called "the Minor," "the Less," "the Younger," or "the Little." St. James the Greater held, with Peter and John, a certain precedence among the Apostles.

St. James the Greater is the patron of Spain and Chile. According to Spanish tradition, James traveled and preached in Spain before he was martyred in Jerusalem. One of the many versions of the tradition holds that after the death of James, his disciples carried out his request that he be buried in Spain.

In the early part of the ninth century — one date given is 813 — a star is said to have miraculously revealed the place where the Apostle was buried in a field in the northwestern region of Spain. A church was built over the spot, and this place is now known as Santiago de Compostela (St. James of the Field of the Star). The finding of the tomb supposedly heartened Spaniards in their war against the Saracens, who had taken over most of Spain at that time.

During the Middle Ages, Santiago de Compostela ranked with Rome and Jerusalem as a major shrine, attracting pilgrims from all parts of Europe. Kings granted safe conduct to all foreigners, and pilgrims on the road to Santiago de Compostela were accorded special protection and hospitality.

After the Moors destroyed the original earthen church built over the tomb in the ninth century, it was replaced with a stone church. The present Romanesque cathedral built on the same site was begun in 1078, consecrated in 1128 and completed in 1211. One of the oldest and most historic hotels in all Europe is the Hostal de Los Reyes Católicos, built in 1501–1511 by King Ferdinand and Queen Isabella to receive pilgrims to the shrine. The hotel stands just across the square from the cathedral.

Whenever the Feast of St. James falls on a Sunday, it is the occasion of a jubilee year (or holy year) in Santiago de Compostela. The holy year is officially begun on the afternoon of December 31, with a ritual opening of the holy door of the cathedral — to signify welcome to all pilgrims. Many ceremonies, religious and festive, occur throughout the year and especially around the saint's feast day in July. Many other Spanish-speaking countries or communities also hold special celebrations to mark the Feast of St. James (or Santiago).

The Spanish influence is also seen in the Indian pueblos of New Mexico, which were the objects of early Spanish missionary efforts. Church events on saints' days are often supplemented by nonchurch events, including indigenous Indian dances with a history that far predates the arrival of the Spanish missionaries. The corn dance, most commonly performed of all the region's Indian dances, is part of the two-day Fiestas de Santiago y Santa Ana, held annually on July 25 and 26, or the nearest weekend, in Taos Pueblo. Santiago's Day dances also customarily take place in Santa Ana, Laguna, and Cochiti pueblos. The July 25 anniversary is also habitually marked by a rooster pull at Acoma Pueblo, where the celebration continues the next day as well, in honor of the parents of the Virgin Mary, SS. Joachim and Anne.

Puerto Rico's Constitution Day

Puerto Rico's most important holiday takes place annually on July 25, the anniversary of its founding as a commonwealth and of the adoption of its new constitution in 1952. By the terms of the constitution, Puerto Rico became a self-governing commonwealth voluntarily associated with the United States. Puerto Ricans retained their US citizenship (granted by the Jones Act in 1917) but were exempt from federal taxes and did not take part in US presidential elections.

Under the 1952 constitution Puerto Ricans were empowered to elect a governor and a legislature (composed of a Senate and a House of Representatives) by direct vote for four-year terms. Until 1948, when the journalist and reformer Luis Muñoz Marín won the first popular election for governor, executive officials had been appointed by the President of the United States, to which Puerto Rico had been ceded by Spain after the Spanish-American War in 1898. Amendment of the Jones Act in 1947 gave Puerto Ricans the right to elect their own governor. Muñoz, who was instrumental in securing commonwealth status for Puerto Rico, voluntarily stepped down from the governorship on January 3, 1965, after four terms in office. During his administration the success of Operation Bootstrap economic programs in raising Puerto Rico's standard of living made the commonwealth a model for underdeveloped nations around the world.

Under the 1952 constitution, which provides for the division of power between executive, legislative, and judicial branches of the Puerto Rican government, islanders also elect a resident commissioner who is sent, with a voice but no vote, to the US Congress in Washington.

Perhaps the most interesting feature of Puerto Rico's commonwealth relationship with the United States is that, while the arrangement is permanent as long as agreeable to both parties, it can be changed by mutual consent. The relationship came about after Puerto Rico's election of 1948 failed to produce a majority in favor either of statehood or of complete independence. The search for a third alternative led the resident commissioner in Washington to introduce a bill giving Puerto Ricans a chance to vote on whether they wanted to prepare their own constitution under a compact with the United States. Congressional passage of the bill was followed by a 1951 referendum in which Puerto Ricans indicated their approval of the idea by a large majority.

Early the next year, Puerto Rican representatives of varying political views met in convention to draft a Constitution. On March 3, 1952, the island electorate approved the document by a vote of more than four to one. On July 3 it was ratified by the US Congress. And on July 25, 1952, the Commonwealth of Puerto Rico and the constitution that established it were proclaimed.

The anniversary of Puerto Rico's change from territorial to commonwealth status is a legal holiday throughout the island. It is marked with speeches, parades, special floats, and exhibits. The celebrations include such events as fireworks displays, speedboat races, and special parties. On July 23, 1967, just two days before the 15th anniversary of Puerto Rico's Constitution, island residents in a referendum confirmed their preference for remaining a commonwealth. The vote was 425,081 in favor of commonwealth status; 273,315 in favor of statehood; and 4,205 for complete independence.

JULY 26

Feast of SS. Joachim and Anne

Although not even their names are certain and nothing about their lives can be historically documented, the parents of the Virgin Mary are honored by many Christian churches as SS. Joachim and Anne.

Saint Anne, or Hannah, in the Hebrew form, is traditionally the mother of Mary, the mother of Jesus. All that is known of her is gained from apocryphal writings dating from about 150. According to the account in these writings, a rich and pious couple named Joachim and Hannah lived in Nazareth. They were childless. When Joachim presented himself at the temple with an offering, he was repulsed and told that men without children were unworthy to enter. Thereupon he went into the mountains to pray for a child. His wife heard of what he had done and she too prayed for a child, vowing to dedicate that child to God. Not long afterward an angel appeared to her and told her that she would give birth to a child who would be blessed by all the world. In due time a child was born and named Mary. Scholars doubt the authenticity of this account, as it is apparently based on the story of the birth of Samuel in the Old Testament. Despite the lack of sound biographical evidence, however, many people have for centuries felt a closeness to Mary's parents, especially to her mother, St. Anne, and years of tradition now furnish the foundation for this veneration.

Veneration of St. Anne was well established among Eastern Catholics by the sixth century and had spread to the West by the eighth century. The Byzantine emperor Justinian I erected a magnificent temple in honor of St. Anne in Constantinople in about the year 550. Justinian II built another in 705. Many churches built in honor of St. Anne throughout Europe in the Middle Ages show the spread of the devotion in the West.

St. Anne, often called the Mother of the Poor, is also the patron of Christian mothers and wives. When medieval work and craft guilds were founded, many groups chose her as their patron. These included miners (in Wales), servants, cabinetmakers, lacemakers, seamstresses, carpenters, broommakers, and linen drapers.

The Feast of St. Anne was instituted probably in 1378 by Pope Urban VI, most likely because of the persistent requests of the English. In 1584 Pope Gregory XIII fixed July 26 as the date of the feast and extended it to the whole Roman Catholic church. Pope Leo XIII, whose baptismal name was Joachim, raised the Feast of St. Anne and that of St. Joachim (then celebrated on August 16) to the rank of second class feasts.

The Episcopalian church honors the two saints on July 26. Subsequent to changes in the Roman Catholic church calendar instituted by Vatican Council II, the Roman Catholic church now celebrates the Feast of both St. Joachim and St. Anne on July 26. Eastern Orthodox churches celebrate St. Anne, or Anna, on July 25. The day is variously designated on Orthodox calendars for the veneration of St. Anna, the mother of the Theotokos — that is, bearer of God — or as the Repose of St. Anne, mother of the Theotokos. Those Orthodox churches that still adhere to the old Julian calendar venerate St. Anne 13 days later, on August 7.

Pilgrims to the Holy Land can visit the tomb of St. Joachim in the Vale of Jehoshaphat, near Jerusalem, in the Church of the Holy Sepulcher of Our Lady, where St. Anne and St. Joseph, husband of the Virgin Mary, were also buried. On the basis of a legend that the body of St. Anne was taken to Apta Julia (now Apt) in Provence, France, the cathedral of Apt became a center of pilgrimage for Christians all over the country. Another renowned French shrine is Sainte Anne d'Auray in Brittany.

The French carried their devotion to St. Anne with them to the New World. Perhaps the most visited shrine in North America is St. Anne de Beaupré, often called "the Lourdes of the New World." The first little church in Beaupré, which is located on the St. Lawrence River about 20 miles from Quebec, was begun in 1658 by a handful of settlers who worked in the face of extreme poverty and constant attacks by Iroquois Indians. Little by little the church went up with each settler helping as best he could. A local farmer named Louis Guimont, who was crippled by arthritis, came one day to add a few stones to "Good St. Anne's Walls," as the people used to call the structure they were building. Guimont, who had great faith in the power of the saint, laid three stones in the foundation and immediately reported that he was cured of his affliction. This was the first of many reported cures at St. Anne de Beaupré.

In 1887 Ignace Bourget, bishop of Montreal, wrote:

This religious shrine [Beaupré] soon became famous for wonderful prodigies. The blind saw, the cripple walked, the paralytic arose, the sick returned home cured after having made their pilgrimage to Good Saint Anne. Before leaving, they hung on the walls of this dear shrine, in token of their cure, the crutches and other objects which had been their support in their infirmities.

Visitors to the huge Romanesque-Gothic basilica can see many crutches, wheelchairs, canes, braces, slings, eyeglasses, and other medical aids left by people who claim they were cured through the intercession of St. Anne with Christ. On May 5, 1887, the Shrine of St. Anne de Beaupré became a basilica, a title given to certain churches because of their antiquity, dignity, historical importance, or significance as centers of worship.

During 1958, the tercentennial year of St. Anne de Beaupré, well over 2 million pilgrims from Canada, the United States, and many other countries visited this shrine and witnessed or participated in the many tercentenary ceremonies, which included candlelight processions, religious services from morning till night, children's days, the christening of three new tercentenary bells, and a solemn novena, which actually is a yearly event. Another tercentenary event was the pilgrimage of Indians from many parts of Canada. Huron Indians had been among the first pilgrims to the shrine in 1658. Other tribes followed after them, and for two centuries Algonquins, Montagnais, Malecites, Abenakis, Micmacs, and Iroquois went to Beaupré each year to make the novena and celebrate the Feast of St. Anne. Sometimes they took with them the remains of relatives whose dying wishes were to be laid to rest in the shadow of St. Anne's shrine. St. Anne de Beaupré is still a popular pilgrimage site, registering over 2 million pilgrims annually.

Devotion to St. Anne is also strong in the United States. At the Shrine of St. Ann at the Roman Catholic church of St. Jean Baptiste at 76th Street and Lexington Avenue in New York City, hundreds attend the novena services held each Tuesday. During the solemn novena, which starts nine days before St. Anne's feast on July 26, services are held four times daily, and there is a candlelight procession each night. Between 700 and 800 people attend each night of the novena, and near its end the church is crowded all day long with people from New York and nearby states, expressing devotion to the saint, asking for her intercession for physical cures or spiritual grace. Many cures and other favors have been reported at this shrine since its inception in 1892, when a clergymen enroute to deliver a relic of St. Anne at Beaupré stopped in New York at St. Jean's. When the priests at St. Jean's asked if they might place the relic in the church to be venerated by the faithful, such huge crowds came that the priest delayed his journey to Beaupré for three weeks. During this period an estimated 200,000 to 300,000 people came, to pray to St. Anne, and many cures were reported. On the last day, a dismal rainy day with violent winds, thousands of people lined the streets around the church, many of them supporting relatives or friends with various afflictions and infirmities. Finally, when the priest could delay no longer, he left with the promise that such devotion to St. Anne would be rewarded, and he obtained another relic that could be permanently kept at St. Jean's. The relic is on view every day of the year at the shrine, which is in the lower church. There, too, crutches, canes, and other prosthetic devices have been left.

In New York City, the Church of St. Ann, at 110 East 12th Street, was designated a National Shrine of St. Ann and official headquarters of the Archconfraternity of the Motherhood of St. Ann by Pope Pius XI on August 26, 1929.

There are shrines to St. Anne in many other American cities, including Fall River and Fiskdale, both in Massachusetts, and in New Orleans. The saint's day is also celebrated in Indian pueblos in New Mexico, where the mass offered in the Roman Catholic churches, which were established by the Spanish, may be followed by indigenous dances performed in the main plaza. At Taos Pueblo, the famous corn dance is customarily part of the annual Fiestas de Santiago y Santa Ana, held annually on July 25 and July 26. The farming pueblo of Santa Ana, named for the saint, also marks the two days. Acoma Pueblo, too, marks both days with varied activity, including the corn dance.

The San Joaquin River and Valley in California were named for St. Joachim (Joaquín in Spanish).

New York Ratifies the Constitution

New York emerged from the American Revolution in a most favored position. Its strategic location, which had made the state a critical objective in the war, promised to bring untold commercial riches. New York City was the best natural ocean port in the United States, and the Hudson and Mohawk rivers offered the easiest route to the vast interior of the new nation.

New York was a proud member of the Union, but its leadership stressed the importance of states' rights and played down the role of the central government. Governor George Clinton was especially eager to exploit New York's potential without interference. He saw no reason for New York to support national programs that would inevitably draw money from his state's coffers to improve the lot of the less fortunately situated states.

George Clinton regarded the Articles of Confederation, which bestowed only minimal powers on the central government, as a suitable frame of government for the new nation. Despite assurances to General George Washington that he would support "every measure which has a tendency to cement the Union, and to give to the national councils that energy which may be necessary for the general welfare," Clinton consistently stymied attempts to increase the powers of the central authorities. In particular, the governor was hostile to legislative proposals that offered the Continental Congress greater control over the customs revenues generated in the port of New York. Clinton agreed that Congress should receive the duties, but demanded that the state alone have the power to levy and collect these taxes.

Alexander Hamilton was the principal opponent of Clinton's parochial view of New York's role in the Union. The governor's young antagonist had served during the Revolution as an artillery officer and as secretary, aide, companion, and confidant to General Washington, and had become well acquainted with the grave problems facing the national government. Hamilton believed that New York's real greatness lay in becoming the cornerstone of a powerful nation rather than in remaining the most prosperous member of a collection of city-states.

In the years immediately following the War for Independence, the deficiencies of the Articles of Confederation became apparent. The central government lacked the authority necessary to resolve elementary interstate problems, and, even worse, the national leaders were virtually impotent in international matters. Unable to command full support from the states, the Continental Congress could neither require the English to fulfill the obligations imposed on them by the Peace Treaty of 1783 nor prevent them from using their former colonies as a dumping ground for exports.

In 1786 Congress called for delegates of the states to meet in Annapolis, Maryland, to discuss methods of strengthening the national government. Hamilton represented New York at the gathering, which emissaries from New Jersey, Pennsylvania, Delaware, and Virginia also attended, and proposed that states bestow greater powers on the national government. Hamilton's exhortation stirred the Continental Congress to call all the states to send delegates to Philadelphia to discuss revision of the Articles of Confederation.

New York's legislature responded to the Congress's request and dispatched Alexander Hamilton, Robert Yates, and John Lansing Jr. to Pennsylvania. Clinton hoped that Yates and Lansing, who shared the governor's view of the Union, would be able to frustrate Hamilton's dreams of a stronger federation. At the convention each state would have one vote, and, if Yates and Lansing cooperated, they could deprive the nationalists of New York's critical support.

At the Constitutional Convention, Hamilton espoused an extraordinarily powerful central government that could appoint state governors and veto state legislation. He even proposed that Presidents and senators hold office for life. Unable to win support for his extreme program, Hamilton accepted the more modest proposals of James Madison of Virginia, who also desired an entirely new frame of government with greatly increased federal powers. Yates and Lansing rejected Madison's suggestions as going beyond the "revision" of the Articles of Confederation in which the New York legislature had commissioned them to participate. Both men withdrew from the convention and returned home with the apparent approval of Governor Clinton. Hamilton had no authority to cast New York's ballot independently, but he remained in Philadelphia and affixed his signature to the constitutional proposal finally adopted by the convention.

On September 28 the Continental Congress transmitted a draft of the Constitution, which required the assent of 9 of the 13 states for adoption, to the several legislatures. In New York the proposed frame of government divided the political leadership and populace. Clinton led the opponents of ratification, and sought to prevent the calling of a ratifying convention. Alexander Hamilton worked vigorously on behalf of the new Constitution and, together with Madison and his fellow New Yorker John Jay, produced the *Federalist Papers*, a series of essays eloquently advocating the nationalist cause.

In January 1788 Egbert Benson proposed in the New York legislature that the state hold a convention to consider the proposed Constitution. The legislature accepted his suggestion, and 61 delegates gathered at the courthouse in Poughkeepsie on June 17. Advocates of ratification were disappointed initially because two-thirds of the body opposed adoption of the new frame of government. Nevertheless, Federalists like Hamilton, Jay, Robert Livingston, Robert Morris, and James Duane immediately undertook the hard task of changing their adversaries' minds.

Hamilton argued that the new Constitution would add strength and vigor to the government without weakening the liberty gained under the Articles of Confederation. Melancton Smith, an adept debater, forcefully presented the Antifederalists' arguments. Smith particularly warned that a far-off national government that had the support of an army and navy and maintained contacts with the nations of Europe would pose a grave threat to popular liberty.

Clinton's supporters apparently had the convention under their control, but Hamilton slowly undercut their position. Besides using eloquent arguments, he established contact with delegates meeting in Constitutional Conventions in Virginia and New Hampshire. When New Hampshire and Virginia became respectively the 9th and 10th states to ratify, Hamilton announced to the Poughkeepsie gathering that the new Constitution would soon go into effect, and warned that New York was in danger of being omitted from the Union.

The defeat of the Virginia Antifederalists, led by Patrick Henry, Clinton's ally, was a severe blow to the New York governor. Support for the opponents of the Constitution quickly waned, and even Melancton Smith became a convert to federalism. Finally, on July 26, 1788, by a vote of 30 to 27, the Poughkeepsie convention ratified the Constitution. Clinton, who had evidently advised his friends to acquiesce in the adoption, on September 13, 1788, officially proclaimed the Constitution as the fundamental law of the United States.

Although the original 13 colonies became states at the time they declared their independence from Great Britain in 1776, they are generally ranked according to the order in which they ratified the Constitution. New York was the 11th to approve the frame of government and thus is considered to be the 11th state.

JULY 27

First Permanent Transatlantic Cable Completed

Telegraphic communications between the United States and Great Britain have been uninterrupted since July 27, 1866, when the spanning of the Atlantic Ocean by underwater telegraphic cable was permanently achieved. There had been a briefly successful cable eight years earlier by means of which Britain's Queen Victoria and US President James Buchanan had exchanged greetings on August 16, 1858. Queen Victoria cabled:

The Queen is convinced that the President will join with her in fervently hoping that the electric cable, which now connects Great Britain with the United States, will prove an additional link between the nations, whose friendship is founded on their common interest and reciprocal esteem.

In reply, President Buchanan warmly echoed the queen's sentiments, praying, too, that

the Atlantic Telegraph might under the blessing of Heaven, prove to be a bond of perpetual peace and friendship between the kindred nations, and an instrument destined by Divine Providence to diffuse religion, civilization, liberty and law throughout the world.

The general public greeted the news of the first transatlantic cable with wild acclaim.

The feat had been accomplished through the cooperation of both governments, with financing and technical support from government and private sectors of both countries, and with the active participation of the navies of both the United States and the United Kingdom. But the driving force for the cable was an individual: Cyrus West Field, an American merchant and self-made man.

Field was born on November 30, 1819, in Stockbridge, Massachusetts, one of the numerous children of the Reverend David Dudley Field and Submit Dickinson Field. At least two of his brothers became prominent lawyers, David Dudley Field in New York City, and Stephen Johnson Field in California and later in the US Supreme Court, of which he was appointed an associate justice in 1863.

Cyrus West Field, however, struck out early into the business world, leaving home at the age of 15 for several years' work in New York City, followed by a stint in Lee, Massachusetts, where he assisted his brother Matthew, a paper manufacturer. In 1840 young Cyrus Field briefly went into the paper business for himself in Westfield, Massachusetts. Not long afterwards, however, he accepted a partnership in the firm of E. Root & Company, wholesale paper dealers in New York City. When the Root establishment failed in 1841, he formed his own firm, Cyrus W. Field & Company. Though he initially was forced to extraordinary exertions in order to pay off the debts of the old firm, in time his enterprise triumphed. Indeed, it was so successful that by the time he was 33, Field felt he had worked hard enough and had accumulated enough money — more than a quarter million dollars — to retire; his intention was to enjoy life and to see the world. He visited Europe with his wife, Mary Bryan Stone Field, in 1849; and in 1853 he took a trip through South America with a friend, the well-known artist Frederick E. Church. In the ensuing years he was to take more than 40 trips to England, but not as a sightseer.

At the family's Thanksgiving dinner in 1853, Field's brother Matthew asked whether he would be interested in a project that intrigued Matthew and a friend, Frederick Newton Gisborne, a Canadian engineer. The project — no doubt inspired by the cable connecting England

and France in 1845 and another connecting Scotland and Ireland in 1853—had as its goal the laying of a submarine telegraph line across the Gulf of St. Lawrence, connecting Newfoundland and the North American mainland, and the establishment of land lines from the gulf to St. John's at the eastern end of Newfoundland. Connecting land lines were to extend also from the Gulf of St. Lawrence south to New York and other eastern cities of the United States. Newfoundland, the easternmost point of North America, was the closest landing for westbound ships from Europe. With luck, fast ships could ply between Ireland and Newfoundland in six days. The submarine cable across the Gulf of St. Lawrence, plus necessary land lines at either end, could speed the communication of transatlantic news and messages — which at that point took between one and two months by surface, over land and sea. Not only did Cyrus Field become interested in the Gulf of St. Lawrence project, but his imagination stretched all the way across the Atlantic Ocean. A transatlantic cable would be his ultimate aim. He had retired from "toil" and at 34 years of age was about to begin the hardest, most important work of his life.

Knowing that the enormous undertaking would require scientific, financial, and government support, he immediately set about communicating with and organizing the various sectors. He talked to the men involved with cables already laid between Britain and France and between Britain and Ireland, among them John W. Brett of the former enterprise, who became his associate. Field also sought advice from others, including Samuel Finley Breese Morse, the artist and inventor who had devised a successful electric telegraph apparatus and a code for transmission, and Matthew Fontaine Maury, the naval officer and oceanographer who was for years head of the United States Naval Observatory and Hydrographical Office in Washington, D.C. For financial backing, Field approached influential friends and neighbors such as Peter Cooper, Moses Taylor, Marshall Owen Roberts, and Chandler White, and, with them, formed the New York, Newfoundland and London Telegraph Company, chartered May 6, 1854, with headquarters in New York.

In the summer of 1856 Field took his family to reside in England, where he had much work to do. In the company of John Brett, he met with Charles Tilston Bright, the young British engineer who was already credited with the submarine cable connecting Scotland and Ireland and whose practical experience led to other underwater telegraphic enterprises. In December 1856 they gathered British financiers and organized the Atlantic Telegraph Company, with headquarters in London. Bright, initially the company's engineer-in-chief and consulting engineer later in the cable-laying project, was knighted for his work in 1858. Field was a director of both the London and New York companies from the beginning. He had stirred up scientific and financial support on both sides of the Atlantic. An additional source of support was the British government, which gave a grant of £14,000 annually for government messages; also helpful was a similar grant from the United States.

The work of establishing land lines in the rugged territory of Newfoundland had already begun. The first submarine cable across the Gulf of St. Lawrence, started in August 1855, was unsuccessful, but a cable was successfully laid the following year; and land lines (which frequently needed repair) connected St. John's (Trinity Bay), Newfoundland, with the submarine cable across the gulf and with land lines from the southern shore of the gulf to New York City and other eastern points in the United States.

In order to proceed with the transatlantic cable, Field went to Washington, D.C., to gain official approval for the project, which many considered either farfetched or impossible. After long delays and debate on Capitol Hill, the cable bill was finally passed and signed on March 3, 1857, by President Franklin Pierce as one of his last official acts.

The United States and Great Britain assigned naval personnel and ships to cooperate in the venture: from the United States, the steamship *Niagara* was attended by the *Susquehanna*. Britain's *Agamemnon* was accompanied by the *Leopard* and the *Cyclops*. Hopes, expectations, and excitement were high. On the eve of the ships' departure for the cable-laying effort, Lord Carlisle, then Lord-Lieutenant of Ireland, spoke eloquently on the historic significance of the occasion.

For that first attempt in 1857, the plan was for the *Niagara*, starting from Valentia, Ireland, to lay out the first half of the cable. Sailing with the *Niagara* was the *Agamemnon*, carrying the second half of the cable. At approximately midpoint in the Atlantic, the two halves were to be spliced and the *Agamemnon* was to continue the laying of the cable to Newfoundland. However, the *Niagara*'s line snapped after only about 350 miles of cable had been laid. The first attempt, thus ended, cost £100,000. Meanwhile, in the economic depression of 1857, Field's personal fortune was depleted. Though not bankrupt, he was no longer wealthy. Still, he continued to work on the transatlantic cable project without pay, refusing a salary offer of £1,000. In spite of his personal reverses, he was able not only to raise capital for the venture, but also to supervise changes in the ships and equipment, including methods and materials to improve cable insulation. For the second cable-laying attempt, the ships were first to splice the cable in mid-ocean and then take off for their respective shores. The mid-ocean meeting took place on June 25, 1858, but the attempt was given up on June 28.

On the third attempt, almost everyone involved with the cable venture, including the directors of both the British and US financing companies, was disheartened. There was no happy send-off when the cable fleet departed. Later, it was reported that "Mr. Field was the only man on board [the *Niagara*] who kept up his courage through it all."

On July 29, 1858, the splice was made in mid-ocean and the ships sailed off as planned, going through heavy weather and high winds; cable engineers, mechanics, and naval personnel, fearful that passing merchant ships might inadvertently damage the cable as it was paid out, scrambled to correct mechanical snags or make navigational maneuvers to compensate for compasses gone awry. On August 14, 1858, when the *Niagara* sailed into Trinity Bay, Newfoundland, the *Agamemnon* was already harbored in Valentia Bay: the first transatlantic cable had been laid. The first shore-to-shore message was sent on August 13 from the British directors to the American directors (of the respective transatlantic cable companies): "Glory to God in the highest and on earth Peace, goodwill toward men." Cyrus Field was in Newfoundland when that message came via cable. However, he and a team of men had to go into the Newfoundland woods, amidst much derision, to repair the land lines before the message could be relayed to New York and other East Coast points. The first through message — received by transatlantic cable at Newfoundland and transmitted via land lines and the Gulf of St. Lawrence cable to the eastern seaboard of the United States — was that from Queen Victoria to President Buchanan on August 16, 1858.

The accomplishment was hailed on both sides of the Atlantic. One account described the enthusiastic reaction in New York City:

Flags went up everywhere, the cannon roared and the church bells rang clamorously while the name of Cyrus Field was greeted with boisterous cheers as the hero of the hour, fit to be named with that of Benjamin Franklin and Columbus. There seemed no limit to the tumultuous rejoicing. New York City was illuminated by a great torchlight parade and a grand public reception was given in honor of [Field] and the other members of the company with the officers of the ships included.

As Field was getting into his carriage to go to the New York reception, he was handed a message cabled from the directors of the London company. When he read it at the reception, the "cheering was half-frantic." No one knew at the time that it would be the last message to be transmitted via that cable. Poor insulation against the sea water was given as the reason for the cable's malfunction on September 1, 1858, after approximately three weeks of operation. People on both sides of the Atlantic who had been at a peak of jubilation were now skeptical and even suspicious. Field and his companies were accused of chicanery and deception. The brief success was brushed aside; some said that no messages had ever crossed the ocean at all and that the whole scheme was a fraud.

For several years, further attempts to lay a transatlantic cable were halted by negative public feeling, lack of financing, and the outbreak of the Civil War. Field himself, however, continued his efforts to restore interest in and gain financial backing for the undertaking. In later years, he described the nadir: "Great was our discouragement and severe also were our struggles to raise money for what seemed to many people an insane venture."

In 1862 Field traveled — in vain — to Boston, Philadelphia, Albany, Buffalo, and New York City (where he addressed the Stock Exchange, the Corn Exchange, and the Chamber of Commerce — all organizations that would benefit greatly in day-to-day business from fast overseas financial communications). Meanwhile, he kept abreast of improvements in cable-laying equipment, giving encouragement wherever he could.

It was not until 1865 that the fourth attempt to span the Atlantic Ocean by electric cable was undertaken. The world's largest steamship, the *Great Eastern*, was engaged by Field, and specially fitted for the cable-laying task. The ship departed from Ireland on July 23. Some 1,200 miles of cable had been laid when, only two or three days from Newfoundland and success, the cable snapped.

Finally, a year later, the fifth attempt was successful. The *Great Eastern* departed from Ireland on July 13, 1866, and on July 27, 1866, Cyrus Field stepped ashore at Newfoundland — only to find that the land lines in the wilderness of Newfoundland again needed repair. However, minutes after the submarine cable had been properly hooked up to the terminal (the optimistic Field had had the terminal, Telegraph House, built at Trinity Bay, Newfoundland, during 1857–1858), it carried the latest news of the Austro-Prussian War to the North American continent, where people erroneously believed, according to very old information, that the warring factions had made peace.

Cyrus Field, who had weathered storms of public hostility and derision worse than any gale at sea, was again greeted as a hero with parades, luncheons, receptions, and medals of recognition from many governments, including those of the United States, Great Britain, France, and Italy. At one banquet — he was being honored by the New York Chamber of Commerce — Field said:

It has been a long struggle. Many times, when wandering in the forest of Newfoundland in the pelting rain or on the decks of ships on dark and stormy nights alone and far from home, I have almost accused myself of madness and folly to sacrifice the peace of my family and all the hopes of life for what might prove, after all, but a dream. It has taken nearly 13 years of ceaseless anxious watching and toil. I have seen my companions falling by my side one after another and feared that I might not live to see the end. And yet one hope has led me on and I have prayed that I might not taste death until the work was finished. That prayer was answered and now, beyond all acknowledgment to me, is the feeling of gratitude to Almighty God.

Field was only 47 at the time.

He had shown that great bodies of water could be spanned by submarine cable — well-insulated cable that could withstand deterioration from the sea — and he inspired others to set about linking nations and continents. Field's colleague and early mentor, Sir Charles Bright, went on to connect countries by submarine telegraph cables laid in the Mediterranean Sea, the Persian Gulf, and the West Indies. Field himself also promoted other transoceanic cables: the most ambitious, perhaps, was the transpacific cable, via Hawaii, to Asia and Australia.

Apart from his cable ventures, the man who had retired in his mid-30s made and lost more than one fortune from the activities of his later life. These included his participation in the financing of the New York elevated railroad lines, his control of the New York *Mail and Express*, and his involvement in the development of the Wabash Railroad. He was a man of reduced circumstances when he and his wife celebrated their 50th wedding anniversary on December 2, 1890. She died the following year, and Field died on July 12, 1892, at the age of 72. They were survived by seven children.

The Civil War and its aftermath had placed many strains on Anglo-American relations; the transatlantic cable helped ease at least some of those strains and renew amity between Great Britain and the United States. Referring to the *Alabama* Claims question and its settlement by the Treaty of Washington in 1871, a British statesman paid tribute to Field and the role of the cable in international affairs:

Undoubtedly there are frequent occasions when it is almost essential to have the means of exchanging ideas with only a few minutes', or at most a few hours' delay, instead of at intervals of weeks. I will venture to say that the Atlantic cable is a great pacific instrumentality, which, by the rapidity with which it enables facts to be made known, and misunderstandings to be cleared up, reduces the danger of war to a minimum; and certainly the experience of the Washington negotiations completely justifies the beautiful lines of the poet [John Greenleaf] Whittier and makes them as true as they are poetic:

> Weave on, swift shuttle of the Lord,
> Beneath the deep so far,
> The bridal robe of earth's accord,
> The funeral shroud of war.

JULY 28

Fourteenth Amendment Proclaimed Ratified

The 14th Amendment, second of three that are commonly called the Reconstruction Amendments to the Constitution, was approved by the Congress on June 13, 1866, submitted to the legislatures of the states on June 16, and declared ratified by the secretary of state on July 28, 1868. Ratification came after most of the states of the former Confederacy first rejected the amendment and then, with ratification a condition for their return to the Union, approved it.

The 13th Amendment had abolished slavery. The 14th Amendment for the first time defined national citizenship — to include blacks, most of whom, in pre–Civil War days, had been slaves in the South. It also guaranteed the personal and property rights of citizens, granting to all persons born or naturalized in the United States equal protection of the laws.

Although the 14th Amendment's main purpose was to guarantee to black Americans in an unquestionably constitutional way the rights enjoyed by other Americans (there had been doubt about the constitutionality of the Civil Rights Act of 1866, which had similar provisions), its terms are general. A clause of the amendment's first, and most-quoted section, forbidding the states to deprive any person of "life, liberty, or property, without due process of law," has also been cited in litigation having nothing to do with black rights, but often bearing instead on property protection and the rights of corporations. Furthermore, there was a long period beginning in 1883 when the intent of the amendment was subverted by a Supreme Court finding that, while the 14th Amendment prohibited infringement of civil rights by the *states*, it did not apply to the infringement of rights by individuals who acted without the help of state authority. With other acts and rulings, this opinion set the cause of civil rights back for decades — until new rights legislation was enacted in the 1950s and 1960s (see May 17, July 2, and August 6).

In its entirety, the first section of the 14th Amendment reads as follows:

All persons born or naturalized in the United States, and subject to the jurisdiction thereof, are citizens of the United States and of the State wherein they reside. No State shall make or enforce any law which shall abridge the privileges or immunities of citizens of the United States, nor shall any State deprive any person of life, liberty, or property without due process of law; nor deny to any person within its jurisdiction the equal protection of the laws.

Of the 14th Amendment's other sections, the fifth (and last) empowers Congress to enforce the amendment's provisions by appropriate legislation. Section 4 pledged the payment of Union debts but forbade the payment of Confederate debts — or, as it was phrased, of "any debt or obligation incurred in aid of insurrection or rebellion against the United States." And section 3 excluded from Congress and from federal and state office any person, "who, having previously taken an oath" in any such capacity "to support the Constitution of the United States, shall have engaged in insurrection or rebellion against the same."

But perhaps the most thought-provoking part of the 14th Amendment is the never-enforced second section, which was overlooked for some 90 years before it began to receive new scrutiny in the 1950s and 1960s. It provides for a proportionate reduction of representation in Congress when a state denies or abridges the right of any citizens to vote in federal or state elections.

Asserting that the 14th Amendment, as a "basis for the recent libertarian decisions of the Supreme Court . . . is now scarcely second in importance to the original Constitution itself," the New York University School of Law in October 1968 was host to a three-day 14th Amendment Centennial Convocation, which it described as the only large-scale celebration of the amendment's centennial and as a "significant event in American life." The first day's program was designed to provide historical background on the amendment, with Associate Justice William J. Brennan Jr. of the US Supreme Court, historian Henry Steele Commager of Amherst College, and law professor Bernard Schwartz of New York University as speakers. The second day's program was devoted to an examination of the amendment's impact in such areas as "personal sanctity" (Justice Walter V. Schaefer of the

Illinois supreme court); political rights (Dean Robert B. McKay of the NYU law school); religious beliefs (Harvey Cox of Harvard Divinity School); expression (Merlo J. Pusey of the Washington *Post*); and equality (Associate Justice Abe Fortas of the US Supreme Court). On the third day, speakers devoted themselves to the theme of Constitutionalism in a Changing World.

The climax of the centennial celebration was the hour-long address that evening by Chief Justice Earl Warren of the US Supreme Court entitled "14th Amendment: Retrospect and Prospect." Referring to "the seriousness of the nation's current racial problems," the chief justice commented that all local, state, and national governmental agencies "must employ their total resources in seeking solutions to the problems of racial hatred and unrest." Warren, a strong champion of human rights, scored 19th century Supreme Court decisions and congressional acts that delayed equality for black Americans. Emphasizing that "the steps we have taken in the last 100 years toward fulfilling the promise of equality have been halting and uncertain," he declared: "We have learned in recent years — and at a cost which this nation cannot long bear — that promises and piecemeal progress are no substitute for true equality."

JULY 29

Feast of St. Martha

The Feast of St. Martha is celebrated by Roman Catholics on July 29. The Protestant Episcopal church calendar notes "Saints Mary and Martha of Bethany" on the same date, which is included in *The Lesser Feasts and Fasts* authorized for trial use by the church's General Convention in 1964.

Martha lived with her brother Lazarus and her sister Mary in Bethany, a village about two miles from Jerusalem, and Jesus Christ was apparently a frequent guest in their home. In the New Testament, the only source of information about St. Martha, the Evangelists Luke and John both mention her. John summed up the relationship between Jesus and this family: "Now Jesus loved Martha and her sister and Lazarus." (John 11:5) It is generally held that Martha was the oldest of the family, and she apparently managed the household.

The Gospel of Luke (10:38–42) records what happened on one of Jesus' visits to Bethany: "A woman named Martha received him into her house. And she had a sister called Mary, who sat at the Lord's feet and listened to his teaching. But Martha was distracted with much serving." Evidently resentful of the fact that she was doing all the work, Martha went to Jesus and complained, "Lord, do you not care that my sister has left me to serve alone? Tell her then to help me." He answered her gently: "Martha, Martha, you are anxious and troubled about many things; one thing is needful. Mary has chosen the good portion, which shall not be taken away from her."

Biblical commentators often emphasize the different personalities of the two sisters, sometimes referring to Martha as a doer and Mary as a dreamer. Because of their contrasting personalities, Martha has come to symbolize the active life and Mary the life of prayer — either in religious orders, active and contemplative, or the active and contemplative facets of every human life.

The New Testament second reference to Martha occurs in the Gospel according to John (11:1–44). When Lazarus became ill, his two sisters sent a message to Jesus asking nothing directly but merely stating, "Lord, he whom you love is ill." However, by the time Jesus reached Bethany, Lazarus had already been in his tomb for four days. Many Jews had come from Jerusalem to Bethany to console the bereaved sisters.

When Martha heard that Jesus was coming, she went and met him ... [saying] "Lord, if you had been here, my brother would not have died. And even now I know that whatever you ask from God, God will give you." Jesus said to her ... "I am the resurrection and the life; he who believes in me, though he dies, yet shall he live, and whoever lives and believes in me shall never die. Do you believe this?" She said to him, "Yes, Lord; I believe...."

After speaking with Jesus, Martha sent for her sister, who fell at his feet weeping and repeated her sister's words

"Lord, if you had been here, my brother would not have died." Then Jesus, deeply moved ... came to the tomb; it was a cave, and a stone lay upon it. Jesus said, "Take away the stone." After praying, Jesus cried with a loud voice, "Lazarus, come out." The dead man came out, his hands and feet bound with bandages, and his face wrapped with a cloth.

The Evangelist John (12:1–3) makes the third and last New Testament reference to Martha. Though brief, the passage shows Martha's role in the family: "Six days before the Passover, Jesus came to Bethany, where Lazarus was, whom Jesus had raised from the dead. There they made him a supper; Martha served, but Lazarus was one of those at table with him."

These three references to Martha in the New Testament comprise the only documentation of her life. Understandably Martha is the patron saint of innkeepers, housekeepers, hotelkeepers, cooks, and laundresses.

There was no cult of St. Martha for almost 12 centuries, and when devotion to her began, it came about by accident. The remains of another Martha, a Persian nun who had been martyred in Asia on June 6, in the year 347, had been carried to southern Gaul for safe burial. Near the end of the 12th century, these remains were discovered at Tarascon in Provence. Stories, passed by word of mouth, soon claimed that the Bethany family, Martha, Lazarus, and Mary, had sailed to France after the death of Christ. This account may have been erroneously reinforced by the fact that there was a French bishop named Lazarus — who lived, however, in the fifth century. At any rate, this story succeeded in drawing some attention to St. Martha, and in the year 1262 the Order of Friars Minor (Franciscans) added her name to their calendar, insuring that she would be remembered in special prayers on July 29 by all Franciscans. Some years later the feast was included in the calendar for the whole Roman Catholic church.

Two Roman Catholic religious communities of women, both founded in Canada, have St. Martha as their patron: Sisters of St. Martha of Prince Edward Island, and Sisters of Saint Martha of St. Hyacinthe in Quebec.

Pony Penning on Chincoteague Island

This is a movable event. See note on page xxvi.

Every year in late July the inhabitants of Chincoteague, Virginia, and thousands of visitors join in the carnival spirit of the Pony Penning Days. Chincoteague is a quiet fishing town on Chincoteague Island, 90 miles from Virginia Beach and 135 miles from Williamsburg via the Chesapeake Bay Bridge-Tunnel. Since 1924, with the exception of several years during World War II, the annual firemen's carnival there has included as its highlight the wild pony penning and sale.

The origin of the wild "ponies" — they are actually stunted horses — is a matter of dispute. They are known to have roamed the small islands off what is now the Virginia and Maryland coast since the 17th century, and various theories account for their presence. Two favorite explanations trace their history back to the early Spanish explorers. One theory holds that the small, wiry horses are the descendants of the survivors of a 16th century shipwreck; its adherents claim that a Spanish galleon carrying a cargo of Spanish mustangs was wrecked off Assateague, the 37-mile-long barrier island parallel to the coast of Maryland and Virginia, whose name — bestowed by the Gingoteague Indians — means "a running stream between." Early settlers in the area supposedly came across the skeleton of the ship. Another widely held theory maintains that early adventurers, perhaps pirates, deposited the ponies on Assateague Island for grazing purposes and for unknown reasons never reclaimed them.

The castaways — solid-colored blacks, sorrels, and bays that were larger and more graceful than Shetland ponies and distinguished by thick curly manes and long flowing tails — roamed the remote sandy island with its low dunes and extensive salt marshes. The scanty diet of salt-marsh grass apparently stunted their growth. Becoming increasingly wild and adventuresome, the rapidly multiplying herd frequently sought refuge from the lashing Atlantic storms by crossing over to nearby Chincoteague Island. Then only a narrow waterway separated Chincoteague from Assateague Island. (The waterway later widened into what is now called the Assateague Channel.)

Unlike barren Assateague Island, the wooded seven-mile-long, mile-and-a-half-wide Chincoteague Island (whose name means "beautiful land across the waters") had been settled since 1671. Jumping the inhabitants' split-log fences, the wild ponies foraged for food in vegetable gardens and corn fields. In an effort to forestall these destructive pony raids, the islanders, sometime in the late 17th or early 18th century, inaugurated the first annual pony roundup and penning. The owner of a section of marshland was generally permitted to claim the wild horses that he had found grazing on his property and offer them for sale.

In subsequent years, numerous mainland colonists, having been informed of the pony penning date (usually around August 10), went to Chincoteague Island to appraise and buy the penned ponies, which had been rounded up from Chincoteague and Assateague islands, and to watch pony races. Former slaves generally roped and branded the unruly ponies and rode them bareback with a wicket or cord for a bridle. Free liquor and food were additional inducements for visitors. Only men were allowed to attend the annual event, which was originally held on the southern end of Chincoteague Island.

The waterway dividing Chincoteague and Assateague islands gradually became too wide for even the intrepid ponies to cross with ease and Assateague, especially, became overrun with multiplying livestock. The increasingly popular pony penning and sale was then routinely supplemented by a "pony swim," during which the horses were forced to cross the Assateague Channel from Assateague to Chincoteague Island.

In 1924, 14 men formed the Chincoteague Volunteer Fire Company. Since their original capital consisted of only $4.16, the volunteers decided to stage an annual carnival in July to raise funds for fire-fighting equipment. To assure continued interest in the island's traditional festivity, the pony penning celebration became the focal point of the two-week carnival program; the date of the sale was firmly set for the last Thursday in July, with the pony swim the preceding day. Concerned lest the wild pony herd eventually become depleted, the firemen established their own breeding herd by buying 80 ponies.

Both the pony penning festival and the spirited horses themselves gained widespread fame when Marguerite Henry, a well-known author of children's books, became an admirer of the Chincoteague islanders and the ponies and wrote several stories about them. *Misty of Chincoteague*, published in 1947 and made into a movie in 1960, brought the Chincoteague horses national prominence.

In 1943 the Chincoteague National Wildife Refuge was established on Assateague Island. It contained 9,030 acres in Virginia and 417 acres of salt marsh in Maryland. The US Bureau of Sport Fisheries and Wildlife agreed to allow the ponies managed by the Chincoteague Volunteer Fire Company to graze and roam at will on the Virginia portion, occupying approximately the southern third of Assateague Island. Today the herd, numbering about 150 adult horses, shares its ancestral home with snow geese, waterfowl, peregrine falcons, and other wildlife. Another, smaller, wild pony herd (of approximately 40 head), on the Maryland portion of the refuge, is owned and managed by the National Park Service of the US Department of the Interior; it is kept as wild and free as possible and is not subjected to an annual roundup and penning. In 1965 the Chincoteague National Wildlife Refuge was incorporated into the 39,500-acre Assateague Island National Seashore in a bill passed by Congress and signed by President Lyndon B. Johnson.

Over the past few decades, the annual Pony Penning Days — the last Wednesday and Thursday in July — have in reality become five full days of activities, an unofficial Pony Penning Week. Visitors tend to arrive early in the week in order to watch the rounding-up and corralling of ponies on Assateague Island, which frequently takes place on Sunday, Monday, and Tuesday; they then witness the pony swim from Assateague to Chincoteague Island on Wednesday, the sale on Thursday, and the "swim to freedom" on Friday, when the remaining horses return to Assateague Island.

Typical of the pony penning festivities was the 45th annual event, held in 1970. The firemen's carnival, which ran from July 17 through August 1, included the usual midway rides, as well as a country music show and other entertainment. The local movie theater showed the film *Misty of Chincoteague* nightly during the two-week period. Although thousands of visitors enjoyed the rides and sampled the famous Chincoteague oyster and clam sandwiches, the climax naturally came with the pony events.

Early in Pony Penning Week, which ran from Sunday, July 26, through Friday, July 31, the firemen donned cowboy garb in preparation for the annual roundup on Assateague Island. These "saltwater cowboys" usually hunt for the foals first, then the mares and stallions. Invariably a few obstinate mares, set upon protecting their offspring, disappear into the saltwater marshes with their foals and cause the firemen many hours of wearisome riding.

On Wednesday, the first official Pony Penning Day, the entire herd — after a three-hour wait for the slack tide — was forced to swim the swift currents of the Assateague Channel. The swim was as usual a little bewildering for the foals, but their dams and sires took the event in stride. The mounted riders guided the group, some 250 to 300 strong, quickly and safely toward Chincoteague Island, where they splashed ashore about five minutes later. Hundreds of spectators lined the Chincoteague Memorial Park shoreline on the east side of the island to watch the proceedings or took seats in the 400-odd boats along the watery route. After a brief rest, the shaggy ponies were herded up Main Street in the town of Chincoteague to corrals at the Chincoteague Volunteer Fire Company carnival grounds.

Beginning at 8:00 A.M. on Thursday, 70 ponies — according to the sponsors, they are docile and easy to train despite their reputation as "wild" — were sold at auction. In 1968 the ponies were sold only at set prices, but public demand forced the resumption of the auction technique. The number of ponies offered usually ranges from 75 to 100, although the total is always carefully assessed to assure that an adequate breeding stock remains on Assateague Island. The ponies up for sale in 1970 went quickly at prices up to $150, some going to dealers, but many to private buyers, especially parents of young children. The proceeds are always used to maintain the fire company and provide for the animals let loose again on Assateague. Each year, however, the firemen give a pony to a member of Congress for presentation to any group or organization. The gesture is a means of thanking people in many states for assistance during the disastrous storm that ravaged the area in 1962 and severely damaged the herd.

In addition to watching the exciting auction, the 1970 crowd relished the seafood and chicken dinners prepared by the women's auxiliary of the fire company. Continuous carnival attractions, wild pony rides, and branding with the fire company's "F" of young ponies that were not offered for sale completed the activities. The remaining wild ponies could be seen at the carnival grounds the morning of Friday, July 31, but in early afternoon the breeding stock was allowed to swim back to Assateague Island for another year of freedom until the following July.

JULY 30

The Battle of the Crater

The harrowing Battle of the Crater, an important event of the Civil War during which the Confederate defenders of Petersburg, Virginia, held firm in the face of a determined Union effort to pierce their lines, took place on July 30, 1864. For many years the anniversary of this day — when Federal troops exploded a large mine under Confederate defense lines, creating an enormous crater that is still visible today — was sporadically marked as Crater Day by organizations of Confederate veterans and sons of veterans.

However, although the centennial of the Battle of the Crater was the subject of special note in 1964, it has been many years since the last regular observance of Crater Day took place. In actual fact, the Battle of the Crater was part of the historic, 10-month siege of Petersburg, whose fall on April 2, 1865, climaxed the last major engagement of the Civil War.

The Battle of the Crater was preceded by other unsuccessful efforts in which Union forces with superior numbers and ample opportunity failed utterly in their attempts to take strategically important Petersburg. One of these onslaughts took place on June 9, 1864, a date that Petersburg still commemorates annually, in the same way that the rest of the South marks Confederate Memorial Day on other dates (see June 9).

Henry Ford's Birthday

Perhaps more than any other, the name of automobile manufacturer Henry Ford has come to be synonymous with mass production. His innovation was efficient use of that cornerstone of production, the assembly line. A pioneer in development of the automobile, Ford "put the nation on wheels" with his Model T. With his cardinal principles of increased efficiency, increased volume, lower prices and higher wages, he brought the automobile, once the toy of the rich, within the reach of the many. Effects of the revolution that he helped put in motion extended beyond his own lifetime, resulting in mass mobility, the growth of suburbs, gigantic highway-building programs, widespread tourism, and a lessening of sectional differences.

On July 30, 1963, the 100th anniversary of Ford's birth was observed in Dearborn, Michigan, with the placing of a historical marker purchased by local schoolchildren at Ford's birth site; speeches by his grandson Henry Ford II and Lenore Romney, wife of the governor of Michigan; and presentation of a pageant, The Man from Dearborn, with a cast of 1,000. The centennial was also the occasion for announcement that the Ford Motor Company would present to the city of Dearborn a 15-acre setting for the $3 million Henry Ford Centennial Library to be constructed by the philanthropic Ford Foundation.

Other centennial fanfare took place at Dearborn's widely visited Henry Ford Museum and Greenfield Village. The village, which was founded by Ford in 1929, grew out of his interest in Americana. It contains over 100 buildings illustrating the life and inventions of 19th century America, among them structures important in the lives of famous Americans, including Ford. The 14 nearby acres, on which the museum is housed in replicas of historic Philadelphia buildings, include exhibits of antique automobiles, fire engines, locomotives, furniture, farm implements, and household articles.

Born on a farm near Dearborn, young Henry Ford spent hours doing farm chores by hard hand labor — and come to an early conclusion that "much might somehow be done in a better way." This observation, fortified by natural bent, led to his interest in mechanics. From the age of 12, he never stopped tinkering. He attended school until he was 15, then became an apprentice machinist in Detroit, where he repaired watches in his spare time, and read with excitement of the new internal combustion hydrocarbon motor that A. N. Otto had invented in Germany. An interval of work on the farm followed, with Ford, who never liked idleness, utilizing his spare moments to experiment with machinery, attend business college, and court a neighbor, Clara Bryant. They were married on April 11, 1888.

The young couple settled in Detroit, where Ford became a mechanical engineer, and later chief engineer, for the Edison Illuminating Com-

pany — and also tinkered in his backyard shop with a two-cylinder internal combustion engine, powered by gas, for which he himself had drawn the diagram. The motor was tested successfully in 1893 — the same year Clara Ford gave birth to a son, Edsel. Three years later, Ford made history by harnessing his engine to a homemade frame mounted on bicycle wheels and driving it to Dearborn. Although his was not the first gas-powered automobile, it was destined to change the face of America as had no other manufacture before it.

Ford left the Edison Illuminating Company in 1899. After brief associations with two groups of investors, and an attempt at developing racing cars, he found new financial backing and organized the Ford Motor Company, with himself as president, in 1903. The young company was hard-pressed financially until introduction, in 1905, of its Model N, bearing a $500 price-tag, which astonished manufacturers of more expensive cars.

But the real heroine in Ford's success story was the Model T — commonly known as the flivver or the Tin Lizzie — which appeared in 1908. The vehicle, beloved as only an ugly duckling could be loved, swept the country. The subject of verse, cartoons and jokes, it was later immortalized in an essay by E. B. White. Whole new industries grew up around it. The company's capital stock was increased to $2 million. By 1911 Ford had more than 4,000 employees, and a new plant in Highland Park, Michigan. Before the demise of the Model T in 1927, 15 million had been sold and Ford's sales had become worldwide.

Ford accomplished this remarkable production feat by his introduction, in 1913, of standardized, interchangeable car parts, and assembly-line techniques whereby moving conveyor belts transported the parts — on which each laborer quickly performed one simple task — from worker to worker. The manufacturing process thus became a constantly moving, integrated, perfectly timed operation. As Ford's precepts of mass production were applied in industries across the land, American industry expanded and the American standard of living rose.

At Ford plants, production soared, along with worker discontent over monotony and increases in production quotas. Ford stabilized his labor force by instituting the highest wages in the industry and introducing the eight-hour day. In the process he doubled the company's profits from $30 million in 1914 to $60 million in 1916. He was meanwhile lowering automobile prices almost annually. His policies resulted in handsome surplus balances, which he largely plowed back into plant expansion. He also found time in 1918 to campaign, unsuccessfully, for the US Senate on the Democratic ticket.

Ford held the company presidency until 1919, the year a new plant was constructed at River Rouge. He then handed his title to his son Edsel. Meanwhile, however, the senior Ford had bought enough stock to control the company and operate it in his own autocratic, suspicious, sometimes reactionary way for many more years.

While competitors were introducing yearly style changes, color variety, and mechanical improvements, Ford defied his management, clinging to the outmoded features of the Model T, available in black only. But by 1927 even he realized it had seen its day. The Model A was introduced in 1928, the V-8 in 1932, and a yearly changeover thereafter — too late, however, to prevent Ford's loss of first place in the industry to General Motors.

Ford's relations with his labor force did not go smoothly. Despite his pioneering wage policies, profit-sharing plan, and paternalistic concern, workers complained about depression-wrought unemployment, wage cuts, and layoffs; about the speed and tension under which they worked; about the company's sociological department, which investigated their private lives; and about its repressive campaign against union organizing. Ford's running battle with labor erupted in violence in 1932 and 1937. It culminated in hearings before the National Labor Relations Board, which found the company guilty of repeated labor violations, and in a bitter strike in 1941. After an NLRB-ordered election in which 70 percent of the workers designated the United Automobile Workers (CIO) as their bargaining agent, Ford finally agreed to a union contract. He was the last major automobile manufacturer to do so.

When the Japanese attack on Pearl Harbor brought the United States into World War II in December 1941, Ford put aside his pacifist convictions to construct his huge Willow Run plant and manufacture airplanes, tanks, armored cars, jeeps, and robot bomb engines for the government. The company was employing well over 100,000 persons, and war production was at its height when Ford was shaken by an event from which he never fully recovered — the death of Edsel, his only child, in 1943. Ford, at 80, resumed the presidency until his grandson Henry Ford II (later chairman of the board) succeeded him in 1945, inaugurating what has been described as the company's period of miraculous rebirth.

Ford himself died of a cerebral hemorrhage on April 7, 1947. He left an empire estimated in the billions. Like his son, he had bequeathed the largest share of his company holdings to the nonprofit Ford Foundation, which the two had established in 1936 for the "advancing [of] human welfare." The foundation, which theretofore had operated modestly, set about its purpose on a vastly enlarged scale in late 1950. The largest private philanthropic institution, in terms not only of its assets but of aggregate grants, the foundation in 1976 donated over $172 million to educational and charitable institutions throughout the world. A handsome 15-story structure of striking design houses the foundation's New York City headquarters. Located at 320 East 43rd Street, the building, erected in 1967, has work space overlooking an interior glass-roofed garden.

Ford also left behind him Detroit's Henry Ford Hospital; several trade and apprentice schools; and his restoration of Longfellow's beloved Wayside Inn, a handsome, barn-red building at South Sudbury, Massachusetts.

JULY 31

All American Indian Days
Sheridan, Wyoming

This is a movable event. See note on page xxvi.

Like other settlements on the western Plains, the ranching and tourist center of Sheridan, Wyoming — where All American Indian Days now takes place annually — did not come into being until after the conflicts between the American Indians and the US Army that blazed across the land in the decade after the Civil War. Founded in 1882, the town was named for General Philip Sheridan, who forced the resisting Plains tribes to settle on reservations and declared intemperately that "the only good Indian is a dead Indian." Nine years later, Sheridan wrote of the Indians with more reflection: "We took away their country and their means of support, broke up their mode of living . . . introduced disease and decay among them, and it was for this and against this that they made war. Could anyone expect less?"

Despite its location in a region where old resentments had lingered, the town of Sheridan also underwent a change — after Lucy Yellowmule, a Crow, was named queen of Sheridan's famous Sheridan-Wyo Rodeo, in 1951. This event in a region characterized by inequalities between Indians and non-Indians brought to the surface of civic consciousness the need for an effort toward mutual understanding and respect. The result was the establishment of All American Indian Days, an interracial human relations project suggested by Sheridan's F. H. Sinclair and soon supported by Sheridan merchants, individual local citizens, and other interested persons throughout the United States.

All American Indian Days, which includes the selection of Miss Indian America, has been held annually since 1953. Attracting some 2,000 Indians from 30 tribes, events are held at the Sheridan County Fairgrounds, with Wyoming's Big Horn Mountains as backdrop. They include a parade, Indian dances, athletic contests, and games, various ceremonials and other tribal presentations, an award to the Outstanding Indian of the Year, and an intercultural service on Sunday in which people of all faiths join in worship.

Although tribes from all parts of the country take part, the nearby Crows, Cheyennes, Sioux, and other Plains Indians usually appear in the greatest numbers. The next largest groups come from the West Coast, mainly from Washington and Oregon, and from the Southwest. Participants encamp in a village of tepees, which is open to visitors after each performance. Another interest point for visitors is a three-day exhibit and sale of traditional and modern Indian arts, crafts, and paintings.

Officially, the three-day celebration is held on the first weekend in August or the last weekend in July. Following the prefestival Miss Indian America Talent Show on Thursday evening, activities begin with an open-pit barbecue customarily held in the tepee arena at 6:00 on Friday evening. This is followed by the big opening night Grand Entry, generally including dancers, a military color guard, bands, and the Miss Indian America entrants. Sports and dance contests immediately follow. The sports and games, which are continued on Saturday and Sunday evenings, include archery, lance throwing, horse races, and the famous Crow version of football, played by teams of handkerchief-linked or hand-holding couples, with only the women allowed to kick the ball. A tepee-construction race is an annual feature, and in recent years there has also been a frybread-making contest, with competitors building their campfires, mixing dough, and frying the bread in front of the grandstand. The dance contests in almost a dozen categories include men's slow and fast war dances, which have their finals on Sunday evening, as do the dances in other categories.

Another major feature — often scheduled for Friday and Saturday evenings — is the presentation by various tribes of some unique ceremony, dance, or pageant. A Saturday morning highlight is the downtown parade, in which prizes are awarded for the best float, best horseback entry, oldest Indian man and woman, and best costumes in several categories.

The celebration of All American Indian Days reaches its conclusion on Sunday night with the selection of Miss Indian America. The winner must be poised, intelligent, and attractive; accomplished in public speaking (she travels thousands of miles and addresses hundreds of groups during her one-year reign); well versed in the culture and traditions of her own and many other tribes; and dedicated to the betterment of Indians.

Although admission is charged for the various afternoon and evening performances, All American Indian Days is a nonprofit undertaking. The effort to improve relations between Indians and non-Indians has brought national recognition and a number of awards to Sheridan. From the beginning, the All American Indian Days observances have been produced through the joint efforts of a host-board of trustees — a non-Indian group that finances and coordinates the undertaking — and an all-Indian executive committee that plans the programs and provides the suggestions on which other Indian-related efforts are based. These include the long-range projects of a charitable corporation known as the North American Indian Foundation. Chartered in 1960 as an outgrowth of All American Indian Days, it receives and administers funds to support programs in areas of Indian need, including education; contributes to the preservation of Indian arts, crafts, and culture; and finances the Miss Indian America contest and the travels of the winner.

Days of '76
Deadwood, South Dakota

This is a movable event. See note on page xxvi.

The history of Deadwood, South Dakota, which is recalled annually in a three-day celebration known as the Days of '76, reads like all Westerns ever filmed, rolled into one. Generally held the first full weekend in August, the observance includes a parade, rodeo, band concerts, and the reenactment of a famous trial. The proceedings are timed to coincide, more or less, with anniversaries of the deaths of two of Deadwood's best-known residents — "Calamity Jane" Canary on August 1 (1903) and "Wild Bill" Hickok on August 2 (1876).

Deadwood, whose name epitomizes the Wild West to many, is nestled in the Black Hills along the once-notorious Deadwood Gulch (which is now its main street). It is 60 miles north of the town of Custer, where an expedition led by the ill-fated Lieutenant Colonel George A. Custer first discovered gold in 1874, setting off a stampede. Although 15,000 prospectors rushed in — deterred only briefly by the fact that the whole area still belonged to the Sioux Indians — they deserted Custer overnight after new and larger deposits of gold were found in Deadwood Gulch late the next year.

During the spring and summer of 1876, Deadwood experienced what some say was the wildest of the great gold rushes. Thousands came with picks, pans, and other paraphernalia of prospecting. Along with the miners came trouble-makers, thieves, desperados, dance-hall girls, Chinese laborers, and assorted frontier characters, followed shortly by ox-drawn freight wagons, grocers, and merchants. In less than a year, more than 200 stores, 70 saloons and gambling houses, and 30 hotels had sprung up.

Violence sprang up, too, usually originating in arguments over gold or women. Bars and dance halls stayed open night and day, and card games went on indefinitely. In rooming houses, beds were so much in demand that men slept in shifts. Claim-jumping, horse thievery, and stage-coach holdups became the order of the day. According to one source, there was a killing almost daily during the lawless first year. And all the while the Sioux, who retained legal rights to the area until 1877, showed their bitter resentment over the encroachment upon their lands by running off livestock, burning fields and cabins, and shooting arrows into intruders.

One of those who came to Deadwood was the legendary "Calamity Jane" Canary, a team-driving, bull-whacking, buckskin-clad woman who took her whiskey straight, was a superb markswoman, swore profusely, rode like an Indian, was tougher than most men, yet cared with infinite tenderness for the sick and needy. Born Dalton or Canary, she was also known as Burke (or Burk), after one of her several husbands.

Also on hand was the cigar-smoking "Poker Alice" Ivers Tubbs, whose gambling house in Deadwood did a rousing business. English-born and the graduate of a select college, she was a consummate gambler, said to have estimated her lifetime winnings at a quarter of a million dollars.

"Deadwood Dick," the daredevil masked rider of dime-novel fame, had his origin in several colorful personalities who bore the name at different times. Another famous resident was "Yellow Doll," a beautiful Chinese woman who lived in a luxurious setting surrounded by mystery until she was brutally murdered with a hatchet. The brilliant young minister Henry Weston ("Preacher") Smith was also short-lived. On August 20, 1876, he set out for a neighboring community, leaving a note tacked to his door: "Gone to Crook City and if God is willing, will be back at 2 P.M." He was found dead a few hours later, ambushed by Indians.

Most famous resident of all was the natty and much-admired stage driver, soldier, scout, and US marshal James Butler ("Wild Bill") Hickok, a renowned quick draw who had diminished lawlessness along the Kansas frontier and won fame as a gunfighter while driving over the Santa Fe and Oregon trails. Preceded by his reputation, he rode into Deadwood in June of 1876, and all who hated violence breathed

easier — until August 2, when Hickok, sitting in on a poker game in Saloon No. 10, was shot from behind by Jack McCall. McCall, incredibly, was acquitted in a trial held the next day but was retried later in the territorial capital and hanged.

Hickok, Calamity Jane, and the rest all are portrayed in the three-mile-long historical parade that initiates the Days of '76 celebration annually on Friday morning of the first weekend in August and is repeated on Saturday morning. After the first section, with the parade marshal, color guard, and local and visiting dignitaries, the whole procession of 1,500 persons and 500 horses, interspersed with floats and bands, is in chronological order. First come the earliest explorers and settlers, then the varied characters of gold rush days, followed by a collection of antique vehicles. Later entries depict the town's first school, first jail, and so on; the arrival of the cowboys associated with the cattle industry, which was important in the area's growth; and the coming of industry and early tourists. Finally there are show officials, saddle club members, and cowboys. (In recent years there has been no Indian participation.)

The cowboys are seen again in the annual Days of '76 championship rodeo, held Friday, Saturday, and Sunday afternoons at the Deadwood Rodeo Grounds, with events like bronco riding, steer wrestling, bull riding and calf roping supplemented by the reenactment of episodes from Deadwood's early days. The rodeo also includes chariot races; cowgirls' barrel racing; specialty acts, drills, and races; and two special events on Sunday — the 4-H calf catching contest and a competition to determine the champion bareback bronco and the top saddle bronco in the Sioux Nation.

The center of town is abuzz evenings with carnival attractions, Sioux dancing, band concerts, and the reenactment of the capture and trial of Jack McCall (nightly throughout the summer at Old Towne Hall). Visitors can also go to see the now defunct Broken Boot Gold Mine; Adams Memorial Museum; Mt. Moriah Cemetery, where Wild Bill Hickok, Calamity Jane, and Preacher Smith are buried; and to Homestake, the Western Hemisphere's largest producing gold mine, in the nearby town of Lead.

Feast of St. Ignatius Loyola

July 31 is celebrated by the Roman Catholic church as the Feast of St. Ignatius Loyola, founder of the Society of Jesus, the Roman Catholic religious order whose members are known as Jesuits. For more than 400 years members of the Jesuit order have distinguished themselves in many fields, most notably in education and missionary work. Jesuits were among the early missionaries in the New World and contributed greatly to the exploration of the North American continent.

The youngest son of a Spanish noble family of ancient origin, Ignatius was born in the Casa Torre of Loyola, Azpeitia, in the province of Guipúzcoa in the Basque region of Spain. He was the son of Beltrán Yañez de Oñez y Loyola and Marina Saenz de Licona y Balde. The probable year of his birth was 1491. Baptized Íñigo in the parish church of San Sebastián, Loyola later took the name of St. Ignatius of Antioch, a first century bishop and martyr whose life he admired.

In his teens, Ignatius of Loyola was appointed page to an important political administrator who was, for a time, treasurer general for King Ferdinand of Spain. In this capacity, Ignatius spent most of his early years in and around the royal court, becoming a very worldly young man with little formal education, whose only interests seemed to be in gaming, affairs of chivalry, and military daring. He manifested no inclination towards religion.

In his mid-twenties, Ignatius was attached to the household of Antonio Manrique de Lara, duke of Nájera and viceroy of Navarre, in whose service he performed successful military assignments. Naturally drawn to the military life, the future saint might well have become a lifetime army officer. However, on May 20, 1521, while defending the castle of Pamplona against a French siege, he was struck by a cannonball, which fractured his leg, and was forced to abandon his military career. Taken to Loyola for his long convalescence, the immobilized Ignatius, out of sheer boredom, asked for books to pass the time. The only reading matter available happened to be religious books — a life of Christ and *The Golden Legend*, a collection of biographies of saints, written in the 13th century.

Although they were, perhaps, odd reading for a worldy military man, the books transformed his life, convincing him that the heroism practiced by the saints was greater than the military heroism to which he had aspired. Ignatius resolved to become a knight in the service of Christ, with the hope of working in the Holy Land converting Moslems. As soon as he was physically able, he made a pilgrimage to the famous Benedictine monastery in Montserrat, amid the mountains northwest of Barcelona, where he made a knight's vigil on March 24–25, 1522, the eve of the Annunciation.

From there he went to nearby Manresa, where he spent 10 or 11 months ministering to the sick at the Hospital of St. Lucy and retiring to the caves in the surrounding area for long hours of prayer and penance, in preparation for the spir-itual life. In Manresa he began writing his *Spiritual Exercises*, a systematic series of meditations that is considered one of the classics of Christian spirituality. For the next 20 or more years, he continued to revise and enlarge the work, to which Pope Paul III gave his approval on July 31, 1548.

In February 1523 Ignatius left Manresa and joined a group of pilgrims going to the Holy Land by way of Rome. After many delays, he landed at Jaffa on September 1, but the hostility of the Turks prevented him from staying. Determined to get the education he would need in his new life, Ignatius returned to Spain.

He began an 11-year program of learning at the age of 33 by going to a school in Barcelona, where he attended classes with elementary-school children. He continued his studies at the Spanish universities in Alcalá and Salamanca, and then went to France to obtain his master of arts degree from the University of Paris in 1534.

That same year on August 15 Ignatius and six companions gathered at the Church of St. Denis in the Montmartre section of Paris and vowed to live in poverty and chastity. The companions, who had been drawn to Ignatius by his powerful personality and spirituality, were Peter Faber; Francis Xavier (a fellow Basque, also studying in Paris, who went on to become the great missionary), Diego Lainez; Alfonso Salmerón; Nicolás de Bobadilla; and Simón Rodriguez. A year later, on August 15, 1535, when the group renewed its vows there were three new members.

From the beginning, St. Ignatius called his little band "the Company of Jesus" (in Spanish, *Compañía de Jesús*, probably after the military companies Ignatius had so admired). The well-known initials S.J. stem from the Latin *Societas Jesu*. The pious fraternity hoped to go to the Holy Land to work among the Moslems, but when the Turkish wars made this impossible, they journeyed to Rome to offer their obedience and their services to Pope Paul III in 1538.

Ignatius, then 47 years old, and several others in the group were ordained into the priesthood. Soon it was decided that the group should become a definite religious order and after long deliberations with his brothers in religion, Ignatius drafted the outline of the new order's rule. On September 3, 1539, in Tivoli, Pope Paul III orally approved the Society of Jesus; later, he solemnly confirmed it in the papal bull *Regimini militantis ecclesiae*, dated September 27, 1540.

On April 7, 1541, Ignatius, against his will, was elected the first general of the Society of Jesus. While his companions were sent away as missionaries, he stayed in Rome consolidating and structuring the society, writing the constitution for the order, directing the admission of new members and carrying on a staggering correspondence — more than 6,000 of his letters have been published.

At first the constitution limited the Society of Jesus to 60 members. However, this limitation was revoked within two years by a papal bull dated March 15, 1543. By the time Ignatius died in Rome on July 31, 1556, there were about 1,000 members in 100 houses in 12 provinces, and Jesuit missionaries were working in many lands, including the East Indies, Ethiopia, and South America.

By 1565 the number of Jesuits had grown to 3,500. In this time of the Reformation and the Counter-Reformation, Jesuits rose to the defense of the Catholic Church in great numbers and strength. Throughout its history, secular observers have pointed out, the Society of Jesus has produced a seemingly endless supply of great schoolmasters, theologians, missionaries, diplomats, administrators, and tacticians, particularly in times of challenge.

However, things did not always go smoothly for the Jesuits. Ignatius himself was several times questioned by officials during the Spanish Inquisition who, try as they might, could find no fault with his simple philosophy. His aim was merely to dedicate his life and his work "to the greater glory of God," which is to this day the motto of the Jesuits. (The phrase is often abbreviated to AMDG from the Latin *ad majorem Dei gloriam*.) In keeping with this aim, it was the will of Ignatius that members of his order be competent and flexible enough to go wherever and do whatever was necessary for the good of the church and the glory of God.

Perhaps for this reason, Jesuits have frequently been found in the midst of controversy — not, they point out, because they have created the controversy but because they try to find viable solutions to problems that others might try to ignore.

Whatever the reason, no religious order has been criticized more vehemently or more frequently than the Jesuits, who have been expelled from more countries, more often (five times from Spain) than any other religious order. Jesuits were suppressed in various parts of the world for most of the latter half of the 18th century. Under great political pressure, Pope Clement XIV finally dissolved the Society of Jesus in 1773. The order literally ceased to exist in the Catholic world, although most of its members continued their duties wherever possible as individuals.

Two monarchs, Catherine the Great of Russia and Frederick the Great of Prussia, refused to recognize or publish the papal brief of suppression, and Jesuits were harbored in both countries.

The Jesuit order was reestablished in 1814 by Pope Pius VII. It soon became, and still is, the largest single religious order in the world, with about 30,000 members including priests, scholastics (men studying for the priesthood), and brothers. The growth of the Jesuits in the United States — from two dozen in 1815 to 1,344 by 1900 — was remarkable. The United States now has more members of the order than any other country in the world, with Spain ranking second. About 700 American Jesuits are assigned to missionary work in foreign countries and among North American Indians and Eskimos. In the United States the order is especially influential in education, with Jesuits training hundreds of thousands of students in high schools, colleges, and universities. American Jesuits also publish a wide variety of periodicals — including *America, The Catholic Mind, Thought,* and *Theology Digest* — and run 30 or 40 retreat houses (most of them called Manresa after the place of Ignatius's retreat in Spain). There, each year, thousands of American men of all ages and walks of life make religious retreats.

St. Ignatius Loyola, the founder of this disciplined and energetic religious order, was beatified by Pope Paul V on July 27, 1609, and was canonized by Paul's successor, Gregory XV, on March 12, 1622. His feast was added to the church calendar in 1623. Three centuries later, in 1922, Pope Pius XI declared St. Ignatius the patron of spiritual exercises and retreats.

The Feast of St. Ignatius is celebrated with special warmth and devotion in Jesuit houses throughout the world. Many Jesuits take their vows or are ordained on that day.

Since St. Ignatius was born in the Basque region of Spain, Basques everywhere have a proprietary interest in him and have taken him as their special patron. In Boise, Idaho, what is said to be the largest Basque colony in North America holds its annual St. Ignatius Loyola picnic on the Sunday nearest to the saint's day. Non-Basque writers sometimes refer to the event as the Basque Festival. There are approximately 4,000 Basques in and around Boise, many of them descended from Basques who first settled in America in 1865. The picnic, which is held at the Municipal Park, is not open to the public.

August

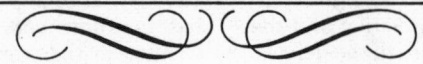

August is the eighth month of the Gregorian, or New Style, calendar now in use and has 31 days. In the ancient Roman calendar, which began in March, August — the sixth month — was called *Sextilis,* a name derived from the Latin word for six, *sex.* Even after the old calendar had been revised, January and February having been added to the start of the year, August, although the eighth month, continued to retain its former name. In 44 B.C. Mark Antony, as consul, had had the name of the month preceding August changed by decree of the Roman senate from *Quintilis* to *Julius* in honor of Gaius Julius Caesar, then head of the Roman state. In the same fashion, *Sextilis* was renamed *Augustus* in 27 B.C. as a tribute to the first Roman emperor, Augustus.

Augustus, who was born in 63 B.C. and named Gaius Octavius (Octavian), was the grandson of Julius Caesar's sister. When Octavian was a youth, he showed such promise that Julius Caesar not only took personal interest in his education, but also designated him as his heir without the boy's knowledge. The young Octavian was pursuing his studies in Illyria when he learned of Julius Caesar's assassination in 44 B.C. He immediately set out for Italy, where he was formally adopted into the Julian clan and received the name Gaius Julius Caesar Octavianus.

Determined to make the most of his inheritance, Octavian was soon accepted as one of the emerging leaders during a very confused political situation. Overcoming considerable opposition, he gained a foothold in the capital city of Rome, secured the consulship in 43 B.C., and then skillfully allied himself with his chief contender for power, Mark Antony. Together with Lepidus, the two leaders formed a triumvirate; then Octavian and Antony fulfilled a vow of vengeance against Julius Caesar's assassins, de-

feating the forces of the conspirators, Marcus Junius Brutus and Gaius Cassius Longinus, at Philippi in Macedonia in 42 B.C. Eleven years later Octavian triumphed over Mark Antony in a naval battle at Actium on the coast of Epirus. He thus cleared the road of all important rivals and without further opposition carried through a final seizure of power. In 29 B.C. Julius Caesar's adopted son was made emperor.

Octavian preferred to regard himself — in public at any rate — as the first citizen *(princeps)* of the Roman state; but he gradually assumed the honors and powers commensurate with his unchallenged political position. On January 17, 27 B.C., for example, the Roman senate granted him the title of honor *Augustus,* meaning "venerable," or "reverend." This designation was adopted by all succeeding Roman emperors.

Since July had been named for Julius Caesar, Augustus thought that a month should bear his own name. The Romans wished to rename September — Augustus' birth month — *Augustus,* but the emperor chose the month following July and decreed that it should be called after himself. The early fifth century Roman writer Macrobius explained Augustus' reasons for this choice:

[After July] Augustus comes next, which formerly was called Sextilis, until it was devoted to the honor of Augustus by a senatus consultum, whose text I have given below: "Since the imperator Caesar Augustus in the month Sextilis entered upon his first consulship [in 43 B.C.] and led three triumphs into the city [the triple triumph for Illyria, Actium, and Egypt on August 13, 14, and 15 in 29 B.C.] and the legions were led down from the Janiculum [one of the seven hills of Rome] and followed his auspices and trust, and since in this month also Egypt was brought under the sway of the Roman people [in 30 B.C.] and since in this month an end was made of the civil wars, and since for these reasons this month is and has been most fortunate for this empire, it pleases the senate that this month be called Augustus.

In addition to conferring his name on *Sextilis,* Augustus supposedly took one day (one version says from February, another from September) to add to his month, making 31 days; he supposedly did not wish to have August number fewer days than Julius Caesar's month of July.

In the third week of August, after the harvesting and planting, the Romans appropriately celebrated the *Consualia,* the festival of Consus, the Roman god of the harvest. Consus, who was probably also the deity of the storage bin and guardian of secrets, was the cult partner of the goddess of sowing and reaping known as Consiva, or Ops. According to yet another hypothesis about his undoubtedly varied functions, Consus was the god of good counsel. He is said to have advised the founder of Rome, Romulus, to abduct the Sabine women (the Sabines were a people who lived in the Sabine Hills of central Italy northeast of Rome), when they came to Rome to participate in the first *Consualia.* Romulus thus gained wives for his womanless supporters. The sanctuary to Consus on the Aventine Hill in Rome was dedicated in 272 B.C. His festival was marked not only by sacrifices there, but also by races in the Circus Maximus, where as a special attraction on this occasion the competing chariots were pulled by mules instead of horses.

Another noteworthy Roman festival, the *Vulcanalia,* took place on August 23 in honor of Vulcan, the god of fire and flame. In an effort for more effective fire prevention, Emperor Augustus had the city of Rome divided into small districts set up to facilitate fire fighting. He was therefore fittingly honored as Volcanus Quietus Augustus (since Vulcan was called upon to prevent fires).

The Anglo-Saxon name for August was *Weodmonath,* or the month when the weeds flourished. The lucky birthstone often associated with August is the carnelian.

AUGUST 1

John Alden Day

This is a movable event. See note on page xxvi.

Plymouth was a small, poor, and relatively short-lived colony. Yet its inhabitants earned a place of special prominence in American history, and few of the Pilgrims are better known than John Alden, the hero of Henry Wadsworth Longfellow's poem *The Courtship of Miles Standish.* Longfellow's narrative poem is without historical

foundation: there is no evidence that Alden ever competed with Standish, who was perhaps 15 years his senior, for the affection of Priscilla Mullens. But John Alden indeed married Priscilla Mullens shortly after the *Mayflower's* arrival on the Massachusetts coast in 1620, and Longfellow was one of their descendants.

Alden was born in eastern England about 1599. Aside from this vague information, nothing is known about his early life. The first definite statement regarding Alden is contained in the reliable history *Of Plimoth Plantation,* written by William Bradford. According to Bradford, the Pilgrims hired the 21-year-old Alden as a cooper or barrelmaker shortly before their departure from Southampton, England. The young man's presence on the *Mayflower* satisfied an act of Parliament that required every seagoing vessel carrying beer to employ a cooper. On the voyage across the Atlantic, Alden kept the beer casks in good repair. And he decided to remain with the settlers after their arrival in the New World.

Before disembarking on the Massachusetts coast, Alden and the 40 other adult male passengers signed the Mayflower Compact, a preliminary plan of government. The youngest to agree to this famed document, he devoted his entire life to the service of the "civil body politic" that the compact advocated. In 1627 Alden was one of the eight "undertakers" who assumed the responsibility for the colony's £2,400 debt. In addition he held many of the most important positions in the colony: he was a member of the colony's council of war in all times of impending crisis; treasurer of the colony from 1656 to 1658; governor's assistant for 44 years; and deputy governor between 1664 and 1665 and again in 1677.

Alden settled first in Plymouth. There he probably built a house similar to those erected by the other Pilgrims: a small, one-room, clapboard structure with a thatched roof. (Contrary to popular belief the first settlers of eastern Massachusetts never constructed log cabins. This type of building did not appear in North America until the Swedes settled in Delaware in the 1640s.) Alden remained in Plymouth until 1627. Then he and a number of colonists, including Myles (or Miles) Standish, determined to set up another town at Duxbury, about 10 miles from the original settlement. The Plymouth General Court approved this plan and in that same year granted Alden 169 acres upon which to establish his farm.

John and Priscilla Alden lived for many years in Duxbury, where most of their 11 children were born. Alden also received a substantial land grant in nearby Bridgewater. On the latter plot, their son Joseph built his home. When their home was destroyed by fire, they temporarily took up their residence with him. In 1653 another son, Jonathan, erected a dwelling, which still stands on the original Duxbury grant. His parents spent their later years in this house, and John Alden, the last surviving signer of the Mayflower Compact, died there in 1687 at the age of 89.

Descendants of John and Priscilla Alden occupied the Duxbury residence for almost three centuries. In 1907, however, the Alden Kindred of America, a society composed of about 800 persons who trace their ancestry back to the Aldens, purchased the home from its last occupant, John T. Alden. The house, located at 101 Alden Street, has been opened to the public periodically since the 1920s; and since 1955 visitors have been welcomed there daily throughout the summer. The dwelling has remained essentially as it was in 1653, and the original gunstock beams and outside clapboards have been preserved. Its furnishings are typical of those used in eastern Massachusetts in the mid-17th century.

Approximately a quarter of a mile from the site of the house, the foundation of the original house built by John Alden has been found. The Alden Kindred have fenced this area and erected a tablet on the site. In addition to maintaining their forebears' place of residence, the Alden Kindred also hold their annual meeting on John Alden Day — the first Saturday in August — at his home in Duxbury. At this time the society considers reports on past and future projects, holds a buffet lunch, and hears a speaker discuss appropriate colonial topics.

Though the exact location of their graves is unknown, both John and Priscilla Alden are buried in Duxbury's Old Burying Ground, as is Myles Standish. The Old Burying Ground is at the junction of Chestnut Street and Pilgrim By-Way. The 130-foot-high Myles Standish Monument, with an observation tower at the top, is on Monument Road in South Duxbury and is part of the Standish Monument State Reservation.

Colorado Admitted to the Union

On August 1, 1876, President Ulysses S. Grant signed the proclamation admitting the Colorado Territory to the Union as the 38th state. Residents of the state have celebrated the event each year since 1908 with their observance of Colorado Day. This is the only annual legal holiday in Colorado other than those of national import. Until 1967 the commemoration took place on August 1, the anniversary of Colorado statehood. On March 3 of that year, however, the governor of Colorado signed a bill making the first Monday in August as Colorado Day.

Colorado Day is observed as a holiday by most state, county, and municipal employees. In other areas of commerce and industry, business is generally conducted as usual, with banks, stores, securities markets, and public libraries functioning normally.

The best-known Colorado Day events take place in Central City, the historic mining town. Central City is considered by many to be the "birthplace" of Colorado: it was near there that John Gregory discovered the celebrated gold deposits on May 6, 1859, in the steep gulch now bearing his name. The area became known as "the richest square mile on earth" until the title was forfeited to another of the state's mining regions, Cripple Creek, 30 years later. The more than $75 million worth of minerals and metals from Central City was of vital importance in keeping the smaller plains settlements alive.

Colorado Day activities, sponsored by the Central City Opera House Association, a private organization, vary from year to year. They generally center about the annual Colorado Day banquet, which has taken place for decades in the famed Teller House, erected in 1872 as the ultimate in sumptuous miners' hotels. Two delegates from each county of the state and dignitaries from Denver, including the governor, are invited to attend. A distinguished speaker usually talks about some aspect of Colorado history.

Colorado Day events have included a statewide historical essay contest for high school students, tours of historic town residences, pageants (with prominent Coloradans participating in re-enactments of events that occurred 100 years before), and special receptions. In 1970, for example, following the Colorado Day banquet at which Avery Brundage, president of the International Olympic Committee, was guest speaker, a reception was held for the delegates and special guests in the Theater Museum, part of the Opera House Association complex, in the Mines Hotel. The 1970 Colorado Day events closed with the guests attending the play *Forty Carats* in the frescoed and crystal-chandeliered 1878 opera house, restored to its original appearance.

Four centuries before the discovery of America by Europeans, sedentary, agricultural cliff dwellers constructed their multistoried "apartment houses" in the canyons of the southernmost region of what is now Colorado. The first Europeans to enter the area were the Spaniards, who traveled from Mexico to Christianize the Indians or seek riches. In the 1540s Francisco Vásquez de Coronado probably touched upon Colorado territory during his quest for the fabled Seven

Cities of Cibola, where the streets were supposedly paved with gold. Throughout the 17th century, small expeditions of Spaniards continued to explore the area, and, as early as 1700, French voyageurs reached the Rocky Mountains. The profitable fur trade also enticed the first American, James Purcell, into the Colorado region in 1803.

The largely uncharted wilderness still remained practically virgin territory for Europeans when the United States gained the vast, vaguely defined region between the Mississippi River and the Rocky Mountains in the Louisiana Purchase of 1803. Several expeditionary parties — including Zebulon M. Pike's (1806), Stephen H. Long's (1820), and John C. Frémont's (1842–1843 and 1845) — were commissioned by the federal government; overland trails were mapped out; and several private forts were constructed; but settlement did not really start in earnest until the United States acquired the rest of Colorado by cession from Mexico in 1848, following the Mexican War. Texas yielded some additional territory in 1850.

Emigrants from Georgia and Kansas entered Colorado as gold seekers in 1858, and Green Russell, a Georgia prospector, found gold in the Little Dry Creek near the south edge of Denver that very year. When the first great gold discoveries were made in the winter and spring of 1859 in Idaho Springs, near Central City, and in Boulder and other places, prospectors flocked to Colorado. The free-for-all days of the mining camps had begun. Horace Greeley, the editor of the New York *Tribune,* was among the first easterners to arrive at the strike near Central City. He vividly described its 4,000 new residents — who slept, cooked and ate outdoors.

The political development during the next two decades was chaotic. In 1858 "Arapahoe county," in which all of Colorado was included, was considered part of Kansas Territory. A delegate was nevertheless dispatched to Washington to secure the admission of an independent territory called Jefferson. After a movement for statehood had been inaugurated, a constitution drawn up, submitted to the people, and rejected, the illegal territory of Jefferson was formed; its provisional legislature managed to operate until Congress passed the bill for territorial status on February 28, 1861. William Gilpin, the first governor, bestowed the name "Colorado" from the Spanish word for *red* or *colored*. The population by that time had risen to 20,798 white males, 4,484 white females, and 89 free blacks. In the 1860s other unsuccessful attempts were made to organize a state government. In 1867 President Andrew Johnson vetoed an enabling act prepared by the Republican party.

Finally an enabling act of Congress, passed March 3, 1875, provided for the admission of the territory as a state. It contained some unusual provisions. It directed as a condition of admission that the constitution should provide by ordinance, irrevocable without the consent of the United States and the people of the state, the following provisions: that perfect religious toleration sould be secured; that the people should disclaim all right to the unappropriated public lands; that the lands should remain at the sole disposition of the United States; that the land in Colorado belonging to citizens of the United States living outside the state should not be taxed at a higher rate than the lands belonging to residents; and that no tax should be levied on lands or property of the United States.

The constitution was framed at a convention held at Denver, from December 20, 1875, to March 14, 1876, and the people of the territory adopted it on July 1, 1876. Independence Day 1876 was one of the most festive days in the history of Colorado, as well as in that of the nation as a whole. While the country's centennial was being elaborately celebrated in Philadelphia, civic societies, various officials, and volunteer fire companies with their fire apparatus bedecked with flags and flowers staged a grand procession in Denver, the capital of the newest state. Thirty-seven girls in white represented the states of the Union. Colorado, as the 38th state, was represented by a girl born in the territory, dressed in a robe of bunting, and adorned with a golden crown and wand.

The final admission proclamation of President Grant was dated August 1, 1876. Colorado, known as the Centennial State since it was admitted 100 years after the Declaration of Independence, observed its own 100th birthday in 1976, along with the 200th birthday of the country. The double celebration was the occasion for enthusiastic commemoration, including extensive reparation of historical properties in Central City and neighboring Black Hawk.

Francis Scott Key's Birthday

Francis Scott Key wrote the words (not the music) of what is now known as "The Star-Spangled Banner," the national anthem of the United States. The occasion for the poem was the British bombardment of Baltimore's Fort McHenry during the War of 1812. Key, on board a British ship in the harbor, where he had been negotiating the release of a friend held prisoner by the British, was an accidental witness to the assault. His anxious watch to see if the fort would remain in American hands at the conclusion of the bombardment on the morning of September 14 and his joyous relief "that our flag was still there" prompted him to set down on paper his stirring lyric (see September 12, Maryland Defenders' Day).

Key was born on August 1, 1779, on his family's estate, Terra Rubra, in Frederick (now Carroll) County, Maryland. His parents were John Ross Key, a well-to-do farmer, and Ann Phoebe Charlton Key. His great-grandfather Philip Key had come to Maryland from England about 1720.

Francis Scott Key attended St. John's College in Annapolis, Maryland, from 1789 to 1796 and after graduation read law in the Annapolis office of Judge Jeremiah Townley Chase of the Maryland general court. One of his colleagues was Roger B. Taney, who, after their studies, accompanied Key on his return to Frederick to set up practice. Taney subsequently married Key's sister, Anne. He became the fifth chief justice of the US Supreme Court.

On January 19, 1802, Key married Mary Tayloe Lloyd, and they had six sons and five daughters. Key moved with his family to the Georgetown area in Washington, D.C. in 1805 and became a law partner of his uncle Philip Barton Key. Slender and erect, Key was an ardent, generous man with a quick logical mind that made him an effective speaker and helped in his extensive practice in the federal courts. A deeply religious person, he gave serious thought in 1814 to entering the clergy. He was a delegate to the general conventions of the Episcopal church from 1814 to 1826 and for many years served as lay reader of St. John's (now Old St. John's) Church in Georgetown.

Key moved from the Georgetown area to downtown Washington in about 1830 and was US attorney for the District of Columbia from 1833 to 1841. In October 1833 President Andrew Jackson sent him to Alabama to negotiate a settlement between the state and federal government over the Creek Indian lands.

On January 11, 1843, while visiting a daughter, Mrs. Charles Howard, in Baltimore, Key died of pleurisy at the age of 63. His body was initially placed in the Howard vault in St. Paul's Cemetery in Baltimore but was transferred in 1866 to Mount Olivet Cemetery in Frederick, Maryland.

Although the flag of the United States is customarily displayed only from sunrise to sunset, there are several exceptions to this rule. The Stars and Stripes flies 24 hours a day over the grave of Francis Scott Key in Mount Olivet Cemetery; at Fort McHenry National Monument and Historic Shrine in Baltimore; and at the Star-Spangled Banner Flag House and 1812 War Museum at 844 East Pratt at Albemarle Street in Baltimore. The flag that so moved Key was begun in this house by a seamstress, Mary Young Pickersgill. One of history's most famous flags, it had 15 stars and 15 stripes and was so huge (30 feet by 42 feet) that Pickersgill had to have the flag moved to a nearby malt house in order to place the stars correctly. The actual flag is on display at the Smithsonian Institution's Museum of History and Technology in Washington, D.C., but a replica of it flies night and day over the house where it was produced.

The Francis Scott Key Museum, in Frederick, occupies part of the Roger Brooke Taney Home, built in 1815, located at 123 South Bentz Street. It can be seen by appointment through the Frederick chamber of commerce. There are monuments to Key at Mount Olivet Cemetery in Frederick; at Fort McHenry and at Eutaw Place in Baltimore; and in Golden Gate Park in San Francisco. What is thought to be the original manuscript of "The Star-Spangled Banner" is on display at the Maryland Historical Society at 201 West Monument Street at Park Avenue in Baltimore.

Herman Melville's Birthday

Novelist Herman Melville was born on August 1, 1819, in New York City. His large family, including an unsympathetic mother and his seven brothers and sisters, moved to Albany, New York, in 1830, after suffering financial reverses. Two years later his father, a once-prosperous importer, died in bankruptcy.

Melville's scant formal education at the Albany Academy ended when he was 15. Then and in later life, however, he read voraciously, beginning with the works in his father's library. He found conventional employment — as a bank and store clerk, as a farmhand, and as a schoolteacher — uninteresting, and in 1837 he chose the sea as the best way to combine adventure with self-support.

His first voyage was in 1839 as a cabin boy on a trader going from New York to Liverpool. On January 3, 1841, he shipped out on the whaler *Acushnet*, which was to provide background for his masterpiece, *Moby Dick*. The vessel was bound for the South Seas from what was then the whaling capital of the world — New Bedford, Massachusetts. There visitors can now follow what is called the Moby Dick Trail to the Seaman's Bethel (the Whaleman's Chapel, still with its prowlike pulpit), other buildings mentioned in the book, and the world's most complete whaling museum, which includes a model whaler that can be boarded. Also of interest is the New Bedford public library's Melville Whaling Room, housing some 20,000 items.

After a year and a half of hardships under the *Acushnet's* tyrannical captain, Melville jumped ship with a companion at the Marquesas Islands, where he passed an idyllic month as the captive of friendly cannibals. He escaped on an Australian whaler to Tahiti, where he participated in a minor mutiny and was imprisoned briefly; wandered through the South Pacific to various other islands; and eventually found his way to Honolulu, where he enlisted as a seaman on the US Navy frigate *United States*. It took him to Boston, where he was discharged in the year from which, he later said, "I date my life" — 1844. It marked the beginning of the writing career on which he embarked almost immediately.

Typee, his first book (1846), based on his experiences in the Marquesas, was a rich brew of exuberance, exciting adventure, the primitive glories of island life and a storytelling knack that Melville — at some times secluded and withdrawn, at others a convivial and delightful raconteur — had exercised in long hours aboard ship. It was an immediate success. The sequel, *Omoo* (1847), a fictionalized version of his adventures in Tahiti, combined hilarity with serious social commentary. Both romances made use of a straightforward reporting style that blurred the line between fact and fancy.

After his marriage in August 1847 to Elizabeth Shaw, daughter of the chief justice of Massachusetts, Melville moved to New York City, where he wrote *Mardi* (1849), a political and moral allegory in which imaginary South Seas islands represented countries of Europe and America. With profound speculation and symbolic beauty, it told of a search for the ideal, but it was hard to understand and poorly received.

Under financial pressure, Melville hastily reverted to what the public had liked before, turning out *Redburn* (based on his voyage to Liverpool) in 1849, and *White-Jacket* (drawing on his experiences aboard the *United States*) in 1850. That year, after attending to publishing business in England and visiting France briefly, he decided to reduce living expenses by moving his family to Arrowhead, a farm, now privately owned, near Pittsfield, Massachusetts. Also in Pittsfield is the Herman Melville Memorial Room of the Berkshire Athenaeum public library. The room, containing first editions, portraits, documents, furniture, and personal items from Melville's home, and materials about him, was established in 1953 "to provide a convenient center for Melville studies," thereby perpetuating his memory "in a useful manner."

It was at Pittsfield that Melville began his friendship with novelist Nathaniel Hawthorne, then living in nearby Lenox, who shared Melville's interest in combining symbolism with romance, and whose probing into the nature of guilt was as out of tune as Melville's own thought with the buoyant optimism then being expressed by Emerson, Thoreau, and other Transcendentalists.

The two men spent long hours together, and Melville, encouraged by Hawthorne's example, embarked on the serious book he was determined to write: *Moby Dick, or, The Whale* (1851), one of the world's great epics, a tale of whales and whaling, God, man and nature. Back of it lay Melville's love of ideal virtues and his deep disillusionment at the apparent heartlessness of nature, the savagery of men, and the seeming indifference of God, who could permit the noble and the unworthy to suffer equal cruelty at the hands of nature. Richly allegorical and with many levels of meaning, the novel told of the mutilated Captain Ahab's maniacal search for revenge against the great white whale that had severed his leg and seemed to him to represent "all evil . . . visibly personified, and made practically assailable." The book failed to achieve wide popularity for its deeper level or as a suspenseful, action-filled tale of adventure.

If preparation of his supreme work had drained Melville of energy, its reception left him disappointed, bitter, in debt to his publishers, and ill. Almost perversely, he sat down to produce *Pierre: or the Ambiguities* (1852), which suggested that, as a guide for man in his perplexity, "silence is the only Voice of our God." Though the book's psychological study of guilt foreshadowed modern novelists, at the time it merely served to further rebuff Melville's readers, who failed to sympathize with an idealistic hero whose good intentions led to incestuous love, murder, and suicide.

Deprived of his public, Melville turned out two largely ignored novels, *Israel Potter* (1855) and *The Confidence-Man* (1857), and collected half a dozen stories (including the powerful "Benito Cereno" and "The Encantadas") in *The Piazza Tales* (1856). He continued to be troubled by illness and financial difficulties.

Seeking solace in religion, Melville traveled to Europe and the Holy Land in 1856–1857. On his return he supplemented his meager income by lecturing. Finally, he sold his farm to a brother in 1863 and moved to New York City, where he was appointed a customs inspector in 1866. He held the post for 19 years, until a bequest placed him in comfortable circumstances. Except for his Civil War poems (*Battle-Pieces,* 1866), the long religious poem *Clarel* (1876), and some other poetry, these were silent years.

When he died, on September 28, 1891, he had lived so long in voluntary seclusion that the event was marked by only a few lines in the press. He left two notable travel diaries and a short novel that he had just completed: *Billy Budd, Foretopman.* Eloquent and subtly symbolic, this celebrated work — another tale of the sea — deals with what Melville saw as the tendency of the forces of evil to triumph over the qualities of innocence and beauty. But although the events described are as tragic as those in *Pierre,* the hero achieved a kind of triumph by remaining true to his better nature even in defeat. *Billy Budd,* which showed Melville again at the peak of his power, revealed the serenity that replaced his earlier bitterness.

Billy Budd was not published until 1924, following the 1919 centennial of Melville's birth and a sudden revival of interest in the South Seas. Melville's reputation continued to grow, and he is now recognized as one of America's greatest novelists.

AUGUST 2

The Pecos Bull
Jemez, New Mexico

One of the pueblo Indian events that reflect the Spanish heritage of the Southwest is the Pecos Bull, which takes place at Jemez Pueblo during the Feast of Porcingula on August 2 and the preceding day. The feast is in honor of the people of now-deserted Pecos, who abandoned that harassed and epidemic-torn pueblo in favor of Jemez in 1838. They took with them the image of their patron saint, Santa María de los Ángeles, whose original shrine was in Portiuncula in Italy and who eventually came to be known as Porcingula.

On the day of the feast, a mass is sung in honor of the saint by Jemez's Roman Catholic priest, who subsequently accompanies her image to the shrine that has been prepared for her in Jemez's middle plaza. Some of the other events that take place during the fiesta have little connection with the Catholic observance, however. The concluding corn dance, for instance, is an Indian prayer for rain and fertility. The people of Jemez perform the dance with some slight variations of their own, although it is similar in its main outlines to the corn dances given, usually also on saints' days, in other pueblos in New Mexico.

The Pecos "bull," which remains active through much of the two days, is a framework creature covered with black cloth, painted with white circles, and superimposed on his impersonator, a dancer in moccasins and ceremonial kirtle. Prancing and weaving, it is prodded with sticks and otherwise besieged by playful men and boys whose movements, together with their prey's responses, mimic a bullfight. In their

dress, words, and mannerisms, the sham matadors also satirize white men — not always gently — for the amusement of their audience.

The hilarity is interspersed with more serious observances. One is the appearance, on the first of the two days, of six Indian priests dressed in white shirts and trousers with red headbands and sashes. Emerging from a ceremonial kiva, they circle the plaza with great solemnity, chanting from time to time according to prescribed ritual before the war captain calls the dancers to the kiva in preparation for the morrow's corn dance. The final day is marked by the Roman Catholic mass and by a feast for the bull and bull-baiters, with the food transported to the table by women carrying baskets and bowls on their heads. The food bearers are clad in black, with bright kerchiefs, and their legs are wrapped in buckskins.

Some time after the mass, and after the feast, the dancing Turquoise People and Squash People emerge in alternating groups from their respective kivas to perform the figures of the concluding corn dance before the bower of the saint.

AUGUST 3

Columbus Sets Sail

Christopher Columbus and the approximately 90 sailors who set forth on August 3, 1492, in three tiny ships to sail the Atlantic rank among the world's great pioneers and adventurers. Lured by the rich East Indies trade, mariners had sought a water route to the Orient for many years before Columbus's voyage. With the encouragement of Prince Henry the Navigator, the Portuguese made significant advances in navigation during the first half of the 15th century and conducted extensive explorations along the western coast of Africa. In 1488 Bartholomeu Dias of Portugal rounded the Cape of Good Hope at the southern tip of Africa, but a mutiny prevented him from continuing on to the Orient. His compatriot Vasco da Gama was the first to sail to India via the African route in 1497.

While the Portuguese concentrated upon finding an eastern water passage to the Orient, Christopher Columbus, a Genoese sailor, made plans for a western voyage. Most educated persons in the 15th century believed the world was round, and Columbus reasoned that by sailing west along 28° north latitude he would eventually reach Japan. In theory he was correct, but Columbus underestimated the distance between Europe and Japan by 8,000 miles and, of course, never suspected the existence of the American continents.

Columbus did not easily find monetary backing for his undertaking. He was refused sponsorship by the Portuguese king, John II, the city of Genoa, and Henry VII of England before King Ferdinand and Queen Isabella of Spain agreed to underwrite his expedition in 1486. It was not until January of 1492, however, when the Spanish war against the Moors was ended with the fall of Granada, that the monarchs were able to finance Columbus's adventurous voyage. In April of that year, arrangements for the expedition were concluded, and under the terms of the agreement, Spain was to acquire "certain islands and mainland in the Western Ocean," and Columbus, named "admiral of all the ocean seas," was appointed governor general with control of trade of any territory he might discover. The Spanish monarchs provided Columbus with three small sailing ships — the flagship *Santa María;* the *Niña,* captained by Vincente Yáñez Pinzón; and the *Pinta,* under Martín Alonso Pinzón. On August 3, 1492, they set sail from Palos in southern Spain (see October 12, Columbus Day).

Nautilus Cruises Under North Pole

The first voyage beneath the North Pole was made by the USS *Nautilus,* an atomic-powered submarine, in August 1958. The *Nautilus* submerged off the northern coast of Alaska, near Point Barrow, on August 1. On August 3, at 11:15 P.M. the ship passed beneath the pole. It was the first time that a ship had reached the North Pole. The vessel resurfaced on August 5 in the Arctic Ocean between Greenland and Spitsbergen. For 96 hours the *Nautilus* had cruised under the polar ice cap, covering a distance of 1,830 miles. At times the ice above was 80 feet thick; the thinnest layer was ten feet thick. The submarine traveled at a depth of approximately 400 feet beneath the ice cap.

The *Nautilus* was the first naval vessel in the world to be propelled by atomic power. Launched at Groton, Connecticut, in 1954 and commissioned in January of the following year, the ship was capable of cruising underwater indefinitely at a speed of more than 20 knots. It was "refueled" (with a new nuclear reactor core) for the first time in March 1957, after cruising over 60,000 miles. In September 1957, on one of three secret trial runs in preparation for the major feat that lay ahead of it, the ship spent five and a half days cruising 1,383 miles under the Arctic ice. By the end of October it had logged a total of more than 100,000 miles, of which almost 70,000 had been traveled underwater.

A transpolar crossing was first attempted by the *Nautilus* in June 1958, but at that time the ice in an area north of the Bering Strait had not yet melted sufficiently to allow passage beneath it. The vessel returned to Pearl Harbor, Hawaii, the port from which it embarked on July 23 for its subsequent successful crossing under the North Pole. Code-named Operation Northwest Passage, the mission was shrouded in secrecy by the US Navy. The public knew nothing of the history-making voyage until August 8, when the success of the operation was dramatically disclosed by the White House.

During the *Nautilus's* cruises beneath the ice, various scientific tests and measurements were made. The salinity and temperature of the water were measured. Ocean depths, to 13,410 feet, were determined by more than 11,000 soundings. In addition, a number of underwater mountain ranges were discovered.

The demonstration of the feasibility of crossing from the Pacific Ocean to the Atlantic Ocean beneath the Arctic ice pack opened the possibility of a new and very much shorter route between the two oceans for such potential commercial vessels as nuclear submarine tankers and freighters. For example, the transpolar route between Great Britain and Japan would be approximately 7,500 miles, as compared with the conventional route by way of the Panama Canal, which totals about 13,800 miles.

Enthusiastic public acclaim, the greatest for any naval hero since World War II, was accorded the captain of the *Nautilus,* Commander William R. Anderson. The success of his pioneering mission enhanced the prestige of the United States at a time when it had been challenged by the Soviet Union's successful launching in October 1957 of the first artificial satellite, Sputnik I, into orbit around the earth. President Dwight D. Eisenhower awarded Anderson the Legion of Merit in a ceremony at the White House. In addition, the Presidential Unit Citation, an award never before given in peacetime, was conferred on the ship's officers and men; Anderson received numerous honors, as both he and his crew were hailed abroad as well as in the United States. He wrote a book entitled *Nautilus 90 North* about the polar voyage.

AUGUST 4

John Peter Zenger Acquitted

Freedom of the press, regarded throughout the world as a cornerstone of liberty, is a constitutional principle of recent origin. Some historians argue that the theory gained acceptance in the Western Hemisphere no earlier than the late 18th century. Until then most political thinkers retained the ancient suspicion that free expression would undermine the commonwealth.

In England, freedom of speech, the antecedent of freedom of the press, originated as a protection for legislators against the monarchy, rather than as a civil right. During the 17th century, English lawmakers twice overthrew Stuart kings to establish this principle. Having guaranteed their liberty of expression by the Glorious Revolution of 1688, the Commons and Lords showed no interest in extending this blessing to the citizenry.

The English boasted that they enjoyed freedom of expression, but construed the term very narrowly. Sir William Blackstone, the 18th century author of *Commentaries on the Laws of England,* stated that freedom of the press "consists in laying no previous restraints upon publications, and not in freedom from censure for criminal matter when published." Blackstone further argued that his position did not inhibit free thought, but simply prevented the dissemination of destructive sentiments.

The government's chief weapon in its war on criticism was the law of seditious libel. Inherently vague, the concept outlawed any comment, true or false, that might lower the popular opinion of the authorities or disturb the peace. Indeed, England's Star Chamber ruled in 1606 that an accurate statement against the government was a worse libel than a deceitful one, for the former created scandal whereas the latter merely breached the peace.

Eighteenth century political and intellectual developments slowly erased age-old theories of free expression and replaced them with a more libertarian attitude. In the American colonies, provincial leaders actively supported the movement insofar as it helped them curb the power of the governors appointed by the Crown to rule over them. As did so many of the colonial struggles for increased liberty, the controversy over freedom of the press produced a number of heroes, of whom John Peter Zenger, the immigrant printer of New York City, is the most famous.

In 1710, at the age of 13, John Peter Zenger immigrated to New York from the German Palatinate, a refugee from the War of the Spanish Succession. His mother later apprenticed him to William Bradford, the first printer in the province of New York. Zenger left Bradford's employ after the older man in 1725 established the *Gazette,* the colony's first newspaper and an organ subservient to the government.

Zenger's independent efforts at printing fared poorly, but his iconoclastic ways pleased the leaders of the party opposed to the government. In 1733 they offered him the financial support necessary to bring out an antiadministration newspaper. Zenger established the *Weekly Jour-*

nal and chose William Cosby, the new governor of New York, as the object of its scorn.

An avaricious man, William Cosby had arrived in New York like a bird of prey. He insisted that the assembly grant him a gift of money beyond his salary and appointed his son secretary of East and West Jersey. In an extraordinarily bold move, Cosby then demanded half of his salary for the time between his appointment in England and his arrival in New York. When Rip Van Dam, who as acting governor had legally earned the money, refused to bow to his wishes, Cosby brought the matter to law. Knowing that he would have no chance before a jury, the governor took the case before the Supreme Court of Judicature, sitting in its juryless exchequer function.

Cosby's attempt to enrich himself by manipulating the legal system so angered Lewis Morris, the chief justice, that he stepped down from the bench and announced that he would sit on no more exchequer cases. The governor removed Morris from his post and installed the more pliable James De Lancey. Morris counterattacked by running for the assembly seat from the town of Eastchester. A veteran of long years in New York and New Jersey politics, he easily defeated Cosby's candidate.

Undaunted and unwise, Cosby continued his assault upon New York's leaders by calling into question the validity of the patents giving them title to vast sections of the colony's acreage. The governor, who really wanted to obtain for his family certain choice locations in the Mohawk Valley, had struck a sensitive spot; the validity of most New York patents was open to question and to challenge them had long been considered a political low blow. The opposition responded by savagely satirizing the administration in Zenger's newspaper.

James Alexander, a noted lawyer and landholder, provided most of the copy that the *Weekly Journal* devoted to the governor and his cronies. Items described the recorder of New York City as a five-foot, five-inch spaniel and the sheriff as a four-foot monkey. Zenger's press worked overtime printing scurrilous ballads denouncing Cosby as a "knave" and rejoicing in the victory of his enemies in the annual elections for the common council.

Dominated by Cosby, the supreme court in the October term of 1734 ordered the hangman to burn Zenger's offensive songs. On November 2, 1734, the governor and council instructed the hangman also to burn four especially insulting issues of the *Weekly Journal,* but pressure from the city officials and the populace forced the executioner to disobey the command. Finally, the sheriff had his slave perform the task.

Governor Cosby's next tactic was to punish Zenger directly. On November 17, 1734, the council had the printer arrested and held incommunicado for three days. James Alexander and another noted lawyer, William Smith, secured a writ of *habeas corpus* and had Zenger brought before the court. Chief Justice De Lancey set the bail at £400, a prohibitively high figure, and cast the printer back into jail.

Zenger spent the next 10 months in confinement, yet every issue of the *Weekly Journal,* save one, made its scheduled appearance. The doughty printer carried on his business by communicating with his wife and servants through the door of his cell, and fulfilled his promise to "entertain" his readers "as formerly." His keepers did not find the witty German amusing.

Meeting in January 1735, the grand jury failed to indict Zenger for any crime. Richard Bradley, the attorney general of New York, then filed an "information," an unpopular means of avoiding the indictment procedure by having a government officer directly accuse the prisoner of a crime. Bradley charged that Zenger was guilty of seditious libel for declaring that the colony's liberties were in danger.

James Alexander and William Smith acted as Zenger's counsel at his arraignment before the supreme court in April 1735. They immediately questioned James De Lancey's right to sit as chief justice, inasmuch as he held his commission at Governor Cosby's pleasure and not on the less political basis of good behavior tenure. Enraged, De Lancey disbarred both Alexander and Smith for contempt and appointed John Chambers as Zenger's attorney. Chambers did a competent job in a delicate situation, and managed to secure for the prisoner a jury sympathetic to his cause.

Attorney General Bradley opened the trial by reading the "information," which included inflammatory statements from the *Weekly Journal.* Chambers, employing the defensive strategy traditional in libel cases, responded that Zenger had not committed a crime because he had not clearly identified the objects of his accusations. Such a beginning forecast a routine trial, but then, in a move worthy of fiction, a man stepped forward and announced that he spoke in behalf of the defendant. The distinguished addition to the *dramatis personae* was Andrew Hamilton, Philadelphia's leading lawyer.

Born in Scotland 59 years earlier, Andrew Hamilton had received his education at St. Andrew's and had been a bencher of Gray's Inn. Zenger's supporters had brought him to New York in secrecy, and his appearance at the trial awed the judges. Indeed, his presence changed the temper of the trial as he refused to conduct the defense along the lines that the prosecutor expected.

Hamilton began by admitting that Zenger printed the two allegedly seditious copies of the *Weekly Journal.* Bradley, referring to a number of old Star Chamber cases in which the court ruled that the truth of printed accusations was irrelevant, proposed that Zenger was obviously guilty of libel. Seeing his opportunity, Hamilton rhetorically asked whether the attorney general desired to resurrect the arbitrary Star Chamber, long dismantled in England, and establish it in New York. The defense attorney then stated that the truth or falsity of Zenger's words was of paramount importance.

Chief Justice De Lancey recognized that the Philadelphian had effectively put Cosby on trial, and quickly tried to undo Hamilton's work: "It is far from being a justification of a libel that the contents thereof are true, or that the person upon whom it is made had a bad reputation," said the judge, "since the greater appearance there is of truth in any malicious invective, so much the more provoking it is."

Stymied by the bench, Hamilton turned to his final recourse, the panel of 12 New York jurors, and summarized his case with an eloquence born of the logic of justice and the emotion of freedom. Remarking that the suppression of evidence itself provided the strongest evidence, Hamilton argued that Zenger's accusations were obviously accurate. The Philadelphian then denounced oppressors who would silence those who opposed them, and called on the jury to strike a blow for liberty against arbitrary authority.

In his charge to the jury, De Lancey ordered the jurors to disregard Hamilton and determine only the fact: had Zenger published the material in question? The bench would then determine the law: was the material libelous? Ignoring De Lancey, the jurors quickly returned a verdict of "not guilty." As Thomas Hunt, the foreman, intoned the words, cheering erupted in the hall, and that night, August 4, 1735, celebrations took place in New York City.

Zenger's trial virtually ended the power of common-law judges and other British officials to harass American newspapers, but it by no means guaranteed freedom of the press. Legislators, who could support printers willing to attack royal governors, readily lost patience with those who exposed their own foibles. Indeed, in the American colonies the legislature proved a worse threat than the judiciary to the press; on numerous occasions assemblies prosecuted printers for publishing their minutes without permission. Not until the passage of the First Amendment to the Constitution in 1791 and the Jeffersonian reaction to the Federalists' repressive Alien and

Sedition Acts of 1798, did the principle of the freedom of the press reach its maturity.

John Peter Zenger spent his imprisonment in the dungeon of the old New York City Hall and stood trial in the same building. The Federal Hall National Memorial, built in 1842 on Wall and Nassau streets to commemorate a later function of the structure, marks the site of Zenger's finest hour. The John Peter Zenger Room, in the present building, contains documents relating to the printer's trial and to the subject of freedom of the press.

AUGUST 5

First Use of the Atomic Bomb

The first atomic bomb used in warfare was dropped on Hiroshima, Japan, at 7:15 P.M., August 5, 1945, Washington time — 8:15 A.M., August 6, Tokyo time — from an American B-29 Superfortress called *Enola Gay* and piloted by Colonel Paul W. Tibbets Jr. Hiroshima, the seaport capital of Hiroshima prefecture, on the island of Honshu in southwest Japan, was the country's eighth largest city and consisted of five islands interconnected by bridges. It was a center of Japanese arts as well as of heavy industry. When the lone Superfortress appeared over the city, there was no alert or rush for shelter, and the inhabitants went about their morning tasks. The *Enola Gay* released its lethal cargo, a bomb (the force of which was approximately that of 20,000 tons of TNT), which descended five miles by parachute and then burst over the target. A flash of blinding intensity and an earthshaking shock followed. Colonel Tibbets reported: "It was like looking over a tar barrel boiling. There was lots of black smoke and dust and rubble. . . . We couldn't see the city at all through the thick layer of dust nor could we see the fires beneath."

It is estimated that out of a population of over 343,000 between 70 and 80 thousand persons died immediately from the blast and fire; 10,000 were missing and never found; and at least 37,000 were injured. The figure rises to a staggering total of almost 200,000 if one counts all those who later suffered from the delayed effects of acute radiation poisoning. Of Hiroshima's total 6.9 square miles, some 60 percent of the city center disappeared: approximately 4.1 square miles were instantly and completely incinerated.

On August 6 (Washington time), President Harry S. Truman was having lunch with the crew on board the cruiser USS *Augusta* on the fourth day of his trip home from the Potsdam Conference in Europe, when he was given a terse but urgent message: "Big bomb dropped on Hiroshima. . . . First reports indicate complete success which was even more conspicuous than earlier test." He then announced the startling news of the atomic bomb. Until that date the existence of the weapon had been a closely guarded secret. In fact only a handful of the thousands of scientists and technicians who developed the first bombs actually knew the ultimate nature of their work.

The research known as the Manhattan Project had been initiated by President Franklin D. Roosevelt, following a warning from leading atomic scientists who had arrived in the United States as refugees from tyranny in their own countries. In 1939 Hungarian-born Leo Szilard was working on the problem of uranium fission at Columbia University with the Italian Nobel Prize winner Enrico Fermi. Frustrated by the slow rate of nuclear research in the United States, Szilard, like other nuclear scientists, was aware that German scientists had already succeeded in splitting the atom, and he was fearful of horrors in store for the free nations of the world if conquest-bent Germany should be the first to develop an atomic bomb. He urged Princeton physics professor Eugene P. Wigner, a fellow Hungarian, to join him in seeking the help of the German-born physicist Albert Einstein in urging the US government to explore the adaptation of atomic fission for military purposes.

At their instance, Einstein composed a now historic letter to Roosevelt on August 2, 1939. World War II had broken out in Europe on September 1, before the letter, with supporting technical documents, was delivered in person to Roosevelt on October 11, 1939, by the Russian-born economist Alexander Sachs, a Szilard acquaintance and Roosevelt friend who served as intermediary. Einstein's letter said in part:

. . . it may become possible to set up a nuclear chain reaction in a large mass of uranium, by which vast amounts of power and large quantities of new radium-like elements would be generated. . . .

This new phenomenon would also lead to the construction of bombs. . . . A single bomb of this type, carried by boat and exploded in a port, might very well destroy the whole port, together with some of the surrounding territory.

Spurred on by Einstein's letter and associated warnings that the Germans were already working on atomic fission, the President initiated a daring enterprise that eventually expended some $2 billion. On December 2, 1942, Fermi and other scientists of the Manhattan Project (which had been placed under the general direction of General Leslie R. Groves) brought about, in a former squash court under the University of Chicago's Stagg Field Stadium, the first self-sustaining nuclear chain reaction. Two immense plants were constructed for the task of producing the bomb: one at Oak Ridge, Tennessee, to separate a uranium derivative known as U-235 and the other at the Hanford Engineer Works, Richland, Washington, to make plutonium. At Los Alamos, New Mexico, a special laboratory under the direction of Dr. J. Robert Oppenheimer was set up to work out the technical problems of fashioning a bomb shell for a weapon that so far existed only in the minds of scientists. The first atomic device was exploded on July 16, 1945, near Alamogordo Air Base, New Mexico.

So secret was the entire process of research and manufacture that Vice President Harry Truman did not learn of the bomb's development until after he had become President, following Roosevelt's death in April 1945. His decision to use the bomb against Japan is the subject of continuing historical debate. Truman wrote that he had made the decision on the basis of evidence that Japan's military leaders would not surrender short of a costly invasion involving the loss of an estimated half million American lives. He was given sharply divided advice about implementing the bomb. Some scientists and political advisers urged that a "demonstration" of the bomb before representatives of the United Nations on some desert island should be afforded the Japanese before the incineration of one of their cities. However, many others argued that American bombers were already pounding Japanese cities, and that the difference between a conventional rain of death and atomic destruction was of no consequence to those killed. Moreover, direct military use of the weapon without specific warning of its nature would provide the United States with a means of saving face if the experiment — at that point yet untried — proved to be a fiasco. It was eventually not only the death toll of Hiroshima that terrified the world, but the prospect that this weapon, which harnessed the energy of the universe, threatened all human existence.

On July 26, 1945, the leaders of the British and United States governments, with the concurrence of Nationalist China, issued the so-called Potsdam Declaration or Proclamation, calling upon Japan to proclaim the "unconditional surrender of all Japanese armed forces, and to provide proper and adequate assurances of their good faith in such action." When the bombing of Hiroshima did not produce the unconditional surrender that the Allies had demanded, a second atomic bomb was dropped about 11:00 A.M., August 9, Tokyo time, on Nagasaki, a railroad terminal and port for Japa-

nese naval and military operations in the Pacific, located on the west coast of Kyushu Island. The bomb fell four miles from the city center in an outlying industrial district; out of Nagasaki's 250,000 inhabitants, it is estimated that more than 35,000 were killed, 5,000 were missing, and 60,000 were injured. The following morning, the Japanese government made known its willingness to offer an unconditional surrender on the basis of the Allies' Potsdam Declaration, with the one proviso that Hirohito remain emperor. The New York *Times* reported in enormous captions the jubilant response of American forces in the Pacific: "GI's in Pacific Go Wild With Joy; 'Let 'Em Keep Emperor,' They Say." The Allies raised no serious objection to the request, provided that the emperor be subject to the supreme commander of the Allied powers. With this decision, the war was all but over. The formal surrender ceremonies took place aboard the battleship *Missouri* in Tokyo Bay on September 2, Tokyo time.

When he first announced the dropping of the atomic bomb on Hiroshima in August 1945, President Truman informed the world of how the American government planned to deal with the new force: "I shall give further consideration . . . as to how atomic power can become a powerful and forceful influence toward the maintenance of world peace." Following the war he placed before the newly organized United Nations a proposal that all humanity be made guardian of atomic power. The USSR vetoed this bold proposal in 1947, since it was working feverishly to develop an atomic bomb of its own, and did not want international inspectors on Russian soil. By 1949 the Russians had created their version of what has come to be known as "the Bomb." But another, more powerful bomb was to come. In 1950 President Truman ordered work begun to develop a hydrogen bomb; the first one was exploded in 1952. One year later Russia also tested an H-bomb.

The anniversary of the dropping of the first atomic bomb is marked with the annual Peace Festival by residents and visitors in the largely rebuilt city of Hiroshima. The commemoration of prayer and remembrance, held each year since 1947 at Peace Memorial Park, is the city's most important yearly event. The date of the first nuclear cataclysm has also been marked from time to time in many other parts of the world. Commemorations have often taken the form of political protest against the use of atomic weapons.

The dawning of the atomic age is also remembered at Bradbury Science Hall of the Los Alamos Scientific Laboratory in Los Alamos, New Mexico. Exhibits, including nuclear reactors, atom smashers, computers, weapons, and equipment for the investigation of space radiation, illustrate research programs dating from the origin of the first nuclear weapons. The displays also focus both on present peaceful applications of nuclear energy and hopes for additional benign uses in the future. Viewable remnants of the first two nuclear catastrophes include the ballistic cases of the 10' x 2' Little Boy uranium bomb dropped on Hiroshima and the 11' x 5' Fat Man plutonium bomb detonated over Nagasaki.

What the exhibits cannot convey is sensory confirmation that the light from an atomic blast is as bright as that of the sun. They can no more than hint at the devastation of a nuclear explosion. Nor can they make it possible for viewers to hear the voice of British Prime Minister Winston Churchill, commenting at Potsdam on news of the successful experimental explosion at Alamagordo, "This is the Second Coming, in wrath." Neither can the exhibits capture the voice of the scientist who witnessed that first detonation of an atomic bomb: "This was the nearest to doomsday one can possibly imagine. I am sure that at the end of the world — in the last millisecond of the earth's existence — the last man will see something very similar to what we have seen."

John Eliot Baptized

John Eliot, "apostle to the Indians," was baptized according to the rite of the Anglican church, at Hertfordshire, England, on August 5, 1604. It is presumed that Eliot was born a few days before, but the exact date of his birth is unknown. At 15 he entered Jesus College at Cambridge University. There he excelled in his studies of the classics, and at the same time became increasingly convinced of the rectitude of Puritan theological teachings. After receiving his bachelor of arts degree in 1622, he accepted a position at the grammar school in Little Badden. His superior at the school was the Reverend Thomas Hooker, the Puritan divine who later founded the colony of Connecticut. Association with Hooker helped strengthen Eliot's commitment to the Puritan way of life, and before long he determined to become a minister and to emigrate to New England.

Arriving in Boston on November 3, 1631, Eliot substituted as the town's spiritual leader during the temporary absence of its regular minister, John Wilson. Upon Wilson's return, the congregation invited Eliot to remain as its teacher, but instead he accepted a similar offer from the newly formed church in nearby Roxbury. For over 60 years Eliot served the congregation faithfully and during that time became one of New England's most loved and admired ministers.

His duties in Roxbury brought Eliot into close contact with the Native Americans of the area, and he decided some time in the early 1640s to attempt to convert them to Christianity. Before this undertaking could begin, however, it was necessary for Eliot to master the Algonquian language. In the absence of phonetic guides and printed vocabularies, this was no easy task. Undeterred, he studied the language diligently for several years under the tutelage of Cochenoe, a Long Island native whom the Puritans had taken captive during the Pequot War of 1637, and by 1646 Eliot became sufficiently fluent to begin proselytizing.

Eliot preached to the Indians for the first time at Nonantum (now Newton), Massachusetts on October 28, 1646. Although he began with a prayer in English, he conducted the major portion of the three-hour service — including a 75-minute sermon on the Ten Commandments — in his listeners' own language. This initial effort was a great success, and within a short time Eliot had converted a number of Indians.

According to Eliot, Christianization was only the first step toward eventual acceptance of the European way of life. For this reason, he argued that it was necessary to establish special villages for the "praying Indians" in order to segregate them from the unconverted and, equally important, to expose them to the basic institutions of English life.

New England Puritans were eager to put Eliot's plan into operation, but lacking funds for such a massive relocation attempt, they were forced to appeal to Puritans in England for financial aid. To attract such support, Massachusetts leaders wrote tracts describing Eliot's success in converting the Indians. These pamphlets circulated throughout England and were largely responsible for the incorporation in 1649 of the President and Society for the Propagation of the Gospel in New England, the organization that bore the chief responsibility for Indian missionary activities in that region until the American Revolution.

In addition to preaching and attracting missionaries and funds for future proselytizing efforts, Eliot sought to aid the Indians by making the Word of God available to them in printed form. In 1654 he published a catechism that served both to summarize Christian religious beliefs and to familiarize the Indians with his written version of their language. But this volume was only a prelude to Eliot's major work. In 1650 he began a translation of the Bible into an Algonquian language. Published in 1663, Eliot's Indian Bible was the first Bible printed in North America.

Until his death on May 21, 1690, Eliot's efforts to Christianize the Indians never flagged. His success was definitely limited, and much of his work was undone by the bitter fighting during King Philip's War, beginning in 1675. But in spite of this, Eliot is noted for his unremitting efforts to share what he considered to be the advantages of his way of life. Eliot's work as a linguist and translator is also noteworthy.

AUGUST 6

Scandinavian Festival
Junction City, Oregon

This is a movable event. See note on page xxvi.

The success of the Scandinavian festival that takes place in Junction City, Oregon — usually on the second weekend in August — lies in its founder's insistence on searching for what was unique in the town's history and the determination to maintain authenticity and avoid commercialism. The result is a four-day celebration that grows logically out of the town's past, has the maximum participation of its 2,500 people, and attracts more than 60,000 visitors each year. The festival was founded out of economic need after a new expressway bypassed the town, taking with it the traffic and the customers that had once frequented the main street.

In 1960, after local businesses began to fail and some of Junction City's stores had become empty shells, G. F. Fletchall, a local physician, searched the area's history for something on which the townspeople could build to enlist the cooperation of local groups, create a better community spirit, and attract visitors. The event that developed takes 10 months of each year to prepare and involves almost everyone in town.

As Fletchall's research reminded him, Oregon, the promised land at the end of the Oregon Trail, is full of history. Sir Francis Drake had seen its impressive coastline in 1577 and Captain James Cook in 1776. Lewis and Clark, who arrived there after an arduous overland journey in 1805, had returned east with glowing reports. A few years later, John Jacob Astor's fur traders had built their trading post at the mouth of the Columbia River. Farther south, the rich farmlands of the valley of the Willamette, a tributary of the Columbia, had attracted the Methodist missionary Jason Lee in 1834; he was followed by settlers from California five years later, and most of the first pioneers who crossed the continent on the Oregon Trail in the 1840s also settled there. Junction City itself was settled in the 1850s. In the heart of the Willamette Valley, it was plotted at a proposed (but never realized)

junction of two railroad lines. Apart from its heritage from pioneer days, the town also figured prominently in development of river and rail transportation during and after the Civil War.

Although any of these developments could have served as the focal point of an observance, it seemed to Fletchall that none of them was really unique to Junction City. What struck him as more distinctive, however, was the town's Scandinavian heritage, which had begun with an influx of Danes from Minnesota at the turn of the century. Attracted by the region's favorable climate and rich farmlands, the Danes became leaders in agriculture and dairying. Their numbers were swelled quickly by the Swedish and Norwegian people who came to the valley from the Great Lakes states and developed its lumbering industry. Fletchall's suggestion for a festival based on the town's Scandinavian background, at first circulated among individual citizens, was relayed in 1961 to the chamber of commerce, which set up a committee and agreed to underwrite the first festival, naming Fletchall as chairman.

The community organized itself into hardworking committees, which made plans for a mall lined with easily dismantled Scandinavian buildings and decorated with more than 100 boxes of red and white petunias. While volunteers constructed the buildings and flower boxes, others made Scandinavian flags and set about researching and sewing the authentic costumes in which a third of the townspeople would appear on opening day. The Community Chorus began rehearsing numbers meanwhile, and a local folk-dance group and Scandinavian band were organized and began practice. A few days before the festival opened in August, workers closed off the designated downtown streets, set up the temporary buildings (where local groups would sell Scandinavian food and craft items), put the flowers in place, erected a dance platform in the center of the mall, and strung the Scandinavian flags and colored lights overhead. They also set up a registration booth where each visitor could choose the Scandinavian nationality he desired and receive souvenir "citizenship papers."

To the surprise of practically everyone, more than 25,000 people, including visitors from 28 states and many foreign countries, visited the town during that first festival. Afterwards, a group of volunteers known as the Vikings was organized to promote future festivals and assume responsibility for preparation. The administrative end is now managed by a board of directors, but the festival's format has remained more or less the same, although local talent has been supplemented by Scandinavian folk groups and other performers from other cities, and the festival now is a Northwest event, attracting visitors from all parts of the country. Programs are still planned with the idea of encouraging everyone to participate, and the original noncommercial emphasis remains, with no charges for admission, events, or entertainment. The festival is supported by memberships in the Scandinavian Festival Association (open to all), gifts from local merchants, and a percentage of revenues from festival booths.

A typical program had each day of the festival designated as a different nationality day: for example, Thursday was Swedish Day, Friday Norwegian Day, Saturday Finnish Day, and Sunday Danish Day. Mornings, which began with pancake breakfasts and flag-raising ceremonies, were devoted to shopping and to the rock, hobby, flower, and arts and crafts shows. For children, there were pony rides, a playgarden known as Børne Haven, and story telling. There were free guided bus tours of the town and surroundings several times daily. Afternoon events included films about Scandinavia; an accordion band and folk dancers performing at the Mall Platform; a show at Festival Park featuring Scandinavian costumes and authentic antique clothing of the late 19th and early 20th centuries. A main meal was prepared by a different organization each day; a Swedish pancake supper was served on one day, a Danish *Festmittag* (seven-course meal) on the next, and Swedish meatballs and a chicken barbecue on the remaining two.

Evening activities in Festival Park included a nightly flag-lowering ceremony, a community songfest, and a pageant. In a simultaneous program on the mall, assorted folk groups meanwhile presented a lively program of singing and dancing. Afterwards, everyone joined in community dancing.

Feast of the Transfiguration

The Transfiguration, the exalting manifestation in which Christ's divinity was made evident to the Disciples Peter, James, and John on a mountaintop, is commemorated by all branches of the Christian church. It is generally celebrated on August 6; a few Eastern Orthodox churches, however, still adhere to the Old Style Julian calendar and observe the Feast of the Transfiguration on August 19. Among Roman Catholics, the Transfiguration is the titular feast of the Lateran Basilica at Rome. Although raised to the rank of a double Class II feast for the whole Roman Catholic church on November 1, 1911, it is now ranked as a feast in the revised Roman Catholic calendar.

Episcopalians, Anglicans and Lutherans are among those who formally mark the occasion, which is considered a minor or "black-letter" commemoration of the Lord. The collect of the Episcopalian *Book of Common Prayer* notes the event's significance:

O God, who on the mount didst reveal to chosen witnesses thine only-begotten Son wonderfully transfigured, in raiment white and glistening; Mercifully grant that we, being delivered from the disquietude of this world, may be permitted to behold the King in his beauty, who with thee, O Father, and thee, O Holy Ghost, liveth and reigneth, one God, world without end.

Members of nonliturgical Protestant churches, such as the Presbyterian, Methodist, and United Church of Christ, also accept the scriptural account of the Transfiguration, although they may not commemorate the day in a specific formal way. Their ministers frequently read the pertinent New Testament passage in the nearest Sunday service, and take the theme of their sermons from its contents.

It is uncertain when the Church first began to celebrate the Transfiguration. The observance apparently originated in the Eastern church, perhaps as early as the fourth century. One tradition claims that St. Gregory the Illuminator, the first metropolitan of Armenia and the founder of the Armenian church, was the first to institute it in the first half of the fourth century. The Eastern Orthodox churches still rank the Transfiguration among their 12 greatest feasts.

The Transfiguration is not mentioned among the feasts of the Western Latin church until well into the Middle Ages. It was officially placed in the Roman calendar only in 1457, when Pope Calixtus III extended its observance to the universal church. An ardent advocate of the holy war against the Moslems, Calixtus III proclaimed the feast in celebration of a great victory of the Western armies over the Turks on August 6, 1456. Led by the Hungarian national hero János Hunyadi, the Christian forces had pushed the Turks back in a battle at Belgrade (then the capital of Serbia), thus staving off the Turkish advance to the west for decades and giving western Europe time to recoup its strained military resources.

The Transfiguration is described in the Gospel of Matthew (17:1–9) in this way:

And . . . Jesus took with him Peter and James and John his brother, and led them up a high mountain apart. And he was transfigured before them, and his face shone like the sun, and his garments became white as light. And behold, there appeared . . . Moses and Elijah, talking with him. . . . A bright cloud overshadowed them, and a voice from the cloud said, "This is my beloved Son, with whom I am well pleased; listen to him." When the disciples heard this, they fell on their faces, and were filled with awe. But Jesus came and touched them, saying, "Rise, and have no fear." And when they lifted up their eyes they saw no one but Jesus only.

Two other Gospels, Mark (9:2–9) and Luke (9:28–36) also relate the occurrence. The "high mountain" upon which it happened has been identified by some scholars as Mount Tabor, the almost 2,000-foot-high mountain located a few miles east of Nazareth in Galilee. Peter refers to it as the "holy mountain" in his account of the Transfiguration in the Second Epistle (1:16–18).

The mysterious transformation of Jesus is traditionally explained as the manifestation of his divine glory in his earthly body. Especially significant was his appearance in conjunction with the two venerable Old Testament figures: Moses, the Hebrew lawgiver and prototype of the Prophets, and Elijah, the Prophet regarded in Jewish tradition as the herald of the coming Messiah. An event of great importance for spiritual and doctrinal reasons, the Transfiguration witnessed by the favored disciples was seen as the fulfillment of the ancient Law.

Voting Rights Act of 1965

After a symbolic ceremony in the rotunda of the Capitol in Washington, D.C., President Lyndon B. Johnson on August 6, 1965, signed into law the Voting Rights Act of 1965, designed to carry out the provisions of a measure that had been enacted 95 years earlier. This was the 15th Amendment to the Constitution providing that "the right of citizens . . . to vote shall not be denied or abridged by the United States or by any State on account of race, color, or previous condition of servitude."

Genuine as the intent of the amendment was, there were in 1965 still parts of the country where blacks and other minorities were prevented from voting — on the grounds (among others) that they had failed to pass literacy tests, failed to interpret sections of the Constitution adequately, failed to locate registrars, or failed to call during registrars' often nebulous office hours — and therefore failed to register. The matter of race was seldom mentioned.

However, there were many who claimed that the denial of voting rights to blacks was deliberate; that different criteria were applied to white and black would-be voters; that the ground for this was race, and no other; and that the 15th Amendment was being violated constantly, deliberately, and by design.

The Voting Rights Act of 1965 had as its goal

the ending of bars to voting everywhere in the nation. Reinforcing the Civil Rights Act of 1964 (see July 2), the new act sought to guarantee the right of every citizen to vote. It specified federal action to prevent local practices that had the effect — whatever the given reason — of denying the right to vote on account of race. In concrete terms, the act called for the suspension of all such devices as literacy tests, constitutional interpretations, registration forms, or required recommendations by registered voters in states and counties where less than 50 percent of adult residents had voted in 1964. It also empowered the US attorney general to dispatch federal examiners to register black voters in those areas if he felt that local registrars were failing to do their job.

As thus spelled out, the law applied principally to Alabama, Alaska, Georgia, Louisiana, Mississippi, South Carolina, Virginia, and parts of North Carolina, but also to scattered counties in Arizona, Idaho, and Hawaii. The new act also directed the attorney general to bring court tests to challenge the constitutionality of poll taxes as a requirement for voting in state and local elections. This provision was directed at the four states — Mississippi, Texas, Alabama, and Virginia — that still had such taxes. Poll taxes as a requirement for voting in federal elections had already been banned with the ratification of the 24th Amendment to the Constitution in January 1964.

Passage of the Voting Rights Act of 1965 was followed by a dramatic upturn in the number of blacks registered to vote. Nearly 250,000 were newly registered by the end of 1965, a third of them by federal registrars, but two-thirds by local registrars who complied with the act.

Dramatic as they were, the figures were less impressive in terms of what remained to be done. Attorney General Nicholas Katzenbach, who was criticized by some for being too fast, and by others for being too slow, in sending federal registrars to areas of low black registration, pointed out the need for intensified registration drives and clear enunciation of demands to vote before the new act could become completely effective. By the beginning of the 1970s, when the variously defined term "black power" had permeated the civil rights movement as a rallying cry, there was still much to accomplish in the field of voter registration. This was true not only in the areas that had been principally affected by the 1965 act, but also in many places where apathy, more than intentional obstacles, had kept people from registering.

The act, extended for five years in 1970, was further extended in 1975, for seven more years. The 1975 legislation widened the coverage to protect voting rights of non-English-speaking minorities — Native Americans, Spanish-speaking Americans, and Asian-Americans.

AUGUST 7

Gulf of Tonkin Resolution Approved

In the years following the end of World War II, the "domino theory," as set forth by President Dwight D. Eisenhower on April 7, 1954, guided American leaders in formulating US policy in Southeast Asia. John F. Kennedy and Lyndon B. Johnson, who succeeded Eisenhower, agreed that if the Communists were victorious in South Vietnam, all of Southeast Asia would fall to the enemy. Both Presidents therefore determined to safeguard South Vietnam from Communist encroachment. Kennedy's years as President witnessed increased US involvement in the small Indochinese nation, and after Congress approved the Gulf of Tonkin Resolution on August 7, 1964, the Johnson administration escalated US military participation in the war in Vietnam.

The United States had become entangled in Vietnam during the last years of French domination of Southeast Asia. At the end of World War II, Vietnamese nationalists, many of whom had become identified with Ho Chi Minh's Communist-dominated Vietminh (or League for the Independence of Vietnam), desired independence for their homeland. France, however, had no intention of surrendering control of Vietnam or any other part of its Indochinese empire. Realizing that neither the United States nor the powers of Western Europe would support a war to stifle a movement for Vietnamese independence, French leaders determined to transform the image of their military efforts into a fight against communism. As part of this undertaking, the French in 1949 set up a quasi-independent government in Vietnam headed by former emperor Bao Dai. The new regime lacked true autonomy and failed to satisfy Vietnamese nationalists, but it accomplished its purpose. United States leaders, anxious after the fall of China to the Communists in 1949 to contain the spread of Red domination, believed the new French-supported Vietnamese government was a bulwark against communism. On February 7, 1950, the United States recognized the Bao Dai government and during the next four years provided some $2.6 billion to assist France "in restoring stability in Vietnam."

Despite such enormous economic aid, France was unable to put down what the Vietminh and those allied with them saw as a struggle for self-determination. In the spring of 1954 France committed its best troops to the protection of the fortress of Dienbienphu in Vietnam's northern province of Tonkin. The French military command believed this tactic would lure the Vietminh into an engagement that would result in a decisive defeat for the insurgents — but their reasoning proved wrong. Supplied with artillery by Red China, the Vietminh beseiged Dienbienphu and captured the fortress on May 7, 1954.

The fall of Dienbienphu marked the end of French military efforts in Vietnam. The Geneva armistice and agreements of July 20 and 21, 1954, provided for a ceasefire in Vietnam and partitioned the war-ravaged nation at the 17th Parallel. Ho Chi Minh and the Communists were given control of the North and the government of Bao Dai was recognized in the South. But the division was to be temporary: the Geneva agreements called also for a free election to be held under international supervision in July 1956 to decide the question of Vietnamese unification.

Unwilling to participate in negotiations with the Communists, the United States did not sign or endorse the Geneva agreements. An official statement was issued, however, warning that the United States "would view any renewal of the aggression in violation of the . . . agreements with grave concern."

In the months following the 1954 armistice, US involvement in South Vietnam deepened. With US approval, Bao Dai selected Ngo Dinh Diem, the nationalist leader of Vietnam's powerful Roman Catholic minority, to be prime minister. American leaders believed Diem would be able to build South Vietnam into a stronghold against communism, and on October 23, 1954, President Eisenhower notified Diem that the United States would assist Vietnam to become "a strong, viable state, capable of resisting attempted subversion or aggression through military means," but in the same message Eisenhower also warned that "the Government of the United States expects that this aid will be met by performance on the part of the Government of Vietnam in undertaking needed reforms."

In October 1955 Diem — after a one-sided, government-controlled referendum ousted Bao Dai — proclaimed himself president of the Republic of Vietnam. The United States immediately recognized the new regime. It also continued its liberal financial assistance to South Vietnam.

The Geneva accords called for a general election to be held in Vietnam in July 1956, but in July of the previous year, Diem announced that his government had not signed the Geneva agreements and therefore was not bound by them; and that no referendum would take place in Vietnam until the conditions for a free election were present in the North. Ho Chi Minh and the Vietminh, who most observers believed would have easily won the election, were eager for the referendum. They repeatedly called upon Diem's Saigon government to enter into discussions so that arrangements might be made for the elections, but the South Vietnamese, with the support of the United States, refused.

Conditions in Vietnam steadily deteriorated. After 1956, Communist guerrillas, popularly known as the Vietcong, began to make raids in the South, and the Diem government proved itself unable to stem the terrorists. Between 1956 and 1960 the United States sent to South Vietnam several hundred military advisers — the first of whom were killed on October 22, 1957, when a bomb exploded in their quarters — and financial aid estimated by some to have averaged as much as $300 million a year. Despite this massive assistance to the Saigon government, the Vietcong gained strength and in December 1960 joined with non-Communist, anti-Diem insurgents, to form the National Liberation Front (NLF) of South Vietnam.

By the autumn of 1961 the NLF had perhaps as much as 80 percent of the South Vietnamese countryside under its influence and so threatened the Diem government that on October 18, 1961, South Vietnam's President Diem declared "a state of emergency." The United States acted quickly to provide assistance. On December 11, 1961, two army helicopter companies, the first US military units to become directly involved in combat support, arrived in Saigon. On December 14 President Kennedy reaffirmed US support of South Vietnam and authorized the addition of 1,500 military advisers to the more than 600 already in South Vietnam.

Throughout 1962 American involvement in Vietnam steadily deepened. By February, the number of US military in South Vietnam climbed to 4,000, and early in March Pentagon officials admitted that American pilots were flying some combat missions there. The United States did not become directly involved in ground fighting during 1962, but by the end of the year, 11,300 American troops were stationed in South Vietnam.

Despite this massive aid, the Diem regime made no progress against the enemy. The Army of the Republic of Vietnam (ARVN) repeatedly proved itself incapable of holding its own against the Vietcong. On one occasion, during January 1963 in the Mekong Delta, 200 Vietcong were able to repulse the advance of 2,000 government troops supported by armor and air units. Moreover, such failings by his military force were not the only problems facing Diem in 1963.

For some time prior to 1963 the Buddhists who formed the majority of Vietnam's population had resented the favoritism Diem showed toward the Catholic minority and had chafed under the oppressive measures carried out by Diem's brother, Ngo Dinh Nhu, who headed the secret police. Then, on May 8, 1963, the police in Hué fired into a crowd demonstrating against an order prohibiting the flying of Buddhist flags during a religious festival. The incident precipitated a major crisis. On June 11 a Buddhist monk immolated himself in Saigon to protest the Hué shooting, and during the summer of 1963 several others followed his example. By August South Vietnam was in such turmoil that Diem declared martial law so that order could be restored.

Only 11 days after martial law was lifted, on September 16, 1963, Diem permitted national elections to take place in South Vietnam. By allowing only candidates who had won prior governmental approval to seek election, Diem totally ignored the months of protest and unrest that had preceded the September 27 canvass. But, in any case, the days of his corrupt and authoritarian regime were numbered. On November 1, 1963, a group of officers in the South Vietnamese armed forces, probably with the tacit approval of the United States, overthrew the Diem government. The following day they murdered Diem and his brother Nhu and set up a military junta to rule Vietnam.

After the downfall of Diem, South Vietnam's internal political situation was chaotic. Worried that the cause of anticommunism might fail, the United States continued to support the Saigon government. On January 1, 1964, Lyndon B. Johnson, who had succeeded to the presidency following the assassination of President Kennedy, assured South Vietnamese leaders: "We shall maintain in Vietnam American personnel and matériel as needed to assist you in achieving victory."

By March and April, high administration advisers were considering what they would come to see as the necessity for a major increase in the American role in Vietnam. Contingency planning for large-scale US involvement in the war went on throughout 1964.

In the spring of 1964 the US Joint Chiefs of Staff prepared a list of possible bombing targets in North Vietnam. During the first half of the year, American advisers provided the South Vietnamese with training and equipment for guerrilla operations, reconnaissance missions, and raids against coastal installations in North Vietnam — all part of a program, code-named Operation 34A, of covert military pressures against the North. In addition, US Navy destroyers secretly patrolled the Gulf of Tonkin, directly east of North Vietnam, conducting reconnaissance, monitoring Communist radio broadcasts, and collecting information about North Vietnamese radar installations. By summer, with the military situation of anti-Communist South Vietnam particularly precarious, the Johnson administration was maneuvering to gain approval for a congressional resolution that would, in effect, authorize undeclared war, should that seem necessary.

The first of two incidents that led to just such a document took place on August 2, 1964, when North Vietnamese PT boats fired on the US destroyer *Maddox* cruising in the Gulf of Tonkin. As it happened, the attack took place just two days after South Vietnamese PT boats had completed a 34A raid against Communist installations in the area, and it is probable the North Vietnamese erroneously believed the *Maddox* to be involved in that action. President Johnson ordered a second destroyer, the *C. Turner Joy*, added to the US patrol and protested the "unprovoked attack" to Hanoi.

A second North Vietnamese attack on the *Maddox* and the *C. Turner Joy*, took place in the same area on August 4 — or was believed to have taken place: there were no visual sightings in the pitch-dark night. President Johnson retaliated by ordering US planes to bomb strategic targets in North Vietnam, the first overt military action undertaken by the United States in the area.

During the critical days of early August 1964 the President acted independently of Congress, but on August 5 he asked that body to promise full support for US forces in South Vietnam in order "to promote the maintenance of international peace and security in Southeast Asia." The response was quick and predictable. At the time, Congress and the American public had no knowledge of 34A missions, nor of any possible confusion surrounding the Gulf of Tonkin incidents. These appeared as clear examples of unprovoked North Vietnamese aggression, and the Gulf of Tonkin Resolution, which Congress passed rapidly on August 7, appeared to be a clearly warranted response.

The resolution, which passed 416 to 0 in the House of Representatives and 88 to 2 in the Senate, gave the President power "to take all necessary measures to repel any armed attack against the forces of the United States and to prevent further aggression." The resolution also stated that "the United States is . . . prepared, as the President determines, to take all necessary steps, including the use of armed force, to assist any member or protocol State of the Southeast Asia Collective Defense Treaty requesting assistance in defense of its freedom."

Although the Gulf of Tonkin Resolution did not authorize a full-scale war in so many words, it was, in effect, a blank check, and US participation in the fighting in South Vietnam dramatically increased in the months following its approval. On November 1, 1964, the Vietcong attacked the US air base at Bien Hoa, about 30 miles outside Saigon. The Joint Chiefs of Staff urged President Johnson to make a "strong response" to this incident. Their proposals included air strikes against North Vietnam; US ambassador to South Vietnam Maxwell Taylor similarly suggested the bombing of "selected targets" in the North.

Johnson did not immediately accept the advice of his military planners, and he appeared to be an advocate of restraint during the presidential campaign of 1964. His Republican opponent, Senator Barry Goldwater of Arizona, spoke more boldly of using force to accomplish US foreign policy objectives. Goldwater's stance may have hurt his candidacy, and Johnson scored a massive victory. But in December 1964, only one month after the election, Johnson approved a contingency plan for air attacks against North Vietnam and even the deployment, if necessary, of ground troops.

On February 7, 1965, the Vietcong attacked the US military advisers' compound at Pleiku. As a result of this operation, 8 Americans were killed and another 109 were wounded. President Johnson immediately ordered retaliatory air strikes against Dong Hoi in North Vietnam. Then the Vietcong on February 10 raided Qui Nhon; this time American casualties numbered 23 dead and 21 wounded. Shortly afterwards, the United States launched a sustained air war, code-named Operation Rolling Thunder. President Johnson announced on February 28 that the bombing of North Vietnamese military targets would continue until the enemy agreed to "a negotiated settlement."

With the arrival of 3,500 marines at Da Nang on March 7 through 9, 1965, US servicemen in South Vietnam totaled 27,000. In April President Johnson authorized the addition of 18,000 to 20,000 men in "military support forces," and by May US troops in South Vietnam numbered 46,500. Despite this commitment of military personnel — all of whom were still officially advisers — the United States tried to initiate a movement toward a peace settlement by halting the bombing of the North in May. When Hanoi failed to respond favorably after five days, the air attacks on North Vietnam were resumed.

On June 9, 1965, American troops — which by the end of the month totaled over 74,000 — were officially authorized to take part in field operations. They participated in their first major "search and destroy" mission on June 28, 1965, and after that date became deeply involved in combat operations throughout South Vietnam. At the end of 1965 the number of American servicemen in South Vietnam had climbed to 184,300, and by that time 1,350 Americans had been killed, 5,300 wounded, and 148 missing or captured.

Estimates of the size of the North Vietnamese army (not including Vietcong guerrillas) in South Vietnam increased from a range of 1,000 to 5,000 at the end of 1964 to 11,000 to 14,000 at the end of 1965. In 1966 the war in Vietnam reached a stalemate: American troops prevented a Vietcong victory, but the United States was not able to defeat the enemy. American planes continued to fly missions over North Vietnam, and on June 29, 1966, began bombing near Hanoi, capital of the North, and Haiphong, its most important port. Meanwhile, US troops were taking over most of the ground offensives from the ARVN. Their "search and destroy" missions, aimed at suppressing guerrilla operations and preventing North Vietnamese infiltration, were only marginally effective. By the end of 1966 there were more than 385,000 US troops in South Vietnam; the number of American dead stood at 6,644 and the number of wounded reached 37,738.

Attempts by the United States to stabilize South Vietnam's internal affairs fared better than its efforts against the Vietcong and North Vietnam. Between the fall of the Diem regime in November 1963 and the coup that on June 19, 1965, established Air Vice Marshal Nguyen Cao Ky as premier and General Nguyen Van Thieu as chief of state, nine governments successively came to power and were overthrown in South Vietnam. Realizing that such political instability severely crippled South Vietnam's ability to crush the Vietcong, their NLF political arm, and their North Vietnamese allies, the United States urged the Ky-Thieu government to draft a constitution and hold national elections. The South Vietnamese leaders agreed, and in September 1967 Thieu was elected as president and Ky as vice president by a plurality of only 34.8 percent of the vote, despite the government's heavy-handed efforts to assure the result in advance. Like their predecessors, Thieu and Ky were for the most part unresponsive to demands for civil liberties and much-needed economic reforms, but they did restore a measure of political stability to South Vietnam.

Meanwhile, as the fighting continued in Vietnam through 1965, 1966, and 1967, a number of peace overtures were made. United Nations secretary General U Thant, President Charles de Gaulle of France, and Pope Paul VI were among the international dignitaries who tried to break the impasse between the United States and North Vietnam during the three-year period. Their efforts were unsuccessful. Several times the United States and North Vietnam also put forth plans, unsuccessfully, for ending the war in Vietnam. North Vietnam insisted that the United States unconditionally halt its bombing before peace talks could begin and demanded that the NLF be represented in negotiations and that the United States unilaterally withdraw its troops from Vietnam. President Johnson on several occasions temporarily halted the bombing of North Vietnam, but the United States agreed to remove military forces from South Vietnam only if North Vietnam also withdrew troops, and the United States repeatedly refused to recognize or enter into peace talks with the NLF.

Through 1967 the numbers of United States and North Vietnamese troops increased in South Vietnam, and the fighting intensified. By the end of the year the number of US forces reached 485,600. In the air the US military flew missions as close as 10 miles from the Chinese border and mined North Vietnamese rivers; on the ground, American forces saw combat in the southern portion of the demilitarized zone separating North and South Vietnam. In the meantime, an estimated 7,000 North Vietnamese regulars infiltrated into the South each month. These troops, together with Vietcong guerrillas, launched coordinated attacks against South Vietnam's major cities on January 30, 1968, the first day of the Tet, or Lunar New Year, truce. During this so-called Tet Offensive, which lasted until February 25, 1968, the Communists controlled the grounds of the United States embassy in Saigon for six hours. They were even more successful in other South Vietnamese cities and were not defeated in Hué until February 24.

As US involvement mounted steadily in the mid-1960s, increasingly large sectors of the American citizenry expressed their disapproval of their nation's participation in the war. College students, many of whom faced the possibility of being drafted to fight in Vietnam, were in the vanguard of those who denounced the war. As early as 1965, "teach-ins" against the war were frequent on college and university campuses, and that autumn thousands of Americans joined in a massive nationwide protest against the Johnson administration's escalation of the war in the year since passage of the Gulf of Tonkin Resolution.

Through 1966 students continued to be the most vociferous protesters against US participation in the war, burning draft cards and staging numerous marches and demonstrations. However, those who overtly protested still formed only a minority of the US population, and their actions were often criticized as illegal or even treasonous. But as hundreds of thousands of young men left their homes to join the fight in Vietnam with no hope of winning an early victory, and as the distant war became an increasingly heavy economic burden on American taxpayers, the ranks of those opposed to US involvement in Vietnam gradually swelled.

Mounting antiwar feeling found political expression as the presidential election of 1968 approached. In November 1967 Democratic Senator Eugene McCarthy of Minnesota announced plans to run in preferential primary elections against President Johnson to give the American people an opportunity to disavow the administration's handling of the war. McCarthy was a vehement critic of American involvement in Vietnam, but he was not well known nationally, and political observers initially believed his candidacy would have little impact. In the early months of 1968, however, the McCarthy campaign, supported by massive numbers of college and university students, gained momentum. In March the Minnesota senator won 42.4 percent of the popular vote in the New Hampshire primary. The election demonstrated the strength of antiwar feeling among American citizens and encouraged Senator Robert F. Kennedy of New York, another opponent of the Vietnam war and brother of the slain President, to enter the 1968 race.

President Johnson did not remain unresponsive to the growing popular desire for peace that had been expressed at the polls, but neither did he accede to demands that the United States immediately end its involvement in Vietnam. On March 31, 1968, the President appeared on television. In his address he announced that US participation in the war would be deescalated: he ordered that bombing raids be halted north of the 20th Parallel and called upon Hanoi to enter into peace negotiations. Then Johnson made the startling announcement that he would not seek, or accept, renomination for the presidency.

Hanoi responded to Johnson's initiative, and in May 1968 formal peace talks opened in Paris. Meanwhile, in the United States, the race for President continued. Following Johnson's refusal to seek another term, Vice President Hubert H. Humphrey of Minnesota announced his candidacy for the Democratic nomination for President. As Vice President, Humphrey was closely associated with the Johnson administration's Vietnam policies and consequently was not so strongly opposed to them as were McCarthy and Kennedy.

During the spring of 1968 McCarthy, Kennedy, and Humphrey fought for convention votes in the Indiana, Nebraska, Oregon, and California primaries. Kennedy's victory in the last of these contests in June 1968 seemingly left him as the leading contender at the upcoming Democratic convention. But only hours after winning the California primary on June 5, he was assassinated.

In late August the Democrats met in Chicago, with antiwar protesters demonstrating in the streets and proclaiming their support for McCarthy and South Dakota Senator George McGovern, another peace candidate, who had joined the race for the nomination shortly after Kennedy's assassination. The demonstrators, however, made little impression on the convention delegates, who bypassed McCarthy and McGovern and nominated the more moderate Humphrey.

Unlike the Democrats, the Republicans had little difficulty selecting their presidential candidate. Early in 1968 Richard M. Nixon had emerged as the leading contender, and in August the Republican National Convention, meeting in Miami, chose him. Nixon did not share the antiwar activists' outrage at the US presence in Vietnam, but he realized that the fighting in Southeast Asia was becoming increasingly unpopular. Accordingly, he promised that if elected he would strive to end the war.

While US voters in 1968 considered the merits of Nixon, Humphrey, and George C. Wallace, the candidate of the American Independent party, the war continued. On April 8, 1968, the United States and its allies began Operation Complete Victory. Described as "the biggest drive of the war so far," the offensive was designed to eliminate enemy forces from the provinces around Saigon. The effort was a dismal failure. Between May 5 and 13, only a few months after the Tet Offensive, the Communists launched a new attack against South Vietnam, and from June 3 to 15 Saigon again became the scene of heavy fighting.

Although the Communists were quickly subdued in the South Vietnamese capital, bitterly fought military actions continued to take place in the provinces of South Vietnam throughout the summer and fall of 1968. Meanwhile, in the United States, the presidential campaign entered its final days. Nixon began the race with a considerable advantage over his Democratic rival, but Humphrey was able slowly to narrow the margin. Humphrey's cause was not hurt when President Johnson announced — five days before the November 5 election—that the United States would cease "all air, naval and artillery bombardment of North Vietnam" on November 1. Voters nonetheless deserted the Democratic administration in sufficient numbers to select Nixon as the nation's next President.

During the first few months of the Nixon presidency, US participation in the war in Vietnam did not abate. In February 1969 the Communists again launched a major offensive in South Vietnam. Nixon responded in March by declaring that the United States "will not tolerate" such enemy aggression, and by warning the North Vietnamese to expect retaliatory measures. At the same time, the number of US troops in Vietname continued to increase, reaching a total of 541,500 by March 1969.

Although many observers interpreted Nixon's election as a mandate to change US policy in Vietnam, it was not until late in the spring of 1969 that he began to outline his plans for concluding the war. Rejecting peace advocates' demands for an immediate end to American involvement, he proposed instead that US troops be withdrawn gradually and that the South Vietnamese army slowly assume the total responsibility for defending its nation. In June 1969, he met with President Thieu of South Vietnam on Midway Island in the Pacific and put his policy of gradual US withdrawal, known as Vietnamization, into operation by announcing that 25,000 American troops would leave Vietnam by the end of August.

Nixon's proposal to "wind down" the war slowly appeared to satisfy many Americans, whom he designated as the "silent majority," but it failed to gain the approval of the more intense advocates of rapid disengagement. Concerned that hundreds of thousands of American soldiers remained in Vietnam, that aerial bombing raids and defoliation continued, and that the Paris peace talks were stagnated, opponents of the war scheduled a number of "moratorium" days during the autumn of 1969. One such demonstration drew some 250,000 persons to Washington, D.C. Nixon's commitment to Vietnamization remained unshaken, however; on November 3, 1969, he reiterated that American troops would be pulled out gradually, according to a timetable that would permit South Vietnamese forces to take over the defense of South Vietnam.

By the end of 1969, up to 100,000 US servicemen were scheduled to depart for home. However, US involvement in Vietnam diminished only slightly in 1970. Indeed, when President Nixon on April 30 of that year sent US combat troops into neighboring Cambodia to destroy Vietcong and North Vietnamese "sanctuaries," peace advocates feared that the war was being escalated again. Strong protests were staged across the nation, most notably on May 4 at Ohio's Kent State University, where national guardsmen reacted to the confusion by opening fire on the crowd of protesters and bystanders. Four students were killed, and several others were wounded.

An outburst of public rage and alarm over the Kent State shootings and the expansion of military operations into Cambodia led Nixon to promise a congressional committee he would withdraw the ground troops from Cambodia by the end of June. Remaining convinced of the value of the Cambodian "incursion," however, he announced in June that it had accomplished its objective of destroying enemy sanctuaries and thereby had hastened the return of American soldiers from Vietnam. The same month, the US Senate, which was less sanguine about the venture, repealed the Gulf of Tonkin Resolution and approved the Cooper-Church Amendment, which prohibited future operations in Cambodia and aid to its military chief of state, Lon Nol, without congressional approval.

The short-lived Cambodian undertaking and the Kent State shootings were not the only events that disheartened the US public in 1970. Reports of atrocities allegedly committed by the South Vietnamese Army and accounts of morale problems and increasing drug use among American troops caused further anguish. Yet not even these stories had prepared the country for the news in 1970 that US soldiers had massacred a large number of civilian men, women, and children at the Vietnamese hamlet of My Lai in March 1968 — an ultimate demonstration, it seemed to many, of the demoralizing and dehumanizing effect of the war.

During 1971 the Paris peace talks and secret negotiations conducted by President Nixon's special foreign policy adviser, Henry Kissinger, failed to resolve basic issues separating the adversaries in Vietnam. Despite the diplomatic stalemate, the process of Vietnamization advanced. In April President Nixon ordered 100,-000 troops withdrawn and in November reduced the American military force in Vietnam by another 45,000, leaving 156,800 US soldiers in the war-wracked Southeast Asian nation.

On June 13, 1971, the New York Times began a series of articles with the headline "Vietnam Archive: Pentagon Study Traces 3 Decades of Growing U.S. Involvement." The articles were based on information contained in a secret, 47-volume study, which Secretary of Defense Robert S. McNamara had ordered in 1967. Copies of the study were smuggled from the archives of the Rand Corporation by Dr. Daniel Ellsberg, a senior research associate at the Massachusetts Institute of Technology, who had served in the Defense Department as an analyst and consultant. Passed by Ellsberg to New York Times reporter Neil Sheehan, the popularly named Pentagon Papers — which Ellsberg himself had helped prepare — revealed to the American public the hitherto secret and seemingly incredible history of US participation in Vietnamese affairs. The Pentagon documents contained information that made clear the importance of the decision by the Truman administration to assist French counterinsurgency efforts in Indochina and demonstrated how US actions during the presidency of Dwight D. Eisenhower had prevented the otherwise inevitable establishment of a pro-Communist government in South Vietnam. The papers showed that President Kennedy had considerably broadened the nation's commitment to Vietnam and that the choice before President Johnson was either to withdraw or to intensify US support. Choosing the latter course, Johnson embarked on a policy of escalation, but, the Pentagon study indicated, his decision was concealed from the American people for a year.

The publication of the controversial Pentagon Papers — first in the *Times*, then, despite the government's attempts to obtain restraining orders, in the Washington *Post* and other newspapers around the country — continued. Ultimately, on June 26, 1971, the Supreme Court ruled in favor of the *Times* and the *Post*, upholding their right to resume publication of the material. The Pentagon Papers strengthened the conviction of peace advocates and turned more Americans against the war, but US involvement in the Vietnam conflict continued through 1971 and 1972. The latter was a presidential election year in the United States, and, for the war-weary citizenry, ending the fighting was again the key issue. In January 1972 President Nixon, who had promised during his 1968 campaign to end the war, and was soon to seek reelection, announced that 70,000 more soldiers would come home from Vietnam by May 1. He also reported for the first time that Henry Kissinger had been engaged in secret negotiations for months, but that North Vietnam had rejected US proposals — which included guarantees of free elections in South Vietnam, the exchange of prisoners of war, and withdrawal of American and other foreign forces within six months of an agreement between the opposing parties.

Steady withdrawals of US troops brought the number of American soldiers in South Vietnam down to 47,000 by July 1, 1972, but a number of incidents in the spring of that year discouraged those who hoped for an early termination of the fighting. In March 1972 the United States, claiming that the North Vietnamese were not negotiating seriously, suspended the formal peace talks in Paris. Soon afterwards North Vietnamese armor and artillery units crossed the Demilitarized Zone and launched a major offensive against the South. In April the United States retaliated by conducting bombing strikes against Hanoi and Haiphong, the first such air raids against major northern targets since Johnson had ordered them stopped in the spring of 1968.

The United States then agreed to return to the peace table.

Diplomatic efforts had barely resumed when, in May 1972, enemy forces took control of Quang Tri, the northernmost province of South Vietnam. In response the United States and South Vietnam announced that they would postpone the Paris negotiating sessions indefinitely, and the United States initiated new measures to stem the northern aggression. On May 8, 1972, President Nixon reported to the American people that he had ordered the US military to mine the harbors of Haiphong and of six other major North Vietnamese ports, and to maintain a naval blockade that would prevent supplies from entering North Vietnam. At the same time, he announced that if the North Vietnamese would agree to the return of American prisoners of war and to an internationally supervised ceasefire, we would "stop all acts of force throughout Indochina and proceed in the complete withdrawal of all forces within four months." Commentators noted that these terms represented a slight departure from previous US peace overtures, because the Americans for the first time did not insist on free presidential elections in South Vietnam after the ceasefire.

Despite the North Vietnamese offensive and American retaliatory measures in the spring of 1972, the North agreed to resume peace talks in July. Private negotiations also were resumed. Initial reports from Paris were discouraging, for the North Vietnamese claimed that the United States was refusing to consider any new proposals for ending the fighting. Nevertheless, two months later, rumors circulated widely that Kissinger and the North Vietnamese representatives were close to reaching an agreement.

Reports in October 1972 from Hanoi, Saigon, and even Kissinger himself, indicated that "peace is at hand." In the United States the news weakened the campaign of the Democratic presidential candidate, Senator George McGovern, an advocate of an immediate end of American participation in the Vietnamese struggle. Nixon overwhelmed McGovern, who lost all the electoral votes except those of Massachusetts and the District of Columbia.

In late November and early December Kissinger and Hanoi's chief representative, Le Duc Tho, met 15 times without reaching a final agreement. Believing that the North Vietnamese were not operating in good faith, President Nixon decided to resort again to force as a means of encouraging serious negotiations. On December 18, 1972, he ordered the resumption of US bombing missions above the 20th Parallel in North Vietnam, including B-52 raids around Hanoi and Haiphong. The air strikes lasted 12 days. During this period 15 B-52s were lost, and 93 American airmen were killed, captured, or missing.

On January 8, 1973, Kissinger and Le Duc Tho resumed their talks in Paris. Thirteen days later Nixon announced "progress" in the peace negotiations, and suspended bombing in all of North Vietnam, as well as mining, shelling, and other offensive actions. Kissinger and Tho held one additional session. Then, on January 23, 1973, President Nixon reported that the representatives had initiated an agreement "to end the war and bring peace with honor in Vietnam and Southeast Asia."

On January 27 representatives of the United States, Hanoi, the Vietcong, and Saigon signed the Vietnam peace pact in Paris. The agreement specified, among other things, that all military prisoners of war and foreign civilians would be released, that the 23,700-man US force in South Vietnam would be withdrawn within 60 days, and that an international force composed of Canadians, Hungarians, Indonesians, and Poles would supervise the truce. North Vietnamese troops already in the South were allowed to remain, but they could not be replaced; and both the United States and North Vietnam agreed to respect "the South Vietnamese people's right to self-determination." The ceasefire went into effect at 7:00 P.M. Eastern Standard Time and brought the United States' longest and most controversial involvement in a war to its conclusion.

Unfortunately the extrication of the United States from the hostilities did not mean that the fighting had stopped. During the spring of 1973 violations of the truce were so frequent and flagrant that representatives of the United States, North Vietnam, South Vietnam, and the Viecong signed a second peace agreement in South Vietnam on June 13, 1973. Called an "amplification and consolidation" of the earlier Paris accord, the new document stipulated that all military actions in South Vietnam end at noon Greenwich Mean Time on June 15, 1973, and that commanders of the opposing forces meet within 24 hours of that time to insure compliance with the truce and to guarantee medical attention for all combatants. It also specified that the United States would no longer fly reconnaissance missions over North Vietnam, would resume minesweeping operations in North Vietnamese waters, and would resume talks regarding aid to North Vietnam.

Even after the second ceasefire, fighting in Vietnam continued. Although neither the South nor the North conducted a major offensive during 1973, the Saigon government estimated that nearly 16,000 South Vietnamese and some 45,000 North Vietnamese and Vietcong died in guerrilla operations and skirmishes between January 27, 1973 and January 27, 1974.

Through 1974 the bloody war continued in stalemate. Troops from the North infiltrated the South and conducted limited offensives against areas controlled by the Saigon government. Meanwhile the United States continued to aid its ally; about 5,000 Americans remained in South Vietnam as civilian advisers, and Congress appropriated hundreds of millions of dollars in military aid. At home the United States endured the long-festering political scandal that in August brought about the resignation of Nixon and the succession of Gerald R. Ford to the presidency.

The major Communist offensive, which many observers had long expected, came in March 1975. Early in the month, Northern troops struck at the Central Highlands provinces of Kontum, Pleiku, and Darlac. In the two weeks of fighting that followed, the Communists severed the two main highways leading from the highlands, took a number of key outposts, captured the provincial capital of Ban Me Thuot, and caused about 100,000 persons to flee to the coast of the South China Sea. The forces of the Saigon government were unable to stem the Communist advance, and on March 18 President Thieu ordered a retreat from the strategic Central Highlands area.

Communist control of the Central Highlands effectively isolated the northern provinces of South Vietnam from the remainder of the nation, and within days of their success in the Highlands the Communists gained command of two-thirds of the northern area of the country. By sacrificing this region, the Saigon government hoped that it would be able to defend the rich and populous southern part of the nation and the narrow strip running northward from Saigon along the coast of the South China Sea to Da Nang or even farther, to Hué. This was not to be.

Through the last days of March and the beginning of April, the Communist forces continued their startling victories. By April 10 the North Vietnamese and the Vietcong had control of Hué and Da Nang in the north and had turned their attention toward isolating Saigon. The situation in South Vietnam was so critical that on April 11 President Ford appealed to Congress for nearly $1 billion in military and humanitarian aid so that the Southeast Asian nation might "save itself." Reaction was favorable to Ford's request for $250 million to be used for humanitarian purposes and for authority to call upon US troops to insure the evacuation of American citizens from Vietnam. But the fact that the South Vietnamese army had already abandoned to the enemy armaments estimated at $1 billion that the United States had previously provided made most representatives to Congress unwilling to approve the expenditure of $722 million for further military assistance.

During mid-April South Vietnam's remaining defenses rapidly crumbled and with 10 divisions of the North Vietnamese army surrounding Saigon, President Thieu resigned on April 21. When the Communists refused to negotiate peace with Thieu's former vice president and successor, Tran Van Huong, he too left office, and on April 28 General Duong Van Minh was sworn in as the new president. Both the North Vietnamese and Vietcong were favorable to Minh, but they would not deal with him until all 1,000 Americans remaining in Vietnam had left. On April 29 US helicopters carried out this emergency evacuation. The following day President Minh announced the unconditional surrender of South Vietnam. After more than three decades of fighting, the loss of 180,000 South Vietnamese troops, an unknown number of Northern and Vietcong forces, and hundreds of thousands of civilians, peace at last came to Vietnam.

AUGUST 8

Charles A. Dana's Birthday

Charles Anderson Dana, one of the most influential newspaper editors in the decades before and after the Civil War, molded public opinion, influenced decisions of government officials, and permanently changed the style of American journalism. Dana, who was to become the first managing editor of an American newspaper, was born in Hinsdale, New Hampshire, on August 8, 1819. When he was nine years old, following his mother's death, he was sent to live with an uncle in Buffalo, New York. He worked from the time he was 12, first on a farm and then as a clerk in his uncle's store, diligently educating himself in his free moments.

His self-education was evidently of high caliber since Harvard accepted him as a regular matriculated student in 1839. Although Dana ranked high in his class during his first term, his eyesight became impaired by the long hours of study, and he left Harvard in 1841. However, 20 years later Harvard gave him an honorary Bachelor of Arts degree as of the class of 1843, the year he would have graduated.

Probably while he was at Harvard, Dana became acquainted with George Ripley, a Unitarian minister and Harvard graduate who preached in Boston from 1826 to 1841. Ripley left Boston in 1841 to start Brook Farm, perhaps the most famous of the numerous experiments in communal living that sprang into existence in the early and middle 19th century.

The concept of Brook Farm — to strive for intellectual freedom and a society of educated, cultivated, and liberal-minded persons in a simple setting away from the competition and distractions of the outside world — appealed greatly to the idealistic Dana, who went to Brook Farm in 1841 and stayed for five years. He and Nathaniel Hawthorne were among the original shareholders of Brook Farm, which comprised 160 acres in West Roxbury, Massachusetts, nine miles from Boston. Dana and Hawthorne served together as the institution's first directors of agriculture, but Hawthorne, unable to write in the idyllic setting, left after six months.

During his years at Brook Farm, Dana worked on the farm, taught German and Greek, sang bass in the choir and wrote for *The Harbinger*, the Brook Farm publication edited by Ripley, and *The Dial*, the literary magazine put out by New England Transcendentalists. After he left Brook Farm, which was soon to fail, Dana wrote for the Boston *Chronotype* in 1846.

Joining the New York *Tribune* in 1847 with a starting pay of $10 weekly, Dana soon rose to be managing editor, second in importance only to the paper's editor and publisher, Horace Greeley. The creation of the post of managing editor was one of Greeley's many contributions to American journalism. Both men had strong personalities, and increasingly they clashed on many points, especially about the Civil War. The friction between the militant Dana and the pacifist Greeley became intolerable and, after 15 years, Dana left the *Tribune* on March 28, 1862.

Secretary of War Edwin Stanton, who had often received Dana's editorial support, immediately appointed Dana as a special investigating agent of the War Department. In that capacity Dana sent Stanton reports from the front — he was present at the campaigns of Vicksburg, Chickamauga, and Chattanooga — gave valuable aid to Generals Ulysses S. Grant and William Tecumseh Sherman, and urged Stanton to name Grant supreme commander of all the armies in the field. Dana served as second assistant secretary of war from 1864 until July 7, 1865, when he resigned from the War Department.

At the close of the war, he edited the Chicago *Republican*. On its failure, he returned to New York in 1868 as editor and part-owner of the New York *Sun*, which he ran with great vigor and independence until his death. Under his leadership, the *Sun* became known as "the newspaperman's newspaper," distinguished by a bright, witty style, fresh reporting techniques, and emphasis on the human-interest story.

However, Dana's erratic editorials showed

that the Brook Farm idealist had become skeptical and cynical. While he could endear himself to newspaper colleagues, he had the reputation of never forgiving a grudge or supposed slight, or of dropping a point. An example was the hotly disputed presidential election of 1876, in which the *Sun* had supported the unsuccessful candidate Samuel Jones Tilden. After the inauguration of Rutherford B. Hayes, the paper persisted in using such references as "His Fraudulency the President."

On October 17, 1897, Dana died at his home on Dosoris Island, Glen Cove, New York, where he had lived with his wife — Eunice McDonald Dana, whom he had married on March 2, 1846 — and their children.

Dana edited one of the most successful anthologies of American verse, *The Household Book of Poetry,* published in 1857. With Ripley he edited the *New American Cyclopaedia* (1858–1863). He also wrote *The Art of Newspaper Making,* published in 1895; *Recollections of the Civil War,* considered by some to be his most valuable book; and *Eastern Journeys.* The last two were published posthumously in 1898.

Feast of St. Dominic

According to the revised Roman Catholic calendar, the feast of St. Dominic, the founder of the Dominicans, or Order of Friars Preachers, which used to be celebrated on August 4, is now commemorated on August 8. It is classed as a memorial. The day is widely observed among Roman Catholics both in the United States and abroad. The former feast date is still marked with great ritual by the Pueblo Indians in the San Domingo Pueblo in New Mexico.

St. Dominic or, in Spanish, Santo Domingo, was born in Calaruega, Castile, in northern Spain, about 1170. It is generally believed that he was a member of the famous and wealthy Guzmán family, his parents having probably been the nobleman Félix de Guzmán and his pious wife, Joanna of Aza. The childhood of Domingo de Guzmán apparently was uneventful; at least very few details about it were recorded. As a young man he studied theology, notably at the University of Palencia. About 1195 he was ordained and served in his native diocese as an Augustinian canon regular at the cathedral chapter of Osma. The gifted young prelate soon became subprior and then prior of the cathedral community.

Prior Dominic most likely remained in Osma until 1203, various unsubstantiated stories of his missions to convert the Moors during this period notwithstanding. In 1203 he traveled with Diego, bishop of Osma, on an embassy for the king of Castile, journeying to the "marches." Of the dozen or so territories then known as marches, it is generally assumed that the Danish march, or Denmark, was their destination. Bishop Diego and Dominic Guzmán then petitioned Pope Innocent III at Rome to release them from their obligations in Osma and permit them to conduct foreign missionary work, possibly in the Dnieper River area of what is now Russia. The pope, deeply concerned about the rapidly spreading Albigensian heresy in Languedoc, southern France, instead recruited the pair as preachers to this troubled area. Bishop Diego became the unofficial leader of a papal mission to the heretics, and Dominic his assistant. A contemporary described Dominic as follows:

Average height, a thin body, a handsome and slightly fresh-colored countenance, hair and beard slightly reddish. . . . From his forehead and . . . lashes a kind of splendor radiated. . . . He remained always smiling and joyful unless he was moved with compassion by some distress of his neighbor. He had long and beautiful hands; a voice that was deep . . . and resounding. . . . His crown of hair was complete, shot through with occasional white hairs.

The mission in southern France was to be the turning point of Dominic Guzmán's life. The Albigensians practiced an extreme form of Manichaeism, believing in the coexistence of two dominating principles — one good, which was of God and equated with light; and one evil, the domain of Satan, or the Evil One, identified with darkness. Holding that spirit, as created by God, was inherently good, the Manichaeans believed that all matter, as the creation of Satan, was essentially evil. Thus material possessions, the eating of meat, marriage, and procreation were regarded as grave sins. The most convinced followed these tenets to their logical conclusion and committed suicide by starvation. The Spanish preachers used astute but basically simple techniques to overcome the movement, which was undermining Christianity and such cornerstones of civil society as the family and the concept of property. Traveling throughout southern France, Guzmán and Diego sought to win converts to the Catholic faith by impressing the heretics not only with high-level intellectual disputation, but also with a poverty, austerity, and mortification of flesh and spirit similar to that practiced by the Albigensians.

Using this approach, Dominic and a small band of followers continued the task of conversion even after Bishop Diego's death in December 1207 and Pope Innocent III's proclamation of full-scale armed warfare against the Albigensians in 1208. A refuge in Prouille, which

Dominic had established in the south of France in 1206 as a place of prayer and sanctification for female converts, served as a base of operations for the dedicated group of preachers.

From this small but intrepid volunteer group, Dominic gained the inspiration to form an order of highly trained priests who would be bound by monastic vows, especially the vow of poverty, but who would also preach in the world. In 1215 he journeyed to Rome to request papal permission to found a new order, which was approved by Pope Innocent and received official approbation in two bulls issued by Innocent's successor, Pope Honorius III, in December 1216. The Order of Friars Preachers, which first established its headquarters in Toulouse, France, embraced several novel features. Although subject to such austerities as lengthy fasting, abstinence from meat, and prolonged silence, the Dominicans were excused from most manual labor; instead they were expected to devote themselves to intellectual studies in preparation for preaching and teaching. The order soon set up houses of study in prominent European centers of learning. Practicing poverty like the newly founded Franciscans, the Dominicans were also mendicants, having no material possessions (except churches and monastic buildings) and no set income.

Dominic spent the last years of his life fostering the Dominican movement throughout western Europe, establishing friaries, notably in France, Spain, and Italy. When he died — exhausted from mortifications and unceasing activity — on August 6, 1221, his order encompassed more than 500 friars and 60 friaries in eight Dominican religious provinces. Pope Gregory IX canonized Dominic in 1234.

Within a few decades the movement had expanded into Russia, Poland, Palestine, and even parts of central Asia. From the mid-14th to the mid-17th century, Dominicans conducted missionary activities in China, India, the Middle East, and Africa. But among the order's most outstanding services was its role in the development of the intellectual life of western Europe in the Late Middle Ages. At the universities, great Dominican scholastics, including Albertus Magnus and Thomas Aquinas, decisively shaped the course of medieval theology and philosophy.

The Dominican order was introduced into the United States shortly after 1800, the first American province being founded in 1805. The order still maintains numerous establishments throughout the country, and many churches have been named for its founder. Dominican priests and nuns, as well as members of the "third order" (which also involves lay members in varying degrees of spiritual activity), carry out the Domini-

can ideal in the fields of education, hospital and missionary work, and religious guidance, and in the pursuit of Christian perfection.

One of the most interesting observances in honor of St. Dominic in the United States takes place on his former feast day, August 4, in the San Domingo Pueblo, located between Santa Fe and Bernalillo, New Mexico. As is true in all of the Rio Grande pueblo settlements, the corn dance, an ancient prayer for rain, is presented on the name day of the saint after whom the Spaniards called the village. The ritual of song and dance follows early morning mass and a solemn procession in which St. Dominic's statue is carried from the church to an outdoor shrine made of skins and cloth. Two groups of dancers, one from each of two kivas (ceremonial chambers), perform alternately in the plaza until sunset. The men, dressed in Hopi ceremonial kirtles with red and green embroidery and fox skins, flourish gourd rattles and sprigs of evergreen, symbolic of everlasting life. The women are clad in black *mantas* (shawls) embroidered in red; scarlet and green sashes; and headdresses of carved wood, which are painted blue and decorated with cloud symbols. The ceaseless stamping and chanting is accompanied by the pantomime and antics of the prank-playing Koshares (clowns representing ancestral spirits).

AUGUST 9

Free-Soil Party Organized

The two-party system in the United States is based on the belief that the problems with which the government deals may be solved by political compromise. For most of the history of the American republic this premise has held true. But in the mid-19th century the national government grappled with the urgent moral issue of slavery, which could not be resolved through the usual method of partisan give-and-take. Political compromise ultimately proved to be impossible. Before the very existence of the federal Union was challenged, however, the course of debate over slavery led to the formation of a significant third party, the Free-Soil party, which first convened on August 9, 1848.

Although abolitionists had denounced slavery prior to the 1840s, the annexation of Texas in 1845 and areas won in 1848 as a result of the US victory in the Mexican War brought a new intensity to their arguments. Opponents of slavery viewed the new territories as regions into which the institution they so detested might be extended. Accordingly, Representative David Wilmot of Pennsylvania proposed in 1846 a prohibition against slavery in any territory that might be taken from Mexico. This Wilmot Proviso failed to win congressional approval, but the expansion of slavery became an increasingly important issue in the years that followed.

The debate over the Wilmot Proviso raised a major constitutional question: did Congress have the power to prevent the extension of slavery to the new territories? Many northerners argued that the national legislature did have the authority to prevent such expansion, and indeed, with the Ordinance of 1787, which banned slavery in the Old Northwest Territory, had already done so. Southerners, on the other hand, denied that Congress possessed such power; they claimed that such interference with slaveholding was a direct violation of property rights guaranteed by the Constitution. And there was yet another viewpoint. A large number of influential westerners supported the doctrine of "popular sovereignty"; according to this theory, the actual settlers of the new territories should be allowed to decide the question of slavery for themselves.

Although the expansion of slavery and the question of Congress's power to prevent its introduction into the territories were the most important issues in the election of 1848, both major political parties tried to avoid taking an absolute stand on these problems. The Democrats chose Senator Lewis Cass, former governor of the Michigan Territory and an advocate of popular sovereignty, as their presidential candidate, while the Whigs selected General Zachary Taylor, the Mexican War "Hero of Buena Vista" to be their standard-bearer. Neither nominee pleased the "Barnburner" Democrats, so called because they were allegedly willing to "burn" down the Democratic "barn" to eliminate the pro-slavery "rats"; or the "Conscience Whigs," who were also strongly opposed to slavery.

Unable to accept either of the candidates offered by the two major parties, the Barnburner Democrats, the Conscience Whigs, and other dissidents determined to form a third party. On August 9, 1848, 465 representatives from 18 states met at Buffalo, New York, to organize the Free-Soil party. The delegates came from varied backgrounds, but, for one reason or another, all opposed the extension of slavery into the territories that the United States had acquired from Mexico.

The Free-Soil party chose Martin Van Buren, the former President of the United States and a Barnburner Democrat, as its presidential nominee, and selected Charles Francis Adams, the son of President John Quincy Adams and a Conscience Whig, as its vice presidential candidate. In their platform, the Buffalo delegates attacked the expansion of slavery into the newly acquired territories, favored the habitation of these areas by bona fide white settlers, and approved certain river and harbor improvements. They summed up the goals of their new party with their slogan Free Soil, Free Speech, Free Labor, and Free Men.

In the November election Van Buren and Adams polled only 291,263 popular votes and failed to carry a single state. But the young party had an important effect on the outcome of the presidential contest. The Free-Soilers drew away so many ballots from the regular Democrats in New York that Cass failed to carry that key state. The lack of unity among Democrats lost him the election.

More significant than the impact of the Free-Soilers on the 1848 election was the lasting effect the party exerted on national politics. Though the party never again garnered as many votes as it did in 1848, when its presidential ticket won slightly over 10 percent of the ballots and elected nine representatives to Congress, the very existence of the Free-Soil party forcefully demonstrated the strength and intensity of the slavery issue, and in the years between 1848 and 1854 it served as an important channel for antislavery sentiment.

The Free-Soil party lasted only six years. In 1852 its presidential and vice presidential nominees, John P. Hale of New Hampshire and George W. Julian of Indiana, won only about five percent of the popular vote. The party never participated in another national contest, for in 1854 its membership found another political home in the newly created Republican party.

Feast of St. Matthias

The Feast of St. Matthias, who was chosen by lot to replace Judas Iscariot as one of the 12 Apostles of Jesus Christ after Judas had betrayed his master, is marked on August 9 by Eastern Orthodox and Eastern Catholic churches. It was commemorated by Roman Catholics on February 24 until the revision of the Roman calendar. The celebration was then moved to May 14 to avoid having it fall in Lent and to place it in Eastertide, close to Ascension Day. The original date is still kept by the Protestant Episcopal and Lutheran churches (see February 24).

Webster-Ashburton Treaty Signed

For more than half a century, the location of the northeastern border between the United States and Canada was disputed. The Treaty of Paris of 1783 specified that the boundary separating the new American nation from its British neighbor to the north extended from the north-west angle of Nova Scotia, viz. — that angle which is formed by a line drawn due north from the source of the St. Croix river to the highlands, along the said highlands which divide those rivers that empty themselves into the St. Lawrence, from those which fall into the Atlantic ocean to the north westernmost head of the Connecticut river — thence down along the middle of that river to the 45th degree of north latitude; from thence in a line due west on that latitude until it strikes the river Iroquois or Cataraqui.

But unfortunately the wording of the 1783 settlement was open to several interpretations, and not until the signing of the Webster-Ashburton Treaty on August 9, 1842, was the issue finally resolved.

Prior to the 1842 treaty, England and the United States made several unsuccessful attempts to settle the border controversy. In 1798 a commission composed of representatives from both nations was able to reach agreement concerning which of several rivers in the disputed area was actually the St. Croix river specified in the 1783 treaty. But efforts in 1803 and 1807 failed to produce a settlement of where the line from the St. Croix reached the highlands. Between 1816 and 1822 the United States and England again tried to resolve this difficulty, but without success. In 1827 the king of the Netherlands agreed to arbitrate the matter. Four years later the king found the 1783 treaty to be "inexplicable and impracticable" and suggested a completely arbitrary division of the disputed territory. The United States refused to accept this compromise.

In the winter of 1838–1839 the boundary dispute threatened to become the cause of armed conflict. Beginning in 1820 the legislatures of Maine and Massachusetts had made extensive grants of land in the Aroostook Valley to US citizens. The British, however, also claimed the rich area, and in 1838 Canadian lumberjacks started cutting timber there. To protect the interests of American settlers, the Maine legislature in January 1839 named Rufus McIntire a land agent and instructed him to expel the Canadian loggers from the valley. On February 12, 1839, the Canadians arrested McIntire. This action and the Canadians' determination to remain in the area resulted in the calling up of militias in both Maine and New Brunswick. The Nova Scotia legislature and the US Congress voted for substantial war appropriations. As preparations for the so-called Aroostook War continued, President Martin Van Buren sent General Winfield Scott to Maine. In March 1839 Scott was able to persuade the governor of Maine and the lieutenant governor of New Brunswick to agree to a truce. The Aroostook War thus ended

without bloodshed, but the boundary issue remained unresolved.

Although the need to establish the northeastern boundary between Canada and the United States became increasingly urgent during the 1830s, several incidents not directly related to the disputed area complicated negotiations between Great Britain and the United States. After the failure of an insurrection in Canada in 1837, rebel leader William Lyon Mackenzie and some of his followers took refuge on Navy Island, which is located on the Canadian side of the Niagara River. The assistance of New Yorkers hostile to the British enabled the Mackenzie group to launch a number of attacks against the Canadian frontier in the fall of 1837, and to prevent further depredations a party of Canadian militia on December 29, 1837, crossed to the American side of the river. They destroyed the steamboat *Caroline*, which had been used to carry supplies and arms to the rebels, and killed Amos Durfee, a US citizen.

Tensions between the United States and Britain over the *Caroline* and several minor incidents began to abate in 1839, but hostilities soon flared again. In November 1840 Alexander McLeod, a Canadian deputy sheriff, boasted in a New York tavern that he had participated in the *Caroline* affair and had personally killed Durfee. New York authorities promptly charged McLeod with murder. On December 13, 1840, the British, claiming that McLeod had acted under military orders, protested his arrest. This admission that the *Caroline* action had received official sanction served only to further antagonize the already excited residents of northern New York, for federal authorities, claiming to have no jurisdiction in the McLeod case, announced they could not comply with Britain's demand for his release. McLeod accordingly was brought to trial. Many observers believed that conviction of the Canadian would have precipitated a serious international crisis. This most dire possibility was averted when a jury found McLeod innocent of Durfee's murder on October 12, 1841. But despite the fortunate outcome of the trial, the McLeod case placed a great strain on Anglo-American ties.

Relations between Britain and the United States further deteriorated late in 1841. Britain had outlawed its slave trade in 1807 and abolished slavery throughout the Empire in 1834, but British efforts to end slaving were seriously hampered because the US ban against the trade was enforced laxly. For decades both nations had harbored ill-feelings regarding slave-trade activities in particular and naval rights in general, and the *Creole* incident intensified these antagonisms. On October 27, 1841, the American brig *Creole* set sail with a cargo of slaves from Hampton Roads, Virginia, on a legal coastal voyage to New Orleans. The slaves revolted, gained control of the vessel, and ordered it to put in at the British port of Nassau in the Bahama Islands. British authorities there arrested and charged several of the slaves with mutiny and murder, but then freed most of them. US Secretary of State Daniel Webster immediately protested the latter action. He asked the return of the "mutineers and murderers and the recognized property" of citizens of the United States, but the British took no action.

Against this background of mutual provocations and minor incidents, Anglo-American relations suddenly took a sharp turn for the better in 1842. In September 1841 Sir Robert Peel had replaced Lord Melbourne as Britain's prime minister, and the new goverment named Lord Aberdeen to head the foreign office. Aberdeen strongly desired to settle the longstanding grievances between England and the United States — most notably the matter of the northeastern boundary — and in the spring of 1842 he sent a special minister, Alexander Baring, the first Baron Ashburton, to Washington to accomplish this end.

Lord Ashburton, the head of the House of Baring, London's great banking institution, and Daniel Webster began negotiations on June 13, 1842. Like the king of the Netherlands before them, Ashburton and Webster concluded that the 1783 Treaty of Paris was too vague to permit a boundary settlement, so they put aside that document and worked out an arbitrary division of the disputed lands. The treaty, which Ashburton and Webster signed on August 9, 1842, and which subsequently received the approval of their respective governments, ended the decades-long controversy over the northeastern boundary and settled a number of other issues. In a supplementary exchange of notes Ashburton unofficially apologized for the *Caroline* and McLeod cases, thereby disposing of these matters.

According to the Webster-Ashburton Treaty of August 9, the British received 5,000 square miles lying north of the Aroostook Valley in what is now New Brunswick — the region needed for the military road connecting Halifax and Quebec. In return the United States gained about 7,000 square miles of the 12,000 in question; Maine retained the Aroostook Valley, and both Maine and Massachusetts were indemnified $150,000 by the United States for abandoning their claims to the area that had been awarded to New Brunswick. In addition, the northern boundary of Vermont and eastern New York State was set at about a half mile north of the 45th Parallel. This gave the United States control of a military outpost accidentally built on

Canadian soil, near the head of Lake Champlain in what is now New York State. The US-Canadian border then followed a previously agreed-upon course through the Great Lakes and their connecting waterways to Lake Superior. A compromise between Webster and Ashburton fixed the border west from there to Lake of the Woods at the present boundary line — giving the United States the 6,500 square miles of northeastern Minnesota that was later found to be the site of the rich Mesabi iron ore deposit. The treaty also established mutual extradition procedures for seven nonpolitical crimes, authorized joint squadrons to suppress slaving along the African coast, and gave the United States the right to navigate the St. John River, which empties into the Bay of Fundy at St. John, New Brunswick.

AUGUST 10

Herbert Hoover's Birthday

Herbert Clark Hoover, a great humanitarian and the nation's 31st President, was born on August 10, 1874, in West Branch, Iowa — which had been founded as a Quaker settlement by his ancestors in 1853. His father, Jesse Clark Hoover, a blacksmith and farm equipment dealer, was descended from Quakers who had settled in Pennsylvania in 1738. The forebears of Hoover's mother — Huldah Randall Minthorn Hoover — were also Quakers, having migrated to New England in 1630.

Herbert Hoover was only six when his father died of typhoid fever. His mother supported three children by sewing. In 1884 she died of pneumonia, and the children were cared for by relatives. Young Hoover went to live in Oregon with an uncle.

After attending a small Quaker academy in Newberg, Oregon, Hoover decided, at 17, to become an engineer. He was accepted in 1891 into the first class at Stanford University. Summers, he worked for the Arkansas and US geological surveys. After specializing in mining engineering and geology, he was graduated from Stanford in 1895.

At that time, the country was suffering an economic depression, and Hoover found that his degree was worth little in the job market. After some difficulty, however, he managed to work as a miner — until the mine went bankrupt a year later. Then, in 1896, he sought work from the mining engineer and entrepreneur Louis Janin. Janin hired Hoover as an office boy but soon sent him to assist in an extensive northern California mining project. The next year Hoover received a job, on Janin's recommendation, as a consulting engineer to develop newly discovered Australian gold deposits for the British mining firm of Bewick, Moreing and Company.

From that time Hoover's fortunes improved. At 24 he was earning the substantial sum of $7,500 per year. His immediate success — he advised that Bewick, Moreing purchase a controlling interest in what became the extremely lucrative Sons of Gwalia gold mine — laid the foundations for what was to become a peerless reputation as a mining consultant. Hoover remained in Australia for two years, until he accepted the challenge of organizing mining and transportation facilities for the Chinese government's Imperial Bureau of Mines. On his way to China, where he would introduce modern mining methods into a creakingly outmoded industry, Hoover detoured to California, where he married his Stanford sweetheart, Lou Henry, on February 10, 1899.

The Boxer Rebellion, an effort to expel colonial powers from China, flared up in 1900, just as the Hoovers arrived. Many were felled during the upheaval, and the rebellion was subdued only by the arrival of an international army representing countries with interests in China. Foreshadowing the kind of initiative that was to make him famous, Hoover took charge of the safety of Westerners trapped by the uprising and managed to obtain food for them.

After the rebellion, China closed its Bureau of Mines, and Hoover in 1901 returned to private industry, becoming a junior partner in Bewick, Moreing. In association with that firm and subsequently he traveled around the world many times in the capacity of mining consultant. It was during Hoover's association with Bewick, Moreing — and in the absence of his senior partners — that a million dollars was embezzled by the company's chief accountant. Though not required to do so by law, Hoover, in a move that became legendary, pledged the company to make good the loss. He took on much of the loss himself, almost going bankrupt in the process.

In 1908 Hoover left Bewick, Moreing to found his own firm. Having recouped his earlier losses, he again had assets of $1 million. By the time he reached 40, his fortune had quadrupled. In 1909 Hoover published the *Principles of Mining*. He and his wife then translated a 16th century tract on mining, Georgius Agricola's *De Re Metallica*, which had previously defied Latin scholars because of its technical nature.

The outbreak of World War I found the Hoovers in England. It also found 120,000 Americans stranded abroad, with their credit cut off. Overnight, Hoover founded an organization to help these unfortunate travelers get home. In the course of the venture, Hoover's group loaned $1.5 million, of which they lost only $300.

For his relief efforts Hoover received public acclaim and was appointed head of the Commission for Relief in Belgium. During four war-torn years this commission moved 5 million tons of food through Allied and German blockades to feed starving millions in Belgium and northern France.

In April 1917 the United States entered the war, and President Woodrow Wilson called Hoover back to the United States to head the US Food Administration. He was given broad powers to regulate food production, foreign food purchases, and food distribution, which he managed without recourse to rationing. Hoover's persuasive powers, abetted by price incentives, resulted in the tripling of American farm production. Hoover authorized the purchase of Cuba's entire annual sugar crop. In order to feed the fighting men, Americans were urged to "hooverize," that is, to consume less food.

Hostilities ceased on November 11, 1918. With the armistice in effect, Hoover was called upon by the Allied governments, Britain, France, the United States, and Italy, to direct relief efforts throughout 30 European countries. Hoover directed the distribution of approximately $3.5 billion to feed and clothe Europeans left without resources by the war. Under this effort, more than 23 million tons of food, clothing, and medicine were made available.

Peace treaties signed by the separate countries during 1919 brought both the war and Hoover's official work to an end. However, with American support he continued his relief efforts, establishing the American Relief Administration and persuading Congress to appropriate $100 million for relief of children. Hoover privately raised another $200 million. He concentrated his efforts in Poland and Rumania, where typhus raged. Then in 1921 famine struck Russia, threatening the lives of 20 million persons, mostly children. The strains between Washington and the new revolutionary government in Russia notwithstanding, Hoover, to whom lives were more important than politics, raised $75 million in relief money. This massive effort continued from 1921 to 1923 and was conducted under the authority of the American Relief Administration.

Popular because of his humanitarian efforts, Hoover was mentioned by both American political parties as a potential presidential candidate. He himself went to the trouble of declaring that he was a Republican, also announcing that he would not be a candidate. Party bosses picked a dark horse candidate, Warren G. Harding.

When elected, Harding appointed Hoover secretary of commerce. It was perhaps Harding's best appointment. Hoover's performance in the cabinet was characterized by high intelligence, administrative ability, a regard for the public trust, and extreme diligence. He remained at his post throughout the administrations of Harding and Calvin Coolidge. As secretary of commerce, Hoover established housing and highway safety programs, began government regulation of the infant radio and aviation industries, and persuaded manufacturers to establish standardization codes for appliance parts. He also offered a program to reorganize the federal government. Harding submitted the proposal to the Congress, but it was turned down. In 1927 Hoover oversaw massive relief efforts for the Mississippi basin area, which had been devastated by floods.

When Coolidge declined to run for the presidency in 1928, Hoover was the obvious choice. He was nominated and entered the campaign against Al Smith, the Democratic nominee. With prosperity apparently available to all Americans after eight prosperous years of Republican administration, it is doubtful that any Democrat could have won. One of the campaign's few real issues, apart from prosperity, was Prohibition. Al Smith, an anti-Prohibitionist and a Catholic from New York City, who supported modification of the Prohibition amendment, was attacked in a scurrilous whispering campaign. To old-line Protestants he represented the poor immigrants crowded together in the nation's cities as a result of the floodtide of immigration of the late 19th and early 20th century. Hoover remained personally aloof from the smears on Smith's religion and took a somewhat ambiguous stand for Prohibition. Though conceding abuses, Hoover proclaimed Prohibition "a great social and economic experiment, noble in motive and far-reaching in purpose." He was elected by a landslide.

The presidency, however, soon turned into a nightmare for Hoover. Only seven months after he entered the White House, the stock market trembled, rallied, and then crashed (see October 29). With the prices of watered or worthless stocks swollen far beyond their real worth by rampant speculation, the confidence upon which speculation had been built suddenly vanished. With no customers for stocks, prices tumbled and panic gripped the financial community. Hoover himself had been worried about the runaway economy and had protested the policy of easy money to the Federal Reserve.

Now, although somewhat alarmed himself, Hoover tried to restore confidence among investors. When the expected upswing in the market never came, however, his optimism rang hollow. An international monetary crisis followed, and banks began to call in loans to repay their foreign debts. Americans, meanwhile, commenced withdrawing their savings. Fear spread across the country, and businesses finally refused to honor their pledges to Hoover on holding wage levels. Wages tumbled. Consumers stopped buying. Factories closed, and unemployment settled in like a dismal nightmare.

During the 1920s, businessmen had been held in awe as the architects of the nation's prosperity. Americans had allowed themselves to be caught up in the spirit of speculation. Many had bought stocks, and many had used credit for purchases of appliances or cars. When the depression came and people were caught short, the financiers were despised as false prophets; and much of the ill-will rubbed off on Hoover and the Republican party, which represented them.

Yet Hoover took bold, even unprecedented action. He prodded businessmen and bankers into promising that they would not retrench wages and investments drastically. He founded the Emergency Relief Organization, and a huge federal loan agency, the Reconstruction Finance Corporation. The latter agency secured loans for businesses, banks, farmers, and even states. However, Hoover insisted that direct relief was not a proper function of the national government. In this, he was relying on the American tradition of voluntarism. So convinced was he of the efficacy of community self-help that he refused to believe advisers who reported widespread hunger throughout the country. Voluntarism failed badly: community and state treasuries were quickly exhausted, businessmen looked after themselves and cut wages, banks called in loans. And everyone blamed Hoover, who, to the end of his term, doggedly vetoed all Democratic social legislation.

Hoover had never been a good politician, and now his impassive countenance led those who were desperate to believe that he did not care about them. Many became furious with the national leadership. There was no lack of food, yet people went hungry. There was coal to be mined, yet people froze. Through no fault of their own, farmers had their mortgages foreclosed. Many were on the verge of taking up firearms to keep their property. When 17,000 unemployed veterans on a Bonus March camped on the Capitol grounds to dramatize their plight, Hoover ordered them evicted. Under the direction of Douglas MacArthur, the veterans were driven out with sabers, drawn bayonets, and tanks.

Renominated at the Republican National Convention in 1932, Hoover defended his policies during the campaign. In a charge that history renders ironic, his Democratic opponent, Franklin D. Roosevelt, accused the Republicans of being spendthrifts. Roosevelt pledged to enact experimental social legislation while spending less than Hoover had. However, the Great Depression was not the main topic of election discussion. Prohibition held the attention of the candidates while nearly 12 million men and women were jobless.

Roosevelt won the election overwhelmingly. A tired and discouraged Hoover had to wait out the intervening months until March as a lame-duck President. During this critical time a final wave of bank liquidations added to the grimness of the scene.

For three years Hoover led a quiet life of fishing and writing but then turned to social criticism, writing and speaking out against New Deal legislation. He pointed out that unemployment was as high as 10 million until the eve of World War II. Until December 7, 1941, when the Japanese attacked Pearl Harbor, Hoover spoke against US involvement in another war. After the attack he offered to help, but was never called upon by Roosevelt.

In May 1945 President Harry S. Truman asked Hoover to make a survey of world food needs. The next year, at the request of President Truman he traveled throughout Europe and Asia, surveying the extent of famine and world food needs. On his return he urged massive relief efforts to feed the starving millions around the world. Again he set out, at 73, to South America. And again he called upon the American conscience to help feed those in need.

Under President Truman and again under President Dwight D. Eisenhower, he was called upon to head the Commission on Organization of the Executive Branch of the Government — the so-called Hoover Commission — to find ways of making the federal government more efficient. It was estimated that the reforms recommended by the two commissions, many of which were adopted, could have saved the government as much as $10 billion a year.

Hoover's years after World War II were devoted to a full schedule of writing, speaking, and performing organizational work for various enterprises. (Mrs. Hoover had died during the war, in January 1944.) He spent many hours working with the Boys Clubs of America and delighted in answering the thousands of letters he received from youngsters. He wrote more than 30 books, including his three-volume memoirs; *The Ordeal of Woodrow Wilson*; the four-volume *An American Epic*, about American relief efforts during and since World Wars I and II; and many "little books," as Hoover called them. These included *On Growing Up* (1962), drawn from his voluminous correspondence with children. At his alma mater, Stanford, Hoover founded the Food Research Institute, the old Student Union, the Graduate School of Business, and the Hoover Institution on War, Revolution and Peace. He was an absolutely tireless worker, and it was to this that he attributed his longevity.

At the Republican National Convention in 1960, the aged Hoover gave a poignant farewell to the GOP. To his remark that this was his last public appearance, the assembled throng shouted, "No, no, no!" As it turned out, Hoover's actual last public appearance was at a New York luncheon for astronaut L. Gordon Cooper Jr. on May 22, 1963. Death came to the former President on October 20, 1964.

The tiny white cottage where Hoover was born in West Branch, Iowa, has been preserved as a national historic landmark. A blacksmith shop, like the one worked by Hoover's father, and a presidential library may also be visited at this site. Nearby, Hoover and his wife are buried on a small knoll overlooking his birth site.

Hoover is also remembered in Palo Alto, California, where the 285-foot Hoover Tower stands over Stanford University's main library. Many of Hoover's papers, assembled in the years since World War I, may be studied there. His name also is perpetuated by Hoover Dam in Boulder, Colorado, which forms Lake Mead, the world's largest artificial lake. During the Great Depression the dam was temporarily renamed Boulder Dam by the Democrats, but it was renamed Hoover Dam by a nonpartisan vote in 1947.

Missouri Admitted to the Union

On August 10, 1821, President James Monroe proclaimed the admission of Missouri to the federal Union. Monroe's action brought an end to the controversy that had erupted shortly after Congress first considered Missouri's application for statehood in 1818. By the so-called Missouri Compromise, Missouri gained statehood with a constitution containing no restrictions against slavery, Maine entered the Union as a free state, and slavery was prohibited in the area of the Louisiana Purchase north of latitude 36°30'. But the compromise was only a temporary solution to the serious problems that stemmed from the existence of slavery in the United States. Former Presidents Thomas Jefferson and John Adams respectively referred to the Missouri controversy as "a fire bell in the night" and "a title-page to a great tragic volume," and their fears were justified, for the same issues that divided the United States in 1820 plunged the nation into the Civil War in 1860.

Missouri, the second state to be created from the vast area of the Louisiana Purchase (see December 20), had passed from French to Spanish control and back again to the French before coming under the jurisdiction of the United States in 1803. During their periods of rule both the French and Spanish had permitted slavery throughout the Louisiana Purchase region, and thus well before 1803 the practice was firmly implanted in Missouri. When the United States purchased Louisiana, it promised by the treaty of cession to protect the liberty, property, and religion of the inhabitants of the trans-Mississippi Purchase area. Most observers assumed that slaves were included in this guarantee of property, but Congress's failure specifically to provide for slavery in its first act pertaining to Louisiana displeased Missourians, and some feared that such silence might "create the presumption of a disposition in Congress to abolish at a future day slavery altogether in the district."

When lower Louisiana — which had been known as the Territory of Orleans — was admitted to the Union in 1812 as a slave state named Louisiana, the huge upper Louisiana region was renamed Missouri Territory. At that time, Representative Abner Lacock of Pennsylvania moved to prohibit the admission of slaves into Missouri Territory. But the United States was on the brink of war with England in 1812, and congressional fears that a restriction on slavery in Missouri might create great dissension throughout the South at a time of crisis caused Lacock's motion to be overwhelmingly defeated. However, an elective legislature for the Missouri Territory was authorized in 1812 and again in 1816, after population in the area had begun to swell with a heavy influx of pioneers in 1815.

In 1817 residents of Missouri began to petition Congress for permission to frame a constitution as a preliminary to statehood. Congress considered the request in 1818 but failed to act upon the enabling legislation reported by a House committee. The inhabitants of Missouri continued to press the issue; in November 1818 they again memorialized Congress for permission to form a state government, and in December 1818 Speaker Henry Clay presented their request to the House of Representatives.

A large number of slaveholding settlers from Virginia, North Carolina, Kentucky, and Tennessee had migrated to the Missouri region after 1803, and there was no doubt that the majority of its residents favored the continuation of slavery. However, Missouri's admission as a slave state was not to be easily accomplished. When the House took up the question of Missouri on February 13, 1819, Representative James Tallmadge Jr. of New York proposed the following amendment to the admission bill:

That the further introduction of slavery or involuntary servitude be prohibited, except for the punishment of crimes, whereof the party shall be duly convicted; and that all children of slaves, born within the said state, after the admission thereof into the Union, shall be free, but may be held to service until the age of twenty-five years.

For several days, the representatives debated the Tallmadge amendment. The antislavery forces argued that any decision made on Missouri would affect not only that state but the entire region west of the Mississippi. Denouncing slavery, they claimed that Congress had the power to require an amendment against slavery in the constitution of any new state admitted to the Union. On the other side, the proponents of slavery, including Henry Clay, countered that "the cause of humanity" necessitated allowing slavery into the West, contending that such expansion would provide more adequate food supplies and living conditions for slaves than were to be had in the South. They also denied that Congress had the right to require prohibitions against slavery in the constitutions of any new states, and they argued that the 1803 cession treaty between the United States and France specifically prevented congressional interference with slavery in any state created from the Louisiana Purchase.

Voting on the Tallmadge amendment, the House approved the measure by February 17, 1819, and then sent it to the Senate, where it faced stronger opposition. In the spring of 1819, 10 slave and 11 free states were represented in the Senate. But the residents of Illinois, which was counted on the side of the predominantly antislavery North, strongly sympathized in 1819 with the South, and both its senators were slaveholders. They opposed the Tallmadge amendment, and their ballots and those of a handful of other northern senators helped the South defeat the antislavery measure in the Senate. On March 2, 1819, the Senate passed the Missouri statehood bill without the defeated Tallmadge amendment; but the following day the House refused to admit Missouri as a slave state, and the 15th Congress adjourned on March 3, 1819, leaving the future status of Missouri unresolved.

By the fall of 1819 admission of Missouri had become a national issue. The debate, no longer confined to Congress or the disputed area, stirred wide interest, and mass protest meetings were held in many northern communities. The question was further complicated because Massachusetts had agreed, in June 1819, to allow its northern section to become the independent state of Maine. Maine applied for statehood shortly after Congress convened in December 1819, and since Maine was to be an additional free state, the North greeted its request with enthusiasm. Moreover, the North, with its larger population, controlled the House, so that it passed the Maine statehood bill by a substantial margin on January 3, 1820.

However, Maine's application for admission to the Union faced strong opposition in the Senate. On December 14, 1819, Alabama had gained statehood. The addition of Alabama made the number of slave states in the Union equal to the number of free states. Since each state sent two representatives to the Senate, and the Illinois senators consistently voted with the South, that region could count on a clear Senate majority of ballots in 1820. And the South had no intention of giving up its control of the Senate by allowing the admission of another free state to disrupt the sectional balance. As early as December 30, 1819, Henry Clay presented an ultimatum to the free states: "If you refuse to admit Missouri also free of condition, we see no reason why you shall take to yourselves privileges which you deny to her — and until you grant them also to her, we will not admit [Maine]."

Maine's application for admission to the Union was thus inextricably tied to the fate of Missouri. On January 3, 1820, the House approved the aforementioned bill admitting only Maine to statehood. But the following month, when the Senate considered the Maine statehood bill, that body added an amendment also allowing Missouri to prepare for statehood by forming a state constitution — one that would have no restrictions against slavery. In addition the Senate also attached to the bill the amendment suggested by Senator Jesse B. Thomas of Illinois:

That, in all that territory ceded by France to the United States, under the name of Louisiana, which lies north of thirty-six degrees and thirty minutes north latitude, excepting only such part thereof as is included within the limits of the State contemplated by this act, slavery and involuntary servitude, otherwise than in the punishment of crimes whereof the party shall have been duly convicted, shall be and is hereby forever prohibited: Provided, always, That any person escaping into the same, from whom labor or service is lawfully claimed in any State or Territory of the United States, such fugitive may be lawfully reclaimed and conveyed to the person claiming his or her labor or service as aforesaid.

In short, the Senate version of the Maine bill was a plan to resolve the 1820 controversy by permitting Missouri to form a constitution with no restriction against slavery, admitting Maine as a free state, allowing slavery to exist in the unsettled regions that today are part of Arkansas and Oklahoma, and outlawing slavery in the remainder of the Louisiana Purchase north of latitude 36°30', which was the southern boundary of Missouri.

The southern majority in the Senate passed the bill joining Missouri and Maine statehood and including the Thomas amendment. But the North was not satisfied with the compromise and used its majority in the House to defeat the Senate compromise plan late in February 1820.

The House rejection of the Senate compromise bill and its subsequent passage on March 1, 1820, of a Missouri statehood bill with an amendment restricting slavery created a stalemate: the Senate would not consider any alternative to its compromise plan, and the House refused to approve the admission of Missouri as a slave state. To attempt to break this deadlock, the Senate requested that a conference committee be set up with the House. The report of the joint committee was made public on March 2, 1820. It recommended (1) withdrawal of the Senate's amendments to the Maine statehood bill that allowed Missouri to form a state government with slavery and that restricted slavery in the Louisiana Purchase; (2) removal of the clause restricting slavery in the Missouri statehood bill passed by the House on March 1, 1820; and (3) addition to the Missouri admission bill of a provision prohibiting slavery in all areas of the Louisiana Purchase north of latitude 36°30', except in the new state of Missouri.

Since northern representatives opposed the admission of Missouri as a slave state and many southern representatives were against a restriction on the expansion of slavery, the House would have defeated the compromise resolutions of the joint congressional committee if they had been voted on as a single bill. For this reason, Henry Clay used his influence to see that each of the committee proposals was voted on separately. Thus Clay was able to gain slim majority votes in the House for each of the recommendations. The Senate also went along with the committee proposals, and on March 3, 1820, a bill was passed admitting Maine to the Union as a free state (effective March 15). On March 6 Missouri gained the right to form a constitution and form a state government with no restrictions on slavery, and on the same day a bill was passed banning slavery from the remainder of the Louisiana Purchase north of latitude 36°30'.

The Missouri Compromise of 1820, as the measures are collectively known, ended the crisis that erupted over the expansion of slavery into new states to be created from the Louisiana Purchase territory and suspended threats of secession, which had been common during the controversy. It did not, however, immediately bring Missouri into the Union as a state. Its constitution had to first gain the approval of both the House and Senate.

In the months following March 1820, a number of northern newspapers and philanthropists, many of whom were Federalists who opposed southern Democratic control of the national government as well as slavery, revived the controversy over Missouri by urging Congress to refuse to admit Missouri to statehood unless its constitution prohibited slavery. In the meantime, Missourians framed a constitution not only permitting slavery but also forbidding free blacks and mulattoes from entering the state and making it illegal for the legislature to free slaves without their owners' consent. These two latter portions of the Missouri constitution served as the basis for the dispute over Missouri that continued into 1821.

On December 12, 1820, the Senate approved a Missouri statehood bill saying nothing specific against the two controversial clauses of its constitution but including the ambiguous proviso that

nothing herein contained shall be so construed as to give the assent of Congress to any provision in the constitution of Missouri, if any such there be, which contravenes that clause in the Constitution of the United States which declares that "the citizens of each State shall be entitled to all privileges and immunities of citizens in the several States."

This so-called Pontius Pilate proviso did not satisfy those who opposed Missouri's gaining statehood with no restrictions against slavery and who were particularly determined to fight against the clauses in the Missouri constitution barring free blacks from the state and impeding the liberation of slaves. Their strength, of course, lay in the House of Representatives, where the North enjoyed a clear majority. On December 13, 1820, the question of Missouri statehood came to a House vote, and on that day it was defeated by the margin of 93 to 79.

Throughout January and February 1821 the Missouri controversy, or the "misery debate," as it was also known, dragged on. During this time a number of compromise plans were put forth, but both sides adamantly refused to yield any ground. The situation was potentially explosive. Southerners felt the North had betrayed the spirit of compromise of 1820 by refusing to admit Missouri to statehood, and in the early months of 1821, some threatened to secede from the Union.

The crisis of 1821, like that of the preceding year, called forth the exceptional talents of Henry Clay. On February 22, 1821, Clay proposed that a joint congressional committee meet to attempt to resolve the Missouri dispute before the 16th Congress adjourned. The entire House was to vote to select the 23 men who would be their representatives to the committee. But before the balloting began, Clay circulated a list of influential southerners and moderate northerners who would be most likely to agree to a compromise, and the House membership chose many of these individuals.

When the joint committee, composed of the 23 representatives of the House and seven members of the Senate, convened, Clay proposed

that Missouri shall be admitted into this union on an equal footing with the original States in all respects whatever, upon the fundamental condition, that the fourth clause of the twenty-sixth section of the third article of the constitution submitted on the part of said State to Congress shall never be construed to authorize the passage of any law . . . by

which any citizen of . . . the States in this Union shall be excluded from the enjoyment of any of the privileges and immunities to which such citizen is entitled under the Constitution of the United States: Provided, That the Legislature of the said State, by a solemn public act, shall declare the assent of the said State to the said fundamental condition and shall transmit to the President of the United States, on or before the fourth Monday in November next, an authentic copy of the said act; upon the receipt whereof the President, by proclamation, shall announce the fact: whereupon, and without any further proceeding on the part of Congress the admission of the said State into this Union shall be considered as complete.

As he had anticipated, Clay was able to influence most of the committee members, and he thereby gained approval of his resolution. On February 26, 1821, he reported his compromise plan to the House, which passed the resolution on that same day. The Senate rapidly followed suit, and the agreement became official on March 2.

Clay's so-called Second Missouri Compromise did not automatically guarantee Missouri statehood. His resolution made the admission of Missouri conditional upon its legislature's promising never to pass laws that would discriminate against citizens (technically including free blacks and mulattoes) of another state. And even after Clay's bill gained the approval of Congress, some northerners hoped that the Missouri legislature would not make such a pledge. They were disappointed in their hopes, however. In June 1821 the Missouri lawmakers made the necessary promise — albeit phrased in defiant and sarcastic language — and on August 10, 1821, President Monroe proclaimed the admission of Missouri as the 24th state of the Union.

So ended the Missouri statehood controversy. However, the issues raised during the uproar would reappear explosively — in the heated debate over the admission of California in 1850, in the bloodshed preceding the admission of Kansas in 1861, and, ultimately, in the Civil War.

AUGUST 11

Feast of St. Clare of Assisi

St. Clare, the first and most famous member of a Franciscan order, was received into the austere religious life by Francis of Assisi himself (see October 4), and under his leadership became the founder of what became known as the Second Order of St. Francis. (There are numerous orders of women Franciscans; all belong to the Second Order of St. Francis.) The feast day of St. Clare, which for centuries was observed by Roman Catholics and also some Episcopalians on August 12, has been moved to August 11, the date of her death in 1253 in the revised Roman Catholic calendar and some other calendars.

A descendant of a noble family of Assisi, Clare heard Francis preaching and felt deeply drawn to his rule of poverty and penance. Since her wealthy family would have been unlikely to approve of her wish to take up this harsh life, she did not ask permission. She was about 18 years old when, on the evening of Palm Sunday in the year 1212, she left home, went to Francis, and declared her intention of dedicating her life to God in the Franciscan way. Francis, who had not started out with a plan to form a religious order, certainly had not anticipated women joining, but he knew Clare was dedicated. He accepted her as a Franciscan, and she exchanged her costly clothing for the coarse tunic worn by the other Franciscans. Francis put her into the care of Benedictine nuns until definite plans could be made, and 16 days later she was joined by her sister Agnes.

Soon the women were established in a little convent near the church of San Damiano in Assisi, where they were later joined by other women, often wealthy and of noble family, who were attracted to the hard life Clare had chosen. Clare's widowed mother and sister Beatrice were among these new Poor Ladies, as they were first called. The members of the religious order started by Clare and Francis are best known today as Poor Clares.

When a group of Benedictine nuns at Monticelli asked to become Poor Clares, Francis sent Clare's sister Agnes to be the abbess at that convent. Clare herself was never to leave San Damiano, of which Francis had appointed her abbess in 1215; yet the ranks of Poor Clares grew not only in Italy but in other countries as well. Clare, who personally practiced great austerities, wrote to one of her Poor Clares in Prague, Czechoslovakia, cautioning her against extremes in austerity, "for our bodies are not made of brass."

Clare outlived Francis by 27 years (he died in 1226 and was canonized in 1228). During most of those years she was ill and often confined to bed. Yet throughout this period she fought for the Primitive Rule, which incorporated the perfect poverty and great austerity that Francis had preached. Although Pope Innocent III in about 1215 granted Clare the "privilege" of taking the vow of poverty, most church leaders felt that absolute poverty was impractical, and subsequent popes insisted on endowing the Poor Clares with the buildings they lived in and providing concessions that made poverty a qualified rather than an absolute state. Clare objected to this as a dilution of the Franciscan ideal. Clare opposed the well-meaning popes and practical church leaders until finally on August 9, 1253, just two days before she died, she received approval from Pope Innocent IV for her own ideal of the Primitive Rule.

The Primitive Rule calls for a strict dietary code, including perpetual abstinence from meat and perpetual fast except on Sundays and Christmas. In addition to the usual vows of poverty, chastity, and obedience taken by other religious, the Poor Clares take a vow of enclosure, never going outside the convent. Necessary contact with the outside world is handled by "extern" sisters, who do not take solemn vows. The Poor Clares devote themselves to the Divine Office, contemplative prayer, manual and mental labor, and lives of reparation and penance for the salvation of the world.

In the United States, two groups of Poor Clares were started in the 1870s — one by a former German countess, the other by a former Italian countess. Both the convents adhered to the Primitive Rule, and from them came 24 monasteries of Poor Clares in the United States.

For all of the austerity Clare gladly embraced, she continued to show warmly human characteristics, and one of the best documented of these was her habit of walking through the convent dormitory after the other nuns had gone to sleep, making sure everyone was all right, and tucking in blankets that had slipped off the sleeping nuns. She loved flowers and, like Francis, perhaps she had a special closeness with animals. There is an authenticated incident that tells of the then-bedridden Clare ordering the convent cat to bring a towel across the room and "not to drag it on the floor like that."

Clare was canonized on August 15, 1255, just two years after she died. She was first buried in the church of S. Giorgio (St. George) in Assisi. In 1257 construction was begun on the Church of Santa Chiara (St. Clare), a Gothic structure with a red-and-white banded facade and an interior of classic simplicity. On October 3, 1260, her remains were transferred to Santa Chiara, where visitors to Assisi go to pay tribute to one of St. Francis's most famous disciples. The feast day of St. Clare is marked by Roman Catholics as a memorial — the equivalent of the former class III feast.

Tishah B'Av

This is a movable event. See note on page xxvi.

Strictly observant Jews mark Tishah B'Av, the ninth day of the Hebrew month of Av (July or

August), as a day of fasting in commemoration of the destruction of the first and second Temples in Jerusalem. The First Temple, built by King Solomon, was destroyed in 586 B.C. by the Babylonians under Nebuchadnezzar. It was rebuilt after the Jews had returned from exile in Babylonia. However, the Second Temple was in turn destroyed by the Romans under Titus in A.D. 70, some 600 years after the first disaster.

According to rabbinic tradition these two catastrophes for the Jewish people occurred on the same day, the ninth of Av. Furthermore, the complete destruction of Jerusalem by the Romans a year after the suppression of the revolt of Bar Kochba (or Bar Cochba) in A.D. 135 is also supposed to have taken place on Tishah B'Av. Thus Tishah B'Av became a day of mourning associated with a number of events in Jewish history and was observed by Jews in particular memory of their loss of national independence in A.D.70 and their second exile and dispersion.

During the Middle Ages the significance of the day increased, especially after the expulsion of the Jews from Spain in 1492 on Tishah B'Av. As the Jews have suffered more persecutions, the importance of this sad day has grown, for there is more pain to remember. In addition to the destruction of the Temples and the ancient loss of Jewish independence, Jews now commemorate the murder of 6 million European Jews under Germany's Adolf Hitler during World War II.

Tishah B'Av is the only Jewish observance, aside from Yom Kippur, during which fasting is continued by the devoutly Orthodox for a full 24 hours. Orthodox Jews not only fast but also mark the day with all the traditional customs of mourning. The synagogue is draped in black. The curtain covering the ark, where the scrolls of the Bible are kept, is removed, and the ark is either left bare or covered with black cloth. The scrolls, too, may be dressed in black. The Book of Lamentations is read during the morning synagogue service and during the synagogue service that begins the observance of Tishah B'Av the previous evening. (All Jewish holy day observances begin at sundown the preceding day.) Special prayers, dirges, and laments called *kinot* are also chanted. For Jews living in Israel this is a special day to pray at the Western Wall (the so-called Wailing Wall) of the Second Temple and the only remnant of the Temple still standing. Reform Jews generally, and some Israeli Jews, do not observe Tishah B'Av because they believe that the Jews are not in exile today and that it would not be desirable to rebuild the Temple and reinstitute its system of animal sacrifice.

AUGUST 12

Hawaii Annexed to the United States

Hawaii, which was formally annexed to the United States on August 12, 1898, attracted American attention as early as the first quarter of the 19th century. Merchants, missionaries, and whalers all found the islands important and made Honolulu a major port before California entered the Union. The American government recognized the usefulness of the islands, and on December 20, 1842, President John Tyler informed Congress that foreign interference in the area would "create dissatisfaction on the part of the United States."

Thoughts of annexing Hawaii formed in American minds even in the days before the Civil War. In 1854 David L. Gregg, a commissioner sent to the isles by President Franklin Pierce, drew up a draft treaty making Hawaii a state, but the administration was reluctant to send it to the Congress. William H. Seward, who served as secretary of state to Presidents Abraham Lincoln and Andrew Johnson and who was responsible for the purchase of Alaska, entertained a similar vision, but also abandoned it for fear of domestic opposition.

Economic ties held the United States and Hawaii in a close commercial union. By a reciprocity agreement of January 30, 1875, the two nations agreed to admit without duty a variety of items, including unrefined sugar. This agreement was a boon to the sugar planters of the islands, who gained an advantage over the planters of other nations in dealing with the United States. In 1887 the governments of Hawaii and the United States agreed to renew the favorable commercial arrangement.

Within a short time, however, unrelated events in the United States and in Hawaii darkened the prospects of the islands' sugar planters, many of whom were of American descent. The McKinley tariff of 1890 deprived them of their trade advantage by authorizing duty-free importation of sugar to the United States from all the nations of the world. And in Hawaii, the strong-willed Queen Liliuokalani succeeded her brother, King Kalakaua, in 1891. She abrogated the relatively liberal constitution that the nonnative residents had persuaded the king to adopt in 1887.

In January 1893 opponents of Liliuokalani conducted a bloodless revolution aimed at establishing a republican government that would seek annexation to the United States. Unbeknownst to his superiors, the US minister in

Hawaii, John L. Stevens, abetted the uprising by calling for sailors and marines from the cruiser USS *Boston* to land in Honolulu. Stevens also raised the American flag in the capital and declared the islands a protectorate of the United States. Secretary of State John W. Foster acted with equal haste to recognize the new republic and signed an annexation treaty on February 14, 1893.

Grover Cleveland, a Democrat, replaced the Republican Benjamin Harrison as President in March 1893 before the Senate concluded debate on the annexation treaty. Doubtful that the revolutionary government represented the will of the native Hawaiian majority, Cleveland withdrew the treaty from the Senate on March 9. Two days later he appointed Representative James H. Blount of Georgia, onetime chairman of the House Foreign Relations Committee, as his emissary to investigate the whole matter. Upon arriving in Hawaii, Blount declared the protectorate ended, and he reported to the President that the Hawaiians did not wish annexation.

Cleveland hoped to restore Liliuokalani to her throne, but the queen's express intention to behead her opponents and the stability of the republican government in Hawaii combined to thwart his ambitions. He passed the problem to the Congress, which coupled a statement renouncing intervention in the islands' affairs with a warning to other powers to follow an equally innocent course. In the summer of 1894 Cleveland extended official recognition to an undemocratic government established by the island's white minority, and the Wilson-Gorman Tariff of that year restored the islands' sugar planters to their former position.

Extracontinental expansionist sentiment grew increasingly strong in the United States in the late 1890s. In 1898 the nation went to war with Spain over the fate of Cuba, where a popular revolutionary movement was being suppressed by an imperialist power. Expansionist Americans, including those who wished to annex Hawaii, found the wartime period an auspicious one to promote their cause.

William McKinley, a Republican who became President in March 1897, favored annexation of Hawaii. He had promised to raise the tariff, but did not want to undo the reciprocity agreement with the islands. Annexation would eliminate any question of conflict. Moreover Japan, angered by immigration limitations leveled against its citizens by the Hawaiians, had threateningly dispatched a cruiser to Honolulu, a show of force that disturbed many Americans. Annexation would prevent any repetitions of such provocations in a locale deemed important to the security of the United States.

In May 1897 McKinley decided to accept Hawaii's request for annexation, and on June 16, 1897, Secretary of State John Sherman signed an annexation treaty with the Hawaiian government. Japan immediately protested the act, but withdrew its complaint in December, when the United States promised to protect the rights of Japanese nationals in Hawaii.

Domestic sugar growers and anti-imperialists heartily opposed the incorporation of Hawaii into the United States, and enough senators agreed with them to make it impossible for the annexationists to gain the two-thirds vote necessary for approval of the treaty. Undaunted, the expansionists turned to another tactic: annexation by a joint resolution of Congress, which required only the support of a simple majority of the legislators. On July 7, 1898, Congress passed and President McKinley signed the Newlands resolution, and on August 12, 1898, Hawaii officially became part of the United States. Congress on April 30, 1900, granted the islands territorial status, which they maintained until 1959, when they gained admission to the Union as the 50th state (see August 21).

Old Spanish Days
Santa Barbara, California

This is a movable event. See note on page xxvi.

As its name suggests, Old Spanish Days, Santa Barbara's big annual fiesta, draws heavily on California's Spanish/Mexican heritage. That heritage dates from 1542, when Juan Rodriguez Cabrillo, a Portuguese navigator in the employ of Spain, discovered California and explored its coast. His exploration, which began with the discovery of San Diego Bay (see September 28, Cabrillo Day) included the discovery of the Santa Barbara area. Cabrillo is said to be buried on nearby San Miguel Island, where he died on January 3, 1543.

Santa Barbara's Old Spanish Days fiesta, which is held for five days, as close as practicable to the full moon in August, actually begins with a number of pre-fiesta events, including a costume breakfast on opening day (Wednesday). Officially, however, Old Spanish Days begins with the Fiesta Pequeña (little fiesta), held on the steps of Santa Barbara's Mission on Wednesday evening. Apart from the Spanish and Mexican songs and dances, which set an appropriate tone for ensuing festivities, the program includes the traditional fiesta blessing, the introduction of St. Barbara (as portrayed by a local citizen), and greetings from such dignitaries as the governor of California, the mayor of Santa Barbara, visiting Spanish or Latin American diplomats, and the fiesta's *presidente* (an outstanding resident named annually).

Santa Barbara Mission, 10th of the 21 Spanish missions built in California by Fray Junípero Serra and his successors, is particularly appropriate for the start of a historically oriented celebration. Founded in 1786, two years after Fray Serra's death, the mission played an important role in the colonization, agriculture, and architecture of California. Fray Serra, who selected its site, was part of the Gaspar de Portolá expedition sent out from Spanish-controlled Mexico in 1769, when Spain — after ignoring Cabrillo's discovery for two and a quarter centuries — decided to colonize California. All of the Spanish missions — the last of which was completed in 1823, a year after Mexico gained its independence from Spain and claimed California as a province — can be seen today, restored or in replica, along California's historic El Camino Real (US 101).

The opening ceremonies of Old Spanish Days at the Santa Barbara Mission are followed by the first of the evening and matinee performances held during the fiesta at the Lobero Theatre. The entertainment customarily features Spanish dancers, singers, and flamenco guitar artists, and a Mexican folklore dance program.

The presentations at the Lobero Theatre are in keeping with a long fiesta tradition, for it was the opening of this theater (on the site of an earlier one) that helped prompt the first Old Spanish Days in 1924. Other impetus for the 1924 fiesta came from the wish of civic leaders to attract summer visitors and the desire to celebrate Santa Barbara's cultural heritage. To this end, they drew on a body of authentic music and dances, which had been painstakingly collected from the region's residents of Spanish descent for a dramatic masque presented several years earlier.

Except for 1925, when an earthquake occurred, the Old Spanish Days fiesta has taken place annually since 1924. Despite contemporary additions, much of the original historical flavor remains intact.

The most important event — the Desfile Histórico, the historical parade, which takes place on Thursday of fiesta week — has been a feature from the start. The parade usually depicts episodes in Santa Barbara's history, represented by floats and other entries from various periods, such as the era of exploration (early Indians; the landing of Cabrillo; the galleon of Sebastián Vizcaíno, who passed nearby in 1602); the Span-

ish period (1769–1822); the era following Mexico's independence from Spain (1822 to 1846); and the coming of the Americans (events subsequent to the arrival of John C. Frémont, who took possession of Santa Barbara for the United States in 1846). Included in the parade are mantilla-draped young women, dashing Spanish *caballeros*, priests, and pioneer Americans; an impressive array of horses, heavy with silver trappings; dozens of marching bands and precision drill teams; and the costumed flower girls who serve as official hostesses for the fiesta.

Although there was no full-scale fiesta in 1925, that year was marked by the introduction of what became a traditional feature — the Old Spanish Days night pageant or play. In later decades this was supplanted by Noches de las Estrellas, with such attractions as the Ballet Folklórico of Mexico; Carlos Montoya, the flamenco guitarist; Sergio Mendes; and Jose Feliciano. The entertainment takes place nightly except Wednesday during fiesta week in the Santa Barbara County Bowl.

Two other highlights of the fiesta are the Cabalgata (the cavalcade) of costumed riders on splendidly outfitted horses on State Street, on Friday afternoon; and the Desfile de los Niños, a children's version of the historical parade, on Saturday morning. It is followed by a Spanish variety show for children in the sunken gardens of Santa Barbara's county courthouse, which is noted for its Spanish-Moorish architecture.

Other traditional features of Old Spanish Days are the Competición de Vaqueros, a rodeo and stock horse show that takes place at the Earl Warren Showgrounds Arena (with nightly presentations and weekend matinees); Noches de Ronda, a Spanish variety show presented nightly in the courthouse gardens; a nightly Mexican-style party with outdoor dancing; and El Mercado, the Spanish marketplace, open night and day in De la Guerra Plaza, opposite City Hall.

Various other events that take place during fiesta week are Saturday's Kiwanis pancake breakfast in Alameda Park; a band concert at City Hall Saturday afternoon; the Fiesta Folk Dance Festival at Santa Barbara High School Boys' Gym Saturday evening; and the harborside Fiesta Arts and Crafts Show, beginning at noon on Sunday. Among other features of Old Spanish Days have been the Fiesta Street Dance, nightly at De la Guerra Plaza; the beachside Enchilada Luncheon on Thursday sponsored by the Lions Club; the Merienda, the Women's Club fiesta party, on Friday; and the outdoor Baile del Mar held Thursday, Friday, and Saturday evenings on West Beach opposite La Playa Field. The latter site is the scene of carnival rides and attractions from late afternoon until midnight on Wednesday and Thursday of Old Spanish Days, and both afternoons and evenings on the weekend. In addition are the popular tours of local gardens and of Santa Barbara's famous adobe dwellings.

AUGUST 13

Lucy Stone's Birthday

Lucy Stone, a leading suffragist and abolitionist of the 19th century, is perhaps best known for her determination to assert her individuality by retaining her family name after marriage. Women who followed her example became known as Lucy Stoners.

A person of "unusual personal magnetism" who was — according to Elizabeth Cady Stanton — first to deeply stir "the heart of the American public . . . on the woman question," Stone was born on August 13, 1818, near West Brookfield, Massachusetts. She was still a child when she became indignant at the second-class treatment accorded women, and she determined to study Greek and Hebrew so that she could decide whether biblical pronouncements on the subjection of women had been translated accurately. In time, she enrolled at the first coeducational college in the country, Oberlin, from which she graduated in 1847. She gave her first lecture on women's rights the same year.

An ardent abolitionist, Lucy Stone was engaged as a regular lecturer by the Anti-Slavery Society in 1848. Although her duties demanded that Saturday evenings and Sundays be devoted to the cause of emancipation of slaves, she also lectured widely on the emancipation of women. Pictured by biographers as approachable, good-natured, and dynamic, she won wide popularity as a lecturer, demonstrating great eloquence and the ability frequently to win unruly, antagonistic audiences to her point of view. The last ability, which once even tamed the club-bearing leader of a mob that was storming the speakers' platform, was particularly remarkable since her most noticeable qualities reportedly were gentleness, complete "womanliness," and a speaking voice notable for its sweet and musical quality. Another facet of her character was noted by her daughter, who described her as "always keenly alive to the beauties of nature" — one who "reveled in all the beauty of the world."

In 1850 she headed the call — signed by many distinguished men and women — for the first national women's rights convention, held in Worcester, Massachusetts. Harriet Taylor, who later married John Stuart Mill, wrote an article about the convention, published in the *Westminster Review*, which marked the beginning of the modern women's rights movement in England. Although the meeting in Worcester had been preceded by others, most notably the one in Seneca Falls, New York, in 1848 (see July 19), they had been more local in scope.

When Stone and the abolitionist Henry Brown Blackwell were married in 1855, they agreed that she, as his equal, would retain her original surname. Her husband joined her in protesting the inequalities of marriage laws of the time and afterward worked with her for woman suffrage.

At the time of their marriage, they drew up a joint statement that said in part:

While acknowledging our mutual affection by publicly assuming the relationship of husband and wife, yet, in justice to ourselves and a great principle, we deem it our duty to declare that this act on our part implies no sanction of nor promise of voluntary obedience to such of the present laws of marriage as refuse to recognize the wife as an independent, rational being, while they confer upon the husband an injurious and unnatural superiority, investing him with legal powers which no honorable man would exercise, and which no man should possess. . . .

We believe that personal independence and equal human rights can never be forfeited except for crime; that marriage should be an equal and permanent partnership, and so recognized by law; that, until it is so recognized, married partners should provide against the radical injustice of present laws by every means in their power. . . .

Thus, reverencing law, we enter our protest against rules and customs which are unworthy of the name, since they violate justice, the essence of law.

Mrs. Stone, as she was called, took a leading part in 1869 in founding the American Woman Suffrage Association, which sought votes for women by organizing to exert pressure on the various state legislatures. In contrast the National Woman Suffrage Association, organized the same year by Susan B. Anthony and Elizabeth Cady Stanton, began its suffrage work with appeals on the national level.

In 1870 Stone founded the *Woman's Journal* in Boston. With her husband she edited the publication beginning in 1872. Later they had the assistance of Alice Stone Blackwell, their daughter, who succeeded them. After 1890, when Stone's American Woman Suffrage Association combined with the Anthony-Stanton group, the *Woman's Journal* became the official organ of the resulting merger — which was known as the National American Woman Suffrage Association. Stone continued her editorial duties until the year of her death, 1893. She died on October 18.

The Reverend M. J. Savage stated in a tribute that Lucy Stone's keeping her own name at marriage was much discussed and much misunderstood. Still true is his point that there was "no law in existence forbidding this. It was done by mutual consent, and was intended as a protest against the idea that a woman's individuality was merged at marriage in that of her husband."

Memorials to the pioneering rights advocate have taken varied forms. The Lucy Stone League, with headquarters in New York City, at 133 East 58th Street, is a center of research and information on the status of women. Opposing discrimination against women in legal, economic, educational, and social relationships, it maintains archives for women and has become identified particularly with problems arising from the desire, felt by many women, to retain their family names at marriage, and to vote, hold property, run for public office, sign contracts, and conduct various enterprises in that name. The league was founded in 1921 by Ruth Hale and Jane Grant, who determinedly kept their own names after marriage (Hale married Heywood Broun, the columnist, and Grant married Harold Ross, founder of *The New Yorker* magazine).

Photographs, historical items, and publications related to Stone's life are in the Quaboag Historical Society Museum in West Brookfield, Massachusetts. Included are her marriage certificate; her personal copy of the New Testament in Greek; Elinor R. Hays's biography *Morning Star;* and *Lucy Stone — Pioneer of Woman's Rights* by Alice Stone Blackwell. Members of the Quaboag Historical Society from time to time make a pilgrimage to Cox's Hill, where Stone's home stood until fire destroyed it in the early 1950s. The riverside Lucy Stone Park in nearby Warren was a project of the women's Tuesday Club, which was formed in 1963 with the aim of stopping pollution of the Quaboag River and preserving the beauty of the surrounding woodland. The undertaking received financial and other support from the Warren Rural Improvement Association and the Conservation Commission. Since its inception, the park, which is jointly maintained by the Tuesday Club and the Lucy Stone League, has been enlarged and improved.

In 1968, the 150th anniversary of Stone's birth, the opening of newly cleared trails was marked (on October 12) by a ribbon-cutting ceremony and addresses by members of the Massachusetts state legislature and conservation leaders. Messages were sent by Secretary of the Interior Walter J. Hickel and Governor Francis W. Sargent of Massachusetts. Representative Margaret Heckler of Massachusetts also sent a message, commenting on the dual devotion of

Lucy Stone to nature and to the rights of women.

Other sesquicentennial events included issue by the US Post Office of a commemorative stamp bearing the likeness of Lucy Stone and a luncheon in her honor held in September by the Lucy Stone League at the Overseas Press Club in New York.

AUGUST 14

The Atlantic Charter

The entry of the United States into World War II was slow and hesitant. Japan's bombing of Pearl Harbor in 1941 (see December 7) finally propelled the country into war against the Axis powers of Germany, Italy, and Japan; but events earlier in 1941 had clearly indicated the direction of American sympathies in favor of the Allies. On March 11, 1941, the Lend-Lease Act went into effect. This act empowered the President to sell, lend, lease, transfer, or exchange war materials, the negotiations to be carried out with any country whose defense he considered vital to US security. Passage of Lend-Lease occurred at a critical stage in the Allied struggle: the strains of the war, which had begun in Europe on September 1, 1939, had depleted the financial resources of Great Britain — then the only major Ally that had not been overrun by Nazi Germany — and without American armaments it would have lacked the equipment needed to continue its fight.

As the Lend-Lease Act provided the material aid necessary for the Allied war effort, the Atlantic Charter supplied the equally essential moral support. The declaration, jointly issued on August 14, 1941, was the outcome of the secret meetings on August 9 to 12, of President Franklin D. Roosevelt and Prime Minister Winston Churchill aboard the US cruiser *Augusta* and the British battleship *Prince of Wales* in Argentia Bay, off Newfoundland. Basically the principles embodied in the charter were those urged by President Woodrow Wilson during the peace conference at Versailles following World War I. The Atlantic Charter denounced territorial aggrandizement and supported the right of people to live under a government of their own choosing. It also supported unrestricted trade and access to raw materials, freedom from want and fear, freedom of the seas, and the disarmament of belligerent nations. The charter did not formally ally or legally bind the two nations, but it demonstrated that the United States and Great Britain shared identical postwar aims. By September 1941 the document had been endorsed by 15 nations.

V-J Day

Since the actual and official conclusions of wars are seldom identical, it is not surprising that there is some confusion as to the exact end of World War II in the Pacific arena. The formal ratification of surrender by Japan took place aboard the battleship *Missouri* in Tokyo Bay on September 2, 1945, Tokyo time, which was September 1, Washington time. President Harry S. Truman proclaimed the following day — September 2 (Washington time) — as Victory over Japan Day, or V-J Day. However, Japan's capitulation had already been announced on August 14, and it is this date that is generally remembered as V-J Day.

As the war in Europe was drawing to a close in April 1945, the Pacific Allied forces were reorganized in expectation of a major push against the chief remaining enemy, the Japanese. General Douglas MacArthur (see January 26) was made commander of all US army forces in the Pacific; Admiral Chester W. Nimitz (see February 24) had command of all US Navy units. The 8th Air Force under Lieutenant General James H. Doolittle and the 20th Air Force under Lieutenant General Nathan F. Twining were joined to form the US Strategic Air Forces under General Carl Spaatz. Lieutenant General George C. Kenney commanded the US Far Eastern Air Force.

During the spring and summer of 1945, the Japanese home islands were subjected to intensive air attacks, among them the massive fire-bomb raid on Tokyo on March 9–10, 1945, in which it is estimated that over 80,000 persons perished. B-29 Superfortresses and other bombers based on land or on navy aircraft carriers carried out systematic bombing attacks on an intensifying scale. They included both high-altitude precision bombing and low-altitude incendiary bombing against Japanese urban centers such as Osaka, Nagoya, and Kobe, and against individual industrial targets. The home islands meanwhile were also subjected to naval bombardment by US and British units, and US submarines took a mounting toll of Japanese merchant vessels and warships. On May 25 the Joint Chiefs of Staff laid plans for an invasion of Kyushu, one of the main islands of Japan; on November 1, 1945, and the Tokyo plains area of Honshu on March 1, 1946.

In mid-July, while attending the Potsdam Conference in Europe with leaders of Great Britain and the Soviet Union, President Truman learned of the successful explosion of the world's first atomic device during a test conducted on July 16 near the Alamogordo air base in New Mexico. On July 26 the heads of state of the United States and Britain, with the concurrence of Nationalist China, issued the so-called Potsdam Declaration or Proclamation calling upon Japan to proclaim the "unconditional surrender of all Japanese armed forces, and to provide proper and adequate assurances of their good faith in such action."

Earlier, on May 8 Truman had already announced that unconditional surrender involved the end of military rule in Japan, but stressed that it did not signify the "extermination or enslavement" of the Japanese. Although by midsummer 1945 Japanese leaders, with the exception of a few militant diehards, were seeking means of ending the war, they were not yet prepared to accept unconditional surrender, especially since neither Truman's May statement nor the Potsdam Proclamation had made clear what the future status of the Japanese emperor or empire would be. On July 28, therefore, the Japanese in effect rejected the Allies' ultimatum. In the meantime the leaders of Japan continued to search for an honorable way to surrender.

Following the dropping of atomic bombs on Hiroshima on August 6, Tokyo time (see August 5) and on Nagasaki on August 9, Tokyo time, the Japanese were unable to cope immediately with the meaning of the new weapon. Faced with utter ruin, they could hardly believe their helpless position. Moreover, on August 8, the Soviet Union had declared war against Japan, a step agreed upon earlier and reaffirmed at the Potsdam conference.

On August 9, the bewildered and divided members of the Japanese Supreme Council for the Direction of War convened and became deadlocked on the course of action, an impasse which even news of the Nagasaki bomb failed to break. They prevailed upon Emperor Hirohito to summon an imperial conference; this was an unprecedented step since the emperor, albeit the titular ruler of the Japanese empire, normally played a passive role in government and only received word of policy decisions that had already been made. Shortly before midnight on August 9, Japan's chief political and military leaders gathered in an underground air raid shelter adjoining the Imperial Library. There, Hirohito, when asked for an opinion, approved the proposal for seeking peace, stating: "I cannot bear to see my innocent people suffer any longer." His prestige carried enough weight to settle the deadlock.

On August 10, the Japanese government made known its willingness to accept an unconditional surrender based on the Allies' Potsdam Declaration, provided the emperor was retained. The Allies raised no serious objection to this request, with the one proviso that "from the moment of surrender the authority of the Emperor and the Japanese Government to rule the state shall be subject to the Supreme Commander for the Allied powers who will take such steps as he deems proper to effectuate the surrender terms." After intense debate, the Japanese accepted the Allied proviso on August 14, 1945. General Douglas MacArthur was then appointed Supreme Commander for the Allied Powers to oversee the occupation of Japan.

At 7:00 P.M., Eastern War Time, August 14, 1945, the moving electric sign on the Times Tower in New York City flashed the words, "Official — Truman announces Japanese surrender," and set off an unparalleled demonstration that was typical on a lesser scale of every city, town, and village in the United States. The terrific roar that greeted the announcement on the Times Tower lasted for 20 minutes and literally deafened the participants. Those in the streets tossed hats and flags into the air, and from those in the windows of adjacent hotels and office buildings came the shower of confetti streamers invariably cast upon the city by New Yorkers in celebration of major events. People began pouring into Times Square from the subways and buses and on foot, and in a short time they were packed so solidly individual movement was impossible. By 10:00 P.M., the Manhattan police estimated that two million persons were in the Times Square area from 40th to 52nd streets between Sixth and Eighth avenues, making an all-time record. The rest of the city displayed equal enthusiasm; Greenwich Village was a madhouse and in Queens thousands staged impromptu parades; Emperor Hirohito was hanged in effigy from electric light poles in the Bronx and other boroughs; everywhere automobiles, taxis, and trucks ran through the streets with passengers perched on the hoods, as well as two-deep inside, their passage accompanied by shouting and horn blowing. The sacred dragon, reserved for the Chinese New Year and considered a symbol of peace, was called out in the narrow, crooked streets of Chinatown and there were four ritualistic, dragon-led processions through Mott, Doyer and Pell streets. The metropolitan fire departments were run ragged answering both real and false alarms turned in by exultant citizens. Even those who stayed off the streets exhibited similar unrestraint by throwing "victory parties" lasting far into the night for their friends. Other cities expressed their joy and relief with the same extravagance; a victory bonfire was started on busy Market Street in San Francisco; servicemen and civilians, men and women, old and young, joined in a conga line on the grass of Lafayette Square across from the White House in Washington, D.C. Throughout the country, in urban, suburban, and rural areas, Americans rejoiced in their hearts, whether or not they took part in the public demonstrations.

No observance of V-J Day since 1945 has compared with the first exuberant event, but August 14 is still commemorated, for example, in the states of Rhode Island and Arkansas, which keep the date as a legal holiday. Rhode Island commemorates the day as Victory Day, while Arkansas calls it World War II Memorial Day. On August 15 (Tokyo time), 1970, the Japanese marked the 25th anniversary of the country's surrender with silent prayer and the tolling of bells; Emperor Hirohito also presided at a memorial service at Budokan Hall near the Imperial Palace; in attendance were some 5,000 relatives of servicemen who had died in World War II.

AUGUST 15

Feast of the Assumption

The Feast of the Assumption of the Blessed Virgin Mary, celebrated on August 15, is a holy day of obligation for members of the Roman Catholic church. From early times, the Assumption, or taking up into heaven, of the Virgin Mary has been commemorated as the greatest of her feasts and one of the chief solemnities of the church year. According to one of the oldest traditions of the church, Mary "departed from this life" and was taken, body and soul, into heaven. The observance of this feast is documented from the second half of the sixth century in the East and from the seventh century in Rome.

In the Roman Catholic church, a saint's feast day is usually the day the saint died, which is considered that saint's "heavenly birthday" since at death the soul would be reunited with God in heaven. In the same way, a memorial feast of the Virgin Mary was held each year with great solemnity and devotion by the monks of Palestine, according to writings of Bishop Theodore of Petra, dated about 529. Traditionally the day of Mary's "dormition" (falling asleep) was observed on August 15. This yearly memorial soon spread throughout the entire Eastern church. In 602 the Byzantine Emperor Mauritius (or Maurice) established the August 15 feast as a public holiday for his entire realm. The feast, then officially designated as the Dormition of the Blessed Virgin Mary, was immediately adopted by Rome under the same title. Because of the ancient traditional belief that Mary's body did not decay, but was taken up to heaven with her soul after her death, the feast began to be known as the Assumption in the seventh and eighth centuries.

The centuries-long tradition of belief in the Assumption was confirmed and given official definition as a dogma on November 1, 1950, by Pope Pius XII, who said: "The Immaculate Mother of God, the ever-Virgin Mary, having completed the course of her earthly life, was assumed body and soul into heavenly glory."

From ancient times, a procession has been a part of the celebration of the Feast of the Assumption. In Jerusalem, even before the 4th century, the procession was formed by the multitude of pilgrims who came to pray at the tomb of the Virgin Mary, and who thus contributed to the institution of this solemnity. In Constantinople, on the Feast of the Rest, or Dormition, of the Blessed Virgin, the procession was held by members of the clergy. In Rome from the 7th to the 16th century, representatives of the senate and others took part in the papal cortege that on August 15 went from the Church of St. John Lateran to the Church of St. Mary Major in a ceremonial procession called the Litany.

Processions remain part of the celebration of the Feast of the Assumption in many regions of the world, especially among Latin peoples.

In rural areas not far from Rome (and also in Sicily) the people have a Bowing Procession. A statue of Mary is carried through the town, symbolizing her sojourn on earth on her way to heaven. The climax of this procession comes when the statue is carried to a ceremonial arch of flowers and boughs, representing the gate of heaven. There another group holds aloft a statue of Christ. Both statues are inclined toward each other three times in a bow of solemn respect. The Christ figure then precedes that of Mary back to the parish church, symbolizing her entrance into heaven, and the people who have participated in those ceremonies, or watched the procession, enter the church for a solemn benediction, which concludes the religious celebration.

From pre-Christian times, medicinal herbs have been gathered in August in many parts of the world. In medieval times, the Blessing of Herbs ceremony was held on the Feast of the Assumption. Many other elemental things are also blessed on this day — farm animals, orchards, meadows, and mountains. In many Latin countries where fishing is an important part of life, the waters and the fishing boats are blessed on the Feast of the Assumption. This custom is still observed in a number of coastal towns in the United States. Among the many Native Americans who observe the Feast of the Assumption are the Pueblos of New Mexico and the Coeur d'Alene Indians. The latter make an annual pilgrimage to the Cataldo Mission church in north-

ern Idaho; the 19th century mission, which Coeur d'Alene workers helped build, is the site of a mass, a picnic, and dancing, open to the public.

Eastern Orthodox churches, maintaining the original title of the feast, celebrate the Dormition of the Mother of God on August 15 (or on August 28 when the Julian calendar is used). It is considered one of the 12 great feasts of the Eastern Orthodox church. The Episcopal church celebrates the Feast of St. Mary the Virgin on August 15.

Natural Chimneys Jousting Tournament

This is a movable event. See note on page xxvi.

The jousting, or ring, tournament, held at Natural Chimneys (located in the Shenandoah Valley approximately a mile north of Mount Solon and 18 miles from Staunton, Virginia) has been an annual event since 1821. Its sponsors claim that it quite possibly has the distinction of being the oldest continuous sporting competition in the United States, a claim that may very well be true. In 1821 the United States was a young nation and most of its traditional sporting events were yet unborn. The first Kentucky Derby, for example, did not run until 54 years later. In any case, the jousting tournament at Natural Chimneys, scheduled for the third Saturday in August, boasts a long and picturesque tradition.

The Natural Chimneys, which rank high among the great natural wonders of Virginia, provide a most appropriate backdrop for the annual jousting meet. The seven colorful and massive limestone monoliths, ranging in height from 65 to well over 100 feet, resemble the ruins of a turreted feudal castle. Weather-beaten from exposure to wind and water, they are honeycombed with water-eroded tunnels, which in two of the chimneys suggest fortress doors. A moatlike stream winding along the plain from which the chimneys rise contributes to the impression. On August 5, 1970, the striking site was purchased by the Upper Valley Regional Park Authority, with the intention of developing the area as a regional park.

Jousting, a test of horsemanship, marksmanship, and balance, was traditionally a form of combat between knights on horseback armed with lances. It was described by the 12th century English chronicler Roger of Hoveden as "military exercises carried out, not in the spirit of hostility, but for practice and display of prowess." Several medieval chroniclers credit a French baron, Geoffroi de Pruelli, with inventing the sport shortly before the battle of Hastings in 1066. But although there is a general consensus that jousting originated in France about the middle of the 11th century, some scholars doubt that it could have been the creation of any one person.

The Catholic church opposed jousting, regarding it as an occasion for unnecessary bloodshed and denied Christian burial to those killed during such combats. King Henry II of England, alarmed at the idea of mass gatherings of unruly knights, found it expedient to forbid the sport during his late-12th century reign. Richard I, his son, lifted the ban, but exacted onerous fees for the required royal license. The church's harsh rules against jousting abated slightly during the late Middle Ages and in any case were usually ignored. Jousters traveled from country to country, challenging and accepting challenges. By the 16th century the tournament had generally become a bloodless meeting with blunted weapons and had taken on the air of a spectacle rather than that of a lethal sport, although accidents occurred.

An attempt was made to revive the custom in 1839, when British lords and ladies, many dressed in authentic costumes of the 14th and 15th centuries, gathered in Scotland at Eglinton, Ayrshire, to watch a three-day gala joust. Each of the 15 "knights" who had entered the lists was attended by squires and men-at-arms and occupied a separate pavilion. A highlight was a mock tilt in which Prince Louis Napoleon (later Napoleon III) participated. Although this event was not continued, starting in 1878 the Royal Naval and Military Tournament featured annual meets in which only British army and navy officers could compete. In the interval between the two world wars, the French also staged jousting contests at Compiègne. Both the British and the French tournaments died out during World War II. The only modern jousting tournament that has functioned steadily in both war and peace is that held at Natural Chimneys.

Legend says that the tournament had its impetus when the hand of a young Virginia woman was sought by two ardent and gallant suitors in 1821. She was unable to decide which suitor to choose, and her uncle suggested that she base her decision, as in the days of King Arthur, upon the outcome of a jousting contest. The bout was to prove skill and horsemanship, but without the mortal danger of the medieval tournaments, when each rider sought to unhorse the other with a penetrating thrust at the breastplate of his mail-clad foe. The course was to be 75 yards in length, with a series of two-inch rings placed on three posts at intervals of 25 yards. The two "knights" were to gallop down the course in the allotted eight seconds and attempt to spear the rings, the one with the greater num-

ber being named the victor and the bridegroom-to-be.

This unique method of choosing a husband aroused the sporting interest of the whole countryside. On the fateful day the suitors met and jousted at Natural Chimneys. At the end of the contest there was food and drink for the spectators, and the winner lifted his betrothed to his saddle, escorting her home amid cheers and good wishes.

It was thereafter decided to make the tournament an annual affair. In 1822 the young men of the community all competed, and the winner crowned his Queen of Love and Beauty.

Although jousting has become popular in a few other US localities, particularly in Maryland and South Carolina, there is no competition so large or tradition-filled as the tournament at Natural Chimneys. Literally thousands of "knights" have galloped down the course since the tournament's inception. Procedure has changed very little over the past century and a half, because local citizens have resisted any major innovations in the program.

The tournament, attended by over 4,000 annually, is heralded by a parade of gaily garbed contestants, usually in riding breeches and flamboyant sports shirts, not suits of mail, although several wear costumes and sashes and wield heirloom lances. After riding around the base of the Natural Chimneys, the "rivals" — who always assume intriguing titles, such as Knight of the Dusty Trail, Knight of the Golden Horseshoe, or Knight of Whiskey Creek — pass through one of the tunnels out onto the jousting green. There, in the shadow of the natural pinnacles, the marshal gives the traditional command, "Charge, Sir Knight!" to the first of the competitors.

The field is always set up as it was in 1821. Each rider must send his charger down the 75-yard course in not more than eight seconds and try to spear the suspended steel rings, with any rider who misses all the rings being eliminated. There are three such passes for a possible total of nine rings in the preliminary runs. In the finals, rings with a one-inch diameter replace the two-inch rings used in the eliminations. Occasionally remarkable skill is exhibited, as in 1936 when a contestant rode the course 7 times and won with a perfect score of 21 rings.

Several relatively minor innovations have been made in recent years. Pony rides, games, and refreshments, for instance, now provide a midway atmosphere. In 1937 the site was first equipped with electricity, thus permitting a night session of the tournament, which usually begins at 8:00 P.M., in addition to the traditional afternoon bout at 2:30 P.M. Of late an honorary queen, sometimes a local resident, sometimes a celebrity, such as a national beauty queen or a movie star, has been chosen to preside over the two meets. Generally seated with her court attendants directly opposite the judge's stand, she opens the event and presides over the competitions until the conclusion of the night contest. Then, following an address, the two winning "knights" from the afternoon and evening tournaments crown their own queens. Beginning in 1940 women were permitted to compete in the tournament.

Panama Canal Opens Officially

On August 15, 1914, the Panama Canal, completed earlier in the year, was officially opened to international sea commerce. The first vessel had traversed the canal seven months earlier (see January 7).

AUGUST 16

Bennington Battle Day

In the crucial summer of 1777 British forces in America undertook a campaign to suppress the rebellion of the colonies against Great Britain. Major General John Burgoyne devised the strategy, which included a three-pronged attack on New York's upper Hudson River valley. Burgoyne himself led the main column of more than 7,000 men south from Canada. On July 5 his men took possession of Fort Ticonderoga, which the Americans had abandoned as the enemy drew near, and then resumed the advance toward Albany.

By the time Burgoyne reached Fort George at the end of July, he realized that his supply line, stretching 185 miles back to Canada, was inadequate for the expedition. His forces badly needed provisions as well as horses to pull wagons and serve as mounts for the 250 German dragoons that the duke of Brunswick had committed to the English cause. Upon the advice of his German subordinate General Baron Friedrich Adolphus von Riedesel, Burgoyne decided to send a detachment into western New England to arouse popular support for the royal government and to obtain large numbers of cattle, horses, and carriages.

Burgoyne designated Lieutenant Colonel Friedrich Baum, the commander of the Brunswick dragoons, to lead the raid. Manchester, in what is now Vermont, was the original objective, but a last-minute intelligence report indicated that the party could more easily capture the stores in Bennington where only 300 or 400

militiamen guarded an American supply depot. On August 11, Baum started his force of 374 Germans, 50 British marksmen, and 300 Tories, Canadians, and Indians toward Bennington, located near the New York border.

On July 24, 1777, the colonial commander in chief George Washington placed Major General Benjamin Lincoln of Massachusetts in charge of the militia units forming east of the Hudson River to oppose Burgoyne. Lincoln performed well, but was unable to win the submission of John Stark, the commander of New Hampshire's 1,500-man contingent. Stark had resigned from the Continental army in March 1777, when Congress failed to promote him from colonel, and accepted New Hampshire's commission as a brigadier general. Lincoln prudently treated the truculent Stark as an ally rather than as a subordinate, approving his plan to operate independently and to harass Burgoyne's rear forces.

General Stark's wanderings took his brigade to Bennington before Baum reached there. On August 13 the militia leader dispatched 200 men to investigate Indian hostilities around neighboring Cambridge in what is now New York State, and the patrol discovered that the Indians were only part of a larger operation. Stark decided to intercept the enemy force, now that he was aware of its existence, and sent word to Lieutenant Colonel Seth Warner to bring his Green Mountain Boys from Manchester to assist in the attempt.

On the morning of August 15 an American forward party made the first contact with Baum's troops at Van Schaick's Mill. The colonists fired one volley and then retreated. The skirmish and the necessity of repairing the burned St. Luke's Bridge across Little White Creek delayed the enemy, but they soon resumed their advance, marching another mile and three quarters to the bridge or ford of the Walloomsac River.

Unenviably, Baum found himself 25 miles from his parent unit and facing a force twice the size of his own. Logic called for retreat; instead, Baum sent a message to Burgoyne requesting a small number of reinforcements, and proceeded to deploy his inadequate band ineptly. The German commander placed 150 men on the far, or enemy, side of the Walloomsac in a hastily constructed earthworks called the Tory Redoubt. He kept his largest contingent, 200 men, in the Dragoon Redoubt on the near side of the river, and scattered the rest of his troops in smaller detachments.

Rain prevented a battle on August 15, but Stark attacked on the afternoon of August 16. He sent 300 rangers and Bennington militiamen to approach the Dragoon Redoubt from the left and attack the enemy's rear guard. Colonel

Moses Nichols simultaneously led 200 New Hampshire men to assault the redoubt from the right. Stark sent another 200 men under Colonels David Hobart and Thomas Stickney to engage the defenders of the Tory Redoubt; the former approached from the left and the latter from the right.

The tactic of double envelopment requires such a high degree of timing and coordination that professional soldiers rarely employ it. Yet Stark's band of rustic military neophytes perfectly executed a double envelopment. Stark then led his main column of almost 1,300 men down the Bennington Road, advising them that "we'll beat them before night, or Molly Stark will be a widow."

The Tory Redoubt and the scattered enemy positions quickly fell, but Baum's dragoons held their ground. Having expended most of their ammunition by 5:00 P.M., the Europeans attempted to cut their way out with their swords. They made some progress, but surrendered when Baum received a mortal stomach wound.

Both Baum and Stark had called for reinforcements, and the arrival of the new troops precipitated the second phase of the battle. Lieutenant Colonel Francis Breymann's more than 650 Hessians came in time to halt Stark's pursuit of escapees from Baum's expedition; but Seth Warner's 350 Green Mountain Boys then made contact with Breymann near what is now Walloomsac, New York. The Germans held their ground until they ran low on ammunition, and then they attempted to retreat. The Americans managed to capture a number of them, but two-thirds of the force slipped away after dark.

Stark reported 14 Americans killed and 42 wounded. Enemy losses totaled 207 dead and 700 captured. Only nine of the Brunswick dragoons managed to get back to Burgoyne. The British commander had lost a tenth of his men and gained nothing. Only slightly daunted, Burgoyne continued down the road that would carry him to total defeat at Saratoga in October. The British defeat there marked the turning point of the American Revolution.

The anniversary of the fighting along the Walloomsac River is a legal holiday in the state of Vermont, where it is known as Bennington Battle Day. Exercises to commemorate the battle are often held on that day at the base of the Bennington Battle Monument, an impressive, 306-foot tower with an observation platform at the top, located in the town of Old Bennington, two miles west of Bennington proper. A statue of Seth Warner stands near the monument. Not far away, the men who fell in the engagement rest in the Old Burying Ground adjoining the Old First Church.

The Bennington Museum, on West Main Street in Old Bennington, is an excellent regional repository, containing relics of early Vermont. It is the home of the Bennington Flag, the earliest extant Stars and Stripes. The numerals "'76" are printed on the flag, centered beneath its 11 stars. The banner saw action in the battle of Bennington, as did four brass cannons captured from the British. (The guns have an interesting history, since the British captured them from the French at Quebec in 1759 and lost them to the Americans in 1777; the Americans later lost them to the British in the War of 1812 — at the battle of Detroit — and recaptured them in 1813 at the battle of Niagara.)

The 208-acre Bennington Battlefield State Park, a national historic landmark, located in New York's Rensselaer County, includes the site of the heaviest fighting. The high ground overlooking Walloomsac affords an excellent view of the site. A bronze relief map indicates the dispositions of the various units that participated in the battle, and other monuments commemorate the service of General Stark and his militiamen. New York State owns the battlefield and the state Department of Education administers it.

AUGUST 17

American Indian Exposition
Anadarko, Oklahoma

This is a movable event. See note on page xxvi.

The American Indian Exposition, opening on the second Monday in August, in Anadarko, Oklahoma, has been called one of the most colorful and comprehensive American Indian events. Entirely Indian in ownership, management, and participation, the exposition, which runs for six days (Monday through Saturday) began simply as a fair for Indian residents of the area. It became a tourist event unexpectedly, when the excitement it generated aroused widespread public interest. It now attracts some 45,000 visitors from across the country each year.

Nor is the widespread interest as new as many suppose. The Anadarko Exposition was 47 years old in 1978.

The 3,000 people who take part in the exposition are members of the 12 tribes officially affiliated with it: Kiowa, Comanche, Delaware, Wichita, Caddo, Kiowa-Apache, Osage, Pawnee, Otoe, Cheyenne, Arapaho, and Fort Sill-Apache. The 12 tribes elect 4 executive officers and 12 directors — one from each tribe — for the exposition each year. They also choose 12 tribal princesses, who reign for a year and appear at the various events.

Participants begin making camp, setting up their brush arbors, teepees, and tents on the east edge of town a few days before the exposition opens. Officially, the exposition begins early Monday afternoon with a parade through downtown Anadarko of several hundred Indians, including the 12 princesses, all in tribal dress. Buckskins, war bonnets, moccasins, and leggings are much in evidence, as are the beads, fringes, feathers, ribbons, and embroidered shawls of the women, whose costumes vary distinctively from tribe to tribe. The princesses are joined by visiting princesses from other tribes and by some of the princesses who will reign over powwows in various parts of the United States during the summer.

After the parade (which is repeated on closing day), everyone adjourns to the fairgrounds for an afternoon performance featuring band music, Indian games, ceremonial dances, horse racing, and contests of skill. The performance, which is repeated with some variations each afternoon, commences with the introduction of the tribal princesses and of visiting state, local, or federal officials. Afternoon high points in one typical year included a Creek Indian stickball game, Indian foot races, special acts — clowns, and hoop, eagle, and ruffle dancers among others — and an egg-throwing contest.

The exposition's evening programs, also at the fairgrounds, are divided evenly between a pageant — usually presented on Monday, Wednesday, and Saturday evenings — and dance events on Tuesday and Thursday. The pageant, which involves members of all the 12 tribes and tells the story of the Indians of the Great Plains and the Southwest, is different each year. In one representative year, for example, the pageant, entitled From Sunrise to Sunset, was written by Libby Littlechief, a Kiowa, and depicted the story of an Indian life from birth to death. Featuring a cast of 135, it was divided into four sections and included all the major dances of the Southern Plains Indians. The first part, after an elaborate processional, dealt with childhood and included the eagle dance and the snake and buffalo dances, as well as the rabbit dance and slow war dance, performed by children. Part two, which dealt with the rituals of entrance into manhood and womanhood, included the shield and ruffle dances, as well as dances and ceremonies connected with courtship and marriage. The next section, called Eveningtide, included a war council and war dances. The fourth and final section included a death chant by the Kiowa warrior Stumblingbear. One of several religious presentations in the two-hour pageant, it was followed by the Lord's Prayer in Indian sign language and by the Kiowa flag ceremony.

The evening programs on Tuesday, Thursday, and Friday are devoted to ceremonial and tribal dances and include several dance contests, among them a tribal contest, a competition for women, and (on Friday) the National War Dance Contest, in which a world champion is crowned. Group and individual dances also are performed and there are various special acts — for instance the Acoma Snake Dancers from Tulsa, who have appeared several times. An additional feature, at one of the late-week evening programs, is the naming of the Outstanding American Indian of the Year. LaDonna Harris, Jim Thorpe, Allie Reynolds, Will Rogers Jr., and Maria Tallchief are among those who have been so honored.

Apart from the exposition itself, there are a number of points of interest in the Anadarko area that are related to American Indians. One is the Anadarko City Museum, sponsored by the local Philomathic Club, in the city hall. Another is the Southern Plains Indians Museum and Crafts Center, at the east entrance to Anadarko on US highway 62. Near it is the National Hall of Fame for Famous American Indians, established in 1952, in which busts of famous individuals of Indian heritage have been placed (Pocahontas, Sacagawea, Osceola, Chief Joseph, and Will Rogers are among those included).

Most visitors also view Indian City USA (about 2 miles south of Anadarko), an outdoor museum in which the villages of seven quite different tribes have been authentically recreated under the supervision of the Department of Anthropology of the University of Oklahoma. There are guided tours and dance presentations daily in summer and on most winter Sundays.

Davy Crockett's Birthday

America's frontier produced numerous folk heroes, few more famous than Davy Crockett. His paternal grandparents emigrated from Ireland, and his father, John Crockett, was born either there or on the voyage to the New World. John Crockett, who took part in the patriot victory at the battle of King's Mountain on October 7, 1780, during the American Revolution, married Rebecca Hawkins, from Maryland. Around 1783 they moved from North Carolina to Tennessee, where Crockett became a tavern keeper.

David, better known as Davy, Crockett was born on August 17, 1786, near what is now Greeneville, Hawkins County, Tennessee. He remained there 13 years but then ran away to avoid a beating. Crockett wandered for three years and made his way to Baltimore before he returned home. He spent his first year back in Tennessee working to pay debts incurred by his father.

The schoolhouse never held a strong attraction for Crockett. He was proud of his lack of formal education and limited his exposure to a short foray into the classroom, made at 18 in an unsuccessful bid to impress a young woman. As a member of Congress, he later would resist an invitation to visit Harvard for fear that the institution might grant him an LL.D., an honor he felt his rustic constituents would translate as befitting a "lazy lounging dunce."

While still a teenager Crockett married Polly Findlay, and, with $15 borrowed from a friend, rented a homestead. Despite his wife's dowry of two cows with calves, Crockett's career as a farmer was a failure, and they moved near the Alabama border. Polly Crockett died around 1815, leaving her husband with three children. He later married Elizabeth Patton, and they had two children.

Adventure and politics suited Crockett. In 1813 and 1814 he served as a scout under General Andrew Jackson in the war against the Creek Indians. Crockett performed his duties well, but left the service early and hired a substitute to complete his enlistment service.

Typically a frontiersman, Crockett was continuously on the move. With his family he went farther west, and became a justice of the peace when Tennessee's Giles County absorbed his new home. His fortunes continued to improve: he became a colonel of the district's militia, and won election to the state legislature in 1821. When the Crocketts migrated to the western border of Tennessee, near the junction of the Obion and Mississippi rivers, he was again elected to the legislature.

Crockett advanced in the political world in 1826, when he won election to the US Congress. If a famous tall tale has any accuracy, he undoubtedly made an impression. "I'm David Crockett," he is said to have announced, "fresh from the backwoods, half horse, half alligator, a little touched with snapping turtle. I can wade the Mississippi, leap the Ohio, ride a streak of lightning, slip without a scratch down a honey locust, whip my weight in wildcats, hug a bear too close for comfort and eat any man opposed to Jackson."

Despite this protestation, Crockett's relationship with Andrew Jackson was not smooth. As a state legislator, Crockett had opposed his former commander's selection as senator from Tennessee, but in 1828 he gave his backing to Jackson's successful campaign for the White House. During their tenures in Washington, Crockett and Jackson frequently clashed. To his credit, Crockett opposed the President's support of Alabama, Georgia, and Mississippi in their violation of the treaty rights of the Cherokee, Chickasaw, Choctaw, and Creek Indians.

Crockett's temerity cost him the 1830 congressional election, but he managed to regain his seat two years later despite Jackson's landslide victory in the presidential contest of 1832. Crockett's success against such odds and his opposition to Jackson's veto of the renewal of the charter for the Second Bank of the United States made him the hero of the antiadministration forces. The Whig party adopted the backwoodsman and in 1834 sent him on a tour of the Northeast.

Life and industry in Philadelphia, New York, and Boston pleased Crockett. He was particularly impressed by the system of factories that his Whig mentors had developed in New England. He thought the mill workers of Lowell, Massachusetts, to be especially blessed: "There is every enjoyment of life realized by these people and there can be but a few who are not happy."

In 1834 Crockett lost his congressional seat for the final time. He remained active in politics temporarily and in 1835 allowed his name to be associated with a scurrilous biography of Vice President Martin Van Buren, whom Jackson had selected to succeed him in office. Crockett's book described Van Buren in abusive terms.

Troubles in Texas fortunately diverted Crockett's attention from political invective. Texas was Mexican territory, but the many Americans who had settled there were anxious to be independent and even to become part of the United States. The Americans revolted in 1835; Crockett went off to join their fight.

The Texans under Sam Houston's leadership cleared the province of Mexican garrisons in 1835, but the enemy soon returned. On February 23, 1836, General Santa Anna appeared with more than 6,000 men before the Texan outpost, the Alamo Mission at San Antonio (see March 6). One hundred and forty-five men, including Davy Crockett, were within the fortress, which Lieutenant Colonel William Travis and James Bowie jointly commanded. Soon 32 additional men came to their aid.

Santa Anna demanded that the fort surrender, but the defenders refused to lay down their arms. "I have sustained a continual Bombardment and cannonade for 24 hours and have not lost a man," Travis answered. "Our flag still proudly waves from the wall. I shall never surrender or retreat. . . . Victory or death."

A siege ensued for 13 days, and on the morning of March 6, 1836, Santa Anna launched his assault. After failing twice the Mexicans breached the walls on the third try. The Texans had not suffered many casualties, but were almost out of ammunition and were physically exhausted. Fighting continued within the fortress, but gradually the Mexicans killed all the defenders. The last position taken was the chapel; there Davy Crockett and 12 other Tennessee volunteers fell.

Although the Alamo originally extended over two and one half acres, only its chapel remains. Each year thousands visit the site of Davy Crockett's death. The mission has been restored, and there is also a museum containing many artifacts pertaining to Texas history.

In Tennessee, places associated with Davy Crockett's life abound. Nine miles from Greeneville is the Davy Crockett Birthplace Park. The 15-acre park overlooks the Nolichucky River, and a limestone slab marks the site where the frontiersman was born. The park includes a replica of the Crockett log cabin, a visitor center, and a picnic and camping area.

In nearby Morristown, where Crockett spent his boyhood, is the Davy Crockett Tavern-Museum. The tavern is a replica of the one kept by Crockett's father, and among its frontier furnishings are a coonskin cap and a Davy Crockett rifle. A covered wagon stands behind the tavern, and a museum in the basement contains early 19th century antiques.

Crockett moved west to Rutherford, Tennessee, in 1821, where a replica of his cabin has been constructed from the original logs on the grounds of the Rutherford High School. The cabin's furniture, tools, and utensils are typical of those used by the pioneers, and a rocking chair made by Crockett is on exhibit. His mother is buried near the cabin.

The state of Tennessee has honored Crockett by dedicating the David Crockett State Park to his memory. Located in Lawrenceburg, the park contains a museum and has facilities for boating, picnicking, tennis, and camping. Always a popular hero of American history, Davy Crockett was the subject of a highly successful 1955 film that spawned a Crockett fad among the young and persuaded millions of children to wear coonskin caps, fringed jackets, and other frontier paraphernalia.

Fulton's Steamboat Sails

Robert Fulton did many remarkable things during his 50 years of life, but he did not invent the steamship as Americans often credit him with doing. He did, however, successfully develop the first steamboat that was commercially practical.

Harnessing steam to power machines had been dreamed of at least since the time of Hero of Alexandria, a Greek mathematician and inventor (circa third century A.D.). Again contrary to public opinion, the first steam engine was not invented by James Watt. Watt, a Scottish instrument maker working at the University of Glas-

gow, discovered some interesting things when he was repairing a steam engine that had been patented in 1705 by Thomas Newcomen and Thomas Savery. In 1769, when Watt patented his improvements on the steam engine, he gave inventors of the world the most practical source of steam power that had been seen up to that time.

Around the world, inventors promptly busied themselves in trying to use steam to power machines and devices of all sorts. Many engineers succeeded in their experiments to power ships by steam. Among these were the Americans John Fitch and James Rumsey, whose steam-powered ships successfully sailed less than two decades after Watt patented his piston steam engine. But it remained for Fulton to make the application of steam power to ships practical enough to be used commercially.

Born on November 14, 1765, on a farm in Little Britain, Pennsylvania, about 22 miles south of Lancaster, Fulton showed great mechanical talent and inventiveness early in his life. When he was 14 he enjoyed going fishing with a group of boys, but he balked at the exertion required to pole the boat out to the fishing spot — so he designed a paddle-wheel vessel. While still in his teens he built a remarkable skyrocket to celebrate Independence Day. He liked talking with craftsmen and watching them work, and he learned much this way, becoming in fact an expert gunsmith while the American Revolution was being fought.

After the war Fulton was apprenticed to a jeweler in Philadelphia. Two or three years later, still in Philadelphia, he became self-employed as a painter of landscapes and portraits, and also of miniatures, which were then very much in vogue. His success enabled him to buy a small farm in Pennsylvania for his mother.

In 1786 he went to London and studied under another Pennsylvania-born painter, Benjamin West. Fulton's paintings had a fairly good reception in England and France, but his own interest turned more and more to canal engineering and machine invention. Consequently abandoning art in 1793, he wrote Treatise on the Improvement of Canal Investigation, which appeared in 1796, but failed to interest either the United States or France in his canal proposals.

In the spring of 1797 Fulton moved to France, where he drew plans for a submarine, using many of the principles of David Bushnell's underwater vessel, which Americans had used in combat, albeit with scant success, in 1776. Fulton submitted his submarine plans to France, explaining that with an underwater vessel that could remain undetected it would be possible to attach an underwater bomb to a British warship and thereby destroy it. France rejected the plans — but Fulton is sometimes credited with inventing the marine torpedo.

In 1800 — a hundred years before the US Navy got its first submarine — Fulton successfully launched his submersible *Nautilus*. He himself stayed in the submerged vessel for six hours, receiving air from an above-water tube. He later improved the *Nautilus* by devising an on-board supply of compressed air, a horizontal rudder, and other refinements that validate the craft as the forerunner of modern submarines. However, the French rejected the *Nautilus*, and Fulton turned to experimenting with steamboats. (Later he tried, but failed, to interest President Thomas Jefferson in his submarine.)

Fulton then went into partnership with Robert R. Livingston, who was appointed as American minister to France in 1801 by Jefferson and helped negotiate the Louisiana Purchase in 1803. Livingston had been experimenting with steamboats and held a monopoly on steamboating in New York waters. He financed Fulton's experiments, and together they launched Fulton's first steamboat on France's Seine River in 1802.

Having spent 20 years abroad, Fulton returned to the United States in 1806, still working on improvements for what he called The Steamboat and what came to be known, prematurely, as Fulton's Folly. On August 17, 1807, a few days after a trial run, Fulton's Folly, with a 24-horsepower Boulton-Watt engine, made its historic trip up the Hudson (or North) River from New York City to Albany. The trip of 150 miles took 32 hours, and the return trip an additional 30 hours. But Fulton had proved it could be done; and regular commercial schedules, beginning in the fall, were advertised for the "North River Steamboat."

Substantially rebuilt, and lengthened from 140 to 149 feet, the ship was registered in 1808 as *The North River Steamboat of Clermont*, which the press shortened to *Clermont*. Clermont was the name of the house in which Fulton married Harriet Livingston, the cousin of his partner. The house, which can be seen today near the Germantown section of Philadelphia, had been built in 1729–1730 by Robert Livingston, Harriet Fulton's great-grandfather, and rebuilt after it was burned by the British in 1777.

Over the next few years more steamboats were built to ply the Hudson River route. Fulton set up an engine works in New Jersey and continued to design steamboats of all sorts, including ferries used on the Hudson and East rivers, which border Manhattan. He designed the *New Orleans*, which accomplished the first steam navigation of central US waterways — on the Mississippi River in 1811. During the War of 1812 Fulton gained acceptance for and built the ship *Demologos*, sometimes called *Fulton the First*, which he conceived as a floating fort to defend New York harbor. It was launched shortly before the war ended in December 1814.

Having spent his comparatively short life making great practical contributions by improving upon the inventions of others, Fulton died in New York City on February 24, 1815. He was among the original group of men honored by inclusion in the Hall of Fame for Great Americans in New York City.

In 1909 a Hudson-Fulton Celebration focused on the discovery of the North River by Henry Hudson in 1609 and the commercial success of Robert Fulton two centuries later. A Robert Fulton commemorative stamp was issued by the US Post Office in 1965, the bicentennial of his birth. Fulton's birthplace — the farmhouse near Lancaster, Pennsylvania — was acquired by the Pennsylvania Historical and Museum Commission.

AUGUST 18

First United States Government Maritime Expedition Sets Sail

Exploration—over land, across seas, and through the skies — has been central to the American experience. The earliest Europeans to visit America conducted extensive expeditions into the continent, and, only decades after the United States achieved independence, the young nation sponsored several western explorations, including those of Lewis and Clark in 1804–1806 and Zebulon Pike in 1806–1807. As increasing numbers of US merchant vessels entered the trade between China and the Pacific Northwest, and whaling vessels made their dangerous voyages to the South Seas, Americans also sought knowledge about the oceans. On August 18, 1838, the first marine expedition sponsored by the federal government set sail from Hampton Roads, Virginia, to survey maritime routes in the Pacific Ocean and South Seas and to make detailed observations of major harbors in those regions.

Lieutenant Charles Wilkes commanded the 1838 expedition. The 40-year-old Wilkes, who since 1833 had headed the Depot of Charts and Instruments in Washington, D.C. (from which later developed the Naval Observatory and the

Hydrographic Office), was well qualified for the task before him. He had personally selected many of the astronomical and other scientific instruments that equipped his squadron of four naval vessels — the *Vincennes, Peacock, Porpoise,* and *Relief* — and two pilot boats — the *Sea Gull* and *Flying Fish.* (All the craft were overage.) The success of the expedition did not depend on Wilkes's talents alone, for noted civilian specialists, including geologist-mineralogist James D. Dana, botanist W. R. Rich, artist Alfred T. Agate, zoologist Charles Pickering, and artist and naturalist Titian Ramsay Peale were among the 440 men who embarked on the 1838 adventure.

The expedition reached Rio de Janeiro on November 24. After a stay of more than three weeks in the Brazilian city, the squadron returned to sea on December 17. Continuing south, it sailed the entire length of South America and rounded Cape Horn — though the *Relief* turned out to be so slow that it had to be left behind in Tierra del Fuego. Below Cape Horn, the explorers sighted the northernmost of the South Shetland Islands and continued south for their first incursion into the Antarctic. The expedition split into two sections for this initial investigation. Under Wilkes's second-in-command, Lieutenant William L. Hudson, the *Peacock* and *Flying Fish* explored the Bellingshausen Sea west of Palmer Peninsula, which points from Antarctica toward the southern tip of South America. The little *Flying Fish* reached as far as 70° S., 107° W. — almost equaling Captain James Cook's earlier record of 71° 10′ S. — before it was stopped by a wall of ice and turned back to meet the *Peacock,* from which it had become separated, at 68° S., 95° 44′ W.

Less successfully, the *Porpoise* and *Sea Gull,* under Wilkes, investigated east of Palmer Peninsula in the ice-filled Weddell Sea, where they experienced the piercing brutal Antarctic cold. They also encountered great beauty: "I have rarely seen a finer sight," wrote Wilkes. "The sea was literally studded with . . . beautiful [ice] masses . . . of pure white . . . all . . . shades of opal, . . . emerald green, and occasionally . . . some of deep black, forming a strong contrast to the pure white."

The long Antarctic winter was now at hand, however, and both sections of the expedition retreated northward. Wilkes, with three vessels, headed for Valparaiso, Chile, where he arrived on April 13. He meanwhile dispatched the *Flying Fish* and the *Sea Gull* to Tierra del Fuego to pick up the *Relief* and escort it around Cape Horn. When the latter ship proved too feeble to be useful and had to be sent home, the two smaller vessels proceeded around the treacher-

ous Horn alone, en route to join the others in Valparaiso. They were separated, however, on April 26, during a severe storm, and the *Sea Gull* was lost and never seen again.

On May 1 the remainder of the expedition — rejoined by the *Vincennes,* which also had remained in Tierra del Fuego during the explorer's first journey into the Antarctic — left Valparaiso and 12 days later arrived at Callao, the seaport of Lima. The explorers remained in the Peruvian capital for more than two months before they departed on July 13, 1839, with their four remaining vessels — the *Vincennes, Peacock, Porpoise,* and *Flying Fish* — taking a westerly course that would permit extensive scientific observations in the South Pacific and the collection of many valuable specimens. The scientists carefully noted the exact location of each of the many small islands they encountered. They also went ashore numerous times, examined the terrain of the islands, and made contact with the inhabitants.

By September 12, 1839, the expedition reached Tahiti. The scientists made extensive surveys of the island, and Lieutenant Wilkes negotiated a commercial treaty with the principal tribal chiefs. On October 10 the American party left Tahiti, and, continuing westward, arrived at Pago-Pago, Samoa, on October 18.

After staying only one day in Pago-Pago, they pushed on to the neighboring island of Upota. There they purchased much-needed provisions, explored the interior of the island, and made detailed observations of the tides. On November 10 they sailed southward and encountered numerous small islands before entering the harbor of Sydney, Australia, on November 27.

The Americans remained in Sydney for almost a month and then on December 26 began an exploring cruise in the Antarctic Ocean. Dense fog and driving rain accompanied the vessels as they made their way south. But on January 10, 1840, the weather cleared and the adventurers caught their first glimpses of icebergs. The following day they came upon even more spectacular ice formations, some of which they estimated to be five miles long and 300 feet high.

On January 19 the explorers sighted land, and during the weeks that followed they confirmed a theretofore undiscovered continent. On several occasions their boats sailed fairly close to the Antarctic land mass, thereby enabling the scientists to observe and gather specimens of the rock and sand of the continent. The discovery that Antarctica was, in fact, a continent was undoubtedly the most spectacular achievement of the expedition, and, in honor of its commander, a large region of the southernmost continent bears the name Wilkes Land.

On February 21 the Americans began their return north, and on March 11 they arrived back in Sydney. The squadron set sail again on March 19, and 11 days later reached New Zealand. Departing from New Zealand on April 6, the expedition made its way northeast and on April 24 put in at Tonga. The Americans continued their journey on May 4 and within two days landed at Levuka in the Fiji Islands.

Desiring to conduct detailed surveys, the expedition remained in the Fiji Islands several months. The initial weeks of the stay were peaceful, but violence erupted on July 24 when Lieutenant Joseph Underwood and a small party went ashore at Malolo to attempt to purchase provisions. At first the natives seemed eager to barter, but when Lieutenant Underwood refused to supply them with muskets and gunpowder they became hostile. They attacked and killed Underwood and Midshipman Wilkes Henry. When Lieutenant Wilkes heard of the killings, he moved quickly to avenge his men. Acting under his orders, a force of 80 Americans landed on Malolo early on July 25, and within hours they devastated the principal village of the island. About 100 natives died in the retaliatory strike before the islanders surrendered on July 26 to the Americans.

When they had completed their scientific observations, the members of the American expedition left the Fiji Islands, on August 11, and after sailing in a northeasterly direction for more than six weeks arrived at the Hawaiian Islands on September 30. The explorers remained there for six months, during which time they collected much valuable data. They descended into the crater of the great volcano of Mount Kilauea and obtained specimens of volcanic rock and lava; they climbed to the summit of Mauna Loa, which is 13,680 feet above sea level, and there unfurled the Stars and Stripes; and they also explored Maui and some of the smaller islands.

From Hawaii the Americans took a northeast course, and on April 28, 1841, they reached the northwest coast of America. During the months that followed, they conducted extensive surveys of the area of Washington and Oregon, and the data provided by these investigations proved extremely useful during the dispute between the United States and Great Britain over the Oregon Territory in the mid-1840s. The area to the south also interested the explorers, and early in September 39 persons, including a naturalist, an artist, and a botanist, began an overland journey to San Francisco. This party made detailed reports on the animals and vegetation they encountered as they proceeded south.

Members of the overland party rejoined the maritime expedition in San Francisco on October

9, 1841, and at the end of October the entire American squadron returned to sea. Proceeding west they secured provisions in Honolulu on November 19, and then went on and reached Singapore on January 22, 1842. They again set sail on February 25 and arrived 13 days later at St. Helena off the west coast of Africa. From St. Helena the expedition continued its circumnavigation of the globe. The American ships crossed the Atlantic, touching at Rio de Janeiro, and finally reached New York City on June 10, 1842.

The report of the 47-month expedition was published in 19 volumes. Wilkes contributed the *Narrative of the United States Exploring Expedition* (5 volumes plus atlas). He also edited the scientific reports and was the author of the hydrography and meteorology volumes. Indeed, he devoted most of his time in the years 1843 to 1861 to preparation of the report.

AUGUST 19

The *Constitution*'s Great Victory

The War of 1812 pitted the young American nation against Great Britain, the mightiest sea power of the era. When hostilities between the two nations began in June 1812, eleven British ships of the line, together with 34 frigates and 52 smaller warships, patrolled American waters. In comparison, US naval resources consisted of only 4 frigates and about 12 other warships capable of fighting on the open sea. The addition of several hundred armed American merchant vessels, which harassed British commerce throughout the war, considerably aided the American effort. But from the start it was clear that the American navy was no match for the British.

English newspapers reflected the contempt the British felt for their adversaries. One paper described the USS *Constitution*, one of the four American frigates, as "a bundle of pine boards sailing under a bit of striped bunting," and claimed that "a few broadsides from England's wooden walls would drive the paltry striped bunting from the ocean."

A few days later the *Constitution*'s performance necessitated a reconsideration of these words. Under the command of Captain Isaac Hull, the *Constitution* sailed from Chesapeake Bay on July 12 to join forces with an American squadron then plying the waters off New York. Along the route a number of British vessels, including the frigate *Guerrière*, sighted the lone American ship and pursued it for three days and two nights. Hull was able to outmaneuver his adversaries, however, and the American frigate escaped to the safety of Boston harbor.

On August 12 the *Constitution* left Boston, and seven days later, while cruising 200 miles off the Maine coast, again met the *Guerrière*. This time a confrontation between the two vessels was unavoidable. The 30-minute battle that ensued resulted in 79 British casualties and the destruction of the *Guerrière;* the Americans, however, suffered only 14 casualties and minor damage to their ship. In fact the *Constitution*'s ability to withstand British attack was so great that one of its gunners allegedly exclaimed "Her sides must be made of iron." Although tradition holds that this is the source of its nickname, Old Ironsides, some claim that the incident merely confirmed its widespread usage. According to them, the name originated at the time of the ship's construction because the oak planking was bent into place without first undergoing the customary steaming and softening process.

A hero's welcome awaited Hull when he returned to Boston. On the other side of the Atlantic, the stunned London *Times* reported, "Never before in the history of the world did an English frigate strike to an American." The *Constitution*'s victory was, indeed, a great boost to American morale, and an equally great blow to British pride. But aside from this, the battle itself had little long-range significance. The regular American navy was too weak to withstand the superior British fleet, and during most of the remainder of the war British ships kept the *Constitution* and the other frigates confined to their home ports.

The contribution of Old Ironsides to American history is not limited to the defeat of the *Guerrière*. The 44-gun frigate was one of the first six warships Congress had ordered built when it reactivated the US Navy in 1794. Launched on October 21, 1797, the ship had served in the Tripolitan War of 1801 to 1805; and several times during the War of 1812 it escaped British surveillance to put a number of enemy vessels out of commission. In 1830 the navy declared it unseaworthy, and it would have been broken up had not Oliver Wendell Holmes's stirring poem "Old Ironsides" gained the ship a last-minute reprieve.

After extensive rebuilding, the *Constitution* returned to service in 1833. For another 22 years it saw active duty, but in 1855 deterioration again reached such an extent that it was retired to the Portsmouth Navy Yard. Partially restored in 1877, it made a final transatlantic crossing in that same year. The *Constitution* sailed only intermittently thereafter, and in 1897 returned to the Boston Naval Shipyard, where it was used as a barracks ship until 1927.

Popular interest in Old Ironsides has lasted into the 20th century. After its restoration in 1931 — a project financed entirely by voluntary contributions — the ship called at 90 US ports on both the Atlantic and Pacific seaboards. The presence of the historic old vessel elicited tremendous response, and in the course of the tour over 4.5 million people turned out to see it. In 1934 the ship returned to Boston, where it has since remained permanently berthed at Pier 1 of the Boston Naval Shipyard. Each year approximately 500,000 persons visit Old Ironsides. The ship, which is the oldest commissioned vessel afloat, was reconditioned again in the 1960s. Although numerous rebuildings have resulted in the virtual replacement of all its original parts, the *Constitution* presents a true picture of a 19th century frigate. Moreover, Old Ironsides contains a display of 30 of its original guns and some of the hardware fashioned by Paul Revere in the 1790s to hold its timbers to the copper plates of the hull.

National Aviation Day

National Aviation Day, observed annually on August 19, celebrates the development made in manned flight. In the years since the 120-foot hop of Wilbur and Orville Wright at Kitty Hawk, North Carolina in 1903 (see December 17), aviation has so advanced that today jumbo jets, with wingspans longer than the total distance covered by that initial experiment, carry passengers across oceans in a few hours. Moreover, the plane has become an increasingly important factor in commerce and warfare, and America's success in the skies has been vital to economic strength and national security.

Even before World War II Americans were fully aware of the magnitude of the airplane's potential. On May 11, 1939, the United States Congress adopted a resolution to set aside a special day each year to commemorate the contributions of the aircraft industry and to stimulate interest in it. In accordance with this legislation, President Franklin D. Roosevelt, on July 25, 1939, proclaimed August 19, the anniversary of Orville Wright's birth, as National Aviation Day and encouraged all US citizens to observe it with appropriate exercises. Senator Jennings Randolph of West Virginia, a member of the House of Representatives in 1939, sponsored the original resolution, and retained his interest in the festivities. He even served as chairman of the Honorary Committee for National Aviation Day in 1967.

The President of the United States annually proclaims National Aviation Day, and in recent years organizations concerned with aviation have sponsored celebrations in about 20 states on August 19 or the following weekend. The aviation manufacturing industry encourages community observances of National Aviation Day by holding open house celebrations at local airports. The public is invited to view flight operations and displays of new and antique aircraft. Other suggested events are parachute jumping, glider and model airplane demonstrations, films, around-the-field plane rides, and sample ground-school flying lessons.

AUGUST 20

Benjamin Harrison's Birthday

Benjamin Harrison, 23rd President of the United States, was born on August 20, 1833, in North Bend, Ohio. He came from a wealthy family of the planter class, heavily involved in politics. Harrison's great-grandfather Benjamin Harrison had been a governor of Virginia and a signer of the Declaration of Independence. The governor's son, William Henry Harrison, who settled in Ohio, became the 9th President of the United States in 1841, a memorable event in the life of his then seven-year-old grandson, Benjamin Harrison. Young Benjamin's father, John Scott Harrison, the eldest son of William Henry, lived on a farm adjacent to the estate of the new President. John Harrison was himself twice elected to the US House of Representatives as a Whig. His second wife, Elizabeth Irwin Harrison, was Benjamin Harrison's mother.

Harrison received private tutoring before entering Farmers' College in Walnut Hills, Ohio. He studied three years at Farmers' College before transferring to Miami University at Oxford, Ohio, from which he received a degree in 1852. Harrison was a good student, especially drawn to political science and history. Following college, Harrison studied law for two years before being admitted to the bar. On October 20, 1853, Harrison married Caroline Lavinia Scott.

In 1854 Harrison established his own law practice in Indianapolis, Indiana. His practice flourished in the burgeoning state capital. Talented as a public speaker, Harrison became involved with the infant Republican party, making addresses on behalf of Republican candidates and policies. He was elected city attorney of Indianapolis in 1857. Three years later, and again in 1864, he was elected reporter of the Indiana supreme court.

After the outbreak of the Civil War, Harrison, in 1862, helped raise the volunteer 70th Indiana Infantry Regiment, and was appointed its colonel. At first his men guarded railroads and took part in minor encounters in Kentucky and Tennessee. In 1864, however, his regiment was attached to the command of General William T. Sherman and engaged in the difficult campaign that culminated with the capture of Atlanta. Harrison's skill in commanding his men won him promotion to the brevet rank of brigadier general. Harrison was diverted from further direct military action by the request of Governor Oliver P. Morton that he return to Indiana to help campaign in the 1864 elections against the "Copperhead" Democrats, who sympathized with the South.

After the war Harrison resumed the practice of law and was soon recognized as one of the leading lawyers of the state. He was noted especially for his excellent memory, eloquent presentation, and analytical mind. He tried for the Republican gubernatorial nomination in 1872 but was not selected. Four years later he was nominated, but not elected. In 1880 Harrison was chairman of the Indiana delegation at the Republican National Convention. He supported the swing of delegates that gave the nomination to James A. Garfield of Ohio. Garfield, when elected, offered him a cabinet post, but Harrison declined it since he had just been elected by the Indiana legislature to serve in the US Senate.

In Washington, Harrison worked assiduously for expansion into the territories and the admission of new states. He also labored for the establishment of a national park system. As a Republican, he supported the party's position in favor of continued high tariffs; but he was instrumental in the passage of the Interstate Commerce Act of 1887 before the expiration of his term. He had lost the support of the Indiana legislature the previous fall and had not been reelected. However, at the Republican National Convention of 1888 he was nominated to run for President. In the election Harrison won over the incumbent, Grover Cleveland, by 233 to 168 electoral votes, even though Cleveland received a larger popular vote.

As President, Harrison pushed ahead with plans to increase the number of states. In April 1889 Oklahoma was opened to new settlers, after the Creek and Seminole Indians were paid to move out. During Harrison's administration, North Dakota, South Dakota, Montana, Washington, Idaho, and Wyoming became states.

During the winter of 1889–1890, representatives of South and Central American countries met in Washington, D.C., in the first Pan American Congress, with the goal of establishing closer ties. However, the Latin American image of the United States did not improve during Harrison's term. One particularly unpleasant incident was a brawl involving US sailors in Chile, which resulted in a forced apology from the Chilean government.

Harrison's administration saw much important legislation. Measures were enacted to strengthen the navy and army. Public clamor for some restraints on the activities of giant "trusts" was placated with the Sherman Antitrust Act. The Sherman Silver Purchase Act satisfied western Republicans, while the McKinley Tariff Act raised tariff schedules slightly for eastern, business-oriented Republicans. In addition a new veterans' pension bill vastly increased payments to Civil War veterans. Unfortunately the effects of the pension, silver, and naval building acts and increased public works projects of Harrison's administration combined with the state of the economy to drain the Treasury's surplus funds. By the end of his term, economic collapse was imminent.

A number of factors led to Harrison's defeat in 1892. Although the United States was rapidly being transformed from an agrarian to a highly urban and industrial country, neither Harrison and the Republicans nor their political opponents took into serious consideration the nation's increasing labor problems — created especially by the floods of new immigrants — or the mounting dissatisfaction of farmers. Labor unrest, Populist farmer movements, and the growing economic malaise led to a call for change in leadership. Then there was the explosive question of civil service, and on this Harrison, though steering an even course, managed to alienate both the Republican bosses with their demands for patronage and those members of the party who were ardent for civil service reform: neither faction felt he had gone far enough in the direction of its choice.

In the presidential election of 1892, Grover Cleveland was again the Democratic nominee. After the balloting was over, Cleveland had received 277 electoral votes, and Harrison had garnered a mere 145.

Although Benjamin Harrison had a relatively good record as President, he alienated many by the coldness of his manner. Acting Attorney General William Howard Taft aptly pinpointed the difficulty in 1890:

The President is not popular with the members of either house. His manner of treating them is not at all fortunate, and when they have an interview with him they generally come away mad. . . . I think this is exceedingly unfortunate, because I am sure we have never had a man in the White House who was more conscientiously seeking to do his duty.

Indeed, conscientiousness and devotion to duty, along with integrity of purpose and high moral principles, were among Harrison's most frequently cited qualities. They were combined in him with legal acumen and loyalty to Republican party principles.

At the end of his term, Harrison returned to his law practice in Indianapolis, handling many important court cases in the ensuing years. He also accepted numerous invitations to make public addresses, and he wrote articles for various magazines. A series of pieces that appeared in the *Ladies' Home Journal* on the nature of the federal government was later revised and issued as a book, *This Country of Ours*, which was used for many years as a standard reference work for schools and colleges. It was republished in England, and the Carnegie Endowment for International Peace had it translated into Spanish and given to leaders in Latin America. The former Chief Executive also published a volume of essays — originally presented as speeches — which appeared under the title *Views of an Ex-President*. Harrison was active on behalf of Republican candidates in the elections of 1894 and 1896. In addition he was chosen to be senior counsel for Venezuela in its boundary dispute with British Guiana. After nearly two years of preparation, he presented the Venezuelan case before an arbitration tribunal in Paris in 1899. Before his impressive closing argument was half finished, the British counsel recognized that defeat was imminent and indicated as much in a message home.

Harrison's first wife had died in the White House in 1892, after suffering a long illness that added to the causes of Harrison's defeat that year by draining the strength and enthusiasm he might otherwise have found for a more energetic presidential campaign. In 1896 he was remarried — to Mary Scott Lord Dimmick, a relative of his first wife. The couple became parents of a daughter Elizabeth; by his first marriage, Harrison had become the father of two children, Russell and Mary. During his postpresidential years, Harrison retained the interest he had always had in the activities of the Presbyterian church. He was an elder of the church for 40 years, he taught a men's Bible class, he was superintendent of a Sunday school, and he was several times a delegate to the General Assembly of the Presbyterian church.

The former President died of pneumonia on March 13, 1901. His burial place was Crown Hill Cemetery in Indianapolis. Harrison's Indianapolis house, completed in 1874, has been designated the Benjamin Harrison Memorial Home; it still stands on North Delaware Street.

AUGUST 21

Hawaii Admitted to the Union

Hawaii, an archipelago valued by Europeans since the 18th century for its beauty and strategic importance, became the 50th state of the United States on August 21, 1959. Captain

James Cook of the British navy was the first European to visit Hawaii, in 1778. Many other Westerners followed, including a large number of American merchants, missionaries, and whalers who migrated to the islands in the 19th century. The Americans eventually gained control of Hawaii's economy and government, and the United States annexed the isles in 1898.

Composed of 132 islands formed by volcanic eruptions, Hawaii is located approximately 2,400 miles west of San Francisco. Hawaii, Oahu, Maui, Kahoolawe, Lanai, Molokai, Kauai, and Niihau are the major islands of the chain, and Honolulu, the capital city, on the island of Oahu, is the heart of the state. Together, the city and county of Honolulu — comprising all of Oahu — are home for more than three-quarters of the state's total population.

Seafaring Polynesians, probably from Tahiti, first settled the islands in the eighth century. Since that time peoples of every race have gone to live in Hawaii. Hawaiians, Chinese, Filipinos, Japanese, and mainland Americans comprise the bulk of the present population.

The US Congress granted Hawaii territorial status in 1900 and in 1919 considered a bill to grant the islands statehood. This initial measure failed, and 40 more years passed before the advocates of statehood achieved success. On March 12, 1959, the US House of Representatives completed congressional action by passing the Hawaiian Statehood Bill, and President Dwight D. Eisenhower signed the bill on March 18. The citizens of Hawaii gave their approval to the act by a margin of nearly 17 to 1 at the June 27 plebescite, and on July 28 elected their first state governor, senators, representatives, and legislators. President Eisenhower brought the long process to its culmination by signing the Hawaiian Statehood Proclamation, which officially admitted the new state to the Union on August 21, 1959. The 50-star US flag became the nation's official standard on the following July 4.

The third Friday in August, approximately the anniversary of Hawaii's admission, is annually marked as a state holiday.

Feast of St. Pius X

Pope Pius X, who in his 1903–1914 tenure initiated extensive changes in eucharistic worship, religious education, canon law codification, and liturgical practice for Roman Catholics, died on August 20, 1914. Already venerated popularly during his lifetime and officially considered a possible subject for canonization as early as nine years after his death, Pius X was beatified on June 3, 1951, by Pope Pius XII. On May 29, three years later, he was canonized, thus becom-

ing only the second pope (Pope Pius V had been canonized in 1712) declared a saint since the 13th century. The feast day of Pius X, originally September 3, was changed in the revised Roman Catholic calendar to August 21, the day following his death date. The strictly Roman Catholic observance, formerly ranked a III Class, is now classed a memorial.

Born Giuseppe Melchiorre Sarto on June 2, 1835, the future pope was the second and oldest surviving son of the 10 children of Giovanni-Battista Sarto, a parish clerk in Riese near Treviso in northern Italy. His formal schooling started in his native village, but he showed such promise that at the age of 11 he was admitted to the high school at Castelfranco Veneto, to which he had to walk five miles. At 16 Sarto, who had been convinced of his vocation to the priesthood since the age of 10, was studying theology at the seminary at Padua when his father died. His poverty-stricken mother, Margherita Sanson Sarto, refused to consider her son's proposal that he abandon his studies to support the large family.

Giuseppe Sarto was ordained a priest in September 1858 at Castelfranco Veneto. For 17 years he served in the diocese of Treviso — from 1858 to 1867 as curate of Tombolo, and from 1867 to 1875 as parish priest of Salzano. Dedicated to working with the poor, Father Sarto regretted deeply his summons in 1875 to become canon of the cathedral of Treviso, rector of the Treviso seminary, and chancellor of the diocese. In a private letter he described his new duties as "a misfortune." Similarly he did not wish to accept a bishopric, refusing that of Treviso in 1880 but finally accepting that of Mantua four years later at Pope Leo XIII's express command.

His outstanding abilities as both spiritual leader and administrator caused Sarto to be created cardinal on June 12, 1893, and nominated patriarch of Venice — three days later. This turn of events made him "anxious, terrified, and humiliated." Although his piety, simplicity, and competence soon endeared him to the local populace, the cardinal-patriarch of Venice disliked the prestige of his office and retained his feelings of inadequacy. He yearned for quiet parish life in a small village. When in early August 1903 the deliberations at the conclave called to elect a successor to Pope Leo XIII unexpectedly turned in favor of the relatively unknown Cardinal Sarto, the unlikely candidate begged the other cardinals: "I am unworthy . . . I am incapable . . . For the love of God, forget me!" He was elected Roman pontiff on August 4 and took the name Pius X.

For the first time in centuries, a pope of peasant stock, a man of the people accustomed to solving difficulties simply and directly, ascended the chair of Peter. Unlike his predecessor, he was mystified by the complicated workings of the papal curia, the subtle techniques of ecclesiastical diplomacy, and the intricacies of international diplomatic activity. As a result, Pius X used a firm, direct approach to all problems, one that proved remarkably effective. One of his first moves was to reorganize the operation of the papal conclave. At the 1903 conclave which had elected him pope, the Austrian emperor Franz Josef (through Cardinal Puzyna, the prince-bishop of Cracow) had signaled his desire to wield the ancient Hapsburg privilege of veto, in opposition to a leading candidate, Cardinal Rampolla, Leo XIII's former secretary of state. After Pius X became pope instead, the possibility still existed that similar pressure might be applied in future elections. In 1904 the new pontiff accordingly issued the constitution *Commissum nobis,* which guaranteed perfect freedom in elections by abolishing the veto. Later, absolute secrecy was required for conclave deliberations.

The new pope was equally decisive when the French government, repudiating the Napoleonic concordat of the early 19th century, began to regulate severely both religious education and church property in France. Rather than accept the proposed, more circumscribed role for the church in France with its attendant dependence on the state, Pius advocated complete separation of church and state. He accordingly urged French Catholics — who unselfishly followed his advice — to sacrifice church property in favor of freedom from civil dominance.

Pius X also made his mark on European politics by attempting to ease the relations between church and state in Italy. They had been very much strained since the unification of the country in 1870, when the Italian kingdom had claimed sovereignty over the traditional Papal States. The pope ceased direct dispute with the government and took the first step toward allowing Roman Catholics to take part once more in Italian politics. At their discretion, Italian bishops could lift the decree of the Holy See prohibiting their congregations from voting in elections.

Deeply convinced of the necessity of vital spirituality in the church, Pius X advocated a thorough revamping of ecclesiastical institutions. He took as his motto *Instaurare omnia in Christo,* "To restore all things in Christ," proclaiming in his first encyclical:

We proclaim that the interests of God shall be our interests and for those we are resolved to spend all our strength and our very life. Hence, should anyone ask us for a symbol and expression of our will, we will give this and no other — to restore all things in Christ so that Christ may be all in all.

Here he laid down his program of the next 11 years, which would reinvigorate the entire church. One of the pope's earliest and most noted spiritual reforms concerned the reception of the sacrament of the Holy Eucharist. In 1905 he decreed that "frequent and daily Communion should be open to all the faithful whatever rank or condition so that no one who is in the state of grace . . . can be lawfully hindered therefrom." He later decreed that children should receive First Holy Communion at an early age, generally about their seventh year.

Among Pius X's other actions that revitalized Catholic piety, learning, and administration were reform of the Breviary, codificaton of canon law, foundation of an institute for scriptural studies, reorganization of the outmoded medieval Roman curia, and reform of public worship as seen in the renewed emphasis upon sacred music, especially Gregorian chant.

Since the pontiff's own intellectual interests were theological in nature, he vehemently opposed the use of secular disciplines in matters affecting faith. He therefore took a particularly strong stand against Roman Catholic intellectuals who advocated modernism, an analytical approach to the Scriptures and questions of dogma. Believing that supernatural truths could not be known with certainty by human reason and that such a rational approach was against orthodox belief, Pius condemned modernism in the decree *Lamentabili sane exitu* of July 1907 and in the encyclical *Pascendi dominici gregis* of September 1907. His move, considered by some as unduly strict, caused consternation and bitterness among Roman Catholic intellectuals and severed the church from modern scholarship. Pius X also recommended intense supervision of professors in seminaries, stricter control of the Catholic press, and sounder education of the clergy.

Pius X never really felt at ease in high office. In many ways he remained the parish priest of his youth, having his sisters move to Rome to do his washing and mending, gathering papal servants together for informal chats, and explaining the Gospel every Sunday in a Vatican courtyard to whoever came to listen. As pope, he was embarrassed by the many formalities of his position. He preferred to carry his own nickel watch to tell time rather than disturb his attendants for such a simple request; and he shed tears on one occasion while lamenting to an old acquaintance, "Look how they have dressed me up!" Pius X remained humble, not only in spirit but also in the frugality of his life. He declared in his will: "I was born poor. I have lived poor, and I wish to die poor."

Early in 1914, Pope Pius X foresaw the great war that threatened to engulf Europe. The conflict erupted in August on the 11th anniversary of his ascension to the papacy. A few days later the pontiff became ill; he died on August 20, saddened by human suffering but unaware of the extent of the coming tragedy of World War I.

AUGUST 22

First America's Cup Race

On August 22, 1851, the schooner *America* triumphed spectacularly in the first of a long series of hotly contested races, the most prestigious in international yachting today. That first competition had its origin in 1850 with an invitation to a New York businessman from a Londoner. He suggested that the Americans send one of their fastest yachts to England to race in a regatta — sponsored by the British Royal Yacht Squadron — that was to be held in conjunction with the Great Exposition opening at the Crystal Palace in London the next year.

Designed by George Steers, the *America*, 101 feet, 9 inches overall, with a waterline length of 90 feet, 3 inches, was especially built by a six-man syndicate of the New York Yacht Club, headed by John C. Stevens, the club's commodore. To hide its speed, the *America* was sailed first to France and then refitted with racing sails. As it sailed for the Isle of Wight, where the regatta was to be held, a British cutter enticed it into a race, which the *America* won, revealing its speed prematurely.

The English then realized that they could not win in an open competition, and there was talk of dropping the challenge to the *America*. Because of pressure from the press and public, however, the schooner was in the end included in the regatta, which took place as scheduled on August 22. The race was against 14 of England's fastest schooners and cutters and was in coastal waters "round the Isle of Wight, inside Noman's Buoy and Sandhead Buoy, and outside the Nab." At the starting gun, the *America* fouled its anchor and had to haul down and reset its swelling sails. But even with the delay it was in fourth place within 15 minutes.

The victorious *America* took 10 hours and 37 minutes to sail the 58 miles. The victory was not without protest, however, for several British yachtsmen claimed that the *America* had not won. The British interpreted the specified race-course "outside the Nab" to mean outside Nab Light, and the Americans, not realizing the difference between Nab Light and Nab promontory, had sailed outside the tip of land but inside the light. However, the Royal Yacht Squadron awarded its Hundred Guinea Cup (its cost equaled about $600) to the *America*, and it has since been known as the America's Cup. Commodore Stevens gave it to the New York Yacht Club in 1857, and despite impressive challenges it remained there into the late 1970s.

The *America* was sold to an Englishman a few months after the race. He raced it for a while but then sold it for junk. The schooner was subsequently reconditioned, however, and during the Civil War was a blockade runner aiding the Confederacy. Found scuttled near Jacksonville, Florida, it was raised by the federal government and then used as a blockade ship. After the war, it was used as a training ship at the US Naval Academy at Annapolis, Maryland.

In 1899 the *America* was at the race, though not in competition, and 1901 was the last year in which it was seen under sail. The *America* spent the next 20 years in a Boston shipyard, and in 1921 was towed to Annapolis. In 1940 it was hauled ashore and blocked up. A protective shed was built for it, but four years later the shed collapsed when two feet of ice and snow landed on its roof; and the 93-year-old schooner was shattered in the crash.

There was no challenge from England for a race to recover the cup until 1870, when the *Cambria* raced a fleet of 23 New York Yacht Club boats, losing to the American ship *Magic* in the single-race competition. In 1871 the United States kept the trophy after winning four out of five races against an English ship. In 1876 and 1881 Canadian ships were the challengers and the United States won both of the two-race series.

British and American ships held competitions in 1885, 1886, 1887, 1893, 1895, 1899, 1901, and 1903, with the United States taking all of the 21 races held during those years. In 1920, in a series lasting 13 days, the American *Resolute* held onto the trophy against the British challenger, Sir Thomas Lipton's *Shamrock IV*, only by winning three in a series of five races. Ten years later the American *Enterprise* defeated Lipton's *Shamrock V* in four races straight. Lipton, who had been the challenger ever since 1899, had meanwhile captured worldwide admiration with his spirit and gallantry, even in defeat. He was 81 when he died, a year after his last challenge.

In the 1934 America's Cup competition, the US contestant, Harold S. Vanderbilt's *Rainbow*, lost two in a series of six races against an English entry. During the next two contests, in 1937 and 1958, the American entries took four races straight against English challengers. In 1962, the first year that Australia competed for the cup, its *Gretel* took one race but was defeated by the American *Weatherly* in four more. Four races were held in 1964, and the American *Constellation* took them all against England. In the competition of 1967 the Australian challenger, *Dame Pattie,* was defeated four races to none by the American *Intrepid.*

The *Intrepid* was victorious for a second time on September 28, 1970, when it won the fifth and final race in a four-out-of-seven series against the Australian yacht *Gretel II.* The United States thus retained possession of the famous cup, which it had held ever since the first international sailing competition in 1851. One hundred fifty spectator boats and Coast Guard patrol vessels watched as the American sloop sailed across the finish line one minute, 44 seconds ahead of the Australian challenger in the 24.3-mile race.

The longest series of races in the cup's history had opened on September 15, 1970, off Newport, Rhode Island, long host to the America's Cup competition. The defending yacht, skippered by Bill (William P.) Ficker and measuring 64 feet, 6 inches in overall length, 47 feet at waterline, took the race against the challenger — 62 feet long, 46 feet at waterline, skippered by Jim Hardy — by 5 minutes, 52 seconds. In the second race the *Gretel II* sailed across the finish line 1 minute, 7 seconds ahead of the *Intrepid.* However, both boats had raised their protest flags within seconds of the start of that race because they had touched each other — in violation of racing rules — and a decision had to be made as to which boat was at fault. The six-man race committee of the New York Yacht Club disqualified the *Gretel II,* awarding the *Intrepid* the second race. The third race, on September 22, was won by the American sloop by 1 minute, 18 seconds. The *Gretel II* took the fourth race on September 24 by overtaking the defending yacht 200 yards from the finish and crossing the line about 3 boat lengths ahead, with a 1-minute, 2-second lead. It thus established the first win for a challenger since 1962; and it was only the seventh race won by any challenger in the history of the America's Cup competition, a total of 73 races. The final race was delayed by fog, extending the competition to a total of 14 days.

The 1970 races were the 21st defense of the America's Cup. The *Intrepid* was the second ship ever to defend the cup twice. The first was the *Columbia,* which sailed in 1899 and again in 1901. The *Intrepid* was rebuilt for the 1970 competition, and was chosen as the American defender that year after winning 22 out of 27 races in a series that began on July 7 against other American yachts. The final trial competition was held August 29, when it took the fifth straight race against the *Valiant.* It was the *Intrepid*'s eighth consecutive win.

The *Gretel II* became the challenger after defeating a French entry, the *France,* in four races straight. On August 28, during the final race of that series, the *France* got lost in the fog and returned to the starting line with only 30 seconds left in the race.

The highly ornate silver trophy that became known as the America's Cup was made in England by Robert Garrard in 1848. It rests in a cabinet of the New York Yacht Club's trophy room. Members say jestingly that if the cup is ever lost, its place in the cabinet will be filled with the skulls of the designer and skipper of the losing ship.

The historic competition for the America's Cup has made that international sailing event the exciting focus of yacht design, development, and racing. The rules of the competition have evolved through the years, with a recurring trend toward boats of greater sail-carrying power, larger rigs, more complicated design, and greater cost.

In the 1800s the yachts of the cup race were varied in size and form. Near the turn of the century the boats tended to great size, with lengths of 90 feet at waterline. The culmination of this trend was the American *Reliance,* 144 feet in deck length and more than 200 feet overall. It was the most powerful and fastest single-masted sailing vessel ever constructed. The less huge but still imposing "J"-class sloops, with a 70-foot waterline, raced for the America's Cup during the 1920s and 1930s. In this class, too, the trend was always toward greater power and increasingly complicated design. But World War II and changing economic conditions made such large and advanced craft far too expensive — the cost of competing on this scale rose from hundreds of thousands of dollars to millions.

It seemed, for a time, as if the competition might not continue. After a lapse of more than two decades, the yachting classic was revived in 1958 with sailing yachts of the 12-meter class — craft with a waterline length of less than 50 feet. Also adopted in 1958 was the policy of not accepting a cup challenge more often than every three years.

The America's Cup races have been held in Newport since 1930. Each year during the event, the town is the center of great social activity and festivity.

In 1967 a 104-foot wooden replica of the original *America* was built and launched at East Boothbay, Maine. It was present at the 1967 defense, and was used in the documentary television film *Sail to Glory* that same year. The film told the story of the ship whose triumph in 1851 marked the start of one of the most celebrated events in international sport.

AUGUST 23

Oliver Hazard Perry's Birthday

Oliver Hazard Perry, the great naval hero of the War of 1812, died on August 23, 1819. According to a number of authoritative sources, he was also born on August 23 – in 1785. Other scholars claim he was born on August 20. All, however, agree on the year of his birth, and on the place, which was South Kingstown, Rhode Island. His father, Christopher Raymond Perry, had enjoyed a long seafaring career both in the service of his country and on merchant vessels, and in 1798 was commissioned a captain in the US Navy. Perry followed in his father's footsteps: at the age of 14 he entered the navy as a midshipman. He completed his first tour of duty aboard his father's ship, the *General Greene*, during the brief naval conflict with France in 1799; he then served in the Mediterranean in 1802–1803, and again in 1804–1805, during the war against the Barbary pirates. Commissioned a lieutenant in 1807, Perry spent his next five years carrying out routine peacetime assignments.

Perry's experience and skill well qualified him to serve his country when hostilities between the United States and Great Britain began in 1812. Given command of US naval forces on Lake Erie early in 1813, he worked at his headquarters in Erie, Pennsylvania, throughout the summer and spring of that year, preparing his small, 10-vessel fleet for combat. By the end of July he was ready to begin operations. But not until mid-August were his ships able to elude the British blockade under the command of Robert H. Barclay and sail across the shallow Erie bar into the open waters of the lake. On August 12 Perry directed his fleet to Put-in-Bay. The bay, which is located 20 miles north of Sandusky, Ohio, gave him an excellent view of enemy ship dispositions, and he remained there almost a month awaiting the next British move.

The confrontation between American and British forces for control of Lake Erie came on September 10, 1813. At sunrise the Americans sighted the approaching six-vessel squadron commanded by Barclay and immediately began preparations to meet its challenge. When the British attack began at 11:45, Perry's 10 ships were ready. The actual fighting proceeded according to the American commander's strategy: his flagship, the *Lawrence*, engaged Barclay's

strongest ship, the *Detroit;* the *Niagara* fought the *Queen Charlotte;* and his remaining smaller vessels sought out their enemy counterparts.

During the ensuing three-and-a-quarter-hour encounter, the *Lawrence* sustained such extensive damage that Perry had to abandon his flagship for the safety of the *Niagara*. After intense fighting, the British counted 41 killed and 94 injured; American casualties numbered 27 dead and 96 wounded. But in the end, the American force proved superior.

Soon after the British surrender Perry sent the famous message "We have met the enemy and they are ours" to General William Henry Harrison, the American commander in chief of the western army. In light of Perry's accomplishment, his description of the event was modest. Perry's victory at the battle of Lake Erie gave the United States lasting control of the lake and enabled Harrison to undertake his successful conquest of Upper Canada.

Perry immediately became a national hero. When news of his victory reached Washington, President James Madison at once promoted him to the rank of captain, and shortly afterwards the US Congress passed a resolution expressing its gratitude. In addition, state and local governments also recognized his great achievement. The legislatures of Pennsylvania and Georgia voted Perry their thanks; Boston and Newport expressed their admiration with a gift of silver plate; and Baltimore, Washington, and Boston held dinners and receptions in his honor.

Perry saw action in several other important engagements during the War of 1812. In October 1813 he assisted in Harrison's capture of Detroit and the successful operation against the British and the Indians in the battle of the Thames. Then he turned his fleet over to Jesse Duncan Elliott, his second in command, and returned to the Eastern Seaboard. In July 1814 the navy placed the 44-gun *Java* under Perry's command. However, the British blockade prevented this ship from leaving Baltimore harbor, and for the remainder of the war the young captain participated only in minor skirmishes with British shippers on the Potomac River.

After the war Perry commanded the *Java's* two-year cruise of the Mediterranean. Upon his return from this tour of duty, the navy placed him in charge of a small fleet being sent on a diplomatic mission to Venezuela and Buenos Aires. This assignment was to be Perry's last. While sailing down the Orinoco River in Venezuela, he contracted yellow fever, and several days later, on August 23, 1819, he died. His crewmen interred Perry's body at Port of Spain, Trinidad, but in 1826 the US government returned Perry's body to Newport, Rhode Island.

Its final resting place is beneath the granite obelisk that the state erected to his memory. Rhode Island honors Perry during its Heritage Month each May by displaying the *Lawrence*'s logbook at the Newport Historical Society.

Perhaps the most outstanding tribute to Perry is the Perry Victory and International Peace Memorial. The monument, which commemorates both the American victory of September 1813 and the many years of peace and unarmed borders between the United States and Canada, is located on South Bass Island in Ottawa County, Ohio. During the summer months, ferries transport many visitors across the four miles of Lake Erie that separate the island from the mainland. Tourists may explore the 22-acre island, but the 352-foot-high concrete and pink Massachusetts granite shaft is the main attraction. An elevator services the observation platform, which is situated just below the 32-foot-high, 11-ton bronze urn that surmounts the Doric-columned memorial. The rotunda at the base of the shaft is also worthy of note. The names of Perry's vessels and of the US sailors who sacrificed their lives during the battle of Lake Erie are carved on its marble, limestone, and granite walls, and the three American and three British officers who died in the conflict are buried in the crypt below.

Erie, Pennsylvania, the site of Perry's headquarters in the spring and summer of 1813, has preserved several places associated with the naval hero. The Perry Memorial House at Second and French streets is open to the public. This house, where Perry stayed, is an excellent example of early 19th century architecture. The Cascade Street Ship Yard is another of the town's points of interest. There, Sailing Master Daniel Dobbins constructed the *Lawrence* and the *Niagara*, the two principal ships in Perry's small fleet. An appropriate marker, located at the corner of Second and Cascade streets, stands 100 yards away from the site of this shipyard.

Although the hull of the *Lawrence* was destroyed by fire when it was displayed at the Philadelphia Centennial in 1876, it is still possible to see a replica of the *Niagara*. In 1912 the Pennsylvania legislature appropriated $75,000 to erect a permanent memorial to Perry as part of the centennial celebration of his great victory. Part of this fund financed the construction of the Perry Monument at Misery Bay, in the northwestern part of Erie Harbor, but the remainder was used to rebuild the *Niagara*. On March 6, 1913, the ship's original hull was salvaged from Misery Bay, where it had been sunk in 1836. During the months that followed, shipwrights fashioned the old timbers into a replica of the *Niagara*, and on June 7, 1913, it was launched.

A second reconstruction of the ship was built in 1963, and since that time many persons have visited the ship at its permanent mooring at Niagara Park in Erie.

In 1963 Erie marked the sesquicentennial of Perry's great victory, with a mammoth celebration from May 29 to September 10. To help carry out the theme of the anniversary, 150 Years of Peaceful Boundaries Between the United States and Canada, representatives of the Royal Canadian Navy attended several events: on June 20 Rear Admiral Desmond William Piers reviewed the military parade, and from July 19 to July 21 the destroyer *Nootka* participated in the festivities. The highlight of the celebration was the pageant From These Shores. This 90-minute spectacular, which was presented intermittently from May 29 through August 17, featured a cast of over 800, all in authentic historical costumes, and concluded each evening with a magnificent fireworks display. As a lasting memento, the Sesquicentennial Headquarters authorized the striking of medals depicting a bust of Perry on one side and the *Niagara* on the other.

Perry's birthplace in South Kingstown, Rhode Island, a building now privately owned, is a local landmark.

AUGUST 24

Feast of St. Bartholomew

St. Bartholomew, one of the 12 Apostles of Jesus Christ, is identified by many scholars with Nathanael (or Nathaniel) in the Scriptures. In listing the Apostles the four Gospels all include Bartholomew, whose name is a form of *bar-Tolmai*, meaning "son of Tolmai, or Ptolemy."

According to St. John's gospel account of the first meeting between Bartholomew and Jesus, Philip, who had already been called to join Jesus and the other Apostles, saw his friend Nathanael (Bartholomew) resting under a fig tree. Philip excitedly reported, "We have found him of whom Moses in the Law and Prophets wrote: Jesus the son of Joseph of Nazareth." Jesus, seeing Nathanael coming, immediately perceived his essential nature and said, "Behold a true Israelite in whom there is no guile." Nathanael, taken by surprise, stammered, "Whence knowest thou me?" Jesus replied, "Before Philip called thee, when thou wast under the fig tree, I saw thee." Amazed, Nathanael answered, "Rabbi, thou art the Son of God, thou art King of Israel." Jesus said, "Because I said to thee that I saw thee under the fig tree, thou dost believe. Greater things than this shalt thou see."

According to tradition, Nathanael spent his

apostolic life preaching in Ethiopia, Persia, and other parts of Asia Minor — including Armenia, where he was martyred, being flayed alive and then beheaded.

The saint's name became linked to an infamous event of the 16th century. This was the St. Bartholomew's Day Massacre, which began on August 24, 1572, initiating the fourth in a series of at least seven civil wars fought in France from 1562 to 1598 and referred to often as the Wars of Religion. The trouble began when the Calvinist Protestant Huguenots held their first French national synod in 1559 and founded a church. Some members of French royalty and nobility accepted the new communion, others adhered to the old, Roman Catholic one — and still others, more political than religious, tried to maintain a balance of power and to sway the king.

When the Huguenot Henry of Navarre (later Henry IV of France) was married to the Catholic Margaret of Valois, sister of King Charles IX, nobility and other important and wealthy people traveled to Paris for the wedding on August 18, 1572. Catherine de Medici, King Charles's mother and regent, seized this opportunity to strike at the powerful Huguenots. She ordered the assassination on August 22 of Admiral Gaspard de Coligny, one of the Huguenot leaders. When this failed, large-scale violence broke out two days later, on the Feast of St. Bartholomew, spreading from Paris to other parts of France. Coligny and countless others, Catholics as well as Huguenots, were killed. The massacre led to the resumption of the civil wars, which had been halted just two years before by the Treaty of Saint-Germain and were to continue off and on until 1598, when Henry IV (now a Catholic) instituted a policy of religious toleration through the Edict of Nantes. The revocation of this edict in 1685 led many Huguenots to resettle in the New World.

AUGUST 25

Feast of St. Louis

Louis IX, after whom St. Louis, Missouri, is named, was one of France's greatest and best-loved monarchs. Born in Poissy, France, on April 25, 1214, he inherited the throne when his father, Louis VIII, died in 1226. Since the new king was still a boy, his mother, Blanche of Castile, was made regent and ruled until 1234, when he came of age. Blanche reared her son carefully, giving him a thorough religious education and teaching him to prefer to die rather than commit a mortal sin. Even after Louis as-

sumed the full prerogatives of the throne, she continued to act as his adviser, and when he went off to the Crusades she again ruled for him.

In May 1234 Louis had married Margaret, or Marguerite, daughter of a count of Provence. In the years that followed they had 11 children.

Renowned for his justice and his charity, Louis came to be regarded as an ideal king. He respected the rights of his subjects, whether peasants or nobles. He fed beggars from his table, washed their feet, and ministered to lepers.

Austere with himself, he was extremely affable to others. Louis's friend and biographer Jean de Joinville wrote: "Often I have seen the good King, after Mass, go to the wood at Vincennes, sit down at the foot of an oak tree and there listen to all who had to speak to him."

A man of great piety, Louis nevertheless did not neglect his duties as king, and France enjoyed unprecedented peace and prosperity under him. Some of the most beautiful examples of Gothic architecture standing today were built during his reign. These include the cathedrals at Chartres, Amiens, Beauvais, and Bourges. Sainte-Chapelle in Paris, containing some of the world's most brilliant stained glass, was built on Louis's personal order. He was also responsible for the formation of the first French navy. Under his patronage, Robert de Sorbon, friend and chaplain to Louis, founded the first endowed college, now called the Sorbonne, of the University of Paris.

The Crusades, started in the 11th century to recover the Holy Land from the Saracens, continued throughout Louis's lifetime and led to his death. In 1244 a treaty with Damascus returned Palestine to the Christians, but that same year Egyptian and Turkish allies captured Jerusalem and drove out the Christians.

Louis, recovering from a serious illness, determined to lead a crusade to help the beleaguered Christian rulers recapture the Holy Land. In 1248, after lengthy preparations, he set forth on what was to be the Seventh Crusade. Captured in 1250, he was ransomed and remained in Asia Minor to strengthen Christian fortifications in Caesarea and Joppa.

He returned to France in 1254 after news of his mother's death in 1252 reached him. He ruled France carefully and wisely for 15 more years. Then, on July 1, 1270, he joined the Eighth Crusade, which was aborted by his death from the plague on August 25, 1270, near Tunis.

He had lived such a holy life that within three years of his death it was proposed that he be canonized. The inquiries into his worthiness continued until 1297, when Pope Boniface VIII proclaimed him to be St. Louis and fixed August 25, the day of his death, as his feast day.

The city of St. Louis was named by the French, who established a trading post on the banks of the Mississippi in 1763, close to the site of the modern Gateway Arch. A statue of the crusader stands in Forest Park.

Pennsylvania Dutch Days
Hershey, Pennsylvania

This is a movable event. See note on page xxvi.

The Pennsylvania Dutch Days observance at Hershey, Pennsylvania — the oldest and largest of the several Pennsylvania Dutch celebrations that now take place annually in the Keystone State — had its inception in 1948, when a class was formed at the Derry Township Evening School in Hershey for study of the fast-disappearing "Pennsylvania Dutch" — that is, German — dialect. When the course was concluded the next spring, members of the class decided to demonstrate their appreciation for it by holding a Pennsylvania Dutch gathering in Hershey Park.

What ensued was a one-day exhibition — the first of many, as it turned out — featuring the possessions of class members and assorted displays. The event, held on August 27, 1949, surprised its sponsors, who had anticipated that 2,500 persons might be interested enough to attend. An astonishing total of 25,000 appeared instead.

Since then the number of visitors that may be expected at the event has grown to approximately 100,000. The purpose remains the same today as at the start: to recreate and bring to public appreciation the arts, crafts, customs, and folklore of Pennsylvania's early German settlers. As at the beginning, the observance is under the aegis of the nonprofit Pennsylvania Dutch Days Committee — made up largely of members of the original Pennsylvania Dutch dialect class and succeeding classes, who volunteer their labors to administer all aspects of the undertaking.

The annual observance, which has received widespread attention, has expanded consistently since its unexpected initial success. It became a three-day affair by popular demand in 1950. A fourth day was added in 1955, a fifth in 1962, and a sixth in 1963. Later, this perennial celebration was scheduled during the last week of July. The 29th annual presentation took place in 1977.

Probably the most outstanding feature of Pennsylvania Dutch Days is the wide array of crafts demonstrations set up in Hershey Park's Sports Arena. Each year, the interior of that large building is hung with some 300 handmade quilts — believed to be the largest exhibit of its kind in the world. Perhaps the most prominent of the floor exhibits is the working demonstration of quilt-making put on by women members of various congregations of the Church of the Brethren in the area. Prizes are awarded for the best products, and funds from the sale of finished quilts go to support the work of the churches.

Since stress is placed on old handicrafts, some of the demonstrations — like flax handling, oak basketmaking, and glass blowing — are seen only infrequently elsewhere. Among the most interesting are pretzel bending and toleware painting. Guilds of artisans also bring to public view such time-honored skills as pottery making, spinning and weaving, cigarmaking, *Fraktur* art, leather crafting, carpetmaking, candle dipping, bookbinding, and the painting of barn signs — the bright, circular decorations often referred to as "hex signs." In 1964 Pennsylvania Dutch Days initiated a unique presentation featuring 48-inch replicas of the "old country" originals for these signs, each displayed with an explanation of how the design originated.

Outside the Sports Arena there are craft and agricultural exhibits and Pennsylvania Dutch food and entertainment. A Farmarama recreates farmyard scenes, showing the implements and paraphernalia of rural life. Hay wagons, corn crib shelters, a meat smokehouse, various types of farm fences, and a wooden pump are all on view, as are the familiar sawbuck, woodpile, and Schnitzelbonk or cutting bench. The village blacksmith can be visited, and a threshing rig can be seen in operation. Among other attractions are farm animals with their young, a pond stocked with ducks and geese, and chicks being hatched in an incubator. In addition there are poultry, hog, cattle, pony, and dairy shows run by state or regional agricultural groups and 4-H Clubs, and the crowning of the Pennsylvania Poultry Industry Queen.

The air in Hershey Park is filled during Pennsylvania Dutch Days with the odor of barbecue demonstrations and of boiling apple butter, in huge, bubbling vats tended by poke-bonneted women. Lectures and seminars on the origins, arts, lore, and folkways of the Pennsylvania Dutch are given daily by experts. There are also related motion pictures and slides, a country auction, an antique show (in downtown Hershey), a church service and hymn sing in Pennsylvania Dutch dialect, and an English-to-Dutch word translation bee.

And there is varied entertainment, although in recent years this aspect has been deemphasized because of lack of suitable space. However, music was provided one year — by Schwab's Dutch Country Band, the Johnnie Schmoker Strolling Band, the Mahoning Valley Variety Band, and the Spring Garden Band of York. Annual events include concerts and variety shows in the bandshell and organ recitals. In addition, the Pennsylvania State Police present a horseback riding exhibition in the Hershey Park Stadium, generally including trick and rough riding, jumping, a dramatic cavalry charge, and precision cavalry and motorcycle drills, as well as a demonstration of the stunts and skills of trained police dogs.

Not least of the celebration's attractions is the famous Pennsylvania Dutch food available both in Hershey Park and in downtown Hershey. Apart from sampling the traditional "seven sweets and sours" and the well-known pretzels, apple butter, shoo-fly pie, and Pennsylvania Dutch barbecued chicken, visitors can choose among snackbar lunches and an abundance of family-style, homecooked, and restaurant meals. They can also visit the zoo, or use the picnic, golf, boating, swimming, and amusement facilities of Hershey Park.

AUGUST 26

Nineteenth Amendment Proclaimed Ratified

On August 26, 1920, Secretary of State Bainbridge Colby proclaimed the 19th (or Susan B. Anthony) Amendment to the Constitution in effect after its adoption by three-fourths (36) of the states. Proponents of woman suffrage rejoiced in this result of 72 years of organized effort. The wording of the amendment is simple and direct: "The right of citizens of the United States to vote shall not be denied or abridged by the United States or by any State on account of sex." Thus, in November 1920, for the first time in the history of the United States, women throughout the country were able to vote in a presidential election.

The cause of woman suffrage had been pressed by isolated reformers since colonial days. A short-lived "first" had come about when the state constitution adopted by New Jersey on July 2, 1776, granted — or seemed to grant — women the vote. What the document actually said was that "all Inhabitants" of the colony who had reached the age of majority and fulfilled certain monetary and residency requirements were entitled to vote. The legislature did away with this convenient and perhaps intentional vagueness by providing in the Act of 1807 that "no person shall vote in any state or county election for officers in the government of the United States or of this state unless such person be a free, white male citizen," an injustice not remedied until the next century.

The organized campaign for woman suffrage in the United States commenced with Elizabeth Cady Stanton (see November 12) and Lucretia Mott, who, with others, called the Woman's Rights Convention at Seneca Falls, New York, in 1848 (see July 19).

Securing the vote became a pressing issue after the end of the Civil War, when women renewed their drive. Rights organizations were formed — the National Woman Suffrage Association of Susan B. Anthony (see February 15 and June 18) and Elizabeth Cady Stanton, and the American Woman Suffrage Association led by Lucy Stone (see August 13), Henry Ward Beecher (see June 24), and others — and annual conventions became a fixed part of their programs.

The constitutional amendments passed after the Civil War had had a direct bearing on the struggle for the woman suffrage amendments. Women were deliberately excluded from the 15th Amendment (see March 30), which established for black males the right to vote, because proponents of that measure feared the less popular female cause might bring defeat to black male suffrage. Earlier, similar reluctance had prevented women from being specifically included in the 14th Amendment (see July 28), another measure intended primarily to establish black rights in the post–Civil War years. But although the second section of the 14th Amendment, which dealt with apportionment, mentioned only "male inhabitants" and "male citizens," the first section, which defined citizenship, did not exclude women in so many words. Instead, the opening sentences simply stated that

All persons born or naturalized in the United States, and subject to the jurisdiction thereof, are citizens of the United States and of the State wherein they reside. No state shall make or enforce any law which shall abridge the privileges or immunities of citizens of the United States. . . .

This seemed plain enough to Susan B. Anthony. It was under this provision that she sought to exercise what she interpreted as her clear right, as a citizen, to vote — in the election of 1872. In so doing, she tested for women the citizenship and voting rights extended to black males by the 14th and 15th amendments. The outcome of her test, which was unsuccessful (although it left her undaunted), was the celebrated case of 1872 (see June 18). The rulings in this and other cases, all the way up to the Supreme Court, leaned on the phraseology in the second section of the 14th Amendment to exclude women from any right to vote. These rulings also left open the possibility for women to be excluded, at the pleasure of the courts, from any of the other protections and benefits of the Constitution.

It was in the Wyoming Territory that women first permanently won the right to vote — in 1869 — largely as a result of the efforts of Esther Morris. The women of Utah also received the right to vote in 1869, although Congress temporarily rescinded that right in 1887. When Utah entered the Union in 1896, however, it was with woman suffrage. Women meanwhile were given the vote in Colorado in 1893 and in Idaho in 1896. Later, referendums extended the franchise to women in the states of Washington (1910) and California (1911). Kansas, Oregon, and Arizona followed suit in 1912, as did Nevada and Montana in 1914. East of the Mississippi, only Illinois gave women the right to vote (in 1913) and then only in presidential elections. Finally New York, which had voted down a suffrage referendum in 1915, passed the measure in 1917.

Many of these voting rights gains were the result of persistent and long-continuing effort by members of the National American Woman Suffrage Association, formed in 1890 by a merger of the two suffrage organizations with which the Anthony-Stanton and Stone-Beecher groups had been associated. But it was uphill all the way. The granting of woman suffrage in individual states was a piecemeal business, slow and hard-won; and the victories were exceptions in a sea of defeats, for state suffrage campaigns fared poorly elsewhere.

Work was also going on toward a federal amendment to guarantee the right to vote for all women in the nation. After 1913 the National American Woman Suffrage Association, long active in this endeavor, was joined in the effort by the National Woman's Party (originally known as the Congressional Union), which under the leadership of Alice Paul played a significant role in achieving passage of the amendment.

That victory, however, did not come easily either. The Anthony Woman Suffrage Amendment, as it was known, was first introduced in Congress in its final form in 1878, but it had been introduced in other versions from 1868 on. It was reintroduced in every succeeding Congress (except the 46th) until 1919, and supporting presentations were patiently repeated before the congressional hearings that were held annually on the measure. The important contributions of women in industry and war work during World War I helped create a climate favorable to their enfranchisement on a national level. Ultimately, the support of President Woodrow Wilson was added to the congressional lobbying, state referendum campaigns, picketing, hunger strikes, and other forms of political pressure that marked the drive for a federal amendment. Congress finally passed the amendment and sent it to the states on June 4, 1919.

Then began the 14-month-long campaign that was necessary before the amendment received ratification by three-fourths of the states. That achievement was another closely-won contest, with Tennessee, the 36th state, granting approval by the narrow margin of one, and that only after intense debate in the lower house of the state legislature. Tennessee's affirmative action, on August 18, 1920, was shortly followed by Secretary Colby's proclamation of the 19th Amendment on August 26. Passage of the amendment brought partial realization of the dream of Mott, Anthony, Stanton, Stone, and other pioneers.

Proponents of full equality for women regard August 26 as an important anniversary. The legislature of Massachusetts, Anthony's home state, took note of the day's importance in 1958, when it provided by law that "the governor shall annually issue a proclamation setting aside the twenty-sixth day of August as Susan B. Anthony Day, recommending its observance by the public in honoring the woman who was . . . organizer, lecturer, campaigner and ardent advocate in the fight for American woman suffrage, and whose unfailing efforts culminated in the prohibition of the denial of the right to vote on account of sex." Although the wording of the proclamations of course varies from year to year, their tenor has not altered markedly from that of the 1964 proclamation in which Governor Endicott Peabody urged citizens to offer appropriate honors:

Whereas, In 1920, exactly one hundred years after the birth of Susan B. Anthony, the Nineteenth Amendment to the U.S. Constitution became law, and gave the women of this nation the right to vote, and

Whereas, Although she did not live to see the success of her efforts, the amendment was ratified largely through the groundwork laid by her many years of work against civil and political discrimination . . . and was known as the Susan B. Anthony Amendment . . . I, Endicott Peabody, Governor of the Commonwealth of Massachusetts, in accordance with Chapter 265 of the Acts of 1958, do hereby proclaim [August 26] as Susan B. Anthony Day. . . .

Adams, Massachusetts, where Anthony's privately owned birthplace is cherished as a historic landmark, is one of the communities where the day is noted. The Adams Free Library, which has Bradford Lambert's portrait of the suffrage leader permanently on display, customarily plans a special exhibit to coincide with the

August 26 anniversary. The Berkshire County Women's Republican Club usually sends flowers or in some other way contributes to the commemorative exhibit.

Both the library and the Women's Republican Club have noted the anniversary since 1958, when efforts by Silvio O. Conte, a state senator who later represented Massachusetts in the national legislature, were successful in establishing August 26 as Susan B. Anthony Day in Massachusetts. The day is usually quietly observed in Adams, but in years of particular significance it is celebrated with special enthusiasm. This was true in 1958, for example, when ceremonies noting the first Susan B. Anthony Day, held on the lawn of her homestead, were marked by speeches and refreshments, and by tributes from national, state, and local leaders.

Another special year was 1970, the 50th anniversary of woman suffrage and the 150th anniversary of Anthony's birth. It was highlighted by Adams's four-day celebration of Susan B. Anthony Days, which began with a parade on Sunday August 23 and was climaxed on Wednesday by first-day-of-issue ceremonies for the postage stamp released by the US Post Office in commemoration of the dual anniversary. The celebration attracted thousands of visitors. Related events included a block dance on Monday evening; a Tuesday afternoon costume parade with children dressed to commemorate the period in which Anthony and her colleagues worked for suffrage; a Tuesday evening fireworks display; and other events, including a first-day-of-issue luncheon and a postal department stamp display. Young people in the region participated in an essay contest on the subject of the women's rights movement.

The first-day-of-issue ceremony, held at the Adams Memorial High School, was sponsored by the League of Women Voters, an organization that dates its existence from the beginning of woman suffrage. It was, in fact, organized in conjunction with the Victory Convention of the National American Woman Suffrage Association following ratification of the 19th Amendment in 1920. When that organization's goal of a federal amendment was achieved, it was dissolved in favor of the new National League of Women Voters, dedicated to promoting the "informed, active participation of citizens in government." Carrie Chapman Catt, who had succeeded such leaders as Stanton and Anthony as president of the earlier organization, became president of the new association, which received its present name — the League of Women Voters of the United States — in 1946. In 1970 the league marked the 50th anniversary of woman suffrage and of its own founding with a year-long, nation-wide celebration, which was formally launched by a White House reception. Events organized by local chapters of the league included birthday parties held with the participation of community leaders and government officials, panel discussions, luncheons, and television interviews.

Legislatures in various states recognized the 50th anniversary of woman suffrage by passing resolutions to laud the achievement. In some cases they held receptions in honor of the occasion. The year was marked by numerous exhibits, including Women and Politics, displayed at the Smithsonian Institution's National Museum of History and Technology. This exhibit traced the attempt to gain the vote for women from the time of Abigail Adams, who urged her husband, John — then in Philadelphia helping to frame the Constitution — to press for the enfranchisement of women.

The specific August 26 anniversary of suffrage frequently is noted by ceremonies at Anthony's grave in Rochester, New York. Another site of observance is the Capitol crypt, originally intended as a memorial over the tomb of George Washington. The circular crypt contains sculptured figures of Anthony, Stanton, and Mott carved from an eight-ton block of marble. Although women's rights advocates who take part in ceremonies in the crypt customarily represent a wide cross-section of organizations, the observances are usually organized by the National Woman's Party, whose members donated the sculpture at the conclusion of the suffrage campaign. The actual presentation at that time was made by the pioneer social worker Jane Addams. Floral and musical tributes and addresses by members of Congress and others are customary features of the observances that take place in the crypt on August 26 and also on other important anniversaries in the history of the women's rights movement.

Women's Equality Day

August 26, the anniversary of the ratification of the 19th Amendment in 1920, is also celebrated as Women's Equality Day — so designated, in the 1970s, by the President. With the ratification of the 19th Amendment, voting became the only right guaranteed by the US Constitution to women, who are nowhere specifically included in that document and who by judicial interpretation have often been excluded from the protections afforded by such measures as the 14th Amendment.

Decisions against women in various courts of the land have extended far beyond the matter of voting. Some unfavorable rulings have been based on the ground that privileges and immunities seemingly guaranteed by the 14th Amendment belong, in actuality, only to citizens of the United States as distinguished from citizens of a particular state. In this way, many unjust and discriminatory state statutes have been upheld as being within the power of the state.

The need for a more inclusive amendment led to a campaign — spearheaded by the National Woman's Party under Alice Paul — for an Equal Rights Amendment. This measure, drafted by Paul, was first introduced in Congress in 1923, by Senator Charles Curtis and Representative Daniel R. Anthony (a nephew of Susan B. Anthony), both of Kansas. The proposal was simple and straightforward — "equality of rights under the law shall not be denied or abridged by the United States or by any State on account of sex." But not until the new wave of feminism in the 1960s did the Equal Rights Amendment receive serious consideration in Congress. On March 22, 1972, the measure was sent for ratification by the necessary three-fourths of the states following that day's favorable Senate vote of 84 to 8, and the earlier House approval, by a vote of 354 to 23, on October 11, 1971. By January 1978 the proposed amendment had been ratified by 35 states; one state, Hawaii, approved the measure a half hour after it had passed the Senate. Ratification by 38 states is required if this amendment is to become part of the Constitution.

Opponents of the amendment, in the 1960s and 1970s, feared that it would destroy the traditional structure of the family and alter sexual mores. In addition, many critics argued that women should not be deprived of the special protections enjoyed under existing laws. Exemption from compulsory military service during wartime was sometimes cited in this context.

Supporters of the amendment argued that because of what the Constitution does *not* say, the legal status of female Americans (except in the matter of voting) remains today as ambiguous as ever. Since the equal rights of women are nowhere specifically established in the Constitution — and have been disallowed where they might have been assumed — American women still live under the shadow of the English common law that the original colonists brought to this country, or, more exactly, under the shadow of that law as it existed when the US Constitution was written. As Dr. M. Carey Thomas, a former president of Bryn Mawr College, phrased it, "Behind every man . . . stands the Constitution; but forever behind a woman is the medieval English common law which places upon her the stigma of inferiority and bondage."

Rebekah S. Greathouse, a former assistant US attorney for the District of Columbia, summed up the situation of married women in 1789 as follows:

A married woman could not contract for the spending of her own money, even though it had been given to her by her parents or earned by her own labor. She owned no personal property, not even the clothes she wore, nor the jewels her husband gave her. She could not sue in the courts for injury to her person. She could not make a will. Her husband could chastise her or restrain her of her liberty. In short, she was her husband's slave, dependent upon his whims, without appeal to any court — and penniless. . . . She had no right to the control or even the society of her own children, as her husband could transfer the guardianship of them to a third person by deed or will. No woman could vote or hold office, and the disabilities of women when married were advanced as reasons for keeping all women out of various professions.

Sir William Blackstone gave the gist of this in one succinct sentence: "The husband and the wife are one and that one is the husband."

Circumstances have altered, but not everywhere and not in all respects. Vestiges of the old common law linger on, in fact and in attitude. Changes that have occurred in the direction of liberation have come as a result of revised public concepts of women's rights, responsibilities, and personhood; judicial rulings in some specific cases in some states and municipalities; and the passage of laws (although women, like minority groups, have discovered that such laws are often difficult to enforce). Inclusion of women in Title VII of the 1964 Civil Rights Act, which prohibits discrimination in employment, was an example of federal law affecting women. The Equal Pay Act of 1963 was another instance, as was Title IX of the Education Act amendments of 1972 with their prohibitions against sex discrimination in education. Less popular with women were the so-called protective laws enacted by, and still on the books of, many states. In limiting the number of hours and the conditions under which women are permitted to work, these laws have also limited earning power and hampered women as much as they have helped them. Moreover, even when genuinely serving the advancement of women, state laws have a built-in disadvantage: they are impermanent, since they are subject to change from one legislature to the next.

The federal Constitution, unchanged with respect to women from the day it was written, except for the 19th Amendment, is still without the egalitarian affirmation of the Charter of the United Nations' declaration of "faith . . . in the dignity and worth of the human person, in the equal rights of men and women"; or the statement in the Universal Declaration of Human Rights, which the UN General Assembly adopted in 1948 (see December 10), that "everyone is entitled to all the rights and freedoms set forth in this Declaration, without distinction of any kind, such as race, colour, sex, language, religion, political or other opinion, national or social origin, property, birth or other status." Missing, too, is the kind of simple rider, almost unique among the states, that is attached to New Jersey's Constitution of 1947: "Whenever in this Constitution the term 'person,' 'persons,' 'people' or any personal pronoun is used, the same shall be taken to include both sexes."

A publication of the Lucy Stone League stressed the fact that "modern woman is still a subordinate citizen in the eyes of the law, and a lesser person in the social framework." Progress has been made, but supporters of the amendment cite the persistence of custom-hallowed inequities in all areas of life: education; employment, promotion, and pay; control of earnings; personal name and identity; property and inheritance rights; criminal justice; credit; guardianship. In traditionally male professions — medicine, engineering, architecture, law, and religion — opportunities for training and careers still lag despite affirmative programs. Marital law and property arrangements constitute a special area for reform; although men are sometimes victimized in alimony decisions, women are more frequently victims of the double standard and have difficulty establishing grounds for divorce. In the matter of property, although much of the nation's wealth is listed in women's names, few women manage great fortunes or hold decision-making positions in industry and finance.

Another continuing concern in many places is discrimination in housing and public accommodation. The National Organization for Women points out that women have frequently been "barred from renting apartments or buying homes on the whim of the landlord or agent" and also that businesswomen often "are at a disadvantage because they cannot frequent the men's restaurants and luncheon clubs where business often is discussed — or they are embarrassed by being forced to sneak up backstairs to attend business meetings at these places."

Organizers of new women's groups have turned to consciousness-raising techniques. Women in consciousness-raising groups discuss their own experiences, feelings, and expectations, in an effort to reassess the traditional "feminine" role. By posing such questions, feminists have heightened public awareness and sensitivity on such issues as the right of women to control their own reproductive lives; establishment of day-care centers for children; an end to credit discrimination based on sex or marital status; and a larger role for women in the power structure of government, business, and society.

August 26 observances of Women's Equality Day — initially suggested by the writer Betty Friedan, a founder and the first president of the National Organization for Women — have taken place in many US cities since 1970. Speaking at the 1970 convention of NOW, Friedan proposed

that on Wednesday, August 26, we call a twenty-four-hour general strike, a resistance both passive and active, of all women in America against the concrete conditions of their oppression. On that day, fifty years after the amendment that gave women the vote became part of the Constitution, I propose we use our power to declare an ultimatum on all who would keep us from using our rights as Americans. I propose that the women who are doing menial chores in the offices cover their typewriters and close their notebooks, the telephone operators unplug their switchboards, the waitresses stop waiting, cleaning women stop cleaning, and everyone who is doing a job for which a man would be paid more — stop — every woman pegged forever as assistant, doing jobs for which men get the credit — stop.

Although the "strike" aspect of the August 26, 1970, anniversary observances fell short of its goal, other activities of the day received wide support. Sponsored by a coalition of women's groups in some 40 cities, events took the form of marches, rallies, and various educational efforts, including demonstrations, skits, public dialogues with civic leaders, self-defense lessons, and the distribution of literature. The day before, President Richard M. Nixon had issued a proclamation noting the 50th anniversary of woman suffrage in the United States and asking Americans "to recognize the great debt we owe to those who dedicated their life's work" to that cause. In New York State, Governor Nelson A. Rockefeller proclaimed the anniversary as Women's Rights Day. In New York City, where Mayor John V. Lindsay proclaimed August 26 Equality for Women Day, a full day of protest and educational activities was climaxed by a march down Fifth Avenue that brought out as many as 50,000 people, and by an evening rally at Bryant Park. Speakers included Eleanor Holmes Norton of the city's Commission on Human Rights, congressional candidate (later Representative) Bella S. Abzug, author Kate Millett, and Betty Friedan, who took occasion to repeat that in the fight against oppression, "man is not the enemy, man is the fellow-victim." Earlier in the day, some of the same speakers, along with writer Gloria Steinem and the city's commissioner of consumer affairs, Bess Meyerson, had addressed a lunch-hour crowd in City Hall Park. The park was also the site of a demonstration day-care center and of dialogues on various issues of concern to women.

In Boston some 5,000 persons congregated on Boston Common, near the State House, for a rally, and approximately 1,000 of them marched through the downtown business area. Included in the line of march were some suffragists who had fought for the vote 50 years earlier (as was also true in the New York City march) and a contingent in academic gowns. The Boston procession included marchers who were chained to typewriters or weighted down with household cleaning equipment, and one group carried a coffin, inscribed with the names of women who had died following illegal abortions.

There were marches and rallies in Washington, D.C., and much stress there was placed on lobbying efforts for the Equal Rights Amendment, which at the time had yet to be passed by Congress. Marchers also carried signs demanding equal opportunity for women to hold high-paying government jobs.

Residents of Baltimore marked the August 26 anniversary with a noontime rally in Center Square, attended by about 1,000 people. In Pittsburgh the day was the occasion for a 13-hour conference on women's rights, sponsored by a coalition of women's groups. Los Angeles took note of the anniversary with several demonstrations, a motorcade, and a rally in the evening. In Detroit it was announced that husbands and friends — who labeled themselves Male Chauvinists for Women's Liberation — would babysit so that mothers of small children could attend the workshops scheduled for August 26. (New York was one of the other cities where a contingent of male supporters — Men for Women's Rights, their banner proclaimed — actively participated.) A noon rally in San Francisco's Union Square attracted some 2,000 persons. Rights advocates in a number of cities devoted themselves to collecting signatures urging passage of the Equal Rights Amendment. Leaflets containing information for women were distributed in Denver, New York, and Philadelphia.

Observances of the 50th anniversary of woman suffrage on August 26, 1970, took almost every conceivable form. This has been the pattern of the observances in the years since. Rallies, speeches, exhibits, luncheons, picnics, and other special events, educational programs, marches, skits, street drama, dialogues, demonstrations related to specific issues, and the distribution of literature are among the activities on August 26, and the precise forms of observance vary widely. In 1973, one of the events scheduled for August 26 — ceremonies at Eisenhower College honoring the first 20 Americans chosen for the Women's Hall of Fame — took place in Seneca Falls, New York, where the movement for equality had its formal beginning in 1848 (see July 19).

Elimination of barriers to equality for women continued to be the goal of concerted effort, national and international, in the 1970s. The United Nations proclaimed 1975 International Women's Year, sponsoring a conference in Mexico City that focused on a world plan of action. The year was extended to a Decade for Women (1976–1985) by the UN. In the United States, a presidential order by Gerald R. Ford established a National Commission on the observance of International Women's Year; the commission's report, "... *To Form a More Perfect Union ...": Justice for American Women* (1976), contained over 100 recommendations and served as a handbook for an unprecedented series of congressionally mandated women's conferences, federally funded at $5 million and organized by the IWY commission (the commission itself operating under the aegis of the US Department of State).

At 56 preliminary state and territorial IWY meetings, open to all, more than 130,000 American women (and a few men) voted on resolutions and delegates to be sent to the National Women's Conference in Houston, Texas. Assembled at that meeting, held November 18–21, 1977, were over 1,400 elected delegates, as well as several hundred commission-appointed delegates at large, embodying diverse age, racial, ethnic, and minority groups; various political and religious beliefs; feminist, nonfeminist, and antifeminist opinions; and the widest possible range of occupations, lifestyles, and socioeconomic classes. Over 10,000 others attended as observers. Former Representative Bella S. Abzug served as presiding officer. Among the noted leaders present as guests and speakers were three First Ladies — Rosalynn Carter, Betty Ford, and Lady Bird Johnson. Media coverage was nationwide as the delegates voted on 26 resolutions on issues affecting women: a national plan of action to be submitted to the President and Congress in 1978. A key resolution was that urging ratification of the Equal Rights Amendment, strongly but not unanimously endorsed by the delegates.

The national conference — the largest convocation of women in the country — had as its theme American Women on the Move. The work of the conference, and of the women's movement, was symbolized by the torch relay begun in Seneca Falls on September 29, 1977. Carried and passed hand to hand by over 2,000 female runners, the torch traveled more than 2,600 miles through 14 states for the opening ceremony at Houston. On November 18 it was presented to Dr. Susan B. Anthony, grandniece of the suffragist, who told the final runners: "You have finished one race — the race begun by our founding mothers at Seneca Falls in 1848. ... We press on ... saying with our one voice as did Aunt Susan when she finished her lifelong race, 'Failure is impossible.' "

AUGUST 27

Lyndon B. Johnson's Birthday

Men of varied backgrounds, abilities, and temperaments have served as President of the United States. Lyndon Baines Johnson, the 36th Chief Executive, brought to the highest office in the land the benefit of impressive political expertise gained during his many years in Congress. Johnson led the nation admirably during the critical period following the assassination of his predecessor, John F. Kennedy, and his vast experience in politics helped bring to fruition several important domestic programs in the months following the tragedy and during his own four-year term in office.

The eldest of the five children of Samuel Ealy Johnson Jr. and Rebekah Baines Johnson, Lyndon was born on August 27, 1908, at his parents' farm near Stonewall, Texas. When he was five years old, his family moved to Johnson City, a town founded in the 1850s by his paternal grandfather, Samuel Ealy Johnson Sr. There the future President attended public schools. In 1924 he was one of the seven members of the graduating class of the Johnson City High School.

Initially uninterested in further study, Johnson spent the next few years wandering and working at various temporary odd jobs. His travels took him as far west as California, but his love for Texas eventually brought him home. In February 1927 he enrolled in Southwest Texas State Teachers College in San Marcos, Texas.

To earn his tuition, Johnson worked as a janitor, as secretary to the president of the college, and as an elementary school teacher. An energetic young man, he also participated in several extracurricular activities: he was a star debater, the editor of the school newspaper, and the founder of a political group on the San Marcos campus. But neither his outside jobs nor his extracurricular interests distracted Johnson from his studies of history and political science, and in August 1930 he received his B.S. degree.

Upon graduation from college, Johnson accepted a post as a teacher of debate in a Houston high school, but politics soon drew his attention from academics. In 1931 he campaigned on behalf of Richard M. Kleberg, a candidate for the House of Representatives, and when Kleberg won the election he rewarded his young supporter by selecting him to be his secretary. Johnson adjusted quickly to life in Washington, D.C. Renewing his acquaintance with Texas representative Sam Rayburn, a friend of his father's (who later served as Speaker of the House), he

learned much about politicking in the nation's capital; and in 1933 he was elected speaker of the organization of congressional secretaries, known as Little Congress.

In 1935 President Franklin D. Roosevelt appointed Johnson as Texas director of the National Youth Administration. Johnson's position in this New Deal agency gave him an opportunity to help approximately 30,000 young Texans to remain in school or to find jobs. In return, many thousands of those aided by the program gratefully remembered the young politician, and they formed a core of loyal supporters when he ran for elective office.

In 1937 Johnson competed against nine other candidates for the seat in Texas's 10th Congressional District, which had been vacated by the death of its incumbent. Running on a New Deal platform that included support for Roosevelt's controversial plan for reorganizing the Supreme Court, Johnson won the special April election. And on the recommendation of President Roosevelt himself, the freshman member of the House of Representatives was appointed to the House Committee on Naval Affairs.

Johnson won reelection to the House in every contest between 1938 and 1948. However, on December 9, 1941, two days after the Japanese attack on Pearl Harbor, he temporarily abandoned his congressional duties and became the first member of Congress to enter active service in the nation's armed forces. Commissioned a lieutenant commander in the US Navy, he was stationed in the South Pacific and was awarded the Silver Star for gallantry before July 1942, when President Roosevelt ordered all members of Congress to return to their posts in the nation's capital.

Although Johnson enjoyed considerable influence in the House of Representatives and sat on such important committees as the House Armed Services Committee and the Joint Atomic Energy Committee, he aspired to a seat in the Senate. In 1948 he won election to the Senate, where his power and influence increased rapidly. In 1951 and 1952 he served as the majority whip, or deputy leader, of the Democratic party in the Senate; and in 1953, at the age of 44, he was elected Democratic floor leader. As floor leader he also automatically assumed chairmanship of the Senate Democratic Conference, the Democratic Policy Committee, and the Democratic Steering Committee. These positions gave him considerable control over such vital matters as legislation schedules and committee assignments.

Between 1955 and 1961 Johnson served as Senate majority leader. The youngest man in history to hold this important post, the 46-year-old Texan was one of the most powerful men in the federal government. By means of political maneuvering, he helped win congressional approval of measures that included the 1957 and 1960 civil rights bills (see September 9 and May 6), the National Defense Education Act, extension of Social Security coverage, and liberal appropriations for defense, foreign aid, and the nation's space program. His stands on issues did not always please all factions of the Democratic party. Many liberals, for example, considered him too moderate on civil rights and too favorable to the interests of the South. But Johnson managed to weather such criticism, and up to the time he left the Senate in January 1961, he continued to exercise extraordinary influence in that body.

In 1960 Johnson sought the Democratic presidential nomination, but the party's convention selected John F. Kennedy instead. The day after receiving the nomination, Kennedy asked Johnson to be his running mate, and much to the surprise of many political observers, the Texan accepted the vice presidential candidacy. Johnson campaigned energetically throughout the fall of 1960. His presence on the ticket undoubtedly won many southern votes for the Democrats, and indeed may have been the decisive factor in the Democrats' victory over the Republican candidates, Richard M. Nixon and Henry Cabot Lodge, in November.

As Vice President, Johnson probably exercised considerably less power than he had as Senate majority leader, and many pundits were quick to remark on his loss of influence. But Johnson was not merely a cipher in politics during his years as Vice President. By means of countless briefings, cabinet meetings, and advisory sessions, he not only remained well informed on foreign and domestic matters, but also was able to help mold the administration's policy in these areas. Moreover, Johnson performed invaluable service for the President by undertaking negotiating missions on his behalf in many capitals of the world.

On November 22, 1963, an assassin's bullet killed President Kennedy in Dallas, Texas. Within a half-hour of Kennedy's death, Johnson stood before Mrs. Johnson, Mrs. Kennedy, and about 25 other persons on the presidential jet, *Air Force One*, at Love Field, Dallas, and took the oath of office as President of the United States. Lyndon Johnson met the greatest challenge of his life with determination and humility, and later that momentous day, when his plane returned to Washington, D.C., he told the American people: "I will do my best. That is all I can do. I ask for your help and God's."

During the days immediately following the assassination of Kennedy, the stunned nation mourned its loss. Then, five days after the tragedy in Dallas, the new President addressed a joint session of Congress. His speech was moving, eloquent, and forceful:

All I have I would have given gladly not to be standing here today. . . .

This nation has experienced a profound shock and in this critical moment it is our duty, yours and mine, as the Government of the United States to do away with uncertainty and doubt and delays and to show that we are capable of decisive action — that from the brutal loss of our leader we will derive not weakness but strength — that we can and will act, and act now. . . .

This is our challenge: Not to hesitate, not to pause, not to turn about and linger over this evil moment, but to continue on our course so that we may fulfill the destiny that history has set for us.

Then Johnson called on Congress to enact the extensive legislative program, including the civil rights bill and the tax reduction bill, that Kennedy had advocated.

The first months of the Johnson administration were a time of exceptional legislative activity. Bills that had been stalled in Congress during the Kennedy years were urgently pressed by the new President; before the 88th Congress adjourned in October 1964, it approved an $11.5 billion tax cut and a civil rights bill that protected voting rights and outlawed discrimination in employment and public accommodations. But not all 1964 legislation stemmed from Kennedy's New Frontier. In 1964 Johnson also called upon the nation to begin a "war on poverty," and in August of that year Congress responded by appropriating $947.5 million for the establishment of a federal Office of Economic Opportunity and an extensive antipoverty program.

In August 1964 the Democratic National Convention unanimously nominated Johnson as its presidential candidate and, at Johnson's urging, chose Senator Hubert H. Humphrey of Minnesota for the second place on its ticket. The Republicans, for their part, selected two conservative members of their party, Senator Barry Goldwater of Arizona and Representative William E. Miller of New York, as their standard-bearers. The November election was a landslide victory for the Democrats, and Johnson defeated his Republican rival by an unprecedented 16 million votes.

In his State of the Union Message on January 4, 1965, Johnson outlined his plan for a Great Society. His program emphasized the need for adequate health care for the aged, preservation of natural resources, the elimination of poverty, increased aid to education, and the establishment of a cabinet-level Department of Housing and Urban Development. In the months that followed, the large Democratic majorities that controlled both houses of Congress gave Johnson enough votes to put a number of Great Society measures into effect. Most notably, Congress passed the Medicare bill, which financed medical insurance through Social Security for those over 65, and the Voting Rights Act (see August 6), which authorized the attorney general to send federal registrars to enroll black voters in states violating the 15th Amendment.

Unfortunately Johnson's conduct of foreign policy did not prove to be as successful as his handling of domestic affairs. His sending of American troops into the Dominican Republic in 1965, in an effort to prevent a Communist takeover of that nation, aroused opposition in many quarters. Even more important, his increasing support of the government of South Vietnam against the opposition of Communist North Vietnam and its guerrilla allies became a major source of concern to many American citizens. This was especially true after February 1965, when he authorized bombing attacks against North Vietnam, and after the sharp increase in the number of US troops in Vietnam that began the same year. These steps followed congressional approval of the variously interpreted Gulf of Tonkin Resolution in 1964 (see August 7), which some observers regarded as vital to the protection of the Free World, while others retrospectively characterized it as a blank check for escalation.

Although developments in several areas, including Vietnam and the Middle East, where the United States and the Soviet Union supported opposing governments, severely tried US-Soviet relations during the Johnson administration, there was no significant deterioration in the relationship between the two nations. Indeed, when Premier Aleksei Kosygin visited the United States shortly after the Arab defeat by Israel in the Six-Day War of June 1967, the Soviet premier and the American President held a summit conference. Meeting in the town of Glassboro, New Jersey, between June 23 and June 25, 1967, the two leaders discussed the situations in Vietnam and the Middle East. Few concrete proposals resulted from these conferences, but the meetings did much to relieve the tensions that had followed the Arab-Israeli war and to renew the spirit of international cooperation.

Despite Johnson's continued efforts to build a Great Society, after 1965 the vast expenditures necessary to support the war effort in Vietnam sapped the resources of the United States, and appropriations for domestic programs suffered. The American people became increasingly divided over Vietnam; a sizable portion of the citizenry opposed the man who had so deeply involved the nation in a conflict that seemed morally dubious and incapable of solution by a clear-cut victory. Large-scale demonstrations against the war took place in many cities and on college campuses, and public opinion polls showed that the President was steadily losing the confidence of the people.

On March 31, 1968, President Johnson addressed the nation over television and radio. To end the fighting in Vietnam, he announced a new peace initiative: he ordered an end to US bombing of most of North Vietnam and invited the Hanoi government to join in a "series of mutual moves toward peace." Then the President made a dramatic statement:

What we won when all of our people united ... must not now be lost in suspicion and distrust. ... I have concluded that I should not permit the Presidency to become involved in the partisan divisions that are developing in this political year.

Accordingly, I shall not seek, and I will not accept, the nomination of my party for another term as your President.

Johnson's startling announcement produced immediate results. Within days the Hanoi government agreed to establish contact aimed at beginning talks that might eventually lead to a peace settlement. Meanwhile the race for the Democratic nomination for President intensified. Vice President Hubert H. Humphrey on April 27 joined previously announced presidential hopefuls Senators Eugene McCarthy and Robert F. Kennedy, the brother of the late President. After the assassination of Kennedy on June 5 Senator George McGovern entered the contest.

The 1968 Democratic convention nominated Humphrey for President and selected Senator Edmund S. Muskie of Maine as his running mate. The Republicans that year chose former Vice President Richard M. Nixon and Maryland governor Spiro T. Agnew as their standard-bearers. Nixon, with only 43 percent of the popular vote, garnered 302 electoral votes as compared with the 191 electoral votes for Humphrey and the 45 of ultraconservative candidate George C. Wallace.

After more than five years as Chief Executive, Johnson left public office in January 1969. The first President from the South since the Civil War (though he regarded himself as a westerner), he had seen the country through the crisis following the Kennedy assassination and had overseen passage of important legislation. Yet his involvement with the unpopular war in Vietnam had cost him much of the esteem that he had earned during his years in government service. Only after the passage of time could his place in history be fairly assessed.

Following the inauguration of Nixon, Johnson and his wife – Claudia Taylor ("Lady Bird") Johnson – returned to their 600-acre LBJ Ranch near Johnson City, Texas. During their years in the White House their daughters, Lynda Bird and Lucy Baines Johnson, had married and presented them with grandchildren. Retirement from public office left the Johnsons with more time for their growing family and an opportunity to record their reminiscences of their time as the First Family. In addition, Johnson was able to oversee construction of the $18.6 million Lyndon Baines Johnson Library at the University of Texas in Austin, which houses some 31 million documents, 500,000 photographs, and memorabilia associated with his 38 years in politics. The library was dedicated in a nationally televised ceremony on May 22, 1971. It stands on a hilltop site, next to Sid Richardson Hall, part of which houses the new Lyndon Baines Johnson School of Public Affairs, opened in September 1970.

On January 22, 1973, the 64-year-old Lyndon B. Johnson died of a coronary thrombosis at the LBJ Ranch. He was stricken suddenly, although he had suffered major heart attacks earlier, in July 1955 and in the spring of 1972. Johnson's last public appearances were characteristic of his dedicated public career: on December 12, 1972, for example, he had acted as mediator in quieting a divisive dispute among civil rights leaders who had gathered for a symposium at the University of Texas; only two days before his death, he had joined his wife in a tree-planting ceremony — part of her beautification program — at Stonewall, Texas, near his family ranch.

Johnson's death occurred at a time when the nation was observing a period of mourning for former President Harry S. Truman, who had died on December 26, 1972. President Richard M. Nixon ordered the flags on government buildings, already lowered in tribute to Truman, to fly at half-staff until February 21. For the sixth time in its history, the United States was left without a living former President.

Respect for Johnson was shown throughout the country. The Texas senate passed a resolution making August 27 a state holiday. In Austin, his body lay in state at the Johnson Library from noon on Tuesday, January 23, until the following morning. During that period, some 32,000 persons filed past the coffin. On January 24, after a 21-gun salute and a brief memorial service, his body was flown in *Air Force One* to Andrews Air Force Base in Maryland. From there the hearse, accompanied by a 30-car-motorcade, traveled slowly to the Capitol. At Constitution Avenue the coffin was transferred to the traditional horse-drawn artillery caisson. The black gun carriage was preceded by some 1,800 servicemen from all branches of the military and trailed by Black Jack, a riderless steed bearing

boots reversed in the stirrups to signify a departed leader. Cars carrying the Johnson family, the party of President Nixon, and various dignitaries ended the cortege, which moved slowly to the muffled cadence of the Marine Band's black-draped drums.

Once the procession had reached the Capitol, the flag-draped coffin was carried through the Senate hallway to the Rotunda, where it was set upon the black catafalque that had borne the coffins of eight other Presidents. Following hymns, prayers, a eulogy by Representative J. J. Pickle of Texas (who held the congressional seat once occupied by Johnson), and Nixon's placing of a wreath at the foot of the catafalque, the Rotunda was opened to the public. Some 40,000 mourners paid homage during the late afternoon and night.

On January 25, which President Nixon had designated as a national day of mourning, memorial services were held throughout the country; many schools, federal, state, and city offices, and stock exchanges were closed. A mid-morning funeral service was held at the National City Christian Church in Washington, D.C., where Johnson had often worshiped. Marvin Watson, who had served under Johnson as postmaster general and as White House appointments secretary, delivered the eulogy. The body was then flown in the presidential plane to Texas for burial in the late afternoon at the LBJ Ranch. The former President had expressed the wish to be buried beside his father, mother, and other relatives in the small, oak-shaded, walled cemetery on the northern bank of the Pedernales River, about 400 yards from his ranch house. The evangelist Billy Graham and former Texas governor John B. Connally spoke at the simple but moving burial service, which was attended by family, neighbors, and close friends from the surrounding hill country.

Thousands visit the site of the former President's home each year, driving along US Route 290 to catch a glimpse of the limestone and wood LBJ ranch houses on the opposite bank of the Pedernales River. But the major attraction is in Johnson City itself. There the modest frame house where Johnson lived as a boy has been restored and is open to the public.

On the first posthumous anniversary of Johnson's birth, August 27, 1973, the US Postal Service issued a memorial stamp bearing his likeness. The site chosen for the unveiling of the eight-cent stamp was the Lyndon Baines Johnson Library. Following this ceremony, members of the late President's family flew to Houston, where the Manned Spacecraft Center of the National Aeronautics and Space Administration (NASA) was rededicated as the Lyndon B. Johnson Space Center in tribute to his longstanding encouragement of the nation's efforts to explore outer space and the spectacular advances in that area made during Johnson's presidency.

In 1974 Lady Bird Johnson dedicated the 15-acre Lyndon B. Johnson Memorial Grove on the Virginia banks of the Potomac River, overlooking Washington, D.C. This national memorial was authorized by the federal government but financed by private contributions. Amid the trees and flowers — the site is within an existing park named earlier for Lady Bird Johnson — is a rough-hewn granite mass inscribed with Johnson's words: "From the grove is a view that will be engraved on my heart forever." Other Texas memorials to Johnson include a bust of him, unveiled in 1975, in front of the Senate chamber in Austin, and an eight-foot bronze statue of Johnson in the Lyndon B. Johnson State Park near Stonewall, across the Pedernales River from the Johnson Ranch.

AUGUST 28

Feast of St. Augustine of Hippo

St. Augustine of Hippo, one of the greatest figures of the Latin church, is one of the four Church Fathers of the West and also a doctor of the church. These titles signify his sanctity, learning, and contributions to Christian life and thought. He is sometimes called Doctor of Grace because of his important writings and teachings on the subject of divine grace. His August 28 feast day, marked since the eighth century, is observed by Roman Catholics as a memorial, equivalent to the former Class III feast.

Augustine was born on November 13 in the year 354 at Tagaste in Numidia, now Souk-Ahras in Algeria. His father, Patricius, was an official of the city and a pagan. He wanted his son to be educated and to enjoy life. His mother, Monica (later canonized), was a Christian. She wanted her son to be educated and to live a life devoted to God. In time, both parents got their wishes.

After Augustine had finished the usual literary studies in Tagaste and in Madaura, a nearby town, his father wanted him to continue his education in the great city of Carthage, an ambition that even wealthier fathers of the time rarely held for their sons. During his 16th year, Augustine lived in idleness at home while his father accumulated enough money to send him away to study.

It was during this period that Augustine began the dissolute life that he was to continue for many years and that he was to condemn so heartily in his *Confessions*, the most famous of his writings. One of the earliest episodes he relates tells how Augustine with a band of other youths stole pears from a neighbor's tree. Later, in Carthage, he took a concubine, to whom he was faithful for many years. As a matter of fact, Augustine was probably living as most of his contemporaries lived. His *Confessions*, full of remorse for his youthful excesses, were written after he had turned to a holy life with as much vigor as he had spent in his earlier pursuits.

About his *Confessions*, St. Augustine said, "The thirteen books of my Confessions praise God, Holy and Good, on occasion of that which has in me been good or evil, and raise up man's understanding and affections to Him: for myself, they did so while they were being written, and now do, when read."

While studying and later teaching rhetoric in Carthage, Augustine put aside all his mother had taught him about Christianity. He sampled many pagan philosophies and finally became a strong advocate of Manichaeanism, a philosophy founded by a Persian in the century before Augustine's birth. The persuasive Augustine, who had fulfilled his teachers' earliest wishes for him to "excel in the tongue science," made many converts to Manichaeanism before he himself, always searching for the truth but not always wanting to accept it, began to have strong doubts about this way of thinking.

Augustine returned to Tagaste and continued teaching there until he was about 29. He then went to Rome and, in 384, to Milan, where he taught rhetoric. There he became much impressed with the thought of an eminent Christian intellectual, Ambrose, bishop of Milan. A Roman born to senatorial aristocracy, Ambrose (who was later canonized) had been a provincial governor, with Milan as his headquarters, before becoming bishop of that city — which was, during most of his episcopate, the capital of the Western Roman Empire.

After the death of Patricius, who, to his wife's great happiness had become a Christian, Monica traveled to Italy to be with her son, always praying for his conversion. After several years of intellectual and emotional conflict within himself and with his educated friends, Augustine resolved to become a Christian. He was baptized by Ambrose on Easter Eve, in 387, to his mother's joy and relief.

Determined to devote his life to God, Augustine, with his friend Alypius and his mother, started back to Africa, traveling from Milan to Ostia, the port of Rome. Before embarking on the voyage across the Mediterranean, however, they rested in a house at Ostia. There Monica told Augustine:

One thing there was, for which I desired to linger for a while in this life, that I might see thee a Catholic Christian before I died. My God hath done this for me more abundantly, that I should now see thee withal, despising early happiness, become his servant: what do I here?

Within a few days, Monica fell ill of a fever and died.

When Augustine returned to Africa, Valerius, bishop of Hippo (now Bône in Algeria), persuaded him to become a priest. Augustine was ordained in 391, was consecrated bishop in 395, and became bishop of Hippo in 396, after the death of Valerius.

As bishop, Augustine made many enduring contributions to the church during the next 35 years. He lived a monastic life with his clergy and strongly encouraged the formation of religious communities. His letters and sermons outlined the basis of the religious and monastic life, emphasizing charity as the foundation for perfection. From his writings evolved the Augustinian rule, now followed by many groups of friars, monks, and nuns.

Having sampled most of the rampant heretical philosophies during his student days, Augustine, as bishop, ably refuted the many heresies that threatened the church, including the Manichaean philosophy. When Rome was invaded by the Vandals in 410, Christianity was blamed for the fall of the Roman Empire. Because of the Christians, their enemies claimed, the gods had been neglected and as a consequence had deserted the Roman Empire.

In his defense of the church, Augustine wrote *The City of God*. In this famous book he asserted that calamity in this world is not due to the neglect of gods. He examined the history and institutions of pagan Rome, distinguished between the City of God and the worldly city, and discussed their respective origins and goals.

The Vandals, spreading out from Rome, were at the gates of Hippo when Augustine died on August 28, 430. A bishop, preacher, and administrator of both church and civil matters, the indefatigable Augustine left a priceless legacy of thought. It survives in 113 books and treatises, and more than 200 letters and 500 sermons.

St. Augustine, Florida, the oldest city in the United States, was named in honor of this saint. Florida had been discovered by the Spanish explorer Ponce de León in 1513. King Philip II of Spain, learning that French Huguenots had settled in this Spanish possession, sent his admiral, Don Pedro Menéndez de Avilés, to expel the intruders. Menéndez first sighted land on St. Augustine's feast day, August 28, 1565, and so named his settlement in honor of the saint. The quadricentennial of the city of St. Augustine was celebrated on September 8, 1965.

AUGUST 29

Oliver Wendell Holmes's Birthday

Oliver Wendell Holmes, the father of the Supreme Court justice of the same name, was one of New England's most versatile men — an author, humorist, poet, lecturer, physician, and ardent conversationalist. He was born in Cambridge, Massachusetts, on August 29, 1809 — the year in which his father, the minister Abiel Holmes, published a historical work entitled *The Annals of America.* Oliver's mother, Sarah Wendell Holmes, was the daughter of the well-to-do Oliver Wendell. She was the second wife of Abiel Holmes, who was a childless widower before his remarriage.

As a youngster, Oliver Wendell Holmes received his education at local schools and then at Phillips Academy, Andover, Massachusetts, for a year. He subsequently entered Harvard in 1825, where his classmates elected him class poet. Just a month before Holmes was graduated from Harvard, a two-year battle between Calvinists and Unitarians came to a head, and his father was ousted from his Cambridge pulpit. Holmes blamed the Calvinists for this bitter blow to his father's pride and career, and for the rest of his life he rarely missed an opportunity to attack Calvinist clergy and doctrines.

After receiving his undergraduate degree, Holmes went on to study law at Harvard. Finding the studies dull (he continued in law for only one year), he turned more and more to writing verse, an avocation he followed for the rest of his life. In 1830 he switched to the study of medicine — and published what is perhaps his most famous poem. This was "Old Ironsides," a tribute to the American frigate USS *Constitution,* which had won a decisive victory in its encounter with the British frigate *Guerrière* during the War of 1812. Holmes's poem stirred the nation to protest the sending of the famous ship to the scrap heap. Preserved, and later restored with money raised by American schoolchildren, the USS *Constitution* today is one of the historical attractions of Boston, where it can be seen at Pier 1 of the Boston Naval Shipyard.

Although he was working hard at his medical studies, in 1831 Holmes was still able to publish "The Last Leaf," another poem that gained great popularity. His conscientiousness having impressed his teachers, he was able to persuade his parents to let him pursue his medical studies in Paris for an additional two years. He found no time for poetry there, however, since he was concentrating on learning his profession. Holmes was influenced by a group of French clinicians who were skeptical about the effectiveness of drugs then widely prescribed. He was to be a lifelong crusader against quackery, rampant in the United States at the time, and his influence acted as a brake against the use of unscientific remedies.

Returning from France in December 1835, Holmes took his degree from Harvard. Although he was thus qualified to practice medicine, his real preference was for teaching, and for 10 years he combined the two. In 1838 Holmes and other physicians founded the Tremont Medical School, where he taught even while carrying on his private practice and serving for two years (1838 to 1840) as professor of anatomy at Dartmouth College in Hanover, New Hampshire.

By 1840 Holmes married Amelia Lee Jackson, whose father, Charles Jackson, was a justice of the supreme judicial court of Massachusetts. They had three children. Their firstborn, Oliver Wendell Holmes Jr. (see March 8), became known as the Great Dissenter in his role as an associate justice of the US Supreme Court. His birth in 1841 was followed by that of a sister, Amelia, in 1843 and a brother, Edward, in 1846.

The senior Holmes was offered the teaching post he really wanted in 1847, and for the next 35 years, until his retirement in 1882, he was Parkman Professor of Anatomy and Physiology at Harvard. As a humorist, he made his lectures amusing. As a well-trained medical man, he encouraged his students to practice medicine on the basis of scientifically proven treatments. Among other things, he introduced the use of the microscope in his classroom. While no original medical discoveries are attributed to Holmes, he lent his prestige and talents to the support of many worthwhile causes, encouraged original research and good methods of practice among American doctors, and spoke out against quackery of all types.

He was awarded the Boylston prize in 1836 for his first medical essay. Entitled "Direct Exploration," this was a convincing argument for the more extensive and frequent use of the stethoscope, an instrument that was then largely ignored in American medicine. His most controversial medical essay — *The Contagiousness of Puerperal Fever*, published in 1843 — indicated that "childbed fever," which caused the deaths of many women, was transmitted from patient to patient by obstetricians. Four years later similar conclusions were published by a young Hungarian physician, Ignaz Semmelweis, who is credited by medical historians with this important discovery. Unfortunately, Semmelweis, ridiculed for publishing his theory and for attempting to have doctors wash their hands before attending women in labor, fled Vienna and committed suicide before his theory was accepted. Holmes, meanwhile, was able to withstand the abuse — perhaps because of his sanctuary in the classroom — and in 1855 he reprinted his original essay with an eloquent appeal to American doctors to acknowledge the facts. Holmes's other medical writings include the books *Homœopathy and Its Kindred Delusions* (1842) and *Currents and Counter Currents in Medical Science* (1860).

Holmes's reputation as a man of letters soon outstripped his reputation as a man of science. His first volume of verses, simply entitled *Poems*, was published in 1836. In Boston, where conversation was recognized as an art, Holmes had no superiors. He loved to talk. Ralph Waldo Emerson noted that Holmes "could always write or speak to order; partly from the abundance of the stream, which can indifferently fill any provided channel."

Holmes was often called upon to address informal groups of friends or colleagues. During the 1840s he became a popular lecturer to wider audiences, regaling the public with his witty observations on almost any subject. The British author William Makepeace Thackeray, after a visit to the United States, declared Holmes to be the best thing he had seen in America.

Holmes's popularity was such that in 1857, when James Russell Lowell was asked to become editor of a new magazine founded by literary Bostonians, he accepted on the condition that Holmes would be a regular contributor. Holmes not only contributed to the magazine, but gave it its name — the *Atlantic Monthly;* and, according to William Dean Howells, the magazine's third editor, "not only named but made it." Many of Holmes's poems and sketches appeared first in the *Atlantic Monthly*, and his three novels were serialized in the magazine before being published in book form. They were *Elsie Venner*, published in 1861; *The Guardian Angel* (1867); and *A Mortal Antipathy* (1885). They have been called the first American psychological novels but were less popular than his other writings, possibly because they were strongly anti-Calvinistic and not in his usual humorous vein.

Probably the most popular prose Holmes ever produced was his series of Breakfast Table sketches, published first in the *Atlantic Monthly* and later collected into books, including *The Autocrat of the Breakfast Table* (1858) and *The Professor at the Breakfast Table* (1860). His most famous poems besides "Old Ironsides" and "The Last Leaf" were "The Chambered Nautilus" and "The Deacon's Masterpiece; or, The Wonderful One-Hoss Shay." He also wrote biographies of some of his contemporaries, including Emerson (1885).

Holmes died in Boston, at the age of 85, on October 7, 1894. He was elected to the Hall of Fame for Great Americans in New York City in 1910.

The Death of St. John the Baptist

A commemoration of St. John the Baptist was observed in Jerusalem as early as the fifth century, probably on August 29, the anniversary of the dedication of the Church of the Precursor of the Lord at Sebaste, Palestine, where John's remains were thought to be buried. In the following centuries, this commemoration became known as the Passion (or Beheading) of St. John the Baptist in Eastern Orthodox and Roman Catholic churches. In the revised Roman Catholic calendar, the commemoration of the death of John the Baptist is designated as a memorial, comparable to the former Class III feast. Although this feast, like other saints' days, marks the death of a saint, it is outranked in liturgical importance by the older Feast of the Nativity of St. John the Baptist (see June 24), which is one of the principal feasts of those Christian churches that commemorate the lives of the saints.

The story of the beheading of John is one of the most dramatic in the New Testament. Herod Antipas, ruler of Galilee, had repudiated his own wife and married Herodias, his niece; she, for her part, had left Philip, Herod's half brother, in order to marry Herod. John the Baptist rebuked Herodias, an ambitious, scheming, and vengeful woman.

According to the New Testament account (Mark 6:17–29), Herodias persuaded Herod to imprison John. In the opinion of the historian Josephus, Herod took this step because he feared John's influence with the people. John was confined in the Machaerus, a luxurious fortress on the border of Herod's territory. He was not illtreated, and was allowed visits from his disciples, who brought him news of Jesus Christ and carried his communications to Jesus. It was John's hope that Jesus would publicly declare himself the Messiah before he (John) died.

It had evidently not been Herod's intention to kill John, but only to quiet him and keep him out of the public eye. But Herod had not reckoned with Herodias.

On his own birthday in about A.D. 29, Herod gave a banquet at which Herodias's daughter Salome danced. Her performance pleased him so much that he offered her anything, including half his kingdom. Salome asked her mother what she should request, and, following her advice, told Herod that she wanted the head of John the Baptist on a platter. Although Herod was loath to grant her request, he kept his word and ordered the prophet's head cut off and placed on a platter.

Although Herodias is the real villain in the scriptural account of the beheading of St. John, her wickedness is usually transferred to her daughter, Salome, in later literature and other art forms. Oscar Wilde's play *Salomé*, written in French, is an extreme example of this tendency, attributing to Salome a perverse and violent passion for the prophet.

Before the play was published, in Paris in 1893 and in English translation in London a year later, Wilde showed it to the actress Sarah Bernhardt. She was so taken with the play that she insisted not only on acting the title role but also on producing the play in London, to which end she rented the Palace Theatre. Three weeks of rehearsals and much time and money had been spent before it was realized that Wilde had not applied for a license for the play. The license was denied, rehearsals were discontinued, and Bernhardt was furious, especially with Wilde. Finally, however, the play was staged in Paris in 1896, and it was well received. In 1905 Richard Strauss wrote his well-known opera based on Wilde's play, which is still popular.

AUGUST 30

Huey P. Long Day in Louisiana

The birthday of Huey Pierce Long, governor of and US senator from Louisiana, has been observed annually in that state since 1937. It was declared a legal holiday by a constitutional amendment ratified by the state's voters in 1936, a year after Long's death from an assassin's bullet.

The eighth child of a family of 10, Long was born on August 30, 1893, near Winnfield, in Winn Parish, Louisiana. There he attended the local school and worked on his father's farm. In his family background there was a strong Baptist evangelicalism and also a back-country Populist animosity to the wealth and sophistication of New Orleans and the planter class.

Huey Long attended Winnfield High School, where he excelled in debate. Financial difficulties compelled him to temporarily give up his ambition to study law, although he was able to attend University of Oklahoma Law School for a semester. Until 1914, when he entered Tulane University Law School, he worked as a traveling salesman.

When Long entered Tulane he had funds to last only a little over seven months, but by hard work he managed to complete the three-year law course in that time. On May 15, 1915, he took a special bar examination and was admitted to the bar. Although Long first set up his law practice in Winnfield, he soon settled at Shreveport.

In 1918 he won appointment to the only state

office from which he was not excluded by a minimum age requirement, state railroad commissioner. In this capacity, and later in 1921 as public service commissioner (when the Railroad Commission became the Public Service Commission), he began his long warfare against public utilities. He succeeded in preventing street-railway rate increases in Shreveport, in reducing telephone rates, and in forcing pipelines to act as common carriers. Long also successfully defended these measures in court when they were attacked.

In 1924, during his service as chairman of the Public Service Commission, Long ran for governor. Although he won much support from the rural parts of the state, Long lost New Orleans and was defeated. Four years later he was elected governor by a large plurality.

A year later a coalition of legislators — including some who were shocked at Long's alleged misconduct and misappropriation of state funds, some who opposed his "occupational" tax on oil refineries, and some who belonged to the Old Regular faction of the Democratic party in New Orleans — impeached Long. However, these forces were unable to secure his conviction. Running for the US Senate in 1930, Long took his case to the people. He blamed the impeachment attack on the Standard Oil Company, one of his favorite targets. He was elected by a majority of 38,000.

With this victory Long also cemented an alliance with the New Orleans Regulars, and entrenched himself in Louisiana by the establishment of a strong political machine. Unwilling to give up the governorship to the politically hostile lieutenant governor, Paul Cyr, Long refused to relinquish his seat. Not until January 1932, when a candidate of whom he approved was elected, did he take his seat in the US Senate.

As governor, Long — despite the opposition of the legislature — made numerous public improvements. He passed a free schoolbook law and expanded the facilities of Louisiana State University. With a $30 million highway fund new roads were built. Long also had constructed at Baton Rouge, the state capital, a magnificent new capitol building. Thirty-four stories high, it stands 450 feet tall and contains 30 varieties of marble. It remains the city's most notable landmark, and visitors flock to its observation tower for a view of the city and its surrounding countryside.

As senator, Huey Long, nicknamed by himself the Kingfish, seemed to many Americans a clown. His stand on the redistribution of wealth was considered extreme, and though as a Democrat he supported Franklin Delano Roosevelt in 1932, by August of 1933 Long was in open rebellion against the administration. A year later the New Orleans Regulars broke with Long over his defiance of the federal administration, and succeeded in electing their candidate mayor of New Orleans.

Long responded by having the Louisiana legislature during 1934–1935 reorganize the state government, creating a virtual dictatorship, unique in US history. By the end of 1935 Long had ended local government in Louisiana and had obtained direct control over the appointment of the militia, the judiciary, the police, firemen, schoolteachers, election officials, and tax assessors. He exercised this control over the state while serving in the US Senate.

Long's strength in his own state, plus the support engendered by his Share-Our-Wealth Society (organized in 1934), which promised a minimum income for every American family, made him a power to be reckoned with as a potential presidential candidate in 1936. Meanwhile, he had found time to write two books — *Every Man a King* (1933) and, optimistically, *My First Days in the White House* (1935).

However, on September 8, 1935, as Long was leaving the state capitol where the legislature was in special session, he was fatally shot by Dr. Carl A. Weiss, the son-in-law of a political enemy. Weiss was killed on the spot by Senator Long's bodyguards. Long died on September 10.

Long's subsequent burial in what is now a sunken garden in front of the state capitol drew some 100,000 people. A statue surrounded with carefully selected inscriptions by and about him stands as a memorial over his grave.

Considered a fascist demagogue by many, Huey Long actually shunned all party ideologies and sought power by any means available. His political activity, often boisterous, vulgar, and extreme, grew out of the agrarian Populist tradition, as did his violent attacks on corporations.

Whatever his shortcomings, Long was revered by the rural people of Louisiana, and his political career marked the beginning of a family dynasty in Louisiana politics. Among his successors in politics have been his son Russell B. Long, also a US senator; a brother, Earl, who was three times elected governor; and two cousins who were elected to Congress.

AUGUST 31

The Charleston Earthquake

The most disastrous North American earthquake ever experienced east of the Mississippi occurred late on August 31, 1886. The epicenter was 15 miles northwest of Charleston, South Carolina, where three-fourths — some say nine-tenths — of the buildings were wrecked or badly damaged. The loss of life in Charleston was variously reported at between 41 and 57 and at 100 in the entire affected area. Property damage amounted to some $8 million. The shock was felt at distant places — Bermuda, Jacksonville, Cuba, New Haven, Dubuque, and even Toronto.

In the Charleston area the quake opened deep cracks in the ground, out of which issued sulfurous clouds. Falling buildings were the principal cause of death. Many of the victims were people who, after the first tremors, rushed out into the city streets expecting to see the end of the world. They were thus exposed to a rain of debris as subsequent shocks brought down walls and roofing.

The 1886 earthquake was recalled in 1977 when unexplained booming sounds in widely scattered regions attracted public attention. Such sounds had preceded the 1886 earthquake. On December 2, 1977, residents of the Charleston area once again heard the booming sounds — the first in a series to occur on the east coast of the United States. The two explosionlike sounds rattled windows. On December 15 two mild quakes in Charleston were preceded by five booms. Two more booms were heard in Charleston on December 20. The booms, records of which date to precolonial times, are a subject of wide controversy in the scientific community. Among the various causes suggested are activity along a fault in the earth's crust, and the explosion of methane gas rising from bodies of water.

September

September is the ninth month of the Gregorian, or New Style, calendar used today and numbers 30 days. As can be seen from its name, derived from the Latin word *septem,* meaning "seven," September was the seventh month in the ancient Roman calendar, which began in March. Even after the Roman calendar had been revised extensively and the year commenced two months earlier—in January—September, then the ninth month, retained its name.

During the time of the Roman Empire, there were numerous attempts to rename September. The months of *Quintilis* and *Sextilis* had been renamed July and August, after Julius Caesar and Augustus, in the first century B.C. Once July and August had taken their places in the Roman calendar, it was not surprising that the Roman senate tried to bestow upon succeeding rulers a similar sign of prestige. It was the custom to vote to each new emperor the honors and prerogatives that his predecessors had held, including the "divine honor" of the honorific month. September was especially open to change since it immediately followed July and August.

Shortly after Emperor Augustus' death in A.D. 14 and early in the reign of his successor, Tiberius (A.D. 14–37), the senate proposed to rename September *Tiberius.* The emperor's refusal seems to have modified but not halted the schemes of his flatterers in the senate. They soon attempted to name his birth month, November, after him, but this time Tiberius supposedly stopped all such adulation with the cutting remark: "And what will you do if there be thirteen Caesars?"

According to the second century Roman biographer Suetonius, in A.D. 37, the start of his reign, Emperor Caligula (A.D. 37–41) had the Roman senate name September *Germanicus* "in memory of his father," Germanicus Caesar (15 B.C.–A.D.

19), a famous Roman general. The change was apparently short-lived, however.

Emperor Domitian, who reigned from A.D. 81 to 96, also tried to rename September *Germanicus,* he himself having adopted this cognomen to commemorate his victories in Germany. Domitian selected September because the *dies imperii,* marking his accession as emperor, fell within that month. Again, however, the change did not survive the tyrannical emperor's death. The early fifth century writer Macrobius commented:

The month September retains its own original name; this month Domitian had usurped with the appellation Germanicus and October with his own name Domitianus. But when it was decreed that the unpropitious word [Domitianus] be erased from every bronze or stone, the months too were freed from the usurpation of a tyrannical appellation.

In yet another move, the Roman senate, probably in A.D. 138, suggested that the inappropriately named September be called *Antoninus* in honor of Emperor Antoninus Pius (A.D. 138–161), who had been born on the 19th day of the month. The emperor refused.

Conspicuously less modest was Emperor Commodus (A.D. 180–192), who about A.D. 191 had the Roman senate approve the renaming of all 12 months in his honor. Each was to be called after an honorary name he sometimes assumed, September being designated *Augustus,* meaning "venerable," or "reverend." The month of August, previously renamed for the first Roman emperor, Augustus, was renamed *Commodus* so as not to cause conflict. However, Commodus's innovations in the naming of months did not long outlast his own short life.

The last Roman emperor to have his name given to September was Marcus Claudius Tacitus, who ruled for the brief period of A.D. 275 to 276. According to an account in his unreliable contemporary biography, "he ordered the month September to be called Tacitus because in this month he was born and also made emperor." The name *Tacitus*, like all others previously bestowed on September, did not long survive.

Moreover, the rapid growth of Christianity by the closing years of the third century and beginning of the fourth — and especially the conversion of Emperor Constantine (A.D. 311–337) — struck a severe blow at the Roman state religion with its worship of the emperor as a god. It spelled doom for the "divine honor" of the honorific month. It therefore also marked the end of attempts to rename September in line with the precedent set by July and August.

The chief events in September were the games in honor of Juno, Minerva, and Jupiter, which were called the *ludi magni* or *ludi Romani*, and which began on September 4.

In Charlemagne's calendar, September was known as the harvest month. The Anglo-Saxon name for it was *Gerst-monath*, or barley month, since barley was harvested then. After the introduction of Christianity it was sometimes called *Halig-monath*, or holy month, in allusion to the birth of Mary, the mother of Jesus, on September 8. It is usually the month of the harvest moon, the full moon nearest the time of the autumnal equinox. It appears above the horizon at about sunset for several days, giving light enough for farmers to continue their harvesting.

SEPTEMBER 1

World War II Begins

World War II, the most cataclysmic event of the 20th century, began in Europe when the forces of Adolf Hitler's Nazi Germany invaded Poland on September 1, 1939. The war stemmed from the territorial ambitions of the land-hungry totalitarian regimes that had developed against the backdrop of worldwide economic disaster in the 1930s and conditions created by the peace terms signed after World War I (see June 28). The capabilities of the faltering and inadequately supported League of Nations (see January 10) proved insufficient to check aggression and prevent war.

The onslaught directed against Poland by the German dictator was preceded by aggression elsewhere. Under Hitler — whose unparalleled brutality would be epitomized by the Nazis' murder, in concentration camps, of 6 million Jews and countless others before the war was over — Germany had earlier remilitarized the Rhineland in 1936, annexed Austria in 1938, and swallowed up Czechoslovakia in March

1939. Germany's partner in what was initially known as the Rome-Berlin Axis was Italy. Under the leadership of the Fascist dictator Benito Mussolini, that country had conquered Ethiopia in 1936 and overrun Albania in April 1939. Militarist-dominated Japan, which would be the third mainstay of the Axis during World War II, meanwhile had been pursuing a policy of territorial aggrandizement in Asia throughout most of the decade, most notably with its occupation of Manchuria in 1931 and the war against China that followed. Known as the Second Sino-Japanese War, it ultimately would merge into World War II.

Abandoning a policy of appeasement, which they at last saw to be futile, Great Britain and France declared war against Germany two days after the invasion of Poland. The distaste of the United States for conflict following World War I had led it into an extended period of isolationism; the United States supplied increasing aid to the British and French Allies but did not enter World War II on their side until Japan's attack on the US naval installation at Pearl Harbor, Hawaii, in 1941 (see December 7). That action precipitated the US declaration of war against Japan the following day (see December 8). Germany and Italy reacted by declaring war on the United States on December 11. On the same day, the US Congress, with only one dissenting vote, responded in kind, issuing a declaration of war against the two European dictatorships.

After untold suffering and bloodshed, and almost incalculable cost, World War II, the greatest and most terrible war that humanity had known, ended in 1945 with victory for the British, Free French, US, and Soviet Allies, who had been joined by many other nations in the course of the conflict. In Europe, the German surrender was signed at 2:41 A.M., local time, on May 7 (8:41 P.M., May 6, East Coast time). After simultaneous announcements by the Allied chiefs of state, May 8 was officially celebrated by Americans as V-E, or Victory-Europe, Day (see May 8); unofficial celebrations had occurred earlier. In the Far East, Allied victory came later in the year, shortly after the first use of the atomic bomb (see August 5). The Japanese willingness to surrender was announced in Washington, D.C., on August 14, 1945, a day since remembered as V-J, or Victory-Japan, Day (see August 14). Formal ratification of the Japanese surrender followed (see September 2).

World War II Ends

World War II, which had begun in Europe on September 1, 1939, with the invasion of Poland by Nazi Germany, ended officially six years later to the day. The conclusion came with the signing of surrender papers by representatives of

Japan, Nazi Germany's Axis partner in the Far East, and the victorious Allies – the United States, Great Britain, Australia, New Zealand, China, Russia, the Netherlands, and France. In Japan, where the surrender ceremony took place aboard the battleship *Missouri*, moored in Tokyo Bay, the date was September 2 (see September 2).

SEPTEMBER 2

Eugene Field's Birthday

Eugene Field, author and journalist, often called the Poet of Childhood, was born in St. Louis on September 2, 1850, although in later life he often gave September 3 as his birth date. The earlier date is probably the correct one. Field was a notorious prankster and practical joker, full of high spirits, and possibly he gave the later date, or so friends surmised, so that anyone who forgot to wish him well could make amends on the following day.

His father, Roswell Martin Field, a Vermont-born lawyer, settled in Missouri in 1839 and was counsel for Dred Scott in his fight for his freedom from slavery. Field's mother, Frances Reed Field, the daughter of a professional musician, was also born in Vermont, although it was in St. Louis that she was married. When she died in 1856, Eugene Field and his brother, Roswell Martin Field Jr., who was just a year younger, were sent to Amherst, Massachusetts, to be cared for by a cousin.

Field went to a private school in Monson, Massachusetts, for a time. In 1868 he entered Williams College in Williamstown, Massachusetts, but did not complete the year. His father died in the summer of 1869, leaving his two sons with a generous inheritance. That autumn, Field enrolled in Knox College at Galesburg, Illinois, and the following year he attended the University of Missouri with his brother, who was preparing for a legal career. During Field's days at the University of Missouri, his contribution of humorous verse to the local newspaper became the first step in his journalistic career. But he was never interested in college, and the only name he made for himself on campus was as a prankster. He never obtained a degree.

Instead of returning to his studies in the fall of 1872, he visited Great Britain, France, and Italy, spending a goodly portion of his inheritance. On his return from Europe he married Julia Sutherland Comstock of St. Joseph, Missouri, on October 16, 1873. They had become engaged two years earlier, when she was just 14 years old. Although her parents had some hesitation about the marriage because of her youth, it proved to be a very happy one. Besides being

a devoted wife and mother to their eight children, she helped keep her husband's business affairs from ruin. They had been married for 21 years when, a year before he died, Field wrote, "It is only when I look and see how young and fair and sweet my wife is that I have a good opinion of myself."

After their wedding trip, on which Field spent the remainder of his inheritance, the couple settled for a time in St. Louis. In 1876 they returned to St. Joseph, where they lived in a rambling two-story brick house painted white and set behind an iron fence. Although the interior of the house has been converted into apartments, the Eugene Field Home is considered one of the landmarks of St. Joseph and is opened by appointment. It is at 425 North 11th Street.

Like his father before him, Field lived in a number of Missouri communities. He went as far west as Denver in pursuit of the right journalistic niche, before he finally settled in Chicago. He held editorial positions on the St. Joseph *Gazette*, the St. Louis *Journal*, the Kansas City *Times*, and the Denver *Tribune*, all in the space of less than 10 years. In 1883 he joined the staff of the Chicago *Morning News* (which was renamed the *Record* in 1890), and his columns appeared in that paper until his death. In fact, he had even completed his column for the day on the day he died – November 4, 1895. Field had lived for some time in Buena Park, a Chicago suburb, and shortly before he died he bought a house there, which he nicknamed the Sabine Farm, since one of the great interests of his later life was the Latin poet Horace, who had lived on the original Sabine Farm in the hills above Rome. Field and his brother Roswell had done rhymed translations or paraphrases of Horace, published in 1892, under the title *Echoes from the Sabine Farm*.

Field's column "Sharps and Flats," which appeared in the Chicago *Morning News*, added much to the development and improvement of newspaper column writing. He served his readers a better quality of prose and more literate and diverse subjects than had previously been available in this type of feature. His humor was whimsical and often subtle. Sometimes his whimsy got him into trouble, as when he attributed the authorship of pieces he had written to well-known personalities of the time.

Field was well loved by his friends, but they often felt concerned that he was wasting his talent in merely amusing himself and them. His deeply devoted brother, who by this time was established as a lawyer, reprimanded him for his constant attempts to be humorous and tried with no success to make him more serious in his work and life.

While most of Field's poetry is now considered superficial and sentimental, it enjoyed great popularity during his lifetime and for many decades after his death. "Wynken, Blynken and Nod" (also called the "Dutch Lullaby") and "Little Boy Blue" have become classics of a sort. Field and the whimsical characters in some of his poems are memorialized in a bronze monument in Chicago's huge Lincoln Park, which also contains statues of such figures as Hans Christian Andersen, Shakespeare, Lincoln, and Beethoven.

While Field was still in Denver, he wrote his most successful humorous poem, "The Little Peach," which was recited or sung by comedians for many years thereafter. Field's own appraisal of it was "popular but rotten." Several of his poems were set to music and were included for many years in the repertoire of concert singers.

Most of Field's books were collections of verse or paragraphs that had first appeared in his columns. These include The [Denver] Tribune Primer, published in 1882; Culture's Garland (1887); A Little Book of Western Verse (1889); A Little Book of Profitable Tales (1890); With Trumpet and Drum (1892); Second Book of Verse (1892); The Holy Cross and Other Tales (1893); and The Love Affairs of a Bibliomaniac (1896). A year after his death, the collected works of Field were published in 10 volumes, with 2 more volumes published in 1901. Also after his death, a public school in Chicago was named for him.

In St. Louis, the poet's childhood home, which is sometimes called the Eugene Field Shrine, is at 643 South Broadway. The three-story brick house was slated for demolition in 1934 until a group of St. Louis citizens intervened. The house was dedicated as the Eugene Field Museum in December 1936. Important Field manuscripts are displayed in the two rooms of the first floor, and clothing and furniture used by Field and his wife when they later lived in the house can be seen upstairs. At Christmas, a recurring theme in Field's writings, the museum is decorated with old-fashioned toys and Christmas ornaments. It is maintained by the St. Louis Board of Education.

World War II Ends: Japanese Surrender

Following the capitulation of Japan in 1945 (see August 14, V-J Day), preparations were begun for formal ceremonies of surrender. Since there was unease about the safety of holding such important formalities on the Japanese home islands with the hostilities so recently ended, it was decided to hold the ceremonies in Tokyo Bay — on the battleship Missouri, surrounded by a large fleet of Allied warships. President Harry S. Truman chose the Missouri for several reasons. It was a new and impressive battleship, was named after his home state, and had been christened by his daughter, Margaret.

The ceremony was held on September 2, 1945. Foreign Minister Mamoru Shigemitsu and General Yoshijiro Umezu signed the surrender papers for Japan. Those signing for the Allies included General Douglas MacArthur and Admiral Chester W. Nimitz of the United States and the representatives of Great Britain, China, the USSR, France, Australia, New Zealand, Canada, and the Netherlands. After the signing was completed, hundreds of aircraft roared over the ships in a massive show of Allied air power. The display was followed by an address broadcast to the United States by General MacArthur, who had been named supreme allied commander to receive the surrender and given responsibility for supervising the postwar occupation of Japan by Allied forces.

The surrender ceremonies marked the end of World War II, history's deadliest and most far-reaching conflict, which had begun in Europe six years earlier (see September 1, World War II Begins).

SEPTEMBER 3

Britain and France Declare War on Germany: World War II

On September 3, 1939, Great Britain and France declared war on Germany in the stand against aggression that became World War II. What was to escalate into the most devastating conflict known had begun two days earlier (see September 1, World War II Begins), when Germany, under the leadership of Nazi dictator Adolf Hitler, invaded Poland. Before its end in 1945 in Europe and Asia, the war would become global in nature, involving many of the nations of the world. The contesting countries were headed by the Axis powers — Germany; Italy under the Fascist dictator Benito Mussolini; and militarist-dominated Japan — and by the Allies — Britain; France; the USSR after it was invaded by Germany in June 1941; and the United States after its naval installations at Pearl Harbor, Hawaii, were attacked by Japan on December 7, 1941.

American involvement in the conflict was followed by a monumental effort by the United States, with human and industrial resources thenceforth devoted to the cause of Allied victory. For the United States, as for every other nation that participated, this most terrible and costly war was a history-changing event.

Henry Hudson Enters New York Harbor

Henry Hudson, who on September 3, 1609 sailed his vessel, the *Half Moon,* into New York harbor, was the first European to explore the river that now bears his name. Sixteenth-century mariners — notably the Italian Giovanni da Verrazano, as well as Portuguese, French, and (possibly) English voyagers — had entered or crossed the river but Hudson was the first to give a full account and to recognize the potential value of his discovery for his sponsors in Amsterdam.

Despite his achievement Hudson remains a mysterious character about whom little information is available. Historians do not know the date of his birth and can give only the approximate time of his death. He is believed to have been an Englishman, to have married a woman named Katherine, and to have fathered three sons, the second of whom, John, accompanied his father on the voyages of discovery and perished with him.

All that is known with certainty about Henry Hudson's career concerns the four journeys of exploration that he undertook between 1607 and 1611. In each instance, a leading company of merchants in either England or the Netherlands commissioned him to find shorter water routes than those then known to the highly prized areas of trade in the Orient. Their trust in Hudson suggests that he was already a capable, experienced, and respected mariner.

In 1607 the English Muscovy Company hired Hudson to search for a northeast passage to China, Japan, and the East Indies across the top of Scandinavia and Asia. On May 1 Henry Hudson, his son John and 10 mariners, aboard an 80-ton vessel, the *Hopewell,* set sail from Gravesend, in the Thames estuary, east of London, and about a month later they reached the Shetland Islands. After spending some time on the east coast of Greenland, Hudson sailed east to Spitsbergen. The voyage produced no discoveries, and the *Hopewell* returned to London in September.

Undaunted by his failure, Hudson set sail in 1608 on a second voyage, again financed by the Muscovy Company, which was to search for a northeast passage to the Orient between Spitsbergen and the two islands called Novaya Zemlya in the Arctic Ocean, north of Russia, or, failing that, to find a strait leading to the Kara Sea. Hudson gathered a crew of 14, including his son John, and in the spring set sail from London in the *Hopewell* from London's St. Katherine's Docks, on the Thames.

It was cold and foggy when Hudson and his men reached the Lofoten Islands on the west coast of Norway a month later. The explorers continued their journey, rounding the North Cape in June. The arduous passage began to wear down the mariners, and Hudson noted at one point in his log that two of his men claimed to have sighted a mermaid. Soon afterward the *Hopewell* encountered an ice pack, which forced the vessel onto a southeasterly course toward Novaya Zemlya, where they landed. Unable after repeated attempts to negotiate an eastward passage through the ice flow, the captain finally gave up and unhappily sailed back to England.

After the second voyage, Hudson went to Holland to discuss the possibility of further explorations with the Dutch East India Company, a commercial group representing merchants from six neighboring areas. The representatives of Amsterdam favored making a pact with Hudson, but the delegates from Zeeland persuaded the organization to delay such an undertaking for at least another year. At that point, the Amsterdam Chamber of the Dutch East India Company, well aware of the French government's desire to obtain Hudson's services, independently made an agreement with the mariner.

Under terms of a contract signed by Hudson on January 8, 1609, the explorer was to seek a northeast passage to the Orient by way of Novaya Zemlya. The Amsterdam Chamber of the East India Company promised to provide Hudson with a well-equipped ship and a crew and paid him 800 guilders ($320). If he returned within a year, the merchants pledged to give him additional compensation, and if he failed to come back, agreed to pay his wife an extra 200 guilders.

Hudson set sail from Amsterdam on April 4, 1609, with a crew of 18 English and Dutch sailors on the *Halve Maen (Half Moon).* The three-masted vessel weighed less than 80 tons, and measured approximately 75 feet in length, 17 feet in breadth, and 10 feet in depth. On the foremast was a square foresail and a foretopsail, on the mainmast a square mainsail and a maintopsail, and on the mizzenmast a triangular rigged sail.

Ice and cold again awaited Hudson in the northern waters and cut short his quest for a northeastern passage. Frustrated once more in his attempts to reach the Orient by way of an Arctic route, he decided to abandon his instructions and try to find a northwest seaway to the East. Equipped with information about the Atlantic coast of America, which Captain John Smith had sent him from Virginia, Hudson reversed his course and sailed for the New World.

The *Half Moon* arrived on the coast of Maine in July 1609. The crew stopped to repair the vessel's torn sails and to cut a new foremast from the abundant timber in the area. For two more weeks the adventurers sailed south, finally reaching a point south of Chesapeake Bay. Then Hudson moved north again and examined Delaware Bay. Still in search of the northwest passage, the captain continued farther north and on September 2 approached New York's lower bay. On September 3 and the following nine days he explored and took soundings in the waters at the mouth of what would be known as the Hudson River. On the 12th, the vessel passed through the narrows, and the mariners dropped anchor at the southern tip of Manhattan Island.

On September 13 the *Half Moon* began its voyage up the Hudson. By the next day the vessel was as far north as Stony Point and on the 15th it sailed past the Catskill Mountains. On September 19 Hudson reached a latitude of 42°20′, or the approximate location of Albany. From there he proceeded north in a small boat to continue his search, in vain, for a northwest passage. The *Half Moon* weighed anchor and began the journey back down the river on September 23. Rain slowed the descent, and the vessel finally reached the site of Hoboken, New Jersey, on October 2.

Hudson recognized the beauty of the river that future generations would call by his name, and Robert Juet, one of the *Half Moon*'s officers, described the valley as "a pleasant land to see." The explorers saw many trees, especially oaks, suitable for shipbuilding, and even found plum trees. The water itself was full of fish, including salmon, mullet, and sturgeon.

Indians frequently paddled out in their long canoes to meet the *Half Moon*. They brought tobacco, grapes, currants, corn, pumpkins, oysters, and the skins of beavers and otters to present to the strangers as gifts or to trade with them for knives, hatchets, and ornaments. Unfortunately, however, not all the encounters with the natives were friendly. On September 6 a band of Indians had attacked four of Hudson's sailors who were investigating Lower New York Harbor in a small boat and killed the Englishman John Colman in the engagement. On October 1, while the *Half Moon* was in the vicinity of the Hudson Highlands, Robert Juet had killed two Indians who had stolen some items from the vessel. The following day, in the area near the Spuyten Duyvil Creek, Indians attacked the ship, but their bows and arrows could not match the crew's guns. About 10 were killed, but none of Hudson's men suffered injury.

On October 4, 1609, the *Half Moon* sailed out of New York Harbor into the Atlantic Ocean for its homeward voyage, arriving at Dartmouth, England, a month later.

In 1610 Hudson set out on his fourth voyage. Sailing this time on behalf of a group of English merchant-adventurers, he again went in search of a northwest passage to the Orient. On April 27, with a crew of 23 men on the bark *Discovery*, he set sail from London, never to return.

Sighting the coast of Greenland on June 4, Hudson continued west and by August 2 passed through the Canadian strait later named for him. On August 3 the *Discovery* entered what would be known as Hudson Bay, which the crew explored for many weeks. Winter soon set in, and in early November Hudson hauled his vessel onto the shore of Rupert's Bay, which soon became frozen. Scurvy and starvation threatened the crew, who sustained themselves by eating frogs and moss until the weather warmed sufficiently to permit hunting parties to search for food.

In the spring of 1611 Hudson explored to the southwest with a few members of his crew. In his absence Robert Juet, who had had a falling-out with the captain, plotted a mutiny. Upon his return to base, Hudson disregarded the hostility of the men and on June 12, 1611, set sail again in search of the elusive northwest passage. On June 23, Juet and others seized Henry and John Hudson and set them, with seven of their supporters, adrift in a small shallop. The mutineers then sailed away. Nothing further was heard of Hudson and his companions; they undoubtedly perished shortly thereafter.

Misfortune followed the *Discovery* on its homeward journey. Eskimos killed several of the mariners. Sickness and starvation took a number of the others, including Robert Juet. Only seven men and a boy were alive when the *Discovery* reached Ireland on September 6, 1611. The survivors of the *Discovery* were never punished for their roles in the insurrection. On July 24, 1618, four of the men were arraigned at Southwark in London, but they pleaded not guilty and won acquittal from a jury.

The most fitting monuments to Hudson are the river in New York State and the bay in Canada that bear his name. In addition a small park at Independence Avenue and West 227th Street in New York City also honors the explorer. Appropriately, the focal point of the park is a statue of Hudson, two times life size, mounted on a tall column and overlooking the river he discovered.

The tercentenary of the exploration of the Hudson River was commemorated — together with the anniversary of the inauguration of steam navigation by Robert Fulton in 1807 — in the Hudson-Fulton celebration of September 25—October 9, 1909. Observances, which took place chiefly in New York City, included voyages up the river by replicas of Hudson's *Half Moon* and Fulton's *Clermont*.

In early July 1976 a flotilla of nine antique vessels from the Netherlands that had participated on July 4 in Operation Sail in the harbor and rivers of New York City began a seven-day journey up the Hudson River to Albany, reenacting Hudson's historic voyage as part of the US Bicentennial celebration.

Treaty of Paris Signed

On this day in 1783 the Treaty of Paris, ending the American Revolution and setting forth terms for the independence of the United States, was signed in Paris by representatives of Great Britain and the United States. The treaty became official when it was ratified by the Continental Congress (see January 14, Ratification Day).

SEPTEMBER 4

Los Angeles Birthday Celebration

The city of Los Angeles traditionally holds an annual birthday celebration on September 4 — with few exceptions — to commemorate its founding on that date in 1781. The moving spirit behind the foundation was Don Felipe de Neve, the Spanish governor of California, who acted in conformity with the Spanish colonial policy that active colonization should start once the mission center and military presidios were established. He recommended to the viceroy of Mexico that a pueblo be built on the spot where, in 1769, a group of explorers and missionaries under Captain Gaspar de Portolá had discovered an Indian village, Yang-na; they had renamed the fertile valley Portiuncula after a chapel in Italy beloved by Francis of Assisi. The establishment of the future city was subsequently ordered by royal prerogative and decree of King Charles III of Spain.

Every detail was worked out well in advance of settlement. An area of four square leagues out of the 17,500-acre tract was set aside and divided into a small plaza surrounded by 7-acre fields for agriculture, pastures, and royal lands to be leased to citizens. On August 18, 1781, the settlers, recruits from Mexico, chiefly the state of Sonora, reached the San Gabriel Mission, the fourth of 21 missions established by Father Junípero Serra, the famous Franciscan missionary. Lying nine miles to the northeast of the planned site, the mission served as a base where the settlers rested and received instruction about where to live, what to build, what crops to grow, and how much time to give to community undertakings. On September 4 the expedition set out for the newly designated pueblo. It included the

44 settlers (11 men, 11 women, and 22 children), Don Felipe de Neve, a detachment of soldiers, and priests and Indian acolytes from the San Gabriel Mission. At the site, the Yang-na Indians gathered to look on as a procession formed and the marchers slowly circled the plaza, invoking God's blessing; the governor gave a formal address, followed by prayers and benediction. Thus the new settlement, named El Pueblo de Nuestra Señora La Reina de Los Angeles de Portiuncula, was one of the few cities planned in advance and ceremoniously inaugurated.

The little pueblo consisted first of dwellings with rawhide doors and paneless windows. It took the settlers three years to erect a simple adobe church on the plaza. The narrow streets became pools of mud in winter and clouds of dust in summer. By 1800 the population of Los Angeles numbered only 315, living in 30 adobe dwellings, with a town hall, guardhouse, army barracks, and grain storehouses.

After Mexico gained independence from Spain in 1821, the settlement experienced frequent political disturbances. In 1835 it was made a city by the Mexican congress, and from 1845 to 1847 it was the capital of California. Once the Mexican War had broken out between the United States and Mexico, the defenders of Los Angeles fled before advancing US troops under Commodore Robert F. Stockton and Captain John C. Frémont. The American flag was unfurled over Los Angeles on August 13, 1846.

After California was granted admission to the Union as a state in 1850, the population of Los Angeles increased with great rapidity, augmented by the California gold rush and later by the completion of the transcontinental railroad, the discovery of oil, and the development of the aircraft and motion picture industries. Between 1890 and 1940, the population grew from 50,395 to 1,504,277, a gain of almost 3,000 percent. Los Angeles eventually became the third largest city in the United States.

The birthday celebration on September 4 originated in 1894. The program varies from year to year, but it is always picturesque. Often the first expedition from the San Gabriel Mission is reenacted in costume, with the governor leading on horseback. Special exercises are usually held at the Pueblo de Los Angeles State Historical Park, which was laid out in the early 19th century after floods had forced the abandonment of the original adobe houses.

Occasionally the birthday celebration is held just north of the Plaza on Olvera Street, where a hand-carved wooden cross commemorates the 1781 founding site. A brick-paved, arcaded lane named for Don Augustín Olvera, who fought against Frémont, Olvera Street was restored in the early 1930s in the manner of a Mexican street, with market stalls, native craft shops, cafes, and restaurants featuring Mexican dishes. Music and street dancing keynote the festivities here, and speakers address the celebrators from the steps of the Avila Adobe, which served as the headquarters of the American army under John C. Frémont.

One of the most elaborate birthday celebrations in Los Angeles history took place from September 4 through 13, 1931, in commemoration of the 150th anniversary of the city's founding. The 10-day affair, heralded by a dance contest in front of Avila Adobe, began with an official opening at City Hall and the placing of a gigantic birthday cake over the fountain at Pershing Square. The title of the grand historical parade, Under Four Flags, referred to the four governments under which Los Angeles has prospered since its official founding in 1781: Spain, Mexico, California, and the United States. The parade featured 18th century Spanish soldiers in velvet suits, silken sashes, and jingling gold and silver spurs; hundreds of horses; covered wagons; stagecoaches; plainsmen; Franciscans; and a 10-year-old girl chosen from one of the city's orphanages to be La Princesita. Paraders marched to the Olympic Stadium, which was decorated with fiesta banners and the four flags of the city's history and transformed into a colossal outdoor throne room where the queen of the fiesta, flanked by 30 ladies-in-waiting, was crowned. The first day's festivities ended with a formal coronation ball and informal street dancing to the music of Mexican troubadours.

The remainder of the festival period celebrated other important anniversaries in Los Angeles history. September 5, Transportation Day, commemorated the 55th anniversary of the city's connection with the East by rail and featured a transportation parade of diverse vehicles ranging from dogsleds to Mexican *carretas*. September 6, the 100th anniversary of the opening of the Santa Fe Trail for trade between Los Angeles and the trading post at Santa Fe, opened with a solemn pontifical mass for 105,000 persons in the Olympic Stadium and closed with evening interdenominational vesper services for 35,000 in the Hollywood Bowl. The highlight of September 7, Labor Day, was a rodeo in the stadium, which evoked old California with its brilliant assemblage of spirited horses and superb equestrians. September 8 was the 160th anniversary of the founding of San Gabriel Mission and the 134th of San Fernando Mission, both of which, conveniently close to Los Angeles, extended hospitality to fiesta visitors. On September 9 the California the Golden parade was staged to mark the 81st anniversary of Cali-

fornia's admission to statehood. The remaining festival days featured a Spanish wedding in the Adobe Plaza Church, erected between 1818 and 1822; an illuminated night parade, Pageant of Jewels; and an air show of army, navy, and commercial planes.

Recent observances of the birthday have included evening programs at Olvera Street featuring music performed in the Kiosko in Plaza Park by a Mexican orchestra; Mexican and Spanish dances; and a fireworks display in front of the Plaza. On the Sunday preceding each anniversary there is a Te Deum mass at the Plaza church.

The Santa Fe Fiesta

This is a movable event. See note on page xxvi.

The anniversary of the reconquest of New Mexico from the Pueblo Indians in 1692, which was first formally celebrated in September 1712, was renewed by the city of Santa Fe in 1919, and is known as the Santa Fe Fiesta. Now generally scheduled for four days, including Labor Day, the fiesta combines both a religious observance and a gala extravaganza.

The historical background of the celebration dates from 1528, when the battered and hungry survivors of Pánfilo de Narváez's expedition to Florida, fleeing across the Gulf of Mexico from hostile Indians, were shipwrecked off the Texas coast. Only four men escaped from the ordeal and managed to reach land, probably Galveston Island. They included Álvar Núñez Cabeza de Vaca, who had served as Narváez's treasurer; and a black Moor known as Esteban, or Estevanico, who had served as guide.

In the nearly eight years that followed, the quartet labored for Indian captors, escaped, and wandered thousands of miles through the rugged terrain of the American Southwest, probably crossing through the areas of New Mexico and Arizona and possibly reaching the Gulf of California. Far south of the Rio Grande, they finally encountered Spaniards near Culiacán. In Mexico, they spread tales they had heard about the Pueblo Indians and the rich northern cities to be conquered, thus giving rise to the myth about the fabled Seven Cities of Cíbola.

Spurred by these accounts, Antonio de Mendoza, the viceroy of New Spain, dispatched an exploring party under the leadership of the Franciscan missionary Fray Marcos de Niza, in 1539. Estevanico, who had become an experienced ambassador to the Indians in the previous years of wandering, went with him as guide and scout. The party, accompanied also by Indian guides, explored southeastern Arizona. Sent ahead as leader of an advance expedition, Estevanico was the first non-Indian to see the region of northwestern New Mexico. He discovered the Zuñi Indians, but the discovery was to cost him his life. At Hawikuh, their westernmost pueblo, the Zuñis, for reasons unknown, killed him. Also killed were some of the Indian guides who had accompanied him.

Three who escaped hastened back to Fray Marcos, some days away, with news of the tragedy. Though he promptly turned back for Mexico, the friar's imagination and credulity were undiminished by the disaster. His unsubstantiated report about a land "rich in gold, silver and other wealth," where people were "very rich, the women even wearing belts of gold," aroused such enthusiasm that a year later, Captain-General Francisco Vásquez de Coronado, with Fray Marcos as guide, set out at the head of a military expedition of 1,500 men. After crossing the deserts, mountains, and forests of southeastern Arizona, they arrived five months later at Hawikuh. When the Zuñis refused to submit to Coronado, he subdued them by force. As it turned out, however, Hawikuh was not one of the golden cities of Cíbola, but a "few hovels of clay and stone built upon a high rock," surrounded by barren land. Coronado, spurred on by yet another fabulous tale — of the wealthy kingdom of Quivira — continued his explorations, probably as far east as the southern part of what is now Kansas. Bitter and disappointed, he returned to Mexico City in 1542, having found no gold in his 3,000-mile march, but having claimed extensive lands for Spain.

Although the legends of riches and glory lingered, a royal ordinance suspended further Spanish exploration — at least as far as government-sponsored expeditions were concerned — of the recently discovered New Mexican area. Five decades were to pass before serious colonization of New Mexico would be attempted. Then, in 1598, Don Juan de Oñate, acting on reports about profitable grazing and mining opportunities there, offered to finance a private expedition. Born into a well-to-do mining family, he could well afford to equip the company of colonists — 130 families and 270 single men — and supply 7,000 cattle.

He established the first permanent European settlement in New Mexico in 1598, at an Indian pueblo that he renamed San Juan de los Caballeros. It was situated at the confluence of the Chama River and Rio Grande, 30 miles north of what is now Sante Fe.

This provisional Spanish capital of New Mexico was later transferred to the west bank of the Rio Grande and named San Gabriel del Yunque. The colony remained there for several years until the viceroy of New Spain ordered Don Pedro de Peralta, the third governor of "the Kingdom and Provinces of New Mexico," to move it farther south. In the winter of 1609–1610, therefore, he built a new capital at a spot known to the Indians as Kuapoga, the "place of the shell beads near the water." This modest mud and stone settlement, located at the base of the Sangre de Cristo Mountains, was proclaimed La Villa Real de la Santa Fe de San Francisco de Assisi — the Royal City of the Holy Faith of St. Francis of Assisi, or Santa Fe, as the name was abbreviated. Work immediately began on construction of a colonial headquarters at Santa Fe. The result, called the Royal Palace, was a long, adobe structure with walls several feet thick, which still dominates Santa Fe's town plaza today. Now known as the Palace of the Governors, it was successively occupied by Spanish captains-general (until 1821, when Mexico won independence from Spain), by Mexican governors (until 1846), and by American territorial governors (until 1907). A carefully restored example of Spanish-Indian architecture, it presently houses the Museum of New Mexico.

By 1617 Spanish villages had spread all along the Rio Grande, and the Franciscan friars who accompanied the Spanish soldier-settlers had erected 11 churches and reputedly had converted 14,000 Indians.

The Spaniards and Indians lived in comparative harmony for 70 years, but dissatisfaction and resentment mounted as some of the Indians were enslaved and compelled to work in the mines and others were slain by zealots because they rejected conversion. In August 1680 the Pueblo Indians, under the leadership of Popé of Taos and with Apache help, rose in revolt. They killed 21 Franciscans and all the other Spaniards they could find. Governor Antonio Otermín, at the head of a small military force, led the remaining colonists in a hasty retreat from the city. The nearly 1,000 survivors crossed southern New Mexico and reached the safety of El Paso del Norte, where the cities of El Paso, Texas, and Juárez, Mexico, now face each other across the Rio Grande. In the meantime, the Indians at Santa Fe "washed away" their baptisms with mud; they sacked and burned the churches and the Royal Palace; and their leader donned a mother-of-pearl crown and drank from an ecclesiastical gold chalice.

After 12 years in humiliating exile, awaiting the appearance of a bold conquistador to win back Santa Fe, the Spanish settlers finally found their man in Captain-General Don Diego de Vargas Zapata y Luján Ponce de León, who had been appointed governor of New Mexico in 1691. Before marching to regain New Mexico for Spain in 1692, de Vargas solemnly vowed that, in return for a bloodless victory, he would have an annual novena to Our Lady offered in thanksgiving. He successfully negotiated a peace agreement with the Indians, and under the royal banner of New Mexico, his troops triumphantly entered Santa Fe on September 14, 1692. With elaborate fanfare, de Vargas took over the Royal Palace.

Soon afterwards he and his men marched south and rounded up the settlers to escort them back to Santa Fe. They also carried back the statue of Our Lady as patroness and queen of New Mexico and Santa Fe, known as *La Conquistadora*, which had been saved from damage in the 1680 uprising. Renewed Indian opposition in 1693, however, soon forced the Spaniards to fight to keep control of the city.

In the years immediately following the reconquest, the inhabitants of Santa Fe continued to hold their traditional fiesta of La Conquistadora on the first Sunday in October, as had been customary before the revolt. At the same time, they commemorated the 1693 battle for the city, when they had prayed before the statue for victory. In 1712 the city council agreed to inaugurate a special fiesta in memory of the 1692 reconquest as well. The lieutenant governor of New Mexico, Juan Paéz Hurtado (acting in place of the governor, the Marqués de la Peñuela), with the governing body of the city, issued a proclamation on September 16. It required "that in the future the said 14th day [of September] be celebrated with Vespers, Mass, Sermon and Public Procession through the Main Plaza. . . . It is our will that it be [henceforth] celebrated for all time to come . . . and . . . we swear [this] in due form of law."

It is not known how long this order was obeyed, since documentary evidence is lacking. It may have been only in 1712 or may have continued for many years afterwards; but in the course of time the fiesta was abandoned.

In the 20th century there was renewed interest in having a fiesta. For several years prior to 1911, the Women's Board of Trade of Santa Fe had been holding an annual festival on the town plaza to raise money for the library. Early in that year, the Reverend James Mythen suggested a commemoration of the important events in the history of the city, and, on July 4, 1911, the women arranged a pageant representing the entry of de Vargas into the city, with more than 100 Indians taking part. It was repeated two or three times in succeeding years, but abandoned because of World War I. It was not until 1919, therefore, that public-minded citizens, aware of the 1712 decree and appreciative of Santa Fe's culturally diverse heritage, began seriously to arrange for an annual celebration. The original

date of the fiesta, set in 1712 for September 14, was changed to the Labor Day weekend when the festivities attracted larger numbers of people and spread over a number of days.

Typical of the fiesta, which has remained basically the same over the past decades, was the 258th anniversary, in 1970. A number of events during late spring and summer led up to the major celebration, which attracted an estimated 70,000 visitors. A fiesta queen was chosen and attended by a royal court. In June, de Vargas's vow of an annual novena to Our Lady was fulfilled. This provided a fitting prelude to the historical part of the Santa Fe Fiesta. The wooden statue of La Conquistadora was carried in a solemn, mile-long procession from its chapel in St. Francis Cathedral to the Rosario Chapel and was returned in another procession after the novena.

The summer horse show, art exhibit, and rodeo contributed to the rising festive spirit. In late August and early September, variety shows and mariachi serenades were nightly features. The Santa Fe Community Theater presented the first performances of the Fiesta Melodrama on September 2 and 3. On Fiesta Eve, a chuckwagon supper was served.

The fiesta itself got off to an early start on Friday, September 4, with the annual 6:30 A.M. de Vargas mass at Rosario Chapel. Among others, the fiesta queen and her court, authentically costumed impersonators of de Vargas and his military staff, and members of the Fiesta Council attended. From 10:00 A.M. to 9:00 P.M., the arts and crafts market near the town plaza featured sidewalk booths exhibiting the work of about 85 local artists. At noon, banners, balloons, carnival rides, and street kitchens offering an endless variety of enchiladas, tamales, and tacos, filled the historic plaza, which is still the social center of the city. From 6:00 P.M. a dance for teenagers, a band concert, and Spanish folk dancing provided entertainment.

The greatest attraction of the day, drawing some 20,000 spectators, was the dramatic "performance" of Zozobra on a hillside overlooking Fort Marcy Park at 8:30 P.M. The burning of this 40-foot effigy of Old Man Gloom symbolizes the banishment of cares and the ushering in of merriment. Two residents of Santa Fe, the dancer Jacques Cartier and the artist Will Shuster — convinced that the fiesta needed an eye-opening start — created the first Zozobra in 1927. Traditionally shaped from paper, chicken wire, and billowing muslin, with a 9-foot head and telephone-pole backbone, the monster flailed his arms, rolled his eyes, and growled at the crowds. As rockets and flares were fired and dry tumbleweed on the hillside was set aflame, the lithe, red-clad Spirit of Fire hurled firebrands at Old

Man Gloom, thus touching off the grand conflagration.

In the center of town, following Zozobra's fiery expiration, the 1970 fiesta queen received her red velvet robe and silver and turquoise crown on the Plaza platform. Fiesta-goers who did not wish to attend the coronation and subsequent Queen's Show (variety entertainment) had their choice of going to either the Fiesta Melodrama at 9:30 P.M. or the Spanish colonial costume ball, El Baile Antiguo.

The festivities on Saturday started with the Desfile de los Niños, commonly termed the Children's Pet Parade, in which youngsters and their animal friends — both in costume — provided a vivid and sometimes hilarious spectacle. Entertainment, rides, teenage and Indian dances, and the arts and crafts market continued throughout the day. At 4:00 P.M. the queen, with her court, presided over the Audiencia con la Reina, a reception for the general public in the plaza. In addition to two performances of the Fiesta Melodrama, the evening program offered dances of all types, from street- and folk-dancing to the traditional Gran Baile de los Conquistadores, at which de Vargas and his staff and the queen and her court mingled with the costumed merrymakers.

To fulfill the religious stipulations of the 1712 decree, a procession and solemn mass and sermon in the Cathedral of St. Francis took place on Sunday morning. In the afternoon, visitors flocked to Fort Marcy Park to enjoy the pageantry of the historic Entrada of 1692, as the 1680 Pueblo Indian revolt and the subsequent bloodless reconquest were reenacted in music and drama. The pageant has been annually sponsored since 1957 by the Caballeros de Vargas, a civic-religious group organized by past portrayers of de Vargas and his men, descendants of the conquistadors, who wished to recall the traditions and history of the Spanish New World. The role of de Vargas — an honor given only to an outstanding young Spanish-speaking man in Santa Fe County — is open to competition, but the final selection is made by secret ballot by the Fiesta Council. The Caballeros de Vargas reenacted the *entrada* as authentically as possible in scenes showing the historical personages, from foot soldiers to de Vargas. They led livestock and baggage trains, dragged cannons, and finally planted the royal banner and cross in the plaza, while the 1712 decree was intoned.

After the pageant, the Sociedad Folklórica presented its customary Merienda, a "fashion show" with heirloom costumes. At 7:00 P.M., following vespers and mass in the cathedral, the impressive candlelight procession wound its way to the Cross of the Martyrs on Fort Marcy Hill,

where a solemn service in memory of the 21 Franciscan friars killed in the 1680 uprising took place.

Following this serious commemoration, it was time for a return to gaiety. Late evening activities included continuous plaza entertainment and the de Vargas ball.

The highlight of the fourth and final day of the fiesta, Labor Day, September 7, was the Desfile de las Fiestas, the general fiesta parade. Staged for more than 50 years, and dubbed the "historical and hysterical" parade, this procession reflects both the glamorous and the humorous in its attractive floats, lively bands and marching units, and caricatures of well-known personages and events. The last official event of the Santa Fe Fiesta was the queen's review of the 1970 celebration, which was held at 8:00 P.M. in the plaza. Then while the mariachis played, the plaza decorations were carefully packed away until the next year's fiesta.

SEPTEMBER 5

The First Continental Congress Convenes

To Britons, the Boston Tea Party, in 1773 (see December 16), was a severe breach of Empire etiquette. The English saw it as a malicious destruction of property and an affront to the British nation rather than as a justified protest against undue taxation and the threat of monopoly. Despite some opposition, most Britons — both politicians and ordinary citizens — thought it necessary to chastise the upstart colonials.

England's response to Massachusetts was the Coercive or Intolerable Acts, a collection of measures designed both as a punishment and as a preventative. The Boston Port Bill of March 31, 1774, closed Boston Harbor until Massachusetts made reparations to the East India Company for the lost tea. The Administration of Justice Act of May 20, which authorized the governor and council of Massachusetts to transfer to England certain trials for capital offenses involving British officials, protected government functionaries from harassment by the colonial patriots. The Massachusetts Government Act, also of May 20, abolished a number of charter rights and severely limited the holding of town meetings. The Quartering Act of June 2 legalized the forced housing of troops in occupied private dwellings in all the colonies. And although Britain did not intend the Quebec Act of May 20 as a punitive measure, the Americans regarded it as one of the Coercive Acts. They resented the legislation — which granted civil and religious liberties to Canada's predominantly Roman Catholic population and extended Canada's borders far to the south — as a threat not only to Protestantism but also to American colonial hopes for westward expansion.

Ships from England brought news of the passage of the Port Act to Boston on May 10; to New York on May 12; and to Philadelphia on May 14. Boston town meetings on May 13 called for all American provinces to suspend trade with England and the West Indies and on June 17 refused to pay the demanded reparation to the East India Company. Dr. Joseph Warren of the Massachusetts Committee of Correspondence gathered signatures for a Solemn League and Covenant, which pledged subscribers to boycott anyone who continued commerce with Great Britain. Royal Governor Thomas Gage's denunciation of the document as a "traitorous combination" only encouraged more people to sign it.

Colonists elsewhere, uninvolved in the Boston Tea Party issue and exempt from the provisions of most of the Intolerable Acts, were not so anxious to resort to extreme measures. Philadelphians met publicly on May 20 and rejected Massachusett's request for suspension of commerce with England. Instead, they suggested that every colony send delegates to a congress specially established to respond to this latest crisis. In New York City on May 23, the patriot committee of 51, under the leadership of Isaac Low, also declined to terminate trade immediately and echoed the call for a Continental Congress. Eighty-nine members of the Virginia House of Burgesses, meeting informally on May 27 in the Long Room of the Raleigh Tavern, reached the same decision as their northern counterparts.

Massachusetts accepted the more moderate position of the other colonies. Its General Court on June 17 appointed five delegates to the congress meeting in Philadelphia in September. Connecticut and Rhode Island also selected representatives during June, and nine more colonies followed suit during July and August; only in Georgia was the royalist government able to prevent the naming of a contingent.

Fifty-six men from 12 colonies convened in what history would recall as the First Continental Congress, which opened in Philadelphia on September 5, 1774. Joseph Galloway, the Speaker of the Pennsylvania assembly, suggested the colony's State House as a meeting place, but the delegates accepted instead the offer by the city carpenters of their own building. The provincial leaders believed that the choice of Carpenters' Hall would be "highly agreeable to the mechanics and citizens in general." The representatives elected Peyton Randolph of Virginia to be the president of the Congress and selected a non-

delegate, the radical Charles Thomson of Pennsylvania, as secretary. They also decided that each colony would have one vote in determining questions and pledged to keep the proceedings secret.

The British Parliament's authority to enact legislation affecting the Americas was the center of debate, until Samuel Adams of Massachusetts introduced a set of resolutions that had been drawn up by Joseph Warren and adopted on September 9 by Suffolk, the county in which Boston is located. On September 17 the First Continental Congress also endorsed these declarations, in a clear victory for its more radical members. The Suffolk Resolves, as they were called, stated that the Coercive Acts were null and void and thus not to be obeyed, and they advised Massachusetts residents to form an extralegal government that would collect taxes but withhold them from the British until Parliament repealed the Intolerable Acts. Even more foreboding were provisions urging the people to arm themselves and organize militia and calling for stringent economic sanctions against England.

Conservative delegates to the Continental Congress tried to recoup their losses by advocating Joseph Galloway's Plan of a Proposed Union Between Great Britain and the Colonies. The Pennsylvanian called for a grand council composed of delegates selected for three-year terms by each of the colonial assemblies. Together with a president-general appointed by the king and equipped with veto power, the provincial congress would form a separate and subordinate branch of the British legislature. Parliament and the council would each enjoy the right to originate legislation concerning America, but both would have to approve each proposal before it could become law. Radical patriots found this measure insufficient to solve their problems, and on September 28 the Continental Congress rejected Galloway's plan by a six-to-five vote and on October 22 expunged all reference to it from the minutes.

On October 14, 1774, the Continental Congress issued its Declaration and Resolves, which made the radical claim that, subject only to the king's veto, the provincial legislatures had the sole right to levy taxes on the colonies and to enact measures affecting their internal polity; Parliament's sphere of action was to be restricted to England and to imperial affairs. The Congress denounced 13 acts of Parliament passed since 1763 as violations of American rights and promised to invoke economic sanctions until their repeal.

The Continental Association, a series of agreements adopted by the delegates to the Congress on October 18, pledged that their colonies would cease all importations from England by December 1, 1774, and also terminate the lucrative West Indian slave trade by the same date. In addition the Association called for the nonconsumption of British goods and certain foreign luxury items, beginning on March 1, 1775, and set September 1, 1775, as the date for ending American exportation to England, Ireland, and the West Indies. Adding teeth to its resolutions, the Continental Congress provided for the establishment of extralegal machinery to force compliance on local citizens through threats of unfavorable publicity and boycotts.

The First Continental Congress adjourned on October 26, 1774, but made plans to reconvene on May 10, 1775, if Great Britain did not act to resolve the crisis. In less than two months the patriot leaders had taken a giant step toward intercolonial unity. Perhaps more important, the Congress's demand that Parliament surrender its voice in American affairs marked an even greater development in the growing movement for independence.

The historic Carpenters' Hall in which the First Continental Congress held its meetings had been erected in 1770 by the Carpenters' Company of Philadelphia, the city's organization of master builders, as the home for their guild. The Carpenters' Company is active today and still uses the building, which is located off Chestnut Street between Fourth and Orianna streets, in Philadelphia's 22-acre Independence National Historical Park. Under an agreement between the company and the US Department of the Interior which administers the park, Carpenters' Hall is open to the public. The City Tavern, where the delegates first assembled when they arrived in Philadelphia, has been restored and functions as a commercial establishment.

Two hundred years after the opening of the First Continental Congress, the historic gathering was reenacted in Carpenters' Hall as political leaders of the 13 original states, including all but two, met in Philadelphia on September 5 and 6, 1974. The gathering, with oratory and preceding and concluding ceremonies, issued resolutions on a number of important current national questions and was climaxed by a banquet at which President Gerald R. Ford was the principal speaker.

Nauvoo, Illinois, Grape Festival

This is a movable event. See note on page xxvi.

The Wedding of the Wine and Cheese, an unusual ceremony borrowed from the south of France, is the climax of the Grape Festival held annually in Nauvoo, Illinois, on Saturday and Sunday of Labor Day weekend. The Wedding is preceded by a pageant depicting the colorful, and sometimes violent, history of Nauvoo, which was once the largest city of Illinois and played an important role in the history of the Mormons. Although the official opening of Nauvoo's Grape Festival takes place on Saturday afternoon, prefestival attractions, especially carnival rides and concessions, are already in full swing on Friday evening.

The Wedding of the Wine and Cheese ceremony is presented on both Saturday and Sunday evening. Other attractions of the festival include a festival queen, who is crowned before the pageant Saturday evening; visiting dignitaries, sometimes including the governor of Illinois; band concerts; a talent show; variety acts; and two parades. The pet (and children's) parade, presided over by a youthful king and queen, takes place on Saturday afternoon. The grand parade, which winds its way through Nauvoo's business district to Nauvoo State Park on the south edge of town, is on Sunday afternoon. Additional festival features have, from time to time, included such events as horse shows, antique car parades, and powered Soap Box derbies. Guided tours introduce visitors to Nauvoo's numerous historic buildings and sites. Especially noteworthy is the Nauvoo Restoration, Inc., sponsored by the Church of Jesus Christ of Latter-Day Saints, which has restored about 10 buildings, including a blacksmith shop and a house once occupied by church leader Brigham Young, and hopes to create "the Williamsburg of the West."

The festival, which is timed to coincide with the local grape harvest, began in 1938 and has attracted as many as 100,000 visitors to Nauvoo, which has a year-round population of slightly over 1,000.

The historical pageant is presented in a natural amphitheater in the state park. It takes place on a sod stage, with a cast of about 200.

Nauvoo's known history begins with the Indian settlement called Quashquema, which a trader found on the spot in 1803. Later it was known as Venus and then as Commerce — the name it had when the prophet Joseph Smith and his band of Latter-Day Saints, or Mormons, arrived in 1839, after being driven out of Missouri.

The Mormons changed the town's name to Nauvoo, built permanent homes (including those of Joseph Smith and Brigham Young) and a temple, and set out to make the community the capital of their faith. As Mormons from the East and converts from Europe (especially England) arrived, the population swelled to a total of about 20,000.

The Mormons' stay was a short one, however, because of the "Mormon war," which began with the excommunication of several prominent members of the church. The suppression and destruction of a newspaper run by two of the excommunicated and controversy over the resulting trial were particular sources of friction. The conflict also involved the antagonism of neighboring non-Mormons, who feared the Mormons' political power and envied their apparent prosperity. By the early summer of 1844, tension was high, with the Mormons' 5,000-man militia under arms in Nauvoo and some 1,500 armed men bent on the Mormons' expulsion gathered in the county.

So emotionally charged was the climate that Governor Thomas Ford took charge of the situation himself. As leader of the sect, mayor of Nauvoo, and commanding officer of the Mormon militia, Joseph Smith offered to surrender on a charge of riot. Having received the promise of protection by the state, he was taken to Carthage, Illinois, to answer the charge, and imprisoned. On June 27, 1844, he was murdered by a mob that attacked the jail.

Although state forces kept peace for a time afterwards, there was further violence in the fall of 1845. On October 1 the Mormons promised to leave Nauvoo the next spring. Their departure, which began in February, was virtually completed by the end of 1846. The best-known of their odysseys in several directions was the one led by Brigham Young, which resulted in the founding of Salt Lake City. Some remained in the Midwest, however, and reconstituted themselves in 1860 as the Reorganized Church of Jesus Christ of Latter-Day Saints, with Joseph Smith III, a son of the founder, as their leader and prophet. The group, which today has headquarters in Independence, Missouri, and numbers more than 150,000 members, remains active in Nauvoo.

After the exodus, Nauvoo had a strangely deserted look until 1849, when the town's empty buildings were occupied by a French communist group, the Icarians. Although their experiment in Nauvoo lasted only seven years, they and the German settlers who succeeded them (along with Swiss, English, and Irish) instituted the grape and wine industry, which, along with the cheese industry introduced later, is a mainstay of Nauvoo today.

The Grape Festival's historical pageant concludes with a picture of modern Nauvoo and with the Wedding of the Wine and Cheese ceremony, which Nauvoo's French settlers originally brought with them from Roquefort, France. Based on a legend describing the discovery of Roquefort cheese, the "wedding" pageant is the story of a French shepherd who left some bread and cheese in a limestone cave and, returning the next year, found that the cheese had acquired a strange blue mold that enhanced its flavor. The result, deliberately produced ever since, was the famous Roquefort cheese.

In the ceremony, the shepherd boy is seen, with milkmaids, cheesemakers, grape cutters, and wine makers. The bride, who represents the wine, comes forward to place the wine on a barrel intended to symbolize the altar. The groom carries the cheese to the same altar. After the chief magistrate has read the marriage contract, he places the scroll on the altar between the wine and cheese. The minister completes the ceremony by placing around all three articles a wooden hoop representing the wedding ring.

Wilhelm Tell Festival

This is a movable event. See note on page xxvi.

Each Labor Day weekend, the townspeople of New Glarus, Wisconsin, a tiny, predominantly Swiss community, cooperate to present Friedrich von Schiller's drama *Wilhelm Tell* and provide an Alpine festival of Swiss entertainment for thousands of visitors. A cast of more than 200 unpaid local residents, in authentic, homemade costumes copied from old Swiss books, performs Schiller's verse classic in both English and German. The play is a retelling of the familiar legend of William Tell, whose defiance of Gessler, an Austrian bailiff, in 1291 is said to have contributed to Swiss independence from Austrian tyranny, even though it cost Tell the harrowing punishment of having to shoot an apple off the head of his own son.

In 1938, when Europe was threatened by Nazi tyranny, the people of New Glarus first determined to set before the world their reminder of Switzerland's successful struggle against oppression. The drama is presented in a natural amphitheater a mile east of town, an outdoor setting that accommodates not only the enormous cast but also the horses, cows, goats, and sheep that add pageantry to some scenes. Costumed folk dancers (who also serve as ushers) perform during intermission, as do Swiss bell-ringers.

The drama is presented three times each Labor Day weekend — in German on Sunday afternoon and in English on Saturday and Labor Day. Starting times have customarily been 1:00 P.M. for the opening entertainment and 1:30 P.M. for the three-hour production itself.

Other weekend events are in a decidedly festive vein. An increasingly popular outdoor art show, at which some 200 professional and amateur artists display their works, takes place in

the village all day Sunday. The traditional Alpine festival is held Saturday and Sunday evenings, usually at 8:00 P.M. in the high school
gymnasium. It offers New Glarus's best talent in
Swiss singing and yodeling. The program in one
typical year included performances by the New
Glarus Yodelers, the Edelweiss Stars, a Swiss
flag-thrower, a trio of Alpine horn-blowers, the
New Glarus Maennerchor (Swiss men's chorus),
and the Alpine Troubadours. To top the evening
off, a free street dance, sponsored by the New
Glarus Business Association, is held at 10:00
P.M. Saturday in the downtown area.

New Glarus has been able to retain its predominantly Swiss characteristics over the years
for several reasons: the town was virtually isolated during its first 42 years of existence — until
a railroad was put through in 1887; many of its
residents are descended from the original Swiss
settlers; and other immigrants have come from
Switzerland more recently.

Newer arrivals, however, have had much more
choice in the matter than the community's 108
original settlers in 1845, who were driven by
famine to leave their home canton of Glarus. Experts, sent on ahead to choose a fertile site for
the new settlement, selected the spot that later
became New Glarus. Those who were to emigrate were given money, raised by the canton
from those who were to stay at home, to pay for
their trip and purchase land, cattle, and supplies
in the new land.

To their new land, now part of the state
known as the nation's cheese capital, the newcomers brought their knowledge of dairy farming and established a thriving cheese industry.
The arrival of the town's original settlers is commemorated by special celebrations every ten
years, generally close to August 16, the anniversary of the actual arrival.

Evidences of New Glarus's Swiss heritage include the large Swiss floral clock at the entrance
to town; a number of Swiss-style buildings;
Swiss delicacies offered by a local hotel and supper club; a Swiss lace factory, which visitors can
tour; and two museums. One of these is the Chalet of the Golden Fleece on Second Street. An
authentic replica of a Swiss chalet, it exhibits
some 3,000 Swiss and other items and is open
daily from April 1 through October 31.

The New Glarus Historical Swiss Museum
Village, sponsored by the New Glarus Historical
Society, is on Sixth Avenue at Seventh Street. It
includes an area landmark, the cheese factory
that has been preserved for more than a century;
and replicas of an early community building, the
first church, a blacksmith shop, a country store,
and a country school. The village is open daily
from May 1 through October 31.

SEPTEMBER 6

Jane Addams's Birthday

It was the particular genius of Jane Addams, the
pioneer social worker, to apply herself to the
cause of bettering the lives of the urban poor.
Having seen the blight of post–Civil War industrialization, she set in motion many social reforms and was responsible, with her associates,
for much important legislation. Her name is
closely linked with that of Hull House, the famous Chicago settlement house that she founded
in 1889.

On September 18, 1964, board members of
the Hull House Association and its affiliated centers met at a luncheon in Chicago to launch a
yearlong 75th anniversary observance celebrating the founding of Hull House — which a telegram from President Lyndon B. Johnson praised
for "a tradition of community activity and social
justice which has few equals." The luncheon
was followed by other events marking the Diamond Jubilee Year in various cities.

An affectionate and tactful person, skilled at
dealing with people, Jane Addams was also a
prominent pacifist, devoting much effort to
crusading for peace during the last two decades
of her life. In 1915 she presided over the International Congress of Women meeting at The
Hague and became president (1915–1935) of
the Women's International League for Peace
and Freedom, which it created. The anniversary
of her birth — September 6, 1860, in Cedarville,
Illinois — is commemorated annually under the
sponsorship of this group.

In 1960 the 100th anniversary of her birth
was the occasion for particularly widespread
observances, many of them spearheaded by the
WILPF and by the National Federation of Settlements and Neighborhood Centers, of which
she was a founder and the first president. President Dwight D. Eisenhower noted the Jane
Addams centennial by proclaiming September
6 a day on which all Americans should pay
her honor. New York renamed its Times Square
Jane Addams Square for a day. Governor Christopher Del Sesto of Rhode Island declared September 25 through October 1 Jane Addams
Week. Governor William G. Stratton proclaimed April Jane Addams Month throughout
Illinois, citing "this heroic woman" who was "a
lifetime crusader for . . . the relief of human suffering" and who "worked vigorously for . . . the
rights of minority groups." In Chicago Mayor
Richard J. Daley proclaimed 1960 Jane Addams
Year; over 1,000 citizens joined the mayor and
the Civic Committee of One Hundred at a
centennial banquet addressed by the poet Archi-

bald MacLeish, a native of Glencoe, Illinois, a suburb of Chicago.

Marked by publication of three related books, the centennial year was also observed by schools, churches, libraries, and civic groups in many other parts of the country and by national organizations with which Addams had worked closely or served as officer or cofounder. They included the AFL-CIO, Urban League, National Recreation Association, YWCA, Camp Fire Girls, Girl Scouts, and associations of social workers. At Rockford College, Addams's alma mater in Rockford, Illinois, there was a two-day centennial program with a dinner, addresses, a presentation of Jane Addams materials to the library, a luncheon at the privately owned Jane Addams homestead in Cedarville, and a ceremony at her grave in Cedarville Cemetery.

Rockford College also honors Jane Addams annually with presentation of its Jane Addams Medal for distinguished humanitarian service. The "incorrigible democrat" is also memorialized annually by presentation of the Jane Addams Children's Book Award of the WILPF, for the child's book of the previous year that best promotes understanding, nonviolence, and a strong faith in people.

The woman whose life set off chain reactions affecting so many others was graduated from Rockford College in 1881. Shortly afterwards she embarked on studies at the Woman's Medical College of Philadelphia but had to give them up because of bad health.

After two years of invalidism, she traveled widely in Europe, and it was this circumstance that affected so much of her later life. Her already awakened social conscience, appalled at an auction of rotten vegetables in London, found hope in another London establishment: Toynbee Hall. What was probably the first settlement house — or community center, or neighborhood house, as it might be called today — had begun in 1884, when the Anglican clergyman Samuel Barnett invited a group of university students to join him and his wife in "settling" in London's deprived Whitechapel area.

Toynbee Hall, as it did for other early visitors, kindled in Addams an interest in settlement-house work. Returning to Chicago, she founded a settlement house dedicated to improving community and civic life. Hull House — formerly the Hull mansion, on Chicago's West Side, which she and Ellen Gates Starr purchased in 1889 — was a pioneer institution. Initially, its main purposes were to give welfare assistance to needy families and combat juvenile delinquency by setting up recreation facilities for slum children. It became a beehive of nurseries and sewing clubs, helped large numbers of the neighborhood's foreign-born to learn English and to become citizens, and opened its doors to union meetings in the early days.

As resident head of the settlement until her death, Addams was noted for her ability to recruit outstanding workers and hold their loyalty as well as for her knack for disarming would-be critics. Her books and articles brought public support, and the work of Hull House influenced the settlement movement throughout the country.

With her associates, Addams affected the course of US legislation, championing woman suffrage and seeking reforms to bring justice to laborers, immigrants, blacks, and children. With other groups, she campaigned against sweatshops and pressed for many of the early welfare laws — the first juvenile court law, for instance, and laws providing for tenement house regulation, factory inspection, the first "mothers' pension," workmen's compensation, and an eighthour workday for women.

As Jane Addams became the recognized leader of social settlement work in the United States, Hull House became one of the largest institutions of its kind in the country. Its facilities for recreation and education—which included a day nursery, a gymnasium, meeting and recreation rooms, a social-service center, and classrooms for adult education — were supplemented by a music school, an art school, a labor museum, a theater, and a summer camp for children. In 1963 the Hull House Association decentralized to operate an expanding program through a number of affiliated Chicago centers with headquarters at the Jane Addams Community Center, 3212 North Broadway. In line with Addams's insistence on flexibility, the association's plans for the future included innovations to meet the needs and challenges of the late 20th century.

The original Hull mansion became the center of bitter controversy in 1961, after the University of Illinois purchased it and surrounding buildings for a slum-clearance project to make way for its new Chicago campus, including the Jane Addams College of Social Work. Widespread fears that the building would be demolished ended in July 1963, when the university announced a $250,000 drive to finance restoration of Hull House to its original state. It now houses a museum, library, and archives.

Jane Addams, who was instrumental in organizing the first White House Conference on Children in 1909, was named the first woman president of the National Conference on Social Welfare in 1910, took an active part in Theodore Roosevelt's campaign for the presidency on the

Progressive party ticket in 1912, and was named chairman of the Woman's Peace Party in 1915. In 1931 she became the first American woman to receive the Nobel Peace Prize, which she shared with Nicholas Murray Butler.

When she died four years later, on May 21, 1935, of cancer, she left a legacy of social progress for which she is still being honored. A bust of Addams in bronze — by Lawrence Taylor, winner of a competition among Illinois artists — was unveiled at the Illinois State Historical Library on January 23, 1964. A statue of her, flanked by figures of St. Paul and Albert Schweitzer, can be seen on the south wing of Riverside Church in New York City.

Labor Sunday

This is a movable event. See note on page xxvi.

In the last decades of the 19th century and in the early years of the 20th, a number of American religious leaders began to stress the role of churches in dealing with the problems of society. Those clergymen who subscribed to the Social Gospel made considerable efforts to make religion relevant and attractive to their congregations. In particular they directed attention to the poor workers who lived in the nation's cities. One of the more important of the Social Gospel ministers was Charles Stelzle. A Presbyterian clergyman who had himself grown up in poverty on the lower East Side of New York City, Stelzle involved himself with the problems of US workers. He organized the national labor department of the Presbyterian Church in the USA; he was superintendent of the Department of Workingmen, later the Department of Church and Labor, of the same denomination from 1903 to 1913; and he served as a delegate to the annual conventions of the American Federation of Labor between 1905 and 1915. In addition, Stelzle, in 1905, initiated the Labor Sunday observance, which still takes place each year on the Sunday preceding Labor Day.

Observance of Labor Sunday began only a few decades after the first celebration of Labor Day in 1882. As superintendent of the Department of Workingmen of the Presbyterian Church in the USA, Stelzle in 1905 called upon the ministry of that denomination to hold services having special relevance for working people on the Sunday before Labor Day. In 1905 commemoration of Labor Sunday was probably confined to Presbyterian churches, but in a short time clergymen of other denominations also acted upon Stelzle's suggestion, and in 1909 responsibility for Labor Sunday arrangements was transferred from the Presbyterian Bureau of Social Service

to the more broadly based Commission on Church and Social Service of the Federal Council of Churches of Christ in America.

Organized labor endorsed Labor Sunday in 1909, when the annual convention of the American Federation of Labor resolved

that the Sunday preceding the first Monday in September be officially designated by the American Federation of Labor as "Labor Sunday," and that the churches of America be requested to devote some part of this day to a presentation of the labor question.

Federation officers appealed to ministers of all denominations to observe the day and requested local unions to cooperate with the churches. As a result, observance of Labor Sunday grew so quickly that by 1914 more than 150,000 clergymen sponsored special services honoring workers.

In more recent years, Catholic and Protestant churches have continued to observe Labor Sunday, while synagogues hold appropriate services on the Saturday preceding Labor Day. Often, church and synagogue bulletins carry a special message on the day of the observance, and sermons take their inspiration from the role and responsibility of the labor movement. In keeping with the theme of the occasion, labor officials are frequently invited to speak, and a labor delegation may take a special part in the religious services. Young people also are involved in the day's events, and Sunday schools and other youth groups hold Labor Sunday observances.

Each year the National Council of Churches, the US Catholic Conference, and the Synagogue Council of America issue special Labor Sunday or Labor Day statements. These messages generally emphasize a common theme — in 1968, for example, all three cited the acute need for equal opportunities in the nation's ghettos. Others since have continued to stress needs of the times. The messages provide thought-provoking topics for Labor Sunday sermons and other presentations and are often used as starting points for discussion groups and seminars that are held in churches and synagogues on Labor Sunday or some related date.

The AFL-CIO also has continued to recognize the importance of Labor Sunday. In some years, the national labor organization has distributed thousands of copies of the three major faiths' Labor Sunday statements to union locals across the country and has suggested that the locals help to organize discussions or other programs dealing with the themes of these annual messages in cooperation with religious leaders. Union locals have frequently acted on this advice, and as a result clergymen and workers have come together – much as Charles Stelzle may have envisioned – to work for justice and the improvement of the American social order.

Lafayette's Birthday

Marie Joseph Paul Yves Roch Gilbert du Motier, Marquis de Lafayette, the French hero of the American Revolution, was born on September 6, 1757. The site of his birth was the 17th century château of Chavaniac in the province of Auvergne.

Lafayette was only two when his father was killed at the battle of Minden during the Seven Years' War, and 13 when he became an orphan with the death of his mother in 1770. The inheritor of a large fortune, Lafayette was married just three years later, to Marie Adrienne Françoise de Noailles, a member of a wealthy and powerful family of the nobility.

Bashful and clumsy, young Lafayette was nevertheless anxious to tread in his father's military footsteps. He joined the King's Musketeers in 1771 and was a dragoon captain when the American colonies revolted against England in 1775. While attending a banquet in honor of the duke of Gloucester in August of that year, the young officer listened enthusiastically to the duke's sympathetic remarks about the American "rebels."

Lafayette later wrote in his memoirs, "At the first news of this quarrel, my heart was enrolled in it." He resigned from active service in June 1776 and through Silas Deane, an American agent in Paris, made an agreement to serve in the colonies without pay but with the rank of major general. The young Frenchman fitted out a ship at his own expense. Despite the obstacles laid in his path by the officially neutral French government – which forbade his departure, issued orders to seize his ship, and even arrested him – Lafayette managed to sail from a Spanish port on April 20, 1777.

With a dozen or so companions, he arrived at Georgetown, South Carolina, on June 13. He found himself amazed at the contrast between America and its people and conditions in France, and from Charleston, South Carolina, soon wrote his impressions to his wife:

What most charms me is, that all the citizens are brethren.
In America, there are no poor, nor even what we call peasantry. Each individual has his own honest property, and the same rights as the most wealthy land proprietor.

Lafayette traveled to Philadelphia, where Congress, on July 31, 1777, accepted his services and resolved that, in view of his "zeal, illustrious family and connections," he should have the rank of major general. Not long afterward he gained the close friendship of General George Washington, to whose staff he was appointed. On September 11 the 20-year-old major general took part in the battle of Brandywine, near Chadds Ford, Pennsylvania. There, Washington suffered defeat in an attempt to prevent the English general, Sir William Howe, from advancing on the strategic city of Philadelphia. Lafayette received his baptism of fire and showed his mettle by rallying the scattered American troops, although he himself had been wounded in the left leg.

Spending the winter at Valley Forge, Lafayette early in 1778 was put in command of a projected invasion of Canada. The expedition was, however, abandoned for lack of supplies. The impatient youth then fought under General Charles Lee at the battle of Monmouth, in New Jersey, on June 28. In August he served as a key liaison officer between the American forces and the French fleet under Count Charles d'Estaing, during and after the unsuccessful attack on British-occupied Newport, Rhode Island.

When war broke out between France and England, Lafayette returned to France, sailing in January 1779, with an elegant sword voted by Congress and a letter of appreciation to Louis XVI. Acclaimed in Paris and at the Versailles court and created a colonel in the French cavalry, he persuaded the French king to send a land and naval expedition to help the Americans. In April 1780, Lafayette returned to the United States to prepare for the expedition's arrival. He accompanied General Washington to West Point, where the young French officer was a member of the court-martial that sentenced to death Major John André, a captured British soldier who had plotted with the American general Benedict Arnold to surrender West Point to the enemy.

Early in 1781 General Lafayette was ordered to Virginia with 1,200 troops, drawn from the New England and New Jersey Continental regiments, to operate against the British. He arrived at Richmond on April 29, just in time to prevent its capture.

Even after he received reinforcements, he had only about 3,000 men to oppose the more than 7,000 troops under the command of the British general Lord Charles Cornwallis – who is said to have written at the time, "The boy cannot escape me." But Lafayette skillfully avoided any decisive engagement and explained in a letter to Washington:

Were I to fight a battle, I should be cut to pieces, the militia dispersed, and the arms lost. Were I to decline fighting, the country would think itself given up. I am therefore determined to skirmish, but not to engage too far, and particularly to take care against their immense and excellent body of horse, whom the militia fear as they would so many wild beasts. . . . Were I anyways equal to the enemy, I should be extremely happy in my present command. But I am not strong enough even to get beaten.

Subsequently, however, Lafayette joined with 800 Pennsylvanians under the command of General Anthony Wayne and, strengthened by local militia, at last offered battle to Cornwallis. After a brisk encounter on July 6 at Green Spring, near Jamestown, Virginia, the British crossed the James River and marched to Portsmouth. There Cornwallis received orders to take up a position at Yorktown.

In 1781, with the additional forces of the French navy under the French admiral François Joseph Paul Comte de Grasse, and a greatly strengthened French-American army, including forces under General Jean Baptiste de Vimeur, Comte de Rochambeau, Washington concentrated 16,000 men around Yorktown. Neatly bottled up, Cornwallis surrendered his army of 7,500 (see October 19). Lafayette won the praise of fellow patriots for distinguishing himself in what proved to be the closing military campaign of the Revolutionary War. In December 1781 the hero sailed for home from Boston, and his direct connection with American affairs ended.

When Lafayette died on May 20, 1834, after more than another half-century of eventful living in France, citizens of the United States were grief-stricken. They observe the anniversary of his death to this day.

However, twice during his lifetime they had an opportunity to express gratitude for his assistance. Once was when he visited the United States from August 4 to December 21, 1784. He was then publicly honored to some extent — at a banquet in Boston's historic Faneuil Hall and elsewhere. However, the trip was primarily that of a private citizen on a personal visit to George Washington, and its highlight was the happy time he spent at Washington's home at Mount Vernon.

In the years that followed, Lafayette was repeatedly urged to revisit his adopted country. Finally, in a message to Congress in December 1823, President James Monroe asked that body to extend a formal invitation. Accepting, Lafayette arrived in New York City on August 15, 1824, aboard the *Cadmus*, and was given a tremendous ovation at Castle Garden. He reviewed the troops, and afterwards a horse-drawn barouche took him to City Hall for an official welcome.

He remained 13 months as a guest of the nation and proved to be an extremely popular ambassador of goodwill for France. Dinners, balls, troop reviews, parades, and milling crowds marked every step of his triumphal tour. During his busy schedule, he laid the cornerstone of the Bunker Hill Monument in Massachusetts. He also visited the US Military Academy at West Point. At a grand banquet there, the speaker, alluding to the desperate days at Valley Forge and recalling that the guest of honor had supplied the barefoot Continental army with shoes, offered a toast "to the noble Frenchman who placed the Army of the Revolution on a new and better footing."

In the course of his unparalleled welcome, Congress voted $200,000 and a township in Florida to Lafayette. Cities and towns in all parts of the country were named for him, including Lafayette in Indiana, New York, and Louisiana. On December 27, 1824, a group of citizens in Easton, Pennsylvania, resolved to establish a college in their community, and to name it after the hero "as a testimony of respect for [his] talents, virtues and signal services . . . in the great cause of Freedom."

Since his tour, the name Lafayette has been bestowed on natural sites: the 5,249-foot Mount Lafayette is the highest peak of the Franconia range of New Hampshire's White Mountains, and Acadia National Park in Maine was first established in 1919 with the name Lafayette National Park. In 1960 the US Navy named a Polaris missile submarine for Lafayette.

Statues of the general and monuments in his honor have been erected in many cities. In Washington, D.C., for example, Lafayette Square, the pleasant park directly across Pennsylvania Avenue from the White House, includes a figure of Lafayette among its memorials to Revolutionary War heroes from abroad. Another of the many examples is the statue of Lafayette in New York City's Union Square. One of the most interesting of all the monuments is in Philadelphia's Monument Cemetery, which is dedicated to the joint memory of Washington and Lafayette.

On February 22, 1932, the bicentenary of Washington's birthday, a replica of Jean Houdon's bust of Lafayette was placed in a special niche opposite the Hall of Fame for Great Americans in New York City. Although the original constitution governing the Hall of Fame had stipulated that no foreign-born citizen could be eligible for election, Lafayette was granted what might be called a posthumous "associate membership" in recognition of his services in the American Revolution. Comte René de Chambrun, representing the family of Lafayette, acknowledged the honor.

An equestrian statue of Lafayette by P. W. Bartlett, presented to France by US schoolchildren in 1908, stands in the courtyard of the Louvre in Paris. To raise the funds for this, October 19, 1898, the 117th anniversary of the battle of Yorktown, at which Lafayette had played such an important role, had been proclaimed Lafayette Day by the governors of various states. In the course of the day, which featured simple patriotic exercises and discussions about the life and character of the marquis, 4 to 5 million children contributed a total of $250,000 to the monument fund.

Elaborate celebrations of Lafayette's birthday have a long, if irregular, history in the United States. On September 6, 1824, for instance, during his triumphal US tour, a rousing banquet was given in his honor by the Society of Cincinnati, composed of officers who had served in the Continental army for at least three years or who had been in service to the end of the war. Lafayette, having received membership from George Washington himself in 1783, had been one of the first members of the order and always held it in esteem. On his 67th birthday, therefore, the remaining veterans assembled at Washington Hall in New York City, which had been splendidly decorated for the occasion.

Lafayette was still in the United States on the occasion of his 68th birthday in 1825, when his old friend President John Quincy Adams honored him at a dinner in the White House. President Adams broke the rule that the President never proposes a toast, with an exuberant "To the 22nd of February and the 6th of September, the birthday of Washington and the birthday of Lafayette."

Once Lafayette had sailed for France, the anniversary of his birth was not observed with any regularity for many years. The centennial of his birth, on September 6, 1857, was commemorated in a quiet way. Cities such as New Orleans and New York reported the event in local newspapers, but only in Boston was it celebrated municipally.

Beginning in 1915, however, when the First World War was being fought, there was much sympathy in the United States for the heroic efforts that France was making to defend itself against German invasion, and there was also much renewed interest in Lafayette. In that year, Maurice Leon originated the idea of celebrating Lafayette's birthday in conjunction with the anniversary of the first battle of the Marne, which had begun on September 6, 1914, and ended with the failure of the planned German thrust against Paris. In the United States, petitions were circulated asking for the proclamation of September 6, 1915, as Lafayette-Marne Day. Articles on the subject appeared throughout the country, and thousands of Lafayette tricolor buttons were sold at that year's Panama-Pacific Exposition in San Francisco, for the benefit of the Lafayette Fund.

Announcing elaborate plans for marking September 6, 1916, William D. Guthrie of the Lafayette Day National Committee wrote:

As Washington declared, the generosity of France to America during the War of the Revolution "must inspire every citizen of the states with sentiments of the most unalterable gratitude." During the course of our history since 1783 the remembrance of that feeling of gratitude has ... seemed ... dim at times, but there are many evidences of its revival in our own day. The heroism and ... sacrifices of the French people during the past two years have reawakened in every section of the United States ... the old feeling of sympathy, affection and gratitude. ... The celebration by Americans on Wednesday, September 6, of the anniversary of the birth of Lafayette is ... singularly fitting and ... should be looked upon as a sacred duty.

The September anniversary was perhaps even more widely commemorated than expected. About 100 newspapers ran editorials, articles, and patriotic drawings featuring Lafayette. The New York *Tribune* of September 6, for example, carried an illustration of Lafayette and Marshal Joseph Joffre, French commander in chief and hero of the battle of the Marne, next to an editorial entitled "Lafayette and Marne Day." At New York City Hall, where Lafayette had been officially welcomed in 1824, special exercises arranged by the Citizens' Committee of 111 members were attended by a large and distinguished audience. French military and diplomatic representatives, including Ambassador Jusserand, were greeted in the Governor's Room to the strains of the "Marseillaise" and the "Star-Spangled Banner," played by the Lafayette Guards' Band. They were escorted to the Aldermanic Chamber, where the portrait of Lafayette executed in 1826 by Samuel F. B. Morse had been placed over the decorated platform. In the course of the day, many persons visited the Lafayette Room at the Morris-Jumel Mansion, once Washington's headquarters; and tricolor wreaths were laid on Lafayette's statue in Union Square. In the evening 350 persons attended a banquet held at the Waldorf-Astoria under the auspices of the France-American Society.

In New Orleans a bust of Lafayette was unveiled in Lafayette Park, and there were special evening ceremonies at the historic Cabildo, or city hall, where the general had been entertained when visiting the city in 1825. The chairman used a gavel made from the branch of a magnolia tree Lafayette had planted at Mount Vernon.

In Rhode Island, many Providence residents attended the exercises staged by the Rhode Island Society of the Sons of the American Revolution in the North Burial Ground, where 200

French soldiers, some of them Lafayette's companions, had been interred. Floral wreaths were placed on the Lafayette Monument in Washington, D.C., while in San Francisco proceeds collected at exercises held by the Friends of France went toward a memorial to Lafayette in the San Francisco Public Library. Three months after the enthusiastic Lafayette-Marne Day celebration of 1916, the general was further honored — when the French Flying Corps' Escadrille Américaine — 180 US volunteer pilots who later would account for 199 enemy planes — was renamed the Lafayette Escadrille.

The United States entered World War I on the side of the Allies on April 6, 1917, and soon joined in resisting the German advance. On July 4, after the first American troops had arrived in France, a battalion of the 16th Infantry Regiment, chosen for its marching precision, paraded through Paris and made a stop at Lafayette's tomb in Picpus Cemetery. It was there that Colonel Charles E. Stanton, chief disbursing officer of the American Expeditionary Forces, uttered the immortal words "Lafayette, we are here."

In 1917 the 160th anniversary of Lafayette's birth was widely observed, with such dignitaries as Theodore Roosevelt and Elihu Root serving as honorary presidents of the committee of arrangements. Events in New York City included a banquet at the Waldorf-Astoria, exercises at Union Square's Lafayette Statue, and the laying of a wreath at the new Lafayette Monument in Prospect Park, Brooklyn, which had been dedicated the preceding May 10 by Marshal Joffre.

Philadelphians warmly welcomed Ambassador Jusserand at Independence Hall. The location evoked memories of Lafayette, who had been received there in 1824. Fittingly enough, his visit had helped to bring what was then known as the Old State House, rotting and threatened with demolition in 1816, back to public attention. It was at about the time of his visit that someone attached to it the name Independence Hall. For the 1917 celebration, a 13-star flag duplicating the one under which Lafayette fought had been made in the Betsy Ross House by 13 French-American girls. There was "a stiffening of the lines of soldiers" while it was dramatically raised at Independence Hall. On the same day a similar flag, sent to France for the purpose, was raised over the Hôtel de Ville in Paris.

On the West Coast, the main feature in San Francisco's 1917 Lafayette-Marne Day celebration was the dedication of the Library of French Thought, a gift of the French government to the University of California. In Los Angeles, Lafayette Day exercises were held at Exposition Park with addresses by several dignitaries, including Mayor Frederic T. Woodman and Louis Sentous Jr., consular agent of France. The day's festivities led to the organization of the Lafayette Society to aid in the fostering of French-American traditions. Moreover, members of the Lafayette Day Committee had secured $4 million in subscriptions to the Second Liberty Loan, one of a series of US government bond issues that helped finance World War I. In many other American cities auctions, at which items related to Lafayette were sold for the benefit of French war relief, highlighted the celebration.

In 1918, during the victorious advance of the Allied armies after the second battle of the Marne in July, the governors of Tennessee, Nevada, Ohio, Massachusetts, Georgia, Indiana, and Puerto Rico issued proclamations calling upon the people to observe the day. Celebrations in major cities, including New York, Washington, Philadelphia, Boston, Milwaukee, Chicago, and Los Angeles, followed patterns that had been established in the two preceding years. In New York, Theodore Roosevelt gave a speech, and 18 airplanes soared above the city in battle formation and dropped cards reading "Lafayette Day, Greetings from the French and American Aviators." In Washington, President and Mrs. Woodrow Wilson were among onlookers who attended the ceremonies at the Lafayette monument near the White House. Meanwhile, the French tricolor — which Lafayette himself had originated in 1789 by proposing the combination of the colors of Paris, red and blue, and the royal white — flew at the University of California at Berkeley, while the chimes of Sather Tower played the French anthem. The occasion was also marked at US Army camps in various locations. As a final tribute to Lafayette in 1918, the American Lafayette Memorial Association restored and furnished his birthplace, the château of Chavaniac.

During the years immediately following the First World War, when Franco-American feeling ran high, September 6 was marked with flag-raising ceremonies in Philadelphia, services at St. Paul's Cathedral in Boston, and exercises at the Lafayette statues in New York City and Washington, D.C. The US Military Academy at West Point, New York, was the scene of impressive festivities in 1920, when the assemblage gathered near a statue of Lafayette — presented the preceding year by the École Polytechnique of France, at which Lafayette's two sons had been educated.

During the 1930s the September 6 celebrations were staged more modestly. The Lafayette Day National Committee urged the display of the tricolor, and French-American societies commemorated the day. In 1932, the 175th anniversary of Lafayette's birth, President Herbert Hoover sent a message to the French government, while in 1934, the centenary of the general's death, Governor Herbert H. Lehman of New-York proclaimed Lafayette-Marne Day statewide. By the 1940s, with the defeat of France at the beginning of the Second World War, even the flag-raising ceremony at Philadelphia's Independence Hall was neglected.

However, by the approach of the 200th anniversary celebration of Lafayette's birth on September 6, 1957, interest in the French hero of the American Revolution had been renewed. In the preceding year, Indiana University had already begun to prepare an 8,500-item exhibit of Lafayette mementos. In February 1957 the New York Historical Society exhibited a punch bowl depicting Lafayette's 1824-1825 visit. In March President Dwight D. Eisenhower accepted the honorary chairmanship of the National Lafayette Bicentennial Committee. At Yale University, Lafayette's own map of the Virginia campaign of 1781 was displayed. And Lafayette College recalled its ties with the marquis at Easton, Pennsylvania — the community designated for issue of a three-cent commemorative stamp on September 6.

On the actual 200th birthday anniversary, the mayors of 21 American towns named Lafayette were invited to tour France and to visit the birthplace of Lafayette. In New York City, New York University's Maison Française held a special exhibit, as did the Pierpont Morgan Library. And President Eisenhower sent a crystal medallion commemorating the bicentennial to President René Coty of France.

On October 26 Count René de Chambrun, a descendant of Lafayette, spoke at Lafayette College about progress on the restoration of La Grange château near Paris, where a vast collection of Lafayette's personal papers and effects, including his 3,000-volume library, had recently been discovered in an attic.

In 1957 the Lafayette Fellowship Foundation was set up to celebrate the bicentennial, "with the basic purpose of strengthening the historic bonds of friendship between France and the United States." Over the next decade or so, the foundation (which is now defunct) invited high-ranking students of the École Nationale d'Administration, France's graduate school for the training of civil servants, to come to the United States for six months of seminars, travel, and conferences; and provided fellowships to allow top French graduate students to complete two-year courses of study at American universities of their choice.

William McKinley Assassinated

One chapter in a tragic history of assassinations, which would deprive the United States of four of its Presidents by 1963, was written on September 6, 1901. The victim was 58-year-old President William McKinley (see also January 29), then six months into his second term as the nation's Chief Executive. Like other Presidents, McKinley was vulnerable to one nearly inescapable requirement of American politics — that the Chief Executive be to some degree accessible to the citizenry. In an effort to maintain personal contact with the electorate, McKinley ignored the warnings of his closest adviser, scheduling a reception that would be open to the public during his September 1901 visit to the Pan-American Exposition in Buffalo, New York. McKinley was struck down by an assassin's bullet only minutes after the reception began on September 6.

McKinley had eagerly anticipated his two-day visit to Buffalo. September 5, the day before the shooting, had been designated President's Day at the Pan-American Exposition, and a record-breaking crowd of 116,000 persons was present at the fairgrounds on that day to catch a glimpse of the Chief Executive. By noon more than 50,000 fair-goers overflowed the vast expanse of the esplanade, and they enthusiastically greeted the President when he entered the fairgrounds amid much pageantry and ceremony. Proceeding along the Triumphal Causeway, McKinley made his way to the flag-draped platform, where he spoke to the throng about the impossibility of the United States' isolating itself from the rest of the world and the necessity for entering into reciprocal trade treaties. The audience responded with a thunderous ovation.

At the conclusion of his speech, McKinley reviewed several military units and then made a brief tour of the fair. He visited the exhibits sponsored by other nations of the Western Hemisphere, was the guest of honor at a luncheon at the New York State Building, and greeted guests at a special reception in the Government Building. Crowds accompanied the President during his day's activities, and McKinley almost encouraged those of his admirers who defied the security officers in their efforts to see him at close range.

After a quiet dinner with John G. Milburn, who as president of the exposition was his host, McKinley and his wife attended a fireworks display at the fairgrounds. They were thrilled by the spectacular pyrotechnics and seemed particularly pleased with the finale, which lit up the sky with a blazing portrait of the President and the greeting: "Welcome to McKinley, Chief of Our Nation." When the display was ended the McKinleys returned to the Milburn mansion, where they retired early.

McKinley wanted September 6 to be "the restful day" of his Buffalo visit. On that morning he and his party traveled to nearby Niagara Falls. After seeing the falls, Mrs. McKinley was overcome by the late summer heat and retired to a suite at the International Hotel. But the weather did not keep the President from enjoying the awesome sights of the falls, and he even ventured up a steep incline in his heavy frock coat to get a better view of the natural wonder.

In midafternoon the presidential party returned to Buffalo so that McKinley might attend the public reception that had been scheduled for 4:00 P.M. in the exposition's Temple of Music. Since the day's activities had already taxed her frail health, Mrs. McKinley returned to the Milburn mansion instead of accompanying her husband during his last official appearance at the fair. The President bade her good-bye at the train station, and, with his secretary, George B. Cortelyou, and Milburn, he proceeded to the Temple of Music.

McKinley's hosts in Buffalo had instituted fairly rigorous security measures to insure the President's safety during the reception. The three secret servicemen who had accompanied him to the exposition took positions close to his place on the receiving line, a squad of exposition police guarded the entrance of the Temple of Music, and several Buffalo detectives stood watch along the aisle leading to the Chief Executive. As an extra precaution, 11 unarmed artillerymen also were stationed in the aisle at the last moment; and they were ordered to scrutinize all persons approaching the President.

Despite the good intentions of those in charge of the reception, the measures taken to safeguard McKinley were not ideal. The artillerymen, who had been hastily added to the security force, had no experience with such work. Indeed, their presence only served to congest the aisle, thereby violating the basic principle of police protection that requires a large space to be kept open before the person being guarded. The secret servicemen also were poorly positioned on that fateful day. Ideally, one agent should have been stationed to the left and just slightly behind McKinley so that he could see each hand outstretched to the President; instead, to facilitate introductions, two secret servicemen were placed opposite the Chief Executive, and the third stood sentry some distance to McKinley's right. And finally, the weather indirectly affected the security of the President. September 6

was a hot, humid day, so many of the fair-goers, who had waited for hours under the blistering sun, carried handkerchiefs, making it impossible for the guards to insist that the hands of all persons near McKinley be empty and clearly visible.

Hours before the reception was to begin, hundreds of people had queued up outside the Temple of Music to await the arrival of the President. Among them was Leon Czolgosz, who carried a .32 caliber Iver-Johnson revolver.

Czolgosz's family had experienced the difficulties that were the common lot of many immigrants in late 19th century America. The senior Czolgosz, father of eight, was a Polish immigrant laborer who moved from town to town in Michigan, then went to Pittsburgh, and finally settled in Ohio. He never had much money, but by drawing on the earnings of his six sons, he was able to buy a farm near Cleveland during the depression of the 1890s.

Leon Czolgosz grew up embittered. The inequities of the American social order appalled him, and he became increasingly interested in socialism. A devotee of Emma Goldman and other anarchists, he looked to violence for redress of the grievances of the American worker and as an outlet for his hostilities.

Radical politics would not have made Leon Czolgosz an assassin had his psychological make-up been more stable. Doubtlessly deranged at the time of the assassination, Czolgosz had always been a loner and became a virtual recluse after suffering a nervous breakdown in 1898. He left his job at a Cleveland wire mill and returned to the family farm, where he ate his meals alone, slept an inordinate amount of time, and dissipated his few waking hours in restless idleness. Newspapers fascinated him, and he pored over the account of the assassination of King Humbert of Italy for countless hours.

In July 1901 Czolgosz left his family's home and, after some wanderings, arrived in Buffalo in time for the Pan-American Exposition. Apparently he did not go there with the intention of killing McKinley, but newspaper stories of the planned reception for the Chief Executive stirred his imagination. Leon Czolgosz hated the adulation reserved for the President. "I didn't believe one man should have so much service," he later said, "and another man should have none."

Having no concern for his own safety, he decided to shoot the President at close range. Czolgosz realized that the reception would provide the best opportunity for such an act, so early on September 6 he joined the crowd waiting to greet McKinley and calmly stood outside until 4:00 P.M., when the doors opened to allow the holiday throng to file past McKinley. As he approached the President, Czolgosz carefully swathed the gun in his hand with a handkerchief. He reached McKinley's place on the receiving line at 4:07 P.M., and without uttering a word to his victim he fired two shots. Czolgosz then tried to escape, but shocked onlookers immediately seized him and might have killed him on the spot, had not the wounded President gasped: "Don't let them hurt him."

One of Czolgosz's bullets ricocheted off the President's ribs, and, minutes after the shooting, when McKinley was examined at the exposition's emergency hospital, it fell from his clothing. The second bullet created a more serious problem, entering the President's abdomen and causing such extensive damage that the first doctors to examine McKinley decided to operate immediately. Working by the light of the setting sun, the surgeons repaired the lacerations in the walls of the President's stomach, one of several affected organs, but they could not locate the bullet itself. An X-ray machine was being exhibited at the fairgrounds, but they made no use of the six-year-old discovery; instead, they merely cleansed McKinley's peritoneal cavity and closed the incision, leaving the bullet embedded in his abdomen. Then the President was taken to convalesce at the Milburn mansion.

McKinley was shot on a Friday, and, during the weekend that followed, Vice President Theodore Roosevelt, most members of the cabinet, and relatives and close friends of the President went to Buffalo to keep their anxious vigil. McKinley's condition was serious, but medical bulletins released on Monday indicated that he was recovering, and those made public on Tuesday led most observers to believe that he was no longer in danger. In fact McKinley's condition seemed so improved that his relatives returned to their homes in Ohio, governmental officials went back to Washington, and Vice President Roosevelt joined his family at a retreat in the Adirondack Mountains of New York State, 12 miles away from the nearest telephone or telegraph.

However, though the President's strong constitution enabled him to rally from the initial trauma of the attack on his life and the surgery that followed, his doctors' optimism for his ultimate recovery was largely unfounded. The possibility of infection along the track taken by the bullet that had lodged in McKinley's body posed a constant threat to his life in this era before antibiotics. The doctors attending him ignored the danger.

For several days McKinley struggled against the gangrene that was spreading through his abdomen. But by Thursday, September 12, his re-

sources were taxed beyond their limits, and his condition deteriorated. Despite the best efforts of his physicians, the Chief Executive continued to fail, and late in the afternoon of Friday, September 13, he realized he was dying and said to his doctors: "It is useless, gentlemen. I think we ought to have a prayer." Mrs. McKinley was brought to her husband's side. The President whispered: "Good-bye, good-bye, all. It is God's way. His will, not ours, be done." Then he began to whisper the words of his favorite hymn, "Nearer My God to Thee."

Mrs. McKinley remained with her husband throughout his last evening, but her own health was so poor that she was persuaded to end her sad vigil some time before midnight. Dr. Presley Rixby, who was the personal physician of both the McKinleys, then took her place at the President's side. For several hours he stood by, helplessly listening to the harsh rasps of the Chief Executive's breathing. Death occurred about 2:00 A.M., September 14.

News of McKinley's death plunged the nation into mourning. A special train carried the President's body back to Washington. There McKinley's remains lay first in the East Room of the White House. They were then transferred to the Capitol, where thousands of citizens went to pay their final respects. When official services concluded in Washington, a funeral procession escorted McKinley's body to the train that would carry the slain President back to his beloved Canton, Ohio.

Final services for McKinley were held at the Methodist Church in Canton. Theodore Roosevelt, who succeeded to the presidency, and many other governmental dignitaries attended the funeral, while the entire nation showed its grief for its fallen leader by observing five minutes of silence. Then McKinley was laid to rest in a temporary vault in the Canton cemetery.

The nation's grief for McKinley had not yet subsided when on September 23, 1901, the trial of his assassin began. After a hearing that lasted only two days, the jury deliberated less than one hour before finding Czolgosz guilty. He was electrocuted on October 29, 1901, at Auburn State Prison in Auburn, New York.

In the years following McKinley's death, numerous localities subscribed thousands of dollars to erect suitable monuments to the late President. The citizenry of Buffalo honored McKinley by dedicating a 69-foot-high marble shaft on the sixth anniversary of his September 5, 1901, speech at the Pan-American Exposition. Other cities, including Columbus, Chicago, Springfield (Massachusetts), and Philadelphia, similarly paid tribute to McKinley, but perhaps the most impressive memorial is the domed white granite mausoleum in Canton. Erected at 7th Street, N.W., at the edge of Westlawn Cemetery, it is set on a grassy hilltop. The circular structure, which has a diameter of 75 feet and is 97 feet tall, rests on platform with a diameter of 178 feet. A stairway broken into four flights ascends the side of the platform, and a 9-foot bronze statue of the President adorns its center landing. At the base of the monument is a rectangular pool of water that is subdivided into five levels over which water flows in four cascades. The monument and the beautiful grounds that surround it are known as the McKinley State Memorial. One element of the neighboring Stark County Historical Center, the cultural and educational complex north of 7th Street, N.W., is the McKinley Museum, which contains memorabilia of the late President. Both the complex and the museum are adjacent to the portion of Canton's outstanding municipal park system, which extends for five miles along West Creek. Elsewhere in Canton, murals in the McKinley Room of the Hotel Onesto on Cleveland Avenue depict events in the life of the former Chief Executive.

Also of interest is the elaborate McKinley Memorial building, of classical contours, designed by McKim, Mead and White in Niles, Ohio, where McKinley was born. It surrounds the likeness of McKinley by sculptor J. Massey Rhind that stands in an open courtyard.

SEPTEMBER 7

Labor Day

This is a movable event. See note on page xxvi.

Industrial workers have played a major role in the emergence of the United States as a world power. Labor has contributed to the general prosperity and has buttressed the nation in times of hardship as well as prosperity. Labor Day, an annual celebration that takes place on the first Monday in September, is not only a federal holiday (applying to federal employees and the federal District of Columbia); by separate legislative action, it has also been made a legal holiday in each of the 50 states. It is also observed in the US Virgin Islands and other US territories and possessions, as well as in the Commonwealth of Puerto Rico. The observance, in recognition of labor's contributions to the nation, is highly prized by America's labor unions and their members, not only as a day of leisure, but also as an occasion for commemorating the labor movement's many victories during the past century.

Unfortunately, employers and the government did not always acknowledge the great contributions of workers; nor did they always even recognize the difficulties they faced. In the wake of the Industrial Revolution, most workers toiled long hours, for low pay and under difficult conditions; lacked any real strength vis-à-vis their employers; and were almost totally without the organization that could improve their bargaining position. Efforts to organize the nation's vast work force began to be more meaningful in the decades following the Civil War. Many of the nation's workers joined the spreading labor union movement. Their struggle for higher wages, better working conditions, and shorter hours was long and arduous. Utilizing such weapons as spontaneous work stoppages, strikes, picketing, and boycotts, they called attention to the harsh conditions under which they lived and worked. Although the unions grew in number and strength, they had only limited success in redressing the grievances of their members. Later, the growth of the ranks of organized labor was further abetted by the (intermittently) more favorable political climate of the 20th century; by the late 1970s the nation's unionized work force numbered 18 million. It is referred to often in the aggregate as Big Labor.

According to a long-accepted version of events, it was at a meeting of an early labor organization, in 1882, that Peter J. McGuire, the founder and general secretary of the new Brotherhood of Carpenters and Joiners, first proposed the idea of setting aside a day to honor labor. McGuire, with other labor leaders, had been influential the previous year in establishing the Federation of Organized Trades and Labor Unions, which was to be reorganized in 1886 as the American Federation of Labor. The son of Irish immigrants, McGuire had himself known the extreme poverty that oppressed many laborers in the years following the Civil War. Forced to leave school and go to work at the age of 11, he had held an assortment of low-rung jobs and, according to his later recollection, "was everything but a sword swallower. And sometimes I was so hungry, a sword — with mustard, of course — would have tasted fine."

McGuire's youthful experiences gave him a deep respect for workers and made him determined to improve their condition. He believed that a day should be set aside to honor laborers and to bring their plight to public attention, and at a meeting of the New York Central Labor Union on May 8, 1882, he made his idea known. McGuire suggested that the labor holiday be celebrated on the first Monday in September because, in his words, "it would come at the most pleasant season of the year, nearly midway between the Fourth of July and Thanksgiving, and would fill a wide gap in the chronology of legal holidays." He also proposed holding a street parade on that day in order to "show the strength and *esprit de corps* of the trade and labor organizations," and then he urged concluding the day's events with a picnic or similar festivity.

The Central Labor Union enthusiastically approved McGuire's idea, and, on September 5, 1882, the first Labor Day observance took place in New York City. The celebration was on a Tuesday, but the change to Monday was made within two years. Apart from this detail, events of the initial Labor Day adhered closely to the plan McGuire had proposed. A parade of some 10,000 workers, "with bands and banners," first marched up Broadway from City Hall to Union Square, and then the participants adjourned to Reservoir Park for a picnic, concert, and orations. According to a reporter for the New York *Herald,* "Fellow workers and their families sat together, joked together and caroused together. . . . Americans, English, Irish and Germans . . . hobnobbed as though the common cause had established closer brotherhood."

Although the 1882 observance was confined to New York City, the idea of setting aside a day to honor laborers quickly gained popularity. In 1884, when the Federation of Organized Trades and Labor Unions, the national labor organization that soon would become the AFL, gave its endorsement to the idea of an annual Labor Day, the occasion was scheduled for the first Monday in September. On that day, parades of workers took place in cities throughout the Northeast. Enthusiasm for the new holiday spread rapidly, and the idea also was endorsed by the Knights of Labor organization. By 1895 Labor Day events were taking place in localities across the nation.

Oregon, on February 21, 1887, became the first state to recognize Labor Day as a legal holiday. The Oregon statute set the first Saturday in June for the labor observance, and this law remained in force until 1893, when the state's lawmakers moved the date of Labor Day to the first Monday in September. In the meantime other state legislatures also had approved statutes establishing the first Monday in September as Labor Day: Colorado, Massachusetts, New Jersey, and New York did so in 1887, and by 1893 the lawmakers of more than 20 other states had legalized the holiday.

In 1893 a bill to establish Labor Day as a federal holiday was introduced in Congress. Both houses gave it their unanimous approval in 1894. On June 28 of that year President Grover Cleveland signed an act making the first Monday in September a legal holiday for federal employees and in the District of Columbia. All of the remaining states and Puerto Rico eventually legalized the day.

Having won legal recognition of Labor Day, workers in the 1890s and early 20th century used the holiday to dramatize their grievances. The large Labor Day parades, which took place in so many cities across the nation, proved to be particularly effective. This was demonstrated by an incident that occurred just before the 1894 parade in New York City. Many of the women garment workers were reluctant to take part in the march, and one of their representatives explained that they were embarrassed because "they have very poor clothes, many of them are little better than rags." "So much the better," was the reply of another delegate. "Let them march in their rags so that the New York public may see how they are treated." And they did march, together with 12,000 other workers, while, according to one newspaper report, "one half of the city" watched.

Such successes convinced union leaders of the value of Labor Day observances to their cause. In 1898 Samuel Gompers (see January 27), the pioneer who served for more than a quarter century as president of the American Federation of Labor, said of the holiday:

It is regarded as the day for which the toilers in past centuries looked forward, when their rights and their wrongs might be discussed, placed upon a higher plane of thought and feeling; that the workers of our day may not only lay down their tools of labor for a holiday, but upon which they may touch shoulders in marching phalanx and feel the stronger for it; meet at their parks, groves and grounds, and by appropriate speech, counsel with, and pledge to, each other that the coming year shall witness greater effort than the preceding in the grand struggle to make mankind free, true and noble.

For many decades Labor Day was, as Gompers noted, a time when laborers came together, discussed common problems, and organized their forces so that they might be better able to carry forward their efforts to obtain fair working conditions and a decent standard of living.

As labor unionism continued to grow in the 20th century, the AFL's insistence on organizing workers by crafts, rather than by industries, left many unskilled laborers outside the movement and troubled those who felt that industrial organization would be more effective. Dissatisfaction peaked in 1935, when a minority of members left the AFL to form a new organization known as the Committee for Industrial Organization (after 1938, Congress of Industrial Organizations), a designation soon abbreviated to CIO. In 1955 a long-hoped-for reunion took place when the two bodies joined to form a single organization — the AFL-CIO.

In addition to the AFL-CIO's later membership of more than 14 million, the ranks of organized labor were swelled by 5 million members of independent unions. Over the years, the organized labor movement — which now encompasses large white-collar and professional unions — has vastly changed US working conditions, not only for union members but in many respects for nonunionized workers as well: by the middle of the 20th century, the circumstances of labor were in marked contrast to those of a century earlier, and most of the nation's industrial workers enjoyed considerable respect, and certain skilled trades a measure of affluence.

With many demands fulfilled — even though there are always new demands, particularly in times of inflation — the emphasis on Labor Day as an opportunity for bringing workers' problems to public attention has diminished, along with the militant tone of some of the earlier observances.

Labor organizations still take special note of the holiday, however. AFL-CIO President George Meany and other labor leaders usually issue special Labor Day statements. These messages generally review developments that have occurred in the labor movement and in the nation at large during the previous year. They also outline some of the major problems with which the working force and the society as a whole will have to cope during the following year.

Labor leaders have also taken advantage of the Labor Day holiday to encourage citizens of the nation to reflect upon the vast strides forward that the industrial workers of the United States have made during the past century. To accomplish this end, the labor organizations make available to radio and television stations a number of tapes and films. These presentations, which have included *Land of Promise*, a 1960 film depicting the history and growth of the American labor movement; *When the Day's Work Is Done*, a 1964 documentary showing the vast contributions industrial workers make to their communities during their leisure hours; and *The Liquid Fire*, a 1966 film based on the life of Samuel Gompers, have been seen by millions of viewers.

Union locals in many areas still sponsor traditional observances of Labor Day. In recent years, mammoth parades and rallies have taken place in such cities as Boston, Cleveland, and Detroit. Thousands of labor union members have participated, and floats and other displays depicting various epochs in labor's fight for just treatment have made these events extremely colorful spectacles. These massive demonstrations are not necessarily annual events, but they are held regularly — particularly in election years, and, understandably, candidates seeking public office often participate in the observances. John F. Kennedy, for example, launched his 1960 campaign for the presidency at a huge rally sponsored by the Michigan AFL-CIO in

Detroit's Cadillac Square. Eight years later, Hubert Humphrey began his unsuccessful quest to occupy the White House by leading a parade of 150,000 marchers up New York's Fifth Avenue.

Labor Day parades and similar demonstrations do not always have political overtones, nor are they confined to the nation's largest cities. Across the country, union locals in smaller cities and towns also sponsor special observances to mark the labor holiday. In keeping with Labor Day's present function as a time for leisure and enjoyment, these events are often part of more extensive festivities during the three-day weekend. On Labor Day in Syracuse, New York, for example, the mayor and labor officials lead a large cavalcade from the city to the nearby New York State Fairgrounds. There, municipal and labor leaders assemble for a luncheon and hear speeches by dignitaries, while the paraders enjoy the sights and exhibits of the state fair, which traditionally begins in late August and continues through the Labor Day weekend. Other state fairs that customarily embrace the Labor Day weekend, with varying degrees of attention officially paid to the holiday, include those of California (at Sacramento), Minnesota (at St. Paul), Nebraska (at Lincoln), Ohio (at Columbus), Oregon (at Salem), and South Dakota (at Huron).

Since 1892 citizens of the northwestern Illinois town of Galesburg have held elaborate Labor Day festivities. In recent years the celebration has extended over the entire three-day weekend, beginning on Saturday evening with a country-and-western show or other entertainment, and concluding on Labor Day with an entertainment program at the Labor Temple. However, the parade on Labor Day morning remains the greatest attraction of the weekend's events. The line of march generally proceeds through Galesburg's business district and features floats, marching bands, drum corps, and equestrian groups.

For more than 25 years, a holiday fete has taken place over the Labor Day weekend in Henryetta, Oklahoma, which many consider one of the strongest union communities in the state. Appropriately, a labor leader generally is the featured speaker at the banquet following the Labor Day parade. During the three-day celebration such varied activities as a band concert, fireworks display, dune buggy races, a shooting exhibition by the Oklahoma Highway Patrol, and terrapin races (to sample one year's program) draw thousands of visitors to Henryetta.

Tiny Francestown, New Hampshire, for well over 50 years has marked the Labor Day weekend with three days of traditional events that typically have included a vesper service, Little League baseball game, tennis tournament playoffs, a magic show, band concert, square dance,

New England-style dinner, games and sale booths on the town common, and the Giant Parade of Floats on Labor Day afternoon.

In Derry, a slightly larger New Hampshire town, a Labor Day festival that originated in 1963 has become so popular that in recent years it has attracted as many as 100,000 visitors. Derry's weekend celebration typically features such attractions as a festival ball with the coronation of a Labor Day queen and presentation of her court, a midway with a ferris wheel, a family picnic, an art show, and a barbecue. The highlight of the Derry festival is the Labor Day parade, with unusual floats and costumes, and emphasis on visiting dignitaries. These are likely to include state officeholders and representatives of the US labor movement, as well as foreign diplomats and labor delegations.

Although a fairly large number of union locals still sponsor parades and other official exercises on Labor Day, others hold less formal functions. Many labor organizations mark the holiday with a family picnic or barbecue. At some of these events, prominent speakers give addresses. But, for the most part, the emphasis during such Labor Day festivities is on entertainment and special events, such as athletic contests for children and adults or the selection of beauty queens.

In addition to the many events sponsored by union locals, countless communities and organizations take advantage of the long weekend and the pleasant weather that usually accompanies it to schedule special festivities that have little or no relation to the labor movement. Some of these celebrations have become traditional Labor Day observances, and their special qualities attract visitors from distant places.

One of the most colorful celebrations on the Labor Day weekend is the four-day Louisiana Shrimp and Petroleum Festival in Morgan City. There are pageants on land and on water, a boat parade, the coronation of a king and queen, a street parade, fireworks, a football jamboree, a swimming meet, a square dance, and a speedboat regatta. The highlight of the festival is the Blessing of the Shrimp Fleet ceremony on Sunday morning. Performing a ritual that dates back to early Christian times in southern Europe, the Roman Catholic clergy on the flagship of the fleet and the spectators of many faiths on the shore join to ask divine protection for the men and boats that will trawl the waters of the Gulf of Mexico for shrimp during the following year.

Another observance that has grown out of local customs takes place at Dorney Park in Allentown, Pennsylvania. This event emphasizes the customs of the Pennsylvania Dutch. Costumed entrants vie in the Pennsylvania Apple

Butter cooking contest, while others enjoy square dances, an ox roast, special shows on the park stage, and a fireworks display.

Persons of Scottish descent are another group holding a special celebration over the Labor Day weekend. For more than a century, Scottish clans have gathered each year on the Saturday and Sunday of the weekend at Santa Rosa, California. Thousands of spectators at the Sonoma County Fairgrounds watch the sporting events, including the hammer throw and caber toss, as well as piping performances, drumming exhibitions, and demonstrations of the Highland fling, reels, and sword dances.

Labor Day is also the date of an auto racing festival at Darlington, South Carolina. The annual Southern 500 Festival at Darlington, one of the largest stock car classics in the United States, takes place on Labor Day itself and is the culmination of the festival, with numerous special events, such as parades, street dances, a barbecue, a golf tournament, and beauty contest.

A unique experience for those who enjoy walking is the general recreational walk across Michigan's Mackinac Bridge that takes place each Labor Day. The five-mile span connecting Michigan's upper and lower peninsulas has been the scene of the walk since the bridge was completed in 1957. Labor Day is the only time of the year when crossing the bridge on foot is permitted, and as many as 15,000 strollers — including the governor of Michigan in some years — have turned out for the event.

Various other types of Labor Day observances take place each year across the United States. Residents of Skagway, Alaska, for example, hold the Sourdough Days celebration, which commemorates "Alaska statehood, Canadian neighbors, and American labor." Inhabitants of Lewes, Delaware, sponsor a marine flotilla parade. The tiny lumbering and plywood center of St. Maries, Idaho, schedules its annual Paul Bunyan Days, with logging events, water show, parade, barbecue, county fair, and horse show, for Labor Day weekend — which is also the time for the Wilhelm Tell Festival, staged annually by the Swiss-descended residents of New Glarus, Wisconsin (see September 5, Wilhelm Tell Festival).

Okeechobee, in south-central Florida, and Ellensburg, Washington, choose Labor Day weekend for their annual rodeos. The village of Milan, Ohio, where the inventor Thomas A. Edison was born, schedules its annual Milan Melon Festival and sports-car hill climb for Labor Day weekend. The weekend is the time also for the Bisbee, Arizona, annual Brewery Gulch Days, complete with melodrama, fiddlers' contest, copper mine tour, art show, pageant, and food fair. One of the most publicized events scheduled over the weekend is New Mexico's venerable Santa Fe Fiesta, a colorful blend of Spanish, Anglo-American, and Indian heritages (see September 4).

Many other nations have set aside days to honor working men and women. However, in most countries it is the traditional May Day that is marked as labor's holiday (see May 1). A few nations — such as New Zealand, where Labor Day is in late October, and Australia, where the date varies from state to state — choose other dates for their labor observances. Only in Canada (where the day has an independent history dating as far back as 1872) and in the United States is the day marked on the first Monday in September. Labor Day on this date, with its past history of militant demonstrations and its present function as a day of leisure is thus a uniquely North American phenomenon. The earliest of the observers of Labor Day in the United States probably never imagined that by the late 20th century the average working person would face the variety of pleasant choices that are available on that holiday today: to attend one or more of the nation's hundreds of Labor Day events, to join the crowds flocking to beaches and resorts, or to enjoy a restful time at home before returning to the routine work schedule of autumn and winter.

Peter J. McGuire, the most prominent of the contenders for the title Founder of Labor Day, died penniless in 1906. Considerable effort has been expended to honor him in the years since.

The Chicago District Council and Affiliated Unions of the Carpenters' Brotherhood contributed a bronze memorial plaque to its headquarters in Indianapolis, Indiana, on April 11, 1910. It was transferred to Washington, D.C., in 1961, when the Brotherhood moved its headquarters there and can be seen in the lobby of the union's building at 101 Constitution Avenue, N.W.

Perhaps the greatest tribute to McGuire is the annual wreath-laying ceremony at his grave in Pennsauken, New Jersey, near Camden, McGuire's home for the last two decades of his life. There, at the large memorial monument and statue dedicated to McGuire, labor and public officials and other notables convene each Labor Day to express their feelings concerning Labor Day, McGuire, and the labor movement in general. Then they adjourn to a nearby restaurant, where the Camden Central Labor Union sponsors a Labor Day luncheon.

To honor the contributions of labor, the US government issued a Labor Day stamp in 1956. It was first made available at Camden on Labor Day. Release of the commemorative stamp came a half century after McGuire's death in 1906.

The Miss America Pageant
Atlantic City, New Jersey

This is a movable event. See note on page xxvi.

What is probably the greatest publicity coup ever contrived by any metropolis, the week-long Miss America Pageant that takes place each September in Atlantic City, New Jersey, has also become something of an American institution. By the time it reaches its climax on the Saturday evening after Labor Day, when millions of viewers watch the crowning of the new Miss America on network television, newspaper stories and photographs devoted to the event have circulated everywhere, and the interest and local pride of much of the nation have been skillfully tapped in advance.

Across the country, thousands of persons have already become involved — if not in the national Miss America Pageant at Atlantic City, then as competitors or volunteer workers in the 3,500 local and state pageants for which the Atlantic City pageant is the prototype and inspiration. Winners at the local level have moved up to the state pageants, which are only slightly less elaborate than the national one. In all, some 70,000 contestants a year compete in the local and state pageants, which are managed by organizations franchised by the national Miss America Pageant. (Most often these are junior chambers of commerce, although they may also be Lions, Kiwanis, or other clubs, private organizations, newspapers, or special pageant-promoting corporations.)

The 50 winners on the state level represent their states in the final, suspense-filled week of judging in Atlantic City, where they customarily arrive on Labor Day.

Miss America aspirants have the opportunity, each year, to compete for scholarships — which in 1977, for example, amounted to more than $1 million — for which state and local contest managers have secured sponsors. Those preliminary contestants who reach Atlantic City compete for scholarships that are worth more than $125,000 annually. At the end of the 1977 pageant, these had reached a cumulative total of over $1 million since the scholarship program had been instituted on the national level by Lenora S. Slaughter, executive director of the Miss America Pageant in 1945 — ensuring much of the pageant's subsequent success in attracting candidates and keeping its image a cut above the mere "bathing beauty" level.

The rewards for participation in the Miss America Pageant include a $20,000 scholarship for Miss America herself; scholarships in the amounts of $10,000, $6,000, $5,000, and $4,000 for the four other finalists; and other scholarships for the five semifinalists, the contestant other candidates name Miss Congeniality and those voted most talented in such areas as singing, dancing, musicianship, and acting. The entrant who becomes Miss America is also compensated with a year of (heavily chaperoned) travel, and personal appearances that bring at least $60,000 in booking fees — and may lead indirectly to a career as model, motion picture actress, or television personality.

From the moment of their arrival in Atlantic City, the Misses Alabama through Wyoming help preserve the wholesome Miss America image by subscribing to a strict set of rules. They may not smoke in public, enter a cocktail lounge, dress immodestly, or — except in the presence of an official pageant hostess — speak to any man or permit interviews or photographs.

The contestants make their first major public appearance in an illuminated parade on Atlantic City's boardwalk on Tuesday evening. Between high school bands and the floats of various business concerns, organizations, and communities, the 50 state contestants ride in convertibles provided by a national automobile manufacturer — a contrast to the elaborately decorated rolling chairs used by contenders in early pageants.

On Wednesday, Thursday, and Friday evenings, large audiences of paying ticket holders excitedly watch the preliminary judging, in which the number of contestants for the Miss America crown is narrowed to ten. On each evening, a third of the aspirants perform in each of the three categories in which they will be judged: evening gown and swim suit appearances, and talent (the category that earns most points). By Friday night, all contenders have appeared in all categories. Their afternoons, meanwhile, have been devoted to the personality interviews by which a panel of well-known judges appraises their poise, personality, articulateness, and ability to carry the responsibilities of the title.

The week's climax comes from 8:30 to midnight on Saturday evening, when the final selecting of Miss America — interspersed with entertainment and once built around such themes as How This Land Can Sing (1971) and Keeping America Beautiful . . . Our Way (1972) and now centering on specially written songs — takes place in a climate of mounting suspense in Atlantic City's Convention Hall. The events, presided over for many years by Bert Parks, are watched in their entirety by a capacity crowd of ticket holders and for the last two hours by a nationwide television audience. Before the marathon is over, the 50 state queens have been presented; the 10 semifinalists — those with the highest cumulative scores from the preliminary competitions — have been introduced and have performed in the evening gown, bathing suit, and talent categories; and five finalists have been announced and submitted to capsule interviews and further judging. The highest point is reached shortly before midnight, with the coronation of the new Miss America, who is serenaded by the host with the traditional "There She Is — Miss America," as she begins her year's reign by walking regally down the runway — smiling, usually, through tears of joy.

The Miss America Pageant was held for the first time in 1921, when bathing beauties from eight cities and states lined up on the beach for judging; yearly through 1927; and again in 1933. Since 1935, when it resumed in the Marine Ballroom of Atlantic City's Steel Pier, it has been an annual event. By 1940, when the pageant moved to Convention Hall, there were 46 aspirants from 30 states and the District of Columbia. Every state in the Union was represented for the first time in 1959.

SEPTEMBER 8

Feast of the Birth of Mary

The feast of the birth or nativity of Mary, the mother of Jesus Christ, is observed on September 8 by the Roman Catholic church. It is also marked on this date by Eastern Orthodox churches, except those that still adhere to the Old Style, or Julian, calendar and observe the feast on September 21. Among the Eastern Orthodox, the feast is known as the Nativity of Our Most Holy Lady, the Theotokas, or simply as the Nativity of the Theotokas.

The Greek word *theotokas* means "god-bearer" or "mother of God." Mary was declared to be *Theotokas* as a result of the early church Council of Ephesus, held in 431. It had been summoned in order to discuss, among other issues, the first major theological controversy over Mary. Nestorius, a Syrian bishop, asserted that Mary was not the mother of the incarnate Son of God; instead, he held that she had given birth only to a human being who was subsequently united to the Son of God. This viewpoint, which detracted from the divinity of Jesus Christ by maintaining that the divine and human natures were not merged into one person in Jesus Christ from the start, was condemned as heretical at the council.

The feast of Mary's nativity seems to be a very old observance, which originated in the East, probably in either Syria or Palestine. At the end of the 5th century, at least in Jerusalem, it held the same prestige as the Assumption (see August 15) as a major Marian celebration. In the 7th century the feast became established in the Roman liturgy, a special service being prescribed with appropriate collects and other prayers. By the 11th century the September 8 feast had spread throughout Christendom.

For centuries September 8 was enjoined as a holy day of obligation for all Christians. The observance was downgraded in 1918. The Assumption of the Blessed Virgin Mary, commemorating the taking up of Mary's body upon her death into heaven, and the Feast of the Immaculate Conception (see December 8), celebrating Mary's preservation from original sin from the instant of her conception, superseded her birthday as the chief Marian feasts. In the newly revised Roman Catholic calendar, the September 8 observance, formerly Class II, is now ranked as a "feast."

Just as the Assumption, celebrated at the peak of the summer harvesting in southern Europe, took on added seasonal significance there as the Feast of Our Lady in Harvest, so in northern Europe, where crops ripened somewhat later, the Feast of the Nativity of Our Lady functioned as the traditional harvest festival. Mary's birthday was regarded as the appropriate time to express thanks to her for the bountiful fields and to beg her protection, lest the rich harvest suffer damage before being fully gathered. The mother of Jesus Christ was also considered the patron of wine-makers, a designation most likely stemming from her important role at the wedding feast at Cana, as related in the second chapter of the Gospel of John. It was she who called the attention of her son to the fact that the hosts had run out of wine, leading him to perform his first miracle: the changing of water into wine.

In the United States, where some of the most fascinating commemorations of feast days are staged in the Indian pueblos of New Mexico, September 8 is an important festive occasion at Laguna Pueblo. Traditional Indian harvest dances are performed in Mary's honor following mass in the Roman Catholic mission church.

September 8 is sometimes regarded as a feast that is implicitly intended to commemorate Mary's parents, traditionally Anne and Joachim, as well as their daughter. The actual feast day of Anne and Joachim, however, occurs in July (see July 26).

The Galveston Hurricane of 1900

Beginning on September 8, 1900, a savage hurricane battered the southern coast of Texas for 18 hours without letup, leaving such destruction that it continues to be ranked among the most devastating North Atlantic hurricanes of the 20th century. Although great damage was done to farms and villages for many miles east and west, the storm wreaked its greatest havoc on Galveston, an island city and key southern port, then with a population of 38,000 persons.

The disaster of 1900 was met with striking fortitude by Galveston's residents, who owed their predicament largely to their geographical location. The city of Galveston lies 48 miles southeast of Houston, on Galveston Island – a sea island some 32 miles long and 2 miles wide, lying in the Gulf of Mexico about 2 miles off the Texas coast, across the entrance to Galveston Bay. Beautiful beaches line Galveston's gulf front, and a major harbor extends on the bay side for 6 miles.

The island was known to Spanish explorers from early times. Cabeza de Vaca is believed to have been shipwrecked in 1528, off either Galveston or the nearby island of San Luis, and from there to have begun wanderings through what are now Texas, New Mexico, and Mexico that eventually inspired other expeditions on the North American mainland. The island and bay were named in 1785 by José de Evía, a pilot sent out to survey the Gulf coast by Bernardo de Gálvez, then Spanish governor of Louisiana and later viceroy of Mexico; Americans later gave the settlement an anglicized form of the name ("Galveztown" – Galveston).

The Spaniards settled the island in 1816, under Luis Aury. But they soon lost control of it to the pirate chieftain Jean Lafitte and his cohorts, who used it as a base from which to prey on the Spanish galleon traffic. The Spanish were unable to curtail Lafitte's plundering, and Galveston remained a nest of looters, buccaneers, slave traders, gamblers, and desperadoes until 1821, when the US Navy ordered Lafitte to leave. He departed, burning Galveston behind him in its first great disaster.

The first English-speaking settlement was established on Galveston Island in 1837, and in 1839 the city of Galveston was incorporated under the independent Republic of Texas. The town grew, despite yellow fever epidemics and recurrent hurricanes, and during the American Civil War it was the largest Confederate port on the Gulf coast. Retaining some of its early flavor, Galveston long held out against Texas anti-gambling laws. Today, however, the city gives few indications of its turbulent past. It is a well-known beach resort, decked much of the year in oleanders and other tropical flowers. Despite the construction of a channel that can take shipping inland to the much larger city of Houston, Galveston remains a major port for cotton and sulphur, with shipbuilding and oil refining as chief industries.

The Galveston storm of 1900 has been called a "tornado," but the accepted American term for severe tropical storms originating, like this one, over West Indian waters, is "hurricane." On September 8 and 9, Galveston was lashed by winds at least up to 120 miles an hour. Since the weather instruments in Galveston broke at that point, the maximum velocity remains unknown. The barometer, meanwhile, fell to 28.48, the lowest on record for the United States up to that time. The storm hurled gulf waters through the sea-level streets with tidal-wave force. For both life and property, the hurricane was catastrophic. As the sky blackened and the wind howled, Galvestonians were trapped on their island. To venture into the storm was to court death (though many acts of heroism were performed). On the other hand, to remain under cover from the swirling waters and raging wind was to risk being helplessly crushed as sheltering structures collapsed.

News reports of the time still capture Galveston's terror. On September 9 the Richmond *Times-Dispatch* alerted its readers to a special bulletin from Dallas:

All Texas is in a keen state of doubt and uncertainty to-night concerning the fate of Galveston Island and city, which are shut off from communication. In everybody's mind is the suspicion that a calamity rests behind the lack of information from the Gulf coast. . . . It is said that the bridges leading from the mainland to the island have been swept away by the terrible fury of the wind and the rolling up of the water in the bay, and if this is so it is not seen how the town could have escaped.

When, after another 24 hours, boats finally were able to make the crossing, the spectacle of flattened and desolated Galveston was worse than anything anyone had imagined. The death toll was continually revised upward during succeeding days, until Galveston's dead were estimated at between 5,000 and 8,000. The need to avoid disease by disposing of the bodies at once was so great that those killed could not be very carefully counted. Many persons who were never found were simply presumed to have been swept out to sea. Somewhere between one-seventh and one-fifth of Galveston's population perished.

In addition, almost all of the buildings were struck, and many disappeared entirely. Property damage was estimated at between $20 million and $25 million. Because the best of the cotton crop was then being shipped out through Galveston, the New York Stock Exchange dipped sharply when rumors of the disaster at Galveston first came in.

Galveston's state was desperate immediately after the storm. Fresh water and supplies had been wiped out; electricity was gone, and telegraphic services cut off; the survivors were unorganized and thoroughly exhausted; and at least 8,000 persons were homeless. Amid civil chaos, vandals began looting and robbing and mutilating the dead. In response, entry to the island was soon tightly controlled, martial law was established, and vandals were summarily shot. As soon as possible, Galveston's mayor and other surviving leaders wired urgent pleas for help to high officials of Texas and the federal government, including President William McKinley, and to newspapers throughout the nation. Assistance poured in. The military garrison at Galveston had suffered no less than the civilian population. The US Army forwarded essential supplies, including thousands of tents for the homeless. Doctors traveled to the stricken city from as far away as New York City. And Clara Barton, the famous nurse, offered her services. All across the land, collections of money and clothes were taken up for the people of Galveston.

After burial of the dead and satisfaction of the community's most elementary wants, a major question confronted the populace: should they remain and reconstruct Galveston, or emigrate to a potentially less dangerous place? Some families left Galveston, but the majority determined to stay. An early decision of the local railroad to rebuild extensive facilities at Galveston boosted morale and insured the city's future as a port.

To guard against repetition of the disaster, the city undertook a major feat of engineering — the raising of the level of the entire city and the building of a reinforced concrete seawall along the Gulf front. Some eight miles long, the wall was 17 feet high (approximately a foot and a half higher than the storm's highwater mark). An eight-lane boulevard now runs on top of the seawall, overlooked by large resort hotels, and at its base lies the Gulf beach. The entire city — now between 6 and 17 feet above sea level — was raised from 1 to 15 feet above its former level, proportional to the seawall's height. The grade was raised by pumping sand from the Gulf. While the work was in progress, houses left standing were propped up on stilts, an elevated structure was built to carry streetcar lines, and planks supported by tall poles were used to form sidewalks. When the fill was completed, paved streets, sidewalks, and streetcar tracks were relaid, and trees and shrubbery were planted. And, to link the city with the mainland, a two-mile steel and reinforced concrete causeway was built across Galveston Bay with a roadway and railroad tracks. Another long causeway now connects the city with Texas City, also on the mainland. Galveston's harbor, which now has berths for 50 ships, also was reconstructed in 1900.

When a second vicious hurricane hit Galveston in 1915, the reconstructions of 1900 held, proving their critical role in the city's survival. Only in 1961 did a hurricane damage Galveston's defenses against the sea so badly that much of the work of 1900 had to be redone.

The people of Galveston changed more than the physical lines of their city in 1900. They also altered their form of government in the aftermath of the storm. Since the mayor and city council were clearly unable to cope with the enormous problems of recovery from the catastrophe, the governor of Texas appointed a five-man commission to govern Galveston during the crisis period. Each commissioner was in charge of a specific phase of the administration, and together they legislated for the whole city. In 1901, the crisis over, Galveston was again ready to elect officials. However, the citizens petitioned the governor to let them retain the commission as their permanent form of government.

The commission form, which became known as the Galveston Plan, was widely adopted in American cities in succeeding years. It gave US cities their first alternative to the traditional but frequently ill-functioning mayor-and-council plan of government. The new arrangement had a flaw of its own, however: in a case in which commissioners split on policy, there was no machinery for resolution. Two decades later, another new form of city government provided a way out of such impasses. This was the manager-and-council plan, which was destined to overtake the commission plan in popularity. Interestingly, this plan also was launched by a catastrophe. Dayton, Ohio, put it into practice as an emergency measure following a severe flood in 1913. Together, the Galveston Plan and the manager-and-council plan were important in helping to mitigate corruption in American city governments during the first half of the 20th century.

St. Augustine, Nation's Oldest City, Founded

The 400th birthday of St. Augustine, Florida, on September 8, 1965, was a reminder of the nation's Spanish heritage — as in the Days in Spain fiesta, which commemorates the city's earliest history annually in August today. At the time of St. Augustine's quadricentennial, many US citizens — whose history books had placed more stress on the 13, predominantly British,

original colonies — found it something of a shock to be reminded that St. Augustine's founding took place 55 years before the Pilgrims ever set foot on Plymouth Rock and 42 years before the historic settlement at Jamestown, Virginia.

Spain's claim to Florida — a huge region that in Spanish minds covered most of the Southeast — dated from 1513, when Juan Ponce de León first passed that way. The later explorations of other Spaniards notwithstanding, the claim rested rather casually in the Spanish grasp until 1564, when a group of French Huguenots established Fort Caroline at the mouth of Florida's St. Johns River (10 miles northeast of what is now Jacksonville). Potentially, this was a splendid spot from which to prey upon Spanish treasure ships, a possibility that was not lost upon King Philip II of Spain. He commissioned his leading admiral, the brilliant Don Pedro Menéndez de Avilés, to drive out the French Protestants and named him proprietor of any colony he managed to establish in Florida.

Menéndez first entered the Bay of St. Augustine on August 28, 1565, the feast day of the saint for whom he named the bay, before sailing north to reconnoiter the French position. Menéndez returned to St. Augustine, disembarking his colonists on September 6 and 7 and ordering hasty fortification against an anticipated French attack. It was not until the next day, September 8, that the Spaniards officially dedicated St. Augustine "with many banners spread, to the sound of trumpets and salutes of artillery." Mass was said, and Menéndez, kneeling to kiss the cross, claimed the land in the name of Spain.

When the French appeared as expected several days later, what Menéndez's chronicler called a miracle took place, although the French undoubtedly called it something else. Before they could enter the harbor, much less attack, their ships were driven off by a hurricane and wrecked. During their absence, Menéndez attacked their half-empty Fort Caroline — now reconstructed as a national memorial — killing 132 Huguenots in one hour. Later he found the shipwreck survivors and had them massacred, "not as Frenchmen but as Lutherans." (Members of a Spanish garrison that Menéndez left behind at Fort Caroline were later hanged by friends of his French victims — "not as . . . Spaniards but as murderers," according to the friends.)

The Spanish victories marked the beginning of two and a half centuries of Spanish rule, interrupted by only a short interval of British control (1763–1783) and not ended finally until July 17, 1821, when Florida formally passed from Spain to the United States under the terms of the Adams-Onís Treaty (see February 22). Since the Spanish period of its history was so much longer than any other, it is not surprising that St. Augustine observances tend to emphasize that era.

This, at any rate, was the case with the city's yearlong, 400th birthday celebration, which took place with the participation of the federal, state, county, and municipal governments and the cooperation both of the Spanish government and of Latin American governments through the Organization of American States. After preliminary events spaced over several months, the anniversary year began in earnest on August 28, 1965. Opening day events included a band concert, open house, and dedication ceremonies for a commemorative stamp at St. Augustine's Castillo de San Marcos, now a national monument. The National Park Service, which administers this fortress, undertook extensive improvements in honor of the quadricentennial. It also reconstructed the Cubo Line, which once protected the city, and restored the city gate area.

Beyond the gate, on historic St. George Street and elsewhere, visitors could see other refurbishing and reconstruction — the restored houses and public buildings of Colonial St. Augustine, which are part of a 20-year, $20 million program to recreate the city as it appeared in the late 1700s and early 1800s. Included in the various house-museums are demonstrations of crafts, among them candle-dipping, weaving, baking, cigar-making, carpentry, and printing. The anniversary-linked reconstruction project, financed by various levels of government with private, corporate, and foundation support, was initiated with the Florida legislature's establishment of the St. Augustine Historical Restoration and Preservation Commission in 1959. The undertaking led President John F. Kennedy to recall how Colonial Williamsburg, Virginia, has symbolized "the bond between English-speaking peoples" and anticipate "how valuable it will be to have a similar symbol of the cultural heritage which came to us from Hispanic-American sources."

National, local, and foreign dignitaries arriving in St. Augustine for the quadricentennial participated in dedication ceremonies that marked the unveiling of restoration projects and opening of exhibits from August 29 through September 5. These included Spain's $350,000 Casa del Hidalgo (now a house-museum and Spanish National Tourist Office) and the Pan American Center, which was officially opened by the secretary-general of the Organization of American States.

For five succeeding evenings, St. George Street was the setting for a large-scale birthday celebration known as Days in Spain — beginning with a costumed procession on Saturday, September 4, and continuing with such features as nightly fireworks displays, a beard contest, Spanish and French sword fighting, continuous entertainment, and offerings of food and games at gaily decorated booths. The fiesta came to a climax with the cutting of an enormous birthday cake bearing 400 candles on September 8.

An earlier highlight of that day was a solemn anniversary mass and founder's commemoration at the Mission of Nombre de Diós, located on the site of Menéndez's landing. Near the mission are the illuminated, 200-foot-high cross of stainless steel, the Votive Church, and the library and research center, which were erected as part of the Catholic Diocese of St. Augustine's $1 million quadricentennial construction program. The library has as a central exhibit the parish records of St. Augustine, dating from 1594 — the oldest records written in what is now the United States.

Paul Green's specially composed symphonic drama, *Cross and Sword*, recounting the history of St. Augustine's first two years, was presented evenings throughout the summer in the 2,000-seat St. Augustine Amphitheater, which was built in connection with the quadricentennial. It has been an annual summer feature ever since. Other quadricentennial-related events were scattered throughout 1966 — until September 8, when the yearlong celebration came to a close as it had begun, with St. Augustine's annual Days in Spain fiesta.

In more recent years, the Days in Spain has continued as an annual birthday celebration, although now it is generally staged in mid-August. The earlier date was adopted because more people are able to attend the fiesta during the summer, before Labor Day and the beginning of the school year. The fiesta, sponsored by the St. Augustine Jaycees, was instituted in the mid-1950s as a relatively small event, but has since expanded in both scope and size. It now continues for four days, and attendance ranges from 20,000 to 25,000 persons.

The Days in Spain originally took place on Aviles Street. In 1964, however, the location was changed to St. George Street — the *Calle Real* of the Spanish colonial period — where restoration of many of the buildings has been carried out. The gracious structures with their balconies and colorful gardens provide an appropriate setting for the Spanish-style fiesta. In addition, banners and flags in the Spanish colors of red and yellow, varicolored Spanish shawls, and gay flower baskets decorate the area in the heart of the old city.

Typical of the fiesta program was the 1972 Days in Spain, held from Wednesday, August 16, through Saturday, August 19. On Wednesday evening the mayor of St. Augustine and the chairman of the St. Johns County Commission officially opened the festivities with a ribbon-cutting ceremony just south of the city gates on St. George Street. Every evening, free entertainment with a Spanish flavor was provided at two stage areas, along St. George Street, and from the overhanging balconies of the old houses. The four hours of entertainment included vocalists, instrumentalists, three dance groups, strolling guitarists, and accordionists. Members of a 12-man Jaycee Sword Fighting Unit, costumed as swashbuckling French and Spanish soldiers, struggled to take possession of Florida by fighting mock duels twice each night along St. George Street, to the delight of the crowds. Another highlight of the festivities was the beard-growing contest, with prizes awarded for the most authentic Spanish-style beards.

In addition to the entertainment, some 40 concession booths, featuring novelties, games, Spanish souvenirs, and a variety of edibles, were run by local civic and religious organizations. One favorite fiesta delicacy is *fromajardis*, a cheese pastry known from colonial times. Cotton candy, Spanish bean soup, foot-long chili dogs, and confetti eggs (*casarones*) were among the other tempting offerings. Adding to the fiesta's interest were the various demonstrations of crafts in some of the restored buildings. Children were treated to pony rides, a puppet show, games, and other amusements. The climax of Days of Spain came on the final evening with the traditional lighting and cutting of an immense birthday cake — this time decorated with 407 candles and a replica of the Castillo de San Marcos. City officials cut and passed out slices to several thousand fiesta-goers.

On the city's anniversary in 1972, a "second" birthday celebration, called La Fiesta de Menéndez, was staged. The festivities began at 9:00 A.M. with a reenactment of Menéndez's landing, staged by the St. Augustine Jaycees at the Mission of Nombre de Diós, and followed by an outdoor mass on the mission grounds. The day's other events included the dedication of a bronze statue of Menéndez, cast from the original, which stands in Avilés, Spain, St. Augustine's sister city and the birthplace of the Spanish leader. The statue was erected in front of St. Augustine's new city hall. Dignitaries from Spain and the governor of Florida presided over an official luncheon, and there was an open house at the Castillo de San Marcos. Evening activities included a dinner and gala ball held at Flagler College in a fund-raising effort to restore the Villalonga House, a colonial structure on St. George Street, which dates from 1800.

SEPTEMBER 9

California Admission Day

On September 9, 1850, President Millard Fillmore signed into law a bill that made California the 31st state of the United States. The act of Congress admitting California to the Union was the culmination of a confused political period extending back into the previous 30 years of California history.

California, once a Spanish possession, had become a Mexican province in the early 1820s, in the wake of Mexico's successful revolt against Spain. The Californios, including several hundred Americans who had migrated to the area, grew increasingly dissatisfied with Mexican rule. They briefly asserted their independence in 1836 and drove out the last Mexican governor in 1845. Under the influence of the American explorer John C. Frémont, a somewhat ragged band of American "revolutionaries" conducted a surprise attack on the Mexican presidio in the pueblo of Sonoma on June 14, 1846. They surrounded the house of the commandant, General Mariano G. Vallejo, and seized the garrison in a practically bloodless battle. The frontiersmen's army then hauled down the Mexican flag, raised its own Bear flag over the drowsy Sonoma plaza, and proclaimed the independence of the province. Designed principally by William L. Todd, cousin of Mary Todd Lincoln, the flag was a piece of unbleached cotton bordered at the bottom by a broad red-flannel stripe. An uneven five-pointed red star was painted in the upper left-hand corner and, to the right of it, the crude figure of a grizzly bear. The animal was so poorly drawn that it was even mistaken for a pig. A motto read: "A bear stands his ground always, and as long as the stars shine we stand for our cause."

The short-lived talk of making California an independent republic came to an abrupt halt three weeks later when the issue merged with a larger question: the US declaration of war on Mexico on May 13, 1846. When the news of the war finally reached California, Commodore John D. Sloat of the US Navy captured the Californian capital of Monterey on July 7, as an act of war; raised the Stars and Stripes over the customhouse; and claimed California as a military possession of the United States. Two days later the Bear flag was hauled down from the Sonoma plaza.

The Treaty of Guadalupe Hidalgo of February 2, 1848, which ended the Mexican War, arranged for the cession of California to the United States. The federal government was therefore obligated to provide a civil government for the region. Settlement of California's political status soon became even more pressing, as news spread that James W. Marshall, while establishing a sawmill for John A. Sutter on the south fork of the American River at Coloma, had discovered the fabulous riches of a mother lode on January 24, 1848. The discovery touched off the California gold rush.

As thousands of easterners migrated to California, the congressional debate about what should be done with this area of great national importance grew bitter and was deadlocked over the question of slavery. The Union had 15 states without slavery, 15 with, and the admission of California to statehood would upset this delicate balance. After a confused period in which Spanish law, American law, and military law were simultaneously administered in California, Brigadier General Benet Riley, the area's military governor, issued a proclamation on June 3, 1849, "recommending the formation of a State constitution, or a plan for a Territorial government." However, the organizers of California — in no mood to wait for congressional agreement — never thought seriously about territorial status. Forty-eight delegates met at a constitutional convention in Colton Hall, Monterey, on September 1, 1849. On October 10 they adopted a state constitution, which was ratified overwhelmingly by the people of California on November 13 and put into effect a month later. On December 15 the state legislature convened at San Jose, and on December 20 Peter H. Burnett was inaugurated as the first governor.

On that same day, Brigadier General Riley issued a proclamation: "A new executive having been elected and installed into office in accordance with the provisions of the constitution of the State, the undersigned hereby resigns his powers as Governor of California." The highest US official in California had recognized California as a state, although legally it had no right to declare itself such without federal action.

The action precipitated an argument that lasted eight months in Congress. Since the founders of California had explicitly included in the constitution adopted at Monterery a clause forbidding slavery forever, the debate was prolonged by proslavery members of Congress, who desperately fought to prevent the admission of a new free state.

From January to September 1850 threats of dissolution of the Union, if California was admitted, were frequently made. The decision in favor of admission was due largely to the flowery eloquence of Senator William Seward of New York, who swayed Senate members with glowing descriptions of California as "the youthful Queen of the Pacific, in robes of freedom gorgeously inlaid with gold," and with this ringing cry:

Let California come in. California, that comes from the clime where the West dies away into the rising East. California, which bounds at once the empire and the continent.

California was finally admitted as a free state in the momentous Compromise of 1850, worked out by Henry Clay. Thus California, cut off from direct contact with the 30 states in the East, entered the Union less than three years after gold had been discovered within its precincts. Sharing a distinction possessed by the original 13 states and Texas, it did not pass through customary territorial status.

News of admission came belatedly to the 92,597 inhabitants of California. On October 18 the ship *Oregon*, having rounded South America's Cape Horn, sailed into San Francisco Bay with guns booming and masts dressed with flags to announce the good tidings. Business halted, and the pioneer city assumed a carnival atmosphere with fireworks and street dancing as the populace celebrated through the night. This riotous spontaneous celebration was considered too undignified to mark the occasion properly; a formal program followed on October 29. A paltry number of spectators watched the big parade on that day, however, since nearly everyone preferred to join in the line of march.

On September 9, 1851, the first anniversary of statehood, the Society of California Pioneers staged literary exercises, an observance repeated yearly until 1874. The Pioneers gained possession of the historic Bear flag after it had been briefly shown in Boston and Washington, D.C., carried it in the 1855 California Admission Day parade, and continued to display it until their organization was superseded on July 11, 1875, by the Native Sons of the Golden West. Dedicated to the remembrance of the history of California, the Native Sons assumed sponsorship of the Admission Day ceremonies. As their first activity, they directed the 25th anniversary celebration in San Francisco in 1875, which included a picnic, dancing, literary exercises, and a parade featuring French Zouaves. The Native Sons also continued to use the Bear flag in fraternal and patriotic ceremonies until the original was destroyed in the San Francisco earthquake and fire of 1906. Its likeness, however, remains a living emblem, flying proudly, especially on Admission Day, since on February 3, 1911, the California legislature adopted it as the state flag.

In 1879 the governor of California gave official notice to Admission Day by proclaiming the day a holiday, a practice continued yearly through 1888, when the 40th anniversary of the discovery of gold aroused great enthusiasm for commemorating the state's past. Admission Day became a statutory holiday the following year. With a brief exception, from September 10, 1953, through September 8, 1955, when the observance was temporarily designated as an optional state holiday, it has remained a mandatory state holiday in California. Public schools, banks, city and state offices and courts are closed, although stores, federal offices and courts remain open, and mail is delivered.

While many Californians use the opportunity to go to beaches and picnic grounds, an official program is sponsored by the Native Sons of the Golden West and assisted by the Native Daughters of the Golden West. The location for this formal observance shifts from year to year. There are also several smaller celebrations on the local level. Many communities in Northern California stage Old West parades, while San Diego commemorates the anniversary with all-day festivities in Old Town Plaza, where the city began in 1769. In addition to mariachi groups and dancing, there is a reenactment of the 1846 flag-raising ceremony, when the Stars and Stripes was unfurled from the plaza for the first time.

Typical of the official five-day program was the 1970 observance in Fairfield, near Vallejo in Solano County. The celebration featured golf, bowling, and softball tournaments on September 5, 6, and 7 and a civic banquet and dance on the evening of September 8. The colorful Admission Day parade began at 10:30 A.M. on September 9 and was followed by a barbecue in West Texas Park.

Two 20th century observances of Admission Day have been much more elaborate: the 75th Diamond Jubilee in 1925 and the Centennial of Statehood in 1950. The 1925 festivities, attended by Vice President Charles G. Dawes, numerous representatives of foreign countries, and officers of British, Japanese, Canadian, and American warships, opened in San Francisco on the evening of September 5 with a Spanish masquerade ball. On September 6 many visitors watched the rowing regatta, drum corps and drill team competitions, and automobile races, and 25,000 attended a fashion show. In the Labor Day parade on Monday, September 7, forty magnificent floats and 30,000 marchers depicted the history of labor and various individual occupations. An estimated 400,000 persons witnessed the army and navy parade on September 8, while on Admission Day itself the Native Sons and Daughters of the Golden West and the Citizens' Committee of the California Diamond Jubilee united to portray California's history in a grand pageant-parade. Floats had such themes as The American Flag Raising at Monterey, 1846, and The Landing of the Ship *San Antonio* at San Diego, 1769. Four of the 21 Franciscan missions established in California under the Spanish were reconstructed faithfully. Included among the 55,000 participants were 45 "covered wagon" babies; descendants of the original Spanish settlers of California; and the great-granddaughter of General Vallejo, riding in his private carriage. The parade, extending for nearly 17 miles and watched by approximately 1.1 million spectators, took five hours and 15 minutes to pass the official reviewing stand. September 10 was devoted to athletic contests, while on September 11 Haydn's oratorio *The Creation* was performed in the Exposition Auditorium. The Diamond Jubilee closed on September 12 with a night parade. Thousands of pounds of colored fire material, burned on the roofs of more than 100 high buildings along the line of march, provided spectacular overhead illumination.

A second great Admission Day celebration took place in 1950, when extensive centennial programs were staged in numerous places throughout the state. In San Francisco an eight-day pageant, entitled California's Fabulous Century, was held on the grounds of the historic Presidio. A record-breaking, six-hour parade portrayed the century of statehood, and a huge birthday cake with three tiers and 100 candles was a major part of the celebration at the city's Civic Center. In Los Angeles the California Story pageant, held for five evenings in the Hollywood Bowl, emphasized the state's admission and utilized a 200-voice civic chorus, 200 square-dancers, covered wagons, and stagecoaches. In Sacramento the Post Office Department presented the governor of California with the new 3-cent stamp commemorating California statehood. From August 1 through September 9 in San Diego, an exhibit at Balboa Park paid tribute to the role of newspaper men and women in the early progress of the state, and a pageant, The Golden Pueblo, highlighted important events in local and state history.

Civil Rights Act of 1957

Following widespread opposition to the 1954 US Supreme Court decision ordering desegregation of public schools (see May 17) and the use, in some places, of economic pressure, intimidation, or violence to delay desegregation and discourage blacks from exercising their right to vote, the US Congress took action aimed at protecting the rights of all. The Civil Rights Act of 1957, the first such measure since the Reconstruction, became law on September 9, 1957.

The law, important in the movement for civil rights that subsequently swept the country, provided the basis for many of the actions taken by the federal government to protect rights; spelled out methods of enforcement for the principles set forth in the 13th, 14th, and 15th amendments to the Constitution; and made clear the role of federal district courts in hearing cases under federal civil rights laws. Specifically, the act gave the US attorney general the power to apply federal court injunctions against any violation, or threatened violation, of individual voting rights. The act also authorized civil contempt proceedings without juries to secure compliance with law. And it eliminated state requirements as qualifications for federal jury service.

Two other important provisions of the Civil Rights Act of 1957 authorized creation of a special civil rights division within the US Justice Department—which subsequently initiated hundreds of legal actions against the infringement or attempted infringement of blacks' rights, and established the six-member, bipartisan US Commission on Civil Rights. The commission was armed with subpoena powers to investigate alleged deprivation of voting rights, examine federal laws and policies in regard to equal protection of the laws, and look into any legal developments constituting a denial of such equal protection.

Valuable as the act was as a tool in the march toward equality, it was not in itself sufficient. It was succeeded by other rights legislation and by alternating setbacks and gains in the continuing drive for civil rights. That drive constituted a major national effort in the third quarter of the 20th century.

SEPTEMBER 10

John Smith Assumes Jamestown Council Presidency

John Smith, one of the first English colonists in America, was born in Willoughby, Lincolnshire, in 1580. He left England at about 16 and became a military adventurer abroad, fighting in wars against the Turks, probably until 1604. On his return to England he developed an interest in the London Company (sometimes called the Virginia Company) and became a member of the company-financed expedition that in 1607

established at Jamestown, Virginia, the first permanent English settlement in America.

Smith, whom historians have alternately criticized for boastfulness and exaggeration and praised for bravery and resourcefulness, had his ups and downs with the other settlers. When they set sail for Virginia in 1606, he was named in the secret sailing orders as a member of the council for the new community. But during the voyage he was charged with sedition and imprisoned, and, when the ship landed and the secret instructions containing his name were opened, it was decided that he had forfeited his right to sit in the council.

During the colony's bleak first year, the settlers were malnourished and wracked by disease. Their gentlemen leaders, unprepared for frontier hardships, were also unaccustomed to work. Smith went out on various foraging expeditions, explored and mapped the country surrounding Jamestown, defended the community, compelled the settlers to work, and warded off starvation by contriving to trade trinkets with the Indians for corn.

He also found time to pen a personal narrative — *A True Relation of Such Occurrences and Accidents of Noate As Hath Hapned in Virginia since the First Planting of that Collony* (1608), the first book published about America and the most respected of his writings. So successful were Smith's undertakings that he was permitted to take his seat in the council in 1607 and was elected its president in July 1608. A friend, Scrivener, acted in Smith's place until his return from an exploratory trip on September 7. Smith assumed his presidential duties three days later, on September 10, 1608.

Though he has been described as "in all but name" the leader of the settlement, his council presidency was short-lived. A new charter was granted for the Jamestown colony in 1609, and Smith, of whom some of the highborn settlers approved and whom others found intolerable, was left out in the reorganization of government.

He returned to England the same year and thenceforth devoted himself to exploration and to written reminiscences, which encouraged interest in the New World and grew more colorful as the years went by. His *Map of Virginia . . . ,* containing a remarkable map and a vivid account of the new land and its original inhabitants, appeared in 1612. Two years later he led an expedition that explored and mapped the American coast from the Penobscot River to Cape Cod. Smith was responsible for the name New England — bestowed on the region at his request by the Prince of Wales; and it is said that such works as his *Description of New England* (1616) proved useful to the Pilgrims on their historic *Mayflower* voyage. In 1615 and 1617 Smith was frustrated in three other attempted voyages to New England. Causes of failure included bad weather and capture by pirates – or the French, according to a conflicting source. In either case, Smith was still able to bring out his *New Englands Trials,* a tract on fisheries, in 1620, and by 1622 had added to it a report of the colony at Plymouth.

The tradition that in 1608, during his stay at Jamestown, Pocahontas, daughter of the Indian chieftain Powhatan, prevailed upon her father to spare Smith's life is not included in the personal narrative Smith wrote at the time. The story, that appeared in Smith's much later *Generall Historie of Virginia, New-England, and the Summer Isles* (1624), oddly parallels his accounts of generous women who saved him from earlier, similar disasters in other lands. It is regarded as perhaps – though not necessarily – an exaggeration of what really happened.

Also fanciful in its own way was the name Pocahontas – given to the young Matoaka by Indians who believed that knowledge of her real name would enable foreign settlers to cast an evil eye upon her. This precaution notwithstanding, she was taken prisoner by the English in 1612. After her conversion to Christianity her name was changed again, this time to Rebecca. A further change of name took place in April of 1614, when she was married to the colonist John Rolfe – a union succeeded by some years of peace between the Indians and the English in Virginia. Two years after their marriage, Pocahontas went with Rolfe to England. A letter attributed to John Smith and dated 1616 called the sterling qualities of Pocahontas (including the disputed story) to the attention of Anne, consort of England's James I. Pocahontas was received with royal honors and presented to the court.

Pocahontas became ill and died as she was preparing to return to America in 1617. If she was born in 1595, as historians hesitantly surmise, she was about 22 years of age at the time. Her husband, John Rolfe – whose discovery of a method for curing tobacco laid the foundation for Virginia's later prosperity – died in Virginia in 1622, probably at the hands of the Indians. Prominent Virginians are numbered among the descendants of Thomas Rolfe, their son.

Smith, who remained in England, survived both John Rolfe and Pocahontas. His literary output included one work against which serious charges of fabrication have been leveled, though not proved: *The True Travels, Adventures, and Observations of Captaine John Smith,* published in 1630. He died in 1631, the year of publication of his last tract – *Advertisements for the Unexperienced Planters of New-England . . . .*

Most of Jamestown Island, where archeological explorations have exposed the outlines of the original settlement, is today part of the 9,430-acre Colonial National Historical Park, administered by the National Park Service. Some 20 acres of the island are owned by the Association for the Preservation of Virginia Antiquities, which cooperates with the Park Service in research and preservation efforts. Open or on view are a visitor center with information, narrated slides, and exhibits; the New Towne area where Jamestown expanded in about 1620; the colonists' first landing site; the ruin of the Old Church Tower, dating from 1639; the Memorial Church, built by the Colonial Dames of America over the foundations of the original; and sculptured likenesses of Pocahontas and John Smith, among other attractions. Replicas of the ships that brought the original settlers are moored at Jamestown Festival Park, which is near the Colonial National Historical Park. Constructed by the Commonwealth of Virginia in 1957, the Jamestown Festival Park is a reconstruction of much of early Jamestown, administered by the Jamestown Foundation.

SEPTEMBER 11

Battle of Brandywine

In the summer of 1777 the British forces in America conducted two vigorous campaigns to end the movement for colonial independence. In New York State General John Burgoyne and Lieutenant Colonel Barry St. Leger undertook an unsuccessful joint operation against the American rebels, leading to the English surrender at Saratoga on October 17. In Pennsylvania General William Howe, the British commander in chief in North America, was able to capture the patriot capital at Philadelphia, after defeating George Washington's troops at Brandywine on September 11.

After leaving his winter quarters at Morristown, New Jersey, Washington in May 1777 had established his troops in a strong position at Middlebrook, New Jersey, where he could thwart any attempt by the British to move directly against Philadelphia from their post at New Brunswick. General Howe, unable to draw the Americans into battle, removed his troops in June to New York City; from there he planned to advance on Philadelphia by sea. On July 23 some 15,000 of his soldiers set sail from New York in more than 260 ships. Howe's armada reached Delaware Bay on July 29 but found the river approach to Philadelphia too well defended. The British general accordingly sailed instead to the head of Chesapeake Bay, where his troops disembarked on August 25. Worn down by the journey and the late summer heat, the British troops then started on the overland trek to Philadelphia.

Howe's peregrinations confused General Washington. However, despite misgivings that his adversary intended to sail up the Hudson River to join Burgoyne and St. Leger, the American commander decided to prepare to defend Philadelphia. When the British army reached Kennett Square on September 10, they found 11,000 rebels on the north side of Brandywine Creek, blocking their advance. The Pennsylvania militia under General John Armstrong defended the American left at Pyle's Ford, Generals Nathanael Greene and Anthony Wayne defended the center at Chadds Ford, and General John Sullivan was stationed at the right.

Howe decided to envelop the American flank, employing the same tactic that had previously given him victory on Long Island. He sent Baron Wilhelm von Knyphausen's division in a feint toward Chadds Ford and commanded General Charles Cornwallis's division to encircle Sullivan. When Knyphausen did not seriously attempt to advance, Washington guessed that Howe had divided his forces and planned a counterattack across Chadds Ford. Unfortunately, however, he gave up the idea when he received intelligence reports that incorrectly stated that Howe was not trying to outflank him.

Cornwallis crossed the Brandywine at Jeffries Ford, above the end of the American right flank, and fell upon Sullivan's men. The rebels fought bravely, encouraged by the presence of Washington and the young French Marquis de Lafayette, who received a leg wound in the battle. When General Greene committed the patriot reserves to Sullivan's aid, Knyphausen was able to cross Chadds Ford against little resistance. The Americans managed to hold their ground until sunset, when they withdrew in confusion.

British casualties totaled over 500, and American more than 1,000. Perhaps Howe could have destroyed Washington's army had he pursued it, but his men were too exhausted to endeavor a chase. The patriots escaped to fight more effectively on other days.

The Commonwealth of Pennsylvania today owns the Brandywine Battlefield, 50 acres of rolling ground in Delaware County, overlooking Chadds Ford and the scene of the conflict to the north and west. The Brandywine Battlefield Park Commission administers the site, which includes well-maintained picnic areas and excellent roads. C. Edwin Brumbaugh, an expert on the early houses of southeastern Pennsylvania, carried out the reconstruction of Washington's headquarters and the restoration of Lafayette's,

both on the grounds of the park. Three periods of American architecture appear in the restoration of the Gilpin house, which was Lafayette's headquarters: the original frame structure dates from the 17th century, the stone addition to the west from the mid-18th century, and the north wing from 1782.

The Navajo Nation Fair
Window Rock, Arizona

This is a movable event. See note on page xxvi.

The giant Navajo fair held annually at Window Rock, Arizona, the capital of the Navajo Nation, is the largest Native American fair in the United States. Not only Navajos but Indians representing many other tribes participate, demonstrating colorful traditional dances and exhibiting a wide variety of clothing, arts and crafts, and other facets of cultures that predate written history. The fair also represents the contribution of Indians to American history and is a practical example of cross-cultural influences between the Navajo people and the modern world.

The first Navajo Tribal Fair took place in 1908 in Shiprock, New Mexico, headquarters of the Northern Navajo Agency; it was the idea of the first superintendent of the agency, William T. Shelton. For many years Shelton had helped and guided the Navajo people, and he was eager to exhibit their products and crafts. The main attractions of the fair, in addition to exciting races and rodeos, were the fine vegetables, canned and preserved foods, improved breeds of animals, arts and crafts, and needlework of the Navajos.

The first Shiprock fair was such a success that it was decided that it would be held on an annual basis. In 1937, because of the ever-growing popularity of this fair, the first Window Rock fair was held, without detracting from the Shiprock event. However, unlike the Shiprock fair (the Northern Navajo fair, held in late September or early October), which continued even through World War II without a break in observance, the Window Rock fair was discontinued during the war and was not restaged until 1951. It has been held every year since then, usually during the second week in September, beginning on a Wednesday or Thursday and ending on the Sunday of that same week.

The Navajos, who make up America's largest Indian nation, have since incorporated much white culture into their three- or four-day fair schedule. A visitor to the fairgrounds on Friday or Saturday night can see an evening performance of Indian songs and tribal ceremonies. In another area, one may participate in a square dance with country and western music. In addition to exhibits of the ancient art of rug weaving and silver jewelry making for which the Navajos are famous, one can also visit the home arts and science exhibitions, the 4-H livestock judging, and the horticulture displays. For those who like excitement, the rodeo is performed every afternoon, and on Friday, Saturday and Sunday, just prior to the rodeo, horse races are held. An interstate parade takes place on Saturday.

With the exception of some corn dishes, the Navajo's native foods are infrequently prepared, except on ceremonial occasions. But the fair offers many samples of traditional meals, barbecues, and the famous fry bread, for which a contest is held, the winner being announced on Sunday.

The Miss Navajo Pageant is one of the most popular attractions at the fair, and the contest begins on the first day. Contestants, wearing the traditional velvet blouse and the long, brightly colored, gathered skirt, range in age from 18 to 25 years and compete in a variety of activities every day through Friday. The crowning of the new Miss Navajo takes place on Friday evening. The winner of the pageant then travels several thousand miles during her reigning year as a representative of the Navajo people.

Although the Window Rock with its fair is a highlight of the Navajo country, there are many other places of interest. Occupying a four-corner area of the Southwest where Arizona, New Mexico, Colorado, and Utah join, the reservation of the Navajo Nation is some 200 miles wide and 135 miles north to south and offers some of the most scenic and breathtaking vistas in the Southwest. A high tableland, it is criss-crossed by spectacular canyons and sprinkled with eroded buttes and other natural formations, one of the most famous being Window Rock itself. The rock has been important for many centuries in the rites and legends of the Water Way Ceremony, and Navajo people call the formation Tse-ghahodzani, or "perforated rock." Years ago it was one of only four places where tribal medicine men went to get water for rain ceremonies. The "window," which was eroded by wind, water, and blowing sand, measures 48.31 feet from top to bottom and 57.28 feet from east to west.

This arid Indian country is a study in contrasts between modern methods of farming, government, and education and the ancient practices of the past. The Navajos, who prefer to call themselves *Diné*, like their ancestors, speak a language of the Athabaskan family. They still occupy the centuries-old *hogan*, which is a unique type of dwelling, built of sturdy logs and mud according to old traditions and religious observances.

Navajo women continue to practice the art and painstaking craft of weaving. When the demand for handwoven blankets decreased, the weavers were persuaded to make heavier pieces suitable for floor coverings. The process is laborious: after the wool is clipped from the sheep, it is washed, carded, spun into yarn, and dyed. The loom is then prepared, and the weaver, without any pattern or guide, begins to weave. A three-by-five-foot rug of modest design and average quality wool requires about 350 hours of work. (Rug designs are without significance; the so-called ceremonial rug is not used in any part of a Navajo rite.) With the passing years, weaving has declined in quantity, though not in quality.

The Navajo Tribal Museum is situated on the south side of Gorman Hall on the fairgrounds. The museum offers geology and archeology exhibits and includes a library and photographic collection as well. It is open to the public from 8:00 AM to 5:00 PM, seven days a week. Adjacent to the museum is the zoo, which was opened in the fall of 1962. Through the years the zoo has expanded to include many of the birds and mammals indigenous to the Navajo country.

SEPTEMBER 12

Maryland Defenders' Day

This day, a legal holiday in Maryland, marks the anniversary of the battle of North Point in the War of 1812. The battle was fought near Baltimore on September 12, 1814 — the day before the unsuccessful British bombardment of Baltimore's Fort McHenry inspired Francis Scott Key to write "The Star-Spangled Banner." The anniversary of the North Point battle — which special exercises in Baltimore and other parts of Maryland commemorate annually on the 12th — is observed more or less in conjunction with the anniversary of Key's composition. That event, which actually took place on September 14, has inspired Maryland and some other states from time to time to designate the 14th as National Anthem Day.

The War of 1812, which some have called the second War for Independence, had been going on since the US Congress declared war on Great Britain June 18, 1812. Despite scattered American successes in the first two years of conflict, the United States lacked the resources to match the naval superiority and other advantages of Great Britain. By late summer 1814, prospects for the young American nation appeared gloomy. The British had instituted a devastating blockade of the eastern seaboard and, under Admiral Sir Alexander Cochrane's plans, were diverting attention from Canadian border–Great Lakes campaigns by attacks on the East Coast. In August the British had attacked Washington and set fire to the White House and other public buildings; and Rear Admiral Sir George Cockburn, in command of British naval forces in the area, had threatened to burn Baltimore.

On September 11, 1814, the British sailed up Chesapeake Bay and entered the Patapsco River. Early the next morning they landed 6,000 troops at North Point, near Baltimore, and then continued up the Patapsco preparatory to bombarding Fort McHenry. That garrison was held by 1,000 troops under Major George Armistead — who would later be rewarded for his defense with an honorary lieutenant colonelcy. General Samuel Smith, a US senator from Maryland, also stood ready, commanding some 13,000 regulars and militiamen who had been assembled to defend the city.

When news of the British landing at North Point reached Smith, he sent Brigadier General John Stricker with a force of about 3,200 to watch the movements of the British and act as conditions required. Stricker accordingly sent ahead about 150 men, accompanied by sharpshooters, to reconnoiter. General Robert Ross, advancing up North Point in command of the British troops, had ridden to the head of his men when the sharpshooters, firing from concealment, killed him.

The British force then moved forward under the next in command and met the first line of General Stricker's army. During this battle of North Point, the Americans fought gallantly for two hours. They then fell back half a mile and waited for a follow-up attack that never came. Toward sunset, they withdrew in unhurried fashion to the defenses on the perimeter of Baltimore. There, joined by reinforcements and still waiting, they spent the rainsoaked night.

Instead of attacking in that direction, however, the British troops halted and camped on the field, also waiting — while their ships stole up the Patapsco River toward Fort McHenry. At six the next morning — the 13th — the ships began their bombardment of the fort from a distance of two miles (the range best suited to their guns). Back on the North Point side of the city, the British troops vainly waited for the bombs to succeed in their work, holding themselves ready to join in what had been planned as an amphibious assault on the fort. But the bombardment, spectacular as it was, was unsuccessful.

Days earlier and miles away, a young American lawyer named Francis Scott Key and an American intermediary named John Skinner had boarded one of the British ships to negotiate release of Dr. William Beanes, a friend of Key's whom the British held prisoner. The negotiations were successful, but at a price: Key and Skinner were held by the British, remaining unwilling witnesses until after the attack on Baltimore.

The bombardment went on for some 25 hours. When it ceased, some time after daybreak on September 14, Key and his friends did not know whether the fort had surrendered. Anxiously, they waited for the day to grow brighter and a breeze to unfurl the limp banner above the fort before they could see through their glasses that it was the American flag. Relieved and inspired, Key exuberantly wrote on the back of an old letter a rough draft of the words that were to become the United States' national anthem. Joyously, they began:

O say can you see, by the dawn's early light,
What so proudly we hailed at the twilight's
last gleaming,
Whose broad stripes and bright stars through the
perilous fight
O'er the ramparts we watched, were so gallantly streaming?
And the rockets' red glare, the bombs bursting
in air,
Gave proof through the night that our flag
was still there:
O say does that star-spangled banner yet wave
O'er the land of the free and the home of
the brave?

That night, in a Baltimore hotel, Key wrote the words out in full. The next morning he read them to Judge Joseph H. Nicholson, his brother-in-law, who had been one of the defenders of the fort. The judge liked them so well that he took them to the press of the Baltimore *American* and had them printed in handbill form under the title of "The Defence of Fort McHenry." The song subsequently appeared in the Baltimore *Patriot* on September 20 and the Baltimore *American* on September 21 with the notation that it was to be sung to the tune of "To Anacreon in Heaven," a popular old English drinking song. Tradition has it that the anthem was first sung in public by actor Ferdinand Durang, either in or in front of McConkey's Tavern, next door to the Holliday Street Theater.

On October 18 — when it finally seemed certain the British would not return, and Baltimore's mayor proclaimed a day of thanksgiving — newspaper advertisements for a production at that theater announced that it would be followed by the singing of "a much admired new song . . . called The Star Spangled Banner." The same title was used for the sheet music, which was published at about the same time.

The popularity of "The Star-Spangled Banner," which evidently was an instant hit in Baltimore, grew more slowly in the rest of the nation. It was often sung by Union soldiers during the

Civil War, however, and although it still competed for attention with such other favorites as "America" and "Hail Columbia," it gained currency, especially in the armed forces, in the post–Civil War decades. In 1904 the secretary of the navy directed that it be played at morning and evening colors throughout the navy. In response to an executive order by President Woodrow Wilson, the army and navy have regarded "The Star-Spangled Banner" as the national anthem ever since 1916. It was not until years later, however, that Congress confirmed that order in an act signed by President Herbert Hoover on March 3, 1931.

Baltimore abounds with reminders of the battles of September 1814; one of the most prominent is the 56-foot Battle Monument at Calvert and Fayette streets, which was begun in 1815, completed in 1825, and surrounded by a landscaped park in 1964. The star-shaped Fort McHenry, one of the few places in the nation where the American flag is properly flown 24 hours a day, is a national monument and historic shrine. Two other places where the flag flies night and day are the Star-Spangled Banner Flag House at Pratt and Albemarle streets, now a museum of the War of 1812, where Mary Young Pickersgill made the Fort's historic flag; and the grave of Key — who died at Baltimore on January 11, 1843 — in Frederick, Maryland. What is thought to be the earliest manuscript of "The Star-Spangled Banner" is on view at the Maryland Historical Society, 201 West Monument Street, Baltimore.

One of the ways in which Defenders' Day is currently marked is by an annual mock bombardment of Fort McHenry on the Sunday nearest September 12. But Baltimore's commemorations of the battles of September 1814 have been going on for a long time.

One notable commemoration was The Star Spangled Banner Centennial in 1914. It began on September 8 with the unveiling of a tablet on the US frigate *Constellation*. (Now restored and berthed at Pier 4, Pratt Street, at the foot of Market Place, the *Constellation*, built in 1797, was the first ship of the US Navy.) The centennial was also marked with the dedication at Fort McHenry of a bronze memorial statue to Major Armistead and an address entitled "The Flag" by Secretary of State William Jennings Bryan, whom President Wilson had appointed to speak for him at the exercises.

Efforts of the National Star-Spangled Banner Commission, organized in the centennial year, to have "The Star-Spangled Banner" accepted as the national anthem continued after the 100th anniversary celebration was over. Another aftermath of the 1914 observance was the use of left-over centennial funds for the erection of a statue of General Smith, unveiled in 1918. It now stands in the center of a small park named for him, at Pratt and Light streets. In 1922 President Warren G. Harding dedicated a monument to Key and the Fort McHenry defenders on the grounds of the fort. Key had previously been honored (in 1911) by a major monument on Eutaw Place at Lanvale Street.

Baltimore's earlier celebrations were surpassed in 1964, when the city marked The Star-Spangled Banner Sesquicentennial with a summer-long series of events. They included historic pageants, special exhibits, band concerts, sailing regattas, jousting tournaments, dances, historic tours, a national baton-twirling contest, an antique automobile rally, horse shows, and county and state fairs.

The celebration reached its climax on Defenders' Day weekend. On Friday, September 11, members of the Society of the War of 1812, holding their national convention in Baltimore in honor of the anniversary, boarded the steamer *Port Welcome* for a daylong tour to Annapolis, the state capital. On Defenders' Day Baltimore's Patterson Park was the setting for a US Army band concert and presentation of the "Story of the Flag" by the US 3rd Infantry ("Old Guard") Fife and Drum Corps. At Navy Dock, Fort McHenry, the assistant secretary of the interior presented a plaque designating the USS *Constellation* a national historic landmark. Governor J. Millard Tawes and other dignitaries were on hand for the ceremony. The sesquicentennial banquet and ball were held that evening in a large hotel.

The conclusion and climax of the summer-long Star-Spangled Banner festival came on Sunday, which was designated a joint observance of Defenders' Day, Constitution Day, and I Am an American Day. It began with the placing of wreaths by distinguished officials, as is customary on Defenders' Day, in the course of a patriotic pilgrimage to the city's numerous monuments and historic sites associated with the War of 1812. The afternoon portion of the program got under way with a band concert in Patterson Park, followed by a massive parade through city streets.

Celebrants who watched the long procession barely had time to prepare themselves for the climactic 150th Defenders' Day ceremony held that evening at Fort McHenry. That presentation began at 6:00, when boats of the Maryland Yacht Club passed in review. At 7:00 there was a concert of patriotic selections by an army band. After presentation of the colors by a color guard of the Maryland National Guard, the army's fife and drum corps repeated its dramatic "Story of the Flag." Later there were speeches by Vincent Godfrey Burns, the poet laureate of Maryland; Governor Tawes; and Baltimore's Mayor Theodore R. McKeldin. A display by Baltimore's fireboats, which came after the retiring of the colors, was followed by more patriotic band selections. Then, in a spectacular finale, the sesquicentennial observance came to a conclusion with the theretofore largest fireworks display in Maryland's history, presented as a reenactment of the bombardment of the fort. When it was over, the many thousands who had witnessed the mock bombardment joined in singing the national anthem. Seldom has it had a more resounding performance.

SEPTEMBER 13

John Barry Day

John Barry, a naval hero of the American Revolution, was born at Tacumshane, County Wexford, Ireland, in 1745. The exact date of his birth is unknown. While he was still young, his father apprenticed him to a ship captain, and when he was 14 he came to America, where he found employment on a ship trading from Philadelphia. Young Barry was hard working and ambitious. By his 21st birthday he had become the master of a schooner, and in the decade prior to the Revolution he commanded many fine trading vessels.

When hostilities between the colonies and Great Britain erupted in 1776, Barry immediately placed his naval skills at the disposal of his adopted homeland. The Continental Congress quickly accepted his aid and ordered him to outfit the first fleet sailing from Philadelphia. The Pennsylvania Council of Safety likewise enlisted Barry's talents and authorized him to build a ship for the province.

As commander of the brig *Lexington*, Barry was responsible for the first capture in battle of a British warship by a regularly commissioned Continental cruiser. The *Lexington*'s seizure of the British tender *Edward* occurred on April 17, 1776. In October of that year, the Continental Congress placed Barry seventh on its seniority listing of naval captains, and put him in command of the *Effingham*. However, the frigate, which was scheduled to put to sea in September 1778, never left the Delaware River. The British occupied Philadelphia before the *Effingham* was completed, and to prevent its capture General George Washington ordered that it be burned.

During the winter of 1777–1778 Barry harassed British supply boats in the lower Delaware River. He then took command of the 32-gun ship *Raleigh*. But ill luck again plagued Barry. Shortly after the *Raleigh* put to sea in September 1778, it encountered a 64-gun British warship and a frigate. A 48-hour chase ensued, and after a hard-fought battle the *Raleigh* was finally captured near the mouth of the Penobscot River in what is now Maine.

In the fall of 1780 Barry was put in command of the *Alliance* and ordered to take Colonel Henry Laurens to France on a diplomatic mission. On his return voyage he encountered two British war sloops, the *Atalanta* and the *Trepassy*. In the ensuing battle he was severely wounded, and the flag of the *Alliance* was shot away. But he continued to fight and forced the enemy to surrender. The captain of one of the ships had been killed, but the captain of the other, when taken aboard the *Alliance*, surrendered his sword. Barry took it and then returned it, saying: "You have merited it, sir. Your King ought to give you a better ship." The *Alliance* sailed for France again in the fall of 1781: after the battle of Yorktown, Barry's ship conveyed the Marquis de Lafayette and the Vicomte de Noailles back to their homeland.

As commander of the *Alliance*, Barry continued to inflict considerable damage on the British fleet until the end of the war. The January 1783 encounter between the *Alliance* and the British frigate *Sybil* is generally regarded as the last significant naval battle of the American Revolution.

Barry continued in the public service after the end of the war and made many suggestions for the improvement of the navy. President Washington, on June 4, 1794, appointed him senior captain of the new nation's naval forces. Although the rank of commodore had not yet been created, the officer in command of more than one ship was popularly known by that title. Barry qualified for this honor since he had twice been in charge of all the US ships in the West Indian waters.

The anniversary of Barry's death on September 13, 1803, is widely commemorated. The governors of Pennsylvania, Rhode Island, and Massachusetts proclaim the day as Commodore John Barry Day, and in New Jersey it is designated by law as "a day of annual special school observance." Philadelphia, Barry's home, faithfully keeps his memory alive. Each year on the Sunday nearest September 13, a number of ceremonies are held throughout the city. The city of Philadelphia sponsors a parade in which delegations from various Irish societies march. After the parade a commemorative ceremony is held at Independence Hall. Then the marchers reconvene at St. Mary's churchyard, where they lay a wreath on Barry's grave.

New York members of the Knights of Columbus also travel to Philadelphia to participate in ceremonies honoring Barry. On the Sunday nearest the anniversary of his death, a delegation from the Barry Council of the Knights of Columbus of Long Island, New York, attends mass at St. Mary's Church and then holds graveside services during which a wreath is traditionally laid. The Commodore Barry Assembly of the Fourth Degree Knights of Columbus of New York City conducts similar observances on the Sunday nearest Memorial Day.

A statue of Barry stands in Franklin Square in Washington, D.C. Thousands of Americans of Irish descent joined the 5,000 sailors and marines and a brigade of midshipmen from the US Naval Academy at Annapolis at its dedication on May 16, 1914. Another statue of Barry stands in Independence Square in Philadelphia. It was donated to the city by the Friendly Sons of St. Patrick on March 16, 1907.

Feast of St. John Chrysostom

St. John Chrysostom, patriarch of Constantinople and one of the great Christian doctors of the East, was one of the learned men of the early Church and is frequently compared with St. Jerome. The son of the commander of the imperial army in Syria, John was born at Antioch, probably between 344 and 347, and he notably influenced Christian thought. He was not called Chrysostom (from the Greek, meaning "golden-mouthed") until about 680. At that time, his reputation as one of the most brilliant orators of his time had survived him by nearly two and three-quarters centuries, and a church council decided to honor him by adding the name Chrysostom.

Since its calendar reform of 1969, the Roman Catholic church has observed the Feast of St. John Chrysostom, as a memorial, on September 13, the day before his death in the year 407. Syrian rite Catholics also observe this date. Those Episcopalians who mark the feast do so on an optional basis, on January 27, the anniversary of the translation of the saint's remains to Constantinople in 438, which was also the date observed by Roman Catholics from the 13th century until their calendar revision. Eastern Orthodox churches similarly commemorate the saint on January 27, but on other dates as well, including November 13, which is the date on which Byzantine and Coptic Catholics also observe his feast.

John's father died when he was a baby, and he was reared by his mother. When he was old enough, he studied oratory under a Roman rhetorician, having decided to become a lawyer. He soon excelled his teacher but felt called to the religious life and gave up law to devote himself to the study of the Bible.

On his mother's death about the year 375, John retired to the desert, near Antioch, and lived in the simplest possible manner as a monk. However, the rigors of his asceticism brought on an illness and he was forced to return to Antioch after some years. He was ordained as a deacon in 381, and as a priest five years later.

His inspired preaching attracted wide attention in the next dozen years, and he was consecrated archbishop of Constantinople in 398. He used the greater part of the revenues of his office for charity and came to be known as John the Almoner because of his concern for the poor. He also sought to bring about reforms in the life of the clergy and berated the wealthy — particularly the court of the Roman empress of the East, Eudoxia, and her husband, the emperor Arcadius — for their lack of charity. In the process he aroused the enmity of both his ecclesiastical and political superiors.

The result was that he was deposed from his archbishopric on false charges by an illegal synod and banished from Constantinople. His banishment was resented by the faithful, however — a circumstance that enraged the emperor and caused John first to be recalled temporarily and then exiled again, to a little town in the Armenian highlands. He was received kindly by the resident bishop, continued his Christian work among the people, and was much visited by his friends. This solace was denied him several years later, when he was ordered into still more distant exile. His destination was to be a town on the coast of the Black Sea, hundreds of miles away, at the very edge of the Roman Empire.

Already ill, John set out on foot to make the journey, but after traveling for three months he could go no farther. With the praise of God on his lips, he died at the chapel of Basiliscus, six miles from Comana, in the Roman province of Pontus (originally part of Cappadocia) on September 14, 407. Some Russian Orthodox churches commemorate the saint on the anniversary of this date.

Not until after his death was John's name officially restored to honor. In the year 438 his body was returned in solemn procession to Constantinople, and the new emperor, Thedosius II, did penance for his parents' offense. The legacy of John Chrysostom for other generations includes a large number of written works — sermons, homilies, commentaries on Scripture, treatises (including a classic one on the priesthood), and more than 200 letters. Declared the patron saint of orators by the Roman Catholic church on July 8, 1908, St. John Chrysostom is revered as a doctor of the church and as a church father by both the Roman Catholic church and the churches of the East. The Protestant Episcopal church honors him by including one of his prayers in its order of service.

SEPTEMBER 14

National Anthem Day

Various states from time to time declare September 14 — the anniversary of the day in 1814 when Francis Scott Key composed the words of what became the United States' national anthem — as National Anthem Day. Usually the observance is by proclamation of the governor. Maryland, where Key penned "The Star-Spangled Banner" after witnessing the unsuccessful British bombardment of Baltimore's Fort McHenry (see September 12, Maryland Defenders' Day) has been in the forefront of observing states.

US Forces Capture Mexico City

On September 14, 1847, US forces under the command of General Winfield Scott gained control of Mexico City. Scott's capture of the "halls of Montezuma" was the decisive campaign of this nation's war against Mexico (see May 13). The conquest led to General Antonio López de Santa Anna's surrender and to Mexico's acceptance early in 1848 of the Treaty of Guadalupe Hidalgo (see February 2). According to that document, Mexico recognized the Rio Grande as its northern boundary and ceded California and New Mexico (then comprising much of the US Southwest) to the United States in exchange for $15 million.

Scott's 1847 campaign against Mexico City followed the route taken by Hernando Cortes during his conquest of Mexico more than three centuries earlier. On March 9, 1847, the American commander landed his force of more than 10,000 men along the beaches southeast of Veracruz. The soldiers then set about establishing their positions in a wide arc to the rear of the city, thereby cutting the port off from the rest of Mexico. On March 22 this undertaking was completed, and Scott demanded the immediate surrender of Veracruz. When the Mexicans refused, the Americans began a land and naval bombardment of the city. After four days of continual shelling, negotiations for surrender started on March 26, and three days later American forces occupied the port.

Having gained control of Veracruz, Scott began the overland trek to Mexico City. With fewer than 9,000 troops the American general set out for the interior capital on April 8. His immediate objective was Jalapa, a town whose location 75 miles northwest of Veracruz and 4,250 feet above sea level made it free from the yellow fever that plagued the coastal lowlands. Proceeding along the national highway, Scott's forces advanced with little difficulty until they were about 20 miles from Jalapa. Then, on April 13, they encountered outlying enemy defenses at Plan del Río, just below the important mountain pass at Cerro Gordo.

Less than two months after his crushing defeat at Buena Vista in northern Mexico, General Santa Anna had reorganized his army and readied his troops to defend the route leading from Veracruz to Mexico City. Choosing to engage Scott's army at Cerro Gordo, the Mexican general used the natural terrain of the area and his 13,000-man force to advantage. He established defenses extending two miles from the high bluff and river (the Río del Plan) on his right, across the national highway to El Telégrafo (or Telegraph Hill, as the Cerro Gordo eminence was sometimes called) and another rise, La Atalaya, on his left.

Although the Mexican troops were well positioned, adroit reconnoitering by Scott's engineers, including Captains Robert E. Lee and George B. McClellan, disclosed a path leading to the enemy's left flank. Scott exploited this passage. After his men had cleared away rocks and underbrush, he moved his artillery along the route. Aided by this firepower, American forces were able to capture La Atalaya on April 17. The following morning, the troops commanded by General Gideon J. Pillow, a former law partner of President James K. Polk, undertook a diversionary attack against the Mexican right flank. Meanwhile the main body of American soldiers assaulted Santa Anna's strongest fortification at El Telégrafo. The struggle was brief. By 10:00 A.M. on April 18 the Mexican army retreated, leaving Scott and his men more than 3,000 prisoners, a large number of arms, and most important, control of the Cerro Gordo pass.

On April 19 Scott's troops marched into Jalapa, and three days later an expedition under the command of General William Jenkins Worth took control of the city of Perote. But as his army moved westward, Scott faced a difficult problem: many of his soldiers were 12-month volunteers, and their enlistments were due to expire in the middle of June. Scott pleaded his case and offered bounties to these volunteers to persuade them to extend their time with the army; but when his efforts failed, he reluctantly decided to release them at once. Thus, during the first week in May, about one-third of his forces returned to the coast, leaving Scott deep within enemy territory with an army of under 7,000 effectives.

Early in May, the forces under Worth continued to advance westward, and on the 15th of the month they captured Puebla. By the end of May, Scott moved his headquarters to that important Mexican city. Awaiting additional troops, Scott's army had to remain in Puebla throughout the months of June and July. During that time the morale of the soldiers sagged badly, but reinforcements gradually came to their assistance, and by early August American troops in Puebla numbered nearly 14,000, including 3,000 who were ill.

Setting forth again on August 7, Scott's army — minus the hundreds of sick who were left behind — reached the Valley of Mexico on August 11. With the arduous journey from the coast behind them, the American forces still faced the most difficult task of actually conquering the Mexican capital. And not all experts were optimistic that they could succeed. Indeed, the Duke of Wellington, who in England closely followed Scott's advance, remarked: "Scott is lost — he cannot capture the city and he cannot fall back upon his base."

Following his defeat at Cerro Gordo, Santa Anna meanwhile had returned to Mexico City. There, having reestablished his political power, he strengthened the capital's defenses and organized the 25,000 troops under his command. By the time Scott's army reached the Valley of Mexico, the Mexican general was well prepared to meet the Americans' assault.

Santa Anna's strategy was to supplement Mexico City's natural defenses. Vast marshlands surrounding the capital made access possible only along a few stone causeways. Santa Anna fortified the most likely of these approaches — at the suburb of Guadalupe Hidalgo to the north and at Mexicalcingo to the south — with infantry and artillery. Between these two sites he erected his strongest defense atop El Peñón, a hill that commanded the main road from the east.

Scott learned of Santa Anna's disposition of his forces through reconnaissance operations. Initially he thought that Mexicalcingo would be the most vulnerable point at which to attack. But last minute intelligence gathered by General Worth's men prompted a change of mind. Scott decided to circle around Lakes Xochimilco and Chalco, which lie east of Mexicalcingo, and attack San Augustín, a town far below Santa Anna's southernmost fortifications.

Taking San Augustín, Scott had the option of attacking north toward San Antonio, where Santa Anna had quickly established defenses, or west across the Pedregal lava field to Contreras, which was defended by General Gabriel Valencia. The American commander chose the latter course, and, on August 19, while Worth feinted toward San Antonio, Pillow's men moved slowly toward Contreras, building a road across the lava as they advanced. By evening the main element of Pillow's force was in position before Contreras, and a smaller portion had occupied the village of San Gerónimo to the west and discovered a ravine leading behind Valencia's position.

Pillow and Scott decided to attack Valencia from the rear. At 3:00 A.M. on August 20, Americans began to advance along the ravine leading from San Gerónimo to Contreras. The Mexicans, who were concentrating on Pillow's diversionary force in front of them, were totally surprised when the enemy struck from behind. The Americans, who lost fewer than 100 men, routed the defenders, inflicting casualties at a ratio of five to one, taking approximately 800 prisoners (including several generals), and capturing 20 artillery pieces and an abundance of ammunition.

With the fall of Contreras, San Antonio was outflanked, and Santa Anna withdrew his forces to Churubusco. The Americans could have advanced directly from Contreras toward Mexico City, but Scott would have had to leave his right flank exposed to Santa Anna. The American commander refused to take the risk and decided to reduce Churubusco before assaulting the capital. The Mexicans stubbornly defended their position against an attacking force, which was weary after the morning's action at Contreras, but by late afternoon Churubusco also fell, and the Americans found themselves within three miles of Mexico City.

His troops defeated twice in a single day, Santa Anna was anxious to delay further battle. The Mexican commander, rejecting a demand by Scott for immediate surrender, indicated interest in an armistice (although he did not use that word) to permit negotiations. Scott, who also desired to give his weary troops rest, agreed. The negotiators talked until September 6, but they could reach no agreement. Angered by the Mexicans' recalcitrance and convinced of their treachery, Scott then declared the armistice terminated.

On September 7, Scott moved north to Tacubaya, from which his forces could attack Mexico City's southwestern defenses. Two objectives lay ahead — the palace of Chapultepec and, at the western end of the park surrounding it, a group of buildings known as Molino del Rey, where the enemy was supposedly manufacturing guns. On

September 8 the Americans assaulted Molino del Rey and took it at the cost of more than 700 men, a tremendous number considering that they found few guns in the foundry, which was no longer in operation.

Scott, with his effective force reduced to some 7,000 troops, hesitated before moving against Chapultepec. On the advice of officers like Robert E. Lee, the American commander considered bypassing the fortress and attacking Mexico City from the south. Finally, the counsel of another young engineer, P. G. T. Beauregard, convinced Scott that he should return to the original plan of attacking the capital from the west.

On September 12 the Americans began to bombard Chapultepec, and on the following morning they assaulted the palace. A division under Brigadier General John A. Quitman advanced from the south, Pillow led his men from the southwest, and Worth's forces came from the west. By 9:30 A.M. Chapultepec had fallen. The attackers pressed on toward Mexico City. Quitman drove for the Belén Gate and Worth for the San Cosmé Gate, and both gained their objectives by nightfall.

Santa Anna decided to save his demoralized troops for another battle, and on the night of September 13 he withdrew his forces to Guadalupe Hidalgo, rather than engage the Americans in battle in the streets of the capital. On the morning of August 14 the Mexico City authorities, after an unsuccessful bid for negotiated terms, surrendered the municipality to the Americans. Quitman occupied the Grand Plaza and raised the US flag over the palace; by 8:00 A.M., Scott and his staff rode triumphantly into the city.

Scott's entry into Mexico City did not immediately bring peace to the capital. For three days, residents waged guerrilla war against the American troops, but their efforts were futile. By September 16 Scott's army had restored order in Mexico City. The American general exacted a levy of $150,000 from the populace. He used $50,000 of this money to assist his troops; the remainder he sent back to the United States with the suggestion that it be used to construct a soldiers' home in Washington, D.C. The federal government complied with the general's request, and the Soldiers' Home that was built in 1851 still stands at 3700 N. Capitol Street.

To all intents and purposes, the capture of Mexico City on September 14, 1847, marked the end of the Mexican War. The war's formal conclusion, however, had to await the signing of the Treaty of Guadalupe Hidalgo early the following February.

SEPTEMBER 15

James Fenimore Cooper's Birthday

James Fenimore Cooper, the first important American novelist, was born on September 15, 1789, in Burlington, New Jersey, and grew up in Cooperstown, New York, on the shore of Otsego Lake where his father, Judge William Cooper, had a large estate. At Cooperstown, which Judge Cooper founded, the family first lived in a log house and later moved into the fine mansion known as Otsego Hall. It was built to the specifications of the judge, a Federalist active in New York State politics and one of the largest property owners of the region.

Otsego Hall was on the edge of frontier wilderness, and young Cooper, born to wealth and position, early became interested in the Indians of the region and the life of the frontiersmen. From this background came his best-known works, the series of novels called The Leatherstocking Tales. (In Cooper's day, Cooperstown villagers used leather to make leggings, aprons, and even petticoats. It was commonplace to see behind a plow a farmhand wearing the leather leggings, or "leatherstockings.")

After receiving his preparatory education in the household of an Episcopal rector in Albany — a Federalist no doubt carefully selected by the elder Cooper — Cooper entered Yale at 13, the youngest in his class. His age notwithstanding, he proved to be the class's best Latin student but showed a lack of discipline. He was expelled in his third year at Yale, reportedly for exploding a charge of gunpowder that he had carefully placed in the lock of a tutor's door.

In an effort to teach his son discipline, Judge Cooper obtained a berth for Cooper as an apprentice seaman. On his return from his first transatlantic voyage, which took more than a year to complete, the young man could regale his family with stories of life at sea. Among other new and exciting experiences, his ship was actually set upon by pirates and boarded for searching. The excitement of this and other adventures probably confirmed young Cooper in his desire for a naval career. In a year or two he received a commission as a midshipman in the US Navy and served in the Atlantic Ocean as well as on Lakes Ontario and Champlain. This phase of his life gave him the foundation for the sea stories he would later write.

On January 1, 1811, Cooper married Susan A. DeLancey, the daughter of a wealthy Tory who lived in Mamaroneck, Westchester County, New York. Resigned from the navy, Cooper took up the life of a gentleman farmer, and might have lived happily in that role had his wife not challenged him to write a book. He often read aloud to her, and one evening as he was embarked on a particularly dull English novel, he stopped in the middle of a paragraph and exclaimed with annoyance that he could write a better book himself. Replied his wife: "Why don't you?" The words launched America's first significant novelist into what was to be his third and true career.

Most English novels of the time were slight, sentimental drawing-room tales. Cooper was to bring adventure, suspense, action, and vigor to the novel. He was to carry America, its frontiers, its people, and their strange customs, dress and manners into the homes of Europeans who were eager for knowledge about the New World, its exotic Indians and adventurous pioneers, and the wonders of its deep forests and varied terrain. Cooper's first attempt, however, was no indication of the success he would have in the future.

Taking up his wife's challenge, he set about writing *Precaution* (1820), a novel of English life with which he was not familiar. Indeed the book, which was a failure, was not very different from the stiff, dull stories he himself had chafed at. But the writing of it had stirred the creative spirit in Cooper, who then definitely determined that this was an occupation he would pursue. He was dissatisfied with his first book and later commented: "Ashamed to have fallen into the track of imitation, I endeavoured to repay the wrong done to my own views, by producing a work that should be purely American, and of which love of country should be the theme."

The first fruit of this wisdom was *The Spy* (1821), a story of the American Revolution with its scene laid in Westchester County. The book was a huge and immediate success, both in this country and abroad, and became more popular than any previous American novel.

In 1823 and 1824 he produced two significant and well-received novels: *The Pioneers*, which introduced the hero Natty Bumppo; and *The Pilot*, the first American sea story. Natty Bumppo is a true son of nature, at home in the forest, and uneasy about civilization's encroachment on the freedom of the wilderness. Cooper himself, intrigued by the character he had created, described Natty Bumppo as "a philosopher of the wilderness" and decided to pursue his career further. Readers, too, wanted more stories about this remarkable character. Thus was laid the foundation for the Leatherstocking Tales, five stories that show the American forests and

plains, first in their primeval splendor known only to Indians; then entered by respectful woodsmen who were, in turn, followed by pioneers and settlers — not all of them respectful; and then vastly changed by the imposition of European culture.

The character of Natty Bumppo reappears throughout the series also under such names as Leatherstocking, Hawkeye, the Deerslayer, the Pathfinder, and La Longue Carabine. Whatever he is called, the character remains the simple, self-sufficient, natural man of integrity, courage, and loyalty, who feels a far closer kinship to the Native American than to the exploitive and greedy whites; an individual who turns his back on the corrupting influence of settlements, choosing to face toward the serenity and abundance of the untrampled wilderness.

By the time Cooper wrote *The Last of the Mohicans*, published in 1826, his popularity at home and abroad rivaled that of the novelist Sir Walter Scott — who warmly welcomed Cooper and his family when they sailed to Europe that same year. The Coopers were to stay in Europe for seven years. During most of this time they traveled; but Cooper, fiercely patriotic and wishing to be identified as an American, and not as an expatriate, obtained the nominal position of US consul in Lyons, France. The appointment did not interfere with the family's travels or with Cooper's writing output, which included *The Prairie* (1827), the third novel in the Leatherstocking series; *The Red Rover* (1827); *The Wept of Wish-ton-Wish* (1829); and *The Water-Witch* (1830). He also wrote a trilogy that, while dealing with social relations in Europe during the Middle Ages, incurred some European displeasure by persistently ranking democracy above aristocracy.

During his stay in Europe, Cooper found himself constantly explaining or defending the United States and things American. His *Notions of the Americans* (1828) gave much information about Americans and their views, but succeeded only in irritating both his American and European readers. Proud as he was of the young republic, he was not as tactful as he might have been when he pointed out in conversation, novels, and expository writings, the superiority of the American way of life over that of Europe's aristocracy.

When, however, Cooper returned home to Cooperstown with his family in 1833, what he saw was not the United States that he had touted with so much pride all over Europe. Perhaps he had been influenced more than he thought by cultivated European society. In any event, his

Federalist dignity was outraged by the "coonskin democracy" of President Andrew Jackson. Never one to mince words, Cooper loosed a torrent of criticism, scolding and lecturing Americans on their faults — and antagonizing many in the process. His writings turned more and more to social criticism and the defense of American principles that he felt were being sorely abused. His books of social criticism included *A Letter to His Countrymen* (1834); *The Monikins* (1835); *Homeward Bound,* a fictionalized account of the American scene as viewed by Americans just returning from a stay abroad, and its sequel, *Home As Found* (both published in 1838); and *The American Democrat* (1838), in which he clearly stated his political principles.

During this same period, Cooper also wrote five books about his travels abroad, which succeeded in raising hackles on both sides of the Atlantic. He gave at least some of his attention again to the pioneers and Indians in such novels as *Wyandotte* (1843) and *The Oak-Openings* (1848). In the trilogy called *The Littlepage Manuscripts,* he followed a New York family through three generations: *Satanstoe* (1845), *The Chainbearer* (1846), and *The Redskins* (1846).

If Cooper had a talent for inventive story telling, he also had a genius for annoying people to the point of infuriation. From the time he returned to the United States and began criticizing political trends and social changes, he sowed seeds of enmity from which he would reap a bitter harvest. As one commentator put it, Cooper became "the most popular author and the most unpopular man in American literature." Newspapers fought back, calling him everything from "snob" to "anti-democratic" and worse. Cooper spent years suing for libel and usually winning, neither of which helped his personal popularity.

He frequently turned to his first love, the sea, during these troubled years and wrote not only fiction, replete with sea chases and battles, but many solid nonfictional works, such as *The History of the Navy of the United States of America* (1839), *Lives of Distinguished American Naval Officers* (1842–1845), and *Ned Myers* (1843), the story of a sailor Cooper had met on his first voyage as an apprentice seaman. Some of the novels of this period, also set at sea, were *The Two Admirals* (1842), *The Wing-and-Wing* (1842); *Mercedes of Castile* (1840); *Afloat and Ashore* and its sequel, *Miles Wallingford* (both 1844); *Jack Tier* (1846–1848); *The Crater* (1847); and *The Sea Lions* (1849), in which Cooper's early religious bigotry, which became a growing affliction in his later life, reached its highwater mark.

Although some of Cooper's many novels fell below his highest standards, others were splendidly original and inventive. The novelist Joseph Conrad described Cooper as "a rare artist . . . one of my masters." Other writers who imitated Cooper or greatly admired him included Balzac, Victor Hugo, and Scott.

It was during years of personal strife and public litigation that Cooper wrote *The Pathfinder* (published in 1840) and *The Deerslayer* (1841). The narrative order of the books in the Leatherstocking series is as follows: *The Deerslayer, The Last of the Mohicans* (1826), *The Pathfinder, The Pioneers* (1823), and *The Prairie* (1827). In all, Cooper produced some 50 works during his 30-year literary career.

Although Cooper never failed to be warmly affectionate to his family, he remained sour toward the public to the end of his days and forbade family and friends to authorize any biography of him. He died on September 14, 1851, the day before his 62nd birthday, and was buried in the Episcopal churchyard in Cooperstown. He was elected to the Hall of Fame in New York in 1910.

In many respects, Cooperstown today is a page out of the American past. Among other things, it has one of the finest collections of American folk art in the country, displayed in Fenimore House, one mile north of Cooperstown. The house, built in 1933 as a private residence, is located on grounds that James Fenimore Cooper once owned. In 1945 Fenimore House, named for the author's maternal ancestors, became the headquarters of the New York State Historical Association, a private membership organization. Besides the treasures of American folk art and J. H. I. Browere's unique, bronze-cast life masks of such persons as Thomas Jefferson, John Adams, Dolley Madison, Lafayette, and Gilbert Stuart, Fenimore House also displays some remembrances of Cooper, including a bust and a portrait of the author, a few of his manuscripts, and other memorabilia.

Three other museums in Cooperstown place even more emphasis on life during the time of James Fenimore Cooper. The Farmers' Museum, almost adjacent to Fenimore House, ranks, in some opinions, with Williamsburg, Virginia, Sturbridge Village, Massachusetts, and Vermont's Shelbourne Museum in its collection of regional Americana, which it preserves in 18 buildings. Here, visitors can tour a farmhouse, country store, blacksmith shop, tavern, printing shop, church, and drugstore, among other buildings; learn about the customs of the times; and see demonstrations of the crafts practiced by farm families in rural villages of 1785–1860.

The Cooperstown Indian Museum displays exhibits on New York State Indians as well as historical and archeological dioramas. It is located on the lakefront at 1 Pioneer Street. More local history is recorded at the Woodland Museum, which has dioramas depicting scenes from *The Deerslayer*, as well as a nature trail, a fossil collection, an aquarium, and wildlife habitat groups in a Bird and Game Building. The Woodland Museum is three miles north of Cooperstown.

Visitors to Burlington, New Jersey, can see the James Fenimore Cooper House at 457 High Street, where the author was born in 1789. The house now contains documents, pictures, and other items of Americana belonging to the Burlington County Historical Society.

William Howard Taft's Birthday

William Howard Taft is the only man in the history of the country who has held both the office of President and the office of chief justice of the United States. His record is remarkable also in that he held public office almost continuously from his early manhood until a few weeks before his death. A huge, affable man, Taft was afflicted with a lifelong tendency to procrastinate. He enjoyed the quiet, orderly, and conservative life of the legal profession, particularly in the judicial aspect, and actively disliked the rough and tumble of politics.

Taft was born in Cincinnati, Ohio, on September 15, 1857, the son of Alphonso Taft, who was attorney general in the cabinet of President Ulysses S. Grant during the last nine months of his second term. Graduated from Yale College in 1878, the second in his class, young William Taft then entered the Law School of Cincinnati College, from which he was graduated in 1880. Although he was admitted to the bar at once, he spent the next year as law reporter on a Cincinnati newspaper.

In 1881, as a Republican party prize for his campaign services, he was appointed assistant prosecuting attorney for Hamilton County, of which Cincinnati is the county seat. He gave up the position the next year, when he was appointed collector of Internal Revenue for the first district of Ohio. After serving in the latter post for about a year, he resigned — following his refusal, on principle, to oust several officeholders according to the "spoils system" of political reward.

Taft took advantage of his leisure for travel in Europe at this juncture, and then resumed his practice of law. He returned to political office in 1885 with his appointment as assistant solicitor for Hamilton County. In 1886 he married Helen Heron, a cultured, capable, and ambitious woman.

The following year Taft was made judge of the Superior Court of Ohio to fill a vacancy, and in 1888 he was elected to complete the term. Aside from the presidency, this was the only elective office he was to hold. Taft himself said that he proceeded in politics by having his "plate the right side up when offices were falling." He resigned his judgeship in 1890 to accept the office of solicitor general of the United States under President Benjamin Harrison.

Two years later, the President appointed him US circuit judge for the Sixth Circuit. Taft accepted the post against the opposition of his wife, who considered the post a poor job with no political future. While still on the bench, Taft also served as dean and professor in the law department of the University of Cincinnati from 1896 to 1900.

In a time of great labor unrest, Taft was to make a number of judicial decisions relating to strikes and injunctions that earned him the enmity of organized labor. Though he granted that huge industrial trusts needed to be restrained, this did not ally him with labor. As a man trained to the law, Taft instinctively mistrusted organizations of workers, who, he felt, were an uneducated rabble bent on overturning the social order.

President William McKinley took Taft from the bench in 1900 and made him president of the Philippine Commission. When civil government was established in the Philippine Islands, he became *ex officio* governor general. The status of church lands in the islands was uncertain, and, in 1902, in a personal interview with Pope Leo XII, Taft arranged a satisfactory settlement under which $7,239,000 was paid for the lands.

He was recalled to the United States by President Theodore Roosevelt in January 1904 to serve as secretary of war. In that capacity, Taft had supervision of the construction of the Panama Canal. Taft became Roosevelt's trusted aide and was granted powers more than commensurate with his official position. Roosevelt, holding to his promise not to run again, used his influence in 1908 to bring about the nomination of Taft as his successor. Taft was elected by a majority of 159 electoral votes over William Jennings Bryan, the Democratic candidate.

As President, Taft recommended the adoption of an amendment to the Constitution that would permit the levying of income taxes. He urged upon Congress the importance of arranging for a national budget apportioning expenditures within the anticipated national revenues. He negotiated treaties with Great Britain and France providing for arbitration of disputes that could not be settled by the ordinary diplomatic means, but when the Senate began to modify them he withdrew the treaties. During his term there was a controversy over the conservation of natural resources, which resulted in the removal of Gifford Pinchot, the chief forester, and the resignation of Secretary Richard A. Ballinger from the Department of the Interior. There was also much dispute over the enactment of the Payne-Aldrich Tariff, which in its final form hardly affected rates at all, but which offended nearly all concerned political factions. Taft's leadership on the tariff issue was, at best, inconsistent, since he had declared himself for higher tariff rates only to reverse himself in a matter of months.

Taft ran for reelection, but a section of his party that called itself "progressive" opposed him on the ground that he was too conservative and reactionary. When the Republican National Convention met in 1912 and gave him the nomination, the Progressives held an independent gathering, known as the Bull Moose convention and nominated Theodore Roosevelt, who had broken with Taft early in his term. Because of the divided opposition the Democrats elected their candidate, Woodrow Wilson.

On his retirement from the presidency, Taft became Kent professor of law at Yale University. As his professional duties did not occupy all his time he lectured frequently and for a year or more wrote editorial articles for the Philadelphia *Public Ledger*. He was elected president of the American Bar Association in 1913 and 1914. He became the first president of the American Institute of Jurisprudence, an organization formed to improve the administration of the law. He favored the ratification of the Versailles Treaty in 1919, regarding the Convenant of the League of Nations as its most important part.

On the death of Chief Justice of the United States Edward Douglass White in 1921, President Warren G. Harding appointed Taft to succeed him. In making his appointment Harding fulfilled a lifelong dream of Taft's, even though Taft had earlier turned down a seat on the Supreme Court offered him by President Theodore Roosevelt. The early rejection was due to the influence of Taft's wife and brother, who wanted him to become President. When the second chance came, however, Taft was glad to accept appointment to the Court.

He enjoyed his work as chief justice. In this capacity he was guided in his thinking by moderate-to-conservative principles. He viewed the more liberal justices, led by Louis D. Brandeis, simply as habitual dissenters. Taft was an excellent legal administrator and revised rules of the Court to end long delays in litigation.

He resigned from the bench on January 3, 1930, because of ill health. He died on March 8 of the same year, and was buried in the Arlington National Cemetery at Arlington, Virginia. His son, Robert A. Taft, later became a US senator,

carrying on the political heritage. He was so famous in his Senate leadership role that he became widely known as Mr. Republican before his own death in 1953.

As the home of generations of distinguished Tafts, Cincinnati is rich in Taft family associations. The Alphonso Taft Home at 2038 Auburn Avenue, birthplace of William Howard Taft, is a national historic landmark. Earlier a boarding-house, it has been restored in recent years. The Taft House Museum at 316 Pike Street, once the home of the President's half brother Charles P. Taft, is an outstanding example of Federal-style architecture, containing a fine collection of European paintings, enamels, and jewelry, and Chinese porcelain.

SEPTEMBER 16

Cherokee Strip Day

On September 16, 1893, a now-famous land "run" opened to settlement the section of Oklahoma that was known officially as the Cherokee Outlet and popularly as the Cherokee Strip. September 16, Cherokee Strip Day, is observed as a holiday throughout the state. The chief celebrations of this historic event, however, take place in Ponca City, Enid, and Perry, Cherokee Strip communities that sprang into existence as a result of the 1893 run.

The Cherokee Indians, one of what were known as the Five Civilized Tribes, have a deep-rooted connection — extending back into the first half of the 19th century — with several parts of Oklahoma, including the "Strip." As early as 1809, some of these Indians, who lived in the southeastern states of North and South Carolina, Georgia, Alabama, and Tennessee, informed President Thomas Jefferson that they wanted to migrate to new hunting grounds beyond the Mississippi River. They were at first given permission to move into the area of Arkansas. Only limited numbers had made the transfer before mounting white pressure — a fever for westward expansion that was intensified by the discovery of gold on Cherokee land — forced the removal of the entire tribe from the eastern United States. In 1838, with the approval of President Andrew Jackson, some 16,000 Cherokees — 4,000 of whom died en route — were prodded along the "trail of tears" (see June 23). A new home awaited them, as it did the four other Civilized Tribes — Chickasaw, Choctaw, Creek, and Seminole — in the vast western region that had been set aside by Congress in 1834 and designated Indian Territory (see November 16, Oklahoma Becomes a State).

In addition to some 7 million acres of land in what is now northeastern Oklahoma, the Cherokees received extensive territory to the west, intended not as a homesite but as a "perpetual outlet" to hunting grounds in what are now New Mexico and Colorado. The "outlet" encompassed more than 6 million acres of land, extending from Keystone to the 100th meridian, then the western border of the United States. North-south, it stretched from the border of what was to become the state of Kansas to a point three miles north of Hennessey.

After the Civil War, the federal government forced the Five Civilized Tribes to relinquish the western half of the Indian Territory. On this land newly at its disposal the US government re-settled, from 1866 to 1883, numerous Indian tribes, especially the nomadic Plains Indians. The Cherokees were required to give up the eastern end of the Outlet, which was then assigned to the Osages; the Ponca, Oto, and Tonkawa Indians, among others, were settled on reservations in smaller sections of the Strip. But a great expanse still remained under Cherokee control.

The range-cattle industry quickly expanded in the 1870s and 1880s. Cowhands, driving longhorns northward from Texas to Kansas across the Indian Territory, soon discovered that the animals thrived on the grassy plain of the Cherokee Outlet. In 1883 the Cherokee Strip Livestock Association, a group of white ranchers, persuaded the Cherokee Nation to lease its unoccupied Strip for $100,000 a year, for five years. The mutually profitable agreement was renewed at its expiration in 1888.

As early as the late 1870s, both cattlemen and homesteaders, realizing the priceless value of the millions of acres of Indian land, began to demand the opening of the Indian Territory to white settlement. Especially desirable were the two "unoccupied" sections: the Unassigned Lands, a 2-million-acre tract in the center of the Indian Territory later known as Old Oklahoma or the Oklahoma District; and the Cherokee Outlet, which, although assigned to the Cherokees, had never been settled. The Unassigned Lands were thrown open to white migration under the 1862 Homestead Act in a run on April 22, 1889 (see April 22, Oklahoma Day). Other sections of western Indian Territory were gradually occupied by white homesteaders in the subsequent runs of 1891 and 1892.

In the meantime, the US government was conducting negotiations to obtain a clear title to the Cherokee Outlet. It terminated the Cherokee Strip Livestock Association's second lease before expiration; abolished the tribal land allotments, which had been granted to several Indian tribes

from the area, in favor of individual allotments; and purchased the Outlet's more than 6 million acres for $8,595,736.

In summer 1893 President Grover Cleveland signed the proclamation opening the region to settlement by means of a land run set for September 16, 1893. Great efforts were made to prevent fraud. Prior to the run, the Strip was carefully surveyed by government engineers and divided into counties of equal size; county seats, townsites, and 160-acre claims were minutely determined. All that was needed to obtain a claim was to be the first to plant a flag stake at a given spot. Thus speed was essential in securing the best plots.

The lure of free land and the thrill of the race attracted an estimated 100,000 prospective settlers. They swarmed along the borders of the rectangular Cherokee Strip in anticipation of the noon opening on September 16. The majority concentrated in the border towns of Arkansas City and Caldwell in Kansas, on the northern side of the Outlet, and Orlando and Hennessey in Oklahoma, on the southern side. Housing, food, water, sanitary facilities, and supplies were inadequate or nonexistent. Eight cavalry troops and four infantry companies guarded the 400-mile border in an effort to protect the area from illegal invasion. But nonetheless some (called "Sooners") managed to slip into the territory just as they had infiltrated the Oklahoma District before the land rush of 1889.

The multitude of impatient land seekers lined up in the neutral zones starting at dawn on September 16. As the burning morning sun climbed higher and higher, the tension became almost unbearable. Tempers flared as men, with their animals and vehicles, jockeyed for position. Precisely at noon rifles cracked, and before the reverberations faded away, the frantic race had begun. The restless, surging crowd charged forward in a whirlwind of dust, as seen in the historic photographs taken within seconds of the starting signal. (W. S. Prettyman, an Arkansas City photographer, had erected a 24-foot scaffold at the border from which to snap the shots; at the last moment, deciding to join the run himself, he left the job to an assistant.)

The eager homesteaders swept over the flat prairie in every available means of conveyance. Many made the race in lumber wagons, buckboards, and buggies, while others went on foot, horseback, and even bicycles. The Atchison, Topeka and Sante Fe Railroad ran 10 special trains across the high Plains south to Newkirk and Ponca (about six miles south of Ponca City). By sunset, 40,000 homesteads of 160 acres each had been claimed throughout the tract, except on the sites allocated for towns, and the exhausted settlers were established in tents or wagon boxes on their own land. Within half a day, "tent-and-shack" cities had sprung up in designated places on the Cherokees' former Outlet.

The run of 1893 was a venture chiefly of young men, the average age of the land seekers being 29 years. Youth was a desirable asset for a pioneer building a home on the stark Plains with only a spirit of adventure and a few meager possessions. The homesteaders erected crude sod dugouts, which furnished some shelter from the fierce winds and violent blizzards that tore over the unprotected grasslands in winter. (About 30 miles west of Enid, a two-room, 1894 sod house — believed to be the only original example of this kind of house remaining in Oklahoma — has been preserved by the Oklahoma Historical Society.) No harvest was possible until the year after the run, and the intervening winter of 1894 was one of bitter poverty. Many homesteaders, as this little ditty indicates, were forced to burn cow and buffalo chips for heat and collect animal bones to sell for $5 a load:

> Picking up bones to keep from starving,
> Picking up chips to keep from freezing,
> Picking up courage to keep from leaving,
> Way out West, in No Man's Land.

The land rush of 1893 was the largest and last of the runs that opened the western Indian lands to white settlement. Land lottery and auction replaced the often violent run, completing the homesteading process in the early 20th century. The Cherokee Strip became part of Oklahoma Territory, which roughly encompassed the westernmost part of the Indian Territory set aside by Congress in 1834. The eastern half of the congressionally designated Indian Territory still retained that name. Subsequently the "twin" territories combined to form the state of Oklahoma in 1907.

The pioneers spirit of '93 is revived each year around September 16, when major celebrations are staged in the Cherokee Strip communities of Ponca City, Enid, and Perry. Ponca City, now a prosperous center of over 20,000, was conceived in the minds of certain farsighted pioneers prior to the run of 1893. The site selected for the settlement was adjacent to the Arkansas River, a freshwater spring, and the railroad; within two or three weeks after the opening of the Strip it was a full-fledged town. Ponca City's three-day program commemorating the September 16 run generally includes band concerts, an old settlers' picnic, rodeo, western dances, and a parade. The parade is a colorful pageant of pioneer life featuring prairie schooners, buggies, floats of all descriptions, and several hundred people on horseback. On occasion a replica of one train that made the run reenacts the 28-mile trip from Arkansas City, Kansas, to Ponca City. The brass-trimmed locomotive pulls bright yellow passenger cars, loaded with colorfully costumed "land seekers."

Enid, formerly a "tent city" born of the seething land rush of 1893, is located in a farming and oil region and has a population of more than 40,000. In 1960 the Sons and Daughters of the Cherokee Strip Pioneers, an organization founded in 1957, took over sponsorship of Enid's annual September 16 festivities. Among the highlights of the present four-day celebration have been a western-type parade and a dinner honoring the remaining living pioneers who made the land run in 1893. Phillips University, a liberal arts college and graduate seminary in Enid, houses the Cherokee Strip Museum, where historic mementos of the run and the pioneer era are displayed. Cherokee Strip museums are also located in the towns of Alva and Perry. In mid-September, the inhabitants of Perry commemorate the opening of the Cherokee Strip with a parade, carnival, rodeo, and square dance.

The Pendleton Round-Up

This is a movable event. See note on page xxvi.

Throughout the West some 600 rodeos are held each year. The roundup in Pendleton, Oregon, staged every year the second full week in September, is among the best known. It is a large-scale and picturesque celebration, reminiscent of the rip-roaring "sin and six-gun" era, when Pendleton was both a cow town and a stop on the Oregon Trail. The small city in the eastern Oregon cattle country is still a cowboy center surrounded by ranches and Indian reservations.

The Pendleton Round-Up started more or less informally in 1910, under the inspiration of Roy Raley, a young Pendleton attorney. Ranchers from a 100-mile area brought their meanest steers, most ornery calves, and wildest bucking horses to the rodeo, held on a gravel bar near the Umatilla River. To everyone's surprise, 4,000 spectators turned out to cheer the first amateur contestants. From the profits, plus $12,500 in donations, a grandstand and bleachers were constructed to accommodate 10,000 persons.

Beginning in 1912, crowds as large as 40,000, from as far away as Chicago and even New York, flocked to Pendleton. When the old wooden grandstand caught fire just a month before opening day in 1940, a new concrete stadium was immediately erected and the show was held as scheduled. Only World War II caused an interruption in the annual competition, which was omitted in 1942 and 1943. Receipts from the roundup have been continuously used for improvement and beautification of the rodeo facilities — which were given to the city — and the surrounding grounds. In 1952 the arena was turfed and lighted to make an all-season sports center for baseball and other community events.

The roundup has changed little over the years, except that bucking, riding, and roping events, now subject to a time limit, move faster. The Pendleton gathering features six major Rodeo Cowboys Association–approved competitions: bronco riding, bareback riding, Brahma bull riding, steer wrestling, calf roping, and steer roping. Ranked one of the four big outdoor shows in the United States in terms of purse money and attendance, the Pendleton Round-Up attracts the outstanding cowboys of the nation. The number of contestants varies slightly from year to year, depending mostly on the extent of national television coverage. Held late in the season, the Round-Up has an important bearing on contestants' rankings for the year.

The second big attraction in Pendleton, held at the same time but under separate management, is the annual Happy Canyon pageant. Since 1910, when he planned the original roundup program, Roy Raley had been intrigued by the possibility of holding a night show as well. In 1913 he and two other Pendletonians, Lee Drake and George Hartman, reacting against the expensive yet poor-quality entertainment at a local district fair, decided to start their own presentation, which they named Happy Canyon. The first shows, in 1914 and 1915, reenacted the activities of the rowdy frontier town. When Happy Canyon moved to better facilities in 1916, Indian pageantry and emigrant train scenes were added. Eventually numerous episodes were woven into an hour-and-15-minute sequence. An anonymous cast of 375 local residents, including 220 Indians, now depicts the story of the Indian West. The acts portray Indian arts, crafts, and daily life before the coming of whites; Sacagawea directing Lewis and Clark to the West; clashes with white settlers; and the Indians' retreat from their hunting regions. Then the scene suddenly changes to the rip-snorting western town of Happy Canyon in the 1840s, where the Cowboy and Cowgirl Mounted Quadrille provides a spectacular finale. The audience is then invited to enjoy western dancing and an Old West atmosphere in the Happy Canyon Dance Hall and to spend there the "legal currency," Happy Canyon Bucks, obtainable at 10 cents each and "good for nothing but fun."

The pageant has become part of the life of the Indian tribes who for the past 50 years have set up their tepees in the campground on the Umatilla River near the roundup and unpacked their family possessions there. They hand down the roles from the old to the young and appear without rehearsal in the moving presentation of their history.

Besides the exciting roundup and colorful Happy Canyon pageant, the visitor to Pendleton can attend numerous special events, as the 1970 program shows. On Saturday, September 12, the annual evening Dress-Up parade, routed through downtown Pendleton to the roundup area, heralded the approach of the main activities — as did the Kick-Off dance, which followed at 9:30 P.M. The large number of contestants made it necessary to supplement the roundup proper by running the first and second preliminary go-arounds on Tuesday, Wednesday, and Thursday.

On Wednesday morning, meanwhile, rodeo fans awoke to the smell of ham, eggs, flapjacks, and coffee, and could enjoy a cowboy breakfast at Stillman Park. The roundup started officially at 1:15 P.M., when mounted flagbearers dashed around the tracks, and the cry "Let 'er buck" signaled the eagerly awaited opening. The day's second major event was the Happy Canyon pageant at 7:45 P.M. In addition visitors participated in an enormous beef barbecue dinner in the arena following the rodeo performance.

The schedule on Thursday, Friday, and Saturday followed basically the same pattern, with the cowboy breakfast at 6:30 or 7:00 A.M., continuation of the preliminary go-arounds at 8:00 A.M., roundup at 1:15 P.M., and pageant at 7:45 P.M. The basic program was supplemented by other events.

On Thursday, for example, the 10:00 A.M. Junior Indian beauty contest, inaugurated in 1961, was open to Indian girls 12 years of age and under, who were camped on the roundup grounds. At 7:00 P.M., the Main Street Cowboys, an organization of professional and business men of Pendleton who serve as official hosts for the week, took over Main Street, as they were to do on Friday night and Saturday morning and evening as well. Their pony and stagecoach rides, clown acts, medicine shows, horseshoeing, saddlemaking, and other crafts proved to be informative and fun for youngsters and oldsters alike. On the same evening, the roundup queen and her court of four princesses were honored at the annual queen's ball in the Happy Canyon Dance Hall.

Special features on Friday began with the 9:00 A.M. American Indian beauty contest, in which Indian girls were judged for beauty and tribal costumes, and on their horses' trappings. The annual Westward Ho! parade, named after the traditional slogan of the pioneers during their migration to the West, followed at 10:00 A.M. Featuring over 1,000 Indians and

1,500 horses, the parade depicts the history of transportation before the automobile. No commercial signs or motorized vehicles are allowed in the line of march. For two hours, every sort of pioneer vehicle, including stagecoaches, hacks, surreys, buggies, buckboards, Indian travois, Mormon carts, and covered wagons pulled by 12 mules on a jerkline, accompanied by costumed drivers and riders, traversed the city, raising as much dust and hullabaloo as might have been found in one of the gold-rush towns of the Old West.

Saturday, the final day of the Round-Up, got off to an eye-catching start with the 9:00 A.M. Indian tribal dancing contest in the roundup arena. The afternoon finals, undoubtedly the most thrilling chapter of the four-day fete, included, besides the six Rodeo Cowboys Association–approved competitions, pony express, wild horse, Indian, cowgirl, and baton races, exhibition "snubbing and bucking," and wild-cow milking.

The Pendleton Round-Up runs with a clocklike precision that belies the tremendous amount of work needed to manage the event. The rodeo continues to be a voluntary activity of resident and local ranchers under the supervision of a board of directors, whose members serve without remuneration for four-year terms. The nonprofit Happy Canyon Company, first incorporated with a capital stock of $600 in 1916, has its own board of directors to conduct the planning, business aspects, and execution of the night pageant.

To help perpetuate the fame of outstanding participants and officials of past years, the Pendleton Round-Up inaugurated a Hall of Fame in 1969. A first among individual western shows, it had honored – as of 1970 – 12 men (and five horses) chosen by a committee on the basis of their performances and contributions.

SEPTEMBER 17

Warren E. Burger's Birthday

President Richard M. Nixon on May 21, 1969, selected Warren Earl Burger to succeed the retiring Earl Warren as chief justice of the United States. Nixon saw in Burger – a man who felt that the rights of the public to protection from crime had been neglected in the previous decade's judicial preoccupation with protecting the rights of the accused – a chief justice who would turn the Supreme Court toward a conservative position more in accord with his administration's stated views. However, although Burger became known for his philosophy of judicial restraint and

his perception of the Court's role as interpreter of existing laws rather than innovator of legal, social, or economic change, it would be erroneous to describe the chief justice, who grew up on the soil of midwestern progressivism, as unalterably conservative. Such simplistic labeling overlooks his inquiring and independent turn of mind – a characteristic shared by most of his predecessors. His appointment as the nation's chief judicial officer, following the many landmark decisions that had sprung from the Warren court, was nevertheless seen as the end of one era and the beginning of another. The Senate confirmed the President's selection on June 9, 1969, and on June 24 Burger was sworn in by Warren as the 15th chief justice of the United States.

Warren E. Burger, a Protestant of Swiss-German extraction, was born in St. Paul, Minnesota, on September 17, 1907. He was the fourth of the seven children of Charles Joseph Burger, who worked variously as a railroad cargo inspector, traveling salesman, and small truck farmer, and Katherine Schnittger Burger. At the age of nine he began to deliver newspapers. Later, when he attended John A. Johnson High School in St. Paul, he played the cornet and bugle and was active in track, swimming, football, hockey, and tennis. He served not only as student council president and editor of the school newspaper but also as head of the student court. During his summer vacations, he worked on a farm in Red Wing, Minnesota, and also held positions at a YMCA camp, where he served as a counselor. He worked, too, as truck driver, lifeguard, and track coach.

Princeton University, impressed by Burger's many activities, decided to overlook his undistinguished academic record and to offer him a scholarship. Burger, whose family's financial status was quite modest, had to turn down the small stipend. Instead he took extension courses at the University of Minnesota from 1925 to 1927 and then entered night classes at St. Paul College of Law (now Mitchell College of Law). Despite having to hold a job – as a salesman for the Mutual Life Insurance Company – while he was studying, Burger managed to earn his LL.B. degree, *magna cum laude*, in 1931 and to rank third in his graduating class.

Burger was an associate until 1935 of the St. Paul law firm of Boyesen, Otis and Faricy, and he was a partner until 1953 of its successor, Faricy, Burger, Moore, and Costello. From 1931 until 1953 he taught at St. Paul College of Law and eventually became professor of contract law. He served also as president of the St. Paul Junior Chamber of Commerce in 1935.

A chronic back ailment prevented Burger

from joining the military during World War II, and from 1942 to 1947 he was a public member of the Minnesota Emergency War Labor Board. In 1948 he gained appointment to the Governor's Interracial Commission and remained on it until 1953. He also became the first president of the St. Paul Council on Human Relations, which was designed to promote understanding between the city police and the black and Mexican-American minorities.

Burger, a lifelong Republican, played an important role in the successful gubernatorial campaign of liberal Republican Harold Stassen in 1938. Ten years later, Burger was floor manager for Stassen's unsuccessful run for the presidential nomination at the Republican National Convention in Philadelphia. Burger served again as Stassen's manager in 1952, but, when the Minnesotan's bid appeared doomed, he switched his support to Dwight D. Eisenhower and helped assure the general's first-ballot nomination in a contest with Robert A. Taft of Ohio.

Upon taking office, President Eisenhower appointed Burger as the assistant attorney general in charge of the Civil Division of the Department of Justice. Burger and his staff of 180 lawyers had the responsibility of representing the government in all civil cases except those involving land or antitrust matters. Among other litigation, Burger successfully handled a number of cases involving maritime affairs for the government, even though he previously had had virtually no experience in that branch of the law. Also while attached to the Department of Justice, Burger, in 1954, was a member and legal adviser to the US delegation to the International Labor Organization in Geneva. In 1955 he represented the government in cases involving Norwegian claims against the United States.

Eisenhower nominated Burger in June 1955 to a seat on the US Court of Appeals for the District of Columbia Circuit, which has appeal jurisdiction over many federal agencies and departments in Washington. The Senate confirmed Burger's appointment, and he took office on April 13, 1956. Burger served on the court for 13 years and established a reputation as a conservative jurist. He was openly critical of several Supreme Court rulings designed to protect the rights of accused persons. He attacked the Durham rule of 1954, which broadened the definition of criminal insanity, and the Miranda decision of 1966, which forbade the police to interrogate a defendant without informing him of his right to remain silent and of his right to legal counsel. In a dissenting opinion on the 1968 Frazier case, in which a robbery conviction was overturned on the ground that the defendant's conviction had been obtained unconstitutionally,

Burger commented on the jumble of "rules, sub-rules . . . and exceptions" that he said had developed from "the seeming anxiety of judges to protect every accused person from every consequence of his voluntary utterances." As a result of recent judicial trends, he added, "Guilt or innocence becomes irrelevant in the criminal trial as we flounder in a morass of artificial rules poorly conceived and often impossible of application."

Richard Nixon in 1967 was impressed by a magazine reprint of Burger's commencement address that year at Ripon College. Unlike some of the Warren court's more intemperate critics, Burger pointed out in the course of that speech that the high tribunal could hardly be held responsible for the sharply rising crime rate. He praised as "long overdue" some of the Court's rulings for the protection of individual rights — such as bail reforms and "assuring a lawyer to every person charged with serious crime." However, he scored neglect of other injustices — such as long court delays and inadequate provision for the rehabilitation of criminals — and deplored the Court's piecemeal, case-by-case approach to the reform of criminal law and procedures. (Burger's own recommendation was a more thorough-going approach via creation of a broad-based advisory committee to study the entire subject of criminal justice and recommend specific changes within the context of the whole.) Shortly after taking office in 1969, President Nixon several times called Burger to the White House for discussion. Since Earl Warren was to retire in June, the President chose Burger to replace him. Herbert Brownell Jr., who was attorney general when Burger was chief of the Civil Division of the Justice Department, Secretary of State William Rogers, and Attorney General John Mitchell concurred in the President's choice.

Conservatives were delighted with the choice, and liberals, who took consolation in Burger's moderate stand on civil rights, resigned themselves to the passing of the Warren court. Some were less sanguine about the appointment, believing that Burger had a flair for controversy that would seriously divide the Court. Allegedly a number of Burger's fellow circuit court justices also considered him unsuited in talent or temperament for the office of chief justice. Despite these doubts, the Senate quickly confirmed the nominee by the wide margin of 74 to 3.

Taking a strong "law and order" stance, the Burger court supported a decision that allows prosecutors to allude to confessions obtained from a defendant unaware of his constitutional right to remain silent. Burger agreed to limit the defendant's rights to cross-examine hostile witnesses by permitting courtroom use of statements by an accomplice who is unavailable to take the stand. Burger approved the use without a court order of listening devices hidden in an informer's clothes, to incriminate a suspect, and he rejected an argument that a guilty plea induced by fear of the death penalty is invalid.

Chief Justice Burger proved somewhat more liberal in aspects of the law not concerned with the prosecution of criminals. He wrote the Court's unanimous decision that ordered the use of pupil busing as well as other techniques to achieve school desegregation. The Burger court declared unanimously that a person cannot be jailed simply because of inability to pay an imposed fine and that job tests that discriminate against blacks and are not directly related to the work to be performed are illegal. On the other hand, the Court authorized residents of communities to veto construction of low-cost housing for the poor, stated that authorities could close public facilities such as swimming pools rather than integrate them, and permitted state governments to cut off welfare payments to recipients refusing to allow caseworkers to visit their homes.

Burger found himself in the minority in several instances, including the important Pentagon Papers case. In 1971 Dr. Daniel Ellsberg, a former government adviser, released to the New York *Times* and Washington *Post* a series of secret documents concerning the history of the Vietnamese war. Federal authorities sought to force the newspapers to cease publication of the papers, and the Supreme Court quickly took jurisdiction in the matter. With President Nixon's two appointees, Burger and Harry A. Blackmun, in dissent, the high bench by a vote of 6 to 3 granted the newspapers permission to continue publication of the sensitive material.

Burger also discussed such subjects as basic rights and emerged as a spokesman for judicial reform. Addressing the American Legal Institute in the spring of 1970, he noted that "in periods of stress there are always some voices raised urging that we suspend fundamental guarantees and take shortcuts as a matter of self-protection." Such advice, Burger warned, usually proved to be unwise. The chief justice emphasized the need for modernization of the nation's court system and urged lawyers and judges to participate in efforts to quicken court procedures so that defendants could be assured of speedy trials. Calling for fundamental improvement of prison conditions, he stressed the need for far greater emphasis on rehabilitation. In the speech that had impressed the President before he appointed the chief justice, Burger had declared:

In part, the terrible price we are paying in crime is because we have tended – once the drama of the trial is over – to regard all criminals as human rubbish. . . . The imbalance in our system of criminal justice must be corrected so that we give at least as

much attention to the defendant after he is found guilty as before. We . . . must proceed, even in the face of bitter contrary experiences, in the belief that every human being has a spark somewhere . . . in him that will make it possible for redemption and rehabilitation. If we accept the idea that each human, however bad, is a child of God, we must look for that spark.

Burger, a tall, white-thatched man who looks, according to some, "the way a Chief Justice should look," was married on November 8, 1933, to Elvera Stromberg. They had two children: Wade Allen, a businessman in real estate, and Margaret Elizabeth, a teacher. The Burgers' home is a pre–Civil War farmhouse on a six-acre tract in Arlington. Burger enjoys sculpturing, painting, and gardening, and is considered a gourmet and connoisseur of wine.

Citizenship Day

Americans set aside many days each year to remember individuals or events closely associated with the development of this nation. Fittingly, on September 17, the anniversary of the signing of the Constitution in 1787, the United States annually calls to mind the most important contributors to the greatness of the republic — ordinary citizens. Citizenship Day, as the celebration is known, provides an opportunity for recalling the rights and obligations of those who enjoy American citizenship, and it is also an occasion when special attention is centered on young adults who have attained legal voting age and on immigrants who have been naturalized during the previous year.

Citizenship Day is the outgrowth of two patriotic celebrations: Constitution Day and "I Am an American" Day. The former observance first took place in Philadelphia on September 17, 1861, shortly after the outbreak of the Civil War. Little is known about the 1861 exercises, aside from the fact that Philadelphians used the anniversary of the signing of the Constitution to reaffirm their devotion to the Union at a time when the secession of many Southern states threatened its very existence.

No other observance of September 17 seems to have occurred until 1887, when Philadelphians marked the centennial of the signing of the Constitution with a mammoth three-day celebration. Buildings throughout the city were draped in red, white, and blue bunting, and an estimated 500,000 visitors, including cabinet members, Supreme Court justices and the governors of several states, joined Philadelphia residents to witness the many patriotic events. Festivities began on September 15 with an industrial parade showing the technological achievements made during the preceding century. The next day President Grover Cleveland arrived in the city and reviewed a parade of 30,000 members of federal and state military units. Later that same day approximately 10,000 persons gathered at the Academy of Music to pay their respects to the Chief Executive at a reception held in his honor. September 17, the third day of the celebration and the actual anniversary of the signing of the Constitution, was devoted to exercises in Independence Square, in front of the building now known as Independence Hall, where the document of 1787 was drafted. President Cleveland was the main speaker on this occasion, and he concluded his address with these words:

As we look down the past century to the origin of our Constitution, as we contemplate its trials and triumphs, as we realize how completely the principles upon which it is based have met every national peril and every national need, how devoutly should we confess with Franklin, "God governs in the affairs of men"; and how solemn should be the reflection that to our hands is committed this ark of the people's covenant, and that ours is the duty to shield it from impious hands. We received it sealed with the tests of a century. It has been found sufficient in the past; and in all the future years it will be found sufficient, if the American people are true to their sacred trust. Another centennial day will come, and millions yet unborn will inquire concerning our stewardship and the safety of their Constitution. God grant that they may find it unimpaired; and as we rejoice in the patriotism and devotion of those who lived a hundred years ago, so may others who follow us rejoice in our fidelity and in our jealous love of constitutional liberty.

Although the initial observances of Constitution Day took place only in Philadelphia, the celebration of September 17 became more widespread during the first decades of the 20th century. Organizations such as the National Security League, the American Bar Association, and the National Society of the Sons of the American Revolution devoted much time and effort to popularizing the observance, and as early as 1919 at least 22 states and 100 cities sponsored special exercises on September 17 or took note of the anniversary in some other way.

The celebration continued to flourish throughout the first half of the 20th century, but in more recent years the observance of Citizenship Day has largely supplanted that of Constitution Day. However, the President of the United States and the governors of several states proclaim the entire week in which September 17 occurs as Constitution Week. During Constitution Week numerous patriotic organizations hold programs designed to acquaint the public with the history of the Constitution, and many schools make special efforts to instruct their pupils in the function and importance of the Constitution.

Of more recent origin than Constitution Day celebrations, but equally important as a forerunner of present Citizenship Day exercises, was the observance of "I Am an American" Day. A 1940 act of Congress set aside the third Sunday in May as "I Am an American" Day, and, during the next 12 years, festivities were held on that day to honor those who, by coming of age or by naturalization, had attained citizenship status. The President of the United States generally issued a proclamation each year recognizing the day, and cities across the nation sponsored special programs. Many localities held public ceremonies at which new citizens took the oath of allegiance, while in other areas pageantry, music, dancing, and speeches were employed to emphasize the importance and significance of the occasion.

As independent celebrations, both Constitution Day and "I Am an American" Day enjoyed widespread popularity. But because of the close relationship between the Constitution and the duties and privileges of American citizenship there was considerable feeling in favor of uniting the two observances. In response to this sentiment, Congress in 1952 approved the resolution and President Harry S. Truman signed the bill joining the two holidays. The new observance, known as Citizenship Day, has been the occasion of special celebration since 1952. And although separate observances of both Constitution Day and "I Am an American" Day have continued in some areas, Citizenship Day exercises have largely superseded these events.

The President annually proclaims Citizenship Day, as do the governors of a number of states. Celebrations of the day, of course, vary from place to place. For example, in 1959 the highlight of the observance in Washington, D.C., was a naturalization ceremony near the Washington Monument. Some noteworthy observances are the annual playlet in Los Angeles, in which local attorneys recreate the signing of the Constitution and the traditional "I Am an American" Day parade held in Baltimore, Maryland, which has attracted as many as 500,000 participants and spectators. Wherever Citizenship Day events occur and whatever their size, the countless programs across the country all stress the rights and obligations that the Constitution bestows upon the nation's citizens.

Baron von Steuben's Birthday

Under Commander in Chief George Washington, 10,000 poorly supplied soldiers of the Continental army suffered through the winter of 1777–1778 in their Valley Forge, Pennsylvania, camp, trying to keep themselves and their new nation alive. Despite the vital patriot victory at Saratoga in October 1777 (see October 17), the

British still held the major cities of New York and Philadelphia and menaced the rebel Congress meeting at York, Pennsylvania. American successes against British and Hessian regulars demonstrated that the colonists were not bumbling rustics, but their inconsistent performance reflected a lack of military finesse and discipline. Friedrich Wilhelm Augustus von Steuben remedied this deficiency after his arrival at the Valley Forge winter quarters on February 23, 1778.

Steuben was born on September 17, 1730, in the fortress at Magdeburg, Prussia, where his father served as an engineer lieutenant in the army of King Frederick William I. Entering the Prussian officer corps at the age of 17, the younger Steuben acted during the Seven Years' War of 1756 to 1763 as a member of the general staff and aide-de-camp to Frederick the Great. The general staff was a sophisticated institution unique to the Prussian military establishment, and Steuben's association with it equipped him with an expertise that would prove invaluable to the patriot cause during the American Revolution.

Discharged from the army with the rank of captain at the conclusion of the Seven Years' War, Steuben became the chamberlain of the prince of Hohenzollern-Hechingen and earned the title of baron. He accompanied the prince to France when financial embarrassments forced the closing of the court in 1771, but by 1776 the burden of his own debts led Steuben to seek other employment. A friend of his in Baden sent Steuben with a letter of introduction to Benjamin Franklin, the American representative in Paris.

Both Franklin and the Comte de Saint-Germain, who was French minister of war, recognized the Prussian's talents and arranged for him to go to America. Hotalez et Cie., a commercial corporation that covertly supplied French aid to the American colonial rebels, paid for Steuben's passage. The wily Franklin, without power to offer the baron a commission, insured his welcome to the colonies by promoting him, in a letter to George Washington, to "Lieutenant General in the King of Prussia's Service."

Steuben arrived in Portsmouth, New Hampshire, on December 1, 1777, and proceeded overland to York, Pennsylvania. The baron impressed the Continental Congress — which accorded him a reception worthy of his bogus status in the Prussian service — by offering to serve as a volunteer in the Continental army with no rank or pay, save compensation for his expenses. If the American cause was successful, he would expect a suitable reward; if it met with disaster, he would make no claim. Congress quickly dispatched him to join Washington at Valley Forge.

The baron's first task was to introduce the Continental army to the intricacies of military drill, a form of training requiring concentration and cooperation and intended to promote unified action. Steuben's inability to speak English inhibited communication with his pupils, but he overcame the obstacle by teaching, praising, and swearing at the soldiers through interpreters. He personally instructed a select company of 100 men, which he then employed as a model for the other units. The rapid progress made by the colonials under their Prussian tutor greatly pleased Washington, and, at his request, Congress on May 5, 1778, appointed Steuben inspector general with the rank of major general. On June 28 the value of Steuben's training was demonstrated in the rout of the British at the battle of Monmouth.

General von Steuben spent the next winter preparing his *Regulations for the Order and Discipline of the Troops of the United States,* a task that language differences made especially difficult. The baron wrote the manual in simple French, and an aide then put it into literary French. A third officer rendered it word for word into English, and another transformed this stilted product into a smoother English translation. The final version became the "blue book" of US military instruction and justified Steuben's sobriquet of Drill Master of the American Revolution.

Administrative ability was another of Steuben's assets. In the winter of 1779–1780 he served as Washington's representative to Congress on matters involving reorganization of the army. More important, the baron developed a system of property accountability that curtailed the egregious waste that bedeviled the American military.

General Nathanael Greene, who replaced Horatio Gates as American commander in the South in the autumn of 1780 after the disastrous defeat at Camden, New Jersey, gave Steuben the responsibility for Virginia, the state on which Greene relied for personnel and military support. Then, after Lafayette took charge of Virginia in April 1781, Steuben exercised his first field command in America, leading one of Washington's divisions at the climactic battle of Yorktown. His knowledge of siege warfare greatly contributed to that victory, which virtually concluded the colonies' successful revolution against British rule.

In 1783 Steuben helped Washington to plan for the future defense of the young United States and to demobilize the Continental army. Washington's last official act as commander in chief of the American forces was to write the baron expressing the depth of his respect for his Prussian aide:

Altho' I have taken frequent Opportunities both in public and private, of Acknowledging your great Zeal, Attention and Abilities in performing the duties of your Office; yet, I wish, to make use of this last Moment of my public life, to Signify in the strongest terms, my intire [sic] Approbation of your Conduct, and to express my Sense of the Obligations the public is under to you for your faithful and Meritorious Services.

Steuben received an honorable discharge on March 24, 1784. He remained in the United States after the Revolution, and the legislatures of Pennsylvania and New York, in March 1783 and July 1786 respectively, granted him American citizenship. A resident of New York City, Steuben was president of its branch of the Society of the Cincinnati, the organization of former Revolutionary War officers, and a member of the board of regents of the state university. He was also president of the community's German Society, which was founded in 1784.

In 1786 New York State bestowed on Steuben 16,000 acres of Mohawk Valley land, north of the city of Utica, and in 1790 Congress granted him a yearly pension of $2,500. In expectation of the government's offering him a large sum of money rather than an annuity, Steuben had allowed himself to assume heavy debts, but Secretary of the Treasury Alexander Hamilton and other friends extricated him through a liberal mortgage of his lands. The New York State legislature designated the baron's lands the Town of Steuben on April 10, 1792. Steuben thereafter spent his winters in New York City and his summers in a log-cabin retreat in the township that bears his name. He died of apoplexy in the latter place on November 28, 1794.

Steuben had desired that his final resting place be an unmarked grave situated on his own property. Although his request was carried out at the time of his death, later generations determined that he merited a more elaborate burying place. When highway construction necessitated the relocation of the grave, his remains were moved to a nearby five-acre wooded area named Sacred Grove. There the massive monument that presently surmounts his grave was dedicated on September 30, 1872.

In February 1931 the state of New York acquired title to 50 acres adjacent to Sacred Grove. Franklin Delano Roosevelt, then governor of New York, the German ambassador Dr. W. von Prittzwitz-Gaffon, and numerous other national, state, and local dignitaries presided at ceremonies dedicating these grounds as the Steuben State Memorial Park on September 12, 1931. Since that date, benefactors have contributed additional land to the park, and New York State has constructed a replica of the baron's log cabin on the premises. The site, located 15 miles north of Utica and 3 miles west of Remsen in the Oneida County Town of Steuben, is open to the public from May 1 to October 1. The Carl Schurz Society of Utica conducts memorial exercises every year at the site, and parking and picnicking facilities are available.

The Steuben Society of America, an organization of US citizens of German descent, is actively engaged in commemorating the Revolutionary hero. Founded in 1919 to encourage civic improvement in this country, the society now has units in many states. These local branches, in accordance with a directive from the society's national council, generally observe the anniversary of Steuben's birth with suitable exercises and encourage other patriotic organizations and officials to participate in the celebrations. The society also presents an annual award to the cadets graduating from West Point, Annapolis, and the Air Force Academy who display the greatest proficiency in the German language.

Valley Forge, Pennsylvania, the scene of Steuben's initial great contribution to the cause of American Independence, also has commemorated the baron. In June 1968, ten years of effort by the Pastorius Unit of the Steuben Society of America culminated in the official opening of the Steuben Quarters and Camp Hospital. The structure, which is located on Route 23, a short distance from the building that served as George Washington's headquarters, has been furnished by the society and is open to the public. In addition, the Valley Forge State Park contains a statue of Steuben that was erected by the National German-American Alliance of the United States of America in 1915. A celebration featuring German music and speeches takes place at the base of this monument each year on September 17.

Ceremonial and monumental tributes to Steuben abound throughout the nation. The New Jersey Park Department maintains the Steuben Home at River Edge, which the state gave to the baron in gratitude for his services. Although Steuben probably never occupied this residence, it is the site of an annual observance sponsored by the Steuben Society on or about September 17. Many cities, including Washington, D.C., Utica, and St. Louis, have statues of Steuben. The German government's contribution of a statue to the St. Louis World's Fair of 1904 was restored and mounted upon a granite pedestal in the city's Tower Grove Park in 1968. Still another landmark associated with the Prussian military leader is the New Windsor Cantonment, located a short distance from Newburgh, New York. This area, where Steuben encamped for a considerable time, has also been the scene of commemorative services.

New York City's Steuben Day parade is perhaps the most colorful observance of the baron's birthday. An annual event since 1958, the two-and-a-half-hour parade takes place on the Saturday afternoon immediately following September 17. Thousands of spectators crowd along the line of march, which generally proceeds from 61st Street up Fifth Avenue to 86th Street and then turns east to end at Second Avenue in the heart of Yorkville, New York's once predominantly German neighborhood. Floats, bands, and military contingents take part in the lively procession, as do large numbers of lederhosen-clad youth and girls in dirndls. The sounds of polka-playing bands alternate with the stirring brass and drums of more martial music. City and state officials and candidates for political office usually watch the merriment from the Fifth Avenue reviewing stand. And in Yorkville, where it all comes to a climax, a joyous spirit prevails. Celebration continues into the dinner hour and beyond, with paraders, families, and onlookers flooding into the area's German restaurants, beer halls, and pastry-laden *Konditoreien*. Since 1967 Chicago also has held a Steuben Day parade on or near the birth date of the Prussian hero of the American Revolution.

SEPTEMBER 18

Capitol Cornerstone Laid

Two years after Congress selected the District of Columbia as the site of the national capital in 1790 (see November 17, Congress Finds a Permanent Home), the district commissioners invited both professional and amateur architects to submit sketches for the city's two most important structures, the presidential residence and the home of Congress. The committee charged with choosing the winning entries quickly recognized that James Hoban's design for the executive mansion was the best plan, and the cornerstone for the building was laid on October 13, 1792. Selection of an appropriate design for the Capitol was more difficult.

The French architect Pierre Charles L'Enfant had already laid out the new federal city, and according to his plans the congressional building would occupy a hill that stood "as a pedestal waiting for a monument." The problem was that none of the designs originally entered in the contest reflected this majestic spirit: some were outlandish; most were mundane. Then, three months after the competition deadline, William Thornton, a physician, painter, and inventor, submitted his drawings. Thornton's work was outstanding. Secretary of State Thomas Jefferson remarked that it "captivated the eyes and judg-

ment of all." The committee agreed and, despite the lateness of his entry, named Thornton the winner of the competition.

During the months that followed, work on the Capitol progressed so rapidly that plans were made to lay the building's cornerstone on September 18, 1793. On that day, the festivities began with a parade. Uniformed members of the Alexandria Volunteer Artillery and the Masonic lodges of Maryland, Virginia, and the District of Columbia escorted President George Washington from Virginia across the Potomac River into Maryland and then on to the President's Square in the federal district. It was a grand occasion. According to one contemporary account, "the procession marched two abreast in the greatest solemn dignity, with music playing, drums beating, colours flying and spectators rejoicing." But participants in the parade had to contend with the primitive condition of the city: before reaching their destination at the top of Capitol Hill, the marchers had to skirt the "great Serbonian Bog," where Pennsylvania Avenue is now, and cross the Tiber Creek by either stepping from stone to stone or balancing along a single log.

In keeping with the custom of the period, elaborate Masonic rituals, dating from the Middle Ages when stonemasons and the Masonic Order were closely associated, formed a major part of the festivities. George Washington — in his dual capacity as President of the United States and acting grand master of Maryland's Masonic Grand Lodge — laid the cornerstone himself. Wearing a Masonic apron allegedly made by the wife of General Lafayette, the first President used a silver trowel and a marble-headed gavel to put the stone in place. Then he attached to it a silver plate that recorded the date of the ceremony as the 13th year after American independence, the first year of his second term, and the year 5793 of Masonry. Prayers and Masonic rituals followed, and the official program concluded with a 15-gun volley by the artillery company.

The 1793 cornerstone was only the first of several such markers laid at the Capitol. On August 24, 1818, the cornerstone for a center section that would connect the north and south wings was laid. Completion of this part of the building six years later made Thornton's original plan for a domed center area, flanked by two wings, at last a reality.

On July 4, 1851, a third cornerstone laying marked the beginning of work on much-needed additions to the Capitol. Since the North and the South had narrowly averted conflict over the perennial problem of slavery only one year before, it is not surprising that the 1851 ceremony combined the theme of national unity with the traditional Masonic rituals. The actual cornerstone laying recalled the 1793 festivities. Using the same trowel and gavel Washington had wielded 58 years before, President Millard Fillmore and B. B. French, the grand master of the Masonic fraternity, set the new stone amid customary civil and Masonic ceremonials. Then Secretary of State Daniel Webster gave the dedication address. In the most famous part of this speech, and, indeed, in the portion that Webster himself selected to be preserved in the cornerstone, the elder statesman voiced the feelings of many of his contemporaries:

If therefore it shall be hereafter the will of God that this structure shall fall from its base, that its foundation be upturned, and this deposit brought to the eyes of men, be it known that on this day, the Union of the United States stands firm; that their constitution still exists unimpaired, and with all its original usefulness and glory.

For almost a century — from 1863, when the work begun in 1851 was completed, until 1959 — no major alterations were made on the Capitol. However, by the mid-20th century the ever-expanding business of the federal government made it necessary to add another part to the building. Greater architectural balance and space for 75 additional Capitol offices were achieved when the center section's East Front was moved forward 32½ feet. Still another cornerstone was laid in the course of this construction. President Dwight D. Eisenhower put the Capitol's fourth cornerstone in place on July 4, 1959. Tradition played an important part in this ceremony: Eisenhower employed the same trowel and gavel Washington and Fillmore had used, and, as in 1793 and 1851, Masonic rituals formed an integral part of the program. The new addition was completed in 1961, with marble replacing the sandstone of the old East Front but following the design of the original sandstone.

SEPTEMBER 19

First Battle of Saratoga

September 19, 1777, marked the first of the two battles of Saratoga. Both battles took place somewhat south of the town of Saratoga, now Schuylerville, New York. Although the first battle — which was fought at Freeman's Farm, just north of Stillwater — was technically a victory for the British, it stopped their forces in their tracks and decisively cut them off from their objective, which had been Albany.

The second battle of Saratoga, which took place on October 7 of the same year, began with a British reconnaissance in force, directed toward the American positions at nearby Bemis Heights. It ended in a British rout, followed by a retreat, and by the historic surrender at Saratoga (see October 17).

Together the two battles constituted the turning point of the American Revolution. Not only had the relatively impoverished colonists defeated the great British army, they also had conducted themselves so impressively that they were able to persuade France to enter the war against England on the American side.

Feast of St. Januarius

The Feast of St. Januarius, or San Gennaro, the patron saint of Naples, falls on September 19, the date of his death as recorded in an early medieval source and as established officially at Rome in 1586. The strictly Roman Catholic observance, formerly considered Class III, is now ranked as an optional memorial.

There is little reliable information either about Januarius or about his martyrdom, although legends and traditions abound. He was apparently a bishop of Benevento in southern Italy who lived at the end of the third century and the beginning of the fourth. Januarius supposedly sought to bolster the faith of four Christians who had been imprisoned for their religious beliefs during the severe persecution launched by Diocletian and Maximian, the joint Roman emperors. About 305 he himself, during a visit to console his fellow believers, was denounced as a Christian and seized.

Accounts of his death vary. According to one of the more authentic, Timotheus, governor of the Campania region of southern Italy, ordered Januarius to be tossed into a fiery furnace, but the bishop is alleged to have remained perfectly comfortable. When the flames did not harm him, he is said to have been thrown to wild beasts in an amphitheater, located perhaps at Pozzuoli. The animals ignored him. Incensed, Timotheus declared that Januarius's immunity was the result of magic and ordered his beheading, at which moment the governor suddenly became blind. Januarius restored his sight, a miracle that swayed 5,000 spectators to profess Christianity. The bishop of Benevento finally met martyrdom by the sword.

The martyr's relics were at first preserved in Benevento, but they were later removed to Monte Vergine and then to Naples, where they are now honored in the cathedral. The oldest extant reference to the saint — that of Uranius (431) — attests to the existence of a cult devoted to Januarius as early as the fifth century. The local inhabitants of the Naples area attributed to his intercession the sudden arresting of an eruption of Mount Vesuvius, the smoldering volcano near Naples. The bishop's relics continued to be venerated throughout the Middle Ages as protection against future upheavals, and Januarius became the patron saint of Naples.

In modern times, St. Januarius has acquired renown not so much because of his obscure life and death, but because of his relics. A silver bust in the cathedral of Naples reputedly encloses his skull, and a flagon-shaped vial contained in a glass reliquary on a jeweled stand contains a substance said to be his dried blood caught by a pious woman onlooker at his martyrdom.

Since the mid-15th century, the relic of his blood has increasingly attracted worldwide attention. About 18 times yearly, especially in May, September, and December, it is exhibited publicly before the silver bust. The anniversary of the translation of the saint's relics to Naples falls in May; September is the feast-day month of the saint; and the December commemoration marks the occasion in December 1631 when the saint is said to have answered the desperate pleas of the residents of his city and protected them from another volcanic eruption. When exposed, the apparently congealed blood liquefies after a time span ranging from several minutes to several hours. The fact that the substance in the vial periodically liquefies is now accepted beyond dispute. How and why this phenomenon happens, however, has been the subject of controversy. Some claim that the transformation is a miracle, a supernatural sign; others hold that a natural scientific explanation must exist and will undoubtedly be unearthed with more thorough investigation.

Not only Neapolitans but also their descendants in the United States celebrate the Festa di San Gennaro — the feast of St. Januarius or San Gennaro — every year around the third week in September. In particular, Italians in New York City stage an impressive celebration in the center of the original Italian neighborhood, known as Little Italy, between Chinatown and Greenwich Village. The combined religious observance and carnival, sponsored by the local Società San Gennaro and run by a committee of the society, usually lasts at least 10 days. It has been held annually since 1926.

Similar to other Italian festivals in New York, such as that of St. Anthony of Padua, but larger and more elaborate, the Festa di San Gennaro attracts thousands of visitors to the 15-block area centering on Mulberry Street, where the rectory of the Roman Catholic Church of the Most Precious Blood is located. The narrow streets of

Little Italy, intermittently filled with music for the occasion, are bedecked with tiara-shaped illuminated arches, colorful sidewalk booths, gaily decorated pushcarts, and carnival equipment. A number of restaurants feature Neapolitan cuisine, but the aroma of Italian specialties pervades every corner of the festival area, tempting all comers to engage in prodigious eating feats by sampling such delights as *calzone* (a pasta-encased, fried combination of ricotta and mozzarella cheese and ham or sausage), *zeppole* (a fried doughnut covered with sugar), cream cakes, and *torrone* (nougat) — not to mention the ever-present sausages and peppers, clams on the half-shell, and pizza. The highlight of the street festival is the float parade and procession. A gold-covered bust of St. Januarius — displayed the rest of the year in the Church of the Most Precious Blood on Baxter Street, a block away — is borne through the streets, while spectators pin contributions of dollar bills or bills of larger denominations to the streamers hanging from the statue to help defray festival expenses. The bust is exhibited in an outdoor shrine at the corner of Hester and Mulberry streets during the course of the festival.

SEPTEMBER 20

Panic of 1873

In associating economic collapse with the stock market crash of 1929 and the subsequent depression, Americans often overlook earlier economic history, including five crises in the 19th century. The "panics," as contemporaries labeled them, of 1819, 1837, 1857, 1873, and 1893 were not so severe as the Great Depression of the 20th century, but they caused considerable hardship. Indeed, the panic of 1873 precipitated one of the longest periods of economic contraction in America, lasting until 1879.

The collapse marked the termination of the period of economic expansion that followed the Civil War. By 1869 the Transcontinental Railroad (see May 10) had linked the coasts of the United States, and numerous new subsidiary routes supplemented the older networks of the eastern half of the nation. The increases in immigration and population provided a strong stimulus to the construction of houses, another major industry that enjoyed peak years in the early 1870s.

By 1873 the tight money market had deprived the railroads of investors. The unnecessary expansion of some lines complicated the problems caused by the scarcity of backers, and, during the first eight months of the year, 25 railroads found themselves unable to pay the interest on their bonds. Such failures darkened economic prospects.

Jay Cooke, the chief financier of the Union effort during the Civil War, fell victim to the railroads' difficulties. In the expectation that European financiers would soon purchase from him bonds worth $100 million, Cooke put money obtained from short-term depositors into the Northern Pacific Railroad, a long-term investment, which was far from completion. When no foreign backers appeared and the depositors called for their money, Cooke was unable to meet his commitments. The failure of the prestigious Jay Cooke and Company on September 18, 1873, precipitated the collapse of numerous other firms in similar circumstances and touched off a banking panic that forced the New York Stock Exchange to close, for the first time in its history, on September 20.

Levelheaded action by New York bankers quickly terminated the financial panic. On September 24 a five-man committee of the New York Clearing House Association took control of the cash reserves of the organization's member banks and used them freely to restore confidence. By September 27 the monetary crisis was over, and in October bankers' cash reserves began to increase.

Although short-lived, the banking panic did serious damage to the economy. Businessmen reduced or canceled orders and were unable to meet their payrolls; unpaid employees bought fewer goods. Added to the unfavorable investment prospects, this temporary interruption of the nation's commerce was enough to cause a full-scale depression.

More than 18,000 business enterprises, including the majority of the nation's railroads, went bankrupt during the depth of the depression in 1876 and 1877. Half a million workers lost their jobs as a result of the collapse, and countless others had their wages lowered. Political theory of that time assigned no responsibility to the government for relief operations, and private charities, inadequate even during good times, could not answer all the pleas for help.

Labor problems increased significantly during the depression. On July 17, 1877, workers on the Baltimore and Ohio Railroad struck to protest wage cuts, and the stoppage quickly spread to other rail lines across the country. Riots occurred in Baltimore, Chicago, and St. Louis, and on July 21, twenty-six people died as a Pittsburgh mob battled the militia and then burned almost $10 million worth of railroad property. Federal troops, dispatched by President Rutherford B. Hayes, finally restored order, but only

the eventual return of prosperity brought real peace to the nation.

The investment outlook improved in 1877, but several short-term factors delayed the advent of recovery. In particular, strikes, rate wars, and legislation inspired by the National Grange farm organization all adversely affected the major industry of railroading. Prosperity finally returned, however, in 1879, when the government's readoption of the gold standard increased business confidence, and crop shortages in Europe provided a strong stimulus to American exports.

SEPTEMBER 21

Autumn Begins (Traditional Date)

Although autumn in some years begins on September 21 in the north temperate zones and although many people think of it in connection with that day, the date varies between September 21, 22, and 23. Most authorities give September 23 as the approximate date of the autumnal equinox (see September 23, Autumn Begins).

Delaware Organized as a State

In the colonial period of America, Sweden, the Netherlands, and England successively ruled the area of Delaware. England gained control of Delaware in 1664, and in 1682 the duke of York gave William Penn, proprietor of the new colony of Pennsylvania, title to the counties of Kent, New Castle, and Sussex, which today comprise the state. Delaware settlers were not pleased with their inclusion in Penn's colony, and in 1704 Penn allowed them to hold a separate assembly, although the governor of Pennsylvania continued to administer the so-called Three Lower Counties.

The American Revolution gave Delaware residents the opportunity to determine their own destiny. Although still technically under the jurisdiction of the governor of Pennsylvania, Delaware sent its own delegates to the Second Continental Congress, which declared the independence of the United States in 1776. In the following August a constitutional convention met to form a government for Kent, New Castle, and Sussex counties. On September 21, 1776, the convention completed organizing the government for the new and autonomous Delaware State. Later, in 1787, Delaware had the honor of being the first state to ratify the Constitution of the United States and consequently won for itself the title of the First State.

Feast of St. Matthew

The Feast of St. Matthew, one of the 12 Apostles and one of the four Evangelists, is observed on September 21 by the Roman Catholic church, the Episcopal church, and some other Protestant churches. The feast is celebrated on November 16 by Byzantine Rites of the Roman Catholic church and by Greek and Russian Orthodox churches (on November 29 if the Julian calendar is used).

St. Matthew was from Galilee, the region that included the towns of Cana, Capernaum, Tiberias, and Nazareth. As a tax collector, he was stationed in Capernaum, where Jesus preached during the early part of his ministry. Matthew is traditionally credited with the authorship of the first book of the New Testament.

In his Gospel (9:9), he records how he was summoned by Jesus: "Now as Jesus passed on from there, he saw a man named Matthew sitting in the tax-collector's place, and said to him, 'Follow me.' And he arose and followed him." The Gospels of St. Mark (2:13) and St. Luke (5:27) give the same report of this incident, except that they refer to the tax collector or publican as Levi. St. Mark further identifies him as the son of Alpheus. However, all three call him Matthew in listing the names of the Apostles in their Gospels, and it is possible that Jesus gave him that name. (Mattai in Aramaic means "gift of God.")

One other incident concerning St. Matthew is recorded by these three Evangelists just after their accounts of Jesus' calling Matthew to be an Apostle. In St. Luke's words (5:28):

And leaving all things, he [Levi or Matthew] arose and followed him [Jesus]. And Levi gave a great feast for him at his house; and there was a great gathering of publicans and others, who were at the table with them. And the Pharisees and their scribes were grumbling, saying to his disciples, "Why do you eat and drink with publicans and sinners?" And Jesus answered and said to them, "It is not the healthy who need a physician, but they who are sick. I have not come to call the just, but sinners to repentance."

As a publican, Matthew's job included collecting taxes and customs duties from everyone, Jews and Gentiles alike. Publicans were especially disdained by scholarly or upper-class Jews for dealing with "unclean" Gentiles, and even handling their money. They were held in such low esteem that it was common to mention "publicans and sinners" in the same breath.

Matthew left his tax and customs records behind when he followed Jesus (Judas was charged with monetary tasks), but his organized habits and orderly way of keeping records show in his clear, ledger-like account of Christ's life. Matthew wrote his Gospel for the Jews in Palestine, bringing in Hebrew background and identifying Jesus as the fulfillment of the prophecies of the Scriptures.

It can be assumed that Matthew was one of the Apostles present at the Last Supper as well as one of the witnesses of the Resurrection and Ascension. The meager record of his life in the New Testament is supplemented by tradition, much of which is of doubtful value, partly because of confusion between Matthew and St. Matthias, who replaced Judas as an Apostle. According to one tradition, St. Matthew was martyred, possibly in Persia, and his body reposes in the Cathedral of Salerno, Italy.

SEPTEMBER 22

Nathan Hale Hanged

Nathan Hale, the son of a prosperous farmer, Richard Hale, and his wife, Elizabeth, was born in Coventry, Connecticut, on June 6, 1755. He entered Yale College at the age of 14 and was graduated in 1773 with high honors. A friend once described Nathan Hale as slightly above average height, blue-eyed, extraordinarily agile, pious, and as having a "rather sharp or piercing" voice. Several tales are still recounted of his athletic prowess, but education attracted him at an early age, and shortly after leaving Yale he accepted a teaching position in East Haddam, Connecticut. He remained there for several months and then moved to New London, where he taught for about a year.

The first skirmishes of the American Revolution ended Hale's academic career in 1775. Five of his brothers battled the redcoats at Lexington and Concord, and Nathan Hale joined the fight on July 6, 1775, when he was commissioned a lieutenant in the Seventh Connecticut militia. Despite his youth — he was only 20 at the time of his enlistment — Hale advanced quickly. By the following summer he had earned the rank of captain and commanded a company of rangers in New York.

Shortly before the battle of Harlem Heights, General George Washington requested a volunteer for an intelligence mission behind enemy lines. Hale agreed to perform the task. Explaining his reasons for accepting the mission to one of his friends, he stated: "I wish to be useful, and every kind of service, necessary to the public good, becomes honorable by being necessary."

Disguised as a Dutch schoolteacher, Hale left the rebel camp at Harlem Heights about September 12. For the next nine days he gathered much information on the position of the British troops, and he was returning to the American entrenchment when he was captured by the enemy.

The British sentries took Hale to Beekman Mansion, the heaquarters of their commander in chief, General William Howe. It was at the mansion that he was allegedly betrayed by his cousin Samuel Hale, who was serving as Howe's deputy commissioner of prisoners. But even without his cousin's testimony there was little doubt that Hale was a spy: when captured he was not in uniform, and he had incriminating papers in his possession. Howe did not hesitate to sentence his prisoner. Without allowing him the benefit of a trial, Howe ordered that Hale be hanged the following day.

As he approached death on Sunday, September 22, the young schoolmaster did not forget his academic training. Inspired by words of the English writer Joseph Addison, "What pity is it / That we can die but once to save our country!," Nathan Hale concluded his speech at the gallows with his own ringing statement: "I only regret that I have but one life to lose for my country."

Connecticut has not forgotten the martyr spy of the Revolution. The state's governor annually proclaims September 22, the anniversary of his death, as Nathan Hale Day. In addition there are several historic areas in the state closely connected with his short-lived career. Visitors to New London may tour the schoolhouse where Hale taught for a year. The 20-by-30-foot frame structure has been moved from its original site to the Old Town Mill on Mill Street, not far from the town's business district. In East Haddam the one-room schoolhouse that was the scene of Hale's first teaching efforts is also open for public inspection.

A popular attraction in South Coventry is the 12-room Nathan Hale homestead. The patriot himself never saw the completed building, since it was finished several months after his death. However, the present structure does stand on the site of his birth, and local tradition persists that part of the ell of the existing house is a remnant of the original birthplace. Many mementos of Hale's life are on exhibit there: the silver shoe buckles that he removed just before he went behind the British lines; a shadow drawing, which is the only known likeness of Hale extant; and his troop records, diaries, and personal letters. The house, which was bequeathed to the Antiquarian and Landmarks Society of Connecticut in 1948, is situated in the midst of the Nathan Hale State Forest. The Society has furnished the homestead and invites the public to visit.

Several statues have also been erected in Hale's memory. The most famous are those located at City Hall Park in New York City, at Yale University in New Haven, and in the Connecticut Statehouse at Hartford.

Preliminary Emancipation Proclamation

On September 22, 1862, several days after Union troops had claimed at least a technical victory in the Civil War battle of Antietam, in Maryland, President Lincoln issued his preliminary Emancipation Proclamation. The proclamation declared his intention to issue another proclamation 100 days later, which would declare free the slaves in those states then deemed to be in rebellion. The result was the great Emancipation Proclamation of 1863 (see January 1).

SEPTEMBER 23

Autumn Begins

According to most sources, autumn begins "about September 23" in the United States and the north temperate zones generally. In actual fact, the season known as autumn, or fall, can start on September 21, 22, or 23. The numerous oscillations and wobbling motions that the earth undergoes, both in its daily rotation on its axis and in its annual elliptical course around the sun, cause the date of the autumnal equinox—which marks the official change of season—to vary slightly each year.

Astronomically the start of the third season of the year, which comes between summer and winter, can be pinpointed precisely. The ecliptic, the plane in which the sun seems to revolve about the earth and in which the earth actually revolves about the sun, is divided into four 90° sections, each of which commences with a specific point: two equinoxes and two solstices. Autumn starts at the autumnal equinox (Latin *aequinoctium*, from *aequus* meaning "equal" and *nox* meaning "night") situated halfway between the summer solstice, the start of summer (see June 21) and the winter solstice, the start of winter (see December 22). The period from the autumnal equinox to the winter solstice has been designated the season of autumn.

Autumn is also said to begin when the sun appears to reach the zodiac sign of Libra, the scales (see Appendix, The Zodiac). That statement is somewhat misleading today since precession—the backward movement of the equinoctial points—has caused a retrograde motion of 30° for over the past 2,000 years. Thus the autumnal equinox, which used to be found in

Libra, is presently in the sign of Virgo, the virgin. Only at the completion of a 25,800-year cycle will the autumnal equinox once more be located in Libra.

It is thought that Libra received its designation as "the scales" from the "balancing" or equality of day and night that occurs at the equinoxes, vernal (see March 21) as well as autumnal. About September 23, the sun appears to reach the intersection of the celestial equator and the ecliptic, having then a celestial longitude of 180° and a declination of 0°. Its rays extend from the North to the South Pole.

During the season of autumn, the sun, having crossed the celestial equator from north to south, leaves that great circle and progresses along the ecliptic south of it. The sun's south declination increases constantly. At the winter solstice, when the sun is said to enter the zodiac sign of Capricorn, it reaches a longitude of 270° and its maximum south declination of −23° 27′. Autumn then ends.

In the Northern Hemisphere, autumn is the shortest season after winter because of the earth's changing velocity in its yearly orbit; the difference in speed is due to the elliptical shape of the orbit and the laws of motion. The earth travels most rapidly in early January and most slowly in early July. Astronomically, autumn comprises the months of September, October, and November in the Northern Hemisphere. In some sections of the North American continent, however, the climate does not necessarily coincide with the astronomical divisions, September often seeming like part of summer and November often wintry. In great Britain autumn is popularly thought to encompass August, September, and October.

Seasonal differences, especially the regular fluctuations in weather, are the result of the tilt of the earth's axis (23½°) as well as of the elliptical nature of its revolution around the sun. When the North Pole points directly toward the sun at the summer solstice, the amount of solar radiation absorbed daily by the surface and atmosphere of the earth is high; so, consequently, are temperatures. By the winter solstice, when the North Pole inclines away from the sun, opposite conditions prevail. Like spring, autumn is therefore a transitional period between the extremes of summer and winter. In the Southern Hemisphere the seasons are reversed, since the South Pole moves in the opposite direction from the North Pole. Astronomical autumn begins there about March 21 and ends about June 21.

The season of autumn has always played a vivid role in the life of the farmer. As the period of harvest, vintage, and fruit gathering it has left an imprint not only on day-to-day living but also on the development of folklore, mythology, and art. The intimate intertwining of art and nature can be seen in the detailed depictions of the autumn months in the French cathedrals; at Reims, for example, in one of the carved stone scenes portraying the calendar year, fermenting wine is being transferred from vats to casks. The season itself was often personified as a female figure bearing grapes.

The harvest moon, the full moon nearest to the autumnal equinox, appears above the horizon at about sunset for a number of days each fall, thereby providing sufficient light for farmers to continue harvesting well into the night.

Lewis and Clark Expedition Completed

When the explorers Meriwether Lewis and William Clark appeared in St. Louis on September 23, 1806 — to the astonishment of a world that had thought them dead — their return from the first recorded overland crossing of the continent was celebrated with excitement in St. Louis, where they were "met by all the village." As the news spread, the entire nation celebrated their return. A century later, the 1905 Lewis and Clark Exposition at Portland, Oregon, honored their achievement, which, according to an exposition pamphlet, had "made possible the acquisition and permanent occupation of . . . the magnificent Golden West" by the United States. The federal government, Oregon and 16 other states, various industries, and 15 foreign countries participated in the exposition, on a 406-acre lakeside site.

The 1954–1956 Lewis and Clark Sesquicentennial was the occasion of observances in towns all along the explorers' trail, particularly in the six northwest states carved from the territory through which they had passed — Washington, Oregon, Idaho, Montana, and North and South Dakota. The parades, dances, and historical pageants that dotted their route at various times during the two-year period were supplemented by other events — such as a 100-mile marathon boat race from Coeur d'Alene, Idaho, and the Ilwaco, Washington, dedication of a marker at the point from which the explorers first saw the Pacific. Particularly notable were the sesquicentennial events that took place the weekend of October 6–9, 1955, in the neighboring towns of Lewiston, Idaho, and Clarkston, Washington. They included a parade, buffalo barbecue, Indian war dance, water pageant, air show, governors' breakfast, and dedication of a Lewis-Clark marker placed by the Daughters of the American Revolution at the Lewiston end of the Interstate Bridge over the Snake River. Another feature of the sesquicentennial was the retracing of Lewis and Clark's route, or sections of it, by many travelers, among them more than 1,000 Boy Scouts.

To anyone familiar with the inquiring mind of President Thomas Jefferson, who had been trying for two decades to bring about exploration west of the Mississippi, his commissioning of the Lewis and Clark expedition in 1803 should have come as no surprise. When Jefferson named Lewis, a fellow Virginian whom he had known as a boy, as his private secretary in 1801, it probably was with this in mind. Captain Lewis, who had been born on August 18, 1774, near Charlottesville, Virginia, had spent several years in the Northwest Territory while serving in the army. He subsequently added to his qualifications for wilderness survival by traveling to Philadelphia to study botany, zoology, and celestial navigation.

Lewis persuaded Jefferson to let him name his friend Lieutenant William Clark as coleader of the expedition. A veteran of frontier service against the Indians, Clark, like Lewis, had served in the army under General Anthony Wayne. Born on August 1, 1770, he was 18 years younger than his noted brother, George Rogers Clark of American Revolutionary fame. Like both Jefferson and Lewis, he came from an old Virginia family, but he had less book learning than either.

With the more than 40 healthy "hardy young men" they had assembled for the expedition, Lewis and Clark spent the winter of 1803–1804 at Wood River, near St. Louis, getting supplies and preparing to follow Jefferson's instructions to explore, observing carefully geographical features, flora, fauna, Indian customs, climate, and commercial possibilities. Before they set out on May 14, 1804, with two dugouts and a 55-foot keelboat, Jefferson had concluded the great Louisiana Purchase, whereby the United States, for $15 million, acquired a vast territory stretching from the Mississippi to the Rocky Mountains.

The explorers followed the Missouri River, whose treacherous current they fought every mile of the way, along what are now the borders between Kansas and Missouri, and Nebraska and Iowa. In Iowa their journey is commemorated in Council Bluffs by a Lewis and Clark Memorial and in Sioux City by the grave of Sergeant Charles Floyd, the expedition's one fatality, who was "taken verry bad all at once" and "died with a great deal of Composure." In South Dakota they are remembered in the naming of Lewis and Clark Lake, formed by the Gavins Point Dam, which was completed in 1957, and by a monument at the Crow Creek Indian Reservation.

By November 2 the explorers had ascended the river 1,600 miles to the Mandan Sioux villages, 60 miles above what is now Bismarck,

North Dakota. There they built Fort Mandan and spent their second winter among friendly Indians who lived in earthen lodges.

In April 1805 the party continued up the hostile Missouri. With them now were two guides, Toussaint Charbonneau and his Shoshone wife, Sacagawea, whom he had bought from slave traders. A native of what is now southwestern Montana, the resourceful Sacagawea traveled with her infant on her back while she served as interpreter and principal guide of the expedition. (A statue of Sacagawea now stands in Bismarck.)

It took the party nearly a month to make portage around the falls near Great Falls, Montana. As they approached the Rocky Mountains, the Missouri took them through a canyon that they named Gates of the Mountains — because of its towering rock walls, which gave the illusion of opening before them and closing behind them like monstrous gates. Today's summer visitors can experience the same sensation via sightseeing boat from a spot 16 miles north of Helena. The explorers also passed the site of Three Forks, at the juncture of three forks of the Missouri River, where annual pageants now recreate episodes from their trip. Meanwhile, they had also passed near what is now called Lewis and Clark Cavern in Montana's Lewis and Clark State Park.

Passing landmarks that Sacagawea recognized from her childhood, the explorers then followed the fork of the Missouri that they named the Jefferson to its source in southwestern Montana. Unable to negotiate the Salmon River in nearby Idaho — it was, in Clark's words, "almost one continued rapid" — Lewis and Clark bartered for horses with a Shoshone chief who turned out to be the brother of Sacagawea.

Detouring 110 miles north through the Bitterroot Range of the Rockies, they were able to turn west through the Lolo Pass. Ill, nearly starved, and plagued by early snow, they were reduced to eating bear oil and candles before they reached the headwaters of the Clearwater River at what is now Orofino, Idaho, 125 miles farther on, and paused to build canoes. So difficult was the terrain that a century of effort was required before the region's isolation could be ended. The Lewis-Clark Highway, US 12, completed in 1962, follows the same route.

The Clearwater led into the Snake, and the Snake into the Columbia River, which carried the explorers westward along what is now the boundary between Oregon and Washington. On November 15, 1805, they finally reached the mouth of the Columbia. Clark recorded the event with understandable elation: "Ocian in view! O! the joy."

On March 23, 1806, Lewis and Clark began

their comparatively rapid trip back to St. Louis. Just east of the Continental Divide they separated, Lewis going north with one party to explore (and name) the Marias River, and Clark going south to explore the Yellowstone. En route he sighted and named a huge rock, Pompeys Pillar (28 miles east of Billings, Montana), which bears the only visible evidence of the expedition — Clark's carving of his own name. Reuniting just below the junction of the Missouri and Yellowstone rivers, Lewis and Clark reached St. Louis on September 23, 1806, bearing with them their remarkable diaries and Clark's excellent maps and drawings.

In providing the first detailed description of the largely unknown territory through which they had traveled, Lewis and Clark gave impetus to the opening of the West, presenting the United States with a valid claim to the Oregon Territory, contributing scientific and geographic knowledge, and ending the long and futile search for an easy northwest passage across the continent by water. They were rewarded with double their promised pay and 1,600 acres apiece of public land. Lewis was appointed governor of the Louisiana Territory. Clark was named superintendent of Indian affairs at St. Louis and became governor of the Missouri Territory, in which capacity he concluded treaties with the Indians after the War of 1812. He lived until September 1, 1838. Lewis, however, died early, probably the victim of foul play, on October 11, 1809, in central Tennessee.

Near what is now Astoria, Oregon, Lewis and Clark built Fort Clatsop, where they spent the winter of 1805–1806. It is now the site of a 125-acre park. During the 1954–1956 Lewis and Clark Sesquicentennial, a reconstruction of the fort was dedicated by Secretary of the Interior Douglas McKay and Governor Paul L. Patterson of Oregon. The "Lewis and Clark party" arrived by water for the occasion, which also featured Indian dances, a barbecue, and the selection of Miss Sacagawea. On August 25, 1963, the reconstructed fort was rededicated in the presence of Senator Maurine Neuberger and Representative Walter Norblad — who had introduced bills establishing it as a national memorial — and the director of the National Park Service, Conrad L. Wirth.

SEPTEMBER 24

John Marshall's Birthday

John Marshall, the fourth chief justice of the United States, was born in Germantown (now Midland), Virginia, on September 24, 1755. He enlisted in the Continental army in 1776, and within a year rose to the rank of captain. Mar-

shall fought in several of the important early battles of the American Revolution — Brandywine, Germantown, and Monmouth — and spent the harsh winter of 1777–1778 at Valley Forge. In 1780 he resigned his army commission and returned to Virginia, where he attended law lectures at the College of William and Mary. Following his admission to the bar in 1781, the fledgling lawyer established his first practice in his native Fauquier County, but after only a few years he moved to Richmond, the state capital, in 1783. There Marshall quickly advanced his legal reputation, and, equally important for the advancement of his career, married Mary Willis Ambler, the daughter of Virginia's treasurer.

Marshall served in the Virginia assembly almost continuously from 1782 to 1797 and was also a representative to the state convention that ratified the federal Constitution. President George Washington offered him the cabinet post of attorney general in 1795 and the position of US minister to France in 1796, but Marshall declined both offices.

Despite this initial reluctance to enter national politics, Marshall did consent in 1797 to go to Paris with C. C. Pinckney and Elbridge Gerry to try to persuade the French to remove restrictions on American commerce. Although this mission failed, it so increased Marshall's renown that he won election in 1799 to the US House of Representatives.

By the end of the 1790s, two distinct political parties had developed in the United States: the Federalists, who advocated a strong national government; and the Democratic-Republicans, who favored a more decentralized system. John Marshall was an ardent Federalist. He served briefly as secretary of state during the administration of John Adams, his copartisan, but, ironically, he exerted his greatest influence when the opposing party occupied the White House. In 1800 Thomas Jefferson, the Democratic-Republican candidate, won the presidency and gained control of the executive branch of the national government. However, just before Adams left office in 1801 he appointed Marshall chief justice of the United States and thereby insured Federalist dominance of the judiciary.

Marshall's accomplishments as chief justice securely established the prestige of the Supreme Court. In the 1803 case of *Marbury* v. *Madison*, he insisted that it was the function of the Supreme Court to interpret the Constitution and to decide whether the acts of Congress and of the state legislatures exceeded the powers delegated to these bodies. In addition he himself wrote many of the most important opinions handed down during his 34 years on the bench, and these decisions reflected his belief in a strong national government.

Marshall's most famous defense of such a system of government is contained in his 1819 opinion in the case of *McCulloch* v. *Maryland:* "Let the end be legitimate, let it be within the scope of the constitution, and all means which are not prohibited, but consist with the letter and spirit of the constitution, are constitutional." This doctrine of "implied powers" has served to extend the powers of the federal government in areas beyond those specifically enumerated in the Constitution.

Marshall's service to his country ended in 1835. Following a stagecoach accident, he was taken to a Philadelphia hospital, where he died on July 6, 1835. The Liberty Bell in the tower of Independence Hall tolled to announce his death.

Visitors to Richmond are welcomed today at the John Marshall House at 810 East Marshall Street. Designed by the great jurist himself, the house contains original paneling and floors, and many family mementos. The Association for the Preservation of Virginia Antiquities maintains the site. The residence Marshall occupied in Washington, D.C., has been bequeathed to the National Trust for Historic Preservation.

SEPTEMBER 25

American Indian Day

This is a movable event. See note on page xxvi.

American Indian Day, dedicated to recognizing and honoring Native Americans and improving their condition, is not a universal holiday in the United States. Various members of Congress have sponsored numerous resolutions to have a single date proclaimed for official nationwide observance, but as of 1977, no definitive action had been taken. The observance and its date are left to the individual states and vary widely.

The states that usually note the day are those that have large Indian populations. Each state has its own version of the day, which is not a religious or ceremonial occasion but rather an event of educational and promotional nature to awaken interest in and knowledge of Native Americans and their achievements. The Connecticut statute proclaiming the day, for example, stipulates that it is to be "suitably observed in the public schools of the state as a day of commemoration for the American Indian and his contributions to American life and civilization."

The fourth Friday in September is the date on which American Indian Day is usually celebrated. As early as 1919, Illinois chose this day, and Arizona, California, and Connecticut are among the states that have followed suit. Other states observe an Indian Day on the second Saturday in May or select a day convenient for their residents. A 1935 Massachusetts statute

provided for the observance of Indian Day but did not immediately specify a date. November 25 was later set aside for the commemoration in 1935 and 1936, but according to a 1939 amendment to the original statute, the governor annually proclaims August 12 as Indian Day. In New York State, American Indian Day customarily occurs in September; the specific date, however, is determined by the governor's office upon the request of Indian groups and varies from year to year. Oklahoma designates the first Saturday after the full moon in September, and the Maine Indian Day, primarily observed on the Penobscot Indian Reservation just north of Old Town, falls in late July.

The origins of American Indian Day extend back to the early 20th century. In 1912 the anthropologist and archeologist Arthur C. Parker, director of the Museum of Arts and Sciences at Rochester, New York, urged that a day should be set aside to honor the American Indian. Dr. Parker, of Seneca ancestry, persuaded the Boy Scouts to adopt his suggestion, and for three years they observed an American Indian Day.

In 1914 Red Fox James of the Blackfeet tribe, now headquartered in Montana, rode a pony 4,000 miles seeking approval for celebrating a day in honor of Indians. The governors of 24 states expressed their sympathy with the movement. Red Fox James presented their endorsements at the White House on December 14, 1914. In 1915 the Society of American Indians, at its annual congress held at Lawrence, Kansas, and attended by 1,250, directed its president, the Reverend Sherman Coolidge, an Arapaho, to call upon the country to observe an American Indian Day on the second Saturday in May. He accordingly issued a proclamation on September 28, 1915, urging recognition of Indian citizenship, and Indian loyalty to the United States. It was the first formal appeal for definite recognition of Indians as citizens. Coolidge concluded:

We call upon our country not only to consider the past but to earnestly consider our present and our future as a part of the American people. To them we declare our needs now and tomorrow as those primarily of Americans struggling for enlightenment and that competency that is consistent with American citizenship. We do avow our hopes and our destiny inseparably united to that of the people of the United States of America and that our hearts and minds are now and forever loyal to our country, which we would serve in our fullest capacity as men and Americans.

In line with this appeal, the first general American Indian Day was observed on the second Saturday in May, when the governor of New York fixed May 13, 1916, for its observance in his state. He called attention to the fact that the Confederacy of the Six Nations of the Iroquois had occupied the region long before it had been taken by white settlers. He also asked for consideration of the present and future needs of Indians living on reservations in the state.

There are sizable numbers of Indians in many states, and at least small numbers in all. Oklahoma, with about 100,000, has the largest Indian population, and it is followed by Arizona, California, New Mexico, and North Carolina. According to the US Census for 1970, there were almost 800,000 Indians in the United States, more than half living on or near reservations in 24 states, and the rest residing in cities and towns throughout the nation.

Some changes for the better have been made in the Indians' condition since the integrationist appeal by Sherman Coolidge. A June 15, 1924, act finally granted US citizenship to all Indians born in this country. By 1926 the failings of the previous 40 years of Indian policy had become painfully evident as the result of extensive governmental investigations. Indians, according to the findings, were generally extremely poor, in bad health with a short life expectancy, poorly educated, and uninterested in serious adjustment to the predominant culture of the nation.

The Indian Reorganization Act of June 18, 1934, was the first major step towards reform of the status of Indians and promotion of their well-being. It provided, among other things, for an end to the disastrous land allotment program of 1887, which had resulted in the dissipation of a large part of tribal land holdings; for augmented self-government and responsibility; for a revolving credit program for land purchases; and for increased educational support. Apart from its aim of raising Indians' deplorable standard of living, the act helped make more possible the preservation of Indian identity and heritage through its provisions for tribal self-government and religious and cultural freedom. Increased civic involvement on the part of Indians, beyond reservation boundaries, followed official recognition of Indians' right to preserve their own culture. It was also becoming apparent that the Indian population, which long had been declining — from an estimated 846,000 in 1492 to 244,437 recorded in the 1920 US Census — had begun to rise. The long-held picture of the "vanishing American" began to fade after the 1930 census noted an Indian population of 332,397.

By 1948 American Indians were able to vote in virtually all states — even those that had long placed obstacles in the way of their exercising this right of citizenship. In 1952 the US Department of the Interior inaugurated a controversial new policy for ending federal control over Indians and reservations. Although some of the tribes reportedly were unprepared for self-government, others were released from federal trust supervision as early as the start of the 1960s. Since the 1950s, federal authorities, besides encouraging Indians to play a decisive role in their own affairs, have sought to promote development of the reservations' natural resources and to assist those Indians desiring relocation to cities and off-reservation jobs. Academic and vocational training has also been intensified as part of the overall goal of self-support. One notable trend has been a marked increase in awareness of Native American identity and heritage and in political activism.

Despite advances, however, the plight of the American Indian is dismal. In 1970 the rate of unemployment among Indians was nearly 40 percent. It has been ascertained that 10 percent of all Indians over the age of 14 have had no schooling, and that over 40 percent of Indian schoolchildren drop out of high school. Indian rates of sickness, poverty, and illiteracy are among the highest in the nation.

In spite of these odds, American Indians have risen to distinction in the business, professional, scholarly, political, cultural, and sports worlds. Among eminent persons of Indian ancestry have been actor and humorist Will Rogers (part-Cherokee); Senator (later Vice President under Herbert Hoover) Charles Curtis (part-Kaw and Osage); ballerina Maria Tallchief (part-Osage); baseball player Allie Reynolds (part-Creek); Olympic champion Jim Thorpe (Sac and Fox); Pulitzer Prize–winning novelist Scott Momaday (Kiowa); author-activist Vine Deloria Jr. (Standing Rock Sioux); anthropologist D'Arcy McNickle (Flathead); singer Buffy Sainte-Marie (Cree); and activist LaDonna Harris (Comanche).

Almost 500 years after the first encounter between immigrant explorers and Native Americans there has begun to be wide awareness, as well as an understanding, of the richness and variety of Indian cultures and the contributions of these cultures to the European-settled New World. Many societies and museums in the United States focus their activities and collections on American Indians. The Institute of American Indian Art was founded at Santa Fe, New Mexico, in 1963. In New York City, the Museum of the American Indian, located at Broadway and 155th Street, was started in 1916 by George Heye, a philanthropist. It was later headed by Dr. Frederick J. Dockstader, a part-Navajo, who has won distinction as an author, anthropologist, and artist. The museum has grown from a nucleus consisting of Heye's personal collections into the largest display of Indian artifacts and effects in the entire Western Hemisphere. In addition to the museum, there are extensive research and library facilities available for qualified scholars.

Balboa Discovers the Pacific Ocean

Vasco Núñez de Balboa, the Spanish discoverer who led the first band of Europeans to the Pacific, was born at Jeréz de los Caballeros in western Spain about 1475. By birth he was a *hidalgo* (gentleman), descended from Galician nobles who had become impoverished. Little is known of his life in the Old World. Perhaps to repair the family fortunes and doubtless also for love of adventure, the tall, handsome swordsman joined the great mercantile expedition to the New World undertaken by Rodrigo de Bastidas in 1501.

The Bastidas group explored the coast of Colombia and the northern coast of the Isthmus of Panama. While linking continents to the north and south, the Isthmus of Panama itself lies in a west-to-east curve. Thus the Caribbean Sea, already familiar to the Spanish by 1500, lies off its northern shore. But off its southern coast lies the Pacific Ocean, unknown to Europe until Balboa and his men discovered it. For Balboa, little came of the Bastidas voyage immediately, but it would assume significance later, and of course it brought him to the New World.

He settled on Hispaniola, the island that Haiti and the Dominican Republic occupy today, and tried farming in the vicinity of Salvatierra. But his plantation was not financially successful. In 1510, to escape his creditors, Balboa had himself smuggled aboard the caravel that was being sent to provision Alonso de Ojeda's new settlement — San Sebastián, bordering the Gulf of Urabá on the north coast of Colombia. It is said that Balboa hid in a cask of "victuals for the voyage," sent from his farm to the ship.

In this bizarre fashion, he joined his second expedition to the South American continent. This time Balboa sailed under Martín Fernández de Enciso, an adventurous lawyer from Hispaniola who had been engaged by Ojeda. On reaching the coast, however, the provisioning party found that Ojeda had vanished. Only 41 survivors remained in the ruined settlement, led by Francisco Pizarro, who later conquered Peru. While Enciso hesitated, the seasoned Balboa urged that the colony sail west to the other side of the Gulf of Urabá. This would put them on the easternmost part of the Isthmus of Panama in the region called Darién, where Balboa had touched earlier with Bastidas. Balboa's proposal was accepted, and the first permanent settlement of Europeans in South America, Santa María de la Antigua del Darién, was established by Enciso's group and the remnant of Ojeda's expedition.

Any impartial observer might have foreseen a struggle for leadership between the ambitious Enciso and Balboa, whose initiative had saved the colony. Predictably enough, it came, and in the end Enciso was deposed, imprisoned, and shipped to Spain under watch of an ally of Balboa's. He would stir trouble for Balboa at the Castilian court, but in the meantime the latter was freed for important leadership in the second stage of Spanish exploration.

The first stage had been capped by the settlement of Hispaniola, which — having served as "the advance base of the conquest" — thereafter declined in vigor and importance. As leader of the Darién colony, Balboa began to bring the surrounding area under Spanish control. In the process he established a reputation for courtesy, kindness, and justice unusual among the conquistadors, though acts of cruelty to the Indians are recorded even of him. On an excursion into the interior, Balboa first heard from an Indian cacique, or chief, of the great sea across the mountains of Darién, and of the gold of Peru. Balboa wrote King Ferdinand V of his conviction that the "Other Sea" and its fabled realms, lay near, and he included the Indians' estimate that 1,000 soldiers would be needed for its discovery. At this news, King Ferdinand was moved to authorize a large crown colony (Castilla del Oro), for which 2,000 new colonists were gathered. (Under Ojeda and his successors, 1,000 men had already died in the fever-ridden swamplands along the Gulf of Urabá.)

Informed, however, that the king was also sending a new governor, Pedro Arias de Ávila (often called Pedrarias Davila) with these reinforcements, Balboa resolved to find the "South Sea" before his replacement could arrive. On September 1, 1513, he set out at the head of 190 Spaniards (one-half his colony) and 800 friendly Indians to cross the Isthmus of Panama. Reaching the summit of the range, Balboa and his men sighted the Pacific on September 25 (the 26th and 27th are sometimes mentioned), 1513. After falling on his knees to give thanks for the new ocean, Balboa sent Pizarro and two other scouts ahead to find the shore. On September 29 Balboa himself arrived at the Gulf of San Miguel. With banner raised and sword drawn, he strode into the waters, claiming the new ocean and all the lands bordering on it for the crown of Castile.

For some months Balboa explored the region in the direction of Panama, visited the Pearl Islands, and learned again of Peru. Reentering Darién on January 18, 1514, he sent messengers to Spain with gifts and the news of his discoveries.

For his success King Ferdinand named Balboa admiral of the South Sea and governor of Panama and Coiba, an island off the southwest coast of Panama. But he still sent Pedrarias to govern Darién. In the interim, Balboa revisited the Pacific a number of times and began to project the conquest of Peru and the exploration of the new ocean.

After his arrival, Pedrarias, cheated of the great discovery, hounded Balboa and prevented his putting to sea for Peru in ships Balboa and his men had built on the Pacific side of the isthmus. The marriage by proxy of one of Pedrarias's daughters to Balboa exacerbated the feud, and late in 1518 Pedrarias lured his rival to Acla, imprisoned him, and had him condemned on a trumped-up charge of treason, with his right of appeal denied. Vasco Núñez de Balboa was beheaded in January 1519.

Thus, at the age of 44, one of the great conquistadors was executed and his explorations brought to an end. His discoveries remained the foundation of others' achievements, however. Balboa's comrade, Pizarro, went on to conquer Peru with blood and fire. And Ferdinand Magellan, spurred by the discovery of another ocean 45 miles west of the Atlantic, sailed south and west around what he presumed to be a great peninsula — South America. It was Magellan who — seven years after Balboa's original sighting — first called the South Sea the Pacific. In the year of Balboa's death Pedrarias established the city of Panama as his capital, and the isthmus soon became the passage for the transport of goods from Peru and Argentina to Spain. Indeed the early Spaniards envisioned cutting a strait through the isthmus — a dream eventually fulfilled with the opening of the Panama Canal in 1914.

More than four centuries after his exploits, Balboa is remembered in the name of a town and district at the Pacific entrance to the canal. Balboa district covers 222 square miles of the Panama Canal Zone, and the town of Balboa is the port for Panama City a mile away. Its large harbor contains a causeway to protect the Pacific entrance to the canal from silting.

In the continental United States the conquistador has as his memorial the famous Balboa Park in the center of San Diego, California. With its main entrance at Laurel Street and Sixth Avenue, Balboa Park encloses 1,400 acres, around which the city has grown since 1870. "Close to being a civic center," the park has been the site of two international expositions — the Panama Pacific (1915) and the California Pacific (1935) — both of which left behind permanent buildings. Especially famous is the Old Globe Theatre erected in 1935 to replicate Shakespeare's Globe Theatre in London. The National Shakespeare Festival is held there every summer in conjunction with a wealth of musical and other cultural events that make up the San Diego Summer Festival from July to September. The California Building, considered a nearly perfect reproduction of Spanish Renaissance architecture, is another notable park building dating from 1935. Its tower is a San Diego landmark. Balboa Park contains diverse museums and acres of landscaped gardens and walks. In addition the San Diego Zoological Garden, a zoo of the advanced, cageless type, is one of its supreme attractions. In this subtropical garden covering 128 acres of the park, animals may be seen in a virtually natural setting. As beautiful as it is famous, Balboa Park offers a 20th century celebration of Vasco Núñez de Balboa's opening the Pacific coast to European exploration and settlement in 1513.

Twelfth Amendment Proclaimed Ratified

The Founding Fathers, in writing the Constitution, wisely made provision for an amending process whereby Americans in the future could modify their handiwork to overcome then unforeseen problems. During the first years of its history, the republic enacted a large number of amendments to correct weaknesses that had become apparent in the original document. Complications in the national election of 1800 inspired the 12th Amendment, which changed the process of selection for the offices of President and Vice President. The Congress proposed the 12th Amendment in December 1803, and it was declared ratified on September 25, 1804.

Article II, Section 1, of the Constitution entitled each state to appoint quadrennially a slate of presidential electors equal in number to its total membership in both houses of Congress. These men, empowered to choose a President and a Vice President, could each cast votes for two persons. The individual who received the greatest number of these electoral votes became President, provided that his total exceeded one-half the number of appointed electors. If no one gained such a majority, or if two candidates managed to do so and obtained an equal number of votes, the House of Representatives had the right to make the final decision. In either case, whether the electors or the House made the choice of the President, the person with the second greatest number of votes became Vice President.

In the 1790s, because of disputes over domestic and foreign policies, two relatively stable political parties emerged. The Founding Fathers, who looked upon parties as unhealthy manifestations of division and selfishness, had not envisioned such a development. The appearance of these disciplined voting organizations played havoc with the electoral system created by the Constitution and in 1800 demonstrated that the original process was already obsolete.

Federalists, as one group became known, favored strong central government and a diplomatic stance friendly to England. Their opponents, the Democratic-Republicans, wanted greater reliance upon local government as a means of preserving civil and individual liberties and generally sympathized with the goals of the French Revolution. President George Washington warned of the dangers of factionalism, but he increasingly sided with the Federalists during his two terms. John Adams of Massachusetts, his Vice President, openly aligned himself with the Federalists, and Thomas Jefferson of Virginia, his secretary of state until 1793, became the leader of the Democratic-Republicans. (Members of the party referred to historically as *Democratic-Republican* called themselves *Republicans*. They were also known as *Jeffersonian Republicans*. The term *Democratic*, originally applied by their Federalist opponents, came to be the popular, and eventually the official, name of the party.)

Washington, elected President in 1789 and 1792 without opposition, announced that he would retire after his second term in office. In 1796 candidates from the two parties vied for the White House for the first time. Many Federalists favored John Adams for President and Thomas Pinckney of South Carolina for Vice President, while almost all Democratic-Republicans supported Jefferson for the office of Chief Executive. The party system had not yet attained maturity, and the division of the electoral vote among 13 candidates demonstrated that voting discipline was weak. Adams managed to win the presidency, but not all his supporters cast their ballots for Pinckney. Democratic-Republicans and independent-minded electors chose Jefferson for Vice President. The Virginian accepted the position and bided his time until 1800 for a second attempt at the White House.

Adams was again the Federalist candidate in 1800, but his even-tempered resolution of America's diplomatic and maritime conflict with France undermined his position with more aggressive Federalists. Alexander Hamilton of New York, for example, worked almost openly to defeat Adams and put Charles Cotesworth Pinckney, the Federalist vice presidential selection, in the White House. Jefferson once more carried the Democratic-Republican banner, and Aaron Burr of New York, who had made the party a powerful force in his state, was his running mate.

Party discipline was rigorous in 1800, and the electors divided their ballots among only five men. John Adams, in defeat, received 65 votes, and Pinckney 64. Rhode Island cast one of its Federalist ballots for John Jay of New York rather than for Pinckney to prevent a tied vote, which would have sent the election to the House of Representatives in the event of a Federalist victory. However, the Democratic-Republicans won the contest, and their electors, lacking this foresight, allowed both Jefferson and Burr to gain 73 votes.

Some Federalists saw the Jefferson-Burr tie as their salvation. Still strong in the House of Representatives, where each state would have one vote, they hoped to be able to give the presidency to Burr, who was the more conservative of the two. Others, like Alexander Hamilton, thought Burr untrustworthy and deceitful and admitted that, in comparison to the New Yorker, Jefferson had some "pretensions to character."

When balloting began on February 10, eight states aligned with Jefferson, six with Burr, and two were divided. To be victorious, a candidate needed the votes of a majority, or 9 of the 16 states. The stalemate continued for 35 ballots until February 16. On that day, Federalist James A. Bayard, the sole representative from Delaware, broke the impasse. Bayard preferred Burr, but thought his cause hopeless. Assured by a friend of Jefferson's, Senator Samuel Smith of Maryland, that the Virginian did not intend to revoke the major pieces of legislation enacted by the Washington and Adams administrations, Bayard agreed to acquiesce in his election. After Bayard declared his intentions, politicians from both parties worked out an arrangement whereby 10 states gave their votes – and the election – to Jefferson without a single Federalist's having cast a ballot in his favor.

Both victors and vanquished learned from the election of 1800 the weaknesses of the Constitution's original system for selecting the President and Vice President. No party wanted to risk losing the fruits of a successful campaign by having a tie force an election into the House of Representatives, where their opponents could block the way to victory. In December 1803 the Congress proposed for the Constitution a 12th Amendment, which provided for distinct ballots distinguishing presidential and vice presidential candidates. The states found the amendment acceptable, and it was declared ratified on September 25, 1804.

SEPTEMBER 26

Johnny Appleseed's Birthday

Even during his own lifetime, John Chapman, one of America's true folk characters, was better known as Johnny Appleseed. An early conservationist and a pioneer in establishing midwestern orchards, he has been called the "patron saint" of American orchards and floriculture. Born September 26, 1774, in Leominster, Massachusetts, Chapman spent most of his life roaming the Middle West, planting orchards from apple seed first obtained in Pennsylvania, or teaching others how to plant and care for apple orchards.

He had nurseries scattered throughout the Midwest — mostly in Ohio, Michigan, and Indiana — and he traveled often, usually on foot, visiting his nurseries and later his orchards to prune and tend them. He gave or sold apple seed or saplings to pioneers heading west, sometimes charging a "fippenny bit" (a coin worth about six cents), but more frequently exchanging the saplings for old clothes or promissory notes, which were never collected. He was more interested in knowing that the saplings would be properly planted and tended, even in areas he would never see. Chapman himself had gone west of the Alleghenies in advance of the pioneer settlements. With two lashed-together canoes bearing apples from the cider presses of western Pennsylvania, he was seen drifting past Steubenville on the Ohio River in 1800 or 1801, his first recorded appearance in the Midwest. By the latter year, he already had a chain of seedling nurseries flourishing throughout Kentucky and Ohio.

One story has it that as Chapman planted seeds, he often remarked, "Maybe sometime someone will come along here and be hungry. Then they will have apples to eat and apples are God's food." And, according to that story, "the settlers who followed him called him blessed." Another account notes that "towns had an uncanny way of springing up wherever he selected an orchard site."

Nature was Chapman's first love. As a boy in New England, he often wandered off on long trips searching for flowers and birds. Early in life, he became a disciple of Emanuel Swedenborg, the eighteenth century Swedish scientist and religious mystic. Chapman was reportedly a Swedenborgian missionary in Virginia for a time. It may have been in Virginia, even then an important apple-growing region, that John Chapman took the first steps toward becoming Johnny Appleseed. It happened, according to one report, after a horse kicked him in the head, whereupon Chapman envisioned heaven as filled with apple trees in bloom. From that time on, he took as his mission the planting of nurseries and distributing of apple seeds and saplings to all who would grow them. One thing is certain: John Chapman became as zealous in planting and caring for apple trees as he was, to the end of his days, in preaching the Scriptures.

In this dual cause, it is estimated he tramped over 100,000 square miles, meeting and becoming familiar to many groups of settlers — those en route to the West and those already settled in the Midwest. He was easily identifiable and unforgettable because of his eccentricities of dress and manner.

For all his walking, Chapman was barefoot most of the time, even in the deep of winter. He wore the roughest of clothes. Over short ragged trousers, his tunic was usually a coffee sack with holes cut out for head and arms. On his head he wore a tin mush pan or iron cooking pot, which he used both as protection from the elements and to prepare the meager fare on which he subsisted.

It is hard to know how much truth rests in the myriad tales told of Johnny Appleseed. One famous story tells of a day when a minister, preaching to his congregation, asked rhetorically, "Where is the man who, like the primitive Christian, walks toward heaven barefoot and clad in sackcloth?" Johnny Appleseed stepped forward, barefoot and clad in sackcloth, as prescribed — with the added touch of his mush-pan hat. He approached the minister, saying, "Here is a primitive Christian!"

While frontier settlers variously regarded Johnny Appleseed as a religious fanatic, a borderline saint, or a dedicated horticulturist, Indians regarded him as a great medicine man. Chapman in his travels did scatter the seeds of many herbs that were thought to have curative powers, such as catnip, rattlesnake weed, horehound, and pennyroyal — all of which are still sold in herb stores. Unfortunately he also scattered widely the noxious weed dog fennel, which he mistakenly thought was effective against malaria.

Chapman would preach the principles of Swedenborg or read from the Bible, often while lying on the floor, to anyone who would listen. As people came to know his goodness and generosity, they tolerated him more, overlooking his eccentricities. His kindness to animals, even to insects and poisonous snakes that bit him, became legendary.

For all his gentle and undoubtedly strange ways, Chapman was also a brave man, as he showed on several occasions during the War of 1812. It is said that after Sir Isaac Brock and his British forces, on August 16 of that year, seized the fort at Detroit then under the American general William Hull, Johnny Appleseed covered a wide area of northern Ohio, relaying the news to the settlers and warning of the probability of Indian raids that would follow.

One authenticated incident explains why Mansfield, Ohio, has a monument to John Chapman. When, in 1812, the British incited the Indians around Mansfield to attack the American frontier settlements, Chapman volunteered to get help from Mount Vernon, Ohio, some 20 to 30 miles away. As he raced through the night, he warned isolated homesteaders on his way. His success in getting reinforcements is credited with averting the raid.

Chapman's home base for more than a quarter century, beginning about 1810, was Ashland County, Ohio, and during some of that time he lived with his half sister in a cabin near Mansfield. The last 10 years of his life, however, he made his home in northern Indiana, where he continued his dedication to missionary and horticultural work. Returning home from a long, cold trek to care for a damaged orchard, the ragclad Chapman was stricken with pneumonia. He sought refuge in William Worth's cabin in Allen County, Indiana, where he died — in March 1845, according to some sources, or, according to others, on March 11, 1847. He is buried in what is now known as Johnny Appleseed Park, near the War Memorial Coliseum in Fort Wayne. Fort Wayne also honors Chapman with a boulder memorial located in the city's 90-acre Swinney Park.

Leominster, Massachusetts, has honored its native son annually since 1962 with Johnny Appleseed Civic Day, held the first Saturday of June each year. A feature of the second Johnny Appleseed Civic Day was the rededication of the monument with which the Leominster Historical Society had marked the site of Chapman's birthplace, off Nashua Street extension.

The monument was embellished with Maurice Kaufman's pictorial representation of Chapman, replacing an older plaque, which had been destroyed by vandals. In 1966 Leominster was chosen to be the site for the first day of issue of a Johnny Appleseed commemorative stamp, selected as the first stamp of the American folklore series. Based on Robert Bode's design, the stamp showed the black and white figure of the pioneer orchardist against the background of a large red apple on a white ground. The ceremony marking the stamp's issue, in which local and state officials and the assistant US postmaster general participated, was held on September 24, the Saturday preceding Chapman's birthday. In 1974 the New York and New England Apple Institute designated the year as the Johnny Appleseed Bicentennial.

The appealing American folk character is also honored elsewhere. In Ashland, Ohio, where Chapman lived for more than 25 years, the Johnny Appleseed Monument, an eight-foot stone shaft, stands at Main Street and Cleveland Avenue. Chapman's contributions are frequently celebrated at the harvest festivals held in apple-growing regions, not only in the Midwest but in all the apple-producing states. As one example, a three-day Johnny Appleseed Festival is held annually in mid-September at Lisbon, one of Ohio's most historic communities, with an apple auction, a queen competition, parades, a variety show, and folk and square dancing.

Chapman's most enduring monuments, however, are the orchards he planted himself. Even today, orchards begun by Johnny Appleseed provide fruit for many and widely scattered markets.

George Gershwin's Birthday

That most "American" of American composers, George Gershwin, whose incorporation of jazz idioms into serious compositions influenced the course of music, is remembered for both his popular songs and his concert works. In addition, his last major work, the opera *Porgy and Bess,* is considered by many to be the best work for the musical theater ever written by an American. His music has such wide appeal that there is probably not a time when it is not being heard somewhere in the world. The year of the 75th anniversary of Gershwin's birth, 1973, was the occasion for particular celebration and commemoration of the accomplishments of one of the 20th century's best-loved composers.

Gershwin was born in Brooklyn, New York, on September 26, 1898, and was officially named

Jacob Gershvin — the family name having been simplified from Gershovitz by his father upon immigration from Russia. His mother, Rose Bruskin Gershvin, was also of Russian birth. Regardless of the name they had given him, Gershwin's family always called him George. When he entered the music field professionally, George changed the spelling of his last name to Gershwin, and the family followed suit.

Far from being pushed by his parents, young George Gershwin came to an awareness of his talent and sensitivity entirely on his own. The boy whose music Arturo Toscanini later was to characterize as "the only *real* American music" studied piano with Charles Hambitzer, who exerted the major influence in Gershwin's musical development. He also studied harmony, theory, and orchestration with Edward Kilenyi. Although he studied at different times with others, these were his most important teachers. As a boy, his seriousness and enthusiasm were unusually intense, and his creativity was apparent very early.

Eager to move into the professional world, Gershwin left school at the age of 15, when he was offered a job as pianist and song plugger for a New York music publisher. He was more interested in composing than in playing, and he got his big break less than four years later when another music-publishing firm put him on the payroll with no other duties than to write songs and show them to the firm for consideration. One of his songs had already been included in a Broadway production by 1916.

The first musical comedy for which Gershwin wrote the entire score, *La, La, Lucille,* was produced in 1919, when he was just 20 years old. A few months later Gershwin's "Swanee" caught the interest of Al Jolson. The popular singer's rendition was such a hit that fans bought more than 2 million records and a million copies of sheet music in a year's time. To this day, "Swanee" remains one of the most popular of all Gershwin's songs.

His name was becoming known, and Gershwin quickly moved into high gear as a composer for musical comedies. Among those for which he wrote all the music were the *George White's Scandals* for the years 1920 through 1924 (songs included "Stairway to Paradise" and "Somebody Loves Me"); *Lady, Be Good!,* produced in 1924 ("Fascinating Rhythm," "Oh, Lady Be Good!"); *Tip-Toes,* 1925 ("That Certain Feeling"); *Oh, Kay!,* 1926 ("Do, Do, Do," "Someone to Watch Over Me"); *Funny Face,* 1927 ("'S Wonderful"); *Strike Up the Band,* 1927, second version 1930 ("Strike Up the Band!"); *Girl Crazy,* 1930 ("Bidin' My Time," "Embraceable You," "I Got Rhythm"); and *Of Thee I sing,* 1931 ("Winter-green for President," "Love Is Sweeping the Country," "Of Thee I Sing"). The last-named, a rollicking political satire, was the first musical comedy to be awarded the Pulitzer Prize for drama.

An original and sophisticated style marked Gershwin's popular music. The lyrics for most of his songs were written by his older brother Ira (though Irving Caesar wrote the words to "Swanee") in a close collaboration in which each sparked the genius of the other.

Jazz held a powerful fascination for Gershwin from the time of his earliest exposure to music. Convinced of its importance as a native American art form, he was determined that it not be confined to the realm of popular music, but incorporated also into serious music. Accordingly, he tried to make the transition.

His first attempt was a one-act jazz-idiom opera called *Blue Monday,* written for the *George White's Scandals of 1922.* Though not rated well artistically, it won some recognition as a trailblazer. (It had been written, under pressure, in just five days.) Because White felt the somber opera did not fit well in the overall production, it was dropped after the first night. It has since been revived several times under the name *135th Street.*

The "king of jazz," Paul Whiteman, who conducted the orchestra for the *Scandals of 1922,* was so excited by the potential he saw in *Blue Monday* that he suggested Gershwin write a new piece for orchestra for a special jazz concert he was planning. Thus was born *Rhapsody in Blue,* for piano and orchestra. It was first performed at Aeolian Hall in New York City on February 12, 1924, with Gershwin at the piano. Music critics were divided in their reactions. Some considered it masterly; others, without merit. But the enthusiasm of the audience was unquestioned.

This thoroughly American work, with its engaging spontaneity and verve, is so widely performed internationally — on records, on radio, in films, and in the ballet theater, as well as in the concert hall — that it is believed to be the most frequently performed of all American orchestral works. It has exerted a strong influence on other composers, leading them to incorporate jazz idioms into large works of traditional form.

With the success of *Rhapsody in Blue,* the New York Symphony Society was persuaded by conductor Walter Damrosch to commission an orchestral work by Gershwin. The resulting Concerto in F, for piano and orchestra, never as well known as *Rhapsody in Blue,* was performed at New York's Carnegie Hall under Damrosch with Gershwin as soloist on December 3, 1925. Its reception was very similar to that accorded his previous work; the audience again gave its vociferous approval, with the concurrence of some music critics and not of others.

Three years later *An American in Paris,* a tone poem for orchestra that included parts for Paris taxi horns, was presented at Carnegie Hall. The premiere was performed by the New York Philharmonic Orchestra, under Damrosch, on December 13, 1928. Mixed reviews again proved no hindrance to its winning a place in symphonic repertoire as well as performances in lighter productions.

The *Second Rhapsody* (1931), for piano and orchestra, and *Cuban Overture* (originally titled *Rumba,* 1932), for orchestra and Cuban percussion instruments, are less important works.

Gershwin's most ambitious and mature work is the folk opera *Porgy and Bess* (1935), with a libretto by DuBose Heyward, based on his novel *Porgy.* Audiences were at first puzzled by its new form, actually somewhere between musical comedy and opera, but as they became familiar with it, the popularity of the opera, written for an all-black cast, grew. Several of its songs — "I Got Plenty o' Nuttin'," "It Ain't Necessarily So," and "Summertime" — became very popular.

Though Gershwin did not live to see it, within a decade the opera had been performed not only throughout the United States but also in Western Europe and the Soviet Union. Then in 1952 the US State Department sent a black company on a goodwill tour of Western Europe, North Africa, the Middle East, Latin America, and the Soviet Union. Everywhere, the enthusiasm of its audiences was overwhelming. So successful was it that the tour lasted almost four years. In Milan *Porgy and Bess* was the first opera by an American-born composer to be performed at the famed La Scala opera house, and the first opera ever to be performed there continuously through an entire week. *Porgy and Bess* has become an international classic.

A brilliant pianist, Gershwin frequently performed as soloist at the premieres or other performances of his works. He also ably conducted his own music, both symphonic works and musical comedies, at various times. During the mid-1930s he was host of a radio program on which he often generously showcased the music of unknown composers in addition to playing, conducting, and talking about his own.

He made a few recordings, of *Rhapsody in Blue* and of songs, some of which survive. Almost all of the many piano rolls he made for player pianos between 1916 and 1925 are owned by collectors.

Gershwin felt drawn to the medium of the motion picture, and wrote scores for three films. Memorable songs from *A Damsel in Distress*

(1937) are "A Foggy Day" and "Nice Work if You Can Get It." *Shall We Dance?* (1937) included "Let's Call the Whole Thing Off," "They Can't Take That Away from Me," and the title song. For *The Goldwyn Follies* he wrote "Love Walked In" and "Love Is Here to Stay." After his death some of his unused compositions were adapted as songs for films, among them "Aren't You Kinda Glad We Did," "For You, for Me, for Evermore," and "The Back Bay Polka," all in *The Shocking Miss Pilgrim* (1947). *An American in Paris* (1951), featuring Gershwin's composition of that title and a number of others, received an Acadamy Award. In addition motion pictures were adapted from his musical comedies and from *Porgy and Bess.*

While working on *The Goldwyn Follies,* Gershwin died suddenly in Hollywood on July 11, 1937, of a brain tumor. He was 38 years old. Despite his untimely death, he left more than 1,000 musical works, which abundantly illustrate the unique Gershwin blend of musical verve, vitality, and brashness with original, sophisticated melodies and ingenious, intricate rhythms.

Gregarious and outgoing, Gershwin loved to be the life of the party. At social gatherings, he invariably spent most of his time at the piano, playing his own music. However, his large ego did not repress an enthusiastic appreciation of works of other composers, and he gave considerable help to many unknown or lesser-known musicians.

Although music was the undisputed center of his life (he did not marry), Gershwin's enthusiastic, dynamic personality found other outlets too. He was an avid participant in games and sports of all kinds — except those in which his hands might be easily injured — and an excellent dancer. When Fred and Adele Astaire needed an exit step during rehearsals of *Lady, Be Good!,* "hoofer George," according to Astaire, came up with one that "turned out to be a knockout applause puller."

Painting also became a passion. With a minimum of instruction Gershwin produced a number of works, including two self-portraits, which were well regarded. His canvases were first exhibited six months after his death. Then in May 1963 an exhibit at Philharmonic Hall in New York City commemorated the 65th anniversary of his birth.

As early as August 16, 1932, the first all-Gershwin concert took place. With the composer participating as soloist for his two rhapsodies, it was performed by the New York Philharmonic Orchestra at the open-air Lewisohn Stadium in New York City. Attendance records at the stadium, which had been presenting summertime concerts for 15 years, were broken that night with 17,845 paid admissions; 5,000 people tried unsuccessfully to get in. It was historically noteworthy in another respect, too, for programs devoted solely to the works of one composer had been few. And it was to be the forerunner of literally thousands of such Gershwin evenings.

From about that time, annual all-Gershwin nights were scheduled at Lewisohn Stadium (until its closing in 1966) and at the Hollywood Bowl in Los Angeles. They have also been presented elsewhere across the United States and abroad, particularly in the open-air shells, bowls, and stadiums where informal concerts stressing light classical fare are held during warm weather. Many have been timed to coincide approximately with the anniversary of Gershwin's death (July 11). Always they draw tremendous, frequently record-breaking, crowds.

Gershwin's life has been the subject of broadcasts and formed the basis of a somewhat fictionalized screen biography entitled *Rhapsody in Blue* (1945).

Special note was taken in 1973 of the 75th anniversary of the composer's birth. New York City alone had two exhibits of Gershwin memorabilia and a film retrospective, *Gershwin on Film*, probably the first retrospective devoted to a composer. By mayoral proclamation, the city celebrated February 28 as George Gershwin Day. A number of new and revised Gershwin biographies and song books were published during the year. New record albums were released, some of them containing some of his less familiar songs. A commemorative eight-cent stamp was issued by the US Post Office.

The largest collection of Gershwin's manuscripts is in the George Gershwin Collection at the Library of Congress, which includes also the work desk he designed for himself and other memorabilia. The library has a George Gershwin exhibition about once a year, and it draws large crowds. Another storehouse of Gershwiniana is the George Gershwin Memorial Collection of Music and Musical Literature at Fisk University in Nashville, Tennessee. Yale University has still another collection.

Between 1946 and 1955 the annual Gershwin Memorial Contest, judged by renowned musicians, was sponsored by B'nai B'rith's Victory Lodge for the best composition by an American; the winning piece, for which the composer received a monetary award, was performed by the New York Philharmonic Orchestra. In 1962 a George Gershwin Scholarship Fund was established by the Juilliard School of Music.

In Gershwin's home borough of Brooklyn, New York, the George Gershwin Junior High School was dedicated in June 1957. Its band and glee club give special concerts of the composer's music at the school and have performed his tunes for such events as the placing of a plaque at Gershwin's birthplace in 1963 and the Gershwin exhibition in 1968. A trust fund was set up by Ira Gershwin in 1964 from which awards are given to 10 of the school's outstanding students each year.

Ira Gershwin also established George Gershwin scholarships for piano at New York's Henry Street Settlement in 1969.

Through the years, George Gershwin has also been honored in many other ways. His name has been given to a Liberty ship (1943), the George Gershwin Theater Workshop Arena at Boston University (1950), the George Gershwin Practice Hut at the Chautauqua Institute (1952), a theater at Brooklyn College (1954), a public elementary school in Chicago (1966), an avenue in Hull, England (1967), and Gershwin College of the State University of New York at Stony Brook (1970).

SEPTEMBER 27

Samuel Adams's Birthday

The New England patriot and politician Samuel Adams, most persistent and most zealous of all the agitators for American independence, was born in Boston on September 27, 1722. The second cousin of John Adams, he graduated from Harvard College in 1740, made a subsequent brief study of law, and failed in several business undertakings, including management of the brewery that he inherited from his father. He served, not outstandingly, as a tax collector in Boston from 1756 until 1764. Like Paul Revere, he meanwhile joined Boston's influential "Caucus Club" and had become powerful in local politics by 1764. But it was with the enactment, that year, of the Sugar Act duties (by which the British Parliament sought to raise money for King George III) that Adams's political star began to rise. In his fiery opposition to that and later measures regarded by the colonists as oppressive — the Stamp Act, the Townshend Acts, the Coercive ("Intolerable") Acts, the provisions for quartering British troops — Adams became as forceful an advocate of liberty as the colonies possessed. In a dozen or more years of pre-Revolutionary activity, he pressed for total independence, worked to set up the Sons of Liberty, took part in the agitation that brought about the Boston Massacre (see March 5), became a leader of the Boston town meeting, organized the Boston

Tea Party (see December 16), and was instrumental in other retaliatory efforts such as the nonimportation of British goods.

Adams, a member (1765–1774) and recording clerk (from 1766) of the lower house of the Massachusetts General Court (the legislature), was a master of political organization. His reputation as an implacable foe of taxation without representation, and as a revolutionary author of newspaper and other writings — including the Massachusetts Circular Letter and such titles as *The Rights of the Colonists as Men, as Christians, and as Subjects* — spread throughout the colonies. He convened Boston's committee of correspondence, a widely copied body that the towns and colonies employed to inform one another of their various anti-British actions and enlist mutual cooperation. A consistent foe of compromise, he stirred the fires of controversy during a period of relative calm in the early 1770s. As a delegate to the Continental Congress (1774–1781) he fought strongly for immediate independence and was one of the signers of the Declaration of Independence. He figured in most of the important events that led to the American Revolution.

The opening incidents of the Revolution took place at Lexington (where Adams and John Hancock were staying at the time) and, with considerably more bloodshed, at Concord, on April 19, 1775 (see April 19, Patriots' Day). When the British governor, General Thomas Gage, in a vain attempt to stem hostilities, offered pardon to all colonists who returned to British allegiance, only Adams and Hancock were excepted from the offer. But as far as practical effects were concerned, the overture might as well not have been made. Adams continued to play an important role while the Revolution dragged on. He was a delegate to the convention that framed the Massachusetts constitution in 1779–1780. After hostilities had ended with independence for the new United States of America, he was also a delegate, in 1788, to the state convention that ratified the new federal Constitution — after Adams's strong anti-Federalist stance had been overcome with the promise of Federalist support for amendments, among them a bill of rights and the assurance that all powers not specifically delegated to the central government would be entrusted to the states. He subsequently served as lieutenant governor (1789–1793) and then as governor (1794–1797) of Massachusetts. In his later years, however, his position of preeminent influence somewhat declined.

On October 2, 1803, six years after his departure from public office, Samuel Adams died in Boston. He was interred in the Granary Burying Ground in Boston. John Singleton Copley's portrait of Adams hangs in the Boston Museum of Fine Arts. A statue of him represents Massachusetts in the Capitol in Washington, D.C.

A bronze statue of Adams, by Anne Whitney, can be seen in Boston, standing in front of historic Faneuil Hall, called the Cradle of Liberty, where he and other patriots met to protest British taxes. The bronze likeness has an air of rugged determination, leaving it to the viewer's imagination to recreate the living presence of the man whose blistering oratory made people forget his rumpled attire, watering eyes, and fidgeting hands.

SEPTEMBER 28

Cabrillo Day in California

In California, September 28 is observed in honor of Juan Rodríguez Cabrillo, the Portuguese explorer who discovered California on that date in 1542. Cabrillo Day was commemorated statewide by official proclamation of the governor of California until the late 1960s, when the issuance of proclamations in California was vastly curtailed as an economy and timesaving measure during the administration of Governor Ronald Reagan, and the Cabrillo Day proclamation was discontinued. Subsequently it became customary for the California senate and assembly to issue concurrent resolutions proclaiming Cabrillo Festival Week. The celebration of the September 28 anniversary is staged primarily in the San Diego area by city and county officials, local schools and churches, Portuguese-American clubs, and the National Park Service of the US Department of the Interior, which has charge of the Cabrillo National Monument, located 10 miles from the center of the city.

Juan Rodríguez Cabrillo, the Columbus of California, was Portuguese by birth. His date of birth is unknown, as is his birthplace, which may, however, have been one of several places in Portugal named Cabril. Cabrillo's last name was apparently a nickname, either assumed by Cabrillo himself or added by contemporaries as a means of differentiating the navigator from others named Juan Rodríguez.

A professional soldier and mariner who served Spain, Juan Rodríguez Cabrillo arrived in Mexico with the expedition of the Spanish conquistador Pánfilo de Narváez in 1520. Participating in the earliest Spanish conquests of the Central American territory, the adventurer accompanied another conquistador, Hernando Cortes, in the capture of Mexico City from the Aztec ruler Montezuma. He later joined an exploratory party into Oaxaca in southern Mexico. Having proved his mettle, Cabrillo was enlisted by the governor of Guatemala, Pedro de Alvarado, to help conquer Guatemala. When the latter set out to explore and conquer the as yet unknown area to the northwest of Mexico, he recruited Cabrillo for the expedition.

Interest in the lands northwest of Spanish Mexico was stimulated not only by pure adventurism and curiosity, but also by widespread rumors, circulating soon after the conquest of Mexico in the 1520s, about the legendary Seven Cities of Cíbola in the fabulous "Isle of California," which were alleged to be far richer than Mexico or Peru. Moreover, the prospect of establishing profitable trade connections with the Orient and of discovering the western mouth of the elusive Northwest Passage — the interoceanic strait that supposedly joined the Atlantic and Pacific oceans — provided additional allure. In the 50 years following Christopher Columbus's discovery of the New World in 1492, slow but steady progress had been made in penetrating the unexplored regions, on both the Atlantic and Pacific sides of the North American continent. In 1513 Vasco Núñez de Balboa discovered the Pacific Ocean — which he termed the South Sea. After the western shores of Central America had been explored, tentative steps were made northwards along the Pacific coast. By 1539 it was clear that Lower California was a peninsula. In the following year, Hernando de Alarcón became the first European to set foot in Upper California when he sailed up the Colorado River from the Gulf of California as far as the Gila River. The stage was therefore ready for Juan Rodríguez Cabrillo, who was to be the first European to touch upon the Pacific coastline of what is now the United States.

Cabrillo apparently assisted Pedro de Alvarado in building the fleet designed for the unexplored northwestern lands. He must have been present when this leader was killed while quelling an Indian revolt on the western coast of Mexico in 1541. The viceroy of New Spain, Antonio de Mendoza, who took responsibility for the fate of the fleet, assigned two lumbering caravels — the flagship *San Salvador* and its consort, the *Victoria* — to Cabrillo. The new commander set sail from Navidad, a small port on the western coast of Mexico, on June 27, 1542. The two vessels crossed the Gulf of California and continued along the western shores of Lower California until, on August 20, they reached Cape Deceit (Cabo del Engaño), at that time the northernmost point touched by previous Pacific mariners. Intrepidly passing beyond into strange seas, Cabrillo's expedition cautiously skirted the untested coastline. Some 90 days away from their

home port, the sailors approached the islands off northern Mexico that are opposite what is now known as San Diego Bay. In the dark, they glimpsed Indian campfires on the high land to the west — the tip of Point Loma, which forms the northern arm of the bay. On the following day, the *San Salvador* and the *Victoria* rounded this lofty point and sailed into one of the outstanding naturally landlocked harbors of the world, which Cabrillo described as a "closed and very good port," and which he named San Miguel. (The name San Diego was applied to the bay in November 1602, by Sebastián Vizcaíno, a Spanish explorer and merchant.) There, on September 28, 1542, the fleet anchored. A handful of its crew disembarked, probably at Ballast Point, a small stretch of land jutting out into the bay. The landing party, although attacked by Indians and suffering three casualties, briefly explored the area. Contacts were later established with the natives. Juan Rodríguez Cabrillo laid claim to the "Isle of California" in the name of the king of Spain and Holy Roman Emperor, Charles V, by planting the imperial flag and bestowing two shirts apiece on two Indian youths.

On October 3 the expedition put out to sea once more to further explore the coast of Upper California. Four days later it reached the islands of Catalina and San Clemente, to which Cabrillo gave the names of his caravels. Passing Santa Monica Bay, as well as the Channel Islands, Cabrillo sailed through the Santa Barbara Channel, past Point Conception, and then far northward beyond Point Reyes north of San Francisco Bay, which he failed to discover.

Driven off course by a severe storm, Cabrillo returned south to winter at what he called Isla de la Posesión, now known as San Miguel Island, the farthest north of the eight Channel Islands off the Santa Barbara coast. He anchored his two ships there on November 23. On January 3, 1543, Juan Rodríguez Cabrillo died on this island, probably as the result of an infection that developed after he had broken a limb sometime earlier on the voyage. He was buried on San Miguel — which his men renamed Isla de Juan Rodríguez — although his grave, possibly located near Cuyler Harbor, has never been discovered.

After Cabrillo's death, his chief pilot, Bartolomé Ferrelo (or Ferrer), assumed command in fulfillment of the dead leader's last request — that the work of the expedition still continue. The *San Salvador* and the *Victoria* accordingly sailed northward along the Pacific coast until March 1, 1543, when they attained their northernmost point, probably the region of the Rogue River in what is now southern Oregon. Separated from its consort during violent storms, which again forced the explorers south, the flagship *San Sal-*

vador subsequently sought shelter in San Diego Bay to await its arrival. Having waited in vain, the crew of the flagship proceeded down the coastline of Lower California to Cedros Island, where they finally encountered the *Victoria* on March 26. Together the two caravels returned triumphantly to their home port of Navidad, Mexico, on April 14, 1543.

The Cabrillo National Monument is located on Point Loma, the 400-foot-high promontory that is the southwesternmost point in the continental United States, overlooking the entrance to San Diego Bay. The monument was established by President Woodrow Wilson on October 14, 1913, as a mere half-acre tract of land, then the smallest of such national monuments. In 1933 the administration of the monument was transferred from the War Department to the Department of the Interior, which through its National Park Service presently maintains it. Cabrillo National Monument was enlarged to 80.6 acres in 1956. It was further enlarged to 144 acres by a presidential proclamation in 1974.

The site includes the Old San Diego Lighthouse, which is known as the Old Point Loma Lighthouse — or, incorrectly, as the Old Spanish Lighthouse. Erected in 1854 as one of several beacons ordered by Congress in 1850 for the newly acquired Pacific region, the lighthouse commenced operations on November 15, 1855. It functioned until 1891, when it was abandoned because its beacon could not be easily spotted from the ocean. Although it was replaced by a modern lighthouse, the historic Old Point Loma Lighthouse survived; the structure is now partially refurnished with antiques from the period of its activity. From its tower can be seen what has been described as "one of the world's greatest seascapes"; there visitors view the Pacific Ocean to the west, Mexico to the south, and to the north and east, the mountains, valleys, and coastline surrounding San Diego. The tower also provides a vantage point for sighting the yearly migration of gray whales.

On Cabrillo Day in 1935, the Native Sons of the Golden West placed a plaque in memory of California's discoverer on the old lighthouse. A 14-foot statue of Cabrillo also memorializes the explorer. A gift to California from Portugal, it stands on an overlook facing San Diego Bay. Carved in Lisbon in 1939 by the distinguished Portuguese sculptor Álvaro de Bree, it was dedicated on September 28, 1949. The visitor center complex at the monument, which includes a permanent historical exhibit, has a glass-enclosed building offering a spectacular view over the harbor and metropolis of San Diego. Just beneath this promontory outlook is Ballast Point, where Cabrillo landed in 1542.

Before the early 1960s, September 28 was usually celebrated in the San Diego area with a modest ceremony at the Cabrillo National Monument at Point Loma. City and county representatives, members of Portuguese-American clubs, schoolchildren, church groups, and occasionally a foreign dignitary gathered in the plaza adjoining the old lighthouse to participate in a brief commemorative program, typically featuring a few short speeches. Beginning in 1963, with the inauguration of the Cabrillo Festival, the traditional ceremony at the monument was continued and the anniversary-day program was gradually expanded into a week-long, community-sponsored event. Five years later the Cabrillo Festival Committee was incorporated with its membership open to all interested persons.

Although certain events have become traditional and occur annually, they are supplemented by special features each year. These were particularly numerous in 1969, when Cabrillo Festival Week played an important role in the observance of San Diego's 200th anniversary. The occasion marked was Father Junípero Serra's founding, in 1769, of the San Diego de Alcalá Mission, beginning the Spanish settlement of California. Portugal contributed greatly to the success of the festival that year, when the Casa de Portugal furnished a large display of Portuguese products, which were exhibited in San Diego's Balboa Park Conference Building throughout September. The Portuguese navy sent two of its newest frigates to San Diego for the entire week of the Festival. Open to the public daily, they were also the scene of two receptions given by Portugal's chief of naval operations — one for the governor of California and the other for civic and community leaders. Other festival week highlights included a fashion show by a well-known Portuguese designer and the premiere of the film *The Voyage of Discovery*, depicting Cabrillo's life and expedition and now on view daily at the Cabrillo National Monument.

More typical was the 1970 Cabrillo Festival, held in San Diego from September 21 through September 27. The seventh such annual event, it commemorated the 428th anniversary of the discovery of the West Coast of the United States. Portuguese-American dancers in ethnic costume along with a Portuguese-American choral group and musicians added a festive Old World flavor to several events during the seven days of celebration. The festival week schedule began with the Monday morning flag-raising ceremony by members of San Diego's Portuguese community in front of the County Administration Building. On Thursday morning the City Council Chambers of the City Administration Building resounded with the clanging of swords and the thump of heavy boots as an authentically costumed Juan Rodríguez Cabrillo and an escort of Spanish soldiers marched in to "reclaim" the lands of California. Cabrillo was accompanied by the Miss Cabrillo Festival Queen, a San Diego County resident of Portuguese descent selected in July. She reigned over all festival events and was honored by the Portuguese government with a two-week visit to Portugal.

The commemorative ceremony at the Cabrillo National Monument took place on the Saturday afternoon nearest September 28 — September 26 in 1970. A US Naval band and choral concert preceded this annual event, staged in the presence of members of Congress, state senators, the mayor of San Diego, and distinguished national and international guests. In addition to several speeches, including one by Secretary of the Interior Walter J. Hickel, the ceremony featured the placing of wreaths at the base of the statue of Cabrillo and the playing of the American and Portuguese national anthems. The climactic social event of the week was a dinner dance held Saturday evening under the joint sponsorship of the Portuguese-American Social and Civic Club and the Cabrillo Civic Club Number 16.

The next afternoon, thousands of San Diegans gathered at Point Loma's Shelter Island to watch the annual reenactment of Cabrillo's discovery of San Diego Bay. The festival flagship *Swift* — a 90-foot wooden caravel — was accompanied by an escort of yachts, motor boats, fireboats and Coast Guard cutters. The landing party, in authentic costumes, consisted of Cabrillo, his soldiers, and a Franciscan friar. After disembarking from the *Swift* in a small boat, they stepped ashore to claim the territory for Spain. The program on Shelter Island that followed the landing included greetings from local and regional officials; a performance by costumed Portuguese-American folk dancers; and Lakota Indian dances to represent the Native American culture discovered by the explorers in the New World.

Frances E. Willard's Birthday

September 28 is designated as Young Crusader Day by the Woman's Christian Temperance Union to commemorate the anniversary of the birth in 1839 of its most distinguished leader, Frances E. Willard (see February 17, Frances E. Willard Memorial Day).

Soon after Willard's death on February 17, 1898, the Kansas legislature passed a law directing that in every public school in the state at least one-fourth of the school day on every September 28 be devoted to exercises in her memory. Frances E. Willard is also honored in the public schools of a number of other states, each state legislature designating the date of observance.

SEPTEMBER 29

Michaelmas Day or the Feast of St. Michael and All Angels

September 29 is the date of what Episcopalians and Lutherans know as the Feast of St. Michael and All Angels, Anglicans call Michaelmas, and Roman Catholics, since their calendar revision, observe as the Feast of SS. Michael, Gabriel, and Raphael, Archangels. (Catholics earlier marked September 29 as the Feast of the Dedication of St. Michael the Archangel; after 1921 they celebrated the feasts of the archangels Gabriel and Raphael, on March 24 and October 24 respectively. The new calendar joined the observances related to the three archangels under the date of September 29 and classed the occasion as a solemnity.) Eastern Orthodox churches celebrate the Feast of St. Michael on November 8, except for those still adhering to the Old Style or Julian calendar, who observe the feast on November 21.

The reasons for honoring Michael and all the angels are fittingly expressed in the Collect for the September 29 feast found in Lutheran hymnals:

O Everlasting God, who hast ordained and constituted the services of angels and men in a wonderful order: Mercifully grant, that as thy holy angels always do thee service in heaven, so by thy appointment they may succor and defend us on earth.

Michael, whose name in Hebrew means "who is like God," is a noteworthy figure in the Jewish, Christian, and Moslem religious traditions. He even finds a counterpart among the Babylonian and Persian angels.

Michael is mentioned several times in the Bible, three times in the Old Testament (but only in a later book after the angelic functions had apparently been distributed among individual angels) and twice in the New Testament. In the Book of Daniel, Michael, described as "one of the chief princes" — presumably of the heavenly host — and "your prince" (of Israel), helps Daniel against the Persian enemy (10:13, 21). The archangel seems to have acted as the protector of the Israelites in their efforts to maintan monotheism in the face of foreign influences (12:1):

And at that time shall Michael stand up, the great prince who standeth for the children of thy people, and there shall be a time of trouble, such as never was since there was a nation even to that same time;

and at that time thy people shall be delivered, every one that shall be found written in the book.

In the New Testament, Michael figures prominently in the Book of Revelations (12:7) as the first archangel, prince of angels, and captain of the hosts of heaven. It is he who when "there was war in heaven" fought "against the dragon," the devil Lucifer and his angels, driving the enemy back until "neither was their place found any more in heaven." The leading archangel figures in the New Testament Epistle of St. Jude (9). Jude, in rebuking those who speak evil of others, wrote that "Michael the archangel when contending with the devil he disputed about the body of Moses, durst not bring against him a railing accusation, but said 'The Lord rebuke thee.'" This refers to an ancient Jewish tradition that Michael concealed the tomb of Moses, and that the devil by disclosing it tried to lead the Jewish people into what is described as "the sin of hero worship." This tradition is probably based upon Deuteronomy 34:6, "And he buried him in a valley in the land of Moab . . . but no man knoweth of his sepulcher unto this day," assuming that Michael was the unidentified figure who took charge of Moses' burial.

The church fathers held the theory that Michael appears many times in the biblical narrative where his name is not mentioned. For example, it was said to be he whom God had "placed at the east of the garden of Eden" with "a flaming sword which turned every way, to keep the way of the tree of life" (Genesis 3:24). It was through Michael that God revealed the Ten Commandments to His people: "And when the voice of the trumpet sounded long, and waxed louder and louder, Moses spake, and God answered him by a voice" (Exodus 19:19). It was the archangel Michael, "his sword drawn in his hand," who "stood in the way" of the soothsayer Balaam "for an adversary against him" (Numbers 22:22). And it also was Michael who routed the army of Sennacherib, the king of Assyria, who was advancing against the cities of Judah: "And it came to pass that night, that the angel of the Lord went out, and smote in the camp of the Assyrians an hundred fourscore and five thousand" (2 Kings 19:35).

In Chapter 20 of the noncanonical Book of Enoch, where the names and functions of the seven chief archangels are given, Michael is described as "one of the holy angels, to wit, that he is set over the best part of mankind and over chaos."

Just as to Jews Michael was the special guardian of Israel, so, too, Christians think of him as the protector of the "true Israel," the Church. The Roman Catholic prayers after Low Mass, for example, include an invocation to the archangel to be "our safeguard against the wickedness and snares of the devil." In Christian tradition, Michael escorts the souls of the faithful departed to the presence of God. The offertory anthem in the Requiem Mass or Mass for the Dead contains a passage in which the archangel is named as the "holy standard bearer" to introduce the departed souls "to the holy light, which thou didst promise of old to Abraham and to his seed."

In religious art, Michael is usually represented as a sword-bearing warrior and hero of battles, with the devil under his foot. Joan of Arc, who in the 15th century helped defeat the English in the Hundred Years' War and was later captured by them and burned at the stake, testified that St. Michael — together with SS. Catherine and Margaret — had appeared to her, urging her to undertake the arduous task of freeing France from English oppression.

It is not known exactly when the veneration of St. Michael the Archangel began, but it undoubtedly extends in the East back to early Christian times. He was the patron saint of the sick among the early Christians. A church bearing his name existed in Constantinople in the early fourth century. By the fifth century, he was being honored in the West as well. Interest in the saint's cult intensified when he supposedly appeared in a vision on the top of Monte Gargano in Apulia, southern Italy, at some time during the reign (492–496) of Pope Gelasius I. A lesser feast long observed by Roman Catholics on May 8, known as the Feast of the Apparition of St. Michael, is no longer noted in the general, or universal, calendar, although the date may be marked in calendars of particular regions or religious orders.

The origin of the September 29 feast of St. Michael the Archangel can be traced to the dedication of a basilica in his honor — shortly before 600 — in the Via Salaria six miles from Rome. Observance of the feast day was confined, at first, to this church and then spread to a gradually increasing number of holy places under his patronage. The cult of the archangel had been firmly implanted throughout Christendom, including Russia, by the Middle Ages. Probably because of the appearance on Monte Gargano, Michael was regarded as the angel of the mountains. Many of the churches and chapels dedicated to him were erected on the tops of hills or mountains in western Europe. Of them the French monastery Mont-Saint-Michel is the most famous.

Mont-Saint-Michel is situated in the English Channel on a tiny granite island one mile from the Normandy coast near Avranches. It is easily accessible on foot at low tide and is also joined to the shore by a causeway. The renowned monastery, which is regarded as one of the finest surviving examples of French medieval architecture, was founded in 708 by St. Aubert, bishop of Avranches. Aubert, according to legend, had three visions of Michael and was commanded to build a shrine and monastery on the rocky spot. The first small oratory, which pilgrims from France and the British Isles soon frequented, was superseded by a Benedictine monastery erected by Richard I, duke of Normandy, in the mid-10th century. Additions and alterations were constantly made, the most radical change coming after a French king, Philip II, or Philip Augustus, had the monastery burned to the ground in 1203, during one of his military campaigns. However, the monarch subsidized the elaborate reconstruction of the monastery. A nucleus of six Gothic buildings — almonry, cellar, refectory, Hall of Knights, dormitory, and cloister — was constructed between 1203 and 1228 and formed a magnificent unit still known as La Merveille. Crowning the summit is a large abbey church, the central tower of which narrows into a spire topped by a figure of St. Michael.

In the late 18th century, during the French Revolution, the monks of the congregation of St. Maur, who had replaced the Benedictines more than 150 years earlier, were ejected from Mont-Saint-Michel, and it was made a prison for political offenders. It remained a prison until 1863, when it was leased to the bishop of Avranches. In 1872 the French government took it over as a national monument and began the work of restoration. It is now one of the most visited tourist attractions in France.

There is also a granite and slate islet off Cornwall, England, resembling Mont-Saint-Michel and known as St. Michael's Mount. In 1047 the last Anglo-Saxon king of England, Edward the Confessor, founded a chapel there and placed it under the protection of the Benedictine abbey in Normandy. The subsequently enlarged edifice was considerably remodeled into a private castle during early modern times and presently belongs to an English noble family.

A great variety of customs grew up about St. Michael's feast day in Western Europe. It became an occasion for feasting, usually on a goose dinner, and for making weather predictions. In England the feast, which was known as Michaelmas, gained prominence as one of the four quarter days on which rents were due and contracts affecting houses and property were assumed or terminated. The annual election of the lord mayor of London, an occasion of high ceremony, still takes place on September 29.

In mountainous areas of Norway cows and goats are customarily herded down from the high pastures to the valley farms on or about St. Michael's Day. Dancing, singing, and feasting generally follow. Similar merriment marks the feast day in other parts of Western Europe. One of the superstitions attached to the day undoubtedly arose as an explanation for the overindulgence, that commonly occurred. According to legend, Satan tramples all the blackberries in the world on the eve of Michaelmas and poisons them. Any ill effects stemming from gluttony can therefore conveniently be laid to berry-eating and thus ultimately to the devil.

The cult of St. Michael spread also to the New World. Annual fiestas in honor of Michael are still staged at the end of September in Puerto Rico, especially in Cabo Rojo, where the archangel is the patron saint.

Until the present century Michael was the only archangel commemorated with a special feast in the Western church calendar, although other angels had long been honored liturgically in the East. In 1921 the Roman Catholic church set feast days for Gabriel and Raphael; both of these feasts, as noted above, were later transferred to September 29.

Gabriel, whose name in Hebrew has been variously interpreted as meaning "man of God" or "God hath shown himself mightily," is the archangel who seems to function as the divine herald. In the Bible he undertakes this role on several occasions, appearing to Daniel in the Old Testament and to Zacharias and the Virgin Mary in the New Testament. To Daniel, Gabriel was sent as the heavenly messenger to interpret the vision of the ram and the he-goat (Daniel 8:15–27), and he later prophesied the advent of the Messiah (Daniel 9:21–25). He made known the impending birth of John the Baptist to Zacharias (Luke 1:11–19), identifying himself as "Gabriel, who stand in the presence of God." In one of the New Testament's best-known passages, the archangel "was sent from God unto a city of Galilee, named Nazareth, to a virgin espoused to a man whose name was Joseph, of the house of David, and the virgin's name was Mary." (Luke 1:26–27). The divine messenger of the Annunciation then foretold the joyous tidings about the coming birth of the child who "shall be great, and shall be called the Son of the Highest" (Luke 1:32).

In the 20th chapter of the Book of Enoch, Gabriel, one of the four great archangels, is described as having been placed "over Paradise, and the serpents, and the Cherubim." According to a generally accepted Christian tradition, Gabriel functions also as the unnamed trumpeter of the Last Judgment, as mentioned in St. Paul's

First Epistle to the Thessalonians: "For the Lord himself shall descend from heaven with a shout, with the voice of the archangel, and with the [trumpet] of God; and the dead in Christ shall rise first" (4:16).

In Christian art, Gabriel is usually depicted either as the heavenly herald of the Annunciation, often bearing a lily to symbolize Mary's purity, or as the trumpeter of the Last Judgment who faces eastward to proclaim the Second Coming of the Lord.

Raphael, whose name in Hebrew means "God heals," is the archangel who figures prominently in the apocryphal Book of Tobit. According to Tobit 12:15, he is "Raphael, one of the seven holy angels who present the prayers of the saints and enter into the presence of the glory of the Holy One." Disguised as a human being under the name of Azarias, he fulfills a threefold mission: as the healer of Tobit; as the companion of Tobias, Tobit's son, on his journey; and as the rescuer of Sara, Tobias's future wife, from the clutches of the demon Asmodeus (Tobit 3:17).

In the Book of Enoch (chapter 20) Raphael is described as "one of the holy angels, who is over the spirits of men"; his function is to heal the defiled earth. He is therefore often identified with the angel in the New Testament who stirred the healing waters of the pool in Jerusalem: "For an angel went down at a certain season into the pool, and troubled the water: whosoever then first . . . stepped in was made whole of whatsoever disease he had" (John 5:2–4).

SEPTEMBER 30

Feast of St. Jerome

The Feast of St. Jerome, one of the greatest scholars of the early Christian church, has been celebrated in Rome on September 30, the date of his death at Bethlehem in 419 or 420, since the seventh century. Jerome is honored by all branches of the Christian church, and his feast day is observed regularly in Roman Catholic churches. In the revised Roman Catholic calendar, it is ranked as an obligatory memorial and was formerly a Class III feast. Perhaps the most noteworthy observance commemorating the saint occurs at the Indian Pueblo in Taos, New Mexico, where the San Geronimo Fiesta is the climax of a nearly continuous yearly round of fiestas, fairs, and ceremonial dances. (The full name of the ancient village is San Geronimo [Jerome] de Taos.) The events, staged usually on September 29 and 30, are attended by thousands of visitors. They generally include the Sun Down dance,

pole-climbing competitions, races, ritual clown antics, and a trade fair.

St. Jerome was born in 347 at Stridon, a town near Aquileia in the extreme northeast of Italy in the border area near the outlying Roman provinces of Dalmatia and Pannonia. Stridon was destroyed by the Goths in the late fourth century, and its precise location is not known. The saint's Latin name was Eusebius Hieronymus Sophronius. His parents were well-to-do Christians.

Jerome received an excellent literary and rhetorical education of the type generally given boys of the upper classes in ancient times. He studied first at Stridon and later at Rome, where he developed into a fine Greek and Latin scholar while living a carefree life. The young man learned grammar from Aelius Donatus, the renowned grammarian of the day, and then mastered the art of rhetoric. The assiduous student frequented the law courts and schools of philosophy. According to his own writings, he often spent his Sundays deciphering inscriptions on the graves of Christian martyrs in the catacombs "hollowed deep in the earth, where the path runs between bodies buried in the walls on either side. All is so dark that one feels the word of the Prophet almost realized: 'Let them go down living into hell.'" Besides acquiring in Rome a lifelong passion for classical education, Jerome gained remarkable skill in writing a pure and forceful Latin.

Although reared as a Christian and apparently a practicing believer since childhood, Jerome was baptized only at the age of 19, probably by Pope Liberius on Easter Saturday, 366. (Late baptisms, however, were not out of the ordinary in the early days of Christianity.) After completing his studies, he visited Trier, the Roman city in the Moselle River valley in what is now West Germany; there, after closely observing the ascetic way of life, he apparently realized his true vocation. About 370 the young scholar became a member of a loosely organized community of priests and laymen at Aquileia.

When the group split in 374, Jerome and a few friends journeyed east to the lands where Christianity had first taken root. They passed through Thrace, Athens, Bithynia, Galatia, Pontus, Cappadocia, and Cilicia to Syria, which to Jerome seemed "like a peaceful harbor open to the shipwrecked sailor." At Antioch, however, Jerome fell dangerously ill. While lying bedridden in the spring of 375, he experienced a dream that affected his entire life. In it, he was dragged before the Divine Judge and heard a voice saying accusingly, "Thou art a Ciceronian, not a Christian." He was then severely beaten.

Jerome, who took the admonition of his dream as a rebuke for his interest in the classics of pagan Rome, underwent an intense spiritual transformation. He resolved to devote the remainder of his life to the study of the Sacred Scriptures. He fled into the desert of Chalcis, some 50 miles southeast from Antioch. There, with "no other company but scorpions and wild beasts," he lived the life of a hermit. As an aid in overcoming violent temptations and poor health, he copied manuscripts and later began to study Hebrew with a Jewish convert to Christianity. Jerome thus started on his lifelong work as a scriptural scholar.

When numerous and sometimes undesirable hermits gathered in the desert about him, Jerome decided to return to Antioch, declaring: "From . . . our cells we condemn the universe; in our sackcloth and ashes, we pass judgment upon bishops. . . . Better to live among wild beasts than among such Christians." At Antioch, Jerome was ordained as a priest, but with the understanding that he would not be required to perform the priestly functions that he believed might prove incompatible with his real vocation. In 379 he traveled to Constantinople to study the Scriptures under the famous Greek theologian Gregory Nazianzen.

Three years later, Pope Damasus I invited Jerome and Gregory to Rome to resolve some Eastern doctrinal disputes. Jerome stayed on as papal secretary. Damasus I soon realized that the scholar's vast erudition might be usefully employed for the good of the church. Since there were in circulation several conflicting and partly erroneous versions of the Scriptures, the pope at first suggested revision of biblical texts. However, it soon became evident that an entirely new translation into Latin of the oldest and most reliable Greek and Hebrew manuscripts of the Bible was needed. Jerome plunged into the task with zeal, publishing the Gospels and the remainder of the New Testament, as well as a new version of the Psalms.

Jerome, an ardent proponent of the ascetic life, found an enthusiastic following among the noble Christian women of Rome, who were leading conventual lives at home. Among those to whom he acted as spiritual adviser and tutor in Hebrew and the Scriptures were Paula and her daughter Eustochium (later saints). Jerome's close friendship with these aristocratic women and his merciless criticism of important Roman personages, including members of the clergy, aroused much resentment. Finally his irascibility and his strong influence on his pupils made him so greatly disliked that after the death of his protector, Pope Damasus I, in 384, Jerome found it advisable to return to the East the following year.

At Antioch, Jerome was reunited with Paula,

Eustochium, and a group of Roman women who wished under his guidance to devote themselves to an ordered, peaceful, and celibate religious life. After traveling to Palestine and Egypt, where they visited the centers of monasticism, the small band eventually settled down near the Church of the Nativity at Bethlehem in Palestine. Paula's wealth was used to construct four monasteries: three for nuns, which Paula superintended until her death in 404, when Eustochium became her successor, and one for monks, over which Jerome presided. The buildings also included a hospice for wayfarers and a school, where Jerome instructed the local children in Greek and Latin.

In these comparatively remote surroundings, Jerome had by the beginning of the fifth century revised and translated almost the whole of the Old Testament, with the exception of the books of Wisdom, Ecclesiasticus, Baruch, and Maccabees 1 and 2. His version gradually superseded all others, and eventually it became known as "the Vulgate," that is, the "popular" edition of the Bible. In 1546 the Council of Trent decreed it the authorized version to be adopted by the Catholic church as the official text. This did not necessarily imply, however, that other versions were to be rejected.

At Bethlehem, Jerome also wrote commentaries on many books of the Old Testament; a church history consisting of biographies of 130 Christian authors, ending with his own; brilliantly penned letters of which over 100 have been preserved; and vigorous controversial works arising largely from contemporary doctrinal disputes. In particular, these concerned the errors of the great Alexandrian scholar Origen, whom Jerome had at first greatly admired, and the Pelagian heresy. Jerome's earlier rhetorical training had given him a powerful ability to voice scathing abuse in the style of the great classical orators and satirists.

The deaths of Paula and especially Eustochium were a severe blow to the scholar. He lamented to a friend:

The sudden falling asleep of the holy and venerable virgin Eustochium has completely crushed us, and it has almost transformed our way of living, for we can no longer carry out our plans in many things, and the fervor of the mind is frustrated by the infirmities of old age.

After a lingering illness, Jerome himself died in September 419 or 420. His body was first interred with those of Paula and Eustochium beneath the Church of the Nativity in Bethlehem. His remains may have been taken in the High Middle Ages to the Church of St. Mary Major in

Rome, but if so, their exact burial spot has long been in doubt. About 1586, his body was supposedly hidden; in 1747 a casket of relics was found, but whether it actually contains Jerome's remains has not been proved.

Jerome is one of the few fathers of the Church to whom canonization seems to have been granted not so much for outstanding holiness as for service to the church. Recalling the saint's explosive temperament and uncharitable critical tendencies, Pope Sixtus V supposedly commented, while gazing at a painting of Jerome beating his breast with a rough rock: "You do well thus to use that stone: without it you would never have been numbered among the saints." Whatever his failings, the learned Jerome must have been endowed with profound spirituality in order to compose his timeless version of the Sacred Scriptures — one that still fulfills the purpose for which it was first commissioned over 1,500 years ago.

In Christian art, Jerome is sometimes shown wearing a cardinal's garb. This depiction, however, which is probably based on his service as papal secretary to Pope Damasus I, is erroneous because in the late fourth century a papal secretary was not a cardinal secretary. The saint is also frequently represented as being accompanied by a lion. The famous legend about Jerome and the lion, which was disseminated in the Middle Ages in Jacobus de Voragine's highly popular *Legenda aurea (Golden Legend)*, was undoubtedly derived from the fact that Jerome had lived both in the Syrian desert and in remote Palestine. It is, however, completely unfounded. According to the legend, Jerome was sitting at the gate of the monastery in Bethlehem when a lion came up to him and held out his paw. Jerome looked at it and found that it was pierced by a large thorn. He removed the thorn, put healing lotions on the wound, bound it up, and had the animal lie down in his cell till it was healed. Thereafter the lion is said to have followed him about like a dog. Jerome told the lion to watch an ass used in carrying firewood so that it might not stray from the pasture. One day while the lion slept the ass disappeared, and the lion returned to the monastery with a drooping head and a look of shame. Jerome thought the lion had killed the ass and made him carry the firewood thereafter. After a time the lion decided to hunt for the missing animal. When a caravan led by an ass passed by, the lion recognized the ass, which had been stolen, and he drove the whole caravan — camels, drivers, and all — into the gate of the monastery. There the men of the caravan admitted that they had stolen the ass. Jerome rejoiced at the proof of the faithfulness of the lion, pardoning the thieves and setting them free.

Mountain State Forest Festival

This is a movable event. See note on page xxvi.

Annually since 1930 (except during World War II), the citizens of the small town of Elkins, West Virginia, have staged the colorful Mountain State Forest Festival. The event is traditionally scheduled for the first weekend in October, when the year-round splendors of the state's mountains are enhanced by brilliant autumn foliage. The purpose of the festival, which has attracted as many as 300,000 people, is not only to tell the nation about Elkins, but also to call attention to the entire state of West Virginia and to foster tourism and draw new industry. Events usually include demonstrations of forestry skills, float and fire fighters' parades, concerts, balls, the coronation of a forest monarch (Queen Silvia), and numerous forest, industrial, and commercial exhibits.

Elkins is situated at an altitude of 2,000 feet in the foothills of the Allegheny Mountains in the eastern part of West Virginia. Like most towns beyond the coastal mountain ridge, it was laid out only after transportation and industry had been developed in the region. Its founding in 1889 and incorporation the following year were due primarily to the initiative of two US Senators, Stephen Benton Elkins, for whom the community was named, and Henry Gassaway Davis. With the dream of developing the natural resources of western Maryland and West Virginia, they built the West Virginia Central and Pittsburgh Railway into the mountains to tap the abundant supplies of coal and timber and facilitate land cultivation. The two senators donated funds for the establishment of Davis and Elkins College, controlled by the Presbyterian Church. Opening in 1904, the liberal arts college expanded rapidly and the campus later moved to the former Elkins estate, which provides a forested hillside setting for much of the Mountain State Forest Festival.

The festival was the idea of George H. Dornblazer of Elkins, who saw the mountainous region as the "Switzerland of America" and envisaged it as a tourist area. His enthusiasm inspired the cooperation of a group of the town's businessmen as well as other West Virginians.

By 1930 development of part of the Seneca Trail — one of the famous Indian trails extending from New York to the Gulf of Mexico — in the nearby Monongahela National Forest had been completed. To mark the event and to call attention to neighboring scenic attractions, the town, under Dornblazer's leadership, began that summer to plan a "fall homecoming." West Virginia's state and national legislators were asked to name young women to serve as princesses in the court of the forest queen, who was to be crowned during the festival. Elkins presented its first, and extremely successful, edition of the Mountain State Forest Festival from October 30 to November 1, with a pageant, games, and a coronation ceremony at which Governor William B. Conley crowned Queen Silvia I.

A year or two later, a one-day horse show was held, and woodchopping contests were introduced to interest and attract the foresters. By 1936, elaborate ceremonies were being staged. It was most appropriate that President Franklin Delano Roosevelt crowned Queen Silvia VII. Under his leadership, the National Forest program had been stepped up in the 1930s and the Civilian Conservation Corps established, a move that greatly benefited the Monongahela National Forest. (CCC workers, operating from as many as 12 camps in the forest from 1933 to 1942, constructed campgrounds, highways, and fire trails, planted trees, and set up watersheds and wildlife preserves under the supervision of Forest Service personnel.) Following an address by President Roosevelt, the 1936 festival continued with a pageant based on the ancient Egyptian myth of creation, with Ra, the sun-god, bringing forth the world out of nothingness. There were sports and contests of several kinds on the second day, and on the third day visitors were escorted over the roads and trails in the forest or were entertained by a horse show and by athletic contests for members of the CCC.

Throughout the years, various activities were added, until the three-day festival expanded into a five-day celebration. Many of these events have remained traditional parts of the Mountain State Forest Festival. In 1962, for example, there were motorcycle hill-climbing competitions and a special Folk Day on which singers, dancers, and musicians presented an afternoon of continuous entertainment. In 1963, the centennial year of the state, soprano Eleanor Steber, a native of Wheeling, was the guest artist for the coronation ceremony; a pageant, A State Is Born, written by Mrs. Bond Davis of Salem and Claire Fiorentino of Davis and Elkins College, depicted the state's 100 years of history; and the Golden Knights, a US Army parachute team, demonstrated free-fall parachuting at the Elkins Municipal Airport. At the 1965 air show, Hollywood stunt fliers presented two hours of aerial action.

For more than three decades, the inhabitants of Elkins have looked forward each fall to welcoming visitors to their festival. Although the endeavor requires some outside assistance from the state government and from industry, schools, churches, and civic clubs, it is chiefly a tribute to the people of Randolph County, who work hard to execute plans, donating countless hours without recompense. (A nonprofit institution chartered in September 1935, the Festival Association employs only one full-time worker, a secretary who handles correspondence throughout the year.)

The 34th festival, in 1970, also marked the 50th anniversary of the Monongahela National Forest, whose 806,000 acres make it one of the largest forests in the eastern United States. The five-day celebration of the dual event began on Wednesday, September 30, with the 9:00 A.M. arrival of the Cass Scenic Railroad, an old logging train pulled by a Shay steam locomotive at a daring 20 miles an hour. This authentic reminder of the state's impressive lumbering history offered 40-minute rides throughout each day of the festival, puffing its way over a six-mile stretch between Elkins and Canfield. (It has been an annual feature of the festival since 1963.) First-day events continued with the opening of craft, industrial, and commercial exhibits for festival visitors at 10:00 A.M.

At 1:00 P.M. a warm welcome was given to the festival queen-to-be, Maid Silvia XXXIV (Susan Staggers), who arrived by Cass Railroad at the Western Maryland Depot. Once in the festival city, Maid Silvia embarked upon a whirlwind round of appearances, starting at 1:30 P.M. with a tour of the schools and continuing through the afternoon with a 4:00 P.M. radio interview. On Thursday she toured the Monongahela National Forest, visited the exhibits and Davis and Elkins College, and attended the annual Distinguished Guest dinner at the National Guard Armory. Russell E. Train, national chairman of the Council on Environmental Quality, was the featured speaker, and Edward P. Cliff, head of the US Forest Service, was a special guest in honor of the Forest's golden anniversary. That same evening, the general public had an opportunity to enjoy the Blue Grass Jamboree at Blue Grass Park, a square dance, or a band concert.

On Friday visitors watched a horse-pulling contest in the morning before the precoronation ceremonies for Maid Silvia at the hillside amphitheater on the Davis and Elkins campus. At 1:00 P.M. the Fairmont State College Falcon Band heralded the approach of the queen and her court with a concert. The Sing-Out Clarksburg group of 40 young people continued with patriotic songs and spirituals. Then trumpets blared as Maid Silvia XXXIV and her court slowly made their way up the pathway. The US Air Force ROTC Cadet Wing of West Virginia University acted as an honor guard. The 40 festival princesses were arrayed in velvet gowns of autumn-leaf hues. Maids of honor, flower girls, and formally clad state and local officials completed the royal party. Following the performance of Franz Schubert's "Who is Silvia?," Governor Arch A. Moore Jr., crowned Queen Silvia XXXIV. A public reception followed immediately and was succeeded by a band concert.

The Grand Ole Opry, an annual event featuring country and western music, was staged at 6:30 P.M. and again at 9:30 P.M. at the National Guard Armory. At 8:00 P.M., with flashlights and wailing sirens, the annual Firemen's Parade began, and volunteer fire fighters displayed shiny antiquated equipment and demonstrated up-to-date improvements. A square dance started at 9:00, and fireworks at 9:30. Queen Silvia continued her schedule of appearances by attending the Royal Forest Queen's Ball at the downtown Elks Club.

The full schedule of events on Saturday presented a challenge to visitors — and to Queen Silvia XXXIV, who was whisked from one festival feature to another. These included many competitions, among them sawing, wood-chopping, muzzle-loading, and fly-casting contests, as well as archery and riding events.

After choosing between a noontime chicken barbecue sponsored by the Elkins Jaycees and a soccer game (Davis and Elkins College vs. Morgan State), visitors converged on the Elkins business district at 2:00 P.M. for what was probably the festival's greatest single attraction — the Grand Feature parade. The 1970 honorary parade marshal was Neil A. Armstrong, the first man to walk on the moon. Joining in the procession with Queen Silvia and her entourage and prominent state and national figures were 50 high school and college bands. Apart from a Little League football game at 7:30 P.M., the rest of the festivities came under the heading of music and dancing — a fiddlers' contest, a cabaret dance for teenagers, and the Mountain State Forest Festival cabaret.

On Sunday morning visitors were welcomed at worship services in Elkins churches. In the afternoon an archery contest and stock car races at the Elkins Speedway provided a climax to the five days of celebration.

October

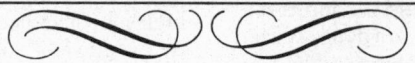

October is the 10th month of the Gregorian, or New Style, calendar used today and has 31 days. It was the 8th month in the ancient Roman calendar, which started in March, as its name, derived from the Latin word for eight, *octo,* indicates. Although the Roman calendar was revised on several occasions, most extensively under Julius Caesar in 45 B.C. (see Appendix, The Calendar), October retained its outmoded name even after it had become the 10th month.

Several efforts were made to rename October in honor of Roman emperors or their wives. The months of *Quintilis* and *Sextilis* had been renamed *Julius* for Julius Caesar and *Augustus* for Emperor Augustus in the first century B.C. Following this precedent, there was an attempt on the part of the Roman senate shortly after the death of Augustus in 14 A.D. to rename October as *Livius* in honor of Livia, the politically influential mother of the new emperor, Tiberius (14–37 A.D.). It was a change that Tiberius refused to sanction, however. Emperor Domitian (81–96 A.D.) renamed October, his birth month, *Domitianus,* after himself, but the change was short-lived. About 138 A.D., the Roman senate proposed that September be changed to *Antoninus* as a tribute to Emperor Antoninus Pius (138–161 A.D.). As an accompanying gesture, the senate suggested that the following month, October, be known as *Faustinus* in honor of Faustina (c. 104–141 A.D.), wife of Antoninus. The emperor rejected both proposals. A fourth name change was projected about 191 A.D., when it was suggested that October be called *Hercules* to honor Emperor Commodus (180–192 A.D.), who sometimes termed himself the Roman Hercules. But none of these actual or attempted changes was permanently successful.

On October 13 the Romans celebrated the *fontalia,* the festival of the fountains, by scatter-

ing flowers over the sources and springs. From October 15 to 19 they honored the war god Mars in a feast known as the *armilustrum.* Held as a counterpart to the festival of Mars celebrated in March and marking the beginning of the season for military campaigns, it was the occasion for sacrificing a horse to the god of war and for purifying the sacred war shields and arms of the Roman army before retiring all weapons for winter.

The Anglo-Saxons had three names for October: *Win-monath,* "wine month," or the time for making wine; *Teo-monath,* "10th month"; and *Winterfylleth,* because winter was supposed to begin with the full moon of October. The lucky birthstones often associated with October are the opal and the aquamarine.

OCTOBER 1

Rosh Hashanah

This is a movable event. See note on page xxvi.

The Jewish New Year, Rosh Hashanah, falls on the first day of the Hebrew month of Tishri (in the course of September or October), which in 1970 corresponded to October 1. Rosh Hashanah is the first of the 10 Penitential Days, which end with Yom Kippur, the Day of Atonement (see October 10). The Hebrew calendar, which is lunisolar, is divided into 12 lunar months of 29 or 30 days each. A 12-month lunar year contains 353 to 355 days. Since a solar year is about 11 days longer than 12 lunar months, seven times in a 19-year cycle a 13th month is added to the Hebrew calendar. The beginning of the new year falls between September 5 and October 5. All other Jewish festivals also fall on different dates of the solar secular calendar from year to year.

Rosh Hashanah is also called the Day of Judgment and the Day of Remembrance because, according to Jewish tradition, on this day God remembers all his creatures and judges humankind. According to the traditional Jewish imagery, on Rosh Hashanah God opens three books in which the deeds of every individual are recorded. One book is for the completely wicked, a second is for the perfectly righteous, and a third for those in between. The righteous are at once inscribed and sealed for life, and the wicked for death. Judgment of the middle group is suspended until Yom Kippur, the Day of Atonement. Thus the customary salutation of Jews on Rosh Hashanah eve is "*Leshanah tovah tikatevu vetichatemu*"–"May you be inscribed and sealed for a good year." In a somewhat different form, this message appears on the New Year greeting cards sent at this time.

Rosh Hashanah, like every day in the Hebrew calendar, starts at sundown on the previous day. In the synagogue the *shofar,* or ram's horn, is blown to mark the beginning of the New Year. The sounds of the *shofar* summon all Jews to meditation, self-examination, and repentance. Reform and Israeli Jews celebrate Rosh Hashanah at special holiday synagogue services for one day from sundown to sundown, as specified in the Bible, while Orthodox and Conservative Jews observe the holiday for two days, according to later tradition. In the afternoon on the first day of the New Year, Orthodox Jews also take part in the ceremony known as *Tashlikh,* going to a nearby body of water where they recite special prayers and symbolically cast away their sins by shaking out their hems and pockets. The name *Tashlikh* derives from the recitation of the first words of Micah 7:19, "you will cast your sins into the sea."

Although Rosh Hashanah and Yom Kippur are Days of Awe, the High Holy Days of the Jewish year, celebration of the New Year is marked by festivity as well as by prayer. Most Jews do not work on Rosh Hashanah. In the evening of the holiday candles are lighted and a holiday meal is served, including bread or apples dipped in honey to symbolize the hope for a sweet new year. The main observance of Rosh Hashanah, though, centers on the synagogue services. Traditionally, the rabbi, cantor, and other officiants wear white garments during the services, and the Torah scrolls in the ark are also clad in white. Two passages from the Bible are read, chapters 21 and 22 of Genesis and chapter 29 of Numbers. The most moving moment occurs when the cantor chants the medieval prayer *Unetaneh Tokef.* This prayer describes vividly the awesomeness of God's judging the world on Rosh Hashanah. But, although men and women stand in awe of God's judgment on this day, they are not helpless, since "repentance, prayer, and charity annul the severe sentence." During the 10 Penitential Days all Jews attempt to amend the wrongs they have committed during the year just passed, for without this action God is not willing to accept their repentance as true.

Jimmy Carter's Birthday

Jimmy Carter (James Earl Carter Jr.), the 39th President of the United States, was born on October 1, 1924, in Plains, Georgia, a small town in the state's southwestern peanut- and pine-growing region. His father, James Earl Carter Sr., was a farmer and grocery store manager, who launched a business reselling peanuts for processing and later served as a representative in the state legislature. His mother, Lillian Gordy Carter — once described by her son as "the most influential woman in my life" — worked as a nurse at the Plains hospital and served in the Peace Corps as a birth-control information specialist in the late 1960s.

The oldest of four children, Jimmy Carter grew up three miles from Plains in a wooden clapboard house in the unincorporated community of Archery. As a boy he worked hard in the fields under his father's strict supervision; in his free time he enjoyed hunting and fishing with the children who lived nearby, almost all of whom were black.

After his graduation from Plains High School in 1941, Jimmy Carter became the first member of his family to attend college. He studied at Georgia Southwestern College in Americus for a year; he then transferred to the Georgia Institute of Technology in Atlanta in order to fulfill the mathematics requirements for admission to the US Naval Academy at Annapolis, where he began an accelerated wartime program in 1943 and graduated 59th in his class of 820 three years later. Shortly afterwards, on July 7, 1946, he married Rosalynn Smith, also of Plains.

Carter proved himself a naval officer of exceptional ability during his two years of service on battleships and five years on submarines. His first submarine commander, Captain John B. Williams of the *Pomfret,* characterized him as a natural leader "who no matter what he does ends up being the boss." Taking postgraduate evening courses in nuclear physics at Union College in Schenectady, New York, the young officer in 1951 joined the nuclear submarine development program sponsored by the Atomic Energy Commission and conducted by Captain (later Admiral) Hyman G. Rickover, a firm chief to whom Carter attributed his insistence on excellence, drive, and discipline. He became a senior officer on the *Sea Wolf*, one of the first atomic-powered submarines.

His father's imminent death from cancer forced Jimmy Carter to make the agonizing decision to take over the family peanut business, then encompassing some 2,500 acres of farmland. He later recalled: "You have only one life, and I began to wonder if I should spend mine engaged in war, even if I could rationalize it as the prevention of war." He resigned his commission as lieutenant in 1953 and moved his family — which then included three young sons, John William, James Earl III, and Donnel Jeffrey — to Plains. By hard work, application of his engineering skills, and bold investments, he eventually built up the enterprise until by 1971 he was grossing an estimated $800,000 yearly.

Widely read and widely traveled, Carter soon became active in local civic affairs, but, torn between his conservative background and liberal inclinations, he frequently clashed with his segregationist white neighbors over racial issues. After the 1954 Supreme Court ruling outlawing racially segregated schools (see May 17), for example, he was the only white man in Plains who would not join the segregationist Citizens Council. His stand resulted in a temporary business boycott of the Carters. As late as the mid-1960s the family stood alone in voting to admit blacks to the town's Baptist congregation and, as Rosalynn Carter remembers, "people wouldn't speak to us in church." (Blacks were not admitted until after Carter's election to the presidency in 1976.)

Jimmy Carter served as chairman of the Sumter County Board of Education from 1955 to 1962, when, angered by the rejection of a school-consolidation plan he had advanced, which had been defeated as an "integration scheme," he became a candidate for the Georgia senate. Although the original ballot count showed that he had lost narrowly, he contested the results on the grounds of voting irregularities. A subsequent suit revealed that he had been beaten by voters "who were dead, jailed, or never at the polls on Election Day," and the outcome was reversed. Elected to a second term in 1964, the senator gained a reputation as a hardworking, moderate liberal concerned especially with educational improvements.

In September 1966 the still relatively unknown politician passed up an almost certain seat in the US House of Representatives to run as a liberal in the Democratic gubernatorial primary. His third-place showing behind segregationist Lester G. Maddox and the liberal former governor, Ellis Arnall, was a bitter disappointment that Carter vowed would be the last of his political career.

During the next four years, Carter prepared methodically for the 1970 gubernatorial campaign, building up an effective political network, polishing his speaking style in some 1,800 statewide addresses, and (with his wife) shaking some 600,000 hands. Skillfully exploiting the weakness of his chief opponent, former governor Carl Sanders, suspected by some of being a pawn of Atlanta wealth, he played up his populist appeal as a simple farmer. He also positioned himself as a rural candidate sympathetic to the views of Governor George Wallace of Alabama and did not hesitate to attract segregationist voters, rationalizing along the lines of one of his favorite quotations by theologian Reinhold Niebuhr: "You can't establish justice in a sinful world unless you win elections." He cautioned Atlanta's black leaders: "You won't like my campaign, but you'll be proud of my record as governor."

Carter's expedient antiestablishment tactics, which some observers viewed as shrewd, others as opportunistic, achieved the results he desired. Supported by Georgia's rural white and urban blue-collar voters, he won a plurality in the September 8, 1970, Democratic primary and two weeks later secured the runoff election against Sanders. In the November 3 general election he easily beat television newscaster Hal Suit, his Republican opponent.

The new governor, long known as a moderate liberal but elected as a conservative, ended whatever doubts he had aroused as to his political viewpoint at his inauguration on January 12, 1971. In his inaugural address he rejected the white supremacy that had traditionally prevailed in Georgia and advocated social and economic progress for blacks and whites alike: "The time for racial discrimination is over. No poor, rural, weak, or black person should ever have to bear the additional burden of being deprived of the opportunity of an education, a job, or simple justice." Carter's ambitious reform program, hailed as a model for the New South, made him, however briefly, something of a national celebrity.

Governor Carter's four-year term was one of hard-won, solid achievement, although some critics contend that in subsequent campaigning he inflated a decent record into an outstanding one. His massive reorganization of the unwieldy and inefficient state bureaucracy streamlined 300 agencies — many of them unstaffed and unbudgeted — into 22 superdepartments. He introduced zero-base budgeting, requiring state officials to justify every program each year. He improved prison and mental-health systems and backed consumer and environmental protection programs. He opened state jobs to blacks, appointing 53 to supervisory boards. In an impressive ceremony at which an integrated audience sang "We Shall Overcome," he had a portrait of Martin Luther King Jr. hung in the Georgia State House, the first black so honored.

During his term of office Carter had an opportunity to observe national politics firsthand. He attended governors' conferences and in Atlanta played host to the country's leading politicians, including the 1972 Democratic presidential aspirants, who sought his support. Later he recalled: "We'd discuss national issues and I decided I knew as much as they did. I started to think about the presidency in human terms, not historical terms." At the July 1972 Democratic convention in Miami he nominated Senator Henry M. Jackson of Washington as a centrist alternative to Senator George McGovern of South Dakota.

In October 1972, however, before McGovern's defeat by President Richard M. Nixon Carter had already started to plan his own 1976 presidential bid with a handful of close advisers. The small Carter executive committee shrewdly focused on what they foresaw as the 1976 picture: a heyday of the antipolitician, a year in which personal character and ideals would count more than issues and statistics. Jimmy Carter's obvious drawbacks as a nonincumbent and as a newcomer to the national scene lacking financial, popular, and party support could be turned into assets.

The aspirant plunged into a total-immersion course in the craft of the presidency. He pondered foreign affairs, traveled abroad on trade missions to meet foreign leaders, and read voraciously on national and international issues. He wrote an autobiography, *Why Not the Best?* He used his honorary chairmanship of the 1974 National Democratic Congressional Campaign to further his political future, monitoring all gubernatorial and congressional campaigns, developing contacts, and seeding Carter for President committees.

On December 12, 1974, one month before the expiration of his term as governor, Jimmy Carter formally announced his candidacy for the presidency. Using the same populist tactics that had won him the 1970 gubernatorial race, he began to stump the nation in January 1975 as if it were Georgia. Having enlisted all close family members — his wife, his three grown sons, and even his eight-year-old daughter, Amy — he ran a Spartan, precision-timed campaign with prodigious gusto. In 99 weeks he gave over 1,500 speeches in 1,000 cities in 50 states, piling up nearly half a million miles of travel and spending in 1975 alone 250 days on the road.

His bid — regarded in most circles as a quixotic assault by "Jimmy Who?" — was at first either ignored or ridiculed by the Democratic establishment. Frequently asked, "Are you serious?," he replied self-confidently: "I don't intend to lose." Pushing his personality, displaying charm, and inspiring confidence, he attacked the "confused, bloated bureaucratic mess in Washington" and called for revival and reform in the wake of Vietnam and Watergate. A staunch Southern Baptist, baptized in 1935 but "born again" spiritually in the aftermath of his 1966 gubernatorial defeat, he effectively employed an evangelistic oratorical approach in promising strong moral leadership to form a government "as decent, as honest, as truthful, as fair, as compassionate and as filled with love as our people are." He proved himself a master of the nuances of the English language, developing the ability to take positions on vexing major issues yet to phrase his statements so carefully as to gain the confidence of conservatives, liberals, and moderates alike.

Entering all but one of the 27 Democratic presidential-preference primaries in 1976, Carter gathered momentum daily. He eventually placed first in 17 of the contests and second in 8, amassing 39 percent of the votes cast — far more than any of the 12 other formally avowed Democratic aspirants. Carter's resounding Ohio primary triumph in June touched off a stampede of key party leaders, still somewhat uneasy about his inexperience, self-sufficiency, and religious fervor, but conceding, as one Illinois regular put it, "He's a machine we didn't make, but he works."

While the former governor of California, Ronald Reagan, and President Gerald R. Ford were still contending for the GOP nomination, Jimmy Carter, on July 14, 1976, overwhelmingly won the Democratic nomination on the first ballot at the party's 37th national convention at Madison Square Garden in New York. The following day he named Senator Walter F. ("Fritz") Mondale of Minnesota as his running mate, a decision reached after a painstaking three-month search. Carter and Mondale, dubbed Grits and Fritz by the press, followed a precise state-by-state fall timetable against their Republican opponents, President Ford and his vice-presidential choice, Senator Robert Dole of Kansas. Carter and Mondale suffered a substantial 30-point slide from their summer poll ratings, partly because of the difficulty of competing with an incumbent. For the first time since the Kennedy-Nixon debates of 1960, two presidential nominees matched issues and images in televised debates: one on domestic affairs on September 23, another on foreign policy on October 6, and a final general debate on October 22.

The contest was rated a toss-up as late as Election Day, November 2. In one of the century's tightest presidential elections, Jimmy Carter won 51 percent of the popular vote against Ford's 48 percent and 297 electoral votes against Ford's 241. Carter made history as the first chief of state from the Deep South since Zachary Taylor of Louisiana was elected in 1848, thereby helping to heal the century-old division between North and South caused by the Civil War. Many political analysts assert that he owed his victory in large part to the massive southern black vote, made possible by the civil rights movement and the federal Voting Rights Act of 1965 (see August 6).

On January 20, 1977, Jimmy Carter assumed office as the President of the United States, optimistic that the strong Democratic majorities in the House of Representatives and the Senate would enable him to push through his bold, many-sided campaign programs, including those for economic recovery, tax and welfare reform, national health insurance, and government reorganization. His first year in the White House, however, was marked by domestic and international troubles: difficult relations with Congress; unabating energy dilemmas; persistent inflation and unemployment; a prolonged coal strike; spreading urban decay; a farmers' protest movement; delayed ratification of the Panama Canal treaties; controversial defense planning and disarmament negotiations; a growing trade deficit and weakening dollar; violations of human rights; conflicts in the Middle East and Africa.

Despite these burdens and despite criticism and investigations of several members of his staff, Carter continued to work confidently and energetically towards the achievement of the goals he had set for himself and for the nation.

Treaty of San Ildefonso

By the Treaty of Fontainebleau of 1762 and the Treaty of Paris of 1763, France gave up all its colonial possessions in North America. Preoccupied with domestic affairs, the French government for several decades showed no inclination to regain its empire. But at the beginning of the 19th century Napoleon I decided to revive his nation's colonial interests in North America. To carry out his plan, the French government forced Spain to accept the Treaty of San Ildefonso of October 1, 1800, by which that nation returned the vast territory of Louisiana, which it had received from France 38 years earlier.

The San Ildefonso Treaty was a secret agreement, and news of the retrocession did not reach the United States until more than a year later. Nevertheless, the transfer of jurisdiction over the area west of the Mississippi River had an important effect on the historical development of the United States.

News that France had regained possession of the Louisiana Territory disturbed President Thomas Jefferson. He feared that French occupation of the area might jeopardize the security of the United States and inhibit this nation's commercial use of the Mississippi River. Thus, as early as 1802, Jefferson instructed Robert R. Livingston, the American minister at Paris (see November 27), to begin negotiations for a tract of land on the lower Mississippi that could be used as a port, or at least for an irrevocable agreement that US citizens would be able to navigate the river freely and deposit their goods at New Orleans. In January 1803 President Jefferson named James Monroe minister plenipotentiary to France to assist Livingston in negotiating these matters. Their task was accomplished with ease, for even before Monroe had reached France in April 1803, Napoleon had already given up the idea of reviving the French colonial empire in North America and was willing to sell the entire province of Louisiana. Discussions over the terms of sale lasted only a few weeks, and on May 2, 1803, the treaty of cession – antedated to April 30 – was signed. According to this document, the United States agreed to pay France $15 million for the vast area between the Mississippi River and the Rocky Mountains. The US Senate approved the treaty on October 20, 1803, and the nation took formal possession of Louisiana later the same year (see December 20).

OCTOBER 2

Major John André Hanged as a Spy

During the difficult years of the American Revolution, countless deeds of valor were performed by patriots to secure the colonies' freedom, and to this day the United States honors the heroes who fought for independence from Great Britain. But the nation's history also records the treachery of General Benedict Arnold. Arnold's traitorous plan, which would have given the British control of the vital Hudson River fortification at West Point, New York, failed, and Arnold himself escaped punishment by fleeing to safety behind British lines. Major John André, the British officer who had plotted with Arnold, was not so fortunate. By order of General George Washington, the commander in chief of the Continental army, André was hanged as a spy on October 2, 1780.

A brilliant young soldier, André first came to the American colonies as a lieutenant in 1774. Captured the next year at St. John's, north of Lake Champlain, during the abortive American campaign against Canada, André spent a year on parole in Pennsylvania before being exchanged and returning to service with the British army in New York City. André's superior officers quickly recognized the young man's abilities; by 1779 he had advanced to the rank of major, and Sir Henry Clinton, the commander in chief of British forces in America, had selected him to be his aide-de-camp and adjutant general.

As Clinton's aide, André had charge of the British general's correspondence with secret agents and informants, the most notable of whom was Benedict Arnold. Beginning in May 1779 Arnold provided the British with important information regarding American defenses, but not until the summer of 1780 did he gain command of West Point and develop the plan to betray that strategic fortification. Using the pseudonyms Gustavus and John Anderson, Arnold and André exchanged considerable correspondence about the plot against the American garrison. Finally, in August 1780, Clinton agreed to pay Arnold £20,000 for his assistance in bringing West Point under British control.

On September 20, 1780, André ventured up the Hudson River on the British sloop *Vulture*, wearing his British uniform so that he could not be charged as a spy if he was captured behind enemy lines. On September 22, before dawn, André was able to go ashore as planned. He and Arnold met in a wooded area across the Hudson from West Point until about 4:00 A.M. and worked out specific details for the British takeover of the garrison.

Fearing detection if he attempted to return to the *Vulture* at daybreak, André decided to wait at the home of a British sympathizer, Joshua Hett Smith, until that night. This delay proved disastrous for him. At dawn on the 22nd, Colonel James Livingston, a Continental officer who had no knowledge of the plot between Arnold and André, meanwhile had ordered his men to fire on the *Vulture*. The British sloop managed to escape down the Hudson, but its retreat left André stranded within patriot territory.

The departure of the *Vulture* forced André to return to the British forces in New York City by an overland route through perilous countryside. Before beginning the trip André decided to remove his scarlet uniform. By so doing he discarded his chief advantage as well as his worst handicap, for although his military garb made him conspicuous, it also guaranteed him protection as a soldier from the reprisals and punishments accorded a captured spy. For his hazardous journey he donned civilian clothes, including a round beaver hat and a long flowing blue cloak, and hid the papers detailing the secrets of West Point's defenses in his boots.

Arnold wrote out special passes so that André would be allowed through the American lines. Then, with Joshua Smith as his guide, André set out at nightfall on Friday, September 22, for New York. Smith accompanied André as far south as the Croton River. There he considered his charge to be beyond all danger, and shortly after dawn, the next day, he left the British major to complete the remaining 15 miles of his journey alone.

André's trip continued without mishap until about 9:00 A.M., when he encountered three volunteer militiamen. John Paulding, Issac Van Wart, and David Williams were probably adventurers acting under a New York law that permitted them to claim any property they might find on a captured enemy. However, when they stopped André, he mistook them for British sympathizers, and in the confusion of the moment he revealed to them his true identity. The militiamen searched their captive, and when they discovered the incriminating papers relating to West Point in his boots, they immediately turned him over to Lieutenant Colonel John Jameson, the commander of American outposts in the region.

During the two days that followed, American leaders slowly unraveled the complicated plot involving Arnold and André. On September 25 Arnold heard of André's capture and managed to flee to safety with the British just hours before General George Washington arrived in the vicinity of West Point and learned of his subordinate's treachery. But André had no hope of escaping punishment. On September 29 a military board consisting of such respected officers as Nathanael Greene, the Marquis de Lafayette, Baron von Steuben, and Henry Knox met to interrogate him. During the hearing, which lasted only one day, the evidence that was presented conclusively indicated that André was guilty of spying.

When Washington heard the board's report, he ordered André to be hanged on October 1. The execution was postponed a day, following General Sir Henry Clinton's request for a delay so that Washington might learn "a true state of facts." But the British general's efforts on behalf of his aide were futile, and Washington could not agree to André's request to be shot as a soldier rather than hanged as a spy. On October 2, 1780, the original orders were carried out, and André met his death on the gallows.

André had been well loved by his fellow soldiers. Following his death, the British army went into mourning. Indeed, he was mourned by the patriots as well. A monument to the soldier who had plotted with Arnold to advance the cause of England was erected in Westminster Abbey, where his remains, transferred there in 1826, subsequently found their final resting place.

First Pan American Conference Convenes

On October 2, 1889, the First International Conference of American States convened in Washington, D.C. At this first Pan American Conference, as the 1889 gathering is more commonly known, representatives from all the nations of the Western Hemisphere, except Canada and the Dominican Republic, came together for the first time. The meeting thus marked the beginning of an effort towards true international cooperation in the Americas.

The hope that the nations of the Western Hemisphere would come together to discuss matters of common interest originated as early as 1826, when Simón Bolívar, the Liberator of South America, invited all the nations of North and South America to the Congress of Panama. Bolívar's dream of establishing diplomatic unity among the nations of the Americas was premature; indeed, the Panama Congress adjourned before the US delegation had arrived. But Bolívar's plan was not forgotten.

Representatives of Latin American countries met several times in the mid- and late 19th century to discuss possible alliances in the event of foreign attack and to deliberate on some aspects of international law. The United States did not take part in these conferences. In 1881, however, during the brief administration of President James A. Garfield, Secretary of State James G. Blaine invited delegates from the nations in the Western Hemisphere to a meeting to consider ways of "preventing war between the nations of America." International difficulties in Latin America and domestic problems in the United States prevented the conference that was scheduled for 1882 from taking place, but interest in the hemispheric meeting soon revived.

In 1888 President Grover Cleveland instructed his secretary of state, Thomas Bayard, to invite the nations to a Pan American conference. Ironically, when the gathering convened on October 2, 1889, James G. Blaine was again secretary of state, appointed by the new President, Benjamin Harrison.

The delegates to the first Pan American Conference met for more than six months, undertook a railroad tour of the United States, and listened to countless speeches. Since most of the countries of Latin America had strong economic ties with Europe, the representatives rejected the plan for a customs union with the United States that Blaine proposed, but on April 14, 1890, they created the International Union of American Republics, an information clearinghouse based in Washington, D.C., which later became the Pan American Union (see April 14). The delegates to the conference also approved a number of recommendations involving sanitary regulations, patents and trademarks, and other matters. Most significantly they established the precedent for later hemispheric cooperation that resulted in the holding of seven other Pan American conferences between 1901 and 1938 and that culminated in the formation of the Organization of American States in 1948. The charter of the OAS was the product of the ninth Pan American Conference — officially the Ninth International Conference of American States — which met at Bogotá, Colombia, from March 30 to May 2 of that year.

OCTOBER 3

George Bancroft's Birthday

George Bancroft, who has been called the Father of American History, was born in Worcester, Massachusetts, on October 3, 1800. The eighth of the 13 children of Aaron and Lucretia Chandler Bancroft, he was descended from old New England families. His forebears included Captain Benjamin Church, the historian of the 1675 war between the Wampanoag Indians and the settlers of New England that has become known as King Philip's War, and "Tory John" Chandler, who served as a judge in Worcester County before fleeing to England during the American Revolution. George Bancroft's father, Aaron Bancroft, also had a notable career; he played a leading role in the Unitarian schism from the Congregational church, served as the first president of the American Unitarian Association, and wrote a biography of George Washington that enjoyed considerable popularity.

George Bancroft attended local Worcester schools before enrolling at Phillips Exeter Academy in Exeter, New Hampshire, at the age of 11. After a two-year stay at that school, he entered Harvard College. He was graduated from that institution before his 17th birthday and then stayed on in Cambridge as a divinity student during the year that followed.

During his years at Harvard, Bancroft so impressed President J. T. Kirkland and a number of professors that in 1818 they arranged for him to continue his studies in Europe. Bancroft's sojourn on the Continent lasted four years. In 1820 he received his Ph.D. degree from the University of Göttingen. He also studied for a time in Berlin, and then traveled through Europe.

In 1822 Bancroft returned to the United States, where he accepted a position as a tutor in Greek at Harvard. He hoped to institute sweeping academic reforms at Harvard, but that institution was not interested in his recommendations for changing its methods of instruction. Instead, Bancroft, with his newly acquired European mannerisms and educational beliefs, became increasingly alienated from his fellow faculty members. By the end of his first year of teaching he had written: "I have found College a sickening and wearisome place."

In association with Joseph G. Cogswell, who also had studied at Göttingen, Bancroft in 1823 founded the Round Hill School at Northampton, Massachusetts. Modeling the school after the German *Gymnasium,* Bancroft and Cogswell tried to put into practice the educational innovations they had seen in operation at Göttingen and other European universities. Round Hill was a bold experiment in educational reform, but it ultimately failed. In 1830 Bancroft sold his interest in the school, and several years later he recorded his dissatisfaction with teaching when he wrote that it "was a kind of occupation to which I was not peculiarly adapted, and in which many of inferior abilities and attainments could have succeeded as well."

As his interest in teaching waned, Bancroft became increasingly involved in politics. On July 4, 1826, he had delivered an address at Springfield, Massachusetts. In this speech on the occasion of the 50th anniversary of American independence, Bancroft emphasized the value of the democratic principles advanced by Thomas Jefferson. This address was the beginning of Bancroft's efforts to propound his democratic beliefs. In the years that followed, Bancroft eloquently defended the actions of President Andrew Jackson and other Democrats in numerous articles that appeared in the *North American Review* and other periodicals.

Through his political writings and his activities in public office, Bancroft made substantial contributions to the American political scene, but it is for his historical works that he is best remembered. Bancroft first made public his idea of writing a history of the United States in 1828. He set out to write "A History of the United States from the Discovery of the American Continent to the Present Time," and by 1834 he had completed the first volume of his ambitious undertaking. The first volume, which treated the development of European colonization of America to 1660, received an enthusiastic reception. With its basic theme that "the spirit of the colonies demanded freedom from the beginning," Bancroft's history, as the historian J. F. Jameson noted, "caught, and with sincere and enthusiastic conviction repeated to the American people the things which they were saying . . . concerning themselves."

During the next 40 years Bancroft completed 10 volumes of his history. The task of writing a history "to the present time" proved impossible, and he carried his unbroken narrative only through the period of the American Revolution. Bancroft's work enjoyed great success. The history went through at least 20 editions and made its author a wealthy man.

Historians in the 20th century have noted important flaws in the work. The underlying thesis of the *History*, that the American Revolution was the inevitable result of the colonists' continuing search for freedom, often caused Bancroft to distort his account of the development of the American colonies. Moreover, he ignored the social growth of the American colonies and often oversimplified complex issues. Despite these shortcomings Bancroft's work remains a classic as much respected for its accurate reflection of the spirit of the United States in the 19th century as for its detailing of the history of the nation during the colonial and Revolutionary periods.

Bancroft's overtly political writings and his *History*, which seemed "to vote for Jackson," marked him for preferment in the Democratic party. In 1834 he was an unsuccessful candidate for election as representative to the Massachusetts General Court from Northampton. Three years later President Martin Van Buren appointed the historian to be the collector of the Port of Boston. In 1844, as a delegate to the Democratic National Convention, he played an important role in gaining the presidential nomination for James K. Polk. Bancroft lost his race for governor of Massachusetts in 1844, but, as a reward for his political services, President Polk selected him to be secretary of the navy. Bancroft held this post for only 18 months, but in that short time he answered a long-felt need by establishing the US Naval Academy at Annapolis, Maryland.

In 1846 Polk appointed Bancroft to be US minister to Great Britain. This three-year service in England strengthened his great affection for America, and he wrote "my residence in Europe has but quickened and confirmed my love for the rule of the people." It also gave him access to important documents in London and Paris relating to the American colonies and the War for Independence. His extensive research in these materials contributed much to the broad international scope of his *History*.

Returning to the United States in 1849, Bancroft took up residence in New York City. For the next 18 years he devoted himself almost exclusively to his *History,* and during this time he completed volumes IV through IX. During this period, Bancroft held no public office, but despite his strong association with the Democratic party, he became a friend and supporter of Republican President Abraham Lincoln. Indeed, Bancroft's relationship with the 16th President was such that he was chosen to deliver the February 12, 1866, memorial address on the life and character of Abraham Lincoln before the House of Representatives.

Bancroft also enjoyed a close association with Lincoln's successor, Andrew Johnson. In 1867 Johnson appointed the historian to be US minister to Berlin. Serving in this capacity for seven years, Bancroft helped resolve questions concerning naturalization and trademarks and assisted in arbitrating the boundary between British Columbia and the state of Washington. He also found time during this stay in Europe to gather material for volume X of his *History,* which was published in 1874.

At the age of 74 Bancroft returned to the United States. He settled in Washington, D.C., in 1874, and for the remainder of his life he resided alternately in the nation's capital and Newport, Rhode Island. The scholar and diplomat was much honored during the twilight of his life, and perhaps the most important of his many distinctions was the Senate's voting to admit him to the floor of its chamber.

Almost to the end of his life, Bancroft continued his historical writing. In 1876 he published a "thoroughly revised edition" of his *History.* Six years later his two-volume *History of the Formation of the Constitution of the United States* was published. He again revised his multivolume *History of the United States,* producing the "author's last revision" of the work between 1883 and 1885. Bancroft completed one other noteworthy volume after his 80th birthday; *Martin Van Buren to the End of His Public Career* was published in 1889.

Bancroft died in Washington, D.C., on January 17, 1891. As a symbol of the nation's grief, President Benjamin Harrison ordered the executive departments in the capital to fly their flags at half-mast. While Bancroft's body was being transported to its final resting place in Worcester, Massachusetts, the cities through which his funeral train passed likewise displayed the flags on their public buildings at half-mast.

The greatest tribute to Bancroft's memory is the continuing respect shown for his massive *History of the United States.* The US Naval Academy has also honored Bancroft by naming its dormitory for midshipmen after him.

OCTOBER 4

Feast of St. Francis of Assisi

St. Francis of Assisi, perhaps the most appealing of all saints, has captured the imagination and affection of generations of people regardless of their religious inclinations or lack thereof. Roman Catholics, Episcopalians, and some other Protestants celebrate his feast on October 4.

Sometimes called God's Troubadour, Francis was born in Assisi in the Umbrian region of central Italy, during the era of European troubadours, in 1181 or 1182. His father, Pietro di Bernardone, was a well-to-do textile merchant who loved France and things French. In fact, Francis' mother, a devout woman who had a marked influence on him, came from a distinguished French family. Reportedly, Francis' father was away on a trip to France when his son was born and given the name Giovanni, or John, at baptism. On his return home, he changed the name of his newborn son to Francesco, or Francis, as a tribute to France. The name was not common in those days, and it was Francis of Assisi who popularized it for succeeding generations of children called Francis or Frances.

In his youth Francis was naturally joyful and impetuous, wholeheartedly throwing himself into whatever activity was before him. He loved to sing and laugh and was extremely generous. His qualities endeared him to his peers and made him their leader in revelry. His father provided him with fine clothes and money.

When he was about 20, Francis was held prisoner for approximately a year during a war between the neighboring hill towns of Assisi and Perugia. The experience of war, the subsequent enforced seclusion, and a serious illness caused him to reexamine his life. He became a little subdued, although not entirely changed. In about the year 1205 he set off southward towards Apulia for another military campaign, but on the way he had a dream that convinced him that Christ was calling him to his service. Turning back to Assisi, Francis shed his erstwhile worldly ways and spent much time in solitary prayer, behaving in a manner his father, who had counted on the young man's entering the family business, could not understand.

While praying in the old Church of San Damiano one day in 1206, Francis heard a voice he took to be Christ's saying, "Go, Francis, and repair my house which, as you see, is well-nigh in ruins." Francis took the appeal literally and, gathering expensive fabrics from his father's stock, sold them to get money to repair the dilapidated Church of San Damiano. This was the ultimate provocation for Francis' father, who had been sorely tried by his son's behavior since his Perugian captivity. Francis was brought before the bishop, in whose presence the father disinherited him. The bishop was no doubt startled when Francis peeled off his clothes and returned them to his father, saying, "Until now I have called you my father on earth. But henceforth I can truly say, Our Father who art in heaven." With this, and wrapped in a cloak hastily provided by the bishop, Francis went off to live in poverty and prayer in the woods of nearby Mount Subasio. He had not forgotten the project to repair San Damiano, however, and went about Assisi gathering stones needed for the job. When it was completed, he began to renovate other old churches, including the Portiuncula, a little chapel of the church of Santa Maria degli Angeli, on the plain below Assisi. In addition to repairing churches, Francis also took upon himself the care of lepers and outcasts.

His enthusiasm, love of God, and reverence for all creation reached the hearts of the people who heard him preach. He so ordered his life that everything he said or did was an affirmation of God. Even when he preached penance, he encouraged it as a positive act, not as a deprivation. For Francis, penance offered more than it asked.

Soon other men chose to join Francis in his way of life, renouncing all material things. They were the first Franciscans, at the time called Penitents of Assisi. In spite of the forbidding-sounding name, the men became known for their high spirits and appreciation of the simple things in life. Like Francis, they were troubadours and went about singing of God's benevolence. Sometimes they were taunted by children or mistreated by adults, but for the most part they were accepted by the townspeople with kindness or tolerance.

In 1209 or 1210 Francis and his group of about 11 men journeyed to Rome, where they told Pope Innocent III of their hope to live according to the Gospels and to go about the country preaching in poverty and humility. Francis apparently had no intention of starting a religious order — indeed he was not even a priest — but only wanted papal approval for the way of life to which he was drawn. The aim of this new way of life, as set forth in Francis' first "rule," was to follow the example of Jesus and to obey his exhortation "Take no gold, nor silver, nor copper in your belts." After consideration, the pope gave oral approval to the Penitents of Assisi to live according to their plan. From this beginning grew the so-called First Franciscan Order, formally known as the Order of Friars Minor or, in English, Lesser Brothers.

Returning to Assisi, Francis and his men roamed central Italy and, in their humility, simplicity, and enthusiasm, drew many people closer to God. Wherever they went, men decided that this serious yet joyous band of ragged, underfed troubadours offered the good life; and the number of Franciscans grew rapidly. The group made its headquarters at the Portiuncula. It was there, on March 18 or 19, 1212, that Francis invested Clare (or Clara), a young noblewoman later to be canonized as St. Clare of Assisi (see August 11), making her the first woman Franciscan and thus beginning the Second Order of St. Francis, a religious order of women. At first called Poor Ladies and later sometimes called Minoresses in England, members of this order are now known as the Poor Clares.

In the early 13th century, Moslems were much in the minds of Christians as a force to be reckoned with; and in 1212 Francis set off to be a missionary in Syria. He was, however, shipwrecked and got no farther than Dalmatia. A year or two later he attempted to go to Morocco, but illness halted him in Spain. In 1219, still anxious to convert Moslems, Francis traveled to the Middle East during the Fifth Crusade. At Damietta, in Egypt, he somehow got through all the guards and formalities surrounding the sultan of Egypt, Malik al-Kamil. Francis was received courteously — but he did not succeed in converting the sultan.

Meanwhile the ranks of Franciscans had increased so remarkably that by about 1217 the order had been divided into provinces. The loosely structured order, which had depended so much on the strong personality of its founder, had developed administrative difficulties brought on by rapid growth, and there was much dissension among the various provinces.

Francis returned from the Holy Land in 1220 to deal with the problems. Never interested in administration, he asked Pope Honorius III to appoint, as protector of the order, Cardinal Ugolino, who later became Pope Gregory IX and had an important formative influence on the order. Also, from that time on, although Francis remained the minister general, there was always a vicar (deputy) who handled administrative matters.

There is no record of the actual wording of the first "rule," or constitution, that Francis had been asked to write when his group was formed. Some say he merely selected three passages from the

New Testament and suggested that his brothers live according to them. In any event, the rule clearly made the Gospel the basis of their simple and ascetic lives. But during Francis' absence and with the remarkable increase in numbers of Franciscans, the rule had been added to and changed many times over, developing with little or no guidance. To formulate a new and more official Franciscan rule, a great assembly of 3,000 friars met at Assisi in 1221. On November 29, 1223, Pope Honorius III approved a revised and definitive rule.

With administrative matters taken care of by a vicar, Francis could devote himself to the things of the spirit. While he wrote to the various Franciscan provinces on matters of spiritual development, he was especially concerned about those men and women who wished to live more perfectly but were not drawn to monastery or convent living. For this majority, Francis developed a Third Order, which enabled people, married or single, to follow their own vocations in life but with an added religious dimension. People from all walks of life, from popes to peasants, became members of the Franciscan Third Order. Later, when many members of the Third Order wanted to live a communal religious life, the Third Order Regular was developed.

Meanwhile, Francis continued to preach throughout the Italian countryside with "no gold, nor silver, nor copper" in his belt. Often, he went off to pray in solitude. It was during one of these periods of prayer, in 1224 on Monte della Verna, that Francis received the stigmata — actual wounds reproducing the five wounds inflicted on the body of Christ at the time of Crucifixion. Francis' stigmatization was the most famous example of this recurring phenomenon. The memorial of the occasion, long marked on September 17 in the universal calendar of the Roman Catholic church, is now regularly observed by the Franciscan order and by option at particular churches.

During the last two years of his life, Francis became almost totally blind, as well as seriously ill, and had to be carried from place to place by companions. He was only 44 or 45 when he died at the tiny Portiuncula chapel. Having begun his career by repairing the physical structure of this and other churches, he ended it after spiritually shoring up the universal church. He was buried, temporarily, in the church of San Giorgio in Assisi on October 4, 1226, the day after his death.

On July 16, 1228, Francis was canonized by Pope Gregory IX (the former Cardinal Ugolino). The next day the pope laid the cornerstone for the Basilica of St. Francis, or San Francesco, also in Assisi, which was to be Francis' final resting place. On May 25, 1230, the saint's body was transferred to the lower church (then almost completed) of the two-tiered basilica. (The upper church was constructed within a decade.) Because church authorities were afraid that his remains would be stolen, the exact location of the grave was kept secret — so secret that it could not be located until 1818. A vault cut into the rock two flights beneath the lower church, his burial place has been expanded into a crypt-church, seen today by many of the hundreds of thousands who visit Assisi each year.

Fittingly, Francis, who all through his adult life showed his love of God by his actions, was named the patron of Catholic Action in 1916. In 1939 he was named patron saint of Italy, a title he shares with St. Catherine of Siena. The 700th anniversary year of his death, 1926, was commemorated in many ways throughout the world as St. Francis Year.

The man who never intended to found an order, but simply wanted to serve God in a special way, is venerated as the spiritual father of the three branches of the First Order, that is, Franciscans, Franciscan Conventuals, and Capuchins; the several branches of the Second Order of Poor Clares, which include Urbanists, Colettines, and Capuchinesses; the Third Order Secular; and the Franciscan Third Order Regular. In addition to the dates of October 4 and September 17, the Franciscan Order also celebrates Pope Innocent III's approval of the rule on April 16; the translation, or moving, of Francis' remains from one burial site to another on May 25; his canonization on July 15; and the finding of his grave on December 12.

Franciscan missionaries have contributed much to many nations, including the United States. Their early influence in the West is well known. The city of San Francisco, for example, was named for the saint, and the city of Los Angeles was named after the church of St. Mary of the Angels, whose chapel, the Portiuncula, was the first headquarters of Francis. Franciscan missions dotted the land, and their work with Native Americans was sometimes the only consideration shown them by European settlers.

St. Francis is still honored in several American Indian settlements. In the Pauma Valley, in San Diego County, California, the Mission San Antonio de Pala, a branch of the famed Mission of San Luis Rey, was founded on June 13, 1816, the feast day of St. Anthony of Padua, himself a Franciscan. Extensive restoration of the mission began in 1954, and it maintains the only mission school for children from seven reservations in the area. The feast of St. Francis, the patron of the Cupenos, is marked at the mission by a children's festival. The celebration begins with a solemn high mass, followed by a religious procession. The afternoon is filled with various entertainments to please the children: tribal dances in colorful costumes and games and contests.

In New Mexico, St. Francis is the patron saint of the city of Santa Fe, where a religious procession is held to commemorate his feast. At the Nambe pueblo a few miles north of Santa Fe, the feast of St. Francis of Assisi is the occasion for an annual fiesta during which the Nambes perform native dances. Farther north, at Ranchos de Taos, a highlight of the Feast of St. Francis is a procession of lights at the St. Francis of Assisi Mission Church. In Arizona the feast is celebrated by the Papago tribe at Sells, on the Papago Indian Reservation southwest of Tucson.

The pure joy St. Francis derived from simple things is probably responsible for two widespread Christmas traditions: the crèche, or manger, representing the birthplace of Christ in Bethlehem, and the singing of Christmas carols. According to his biographer Thomas of Celano, who completed an account of Francis' life within a few years of the saint's death, Francis decided to spend Christmas in 1223 with a good friend in Greccio, Italy. Francis gave his friend specific instructions to prepare a special outdoor Christmas celebration: "I want to enact the memory of the Infant who was born at Bethlehem, and how He was deprived of all comforts babies enjoy; how He was bedded in the manger on hay, between an ass and an ox. For once I want to see all this with my own eyes."

The friend complied with this unusual request. Franciscan friars came from many communities, and the men and women of the area brought torches and candles to brighten the night. When Francis arrived, he rejoiced. In his biographer's words, "The crib was made ready, hay was brought, the ox and ass were led to the spot. . . . Greccio became a new Bethlehem. . . . The crowds drew near and rejoiced in the novelty of the celebration. . . . As they sang in praise of God the whole night rang out with exultation." Francis, dressed in his deacon's vestments — it is said that out of humility he never attempted to become a priest — assisted the priest who sang the solemn mass at the crib. Then Francis "preached a delightful sermon to the people who stood around him, speaking about the nativity of the poor King and the humble town of Bethlehem." From that time on, the crèche has been a familiar sight in many Christian countries.

The gaiety and joy of Francis was clearly seen in his love and pleasure in celebrating Christmas with song. He is often credited with introducing the joyous custom of caroling. In this spirit, early Franciscans composed Italian Christmas carols, and the practice of singing carols is said to have spread from Italy to other European countries.

Francis, who loved animals because they, too, were God's creatures, started another custom, still honored in parts of Europe and Scandinavia — that of extending special kindness to animals at Christmas. He urged farmers to provide their oxen and asses with extra rations of corn and hay at Christmas, "for the reverence of the Son of God, whom on such a night the Blessed Virgin Mary did lay down in the stall between the ox and the ass." No creature was omitted from his feeling that all creation should rejoice at Christmas: "If I could see the Emperor," he said, "I would implore him to issue a general decree that all people who are able to do so shall throw grain and corn upon the streets, so that on this great feast day the birds might have enough to eat, especially our sisters the larks."

Francis had great affection for songbirds, especially larks. It is said that he delivered his "Canticle of the Creatures," sometimes called the "Canticle of the Sun," to an audience of birds. Excerpts from this famous work show the true spirit of Francis and explain the way he viewed the things of this world:

Praised be my Lord God with all His Creatures, and especially our brother the sun, who brings us the day and who brings us the light; fair is he and shines with very great splendor; O Lord, he signifies to us Thee!

Praised be my Lord for our sister the moon, and for the stars, the which He has set clear and lovely in heaven.

Praised be my Lord for our brother the wind, and for air and clouds, calms and all weather by which Thou upholdest life in all creatures —

Praised be my Lord for all those who pardon one another, for His love's sake, and who endure weakness and tribulation; blessed are they who peaceably shall endure. For Thou, O Most Highest, shalt give them a crown!

It is said that the birds listened to this paean of joy so quietly and with such great attention that Francis chided himself for not having preached to them sooner.

Rutherford B. Hayes's Birthday

Rutherford Birchard Hayes, the 19th President of the United States, was born in Delaware, Ohio, on October 4, 1822. He was the son of Rutherford Hayes and Sophia Birchard Hayes. The senior Rutherford Hayes, who died before his namesake was born, had migrated from Vermont, where he had managed a country store of which he was part owner. Hard times after the War of 1812 impelled him to join the westward migration, and he and his wife settled in Ohio, where he became a farmer and whiskey distiller.

With the death of his older brother, by drowning, the younger Rutherford Hayes became the only son in the family when he was only two. The subsequent pampering of the child by his mother and sister profoundly influenced his early life. Especially important was his attachment to his sister, Fanny. Balancing the female family environment were the guidance and aid provided by his uncle Sardis Birchard. The boy had a keen mind, and Birchard gladly paid for his education.

After attending the Methodist Academy in Norwalk, Ohio, he studied at Isaac Webb's private school in Middletown, Connecticut. He then continued his studies at Kenyon College in Gambier, Ohio, from which he was graduated in 1842. Influenced by his sister's enthusiasm, he decided to become a lawyer and statesman. To this end, he read law in the office of Sparrow and Matthews in Columbus, Ohio, and then studied for a year and a half at Harvard Law School, from which he was graduated in 1845.

Returning to Ohio, Hayes was admitted to the bar in March 1845 and established a small practice in Lower Sandusky (now Fremont), where his uncle maintained a home and where Hayes himself would later live. During his five-year stay in this small community, he carried on a minimal legal practice while devoting much time to diverse studies. When the Mexican War erupted in 1846, Hayes almost volunteered, thinking the change of climate might cure a bronchial infection he had contracted. However, his doctor advised against the adventure. In 1848 Hayes visited Texas. Although he found the frontier rough, what he saw of slavery did not seem cruel to him.

Early in 1850 Hayes moved his law practice to Cincinnati, Ohio, where his career soon flourished. He joined several literary and fraternal societies and made many friends. In 1851 he declared himself a Whig, and in 1852 he campaigned for the Whig presidential nominee, Winfield Scott. Later the same year, on December 30, Hayes married Lucy Ware Webb, whom he had loved since boyhood. They had seven sons, of whom only four survived infancy, and one daughter.

In 1854 the young lawyer and his growing family moved into a comfortable house, purchased with the aid of his uncle. In the same year, Hayes left the regular Whig party and, like other radical or "conscience" Whigs, joined the new Republican party. He served as volunteer counsel for the Underground Railroad, which aided escaped slaves in their flight to Canada. During the height of the Kansas-Nebraska conflict, in 1855, Hayes supported the Free-Soilers against the proslavery faction. In 1856 he attended the convention of Ohio state Republicans, which gave its support to John C. Frémont. At the subsequent Republican National Convention in Philadelphia, Frémont became the new party's first presidential candidate. As a Republican, Hayes opposed the extension of slavery, but not the existence of the institution itself.

Hayes actively entered politics on his own behalf in 1858, when he ran successfully for the post of city solicitor of Cincinnati. He held this post until the outbreak of the Civil War in 1861, when he joined the Union army as a major. During the war he distinguished himself for bravery and was wounded five times. By 1864 he had advanced his rank to brigadier and the next year was breveted major general of volunteers. While Hayes was still in the army, he was elected to the national House of Representatives. Resigning his army position, Hayes served two terms. He left Congress in 1867 to run for governor of Ohio. He won the election and held office from 1868 until 1872 as a reform governor.

After two terms, Hayes retired to the estate at Fremont, Ohio, which had been bequeathed to him by his uncle. It was not a long retirement, however. Since the Democrats had carried the state in 1873, the Republicans persuaded Hayes to run for governor again in 1875. He campaigned on a platform pledged to "sound money," opposing Democratic calls for increased issuance of greenbacks, or fiat money, and won by a large majority.

His decisive victory thrust Hayes into national prominence, and when the Republican National Convention met in Cincinnati the next year, it nominated Hayes, who triumphed over the supposed front-runner, Senator James G. Blaine of Maine. The campaign of 1876 was a singular one. Both Democrats and Republicans ran on reform tickets, pledging to clean up the corruption associated with the administration of the incumbent Republican President, Ulysses S. Grant. Hayes had been an effective reform governor in Ohio, while his Democratic opponent, Samuel J. Tilden, was known as the reformer who had smashed the notorious Tweed Ring before becoming governor of New York.

The election brought no clear-cut decision. The Democrats proclaimed themselves the winners, but the Republicans claimed a narrow victory on the basis of disputed returns from South Carolina, Florida, Louisiana, and Oregon. Without the disputed states, Tilden had 184 electoral votes — a single vote short of election. Only if Hayes received all of the disputed states could he claim necessary 185 electoral votes — and the presidency. The popular vote, however, favored

Tilden by 250,000 votes, even with the disputed states counted as Republican.

The emotions aroused by the dispute over the election results were tremendous. Southern Democrats threatened to march on Washington if they were denied the presidency. Talk of a new civil war continued throughout the winter. The tension was heightened by the economic depression that then gripped the nation.

In Florida, South Carolina, and Louisiana, which were still undergoing Reconstruction, election boards staffed by Republicans had discounted many Democratic votes on grounds of intimidation and fraud. Such charges were often true, but it is nearly impossible to know exactly how many votes were manipulated, or who manipulated them, since both parties were guilty of intimidation, bribery, and other irregularities. In any event, two different sets of election returns were reported from these three states, as well as from Oregon.

The first attempts at compromise late in 1876 broke down quickly. In January 1877 Congress passed a bill establishing an electoral commission of 15 members to settle the matter. The commission idea was supported by the Democrats, who felt it was their best chance to reverse some of the returns in which Republicans claimed victory. The bipartisan commission was to have five senators — three Republicans and two Democrats; five representatives — two of them Republicans and three Democrats; and five members of the Supreme Court. In the last category, two Republicans and two Democrats were chosen. They, in turn, chose the last member, settling upon a liberal Republican, Justice David Davis, who was seen as a potential arbiter between opposing parties of the commission. On his election as senator by Illinois voters, however, Davis resigned suddenly, upsetting the commission's expected makeup. The much more partisan Justice Joseph P. Bradley, chosen to replace him, was a Republican who joined other commission members in what was from then on a purely political approach to voting — eight Republicans to seven Democrats on all questions.

On February 1 the two houses of Congress, meeting jointly, began to count the electoral votes, proceeding alphabetically state by state. When the counting reached the first disputed state, Florida, the electoral commission was called upon to adjudicate. The question before the commission was whether to investigate beyond the election return information then available. Democrats hoped to investigate charges of election-board fraud and thus throw out enough Republican districts to win at least one disputed state. However, the commission members, voting along party lines, decided against investigating

the disputed count and accepted the Republican version of the Florida election returns. This vote established the commission's precedent for dealing with the other disputed states.

To reestablish their bargaining position, the Democrats began filibustering tactics to delay the vote count. The possibility that the March 4 presidential inauguration date might arrive with no President yet chosen became a distinct threat, as public positions hardened on all sides.

Both parties sent "visiting statesmen" to the South in an effort to win support in the disputed states, and other discussions took place in Washington. Supporters of Hayes allegedly met secretly with a number of southern Democratic politicians, whose concern for ending Reconstruction and restoring white supremacy to the South overrode even their desire to secure the presidency for their party. Although Hayes later disclaimed knowledge of any such bargain, the two groups reportedly agreed that the election must be concluded peacefully in Hayes's favor, in exchange for an end to Republican military domination of the South with the withdrawal of the last federal troops. There were said to have been other inducements as well, including the clear intimation of forthcoming Republican support of federal aid for southern railroad construction. Democrats, for their part, agreed to end the threatened congressional filibuster and assured Republicans that they would protect, without troops, the rights of blacks in a post-Reconstruction South. The assurance was dubious at best, however, since most whites, in both the North and South, were concerned more with settling the election and ending Reconstruction than with advancing black rights.

Though they added little to either the current or future security of the nation's recently freed blacks, the various compromises of 1877 ended the election deadlock. The electoral count was completed, and Hayes was declared President on March 2, 1877. Since the then customary Inauguration Day, March 4, would have fallen on a Sunday, he was sworn in informally on Saturday, March 3, and took the oath of office officially on Monday, March 5.

Shortly afterwards, he withdrew the last federal troops from the South — from South Carolina on April 10 and from Louisiana on April 24. With this action, the already waning Reconstruction effort came to an official end. The conciliatory policy of the Hayes administration toward the defeated South hastened that region's slow economic recovery from the devastation of the Civil War and freed it from the excesses of the carpetbag regimes, the last of which disappeared with the troops.

To ensure the actual ending of military Reconstruction by Hayes, Democrats meanwhile sabotaged an army appropriations bill. For this reason, Hayes had to deal throughout 1877 with an unpaid army. Economic depression and the opposition to federal spending that grew out of the Grant administration scandals effectively ended support for southern railroad construction.

Hayes proceeded to institute civil service reforms but met stiff opposition from members of the Stalwart wing of his own party, who had entrenched themselves in positions of power during and after the Civil War. Roscoe Conkling of New York led the antireform forces.

Economic reform was another important issue during the Hayes administration. Although the country continued to suffer from a depression, Hayes refused to allow government intervention in economic matters. His insistence on sound, or uninflated, money enraged debtor classes. A number of economic panaceas were current, of which the "silver heresy," urging a return to bimetallism, was the most powerful. Early in 1878 Congress passed the Bland-Allison Act over Hayes's veto. This legislation made silver legal tender along with gold and provided for the government's mandatory purchase of $2 million to $4 million worth of silver bullion every month and its coinage into silver dollars. The inflationary impact of the bill was lessened by the conservative administration of the act by the secretary of the treasury.

Hayes's announcement at the time of his nomination that he would serve only one term as President relieved him from much pressure to run again. Some said he probably could not have been reelected in any case. However, though he was never popular with certain elements — Democrats never got over their bitterness at the outcome of the disputed election of 1876, and professional Republican politicians found the honest, conscientious Hayes less than pliable — the President had come to be esteemed by those who recognized his genuine concern for the country and saw in him an able executive.

On his retirement in 1881, Hayes returned to his estate at Fremont. He expanded his house and collected an impressive library. When not reading, Hayes busied himself with many philanthropic enterprises. He was president of the American Prison Association from 1883 until his death, and served as president of the board of trustees of the John F. Slater fund to aid the industrial education of southern blacks. As a member of the board of the Peabody Education Fund, he promoted the improvement of southern education.

Hayes died on January 17, 1893, at Fremont, where he is buried. His heirs deeded the 25-acre Fremont estate at 1337 Hayes Avenue to the state of Ohio and erected a memorial museum and library on the grounds with an endowment of $500,000. The estate, known as Spiegel Grove, now constitutes the Rutherford B. Hayes State Memorial. Hayes's 20-bedroom home is still occupied by his descendants, but the estate grounds and the Hayes library and museum are open to the public.

OCTOBER 5

Chester A. Arthur's Birthday

Chester A. Arthur, the 21st President of the United States, was born on October 5, 1829, probably in Fairfield, Vermont. His father, Reverend William Arthur, an immigrant from the north of Ireland, was a Baptist preacher; his mother, Malvina Stone Arthur, was a native Vermonter. Little is known of Chester Arthur's youth. The family changed residence five times during his first nine years. He was graduated with honors from Union College in Schenectady, New York, in 1848, having entered with advanced placement as a sophomore and having worked his way through by teaching school.

Arthur then took a position as a schoolteacher at North Pownal, Vermont, and studied law in his spare time. In 1853 he took an apprentice position in a New York City law office. One year later he was admitted to the bar. Arthur's family background, which was strongly Whig and abolitionist, led the young lawyer into a number of notable cases. He was associated with a well-known American lawyer and statesman, William Maxwell Evarts, in the Lemmon slave case, which involved eight slaves who had been taken to New York by Jonathan Lemmon of Virginia. Lemmon had expected to sail to Texas with them. A writ of habeas corpus was obtained in behalf of the slaves, and a New York court — with Arthur serving as special counsel for the state of New York — established that slaves passing through a free state automatically became free and ordered their release. The case was eventually taken to the US Supreme Court, which sustained the action of the New York court. Arthur also won a decision that forced streetcar operating companies in New York City to accommodate black passengers equally with whites.

On October 25, 1859, Arthur married Ellen Lewis Herndon, who bore three children before she died of pneumonia in 1880. Drawn to politics, Arthur had been an active member of the Republican party from the time of its founding in 1854. He served as a delegate to the convention at Saratoga, New York, that organized the state Republican party and became increasingly involved in the party's local affairs. Arthur also joined the state militia. When the Civil War broke out in 1861, he was serving as engineer-in-chief on the staff of the governor of New York, Edwin D. Morgan. He was charged with the immense task of recruiting, training, equipping, and dispatching soldiers from New York City to the front to serve in the Union army. Arthur was promoted successively to inspector general and quartermaster general of the state. In January 1863 he retired to his private law practice.

In 1871 President Ulysses S. Grant appointed Arthur collector of customs for the Port of New York, a post that was considered one of the most desirable patronage appointments available. From this position Arthur was expected to give jobs to those who faithfully worked in the interest of the Republican party. He served as an efficient and — within bounds of the then prevalent spoils system — honest official. However, in 1877, the new Republican administration of President Rutherford B. Hayes set out to institute certain civil service reforms. Hayes directed that civil service employees abstain from political involvement. Arthur, together with his political boss, New York's US Senator Roscoe Conkling, decided to fight Hayes on the patronage issue. The Tenure of Office Act of 1867 prevented Hayes from removing Conkling's supporters outright. However, during the congressional recess in 1878, Hayes suspended Arthur, among others, and made interim appointments. The next session of the Senate refused to overturn Hayes's decision. Although Hayes had won his battle to have Arthur and other Conkling men removed from office, Conkling himself and the New York Republican machine became even more powerful in politics.

In 1880 Arthur attended the Republican National Convention at Chicago as a delegate-at-large. The New York delegates numbered themselves among the Stalwarts who wished to renominate Grant for a third term (Hayes declined to run for reelection). However, James A. Garfield of Ohio was nominated. In an effort to retain the support of the disenchanted Stalwarts, Arthur was chosen as Garfield's running-mate. Despite this effort at reconciliation, the Conkling Republicans gave only grudging support to the ticket. In fact, Conkling had advised Arthur to thrust aside the offer "as you would a red-hot shoe from the forge." But Arthur, convinced that "the office of Vice President is a greater honor than I ever dreamed of attaining," stood firm. Misgivings were voiced throughout the nation over the selection of such a reputed spoilsman as the Republican vice presidential

running-mate, but as E. L. Godkin, editor of the *Nation,* argued: "There is no place in which his powers of mischief will be so small as in the Vice Presidency. . . . It is true General Garfield . . . may die during his term of office, but this is too unlikely a contingency to be worth making extraordinary provision for." The Republicans won the election by a narrow margin. Garfield's policy of office appointments did not meet with Conkling's approval, and a power struggle ensued. Arthur was not strictly loyal to the President during the contest. After Senator Conkling had resigned in protest over an appointment to the collectorship of the Port of New York, Arthur even went to Albany in an unsuccessful attempt to use his influence in behalf of Conkling's reelection.

Garfield had scarcely won his battle against Conkling when on July 2, 1881, he was shot by a crazed office-seeker, Charles J. Guiteau. When Garfield died on September 19, Arthur took the oath of office as President in his own house in New York City and again three days later in Washington before the chief justice of the United States. Arthur had become the Chief Executive under a good deal of public apprehension, since he was known as a political maneuverer through his longtime association with Roscoe Conkling. Furthermore, Garfield's assassin claimed to be a Stalwart who wanted Arthur to become President.

Despite such an inauspicious beginning, Arthur tried his best not to be a factionalist President. In 1882 he vetoed a bill to restrict Chinese immigration, asserting that it violated existing treaties with China. He also refused to sign a river and harbor development bill on the grounds that it would squander over $18.7 million of public funds, by improperly using some of the allocated money for insignificant local projects. A major political issue of this time was the large surplus of funds flowing into the US Treasury, a surplus largely the result of high tariffs continued since the Civil War. Some of the funds were used for increased public works projects and for rebuilding and enlarging the US Navy. Democrats pushed to have the tariffs lowered. Despite recommendations for downward revision from a special commission, supported by Arthur, another high protective tariff was passed in 1883.

Wherever they turned, the Republicans seemed to be setting up conditions for Democratic victories at the polls. In 1882 Arthur himself committed what has been since regarded as the greatest political mistake of his administration. He insisted upon the nomination of his secretary of the treasury, Judge Charles J. Folger, for the governorship of New York. The Democrats nominated Grover Cleveland, the reform Democratic mayor of Buffalo, and denounced federal interference in state elections. Cleveland won the election, partly on the strength of public annoyance with Arthur's role in the contest. Yet, although the President continued to support political bossism to a certain extent, he also strongly backed the reform Civil Service Act of 1883.

At the Republican National Convention of 1884, Chester A. Arthur's name was presented for renomination, but the President lost to James G. Blaine (who in turn lost the election to the Democratic reform candidate, Grover Cleveland). For many years, Arthur's lack of success was attributed to his political obstinacy, weak support in New York State, factionalism within his own party, and widespread Republican losses throughout the country. However, evidence found in 1972 revealed that Arthur had been afflicted with a serious kidney ailment from the earliest days of his presidency. Historians now feel certain it was his knowledge of this illness — which was to prove fatal — more than any other factor, that prevented him from promoting his own reelection.

Although his administration was far from a political success, Arthur — a tall, stout, handsome, and socially correct man, "usually wearing a Prince Albert coat, buttoned closely in front, with a flower in the upper button-hole and the corner of a colored silk handkerchief visible from a side pocket" — impressed his contemporaries not only by fitting the image of a President, but also by doing a far better job than most of his detractors had imagined feasible given the circumstances. He proved to be a good administrator and, despite some political blunders, a competent executive.

After the end of his term of office in 1885, Arthur returned to New York City, where he died less than two years later, on November 18, 1886. He was buried in Albany, New York. The five-story brownstone town house at 123 Lexington Avenue, where he lived in New York City, is now privately owned and has been designated a national historic landmark.

Tecumseh's Death

Tecumseh, the Shawnee chief and statesman whose federation of American Indians was almost successful in halting the white intrusion into the Indian lands that now make up the United States, was a heroic figure, respected by both Indians and settlers for his integrity, dignity, and towering leadership. He was born probably in 1768 in a Shawnee village near what is now Springfield, Ohio. His brother Tenskwatawa, popularly called the Prophet, became known as a religious mystic.

As a youth, Tecumseh roamed far in hunting expeditions through what whites soon named the Northwest Territory — including what are now Ohio, Indiana, Illinois, Michigan, and Wisconsin. It was a period in which various Indian tribes, backed by the British in Canada, sought to check the territorial expansion of the new United States. The aim was to contain frontier settlements south of the Ohio River. Tecumseh himself participated in attacks on US nationals traveling down the river. A skilled warrior, he became noted for his role in the Northwest border wars. He also became noted for his humanitarianism, exhibiting clemency toward captives and persuading the Shawnees to abandon their practice of torturing prisoners.

As pioneer settlements spread north of the Ohio River, Indian opposition stiffened — and was met by various expeditions sent out by the US government. One of these, headed by General Anthony Wayne in 1794, administered a defeat to the Indians at Fallen Timbers, Ohio, and paved the way for the Treaty of Greenville, which was signed the next year. But although the treaty opened much of Ohio and other scattered tracts to white settlement — supposedly clarifying the boundary between Indian and non-Indian lands in the process — all did not go smoothly. In the ensuing conferences between Indians and settlers, Tecumseh, by virtue of his eloquence, determination, and restraint, became a leading figure by 1800.

Tecumseh foresaw the trend of history more clearly than the leaders of many other tribes, realizing that if the Indians were to remain strong they could afford to retreat no further. Backed by long Indian tradition, he argued that since all tribes held their grounds in common, no one tribe or chief had authority to sell or cede land without the agreement of all. He felt one might with as much logic attempt to sell the air or clouds, also natural gifts. Therefore, he held, no sale or cession of Indian lands could be valid without a consensus of the tribes.

When the US government — particularly in the person of William Henry Harrison, governor of the large Indiana Territory, which had been carved from the old Northwest — ignored this stand, Tecumseh and his brother Tenskwatawa set about organizing a vast confederation of Indian tribes, which they hoped would stem the whites' advance. The program began with organization of certain groups of Shawnees into what was called "the Prophet's town," initially located near Greenville, Ohio, and later transferred to a spot near the juncture of the Tippecanoe and Wabash rivers, a few miles above the site of Lafayette, Indiana.

Tecumseh — whose mission was made more urgent by the treaties of 1804 and 1805, calling for further cessions of Indian lands — traveled from Wisconsin to Florida urging other tribes to join his confederation. Growth of his coalition was disquieting to Northwest settlers, although the brothers, in conference with Governor Harrison, expressed their intention to keep peace. The pledge of peace depended on abandonment of certain cessions of Indian territory — particularly the 1809 agreement that took from the Indians their best hunting ground — and on acceptance of Tecumseh's principle concerning the common ownership of land, which Governor Harrison refused to consider.

Even so, it was not Tecumseh's wish to have war. Just before he was called away on a trip to the south in 1811, he cautioned Tenskwatawa against allowing himself to be drawn into any military engagement. When Tecumseh left, peace was still possible, and the chance that he might consolidate his federation and win acceptance for his point of view was still excellent.

Governor Harrison, however, chose the period of Tecumseh's absence for a hostile move. On November 6, 1811, he camped with 1,000 men about a mile away from "the Prophet's town." With perhaps understandable apprehension, Tenskwatawa decided against leaving matters to chance. He attacked the encampment at dawn on November 7, thus beginning the famous battle of Tippecanoe. By the end of the next day, Harrison had surmounted heavy losses to force the Indians back and raze their village. (Nearly three decades later the battle furnished a slogan, Tippecanoe and Tyler Too, on which Harrison and his running-mate successfully campaigned for the presidency and vice presidency of the United States.) The battle caused the loss of Tenskwatawa's personal influence and largely destroyed the confederacy built by Tecumseh. At an Indian council in May of the next year, Tecumseh sadly defied any "living creature to say we ever advised anyone . . . to make war on our white brothers." Governor Harrison, he pointed out, "made war on my people in my absence."

With little time to rebuild his fortunes before the War of 1812, Tecumseh sided in that conflict with the British, a position from which he hoped to obtain some advantage for his people. He received the rank of brigadier general in the British army and commanded 2,000 Indian allies. When British fortunes took a turn for the worse, after Oliver Hazard Perry's victory in the battle of Lake Erie, Tecumseh reluctantly covered the retreat of Colonel Henry Proctor, whom he mistrusted and regarded as a coward. "You always told us, that you would never draw your foot off British ground," said Tecumseh to Proctor, "but now . . . we see you are drawing back. . . . Our lives are in the hands of the Great Spirit. We are determined to defend our lands, and if it be his will, we wish to leave our bones upon them."

Tecumseh's words forced Proctor to take a stand against the Americans near Chatham, Ontario. In the ensuing engagement, known as the Battle of the Thames, on October 5, 1813, the Americans under Harrison were victorious. As if by premonition, Tecumseh, who lost his life, had prepared for the battle by shedding his British uniform in favor of his native buckskins. His death marked the end of the last desperate stand of the Indians of the northeastern United States against the steady westward advance of white pioneers.

OCTOBER 6

Daniel Boone Festival
Barbourville, Kentucky

This is a movable event. See note on page xxvi.

Honored at the Daniel Boone Festival, which is held each October in Barbourville, Kentucky, are the pioneer frontiersman Daniel Boone (see June 7) and the Cherokees who arrive for the annual signing of the Cane Treaty. The festival, for years a four-day event, has been expanded to run from the first Saturday in October through the following Saturday.

Barbourville, a community of several thousand people, is located on the historic Wilderness Road — the trail that Boone and 30 woodsmen carved through the Appalachian Mountains for the Transylvania Company in 1775. The trail, which ran from eastern Tennessee, through the Cumberland Gap, and into what became the state of Kentucky, was soon extended all the way to the Ohio River. (It is usually spoken of as also including the connecting and earlier trails that ran down the Valley of Virginia.) Although Boone did not discover the strategic Cumberland Gap himself — its existence had been known of since 1750 — the Boone party was the first to pierce the mountains and lead the way for settlement beyond the eastern seaboard. For the next 50 years, it was Boone's Wilderness Road, with the Ohio River as its only alternate, that opened the lands of the interior for the westward migration by which this country was settled.

The Indians who take part in the Daniel Boone Festival at Barbourville are from the Cherokee Indian Reservation at Cherokee, North Carolina. They are rare among Native Americans in actually living on, or near, land that belonged to their ancestors – in this case at the entrance to Great Smoky Mountain National Park. Now constituting the Eastern Band of Cherokee, they are descendants of the handful who hid in their beloved Smoky Mountains to escape forced removal to Oklahoma in 1838 and 1839 over the notorious Trail of Tears (see June 23, "Unto These Hills," Cherokee, North Carolina).

As Boone and his party cleared and marked their trail to the interior, they passed the rolling canelands of Kentucky, where the town of Barbourville was to spring up in 1800. The cane, still growing along the banks of the meandering Cumberland River, is one of the reasons for the festival, which features the annual signing of the Cherokee Cane Treaty. This treaty provides for gifts of the cane to the Cherokees so that they can make baskets from it, as their ancestors did, and is an attempt to aid the Indians' handicrafts industry.

The Daniel Boone Festival, founded in 1948, attracts an attendance of some 15,000 people. In one typical year, before the program was expanded, the Daniel Boone Festival began on Tuesday evening with a variety show at the Barbourville High School Gymnasium. Sponsored by the Barbourville Junior Study Club, it featured the Miss Daniel Boone Festival; Miss Kentucky Rifle; the miniature King and Queen – two youngsters named Little Daniel Boone King and Little Miss Daniel Boone; and the winner of the Boone Festival Queen's Race. The arts and crafts exhibitions, which continued throughout the festival, opened on that day. The big Thursday evening program at the Union College Physical Education Building included a pageant portraying episodes from the life of Daniel Boone, as well as the coronation of Miss Daniel Boone Festival and of other festival royalty.

The Daniel Boone Festival Feast, preceding the signing of the Cane Treaty, took place on Friday evening. The feast, held in the Barbourville Armory, was an old-fashioned barbecue, with beef, pork and venison and a variety of pioneer and Indian foods, among them Indian corn and Kentucky hot biscuits. After dinner came the signing of the treaty followed by the smoking of peace pipes. There was an official welcome to the visiting Cherokees and a program of dances by their nationally known dancers. Other high points included the awarding of a citation to Barbourville's oldest ablebodied citizen, the presentation of an outstanding citizen award, and the recognition of distinguished guests, among them a descendant and namesake of the original Daniel Boone.

The Long Rifle Shoot took place the next morning at Knox High School's Lay Field. This annual event originated in an attempt to settle a dispute as to whether the long rifle of frontier days should be named for Pennsylvania (where it was originally manufactured) or for Kentucky (whose frontiersmen excelled in its use). A Pennsylvania team pressed its claim unsuccessfully for two years before relinquishing the official Kentucky long rifle to Kentucky's governor in 1964. Since then, Kentucky teams have matched their skills with those of teams from other states at the annual festivals.

The annual rifle shoot was preceded by a gigantic pancake breakfast, sponsored by the Kiwanis Club, a horseshoe-pitching contest and demonstrations of Indian dances and skills. Following the rifle shoot and a lunch intermission, the scene shifted to Barbourville's Court House Square for a series of old-time contests. Emphasis was on such favorites as hog calling, woodchopping, and fiddling.

The two-mile-long Daniel Boone Festival parade, which followed, was a colorful procession of bands, floats, covered wagons, pioneer-costumed paraders (many with beards and coonskin caps), Indians, walking horses, and mule teams. A musical program was presented after the parade. The festival reached its climax and conclusion on Saturday evening, when everyone joined in a lively square dance and an outdoor dance for teenagers.

British Capture Forts Clinton and Montgomery

British strategists in 1777 devised a three-pronged attack to defeat the American armies in the state of New York and to crush the colonists' efforts to gain independence. General John Burgoyne was to lead the main column south from Canada down the Lake Champlain Valley to the upper Hudson River. Colonel Barry St. Leger was to head an auxiliary force east from Oswego through the Mohawk Valley. General William Howe was to bring a strong army from New York City up the Hudson.

The English did not execute their plan well. General Nicholas Herkimer and his fellow officers led the colonists to victory over St. Leger at Oriskany and Fort Stanwix, New York, in

August, and General Thomas Gates produced another American victory by October 17 over Burgoyne at Saratoga (see October 17). General Howe, who captured Philadelphia from the American colonists in late September, failed to return to New York in time to take part in the operation. Only General Henry Clinton, commander of the British garrison in New York City, who captured Forts Montgomery and Clinton on October 6, pursued the mission with any success.

When William Howe sailed for Philadelphia on July 23, Clinton remained in New York City with 4,000 regular and 3,000 American Tory troops to defend the vital urban center. Envious of Burgoyne and Howe, Clinton resented his inactive position of conducting "a damned starved defensive," and he feared that the rebels under General George Washington could, with a concerted effort, annihilate his position. Clinton unhappily stayed in New York City during July and August awaiting an American assault and avoiding offensive operations.

By September Burgoyne was encountering stiff resistance, and he asked General Clinton for assistance. The latter, who expected reinforcements to arrive from England shortly, promised on September 12 to move against the Hudson Highlands within 10 days. General Burgoyne, receiving this assurance on September 21, two days after the first battle of Saratoga, unwisely decided to delay an operation that might have opened the road to Albany, and instead bade Clinton to act as soon as possible.

Clinton's objectives were Forts Montgomery and Clinton, located astride Popolopen Creek in the Hudson Highlands. Only 45 miles north of New York City, the Highlands, which rise more than 500 feet along the west side of the Hudson, are the highest ground in the Hudson, Mohawk River, and Lake Champlain area, and form a natural barrier of easily defensible terrain. The Americans recognized that control of this area could make possible control of the Hudson River, and as early as 1775 the Continental Congress acted to encourage the erection of fortifications.

Fort Montgomery lay north of Popolopen Creek and was a good position from which to harass shipping going up the Hudson. Its breastworks were strong facing the river but weak on the western side. Fort Clinton lay north of Bear Mountain and on the south side of the deep Popolopen gorge. Fort Clinton was smaller but stronger than Fort Montgomery and was essential to the latter's protection. The land defenses to the two redoubts followed rugged, defensible defiles, and a system of riverine obstructions, including a log boom and a great iron chain,

stretched across the Hudson from Fort Montgomery to a point called Anthony's Nose on the eastern shore. A flotilla of a sloop, two galleys, and two frigates, the *Montgomery* and the *Congress*, supplemented the river defenses.

The reinforcements for General Clinton arrived around September 24, placing his total strength in regulars at 2,700 British and 4,200 Hessian troops. On October 3, somewhat later than promised, Clinton moved north with 3,000 men from New York City up the Hudson River. The attacking force landed on the evening of October 5 at Verplanck's Point, which was across the river and southeast from Forts Clinton and Montgomery.

Major General Israel Putnam, the American commander in the Highlands, had approximately 1,000 Continental soldiers and 400 militiamen on the east side of the river. Clinton immediately engaged a small contingent of these rebels and routed them from their outpost. Putnam quickly drew his men back several miles and called for reinforcements from the west side of the river. The American response, which reduced the number of defenders at Forts Clinton and Montgomery, perfectly suited the British plans.

Leaving 1,000 troops on the east side of the Hudson in order to keep Putnam distracted, General Clinton took the major portion of his force across the river to Stony Point, under the cover of the dawn fog on October 6. Following a Tory guide named Brom Springster, the British and the Hessian soldiers moved quickly through an 850-foot-high pass called the Timp to a trail junction at Doodletown, within two and a half miles of Fort Clinton. There, after driving off a small American patrol, Henry Clinton divided his forces. He sent 900 men west around Bear Mountain to cross Popolopen Creek and attack Fort Montgomery from the rear; the remainder moved to a position from which they could attack Fort Clinton from the south, and there they waited for the encircling column to complete its seven-mile trek.

Scouts reported the British landing at Stony Point to Governor George Clinton, the American commander of Forts Clinton and Montgomery (and no relation to the attacking Sir Henry). The governor had hurried south from Esopus (now Kingston) to direct the defense as soon as he received word of the enemy's approach from Putnam. Governor Clinton dispatched two delaying forces to the Doodletown area, but the British repulsed both of them. The American commander then sent Captain John Fenno with 100 men and an artillery piece to engage the attackers about a mile from the fort. The British and Hessians forced the patrol from its primary position and captured Fenno; the American pickets retreated to a secondary line and finally fell back to Fort Montgomery.

By 4:30 P.M. the offensive columns had reached their positions before Forts Montgomery and Clinton. Lieutenant Colonel Campbell commanded the British units at Fort Montgomery. From north to south were the 52nd Regiment, a group of New York Volunteers, Colonel Beverley Robinson's 400 Loyal Americans, Emmerich's Hessian Jägers, and the 57th Regiment. Campbell suffered fatal wounds in the attack, and his angry soldiers refused to show mercy as they routed the Americans. The attackers spared some of the garrison, however; and others among the defenders, including Governor George Clinton, the commander of Fort Montgomery, managed to escape to the south or across the river.

Sir Henry Clinton directed the costly, successful assault on Fort Clinton, which was under the command of General James Clinton, the brother of the governor of New York. Lacking room to maneuver, the British general committed the bulk of his forces to a frontal attack on the strongly defended southern face of the fort. The flank companies of the 26th Regiment, a dismounted troop of the 17th Light Dragoons, and some Hessian chasseurs followed in the second wave. The 63rd Regiment circled west to attack from the northwest, and the battalion companies of the 7th Regiment and a German battalion provided a reserve.

Losses were heavy on both sides during the assaults on Forts Clinton and Montgomery. The British may have lost as many as 300 men, including at least 18 officers and 169 enlisted men killed. Approximately 250 of the more than 600 Americans in the forts were killed, wounded, or missing, and the British captured 67 guns and many supplies. The Americans also lost their river flotilla, which was unable to escape north against the wind and was burned after dark.

On October 7 Clinton seized Fort Constitution north of Forts Clinton and Montgomery and across the river from West Point. Then, in response to pleas from Burgoyne, Clinton sent General John Vaughan with 1,700 men and Sir James Wallace with a flotilla north to assist him. Vaughan and Wallace burned Esopus on October 16 and proceeded to Livingston Manor 45 miles south of Albany. Putnam fell back before the advance of Vaughan and Wallace and placed his forces across their route to Burgoyne. Vaughan and Wallace reported the situation to Clinton, who had in the meantime received orders to abandon the Highlands and send reinforcements to Howe in Philadelphia, and he instructed them to return toward New York City.

So ended the futile British 1777 campaign in New York.

Feast of St. Thomas the Apostle

The feast of St. Thomas the Apostle, the biblical "doubting Thomas," is celebrated on October 6 by those Eastern Orthodox churches that follow the New Style, or Gregorian, calendar, and on October 19 by Eastern Orthodox churches that still adhere to the Old Style, or Julian, calendar. Roman Catholics, Episcopalians and some other Protestants celebrate the feast on July 3 (see July 3).

OCTOBER 7

James Whitcomb Riley's Birthday

James Whitcomb Riley, the Hoosier Poet, was one of the few American poets to become wealthy and, during his lifetime, to gain renown. His popularity was such that he received without delay a letter that Mark Twain had sent from Vienna, addressed to the "Practicing Poet, and a dern capable one, too, Indianapolis, Indiana."

The title Hoosier Poet was bestowed on Riley not only because he was born and lived most of his life in Indiana but also because he so colorfully portrayed, with sympathy and humor, the inhabitants of the region. His universally appealing poems truly depicted their behavior in everyday situations and their feelings about basic issues. For his down-to-earth quality and his interest in "ordinary folk," Riley was sometimes called "the poet of the common people" or "the people's laureate." Many, though not all, of his poems and prose pieces were written in a Hoosier dialect, and it is perhaps for these that he is best remembered. Although he was a regional poet, his fame spread throughout the country, and his Hoosier-flavored pieces were as well received in large cities as they were in the small towns of Indiana. He wrote over a thousand poems, which were published in a number of collections in the 1880s and 1890s.

The third of six children, Riley was born on October 7, 1849, in Greenfield, Indiana, about 20 miles from Indianapolis, where he later took up permanent residence. His father was a respected lawyer, but the legal profession did not appeal to the younger Riley, whose ambition was to be an actor. Never very good at academic subjects, he dropped out of school at 16 and joined an itinerant group of young sign painters who called themselves the Graphics and, according to Riley, "covered all the barns and fences in the state with advertisements." Later he was a traveling musician and jack-of-all-trades with patent medicine shows, an important source of entertainment for country people of the time.

Riley got his first taste of professional acting by taking part in these skits, whose purpose was to attract crowds. After the free entertainment for which they had gathered, the townspeople would be offered, in colorful terms, the various nostrums being sold. Not only did Riley act, fiddle, sing, and recite in these entertainments; he also composed many of the skits used. The traveling also brought him into close contact with the Hoosier dialect, which was more pronounced in the rural areas. Later Riley was to say that once during his itinerant days he had returned home to study law but soon ran away again because "my health was bad — as bad as I was."

After approximately 10 years of this traveling life, Riley took a job with a newspaper, the *Democrat*, published in Anderson, Indiana, not very far from Greenfield. He began to write verse but was frustrated in his attempts to get it published. He had great confidence in his work, however, and felt that it was being rejected not because of its quality but because its author was not well known.

To prove his point, Riley thought out and executed an elaborate prank, which came to be known as the "Leonainie hoax." Using the style of Edgar Allan Poe, he wrote a poem called "To Leonainie." A newspaper editor in Kokomo, Indiana, apparently privy to the hoax, printed a story of the "discovery" of the poem, which was handwritten on a flyleaf of a book known to have been published during Poe's lifetime; the story suggested that the poem was possibly an unpublished work of Poe's.

The account caused greater stir than Riley had hoped. Scholars and literary people all over the country became interested, and many of them were ready to authenticate the poem as Poe's. When the truth was told, however, their fury was unleashed. Riley was called unethical and a fraud. Many other humiliating terms were applied to him as his joke backfired in a manner he had never anticipated. Dismissed from his newspaper job (the spurious poem had appeared in a rival paper), he felt that he would never be able to hold his head up in public again.

To make a living, Riley went back to sign painting and life as a minstrel with medicine shows, but — perhaps because of his remorse over the Leonainie hoax and the fact that he was now older — his exuberance for life on the road

was gone. In the midst of his gloom, however, a letter arrived from the editor of the Indianapolis *Journal*, offering to publish his poetry.

The letter changed Riley's life. He moved to Indianapolis and from 1877 to 1885 wrote poems that were published in the *Journal*, at first under the pen name of Benjamin F. Johnson of Boone. In 1883 the first collection of his poems was privately published under the title *The Old Swimmin'-Hole and 'Leven More Poems*. One of the poems in this collection, "When the Frost Is on the Punkin," became one of his best known.

The book helped to broaden Riley's fame, and in 1887 he was invited East to participate in readings, very popular at the time, with such famous writers as Mark Twain, William Dean Howells, George W. Cable, Frank R. Stockton, and Edward Eggleston, the author of *The Hoosier Schoolmaster*. Riley's first appearance was in New York City's Chickering Hall, where James Russell Lowell heard Riley read his own poetry. In introducing him the next day, Lowell admitted that, though he previously had been unacquainted with Riley's work, he had been so impressed by the recitation that he had spent the night reading Riley's poetry. "Today," Lowell declared, "in presenting him, I can say to you of my own knowledge that you are to have the pleasure of listening to the voice of a true poet."

With this warm praise from the highly respected Lowell added to the deafening applause of appreciative eastern audiences, Riley's fame grew, and he received more invitations to appear on the lecture circuit. Soon he teamed up with Edgar Wilson Nye, the American humorist and journalist better known as Bill Nye, and they became the most popular lecturers of the time. Their effect on their audiences was summed up in the couplet "Nye and Riley, Riley and Nye! Grin and chuckle, sob and sigh!" The two men also collaborated on a book, *Nye and Riley's Railway Guide* (1888).

In 1893 Riley, who had lived in hotels and boardinghouses since he left home, moved to the house at 528 Lockerbie Street in Indianapolis, where he spent the rest of his life. His feelings for the home and neighborhood can be seen in his poem "Lockerbie Street." It begins with the words "Such a dear little street it is, nestled away,/From the noise of the city and heat of the day." And it ends, "For no language could frame and no lips could repeat/My rhyme-haunted raptures of Lockerbie Street."

Riley never married, but he did not lead a lonely life. His home was visited often by neighborhood children and by many adult friends, including famous writers and other celebrities who were frequent houseguests. He had a special feeling for children and wrote many poems for and about them. They reciprocated his affection. Sometimes the very dignified-looking Riley, impeccably dressed with his carnation boutonniere and carrying his gold-headed cane, would stop to play games with the children on the street. He was sometimes called the Children's Poet. His dedication of one of his most famous poems, "Little Orphant Annie," could be applied to all of his writings for young readers. It was "inscribed with all faith and affection — To all the little children: — The happy ones; and the sad ones; The sober and the silent ones; the boisterous and glad ones; The good ones — Yes, the good ones, too; and all the lovely bad ones."

Riley received many public honors in his lifetime, including a number of honorary degrees, election to the American Academy of Arts and Letters, and the gold medal for poetry of the National Institute of Arts and Letters. He also received personal honors, which he thoroughly enjoyed — tributes from little friends or having parents name their children after him. (One family awarded the names James, Whitcomb, and Riley to newborn triplets.)

In 1911 schools in Indiana and New York City staged special programs in celebration of Riley's birthday. In 1912 the celebrations became more widespread, and the town of Greenfield — Riley's birthplace — proclaimed Riley Day. The following year Riley Day was proclaimed by Anderson, Indiana, and Cincinnati, Ohio, and by Indiana University and other places Riley frequently visited. On his birthday in 1913, the schoolchildren of Indianapolis formed a procession on Lockerbie Street, passing the poet's house. Thus began the Riley birthday celebrations, which continued annually at the Lockerbie Street house until the location was changed in the 1960s.

In 1915 Governor Samuel Moffett Ralston of Indiana issued a proclamation making Riley's birthday a day of statewide celebration. That year a festival was staged in Indianapolis on the afternoon of Riley's birthday. Several of his poems and pieces were recited, narrated, danced, sung, and acted out in pantomime. Throughout the state, addresses were made in his honor, and his poems and readings were recited by schoolchildren, bringing to life many of the friendly and familiar characters he had created — including Little Orphant Annie, Old Aunt Mary, Tradin' Joe, Uncle Sidney, and Squire Hawkins.

In the evening, Charles W. Fairbanks (Vice President in Theodore Roosevelt's administration) served as toastmaster for a dinner in Riley's honor. President Woodrow Wilson sent the following message to those present at the dinner:

"I wish that I might be present to render my tribute of affectionate appreciation to him for the many pleasures he has given me along with the rest of the great body of readers of English. I think he has every reason to feel on his birthday that he has won the hearts of his countrymen."

It was the climax of an exceptional birthday celebration, which, as it turned out, was Riley's last. He died in Indianapolis on July 22, 1916. He is buried in Crown Hill Cemetery, beneath an imposing marble monument supported by Grecian columns on the highest point of land overlooking Indianapolis.

The James Whitcomb Riley Memorial Association purchased Riley's house on Lockerbie Street. In addition, as an appropriate memorial, the association built and maintains the widely noted James Whitcomb Riley Hospital for Children, part of the Indiana University Medical Center in Indianapolis. The hospital opened its doors on Riley's birthday in 1924. Two important additions dedicated in 1965 and 1971 were part of a long-range expansion and modernization program.

The Riley Hospital for Children is now the site of annual celebrations in honor of the poet's birthday. Sponsored by the Riley Memorial Association, the festivities include entertainment for the hospital children, with a birthday party for all ambulatory patients and gift to each child "from Mr. Riley." The observance is held in cooperation with the Riley Hospital Cheer Guild. The association also cosponsors the James Whitcamb Riley Camp — at Bradford Woods in Indiana's Morgan County — which provides two weeks of camping for over 150 physically handicapped children each summer.

A different kind of Riley shrine is the Indianapolis Public Library, completed in 1917 — a handsome specimen of Greek revival architecture for which Riley in 1911 presented a portion of land then valued at $75,000. Elsewhere in Indianapolis, the John Herron Museum of Art, at 110 East 16th Street, contains a portrait of the Hoosier poet by John Singer Sargent. Riley's name is also memorialized in the James Whitcomb Riley Center, an urban renewal project in Indianapolis.

However, the structure that most accurately captures the flavor of the poet's life is the house he loved so much on Lockerbie Street. With its outstanding collection of Victorian furnishings intact, the building, which was declared a national historic landmark during the 1963 Riley birthday observance, is visited by thousands annually.

During the last few years of his life, Riley enjoyed the birthday celebrations staged in Indianapolis in his honor, and – perhaps a day or two later – drove the 20 miles to Greenfield, where local children were excitedly awaiting his arrival for the start of *their* celebration of his birthday on the courthouse lawn. As Riley's car came into view, his young admirers clustered at the curbside and tossed flowers at the poet. It would be hard to know who enjoyed the birthday parties more, Riley or the children.

Greenfield has celebrated the poet's birthday since 1911. The annual festivities are held on a weekend near October 7. Following a dinner given by the Hancock County Historical Society on the preceding Sunday, the Riley Festival begins with the annual parade of flowers. Children from the first six grades of Greenfield's schools gather at the Riley Elementary School to form their procession and from there march to the courthouse, where they place flowers at the poet's statue. The parade of children is led by high school and junior high school bands.

The downtown shopping center is the site of many Riley Festival events, including a popular flea market on the courthouse lawn. Civic organizations and retail merchants participate by sponsoring gaily decorated stands and booths, where townspeople and visitors are offered goods, services, or an opportunity to participate in a philanthropic project. Local service clubs generally sponsor a variety of contests. A typical year featured poster, talent, and costume contests, a bicycle race, and a queen competition in all the county high schools. An art show and festival parade built around Riley themes rounded out the commemorative activities.

Nostalgic store window displays center on old-fashioned motifs. Women in period costumes welcome visitors to the Riley Old Home on West Main Street and in the afternoon serve punch and cookies. Tape-recorded recitations of Riley works are played, and books by Riley are displayed and sold in the Old Home.

Thousands of visitors, many of them schoolchildren, visit the Old Home each year. The house, built by the poet's father when young Riley was a very small boy, is where "Little Orphant Annie" shooed "the chickens off the porch." It is maintained by the Riley Old Home Society of Greenfield and is open to the public from May 1 to November 1.

Second Battle of Saratoga

The second battle of Saratoga, which resulted in a resounding British defeat at the hands of colonials and marked the turning point of the American Revolution, took place on October 7, 1777, in the vicinity of Bemis Heights, about three miles north of what is now Stillwater, New York.

The site is marked by Saratoga National Historical Park.

Both battles and the park took their name from the town of Saratoga, a few miles farther to the north. Confusingly enough for today's visitor, Saratoga, which dated from 1689, no longer exists. It was burned by Indians in 1745 and supplanted by Schuylerville in 1831. However, as much of the place as survived was still known as Saratoga when it served as the site of General John Burgoyne's historic surrender to General Horatio Gates on October 17, 1777 (see October 17, British Surrender at Saratoga).

OCTOBER 8

John Clarke's Birthday

John Clarke, a founder of the colony of Rhode Island and a pioneer of religious liberty in America, was born in Westhorpe, Suffolk, England, on October 8, 1609. One of eight children, Clarke was the son of Thomas Clarke and Rose Kerrich Clarke.

Probably equipped with a university education, he arrived in America in 1637, landing in Boston in November, just after the General Court of the Massachusetts Bay Colony had taken action to purge the colony of antinomianism, a belief that human salvation depends on faith in the Gospel's message of redemption rather than on rules of behavior. Clarke allied himself with Anne Hutchinson, William Coddington, and other condemned antinomians who were banished from the colony. The exiles fled to Exeter, New Hampshire, and then, in the spring of 1638, a party of them, including Clarke, journeyed to Roger Williams's newly established settlement of Providence in the Narragansett Bay area. After conferring with Williams, they decided to buy Aquidneck (later Rhode) Island in Narragansett Bay from the Indians and settle on it. During the year they founded Pocasset (now Portsmouth) in the northern part of the island, and in the spring of 1639, Clarke, Coddington, and others moved south and established Newport, where Clarke practiced medicine and served as pastor of the church he helped to organize, subsequently referred to as the First Baptist Church. A fourth Narragansett Bay settlement, on the mainland like Providence, was Warwick, founded by Samuel Gorton and settled in 1643.

Among the leaders of the Narragansett Bay settlements, Clarke aligned himself against Coddington and on the side of Roger Williams in support of a political union of the settlements. He also favored religious liberty and, along with

Williams, is given credit for the democratic character of the code of laws adopted by the Providence Plantations, the name given to the union — in 1647 — of the Narragansett Bay settlements under a patent Williams obtained from the British parliament in 1644.

In 1651, after Coddington had gained English permission to annul the patent and withdraw Aquidneck and another island from the Providence Plantations colony, Clarke went to England with Williams to get the charter reinstated. They succeeded, and Williams returned to America in 1654. Clarke, however, remained in England for 10 or more years to represent the interests of the colony and was largely responsible for securing from King Charles II in 1663 a new charter that reconfirmed the corporate existence of the colony — designated in the new charter as Rhode Island and Providence Plantations — and proclaimed religious liberty within its jurisdiction in words that are inscribed in part on the south front of the State House in Providence:

. . . to hold forth a lively experiment that a most flourishing civil state may stand and best be maintained . . . with full liberty in religious concernments.

The provisions of this charter were incorporated in the constitution of the state and were in force until 1842, when a new constitution was adopted.

On Clarke's return to Rhode Island he served in the general assembly from 1664 to 1669 and was deputy governor for three terms. He died on April 28, 1676, and is buried in a small walled cemetery located on West Broadway in Newport, on part of his original land. Trustees of his estate marked his gravesite with a monument in 1840. There, each year on the Sunday nearest Memorial Day, the Baptist church descended from his original congregation holds a small ceremony and places flowers on his grave. Clarke is honored in the full name of this church, now officially designated as the United Baptist Church John Clarke Memorial and located at 30 Spring Street, Newport, in its third home, a building constructed about 1845. At the time of the church's 300th anniversary in 1938 — the occasion for "A Hero of Conscience: A Dramalogue of John Clarke and Early Newport," written by Clarence M. Gallup — the group was still known as the First Baptist John Clarke Memorial Church. Newport's early leader and pioneer for religious freedom has also been remembered in the naming of both the John Clarke School, a public elementary school on Newport's Mary Street, and the John Clarke Science Building, which was dedicated on July 8, 1963, at Rhode Island College, Providence.

OCTOBER 9

The Chicago Fire

Sunday, October 8, was an unusually warm day in Chicago, like too many others in the summer and fall of 1871. City officials were worried. Buildings were predominantly wooden, and less than one-quarter of the normal amount of rain had fallen in the preceding months. The fact that many woodworking industries made the city their home only amplified the tinderbox effect. And a spectacular fire that claimed four blocks on the night of October 7 added to the uneasiness.

On the evening of October 8, Daniel ("Pegleg") Sullivan, a drayman, spent a few minutes visiting his friend Patrick O'Leary, a laborer, and his wife, Catherine, at their home at 137 DeKoven Street. Then he went across the street and sat down in front of his own house to enjoy the evening breeze. The sight of flames inside the O'Learys' barn ended his relaxation; Sullivan rushed to the building and managed to rescue a calf, but not much else could be done.

The firewatcher spotted the blaze from his tower, but misjudged its location by a mile. He soon recognized his error, but more valuable time was lost when the alarm operator, for some inexplicable reason, temporarily refused to revise the telegraph message. The flames, aided by a high, veering wind, spread quickly. The fire traveled two and a quarter miles across the air in six and a half hours and continued through the next day. The use of explosives to raze buildings and create a firebreak brought the conflagration under control on the city's south side on October 9. On the north side, where the waterworks were soon destroyed in the disaster, the flames licked their way almost out to the prairie before a rainfall finally quenched them. In 27 hours the Chicago fire had burnt across 2,000 acres, destroying 18,000 buildings and causing $196 million in property damage. At least 300 Chicagoans lost their lives, and 90,000 out of a population of approximately 300,000 found themselves homeless.

Speculation about the origin of the fire began while Chicago was still ablaze. Some said that Mrs. O'Leary was milking her cow when the animal kicked over a lamp and set the straw in the barn on fire. Others noted that a party had been in progress next door at the McLaughlins' to welcome the brother of Mrs. McLaughlin, who had recently arrived from Ireland. Perhaps some of the guests had been in the O'Learys' barn and disturbed the much-maligned cow. A few malicious people accused Mrs. O'Leary of intentionally starting the blaze in revenge for being taken off the relief rolls, though in reality she had never received public assistance. Daniel Sullivan, the only eyewitness, did not see anyone in the vicinity, and so all that historians can say with certainty is that the fire began in the O'Learys' barn. Curiously, the O'Leary house survived the disaster with only slight damage.

Chicagoans quickly rebuilt their metropolis. They restored the business district within a year; and by 1893 the city was ready to become the site of a great World's Fair. Success buoyed the spirits of the populace, and on each October 9 they commemorated the tragedy with parades and other festivities. In 1911 the Fire Marshals Association of North America suggested a more serious motif for the celebrations, and so the 40th anniversary became the first Fire Prevention Day. On recommendation of a National Fire Protection Association committee, the observance was extended in 1922, and President Warren G. Harding and the governor-general of Canada proclaimed Fire Prevention Week. Both nations have continued the practice, and Fire Prevention Week is marked each year during the Sunday through Saturday period in which October 9 falls. The chief executives· of the United States and Canada issue proclamations, as do many governors and mayors.

Leif Erikson Day

In the ninth century the Vikings emerged from the isolation of their native Norway and began a series of invasions that radically altered the course of world history. For 200 years the Norsemen — or Northmen — plundered and pillaged the towns and coastlines of France, Portugal, Spain, Italy, and the British Isles. They established settlements in some of these areas, and eventually gained dominance of the northern region of France, now known after them as Normandy. William the Conqueror, the most famous of the French Normans, invaded Britain in 1066 and quickly brought the English kingdom under his control.

Ability to sail the seas and a thirst for adventure made the Norsemen powerful. They not only raided communities in Europe but dared to venture across uncharted seas to seek out little-known lands. Proceeding west from Norway, the intrepid Vikings established settlements in the Shetland, Faroe, and Orkney islands during the eighth century and set up a colony in Iceland in 874. Eric the Red, an exile from Iceland, discovered Greenland in the early 980s. After exploring its lengthy coast for several years, he went back to Iceland and, returning to Greenland with colonists, established two settlements in the western part of the island. These communities lasted for several centuries, and ruins remain as mute testimony to the Norse occupation of Greenland.

The Norse settlements definitely extended as far west as Greenland in the pre-Columbian era, and there is interesting evidence that Viking ships may have reached the North American coast during the same period. According to Icelandic sagas, Leif the Lucky, the son of Eric the Red and thus also known as Leif Ericson (or Erikson), sailed west from Greenland in about A.D. 1000 and discovered a land rich with wild grapes and wheat, which he named Vinland. In the centuries since, there has been much conjecture as to the identity of Vinland. Varied theories have located it anywhere from Newfoundland to Virginia, with New England one of the favored guesses. The Icelandic sagas go on to relate that in the years following the discovery of Vinland, Leif's brother, Thorvald, returned to explore the coast of the continent, and that Thorfinn Karlsevni, a Norse trader, attempted to establish a colony in the western land.

Although the sagas contain intriguing evidence that Leif Ericson reached the New World prior to Columbus, they were transmitted orally for more than 200 years before being written down in the 13th century. It is therefore not surprising that a number of contradictions and discrepancies appear in them. For example, what is known as the Greenland saga relates that Leif Ericson purposefully set out for the North American coast, guided by the records of Bjarni Herjulfson, a Norse navigator who purportedly sighted the land in 986; the Karlsevni saga relates that Ericson was blown off course and came upon Vinland accidentally. To confuse matters further, the sagas use the same terms to identify the discoveries of Leif and Thorvald Ericson that are employed for the finds of Karlsevni; but variations in geographical descriptions suggest that Karlsevni and the Ericsons probably explored different regions.

Because of the serious discrepancies in the different sagas, historians have been unwilling to accept folklore as proof of the Norse discoveries and have tried to verify theories of Viking exploration in North America by other means. As the seafarers left no written documents about their adventures, archeological clues have been sought. Several findings support the thesis that the Vikings were the first Europeans to set foot in North America. Noted among these discoveries are a stone tower in Newport, Rhode Island; the Kensington Stone, found near Kensington, Minnesota, which bears supposed runic inscriptions dated 1362; and a sword, ax head, and shield grip from about A.D. 1000, which were uncovered in Beardmore, Ontario. Opinion is sharply divided on the authenticity of these finds, and a number of experts believe the relics to be spurious.

At least two discoveries uphold the belief that Vikings came to American shores before Columbus. In 1963 Dr. Helge Ingstad reported finding the remains of a Norse settlement near L'Anse aux Meadows in Newfoundland. Working with a number of scientists, Ingstad unearthed traces of nine Norse structures and, by means of radiocarbon tests, verified that the site had been occupied around A.D. 1000. Although there is no proof that Leif Ericson himself ever visited L'Anse aux Meadows, most experts agree that the ruins are of pre-Columbian Norse origin.

For many years Norwegian-Americans worked through such organizations as the Leif Erikson Association to establish October 9 as Leif Erikson Day. Their efforts were rewarded in 1964 when President Lyndon B. Johnson proclaimed October 9 as Leif Erikson Day. Since 1964, a presidential proclamation has been issued annually on October 9, and in 1968 the Post Office Department issued a Leif Ericson commemorative stamp.

The governors of several states also issue proclamations on October 9, and states with a large Norwegian-American population, such as Washington, Minnesota, Wisconsin, and New York, hold observances on the day. The Sons of Norway, a fraternal organization of Norwegian-Americans, regularly commemorates Leif Erikson Day. Its lodges sponsor dinners, dances, and special meetings on October 9.

OCTOBER 10

Yom Kippur

This is a movable event. See note on page xxvi.

The Day of Atonement, Yom Kippur, is the last of the 10 Penitential Days which mark the beginning of the Jewish New Year (see October 1, Rosh Hashanah). Yom Kippur is observed on the 10th day of the lunar month of Tishri (in the course of September or October), which fell on October 10 in 1970. Jews traditionally consider Yom Kippur the Sabbath of Sabbaths, the holiest day in the Jewish year. It is a day of prayer and fasting to obtain forgiveness of sins and reconciliation with God through sincere repentance. The Day of Atonement is devoted to the regeneration and renewal of moral and religious life.

Before the destruction of the second Temple in Jerusalem in A.D. 70 (see August 11, Tisha B'Av), an elaborate ceremonial was practiced, including the offering of sacrifices. The ceremonial is described in chapter 16 of Leviticus, the portion of the Bible read during the Yom Kippur synagogue services.

Today, the ancient sacrificial ceremony is recalled by the repetition in the synagogue of a special service: of the *Avodah* (literally "sacrificial service"). The *Avodah* service describes in poetry and prayer the ritual of confession and sacrifice that the High Priest performed when the Temple was standing. The High Priest recited three confessions of sins — one for himself and his household, one for the whole community of priests, and one for the entire Jewish people. The third confession was accompanied by the ritual of the scapegoat, during which the High Priest confessed the sins of Israel while resting his hands on the head of a goat. The priest then sent the scapegoat to die in Azazel, the wilderness.

Since the destruction of the Temple, the importance of individual repentance has been stressed. One of the readings from the Bible on Yom Kippur is Isaiah 57:14–58:14. It teaches that external signs of repentance are not acceptable to God; only a change of heart that affects one's relations with others is true repentance.

The Day of Atonement is observed in modern times by synagogue services that begin in the evening of the preceding day with the chanting of the Kol Nidre. This moving prayer asks for the remission of unfulfilled vows to God, specifically including those made under duress, and indicates the petitioner's desire for a new beginning. It is a tenet of Jewish belief that the remission does not apply to unfulfilled obligations between people. For these or other wrongs, it is incumbent upon the individual to seek the pardon of those wronged. By custom, the day before Yom Kippur is therefore given over to the mutual asking of forgiveness. (Some Reform Jews do not chant the Kol Nidre but begin the evening service by reciting Psalm 130, as was done in biblical times.)

Traditionally, the scrolls in the ark are clothed in white, and white garments are worn by the rabbi and the cantor during the Yom Kippur synagogue services, which continue for the whole day. The souls of the dead are included in the community of those remembered on this day. Many Jews visit cemeteries and make special charitable gifts during the days before Yom Kippur. On the day itself, traditional Jews customarily light two candles — one in memory of the dead and the other for the living. The synagogue services include a special *Yizkor* (literally, "He will remember") service in memory of the dead. The last section of the synagogue services is the emotion-filled *neilah*, or closing, service of the day, which takes place just before sunset. This service is interpreted to mean the closing of the heavenly gates, at the sealing of the divine judgment.

The Day of Atonement services end with the confession of faith and the blowing of the *shofar* (ram's horn). For some, the break-the-fast dinner that follows may be hearty and include traditional foods: the braided bread known as *challah*, chicken soup, wine, honey or sponge cake, and *taglach* – a sweet pastry containing nuts, honey, and cinnamon.

Geauga County Apple Butter Festival
Burton, Ohio

This is a movable event. See note on page xxvi.

For two days each October the small community of Burton, Ohio, turns back the clock for an authentic demonstration of the skills of an earlier day. The occasion is the Geauga County Apple Butter Festival, sponsored by the Geauga County Historical Society, and the principal skill demonstrated is the making of apple butter. The festival takes place usually on the second weekend in October.

An air of commercialism, which pervades some festivals, is absent from the Burton event. Also missing are the usual contests, beauty queens, and specially-invited notables. Although most of the events are related to apples and apple products, there also are craft demonstrations, employing antique implements.

Participants turn out for the festival in clothes like those of the pioneers who settled Burton in the early 1800s, the women in shawls and poke bonnets, the men in overalls and broad-brimmed hats. Some members of a nearby Amish community also appear in traditional clothing, and visitors occasionally turn up in resurrected Civil War uniforms or other finds from local attics.

The atmosphere of nostalgia is in keeping with the interests of the museum and Pioneer Village maintained by the historical society. The festival is held on the museum grounds. Part of the museum's main building originally housed the family of Thomas Umberville, who became Burton's first permanent settler in 1798, a year after the town was first laid out. Today the building constitutes part of Pioneer Village, along with a dozen or so other structures, which have been moved in as representative examples of early architecture.

Preparations for the festival begin well in advance, with the interminable job of peeling enough apples to satisfy festival demands. All over Geauga County, hand-operated presses work to produce the cider – boiled and unboiled – which is an indispensable ingredient of apple butter. Next, antique 15-gallon caldrons of iron or copper, blackened by long use, are set up on tripods over smoldering fires. As the festival gets under way, the fires are brought to a blaze, and the caldrons are filled with the apples and cider. Thenceforth, from early morning to late afternoon, volunteers continuously stir the aromatic mixture with long wooden ladles. The resulting apple butter, as well as the apple cider and fresh apples, is then sold to festival-goers.

Coinciding with the festival, which is usually attended by about 30,000, is the annual ox roast sponsored by the Burton Volunteer Fire Department. In addition, the log cabin on the village green offers for sale such items as maple sugar, maple syrup, and maple cream.

The museum's country store features penny candy, jams, produce, baked goods, and dried foliage. Guests can also see the blacksmith's shop, the potter's shop, and the one-room schoolhouse. In the Law House — formerly the residence of one of Burton's founders — visitors can watch demonstrations of spinning, weaving, and rug hooking and braiding.

For children, favorite attractions are an antique hearse and vehicles on which they can ride. These include an ox-cart, a surrey, and a steam engine.

The Geauga County Apple Butter Festival had its beginning in 1949, when it was decided to include the making of apple butter, simply as an added feature of a regular museum open house. The popularity of this colorful demonstration grew so rapidly, however, that the main event soon became an apple butter festival rather than an open house. Proceeds of the festival go to the Geauga County Historical Society for the purchase of antiques or for other projects.

Oklahoma Historical Day

Oklahoma Historical Day was inaugurated in 1939 by the state legislature, which passed a resolution directing the governor to proclaim October 10 of each year as a day for commemorating the anniversary of the birth, in 1758, of Major Jean Pierre Chouteau, the Father of Oklahoma. In 1796 Chouteau established at Salina the first permanent non-Indian settlement within the boundaries of what is now the state of Oklahoma. As early as 1740, French traders and trappers had made settlements in other sections of the state, but these small outposts had all been abandoned by the beginning of the 19th century, making Chouteau's subsequent outpost the first that lasted.

Chouteau's birth date is a legal holiday in Oklahoma. In schools and other educational institutions throughout the state, it is usually marked by special programs that implement the 1939 resolution by reviewing, in the words of the governor's 1970 proclamation, "the state's constructive history from the establishment of the first permanent settlement to the present." In 1945 the state legislature set up the Oklahoma Day Historical Committee, always appointed by the Oklahoma Historical Society, to organize and stage a major annual celebration at Salina on October 10.

Typical of the observance at Salina was the 1970 program. (This Mayes County community began its observance of the day two years before the legislature's 1939 resolution.) A crowd of several thousand spectators watched the day's activities, which included sports events, a fiddlers' contest, a children's costume competition, and a street parade. The highlight was the "Chouteau Day" presentation, held in the early afternoon at the Salina High School parade grounds. Groups from various sections of the state presented song and dance acts and twirling and drill-team exhibitions. The Jean Pierre Chouteau Pioneer Club held a drawing for a cash award among its members. The club, whose membership was originally limited to those pioneer residents of Oklahoma who had lived in the area since territorial days, is now open to any person who has continuously resided in the state for at least 40 years.

Much of the early history of Oklahoma is connected with the French family named Chouteau. In 1794 Major Jean Pierre Chouteau took command of the newly constructed Fort Carondelet on the south bank of the Osage River in what is now Missouri. The fort was intended to protect white settlers in the region west of St. Louis from the Indian attacks stimulated by intertribal hostility between the Osages and various other tribes that resented Osage dominance. Major Chouteau and his half brother René Auguste took over a virtual monopoly of the fur trade with the Indians of the area, especially the Osage. Spain, which then owned the vast central region known as Spanish Louisiana, at first left them undisturbed. Later, however, the Spaniards granted extensive fur-trading rights in the area to a young New Orleans-born Spaniard named Manuel Lisa (or Liza) and his French associates, thus threatening to close down the Chouteau trade.

Not easily thwarted in his plans, Major Chouteau began to scout around for another base of operations for his profitable business. In late March 1796 he formed a party of French hunters and traders and headed southwest from Fort Carondelet into what was then unknown country. Some 400 miles from the fort, he came upon a sizable river, which the Indians called Neosho. Chouteau ordered his men to follow *cette grande rivière* and thus unwittingly gave the Neosho River the name it bears today — after crossing into Oklahoma from Kansas — the Grand River. Following this river south, the major found a site for his new trading post. Located near a freshwater spring and a ford across the Grand River, it also had convenient access to the extensive water network via the Grand, Arkansas, and Mississippi rivers to the New Orleans markets.

One part of the Chouteau party erected a cabin at the site of Salina to serve as a headquarters and trading post, while another group set out to explore the surroundings. Despite the ideal location of the post, Chouteau was dismayed to learn that within hundreds of miles there were no Indian villages with which he could trade.

Forced to leave their campsite near the Grand River at least temporarily, Chouteau and his men returned to Fort Carondelet. The major still schemed to salvage the family's lucrative Indian trade, and he skillfully used his power, wealth, and position to create dissension among the Osages. He persuaded one faction of the tribe to move its villages southwest into the country around the Grand, Arkansas, and Verdigris rivers and agreed to establish trade with them at the little campsite (Salina) that he had already selected. As soon as the Osages started to move into the area in 1802, the major personally oversaw the reestablishment of the remote outpost. Several thousand Osages were soon shooting and trapping in their new hunting grounds, providing Chouteau's trading post with an abundant supply of pelts. The furs, as Major Chouteau had anticipated, were then piled onto rafts or flatboats and floated down the river network to New Orleans.

Meanwhile, in 1800, France had acquired the territory known as Louisiana by the secret Treaty of San Ildefonso. In 1803 the United States, through the Louisiana Purchase, bought the huge tract, which included Oklahoma. Chouteau frequently visited his "American" trading post from 1802 to 1817, when he passed its supervision over to his oldest son, Auguste Pierre. The major retired from the fur trade about 1820, but his descendants for several generations continued to be active not only in expanding the fur trade, but also in settling other places within what is now Oklahoma, such as Vinita and Chouteau.

OCTOBER 11

Pulaski Day

The ideals and adventure of the American Revolution inspired a number of noteworthy Europeans to take up arms and fight for the independence of the 13 American colonies. Men such as the Marquis de Lafayette of France, Baron Friedrich von Steuben of Germany, and Thaddeus Kosciuszko of Poland rendered valuable assistance to the colonists during the war against Great Britain. Several representatives of foreign nobility lost their lives while attempting to win this nation's freedom. Count Casimir Pulaski was one of those heroes.

Born in Warka, Poland, about 1748, Pulaski was the son of Count Joseph Pulaski, an ardent nationalist and the founder of the Confederation of the Bar, an organization that attempted to prevent foreign domination of Poland in the mid-18th century. In 1767, at the age of 19, Casimir Pulaski joined the fight to preserve the independence of his homeland. He fought bravely for several years and scored a number of victories. But the Polish army was no match for its stronger adversaries. In 1772 Prussia, Russia, and Austria partitioned Poland. Pulaski's estate was confiscated, and the young nobleman was forced to seek refuge in Turkey.

For three years Pulaski tried to persuade Turkey to attack Russia, but his efforts failed, and in 1775 he went to Paris. Mutual acquaintances there brought Pulaski together with Benjamin Franklin and Silas Deane. The American commissioners were impressed by Pulaski's military background and believed he might substantially aid the patriot cause. Penniless and in need of employment, Pulaski readily agreed to their suggestion that he fight on behalf of the Americans. With a letter of introduction from Franklin to George Washington, the commander in chief of the Continental army, the Polish count sailed from France in June 1777.

Pulaski arrived in America just as the Continental army was being reorganized to include four regiments of dragoons. When Washington heard of Pulaski's considerable experience with the Polish cavalry, he recommended that Pulaski be given command of the new mounted units. On September 15, 1777, the Continental Congress appointed Pulaski to the rank of brigadier general and named him to the post of Commander of the Horse.

After taking part in the battle of Germantown on October 4, Pulaski spent the winter of 1777 doing outpost duty at Trenton and Flemington, New Jersey. With General Anthony Wayne he also conducted several expeditions designed to obtain provisions for the Continental soldiers, then in their harsh winter quarters at nearby Valley Forge, Pennsylvania. But his association with the army was not happy. Unable to speak English and unwilling to subordinate himself even to Washington, Pulaski failed to maintain the respect of the troops under his command. In March 1778 he resigned from the army.

With the permission of Congress, Pulaski then raised an independent cavalry corps. Still things did not go well for him. In September 1778, after he complained that he was "languishing in a state of inactivity," Congress ordered his unit to guard American supplies at Little Egg Harbor, New Jersey. Pulaski saw combat at Little Egg, but unfortunately a surprise British attack early in October 1778 almost destroyed his volunteer legion. The following month the young Pole was sent to Minisink on the Delaware River to protect the inhabitants of the area from Indian attack. This new assignment did not please him; on November 26 he wrote that he had "nothing but bears to fight."

After 1778 the scene of the major military confrontations between the British and the patriots shifted to the South. Under orders from Congress, Pulaski proceeded to South Carolina in February 1779 to assist General Benjamin Lincoln, the American commander of the Southern Department. This change in the theater of his operations did not relieve Pulaski's frustration. In May 1779 the British under the command of General Augustine Prevost badly defeated Pulaski's cavalry corps, and in August Pulaski again complained to Congress of "ill treatment."

Despite his dissatisfaction, Pulaski continued to fight for the patriot cause. During the unsuccessful American attempt to wrest Savannah, Georgia, from British control on October 9, 1779, Pulaski led a gallant, if perhaps foolhardy, cavalry attack against the enemy defenses. He was mortally wounded during this heroic action and died on October 11, 1779, aboard the brig *Wasp*.

Although largely ignored in the 19th century, the commemoration of the anniversary of Pulaski's death received increasing attention in the early 20th century. The Military Order of Pulaski, which was formed in 1915, originated observances of October 11, and groups such as the Polish National Alliance and the Polish Army Veterans Association lent much support to these celebrations. The President of the United States annually proclaims October 11 as Pulaski Day, and a number of governors and mayors similarly mark the occasion.

Many cities include a parade in their celebrations of the day, but the largest one takes place in New York City. On the Sunday nearest October 11, over 100,000 Polish-Americans parade up Fifth Avenue. Young girls wear traditional white dresses with black velvet vests and ribbon streamers; bands provide lively musical entertainment; and numerous floats recall great Polish historical figures. Municipal and state officials generally march in the parade or sit in the reviewing stand.

Count Casimir Pulaski is permanently honored in several places in the United States. Visitors to the Savannah area in Georgia may tour Fort Pulaski National Monument on Cockspur Island, 15 miles east of the city. The fortification was constructed between 1829 and 1847 and served as a Confederate stronghold during the Civil War. In Savannah, Pulaski Square and a monument in Monterey Square honor him. Another memorial to the Polish general stands at Valley Forge, and Pulaski Skyway, a four-lane elevated highway in New Jersey, is named in his honor. In addition, small communities in several states (Mississippi, New York, Tennessee, and Virginia) and counties in Arkansas, Georgia, Illinois, Indiana, Kentucky, Missouri, and Virginia all bear the name of Pulaski.

Eleanor Roosevelt's Birthday

Anna Eleanor Roosevelt, who became, in the words of President Harry S. Truman, the "First Lady of the World," was born on October 11, 1884, in New York City. The niece of President Theodore Roosevelt and the socially conscious wife of President Franklin Delano Roosevelt (see January 30), Eleanor Roosevelt, through the force of her personality and the compassion of her convictions, became a prominent figure in her own right. By the time of her death at the age of 78 on November 7, 1962, she had traveled to all corners of the earth to speak and act on behalf of peace and amity among nations and peoples.

Eleanor Roosevelt was born a member of America's upper class. Her parents, Elliott and Anna Livingston Hall Roosevelt, were descendants of wealthy old New York families. Claes Van Rosenvelt had arrived in America from the Netherlands in the 1630s, when Manhattan Island was the Dutch colonial city of New Amsterdam, and Robert Livingston had come to New York from Scotland in the late 1600s. Both immigrants became the progenitors of impressive clans, and the Livingstons contributed several leaders of the American movement for independence.

Anna Livingston Hall Roosevelt was a beautiful socialite unable to hide her disappointment in the plain appearance of her daughter, whom she called Granny. In a family noted for its attractive women, Eleanor Roosevelt was an exception, the "ugly duckling," as her aunts reminded her. Sharing the values of her society, Eleanor Roosevelt became self-conscious and withdrawn.

Sportsman Elliott Roosevelt, the older brother of Theodore Roosevelt, doted on his daughter, calling her Little Nell and offering her the affection that her mother could not give. Unfortunately, however, he was an alcoholic who later spent much time in sanitariums. Her mother died of diphtheria when Eleanor was eight years old. After her father died two years later, she and her younger brother went to live with their maternal grandmother, Mrs. Valentine Gill Hall. They resided in a brownstone on West 37th Street in New York City most of the time, but spent several months each year in a brick mansion at Tivoli-on-Hudson, where Eleanor had no friends of her age, and which she found particularly tedious and lonesome.

Her grandmother had a narrow conception of the education appropriate for a young lady, centering her granddaughter's early training on such social and homemaking arts as playing the piano and darning socks. Fortunately, when she was 15, Mrs. Hall agreed to send her to the Allenswood school in London, which was run by a Frenchwoman, Marie Souvestre. A staunch political liberal, Souvestre emphasized the rights of the individual and the necessity of acting with complete fairness. Eleanor Roosevelt spent three years under her tutelage and toured the Continent with her.

Returning to the United States at age 18, Eleanor Roosevelt made her debut into New York society at the Assembly Ball, where she was abashed to discover that she knew hardly anyone. She found the role of debutante unsatisfying, later stating that "that first winter, when my sole object in life was society, nearly brought me to a state of nervous collapse." She decided to devote herself to the aid of the less fortunate, and soon took a position teaching at the Rivington Street Settlement House in Lower Manhattan.

Franklin D. Roosevelt, who had known her slightly before she went to Europe, entered her life seriously during these years. A student at Harvard, he found in his fifth cousin once removed those qualities that later endeared her to the world. In 1903 the couple announced their engagement, but out of respect for the wishes of Franklin Roosevelt's strong-willed mother, they prolonged their engagement until March 17, 1905, when they were married at the home of relatives on Manhattan's upper East Side. Theodore Roosevelt, fresh from his presidential inauguration, gave the bride away, and the Reverend Endicott Peabody, headmaster of the exclusive Groton School, conducted the ceremony. The wedding was a gala affair, with the President attracting as much attention as the bride and groom.

Then a law student at Columbia University, Franklin Roosevelt had time only to take his bride for a week's honeymoon at the family estate in Hyde Park, New York. Later the newlyweds made a trip through Europe, visiting London, Paris, and Venice. On their return they lived on East 36th Street in New York City in a house rented for them by his mother, who lived only three blocks away. The Roosevelts had six children, born within 11 years: Anna Eleanor; James; Franklin Jr., who died in infancy; Elliott; a second Franklin Jr.; and John. As expected, the young wife was also a dutiful daughter-in-law; she drove with her mother-in-law every afternoon and took at least one meal with her daily.

Franklin Roosevelt entered politics six years after their marriage and won election to the New York State Senate. In 1913, when President Woodrow Wilson named him to be assistant secretary of the navy, Eleanor Roosevelt accompanied him to Washington. There she began to emerge as a public figure with the onset of World War I. "I went into the canteen," she said, "and I suddenly began to understand. We were sending men to fight who had no idea where they were going or why. And that was the beginning of a lot of education for me."

Horrified by the poor medical treatment that the government gave sailors and marines at St. Elizabeth's, the federal psychiatric hospital, she insisted that the secretary of the interior obtain a larger appropriation for the hospital from Congress. She also persuaded a charitable organization to contribute $500 for occupational therapy for the patients and the Red Cross to build a recreation room.

Newly aware of political issues, she was with her husband in Europe during Wilson's triumphal postwar visit, and they returned to the United States on the same ship as the President. A supporter of the League of Nations, she was disappointed when Congress refused to commit the United States to the international body. She suffered further disappointment in 1920 when the Republican ticket of Warren G. Harding and Calvin Coolidge defeated the Democratic slate with James M. Cox as the presidential candidate and her husband as the candidate for Vice President.

The year 1921 brought personal tragedy to the Roosevelts, when Franklin Roosevelt contracted poliomyelitis while vacationing at their summer home on Campobello Island, New Brunswick, Canada. Although his mother expected him to retire as an invalid to Hyde Park, his wife was determined that he remain in public life. To renew his interest in politics, she became active in the field herself. She joined the board of the League of Women Voters, participated in the work of the Women's Trade Union League, and assumed an active role in the state committee of the Democratic party.

Regaining his political enthusiasm, Franklin Roosevelt in 1924 managed Alfred E. Smith's unsuccessful bid for the Democratic presidential nomination. In 1928 he successfully put Smith's name in nomination, and Eleanor Roosevelt directed the women's campaign committee. Smith lost the election to Herbert Hoover, but Franklin Roosevelt won the gubernatorial race in New York.

She maintained an amazing pace of activity while her husband was governor. Three mornings a week, she taught civics at the Todhunter School in New York City, a private school for girls, of which she was part owner. She also devoted evenings to political work. She passed the other four days of the week in Albany or in Hyde Park, where she and Marion Dickerman had started the nonprofit Val-Kill furniture factory to give disabled men employment manufacturing copies of early American furniture.

In 1932, with the nation in economic collapse, Franklin Roosevelt won the presidency of the United States and began preparing his New Deal programs to combat the Great Depression. In Washington, Eleanor Roosevelt attained national prominence and held unprecedented weekly news conferences. She toured the nation inspecting projects for her disabled husband. During her first eight years in the White House she averaged 40,000 miles of travel annually, and her peripatetic ways inspired comedians' wit and cartoonists' pens. At home she made the White House a less forbidding place than previously — one where grandchildren and pet dogs were always welcome.

Many criticized her for her sympathy with left-wing groups. She dissociated herself from any connection with several organizations that proved to be controlled by Communists but continued to defend the right of individuals to maintain their political convictions. Her championship of the rights of blacks also raised the hackles of some, but she remained adamant in her pursuit of racial justice and even resigned from the Daughters of the American Revolution when that organization refused the use of Washington's Constitution Hall for a concert by the contralto Marian Anderson.

World War II changed the focus of her activity. In 1942 she went to England to visit American training bases, becoming the first wife of a President to go abroad alone and the first to fly across the Atlantic. During the remainder of the war, she also served as assistant director of the Office of Civilian Defense and traveled to remote areas of the world to see troops in the war zones and comfort the wounded.

Eleanor Roosevelt's days in the White House ended with the death of her husband on April 12, 1945. She remained, however, in the public eye. In 1945 President Harry S. Truman appointed her as a delegate to the first General Assembly of the United Nations. The next year she chaired the Commission on Human Rights of the UN Economic and Social Council, serving until April 1951. She played an important role as one of the chief authors of the Universal Declaration of Human Rights, designed to define fundamental rights and freedoms for peoples throughout the world. The declaration was unanimously adopted by the UN General Assembly in 1948 (see December 10). It is regarded today as one of the landmark documents of human dignity, even though ratification by UN member-nations of the related Covenants on Human Rights — designed to enforce the declaration's provisions — proved to be a far slower process, which has not yet been completed. President Dwight D. Eisenhower selected a new UN delegate, but John F. Kennedy returned her to the international body.

Eleanor Roosevelt remained active in Democratic politics after her husband's death. She supported the unsuccessful bids of Adlai E. Stevenson for the presidency in 1952 and 1956, and endorsed the victorious candidacy of Kennedy in 1960. In New York State, she cast her lot with the liberal reform wing of the party.

On September 26, 1962, she entered Columbia Presbyterian Medical Center, where it was found that she suffered from anemia and a lung infection. Although she was returned to her home, she proved unable to overcome her illness and died on November 7, 1962, four weeks after her 78th birthday. Upon learning of her death, President Kennedy said:

One of the great ladies in the history of this country has passed from the scene. . . . Our condolences go to all the members of her family, whose grief at the death of this extraordinary woman can be tempered by the knowledge that her memory and spirit will long endure among those who labor for great causes around the world.

Eleanor Roosevelt was buried on November 10, 1962, next to her husband at Hyde Park. Besides the Roosevelt family, President Kennedy, Vice President Lyndon B. Johnson, and former Presidents Harry S. Truman and Dwight D. Eisenhower attended the services. Leading figures from the days of the New Deal and representatives of the United Nations also were present.

Reverend Gordon L. Kidd, rector of St. James Episcopal Church in Hyde Park, conducted a private funeral service at the church before the interment. The ceremony included her favorite prayer, by St. Francis of Assisi, and her favorite hymns. During his brief eulogy, Dr. Kidd said, "The entire world becomes one family orphaned by her passing." A week later, thousands of her friends, admirers, and UN colleagues heard a longer eulogy, one that became famous, delivered by Adlai Stevenson, then US representative to the United Nations. The occasion was the memorial service to which the public was invited, at the Cathedral of St. John the Divine in New York City.

Governments and individuals continued to offer tribute to Eleanor Roosevelt in the years following her death. President Kennedy on April 24, 1963, signed legislation chartering the Eleanor Roosevelt Memorial Foundation. It was stated that the foundation would attempt to carry on her work for world peace, human rights, the underprivileged, emotionally disturbed children, and cancer research. In October 1964 the foundation sponsored dinners in New York, Washington, and Chicago to commemorate what would have been her 80th birthday and to raise money for the construction of two new Eleanor Roosevelt wings at the Roosevelt Library in Hyde Park. In New York, 1,500 people heard speeches by Adlai Stevenson, Chief Justice Earl Warren, and UN Secretary General U Thant at a $100-a-plate dinner.

On October 11, 1963, the 79th anniversary of her birth, the US Post Office had issued a five-cent stamp bearing her likeness. Ten days later, some 2,600 persons gathered at New York's Philharmonic Hall for an evening in memory of Eleanor Roosevelt, at which Stevenson and U Thant were guest speakers. In November 1965 *The Eleanor Roosevelt Story*, an hour-and-a-half documentary film written by Archibald MacLeish, and narrated by MacLeish, news commentator Eric Sevareid, and Mrs. Francis Cole, a cousin of Eleanor Roosevelt, was presented in theaters.

The United Nations, which remained Eleanor Roosevelt's best hope for world peace, honored its champion in 1966. On April 23 the organization dedicated a memorial to her in New York City. The monument consists of a granite slab 4 feet wide and 10 feet high and a semicircular granite bench set in a grove of trees in the UN garden. The slab is carved with a flame and a quotation from Adlai Stevenson's eulogy: "She would rather light a candle than curse the darkness and her glow has warmed the world."

Among the many monuments to Eleanor Roosevelt are the books and articles that she wrote. For many years she wrote a daily newspaper column entitled "My Day," and she also contributed a question-and-answer feature in the *Ladies' Home Journal* and later in *McCall's* magazine. Her books included *You Can Learn by Living* (1960) and *India: The Awakening East* (1953). She also wrote four volumes of autobiography: *This Is My Story* (1937), *This I Remember* (1949), *On My Own* (1958), and *The Autobiography of Eleanor Roosevelt* (1961).

Harlan Fiske Stone's Birthday

Harlan Fiske Stone, the 12th chief justice of the United States, was born at Chesterfield, New Hampshire, on October 11, 1872. His father, Frederick Lauson Stone, was a farmer who encouraged his sons to make agriculture their occupation. In 1874 Frederick Stone moved his family to Amherst, Massachusetts, so that his eldest son might attend the state agricultural college (now the University of Massachusetts).

His younger son, Harlan, grew up on the family farm, where he spent many hours doing such chores as milking and plowing. Originally he too planned to become a farmer. He even left high school after his second year and enrolled at the agricultural school. But Stone's days there as a student were few: before long his pranks led to his expulsion.

Stone's admission to Amherst College, in the same town, in 1890 was the turning point in his life. During his four years there he achieved an outstanding record. Among other distinctions, he served as class president, was a member of the football team, and won election to Phi Beta Kappa. After graduation in 1894, he taught in a neighboring community for a year and then entered Columbia Law School in New York. Admitted to the bar in 1898, he began his legal practice with the New York law firm of Sullivan and Cromwell and joined the Columbia faculty as a lecturer in that same year.

Both as a practicing attorney and as an academic, Stone enjoyed great success. In 1905 he became a senior partner in the firm of Satterlie, Canfield, and Stone. During the next 18 years he remained an active member of this firm, although for much of the period this practice was not his only concern: in 1907 and from 1910 to 1923 he also served as dean of the Columbia Law School. In 1923 Stone resigned both positions and rejoined Sullivan and Cromwell, plan-

ning to devote himself to the large corporate practice for which the firm was renowned.

This was not to be, however; for it was public rather than private service that was to give Stone the opportunity to utilize his legal talents fully. In 1924 President Calvin Coolidge appointed Stone attorney general of the United States. Although he held this office for only one year, he initiated reforms that salvaged the reputation of the Department of Justice from the depths into which it had fallen as a result of the scandals of the Harding Administration. The following year Coolidge named Stone associate justice of the Supreme Court.

Justices who were inclined to be conservative in outlook and predisposed toward the interests of big business dominated the Supreme Court throughout the 1920s. To those interested in social change, Stone's background seemed to indicate that he too might be "another tool of Wall Street," and when his appointment was announced they feared that yet another reactionary voice had been added to the Court. But they could not have been more in error.

During Stone's 21 years on the bench, three basic areas of law preoccupied the Supreme Court. In the 1920s the main issue before the tribunal was the extent of power an individual state had to alter its economic system by regulation, prohibition, and taxation; in the 1930s the constitutionality of New Deal legislation that sought to change the nation's economic and legal order was the burning issue; and in the 1940s the most noteworthy cases before the Court concerned the validity of wartime measures such as martial law and military courts. Stone wrote more than 600 opinions and dissents dealing with these matters, and an examination of his record shows how closely he aligned himself with the liberal members of the Court.

From the time of his appointment to the Court in 1925 until 1937, Stone and some fellow justices — Oliver Wendell Holmes Jr., Louis Brandeis, and, after Holmes's retirement in 1932, Benjamin Cardozo — rendered opinions that earned for them the sobriquet of "the three great dissenters." While the other members of the Court were guided by conservative inclinations and, therefore, struck down every legislative innovation designed to change the social order, the dissenters based their opinions on the judicial theory originally put forth by Holmes and Brandeis. These two justices had long argued that individual judges should refrain from invalidating legislation merely because they personally opposed it and instead should allow statutes to remain in effect if any reasonable basis could be found to support them. The 1936 case of *United States* v. *Butler* provides the best example of

Stone's acceptance of the Holmes-Brandeis position. Had Stone been a member of Congress, he would have worked vigorously to prevent the passage of the legislation in question, which was the New Deal measure known as the Agricultural Adjustment Act. He upheld the statute, saying: "While unconstitutional exercise of power by the executive and legislative branches of the Government is subject to judicial restraint, the only check upon our own exercise of power is our own sense of restraint."

In 1937 several of the more conservative justices retired from the Supreme Court, and President Franklin D. Roosevelt selected liberals to fill the vacated positions. This change in the Court's membership resulted in a corresponding change in its rulings. Post-1937 decisions reversed previous opinions, and the majority of the Court after that date accepted many of the positions that Holmes, Brandeis, Stone, and Cardozo had taken in their earlier dissents.

When Chief Justice Charles Evans Hughes retired in 1941, President Roosevelt named Stone as his successor. Stone served five years in this office. He was delivering a dissenting opinion in the case of *Girouard* v. *the United States* when he became fatally ill. He died on April 22, 1946, in Washington, D.C.

OCTOBER 12

Columbus Day

This is a movable event. See note on page xxvi.

The identity of the first Europeans to visit the shores of America is uncertain. The Irish may have reached what is now Canada in the 9th or 10th century, and two Norse sagas report that Leif Ericson (see October 9), son of Eric the Red, reached Vinland, an area of wild grapes and self-sown wheat located west of Greenland, about 1000 A.D. But if the Irish or the Norse were the first Europeans to set foot in the Americas, neither had any lasting impact on the land or its natives. It was only with the voyage of Christopher Columbus in 1492 that effective European exploration and colonization of the New World commenced.

Little is known about the commander of the momentous 1492 expedition. Most historians believe Christopher Columbus, or, in Italian, Christoforo Colombo, was born in Genoa in 1451. His father, Domenico Colombo, was a weaver, and the future navigator may have followed his father's trade during his youth. He very likely went to sea sometime around 1472.

Columbus arrived in Portugal in 1476 after narrowly escaping death during a naval battle. The young seaman made a number of voyages under the Portuguese flag during the following years and visited England, the African Gold Coast, the Madeira Islands, and the Azores. In 1479 or 1480 he married Felipa de Perestrello, the daughter of the captain of Porto Santo, one of the Madeiras.

Unfortunately, Portugal failed to offer Columbus support for his most daring venture. Like many mariners of his time, Columbus dreamed of gaining fame and wealth by finding a water route to the Orient. In 1484 he asked King João II of Portugal to provide financial backing for his plan to reach the East Indies by sailing west. The king refused.

Most educated persons of the 15th century believed the earth to be round and accepted Columbus's plan as theoretically possible. Nevertheless, the best geographers correctly calculated that 10,000 miles lay between Europe and the East Indies, and few were convinced that ships could successfully complete so arduous a voyage. Columbus disagreed, claiming that only 2,400 miles separated the continents, and his gross underestimation was the source of much of his self-confidence and courage.

For years Columbus was unable to obtain financial support for his adventurous undertaking. Then, in 1492, King Ferdinand and Queen Isabella of Spain agreed to sponsor his voyage. The Spanish monarchs met all of Columbus's demands: they provided him with three ships, named him Admiral of the Ocean Sea, and appointed him viceroy of any territory he might discover. On August 3, 1492, Columbus and his 90-member crew sailed from Palos, Spain, aboard the *Niña*, the *Pinta*, and the *Santa María*. They carried with them a letter from Ferdinand and Isabella addressed to the Grand Khan of China.

Columbus's transatlantic crossing was relatively easy. From Spain his three ships sailed to the Canary Islands, off the coast of Africa. There they took on additional provisions and on September 6 began their voyage west. At first the northeast trade winds wafted the caravels briskly along, but then unfavorable breezes and calms slowed their progress. For more than a month the vessels sailed, almost 2,700 miles, without sighting land. The sailors became mutinous, and in early October they tried to persuade Columbus to turn back. The commander remained steadfast, vowing that he would continue the voyage until, with God's help, he found the Indies.

The expedition maintained its westward course, and within a few days Columbus believed he had accomplished his purpose. At 2:00 A.M.

on October 12, one of the lookouts on the *Pinta* spotted land — probably the island of San Salvador (also named Watling or Watlings Island) in the Bahamas. Later the same morning, Columbus and his captains went ashore. Columbus — who reported that the natives called the island Guanahani — gave it the name of San Salvador. He also planted a cross there — as a symbol, he later explained to Ferdinand and Isabella, "that Your Highnesses hold the land for your own."

Believing he had reached the East Indies, Columbus called the inhabitants of San Salvador "Indians." The aborigines Columbus encountered were, in fact, members of the Arawak tribe, and although they lacked the gold and riches the European adventurers craved, they were peaceful and helpful. Several learned to speak Spanish and served as guides during the remainder of the voyage.

After exploring the Bahamas for several weeks, the expedition arrived in Cuba on October 27. On that island, the crew members were amazed to see "many people with a firebrand in the hand . . . to drink the smoke thereof," but were disappointed in their hopes of finding gold and the other reported treasures of the Orient. Columbus and his men left Cuba on December 5, and on the following day they reached the island of Hispaniola (still referred to as Santo Domingo, its name in Spanish colonial days), which today comprises Haiti and the Dominican Republic. They remained there for more than a month, and after the wreck of the *Santa María* on a reef off the island on December 25, they established a trading-post colony, which they named Navidad.

Leaving a contingent behind at Navidad, the *Niña* and the *Pinta* began the return voyage to Spain on January 16, 1493. Two severe storms battered the vessels on the long trip, but, after stops at the Azores and Lisbon, the ships finally arrived at their home port of Palos, Spain, on March 15. Columbus, having dispatched from Lisbon a letter telling Ferdinand and Isabella of his discovery of the "Indies," was invited to proceed without delay to the Spanish court at Barcelona, where he received an enthusiastic welcome.

Columbus made three more voyages to the New World. He visited Trinidad, Puerto Rico, Martinique, and Panama. But his failure to find gold or silver in any of these places caused the Spanish monarchs to lose interest in his expeditions. He spent the last years of his life in relative obscurity. He died in Valladolid, Spain, on May 21, 1506, still believing he had discovered a new route to the Orient.

Interred first in Spain, Columbus's body was transferred around 1540 to a crypt in the cathedral at Santo Domingo, capital of the Dominican Republic. In the centuries that followed, the remains of the explorer were supposedly redeposited, first in Havana and then in Seville. In 1877, however, a casket was found in the Santo Domingo cathedral with an inscription indicating that it contained Columbus's bones. The authenticity of this find was never established, but in 1892 a monument was erected in the cathedral. Both Santo Domingo and Seville claim the honor of being the burial place. Santo Domingo is said to be the oldest continuous European settlement in the Americas.

The landing of Columbus was not only a great feat but an event that was to change the history of the world. Italy and Spain take just pride in his accomplishment, and observances of the October 12 anniversary are widespread in both countries. Churches hold special religious services, and, in a lighter vein, fireworks displays and festivals also are frequently held. Some areas annually sponsor special reenactments.

Almost all of the nations in the Western Hemisphere mark the anniversary of Columbus's landing in the New World. The Spanish-speaking countries hold religious exercises and festivals, and, like Spain, at least one of them — Mexico — honors Columbus as part of the celebration of Día de la Raza, or Day of the Race. North of the Rio Grande, commemorations tend to have a more secular and sometimes also a political tone.

The first observance of October 12 to take place in the United States occurred in New York City in 1792. That year the Society of St. Tammany (also known as the Columbian Order) sponsored a dinner and organized elaborate ceremonies for the 300th anniversary of Columbus's voyage. As part of the decorations for the event, the society erected a monument in its headquarters. It was only a temporary structure, but it is generally believed to have been the first memorial raised to Columbus in this country.

The 1792 observance attracted only limited interest, and little, if any, notice of October 12 was taken in the United States during the century that followed. However, in 1892 the nation readied a massive celebration to honor Columbus on the 400th anniversary of his landing at San Salvador. President Benjamin Harrison issued a proclamation calling upon citizens to participate in commemorative services and requested schools to organize programs. The American people responded enthusiastically, and many localities sponsored special festivities. Unfortunately, preparations for this country's greatest tribute to the discoverer, the Columbian Exposition, were not completed by 1892; it was not until the summer of 1893 that the gates of the great fair opened in Chicago. The celebration held at the exposition on October 12 of that year was the most elaborate arranged up to that time.

During the first decade of the 20th century, the Knights of Columbus (a Roman Catholic society for men founded in 1882) repeatedly urged state legislatures to declare October 12 a legal holiday. In 1905 the governor of Colorado issued a proclamation calling on the people of the state to commemorate the day and the next year the mayor of Chicago made a similar request of the residents of that city. But it was not until 1909 that New York became the first state to pass legislation declaring Columbus Day a holiday. Elaborate festivities marked New York's 1909 celebration of October 12. The crews of two Italian cruisers joined more than 60 Italian-American societies in a parade, and then Governor Charles Evans Hughes addressed the Knights of Columbus and others in Carnegie Hall.

Within a few years other states followed New York's lead, and October 12 became a legal holiday in more than 30 states. Not all refer to it as Columbus Day, however: the anniversary is known as Landing Day in Wisconsin and as Discovery Day in North Dakota and Indiana; and it is celebrated in conjunction with Farmers' Day in Florida and with Fraternal Day in Alabama. For many years American presidents proclaimed October 12 as Columbus Day, but in 1968 President Lyndon B. Johnson signed a law designating the day as a federal holiday for the first time and setting the day of its observance as the second Monday in October in accordance with the new federal policy of scheduling three-day weekends. The legislation, which became operative in 1971, affects only District of Columbia employees and residents and federal employees, but many states have amended their holiday laws so that they conform.

Celebrations of Columbus Day in the United States are countless. Most localities sponsor special programs to mark the day, and virtually every school holds exercises on the day. Parades, patriotic ceremonies, and addresses are popular ways of honoring Columbus.

In New York City, a mammoth parade up Fifth Avenue has become a Columbus Day tradition. Over 100,000 persons, including Italian-American groups and members of the Knights of Columbus, customarily participate in this event. Local, state, and even national political leaders and candidates generally march in or review the procession, and later in the evening they attend a Columbus Day dinner in one of the city's larger hotels.

In Boston October 12 ceremonies usually begin with a Columbus Day anniversary mass. After this, municipal officials lay a wreath at the foot of the statue of Columbus in Louisburg Square. They then join the bands, veterans groups, military units, and other participants in the city's annual Columbus Day parade. The line of march, which has numbered as many as 8,000, proceeds along a four-mile route from the city's Back Bay section to the North End. As in New York, politicians play a prominent part in the event.

Each year Asbury Park, New Jersey, sponsors a pageant depicting the landing of Columbus on the Sunday nearest October 12. As municipal bands play suitable music, the program opens with Columbus — portrayed by a city employee — disembarking from a longboat. "Indians" emerge from the simulated village set up on the beach and welcome the explorer. Then the mayor addresses the assembly, a member of the local Sons of Italy lodge lays a wreath at a bust of Columbus, and sometimes a representative of the Italian government speaks.

In Los Angeles, the flag of Italy flies over the city hall on October 12, and an Italian movie star usually participates in the flag-raising ceremonies. To the north, the annual Columbus Day parade and the Festa Italiana are held in San Francisco to commemorate the discovery of the New World. On the weekend preceding or following October 12, San Francisco also stages such events as a pageant depicting the coronation of Queen Isabella, a waterfront cavalcade representing highlights of Columbus's life, and the North Beach Street Fair. Also included in a typical schedule of activities are ceremonies at the statue of Columbus on Telegraph Hill, a Columbus Day banquet, and a ball.

The numerous observances of Columbus Day are only part of the tribute this nation has paid to the explorer. The federal capital district, many cities and towns, and a major university bear his name. Poetically and symbolically, the appellation Columbia is used to refer to America or the United States, and a classically draped female figure, similarly named, provides visual representation.

Statues honoring Christopher Columbus adorn many localities. A few of the more noteworthy are the likenesses in Fairmont Park, Philadelphia, which Italian residents of the city financed in 1876; the towering figure in New York City's Columbus Circle; and the 20-foot-high, 7,000-pound bronze statue that the city of Genoa presented to Columbus, Ohio, in 1954. In the last-named city, the annual Columbus Day celebration is a four-day observance with a parade, fireworks, and varied entertainment.

Most of the areas of the New World that Columbus explored are today under the control of other nations, but Columbus disembarked in at least one place where the flag of the United States now flies. On his second voyage he went ashore at St. Croix in the Virgin Islands. The spot where he is believed to have stepped ashore is known as the Columbus Landing Site and is situated four miles west of Christiansted. The government of the Virgin Islands owns the five acres where Fort Sale once stood, and the remainder of the area is privately owned.

University of North Carolina Day

University Day is a traditional observance on October 12 each year at the University of North Carolina, at Chapel Hill. The celebration commemorates the laying of the cornerstone of Old East, the first building, on October 12, 1793. Provided for in the state constitution of 1776, the university was chartered in 1789 and formally opened, as the first state university in the United States, in 1795.

The ceremonies have varied from year to year. One of the past features was a short pageant depicting the laying of the cornerstone. More recently the day has been observed by an assembly of students, a faculty procession, and a speech by some person of note. Speakers have included President Nathan M. Pusey of Harvard, President Robert F. Goheen of Princeton, and President John F. Kennedy. As a part of the annual program there is a responsive reading and a moment of silence in memory of alumni who have died since the previous anniversary.

An account of the proceedings on October 12, 1793, when the cornerstone of the building now known as Old East was laid, records that a long procession marched toward the site previously selected by a board of commissioners. The charter provided that the site not be within five miles of the permanent seat of government or any courthouse, a prohibition occasioned by earlier rowdyism during court week. Among the many localities considered, Chapel Hill appeared the most suitable and was eventually chosen, in part for the donations of land offered, totaling nearly 1,200 acres, and in part for its accessibility at the crossing of the "great roads" from Petersburg to Pittsboro, and from New Bern toward Greensboro and Salisbury. A chapel of the Church of England stood at the northeast corner of the crossroads, which was situated on a plateau, and from this place derived the name Chapel Hill. The plateau was covered with primeval forest except for small clearings and a narrow branch road, along which marched the body of distinguished and public-spirited sponsors, attended by a large crowd. The orator of the day, Dr. Samuel E. McCorkle, was one of the most noted

educators of his time and a member of the first board of trustees of the new university.

During its early years, the institution struggled with both penury and the condition of lawlessness then rife in the region. Judge Archibald Murphy, one of the first students and later a professor at the university, reported in 1827 that before the University of North Carolina came into existence there were not more than three schools in the entire state at which the rudiments of a classical education could be acquired. Libraries were practically nonexistent except as the private property of a few professional men. The first class to be graduated contained only 7 students; however, by 1858 a class of 96 was graduated and, after the setback of the Civil War, the university resumed a slow but steady growth.

The university is situated on a campus of over 600 acres and has a plant with a value of approximately $100 million. The library contains over a million bound volumes.

Other branches consolidated with the University of North Carolina, by act of the state legislature in 1931, are two formerly separate institutions now known as the North Carolina State College of Agriculture and Engineering at Raleigh, established in 1887, and Woman's College of the University of North Carolina at Greensboro, founded in 1891. Of more recent vintage are the University of North Carolina at Charlotte, established in 1946, and the also affiliated Baston Technical Institute in Gastonia, 1952. Together the several branches have an enrollment of over 100,000 students.

OCTOBER 13

White House Cornerstone Laid

In 1790 the US Congress rejected the established urban centers of New York and Philadelphia as locations for the permanent seat of government and instead chose to express the youth of its nationhood by placing the federal capital in a new city. Although the site chosen for this massive undertaking was a rather bleak and unpromising stretch of land along the Potomac River, Congress determined to transform the area into a metropolis. To insure the success of this project, nothing was left to chance. Congress selected the outstanding French engineer Pierre Charles L'Enfant to superintend the overall design of the city, and it announced an open competition in which other architects were invited to submit plans for the Capitol and the President's home.

The design of the Chief Executive's house

captured the imagination of many; even Secretary of State Thomas Jefferson submitted a plan. From numerous entries, Congress selected that of James Hoban, an Irish architect living in Charleston, South Carolina. Hoban envisioned the presidential mansion as a Georgian country seat. His winning design featured a hipped roof, balustrade, and alternating window arches — characteristics typical of the Palladian architectural style then enjoying widespread popularity in Europe.

The cornerstone of the presidential residence was laid on October 13, 1792, thereby making it the first federal structure in the national capital. Initial plans called for its completion within eight years, so that it would be ready when the government relocated to Washington in 1800. This deadline was not met, however, and the building was still unfinished when it received its first occupant, President John Adams, on November 1, 1800. The primitive condition of his new living quarters does not seem to have unduly dismayed Adams. Only one day after he moved in he wrote to his wife, Abigail, the inspiring words that President Franklin Delano Roosevelt later ordered carved on the mantel of the State Dining Room:

I pray Heaven to bestow the best of Blessings on this House and all that shall hereafter inhabit it. May none but honest and wise Men ever rule under this roof.

Every President of the United States since Adams has occupied the residence at 1600 Pennsylvania Avenue. Since then, the building itself has undergone a considerable transformation. Only a few years after its completion, the entire interior of the house was destroyed when the British burned Washington on August 24, 1814. Reconstruction of the White House began immediately under the supervision of its designer, Hoban, and the building was again ready for occupancy in 1816. The South Portico was added in 1824, the North in 1829; and throughout the remainder of the 19th century, various Presidents altered the house to suit their personal preferences and the changing styles of the times.

The presidential mansion assumed its present appearance during the administration of Theodore Roosevelt. Commissioned by him in 1902, the famed architectural firm of McKim, Mead, and White rid the building of the Victorian trappings so favored by the late 19th century Presidents and renovated the house in the French classical style. They relieved its overcrowded condition with the addition of the West Wing, which houses various executive offices that had previously occupied space in the original struc-

ture. But the administration's influence on the building was not only architectural: in 1902 Roosevelt also made its popular name, the White House, the official designation of the President's home.

Structural weaknesses necessitated a total renovation of the White House in 1948. In the course of this four-year project, the entire interior of the building was removed, and a new basement and foundation were constructed under its original walls. The interior was then reinstalled with only one major deviation from the 1902 design: the main stairway was redirected from the Main Hall into the Entrance Hall.

Although more than a million visitors tour the public rooms of the White House each year, it is only within recent times that adequate attention has been paid to their furnishings. In 1961 Jacqueline Kennedy, wife of President John F. Kennedy, created two committees to select appropriate furnishings and paintings to grace the historic building. The work of these committees beautified the house immeasurably. The committees acquired numerous antiques to supplement the pieces that were originally purchased for the White House. In particular, they sought items dating from the early 19th century, since very few things associated with the presidential mansion during that era have survived. Substantial additions have also been made to the White House Art Collection so that it now includes works representative of every genre of American painting. But its most prized possession still remains the Gilbert Stuart portrait of George Washington — saved from the advancing British by Dolley Madison in 1814 and now hanging in the East Room. This is the only object that has been in the house since the time of its first occupancy in 1800.

OCTOBER 14

Dwight David Eisenhower's Birthday

Dwight David Eisenhower, who won his place in history on the battlefields of Europe and in the White House of the United States, personified for many the best aspects of the American tradition. The general and president was descended from a family that traces its lineage back to the colonial period. The victims of religious persecution in their native Catholic Bavaria, Eisenhower's forebears emigrated to America in the early 1730s. They settled on the Susquehanna River near Harrisburg, Pennsylvania, in 1732 and there helped organize the branch of the pietist Mennonite sect that became known as the River Brethren. A plain, hardworking people, the Eisenhowers remained among the Brethren in the Pennsylvania Dutch region for almost a century and a half.

The lure of the West, however, proved to be an irresistible attraction for the Reverend Jacob Eisenhower and his family, who in 1878, together with other members of the River Brethren, moved to Kansas. The Eisenhowers settled on a 160-acre farm in Abilene, and shortly after their arrival, their son, David, met Ida Elizabeth Stover. In 1885 the couple was married in the United Brethren Church in Lecompton, Kansas.

After several business failures in Abilene, David Eisenhower took his wife and two young sons to Texas. He found employment as a mechanic in the Cotton Belt Railroad shops at Denison, and there, only a short distance from the railroad yards, his third son was born on October 14, 1890. Christened David Dwight Eisenhower, he was known instead as Dwight David Eisenhower in accordance with the wish of his mother, who wanted to distinguish her son from his father and spare him the nickname Dave.

In 1892 the Eisenhowers returned to Abilene. Their life-style was typical of that enjoyed by numerous other midwesterners at the turn of the century. David Eisenhower supported his growing family by working in a local creamery; his six sons attended nearby schools and helped their mother care for their small vegetable garden and their chickens. It was a happy household, strongly influenced by the strict religious training the elder Eisenhower imparted to his sons.

Although Dwight Eisenhower, or Ike, as he became widely known, did well in high school, he graduated with no definite plans regarding his future. For a year, he held several odd jobs, including a brief stint as a semiprofessional baseball player. But not until he took the competitive examinations for the service academies — West Point and Annapolis — did he exhibit a real enthusiasm for his undertakings.

At the time, young Eisenhower would have preferred to attend Annapolis, and, indeed, he finished first in the examination for that school. However, shortly after he received the appointment to the academy, he discovered that he would be several months beyond the age limit at the start of the next academic year. But the candidate who had placed first in the competition for West Point turned down his appointment, and Eisenhower, who had been second, was selected to fill the vacancy.

On July 1, 1911, Eisenhower began his studies at West Point. At first it seemed as though athletics rather than the military might be the young cadet's calling. He earned his varsity letter in both baseball and football, and, until a knee injury ended his football career, many considered him one of the most promising backs in the East. His academic record was less distinguished: at graduation Eisenhower placed 61st in a class of 164. But the Class of 1915 was not composed of mediocre students: 59 of its members became generals, earning a total of 111 stars, and it is remembered as "the class the stars fell on."

Commissioned a second lieutenant in June 1915, Eisenhower began his active military career with the 19th Infantry Regiment at Fort Sam Houston in San Antonio, Texas. During his first tour of duty in Texas, he met Mamie Geneva Doud. After a brief courtship, they were married on July 1, 1916, at her parents' home in Denver, Colorado.

Eisenhower did not participate in the actual fighting in World War I. During the first year after the United States entered the conflict in April 1917, he held several minor posts at army installations in the United States. His real contribution to the war effort came in 1918, when the 28-year-old captain took command of the Camp Colt tank training center at Gettysburg, Pennsylvania. His assignment was to instruct the soldiers in the methods of tank warfare. This was not an easy task, since the tank had not been used in actual combat prior to World War I. But the extent of Eisenhower's success in achieving his purpose can be gauged from the fact that he received the Distinguished Service Medal for his "unusual zeal, foresight, and marked administrative ability in the organization, training, and preparation for overseas service of technical troops of the Tank Corps."

In 1920 Eisenhower, who had advanced to the temporary rank of lieutenant colonel during the war, received the permanent commission of major. During the next five years he competently performed routine peacetime assignments in this country and in the Panama Canal Zone, but not until 1925 did he really begin to distinguish himself. In August of that year the army selected 275 officers, including Eisenhower, for training at its Command and General Staff School at Fort Leavenworth. Eisenhower excelled at the school; in fact, the following June he graduated at the top of the class.

Although there was no doubt of Eisenhower's superior ability for military organization after 1926, there was little demand for such talents during the isolationist 1920s. The United States, which had just finished fighting "the war to end war," showed a keener interest in honoring the memory of the soldiers who had sacrificed their lives in World War I than in maintaining the nation's military preparedness. And Eisenhower's next major assignment reflected the country's preoccupation: from 1927 to 1929 – except for the brief period when he attended the Army War College – he served with the American Battle Monuments Commission, preparing a guide to American battlefields in France.

Eisenhower served as assistant executive officer to the assistant secretary of war from 1929 to 1933. During that time he helped establish the Army Industrial College and drafted a plan for industrial mobilization in time of war. The latter work came to the attention of the chief of staff of the army, General Douglas MacArthur, and so impressed him that in February 1933 he appointed Eisenhower the senior aide on his personal staff. Moreover, two years later, when MacArthur went to the Philippine Islands as military adviser to the new commonwealth, Eisenhower accompanied him as senior military assistant.

Returning to the United States in 1939, Eisenhower, who had been commissioned a lieutenant colonel in 1936, rapidly advanced as the country mobilized for possible entry into what was soon to be known as World War II, then being waged in Europe between the Axis powers led by the Nazi Germany of Adolf Hitler and the Allied nations headed by Britain and France. In March 1941 he won the rank of temporary colonel, and three months later he was named chief of staff for the Third Army. This body engaged in the extensive war games that took place in Louisiana during the early fall of 1941, and Eisenhower's leadership throughout the greatest peacetime "war" in history was so outstanding that one reporter wrote: "His work in those maneuvers was brilliant, so much so that he was noted and marked for future use by General George C. Marshall, Chief of Staff." On September 29, 1941, Eisenhower was promoted to the temporary rank of brigadier general.

Eisenhower's career was changed abruptly when Japan, Germany's Far Eastern ally, bombed the US naval base at Pearl Harbor, Hawaii, on December 7, 1941, precipitating US entry into World War II. A week later Marshall ordered Eisenhower to Washington, D.C. Throughout the spring of 1942, he held several key organizational positions. Although Eisenhower had never led troops in combat, he so impressed the Washington authorities with his abilities and tact in carrying out his assignments that on June 25, 1942, Marshall named him commanding general of US forces in the European Theater of Operations with the temporary rank of lieutenant general.

Eisenhower arrived at his headquarters in London in July 1942 and almost immediately began preparations for the Allied invasion of North Africa. One of his major tasks during the months of planning and combat that followed was to conciliate the various Allied officers participating in the project. Under such trying circumstances, the general's personal charm and genuine friendliness proved to be one of his greatest assets, and, apart from a few abrasive incidents, Eisenhower managed to promote harmony among British, French, and American military leaders.

Named Allied commander in chief, North Africa, on August 14, 1942, Eisenhower in November moved his headquarters to Algiers, where he directed operations against the German general Erwin Rommel and his Afrika Korps. The battle of North Africa was hard-fought. The Allies suffered several critical reverses during the initial months of fighting, and not until February 1943 did the tide turn. From that point on, however, the Allies gradually gained control. By the following May 13, the German and Italian troops in Tunisia had surrendered, and the conflict had officially ended. Eisenhower had won his first military campaign.

Eisenhower next turned his attention to the other side of the Mediterranean. He directed the amphibious attack on Sicily in July 1943, which led to its surrender the following month. He also prepared for and directed the early stages of the invasion of Italy. This operation remained necessary even after Allied successes in Africa and Sicily, coupled with the imminent invasion, resulted in the deposition of Hitler's ally Benito Mussolini, the Fascist leader of Italy, and led to the surrender of Italy on September 3, 1943.

Though the surrender officially removed the southern partner of the Berlin-Rome Axis from the conflict and increasingly made it possible for Italian anti-Fascists to offer the Allies assistance, it did not remove the German troops, who immediately took control of Italy. On the same day that Italy surrendered, therefore, Allied landings commenced in the "toe" of Italy. They were followed, six days later, by other landings in the Gulf of Salerno; and then by two months during which the Allies advanced to the German's well-fortified Gustav Line, above Naples.

The liberation of Italy was a long, painful process that lasted throughout 1944 and into the spring of 1945. Eisenhower, meanwhile, had other tasks to perform. His most important contribution to the war effort was yet to come, and, as he first learned privately on December 10, 1943, it would take him far north of Italy – where he would be succeeded as supreme Allied commander by a British officer, General Sir Henry Maitland Wilson.

On Christmas Eve 1943 President Franklin D. Roosevelt made public Eisenhower's new assignment: he had been selected as supreme commander of the Allied Expeditionary Forces then preparing to invade Nazi Germany's Fortress Europe. In making the announcement, Roosevelt noted: "The performances in Africa, Sicily, and Italy have been brilliant. He knows by practical and successful experience the way to coordinate air, sea, and land power." The President did not overstate Eisenhower's qualifications, and a successful invasion of Western Europe required just such a leader.

D day, in 1944 (see June 6), proved to be one of the most important days of Eisenhower's life. Although weather conditions were far from perfect — an approaching storm had already delayed the operation that had originally been scheduled for the previous day — Eisenhower decided to proceed with the invasion. His judgment proved correct. Eisenhower encouraged the soldiers with stirring words: "You are about to embark on a great crusade." Then a vast fleet carried the thousands of Allied troops across the English Channel to northern France. This amphibious landing, combined with a heavy air attack, caught the enemy off guard, and, after hours of bitter fighting, the Allies established several crucial beachheads in German-occupied Normandy.

Securing these footholds in France allowed the Allied campaign against the Axis to accelerate. By the end of August 1944, Paris had been liberated, and within another month German control of southern France also had ended. The Allied cause suffered a setback when Nazi troops briefly rallied at the Battle of the Bulge in December 1944. But this was to be Hitler's last major counterattack. By February 1945 the Allied forces had resumed their offensive. In March they entered Germany, and at 2:41 A.M. on May 7, 1945, General Alfred Jodl of the German army unconditionally surrendered at Eisenhower's headquarters in a schoolhouse at Reims, France. The next day, May 8, when the surrender became effective, was celebrated as V-E — Victory in Europe — Day (see May 8).

In recognition of his services in defeating the Nazis, many countries bestowed honors upon Eisenhower. Premier Joseph Stalin invited him to Moscow to present him with the Order of Victory, the USSR's highest award, and the Order of Suvarov, the nation's highest military decoration. In Paris, General Charles de Gaulle hailed Eisenhower as a Fellow of the Liberation, and the French government awarded him the Cross of Liberation. At Buckingham Palace, King George VI expressed Britain's gratitude by investing the general with the Order of Merit, and the city of London added its thanks by giving him the Freedom of the City of London. Many other nations also paid tribute to his achievements.

When Eisenhower returned to the United States in June 1945, more than a million persons lined the streets of Washington, D.C., to catch a glimpse of their hero; a joint session of Congress praised him; and President Harry S. Truman awarded him his second Oak Leaf Cluster and a citation that read:

In accomplishing this great victory, his modesty, his impartiality, and his sound judgment, together with his great abilities as a soldier and a diplomat, have won the confidence and admiration of the American people.

The largest outpouring of popular feeling occurred in New York City, where an estimated 4 million spectators viewed the ticker-tape parade honoring Eisenhower. Less massive celebrations held elsewhere throughout the country were no less heartfelt. For example, elaborate ceremonies greeted the general when he returned to his alma mater, West Point; and Denison, Texas, and Abilene, Kansas, honored him by purchasing, respectively, his birthplace and the site of his family's home.

In the late summer of 1945 Eisenhower returned to Germany, where he assumed his duties as commander of the US occupation forces and as military governor of the zone occupied by the United States. His stay was brief. On November 20, 1945, President Truman ordered his recall, and named him to succeed General Marshall as the army's chief of staff. Eisenhower held this position until his resignation on February 7, 1948. Three months later, the five-star General of the Army — he had attained this highest rank on April 11, 1946 — retired from the armed services.

The American citizenry has a long tradition of proposing its great military heroes for the presidency, and Eisenhower was no exception. As the 1948 presidential election approached, he was sought out as a presidential nominee by both the Democratic and the Republican parties. He expressed no interest, however, declaring: "I am not available for and could not accept nomination for high public office."

Eisenhower instead became the president of Columbia University on June 7, 1948. His background was ill suited for this role, and many observers believed that his talents could be more fruitfully employed elsewhere. Authorities in Washington, including President Truman, apparently agreed. At their request, Eisenhower took a leave of absence from the university to serve as the temporary chairman of the Joint Chiefs of Staff. He then permanently resigned his university post in 1950 to assume command of the military forces of the newly created North Atlantic Treaty Organization (NATO).

From 1950 to 1952 Eisenhower labored to strengthen the military defenses of Western Europe against the possibility of future Communist aggression. Meanwhile, Republican leaders in the United States, convinced that the general's candidacy would give their party its best chance for success in the 1952 presidential election, waged a two-year campaign to persuade the general to accept the nomination. Finally, on January 7, 1952, Eisenhower agreed to consent, if he heard a "clear-cut call to political duty."

Eisenhower's chief rival for the Republican nomination was the widely respected Senator Robert A. Taft of Ohio, popularly identified as Mr. Republican. Known for his conservative policies, Taft had strong support when the Republican delegates convened in July 1952. But Eisenhower's backers were determined to win the nomination for their more moderate candidate. Under the leadership of New York's Governor Thomas E. Dewey, they managed to swing several key delegations to Eisenhower, and with these crucial votes the general won the nomination after only one ballot. As the party's vice presidential candidate, the convention then approved Eisenhower's choice of Richard Milhous Nixon, then a California senator.

The personalities of the two major candidates for the presidency in 1952 could not have been more different. The American people responded warmly to Eisenhower's infectious grin, and they eagerly voiced cries of "I Like Ike" throughout the country. Their reaction to his Democratic rival, the governor of Illinois, Adlai E. Stevenson, was more reserved. Stevenson's aloof manner and his reputation as an intellectual aroused little popular enthusiasm. On election day, these personality differences and the country's desire to end the Democrats' 20-year tenure of the White House resulted in an overwhelming victory for Eisenhower. The former general won almost 34 million popular votes and 442 votes in the electoral college. His opponent received only 27.3 million popular votes and 89 electoral votes.

Even before his inauguration Eisenhower fulfilled one campaign promise. The Truman administration's inability to extricate the country from the highly unpopular Korean conflict was perhaps the Democrats' greatest political liability. Eisenhower had taken advantage of this situation. Speaking in Detroit on October 24, 1952, he had pledged that, if elected, he would go personally to the combat area before the following January. The President-elect was true to his word; during a tour of Southeast Asia in early December 1952, he spent three days on the battlefields of Korea.

Most military experts attribute the July 27, 1953, armistice, which ended the fighting in Korea, to the change of presidential administrations rather than to Eisenhower's personal diplomatic efforts. But that his action had a tremendous psychological effect on the American people cannot be denied. In the early 1950s American citizens were increasingly confused by their inability to control their nation's postwar destiny; Eisenhower's apparent success in Korea gave them increased confidence in the ability of their new Chief Executive to guide the country through a period of international uncertainty.

On January 20, 1953, Dwight David Eisenhower became the 34th President of the United States. His first term in office witnessed a general relaxation of tension in both domestic and foreign affairs. Although the conclusion of the war in Korea was the outstanding achievement of his first administration, other policies and actions were also noteworthy, among them his designation of Earl Warren as the nation's 14th chief justice, an appointment that was to have far-reaching consequences. Prior to Eisenhower's election, many of his critics had argued that selection of the Republican presidential candidate would mean the country's return to isolationism in world affairs and the end of social welfare legislation at home. However, Eisenhower's years in office proved that these fears were ill-founded. Eisenhower curtailed neither international involvements nor social welfare programs. In fact he extended American participation in both areas: Eisenhower's "Atoms for Peace" proposals of 1953 and his "open-skies inspection" program in 1956 were important steps toward global cooperation; his sponsorship of wider social security benefits and increased minimum-wage requirements substantially advanced the social legislation begun under the New Deal of Franklin D. Roosevelt and the Fair Deal of Harry S. Truman.

Although the President had suffered a heart attack in September 1955 and underwent major intestinal surgery the following June, his doctors declared him physically fit to seek reelection in 1956. The Democrats again nominated Stevenson for President, but his campaign in 1956 was no more successful than it had been in 1952. Under Eisenhower's leadership the American people had enjoyed four years of peace and prosperity, and they did not forget this on election day. They gave Eisenhower 35.5 million popular votes — until then the largest number ever won by any presidential candidate — and 457 electoral votes. Stevenson won only 26 million popular votes and 73 votes in the electoral college.

Eisenhower's second term was fraught with crises. The South resisted the Supreme Court's 1954 order to integrate its schools; the national economy entered a three-year recession; the Soviet Union orbited Sputnik I, the first artificial earth satellite; and the Russians captured an American U-2 reconnaissance plane in the act of violating Soviet airspace. Confronted with these great problems, Eisenhower's reaction was not passive. In 1957 he sent federal troops to Little Rock, Arkansas, to force compliance with the Supreme Court's desegregation order, and signed the first Civil Rights Act since Reconstruction (see May 17). In February 1958 he announced the launching of a small American satellite; and shortly after the U-2 incident in 1960, he promised to end this country's espionage flights. But to many Americans these efforts represented only stopgap measures. Eisenhower failed to commit himself publicly to integration as a moral necessity; his attempts to restore the nation's prosperity were ineffective; and he could neither quiet American fears regarding the country's so-called space lag nor repair the damage done to US-Soviet relations by U-2 flights.

He did, however, issue a warning that would be often quoted with increasing urgency throughout the next decade, that would give him a reputation for prescience, and that was all the more remarkable for being voiced by a military man. In the warning, issued just before he left the White House, and before the country had become deeply involved in the unpopular war in Vietnam, which claimed much industrial output during the late 1960s, he spoke of something "new in the American experience" — the "conjunction of an immense military establishment and a large arms industry." Said Eisenhower:

We recognize the imperative need for this development. Yet we must not fail to comprehend its grave implication. . . . In the councils of government, we must guard against the acquisition of unwarranted influence, whether sought or unsought, by the military-industrial complex. The potential for the disastrous rise of misplaced power exists and will persist.

Immediately after the inauguration of John F. Kennedy as President, in January 1961, Eisenhower took up residence at his 230-acre farm in Gettysburg, Pennsylvania. In March 1961 Congress restored his rank of General of the Army, and after that date he preferred to be addressed by his military title. He enjoyed an active retirement, spending much time at his office at nearby Gettysburg College. There he prepared his two-volume memoirs, *The White House Years;* compiled a series of personal anecdotes, *At Ease: Stories I Tell My Friends;* prepared numerous speeches for delivery at Republican gatherings; and responded to calls for advice from his suc-

cessors, Presidents Kennedy and Lyndon B. Johnson. He also found time for his two favorite hobbies, golf and painting.

Poor health plagued Eisenhower after 1965. He suffered two heart attacks in that year, underwent surgery to correct a gall-bladder condition in 1966, and required hospitalization for stomach and prostate gland ailments in 1967. On May 14, 1968, he entered Walter Reed Hospital in Washington, D.C., to recuperate from a heart attack that he had suffered a few weeks earlier. During the 10-month stay that followed, the general endured three more heart attacks, repeated episodes of ventricular fibrillation, and surgery for the removal of an intestinal obstruction. The accumulated effect of these illnesses at last took their toll. Dwight David Eisenhower died on March 28, 1969.

The United States paid its respects to Eisenhower in the days following his death. In Washington, D.C., a three-day state funeral honored the fallen leader. The services began on Saturday morning, March 29, when the closed coffin bearing his body was taken to Bethlehem Chapel of the Washington Cathedral for brief ceremonies attended by members of his family and close friends. The public was allowed to pay its last respects throughout the remainder of the day.

The following afternoon a hearse and then a horse-drawn artillery caisson carried Eisenhower's coffin from the cathedral to the Capitol, where eight servicemen bore the casket into the Capitol Rotunda and placed it on the velvet-covered catafalque that had served earlier as the bier for Abraham Lincoln, John F. Kennedy, and Herbert Hoover. At the conclusion of the half-hour ceremony in the Rotunda, the throngs of mourners waiting outside were permitted to enter the great domed chamber. It is estimated that about 55,000 persons, including Eisenhower's World War II comrades Charles de Gaulle, the French president, and Lord Mountbatten of England, filed past the funeral bier during the next 13 hours.

President Richard Nixon proclaimed March 31, 1969, as a national day of mourning. At 4:00 P.M. that day, the coffin containing Eisenhower's body was returned amid highest military honors to the cathedral, where President and Mrs. Nixon, members of the Cabinet and Congress, many US governors and mayors, and 191 dignitaries representing 78 countries were among those who attended the simple Episcopalian-Presbyterian rites. The service, which had been approved by Eisenhower and his family more than a year before, emphasized the Christian belief in eternal life for those who serve God. The coffin was then taken to Washington's Union Station, where it was placed aboard a train for the journey to the Eisenhower Center in Abilene, Kansas. Thousands lined the track as the train proceeded westward. Burial took place on April 2, in the crypt of the chapel at the Eisenhower Center, after religious services and military ceremonies, including a 21-gun salute and the sounding of taps.

Since that time, thousands of tourists have flocked to Abilene to visit the center. After paying their respects, most persons then explore the other three buildings of the center. These are the original Eisenhower family home, a two-story white frame house at 201 Southeast Fourth Street, containing family memorabilia and furnishings from the period of Eisenhower's mother; the library, housing both public displays of historic material and some 16 million pages of official Eisenhower administration papers, which may be seen only on written application to the library's director; and the Eisenhower Center museum, repository for the largest collection on view of items pertaining to Eisenhower's life and career. The nonprofit Eisenhower Foundation maintains the center, which is open to the public.

Eisenhower's 230-acre farm at Gettysburg was deeded on November 27, 1967, to the US government. Although it was designated as the Eisenhower National Historic Site on that same day, the farm was not open to the public during Eisenhower's lifetime. In June 1969 the National Park Service, which administers the area, announced that it would remain closed to the public during Mrs. Eisenhower's lifetime use of the property.

In addition to the places and mementos associated with the life and achievements of Eisenhower, several memorials were specifically planned in his honor. At Johns Hopkins University in Baltimore, the editing of Eisenhower's personal letters and papers began in 1963; five volumes, subtitled *The War Years*, were published in 1970. Other lasting tributes include the Eisenhower Theater of the John F. Kennedy Center for the Performing Arts in Washington, D.C., and Eisenhower College in Seneca Falls, New York — where Eisenhower, at the 1963 ground-breaking ceremonies, defined the liberal arts college as "the key to the understanding and exercise of real citizenship."

OCTOBER 15

Sukkot

This is a movable event. See note on page xxvi.

In the Jewish calendar, the first full day of Sukkot (the Feast of the Tabernacles or Booths), is the 15th day of the lunar month of Tishri (in the course of September or October). Sukkot, like all other Jewish holidays, begins at sundown on the preceding evening. In 1970 the 15th day of Tishri coincided with October 15. The holiday lasts for eight days although only the first two days and last two days are considered full holidays by Orthodox and Conservative Jews. Reform Jews celebrate the first and last days only as full holidays. The last day of Sukkot is called Shemini Atzeret, the Eighth Day of Solemn Assembly. During the Middle Ages a ninth day had the name Simhat Torah, the Rejoicing in the Law. Today Orthodox and Conservative Jews continue to celebrate Simhat Torah as a separate holiday. In Israel Simhat Torah is observed together with Shemini Atzeret on the eighth day of Sukkot. Reform Jews similarly observe Simhat Torah and Shemini Atzeret on the same day (see October 22, Shemini Atzeret).

Although the precise origins are uncertain, it is generally believed that the observance of Sukkot began after the Jews had ended their 40 years of wandering in the wilderness and had entered the Promised Land of Canaan. Sukkot is one of the three great pilgrimage festivals — the others being Pesach (Passover), and Shavuot (the Feast of Weeks) — during which all male Jews were supposed to go to the Temple in Jerusalem. Since Sukkot occurs at the end of the fruit and wine harvest, it was one of the three important harvest festivals in ancient times. In the Bible it is referred to as Hehag, literally "The Festival." Sukkot is one of the many festivals of thanks that predate the first thanksgiving observance of the Pilgrims in New England.

Sukkot is also referred to in the Bible as Hag HaAsif, the Feast of the Ingathering, and as Hag HaSukkot, the Feast of the Booths. These two names reflect the dual quality of the holiday. Although originally it was only a joyous harvest festival — the *zeman simhatenu,* or "time of our rejoicing" — later a historical significance was added to the holiday. The custom of dwelling in booths during Sukkot, though originally probably connected with the harvest, came to commemorate Israel's dwelling in tents during the 40-year wandering in the wilderness. The commandment is given in Leviticus 23:42-43: "Ye shall dwell in booths seven days. . . . That your generations may know that I made the children of Israel to dwell in booths, when I brought them out of the land of Egypt."

According to Jewish teaching the booth, or *sukkah,* used during Sukkot must be built especially for the festival, and so thatched as to be a protection against the sun by day while allowing the stars to shine through at night — so that one can see the heavens and direct one's heart to God. In ancient times the booth served as a dwelling place for the entire seven days, and all males were supposed to live in booths unless prevented by illness or other valid cause. For seven days the booth was his home, and the true house became only a temporary home. The booth's fragility symbolized the brevity and insecurity of all human life and especially the transitory character of Jewish life throughout most of history. The memory of the wandering in the wilderness reminded Jews at this time of thanksgiving of how dependent upon God they were. Even for those who had better harvests than their neighbors — in modern terms this might translate as greater wealth — the command that during Sukkot all Jews should live in booths — which had to conform to certain dimensions — emphasized the equality of all people before God, as in the days in the wilderness.

With the destruction of the second Temple by the Romans in A.D. 70, many of the ancient customs of Sukkot, especially those having to do with the Temple's sacrificial ritual, were abandoned, but the command to dwell in booths remained obligatory. Today, intemperate climate or city congestion may modify custom so that booths are sometimes built indoors. As far as possible, however, the ancient ways are retained. Jews build their booths in their backyards, on their roofs or in the courtyards of synagogues, and at least say a *kiddush*, or blessing, and have something to eat while inside the booths.

The services held in synagogues on Sukkot also retain some of the old customs or customs derived from the older time. The ancient procession around the altar in the Temple, for example, has been replaced by a procession in the synagogue. Members of the congregation carry the "four species" — branches of palm, myrtle, and willow bound together to form a *lulav*, and a citron, called an *etrog*. In addition to the regular weekly Bible reading, the Book of Ecclesiastes is read on Sukkot.

The seventh day of Sukkot is called Hoshana Rabbah (literally "the great hosanna"). A procession is held seven times around in the synagogue on this day. At the end of the procession, willow branches are beaten against the floor, a ritual performed in ancient times in hope of obtaining rain for the coming year. Hoshana Rabbah became an important holiday during the Middle Ages, when it acquired the characteristics of a second Day of Atonement (see October 10, Yom Kippur).

Feast of St. Teresa of Ávila

The Roman Catholic church observes October 15 as the Feast of St. Teresa (or Theresa) of Ávila. Teresa was a Spanish mystic and religious reformer, and — with St. Catherine of Siena — one of the first two women to be declared a Doctor of the Church. That honor came to her in 1970, nearly four centuries after her death.

Born Teresa de Cepeda y Ahumada in Ávila, Spain, on March 28, 1515, she was a natural extrovert and early showed great enthusiasm for religion. When she was seven, she set off with her brother Rodrigo for Moorish territory, where they hoped to be beheaded and thus become martyrs for the faith. Their heroic plans were aborted when an uncle found them on their way out of the city and returned them to their home.

The home was a comfortable one, with well-to-do parents and a large and loving family. When Teresa was 13, however, her mother died, leaving 10 children. The loss affected Teresa deeply.

As a teenager, Teresa was a boarding student for about two years at a convent run by Augustinian nuns. She entered the Carmelite convent of the Incarnation in Ávila on November 2, 1535, and was given the name Sister Teresa of Jesus. Less than two years after receiving the Carmelite habit in 1536, she became ill and had to take temporary leave from the convent. Over a long period that followed, her father took her to various healers; when their attempts failed, he took her home to Ávila in July 1539. On August 15 of that year, she went into a coma so deep that she was feared dead. She revived after four days, but her legs were paralyzed for three years afterwards.

Although Teresa resumed religious life, it seems that her early fervor and enthusiasm left her for the better part of two decades. In her writings, she herself discussed the mediocrity of her spiritual life during this period. Nonetheless, she underwent mystical experiences, including visions.

When she was about 40 years old, Teresa developed a deeper religious feeling and began to look seriously at the lax religious life she was leading, which, indeed, was not exceptional in her convent or in many others. Although there was nothing particularly scandalous or corrupt, Teresa felt that neither was there anything particularly religious about convent life as it was then lived. The convent was in some ways a boardinghouse with a religious overtone. The nuns could keep their property and material wealth, and they could come and go as they pleased.

To Teresa's new way of thinking, the freedom then customary in convents was not conducive to prayer or to spiritual recollection and meditation. There was no restriction on visitors, whose constant presence precluded a serene and prayerful atmosphere. In addition, the nuns had to go to their parents or relatives for their daily meals, since the convent itself supplied only bread. Instead of providing a well-ordered routine, the convent life of the time was disorganized and distracting.

Teresa set about her reforms of religious life

in order to provide the proper atmosphere for spiritual recollection and to make it possible for nuns to lead more prayerful lives. She advocated keeping the communities of religious small, preferring about 21 nuns to each convent; and, accordingly, she favored the building of more small convents, rather than retaining the large convents then prevalent, with 100 or more nuns in each. Many of her reforms were merely a return to the austerities upon which the Carmelite order had originally been based. Other factors she felt to be important were strict poverty, the cloistered life, many hours of daily solitude, and two hours daily of mental prayer, in addition to communal prayers.

At first, Teresa's ideas of reform were not universally popular, and while she could be charming and tactful, her direct, sometimes blunt, manner often antagonized people. Fortunately, she had great courage and a forceful personality. She was able to adapt to different circumstances or somehow manage to have them adapt to her. She showed a great talent for overcoming obstacles when she felt certain that she was right.

Thus, against much opposition, Teresa succeeded in founding her first reformed convent, dedicated to St. Joseph, on August 24, 1562, at Ávila. There, four novices received the habit of the Discalced Carmelites. The word *discalced*, derived from the Latin, means "without shoes"; it is often part of the proper name of religious orders whose members go barefoot or wear sandals, usually as a mark of poverty and an indication of the austerity of the order.

Teresa went on to establish a total of 17 small religious communities, which were scattered throughout Spain. Although her health sometimes failed her, her sense of humor apparently did not. One of the most popular stories told about her concerns her difficult return to Ávila after a particularly arduous trip, undertaken for the greater glory of God. In a driving rainstorm, her carriage struck a rock and was overturned, landing its weary passenger in a great puddle. Wet, muddy, tired, and exasperated, Teresa looked up to heaven and said, "Well, Lord, if this is how you treat your friends, it's no wonder you have so few of them."

It was this down-to-earth practicality in combination with her life of prayer and mysticism that made Teresa the successful and beloved reformer that she was. She was the author of many books, letters, and other writings; and her natural liveliness and spontaneity are apparent in her literary style. The writing earned for Teresa the admiration of popes, founders of religious orders, and other scholars and theologians who unofficially bestowed upon her the title Doctor of

the Church long before the title was made official in 1970. The title Doctor of the Church is conferred upon ecclesiastical writers who have attained great sanctity and whose writings or teachings have benefited the whole Catholic church.

Although her mystical experiences were an important part of her life, Teresa never unduly stressed her spiritual ecstasies and visions. Her writings reveal her own human faults with great forthrightness, humor, and honesty. Her confessors asked her to commit to paper an account of her spiritual experiences. In obedience to them she wrote her *Life* (1562–1565). It was the first and longest of several autobiographical works she produced. Chief among her other writings are *The Interior Castle*, written about 1577, describing the seven stages of mystical prayer, and *The Way of Perfection*, instructing her nuns in the technique of prayer. These three books are considered religious classics.

In 1582 Pope Gregory XIII, in his reform of the calendar, had ordered the suppression of 10 days to rectify calendar errors. According to his plan, October 4, 1582, was followed by October 15, 1582. It was during the night of October 4–15, 1582, that Teresa died at Alba de Tormes, where her body was interred.

On April 24, 1614, she was beatified by Pope Paul V, at which time she was called Blessed Teresa. Three years after her beatification, the Spanish parliament proclaimed her patroness of Spain, bestowing an honor usually reserved for canonized saints. But there was no doubt of Teresa's sanctity. She became St. Teresa on March 12, 1622, when she was canonized by Pope Gregory XV.

Each year on October 15 Ávila holds an enormous celebration in honor of its great saint, with religious services, parades, dances, games, feasts, and with colorful banners, flowers, and other decorations everywhere. Even the community's donkeys are ornamented — with flowers, ribbons, and sometimes straw hats.

Ávila is the capital of the province of Ávila in central Spain, about 65 miles from Madrid. The walled city is considered one of the finest extant examples of European medieval towns. Landmarks associated with St. Teresa include the Convent of the Incarnation and a church built on the site of the house where she was born.

St. Teresa of Ávila is sometimes colloquially referred to as the Big St. Teresa, to distinguish her from St. Teresa of Lisieux (Thérèse de Lisieux), a 19th century French Carmelite nun and author. Unlike St. Teresa of Ávila, St. Thérèse of Lisieux was a quiet person who never left her convent.

OCTOBER 16

Noah Webster's Birthday

Lexicographer, as defined by *Webster's New Collegiate Dictionary*, is "an author or editor of a dictionary." But this modest definition does not do justice to Noah Webster or to his monumental contribution to the standardization of American spelling and pronunciation. Although he wrote many textbooks for schoolchildren, his most noted work, which took him 20 years to complete, was his *American Dictionary of the English Language*, published in 1828. A staunch patriot, he believed that a cultural declaration of independence was as important as a political one.

Born in West Hartford, Connecticut, on October 16, 1758, Noah Webster was a descendant of distinguished Yankee families. His mother, Mercy Steele Webster, was the great-great-granddaughter of William Bradford, the second governor of the Plymouth colony; his father, Noah Webster, was descended from John Webster, a founder of the Connecticut colony, who became governor in 1656. One of five children, Webster was steeped in the traditions of his New England heritage.

Even as a small child Webster showed an interest in books. He received his early education from the Reverend Nathan Perkins and later from a local Hartford teacher. Webster entered Yale in 1774 — a decision that placed an additional financial burden on his family, necessitating the mortgage of his father's 90-acre farm. The Revolutionary War broke out two years later, and although he served as a volunteer, Webster managed to complete his studies within four years, graduating in 1778 with a B.A. degree. After his graduation, he decided on a law career, but because his father could not provide further financial aid, he was forced to earn his living by teaching while he studied law in his spare time. In 1781 he passed his bar examinations at Hartford; he continued to teach, however, and did not actively practice law until 1789.

During this period, he taught school in Goshen, New York, and came to realize the critical need for American textbooks. Between 1782 and 1785 he wrote his first textbook, *A Grammatical Institute of the English Language*. Intended for use by schoolchildren, it consisted of three parts: a grammar, a reader, and — most famous and widely used — *The American Spelling Book*, known as *Webster's Spelling Book* or the "Blue-Backed Speller." The great success of the spelling book was due largely to Webster's innovative use of American spelling and pronunciation, as well as to its patriotic theme. Although the speller was the most successful, selling as many as 60 million copies by 1890, the reader also had a number of editions. To the 1787 edition of the reader he had added "some American pieces under the discovery, history, wars, geography, economy, commerce, government, of this country . . . in order to call the minds of our youth from ancient fables & modern foreign events, and fix them upon objects immediately interesting in this country."

Because he was unable to copyright his works in 13 states, Webster became aware of the need for a uniform national copyright law. In 1782, in his early twenties, he began to work for legislation to that end, and he spent the next six years traveling throughout the country lobbying, lecturing, and corresponding with many state legislators. To help defray the expenses he incurred during this fight for the copyright law, Webster taught, gave singing lessons, and wrote many pamphlets. His efforts drew him into politics, and he soon earned the reputation of being an avid Federalist. In 1785 he wrote "Sketches of American Policy," a pamphlet advocating strong central government that brought him to the attention of George Washington and James Madison. Webster's lobbying efforts were not in vain, and in 1790 Congress enacted a national copyright law.

While agitating for the copyright legislation, Webster lectured in Philadelphia and had the opportunity to meet Benjamin Franklin. Their mutual interest in simplified spelling led to prolonged correspondence as well as periodic visits by Webster to Philadelphia. During one of these visits he was introduced to Rebecca Greenleaf, the daughter of a Boston merchant. They were married in Boston on October 26, 1789, and subsequently had two sons and six daughters.

Webster practiced law in Hartford from 1789 through 1793. His first interests, however, were journalism and lexicography. Giving up his legal career in Hartford, he founded two Federalist newspapers in New York, the *Minerva* (later the *Commercial Advertiser*), and a semiweekly, the *Herald* (later the *Spectator*). In 1798 he moved to New Haven, his interest in the newspapers by then having waned. Eventually the financial success of his early schoolbooks enabled him to retire, and in 1803 he gave up journalism totally and turned all of his attention to lexicography.

For the next three years he worked on *A Compendious Dictionary of the English Language*, issued in 1806. This was to be the forerunner of *An American Dictionary of the English Language*, which proved to be one of the most outstanding publications of the time. Webster labored for 20 years in the compilation of his dictionary, spending a year (1824–1825) in England and France doing research. Published in two volumes in 1828, it contained 70,000 entries, with 5,000 new words and nearly 40,000 definitions that had never appeared in any other dictionary. It included many nonliterary words, technical terms, and "Americanisms" and favored American rather than British spelling. Despite the weakness of its etymologies, Webster's dictionary was a landmark work and a great scholarly achievement. Its only competitor in the United States was the dictionary compiled by Joseph Emerson Worcester, whom Webster charged with plagiarism, precipitating the "War of the Dictionaries." Unfortunately, the great dictionary was less successful financially than his earlier works. After his death the rights were purchased from his estate by George and Charles Merriam.

In 1812, while compiling his dictionary, Webster moved from New Haven to Amherst, Massachusetts. In 1822 he returned to New Haven, where he lived the remaining years of his life.

By the time he died in 1843 at the age of 84, Webster had added to his lexicographical works several more dictionaries with abridgments and revisions. His broad range of interests is evidenced in other publications, including *A Brief History of Epidemic and Pestilential Diseases* (1799); *Historical Notices of the Origin and State of Banking Institutions and Insurance Offices* (1802); *Origin, History, and the Connection of the Languages of Western Asia and of Europe* (1807); *A Philosophical and Practical Grammar of the English Language* (1807); *Experiments Respecting Dew* (1809); *History of the United States* (1832); a revision of the Authorized Version of the Bible (1833); and numerous political pamphlets and informal essays.

A public-spirited citizen throughout his life, Webster was active over the years in many offices and organizations. He served as committeeman of his Hartford school district; alderman in New Haven and judge of the county court; member of the Connecticut and Massachusetts legislatures; director of the Hampshire Bible Society; and vice president of the Hampshire and Hampden Agricultural Society. He was also a founder of Amherst Academy and Amherst College, as well as of the Connecticut Academy of Arts and Sciences. In New Haven he worked to bring about an adequate water supply and to have trees planted along the streets.

The West Hartford birthplace of Noah Webster, at 227 South Main Street, has been named a national historic landmark. The privately owned two-story frame house, which dates from about 1676, is characteristic of late 17th century New England colonial architecture.

OCTOBER 17

British Surrender at Saratoga

John Burgoyne possessed political, martial, and literary abilities, and used all three to gain command of the British campaign against the American rebels in the summer of 1777. Born in 1722 into a distinguished Lancashire family and married in 1743 to Lady Charlotte, the daughter of the earl of Derby, he had connections that guaranteed his advancement in the British army. Burgoyne organized that service's first light-horse units and served with distinction in Portugal in 1762. Having won promotion in 1772, he came to America in May 1775, accompanying William Howe and Henry Clinton as the junior of three major generals.

Burgoyne, known as Gentleman Johnny for his love of high living, was also noted for his humane treatment of the troops serving under him. However, he lacked similar consideration for his superiors. He wrote frequently to England to criticize the actions of the other British generals in America, especially the commander in chief, Thomas Gage. After the 1776 campaign, Generals Burogoyne and Clinton returned to England to sit for a time in Parliament and to advance their careers. Burgoyne managed to outdo his rival Clinton, and won the assignment of leading the next summer's expedition in the colonies.

British strategy for the campaign grew out of Burgoyne's "Thoughts for Conducting the War on the Side of Canada," submitted on February 28, 1777, to the king and Lord George Germain, the secretary of state for the colonies. Burgoyne was to lead the main body of British troops south from Canada by way of Lake Champlain, capture Fort Ticonderoga, New York (which Ethan Allen and his Green Mountain Boys had wrested from the British just two years earlier), and proceed to Albany. Lieutenant Colonel Barry St. Leger, meanwhile, was to conduct a diversionary operation in the Mohawk valley, which he would approach from the west via Lake Ontario, and then join Burgoyne at Albany. General William Howe, the commander of the third prong of the offensive, was to bring a large number of men up the Hudson valley from New York City to meet the other two British columns. The objective was to wipe out the patriot forces in centrally located New York, thus splitting the newly formed nation into isolated halves.

On June 17 Burgoyne left St. John's, Canada,

with a force of 7,700 British, Germans, Canadians, Tories, and Indians. His column reached Ticonderoga by June 30 and forced the American defenders under Major General Arthur St. Clair to evacuate the fort on July 5. Burgoyne resumed his trek southward and experienced many trials, as natural obstacles and others set up by the Americans slowed his progress. The expedition soon ran short of supplies; to obtain the necessary provisions, Burgoyne sent a party of German dragoons under Lieutenant Colonel Friedrich Baum to raid an American storehouse at Bennington, in what is now Vermont. Colonials under General John Stark severely defeated the Hessians in the battle of Bennington (see August 16), leaving Burgoyne without the additional supplies he needed and bereft of one-tenth of his original strength.

Considering the fate of the other two British columns, General Burgoyne would have been wise not to press on to Albany. St. Leger left Oswego, New York, on July 26 with a British force of 1,800 Loyalists and Indians. On August 3 he reached and besieged Fort Stanwix on the Mohawk River. At nearby Oriskany on August 6 a detachment under Mohawk chief Joseph Brant defeated General Nicholas Herkimer's American relief force, but Major General Benedict Arnold managed to bring 1,000 volunteers to the aid of the beleaguered patriot garrison. St. Leger had no choice but to terminate the siege and withdraw, especially after an American ruse caused his Indian allies to desert him.

General Howe, meanwhile, left New York City with 15,000 troops on July 23, but rather than march up the Hudson valley as originally expected, he sailed for an attack on Philadelphia. Howe, who had succeeded General Gage as the British commander in chief in America, had won approval for this plan from Lord Germain, who expected the general to complete the operation in time to aid Burgoyne. However, the British did not occupy Philadelphia until September 26, much too late to be able to return to the New York campaign.

Despite these difficulties, Burgoyne imprudently decided to complete his mission. On September 13 he crossed the Hudson to its west bank near Saratoga (now Schuylerville), New York, 32 miles north of Albany. A month later Burgoyne and those of his men who remained were to return to Saratoga under other circumstances. In the meantime, however, the British column, reduced to 6,000 by the Bennington defeat and Indian desertions, continued a short distance south to the vicinity of Bemis Heights, where the Americans were encamped, three miles north of what is now Stillwater, New York.

Major General Philip Schuyler had conducted the patriot defense of the upper Hudson region until August 4, when Congress, for political reasons, had replaced him with General Horatio Gates. The new American commander had arrived on August 19, and on September 12 had moved his army north from Stillwater to well-entrenched positions on Bemis Heights. There he and his 7,000-man force lay in wait for the British attack.

General Burgoyne decided to attempt a reconnaissance in force to test the colonists' strength. On September 19, in the first battle of Saratoga, Burgoyne sent 2,200 men under General Simon Fraser out on the right flank to sweep the Freeman's Farm area. Major General Baron Friedrich Adolphus Riedesel was to move south with 1,100 men along the Hudson River road on the left flank. Burgoyne accompanied the center column of 1,100 troops, whose mission was to move south and then westward to make contact with Fraser.

Gates made no countermove until Major General Benedict Arnold persuaded him to send Colonel Daniel Morgan's Virginia riflemen and Major Henry Dearborn's light infantry out from his left flank to make contact. Morgan's marksmen surprised the British center column's advance guard and picked off all of its officers as they stood near the cabin of Freeman's Farm. Burgoyne quickly brought up the rest of the center force and dispersed it along the northern edge of the farm. Seven more American regiments meanwhile joined Morgan and Dearborn, and the colonists took their positions on the southern side of the farm. The opposing forces fought inconclusively for almost four hours.

About 5:00 P.M. Riedesel received a call from Burgoyne for reinforcements. Riedesel detached 500 men from his column to aid his commander. When the fresh troops arrived, Burgoyne counterattacked, and the Americans retired to their quarters as darkness fell. Burgoyne held the field and could claim the victory, but the British had been stopped in their tracks with casualties totaling 600 to the Americans' 319. The British forces might have suffered even greater losses had Gates had the sense to use some of the 4,000 men he had kept on Bemis Heights to attack the approximately 900 men Riedesel had left behind to guard the supply train.

Burgoyne wanted to attack the confused Americans in force on September 20, but Fraser asked for a day's respite for his tired troopers. The next day Burgoyne received a letter from his old rival, Lieutenant General Henry Clinton, whom Howe had left in New York City, offering to make a diversionary attack against the Hudson Highlands. The British commander thereupon canceled his plans in order to await the outcome of Clinton's venture — which resulted in the British capture of Forts Clinton and Montgomery, far downstream, and the burning of Kingston, but did not materially help the hard-pressed Burgoyne.

American strength rose after the first battle of Saratoga, reaching 11,000 by October 7. The colonists continuously harassed Burgoyne's position, and his numbers fell to 5,000 regulars as desertions increased. Finally Burgoyne decided to undertake another reconnaissance in force. If he found the enemy vulnerable he would attack in force on the following day; if not, the British would retreat to another position.

Divided into three columns, about 2,100 British troops left their entrenchments on the first Saratoga battlefield on the morning of October 7, 1777. After a short march, the main body of 1,500 men formed a 1,000-yard line on high ground near Mill Creek. The earl of Balcarres held the right with light infantry, while Major John Acland's British grenadiers were on the left. Riedesel's men formed the center of the British line. General Fraser commanded 600 auxiliaries in a wooded area protecting the right flank.

The British dispositions would have been excellent had the enemy been a European opponent used to frontal attack. The Americans, however, chose to approach through the woods, which covered both flanks. In mid-afternoon General Enoch Poor's 800 men struck Acland's flank, routed the grenadiers, and captured the wounded major. Daniel Morgan's riflemen attacked the right flank, drove off Fraser's auxiliaries, turned the enemy's line, and with the aid of Dearborn pushed back Balcarres's forces.

Riedesel's Germans held their ground, unaware that Sir Francis Clerke had been mortally wounded and captured while trying to bring them Burgoyne's order to retreat. As other American units put pressure on the German flanks, Brigadier General Ebenezer Learned's brigade approached them from the front. At that moment, General Benedict Arnold, who that day was without a command — Gates had relieved him after a quarrel — rushed forward and, without authorization, took over control of Learned's brigade. The Germans managed to withstand the colonists' first assault, but then fell back to the Balcarres Redoubt.

Arnold's aggressiveness brought the Americans victory. When an attack on the Balcarres Redoubt failed, Arnold led Learned's men in an attack that overran the fortified cabins located between the Balcarres Redoubt and that of Lieutenant Colonel Heinrich von Breymann, German ally of the British. Then Arnold rushed to the other flank of Breymann's Redoubt and led four regiments in an assault that routed the defenders. One of Breymann's own soldiers shot the German to death after he had used his saber on four men to increase their efforts.

By day's end, British losses reached about 600, while the Americans' totaled approximately 150. Arnold's efforts made Burgoyne's position untenable and forced him to fall back to the Great Redoubt. On the night of October 8 the British forces slipped away from the camp and past the sleeping 1,300 Massachusetts militiamen under Brigadier General John Fellows, whom Gates had dispatched to prevent Burgoyne's escape to the north. By the night of October 9 the British reached Saratoga, where Burgoyne decided to rest his tired soldiers.

Gates took up the chase on October 10 and quickly caught up with his enemy. Instead of pushing his way back to Canada, Burgoyne had unwisely clung to his strong defensive position at Saratoga and established his troops there. By October 12 the Americans had enveloped his forces except on the north. At a council of war Burgoyne and his men decided to try to escape that night toward the open side. However, the arrival of Brigadier General John Stark of New Hampshire closed the northern route before the British could withdraw. Burgoyne had no choice but to surrender.

Negotiations over the conditions of surrender consumed several days. On October 13 Burgoyne offered to discuss terms but rejected Gates's demand for unconditional surrender. The British commander on October 15 asked that his men be paroled if they agreed not to serve again in North America during the war. Gates agreed, but his insistence that the British quickly leave their positions indicated to Burgoyne that the Americans feared Clinton might attack them from the rear. In reality, however, Clinton, after scoring his lower Hudson successes, had not pressed farther north, but instead had returned to New York City for reinforcements. Gates agreed to Burgoyne's request that the agreement be called a convention rather than a capitulation but, tired of the British commander's delaying tactics, demanded on October 16 that he surrender or fight. Still thinking that Clinton might be coming to save him, Burgoyne reluctantly submitted. On October 17 Burgoyne surrendered his sword to Gates, and the American graciously returned it. The British soldiers laid down their arms, signifying the end of Burgoyne's campaign.

Historians have described the two battles of Saratoga as the turning point of the American Revolution. In the course of the conflict, the colonials had defeated a great British army and saved themselves from disaster. Moreover, the victory gave the United States a psychological lift and led France to ally with the young nation against England, its traditional rival.

The creation of Saratoga National Historical Park, on the site of the American victory, was authorized by Congress on June 1, 1938. Completed on June 22, 1948, the park — 28 miles north of Albany on US Route 4 and New York Route 32 — is just above Stillwater, New York. It includes 5,500 acres, of which the federal government owns 2,432.35 and the state 3,067.65. The National Park Service of the US Department of the Interior administers the site. The visitors' center houses a museum containing memorabilia of the encounters and offers an audiovisual program to supplement the story told by exhibits. Signs and markers located at numerous spots in the park help the visitor to understand and visualize events connected with the battle.

Several original and reconstructed buildings dot the landscape of the park. The Neilson house on Bemis Heights, which served as the quarters of Generals Benedict Arnold and Enoch Poor, has been restored. Nearby stands a reconstruction of the Americans' stone powder magazine. A reconstruction of one of Freeman's cabins is situated on the Freeman farm. The National Park Service has also restored the General Philip Schuyler House in Schuylerville, which is frequently referred to as Old Saratoga. The house was built after Burgoyne's surrender to replace the family's home, burnt by the British on October 10, 1777. Also in Schuylerville is the Field of Grounded Arms, where the surrender ceremony took place. There, in the 50-to-60-acre field, Burgoyne's surviving men marched out of camp "with the Honors of War," and piled their arms near the edge of the Hudson. Most of the field remains open, in part privately owned, and in part owned by Schuylerville, so that the area is available for recreation.

Visitors can also see the Saratoga Battle Monument, which overlooks the Hudson at Victory Mills, just north of Schuylerville. In Saratoga National Historical Park, other monuments also commemorate a number of the men who fought at Saratoga. One erected on Bemis Heights in 1936 recalls the contribution of Thaddeus Kosciuszko, the Polish military engineer who selected and fortified the American lines. The Arnold monument on the site of Breymann's Redoubt is the most unusual; centered around a sculptured left military boot, it commemorates a leg wound the general received while leading charges against the enemy strongholds. Also within the bounds of the park is the American Soldiers Monument, a stone shaft erected in 1931 by the Daughters of the American Revolution of New York State to memorialize those colonists who fell in the battle.

Schuylerville and the other small communities in the vicinity of the battle site began preparations for celebrating the Bicentennial of the American Revolution long before 1976. To commemorate the 190th anniversary of the battles of Saratoga in 1967, Revolutionary War Celebrations, Inc., which was organized in Schuylerville, drew up a varied program. On October 7, the anniversary of the second battle of Saratoga, the town dedicated a museum recalling local historical events and the battle. The town was also the site of a large parade. Larger-than-life plywood representations of British and American drummer boys decorated Broadway, the town's main street. For the celebration, bronze souvenir coins depicting General Arnold's boot were minted — the first of a series of commemorative Saratoga coins.

John Trumbull's painting of Burgoyne surrendering to Gates decorates the US Capitol Rotunda in Washington, D.C.

OCTOBER 18

Alaska Day

Alaska Day, an official holiday in the 49th and geographically largest state, commemorates the formal transfer of Alaska from Russia to the United States. That event was the culmination of several months of diplomatic maneuvering (see March 30, Seward's Day). The transfer took place at Sitka on October 18, 1867.

Each year the transfer ceremonies are reenacted as part of a three-day festival in Sitka, the last headquarters of czarist Russia in Russian America — as Alaska was then called. Alexander Baranof, the first Russian governor of Alaska, had established Sitka as the capital in 1799 (Juneau has held that distinction since 1906).

The last Russian governor, Prince Dmitri Maksoutsoff — like most of the Russian settlers — bitterly opposed the sale of Alaska. He refused permission to land to the 250 American troops sent for the transfer ceremonies. Eager to get ashore after a rough three-week voyage from San Francisco, the troops had to spend an additional 10 days confined to their ship off Sitka — until the arrival of the Russian and American commissioners authorized to carry out the formalities.

At the appointed hour the commissioners, Russian and American military personnel, local dignitaries, Indian chiefs, and civilians gathered at Castle Hill near the official residence of the Russian governor. The ceremony was to be simple. During alternate salutes by Russian and American guns, the czarist flag was to be lowered, the Stars and Stripes raised, and the formal words of transfer and acceptance spoken by the commissioners, Captain Alexei Pestchouroff from St. Petersburg and General Lovall H. Rousseau from Washington. Princess Maksoutsoff, wife of the governor, waited to receive the Russian ceremonial flag.

In an effort to ease the emotion-charged transfer and as a courtesy to the Russian colonists who were losing their adopted home, the tactful General Rousseau had asked that no cheers be given. But despite Rousseau's considerations, the Russians found the occasion a sad one.

As they watched the ceremonies begin, they saw the wind-whipped Russian imperial double eagle wrap itself around the flagstaff and catch in the halyards, as if refusing to be displaced. After much tugging and manipulation of the ropes and equally futile attempts by seamen to climb the 90-foot flagpole, a boatswain's chair was hastily made of rope, and a seaman was hoisted to the banner.

When the seaman finally retrieved the wind-torn flag, he either fumbled or misunderstood shouted orders to bring it down. Instead the flag was dropped and a strong gust swept it onto Russian bayonets. The tattered double eagle was subsequently presented to a weeping Princess Maksoutsoff.

By contrast, today's annual celebration of Alaska Day in Sitka is a joyous event. The Russian flag is lowered without complications, and the Stars and Stripes raised to cheers and jubilation. The reenactment is one of the highlights of the festival, which includes a pageant, parades, a ball, and band concerts. A historical pageant, In This Place, is staged at the Centennial Building, tracing the story of the Russian colony at Old Sitka and Sitka from its founding to October 18, 1867. The Centennial Building is also the setting for the Baranof ball, with women appearing in post–Civil War gowns and men sporting "prospector" beards grown for the occasion. But the climax of the annual Alaska Days comes on October 18 with the grand parade, featuring floats, bands, and military units, and with the reenactment of the transfer ceremony.

The Sitka festivities were embellished and prolonged during 1967 when, with a statewide, yearlong celebration, Alaska marked the centenary of its purchase — or at least the centenary of its transfer. (Because of the tardiness of Congress, Russia was not actually paid the purchase price until 1868.)

While each area of Alaska planned its local schedule of centennial events, Fairbanks was the site of the official Alaska Centennial Exposition during the summer of 1967. Since the exposition site bordered the Chena River, activities there were abruptly curtailed on August 15, when the river overflowed and flooded Fairbanks. But two and a half months of celebration and exhibitions had already taken place on schedule.

Among other attractions, the exposition featured two geodesic domes housing exhibits on historical, industrial, agricultural, and commercial aspects of Alaska. There was entertainment, including Broadway musicals performed by a resident stock company and some native contests — blanket tosses, seal-hook throwing, kayak racing, and seal skinning. Eskimo, Indian, and Aleutian art, artifacts, and ceremonial masks were displayed. Visitors could tour a zoo and the Bonanza amusement park. In Mining Valley they were reminded of the various gold rushes that drew US settlers to Alaska during the 1880s and later. They could also pan for gold (and keep what they panned). And they could see the stern-wheeler steamer *Nenana* in a gold rush town whose authentic buildings had been transported to the centennial site. At the exposition's Native Village, fair-goers could view Eskimos in native costumes and visit log cabins, Eskimo sod huts, and a summer house walled with walrus skins. Many of the Fairbanks exposition structures were intended to be permanent, and after a major, postflood cleanup operation during the winter months they were again on view by 1968.

Two events that take place annually in Fairbanks were added to the city's centennial celebration. They were the big Golden Days festival, which commemorates the community's beginnings with five days of costume parading, street dancing, contests, entertainment, and varied festivity; and the Eskimo Olympics, with Eskimos from all over the Arctic competing in sports and skills unfamiliar to other Americans.

Centennial-year celebrations were also going on throughout the rest of Alaska. Highlighting local observances were pageants depicting the heroic Vitus Bering discovering Alaska, or the original flag raising at Sitka and other events of historical importance. Gold prospectors got their due in commemorations of gold finds. Sports contests featured beluga whaling; muktuk (whale skin) eating; log rolling; and kayak, ski, dogsled, mountain-climbing, and crab races. One of the events not often duplicated in the 49 other states was a rodeo program that included a "chicken, moose, caribou and bear barbecue."

Alaska's road to statehood was a long one. After control passed from Russia to the United States, it was governed first by the US Army and then by the US Navy. In 1884 Congress designated the region a "district" under civil authority, and so it remained until August 24, 1912, when it was organized as a territory. The territorial status remained in effect until 1959, when Alaska was admitted to the Union as the 49th state (see January 3).

Feast of St. Luke the Evangelist

The Feast of St. Luke the Evangelist is observed on October 18 by Roman Catholics, some Protestants — notably Episcopalians and Lutherans — and most Eastern Orthodox churches. St. Luke is traditionally regarded as the author of the third Gospel and of the Acts of the Apostles.

Very little is known about Luke. He was probably a Greek-speaking Gentile and, for some time at least, was associated with the city of Antioch, since he seemed to be familiar with the early Church in Antioch. According to the Church historian Eusebius, whose life bridged the third and fourth centuries, Luke was a Syrian born in Antioch. No one has proved or disproved that statement.

Like Paul, with whom he was closely associated, Luke never actually met Jesus but, after the Crucifixion, was one of the early converts to Christianity. The fact that his writings are the most literary of the Gospels is an indication that Luke was well educated.

In writing the Acts of the Apostles, Luke sometimes employed the first person plural, and from this it is assumed that he accompanied Paul for part of his second and third missionary journeys. One example of Luke's use of the term "we" is in his account of Paul's shipwreck off Malta and subsequent sojourn on that island.

Luke traditionally has been considered a medical doctor by profession, no doubt because in his letter to the Colossians (4:14), Paul refers to Luke as the "beloved physician." In his Epistles, Paul mentions Luke by name on two other occasions. Once, in closing his letter to Philemon, Paul speaks of Luke by name as one of his "fellow workers" who send greetings to Philemon. Again, in 2 Timothy 4:11, when Paul is asking Timothy to join him, he notes that others have left, and that "Luke alone is with me."

It is possible that Luke knew Paul before either of them became Christians, but whether, as is sometimes held, the two met at the university in Tarsus as students or whether it was Paul who baptized Luke is nowhere documented. It is probable, however, that Luke joined Paul on his second missionary journey in about A.D. 50 but remained at Philippi when Paul continued his journey. Luke again joined Paul on his travels in about A.D. 57 and from then on was a fairly constant companion to Paul in his travels throughout Asia Minor, finally accompanying him on his trip to Rome for trial.

While Paul was in prison, Luke apparently continued his research for his writing of the Gospel, speaking with people who remembered Jesus and could give firsthand accounts of events in his life and describe the early Church. Luke escaped Nero's persecutions, which presumably made martyrs of Peter and Paul; and tradition has it that he lived his remaining years in Greece. According to a second century writer, it was there that Luke, "serving the Lord faithfully, unmarried and childless . . . died at the age of 84 in Boeotia, full of the Holy Spirit."

It is widely held that one of the people Luke interviewed, perhaps at greater length than any other witness, may have been Mary, the mother of Christ. Certainly many of the details that are recorded by Luke and by no other Evangelist seem ones that only Mary could have supplied.

In any event, Luke made a number of unique contributions to the New Testament. Readers are indebted to him for handing down the compelling parables of the Good Samaritan (Luke 10:33–37) and the Prodigal Son (Luke 15:11–32), among others. And he is the only Evangelist to provide (in the first two chapters of his Gospel) certain information about the conception, infancy, and childhood of Jesus.

The events that Luke alone describes include the Annunciation, the announcement by the Archangel Gabriel that Mary had been chosen to be the mother of Christ. The words of Luke's account of this event are familiar to all Christians. They are the basis for two Roman Catholic prayers, the "Hail Mary" (or *Ave Maria*), and the Angelus, said morning, noon and night and signaled by the chiming of church bells as a reminder to say the prayer. It is called the Angelus because the prayer begins, "The Angel [*Angelus* in Latin] of the Lord declared unto Mary. . . ."

Luke also gives the only Gospel account of the Visitation — Mary's visit to her kinswoman Elizabeth, who in a few months would give birth to John the Baptist. One of the most beautiful prayers in Christendom, the Magnificat, also appears in this passage. It comes after Elizabeth, hearing Mary's greeting, "was filled with the Holy Spirit and exclaimed . . . 'Blessed are you among women, and blessed is the fruit of your womb!'" Mary's modest reply, the paean of praise now known as The Magnificat, begins with these words:

My soul magnifies the Lord,
and my spirit rejoices in God my Savior,
for he has regarded the low estate of his handmaiden . . .
for he who is mighty has done great things for me,
and holy is his name.

Luke is also the only Evangelist to describe the Presentation of the child Jesus in the Temple, according to Jewish custom — and to relate how, at a later time, he was found in the Temple by his anxious mother, Mary, and her husband, Joseph, after they had discovered him missing during their homeward journey to Nazareth following their celebration of Passover in Jerusalem. It was after a three-day search that they found him, sitting among the teachers, who were amazed at his questions and answers. Like Matthew, Luke also tells of the Nativity, but his account provides additional details.

These five events — the Annunciation, the Visitation, the Nativity, the Presentation, and the finding of Jesus in the Temple — have been the subject of many famous paintings. For Roman Catholics, they make up what are called the five joyful mysteries of the series of prayers known as the Rosary.

Although no one can say when Luke first decided to write the records that would eventually be known as the Gospel of Luke and the Acts of the Apostles, he apparently spent a long time, perhaps two or three decades, gathering information. The actual writing is now thought to have taken place between A.D. 70 and 90.

Both records are addressed to a certain Theophilus, about whom nothing is definitely known, but who has been variously described as a man of conspicuous rank or office, or as Luke's patron, or simply as a fellow Christian, or one instructed in the faith if not already baptized. It is also logical to conjecture that the name does not refer to an individual but instead represents all seekers of the truth, since *Theophilus* in Greek means "one who loves God."

In the opening lines of his Gospel, Luke gives Theophilus the reasons for his writing this record:

Inasmuch as many have undertaken to compile a narrative of the things which have been accomplished among us, just as they were delivered to us by those who from the beginning were eyewitnesses and ministers of the word, it seemed good to me also, having followed all things closely for some time past, to write an orderly account for you, most excellent Theophilus, that you may know the truth concerning the things of which you have been informed.

That Luke succeeded in writing "an orderly account" is obvious. Tracing the life of Christ, Luke's Gospel moves inevitably from Nazareth toward Jerusalem. In like manner, the Acts of the Apostles, tracing the early spread of Christianity, moves from Jerusalem to Rome. Because Luke carefully records Christ's promise to send the Holy Spirit to sanctify and guide his Church and then goes on to document the fulfillment of

that promise in the Acts of the Apostles, this book is sometimes referred to as the Gospel of the Holy Spirit. This supplement to the Gospels covers a period of about 35 years, ranging from the time of Christ's Ascension to the second year of Paul's imprisonment in Rome.

Luke's emblem is a winged ox. It is perhaps appropriate that the ox, a sacrificial animal, should be the symbol of the Evangelist whose Gospel begins and ends in the Temple. Luke opens his account with the story of Zachariah, a priest in the Temple and the father of John the Baptist. After a brief account of the Ascension, Luke concludes his Gospel by noting that Christ's followers, having witnessed the Ascension "worshiped him, and returned to Jerusalem with great joy and were continually in the temple blessing God." Although Luke literally begins The Acts of the Apostles where he has left off in his Gospel, addressing his words to Theophilus and then giving a more complete description of the Ascension, the book of Acts is separated from the third Gospel by the Gospel of St. John.

St. Luke is the patron saint of physicians and artists; other emblems used for him are a brush and palette. As far as is known, he was not an artist himself, though he is often depicted as such in fiction. However, he created rich images with his words; and his contribution to the New Testament is major.

OCTOBER 19

Feast of St. Isaac Jogues and Companions

The Feast of St. Isaac Jogues and Companions, observed by Roman Catholics, commemorates eight French Jesuit missioners and martyrs who became the first canonized saints of the North American continent. The eight, all killed between 1642 and 1649, are known collectively as the North American Martyrs. Three of them, Isaac Jogues, René Goupil and Jean Lalande, were killed in what is now New York State. The other five, Jean de Brébeuf, Antoine Daniel, Gabriel Lalemant, Charles Garnier, and Noël Chabanel, were killed in New France (now Canada). With two exceptions, they were all priests. Goupil and Lalande had joined the missionaries as lay helpers. At some time between his arrival in the New World in 1640 and his death two years later, Goupil — who had studied surgery in Orléans — took the vows of a Jesuit brother.

The story of the North American Martyrs must be seen in the light of the times. In the 17th century and much of the 18th, France and England were continuously battling over possession of

Canada. In this conflict the Iroquois people of the region were usually allied with the British, more out of hatred for the French than affection for the British.

The French missionaries made their headquarters in New France in what is now the province of Ontario. It was their intention to bring the gospel of Christ to the native peoples of the New World. The Iroquois were a confederation of five tribes that stretched across territory including present New York State, with the Mohawks on the east and the Senecas on the west and the Oneida, Onondaga, and Cayuga tribes in between.

The belligerent Iroquois had vowed extermination of the more peaceful Hurons, who at that time were settled between Lake Simcoe, north of the eastern part of Lake Ontario, and Georgian Bay to the west. During the years that the French missionaries were working — mostly among the Hurons — the Iroquois repeatedly sent war parties into Huron territory, until the Hurons were decimated or fled to new settlements. Finally, in 1649, the same year the last four of the martyrs were killed, the Iroquois succeeded in permanently disrupting the Huron confederacy.

The Jesuits (or Blackrobes, as the Indians called them) made their missionary center at Fort Sainte Marie, today marked by the Martyrs' Shrine in Midland, Ontario, about 90 miles north of Toronto. (The Canadian government has restored the whole settlement as it was from 1639 to 1649.) Father Isaac Jogues had helped in the building of the old fort, which was destroyed in the Iroquois invasion of 1649. It was from Fort Sainte Marie that the Jesuits set out for their Huron missions scattered throughout the wild countryside.

The year 1642 was a particularly bad one in the land of the Hurons. The harvest had been poor, illness was rampant, and clothing was scarce. Even though the Iroquois posed a threat, an expedition had to be sent to Quebec for supplies. The 600 miles of land and water from Fort Sainte Marie to Quebec were in rugged territory made more dangerous by the Iroquois presence in the area. Father Isaac Jogues led the expedition, which left in June 1642 and arrived in Quebec in mid-July.

On August 1 he and about 40 others — including René Goupil and a few other Frenchmen, and some high-ranking Huron converts, including a chief and a noted medicine man — headed back for the mission with their canoes heavily laden with supplies. The next day they heard the dreaded Iroquois war cry and were immediately set upon by 70 Mohawks in 12 canoes. Fighting ensued, but the mission convoy was outnumbered. The Mohawks took their captives

and booty back to their village of Ossernenon (now Auriesville), New York. During the 12-day trip from the banks of the St. Lawrence to the banks of the Mohawk River, the Mohawks tortured their prisoners, especially the hated French and most especially Father Isaac Jogues.

When they arrived at Mohawk territory, the captives were dragged from village to village with the inhabitants of each community inflicting additional brutalities. The captives who did not die were given as slaves to Indian families. For a while Jogues and Goupil were kept in a kind of public slavery.

It was six weeks before their wounds were even partially healed. Gradually the two men were given some degree of freedom in and around the stockaded village. Sometimes they were permitted to go a short distance up a hill, where they prayed together.

In the village itself there was one rather quiet cabin, where Goupil sometimes went to pray. One day while he was there a small child came in, and Goupil, who dearly loved children, playfully put his hat on the child's head and made the sign of the cross over him. Just as that moment the child's grandfather chanced to look in. He thought the "dog of a Frenchman" was bewitching the child. Enraged, he drove Goupil out of the cabin and plotted to have him killed outside the palisades.

A few days later Goupil and Jogues went to their "hill of prayer" outside the stockade. Evidently sensing their new danger, they offered themselves to God as martyrs. As they came down the hill, reciting the Rosary, two Indian warriors approached and ordered them back to the stockade at once. The two continued saying the Rosary as they walked downhill with the warriors close behind. Then one of the warriors drew a hatchet from beneath his blanket and struck at Goupil's head. Goupil fell to the ground and was attacked a second time. Jogues, seeing the hatchet, knelt down to pray, sure that he would be treated in like manner. Instead he was told to stand. He rushed to his dying companion, and while he was administering absolution, he was thrust aside as the Indians cleft Goupil's skull. Thus died the first North American Martyr, on September 29, 1642. Father Jogues later wrote a biography of René Goupil, the only North American Martyr whose life was recorded by another of the martyrs. It has been translated into English. The original is in the Collège Sainte-Marie in Montreal.

For more than a year, Jogues remained a slave of the Mohawks, forced to do the heaviest work, often in bitter cold, on hunting and fishing trips. Some of the Indians began to respect him, however, for his bravery, endurance, and good spirits. Although the Dutch at Fort Orange (now Albany) offered to ransom Jogues for the then substantial sum of $200, the Indians refused. Once in a while Jogues was able to minister to other Christian captives, comforting them and hearing their confessions. On one occasion, when a woman was being burned at the stake, Jogues rushed into the flames to baptize her.

Finally, in August 1643, he escaped. Somehow, after a fishing trip, he had reached the Dutch Fort Orange ahead of the Indians and had been persuaded, after much urging, to seek freedom. When the Indians reached the fort, they threatened to burn it down if their prisoner was not returned to them. The Dutch, stolidly ignoring the threat, moved Jogues from one hiding place to another until he could be smuggled aboard a ship.

One of those largely instrumental in Jogues's escape was a Dutch Reformed minister at Fort Orange who boarded the ship with Jogues and provided him with clothing and food. At New Amsterdam, Jogues was entertained by Governor William Kieft while he waited for a ship to take him overseas.

On November 5 Jogues set sail for France by way of England. After escaping pirates on the high seas, robbers in port, and Puritan persecutors in England, he was taken across the English Channel by a French collier. He reached France in time to attend Mass in a Breton church on Christmas morning. After a 10-day trip on horseback, he arrived at the Jesuit college at Rennes, where his fellow Jesuits — who had long given him up for dead — did not at first recognize him.

Much to his embarrassment — for he was a humble man — Jogues was received with acclaim wherever he went. The French queen, Anne of Austria, kissed his hands, which had been mutilated, and people everywhere looked upon him as a saint and a martyr. Pope Urban VIII granted Jogues the one gift he had longed for: permission to say the mass despite the handicap presented by his deformed fingers. In a few months he was back in New France, anxious to continue his work.

Tired of the perpetual war, the Mohawks notified the governor of New France that they wished to make peace with the French. In May of 1646 Jogues, wearing civilian clothes, was sent down to the Mohawk country as the French ambassador of peace. En route he discovered Lake George on May 30, 1646. Since it was the eve of the Feast of Corpus Christi, he named it Lac du Saint Sacrement, or Lake of the Blessed Sacrament. The name was retained until 1755, when Sir William Johnson, a British colonial leader, renamed it Lake George in honor of England's King George II.

The peace council in the chief Mohawk village ended happily and, before he returned, Jogues, who hoped to establish a permanent mission among the Mohawks, stopped at Ossernenon. Then he returned to Quebec to report to the governor of New France on the successful negotiations.

Although Jogues himself felt certain that God wanted him to labor and die among the Mohawks, his Jesuit superiors in New France were understandably hesitant to send him back to Ossernenon. But the Huron council decided to send a peace mission of its own to the Mohawks and requested that Father Jogues accompany their representatives. Jogues, determining to go chiefly as a missioner, and only secondarily as a peace legate, replied, "I shall go, but I shall not return." He asked for a mission assistant who "must be virtuous, docile to direction, courageous, willing to suffer anything for God." The young layman who accepted the challenge was Jean Lalande, who had recently come from Dieppe, France, to dedicate his life to helping the Jesuits in New France.

On September 24, 1646, three canoes left Three Rivers (Trois Rivières) on the St. Lawrence River between Quebec and Montreal. One carried Hurons of the peace mission, one transported returning Mohawks, and the third carried Jogues, Lalande, and the Huron spokesman. By the time they reached Lake Champlain, however, the Mohawks and Hurons had abandoned the party in fear.

As Jogues and Lalande approached Ossernenon, they were received with sullen expressions by a small group of Mohawks who then vanished. Suddenly a great number of Mohawks appeared, attacked Jogues and Lalande, ripped their clothing, and dragged them to the village. The two missioners were rescued by the friendly Wolf clan of the Mohawks and learned that some of the warriors — notably the Bear clan — blamed the Jesuits and their "sorcery" for the blight and pestilence that the Indians had recently suffered. The Wolf clan and the Turtle (or Tortoise) clan spoke on behalf of the Frenchmen, and the next day Jogues was allowed to defend his position and refute the Bear clan's charges before the council of chiefs. The chiefs then went to the capital village, six miles away, where they deliberated the fate of the missioners and ultimately declared them innocent.

But it was too late. While the chiefs were deliberating, a warrior from the Bear clan entered Jogues's cabin and invited him to a feast. Since refusal of such an invitation would give offense, Jogues decided to follow the warrior to the lodge of the Bear chief. As he stooped to enter the door of the lodge, he was killed with a tomahawk. The date was October 18, 1646. The next morning Lalande met the same fate.

Jogues had often expressed the desire to suffer martyrdom. Therefore, when in the spring of 1647 his Jesuit companions in New France heard of his death, they celebrated the Mass of Thanksgiving instead of the usual Requiem Mass. For five of these Jesuits in New France, their own martyrdom was not far off.

On July 4, 1648, Father Antoine Daniel had just celebrated Mass at the Huron village of Teanaustaye, near what is now Hillsdale, Ontario. All the Huron warriors were away from the village when the Iroquois attacked women, children, and old men. Daniel hurriedly baptized those who came to him and urged them to escape through an opening in the palisade. The invaders set fire to the village and killed those who had not escaped in time. Daniel, still wearing his Mass vestments, came out of the chapel to meet the Iroquois. For a moment, stopped by the sight of the priest as he calmly approached them, the Iroquois merely stared. Then they sent a shower of arrows at him, and a gunshot stopped his heart.

Father Jean de Brébeuf, at 56 the oldest French missionary in Canada, was one of the first Jesuits sent from France — in 1625 — to work among the Indians. On March 16, 1649, he and Father Gabriel Lalemant were captured during an Iroquois raid into Huron territory and martyred in the village of St. Ignace, not far from Fort Sainte Marie. Brébeuf died under torture that day and Father Lalemant the following morning.

Father Charles Garnier met martyrdom on December 7, 1649, in another Iroquois raid. Alone among his Huron converts and friends in the village of St. Jean, he blessed and baptized them and urged them to flee the oncoming Iroquois. As he ran from house to house, an Iroquois shot him three times, tore off his cassock and his black robe, and rushed off in pursuit of the fleeing Hurons. The priest recovered sufficiently to try to drag himself towards a mortally wounded Huron to give him absolution, but before he could reach his convert he was killed.

Garnier's companion, Father Noël Chabanel, was away at the time and never returned. Later a Huron confessed that out of hatred for the faith, which he blamed for all his misfortunes, he had killed Chabanel as he was returning to the mission on December 8, 1649, and had thrown the body into the Nottawasaga River in Ontario.

Remains of three of the eight North American Martyrs — Jean de Brébeuf, Gabriel Lalemant, and Charles Garnier — were partially recovered and enshrined in reliquaries at the National Shrine of the North American Martyrs in Auries-

ville and in its Canadian counterpart, the Martyr's Shrine in Midland, Ontario.

In 1884 General John S. Clark, a Seneca archeologist of New York State, announced that he had found evidence that Ossernenon, on a bluff overlooking the Mohawk River, had occupied the site on which the village of Auriesville had been built years later. Because Jogues and his two companions had been martyred there, 10 acres of land were purchased by a benefactor, and a tiny chapel, named Our Lady of the Martyrs, was erected in 1885.

The first pilgrims — about 400 Catholics from eastern New York State — went there on August 15, 1885, and knelt in the grass outside the chapel, which had room inside only for the priest and acolytes. The shrine's fame has grown over the years. The eight martyrs were canonized by the Roman Catholic church on June 29, 1930. The present shrine was begun that same year.

The original 10 acres have been increased to 600, and a circular church, called the Coliseum, seating 6,700, was built with four rustic altars to accommodate worshipers. A crucifix has been erected on the hill where Jogues and Goupil frequently prayed. The turbulent and wild countryside of 300 years ago has become a place of peace where pilgrims can make their devotions outdoors and meditate before numerous small shrines on the grounds. Visitors can also see the Indian museum named after Kateri Tekakwitha (or Tekawitha), known as the Lily of the Mohawks, a convert to Christianity who was born at Ossernenon 10 years after Jogues and Lalande were martyred there. Her father was a Mohawk chief of the Turtle Clan, and her mother was a Catholic Algonquin. Kateri Tekakwitha died in Caughnawaga, founded in 1667 in the St. Lawrence country of Canada as a refuge for Iroquois converts. A statue of Tekakwitha occupies a prominent place on the grounds of the Martyr's Shrine at Auriesville. She and Jogues are both represented on the bronze doors of St. Patrick's Cathedral in New York City.

Mohawk descendants of Ossernenon-Auriesville's 17th century inhabitants have traveled annually from Caughnawaga for a pilgrimage to the shrine in Auriesville. The high point of the Mohawk pilgrimage takes place on the Sunday before Labor Day, when the native language mass is sung.

Some 200,000 people annually visit the Auriesville shrine from May to October. On special "national" days, Italians, Poles, Slovaks, and others hear the story of the martyrs in their own languages. The National Shrine of the North American Martyrs is under the care of the Jesuits.

The Martyrs' Shrine at Midland, Ontario, is on the site of old Fort Sainte Marie, which the early

Jesuits made their mission center. Before the site of the old fort was fixed in 1925, a small chapel was built, in 1907, at the nearby old Mission St. Ignace to mark the martyrdom of Fathers Jean de Brébeuf and Gabriel Lalemant. The feast, formerly commemorated on September 26, was moved to its present date following the Second Vatican Council of 1962–1965. Since the revision of the Roman Catholic calendar became effective in 1972, the day has been marked in the United States as an optional memorial.

Peggy Stewart Day

The Boston Tea Party, the most famous demonstration against the British Tea Act of 1773 (see December 16), inspired violent resistance to the hated legislation in several other American localities as well. In April 1774 the Sons of Liberty dumped tea into New York harbor, and in June and again in September of the same year mobs forced a Portsmouth, New Hampshire, merchant to reship his cargoes of tea to Nova Scotia. Then in December 1774 patriots in Greenwich, New Jersey, set fire to a tea shipment. Similar public outrage met efforts to land the dutied leaves at Annapolis, Maryland, and it was there that one of the most serious disruptions of 1774 took place.

On May 14, 1774, the *Peggy Stewart* left London carrying more than a ton of tea that Thomas C. Williams had consigned to his brothers and business partners, James and Joseph, in Annapolis. Williams's action was ill advised. Even before the brig had reached its destination, J. J. Johnson, the London agent for another Annapolis firm, wrote home: "I would not be surprised to hear that you made a Bon Fire of the Peggy Stewart as I have a hint that a certain T[homas] W[illiams] has ship'd Tea on Board of her." Johnson accurately prophesied the fate of the vessel and its cargo.

When the *Peggy Stewart* arrived in Annapolis on October 14, 1774, its owner, Anthony Stewart, tried first to enter the ship and all the cargo except the tea at the customhouse. The customs official, however, ruled that the entire cargo had to be entered; Stewart yielded to his demand and paid the duty on the tea. News of this action enraged the local patriots, and the Annapolis Committee of Observation immediately called a meeting to deal with the emergency. Some of those present at this gathering wanted to land and burn the tea without further discussion, but others objected. They argued that no action should be taken on a matter of such importance without consulting all the inhabitants of Anne Arundel County, in which Annapolis is located. The latter opinion prevailed: the October 14

convocation called a town meeting for October 19 and ordered a guard be posted on the brig to prevent any attempts to land the tea.

Both the local committee and Stewart used the next five days to persuade the public of the rectitude of their respective positions. The patriots circulated handbills throughout the county, advising the populace that Stewart's actions had jeopardized their liberties. Stewart replied to this charge with a detailed explanation. In defense of his behavior, he disclaimed ever having any interest in the cargo of the *Peggy Stewart*. He argued that the presence of more than 50 passengers aboard his leaky ship had bound him "both in humanity and prudence to enter the vessel and leave the destination of the tea to the Committee."

Stewart's claims had little effect on the citizens who gathered in Annapolis on October 19, 1774; before that date they had judged Stewart and the Williams brothers guilty of offensive behavior. The meeting concerned itself only with obtaining the offenders' signatures on a prepared apology and determining an appropriate punishment. The first matter presented no problem: Stewart and the Williams brothers readily agreed "to acknowledge that we have committed a most daring insult and act of the most pernicious tendency to the liberties of America." Less easily determined was the matter of punishment.

Although the populace unanimously voted to burn the tea, this did not satisfy "the gentlemen from Elk Ridge and Baltimore Town," who called for total destruction of the *Peggy Stewart*. Seven-eighths of the assembly rejected this demand, but the extremists would not be denied. Throughout the day of October 19, they repeatedly threatened Stewart's home and family. Finally, to prevent further violence, the shipowner agreed to burn his vessel.

Accompanied by the Williams brothers and some of the radical patriots, Stewart boarded his ship and sailed to Windmill Point, where he ran it aground. There, in a wide, level area, lying between the present-day harbor and the US Naval Academy's Bancroft Hall, Stewart personally set his brig and the entire cargo aflame. The ship "burned to the water's edge." More than a century later, when the harbor was dredged to allow for the expansion of the academy, the charred remains of the *Peggy Stewart* were found. Several of the timbers are in the possession of the Maryland Statehouse.

The patriots' harassment of Anthony Stewart temporarily ceased after the destruction of his vessel. But prior to the incident, Stewart had been considered a Tory, and after his experience he again took up his opposition to "the enemies of Government." The patriots in turn resumed their tactics. They hanged and burned Stewart in effigy throughout the county, and they eventually forced him to leave his wife, family, and property for the safety of England.

The *Peggy Stewart* Tea Party, unlike its counterpart in Boston, provoked no response from the British government. England was then attempting to strengthen Loyalist feeling in the southern colonies, and retaliatory measures might have alienated many potential supporters. In addition there was a basic difference between the tea parties at Boston and Annapolis. In the former harbor, the patriots had destroyed tea belonging to the East India Company; in the latter, the actual owners of the brig and tea had set their goods aflame.

Maryland has kept the memory of the *Peggy Stewart* incident alive. A mural in the statehouse depicts Stewart holding a blazing torch to his brig. The shipowner's home still stands on Hanover Street in Annapolis, although its exterior has been radically altered. Moreover, various patriotic organizations in the state, such as the Colonial Dames of America and the Daughters of the American Revolution, annually celebrate the anniversary of the *Peggy Stewart* Tea Party; in fact the Annapolis chapter of the latter organization has adopted the name of the vessel for its own use.

Yorktown Day

At 2:00 P.M. on October 19, 1781, Lieutenant General Lord Charles Cornwallis's more than 7,000 British and Hessian troops unhappily tramped down the Hampton Road outside Yorktown, Virginia, to surrender themselves to their American and French adversaries, commanded by General George Washington. There is a tradition that the British band played "The World Turned Upside Down," and indeed the world had altered; the colonial victory at Yorktown marked the death knell for British control of the 13 American colonies. The peace treaty recognizing American independence was not signed until September 3, 1783, nor ratified until January 14, 1784, but the sporadic fighting that occurred in the intervening two years was anticlimactic.

The battle of Yorktown took place partially because of disunity within the British high command. After General Sir Henry Clinton, the chief of the royal forces in America, captured Charleston, on May 12, 1780, he returned to New York City and put Lord Cornwallis in charge of the southern district, with strict orders to protect South Carolina. Clinton believed that the British should remain on the defensive, holding key cities like New York, Charleston, and Savannah until the acquisition of 10,000 reinforcements would make possible more positive action. The younger, more adventurous Cornwallis wanted to invade North Carolina, and his impressive defeat of the colonists under General Horatio Gates at Camden, South Carolina, on August 16, 1780, won him the support of the inept Lord George Germain, the secretary of state for the colonies. Defeats in South Carolina at Kings Mountain (October 7, 1780) and Cowpens (January 17, 1781), and a Pyrrhic victory in North Carolina at Guilford Court House (March 15, 1781), thwarted Cornwallis's plans for that region, and so he took his army to Virginia, where he established a base on the York River at Yorktown.

The patriot victory there resulted in large measure from well-coordinated American and French operations. Forces under Washington and Jean Baptiste Donatien de Vimeur, comte de Rochambeau, spent the early summer of 1781 unsuccessfully probing Clinton's defenses near New York City. Then word arrived on August 14 that admiral François Joseph Paul, comte de Grasse, would bring his French fleet and more than 3,000 troops to the Chesapeake area and remain there for joint operations until the middle of October. Washington seized the opportunity to trap Cornwallis: he advised the Marquis de Lafayette, who was in Virginia with a large number of troops of the Continental army, to keep the English bottled up on the Yorktown Peninsula. The American commander prepared to move south. On August 21, some 7,000 allied troops, including Rochambeau's 5,000 Frenchmen, left their New York encampments and, slipping past Clinton, sped off to Virginia. On September 5 Admiral de Grasse defeated the British fleet under Sir Thomas Graves off the Chesapeake Capes, and on September 9 Admiral Paul François Jean Nicolas, vicomte de Barras, arrived safely from Rhode Island with siege artillery and provisions. Cornwallis was doomed. The French and American forces slowly enveloped the British positions and by October 6 were ready to begin siege operations. In a night attack on October 15 they captured several strategic positions, and on October 17 Cornwallis asked for terms. As demanded, all his men surrendered two days later.

Washington's aide-de-camp, Lieutenant Colonel Tench Tilghman, officially informed the Continental Congress, assembled in Philadelphia, of the nation's good fortune. Land and naval gun salutes, fireworks, and thanksgiving services conducted by a congressional chaplain, the Reverend Mr. Duffield, in the Dutch Lutheran Church highlighted the celebration of the victory in the capital. The Congress voted special honors to the French commanders, Rochambeau and de

943

Grasse, and to Washington, who, with his wife, Martha, received a warm reception in Philadelphia in November.

Congress on October 29 resolved to erect a marble monument to commemorate the battle of Yorktown, but more urgent matters prevented immediate action. For years many towns celebrated the October 11 anniversary; in Massachusetts, a "Cornwallis," which James Russell Lowell described as "a sort of muster and masquerade," annually recalled the surrender. The approach of the Yorktown Centennial and an outpouring of petitions from historically minded citizens prompted Congress finally to take action on June 7, 1880, to create the memorial. The order of the Ancient Free and Accepted Masons opened the four-day centennial celebration on October 18, 1881, by laying the cornerstone of the Yorktown Monument to the Alliance and Victory. It was completed by 1884. Inscriptions on the base dedicate it as a memorial to the victory, describe the action, celebrate the French alliance, and summarize the peace treaty. The podium, sculpted in the form of a drum, carries the words "One country, one constitution, and one destiny." A granite shaft, decorated with one star for each state in the Union in 1880, rises from the podium, and a sculptured figure of Liberty — replaced in 1956 after the original was damaged in an electrical storm — stands atop the column.

The people of Yorktown have celebrated their day every year since 1881. On the 150th anniversary, in 1931, President Herbert Hoover participated, as did descendants of Lafayette, Rochambeau, and Baron von Steuben, and the then Lord Cornwallis unveiled a bust of his forebear. In 1930, shortly before the impending sesquicentennial, Yorktown Battlefield was established by presidential proclamations as part of Colonial National Monument, which six years later became Colonial National Historical Park. As subsequently enlarged, the park, comprising 9,430 acres, includes Yorktown battlefield; most of nearby Jamestown Island, which was the site of the first permanent English settlement in America; a 22-mile parkway leading from these historic shrines to the famous restoration of Colonial Williamsburg; and the Cape Henry Memorial.

Administered by the National Park Service, the park is visited by thousands annually. Yorktown Day is an occasion of special interest there. Each October 19 the National Park Service conducts a patriotic service at Yorktown Monument in the morning and exercises on the battlefield in the afternoon. Military parades, pageantry, and occasionally participation by French units are part of the festivities. A particularly large celebration was held on Yorktown Day in 1957 in conjunction with the commemoration of Virginia's 350th anniversary. Queen Elizabeth II of England and Prince Philip were among the scores of distinguished guests at Colonial National Historical Park.

OCTOBER 20

Convention of 1818 Signed

On October 20, 1818, representatives of the United States and Great Britain signed a convention in London. The terms of this agreement established the northernmost limits of the Louisiana Purchase by setting the boundary between the United States and Canada at the 49th parallel from the Lake of the Woods west to the crest of the Rocky Mountains. In addition the 1818 document provided that Oregon country, west of the Rockies, would remain open to settlement by both US and British citizens for 10 years without either nation's forfeiting its territorial claim in the Pacific Northwest.

The convention of 1818 also dealt with matters not directly related to territorial disputes. One article granted American citizens fishing rights in the coastal waters of Labrador and Newfoundland. Another renewed the commercial agreement of 1815 that permitted the United States to trade in the East Indies and ended discriminatory duties on imported goods.

MacArthur Returns to the Philippines

In the three weeks after the Japanese attack at Pearl Harbor, the Philippine Islands were the scene of heroic defenses led by General Douglas MacArthur (see January 26) and Major General Jonathan M. ("Skinny") Wainwright. When Manila and Cavite fell to the Japanese on January 2, 1942, the American and Filipino forces withdrew to the Bataan Peninsula, where they resisted a siege for three months. Bataan fell on April 19, and the defenders retreated to Corregidor Island in Manila Bay. Finally, on May 6, Wainwright surrendered Corregidor and its garrison of 11,500.

During the battle for the Philippines, President Franklin D. Roosevelt had directed General MacArthur to leave the islands for Australia, where he was to become supreme commander of Allied forces in the Southwest Pacific Area. MacArthur left Corregidor by PT boat on March 11 and reached Australia on March 17. Arriving in Australia, MacArthur told reporters of his determination to retrieve Allied losses: "The President of the United States ordered me to break through the Japanese lines and proceed from Corregidor to Australia for the purpose, as I understand it, of organizing the American offensive against Japan, a primary object of which is the relief of the Philippines. I came through and I shall return."

MacArthur fulfilled his promise two and one half years later, on October 20, 1944, when he waded ashore at Leyte Island on the first day of the American invasion of the Philippines. The general had a deep attachment to the islands that went far beyond his professional interests as a soldier. In 1900 his father, Major General Arthur MacArthur, had become the military governor of the Philippines and had led the American forces that suppressed the nationalist guerrillas of General Emilio Aguinaldo. The younger MacArthur had courted his second wife in Manila and their son was born there in 1938.

American strategy, developed in the early days of World War II, called for two lines of advance against the Japanese. Admiral Chester W. Nimitz, commander in chief of Pacific Ocean Areas, was to attack westward from the Hawaiian Islands. General MacArthur was to proceed northward from Australia. Early in 1944 forces within MacArthur's Southwest Pacific command fought to secure Papua (the southeastern section of New Guinea), seized the Admiralty Islands, and began a series of amphibious assaults along the northern coast of New Guinea. In the Central Pacific Area, forces under Nimitz's command took the Gilbert Islands late in 1943 and invaded the Marshall Islands early in 1944. Meanwhile, additional bloody encounters, including the struggle for the bitterly contested western Solomon Islands, were taking place in other areas of the Pacific. By March 1944 the Joint Chiefs of Staff in Washington, D.C., agreed that the Allies could soon return to the Philippines, and they proposed November 1944 as the date for an invasion of Mindanao, the southernmost large Philippine island.

During the spring and summer of 1944, MacArthur continued his offensive across the northern coast of New Guinea, leapfrogging his forces in a series of amphibious operations, supported by air cover from Nimitz's carriers. By the end of July MacArthur was at New Guinea's northwest tip.

Meanwhile, Nimitz moved farther westward across the Central Pacific. His carrier forces defeated the bulk of the Japanese fleet on June 19 and 20 in the battle of the Philippine Sea. His army and marine divisions took the island of Saipan in July and then stormed Guam. By mid-September, with the invasions of Morotai and the Palau Islands, the stage was set for the retaking of the Philippines.

Flying in support of the Morotai and Palau landings, Admiral William Halsey's carrier planes bombed the central Philippines on September 12 and 14. The Japanese offered little resistance, and Halsey recommended that MacArthur and Nimitz change the next major objective from Mindanao in the southern Phillipines to Leyte. More centrally located, Leyte offered the Allies potential air and logistical bases from which to carry out further operations. The target lay beyond the reach of land-based planes, but Nimitz offered to make aircraft carrier support available. MacArthur immediately agreed to the proposal and set October 20, 1944, as the new date for his return to the Philippines.

Coordinated army and navy operations underlay the Leyte plans. Lieutenant General Walter Krueger's US Sixth Army, with over 200,000 men, was responsible for the actual invasion of the island. The US 7th Fleet had the assignment of transporting Krueger's troops and of providing direct naval and air support. Lieutenant General George C. Kenney's bombers from Morotai, China-based B-29 bombers, and Admiral Halsey's Third Fleet carrier planes were to attack Japanese air power on Formosa (Taiwan), on the northern Philippine island of Luzon, and in the Netherlands East Indies.

On October 17, 1944, a US Army Ranger battalion landed on Dinagat and Suluan, two of several small islands that guard the entrance to Leyte Gulf, but poor weather conditions forced postponement of further landings until October 18. Minesweepers began operations to clear the waters for the troop carriers, and on October 20, after a two-hour naval bombardment, the full invasion began. At 9:30 A.M. the 21st Regimental Combat Team captured the Panaon Strait. One half hour later, four divisions landed in Leyte Gulf.

Behind the third assault wave of American troops, MacArthur waded ashore on Leyte with the Philippine President, Sergio Osmeña. Standing in pouring rain on the island, MacArthur spoke by radio: "People of the Philippines: I have returned. By the grace of Almighty God, our forces stand again on Philippine soil — soil consecrated by the blood of our two peoples." Reporting that President Osmeña was with him, MacArthur urged the Filipinos to rally to him: "Let the indomitable spirit of Bataan and Corregidor lead on . . . In the name of your sacred dead, strike! Let no heart be faint. Let every arm be steeled. The guidance of Divine God points the way. Follow in His Name to the Holy Grail of righteous victory."

Initially the Japanese expected to make the northern island of Luzon their main defensive position in the Philippines, and so only their 16th

Division met Krueger's Sixth Army. On October 21, however, General Tomoyuki Yamashita, the Japanese commander in the Philippines, decided to focus his efforts on Leyte and immediately began to send 45,000 reinforcements to the western port of Ormoc. In addition the Japanese decided to commit their badly depleted combined fleet in an attempt to destroy the American landing operation.

The Japanese naval undertaking — Sho-Go ("victory operation") — was a desperate gamble, dependent on deception for success and reflecting in its tactics the weakened state of Japanese naval air power. The Sho-Go Plan involved splitting the combined fleet into four groups, one of which, called the Main Group, consisted mostly of carriers (but with few aircraft). The mission of the Main Group was to act as bait to lure Halsey's Third Fleet northward away from Leyte, while three other groups of combat ships — the First and Second Attack Forces and C Force — were to head into Leyte Gulf from two directions in a pincer movement designed to destroy the American transport supporting MacArthur's landings.

Early on October 23, American submarines encountered Vice Admiral Takeo Kurita's First Attack Force west of Leyte and sank two cruisers. On the alert, planes from Halsey's Third Fleet soon discovered and bombarded both the First Attack Force and C Force. So effective were the American planes that Kurita reversed course, a decision that destroyed the coordinated timing necessary to the planned pincer maneuver and encouraged Halsey to go after the Main Group of carriers.

While Halsey moved north, the US Seventh Fleet, under Vice Admiral Thomas C. Kinkaid, took its position in the Surigao Strait, and at 2 A.M. on October 25 smashed the Japanese C Force, sinking all its vessels except one destroyer. The Japanese Second Attack Force withdrew without offering battle.

Much to the dismay of the Americans, Kurita soon reappeared. After Halsey's departure to the north, the Japanese commander had again turned his First Attack Force eastward and on the night of October 24 passed through the San Bernardino Strait north of Leyte. Kurita then turned south against the US Seventh Fleet, which had just routed the Second Attack and C Forces. The Seventh Fleet, which mistakenly thought that Halsey was still guarding the San Bernardino Strait, was taken by surprise. The Americans fought heroically but were in danger of annihilation. Fortunately, Kurita, who by this time had learned of C Force's destruction and feared attack from land-based aircraft, made an incorrect decision and ended the action by withdrawing without pursuing his advantage.

Halsey's Third Fleet followed the Japanese Main Group 150 miles to the north. On the morning of October 25, Halsey engaged the Main Group off Cape Engaño and sank all four Japanese carriers, three destroyers, and one cruiser. The Third Fleet then returned to the vicinity of Leyte.

The battle of Leyte Gulf was a disaster for the Japanese. So desperate had their naval situation become that they began to use suicidal kamikaze tactics. The victory that the US Third and Seventh fleets achieved secured American control of the Pacific waters for the remainder of the war.

On the ground, Japanese lines hardened with the arrival of reinforcements from Luzon, but General Yamashita recognized that the outcome of the battle of Leyte Gulf made an American victory on the ground inevitable. Yamashita decided to withdraw Lieutenant General Sosaku Suzuki's remaining troops to the northern island of Luzon for a final stand, but the military leadership in Tokyo overruled him. Faced with an impossible task, Yamashita continued to send aid to Suzuki, who, in turn, made plans to drive the invaders from Leyte.

Lieutenant General Krueger was determined to reduce the stiffened Japanese resistance in Leyte with a two-pronged offensive against the key western port of Ormoc, through which fresh enemy troops were entering the island. On November 16, after a prolonged battle US troops took the village of Limon, which controlled an important approach to Ormoc. On November 22 the 7th Division moved to Balogo on the southwest coast of the island and began a march north. On December 7 the Seventh Fleet landed the 77th Infantry Division at Deposito, even closer to Ormoc, and three days later, units of the 77th Infantry entered the port.

The Americans had secured the rest of Leyte by the end of the year. The First Cavalry and the 32nd Infantry divisions moved south to join the 77th Division at Libungao on December 20. West of Ormoc, a battalion of the 77th Division seized Palompon, the last Japanese-held port on Leyte, on Christmas Day, 1944. The campaign for Leyte cost the Americans 15,584 casualties and the Japanese well over 70,000.

While the fighting in Leyte was going on, General MacArthur laid complex plans for the capture of Luzon, the large northern Philippine island, which the Japanese held with 250,000 troops, although lacking air and naval support. The first part of the operation, designed to mislead the Japanese as to the location of the main

US assault, was to be the seizure of a stepping-stone, the island of Mindoro, which lies north-west of Leyte and south of Luzon. The second part of the operation called for General Krueger's Sixth Army to go by sea clear around to the northwest coast of Luzon and make the main amphibious landing at Lingayen Gulf. Nimitz's Seventh Fleet was to provide air and naval support for the invasion, which was scheduled to begin on December 20, 1944.

Operations on Leyte took longer than expected, however, and MacArthur was forced to delay implementation of his Luzon plan. A brigade-size task force landed on Mindoro on December 15, and by December 23 two airfields were in operation on that island. On January 9, 1945, Krueger's Sixth Army began to land at the Lingayen Gulf beaches. By the end of the month the Americans had penetrated deeply into the interior of Luzon. Krueger's XIV Corps, commanded by Major General Oscar W. Griswold, had captured Clark Field, and one regiment of the Corps had advanced southward as far as Calumpit, less than 30 miles north of Manila.

MacArthur's attention now turned to the recapture of the Philippine capital. On January 29 the US XI Corps landed at San Antonio to secure Subic Bay and block off the Bataan Peninsula. Then, on January 31, the 11th Airborne Division made an amphibious landing at Nasugbu, southwest of Manila, and began a drive toward the capital. By February 3, two vanguard columns from the First Cavalry reached the outskirts of the city, liberated 3,500 Allied internees held at the University of Santo Tomás, and seized Malacañan Palace, the official residence of the president of the Philippines. A regiment of the 37th Infantry took control of Bilibid Prison on February 4 and set free 1,300 more military and civilian captives.

General Yamashita had not wanted Japanese forces to attempt to hold Manila, but the naval commander there decided to conduct a frantic defense of the city. Reluctantly, MacArthur in mid-February allowed the unrestricted use of artillery to rout the determined foe. By February 14 the 1st Cavalry, which had approached from the north, and the 11th Airborne, which had arrived from the south, made contact. The Japanese in Manila were virtually trapped. The 37th Division then drove the Japanese back into the old walled city of Intramuros and eliminated the final resistance in Manila by March 4.

Even as the fighting raged, MacArthur reestablished the Philippine government. On February 27, 1945, MacArthur announced the restoration of the constitutional government of President Osmeña in a ceremony at the Mala-cañan Palace, which fortunately had survived the fighting intact.

Japanese resistance continued, however, after the fall of Manila, and it was not until July 5, 1945, that MacArthur could announce: "All the Philippines are now liberated." Even then the Philippine campaign was not totally concluded: extensive mopping-up operations continued until Japan's general surrender the following month (see August 15). The enemy had fought an effective delaying action that tied down several American divisions and caused 62,143 ground casualties within MacArthur's command. The Japanese paid an even heavier price; the fighting in the Philippines destroyed the remnants of their navy and air force and cost them nearly 450,000 ground troops.

On October 20, 1969, twenty-five years after the actual event, MacArthur's historic return to the Philippines was reenacted by Filipino and American officials and some 200 Filipino soldiers who swarmed ashore on Leyte's Red Beach. The soldiers repeated the planting of the Filipino and American flags on the beach. President Ferdinand Marcos of the Philippines, speaking at the anniversary ceremonies, referred to the 1944 landing and the cooperation of Filipino and American soldiers in liberating the islands from the Japanese as "one of the most luminous chapters in the history of Philippine-American friendship." President Marcos and US Ambassador to the Philippines Henry A. Byroade then laid the cornerstone for a MacArthur memorial just off the beach where the general had gone ashore, fulfilling his pledge to return to the Philippines. Also participating in the ceremonies was Foreign Secretary Carlos P. Romulo of the Philippines, who, as brigadier general and aide to MacArthur, had waded ashore with him at the time of the original landing.

OCTOBER 21

Electric Light Bulb Perfected

On October 21, 1879, Thomas Edison and his associates at Menlo Park, New Jersey, tested an incandescent light bulb that burned for a recorded 13½ hours. Their experiment demonstrated the feasibility of electric lighting and thus marked the beginning of a new era.

Edison was not the first to try to devise an electric light bulb. During the half century preceding his achievement, scientists throughout the world had attempted to develop a practical technique for electric lighting. Experiments in England, Russia, and the United States led to devices that utilized platinum or carbon conductors enclosed in glass globes or tubes. But the results were disappointing for the earlier incandescent lamps burned for only a few moments.

Edison himself briefly experimented with electric lighting in 1876 and again in 1877, but both times he abandoned the project without making any significant discoveries. In 1878, however, his interest in electric light revived. He felt frustrated with the work on the phonograph that had been occupying his attention, and he later recalled, "Just at that time I wanted to take up something new." With the encouragement of Grosvenor P. Lowrey, the general counsel for Western Union, and Professor George F. Barker of the University of Pennsylvania, he launched the investigation that ultimately produced one of the world's greatest inventions.

Before beginning his own experiments, Edison carefully studied the work of others. He also traveled to Ansonia, Connecticut, in September, to see a display of electric arc lights. This exhibit greatly impressed Edison, but it did not convince him of the utility of the arc light, and he commented to his host, William Wallace, "I believe I can beat you making the electric light. I do not think you are working in the right direction."

Late in the autumn of 1878 Edison gave a press interview at which he made public his intention to devise an electrical system capable of lighting New York City. At the time that Edison made his announcement, electric arc lights had been installed in several areas, including the Avenue de l'Opéra in Paris and John Wanamaker's department store in Philadelphia. These lights burned in open globes, emitted a blinding glare and noxious odors, and were wired to the dynamo in series, so that they could not be individually operated. Edison was convinced that further work with arc lights would not produce a practical means of household lighting. He proposed to create an entirely different electric lighting system, one that would be modeled closely on the gas lighting systems that then illuminated many American cities.

Edison's plan seemed visionary. The gas lighting systems then in existence permitted a central gashouse to supply energy via gas mains and smaller branch pipes to thousands of individual jets that could be individually turned on or off. To develop a similar electrical lighting system, Edison not only had to produce a workable light bulb, but had to deal with much more perplexing problems involving electrical resistance, distribution of power, and fluctuating pressure in electrical conductors.

Confident that he could overcome these prob-lems, Edison began work on his project. By choosing to create an entire lighting system rather than a single device, he gained a perspective that eventually allowed him to resolve the difficulties that had stymied other inventors and scientists. He was forced to consider problems of power distribution and consumption that his predecessors had more or less ignored. They had wired their devices to the power source in series and had constructed low-resistance lights that consumed large quantities of current. Edison realized that such apparatuses were impractical for the lighting network he envisioned, and he determined to investigate other possibilities. He turned his attention to parallel wiring, which would permit each unit to operate independently of the others in a circuit, and he began work on a high-resistance incandescent light bulb that would use very little current.

To finance the search for a practical means of lighting, Edison's friend and financial adviser, Grosvenor Lowrey, persuaded some of the wealthiest people in the United States to invest in the project. In the autumn of 1878 the Edison Electric Light Company was formed to "own, manufacture, operate and license the use of various apparatus used in producing light, heat and power by electricity." In return for agreeing to assign to the corporation any invention or improvement he might make in electric lighting during the following five years, Edison received 2,500 shares of company stock; for their part, such important financial figures as W. H. Vanderbilt, Western Union president Norvin Green, and J. P. Morgan partner Eggisto Fabbri agreed to subscribe $50,000 for Edison Electric's remaining 500 shares of stock.

To create a high-resistance incandescent light bulb, Edison first had to find a material that could sustain high temperatures without fusing, melting, or burning out. Although he had gained a substantial knowledge of the uses of carbon from his work with the phonograph, he was unsuccessful in his initial experiments using strips of carbonized paper for the "burner" (or partial conductor) in a glass globe that he had partially exhausted of air. Similarly fruitless were his efforts, also in the autumn of 1878, to make a burner of platinum wire. But these attempts made Edison aware of the need to produce a greater vacuum in his glass container and to calculate the exact resistance in ohms of potential burner materials.

Although Edison originally boasted that his lighting system would be completed within six weeks, the project proved much more complicated than he had expected. By the end of the winter of 1878–1879, he and his associates at Menlo Park had experimented with a wide variety of materials in their search for a suitable burner. With the new Sprengel pump, they had raised the vacuum in their glass globes to within one or two millimeters of full exhaustion of air, and in addition they had completed extensive mathematical calculations of electrical conductors, lamp resistance, and dynamo capacities. Their efforts yielded much valuable data, but considerable work remained ahead.

Throughout the spring and summer of 1879, Edison's team concentrated on three major problems: the development of a dynamo that could power their new lighting system, which would require a constant-voltage current in a multiple circuit; the production of a higher vacuum in the glass globe of their lighting device; and the search for a perfect incandescent material. By the autumn of 1879 they had completed work on a dynamo that converted steam power into electrical energy with 90 percent efficiency, and they succeeded in excluding all but a one-millionth part of an atmosphere from their light globes. But experiments to find a suitable illuminant continued.

After attempting to use more than 1,500 materials for the burner in his light, Edison, by the summer of 1879, had resumed his work with carbon, the element with the highest melting point. His earlier work with carbon had been unsuccessful because carbon in its natural state is porous and tends to absorb gases. However, during his year of experimentation, Edison had learned that it was possible to expel occluded gases by sending a current through the burner material and heating it at the same time that air was being pumped out of the glass globe of the light bulb. This procedure gave the burner substance a greater resistance to high temperature. It allowed Edison to construct a light with a platinum burner capable of burning for over an hour, and, more important, it permitted him to perfect the light with a carbon illuminant, the precursor of today's modern light bulb.

Contrary to popular opinion, Edison did not solve the problems of electric illumination by accident or by unscientific methods. Months of mathematical calculations of voltage, current, conductor resistance, and other factors led Edison to conclude that a carbon filament was best suited for use as the illuminant. Then, with his associates at Menlo Park, he further estimated that the carbon burner should be only one sixty-fourth of an inch in diameter and about six inches long. But the construction of such a thin burner from a substance as crumbly as carbon proved to be extremely difficult.

For months the scientists experimented with threadlike carbon filaments. By October 1879, feeling that success was near, they worked around the clock. After hundreds of tests, their labors were rewarded on October 21. Using a filament of ordinary cotton thread that had been packed with powdered carbon in an earthenware crucible and then heated to a high temperature, Edison began the ninth of a series of experiments. At 1:30 A.M. he attached the filament to a power source. Thirteen and one half hours later, at 3:00 P.M. the following afternoon, the light was still burning.

The light that glowed for at least the 13½ hours recorded in the Menlo Park notebooks demonstrated the feasibility of electric lighting. In other sources, there is frequent reference to a lamp that burned for as long as 40 hours — possibly another early accomplishment, but one not recorded in the notebooks. In any event, the significant recorded breakthrough came on October 21, 1879.

The success did not end Edison's search for an even more perfect burner substance. During the weeks that followed, he and his associates made carbonized filaments from innumerable materials, including celluloid, coconut shell, and even hairs clipped from the beard of staff member J. U. Mackenzie. But it was bristol cardboard that proved best suited for use as the filament in the electric light. Edison's first experiments with this material produced a lamp that burned for 170 hours, and he was confident that he could perfect this device so that it would stay incandescent much longer.

On December 21, 1879, the New York *Herald* made public Edison's successful experiment of October 21. The announcement was greeted with amazement, and the Wizard of Menlo Park was acclaimed in all parts of the world. Much work, even the necessity of inventing other new electrical appliances, still remained before Edison's dream of lighting New York City could come true. But by December 1879 he had solved the greatest of the problems facing those who attempted to devise a practical system of electric lighting.

OCTOBER 22

Cuban Missile Crisis

In a televised address on October 22, 1962, President John F. Kennedy declared that the United States would take whatever steps were necessary to force the removal from neighboring Cuba of offensive weapons and installations — missiles, launching sites, and jet bombers — that had been placed there by the Soviet Union. Pending compliance with this demand, Kennedy announced imposition of a naval "quarantine" to prevent the further importation of offensive weapons into Cuba.

Failing compliance, the President added, the quarantine — in effect a limited blockade — would be merely an initial step. Furthermore, he declared, it would be US policy to regard "any nuclear missile launched from Cuba against any nation in the Western Hemisphere as an attack by the Soviet Union on the United States requiring a full retaliatory response on the Soviet Union."

With the threat of nuclear confrontation between the world's two greatest powers, the quarantine went into effect on October 24. For five long days, during which several Cuba-bound Soviet vessels altered their course, the world held its breath. Finally, on October 28, Soviet Premier Nikita Khrushchev informed Washington that the weapons regarded by the United States as offensive would be removed as quickly as possible.

The decision apparently was news to Cuban premier Fidel Castro, the revolutionist and subsequently avowed Marxist who had come to power in 1959. Castro's denunciations notwithstanding, it appeared that the offensive missiles had been removed and the missile bases dismantled by November 20, 1962, and the bombers removed by early December — developments preceded by the visits to Cuba of United Nations Secretary-General U Thant, who played a key role in negotiations, and Soviet First Deputy Premier Anastas I. Mikoyan.

Premier Krushchev was turned out of power in October 1964 — for various reasons, including failures in domestic agriculture. One of his "errors," however, was reported to have been the Cuban missile episode.

Shemini Atzeret

This is a movable event. See note on page xxvi.

Although the Jewish observance Shemini Atzeret actually is the eighth day of Sukkot (see October 15), it is celebrated as a separate holiday, dedicated to the love of God. Literally, Shemini Atzeret means Eighth Day of Solemn Assembly. On this day in ancient times prayers for rain were recited, a practice continued in Orthodox services today. The first day of Shemini Atzeret also is one of four Jewish holidays during which the *Yizkor* — memorial rite for the dead (members of the immediate family, friends, relatives, and in recent decades the martyred six million Jewish victims of Nazism) — is observed. (This service is also held on Yom Kippur; on the second day of Shavuot; and on the last day of Passover.)

Orthodox and Conservative Jews (and some Reform Jews) celebrate the second day of Shemini Atzeret as Simhat Torah, the Rejoicing in the Law. The festival is dedicated to the completion of the year's cycle of reading from the Torah (Pentateuch) and the beginning of the annual cycle again, thus affirming that the study of God's word is an unending process. The process of reading from the Torah continues throughout the year in all synagogues. A portion from the Pentateuch and a portion from the Prophets are read each Sabbath until on Simhat Torah the last portion — the concluding section of Deuteronomy — is read and the entire Pentateuch completed. The new cycle begins immediately, at the same service, with the reading of the first portion from the Pentateuch — the opening section of Genesis.

On Simhat Torah the scrolls of the law are taken from the ark and carried around the synagogue, amid great rejoicing. Members of the congregation — men and women — touch the Torah, as a blessing. Children walk in the procession carrying banners and flags, often with an apple on top of the flagstick. Sweets and candies are distributed after the service. Simhat Torah is one of the happiest days of the whole joyful period of Sukkot. In Orthodox and Conservative synagogues, there is actual dancing while the scrolls are carried around. An attempt is made to allow every male over the age of thirteen to participate in this carrying of the scrolls. In Hasidic communities such as that of Brooklyn's Williamsburg district, people come from distant areas to behold the joyful sight of sedate, elderly men (and others as well) singing and dancing in the street on Simhat Torah.

OCTOBER 23

Francis Hopkinson Smith's Birthday

Francis Hopkinson Smith, one of the most versatile Americans of his generation, was born in Baltimore, Maryland, on October 23, 1838. A maternal great-grandfather, Francis Hopkinson, was a poet and a signer of the Declaration of Independence; his father, Francis Smith, distinguished himself as a musician, philosopher, and mathematician. The younger Smith continued his family's tradition of wide interests and gained fame as an engineer, artist, and writer.

Financial necessity forced Smith to begin his career as a shipping clerk in his brother's iron foundry, but neither Baltimore nor his brother's business held a lasting attraction for him. Shortly after the Civil War, he moved to New York, where he set himself up as an engineer. His enterprise flourished and he won important government contracts, including those for the Block Island breakwater, the foundation of the Statue of Liberty, and the Race Rock Lighthouse. Smith considered the latter structure his greatest engineering achievement, and, indeed, the lighthouse, situated in the rough waters six miles off the coast of New London, Connecticut, demanded the utmost use of its designer's innovative and technical abilities.

Engineering was Smith's occupation, art his passion. A proponent of "art for its own sake and not as a mere means of making money," he believed that a clear-cut distinction between art and earning a livelihood would keep the former "high and noble, [a man's] worthiest and best expression." For 30 years Smith lived by this dictum, devoting his work week to engineering and his spare time to art. His European vacations provided him with his best opportunities to indulge his artistic interests. During one stay in the Mediterranean region he completed 53 pictures in an equal number of days. But despite the relatively brief periods he allowed for painting, Smith's works are not without artistic merit. He is best known for his watercolors of Venice, but perhaps even more perceptive are his charcoal studies: *Charcoals of New and Old New York, In Thackeray's London,* and *In Dickens's London.*

At the age of 53 Smith published his first fictional work, *Colonel Carter of Cartersville.* This collection of tales about an impoverished aristocrat in the post–Civil War South proved so successful that its author gave up his engineering business and turned to writing as a full-time career. Smith wrote many novels, short stories, and travel accounts during the next two decades. Some of these works are semi-autobiographical, but all reveal his special talent with the anecdote and the local color sketch. He died in New York on April 7, 1915.

Simhat Torah

This is a movable event. See note on page xxvi.

The happy occasion of Simhat Torah (Rejoicing in the Law) is observed by Orthodox and Conservative Jews as a second day of Shemini Atzeret and by Reform Jews concurrently with Shemini Atzeret (see October 22).

OCTOBER 24

Pennsylvania Day

Pennsylvania's history begins with the man whose name it bears. William Penn, the son of the wealthy and influential Admiral Sir William Penn, was born in London on October 24, 1644. His father was a creditor and close friend of both King Charles II and his brother the duke of York, who later became James II.

Such connections would have guaranteed young William Penn's worldly success, but he forsook these advantages for the sake of conscience. He associated himself with George Fox's Society of Friends, commonly called by the then derogatory sobriquet Quakers, and came to know the opprobrium reserved for that radical religious group. Christ Church in Oxford expelled the 18-year-old Penn when he interfered with the college's divine service in protest against the established Anglican religion. To correct such theological views and behavior, the senior Penn severely thrashed his son and then sent him on a European tour designed to revive his worldly interests. Penn temporarily disavowed Quakerism, but by 1668 he had rejoined the sect.

Dismayed by the excesses of Restoration England, the Quakers, like so many 17th century dissidents, longed to establish a moral oasis in the New World. And Penn had the means by which the dream of a Quaker colony could become a reality. His father's death in 1670 left him with a large fortune, including a claim of several thousand pounds against the crown. Travels through northern Europe in 1676 convinced Penn that there was a sufficient number of Quakers and other religious dissidents to populate a new colony. In 1680 – perhaps in lieu of requesting the unpaid royal debt – he petitioned Charles II for a grant of land in America.

The king's response was favorable, and, despite the opposition of Parliament, Penn received in March 1681 absolute title to the territory between 43° and 40° north latitude extending west of the Delaware River through five degrees longitude. The following year the duke of York added the three Delaware counties of Newcastle, Sussex, and Kent to Penn's jurisdiction in return for an annual rent of five shillings and a "rose to be paid on the Feast of St. Michael the Archangel." This exchange was the precedent, no doubt, for several colorful "rose rent" ceremonies annually enacted in Pennsylvania today.

Penn received his grant at a time when England was becoming interested in exerting more control over its American colonies. For this reason, Penn's charter contained several restrictions not included in earlier grants: Laws could be enacted only with assembly approval, and none could be passed that were contrary to those of England; decisions of provincial courts could be appealed to the crown; strict obedience to the Navigation Acts was to be maintained;

and Parliament's theoretical right to tax the colony was affirmed in a rather ambiguous clause.

Penn was free to establish any form of government that would not violate the charter restrictions. His first "frame of government," which he wrote in 1682 while still in England, provided for a governor (Penn himself or his appointee) and a bicameral legislature elected by the freemen of the colony. The upper house, or council, of 72 members had the power to initiate all bills, and an assembly of 200 to 500 representatives could either approve or reject the proposed legislation. The franchise was open to all men who held a small amount of land or paid taxes. In 1683 a second frame of government reduced the council and assembly to 18 and 32 members respectively, after it became apparent that their original size prevented efficient operation.

Penn's foresight and planning insured the success of his colony. To attract settlers to the area, he published in 1682 a pamphlet entitled *Some Account of the Province of Pennsylvania*. The tract, which was translated into German, French, and Dutch and distributed throughout Europe, guaranteed complete religious freedom to all believers in God and offered liberal terms for obtaining land. Penn himself visited his colony in 1682. During his two-year stay he supervised the planning of the city of Philadelphia. But even more important, his insistence that the colonists treat the Indians well inaugurated what was to be a 70-year period of good relations between the newcomers and the Native Americans.

Penn returned to England in 1684 in an attempt to settle his dispute with Lord Baltimore over the boundary between Pennsylvania and Maryland. Despite his absence the colony flourished. Peopled by immigrants from the British Isles, Holland, the Rhineland, and France, Pennsylvania's population grew from about 1,000 in 1682 to 12,000 in 1689. The economy of the colony also thrived as its exports of wheat, beef, and pork found ready markets in the West Indies.

In 1699 Penn returned to his colony, and on November 8, 1701, he issued the Charter of Privileges, the constitution by which Pennsylvania was governed until the American Revolution. This plan provided for a unicameral legislature elected by the freemen and a governor appointed by the proprietor. All laws needed the approval of both the assembly and the chief executive before becoming effective. The Charter of Privileges also explicitly guaranteed religious freedom to all believers in the "One Almighty God."

The controversy over his colony's southern boundary again called Penn back to England in 1701, but he was unable to reach a satisfactory settlement. (The matter was not settled until 1764, when the surveyors Charles Mason and Jeremiah Dixon established their famous line at 39°43′26″.) During his tragic declining years, the agents Penn had entrusted with his fortune cheated him, and he fell deeply into debt. His financial condition deteriorated so seriously that he was forced to spend a number of months in debtors' prison. In 1708 his insolvency forced him to mortgage Pennsylvania to trustees. Three years later Penn suffered his first stroke, and the following year two additional attacks left him an invalid. He was virtually helpless until his death in 1718.

Pennsylvanians have been faithful to the memory of the founder of their commonwealth. In 1932 the 250th anniversary of the arrival of Penn on the banks of the Delaware was celebrated. Preceded by a lesser observance the previous year, it was actually the second celebration of what has since become known as Pennsylvania Day. Governor Gifford Pinchot, setting a pattern for his successors, proclaimed October 24, 1932, William Penn Commemoration Day. Ceremonies honoring Pennsylvania's founder were highlighted by radio addresses by the heads of several European countries and a special letter written by President Herbert Hoover. Moreover, interest in the anniversary was not limited to the commonwealth; a pageant at Jordans, Buckinghamshire, England, where Penn and his family are buried, also commemorated the founding.

The tercentenary of Penn's birth in 1944 was also celebrated in many areas. More than 2,580 exercises were held in his honor throughout 19 states. In Pennsylvania, over 1,500 schools participated in the festivities, and most added to the beauty of the state by planting and dedicating the state's tree, the hemlock, to the memory of the founder. What was perhaps the most outstanding contribution of Penn — his plan for religious freedom in his colony — was commemorated on October 22, 1944. On this day, designated Toleration Sunday, an estimated 15,000 religious leaders throughout the state paid tribute to Penn. Many publications were commissioned to provide a record of the proceedings, including *Remember William Penn, 1644–1944*, an illustrated volume published by the commonwealth and released through Pennsylvania's Historical and Museum Commission in Harrisburg.

In recent years the week of October 24 has been proclaimed Pennsylvania Week by the governor. Celebrations are generally local, rather than statewide. The present Penn commemoration on and around October 24 was preceded by a similar earlier observance, authorized by law in 1927 but scheduled for March rather than October. Earlier — in 1916 and previous years — October 14 (Penn's birth date by the Julian, or

Old Style, calendar) had been informally celebrated.

Visitors to Philadelphia today are surrounded by reminders of the city's founder. The most prominent of these is the huge statue of Penn atop the City Hall Tower. Less well known are the treasures housed by the Historical Society of Pennsylvania. These holdings include a letter Penn wrote to "the King or Kings of Indians" before he left England and a wampum belt that he received from the Indians as a token of goodwill. On display at the Pennsylvania Academy of Fine Arts is the painting *Penn's Treaty with the Indians* by the Quaker artist Benjamin West. Although the scene that West depicted probably never actually occurred, the work accurately conveys the bond of friendship and mutual trust between Pennsylvania's proprietor and the Native Americans.

Harrisburg, the state capital, is the home of the William Penn Memorial Museum, which opened in 1965. This five-story circular structure houses Janet de Coux's 18-foot, 3,800-pound bronze casting of the state's founder. The 90-by-24-foot mural by Vincent Maragliotti depicting the history of the state's attempt to fulfill Penn's ideals of freedom and justice, as well as the original charter that Penn received from Charles II in 1681, may also be seen there.

A reconstruction of Pennsbury Manor, Penn's home on the banks of the Delaware near Morrisville, can be visited today. Penn's cousin and deputy governor, William Markham, selected the site for the house prior to the proprietor's arrival in the New World. On July 15, 1682, Penn himself purchased this land from the Delaware Indians for 350 fathoms of wampum, 300 guilders, and English goods. Construction of the manor was quite advanced before Penn's departure in 1684, and it continued throughout his 15-year absence. When its owner returned to America in 1699 the house was ready, and for two years the Penn family resided in the gracious three-story brick home. Following Penn's return to England, however, the manor fell rapidly into ruin.

The 1932 celebration of Penn's birthday provided the impetus for restoring Pennsbury Manor. At a ceremony on October 23, 1932, Charles Warner presented the commonwealth with the deed to the nine acres upon which the manor's original buildings had stood. Subsequent excavations of the site unearthed such items as original bricks, nails, glass, and the delft tiles that had surrounded the fireplaces. The cornerstone of the new manor was laid in April 1938, and the house and outbuildings were reconstructed in accordance with plans indicated by the remains and by Penn's written instruction to his deputies

in America. Within a decade the project was completed, and visitors can now view the entire manorial complex, which includes the bake and brew house, smokehouse, icehouse, and barn. Pennsbury Manor is situated on almost 40 acres of landscaped gardens and walks. Though few original pieces were uncovered during the excavations, most of the house's furnishings are period antiques.

United Nations Day

In World War II approximately 25 million to 30 million military personnel and civilians died, and property damage was so great that it was impossible to estimate. No war in history had ever produced such appalling statistics. Even before the fighting ended, the Allied leaders recognized their obligation to attempt to prevent a repetition of this tragedy. Toward this end, they began preparations for the creation of a new international organization designed to help maintain world peace.

As early as October 1943 the foreign ministers of Great Britain, the Soviet Union, and the United States met in Moscow and agreed to establish a new peace-keeping organization. During the following year a number of conferences of the so-called United Nations — that is, those countries that had agreed to cooperate in the fight against the Axis powers according to the principles laid down in the Atlantic Charter (see August 14) — dealt with specific problems arising from the war. To aid countries that had fallen under Axis control, the UN Relief and Rehabilitation Administration was set up on November 9, 1943; to restore and expand educational opportunities, the UN Organization for Educational and Cultural Reconstruction was proposed in April 1944; and to stabilize international finances the UN Monetary and Financial Conference, otherwise known as the Bretton Woods Conference, was held from July 1 to July 22, 1944.

The first discussions concerning the actual establishment of the proposed international peace-keeping organization took place at the Dumbarton Oaks estate in Washington, D.C. Meeting between August 21 and September 27, 1944, representatives of the United States, Great Britain, the Soviet Union, and Nationalist China considered various problems pertaining to the structure of the new agency. The results of these talks, which were released in October 1944, became the basis for the UN Charter.

Only one major question, voting procedure in the UN Security Council, remained unresolved after October 1944. At Dumbarton Oaks the Soviet delegates had insisted that the permanent members of the Security Council should have the right to bar discussion of disputes in which they were involved. The United States would not accept this plan.

On February 3 and 4, 1945, President Franklin D. Roosevelt, Prime Minister Winston Churchill, and Premier Joseph Stalin met at Yalta, in the USSR, considering, among other issues, the organization of the United Nations and the critical voting procedure problem in the Security Council. Their talks produced important results: the Soviet Union was allowed three votes in the General Assembly since the Ukraine and Byelorussia (White Russia) were to be considered independent nations for voting purposes. But even more important, the Russians abandoned their former demands and agreed to a voting formula that allowed each permanent member of the Security Council veto power over the final decisions rather than over the discussions of that body.

With the Big Three powers in agreement on all major issues concerning the structure and organization of the United Nations, representatives of 46 nations gathered at the Opera House in San Francisco on April 25, 1945, to draft the organization's charter. The document, which they unanimously approved on June 26, 1945, provided for the six chief organs of the United Nations: the General Assembly, or policy-making body; the Security Council, which in theory functions in continuous session to resolve international military and political problems; the Economic and Social Council, which is entrusted with the preservation of fundamental human rights and freedoms; the International Court of Justice, which mediates legal disputes between countries; the Trusteeship Council, which administers the trust territories; and the Secretariat, or administrative agency.

Ratification of the UN charter by the signatory nations was swift. Even the US Senate, which had rejected the League of Nations three decades earlier, acted quickly and on July 28, 1945, approved US membership. By October 24, 1945, the requisite 29 nations, including the five permanent members of the Security Council — Great Britain, France, the United States, the Soviet Union, and China — had ratified the charter, and it was on that day that the United Nations came into formal existence.

Since its establishment, membership in the United Nations has risen to more than 140. Although its efforts to preserve peace have not always been successful, the organization has served as an important international forum dealing with such crises as the conflicts in Korea, the Suez Canal, the Middle East, and Vietnam. The United Nations has also made significant progress toward restricting the production and testing of nuclear armaments.

Working through specialized agencies — for example, the World Health Organization and the United Nations Children's Emergency Fund (UNICEF) — the United Nations also advances humanitarian causes, including the improvement of living standards and the elimination of disease, two goals also promoted by UNESCO (United Nations Educational, Scientific, and Cultural Organization), which seeks, by furthering education and the free exchange of ideas and achievements, to diminish social, religious, and racial tensions throughout the world.

United Nations headquarters are located in New York City. The architecturally striking complex, situated on First Avenue between 42nd and 48th streets, is one of the city's most visited attractions. At the General Assembly building, the public may attend the regular sessions of that body, which usually begin on the third Tuesday in September. Guided hour-long tours also acquaint visitors with the Conference Building, where the Economic and Social Council, the Trusteeship Council, and the Security Council convene in modern chambers that were the gifts of three Scandinavian nations. Another high point of the tours is the tall, glass-walled Secretariat building, where the administrative work of the organization is done. Access to the Dag Hammarskjold Library is more limited; only those engaged in professional or doctoral research projects may obtain permission to use this facility.

UN associations have been set up in more than 60 member countries to publicize the organization's work. In the United States, the American Association for the United Nations and the US Committee for the United Nations worked independently for many years to encourage support for the UN's undertakings. In the early 1960s these two groups merged to form the nonprofit, nonpartisan, privately-run United Nations Association of the United States of America. This group makes available numerous publications and programs and serves as the chief coordinator of this country's annual United Nations Day observances.

In accordance with the October 31, 1947, declaration of the General Assembly, each member nation annually observes October 24 as United Nations Day. The United States is no exception. Every year countless commemorations mark the nationwide celebration, and in some areas the entire week in which October 24 occurs is known as United Nations Week.

Since 1948 the President of the United States has issued a proclamation encouraging the citizens of this country to participate in United Nation Day observances. Under the direction of the national chairman for United Nations Day, who is annually appointed by the Chief Executive, the UN Association each year distributes approximately 1 million copies of the presidential proclamation to state and muncipal leaders and urges observance of the day. A majority of US governors customarily issue United Nations Day proclamations. They also appoint United Nations Day directors, as do individual communities across the nation.

Observances of United Nations Day and Week are varied. Many localities sponsor parades, international fairs, and dinners featuring the foods of numerous countries. In New York City, UN delegates and their spouses may attend the annual United Nations Day ball. In Washington, D.C., the chiefs of the diplomatic missions to the United States are invited to the annual UN concert. But the activities of United Nations Day and Week are not intended merely to entertain. Pertinent debates, film showings, and discussions are also held in many areas to acquaint the public with the workings of the international organization.

In many states schools pay tribute to the United Nations during United Nations Day and Week. Folk festivals featuring the authentic music, songs, and dances of different countries are popular in some regions. Many educators organize programs on other member nations and encourage their pupils to learn about their geography, products, cultures, and governments. Many schools also hold discussions and display special exhibits on the role of the United Nations in world affairs.

OCTOBER 25

Richard E. Byrd's Birthday

An attitude of determination and a searching gaze are portrayed in the first of the statues lining the Avenue of Heroes, which flanks Memorial Avenue between Arlington National Cemetery in Virginia and the bridge to Washington, D.C. The bearing of the statue is entirely appropriate to the subject — Admiral Richard E. Byrd, the pioneer aviator and explorer of the Antarctic, who is buried in Arlington Cemetery. The eight-foot bronze by Felix de Weldon was commissioned by the National Geographic Society at the behest of Congress, which authorized the monument soon after the explorer's death in 1957. It was presented by the Society at dedication ceremonies on November 13, 1961, and accepted for the nation by Lyndon B. Johnson, then Vice President, who described Byrd as "one of the great Americans of our time," "a man who lived life to the hilt" and "discovered . . . that happiness comes only from striving in a worthwhile cause." Other dedication day speakers were Secretary of the Navy John B. Connally Jr., who announced that the guided missile destroyer USS *Richard E. Byrd* would be launched in February 1962; and another member of Virginia's noted Byrd family, the explorer's brother, Senator Harry F. Byrd. During his own lifetime, Byrd was the recipient of many honors, including some of the nation's most cherished decorations and numerous honorary degrees, foreign awards, and society memberships.

Richard Evelyn Byrd, who was born on October 25, 1888, in Winchester, Virginia, began exploring early — by traveling around the world alone when he was 12. After attending the Shenandoah Valley Military Academy, Virginia Military Institute, and the University of Virginia, he entered the US Naval Academy at Annapolis. Elected president of his class while a plebe, he was also a member of the football squad and gymnastics team — pursuits that resulted in fractures of his right foot and ankle. They caused him to miss his semiannual examinations and led to a months-long bout with the ankle injury and a race to catch up with his studies. Years after his graduation in 1912, he recalled that "this terrific struggle . . . to graduate taught me a great lesson — that it is by struggle that we progress."

Byrd was assigned to active navy duty, but his injured leg proved too weak for standing long watches, which caused pain throughout his body. He was retired for physical disability in March 1916 but recalled two months later. In his new assignment he worked night and day to organize the US Navy's Commission on Training Camps and worried that he would not see combat duty. The resulting strain on his health was severe. He lost 25 pounds and was ordered by a medical board to take a leave.

He had, however, won the board's permission to learn to fly when he was well. The prospect, which excited him, was better than any medicine. He was pronounced in perfect health two months later, reported to the Naval Aeronautic Station at Pensacola, Florida, and was a full-fledged naval aviator by the spring of 1918. "From that moment . . . ," he later wrote, "my ambition was to make a career out of aviation. Not merely in the sense of routine flying, but rather in the pioneering sense."

During World War I, Byrd commanded the US air patrol operating from Canada. In administrative positions, he subsequently devised several instruments for aerial navigation and played an important role in the development of naval aviation reserves and in the enactment of navy-oriented legislation, including that creating the navy's Bureau of Aeronautics.

His career in polar exploration began in 1925, when he was named commander of the naval aviation unit accompanying Donald B. Mac-Millan's expedition to the North Polar regions, sponsored by the National Geographic Society. The next year, Byrd and Floyd Bennett returned to the area and on May 9, 1926, became the first men to fly over the North Pole. Byrd received the Congressional Medal of Honor, the Distinguished Service Medal, and the society's Hubbard Medal. He was praised for his courage, vision, and persistence by President Calvin Coolidge in an address to National Geographic Society members, and he was promoted to the rank of commander. He recorded his experiences in *Skyward* (1928). A year later Byrd and three companions were saluted by New Yorkers with a ticker-tape parade up Broadway after making the first nonstop flight to Europe by a multi-engined plane.

Described as "straight as a jack staff, handsome, and forthright," with an appealing enthusiasm and warmth, the aviator won additional support from the National Geographic Society for his first expedition to Antarctica (1928–1930). His party set out from New York on August 25, 1928, and in December established a base, Little America, from which Byrd and three others made the first flight over the South Pole on November 29, 1929. The expedition also mapped some 150,000 square miles of Antarctica and discovered what are now called Rockefeller and Edsel Ford mountain ranges and Marie Byrd Land (named for Byrd's wife). Promoted to the rank of rear admiral, Byrd received the society's special medal of honor from President Herbert Hoover and released a report, *Little America*, in 1930.

His second Antarctic expedition (1933–1935), also with the backing of the National Geographic Society, resulted in scientific research and the exploration of more than 450,000 square miles of territory. Byrd, who journeyed 123 miles south of the expedition's main Antarctic base to spend a solitary five months making weather observations in a shack beneath the ice, almost lost his life through carbon monoxide poisoning from a defective stove. Knowing his men would risk their lives if they came to rescue him, he refused to send for help, sometimes crawling on his hands and knees to make regular radio reports. He was finally rescued after his faltering signals inadvertently warned of trouble. Welcomed by President Franklin D. Roosevelt on his return, Byrd subsequently published *Discovery* (1935),

telling of the expedition, and the eloquent and poignant *Alone* (1938).

In 1939–1940, Admiral Byrd returned to Antarctica as commander of a government-sponsored expedition that was set up in conjunction with the US Antarctic Service, established by President Roosevelt (but abandoned with the onset of World War II). Expedition achievements included aerial surveys of some 100,000 square miles and the discovery of five mountain ranges, an important peninsula, and five islands.

Byrd was assigned secret duties during World War II, including strategic planning for the chief of naval operations, inspection of advance bases before the US Marine invasion of Guadalcanal, and study of US forces in Europe. After the war, in 1946 and 1947, he headed 4,200 men in what was then the largest expedition ever sent to the Antarctic and which discovered more territory than any had previously – 1.7 million square miles. Sponsored by the US Navy, the expedition also tested equipment and made weather and geological observations. Byrd himself again flew over the South Pole and reported that he had photographed from the air "all major gaps in our maps" of Antarctica's coast.

In 1955 Byrd was placed in command of all US Antarctic activities, and in 1955–1956 he returned to Antarctica as head of the first phase of the Operation Deepfreeze expedition dispatched by the United States in connection with the observation of International Geophysical Year (1957–1958). While there he made his third flight over the South Pole. When he returned home for the last time, in March 1956, huge reaches of Antarctica had been explored and charted. Largely because of his work, the American effort in Antarctica was to continue.

The Admiral of the Ends of the Earth, as Byrd was affectionately dubbed, died in Boston on March 11, 1957. An exhibit comprising some of the items he carried with him on his flight over the North Pole and a bust of him by Felix de Weldon can be seen in Explorers Hall at 17th and M streets, N.W., Washington, D.C., the handsome headquarters building of the National Geographic Society, dedicated in 1964.

OCTOBER 26

Erie Canal Opens

In the years after the War for Independence, Americans began intensive exploration of the interior of their vast nation. Numerous barriers confronted them, but the presence of the long Appalachian mountain chain separating the coast from the frontier threatened to be the greatest obstacle to western settlement. How could inland territories and states develop to maturity if geographical conditions prohibited quick and economical communication and commerce with the established eastern section of the nation? The opening on October 26, 1825, of New York State's Erie Canal, which linked the Great Lakes with the Hudson River and thus with the Atlantic Ocean, provided the most successful early solution to the problem. At the same time, it helped make New York City the major commercial center to which goods were sent for distribution elsewhere in the United States.

Geographically, New York was the 19th century key to the inland empire of America. The Hudson River, passable north from New York City almost 150 miles to Troy, was the only navigable waterway through the Appalachians. Westward from there, the Mohawk Valley pointed the way to the Great Lakes along a chain of natural waterways.

Colonial New Yorkers had as early as 1768 considered plans to develop their waterways, but the coming of the American Revolution forced postponement. Interest rose again after independence was won, and in 1792 the New York legislature, under the prodding of Governor George Clinton, chartered the Western Company and the Northern Inland Lock Navigation Company to connect the Hudson River with Lake Ontario and Lake Champlain respectively. The Northern Company did little, and the Western built a series of short stretches of canals at portages rather than a continuous waterway. The efforts improved communications somewhat, but the overall effect may have been to discourage the undertaking of a more daring enterprise.

Spurred by a suggestion of President Thomas Jefferson in 1805 that surplus federal revenues might be applied to improving canals and roads, New Yorkers began thinking of a greater canal. In January 1809 James Geddes, salt producer, lawyer, surveyor, and later a member of Congress, reported that the best path for an artificial waterway in New York lay along a channel made to cut directly across the center of the state from the northern end of the Hudson River to Lake Erie. Joshua Forman, the Onondaga assemblyman who had introduced the legislation commissioning Geddes's study, brought the document to Jefferson's attention, but the retiring President rejected the idea of building a canal through 350 miles of wilderness as economically unfeasible.

Despite the lack of federal cooperation, New York continued to contemplate building the gigantic waterway. In 1810 Jonas Platt, the minority leader in the New York State Senate, and Thomas Eddy, treasurer of the Western Inland Lock Navigation Company, persuaded De Witt Clinton, nephew of George Clinton and a spokesman for the state senate majority, to introduce legislation establishing a commission to lay plans for a canal that would connect the Hudson River with Lakes Erie and Ontario. Distinguished New Yorkers, including Clinton, Eddy, Stephen Van Rensselaer, Simeon De Witt, William North, Peter B. Porter, Robert R. Livingston, and Robert Fulton, made up the commission. In March 1812, in spite of the unavailability of federal funds, the commission reported in favor of immediate construction of the canal system. Their support stirred the popular enthusiasm necessary for the project.

However, the War of 1812 with Great Britain delayed further consideration of the canal scheme until 1815. In December of that year Jonas Platt and Thomas Eddy prompted De Witt Clinton, then serving as mayor of New York City, to write the famous New York Memorial. Purportedly the work of a committee, the document rekindled enthusiasm for the project and encouraged other communities to issue similar manifestos. More than 100,000 residents of the state signed petitions encouraging the legislature to undertake construction.

In 1816 the state assembly approved the project, but the senate, influenced by members from New York City who myopically saw the venture as beneficial only to upstaters, prevented the immediate commencement of work. Supporters of the canal spent the remainder of the year making additional studies and surveys. Early in 1817 the commissioners reported that the canal to Lake Erie would be 353 miles long and would have 77 locks to compensate for an aggregate rise and fall of 661 feet. The canal would cost $4,881,738, and another, shorter, waterway to Lake Champlain would require $871,000.

After finally winning legislative approval, the builders broke ground on July 4, 1817, during ceremonies held west of Rome. They then began construction on a portion of the central section of the canal between Rome and Utica. When work in this area neared completion in 1819, the legislature authorized extension of the waterway west to Lake Erie and east to the Hudson River.

Actual construction was in the hands of "amateurs." Benjamin Wright, master of the Erie project, and James Geddes, whose responsibilities included supervision of the Champlain sector, had little engineering experience but used their expertise as surveyors and knowledge garnered from personal inspections of thousands of miles of canals in England to perform the construction miracle of their era. Geddes, who was over 60 years of age at the completion of the work, subsequently also surveyed a route for the Chesapeake and Ohio Canal. Wright, in his 50s at the completion of the Erie waterway, was later chief engineer of the Chesapeake and Ohio project. He and the two men's younger associates came to be regarded as the leading engineers in the United States.

"Amateurs" also supplied the money to build the canal system. On March 3, 1817, President James Madison, as his last official act, vetoed the Bonus Bill, which would have turned over federal money to the states for internal improvements. Stymied in Washington, New York decided to finance its efforts by stock issues. Initially the scheme held little appeal for the wealthy, and the preliminary funds came from New Yorkers of moderate means and from the Bank for Savings, which pooled the small deposits of workers. Only when the canals were partially completed and were making excellent progress did the affluent of the United States and Europe invest unstintingly.

On October 22, 1819, the *Chief Engineer*, named in honor of Benjamin Wright, became the first boat to sail on the canal. Provoking cheers from all who saw it along the route, the boat proceeded the short distance eastward from Rome to Utica and made the return voyage on the following day. Navigation on the completed central section of 96 miles began in May 1820, and on July 4 Syracuse was the scene of an official celebration of the event. More elaborate festivities took place in the fall of 1823, when New Yorkers marked the completion of the Champlain Canal and the remaining portions of the Erie between the Genesee and Hudson rivers.

Construction proceeded apace and the workmen, many of whom were Irish immigrants, were able to finish their tasks in 1825. The people of New York began to plan ceremonies to commemorate the achievement of this modern wonder. On October 26 De Witt Clinton, then governor, and other dignitaries embarked on the *Seneca Chief* at Buffalo, chosen after much argument to be the western terminus of the waterway, for the first voyage on the fully opened canal. A battery of 500 cannons passed the news of the event from Lake Erie to New York City in 90 minutes as gunners fired each cannon in sequence upon hearing the report of the blast from the neighboring weapon.

Cheering crowds on the banks, fireworks displays, and ceremonies at several towns along the route enlivened the journey of the dignitaries, which ended with mammoth festivities in New York City on November 4. On that day the *Seneca Chief*, other boats that had accompanied it along the route, and a number of additional craft formed a circle off Sandy Hook. Governor Clinton performed a "marriage of the waters" by pouring a keg of Lake Erie water into the Atlantic Ocean to mark the union of the Great Lakes with the sea. Then he proceeded to pour into the ocean water from 14 great rivers of Asia, Africa, Europe, North America, and South America to symbolize the commerce of the United States with all nations. Dr. Samuel Latham Mitchill, a noted physician, naturalist, and legislator, concluded the festivities with some fitting remarks. While Governor Clinton was performing the marriage of the waters at sea, New Yorkers participated in a five-mile procession through the streets of the city. The celebrations, carried on for three days, were climaxed with a ball.

The Erie Canal was an immediate success. By 1830 annual revenues exceeded $1 million. Land values soared along the route, and cities like Buffalo, the western terminus, and Rochester, located at the junction of the canal and the Genesee River, grew at an astounding rate.

Encouraged by the bonanza, New Yorkers wasted money building a number of unnecessary lateral waterways connecting relatively unimportant locales with the main canal. These auxiliary projects were a tremendous financial burden. Afterward the development of the railroad network, especially the New York Central Line, proved to be too great a challenge to the canal. Weakened by unwise management, the Erie Canal was unable to compete with the quicker, more efficient trains and, after the conclusion of the Civil War, declined to an unimportant position in the state's economy.

Before that time, however, the waterway had facilitated emigration to the Old Northwest, made the agrarian produce of the Great Lakes region available to eastern markets, and contributed to the establishment of a number of the nation's major cities. Later, as the population and industrial growth of the Midwest increased freight shipments to more than the railroads could handle easily, demand grew for the canals across New York State to be made more usable. The Erie and connecting canals, expanded, improved, and in some portions rerouted, were converted into what is today known as the New York State Barge Canal, begun in 1905 and completed in 1918.

OCTOBER 27

Theodore Roosevelt's Birthday

Navy Day

Endowed with strength and resolve, Theodore Roosevelt provided fitting qualities of leadership for the United States in the opening years of the 20th century. As cowboy, cavalry colonel, and Chief Executive, TR, as he was called, fought vigorously for what he believed to be right. His brashness alienated some, but his gameness won the hearts of all.

Theodore Roosevelt was born on October 27, 1858, at 28 East 20th Street in New York City, the place to which his paternal Dutch ancestors had emigrated more than two centuries earlier. Claes Martenszen Van Rosenvelt came to Dutch New Amsterdam in the 1640s; his son Nicholas was a flour bolter and became a municipal alderman in what by then was British New York. The family remained prominent, and the future President's father, also named Theodore, was a man of considerable wealth and importance in civic affairs.

Martha Bulloch Roosevelt, the younger Theodore Roosevelt's mother, was the daughter of James Stephen Bulloch of Roswell, Georgia. A descendant of Archibald Bulloch, the first president of the Georgia Provincial Congress, she was of Scotch-Irish and Huguenot lineage. To her in-laws' cosmopolitan burgher qualities, she added the traditions of the southern aristocracy.

Handicapped in childhood by asthma and poor eyesight, young Theodore Roosevelt became conscious of his physical shortcomings and undertook strenuous body-building activities. He taught himself riding, shooting, and boxing, and maintained a devotion to these sports throughout his life. His efforts to compensate for his early maladies affected all facets of his character and contributed to his aggressive philosophical outlook and political behavior.

Anxious about their son's delicate constitution, Roosevelt's parents employed tutors for his education and afforded him opportunities to travel. He was graduated from Harvard in 1880 as a member of Phi Beta Kappa. Legal studies first attracted the young graduate, but he soon turned to literature and history, publishing in 1882 the first of his 30 books, *The Naval War of 1812.*

In addition to his literary efforts, Roosevelt participated in New York City's Republican Reform Club. His impressive credentials attracted the attention of the party's leadership, and in 1881 he was elected assemblyman from New York's 21st district. During his tenure in this post, Roosevelt gained extensive newspaper coverage for his support of workers' relief and good government legislation.

The year 1884 was a painful one for the young politician. On February 14 Alice Hathaway Lee, whom he had married on October 27, 1880, died — only 12 hours after the death of his mother. Despondency over these personal losses as well as his failure to prevent the presidential nomination of James G. Blaine at the Republican National Convention in Chicago led Roosevelt to withdraw temporarily from politics.

With his baby daughter, Alice, Theodore Roosevelt retreated to his ranch lands in the Dakota Territory. He found solace in the cattleman's life and had time to continue his historical writing. His *Hunting Trips of a Ranchman* appeared in 1885 and a biography, *Thomas Hart Benton,* in 1886.

In the latter year the campaign trail lured Roosevelt away from the West for candidacy in the New York mayoral election. However, Abram S. Hewitt, a liberal Democrat, won the contest; and Henry George, who advocated a single tax on land, ran second; Roosevelt was an unimpressive third. Later in the same year, on December 2, he married Edith Kermit Carow, whom he had known since childhood.

Benjamin Harrison's victory in the 1888 national election brought the Republicans — and Roosevelt — to Washington: the new President recognized the New Yorker's contribution to his campaign by naming him to the Civil Service Commission. In this capacity, Roosevelt worked hard to curb spoilsmen and to protect competent government employees, and during his six-year sojourn in the capital he greatly increased his knowledge of politics and politicians.

William L. Strong, a Republican reform mayor, called Roosevelt back to New York in 1895 to become president of the Board of Police Commissioners. Roosevelt's fervor and his newsworthy personality drew attention to the crime, graft, and poverty that plagued the city. His two years in office alienated corrupt politicians and even dismayed many of New York's police officers, who were unaccustomed to such zealous leadership.

In 1897 Senator Henry Cabot Lodge of Massachusetts persuaded the new President, William McKinley, to appoint Roosevelt assistant secretary of the navy. An advocate of sea power, Roosevelt — as acting secretary in the absence of John D. Long — on February 27, 1898, anticipated the war with Spain by ordering Admiral

George Dewey to prepare his squadron for possible offensive operation in the Philippines. After the Spanish-American War had commenced (see April 24), Roosevelt resigned his post on May 6, 1898, to take an active part in the fighting.

Cuba, San Juan Hill, and Theodore Roosevelt are inseparable in history. He shared to the full those intellectual and psychological attitudes of patriotism and strong national pride that led to war with Spain. He advocated a strong United States and agreed with Admiral Alfred Thayer Mahan's contention that a powerful Navy and extracontinental bases in such places as the Philippines and Cuba were necessary. Finally, Roosevelt believed that the United States must act in the support of justice; without guile he could exhort his men at the base of San Juan Hill: "Gentlemen, the Almighty God and the Just Cause are with you. Gentlemen, Charge!"

Roosevelt's charging troops were the First US Volunteer Cavalry, a unit raised by Colonel Leonard Wood and Roosevelt himself. Originally ranked as a lieutenant colonel, Roosevelt became colonel and commander of this regiment nicknamed the Rough Riders, when Wood was promoted. Roosevelt's martial exploits and his complaints about the unsanitary and unhealthful conditions under which the soldiers had to live made him an overnight hero. He subsequently contributed to his growing fame through his account of his experiences in the largely autobiographical *Rough Riders* (1899), a book that "Mr. Dooley," the whimsical Irishman created by humorist Finley Peter Dunne, wanted to entitle "Alone in Cuba."

Meanwhile, Thomas Collier Platt, the "Easy Boss" of New York's Republican party, saw in the returning hero the answer to a politician's prayer. He knew that only Roosevelt could keep the governor's mansion in the control of the GOP, which had been discredited by scandals in the administration of the state's canals and its civil service system. Platt persuaded the party's reluctant regulars to support the patrician reformer as the Republican candidate for governor in the election of 1898, and Roosevelt accepted the nomination.

Roosevelt and his escort of Rough Riders opened the campaign with a tour of the state; as the candidate of the unpopular incumbent organization, Roosevelt spoke more of Cuba than he did of New York. Augustus Van Wyck, his Democratic opponent, attacked the Republican record and seemed the likely victor until Tammany Hall boss Richard Croker unwisely blocked the renomination of Supreme Court Justice Joseph F. Daly, a noted jurist with 28 years' service on the bench and antimachine proclivities. Roosevelt immediately turned the tables on the

Democrats and gained the allegiance of reformers from both parties by his assaults on "Crokerism." In November Roosevelt won by 18,000 votes.

Governor Roosevelt became a proponent of progressivism, the political reform movement of the turn of the century. He supported legislation to improve the civil service system, ameliorate working conditions in factories and other places of employment, and protect inhabitants of tenement houses. The new governor managed to overcome the opposition of Platt and the Republican party to achieve enactment of a measure levying taxes on public-service corporations.

Roosevelt never broke with Platt, but his independence unnerved even the Easy Boss. By 1900 Platt, wanting to remove the headstrong Roosevelt from his bailiwick, persuaded a hesitant President William McKinley to take him as his second-term running mate in the national election. The governor's active campaign offset the efforts of William Jennings Bryan, the vigorous Democratic presidential candidate, and ensured a Republican victory in November.

On September 6, 1901, Leon Czolgosz, an anarchist, shot President McKinley at a public reception at the Pan-American Exposition at Buffalo, New York. Eight days later McKinley died, and Theodore Roosevelt, at the age of 42, became the youngest Chief Executive in the history of the United States. Roosevelt's accession brought progressivism to the White House and important changes to the nation.

An accidental President dealing with a conservative Congress, Roosevelt prudently chose not to seek the immediate enactment of a program of progessive legislation. Instead the President achieved constructive results and greatly increased the powers of his office through executive action based on existing legislation. Roosevelt became the first of the strong presidents of the 20th century.

President Roosevelt's first years in office coincided with the high point of the period of consolidation in American industry. Many progressives, fearful of the threat to free enterprise, wanted to arrest the trend of incorporation, but Roosevelt recognized the process as inevitable. Rather than destroy the new economic monoliths, he preferred to regulate their activities for the public welfare. He avoided asking congressional conservatives for additional statutes and instead discouraged malefaction by vigorous exercise of federal powers against improper corporate behavior — a policy that became known as the Square Deal.

In 1902 the President ordered the Justice Department to seek the dissolution of the Northern Securities Company, which monopolized the railroads of the Pacific coast. The conglomerate — which united the interests of J. P. Morgan, James J. Hill, and E. H. Harriman — proved a popular and easy target. The Supreme Court in 1904 upheld the government's casè under the Sherman Antitrust Act of 1890 and established precedents for future government action against the American Tobacco Company, meat packers, and Standard Oil.

Roosevelt earned a reputation as a "trust buster," but actually preferred less dramatic approaches to business. Typically, he sought arrangements like his 1905 "gentlemen's agreement" with Judge Elbert H. Gary, chairman of the board of United States Steel, whereby the corporation promised to open its records for government inspection and to correct abuses in return for immunity from prosecution. Such accords greatly increased presidential influence and marked an advance for the public interest.

Roosevelt's response to labor unrest likewise bypassed Congress, increased the powers of his office, and aided workers. Seeking higher wages, an eight-hour day, and recognition of their union, John Mitchell's United Mine Workers in June 1902 struck the anthracite coal industry. The miners acted with restraint and offered to submit to arbitration, but the operators, who were allied with railroad and Wall Street interests, adamantly refused to negotiate. George F. Baer of the Reading Railroad claimed that God supported the employers, and the strike dragged on through the summer.

As winter approached, Roosevelt decided to intervene to insure an adequate fuel supply for the nation. Early in October the President summoned both miners and operators to the White House. Mitchell displayed a mood of enthusiastic cooperation, but the owners, angered by Roosevelt's implicit recognition of the union, demanded that the government use troops to break the strike. The President's warning that he might use the US Army to seize the mines from the operators was effective, and management soon reopened the pits. The settlement, determined by a government commission in 1903, granted the workers a 10 percent raise and a nine-hour day.

Progressive but prudent, Roosevelt did not alienate the conservative magnates of the Republican party with his first-term liberalism. He faced no serious opposition for the GOP's 1904 presidential nomination, and in November he defeated Judge Alton B. Parker of New York, the conservative Democratic candidate, by more than 2.5 million votes. As one wry commentator observed: "Parker ran for the presidency against Theodore Roosevelt and was defeated by acclamation."

Fortified by the popular vindication of his Square Deal policies, Roosevelt in his second term prodded Congress to enact a comprehensive program of progressive legislation. The lawmakers rejected many of his proposals, especially those that would have benefited labor, but they grudgingly surrendered a few major points. The Hepburn Act of 1906 authorized the Interstate Commerce Commission to examine railroad records and set carrier rates; and the Pure Food and Drug Act outlawed the production and sale of adulterated merchandise.

Roosevelt was characteristally aggressive in the field of foreign relations and continued the trend toward greater American involvement in world affairs. In 1905 he played a leading part in the Portsmouth (New Hampshire) Peace Conference, which brought an end to the Russo-Japanese War. As results of his efforts, American interests in the Far East were protected and he became the first American recipient of the Nobel Peace Prize. In 1906 he actively supported the Algeciras Conference, which guaranteed Moroccan independence and averted a Franco-German clash over North Africa.

In regard to Latin America, Roosevelt conducted himself in accord with his dictum "Speak softly and carry a big stick." When the government of Colombia rejected as inadequate an American offer of $10 million to build a canal across its isthmian territory, Roosevelt tacitly supported a 1903 revolution by Panamanian nationalists willing to accept the offer. By the Hay-Bunau-Varilla Treaty of 1903, the United States guaranteed Panama's independence from Colombia in return for control of a 10-mile-wide zone across the isthmus.

Threats by European nations to collect by force debts owed their nationals by Latin American governments deeply upset the President. He countered these threats by promising that the United States would take action when other New World nations proved unable or unwilling to meet their obligations. This "Roosevelt corollary to the Monroe Doctrine" changed the US role from that of guardian against European interference to that of hemispheric police officer.

President Roosevelt picked Secretary of War William Howard Taft to succeed him as the Republican leader. Taft received the party's presidential nomination in 1908 and defeated his Democratic opponent William Jennings Bryan by more than 1 million votes. With the White House secure in the hands of a trusted associate, Roosevelt set off for an African safari vacation.

In his first years in office, Taft turned for support to the Republican old guard conservatives rather than to the Roosevelt liberals. The new President supported the high Payne-Aldrich tariff, dismissed Chief Forester Gifford Pinchot, an ardent conservationist who intemperately attacked Taft's policies, and severely chastised progressives who tried to oust House Speaker Joseph Cannon. When Roosevelt returned in March 1910 he found himself in the middle of the party controversy.

At Osawatomie, Kansas, in August 1910 Roosevelt placed himself firmly on the side of the progressives and called for a comprehensive legislative program that he termed the New Nationalism. He argued that the federal government needed the power to regulate for the public good the behavior of the giant corporations that had recently developed. He also advocated laws designed to aid workers and the socially disadvantaged.

Unable to settle their differences, Taft and Roosevelt fought each other for the 1912 Republican presidential nomination. As the incumbent, Taft was able to secure the honor through shrewd use of the party machinery. Roosevelt and his supporters formed a new coalition, the Progressive, or "Bull Moose," party, based on a platform of the New Nationalism.

The Democratic candidate, Woodrow Wilson, received 435 electoral votes and defeated the divided Republicans in the November contest. Roosevelt ran second with 88 votes, and Taft a poor third with only 8. Wilson's New Freedom philosophy closely resembled Roosevelt's, except that the victor emphasized preserving competition in business and arresting rather than just controlling the growth of giant corporations.

In Roosevelt's opinion, Wilson was as poor a President as Taft, especially in the realm of foreign affairs. During his first term Wilson cautiously maintained a policy of US neutrality during World War I, which erupted in Europe in 1914. Roosevelt disdained the President's unwillingness to arm the United States and increasingly favored open American aid to the Allied powers. In 1916 he strongly supported the unsuccessful bid of Republican candidate Charles Evans Hughes to unseat the incumbent.

The United States finally entered the war in 1917, and Roosevelt's four sons served in Europe; Quentin Roosevelt lost his life in 1918 while flying over France. Roosevelt offered to raise a division and lead one of its brigades, but Wilson, following the military's advice to leave the fighting to the professionals, rejected the offer. Soon after the war, on January 6, 1919, Roosevelt died in his sleep.

Memorials to the 26th President abound throughout the United States. Both the four-story Greek revival brownstone at 28 East 20th Street in New York City, where Roosevelt was born, and his Victorian home at Sagamore Hill

in Oyster Bay, Long Island, where he died, are national historic sites administered by the National Park Service. The Theodore Roosevelt Association donated the two buildings to the federal government in 1963 "to keep alive for future generations the life, the standards and the ideals of Theodore Roosevelt."

Perhaps the most fitting tribute to Roosevelt's interest in conservation is the Theodore Roosevelt National Memorial Park in North Dakota. Its 70,436 acres are located in the Badlands and include part of the Elkhorn Ranch, which Roosevelt himself established in 1884. Deer, antelope, and a herd of buffalo graze throughout the extensive acreage.

In neighboring South Dakota two areas honor Roosevelt. At Mount Theodore Roosevelt, a 5,676-foot peak near Deadwood, stands the Theodore Roosevelt Monument. The best-known memorial to Roosevelt in the state is a likeness that — together with those of George Washington, Thomas Jefferson, and Abraham Lincoln — was carved on the face of Mount Rushmore, near Keystone, by the sculptor Gutzon Borglum.

In Washington, D.C., the Theodore Roosevelt Memorial is one of the newest attractions. On October 27, 1967, President Lyndon B. Johnson unveiled Paul Manship's 17-foot-high bronze statue of the 26th President. It is the focal point of the 3-acre memorial, which is open to the public, located on the wooded, 88-acre Theodore Roosevelt Island in the Potomac River. Designed by Eric Gugler, the memorial also includes a huge paved plaza, two fountains, and four 20-foot-high tablets bearing Roosevelt's words.

An enduring memorial of a different sort originated with a contemporary newspaper cartoon of a bear cub — an allusion to the President's interest in conservation and wildlife. Small stuffed bears soon acquired Roosevelt's nickname, and the ever popular toys continue to be known as "teddy bears."

The various parks named for Roosevelt and the historic sites associated with his life help keep the American people aware of Roosevelt's most significant contributions to the nation. However, Roosevelt's bold and adventurous spirit was also largely responsible for popularizing the rodeo in the United States, and one town annually celebrates this fact: Roosevelt introduced the rodeo in the small town of Las Vegas, New Mexico, in 1898; ever since that date the town has annually held the Teddy Roosevelt Rough Riders and Cowboys Reunion. The event generally lasts for several days in late June or early July, and it is recognized as the oldest regular rodeo in the Southwest.

Roosevelt's efforts as secretary of the navy greatly strengthened that branch of the armed forces, and his birthday coincides with the date upon which the Continental Congress in 1775 received the "bill providing for the creation and establishment of a Fleet." It is therefore appropriate that the Navy League of the United States, a civilian organization founded to promote the role of sea power in the nation's defense, has since 1922 selected October 27 for its observance of Navy Day.

Other organizations – among them Rotary clubs and the Naval Reserve Association – also may sponsor Navy Day events. The navy, which sees the day as an opportunity for stimulating *esprit de corps*, encourages both internal observance of the day and the cooperation of naval units with civilian organizations that plan ceremonies to mark the occasion. At their request, naval units are urged to provide speakers or participate in luncheons, dinners, birthday balls, and other related events. They are also encouraged to undertake Navy Day troop unit reviews and to dress ships and hold open house aboard ships and at naval stations. To support these efforts, various governors and mayors issue proclamations, and the public schools of some states hold special programs.

At least one locality celebrates the week of October 27 as Navy Week: Each year National City, California, a town near the massive San Diego Naval Base, expresses its appreciation of the navy by holding dances, concerts, and other events during the week of October 27.

OCTOBER 28

Czechoslovak Independence Day

On October 28, 1918, the Republic of Czechoslovakia was founded. After its establishment, October 28, known as Czechoslovak Independence Day, was elaborately celebrated in Czechoslovakia until the Communist seizure of power there in 1948. The anniversary of the proclamation of Czechoslovak independence has been commemorated in other countries, especially by persons of Czech and Slovak descent.

In the United States the day is noted with special banquets, addresses, religious services, rallies, cultural programs, and the laying of a wreath at the tomb of President Woodrow Wilson at Washington Cathedral in Washington, D.C. (Wilson was influential in securing backing and recognition for a nation of Czechs and Slovaks during World War I.) Communities with large Czech or Slovak populations such as New York; Los Angeles; Newark, New Jersey; and Masaryktown, Florida, usually mark the occasion.

The President of the United States frequently has proclaimed the anniversary and stressed the contributions of Czech- and Slovak-Americans; several state governors annually proclaim Czechoslovak Independence Day and in some cases are following a tradition of many years.

The idea of independence for this east central European area was not new in 1918. The kingdom of Bohemia enjoyed a flourishing independent status during much of the Middle Ages. But as a result of defeat in the Thirty Years War (1618–1648) at the hands of the Austrian Hapsburg emperors, the region was virtually deprived of political independence and incorporated into the Hapsburg state. Although nationalist sentiments were systematically suppressed over the years, there were always a few patriots who never completely abandoned the dream of recovering independence.

The nationality question in east central Europe – most of which, including the Czech and Slovak sections, was included in the multinational Austrian Empire ruled by the Hapsburgs – became increasingly important as concept of nationalism and the right of self-determination advanced in the 19th century. Especially during the revolutionary year of 1848, the Czechs, politically aware of their past sovereignty, started to voice strong opposition to those who wished to maintain, at any cost, hegemony over the non-German components within the Hapsburg empire.

The outbreak of World War I offered the Czechs an opportunity not only to air their grievances, as in the past, but also to strive actively for independence through passive resistance, the formation of Czech military units on the Allied side, and the organization of clandestine groups planning decisive moves if and when the right moment arose. The brunt of the independence struggles fell upon Czech and Slovak political exiles in the Allied and neutral countries. These people used diplomatic, military, and propagandist means to achieve their goal.

Prominent among the exiles was Tomáš Garrigue Masaryk (1850–1937), a professor of philosophy at the Czech University in Prague, who for years had been a staunch foe of Hapsburg political domination. As early as 1907 he had been elected a member of the Austrian parliament in Vienna as leader of his own political party – whose platform stressed, above all, the national sovereignty of his country. Away in Italy at the start of World War I, Masaryk, having been advised in December 1914 of his impending arrest by the Austrian police upon his return home, wisely stayed abroad. He sought refuge in Paris and later in London. He and another Czech leader, Eduard Beneš, were determined to bring the Czech question to international attention. The formation of the Czech Committee Abroad was the opening step.

On November 14, 1915, Masaryk, leaders of Czech groups in the Allied countries, and Czechs and Slovaks in the United States signed a manifesto, which was significant as the first official statement made abroad in support of Czecho-Slovak freedom from Austria-Hungary. At the start of the next year, Masaryk's committee became known as the National Czech and Slovak Council. Masaryk, as its president, traveled widely during the war years to win support for his cause, the success of which was already evident in January 1917, when the Allies advocated as one of the top-priority war aims the end of foreign domination in what was to become Czechoslovakia.

In spite of repression and widespread arrests, the liberation movement grew at home as well as abroad. At the so-called Epiphany Convention of January 6, 1918, leaders in Prague issued a manifesto calling for a sovereign state "within the historic boundaries of the Bohemian Lands and of Slovakia." In May 1918 Masaryk — whose wife, Charlotte Garrigue, was an American — paid a visit to the United States, where he was greatly respected and admired. He elicited both financial aid and sympathy for the cause of Czech independence. His movement received further support in the Lansing declaration of May 29, which expressed American approval of the anti-Hapsburg resolution promulgated by the Congress of Oppressed Nationalities in Rome earlier that year.

From then on, events moved quickly. On June 3, 1918, the Allied War Council at Versailles announced its willingness to back the Czechs' political aspirations. Then the Allied powers recognized Masaryk's National Council as the de facto government of the future Czechoslovakia — first France on June 29, then Great Britain on August 9, and finally the United States on September 3.

The impending defeat of the Central Powers in the fall of 1918 presented an opportune moment for action within the Czech territory. On October 27 the last Austro-Hungarian foreign minister, Count Julius Andrassy, replied favorably to President Woodrow Wilson's note urging that the nationalities of the empire be allowed to determine their own political future. On October 28 the National Committee in Prague proclaimed independence and took over the administration of an "independent Czechoslovak state." A Slovak assembly at Turciansky Svaty Martin on October 30 declared itself in favor of Slovakia's participation in the new state. On November 13, 1918, the National Committee promulgated an interim constitution; the following day Masaryk was unanimously elected president of the new nation at the first meeting of the National Assembly. He was subsequently reelected three times, in 1920, 1927, and 1934 (at the age of 84), but he resigned in December 1935 because of age.

The Treaty of Paris of 1919 finally confirmed the frontiers of Czechoslovakia, which included all or parts of Bohemia, Moravia, Silesia, Slovakia, and Ruthenia. The First Republic survived until October 1938 when, following the Munich agreement, it was forced to cede much of its territory to Nazi Germany, and later also to make cessions to Poland and Hungary. The short-lived Second Republic was a satellite of Germany. On March 15, 1939, Adolf Hitler's armies occupied the western portion of what was left of Czechoslovakia. Hitler transformed this section into the Protectorate of Bohemia and Moravia, which was then incorporated into the German Reich. Slovakia became a nominally independent satellite state of Germany. Following the Allied defeat of Nazi Germany in May 1945, near the close of World War II, Czechoslovakia was restored as an independent state. The Communist seizure of power in February 1948 turned it into a Soviet satellite.

Statue of Liberty Dedicated

Since its dedication on October 28, 1886, the magnificent Statue of Liberty, which stands in New York Harbor, has welcomed millions of immigrants, foreign visitors, and citizens returning to the United States from abroad. The idea for such a statue originated in France during the early 1870s. Having just adopted a republican form of government, the French people wanted to pay special tribute to the United States, the first modern republic, on the occasion of its 100th anniversary in 1876. The gift chosen to symbolize the lasting friendship between the two countries was Frédéric Auguste Bartholdi's statue *Liberty Enlightening the World*. In 1875 the newly organized Franco-American Union began to solicit contributions to finance the statue's construction, and by the time of its completion in 1884 the French people had donated the entire cost of $250,000.

Bartholdi himself selected the 12-acre Bedloe's Island (renamed Liberty Island in 1960) as the permanent site for his statue, and the United States Congress agreed to its being used for this purpose. To provide a suitable base for the 225-ton figure, Americans subscribed $350,000. This money financed the building of a concrete and granite pedestal, and in 1886 the Statue of Liberty was placed upon this structure to begin its symbolic vigil in New York Harbor.

Approximately 800,000 persons visit Liberty

Island each year. Boats leave Manhattan's Battery Park for the island frequently during the day, and those who make the 1.6-mile trip to inspect the statue at close range are well rewarded for their efforts. The main point of interest is the hollow interior of the statue. An elevator takes sightseers to the top of the pedestal, but from there those who wish to venture higher, up into the statue itself, must walk. A climb of 168 steps leads to the statue's head, where there is an observation platform. On a clear day, this platform affords a magnificent view of the harbor and the New York skyline. The right arm and the torch are no longer open to the public.

A bronze plaque was affixed to the pedestal of the Statue of Liberty in 1903. On this tablet is engraved the famous excerpt from "The New Colossus" by Emma Lazarus:

> Give me your tired, your poor,
> Your huddled masses yearning to breathe free,
> The wretched refuse of your teeming shore,
> Send these, the homeless, tempest-tossed, to me:
> I lift my lamp beside the golden door.

In 1937 the statue, which with its pedestal is 305 feet high, was declared a national monument, and since that time the National Park Service has administered the site. In 1964 the Park Service began construction on the American Museum of Immigration at the base of the statue. Opened in 1972, the museum contains an exhibit hall where dioramas, paintings, and other materials depict the contributions of the various national and ethnic groups to American history.

OCTOBER 29

The Panic of 1929

Black Tuesday, October 29, 1929, is usually considered the date of the great stock market crash. Trading on that day culminated an almost week-long period of falling prices on the New York Stock Exchange. The Wall Street collapse was the most significant indicator of the depth of the economic depression that the United States and the rest of the world were then entering.

The American economy had done well during the most of the 1920s, and popular faith in the ability of capitalism to insure prosperity was strong. Increasing prices on the stock market reflected this optimism. In the latter half of 1924, a boom period began, which continued through 1925 and, after a setback in 1926, gained speed in 1927. Unfortunately, however, the character of the expansion changed, and during 1928 the upward spiral no longer reflected solid economic gain but rather an inordinate amount of speculation.

Two mechanisms satisfied the public craving for common stock during this period: investment trust companies, approximately 450 of which appeared in 1928 and 1929, marketed securities to the public under new names and put the proceeds into previously existing companies. This procedure, however, ended the traditional relationship between the volumes of corporations' outstanding securities and their assets. In 1929 alone, investment trust companies sold $3 billion in securities. Brokers' loans, meanwhile, enabled people to buy stocks on margin, paying a fraction of the owed price in cash and using the purchased securities as collateral for the rest. Always part of market operations, these brokers' loans reached an unprecedented volume of almost $6 billion in 1928 and made possible large-scale speculation.

Far fewer than 1 million of the 120 million people then living in the United States had ever engaged in stock-market speculation, but most of the populace participated in the mania vicariously, if not directly. Normally countervailing forces failed to oppose the unhealthy trends. Even the banking community, a bastion of financial responsibility, contributed to the boom through its newly organized securities outlets. The statement by Yale economics professor Irving Fisher that "stock prices have reached what looks like a permanently high plateau" reflected the optimism common in academic circles.

As always, however, the law of supply and demand is Wall Street's law of gravity, ruling that stocks that go up in value without adequate reason must assuredly go down. And almost anything could precipitate the end of a speculative boom, which — being partly psychological in origin — could easily be terminated by a crisis of confidence.

By late 1929 there were several factors that may have produced the crisis. After June 1929 the indices of industry and factory production had begun to decline, and this may have adversely affected investments. British authorities disclosed in September that Clarence Hatry, one of the world's most influential financiers, had engaged in fraudulent practices. (Hatry's empire collapsed and he later went to prison.) In October 1929 the Massachusetts Department of Public Utilities refused to allow the Boston Edison Company to split its stock four to one and charged that the firm's securities were overvalued and not worth buying.

Whatever the deep-rooted causes, the stock market had begun to falter after Roger W. Babson, on September 5 at his Annual National Business Conference, predicted an impending crash. That day the market suffered the "Babson Break," with the New York *Times* industrial averages reporting a 10-point loss. For the next few weeks Wall Street prices were uneven, but the bull market was definitely finished. The volume of transactions increased, and by October 21 the New York Stock Exchange ticker, unable to keep pace with the flow of business, fell behind one hour and 20 minutes. In the last hour of trading on October 23, some 2.6 million shares changed hands as prices fell sharply.

Wall Street was in trouble, and the crisis became panic in the morning hours of October 24, Black Thursday. By 11:00 A.M. so many stockholders were trying to sell that they could not find buyers. But Thomas Lamont of the J. P. Morgan banking house and other financial leaders pooled their institutional resources to arrest the decline. Their action restored confidence, and by the close of the trading period the market regained enough strength so that industrial averages declined, overall, only a third of the loss of the previous day.

Stock prices held their own on Friday and during the short session of Saturday, but they tumbled again on Monday, October 28. The New York *Times* industrial averages fell 49 points, more than in the entire previous week. This time even the bankers could not counteract the urge to sell. In the first weeks of the decline the small investors had borne the brunt of the decline; now the wealthy began to feel its effects.

Commentators have dubbed October 29 Black Tuesday. That day, 16,410,030 sales took place, driving the industrials down another 43 points — to a level that erased all the gains of the past year. The investment trusts suffered most. Later days brought worse news, with the nation headed for disaster.

In response to the collapse, corporations and out-of-town banks withdrew over $2 billion from Wall Street; but the New York banks boldly increased their loans by about $1 billion, preventing an even greater catastrophe. Thus, despite the enormous drop in stock prices, no money panic ensued. The New York banks, in conjunction with the Federal Reserve Bank, met all legitimate demands for credit, and the liquidation was carried out on as orderly a basis as the severity of the crisis permitted.

It is generally thought that a rash of suicides followed the collapse of the market. Some killed themselves after the crash, and such tragedies naturally received widespread attention in the newspapers. Yet fewer Americans took their own lives in the months of October and November 1929 than had done so during the boom months of the summer. Contrary to popular belief, most of those who ended their lives chose means other than leaping from tall buildings.

OCTOBER 30

John Adams's Birthday

John Adams, the son of John and Sarah Boylston Adams, was born on October 30, 1735, in the part of Braintree, Massachusetts, that has since been incorporated into the city of Quincy. The Adams family, descended from Henry Adams, who reached America in 1640, had remained obscure farmers and village officials until John's father married into the prominent Boylston clan. John Adams, the first member of the family to attend college, was graduated from Harvard in 1755. Originally he had planned to become a minister, but doubts about certain Calvinistic tenets caused him to put aside this career; in 1758 he instead gained admittance to the Massachusetts bar. Six years later, Adams wed Abigail Smith, the daughter of Reverend William and Elizabeth Quincy Smith. In the years that followed, Abigail Adams was a constant support to her husband, and her association with the leading families of the colony undoubtedly also helped his career.

The aspiring lawyer and politician took an interest in local affairs, but it was not until the Stamp Act Crisis that Adams assumed a leading role in the patriot cause. He attacked the taxation measure in a series of articles published in the Boston *Gazette* in 1765, and wrote the resolutions by which Braintree instructed its representatives in the colonial assembly. He gained prominence as other towns adopted his directives. John Hancock chose Adams to defend him against smuggling charges, and Adams was elected to the Massachusetts General Court in 1769.

Adams rarely allowed his patriotism to interfere with his sense of justice and responsibility. While many of his associates sought to extract all possible propaganda value from the Boston Massacre of March 1770 (see March 5), Adams and Josiah Quincy acted as defense attorneys for Captain Preston and the six other British soldiers accused of murder. Preston and four of the men won acquittals, and the other two, convicted of manslaughter, received only token punishment.

The British saw the value of a man like Adams and offered him the position of advocate general of the admiralty court. But Adams, interpreting this gesture as an attempt to dissociate him from the patriot movement, declined the post.

Pen and paper were his early weapons in the struggle against Great Britain. In 1774, as "Novanglus," he engaged in debate in Boston newspaper columns with Daniel ("Massachusettensis") Leonard, a Tory adversary. Elected to the First Continental Congress, Adams helped write the address to King George III and the Declaration of Rights. As a member of the Second Continental Congress he put his pen aside, and on June 7, 1776, he seconded Richard Henry Lee's resolution in favor of severing American ties with the British Empire. He was a member of the committee that drafted the Declaration of Independence, and it was on his motion that George Washington was appointed General of the American army.

Adams became chairman of the Board of War and Ordnance and served in Congress until late in 1777. On November 28 of that year the government nominated him to replace Silas Deane as a commissioner to France, and on February 13, 1778, he and his son, the 10-year-old John Quincy (see July 5), set sail across the Atlantic. Adams's experiences there soon convinced him that a sole envoy could represent American interests better than a commission, and in mid-1779, with congressional approval, he returned home, leaving the task to Benjamin Franklin.

Adams remained in America only long enough to draw up a state constitution for Massachusetts, and in November he set off again for Europe as minister plenipotentiary to negotiate treaties of peace and of amity and commerce with Great Britain. The times were not auspicious for such gestures, however, and Adams made no overtures to the English. Congress in December 1780 made him minister to Holland, and in 1782 he won that country's recognition of, and financial support for, the United States. With Benjamin Franklin and John Jay, Adams negotiated the Paris Peace Treaty of 1783, which guaranteed American independence and officially ended the Revolution (see January 14, Ratification Day). From 1785 to 1788 he served as the fledgling nation's first envoy to Britain.

In April 1789 George Washington took office as the first President of the United States under the new Constitution, and John Adams became his Vice President. The Massachusetts patriot thought his post was "the most insignificant office that ever the invention of man contrived or his imagination conceived," but during his term, as president of the Senate, he cast 20 deciding votes, a mark yet to be matched. Adams retained the vice presidency in the 1792 election and in 1796 was the logical choice of the Federalist Party to succeed the retiring President Washington. Alexander Hamilton, knowing he would have little influence in an Adams administration, tried unsuccessfully to turn the election to Thomas Pinckney of South Carolina, the Federalists' original choice for the vice presidency. But Adams won the contest, and Thomas Jefferson, a Democratic-Republican, became his Vice President.

The presidency of John Adams covered four bitter years. The powerful Hamilton never accepted him, and other Federalists were scandalized by his efforts to establish amicable relations with France, their faction's traditional *bête noire*. Adams was not responsible for the Alien and Sedition Acts, but many also blamed him for these antilibertarian measures. He became extremely unpopular, thereby allowing the Democratic-Republican candidates, Thomas Jefferson and Aaron Burr, to sweep to an easy victory in the election of 1800. The dejected loser left Washington without attending his successor's inauguration. He took no further part in public affairs beyond writing letters and articles. The enmity that had arisen between him and Jefferson because of political differences was removed in the course of time, and the two men engaged in correspondence for years, exchanging reminiscences and expressing their views on current affairs.

Adams's death, on July 4, 1826, occurred only a few hours after the death of Jefferson in Virginia. The nation's second President was buried in the crypt of the First Parish Church (Unitarian) in Quincy, Massachusetts. Beside the pulpit in the church there is a commemorative inscription on a marble tablet surmounted by a bust of him. On the other side of the pulpit is a similar tablet to the memory of his son, John Quincy Adams, the sixth President of the United States, whose body lies beside that of his father.

The church is not far from the famous Old House — now the Adams National Historic Site — at 135 Adams Street, where John Adams spent his later years and where generations of distinguished Adamses lived after him. Now administered by the National Park Service, the house, which Adams purchased in 1787, was presented to the US government in 1946 by members of the family. Not remarkable architecturally, it is a gem of history. It tells much, not only about the family that owned it but also about the style of life of many early Americans. There are, for instance, portraits of George and Martha Washington for which John Adams paid the painter Edward Savage $46.67. Among the interesting Adams memorabilia are the cradles of two Presidents and a chair to whose bottom a note is tacked. The message, signed by the historically minded John Quincy Adams, states: "Father was seated in this chair when he was stricken, July 4, 1826."

Travelers to Quincy can also visit the houses in which John Adams and his son were born, still standing today at numbers 133 and 141 Franklin Street. The two steeply roofed, saltbox dwellings, known locally as the "little red houses," date from the 17th century and are registered national historic sites.

In March 1975 a monument to Adams was unveiled in the Massachusetts State House in Boston. Publication of the projected 100-volume Adams Papers series — papers of John Adams and other members of the distinguished Adams family — was undertaken by the Harvard University Press with a subsidy from the National Historical Publications and Records Commission.

OCTOBER 31

Halloween

Few holidays have a stranger or more paradoxical history than Halloween. As the vigil of All Saints' Day — also known as Hallowmass or All Hallows' Day (see November 1) — Halloween is the eve of one of the most important feasts of the church year, solemnly observed by Roman Catholics, Anglicans, and Lutherans. However, some of the customs traditional to Halloween commemorate rites and creatures that Christianity has over the centuries adamantly opposed: auguries, ghosts, witches, goblins, and fairies. In many countries of Western Europe, such as France, Spain, and Italy, All Hallows' Eve is observed only as an austere religious occasion with extra masses and prayers at the graves of deceased relatives and friends; but in the British Isles and, especially, in the United States Halloween is primarily regarded as a night of merrymaking, superstitious spells, fortune-telling, games, and pranks. To understand this curious mixture of the religious and the secular, and to realize how the varied customs of Western Europe have affected the American celebration of Halloween, it is necessary to trace the remote origins of the holiday.

It is generally accepted that Halloween in its more popular or folk aspects represents a combination of druidic practices and classical Roman religious beliefs. These ancient influences are inferred both from the predominance of nuts and apples as customary Halloween foods and from the important part played by ghosts, black cats, witches, and skeletons. Halloween has clear connections with the primitive and sometimes savage rites of the priestly druids in the pre-Roman, pre-Christian Celtic communities of Northern and Western Europe, especially in Ireland and Scotland. The Celtic order of druids, which had originated in Gaul in the second century B.C., performed mystical ceremonies in honor of the great sun god at various sites.

The Celtic year ended on October 31, the eve of *Samhain* ("summer's end"), and on this occasion the white-robed priests celebrated a joint festival for the sun god and the lord of the dead. In the agrarian sense, the last day of October was the festival of the waning year. After the ripened grain had been gathered, the sun was thanked for the harvest and given moral support for the coming battle with darkness and cold. Cattle were brought back from the meadows to the stalls. The *Samhain* rites were intended to offset the blight of winter with its perils and anxieties for people and beasts alike. *Samhain* was also an occasion for feasting, when the food supplies amassed in summer were first opened.

On this night, Celtic householders extinguished the fires on their hearths and gathered at a designated circle, where the priests solemnly quenched the sacred altar fire. Having rubbed together pieces of sacred oak to kindle a new fire on the altar, the priests passed on the sparks to light great bonfires on the hilltops — similar to those of Midsummer Eve — to honor the sun god and frighten away any lurking evil spirits. The head of each family received live embers to kindle a new fire on his hearth, which was to last until the next autumn festival. Blessed fire was thought to protect the home from danger throughout the year.

The Celts also believed that on October 31 the lord of the dead assembled the souls of all those persons who had died in the previous year, each having been required to expiate his sins by dwelling in the body of an animal. The lord then decreed what forms the dead persons should inhabit for the coming 12 months or perhaps admitted some to the druidic equivalent of heaven. Moreover, the spirits of the departed were believed to be allowed a brief visit to their relatives in search of warmth and comfort as winter approached.

Since, it was claimed, the departed souls roaming abroad sometimes played tricks on October 31, the druids sought to appease them — and simultaneously honor the sun god — by sacrificing horses and also human beings. Although such practices were outlawed by the Romans in A.D. 61, during their rule of Britain, the ancient Celtic rites survived for centuries in attenuated form: for example, horses continued to be sacrificed at *Samhain* as late as A.D. 400. Even after Christianity had spread over Europe and the British Isles and the pagan temples had been consecrated to Christian uses, oxen were sacrificed on October 31 "in honor of the saints and sacred relics." In medieval Europe, black cats — chosen as victims in the belief that they were witches in disguise — were burned on that day.

The modern observance of Halloween also reflects slight influences from the Roman festival honoring Pomona, the goddess of fruits, especially in the use of fruit and nuts for divination. A grove near Ostia, Italy, was dedicated to the goddess in ancient times, and a harvest festival was held there about November 1. It is supposed that offerings of the winter stores of nuts and apples were made to her and that the deities of fire and water were propitiated to aid in the growth of the crops.

The process of incorporating October 31 into the Christian calendar as All Hallows' Eve took several centuries. The idea of honoring numerous martyrs and, eventually, saints, on a common day had grown out of the fact that there were fewer days in the calendar year than there were saints to venerate. In keeping with this idea, during the fourth through the seventh centuries, various localities observed a day for venerating all martyrs at one time – usually in the spring of the year. It was not until the eighth century that Pope Gregory III moved the feast to November – probably to offset the residual paganism of the old *Samhain* rites. It was a century later, however, before Pope Gregory IV placed All Saints' Day in the church calendar, decreeing that the day and the vigil – All Hallows' Eve – be generally observed. Even after that, however, the Christianizing of the observance took time.

Outside the church, the conviction that Halloween was the gathering time for unsanctified spirits persisted and found an outlet during the Middle Ages in the witchcraft cult devoted to the worship of Satan. The cult included periodic meetings, named witches' Sabbaths, which were popularly thought to be given over to orgies and revelry and to which the witches allegedly flew on broomsticks, accompanied by their black cats. The most important witches' sabbath, aside from May or Walpurgis Eve, was All Hallows' Eve, when the Prince of Darkness supposedly mocked the feast of the saints with unholy rites.

The opinion of the Church on witches varied during the early Middle Ages. At one time it regarded belief in witches as a delusion and at another it accepted the existence of witches and condemned contact with them as a form of traffic with the devil. By the end of the 15th century, however, it had adopted a policy of punishing witches with extreme severity. A papal bull against witchcraft was promulgated in 1484. During the following two centuries, thousands of people were accused of practicing witchcraft, tortured into confessing, and burned.

There were many persecutions for witchcraft in America in the 17th century in the colonies of Massachusetts, Connecticut, and Virginia. Through the influence of the intolerant Cotton Mather, the New England Puritan minister, the campaign against witches was especially intensive in Salem, Massachusetts.

As the 18th century dawned, belief in witchcraft was slowly abating. As late as the 1720s, a woman in Scotland was judged guilty of sorcery and sentenced to death. Although the English and Scottish laws against witchcraft were repealed in 1736, even Blackstone's renowned *Commentaries on the Laws of England* in 1765 stated plainly that the existence of witchcraft "is a truth to which every nation in the world hath in its turn borne testimony." However, John Wesley, the founder of Methodism (1703–1791), expressed regret that men of learning "have given up all accounts of witches and apparitions as mere old wives' fables."

Halloween folk customs of pagan origin continued to flourish in Ireland, Scotland, Wales, and parts of England well into the 18th century and in some instances into the 19th. Country people, especially those in isolated locations, practiced the ancient methods of dispersing the "spirits," who they believed were out on Halloween stealing milk, harming cattle, and destroying crops. They therefore lighted bonfires on hilltops on October 31 and set pitchforks plaited with straw on fire to singe the brooms of lurking witches.

Since the prospect of facing a ghost alone was not pleasant, country folk huddled together in groups on that fearful night. To while away the time – because no one dared to relax and sleep – they related their experiences with strange noises and spooky shadows and played traditional games, such as bobbing for apples. They also feasted on the new crop of apples and nuts.

Halloween was the time when the invisible world of the spirits was closer than at any other point in the year. Since spirits supposedly could help one predict the future, various methods of divining the future were used on Halloween and the results were accepted in all seriousness. They concerned such questions as the identity of future spouses, the chances for wealth or good fortune, and the identity of those who would die during the coming months. Welsh peasants peeked through the keyholes of the church door, convinced they would see apparitions of those who would soon die. In Scotland each member of the family put a stone in the fire and marked a circle around it. When the fire was burned out, the ashes were raked over the stones. If any stone was found misplaced in the morning or if there was a footprint near it, it was believed that the person to whom the stone belonged would die within the year.

One of the dishes served at supper in Ireland on Halloween was known as *callcannon*, or *colcannon*. It consisted of mashed potatoes, parsnips, and chopped onions. A ring, a thimble, a china doll, and a coin were stirred into it and the one who found the ring when the *callcannon* was served was to be married within a year; the finder of the doll would have children; the one who got the thimble would never marry; and whoever was fortunate enough to get the coin would have wealth. This was varied, sometimes, by baking a ring and a nut in a cake. The one whose slice of cake contained the ring would marry, and the finder of the nut would marry a widow or a widower — unless the kernel of the nut was shriveled, in which case the finder would never marry.

The discovery of marital prospects was also sought — by burning nuts in the coals in the fireplace. A young woman would put three nuts in the coals, naming one for herself and the other two for admirers. If one of the nuts burned quietly beside that named for the woman, it meant that that man was true to her; but if the nuts separated there would be no lasting happiness beween her and either of the contenders. Another test used by lovers was the sowing of hempseed. The idea was to take a handful of the seed and go out into a field and sow it, while repeating this rhyme:

> Hempseed, I saw thee,
> Hempseed, I saw thee,
> And her that is to be my true love,
> Come after me and draw thee.

If the sower had the courage to look back over his shoulder, he would see the apparition of his true love following him and reaping hemp.

In another charm, a girl would throw a ball of blue yarn out the window after dark and hold fast to one end of the yarn. Then she would wind it over her hand from left to right, or widdershins, and repeat the Creed backwards. If this charm worked, the end of the yarn still out the window would be held by someone so that she could wind no more. Then the girl would ask, "Who holds?" and the name of her sweetheart would be wafted through the window by the wind.

Halloween also was the time when young people went in pairs into the fields blindfolded and pulled up cabbages. The size and shape indicated the appearance of the future husband or wife. The stalks were placed over the door and numbered. And if, for example, a youth was the third person entering the door, his name would be the name of the husband of the girl whose stalk was number three. It was believed that if a girl went into her room at midnight on the fateful eve, sat down before her mirror, cut an apple into nine slices, and held each slice on the point of her knife before eating it, she might see in the mirror looking over her shoulder the face of her future lover and he would ask for the last slice. In 1786 the Scottish poet Robert Burns described in "Halloween" a party in which many ancient customs were followed by the young people, but with a touch of skepticism not characteristic of the earlier days.

Pranks and mischief were also common in rural areas of the British Isles on October 31. Roaming groups of merrymakers — in some places dressed in masks and the clothing of the opposite sex — played tricks on neighbors: stealing gates, blocking house doors, and covering chimneys with turf so that smoke could not escape. Blame for the resulting chaos was naturally placed on the "spirits."

Although a few of the original customs are still practiced today in the British Isles on Halloween, most have been forgotten. Transplanted to the New World, however, some of the old traditions have been revitalized and fostered with perhaps even more enthusiasm than was once evident in the Old World. Widespread observance of Halloween nevertheless came relatively late to the United States. Most of the early settlers, the majority of whom were Protestant, did not observe All Saints' Day or Halloween. October 31 had little significance in colonial days, although records show that some New World English kept up the secular side of the evening with apple ducking and apple snapping, a game using a suspended twirling stick with an apple on one end and a lighted candle on the other, the object being to bite the apple without being burned.

In pioneer days, some Americans celebrated Halloween with corn-popping parties, taffy pulls, and hayrides. Farmers, especially, gathered on what they termed Snap Apple Night or Nutcrack Night to play some of the customary divination games. However, all these Halloween practices were scattered and regional until the great Irish immigration in the 1840s, following the Irish Potato Famine. The Irish brought with them not only the religious observances of All Saints' Day and Eve, but also the folklore remnants of the eve of *Samhain* (until recently October 31 was still called Oidhche Shamhna in Ireland) and the traditional mischief of their "fairy folk," or "little people." In fact, one of the most popular and enduring features of Halloween, jack-o'-lanterns, are primarily an Irish tradition. In Ireland, oversized rutabagas, turnips, and potatoes — instead of pumpkins, which were not available — were hollowed out, carved into hideous faces and illuminated with candles, to be used as lanterns at Halloween celebrations.

The name *jack-o'-lantern* supposedly came from an Irish tale of a man named Jack who was notorious for drunkenness and for being stingy. One evening at the local pub, the Devil appeared to claim his soul. Jack skillfully persuaded the Devil to "have one drink together before we go." To pay for his drink, the Devil turned himself into a sixpence, which Jack immediately snatched. He put it into his wallet, which had a catch in the form of a cross, thus preventing the Devil from escaping. Jack eventually released the Devil on condition that the latter leave him in peace for another year. Twelve months later, Jack played another practical joke on the Devil, letting him down from a tree only on the promise that he would never pursue him again. Finally, Jack's body wore out. Barred from heaven because of transgressions and from Hell because of the pranks he played on the Devil, Jack in desperation begged the Devil for a live coal to light his way out of the dark. Jack put it into a turnip he was chewing and, as the story goes, is condemned to walk the earth with his lantern until Judgment Day.

By the late 1800s, Halloween had become a national observance in the United States, characterized by games, divinations, parties, and especially the custom of going "trick-or-treating" dressed in weird masks and costumes.

There are several theories about the origins of trick-or-treating. One claims that the practice stems from the custom of "souling" or "soul-caking," when Englishmen went around on All Saints', and especially All Souls', Day to beg for soul cakes (square buns with currants) in remembrance of the dead. Those begging promised extra prayers for the dead relatives of the donors.

However, the contemporary custom of trick-or-treating also resembles an ancient Irish practice on Halloween, when groups of peasants went from house to house, asking for money for which to buy luxuries for a feast and demanding that fatted calves and black sheep be prepared for the occasion. These contributions were often requested in the name of Muck Olla, a druid deity, or St. Columba (a monk who in the sixth century converted the Picts and founded a monastery on Iona off the Scottish coast). Prosperity was assured liberal givers, and threats were voiced against those who were stingy.

Another possibility is that trick-or-treating, as well as masquerading, is derived from the "penny for the Guy" practice in England on November 5, when Guy Fawkes Day festivities — commemorating the foiling of the 1605 Gunpowder Plot to blow up King James I and Parliament — include begging and dressing up in costumes. Some scholars claim that masquerading on Halloween is derived from the medieval practice of celebrating All Hallows' Day with a procession around the church in which the local populace sometimes dressed as angels, patron saints, or even devils.

According to tradition, the fairy folk or little people whom the Irish brought with them to the New World were expected to be particularly mischievous on Halloween. Their influence soon spread in energetic, 19th century US communities, where practical jokes furnished welcome and not-so-welcome diversion. When house and street numbers were changed, fences built across roads, animals hidden, water faucets opened, and store and house windows soaped, people good-naturedly said "the fairies or goblins must have done it."

In the course of the 20th century, Americans have become less tolerant of pranks, which have often descended into vandalism. Especially after World War II, "harmless" jokes, originally intended as good fun, turned into acts of lawlessness, such as slitting tires and breaking street lights. Civic authorities and private citizens alike, concerned about increasing rowdiness and costly property damage, issued warnings about vandalism and attempted to deal with the problem by educational means and stricter law enforcement.

Community Halloween festivals, sponsored by local merchants, civic groups, and schools, especially PTAs, have done much to curtail the widespread vandalism. Even as early as 1908, some communities sought to prevent damage by giving Halloween parties for children. However, it was apparently the residents of Anoka, Minnesota, who organized the first citywide, supervised party in the early 1920s. Similar celebrations were soon inaugurated in diverse places. In most communities, observances at schools, parks, and downtown areas included costume parades — often with prizes for the scariest, funniest, and most original garb. These were supplemented by dramatic skits, carnival booths, refreshments (the ever-popular candied apples, popcorn, candy corn, and peanuts), and such games as the traditional bobbing for apples. Merchants invited young people to soap the windows of their stores and offered prizes for the best soap drawings with Halloween themes.

Some Halloween festivities have grown through the years to become major attractions. In Allentown, Pennsylvania, for example, the annual Halloween parade, held on the Tuesday evening nearest October 31, has been staged for more than 50 years. Watched by over 80,000 people during its 20-block march, it usually has 20 divisions, each headed by a band or musical group followed by marching formations and floats. Since 1923 the inhabitants of Anaheim, California, also have channeled Halloween enthusiasm into an enterprising community celebration. One of the highlights is the pageant parade traditionally scheduled for the Saturday preceding October 31. The event, which has developed into one of the most outstanding night parades in the West, is often attended by more than 150,000. A typical annual program at Anaheim also includes a Kiddies' Parade (in which over 6,000 costumed schoolchildren participate), a costume ball, stage entertainment, costume judging, display-window decorating contests, a Pumpkin Bowl football game, and a community costume breakfast in a city park.

The trend towards manipulating, rather than celebrating, folk festivals such as Halloween may be indicative of a declining interest in fantasy and imagination. Halloween has now become what sociologists term a "degenerate" holiday, the folk vitality of witches, divinations, and the black arts having long receded into the past. But the decline in its significance has not affected small children, who still enjoy ringing doorbells and shouting "Trick or treat!" Yet even here, the practice of begging for coins, apples, candy, and trinkets has often been transformed into a good deed instead of mere merriment. Swarms of exuberant youngsters still dress up in traditional costumes, but they are likely to chant "Trick or treat for UNICEF" (the United Nations Children's Fund).

This worthwhile Halloween project started in 1950, when the children in a Sunday school near Philadelphia sent UNICEF the $17 they had collected trick-or-treating. The idea caught on, and, with the assistance of parents, teachers, and religious leaders, it has expanded until in the 1970s over 3 million American children in 13,000 communities in all 50 states and at service installations abroad were involved in the effort. A presidential proclamation of October 27, 1967, covering all successive years, made October 31 National UNICEF Day in the United States.

"Trick-or-treating for UNICEF" usually ends on a festive note, as the youngsters gather for parties at the collection centers. After emptying their orange-and-black cartons into a huge witches' caldron, they are "treated" to cake and candy, play games, and are awarded prizes for the best costumes.

Nevada Day

The territory of Nevada was admitted to the Union as the 36th state on October 31, 1864, by proclamation of President Abraham Lincoln, issued in accordance with the provisions of an act passed on March 31 of that year. The anniversary of Nevada's admission is a legal holiday in the state and is observed by the display of flags on all public buildings. The major Nevada Day festivities take place in Carson City, the state capital since 1864, which is located 30 miles south of Reno. They center on the big Admission Day parade, which has been held annually since 1938. An Indian pageant, an 1864 costume ball, the coronation of Miss Nevada Day, and other events traditionally round out the occasion. The Nevada Day celebration has expanded each year — with participants and onlookers coming from nearby states as well — until the activities are at present spread out over an entire week, culminating with the October 31 parade.

An impressive celebration was staged in 1964, when Nevada marked its centennial of statehood. Observances were held in each of the 17 counties; and groups such as the singing ensemble "The Centennial Belles," performed at civic and community meetings throughout the state. But Carson City was the scene of the most elaborate fete. The full program of centennial events, including the grand centennial ball, coronation of Miss Nevada Centennial, rodeo, and fashion show featuring 100 years of wedding dresses, was, as usual, highlighted by the anniversary procession, only this time it was called the grand centennial parade. A special Indian program featured an all-Indian parade in which tribe members from several western states participated; an Indian trade fair; and an Indian princess contest. Coins, flags, historical documents, and a number of items connected with Nevada's 100th anniversary were sealed in the metal centennial capsule, to remain unopened until the bicentennial Nevada Day, October 31, 2064.

More typical of the Nevada Day festivities was the 1970 program marking the 106th anniversary of statehood. The celebration began on Saturday, October 24, and reached a high point with the Nevada Day parade the following weekend. Events early in the week included an 1864 costume ball, as well as motorcycle races, an art exhibit, the fall classic football game, coronation of Miss Nevada Day, the Kiwanis Club pancake breakfast, and the Nevada Day horse show. The eagerly anticipated grand parade, which got underway at 11:00 A.M. on Saturday, October 31, attracted an estimated 20,000 persons to the capital city and lasted more than two hours. The 200-odd participants included beauty queens, marching bands, mounted units, and military cadets; dozens of floats depicted the theme Recreation Unlimited. Immediately following the parade, the Carson Indian Colony staged its annual Indian festival and barbecue in Governor's Field. Indian arts and crafts were exhibited, and there were Indian games and a pageant depicting events in early Nevada history, before the coming of Europeans.

In an early afternoon ceremony at the Capitol on October 31, the governor of Nevada presented awards to the nine winners selected in the annual Nevada Day historical essay contest.

The contest has been sponsored each year since 1959 by the Nevada Day Committee. The winners in the various school districts are chosen by their local superintendents or teachers. Their essays and photographs are published as the major editorial material in each Nevada Day souvenir program. Later on in the day, the Whiskerino contest entrants vied for the prizes awarded for the grayest, reddest, heaviest, longest, and fanciest beards. Square dancing, a teenage dance, and a horse show concluded the weekend activities.

The history of Nevada before it entered the Union reflects — perhaps even more than that of most states — the important role played by geographical and physical, as well as human, factors. Formed as a result of turbulent geological upheavals, Nevada is a land of picturesque contrasts: vast arid stretches of sagebrush and creosote bush, lofty mountains extending north to south, and relatively few rivers. Its early inhabitants, the Basketmakers, and later the Paiute, Shoshone, and Washoe tribes, were preoccupied with eking out a meager living. The sparse population existed on a diet of wild animals, insects, and plants.

The first white men to enter the region of Nevada are said to have been Franciscan missionaries en route from Mexico to California in the 1770s. Fray Francisco Garcés probably passed through what is now the extreme southwestern part of the state. Fray Silvestre Vélez de Escalante may have crossed the eastern edge in search of a new route to the coast. Their reports about the forbidding wilderness of mountains and semidesert were sufficient to discourage further exploration for almost 50 years.

Only in the 1820s and 1830s did American and Canadian fur traders and trappers penetrate the unknown region for beaver pelts. Peter Ogden and other members of Hudson's Bay Company, trading out of the Oregon country, crossed into what is now Nevada from the north and discovered the Humboldt River valley. Jedediah Smith, an American Fur Company trader from St. Louis, traversed the area of the present state while journeying from the Mississippi to the Pacific. Another adventurer, Joseph Walker, scaled the precipitous Sierra Nevadas into California. During 1843–1845, Captain John C. Frémont, guided by the renowned frontier scout Kit Carson (after whom the capital city was named), conducted the first systematic exploration of the region. Writing in 1846, a trapper, James Clyman, still characterized the area as one of the "most STERILE BARREN countrys I have ever traversed . . . [having the] most thirsty appearance of any place I ever witnessed."

In the 1840s, emigrant trains and gold seekers hurried across the inhospitable territory on the trail to California. At the end of the Mexican War, the territory from which Nevada was formed came into the possession of the United States by the Treaty of Guadalupe Hidalgo on February 2, 1848 (see February 2). Since it was adjacent to the Mormon commonwealth that was just being formed in the Salt Lake City area, Nevada was included in the vast Mormon "state" of Deseret proclaimed by the Mormon leader Brigham Young in March 1849. The Mormons soon established a trading post and base for exploration in the Carson River valley. Known as Mormon Station and later as Genoa, it was the first permanent white settlement in Nevada.

When the US government rejected the Mormon claim to Deseret, most of the area of Nevada was included in the newly organized territory of Utah in 1850. Salt Lake City, seat of the Utah territorial government, however, proved to be too far distant to provide adequate political control and military protection for the area's westernmost inhabitants. As early as 1851, therefore, these settlers tried to form a more satisfactory — and preferably, in their eyes, a more independent — form of government. In 1854 the Utah legislature quashed all such attempts by including the settlements of the western Utah territory in a newly created Carson County. In 1859 the people of Carson County made an abortive attempt to form a state government of their own.

In general, life in the area had remained quiet until 1859, when Nevada's huge mineral wealth, missed even by the gold-hungry Spaniards, was discovered. The famous Comstock Lode, one of the richest silver deposits ever tapped, yielded precious metal worth hundreds of millions. Near its site, the little settlement of Virginia City mushroomed overnight as news of the strike spread like wildfire. In its heyday, Virginia City boasted a population of 30,000 — and 106 saloons. Mark Twain, who was a Virginia City inhabitant from 1862 to 1864, vividly depicted the wild Nevada Days in *Roughing It*. He also left little doubt that although the mining boom had unearthed riches underground, the area's physical attractiveness had not improved:

I overheard a gentleman say the other day, that it was "the d——dest country under the sun" and that comprehensive conception I fully subscribe to. It never rains here, and the dew never falls. No flowers grow here, and no green thing gladdens the eye. The birds that fly over the land carry their provisions with them. Only the crow and the raven tarry with us.

The influx of easy-money men and the lack of effective federal control made lawlessness rampant in the raucous mining towns. In a move partly designed to impose law and order, Congress divided the territory of Utah on March 2,

1861, and out of its western portion created the territory of Nevada. (The name, originally designating the snow-capped Sierra Nevada, means "snow-clad" in Spanish.) An effort to achieve statehood in 1863 failed. By the following year, however, it had become obvious that two more Republican senatorial votes were required to push through such legislation as the long-contested 13th Amendment, formally abolishing slavery. In a maneuver designed to bolster antislavery legislation, Nevada attained statehood on October 31, 1864, a mere three years after gaining territorial status. Even then, the "battle-born" state formed during the dark days of the Civil War was considerably short of the 60,000 population theoretically necessary for entry into the Union. In 1866 Nevada reached its present boundaries by acquiring its southern tip from New Mexico and eastern lands from Utah.

The history of Nevada since its admission to statehood has been in great part dependent upon the fate of its mines. The Silver State, as it is also called, boomed during the 1860s and 1870s. The Comstock Lode production reached a high of $36 million in 1878. But in the late 19th century, the area's economy was deeply shaken by mining depressions and fluctuations in the value of precious metals. Only eerie ghost towns recalled the days of the big strikes; instead the state developed its cattle ranching and sheep grazing potentials.

In 1900 the discovery of a new gold and silver belt in southern Nevada, amidst the cactus and sagebrush at such places as Tonopah and Goldfield, spurred prosperity. Large-scale copper production was initiated about 1908. Although mining still remains a multimillion-dollar industry, Nevada has become famous in the 20th century as a tourist and resort center noted for its legalized gambling, speedy marriages and divorces, glittering entertainment, and impressive natural phenomena.

Protestant Reformation Day

All Saints' Eve, October 31, in the year 1517 was the fateful date on which Martin Luther, the German religious reformer, nailed his 95 theses to the door of the castle church in Wittenberg. His challenge to some of the doctrines and practices of the Roman Catholic church gained such rapid and widespread support among all classes of people throughout western Europe that the ensuing religious revolt, which came to be known as the Reformation, ended the role of the pope as the head of all of Western Christendom and brought about the formation of the Protestant churches. Consequently, October 31 is observed as Reformation Day by most Protes-

tant denominations. It is also often marked by special services, particularly in Lutheran churches, on the last Sunday of October (Reformation Sunday).

Martin Luther was born in Eisleben, Saxony, on November 10, 1483, the son of a poor miner. At the age of 13 he was sent to school in Madgeburg and then, for three years, attended St. George's school in Eisenach. In return for free lodging and schooling and for being permitted to beg from door to door for his bread, he sang in the church with which the school was connected. At the age of 18 he entered the University of Erfurt, from which he received his bachelor's degree at 19 and his master's degree three years later. In accordance with his father's wishes, Luther began the study of law in 1505. It is said that at that time, while returning to Erfurt after a visit to his parents, he was caught in a violent thunderstorm and was so thoroughly frightened that he vowed to St. Anne, mother of the Virgin Mary, that if he was saved he would become a monk. Even as a young boy, Luther had had a strong religious inclination. He left the university and entered the Augustinian friary in Erfurt, allegedly two weeks after the thunderstorm.

In due time Luther took the vows of poverty, chastity, and obedience, and in 1507 he was ordained a priest. He studied and taught during the next few years, both at the University of Wittenberg and at his alma mater at Erfurt. During a visit to Rome on business for the Augustinian order in the winter of 1510–1511, he was scandalized by the luxury and vice he found there. In 1511 or 1512 he returned to Wittenberg, and for the remainder of his life he preached in the parish church there and held the chair of professor of biblical exegesis at the university. He was awarded a doctorate in theology in 1512.

Deeply troubled about his own unrighteousness and about the church's teaching that salvation could be gained through good works, including the purchase of indulgences, Luther went through a long period of spiritual searching. Through deep study of the Scriptures, particularly the Epistles of St. Paul, he came to believe that God freely forgives sins because Christ died for all human sins. Since God's forgiveness is a gift, Luther reasoned, it cannot be gained by good works but only by faith. As he became firm in these beliefs, Luther began to teach them.

At about this time a German Dominican monk, Johann Tetzel, was traveling through Germany granting indulgences to all who contributed to a fund for the rebuilding of St. Peter's basilica in Rome. Preaching the importance of buying indulgences not only for the living but also for the dead, he reached the neighborhood of Wittenberg in 1517. Convinced that the granting of indulgences was doctrinally wrong, and that the selling of them heaped abuse upon error, Luther posted his challenging 95 theses in the hope that they would bring about public debate. He had no thought at this time of opposing the overall authority of the Roman Catholic church. The theses were written in Latin but were soon translated into German. Within two weeks they had been printed and circulated throughout Germany, and within a month word of them had spread through western and southern Europe. They were received with great enthusiasm by those who had long sought relief from their economic exploitation by the church as well as an end to the corruption within it.

Luther was ordered by Pope Leo X to recant, and various church authorities attempted to compel him to do so. He refused each time, saying that he would recant only if proved wrong by Holy Scripture. An agreement was arranged in 1519 whereby both Luther and his critics were to maintain silence while the issue was arbitrated by German bishops. However, the agreement was broken during the year when the Catholic theologian Johann Eck challenged Luther to a debate in Leipzig. Luther accepted, and the debate brought the issue again to public attention.

He then gained wider support for his views by the publication of three pamphlets in which he set forth his arguments and his program for reform. These treatises, entitled *An Address to the Christian Nobility of the German Nation, The Babylonian Captivity of the Church,* and *The Liberty of a Christian Man,* were all published in 1520. In them Luther propounded his fundamental doctrine of justification by faith alone, attacked the belief in the supremacy of the pope and the assumption by the church of the role of sole intermediary between God and Christian man, suggested that the German rulers establish a national church free from Roman domination, and denounced clerical celibacy and monastic life. He held that the Bible, not the Church, was the true source of religious authority.

In the same year, 1520, Leo X moved to excommunicate Luther, issuing a bull that condemned the priest for heresy but permitted him a final opportunity to recant within 60 days. When the bull reached him in Wittenberg, Luther, accompanied by faculty members and students of the university, took both the bull and a copy of the canon law to a meadow and burned them in a bonfire. In the wake of Luther's intransigence, a formal bull of excommunication was issued by the pope. Instead of executing it,

though, Holy Roman Emperor Charles V ordered Luther to appear before the Diet of Worms in April 1521 to defend himself. Still refusing to recant, Luther and his supporters were found guilty by the diet and placed under the ban of the empire. However, at the behest of Luther's ruler and protector, the elector of Saxony, Frederick III, Luther was seized upon leaving Worms and taken for protection to the Wartburg, a castle near Eisenach. His identity was concealed during his stay there, and he was known as the Knight George.

Only because of the tremendous amount of support he received was Luther able to act so boldly and with such freedom. He had numerous supporters among both the lower and upper classes, including professors, monks and members of the lower clergy, and rulers. Of particular importance was the protection given him by Frederick. One of the aspects of the program proposed by the Lutherans — or Evangelicals, as Luther preferred that he and his followers be called — was the placing of the church under civil authority, a proposal that appealed to ruling houses as well as to all those caught up by the rising spirit of nationalism.

During almost a year spent in hiding in the Wartburg, Luther began his translation of the New Testament from Greek into German and also wrote a number of pamphlets, which were banned but nevertheless had wide circulation. Meanwhile Charles V had become involved in war with France and was giving no attention to the developing religious revolt. In 1522 Luther left the castle to return to Wittenberg. Two years later the Peasants' War broke out. In their demands for the redress of economic and other grievances, the leaders of the Peasants' War cited Lutheran teachings and biblical quotations. Luther, who did not approve of the use of his religious doctrine to support such a major revolt against the existing economic system, tried to effect a compromise between the peasants and their landlords. When the peasants refused and continued in their violent rebellion, Luther denounced their actions in a pamphlet, *Against the Murdering, Thieving Hordes of Peasants,* and called upon the landlords to subdue them by any means. Not surprisingly, this action lost Luther the support of many peasants. The revolt was ruthlessly crushed in 1525.

Having previously taken a stand against the need for celibacy of the clergy, Luther, in 1525, married Katharina von Bora, a former nun who had renounced her vows as a result of his teachings. They enjoyed a happy marriage and had six children (one of whom died in infancy).

Lutheranism had grown so strong in Germany by this time that the Diet of Speyer, convened in

1526, decided to allow those German princes who desired to practice Lutheranism to do so for the time being. A Catholic majority at the second Diet of Speyer overturned that decision in 1529. The Lutherans protested this retraction of religious freedom and thereby became known as "Protestants," a term later broadened to cover all of the Christian denominations formed as a result of the Reformation.

In the hope that compromise was possible, the following year Charles V asked Luther and his supporters to submit a summary of their views and ideas for reform to an imperial diet that was to meet in Augsburg. The statement, prepared by the German scholar and religious reformer Melanchthon, reaffirmed that the Lutherans were seeking not to separate themselves from the Roman Catholic church but to correct what they considered to be abuses and incorrect interpretation of doctrine within the church. This Augsburg Confession — which is still a basis of Lutheran doctrine — was strongly opposed by the emperor and most of the members of the diet.

Expecting that their opponents would now try to crush them by force, the Protestant rulers of such German states as Hesse, Saxony, and Brandenburg, along with various free cities, met at Schmalkalden to form a league for common defense. Again, however, the attention of the emperor was distracted by his involvement in foreign conflicts, this time to such a degree that the six-month truce with the league to which he consented in 1532 lasted until 1546. In the latter year he brought military force to bear and was initially successful. But a satisfactory, workable means of reestablishing the authority of the Roman Catholic church over half of the German population — so widely had Protestantism taken hold — was extremely difficult to find. Time dragged on until the defection of one of the emperor's principal supporters, Maurice, duke of Saxony, in 1551, gave the real victory to the Protestants.

By the terms of the Religious Peace of Augsburg (1555), each of the rulers of the several hundred German states was permitted to choose either Roman Catholicism or Lutheranism. The inhabitants of each state were bound to practice the same religion as their ruler; if they did not wish to practice his religion, they could move to a state in which the ruler's religious preference was the same as their own. With this accord, official consent was given for the first time to the establishment within Western Christendom of a church other than the Roman Catholic church.

Luther, meanwhile, had continued his activities, and in 1529 had published his *Small Catechism*, which is still held basic to the Lutheran faith. He also finished, in 1534, his translation of the Bible from Greek into German. Some of the poor university students who were frequent guests in Luther's home found his conversation so entertaining that they wrote down everything they heard him say. Their material was later published as *Table Talk*. Luther died during a visit to the town of his birth, Eisleben, on February 18, 1546, before the outcome of the upheaval inadvertently begun by him was determined.

Numerous buildings associated with Luther still stand, despite the great destruction wrought in Germany during World War II. In Eisleben the house in which he was born is now a museum devoted to him. The house in which he died is maintained as a memorial. During his school years in Eisenach Luther was a protégé of Ursula Cotta. Although the Cotta mansion suffered bomb damage during World War II, the room used by Luther remains intact. Buildings of the former Augustinian monastery at Erfurt, where he stayed from 1505 to 1508, have been damaged but still stand.

In Wittenberg the castle church and its door, to which Luther nailed his 95 theses, may be visited, as may the parish church where he preached for 35 years. Luther's tomb is in the castle church. His home contains a museum. A statue also honors the reformer, and an oak tree marks the alleged place where he burned the papal bull that condemned him for heresy.

Worms, the seat of the imperial diet that in 1521 ordered Luther to recant, is now the site of one of the most famous memorials to him. In this monument, Luther is depicted with his hands on the Bible, uttering these words: "Here I stand. I cannot do otherwise. God help me. Amen." Surrounding the representation of Luther are statues of other figures important to the Reformation. The Wartburg sustained some war damage, but not in the area in which the reformer lived and worked. His table and drinking vessel and various memorabilia — as well as the armor of "Knight George" — are still there.

During the late 1960s the character of the observances of Reformation Sunday changed considerably. Previously, emphasis had been largely upon the celebration of the anniversary of a historical event, with the ideas of the Reformation being considered in their 16th century context, rather than with the thought that they might be relevant to the current time. But Protestant thinking in this regard changed, at least partly in response to the searching self-examination conducted by the Roman Catholic church in its ecumenical Second Vatican Council (Vatican II) in the early 1960s. During this period the Catholic church accepted some of Luther's ideas as valid, and approved certain changes, such as the translation of the liturgy into the vernacular. Some of the changes adopted by Catholics went further than some Protestant churches had gone in making church services relevant to contemporary concerns. As Protestants, too, began to look inward, they felt a need to revise traditional Reformation Day observances to stress the continuing necessity for reform within their churches and within individuals. In addition, they placed emphasis on the common origin and close similarity of beliefs held by the Roman Catholic and Protestant faiths, and in many cases expressed a desire for closer ties between the two.

Traditionally included in Reformation Sunday services is Luther's great hymn "A Mighty Fortress is Our God." One of the Bible readings Lutherans customarily hear on that day is John 2:13–17, which tells of Jesus' driving the money-changers from the Temple in Jerusalem. Because of their direct ties to the reformer, Lutherans have had greater interest in observing the day than have some other sects. Nevertheless, in many places all Protestant churches participate in communitywide services, often held in schools or theaters that can accommodate large numbers.

The 450th anniversary of the beginning of the Reformation was celebrated in 1967 in the United States with great spirit, born of a widely felt desire to imbue the observances with new life and an ecumenical emphasis. Perhaps the most remarkable aspect of the observances was the active participation around the country of Roman Catholics, including members of the clergy. For example, in a Reformation Day program at the Church Center for the United Nations, both Roman Catholic and Protestant speakers probed the topic "Reformation Past and Present." At Princeton University, a joint Protestant–Roman Catholic service was held for the first time since the university's founding 221 years before. Dialogue between Catholics and Protestants took place in many parts of the country, and there were special concerts, rallies, pageants, art exhibits, dramatic programs, radio and television coverage, and presentations of a full-length film entitled *Martin Luther*. Of particular note were performances of Felix Mendelssohn's *Reformation* Symphony.

Reformation Sunday is still observed with special worship services, special Sunday school lessons, and special musical programs. Considerable weight is being given to persistent efforts to bring Christians closer together. The dialogue between Protestants and Catholics that gained such momentum in 1967 has continued. And, four and a half centuries after its condemnation of Martin Luther as a heretic, the Roman Catholic church began to reappraise its view of the Augustinian friar who was responsible for the birth of Protestantism.

November

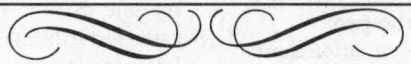

November is the 11th month of the Gregorian, or New Style, calendar in use today and numbers 30 days. As its name — derived from the Latin word *novem*, or "nine" — indicates, November was the ninth month in the old Roman calendar, which began in March. Even after the ancient Roman calendar had been revised extensively and the year began two months earlier — in January — November, like September, October, and December, retained its traditional but inappropriate name.

The Roman senate, however, sought to rename November in the early first century A.D. In the first century B.C., *Quintilis* and *Sextilis*, the fifth and sixth months of the old Roman calendar, had been renamed *Julius* and *Augustus*, after the dictator Julius Caesar and the first Roman emperor, Augustus. Once the names *Julius* and *Augustus* had been accepted, it was only natural that the Roman senate should attempt to flatter succeeding rulers by naming months in their honor as well. September, October, November, and December were particularly subject to change since they not only followed July and August, but had in addition inaccurate and outmoded names. The senate therefore proposed naming November *Tiberius* in honor of the second Roman emperor, Tiberius, who ruled from A.D. 14 to 37.

Since Tiberius was stern and withdrawn, uninterested in imperial trappings and flattery, it was not surprising that the Roman senate failed in its attempt to honor him with a month named *Tiberius*. The senatorial body first tried to rename September *Tiberius* and October *Livius* in honor of his mother, Livia, the first Roman empress. (Livia's second husband was Augustus, who had made his stepson Tiberius his heir and successor.) Tiberius rejected the senate's efforts, and the senators concluded that the emperor had been displeased because his month had been coupled with the naming of a month for

Livia, who, although once politically influential, was increasingly in her son's disfavor.

Deciding that Tiberius might accept the honor if the tribute was extended to him alone, the senate selected November — since Tiberius had been born on November 16 — in a second attempt to honor him. The principle of choosing the ruler's birth month had been laid down in the case of Julius Caesar and proposed, although rejected, in the case of Augustus. However, the senate's second proposal merely aroused the wrath of Tiberius. He again declined the honor, remarking sarcastically: "And what will you do if there be 13 Caesars?"

In a much less modest fashion, Emperor Commodus (A.D. 180–192) forced the Roman senate, in about 191, to consent to the renaming of all 12 months after himself. Each was to be designated with one of his honorary titles. November was to be called *Romanus* ("the Roman"), according to one contemporary historian or, according to a less reliable account, *Exsuperatorius*, signifying that Commodus surpassed all men. However, the new calendar names did not outlive the rule of Commodus.

The Anglo-Saxons called November *Windmonath*, or "wind-month," since the winds blew furiously during this season. The month was also designated *Blod-monath*, or "bloody month," since it was the time for slaughtering animals for winter food. The lucky birthstone often associated with November is the topaz.

NOVEMBER 1

All Saints' Day

November 1, All Saints' Day, is a feast observed by Roman Catholics, as well as by Episcopalians, Lutherans, and some other Protestant denominations, in honor of all the saints blessed in heaven, whether known or unknown. The day also used to be called All Hallows' Day or Hallowmass from the Old English word "hallow," meaning "sanctify." In the Roman Catholic church, All Saints' Day — a feast of highest rank, or solemnity — is considered one of the most important observances of the church year. It is a holy day of obligation on which all Catholics are obliged to attend mass. The feast is the first day of the octave that enhances it— an eight-day period during which special prayers, such as the special preface for All Saints' Day, are said every day. It is preceded by a vigil of preparation on the evening of October 31.

Strangely enough, it is this vigil, All Hallows' Eve, or more familiarly Halloween, that has become the most widely known feature of the observance. All Hallows' Eve was originally intended to be celebrated entirely as a religious occasion with prayers and extra masses, as on the eve of any great feast, and is still commemorated in this fashion in many European and Latin American countries. But throughout the Middle Ages, especially in the British Isles, the old Celtic religious and folk ways connected with the pagan celebration of *Samhain* lingered on alongside the ecclesiastical celebration. Today in Great Britain, Ireland, and the United States, October 31 has lost its serious religious tone and is primarily regarded as a night of merrymaking, games, and parties featuring macabre and superstitious themes (see October 31).

The origin of All Saints' Day is probably to be found in the common veneration of all who either suffered martyrdom in groups or whose names were unknown. As early as the fourth century, following the persecutions under the Roman emperor Diocletian and his predecessors, it was suggested that there be a special day to commemorate all the martyrs — the first saints publicly venerated by the early Church — since the year was not long enough to assign an individual day for the veneration of each martyr. The Eastern churches have observed such a day (on various dates) since the fourth century. St. John Chrysostom (A.D. 345–407), the Greek Father of the Church and later bishop of Constantinople, preached a sermon every year to commemorate all the saints.

In 609 Pope Boniface IV consecrated the Pantheon in Rome — formerly the Roman temple of all the gods — to the Virgin Mary and all martyrs, and he designated the first observance of the feast for May 610. In conjunction with the Church's attempt to displace or suppress preexisting pagan cults, Pope Gregory III (731–741) changed the feast from May to November — and enlarged it to embrace all saints as well as martyrs — when he consecrated a chapel in St. Peter's

Basilica at Rome to all the saints. Although the change of date was presumably to combat the lingering *Samhain* rites, some scholars hold that November was selected so that the multitude of pilgrims flocking to Rome for the feast of the saints could be fed from the fall harvest. In the 830s, Pope Gregory IV (827–844) established the feast in the church calendar as All Saints' Day and required its observance — and the observance of its vigil, All Hallows' Eve — by all churches. Pope Sixtus IV (1471–1484) added the octave.

After the Reformation, in the 16th century, the feast was generally retained by Protestants — in varying degrees of observance — although among some denominations it either was not adopted or soon ceased to be celebrated. In the Church of England, for example, All Saints' Day is still a meaningful and moving occasion; the collect in the Book of Common Prayer aptly expresses its significance:

O Almighty God, who hast knit together thine elect in one communion and fellowship. . . . Grant us grace so to follow thy blessed Saints in all virtuous and godly living, so that we may come to those unspeakable joys which thou hast prepared for those who unfeignedly love thee.

Throughout the predominantly Catholic countries of Europe and in Latin America, All Saints' Day is now widely observed in churches with flowers, lighted candles, and joyful music to glorify the saints. At nightfall, however, November 1 (which is also All Souls' Day Eve), takes on a more subdued tone. Cemeteries are usually decorated in preparation for the commemoration of the dead on the next day, the solemn Feast of All Souls (see November 2). In Puerto Rico, many go to the churches and cathedrals on All Saints' Day and visit cemeteries, where they place lighted memorial candles on the graves.

In the United States, All Saints' Day is observed with similar traditional ceremonies, in addition to religious services, in sections where Roman Catholics predominate. In Louisiana, for instance, where many areas are predominantly Roman Catholic, the day is a legal holiday. In New Orleans — a city with French and Spanish customs and culture dating from the early 1700s, people crowd the cemeteries from sunrise to nightfall. The graves, covered by a blanket of chrysanthemums, turn into flower beds. As they are being decorated, mourning and weeping present a contrast with gossip and commerce, as vendors sell peanuts, taffy, pralines, and even toy skeletons to create a strange atmosphere of solemnity and festivity on the state holiday.

All Saints' Day also receives particular attention in other sections of southern and southwestern Louisiana. The country around St. Martinville, west of New Orleans, is inhabited by descendants of Acadian families driven from eastern Canada in the mid-18th century. These Cajuns, as they are popularly termed, are still French-speaking and, with few exceptions, Roman Catholic. In the traditional French manner, they place colorful wreaths and bouquets in even the most remote and unpretentious cemeteries of the region. As the evening of November 1 falls, hundreds of candles illuminate the graveyards as the faithful turn their thoughts to the Feast of All Souls' Day.

NOVEMBER 2

All Souls' Day

All Souls' Day which is celebrated on November 2, is primarily a feast of the Roman Catholic Church to commemorate the faithful departed — those who died members of the faith — especially those believed to be still suffering in purgatory. The observance is based on the Catholic doctrine that "the souls which on departing from the body are not perfectly cleansed from venial sins, or have not fully atoned for past transgressions are debarred from the Beatific Vision" until they have purged themselves of sins in purgatory. The faithful on earth — known as the Church Militant — are believed to be able to help these souls — the Church Expectant — to become members of the Church Triumphant in heaven, through prayers, alms, good deeds, and the sacrifice of the Mass.

The Office of the Dead is recited, and the mass is a requiem — requiem is a form of the Latin word *requies*, meaning "rest," and is used in the introductory prayer, "Grant unto them eternal rest . . . ." All Souls' Day is not a holy day of obligation, but many Catholics attend mass on this day and receive special indulgences applicable to the souls in purgatory. Aside from Christmas, All Souls' Day is the only day of the church year on which priests are given permission to celebrate three masses, a privilege granted by Pope Benedict XV in 1915.

Numerous ancient civilizations practiced the custom of setting aside a day or a longer period every year for the purpose of praying for all the dead. General prayers were also said to intercede for particular groups of the departed — for example, a slain regiment. A passage from the apocryphal Second Book of the Maccabees (12: 43–46) records the single Jewish precedent for offering prayers for the dead:

He [Judas Maccabaeus] sent twelve thousand drachmas of silver to Jerusalem for sacrifice to be offered for the sins of the dead, thinking well and religiously concerning the resurrection. For if he had not hoped that they that were slain should rise again, it would have seemed superfluous and vain to pray for the dead. . . . It is therefore a holy and wholesome thought to pray for the dead, that they may be loosed from sins.

The deceased were prayed for from the earliest days of Christianity; their names were entered in the tablets, known as diptychs, containing the lists of the departed, by both the Eastern and Western churches. Starting in the sixth century, the Benedictine monasteries held an annual remembrance of deceased members of the order at Pentecost.

The institution of a special feast of general intercession was probably the work of Odilo, an 11th century abbot of Cluny, France. Renowned for great spirituality (he is venerated as a saint), Odilo displayed equally great administrative talents. He is said to have been the first to prescribe — some time about 998 — that a common commemoration of the dead should be made in his religious community, and in other Cluniac monasteries, on November 2, the day following the Feast of All Saints (see November 1). The Feast of All Saints had been moved from May to November in the 8th century, most likely to displace the pagan celebration of *Samhain* on October 31 (see October 31, Halloween); its formal observance as All Saints' Day had been required of all Christians in the 9th century. Odilo undoubtedly chose November 2 in a deliberate attempt to continue the process of neutralizing the lingering pagan rites practiced at this time of the year. Even after Odilo's death on January 1, 1048, his observance continued to spread throughout Western Europe, through the efforts of the Cluniac monks.

A well-known center of religious revival and reform, Cluny, founded as a Benedictine abbey, grew to become the nucleus of a great order, embracing by the mid-12th century hundreds of monasteries in all sections of Europe and even in the Holy Land. Moreover, its influence in spiritual matters, including its advocacy of All Souls' Day, extended far beyond the actual order, and additional monasteries, such as the renowned Benedictine houses of Subiaco and Monte Cassino in Italy, adopted its customs. The feast of All Souls had become practically universal in Western Europe by the end of the 13th century and was adopted by Rome in the 14th.

The 16th century Protestants, although generally respecting All Saints' Day, sharply attacked the observance of All Souls' Day for a number of doctrinal reasons, especially since it revolved around a belief in purgatory, which they rejected. They also held that the practice of soliciting money for votive masses on November 2 to pray souls out of purgatory had been abused to a scandalous extreme. The Feast of All Souls was therefore, with few exceptions, generally abolished among Protestants. Now, however, the day is slowly being revived in some circles, notably in Anglo-Catholic churches. Among all who observe it, it has come in modern times to have a more general meaning, not as a special day to pray for souls in purgatory, but as an occasion to commemorate the faithful departed in general.

For Roman Catholics in Western Europe, All Souls' Day is a time of great solemnity; the church service on that day is often referred to as the "black vespers," especially in southern Europe, since the churches are draped in black, and worshipers wear black clothing, heightening the funereal mood. On November 1, the eve of All Souls' Day, the thoughts of European Catholics have already turned to the dead. Graveyards are decorated with offerings of flowers and candles are lighted in memory of the dead. Relatives gather to hold family reunions, remembering their dead kin.

There are many customs peculiar to All Souls' Day that have survived from popular folklore or pagan beliefs and that vary slightly from area to area. In northern and central Europe, for example, it is a popular folk belief that the dead revisit their homes on All Souls' night and eat the food of the living. Candles are left burning and offerings of "soulcakes" — square buns with currants — are placed on tables. In some areas, such as Brittany, people crowd the cemeteries after dark to kneel bareheaded at family tombs and pour libations on the graves.

In the British Isles, the custom of "souling" was once widespread. On All Souls' eve, "soulers" went from house to house to utter prayers for the dead and beg alms in the form of soulcakes while singing "A soulcake, a soulcake, have mercy on all Christian souls for a soulcake!" According to an age-old superstition, "the more cakes you eat on this night, the more souls you can save from purgatory."

In Italy the traditional food is the *fave dei morti*, "beans of the dead," the name given to bean-shaped cakes eaten on the occasion. Sicilian children who pray for deceased relatives receive toys and sweets, supposedly from the *morti* or souls of the family dead.

In Mexico a combined three-day observance celebrates All Saints' and All Souls' days from October 30 through November 2. November 1 is also given over to mourning for dead children. November 2 is the *Día de los Muertos*, the Day of the Dead, when families pray for souls of the dead and visit cemeteries with flowers and eat picnic lunches at the graves. Even the grimmer attributes of death are turned into motifs for toys and foodstuffs. Children delight in sugar-coated loaves of bread with gruesome decorations and candles shaped like skulls, caskets, bones, and skeletons. One of the most moving rites to mark the Day of the Dead is the night-long vigil on the island of Janitzio in Lake Pátzcuaro west of Mexico City. After midnight, religious Tarascan Indians scatter marigold petals on family graves; set up candles and fruits and pastry for dead relatives; and either remain in meditation or recite prayers throughout the night.

Several of the customs peculiar to All Souls' eve and All Souls' Day elsewhere in the world have survived in those parts of the western United States in which an intermingling of Indian religious customs and Spanish Catholic ritual has taken place. On November 2, for example, the impressive Night of the Candle ceremony is celebrated on the Indian reservations of Pala and Rincon east of Oceanside, California. During the day the inhabitants decorate the graves, place candles on them, and sing Spanish hymns while the priest blesses each individual grave. As dusk falls candles are lighted, illuminating the cemetery.

Spanish customs are also evident in New Mexico, where the All Souls' Day feast is marked with old traditions in Santa Fe, Spanish-American villages, and especially in many of the Indian pueblos. Although in nearby Mexico All Saints' and All Souls' Days are generally combined as a single celebration for the dead, Pueblo Indians generally observe All Souls' Day on November 2. Only Isleta, south of Santa Fe, observes All Saints' Day, while the Day of the Dead is commemorated in pueblos throughout northern and central New Mexico, such as Jemez, San Felipe, Taos, Cochití, and San Juan — the Hopi pueblos alone excepted. One of the most elaborate observances takes place at Cochití, the northernmost of the Keresan-speaking pueblos along the Rio Grande west of Santa Fe. Late in the 17th century, the Indians here were converted to Roman Catholicism by Spanish missionaries and Mission San Buenaventura de Cochití, built in 1694, is still preserved amidst the one-story adobe houses around the plaza. The few hundred inhabitants still maintain their ceremonial organization, ancient Indian rites, and traditional dances.

The Cochití Pueblo Indians refer to November 2 as Their Grandfathers Arrive from the West, or the Dead, feast. Each family fasts and deposits in the church a large quantity of food for the returning dead — wheat, corn, beans, peas, watermelons, tortillas, wheat-root bread, or boiled meat; bowls of food for the ghosts of the dead are set out in the corner of each house as well. The door of the house is left open for them. In order that the visiting spirits may be satisfied that their kin are prosperous, the material wealth of the household, in blankets, shawls, clothing, or jewelry, is displayed on the walls, and horses and other livestock are locked up in the corrals, where they can easily be seen. Candles are placed in both the church and the houses, lest the dead burn the fingertips of those who fail to light their way. The women stay at home, but the men congregate in the ceremonial chamber known as a *kiva*, where they sing all night and cut food into small pieces to throw outside for the dead. Members of societies assemble separately. The All Souls' Night Kachina Society members, for example, move from house to house, staying a few minutes in each to entertain the ghosts of the dead with their dances.

Similar ceremonies are also held at other New Mexico pueblos. At Taos Pueblo food and water are taken to graves in the churchyard, where candles are burned and the church bell rings all night. At Santo Domingo, the "grandfathers" who are expected to come from the west are "fed" at noon on November 2. Every person digs a hole beyond the town limits, burying in it a bundle of food and feathers and exclaiming: "Here eat, Grandfathers! After you eat, bring us crops!" On All Souls' night, the men sit around a bonfire and sing, despite the accompaniment of church bells, which peal until dawn. At the Zuñi Pueblo in west central New Mexico, Grandmothers' Day is the equivalent of All Souls' Day and is celebrated toward the end of October or beginning of November, after the crops have been harvested. Men and boys go from home to home singing and receive food, and both men and women make food offerings to the dead.

Warren G. Harding's Birthday

Warren Gamaliel Harding, the 29th President of the United States, was born on November 2, 1865, in Blooming Grove, Morrow County, Ohio. He was the eldest of eight children of Phoebe Elizabeth Dickerson Harding and George Tryon Harding, a farmer and later a physician. The young Harding studied at Ohio Central College for three years, leaving in 1882 and moving with his family to Marion, Ohio. He taught school and studied law for a year.

Having learned the printer's trade by working at the Caledonia *Advertiser*, Harding was hired by the *Democratic Mirror* in Marion in 1884. Irritated by the Democratic bias of the paper, however, he quit his job. With a partner he purchased the bankrupt Marion *Star* for $300. Harding soon bought out his partner's share and set out to make his enterprise a commercial success. Florence Kling De Wolfe, a widow who became Harding's wife on July 8, 1891, assisted him on the *Star*. Together they made the paper grow as the town grew. (It was appraised at about $500,000 after Harding's death.)

Harding's interest in politics steadily increased. Winning a seat in the Ohio senate in 1898, he served two terms there. In 1903 he was successful in his bid for election as lieutenant governor of Ohio. When his term ended two years later, Harding went back to his newspaper. He ran for governor in 1910 but was defeated by the Democratic candidate. Having earned a reputation as a forceful speaker and regular party man, he was chosen by President William Howard Taft to make the Republican National Convention nominating speech in 1912.

Elected to the US Senate in 1914, Harding began to draw some notice, especially among fellow politicians. He thus earned the temporary chairmanship of the Republican National Convention of 1916, at which he gave the keynote speech.

As a senator, Harding was unexceptional. In foreign affairs he attacked Wilson's policy of restraint when American business interests in Mexico were threatened during the upheavals caused by the Huerta-Carranza conflict and related events in that country. He approved the American declaration of war against Germany in 1917 and also favored various supporting measures, including provisions for a military draft and the repressive Espionage Act of 1917. After the war he followed the isolationist views of Senator Henry Cabot Lodge on foreign policy, including disapproval of President Woodrow Wilson's proposal to include the Covenant of the League of Nations in the Treaty of Versailles, which officially concluded World War I.

In domestic policy, Harding was a defender of big business. He supported protective tariffs and voted against high taxes on excess war profits. He voted in favor of the 18th (prohibition) amendment but never felt constrained to stop his own heavy drinking. Throughout his career Harding enjoyed a gregarious, clubroom atmosphere; poker games, drinking, and other forms of night life remained part of his social style until his death.

His loyalty to the Ohio Republican machine

won him a dark-horse nomination for the presidency at the 1920 convention. As his political mentor, Harry M. Daugherty, had predicted, he was chosen in a "smoke-filled room" by a handful of party bosses, after being asked to swear that there was nothing in his past to keep him from accepting the nomination.

The selection of Harding was greeted with scorn or indifference by the press. However, in the actual election campaign he fared better. He straddled, and as far as possible ignored, the controversial League of Nations issue, while his Democratic opponents, James Cox and Franklin D. Roosevelt, crusaded for the league. Harding campaigned for high tariffs, curbs on immigration, and a deflationary economy. Having supported the 19th (woman suffrage) amendment and the prohibition amendment, Harding reaped much of the new female vote. Thus after a colorless, boring campaign, he won the election by large electoral and popular majorities.

Harding was, by all accounts, an ordinary man who people thought would bring "normalcy" back to a country disillusioned with the shattered idealism of World War I. However, Harding brought incompetence to the highest levels of government. His cabinet was a mixture of excellence, corruption, and mediocrity. Three of his top appointments — Charles Evans Hughes (see April 11) as secretary of state, Andrew W. Mellon as secretary of the treasury, and Herbert Hoover as secretary of commerce — were above reproach. Other appointments, however, were based on personal friendship or political debt rather than on qualification for office. The predatory "friends" who surrounded the genial, well-meaning, and far from vigilant President — political cronies and hangers-on who came to be known as the Ohio Gang — were quick to take advantage of their posts for personal gain. Though neither the enormity of their individual greed nor the pervasiveness of corruption within the administration came to light until later, they eventually cast a cloud over Harding's posthumous reputation.

Most notorious was Secretary of the Interior Albert B. Fall, who, with the passive cooperation of US Navy Secretary Edwin M. Denby, illegally transferred naval oil reserve lands — including the Teapot Dome preserve in Wyoming — to Interior Department control and then leased the land to private oil companies with a substantial reward for himself. In time, their conspiracy brought prison sentences for both Fall and oil magnate Harry Sinclair. The administration's attorney general, Harry Daugherty, Harding's longtime political backer, meanwhile was also busy. A Senate committee later found him guilty of misconduct, including the illegal sale of liquor permits and pardons to violators of prohibition

statutes. (He narrowly escaped incarceration when a jury could not reach agreement.) Daugherty's crony Jesse Smith, an eventual suicide, had a desk but no official duties in the Department of Justice. He has been variously described as dispenser of graft and as prime "fixer" of the administration. Gaston B. Means, who also held office in Daugherty's Department of Justice, eventually served time in prison for selling liquor permits. Means afterward reported that he had collected and passed on to Jesse Smith some $7 million in bribes from bootleggers. Harding's choice to administer the Veterans' Bureau, a chance acquaintance known as "Colonel" Charles R. Forbes, went to Leavenworth after bilking the nation of at least half the bureau's congressionally appropriated funds and amassing huge sums from kickbacks, rebates, and other graft.

Holders of lesser posts were also guilty of corruption. Dishonesty and incompetence at all levels defrauded the government of millions of dollars, as bootlegging, blackmail, and influence-peddling burgeoned during Harding's term of office.

The growing scandals of Harding's administration were not counterbalanced by a notable record of legislative or executive action. Probably the outstanding accomplishment of his presidency was the 1921 Washington Conference called at the behest of Secretary Hughes to discuss future limitation of the size of their navies by the major world powers. The meeting resulted in the signing of 9 treaties concerning armaments and territory. Another achievement was the establishment of a federal Bureau of the Budget to coordinate the piecemeal procedure whereby each federal department applied independently to Congress for the funds it thought it needed. A kind man, Harding is also remembered for his presidential pardon of several persons, including the Socialist Eugene V. Debs. They were among many who had been imprisoned under provisions of the stringent Espionage and Sedition acts during World War I, when a wave of intolerance, zealous patriotism and fear of leftists had swept the country. For the most part, "normalcy" meant isolationism and *laissez-faire*. Though he was one of the most inept Presidents, Harding was not himself dishonest. His tragedy was that of an ordinary man submerged by extraordinary burdens and betrayed by people he thought were his friends.

Word of his administration's rampant corruption apparently reached the gullible President early in 1923. Aware that the scandals would surely soon break — as had reports of his illegitimate daughter, born to Nan Britton in 1919 — the distraught Harding left Washington on an official visit to Alaska in June 1923 with his wife and a few friends. During his return trip he was stricken by what was diagnosed as ptomaine poisoning. He stopped in San Francisco to rest but developed bronchopneumonia and then died on August 2 of an embolism.

Not long afterward, the Teapot Dome scandal and news of other Harding administration corruption became public. At the time of his death, however, most of the corruption had yet to reach the light, and Harding, a genial and likable man, was mourned throughout the nation.

After a state funeral in Washington, Harding was buried at Marion, Ohio, on August 10, 1923. A memorial association was almost immediately organized to provide a monument over his grave. With contributions from schoolchildren and others a fund of more than $800,000 was raised. This, through interest and other accretions, reached about $1 million before the monument was dedicated. It is an open structure 102 feet in diameter, surrounded by columns of Georgia marble. The bodies of the President and his wife, who died on November 21, 1924, are buried in a vault beneath the floor. The 10-acre Harding Memorial, at US Route 23 and McKinley Park Boulevard, was dedicated on June 16, 1931, with an address by President Herbert Hoover. Calvin Coolidge, who had become President upon the death of Harding, officiated.

Also at Marion is the restored house Harding built for his wife at 380 Mt. Vernon Avenue, now known as the Warren G. Harding Home and Museum, which is open to visitors.

North Dakota Admitted to the Union

As a result of political feuding between the northern and southern parts of the Dakota Territory, North Dakota and South Dakota were admitted to the Union as separate states on November 2, 1889. The two areas had been unable to agree on a capital city, and the argument had grown increasingly more heated during the 1870s and 1880s. Thus North Dakota, with its capital at Bismarck, became the 39th state of the United States, and South Dakota (see November 2, South Dakota Becomes a State), with its capital at Pierre, became the 40th.

At the time of the first recorded visit by a white man to the region now constituting North Dakota, that of the French-Canadian explorer Pierre Gaultier de Varennes, Sieur de La Vérendrye, in 1738, approximately 10 tribes of Indians inhabited the area. Some, such as the Mandan, Arikara, and Hidatsa, lived in villages and were farmers. Their willingness to share their agricultural knowledge with Europeans to whom maize and other indigenous crops were unknown, proved a boon to the economy of the northwestern section of the country. Other tribes, including the Assiniboin, Crow, and Dakota (known also as the Santee Sioux), for whom the territory and state were named, were nomadic. They hunted bison, whose meat provided food and whose skin they used for clothing and tepees. The Cheyenne and Cree tribes, also in the region, were seminomadic.

After La Vérendrye, the next Europeans to visit the area (in 1742) were two of his sons, Louis Joseph and François. They renewed his attempt to establish a trade route from Manitoba, Canada, to the Pacific coast. However, they turned back after traveling as far as the Big Horn Mountains in what is now Wyoming. No further penetration of the North Dakota region was made by Europeans until the latter part of the 18th century, when fur trappers discovered the abundance of wild game — including elk, antelope, and deer — and hastened to take advantage of such a vast source of wealth.

The central and southwestern area of what is now North Dakota formed part of the territory of Louisiana, which passed from French to Spanish control by the secret Treaty of Fontainebleau in 1762; Britain controlled the rest of the area. The North West Fur Company, a privately owned British fur-trading company, built the first trading post in 1797 at the confluence of the Pembina River and the Red River of the North, in the extreme northeastern corner of North Dakota. Numerous fur-trading posts were subsequently established in the British region by various companies, including the Hudson's Bay and North West Fur companies. British fur traders operated not only in the British-dominated valley of the Red River, but also along the Missouri River, where Spain permitted them to do a certain amount of trading with the Indians. Spanish fur traders were also active.

Even after the secret Treaty of San Ildefonso, which returned the whole vast Louisiana region to France in 1800, Louisiana temporarily remained under Spanish administration. When the United States acquired the huge Louisiana area through the Louisiana Purchase in 1803, what had been the Spanish-held part of North Dakota was transferred to US sovereignity. Meriwether Lewis and William Clark were promptly dispatched by President Thomas Jefferson to explore the newly acquired territory, which had doubled the size of the United States. By the fall of 1804 they reached the point on the eastern bank of the Missouri River — about 14 miles west of what is now Washburn, North Dakota — where they build Fort Mandan. Today a historical marker designates the site of the fort, and a replica of it has been constructed by the McLean County Historical Society.

During the winter Lewis and Clark spent at the fort, the friendly Hidatsa and Mandan Indians provided supplies for the continuation of their journey to the Pacific coast. Also of great value was the information they provided, as well as the presence of Sacagawea, a Shoshone who had been captured by the Hidatsa. The Hidatsa sold her to Toussaint Charbonneau, a Canadian trapper, who then married her. Both Charbonneau and Sacagawea acted as interpreters for Lewis and Clark, but Sacagawea's greatest contribution to the success of the expedition was her ability to guide the party through her home area and procure needed horses from her fellow Shoshones. (A statue honoring Sacagawea stands on the gounds of the state capitol in Bismarck.)

Scottish immigrants led by a member of the Hudson's Bay Company, Thomas Douglas, the earl of Selkirk, came by way of Canada in 1812 to attempt to establish at Pembina the first permanent settlement in the region. So bitter was the rivalry between the various fur-trading companies, however, that the settlers were twice driven from their homes by members of the North West Fur Company before Pembina could be established as a permanent settlement. A state park at the site now contains the Pembina State Historical Museum, which houses exhibits relating to the early history of North Dakota.

Meanwhile, Great Britain had refused to recognize American sovereignty in the area, claiming the territory for itself. The US victory in the War of 1812 was a severe blow to Britain, and it formally gave up the claim to the region in 1818, when an agreement between the two countries fixed the 49th Parallel as the boundary between the United States and British North America from the Lake of the Woods west to the Rocky Mountains — establishing in the process what serves today as the northern boundary of North Dakota.

From the time of the Lewis and Clark expedition, the Missouri River had been a main avenue of transportation for the fur traders. For almost three decades small boats plied its waters. Then, in 1832, they were joined by the *Yellowstone*, the first steamboat to navigate within the area of North Dakota. The steamboat traveled as far as Fort Union, which had been built in 1828 by the American Fur Company of the financier John Jacob Astor, the same trading company that owned the *Yellowstone*.

Fort Union was located close to the western border of North Dakota, at the confluence of the Yellowstone and Missouri rivers. For four decades it was the largest and most important trading post in the upper Missouri region, and it also served as the gathering place for Indian tribes, artists, scientists, and missionaries. (Its location is now noted by the 380-acre Fort Union Trading Post, a national historic site.) The romance and adventure of the newly important area drew such men as John James Audubon, the ornithologist and painter of birds, and George Catlin, the American artist and author who painted hundreds of Indian portraits and scenes from life. Their various works, including journals, provide valuable historical material on the North Dakota area.

Settlement of the region was slow, the fur traders had it virtually to themselves for a long time. The Dakotas, more warlike than other tribes, particularly resented the incursion of the whites and resisted their attempts to wrest the land from them and place them on reservations. Because of the hostility between the whites and the Indians, a number of military posts were established. The first was Fort Abercrombie, built in 1857 on the Red River at the eastern border of the state. The original guardhouse can be seen today, along with reconstructed blockhouses and a stockade, within the Fort Abercrombie State Park. Several of the original buildings of Fort Totten (established in 1867) still stand; the fort is one of the few of the period to remain in such good condition. The Fort Totten Historic Park, in the northeastern part of the state, 14 miles south of Devils Lake, also numbers among its attractions a pioneer museum and musical presentations. Whitestone Battlefield State Historic Site commemorates a major battle with Indians fought in 1863. Relics of the engagement are preserved in a museum at the site, which is located about 28 miles northwest of Ellendale, in southeastern North Dakota.

Sitting Bull, after the encounter at Little Big Horn in 1876 (see June 25), sought refuge in Canada. In 1881 he decided to accept a promise of amnesty from the United States government, and he and his remaining followers returned to the United States. They surrendered in present North Dakota, at Fort Buford, a military post that had replaced Fort Union after 1866. Two of the fort's original buildings remain at the Fort Buford State Historic Site.

As the number of military posts grew and the Indians were subdued or pushed farther west, the flow of settlers into the Dakota region increased. The homestead laws passed by Congress beginning in 1862, which permitted settlers to claim up to 160 acres of land without paying, were a powerful incentive to settlement of the frontier areas. Completion of the Northern Pacific Railway as far west as the North Dakota-Montana border in 1881 provided another strong impetus. Farming in the eastern part of the state and ranching in the western part were both large-scale operations for some time, but gradually many of the large holdings were broken up.

Among early settlers was Theodore Roosevelt. He was attracted in 1883 by the opportunity to hunt bison and other big game in the Badlands of southwestern North Dakota, and while there he developed an interest in ranching. He bought two ranches, the Maltese Cross and the Elkhorn, and made his home there from 1884 to 1886. The Theodore Roosevelt National Memorial Park has been established in recognition of his concern for the conservation of natural resources. In the 70,436-acre park, through which bison and other game still roam, are a museum, the cabin Roosevelt used on the Maltese Cross Ranch, and the Elkhorn Ranch Site.

In whole or in large part, the region of North Dakota was successively included in the Missouri, Michigan, Wisconsin, Iowa, Minnesota, Nebraska, and Dakota territories. In 1868 Dakota Territory, which originally included Montana and Wyoming, was reduced in size to include only North Dakota and South Dakota, an area inhabited at that time by about 300,000 persons.

Controversy had erupted over the location of the territorial capital following the formation of Dakota Territory in 1861. Yankton, in the south, was the first capital, but a number of other towns were eager to displace it. The controversy evolved into a north-south dispute, which was intensified by the selection of Bismarck, in the north, as the new territorial capital in 1883. As a result of the conflict between the two sections, the north and south were admitted to the Union as separate states. The admission of North Dakota (with its capital at Bismarck) and South Dakota was proclaimed by President Benjamin Harrison on November 2, 1889.

James K. Polk's Birthday

James Knox Polk, the 11th President of the United States, was the eldest son of Samuel and Jane Knox Polk. Samuel Polk was a farmer and surveyor by trade. His Scotch-Irish ancestors were named Pollock, which was shortened to Polk for convenience. James Polk was born November 2, 1795, in Mecklenburg County, North Carolina. His mother was a devout and intelligent woman, formal in her relations with other people.

James Polk grew in his mother's mold. Frail from early youth, he channeled his energies into study. In 1806 the family moved to the valley of the Duck River in Tennessee's Maury County. After preparation at subscription academies, Polk entered the University of North Carolina in 1815 as a sophomore. At school he was serious, meticulous, and tireless in his devotion to his studies. Upon graduation in 1818 he won his school's honors in mathematics and classics.

Polk returned to Tennessee and began to study law at Nashville in the office of Felix Grundy — one of the members of Congress known as War Hawks, whose bellicose attitude helped cause the War of 1812 with England. Young Polk worked hard and was admitted to the bar in 1820. Returning home to Maury County, he established a law practice in the town of Columbia. His intelligence and diligence quickly brought him success.

After three years of law practice, he entered the state legislature in 1823. In politics a loyal Democrat, Polk applied his talents with effect. He quickly established a reputation as a well-informed, persuasive speaker. His political principles were modeled after those of Thomas Jefferson. Polk rapidly entered the orbit of Andrew Jackson. They grew to be friends and maintained a close political relationship until Jackson's death. Jackson was an extrovert and popular; Polk was reclusive, meticulous, and a faithful lieutenant.

On January 1, 1824, James Polk married Sarah Childress, of Murfreesboro, Tennessee. She was a cultured woman who was to smooth her husband's public relationships throughout their marriage.

In 1825 Polk advanced to the US House of Representatives. Consistently reelected, by 1832 he was leader of the Democratic forces in Congress.

In that year, Jackson began a war against the Bank of the United States. Being a partisan of the South and the emerging West, Jackson distrusted the bankers of the Northeast. In particular he did not like their policy of holding a tight rein on bank loans in an effort to discourage rampant speculation. Polk emerged as Jackson's congressional spokesman on the bank issue. As a member of the powerful House Ways and Means Committee, Polk entered a bill to sell out government stock in the national bank. However, the committee as a whole decided that there was no proper cause for governmental attacks on the bank. Jackson subsequently followed Polk's suggestion to withdraw government deposits from the bank.

Polk, as chairman of the House Ways and Means Committee since December 1833, continued to defend Jackson's course ably and faithfully. Jackson won his skirmish with the bank, but lost the overall battle, inasmuch as the net effect of destroying the Philadelphia-based bank was to move the banking center of the United States farther north to New York, which was not at all what he had intended.

In 1834 Polk opposed John Bell for the office

of Speaker of the House. Bell won by joining with the anti-Jackson forces. Polk refused to go against Jackson and lost his fight for the speakership. However, he stood for the position the following year and won. He served as speaker from 1835 to 1839, during which time he was the whipping boy for a collection of anti-Jackson Whigs and Nullifiers. Polk customarily did his legislative homework better than any of his adversaries, however, and his excellence, in addition to his aloofness, provoked some opponents to envious rage.

Bowing to his party's needs, Polk agreed to oppose the Whigs for the governorship of Tennessee. He won the election, serving as a competent governor from 1839 to 1841, but lost subsequent campaigns for reelection in 1841 and 1843.

In 1840 the Whigs, making political capital of the panic of 1837, which had been rooted in Jacksonian speculative banking, elected William Henry Harrison as President. Harrison died a month to the day after his inauguration, and his Whig Vice President, John Tyler, became President. Senator Henry Clay was the national leader of the Whigs, however, and was nominated as their presidential candidate in 1844.

Former President Martin Van Buren seemed destined to represent the Democrats. However, early in 1844 both Clay and Van Buren made public statements designed to remove from the forthcoming election the touchy issue of the annexation of Texas. That ill-defined region, whose southern boundary was still a matter of dispute, had belonged to Mexico before it declared itself an independent republic in 1836. Largely settled by Americans, at first with Mexican encouragement, Texas now sought annexation by the United States.

The elderly Andrew Jackson still ran the Democratic party, and as an expansionist he would not countenance Van Buren's heresy in opposing the annexation of Texas. Instead Jackson rewarded Polk's devotion to Democratic party policies, which now included expansionism, by supporting him over Van Buren. At the Democratic National Convention in 1844, Van Buren accordingly was passed over for Polk, who became the nation's first dark-horse presidential candidate.

In spite of his 14 years in Congress, people asked derisively, "Who is James Polk?" Polk ran on a Democratic platform advocating the "reannexation" of Texas and "reoccupation" of Oregon. His Whig opponents were a divided party, at best merely a collection of old National Republicans, new antislavery forces, and anyone else who had opposed Jackson. Many Whigs also refused to vote for Henry Clay as their party's candidate because of his evasiveness on the issue of the expansion of slavery.

Polk entered the White House in 1845 with a very clear conception of what he wished to accomplish: "one, a reduction of the tariff; another, the independent treasury; a third, the settlement of the Oregon boundary question; and lastly, the acquisition of California."

Polk wanted simply to buy California, and he was willing to bully Mexico into selling. However, the annexation of Texas — which had been effected under President Tyler days before Polk's inauguration — stood as a roadblock between Polk and California, and it was the Texas question that brought on war with Mexico in 1846 (see May 13). Although Mexico remained in a constant state of internal confusion during those years, the Mexican War was to last through much of Polk's term and sap the energy of the hardworking, dedicated President.

More than a decade of talk about the annexation of Texas had taken place before the step actually came. The foremost domestic reason for the long inaction was the issue of slavery. Sentiment had grown in the North that blacks and the institution of slavery should be excluded from new territories. Simultaneously the opinion had grown in the South that the industrializing North was living off the South by imposing high tariffs that prevented the agricultural South from buying manufactured items cheaply from Britain. Thus the North and South each watched events jealously to guarantee that the other did not gain in political power. The emerging West held the balance of power and was courted and fought over by both North and South. In 1820 the Missouri Compromise had been worked out to establish the northern boundary of slavery in new territories at 36° 30' latitude.

However, the issue of slavery, then thought settled, was raised again by Texas. Mexico had outlawed slavery in 1831. Southerners were worried that Texas would become a free state. Although there were then 13 free states and 13 slave states, only Florida was sure to enter on the slave roster, while Wisconsin, Minnesota, and Iowa would eventually enter as free states.

Just before leaving the White House in March 1845, President Tyler had persuaded Congress to offer annexation to Texas. Mexico, understandably, had been angry when its rebellious northern province earlier declared itself independent. Now, when the United States offered annexation to Texas, Mexico's minister left Washington in a fury.

In November 1845 President Polk sent John Slidell, a politician and diplomat, to Mexico to try to establish the Texas boundary at the Rio

Grande and to buy California and New Mexico. The Mexican government was in turmoil and refused to receive Slidell. In January 1846 Polk ordered General Zachary Taylor to occupy the land between the Nueces River and the Rio Grande. In the eyes of Mexico, this was a provocation since Mexico had always considered the more northerly Nueces as the southern boundary of Texas — a position conflicting with the Texan view, which held that Texas extended all the way to the Rio Grande. Taylor's army moved, expecting the Mexicans to attack.

With this background, President Polk decided to ask Congress to declare war on Mexico. The evening after informing his cabinet of his decision, Polk received news that Mexican forces had attacked a party of Taylor's men. Thus bolstered in his position, the President presented his request for a declaration of war to Congress on May 11, 1846. Congress declared war two days later.

Public support for the venture was not widespread. Though the South and Southwest were eager in their backing, Northerners felt that the war, as a resolution of the Massachusetts legislature put it, was "wanton, unjust and unconstitutional." A junior representative from Illinois, Abraham Lincoln, put forth a cogent critique of what was becoming known as Polk's War.

There was talk that Britain might come to Mexico's aid. The origin of this was the smoldering dispute between Britain and the United States over their joint occupation of the Oregon territory. Both countries adamantly and unrealistically claimed the entire area. With one war already on his hands, Polk avoided another war by using firm diplomacy. A treaty signed with Britain in June 1846 established a compromise boundary at the 49th Parallel (see June 15, Oregon Treaty Ratified).

California was an exotic gem that Americans desired, even though they knew very little about the area. Polk, too, wanted to annex California. Through a member of his cabinet in Washington and by way of the American consul in California, the suggestion was allowed to reach the West Coast that Californians might like to follow the example of Texas. Not long afterwards, Captain John C. Frémont, the explorer, reached California, ostensibly to make a topographical survey, but actually with secret instructions for action in the event of war between the United States and Mexico. Ulimately Frémont joined forces with the American settlers who had carried off the Bear Flag Revolt (probably with his encouragement) in the Sacramento Valley. When news arrived that war had broken out with Mexico, he joined other Americans — Colonel Stephen W. Kearny, advancing from New Mexico, and Commodore John D. Sloat and his successor, Commodore Robert F. Stockton, who arrived via the Pacific — in seizing control of California.

But once again the specter of slavery arose. On August 8, 1846, Polk had asked Congress for a secret appropriation of $2 million to defray "any extraordinary expenses which may be incurred in the intercourse of the United States and foreign nations." Rumor held that the money was earmarked as a bribe to persuade the Mexican general Santa Anna to sell California. The "persuasion" was unsuccessful, but while the matter was before Congress, the Pennsylvania legislator David Wilmot tried to add a proviso to the appropriation bill that would prohibit slavery in any former Mexican territory acquired by treaty or purchased with the money. Polk instead proposed that the Missouri Compromise line simply be extended to the Pacific — a compromise that offended abolitionists and slaveholders alike. Congress ultimately avoided the issue, and the Wilmot Proviso was defeated; but the Pandora's box of slavery had been opened once again.

Yet the problem was put aside for the moment when the Mexican War was concluded by the Treaty of Guadalupe Hidalgo, signed near Mexico City in 1848 (see February 2, Mexican War Ends) and ratified by the Senate on March 10 of the same year. By the terms of the treaty, the United States won Texas with a southern boundary at the Rio Grande. The treaty also gave the United States the right to purchase, for $15 million, California and New Mexico. In addition the United States agreed to assume all Mexican debts to Texas citizens.

Throughout these events Polk was vilified for political intrigue, apparently with little justification. However, his excessive secrecy and personal attention to minute details of government gave the impression of a manipulative schemer. Polk, in fact, worked hard at his task as President and expended no effort solely to improve his public image. Before leaving the White House, he pushed through the enactment of lower tariff schedules known as the Walker Tariff of 1846. In the same year he also saw through Congress the Independent Treasury Bill, which reestablished a national financial system that was not supplanted until the establishment of the Federal Reserve System in 1913.

The systematic Polk had thus achieved all four of his presidential objectives. But in the process, he literally worked himself to death. Succeeded in the presidency by the victorious general of the Mexican War, Zachary Taylor, Polk left the White House a shadow of his former self. Three months later, on June 15, 1849, he died at the age of 54. He was buried at his Nashville, Tennessee, home – Polk Place. In 1893 he was re-buried, with his wife, on the grounds of the Tennessee state capitol.

The Polk Memorial Association acquired the childhood home of Polk in Columbia, Tennessee, and has preserved it as a shrine. It was formally opened on November 23, 1929. In it are deposited historical and personal relics. Polk's birthday is still observed by the association with a luncheon or coffee in Nashville, at which time there is a joint meeting of members of the Polk Memorial Association of Nashville and the Polk Memorial Auxiliary of Columbia. The home of Polk's parents in Columbia and the house next door, where his two sisters lived, contain mementos and documents of the presidential years. The home, built by Samuel Polk in 1816, is of brick with French windows and balconies. Gardens link this house with the one built by Samuel Polk for his daughters. The houses, at 301 West 7 Street, have been restored by the Polk Memorial Association and are open to the public. In Raleigh, North Carolina, on the six-acre landscaped Capitol Square, stands an equestrian statue honoring Polk.

South Dakota Admitted to the Union

Along with North Dakota, South Dakota joined the Union on November 2, 1889. The proclamation issued by President Benjamin Harrison made South Dakota the 40th state (North Dakota was officially the 39th – see November 2, North Dakota Becomes a State). The region comprising the two states had been united as the Dakota Territory, and had it not been for the protracted and bitter wrangling over the choice of a capital city it might well have been admitted to the Union as a single state.

Ancestors of the Indians who were found inhabiting the South Dakota area by the early explorers are known to have lived in that area, at least in the part that lies east of the Missouri River, prior to A.D. 1200. These people are known as Mound Builders, from their custom of building mounds of earth in which to bury their dead. The Arikara Indians were living in villages and farming near the Missouri River when the first Europeans of whom there is record, Louis Joseph and François de La Vérendrye, passed through South Dakota in 1742 and 1743. Starting out from Manitoba, Canada, these two sons of the French-Canadian explorer Pierre Gaultier de Varennes, Sieur de La Vérendrye, were searching – unsuccessfully – for a route to the Pacific Ocean. In 1913 children found a lead plate buried in 1743 on a hill overlooking the Missouri River, opposite what is now the city of Pierre, by the La Vérendrye brothers to establish a French claim to the region. (A small monument now marks the spot where the plate was discovered.)

After 1750 the Dakota (or Santee Sioux) Indians, for whom the state is named, became numerous in South Dakota as the increasing number of whites in Minnesota forced them westward. The movement of whites into the South Dakota area was very slow, however. Fur trappers began to filter in during the latter part of the century, when the region was under Spanish rule. In 1803 the United States acquired title to the land as part of the Louisiana Purchase. For the first time in more than half a century, explorers penetrated the region. At President Thomas Jefferson's behest, Meriwether Lewis and William Clark led an expedition that explored the vast unknown territory acquired in the Louisiana Purchase. During the westward journey from St. Louis to the coast of Oregon, the Lewis and Clark expedition crossed South Dakota in 1804; it again traversed the area on its return trip in 1806.

The success of the expedition prompted more trappers to seek their fortunes in new territory. Trading posts sprang up all over South Dakota, particularly on the banks of the Missouri River. One of the leading posts, Fort Pierre, was established in 1817. By coincidence, it was erected on the site where the La Vérendrye brothers had planted their lead plate 70 years earlier. Fort Pierre was rebuilt by a subsidiary of the American Fur Company in 1832, a year after the same company had inaugurated steamboat travel on this section of the Missouri River. The fur trade boomed during the next two decades, but no settlements were established. In 1856 an attempt was made by land speculators to create a settlement in southeastern South Dakota, at the falls of the Big Sioux River. The uprising of the Sioux in neighboring Minnesota in 1862 forced the settlers to flee.

Gradually the Indians relinquished title to various parts of their lands; the whites tried to persuade or force them onto government reservations. Most notable of the Indian leaders who resisted giving up their freedom or land was the powerful Sioux chief Sitting Bull. However, in 1881 he decided he could no longer hold out, and he surrendered to US authorities. Settled on the Standing Rock Reservation, he was arrested by Indian guards on December 15, 1890, as a precaution against mounting Sioux unrest – and shot and killed in the ensuing fighting. His burial place is three miles west of Mobridge, in the north-central part of the state, near the spot where he was killed.

Yankton had been established as a permanent settlement in 1859, as was Vermillion later the same year. Despite passage a few years later of the federal homestead laws, which permitted a citizen to take possession of 160 acres of land without payment, fewer than 12,000 settlers migrated to South Dakota during the 1860s. The continuing Indian-white conflict was a restraining influence at that time. During the following decade a number of factors combined to increase the settlement rate. Much of the Indian resistance collapsed. Access to the area was eased tremendously by construction of a railroad line from Sioux City, Iowa, which reached Yankton in 1872, was continued northward through the eastern part of the state, and reached Watertown in 1878. Rain alleviated the drought conditions that had prevailed previously. Numerous northern European immigrants made their ways across the country to settle in the area east of the Missouri River.

In addition, reports of gold lured many to the Black Hills of western South Dakota. Members of an expedition led by General George A. Custer discovered the precious metal there in July 1874 and thereby set in motion a gold rush. Because the Black Hills were within the great Sioux Reservation established by treaty between the US government and the Sioux in 1868, the government tried to prevent whites from entering the area while it sought to persuade the Indians to cede the territory. When the Sioux refused and a geological expedition in 1875 reported that the gold deposits were valuable, the government ceased its attempts to keep miners from the Black Hills. The following two years saw the peak of the rush.

This invasion of their lands was deeply resented by the Sioux, and hostilities flared. Custer himself was killed, as were all of the men in his command, in the engagement known as the battle of Little Big Horn fought in Montana in 1876. In other battles, though, the Sioux were defeated, and in 1877 they were forced to cede the Black Hills region to the US government.

In December 1874 the first miners had reached the vicinity of what is now the town of Custer. (Custer is now headquarters for the Black Hills National Forest, which encompasses 1,527,000 acres of South Dakota and Wyoming. Each year during the last week of July the anniversary of the discovery of gold is celebrated in Custer with a historical pageant depicting important events in the Black Hills region. Original mining equipment may be seen in the town in the Black Hills Museum of Mining and Minerals.)

Another old mining town is Deadwood, in which all but the main street is built on the slopes of a canyon. (Deadwood is the site, during the first weekend of August, of the annual Days of '76, during which gold-rush scenes are recreated and a western rodeo is held. The Adams Memorial Museum in Deadwood has exhibits relating to the early mining days.)

Even more valuable gold deposits were found in the vicinity of Deadwood and of Lead, where in 1876 the Homestake Lode was discovered. In operation for a century, the Homestake Mine is the largest in the Western Hemisphere and one of the largest in the world. (Tours through the surface workings are conducted through much of the year.)

What has been called the last major military encounter in the United States between government forces and Indians took place on December 29, 1890, at a spot that is now the site of the tiny town of Wounded Knee on the Pine Ridge Indian Reservation in southwestern South Dakota, a few miles above the border with Nebraska. A band of 350 hungry and ill-clothed Oglala Sioux, including 230 women and children, had left their reservation, in defiance of government orders, for a peaceful meeting with another group of Indians. They were intercepted by a US cavalry unit, to which they surrendered without resistance.

Camp was made for the night at Wounded Knee. While soldiers were confiscating the Indians' weapons the next morning, a shot rang out. Immediately wholesale shooting began. The Sioux were virtually unarmed; about 250 men, women, and children were killed. Twenty-five or more soldiers died, mainly from their own crossfire. At Wounded Knee there are markers telling of the massacre, and in the graveyard a memorial erected by relatives of Indians who were killed. An Indian museum and a trading post are located there.

The area now forming South Dakota, North Dakota, Montana, Wyoming, and part of Idaho became in 1861 the newly created Dakota Territory. The capital was at Yankton, in what is now South Dakota. (Yankton has a historical museum devoted to exhibits concerning the territorial period.)

In 1868 the Dakota Territory was reduced in size to include only South Dakota and North Dakota. Controversy raged over the location of the capital, both between the northern and southern parts of the territory and among various cities. By 1883 the southern part had already drawn up and approved a constitution and was eager for separate statehood. The more populous northern part wanted admission of the entire territory as one state.

Through electing state officers and a state legislature, in anticipation of gaining separate statehood, the citizens of the southern area indicated their preference for the Republican party. In the US Congress, at the time, the Republicans held only a slim majority of seats. Being loath to see that majority increased, the Democrats vigorously opposed granting separate statehood to South Dakota. The issue was not resolved until after the elections of 1888, which gave the Republicans firm control of Congress as well as of the presidency, thus guaranteeing victory to the South Dakotans.

Legislation permitting the division of the Dakota Territory was passed in February 1889. A revised state constitution that met congressional demands was adopted in May of the same year, and on November 2 South Dakota and North Dakota were separately granted statehood. Pierre was named the capital of South Dakota, and it has remained so even though between 1890 and 1904 its status was challenged by no fewer than six other cities.

NOVEMBER 3

General Election Day

This is a movable event. See note on page xxvi.

Voting is both a right and, many feel, an obligation of US citizenship. The power of the people to choose those who guide their public affairs is one of the chief blessings and ultimate safeguards of democracy. Americans who recognize this responsibility to vote cast their ballots for local, state, or national candidates in every election.

The date reserved for elections varied from state to state during the early years of the nation, but in 1845 the US Congress took an important· step toward establishing uniformity in federal contests by decreeing the Tuesday after the first Monday of November to be the legal day, every four years, for the selection of presidential and vice presidential electors. An 1872 federal statute set the same day for the biennial election of members of the House of Representatives, and since the ratification of the 17th Amendment in 1913, US senators have also been popularly elected on that day.

The US Constitution gives each state the right to establish voting qualifications for federal electors, and at various times states have enfranchised only those persons who could meet property ownership, age, sex, residence, or other requirements. However, the adoption of several amendments to the Constitution in and since 1870 has considerably limited the restrictions states may set. The 15th Amendment (see March 30) enfranchised those who had previously been denied voting rights because of "race, color, or previous condition of servitude"; the 19th (see

August 26), enfranchised women; the 23rd (see March 29) extended the vote for President and Vice President to residents of the District of Columbia; and the 24th (see February 10) prohibited payment of a poll tax as a requirement for voting in national elections. In addition the Voting Rights Act of 1965 (see August 6) outlawed literacy tests and similar devices that had been used to deny the ballot to qualified voters and enabled the US attorney general to send federal registrars into states and counties in which less than one-half of the voting-age population was registered. This legislation was due to expire in 1970, but in that year Congress not only extended its life for another five years but added a provision granting the right to vote to 18-year-olds. Later in 1970 the Supreme Court upheld the right of Congress to enfranchise those between 18 and 21 in federal elections, but ruled that states could set the voting-age requirement for state and local contests. In 1971 the 26th Amendment enfranchised 18-year-olds in all elections (see June 30).

Despite efforts to extend the franchise, large numbers of American citizens each year do not vote. To encourage their residents to vote, many states have made Election Day a legal holiday or a half holiday, and even where the day is not a legal holiday numerous businesses give their employees the day off. Organizations such as the League of Women Voters conduct massive campaigns each year to educate Americans on the necessity of registering and the importance of voting. Distinguished public figures urge eligible voters to go to the polls, and most schools hold special programs designed to acquaint future voters with their rights and responsibilities.

In the 20th century, population growth, educational campaigns, and the easing of restrictions on voting qualifications have vastly increased the size of the electorate, but the advances of technology have radically reduced the time required to tabulate the vote. In years past, the counting of handwritten election ballots was a tedious task requiring days, or even months. Today, voting machines have replaced written ballots in most places; and these, together with advanced tabulating systems, provide results with great speed. Television and radio stations generally preempt their regular programming schedules on the night of Election Day, and they broadcast the results of national contests — as well as those of any state and local elections.

Edward Douglass White's Birthday

Edward Douglass White, the ninth chief justice of the United States, was the son of Edward D. and Catherine Ringgold White. He was born in

Lafourche Parish, Louisiana, on November 3, 1845, the great-grandson of an Irish immigrant. The White family became increasingly successful in its adopted land; Edward White's father was prominent in his state's public life.

A Catholic, White attended Mount St. Mary's College in Emmitsburg, Maryland, and Georgetown College in Washington, D.C. He left the capital at the onset of the Civil War to return home and enlist in the Confederate Army. Union troops captured him after the fall of Port Hudson in 1863, but soon freed him on parole after he promised not to take up arms again.

White studied law after the Civil War and gained admission to the Louisiana bar in 1868. Entering politics, he won election to the state senate in 1874 and served as a judge on the state supreme court from January 1879 to April 1880. The state legislature selected White as US senator, and he assumed that post on March 4, 1891.

A bitter feud between two New Yorkers, President Grover Cleveland and Senator David B. Hill, made possible White's elevation to the US Supreme Court. When Justice Samuel Blatchford of New York died in 1893, Hill thwarted Cleveland's attempt to name one of his associates from New York to the Court. Invoking senatorial courtesy, the custom by which the Senate grants its members practical vetoes over appointments of residents from their home states to important federal posts, Hill prevented the confirmation of both William B. Hornblower and Wheeler H. Peckham. Knowing that Hill could not employ the same machinations against a fellow senator, Cleveland next nominated White, who took his seat on the bench on March 12, 1894.

In 1910 President William Howard Taft surprisingly bypassed his own appointee to the bench, the outstanding Charles Evans Hughes, to select White as chief justice of the United States. Historians tend to explain the nomination of the Louisiana Democrat as an attempt by the Republican President to make political inroads in the solidly Democratic South. White served in the highest judicial post until his death in Washington, D.C., on May 21, 1921.

During his tenure as associate and chief justice, White passed judgment in many vital cases, particularly in the fields of labor relations and commercial regulation. He opposed attempts by workers to gain better conditions through organization but made some allowance for governmental programs to improve their lot. In cases affecting big business, White consistently found unconstitutional the attempts of the Progressives to stem the growth of giant corporations.

In 1894 Eugene V. Debs, the president of the American Railway Union, defied a federal court injunction and led a strike against the Pullman Company. White concurred in the decision (*In re Debs,* 1895) that sustained the power of the government to issue injunctions in labor disputes and upheld the citation of Debs for contempt. The Court based its opinion on the railroads' importance in interstate commerce and the transportation of the mails.

The Court in *Adair* v. *United States* (1908) declared unconstitutional the provision of the Erdman Act of 1898, which protected the rights of employees of interstate railroads to join unions. White concurred in this decision and in the finding of *Loewe* v. *Lawler* (1908) that a boycott by workers to force unionization constituted a conspiracy in restraint of trade. The latter suit, popularly known as the *Danbury Hatters'* case, marked the first application of the Sherman Antitrust Act of 1890 to labor organizations.

White displayed a somewhat more favorable attitude toward legislation that protected individual workers. In *Locher* v. *New York* (1905) he unsuccessfully supported the constitutionality of a state law limiting the hours of bakery employees, but in *Bunting* v. *Oregon* (1917) he concurred in a decision that made void a similar law. White gave his most important decision in the case of *Wilson* v. *New* (1917), which upheld the constitutionality of the Adamson Act. The Court justified the measure, which granted interstate railway workers an eight-hour day, as a necessary emergency expedient to prevent an interruption of service.

White saw little necessity to use the Sherman Antitrust Act against its intended targets, the large corporations that developed at the end of the 19th century. He concurred in the case of *United States* v. *E. C. Knight Company* (1895), which limited the law's jurisdiction over manufacturing, as contrasted with commerce. In the *Northern Securities Company* case (1904) he dissented from the majority opinion, which rejuvenated the Sherman Antitrust Act by dissolving a major railroad holding company.

Chief Justice White's most famous decisions, however, came in 1911, in the cases of *United States* v. *American Tobacco Company* and *Standard Oil Company of New Jersey et al.* v. *United States.* In these instances he argued that the "rule of reason" should be applied to the Sherman Act so that only those corporations that most "unreasonably" restrained trade would be chastised. The Court dissolved Standard Oil and reorganized the American Tobacco Company (though White's interpretation weakened the antitrust movement).

NOVEMBER 4

Feast of St. Charles Borromeo

The feast of St. Charles Borromeo, one of the most distinguished and devout ecclesiastics of the Roman Catholic church in the 16th century, is a strictly Roman Catholic observance. It falls on November 4, the day after the saint's death date of November 3, 1584. Formerly ranked as a Class III feast, it is now classed as an obligatory memorial in the Roman Catholic calendar. Many Roman Catholic churches throughout the world are named for this saint, who is often regarded as the epitome of the ideals of the Catholic Counter-Reformation.

Carlo Borromeo was born at Arona on the shore of Lake Maggiore in northern Italy on October 2, 1538. He belonged to a distinguished family, being a son of a noble and wealthy Lombard count, Gilberto Borromeo, and of Margherita de' Medici. The young Borromeo was religiously inclined and, as the second son in his family, was early destined for service in the church. At the age of 12, his father allowed him to receive the tonsure and not long afterwards, with the backing of other relatives, made him titular abbot of the wealthy monastery of SS. Gratiano and Felino at Arona. He then studied under a tutor in Milan and at the age of 14 entered the University of Pavia, where he eventually completed a doctorate in canon law in 1559. His father meanwhile had died in the summer of 1558, and he was asked to take charge of the family estates, since his older brother, Federigo, showed little administrative ability.

Pope Paul IV died in the summer of 1559, and the conclave of cardinals elected Borromeo's maternal uncle, Cardinal Giovanni Angelo de' Medici, as pontiff after a session of nearly three months. He took the name of Pius IV. The following January, the new pope called his young nephew, whose acumen and scholarship he admired, to Rome. On January 31, 1560, at the age of 21, Borromeo was given the title of cardinal-deacon of the Church of SS. Vito and Modesto in Rome. Although he was not yet a priest, he soon became administrator of the archdiocese of Milan, upon the resignation of its archbishop. That year his uncle named him archbishop, a title that was reconfirmed formally in 1564.

In the meantime, the shower of ecclesiastical preferments continued as Borromeo became papal legate of Bologna, Romagna, Ancona, and other sections of the Papal States, as well as protector of the kingdom of Portugal, Lower Germany, the Catholic Swiss cantons, and various religious orders such as the Franciscans and Carmelites. Despite his extreme youth, the pope's favorite was entrusted with the highly responsible position of papal secretary of state, in which function he supervised all official papal correspondence.

The inexperienced but brilliant cardinal-deacon fully justified his uncle's confidence. He handled all assignments skillfully, especially the difficult negotiations connected with the reassembling of the Council of Trent — often considered the greatest and most productive council held in the West by the Catholic church and certainly the keystone to the reforms that took place following the Protestant Reformation in the early 16th century. The second session of the reforming body had hastily adjourned in 1552, because of the imminent approach of the Protestant forces under the German general Maurice of Saxony. Whereas Pope Paul IV had shown lukewarm interest in reconvening the assemblage, Pius IV and his secretary of state were eager to resume deliberations as soon as possible. They struggled against immense odds to secure the necessary approval of the Holy Roman Emperor and the French monarch, as well as the churchmen involved. At the opening of the third session, called for Easter Sunday, April 6, 1561, only four bishops appeared. The session was postponed until January of the following year. When it did convene, it was undoubtedly Charles Borromeo's almost superhuman tact, judgment, and diplomacy that caused all present to put aside personal rancors and work assiduously toward compiling a statement of traditional Catholic doctrine that would be clear and unequivocal in view of the challenge raised by the Protestant Reformation. Under his inspiration and guidance, the council formulated definitive decrees and definitions on such matters as purgatory, veneration of relics, indulgences, and the doctrine of the Holy Eucharist, making clear what was considered orthodox and what heretical.

In the meantime, upon the death of his elder brother Federigo in 1562, Charles Borromeo had become the head of his family. He looked upon the death as a warning to devote himself entirely to religious matters. His family, however, urged him to abandon his ecclesiastical activities and to marry. The pope may have even suggested such a step. His nephew was, after all, only a cardinal-deacon, who could easily be released by papal dispensation from the vow of chastity. But Charles Borromeo, although still a man of culture and taste who hunted, played the cello, and enjoyed perusing his vast private library, resisted all importunities. In July 1563 he was ordained a cardinal-priest, and he was consecrated a bishop in September of that year.

After the Council of Trent had ended in 1563,

Borromeo was at first busy in Rome with affairs of state, and Pius IV did not permit him to assume residence in the Milan archdiocese, which he headed, until September 1565. Even then he was soon called back to Rome to attend the pope on his deathbed and participate in the election of a successor. Only in April 1566, at the age of 28, was Cardinal Borromeo able to devote himself to his duties as archbishop of Milan.

In line with the recommendations on the pressing need for reform of the pastoral episcopate set down at Trent, Charles Borromeo was determined to become a model ecclesiastical administrator in the new style. He was so successful in effecting reform in both the diocese and province of Milan (he held 6 provincial and 11 diocesan synods during his administration) that his episcopate soon served as an example throughout Catholic Europe. He was active in correcting abuses in monasteries and convents and in instilling in priests a greater appreciation of the importance of the spiritual life. The cardinal instituted a number of colleges and seminaries, acting as a benefactor of the English College for training clergy at Douay in northern France, and was a firm supporter of religious orders such as the Jesuits and Barnabites. In fact he was so uncompromising in his moral principles and so zealous in suppressing abuses that he aroused the antipathy of a group of discontented members of the Order of the Humiliati. A plot was conceived against him, resulting in the firing of a pistol at him while he was at evening prayer in his palace in 1569. The dramatic assassination attempt failed, and he was not even wounded. The plotters, however, were handed over to the civil authorities for execution.

The great churchman also interested himself in the religious life of the laity. He constantly traveled throughout his vast diocese, which stretched north into what is now Switzerland, preaching and administering the sacraments even in the most isolated Alpine valleys. The revival of Catholicism in the Swiss sections under his jurisdiction ranks as one of his outstanding achievements. In a move to help improve the common people's religious knowledge, Charles Borromeo also strengthened and reorganized the Confraternity of Christian Doctrine for the instruction of children in religious matters. This step has frequently been described as the beginning of what has come to be known as the Sunday school.

Borromeo lived by the motto "Reform we must begin by reforming ourselves." Soon dispersing his immense private fortune among the needy, he set an example to his congregation by living simply and selflessly. Always ready to minister to the sick, he rose to heroic standards during the great plague that raged in Milan from 1576 to 1578. When the disease first broke out, he was convinced that it had been sent by God as a punishment for the sins of the people, but he devoted himself to the care of the stricken after making his will and preparing himself for death. He even decided to do penance for his flock and, for example, walked barefoot in a procession with a rope about his neck. A Capuchin who worked by his side during the dark days of the late 1570s, wrote:

> He fears nothing. . . . It is true that he exposes himself much to danger but as so far he has been preserved by the special grace of God, he says he cannot do otherwise. Indeed the city has no other help and consolation.

Self-mortification, strenuous administrative duties, an overwhelming correspondence, pilgrimages, pastoral visits, and relentless demands for his advice and intervention all took their toll over the years on the cardinal's health and strength. Charles Borromeo became critically ill in October 1584, but he continued the performance of his duties until his strength was exhausted. He died on November 3, at the age of 46. The Milanese immediately began to venerate him as a saint and kept the anniversary of his death as though he had been canonized. On November 1, 1610, only 26 years after his death, Charles Borromeo was declared a saint by Pope Paul V, and his feast day was soon placed in the Roman calendar for November 4.

Will Rogers Day in Oklahoma

In Oklahoma the birthday of one of America's best-loved humorists, William Penn Adair Rogers, is celebrated as a legal holiday. Observance of Will Rogers Day is officially by proclamation of the governor.

Will Rogers was born on November 4, 1879, in Indian Territory, halfway between the towns of Claremore and Oologah in what is now Oklahoma. "I usually say I was born in Claremore for convenience, because nobody but an Indian can pronounce Oologah," he quipped. He was of Cherokee extraction on both sides of his family, and his father, Clem Vann Rogers, was prominent in the affairs of the Cherokee Nation. As Will Rogers told his audiences, "My ancestors didn't come over on the *Mayflower* — they met the boat."

As a youth he became expert at roping calves. After completing his formal education, including a brief period at the Kemper Military School in Boonville, Missouri, he worked as a cowboy, rope artist, and rough rider, traveling as far as

Argentina, South Africa, and Australia, and appearing in steer-roping contests and Wild West shows.

Twirling a lariat, he made his first New York City vaudeville appearance in 1905 at Madison Square Garden. It was the beginning of a notable career in show business. He discovered accidentally that talking informally to the audience was a good accompaninent to his rope tricks. The image he projected was of a warm, homespun, gum-chewing, and, as he put it, "natchell" man. In his comments and jokes about current events the humorist delighted listeners by exposing smugness, bias, and hypocrisy wherever he saw them. By 1915 he had achieved stardom on the stage; beginning in 1916 he appeared in a number of Ziegfeld *Follies* presentations. His popularity continued to grow as he subsequently starred also in motion pictures, wrote syndicated newspaper articles, lectured, performed frequently on the radio, and wrote several books in which shrewd observations on life and politics were clothed in his inimitable dry wit. The warm-hearted Rogers, who became famous as the "cowboy-philosopher," was known also as one of the foremost air travelers of his day. He died on August 15, 1935, with a fellow Oklahoman, the noted aviator Wiley Post, in an airplane crash near Point Barrow, Alaska. The Will Rogers and Wiley Post Monument was erected at the site.

The first observance of Will Rogers Day took place on November 4, 1947, centering on the Will Rogers Memorial one mile west of Claremore. The Claremore Chamber of Commerce, the Oklahoma Will Rogers Memorial Commission, and the Variety Club International sponsored the celebration, of which the chief feature was an hour-and-a-half parade with 16 bands. Distinguished guests included Governor Roy J. Turner; former governors Robert S. Kerr and Leon C. Phillips; the poet Edgar A. Guest, a friend of Rogers; Bob Hope, the comedian; and Will Rogers Jr. Approximately 25,000 persons were present, many of whom were from distant parts of the country.

Will Rogers Day, which continues to be sponsored by the Claremore Chamber of Commerce and the Will Rogers Memorial Commission, is still observed in a similar manner, with a guest speaker and downtown parade. As many schoolchildren as possible are involved so that they may become better informed about the humorist's life and works. In addition, the Pocahontas Club, whose members are women of Indian descent, presents a program during the day and lays a wreath at Rogers's tomb.

The Will Rogers Memorial, which was dedicated on the anniversary of his birth in 1938, is a museum containing possessions and memorabilia of Rogers. On the base of the Jo Davidson statue of him in the foyer of the building are engraved his famous words: "I never met a man I didn't like." Another statue cast from the same mold can be viewed in the Capitol in Washington, D.C., where it was placed by the state of Oklahoma in 1939. Another honor bestowed by his native state is the naming of the Will Rogers World Airport in Oklahoma City.

Rogers and his wife, Betty Blake Rogers, are buried in crypts beneath a marble sarcophagus in the garden of the Will Rogers Memorial. Opposite the memorial, which is one of the nation's most frequently visited shrines, is Will Rogers Park. Nearby is the restored Will Rogers Home, the frontier ranch house in which he was born. An annual Will Rogers Rodeo is held in Claremore in June.

The home in Pacific Palisades, California, in which Rogers and his wife and three children lived at the time of his death, is now a part of the large Will Rogers State Historical Monument. Both the home, which is maintained as a museum substantially as the family left it, and its park, in which polo is played, are open to the public.

The Will Rogers Memorial Hospital and Research Center in Saranac Lake, New York, served actors with pulmonary ailments from the 1930s until 1975. In 1977 the hospital's equipment was moved to the Burke Rehabilitation Center in White Plains, New York, under an affiliation agreement with the New York Hospital–Cornell Medical Center, and the Will Rogers Institute was established. Operated by the Will Rogers Memorial Fund, the institute sponsors patients into Burke; conducts research; and produces health education tapes and films for television, radio, and movie theaters.

NOVEMBER 5

John Dickinson Writes First of the "Farmer's Letters"

On November 5, 1767, John Dickinson wrote the first of the series of his famed "Letters from a Farmer in Pennsylvania to the Inhabitants of the British Colonies." According to the 19th century literary historian Moses Coit Tyler, publication of the "Farmer's Letters" was "the most brilliant event in the literary history of the [American] Revolution." But aside from their literary merit, the essays are important because they set forth the strongest constitutional arguments for the colonists' opposition to the hated Townshend Acts of 1767.

In the years following the Treaty of Paris of 1763, the British government tried repeatedly to force the American colonies to bear the expenses of their own defense. In 1764 Parliament passed the Sugar Act, which increased the duties on foreign refined sugar and other non-British goods. The next year Parliament passed the Stamp Act, levying the first direct tax on the American provinces by requiring tax stamps to be affixed to various articles, including newspapers, pamphlets, almanacs, legal documents, and playing cards.

The colonies protested the Sugar Act by pledging not to import the goods subject to the additional duties specified by that legislation, and their resistance to the Stamp Act was even stronger. Secret organizations, most notably the Sons of Liberty, forced the resignation of all stamp agents in America; the Stamp Act Congress, meeting in October 1765, prepared resolutions demanding the repeal of the act; and colonial merchants refused to import European goods until the stamp tax was ended. The last measure was the most effective. British merchants whose businesses suffered because of the nonimportation agreements appealed to Parliament to repeal the Stamp Act, and in March 1766 that body agreed to their demands.

Just over a year after the repeal of the Stamp Act, the British government again tried to raise revenue from the American colonies. Persuaded by Chancellor of the Exchequer Charles Townshend that the Americans might accept taxation if it was an "external" levy on trade, Parliament in June 1767 approved import duties on glass, lead paints, paper, and tea. To enforce the collection of these duties, the so-called Townshend Acts set up an American Board of Commissioners of Customs in Boston and established vice-admiralty courts, whose judges were to be paid from the fines and judgments collected from colonials violating the new legislation. The acts also suspended the New York Assembly until that body agreed to comply with the Quartering Act of 1765, which required colonial governments to provide barracks and other necessities for the British troops garrisoned in America.

The American colonists refused to accept the Townshend Acts. In the autumn of 1767 the major Atlantic seaports turned again to nonimportation to force Parliament to rescind the new duties. And as the major provincial cities agreed to ban foreign goods, John Dickinson took up his pen on November 5, 1767, to warn his fellow colonists of the dangers of the Townshend Acts.

Dickinson, who was born on November 8, 1732, was fairly typical of the conservative businessmen and other personages who led the opposition to the Townshend Acts. The son of a gentleman farmer, he studied law in Philadel-phia and London, served in the Assembly of the Lower Counties (the lower legislative house of Delaware), and then won election to the Pennsylvania legislature.

Reflecting the substantial position and conservative nature of their author, the "Farmer's Letters" firmly opposed the Townshend Acts but did not advocate any radical or violent measures to force their repeal. Dickinson recognized force as an ultimate avenue of redress, but he eloquently stated that "the course of Liberty is a cause of too much dignity to be sullied by turbulence and tumult." Instead he urged the colonists to "behave like dutiful children, who have received unmerited blows from a beloved parent. Let us complain to our parent; but let our complaints speak at the same time the language of affliction and veneration."

Although Dickinson counseled his fellow Americans to use moderate means to oppose the Townshend Acts, his "Farmer's Letters" were an important step in the colonists' efforts to set forth the exact nature of their relationship with England. From the arguments that had been put forth by the Americans at the time of the Stamp Act controversy, Charles Townshend and other government officials in London had concluded that the colonists would not accept direct taxation, such as the stamp tax, but that they would agree to an indirect tax such as was established by the Townshend Acts. Dickinson, however, denied the distinction between direct and indirect taxation. He agreed that Parliament had the authority to impose import duties on the colonies for the purpose of regulating the trade of the British Empire, but he argued that Parliament had no right to pass legislation, such as the Townshend Acts, that was intended primarily to raise revenue. Dickinson also took Parliament to task for suspending the New York Assembly, and he warned the Americans that this action was a threat to the liberties of all the colonies.

Printed anonymously in the *Pennsylvania Chronicle* from the end of November 1767 through January 1768, the "Farmer's Letters" were quickly recognized to be the work of Dickinson. Moreover, the cogent arguments against the Townshend Acts presented in the essays made Dickinson's work extremely popular. They were published in all but 4 of the 25 newspapers then printed in the colonies and then as a pamphlet went through at least eight editions in America. They were also published and circulated throughout Europe.

So popular were the "Farmer's Letters" that colonial town meetings, grand juries, and other groups voted Dickinson public thanks, and the College of New Jersey (later Princeton University) granted him the degree of doctor of laws.

The "Farmer's Letters" made Dickinson one of the most respected political theorists in the 1760s and 1770s. He was a member of the First and Second Continental Congresses. In 1776 Dickinson believed conciliation with Great Britain might still be possible, and he refused to sign the Declaration of Independence. But once the colonies determined to separate from Britain, Dickinson joined in the fight for independence. He also served in Congress during the American Revolution, was elected president of the Supreme Executive Council of Delaware in 1781, and held a similar post — equivalent to governor — in Pennsylvania from 1782 to 1785. In 1787 he represented Delaware at the Constitutional Convention. Indeed, particularly through the series of letters that he wrote under the name of Fabius, he was influential in securing the adoption of the new federal Constitution in his two home states: Delaware and Pennsylvania, respectively, were the first two states to ratify the new frame of government.

Dickinson published two volumes of his writings in 1801, under the title *The Political Writings of John Dickinson, Esq., Late President of the State of Delaware and of the Commonwealth of Pennsylvania.* Dickinson College in Carlisle, Pennsylvania, chartered in 1783, was named in his honor. Founded 10 years earlier as The Grammar School, the institution began celebration of its 200th anniversary in September 1972.

Dickinson, whose powerful, well-reasoned writing earned him the title Penman of the Revolution, died in Wilmington, Delaware, on February 14, 1808, and was buried in the Friends' burial ground there. The surviving building most closely associated with him is the colonial plantation house built by his father, five miles southeast of Dover, Delaware. Now owned by the state of Delaware and open to the public, it has been designated as a national historic landmark. Dickinson lived there until he was 18, and at various times afterwards, although his career as a public figure kept him in Wilmington and Philadelphia during most of his later life. When the house was restored after it was gutted by fire in 1804, the restoration was under the close supervision of John Dickinson himself.

NOVEMBER 6

John Carroll Appointed First Roman Catholic Bishop in the United States

On November 6, 1789, the see (or diocese) of Baltimore was established when John Carroll received his official appointment as bishop of Baltimore, thus becoming the first Roman Catholic bishop in the United States.

The Carrolls were a wealthy and distinguished family. John Carroll's brother Daniel signed the Constitution of the United States, and his cousin Charles Carroll of Carrollton (as he styled himself) signed the Declaration of Independence.

Sometimes called the Father of the Church in America, John Carroll was born in Upper Marlborough, Maryland, on January 8, 1738. He received some of his early education at Bohemia Manor, a Jesuit elementary school in northern Maryland. Subsequently — since there were no Catholic high schools and few secondary schools that would take Catholics in that era of religious intolerance — when he was 13 years old, he was sent abroad with his cousin Charles to St. Omer's, a well-known school run by English Jesuits in French Flanders. Charles Carroll completed his education and returned to America in 1765; but John Carroll entered the Jesuit order in Belgium in 1753 and was ordained, probably in 1769 after the traditionally lengthy Jesuit training.

After traveling extensively in Europe (1771–1773) as tutor to the son of a British peer, Lord Stourton, Carroll was back at the Jesuit house in Bruges in the summer of 1773 — when news arrived that the Society of Jesus (the Jesuits) had been dissolved by papal action on July 21, 1773. Carroll remained at the religious house until the following October, when government officials invaded it and Carroll was arrested. Lord Arundell of Wardour intervened, and Carroll went to England to serve as family chaplain at Wardour.

In 1774 Carroll returned to America, where he lived with his aged mother at Rock Creek, Maryland, performing his priestly duties and ministering to the spiritual needs of people in the area. From the time he returned to America, he dedicated himself to two goals, both of which he saw achieved in his lifetime. As an American, he was a staunch advocate of American independence — as were all the members of his family; as a priest, he hoped to organize the Roman Catholic clergy in America for a more effective ministry.

At the request of the Continental Congress, in 1776 John Carroll accompanied his cousin Charles Carroll, Samuel Chase, and Benjamin Franklin to Canada to ask Canada either to join with the colonies in their fight for independence from Britain or at least to remain neutral. The mission failed, and the discouraged Americans made the long journey home, Carroll returning to Philadelphia with the ailing 70-year-old Franklin, who thanked him for his "friendly assistance and tender care."

In 1784, when the pope moved to appoint a vicar general for the Roman Catholic clergy in the United States, it was on Franklin's recommendation that John Carroll was named "head of the missions in the provinces . . . of the United States."

After receiving his episcopal appointment in 1789, Carroll went to England to be consecrated by Bishop Charles Walmesley on August 15, 1790, in Lulworth Castle Chapel, Dorset. He returned to America as a consecrated bishop with a diocese — then the only see in the United States — that stretched from the Atlantic Ocean to the Mississippi River and from Canada to Florida.

Even before he had received any official authority, Carroll had set about his life's work of building schools and seminaries and encouraging the formation of religious orders of men and women. In 1789 he founded an "academy" at "George Town on the Patowmack River, Maryland," the first Catholic college in the United States. Carroll lived to see Georgetown raised from college to university rank in 1815.

In 1791 he founded St. Mary's Seminary in Baltimore, the first Catholic seminary in the United States. (St. Mary's was closed in 1969, but the chapel dedicated by Bishop Carroll in 1808 and renovated in 1968 can be visited in Baltimore on Paca Street.)

Carroll was recognized not only as a founder of Catholic schools, but also as a patron of all educational institutions. He served on the boards of several secular schools and colleges. A number of educational centers have been named for him, the oldest and most notable being Cleveland's John Carroll University, founded by Jesuits in 1886.

He was also the president of the Baltimore Library Company from its inception until his death and established its printed catalog, a great educational aid. In 1785 George Washington and John Carroll both received honorary degrees at the second annual commencement of Washington College, Chestertown, Maryland.

The first American bishop visited the first American President in retirement at Mount Vernon; and after Washington's death, Carroll preached a eulogy for him at St. Peter's Church in Baltimore on February 22, 1800.

Bishop Carroll laid the cornerstone of the Cathedral of the Assumption (now a basilica) on July 7, 1806, but he did not live to see the completion, in 1821, of the building he had helped to design with architect Benjamin H. Latrobe. The old cathedral is at the corner of Cathedral and Mulberry streets in Baltimore.

In recognition of his patriotism, Carroll was invited to speak at the 1815 laying of the cornerstone of the first Washington Monument to be built (at Charles and Monument streets in Balti-more), but poor health forced him to decline the offer. The priest and patriot, who had been made an archbishop on April 8, 1808, died on December 3, 1815, and was buried in the chapel of St. Mary's Seminary in Baltimore. In 1824 his body was removed to the cathedral.

The year before he died, Carroll, who for years had worked for the restoration of the Society of Jesus in America, had the great joy of knowing that the society was restored throughout the world. A portrait of Bishop Carroll painted by Gilbert Stuart is at Georgetown University, in Washington, D.C. The portrait was reproduced on memorial cards given out to mark the university's 1965 celebration of Founder's Day. The portrait appeared on one side of the card, and on the other was a prayer written by Bishop Carroll in 1791. Under it was the printed notation: "For John Carroll, Georgetown and the Jesuit Fathers, let us be thankful."

NOVEMBER 7

Harvard Established

On November 7, 1636 — or October 28, according to the Julian, or Old Style, calendar then in use — the General Court of Massachusetts ordered the establishment of a "schoale or colledge" and appropriated £ 400 for it. This was an impressive amount for the Massachusetts Bay Colony, whose founding had taken place less than 10 years earlier and whose population of under 10,000 had scarcely secured the necessities of life. In fact, the appropriation represented more than half the entire colony's tax levy for 1635 and almost one quarter for 1636.

Since educated clergymen were essential in the theocratic Puritan colony, the establishment of a higher institution of learning was necessary. As *New Englands First Fruits*, published in 1643, put it:

After God had carried us safe to New England, and wee had builded our houses, provided necessaries for our liveli-hood, rear'd convenient places for Gods worship, and setled the Civill Government: One of the next things we longed for, and looked after was to advance *Learning* and perpetuate it to Posterity; dreading to leave an illiterate Ministery to the Churches, when our present Ministers shall lie in the Dust.

The first step in this direction was the General Court's order of 1636. The November 7 order did not determine the type of institution to be established — whether a boys' boarding school, a college of university standing, or something in between; — but it stipulated that "the next Court [is] to appoint wheare and what building." The following session, which met at Boston on December 17, 1636, had more pressing business at hand: Indian attacks and the religious dissent of Anne Hutchinson and her followers. It was thus not until the meeting of the General Court on November 25, 1637, that the college was "ordered to bee at Newetowne," as Cambridge, Massachusetts, was then known. The founders had probably been influenced in their conception of a university site by the gardens, lawns, and water walks of Oxford University and, even more, of Cambridge University, where as many as 70 of the leading men of the colony had been educated. Wishing to find a place level enough for building and protected from the winds and sea, they decided upon Newtown. This fortified capital of the colony, a "spacious plain more like a bowling green than a Wilderness," was nestled between the salt marshes and low hills of the placid Charles River between Charlestown and Watertown.

On December 1 the session appointed the first board of overseers, consisting of Governor John Winthrop, Deputy-Governor Thomas Dudley, four other magistrates, and six ministers. Presented with the tremendous task of setting up a college that existed only on paper, without property, officers, or students, the board courageously hired a "professor" in late November or December: Nathaniel Eaton, a seemingly qualified man of 27 who had attended Trinity College, Cambridge University, although he had not received a degree.

On May 12, 1638, the General Court ordered "that Newetowne shall henceforth be called Cambridge," after the English university. Sometime before June 19 the board housed Eaton and his family in the Peyntree House, which had been described earlier as "one House with a backside and garden about halfe a rood, one Cowhouse with a backside aboute one acker in Cowyarde Rowe." Thus the doors of the first college and what was to become one of the outstanding American educational institutions opened in 1638 — probably in July or August and certainly by early September.

On September 17 a letter from Edmund Browne at Boston addressed to Sir Simonds d'Ewes proudly stated that "wee have a Cambridge heere, a College erecting, youth lectured, a library, and I suppose there will be a presse this winter." One week later, on September 24, 1638, a young Puritan immigrant, John Harvard, died in Charlestown. It was then learned that, according to *New Englands First Fruits*, it had "pleased God to stir up the heart of ... Mr. Harvard ... to give the one halfe of his Estate (it

being in all about £ 1,700) towards the erecting of a Colledge, and all his Library." Although John Harvard did not initiate the institution, secure its charter, or provide money to set the college in operation, he was its first benefactor. On March 23, 1639, the General Court, meeting at Boston, "ordered, that the college agreed upon formerly to bee built at Cambrige shalbee called Harvard Colledge."

The dozen or so students of Harvard College studied and lived in the single frame Peyntree House in College Yard. The harsh punishments and scanty diet, which characterized Master Nathaniel Eaton's regime, were exposed in 1639 at a public trial, at which Mrs. Eaton, for example, confessed as follows:

And for the bad fish, that they had it brought to table, I am sorry there was that cause of offence given them. I acknowledge my sin in it. And for their mackerel, brought to them with their guts in them, and goat's dung in their hasty pudding, it's utterly unknown to me, but I am much ashamed it should be in the family, and not prevented by myself or servants, and I humbly acknowledge my negligence in it.

In 1640 the almost defunct college received new life with the selection of Henry Dunster, a Cambridge graduate who was soon to prove himself a remarkable teacher and administrator, as president. The first commencement took place in 1642, and by the time Harvard celebrated its first centenary, 1,248 men had received degrees.

Although the main intended function of Harvard College was to provide clergymen for the colonies, graduates actually entered all walks of colonial life. The charter of 1650 dedicated the institution to "the advancement of all good literature, arts, and sciences" and to "the education of the English and Indian youth ... in knowledge and godlynes." Liberal arts courses were modeled upon those at Oxford and Cambridge, and before long the college had built up a solid curriculum in mathematics and the physical sciences. Harvard had received generous contributions from abroad for the special purpose of educating the "savages." Although a good number of Native Americans were students, only one, Caleb Cheeshahteaumuck, was awarded a bachelor's degree, in 1665.

By the turn of the century, the college's growing liberalism alarmed strict conservatives, such as the Reverend Solomon Stoddard of Northampton, who wrote that "Places of Learning should not be Places of Riot and Pride; tis not worth the while for persons to be sent to the Colledge to learn to Complement men and Court Women."

Since the board of overseers had proved too

unwieldy to run an educational institution, the Massachusetts General Court, at President Dunster's request, granted Harvard a corporate charter in 1650, under which the university still operates. The document created a self-perpetuating corporation — the first in North America — composed of Harvard's president and treasurer and five fellows, empowered to function as the executive of the college, subject to veto by the board of overseers in matters of major importance. Known as The President and Fellows of Harvard College, it controls funds, holds property and investments, retains copyrights, makes contracts, appoints all officers, and awards degrees. The board of overseers at first jointly represented the state and the church. During its early history, the college was closely allied with the Congregational Church (later with the Unitarian), although the state, as founder and patron, long considered it a state institution. By 1851, however, representation of the clergy on the board of overseers had ceased to be obligatory. Financial help and dependence upon state agencies gradually died out until, in 1865, all connections were formally severed. Starting with John Harvard, Harvard College was increasingly supported by private contributions. At present, overseers are elected in groups of five, for six-year terms, by mail ballot of all alumni. They include among them Harvard's president and treasurer ex officio.

During the second half of the 19th century especially, Harvard experienced a period of unprecedented development under the presidency of the noted educator Charles W. Eliot. Although the college continued to be the hub of intellectual activity, Harvard became after 1869 a university in the highest sense. Schools that had previously been established — Medicine in 1782, Divinity in 1816, Law in 1817, and Dental Medicine in 1867 — were raised to graduate level, and others were founded: Arts and Sciences in 1872, Business Administration in 1908, Education in 1920, Public Health in 1922, Design in 1936, and Public Administration — now named the John Fitzgerald Kennedy School of Government — in 1937. Radcliffe College, established in 1879 as an institution of higher learning for women, is officially connected with Harvard. It received its present name in 1894, in honor of Ann Radcliffe, who had given Harvard College its first scholarship in 1643.

The first benefactor of Harvard remains an elusive figure historically, on whom more research effort has been expended than on the entire early history of Harvard College. Even today only the bare outline of John Harvard's life, drawn from wills and other legal documents, is known. John Harvard came from a fairly well-to-do family, whose members for centuries had been butchers in the Southwark section of London. He was the second son of Robert Harvard — who owned his own business and several properties, including the profitable Queen's Head Tavern — and Katherine, the daughter of Thomas Rogers, a cattle dealer and alderman of Stratford-upon-Avon. The exact date of John Harvard's birth is unknown. His baptism took place in St. Saviour's Church in 1607 on December 9 (November 29, Old Style calendar). Given the customary three-day interval between birth and baptism, it is assumed that he probably was born on December 6, 1607.

There is no record of John Harvard's activities until 1625, when his father and four of his brothers and sisters died in the plague. On December 29, 1627, John Harvard was admitted to Emmanuel College, Cambridge University. By 1635 he had received both a B.A. and an M.A. degree. He married Ann Sadler on April 29, 1636.

In at least four documents he is described as "clerk," long an equivalent for "cleric," but there is no record of his ordination or evidence that he enjoyed a church living. He was the recipient of his family's fortune by spring 1637, after the death of both his mother and his older brother, Thomas.

John and Ann Harvard were already contemplating emigration to New England at this time, undoubtedly for religious reasons rather than economic gain. Harvard sold some of his possessions and collected his debts, the last one on June 7, 1637. The Harvards probably sailed for America on board the *Hector*, which arrived in the Massachusetts Bay Colony on July 6. They settled in the village of Charlestown, then consisting of 150 "comly and faire" houses with gardens and orchards, where they were admitted as inhabitants on August 11. The young couple either built or purchased a home on Town or Windmill Hill, which must have been one of the best houses available, since it was later used as a parsonage.

On November 12, 1637, John Harvard made an appearance before the Massachusetts General Court and was "made free and tooke the oath of freedome"; four days later, both he and his wife were admitted as members of the First Charlestown Church. Although engaging in cattle raising, John Harvard apparently used his formal education as well. He was a member of a committee "to consider of some things tending towards A body of Lawes" and became an assistant to the pastor and a teaching elder of the First Church. On September 24, 1638, a little more than a year after his arrival, he died of "a consumption" and bequeathed his library of

400-odd volumes and £779 17s. 2p. to the college at Cambridge that was soon to bear his name.

Harvard graduates have continued to pay their respects to their first benefactor in various ways. In England, the chapel at St. Saviour's Church (now Southwark Cathedral) has been restored as the Harvard Memorial. In Stratford-on-Avon, the house in which his mother lived has been purchased and preserved as a memorial at which Harvard graduates and other visitors are cordially received. In Boston there is a John Harvard Mall on Town Hill, where his house once stood, and the steps to the hillside church in which he preached have been partially preserved. John Harvard's grave in Boston's Phipps Street Burial Ground is marked with a granite obelisk, erected by alumni of the university in 1828.

Arrangements for designing and erecting a seated portrait statue of Harvard by Daniel Chester French, the famous American sculptor, were made in 1883. The statue, which was donated by Samuel J. Bridge, was unveiled with appropriate exercises on October 15, 1884. Soon becoming a landmark, as well as the butt of student pranks, it still stands in Harvard Yard. (The Yard, as the original campus is called, is a tree-shaded, walled enclosure with residence halls, lecture halls, and other structures in stately red-brick Georgian style.) For many years it was the custom of the Harvard Memorial Society to decorate the statue, stage brief exercises, and gather in Appleton Chapel for brief commemorative services at regular morning prayers, on the anniversary of what was assumed to have been John Harvard's birth date by the Old Style calendar, November 26.

The celebration varied in elaborateness from year to year. Especially notable was the widely attended tercentennial observance in 1907. President Charles W. Eliot presided over a dinner in Memorial Hall, attended by more than 500 alumni, representing the Harvard clubs of all parts of the country. Three days later there was a student torchlight procession. On the occasion of the 350th anniversary of John Harvard's baptism, November 29, 1957 — again, this anniversary was observed by the Old Style calendar — George A. Buttrick, preacher to the university, conducted prayers honoring John Harvard in Appleton Chapel, and the Widener Library opened an exhibit honoring the benefactor. On the same day in England, the Harvard Club of London gave a reception following a commemorative address by the bishop of Southwark in Southwark Cathedral.

Harvard University, an enormous educational complex with a huge endowment, has over the years acquired unique prestige and influence. It is the alma mater of notable Americans in politics, law, science, literature, the arts, business and finance, education, and religion. Among its distinguished graduates are John Adams, Franklin D. Roosevelt, John F. Kennedy, Ralph Waldo Emerson, Henry James, and Oliver Wendell Holmes. Its faculty often provides cabinet officers and presidential aides and advisers. Many foreign students, including potential government leaders, are sent to Harvard.

Whereas Harvard College excels as an undergraduate institution, the university is renowned too for its professional schools. It is served by rich art collections, advanced science facilities, and the largest university library in the world, with a collection of over 8 million volumes.

Battle of Tippecanoe

In the tragic and irreconcilable struggle between Native Americans and westward advancing white settlers, the battle of Tippecanoe, fought on November 7, 1811, is one of the most historic episodes.

Even before the American Revolution, the colonists had looked longingly toward the fertile trans-Appalachian lands, but the British by the Proclamation of 1763 had restricted their settlements to the seaboard area east of the mountains. The winning of American independence in 1783, however, ended the British prohibition against westward expansion. By the Treaty of Paris of 1783 Great Britain ceded to the United States the entire area east of the Mississippi, and the new American nation immediately began preparations to occupy the trans-Appalachian region. As early as 1784 plans were made for organizing the Northwest Territory — the area that is now composed of Ohio, Indiana, Illinois, Michigan, and Wisconsin — and by 1787 the Northwest Ordinance that established a government for the territory gained congressional approval.

The region between the Appalachians and the Mississippi was already occupied by dozens of Indian tribes, but the US government reasoned that the natives had forfeited their claim to the land by fighting on the side of the British during the American Revolution. Consequently, between 1784 and 1786 the Americans forced numerous tribes in the Northwest to sign treaties giving over their acreages to the US government as war reparations.

By 1786 Indian tribes had begun to resist the encroachment on their lands. The US government, in turn, realized that it could afford neither the vast military expenditures necessary to coerce the Indians into relinquishing their lands nor the unfavorable foreign reaction that would accompany such a policy. Thus, after 1786, the United States adopted a new approach to westward expansion. Returning to the British and colonial practice of acknowledging the Indians' right of soil, the government determined to purchase Indian lands and to set the boundaries of such territorial acquisitions by means of formal treaties.

The government's new policy tacitly assumed that the Indians would willingly agree to sell their lands and accept the whites' way of life. Indeed, part of the rationale used to justify their acquisition of Indian territory was that the introduction of such European concepts as individual ownership of property, and European methods of intensive agriculture, animal husbandry, and domestic manufacture would ultimately benefit the Indians.

The assumption was unrealistic.

The Indians did not want to abandon either their lands or their ways of life, but the relentless influx of white settlers into the Northwest Territory seemed to offer few alternatives. The military victory of General Anthony Wayne at Fallen Timbers in 1794 forced them to agree in 1795 to the Treaty of Greenville, which gave the United States control of sections of eastern and southern Ohio, a strip of land in Indiana, and scattered other tracts. Even this major cession did not long satisfy the lust for rich trans-Appalachian lands, however. The young nation was determined to expand westward, and between 1801 and 1810 a number of tribes were tricked or coerced into agreeing to a series of treaties that ceded to the United States a total of 110 million acres in the Ohio Valley.

During the first decade of the 19th century, pioneer settlements in the Northwest increased, and incidents of violence likewise became more frequent. Against this background two Shawnee leaders, Tecumseh and his brother, Tenskwatawa, who was known as the Prophet, attempted to unite the various Indian tribes against their common enemy. Tecumseh argued that the vast unsettled trans-Appalachian regions belonged in common to all the tribes and that no individual chief or tribe could sell or cede land. Tenskwatawa urged his fellow Indians to cast off all white influence and goods — particularly alcohol — and return to their own ways.

To resist the whites' advance, Tecumseh tried to organize all the northwest tribes into one confederation. But as he worked to unite the Indians, William Henry Harrison, the governor of the Indiana Territory, continued his relentless efforts to bring more Indian lands under federal control. When, in 1809, he persuaded the Delaware, Potawatomie, Miami, and Eel River

tribes to accept the Treaty of Fort Wayne, agreeing to cede large areas in Indiana to the US government, Tecumseh's followers became enraged. By 1810 Indian-white relations in the territory had deteriorated to such an extent that Harrison on several occasions reported that war between the two groups seemed imminent. In his reports to the federal government, Harrison tended to blame the activities of British agents for the hostility of the Indians; but in reality the cessions of 1809 seem to have caused the climate of tension.

In July 1811 Tecumseh tried to intimidate Harrison by warning him of his intention to enlist aid from the southern tribes. Tecumseh's plan convinced Harrison of the necessity of taking military action against the Indians, and he selected Prophetstown, the village some of Tecumseh's followers inhabited near the junction of the Tippecanoe and Wabash rivers as his target. Harrison waited until Tecumseh had left the village for a southern trip. Then, on November 6, 1811, he and 1,000 soldiers advanced to within a mile of Prophetstown. Thus menaced, the apprehensive Indians attacked Harrison's encampment at dawn on November 7.

Recoiling from the initial blow, Harrison's men were able to turn the Indians back and to raze their village. However, neither side scored a decisive victory; and the two contesting forces suffered about an equal number of casualties.

The battle of Tippecanoe had both short- and long-range consequences. Most immediately, the encounter served to convince the white settlers that the British were responsible for supplying Tecumseh's followers. This feeling resulted in renewed cries for the conquest of Canada as the best means of safeguarding the frontier. The Indians, for their part, saw the battle as additional evidence that the United States would be satisfied with nothing less than complete control of the Northwest lands. This realization prompted many tribes of the region that had hitherto remained neutral to ally themselves with the British when the War of 1812 broke out in June 1812. The one-day skirmish at Tippecanoe also produced a hero: William Henry Harrison's so-called victory brought him to national prominence, and in 1840, with the slogan Tippecanoe and Tyler Too, he won election as President of the United States.

NOVEMBER 8

Montana Admitted to the Union

On February 22, 1889, Grover Cleveland signed the Omnibus Statehood Bill, which authorized the admission of Montana, North Dakota, South

Dakota, Washington, Idaho, and Wyoming to the Union. The Montana territorial government immediately completed the legal steps required by the US Constitution, and Montana was officially proclaimed the 41st state on November 8, 1889.

The residents of Montana Territory had desired admission to the Union for some time, but earlier efforts in the direction of statehood had been less successful. Although a constitutional convention had been held in Helena in 1884, it was ignored by the Congress in Washington and came to nothing. With enactment of the enabling legislation of February 22, 1889, however, a new constitutional convention met in Montana on July 4, 1889, and by the middle of August completed a frame of government for approval by the citizenry. On October 1 the people ratified the document by a wide margin and then chose their first state officials. Joseph K. Toole, who had served as the territory's delegate to Congress, became the first governor.

Republicans and Democrats sitting in the first legislature were unable to agree on the choice of US senators for the new state. Each of the deadlocked parties attempted to appoint two of its members to the prestigious posts. The Republicans named Wilbur F. Sanders and T. C. Power, and the Democrats selected W. A. Clark and Martin Maginnis. In Washington, the Senate declared Sanders and Power the rightful winners. This was not the end of the story, however, for the question of who should represent Montana in the Senate would continue to arouse controversy for well over a decade.

Also controversial was the choice of a state capital, with Helena emerging as the victor after several years of contention. The town had become the seat of the territorial government in 1875, but in the intervening years several other communities had developed as worthy challengers to its preeminent position. Unable to agree on a site for the capital, the delegates to the constitutional convention put the issue before the voters in 1892. No town won a majority that year, but the people finally resolved the problem in 1894 by selecting Helena over its rival, Anaconda. The mining magnate W. A. Clark reportedly spent a minimum of $500,000 in support of Helena's bid, and Marcus Daly of what later became the Anaconda Copper Mining Company expended over $2.5 million on behalf of Anaconda.

In 1895 the Montana legislature appointed a commission to select a site for the statehouse. A year later, construction began at an unpopulated location approximately one mile east of the famous Last Chance Gulch, where prospectors had made a rich gold strike in 1864. The men

completed work on the central portion of the capitol in January 1902, and W. A. Clark was one of the orators at the dedication of the building on July 4, 1902.

Mount Holyoke College Founder's Day

This is a movable event. See note on page xxvi.

Mount Holyoke College, an independently endowed, nonsectarian liberal arts college for women, is located in the town of South Hadley, Massachusetts, in the Connecticut River valley. Founded on November 8, 1837, by Mary Lyon, it is the "oldest institution for the higher education of women" in the United States. Although not the first institution of its kind to be granted a college charter, it was the forerunner in offering young women an education conforming to college standards. In commemoration of its founding and its importance in the history of American education, the Sunday nearest November 8 has traditionally been observed as Founder's Day since 1891.

Mary Lyon, one of the pioneers in the higher education of women, was born on a farm near Buckland, Massachusetts, on February 28, 1797. Her father, Aaron Lyon, died when she was less than six years old, leaving seven children to the care of his wife. In 1817, with savings earned from spinning and weaving, Mary Lyon attended the Sanderson academy in Ashfield, Massachusetts, and later studied at the academy in Amherst, Massachusetts. At both she displayed extraordinary intelligence: it is said that she mastered Latin grammar between a Friday afternoon and the close of school the following Monday. With an apparently insatiable thirst to acquire and impart knowledge, she taught school during the intervals of her study at the two academies.

In 1821, when she was 24, Lyon shocked her friends — who thought she was too old for school — by entering the seminary conducted by the Reverend Joseph Emerson in Byfield, Massachusetts. She remained there for two terms and then became associate principal of the academy in Ashfield. In 1824 she accepted a position as teacher at the Adams Female Academy in Londonderry, New Hampshire. When the 19th century custom of making girls remain at home in winter provided a respite from teaching at Londonderry, the indefatigable Lyon taught at her own winter school in Buckland. She terminated this venture in the late 1820s, however, when Zilpah P. Grant, a fellow student at Byfield, opened a seminary in Ipswich, Massachusetts, and asked Mary Lyon to be her assistant.

During the entire course of her own studies,

Lyon had also made the most of her few opportunities to participate, at least informally, in men's education: she attended natural history lectures at Amherst College and studied chemistry at what is now the Rensselaer Polytechnic Institute.

During these 13 years of teaching at financially insecure seminaries at which girls acquired a smattering of knowledge, Mary Lyon became convinced that there should be a seminary for young women that was not dependent for its existence upon the life of the person who opened it — a school, with a board of disinterested trustees, that will "outlive the teachers and the principal," "a permanent institution consecrated to the training of young women for usefulness [and] designed to furnish every advantage which the state of education in this country will allow." She herself had experienced the hurdles then facing any woman who desired an education that was at once sounder in content and more serious in its aim than the curriculum of "ornamental" subjects offered in the typical female seminaries of the period. Moreover, these ladies' seminaries, as they were characteristically called, were conducted for the daughters of the well-to-do. Lyon wanted a seminary so conducted that "the rich will be glad to avail themselves of its benefits, and so economical that people in very moderate circumstances may be equally and as fully accommodated."

Reinforcing her own enthusiasm with common sense, she set about the task of securing the necessary financial aid for her plan. On September 6, 1834, a group of men interested in the project met with her at Ipswich to consider ways and means for founding the seminary she envisioned. For the next two years she was the guiding spirit for the coworkers in a fund-raising campaign as donations ranging from $1,000 to 6 cents trickled in.

At this point in her life, Judge Laban Wheaton of Norton, Massachusetts, and Laban Wheaton Jr., his son, offered Mary Lyon the principalship of the girls' school they were establishing in memory of the judge's recently deceased daughter, Elizabeth. Already too much involved in her own project to accept the position, she was able to oversee the planning, and the opening, in 1835, of the Wheaton Female Seminary — now Wheaton College, a four-year liberal arts college for women, located on a 250-acre campus — under Principal Eunice Caldwell, whom she had selected. Lyon taught some of the first classes at Wheaton and visited there in the summer of 1836, "to see how the new house comes on," — the boardinghouse she had "fairly talked into being." Mary Lyon Hall, a classroom building still standing at Wheaton, dates from 1849 and was named in her honor in 1913.

Mary Lyon's own plans were meanwhile progressing, with the selection of a seminary site in South Hadley in 1835. Having overcome indifference and antagonism in persuading a reluctant public that women should have educational opportunities comparable to those offered to men at Harvard and Yale, she was able to write on October 9, 1836:

I have lived to see the time, when a body of gentlemen have ventured to lay the cornerstone of an edifice which will cost about $15,000, and for an instition for females.

She predicted that "this will be an era in female education. The work will not stop with this institution."

After nearly four years of preparation and fund raising, the Mount Holyoke Female Seminary was opened on November 8, 1837, nearly two years after the original charter had passed the Massachusetts legislature, on February 11, 1836. Its beginnings were inauspicious. The first building, a four-story structure located 40 rods from the village church in the heart of South Hadley, was not yet finished: windows were without blinds; walls were mostly bare; much of the furnishings had been delayed by storms; and landscaping was nonexistent. Yet the letters of the first 80 students accepted evinced excitement and a spirit of adventure.

Admission requirements were strict, and the entrance age was set at 17. The original course of study, modeled largely on the systematic curriculum offered at Amherst College, included mathematics, English, science, philosophy, and Latin. Music and modern languages were added later. There was no course in domestic science, for Mary Lyon did not think that subject had a proper place in a literary institution; to reduce the cost of operating the seminary, however, she had the students do the housework, doubtless assuming that they had learned how to do it in their own homes. A diploma was given after three years of study at the new institution, but Lyon anticipated its evolution into a four-year curriculum (which came in 1861). The teachers were women, with visiting male faculty members from Williams and Amherst colleges supplementing the instruction of the resident faculty.

Mary Lyon had no doubts about the lasting success of her endeavors and always spoke of Mount Holyoke's original building — which was swept by fire in 1896 — as "the first building." Indeed the seminary was immediately popular: at the beginning of only the second year, 400 young women seeking admission had to be turned away for lack of room.

Serving as president of Mount Holyoke for

nearly 12 years on a salary of only $200 a year, Lyon enlarged and expanded the facilities until the seminary earned a national reputation for its high standards. She died on March 5, 1849, and was buried on the grounds of the institution, whose "stones and bricks and mortar," she had said, "speak a language which vibrates through my very soul."

The Mount Holyoke Female Seminary set the pattern for future independent women's colleges. Female seminaries, modeled on the institution and upon the educational principles expressed in Mary Lyon's major work, *Tendencies of the Principles Embraced and the System Adopted in the Mount Holyoke Seminary* (1840), sprang up in the United States and abroad. For her contributions in opening to women the highest educational opportunities, Mary Lyon became in 1905 the first woman to be elected to the Hall of Fame.

Mount Holyoke received a charter as a seminary and college in 1888. Between 1888 and 1893 some students were earning degrees, while others were not. In 1893, when all students were fulfilling the requirements for the A.B. degree, Mount Holyoke received a charter exclusively as a college.

Especially notable among its succession of capable presidents was Mary Emma Woolley, who served from 1900 to 1937, and who is also known for her activities as a crusader for women's political rights and as a US delegate to the 1932 international disarmament conference at Geneva.

Located within 10 miles of Amherst, Smith College, the University of Massachusetts, and Hampshire College, Mount Holyoke takes part in what is formally named the Five-College Cooperation, in which the five institutions pool their educational resources in specific areas. Mount Holyoke is also a member of the Twelve-College Exchange (Amherst, Bowdoin, Connecticut, Dartmouth, Smith, Trinity, Wellesley, Wesleyan, Wheaton, Williams, and Vassar), in which students can spend a year or semester studying at one of the other member colleges.

Founder's Day at Mount Holyoke, traditionally observed on the Sunday nearest November 8, is now part of Founder's Day Weekend. Originally including a morning church service and purely religious in tone, the observance has become more secularized over the years. The present observance, which takes place in the Abbey Memorial Chapel, commemorates not only Lyon, but also faculty and staff members, students, or trustees who have died during the previous year. It usually includes hymns, prayers by the dean of the college chapel, and an academic procession. Special events, such as dedications of new buildings, are sometimes scheduled for Founder's Day, and honorary degrees are generally presented at that time instead of at commencement.

As a permanent memorial to Mary Lyon, Mount Holyoke's main administration building is named in her honor. It stands on the site of the original seminary building, erected in 1837.

United States Troops Land in North Africa

North Africa, key to the Middle East and the Mediterranean Sea, was a prized objective of both Allied and Axis forces in World War II. At the beginning of the conflict, Great Britain, which held the Suez Canal and had regional military headquarters in Egypt, enjoyed an advantageous position; but operations by the Axis powers of Italy and Germany soon threatened British control. Only the American invasion of North Africa led by General Dwight D. Eisenhower on November 8, 1942, guaranteed the outcome in favor of the Allies.

Italy, the weakest of the Axis powers, was the first to attack the Allied North Africa bastion. Encouraged by early successes of the Nazi dictator Adolf Hitler in Western Europe, Italian dictator Benito Mussolini in September 1940 dispatched Marshal Rodolfo Graziani to invade Egypt from Libya, the adjacent Italian colony. Despite his superior numbers, Graziani was reluctant to engage the enemy and after his initial advance assumed a defensive posture. Under General Archibald P. Wavell, Allied troops from Britain and the Commonwealth nations of Australia, India, New Zealand, and South Africa pounced on the immobile Italians in December 1940; within two months they had moved 500 miles and crushed nine of the Italian divisions.

Fearful of losing all North Africa, Hitler persuaded Mussolini to accept German assistance on the battlefield. In March 1941 General Erwin Rommel and part of his Nazi Afrika Korps arrived in Tripoli and resuscitated the Axis war effort in the region. Beginning with a raid on El Agheila on March 24, German and Italian units swept eastward across Libya. It was not until late fall in 1941 that the British, who had been taken by surprise by the invasion, managed to regroup; then, in December, they drove Rommel all the way back to his starting point at El Agheila.

Rommel, early in 1942, began his second relentless offensive. By the end of the first week of July he had pushed the British into their last stronghold, El Alamein, only 60 miles from the Egyptian city of Alexandria, which served as operations base for the British Mediterranean fleet. At El Alamein Lieutenant General Bernard L. Montgomery assumed command of the British Eighth Army, and his vigorous reorganization of the battered units soon restored their confidence. Determined to seize the initiative, Montgomery on October 23 hurled his revitalized forces against the Germans and Italians. The British broke the Axis lines, won the battle of El Alamein, and sent Rommel racing westward toward Tunisia.

After delaying temporarily to regroup his troops, Montgomery continued his spectacular offensive by chasing Rommel some 1,300 miles across North Africa. On January 23, 1943, the British entered Tripoli, and the Germans retreated to a defensive position at Mareth. By this time, Hitler's soldiers were feeling tremendous pressure — not only from the British forces on the east, but also on the west from the Allied units that had landed behind them in North Africa in November 1942.

Entry of the United States into World War II in December 1941 had given the hard-pressed opponents of Nazism new hope of ultimate victory. Both the British and their Soviet allies wanted the Americans to enter combat as soon as possible, in order to relieve their own weary soldiers of part of the burden. One proposal, favored by American military planners and by the Russians, was for an early cross-Channel invasion of continental Europe. However, President Franklin D. Roosevelt of the United States and Prime Minister Winston Churchill of Great Britain vetoed this plan as too rash. In July 1942 they instead chose French North Africa as a more vulnerable invasion target and planned the undertaking for fall.

On August 14 Eisenhower received the title of commander-in-chief, Allied Expeditionary Force, and assumed responsibility for the North African operation. Eisenhower, in an early display of the coordinating abilities that made him invaluable, gained a major victory before a shot was fired by establishing an Allied Forces Headquarters at which the military commanders of cooperating nations learned to interact smoothly. Major General Mark Clark of the United States was Eisenhower's acting deputy commander-in-chief, and Admiral Sir Andrew B. Cunningham of Great Britain served as overall naval commander. Brigadier General James H. Doolittle directed American air units, and Air Marshal Sir William L. Welch led the British units.

Casablanca, Oran, and Algiers, politically important cities, became invasion targets. A separate task force received the mission of taking each of these hubs in the rail, highway, and communications systems of French North Africa. The Western Task Force, composed of American troops, was to leave the United States and sail directly to Casablanca. The Center Task Force, also American, but with naval and air components that were largely British, was to embark from England and proceed to Oran. And the Eastern Task Force, including British as well as American troops, was to depart from Britain and attack Algiers. Having secured their objectives, the Western and Center groups were to be ready to invade Spanish Morocco if it became necessary to repel a possible German invasion launched from Spain. The Eastern Task Force would become the British First Army under Lieutenant General Kenneth A. N. Anderson and would move east to Tunisia.

D day for Operation Torch, the code name for the invasion, was November 8, 1942. By November 7 the Western Task Force was in position, and the ships of the Center and Eastern groups moved past Oran and Algiers — as if to approach Malta or the Suez Canal — and then swung sharply south toward their real objectives under cover of darkness. As midnight of November 7/8 passed, the men aboard the transports made their final preparations for battle. At each of the three landing sites, tactics would be similar, as the commanders planned to place units on the coastal flanks of the targets and then take them by envelopment.

Elements of Major General George S. Patton's Western Task Force hit the beach between 4:00 A.M. and 6:00 A.M. on November 8. Hopes that pro-Allied French officers in Morocco would not oppose the invaders proved unfounded, and French colonial troops stoutly resisted the Americans. Major General Ernest Harmon's men had seized Safi, below Casablanca, by 10:15 A.M. on November 8. They took Marrakesh the following day, and Mazagan on November 11. On the opposite flank, to the north of Casablanca, the Third Division took Fédala by the afternoon of November 8 and overran the Port of Lyautey airfield on November 10. Patton requested the surrender of Casablanca, and the French commander, after initially rejecting the demand, gave up the struggle on November 11 at 7:00 A.M. on orders from his superiors in Algiers.

At Oran Major General Lloyd Fredendall landed his Center Task Force at approximately 1:30 A.M. on November 8. A direct assault on the city's harbor was a costly failure, but in general the Americans made excellent progress. Fredendall's men enveloped Oran, and on November 10 at 12:30 P.M. the city surrendered.

British and American troops of the Eastern Task Force met only light resistance at Algiers, because pro-Allied French soldiers managed to seize power in the city at the critical moment. By the time adherents of the collaborationist Vichy French government regained the upper hand, they were already doomed. By nightfall of November 8 the Allies were in control and had taken Admiral Jean François Darlan, the commander of the Vichy forces, into protective custody.

Soon after his confinement, Admiral Darlan issued orders for a cease-fire. Marshal Henri Pétain, the aged chief of state, at first accepted Darlan's action; but, under pressure from Premier Pierre Laval, Pétain withdrew his approval. Darlan temporarily canceled his cease-fire order but quickly reinstated it upon the demand of Eisenhower's deputy, Major General Clark.

Hitler, on November 9, demanded full authority from the puppet Vichy regime to land German troops in French North Africa. Enraged by the behavior of Darlan and Pétain, he then extended the Nazi military occupation of France into the southern region, which had previously retained some autonomy. At that point Darlan openly broke with his superiors and ordered his soldiers to cooperate with the Allies against the Axis.

Hitler saw the danger to Rommel's troops that the Allied invasion posed and immediately sent supplemental forces to Tunisia. French commanders, steadfastly loyal to Pétain or confused by the contradictory directives that had been issued by Darlan and the Vichy government, allowed Axis troops to enter the colony in large numbers. General Walther Nehring arrived in Tunis on November 16 to assume command of the German and Italian units and held control until General Jürgen von Arnim replaced him on December 9.

Terrain suitable to their defensive needs was Tunisia's chief attraction for the Germans. The eastern and western dorsals of the Atlas Mountains form an inverted "V" running southwest from the capital at Tunis. From this stronghold, the Germans hoped to expand their area of control and stop the Allied pincers movement.

After taking Algiers, Anderson's First Army moved east into Tunisia, as planned. In actions on November 23 and 25, the Allies proved unable to break through the German lines. Actions of the German Luftwaffe, or Air Force, as well as supply difficulties and the oncoming winter then combined to deprive the Allies of the initiative.

Taking the offense in early December, Nehring forced the salient northern section of the Allied lines closest to Bizerte and Tunis to retreat westward. On January 2 his successor, General von Arnim, the new commander, attacked the French XIX Corps in the center of the Allied front and captured Fondouk. On January 18 he battered the French in the Bou Arada and Robaa areas, slightly to the north. Von Arnim smashed the French for a third time on

January 30 at Faid, and by February 14 the Germans held the high ground along the eastern dorsal.

Rommel joined von Arnim in February to initiate a dual offensive against the Allies' western pincer. On February 14 Von Arnim seized Sidi-Bou-Zid west of Faid, in the south central region of the Allied lines; and on February 15 Rommel, operating on the southern front, entered Gafsa unopposed. Anderson ordered his troops to withdraw to the Western Dorsal, but to secure Kasserine, Sbeitla, and Feriana. The last two sites fell to the Germans on February 16 and 17, respectively, forcing the Allies to move additional units forward to block the all-important mountain passes at Sbiba and Kasserine. Intending to exploit the more successful of the two ventures, Rommel on February 19 assaulted both Kasserine and Sbiba, but the British and Americans held fast.

Recognizing his failure on the western front, Rommel returned to the east to meet the latest challenge from Montgomery's Eighth Army — which had been making ready for a final assault on Mareth. Rommel hoped to disrupt the Allied preparations, but his encounter with superior forces at Medenine proved disastrous for him, and the Germans lost more than one third of their tanks. Severely ill, Rommel left Africa on March 9, never to return.

Allied units in the east and west began coordinated offensive operations in March. General Patton on March 6 took command of the United States II Corps, which had fought poorly in the Sidi-Bou-Zid and Kasserine period, and quickly restored the men's confidence. The II Corps then seized Gafsa and managed to divert Axis attention from the Eighth Army — which on March 20 broke through the German-Italian defenses southwest of El Hamma. By April 6 Montgomery and Patton were able to link up north of El Hamma, thus establishing a solid Allied line across the neck of Tunisia and trapping the enemy between themselves and the sea.

General Harold R. L. G. Alexander, commander of the British Eighteenth Army Group (comprising the First and Eighth armies) masterfully coordinated the final stages of the Tunisian campaign. He moved the II Corps from the northern sector of the front to the northern area, along the Mediterranean flank. Major General Omar N. Bradley took charge of the II Corps as Patton returned to Morocco to prepare the Seventh Army for the planned invasion of Sicily (see July 10). Anderson's First Army stood in the center and Montgomery's Eighth Army held the south.

Victory escaped the Allies in April. Montgomery on April 19 unsuccessfully attempted a diversionary attack. The main thrust by Anderson also was incapable of cracking the German and Italian lines. Only in the north, where Bradley was facing weaker opposition, did the Allies make major gains.

Anderson's First Army, reinforced with additional units, achieved overwhelming superiority and on May 6 launched an assault that drove the Germans back toward Tunis. Elements of Bradley's II Corps undertook simultaneous actions in the north. On May 7, 1943, the major cities of Tunis and Bizerte fell to Anderson and Bradley, respectively. The Allies continued mop-up operations in the following days, and on May 13 Montgomery accepted the surrender of the Italian First Army. In all, the Allies took approximately 275,000 prisoners, including top commanders, in the last week of fighting. When it was over, North Africa was free of the Axis menace; the Mediterranean was open to Allied shipping; and the Americans and British continued their preparations for the invasion of Sicily.

NOVEMBER 9

The Great Northeast Power Failure

Tuesday, November 9, 1965, was an average autumn workday in the northeastern United States. But, as evening approached, chaos replaced the usual patterns of activity in the region. Many elevators carrying workers to the ground from the heights of Manhattan's steel and glass office towers suddenly suspended their hapless riders between floors. Subways rumbling through tunnels and commuter railroads clicking along suburban tracks pulled to unscheduled stops, stranding their human cargoes. In homes across the Northeast, lights dimmed to darkness, and heating elements on electric ranges lost their glow and cooled, delaying the preparation of evening meals. November 9 was no longer a typical day: darkness and an eerie quiet settled on the northeastern United States and southeastern Canada. The great power blackout had begun.

The electrical difficulties that produced the largest power blackout that history had ever known started at the Sir Adam Beck II generating plant in Queenston, Ontario. Shortly after 5:00 P.M., its system of circuit breakers and primary and secondary relays protecting the plant's five high-tension lines sensed that one of the lines was overloaded. To safeguard this line, the system cut off power along this artery and diverted the electrical energy to the four remaining lines. This shift had disastrous consequences.

The other four lines already were carrying close to capacity loads and could not accept the additional surge of power; so, within seconds, the protective system closed off all four lines.

The shutdown of the Queenston plant resulted in 1.7 million kilowatts of electricity being diverted back along the interconnected grid of power networks that serviced southeastern Canada and the northeastern United States. The high-tension lines of this grid, which were already carrying heavy loads to meet the great dinner-hour demand for electricity, could not absorb this additional power. Their protective systems were activated, and power was cut off along the major cables serving the Northeast.

The effect of the shutdown was quickly felt. Rochester, New York, lost its electric service at 5:17; Boston fell into darkness at 5:18; and New York City's lights went out between 5:24 and 5:28. Eight states (New York, Massachusetts, Connecticut, Rhode Island, and parts of New Hampshire, Vermont, Pennsylvania, and New Jersey) and the province of Ontario, Canada — an 80,000-square-mile area with more than 30 million inhabitants — were left without electric power.

Ordinary citizens of the affected area had no way of knowing that a breakdown in the vast electric system was responsible for the sudden darkness, and in the first minutes of the blackout some thought themselves responsible for the power failure. An 11-year-old New Hampshire boy, who had struck a telephone pole with a stick just as the lights around him went out, confessed to his mother that he was to blame for the blackout. In similar fashion, a woman in Manhattan who had been repairing some electric wires believed she had caused the failure. But soon transistor radios reported the great extent of the blackout. Many believed that the United States had been sabotaged. So prevalent was this idea that a Cuban official at the United Nations felt obliged to declare to one of the US delegates: "You can't blame me. I was right here all the time."

However, the need to deal with the emergency kept most persons from dwelling on dire possibilities concerning the power failure's origins. None of the numerous electric devices that people have come to rely on in the 20th century could operate the evening of November 9, 1965. In their absence, the inhabitants of the Northeast needed great ingenuity and goodwill, and they displayed both these qualities during the trying hours of the blackout.

Occurring only minutes after many workers in New York had ended their day, the blackout severely hampered home-bound travel. Without lights to control the flow of traffic, automobiles jammed intersections, and driving became extremely hazardous. Scores of volunteers, however, helped relieve the emergency situation. Students, business executives, shopkeepers, and office personnel — individuals from all walks of life — spontaneously took it upon themselves to direct traffic, with the help of flashlights.

Less easily solved were the problems confronting the thousands of working people who relied upon subways and commuter railroads for transportation. The power failure left thousands of people who had already begun their homeward journeys stranded in dark, overcrowded cars in subway tunnels and along deserted railway tracks. For the most part, the persons involved adjusted rapidly to the crisis. They sang, played word-games and, in one stalled subway car, even joined in calypso dancing while awaiting their rescuers.

More uncomfortable and worrisome was the plight of the hundreds of people who were trapped in elevators by the power failure. In New York City's Empire State Building alone, 13 elevators carrying a total of 96 passengers had stopped between floors. But they waited patiently as firefighters broke through walls to their stalled cars.

As the minutes of the power failure stretched into hours, many who had not yet begun their homeward journeys realized that they would not reach home that night. Since hotels filled to capacity very soon after the onset of the blackout, stranded commuters had no choice but to pass the night in such unlikely places as business offices, department-store furniture displays, church pews, and railroad stations. For the most part they accepted their fate with good humor; by candlelight they ate meals provided *gratis* by many restaurants.

Meanwhile, those fortunate enough to enjoy the security of their own homes during the blackout also faced considerable difficulties. Without lights or electrical appliances, residents had to rely upon their own resourcefulness to prepare dinner. They dug out unused birthday candles and half-burned tapers that had been put away "for an emergency," and by these flickering lights prepared the evening meals in living-room fireplaces or with barbecue sets that had remained idle since the last days of summer.

A sense of adventure permeated the chill autumn evening of November 9, as the blackout disrupted the routine lives of the more than 30 million inhabitants of the Northeast. Seeing a chance to make a quick profit, a few opportunists gathered flashlights and candles and then sold them on street corners at many times their normal values. They were far outnumbered, however, by people who helped neighbors and

strangers alike to weather the difficulties of the power failure without thought of remuneration.

But the blackout posed critical difficulties for some individuals. As the lights dimmed, hospitals turned to their emergency-generating systems for power, and some institutions found that such equipment was inadequate or not available. To ease the medical crisis, police and other volunteers rushed dry ice to blood banks to prevent plasma from spoiling; they manually operated such life-sustaining devices as iron lungs; and they helped attach electrical equipment in hospital coronary units to temporary sources of power. Operating rooms in which delicate procedures were in progress were especially tense during the blackout. Yet surgery — including a corneal transplant, a lung removal, and even a craniotomy — was successfully performed by the light of battery-powered lamps. Dozens of babies also made their way into the world during the dark hours of November 9.

The cloak of darkness and the failure of electric alarm systems that accompanied it also presented problems for law-enforcement officials. To prevent high incidence of theft and other crime, most off-duty police were recalled to service to patrol the streets, and many private citizens performed similar services. These emergency precautions — and no doubt the unexpectedness of the blackout — not only curtailed looting and robbery, but resulted in less violent crime during the power failure than was typical of an average day.

The blackout, which disrupted the lives of so many millions of people, lasted only a few hours. Forty minutes after the power failure began, electric service was restored to Buffalo, New York, and within four hours the lights were on again in Rochester, New York; Toronto, Ontario; and Providence, Rhode Island. New York City, however, remained in darkness for a longer period of time. Not until 5:28 A.M. — exactly 12 hours after the blackout had begun — did the city again have electric power.

The day following the power failure, reminders of the blackout surrounded the inhabitants of the Northeast. The New York and American stock exchanges opened 65 minutes late. Approximately one-third of the affected area's labor force failed to report for work, and major retail stores noted a similar percentage drop in their business. Post offices faced mountains of unsorted mail, and banks coped with hundreds of thousands of uncanceled checks. The abrupt stoppage of power had ruined goods in numerous manufacturing plants and food processing facilities — bakeries in New York State alone lost 300,000 loaves of bread. In many instances the remains of such damaged merchandise had to be cleared away before workers could begin to re-establish their normal routines.

The US Federal Power Commission immediately began an investigation of the vast power failure. Within weeks it pinpointed the source of the blackout as the difficulties at the Queenston, Ontario, plant. Investigating authorities also warned electric companies involved of the danger of inadequate power-generating facilities and recommended that more efficient safeguards be used to protect the vast electrical grid system in the future.

Since 1965 electrical suppliers have instituted many reforms suggested by the investigators. At least in the northeastern United States, however, power difficulties have not ended. The constantly growing demand for electrical energy, coming at a time when ecologists warn of the dangers to the environment of increased facilities, presents almost unsurmountable problems. Since the blackout in 1965, residents of the Northeast have experienced numerous power reductions, or brownouts, as they are more commonly called, and some areas have even had total blackouts. New York City and Westchester County experienced a devastating 25-hour blackout on July 14–15, 1977.

NOVEMBER 10

Marine Corps Birthday

Marines have constituted a strong element of US naval strength from the time of their first existence in the 18th century. In engagements at close quarters they defended the vessels on which they sailed by firing their muskets from positions in the ships' rigging, and they formed the landing parties that attempted to board the enemy's craft. Specialists in amphibious assault landings, the marines also acted as shock troops; they have maintained this role as their primary function in modern warfare.

Americans saw duty as marines in the later colonial wars. During the War of Jenkins' Ear, from 1739 to 1742, the 43rd Regiment of Foot, more popularly known as Gooch's Marines in honor of its colonel, fought against the French in the West Indies. Provincials also served as marines aboard privateers during the French and Indian War, from 1754 to 1763.

Several colonies raised units of marines at the outbreak of the War of Independence in 1775. A detachment from Connecticut, known in US Marine folklore as the Original Eight, took part in the capture of Fort Ticonderoga, New York, on May 10, 1775. The Continental Congress resolved to raise its own marine force on November 10, 1775. According to the act of this date, two battalions composed of men who were "good seamen or so acquainted with maritime affairs as to be able to serve to advantage by sea when required" were authorized. John Hancock, the president of the Continental Congress, appointed Captain Samuel Nichols the first commandant of the corps.

Captain Nichols set up his headquarters at the Tun Tavern at Water Street and Wilcox Alley in east Philadelphia and began to recruit marines. The hostelry's proprietor, Robert Mullan, received a commission as captain, and carried on the task of recruiting throughout the Revolutionary War.

Curiously, the first marine detachment to serve under the auspices of the Continental government antedated the November 10 resolution. When, on June 10, 1775, the Congress took control of all American military forces on Lake Champlain, it also assumed responsibility for a group of 17 Massachusetts provincial marines under Lieutenant James Watson, who were part of the ship's complement of the *Enterprise*. These troops also fought in the battle of Valcour Island in October 1776.

Continental marines rendered important service to the Revolutionary cause. In March 1776 some 200 marines spearheaded a raid on a British ammunition and matériel depot at Nassau in the Bahamas, and in December 1776 and January 1777 marines from the *Hancock* participated in the battles of Trenton and Princeton in New Jersey. The following autumn they assisted in the unsuccessful defense of Philadelphia. Marines fought on American soil in many other encounters during the Revolution, and some served with John Paul Jones in his attack on Whitehaven, England, in April 1778.

Congress, in 1785, after the conclusion of the Revolution, disbanded the Continental navy and marines for reasons of economy. In 1794, in response to the harassment of American shipping by the Barbary pirates, the government reconsidered and ordered marines assigned to every vessel built at its direction. Finally, on July 11, 1798, Congress established the US Marine Corps as an individual service under the secretary of the navy.

Marines have participated in every war in which the United States has been involved and have accomplished more than 300 landings on foreign shores. They fought in the Tripolitan War against the Barbary pirates from 1801 to 1805, in the War of 1812 against England, in the Mexican War from 1846 to 1848, and in the Civil War. With the further expansion of American interests abroad in the 19th and 20th centuries — especially in Latin America — marines played an important role in quelling local disturbances and conflicts. The familiar "Marine's Hymn" lines "From the halls of Montezuma/To the shores of Tripoli" allude to the wide range of conflicts in which the Marines have been involved.

During both world wars the marines were engaged in major combat operations. In World War I they fought in France at Belleau Wood, Blanc Mont, the Meuse-Argonne, St. Mihiel, and Soissons. Marines spearheaded the landings at Guadalcanal, the first American offensive in World War II, and saw action in such other famous battles of World War II as those at Tarawa, Peleliu, Iwo Jima, and Okinawa. By 1945 the marines included six divisions, four air wings, and supporting troops.

After World War II the marines remained an important element in the US defense establishment. They fought in the Korean conflict of 1950 to 1953, participating in the Inchon landing under General Douglas MacArthur and originating the technique of helicopter assaults. In the Vietnam War the marines again played a critical role in American land, sea, and air efforts.

Since 1921 the Marine Corps has officially celebrated November 10 as the Marine Corps' birthday. The location and circumstances of particular marine units influence observances of the event, but generally a passage from the *Marine Corps Manual* and a special message from the commandant are read aloud. Whenever possible the cutting of a birthday cake is included in the day's festivities, and the oldest and youngest marines present receive the first and second pieces of the cake.

On November 10, 1925, special observances in Philadelphia marked the 150th anniversary of the founding of the corps. The day's events included a parade, a dinner, and a ball. As part of the celebration, the Marine Corps also placed a bronze tablet at the site of Tun Tavern (which was razed in 1900).

In June 1926 the Marine Corps erected a replica of Tun Tavern at the Philadelphia Sesqui-Centennial Exposition Grounds, which served as Corps headquarters during the observance. On June 2 the Sojourners, an organization of Master Masons who are commissioned or warrant officers in the armed services, paid tribute to the beginnings of the Marine Corps by unveiling a plaque at the site of the original tavern.

At Independence National Historical Park in Philadelphia, New Hall, which was built in 1790 and served as the headquarters of the War Department from 1791 to 1792, has been reconstructed and today houses the Marine Corps

Memorial Museum. Many items pertaining to the history of the Corps are on display, and the exhibits are open to the public.

The battle of Iwo Jima, which was spearheaded by the marines, is commemorated by the US Marine Corps War Memorial, located a few hundred yards north of Arlington National Cemetery. The bronze statue, which was executed by Felix de Weldon from a celebrated photograph by Joe Rosenthal, depicts the raising of the American flag on Mt. Suribachi on Iwo Jima. Dedicated on November 10, 1954, the memorial was presented to the United States by friends and members of the US Marine Corps. The 200th anniversary of the Corps was marked in a ceremony at the Iwo Jima statue on November 10, 1975. President Gerald R. Ford hailed the marines, who "for two centuries have heard and heeded the call of the country."

NOVEMBER 11

Veterans Day

At 11:00 A.M. November 11, 1918, an armistice between the Allies and Central Powers ended the fighting of World War I. As the guns of the victors and the vanquished fell silent, the "war to end wars" became history. And once again the people of the world enjoyed the blessing of peace.

News of the cease-fire produced mammoth celebrations. Bells pealed, whistles blew, and millions whispered prayers of gratitude. Parisians thronged the broad boulevards of their city to demonstrate their happiness, while in London thousands flocked to the royal palace and to the residence of the prime minister to sing and cheer. In the United States, observances of the joyous occasion were equally enthusiastic. In New York City, for example, more than 1 million people jammed Broadway, crowds paraded and danced through other thoroughfares, and tons of ticker tape showered out of windows in the Wall Street area.

The November 11 armistice was a cease-fire, leaving vast problems unresolved. Over 10 million were dead, huge areas of Europe lay in ruins, and a satisfactory peace settlement was yet to be negotiated. The proclamation issued on November 11, 1919, by President Woodrow Wilson reflected the pride this nation took in aiding the Allied military victory:

We were able to bring the vast resources, material and moral, of a great and free people to the assistance of our associates in Europe who had suffered and sacrificed without limit in the cause for which they fought. Out of this victory there arose new possibilities of political freedom and economic concert. The war showed us the strength of great nations acting together for high purposes, and the victory of arms foretells the enduring conquests which can be made in peace when nations act justly and in furtherance of the common interests of men.

To us in America the reflections of Armistice Day will be filled with solemn pride in the heroism of those who died in the country's service and with gratitude for the victory, both because of the thing from which it has freed us and because of the opportunity it has given America to show her sympathy with peace and justice in the councils of the nations.

Yet the difficulties encountered in attempting to cope with the aftermath of the war produced a sober atmosphere throughout the world in the year that followed the end of the fighting. Many nations noted the first anniversary of the World War armistice on November 11, 1919, with veterans' parades, secular and religious programs, and two minutes of silence in honor of the war dead.

Two years after the 1918 armistice, France and England observed the anniversary by paying tribute to their soldiers who had died in the war. During the dark days of fighting, many soldiers were buried in unmarked graves. In 1920 the French selected one such unidentified French soldier, interred him in a sarcophagus beneath the Arc de Triomphe in Paris, and lit a perpetual flame over his tomb. That same year Great Britain also chose an unknown British soldier and with much reverence buried him near the tombs of English royalty in Westminster Abbey.

On November 11, 1921, the United States, following the example of England and France, honored its war dead. Months before, the remains of an American soldier had been disinterred in France and taken to the city hall at Châlons-sur-Marne, where they were placed in a casket inscribed "An unknown American soldier who gave his life in the great war."

After a transatlantic voyage aboard the cruiser *Olympia,* the body of the American Unknown Soldier arrived in the United States early in November 1921. The remains lay in state in the rotunda of the Capitol in Washington, D.C., for three days. Then, on November 11, the body of the Unknown Soldier was taken to its final resting place at Arlington National Cemetery in Virginia. Floral tributes and wreaths from all parts of the world decorated the gravesite; and foreign diplomats, members of all branches of the US armed services, and national dignitaries, including President Warren G. Harding, were present for the interment. At 11:00 A.M. — the time the armistice had gone into effect three

years earlier — the casket was lowered into the tomb. Above it subsequently rested a block of white marble, bearing the inscription "Here rests in honored glory an American soldier known but to God."

During the 1920s, annual observance of the armistice became traditional on both sides of the Atlantic. In England and Canada the commemoration came to be known as Remembrance Day; in the United States it was called Armistice Day, or, less commonly, Victory Day. The anniversary did not become a federal legal holiday in this country until 1938, but as early as 1926 Congress adopted a resolution directing the President to issue an annual proclamation calling on citizens to observe the day.

From the beginning, commemorations of the November 11 armistice have paid special tribute to the soldiers who died during World War I. Wherever the day has been observed, civic and religious ceremonies have recalled the sacrifices of the war dead. Their graves have been decorated, and, throughout the world, small red artificial poppies have been worn to honor the deceased of World War I. (Poppies became symbolic because they grow wild in the fields of Europe; the famous war poem "In Flanders Fields" alludes to the profusion of the blossoms.) In the United States, the American Legion for many years sponsored a special observance on Armistice Day. At 11:00 A.M., buglers played taps at main intersections in many localities, and for two minutes all traffic and business stopped as citizens called to mind those persons who had fallen in the war.

In 1968 the 50th anniversary of the 1918 cease-fire was especially noted. In the United States, veterans' groups sponsored parades in many localities; President Lyndon B. Johnson released a statement expressing hope "for the day when all the guns of battle will be stilled"; and a presidential representative laid a wreath at the Tomb of the Unknown Soldier — which in 1958 had become the Tomb of the Unknowns with the addition of the bodies of two other unknown servicemen, killed in World War II and the Korean War.

Although special anniversaries such as the 50th have received considerable attention in recent years, the most widespread tributes to those who fought in World War I and observance of the 1918 cease-fire occurred in the 1920s and 1930s. Most people who had lived through World War I believed that such a massive and bitter conflict could never again take place. But the outbreak of World War II in 1939 shattered such hopes. The second global war resulted in more than twice as many deaths as the first and produced such vast material destruction that its extent was almost incomprehensible. For those who experienced the holocaust of World War II, the anniversary of the November 11 armistice that ended World War I ceased to have relevance; it could no longer be considered the beginning of an era of lasting peace but was instead the date marking the start of an all too brief interlude of tranquility.

During the early 1950s, celebrations of the 1918 cease-fire received little attention. However, considerable enthusiasm was shown for the occasional November 11 observances in honor of all persons who had fought for their country — in World War II and the Korean War, as well as in World War I. In response to this change in attitude, many organizations, particularly veterans' groups, urged that the November 11 holiday be set aside as a day to pay tribute to all those who had served in this nation's armed services. In 1954 Congress passed and President Dwight D. Eisenhower signed a bill specifying that Armistice Day would thereafter be known and commemorated as Veterans Day.

Still another change was made in the November 11 observance in June 1968, when President Johnson signed a law making Veterans Day one of the federal holidays to be observed on a predetermined Monday, to provide Americans with additional three-day holiday weekends. The law, which went into operation in 1971, transferred the observance of Veterans Day from November 11 to the fourth Monday of October. However, veterans' organizations did not approve of the movable date, and much confusion resulted. Most states had reverted to the original date by 1977. In 1975 Congress authorized a federal changeover to take effect in 1978.

The nation's principal observance of Veterans Day still appropriately takes place at Arlington National Cemetery, where the Tomb of the Unknowns symbolizes the country's desire to honor all the war dead. Throughout the year sentries maintain a constant vigil at the grave site; and since 1960, a flaming torch that was lighted in Antwerp, Belgium, and then brought to the United States has burned to honor those who died in the service of the United States. At 11:00 A.M. on Veterans Day, a traditional program begins. After a moment of silence is observed, taps is sounded, and the President or his representative places a wreath on the shrine. The dignitaries at the grave site then go to the oval amphitheater behind the tomb, where representatives of the armed forces and several thousand spectators hear an address by a prominent public figure and attend other solemn ceremonies.

Veterans' groups, of course, are responsible for many of the day's events, perhaps the largest of which takes place in New York City. The American Legion sponsors a morning parade in which veterans, accompanied by brass bands playing martial music, pass down Fifth Avenue from 39th Street to the Eternal Light in Madison Square Park at Fifth Avenue and 24th Street. The line of march reaches its destination by 11:00 A.M. so that ceremonies in the park can coincide with the time at which the 1918 cease-fire began. Several dignitaries, sometimes including the mayor, take part in the Madison Square proceedings. Later in the day, the Veterans of Foreign Wars also holds a parade. The line of march extends down Park Avenue South from 23rd Street to Union Square at 14th Street. In Union Square Park, wreaths are laid at the base of a World War I monument, and a high-ranking municipal official offers appropriate remarks.

Veterans Day observances take place in virtually every locality in the United States. Some are held in places particularly associated with an American war effort — for example the USS *North Carolina* Battleship Memorial, a restored World War II ship docked in Wilmington, North Carolina, is the scene of annual Veterans Day ceremonies — while other events of the day occur in town halls, parks, or churches. Most exercises include such elements as parades, speeches, military balls, or religious commemorations. The Kiowa Indian Veterans Day celebration, a two-day event that takes place at Anadarko, Oklahoma, has several special features, the most outstanding of which is a pre-Columbian ceremony that warriors of the Ton-Kon-Koj perform in honor of the Kiowa who fought in World War II. But wherever and however Veterans Day is observed, all the day's programs have one common theme: they are means of paying homage to the hundreds of thousands of men and women who have sought to defend their country and its allies and have devoted their efforts to the preservation of freedom.

Martinmas

Martinmas ("Martin's mass") is the feast day of St. Martin of Tours. According to ancient custom, it falls not on November 8, the date of Martin's death, but on November 11, the day on which he was buried in Tours, France. Martinmas is observed by the Roman Catholic church as a memorial (the equivalent of the former Class III feast). Celebrated at Rome since the sixth century, it was an extremely popular feast in the Middle Ages and is thus an observance overflowing with religious and folk traditions in many countries of the Old World. To a limited extent, European immigrants have brought the legends and customs connected with the feast to the United States.

Martin of Tours was born at Sabaria in the Roman province of Pannonia (now Szombathely, Hungary) in about 316. His father was a military tribune who, when Martin was still young, was transferred to Pavia, Italy. The boy accompanied his father and, when he had reached the age of 15, reluctantly enlisted in the Roman army in accordance with the regulations for military service. Although both his parents were pagans, Martin began to take instruction in the Christian faith at the age of 10 and was so generous that he gave away whatever he had to those in greater need than he.

Sulpicius Severus, Martin's disciple, recounts in his widely read contemporary biography of the saint the well-known story, frequently portrayed in art, of how Martin — at the gates of Amiens in Gaul where his regiment had been sent — saw a half-naked beggar shivering in the cold. Martin took off his own cloak, cut it into two parts, put one part over the beggar, and donned the other. He patiently bore the jeers of his fellow soldiers who laughed at his scanty cloak. According to the account, the following night Martin had a vision of Christ, clad in the part of the cloak that he had given to the beggar, saying to the angels: "Martin, the catechumen, hath clothed me in his garment." The piece of the cloak that Martin had kept was preserved in the oratory of the early medieval Frankish kings, who regarded the saint as their patron. In addition, a few centuries later, the right to possess this precious relic caused the name "Capetian" (from the Latin cappa, "cloak") to be bestowed on the illustrious French dynasty that ruled from 987 to 1328. Moreover, the place in which Martin's cloak was deposited came to be called a chapel (in Latin cappella, "short cloak").

Soon after his vision, Martin was baptized. After a time he asked permission to resign his army commission, explaining: "I am a soldier of Christ; it is not lawful for me to serve." Accused of being a coward, he volunteered to stand unarmed in the front line. The enemy surrendered before engaging in battle, but Martin was discharged anyway, probably about 339. He then joined the admiring circle around Hilary of Poitiers. After being ordained in a minor rank of the clergy, Martin passed the next few years in a number of places in western Europe, including a small island off the Ligurian coast near Genoa, Italy. In 360 he returned to Gaul, where he obtained permission from Hilary to live as an ascetic recluse at Ligugé, some distance from Poitiers. His modest cell there soon became the nucleus of a community of similarly dedicated men.

After 10 years of asceticism and penitential discipline, combined with active preaching and proselytizing, Martin, whose saintliness and miracles had been widely discussed, was an acclaimed choice for the vacant bishopric of Tours. Only a few nobles and higher ecclesiastics ex-

pressed dissenting opinions against "a man so contemptible with dirty clothes and unkempt hair." Against his will, Martin was consecrated bishop of Tours in 371. Loath to relinquish monastic life for the trappings of the bishopric, he resolved to continue his previous mode of existence. His biographer noted that

with unswerving constancy, he remained the same man as before. There was the same humble heart and the same poverty-stricken clothing; and, amply endowed with authority and tact, he fully sustained the dignity of the episcopate without forsaking the life or the virtues of a monk.

The new bishop moved to a hut in a practically inaccessible spot along the banks of the Loire River, outside of Tours. But he soon found himself the leader of a colony of 80 disciples, the core of the renowned monastery of Marmoutier.

Christianity had barely made an impression on the rustic inhabitants of the countryside surrounding Tours, and Martin was unceasing in his efforts to root out paganism. Active even as an octogenarian, he fell mortally ill at Candes, a village in his diocese, where he died on November 8, 397. Three days later his body was removed to Tours, which became a much-frequented sanctuary.

Martin's reputation as a great wonder-worker soon grew. The sixth century Frankish historian Gregory of Tours lists 206 miracles worked by Martin after his death. Martin of Tours became one of the first saints who had not suffered martyrdom. Although, as the father of French monasticism and the evangelizer of Gaul, he was of immense importance in France, his deeds as missionary, preacher, and founder of monastic communities stimulated enthusiasm and veneration from Ireland to the Middle East. Numerous churches were named in his honor, of which the most famous is perhaps St. Martin in the Fields in Trafalgar Square, London.

As the patron of tavern keepers, beggars, and wine growers, and the friend of the poor, Martin was traditionally a convivial saint much beloved in the rural communities of Western Europe. Moreover, his feast day fell at a convenient time for country people, who were ready to celebrate after the hard work of harvesting and making new wine was over. Mid-November was also the time in which animals were customarily slaughtered to provide meat for the winter. Thus there arose the traditions of revelry, bonfires, processions, and — especially — feasting on Martinmas, which are still being carried on in many European countries.

The dinner essential to the occasion is roast goose, stuffed with such ingredients as apples, sauerkraut, green cabbage, or prunes. According to an old Czech proverb, "On Saint Martin's Day the goose family is crying"; and in Sweden, Martinmas is called Martin's Goose Day. A goose is mentioned in connection with St. Martin as early as the 12th century: The annals of the German monastery of Corvey state that in 1171 Othelricus of Svalenberg presented a solid silver goose to the monks on the feast day.

The reason Martin and a goose are linked is obscure. Most likely, the roast goose dinner on Martinmas became traditional because geese were plentiful and well fattened at harvest time. But several legends provide more colorful explanations. One version is that Martin, horrified at the thought of being elected bishop of Tours, hid in a barn to escape messengers sent to notify him of the news. A goose there honked so much at the intrusion that the racket gave away Martin's hiding place. Other theories trace the goose eating to the Roman practice of killing a goose as an annual sacrificial offering for the harvest; or to the early Germanic custom of sacrificing a bird to Wotan, the chief of the gods. Most improbable of all is the legend that Martin died after eating an entire roast goose at one sitting. At any rate, the traditional feasting on roast goose on November 11 continues not only in Europe but also in the United States. Especially in large cities such as New York, ethnic restaurants sometimes feature roast goose and all the trimmings on Martinmas and are much frequented by persons of European descent.

In Germany, Martinmas is a festival celebrated not only by Roman Catholics but by Protestants as well, since Martin Luther, who was born on the Eve of Saint Martin — in 1483 — was baptized Martin in honor of the saint.

Martinmas has traditionally been a day associated with weather prophecies. For example, "If St. Martin's Day be bright and sunshiny, or if the trees and vines still retain their foliage, there will be a cold winter. But if there be frost before Martinmas, the winter will be mild." Similarly, "If the goose walks on ice on Saint Martin's Day, she'll wade in mud at Christmas." In England the counterpart of the American "Indian summer" sometimes comes in mid-November and is termed "St. Martin's Summer."

Washington Admission Day

The Oregon Treaty, ratified by the US Senate on June 15, 1846, amicably terminated a long dispute with Great Britain over the location of the Canadian-American border west of the Rocky Mountains. The Americans, who claimed Pacific territory as far north as 54°40′ north latitude, and the British, who wanted to restrict the expanding young United States to a much more southerly 42°, compromised on a dividing line set at the 49th Parallel. On August 13, 1848, Congress organized the Oregon country below that line into a territory. A sizable region, the new Oregon Territory included what were to be the states of Idaho, Oregon, and Washington, as well as parts of Montana and Wyoming.

In 1844 Michael T. Simmons and John R. Jackson led a group of settlers, including George W. Bush, a mulatto, to Oregon. When the party discovered that an enactment of the Oregon Provisional Government banned persons of black ancestry from residence in the region, they crossed the Columbia River and in 1845 established the first American communities in the area of Washington. The land, although still part of the Oregon country, was beyond the effective control of the government. Simmons settled at New Market or Tumwater (now Olympia, the state capital); Jackson established his home on the Cowlitz River; and Bush selected what became known as Bush's Prairie for himself.

Few immigrants ventured across the Columbia River in the first years of settlement. The ratification of the Oregon Treaty encouraged the pioneers, but the slaying of the Whitman missionary family by Cayuse Indians at Waillatpu in 1847 frightened away many would-be settlers. The discovery of gold in California diverted still more people from the Puget Sound region, and by 1849 a census by Governor Joseph Lane of the Oregon Territory located only 304 pioneers above the Columbia.

American troops established a fort at Steilacoom in 1849, and their presence insured security for prospective settlers. Economic opportunity proved to be an even greater inducement to the pioneers, who found in growing California a market for the food, fish, and timber that were so plentiful north of the Columbia River. The region developed quickly in response to these stimuli, attaining a population of 1,049 whites by the 1850 census.

Settlers pushed north along Puget Sound in 1851 to what is now Alki Point, but found the location inadequate as a port. The following spring they established a town along the inside shore line of Elliott Bay and named it in honor of Chief Sealth of the Duwamish Indians, though they corrupted his name in the process. Seattle, as they called it, enjoyed an excellent harbor that guaranteed its prosperity.

The residents north of the Columbia River soon became unhappy under the jurisdiction of the Oregon Territorial Government. In order to take care of legal and other matters, they had to travel across many arduous miles of the Pacific Northwest to the territorial capital, located south of the river, first at Oregon City and later at Salem. Furthermore, the legislature, in which the north was underrepresented, neglected to build roads or perform other essential services in the Puget Sound area. On the other hand, the larger southern population found the attention-demanding northerners a nuisance. Both groups saw that the answer to the problem was a separate government for the upper region.

Northerners held a convention at Cowlitz Landing in August 1852 to petition Congress for territorial status, and in the fall the new Olympia *Columbian* added its support to the campaign. On November 25, 1852, a second convention met at Monticello, and the 44 elected delegates repeated the call for the organization of the Territory of Columbia. In Congress Joseph Lane, the Oregon representative and former governor, also advanced the cause of northern independence.

On February 8, 1853, Congress began to discuss a bill to create the Territory of Columbia. Representative Richard Henry Stanton of Kentucky suggested the area's name be changed to Washington to honor the nation's first President. The legislators passed the amended measure on February 10, and President James K. Polk signed it on March 2, 1853. The new Washington Territory included the land from the Pacific Ocean to the crest of the Rocky Mountains between the 49th and 46th parallels of north latitude, except where the Columbia River formed the south boundary.

Congress in 1863 created the Territory of Idaho in response to appeals for their own government made by settlers living in Oregon and Washington east of the Cascade Mountains. Inspired by the Idahoans' success, the residents of the Walla Walla region, also east of the Cascades, agitated for separation from Washington and its distant capital at Olympia: in 1876 Congress rejected a bill to annex Walla Walla to Oregon. The discussions surrounding the proposal, however, prompted western Washingtonians, who were anxious to keep their boundaries intact, to work vigorously for statehood. In response to their efforts, the Washington territorial legislature called for the election of delegates to a constitutional convention to meet in Walla Walla.

The convention assembled at Walla Walla on June 11, 1878, and by July 27 had drawn up a constitution that the voters approved at the next election. After ratification Thomas Brents, the territorial representative, asked Congress to admit Washington to the Union with the Walla Walla document as the state's basic law. Congress rejected this appeal for two reasons: there was no direct railroad connection with the territory, and it was feared that the region's small population of 75,000 might prove unable to support its own government.

Along with several other territories, Washington frequently requested statehood during the 1880s. Congress, fearful that multiple admissions might upset the equilibrium established between the Democratic and Republican parties, turned aside all these motions. In 1889, however, a lame-duck Democratic Congress agreed to admit Montana, North Dakota, South Dakota, and Washington to the Union.

The enabling act, appropriately passed on George Washington's Birthday — February 22, 1889 — required the territory to call a constitutional convention. The voters ratified the frame of government devised by the gathering and submitted it to President Benjamin Harrison. He approved the document and on November 11, 1889, proclaimed Washington a member of the United States.

Washington annually observes Admission Day (as well as Veterans Day) on November 11. Grammar and high schools are closed, but state law requires that they hold special events on the preceding Friday to promote loyalty and devotion to the laws and institutions of Washington. These programs emphasize the rigors of frontier life and major events in the history of the territory and state.

In 1939 Washington celebrated its golden jubilee. The state legislature inaugurated the commemoration on February 22 with a program highlighted by a message from President Franklin D. Roosevelt and a proclamation by Governor Clarence D. Martin. A tribute to Washington's pioneers formed the theme of the 50th anniversary year. Washington in 1964 marked its diamond jubilee with similar appropriate ceremonies.

NOVEMBER 12

Elizabeth Cady Stanton Day

Elizabeth Cady Stanton Day, November 12, marks the anniversary of the birth of one of the pioneers in the field of woman's rights, in 1815 in Johnstown, New York. The daughter of a judge, Elizabeth Cady learned in her father's law office of the discriminatory laws affecting women. She was educated at one of the first institutions to provide improved education for women, the Troy Female Academy, now known as the Emma Willard School.

In a ceremony omitting the then customary

word "obey," she was married in 1840 to the journalist and abolitionist Henry Brewster Stanton. That same year they attended the World International Anti-Slavery convention in London. Also in attendance was the Quaker social reformer Lucretia Coffin Mott. Their indignation when female delegates were excluded from the floor of the convention prompted the two women to organize and work for equality.

With others, they sent out the call that resulted in the first woman's rights convention, held at Seneca Falls, New York, in 1848 (see July 19). For it, Stanton drew up her famous bill of rights for women, demanding redress of wrongs and inequities. She insisted (without Mott's approval, however) that the declaration include what became the first organized demand for woman suffrage in the United States.

It was in 1851 that Stanton, a brilliant orator and capable journalist, first met the dynamic Susan B. Anthony (see February 15). The meeting marked the beginning of a half-century's working partnership: Stanton served as writer and editor, Anthony as business manager, both as untiring lecturers. With Parker Pillsbury they issued *The Revolution*, a women's rights publication, from 1868 to 1870. In 1869 they organized the National Woman Suffrage Association. Stanton served as president of the organization from its founding until 1890, planning suffrage campaigns, appearing before legislative committees, and speaking in favor of liberal divorce laws and complete political, legal, and industrial equality for women. When her association merged with Lucy Stone's American Woman Suffrage Association in 1890, Stanton served for two years as president of the resulting consolidation, which was named the National American Woman Suffrage Association. She was still in the forefront of the movement for women's emancipation when she died, on October 26, 1902, in New York City — 18 years before the 19th Amendment to the Constitution, granting women the right to vote, became law in 1920 (see August 26). Her book *Eighty Years and More* was published in 1898.

The 1941 proclamation by which Governor Herbert H. Lehman of New York declared November 12 Elizabeth Cady Stanton Day is on display in the Johnstown Historical Society museum, located at 17 North William Street, as is a bronze plaque that formerly marked the site of her birthplace (now occupied by a bank). At Seneca Falls, the now privately owned Elizabeth Cady Stanton House and a portion of the church in which the first women's rights convention was held, both identified by state markers, still stand. The Seneca Falls Historical Society museum, at 55 Cayuga Street, has an Elizabeth Cady Stanton Room containing assorted women's rights memorabilia and an organ-piano and desk that belonged to Stanton.

NOVEMBER 13

Edwin Booth's Birthday

Edwin Thomas Booth, the famous 19th century Shakespearean tragedian and one of the most distinguished American actors of all time, was born on a farm near Bel Air, Maryland, 23 miles from Baltimore, on November 13, 1833. He was the son of Junius Brutus Booth, an English actor who had settled in the United States in 1821, and Mary Ann Holmes. Edwin Booth was named for Edwin Forrest, the American tragedian and for Thomas Flynn, an English comedian, and old family friend. In later years he dropped the second name.

While he was still a young boy, Edwin Booth traveled about the country on theatrical tours with his father, who, continuing the successes he had scored in London, won acclaim from American theatergoers as well. On September 10, 1849, when he was not yet 16 years old, young Booth made his stage debut at the Boston Museum, playing the minor role of Tressel to his father's Richard III in William Shakespeare's *Richard III*. He then performed occasional juvenile parts with his father. The aspiring actor himself appeared as Richard III in April 1851 at the National Theater in New York City, after his father, often drunk and eccentric in behavior, had refused to perform. The next year Edwin Booth went with his father to California and acted with mixed success in various plays.

It was not until after the elder Booth's death on November 30, 1852, that Edwin Booth slowly gained recognition in his own right. In 1854 he ventured to Australia with Laura Keene, an English actress who had recently come to the United States. The troupe was unsuccessful, and Booth returned via Hawaii to California, where in 1856 he captured the public's imagination as the leading man of a stock company in Sacramento. He played in the West until September 1856.

Booth was now an experienced actor who not only exhibited the talents of his father but also had improved upon the latter's acting techniques by adopting a more subdued and natural manner, foreshadowing 20th century histrionic realism. Feeling himself ready to return to the East, he first toured the southern states. Then in Boston, on April 20, 1857, he scored a brilliant success as Sir Giles Overreach in Philip Massinger's *A New Way to Pay Old Debts*, which was hailed by the critics. According to one writer, the performance was a great triumph: "Young Booth's success was decided. . . . It brought back the most vivid recollections of the fire, the vigor, the strong intellectuality which characterized the acting of his lamented father." This and other triumphs in various eastern cities, such as his appearance as Richard III in New York City on May 4, 1857, lifted Booth to the top of his profession.

On July 7, 1860, the popular actor married Mary Devlin, a charming young actress whom he had first met in November 1856 while rehearsing Romeo to her Juliet. The couple soon sailed to England, where Booth filled engagements in London, Liverpool, and Manchester, and where their daughter, Edwina, was born in September 1861. The English engagement, although receiving mixed reviews, added to Booth's prestige at home. Upon returning to the United States in August 1862, the actor played to packed audiences at New York City's Winter Garden Theater until the death of his 22-year-old wife in February 1863 caused his brief retirement from the stage.

In 1863 Booth became comanager of the Winter Garden and presented a number of lavish Shakespearean productions. His *Julius Caesar* of November 25, 1864, starred Booth and his two brothers, Junius Brutus Booth Jr. and John Wilkes Booth, as Brutus, Cassius, and Mark Antony respectively. From November 26, 1864, to March 22, 1865, Edwin Booth portrayed Hamlet in a now legendary run of 100 consecutive nights. This dramatic feat, however, was soon followed by personal tragedy: on April 14, 1865, Southern sympathizer John Wilkes Booth assassinated President Abraham Lincoln in Ford's Theatre in Washington, D.C. Much later, Edwin Booth told a fellow actor, Joseph Jefferson, that at the news "it was just as if I was struck on the forehead with a hammer." At first he vowed never to act again and retired from the stage for nearly a year. When his return appearance at the Winter Garden was announced for January 3, 1866, the New York *Herald* inquired: "Will Booth appear as the assassin of Caesar? That would be, perhaps, the most suitable character." But Booth playing Hamlet was welcomed heartily with a standing ovation.

As manager of the Winter Garden, the handsome, black-haired actor continued to stage sumptuous productions until a disastrous fire at the theater in March 1867, in which he lost scenery, his library, and his entire theatrical wardrobe, including prized costumes that his father had worn. Although the destruction was esti-

mated at about $40,000, the 34-year-old Booth vowed, "If I live and don't lose my grip in five years I'll be rich." He recouped his losses and started to build his own theater at 23rd Street and Sixth Avenue in New York City, which opened as Booth's Theater on February 3, 1869.

The seasons of 1869 through 1874 rank as epoch-making in American theater annals, with Booth playing his beloved Shakespearean roles of King Lear, Othello, Iago, Brutus, and other favorites, supported by leading actors and actresses. Unfortunately he lacked business acumen and experience and relied on unqualified financial advisers. Despite excellent box-office receipts, the theater failed in the panic of 1873–1874 and declared bankruptcy on January 26, 1874. Booth once more repaid his debts and intrepidly pursued his career, touring the United States between 1873 and 1879. However, his personal life became increasingly difficult as his second wife, Mary McVicker, an actress whom he married on June 7, 1869, showed signs of mental illness following the death of their infant son, Edgar.

Between 1880 and 1882, Edwin Booth appeared in England. He won praise for his interpretation of King Lear; he also costarred with the renowned English actor Sir Henry Irving at the Lyceum Theatre in London between May 2 and June 10, 1881, when the two stars alternated in the roles of Othello and Iago to frenzied acclaim. After his wife's death, Booth toured Germany and Austria in 1883, performing in English with a German cast. His portrayals of Lear, Othello, and Iago, for which he was greeted with wild enthusiasm and crowned with gold and silver laurel wreaths, represented the peak of his career. In 1886 Booth concluded a business and acting contract with the American actor Lawrence Barrett. He appeared in repertory performances in New York City from 1887 until Barrett's death in 1891, but the decline in his abilities became increasingly evident, although he was still regarded as one of the great actors of his day. Booth's last stage appearance was at the Brooklyn Academy of Music's performance of *Hamlet* on April 4, 1891.

The cherished wish of Booth's later years was to found a first-rate club, in New York City, mainly for actors, which would serve as a social meeting place. He bought the Clarkson N. Potter house at 16 Gramercy Park South and hired Stanford White to remodel it into a clubhouse. He also filled it with a noteworthy collection of theater relics and portraits, reserving for his own use a suite of rooms on the fourth floor. "The Players" was incorporated on January 7, 1888, by 14 men of theatrical and nontheatrical backgrounds, including, for example, Mark

Twain and General William T. Sherman. Edwin Booth was elected the club's first president. He died there on June 7, 1893.

November 13, the anniversary of the birth of Edwin Booth, has been observed by The Players ever since 1893, when the group held a memorial service in the concert hall of Madison Square Garden on his birthday. Joseph Jefferson, who had succeeded Booth as president of the club, presided over the gathering, which had attracted thousands, and made a moving address on the personality and career of his lifelong friend. Other addresses were delivered by the actors Sir Henry Irving and Tommaso Salvini and the journalist Parke Godwin. The poet and critic George E. Woodberry read an elegy that he had written for the occasion, and the New York Symphony Orchestra, under the direction of Walter Damrosch, played Handel's *Dead March from Saul*, a selection that Booth had chosen for his performance of *Hamlet*.

The Players sponsored a Booth memorial window in the nearby Little Church Around the Corner, which was unveiled in June 1898. On November 13, 1918, the club erected a statue in Gramercy Park by Edmond T. Quinn depicting Booth in the role of Hamlet. The dedicatory service, during which Edwin Booth Grossman, Booth's grandson, unveiled the statue, was described in the *Evening Post* as an "unusual little ceremony, held in the exclusive, old park in the bleak November weather. . . . Great numbers of players, old ones to whom Booth is a personal memory, young ones to whom he is a professional tradition, filled the park benches which were drawn close about the statue, and stood in groups about the park." A few years later a bust was erected in New York's Hall of Fame for Great Americans in honor of the tragedian.

Each November 13 the president of The Players presides at a luncheon and introduces the guest of honor, who makes a brief informal address in keeping with the occasion. Following the speech, they gather in Gramercy Park, where the traditional wreath is placed at the foot of Booth's statue.

Feast of St. Frances Cabrini

Francesca Xaviera Cabrini, known as Mother Cabrini, was the first American citizen to be proclaimed a saint of the Roman Catholic church. Her feast, previously celebrated on the day of her death, December 22, is now observed on November 13, which was the day she was beatified in 1938. She was born on July 15, 1850, in the village of Sant'Angelo Lodigiano, in the Lombard region of northern Italy.

Although she was the 13th child of her pious parents, Francesca Maria, as she was christened, was only the 4th to survive; and she looked so fragile at birth that immediate baptism was advised. Her frail health was to be a lifelong burden, although it seemed more of an obstacle in the eyes of others than it did in hers.

Her father, called by friends and neighbors the Christian Tower because he was physically tall as well as a pillar of Christian virtue, read or told his children lives of holiness as exemplified by the saints, especially adventurous missionaries in foreign lands. Early in life, Francesca Cabrini decided that she wanted to go to China as a missionary nun when she grew up. At her confirmation, when she was seven, she took her name from the great Jesuit missionary St. Francis Xavier.

When she was old enough, Cabrini sought admission to a convent but was refused because of her poor health. Later, she again sought admission to two convents but was turned down by both. At 18 she had finished her education and earned the certification necessary for teaching. Following the death of her parents soon afterwards, she performed acts of charity in her native village and, when it suffered a smallpox epidemic, cared for the sick and dying until she herself fell ill with the disease.

She subsequently was offered a temporary teaching job in the nearby village of Vivardo, where she remained for two years. When the Vivardo pastor was transferred to the town of Codogno and found himself with a problem concerning an orphanage for girls, he sent for Cabrini. The dismal orphanage, unclean and located in the midst of tenements, factories, and open sewers, was being mismanaged by an ill-tempered, larcenous woman, who not only mishandled the funds but mistreated the girls. Young Cabrini was to spend six of the worst years of her life in this dreadful place, but later she would seek out the woman who had made her life burdensome and thank her for the experience as if it had been a gift. In the meantime, she worked to clean the filthy building and took loving care of the orphans, some not much younger than she was.

After three years she again asked permission to take religious vows, as did seven of her charges. On September 14, 1877, the eight took the religious vows of poverty, chastity, and obedience. She herself was appointed superior of the orphanage and became known as Mother Cabrini. With her fellow religious, she lived for three more miserable years at the orphanage, still plagued by the manager, who taunted and insulted them in coarse language. Finally, after Francesca Cabrini explained the situation as charitably as possible to the bishop of the region, he disbanded the orphanage and — knowing her dream to be a missionary — directed her to found a missionary order of sisters, since there was none in the area.

The order became a reality in 1880, when she founded the Missionary Sisters of the Sacred Heart and moved with her sisters in religion to an abandoned monastery in the Codogno countryside. Overjoyed as she was at this opportunity, Mother Cabrini could not abandon the orphans, whom she consequently took with her. The first house of her order accordingly became a combined orphanage and convent. Rescued from their cramped, unhealthy, and dilapidated former orphanage, the children had their fresh air, flowers, grass, and trees, and Mother Cabrini had her dream.

Within a year the building had to be enlarged to accommodate more orphans and more young women who wanted to join Mother Cabrini's missionary institute. Estimates from building contractors far exceeded the money she was allowed for the expansion, so Mother Cabrini bargained for lower prices. Then she and her nuns carefully watched the workmen as they plied their different trades. After the masons, for example, had left for the day, the nuns and students would mix mortar and lay bricks. They laughed and sang as they got sore muscles, but the building went up faster and more cheaply. Throughout her life thereafter, Mother Cabrini often donned workclothes and a large straw hat and took an active part in building or renovating many edifices.

This first school and orphanage in the Codogno motherhouse soon became known for its efficiency, high quality of teaching, and spiritual character. Requests came from other towns and cities for Mother Cabrini to found schools, orphanages, and branches of the motherhouse. By 1887 she had founded seven houses.

Then 37, she felt it was time to establish her missionary institute in Rome and seek papal consent to establish foreign missions. Her longtime adviser, Monsignor Antonio Serrati, discouraged her several times, but he could not deter her. On September 24, 1887, she and a sister-companion boarded a train for Rome. There they were again discouraged, this time by the cardinal-vicar, and advised to return home. Instead, Mother Cabrini simply remained in Rome and pressed her case with the cardinal-vicar whenever she could. Finally, on October 22, he asked her to start not one but two houses — a free school in Rome and a nursery in a suburb.

Five sisters came from the motherhouse in Codogno to help in this new enterprise, for which Mother Cabrini rented an unfurnished apartment on Rome's Via Nomentana. For a while the nuns slept on straw and ate from a makeshift table of boards and boxes. They begged and borrowed and hunted through junkshops for whatever they could not make themselves. With hammer and saw, paint and brush, they made a chapel of one of the rooms. Poor as they were, the impact they made as teachers and nuns was great. On March 12, 1888, Mother Cabrini received papal recognition and approval of her institute and the missionary work she had so long dreamed of doing.

One of the people who assumed an unexpected importance in Mother Cabrini's life was Giovanni Scalabrini, bishop of Piacenza, whom she had met when she opened a college in that city. He had taken as his special concern the cause of the impoverished Italians who were then emigrating en masse. After a visit to the United States, where he had seen the conditions under which they were living, he returned to Italy and founded the Pious Society of St. Charles (Borromeo) — a religious order often referred to as the Scalabrinian Fathers — to help Italian emigrants. Some of his priests had just opened a small church in the Italian section of New York City, and Bishop Scalabrini appealed to Mother Cabrini, saying, "The spiritual and social plight of our people in America is beyond belief.... America needs your Missionary Sisters of the Sacred Heart, for there are prodigious works of light to be done." Some months later he told her he had spoken with Archbishop Michael Corrigan of New York City, who wanted her to help with Italian orphans there.

It was her first offer of a foreign mission assignment, and it was in direct conflict with her lifelong resolve to devote herself to missionary work in China. She accordingly at first refused but was soon forced by circumstances to consider the question more seriously.

On the morning she was to have her long-awaited first private audience with Pope Leo XIII, Bishop Scalabrini met her en route with word he had received from Archbishop Corrigan — that an orphanage was waiting for her in New York. Thus confronted, she decided to place the question of what she should do before the pope.

Leo XIII was 78 and had been pope for 10 years before Mother Cabrini met him. His ideas for social reform, based on the dignity of labor and the dignity of the laborer, were well known. After speaking of her Missionary Sisters of the Sacred Heart and referring to her dream of work in China, he made her decision for her with these words:

The house and family of western civilization must first be put in order. . . . There are sad truths you will learn by seeing with your own eyes. . . . Hundreds of thousands of our Italian souls in America have become lost and battered sheep, isolated from Christ, understanding, and ordinary decency. . . . My Daughter, your field awaits you not in the East, but in the West. . . . Go to America. Plant there and cultivate the beautiful fruit of Christ!

On March 23, 1889, Mother Cabrini and six of her missionary sisters sailed from the French port of Le Havre, on a ship carrying 1,300 passengers. Of the 900 emigrants in steerage, 700 were Italian. During the voyage Mother Cabrini talked to many of them, and by the time the ship reached New York on March 31, she had some practical understanding of their hopes and severe problems.

When Mother Cabrini and her nuns landed, there was, strangely, no one to meet them. Although they knew little English, they found their way to the Scalabrinian rectory, where they were received cordially but with obvious surprise: the orphanage that supposedly awaited Mother Cabrini in New York had never materialized; and a letter from Archbishop Corrigan, instructing her to defer her trip, had not arrived in Italy before her departure.

He voiced his thoughts personally to her the next day:

It is a great pity you crossed the ocean for nothing. You cannot possibly know the complexity of prejudices and obstacles here that stand in the way of organized aid for Italian immigrants. It may be a long time before we are in a position to open an orphanage. The problem is too big for you. I see no other and better solution than for you to return to Italy. I'm sorry.

Mother Cabrini turned pale but listened respectfully. Then she firmly explained to the archbishop that she had come to America by order of the pope. "America is my ordained mission. . . Excellence, in all humbleness I must say, in America I stay." In the face of this determination, the archbishop smiled, arranged for lodgings for the nuns at a nearby convent and gave permission for them to start a small school for Italian children in the church run by the Scalabrinian Fathers.

By speaking with the Italian families who brought their children to the school and others who did not, Mother Cabrini saw, as the pope had foretold, the terrible plight then suffered by Italian emigrants in the United States. Many of these poor people — now burdened with the necessity of repaying the cost of their passage — had been enticed from their homes with the offer of a paradise by companies whose main aim was to exploit them as cheap labor. Their living and working conditions were appalling. Fre-

quently several families were crammed into sleeping quarters big enough for only one family, and plumbing facilities were nonexistent, faulty, or shared by an entire tenement building. Wages were poor and working conditions so dangerous that wives and children often became widows and orphans. Young children, another source of cheap labor, were mercilessly exploited.

Mother Cabrini became surer of her mission with each passing day. In three weeks she had rallied enough support to persuade the archbishop to allow her to open the orphanage she had come to open. On May 3, 1889, Archbishop Corrigan celebrated mass in the first American orphanage of the Missionary Sisters of the Sacred Heart. To support their undertaking, the sisters canvassed Italian families and shopkeepers, begging for clothes, furnishings, and food for their orphans. A newspaper report of May 1889 described

young ladies with radiant faces dressed in plain black religious hoods and robes . . . seen coursing the overcrowded streets of Little Italy. . . . These young nuns hardly speak English. The Directoress of their congregation is "Madre Francesca Cabrini," a diminutive, youthful lady with great eyes and an attractive smiling face. She does not know the English language, but she knows the universal language of the human spirit.

Although Mother Cabrini did learn English, she never lost either her Italian accent or her fluency in the "language of the . . . spirit." She went on to establish orphanages, schools, and hospitals in many cities in the United States; in other countries of North, Central, and South America; and in Europe, Australia, and the Middle East. More often than not, her plans seemed haphazard and impossible of completion to builders, real estate men, members of the church hierarchy and others. She replied to such doubts by echoing the words of St. Paul in Philippians 4:13 — "I can do all things in him who strengthens me."

People of diverse religions and national origins contributed generously to Mother Cabrini's many projects for teaching the young and caring for the sick and orphaned. The first hospital she founded in America, Columbus Hospital in New York City, was begun with 10 patients and a donation of $250 in 1891. Four years later, there was a new hospital with more than 100 beds, a full-time professional staff, and all the necessary modern equipment. Seven decades later the hospital was embarked on a new expansion program, to give it a capacity of more than 400 beds. By that time, the hospital was printing its instructions and patient schedules in Spanish and Chinese, as well as in English and Italian.

In every city in which she had established an orphanage, school, or hospital, Mother Cabrini and her sisters also visited prisoners. Sing Sing in New York State was the first prison they visited, and there they realized how much comfort they could bring to the prisoners, even those facing execution.

In Seattle, where she established another Columbus Hospital, Mother Cabrini became an American citizen in 1909. From 1889 to 1912, despite her poor health, she traveled hundreds of thousands of miles by ship, by train, and on foot, even crossing the Andes on muleback. For the last five years of her life, she confined her extensive travels to the United States. She was in Chicago, where she had started one school and two hospitals, when she died on December 22, 1917. In the 67 years of her life, she had established 67 houses in many parts of the world. She was canonized by Pope Pius XII on July 7, 1946.

A shrine to Mother Cabrini is in the National Shrine of the Immaculate Conception in Washington, D.C., and her image is on one of the bronze doors of St. Patrick's Cathedral in New York City. She is buried under the altar of the chapel at Mother Cabrini High School, at 701 Fort Washington Avenue in the Washington Heights area of New York City. The shrine is visited throughout the year. Cabrini Boulevard, also in that area, was named for her.

The feast day of St. Frances Xaviera Cabrini is commemorated with great devotion and joy, both there and at every establishment of the Missionary Sisters of the Sacred Heart.

NOVEMBER 14

First US Bishop Consecrated

A year after the signing of the peace treaty ending the American Revolution, Samuel Seabury was consecrated by Episcopalian bishops in Scotland, on November 14, 1784, as the first US bishop. Most of the congregations in the former American colonies that had been a part of the Church of England were by then calling themselves Protestant Episcopal, and in the following year they held an organizing convention for the newly forming Protestant Episcopal Church.

Seabury was born in North Groton, Connecticut, on November 30, 1729. His New World roots went back almost a century; one of his ancestors, John Seabury, was among the earliest American colonists, having arrived in Boston from England in 1639. Samuel Seabury spent most of his childhood in Connecticut, until in 1742 he and his family moved to Hempstead, Long Island, New York. The son of a minister of the same name, Seabury wanted to devote his life to the same work. His father supervised his early education.

When the junior Samuel Seabury was graduated from Yale College in 1748 with a bachelor of arts degree, he was too young to be ordained. He therefore studied theology and medicine under his father — who was also a physician — and served as a catechist in Huntington, Long Island. In 1752–1753 he completed his medical education at the University of Edinburgh in Scotland, and in London in December 1753 he was ordained a priest of the Church of England.

The Society for the Propagation of the Gospel named Seabury a missionary to New Brunswick, New Jersey, a post he took up on his return to America in 1754. Christ Church was his assigned parish. He was married to Mary Hicks of Staten Island, New York, in 1756. During the next 20 years he also, successively, served Grace Church in Jamaica, Long Island, and St. Peter's Church in an area of Westchester County, New York, that later became part of New York City's borough of the Bronx. Besides putting his medical training to good use, in Westchester he assumed the additional role of schoolmaster. In the early 1760s he was awarded master's degrees by King's College (now Columbia University) and Yale.

Very soon after returning to the colonies, Seabury had begun to involve himself in the developing civil and religious controversies between Great Britain and the American colonists. As a priest of the Church of England he was a faithful servant of the king. In addition, he believed firmly that the colonies would benefit most by remaining attached to Britain and using peaceful, legal means to seek resolution of their differences.

Seabury wrote newspaper articles and pamphlets, clearly and emphatically putting forth his views. An able defender of the monarch, he quickened his activities in behalf of the king as the rift between Britain and the colonies deepened. Four pamphlets he wrote during this later period bear the pseudonym A. W[estchester]. Farmer and are appropriately written in the language of an educated farmer rather than that of a clergyman. One of them aroused so much indignation that in Connecticut copies were tarred, feathered, and nailed to whipping posts; the tract was also publicly burned. Rebuttals to Seabury's pamphlets were written by Alexander

Hamilton, then an undergraduate at King's College and later one of the principal figures in the founding of the new republic.

When the first shots of the Revolution were fired, at Lexington and Concord in April 1775, Seabury and other Loyalists went into hiding. He soon emerged, despite that fact that he had publicly identified himself as a Tory leader. In November he was seized and imprisoned in New Haven, Connecticut, for about a month. Freed, he returned to Westchester, but after eight months he decided to seek safety on British-held Long Island.

His familiarity with Long Island and Westchester qualified Seabury to serve as a British army guide for those areas. He served also as chaplain to both the Provincial Hospital in New York and the King's American Regiment, and also as physician to the New York City Almshouse. As a result of the influence of Loyalist friends, at this time Seabury was granted the degree of doctor of divinity by Oxford University, in England. He and his family lived in New York City during most of the conflict, even after the Society for the Propagation of the Gospel in 1777 appointed him missionary to Staten Island (not then a part of New York City).

Despite the strength of his loyalty to Britain before and during the Revolution, after the conclusion of the war Seabury gave his full allegiance to the new country. Because in England church and state were bound together, the churches established in the 13 colonies now needed to organize themselves on a new, independent basis. While a part of the Church of England, they had been within the jurisdiction of the bishop of London.

On March 25, 1783, the Episcopal clergy of Connecticut, while meeting in Woodbury, elected Seabury their first bishop. In early June he sailed for England to request consecration by the English bishops. However, his allegiance to the United States and other points concerning church and state relationships proved to be large obstacles. Seabury waited in England for a year (having to himself bear all expenses), hoping that action permitting his consecration would be taken. Finally he appealed for consecration to the Scottish Episcopalian bishops, who themselves took no oath of allegiance to the monarch. They consented, and on November 14, 1784, Seabury was consecrated bishop in Aberdeen. A "free and valid episcopate," in Seabury's words, had been secured for the Episcopal church in America.

The following summer he returned to the United States, and from that time until his death he served as bishop of Connecticut (and, from 1790, of Rhode Island) and as rector of his father's old church, St. James' in New London, Connecticut.

Some dispute arose over the recognition of Seabury as a bishop, mainly because of the method of his consecration but partly because of his former Loyalist sympathies. But at the General Convention of 1789, at which the organization of the Protestant Episcopal Church was completed, he was formally recognized as a bishop. By that time an act of Parliament had made it possible for English bishops to consecrate (in 1787) two additional bishops for the United States. The English and Scottish branches of the Anglican Church were thus united in the American Church.

In line with an agreement made by Seabury with the Scottish bishops that he attempt to persuade the American Church to adopt the Scottish Communion office, he successfully proposed the inclusion in the Eucharistic office of an invocation of the Holy Spirit to sanctify and bless the elements. This change was included in the revised Book of Common Prayer, referred to as the American Prayer Book, adopted by the General Convention in 1789. Seabury's influence on the framing of the church's constitution was also great.

Seabury plunged into the work of building up the church. During the Revolution some clergymen with Loyalist leanings had returned to England, leaving their pastorates empty. Until Seabury's consecration, an American wishing to become a priest had to make a long and hazardous journey to England to be ordained. Within less than six months of taking up his duties in New London, Seabury had ordained 12 priests. In a historic ceremony, he joined with the three other American bishops on September 17, 1792, in performing the first consecration to take place in America.

A simple, humble man with strong faith, throughout his life Seabury had worked with great determination to expand the influence of the church. During his episcopate his efforts met with considerable success. Upon his death in New London on February 25, 1796, one of his six children, Charles Seabury, succeeded him as rector of St. James' Church. Samuel Seabury was buried in the public burying ground in New London, but his remains were later transferred to lie beneath the altar of St. James' Church.

Seabury's memory has been honored in many ways. The Glebe House in Woodbury, Connecticut, in which Seabury was nominated bishop by the Connecticut clergy, has been restored. It is considered an important shrine of the Protestant Episcopal Church and may be viewed. A plaque commemorating the historic consecration was placed by American and Scottish churchmen near the spot where the ceremony took place in Aberdeen. In addition, the Seabury-Western Seminary in Evanston, Illinois, was named for him, as were Seabury House, an Episcopal conference center in Greenwich, Connecticut; Seabury Press, the publishing arm of the church; and the Seabury Series, the official guides for Episcopal church schools.

The 150th anniversary of Seabury's consecration was marked with thanksgiving by the church in 1934. Actually, the diocese of Connecticut had begun the commemoration the previous year by marking (on March 25) the 150th anniversary of Seabury's election with a Communion service and, later in the day, a pageant in which the bishop of Connecticut and other clergymen took part.

Observances in 1934 began with an official welcome to the bishop of Aberdeen, a guest of honor, by a joint session of both houses of the General Convention on October 16. On the following Sunday, October 21, a Thanksgiving Eucharist for the gift of the episcopate to the American Church was celebrated in Atlantic City, New Jersey. Services similar to this one were held throughout the church on one of two Sundays, that preceding or that following November 14.

A number of special observances took place in New Haven, Connecticut. On the eve of the anniversary, November 13, a dinner in honor of the bishop of Aberdeen also included as speakers the bishop of Connecticut, the governor of Connecticut, and Samuel Seabury, a great-great-grandson of Bishop Samuel Seabury and an eminent lawyer and judge. The next morning a memorial Communion service was celebrated in New Haven's Trinity Church, as it was in Episcopal churches across the country. Following the New Haven service, the bishop of Aberdeen addressed a mass meeting in Yale University's Sprague Hall. A trip was made to the Glebe House in Woodbury in the afternoon.

In Providence, Rhode Island, a service of thanksgiving and commemoration was held in the Cathedral of St. John on Sunday, November 18.

Through the month of November the Sterling Library at Yale displayed Seabury memorabilia. Included in the exhibit were the original concordat between Seabury and the Scottish bishops, Seabury's miter, his original prayer book containing his handwritten notes about changes that he proposed and that were incorporated in the American Prayer Book, and correspondence, pictures, and drawings pertaining to his life and work.

NOVEMBER 15

Articles of Confederation Adopted

Even prior to the Declaration of Independence, the Founding Fathers, realizing that interregnum too often equated with anarchy, began to lay plans to establish a new governmental structure. Indeed, when Virginia's Richard Henry Lee first introduced his resolution for independence on June 7, 1776, he also suggested that "a plan of confederation be prepared and transmitted to the respective colonies for their consideration and approbation." The Second Continental Congress, meeting at Philadelphia, responded quickly to this proposal and on June 12 appointed a committee under John Dickinson's leadership to accomplish this task.

Formulating a system of government acceptable to the various colonies presented difficult problems. The colonies, diverse in their origins and circumstances, were reluctant to establish any form of government that would compromise their individual social traditions and economic interests. Most important, each province jealously guarded its political autonomy. Several attempts to centralize colonial administration had failed in the past: the short-lived Dominion of New England had ended with the Glorious Revolution in 1688, and as late as 1754 the provinces had rejected the Albany Plan of Union, devised by Benjamin Franklin to increase wartime security and flexibility.

The "Articles of Confederation and Perpetual Union," which Dickinson's committee presented to Congress on July 12, 1776, reflected the colonies' distrust of a strong central government. The plan vested power in a Congress in which every state would be represented according to population, restricted this legislature's authority to certain vital matters, and made no provision for a viable national executive. No legislation could be enacted without the agreement of 9 states, and the assent of 13 was required to amend the articles.

Direction of the American Revolutionary war effort commanded most of the Continental Congress's attention during the months that followed, and only intermittently did that body consider the proposed plan of confederation. These occasional debates did, however, produce one major change in the articles: on October 7, 1777, Congress provided that each state would have one vote in the legislature of the new government. The small states, which had objected to the original recommendation to apportion each state's representation according to its population, now found the proposed articles acceptable. On November 15, 1777, the Continental Congress formally adopted the frame of government and two days later sent the articles to the individual states for ratification.

The Articles of Confederation could not become operative without the unanimous approval of the 13 states, and by February 1779 all but one had given their consent. Maryland, the lone holdout, refused to ratify until the seven states whose colonial charters gave them claims to western lands agreed to transfer jurisdiction over those areas to the national government. As the spokesman for the six "landless" states, Maryland contended that the states' common war effort justified its demand that the unsettled territories be "considered as common property, subject to be parcelled by Congress into free, convenient, and independent governments." Two years passed without compromise, but finally, on January 2, 1781, the legislature of Virginia, "preferring the good of the country to every object of smaller importance," agreed to cede its western lands to the federal government. Within a month, New York and Connecticut followed the example. Although the other states did not surrender their western claims until later, these demonstrations of good faith persuaded Maryland to sign the articles on February 27, 1781.

Formal ratification of the Articles of Confederation occurred on March 1, 1781, as Philadelphia church bells tolled, and the *Ariel,* under the command of John Paul Jones, sounded a 21-gun salute. Although the articles proved within a few years to be inadequate to the needs of the new nation, necessitating the drafting of the present US Constitution (see June 21), the country's "first constitution" was an important step toward the permanent states.

NOVEMBER 16

Oklahoma Becomes a State

On November 16, 1907, President Theodore Roosevelt — appropriately using a quill pen fashioned from an eagle feather found in the Kiamichi Mountains of southeastern Oklahoma — signed the proclamation admitting Oklahoma into the Union as the 46th state. In 1921, 14 years later, November 16 was officially designated Oklahoma Statehood Day.

At first, the day seems to have been celebrated largely by local patriotic groups throughout the state. In 1927, however, the newly formed Oklahoma Memorial Association included among its objectives "To celebrate annually our natal day — November 16, as a memorial to statehood." On the 21st anniversary of statehood, in 1928, the association sponsored its first annual observance of the day. The ceremony in the capital of Oklahoma City featured a 1,000-pound birthday cake decorated with the state seal and scenes from Oklahoma's history; an oil derrick and 21 candles crowned the top tier. The first inductions into the Oklahoma Hall of Fame also marked the occasion. Ever since then, famous Oklahomans, chosen by the Oklahoma Memorial Association, have been received into the Hall of Fame at an elaborate statehood banquet in the capital.

Both the silver jubilee of statehood in 1932 and the golden anniversary in 1957 featured especially impressive banquets and parades. In 1957, the week of November 11 through 16 of each year was designated as Oklahoma Week by the Oklahoma legislature. Eight years later the legislature also stipulated that November 16 was to be observed in public schools throughout the state with any "program that is deemed fit to commemorate Oklahoma history and the achievements of the State of Oklahoma from a historical viewpoint." In 1968 the day was also designated official Oklahoma State Flag Day.

Statehood Day is occasionally observed even outside the boundaries of the state. In a colorful ceremony attended by Oklahoman officials and visitors, Washington Cathedral in Washington, D.C., pays annual tribute to Oklahoma on November 16, just as it honors various other states throughout the year. The royal blue state flag with its peace pipe and ceremonial drum, symbolic of Oklahoma's rich Native American heritage, is ceremoniously carried up the aisle of the nave to stand beside the Stars and Stripes at the top of the chancel steps.

The history of Oklahoma from the early days of its discovery to 20th century statehood is inextricably woven with the fate of the Native Americans who inhabited its territory. Oklahoma, fittingly enough, derives its name from the Choctaw words *okla,* "people," and *homma,* "red." Indians are known to have inhabited the area of the state long before recorded history. About A.D. 1200, a pre-Columbian Indian civilization, which closely resembled the highly developed Mayan culture of Mexico, flourished there. Apparently this region, a section of which has been described as a "cradle of civilization in North America," witnessed the rise and disintegration of several advanced cultures before the first Europeans arrived in the area.

In the early 1540s, Captain-General Francisco Vásquez de Coronado, at the head of a military expedition of 1,500 men, probably crossed what is now Oklahoma in his quest for the supposed riches of the mythical kingdom of Quivira. He found no gold, but before returning to Mexico City in 1542 he claimed the vast region he had traversed, including Oklahoma, for Spain. Shortly before his death that year, another Spanish explorer, Hernando de Soto, may have journeyed up the Arkansas River into Oklahoma. At the beginning of the next century, Juan de Oñate, having established the first settlement in the area of New Mexico, went off in search of Quivira and led a party across Oklahoma into Kansas.

Although other Spanish explorers and traders visited the area in the early 17th century, permanent settlement was not attempted. In fact, Spain lost its claim to the French, who, as a result of expeditions by Louis Joliet and Robert Cavelier, Sieur de La Salle, claimed all of the vast region called Louisiana in 1682. By the secret Treaty of Fontainebleau in 1762, the French ceded to Spain that part of Louisiana west of the Mississippi River. Within a half century, the Spanish returned this huge area to France in the secret treaty of San Ildefonso of 1800. On December 20, 1803, the United States gained possession of the region — including all of Oklahoma except the northwestern panhandle — in the Louisiana Purchase.

Oklahoma had been explored by various French traders and trappers, especially by the Chouteau family of St. Louis. In 1796 Major Jean Pierre Chouteau selected the site of Salina as a suitable location for his thriving trade with the Osage Indians (see October 10, Oklahoma Historical Day), thus establishing the first permanent white settlement in the state. But colonization was slow, and the land continued to belong to the scattered Plains tribes — the Osage, Kiowa, Comanche, Apache, and Wichita, among others. In the early 19th century, the wild unsettled region was unknown to most people save for a few travelers, traders, and official explorers, especially Stephen H. Long. In 1824 Colonel Matthew Arbuckle constructed Forts Towson and Gibson, the first military outposts in Oklahoma.

The Indian Territory was established by Congress in 1834 as the home for the Five Civilized Tribes: Choctaw, Chickasaw, Creek, Seminole, and Cherokee, all victims of white expansion in the eastern United States. The territory originally comprised all of Oklahoma, with the exception of the panhandle. In the 1830s and 1840s, some 5,000 Choctaws of Mississippi and Louisiana and 4,000 Chickasaws of Mississippi were removed to that eastern section of the Indian Territory that lay south of the Canadian and Arkansas rivers. Some 16,000 Cherokees from North and South Carolina, Georgia, Alabama, and Tennessee — about 4,000 of whom died of hardship on the march — were prodded along what is called the Trail of Tears to their new home in the Indian Territory. They settled the broad northern strip, except for a small block of land in the northeastern corner that had been set aside for the Quapaw Agency. Finally some 20,000 Creeks of Georgia and Alabama and 3,000 Seminoles of Florida were forced into the Indian Territory. They occupied the remaining middle section between the Cherokees on the one hand and the Choctaws and Chickasaws on the other.

Those Indians who settled the rolling wooded hills and prairies of the eastern part of the Indian Territory adapted well to the new conditions. Making great advances in agriculture, livestock breeding, flour milling, and handicrafts, the prosperous tribes were soon skillfully managing their own affairs. They each formed a separate "Indian republic," developing sophisticated political organizations. Only the Seminoles failed to draw up a written constitution and laws. The Cherokee Nation — possessors of a written language with an 85-character alphabet invented in about 1821 by their renowned leader Sequoyah — attained a particularly high cultural level. Sequoyah, who joined his people in the Indian Territory, saw knowledge of his alphabet spread throughout the Cherokee Nation. In addition, a newspaper appeared in both English and Cherokee.

Although the Five Civilized Tribes fought briefly with the Plains Indians, especially the Osages, they settled down peacefully to raise corn and cotton, often using slave labor. However, the Civil War proved to be a major disaster for the tribes, even though no large-scale conflict was waged on Indian Territory soil. The issue of slavery sharply divided the Five Tribes. Most of their members, as slaveholders of southern background, sided with the Confederacy, while the remainder clung to the Union. Minor but violent internal civil wars tore the Indian Territory asunder. Confederate General Stand Watie, a Cherokee, did not surrender to the Federals stationed at Fort Towson until June 23, 1865, thus gaining fame as the last rebel commander to put down arms.

Following the Civil War, the US government acted promptly to negotiate new treaties with the Five Civilized Tribes. Partly as punishment for southern supporters and partly on the grounds that the extensive tribal holdings should be shared with freed slaves and other Indian tribes, the original Indian Territory was divided. The Cherokees reluctantly granted the United States permission to assign what had approximately been the western half of their territory to new tribes. The Seminoles, Creeks, Choctaws, and Chickasaws concluded similar agreements.

From 1866 to 1883 the federal government

made a number of small grants from the vast new land. Displaced tribes such as the Delawares and Shawnees and nomadic Plains Indians such as the Osages, Kansas, Wichitas, Iowas, and Kickapoos were settled. Moreover, the US Army rounded up other Plains tribes — Comanches, Kiowas, Cheyennes, and Arapahoes — and gave them land in the southwestern quarter of Oklahoma. Of the portion of Indian Territory that had been ceded to the United States, there soon remained only one major unassigned land block. It was a choice area of approximately 2 million acres situated near the center of the Indian Territory. The unoccupied region came to be known as the Unassigned Lands, Oklahoma District, or Old Oklahoma.

As the great tide of westward expansion gained momentum after the Civil War, the Indian Territory, once thought worthless and best "given to the Indians," became attractive to settlers (see April 22, Oklahoma Day, and September 16, Cherokee Strip Day). The homesteading process, involving approximately 17 million acres, was completed at the beginning of the 20th century. The chaotic inpourings of settlers, besides pushing the Indians into ever-diminishing tribal lands, also caused grave disruptions in the traditional tribal ways of life.

In 1890 Oklahoma Territory was created out of that part of the Indian Territory situated south of the Cherokee Outlet and west of the eastern area still occupied by the Five Civilized Tribes. It also included the panhandle, the 34-mile-wide and 167-mile-long strip taken from Texas in 1850, which had since then remained outside the boundaries of any legally constituted state or territory. Much to Congress's embarrassment, it had simply been overlooked. Known as No Man's Land or Public Land Strip on maps, it had attracted some squatters and many outlaws. Its residents had even attempted to seek independent statehood for the area — larger than Connecticut — under the name Cimarron Territory.

During the 17 years between 1890 and statehood, Oklahoma Territory expanded rapidly. Eventually it included all lands acquired by the United States after the Civil War and ceded to the various Indian tribes from 1866 to 1883. In the southwest corner of the area, Greer County, claimed by Texas, was appended to Oklahoma Territory by a US Supreme Court decision.

The lands of the Five Civilized Tribes in the eastern part of what is now Oklahoma were called the Indian Territory, although this obviously was a much smaller region than what was designated as Indian Territory in 1834. The Five Civilized Tribes were allowed to live there under their own governments, provided they re-

tained their tribal structure. But the numerous whites who had penetrated the area demanded the abolishment of both the tribal governmental structure and the tribal landholding system. In 1893 the US Congress appointed the Dawes Commission to persuade the five tribes to accept the dissolution of their tribal government in favor of government from Washington and to implement the policy of breaking up the tribal lands into individual tracts. Although the Indians naturally condemned such actions, the policies were enforced. Reservation land remaining after the allotment was sold to white settlers. Of the 30 million acres that had originally been granted the Indians in 1834, less than 2 million were in Indian hands on the eve of statehood.

A bid for statehood began as early as 1891 in Oklahoma Territory, with frequent conventions being held in successive years in Oklahoma City, El Reno, Purcell, Kingfisher, Shawnee, and finally Guthrie. In Indian Territory, agitation for statehood started on a large scale only in 1905. After the tribal land divisions had been implemented and Indian "assimilation" hastened, Congress enpowered the "twin territories" to apply for admission to the Union as a single state. Two Osage delegates and 55 from each of the two territories formulated the constitution at the convention that met at Guthrie on November 20, 1906. The document was completed on April 22, 1907, and its approval was voted by the people of the region on September 17. On November 16, 1907, Oklahoma, with a population of 1.5 million, became the 46th state. On the first "statehood day," Charles N. Haskell was duly inaugurated first governor at Guthrie, the new state capital. The event had been preceded by the symbolic wedding of the Oklahoma and Indian territories. A woman of Cherokee descent played the "bride," Miss Indian Territory, while an Oklahoma City businessman represented "Mr. Oklahoma."

The state of Oklahoma prospered, continuing its rapid transition from tents and tepees to flourishing towns, towering oil wells, and productive farms and ranches. Oklahoma's rich Indian heritage, however, is perhaps the state's greatest asset. Today over 98,000 Indians from about 60 tribes embracing every walk of life live within its boundaries. Numerous Indian monuments remind the visitor to the state of its unique background. At Sallisaw, for example, Sequoyah's one-room log cabin erected about 1829 has been preserved by the state. Tsa-La-Gi — south of Tahlequah, which became the capital of the Cherokee Nation in 1839 — is a recreated 18th century Cherokee village welcoming visitors. In addition to basket-making demonstrations, ceremonial dances, and games, the dramatic story of the Cherokees, entitled *The Trail of Tears*, is presented there each summer by the Cherokee National Historical Society.

NOVEMBER 17

Congress Finds a Permanent Home

Before its first session at the Capitol, in Washington, D.C., on November 17, 1800, Congress — like its predecessors during the Revolutionary period — met in a number of locations.

America in 1774 was comprised of 13 mainland colonies and approximately 2.5 million people. Only five percent of the population lived in communities of more than 2,000 residents, but these urban areas greatly influenced politics, commerce, and intellectual life. Philadelphia, with 28,000 residents, was America's foremost city, having surpassed Boston during the course of the 18th century. New York City ranked second.

Politics and practicality made Philadelphia the first capital of the United Colonies. Britain's imposition of the what came to be known as the Intolerable Acts on Massachusetts as a punishment for the Boston Tea Party of December 16, 1773, prompted Bay Colony legislators to seek stringent economic sanctions against Britain. More moderate patriot leaders instead sought to contain the radicals and called a Continental Congress (see September 5) to develop an appropriate American response. They chose Philadelphia to be the site of their gathering, as it was both geographically and politically located in the center. Furthermore, Philadelphia, unlike New York and Boston, was free from garrisons of English troops.

Twelve colonies sent 56 representatives to the First Continental Congress; only Georgia sent no delegate. Joseph Galloway, the conservative speaker of the Pennsylvania assembly, suggested that colony's statehouse as a meeting chamber, but the convention members accepted instead the carpenters' offer of their own building. They foresaw this decision as "highly agreeable to the mechanics and citizens in general." The First Continental Congress accordingly met at Carpenters' Hall from September 5 to October 26, 1774, having resolved to reconvene on May 10, 1775, if British harassment continued.

Meanwhile, what was to develop into the American Revolution had commenced. It began with bloody encounters between American militiamen and British regulars at Lexington and Concord, Massachusetts, on April 19, 1775. In the face of the worsened situation, the colonies held fast to their intention to meet again. The Second Continental Congress convened on May 10, 1775, as planned. This time it held its sessions in the Pennsylvania State House, now known as Independence Hall. Over one year later, on July 4, 1776, in the same hall, the delegates voted to accept Thomas Jefferson's Declaration of Independence, which officially renounced America's allegiance to Great Britain.

Military weakness threatened to invalidate American claims to independence. General Sir William Howe's troops occupied New York City on September 15, 1776, and by November George Washington's men were in flight across New Jersey. On December 11 the British chased the rebels into Pennsylvania, and Congress on December 12 decided to abandon its hazardous position in Philadelphia. In the following months Henry Fite's three-story brick house in Baltimore, Maryland, served as Congress's home.

However, American forces soon scored surprise victories in New Jersey — at Trenton on December 26, 1776, and at Princeton on January 3, 1777. The successes secured that colony for the patriots and bolstered morale in neighboring Pennsylvania. Congress soon left its Baltimore refuge and returned to Philadelphia on March 4.

In the summer of 1777, however, General Howe sailed with 15,000 men against Philadelphia. Congress kept diligently at its work as long as possible but on September 19 again fled the city. The representatives met on September 27 in Lancaster, Pennsylvania, and the next day moved on to York, Pennsylvania, where they convened on September 30. Howe, meanwhile, captured Philadelphia on September 26. The rebel legislators endured their exile until the British evacuated the city in June 1778; then, on July 2 of that year, they returned to Philadelphia.

Congress remained at Philadelphia for the remainder of the Revolution. Later, a demonstration by 300 American soldiers seeking redress of various grievances prompted the body to remove to Princeton, New Jersey, on June 24, 1783. While there, Congress met in the faculty room of Princeton College, in Nassau Hall, which is still standing. Under a plan requiring alternate sessions in Annapolis and Trenton, the legislature adjourned on November 3, 1783, to go to Maryland. The delegates met in Annapolis from November 26, 1783, to June 3, 1784, and at Trenton from November 1 to December 2, 1784. New York City was the final seat of the Congress meeting under the Articles of Confederation, with sessions held there from January 11, 1785, to March 2, 1789.

The Constitutional Convention, held at Philadelphia in the summer of 1787 (see May 25), devised a new frame of government under which elections were held in late 1788. On March 4, 1789, the new Congress convened in New York City, but it did not obtain a quorum until April. Both the Senate and House of Representatives met at Federal Hall at the intersection of Wall and Broad streets in lower Manhattan. The building had long served as the New York city hall, but the French architect Pierre Charles L'Enfant refurbished it at a cost of $50,000 to suit the needs of its new tenants.

Political exigencies soon had the peripatetic Congress on the move again. On January 14, 1790, Secretary of the Treasury Alexander Hamilton delivered his "First Report on the Public Credit," in which he advocated that the federal government take the responsibility for $21.5 million of debts incurred by the states during the Revolution. Hamilton believed the assumption of debts would increase world confidence in the United States and would also strengthen the central government by connecting its well-being with that of the businessmen who held most of the public debt.

Southerners, fearful of national encroachment on state powers, effectively blocked the assumption plan, which Hamilton saw as vital to the American economy. He finally won the support of Secretary of State Thomas Jefferson and Representative James Madison, the Virginians who led the opposition, by agreeing to have the national capital relocated to a more southern area. On July 10, 1790, the House of Representatives authorized the President to pick a 10-mile-square district, within a 105-mile stretch on the Potomac River's banks, to be the site. Philadelphia would serve as the interim capital until 1800.

On December 6, 1790, Congress accordingly began a decade's tenure in Philadelphia, meeting at the county courthouse at Sixth and Chestnut streets, just west of the Pennsylvania State House. The representatives met on the first floor of the building and the senators on the second. The structure, donated by the state for the use of the legislature, became known as Congress Hall. Pennsylvania also built a President's House on Ninth Street between Elm and Chestnut streets, in which the Chief Executive resided. The commonwealth hoped, in vain, that its generosity would persuade the federal government to remain in Philadelphia.

President George Washington spent two weeks in October 1790 inspecting possible locations for the nation's capital along the Potomac River. He finally chose a spot on the east bank, as far south as the congressional mandate allowed. The site included land in both Maryland and Virginia, but the city was to be autonomous.

The government then bought the property from its owners for $66.50 an acre, which was five times the market value.

Three commissioners, including Associate Supreme Court Justice Thomas Johnson of Maryland, supervised the development of the capital, which, they made known in 1791, would bear the name of Washington. Major Pierre Charles L'Enfant designed the city by imposing a series of avenues radiating from circles on a grid of numbered and lettered streets. Thomas Jefferson selected the locations for the Capitol, the seat of the Congress, and for the White House.

The layout of Washington reflects the plan for a government of separate, balanced branches, which the early national leaders envisioned. No one location dominates the city; three centers, assigned respectively to the President, Congress, and the Supreme Court, vie for attention. Networks of avenues radiate from both the White House and the Capitol, thus providing the executive and legislature with equal access to the nation. A single broad avenue, symbolic of the formal communication between separate entities, joins the two sites. The Supreme Court, originally located in the Capitol with the two houses of Congress, now stands properly aloof, connected directly with neither of its coordinate branches.

Some extreme Antifederalists had fearfully envisioned a powerful central government, ensconced in a fortress capital and sending forth armies to prey on the countryside. On the contrary, Washington was a servant city. Its centers were easily accessible by wide avenues, and the seat of government was militarily indefensible. The plans for the capital did not even provide room for large-scale economic development; the community was dependent on the nation for its sustenance.

Congress met in Washington for the first time on November 17, 1800. In the same year, John Adams moved into the White House. The capital had an appropriate frontier quality: President Adams swam in the Potomac before breakfast, and his wife, Abigail, dried the family laundry in the East Room. On March 1, 1801, Thomas Jefferson became the first Chief Executive to be inaugurated in the new city.

The Capitol is an impressive example of early American governmental architecture. The 432-room structure, which covers three and a half acres, is 751 feet long, 350 feet wide, and 287 feet high. Thomas Crawford's bronze statue of Freedom, erected to the accompaniment of a 35-gun salute on December 3, 1863, surmounts the Capitol dome.

As a winner of a competition held for that purpose in 1792, William Thornton, a physician and self-taught architect, was selected by President Washington to design the Capitol, notwithstanding the fact that his entry arrived months after the competition had closed. Thornton shares the credit with French architect Étienne Hallet (also known as Stephen Hallette) for the basic conception of a central dome flanked by north and south wings. Retained to supervise the execution and revision of Thornton's plans, Hallet sought to introduce changes and was dismissed in 1794. President Washington himself had meanwhile laid the cornerstone in 1793, and construction proceeded under various hands for years. The architect Benjamin H. Latrobe, working from 1803 to 1817, modified the original plans, making them more practical, although not without protest from Thornton. Charles Bulfinch, who succeeded Latrobe in 1817, completed the structure in 1830. Thornton died in 1828, before the Capitol was completed.

The north wing, the first one finished, originally served as quarters for the House of Representatives, the Senate, and the Supreme Court. In 1807 the House moved to the new south wing, leaving the north section to the Senate. A wooden walkway joined the two wings. British soldiers burned the Capitol, the White House, and other Washington buildings on August 24, 1814, during the War of 1812. Men quickly went to work to reconstruct the Capitol, and by December 1819 it was again ready for occupancy, with its north and south wings restored. The central portion of the Capitol, which Bulfinch had begun in 1818, included the east and west fronts and central rotunda. Topped with a copper-covered wooden dome, the rotunda was virtually completed by 1824.

In 1849 Congress authorized plans for vastly extending the north and south wings and adding a new, massive dome to match the building's new proportions. Thomas Walter's blueprint avoided the cost of raising the level of Capitol Hill on the south and west by placing the new additions — now containing the House and Senate chambers — at right angles to the original wings and erecting the dome off-center, almost over the eastern portico. The new legislative chambers were essentially completed by 1859. Construction on the 4,500-ton cast- and wrought-iron dome began in 1855 and continued until completion in 1863.

The Capitol then remained undisturbed until 1959, when the east front was moved forward 32 feet to provide greater architectural balance. The new exterior is an exact replica of the old, which now forms an interior wall. The renovation, completed in 1961, also provided space for 75 extra offices.

The chamber of the House of Representatives in the Capitol's south wing measures 93 feet by 139 feet and is the largest legislative hall in the world. Since 1823, portraits of Washington and Lafayette have flanked the rostrum. Medallions located around the room honor men who have made significant contributions in the history of law. The Senate chamber in the north wing of the Capitol retains 45 desks dating from 1839. Busts of the first 20 Vice Presidents rest in niches around the walls.

The original House of Representatives, south of the Capitol's central Rotunda, is now known as Statuary Hall and contains figures of eminent men and women from every state. A bronze plaque marks the spot where John Quincy Adams, who returned to Congress after his presidency, collapsed and died. The old Senate Chamber, north of the Rotunda, served as the quarters of the upper house until 1859 and then of the Supreme Court until that body obtained its own building in 1935. The Capitol is open to the public.

Several Philadelphia buildings that served as headquarters for branches of the federal government stand in Independence National Historical Park. The site, which is administered by the National Park Service, contains 21.84 acres, 16.13 of which are federal property. Independence Hall, in which the Second Continental Congress met and signed the Declaration of Independence, is in the heart of the park. Congress Hall, in which the national legislature convened from 1790 to 1800, and the old Philadelphia City Hall, which housed the First US Supreme Court and the First Bank of the United States, are also located in the park, as is the attractive and compact Carpenters' Hall, in which the First Continental Congress met.

In New York City, the Federal Hall National Memorial Building at Wall and Broad streets stands on the site of the old Federal Hall, which housed the Continental Congress from 1785 to 1789 and the US Congress in 1789 and 1790. Built in 1842 in Greek Revival style, the structure was built as a customhouse. Later it served as a federal Sub-Treasury, and it housed other federal departments in the interval between. It was designated a national historic site on May 26, 1939. John Quincy Adams Ward's statue of George Washington, which rests on the steps leading to the building's Wall Street entrance, commemorates the Virginian's inauguration as the nation's first President. That momentous event took place on a balcony of the old Federal Hall — not in March 1789 as intended but, because of Congress's difficulty in securing a quorum, on April 30, 1789.

Anne Hutchinson Banished

The founders of Massachusetts Bay Colony were convinced of the necessity of establishing a model society — or, in John Winthrop's words, "A City upon the Hill" — that would serve as a symbol of righteousness to a decadent world. Theological ideals would not remain vague abstractions in the colony envisioned by the Puritan leadership, but would be the very basis of the social order. In 1630 the Massachusetts Bay colonists arrived in New England, determined to make their dream a reality; within seven years, two later arrivals, Roger Williams and Anne Marbury Hutchinson, had jeopardized the very existence of the "community of saints."

Dissent had no place in a colony convinced of its own rectitude and struggling to make its religious beliefs the foundation of its governmental system. In 1636 Roger Williams so disrupted Massachusetts Bay with his unorthodox teachings that the Puritan leadership banished him to Rhode Island. The following year Anne Hutchinson, the wife of William Hutchinson, a wealthy merchant, and the mother of 14 children, posed another serious threat.

A great admirer of John Cotton, Hutchinson with her family had followed that great Puritan divine to New England in 1634. Born in Alford (Lincolnshire), England in 1591, Anne Hutchinson was a woman of keen intellect. Shortly after her arrival she began to hold weekly meetings in her home during which she discussed and explained Cotton's sermons of the previous Sunday. Before long these sessions also gave her an opportunity to air her own theological opinions. Her most serious deviations from Puritan orthodoxy were her insistence that "works," or outward behavior, were not an indication of personal salvation and her claim that every convert came to know the will of God through direct personal revelation. The leaders of the Puritan colony felt that such tenets, taken to their logical conclusions, jeopardized their "errand into the wilderness" by justifying activities detrimental to the social order and by deemphasizing the role of the ministry. They immediately acted to eliminate the threat to their community.

The first efforts against Anne Hutchinson were circumspect, for her followers, the Antinomians, numbered among their ranks such influential personages as Sir Henry Vane, the governor of the colony, and the Reverend John Wheelwright, a leading Boston minister and the brother-in-law of Anne Hutchinson. In January 1637 the Massachusetts General Court found Wheelwright guilty of sedition and contempt, but it delayed his sentencing pending the outcome of the 1637 gubernatorial election. To improve the chances of an anti-Hutchinson victory, her opponents had moved the site of the balloting from pro-Antinomian Boston to Newtown (now Cambridge). This stratagem was a success. On May 27, 1637, the freemen elected John Winthrop to succeed Henry Vane.

With the anti-Hutchinsonians in control of the colony's government, action against the Antinomians intensified. The definition of Puritan orthodoxy formulated by the synod of 25 ministers at Newtown on August 30 left no doubt that Hutchinson's teachings were heretical. On November 12 the General Court banished Wheelwright from the colony and ordered his sister-in-law to stand trial on similar charges of sedition and contempt.

In the earlier stages of her trial it seemed that Anne Hutchinson would be able to outwit her adversaries, but in the final days of the proceedings, her insistence that she had direct personal revelation from God clinched the government's case against her. On November 17 the General Court ordered her banished.

Because of the harsh New England winter, Hutchinson was allowed to remain in the colony until spring. In March 1638, however, she was excommunicated in an ecclesiastical trial after she refused to recant. Soon after, she departed from Massachusetts.

The Hutchinson family and many other Antinomians sought refuge in Roger Williams's settlement in Rhode Island and on March 7, 1638, founded Pocasset (now Portsmouth). After her husband's death in 1642 Anne Hutchinson moved to New York — first to Long Island and later to the area of what is now New Rochelle. Sometime in either August or September 1643 the religious leader and all her family except one daughter were killed by Indians.

NOVEMBER 18

Asa Gray's Birthday

Asa Gray, America's leading botanist and taxonomist and a great popularizer of botany in the United States, was born on November 18, 1810, at Sauquoit in Oneida County, New York, to Moses Gray, a tanner and prosperous farmer, and Roxana Howard Gray. He was the oldest of eight children and attended school in Clinton, nine miles away.

Asa Gray's first training in science came from James Hadley, a professor of chemistry and *materia medica*, in 1825–1826. Two years afterwards, he was drawn to an article on botany in Brewster's *Edinburgh Encyclopaedia* and bought a botany handbook of his own, which he studied through the winter. That spring, at the age of 17, he first began collecting and identifying plants. In 1831 Gray was graduated from the Fairfield (New York) Medical School as a medical doctor, but he never practiced medicine. Beyond this point, he was self-educated in science or educated by senior colleagues. He delivered lectures on botany at the medical school the summer after graduating and from 1832 to 1835 taught science at Bartlett's High School at Utica, New York.

By correspondence he came to know John Torrey, a New York City physician who was a distinguished botanist and mineralogist then engaged in pioneer work discovering, studying, and systematizing plants of North America. In particular, Torrey was classifying and publishing reports on plant specimens forwarded by a series of western exploratory expeditions sponsored by the US government. During summers and on leave from his post in 1835, Gray served as Torrey's companion on several botanical field trips and as his assistant in New York City.

In 1836 Torrey secured for Gray the position of curator of the New York Lyceum of Natural History (which in 1876 became the New York Academy of Sciences). Between 1838 and 1843, Torrey and Gray collaborated on the epoch-making *Flora of North America* — a work in which Gray helped revise Linnaeus's procedure for classifying plants in favor of a more elegant classification, based chiefly on fruit anatomy instead of gross morphology, such as similarity of leaf shapes. Torrey and Gray's system continues in use, although, increasingly in the 20th century, genetic evidence of evolutionary development has supplied the definitive indicators of plant relationships.

In 1836 Gray published his *Elements of Botany*, the first of a distinguished series of botany textbooks that helped to popularize the study of botany in the United States. His *Botanical Text-Book for Colleges, Schools and Private Students* followed in 1842. Renamed *Structural Botany* in the sixth edition (1879) after much development and revision, this work is still of value. Gray's other publications include *First Lessons in Botany and Vegetable Physiology* (1857); *How Plants Grow* (1858); *Field, Forest and Garden Botany* (1869); *How Plants Behave* (1872); and a second *Elements of Botany* (1887).

Gray accepted the professorship of botany at the newly founded University of Michigan in 1838 and went to Europe to purchase books for the new school. While there he also pursued his botanical studies, visiting Switzerland, Austria, Bavaria, Italy, France, and England and forming lifelong friendships with European botanists. He never actually took up his duties at Michigan, because he was appointed Fisher Professor of Natural History at Harvard in 1842, a chair he held for 46 years. Gray rapidly made Harvard the nation's center of botanical investigations, creating the department of botany and training many who were to become outstanding botanists. Through wide exchanges he established an herbarium that developed into the largest and most valuable in the country, later named the Gray Herbarium in his honor. He also founded a botany library and replanned the small garden that was already there.

In 1848, the same year in which the Swiss naturalist Louis Agassiz became a colleague at Harvard, Asa Gray married Jane Lathrop Loring. The Grays' home in the Harvard Botanical Garden became a meeting place for botanists from all over the United States and from Europe. There colleagues came to seek advice about classifying plants. Gray's efforts toward systemizing the flora of North America had put him at the head of American botanists and in the company of the world's most eminent naturalists.

His most important work, *Manual of the Botany of the Northern United States*, first appeared in 1848 and through many revisions remained the most popular manual among American botanists. The eighth (centennial) edition (1950), largely rewritten and expanded by M. L. Fernald and others, and entitled *Gray's Manual of Botany*, continues to be the standard reference work for the flora of the United States east of the Rockies. Asa Gray also contributed many book reviews, notes, and short biographies to the *American Journal of Science*. Valuable treatises are included among these articles, and the whole amounts to a fine history of botany over 50 years. Gray's clear, graceful, and precise style did much to extend his influence.

In the field of plant geography Gray was both a pioneer and a masterly synthesizer. His monograph of 1859 on the botany of Japan was of far-reaching importance and contributed significantly to Gray's world reputation. The elaboration of the descriptive botany of North America, however, was Gray's consummate and most sustained achievement. The crowning work in this endeavor, along with the *Manual of Botany*, was the *Synoptical Flora of North America* (1878). Two other signal volumes were his contributions to the *United States Exploring Expeditions during the Years 1838–42*, volume XV (1854–1857) and volume XVII (1874).

In America, Gray was an early and constant supporter of Charles Darwin's theory of the evolution of species by natural selection. Darwin first outlined his theory to Asa Gray in a celebrated letter of September 5, 1857, and sent him one of the three advance copies of the *Origin of Species*. For years afterwards, they corresponded, as Gray's *Darwiniana* (1876) testifies. While remaining a theist who subscribed to the Nicene Creed (which he cited as his own definition of his Christianity), Gray openly announced his belief that existing species, including humans, derived from previous species, rather than being special creations of God. But although he defended Darwin's theory against those who insisted that it was contrary to the teachings of the Bible, Gray did not follow certain contemporaries in making Darwinism a substitute religion. He remained a critic as well as an advocate of the theory of natural selection and formed conclusions about plant variations that pointed toward Gregor Mendel's and Hugo De Vries's later discoveries in plant genetics.

Asa Gray was very active in the scientific organizations of his day, some of which are still highly influential. He helped found the National Academy of Sciences in 1863 "to investigate, examine, experiment and report upon any subject of science or art desired by any department of [the US] Government." He was president of the American Academy of Arts and Sciences for the decade from 1863 to 1873, and in 1872 he was also president of the American Association for the Advancement of Science. From 1874 until his death in 1888, Asa Gray was one of the 14 regents of the Smithsonian Institution in Washington, D.C. He was also a member of the Royal Society of London and received honorary degrees from Oxford, Cambridge, and Aberdeen universities. Many humbler scientific groups also counted Gray a member.

An admirer among contemporary western explorers named Grays Peak, rising 14,270 feet on the line between Clear Creek and Summit counties, Colorado, on the Continental Divide, in Asa Gray's honor. Graymount (or Graymont), a town near its foot, was a significant mining center and later a popular resort. Today it is defunct, but visitors still go to the area below Grays Peak to the Arapahoe Basin, a winter sports area some 70 miles west of Denver.

Gray died at the age of 77 in Cambridge, Massachusetts, on January 30, 1888, and was buried in Mount Auburn Cemetery. Twelve years later he was elected to the Hall of Fame for Great Americans. Visible in the bronze bust of Gray, which was unveiled at the Hall of Fame in New York City on May 21, 1925, are the simplicity, friendliness, and gentle humor that made the great scientist and teacher so beloved.

NOVEMBER 19

James A. Garfield's Birthday

James Abram Garfield, the 20th President of the United States — the last to be born in a log cabin and the second to be assassinated — was born on November 19, 1831, in the tiny frontier community of Orange, Cuyahoga County, Ohio. The youngest of five children, he was the son of a farmer, Abram Garfield, who was 33 years old when he died in 1833, leaving his family in poverty. Eliza Ballou Garfield, the future President's mother, managed through great perseverance to rear and educate her children.

By the time he was midway through his teens, James Garfield had determined to acquire a college education. In view of his continuing struggle with poverty, the resolve necessitated his combining his studies with hard work. He held a number of jobs — as a teacher, a carpenter, and a farmer — and attended the Western Reserve Eclectic Institute (subsequently known as Hiram College) in Hiram, Ohio. He later entered Williams College in Williamstown, Massachusetts, from which he was graduated in 1856. Upon graduation he returned to the institute, where he taught ancient languages and literature. Within a year he had risen to become president of the institute. At about this time, Garfield became a lay speaker for the Disciples of Christ, and in 1858 he was married to a childhood friend and former fellow student, Lucretia Rudolph.

Entering politics during this same period, Garfield supported the Free-Soil movement and was drawn to the new Republican party. Having shown himself an effective speaker against slavery in 1857 and 1858 — he later would be known as a brilliant orator — he successfully ran for a seat in the Ohio state senate in 1859 on the Republican ticket. He meanwhile had learned enough law to be admitted to the bar.

With the outbreak of the Civil War in 1861, Garfield used his powers of persuasion to recruit a regiment — the 42nd Ohio Volunteer Infantry — composed largely of his former pupils. He himself became its lieutenant colonel and then colonel. Although without military training, but adept at grasping from manuals the principles of drilling and the responsibilities of various military assignments, Garfield readied his troops for combat. He led his men against Confederate forces at Middle Creek in Kentucky. As a result of his victory, he was raised to the rank of brigadier general of volunteers, one of the youngest Union officers to achieve such rank. In Tennessee he took part in the fighting at Shiloh in April 1862, and in September 1863 he served creditably at Chickamauga as chief of staff under General William S. Rosecrans in the Army of the Cumberland. Although rewarded with a promotion to major general of volunteers, Garfield resigned his commission to serve in the US House of Representatives, to which he had been elected in 1862. He took his seat in Congress in December 1863.

The studious and hardworking Garfield, of commanding height, powerful in debate, and an accomplished parliamentarian, won reelection eight times in succession, serving in the House of Representatives a total of 18 years. His rise within Congress was steady. At first serving on the committee on military affairs because of his battlefield experience, Garfield later became an expert on fiscal affairs and was a member of both the Committee on Appropriations and the Committee on Ways and Means. Although usually a supporter of Republican policies, his backing of the protective tariff was at best lukewarm — too lukewarm to suit some of his manufacturer constituents in the industrially burgeoning state of Ohio. He showed his independence in a different way when enthusiasm for the issuance of inflationary, nonredeemable greenbacks flooded the region of the Old Northwest, overlooking his Ohio constituents' preference and supporting the Republican sound-money policy, which called for a resumption of specie payments.

Garfield's most difficult campaign for reelection to Congress came in 1874, when attempts were made to link him with two possible conflict-of-interest situations. One of these was the Crédit Mobilier scandal, in which some potentially influential members of congress received "gifts" of stocks; however, the charges that Garfield had benefited similarly were vague and were never proved. Garfield's defense of himself overcame the suggestion of scandal. His career continued its upward course with his reelection. By this time he had become one of the leading Republicans in the House of Representatives; by 1876, when he became the minority leader of that body, he was without rival as the leading House Republican.

Garfield played a central role during the disputed presidential election of 1876. He served as a "visiting statesman" to oversee the vote count in Louisiana, one of four crucial states that had sent in two conflicting sets of election returns; and he was instrumental in working out the compromise legislation passed by Congress on January 29, 1877, establishing a bipartisan electoral commission to check disputed state returns. To that point, the choice of a President had hovered inconclusively — depending on which way the disputed electoral votes were counted — between the two principal contenders, Republican Rutherford B. Hayes and Democrat Samuel J. Tilden. Garfield served on the commission as one of the two House Republicans and voted with the majority in favor of Hayes, who was named President.

In 1880 the Ohio legislature elected Garfield to the US Senate, but he was destined never to serve in that post. At the Republican National Convention that year, delegates became deadlocked between the presidential choices of two factions of the party — the powerful James G. Blaine, leader of the so-called Half-Breeds, and former President Ulysses S. Grant, favored by the Stalwarts. On the 36th ballot the convention swung behind Garfield, who had been the manager for the candidacy of Ohio's John Sherman (brother of Union General William Tecumseh Sherman). To placate the party's Stalwart faction, Chester A. Arthur was chosen to contend for the vice presidency as Garfield's running mate. In organizing his campaign and later, however, Garfield found that even Arthur's placement on the ticket had not satisfied the Stalwarts. The popular vote was extremely close, Garfield being elected by a plurality of less than 10,000 votes over his Democratic rival, Winfield Scott Hancock. In the electoral college, Garfield received 214 votes, and Hancock 155.

After his inauguration — during a heavy snowstorm — on March 4, 1881, Garfield began to make appointments designed to conciliate every section of the Republican party. But Senator Roscoe Conkling of New York, the leader of the Stalwart forces, still was unhappy. Garfield won his fight for independence in presidential appointments, and Conkling resigned his Senate seat.

Before Garfield was able to devote his full attention to affairs of state, he was struck down by an assassin. En route to his 25th class reunion at Williams on July 2, 1881, he was on his way to his train at the old Baltimore and Potomac Railway Depot in Washington when he was shot by Charles J. Guiteau, a disappointed office seeker and Stalwart supporter (see July 2). Guiteau said that he shot Garfield to make Arthur President. After he was shot, Garfield was unable to transact even the minimal functions of his office. With Congress not in session and the cabinet deliberating on the status of Vice President Arthur and whether he should be named temporary, or even permanent, President, a constitutional crisis arose. As the weeks rolled by, hopes persisted that Garfield might recover. In an attempt to aid his recovery by removing him from the Washington heat, the President was taken to the seaside resort of Elberon, New Jersey. Although Garfield clung courageously to life he was, finally, the victim of an infection that spread along the track the assassin's bullet had taken, compounded at the end by pneumonia. The President died at Elberon on September 19, 1881.

Garfield's assassination made him a political martyr, and the stricken nation mourned deeply. One funeral was held in Elberon, followed by a state funeral in Washington, and a third funeral and interment in Cleveland. The President's family was provided for by a fund established by his friends. The assassin was tried, found guilty, and, on June 30, 1882, hanged.

In Mentor, Ohio, stands Garfield's last home, Lawnfield, which has been restored as a memorial. The elm-shaded Victorian house contains many of the President's books and personal effects. The grounds also encompass the small building Garfield used as a one-room campaign office in 1880 and a replica of the log cabin in which he was born.

Lincoln's Gettysburg Address

Military victory is paradoxical; the impression of success is tempered by the knowledge of loss. In the Civil War, the Northern, or federal, army defeat of the Southern, or Confederate, opponents at the battle of Gettysburg in July 1863 (see July 1) contributed significantly to the preservation of the American Union. During the three days from July 1 to 3, more than 3,000 Federal troops died on the Pennsylvania field, falling beside almost 4,000 Confederates.

To commemorate a paradox, it is necessary to retain the paradox; fittingly, the North chose to establish a military graveyard for Union soldiers at the site of its Gettysburg victory. The commission in charge of the project planned appropriate services to accompany the consecration of the cemetery on November 19, 1863. They invited numerous dignitaries to the solemnities and asked former Senator Edward Everett of Massachusetts, a noted orator, to deliver the major address.

President Abraham Lincoln, to the surprise of the commission, accepted their courtesy invitation to attend the ceremonies. The chairman, David Wills of Gettysburg, accordingly on November 2 asked him to deliver "a few appropriate remarks" on the occasion. Lincoln again agreed, although he had little time to prepare his speech.

Secretary of State William H. Seward, Secretary of the Interior John P. Usher, and Postmaster General Francis P. Blair accompanied President Lincoln when he left Washington on November 18 for the journey to Gettysburg. The train ride consumed the entire day, and the President alighted at several stops to greet the citizenry. Contrary to popular belief, Lincoln evidently did no work on his speech during the trip to Pennsylvania.

Chairman Wills greeted the presidential party at the Gettysburg station and escorted it to his home. Serenaders and bands gathered outside the Wills house on the town square and called for Lincoln to make an appearance. The President stepped outside, spoke for a few minutes, and then returned to dinner. About 9:00 P.M. Lincoln went upstairs to his room.

Owing to the pressure of war and politics Lincoln had written only part of his address before he left Washington. He did some more work on it on the evening of November 18, before going to bed around midnight. He spent another hour on the morning of November 19 completing his preparation. He then rolled up the two-page statement, tucked it into his tall hat, and left the Wills house to join the procession to the cemetery.

The prayers that began the ceremonies at the burying ground reflected the solemnity of the event and set the tone for Edward Everett's address. The 69-year-old statesman drew for his oration on his lifetime of varied experience as a minister, professor of Greek, and president of Harvard University. The Massachusetts statesman spoke for two hours, ranging in subject matter from the heroes of ancient Greece to a detailed account of the battle of Gettysburg.

The singing of an ode followed Senator Everett's address, and then the President approached the rostrum. Lincoln delivered his 270-word message within two minutes and resumed his seat. Most of the crowd missed his words entirely; expecting the Chief Executive to speak for a longer period, they had allowed themselves to be diverted by the activities of a photographer attempting to take a picture of the President.

Few among the audience recognized the greatness of Lincoln's speech. Secretary Seward kindly said "his speech was not equal to him." Most major newspapers concentrated on Everett's address and ignored the President's words. The Chicago *Times* was critical: "The cheek of every American must tingle with shame as he reads the silly, flat, and dishwatery utterances of the man who has to be pointed out to intelligent foreigners as the President of the United States." The London *Times* thought that a speech "more dull and commonplace it would not be easy to produce."

However, simple words best explain important events, and Lincoln's phrases had captured the meaning of Gettysburg and the Civil War. The stench of the still-unburied horse carcasses perhaps stifled thoughts of martial glory on that day. Lincoln spoke instead of the sacrifice of the men who had died that a nation might live, drawing from his reading of the King James version of the Bible the eloquence to express his theme:

Fourscore and seven years ago our fathers brought forth on this continent a new nation, conceived in liberty, and dedicated to the proposition that all men are created equal.

Now we are engaged in a great civil war, testing whether that nation, or any nation so conceived and so dedicated, can long endure. We are met on a great battle-field of that war. We have come to dedicate a portion of that field as a final resting-place for those who here gave their lives that the nation might live. It is altogether fitting and proper that we should do this.

But, in a larger sense, we cannot dedicate — we cannot consecrate — we cannot hallow — this ground. The brave men, living and dead, who struggled here, have consecrated it far above our poor power to add or detract. The world will little note nor long remember what we say here, but it can never forget what they did here. It is for us, the living, rather, to be dedicated here to the unfinished work which they who fought here have thus far so nobly advanced. It is rather for us to be here dedicated to the great task remaining before us — that from these honored dead we take increased devotion to that cause for which they gave the last full measure of devotion — that we here highly resolve that these dead shall not have died in vain — that this nation, under God, shall have a new birth of freedom — and that government of the people, by the people, for the people, shall not perish from the earth.

Later critics have thought more favorably of the Gettysburg Address. Lord Curzon, the chancellor of Oxford University in England, speaking one-half century after that cold November day, expressed the general modern evaluation: "The Gettysburg Address is far more than a pleasing piece of occasional oratory. It is a pure well of English undefiled. It sets one to inquiring with nothing short of wonder 'How knoweth this man letters, having never learned?' The more closely the address is analysed the more one must confess astonishment at its choice of words, the precision of its thought, its simplicity, directness, and effectiveness."

The Gettysburg National Cemetery lies along Pennsylvania State Route 134. It contains 20.55 acres, 15.55 of which are federally owned. Buried within its precincts lie 4,569 men, 979 of whom are unidentified. The 60-foot-high Soldiers National Monument, dedicated on July 1, 1869, stands at the spot from which Lincoln delivered his speech. The Gettysburg Address Memorial, erected in 1912, is located at the western end of the grounds. It is the only monument in the world dedicated to a speech.

The master bedroom of Judge David Wills's house, where Lincoln worked on his speech, has been preserved as it was in 1863. The building, situated on Lincoln Square in Gettysburg, is now the Lincoln Room Museum. A huge plaque, made from woods of eleven places connected with Lincoln's life and inscribed with the words of the Gettysburg Address, is another feature of the museum.

The two earliest drafts of the address are now in the Library of Congress. Three other copies in Lincoln's handwriting are extant. One is located in the Lincoln Room of the White House. The Illinois State Historical Library and Cornell University own the other two.

Each year Gettysburg observes the anniversary of the address. On the Saturday closest to November 19 the Auxiliary of the Sons of Union Veterans and its allied organizations hold a banquet. On November 19 the Lincoln Fellowship of Pennsylvania holds a luncheon at which such notable persons as Civil War historian Bruce Catton and poet and Lincoln biographer Carl Sandburg have spoken. After a military parade to the National Cemetery, there is a commemorative program at the site of the Gettysburg Address.

November 19, 1963, the centennial of the Gettysburg Address, was the occasion of a special three-day celebration. The Gettysburg Centennial Commission in conjunction with Gettysburg College planned the program for November 17 and 18. On Sunday afternoon, November 17, Secretary of State Dean Rusk delivered a speech. That evening David Donald, professor of history at Johns Hopkins University, presented a paper on Lincoln's address, and the Gettysburg College choir offered a musical program. On Monday evening a panel moderated by Alistair Cooke discussed Dr. Donald's essay.

Tuesday's observances were the highlight of the centennial. A luncheon at a hotel in Gettysburg honored the Lincoln Fellowship of Pennsylvania on its 25th Anniversary. James I. Robertson Jr., the executive secretary of the Civil War Centennial Commission, was the speaker, and Governor William W. Scranton of Pennsylvania an honored guest.

The military parade followed the same route as had its counterpart 100 years earlier; the line of march proceeded from Lincoln Square to the National Cemetery about one mile away. As in 1863, the Marine Band was at the head of the marchers. A battalion from the "Old Guard" regiment of the Third US Army followed the band. This regiment, the oldest in the army in continuous service, saw action at the battle of Gettysburg. Troops of Pennsylvania's 28th National Guard Division and its band also participated in the parade, as did the full cadet corps and band of the Valley Forge Military Academy.

A Protestant bishop and the pastor of a local Catholic church offered prayers at the cemetery. Marian Anderson, an opera star and a descendant of slaves, sang two selections. Another descendant of slaves, E. Washington Rhodes, the editor and publisher of the Philadelphia *Tribune,* called for statesmanship like Lincoln's to break down the walls of racial hostility in the United States. Governor Scranton said that he hoped the commemoration would help the American people "to find increased devotion for the unfinished cause of human freedom."

President John F. Kennedy, who was unable to attend the ceremony, sent a message that was read to the gathering. He warned that "the obligations of keeping ours a government of and for the people are never-ending." Former President Dwight D. Eisenhower delivered the main address. He called for all Americans "to defend, protect and pass on unblemished to coming generations the heritage, the trust that Abraham Lincoln and all the ghostly legions of patriots of the past have, with unflinching faith in their God, bequeathed to us — a nation free, with liberty, dignity and justice for all."

NOVEMBER 20

Holiday Folk Fair
Milwaukee, Wisconsin

This is a movable event. See note on page xxvi.

Capitalizing on one of its great natural resources —the polyglot population that it has been attracting ever since the 1830s and 1840s—Milwaukee takes pride in the fact that people of some 45 different ethnic backgrounds participate in its annual Holiday Folk Fair. The fair, which is held during the weekend before Thanksgiving, is sponsored by the International Institute of Milwaukee County in cooperation with the various nationality groups and (since 1964) the Pabst Brewing Company.

A colorful amalgam of the food, folk dances, music, and handicrafts of many lands, it has as its setting Milwaukee's Auditorium and Arena at West Kilbourn Avenue and North 4th Street. In recent years it has been drawing an annual crowd of more than 60,000 from all parts of Wisconsin and the surrounding states. Among the visitors, who come from as far away as New York and San Francisco, are school classes, travel clubs, and chartered busloads of Girl Scouts.

Today's crowds are in marked contrast to those of the Holiday Folk Fair's first year, 1944, when the audience was a mere 3,000 — fewer than the 4,000 volunteers who now help to put on the fair each year.

The visitors of 1944 braved a snowstorm to attend the one-day event, which was held in Milwaukee's Public Service Building on December 10. People of 15 nationalities took part in that first undertaking, which offered guests a single meal, some cluttered exhibits, and a limited program of ethnic entertainment.

The idea — that the efforts of various ethnic groups might be pooled in one yearly, cooperative effort to display, preserve, and promote pride in the city's diverse cultural heritage — originated in the minds of a dozen committee members who had met at the International Institute earlier in the year to discuss such a possibility. What at first seemed like insuperable problems of administration and financing were overcome when the International Institute offered to assume these responsibilities and the leadership in overall planning. The step was in keeping with the purposes of the institute, an organization devoted to helping immigrants with naturalization procedures, living accommodations, job-hunting, English lessons, and adjustment to their new community and country as useful citizens. The institute, founded in 1930, also tries to promote pride in the foreign traditions and cultural heritage that the newcomers have brought with them.

The fair grew slowly. It moved to the Auditorium in its second year. In 1947 it was extended from one to two days. In 1959 it overflowed into the Arena, and in 1964 Friday evening was added to the fair. Eventually a small profit was realized, and rules were set up for its use. No individual may benefit. All profits go to charitable, educational, or cultural institutions, or to churches.

High among the attractions of today's Holiday Folk Fair are the more than 35 cultural exhibits, like small folk museums, which include treasured heirlooms. Although the displays differ from year to year, representative examples have included demonstrations of Polish Easter egg decoration, of linen-making in an Irish cottage, and of Norwegian rosemailing in an artist's studio; a family from Czechoslovakia stripping feathers for pillows; a craftsman making traditional Latvian amber and silver jewelry; a young woman fashioning Japanese origami birds in a bower of cherry blossoms; a Swedish immigrant creating wrought-iron candlesticks by ancestral methods in a blacksmith shop. Other folk art can be seen in the fair's World Mart, a series of booths at which articles from some 35 nations can be purchased.

A prime feature of the fair is the traditional food of the participating groups, served in two international sidewalk cafes. There, fairgoers can sample an astonishing range of delicacies including sauerbraten, pilaf, shish kebab, blintzes, tamales, barbecued ribs, knishes, stuffed grape leaves, borscht, spinach pie, and goat's milk cheese. Among pastries, there are baklava, cannoli, strudel, and Vienna torte, as well as Chinese fortune cookies, Irish scones, gugelhupf, and Polish love knots. Candies may be sampled at the International Candy Counter or the American Pantry. Snacks and beverages are available at the Old World Beer Garden, which features dancing by visitors and continuous ethnic entertainment, or at the cafe, East and West.

Each year the Holiday Folk Fair honors a different ethnic group, which selects a Miss Holiday Folk Fair. Among the peoples honored in recent years are American Indians, Germans, Danes, Japanese, Slovaks, Serbians, and Italians. The Folk Spectacle — the program presented five times (including each evening) during the fair, presents some 25 folk dance groups within a storytelling pageant for which the honored group provides the cast. Generally, the program centers around the group in question, as the titles of some typical Folk Spectacles indicate: Swift Feather [an American Indian] Seeks a Bride; Poor Janosik [a Slovak folk hero] Is Dead; The Land of [Danish] Tivoli; and Lincoln's [German-born] Friend [Carl Schurz]. The program, which originated as little more than a costume parade, later became a folk dance recital. Now, however, its dances, which are performed by several hundred costumed folk dancers, are woven into a dramatic story built around the national motto, E Pluribus Unum (One out of Many). The production Our American Freedom, presented in one representative year, can serve as an example. It included tableaus in which members of nationality groups depicted such historic events as the signing of the Declaration of Independence, Washington's inauguration, Lincoln's Emancipation Proclamation, an early election campaign, the conferring of citizenship upon a group of new Americans, and the traditional finale, in which all the participants come together for the salute to the flag. The tableaus were interspersed with the performances of folk dancers in rich variety — among them, feather-shaking, bell-ringing American Indians; heel-clicking, whirling Hungarians; veiled Armenians; shouting, thigh-slapping Bavarians; and leaping, running, clowning Ukrainians.

Before the Friday evening performance of the Folk Spectacle, distinguished guests are introduced, and an award is presented to an outside organization that has made a signal contribution to the year's success. Representative recipients have been the Milwaukee health, fire, and police departments and the Milwaukee County Park Commission. On Saturday afternoon, youngsters put on a less elaborate version of the evening entertainment. Awards for excellence in folk dancing and cultural exhibits are presented at ceremonies preceding the final Sunday night performance.

NOVEMBER 21

North Carolina Ratifies the Constitution

On November 21, 1789, North Carolina became the 12th state to ratify the US Constitution. More than a year earlier, North Carolina had been the first state to refuse to accept the new frame of government. The ratification left only Rhode Island still outside the continental union.

Early in January 1787 in the final days of the North Carolina legislative session Governor Richard Caswell presented to the representatives a letter from the governor of Virginia urging North Carolina's "zealous attention to the present American crisis." Prodded by men like Richard Caswell, William R. Davie, Richard Dobbs Spaight, William Hooper, John Gray Blount, and Archibald Maclaine, the legislators decided to send a delegation to the Constitutional Convention that was to open in Philadelphia in May 1787. They selected two leaders of the conservative faction, William R. Davie and Richard Dobbs Spaight; two political moderates, Richard Caswell and Alexander Martin; and the acknowledged radical spokesman Willie Jones. Governor Caswell, unable to participate because of ill health, appointed William Blount in his stead and replaced Willie Jones with Hugh Williamson, the former having refused to serve without giving a reason.

According to contemporary accounts, North Carolina's representatives were among the less prominent members of the convention. William R. Davie, an attorney and planter, was in his early thirties, and was popular but not prominent. Richard D. Spaight, a wealthy planter, was less than 30 years old. William Blount, a merchant and planter, was regarded as "plain, honest and sincere." Alexander Martin, a lawyer, planter, and former governor, had been dismissed from the army for cowardice at the battle of Germantown. Hugh Williamson had been a preacher and professor of mathematics at the College of Philadelphia before he became a medical doctor; he was fond of debate but was not a good speaker. All five had served in the American Revolution; all except Alexander Martin sat in the Congress of the Confederation; and William Davie, Alexander Martin, and Hugh Williamson were college graduates.

William Blount and Alexander Martin were silent and inactive at the convention, and neither made a speech or served on a committee. William Davie was a member of the committee that devised the Great Compromise authorizing each state to send a number of representatives proportional to its population to the lower house of the new Congress and to have equal representation (later defined as two senators per state) in the upper House. Richard Spaight opposed the Great Compromise but suggested the election of senators by the state legislature. Hugh Williamson, who made 73 speeches, proposed the six-year term for senators and acted as spokesman for the North Carolina contingent.

North Carolina was the fourth most populous state in 1787, but on the critical question of the distribution of seats in the Congress, it voted with the smaller states in favor of equal representation in the Senate. Members of the delegation, all of whom owned slaves except Williamson, supported the three-fifths compromise under which five slaves counted as three freemen for purposes of apportioning representation and taxation. They also agreed with the decision to prohibit the cessation of the slave trade for 20 years and to forbid the taxation of exports. At the conclusion of the convention, William Blount, Richard Spaight, and Hugh Williamson signed the Constitution on behalf of their state, but William Davie and Alexander Martin, who had been absent for several weeks, did not affix their names.

Governor Richard Caswell presented the proposed Constitution to the state legislature on November 21, 1787, the second day of its new session. On December 5, the day set aside for discussion of the document, the lawmakers debated. On December 6 both Houses requested all taxpayers to select, at the March 1788 elections, delegates for a ratifying convention that met on July 21, 1788, at Hillsboro.

Federalists and Antifederalists waged spirited and occasionally vicious campaigns in the months before the March elections. Supporters of the Constitution from Pennsylvania sent masses of literature into North Carolina, but North Carolinian James Iredell, who later served for nine years as an associate justice of the US Supreme Court, provided the most cogent arguments for ratification. He described the "disordered and distracted" state of the country under the Articles of Confederation and suggested that only a "united, vigorous government" could offer salvation. He pointed to the new Constitution's system of popular representation, its

checks against the abuse of power, its sensible procedures for amendment, and the "many provisions calculated to make us as much one people as possible." Arguing that union was the "watchword of American liberty and safety," Iredell pleaded that "our strength consists in union, and nothing can hurt us but division."

Antifederalists claimed that the establishment of a strong national government would lead to the disintegration of the states, that the spirit of the Constitution favored industry and commerce rather than agriculture, and that the absence of a bill of rights could have grave consequences for individual liberties. Some of the Antifederalist evaluations were extravagant. Timothy Bloodworth insisted that the new government would be an "autocratic tyranny, or monarchial monarchy," and the Baptist preacher Lemuel Burkitt of Hertford County predicted that the national capital would be a walled city housing a standing army of at least 50,000 men, who would be at liberty to plunder and pillage.

Opponents of the Constitution won a massive victory in the March elections. Although 11 states had already ratified the proposed frame of government, the Antifederalists were sure of success in North Carolina. When the ratification convention met on July 21, Willie Jones suggested that the meeting vote and adjourn on the first day, because to delay the inevitable outcome was to waste the public money. The Federalists managed to prolong the convention for 11 days, but then by a vote of 184 to 84 delegates declared that North Carolina would not ratify the Constitution until a bill of rights had been presented to the Congress and to a second Constitutional Convention. On August 4 the North Carolina ratification convention adjourned without setting a date to meet again.

North Carolina Federalists were undaunted by the defeat and immediately began circulating petitions for a second ratifying convention. The state senate in November called for another convention, and, although the lower house concurred, the Antifederalists in that body managed to postpone the date of the proposed gathering for a year. The legislators chose to convene in Fayetteville in November 1789.

While North Carolina remained aloof, the new federal government began functioning in the spring of 1789. George Washington, who enjoyed great popularity in North Carolina, became the first President that April, and national authorities engaged in none of the tyrannical practices predicted by the vehement Antifederalists. The US Congress even proposed 12 amendments to the Constitution, designed to safeguard individual liberty; 10 of those resolutions eventually formed the Bill of Rights.

Friends of the Constitution in North Carolina used the months before the August 1789 elections to educate the public about the advantages of the new government. They succeeded magnificently and defeated the Antifederalists in the August canvass, which selected representatives to the November 1789 ratifying convention. Of the 102 delegates chosen in 1789 who had also served at the Hillsboro convention of 1788, 39 were re-elected as Federalists, and 20 converted to the support of the Constitution in the interim; the Antifederalists reelected 43 men. Of the 169 new delegates, 135 were Federalists.

North Carolina's second convention opened on November 16, 1789. The caucus lasted only five days, and on November 21, 1789, North Carolina became the 12th state to ratify the Constitution. The final vote was by the decisive margin of 194 to 77. No doubt the election of George Washington, the proposal of the Bill of Rights, and the state's sense of isolation from the rest of the Revolutionary states strongly influenced the final decision.

North Carolina and the other 12 colonies that formed the original Union under the Articles of Confederation became states when they declared their independence in July 1776. For practical considerations, however, historians determine the chronology of the entrance of these states by the order in which they ratified the Constitution. Thus North Carolina is said to be the 12th state to join the United States of America.

NOVEMBER 22

John F. Kennedy Assassinated

On Friday, November 22, 1963, John Fitzgerald Kennedy, 35th President of the United States (see May 29), was shot as he rode through the streets of Dallas, Texas. Kennedy had gone to Texas to help mend a dispute between factions of the state Democratic party, whose unified strength he would need in his anticipated bid for reelection in 1964. The President also hoped to address and win over the people of Texas, many of whom were conservatives opposed to him because of his espousal of liberal causes such as civil rights.

President Kennedy landed at Love Field in Dallas on the morning of the November 22 and mingled happily with the throng of people there to meet him. With his wife, Jacqueline Bouvier Kennedy, he entered an open limousine with Texas governor John Connally, Mrs. Connally, and a Secret Service agent for the motorcade.

Large crowds cheered the Chief Executive on his journey, and his apparent rapport with the Texans greatly pleased him. Mrs. Connally even turned to her guests and stated that the people lining the roadway exemplified the true affection that Texans felt for Kennedy.

Official investigators later reconstructed events as follows: As the cars turned left at Houston Street onto Elm Street, Lee Harvey Oswald peered down at the motorcade from a sixth-floor window in the Texas School Book Depository. Placing a high-powered Italian rifle with a telescopic sight to his shoulder, Oswald fired three shots at the vehicle bearing the Kennedys and Connallys. Two shots struck the President, one in his head and the other in his neck. One of the bullets, probably the one that struck Kennedy in the neck, also wounded Governor Connally after passing through the President.

The motorcade sped to Parkland Memorial Hospital. Doctors at the hospital worked desperately but to no avail to revive the President. Father Oscar L. Huber administered the last rites of the Roman Catholic church to the dying President, and Dr. William K. Clark pronounced him dead as of 1:00 P.M. central standard time.

Lee Harvey Oswald, who allegedly fired the shots that killed the President, had led an unhappy life. He did not fare well as a student or with his classmates, who remembered him as a bookish "loner." As a high school drop-out, he joined the Marine Corps, where he was again an outsider and unpopular with fellow servicemen. After his mother suffered an injury, he obtained a hardship discharge to support her but remained at home for only a few days before he went to New Orleans and obtained work on a freighter, which took him to the Soviet Union in October 1959. Oswald, who had been attracted to communism for several years, declared that he was renouncing his US citizenship and obtained a work permit. He was distrusted by many Russians, however, and he again became an outsider. With his Russian wife, Marina Nikolaevna Prusakova Oswald, he returned in June 1962 to the United States, where he lived briefly in Fort Worth, Dallas, and New Orleans before returning to Dallas in 1963. He began work at the Texas School Book Depository on October 16, 1963.

According to official reports, Oswald fled the depository after the assassination and made his way to his rooming house by bus, taxicab, and foot. He quickly left the rooming house and was next seen about a mile away at 10th Street and Patton Avenue, where police officer J. D. Tippit stopped the suspicious-looking young man. Oswald spoke briefly to Tippit and then shot the officer four times with a revolver. Having killed Tippit, Oswald fled to the Texas Theater, a movie house, where the police apprehended him after a struggle.

Dallas officials arraigned Oswald for the murders of Kennedy and Tippit, but he denied participation in the deeds. The public may never know much more about Oswald because the 24-year-old suspect soon met his own violent end. On November 24, as police officers were escorting Oswald through the basement of the police headquarters to a vehicle waiting to take him to the County Jail, Jack Ruby, a Dallas nightclub owner, broke through the guards and shot him to death. Ruby, convicted of murder, later died of cancer in prison.

Rumors that there had been a conspiracy to kill President Kennedy spread quickly after the assassination, particularly in the wake of Oswald's death. Lyndon B. Johnson, who succeeded Kennedy as President, appointed a commission headed by the chief justice of the United States, Earl Warren (see March 19), to investigate the tragedy. After months of study, the Warren commission concluded that Oswald had been the sole assassin, motivated by the irrational workings of his own mind. Many remained unconvinced, believing that not all the facts had been revealed, and demands for further investigation and disclosure were still being made more than a decade later.

News of Kennedy's death spread quickly and shocked people throughout the world. Not only Americans but people of all nations everywhere expressed their sorrow and sense of loss. More than 1,000 Londoners made their way to the American embassy at Grosvenor Square. Ten thousand Poles signed the condolence book at the American embassy in Warsaw. In Russia, Premier Nikita Krushchev and his wife signed the condolence book at Spaso House, the residence of the American ambassador in Moscow. In Rome, Pope Paul VI decried the human "capacity for hate and evil."

American television networks suspended all commercials and devoted their complete attention to covering the tragedy and the events leading to President Kennedy's funeral, which was held on Monday, November 25. Approximately 175 million viewers in the United States watched the events of the weekend on their television sets. Countless more persons in 23 foreign countries followed the proceedings by means of US communications satellites.

The events of the long weekend began with the return of the President's body to Washington, D.C. The Secret Service escorted Jacqueline Kennedy and the slain leader's body to the presidential plane at Love Field. On board, Judge Sarah Hughes administered the presidential oath of office to Vice President Lyndon B. Johnson, who had accompanied Kennedy to Texas. After the ceremony, Johnson ordered the pilot to return the plane immediately to the federal capital.

Air Force One, the presidential plane, touched down at Andrews Air Force Base near Washington shortly after 6:00 P.M. A hydraulic lift lowered the casket to the ground, where a waiting ambulance carried the body to Bethesda Naval Hospital for burial preparations. At 4:25 A.M. the ambulance returned the President's body to the White House.

On Saturday, November 23, President Kennedy's body lay in repose in the East Room of the White House. Numerous dignitaries paid their last respects. Meanwhile, under the calm, purposeful guidance of Jacqueline Kennedy, scores of persons worked to complete plans for the funeral ceremonies.

On Sunday morning, tens of thousands lined the streets leading from the White House to the Capitol, where Kennedy's body would lie in state until the following day. At 1:10 P.M. the cortege accompanying the President's body stepped off from the Executive Mansion. First came an honor guard of District of Columbia policemen, followed by the escort commander and the chiefs of the US Army, Navy, Air Force, Marine Corps, and Coast Guard. Next, leading the caisson that bore the President's casket, marched a company of navy men escorting the flag, and three representatives of the nation's clergy.

Six gray horses pulled the caisson, which was flanked by an honor guard of 24 military representatives. The pallbearers, with a sailor carrying the presidential flag, followed. Last in line was a riderless black gelding. A black-handled sword in a silver scabbard hung from the saddle, and polished black boots were thrust reversed in the stirrups in an age-old representation of a fallen leader.

When the cortege reached the Capitol, the navy band played "Ruffles and Flourishes," "Hail to the Chief," and the navy hymn as the pallbearers carried the casket up the East Front steps. Inside the Capitol Rotunda, they placed the casket on a catafalque built almost 100 years earlier to hold the body of Abraham Lincoln. Senate Majority Leader Mike Mansfield, House Speaker John W. McCormack, and Chief Justice Earl Warren offered eulogies, and then the great bronze doors of the Capitol were opened to the public.

Almost a quarter of a million people passed by

the Kennedy bier in the 21 hours the Capitol doors remained open. Many persons remained in line throughout the cold Washington night. Reluctantly, officials closed the building at 9:00 A.M., turning away an additional 12,000 people.

On Monday morning the pallbearers took the casket down the steps of the Capitol and placed it again on the caisson. The cortege returned briefly to the White House, where the final day's journey began. From the White House, members of the Kennedy family accompanied the caisson to St. Matthews Cathedral. Eight heads of state, 10 prime ministers, and representatives from 100 countries followed the entourage on foot to the church.

Richard Cardinal Cushing of Boston, a close friend of the Kennedy family, offered the requiem mass. The Most Reverend Philip M. Hannan, auxiliary bishop of Washington, offered a eulogy at the conclusion of the service. Then, at 1:30 P.M., the cortege resumed its march to Arlington National Cemetery. At the gravesite, 50 jet planes of the air force and navy, each representing one of the nation's 50 states, flew overhead in formation. The apex of the last "V" formation was empty, symbolizing the loss of a fallen leader. *Air Force One*, trailing the 50 planes, dipped its wings in a salute as it passed over the site.

The pallbearers placed the coffin above the grave. Irish officer cadets, carrying their weapons upside down, executed a manual of arms traditional to Irish military funerals. The Marine Band played the "Garry Owen."

Cardinal Cushing offered the final prayers of interment and led the mourners in prayer. Cannons and riflemen then fired the echoing volleys of a 21-gun salute, and a bugler sounded taps. Finally, the military pallbearers folded the American flag that had rested on the casket and presented it to Jacqueline Kennedy, who, assisted by the President's brothers, — Robert F. Kennedy, then serving as US attorney general, and Edward M. Kennedy, senator from Massachusetts — lit an eternal flame beside the grave.

For more than three years Kennedy's remains lay at the picket-fenced gravesite where he was interred in November 1963. John Carl Warnecke, an architect commissioned by the Kennedy family, meanwhile designed a permanent grave, about 20 feet away, to which Kennedy's remains were transferred in March 1967. Buried with him are his son Patrick, who died shortly after his birth in August 1963, and his unnamed daughter, who was stillborn in 1956.

Many nations have honored President Kennedy. Some issued commemorative stamps. Ireland built several memorials, including an arboretum near the Kennedys' ancestral home in County Wexford. Great Britain set up a memorial at Runneymede, the location of the signing of the Magna Carta, 20 miles southwest of London. In Israel the Kennedy Memorial Forest, with its symbolic monument representing a truncated tree, is located on Mount Orah, near Jerusalem.

American towns, cities, and states have also paid homage to the slain President. Dallas dedicated a memorial designed by Philip Johnson and located approximately 200 yards from the place of the assassination. Philadelphia erected a bronze plaque in Independence Hall commemorating a speech on the interdependence of nations given by Kennedy on July 4, 1962. New York City unveiled a bronze bust of the President at the Grand Army Plaza in Brooklyn in May 1965.

Governments and individuals from all walks of life have attempted to honor the President in countless ways. Cape Canaveral, Florida, the site of US missile launches into space, was renamed Cape Kennedy in recognition of the President's support of the space program and his determination that this nation would place a man on the moon — as it did — before the end of the 1960s. (The original name was restored in 1973.) New York City renamed Idlewild, its great international airport, in Kennedy's memory. Almost every major city in the world renamed at least a street to commemorate the fallen leader, and there are schools bearing his name spread across the nation.

President Lyndon B. Johnson on December 2, 1964, broke ground in Washington for the John F. Kennedy Center for the Performing Arts, using a gold-plated spade that also had broken ground for the Lincoln and Jefferson memorials. The center, designed by Edward Durrell Stone and including an opera house, concert hall, two theaters, and a cinema, had its premier performance in September 1971.

President Johnson proclaimed November 22, 1964, the first anniversary of Kennedy's death, a Day of National Rededication, and memorial services were held throughout the land to mark the occasion. Since then the day customarily has been noted in the press and on radio and television. It also has been marked by memorial masses, and by countless gestures by individual Americans, including visits to the Kennedy graves at Arlington. In Massachusetts, by a 1968 act of the state legislature, the last Sunday in November is annually proclaimed by the governor as John F. Kennedy Day.

A huge collection of printed and audiovisual material relating to Kennedy is housed in the John F. Kennedy Library, which is temporarily located at the Federal Records Center in Waltham, Massachusetts. Included in the depository's collection, much of which is open to researchers, are personal papers and official files, sound recordings, films, and books and periodical literature by and about Kennedy. Groundbreaking ceremonies for a permanent library building took place at the Boston campus of the University of Massachusetts in 1977.

NOVEMBER 23

Franklin Pierce's Birthday

Franklin Pierce, the 14th President of the United States, was born on November 23, 1804, in Hillsboro, New Hampshire. His mother, Anna Kendrick Pierce, and his father, Benjamin Pierce, were of English ancestry. Benjamin Pierce, who had served in the colonial forces during the American Revolution, was a successful Democratic politician, and he educated his son for the career of statesman. In 1824 Franklin Pierce was graduated from Bowdoin College in Brunswick, Maine, and by 1827, after studying law under Levi Woodbury — the New Hampshire governor and legislator who later served as associate justice of the Supreme Court — he was admitted to the bar of Hillsboro County.

Beginning in 1829, Franklin Pierce served in the New Hampshire legislature, known as the General Court, having come to office in the same election that saw his father elected governor of the state for a second term. Franklin Pierce was only 25 years old at the time. Yet within two years he was speaker in the legislature. He continued his steady political ascent when, in 1833, he became a member of the US Congress. His two terms in the House of Representatives were followed by five years in the Senate.

During his congressional years, Pierce was a faithful Jacksonian Democrat. However, he opposed federally financed internal improvements sponsored by Jacksonian politicians. Pierce was a handsome, erect man of honesty and unfailing courtesy. All who knew him came to like him as a man. He was not notable as an orator, but he did much conscientious committee work. Though he was from a state in which antislavery feelings were strong, Pierce himself had no ideological misgivings about the institution. On the contrary, he felt that the abolitionists were fanatics bent on destroying the Union.

While a representative in Congress in 1834 Pierce married Jane Means Appleton, the daughter of a former president of Bowdoin. A chronic invalid who suffered from tuberculosis, Jane Pierce disliked politics and her husband's involvement in the gala life of official Washington.

Under her prodding, Franklin Pierce resigned from the Senate in 1842. He returned to Concord, New Hampshire, and soon established a flourishing business as a lawyer. He prepared his cases well and excelled in lucid, forceful presentations before juries.

For five years after leaving the Senate, Pierce was the strict leader of New Hampshire's Democratic party. On one occasion, however, his tight rein on the Democrats worked to the detriment of the party. Pierce "disciplined" a local Democrat for opposing US annexation of Texas. However, New Hampshire voters were not in favor of the adventure against Mexico and voted the Democrats out of office in 1846, creating their first defeat in 18 years. In reward for his party loyalty, Pierce became federal district attorney in Concord. He declined President James K. Polk's subsequent offers of posts as US attorney general and as senator to fill an unexpired term.

In 1847 Pierce entered the army as a private to fight in the Mexican War. Before long he became a colonel and, shortly thereafter, was appointed a brigadier general of volunteers. He marched his men from Veracruz to join in General Winfield Scott's attack on Mexico City, but owing to various circumstances he never saw battle himself.

Returning to New Hampshire, Pierce continued to control the Democratic state machine. When he withdrew party support from John Atwood, the Democratic nominee for governor, on grounds that Atwood did not approve of the Democrats' Fugitive Slave Act, Southern Democrats took note of Pierce's support of slave owners' interests.

Levi Woodbury, who died in 1851, had been regarded by New Hampshire Democrats as a front-running candidate for President. After Woodbury's death state party leaders began to discuss Pierce as a possible candidate. During the Democratic National Convention of June 1852, the active candidates — James Buchanan, Stephen Douglas, William Marcy, and Lewis Cass — divided the votes, and a deadlock developed. Pierce was put forth as a dark-horse compromise candidate, and on the 49th ballot the convention suddenly united to back him. The national campaign was totally without discussion of substantive issues. Nearly any Democrat could have won the election, so divided were the Whigs over the question of the expansion of slavery. Pierce received 254 electoral votes to 42 for the Whig candidate, General Winfield Scott.

As President, Pierce advocated expansionism in foreign affairs to the point of being internationally provocative. Pierce permitted filibustering adventurers to attack Cuba. Southern slave-owners, meanwhile, pressed for the acquisition of that island — which had long been eyed by expansionists — regarding it as a potentially rich slave territory. In response to filibustering provocations, Spain began to search suspicious American ships. An incident occurred in 1854, and Southerners pressed for war. However, Spain apologized, thus undercutting any grounds for hostilities. With Pierce's knowledge, his ministers to Spain, England, and France drew up a statement urging the United States to buy Cuba, and to take it by force if Spain refused to sell. The news of this supposedly confidential Ostend Manifesto, as it came to be called, was leaked to the press, causing a scandal. Pierce proceeded anyway with his plans to try to buy Cuba from Spain, but he was rebuffed by an indignant Spanish government. The President also initiated negotiations for the acquisition of Hawaii, Alaska, and a naval base at Santo Domingo.

Pierce showed little initiative in dealing with the volatile problem of sectionalism. The issue of the expansion of slavery was moving ominously into the spotlight of domestic politics, but the phlegmatic Pierce all but ignored the dangers. Initiative was mainly taken by Stephen Douglas, the Democratic senator from Illinois. Even though in 1853 Pierce had secured the Gadsden Purchase of land from Mexico to facilitate a southern transcontinental railroad, the midwestern Douglas wanted to reroute the proposed rail line to a central continental route that would run through his state of Illinois.

To accomplish this, and generally to stimulate the growth of the northwest, Douglas proposed that Congress organize the Great Plains area. To this end, he introduced the Kansas-Nebraska Bill in January 1854. To lure Southern support, he proposed to repeal the Missouri Compromise that Henry Clay had helped frame in 1820, prohibiting slavery in any of the Louisiana Purchase north of latitude 36°30′ — except Missouri. This call for repeal of the Missouri Compromise stimulated antagonism that had simmered since (and before) passage of another Clay triumph, the series of resolutions known as the Compromise of 1850. Southerners and Northerners alike were unhappy with portions of Clay's formula for the resolution of sectional differences. Northerners refused to support the Fugitive Slave Act, which was part of the Compromise of 1850, while Southerners felt cheated by the provision for California's entrance into the Union as a free state. Douglas planned to make the repeal of the Missouri Compromise palatable to all by allowing the actual settlers of the new territories to decide for themselves whether they would or would not allow slavery within their borders.

Pierce lined up enough Democrats behind Douglas's Kansas-Nebraska Bill to secure its passage by May 1854. So bitter was the debate it engendered between proslavery and antislavery forces that the proposed transcontinental railroad was, for a time, all but forgotten. Also forgotten was the fact that part of the Kansas-Nebraska territory did not even belong to the United States. It had been signed over to Native Americans "forever," though they were pushed aside soon after the agreement and their sustenance, the bison, was hunted to near-extinction by white adventurers.

Most of the new trouble centered on Kansas, which (like Nebraska) was organized in 1854. When the new territory was opened to settlement, Missourians streamed across the border, as did immigrants from the Southern states and from New England — each group determined by sheer numbers to make its view on slavery prevail. What ensued was a period of violence and intimidation — the era of "bleeding Kansas," in effect a rehearsal for the Civil War that would wrack the entire nation before a decade had passed.

When an election for a Kansas territorial legislature was held in 1855, thousands of proslavery Missourians illegally crossed the border to vote. Not surprisingly, the proslavery ticket carried the election, even though the territorial governor set aside the results in six districts and ordered a new election. The proslavery men won Pierce's recognition and set up a technically official government, while the Free-Soilers, who had triumphed in the second election, set up a rival government. In 1856 a local civil war erupted between the two factions. Members of the proslavery group attacked and partially destroyed the antislavery stronghold of Lawrence on May 21. Three days later a group of antislavery men, led by the moral absolutist John Brown, retaliated by killing five proslavery men on Pottawatomie creek. The resulting uproar precipitated violence between abolitionist guerrilla bands and armed companies of proslavery men that continued through the month of June. Meanwhile, it was revealed that various Kansas leaders supported by Pierce had indulged in land speculation; they were replaced by the President. Pierce appointed a second governor of Kansas, and then a third, placing federal troops at his disposal. With this help, the local warfare was finally quelled, but the controversy had blighted much of Pierce's administration.

Although the President hoped for his renomination, his administration was so deeply identified with the politically hot issue of Kansas that the Democrats decided instead upon James Buchanan, who had not been involved on either side in the Kansas conflict. Although sorely disappointed, Pierce remained a faithful party servant and worked to defeat the new Republican party.

After relinquishing the presidency on March 4, 1857, Pierce toured Europe for three years before settling down in Concord, New Hampshire. After the 1860 election, he opposed both Southern secession and Republican efforts to prevent secession. He attacked the Republican Abraham Lincoln for enlarging the power of the presidency, even in light of the crisis that befell the nation with the outbreak of the Civil War in 1861. With offended Republicans added to the Northern Democrats who had been alienated earlier by his prosouthern policies in Kansas, Pierce became increasingly unpopular. Public opinion was influenced by his lack of imagination and his phlegmatic attitude toward decision making. He died on October 8, 1869.

The Franklin Pierce Homestead, northwest of Hillsboro, New Hampshire, consists of a two-story white colonial house. It contains many Pierce family belongings and has the original scenic wallpaper and stenciling. The homestead, which is open to the public, has been declared a national historic landmark. The house in Concord that Franklin Pierce owned and occupied from 1842 to 1848 was moved in 1971 from Montgomery Street to a new site on North Main Street in a historic part of town near the New Hampshire Statehouse.

Stamp Act Repudiated

On November 23, 1765, the court of Frederick County, Maryland, ordered that its business should be carried on without the use of the stamped paper required by the Stamp Act, which King George III had approved the previous spring (see March 22). The anniversary of this repudiation, which is a half holiday known as Repudiation Day, has been celebrated for many years in Frederick, the county seat. A tablet has been set up in the courthouse commemorating the action of the men who refused to recognize the validity of the law. Each year the Daughters of the American Revolution meet in the courthouse on or about November 23, when the original decision is formally read by the clerk of the circuit court. The bylaws of Sergeant Lawrence Everhart Chapter of the Sons of the Revolution of Frederick provide that the chapter shall meet annually on the anniversary and celebrate the courageous act of the county court.

In his action of March 22, 1765, King George approved an act of Parliament that extended to the American colonies the stamp tax, a means of raising revenue that had a long history in England. The legislation required that tax stamps of varying values be affixed to numerous documents and commodities, such as legal papers, school diplomas, liquor permits, and lawyers' licenses. The press was especially burdened as the tax on newspapers and pamphlets was based on the number of printed sheets in each publication, as well as on each advertisement. The law required payment in sterling, which increased these costs by at least a third, as colonial currencies were worth less than that of Britain. Magistrates in juryless vice-admiralty courts were to sit in judgment on those who attempted to evade the duty.

The Stamp Act was the wrong measure at the wrong time. The colonies were experiencing a depression after the end of the French and Indian War, and their economies could not withstand this additional strain. The law struck all areas of the country, transcending sectionalism, and most affected the articulate and influential. American response was quick and hostile.

In Virginia's House of Burgesses, the young firebrand Patrick Henry rose on May 29 to remind King George of the fate of Caesar and, more recently, of Charles I. The burgesses then declared that only they could levy a tax on Virginians. The Massachusetts General Assembly took James Otis's suggestion and proposed on June 6 that all the colonies meet in New York City. Delegates from nine colonies met there from October 7 to 25; their position was moderate but firm. John Dickinson of Pennsylvania expressed their thoughts in a "Declaration of Rights and Grievances," which stated that taxation without representation violated the colonists' rights as British subjects. Since the colonies could not feasibly send representatives to Parliament, the declaration held, only their own provincial legislatures could rightfully levy taxes on them.

Some colonists showed their displeasure with more than words. Sons of Liberty bands, sometimes led by prominent citizens, appeared in every seaport to terrorize the government. In Boston on August 15 a mob forced the stamp act agent Andrew Oliver to resign; on August 26, a mob burned the vice-admiralty records and ransacked the fashionable home of Chief Justice Thomas Hutchinson, destroying his library and manuscripts. On November 1, the day when the Stamp Act legally became effective, New Yorkers chased Lieutenant Governor Cadwallader Colden to a refuge aboard a British warship in the harbor and burned the stamped papers.

Colonial merchants devised perhaps the most effective action against the new tax. In New York, Philadelphia, and Boston they vowed to do no business with Britain until Parliament repealed the Stamp Act. This American boycott adversely affected English merchants, who therefore agitated for repeal. In Parliament William Pitt argued on behalf of the colonists, and the new ministry of the marquess of Rockingham rescinded the Stamp Act in March 1766.

There was rejoicing in the colonies. New York held a public party and erected statues to George III and Pitt. Amid these joyous displays of loyalty, Parliament's passage of the portentous Declaratory Act claiming jurisdiction over the colonies — a position unacceptable to the Americans — was overlooked.

NOVEMBER 24

Zachary Taylor's Birthday

Zachary Taylor, the 12th President of the United States, was born November 24, 1784, in Orange County, Virginia. He was the third son of Richard Taylor and Sarah Strother Taylor. Richard Taylor, whose ancestors had immigrated from England in the 1630s, had served as a lieutenant-colonel on the staff of George Washington.

When Zachary Taylor was still an infant, the family moved to Louisville, Kentucky, where they lived a rugged frontier life. Richard Taylor decided that his third son was to be a farmer, while his second son was given the privilege of embarking on an army career. All this changed, however, in 1808, with the sudden death of the elder brother.

The tragedy liberated Zachary Taylor from the farm. Meanwhile, in 1806, he had served briefly as a volunteer in the Kentucky militia. Two years later he was commissioned a first lieutenant in the 7th US Infantry.

While on a leave in June 1810 he married Margaret Mackall Smith of Calvert County, Maryland. Their marriage brought them six children. Of their five daughters, only three survived infancy. Their only son, Richard Taylor, became a general in the Confederacy.

In 1810 Zachary Taylor was promoted to captain, and the following year was given command of Fort Knox in the Indiana Territory under the territorial governor, William Henry Harrison. During the War of 1812 against England, Taylor continued to serve on the northwest frontier. As captain in charge of Fort Harrison, also in Indiana, he was involved in a desperate battle on September 4, 1812, when his 50 troops fought off 400 Indians. For his leadership in this battle, Taylor was breveted a major.

During 1813 Taylor assisted in defending the frontier from Indiana to Missouri. In the summer of 1814 he was given the assignment of destroying the towns of hostile Indians at the juncture of the Rock River and the Mississippi. Defeated by Indians and their British allies in an engagement in what is now the Davenport, Iowa, Credit Island park area, Taylor retired down the Mississippi to the mouth of the Des Moines River, where he directed the construction of Fort Johnson before returning to the command of Fort Knox in Indiana. After the war's end late in 1814 and the disbanding of forces the following June, Taylor's rank was reduced back to captain. Declining further service in the army at that time, he resigned and returned to his family's farm in Louisville.

Only a year later, President James Madison restored Taylor to the rank of major. Taylor accepted the commission and joined the 3rd Infantry in Green Bay, Wisconsin. Thus began 15 years of garrison duty.

During this time, Taylor was transferred from place to place over much of the United States. In 1819 he went to New Orleans for garrison duty as lieutenant colonel of the 4th Infantry. This assignment was followed by four transfers in four years. He subsequently served briefly in Louisville in 1824; and then went to Washington, D.C., as a member of a military board. His next orders took him to Baton Rouge, Louisiana, for two years. Then, in 1829, he was appointed Indian superintendent at Fort Snelling, on the site of St. Paul, Minnesota — where the old fort's Round Tower, now a military museum, stands in Fort Snelling State Park.

Taylor received a promotion to full colonel in charge of the 1st Regiment at Fort Crawford (now Prairie du Chien, Wisconsin) in 1832. While Taylor was stationed there, a young lieutenant named Jefferson Davis fell in love with his daughter, Sarah Knox Taylor, and eventually married her against her father's wishes.

By the 1830s and 1840s, white settlers' ever-present land hunger had grown to voraciousness. As the tide of settlement moved relentlessly westward, the eagerness of pioneers and land speculators to push the Native Americans out of their homelands had grown more insistent. Indeed, the goal of driving all Indians west of the Mississippi had become national policy — an end pursued by enforced treaties of cession or by more drastic means when these failed. Hostilities between settlers and Indians were inevitable, not only because land claims were often in conflict but also because the so-called land cessions were often negotiated by chieftains who lacked tribal authority to make such treaties and because many settlers unscrupulously violated the terms of even valid treaties.

As the appetite for land grew and instances of treachery, treaty violation, and misunderstanding multiplied, the conflict grew, particularly in areas in which the Indians attempted to take a stand against settlement. As a result, the US Army, of which Taylor was a part, spent much of its time dispossessing and killing Indians in the 1830s and 1840s.

In Illinois, for instance, the Sauk and Fox tribes had lost their cornfields to white squatters and were ordered by Governor John Reynolds to leave the state. The Sauk leader Black Hawk, — whose autobiography later became an American classic — led the tribes westward across the Mississippi under the governor's threats. However, the Sioux beyond did not welcome Black Hawk's people, and winter nearly ended their existence. Forced by hunger and the desire to reclaim their land, Black Hawk and his band of perhaps 1,000, including women, children, and old people, recrossed the Mississippi in the spring of 1832, searching for land on which to plant a corn crop. The settlers reacted with terror. Governor Reynolds called out the militia and had the starving Indians hunted down and shot. Black Hawk State Park at Rock Island, Illinois, is a memorial to this ugly episode, which is known as the Black Hawk War. During the conflict, Taylor served as a regimental commander in charge of 400 regular troops under the overall command of General Henry Atkinson. The Indians retreated north along the Rock River — their leader is portrayed by Lorado Taft's huge statue today overlooking their route from the river bluff at Oregon, Illinois — and then turned west. They met their final defeat on August 2, 1832, at the battle of Bad Axe in what is now Wisconsin, where they were cut down while trying to cross the Mississippi. Black Hawk himself escaped but was captured a few days later. It was Taylor who accepted his surrender. The surrender was later commemorated in the naming of the town now standing near the site — Victory, Wisconsin.

Having acquired some experience in Indian warfare, Taylor was sent to Florida in 1837 to track down Seminoles in the operation known as the Second Seminole War. A relatively new group whose name was first used about 1775, the Seminole tribe had been formed by the inter-marriage of fugitive Creeks and the harassed remnants of other tribes — Oconee, Apalachicola, Hitchiti, Yamasee, and Yuchi among them — who had been pushed out of the Southeast and had taken refuge in the northern part of Spanish-held Florida. Their tenuous position there was further compromised by their giving haven to some fellow fugitives: slaves from nearby Georgia and South Carolina, who flocked south when they learned that the Seminoles would shelter them and often intermarried and became part of the tribe.

The wrath of white slaveholders notwithstanding, the Seminoles for the most part lived a peaceful agricultural existence — though it had been interrupted by the First Seminole War in 1816–1818. This included the incursion of a federal government expedition against a group of resisting Indians and runaway slaves thought to threaten the Georgia border and a high-handed foray led by Andrew Jackson. Sent to pursue hostile elements across the Florida border in 1818, Jackson had enthusiastically exceeded his instructions. His arbitrary execution of two Britons said to be aiding the enemy created an international incident. Jackson's emphatic show of force had much to do with persuading Spain to agree the next year to give up Florida to the United States.

Two decades later, the Seminoles' peaceful existence was shattered again. Aided by settlers' continuing appetite for new land, slave owners seeking to prevent defections were able to pressure the government at Washington into a removal plan for the hospitable Seminoles. In 1832 a few Seminole chiefs were accordingly persuaded, some by bribery, to sign a treaty providing for the mass removal of their tribe west of the Mississippi. However, the tribe as a whole repudiated the treaty. Under the leadership of the famed Osceola — whose later capture came only as the result of base trickery — they refused removal and retired to the comparative safety of the Everglade swamps in southern Florida. From this stronghold, where a handful of their descendants live today, the Seminoles employed guerrilla tactics to inflict what damage they could on their enemies.

For 10 years the US Army conducted a persistent Indian hunt through the disease-ridden subtropical swamps. It was a costly and discouraging affair for all concerned. All but a few Seminoles were killed or dispossessed; 1,500 army men lost their lives; and the government, though victorious, spent $20 million in the undertaking. Most of the Seminoles who survived the war were eventually removed to Oklahoma.

In comparison with predecessors on the Florida front Taylor was successful, since he managed to force the Seminoles into one pitched battle. This was at Lake Okeechobee in December 1837. For his victory there, he won promotion to brigadier general and the applause of an adoring public, which fondly dubbed him Old Rough and Ready. But another two years of pursuing Indians convinced Taylor that the

Florida Everglades represented a dead end for him professionally, and in April 1840 he asked to be relieved.

Assigned to the command of the military department of the Southwest, he was transferred to headquarters at Baton Rouge. Hoping to remain for some time, and looking ahead to retirement, he purchased a house and settled there with his family. He also bought a plantation, which he named Cypress Grove, near Rodney, Mississippi, thus entering the ranks of slaveholders. The plantation, however, proved to be a bad investment, as it flooded nearly every spring.

Within a year, Taylor was ordered to duty in Arkansas, where he remained for three years. Then in May 1844 anticipated developments in Texas led to Taylor's assignment to Fort Jesup in nearby western Louisiana. His subsequent assignments in the Southwest were to involve him in the Mexican War (see May 13). And his role in that conflict would once again bring him public adulation, and set him firmly on the road to the presidency.

American settlers in Texas had declared their independence from Mexico in 1836. Mexico was unable to challenge the existence of the Republic of Texas, and annexation by the United States was sought by many. Late in 1845 Texas accepted a congressional resolution providing for annexation. In May 1845, some two months after passage of the resolution, President James K. Polk had ordered Taylor to prepare to expel "invaders" – meaning Mexicans – from Texas. The next month, Taylor was ordered to organize a site from which to move upon the Rio Grande, in a step to establish it as the southern boundary of Texas.

As a preliminary move, Taylor accordingly advanced into Texas with an army of 4,000 in late July, setting up a base near Corpus Christi. This was at the mouth of the Nueces River – which Mexico claimed as its northern boundary. Then, in January 1846 Taylor was ordered into the disputed territory farther south. He moved in March to Point Isabel, located on the Gulf of Mexico near the mouth of the Rio Grande. There he established a supply depot known as Fort Polk. Elements under Taylor's command also established Fort Texas – soon known as Fort Brown – on the site of what is now Brownsville, Texas. This was a few miles inland on the Rio Grande, at a point opposite Matamoros, Mexico.

On April 24, 1846, a unit of Mexican cavalry moved north across the river from Matamoros. Taylor sent out a reconnoitering party of dragoons late the same day. The dragoons were surrounded the next morning and surrendered after suffering several casualties. Taylor sent word of this engagement to Washington. The news arrived on May 9 – after President Polk had decided to declare war, but still in time to provide a *casus belli*. Polk called for war with Mexico, and Congress assented on May 13, 1846.

In the meantime, Taylor was already pressing on with the fighting. In early May he had marched part of his troops from Fort Brown to Point Isabel on the seacoast, where they worked to strengthen Fort Polk and picked up supplies and ammunition. On their return they were intercepted at Palo Alto by a Mexican force three times as large. On May 8 Taylor attacked the Mexicans and drove them back with heavy Mexican and light American casualties. The Mexicans retreated to more secure defensive positions nearby, closely pursued by the Americans, who occupied a neighboring ravine known as the Resaca de la Palma. There the armies battled again on May 9. In confused hand-to-hand fighting the Mexicans were routed, fleeing across the Rio Grande to Matamoros and suffering appalling casualties en route. On May 18 the American army moved upon Matamoros and discovered that the Mexicans had fled.

When news of these victories reached Washington, President Polk breveted Taylor major general. Congress awarded Taylor with two gold medals. Old Rough and Ready was again a hero in the United States, and people began to mention his name in connection with the presidency.

This popularity escaped neither Taylor's nor Polk's attention. As a Democratic President, Polk had a number of political problems to contend with. Since the war had broken out during his administration, it was politically imperative that it be brought to a successful end before the next presidential election, lest it provide fuel for a Whig campaign. However, the only generals capable of conducting the war, Winfield Scott and Zachary Taylor, were both Whigs.

As Polk anticipated, both generals were soon looked upon as potential presidential candidates by the Whig party. Polk exhibited little confidence in Taylor's military judgment, and as the President and his secretary of war commenced supervision of every detail of the war from Washington, Taylor began to voice his suspicion of a conspiracy to keep him from success.

During the summer of 1846 Taylor kept his army stationary while building up his troop strength, complaining all the while about the low quality of his new recruits. Then, on September 20, Taylor led his army in an unauthorized attack on Monterrey, Mexico, driving within the city walls after four days of costly fighting. Considering the cost of total victory too dear, Taylor agreed to an eight-week armistice rather than an unconditional surrender. Polk, more than ever convinced of Taylor's incompetence, was furious about the armistice and ordered the pact abrogated.

Matters grew still hotter when a private letter written by Taylor on November 5, attacking Polk and defending himself, found its way into the newspapers. Not only did the letter expose the argument between the President and general, but it also revealed the administration's war plans for an offensive on Mexico City, of which Taylor disapproved.

Early in 1847 Polk sent Taylor a severe reprimand and ordered him not to advance beyond Monterrey. Deliberately disobeying this order, Taylor advanced to Saltillo with close to 5,000 men. They met 15,000 or more Mexicans at nearby Buena Vista on February 22, 1847. The Mexicans held the advantage until, badly mauled by artillery and sharpshooting, they withdrew under cover of darkness during the night of February 23–24. In the hands of Whig newspapers north of the border, the Americans' defensive stand at Buena Vista became a major triumph for Taylor. It was the last major battle in the north of Mexico. Taylor was now a national idol. A thankful Congress awarded him another gold medal, even though Polk refused to praise his victory. General Scott was given charge of the planned attack on Mexico City, and was empowered to draw upon Taylor's army for additional personnel.

Taylor, now convinced that he was being victimized for political purposes, took a leave of absence. He returned home in November 1847, and after his initial reluctance had subsided, became available for the Whig presidential nomination. At the Whig national convention in June 1848 Taylor was nominated on the fourth ballot over such leaders as Henry Clay, Daniel Webster, and General Scott.

Taylor's advantages as a presidential nominee were enormous, for he was uncommitted on every important issue. The South remembered that he was a slaveowner, and the entire country worshiped him as a fiery military hero. Taylor won the election over Democrat Lewis Cass by approximately 140,000 votes.

After entering the White House in March 1849 Taylor lived for only 16 months. His brief presidency was unexceptional but competent, as his honesty and common sense, together with a sense of purposeful determination, triumphed over his limited educational background and lack of experience in politics. Most notable, perhaps, was his judicious handling of the slavery issue at a time when the whole country was preoccupied with the question of extension of slavery into the new territories and states being carved out of the West. While assuring Southerners that there would be no attack on the institution of slavery where it already existed, Taylor favored the admission of California as a free state and dampened threats of secession by indicating his determination to preserve the Union at all costs, with force if necessary. Unfortunately, he did not live to see the passage of Henry Clay's Compromise of 1850, which for the time assuaged sectional tensions.

On the foreign front, the most important achievement of Taylor's administration was the signing by Great Britain and the United States of the Clayton-Bulwer Treaty, whereby both countries neutralized the Central America zone in which each wished to construct a canal. Ratifications of the treaty, which the United States signed in April 1850, were exchanged early in July. By then Taylor had discovered that three members of his cabinet were involved in financial conflict-of-interest situations that threatened to become scandalous. As a result of this discovery, he decided to reorganize his entire cabinet.

However, Taylor's plans were unexpectedly cut short. On July 4 he succumbed to the heat at a groundbreaking ceremony for the Washington Monument. That night he had a fever, and on July 9, 1850, he died of what has been variously called cholera morbus and acute gastroenteritis.

Zachary Taylor was buried in the family plot on Brownsboro Road, seven miles east of Louisville, Kentucky. In 1928 the federal government established this site as the Zachary Taylor National Cemetery. The family plot is now surrounded by a national military cemetery.

In 1934 the Southern Society of New York marked the 150th anniversary of Taylor's birth. President Franklin D. Roosevelt served as the honorary chairman of the committee charged with arranging the sesquicentennial celebrations, which included a dinner at the Waldorf-Astoria Hotel. Of Taylor's boyhood home, Springfield, at 5608 Apache Road in Louisville, only the two-story brick dwelling remains. The building is now privately owned and is not open to the public.

NOVEMBER 25

Andrew Carnegie's Birthday

Andrew Carnegie's rags-to-riches life is one of the greatest success stories in American history. Born in Dunfermline, Scotland, on November 25, 1835, Carnegie knew extreme poverty as a youth. His father, William Carnegie, worked as a hand loomer. But at a time when power-driven machinery was rapidly replacing skilled workers in the textile industry, the senior Carnegie's talents were not in demand. To increase the family income, the future industrial magnate's mother, Margaret Carnegie, bound shoes and kept a sweet shop, but her earnings were meager.

Reports of better opportunities from relatives who had emigrated to the United States attracted Margaret Carnegie. Despite her husband's reluctance to leave their native land, she sold all their household goods and borrowed £20 to raise money for the passage across the Atlantic. On May 19, 1848, her efforts were rewarded; William and Margaret Carnegie together with their two sons — Andrew, aged 12, and Thomas, who was then 4 — set sail from Glasgow.

After traveling for two months, the family settled in Allegheny (now part of Pittsburgh). During his first year in the United States, Andrew Carnegie worked as a bobbin boy and engine tender in a local textile factory. He earned only $1.20 a week on his first job, but his fortunes gradually improved.

At the age of 14, Carnegie became a messenger for the Pittsburgh telegraph office. This job paid more than twice as much as the one he had held previously, and, more important, it gave him an opportunity to learn how to send and receive messages. Carnegie proved to be an apt pupil. In fact, he was one of the first telegraphers in this country to be able to read Morse Code.

Within a short time Carnegie was promoted to the position of telegraph operator. His work was outstanding, and one of his most frequent customers, Thomas C. Scott, the superintendent of the Pennsylvania Railroad, was quick to recognize his ability. In 1853 Scott hired the 17-year-old Carnegie to be his private secretary and personal telegrapher.

From 1853 to 1865, Carnegie's connection with the Pennsylvania Railroad and his close association with Scott rapidly advanced his career. In 1860 Scott became a vice president of the railroad, and his young protégé was named superintendent of the Pittsburgh division. The following year the Civil War began. So essential to the success of the Northern effort was the transportation of troops and supplies by rail that Scott was appointed assistant secretary of war. Carnegie, in turn, was selected to be the superintendent of the eastern military and telegraph lines.

Throughout the war, Carnegie rendered valuable service to the Union cause, but at the same time he also devoted himself to his private business interests. His successful introduction of sleeping cars on the Pennsylvania Railroad brought him his first fortune, since he owned one-eighth of the stock in the company that held the Pullman patents. He also invested in the recently discovered oil fields in Pennsylvania, and in 1862 he reorganized the Keystone Bridge Works so that within a short time the company was profitably constructing iron bridges that greatly improved railroad safety.

In 1865 Carnegie resigned his $200-a-month job with the Pennsylvania Railroad in order to give his full attention to his oil, iron, and other business activities. By 1868 his yearly income averaged $50,000, but his interests were still diversified. He established the Union Iron Mills in 1868, sold railroad securities on commission to European buyers, and retained his oil and bridge construction holdings.

By 1873 Carnegie had begun to concentrate his investments in steel. Prior to the Civil War the metal had been produced on a very limited scale in the United States, and, contrary to popular belief, the war had further retarded expansion of the industry. Economic recovery and the boom in railroad building in the 1870s, however, resulted in a greater demand for steel than could be met by foreign imports. Carnegie realized the vast potential of the steel industry. In 1873, according to his own words, he put "all his eggs in one basket," using all his financial resources to establish the J. Edgar Thomson Steel Mills.

Carnegie's gamble made him a millionaire. During the last three decades of the 19th century, the United States became the world's chief producer of steel. Foresight and a genius for organization yielded Carnegie enormous profits from this rapid expansion. By 1900 the Carnegie Steel Company virtually controlled the industry in this country, and Carnegie's share of the profits amounted to $25 million.

The employees of Carnegie's steel mills did not always share his success. While Carnegie was in Europe in 1892, the president of his Homestead plant violated its contract with the Amalgamated Association of Iron and Steel Workers and announced a wage cut. When the union members refused to accept this, the factory was shut down, and 300 Pinkerton detectives were hired to protect it. This action outraged the workers. They attacked the Pinkerton men, and order was not restored until the state militia intervened. The unsuccessful five-month strike that ensued had far-reaching consequences; it retarded unionization of steel workers for 40 years.

In 1901 the newly formed US Steel Corporation bought Carnegie's company. Carnegie retired and received $250 million in 5 percent, 50-

year bonds for his share in the business. For the remainder of his life, the great steel tycoon devoted himself to philanthropy.

In his book the *Gospel of Wealth*, Carnegie articulated his belief that a man with excess riches was "the mere trustee and agent for his poorer brethren." He lived according to this dictate. Before his death in 1919, he had given away $311 million.

Carnegie is best known for his beneficence to public libraries. He was convinced that libraries "are entitled to a first place for the elevation of the masses of the people," but he also believed that "unless a community is willing to maintain libraries at the public cost, very little good can be obtained from them." For this reason Carnegie gave only library buildings and required local governments to provide them with books and operating funds. Many localities agreed to these stipulations, and Carnegie — and after his death the Carnegie Corporation — contributed more than $56 million for the construction of libraries.

But libraries were not the only recipients of Carnegie's generosity. In 1900 he founded the Carnegie Technological Schools in Pittsburgh, to train young people for jobs in industrial society. In 1912 the schools became the Carnegie Institute of Technology, one of the country's leading study and research centers. In 1967 Carnegie Tech, as it was popularly known, merged with Mellon Institute to form the distinguished Carnegie-Mellon University. In addition Carnegie gave approximately $20 million to such schools as Cooper Union, Berea College, and the Hampton Institute in the United States, and an estimated $10 million to several universities in Scotland so that students with limited financial resources could receive a college education.

Moreover, Carnegie knew that his desire to advance higher education could succeed only if professorships were financially attractive. Thus the Carnegie Foundation for the Advancement of Teaching and its successor organizations have contributed more than $29 million to provide pensions and retirement insurance for staff members of many colleges and universities throughout the country.

Carnegie also used his fortune to promote international understanding. He built both the Peace Palace at The Hague (see April 20), which serves today as the seat for the International Court of Justice, and the Pan American Union Building in Washington, D.C., a center (see April 14) for promoting closer inter-American relations. His gift of $10 million founded the Carnegie Endowment for International Peace.

Pittsburgh, the scene of Carnegie's success, owes much to the steel magnate. His greatest contribution to the city is the Carnegie Institute, which is located at 4400 Forbes Street. The institute houses the Carnegie Library, the Museum of Art, the Museum of Natural History, the Division of Education, and the Carnegie Music Hall.

The dedication of the Carnegie Library in November 1895 was followed by the annual observance of founder's day at the institute. At the end of the 19th century and in the opening decades of the 20th, the annual program fell on various dates in October. The occasion customarily marked the opening of an international art exhibit and included appropriate speeches by distinguished national leaders. More recently, the celebration of Founder-Patrons Day — as it has been called since 1951 — has changed somewhat. The date of the observance is now set for the third Thursday in October. International displays are still featured every three years, but in other years the program has highlighted the art of one country.

Carnegie's other philanthropies were varied: gifts for church organs, for Carnegie Hall in New York City, for the Carnegie Institution of Washington, and for the Hero Fund — which was established to provide for the dependents of men who died saving others. In 1911 he founded the Carnegie Corporation of New York, which works "for the advancement and diffusion of knowledge and understanding."

Carnegie lived in quiet luxury after his retirement. He spent six months each year at his castle, Skibo, in Scotland, and he owned a magnificent mansion on Fifth Avenue in New York City. (The mansion now houses the Cooper-Hewitt Museum of Decorative Arts and Design.) He died on August 11, 1919, aged 84, at Shadowbrook, his summer home in Lenox, Massachusetts. He was survived by his wife, Louise Whitfield Carnegie, and one daughter, Margaret Carnegie Miller.

Evacuation Day

By the time the United States and Great Britain signed the Treaty of Paris of 1783, which ended the American Revolution, British forces occupied only two points along the Atlantic coast of the new American nation: a lumber area at the mouth of the Penobscot River in what is now Maine, and New York City. The British had captured New York in September 1776 and made it their headquarters and base of operations. They then controlled Manhattan Island, Staten Island, Long Island, and points along the New Jersey side of the Hudson River.

Most of New York's population fled in 1776 while battles raged in the vicinity, but after the British wrested the port from the colonial rebels, many Tories returned to their homes in the city. During the Revolution, Loyalists, doubtful Whigs, and refugees gravitated to New York. A number of silent patriot sympathizers also remained there under the thumb of the British garrison. But whatever their political preference, all lived under harsh conditions aggravated by sickness, by lack of supplies, and by fires in 1776 and 1778, which destroyed a total of almost 600 buildings.

Soon after the announcement of peace in April 1783, patriot supporters began to return to the city in large numbers, and under strict regulations secured their former houses and lands. Tories, who feared reprisals or who were unwilling to accommodate themselves to the new order, left the city in large numbers. Brook Watson, the British commissary general, reported that between January and November 1783 a total of 29,244 men, women, and children abandoned New York on British vessels bound for Canada or Europe.

Sir Guy Carleton, who became the British commander in chief in the concluding stage of the war, had the delicate assignment of suspending hostilities and protecting Loyalists while withdrawing the remaining British forces. When news of the peace arrived, Carleton acted to facilitate the evacuation of New York City by disbanding the Loyalist units and dispatching a number of regulars to the West Indies, Nova Scotia, and England. By November only slightly more than 6,000 troops remained in the port.

General George Washington met Sir Guy Carleton in May 1783 on board the *Greyhound*, anchored off the Hudson River town of Dobbs Ferry, to discuss the evacuation of New York. Carleton assured Washington that the British would leave as soon as Rear Admiral Robert Digby's fleet completed removal of those Tories who wished to leave the United States. Eventually the two men agreed on November 22 as the final day for the withdrawal operation, but rain caused a postponement until November 25.

General Washington, who had disbanded nearly all the Continental army at Newburgh and West Point, New York, was ready to occupy New York City with a small force as soon as the British departed. On November 19 Washington arrived at Day's Tavern (at what is now 125th Street and Eighth Avenue) in the company of Governor George Clinton and several other army officers and state officials. The contingent of approximately 85,000 regular army soldiers who were to occupy the city camped at McGowan's

Pass (now 110th Street and Fifth Avenue). The troops under the command of Brevet Brigadier General Henry Jackson of Boston were veterans of the long war, the infantry belonging to the Massachusetts line and the artillery to New York.

On Evacuation Day, November 25, 1783, two processions took place. The military paraded into the city to occupy it officially and to relieve the British garrison of control. Then Washington and state officers entered the city to take legal possession of it by virtue of their political authority.

At 8:00 A.M. on November 25 the military units began their march down the Old Post Road into the Bowery, where they halted. At 1:00 P.M., after a British officer announced that the last British guards had withdrawn, the parade resumed. A troop of dragoons commanded by Captain John Stakes led the marchers. An advance guard of light infantry, the artillery, the battalion of light infantry, the 2nd Massachusetts Regiment, and a rear guard composed the rest of the line. The soldiers passed from the Bowery to Chatham Street and then turned down Queen Street. Now known as Pearl Street, Queen Street was the principal business thoroughfare of the city in the 18th century and was also the site of many fine homes. The paraders turned west onto Wall Street and proceeded to Broadway. They halted opposite Cape's Tavern at the northwest corner of Rector Street to await the arrival of the dignitaries.

One company of light infantry and one of artillery then proceeded down Broadway to take official possession of Fort George, raise the American flag, and fire a 13-gun salute. Upon arrival there, the Americans found themselves the victims of a practical joke by the British, who had greased the flagpole and removed the halyards. A sailor made three unsuccessful attempts to climb the slippery pole. Finally he filled his pockets with spikes and managed to ascend the pole by driving the nails into the wood as foot-holds as he climbed. When the sailor reached the top he installed new halyards, and an artillery officer raised the flag. The Americans then fired their salute, as the British and Hessians watched and listened from their ships in the harbor.

The parade of civilian officials, led by Captain Delavan's Light Horse, followed the route taken by the soldiery. General George Washington and Governor George Clinton led the dignitaries on horseback. The lieutenant governor, members of the council of the temporary government of the city, General Henry Knox and other army officers, citizens on horseback, the speaker of the assembly, and citizens on foot followed in that order. Following speeches, the governor gave a formal dinner at Fraunces Tavern, where 13 toasts were offered to commemorate the occasion.

Governor Clinton established himself in the DeLancey mansion on Queen Street and began to conduct the affairs of government. On December 2 a public fireworks display took place at the Bowling Green. Two days later, in a most touching scene, George Washington bade farewell to his troops at Fraunces Tavern. Finally, on December 11 the activities concluded appropriately with a national day of public thanksgiving observed with a number of religious programs.

For decades after the departure of the British from New York City, patriot organizations sponsored special celebrations to commemorate the event. These observances lapsed during the first and middle years of the 20th century, but the approach of the bicentennial of the American Revolution revived interest in Evacuation Day ceremonies.

In 1970 several organizations including the American-Irish Historical Society, the Irish Institute, the Sons of the American Revolution, the New York City National Shrines Associates, and the New York City Revolutionary Bicentennial Citizens Committee combined Evacuation Day observances with special ceremonies honoring Hercules Mulligan. Mulligan, a tailor who served as a secret agent for the Continental army during the British occupation of New York, provided much important information to the patriots throughout the Revolution. George Washington personally recognized Mulligan by breakfasting with him on the morning after American forces reoccupied the city, and almost two centuries later, on November 24, 1970, the aforementioned societies paid tribute to Mulligan by unveiling a plaque at the site of his house at 160 Water Street, where a skyscraper stands today. Willliam B. Mulligan, a direct descendant of the tailor and patriot, unveiled the plaque, the US Army band played patriotic music, and color guards from the various armed services also participated in the ceremonies.

In 1971 the New York City American Revolutionary Bicentennial Committee, the New York City National Shrines Associates, the Battery – Castle Clinton Monument Association, the Sons of the Revolution, the US Flag Foundation, and the New York Chapter of the Association of the US Army noted Evacuation Day with observances in New York's Battery Park. The color guards of the Sons of the Revolution, of the various branches of the armed forces, and of the American Legion and the New York City Fire Department took part in ceremonies; the US Army band provided appropriate music, and speakers added pertinent remarks. The Battery Park observances were the first in a series planned for annual observance during the Bicentennial commemoration of the American Revolution.

NOVEMBER 26

Thanksgiving Day

This is a movable event. See note on page xxvi.

Every year on the fourth Thursday of November the people of the United States pause to express their gratitude for the bounty and good fortune that they enjoy both as individuals and as a nation. Thanksgiving Day is a legal holiday, observed everywhere throughout the United States and in US territories, as well as in the Commonwealth of Puerto Rico. Customarily, the President of the United States issues a proclamation of Thanksgiving Day, and the governors of many of the 50 states often add their own messages.

Although Thanksgiving is one of the most popular holidays in the United States, the idea of setting aside a day to express gratitude for good fortune did not originate in this country. In ancient times many peoples held special festivals in the autumn to give thanks for bountiful harvests. The Greeks honored Demeter, their goddess of agriculture, with a nine-day celebration, and in a similar fashion the Romans paid tribute to Ceres (identified with Demeter). After the crops had been gathered, the Anglo-Saxons rejoiced at a "harvest home," which featured a hearty feast. In Scotland the harvest celebration was known as a *kirn* and included special church services and a substantial dinner. Since biblical days, Jews have given thanks for abundant harvests with the eight-day Feast of Tabernacles, an observance that continues to the present era (see October 15). From ancient times, it also was common for people to set aside special days on which to give thanks for military victories, for deliverance from epidemics, and for other occasions of good fortune.

Thus, since most of the settlers who came to America probably had known some form of thanksgiving day in their homelands, it is not surprising that they transplanted this custom to the New World. The first thanksgiving day service in what was to become the United States was the one held on August 9, 1607, by colonists en route to found the short-lived Popham Colony at what is now Phippsburg, Maine. After their two ships had reached one of the Georges Islands off the Maine coast, the Reverend Richard Seymour led the group in "gyvinge God thanks for our happy metinge & saffe aryval into the country."

The first permanent English settlement in America was founded at Jamestown, on the James River in Virginia, also in 1607. After the tobacco introduced there in 1612 proved to be a successful crop, plantation settlements, or "hundreds" — an early British designation for areas smaller than counties — sprang up elsewhere along the banks of the James. As early as December 4, 1619, the settlers at one of them — Berkeley Hundred — set aside a day to give thanks for the survival of their small company. The settlers at Berkeley, between what are now Richmond and Charles City, observed December 4 each year with special religious services until 1622, when a conflict with Indians almost devastated the colony. Records of the Virginia observances are scant, and for many years most persons were unaware of their existence. Today, however, a special Thanksgiving Festival lasting several days takes place annually at the site of the original. Civic ceremonies, church services, and a football game are among the scheduled events, but the culmination of the festival is a pageant reenacting the thanksgiving of 1619.

Although the Berkeley thanksgiving was probably the first full celebration of its kind by colonists in the New World — the "first official" thanksgiving is a term favored by some — it was another thanksgiving, which took place in Plymouth Colony in 1621, that set the pattern for present-day observances. After landing on the bleak New England coast in 1620, the Pilgrim band had endured tremendous hardships (see December 21, Forefathers' Day, and May 19, William Bradford's Death). During the winter of 1620 about half the 101 passengers of the *Mayflower* died. But those who survived persevered. In the spring and summer of 1621 they constructed a number of wooden houses, and with the aid of Squanto, a Pawtuxet Indian, they planted and cultivated fields of corn and barley. In the fall the Pilgrims gathered a rich harvest, and Governor Bradford proclaimed a day of thanksgiving.

The first Pilgrim thanksgiving probably occurred some time in the middle of October 1621. Governor Bradford "sent four men fowling, so they might in a special manner rejoice together after they had gathered the fruit of their labor." According to Bradford's history *Of Plimoth Plantation*, the hunters brought back a "great store of wild Turkies," and to this were added lobsters, clams, bass, corn, green vegetables, and dried fruits.

The Pilgrims invited Massasoit, the chief of the Wampanoag tribe, to share their feast. Massasoit enthusiastically agreed to attend the celebration, but when he unexpectedly brought along 90 companions the Pilgrim settlers feared that the natives would consume their entire winter larder. Fortunately, however, Massasoit recognized their difficult position and sent his hunters into the forest. They returned with five deer, and the feast began.

For three days the Pilgrims and the Wampanoag shared the bountiful feast. The militia under the leadership of Captain Myles Standish drilled and fired their muskets and cannon to entertain their guests, and in turn the Wampanoag delighted their hosts with demonstrations of their traditional dances. The group also competed in foot races and other athletic contests.

The Pilgrims did not celebrate a thanksgiving in 1622. But in 1623, after a rainstorm ended a summer drought and saved the settlers' crops, the Plymouth populace again observed a day of thanks, probably toward the end of July. And in November after the crops were gathered, Governor Bradford ordered that "all the Pilgrims with your wives and little ones, do gather at the meetinghouse, on the hill, . . . there to listen to the pastor, and render thanksgiving to the Almighty God for all His blessings."

The Pilgrims never set a regular Thanksgiving day, although they held such observances at various times. A law of November 15, 1636, permitted the governor "to command solemn days of humiliation by fasting, etc., and also for thanksgiving as occasion shall be offered." In the decades that followed, harvest festivals were held sporadically in the area around Boston, in the Massachusetts Bay Colony to the north; and in 1665 Connecticut observed a solemn day of thanksgiving on the last Wednesday of October. Beginning in 1644, the Dutch residents of New Amsterdam set aside special Thank Days, and this custom continued even after the British captured the city and renamed it New York in 1664. Typically, though, the early thanksgiving celebrations were to be found in New England. Other colonists in other areas may also have marked thanksgiving occasions of one kind or another, but these were local, isolated events.

Appropriately, the War of Independence, during which the 13 colonies joined in a common effort for the first time, also caused the first Thanksgiving Day to be observed simultaneously. throughout all the colonies. The occasion for the celebration was the patriot victory over the British at Saratoga in October 1777. So important to the rebel cause was this battle that Samuel Adams called upon the Continental Congress to declare a national day of thanks. On

November 1, 1777, the Congress approved Adams's proclamation, setting December 18, 1777, as a day of "Thanksgiving and praise," and the residents of the colonies enthusiastically observed the day with prayers and feasts.

In the course of the American Revolution, the Continental Congress called for a number of days of thanksgiving, although none was observed by all the colonies. A number of local thanksgiving celebrations took place, the most notable of which was at the headquarters of the Continental army at Valley Forge, Pennsylvania, after General George Washington received news that France had allied with the colonies. To celebrate the alliance, Washington ordered his troops to assemble on May 7, 1778. Ceremonies began with the army chaplains offering prayers of gratitude. Then the general reviewed the troops; 13 cannons fired a salute; and the soldiers shouted "Long live the king of France and the American states." After the day's festivities concluded, the troops enjoyed a hearty dinner, and the French officers and other guests attended an outdoor banquet.

The end of the American Revolution in 1783 secured independence of the 13 American colonies, and the adoption of the Constitution established a viable government that began to function in 1789. Both the Revolutionary War and the formulation of the Constitution were massive undertakings, and to celebrate their successful outcomes, Washington, who by then had become the first President of the United States, proclaimed Thursday, November 26, 1789, a day of national thanksgiving. At the request of the President, citizens assembled in churches that day and thanked God for his beneficence.

In 1795 Washington proclaimed another day of thanksgiving, but after that the national celebration of the holiday lapsed. New Englanders, however, continued the custom of holding harvest feasts each autumn, and in other parts of the country, days of thanksgiving were also observed. In 1769, meanwhile, some Spanish colonists in California set aside July 1 as a day to give thanks after surviving the many hazards that had accompanied their settlement of San Diego. Years later a more traditional thanksgiving was held at Portsmouth House in San Francisco, where a superb dinner was served; and in 1849, shortly before gaining statehood, Californians observed Thanksgiving on October 24.

The establishment of a national Thanksgiving Day on a permanent annual basis was largely the result of the work of Sarah Josepha Hale. Beginning in 1827, when she was editor of the *Ladies' Magazine* in Boston, she began to urge the observance of a uniform day throughout the country to express thanks for the blessings of the year. She continued her agitation in a desultory manner until the *Ladies' Magazine* was consolidated with *Godey's Lady's Book*. As editor of *Godey's*, a magazine with a circulation of 150,000 and the largest periodical of its kind in the country, she wrote editorial after editorial in support of an annual Thanksgiving Day. She also wrote personal letters to the successive Presidents and to the governors of all the states and succeeded in persuading many of the latter to fix the last Thursday in November as a day of thanksgiving. Hale's last editorial on the subject appeared in September 1863 and said in part:

Would it not be a great advantage, socially, nationally, religiously, to have the day of our American Thanksgiving positively settled? Putting aside the sectional feelings and local incidents that might be urged by any single State or isolated territory that desired to choose its own time would it not be more noble, more truly American, to become national in unity when we offer to God our tribute of joy and gratitude for the blessings of the year?

Hale's editorial appeared at a significant moment. The Civil War divided the nation into two armed camps in 1863. For more than two years Northern and Southern forces had clashed, and, only weeks before the editorial appeared, hundreds of Union and Confederate soldiers had died at Gettysburg. Despite the staggering loss of human life, the battle of Gettysburg was an important victory for the North. The result produced great rejoicing throughout the North, and this general feeling of elation, together with the clamor produced by Hale's editorials, undoubtedly prompted Abraham Lincoln to issue the proclamation on October 3, 1863, setting a last Thursday in November 1863 as a national Thanksgiving Day.

Lincoln's proclamation, expressing both his gratitude for God's blessings and his hope that the terrible war would come to a speedy end, entreated Americans not to forget that prosperity and freedom were God's gifts.

It has seemed to me fit and proper that they should be solemnly, reverently and gratefully acknowledged as with one heart and one voice by the whole American people. I do, therefor, invite my fellow citizens in every part of the United States, and also those who are at sea and those who are sojourning in foreign lands, to set apart and observe the last Thursday of November next as a day of thanksgiving and praise to our beneficent Father who dwelleth in the heavens.

Ever since 1863, Thanksgiving has been observed annually; and for three-quarters of a century it was scheduled, with only two exceptions, for the last Thursday of November. President Andrew Johnson designated the first Thursday in December as Thanksgiving in 1865; and President Ulysses S. Grant selected the third Thursday in November for the observance in 1869.

A more controversial exception came in 1939. President Franklin D. Roosevelt issued a proclamation setting November 23 — rather than November 30, which was the last Thursday in November that year — as Thanksgiving Day. Roosevelt's action was not favorably received. Despite the proclamation, many states observed Thanksgiving on November 30, and even where celebrations were held on November 23, citizens expressed dissatisfaction with the change. Roosevelt himself realized in the spring of 1941 that he had erred, and he announced that, beginning in 1942, his innovation of marking Thanksgiving on the next to last Thursday in November would be abandoned. Congress formalized this decision in December 1941 with a joint resolution that placed the holiday thenceforth on the fourth Thursday in November.

Thanksgiving has become one of the best loved and most widely celebrated holidays in the United States. Each year citizens across the land pause to give thanks. In time of war, when large numbers of armed forces personnel have been overseas, Americans have even observed Thanksgiving Day in foreign lands. One of the most impressive of many foreign Thanksgiving services took place in 1942 at Westminster Abbey in London. More than 3,500 American troops who were stationed in England during World War II jammed into the historic church and participated in services that included the singing of "The Star-Spangled Banner" and "America the Beautiful." The special service of thanksgiving was the first service other than a Church of England ritual to be held at the abbey's altar in nine centuries.

Whether in Westminster Abbey or in a local house of worship, Thanksgiving is an occasion on which people assemble to express their gratitude to God. Many churches and synagogues hold special services on the day or preceding evening, and interfaith observances have become increasingly popular in recent years. The fruits of the harvest, traditionally distributed to the poor afterwards, are often used to decorate places of worship (as well as schools and other places of public gathering). Thanksgiving sermons stress the need for gratitude and for regarding material possessions appropriately. One of the readings from Scripture frequently heard at Thanksgiving comes from the eighth chapter of Deuteronomy, in which Moses reminds his listeners that they must not forget God:

Man does not live by bread alone, but . . . by everything that proceeds out of the mouth of the Lord. . . . Take heed lest you forget the Lord your God, by not keeping his commandments . . . lest, when you have eaten and are full, and have built goodly houses and live in them, . . . and your silver and gold is multiplied, . . . your heart be lifted up, and you forget the Lord your God.

Another is from the sixth chapter of Matthew, in which Jesus says to his followers:

Therefore I tell you, . . . do not be anxious, saying "What shall we eat?" or "What shall we drink?" or "What shall we wear?" For . . . your heavenly Father knows that you need [these things]. But seek first his kingdom and his righteousness, and all these things shall be yours as well.

One hymn often sung at this time, set to a traditional Dutch melody so familiar that it is synonymous with Thanksgiving to many, begins with the words "We gather together to ask the Lord's blessing." Others frequently heard preserve the traditional harvest theme:

Come, ye thankful people, come,
Raise the song of harvest home:
All is safely gathered in,
Ere the winter storms begin;
God, our Maker, doth provide
For our wants to be supplied;
Come to God's own temple, come,
Raise the song of harvest home.

Another well-known Thanksgiving hymn begins with words that epitomize as well as any the fundamental significance of the observance:

Now thank we all our God
With heart and hands and voices,
Who wondrous things hath done,
In whom His world rejoices.

Thanksgiving has always been a day on which families come together for a sumptuous dinner. Just as the Pilgrims in Plymouth enjoyed "a great store of wild Turkies," many Americans now feast on the domesticated descendants of these birds. Dressing, sweet potatoes, squash, creamed onions, and cranberries generally complement the turkey, as does a vast array of other culinary attractions. Pumpkin and mincemeat pies are the favored desserts of the day, with Indian and plum puddings as close seconds.

Many special events are held on Thanksgiving and the following weekend. It is traditionally a period for professional and college football games, some nationally televised.

Among the local traditional Thanksgiving

celebrations is the annual two-day fund-raising festival held at Pilgrim Place, a home for retired Christian workers in Claremont, California. For the occasion, residents of the home wear colonial dress, and visitors may partake of a turkey dinner, explore the many exhibits, and see a pageant, Pilgrims Triumphant, that traces the history of the Pilgrims from Scrooby, England, to their first thanksgiving in Plymouth.

Plymouth, Massachusetts, is, appropriately, the scene of special Thanksgiving festivities. Places of importance in Plymouth history, including several 17th century houses and Pilgrim Hall, a repository of many Pilgrim artifacts, are regularly open, but the public is extended a special welcome, and refreshments are served on Thanksgiving Day. The highlight of Plymouth's celebration is a procession entitled The Pilgrim's Progress. Each of the 52 Pilgrims who survived the first winter in New England is represented by a Plymouth resident dressed in a replica of 17th century garb. The line of march begins at the Plymouth waterfront near the reproduction of the first house and, to a slow drum beat, proceeds up Leyden Street to Burial Hill, the site of Plymouth's first fort-meetinghouse. After reaching Burial Hill, the marchers and spectators generally attend services at the First Church, which stands on the hill on the site of the original Pilgrim Church.

Although Thanksgiving Day is generally a peaceful time in Plymouth, the holiday has been marked by American Indian demonstrations protesting unjust treatment. The first occurred in 1970, when about 25 Indians observed a day of mourning. Dressed in native garb, they first gathered in front of the statue of the Indian chief Massasoit, which overlooks Plymouth Harbor. Then they buried Plymouth Rock under mounds of sand and ripped the colors from the replica of the *Mayflower* that is moored in the harbor.

While Thanksgiving is a holiday in its own right, it is also the unofficial beginning of the Christmas season, and in many places it is the only day on which Santa Claus comes to town. On Thanksgiving Day in 1920, Gimbel Brothers sponsored the first toy parade in Philadelphia, and ever since that date the department store has organized a gigantic Thanksgiving parade featuring floats, mammoth balloons, and college and high school bands.

Many other cities followed the lead of Philadelphia; the best known and largest Thanksgiving toy parade takes place in New York City. On a lesser scale, holiday parades also take place in smaller cities and towns around the nation, but wherever a toyland parade is held, Santa Claus is the guest of honor — much to the delight of the children who throng the line of march.

NOVEMBER 27

Robert R. Livingston's Birthday

Robert R. Livingston, a distinguished jurist, statesman, and political leader during and after the American Revolution, and the man who administered the oath of office to President George Washington, was born in New York City on November 27, 1746. He was the eldest son of Judge Robert R. Livingston and Margaret Beekman Livingston. Born into a family that had attained prominence soon after establishing its roots in the American colonies in the latter part of the 17th century, the younger Robert Livingston became the most important of the numerous members of the family who were public figures in his day.

After completing his education at King's College (now Columbia University) in 1765, he studied law privately. In 1770, the year in which he was admitted to the bar, he married Mary Stevens, the sister of the inventor John Stevens. The couple had two daughters. Livingston was later associated with Stevens in experiments relating to the development of steam navigation. Livingston and John Jay, who subsequently served as the first chief justice of the United States, were law partners for a time. In 1773 Livingston was appointed by the British government to the judicial post of recorder of New York City. However, because of his sympathy with the goal of independence, he was removed from office in 1775.

Livingston was elected a delegate that year to the Continental Congress. In the next decade in intermittent membership in the Congress, he made many valuable contributions in widely diverse areas. Perhaps in hopes of exerting pressure on the New York Provincial Congress, which had not yet authorized its delegation to vote in favor of independence, the Congress named Livingston one of five delegates appointed to draft a declaration of independence. Most of this task was performed by Thomas Jefferson. Because the New York delegation was still not authorized to vote "yea," it abstained from voting when the Lee resolution for independence was adopted by the Continental Congress on July 2, 1776, and when the final version of the Declaration of Independence was adopted two days later (see July 4) by an otherwise unanimous vote. On July 9 the newly elected New York Provincial Congress endorsed the declaration. Livingston was in New York as a member of that body on August 2 when the Declaration of Independence was signed by most of the delegates to the Continental Congress. His signature was never added, despite his membership on the committee to draft the document.

During this period Livingston served in the Continental Congress on military and finance committees, among many others, and on the committee charged with working out a plan of confederation for the colonies. He played an important role in the drafting of the first New York constitution, in 1777, and then served on the commission that governed after the constitution was adopted but before it took effect. One provision of the constitution, proposed by Livingston, was the creation of a council of revision having veto power; the council consisted of the governor, the chancellor, and the justices of the supreme court. Livingston was appointed to the judicial post of chancellor, which he held until 1801. According to Jefferson, he was "one of the ablest of American lawyers." In the council of revision, measures he opposed included the confiscation and alienation laws directed against the Loyalists; those conferring special powers on the magistracy, with possible resultant loss of freedom by citizens; and one to eliminate slavery in New York. Livingston returned to the Continental Congress from 1779 to 1781, and again he worked diligently and constructively on various committees, including ones concerned with military affairs, foreign affairs, finance, and legal organization.

The Congress created a department of foreign affairs in 1781, and on August 10 Livingston was elected its secretary. His organization and operation of the department were efficient, in contrast to the methods previously used by the Congress. During the peace negotiations with Great Britain, initiated in 1782 in Paris, Livingston sent the American negotiators many recommendations and considerable material for discussion. Among his concerns were boundaries, fishing rights, and West Indian trade, and he took a stand against the repatriation of Loyalists. His suggestions for minor changes in the provisional draft of the treaty were included in the final version. In December 1782 he resigned, offering the reason that his expenses as foreign secretary were $3,000 a year greater that his salary. Dissatisfaction with congressional actions in the area of foreign affairs may also have prompted his resignation. The Congress was reluctant to accept it, however, and persuaded him to remain in office until May 1783. In 1784–1785, he again served as a member of the Continental Congress.

Because of fear that the proposed federal government would interfere with commerce, the New York delegation to the Constitutional Convention of 1787 opposed the newly drafted federal constitution. Livingston's efforts were probably second only to Alexander Hamilton's in gaining ratification of the constitution by New York at a special convention the following year. In his capacity as chancellor of New York, Livingston administered the presidential oath of office to George Washington on April 30, 1789. After the formation of the federal government, Livingston, unhappy at having received no patronage and differing on financial policy with Hamilton (who had become secretary of the Treasury), led his family group in joining the Antifederalists. In a contest for the governorship of New York in 1795, he was defeated by Chief Justice John Jay, even though the latter was in England at the time, negotiating what came to be known as Jay's Treaty.

Livingston had declined the post of minister to France when it was offered to him in 1794 by Washington, but he accepted it when President Thomas Jefferson offered it in 1801. He acted firmly, even boldly, as a negotiator. With the help of James Monroe, who had previously served as minister to France, he concluded in 1803 the purchase of the vast territory of Louisiana (see December 20).

After his resignation in 1804, Livingston retired to his estate, called Clermont, in New York. He was an influential experimenter in scientific agriculture, and in 1791 had with other landowners founded the Society for the Promotion of Agriculture, Arts, and Manufactures (known later as the Society for the Promotion of Useful Arts) to urge and adopt improved methods. His interest in the possibilities of steam navigation led him to aid various experimenters, including Robert Fulton, whose *Clermont,* named for Livingston's home, became in 1807 the first successful steam-propelled vessel. For some years Livingston and Fulton held a joint monopoly in steam navigation in New York State, a monopoly that was very unpopular and bitterly contested. The resulting legal conflicts were not resolved until after Livingston's death — at Clermont, New York, on February 26, 1813.

NOVEMBER 28

The Teheran Conference

The Allied decision to carry out Operation Overlord, thus opening a second front in Western Europe during World War II, was made at the Teheran (Tehran) Conference, held from November 28 to December 1, 1943. At this historic conference of the Big Three heads of state — President Franklin D. Roosevelt, British Prime

Minister Winston Churchill, and Soviet Premier Joseph Stalin — the American and Russian leaders met for the first time, in Teheran, the capital of Iran.

During previous conferences, Roosevelt and Churchill had discussed the idea of launching an invasion from Great Britain across the English Channel into northern France. Such a move, long urged by Stalin, was expected to put considerable additional pressure on Nazi Germany, which had been fighting along an extended eastern front ever since its invasion of the Soviet Union in June 1941. The plan would necessitate diversion of German troops not only from that sector but probably also from Italy, where Allied forces were trying to advance northward.

When Roosevelt and Churchill met in mid-January 1943 at Casablanca, Morocco (site of one of the three Allied landing points during the invasion of North Africa just two months earlier), they agreed that they would not be militarily prepared to open a second front that year. By the time of their next meeting, in Washington, D.C., in May, Roosevelt and his American advisers were eager to formulate plans for a cross-Channel invasion of France the following spring. Agreement was reached on a target date of May 1, 1944. Plans for the operation (code-named Overlord), which had been prepared by a joint Anglo-American staff, were considered by the President and the prime minister at a conference in Quebec, Canada, in August. There were differences of opinion, but the importance of the cross-Channel invasion and the target date were reaffirmed.

At a meeting in Cairo, Egypt, in November, immediately preceding the Teheran Conference, Churchill proposed delaying Overlord until about July 1 in order to concentrate more effort in Italy and the Mediterranean. The Americans were dubious about British proposals to expand Mediterranean involvements.

Stalin was joined in Teheran by Roosevelt and Churchill on November 28, and his insistence that the principal emphasis of the European war in 1944 should be a second front strongly influenced the final decision. A new target date of late May or early June was set. For some time the sorely pressed Russians had been insistent, contending that because of the lack of another major front, their troops were virtually the only ones engaging the German military might in Europe. During the conference, Stalin also endorsed a plan for an approximately concurrent invasion of southern France, to which the other leaders agreed. Churchill was particularly eager to reopen the Mediterranean sea routes to the Soviet Union through the Bosporus and Dardanelles straits, which were controlled by neutral Turkey. He obtained from Stalin a prom-

ise to support Turkey if the latter could be induced to enter the war on the side of the Allies.

On June 6, 1944, the second front was opened as Allied forces crossed the English Channel to land on the beaches of Normandy, in northern France (see June 6, D Day). The proposed assault on southern France was postponed, however, in order not to take men and equipment from the offensive then under way in Italy; the southern invasion was actually begun on August 15 by a combined US-French army. As for British hopes concerning Turkey, they were dashed by what were considered outrageously large Turkish demands for military aid in return for the abandonment of neutrality.

The conferees at Teheran also discussed postwar plans. Formal assurance was given to their host country, Iran, of their respect for its "independence, sovereignty, and territorial integrity" — even though Great Britain and the Soviet Union had been vying for spheres of influence in the area. The two countries had occupied Iran in August 1941 to prevent its possible takeover by Germany and to provide a route for shipment of supplies from the West to the Soviet Union. In 1943 Iran protested that the USSR had isolated the area they were occupying, preventing contact between it and the rest of the country. The Teheran agreement ostensibly rectified the situation, but in reality it did not. After the end of the war, in 1945, an allegedly Soviet-fomented rebellion broke out in the region. Not until a number of international protests had been lodged did the Soviet Union withdraw its troops from Iran, in 1946.

Of major significance was the announcement by the Big Three at Teheran of their determination to see established an international body dedicated to maintaining worldwide peace and security. They also pledged themselves to a policy of nonintervention in the internal affairs of other countries. The idea for such an organization, which also had the approval of Nationalist China, was first publicly outlined a month earlier by the foreign ministers of the United States, Britain, and the Soviet Union during a meeting in Moscow. The concept took root and came to fruition a year and a half later in the founding of the United Nations.

NOVEMBER 29

Advent Begins

This is a movable event. See note on page xxvi.

The season of Advent, observed in most Christian churches, is a preparation for the feast of Christmas, which celebrates the birth of Jesus Christ on December 25 — just as the Lenten season is a preparation for Easter. One of the major divisions of the Christian year, Advent lasts for four weeks or a little less. It begins on the Sunday nearest St. Andrew's Day, November 30, and includes the four Sundays before Christmas.

The word Advent is taken from the Latin *adventus,* meaning "coming" or "arrival." Eastern and some Western churches first observed Advent as an ascetic period of preparation for the feast of the Epiphany — which, in commemorating the manifestations of Christ's divinity, originally celebrated both his birth and his baptism. In the fourth century, however, the Western churches under Rome fixed upon December 25 for a separate commemoration of Christ's nativity. Later in the same century the Eastern churches followed suit, introducing the separate observance of the Nativity on December 25.

The observance of the Advent season eventually underwent a corresponding shift in time. Thus, when Advent was first adopted by Rome, it was as a liturgical (not penitential) season in preparation for Christmas (not Epiphany). This was probably some time in the sixth century.

In the Middle Ages, the faithful fasted during Advent, which was called "the Christmas Lent." Fasting is no longer required, but the liturgical color — purple — is a reminder of the somewhat penitential aspects of Advent, which have for the most part given way to a mood of expectation directed toward the celebration of the Coming of Jesus Christ.

Since the 9th or 10th century, Advent has marked the beginning of the church year in Western churches. However, the Greek Orthodox church and the Byzantine Rite of the Catholic church begin their ecclesiastical year on September 1. Other Eastern Orthodox churches open their liturgical year on September 1 or September 14, depending on whether they follow the Gregorian or Julian calendar.

Advent is regarded as a season in which the faithful should prepare themselves for the three Comings of Jesus Christ — on December 25, at the Last Judgment, and in their daily lives. Therefore, it is a joyous remembrance of the past — the historical event of the first Christmas; an anticipation of the future — the Second Coming at the end of time; and an awareness of the continual Coming of Jesus Christ in individual lives and of his constant gift of grace.

Special liturgical services, and prayers that emphasize the themes of anticipation of and preparation for the birth of Jesus characterize Advent. Especially traditional to the season — although still more widespread in Western Europe than in the United States — is the Advent wreath, a simple circle of greenery in which four candles, one for each week of Advent, are placed. Each candle is lighted in turn on each of the Saturdays or Sundays in Advent. Also traditional, in homes and elsewhere during the season, is the beautifully decorated Advent calendar, especially popular with children, on which a windowlike flap of paper is folded back every day to reveal a holiday symbol and to heighten the atmosphere of anticipation. The culmination of the Advent season comes with the religious services and other activities of Christmas Eve (see December 24).

Morrison Remick Waite's Birthday

Morrison Remick Waite, the seventh chief justice of the United States, was born in Lyme, Connecticut, on November 29, 1816. His father, Henry Waite, was a descendant of a 17th century Massachusetts family and a chief justice of Connecticut. His mother, Maria Selden Waite, was a granddaughter of Colonel Samuel Selden, who earned distinction in the American Revolution.

Waite was graduated from Yale College in 1837 and in the following year migrated to Maumee City, Ohio, where he read law in the office of Samuel M. Young. He gained admission to the state bar in 1839 and joined Young's firm. In 1850 Young moved the office to Toledo, Ohio; shortly afterwards, when he retired, Morrison Waite and his younger brother, Richard, took over the practice. The elder Waite brother was a specialist in real estate matters and his services were often used by railroad companies.

Politics intermittently attracted Morrison Waite's attention. In 1840 he supported the successful Whig Presidential candidate, William Henry Harrison, but he lost his own bid for a congressional seat later in the decade. In 1849, however, Waite won election to the state legislature, where he served one term. During the Civil War he agitated on behalf of the Union cause and in 1862 ran unsuccessfully for Congress as a Republican.

England's construction of cruisers for the Confederacy prompted the United States to seek reparations after the war. In 1871 President Ulysses S. Grant appointed Caleb Cushing, Waite, and a Yale classmate of Waite's, William M. Evarts, to present the American case in Geneva, Switzerland, before an arbitration commission established to settle the issue amicably. Waite and his colleagues deftly handled these *Alabama* Claims negotiations (see April 7), and the United States eventually received $15.5 million in damages.

Upon his return from Geneva, Waite won election to the Ohio constitutional convention of 1873 and served as its president. On January 19,

1874, President Grant nominated him as chief justice of the United States, and, despite his lack of judicial experience, the Senate unanimously confirmed his selection. Waite led the Supreme Court for 14 years and personally delivered its opinion in more than 1,000 cases, a number of which concerned such diverse areas as states rights, civil and personal liberties, and business regulation.

During Waite's tenure as chief justice, the Court severely limited the scope of legislation seeking to protect blacks. In 1876, in the *United States* v. *Reese,* it held invalid several sections of the Ku Klux Klan Act of 1870. Also in 1876, in the *United States* v. *Cruikshank,* the Court ruled that the 14th Amendment did not authorize Congress to enact positive legislation to secure civil rights. Two years later, in *Hall* v. *DeCuir,* the Court nullified, as an undue interference with interstate commerce, a Louisiana Reconstruction act that forbade racial discrimination by common carriers. And in 1883 the Court's finding the Civil Rights Act of 1875 unconstitutional virtually halted the federal government's efforts to end discrimination against blacks until 1954. Not until that year, in its historic school desegregation decision, did the Supreme Court again act meaningfully to protect the rights of black Americans.

Waite's most famous decision came in *Munn* v *Illinois,* one of the six Granger Cases decided in 1877 — in which he found that Illinois could establish rates for grain elevators and railroads in interstate commerce as a legitimate use of the "police power." Borrowing from an argument of Sir Matthew Hale, a 17th century lord chief justice of England, Waite asserted that the state had the right to regulate private utilities associated with a public interest.

In 1878, the chief justice became involved with the difficult case of *Reynolds* v. *United States,* which concerned the Mormon practice of polygamy. Did a congressional law that prohibited the custom in the territories violate the religious freedom of the Latter-Day Saints as guaranteed by the First Amendment to the Constitution? Waite argued that the law was valid because the Bill of Rights protected only the freedom to believe in polygamy as a principle, and not to practice it as a contravention of existing statutes.

The Waite court also decided several important cases in international law. In the Wildenhus case, it upheld the right of New Jersey to exercise jurisdiction in the instance of a murder committed aboard a Belgian merchant vessel docked in New Jersey waters. The Court thus guaranteed that local authorities could control matters that would disturb their peace. Referring in an-

other instance to the "necessary and proper" clause of the Constitution, the chief justice stated in *United States* v. *Arjona* that Congress could punish the counterfeiting of foreign securities.

Republican leaders suggested Waite as a possible presidential candidate, but he refused to use his office as a stepping stone to the White House. On the other hand, Waite participated actively in civil affairs as a trustee of the Peabody Educational Fund and a member of the Yale Corporation. He attended the Protestant Episcopal church in Washington, D.C. and served as one of its vestrymen.

Morrison Waite married a second cousin, Amelia C. Warner of Lyme, Connecticut, on September 21, 1840. They had five children, one of whom died in infancy. Waite himself died in Washington, D.C., on March 23, 1888, of pneumonia.

Marcus Whitman's Death

November 29 marks the anniversary of the death of Marcus Whitman, one of the early missionaries to the Native Americans of the Pacific Northwest, who was killed in 1847 by Cayuse Indians, among whom he had worked for 11 difficult years. A physician, Whitman began his missionary work in 1836, when, under the auspices of the American Board of Commissioners for Foreign Missions, he established a mission among the Cayuse at Waiilatpu, "The Place of the Rye Grass," in what is now southeastern Washington. On November 29, 1847, over a decade of hard work and uncertainty finally came to an end when the Cayuse, in a violent eruption of growing hostility toward the white settlers, attacked the Whitman mission, killing Whitman, his wife, and 12 others at the mission.

The mission itself was razed to the ground, and 49 persons, mostly women and children, were taken captive. Only a few escaped to tell the story of the massacre and to bury the victims in a common grave just north of the mission site. The captives were eventually ransomed, but the white settlers of the region, enraged by the killings, organized themselves as the Oregon Volunteers and fought the Cayuse, all but annihilating the tribe. As more unrest followed, Protestant missions in the Oregon country were closed, not to be reopened until years later.

In 1859, when the conflicts in that part of the country had subsided, Cushing Eells, a missionary and friend of Whitman, returned from his place of refuge in the Willamette Valley and went to Waiilatpu. Deeply moved by the sight of the mission ruins and the unmarked grave, he resolved to honor the memory of his slain friend in some worthy way. That same year he founded a school for Christian instruction and named it the Whitman Seminary. Originally intended to be built on the mission grounds, the seminary was finally established at the rapidly growing community of Walla Walla, some seven miles east of the mission site. The school grew to become Whitman College and now houses the Whitman Museum, which holds, among other frontier mementos, the diary of Whitman's wife, Narcissa Prentiss Whitman. The story of the Whitmans and the founding of the college is retold in the annual orientation talk given to Whitman College freshmen.

In 1897, the 50th anniversary of the Whitman tragedy, a shaft erected in memory of the Whitmans was dedicated, and the remains of the massacre victims were transferred to a nearby new marble vault with the names of the slain inscribed on the slab. Situated just north of the mission grounds, the 27-foot Whitman Memorial Shaft rests high on the hill where Narcissa Whitman used to await her husband when his work took him away from the mission.

In 1931 the grounds around the monument were beautified by the Walla Walla chapter of the Daughters of the Revolution, which was assisted by the Kiwanis Club, but the mission site was not developed until the early 1960s. Established in 1940 as the Whitman National Monument, the mission became part of the National Park Service in 1963 and was renamed the Whitman Mission National Historic Site. By that time the mission grounds, which had been partially excavated included the foundation ruins of the mission buildings and the old channel of the Walla Walla River, where Alice Clarissa Whitman, the Whitmans' only child and the first white girl to be born in the Oregon country, drowned in 1839. None of the buildings was restored, and the only original structure that remained was the gristmill, which the Cayuse themselves needed and therefore left intact.

Other additions to and restorations of the mission site were dedicated on June 6, 1964, in a ceremony that included the laying of a wreath at the Great Grave by an Indian girl. The Whitman National Historical Site also has a visitor center and museum, a restored millpond, an irrigation ditch and mission orchard, and part of the old Oregon Trail, which for two years ran directly past the Whitman mission. When, after 1844, the main trail bypassed the Waiilatpu station, many weary settlers still made the detour to the welcoming mission to rest, replenish sup-

plies, and make repairs before continuing their long trek west.

Apart from the annual Memorial Day service that is held at the Great Grave by the Sons of the American Revolution, there are no ceremonies held on a yearly basis at the Whitman mission site. However, in 1936, there was a centennial celebration commemorating the Whitmans' arrival at Waiilatpu, and in 1947 the 100th anniversary of the massacre was observed with ceremonies. The memory of Whitman was honored in a lasting way when a statue of him was erected on the Witherspoon Building, the headquarters of the United Presbyterian Church in Philadelphia. The state of Washington also paid tribute to one of its most notable historical figures by contributing the statue of Marcus Whitman that now stands in the Capitol's Statuary Hall in Washington, D.C.

Marcus Whitman was born at Federal Hollow (now Rushville), New York, on September 4, 1802. After a preliminary education, he studied medicine and graduated from the Fairfield, New York, medical school in 1832. After three years in medical practice, Whitman decided to devote himself to missionary work at a time when the churches in the East were beginning their efforts to convert the American Indians of the Pacific Northwest. As early as 1834, a young minister named Jason Lee had already established a Methodist mission in the Willamette Valley in Oregon. Whitman offered his services to the American Board of Commissioners for Foreign Missions, in Boston, representing Presbyterian, Congregational, and Dutch Reformed churches, and in 1835, together with a Presbyterian minister, Samuel Parker, was sent by the board to explore the Oregon country for possible mission sites. The two men traveled with a fur caravan as far west as Idaho, found the prospects for mission work favorable, and parted. Parker continued west and eventually returned to the East on a ship of the Hudson's Bay Company. Whitman returned directly to the East for equipment and missionary workers.

Before he embarked on his journey with Samuel Parker, however, Whitman had become engaged to Narcissa Prentiss, a young woman who also had applied to the American Board for a missionary assignment. Her family home still stands in the village of Angelica in western New York State, where she and Marcus Whitman were married on February 18, 1836.

Encouraged by his report, the American Board commissioned Whitman and a new recruit, Henry H. Spalding, to found a mission in the Pacific Northwest. On February 19, 1836, the morning after their wedding ceremony, the

Whitmans departed on their long journey into the distant and still unknown West. Accompanying them were the Reverend Henry Spalding and his wife, Eliza Spalding. The long trip took the two couples up the Mississippi River by paddle steamer and on horseback with a fur caravan across the Great Plains. Then, in July 1836, the group reached the Rocky Mountains. The pass over which they crossed the Continental Divide is now marked by a stone slab reading "Narcissa Prentiss Whitman, Elizabeth Hart Spalding, First White Women to Cross this Pass, July 4, 1836."

Once over the Rockies, the group followed the course of the westward-flowing rivers and reached Fort Vancouver on September 12, 1836. While the women remained at the fort, Marcus Whitman and Henry Spalding left to find suitable sites for their missions. Whitman established his mission among the Cayuse at Waiilatpu on the Walla Walla River, while the dour Spaldings, who did not get along with the Whitmans, settled some 110 miles east among the Nez Percé at Lapwai, near Lewiston, Idaho. It was at the Lapwai mission that the first printing press in the Pacific Northwest was set up in 1839.

In December 1836 the Whitmans established their first quarters in Waiilatpu in a small, poorly equipped log lean-to. Soon they were teaching the Cayuse their methods of farming and cattle raising, but the tribe was reluctant to learn. Missionary efforts were also met with indifference. However, the mission continued to grow and by the end of 1841 could boast a large new mission house, a mill, a blacksmith shop, and the Gray house, the home of the mission mechanic, which after 1842 was used as shelter by the large number of migrants traveling over the Oregon Trail.

Three years after Whitman had established his Waiilatpu station, three other missions were opened by the American Board in what is now eastern Washington and central Idaho. In 1842, however, growing dissension among the missionaries and lack of funds caused the board to order all but one of the missions closed. The Spaldings were to return East, while the Whitmans were to move to Tshimakain, a mission established by Elkanah Walker and Cushing Eells near what is now Spokane.

Reluctant to abandon his mission and convinced of the promise that the Oregon country held for future settlers, Whitman undertook to travel back east to present his case to the board. On October 3, 1842, with a white companion, an Indian guide, and several pack mules, he left Waiilatpu and began his long winter journey.

Traveling part of the way on horseback and part by wagon, Whitman reached St. Louis on March 9, 1843, and from there continued to Washington, D.C., New York, and Boston.

In Washington he was able to alter the unfavorable attitude toward the Oregon country then officially held in the capital by reporting on the vast untapped natural resources of the Pacific Northwest, and in Boston he persuaded the board to rescind its orders to close the missions. His trip to the East a success, Whitman joined the Great Migration to the West and helped guide some 1,000 settlers and 120 wagons over the Oregon Trail and into the Oregon country. On October 10, 1843, this party became the first substantial wagon train to reach Oregon.

As the number of white settlers grew, so did dissension and unrest in the Oregon country. By 1847 the provisional government set up by the settlers after the 1846 boundary settlement with Great Britain was troubled by factional disputes. Moreover the tension between the Protestant and Catholic missions further alienated the Northwest Indians, who were already watching the incoming white settlers with growing alarm. The Cayuse grew more antagonistic as more whites arrived on their lands. Disputes erupted over land, pasture, and game.

Finally, the Cayuse fell prey to disease. With the white settlers of 1847 came the measles, to which the Cayuse had no resistance. In a short time the disease spread, killing half the tribe. Blaming the missionaries for their misfortune, a group of Cayuse attacked the Waiilatpu mission, killing 14 white persons, among them Marcus and Narcissa Whitman.

NOVEMBER 30

Feast of St. Andrew

According to tradition, St. Andrew, the brother of Peter and one of the 12 disciples of Jesus Christ, was martyred on November 30, but the year of his death is disputed, with estimates ranging from A.D. 60 to 70. The day is observed by Eastern and Western branches of the Christian Church. Roman Catholics rank the observance — which has been celebrated at Rome since the sixth century — as a feast (formerly Class II). Andrew's name is mentioned two times in the liturgy of the Mass, once in the canon and once in the embolism — prayer for deliverance from evil — following the Lord's Prayer. Eastern Orthodox churches also observe the Feast of St. Andrew the Apostle, or Andrew the First-Called, on November 30, except for those still adhering to the Julian, or Old Style, calendar, which celebrate the occasion on December 13. Some Protestant churches, notably the Episcopalian and Lutheran, also observe St. Andrew's Day. The Episcopal Book of Common Prayer contains this appropriate collect:

Almighty God, who didst give such grace unto thy holy Apostle St. Andrew, that he readily obeyed the calling of thy Son Jesus Christ, and followed him without delay; Grant unto us all, that we, being called by thy holy Word, may forthwith give up ourselves obediently to fulfil thy holy commandments. . . .

There are in the New Testament few details about Andrew, whose name in Greek means "manhood" or "manly." He was born in the town of Bethsaida in Galilee (John 1:44) and was a follower of John the Baptist, through whose influence he became a disciple of Jesus. According to the famous incident related in John 1:35–40, Andrew probably has the distinction of being the first of the disciples to be chosen, hence his title the First-Called: "And looking upon Jesus as he walked, he [John] saith, Behold the Lamb of God! And the two disciples heard him speak, and they followed Jesus. . . . One of the two . . . was Andrew, Simon Peter's brother."

Andrew then introduced Jesus to his brother, Simon Peter (John 1:41–42), and they both joined themselves to him. However, the brothers, who were fishermen, apparently were not formally called to follow Jesus until the occasion when, while they were casting their nets into the Sea of Galilee, they obeyed a command from Jesus to drop their nets and follow him (Matthew 4:18–19 and Mark 1:16–18).

Andrew seems to have been a likable and humble man who, despite the paucity of specific references to him in the Gospels, was probably one of the most active Apostles. It is recorded that on the occasion of the feeding of the 5,000, it was Andrew who remarked: "There is a lad here who hath five barley loaves and two small fishes, but what are they among so many?" (John 6:5–9). After Jesus' triumphant entry into Jerusalem, "Philip cometh and telleth Andrew: and again Andrew and Philip tell Jesus" (John 12:20–22) that gentile Greeks wished to speak with him. Andrew was certainly present at the Last Supper. He also ranked as a member of the inner circle of disciples, which also included Peter, James, and John, to whom Jesus made known the secrets of his Second Coming, and of the final judgment of mankind (Mark 13:3–4). Andrew presumably was among those who wit-

nessed the Ascension and was among those present on the Day of Pentecost.

It is supposed that after Pentecost Andrew, fulfilling the command of Jesus to go "into all the world, and preach the gospel to every creature" (Mark 16:15), went forth to preach Christianity among the nations, but there is no authentic record of his travels. The late third and early fourth century church historian Eusebius of Caesarea, relates in his *History of the Church* that Andrew preached in Scythia. The famous fourth century Greek church father St. Gregory Nazianzen, claimed that he went to Epirus in northern Greece. The learned doctor of the church St. Jerome wrote that Andrew preached in Achaia in southern Greece. According to tradition, Andrew also served as a missionary in Cappadocia, Galatia, Bithynia, Thrace, Macedonia, and Russia. His connection with Russia, where he has been honored as a patron saint, is based on a tradition that he journeyed as far east as Kiev in the Ukraine. The medieval belief that Andrew eventually settled in Constantinople, where he established a church, apparently is unfounded, but it is generally agreed that he was in Greece, and many sources say that he was crucified at Patras in Achaia.

The details of the martyrdom of Andrew are equally shrouded in mystery. He most likely aroused — probably through his preaching of Christianity — the wrath of the local Roman official. Legend holds that at his own request the saint, too humble to die in the same fashion as his Lord, was crucified on an X-shaped cross, the *crux decussata*, now known as the St. Andrew's Cross. He supposedly lived for two or three days in this position, preaching all the time to onlookers.

The alleged bones of the martyr apparently were first deposited in Patras. Then, according to one version, in the mid-fourth century they were removed to Constantinople, and at the beginning of the 13th century to Amalfi in southern Italy, where some claim they are still preserved in the cathedral. Another version holds that after a fourth century Roman emperor had announced his intention of translating the relics to Constantinople, angels appeared in a dream to St. Regulus, the guardian of Andrew's remains at Patras. They commanded Regulus to take some of the bones to the "far land of the Picts" (part of what is now Scotland). After a two-year voyage, the vessel on which Regulus was traveling from Greece reportedly was cast up upon the Scottish coast near what is now the town of St. Andrews. Regulus erected a church to house the relics and preached Christianity to the Picts. Today the town is the seat of the famous St. Andrews University, founded in the early 15th century and named in the apostle's honor.

Probably about the mid-eighth century, Andrew was named the patron saint of Scotland. During the Middle Ages, the Scots, determined to preserve their ecclesiastical independence and prevent control of the Scottish churches by English archbishops, supported their stand in a protest to the pope by invoking the honored position and special privileges of the "chosen nation" of St. Andrew:

Jesus Christ brought the nation of the Scots, . . . almost FIRST to His most holy Faith. It was His desire to confirm them in the Faith by no other than his first Apostle, Andrew; and him the nation desires to be always over the people as their protector.

Legend claims that a Scottish king, about to engage in battle against his enemies, saw a white cross — the St. Andrew's Cross — against the blue sky. Regarding what he had seen as a favorable sign, the king (who was indeed victorious in the fight) adopted as his battle symbol a white X-shaped cross on a blue field, thus originating the St. Andrew's banner. This banner became Scotland's national flag. In 1707, after the union of England and Scotland, it was embodied in the flag of the United Kingdom, the British Union Jack, on which were superimposed the broad red cross of St. George, the patron saint of England, and the narrow red cross of St. Patrick, the patron saint of Ireland.

In 1687 King James II of England established the Most Ancient and Most Noble Order of the Thistle in honor of St. Andrew. The order, which still exists, has, according to a revised 1827 statute, only 16 members, who, on ceremonial occasions, don dark blue velvet hats and green cloaks with hoods of silk and velvet and wear a badge displaying St. Andrew and his cross against an elongated eight-pointed star.

St. Andrew is also patron of organizations of Scots and men of Scottish descent in all parts of the world, who have founded St. Andrews societies for the relief of poor and needy Scotsmen. Besides collecting and distributing charitable funds, members of the regional societies promote social ties by staging elaborate banquets annually on November 30. The banquet is traditionally an all-male event — women are permitted to enjoy the feast and listen to the speeches only in the gallery boxes. As is customary on most festive Scottish occasions, the "king of the feast" is usually the much-beloved haggis, now regarded as an exclusively Scottish dish. Described by the great 18th century Scottish poet Robert Burns as the "great chieftain o' the pudding race," it is a mixture of finely ground and seasoned heart and liver of a sheep or calf, sewn in the stomach of the animal and boiled.

In the American colonies, to which many Scots migrated, the Scots' Charitable Society of Boston was organized as early as 1657. The St. Andrew's Club of Charlestown, South Carolina (later the St. Andrew's Society of Charleston) was founded in 1729. A St. Andrew's society was organized in Philadelphia in 1749 and one in Savannah in 1750.

The way in which the structure and program of events sponsored by the individual societies grew can perhaps be illustrated by a brief glance at the history of one of the oldest and most prominent St. Andrew's societies in the United States. Scotsmen in New York City instituted their St. Andrew's Society in 1756. They adopted a constitution based upon that of the Philadelphia organization, and put the government of the society in the control of a president, vice president, treasurer, secretary, and a board of four assistants. The 47 original colonial founders, who held important professional and business positions, belonged to eminent New York Scottish families. The first president, for example, was Philip Livingston, who had served as a delegate to the First Continental Congress and had signed the Declaration of Independence; he also took an active part in founding King's (now Columbia) College in New York City.

The New York St. Andrew's Society centennial, in 1856, was marked by a sumptuous banquet consisting of about 400 dishes. In the bicentennial year of 1956, a scholarship fund was initiated to facilitate exchanges of Scottish and American graduate students. Throughout the year, a series of events commemorated the society's founding, including exhibits of Scottish books and manuscripts in New York City museums and libraries, special church services, a festive Grand Ball, and finally the anniversary banquet, held on November 30 at the Waldorf-Astoria Hotel. (The date of the celebration may vary slightly from year to year.)

Mark Twain's Birthday

Mark Twain, possessor of the best-known pen name in American literature, was born Samuel Langhorne Clemens in Florida, Missouri, on November 30, 1835. A wit and raconteur, he liked to point out that he had come into this world in the same year that Halley's comet had made one of its rare appearances. In 1909 Twain looked ahead to the expected reappearance of the comet the next year and remarked that it would be the greatest disappointment of his life if he did not go out with it. Halley's comet did, indeed, reappear on April 20, 1910, and Twain died the next day — at Stormfield, his home in Redding, Connecticut.

Mark Twain's father, John Marshall Clemens, was a lawyer and merchant, proud of his Virginia ancestry. His mother, Jane Lampton Clemens, was also of Virginia ancestry. Twain was their third son and fifth child. When he was four years old, the family moved to Hannibal, Missouri, on the Mississippi River, not far from his birthplace. In Hannibal, Judge Marshall, as his father came to be known, was one of the most respected members of the community, although he was never well off financially.

After his father's death in 1847 Samuel Clemens then 12, went to work in the village newspaper shop to learn the printer's trade. At 17 he traveled about the country, working as a journeyman printer in St. Louis, New York, Philadelphia, and Keokuk, Iowa, where his older brother Orion had a newspaper. Twain left Keokuk in 1856 and headed for Brazil, determined to make a fortune. He got as far as the Mississippi River. After spending the winter in St. Louis and Cincinnati, he boarded the riverboat *Paul Jones* and headed down the Ohio River to New Orleans.

The trip reawakened Twain's boyhood desire to be a riverboat pilot on the Mississippi, and he persuaded Horace Bixby, pilot of the *Paul Jones*, to take him on as an apprentice. The agreement marked the beginning of Twain's four happy years on the Mississippi, the last two and a half of them as a licensed pilot.

When the Civil War interrupted river traffic, cutting short his new career, Twain returned to Hannibal, where he temporarily drifted into a company of Confederate volunteers. Despite the geographical accident of his southern birth, however, his sympathies were with the Union and he left the volunteers after two weeks.

After his brother Orion was appointed secretary of the new Nevada Territory, Twain became his assistant. The two set off from Missouri on July 25, 1861, on a 20-day stagecoach journey to Carson City, Nevada's capital, which then had a population of 2,000.

By December of that year, Twain had succumbed to the prospecting fever then rampant in Nevada and set off in hope of finding silver or gold. His mining camp days added greatly to the riverboat education that was to influence his later writing to a marked degree. Financially, however, they added nothing, so he went on to Virginia City, Nevada, in 1862 and became a reporter on the *Enterprise* there. It was in that paper, on February 3, 1863, that the first use of the pen name Mark Twain was recorded, though he used it only for his features at first and signed his straight news stories Sam Clemens. The term "mark twain" had become familiar to him during his days on the Mississippi

River, when the riverboat leadsmen would call it out to indicate that the depth of water was two fathoms — or 12 feet — and therefore safe.

In 1864 he went to California to work as a reporter on the San Francisco *Morning Call* and while there he wrote the first of his famous short stories, "The Celebrated Jumping Frog of Calaveras County," based on an old tale he had heard while visiting the mining town of Angel Camp, California. Today, thanks to him, Angel Camp is the site of a competition of sometimes breathtaking suspense—the widely noted Jumping Frog Jubilee, which, with surrounding events, takes place annually in May, during the Calaveras County Fair. Indeed, the frog story, as told by Twain, inspired the rash of jumping frog contests that are a phenomenon of contemporary American life — among them the one staged annually in April at Del Mar in southern California. Twain's version of the frog tale was first printed in a New York newspaper, *The Saturday Press*, on November 18, 1865, and was reprinted in all parts of the country. Now Twain could say he was read from coast to coast, and newspapers were eager to publish his contributions.

Commissioned by the Sacramento *Union*, he sailed to the Sandwich Islands (now Hawaii) and sent back stories of the island's history, people, and geographical wonders. His articles broadened his reputation, and on his return he lectured in the West on the Sandwich Islands and his experiences there.

As the special traveling correspondent for the newspaper *Alta California*, Twain next set off for Europe. First, however, he wanted to visit his family in St. Louis and stop also in New York. There, in a lecture timed to coincide with the May 1867 publication of his first book, *The Celebrated Jumping Frog of Calaveras County and Other Sketches*, he beguiled an audience at Cooper Institute (now Cooper Union), then the largest hall in New York. News reports of his success there assured his future as a lecturer.

The next month, Twain joined a party of travelers who were to take the widely publicized first pleasure cruise from America, to visit Europe and the Paris Exposition, and go on to the Holy Land. The *Quaker City* carried 67 passengers, including many clergymen and 12 reporters besides Twain. One of the passengers was 18-year-old Charles J. Langdon, son of a wealthy businessman from Elmira, New York. Langdon showed Twain a picture of his sister Olivia, and, as Twain was to say later, from that moment she was never out of his mind. They met for the first time in December 1867 and on their first evening out together, in January 1868, went to hear Charles Dickens lecture at Steinway Hall in New York. They were married in Elmira on February 2, 1870, and subsequently settled in Hartford, Connecticut, where they had three daughters and a son (only one of the children was to survive Twain).

During his trip to Europe and the Holy Land, Twain meanwhile had sent back almost a quarter of a million words, including 53 letters to the *Alta California*, six to the New York *Tribune*, and three to the New York *Herald*. The trip also resulted in his rollicking and tremendously popular book *Innocents Abroad*. Drawn from the letters, it was published in 1869 and established him as a national figure. It was followed by *Roughing It* (1872), which described his experiences and the people he had met in the West and in the Sandwich Islands; a satirical novel called *The Gilded Age* (1873), written in collaboration with Charles Dudley Warner; and *Mark Twain's Sketches, New and Old* (1875). Twain's boyhood adventures in Hannibal and on the Mississippi River inspired his two most famous novels, *The Adventures of Tom Sawyer* (1876) and *The Adventures of Huckleberry Finn* (1884), as well as the autobiographical *Life on the Mississippi* (1883). Among his other still popular works are *A Tramp Abroad* (1880) and *A Connecticut Yankee in King Arthur's Court* (1889). Punctuated with irreverence and dotted with the colloquial speech that he introduced to American fiction, his works recalled an exciting period of American history, bringing to life the intriguing frontier figures who roamed near the Mississippi and in the West or revealing the Old World as seen through his own undeferential, New World eyes. Characteristically, his writing is laced with his own outspoken brand of satire, a pretense-puncturing humor, and a carefully contrived artlessness, all combined in the quintessentially American idiom that became his hallmark.

As his reputation became secure, Twain alternately wrote and made remunerative appearances on the lecture platform, for which he received increasing acclaim — after surviving an initial attack of stagefright so severe he thought it would kill him. Between his prolific written output and his American and European lecture tours, Twain made a fortune — three, in fact, in the course of his lifetime.

He was, however, also adept at losing money: all his life, he was to be taken in by get-rich schemes or unsuccessful gadgets and inventions that he financed, sure of the wealth they would bring. In one spectacular wrong guess, he supported for years the invention of a typesetting machine that never worked out; but he turned down the requests, and even pleas, of Alexander Graham Bell to take shares in Bell's invention of the telephone. Not satisfied with his dealings with publishers, Twain established a publishing business of his own in Hartford. Between the typesetting machine and the publishing venture, he went bankrupt in 1894. In order to pay his debts, he made a lecture tour around the world in 1895–1896 and succeeded in meeting the claims of his creditors in full by the end of 1898. Then, already over 60, he set about making his third fortune.

Twain's friend Colonel George Harvey was president of the publishing firm of Harper and Brothers as well as editor of *Harper's Weekly* and the *North American Review*. In 1903 Twain signed a contract with Harper and Brothers (now Harper and Row) for the publication of all his books. He was guaranteed $25,000 a year but always got more, sometimes twice as much. (As late as 1959, Harper was to bring out a new edition of Twain's posthumously published *Autobiography*, with previously unpublished material edited and arranged by Charles Neider.)

In 1905, to celebrate Twain's 70th birthday, George Harvey arranged an elaborate celebration, including a dinner at Delmonico's in New York City. Nearly 200 of the nation's most distinguished people, including many writers, attended. Twain received many other honors during his lifetime, including honorary degrees from Yale and the University of Missouri, as well as one from Oxford University, which he prized most of all. Even though he had given up traveling by then, he crossed the Atlantic for that honor in 1907 and in the course of the trip was received by King Edward VII and Queen Alexandra. He also met a fellow author and iconoclast, George Bernard Shaw.

Twain was elected to the Hall of Fame for Great Americans in 1920. His boyhood home, at 208 Hill Street in Hannibal, a two-story, carefully restored, white frame structure that has been designated a national historic landmark, stands next to the gray stone Mark Twain Museum, which houses much Twain memorabilia. Across the street is the home of Laura Hawkins, upon whom Twain based the character of Becky Thatcher in *Tom Sawyer*. These buildings are open to the public year round, except for New Year's Day, Thanksgiving, and Christmas.

Adjoining the Twain house on the other side is what may be the world's most celebrated whitewashed board fence — inspiration for the famous fence-painting incident in *Tom Sawyer*. A board fence put up in front of the original now serves annually in the National Tom Sawyer Fence Painting Contest, held in Hannibal since 1959. The contest takes place on the Saturday nearest July 4 and draws thousands of contestants, who are judged not only on the speed and quality of their painting but also on their costumes. It is the highlight of Hannibal's annual Tom Sawyer Days, an event that has taken on some of the attributes of a state fair. There is also a Tom and Becky contest, in which Hannibal's seventh graders compete on the basis of costume, appearance, and personality. The winners represent the town at various functions throughout the year.

A bronze statue of Tom Sawyer and Huckleberry Finn, cast life-size by F. C. Hibbard, stands at the foot of the hill at Main and North streets in Hannibal. The Mark Twain Cave of Tom, Becky, and Injun Joe, two miles south of town, is another popular attraction. Hannibal also boasts other Twain associations. Perhaps the greatest of these is the Mississippi River itself, beautifully visible from the bluffs of Riverview Park. It is said that the stretch of the river between St. Louis and Hannibal has not changed greatly since the time of Twain, whose statue is appropriately on view at the park's Inspiration Point.

Thirty or so miles from Hannibal is Mark Twain State Park in Florida, Missouri, where the Mark Twain Birthplace Shrine is located. Visitors can see the frame cabin in which Twain was born as well as a library and museum housing material collected by the Mark Twain Research Foundation.

The house in Hartford, Connecticut, in which Twain spent two decades of his life, is also open to the public. Many of the rooms have been restored to look as they did during Twain's lifetime. The house, a national historic landmark, is located at 351 Farmington Avenue and is under the supervision of the Mark Twain Library and Memorial Commission. On or near his birthday, it is sometimes the site of a party for members of the Mark Twain Memorial, who have worked to sponsor the restoration.

Mark Twain is buried with his wife and children in Elmira, New York, where the family spent many summers at Quarry Farm. Travelers can visit the campus of Elmira College and see the study — modeled on the pilothouse of a Mississippi riverboat — in which Twain wrote some of his most famous works. The Strathmont Museum in Elmira has a Mark Twain exhibit emphasizing his local summer residence.

In 1908 Twain founded a library in Redding, Connecticut, his last home, and donated many books from his own library to it. It is now operated by the Mark Twain Library Association.

December

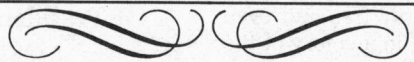

December is the 12th month of the Gregorian, or New Style, calendar in use today and has 31 days. In the ancient Roman calendar, the year began in March and was divided into 10 months, of which December — derived from the Latin word *decem*, or "ten" — was the last. Even after the Roman calendar had been extensively revised, with two added months, January and February, placed at the beginning of the calendar, December retained its inappropriate name.

In A.D. 191 there was a short-lived attempt by Emperor Commodus (180–192) to rename all the months in his honor. According to one ancient source, the emperor had the Roman Senate change December to *Transcendent;* according to another, he ordered that the month should be known as *Amazonius* out of devotion for his mistress, Marcia, who dressed in the garb of the Amazons, the legendary tribe of female warriors.

The *Saturnalia* was the most prominent Roman festival held in December. It had originally been celebrated on December 17, but was gradually extended for seven additional days to December 24, thus encompassing the time of the winter solstice. Almost nothing is known about the original form of the Saturnalian rituals. They were undoubtedly connected with agriculture, since their timing coincided with the completion of the autumnal sowing at the onset of the coldest season of the year.

As its name indicates, the *Saturnalia* honored the Roman god Saturnus (Saturn in English). According to the most widely accepted theory, Saturnus — whose name is derived from the Latin word *satus*, or "sowing" — was the god of planting or sowing. He was also a mythical king of Latium in southern Italy who introduced agriculture into the area. In earliest times, Saturnus apparently became identified with the Greek god Kronos (Cronus in Latin), and his cult took on Greek features.

In Greek legend, Kronos was the youngest of the giant Titans, who were the children of Uranus (Heaven) and Gaea (Earth). He led the Titans in revolt against Uranus and ruled the world in the Golden Age of peace and prosperity. Having fathered the mighty Olympian gods, such as Zeus, Poseidon, Demeter, and Hera, Kronos discovered that he was destined to be overthrown by one of his offspring. He therefore ate all but one of the infants, having been duped into swallowing a stone in place of Zeus. Zeus, as predicted, defeated Kronos in battle and gained control of the world. Kronos reputedly made his way to Rome, where he was well received by Janus, the Roman god of doorways, and where his rites were duly celebrated.

The *Saturnalia*, which evidently either became confused with or drew heavily upon the rites in honor of Kronos, strongly resembled Kronos's agricultural festival in Greece known as the *Kronia*. The lively Roman festivities for Saturnus embodied the merriment and relaxed mood characteristic of harvest-time celebrations. The Romans gave themselves up to reveling, feasting, gambling with dice (otherwise generally forbidden), and rioting. All commercial transactions, public and private, were in abeyance. Law courts and schools were closed. The Roman senate did not sit, and on the first day of the *Saturnalia*, after a young pig had been sacrificed in the Temple of Saturn in the Roman Forum, the senators put aside their togas to wear a light upper garment known as the *synthesis*, which was more in line with the rustic peasant origins of the occasion. Executions, military campaigns, and even daily household chores were suspended. Social distinctions disappeared as all persons greeted one another with a cheerful *Io*

Saturnalia ("Hurrah Saturnalia"). The Romans exchanged presents; the traditional ones were wax candles and little terra-cotta dolls, perhaps some long-forgotten survivals — like the Yule log fire in northern Europe — of ancient festivals of light at this gloomiest time of the year. Even the statue of Saturn in his temple in the Roman Forum, which usually had woolen ties around its feet — presumably to prevent it from escaping — was unbound so that the god could participate in the merrymaking.

The most striking note of the *Saturnalia* was the unusual reversal of the established ranks of society. Slaves were temporarily free and even waited upon by their masters, in memory of the mythical Golden Age, when all men were equal.

In the eastern provinces of the Roman Empire especially, a mock king was chosen by lot to rule as Saturnus and preside over the festival. He issued comic commands and in general was expected to behave ludicrously. The custom continued into the Christian era. As late as A.D. 303, a Christian soldier named Dasius was executed in Ancona, Italy, for refusing to portray Saturnus at the *Saturnalia*.

The ruins of the Temple of Saturn are still preserved in the Roman Forum. Although there are some fragments remaining from the earliest temple of 497 B.C. and from another erected in 42 B.C., the most extensive remains date from a hastily constructed fourth century temple in his honor. The inscription on this final building does not even refer to the god himself. Although Saturnus was primarily an agrarian deity, his temple, situated conveniently near the senate house, was used by the senators of Republican Rome to house the state money in hope that a temple at least might escape plundering in wartime. The Temple of Saturn thus eventually served as the official *Aerarium* or state treasury at Rome.

The Anglo-Saxons called December *Wintermonath,* or "winter-month"; the Christian Saxons called it *Heligh-monath,* or "holy-month," in allusion to the birth of Christ on December 25. Germans still term December *Christmonat.* About December 21 the winter solstice occurs when the sun reaches the Tropic of Capricorn. The lucky birthstone often associated with December is the ruby.

DECEMBER 1

Montgomery Bus Boycott Starts

Under the leadership of the Reverend Martin Luther King Jr. (see January 15), black citizens of Montgomery, Alabama, in 1955 began what was to be a 381-day boycott aimed at the desegrega-

tion of Montgomery's public buses. The boycott began on December 1, when a black woman, Rosa Parks, refused to give up her bus seat to a white male. The peaceful boycott resulted in the bus company's loss of 65 percent of its usual income. In response to a November 13 Supreme Court decision prohibiting bus segregation, desegregated service finally was begun in Montgomery on December 21, 1956.

The boycott, which first brought King world attention, was the opening engagement in what became a nationwide civil rights drive.

Presidential Election of 1824 Deadlocked

On December 1, 1824, the deadlocked 1824 presidential election involving four candidates — John Quincy Adams (see July 11), Henry Clay (see April 12), William Harris Crawford, and Andrew Jackson (see March 15) — was turned over for settlement to the US House of Representatives. It was the result of the seemingly clear but actually ambiguous method of electing the President of the United States stipulated in the US Constitution.

In 1787, following lengthy debate, the framers of the Constitution agreed on the method: "Each State shall appoint, in such a manner as the Legislature thereof may direct, a number of electors, equal to the whole number of Senators and Representatives to which the State may be entitled." It was expected that the electors would — since there was no constitutional provision for a national slate of announced candidates — cast their ballots for individual choices. It was also assumed that only rarely would any one candidate obtain a majority of all the electoral votes cast. The House of Representatives, voting by states with one vote per state, was therefore empowered to elect the President from among the five candidates who had amassed the greatest number of electoral votes. "After the choice of the President," the constitutional provision continued, "the person having the greatest number of votes of the electors shall be the Vice President."

In the course of the early political history of the United States, the electoral system was increasingly subjected to stresses and strains. At first electing the President was very simple. In 1788 and 1792, George Washington was the only candidate seriously considered. But as political parties began to emerge starting in the mid-1790s, congressional party caucuses began to decide upon a candidate and recommend him to the electors. There was generally an undisputed electoral majority.

In 1800, for the first time, the election procedures stipulated in the Constitution were put to a test and the vote went to the House of Representatives. The Constitution provided that the "electors shall . . . vote by ballot for two persons," — without providing that they stipulate whether the votes they cast were for the President or Vice President. Seventy-three electoral votes had been cast for Thomas Jefferson, around whom the new Republican (or Democratic-Republican) party had formed, and 73 votes had gone to Aaron Burr, Jefferson's fellow Republican. Although Burr disclaimed ambition for the presidency, the Constitution required that the tie be settled by the House of Representatives. A prolonged and exhausting House deadlock was broken only on the 36th ballot, on February 17, 1801, and Jefferson was declared elected.

The 12th Amendment, which was ratified in 1804, enjoined the electors to vote separately for President and Vice President and also reduced to three the number of candidates from among whom the House decision was to be made.

The election of 1824 reflected several new trends in American politics: increased opposition to the congressional caucus as a means of selecting the presidential candidate, dissolution of former party distinctions and the gradual transition to new party groupings, and mounting sectionalism as seen in the candidates themselves and in voter alignment. South Carolinian John C. Calhoun, President James Monroe's secretary of war, declared his candidacy as early as 1821. In July of the following year, the Tennessee legislature nominated Andrew Jackson, a popular military personality who represented the interests of the West and the "common man" everywhere. After doing so, the legislature charged in a formal complaint that the congressional caucus procedure was invalid because the Constitution had not empowered Congress to endorse a candidate for electoral approval. Other states imitated Tennessee's action. The Kentucky legislature nominated a native son, longtime Speaker of the House Henry Clay, in November 1822. New Englander John Quincy Adams, son of the second President and Monroe's secretary of state, was subsequently nominated in Boston.

When the congressional caucus finally assembled in early 1823, only 66 representatives met. This rump assembly nominated as its choice the Georgia politician William Harris Crawford, Monroe's secretary of the treasury. The Crawford selection did not meet the approval of the state legislatures. Support for Crawford was further weakened when he suffered a stroke several months later and became physically unfit for the presidency.

The candidates, who were outspoken on the issues of cheap public land, tariffs, and internal improvement, waged a lively campaign. Since a uniform election day in all states had not yet been set by law, the election extended from October 29 to November 22. Andrew Jackson received the highest number not only of popular votes but also of electoral votes (99), with Adams second (84), and Crawford and Clay trailing with 41 and 37 respectively. John Calhoun, who had decided to run as Vice President on both the Adams and Jackson tickets, amassed a clear majority of 182 electoral votes out of the 260 cast (with one elector failing to vote). However, Jackson had received only a plurality, not the required majority of electoral votes.

On December 1, 1824, the presidential election therefore went for decision to the House of Representatives for the second time in the nation's history. Henry Clay, who had been automatically eliminated from the race as holder of fourth place, nevertheless wielded enough power to decide the election outcome by swinging his congressional support in favor of one of the remaining three contenders. Although Clay was ardently wooed by all the candidates, he favored John Quincy Adams — Crawford's bad health and Jackson's popularity in the West, which competed with Clay's own, weighing against them in his eyes. Moreover, Adams's nationalist politics most closely conformed to Clay's political ideals.

Early in January 1825, Clay advised his supporters to cast their ballots for Adams. On February 9 of that year, the House of Representatives — with a vote of 13 for Adams, 7 for Jackson, and 4 for Crawford — elected Adams as the sixth President of the United States.

The controversial 1824 election had several important side effects. The Jeffersonian Democratic-Republican party split into two factions, the Adams-Clay group becoming the National Republicans, and the supporters of Jackson retaining the old name as Democratic-Republicans. Jackson, particularly chagrined at having been deprived of the presidency after initially winning the largest number of electoral and popular votes, began to lay plans for the 1828 presidential election. Adams's appointment of Clay, whose support had won him the presidency, as secretary of state gave currency to allegations made earlier that Clay and Adams had fashioned a "corrupt bargain." Although the charges were never substantiated, the accusation cast a blot on Clay's public image during the rest of his career.

Since 1824 the necessity has not arisen again for the House of Representatives to elect the President of the United States.

DECEMBER 2

The Monroe Doctrine Promulgated

President James Monroe, in his annual message to Congress on December 2, 1823, announced the opposition of the United States to the extension of the control of European powers over territory on the American continents in what has come to be known as the Monroe Doctrine. European activities in the Western Hemisphere precipitated this action. On the Pacific Coast of North America the Russians, who had been fishing and trading furs in the area since the 1741 explorations of Vitus Bering, claimed in 1821 all the area north of the 51st Parallel and forbade ships to enter the coastal waters. The following year the members of the Quadruple Alliance — Austria, Prussia, France, and Russia — met at Verona and considered sending French troops to the newly liberated Latin American republics in an effort to restore Spain's "legitimate rule" there.

Under these circumstances, the United States could not remain silent. The only question was whether it should act unilaterally or in concert with Great Britain. During the Latin American wars of independence Britain had established a most profitable trade with the former Spanish colonies. Since it would lose these newly won markets if the area returned to European control, Britain opposed the restoration of Spanish rule. In 1823 the British foreign minister, George Canning, attempted to win US support for a joint statement opposing French intervention in South America and guaranteeing that neither signatory power would ever annex any part of the former Spanish empire.

The British suggestion elicited a mixed reaction in the United States. Former Presidents Thomas Jefferson and James Madison, Monroe's unofficial advisers, welcomed the plan. However, Secretary of State John Quincy Adams argued that it would better serve the United States to act independently. Adams's logic was persuasive; unlike Great Britain, the United States had already recognized six of the Latin American republics; this nation received no benefits from Great Britain's Latin American trade; and, perhaps most important, the United States had no desire to relinquish the possibility of one day adding Cuba to its domain.

President Monroe sided with Adams. His message of December 2, 1823, was a unilateral declaration of the United States' intention to safeguard the territorial integrity of the Americas. To the Russians he directed the warning that "the American continents . . . are henceforth not to be considered as subjects for future coloniza-

tion by any European powers." And then, referring to the proposed action to assist Spain in recovering control over its former colonies, he said:

> With the governments who have declared their independence and maintained it . . . we could not view any interposition for the purpose of oppressing them or controlling in any other manner their destiny by any European power in any other light than as the manifestation of an unfriendly disposition toward the United States.

At the time of its promulgation, the Monroe Doctrine attracted little attention. The United States had not even been able to safeguard its own capital from invasion during the War of 1812. How would it be able to protect the entire Western Hemisphere only 10 years later? It was not until the United States became a world power that the true significance of Monroe's statement was known. It was then used to justify such actions as the diplomatic pressure on France that led to the withdrawal of Napoleon III's French troops occupying Mexico City; President Grover Cleveland's arbitration of the Venezuelan boundary dispute between Great Britain and the United States; and President John F. Kennedy's stand against the establishment of Russian missile bases in Cuba in 1962.

DECEMBER 3

Illinois Admitted to the Union

Throughout the 19th century the people of the United States pushed the borders of their nation relentlessly westward. The Old Northwest Territory attracted settlers early in the century, and between 1810 and 1820 tens of thousands of settlers flocked to the territory. The population of Illinois alone multiplied so quickly that on December 3, 1818 — only nine years after gaining territorial status — Illinois was admitted to the Union as the 21st state.

One major obstacle blocked the admission of Illinois to statehood in 1818. As a part of the Old Northwest Territory, Illinois had to adhere to the regulations of the Northwest Ordinance governing the creation of states from the territory. The 1787 ordinance stipulated that a population of 60,000 free inhabitants was required before an area could be admitted as a state. However, in 1818 Illinois had little more than 40,000.

Nevertheless, Daniel Cook, a young lawyer and the publisher of a small newspaper in Kaskaskia, worked at that time to make Illinois the 21st state of the Union. On November 20, 1817, he wrote the first of a series of editorials in his paper, *The Western Intelligencer*, urging that

Illinois gain statehood before slave-holding Missouri. Cook discovered that it was possible under certain circumstances for a territory to become a state with a population of only 35,000, and since Illinois had over 40,000 residents he urged the territorial legislature to apply for statehood. Cook's arguments impressed the territorial legislators, and they even incorporated quotations from his editorials in the official request for statehood that they sent to Congress.

Congress approved the application, and on December 3, 1818, President James Monroe signed the act of administration that made Illinois the 21st state. Kaskaskia served as the first capital of the state, but in 1820 the seat of government was moved to Vandalia. Seventeen years later the capital was permanently moved to Springfield.

Daniel Cook had an important role in the state's early history. He served as the state's first attorney general and was elected to several terms in the US House of Representatives before he died in 1827 at the age of 33. In gratitude for his tireless efforts on behalf of his home state the Illinois legislature in 1831 named a new county that it had just created in his honor. Cook County has proved to be a substantial memorial to Daniel Cook for it is today the location of the metropolis of Chicago.

In 1968 Illinois celebrated the 150th anniversary of its admission to the Union. Sesquicentennial events officially began one day after the actual anniversary, on December 4, 1967. Many activities took place throughout the state on that day, but most notable were the raising of a 21-star flag over the Chicago Civic Center and the opening of a yearlong exhibit, A Half Billion Years of Illinois History, at Chicago's Field Museum of Natural History.

Throughout the year the Carson Pirie Scott department stores in Chicago and other cities sponsored a special show. The show consisted of 15 miniature rooms modeled after such historic places as Carl Sandburg's birthplace in Galesburg, Jane Addams's office at Hull House in Chicago, and the red velvet Silver Dollar Barber Shop of 1875 in the Palmer House Hotel in Chicago. The four-foot-long recreations toured the department store branches in Illinois and were also displayed at the governor's mansion in Springfield.

Illinois, dubbed the Land of Lincoln, also scheduled a number of important events on Abraham Lincoln's birthday, February 12. At Shawneetown, the location of the oldest post office in continual operation in Illinois, first day of issue ceremonies were held for an Illinois commemorative stamp, and an address, "Lincoln, the Postmaster," was given. Other events of the day included a program commemorating the Lincoln-Douglas debates at Mattoon, tours of the appellate court at Mount Vernon, where Lincoln pleaded several cases, and a tour to the Old State House at Vandalia.

Numerous activities were also held on July 4, 1968. Most localities throughout the state sponsored old-fashioned Independence Day celebrations, but particularly lavish festivities took place at Kaskaskia State Park, the site of the first state capital. The day's events included a parade and luncheon at Steeleville and a spectacle, Illinois Under Five Flags, which featured drama, musical programs, orations, and fireworks.

As one of the projects of the sesquicentennial year, the Old State House in Springfield was restored to its mid-19th century appearance. The Illinois State Historical Library took up quarters in the basement of the former state capitol, where it houses a valuable collection, including a handwritten copy of Lincoln's Gettysburg Address. Constitution Day, August 26, 1968, was chosen for the dedication of the building in which Lincoln in 1858 had declared that "a house divided against itself cannot stand," and in which his body had lain in state after his assassination in 1865. The Old State House is open to the public and attracts tens of thousands of tourists each year.

December 3, 1968, the last day of the sesquicentennial, was celebrated as Statehood Day throughout Illinois. Public schools held special convocations, and awards were presented to the winners of the Sesquicentennial Commission's literary competition.

Gilbert Stuart's Birthday

The work of Gilbert Stuart, who made his reputation during the earliest years of the republic, has never lost its place in the front rank of American portrait art. Although Stuart painted hundreds of portraits, including those of the most distinguished men of England, Ireland, and America during the late 18th and early 19th centuries, he is best known for his life portraits of George Washington, one of which adorns the US one-dollar bill. Almost every portrait of George Washington seen in classrooms, courtrooms, and other government buildings is a reproduction of a Stuart portrait.

The artist's father, also named Gilbert Stuart, had emigrated from Perth, Scotland, to Rhode Island, where he planned to manufacture snuff, and married Elizabeth Anthony, the daughter of a well-to-do landowner of Middletown, Rhode Island. With the support of two partners, Stuart built a snuff mill at the junction of the Mattatoxet stream and the Pattasquamscott tidal river, in North Kingstown. The gambrel-roofed building, which can be seen today, included living quarters for the Stuart family. The Stuarts' son, Gilbert, was born there December 3, 1755.

The snuff-manufacturing venture was not a success, and in 1761 the elder Stuart sold his share in the mill and moved with his family to Newport, Rhode Island, where young Gilbert Stuart grew up. Stuart taught himself to draw during these years, and, according to a classmate, by the time Stuart was 13 he was copying pictures and a while later drawing portraits.

A mediocre Scottish artist, Cosmo Alexander, went to Newport in about 1769 and became Gilbert Stuart's art teacher. Stuart accompanied his teacher to Edinburgh, where Alexander died on August 25, 1772. After unsuccessful attempts to support himself, Stuart, not yet 20, reportedly worked his way back to America on a coal ship bound for Nova Scotia in 1773 or 1774.

At home once again, he painted and studied music, for which he also showed a definite talent. However, the American colonies of that revolutionary time did not foster the study of art, and young Stuart again crossed the Atlantic, reaching London probably in November 1775.

All his life — even when he was acknowledged as one of the most successful and talented portrait artists of his time — Stuart was to have money problems. When he arrived in London, he tried to support himself by working as a church organist, probably at St. Vedast's Church in Foster Lane. After a period of privation, he wrote a letter in which he described himself as "just arrived att the age of 21 . . . without the necessarys of life," his "hopes from home Blasted and incapable of returning thither." The letter was a plea for help addressed to Benjamin West, the American painter in London who had advised and befriended many young artists.

The plea brought an immediate response from West. Stuart became his pupil and moved to 22 Villiers Street, not far from West's house on Newman Street. Later, probably during the summer of 1777, Stuart moved into West's house, where he remained for five years as a student and member of the West household.

The Pennsylvania-born West had tremendous influence in London and in the world of art. He had been a founder of the Royal Academy of Arts and had the patronage of King George III, who had appointed him historical painter to the king. West's studio was regularly filled with artists from many countries and patrons.

Stuart contributed one portrait to the Royal Academy in 1777, three in 1779, two in 1781 and four in 1782. By 1781 he had already re-

ceived favorable notice from critics, and the next year he received public acclaim for his full-length *Portrait of a Gentleman Skating,* for which his friend William Grant of Congalton had posed. Shortly after this success, Stuart moved into rooms of his own at No. 7 Newman Street.

In 1783 he sent nine portraits to the Exhibition of the Incorporated Society of Artists. He was clearly on the road to professional glory, if not financial stability. His list of patrons over the next five years was impressive. In an era in which British painters had brought portraiture to its peak, Stuart, at the age of 32, ranked with the greatest of his time — Thomas Gainsborough, Sir Joshua Reynolds, George Romney, and Allan Ramsay. Stuart was also commanding huge fees, on a par with these acknowledged British masters, with the possible exceptions of Gainsborough and Reynolds. However, since Stuart ignored business matters and never kept books, he sometimes did not know whether he had been paid for the portraits he painted. This lack of attention to credit and debit ledgers was to have serious consequences.

In 1785 Stuart exhibited at the Royal Academy for the last time. Already known for his lavishness, he rented an expensive house in New Burlington Street, employed a French chef, and entertained on a grand scale, hiring professional musicians even for occasions on which he himself played for his guests, as he enjoyed doing.

He married Charlotte Coates, the daughter of a physician, on May 10, 1786. Although Stuart was successful, charming, and well mannered, the Coates family did not approve of the match. Twelve children were born of the marriage.

Stuart, still in his early thirties, had risen to the top of his profession. However, his extravagant spending outran his substantial fees, and, to avoid debtors' prison, he fled to Ireland, probably early in the summer of 1787. He was an immediate success in Dublin, but within five or six years his overspending and neglect of business details again put him in an impossible financial situation.

In late 1792 or early 1793, he sailed for New York, arranging to paint the portrait of the ship's owner in exchange for passage. While on the ship, Stuart reportedly explained that he hoped to make his fortune (and enough to pay his creditors in England and Ireland) by painting portraits of Washington and selling reproductions of them. It was an idea that stemmed, apparently, from his days in London, when John Boydell, a leading printseller, commissioned Stuart to paint a series of the best-known contemporary painters and artists, including Reynolds and West. Boydell then had plates engraved of Stuart's portraits, from which he produced and sold prints. Stuart later painted many replicas of his originals — including as many as 75 of at least one of his Washington portraits — but he evidently never followed through on the engraving method of replication.

Stuart never lacked for commissions. After working in New York for about a year, he went, in November 1794, to Philadelphia, then the cultural and political center of the United States. Although he is best known for his portraits of distinguished, and usually old, men, in Philadelphia he painted a superb series of portraits of women. It was also in Philadelphia that Washington posed for Stuart's first two life portraits of him. The first, known as the Vaughan Type, showing the right side of Washington's face, was painted in late winter 1795. The second portrait, known as the Lansdowne Type, a life-size standing figure of Washington showing the left side of the face and the right hand outstretched, was begun in April 1796.

Stuart's Philadelphia studio became so overrun by visitors, patrons, and would-be patrons, that the beleaguered artist could not work. He moved to Germantown (now part of Philadelphia) in mid-1796. That fall, at the request of Martha Washington, he painted a third life portrait of the President. Called the Athenaeum Head, it depicts Washington's face, eyes front, but details of clothing — the stock and coat — are not complete. Although Stuart could skillfully draw such difficult details as lace as well as any artist, and on occasion did so with a few flicks of his wrist to prove it, he often left a portrait unfinished, especially if he was pleased with it. Sometimes Stuart liked a commissioned portrait so well that he kept the original for himself. Martha Washington, in fact, had to settle for a replica of the Athenaeum Head. Stuart kept the original until his death.

In 1803, after Washington, D.C., had become the national capital, Stuart moved there. In his studio at F and 7th streets he painted the portraits of many of this country's leaders, including Thomas Jefferson, James Madison, and James Monroe. Stuart was, as one contemporary put it, "worked to death" in Washington.

He moved to Boston in the summer of 1805 and spent the rest of his life painting, even though he was in failing health for the last few years and was especially depressed by signs of paralysis in his left arm. He had an attack of gout in the spring of 1828. On July 9 of the same year, he died at the age of 72, still in debt, in his home on Essex Street. Survived by his wife and four daughters, Stuart was buried in the Central Burying Grounds on Boston Common. He was one of the original members elected to the Hall

of Fame for Great Americans, in New York, in 1900.

Visitors to Rhode Island can see Stuart's birthplace on Gilbert Stuart Road, northwest of Saunderstown. The wooden waterwheel and machinery of his father's snuff mill have been restored, and antique furnishings are on view in the living quarters. In Wickford, about five miles north of the birthplace, sightseers can visit St. Paul's Episcopal Church, built in 1707, where Stuart was baptized on April 11, 1756. Across Narragansett Bay in Newport, where Stuart grew up, visitors can see Stuart's full-length portrait of Washington in the Old Colony House, built in 1739 and now located on Washington Square.

The Athenaeum Head of Washington is in Boston's Museum of Fine Arts. Several Vaughan Types and one Athenaeum Head are in the Metropolitan Museum of Art in New York City, which has over 20 portraits by Gilbert Stuart.

DECEMBER 4

George Washington Takes Leave of His Officers

George Washington served as the commander in chief of the Continental army throughout the course of the American Revolution. But after the 13 colonies achieved independence, he had no desire to retain his powerful post. The general believed that his usefulness to the nation ended on December 4, 1783, when the last British troops set sail from New York harbor. On that day he prepared to take leave of the army and return to his beloved Mount Vernon in Virginia.

Before leaving New York City, Washington had one last meeting with his officers. At noon on December 4, most of the army officers in the city and its environs gathered at Fraunces Tavern in lower Manhattan. The general's farewell was brief:

With a heart full of gratitude, I now take leave of you. I most devoutly wish that your later days may be as prosperous and happy as your former ones have been glorious and honorable.

Deeply moved by these words the men drank their wine, and then Washington continued. "I cannot come to each of you, but shall feel obliged if each of you will come and take me by the hand." General Henry Knox, his successor as commander in chief, approached first. Emotion so gripped Washington that he wept openly and embraced Knox and, then in turn, each of the other officers. One participant many years later described the farewell:

Such a scene of sorrow and weeping I had never before witnessed. . . . The simple thought that we were then about to part from the man who had conducted us through a long and bloody war, and under whose conduct the glory and independence of our country had been achieved, and that we should see his face no more in this world seemed to me utterly insupportable.

After embracing the last officer, Washington went to the door of the tavern and raised his arm in a silent farewell. Then he stepped outside. An honor guard lined the route to Whitehall, where a barge awaited him, and crowds had assembled along the path to pay him tribute. Washington was too moved to attempt to speak. He walked quickly to the wharf and boarded the barge. As the vessel departed he stretched out his arms to bid good-bye to all assembled.

From New York, Washington went by barge to Paulus Hook (now in Jersey City). There a small cavalcade waited to accompany him to Philadelphia and then to Annapolis, Maryland, where the Congress was meeting. Both Philadelphia and Annapolis marked his arrival with special festivities and celebrations. But the glory of a military hero that was accorded Washington was overshadowed by his wish to return to civilian life. On December 23 he surrendered his army commission to the Congress.

A building known as Fraunces Tavern still stands at the corner of Pearl and Broad streets. A tasteful reconstruction of the 1719 building, financed in 1907 by the Sons of the Revolution, represents the period in question but does not duplicate the original structure. The public is welcome to visit the Long Room on the second floor, where Washington met his officers. There is a small museum with Washington memorabilia, scenes of the general's farewell, and items dating from the Revolution. A restaurant still operates on the main floor. Although it and the museum generally are closed on Sundays and holidays, both remain open on Washington's Birthday.

DECEMBER 5

Twenty-first Amendment Proclaimed Ratified

Prohibition represented the most ambitious effort ever undertaken in the United States to pass federal legislation affecting personal morality. The "noble experiment," as President Herbert Hoover characterized the outlawing of liquor, began in 1920, one year after the 18th Amendment — prohibiting the sale, import, and export of alcoholic beverages — was declared ratified (see January 16). It ended on December 5, 1933, when the requisite three-fourths of the states approved the 21st Amendment, thereby repealing the 18th.

The 18th Amendment had remained in effect for 13 years. To put the amendment into operation, Congress had passed the National Prohibition Enforcement Act, also known as the Volstead Act, in October 1919. This act outlawed any beverage containing alcohol in excess of one-half of one percent and created the Prohibition Bureau under the administration of the Bureau of Internal Revenue to insure compliance with the law.

However, efforts to enforce the 18th Amendment and the Volstead Act proved to be time-consuming, expensive, and ineffective. At its maximum strength, the Prohibition Bureau numbered only 3,000 agents. Lacking sufficient staff and failing to get wholehearted public cooperation, the bureau could do little to curb the massive illegal traffic in alcoholic beverages that flourished in the United States during the 1920s and early 1930s.

Both individual citizens and organized criminals violated Prohibition laws. Many persons made liquor for their personal consumption and concocted "bathtub gin" from grain alcohol diluted with water and flavored with juniper and other oils. During the 1920s such operations occurred in countless homes and only rarely aroused the attention of federal agents. More serious and of primary concern to law-enforcement authorities was the large-scale, criminal-controlled traffic in alcoholic beverages.

Despite Prohibition legislation, large segments of the populace continued to demand liquor, and crime syndicates were quick to realize the profitability of catering to the thirst for illicit drinks. The sale of smuggled foreign liquors or illegally distilled domestic spirits soon became a multimillion dollar enterprise. So lucrative were its receipts that gangland leaders claimed monopolies of liquor sales in particular areas and conducted limited, but bloody, battles with other mobsters who dared to challenge their control. Across the nation criminal elements openly flouted the laws, but nowhere was their defiance as blatant as in Chicago. There, under the leadership of the notorious Al Capone, an underworld empire made a mockery of the law by bribing city officials, bombing the warehouses and hijacking the delivery trucks of competitors, and even gunning down possible opponents in public places.

As incidents of criminal violence became more frequent and disregard for the Prohibition law more flagrant, many who had supported antiliquor legislation reconsidered their position. In 1928 Prohibition became one of the major issues of the presidential campaign when the Democrats selected a "wet" candidate, Alfred E. Smith of New York, and the Republicans chose a "dry" standard-bearer, Herbert Hoover of Iowa. Several factors influenced the outcome of the election: Hoover represented the agrarian, Midwest, Protestant tradition; Smith was an Irish Catholic and a product of Manhattan's Lower East Side. But, at least to some degree, Hoover's overwhelming victory against Smith indicated that the nation was not yet ready in 1928 to abandon Prohibition.

Realizing the difficulty of enforcing Prohibition, Hoover in 1929 appointed an 11-man Law Observance and Enforcement Commission headed by a former attorney general, George W. Wickersham, to explore the problem. Almost two years later, in January 1931, the investigative body issued its report. The commission detailed the extensive breakdown of law enforcement resulting from Prohibition and noted that the great profits of the illegal liquor traffic and the public hostility to the law made effective compliance with the 18th Amendment almost impossible. In seeming near self-contradiction, however, the commission at the same time recommended that the ban on alcoholic beverages be continued.

Prohibition continued in effect throughout Hoover's administration, but the election of Franklin Delano Roosevelt in 1932 doomed the 18th Amendment. Even before the elaborate procedures necessary to end Prohibition could be completed, Roosevelt recommended and Congress approved the Beer-Wine Revenue Act on March 22, 1933. This legislation amended the Volstead Act and legalized the sale and manufacture of wine, beer, ale, and porter containing no more than 3.2 percent alcohol by weight or 4 percent by volume.

On February 20, 1933, Congress passed the 21st Amendment and sent it to the states. Less than nine months later, the necessary three-fourths of the states had approved the legislation, and on December 5, 1933, the amendment was declared ratified. The 21st Amendment returned the control of liquor to the states, and all but seven decided to end the total ban on alcoholic beverages. By the 1950s, however, even these had rescinded their laws against liquor, although some states still allow localities the option of prohibiting the sale of alcoholic beverages within their own jurisdictions.

Martin Van Buren's Birthday

Martin Van Buren, the eighth President of the United States, was born on December 5, 1782, at Kinderhook, in upstate New York. His great-grandfather, Maes Van Buren, established the family in the region in 1631, having emigrated from Holland to settle as a leaseholder on the Van Rensselaer Manor. Abraham Van Buren, the father of the future president, earned a comfortable living as a small farmer and tavern keeper. Keenly interested in politics, he also fought in the American Revolution and held such minor local offices as town clerk.

Martin Van Buren attended local schools until, at 14, he became a clerk in the law office of Francis Silvester, a staunch Federalist. Even at this early age, Van Buren did not share his employer's political sympathies, and he spent his free moments eagerly reading the literature of the opposition Democratic-Republican party. In 1800 he worked diligently for the election of his party's candidate, Thomas Jefferson, and the following year he went to New York City, where he completed his legal studies with a fellow Democratic-Republican, the young William Peter Van Ness.

After his admission to the bar in 1803, Van Buren returned to Kinderhook to practice law with his half brother, James I. Van Alen. His political activities on behalf of the Democratic-Republican party gained Van Buren appointment as the surrogate of New York's Columbia County in 1808. The young lawyer won election as state senator in 1812, and he used the following nine years in that office to build a coalition opposed to the policies of De Witt Clinton, governor of New York. So successful was this undertaking that Van Buren's friends in the legislature, or the Albany Regency, as they were better known, became strong enough to elect him to the US Senate in 1821. His enemies, however, attributed his rapid rise to deviousness rather than political acumen and branded the small-statured legislator the Red Fox of Kinderhook and the Little Magician.

Van Buren arrived at the center of national politics at a time when the Democratic-Republican party was splitting into several factions. In the presidential contest of 1824, the New York senator supported William Crawford, the choice of the traditional party caucus, in preference to the other candidates — Henry Clay, Andrew Jackson, and John Quincy Adams. Adams won the disputed election and in his inaugural address called for a broad program of federally sponsored internal improvements on the model of the "American system" advocated by Henry Clay of Kentucky. Van Buren, whose home state had built the Erie Canal with its own resources, philosophically opposed such nationally financed projects; and during Adams's years in office Van Buren increasingly found himself drawn to Andrew Jackson.

Van Buren ran for governor of New York following the death of De Witt Clinton in 1828. He won the election, but after serving only three months resigned to become the secretary of state of the new President, Andrew Jackson. As a member of the cabinet, Van Buren was the President's most trusted adviser. Indeed, he gained favor with Jackson at the same time that the issue over the doctrine of nullification drove Jackson and his Vice President, John C. Calhoun, far apart. In 1831 Van Buren resigned as secretary of state. His hope, in the wholesale cabinet resignations that protocol would then require, was to allow Jackson to eliminate Calhoun's supporters from his cabinet — as Jackson proceeded to do. Van Buren was then named minister to Great Britain. This and other signs of favor clearly showed that Jackson had chosen Van Buren to succeed him in the presidency.

Shortly after his arrival in England, the nomination of Van Buren for the post of ambassador went before the Senate for confirmation. Since that body deadlocked on the issue, it was left to Calhoun to cast the deciding ballot. As expected, Calhoun voted against it, and the nomination was rejected.

Van Buren returned to the United States in May 1832, several days after the Democratic party — whose name had been shortened from Democratic-Republican — had nominated him for Vice President on the ticket headed by Jackson. The two men won the election easily and during the next four years amply demonstrated their political compatibility. Van Buren strongly supported Jackson's stand against nullification and against federally financed programs of internal improvements. But even more important in gaining the confidence of the President was his assistance in eliminating the Second Bank of the United States, an institution Jackson thought monopolistic and evil.

With Jackson's second term almost completed, Van Buren became the Democratic candidate for President in 1836. The new Whig party, lacking a leader with national popularity in 1836, ran several candidates with strong sectional appeal in order to prevent Van Buren's getting a majority of electoral votes. Their strategy was based on the fact that, if no candidate won the needed majority of electoral votes, the House of Representatives, in which anti-Jacksonians were strong, would choose the President. This maneuver, however, failed to overcome Jackson's strong support of his Vice President, and Van Buren won the election with a narrow margin of popular votes and 170 of the 294 electoral votes.

Two months after Van Buren took office as President, the panic of 1837 swept the country. Precipitated by overspeculation, the panic caused many bankruptcies and much human suffering. The new President responded to the economic catastrophe with the Independent Treasury system, which he first outlined to Congress on September 5, 1837. In this message, Van Buren proposed to transfer all government specie from state banks and private businesses to federal depositories throughout the country. The attempt to completely divorce public finance from the vagaries of the private sector of the economy won the approval of the Senate in October 1837, but it was not approved by the House until June 1840. And even this victory was short-lived: the Independent Treasury Bill was repealed the following year.

As 1840 approached, Van Buren's chances of winning another four-year term were slim. The business depression was the greatest cause of the President's loss of popularity. In addition, the administration's refusal to annex independent Texas and the bloody war to remove the Seminoles from Florida alienated large sectors of the electorate. The Whig candidate, William Henry Harrison, labored under none of these disadvantages. As the hero of the battle of Tippecanoe, Harrison, who had little political experience, merely capitalized on the great popular appeal he had shown during the election of 1836. The Whigs' "Log Cabin and Hard Cider" campaign introduced such paraphernalia as placards, slogans, floats, and demagogic oratory into presidential electioneering. And although these innovations resulted in the most unrestrained presidential contest up to that time — one notable for its mudslinging — they also brought the Whigs overwhelming victory: Harrison won 234 electoral votes to Van Buren's 60.

Although Van Buren returned to Kinderhook after the election and devoted himself to the renovation of his nearby Gothic-style home, Lindenwald, he did not retire from public life in 1840. His prediction (accurate) that annexation of Texas would involve the United States in a war with Mexico lost him the 1844 Democratic presidential nomination. But four years later the Free-Soilers, a new party organized to prevent the extension of slavery into the territory acquired from Mexico as a result of the war, chose Van Buren to head their ticket. He failed to carry a single state, but his presence in the race drew essential support away from the regular Democratic candidate, Lewis Cass, and contributed to the victory of the Whig nominee, Mexican War hero Zachary Taylor.

Although Van Buren's active participation in political life ended with the 1848 election, his interest in the affairs of government never wavered. Becoming increasingly disenchanted with the Free-Soilers, he rejoined the Democratic party in 1852. Ardently opposing secession, he was deeply shocked by the Civil War. Since he died at Kinderhook on July 24, 1862, he did not live to see the restoration of the Union that he had served for so long. Funeral services for him were held in the local Dutch Reformed Church, and he was buried in Kinderhook cemetery. Lindenwald, now privately owned, is a national historic landmark.

DECEMBER 6

Feast of St. Nicholas

The feast of St. Nicholas, one of the most popular saints of Christendom, is observed by Protestant, Eastern Orthodox, and Roman Catholic churches on December 6 (or, if the Julian calendar is used, December 19). Very little is known about the saint, save that he was bishop of Myra in Lycia, Asia Minor, in the area that is now southern Turkey. It is supposed that he was born at Patara in Lycia. He died in Myra in the fourth century and was buried in that city's cathedral, which soon became a famous place of pilgrimage.

In the 11th century, Saracens invaded the area, and Christian holy places and shrines were threatened. Christians from the seaport of Bari, in southern Italy, sneaked into the cathedral of Myra and stole the sacred remains of St. Nicholas. They took them to their own city, where they built a basilica in his honor. Thereafter, devotion to St. Nicholas, which had been strong in the East, quickly spread through the West. The saint's body was reinterred in the newly built Romanesque basilica, and Bari became a popular shrine for pilgrims from all over Europe and Asia — particularly from Russia, where veneration of St. Nicholas was stronger than in any other country. St. Nicholas is the patron saint of Russia and of Greece.

There are many legends about St. Nicholas, who is sometimes called St. Nicholas of Myra, St. Nicholas of Bari, or St. Nicholas the Wonderworker. One legend is that he inherited great wealth and devoted it to charity. An instance of his benevolence is related in the legend concerning a nobleman of his city who had become so poor that he contemplated allowing his three daughters to become prostitutes. When he heard of this, Nicholas went secretly to the nobleman's home three nights in succession. Hiding outside the window, he threw a bag of gold into the daughters' room on each visit, thus providing a dowry for each of the girls and saving them from disgrace. This incident is supposed to be responsible for St. Nicholas's connection with the giving of gifts.

It used to be the custom in various parts of Europe for parents to put gifts of sweetmeats and toys in the shoes or stockings of their children on St. Nicholas's Eve. In convent boarding schools, the young women students would leave their stockings at the door of their respective abbesses' rooms, with notes recommending themselves to the generosity of St. Nicholas — the forerunners of letters to Santa Claus. The next morning the abbesses would summon their charges and show them their stockings filled — supposedly by St. Nicholas — with sweetmeats. Even today, the Netherlands, Switzerland, Germany, and some other European countries maintain the annual tradition of gift-giving on December 5, St. Nicholas's Eve, or December 6, the feast day of St. Nicholas.

Still another legend is that three children, butchered by an innkeeper and put into a brine tub, were miraculously restored to life by the intervention of Nicholas. He is also said to have saved sailors in distress at sea and men unjustly condemned to death. In many pictures, Nicholas is represented bearing three purses to symbolize his generosity — the round bags of gold he provided as the triple dowry. By tradition, the three round bags evolved into the three balls that today are the sign of pawnbrokers. Indeed, St. Nicholas is the patron saint of pawnbrokers, as well as of brides, children, sailors, jurists, brewers, coopers, and travelers. Many churches in the United States and Europe are named for him.

The St. Nicholas Society of the City of New York holds its annual dinner on St. Nicholas's Day. The society was founded at the suggestion of Washington Irving, its first secretary. Many of Irving's most famous works were based on the legend and folklore of the early Dutch settlers of New York City and its surrounding area. In 1832, on his return to New York from Spain, where he had served as US minister, a dinner was given in Irving's honor. In the course of his dinner address, he remarked that there was a St. Andrew's Society for Scotsmen, a St. George's Society for Englishmen, and a St. Patrick's Society for Irishmen, but that there was no society for Dutchmen and their descendants. He proposed the organization of such a society, and the St. Nicholas Society was organized on February 28, 1835. St. Nicholas was adopted as the patron saint of the society because he had been particularly dear to the Dutch founders of the city. The ship that had brought many of them to America had a statue of the saint on its deck, and the first church built in the city was dedicated to him.

To this day, the name of St. Nicholas is seen in many places in New York: it is the name of a busy thoroughfare; various retail establishments; and churches, including St. Nicholas Carpatho-Russian Orthodox Greek Catholic Church, at 288 East 10th Street, and St. Nicholas Russian Orthodox Cathedral, at 15 East 97th Street. The cathedral, which follows the old Julian calendar, celebrates the feast of its patron on December 19, when the solemn liturgy is celebrated in Old Church Slavonic and a dinner is held — usually on the Sunday before December 19. The cathedral's women's organization, the St. Nicholas Sisterhood, prepares the food in the church hall in which the dinner is held. It is attended by more than 100 parishioners.

The feast of St. Nicholas is observed in a special way in Wilton, Connecticut, owing to the efforts of Wilton residents who have lived in Europe and are interested in Old World customs — most notably in the celebration of St. Nicholas's feast. An unusual retinue is seen on Wilton streets on St. Nicholas's Eve. A white-bearded St. Nicholas, wearing the red robes and miter of a bishop, is seated on a white horse, led by a squire. Preceding him is a man in Moorish costume, a reminder that St. Nicholas was bishop of a see in Asia Minor. Also in the procession is a girl in Dutch costume, a reminder that this annual spectacle is often portrayed in villages of the Netherlands. As the group goes through the town, its members hand out gifts, candy, and fruit to children. The entourage then proceeds to the Community Nursery School and Center Elementary School, where St. Nicholas dismounts, enters the classroom, and solemnly consults his book containing the records of which children have been well-behaved during the year. Then, to the children's immense relief and delight, he gives presents to all.

The Dutch settlers of New York no doubt retained their Old World custom of giving gifts on the feast of St. Nicholas, or Sinterklaas. In his stories about Sinterklaas, Washington Irving made the saint out to be a rather somber winter spirit, and in pictures drawn at the time, Sinterklaas looked more like a Dutch gnome, perhaps because he was popularly connected with feats of magic — such as making gifts appear during the night.

Over the years, non-Dutch Americans adopted Sinter klaas, who became Santa Claus in American speech and was portrayed as a cross between the original St. Nicholas and the British Father Christmas — neither of whom was particularly rotund. During the 1800s Thomas Nast, the famous political cartoonist, created a merry-looking Santa Claus, more like King Cole dressed in winter furs. Years later this figure had added

girth as well as mirth to his image. Santa Claus as represented today thus is largely an American contribution to the world.

DECEMBER 7

Delaware Day

Delaware, whose 2,057 square miles make it the second smallest state in the Union, was one of the original 13 colonies. Henry Hudson, an Englishman sailing in the employ of the Dutch East India Company, explored the coastline of Delaware in 1609. In the following year a storm blew Samuel Argall's ship into its bay; that Virginia captain called the body of water Delaware Bay in honor of his colony's governor, Thomas West, Lord De La Warr.

Thirty Dutch citizens, who sailed in 1631 from the town of Hoorn under Captain Peter Heyes in *De Walvis* (The Whale), became the first Europeans to settle in Delaware. This initial colonization effort ended in disaster. For reasons that are unclear, in 1632 Lenni-Lenape Indians killed the Dutch band and destroyed their settlement at Zwaanendael, which today is the site of the city of Lewes.

Six years after the Dutch failure, the Swedes attempted to establish a colony in Delaware. About March 29, 1638, Captain Peter Minuit, former governor of the Dutch colony of New Netherland (later New York), led members of a two-vessel Scandinavian expedition ashore near what is now Wilmington. The settlement, which they named Fort Christina in honor of their queen, flourished; and during the next 17 years, 12 more expeditions took Swedes to the area.

At the command of Peter Stuyvesant, the doughty governor of New Netherland, the Dutch wrested control of New Sweden from the Scandinavians in 1655. The Dutch reorganized Fort Casimir, their own former trading post, as New Amstel (now New Castle). But even more important, they introduced town and village government to the colony and set up judicial districts or counties.

Within a decade, England ended the Netherlands' control of the settlement. In 1664, during the Second Anglo-Dutch War, the duke of York, who later became King James II of England, dispatched expeditions to capture enemy settlements in the New World. This task proved easy: New Netherland itself surrendered to Colonel Richard Nichols without any bloodshed, and New Amstel capitulated to Sir Robert Carr after only one brief skirmish.

On August 24, 1682, the duke granted title to the three counties west of the Delaware River and Bay — now Kent, New Castle, and Sussex counties — to William Penn, the proprietor of the newly founded Quaker colony of Pennsylvania. In his Frame of Government of 1683, the Quaker leader incorporated the Three Lower Counties into his commonwealth. This action embroiled Penn in a decades-long dispute with Charles Calvert, the third Lord Baltimore, and the proprietor of the neighboring colony of Maryland, who also claimed jurisdiction over the area. In 1760 the descendants of the original protagonists finally agreed to arbitrate this quarrel, and the English surveyors Charles Mason and Jeremiah Dixon, working between 1763 and 1767, devised the Mason-Dixon Line, setting the Pennsylvania-Maryland boundary at approximately 39°43′ north latitude.

Pennsylvania was a poor guardian of Delaware. The Quaker legislators' indifferent reaction when French and Spanish pirates attacked the little colony during King William's War of 1689–1697 prompted Delawareans to petition for their own government. In 1704 they won the right to hold their own assembly at New Castle, and six years later they gained their own executive council. Penn, however, retained the right to name a single governor to administer both Pennsylvania and Delaware. This arrangement lasted until the American Revolution. When the Three Lower Counties declared their independence of Great Britain in 1776, they also threw off this last vestige of Pennsylvanian control and became an entirely separate state.

After the Revolution, Delaware became one of the first states to espouse revision of the Articles of Confederation. John Dickinson of Delaware, formerly a Pennsylvanian, presided at the Annapolis (Maryland) Convention of September 1786, at which Delaware, New Jersey, New York, Pennsylvania, and Virginia called for a meeting of all the states to revise the articles. It was in response to this request that the Constitutional Convention gathered at Philadelphia in May 1787 (see May 25).

Richard Bassett, Gunning Bedford Jr., Jacob Broom, Dickinson, and George Read represented Delaware at the Philadelphia convention during the summer of 1787. Bedford, Dickinson, and Read worked vigorously to preserve the rights and power of the less populous states *vis-à-vis* their stronger neighbors. Their efforts were rewarded when the delegates at last agreed to a bicameral national legislature in which each state would have two votes in the Senate and a number of votes proportional to its population in the House of Representatives. With the great problem of representation resolved, the delegates quickly compromised their other difficulties. They signed the Constitution on September 17, 1787, and sent it to the states for ratification 11 days later.

On October 24 of the same year, the Delaware legislature called for a ratifying convention to meet in Dover on December 4. In accordance with the legislature's plan, each of Delaware's three counties held special elections on November 26 and selected 10 representatives to the December gathering.

The convention met on December 4 at the old State House, and the delegates chose James Latimer, an active patriot, to preside. Delaware's leading men were strong nationalists; many were originally from Federalist Philadelphia, and all were aware of the benefits that their small state could gain from participation in a strong country. On December 7, 1787, with 30 delegates unanimously agreed, Delaware became the first state to ratify the Constitution and thus to enter the Union. The original Ratification Resolution and other supporting documents approved by this convention are on display at the state's Hall of Records in Dover.

Delaware is justly proud of its sobriquet, The First State. The legend "December 7, 1787" is emblazoned on the state flag, which the Delaware legislature adopted on July 24, 1913. At national events such as presidential inaugurations, Delaware receives special recognition of its primacy, for contingents from the little state always occupy the first position in the line of march.

For many years, patriotic and civic organizations in Delaware held observances to commemorate the state's ratification of the Constitution. In 1939 E. Paul Burkholder, a rural school supervisor of Sussex County and a member of the Delaware senate, proposed to that body that the legislature designate December 7 as Delaware Day, an annual celebration of Delaware's ratification as well as of its entire history. The lawmakers quickly endorsed the Burkholder proposal and directed the governor to appoint a commission to encourage the observance in each of the state's three counties.

During most years, simple festivities mark Delaware Day. The commission suggests a format that includes singing "The Star-Spangled Banner," "America," and "Our Delaware." Participants recite the Pledge of Allegiance and Herman Hanson's poem "Our Heritage" and listen to the reading of the governor's Delaware Day proclamation. There is usually a guest speaker and readings from the Delaware Day Commission's historical bulletin, describing some facet of the state's past.

On December 7, 1962, Delaware commemorated the 175th anniversary of ratification with a special program. The Delaware Day Commission, in conjunction with the Delaware Society of the Sons of the American Revolution, sponsored a reenactment of the state's ratification convention at the capitol (Legislative Hall) in Dover. Governor Elbert N. Carvel and other state notables, along with members of the Kent County Theatre Guild, took the parts of the various delegates to the December 7, 1787, convention.

Pearl Harbor Day

The background of the Japanese attack on Pearl Harbor, on December 7, 1941, which precipitated the US entry into World War II (see December 8), goes back to the period after World War I. In the years following that conflict, Japan sought to become the dominant nation in Asia. An industrialized, heavily populated nation controlled by military leaders, it cast covetous glances at China, its gigantic but weak neighbor. In 1931 the Japanese seized the Chinese province of Manchuria, which had valuable ports and natural resources. The invasion, which was condemned by the League of Nations, was only the first of a series of aggressive acts against China. They culminated in the Second Sino-Japanese War, with full hostilities breaking out in 1937 and eventually merging into World War II.

China was only the first objective in the establishment of what the Japanese envisioned as the Greater East Asia Co-Prosperity Sphere. Japan hoped ultimately to include English, French, Dutch, and Portuguese possessions in the Far East and the Pacific. And events in Europe provided a perfect opportunity: when World War II broke out in 1939, the Japanese decided to move against the vulnerable and oil- and rubber-rich European colonies.

Japan's imperialistic designs soon brought it into a confrontation with the United States. American interest in the Far East had developed in the 19th century, particularly after its acquisition of the Philippine Islands in the Spanish-American War. The US government was eager to maintain strong economic connections with Asia and urged all nations to agree to an Open Door policy of free trade with China. Tokyo's aggression against China threatened America's principles and interests, and Japan's aspirations to capitalize on the outbreak of a European war only exacerbated the situation.

Not all Japanese leaders desired war with the United States. Early in 1941 the premier, Prince Fuminaro Konoye, dispatched Admiral Kichisaburo Nomura to Washington to discuss a détente with the American secretary of state, Cordell Hull. Nomura was an inexperienced diplomat unfamiliar with the English language, but he was a spokesman for the Japanese navy, which was more inclined than the army to seek accommodation with the United States. Both Nomura and Hull seriously sought a peaceful resolution of the nations' differences, but misunderstandings and real conflicts of interest doomed their efforts.

In the summer of 1941 the Japanese began to make final plans for military assaults on the Asian colonies of the Western powers. Although Tokyo had hoped to avoid conflict with the United States, Americans were resolute in their demands for Japanese withdrawal from China and froze all Japanese assets in the United States when Japan occupied French Indochina. With some mixed feelings, the men directing Japan's destiny decided that their country would have to engage the American colossus in combat.

By mid-August 1941 Japanese strategists had drafted their plans of operation. The army and navy would simultaneously attack the Philippines and Malaya and then proceed against the Dutch East Indies. The maneuvers would require precise timing and coordination, but they offered the best flank security for the attackers and promised to provide the maximum element of surprise. During September the Japanese military worked to complete the details of the program and decided to include an attack on the American naval base at Pearl Harbor, Hawaii.

Admiral Isoroku Yamamoto, commander of the Combined Fleet, was the originator of the idea of an attack on Pearl Harbor. Yamamoto argued that the destruction of the American fleet was essential to guarantee the success of the invasion and occupation of Malaya and the East Indies. Japan had little hope of winning a protracted war with the United States, but it felt that the incapacitation of the US Pacific Fleet might lead the Americans to a quick settlement favorable to Nipponese aspirations in Asia. Although some Japanese naval strategists thought Yamamoto's idea too risky, opposition collapsed when the gifted admiral threatened to resign. In mid-October 1941 the Tokyo government formally adopted the plan for the attack on Pearl Harbor.

Premier Konoye still hoped to achieve concord with the United States, but he was working under a severe time limit. Japanese oil reserves were dwindling, and the approach of winter demanded the completion of tactical operations as soon as possible. Delay might force postponement until spring, when the Russians could use the favorable weather to attack the Japanese in Manchuria. Under pressure from the military, the Konoye government resigned on October 18, 1941, and General Hideki Tojo became prime minister.

Tojo determined that if Japan and the United States did not reach an agreement by November 29, he would set the war plans in motion. The date passed without a settlement, and on December 1, at a conference in the presence of the emperor, the military received formal approval of its decision to attack on X-Day — December 7 in Hawaii and the United States (December 8 by Japanese standard time). On December 2 Admiral Yamamoto's flagship, which on November 25 had set sail from the Kurile Islands with the rest of the Pearl Harbor Striking Task Force, sent out the message "Niitaka Yama Nabore" ("climb Mount Niitaka"), the prearranged signal to proceed with the attack on Hawaii.

By late November 1941 President Franklin D. Roosevelt and his advisers had recognized the signs of crisis and accepted the strong possibility of war with Japan. Both political and military leaders anticipated that the Japanese might launch an attack within a few weeks, but they believed that any such operations would take place in the Far East. On November 24 and November 27 the US War and Navy departments dispatched messages to Pacific commanders, warning them of the possibility of an imminent "surprise aggressive movement in any direction," including an attack on the Philippines or Guam. Although the directives stressed the hazards of the situation, they implied that sabotage attempts were the primary danger to the Hawaiian command.

Lieutenant General Walter C. Short, the army commander in the Hawaiian area, took action to insure the islands' internal security. General Short issued Alert Number 1, a standard directive that increased the number of men on guard against sabotage and subversion. He also ordered the army's new radar equipment into operation between 4:00 and 7:00 A.M., the most likely hours for a carrier-based air raid. However, Short did not consider such an assault probable and decided not to promulgate Alert Number 2, which pertained to procedures against air and surface bombardment, or Number 3, which concerned invasion defenses.

Rear Admiral Husband E. Kimmel, the naval commander in Hawaii, reacted in the same manner as his army counterpart. The fleet remained conscious of the danger of sabotage and instituted a careful antisubmarine patrol, but it dismissed the possibility of a total attack. Kimmel refused to send 50 available patrol planes on long-range reconnaissance missions from the island of Oahu; these aircraft might have provided an early warning of the approaching Japanese Task Force.

Although Short and Kimmel were close friends, they were unaware of each other's plans. This lack of coordination was symptomatic of the poor liaison among the ground, air, and naval elements in the Pearl Harbor area. Neither Short nor Kimmel expected an attack on the installation, and each preferred to devote his men's efforts to training for the operations that would be needed in case of unlimited war — rather than to performing supposedly unnecessary defensive exercises.

In the first week of December, Japan's Striking Task Force, composed of six aircraft carriers with more than 360 airplanes, two battleships, two heavy cruisers, six destroyers, and three submarines, continued across the Pacific Ocean. By December 6 the raiders were 500 miles north of Oahu. From this area they turned south toward their planned launching point, some 200 miles from their intended target. In the meantime, 25 Japanese submarines, which were to attack *en masse* if the approaching carrier group was discovered, gathered in the waters south of Pearl Harbor.

At 6:00 A.M. on December 7 the first Japanese attack plane took off from a carrier deck for the two-hour flight to Pearl Harbor. At 7:30 A.M. Hawaii time — 1:00 P.M. in Washington — the Japanese emissaries in the US capital were to announce their nation's decision to go to war and thus prevent accusations of a sneak attack. The strategem failed, however, when Japanese officials in Washington were slow in decoding the final message from Tokyo. By the time the diplomats Kichisaburo Nomura and Saburo Kurusu arrived at the State Department to announce the severance of relations, it was 2:05 and bombs were already falling on Hawaii.

American leaders in Washington were not surprised by the declaration of the Japanese envoys. Through a procedure known as MAGIC, the US government had broken the Japanese code system and could routinely decipher even the most highly classified messages. On the morning of December 7 the Americans intercepted the final section of a 14-part communication from Tokyo, which advised the Japanese embassy in Washington of the decision for war. Chief of Staff General George C. Marshall ordered the army to pass the information to the Hawaiian command, but, owing to communication problems, the warning did not reach Hawaii until the attack on Pearl Harbor was under way.

Deprived of last-minute intelligence from Washington, the military in Hawaii compounded its misfortune by failing to recognize telltale signs of an imminent attack. The commander of an American destroyer and an airplane pilot each spotted and engaged one of the two-man midget submarines dispatched by the Japanese to penetrate Pearl Harbor and advise the approaching Japanese planes. The navy began to investigate the reports of these engagements but did not inform the army of the encounters. In two separate instances, US radar operators picked up large flights on their screens, but junior officers on duty assumed the planes to be from American carriers cruising in the vicinity and did not inform their headquarters.

At 7:55 A.M. the first wave of Japanese aircraft, including 49 high-level bombers, 51 dive bombers, 43 fighters, and 40 torpedo planes, struck Pearl Harbor. A second wave, consisting of 54 high-level bombers, 80 dive bombers, and 36 fighters, appeared just before 9:00 A.M. and continued its deadly work until 9:45 A.M. Finally the assault ended, and the Japanese pilots returned in triumph to their carriers.

American naval vessels, moored side by side in order to limit the possibility of sabotage, and aircraft, lined nose to nose on the ground for the same purpose, had been easy targets for the fliers. Eight battleships, three light cruisers, and eight other naval vessels were destroyed or damaged. The Americans lost almost every plane at the Kaneohe Seaplane Base, the Ewa Marine Air Station, and the Ford Island Naval Air Station. The Japanese wrecked about half the bombers at the army's Hickam Field but failed to inflict significant damage on the repair shops and gasoline storage tanks.

A total of 2,403 American sailors, soldiers, marines, and civilians died in the attack on Pearl Harbor, and an additional 1,178 suffered wounds. The destruction of the battleship *Arizona* by the explosion of a 16-inch shell bomb in the forward magazine accounted for almost half of the fatalities. The Japanese announced the loss of 55 of their fliers and 9 of the 10 men aboard their midget submarines; the sole surviving Japanese seaman became America's first prisoner in World War II.

The day following the Pearl Harbor attack, President Roosevelt appeared before a joint session of Congress. Declaring that December 7 was "a date which will live in infamy," Roosevelt reported the Japanese attack on Hawaii — and on Malaya, Hong Kong, Guam, Wake Island, Midway, and the Philippine Islands the same day — and asked Congress for a declaration of war. Only one legislator (Representative Jeannette Rankin of Montana) rejected his request, and the United States entered the second global war of the 20th century.

December 7, 1941, remains indelibly etched in the memory of Americans everywhere. In formal commemoration, the governors of Alabama, New Jersey, North Carolina, Tennessee, Vermont, and Wisconsin, among others, and the mayors of New York City and many other municipalities proclaim December 7 as Pearl Harbor Day or Pearl Harbor Remembrance Day. A number of annual memorial services also call to mind the disastrous attack. Public officials and representatives of veterans' groups lay wreaths at a variety of places, including the Tomb of the Unknowns at Arlington National Cemetery in Virginia and the World War II East Coast Memorial in Battery Park, New York City. Thousands of veterans, including members of the Pearl Harbor Survivors Association, take part in ceremonies at the National Memorial Cemetery of the Pacific, located in the Punchbowl Crater in Honolulu and at memorials and US naval and military installations elsewhere.

Pearl Harbor is the site of the major monument to the men who died in the bombardment. On December 4, 1962, the US Navy dedicated a gleaming white marble and concrete shrine built on top of a section of the rusting hulk of the USS *Arizona*, which juts out of the harbor waters. The Stars and Stripes flies over the *Arizona's* stern, signifying that the sunken battleship, which holds entombed 1,102 officers and sailors, remains a commissioned vessel of the US fleet.

DECEMBER 8

Feast of the Immaculate Conception of Mary

The Feast of the Immaculate Conception celebrates the preservation of the Virgin Mary from the stain of original sin from the moment of her conception in her mother's womb. It is considered by Roman Catholics one of the most important feasts honoring the mother of Jesus.

The meaning of the feast is perhaps best summed up in a prayer from the Roman Catholic liturgy for December 8:

O God, by foreseen merits of the death of Christ, you shielded Mary from all stain of sin and preserved the Virgin Mother immaculate at her conception so that she might be a fitting dwelling place for your son.

According to the tenets of the Roman Catholic church, only Christ and his mother were so preserved from original sin.

Some other Christian churches celebrate the conception of the Virgin Mary, but only Roman Catholics have proclaimed the dogma of the Immaculate Conception. For Roman Catholics, the feast is a holy day of obligation, that is, attendance at mass is expected.

Strangely enough, Rome was one of the last places to celebrate the feast — which had its origins in the Eastern churches in about the eighth century. It was then called, as it still is by the Eastern churches, the Conception of St. Anne, meaning St. Anne's conception of Mary.

The feast was extended to all provinces of the Byzantine Empire, which included southern Italy. According to some historians, from the Byzantine provinces of Italy it was introduced to other parts of Western Europe by the conquering Normans. The Normans adopted the feast so enthusiastically that during the Middle Ages it was known as the Feast of the Normans.

In both East and West, popular devotion to the feast was far ahead of official recognition. In the East, where it had been celebrated (on December 9) since at least the eighth century, it was not until 1166 that the Emperor Manuel Comnenus recognized it as a public celebration and declared it a holiday for all of the far-reaching Byzantine Empire.

In the West the feast had been celebrated as early as the 9th century in Ireland (on May 3) and as early as the 11th or 12th century in England (on December 8). From England, the celebration spread to France and Germany.

While the church at Rome was aware of the regional celebrations and allowed the feast to be introduced wherever local church authorities chose, Rome itself neither celebrated nor officially recommended the feast until many centuries had passed.

In 1476 or 1477, Pope Sixtus IV introduced the feast in Rome, allowing but not commanding its celebration locally. Early in the 18th century, probably in 1708, Pope Clement XI prescribed it as an annual feast to be celebrated on December 8.

It was declared a holy day of obligation in 1854, at the time when Pope Pius IX solemnly defined the dogma of the Immaculate Conception of Mary, thus giving official recognition to a belief held for centuries by the faithful.

A special mass and office for this feast were prescribed in 1863, nine years after the doctrine of the Immaculate Conception had been formally promulgated by the Roman church. Even before the doctrine was officially defined, bishops in America in 1846 proclaimed Mary patroness of the United States under this title. The National Shrine of the Immaculate Conception in Washington, D.C. is visited by many tourists each year.

To celebrate the centennial of the proclamation of the dogma of the Immaculate Concep-

tion, Pope Pius XII declared 1954 a Marian Year, designating it a year of special devotion to Mary.

The feast is listed in Eastern Orthodox calendars as the Conception of the Ever-Virgin Mary by Anne, or the Conception of St. Anna, the mother of our Lady. In Puerto Rico, where the largely Roman Catholic population observes the day as the Fiesta de la Inmaculada Concepción de María, solemn worship in churches is supplemented by gaiety outside. Humacao, Guayanilla, Las Marías, Las Piedras, Vega Alta, and Vieques are among the towns likely to hold annual festivities, with public dancing, singing, and colorful celebrations in the town plazas.

United States Enters World War II

On December 8, 1941, the day after Japan's surprise attack on US naval installations at Pearl Harbor, Hawaii (see December 7), President Franklin D. Roosevelt went before a joint session of Congress at 12:30 P.M. to report events of the attack and request a declaration of war against Japan. The nation held its breath as citizens everywhere listened to the President's words over the radio. Retiring to their separate chambers, the two houses of Congress acted with unprecedented speed. The Senate adopted the war resolution at 1:00 P.M., and the House of Representatives approved it 10 minutes later. Only one legislator, Representative Jeannette Rankin of Montana, voted against the resolution. The document was signed by the President at 4:10 P.M.

Germany and Italy, the European members of the Axis pact that Japan had formally joined the previous year, responded by declaring war on the United States on December 11, 1941. On the same day, the United States declared war on the two European dictatorships. In so doing, the United States joined the British, French, Soviet, and other Allied nations in the monumental struggle, which was ultimately victorious against the Axis powers (see May 8, V-E Day; August 14, V-J Day; and September 1, World War II Ends, Japanese Surrender).

DECEMBER 9

Battle of Great Bridge

In the years after 1763, Virginia, the most important of the southern provinces, shared with its northern neighbors an increasing hostility to Britain's attempts to reorganize the administration of the colonies. Virginians avoided the confrontations with British authorities that were so common in Massachusetts, but their political philosophy gradually became radical. Firebrands like Patrick Henry, intellectuals like Thomas Jefferson, and political leaders like Edmund Randolph all eventually recognized the necessity for independence.

Parliament's enactment of the Coercive, or Intolerable, Acts in 1774 to punish Massachusetts for the Boston Tea Party accelerated Virginia's estrangement from Britain. The General Assembly of Virginia protested the legislation and ordered that June 1, 1774, be a day of fasting and prayer. In response to this boldness, the royal governor, John Murray, earl of Dunmore, dissolved the assembly, including the representative House of Burgesses, but the burgesses continued to meet extralegally at the Apollo Room of the Raleigh Tavern in Williamsburg and called for a provincial convention to assemble on August 7.

The first Virginia Convention extended the commercial nonintercourse policy to include the nonpayment of transatlantic debts and chose delegates to the First Continental Congress. Among the representatives chosen were Richard Bland, Benjamin Harrison, Patrick Henry, Richard Henry Lee, Edmund Pendleton, Peyton Randolph, and George Washington. The convention also published Thomas Jefferson's *A Summary View of the Rights of British America*, which renounced Parliament's authority to legislate on internal or external matters affecting the colonies and suggested that only through the king were the colonies bound to Britain.

Angered by the failure of words to persuade the authorities in England and outraged by the hardships endured by Massachusetts under the Intolerable Acts, Virginia held a second convention at St. John's Church in Richmond in March 1775. The delegates were more militant, and Patrick Henry set the tone with his famous peroration "I know not what course others may take, but as for me, give me liberty, or give me death!" The convention urged the development of manufacturing to render the colonies less dependent on Britain and adopted Henry's resolution for "embodying, arming and disciplining" the Virginia militia.

Lord Dunmore felt that he had to take action to quell the sedition, and on March 28, 1775, he ordered civil officials to prevent the appointment of delegates to the second Continental Congress, scheduled for May. Unfortunately for the governor, the native leaders were so united behind the work of the provincial conventions that they would not comply with his directions. Dunmore was politically impotent, and resort to use of military force became his only hope.

Sailors were the only British military personnel stationed in the area of Virginia. In mid-April Dunmore quietly took a contingent of them to the governor's residence in Williamsburg. In the early hours of April 21, these sailors under the command of Captain Henry Collins pilfered a great quantity of powder from the public magazine. Angered by Dunmore's action, Williamsburg militiamen prepared to march on his home, but Peyton Randolph, the Speaker of the House of Burgesses, persuaded them to offer only written protestations. Dunmore answered their complaints with a promise to restore the powder and an explanation that he had taken the powder to be ready to suppress a rumored slave insurrection in Surry County.

Few Virginians were satisfied by Dunmore's statement. Cavalrymen gathered at Fredericksburg to move against the capital, but Peyton Randolph and George Washington sent them messages advising against violence. The Fredericksburg citizenry heeded the counsel of these eminent patriots, but the Hanover County militia was more rash. Led by Patrick Henry, the Hanover men marched to the vicinity of Williamsburg and sent Carter Braxton into the capital to demand the return of the powder. Dunmore was enraged and warned Dr. William Pasteur, the mayor of Williamsburg, that "by the living God if an insult is offered to me or to those who have obeyed my orders, I will declare freedom to the slaves and lay the town in ashes!" The governor calmed himself temporarily, however, and on May 4 gave the colony £330 in restitution for its powder, but, as soon as the Hanover army disbanded, he outlawed Henry.

On May 12 Governor Dunmore called for a session of Virginia's general assembly to consider the proposals of Britain's prime minister, Lord North, for reconciling Britain and the colonies. The delegates met on June 1 but received the suggestions hostilely. Upset by the resoluteness of the Virginians and by news of armed clashes in the northern colonies, Dunmore promptly dispatched his wife and children to the safety of the warship *Fowey*. Soon afterwards, deciding to leave Williamsburg himself, he joined their refuge, declaring the ship to be the new seat of government. With Dunmore away from the city, the burgesses rejected North's plan on June 12 and on June 20 adjourned for the last time. In July the third extralegal Virginia Convention assembled and took over direction of the province's affairs.

Dunmore made his way to Norfolk, Virginia's commercial center, where he gathered a flotilla and a small army of Loyalists. Safely ensconced in the port, he was able to strike at Virginians who challenged the royal authority. On October 24 and 25 he sent a naval force to destroy Hampton in retaliation for the burning and looting of a government sloop by residents of that community. On November 7 Dunmore declared martial law. He also offered to free the slaves and the indentured servants of American rebels. The governor even raised a force composed of several hundred slaves captured and enlisted by him and called Dunmore's Ethiopians.

Patriot leaders recognized that they had to oust Dunmore from Norfolk, lest all southeastern Virginia become a haven for Tories. The Virginia Committee of Safety ordered Colonel William Woodford to march on the town with his 3rd Regiment. This decision quickly led to the battle of Great Bridge of December 9, 1775, the first encounter of British and American soldiers since Bunker Hill and the first engagement of the Revolution fought in Virginia.

Governor Dunmore chose to meet the advancing Americans at Great Bridge, about nine miles from Norfolk. He established a virtually impregnable position by fortifying one end of a long causeway that covered a defile and was surrounded by tidal swamps. When Colonel Woodford arrived in the area he built a redoubt at the other end of the causeway and stationed a Lieutenant Travis with 90 men to defend it. The patriot colonel and the rest of his force, which included John Marshall, the future chief justice of the United States, remained on a hill about 400 yards away.

For some unknown reason, perhaps a loss of patience, Dunmore decided to attack the Americans first. By choosing to assume the offense, Dunmore surrendered the advantages natural to the defense in such terrain. To lead the frontal attack down the long, narrow causeway, the governor dispatched Captain Fordyce with 60 grenadiers and approximately 140 regulars. Colonel Samuel — or, in some accounts, William — Leslie with a contingent of some 230 slaves and Virginia Loyalists formed the reserve.

Failing in his first advance, Captain Fordyce regrouped his men and brought up two cannons for support. Again he moved down the causeway toward the American redoubt. Lieutenant Travis held his fire so long that Fordyce became convinced that the rebels had deserted their position. Led by Fordyce, who cheered "The day is our own," the British charged the American fortification only to be met by a last-minute barrage from the outnumbered patriots. Fordyce and a large number of his men were killed; others retreated to their nearby fortifications, from where they returned by night to Norfolk. British losses in the battle of Great Bridge reached a total of 62; the only American casualty was a soldier wounded in the hand. Woodford continued his march to Norfolk, which he en-

tered on December 13. Colonel Robert Howe, who meanwhile had arrived with his 2nd North Carolina Regiment, took command of the town on December 14.

Before the Americans reached Norfolk, Lord Dunmore took refuge with a large number of Tories on board ship. The rebels refused his demands for provisions, and he threatened to retaliate by bombarding the town. On January 1, 1776, Dunmore made good his promise by turning his naval cannons on Norfolk and by sending marines ashore to burn the warehouses. In return, the rebels burned the homes of leading Tories. Soon fires roared out of control in much of the port. What remained of Norfolk was virtually destroyed the following month to prevent the British from using it again.

After the initial burning of Norfolk, Dunmore had established a beachhead there, but the governor returned to his ships after the Americans prevented him from moving inland. In May Major General Charles Lee arrived in Norfolk and drove Dunmore's flotilla away after a ship-to-shore skirmish. The governor took his collection of British troops, Loyalists, and slaves to Gwynn's Island off Virginia's Mathews County, then to Maryland, and finally out to sea, leaving America forever.

Lord Dunmore was the last royal governor of Virginia. His lack of sympathy for the American cause drove many Virginians to ally themselves with the disgruntled citizens of other colonies, and his military activities brought them to open revolt. The battle of Great Bridge marked not only the end of Dunmore's tenure in Virginia but also the beginning of the War of Independence in the South.

DECEMBER 10

Emily Dickinson's Birthday

It would surprise Emily Dickinson, the New England recluse whose passion for life spilled out in brief verses of compressed incandescence, to find herself acclaimed today as one of America's greatest poets. She was virtually unknown in her own quiet lifetime, which began on December 10, 1830, in a house that still stands in Amherst, Massachusetts. Her father, Edward Dickinson, for whom she felt affection and awe, was a lawyer, active in politics and the treasurer of Amherst College. According to one of her letters, he was "too busy with his briefs to notice what we do." Her mother, Emily Norcross Dickinson, did not, in the words of her daughter, "care for thought." Although she grew up with her brother, William, and sister, Lavinia,

Emily Dickinson's more frequent companions came to be "hills, . . . the sundown," and her own soul. It was, nonetheless, a close-knit family, no member of which ever strayed far. William, when he married, moved next door. Emily and Lavinia, neither of whom ever married, lived all their lives at home.

By her own description, Emily Dickinson was "small, like the wren," with hair that was "bold like the chestnut burr." Her eyes were "like the sherry in the glass that the guest leaves." Letters she wrote as a teenager revealed her as interested, eager, and outgoing, with an affinity for people and books. Although she has been described since as "this last pale Indian-summer flower of Puritanism," given to inward reverie, she was reputed to be a lively conversationalist, full of wit and vivacity, as well. She attended Amherst Academy intermittently until she was 16, when she went away from home for the first time.

This was to Mount Holyoke Female Seminary in nearby South Hadley, where she completed a year's study before returning home abruptly in 1848. Only rarely again in her lifetime did she travel — in 1855 to visit her father, then serving in Congress in Washington, D.C.; and in the summers of 1864 and 1865 for treatment of an eye ailment in Boston and Cambridge.

After her departure from Mount Holyoke, her parents' home and gardens became increasingly, then exclusively, her world. With the exceptions noted above, she lived and died without leaving the green hills of Amherst. To one of her vibrant appreciation, it was small confinement. As she wrote later, "I never saw a moor,/ I never saw the sea;/ Yet know I how the heather looks,/ And what a wave must be." Beneath her quiet exterior raged an inner life that was both rich and intense. She found, as she put it, "ecstasy in living," and in nature: "Inebriate of air am I,/ And debauchee of dew,/ Reeling, through endless summer days,/ From inns of molten blue." Though she described her family as "religious, except me," she was, in fact, deeply so, and a vein of mysticism runs through her work.

Her first few poems were written with the encouragement, long cherished later, of Benjamin Newton, a law student in her father's office, who moved away in 1850, married, and died soon afterwards. But it was not until Emily Dickinson was about 30 that she began writing poetry in earnest. Her poems recorded with exquisite precision and economy her uniquely phrased thoughts. Ecstatically or ironically, playfully, at times sadly, she dealt with permanence and transiency, life, death, love, and the adventures of the human soul, which she discovered "unto itself/ Is an imperial friend,/ Or the most agonizing spy/ An enemy could send."

In April 1862 Dickinson responded to an article in the *Atlantic Monthly* by the critic and clergyman Thomas Wentworth Higginson, sending him four carefully selected poems with a question that initiated their lifelong correspondence: "Are you too deeply occupied to say if my verse is alive?" Though intrigued by her ingenuity and the originality of her thought, Higginson, like others, was too confused by her unconventionality of expression to consider her ready for publication. His replies, encouragement, and continuing interest nonetheless were of importance to her. Some years later, one of her letters let him know how much. "You were not aware," she wrote, "that you saved my life."

By 1866 the flow of her poetry had almost stopped. Although she wrote occasional verses for the rest of her life, she devoted far more energy to correspondence, which became her only contact with the outside world. After 1870 her seclusion was virtually complete. Years went by in which she did not cross her doorstep. She continued to dress entirely in white, as had been her practice for some years.

Her father died in 1874, and her mother became an invalid the next year. During a brief respite from personal tragedy, from 1877 until 1884, a mutual love grew out of Emily Dickinson's old acquaintanceship with Judge Otis B. Lord of Salem, Massachusetts, a widowed friend of her father's who visited often and corresponded regularly. Meanwhile, the other correspondents whose friendship-by-mail she had cherished for years had died — the noted Reverend Charles Wadsworth of Philadelphia and San Francisco; publisher Samuel Bowles of the *Springfield Republican* and his associate, Josiah Holland, who later founded *Scribner's Monthly*. Her mother also died in 1882, after seven years of invalidism. With the death of her beloved Judge Lord in 1884, Emily Dickinson was overtaken by "nervous exhaustion." In 1885 came the death of author Helen Hunt Jackson, the Amherst-born contemporary who — though she was only a slight acquaintance — had been alone among literary lights of the day in recognizing Emily Dickinson's true stature as a poet. After this, the woman who had written of the soul that "selects her own society,/ Then shuts the door" was more and more confined to her own room, or bed. She died on May 15, 1886, leaving hundreds of unpublished poems.

Even her sister Lavinia was astonished by their number. She determined to find a publisher and persuaded Higginson, somewhat against his own judgment, to prepare a slim volume, which he did with the help of Mabel Loomis Todd. Thus, *Poems by Emily Dickinson* appeared in 1890, to the accompaniment of critical confusion and public delight. It was followed by *Poems:*

Second Series (1891); two volumes of letters (1894); *Poems: Third Series* (1896); *The Single Hound* (1914); *Further Poems* (1929); *Unpublished Poems* (1932); and *Bolts of Melody* (1945). The Jones Library in Amherst has a noteworthy Dickinson collection.

The 14-room brick house in which Emily Dickinson spent so much of her life is at 280 Main Street in Amherst. The building, privately owned, has been designated a national historic landmark.

Thomas H. Gallaudet's Birthday

Thomas H. Gallaudet, the pioneer teacher of the deaf in the United States, was born on December 10, 1787, in Philadelphia, of Huguenot ancestors who had fled to America from France at the time of the revocation of the Edict of Nantes. When he was 13 years old, his family moved to Hartford, Connecticut.

Gallaudet was graduated from Yale in 1805. During the next seven years he divided his time among studying law, teaching, working in a business office, and traveling for his health. He then decided to study for the ministry and was graduated from Andover Theological Seminary in 1814.

Becoming acquainted with a deaf child named Alice Cogswell at about the time of his graduation, he urged her father to hire a special teacher for her. The father, joining with others, responded by sending Gallaudet to Europe to learn the methods in use there for teaching the deaf. Gallaudet accordingly spent several months studying under Abbé Sicard at the Royal Institute for Deaf Mutes (Institut Royal des Sourds-Muets) in Paris. He also visited England, where he studied the teaching methods of Thomas Braidwood and of the latter's successor, Joseph Watson.

Gallaudet returned to America in 1816 with the brilliant educator Laurent Clerc — himself deaf, who had studied and taught at the Royal Institute for Deaf Mutes. With the aid of Clerc, Gallaudet raised the money to open the first free school for the deaf in the United States, in Hartford, the next year. Initially named the Connecticut Asylum, it later became the American Asylum. Made principal of the school, Gallaudet held the post for 13 years. Apart from his pioneering work with individual pupils, he made important contributions in training others who founded similar schools.

Other members of Gallaudet's family shared his interests. His oldest son, also named Thomas, became a minister to the deaf; and his youngest son, Edward Miner Gallaudet, opened a school for deaf mutes in Washington, D.C. The upper branch of this school developed into Gallaudet College. The institution was named for the senior Gallaudet, who died in Hartford on September 10, 1851.

Human Rights Day and Week

December 10 is observed as Human Rights Day by most member countries of the United Nations. The celebrations mark the anniversary of the unanimous adoption of the Universal Declaration of Human Rights by the UN General Assembly on December 10, 1948.

In the United States, the observance is known as Human Rights Week and extends from December 10 through 17 in order to include another important rights anniversary — December 15, the date on which the Bill of Rights became part of the US Constitution in 1791 (see December 15). Widely observed, Human Rights Week is customarily bracketed by presidential proclamations designating December 10 as Human Rights Day and December 15 as Bill of Rights Day.

City, county, and state officials across the nation are invited to issue proclamations in recognition of the observance, and citizens are invited to organize their own community committees to channel the participation of all local groups and organizations interested in human rights. Participation is sought by religious leaders, educators, political figures, and local officials, who customarily stress human rights themes in their public addresses at this time; and by educators at all levels, who focus on human rights in school assembly programs during this period. Many teachers choose this week for study and discussion of the Universal Declaration of Human Rights and the Bill of Rights, and some examine individual state constitutions as well.

The purpose of all the observances is to foster understanding of the meaning of these landmark documents of human dignity in specific terms. Rights and freedoms are stressed in press and broadcasting media during Human Rights Week, and pertinent displays are seen in schools, libraries, and elsewhere. Often the exhibits are highlighted by full-text displays of the Universal Declaration and the Bill of Rights.

Major anniversary years are, of course, the object of particular attention. This was the case in 1968, which marked the 20th anniversary of the UN declaration. With the intention of intensifying efforts in the field of human rights, the UN General Assembly designated 1968 as the International Year for Human Rights.

In the United States, 1968 accordingly was also declared as Human Rights Year in a proclamation of President Lyndon B. Johnson. He selected the birthday of Eleanor Roosevelt (see

October 11), who had a large role in securing adoption of the UN declaration, to issue his proclamation. And he chose the birthday of another leading exponent of freedom, President Franklin D. Roosevelt (see January 30), to sign the executive order by which he established the Presidential Commission for the Observance of Human Rights Year. The commission, Johnson pointed out, was appointed to increase Americans' understanding of the principles of human rights; to focus the activities of federal, state, and local bodies that share its purpose; to enlist "the cooperation of educational institutions, foundations, and the mass media, as well as civic, labor, and other organizations"; and to conduct appropriate studies, meetings, and other activities to provide for the nation's effective participation in the yearlong observance.

At the United Nations, the 20th anniversary of its declaration was marked on December 9 by a special commemorative session of the General Assembly, and on December 10 with a concert performed by the Minnesota Orchestra. Held in the General Assembly chamber, it was attended by an array of international luminaries. A Human Rights Cantata, commissioned specifically for the occasion by UN Secretary-General U Thant, was performed by the Augsburg College Choir of Minneapolis. Entitled "Yes, Speak Out, Yes," it was composed by Cristobal Halffter to a text by Norman Corwin. Simultaneously and throughout the International Year for Human Rights, more than 64 member countries of the United Nations also held special celebrations or enacted measures to commemorate the 20th anniversary of the declaration. In 1973 the 25th anniversary was observed with a special session of the General Assembly, and commemorative UN postage stamps were issued. The December 10 anniversary is observed annually throughout the world and at the New York headquarters of the United Nations, where speeches, ceremonies, and a concert are customarily presented in honor of the occasion.

The story of how the United Nations' Universal Declaration of Human Rights came into being is not generally known:

When the charter for establishment of the United Nations was drawn up at San Francisco in 1945, it contained repeated references to the "human rights and fundamental freedoms" that it sought to support, and it called upon member nations to promote and encourage such rights in cooperation with the world body. However, since the document nowhere spelled out exactly what these rights and freedoms were, it became necessary to frame such a definition before nations could be expected to promote and encourage them in any very specific way.

The UN Commission on Human Rights was therefore called upon to prepare a statement of principles that could serve as a universal standard. As set forth in 30 articles, the enunciated principles became known as the Universal Declaration of Human Rights. Two of the document's chief authors were Charles Malik, Lebanon's representative to the UN; and Eleanor Roosevelt, US delegate to the UN, who was the first to chair the Commission on Human Rights. Only Saudi Arabia, the Union of South Africa, and six Soviet bloc nations abstained from the vote that resulted in unanimous adoption of the Universal Declaration of Human Rights by the General Assembly of the United Nations on December 10, 1948.

Basic principles of the Universal Declaration are embodied in the following sections:

Article 1. All human beings are born free and equal in dignity and rights. They . . . should act towards one another in a spirit of brotherhood.

Article 2. Everyone is entitled to all the rights and freedoms set forth in this Declaration, without distinction of any kind, such as race, colour, sex, language, religion, . . . opinion, national . . . origin, property, birth. . . .

Article 3. Everyone has the right to life, liberty and security of person.

Article 4. No one shall be held in slavery or servitude. . . .

Article 5. No one shall be subjected to torture or to cruel, inhuman or degrading treatment or punishment.

Article 7. All are equal before the law and . . . entitled . . . to equal protection of the law. . . .

Article 10. Everyone is entitled . . . to a fair and public hearing by an independent and impartial tribunal, in the determination of . . . any criminal charge against him.

Article 11. . . . Everyone . . . has the right to be presumed innocent until proved guilty according to law in a public trial [with] all the guarantees necessary for his defence. . . .

Article 12. No one shall be subjected to arbitrary interference with his privacy, family, home or correspondence, nor to attacks upon his honour and reputation. . . .

Article 13. . . . Everyone has the right to leave any country, including his own, and to return to his country. . . .

Article 14. . . . Everyone has the right to seek and enjoy in other countries asylum from persecution. . . .

Article 18. Everyone has the right to freedom of thought, conscience and religion. . . .

Article 19. Everyone has the right to freedom of opinion and expression; this right includes freedom to hold opinions without interference. . . .

Article 20. . . . Everyone has the right to freedom of peaceful assembly and association.

Article 21. Everyone has the right to take part in the government of his country, directly or through freely chosen representatives. . . .

... The will of the people shall be the basis of the authority of government; this will shall be expressed in periodic and genuine elections which shall be by universal and equal suffrage and shall be held by secret vote....

Article 23. ... Everyone has the right to work, to free choice of employment, to just and favourable conditions of work....

... Everyone, without any discrimination, has the right to equal pay for equal work....

In addition to drafting the declaration, the Commission on Human Rights was charged with the task of preparing treaties — the Covenants on Human Rights, as they are known — by which member nations could undertake as a binding legal obligation the enforcement of the provisions of the Universal Declaration. Ratification of the two implementing covenants — one on the economic, social, and cultural rights involved, and the other on civil and political rights — by the whole, huge roster of UN member nations has been slow; even today, the process is far from complete. That fact notwithstanding, the unanimously accepted Universal Declaration of Human Rights remains a towering achievement as a statement of ideals and declaration of purpose — one that not only recognizes civil and political rights that had been set forth earlier in democratic constitutions, but also sets forth and defines as rights a number of economic, social, and cultural requirements. As such, it is one of the landmark documents of human dignity, and of the worth, equality, and rights of individuals.

Mississippi Admitted to the Union

The Territory of Mississippi, organized in 1798, produced two states: Mississippi, the 20th state, and Alabama, the 22nd. Alabama became a territory in its own right on March 3, 1817, and nine months later, on December 10, the parent territory of Mississippi was admitted to the Union as a state by a vote of Congress. There are no annual observances to mark Mississippi's admission but in the state's centennial year of 1917, a program of speeches, music, and special ceremonies was arranged in Jackson, the capital, on December 10. Among the featured events were an address by Governor Theodore G. Bilbo; the unveiling of the Woman's Confederate Monument on the grounds of the state capitol; and a Masonic ceremony centered on placing a memorial tablet in the Old Capitol Building, which had been converted into a state historical museum when the seat of government was removed to the present capitol building on its completion in 1903. Sealed behind the tablet was a metal box containing historical items. Music for the occasion included a song, "Mississippi," with words and music written especially for the centennial. Fifty years later, Mississippi's sesquicentennial year of 1967 served as the occasion for undertaking several projects to publicize the history of the state and preserve its documents. Under arrangements made with the Department of Archives and History, a documentary film — *Mississippi: Prologue to Statehood* — was produced, and a sesquicentennial issue of the *Journal of Mississippi History*, devoted to articles on the origin of the state and its admission to the Union, was published in November. In December a sesquicentennial postage stamp was issued at Natchez, the state's first capital, and a platinum medal commemorating the anniversary was presented to the Old Capitol Building museum in Jackson, where special statehood exhibits were displayed throughout 1967. The state legislature marked the anniversary in its own way, by passing an appropriation of $1,120,000 for a new archives building.

The region now occupied by Mississippi was once the homeland of the people known as Mound Builders, whose archaeological remains and earthworks excited wonder and admiration when Europeans first encountered them. Scattered about the state even today are ancient, artificially built hillocks, some rising as high as 60 feet and some covering several acres of ground. The mounds were used as burial sites and perhaps also as sites for temples and fortifications and places of refuge when the Mississippi River and its tributaries flooded the valleys. The Mound Builders also left many artifacts, including agricultural implements, pottery, stone and wood carvings, and jewelry, much of it excellently crafted and suggesting the influence of Mexico's pre-European civilizations. The Mound Builders' culture along the lower Mississippi River apparently flourished between A.D. 900 and 1500, and it seems to have been in a decline by the time Europeans arrived in the region. The Mound Builders are thought to have been ancestors of the Indians encountered by European explorers.

At the time of European exploration, the region was inhabited by an estimated 30,000 Native Americans. Of these, the most important tribes were the Chickasaw in the north, the Choctaw in the central and southern parts of the region, and the Natchez along the Mississippi River. The first Europeans known for certain to have set foot in what is now Mississippi were a company of Spanish gold hunters led by Hernando de Soto, who arrived in 1540. Battered and exhausted by intermittent warfare with the Indians as they journeyed inland from the Atlantic coast, de Soto's company entered Mississippi a few miles north of what is now

Columbus. Continuing westward, they came upon the Mississippi River, somewhere near what is now the northwestern boundary of the state, on May 8, 1541. After exploring the region west of the Mississippi, de Soto's company returned to the river. There, on its banks, their leader died on May 21, 1542, and his body was committed to the waters of the river near Natchez. Since no gold was discovered, Spain had little interest in the region de Soto explored, and it was left undisturbed by Europeans for more than a century.

In 1673 a priest and a trader from New France (Canada), Father Jacques Marquette and Louis Joliet, descended the Mississippi River as far south as the mouth of the Arkansas River, and their accounts of the journey inspired further exploration by René Robert Cavelier, Sieur de La Salle, who in 1682 claimed the entire Mississippi watershed for France and gave it the name Louisiana, in honor of Louis XIV, king of France. Other French explorations followed, and in 1699 Pierre Le Moyne, Sieur d'Iberville, founded the first permanent colony in the lower Mississippi valley. The settlement that grew up near the fort, which acquired the name of Biloxi from a local Indian tribe, alternated with Fort Louis de La Mobile, a settlement soon removed to the site of Mobile, Alabama, as the seat of government for French Louisiana until 1723 — when New Orleans (Louisiana) became the capital of the French colony. In 1704 the first "casket girls" — poor young women with trousseaux supplied by the French government — were brought over from France as wives for the settlers, and the European population began to spread from Biloxi and to establish new trading posts and forts, including Fort Rosalie, which became the nucleus of the city of Natchez.

Soon trouble over ownership of the land arose between the French and the Indians as well as between the French and the English, who claimed a part of the Mississippi region as lying within the so-called Carolina grant made in 1629–1630 to Sir Robert Heath by King Charles I of England. Because of these difficulties and unwise administration, the colony was unprofitable for France, and at the end of the French and Indian War in 1763 all of the French Louisiana territory east of the Mississippi River (except New Orleans) came under British rule. The southern third of what is now Mississippi and Alabama were incorporated in the new British province of West Florida — occupied by Spain during the American Revolution. Mississippi took almost no part in that conflict. Under the Treaty of Paris of 1783, which officially ended the Revolutionary War, Great Britain recognized

US claims to land south to the 31st Parallel — including much that had been part of West Florida — although Spain refused to recognize this boundary until 1795.

On April 7, 1798, the Mississippi Territory, comprising the southern portions of present Mississippi and Alabama, was created by act of Congress. The territory was enlarged in 1804 and 1812, so that it came to encompass all of what are now the states of Mississippi and Alabama. Natchez was the territorial capital until February 1, 1802, when the seat of government was moved to the nearby town of Washington. The territorial period was made stormy by conflicts with the Indians, the divided allegiances of inhabitants (who included pro-British, pro-French, and pro-United States factions), border warfare with the Spanish, and the War of 1812.

In March 1817 Mississippi Territory was reduced when its eastern part was organized as a separate territory of Alabama. The western part adopted a state constitution on August 15, and on December 10, 1817, Congress voted the new state of Mississippi into the Union. The first state governor was David Holmes, the former territorial governor, who served until 1820, and the government held its legislative sessions at Natchez and Washington during the early years of statehood. In 1821 a legislative commission appointed to locate a permanent state capital chose as its site Le Fleur's Bluff on the Pearl River, which was renamed Jackson in honor of Andrew Jackson. The legislature convened at Jackson for the first time in January 1822.

When the issue of union or secession became critical after the election of Abraham Lincoln as president in 1860, Mississippi voted to secede from the Union, on January 9, 1861. It thereby became the second state of the Confederacy. One of Mississippi's former US senators, Jefferson Davis, became the first and only president of the Confederate States of America.

A number of Civil War battles were fought in the state, including the campaigns against Vicksburg, which were climaxed by a 47-day siege that forced the surrender of the city on July 4, 1863. After the fall of Vicksburg, most of the Confederate troops within the state were moved elsewhere, and Union forces met with little effective resistance when they raided Mississippi, burning buildings, wrecking railroads, destroying property, and confiscating provisions. By the time the last Confederate force in Mississippi surrendered, on May 4, 1865, the state was in ruins, and its manpower was critically depleted. (Of the approximately 80,000 who went to war only about 28,000 returned, and many of the survivors were disabled.) Ranking fifth in per capita wealth before the war, Mississippi dropped to last place in the postwar period.

During the first months after the fall of the Confederacy President Andrew Johnson attempted to follow the policy of reconciliation begun by Lincoln. Mississippi, like the other Southern states, was provisionally administered by a presidentially-appointed governor who called a constitutional convention that passed an amendment abolishing slavery and arranged for a general election in the latter part of 1865. However, the officials elected in Mississippi and elsewhere in the South showed little inclination to promote political, economic, or social equality for blacks. While they continued to deny the vote to blacks, they demanded increased representation in Congress on the grounds that the recognition of citizenship for blacks had enlarged their constituencies. Angered by the unrepentant Southern attitude and also fearful that the Democratic party would regain political dominance with the support of a revived and predominantly Democratic South, the Republicans in control of Congress moved to disqualify the Southern leadership under the newly enacted 14th Amendment, which defined citizenship to include both blacks and whites, sought to guarantee the civil rights of blacks against unfavorable legislation by the states, and demanded equal protection under the law, regardless of race. On March 2, 1867, the first Reconstruction Act was passed, challenging the constitutionality of all the Southern governments (except Tennessee) and dividing the South into five districts under military commanders who were to remain in charge of the various states until each state had fulfilled certain conditions. These included the election, with black participation, of delegates to a convention that would frame a new constitution and establish a new state government providing for black male suffrage. Another requirement was the ratification of the 14th Amendment by the new state legislatures. When these conditions had been met by a state it was eligible for restoration to the full privileges of statehood. Mississippi, which was placed in the Fourth Military District, was one of the last three states to comply. Finally, in November 1869, a new state constitution, which abolished slavery and extended the franchise to black citizens, was ratified. On February 23, 1870, Mississippi was restored to its former status within the Union.

The constitution of 1869, however, eventually was superseded by that of 1890, a far more restrictive document, and the one still in force today, in amended form. Some of its features were copied in other states of the former Confederacy. The literacy test that the new Mississippi constitution prescribed for voters was so administered as to effectively prevent black suffrage for many decades. The lingering effects of the provision are still felt, despite the voter registration campaigns instituted after enactment of the Voting Rights Act of 1965 (see August 6).

Treaty of Paris of 1898 Signed

The Treaty of Paris of 1898, which set forth terms for the conclusion of the Spanish-American War (see April 21) was signed on December 10, 1898. It was subsequently ratified by the US Senate on February 6, 1899, and signed by the President four days later.

Wyoming Day

On December 10, 1869, John Campbell, the governor of the Wyoming Territory, approved an act granting the women of the territory the right to vote. As the first law in the history of the United States explicitly to grant suffrage to women, this landmark legislation is a source of great pride to the people of Wyoming. Each year the governor of the state proclaims December 10 to be Wyoming Day, and schools, clubs, and civic organizations throughout Wyoming observe the day with ceremonies that commemorate the history of the state and foster the loyalty and good citizenship of its people.

Esther Hobart Morris was, in large part, responsible for Wyoming's 1869 suffrage law. A native of New York State, she was orphaned at the age of 11 and worked for a number of years as a milliner. When she was 28, she married Artemus Slack, a civil engineer. A few years later Slack died, leaving his wife a tract of land in Illinois. She went west to claim her inheritance, but Illinois property laws, which resembled those of many other states, discriminated against women and thus prevented her from obtaining a satisfactory settlement of the estate.

Esther Slack's experience with Illinois property laws made her an ardent advocate of equal rights for women. She avidly followed the teachings of such feminists as Susan B. Anthony, Elizabeth Cady Stanton, and Lucretia Mott. Her interest in women's rights did not wane after her second marriage, to John Morris, in 1845.

News of a rich gold discovery in South Pass lured John Morris and his three sons to Wyoming about 1867, and his wife joined them there in either 1868 or 1869. At about the same time that she arrived in her new home, Wyoming gained territorial status. The first election to choose a representative to the new territorial legislature was scheduled to take place in South Pass on September 2, 1869, and Esther Morris recognized that this election was an opportunity to advance the cause of equal rights for women.

A few days before the election was to take place, she invited the Democratic candidate, Colonel William Bright; his Republican opponent, Captain H. G. Nickerson; and about 40 other residents of South Pass to her home. After serving tea, Esther Morris asked each candidate to pledge that if elected he would introduce and support a bill giving the vote to the women of the Wyoming Territory. Both Bright and Nickerson agreed to the proposal.

The Democrats swept the 1869 Wyoming election, including South Pass. Bright was elected and at the territorial capital of Cheyenne he kept his promise to Esther Morris. On November 28, 1869, he introduced into the Council, or upper house of the legislature, a bill granting voting rights to women. The other legislators at Cheyenne treated the bill as a joke. The members of both the Council and the House raucously debated its merits, and then, perhaps believing that the bill might prove embarrassing to Governor Campbell, a Republican, they unexpectedly approved it.

The Democratic legislators expected Governor Campbell to veto the bill, but on December 10, 1869, he signed the act into law. Campbell's action did not please some of the male residents of Wyoming. One lawmaker toasted the new women voters: "To the lovely ladies, once our superiors, now our equals!" In South Pass another dissatisfied man, Justice of the Peace R. S. Barr, announced his resignation effective "whenever some lady shall have been duly appointed to fill the vacancy." To Barr's surprise, his resignation was immediately accepted, and, appropriately, Morris was appointed as his replacement, thereby becoming the first woman to serve as a justice of the peace.

Despite male apprehensions about allowing women to vote, the women of Wyoming exercised their newly won political rights. In fact, even before an election occurred in which the women might cast their ballots, Judge H. J. H. Howe, in March 1870, impaneled five women for the grand jury and six for the petit jury in the second district court in Laramie. These first women jurors attracted world attention. Newspaper correspondents came to Laramie to report the proceedings, and the king of Prussia cabled President Ulysses S. Grant to congratulate him on the "progress, enlightenment and civil liberty in America."

Women voted, served on juries, and, in the case of Esther Morris, even held public office during Wyoming's territorial period. After being admitted to the Union in 1890, Wyoming continued to lead the nation in opening full political participation to women: in 1911 Susan Wissler of Dayton, Wyoming, became one of the first women in the United States to serve as mayor; and in 1924, when Nellie Tayloe Ross became the governor of Wyoming, she was the first woman in the nation ever to serve in that office.

For her part in bringing about Wyoming's female suffrage legislation, Morris has been called the Mother of Woman Suffrage in the state. She has also been recognized outside Wyoming. In 1960 a statue of Esther Morris was unveiled in the Capitol's Statuary Hall in Washington, D.C. The inscription under the likeness reads:

Esther Hobart Morris — Proponent of the Legislative Act in 1869 which gave distinction to the Territory of Wyoming as the first government in the world to grant women equal rights.

DECEMBER 11

Indiana Day

Indiana began as part of the Northwest Territory, located north and west of the Ohio River and east of the Mississippi. Originally settled probably by prehistoric Mound Builders, then by Miami Indians before French fur trappers arrived in the 1670s, the area became a British possession in 1763 by the terms of the Treaty of Paris, which ended the French and Indian, or Seven Years', War. On February 25, 1779, during the War of Independence, American militiamen under Lieutenant Colonel George Rogers Clark captured Vincennes, the region's most important town, and the United States took title to the area by the Treaty of Paris 1783, which concluded the Revolution.

On July 13, 1787, Congress (functioning under the Articles of Confederation) passed the Northwest Ordinance, placing the territory under a federally appointed governor, secretary, and three judges. Congress provided that when 5,000 free male adults had taken up residence in the region, the people could establish an elected bicameral legislature. Eventually, as planned in the ordinance, a number of states would be carved from the Northwest Territory. From three to five were envisioned. As things worked out, the number ultimately reached the maximum five: Indiana, Illinois, Michigan, Ohio, and Wisconsin. (A portion of Minnesota also was originally part of the Northwest Territory.)

General Anthony Wayne's victory over the Indians under the Miami leader Little Turtle, on August 20, 1794, at Fallen Timbers (on the rapids of the Maumee River near what is now Toledo) removed an early obstacle to the settlement of the Northwest Territory. Immigrants quickly moved into the secured land, and on October 28, 1798, Arthur St. Clair, the first governor of the Northwest Territory, authorized the election of a legislature. Both houses of the new body met for the first time on September 24, 1799, and on October 3 chose William Henry Harrison as the territory's delegate to Congress.

In his year at the national capital, Harrison brought to Congress's attention the inability of the three federal judges to provide adequate court service for the sprawling Northwest Territory. At his suggestion, on May 7, 1800, Congress subdivided the region. The part including present Ohio and part of lower Michigan retained the title of Northwest Territory, and the remainder of the vast area became the Indiana Territory, with its capital at Vincennes. President John Adams appointed Harrison, the descendant of two well-known Virginia families, to be the first governor.

Slavery became a major issue in Indiana politics in the first decade of the 19th century. With the support of Governor Harrison, a convention met at Vincennes in December 1802 and petitioned Congress to repeal the clause of the Northwest Ordinance that outlawed slavery in the territory. When Congress rejected the appeal, the territorial government evaded the ordinance by enacting a system of black and mulatto indentured servitude based on assignable contracts between masters and servants.

Indiana's population grew steadily, and, in accord with a proclamation by Governor Harrison, the people of the territory elected their own assembly on January 3, 1805. Antislavery forces were strong in the legislature, and in October 1808 the second territorial assembly refused to petition Congress for a modification of the ban on the institution. Harrison, who continued to associate himself with the proslavery faction, found himself increasingly at odds with a number of the delegates.

On January 11, 1805, Congress had detached the Michigan Territory from Indiana. Settlers in the western part of the Indiana Territory likewise sought their independence. Eastern Indianans, who opposed the proslavery attitude of the territory's western residents, also favored separation. Indiana's representative in Congress, Jesse B. Thomas, obtained a solution agreeable to all: on February 3, 1809, Congress again divided Indiana, creating an Illinois Territory from its western portion.

The fifth Indiana General Assembly, which met from August 15 to September 10, 1814, petitioned Congress to grant statehood to the territory. On April 19, 1816, President James Madison approved an enabling act authorizing Indiana to devise a state constitution and promising admission to the Union. In quick response to Madison's action, 43 Indianans on June 10, 1816, began a constitutional convention at Corydon, which had become the territorial capital in 1811.

The Indiana constitution clearly banned slavery forever from the proposed state. To placate the proslavery forces and insure their support for the document, the framers validated existing indenture agreements. As was common in that period, many whites felt an aversion to blacks equal to their distaste for slavery, and blacks were forbidden to vote or serve in the militia.

Indiana's constitutional convention completed its work on June 29, 1816. On December 11, 1816, President Madison approved a congressional resolution admitting Indiana to the Union. Jonathan Jennings became the state's first governor, William Hendricks its first congressman, and James Noble and Waller Taylor its first senators.

In February 1925 Indiana's 74th General Assembly declared December 11 to be Indiana Day, an annual celebration of the state's acceptance into the Union. Although it is not a legal holiday, there is some sporadic observation of the anniversary. Indiana schools are especially active in the commemoration.

Indiana's sesquicentennial, 1966, was extraordinarily festive. The observances began on April 19, the day on which President Madison had authorized the framing of a state constitution, and continued to Admission Day on December 11. At Corydon, Indianans reenacted the signing of the state constitution on June 23; and from June 23 to 25 and July 1 to 3 a pageant was held depicting life in the period of early settlement. Festivities surrounding the famous Indianapolis 500 auto race, held annually on Memorial Day, also included sesquicentennial events, as did the state fair, held in Indianapolis from August 26 to September 5.

Although Indianapolis became the capital of Indiana in 1824, replacing the less conveniently located Corydon, the old seat of government still retains many vestiges of its period as capital. The trunk of the Constitutional Elm stands where the tree gave shade to the pioneer legislators as they assembled below it to sign the state's first frame of government. Also still standing in Corydon is the original capitol building, now restored as a state memorial. A two-story, three-room, blue limestone structure, it was built in 1812. Located on Old Capitol Avenue, the building that housed the territorial and state governments from 1813 to 1825 is now a center of interest for tourists.

DECEMBER 12

John Jay's Birthday

John Jay, the first Chief Justice of the United States, was born in New York City on December 12, 1745. One of the eight surviving children of Peter and Mary Van Cortlandt Jay, the future jurist was descended from two of the most important families in the colony of New York. His Dutch Van Cortlandt forebears had been among the original settlers of New Amsterdam and had gained wealth and power through their landholding and trading activities; the Jays traced their lineage to Augustus Jay, a Huguenot exile who sought refuge in New York about 1686 and became an influential merchant. John Jay's father also was a well-established businessman, and he provided his son with an excellent education. Young Jay studied first with private tutors and then entered King's College (later Columbia). He was graduated in 1764.

After studying in Benjamin Kissam's law office, Jay gained admission to the bar in 1768. Five years later he served as secretary to the royal commission charged with settling a boundary dispute between New York and New Jersey. In 1774 the young lawyer married Sarah Van Brugh Livingston, daughter of William Livingston, who later became the Revolutionary governor of New Jersey.

The crises preceding and culminating in the American Revolution called forth Jay's considerable political talents. A man of wealth, he tended, like many of his station, to favor a continuation of the colonies' ties with England. As a member of New York's Committee of Fifty-one and as a delegate to the First and Second Continental Congresses, he espoused conservative solutions to colonial problems. Jay was attending a provincial congress in New York when the Declaration of Independence was adopted and therefore did not vote for the resolution. But he accepted the action of the Congress, and in the months and years following July 1776 he worked unreservedly for the cause of independence.

During the years immediately following the colonies' break with Great Britain, Jay directed his attention toward strengthening support for the Revolution in New York. He worked to gain the state's ratification of the Declaration of Independence in 1776 and was chairman of the committee that formulated New York's new state constitution in 1777. Until 1779 he served as chief justice of New York.

In December 1778 Jay returned to the Continental Congress. He was elected president of that body on December 10, 1778, and held the post until September 1779, when he was selected to be minister plenipotentiary to Spain. In Madrid from 1780 to 1782 Jay was not able to gain Spanish recognition of the independence of the United States and succeeded only in obtaining a loan of $170,000.

In the spring of 1782 Benjamin Franklin called Jay to Paris. There, with Franklin and John Adams, he served as a joint commissioner entrusted with the task of negotiating a peace treaty with Great Britain. In this post Jay was instrumental in persuading Franklin to agree to a preliminary peace settlement without first obtaining concurrence from the French government.

When the final peace treaty was concluded in 1783, Jay was offered the appointment of minister to either Great Britain or France. He declined both positions and returned to the United States, intending to resume his private law practice. However, on his arrival on July 24, 1784, he learned that Congress had named him as secretary of foreign affairs.

Jay conducted the foreign relations of the United States for the next six years. This experience convinced him of the inadequacy of the Articles of Confederation and made him an enthusiastic supporter of a stronger central government. In 1787–1788 Jay together with James Madison and Alexander Hamilton published *The Federalist* essays — the most forceful argument for ratification of the Constitution and perhaps the most brilliant exposition of American constitutional theory ever written.

In 1790 George Washington appointed Thomas Jefferson secretary of state, and Jay became the first chief justice of the United States. He handed down in 1793 the most famous opinion of his five years on the bench. In the case of *Chisholm* v. *Georgia*, Jay and the majority of the court ruled that two citizens of South Carolina could recover damages from the state of Georgia. This decision created an immense furor, since many state legislatures interpreted it as an infringement on their sovereignty. As a result of the states' protests, the 11th Amendment to the Constitution (see January 8), which prohibits a citizen of one state from suing another state, was proposed by Congress. It was ratified in 1798.

In 1794 war with Great Britain threatened because of numerous American grievances. England refused to vacate the Northwest military posts, thus impeding American settlement in the

West and maintaining control of the fur trade, and impressed American seamen after seizing their vessels. The President named Jay special envoy to negotiate these problems, and, on November 1, 1794, he succeeded in making a treaty with Great Britain.

The Jay Treaty was a compromise measure. Together with a number of other concessions, it provided for the British withdrawal from the Northwest positions by June 1796, but it ignored other pressing problems such as impressment, British agitation of the Indians, and the return of the slaves taken during the Revolution. The treaty met with strong resistance at home and only after a long debate did the Senate finally ratify it on June 24, 1795.

By using questionable electioneering practices, George Clinton defeated Jay in the New York gubernatorial election of 1792. Three years later, however, the Federalists succeeded in winning this post for Jay, and he served as governor of New York until 1801. Refusing to become a candidate for a third term, he retired at the age of 56 to his 800-acre estate at Katonah, New York, in the township of Bedford. There, Jay indulged his interests in horticulture and theology, and as an ardent abolitionist perhaps aided the underground railroad until his death on May 17, 1829.

The New York State Department of Education completed the restoration of the Katonah estate in 1965. There, the public may see the front porch on which Jay inspired James Fenimore Cooper to write *The Spy*; browse through a library containing more than 2,000 books and 6,000 manuscripts; and admire the large collection of period furniture on display. Columbia University, which holds the largest collection of Jay papers, published in 1975 the first of three volumes of selected letters to and from John Jay. Other noteworthy commemoratives of the university's distinguished alumnus are John Jay Hall, an undergraduate campus residence opened on February 12, 1927, and a stained-glass window at Livingston Hall. The John Jay College of Criminal Justice of the City University of New York also honors the first chief justice.

Feast of Our Lady of Guadalupe

The Feast of Our Lady of Guadalupe, which falls on December 12, is celebrated by Roman Catholics in the United States and Mexico. Although the observance is not included in the revised universal Roman Catholic calendar, it is commemorated as a memorial in the liturgical calendar that was adopted for use in all dioceses of the United States at the November 1971 National Conference of Catholic Bishops and confirmed by the Congregation for Divine Worship in December of the same year. December 12 is a holy day of obligation throughout Mexico and ranks among the most important Mexican religious holidays.

On the December 12 anniversary, thousands of pilgrims — some making their way to the main altar on their knees with arms outstretched — attend services at the flower-bedecked Basilica of Our Lady of Guadalupe on the outskirts of Mexico City. Outside the shrine, the church grounds are thronged with visitors who enjoy the song and dance groups, amusements, firecrackers, and concession booths that mark the occasion, in addition to the numerous religious services and processions. In Ponce, Puerto Rico, where Our Lady of Guadalupe is the local patron saint, there is an annual festival in her honor, featuring dancing, concerts, and fireworks.

In the United States, December 12 is elaborately observed in the Southwest, where Spanish influence prevails. The feast is noted at a number of Indian pueblos in New Mexico. For example, evening ceremonies honoring Our Lady of Guadalupe that are staged on December 11 at the Pueblo de Taos a few miles north of Taos feature an impressive torchlight procession after vespers. Near Las Cruces, Tortugas Indians participate in a three-day pilgrimage and celebration on December 10, 11, and 12. At the Jemez Pueblo, Matachines perform a variety of Indian ceremonial dances. A repertory of these dances is often given at church grounds and plazas in New Mexico and in neighboring southwestern states such as Texas and Arizona. Such traditional favorites as the arc and arrow, gourd, braid, feather, palm, owl, or snake dances may be included. Sometimes the festivities also include talent shows, raffles, and fair booths.

The religious ceremonies at Our Lady of Guadalupe Church in San Diego, California, are representative of the type of homage paid to the Virgin on December 12 in various churches throughout the Southwest. Some 1,500 persons usually attend one of several masses in the rose-adorned church, and there are other events, such as the singing of the "Mañanitas" or "good morning song," to the Virgin and the singing of mariachis. The Old Mission San Luis Rey near San Diego generally pays tribute to Our Lady of Guadalupe with a solemn mass and a procession in which the participants bear religious banners and a flower-covered platform with statue of the Virgin.

For many years Our Lady of Guadalupe Church in San Antonio, Texas, held a procession around the nearby streets on the Sunday nearest to December 12. Afterwards Indian dances were performed in the churchyard. Starting in 1970, however, the feast day celebration was expanded under the guidance of the Roman Catholic auxiliary bishop of San Antonio, Patrick Flores. Now a citywide event known as Festival Guadalupaño, it is held in the Hemisfair Arena at the Convention Center on the Sunday nearest the feast. The program usually includes a solemn mass with the bishop and priests of the archdiocese of San Antonio participating, mariachis, and other entertainment, such as Mexican dances, and songs and poems honoring the Virgin. At Our Lady of Guadalupe Church on the actual feast day, mariachis sing the "Mañanitas" as early as 4:00 A.M., after which priests and parishioners celebrate a mass commemorating the anniversary of the miracle of Our Lady of Guadalupe.

The legend of Our Lady of Guadalupe is one of the most interesting in the religious history of North America. According to the story, an Aztec named Cuauhtlatohuac, who had recently been converted to Christianity and baptized Juan Diego, was hurrying down Tepeyac Hill a short distance to the north of Mexico City, to attend mass on December 9, 1531, when the Virgin Mary appeared to him. She told him to tell his bishop to have a sanctuary built in her honor where she was standing — reputedly the site of a recently leveled temple to an Aztec fertility goddess of the earth and corn. Although she appeared to Juan Diego twice more at the same place within the next few days to receive an answer, none was immediately forthcoming since the local bishop at first remained highly skeptical of the Aztec's tale. Finally he told Juan Diego to ask the vision for a sign to prove that she was the Virgin.

At daybreak on December 12 Juan Diego, fearful that a sick uncle for whom he was caring was dying, hastened to seek help in Mexico City. To avoid the Virgin, he went around Tepeyac Hill, but she met him at the bottom and asked, "What road is this thou takest, son?" Juan Diego explained his mission to her. Calling herself Holy Mary of Guadalupe, she cured his uncle and again told him to go to the bishop with the message about the sanctuary. For a sign she told him to go up on the rocky, wintry hillside and gather roses, although it was not the season when roses were in bloom. He went and gathered the blossoms in his long cloak of coarse cloth. The Virgin arranged the roses and told him to keep them out of sight and untouched until he reached the bishop.

When Juan Diego arrived at the episcopal residence, he unfolded his cloak, and the roses fell out; to his astonishment the bishop and his at-

tendants were kneeling before him. There on the cloak, it is said, was a life-size picture of the Virgin as he had seen her. The picture, which is still preserved, is painted on two strips of coarsely woven cactus fiber sacking about 70 inches long and 18 inches wide, sewn together with the seam running through the middle of the figure. The dark-skinned Virgin is wearing a blue-green mantle decorated with more than 40 golden stars, and a rose-colored, figured tunic beneath the mantle. She is surrounded by the golden rays of the sun and is resting on a crescent supported by an angel. Her eyes allegedly reflect the images of those men, including Juan Diego, who were present when the cloak was first unfolded.

Reports of the miracle spread quickly and resulted in mass conversions among the Indians, who had previously been relatively lukewarm in converting to Christianity. A small shrine was first built in 1532 on the spot where the Virgin reportedly stood. In 1622 a more elaborate structure was erected, and a much finer one was built in 1709. During the 18th century other edifices were constructed at the same site, including the Chapel of the Little Hill, where Juan Diego had gathered winter roses. A new shrine will replace the 18th century basilica, which, in addition to being too small to accommodate the masses of pilgrims, is suffering irreparable damage through sinkage into the subsoil.

After careful inquiry, Catholic authorities confirmed the authenticity of the religious tradition. In the mid-18th century Pope Benedict XIV named Our Lady of Guadalupe the patroness of New Spain. As the devotion grew, the Virgin was invoked for help in natural disasters and sickness. When discontent with Spanish rule erupted into open rebellion in Mexico in the early 19th century, the revolutionary leader Father Miguel Hidalgo y Costilla fought under a banner bearing her image in the 1810 War of Independence and instructed his soldiers to shout her name as a battle cry. In 1910 Pope Pius X named her patroness of Latin America. Our Lady of Guadalupe subsequently was designated as patroness of the Americas by Pope Pius XII in 1945.

Pennsylvania Ratifies the Constitution

Pennsylvania, on December 12, 1787, became the second state to ratify the Constitution of 1787. The Keystone State's quick acceptance was an important step in the adoption of the new frame of government. But the rapid approval was evidence more of the political acumen of the proratification forces than of unanimity within the state.

On September 17, 1787, the members of the Constitutional Convention meeting in Philadelphia had concluded their labors and remitted their work to the Congress, which was then functioning under the Articles of Confederation and meeting in New York City, the nation's first capital. The national representatives on September 28 gave their assent and sent the proposed Constitution to each of the 13 states, formerly the colonies of Britain. In each state the legislature was asked to call a special convention to examine the proposal and to vote on ratification.

In Pennsylvania, pro-Constitution forces were ready to act immediately. The Federalists, or supporters of the new frame of government, controlled the state legislature in 1787 and were anxious to pass the resolution required to set up a ratifying convention before the end of the session on September 29. If the Federalists had failed to make the enactment, the opponents of the Constitution would have gained invaluable time to organize their forces and might have even been able to gain control of the legislature. Such a development could have delayed or made impossible ratification in Pennsylvania and might have doomed the adoption of the new Constitution.

As soon as the Congress decided to send the Constitution to the states, William Bingham of Pennsylvania sent off an express rider from New York to Philadelphia with the news. But even before the horseman reached the Quaker City with official notification, George Clymer, on the morning of September 28, had proposed in the Pennsylvania legislature that a state convention of deputies, chosen by the voters on the same day and in the same manner as members of the next general assembly, be called to meet at Philadelphia. Robert Whitehill from Cumberland County protested that no word had yet arrived from the Congress and noted that Clymer's proposal violated the traditional procedure of notifying the assembly beforehand of the intention of submitting an important measure, of making the matter the order of the day, and of reading the bill three times.

Despite the objections of Whitehill, the Federalists won approval, by a vote of 43 to 19, for a convention to meet at Philadelphia. Satisfied with their efforts, the deputies then decided to take a recess until 4:00 P.M. before considering the manner of selecting the delegates and the date for their election.

Antifederalist leaders used the hours before the afternoon session to plan their strategy. They concluded that their best hope lay in obstructing the conduct of the legislature until the final adjournment scheduled for the following day. These opponents of the Constitution could count only 19 men in their ranks, but if all stayed away from the meetings of the assembly, the 69-man body, from which several were already absent, would not be able to obtain the quorum of 46 members necessary to carry on business.

Only 44 deputies appeared at the afternoon session. The Speaker ordered the sergeant-at-arms to summon the absentees, but the Antifederalists would not heed the messenger. Lacking a quorum, the Speaker had no choice but to adjourn the assembly until the following morning, September 29, the final day of the session.

By the opening of the morning session, the rider sent by Bingham had delivered the congressional resolution, but still the Antifederalist delegates stayed away. The Speaker again dispatched the sergeant-at-arms and the assistant clerk to round up the recalcitrant. The officers went first to the house of Major Alexander Boyd, where the opposition made their headquarters, and found there James M'Calmont of Franklin County and Jacob Miley of Dauphin County. When M'Calmont and Miley refused to return to the State House with the sergeant and the clerk, a mob of citizens who favored the Constitution broke into the representatives' lodgings and dragged them through the streets to the assembly chamber. With the two unwilling and disheveled Antifederalists present, the legislature finally had a quorum and set the election of delegates to the Constitutional Convention for the first Tuesday in November.

Antifederalists and Federalists in the interim between the adjournment of the legislature and the election of the convention delegates vied with each other to produce arguments designed to win the support of the populace. Samuel Bryan, a leading Antifederalist, was perhaps the anonymous author of the letter of "Centinel," which appeared in the *Independent Gazeteer or Chronicle of Freedom,* a Philadelphia publication edited by Eleazer Oswald, an immigrant from Great Britain who fought on the side of the patriots during the American Revolution. Peletiah Webster, a graduate of Yale and a political essayist, and James Wilson, who had been a member of the Constitutional Convention, were the chief spokesmen of the Federalists.

Opponents of the Constitution feared the extensive powers it gave the central government. They argued that the new frame of government was not a confederation but an undesirable government over individuals, that threatened to destroy the sovereignty of the states that was so well protected by the Articles of Confederation.

Of equal importance, the Congress had direct powers over the lives, liberties, and properties of all citizens, and yet the Constitution offered no bill of rights to prevent governmental abuses.

Supporters of the Constitution countered the Antifederalist arguments point by point. Wilson stated that the Congress, rather than being an omnipotent body, enjoyed only those powers expressly granted to it in the Constitution. The new government, moreover, posed no threat to the states in his view; indeed, the legislatures of each state were to choose its federal senators and indicate the mode of selection of electors of the President.

Federalists swept to victory in the elections for the Pennsylvania Assembly and Council, which preceded by a month the selection of delegates to the ratifying convention. Their success proved to be prophetic of the outcome of the later elections, which took place on November 6. In Philadelphia, which selected five delegates to the convention, the supporters of the Constitution crushed their opponents. The leading Federalist candidate drew 1,215 votes, the lowest vote for a Federalist was 1,157; the leading Antifederalist won only 150 votes. As a ruse, the Antifederalists placed Benjamin Franklin, a supporter of the Constitution, on their ticket. His name drew 235 misplaced Antifederalist votes.

Pennsylvania's ratifying convention opened on November 21 at the State House in Philadelphia, with 60 of the 69 elected delegates in attendance. The opposing sides spent a week arguing about procedures and then devoted two more weeks to a detailed discussion of the proposed Constitution. Finally, on December 12, the members of the convention cast their ballots, 46 in favor of the new government and 23 against it. The following day the convention, joined by the president and vice president of Pennsylvania and all the state dignitaries, both civil and military, went in procession to the State House and read the ratification ordinance to a gathering of the citizenry. On December 15 the convention adjourned.

Among the 13 former British colonies, the order of obtaining statehood is usually calculated on the basis of date of ratification of the Constitution. Thus Pennsylvania, which ratified only five days after Delaware, is usually listed as second in tabulations that place the 50 states in order. With certain exceptions, most states that joined the Union after the original 13 followed the procedures set forth in the Northwest Ordinance of July 1787. Pennsylvania and others of the original 13 thus bypassed the later and more usual procedure whereby an area passed through a territorial status before being admitted to the Union as a state.

DECEMBER 13

Feast of Santa Lucia

The Feast of Santa Lucia, or St. Lucy, the early Christian virgin martyr, is an occasion for great festivities in Italy, in Scandinavia — especially in Sweden and to a lesser extent in Norway — and in those parts of the United States in which Swedish immigrants settled and their descendants still observe traditional customs.

There are many conflicting legends about the life of St. Lucy. According to the most likely accounts, she was born about 283 in Syracuse, Sicily, to wealthy Christian parents. As a young girl she became very much involved in works of charity. Betrothed to a pagan, she helped the poor even to the extent of distributing her wedding dowry among them. Vengeful either because of his fiancee's generosity or perhaps because she wished to break her engagement and remain a virgin, Lucy's suitor denounced her as a Christian to the Roman authorities during the severe religious persecutions of the Roman emperor Diocletian in the early fourth century.

Some legends hold that Lucy was tortured, when she refused to sacrifice to the Roman gods, by having her eyes gouged out (and that her sight was then miraculously restored); others hold that she herself tore out her eyes since their beauty caused her to be desirable to men. The Roman prefect reportedly sentenced her to be burned at the stake, but when the fire did not harm her, she is said to have died by the sword. Her death date is traditionally held to be December 13, 304. Lucy's supposed relics were eventually taken to Venice, where they are still preserved in the Church of Santa Lucia; her eyes are allegedly kept in the Church of San Giovanni Maggiore in Naples.

Lucy quickly became one of the favorite female saints of the Christian Church. Because of her name — derived from the Latin lux, or "light" — she was honored as the patroness of street lamp lighters. Those who suffered from eye diseases, especially imminent blindness, invoked her intercession as the protector of the eyes, "the light of the body." In medieval art, Lucy is therefore often depicted holding a torch or lamp or carrying a plate on which lie two eyeballs.

The Feast of St. Lucy was observed on December 13 at Rome starting in the sixth century. (In the revised Roman Catholic calendar, her feast, still observed on this date, is classed as a memorial.) In Syracuse — where Lucy is the patron saint of the city — the day has long been celebrated with bonfires and torchlight processions. Fires, processions, and illuminations also mark the day in other Italian cities. In Venice gondoliers sing the popular Italian song "Santa Lucia" in her memory.

But it is in Scandinavia, notably Sweden, that the cult of St. Lucy took root in medieval times; its ramifications extend into the Swedish folklore of the modern era. The feast happened to coincide — before the inauguration of the Gregorian calendar reform in the 16th century — with the period of the old pagan midwinter solstice, the shortest time of the year, when the forces of darkness seemed to prevail in northern Europe. The commemoration, with Lucy regarded as a symbol of light and renewed hope, offered an appealing substitute for the primitive pagan rituals aimed at assuring the sun god's return. Several of the ancient fire and light traditions of the northern Yuletide, for example the burning of candles and bonfires, became customary features on December 13.

The legends about Lucy merged above all with the folk traditions of the Värmland region of western Sweden. It was related that during a time of great famine, a young girl was seen on board a ship on Lake Vänern. Dressed in white with a halo of light illuminating her head, she distributed food and drink to the starving populace. (A similar legend was told in Syracuse, where, through Lucy's intervention, a ship appeared laden with wheat to save the city from starvation.)

The tales about Lucy spread to all districts of Sweden and survived in the popular imagination long after the Protestant Reformation of the 16th century and the calendar reform had abolished the original religious and secular significance of her December 13 feast. School records in Stockholm, for example, reveal a Lucia observance in 1655.

Over the centuries, the feast day, or *Lucia-dagen*, was gradually transformed into an occasion for family festivities and for the custom of the Lucia Bride, or *Lussibrud*. At dawn a girl in each Swedish family, usually the eldest daughter, dresses in a long white robe, brilliant red sash, and lingon-leaf crown with seven burning candles, to represent the saint. Awakening the rest of the family, she sings the melody "Santa Lucia," as she serves them coffee and *lussekatter* — X-shaped saffron buns resembling cats' heads.

The December 13 celebration begins the Swedish Christmas season and is a joyful occasion throughout the country. Each community, city, and province selects its own Lucia, who serves the typical coffee and food at schools, hospitals, and other public institutions. Often she is accompanied by attendants dressed in white gowns and by white-clad "star boys" (*stjärngossar*) with peaked silver caps, one of whom bears a star paper lantern. A national Lucia, selected from contestants throughout Sweden, is honored

in Stockholm on December 13 with a street procession, an official welcome by city officials, a dinner at the city hall, and a Lucia Ball.

Swedish customs associated with December 13 were brought to the United States by early immigrants, and Lucia Day is a widely celebrated festivity in Swedish communities throughout the country. Swedish organizations and church groups in places with large Swedish populations stage authentic Swedish Lucia festivals.

Typical of the celebrations in the larger metropolitan areas is the Chicago festivity. Practically every Swedish club or organization in the city has its own festivities and Lucia bride, and a major citywide festival at the downtown Civic Center is arranged for the late afternoon of December 13 by the Central Swedish Committee of the Chicago Area. Dignitaries generally include the Swedish consul general in Chicago and the mayor or a personal representative. After a program of music, the name of the year's Lucia is drawn by lot from among the numerous entries representing social clubs, religious organizations, and other institutions in Chicago. The winner is crowned with a golden crown handmade in Sweden. The traditional coffee and sweets are then served to the crowd, which usually numbers about 300 to 400 persons.

The American Swedish Historical Museum in Philadelphia has been the site of an annual Lucia festival since 1937, staged by the museum's women's auxiliary and usually held on the Saturday nearest December 13. Some 100 adults and children, all members or relatives of members of the museum, present Swedish Christmas songs, folk dances, and the climactic Lucia procession to an audience of about 1,000 persons. The celebration is given in conjunction with a Jul Mart, at which Christmas items and baked goods are sold.

Since 1952 the Swedish Historical Society of Rockford, Illinois, has staged a Lucia program, generally on the Saturday nearest the feast day, at the Erlander Home Museum, which it owns and maintains. There are usually three performances, attracting several hundred persons, that feature Swedish costumes, music, and recitations, with emphasis on the Christmas and Lucia stories and the abounding love of the season. There, too, is a Jul Mart. Throughout the years, the Lucia has been selected by various criteria, such as participation in Swedish classes at a local high school, contributions to Swedish culture, or a demonstrated interest in things Swedish — for example, as active membership in one of Rockford's many Swedish societies.

Lindsborg, Kansas, has as its Lucia a high school senior who is also a member of the community's Swedish folk dance group. After being crowned on December 13, the Lucia and her attendants and star boys proceed downtown to offer coffee and buns to Christmas shoppers. *Luciadagen* is also observed at Lindsborg's Bethany College — but beginning at a far earlier hour, when freshmen in the women's residence halls are awakened by a 3:00 A.M. visit from a white-clad student Lucia bearing the traditional refreshments. The Feast of Santa Lucia is also enthusiastically noted in the Minneapolis-St. Paul area and in such West Coast communities as Seattle and San Diego, among other areas.

DECEMBER 14

Alabama Admitted to the Union

Alabama, on December 14, 1819, became the 22nd state to enter the Union. Although the anniversary is not observed as an annual event, Alabama marked the sesquicentennial of its statehood in 1969 with a yearlong Alabama 150 celebration.There were spring tours of historic homes and beautiful gardens in Greensboro, Tuscaloosa, and Selma; a number of formal balls, including a grand ball held at Selma's historic Sturdivant Hall in April; an antebellum ball held in Demopolis at Bluff Hall in October; and a reenactment of a lavish 1825 ball for the visiting Marquis de Lafayette, which was held in Montgomery during December.

Pageants were produced in a number of localities, commemorating events, both historical and legendary, in the state's history. Honoring the Indian past was a Scottsboro spectacle, Return of God's Mountain, presented for a week in August at an outdoor amphitheater on Sand Mountain. Invited guests included Indians whose ancestors had been driven out of Alabama to the West in the early 1800s, and a pipe of peace was lighted for the occasion. Another pageant with an Indian theme was Gadsden's Noccalula Falls Indian Maiden Festival, held September 19 to 21 in memory of a legendary Indian woman who leaped from the 90-foot falls when separated from her lover. The theme of European settlement inspired Baldwin County's production The Fourteenth Colony, staged for a week in June at historic Fort Morgan on Mobile Bay. Starting with the Welsh Prince Madoc whose legendary visit in 1170 is held by some to have been the first by a white man to the area, the pageant featured a procession of Spanish, French, British, and American explorers and settlers and portrayed the burning of Fort Mims by the Creeks in 1813. The aftermath of the burning of the fort, the battle of Horseshoe Bend, in which the forces of Andrew Jackson defeated the Creeks, was the subject of Alexander City's presentation, The Day the River Ran Red, held at Wind Creek Park on two weekends in late May and early June.

Probably the most festive month in the 150th anniversary year was July. In the first week of the month, a flotilla of decorated boats from five southeastern states sailed through the Tennessee Valley Authority locks and lakes on the Tennessee River. The fleet, sponsored by the Alabama Mountain Lakes Association, went from Pickwick Dam through Wilson, Wheeler, and Guntersville lakes, pausing en route to be welcomed with receptions, picnics, and fish fries. Also during July, five counties sponsored a celebration with tableaux, songs, dances, and fireworks, held at the Alabama State Fairgrounds in Birmingham; Gadsden held a water pageant featuring Alabama music and history on the Coosa River; and spectacles were produced at Decatur and at Florence, which also held a W. C. Handy Festival honoring the Father of the Blues, who was born in Florence. Huntsville, the scene of Alabama's constitutional convention in 1819 and the first state capital, displayed the original state constitution at the Madison County Court House from May 3 to the end of the anniversary year on December 14 and held a special celebration on July 5. A commemorative stamp issued in honor of the sesquicentennial of Alabama's statehood was first released at Huntsville.

Alabama's existence as a state represents but a brief period in the span of its history. The region has been populated for at least 8,000 years, which is the age of the earliest known relics of human habitation found in rock caves within the state. The people who left the relics seem to have depended on hunting and fishing, and their main food must have been mussels, judging from the piles of shells found at the sites of habitation.

In the period before the Europeans came, Alabama was the home of Mound Builders who left distinctive flat-topped mounds that probably were the sites of wooden temples, along the Alabama rivers. They grew corn and other crops, made excellent pottery and fine jewelry, worked copper, carved stone figurines with considerable skill, wove cloth, and generally left evidence of a high state of cultural development.

The largest Indian tribes encountered by the first European visitors were the Choctaws along the Gulf Coast in southwestern Alabama, the Creeks in the southeastern and central parts, and the Cherokees and Chickasaws in the north. So far as is known, the first Europeans to arrive were the Spaniards, notably the companies of Alonzo Álvarez de Piñeda in 1519 and of Pánfilo de Narváez in 1528, both of whom sailed along the Gulf Coast and came into contact with the Indians there. The first white men to penetrate inland were Hernando de Soto of Spain and his troop of 900 armored soldiers, who entered the northern part of Alabama looking for gold in 1540. Their aggression aroused the resistance of Indians they encountered, and in southwestern Alabama, they fought the Choctaws, led by Chief Tascalusa, burning their village and winning a victory that cost the Indians dearly in human lives.

After the Spaniard Tristán de Luna tried and failed to start a permanent settlement on Mobile Bay in 1559–1561, the region was not troubled by European interference for about a century. Eventually, however, the French penetrated the region, lured by the abundance of beaver, the fur of which was highly valued in Europe. In 1699 Pierre Le Moyne, Sieur d'Iberville, claimed the region for France, and in 1702, his brother, Jean Baptiste Le Moyne, Sieur de Bienville, established Fort Louis de la Mobile, which was the first permanent white settlement in Alabama. Because of flooding, the settlement was moved downriver in 1710–1711 to the site of Mobile, which was the capital of French Louisiana until 1719, when France went to war with England and Spain and moved the government to Biloxi, where there was less chance of an attack.

The year 1719 was also notable as the date of the first arrival of slaves, an event that encouraged French settlers to clear land for indigo and rice plantations. Nevertheless, the main economic pursuit of the French continued to be trading in furs. In this activity, they faced competition from the British, who established close trading relations with the Chickasaws. Throughout the mid-1700s, the British and French vied for control of the fur trade. The contest merged into the French and Indian Wars and finally was settled in favor of the British in 1763, when the French ceded Canada and all their possessions east of the Mississippi River to Britain by the Treaty of Paris of 1763.

During the American Revolution, a British garrison held the country around Mobile until 1780, when the governor of Spanish Louisiana forced the British to surrender. By the Treaty of Paris of 1783, which ended the American Revolution, and by a related treaty with Spain, Britain ceded northern Alabama to the United States; and southern Alabama, including Mobile, went to Spain. In 1785 a boundary dispute arose between Spain and the United States, and it was not until 1795 that the Treaty of San Lorenzo settled the southern boundary of the US territory at the 31st Parallel, lying about 26 miles above Mobile. By an act of Congress in 1798, land lying above the 31st Parallel between the Chattahoochee River on the east and the Mississippi on the west was organized as the Mississippi Territory, which at first had its northern boundary at 32°28′ north latitude but was extended to the 35th Parallel in 1804, so that the territory included most of what are now Mississippi and Alabama.

After negotiating the Louisiana Purchase with France in 1803, the United States claimed, but Spain still controlled, the Mobile region. The United States did not annex the area until 1813. At that time most of the land in what is now Alabama, in practical fact, was still in the possession of Indian tribes. Embittered by the whites' treatment of them, members of one of the most important tribes, the Creeks, killed about 500 persons at Fort Mims in August 1813. Ultimately, Andrew Jackson, with his Tennessee riflemen and his Indian allies, ended the Creek War, as it was known, by subduing the Creeks at the battles of Talladega on November 9, 1813, and Horseshoe Bend on March 27, 1814. The site of the latter victory, which extracted from the Creeks the cession by treaty of millions of acres of land, is now known as Horseshoe Bend National Military Park. The decisive crushing of the Creeks paved the way for the removal of most of Alabama's Native Americans from the territory to west of the Mississippi River and opened to white settlement a large area of the Old Southwest.

With the influx of settlers after the removal of the Indians, the population of the region swelled. On March 3, 1817, Alabama was separated from Mississippi and organized as a territory on its own. Two years later, on March 2, 1819, Congress authorized the Alabama Territory to draft a state constitution. This was done at a constitutional convention meeting from July 5 to August 2, 1819. The first Alabama state legislature convened on October 25 of that year, and on November 9, the territorial governor, William Wyatt Bibb, was chosen as the first state governor. Alabama was admitted to statehood on December 14, 1819, by an act of Congress, approved by President James Monroe. The seat of government was Huntsville from that time until 1820; since then, Alabama has had three other capitals: Cahaba (the ruins of which are located near Selma) from 1820 to 1826; Tuscaloosa, from 1826 to 1846; and Montgomery, from 1846 to the present.

Following the election of President Abraham Lincoln in 1860, a special state convention convened at Montgomery and, on January 11, 1861, passed an ordinance of secession, making Alabama the fourth state to declare its secession from the Union. On February 4 Montgomery became the site of a conference of six Southern states (Alabama, Georgia, Florida, Louisiana,

Mississippi, and South Carolina) that created the provisional government of the Confederate States of America. The city was the seat of the new Confederate government until June of that year, when Richmond, Virginia, became the Confederate capital. At the end of the Civil War, Alabama was occupied by Union troops, and a constitutional convention met in September 1865, which revoked the ordinance of secession, ratified the 13th Amendment, abolishing slavery, and adopted a new constitution. A new governor and a legislature were chosen, which were recognized under President Andrew Johnson's liberal conditions for Reconstruction.

In 1866, however, this Alabama legislature, along with those of most other Southern states, refused to ratify the 14th Amendment. Under the more stringent congressional plan of Reconstruction by then in force, a prerequisite for restoration to the Union was ratification of the 14th Amendment, which defined citizenship to include not only whites but blacks; demanded equal protection of the laws for all persons; forbade deprivation by any state of any person's "life, liberty, or property, without due process of law," and disqualified for office Confederates who had formerly held office. Congress responded to the recalcitrance of Alabama (as to that of other states) by refusing to seat its chosen representatives to Congress. It also passed the Reconstruction Acts of 1867, placing Alabama and other Southern states under military rule and calling for new constitutional conventions, which were to provide for state governments guaranteeing the vote to black males and ratifying the 14th Amendment. Delegates were to be elected by universal male suffrage. On June 18, 1868, after a new convention of Alabamans, operating within this framework, had drawn up a new state constitution and a new legislature had ratified the 14th Amendment, Alabama's rights and privileges of statehood were restored.

George Washington's Death

Like the legendary Roman hero Cincinnatus, George Washington returned to his farm after serving his country in its time of need. Mount Vernon, Washington's estate in Virginia, was a working plantation. From the time of his retirement as President in 1797 until his death two years later, Washington devoted himself to this property.

On December 12, 1799, Washington set out on horseback. The day was cold, and rain and snow fell alternately. But he ignored the unfavorable weather and for five hours inspected several areas of his plantation. He returned from his ride with snow clinging to his hair and clothing.

The following day Washington complained of a "trifling" sore throat. The discomfort did not deter him from his work. That afternoon, when the storm ended, he went outdoors and marked the trees on the front lawn that he wished cut down. By dinner time his cold was perceptibly worse, and when he attempted to read aloud that evening he was quite hoarse.

By the morning of December 14 Washington's breathing was labored and his speech almost unintelligible. Every effort was made to relieve his condition. Three doctors applied standard remedies and bled him four times. But it was to no avail. Washington realized this and late that afternoon said: "I feel myself going. I thank you for your attention. You had better not take any more trouble about me; but let me go off quietly; I cannot last long." Several hours later, shortly after 10:00 P.M., he died.

Funeral services took place on December 18. At 3:00 P.M. a solemn procession, which included military personnel, members of the clergy, and representatives from Masonic lodges, as well as friends and relatives, accompanied his casket to the burial vault at Mount Vernon. In the procession was the general's horse, fitted with holsters and pistols. At the vault the Reverend Thomas Davis read the Order of Burial from the Episcopal Prayer Book. There was a brief eulogy, and then Dr. Elisha Dick, grand master of the Alexandria Masonic Lodge, conducted full Masonic rites. When these were concluded, cannons mounted on a schooner in the Potomac River began firing, and 11 artillery cannons behind the vault retorted. Then there was silence. Washington's funeral had ended and all departed.

Grief over Washington's death was not limited to those at the burial site, nor did it end with his interment. Across the Atlantic, one London newspaper prophesied: "His fame, bounded by no country, will be confined to no age"; and in honor of the American President, units of the British fleet blockading the harbor at Brest France, dropped their ensigns to half-mast. In Paris Napoleon Bonaparte ordered a 10-day requiem, and in Amsterdam funeral music filled the air.

"The whole United States mourned him as a father," said one admirer. At least 300 eulogies were given in 185 different American towns between the time of his death and February 22, 1800, and so many citizens wore mourning that black goods were reportedly scarce even as late as July 1800.

When news of Washington's death reached Philadelphia on December 18, 1799, Congress recessed. The temporary capital of the nation observed December 26 as a formal day of mourning. At dawn on that day 16 cannons began firing and continued to boom every half hour until 11:00 A.M., when a procession of troops marched to the Lutheran Church. There, Representative Henry Lee of Virginia enunciated a description of Washington that was to become immortal:

First in war, first in peace and first in the hearts of his countrymen, he was second to none in the humble and endearing scenes of private life. . . . The purity of his private character gave effulgence to his public virtues.

As a lasting memorial to Washington, Congress voted to build a marble monument in the Capitol Building then being constructed in Washington, D.C. The legislators also wanted the seat of government to be the final resting place of the first President. A crypt was provided beneath the building's dome, and Martha Washington agreed to the transfer of her husband's remains. But the plan was never carried out. Instead a new vault was constructed at Mount Vernon according to instructions Washington himself had given before his death. When it was completed in 1831, the bodies of George and Martha Washington (she died in 1802) were moved to this tomb. Approximately 500,000 persons each year visit the grave site.

DECEMBER 15

Bill of Rights Day

Responding to numerous calls for a bill of rights, nine states by December 15, 1791, had ratified the first amendments to the US Constitution of 1787. With this approval of three-fourths of the states, the amendments became part of the law of the land. Many had criticized the members of the Constitutional Convention for giving the national government too much strength and, conversely, doing little to guarantee individual liberty and to protect states' rights. Even supporters of the Constitution realized the need for such amendments. In 1787 Thomas Jefferson, who as minister to France was witness to the abuses of that absolute monarchy, had written to James Madison that "a bill of rights is what the people are entitled to against every government on earth." (Jefferson's fellow Virginian, often referred to as the Father of the Constitution, played a leading role in the framing and adoption of the Constitution.) The demand for a series of guarantees of individual and state rights was so strong that the Constitution itself did not receive the necessary approval of three-fourths of the states until assurances were given that the essential amendments would be forthcoming.

The first Congress of the United States, which convened in New York on March 4, 1789, considered 145 proposed amendments, and on September 25, 1789, submitted 12 of these to the states. The 10 that gained approval are known collectively as the Bill of Rights — one of the landmark documents of human freedom. They provide the individual with protection against such abuses as unreasonable search or peacetime quartering of soldiers. And they provide positive guarantees whose importance to the individual citizen can hardly be overstated. Thus were secured such basics of a democracy as freedom of religion, speech, and press; the right of peaceful assembly; the right of petition; the right of private property; the right to trial by jury; and the right of a defendant "to be informed of the nature and cause of the accusation; to be confronted with the witnesses against him; . . . and to have the Assistance of Counsel for his defence." The Fifth Amendment, which has figured as prominently as any in subsequent court proceedings, provides protection against double jeopardy, and adds significantly: "Nor shall [any person] be compelled in any criminal case to be a witness against himself."

While most of the Bill of Rights provides for the protection of individual rights, the 10th Amendment is concerned with states' rights: "The powers not delegated to the United States by the Constitution, nor prohibited by it to the States, are reserved to the States respectively, or to the people." Since its passage, it has provided the basis for most of the judicial interpretations of the Constitution that have served to limit the power of the federal government.

The 150th anniversary of the adoption of the Bill of Rights, in 1941, found the world arming against the totalitarian oppression of the Axis powers, and the democratic ideology of the first 10 amendments provided a major source of inspiration in this fight. In January 1941 President Franklin D. Roosevelt enlarged upon the guarantees of the Bill of Rights when he proclaimed freedom of speech, freedom of worship, freedom from want, and freedom from fear to be the birthright of all peoples of the world. Later that year he designated December 15, 1941, as Bill of Rights Day and called upon Americans to observe it with suitable patriotic ceremonies. Presidents have issued proclamations designating December 15 as Bill of Rights day annually since 1962, and the governors of a number of states take similar action.

Since the adoption of the Universal Declaration of Human Rights by the United Nations in 1948 (see December 10), Presidents have also customarily proclaimed December 10 as Human Rights Day and urged public participation in marking the week that embraces both anniversaries as Human Rights Week. Ceremonies emphasizing the principles of the two great declarations highlight observances of the week. Across the country, community leaders, school and church authorities, patriotic organizations, PTA's, and members of service and fraternal groups are among those who cooperate in planning programs in honor of the dual commemoration. Speeches delivered at this time deal with the importance of freedom and the great historic contributions to its preservation. Essay contests, which are also a frequent part of the observance, deal with similar themes, as do newspapers, magazines, and radio and television programs, which generally carry related features.

In some places, the commemoration has added significance. This is true in Massachusetts, where by act of the legislature the period of December 8 through 15 has been known as Civil Rights Week since 1952. It is so designated in honor both of the adoption of the Bill of Rights on December 15, 1791, and the adoption of what was to become the state's first code of laws — the Body of Liberties — on December 10, 1641.

The actual dates of Human Rights Week generally extend from December 10 through 17. Though observances within that period may vary from place to place, all of them have in common a single purpose: commemoration of such landmark stands for freedom as the Bill of Rights and the UN Human Rights Declaration.

DECEMBER 16

Boston Tea Party

Tension marked the relationship between Britain and its American colonies in the years between the Stamp Act Crisis of 1765 (see March 22) and the Boston Massacre in 1770 (see March 5). After that the situation eased, as some sources of provocation disappeared. In January 1770, for instance, Lord Frederick North took over leadership of the British government and on April 12 obtained King George III's assent to the repeal of the Townshend Act taxes on glass, lead, paints, and paper. Although a three-penny levy on tea remained in force under the Townshend Act, the colonists' nonimportation campaign petered out after this relaxation. The appointment in August 1772 of North's stepbrother, William Legge, the pro-American earl

of Dartmouth, as secretary of state for the colonies in place of the earl of Hillsborough further improved relations. Still, differing English and American viewpoints, aspirations, and interests made future conflict almost inevitable.

In 1773 the British government determined to save the East India Company, which, although virtually bankrupt, was vital to the preservation of Britain's influence in India. The means chosen was the Tea Act, which authorized the Company to sell 600,000 pounds of surplus tea directly to consignees in America without first offering it at auction in England. Furthermore, the Tea Act provided for the remission of all British duties on tea exported to the American colonies, save for the Townshend levy, after May 10, 1773. The act put the East India Company in the enviable position of being able to sell its leaves more cheaply than could the colonial merchants who obtained them from middlemen in England. In fact the company could undersell even those Americans who smuggled the commodity from Holland.

Opposition to the plan was vehement in the American colonies. Broadsides charged that the East India Company would monopolize the tea trade and then take over all commerce. This argument soon became minor as the patriots learned from informants in England that the true intent of the act was to encourage acceptance of the Townshend tea taxes by making the company's dutied tea cheaper even than smuggled substitutes. Central to the colonists' opposition was the realization that if they acquiesced to one Parliamentary levy, the home government would then have a precedent to support future financial demands.

Pressure from militant colonial leaders prompted the resignation of the East India Company's consignees in New York and Philadelphia. In Boston the situation was different, however, since Governor Thomas Hutchinson gave full support to the government's plan. His sons, Elisha and Thomas, were tea agents in the city. The younger Thomas was married to the daughter of Richard Clarke, who, along with his sons Jonathan and Isaac, was another major consignee. Benjamin Faneuil and Edward Winslow, other prominent Bostonians, also represented the company.

On November 2 the Massachusetts Sons of Liberty sent messages to the tea agents to appear at noon of the next day at Boston's Liberty Tree to resign their commissions. When the men failed to appear, the patriots unleashed the town mob, which, hurling mud and stones, invaded the lower floor of the building in which the consignees were meeting.

Boston's selectmen then called a town meeting for Friday, November 5. Chaired by the radical patriot John Hancock, the gathering denounced the Tea Act and called for the resignations of the consignees. Hancock and three other delegates confronted the agents but were unable to influence them. Shortly afterward, on November 17, Captain James Scott, the commander of Hancock's ship, *Hayley,* arrived with news that four shiploads of tea were en route to Boston. That evening a group of Bostonians demonstrated outside the Clarkes' residence and then smashed windows when someone fired a shot at them.

Persistent harassment diminished the consignees' zest for the struggle. On November 18 they rejected another demand by the town meeting for their resignations, but then they asked the provincial government to take responsibility for the tea until conditions allowed it to be disposed of. The patriots who controlled the Massachusetts Council — one of the few upper houses in the colonies elected by the lower house of the legislature — were unwilling to permit this and refused to consider the request. The royalist Governor Hutchinson, meanwhile, dared not take action without the support of his advisers. Finally the consignees agreed not to unload the expected cargoes, at least until new instructions from England allowed them to offer some concessions to the patriots.

Crisis became imminent when the *Dartmouth,* laden with 114 chests of tea, sailed into Boston harbor on Sunday, November 28. The law allowed a 48-hour delay in reporting the arrival of a vessel to the customhouse, and the Boston patriots prevailed upon Francis Rotch, the son of the ship's owner, Joseph Rotch, to take full advantage of the respite. In the interim they hoped to persuade Hutchinson to allow the *Dartmouth* to return to England without registering, without unloading the tea — and especially without paying the Townshend duty.

On Monday morning, posted bills called Bostonians to meet at the red brick Faneuil Hall with the words: "Friends! Brethren! Countrymen! The Hour of Destruction or Manly Opposition to the Machinations of Tyranny stares you in the Face." This was not a town meeting duly called by the selectmen but an extralegal gathering at which all Bostonians and their neighbors were welcome. When 5,000 appeared at the hall, the meeting adjourned to the more commodious Old South Meeting House not far away. The citizens resolved to send back the tea without paying the duty. They also once again demanded that the consignees resign; but the agents refused and left the town for safer quarters.

The royalist authorities were unimpressed by this demonstration of public disapproval, and so, on Tuesday, November 30, the ship's captain, James Hall, had to report the *Dartmouth*'s arrival to customhouse officials. Since payment of

the Townshend duty was not mandatory until December 17, twenty days after the vessel reached Boston, the authorities decided it was in the interests of peace to delay the payment as long as possible. At the request of the provincial Committee of Correspondence, Captain Hall meanwhile docked close to the city at Rowe's Wharf and then at Griffin's Wharf, where — as the colonials clearly saw — the government's guns at Castle William could not support any forcible attempt to unload the tea.

During the first two weeks of December two other ships, the *Eleanor* and the *Beaver,* carrying 114 and 112 chests of tea respectively, arrived at Griffin's Wharf. The fourth expected vessel had run aground before reaching the Boston harbor, but its cargo remained intact. Although the presence of additional ships aggravated the situation in Boston, the earliest arrival remained the focal point: since the *Dartmouth*'s 20-day grace period would expire first, its fate would determine the outcome of the crisis.

The patriots hoped that shipowner Rotch would take his vessel and its cargo of tea back to England and in November had exacted a promise to that effect from him. Perhaps having discovered that the authorities could seize his ship if he left the port without receiving their clearance, Rotch, however, made no attempt to set sail. On December 14, three days before the deadline, the colonists accordingly haled him before another mass meeting at the Old South Meeting House and demanded that he request permission to sail.

The harried shipowner obediently appealed for clearance to customs collector Richard Harrison, but the officer refused to grant it. Harrison argued that the ship was registered at the customhouse and could not leave Boston until someone paid the duties on its cargo of tea.

At 10:00 A.M. on December 16 more than 5,000 Massachusetts citizens gathered again at the Old South Meeting House. Rotch reported his failure to gain clearance, and the convention told him to go directly to the governor for an authorization to leave. Hutchinson, adamant throughout the crisis, rejected the shipper's request. The mass meeting reconvened that afternoon and heard Rotch report another rebuff.

Finally, the rebellious firebrand Samuel Adams rose to his feet and declared that he did not know what recourse was left to save the country. As if on signal, a group of men disguised as Indians appeared at the door at that very moment. Soon the hall filled with cries of "The Mohawks are come!" and "Boston harbor a teapot tonight."

It was about 6:00 P.M. when the meeting disbanded and the participants rushed out into the darkness. Led by the "Indians" they made their way to Griffin's Wharf. Between 30 and 60 men, divided into three competently commanded groups, boarded the *Dartmouth*, the *Eleanor*, and the *Beaver*. While a large, orderly crowd watched from the shore, the men went to work. They hoisted the tea chests out of the holds and onto the decks, smashed them, and heaved both contents and containers over the sides.

The tea leaves quickly filled the shallow water in which the ships were resting. The patriots completed the Boston Tea Party within only three hours, yet they managed to destroy more than 90,000 pounds of leaves worth approximately £9,000.

The authorities did not interfere since they could not have done so without injuring many. But the patriots soon had to face the consequences of their venture. Although the East India Company calmly accepted the fate of its tea, asking only that the British government compensate its losses, George III did not view the situation with the same equanimity. Many Britons supported him in his wrath: Boston, long considered a trouble spot, had gone too far in its protests. Tired of being conciliatory, the king determined to coerce the city into obedience.

The earls of Gower and Sandwich, both members of an anti-American faction, dominated the deliberations on the fate of Boston by the seven-member British ministry that handled American colonial affairs. They devised a program to punish the colonists, which the British Parliament enacted on March 25, 1774, as the Boston Port Bill.

This piece of legislation, the first of the Coercive, or Intolerable, Acts, closed the port of Boston until the residents paid for the lost tea. Only ships bearing food, fuel, and military supplies could unload in Boston Harbor, and even these vessels had to report first to Salem, Massachusetts, the town to which the customhouse had been moved. The other Intolerable Acts were the Administration of Justice Act of May 20, 1774, enacted to protect British officials from harassment in provincial courts; and the Massachusetts Government Act, enacted on the same day, which seriously curtailed the colony's charter rights and gave the crown-appointed governor extensive power.

These attempts to coerce the colonists were doomed to failure. Angered rather than intimidated, Americans throughout the colonies united behind their fellow citizens in beleaguered Boston and continued on the road to independence.

The Boston Tea Party is one of the best-known events in American history, and the people of Massachusetts proudly recall it. On June 28, 1964, they made a reenactment of the event part of the program for Massachusetts Day at the New York World's Fair. Governor Endicott Peabody was present as members of the Massachusetts National Guard, dressed as Indians, boarded a square-rigger at the World's Fair Marina and dumped 4 cases of tea and 20 cases of green sawdust into the water. This time the ship involved was the HMS *Bounty*, which had been built for the motion picture *Mutiny on the Bounty*.

In Boston a bronze plaque marks the site of Griffin's Wharf, where the Tea Party took place. Once affixed to the old J. P. Manning Building, the commemorative tablet now is found near the entrance to the Sheraton Building on Atlantic Avenue. The bicentennial of the Boston Tea Party was celebrated in 1973 with a reenactment of the event aboard the brig *Beaver II*, a privately built reconstruction of one of the vessels in the actual Tea Party.

On July 4, 1973, a block of four commemorative stamps was issued by the Postal Service. Each stamp was a design unit in itself, but the four combined to depict a complete scene showing the dumping of the tea into the harbor.

In 1974 a privately owned complex including the Boston Tea Party Ship *(Beaver II)* and Museum was opened at the Boston waterfront at the Congress Street Bridge.

Old South Meeting House, where the Tea Party was planned, suffered extensive damage during the siege of Boston in the American Revolution. After the war, restoration of the building was begun, and there were numerous structural changes in the 19th century. The Old South Association maintains the Meeting House — which is at Washington and Milk streets and open to visitors — and, with its limited financial resources, has undertaken some attempts at restoration.

The Boston Tea Party Chapter of the National Society of the Daughters of the American Revolution celebrates the anniversary of the event each December 16. If the day falls on Sunday, there is a formal service in the Old South Meeting House to which the governor, mayor, representatives of patriotic organizations, and the public are invited. Otherwise, it is customary to hold a reception in honor of the society's state officers, followed by a luncheon and program.

Only two of the original tea chests still exist. One, oddly enough, is located in San Antonio, Texas. The Boston Tea Party Chapter of the Daughters of the American Revolution owns the other and keeps it at the chapter's charter room in Medford, Massachusetts.

The New Madrid, Missouri, Earthquake

The residents of New Madrid, Missouri, on December 16, 1811, experienced a devastating earthquake, which was followed by two major shocks, on January 23 and February 7, and nearly 2,000 aftershocks. Because of favorable circumstances, only two lives were lost. Scientifically, however, the event ranks in severity and in size of the area affected with the great Alaska quake of March 27, 1964, and the San Francisco quake of April 18, 1906. Although these two resulted in far greater loss of life and property, the earthquake and following shocks centered near New Madrid were felt over a far wider area — all the way from Canada to the Gulf coast — than most coastal earthquakes.

DECEMBER 17

John Greenleaf Whittier's Birthday

John Greenleaf Whittier, the New England poet, politician, journalist, and abolitionist, was born on a farm near Haverhill, Massachusetts, on December 17, 1807, the second of four children in a Quaker household. Largely self-educated, Whittier had scant formal schooling. His strongest intellectual influences were his religion and his lifelong love of reading.

He was especially drawn to poetry, and when he was about 14 was greatly impressed by the works of the Scottish poet Robert Burns, who had affectionately and accurately depicted the life of his fellow rural Scots in the 18th century. Temperamentally, the two men were poles apart except that both evinced an innately democratic spirit. Beyond this, their only similarities were that they were both the sons of poor farmers, both largely self-educated, and both omnivorous readers. Nevertheless, Burns's influence on the young American poet was great, and Whittier began writing of his rural New England surroundings and background, thus becoming a pioneer in American regional literature.

In 1826 one of his two sisters sent a copy of his poem "The Exile's Departure" to the Newburyport (Massachusetts) *Free Press*, a newspaper edited by the abolitionist William Lloyd Garrison. Only two years older than Whittier, Garrison encouraged him to continue writing. In 1827, while studying at the newly established Haverhill Academy, and later, Whittier continued his contributions to Garrison's and other publications. His father, however, had convinced Whittier that while poetry might be an acceptable avocation it was hardly a practical livelihood.

He accordingly embarked on a journalistic career in Boston in 1829, accepting the editorship of the *American Manufacturer*, which he secured through Garrison. A long-lasting friendship had meanwhile developed between the two young men, who shared strong antislavery convictions. Whittier's editorial post in Boston — the start of an editing career that was to occupy him intermittently over the next three decades — was soon followed by a position in Hartford, Connecticut, where he served from 1830 to 1832 as editor of an influential Whig journal, the *New England Weekly Review*. Throughout this period he continued to write verses, sketches, and tales of New England, and his first volume, *Legends of New England*, was published in 1831.

When he resigned from the Hartford post, he returned to live for a time with his family in Haverhill. His father had died, his own health was poor, and he felt discouraged because he had not received literary recognition.

In an effort to analyze the reasons for what he considered his failure, Whittier, barely 25 years old, concluded that he had not been properly dedicated to the high ideals of his Quaker beliefs, but had let self-interest and vanity take priority. He determined to devote himself to humanitarian endeavors, and for the next decade he immersed himself in the abolitionist cause. Although he did not entirely give up his own literary endeavors, these were of secondary importance during this period of Whittier's life. As he himself said, he "left the Muses' haunt to turn the crank of an opinion mill."

Led by his zeal for social reform, Whittier entered politics actively in 1832. For several years he followed the extreme view of abolitionism held by his friend Garrison. Whittier's antislavery writings, including the widely read militant pamphlet *Justice and Expediency*, which he published at Garrison's urging in June 1833, soon made him one of the best known champions of the abolitionist cause. Like Garrison, who had been prominent among founders of the New England Anti-Slavery Society early in 1832, Whittier was a delegate to the meeting of abolitionists from various states who gathered at Philadelphia in December 1833 to organize the American Anti-Slavery Society.

He thereafter devoted himself to abolition and during those years traveled to various places to promote the cause and became a familiar lobbyist in Boston and Washington. He served one term, meanwhile, in the Massachusetts legislature, during 1835, although he was not well enough to continue in the post after being elected for a second time. He spent from May to December of 1836 as editor of the *Essex Gazette*. Having sold the family farm, he moved, during that period, to a new home in Amesbury, Massachusetts, with his mother and sister. He lived there, except for intervals, during the next 40 years; and even after his move to Danvers, Massachusetts, in 1876, Amesbury remained his legal residence.

Two of his absences from Amesbury were in the spring of 1837, when he spent six months in New York City as a corresponding secretary of the American Anti-Slavery Society; and from March 15, 1838, to February 20, 1840, when he was editor of the *Pennsylvania Freeman* in Philadelphia. On May 17, 1838, Pennsylvania Hall, containing the *Freeman's* offices, was burned to the ground by an antiabolitionist mob.

In 1840 Whittier was forced by ill health to return home to Amesbury, the center of his activities for most of his remaining productive years. Although he continued to be active in the abolitionist movement, he was among those who by 1840 had broken with the intemperate Garrison. In contrast to his mentor, who abjured politics and relied solely on moral persuasion to make his point, Whittier felt that more could be achieved through politics than polemics. He aided in founding the short-lived antislavery Liberty Party in 1840, many of whose members helped establish The Free-Soil party eight years later. Whittier also was among the first to urge formation of the new Republican party, in which Free-Soilers and antislavery Whigs and Democrats joined in 1854.

In the years that followed, he continued his abolitionist writings but turned more and more to his own literary career, finding an increasing acceptance in publishing circles. In 1843, along with Nathaniel Hawthorne and Edgar Allan Poe, Whittier was represented in *The Pioneer,* the new but short-lived literary magazine begun by James Russell Lowell, and that same year he published *Lays of My Home and Other Poems.* In the two succeeding decades, Whittier published five volumes of prose, including the semi-fictional *Leaves from Margaret Smith's Journal in the Province of Massachusetts Bay* (1849) and eight volumes of poems. These included *Voices of Freedom* (1846); *Poems* (1849), which included the long-remembered "Proem"; *Songs of Labor* (1850); *The Chapel of the Hermits* (1853); and *Home Ballads, Poems and Lyrics* (1860), which contained the well-known "Skipper Ireson's Ride" and "Telling the Bees."

For 13 years beginning in 1847, Whittier meanwhile was corresponding editor of the *National Era,* published in Washington, D.C., in which most of his poems and articles of that period first appeared. This was the antislavery publication that created a sensation by introducing *Uncle Tom's Cabin* by Harriet Beecher Stowe to the public in 1851–1852. Whittier also had a long association with the *Atlantic Monthly,* to which he became a frequent contributor after it was established in Boston in 1857. He wrote also for the *Independent,* which was launched in New York in 1848.

With words streaming from his pen, the man who at 25 had felt rebuffed and deprived of literary recognition became in later life almost legendary in his popularity. Along with Henry Wadsworth Longfellow, Whittier became a "household poet" in the United States and England. In 1858 he was elected an overseer of Harvard, which then honored him with a master's degree in 1860 and a doctorate in 1886. Whittier was a member of the famous Saturday Club of Boston, and his 70th and 80th birthdays were celebrated as literary events. In 1888–1889, his complete works were collected in seven volumes.

He himself viewed his success as a justification of a consecrated life, and as an old man he advised a young boy, "My lad, if thou wouldst win success, join thyself to some unpopular but noble cause." His dedication to Quaker beliefs, which had made him such a militant and eloquent advocate of justice and tolerance earlier in life, made him the poet of faith, comfort, and joy in his later years. He was often referred to, appropriately enough, as the Quaker Poet, and many of his poems are sung as hymns in churches of various denominations. It was during these more tranquil years that Whittier was first called "America's finest religious poet" and the Balladist of New England.

For many decades after his death, schoolchildren recited his poems in classrooms, at special programs, and in declamation contests. Among the best-known of these poems are "Barbara Frietchie," part of *In War Time and Other Poems* (1864); and "Maud Muller" and "The Barefoot Boy," both included in *The Panorama and Other Poems* (1856). His most highly praised work, *Snow-Bound,* the New England idyll evoking his childhood days, was published in 1866.

Although Whittier was unquestionably an important voice in his own time, his popularity as a poet has declined in recent decades. His technical skill never matched his sincerity, a point he himself recognized as early as 1849, when he expressed in "Proem" the hope that he could atone for his artistic limitations by "a hate of tyranny intense" and a sympathy for "his brother's pain and sorrow." He made no claims to poetic greatness but preferred rather to be remembered as a champion of human rights.

He was elected in 1905 to the Hall of Fame for Great Americans in New York City. A bust of Whittier was unveiled there on May 10, 1928, by James Weldon Johnson, the author, diplomat, and longtime secretary of the National Association for the Advancement of Colored People.

The bust was the gift of the American members of the Society of Friends, or Quakers.

Although Whittier always kept in touch with his old home town of Amesbury, he moved in 1876 to Danvers, Massachusetts, where he lived for the rest of his life. He usually spent the summer months in New Hampshire, where he died at Hampton Falls on September 7, 1892. He was buried in Amesbury, where visitors today can tour the privately owned Whittier Home, now a national historic landmark, at 86 Friend Street, and see, virtually unchanged, the garden room in which Whittier wrote *Snow-Bound* and many other works. The setting for *Snow-Bound* was the Whittier farm — now known as the John Greenleaf Whittier Birthplace — which can be visited, three miles northeast of Haverhill.

Whittier was honored by the naming of Whittier, California, in 1887 Whittier College, and Whittier State School for Boys.

Wright Brothers Day

On the chilly morning of December 17, 1903, the Wright brothers managed to get their faltering flying machine off the ground near Kitty Hawk, North Carolina, thereby becoming the first men to fly and control a powered heavier-than-air machine. On the day they made history, overcoming their neighbors' conviction that they were crazy, Wilbur Wright, who had been born on April 16, 1867, near New Castle, Indiana, was 36; and Orville Wright, born in Dayton, Ohio, on August 19, 1871, was 32.

The sons of Milton Wright, a bishop of the United Brethren Church, the brothers, both excellent mechanics, opened a shop in Dayton in 1892, where they at first sold and repaired bicycles and then also designed and manufactured them. In their spare moments they avidly read accounts of scientific advances. Of particular fascination to them were the experimental glider flights, in Germany, of the pioneering Otto Lilienthal, whom they always afterwards regarded as their greatest inspiration.

After reading about Lilienthal, the Wrights developed a strong interest in gliding as a sport, and their investigations into the field of flight, beginning in 1896, stemmed from this interest. Planning to construct a captive glider that would be capable of carrying a man, they first experimented for several years with kites.

The Wright brothers were not the first to conduct aeronautical experiments. Clement Ader of France, Sir Hiram Maxim of England, and Samuel P. Langley of the United States each independently built and tested a flying machine, but all failed because they lacked a basic knowledge of the laws of aerodynamics. The same was true of glider experimenters like Lilienthal and Octave Chanute of the United States, from whom the Wrights also learned much.

Although Lilienthal had balanced his gliding apparatus by shifting the weight of his body, the Wrights doubted that this method could be expanded sufficiently to meet the needs of flight. Instead they surmised that a glider should be constructed so that its right and left wings could be presented to the wind at different angles for lateral balance. This they determined to accomplish by warping or twisting the tips of the wings. Their system, employing a cable arrangement whereby the wing tips could be moved, was patented. It represented an innovative solution to the problem of control in flight (predating the aileron control developed by Alexander Graham Bell and his associates). Together with other theories, the Wrights incorporated their device for lateral control into both the model glider with a five-foot wing span, which they constructed in 1899 and flew like a kite, and the man-supporting glider, which they built in 1900.

Searching for a secluded spot at which they could test the latter away from onlookers' jeers, they studied wind records of the US Weather Bureau. Their research, and a letter of inquiry to a local postmistress, revealed the area around Kitty Hawk, North Carolina, as a region of steady winds, level sands, and solitude — ideally suited to their purposes.

Arriving there in September 1900, they tried out their first glider. A year later they returned with a larger version of their glider. This time, they built a camp just north of Kill Devil Hill, still near Kitty Hawk.

Their gliding experiments were not an instant success. Mysteriously, their gliders achieved far less lifting power than existing wind pressure tables had led them to expect. This fact led to their conclusion that calculations based on existing data could not be trusted.

Thus thwarted, the Wrights faced the necessity of starting from scratch to obtain their own information. Returning to Dayton, they constructed a wind tunnel at their bicycle shop. There they investigated the aerodynamic properties of various airfoils, testing more than 200 kinds of miniature wing surfaces in various wing and biplane combinations. The Wrights, who were the first to test miniature wings accurately, sought in this way to determine correct values for lift, drag, and center of pressure. In the process they drew up valuable tables of wind pressure and drift. Indeed, from the figures they compiled, it was for the first time possible to design an airplane that could fly. As a result of their experiments, the Wrights also realized that a sharp front edge for an airplane wing was inferior to a curved surface. And they learned, too, that it was inefficient to employ the cambered type of wing then advocated by others.

Armed with their new knowledge, they returned in 1902 to Kill Devil Hill with an improved glider, constructed according to their own figures on wind pressure. Incorporating both their control system and their own wing design, it also included a vertical steering rudder and had a wing span of 32 feet. It was vastly superior to their earlier model, as they soon discovered: many of their glides were of more than 600 feet and against a stiffer (36 miles per hour) wind than any previous glider had ever challenged. With the 1902 glider, which they flew nearly 1,000 times, the Wrights solved most of the problem of equilibrium.

The basic problems behind them, they now felt ready to build a powered machine — the historic *Flyer,* a biplane of 40-foot wingspan with which they would return to Kill Devil Hill in 1903. An adaptation of their successful glider, the new aircraft incorporated a four-cylinder, 12-horsepower engine weighing 170 pounds, which the Wrights had built themselves. It also boasted the first propellers ever constructed for which performance actually could be predicted. Their design was based on the brothers' own calculations. Altogether, counting the weight of its pilot, the new machine weighed 750 pounds. The experiments leading up to it, from 1899 through 1903, cost the Wrights about $1,000.

It was September 1903 before the Wright brothers returned to their camp at Kill Devil Hill — and it was December 14 before mechanical problems and bad weather were over and they were ready to fly. Winning a toss of a coin for what he referred to as the "first whack," Wilbur Wright climbed aboard. But his first trial was abortive, ending suddenly after three and a half seconds in the air: he had turned the craft upward too suddenly, before it acquired sufficient speed, and it stalled and fell the short distance to earth. Two days of repairs were needed after this.

On the morning of December 17, the brothers were ready to try again. Though they were temporarily daunted by the wind, which was blowing at between 21 and 27 miles an hour, they determined to proceed when it failed to die down. On level ground at the base of Kill Devil Hill, they laid a 60-foot track, which headed straight into the wind. This time it was the turn of Orville Wright, who lay in the control mechanism on the lower wing, beside the engine. "After running the motor a few minutes to heat it up," he subsequently reported, "I released

the wire that held the machine to the track, and the machine started forward into the wind." A handful of persons witnessed the historic trial — in addition to Wilbur Wright, who first walked and then ran alongside the plane, steadying the wing until the craft rose of its own power and, for 12 glorious seconds, flew over the sands near Kitty Hawk. When the plane came to rest on the ground, 120 feet from its starting point, a dream had come true that had preoccupied many over the ages: men at last were able to fly. As Orville Wright put it: "This flight lasted only 12 seconds, but it was nevertheless the first in . . . history . . . in which a machine carrying a man had raised itself by its own power into the air in full flight, had sailed forward without reduction of speed, and finally landed at a point as high as that from which it started."

During the remainder of the morning, the brothers alternated as pilots for three more successful flights. Each flight longer than the last, the series culminated with Wilbur's flight of 852 feet in 59 seconds — the last *The Flyer* would ever make: as the brothers and onlookers stood discussing the day's events, a gust of wind caught the craft, turning it over and over and damaging it badly, though by then everyone was too excited to care very much.

The site of the epoch-making flights and the glider experiments that led up to them is now designated as the Wright Brothers National Memorial, a 425-acre area administered by the National Park Service. Its most prominent feature is a 60-foot-high gray granite pylon atop Kill Devil Hill. Not far away, a granite boulder marks the takeoff point for the first flight. Its course, and that of the other three flights of December 17, 1903, are indicated for visitors to see. Nearby are reconstructions of the Wrights' living quarters and hangar — built in 1953 for the 50th anniversary of the flights. A visitor center, dedicated on December 17, 1960, is also nearby, housing pertinent exhibits and a full-sized reproduction of the Wrights' famous plane. The reproduction was presented in connection with the 60th anniversary of powered flight in 1963. The original plane is in Washington, D.C., as part of the collection of the National Air and Space Museum, which Congress created in 1946 as a bureau of the Smithsonian Institution.

In view of the fact that these remarkable flights of December 17, 1903, signaled the beginning of a new era, it was odd that only three newspapers gave the event any coverage. Undaunted, the brothers returned to Dayton, where they constructed a more sturdy machine. They tested it by flying around and around a cow pasture near Dayton — Huffman Prairie, where the handsome Wright Brothers Memorial monolith now stands. There, on October 5, 1905, they established a record (one of many to come) by keeping their improved craft in the air for 24 miles of circular flight, which they accomplished in 38 minutes. Although they obtained a patent for their plane in 1906, finding a market for their invention was difficult. The Wrights were obliged to devote much time and effort in the next few years to promotion and negotiation. They were among those submitting bids to construct a flying machine for the US Army — and alone in fulfilling the assignment. Meanwhile, they conducted numerous record-breaking demonstration flights. In one, at Fort Myer, Virginia, on September 9, 1908, Orville Wright remained airborne for 62 minutes, during which time he made 57 complete circles at a height of 120 feet — setting several records at once. Wilbur Wright conducted other record-breaking flights in France, also in 1908, and arranged for sale to a syndicate there of rights to manufacture the plane in France.

Not until after these widely heralded demonstrations did the brothers at last receive the acclaim for their achievements that might have been expected earlier. Their newly won fame then precipitated a flood of news stories, decorations, honors, and attention from monarchs and other dignitaries, which left them singularly undistracted from their main goal of producing and assuring the manufacture of a practical machine. Finally, in 1909, the US Army accepted their plane. The same year — in the wake of the favorable impression created by Wilbur Wright's spectacular demonstration flights around the Statue of Liberty and up to Grant's Tomb during that year's Hudson-Fulton celebration in New York — the brothers at last were able to form the American Wright Company. Later negotiations provided for manufacture of Wright airplanes in England, Germany, and Italy.

It was as president of the Wright Company that Wilbur Wright spent his few remaining years. He died of typhoid fever at the age of 45, on May 30, 1912, in Dayton, in the house in which Orville Wright had been born and in which both brothers had grown up. The building has been moved since, together with the Wright cycle shop, to the much-visited Greenfield Village, the collection of nearly 100 historic buildings established, along with his museum of Americana, by Henry Ford at Dearborn, Michigan. In Indiana, the site of the farm in which Wilbur Wright was born is preserved today as the Wilbur Wright State Memorial (though the building itself was long ago destroyed by fire).

Off Indiana Route 38, it is east of New Castle and northeast of Millville. Nearby, the Wilbur Wright Monument also can be seen — on Indiana Route 3, a mile north of New Castle.

Orville Wright, who outlived his brother by many years, sold his interest in the Wright Company in 1915 but continued to work in research and as a consulting engineer. His birthday is observed as National Aviation Day (see August 19). Orville Wright died on January 30, 1948, also in Dayton, at the age of 76. Both brothers were subsequently elected to the Hall of Fame in New York City — Wilbur Wright in 1955 and Orville Wright in 1965 — sooner than the mandatory 25 years after death, so that a bust of him might be placed there with that of his brother.

The Wright brothers are commemorated annually on December 17, the anniversary of their epoch-making first powered flight. The date has been observed in one way or another, and under various titles, almost ever since the flight. A joint resolution approved by Congress in 1963 officially designated December 17 of each year as Wright Brothers Day and requested the President to issue annually a proclamation inviting the people of the United States to observe the day with appropriate ceremonies and activities.

Among the more notable annual observances is a Wright Brothers dinner held in Washington, D.C., by the National Aeronautic Association, founded in 1905, which is composed of several thousand persons interested in the progress and development of aviation. The NAA, which supervises sporting aviation competitions and oversees official world and American records in aeronautics and astronautics, chooses the occasion of the Wright Brothers dinner for the award of the Wright Brothers Memorial Trophy to a civilian for outstanding contributions to American aviation. The city of Los Angeles also makes an award — of the Kitty Hawk Trophy — at a dinner in observance of Wright Brothers Day.

Two of the major events connected with Wright Brothers Day takes place, appropriately, at the site of their historic flights near Kitty Hawk and at Dayton. The celebration, including a traditional flyover and ceremony, has been held at the Wright Brothers National Memorial annually on December 17 since 1932. The flyover by military aircraft, which is an integral part of each ceremony, is scheduled for 10:35 A.M. — the time of the original flight on December 17, 1903. The program also customarily includes music, an invocation, and the playing of the national anthem; a welcome by state, county or local officials; remarks by distinguished speakers; and a memorial wreath laying at the First Flight Marker. The ceremonies are followed by the Wright memorial luncheon in nearby Nags Head, arranged by the Kill Devil Hills Memorial Society, which dedicates itself to fostering the memory of the Wrights' achievements and promoting public understanding of aviation. Speakers at the morning ceremonies and at the luncheon vary from year to year, but they have included such dignitaries as the governor of North Carolina, the director of the National Park Service, famous aviators and astronauts, national and state legislators, military officers, and officials of aviation and aeronautics associations.

Tributes to the Wrights have been very lavish on important anniversaries such as the 50th, in 1953, when the North Carolina observance extended over four days. Sponsored by different groups, each day's memorial observance commenced with a procession to the monument at the top of Kill Devil Hill, where it continued with the placing of wreaths, the playing of taps, and a memorial flight. On the first day, which was designated as Pioneers and Private Flyers Day, the ceremony was followed by the dedication of the reconstructed Wright buildings there, a glider salute by the Soaring Society of America, and a pilgrimage to the Wrights' 1900 glider camp site nearby, where a flag and wreath ceremony was held. The ceremony of the second day, which was known as Industry Day, included, in addition to the customary memorial flight, a World Flag Raising ceremony and an International Goodwill Flight by the Georgia Air National Guard, followed by a second glider salute by the Soaring Society. The memorial ceremony on the third day — Defense Day — was followed by an impressive aerial review. It comprised an air rescue mission performed by the Elizabeth City (North Carolina) Coast Guard Air Station; an Airpower Fly-by in which planes of the armed services took part; a demonstration of Flight Perfection by Air Force Thunderbirds; and a jet helicopter test put on by Bensen Aircraft of Raleigh, North Carolina.

Some of these features were repeated on the fourth and final day, when the usual morning memorial was expanded into a big golden anniversary ceremony — including such features as a demonstration of skywriting; a special Wreath Flight by the US Coast Guard; the traditional memorial flight — this time by the US Navy; a reenactment of the Wrights' first flight; an airpower review by planes of the US Marine Corps, Army, and Air Force; and the arrival of a British Canberra jet bomber flown from London for the occasion. Perhaps the best known of the celebrities who gave addresses that day was the air ace Lieutenant General James H. Doolittle. Sunrise and sunset patrols were flown by the Civil Air Patrol on each of the four days as a gesture of added respect.

The 60th anniversary, in 1963, featured a two-day observance, which had as its most famous guest the astronaut John H. Glenn Jr., who in early 1962 had become the first American to orbit the Earth. Colonel Glenn was moderator of a special Flight Seminar for Youth, held on the morning of December 16. A highlight of the anniversary took place that afternoon, when a ceremony at the visitor center featured the presentation to the national memorial of the exact reproduction of the Wright brothers' airplane, which had been constructed on a volunteer basis by members of the Washington, D.C., section of the American Institute of Aeronautics and Astronautics. A glider aerial tribute followed — and then a procession to the First Flight Marker, where a wreath-laying ceremony took place. This was followed by the traditional memorial flyby, and by a program of aerial demonstrations and aerobatics. Later, two receptions and banquets took place simultaneously in Nags Head and Kill Devil Hills, with Secretary of Commerce Luther H. Hodges addressing each group.

The next day was marked by the dedication of the First Flight Airport, with a 3,000-foot runway for the use of light planes. The morning-long program, which began with the lighting of a signal flare, and a band march down the runway, included anniversary remarks by the chairman of the Civil Aeronautics Board, the commander of the Tactical Air Command, and Secretary Hodges; there followed words of dedication from the governor of North Carolina, the director of the National Park Service, and the deputy administrator of the Federal Aviation Agency. A runway ribbon-cutting ceremony was performed by special aircraft carrying the official dedication party. This was followed by a performance of precision aerobatics, a gyrocopter demonstration, and flybys and demonstrations by military aircraft. Then came the first official takeoffs from the new runway, and a silent flight finale by pilots of the Soaring Society of America.

In another major observance, Dayton has been commemorating the December 17 Anniversary of Powered Flight annually since 1904. The day's events begin with a motorcade to Woodland Cemetery, where Wilbur and Orville Wright are buried. Customarily taking part in the motorcade are local officials and the ranking general from Wright-Patterson Air Force Base — the giant complex outside Dayton that includes the site of Huffman Prairie, where the Wrights made early test flights. Participants in the motorcade join in laying wreaths on the brothers' graves. Prayers are offered by a local clergyman and a salute is fired by a rifle squad from Wright-Patterson. After the sounding of taps, which concludes the graveside ceremony, the police-escorted motorcade proceeds to the handsome Wright Brothers Memorial north of Wright Field. There, other wreaths are laid and memorial addresses are given by visiting officials. The other principal ceremony in Dayton is the addition each year to the Aviation Hall of Fame of four notable contributors to aviation. Chartered by Congress, the Hall of Fame, which came into being in 1962, is housed in the US Air Force Museum at Wright-Patterson Air Force Base.

The enshrinement ceremonies, as they are called, have evolved into a black-tie dinner held annually in Dayton, with a celebrity master of ceremonies and distinguished guests famous in aviation and related fields. A representative of the Dayton Chamber of Commerce initiates the enshrinement ceremonies by stressing the importance of the Wrights' contributions and voices Daytonians' appreciation of them. Each of the newly elected persons, who will thenceforth be represented by a plaque in the Aviation Hall of Fame, is then the subject of an illustrated presentation talk.

Among those included in the Aviation Hall of Fame are Samuel P. Langley, Charles A. Lindbergh, and Richard E. Byrd. The very first to be honored were Wilbur and Orville Wright, "whose unfailing devotion to [their] task," as their citation says, "unlocked the secret of powered flight and freed man forever from the limitations of the land and sea."

DECEMBER 18

Lyman Abbott's Birthday

Lyman Abbott, the American clergyman, editor, and author who became one of the best known religious leaders of his time, was born in Roxbury, Massachusetts, on December 18, 1835. He was the son of Jacob Abbott, a teacher and author of 180 books for boys, including 28 volumes in the then well-known Rollo series. The family moved to Maine when Lyman Abbott was about three years old.

After studying law at New York University, Abbott was graduated in 1853 and practiced his profession for about two or three years. In New York he was greatly influenced by the famous Congregational preacher Henry Ward Beecher, pastor of Brooklyn's Plymouth Church, who was also an editor, author, and public speaker.

Shortly after Abbott's marriage to Abby Frances Hamlin in 1855, he decided to abandon law for the ministry and began a course of private study to that end. Ordained in 1860 by a Congregational council in Maine, Abbott became pastor of a church in Terre Haute, Indiana, from 1860 to 1865; when he returned east to take up the pastorate of a Congregational church in New York City. After the Civil War, Abbott actively participated in reconstruction work through a group of clergymen and laymen interested in providing freedmen's aid, for blacks in the South who needed assistance either in relocating or in adjusting to a new life in the same region.

From the beginning of his clerical life, Abbott had supplemented his ministerial income with literary and editorial work. In 1876 he joined *The Christian Union*, sharing editorial duties with Henry Ward Beecher, who had been editor of the weekly since 1870. Since Beecher was then involved with many outside interests, Abbott more or less took over the editing of the magazine within a short time. In 1893 he changed its name to *The Outlook*. Under his editorial guidance, the publication had become the leading religious weekly in the country, during a period when religious publications were among the most influential media of communication in the United States. For Abbott, it was an effective channel for his views on religion, politics, social problems, and scientific progress for the rest of his life.

Beecher died in 1887, and Abbott succeeded him in 1888 as pastor of the Brooklyn Plymouth Church, which continued to prosper under his leadership. Abbott, in his sixties, resigned the pastorate in 1899 and spent the remainder of his life directing *The Outlook* and lecturing throughout the country. Although he became a nationally known platform and pulpit speaker, his major and most effective role was in religious journalism. In addition to his work on *The Outlook* for 46 years, he wrote nearly 40 books, championing the New Theology and a modern rational stance in American Christianity. He greatly influenced religious thought in the United States. In such books as *The Theology of an Evolutionist* (1897), he assumed the role of mediator between rigid religious views and the current scientific thought that seemed to threaten those views. His other books include *Dictionary of Religious Knowledge* (1902), *Christianity and Social Problems* (1897), *The Rights of Man* (1901), *Industrial Problems* (1905), *The Spirit of Democracy* (1910), *America in the Making* (1911), and *Reminiscences*

(1915, revised 1923). His devotional books include *The Other Room* (1903) and *The Great Companion* (1904). He also wrote *What Christianity Means to Me* (1921) and a biography of the man who had been his inspiration to enter the ministry and whose career was paralleled by his own in so many ways, *Henry Ward Beecher* (1903).

Abbott was interested in the growing industrialism of his times; he was a leader in the Social Gospel movement and one of the most influential members of the liberal wing of Protestant churches. He died in New York City on October 22, 1922, a few months short of his 87th birthday.

New Jersey Ratifies the Constitution

New Jersey on December 18, 1787, became the third state to ratify the US Constitution. Only Delaware and Pennsylvania, which had ratified on December 7 and December 12 respectively, had accepted the new government more quickly. Jerseyans had long been critics of the Articles of Confederation, which preceded the Constitution as a frame of government, and every delegate to the state convention called to vote on the matter cast his ballot in favor of the new constitution.

New Jersey was a prosperous state in the 1780s but was not fortunate in its geographical location. A diversified system of agriculture gave a strong foundation to the economy, which also included a number of industrial establishments, such as eight iron furnaces and hundreds of saw and gristmills. But, unfortunately, commerce flowed through either New York City to the north or Philadelphia to the south.

New Jersey's commercial dependence on New York and Pennsylvania was its principal reason for dissatisfaction with the Articles of Confederation. Under that system the states, rather than the central government, had the right to control commerce, and Jerseyans consequently paid import duties to both New York and Pennsylvania, as well as heavy taxes to support their own state's effort to meet the interest on the national and state debts.

New Jersey hoped that — under a new constitution — the national government would relieve the state of an enormous burden by collecting all commercial duties and using the receipts to erase both the national and state debts. If, in addition, a stronger central government provided for better national defenses, New Jersey, which suffered greatly in the American Revolution, would have further reason to celebrate.

Delegates from New Jersey, Virginia, Pennsylvania, Delaware, and New York took part in the Annapolis Convention of September 1786, which sought to improve the Articles of Confederation. The five states empowered their representatives to discuss commercial problems, and New Jersey suggested that they consider other important matters as well. Spurred by New Jersey's willingness to consider broad changes and recognizing that such alterations could be made only through joint efforts of all 13 states, the Annapolis conferees eschewed independent action and called for a convention "to render the constitution of the Federal Government adequate to the exigencies of the Union."

New Jersey appointed six delegates to the Constitutional Convention, which opened in Philadelphia in May 1787. They were able but not brilliant. David Brearley, 41 years old, was the chief justice of the state. William C. Houston was a lawyer and had been a professor of mathematics at Princeton. William Paterson had been a member of the Continental Congress and attorney general of the state for 11 years. William Livingston was the governor of New Jersey, a post he held until his death in 1790. Captain Jonathan Dayton, who had served with distinction in the Revolution, was a member of the state legislature and, at 26, was one of the youngest delegates. Abraham Clark, the sixth representative, never attended the Philadelphia sessions.

On May 29 Governor Edmund Randolph of Virginia presented a series of resolutions designed to become the basis of any new constitution. This Virginia Plan was strongly nationalist, and its critical provision called for a bicameral legislature with each state represented in both houses in proportion to its contribution of taxes to the national government or to the number of its free inhabitants. The smaller states objected vehemently to the Virginia proposals, and New Jersey offered an alternative solution to the convention.

Speaking on behalf of the New Jersey delegation, William Paterson on June 15 laid before the delegates at Philadelphia the New Jersey Plan for a revitalized union. The plan offered Congress additional powers to raise revenue by import duties, stamp taxes, postal charges, and enforceable requisitions upon the states. Congress would also gain the authority to regulate trade and commerce, and its acts and treaties would become the supreme law of the land. The plan also provided for a vetoless executive branch, composed of several individuals and elected by Congress. The Congress would be able to appoint a supreme tribunal with original jurisdiction in cases of impeachment and appellate jurisdiction from states in maritime disputes, cases involving foreigners or treaties, and acts for the regulation of trade or the collection of the federal revenue. The nine resolutions contained in New Jersey's proposal embodied important amendments to the Articles of Confederation, but made no provision for changing the unicameral structure of the Congress or its equal — as opposed to proportional — representation for each state.

Compromise ultimately produced a solution acceptable to supporters of the Virginia and New Jersey plans. On June 11 Roger Sherman of Connecticut suggested a two-house national legislature with representation proportional to population in the lower house but with each state having an equal vote in the upper chamber. On July 12 the convention agreed that each state's representation in the lower house be based on the total of its white population and three-fifths of its black population. On July 16 the delegates agreed as well that each state would have an equal vote in the Senate. Having solved the critical question of equal versus proportional representation in the national legislature, the Constitutional Convention at Philadelphia was able to conclude its work by September 17.

By a unanimous vote taken on November 1, 1787, the New Jersey legislature called for the election of a state convention to evaluate the Constitution. Late in November those citizens qualified to vote in Assembly elections selected 39 men, three from each county, to attend the ratifying caucus. The delegates assembled in Trenton on December 11 and remained in session one week. After discussing the document section by section, the delegates, on December 18, voted to adopt the new frame of government and affixed their signatures to two copies of it, one sent to Congress and the other retained by New Jersey. As with others of the 13 original states, the date of New Jersey's ratification of the Constitution is commonly used as the date of its statehood; in most lists enumerating the 50 states chronologically, New Jersey therefore appears as the third state.

Thirteenth Amendment Proclaimed Ratified

Although the Emancipation Proclamation, issued by President Abraham Lincoln under his authority as commander in chief of the armed forces on January 1, 1863, proclaimed free the slaves in those states and parts of states that were then in rebellion, slavery still existed in some parts of the country as the Civil War drew to a close. There was still slavery in those slave-holding border states that had never declared secession from the Union and in those parts of

the South that had been under Union control when Lincoln issued his proclamation.

To extend abolition of slavery to these areas and secure full congressional sanction for the provisions of his proclamation, Lincoln urged that Congress propose an amendment to the Constitution that would prohibit slavery in all parts of the nation. After congressional passage (following bitter debate) on January 31, 1865, Lincoln gave his signature to the measure on February 1 and it was sent to the states. The anniversary of the President's signing of the document now is designated as National Freedom Day by presidential proclamation (see February 1). Final ratification by 27 states — the necessary three-fourths — was proclaimed officially by Secretary of State William H. Seward on December 18, 1865.

The text of the 13th Amendment to the Constitution is as follows:

SECTION 1. Neither slavery nor involuntary servitude, except as a punishment for crime whereof the party shall have been duly convicted, shall exist within the United States, or any place subject to their jurisdiction.

SECTION 2. Congress shall have power to enforce this article by appropriate legislation.

DECEMBER 19

Washington Encamps at Valley Forge

British military plans for 1777 called for a three-pronged advance to converge near Albany, New York, to crush the American rebel army, isolate New England, and quickly dampen the American Revolution. General John Burgoyne was to push down from Canada through Lake Champlain, General Barry St. Leger was to come from Oswego through the Mohawk Valley, and General William Howe was to drive north up the Hudson River from New York City. The colonists thwarted St. Leger's efforts and captured Burgoyne's entire force at the battle of Saratoga (see October 17). Howe never reached the intended rendezvous, as he directed his interest instead to an assault on the city of Philadelphia, the seat of the Continental Congress.

The undertaking took longer than Howe expected. Embarking from New York City with 15,000 troops on July 23, he did not land at Head of Elk, near modern Elkton, Maryland, until August 25. It was not until September 11 that he defeated the men of General George Washington, who were blocking the road to Philadelphia at Brandywine Creek. And it was not until September 26 that the British captured the city and forced the American Congress to flee to York, Pennsylvania. Washington's counterattack at Germantown on October 4 was a failure, and after several more minor engagements, he withdrew his forces to their winter quarters at Valley Forge.

On December 19, 1777, the Americans arrived at their inhospitable campsite, a spot selected by "a speculator, a traitor, or a council of ignoramuses," according to Major General Johann Kalb, a Bavarian volunteer. Militarily, however, the location was desirable, being close to water and surrounded by a forest, which could provide fuel and materials for shelter. Even more important, Valley Forge lay between the American Congress at York, and the hostile British forces 20 miles away in Philadelphia.

Valley Forge, in American historical lore, has justly become synonymous with sacrificial suffering. The winter itself was mild, but the men suffered from lack of food and clothing. Disease, hunger, and exposure claimed the lives of 3,000 of the 11,000 men at the Pennsylvania winter quarters.

The rebels lived in makeshift quarters until they completed building temporary huts in mid-January. Many could not even help in the construction because their lack of clothing made them unfit for winter duty. On December 23 Washington complained to Congress that 2,898 of his troops were "bare foot and otherwise naked." "The want of clothing," the commander stated, "added to the rigor of the season, has occasioned [the men] to suffer such hardships as will not be credited but by those who have been spectators." General Anthony Wayne complained that "the whole army is sick and crawling with vermin." Frostbite naturally preyed upon the ill-clad soldiers, and the Marquis de Lafayette noted that amputations were frequent.

Three times during the winter, provisions gave out, and during one week in March 1778 each soldier received only three ounces of meat and three pounds of flour. Over 1,500 horses died of starvation during the crisis. Foraging expeditions by the Americans, as well as by the British in Philadelphia, laid bare the neighboring countryside. Washington was reluctant to alienate the inhabitants by commandeering supplies, but occasionally a farmer had to hand over his seed grain supply at the point of a bayonet.

Greed and bureaucratic inefficiency were at the root of the suffering at Valley Forge. While the soldiers starved, Pennsylvania farmers delivered their grain to Philadelphia, where they could obtain cash payments from the British; and New Yorkers sent their produce to New England civilians. Private contractors profited by using government wagons to ship iron and flour out of Pennsylvania, while pork earmarked for Washington's men rotted in New Jersey for lack of transportation.

Congress, alarmed by the situation, revamped the military supply system during the winter. Joseph Wadsworth of Connecticut became commissary general and for the remainder of the war ably conducted the procurement of provisions. Nathanael Greene, one of Washington's most capable subordinates, took over the office of quartermaster general from the inept Thomas Mifflin. Greene performed so well that Washington's men fared much better in the next winter quarters at Morristown, New Jersey, in weather more severe than that at Valley Forge.

Despite the hardships, the American soldiers remained steadfast. Occasionally the troops chanted ominously "no pay, no clothes, no provisions, no rum," but desertion did not become a major problem; indeed, it decreased when the shortages were most grave. History has confirmed the accolade bestowed by John Laurens, Washington's volunteer aide-de-camp, who spoke of "those dear, ragged Continentals whose patience will be the admiration of future ages."

An army stronger in ability as well as in spirit developed at Valley Forge. Major General Friedrich von Steuben, a Prussian volunteer, used the long winter hours to train the soldiers in modern formations and tactics (see September 17). The soldiers learned the lessons well and repeatedly put them to use when they resumed their campaigns in the spring of 1778.

The Valley Forge reservation now comprises over 2,000 acres. Located 22 miles from Philadelphia, the park is a major tourist attraction. Each year approximately 1.5 million visitors travel to the area, which is particularly beautiful in the spring when the dogwood trees are in bloom. The National Park Service assumed control of the site, formerly a state park, in 1977.

The state of. Pennsylvania. has attempted to restore the park as it was in the winter of 1777. The earthworks have been preserved and reproductions of some of the huts occupied by the soldiers have been erected. Reconstructed too is the one-room log cabin that served as the Continental army's hospital. But one of the major attractions is an original building. The two-story stone farmhouse that Washington used as his headquarters is still standing and is furnished with items the general used during his stay.

The federal government has put up a memorial arch on one of the hills and there are other monuments on the grounds. Just outside the park stands a memorial chapel built in the Gothic style. It contains stained glass windows of great beauty. The Cloister of the States, with 13 bays representing the 13 original states, adjoins the chapel, and a stone tower nearby holds a carillon that tolls regularly throughout the day. There is also a museum maintained by the Valley Forge Historical Society.

One relic of the 1777 encampment has an interesting history. During the so-called log cabin and hard cider presidential campaign of General William Henry Harrison in 1840, Matthias Pennypacker of Phoenixville, Pennsylvania, decided to build a cabin from the logs that had been taken from the Valley Forge huts. He found only one in sound condition, but he built a cabin and used this log in it. He then mounted the cabin on a wagon and drove it about the country to arouse support for Harrison's candidacy. At the close of the campaign, Pennypacker preserved the log. It was safely guarded by his son and grandson. Joseph P. Stockwell obtained it from the grandson and in 1935 presented it to the Pennsylvania chapter of the Sons of the American Revolution. In January 1936, it was deposited with the Pennsylvania Historical Society, where it is preserved along with many other relics of the Revolutionary War.

DECEMBER 20

Louisiana Purchased

Thomas Jefferson's most foresighted act as President may have been the Louisiana Purchase of 1803, which added approximately 828,000 square miles of land between the Mississippi River and the Rocky Mountains to the domain of the United States. The acquisition doubled the size of the young nation and guaranteed American control of the Mississippi River and the port of New Orleans. The government ultimately carved all or parts of 13 of America's heartland states from the region: Louisiana, Arkansas, Missouri, Iowa, Minnesota, Oklahoma, Kansas, Nebraska, the Dakotas, Colorado, Wyoming, and Montana.

France was the original European owner of Louisiana. In 1682 Robert Cavelier, Sieur de La Salle, completed exploration of the Mississippi River and claimed for France "possession of that river, of all the rivers that enter into it, and all the country watered by them." He then named the region Louisiana in honor of Louis XIV. The French won general recognition of their title to the area from their chief colonial rivals, the British, by the Treaty of Utrecht of 1713, which ended the European War of the Spanish Succession.

La Salle's original claim included lands west of the Mississippi River to the Rocky Mountains

and as far east as what is now Kentucky, Tennessee, and West Virginia. Worn down by the continuing colonial wars of the 18th century, the French government proved unable to retain control of this vast area. By the Treaty of Fontainebleau of November 3, 1762, France compensated Spain for assisting in the unsuccessful French and Indian War of 1754 to 1763 against the British by ceding her all of Louisiana west of the Mississippi, as well as the Isle of Orleans, east of the river. By the Treaty of Paris of February 10, 1763, which ended the French and Indian War, the British received the remainder of Louisiana east of the river except for the city of New Orleans.

France had not permanently lost interest in the American continent and under Napoleon Bonaparte sought to regain some of its former colonies. By the secret Treaty of San Ildefonso in 1800 (see October 1), Spain returned the Louisiana territory west of the Mississippi to France; and the Treaty of Madrid of March 21, 1801, reconfirmed the retrocession. Napoleon probably envisioned the region, which remained temporarily under Spanish administration, as a source of food and supplies for the sugar plantations that he hoped to foster in the West Indies, notably on the French-colonized Caribbean island of Santo Domingo (now Hispaniola, divided between Haiti and the Dominican Republic).

Rumors of France's resumption of title to Louisiana gravely upset American westerners, whose prosperity depended on free navigation of the Mississippi. Spain was a weak power, and by Pinckney's Treaty of 1795 had permitted US citizens to sail the river freely and to use New Orleans as a port of deposit. France appeared to be a greater threat, and Napoleon aggravated fears by dispatching 20,000 troops to the Caribbean, under General Charles Leclerc, to suppress a native rebellion on Santo Domingo.

Jefferson recognized that the United States must protect its interests, and in April 1802 he instructed Robert Livingston, the American minister to France, to attempt to buy New Orleans and the Floridas from Napoleon. In October 1802 news that the still-present Spanish intendant had suddenly revoked the US right of deposit at New Orleans prompted the President — who incorrectly blamed the French for this decision — to send James Monroe to Paris as minister plenipotentiary with authority to offer Bonaparte $10 million for New Orleans and the Floridas. Monroe's instructions directed him to undertake negotiations to improve Anglo-American relations if the French proved uncooperative.

Circumstances combined to make Monroe's

mission extraordinarily successful. In the Caribbean, yellow fever and the insurgents of the Haitian liberator Toussaint L'Ouverture had virtually wiped out Leclerc's expeditionary force, and Napoleon, preparing for military action in Europe, could spare no more troops for the New World. In order to raise money and to deprive the British of a priceless but defenseless target, Napoleon decided to offer the whole of Louisiana to the United States for a pittance.

Talleyrand, the French foreign minister, on April 11, 1803, presented Napoleon's offer to Livingston. That diplomat, however, decided to wait for Monroe, who arrived the following day, before committing his government. Monroe and Livingston determined that, although their instructions did not cover such an unexpected development, they dared not allow the opportunity to slip away. They quickly entered negotiations, and on May 2 signed a treaty antedated April 30 with the French by which the United States was to pay $15 million for the entire Louisiana territory.

Jefferson thought that the government lacked power under the Constitution to add new territory to the nation, but he feared that adoption of an enabling amendment would consume too much time and endanger the transaction. Finally he decided that since "the good sense of the country" wanted Louisiana, "the less we say about constitutional difficulties the better." On October 20, 1803, the Senate ratified the treaty, and on December 20 the United States took formal possession of Louisiana. Never, as the historian Henry Adams wrote years later, "did the United States government get so much for so little."

Early exploration of the land acquired in the Louisiana Purchase began with the Lewis and Clark expedition of 1804 to 1806 (see September 23). Having received Congressional approval early in 1803 for a venture designed to establish friendly relations with the Native Americans and to encourage commerce, President Jefferson named his secretary, Meriwether Lewis, and Lieutenant William Clark to lead the trailblazing scientific party. On August 31, Lewis and Clark began their descent of the Ohio River. They spent the winter in quarters that they set up near St. Louis.

With their more than 40 companions, Lewis and Clark resumed their trek on May 14, 1804, beginning the expedition proper with their ascent of the Missouri River, which stretched across much of the Louisiana territory. They spent the winter of 1804–1805 in the area of present North Dakota. In the spring of 1805 the adventurers set out to cross the Rocky Mountains. On November 7, after seven harrowing months, they came within sight of the Pacific Ocean. The expedition returned to St. Louis on September 23, 1806, having paved the way for the ultimate settlement of the West.

Appropriately, St. Louis, the starting point and terminus of the Lewis and Clark journey, has had the most outstanding commemorations of the Louisiana Purchase. The famous St. Louis World's Fair, which ran from April 30 to December 1, 1904, had as its official title The Louisiana Purchase Exposition and marked the centenary of the acquisition. In 1966 the city commemorated its role as entrance point to the West for countless 19th century pioneers by the completion of the 62-story-tall Gateway Arch in the Jefferson National Expansion Memorial.

In 1933 Mayor Bernard F. Dickmann and civic booster Luther Ely Smith had conceived the idea of a riverfront memorial in St. Louis commemorating the city's role in westward expansion, and in 1935 President Franklin D. Roosevelt declared the land a national historic site. World War II and lack of funds delayed the project, but in 1947 the coordinators finally adopted architect Eero Saarinen's design for a huge, inverted catenary arch as a suitable monument. The MacDonald Construction Company began building the 630-foot-tall stainless steel arch in 1962. Upon completion in 1966, the Gateway Arch became the tallest monument in the world except for the Eiffel Tower.

Gateway Arch is the focal point of the Jefferson National Expansion Memorial, a $29 million forty-block area on a once slum-filled waterfront. Nearby, the Spanish Pavilion, a feature of the New York World's Fair of 1964–1965, has been reconstructed as a reminder of Spain's role in the New World.

Elsewhere in the city, Forest Park is the site of the Jefferson Memorial, housing (apart from other items) exhibits pertaining to the history of St. Louis, Missouri, and the West. They include original documents of the Louisiana Purchase.

Shreveport, Louisiana, for more than a quarter century has annually commemorated the signing of the Louisiana Purchase Treaty with the Holiday in Dixie. The 10-day celebration, which occurs in the latter part of April, has attracted as many as 250,000 persons. Festivities included are parades, balls, a queen's pageant, flower and art shows, square dancing, a yachting regatta, various competitions, musical and sports events, a carnival midway, and an air show.

DECEMBER 21

Winter Begins (Traditional Date)

Many people think of December 21 as always being the first day of winter in the north temperate zones. In fact, however, the season can also begin one day later. Most authorities give December 22 as the approximate date of the winter solstice (see December 22).

Forefathers' Day

Plymouth Rock has always symbolized America's historic role as a refuge for persecuted peoples, and as such it is a particularly cherished landmark. There, on December 21, 1620, a scouting party sent out from the *Mayflower* went ashore and explored the area of eastern Massachusetts where the second English colony in North America would be set up. The Pilgrims who settled Plymouth — unlike the colonists at the first English province in Jamestown, Virginia — were seeking freedom, not fortune. Disenchanted with the established Anglican Church of their homeland, they hoped to find a place in the New World in which they could build a model community in accord with their beliefs. Forefathers' Day, observed annually on December 21, commemorates their courageous quest.

"Pilgrim" aptly describes the little band that sailed aboard the *Mayflower* seeking a new home, but it does not indicate the group's theological principles. Specifically, they were Separatist Congregationalists. Like the Puritans who settled Massachusetts Bay in 1630, the Pilgrims were Protestants who believed that the authority of the church rested with the people gathered in each parish or congregation, and they were similarly disturbed by the rites and the hierarchical government of the Anglican church. But the Puritans and Pilgrims disagreed on the means to bring about church reform: the former sect thought the Church of England was a basically good institution from which the vestiges of Roman Catholicism might be purged; the latter group considered it an ungodly organization from which they must separate themselves to insure their continued moral integrity.

The Pilgrim congregation originally came together at Scrooby Manor in Nottinghamshire, England, shortly before 1606. Most of the 50 or 60 Scrooby worshipers were tenant farmers. They had the advantage of outstanding leaders: William Brewster was bailiff of the manor and had attended Cambridge University; John Robinson, the pastor of the congregation, had earned two degrees from the same institution and was a brilliant preacher; and young William Bradford showed promise of his value to the Pilgrim cause (see May 19).

In 1606 neighbors hostile to the religious radicalism of the Scrooby Church reported its doctrinal and procedural irregularities to the Anglican authorities. The royal officials reacted vehemently to this news, and they arrested and fined some members of the congregation in an effort to force them to conform to the practices of the Church of England. But such harassment did not lead the little band at Scrooby to abandon its beliefs. Instead the congregation decided to leave England and go to Amsterdam, which had already received groups of Separatists. The English ecclesiastical authorities at first resisted the plan, but in 1607 their opposition was overcome and Robinson led the members of his flock to their Dutch refuge.

Although Amsterdam offered the Pilgrims work and religious freedom, the English Separatists were displeased by the multiplicity of sects in that tolerant city. Robinson and the other leaders became particularly disturbed when they realized that some of the earlier Separatist immigrants to Holland had begun to accept the tenets of the Dutch Protestant Church. To keep their coreligionists free from the taint of heresy, they decided that the congregation must move again. In 1609 the Pilgrims set out for Leiden, a city with less religious controversy and diversity.

The entire Pilgrim congregation remained in Leiden for 11 years, but some of its members were discontented. Bradford cited several reasons for their unhappiness in his history *Of Plimoth Plantation:* they feared becoming involved if war erupted between Holland and Spain; they found it difficult to earn a living in Leiden; they longed to be under English rule; they believed their children were falling under the influence of the worldly Dutch; and they wanted a chance to preach their faith to others. Some members of Robinson's congregation were so dissatisfied that by 1617 they were ready to undertake another move. Since America offered the best opportunity for the Separatist band to live according to its beliefs, Deacon John Carver and Robert Cushman returned to England in 1617 to obtain permission and financial support for a settlement in the New World.

In 1620, after three years of negotiations, arrangements for the new colony were completed. Not all of Robinson's congregation wanted to settle in the New World. The majority decided to remain in Leiden, and the pastor himself agreed to stay with them. But about 35 church members were eager to go to America, and under the leadership of Bradford and Brewster they journeyed from Delftshaven to England aboard the *Speedwell* in July 1620.

In England the *Mayflower*, bearing about 65 persons, most of whom did not share either Puritan or Separatist beliefs, joined the expedition. The *Mayflower* and the *Speedwell* left Southampton for the New World in August 1620, but the *Speedwell* proved to be unseaworthy, and it was decided that the former vessel would sail alone, bearing all persons who still wished to make the trip. The *Mayflower* departed from Plymouth (where the last unsuccessful repairs on the *Speedwell* had been attempted) on September 16, 1620, with about 102 passengers and crew.

On November 19, after 64 days at sea, the Pilgrims reached the coast of Massachusetts. The passengers of the *Mayflower* had originally intended to settle on land controlled by the Virginia Company (sometimes called the London Company), from which they held a charter. But either storms, shoals, faulty navigation, sheer joy at the sight of land, or perhaps doubt about the legality of their patent caused a change in their plans. Instead of proceeding south to the territory under the jurisdiction of the Virginia Company, they decided to remain in Massachusetts, and on November 21 they anchored at what is now Provincetown on the tip of Cape Cod.

Since Massachusetts lay north of the territorial limits of the Pilgrim's charter, their leaders technically had no powers of government in the area. However, the Pilgrim Fathers knew that they would have no chance to establish their envisioned community without at least recognition of their *de facto* authority by everyone aboard the *Mayflower* — including those who did not share their religious convictions. Consequently, before anyone could disembark, they drew up a document for the self-government of the colony they were about to found. By its terms the signatories constituted themselves as a body politic and promised submission to whatever just and equal laws should thenceforth be enacted by common consent for the good of all. The agreement, signed on November 21 by 41 male passengers, was the famous *Mayflower* Compact.

The Pilgrim leaders then turned their attention to finding a suitable place for their settlement. For almost a month, parties from the *Mayflower* explored Cape Cod without success. Then, on December 21, 17 Pilgrim scouts went ashore at Plymouth. Tradition holds that they first stepped on Plymouth Rock, and this may be true, since the size, shape, and probable location of the boulder would have facilitated their landing. In any case they were impressed with the harbor and the region adjoining it.

After the scouting party returned to the *Mayflower* and disclosed its favorable findings, three more explorations were undertaken at Plymouth. These expeditions confirmed the original report, and on December 30 the Pilgrims voted to settle there. The *Mayflower*, carrying most of the colonists, then sailed southwest from Provincetown, and on January 5, 1621, arrived in Plymouth Harbor.

Life in Plymouth was not easy. Disease and exposure to the cold claimed the lives of almost half of the settlers during their first winter in Massachusetts. Nevertheless, those who survived remained steadfast in their hope of establishing a colony where they would be free to worship according to their beliefs. By the spring of 1621 the first buildings were completed and the first crops were planted.

Plymouth was never a particularly prosperous colony, and in 1690 it was absorbed by its more powerful neighbor, the Massachusetts Bay Colony, which Puritans under John Winthrop had founded to the northwest. Yet the ideals and the devotion of the Pilgrims to their beliefs have inspired all Americans. To honor the memory of the hearty Plymouth settlers, a number of organizations each year hold special Forefathers' Day observances to commemorate the landing of the first Pilgrims in Plymouth.

Forefathers' Day exercises date from 1769, when the Old Colony Club of Plymouth marked the anniversary of the Pilgrims' landing with a dinner. Guests ate Plymouth succotash and other native dishes, drank toasts in honor of the Forefathers, and heard a program consisting of appropriate speeches. The Old Colony Club's observance was held only 15 years after the New Style calendar went into effect in the American colonies, adding ten days to all dates before 1700 and 11 days to all those after 1700. According to the Old Style dating system, which had been in use in 1620, the Pilgrims arrived in Plymouth on December 11, 1620. Thus, 10 days should have been added, making the New Style date of the event December 21. But those in charge of the 1769 proceedings mistakenly added 11 days to the 1620 date and so the first observance occurred on December 22. Until the Old Colony Club disbanded for political reasons during the American Revolution, it continued its Forefathers' Day ceremonies on December 22, and when it reorganized almost a century later, about 1875, the tradition of honoring the Pilgrims on December 22 was resumed. This practice has continued in recent years. At dawn on December 22 club members, wearing top hats and led by a drummer, march down the main street of Plymouth. After firing a small cannon or salute gun, they retire to their club rooms, where they ward off the New England winter chill with breakfast and toasts to the Pilgrims.

Although the Old Colony Club celebrates Forefathers' Day on December 22, most organizations observe December 21. New Englanders who have migrated to other parts of the nation have formed New England Societies in many places, and a number of these groups take note of the anniversary of the Pilgrims' first landing at Plymouth. In addition, all the 50 state societies (plus that of the District of Columbia), that comprise the General Society of Mayflower Descendants mark the occasion. All members of these societies are descended from one or more of the passengers of the *Mayflower*, and on or near December 21, which they refer to as Compact Day, they hold special meetings to honor their forebears.

However, the main observance of Forefathers' Day is that of the Pilgrim Society, founded in 1820 by persons interested in the history of Plymouth, to fill the gap left by the dissolution of the Old Colony Club. The society holds its annual meeting on December 21, and a traditional dinner of succotash and a stew of beef, chicken, hulled corn, beans, and turnips is served. On these occasions notable speakers such as Daniel Webster, Edward Everett, Rufus Choate, and Charles Sumner have addressed the members, and William Cullen Bryant once wrote a poem to be read at a Forefathers' Day celebration. In years past, a church service and a gala ball were also included in the commemoration, but these events no longer take place.

Although Forefathers' Day is a time of special remembrance in Plymouth, the town's numerous places of historic interest attract thousands of tourists throughout the year. Plymouth Rock is, of course, the most popular site, and it has long been the object of very special feeling. For a Forefathers' Day celebration in 1774, twenty yoke of oxen dragged the top half of the rock from Plymouth Harbor to the Town Square. It remained there, at the foot of the Liberty Tree, until 1834, when it was moved several blocks north to the front lawn of Pilgrim Hall. Finally, in 1880, the top half of the rock was returned to its original waterfront position and reunited with the bottom section. A "monumental canopy" was erected over the rock, but this covering was replaced in 1921, when the National Society of Colonial Dames of America donated the columned portico that has since protected the famed boulder.

In addition to Plymouth Rock, numerous other points of interest help visitors understand the history of the Pilgrims. Pilgrim Hall, located on Main Street in Plymouth and maintained by the Pilgrim Society, contains many possessions of the *Mayflower*'s passengers and their descendants. William Bradford's chair, the swords of Captain Myles Standish, and the portrait of Governor Edward Winslow are among the many items on exhibit. The building also houses the Pilgrim Hall Library, an extensive collection of works pertaining to the history of Plymouth.

Plimoth Plantation, just outside of Plymouth, is a recreation of the Pilgrim town as it appeared in 1627. Numerous clapboard houses and a fort-meetinghouse make up the small village, and costumed guides are on hand to demonstrate many 17th century arts and crafts. Another educational replica in Plymouth is the *Mayflower II*, which is berthed at the town's harbor from mid-April through Thanksgiving week. Built in England in 1956 and sailed to the United States in 1957, the vessel is typical of 17th century merchant vessels. Exhibits and guides aboard the ship acquaint visitors with the difficult circumstances the Pilgrims must have encountered during their transatlantic crossing. Plimoth Plantation, a nonprofit educational foundation, owns and operates both the Plantation and *Mayflower II*.

Monuments abound in Plymouth, but none is more impressive than the National Monument to the Forefathers. The 81-foot statue of a heroic figure of Faith, pointing toward heaven, stands on the top of a hill behind the town. Dedicated in 1889, the monument also depicts in marble bas-relief the Pilgrims' departure from Holland, the signing of the Mayflower Compact, their landing at Plymouth, and their treaty with Massasoit, the chief of the Wampanoags (see March 22).

Special anniversaries of the *Mayflower*'s voyage have prompted large-scale celebrations. On the 350th anniversary, in 1970, festivities were held in both England and America. Plymouth, England, scheduled numerous events such as ox and ram roasts, football games, fireworks, folk sings, and parades during the five-month interval beginning in May 1970 that was set aside to mark the anniversary. In Plymouth, Massachusetts, commemorative exercises featured exhibitions, tours of historic places, parades, and musical, dramatic, and religious performances. The program began in September 1970 with a mammoth four-hour parade of military units, marching bands, historical floats, and fife and drum corps, which brought an estimated 100,000 visitors to the small town. Festivities continued for more than a year and concluded on November 27, 1971, the 350th anniversary of the first thanksgiving.

Feast of St. Thomas the Apostle

The Feast of St. Thomas the Apostle is marked on December 21 by Episcopalian, Lutheran, and some other Protestant churches. Until the reform of the Roman Catholic calendar went into effect, Roman Catholics also celebrated the feast on that date; more recently, however, they have venerated St. Thomas on July 3, reputedly the date of the transfer of his relics. Eastern Orthodox churches celebrate the feast on October 6, or 13 days later where the Julian calendar is used.

Thomas was one of the 12 Apostles chosen by

Jesus Christ. He may have been a twin, since he was called Didymus, which in Greek means "twin." Beyond that, very little is known about his life, but some idea of Thomas can be obtained from the New Testament accounts.

Although Thomas, like many of his contemporaries, was confused about the mission of Jesus Christ, he was fiercely loyal to his master, as is shown in the story of events preceding Jesus' raising Lazarus from the dead. When Lazarus died in Bethany, Jesus set off for that village even though the people there were hostile to him and "were but now seeking to stone" Jesus, as the Apostles quickly pointed out, hoping to deter him. But when he would not be deterred, as the Gospel story says, "Thomas, called the Twin, said to his fellow disciples, 'Let us also go, that we may die with him' " (John 11:5–16).

In so saying, Thomas indicated that he was ready to die for Jesus, even though he still did not understand his master's actions or reasons. Thomas's willingness to admit he did not understand elicited from Jesus one of the most widely repeated biblical quotations. It is related that at the Last Supper Jesus had said to the Apostles gathered with him:

"Let not your hearts be troubled; believe in God, believe also in me. In my Father's house are many rooms; if it were not so, would I have told you that I go to prepare a place for you? And when I go and prepare a place for you, I will come again and will take you to myself, that where I am you may be also. And you know the way where I am going."

The narrative continues as Thomas, still uncomprehending, asks outright: "Lord, we do not know where you are going; how can we know the way?" Jesus replied, "I am the way, and the truth, and the life; no one comes to the Father, but by me." (John 14: 1–6).

This Apostle Thomas has been dubbed Doubting Thomas because of New Testament accounts of events that happened shortly after the Resurrection. Mary Magdalene and the Apostles Peter and John had discovered the empty tomb of Jesus in the early hours of the Sunday morning after Good Friday. On the evening of that first Easter, Peter and John had gathered with the other Apostles in a closed room to discuss the puzzling events. Suddenly Jesus appeared in the room with them, showed them the wounds in his hands and side, and spoke with them. However, according to the report of the events given in the Gospel of John (20:24–28) "Thomas . . . was not with them, when Jesus came. So the other disciples told him, 'We have seen the Lord.' But he said to them, 'Unless I see in his hands the print of the nails, and place my finger in the mark of the nails, and place my hands in

his side, I will not believe.' Eight days later, his disciples were again in the house, and Thomas was with them. The doors were shut, but Jesus came and stood among them, and said, 'Peace be with you.' Then he said to Thomas, 'Put your finger here, and see my hands; and put out your hand, and place it in my side; do not be faithless, but believing.' Thomas answered him, 'My Lord and my God!' ' "

Following the Resurrection, the Ascension of Christ, and their receiving of the Holy Spirit at Pentecost, the Apostles all stayed and preached for a while in Jerusalem. After a time many of them left Jerusalem to preach to people of other nations, as Jesus had commissioned them to do. According to tradition, Thomas traveled east, spreading the gospel to the regions between the Caspian Sea and the Persian Gulf, eventually reaching India. To this day, in southwest India, along the Malabar Coast, there are people who call themselves Thomas Christians, or Christians of St. Thomas and claim Thomas as the founder of their church. Many of these people live in Kerala, the smallest state in India, where one-third of the population is Christian.

Although there is little historical confirmation of the events of Thomas's life or death, it is thought that he was martyred in Madras, in southeast India. He is considered the patron saint of the East Indies. Thomas may have been a house builder or carpenter before, or even after, his apostleship. He is often depicted holding a carpenter's rule and square and is the patron saint of architects.

Veiled Prophet Ball and Parade in St. Louis

This is a movable event. See note on page xxvi.

For almost a century, the Veiled Prophet organization of St. Louis, Missouri, staged an annual ball and parade in the city in early fall. In 1970 it changed this tradition by scheduling its elaborate ball on Monday, December 21, while holding its colorful parade on Saturday, September 26. Both events have become very much a part of St. Louis life over the years, the ball as a private affair attended only by socially prominent guests, the parade as a gala spectacle viewed by half a million onlookers.

The history and membership of the Veiled Prophet organization, as well as many details behind the two public events it sponsors, are deliberately wrapped in mystery. But a few facts are known to the general public. On March 20, 1878, a group of about 20 influential businessmen of St. Louis met at the Lindell Hotel to consider what could be done to encourage civic pride and promote tourism. In view of the widespread mood of post–Civil War despondency and the additional deterrent of a yellow fever epidemic raging in the Mississippi Valley, they were especially interested in finding some livelier way than the usual trade procession to promote the annual October Mechanical and Agricultural Fair. Several of them had just returned from the New Orleans Mardi Gras on Shrove Tuesday of 1878. The lavish masques, processions, and mystic organizations there suggested the possibility of similar festivities in St. Louis.

The civic-minded citizens were drawn to the idea of the mystic pageant, which had been so highly successful not only in New Orleans but also in other cities such as Mobile, Alabama. Charles E. Slayback, a leading grain broker who had formerly resided in New Orleans and was still a member of the Mistick Krewe of Comus there, obtained the consent of those present to purchase $8,000 worth of floats from his fellow members in the mystic organization. His brother, Alonzo William Slayback, proposed that an annual pageant and ball be presided over by His Mysterious Majesty, the Veiled Prophet of Khorassan.

The story of this powerful and mysterious ruler was told in the first part of a then very popular poetical tale, *Lalla Rookh,* which had been written in 1817 by the Irish poet Thomas Moore. Moore's inspiration for the Veiled Prophet episode came from the real-life figure of Hashim ibn-Hakim, surnamed al-Mokanna, or "the Veiled," who was the founder of an Arab sect in the province of Khorassan, Persia, in the eighth century. The religious leader had worn a silver gauze veil to conceal his hideously disfigured face. He had convinced his followers, however, that the veil hid magnificent goodness and was intended "to dim the lustre of his face."

Moore placed the veiled prophet and chief in a luxurious palace, where as a villainous religious fanatic he lures men from the path of righteousness into damnation. His high priestess, Zelica, has gone mad because of the death of her soldier-lover and has therefore become a wild-eyed zealot. Moore concluded the poem with a historically accurate account of the Veiled Prophet's death. When Sultan Mahadi's troops marched against the prophet's stronghold, he poisoned all his followers at a banquet before committing suicide himself.

As the hero of the St. Louis festivities, this unsavory Veiled Prophet is annually transformed into a wondrous but still mysterious monarch. Ruling benignly over a Court of Love and Beauty, he dons a veil only to keep his identity secret and turn attention from his own person to the events over which he reigns.

When first proposed, the theme and goal of the proposed Veiled Prophet Order aroused keen interest in St. Louis. Some 200 members of the secret society were initiated into the organization during the summer of 1878. To be eligible for membership, a candidate had to be a resident of St. Louis, over 25, of good character, and willing to assist on any project. A secret committee then considered his application, rigidly examining his personal qualities and business or professional standing.

The First Magnificent Midnight Parade and Grand Tableaux and Ball took place on the Tuesday after the first Monday in October — October 8, 1878. The Veiled Prophet entered his kingdom with fanfare, arriving on an ornate Mississippi River barge accompanied by his boisterous krewe. Together with four masked courtiers of his immediate entourage — two high priests, an almoner, and a herald — he led the parade through the city center. The 17 crude floats, pulled by horses, centered on the theme of the world's advancement, with such titles as the Glacial Period, Primitive Life, Industry, and Wealth. Oil torches with tin reflectors, supplemented by Roman candles, supplied the illumination. Enterprising businessmen along the route also burned Greek fire — an incendiary material used in ancient and medieval warfare — when the procession passed their stores.

At the end of the parade, a group of men welcomed His Mysterious Majesty, the Veiled Prophet, and escorted him to the gala ball in the Merchant's Exchange Building. On October 9, 1878, an editorial in the St. Louis *Evening Post* commented on the "magnificent and unqualified" success of the Veiled Prophet's first appearance.

Ever since, the prophet has graced St. Louis with a yearly visit, with the exception of two years during World War I and four years during World War II. His ball and parade rapidly increased in popularity. Their fascination spread far beyond the city limits. As early as 1880, for example, 595 railroad coaches were needed to transport visitors to St. Louis, and in the following year, out-of-towners numbered about 64,500.

Except in date, the ball and parade have changed little in essential character over the years. From 1878 until 1923 the two events took place on the same evening in early October. For the next 26 years the ball was scheduled on the evening following the parade, and from 1950 through 1969 on the evening preceding it. In 1963 the ball and parade were shifted from midweek to Friday and Saturday.

In 1970 the Veiled Prophet organization separated the two events, holding the parade

— as it remains today — on the last Saturday in September, as part of a new civic Fall Festival. The ball was shifted to an evening close to Christmas, a time when the young women invited would be likely to be home from college for the holidays.

The Veiled Prophet festivities have of course changed with the times. Beginning in 1909, the parade floats, although still drawn by horses, were built on flatbed trolley cars and illuminated with overhead trolley wires. They became motor drawn only in 1946, when it proved impossible to obtain the 100 horses that would have been needed. At the same time, the floats were equipped with specially built generating plants to provide electricity for the thousands of multicolored lights. At first, prominent artists painted sketches for each year's floats, which were then constructed by the Veiled Prophets' own artisans. Starting in 1967, however, designs have come from a competition held in the city's high schools each spring.

The central themes chosen for illustration have varied greatly since 1878. Many have focused on St. Louis and its history.They have included, for example, The Four Seasons, The New Spirit of St. Louis, and, in 1976, the bicentennial of US independence, A Salute to America.

In the past, the 20-odd floats were usually manned by the prophet's madcap krewe — leading business, industrial, and professional men of the city, costumed and masked to conceal their identity. But the flavor of the parade has changed somewhat with the introduction of movie and television personalities, beauty queens, and local and out-of-town marching bands; moreover, the Veiled Prophet himself no longer makes an appearance. In 1970, the parade was expanded to include civic and community floats as well.

Like the parade, the annual ball has grown during its century-long history to become the city's biggest social event. In 1878 and for a few years afterwards, the Veiled Prophet presided alone at the gala occasion, choosing a "belle of the ball" for the first dance. It was not until 1885 that the name of his partner was publicly announced. In that year she was Virginia Joy. In 1887 President and Mrs. Grover Cleveland were present at the ball. Mrs. Cleveland sat on a throne beside the mysterious monarch, and it was probably her presence that suggested the selection of a Queen of Love and Beauty. In 1894 the first queen to be officially crowned was Hester Bates Laughlin, on whose head was placed a copy of the state crown of Queen Victoria of England. Fashioned of gold and studded with brilliants and imitation emeralds and ru-

bies, it was set on an ermine band. In 1895 the queen received a gold crown set with real jewels, a custom that continued until 1909, when the queen chosen was presented with a platinum crown. It was topped with an egret-like plume and set with sapphires, diamonds, and oriental pearls. Today's queens still receive platinum crowns, which vary in design only slightly from year to year. Since the early 20th century, the queen has been allowed to keep her crown as a souvenir.

In the course of the 20th century, the Veiled Prophet ball has come to be the occasion at which debutantes are presented to society. The queen is accorded "regal honors" during her yearlong reign over the city until the prophet's return the following year. In 1923 at least 100 maids and ladies of honor constituted her court and a guard of honor — then World War I veterans — was added. In 1909 the ball moved from the Merchant's Exchange to the Coliseum, then to Kiel Auditorium in 1936. The Queen of Love and Beauty was invited to a supper following the ball for the first time in 1909, and since then the formal queen's supper has become an integral part of the traditional ceremonies.

In 1970 the ball was held on Monday, December 21. Although no longer the opening event of the St. Louis social season, the formal ball was as lavish as ever. Kiel Auditorium was transformed into the regal throne room of the court of Khorassan. Attended by thousands of guests, the festivities started at 7:30 P.M. with a one-hour concert of popular and semiclassical music by the Veiled Prophet Symphony Orchestra. At 8:30 P.M. past Veiled Prophet queens, wearing their crowns, were escorted to a special box. The prophet's boisterous krewe — dressed in masks and costumes — entertained the audience with rollicking pantomimes and dances. After their crowd-pleasing capers, the traditional promenade began.

First the ladies of honor (wives of prominent St. Louis residents) and maids of honor (debutantes) made the stately walk down the length of the hall and took their seats on the terraces on either side of two thrones. The retiring queen, the guard of honor, and the eagerly awaited Veiled Prophet, dressed in flowing blue, gold, and white robes and a golden helmet crown, followed. Four special maids of honor were summoned by the prophet's four herald-trumpeters to enter and receive diadems from His Mysterious Majesty.

Next, the curtains of the grand entrance parted to reveal the 1970 queen. Clad in a white gown with a long train and carrying a huge bouquet of some 400 orchids, the queen made a deep curtsy to acknowledge her subjects' acclaim and promenaded to the dais at the far end of Kiel Auditorium. There, having skillfully executed a difficult obeisance before the enthroned monarch, she received the crown and the gold scepter passed on by the retiring queen. The elaborate ceremonies closed with a courtly recessional as members of the royal court departed. The remaining guests danced until nearly midnight.

Shortly before that hour, the queen and her four special maids reappeared in the foyer of the Chase-Park Plaza Hotel. After pausing for photographs and radio and television interviews, they took their places of honor in a receiving line under green moiré arches dotted with silver sparkles and tiny orchids. At midnight, emissaries of the Veiled Prophet escorted the five guests of honor along a crimson carpet to the hotel's mammoth Khorassan Room for the queen's supper. The imposing dinner for some 1,500 persons was, as usual, held to honor the young women presented that evening (who attended the supper with escorts), as well as members and guests of the Veiled Prophet organization.

As an innovation in 1970, the maids of honor, formerly grouped for the supper at the foot of the queen's dais, were seated at special tables scattered throughout the Khorassan Room and marked by silver and pink umbrellas hung with mirrored tassels. The four special maids occupied places of honor next to the queen, who, with her two escorts, was royally enthroned under a pagoda-style silk awning decorated with purple and gold ostrich plumes. By tradition, the Veiled Prophet does not appear at the supper. The party lasted far into the early hours of the morning as the young people danced to the music of a rock group and relaxed in the pseudo-oriental splendor provided by a "night in Khorassan."

DECEMBER 22

Winter Begins

In the United States and the north temperate zones generally, winter starts, as most sources put it, "about December 22." Actually the fourth and coldest season of the year begins on either December 21 or December 22. The precise moment at which the sun reaches the winter solstice, formally signaling the change of season, varies slightly each year as a result of the many oscillations the earth undergoes during its annual elliptical journey around the sun and its daily rotation on its axis.

Like the other three seasons, winter has an exact astronomical beginning. The ecliptic, the plane in which the sun seems to revolve around the earth and in which the earth actually revolves around the sun, is divided into four equal 90° sections, each having a specific starting point. Whereas spring and autumn commence at the vernal and autumnal equinoxes respectively, winter and summer begin at their respective solstices. The winter solstice (Latin *solstitium* meaning solstice, from *sol* meaning sun and *sistere* meaning to stand still) is situated midway between the autumnal equinox, the start of autumn (see September 23), and the vernal equinox, the start of spring (see March 21). The amount of time the sun requires to traverse the 90° section from the winter solstice to the vernal equinox is known as the season of winter.

Winter is also said to begin when the sun enters the 10th sign of the zodiac — Capricorn, "the Goat" (see Appendix, The Zodiac). This assertion is, in fact, anachronistic. At the time of Hipparchus, the second century B.C. Greek astronomer who laid the basis of the zodiacal system, the winter solstice began at Capricorn; however, precession, as the retrograde motion of the equinoctial points on the ecliptic is called, has caused each of the 12 constellations of the zodiac to move 30° backwards during the course of the past 2,000 years. The winter solstice is now located in the constellation Sagittarius or "the Archer." Only at the completion of a 25,800-year cycle will it once again be situated in Capricorn.

In the Northern Hemisphere the sun shines most weakly at the time of the winter solstice because it then attains its southernmost position in the heavens. At its maximum southern declination (a term used by astronomers to correspond with terrestrial latitude), the sun extends its rays across and beyond the earth's South Pole as far as −23°27'; similarly, its rays fall 23°27' short of the North Pole, striking only the near side of the Arctic Circle. At the same time, the sun has a longitude of 270°. Thereafter for a few days the sun seemingly "stands still" — so much so that the times of sunrise and sunset differ imperceptibly and the days appear to be of equal length. During the remainder of winter, the sun's south declination continuously diminishes until the vernal equinox, at which time the sun reaches both a longitude of 0° and a declination of 0°, thereby completing the yearly cycle of the seasons.

Winter is the shortest season in the Northern Hemisphere. About January 2, when the earth reaches its perihelion (the point in its orbit that is nearest the sun), it is moving at its greatest speed; when it reaches its aphelion (most distant point from the sun) about July 6, it is traveling at its slowest. Both the orbit's elliptical shape and the laws of motion cause this variation in velocity during the earth's yearly orbit. In North America, the season includes the months of December, January, and February; the astronomical divisions do not, however, always coincide with meteorological conditions, and in some parts of the continent November and March have virtually winter climates. In Great Britain, winter is commonly held to include November, December, and January.

The difference in the seasons, especially the variation in weather, is due to the 23½ ° tilt of the earth's axis and to its elliptical revolution around the sun. About December 22, the North Pole is inclined directly away from the sun. Since the sun's rays are slanted, the earth's atmosphere and surface are exposed to a low amount of solar radiation daily. Consequently, temperatures are cold, even freezing. The most extreme cold wave generally occurs at about the beginning of February. In the Southern Hemisphere, as the result of the reverse movement of the South Pole, the seasons are also reversed: astronomical winter begins there about June 21 and ends about September 23.

Winter has a distinct character in the Northern Hemisphere above the Tropic of Cancer. As the season of dormancy, darkness and cold, it greatly impressed the ancients, who regarded this period of the year as a time of crisis during which the deities of the upper world struggled against the spirits of chaos and evil to assure the return of light, warmth, and fertility. Many pre-Christian seasonal traditions marked the winter solstice, as people of various cultures observed what they deemed to be a significant religious occasion. Huge bonfires were an integral part of elaborate solar rites. As the days slowly lengthened and gave promise of eventual spring, a less solemn and more festive mood ensued. The Romans feasted at the Saturnalia (see December); worshipers of the Persian sun-god Mithras celebrated December 25 as the *dies solis invicti nati*, "birthday of the invincible sun." The date of Christmas was probably fixed arbitrarily for this same day because it coincided with and offered competition to these pagan festivities (see December 25).

The winter solstice played an important role not only in mythology and religion, but also in art and literature. Early basilicas and medieval cathedrals, for example, were frequently adorned with symbolic representations of the seasons and of the individual months; some of the carved stone scenes depicting the calendar year show winter as a season of contrasts between the laborious preparations for the rough wintry days ahead and the Christmastide revelries.

James Oglethorpe's Birthday

The American continents attracted Europeans in the 16th, 17th, and 18th centuries for a variety of reasons. Some sought religious freedom, some wanted high adventure, and some were in search of an easy fortune. But none of these motives brought James Oglethorpe, the founder of Georgia, to the New World; Oglethorpe came to America imbued with the altruistic desire to found a colony in which the downtrodden and oppressed debtors of England might prosper and become useful and productive citizens.

James Edward Oglethorpe, the son of Sir Theophilus and Lady Eleanor Wall Oglethorpe, was born on December 22, 1696, in London. The future philanthropist was educated at Eton and attended Corpus Christi College of Oxford University before abandoning his formal education in 1715 to seek adventure on the European continent. Oglethorpe passed some time in Paris during 1716, served as aide-de-camp to Prince Eugene of Savoy during his campaign against the Turks in 1717, and spent 1718 and much of 1719 in Saint-Germain, France, and in Urbino, Italy, at the quasi court of James Stuart, called the Old Pretender, the son of exiled King James II of England. In 1719 he returned to England, where he took up residence at the family's estate at Godalming, Surrey.

Continuing a tradition of parliamentary service established by his father and two older brothers, Oglethorpe won election to the House of Commons in 1722. He served as a member of Parliament for 32 years. During that time he consistently supported programs that strengthened the British Empire and became increasingly involved with the problem of penal reform, a need for which he first became aware of when a friend was placed in debtors' prison and died there of smallpox, amid appalling conditions.

Service as chairman of a parliamentary committee investigating prison conditions in England further convinced Oglethorpe of the deplorable state of that nation's penal system. The large number of persons who were in jail because of their inability to pay small debts particularly horrified him, and the reports of his committee in 1729 and 1730 resulted in limited penal reform and in the release of several thousand debtors from confinement. But Oglethorpe realized that it was not enough merely to set these debtors free. He believed that the impoverished needed an opportunity to begin a new life, and he knew that such a chance was not to be had in England in 1730 since unemployment was already a major problem. Thus, as a means of bettering the condition of the oppressed, he conceived of the bold plan of establishing a new colony in America as a haven for debtors.

Oglethorpe's humane proposal coincided with

the designs of the British government. During the first decades of the 18th century, the Spanish, who controlled Florida, had been a continuing threat to the safety of Britain's southern colonies. To protect these settlements a proposal had been made as early as 1717 to create a new colony that would act as a buffer between South Carolina and Florida; Oglethorpe's desire to establish a new settlement in America gave the government a chance to make this plan a reality.

A parliamentary charter of June 9 (O.S.) or June 20 (N.S.), 1732, named Oglethorpe and 19 other associates "Trustees for establishing the colony of Georgia in America." According to the provisions of this document, the trustees were given control of all the area between the Savannah and the Altamaha rivers extending westward from the sources of these rivers to the Pacific Ocean. But unlike previous British colonial charters, Georgia's charter did not allow the trustees to own land in the new colony or in any other way profit from the venture. Instead they were to hold the colony as a trust for 21 years for the purpose of securing its future and then at the end of that period return control of Georgia to the crown.

An intensive campaign in the summer and fall of 1732 to raise money for the new colony proved so successful that by November 1732 the first settlers were able to embark on what has been called "the greatest social and philanthropic experiment of the age." Oglethorpe himself led the first band of about 35 families across the Atlantic. Landing at Charleston, South Carolina, on January 13, 1733, the Georgia colonists then proceeded southward and on February 12 arrived at the site of Savannah.

Under Oglethorpe's leadership the Georgia colonists maintained friendly relations with the Native Americans. Even before the building of Savannah was completed, Oglethorpe sought out the leaders of the Creek people who inhabited the region. The Englishman and the chiefs came together in Savannah in May 1733 and at this meeting made an agreement by which the Creeks sold a portion of their lands to the newcomers and promised to cease dealing with the Spaniards; in return, Oglethorpe acquiesced in establishing certain joint trade regulations with the Creeks.

Oglethorpe administered the colony for most of its first two years. During that time the population of Georgia grew rapidly — and not merely because of the influx of English debtors. Neither Oglethorpe nor any of the other trustees had wished to restrict immigration to the colony. Thus, in the first years of its existence, Georgia attracted considerable numbers of non-English dissidents — among them Lutherans from Austria and Moravians from Germany, as well as a group of Scottish Highland Presbyterians.

Oglethorpe returned to England late in 1734 to secure additional funds, but he revisited Georgia in 1735–1736 and again from 1738 to 1743. In keeping with the colony's function as a buffer against Spanish attack, he built fortifications in 1736, including what is now known as Fort Frederica National Monument, on St. Simons Island at the mouth of the Altamaha River; he also instituted a program of military training. In addition, Oglethorpe made some attempts at city planning — a fact that accounts for the profusion of green parks, open spaces, and carefully laid-out squares in present-day Savannah. But while he was occupied with these duties, Oglethorpe never lost sight of his primary purpose, and at all times he was determined to transform the settlers into productive members of society.

During much of his last stay in Georgia, Oglethorpe was occupied with the War of Jenkins' Ear between Great Britain and Spain. Among other things, he led an unsuccessful expedition against Spanish-controlled Florida in 1740, and at the battle of Bloody Marsh, near Fort Frederica, in 1742, he crushed the Spanish counterattack against Georgia. The latter defeat ended Spanish attempts to control Georgia and insured the colony's survival.

Georgia successfully served as a buffer between Britain's southern colonies and Spanish Florida, but the colony never fulfilled its trustees' dream that it would become a place in which disadvantaged persons might enjoy useful and productive lives. Much of this failure was caused by the trustees. In planning the new colony, they mapped out a Utopian blueprint: they limited the amount of land each settler might hold to 50 acres and overlooked the fact that such an area of the Georgia pine barrens was inadequate to support a family; they nobly banned slavery and made Georgia incapable of competing with neighboring slaveholding colonies; and they encouraged the production of such items as silk, failing to comprehend that these were unsuited to the Georgia climate. During the 1740s the trustees were forced to make several important modifications in their original plans, but as a trusteeship Georgia never prospered, and in 1752 — one year before their charter expired — the trustees returned control of the colony to Britain.

In 1743, as the failure of Georgia under the trusteeship was becoming increasingly apparent, Oglethorpe went back to England. Shortly after his return he faced a court-martial, but the charges against him were found to be "frivolous . . . and without foundation." He never returned to Georgia.

In 1745 Oglethorpe gained the rank of major general but was court-martialed — and acquitted — on charges of inept leadership in a campaign to put down a rebellion in the north in that same year. He was made a lieutenant general in 1746 and was breveted a full general in 1756. He lived the remainder of his life in England, surrounded by such notable friends as Samuel Johnson, James Boswell, Oliver Goldsmith, Horace Walpole, and Edmund Burke.

James Oglethorpe died at the age of 88 on June 30, 1785. He was buried in the chancel of Cranham Church, Essex, since burned and supplanted by a new church edifice. The body of Oglethorpe, with that of his wife, remains in the original vault beneath the church.

Oglethorpe University, named for the founder of Georgia, was established in 1835. It is situated in DeKalb County, just north of Atlanta. Also bearing the name of Oglethorpe is the General Oglethorpe Oak, a splendid specimen of Georgia's state tree, located in Darien, Georgia.

DECEMBER 23

Federal Reserve System Established

The Federal Reserve System, the central bank of the United States — actually comprising 12 regional banks coordinated by a central board of governors in the nation's capital — was established by the Owen-Glass Federal Reserve Act, which became law on December 23, 1913. Creation of the Federal Reserve was prompted by flaws in the then existing National Banking System (see February 25). Among these were lack of a central bank, inelasticity of both currency and credit, dispersed legal reserves that were sometimes subject to speculative use, and inadequate check-clearing facilities. As originally established and as modified since — particularly by laws enacted during the banking crisis of the early 1930s — the Federal Reserve System is designed to serve as the fiscal agent and depository of the federal government; to integrate and effectively supervise the nation's banking system (previously composed of thousands of independent banks functioning in widely divergent ways); to provide an elastic currency whose supply expands and contracts with changing business needs; to rediscount commercial paper; and, by controlling the availability of credit, to promote sound economic conditions that foster orderly growth, stability of the dollar, and a long-range balance in international payments.

In order to favorably affect the flow of money and credit in the United States, the Federal Reserve, or Fed, as it is popularly known, uses its authority to fix reserve requirements for its member banks, establish discount rates, and set margin requirements.

Establishment of the Federal Reserve System, which was simply superimposed on the old National Banking System, marked the beginning of a new era in the financial history of the nation. National banks were required to join immediately by subscribing 3 percent of their capital and surplus for stock in the Federal Reserve System and holding an additional 3 percent subject to call. (Specifically, a national bank bought stock of the federal reserve bank in whose district it was located.) For state banks, joining or not joining the Federal Reserve System was a matter of choice. Many did, by meeting certain basic conditions, which also applied to the national banks. These had to do with meeting minimum capital requirements; maintaining — on deposit with the regional federal reserve banks — legally required reserves against deposits; adhering to certain limitations on loans; and submitting to examination by federal reserve banks.

After enactment of the Owen-Glass Act on December 23, 1913, the Federal Reserve System actually began to operate, under supervision of the seven-member board of governors appointed by the President, on the following November 14. The 12 federal reserve bank cities and their district numbers are 1 — Boston; 2 — New York; 3 — Philadelphia; 4 — Cleveland; 5 — Richmond; 6 — Atlanta; 7 — Chicago; 8 — St. Louis; 9 — Minneapolis; 10 — Kansas City; 11 — Dallas; and 12 — San Francisco.

Today, the federal reserve notes that the system is empowered to issue constitute the country's chief form of paper money. They are issued in denominations of $1, $5, $10, $20, $50, $100, $500, $1,000, $5,000 and $10,000, though the $100 note is the highest denomination printed since 1945 as there is little demand for the larger notes.

Other forms of paper money that are still in use to a lesser extent than the federal reserve notes are US notes and silver certificates. Today, however, US notes received on any account by the treasurer of the United States are reissued in the denomination of $5 only. Silver certificates, though still in general circulation — principally in denominations of $1, $5, and $10 — have not been issued since October 1964.

All of the nation's money is manufactured by the US Treasury Department, either through the Bureau of the Mint, which produces coins (see April 2), or through the Bureau of Engraving and Printing. The latter facility, at 14th and C streets, S.W., in Washington, D.C., prints paper money at an average rate worth $40 million a day, in addition to turning out US stamps and bonds.

The Federal Reserve System also maintains a nationwide check-clearing and collection system (supplementing the clearinghouse operations within individual cities), which is of great practical convenience to individual bank depositors and largely eliminates the necessity for shipping currency between banks, since most of the nation's enormous daily clearing operations can be done on paper.

Hanukkah

This is a movable event. See note on page xxvi.

Hanukkah, the Jewish festival also known as the Feast of Dedication and the Festival of Lights, begins on the 25th day of the Hebrew month Kislev (November or December), which fell on December 23 in 1970 (though the actual observance, as with all Jewish holidays, began at sundown of the preceding day). The holiday continues for eight days, as does Sukkot, on which the original celebration of Hanukkah was modeled. The observance of Hanukkah was instituted in the year 165 B.C. by Judah the Maccabee at the successful conclusion of his three-year war against the Syrians, culminating in the rededication of the Temple in Jerusalem.

The Temple had been desecrated as part of a program of forced Hellenization undertaken by the Syrian-Greek king Antiochus IV Epiphanes. The efforts of Antiochus to suppress the Jewish religion and to institute pagan worship were resisted by a small group of Jewish nationalists originally led by Mattathias of Modin and, after his death, by his eldest son, Judah the Maccabee. Using guerrilla tactics, they defeated Antiochus's large army and regained control of the Temple. After the Temple had been cleansed, the rededication of the altar — on the 25th of Kislev — was celebrated with sacrifices and songs of praise — *Hallel* — similar to those sung on Sukkot, and the Maccabees decreed that a similar celebration was to take place each year, beginning on the anniversary of the rededication.

After the final destruction of the Temple by the Romans in A.D. 70 and the complete loss of Jewish national independence, the spiritual aspect of this holiday was emphasized. According to a rabbinic tradition, the custom of observing Hanukkah for eight days by kindling one light on the first night and one more each successive night arose from the miracle which was supposed to have occurred at the rededication of the Temple. This story says that when Judah went to rekindle the eternal light that was supposed to burn continuously in the Temple (today all synagogues have a *Ner Tamid* or "Eternal Light," hanging in front of the Ark) he could find only one small cruse of consecrated oil that had not been desecrated by the Greeks.

This small cruse of oil, only enough to burn for one day, actually lasted eight days, until new oil could be prepared and consecrated.

Today, Jews still observe Hanukkah by lighting one candle on the first night, two on the second, three on the third, and so on until on the last night all eight candles are burning. The candles are placed in a menorah, or candelabrum, which contains holders for nine candles. The ninth candle is called the *shammash*, the servant, and is used to light the other candles. The lighted menorah may be placed in a window so that passersby in the street can see it. The menorah stands as a symbol of freedom, of the Jews' love of liberty, and of their willingness to fight for their freedom of conscience in what was the first recorded war for religious freedom. The Hanukkah lights also symbolize the light of faith, which continues to grow even if only a small group of believers remains.

When the candles are lit each night a special blessing is recited:

Blessed art Thou, O Lord our God, King of the Universe, who hast sanctified us by Thy commandments and commanded us to kindle the Hanukkah light.
Blessed art Thou, O Lord our God, King of the Universe, who performed wondrous deeds for our fathers in ancient days at this season.

Because it is forbidden to do any work by the light of the Hanukkah candles, the time during which the candles burn is usually spent singing songs and playing games. Most special Hanukkah games involve the *dreidel*, a four-sided top with one of the Hebrew letters *nun*, *gimel*, *hay*, and *shin* on each side. The letters stand for the saying: "Nes gadol haya sham," "A great miracle happened there." In Israel today, the last word of the saying has been changed to *Po*, so that it reads "A great miracle happened here."

Although Hanukkah is only a minor Jewish holiday (except for the brief time when the candles are burning there is no prohibition against working) and although historically speaking for Jews it is a relatively late holiday, it has recently become important because of the establishment of the State of Israel. The creation of Israel has led to a renewed stress on the national aspects of Hanukkah: the liberation that the Jews won, and the fact that it was a victory of the few over the many and of the weak over the strong. At Hanukkah in Israel, large menorahs are lighted on top of public buildings, and a special torch is carried from the village of Modin, where the Maccabees' revolt first started, to Jerusalem. In New York City a Hanukkah Festival of Lights is held by Jews each year to raise money toward the support of Israel.

Among some people, Hanukkah has also received more emphasis than it once had because it happens to fall at the same time of year as the Christian observance of Christmas. The proximity to Christmas has tended to bring stress on the festive part of Hanukkah, especially the exchanging of gifts. Children traditionally receive Hanukkah *gelt*, or money, and other gifts. Parties are held at which the special holiday food *latkes* (potato pancakes) are eaten.

Although Hanukkah is celebrated mainly at home among family and friends, special synagogue services are held as well. These services include reading from the First and Second Books of the Maccabees, in which the story of the revolt is chronicled. The Torah reading, Numbers 7:1 through 8:4, which describes the dedication offering of the princes of Israel, and the singing of Hallel, emphasize the spiritual victory of the Maccabees — the importance of religious liberty and of the survival of Judaism.

Joseph Smith Jr.'s Birthday

Joseph Smith Jr., the founder of the Church of Jesus Christ of Latter-Day Saints, unofficially known as the Mormon Church, was born in Sharon, Vermont, on December 23, 1805. He was the fourth child of a farmer, Joseph Smith Sr., and Lucy Mack Smith. The child was born into an insecure world, and he never escaped in his lifetime of 38 years. By his fifth year, his impoverished family had moved three times. They settled in Palmyra, New York, in or about 1816 and after living there a short time purchased a tract of land a few miles farther south, near Manchester. Owing to their financial straits, the boy's education was limited to reading, writing, and elementary arithmetic.

In the early 19th century, western New York was the scene of intense religious revivalism. Evangelists of a multitude of sects competed for the attention and loyalty of a rough and roving frontier population. This Pentecostal period was one of the most fertile in US history for the emergence of prophets, but only one of them was destined for lasting fame. A century after his death, Joseph Smith had a million followers who held his name sacred and his mission divine.

The road that led Joseph Smith to the career of prophet and church founder began in the spring of 1820, when the 14-year-old boy, always a dedicated student of the Bible, was uncertain about which denomination to join. He later wrote:

In the midst of this war of words and tumult of opinions, I often said to myself: "What is to be done? Who of all these parties are right, or are they all wrong together? If any of them be right, which is it, and how shall I know it?"

He searched the Scriptures and discovered a passage from the book of James (1:15): "If any of you lack wisdom, let him ask of God, that giveth to all men liberally, and upbraideth not; and it shall be given him."

Smith then retired to a wooded spot near his home and prayed for divine guidance. According to his account, he beheld a pillar of light over his head, from which appeared two personages floating in the air. One of them called him by name and pointed to the other saying, "This is my Beloved Son. Hear Him." Overcoming his fear, the young boy asked which denomination held the truth and was told not to affiliate himself with any, for "they draw near to me with their lips but their hearts are far from me."

On September 21, 1823, Joseph Smith had a second vision, in which he said, an angel named Moroni appeared to him, revealing the hiding place of some golden tablets containing the history of the ancient people of America and the fullness of the Gospel of Jesus Christ. The next day, according to Smith's account, the angel guided him to a hill, which, he was told, was anciently called Cumorah and which was located between Palmyra and Manchester, not far from the Smith home, where he found the plates but was not allowed to take them away with him. On the anniversary of this date, September 22, for the next three years he visited the hill and saw the plates, but was told each time that it was too soon to reveal them to the world.

On January 18, 1827, Joseph Smith married Emma Hale, the daughter of Isaac Hale, a Pennsylvania farmer. On September 22 of that year he visited the hill again and was allowed to take the plates away with him. With them came "two stones in silver bows — and these stones, fastened to a breastplate, constituted what are called the Urim and Thummim, by which he was to translate the mysterious pictographic characters on the plates. Nearly three years were spent in the task, which was performed by Joseph Smith with the assistance of schoolteacher Oliver Cowdery, among others.

The record drawn from the plates accounted for some 1,000 years of pre-Columbian American history. It concerned lost tribes from a colony of Israelite origin, whose members were said to have lived in the Western Hemisphere from about 600 B.C. to A.D. 421 and to have been the ancestors of Native American Indians. According to this account, the descendants of the Israelite settlers split into two factions — the Lamanites, who turned to idolatry and wickedness, and the God-fearing Nephites, who remained true to the teachings of the Lord. In about A.D. 400, before their civilization was destroyed by the warfare that eventually raged between the two groups, Mormon, the last illustrious Nephite prophet, compiled the history of his people found on the golden plates. In part an abridgment of earlier records, Mormon's account also relates scriptural truths revealed to his people by the risen Jesus Christ, who visited them in America, and it included as well the prophecies and genealogies of ancient Israel. It was this record that Mormon is said to have entrusted to his son Moroni — who "hid it up unto the Lord" in Cumorah Hill. There it reportedly was found by Joseph Smith some 1,400 years later.

Smith's translation of this work was published in Palmyra in 1830, under the title *The Book of Mormon.* The first edition of 5,000 copies was financed by Martin Harris, a friend of Smith's who, with Oliver Cowdery and David Whitmer, was also one of three witnesses testifying to the plates' authenticity: "We have seen the plates . . . and we also know that they have been translated by the gift and power of God, for His voice hath declared it unto us." Eight additional witnesses also testified to viewing and "hefting" the golden tablets.

While the translation was in progress, according to Smith's account, John the Baptist appeared to him and Oliver Cowdery, on May 15, 1829, and made them priests after the order of Aaron. Less than a year later, Smith also reported, Peter, James, and John conferred upon them what is known as the Melchizedek priesthood. Thereupon, they began to make converts and to found a church, which was organized as a legal entity by Joseph Smith and five associates at Fayette, Seneca County, New York, on April 6, 1830, as the Church of Jesus Christ of Latter-Day Saints (see April 6). Within a month it numbered 40 members.

Attracting its first converts from the rural areas of New England especially, the church rapidly gained members but was also confronted by prejudice, hostility, and even threats of violence. Convinced that the church would never flourish in such an environment, Joseph Smith asked God for advice, which he said came in the form of a revelation: "That ye might escape the powers of the enemy, and be gathered unto me a righteous people, without spot and blameless, I give unto you the commandment that ye should go to Ohio." In 1831, the planned exodus to Kirtland, Ohio, got under way. As a contemporary observer wrote:

Kirtland presented the appearance of a modern religious Mecca. Like Eastern pilgrims the converts came full of zeal for their new religion. They came in rude vehicles, on horseback, on foot. They came almost any way, filling on their arrival every house, every shop, every barn to the utmost capacity.

There, the first "Stake of Zion" was established, the first temple erected, and the organization of the church perfected, as befitted a rapidly expanding aggressive theocracy.

Groups of Mormons also settled in Jackson County, Missouri, soon designated the site for their City of Zion, the New Jerusalem. Bitter political, social, and religious differences, however, forced them to seek refuge in the surrounding counties in late 1833. In Ohio, the Kirtland Safety Society, an unchartered church-supported financial organization, survived only long enough to absorb the life savings of its depositors, failing in the nationwide monetary panic of 1837, and causing open insurrection in church ranks. When it had become evident that Joseph Smith's career in Ohio was drawing to an inglorious close and that his religion had not found its proper habitat, the Latter-Day Saints under his leadership swept westward to join their brethren in Missouri. There clashes with the Gentiles, as the Saints called non-Mormons, convinced Governor Lilburn W. Boggs that "the Mormons must be exterminated or driven from the state." In 1838, despite the onset of winter, he summoned the militia to forcibly evict some 12,000 to 15,000 Mormons. They left behind them property valued at about $200 million. Smith, having surrendered himself as a "hostage," soon escaped from jail — and probably hanging — to return triumphantly to the faithful, who awaited him in Illinois.

After their mid-winter flight from Missouri in 1838–1839, the Mormons took refuge on the banks of the Mississippi a few miles above Warsaw, Illinois. Smith and his followers settled there in the town of Commerce, which they renamed Nauvoo, which, he claimed, "means in Hebrew a beautiful plantation." Amidst swamps and tangled growth, the Mormons quickly built the biggest city in the state. Converts, especially from England, swelled the population to 20,000, and with a temple finished, a university planned, and a generous charter from the Illinois legislature, Joseph Smith as mayor of Nauvoo might well have been satisfied. But in 1844 he announced his candidacy for the presidency of the United States.

However, events that completely obscured all political ambitions soon overtook him with overwhelming rapidity. On July 12, 1843, Smith had a revelation in favor of the practice of polygamy. A schism developed in the church, and the practice of polygamy, together with other policies, was denounced by a newspaper, the Nauvoo *Expositor,* which was started by the excommunicated schismatics to expose Smith and defend themselves. The paper was suppressed and the printing plant destroyed on order of Smith and his municipal council.

Since the surrounding countryside had been aroused to fury by these arbitrary acts of suppression, Smith, who was lieutenant general of the Nauvoo Legion, instructed his troops to protect the city and was consequently charged with treason. The owner of the suppressed paper obtained an order in Carthage, the county seat, for the removal of Smith to that town on the charge of riot. Having little confidence that he would be granted a fair trial there, Smith submitted his case to another court, which acquitted him. Upon learning that his appearance in Carthage was nevertheless required, he contemplated fleeing to the Rocky Mountains. The combined protests of his wife and church associates, as well as a guarantee of protection by the governor of Illinois, persuaded Joseph Smith and his brother Hyrum to go to Carthage, where they were jailed. On June 27, 1844, a mob with their faces smeared with lampblack, stormed the jail and murdered the two Smiths.

Although their leader's death was an unspeakable shock to the more than 50,000 Mormons, the Church of Jesus Christ of Latter-Day Saints did not disintegrate as anticipated. But a serious dispute over succession followed. One faction, having undertaken a partial reorganization in Beloit, Wisconsin, in 1852, eventually chose Joseph Smith 3rd, son of the founder, as head of what was termed the Reorganized Church of Jesus Christ of Latter-Day Saints (which is now headquartered in Independence, Missouri). Another faction, led by an elder of the church, James Jesse Strang, migrated to Beaver Island, Michigan. (Strang was subsequently crowned King of Beaver Island by his followers, thereby ruling the only monarchy ever created within the boundaries of the United States.) However, the majority of Mormons recognized Brigham Young, the senior member of the church's Council of the Twelve Apostles, as the new leader.

As early as 1842, Joseph Smith had apparently predicted that "his people could yet be driven to the Rocky Mountains where they would build a city of their own, free from molestation." The persecution and mob violence encountered by the Mormons at Nauvoo made it increasingly clear to Brigham Young and other church authorities that such a move was now inevitable. Convinced that the Mormons must seek a new refuge in the Far West, Young began to oversee the exodus early in 1846. As rapidly as companies could be organized, the Mormons took the trail for the unknown land of freedom. After enduring innumerable hardships, the first stalwart band of pioneers entered the valley of the Great Salt Lake and laid out a new city there on July 24, 1847. Before 1869, about 80,000 members of the church were to follow in their footsteps.

Numerous historical sites in the northeastern United States commemorate the places in which Joseph Smith Jr. spent his youth and founded his church. A tall monument of polished stone marking his birthplace in Sharon, Vermont, was dedicated on the centennial of his birth on December 23, 1905. On Stafford Road near the village of Palmyra, New York, stands the Smith homestead that was built by members of the family in the 1820s. Near the homestead is the Sacred Grove, where Joseph Smith had his first vision. Just north of Palmyra is the Martin Harris home, an early 19th century farmhouse, which was the property of the prominent church supporter. One of the more impressive Mormon sites is Hill Cumorah, located four miles south of Palmyra. A 40-foot monument topped by a gold-covered statue of the angel Moroni marks the area in which the sacred records are said to have been buried and revealed to Smith.

The 300-foot-high hill, surrounded by farmland, is the location of a religious pageant sponsored by the Church of Jesus Christ of Latter-Day Saints. Begun in 1937 and presented annually since then except for a brief interruption during World War II, the production has grown from a modest enactment of a few episodes in *The Book of Mormon* to become one of the outstanding annual religious dramatic presentations. It is now staged on six evenings in late July or early August. The pageant, which is formally called America's Witness for Christ, has attracted over 100,000 spectators.

Preceded by an 8:00 P.M. record concert by the famed Salt Lake Mormon Tabernacle Choir, the hour-and-a-half drama, presented on five major stages and 20 smaller ones, begins at 9:00 P.M. Despite its overwhelming sound effects, theatrical lighting, and lavish costumes, it remains a religious experience. There is no commercialism, admission is free, and onlookers are not permitted to smoke or applaud. The cast of over 500 persons is composed of volunteers, many of them serving as missionaries in New York State for two-year periods, others from as far away as Utah and California.

The script for the pageant is based on *The Book of Mormon*. It depicts the rise and fall of the pre-Columbian civilization that the Mormons believe existed in America between 600 B.C. and A.D. 421. Scenes flash from wars, rebellions, and martyrdoms of prophets, to divine miracles and visions as the ancient inhabitants obey or reject the commands of God. Worthy prophets predict great events to come: the birth of Christ, his ministry, and crucifixion. A climactic episode occurs when the Savior, after his resurrection in Jerusalem, appears to his "other fold" in America, and the entire cast slowly advances, with extended arms, up the hill toward the Christ figure.

In 1970, which was the 140th anniversary of the establishment of the church, 1,000 Mormons gathered in late July to dedicate a new church visitors' information center. The open field that was the setting for this gathering was the site of the log cabin of Peter Whitmer in Fayette, New York, where the Church of Jesus Christ of Latter-Day Saints was formally organized in 1830.

DECEMBER 24

Christmas Eve

Like the celebration of Christmas Day (see December 25), the observance of Christmas Eve, or the Vigil of Christmas, on December 24, is a combination of the religious and the merely festive. Whatever popular and even pagan customs have been added to it, however, it is essentially a time of joyous celebration in honor of the birth of Jesus Christ. December 24, which is primarily a day of preparation for the major feast of Christmas, is the culmination of the pre-Christmas Advent season, that period of anticipation and preparation that begins approximately four weeks earlier (see November 29).

The focal point of the Christmas Eve religious celebration is the service of worship held by Christians of all denominations. Some of the services begin at midnight, like the communion service held by Episcopalians, the vigil of Eastern Orthodox churches, and the *missa in nocte*, or "mass at night," of Roman Catholics. The latter is the first of three masses that priests are permitted to say on the feast of Jesus' birth, and it is usually a resplendent service with the celebrant dressed in white and gold vestments and accompanied by an array of acolytes. The choice of the midnight hour is in correspondence with the assertion by many that Jesus was born at or near this hour.

Protestant denominations vary in the timing of their Christmas Eve worship services, which may commence as late as midnight, but may instead be vesper services held in the earlier part of the evening. Some non-Protestant churches hold both vesper and midnight services. Christmas Eve services are very likely to be lighted by candles, the flickering illumination constituting for many a treasured Christmas Eve tradition, along with the profusion of evergreens and poinsettias that decorate the churches. Choral pieces, such as selections from George Frederick Handel's *Messiah*, are often presented, and traditional Christmas carols are sung in churches. Some of the carols whose titles most typify the gladness of the occasion are "Hark, the Herald Angels Sing," "O Little Town of Bethlehem," "Joy to the World," "O Come, All Ye Faithful," and, probably the best-known of all, "Silent Night."

For centuries, the major religious observance on Christmas Eve has been celebrated in the small town of Bethlehem, located only a few miles from Jerusalem in an area that was part of the original biblical land of Palestine. Traditionally known as the birthplace of Jesus, the town was regarded as a holy spot by Christians as early as the second century. Constantine the Great, who in the early fourth century was the first Roman emperor to embrace Christianity, had a church built on the site asserted to be Jesus' birthplace. The original structure of the Church of the Nativity, completed in 333, later underwent many transformations, especially under the sixth century Roman emperor Justinian.

Disruptive quarrels for control of the sanctuary have wracked the various Christian churches for hundreds of years. The nave of the Church of the Nativity is now owned jointly by three Christian churches — Orthodox, Armenian, and Roman Catholic — as is the Grotto of the Nativity, the crypt beneath the church that is reputed to be the original manger area. The three churches in turn hold elaborate Christmas services in the church, the Roman Catholic mass beginning just before midnight on December 24. Flocks of pilgrims from all over the world descend upon the small town. Since the church is not spacious enough to accommodate all the visitors, a closed-circuit television network usually transmits the observance on a screen erected in nearby Manger Square. Elaborate press and radio broadcasting facilities are also imported for the occasion. The highlight occurs at midnight, when, amidst the tumultuous pealing of bells, a carved wooden figure of the Christ Child in swaddling clothes is reverently laid in a manger in the Grotto of the Nativity. Members of various Protestant faiths that do not share in the sanctuary meanwhile participate in an outdoor service held a short distance outside the town in Shepherds' Field, where, tradition holds, the shepherds kept watch over their flocks on the first Christmas Eve.

In Christian households throughout the world, Christmas Eve is celebrated in an atmosphere of spiritual rejoicing and reunion. Christmas Eve observances, especially in Western Europe, generally follow a similar pattern. The entire family celebrates December 24 with a mixture of churchgoing, feasting, and merrymaking. Candles, Yule logs, and Christmas trees decorate the houses, and in some countries the eve is regarded as the customary time to open gifts. There are various national variations: the Danes, for example, leave a bowl of rice and milk to appease the Christmas gnome, a little old bearded man in gray, with a red pointed cap, who is said to dwell in the attic or barn and who bestows good and bad luck. In France and Italy, the preparation of the crèche or presepio — the manger scene in which small figures represent Jesus, Mary, Joseph, the animals, angels, and shepherds — is an annual Christmas Eve event. The French in particular hold an informal family gathering at which the réveillon or late supper is served after midnight mass.

In the United States, Christmas Eve is an occasion for family gatherings, for Christmas lights, for decorated Christmas trees, and for the hanging of stockings from fireplace mantels by children who hope they will be filled with gifts by Santa Claus before morning. In American families whose children have grown up, Christmas Eve, rather than the more customary Christmas Day, sometimes is the time for the exchange of Christmas gifts, given in the tradition of the Three Wise Men who, according to the biblical account, brought gifts to honor the infant Jesus. Even more than the preceding days, Christmas Eve also is the time for the singing of Christmas carols, particularly by church and other choral groups, which often go from house to house, and to institutions housing the ill and shut-in, with their serenades of carols. The practice of caroling, common on the continent of Europe in the Middle Ages, came to the United States largely from England, where the still-observed practice, by strolling bands of waits (minstrels), was at its height in the 15th and 16th centuries.

Christmas Eve in the United States is also marked by some modern American innovations, such as the exciting torchlight ski procession down Dollar Mountain at the popular resort of Sun Valley, Idaho. But the majority of customs are ultimately derived from foreign traditions, imported by immigrants of various nationalities. In Louisiana, both in major cities such as New Orleans and in the countryside, Roman Catholic French-speaking Creoles — like their French ancestors — assemble en famille on Christmas Eve. The messe de minuit, "midnight mass," is elaborately celebrated at the three-spired St. Louis Cathedral in the heart of New Orleans; but worshipers crowd even the most isolated parish church to rejoice at Jesus' birth and sing their favorite hymn, "Minuit, Chrétiens" ("Midnight, O Christians"). They then hurry home for the customary réveillon, a family meal typically consisting of eggs, sweet bread, and delicately flavored daube glacé, a type of jellied meat, prepared with cloves and bay leaves, which was, it is asserted, "taken on a trip to heaven." Wine or rum cake and strong black coffee complete the repast.

In the American Southwest, especially in the Mexican border areas, the heritage stemming from the former Spanish rule results in a number of customs connected with Christmas Eve. One tradition that tenaciously survives is the performance of Spanish-language plays, drawn from the morality plays of medieval Spain and colonial Mexico. They were once staged for the religious edification of Native Americans by the early New World Spanish friars, as a way of overcoming the language barrier. Two of the most popular presentations given, usually during the two weeks before Christmas, involve Christmas Eve themes: Los Pastores (The Shepherds), the story of shepherds who brought gifts to the Christ Child, and Las Posadas (The Inns), the account of Mary and Joseph's search for lodgings. The plays are now rarely performed by Spanish-speaking villagers, as in the past, but are presented mostly by Sunday school groups, by little-theater performers, and sometimes by families that know Spanish and cherish the Spanish heritage. Most commonly, the productions are staged in New Mexico: in Santa Fe, Albuquerque, and the vicinity of Las Cruces (especially in Mesilla, a historic Mexican-style village). Occasionally they may also be seen at some of California's reconstructed, restored, or preserved missions extending from San Diego in the southernmost part of the state to Sonoma some 40 miles north of San Francisco. Olvera Street, the oldest street in Los Angeles, preserved as a Mexican street market, is the site of Las Posadas annually.

Although sheepherders seldom light bonfires on hilltops on December 24, a Christmas Eve custom that still exists in the Southwest is that of burning luminarias — little fires or candles stuck in sand in paper bags — to light the path of Mary and Joseph. The paper-bag lanterns (called luminarias in the southern part of New Mexico, farolitos in the north) can be seen in profusion in such communities as Santa Fe, Española, and Tularosa. The Albuquerque Chamber of Commerce sponsors a Christmas Eve bus tour past the city's flickering lanterns, which border sidewalks, walls, and roof edges. Another outstanding display is staged at the Taos, New Mexico, Indian Pueblo, where the ancient multi-storied living quarters glow with innumerable pine bonfires.

The observances called Las Posadas are based on the scriptural account of Mary and Joseph's search for room at an inn (posada) just before the birth of Jesus. Men, women, and children reenact the journey from Nazareth to Bethlehem on each of the nine evenings from December 16 through Christmas Eve. The procession of candle-bearing friends and relatives wanders from door to door trying to find shelter, singing songs and reciting traditional verses: "In heaven's name, I beg shelter: My wife can go no further tonight." Finally the group reaches the house, at which the nightly party is given. The host at first feigns reluctance but eventually relents and receives his guests with this welcome:

Enter, holy pilgrims,
And receive as a mansion,
Not our humble dwelling place
But our humble hearts. . . .

After praying and singing before the *nacimiento*, the colorful manger scene, the poor pilgrims change into festive party-goers. The climax of the celebration is the festivity surrounding a piñata, a lightweight pottery jar covered with colored papier-mâché in the shape of a donkey, bull, star or other design and stuffed with small presents such as oranges, candy, and nuts. It is hung from the ceiling or above a doorway, and the guests, above all the delighted children, are blindfolded, given a stick, and spun around before being allowed a chance to whack at the piñata. Eventually someone breaks it, and the shower of goodies falls to the floor to close the party with a hilarious scramble. On the last night of this pre-Christmas hospitality, Christmas Eve — the *noche buena* or "good night" — the piñata party is followed by a midnight mass and dazzling fireworks.

In New Mexico's Rio Grande and neighboring pueblos, such as Acoma, Laguna, Santo Domingo, and Tesuque, the mixing of non-Christian Indian rites and Christian customs introduced by the Spanish has created unique Christmas Eve traditions. Following midnight mass in the Roman Catholic mission churches, which have been a feature of the pueblos since the time of Spanish control, ancient Indian ceremonial dances are often performed. Indians of the San Felipe Pueblo, for example, dress as animals of the hunt — mountain sheep, bison, deer, and antelope — to execute intricate steps to the vigorous beating of drums. San Ildefonso also is the scene of a ceremonial dance on December 24. An impressive torchlight procession honoring the Virgin Mary takes place at Taos after vespers on Christmas Eve, while at Isleta, 12 dancers perform as a group in the mission church and then individually kneel to pray before statues of the Virgin and Jesus Christ before ritually withdrawing.

Moravians in Pennsylvania and North Carolina carry out a very different type of foreign tradition imported by their European forebears. In the mid-15th century the Unitas Fratrum, or "Unity of Brethren," was formed as an evangelical sect in Bohemia and Moravia (now Czechoslovakia) by some followers of John Hus, the Bohemian pre-Reformation religious leader of the late 14th and early 15th century. At the height of its development in the early 17th century, the religious society was almost exterminated following the victory of Ferdinand II, the militant Catholic Hapsburg emperor, in the Battle of White Mountain in 1620 during the Thirty Years' War.

The Moravians who survived persecution, the Hidden Seed, at first continued to worship secretly in Moravia. They later fled to safer refuge in German Saxony, settling near the estate of Count Nikolaus Ludwig von Zinzendorf at Berthelsdorf. The devout count allowed the refugees to found the village of Herrnhut on his land in the 1720s and eventually acted as their patron and leader. When persecution soon imperiled the community again, bands of immigrants sailed to the American colonies. The first company, which arrived in Georgia in 1735, later resettled in Pennsylvania, where their ranks were soon bolstered by other groups of Moravian immigrants. Here they founded thriving communities.

One of the earliest Moravian celebrations of Christmas Eve was held on December 24, 1741, at the place now known as Bethlehem, Pennsylvania. The count, who had recently arrived in America on a visit, was struck during Christmas Eve devotions with the similarity of the crude log cabin in the wilderness to the stable in which Christ had been born. Impulsively grasping a lighted candle, he led the assembled Brethren to the section of the shelter in which the cattle were housed. His singing of the old German hymn "Not Jerusalem, Lowly Bethlehem," suggested the name of Bethlehem for the frontier settlement.

In the fall of 1752 pioneering Moravians led by Bishop August Gottlieb Spangenberg left Pennsylvania to seek a site for a new settlement in North Carolina. The exploratory party claimed possession of an immense tract of land situated well beyond the frontier. In the first temporary center, named Bethabara (in Hebrew, "House of Passage"), the Moravians, as at Bethlehem, Pennsylvania, 11 years earlier, celebrated Christmas Eve in a small log cabin. Within a few years, the Brethren had founded other planned communities, including Salem (in Hebrew, "Peace"), which soon developed into the economic and cultural center of western North Carolina.

Today, both Bethlehem, Pennsylvania, and Old Salem, North Carolina (the latter now a historical restoration at which the Moravian way of life is being preserved for posterity), remain closely associated with the Christmas season and with Christmas Eve in particular. Known as America's Christmas City, Bethlehem stages a dignified observance that is marked by impressive religious services on December 24. The community continues the Old World tradition of "putzing" (from the German *putzen*, "to decorate") by making and displaying figures depicting the Nativity and country life surrounding the manger. The amount of work can be immense, depending upon the size of the scene; for example, the annual community crib, which is unveiled only on Christmas Eve, one year involved 800 pounds of sand, 12 bushes of moss, 64 tree stumps, 40 trees, 200 animal figures, and 48 angels.

As early as October, Moravians in both Bethlehem and Old Salem begin using old-fashioned molds and techniques to make the beeswax candles that will be handed out during the traditional Christmas Eve services, the love feast, and the vigil. The Moravian love feast — consisting of music, meditation, and partaking of a simple meal in the manner of early Christians — was first celebrated in Herrnhut, Saxony, in 1727. Held traditionally on the afternoon of December 24, it is primarily a service for the children of the congregation, who are grouped in the first pews of the church. Following the singing of several hymns, men and women serve the love feast of soft sweet buns and mugs of steaming weak coffee to each child. At the conclusion of the service, the servers return with trays of lighted candles that have been decorated with brightly colored paper frills or "petticoats" to catch the hot wax. Every child receives a candle, the symbolic reminder of the birth of Jesus Christ, the Light of the World.

After a pause of a few hours for family gatherings at home the Moravian congregation assembles again at 7:30 P.M. for the Christmas Eve Vigil. This observance is devoted almost entirely to music, alternately performed by a Bach choir, the congregation, or the children. A high point occurs when a Sunday school child sings antiphonally with other boys and girls a favorite hymn regarded as the keynote of the Moravian Christmastide:

> Morning Star, O Cheering Sight!
> Ere Thou cam'st, how dark earth's night!
> Jesus mine, in me shine;
> Fill my heart with love divine.

During the very moving vigil the church lights are dimmed except for a single center star over the picture of the Holy Family. Near the conclusion of the vigil, the choir sings "Behold! A great and heavenly light from Bethlehem's manger shineth bright . . ." and sacristans hand out lighted candles to the entire congregation.

Christmas pageants are presented throughout the United States during the weeks preceding December 25, but several unusual displays have obtained nationwide prominence and attract an especially wide audience. One of the most popular has been staged every Christmas Eve since 1931 at the Hot Springs National Park at Hot Springs, Arkansas. It is advertised as the country's "only outdoor Christmas pageant in a national park." Elizabeth Bowe Sims, music director of the local high school, conceived the idea when the hitherto traditional indoor candlelight service had become overcrowded. The first simple carol sing by local white-robed choral groups and music students was held outdoors in Arlington Park at the north end of holly-tree-lined Bath House Row. Above the park towers the impressive Hot Springs Mountain.

Over the years the carol sing has grown into a major 35-minute production sponsored by the National Park Service and the local chamber of commerce. The natural shelves of the Hot Springs bluffs provide two stages, the higher for tableau figures, the lower for the now highly trained chorus. As a spectacular start to the evening presentation, the white-robed singers wind down a narrow mountain trail in candlelight procession. A narrator recites the scriptural account of the Nativity, which is reenacted in six scenes on the upper stage, interspersed with favorite carols and organ music.

In a tradition stretching back to the early 20th century, the mining town of Madrid, New Mexico, located 20 miles from Santa Fe, celebrates the Christmas season in grand style. On the afternoon of December 24, the Nativity story is presented by means of a huge diorama and oil paintings against a setting of miles of sparkling Christmas trees. The practice, now prevalent, of erecting complex Nativity scenes in such New Mexican mining towns as Gallup, Lovington, and Raton is thought to have originated with Welsh, Cornish, and Mexican miners. In Raton, for example, a deep canyon on the outskirts of town is annually transformed into a brilliantly lighted town of Bethlehem. Various Nativity figures, skillfully graduated in size, are illuminated in sequence to simulate movement.

In the tiny rural community of Bethlehem, Kentucky, the Baptist, Methodist, and Point Pleasant Christian churches have since 1960 annually presented a living Nativity scene. Practically all of the 200 inhabitants participate in one way or another in this tableau depicting the traditional stable manger scene. Some play parts; others build the rustic crèche out of rough poles, plywood, and tarpaulin; still others sew costumes or direct the visitors who take the narrow back roads of central Kentucky to see the portrayal of Mary and Joseph, the shepherds, Wise Men, and angels. A doll serves as the Christ Child as 36 richly costumed townspeople (12 per hour) stand motionless despite the chilling cold to cover the three-hour nightly tableau. The presentation, staged on four evenings from December 22 through December 25, is enhanced by recorded carols and scriptural readings.

Customs and dates for Christmas gift-giving vary widely from country to country, as do the supposed donors of the gifts. Depending upon the place, the gifts allegedly are delivered by elves, angels, the Christ Child, and even by "Jesus' camel." Alternatively, they are said to be provided by the Three Kings or Wise Men, or by St. Nicholas or his derivative, Santa Claus — who in the last two centuries has become the best-known giver of gifts, not only in the United States and parts of Europe, but also in Australia and other southern areas whose warm December climates seem no deterrent to the winter-clad Santa.

In England and the United States, Christmas morning is traditionally the time for opening gifts, although the gifts generally arrive on Christmas Eve. In Britain, the period of Christmas gift-giving is extended to include the first weekday after Christmas, known as Boxing Day, when Christmas gifts or boxes are given to employees, mail carriers, messengers, and others. In Scandinavian countries Christmas Eve is the designated time for opening presents, which often are borne by an impersonator of the Christmas gnome — Jultomten or Julenisse — who is found throughout Scandinavia.

However, in many countries of Europe and Latin America, although there may be token gifts — often in the form of edible treats — on Christmas morning or Christmas Eve, they are overshadowed by another major gift-giving date which, although separated in time, is related either to the Christmas story or to a Christmas custom. In Italy and Spanish-speaking countries, for example, it is on the Epiphany or Three Kings' Day (see January 6) that presents are exchanged, and it is the Three Kings (or, in Italy, the *befana* — the old woman who missed her opportunity to visit the infant Jesus) who bring them.

In many other places, including the United States, as well as much of northern Europe, gift-giving habits ultimately derive from the early medieval account of St. Nicholas, a stern but kindly bishop who lived in Asia Minor in the fourth century. According to legend, Nicholas learned that the father of three young women was planning to allow them to solicit in order to provide dowries. So one night Nicholas filled three bags with gold and threw them into the windows of the rooms occupied by the young women, who soon were happily married. Unexpected gifts were thereafter said to come from St. Nicholas, whose feast day occurs early in December (see December 6).

Not surprisingly, therefore, it is on December 6, the feast day of the saint, or December 5, its eve, that the benign bishop, bearing gifts, and sometimes promising more, for the well-behaved, at Christmastime — makes his appearance in many countries of Europe. This is true in Germany and Switzerland (though in both of those countries Christmas Eve itself surpasses the saint's day as a gift-giving occasion). The good bishop, laden with treats, also appears on December 5, and leaves gifts to be discovered on December 6, in France, Belgium, Luxembourg, and the Netherlands.

When the Dutch settled what was to become New York, they brought with them the concept of an annually reappearing St. Nicholas or, as they called him, Sinterklaas. From there it was an easy step for succeeding generations of Americans to alter his name to Santa Claus.

But not until the 19th century, in New York City, was the figure of the tall, saintly bishop, now so intimately connected with Christmas Eve, recast in the form of the jovial gentleman complete with sleigh and reindeer. The transformation was the result of one poem and one illustration, the work of two unlikely men: a serious classical scholar and a political cartoonist.

Clement Clarke Moore, a professor of Greek and Oriental literature who had been appointed to the General Theological Seminary in New York City, put the Santa Claus myth into the form in which it is now accepted in the United States. Although opposed in principle to the frivolity of Christmas, in 1822 he composed a poem, now known as "A Visit From St. Nicholas," to please his children. Inspired by his surroundings on a snowy Christmas Eve in Manhattan, he made up the 56 lines on his way home from a market trip to buy a Christmas turkey. Santa's sleigh and bells were suggested by the jingling of his own horse and sleigh, while his famous description of St. Nicholas was apparently derived in part from the appearance of a farmer friend, Jan Duyckinck.

Moore read the poem to his children that very evening. It begins, as everyone knows:

'Twas the night before Christmas, when all through
    the house
Not a creature was stirring, not even a mouse;
The stockings were hung by the chimney with care,
In hopes that St. Nicholas soon would be there;
The children were nestled all snug in their beds,
While visions of sugar-plums danced in their heads;
And Mamma in her 'kerchief, and I in my cap,
Had just settled our brains for a long winter's nap;
When out on the lawn there arose such a clatter,
I sprang from my bed to see what was the matter.
Away to the window I flew like a flash,
Tore open the shutters and threw up the sash.
The moon on the breast of the new-fallen snow,
Gave the lustre of mid-day to objects below,
When, what to my wondering eyes should appear,

But a miniature sleigh and eight tiny rein-deer,
With a little old driver, so lively and quick,
I knew in a moment it must be St. Nick.

Moore went on to name the reindeer —
Dasher, Dancer, Prancer, Vixen, Comet, Cupid,
Donder, Blitzen — tell how they landed on the
roof, how St. Nicholas bounded down the chimney with his pack of toys, and what he looked
like:

His eyes — how they twinkled! his dimples, how
      merry!
His cheeks were like roses, his nose like a cherry!
His droll little mouth was drawn up like a bow,
And the beard on his chin was as white as the snow;
The stump of a pipe he held tight in his teeth,
And the smoke it encircled his head like a wreath;
He had a broad face and a little round belly,
That shook when he laughed, like a bowl full of jelly.
He was chubby and plump, a right jolly old elf.
And I laughed, when I saw him, in spite of myself.

The verses were a great success. A cousin
was so enthralled that she copied the poem into
an album, which she later showed to a friend,
Harriet Butler, the daughter of the Reverend
David Butler, rector of St. Paul's Church in Troy,
New York. Harriet Butler in turn took the poem
to the editor of the Troy *Sentinel*, which printed
it on December 23, 1823, with a complimentary
introduction. A copy of the newspaper was sent
to Moore, who was annoyed that the verses that
he had written to amuse his children were
printed. They were soon reprinted by newspapers in other parts of the country and republished during the Christmas seasons of succeeding years.

In 1829 the editor of the Troy *Sentinel*, in response to many inquiries, announced that the
poem had been written by a gentleman who belonged "by birth and residence to the City of
New York," and who was "of more merit as a
scholar and writer than many of more noisy pretensions." In 1837 the work was included in *The
New York Book of Poetry*, and Moore soon publicly admitted that he was its author. He included it in his collected poems in 1844. Since
then "A Visit From St. Nicholas" has been reprinted innumerable times.

In 1910 Milo H. Gates, first vicar of Trinity
Parish's Chapel of the Intercession at 550 West
155th Street in New York City, whose churchyard is the site of Clement Clarke Moore's grave,
inaugurated an annual observance commemorating the author. Every December 24, after a
recitation of the famous verses, Moore devotees
and boys and girls stage a pilgrimage with
lighted lanterns to his grave, where they lay a
wreath, sing carols, and pray.

In the early 1860s, the cartoonist Thomas
Nast drew for *Harper's Illustrated Weekly* a
Santa Claus in line with Moore's characteriza-
tion: a round, bearded figure with a red, ermine-
trimmed suit, wide leather belt, and shiny boots.
Nast's caricature was so popular that he con-
tinued to depict various scenes with Santa
Claus every Christmastime for nearly 30 years.

Undoubtedly the combination of Moore's
poem and Nast's illustrations helps children to
accept the Santa Claus myth, but as they grow
older they begin to have doubts. One child in
1897 wrote to the New York *Sun* asking whether
there is a Santa Claus. The answer, written by
Francis P. Church and printed as an editorial,
has become almost as famous as Moore's poem.
The now celebrated exchange follows:

We take pleasure in answering thus prominently
the communication below, expressing at the same
time our great gratification that its faithful author is
numbered among the friends of the *Sun*:

Dear Editor —
    I am eight years old. Some of my little friends
say there is no Santa Claus. Papa says "If you
see it in *The Sun* it's so." Please tell me the truth,
is there a Santa Claus?
                              VIRGINIA O'HANLON

Virginia, your little friends are wrong. They have
been affected by the skepticism of a skeptical age.
They do not believe except they see. They think that
nothing can be which is not comprehensible by their
little minds. All minds, Virginia, whether they be
men's or children's, are little. In this great universe
of ours man is a mere insect, an ant, in his intellect
as compared with the boundless world about him, as
measured by the intelligence capable of grasping the
whole of truth and knowledge.

Yes, Virginia, there is a Santa Claus. He exists as
certainly as love and generosity and devotion exist,
and you know that they abound and give to your life
its highest beauty and joy. Alas! how dreary would
be the world if there were no Santa Claus! It would
be as dreary as if there were no Virginias. There
would be no childlike faith then, no poetry, no romance to make tolerable this existence. We should
have no enjoyment, except in sense and sight. The
eternal light with which childhood fills the world
would be extinguished.

Not believe in Santa Claus! You might as well as
believe in fairies. You might get your papa to hire
men to watch in all the chimneys on Christmas eve
to catch Santa Claus, but even if you did not see
Santa Claus coming down, what would that prove?
Nobody sees Santa Claus, but that is no sign that
there is no Santa Claus. The most real things in the
world are those that neither children nor men can
see. Did you ever see fairies dancing on the lawn?
Of course not, but that's no proof that they are not
there. Nobody can conceive or imagine all the wonders there are unseen and unseeable in the world.

You tear apart the baby's rattle and see what

makes the noise inside, but there is a veil covering the unseen world which not the strongest man, nor even the united strength of all the strongest men that ever lived could tear apart. Only faith, poetry, love, romance, can push aside that curtain and view and picture the supernal beauty and glory beyond. Is it all real? Ah, Virginia, in all this world there is nothing else real and abiding.

No Santa Claus! Thank God! he lives and lives forever. A thousand years from now, Virginia, nay, ten times ten thousand years from now, he will continue to make glad the heart of childhood.

War of 1812 Ends
Treaty of Ghent

The Treaty of Ghent, concluding the War of 1812 (see also June 18) between the United States and Great Britain, was signed by representatives of the two countries, meeting at the Belgian city of Ghent on Christmas Eve in 1814. Ironically enough, communications were such that the war's last engagement — the battle of New Orleans (see January 8) — was not fought until January 8, 1815, after peace supposedly had been restored. Officially, however, it was the Treaty of Ghent that brought the conflict to a close.

Although historians have often referred to the War of 1812 as an inconclusive conflict that settled none of the issues over which it supposedly had been fought, it had important results, directly and indirectly. Its conclusion found the young American nation, until then a loose cementing of disparate geography and interests, unified for the first time. Also for the first time, the new country was firmly established in the eyes of the world, a nation among nations, to be regarded seriously as a separate, permanent, and independent entity. It also had developed a naval tradition that would prove valuable in its further development.

Directly or not, the War of 1812 removed most of the remaining barriers to westward American expansion — such as British incitement of Indian warfare on the frontier. Indeed, the battle of the Thames had broken the power of the Indians of the Northwest and shattered their confidence in the British. Americans, emerging from the War of 1812 with a new sense of nationalism and an eagerness to settle the continent's vast western lands, proceeded to concentrate their attention on that huge undertaking.

Although some years remained before 1853, when the Gadsden Purchase brought the conterminous United States to its present dimensions, the push to the Pacific was on. With the addition of Alaska — a territory since 1867 and a state since January 3, 1959 — and Hawaii — annexed in 1898 and a state since August 21, 1959, the United States reached its present boundaries.

DECEMBER 25

Christmas Day
Feast of the Nativity of Our Lord

For Christians, Christmas, commemorating the birth of Jesus Christ, is an important religious event, marking the gift from God described in the New Testament: "For God so loved the world, that he gave his only-begotten Son" (John 3:16). In Christian liturgical calendars, only the feast of Easter, commemorating the Resurrection of the Lord, outranks the Nativity in spiritual significance. Christmas, however, is certainly the most popularly observed occasion of the church year.

Throughout Christendom, churches decorated with evergreens and poinsettias reverberate at Christmastime with special Christmas hymns, oratorios, and carols, scriptural readings describing the first Christmas, and sermons about the Nativity. In addition to religious services during daylight hours, services by candlelight — vespers, or vigils beginning on Christmas Eve — are a cherished part of the glad observance. For Roman Catholics, December 25 is a holy day of obligation, on which all must attend one of the three masses priests are permitted to say in honor of the occasion. These usually begin at midnight on the 24th; at dawn on the 25th; and later on Christmas Day. Protestant churches customarily celebrate Christmas with a special service on the Sunday morning preceding December 25, as well as with a service on Christmas Eve and a third joyous service of worship on Christmas morning. Eastern Orthodox Christians celebrate the Divine Liturgy on Christmas Day, and also in services that begin late on Christmas Eve and continue past midnight. In the case of some Eastern Orthodox churches, notably the Russian, the last-mentioned observances constitute an all-night vigil beginning at midnight on Christmas Eve. Although the majority of Eastern Orthodox churches now celebrate the Nativity on December 25, those that still adhere to the old Julian calendar — including many of the Russian Orthodox churches — mark the occasion 13 days later, on January 7.

Over the centuries, Christmas has become a holiday as well as a holy day. In its social or festive aspect, December 25 is a curious hybrid of the seasonal traditions of numerous peoples: Persian, Roman, Norse, Gothic, and Anglo-Saxon, among others. At first glance, the staggering display of customs seems to have little indeed to do with the birth in a stable at Bethlehem two thousand years ago. Turkey dinners, glittering trees, greeting cards, elaborate store window displays, bell-ringing Santa Clauses on street corners, Yule logs, gaily wrapped gifts — all these and much more make up the special atmosphere of Christmas.

On the other hand, not everyone necessarily regards Christmas as an eagerly anticipated time of joyfulness. Ogden Nash, for example, once commented: "Roses are things which Christmas is not a bed of them"; and George Bernard Shaw observed: "Christmas is forced on a reluctant . . . nation by . . . shopkeepers and the press." But regardless of what modern-day critics may say about the commercialization, worship of Santa Claus, excessive eating, and financial drain that Christmas has undeniably also come to embody, December 25 is well entrenched, both as a much-loved social institution and as an occasion for spiritual rejoicing.

The story of the birth of Jesus is told in the Gospel of Luke (2:1–19) in this way:

And it came to pass in those days, that there went out a decree from Caesar Augustus, that all the world should be taxed. . . . And all went to be taxed, every one into his own city. And Joseph also went up from Galilee, out of the city of Nazareth, into Judea, unto the city of David, which is called Bethlehem, (because he was of the house and lineage of David), to be taxed with Mary his espoused wife, being great with child. And so it was, that, while they were there, the days were accomplished that she should be delivered. And she brought forth her firstborn son, and wrapped him in swaddling clothes, and laid him in a manger; because there was no room for them in the inn.

And there were in the same country shepherds abiding in the field, keeping watch over their flock by night. And lo, the angel of the Lord came upon them, and the glory of the Lord shone round about them; and they were sore afraid. And the angel said unto them, "Fear not: for, behold, I bring you good tidings of great joy, which shall be to all the people. For unto you is born this day in the city of David a Saviour, which is Christ the Lord. And this shall be a sign unto you; Ye shall find the babe wrapped in swaddling clothes, lying in a manger."

And suddenly there was with the angel a multitude of the heavenly host praising God, and saying, "Glory to God in the highest, and on earth peace, good will toward men."

And it came to pass, as the angels were gone away from them into heaven, the shepherds said one to another, "Let us now go even unto Bethlehem, and see this thing which is come to pass, which the Lord hath made known unto us."

And they came with haste, and found Mary and Joseph, and the babe lying in a manger.

Although December 25 is observed as the anniversary of the birth of Jesus, the exact date has never been known. Partly for this reason, Christmas was not one of the earliest feasts of the Christian church, since there was at first no general consensus about when the anniversary should be observed — or even whether it should be observed. In fact, many early Christians were convinced that such a divine being could not have had a natural birth; and in any event the observance of birthdays generally was wholly condemned as a pagan custom repugnant to Christians. It was in this vein that Origen, the African church father and philosopher, wrote in A.D. 245 that it was sinful even to contemplate observing Jesus' birthday "as though He were a King Pharaoh."

Proposals for marking the birth date of Jesus — and attempts to determine what it was — nonetheless persisted. The memorable Gospel passages furnished few clues, although some scholars have theorized that if, as Luke relates, the shepherds kept watch outdoors in the fields, the birth must have occurred during a warm season: in winter the sheep were usually penned at night in folds. Early Christian theologians in Egypt reportedly fixed the date as May 20; other churchmen are said to have chosen late March or April dates, approximating the time of the Jewish Passover, or January 1, coinciding with the Roman new year under the calendar then in use. In fact, dates in almost every month in the year were suggested by reputable scholars at one time or another. The most frequently put forth, however, were March 25 (which eventually became known as the Feast of the Annunciation or Lady Day), December 25, and January 6.

What seems clear is that early observances connected with the birth of Jesus took place in scattered places on various dates; that January 6 emerged as the date most pertinent to the development of the Christmas observance we know today; and that it was at first usually a dual celebration noting both the birth and the baptism of Jesus. Known as the Epiphany, meaning appearance or manifestation, the January 6 observance — often referred to since as "Little Christmas" — originated in the churches of the East, at least by the beginning of the third century. The earliest record of any celebration comes from Clement of Alexandria, the Greek theologian, who mentions, about A.D. 200, that members of a certain sect in Egypt had commemorated Jesus' baptism on January 6 (or 10).

It was considerably later, and in the western part of the Roman Empire, that a separate celebration of Jesus' birth was introduced by the church at Rome. A Christian chronography (almanac) issued in A.D. 354 showed the existence of such a commemoration and also indicated that the observance had been instituted some two decades earlier.

Even though controversy still surrounds the actual historical date of Jesus' birth, the December 25 date has long been accepted by most Christian churches. Modern scholars agree, however, that it was selected arbitrarily for practical purposes rather than as a matter of chronological accuracy: the date happened to coincide with the winter solstice — December 25 by the calendar then in use — and thus also coincided with the numerous pagan celebrations connected with the solstice.

The solstitial festivities, which much predated Christianity, cut across several cultures. A number of ancient peoples regarded this time of year as a period of crisis in which the deities of the upper world fought the spirits of disorder and darkness. The Mesopotamians, for instance, performed special rites to support their god Marduk in his grim battle against the powers of chaos. The Greeks offered sacrifices in their temples, believing that their chief god, Zeus, was renewing the struggle against Kronos and the Titans. As victory approached and the lengthening days gave hope of a distant but sure spring, a festive mood ensued. Also during the solstice season, the Romans celebrated the boisterous feast of the *Saturnalia* in honor of Saturn, the god of agriculture. The followers of the Persian sun god Mithras, whose cult in Rome vied with Christianity as the most popular religion, observed December 25 as *dies solis invicti nati*, "birthday of the invincible sun." And at approximately the same period, Jews observed, as they still do, the holiday of Hanukkah, celebrating the rededication of the Temple in Jerusalem.

It was only logical for early Christian leaders to wish to offer competition to the winter festivals being celebrated at what had long been deemed a vital religious time and to make that period a Christian feast commemorating the birth of Jesus. Acceptance of the December 25 date initiated at Rome for the observance of the Nativity spread gradually throughout Western Europe, and more slowly in the East. After the Eastern churches had adopted the observance of December 25 as Christmas in the latter part of the 4th century (and subsequently), the Western church took up the observance of the Epiphany on January 6. The feast of Christmas continued to spread slowly. Not until 813 did it extend to the region of Germany on a large scale, and it reached Norway as late as the 10th century.

For several centuries, December 25 was purely a church anniversary, kept with appropriate religious services and later with banquets and perhaps the exchange of simple presents, such as candles and clay dolls. But as Christianity advanced in northern Europe, the local customs connected with the winter solstice rites began to blend with the Christian observance. Several church fathers condemned the assimilation as potentially dangerous and reiterated Augustine of Hippo's fourth-century warning: "We hold this day holy, not like the pagans because of the birth of the sun, but because of him who made it." But the majority of the missionaries who penetrated Western Europe after the decline of the Roman Empire preferred to follow the tolerant ruling of Pope Gregory I the Great. The pope instructed Augustine of Canterbury, whom he sent to England in 596, to observe old customs, infusing them with Christian significance to propagate the faith, "for from obdurate minds it is impossible to cut off everything at once." On this liberal policy hinged the continuation of numerous traditional customs now connected with Christmastide.

The pagan traditions adapted "to the praise of God" included the lighting of candles, blazing Yule logs, and huge bonfires to speed the sun on its way at the time of its yearly "rebirth." These practices easily tied in with the Christian concept of Christ as the Light of the World. During the awesome solstice season of dread and festivity, the pagans filled their houses with evergreens, mistletoe, holly, and ivy, believing their greenness in midwinter to be evidence of special power defying winter's ability to kill.

The use of mistletoe at Christmastime is without doubt traced to the druids, who regarded it with reverence long before the Christian era. In celebration of the winter solstice, they gathered mistletoe, piled it on the altar, and burned it in sacrifice. Sprigs of the yellow-green leaves and waxen white berries were distributed among the people and hung up in their houses. The plant was regarded as a symbol of future hope and peace. Whenever enemies met under the mistletoe they would drop their weapons and embrace. The still current custom of kissing under the mistletoe may have grown out of this ancient practice.

Christians continued to use greenery in decorating their halls and homes at Christmastime and found the bonfires convenient for disposing of the boughs and sprigs. The legend soon developed that Jesus' crown of thorns had been fashioned from holly, whose berries, originally white, turned brilliant red when pressed on the Son of God's forehead.

As Christianity spread throughout Western Europe in the early Middle Ages, Christmas — the English name dates from the 11th century, when the feast was termed *Cristes Maesse* — grew into a great popular festivity. Coming at a time during which common folk had some of their rare leisure, between fall harvesting and spring sowing, to enjoy prolonged merriment, it quickly developed into a boisterous period of singing, hunting, gambling, and feasting. From very early times, the offering of food and drink had been regarded as a sign of hospitality and good will. Accordingly, steaming beverages, especially spiced ale or beer, known as *wassail* — the term derived from the Middle English *waes haeil*, "be thou well" or "to your health" — were served ceremoniously and in copious quantities to warm chilled bones during the holiday season. Occasionally a boar's head, complete with tusks, was also served.

Christmas festivities were nowhere more lavishly and joyously celebrated than in medieval England. King Arthur allegedly observed the first recorded English Christmas in 521, but it was not until the 11th century, when Norman influence came to England with William the Conqueror, that a note of formality entered into the previously unruly Yuletide observance. Impressive masses, splendid tournaments and pantomimes, hunting parties, and prodigious feasts were staged. In 1252, for example, King Henry III of England commanded that 600 oxen — to be served with salmon pie, roast peacock, and flowing wine — be slain for his Christmas guests.

To organize entertainment for royalty and nobles during this glorious season, a court director known as the Lord of Misrule supervised masquerades in which costumed mummers arrayed themselves as exotic animals and mythological beasts. By the 12th century, the giving of gifts — stemming ultimately from the scriptural account of the Three Magi, who offered gold, frankincense, and myrrh to the Christ Child (Matthew 2:11) — had become common on Christmas as well as at New Year's. In 1236 the king of France sent the king of England a live elephant.

Today's commercialization of Christmas and excessive eating are pale in comparison with the much more hedonistic medieval celebration. Feasting and revelry were not confined to a single day. They lasted at least to Twelfth Night, the Vigil, or Eve, of the Epiphany, so called because it was the 12th night after Christmas, counting December 25 as the first day. In some cases, the festivities extended for five weeks from Christmas to Candlemas, when Jesus had been presented in the Temple (see February 2). Liturgically, moreover, the season had started still earlier, with Advent at the end of November, and it continued until the beginning of the pre-Easter cycle on Septuagesima Sunday.

Although medieval people celebrated the feast of the Nativity with energy and license, new religious notes were gradually introduced as well. In Greccio, Italy, on Christmas Day 1223, St. Francis of Assisi (see October 4) recreated the Nativity outdoors with actors, live animals, and a natural setting, with only the baby Jesus represented by a wax figure. The crèche in both simple and ornate forms became a beloved Christmas tradition in homes and churches, as it remains today.

Despite clerical admonitions concerning the seasonal excesses in eating, drinking, and other earthly delights, Christmas continued in much the same spirit until the 17th century. The Protestant Reformation in the 16th century slightly toned down the Yuletide revels, but it was left to the English Puritans to push through radical changes in the season. They were dismayed by the dangerous pagan atmosphere, commenting that "there is nothing else used but cardes, dice tables, maskyng, mumming, bowling, and such like fooleries" and that men in liveries of "light wanton colour" even charged into church during services, "their belles iynglyng, their handkerchiefes swyngyng about their heades like madmen."

Once the Puritans had risen to power in England in 1642, Parliament soon decreed that on the day "commonly known as Christmas, no observance shall be had, nor any solemnity used or exercised in churches in respect thereof." Town criers shouted "No Christmas!" and the populace was ordered to work as usual. Even plum puddings and mince pies were outlawed as heathen customs.

When the repressive Puritan Commonwealth ended with the restoration of King Charles II, Christmas, which had gone underground, emerged once more, but shorn of much of its lavishness. Dissenters continued to ridicule the feast, calling it Fooltide instead of Yuletide. The festivities, which thenceforth became social rather than ceremonial, and bourgeois rather than royal, gradually focused on the home, family, and friends.

A number of new Christmas traditions were introduced in the 17th, 18th, and 19th centuries, including the tree and the greeting card. The Christmas tree, as it is now known, originated in Germany, although its history — like that of other Christmas customs — goes back to antiquity, when trees were worshiped as spirits. The Egyptians erected green date palms indoors during their winter solstice rites. The Romans hung trinkets on pine trees during the *Saturnalia*. The druids placed candles, cakes, and gilded apples in tree branches as offerings.

Some scholars trace the modern Christmas tree back to the fir tree erected by Boniface — the 8th century English missionary who was known as the Apostle of Germany — in place of the so-called sacred oak of Odin to which the pagans had offered sacrifices. Others connect it with the fir tree — hung with apples to symbolize the "paradise" tree of the knowledge of good and evil — which was used as a stage prop in 15th century German plays performed at Christmastide. Still others give credit for its origin to Martin Luther, the 16th century Protestant reformer. He supposedly was walking home one clear winter evening, when he noticed brilliant stars twinkling amidst the evergreen trees. To recapture the loveliness of the scene for his family, he erected a tree at home and placed lighted candles on its branches. (Two other historical references to Christmas trees, however, give accounts of very early 16th century celebrations in Latvia and Estonia, not Germany.)

A forest ordinance from Ammerschweier, Alsace, dated 1561, states that no burgher "shall have for Christmas more than one bush of more than eight shoes' length." An early account of a decorated tree was written in 1605: "At Christmas time in Strassburg they set up fir trees in the rooms, and they hang on them roses cut of many-colored paper, apples, wafers, gilt, sugar. . . ." Although the *Christbaum,* or Christ tree, did not meet with unanimous acceptance, by the 1700s the idea was firmly imbedded in Germany. The custom spread slowly throughout other parts of Western Europe, being popularized in England only in the 1840s by Prince Albert, Queen Victoria's German consort. The royal family's gigantic tree, bedecked with wax tapers and sweetmeats, set the trend for the rest of Great Britain. Only as late as 1860 did glass baubles replace edible and handmade ornaments. In the early 20th century, brightly colored electric lights replaced burning candles.

Soon after the inauguration of England's penny post in 1839, one of the newer Christmas traditions originated: the sending of cards to friends and relatives. A card made for Sir Henry Cole in 1843 by J. C. Horsley, a member of the Royal Academy, is usually regarded as the first greeting of its kind. About 1,000 copies of it were sold. The custom of sending cards became more popular in the 1860s, and even then it was not widespread. In the course of time, the English royal family adopted the practice and employed distinguished artists to paint appropriate pictures that were reproduced in color. The custom then spread over the rest of Europe and to America.

It was during the Victorian age (1837–1901), that the observance of Christmas began to assume its present character. The old traditions that combined with technological improvements in the fields of transportation and production spawned the glitter and hustle and bustle of the modern festival. And nowhere are these aspects more evident than in the United States.

A rich blend of customs and traditions has made Christmas in the United States a celebration of remarkable fascination. To a certain extent, of course, December 25 with its turkey dinner, presents, and tree has become homogeneous from East to West and North to South. But in numerous areas of the country, traditional European customs are still practiced in strong ethnic enclaves.

Perhaps most interesting is the retention of customs that have died out in Western Europe. For example, the people of the remote mountain districts of Georgia, Tennessee, and Kentucky continue to commemorate Christmas with ancient, moving carols, long forgotten in their countries of origin. And the inhabitants of cut-off sections of the Ozarks and Atlantic coastline still cling to the Old Christmas Day, January 6.

From the beginning of the main thrust of this country's colonization in the early 17th century, the concept and traditions of Christmas varied widely among the different groups of settlers. Some of the transplanted groups, especially in New England, adopted a severely repressive attitude; others, especially in the South, enjoyed all the gracious pleasures of a festivity with aristocratic overtones.

The country's first clearly recorded Christmas was that of 1607 — if one excludes an isolated religious service, feast, and sports events held in 1604 by the French, who tried unsuccessfully to found a permanent settlement on St. Croix Island off the coast of Maine. The observance of 1607 was at Jamestown, Virginia, where about 40 survivors of the 100 original settlers commemorated the day in the crude wooden chapel of their fort. But rather than a time for heedless gaiety, it was an occasion marked by uncertainties of survival in the wilderness. Their leader, Captain John Smith, was absent, having undertaken the hazardous mission of securing corn from the local Native Americans. Later, however, after the first trying year, the Virginians feasted and rejoiced:

The extreame winde, rayne, frost and snow caused us to keepe Christmas among the salvages where we were never more merry, nor fed on more plenty of good Oysters, Fish, Flesh, Wilde fowl and good bread, nor never had better fires in England.

Southerners, especially the gentlemen farmers, continued to nurture Christmas, regarding it as both a sacred religious period and a time for relaxation. They implanted numerous Old World traditions — such as caroling, the Yule log, and using decorative greenery — and also added to the genteel social celebration their own regional variations. Fried oysters, eggnog, and a Christmas morning hunt for foxes and other game were among the innovations. French settlers in Louisiana introduced the custom of setting off firecrackers and firearms to welcome the Prince of Peace. It spread rapidly to many other Southern localities; today fireworks are still regarded in some parts of the South as an indispensable accompaniment of Christmas. Also traditional in Louisiana are Christmas Eve bonfires that burn all night along the Mississippi from Baton Rouge to New Orleans — a means, it was said, of lighting the way for Father Christmas.

A carnival atmosphere of revelry prevailed among the slaves, who — since December was a slow work season — were on holiday as long as the Yule log burned, sometimes a week or more. The Christmas season became the time for full houses and full larders, the social season for meeting friends and even for weddings. It is not surprising that the first three states to proclaim December 25 a legal holiday were Louisiana and Arkansas (1831) and Alabama (1836).

In stark contrast to the southern Christmas revelers, New Englanders, like the Puritans in England, tried hard to stamp out the "pagan mockery" of the observance, penalizing any frivolity. William Bradford's history *Of Plimoth Plantation* recounts that the Pilgrims who started their colony on Christmas Day 1620 worked hard building houses on the occasion — "no man rested all that day"; but the kindly captain of the *Mayflower* at least caused them to "have some Beere." The following year, Governor Bradford found a newly arrived contingent of colonists

at play, openly; some pitching the barr and some at stoole-ball, and shuch [*sic*] like sports. So he went to them . . . and tould them that was against his conscience, that they should play and others worke. . . . Since which time nothing hath been attempted that way, at least openly.

In 1659 the General Court of Massachusetts enacted a law making any observance of December 25 a penal offense; Massachusetts Bay Colony Puritans were subjected to a five-shilling fine for "observing any such day as Christmas." Although the law was repealed in 1681, in deference to the Puritan tradition many years passed before widespread Christmas festivities were held in New England. The solemn note continued until the 19th century, when the influx of German and Irish immigrants undermined the Puritan legacy. By 1856 the poet Henry Wadsworth Longfellow commented: "We are in a transition state about Christmas here in New England. The old Puritan feeling prevents it from being a cheerful hearty holiday; though every year makes it more so." And in that very year, Massachusetts finally proclaimed Christ-

mas a legal holiday. (In 1890 the new Oklahoma Territory was the last region in the continental United States to take this action.)

The Christmas tree, introduced into America during the Revolutionary War by Hessian troops homesick for Germany, was customary among German settlers in Pennsylvania by the early 19th century. But only in the mid-1800s did the idea spread, especially when a picture of Queen Victoria's elaborate tree appeared in *Godey's Lady's Book,* the fashionable women's magazine of the day. In 1856 President Franklin Pierce set up the first Christmas tree inside the White House. In 1923 President and Mrs. Calvin Coolidge began the custom of lighting a National Christmas Tree on the White House grounds.

Following the appearance of colored electric lights in the early 1900s, the custom of setting up a Christmas tree in a prominent place and decorating it with colored bulbs was adopted in many American cities. With all-weather wiring on the market, Californians started the American custom of outdoor community Christmas trees. The inhabitants of San Diego lighted a pine tree in 1904. Five years later, Pasadenans selected a tall evergreen on Mount Wilson, decorated it with lights and tinsel, and loaded it with gifts, which were distributed on Christmas Day. In 1912 trees were first set up in New York City, Cleveland, and Boston. And in 1914 a tree was placed in Independence Square in Philadelphia.

All over the country communities now vie in displaying trees. Since 1929, Wilmington, North Carolina, for example, has lighted what it claims to be the world's largest living Christmas tree, a 300-year-old water oak. Bothell, Washington, contends that its Douglas fir ranks as the largest living Christmas tree, while Tacoma, Washington, advertises that it sets up the country's tallest cut tree. On April 28, 1926, the US Department of the Interior named the giant General Grant sequoia in Kings Canyon National Park, California, the nation's official Christmas tree. At special Christmastide ceremonies, high school choirs generally sing carols around its base. The village of Christmas, Florida, located 25 miles west of Cape Canaveral, maintains a fully decorated tree throughout the year, and Charlotte, North Carolina, has a famous Singing Christmas Tree, 27 feet 8 inches high, with the singing provided by the 115-member Charlotte Choral Society. A real evergreen tops the singers, making a total height of at least 32 feet.

In recent years, the Christmas tree has undergone an immense transformation with the introduction of artificial trees, which — as of the early 1970s — accounted for an estimated one-third of all trees in homes and offices, their popularity ascribed both to convenience and to the ecology movement. As for real trees, the multimillion dollar business in the United States offers more than 60 different types of tree, ranging in size from 2 to 20 feet and in species from Scotch pine and Douglas fir to cedar. Indeed, the display of trees and other evergreens for sale at shopping centers across the nation is one of the characteristic sights of the Christmas season.

Since the early 1930s, the use of outdoor electric lights has spread from Christmas trees to homes and public buildings. Greater Kansas City, for example, which sponsors a nine-day pre-Christmas carnival, is also the site of a Candy Cane Lane of some 20 to 30 houses that have displayed coordinated decorations over the years. St. Louis's Northwest Plaza of 100 stores is illuminated in a special lighting ceremony at the end of November. Temple Square in Salt Lake City blazes with 100,000 flickering lights. Natchitoches, Louisiana, which began to use street and river lights to express the holiday spirit in 1927, presents another of the country's most colorful spectacles, with a 30-block display of red and green lights during its annual Christmas festival.

Typical of big-city Christmas atmosphere are the festivities in New York City, where decorations begin to appear even before Thanksgiving, and multiply as Christmas approaches. Twinkling lights on skyscrapers, often in the form of crosses; the enormous, 75-foot star atop the Pan American Building; the Christmas tree at Rockefeller Center; the sparkling row of lighted trees along Park Avenue; the department store windows; carol programs; and Christmas shows like the New York City Ballet company's production of *The Nutcracker Suite* — all these contribute to the excitement and movement that give a special flavor to the city's Christmas. Pastry shops in Little Italy, Little Hungary, and Yorkville feature smoked sausages, foot-high gingerbread houses, rich fruit cakes, and other seasonal treats. Santa Clauses appear in department stores and on midtown streets. Church choirs perform special oratorios, including George Frederick Handel's *Messiah*.

Throughout the country, other cities usher in December 25 with similar fanfare. In Philadelphia, a gigantic tree in City Hall Courtyard and other Yuletide trappings transform the downtown area. Snowless St. Petersburg, Florida, offers Christmas decorations on a scale that few northern cities can surpass. Its Tampa Bay waterfront, covering an entire block appropriately dubbed Christmas Park, features a 60-foot tree and Christmas scenes with piped-in music. At the end of Municipal Pier, live deer prance in a "winter snow" scene. For more than two decades, Tampa, Florida, has attracted visitors with

its Christmas Card Lane, an exhibit of giant billboard-size greeting cards drawn by local art students. In Michigan, Grand Haven's Dewey Hill, just across the Grand River from the downtown area, is the site each Christmas of what is claimed to be the world's largest Nativity scene. It covers an area larger than a football field and includes, for example, 32-foot-high camels. Nearby is the immense, electronically operated musical fountain, which features a special Christmas program.

Chicago staged its 29th annual Christmas Around the World festival at the Museum of Science and Industry in 1970. Trees, crèches, concerts, and pageants represented the many ways Christmas is celebrated across the globe, and the museum's dining room offered national dishes of the "country of the day." Each year the Cable Car Carollers in San Francisco board the city's famous cable cars to sing to shoppers and residents during the two weeks before Christmas. In Boston the old Irish tradition of placing candles in the windows to light the way for the Christ Child was introduced in 1910. Mrs. Ralph Adams Cram, who lived in the Beacon Hill section, persuaded some of her friends to join her in the window-lighting custom and in singing carols from house to house. Residents and wandering carolers still carry out the tradition, converging eventually on Beacon Hill's historic Louisburg Square.

Bethlehem, Pennsylvania, a city founded by Moravians, has long been integrally associated with Christmas. It received its name on Christmas Eve, 1741, and is fittingly known as America's Christmas City. Since numerous houses and public buildings display candles in windows, Bethlehem is also known as the Christmas Candle City of America. Except for the rush caused by the large numbers of people who have Christmas cards posted from the city, Bethlehem stages a quiet and dignified Christmas observance. A huge five-pointed Star of Bethlehem on top of South Mountain overlooks the city; the longest of its eight rays measures 81 feet. A community tree is annually lighted on Hill-to-Hill Bridge over the Lehigh River. Impressive Moravian religious services are held on Christmas Eve, when, also, the elaborate community crèche is unveiled (see December 24).

Across the land pre-holiday parades — with television and other show business personalities, reindeer, elves, and Santa Claus — have become annual events in December or late November. (In some warm weather coastal communities there are water parades of decorated and lighted boats as well.) Also associated with Christmas is the poinsettia with its crimson star-shaped blossom, which was introduced into the United

States from Mexico by Joel R. Poinsett, the first American minister to Mexico. The plant, which Mexicans called "flower of the holy night," is seen everywhere in the United States at Christmastime, most notably at San Diego's annual Poinsettia Festival.

Among the more unusual Christmas traditions is the Texas Cowboys' Christmas Ball, held in Anson, Texas, on several evenings before December 25, which dates from the "one grand sworray" that the manager of the local Morning Star Hotel held for cowboys of the region in 1885. The heel-and-toe polka, waltz, Virginia Reel, schottische and other favorite dances — played on the banjo, tambourine, fiddle, and bass viol — were so successful that the ball became a town institution in the late 19th century. Today's guests dance the same numbers as at the first ball and wear the pioneer dress of the 1880s and 1890s.

Another unique event is the Sheepherders' Overall Dance staged at Christmastime by the large group of Basque herders who live in the Boise, Idaho, area. Originated in 1929 to provide entertainment for the local Basques coming home from the hills for the holidays, the dance features such ancient Basque dances as the *jota*, *porrosolda*, and *arreska*. Except for a selected group of outsiders, the annual fete is not open to the general public.

In the Southwest, especially in New Mexico, the long tradition of Spanish rule has resulted in a number of holiday customs also found in Latin America. Among them are the lighting of *luminarias* — candle-and-paper bag lanterns or (in northern New Mexico) small bonfires — to light the path of Mary and Joseph; *Las Posadas*, nine nights of pre-Christmas observance and hospitality in which Mary and Joseph's search for shelter is reenacted and guests are welcomed at homes; and performances of *Los Pastores*, medieval morality dramas based on Christmas themes.

In the Rio Grande pueblos of New Mexico, non-Christian Indian rituals combine with Christian Christmas beliefs introduced by the Spanish to create traditions unique to the area. Ancient Indian ceremonial dances, which are also performed as the climax of the Christmas Eve festivities (see December 24), are common occurrences on December 25 and successive days at most of the area's pueblos. Although they are now presented on a Christian feast day, the dances — which seem to have once marked the winter solstice — are performed "in the way of the ancients," as they have been for centuries. They may include buffalo, deer, or harvest dances, or the basket or rainbow dance. Evidence of Spanish influence is the *matachines*, a

Christmas dance at such pueblos as Santo Domingo, San Felipe, Cochití, San Juan, and, in alternate years, Taos.

Also in part indigenous is the observance of the Alaskan Eskimos, who celebrate Christmas in Arctic villages in the way of their ancestors, with a feast of reindeer and seal blubber with blueberries, as well as with sports events such as snowshoeing, wrestling, dog-team racing, and broad jumping.

A recent, but rapidly growing, innovation is the trend to enjoy an old-fashioned Christmas in the country's historical restorations. The leader in the field is Williamsburg, Virginia, the once-flourishing 18th century capital of the royal colony of Virginia. Eighty-five buildings and 50 houses and outbuildings there have been restored to their original condition through the efforts of John D. Rockefeller Jr. The idea of celebrating the December holidays in the manner of colonial days started on a modest scale in 1934, when outdoor lights illuminated eight evergreen trees. The following year a few candles were set in the windows of the historic buildings, gradually leading to the present-day "white lighting" for which Williamsburg is renowned. The lighting ceremony takes place on December 20. Children form a Singing Candles procession, headed by a night watchman and a fife and drum corps, and walk from the Governor's Palace along the length of the Duke of Gloucester Street in the heart of the restoration. Some 2,000 candles twinkle in the windows of the garland- and holly-adorned houses along the way, as the watchman calls out "Light your candles!" in the winter dusk.

The grand illumination sets off 60-odd Christmastide festivities. Included among the events are candlelight concerts of 18th century music in the Governor's Palace ballroom and Bruton Parish Church; Yule log and wassail festivities; street caroling; fireworks and cannonades in the colonial style of noise-making; and old-fashioned sports such as fencing, hoop-racing, and cudgeling.

Greenfield Village in Dearborn, Michigan, recreates American life of the 17th, 18th, and 19th centuries on a 260-acre tract containing more than 100 historic structures from all over the United States. At Christmastime, sleigh rides, exhibits of traditional Yuletide customs, and special tours through the holiday-decorated buildings are featured. The 19th century coastal village in Mystic, Connecticut, recreated by the Marine Historical Association to demonstrate the life-style of the sailing-ship era, not only lights and decorates its vessels and buildings, but also stages the week before Christmas a community carol sing that usually attracts about

2,000 carolers. The farm museum at Landis Valley, Pennsylvania, presents "Christmas at Landis Valley" as an annual event, generally on the third Tuesday evening in December, with costumed choral and instrumental groups, a torchlight procession, blazing fire, and mulled cider.

In an atmosphere of even more ancient historic tradition, several communities in the United States emulate pagan and early medieval Christian customs. In Rochester, New York, discarded Christmas trees, stacked 25 feet high along Lake Ontario, are annually set afire in a raging Twelfth Night bonfire. The inhabitants of Palmer Lake, Colorado, hold a yearly Yule log hunt in the nearby mountains the Sunday before December 25 and then haul the choice log to their city hall for burning. Trinity Episcopal Cathedral in Cleveland, Ohio, is among several churches that stage an Old English Christmas; against a decor of traditional greenery, an impressive Boar's Head and Yule Log Ceremony is presented — modeled after the ritual at Oxford, England — with a trumpeter, trenchermen, crimson-costumed yule sprites, five choirs, and a soloist who sings the 16th century Boar's Head carol: "The boar's head in hand bear I,/bedecked with bays and rosemary;/and I pray you, my masters, be merry. . . ."

In Puerto Rico and the US Virgin Islands, Christmas is a widely observed holiday, combining traditional island customs with those of today, including Santa Claus and imported trees. Pageants and parties often extend from early December into January, culminating with the feast of the Three Kings on Epiphany (see January 6). In Puerto Rico, singers and musicians strumming guitars and other instruments wander from house to house singing ancient carols known as *aguinaldos*. These strolling carolers are sometimes asked inside to sample special Christmas dishes such as rice pudding and roast pig.

The contemporary Christmas Festival on St. Croix in the Virgin Islands stems ultimately from the island festivities staged there in slaveholding times, when Christmas was the only celebration slaves were allowed to enjoy. After slavery had been abolished there in the mid-19th century, the elaborate native holiday customs died out. Anxious to reintroduce and preserve the local heritage of song and dance, the St. Croix Women's League revived the spice and gaiety of the communal fete in 1952. The Christmas Festival opens with the coronation of the festival queen and reaches a climax with the Three Kings' Day parade on January 6. The festivities generally include a children's parade, horse races, steel band competitions, carol singing, choir concerts, and community tree ceremonies.

In the 20th century, Christmas, in all its varied aspects, has indeed become a nationwide celebration in the United States. It is undoubtedly the most widely observed holiday of the entire year. Statistics indicating the widespread use of Christmas cards — some 2.5 billion in 1970 — are an index of its universality.

Clara Barton's Birthday

The indefatigable Clarissa Harlowe Barton, founder of the American Red Cross, was born on December 25, 1821, on an Oxford, Massachusetts, farm to Stephen and Sarah Stone Barton. An acutely shy girl, she received most of her education from her older brothers and sisters and began a career in teaching at the age of 15, when her mother acted on advice that the way to cure shyness was to "throw responsibility upon her. As soon as her age permits, give her a school to teach."

The prescription contributed to the initiative, self-confidence, and abundant determination that — interspersed with periods of nervous prostration — were to characterize her later life. After a period of study at the Liberal Institute in Clinton, New York, in 1851, she accepted a teaching position in Bordentown, New Jersey, where her fierce energy, and the kind of one-woman campaign for which she was to become noted, led to the abolishment of the fees that pupils had paid to attend school. With establishment of a free system came an enormous increase in student enrollment, overwork, construction of a larger school, opposition to a woman's heading it, and the appointment of a male principal, followed shortly by Barton's resignation, and an attack of nervous exhaustion. In 1854 she made a therapeutic move to Washington, D.C., where she served as a clerk in the US Patent Office until the outbreak of the Civil War.

Her work in providing nursing and supplies for the war wounded began with her aid to the men of the 6th Massachusetts Regiment, who straggled into Washington in April 1861. Later, learning of more war suffering, she ran an advertisement for medical and other supplies in the Worcester (Massachusetts) *Spy* and set up her own distribution agency to deal with the resulting deluge. With her characteristic flair for the practical, she recognized the need for rushing the provisions to the places where they were most needed and set about securing transportation and permission to pass through the lines, board the sick transports, and minister to the wounded at the front. As the war ground on, she labored heroically, first from Washington headquarters and subsequently in action around Charleston, on the battlefield of the Wilderness, at Fredericksburg, and with the Army of the James, acting for a time as superintendent of nurses under the command of General Benjamin Butler. On the whole, however, hers was an unofficial, uncompensated, and single-handed endeavor — including service at the battle of Antietam, where army surgeons were dressing soldiers' wounds with green corn leaves when she arrived with her supplies. During the 1962 centennial commemoration of Antietam, a Clara Barton memorial was erected on Mansfield Avenue just east of Maryland's Route 65, near the spot where she had appeared amid the battle's shot and bursting shells.

Her work attained a more official status after the war, when she organized the government's Bureau of Records in Washington and supervised its search for missing soldiers. In 1869 she was overtaken by one of her periods of failing health and went to Europe for a rest — which was abruptly terminated by the outbreak of the Franco-Prussian War the next year. Once again she plunged into war service, this time in association with the International Red Cross, which had been founded at Geneva in 1863 and officially sanctioned by the 1864 Geneva Convention, the first of four so-titled international agreements for the protection of war victims. During the war she helped establish hospitals and distributed supplies in Paris, Belfort, Montpellier, Strasbourg, and Lyons — finding time en route to set up programs of paid work for destitute women in the last two places. Meanwhile, Red Cross officials in Geneva had asked her to see why the United States, then habitually aloof from European treaties, did not join in the Geneva Convention.

Barton returned home in 1873 with a burning desire to establish an American branch of the Red Cross and bring the United States into the convention. The thought stayed with her during a long period of nervous invalidism, including her 1876 move to Dansville, New York, where she first lived in a sanatorium and then purchased her own home. In 1877 she wrote to Switzerland inquiring whether the Red Cross would approve efforts to organize an American branch, adding that if no person was under consideration for the job she would herself be willing to head such an undertaking. The first local chapter was founded in Dansville.

The Red Cross sent her instructions on procedure and a letter, addressed to President Hayes, which invited the United States to join the Geneva Convention and announced appointment of Clara Barton as the active working head of the Red Cross in America. Thus armed, she embarked on a round of letter writing, appointments with officialdom, and pamphleteering to the public and Congress. Her campaign finally

achieved its goal with Senate confirmation of the Geneva Convention in 1882. In anticipation of this approval, a National Society of the Red Cross was formed in 1881, with the determined Barton as its first president.

In 1884 she was responsible for introduction at the Geneva International Conference of the "American Amendment," specifying that in addition to its war work, the Red Cross was to offer humanitarian relief also during natural disasters. It was the first of several international conferences at which she represented the United States.

Meanwhile, Barton lived through some glorious days of service, directing the American Red Cross's relief work in the 1880s and 1890s and in most cases personally visiting the scenes of war and disaster. Included in the tragic roster were the yellow-fever pestilence in Florida in 1887; the Johnstown, Pennsylvania, flood in 1889; the Russian famine in 1891; and the Boer War from 1899 to 1902. She journeyed to Turkey after the atrocities against Armenians that took place in 1896, and during the Spanish-American War of 1898 she sailed to Cuba, at age 76, with a cargo of supplies. She meanwhile wrote several books on the Red Cross and, at 79, spent six weeks on the scene of the 1900 flood in Galveston, Texas. It was the last work she directed personally from the field.

One of the best known women of the 19th century and a leading figure in public life, Clara Barton supported the campaign for female voting rights and enjoyed the friendship of suffragist leaders. She also showed interest in Christian Science and spiritualism. Her writing — diaries, letters, books — was voluminous.

Barton retired at 82 amid a controversy involving poor business management and her difficulty in sharing responsibility with coworkers. She spent the last eight years of her life at her Victorian-style home in Glen Echo, Maryland, where she died on April 12, 1912. Though her home was scheduled for demolition in early 1963, it was later saved by the Friends of Clara Barton, a nonprofit group that raised funds to purchase the house as a memorial to one woman's accomplishment of the improbable. Just outside Washington, D.C., the 38-room house, now a national historic site administered by the National Park Service, was for seven years headquarters of the American Red Cross.

In the late 1970s, membership in the American Red Cross numbered over 30 million persons. In addition to furnishing relief in some 300 foreign and domestic disasters each year, the organization serves members and veterans of the armed forces and conducts an extensive program of local community services through several thousand local chapters. Included are civilian and military hospital aid; a blood program, including research, which secures millions of volunteer blood donations each year; a vast program of training courses in first aid, water safety, and home nursing; and first aid on the nation's highways.

DECEMBER 26

Feast of St. Stephen

Stephen, the first Christian martyr, has been venerated since his death in about A.D. 35. Because he was the first person to lose his life as a result of professing faith in Jesus Christ — and since the exact date of his death is not known — St. Stephen's feast day came to be observed on December 26, the day after the anniversary of the birth of Christ. It is still celebrated on that day by Roman Catholics, Episcopalians, and Lutherans. Eastern Catholics and members of the Eastern Orthodox Church observe the Feast of St. Stephen on December 27. Those few bodies of the Orthodox Church that still adhere to the Julian, or Old Style, calendar observe his feast 13 days later, on January 9.

According to biblical accounts, in the belief that the Second Coming of Jesus was imminent, the 12 Apostles and other early Christians had disposed of their belongings and were living communally in Jerusalem. As the community grew in size, it became too difficult for the Apostles to attend personally to all of the day-to-day needs of the people. Therefore, as it is recounted in the sixth chapter of Acts of the Apostles, the Apostles called everyone together and asked that they select from among themselves "seven men of honest report, full of the Holy Ghost and wisdom, whom we may appoint over this business." Stephen and six others were chosen and presented to the Apostles, who prayed and laid their hands upon them, thus making them the Church's first deacons.

Almost nothing is known of Stephen's earlier life. He was Jewish, he spoke Greek, and evidence suggests that he was educated in Alexandria, Egypt. He was a fervent Christian. After the appointment of the deacons, the number of believers increased, and "Stephen, full of faith and power, did great wonders and miracles among the people." An ardent preacher, he also debated in some of the synagogues, confounding his listeners by his reasoning. In anger, his enemies persuaded witnesses to say falsely that they had heard him speak blasphemously against Moses and against God.

Stephen was arraigned before the Sanhedrin, the supreme council of the Jews. In a long speech in his own defense, he recounted the history of the children of Israel and concluded with a vigorous denunciation of his accusers, as recounted in Acts (7:51):

Ye stiffnecked and uncircumcised in heart and ears, ye do always resist the Holy Ghost: as your fathers did, so do ye. Which of the prophets have not your fathers persecuted? And they have slain them which shewed before of the coming of the Just One; of whom ye have been now the betrayers and murderers.

Although the council members were violently angry, Stephen, looking up, told them: "Behold, I see the heavens opened, and the Son of man standing on the right hand of God." Seemingly unable to contain their rage, the members of the Sanhedrin immediately took Stephen to a spot outside the city walls, where they stoned him to death. As he was dying, Stephen prayed for forgiveness for his executioners, asking "Lord, lay not this sin to their charge."

Among the witnesses to the stoning was Saul of Tarsus, a young, militant anti-Christian who believed Christianity posed a threat to Judaism. Not only did he consent to Stephen's death, but he held the coats of those who participated in the stoning. The experience affected him deeply. Not long afterward, following a dramatic conversion to Christianity, Saul became the Apostle known as Paul. Stephen's influence on Paul is described in this way by St. Augustine: "If Stephen had not prayed, the Church would not have gained Paul."

The biblical record of Stephen is contained in the sixth, seventh, and eighth chapters of the Acts. Portions of the sixth and seventh chapters are customarily read in churches on his feast day, and it is usual at this time for stress to be placed on prayers in which the faithful ask God to help them to love and pray for their enemies, as Stephen did.

Stephen's burial place was not known. In 415 a priest named Lucian found what he believed to be Stephen's bones in Caphar Gamala, north of Jerusalem. They were disinterred and placed in a church on Mount Zion. Subsequently they were removed to a church built on the spot where, according to tradition, Stephen had been stoned, outside the Damascus Gate of Jerusalem. Various churches dedicated to the martyr have succeeded the original one on this site; at present the Basilica of St. Stephen stands on the ancient foundation. A later tradition suggested that the stoning of Stephen took place east of the city, in the Valley of the Kidron. An eastern gate of the Old City is therefore named St. Stephen's Gate in his memory.

Because he was killed by stoning, Stephen became the patron saint of stonecutters. Also related to the manner of his death was a custom based on an Irish legend. According to the legend, Stephen would have escaped from his captors had they not been awakened by the chirping of a wren. Wrens were therefore stoned — to death, in many cases — each year on St. Stephen's feast day in Ireland, on the Isle of Man, and in parts of England. This custom of "hunting the wren" was finally abandoned as a result of the influence of the Society for the Prevention of Cruelty to Animals.

Battle of Trenton

The months following the issuance of the Declaration of Independence on July 4, 1776, were not auspicious ones for the cause of the American Revolution. In August and September General William Howe, the British commander in chief, drove General George Washington, his American counterpart, from Long Island and New York City. The Virginian retreated north to Westchester County, and, after the battle of White Plains on October 28, he led his war-weary band to Fort Lee, New Jersey. When Lord Charles Cornwallis menaced that outpost with 12 regiments, the colonists surrendered it without a struggle and fled to Newark. From there they went to New Brunswick and then to Trenton, staying one step ahead of their enemies.

Washington knew he could not hold New Jersey. On December 7 he assembled his men and supplies and ferried them across the Delaware River to Pennsylvania. To prevent pursuit, the Americans destroyed as many boats as possible along a 75-mile stretch of the lower Delaware. In any event General Howe determined not to follow his quarry and ceased operations for the winter. He thought of withdrawing to the Newark area, but deployed farther forward with principal posts at Bordentown, Pennington, and Trenton, New Jersey. Such an alignment was militarily less secure, but the British wanted to provide security for the Loyalists in the region and in any event were contemptuous of American military ability.

The patriots gained strength in Pennsylvania. General John Sullivan brought 2,000 men to Washington's assistance, and General Horatio Gates arrived with 500 more. A thousand Philadelphia Associators under Colonel John Cadwalader joined the encampment as did a regiment of Maryland and Pennsylvania Germans under Colonel Nicholas Haussegger. By December 25 General Washington had about 6,000 men ready for combat.

Several factors prompted the American command to launch an attack almost immediately. For one thing, Washington wanted to take advantage of his relative abundance of personnel because the expiration of enlistments on December 31 would reduce the army to 1,400. He also expected the British to attack across the Delaware as soon as the river froze enough to support troops and wanted to disrupt their organization before that time. Finally, the enemy was vulnerable, especially at the Trenton outpost.

Colonel Johann Rall, a Hessian, commanded the British forces at Trenton. Rall was a reputable soldier but thought so little of the rebels that he neglected to take fundamental defensive measures. Contrary to orders, he built no fortifications and sent out no reconnaissance patrols. On the night of December 25 he and his men celebrated Christmas so heartily that the drunken commander had to be carried to bed.

Washington chose the same night to begin a three-pronged attack on Trenton. General James Ewing was to cross at Trenton Ferry with 1,000 militia and cut off a line of retreat by occupying the south bank of the Assunpink Creek. Colonel Cadwalader with 2,000 men was to launch a diversionary attack on Bordentown. Neither of these wings was effective; Ewing could not accomplish the crossing, and Cadwalader arrived too late.

The main column was composed of the 2,400 veterans of Generals John Sullivan and Nathanael Greene. Washington planned to lead it across the Delaware at McKonkey's Ferry (now Washington Crossing) and attack Trenton from the north. General John Glover's regiment of Marblehead, Massachusetts fishermen — who had skillfully evacuated Washington's men from Long Island on August 29 to 30 — now carried them across the river in Durham boats, which normally carried bulk freight. The arduous crossing began at 11:00 P.M., but snow, cold, strong currents, and floating ice delayed its completion until 3:00 A.M.

The patriots began their march about 4:00 A.M. At Birmingham they divided into two columns, one taking the Pennington Road to approach Trenton from the north and the other following the river road to attack from the west. Greene commanded, and Washington accompanied, the former which included the troops of Gererals William Alexander ("Lord Stirling"), Hugh Mercer, and Adam Stephens. Sullivan headed the latter column, which contained the men of Generals John Glover, Arthur St. Clair, and Winthrop Sargent.

At 8 A.M. the battle commenced. The hours lost in crossing the Delaware deprived the Americans of the advantage of attacking at daybreak but did not rob them of the element of surprise. Rall and the main body of his troops were still enjoying a morning-after sleep when the firing began. American artillerists under

Captains Alexander Hamilton and Thomas Forrest quickly silenced the enemy's guns, while the foot soldiers drove the Hessians in outlying sectors back into Trenton.

Bitter close combat marked the fighting in Trenton. The Hessians withdrew to the east of the town and found themselves encircled. Some 300 to 500 managed to escape, but 918 surrendered to the rebels. Twenty-two Germans were killed, including Colonel Rall, and 84 were wounded. Historians differ on how many Americans lost their lives, although it is agreed that no more than four fell at Trenton. Captain William Washington and Lieutenant James Monroe (later President of the United States) were among the few wounded.

Washington decided to return to Pennsylvania, as his men were exhausted and the other columns had not been successful in their missions. The withdrawal consumed another day, and it was just as arduous as every other phase of the battle. The British historian George Otto Trevelyan thought the effort worth while, noting that "it may be doubted whether so small a number of men ever employed so short a space of time with greater or more lasting results upon the history of the world."

Celebrations commemorating the battle of Trenton have taken place frequently since 1776. Those for the 125th anniversary in 1901 were noteworthy. Army and veteran units from Pennsylvania and New Jersey held a reenactment of the engagement and, after the sham battle, participated in a parade with other civic organizations. Governor Foster M. Voorhees of New Jersey and Woodrow Wilson, then a professor at Princeton, gave addresses highlighting the ceremonies. In 1926 the New Jersey Historical Society held a parade and dinner to observe the 150th anniversary; President Calvin Coolidge and the governors of the 13 original states were among those invited.

Since 1953 the annual commemoration has centered around a reenactment on December 25 of Washington's crossing of the Delaware River. St. John Terrell, an actor, producer, and founder of the summer Music Circus at Lambertville, New Jersey, inaugurated this observance, taking the part of George Washington each year. The ceremonies begin in Bucks County, Pennsylvania, at the Washington Crossing State Park with the lowering of the American flag to the sound of taps. Before embarking, Washington performed this same service in honor of Captain James Moore, who died on December 24, 1776, of camp fever. At the nearby tavern that served as the American headquarters, the boat and its crew are described. The costumed actors perform the crossing in

a specially made Durham boat. While rowing they try to maintain the grouping depicted in the painting *Washington Crossing the Delaware*, done 75 years after the event by the German-American artist Emanuel Leutze. Vermont's Green Mountain Boys sit in the bow, while Gloucester fishermen from Massachusetts man the oars. General Washington is represented standing with one foot on the gunwale. Near him are persons portraying General Henry Knox and Lieutenant James Monroe. Monroe carries the 13-star flag of the young republic — a curious anachronism, as the banner had not yet been adopted in 1776.

In 1976 the annual reenactment was part of the 10-day finale celebration that climaxed New Jersey's Bicentennial observance. Included, in addition to the customary re-creation of Washington's crossing, were reenactments of the New Jersey events of the next 9 days — among them the battles of Trenton and of Princeton (see January 3) — that marked a turning point in the American Revolution. Participants in the reenactments included more than 1,000 members of historical societies from some 20 states.

Both sides of the Delaware River have memorials to the battle of Trenton. Pennsylvania's 714-acre Washington Crossing State Park surrounds the area from which the Americans started on their mission, and a monument marks the embarkation point.

The public may visit the restored Thompson-Neely Farmhouse near the Delaware River in which Washington, Knox, and Alexander planned the attack on Trenton. A red cedar tree now standing behind the house was there in 1776. Captain James Moore is buried near the house, as are 20 unknown Continental soldiers. A flagpole surrounded by 13 stones, one from each of the original states, marks the site of the unknown heroes.

Bowman's Hill, on which the patriots established their lookout point, is located in the Washington Crossing State Park. A 110-foot-high stone observation tower now stands atop the hill. A wildflower preserve with well-marked trails and a large picnic area is an additional tourist attraction in the area.

McKonkey's Ferry House in Washington Crossing is the first memorial encountered on the New Jersey side. There Washington and his aides waited for the completion of the troops' crossing. Its restored taproom, kitchen, and a bedroom are open to the public.

In Trenton, today's travelers can visit the Old Barracks on South Willow Street. Public resentment over the quartering of troops in private houses during the French and Indian War led colonial authorities to build the barracks in 1758.

British, Hessian, and American troops used it at various times during the American Revolution. The building was sold after the war, and much of it was demolished in the course of time. The Old Barracks Association, founded in 1902, has preserved the remainder. The association gave the property to New Jersey in 1917 but continues to administer it. Period currency, documents, and firearms are on display.

The Battle Monument State Historic Site at North Broad Street and Pennington Avenue is Trenton's chief memorial. Located where Washington stationed his artillery, it is the highest point in the city. A statue of Washington surmounts the 155-foot granite shaft. Three bronze bas-reliefs illustrating the battle scene decorate its base. There is an observatory at the top.

DECEMBER 27

Feast of St. John, Apostle and Evangelist

The Feast of St. John, Apostle and Evangelist, is celebrated by Roman Catholics, Episcopalians, and Lutherans on December 27 and by Eastern Orthodox churches on May 8. St. John is by tradition called the Beloved Disciple in allusion to the anonymous "disciple whom Jesus loved" mentioned in the Fourth Gospel, long attributed to John. He is also called St. John the Divine, that is, the theologian, because of the theological aspects of the writings ascribed to him, especially the famous opening words of the Gospel of John:

In the beginning was the Word, and the Word was with God, and the Word was God. He was in the beginning with God; all things were made through him, and without him was not anything made that was made. In him was life, and the life was the light of men. The light shines in the darkness, and the darkness has not overcome it.

St. John is also traditionally reputed to have been the author of three New Testament Epistles and the Book of Revelation or Apocalypse. He is thought to have done his writing in the decade before he died, at a very old age, in about the year A.D. 100. The works are remarkable for a sublime and soaring quality — like the eagle, which appears in art as St. John's symbol.

However, 20th century scholarship has cast doubt on whether John actually was the author of these works, though without entirely discrediting the traditional attribution. The matter is still debated by scholars, and many theories have been put forward as to the authorship of the writings. Since some clues to John's biography are included in these works, certain questions about some events of his life are raised. Though the facts are not numerous, however, more is known about this pillar of the early Church than about many other saints.

John and his older brother, James, also later canonized and known as James the Greater, were the sons of Zebedee, a fisherman who lived by the Sea of Galilee, perhaps in Bethsaida, and of Zebedee's wife, who was probably Salome, one of the women at the foot of the cross when Jesus was crucified. John and James were among the first apostles to be chosen by Jesus, just after Peter and his brother Andrew. The story is told in Matthew 4:18–22:

As he walked by the Sea of Galilee, he saw two brothers, Simon who is called Peter and Andrew his brother, casting a net into the sea; for they were fishermen. And he said to them, "Follow me, and I will make you fishers of men." Immediately they left their nets and followed him. And going on from there he saw two other brothers, James the son of Zebedee and John his brother, in the boat . . . mending their nets, and he called them. Immediately they left the boat . . . and followed him.

From that time on, John and his brother, James, together with Peter, were present at most of the important events of Jesus' life, including such momentous and relatively private ones as the Transfiguration and the Agony in Gethsemane.

In spite of their closeness to Jesus, it took some time for the sons of Zebedee to understand their master's message of love and peace. Although John is often pictured as a mild-mannered old man or a younger man languishing on the breast of Jesus at the Last Supper, John and his brother were nicknamed Boanerges, or Sons of Thunder, by Jesus, who often had to rebuke them for their zeal and rash impulses — as when a Samaritan town would not receive Jesus and his disciples, and James and John asked their master if he wanted them to "bid fire come down and consume" the villagers.

Their seniority among the Apostles and their closeness to Jesus may have made the sons of Zebedee a little brash, too, according to an incident related in Mark 10:35–45. It was near the end of Christ's ministry on earth, and John and James "came forward . . . and said to him, 'Teacher, we want you to do for us whatever we ask of you.'" That in itself probably seemed presumptuous, but when Jesus asked what they wanted, they reportedly replied, "'Grant us to sit, one at your right hand and one at your left, in your glory.'" Understandably, the other Apostles were aroused to indignation by the request.

There is, however, no doubt that Jesus loved John in spite of his having to rebuke the sons of Zebedee so often. If John can be identified with the Beloved Disciple, one of the passages profoundly illustrative of this is to be found in John 19:25–28. The verses relate how, while he was dying on the cross, Jesus entrusted Mary, his mother, to the care of an unnamed disciple in simple, matter-of-fact words: "When Jesus saw his mother, and the disciple whom he loved standing near, he said to his mother, 'Woman, behold your son!' Then he said to the disciple, 'Behold, your mother!' And from that hour the disciple took her to his own home."

It is related that after the Resurrection and Pentecost, John often preached and traveled with Peter and was at least once arrested with him. The incident and its cause are reported in detail by Luke in Acts 3 and 4, and the passage, while it does not describe the physical aspects of Peter and John, does indicate the impression these two fishermen made on the learned and cultivated religious and civil authorities at Jerusalem: "Now when they saw the boldness of Peter and John, and perceived that they were uneducated, common men, they wondered; and they recognized that they had been with Jesus."

After his brother James was martyred — probably in A.D. 42 or 44 — John apparently left Palestine and traveled through Asia Minor, teaching Christ's message and establishing the Church there. He was considered the head of all Christian communities in Asia Minor. During one period of persecution, he was exiled to the island of Patmos in the Aegean Sea. Those who ascribe to John the Apocalypse or Book of Revelation, a highly symbolic view of things to come, hold that it was while he was on Patmos that he experienced the revelations related in that work.

Apart from the period of exile on the island, John apparently spent much of his later life in Ephesus, where he died, the only Apostle to die a natural death. He had lived a long life. He had been given enough time and grace to become a mellower, gentler theologian who, though uneducated, expounded Jesus' religious teachings in clear fashion.

According to St. Jerome, when the evangelist was very old and too weak to preach he still was visited by crowds of pilgrims who had traveled far to see the only living Apostle and to seek wisdom from him. For them, Jerome states,

John compressed to their essence the teachings of Jesus in these words: "Little children, love one another. That is the Lord's command: and if you keep it, that by itself is enough." The message is strikingly similar to that expressed in the first Epistle of John (4:8): "He who does not love does not know God; for God is love."

DECEMBER 28

Feast of the Holy Innocents (Childermas)

December 28, the Feast of the Holy Innocents, commemorates the innocent male child-martyrs of Bethlehem and its surroundings who were slaughtered by King Herod the Great's soldiers just before the beginning of the first century A.D. The king of Judea, fearful that the Infant Jesus — the "King of the Jews," of whose birth he had learned through Wise Men from the East — would be a contender for the Palestinian throne, had ordered the massacre of all baby boys two years old and under, in an effort to kill his supposed rival. The traditional anniversary was formerly known in the Western world, under its ancient designation of children's mass (Childermas in England).

The Church began to celebrate the feast not later than the end of the fifth century. It set the date for the observance arbitrarily, since no definite information was available about when the incident had taken place — except that it must have occurred within two years of Jesus' birth: males older than two remained unharmed. However, the date of the Nativity was itself highly speculative. Early churchmen therefore contented themselves with commemorating the little ones, the first martyrs who had suffered death in place of the Infant Jesus, within the Octave (eight days) of Christmas. In Christian art, the slaying was already represented in a fifth century mosaic on an arch in the basilica of Santa Maria Maggiore in Rome.

At present, the day is commemorated by Roman Catholics, Episcopalians, and Lutherans. Most of the less liturgical Protestant churches pass over or only briefly note the feast. The Collect specified in the Episcopal Book of Common Prayer for this day aptly intones the spirit of the occasion:

O Almighty God, who out of the mouths of babes and sucklings hast ordained strength, and madest infants to glorify thee by their deaths; Mortify and kill all vices in us, and so strengthen us by thy grace, that by the innocency of our lives, and constancy of our faith even unto death, we may glorify thy holy name. . . .

Eastern Orthodox churches set aside December 29 in honor of the children, except for those that still adhere to the Julian, or Old Style, calendar and observe the feast 13 days later.

The story of the massacre of the innocents is told in the second chapter of the Gospel of Matthew. In most churches that note the occasion, the prescribed Gospel reading for the day is generally given as Matthew 2:13–18, but the complete account of the original event may be found in Matthew 2:7–18. The Wise Men of the East had arrived in Jerusalem and had made inquiries concerning the birth of the "King of the Jews," which had been made known to them by the appearance of his star. Herod ordered the Wise Men to search for the Infant Jesus in Bethlehem, saying that he wanted to know where to worship him. When they found Jesus, they gave him gifts and worshiped him. Warned in a dream not to go back to Jerusalem, they returned home. Then an angel appeared to Joseph in a dream, saying, "Rise, take the child and his mother, and flee to Egypt . . . for Herod is about to search for the child, to destroy him." They departed for Egypt, where they were to remain until Herod's death.

Then Herod, when he saw that he had been tricked by the wise men, was in a furious rage, and he sent and killed all the male children in Bethlehem and in all that region who were two years old and under, according to the time which he had ascertained from the wise men. Then was fulfilled what was spoken by the prophet Jeremiah: "A voice was heard in Ramah, wailing and loud lamentation, Rachel weeping for her children; she refused to be consoled, because they were no more."

Some modern scholars tend to doubt the historicity of the biblical account. They often regard it — with such wondrous elements as the star of Bethlehem and the Wise Men — as a type of literary midrash, or interpretive commentary, with strong emphasis on the spirit of the passage, rather than on its literal interpretation. They therefore think of it not as a historical narrative but as a symbolic story, the theological meaning of which far outweighs its factual authenticity. In their opinion, the Evangelist wished to emphasize the wordly resistance to Jesus' spiritual mission and took inspiration from a midrash of Deuteronomy 26:5–8. Just as Laban the Aramaean attempted to wipe out the family of Jacob, or Israel, in the Old Testament, they assert, so did Matthew in the New Testament deliberately make Herod the Great try — by massacring the Holy Innocents — to prevent the coming of

Christ, the Messiah or new "Jacob-Israel," who would lead God's new Chosen People. The parallel, some modern critics contend, is further underlined since Rachel, Jacob's wife, figures in Matthew 2:18 as a chief mourner.

Scholars also point out that Matthew's episode cannot be substantiated in any other contemporary source. Above all, Flavius Josephus (A.D. 37/38–95?), the noted Jewish historian of the era, who, in his *Antiquities of the Jews,* listed other crimes committed by Herod, did not mention the incident. On the other hand, it must be remembered that Herod the Great — 73(?)– 4 B.C. — had a cruel streak in his character; as he grew older, he became pathologically jealous and suspicious and during the last years of his reign was undoubtedly insane. He ordered so many horrifying atrocities, including the execution of three of his sons and one of his wives, that even a mass killing of children may not at the time have been considered especially unusual.

Moreover, the number of infants slain has been variously estimated. Some Eastern Orthodox churches, including the Greek and Russian Orthodox, put it at 14,000 boys. The Syrian liturgy refers to the 64,000 Holy Innocents. Medieval authors based their improbable estimate of 144,000 on a passage in the Book of Revelation (14:1–5, which is the customary Epistle of the feast).

Medieval artists invariably played up the horror and brutality of the episode by grossly exaggerating the numbers involved. Modern scriptural specialists have reduced the number to correspond with the probabilities. Since Bethlehem was a small town, they have conjectured on the basis of its likely population at the time of Jesus' birth that not more than 15 or 20 infants could have been killed. Some experts reduce the number even further.

Despite the bloody depictions of the massacre in the art and literature of the Middle Ages, December 28 became in some sections of the West a happy occasion reminiscent of April Fool's Day. The youngest monk and nun in monasteries and convents were given leave to exercise authority as "abbot" and "abbess" for 24 hours. Children were temporarily permitted to "rule" the house and play practical jokes on their parents and relatives. In Belgium, for example, where legend claims that two of the innocents were buried in the province of Namur, boys and girls still boisterously "lock up" adults on this feast day, they then require them to pay a ransom consisting of candy, money, an orange, or a toy. Mexican "innocents" celebrate the Día de los Inocentes by "borrowing" a cherished memento or money from grown-ups and substituting a worthless trifle in its place. In Thuringia, now in East Germany, children celebrate the Feast of the Holy Innocents (Allerkindertag) with a tradition known as "whipping with fresh greens," which may stem back to a pagan purification ritual to scare away evil spirts. Taking branches and switches, they "whip" passersby and ask for monetary "contributions."

On the other hand, there is a popular superstition, especially in England, that December 28 is an unlucky day. In medieval times, when the feast was known as Childermas, marriages, promises, or other binding obligations were carefully avoided at this time. A 15th century king, Edward IV of England, for example, put off his coronation, set for December 28, until the next day. The feast was equally unlucky for English children, who were formerly beaten in bed on Childermas morning in remembrance of Herod's deed. This custom, which survived into the 17th century, even spread to the English colonies in the New World. An early New England Puritan noted: "It hath been a custom to whip up the children on Holy Innocents' Day morning, that the memories of this murther might stick the closer." In some sections of England, even today, Holy Innocents' Day is known as Cross Day. In outlying districts church bells may still be muffled and altars draped in black or purple as signs of sorrow. In line with the Old English superstition that no venture begun on December 28 ever flourishes, natives of Shropshire often say of an abortive enterprise that it "must have begun on Cross Day."

In medieval England, as well as in France and Germany, a "boy bishop," having been chosen on the Feast of St. Nicholas, took possession of a cathedral, presided at liturgical ceremonies on that occasion, and reigned through the Feast of the Holy Innocents on December 28. He customarily officiated in the bishop's seat, while "boy ministers" sat in the choir stalls normally occupied by canons. Together they performed all church offices — except the mass — until the religious mockery was condemned by the Council of Basel in 1431. In England, however, the traditional custom lingered on until the time of Queen Elizabeth I. The Statutes of St. Paul's School of 1518 obliged scholars to appear at St. Paul's Church on Childermas Day to "hear the Childe Bishop preach" and contribute one penny to the "Childe Bishop."

Iowa Admitted to the Union

A scant 13 years after the establishment of its first permanent settlement, at Dubuque in 1833, Iowa gained admission to the Union. In fact, having adopted a constitution in 1844, the people of the region had been seeking admission for two years before the proclamation making Iowa the 29th state was signed by President James Polk on December 28, 1846.

The remains of a prehistoric Indian civilization that existed more than 1,000 years ago have been found in the northeastern corner of the state, along the Mississippi River. (The site has been preserved as the Effigy Mounds National Monument, which covers about 1,500 acres.) Some of the mounds built by these early people are in the form of birds and animals.

The first Europeans to visit what is now the state of Iowa were the French explorers Father Jacques Marquette and Louis Joliet, who had been commissioned by the governor of Canada to explore the Mississippi River. During their voyage down the river, part of which now forms the eastern boundary of the state, their expedition reached Iowa in June of 1673. At that time the area was inhabited by various Siouan tribes, including the Iowa, from whom the state was to take its name. They lived in earth lodges in villages, doing some farming and also hunting bison. Subsequently these tribes were largely displaced by Indians of Algonquian stock, including the Sauks and Foxes, whose economy was similar. Some exploration of the Iowa region was carried out in 1680 by the Flemish missionary Father Louis Hennepin, who led an expedition that was also principally concerned with exploring the Mississippi. Joliet's notes were lost, but both Marquette and Hennepin published accounts of their travels.

France formally claimed the Mississippi valley region, which it called Louisiana (Louisiane), in 1682. No settlements were made in the area comprising Iowa, and in 1762 France ceded that region and a vast amount of other territory lying west of the Mississippi to Spain. Not until another 34 years had passed did Spain make the first land grant in Iowa territory. At that time (1796), about 189 square miles of land were given to a French Canadian, Julien Dubuque, who had settled in the area in 1788, received permission from the Fox Indians to mine the valuable lead deposits, and established a trading post. After Dubuque died in 1810, however, no one remained at his settlement. His land included the site on which the city of Dubuque was later founded. His burial place, on the south edge of the city, is marked by the Julien Dubuque Monument, a circular tower built in 1897. Set in a park of nearly 18 acres and overlooking the Mississippi River, it is on the site of Dubuque's mine.

During the period of Spanish sovereignty, only two additional land grants were made; neither became the site of a permanent settlement. Then, France induced the king of Spain to return the Louisiana territory ceded in 1762. This was accomplished by the secret Treaty of San Ildefonso in 1800. Despite the treaty provision that France would not subsequently relinquish ownership of Louisiana to any country other than Spain, it negotiated the sale of the entire vast region to the United States in 1803. Known as the Louisiana Purchase, this transaction added more than 800,000 square miles to the area of the United States, the largest single acquisition ever made by this country.

Having acquired this immense tract of land, much of which was known only to the Native Americans who lived on it, President Thomas Jefferson designated Captain Meriwether Lewis and William Clark to organize an exploratory expedition. While the Lewis and Clark expedition was traveling up the Missouri River (which now forms the western boundary of Iowa) in 1804, one of the staff, Sergeant Charles Floyd, died and was buried on the Iowa side of the river. The Floyd monument in Sioux City honors him, as does the name of the village of Sergeant Bluff.

Beginning in 1805, what is now Iowa formed part of various administrative territories of the United States. It was first included in Louisiana Territory from 1805 to 1812, when that huge region was renamed Missouri Territory. That name held until 1821, when a portion of the area was admitted to the Union as the state of Missouri. For the next 13 years the remainder of the former Missouri Territory, including Iowa, was an unorganized area of the United States. Then, from 1834 to 1836, what is now Iowa was part of Michigan Territory; later, from 1836 to 1838, it was included in Wisconsin Territory. In the latter year, Congress separated Iowa and certain other land — north to Canada and as far west as the Missouri River — from Wisconsin Territory and constituted it as Iowa Territory.

A third of the 19th century passed before the Indians living in the Iowa area saw many settlers; meanwhile, warfare erupted frequently among the various tribes. Settlers slowly began to drift into Iowa beginning about 1830. The rate of settlement increased rapidly when opposition to the white incursion by a number of tribes under the leadership of the Sauk chief Black Hawk was ended by their defeat in 1832. Immediately after this so-called Black Hawk War, the Indians were forced to cede almost 9,000 square miles of territory on the Iowa side of the Mississippi River. Settlers lost no time in establishing towns along the riverbank. Dubuque was the first permanent community to be founded, in 1833. Burlington and Davenport were among the other earliest settlements.

Bit by bit, during the 20 years following Black Hawk's defeat, the Indians gave up their claims to land in Iowa. A population count in 1836 revealed that 10,531 whites had already settled in the region. Within the next four years, 43,112 were making their home in Iowa. Burlington served as the temporary capital of Iowa Territory when it was organized in 1838. In the following year a site on the Iowa River about 30 miles from the Mississippi was selected and laid out as the permanent capital, to be called Iowa City.

Sentiment for statehood developed swiftly. By 1844 a constitution had been framed, and application had been made for admission to the Union. Discussion and debate in the US Congress concerning the acceptability of the Iowa constitution and the proposed boundaries of the new state consumed two years' time. A new constitution was adopted in 1846. Finally, on December 28, 1846, the state of Iowa was formally created, with Iowa City as its capital. The remainder of the territory was divided, some years later, among the new states of Minnesota, North Dakota, and South Dakota.

The area around Des Moines, in the south-central part of the state, had been opened for settlement in 1845, and in 1857 the city of Des Moines replaced Iowa City as the state capital. The Old Capitol in Iowa City, which now houses administrative offices of the University of Iowa, is of architectural as well as historic interest.

DECEMBER 29

Andrew Johnson's Birthday

Andrew Johnson, whose term as the nation's 17th President was among the most troubled in the history of the country, was born in Raleigh, North Carolina, on December 29, 1808. He was the younger son of Mary McDonough Johnson and Jacob Johnson, a sexton and bank porter who died when the boy was only four years old. Although his mother remarried, the family was not well off, and Andrew Johnson was apprenticed to a tailor at 14. His apprenticeship did not permit time for regular schooling, but Johnson studied on his own.

In 1826 he moved with his mother and stepfather to Tennessee, where they eventually settled in Greeneville. He is still honored by that state's annual designation of Andrew Johnson Week, in March, and Andrew Johnson Day, on April 15. On May 17, 1827, Johnson married Eliza McCardle. Their marriage brought them five children. His wife helped Johnson study arithmetic and English. He also joined a debating society of students from Greeneville College to improve his public speaking. In 1828 he organized a party of working men in opposition to the planters. Elected alderman in Greeneville, Johnson served two years. In the meantime he had bought his own tailor shop and had established a good local business.

Politics now began to crowd into the center of Johnson's life. In 1830 he was elected mayor and served for three terms. He then successfully ran for the state legislature, starting his term there in 1835. He was defeated for reelection in 1837 but won again in 1839. During his tenure in the Tennessee legislature, Johnson emerged as a Jacksonian Democrat with a special hatred for aristocratic privilege. He moved up to the state senate in 1841 and two years later was elected to the 28th Congress in Washington as a representative from Tennessee. He stayed in the House of Representatives 10 years, until his district was gerrymandered by Whigs.

During his decade as a representative, Johnson was strongly antiabolitionist. Yet simultaneously he was extremely forward-looking in his views on democratizing government. At all times he supported the interests of poor white people against the wealthy planter class. He called for direct election of senators, popular election of federal judges, and abolition of the electoral college. He widened his following through his advocacy of homestead legislation to provide free land for settlers, a stand designed to appeal to both eastern workers and westerners.

In 1853 Johnson was elected governor of Tennessee. Running for reelection in 1855, he won as a moderate against the anti-immigrant American (or Know-Nothing) party. While governor, he pushed through Tennessee's first state tax in support of public education. He also obtained authorization for a state board of agriculture and a state library. In 1857 the Tennessee legislature sent him to the US Senate.

In April 1860 Johnson's name was put forward for presidential nomination at the Democratic National Convention in Charleston, South Carolina. When the regular Democratic convention refused to include a proslavery platform, the Southerners left and refused to support Stephen A. Douglas, who became the party's regular nominee. Though initially indecisive, Johnson finally chose to support the Southerners' nominee, John C. Breckinridge.

Immediately after Abraham Lincoln was elected President, a wave of secessionist sentiment swept the South. On December 18, 1860, at the time of the South Carolina secession convention, Johnson bravely delivered a speech in the Senate supporting the principle of federal union. The announcement of the secession of South Carolina on December 20 was followed by that of six other Southern states. Together they formed the Confederate States of America, later expanded with the admission of four more Southern states and commonly referred to as the Confederacy.

Johnson remained conspicuously alone when every other Southern senator withdrew from the Senate. Although he was reviled as a traitor by most Southerners, Northerners hailed him as a second Andrew Jackson for his support of union above all else. On July 24, 1861, some three months after the Civil War had begun, Johnson introduced a resolution in a special session of the Senate, which declared union and the preservation of the Constitution to be the only war aim of the North. During the winter of 1861–1862 he served on the important joint committee on the conduct of the war.

In March 1862 Johnson sacrificed his relatively powerful Senate position to accept President Lincoln's appointment as military governor of Tennessee. Unfortunately for Johnson, however, the Union-oriented eastern portion of Tennessee was overrun by the Confederates and remained in their hands until 1863. Thus he could exercise his official powers only in western Tennessee, an area whose residents were hostile to the Union. Under his guidance, western Tennessee became something of a laboratory for his later moderate views on the reconstruction of the defeated South.

During the summer of 1864, an election year, the Civil War was not going well for the North. Faced with the distinct possibility that Northern Democrats might win the presidential election, the Republican party looked for ways to broaden its popular support, renaming itself the National Union Party to attract war Democrats. The sectional image of the party was further modified with Johnson, a war Democrat, as the vice presidential candidate on the ticket with Lincoln. Although the Republicans won the election, Johnson's health had been badly sapped by the strenuous campaign. Though still ill (probably with malaria), at the President's request he dragged himself to the inauguration, steadying himself with a drink that severely affected him and resulted in a display of intoxication later used as a political bludgeon by his enemies.

Lincoln was shot on April 14, 1865, and when he died the following day, Johnson became President. Since the Civil War had been virtually concluded five days earlier by Lee's surrender at Appomattox Court House (see April 9) after four years of bloody conflict, Johnson found himself facing the unprecedented task of reuniting the divided country.

In the word "unprecedented" lies the heart

of the problems of the Reconstruction era. The Constitution did not anticipate or provide for the possibility of secession. Thus, Reconstruction had to be effected with no guidelines to the solution of important questions. Were the Southern states to be regarded as conquered territory, or as states temporarily out of proper order? How should individual Confederate leaders be dealt with: should they lose not only political power but also economic power as well? What was the status of freed blacks? Did freedom from slavery imply legal, economic, and social equality with whites?

Questions such as these required resolution, and a power struggle developed between the President and Congress over who should make the decisions. Johnson's first statements were approved by Northern public opinion. "Treason must be made infamous and traitors must be impoverished," said the new President, a statement that made the Radical Republicans (who did not then control Congress) feel that Johnson would be easier to deal with than Lincoln, whom they had considered too lenient in his attitude toward the South. The Radicals were, however, to be surprised. Congress left Washington for the summer, and the Union armies were quickly disbanded. Immediately, Johnson began to formulate a plan for presidential reconstruction of the South. It was his aim to complete the mechanics of restoring the Southern states to what Lincoln had called their "proper practical relation with the Union" before Congress reassembled in December 1865. ("Readmission" to the Union, the term often used, was not the issue, since the federal government had never recognized the right of the Confederate states to secede.)

On May 29, 1865, Johnson issued a proclamation embodying an amnesty plan along lines drawn by Lincoln. Amnesty was provided for those who would swear allegiance to the Constitution and the Union and to the provisions of the 13th Amendment, forbidding slavery (see December 18). However, former high officeholders of the Confederacy, those who had mistreated prisoners of war, and those whose taxable wealth was over $20,000 were generally barred from pardon. The exclusion of propertied Southerners was Johnson's own special provision in the hope of giving power to small farmers.

But soon many wealthy Southerners, including those who had formed the leadership of the Confederacy, were streaming into Johnson's office seeking special pardons, and the President was liberal in granting such requests.

Among Johnson's other early actions as President was his recognition of the new loyal governments set up under Lincoln in the four states of Arkansas, Louisiana, Tennessee, and Virginia. Johnson then went on to organize provisional governments for the seven remaining states of the former Confederacy. In another important action, on December 25, 1865, he issued a general pardon for the offense of treason.

By this time, most of the Southern states had satisfied Johnson's liberal criteria for restoration of the privileges of statehood. He also decreed that loyal Southerners could determine the qualifications for their own offices. None of these moves endeared Johnson either to the congressional Radicals or to the moderate Republicans, who were increasingly supporting them.

Therefore, when Congress returned to Washington in December 1865, its members were already alarmed over Johnson's apparent *fait accompli*. Under the presidential policy, it was expected that conventions of delegates pledged to support the Union, the Constitution, and the laws concerning emancipation would be called by the provisional governors in the Southern states for the purpose of repudiating secession, reframing state constitutions, and preparing for restoration to the Union. These conventions were also expected to accept emancipation and to repudiate Confederate war debts.

The unease of Northern representatives to Congress was exacerbated, however, when the state conventions showed disdain for the opinions of the Northern victors by watering down state resolutions regarding rejection of slavery and secession, and in other ways. The image of Southerners as unregenerate rebels grew as legislatures of the former Confederate states passed "black codes," which, to many eyes, effectively reduced blacks to the level of serfs. Many Northerners regarded the new rules as de facto slavery, whereas to Southern whites, the codes were merely regulations needed to meet a new and difficult situation.

None of this interested Johnson, who considered Reconstruction now complete — but was to learn otherwise. The actions he had taken during the congressional recess had begun to erode his working relationship with Congress. That body would not immediately allow the seating of the newly elected Southern congressmen who, under Johnson's Reconstruction program, now stood ready to represent their states in Congress when statehood privileges were restored. In its fear that too many of the South's former leaders were returning to power and that emancipation was not being accepted in good faith, Congress created a joint committee to study all bills pertaining to Reconstruction — thus serving notice that it did not consider the matter closed.

In February 1866 Congress also passed a bill to continue the existence of the year-old Freedmen's Bureau, a government agency with military authority to protect the civil rights of blacks throughout the South. Johnson promptly vetoed the bill on February 19, arguing that the federal government had no authority to impose military law during peacetime. He thus held the position that Congress could not override the black codes of the Southern states.

Three days after delivering his veto of the Freedmen's bill, Johnson spoke to a Washington's Birthday gathering. Unwisely, he allowed his audience to prod him into accusing Radical leaders Thaddeus Stevens, Charles Sumner, and Wendell Phillips of something close to treason. Such intemperate statements went far toward convincing Congress that Johnson was worse than merely foolhardy.

In the meantime, reports reached Washington that attempts by blacks at political and economic organization were being met with intimidation in many parts of the South. In response to this, Congress passed a civil rights act and, after Johnson's veto, repassed it on April 9, 1866. This act defined citizenship to include black men as well as white and asserted the right of the federal government to override state governments for the protection of citizens' rights.

Johnson's veto — on grounds that the Constitution did not warrant such an extension of federal power — was something of a surprise, as the bill had been regarded by many as a moderate compromise measure. Overwhelmingly, moderates and cabinet members had urged the President to sign the bill. When he refused, the gulf between himself and Congress became complete.

Many congressmen also feared that the bill might indeed be unconstitutional, and so the 14th Amendment, containing many of the same provisions, was drafted (see July 28). Apart from defining citizenship to include all persons, the 14th Amendment was designed to solve yet another vexing problem. With slavery abolished, the Constitution's "three-fifths" provision — that, in apportioning representatives among the states according to population, five slaves were to be counted as equivalent to three whites — had become obsolete. With the 14th Amendment's provision that apportionment was to be on the basis of a state's total population, excluding Indians not taxed, came the prospect that the South might gain in congressional representation.

That the Civil War might actually result in increased political power for the South was more than Northern congressmen would countenance. Motivated partly by an altruistic desire to safeguard for blacks the gains won in the war, but

also by a purely selfish wish to keep their own party in power, the Radical Republicans therefore wrote into the amendment a provision for reduced representation for states barring male citizens from voting in federal elections. The amendment did not guarantee black suffrage, but it thus theoretically penalized states with large black populations for withholding that right — as most of them still did, along with some Northern states whose black populations were so small that they would not have been affected by the provision. The Reconstruction-bent Congress then made acceptance of the 14th Amendment a prerequisite before Southern states could have their statehood privileges restored. In June 1866 the amendment passed through Congress and went to the states for ratification.

Throughout the spring of 1866, meanwhile, violence against Southern blacks had become more widespread. During May, roving bands of white men burned and shot up the black section of Memphis, Tennessee. By July Congress had passed a new Freedmen's Bill over Johnson's veto. The need for such an agency was immediately evident, for on July 30, white mobs and policemen trapped a political gathering of blacks inside a meeting hall in New Orleans, Louisiana. A merciless hail of bullets through windows and doorways killed 40 people and wounded 136 others.

Incidents such as the New Orleans massacre were used as emotional political material by Radical Republicans for the congressional election campaigns of 1866. In those campaigns, the moderate Republicans might have joined forces with moderate Democrats had Johnson not pushed them into the camp of the Radicals. Thus Johnson's intransigence spelled the end of the wartime Union party.

A good many other people were put off by Johnson's "swing around the circle," the disastrous speaking tour he undertook to help the congressional campaigns of moderate Southern and Northern Democrats, whom he saw as members of a potentially useful coalition sympathetic to his views. Accompanied by various dignitaries, including General Ulysses S. Grant, Johnson set out on the 19-day tour of key Northern cities on August 28 — and made the mistake of repeating one set speech everywhere he went. With national newspapers reporting his past speeches ahead of him, he appeared, at best, unimaginative in his defense of his policies. At the same time, many Radical Republicans were denouncing him as a drunkard and a traitor. Although he was neither, both charges were calculated to win votes for the Radicals.

Their tactics won support in the North, and the voters elected a Congress that was overwhelmingly controlled by the Radical Republicans. The new Congress was even more determined than the old to push through a tough Reconstruction program over Johnson's expected vetoes and did precisely that. An alienated Johnson now became an essentially passive political personality without powers of leadership.

In the months that followed, the defeated South — with the exception of Tennessee, whose restoration to the Union had won congressional approval in 1866 — was placed under martial law. The first Reconstruction Act, of doubtful constitutionality and passed over a presidential veto on March 2, 1867, declared other existing state governments illegal and divided the South into five military districts, each under the control of a major-general with an armed force under his command. To achieve restoration, each state was required to hold a constitutional convention, whose delegates were to be elected by universal suffrage of adult males, both black and white. Excluded from voting were all former Confederate leaders — in effect most of the prior governing class. The states were also required to adopt new constitutions that guaranteed black suffrage and were in harmony with the federal Constitution; to obtain congressional approval of these documents; and to ratify the 14th Amendment.

When the affected states failed to take prompt action along these lines, a second Reconstruction Act, passed on March 23, 1867, authorized military commanders to institute the mechanics of setting up the new state governments, beginning with the enrollment of voters. A third Reconstruction Act, passed on July 19, 1867, further enlarged the duties and powers of military commanders, totally subjecting state civil administrations to their authority. The fourth Reconstruction Act, enacted on March 11, 1868, was designed to keep Southern white voter boycotts from nullifying election results, providing, as it did, that a majority of those voting, regardless of their number, was sufficient to ratify the new state constitutions. Not by accident, these acts and related measures were so designed as to thwart control of the military governments in the South by the President, who had exercised this power by virtue of his position as Commander in Chief. He was now required to give orders not to the army directly but through General Ulysses S. Grant, over whom he was expressly (and unconstitutionally) denied any meaningful authority.

Simultaneously, throughout 1867 a congressional movement was under way to remove Johnson from office by impeachment. Throughout the Reconstruction period, efforts of the legislative branch of government to dominate the executive and judicial branches raised grave constitutional questions. It was clear that the Radical attempts at impeachment were an effort to make the President responsible not only to the people but also to the people's representatives in the legislative branch of government. The impeachment proceedings were power politics, pure and simple. Johnson's moral reputation emerged unscathed from these events, for the Republicans could find no moral or legal pretext for a trial. The first step — a House resolution calling for an investigation of Johnson's record with an eye to impeachment — was initiated in January 1867, but the matter was dropped in December for lack of evidence.

In the meantime a new pretext for impeachment was being generated. In March 1867 Congress passed a Tenure of Office Act prohibiting the President from dismissing without Senate consent any official appointed by and with Senate approval. Unconstitutional as it was, this unprecedented invasion of presidential prerogative was interpreted by many Radicals as extending even to a cabinet member like the Lincoln-appointed secretary of war, Edwin M. Stanton, a Radical Republican who had opposed Johnson at every opportunity. A power struggle ensued when Johnson determined to remove this thorn from his cabinet. On August 12, 1867, he dismissed Stanton and appointed Grant in his place. The Senate reacted by declaring the removal illegal and on January 13, 1868, ordered Stanton reinstated.

Grant, who had agreed to sit in Stanton's place ad interim, now went back to his military duties. Johnson thought that the general had agreed to stay in the post permanently and was furious when Grant stepped down to allow Stanton to return. Johnson's wrath drove the politically uncommitted Grant over to the Radical side and provided the Republicans with a war hero to run for the presidency in 1868.

On February 21, 1868, Johnson replaced Stanton with another general, Lorenzo P. Thomas. With the President's dismissal of Stanton as a pretext, Congress opened impeachment proceedings on February 24, 1868, setting forth on March 2 and 3 a list of "high crimes and misdemeanors," which, when stripped of their verbiage, boiled down to little more than a complaint about his failure to obey the unconstitutional Tenure of Office Act. Radical pressure almost succeeded in moving two-thirds of the senators to support impeachment, and the trial ended in May 1868, only one vote short of conviction. Johnson therefore served out his term but during his remaining year in office was virtually powerless. A bitter and defeated man, he was hated by Northerners as a symbol of their inability to reconstruct the South to their own specifications.

Johnson returned to Tennessee in 1869 and lost his bid for a Senate seat. In 1872 he ran for a seat as representative-at-large but lost again. Though weakened by an attack of yellow fever in 1873, Johnson won his bid for a position as senator in 1874, thus becoming the first man to return to the Senate after serving as President. He went to Washington in March 1875; but, while visiting a daughter in Tennessee soon after the Senate's summer adjournment, he suffered a paralytic attack and died on July 31, 1875. Within two years after his death, the Reconstruction program against which he had fought so hard had also been terminated, with the removal of the last Federal troops from the South after the inauguration of President Rutherford B. Hayes following the disputed election of 1876.

Andrew Johnson was buried in Greeneville, Tennessee, as were other members of his family. His grave, marked by an eagle-capped stone, is now part of the Andrew Johnson National Historic Site, established on April 27, 1942. The site, open to the public, also contains Johnson's two Greeneville homes and his tailor shop. South of Greeneville is an 8,000-acre wildlife preserve, named in his honor the Andrew Johnson Wildlife Area.

The tiny, gambrel-roofed building in Raleigh, North Carolina, in which Johnson was born, was moved from its original location on Fayetteville Street to Pullen Park, adjacent to the North Carolina State University. More recently, the house was moved again — to Raleigh's historic Mordecai Square. Elsewhere in Raleigh — in the six-acre square on which the state capitol is located — stands an equestrian statue honoring the three Presidents born in North Carolina: James K. Polk, Andrew Jackson, and Andrew Johnson.

Texas Admitted to the Union

Some 11 years after Texas' declaration of independence from Mexico (see March 2) and six months after the annexation of Texas by the United States (see March 1), the former republic became the 28th state to enter the Union, on December 29, 1845. (See also March 6, Alamo Day; April 21, San Jacinto Day; and May 13, Mexican War Begins.)

From 1845 until Alaska's admission to statehood on January 3, 1959, Texas remained the largest of all the states, even though sizable portions of its original land area were siphoned off to New Mexico and Colorado, and small portions became part of Oklahoma, Kansas, and Wyoming in the intervening years.

Woodrow Wilson's Birthday

Woodrow Wilson, the 28th President of the United States, was born in Staunton, Virginia, on December 29, 1856. His mother, Janet Woodrow Wilson, was of Scottish descent. His father, Joseph R. Wilson, was a Presbyterian minister descended from Scotch-Irish immigrants.

Although Joseph Wilson had been reared in Ohio, he moved to Virginia three years before the birth of his third child and first son, Thomas Woodrow Wilson. Following the rising professional fortunes of Joseph Wilson, the family moved around the South, finally settling in Wilmington, North Carolina, in 1874. Woodrow Wilson attended Davidson College in North Carolina for one year. Another year of home study prepared him to enter the College of New Jersey (renamed Princeton University in 1896), from which he was graduated in 1879.

Already aspiring to the life of a statesman, Wilson entered the University of Virginia to study law, as he considered it a prerequisite to high public office. He was subsequently admitted to the bar, but, after an unsuccessful year in private law practice, he reentered academic life. At Johns Hopkins University, where he embarked on graduate studies in history and government, he wrote a doctoral dissertation titled "Congressional Government." When this work was published, it was received with some acclaim.

On leaving Johns Hopkins in 1885, Wilson married Ellen Louise Axson. For the next three years he taught history and political economy at Bryn Mawr College. He also taught a single year at Wesleyan University and then was appointed professor of jurisprudence and political economy at Princeton.

Cultivating a forceful and felicitous lecture style, he earned a rising reputation among his colleagues and in 1902 was elected president of the university. During his eight years in that post he worked to raise academic standards, reorganizing the curriculum and introducing the preceptorial system, which was designed to bring students and instructors into a closer and more intellectually stimulating relationship, with emphasis on individual guidance by tutors working with small groups of students. He also sought to democratize the student body and to subordinate the social aspects of student life, deemphasizing the influence of the exclusive undergraduate clubs. This aroused bitter opposition, as did his Quad Plan to divide the university into smaller segments or "quadrangles." With controversy building on controversy, he also became involved in a dispute surrounding the location of the new graduate college and found himself on the losing end of a power struggle with the man chosen to be its dean.

Wilson's speeches on public affairs meanwhile had won favorable attention far beyond Princeton, and his difficulties there had brought him before the public as a champion of democratic principles and defender of the underdog. During his Princeton tenure, Wilson's scholarly writings had been published by Harper & Brothers, then headed by Colonel George B. M. Harvey. Sensing an opportunity, Harvey, an early Wilson admirer, at this point pressed on the New Jersey Democratic organization the desirability of Wilson as a candidate for governor of New Jersey. Machine politicians who thought he would be naive and malleable in office accepted the idea.

Wilson, discouraged by the dim outlook for his program at Princeton, was offered the nomination in September 1910. He resigned the presidency of the university in October, campaigned vigorously, and won the election on a reform platform. Confounding the machine and delighting liberals, he followed no advice but his own in office and achieved a record of reform legislation that brought him nationwide admiration.

Harvey began to urge on Wilson the idea of seeking the Democratic nomination for President. (He was probably the first to put forward the name of Wilson as a presidential possibility, having done so as early as 1906.) Though he later would come to disagree with Wilson's policies, Harvey worked behind the scenes for over a year, rounding up national delegate strength for Wilson. Also contributing important support was Colonel Edward M. House, later one of Wilson's closest advisers.

Placed in nomination at the 1912 Democratic National Convention, Wilson disavowed Tammany aid. He won the decisive support of William Jennings Bryan on the 14th ballot and became the party's nominee on the 46th. With the Republicans weakened by Theodore Roosevelt's bolt from their party, Wilson won the election by the largest electoral majority ever amassed up to that time, even though his popular vote was less than half of the ballots cast.

As a domestic leader, Wilson guided through Congress reforms in several areas. The measures passed during his administration, some of which were to have lasting importance, included the Underwood Tariff Act, which established the Federal Trade Commission, and the Clayton Anti-Trust Act. They also included the Federal Reserve Act of 1913 (see December 23), the sweeping measure of currency reform that was to become a cornerstone of the nation's financial structure.

Military squabbles with Mexico and the coming of World War I in Europe diverted his attention to foreign affairs. Wilson tried to be neutral in the war, hoping that he could bring the warring nations to the peace table. Even after a German submarine sank the *Lusitania*, with the loss of over 100 American lives, he declared that despite provocation, a nation might be "too proud to fight." A strongly worded note brought assurances from Germany that civilian, neutral shipping would not be sunk without warning. However, Wilson, along with most Americans, looked upon the British and French as old friends.

Wilson defended his policy of restraint during the presidential campaign of 1916. His party hailed him as the leader who "kept us out of war." Even so, the election was so close that Wilson went to bed on election night thinking that he had lost and planning to arrange for the immediate transfer of office to his opponent. In the morning, however, he awoke to find that he had won by a very slim majority.

After the election Wilson renewed his diplomatic peace efforts, but could not persuade the two sides to negotiate. At this point, Germany decided that the military advantage of unrestricted submarine warfare outweighed the danger of probable US intervention. With the resumption of submarine attacks on American ships, Wilson, on April 2, 1917, asked Congress for a declaration of war. Congress complied with his request four days later. A draft bill was passed, and about 4 million men were put in training in the ensuing months. Some 2 million Americans sent to France participated in the bloody battles of World War I before the hostilities ended with the armistice of November 11, 1918.

With his wartime addresses stressing a noble conception of the war's purpose as "the ultimate peace of the world," the war to make the world "safe for democracy," Wilson did much to strengthen resolve at home and encourage Europe to look to him for salvation. Best known of all his utterances was his address to Congress on January 8, 1918, outlining the Fourteen Points he recognized as necessary for peace. With the world's potential for peace buttressed by his moral strength, he was at the peak of his influence in the following months.

When the hostilities ended, Wilson arranged to go to Europe to attend the peace conference. Sailing on December 4, he was received in London, Rome, and Paris with great enthusiasm. When the conference assembled at Versailles in January, he proposed that the peace treaty contain the covenant of a League of Nations with provisions for averting war in the future. Through diplomatic pressure, Wilson forced his general peace plan on unwilling allies. Even though the vindictive feelings of the victorious Allies, their secret treaties, and the social unrest on the Continent made specific implementation of his idealistic guidelines all but impossible, compromises were made and Wilson returned from Europe with what he considered a partial victory for principled statesmanship.

But Wilson, whose party had already suffered losses in the congressional elections of 1918, alienated additional support at home by declining to add to the proposed peace treaty even those guarantees of American sovereignty that would have satisfied his opponents. By absolutely refusing to compromise, he assured the Senate defeat of both the treaty and the League of Nations Covenant.

On September 25, 1919, during a strenuous national tour in which he tried to win popular support for his plan, the President collapsed and was forced to return to Washington. A week later he suffered a stroke which largely prevented him from transacting official business and from which he never fully recovered, although he remained technically in office until March 4, 1921.

On his retirement, he and his second wife, Edith Galt Wilson (he was widowed in 1914 and remarried in 1915), moved to the red brick, Georgian-style house at 2340 S Street, N.W., in Washington's Embassy Row section, where he lived until his death on February 3, 1924. The home, restored and open to visitors, was designated as a national historic landmark in 1964. It is filled with Wilson mementos, including the open typewriter, reading glasses, and pillbox that were beside the bed where he died.

Less than a year after his death, the Woodrow Wilson Foundation, established several years earlier in his honor, chose Wilson's birth date for the first of a series of distinguished awards that it presented from time to time over the years, until 1963, to leaders who were deemed to have contributed to the realization of Wilson's ideals. Elihu Root, Bernard Baruch, Harry S. Truman, George C. Marshall, and James B. Conant were among their number. Establishment of the foundation, with the contributions of over 200,000 persons, as a permanent memorial to Wilson was inspired by the award to Wilson of the Nobel Peace Prize in 1920.

During 1956, the Woodrow Wilson Foundation played a major role in the worldwide observance of the 100th anniversary of Wilson's birth, and it has carried on throughout its existence a varied program to promote his ideals.

Since 1957, however, the resources of the foundation have been concentrated on the task of collecting, editing, and publishing the definitive edition of *The Papers of Woodrow Wilson* in a joint project with Princeton University and the Princeton University Press. The first volume of the multivolume collection was published in 1966.

The Princeton campus abounds with Wilson associations, including the Woodrow Wilson School of Public and International Affairs, whose striking colonnaded building, designed by Minoru Yamasaki, was dedicated in 1966 with President Lyndon B. Johnson as the chief speaker. There are also the Jo Davidson bust of Wilson in Firestone Library, the inscriptions at the entrance of Corwin Hall, and the Woodrow Wilson Professorship of Literature and the Woodrow Wilson Prize, awarded each year to an alumnus who has shown outstanding dedication to — in Wilson's phrase — "the Nation's service."

Perhaps the most interesting development, and one not without its ironies, was the 1958 founding of the Woodrow Wilson Society, offering, in effect, a social and intellectual alternative to the "eating clubs." In 1967 Woodrow Wilson College — named to recognize Wilson's early support of the quadrangle idea — was formed with this group as a nucleus. Providing unified residential, study, dining, and social facilities for students, the college comprises Wilcox Hall and the surrounding quadrangle of dormitories.

In Geneva, Switzerland, once the home of the League of Nations (see January 10), Wilson is twice memorialized — by the plaque on the lakeside Palais Wilson, the original building of the league, and by the bronze globe in the gardens of the magnificent structure designed as the league's permanent headquarters. The building now houses the central European offices of the United Nations, which in time succeeded the league.

The Woodrow Wilson International Center for Scholars, founded by Congress in 1968 as the nation's memorial to President Wilson, is located in the main building of the Smithsonian Institution in Washington, D.C. The center awards fellowships for research at the Smithsonian on fundamental political, social, and intellectual issues.

Wilsonians also find interest in the Woodrow Wilson Birthplace, the Greek Revival one-time parsonage in Staunton, Virginia, where Wilson spent his first year. Enhanced with original furnishings and mementos, it is open to the public. Also preserved is Wilson's boyhood home in Columbia, South Carolina, built by his father.

DECEMBER 30

The Gadsden Purchase

Although the Treaty of Guadalupe Hidalgo, which ended the Mexican War in 1848 (see February 2), settled the major difficulties between the United States and Mexico, a number of problems arose within a few years of the signing that necessitated further negotiations between the two countries. Mexico charged that the United States had failed to deal effectively with continuing Apache raids south of the Rio Grande — a violation of Article XI of the treaty — and demanded reparations of $15 million to $30 million. The United States, for its part, wanted control of an area in the Southwest to which both countries laid claim.

The dispute over this territory — today the southern sections of Arizona and New Mexico — began because of an ambiguity in the 1848 treaty. That treaty had definitively fixed the international boundary from El Paso, Texas, east to the Gulf of Mexico; but west of El Paso, the exact location of the line of demarcation was in doubt. The area in question was important to both the United States and Mexico: the former nation wanted it as a possible route for its transcontinental railroad; the latter country could ill afford further territorial losses to its northern neighbor.

Promoters of the southern transcontinental railroad route had the strong support of Secretary of War Jefferson Davis. The Mississippian, who later served as president of the Confederacy, arranged to send James Gadsden, a South Carolina railroad president, as US minister to Mexico in May 1853. Gadsden's primary objective was to obtain the territory needed for the southern railroad route, but he was also authorized to bargain for any additional land the Mexican president, General Antonio López de Santa Anna would agree to sell.

On December 30, 1853, Gadsden completed successful negotiations with Santa Anna. He had persuaded the Mexicans to agree to the abrogation of Article XI of the 1848 treaty and to give up their claims against the United States. But even more important, he had succeeded in purchasing the Mesilla Valley and 19 million acres south of the Gila River for $15 million.

The US Senate reduced the payment to $10 million, and the land cession was proportionately lessened to about 29,640 square miles, but this smaller area included all of the territory needed for the transcontinental railroad. (The first transcontinental railroad was not built along this route, however; not until several decades after the Civil War was construction of the southern railroad route completed.) Gadsden's

treaty was proclaimed in June 1854, and the boundary between the United States and Mexico has not been altered since that date.

DECEMBER 31

New Year's Eve

The approach of the New Year has been celebrated on the evening of December 31 since colonial times in the United States. Here, as in many other lands all over the world, the custom of greeting the hour of midnight by ringing bells, blowing horns, clashing gongs, tooting whistles, shooting firearms, and throwing confetti is widespread. New Year's Eve parties, usually extending into the early hours of New Year's Day (see January 1), have become traditional, as friends and relatives gather in homes, hotels, restaurants, and other city centers to bid the old year farewell and welcome in the new. Church services, with quiet meditation and hymn or carol singing, also mark the occasion. So does the traditional making of New Year's resolutions, by which each individual determines to live in an exemplary way, or at least an improved one, in the new year.

Some of the New Year's Eve traditions rank among the oldest customs known. The raucous din — which is said to have originated in Babylonian and Indian new year's observances — is a relic of the ancient past, when the need was felt to frighten away the spirits believed wandering the earth at the year's change. In northern and central Europe, ancient folk beliefs hold that prowling devils must be decisively routed on the last night of the year with mummery and noise. Men and boys still masquerade in grotesque headdresses and costumes hung with large bells, clowning and dancing to scare even the most obstinate of demons. Various Western European countries bury, burn, or drown the passing year in effigy. In Scotland, a dummy called the Auld Wife is ignited, while in remote parts of the British Isles, huge bonfires are lighted to "burn out the old year." Austrians drown a straw figure known as The Death. Other quaint customs — grown men riding hobby horses up and down the streets of German villages at midnight or Northumberland men marching with pans of blazing tar on their heads in Allendale, England — are still reminiscent of ceremonies practiced on New Year's Eve since ancient times.

All over Europe, parties, beginning late on New Year's Eve and stretching well past midnight, bring family and friends together to welcome the New Year. While waiting for the last long minutes of the old year to tick out, party-goers play old-fashioned games, sing folk songs, and engage in divination. Molten lead is poured from a ladle into a bowl of water and the shapes in which the lead hardens determine the particular fortune. The custom of opening the Bible and foretelling the future from the text on which the forefinger of the right hand rests is also common. Traditional foods are served. In Germany and the Scandinavian countries, herring reputedly brings good luck; cabbage, plenty of silver; and carrots, gold. In Scotland, black bread and whiskey are to be consumed on Hogmanay, as the major Scottish holiday of December 31 is termed. The Spanish customarily eat a small bunch of grapes, symbolizing abundance, one grape per stroke of the clock until the 12 chimes have sounded. In the United States, "Hopping John," a repast of dried peas, rice, and salt pork, hog's head, or ham knuckle, is considered a good-luck omen. Of the beverages abundantly consumed on New Year's Eve, champagne is the traditional favorite. At the stroke of midnight, good wishes and kisses are exchanged and toasts are drunk. In the British Isles, the custom of "first footing" — competing to be the first to cross a friend's threshold — follows.

As is true in the United States, some Europeans prefer a more private farewell and greeting at the year's change and spend a quiet evening at home. In some cities, however, enormous throngs of celebrators, bursting with gaiety and good will, crowd the streets. The inhabitants of Edinburgh, for example, assemble outside the Tron Kirk; for those in London, Piccadilly Circus, Trafalgar Square, and St. Paul's Cathedral are favorite gathering places. As the clock strikes midnight the growing excitement erupts in a hearty display of handshaking, toasting, hat throwing, dancing, and the singing of the nostalgic Scottish song traditionally associated with New Year's Eve, "Auld Lang Syne," which was revised from a much older version by Robert Burns.

A moving Old World custom that has been brought over to the United States is the tolling of the passing year with muffled bells immediately before midnight; then, at 12:00, the unmuffled bells joyously proclaim the start of the new year. But perhaps most beautiful is the night watchman's traditional verse, resounding at midnight in small European villages:

In the name of the Lord
The Old Year goes out the door.
This is my wish for each of you.
Peace forever and Praise to God, our Lord.

In many countries of continental Europe, December 31 is known as St. Sylvester's Day, since it is the feast day of Pope Sylvester I (314–335).

It has its own peculiar traditions as well, especially in Belgium, Germany, France, and Switzerland. For example, the boy or girl who rises last on the final day of the year is mockingly called a "Sylvester." Churches are generally crowded, and, in France, the country people sometimes drive their cattle to the church entrance, where the priest prays for the animals' well-being during the months ahead. In Funchal, Madeira, the noise of a fireworks display resounds over the bay to the delight of the inhabitants and the passengers on board the ocean liners that make a special call to witness the celebration.

In the United States, feasting, drinking, party-going, and noisemaking are traditional ways of "bringing in" the new year. Only during Prohibition, in the 1920s and early 1930s, did New Year's Eve tone down and become a time primarily for small private parties. But with the repeal of the Prohibition amendment in 1933, it again took on the old-time flavor. The widespread drinking characteristic of the evening has today elicited such innovations as the hangover clinic and free coffee service for drivers along major highways.

The explosion of high spirits is especially loud in New York City. Regularly since the early 1900s, masses of revelers, some wearing funny hats and festooned with confetti, have pushed into Times Square and along Broadway to "whoop it up." Excitement mounts when, just before midnight, a glowing 100-pound ball with 185 lights slowly descends a 100-foot pole atop the One Times Square Building to mark the last seconds of the passing year. At 12:00, it hits bottom, and pandemonium breaks loose. The throbbing multitude shouts, stamps, waves, and bursts into "Auld Lang Syne" as the 10-story-high sign on the facade of the tower (originally known as the New York Times Tower and later as the Allied Chemical Tower) proclaims the new year.

Since 1967 New York City has sponsored an annual New Year's Eve celebration at the Bethesda Fountain and in front of the bandshell in Central Park. Colored lights, balloons, bells and dancers in festive dress provide a festive atmosphere, and holiday beverages such as wine punch and rum cider are available at stands. In addition to music, singing, and bell ringing, there is a magnificent display of fireworks at midnight.

Although New York City's exuberant welcome to the New Year is perhaps the best known New Year's Eve event in the United States, other sections of the country have their own traditional ways of greeting January 1. In Miami the gala New Year's Eve celebration centers upon the King Orange Jamboree Parade, traditionally the last parade of the year, which is staged as one of the major attractions surrounding the Orange Bowl Football Game. Pikes Peak, the famed Colorado mountain, is the scene of an annual New Year's Eve fireworks display. Climbing the 14,000-foot peak in severe cold and heavy snow to set off the midnight fireworks is a strenuous ritual; it undoubtedly would astonish Lieutenant Zebulon M. Pike, who wrote the first extensive descriptions of the peak in 1806 and predicted that it would never be scaled. The New Year's Eve trek was conceived and executed by five men who formed the Ad a Man or AdAmAn Club in 1922. As the name indicates, the organization adds only one member each year, initiating him with the exhausting climb to the summit. Weather permitting, the unique welcome to the New Year is visible from Colorado Springs.

The residents of Cherryville, North Carolina, still practice the traditional New Year's custom introduced by the town's original German settlers. Each year they "shoot in the New Year," just as, for example, the inhabitants of Berchtesgaden, Germany, stage a New Year's Gun Salute. The men of Cherryville fire ancient blackpowder muskets, as they proceed from orchard to orchard from midnight until noon on January 1. The ritual probably stems from an old rite to bring fertility to fruit trees in the coming year. It had its counterpart in post–Revolutionary New Year's celebrations in Philadelphia, where the custom of "shooting in" the new year with as much din as possible contributed to the origins of the city's famous Mummers' Parade on New Year's Day (see January 1).

In addition to the secular celebrations, beautiful carillon concerts ring in the new year. In New York the historic chimes of Old Trinity Church at the head of Wall Street, for example, peal forth every year while its congregation kneels in prayer. Many religious denominations hold special services on New Year's Eve from late in the evening until midnight. John Wesley, the English founder of the Methodist church, established the "watch-night" service as a time for worshipers to review their past, give solemn thought to the future, and rededicate themselves to Christian ways. In England, the first watch-night was conducted about 1742 and became especially popular in the 19th century. St. George's Methodist Episcopal Church in Philadelphia held in 1770 what has been called the first such service in America. The custom has since been adopted by a number of Protestant denominations throughout the country. At Roman Catholic churches, holy hours are held to mark the advent of the new year.

George Marshall's Birthday

George Catlett Marshall, one of the most prominent American soldiers and statesmen of the 20th century, was born on December 31, 1880, in Uniontown, Pennsylvania. He was one of the four children of George Catlett Marshall, a successful entrepreneur in the coal and coke industries, and his wife, Laura Bradford Marshall. The younger George Marshall was destined to become the first five-star general in the history of the United States and to hold the vital posts of chief of staff of the army, secretary of state, and secretary of defense.

Upon his graduation from high school, Marshall tried to obtain a congressional appointment to the US Military Academy at West Point, but the Republicans who dominated his region of Pennsylvania had little use for the petitions of a boy whose father was a Kentucky-born Democrat. In 1897 Marshall instead entered the Virginia Military Institute, one of the foremost private military colleges, where he developed into an excellent scholar, athlete, and soldier. Academically he ranked 15th in his class, and he played football well enough to be named a tackle of the All-Southern team. Marshall's fellow students in his final year at VMI selected him for the highest cadet rank, senior first captain.

Graduating from college in 1901, Marshall accepted a commission in February 1902 as a second lieutenant in the army. He served in the Philippine Islands with the 30th Infantry Regiment until its return in 1903 to the Oklahoma Territory. After several years of assignments in the West, the young lieutenant attended the Infantry-Cavalry School at Fort Leavenworth, Kansas, from which he graduated with honors in 1907. The army promoted him to first lieutenant in March 1907 and selected him to remain at Fort Leavenworth as a student at the prestigious Army Staff College. He graduated at the head of his class in 1908 and spent the following two years as an instructor at the school, teaching men who were often his senior in age and rank.

By 1913 Marshall had completed tours with the Massachusetts National Guard and with the 4th Infantry, and in that year he returned to the Philippines. World War I soon began, and during training exercises designed to improve the army's defensive position in the islands, Marshall demonstrated his abilities as a planner and won acclaim as a master of tactics. He became aide-de-camp to General Hunter Liggett, and upon returning to the United States in 1916, he assumed the same role for General James Franklin Bell, a former army chief of staff. Bell thought highly of Marshall, whom he described as "the greatest military genius since Stonewall Jackson."

Marshall, who won promotion to captain in 1916, was a member of the US Army General Staff at the time of America's entry into World War I in April 1917. In July 1917 he accompanied the 1st Division to France and in the following months served as its operations officer. Marshall laid the plans for actions that took place in the fall of 1917 east of Lunéville, and in the first half of the next year at the Saint-Mihiel, Picardy, and Cantigny battle areas. In the summer of 1918 he moved to the headquarters of the American commander, General John J. Pershing, where he formulated plans for the Saint-Mihiel offensive. Later in the war Marshall became chief of operations for the First Army and chief of staff for the VIII Army Corps.

In September 1919 Marshall returned to the United States as aide-de-camp to General Pershing, a post he held until 1924. Well aware of how lack of military preparation had hindered American efforts in World War I, the two men proposed the establishment of a trained army of 450,000 men. The National Defense Act of 1920 incorporated the idea, but Congress never appropriated the funds necessary to implement it.

The interwar period of the 1920s and 1930s brought Marshall a variety of assignments. He served three years, beginning in 1924, with the 15th Infantry in Tientsin, China, and returned to the United States to become an instructor at the Army War College in Washington, D.C. During a tour as assistant commandant of the Infantry School at Fort Benning, Georgia, from 1927 to 1932, he introduced and developed new techniques and concepts in the training of enlisted men and officers. He then undertook successive posts as senior instructor to the National Guard and as the commander of the Eighth Infantry and of the Fifth Infantry Brigade.

Marshall rose slowly in rank during the interlude of peace. He had attained a temporary colonelcy during World War I but reverted to captain at the end of the conflict. In 1920 he became a major, in 1923 a lieutenant colonel, and in 1933 he achieved the regular rank of colonel. General Douglas MacArthur, army chief of staff from 1930 to 1935, who stressed the importance of combat command experience in the development of a leader, prevented the promotion of staff officer Marshall to general. In October 1936, after MacArthur's brief retirement from the army, Marshall finally gained the coveted single star of a brigadier general.

Marshall quickly became chief military adviser to President Franklin D. Roosevelt in the months prior to US entry into World War II. In mid-1938 US Army Chief of Staff Malin L. Craig and Assistant Secretary of War Louis Johnson persuaded the Chief Executive to make Marshall assistant chief of staff in the army's War Plans Division. Marshall rose to the position of deputy chief of staff in October 1938 and became acting chief of staff the following July. On the advice of General Pershing, Roosevelt, in September 1939, passed over 34 more senior general officers and appointed Marshall chief of staff with four-star rank.

Marshall masterfully directed the American armed forces during World War II. He built a fighting machine of more than 10 million men and provided the supplies necessary for its mission. The general also chose able leaders for the army, including Dwight David Eisenhower, from the younger and more vigorous members of the officer corps. In recognition of Marshall's efforts, President Roosevelt in December 1944 made him the first American officer ever to wear five stars and to bear the rank of General of the Army.

Strategically, Marshall advocated an Allied cross-Channel invasion of Europe as the quickest means to defeat Hitler. He staunchly opposed British Prime Minister Winston Churchill's proposals for peripheral attacks and thrusts into the soft southern European underbelly. Ultimately, the Allies implemented Marshall's plan in Operation Overlord, beginning on D Day — in 1944 (see June 6). Marshall hoped to command the forces that landed on the Normandy beaches, but Roosevelt, who protested he would not be able to sleep at night with his chief of staff out of the country, named Eisenhower to the post.

President Roosevelt depended on Marshall as a trusted adviser in diplomatic as well as military affairs. In August 1941 Marshall accompanied the Chief Executive to his seaborne rendezvous off the coast of Newfoundland with Churchill, a meeting which resulted in formulation of the Atlantic Charter. Marshall also assisted Roosevelt at wartime conferences with Churchill and other Allied leaders at Casablanca, Quebec, Cairo, Tehran, and Yalta.

Harry S. Truman, who succeeded Roosevelt as President in 1945, continued to employ Marshall as a diplomat. After the conclusion of the European phase of World War II, Truman took Marshall to the Potsdam Conference, at which the American President discussed plans for peacetime with Prime Minister Anthony Eden of Great Britain and Premier Joseph Stalin of the

Soviet Union. In November 1945 Truman dispatched Marshall, who had recently retired as chief of staff, to China to mediate between the Nationalist government of Generalissimo Chiang Kai-shek and its warring Communist rivals under Mao Tse-tung. Marshall stayed in China until January 1947, but he was not able to bring together the opposing sides.

Marshall served as Truman's secretary of state from 1947 until 1949. In this capacity, he devised what the world came to call the Marshall Plan. Officially, it was titled the European Recovery Plan, a program that ultimately granted to war-torn nations more than $17 billion to rebuild their economies. Explaining the program in a speech at Harvard University, Marshall stated:

Our policy is not directed against any country or doctrine but against hunger, poverty, desperation and chaos. . . . We know that . . . the destitute and oppressed of the earth look chiefly to us for sustenance and support until they can face life with self-confidence and assurance.

Democratic and Republican members of Congress made the program a major part of the nation's foreign policy. (Later the term "Marshall Plan" was often employed to describe other proposals for economic development programs, domestic or foreign, designed to promote or restore self-sufficiency.)

General Marshall assumed the post of secretary of defense for Truman in 1950 and was responsible for rebuilding US armed forces to meet Communist aggression in Korea in concert with other members of the United Nations. In September 1951 Marshall resigned from the cabinet and retired to his estate in Leesburg, Virginia. During the 1950s Senator Joseph McCarthy assailed Marshall as a pro-Communist, but his baseless slurs did not mar the general's reputation.

Marshall lived out his retirement near Pinehurst, North Carolina, with his second wife, Katherine Tupper Brown Marshall, whom he had married in 1930. His first wife, Elizabeth Carter Coles Marshall, whom he married upon graduation from VMI, had died in 1927. Marshall died at age 78 on October 16, 1959, at Walter Reed Army Hospital in Washington, D.C.

During his lifetime, he won decorations from the United States and from 16 foreign nations. In 1953 he became the only professional soldier ever to win the Nobel Peace Prize. After the general's death, the nations of the world continued to honor him. In the fall of 1964 the people of West Germany dedicated the Marshall Memorial Fountain in Frankfurt as a token of their gratitude for aid given under the Marshall Plan to their defeated homeland after World War II. Created by private initiative, the fountain consists of three reclining female figures, the graces Aglaia, Thalia, and Euphrosine, who symbolize giving, taking, and thanking. These figures are grouped around a large center fountain, encircled by 50 smaller jets of water, which represent the states of the United States.

In 1953 Harry S. Truman suggested the establishment of a George C. Marshall Research Foundation to keep future generations of Americans aware of the contributions of the great soldier-statesman. In 1961 the foundation began to raise $2.5 million to erect and endow a George C. Marshall Research Library. Construction started in 1963 under the direction of Alonzo H. Gentry, the architect of the Truman Library in Independence, Missouri. On May 23, 1964, President Lyndon B. Johnson and former Presidents Truman and Eisenhower participated in the dedication of the stucco and stone building, located between the campuses of Washington and Lee University and the Virginia Military Institute in Lexington, Virginia.

The George C. Marshall Research Library houses the papers and records of the general and of several of his associates, including General Leonard Gerow, who commanded the XV Army in Germany during the closing days of World War II. Designed primarily as a center for scholarly study, the library incorporates a variety of attractions for the public. It contains a museum, in the main lobby of which is a bronze bust of the general, as well as a collection of flags associated with his career. The south wing of the building presents a pictorial display of Marshall's life from his birth until his appointment as chief of staff. A World War II room with an electrically illuminated 9-by-12-foot map tracing the course of the conflict drew more than 10,000 visitors in the library's first year of operation.

Appendix

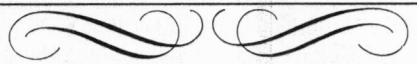

The Calendar

The word *calendar* comes from the Latin *calendarium*, or "account book," derived from *calendae* or "the calends," the first day of the ancient Roman month, on which accounts were due and on which the priests of Rome called the people together to proclaim — *calare* — that the new moon had been sighted. In English a calendar means, abstractly, a people's settled system of reckoning the passage of time in days. Thus, it is by the calendar that the beginning and length of the years, and their subdivision into parts, such as months and weeks, are established for the community over the long term. (See below, The Era and The Days of the Week and also the articles on each of the 12 months in the main text.)

Concretely, a calendar is a table constructed for handy reference, showing the division of the days of a given year into months and weeks and the date of each day. Calendars laden with detailed notes concerning the weather, holidays, and other social matters are usually called almanacs.

All calendars have been based on some combination of celestial observation and observance of the pattern of human activities and rituals. More than once, improved astronomical data have initially conflicted with deep conservatism about the "sanctity" of the calendar, based on its foundation in ancient religious beliefs and social customs. In fact, the astronomical computations necessary to construct calendars have presented stargazers with problems at every stage. To amass accurate long-term readings of the positions of the heavenly bodies and of the sun's shadow is a delicate task extending over many generations. In addition, three major natural phenomena challenge the ingenuity of calendar makers.

The first challenge is the difficulty that the moon's cycle of waxing and waning — so striking in its regularity that it provided early peoples with their first effective subdivision of time beyond the alternations of night and day — is not expressible in whole days. On the contrary, the lunar cycle has an average length of slightly more than 29½ days, with a possible variation of as much as half a day from this average because of the moon's elliptical orbit, and these variations are not readily predictable without extensive astronomical records. These irregularities have always posed serious difficulties to experts in calculating the length of future lunar months. Ordinarily, the problem was solved by alternating months of 29 and 30 days and ignoring the fact that the appearance of the new moon often did not coincide with its designated date in the calendar. This is the basic rule in the Chinese, Jewish, and Muslim calendars.

The second and third challenges became apparent only as people gradually came to need a longer unit of time than the moon's cycle (one lunar month) to regulate group life. The cycle of the seasons, important to all even in very simple economies, naturally attracted attention. The seasons are governed by the sun rather than the moon, so that observers were gradually led to estimate the exact length of the sun's cycle. This was a very difficult feat and one not accomplished in an entirely satisfactory way before the 16th century A.D. But even methods that were only fairly sophisticated revealed that the solar or tropical year was not expressible in whole days, any more than the moon's cycle had been. In fact, one solar cycle requires 365 days, five hours, 48 minutes and about 46 seconds, or roughly 365¼ days.

Long before observations of the sun were so precise, agriculturalists formed an approximate idea of the length of the solar cycle and faced the problem of how to combine it with their existing moon-based calendars. Once again human beings were confronted with a natural incommensurability: lunar and solar cycles are not readily expressible in terms of each other. In terms of complete lunar months, the closest approximation to the sun's cycle of 365¼ days is 12 moon cycles (lunations) or a little more than 354 days — about 11 days too few. As a result, in a purely lunar calendar, such as that required by the prophet Mohammed in the Koran, the months cannot be held in fixed relation to the solstices and equinoxes, the mileposts of the solar (or tropical) year. Instead, the months will arrive progressively earlier in each solar cycle, until at length their names will have circled through all the seasons. To avoid this instability certain important moon-based calendars, such as the Chinese, were early converted to "lunisolar" calendars, in which the lunar months are periodically returned to a stable place in the seasonal cycle by the insertion of an additional lunar month in the calendar every few years — a procedure known as intercalation. The resulting calendar has months of nearly equal length, closely approximating the actual lunations, but its "years" are of varying length and do not reproduce the solar cycle exactly except over a period of several calendar "years." In certain civilizations, however, observers became particularly attentive to the sun's cycle and devised a truly solar calendar (discussed below). That out of these astronomical dilemmas we should have arrived today at our finely calibrated Gregorian calendar is a tribute to the astronomical and political skills of many generations.

At least as early as the third millennium B.C., Egyptian sages had calculated the solar cycle exactly enough to devise a yearly calendar of 365 days (12 months of 30 days each plus 5 extra days added as festival days at the end of the year). In the third century B.C. later Egyptian experts attempted to introduce a sixth extra day into every fourth year to reflect new computations that gave the solar year more accurately as 365¼ days. But the Egyptian people proved obdurate and rejected this proposed "leap year."

The earliest Roman calendar was a crude arrangement of 10 lunar months, beginning with March (Martius), plus an indeterminately long, unnamed period during the winter, when agriculture was moribund. In time, two new months, *Januarius* and *Februarius*, were created out of this unnamed period and added at the end of the year. March continued as the first month of the year for a long period — until 153 B.C., when the Roman state decreed that the new year thenceforth would begin on January 1. The result (even though the people were slow to embrace the year's new official beginning) was the calendar from which the names and order of our present months descend.

Intercalation of days was necessary from time to time, however, to realign this Roman calendar with the equinoxes. Unfortunately those whose duty this was had so abused their office — often adding or subtracting days merely for political reasons — that by the time of Julius Caesar's rule the Roman calendar was thoroughly scrambled, with January falling in autumn and the lengths of years highly unpredictable. A gifted administrator, holding among other titles that of high priest, Caesar determined to reform the calendar so that it would be as nearly self-correcting as possible. In 46 B.C., on advice of the astronomer Sosigenes, a Greek from Alexandria, Caesar reshaped the Roman calendar, basing it upon the Egyptian solar year; he kept the old Roman month names but assigned the months an unequal number of days.

In setting aside the lunar basis of the calendar, Caesar made it necessary for Sosigenes to annex to the new calendar a separate system for calculating the moon's cycles to guide the dating of festivals dependent on the moon's changes. Sosigenes apparently chose the 19-year Metonic lunar cycle from Greece, and he gave his lunar calculations the starting point of March 1 in the solar year.

Caesar's calendar, known as the Julian calendar, went into effect in 45 B.C. It ordained that three successive "common years" of 365 days should be followed by a fourth year with an extra day intercalated in the month of February to make a total of 366 days (see February 29, Leap Year). In this way the real solar year, estimated by Sosigenes at 365¼ days, was systematically expressed in calendar years of whole days. By intercalating 90 days in the year 46–45 B.C., Caesar also made spring begin once more in March.

The Julian reform also reaffirmed January 1 as the start of the Roman calendar year. But it should be noted that neither this new year's date nor the Latin month names were adopted in the Eastern portion of the Roman Empire. Furthermore, after Christianity became the official religion of the Roman Empire, and imperial rule declined in the West, the use of the Julian calendar did not always involve keeping January 1 as the beginning of the new year in the West. During the Middle Ages, in fact, various dates were used to start the calendar year in different localities (see January 1).

The problems that finally led in the 16th century to major overhaul of the Julian calendar are most often discussed in their purely civil aspects in modern reference works. Contemporaries, however, actually were more keenly perturbed in their religious than in their civil life by the astronomical errors that made the reform necessary. Specifically, Christians were troubled by the effects of cumulative error on the Church's Easter calendar. To grasp how important it was to calculate the date of Easter correctly, the centrality of the Feast of the Resurrection of Jesus Christ to Christian faith and worship must be understood (see March 29, Easter Sunday). In addition, in the 16th century most Europeans did not generally perceive any cleavage between religious truth and what would today be called scientific truths. If the Church could be wrong about the date of Easter, some asked, might it not be mistaken also about more profound matters? The clergy and Christian governments thus had strong incentives to provide a calendar by which Easter would be reckoned accurately.

Correct calculation of successive Easters was a vast challenge since it involved adjustments in computing both the solar and the lunar cycles used under the Julian calendar. The chief difficulty stemmed from an error in Sosigenes' original reckoning of the length of the solar year: the Earth actually takes 11 minutes, 14 seconds less than 365¼ days to orbit the sun. As a result the vernal equinox, which marks the beginning of spring (which in Caesar's time had fallen on or about March 25) did not hold stable in the Julian calendar but slipped backward over the centuries, until by the 16th century it was occurring on or about March 11. This lag, while annoying in an agrarian society used to associating the seasonal changes with certain months, would not have been regarded so seriously had it not been that in the early centuries of Christianity the reckoning of Easter, the most important date in the year, had come to depend upon the date of the spring equinox — in order to avoid celebrating Easter twice in one year.

It is frequently asserted that the rule for the computation of the date of Easter was solemnly set down at the great Ecumenical, or General, Council of Nicaea in A.D. 325. While this statement involves considerable telescoping of history, since the council passed no canon on the subject and its synodical letter was not explicit on many points, important elements of the rule that later came to predominate appear to have been agreed upon at the council. In any case, in later centuries both the Western and Eastern Orthodox churches invoked the authority of the Nicene Council for their Easter rule, which came to be formulated as follows: Easter is to be celebrated on the first Sunday after the first full moon on or after the vernal equinox (taken as March 21). (In contrast to the churches of the West, Eastern Orthodox churches insist that the rule requires, in addition, that Easter must always occur after the Jewish Passover; in many years, therefore, the Western and Eastern Orthodox churches celebrate Easter on different dates.)

This rule made calendrical projection of the future dates of Easter highly complex because it combined solar with lunar calculations: accurate solar computation was necessitated by the pegging of Easter to the vernal equinox, as dated at the time of the Council of Nicaea, while the rule's attention to the full moon of the Passover — which the Gospels report Jesus and his disciples had celebrated the night before the Crucifixion (see March 27, Good Friday) — required careful reckoning of the lunar cycles.

Despite an elaborate apparatus of "epacts," "golden numbers," and "dominical letters," Christian scholars in the West, from at least the 8th century, noticed that observable astronomical events did not always square very well with their computations in the Easter tables. The most striking empirical check — one that could be performed by anyone — was the comparison of the date of the actual appearance of the new moon that became full just before Easter with its expected date in the Easter tables. By the 16th century the astronomers' mean Easter new moon was arriving from three to five days ahead of its projected calendar date, with the result that 12 times in that century Easter was in reality celebrated one entire lunation too late. The source of this error traced to the assumption of earlier astronomers that the 19-year Alexandrian (or Metonic) lunar cycle was exactly the same length as 19 solar years in the Julian calendar. Thus at the end of 19 solar years, a fresh lunar cycle was assumed to begin precisely when the new solar year started. The lunar cycle thus was believed to be self-correcting in relation to the sun's cycle every 19 years. In fact, however, after 19 Julian years, real lunar time lagged behind solar time by about 1½ hours. This discrepancy had mounted up over the centuries, causing religious authorities the concern they experienced because the Church was being ridiculed for incompetence in astronomy.

As early as the 13th century, proposals for calendar reform were made, and in the later Middle Ages the papacy began to take the problem seriously, but further astronomical knowledge was needed. The calendar reform finally promulgated by Pope Gregory XIII on February 24, 1582, in his bull *Inter Gravissimas* rested on Nicolaus Copernicus's new mathematical calculations of the motions of the heavenly bodies. The reform, especially in its lunar aspects, was the work of Aloysius Lilius, who had been a physician at the University of Perugia, and, in its solar aspects, of the German Jesuit mathematician Christopher Clavius, who incorporated Lilius's work into the calendar reform.

As for the solar cycle, the new Gregorian calendar provided that three leap years should be suppressed in every 400 years to balance out the 11-minute, 14-second surplus per year provided by the Julian reckoning of the year at 365¼ days. Thus, the Gregorian solar rule is that century years shall be common years instead of leap years, except when the year number is divisible by 400. Therefore, in the Gregorian calendar, 1700, 1800, and 1900 were not leap years, but the year 2000 is a leap year. In translating Julian dates to their Gregorian equivalents, the following table is useful. For dates

from October 5, 1582, through February 28, 1700,
add 10 days
from February 29, 1700, through February 28, 1800,
add 11 days
from February 29, 1800, through February 28, 1900,
add 12 days
from February 29, 1900, through February 28, 2100,
add 13 days

In an effort to preserve the "Nicene" Easter rule intact, and also to avoid having to change all the missals and breviaries of the Roman Catholic church, the Gregorian calendar reformers decided to restore the mean vernal equinox to March 21, its calendrical date at the time of the Council of Nicaea, rather than to March 25, its position in the Julian calendar during the lifetime of Jesus. To accomplish this, Pope Gregory XIII ordered that 10 days be omitted from the calendar in 1582: Thursday, October 4, was to be followed directly by Friday, October 15, in that year. The reformers also instituted January 1 as the beginning of the new year as in Roman times, but they did this for religious reasons. Despite the civil year's beginning on January 1 under the Roman emperors, the early Christian church's Alexandrian lunar cycle had begun on March 1 of the Julian calendar. Now, by making the lunar year and the solar (civil) year begin on the same date, the calendar reformers were able for the first time to include Septuagesima Sunday and Ash Wednesday (see February 11) in the *same* lunar year as the Easter Day these observances prepared the way for. To calculate future dates of Easter, the reformers created new lunar tables starting from January 1, ingeniously devised to reflect new computations of the earth's and the moon's motions — thereby rectifying the flaw in the Metonic or Alexandrian lunar computations so closely associated with the Julian calendar.

The Gregorian calendar had to win acceptance in a Europe bitterly divided by the Protestant Reformation. It was accepted almost immediately in lands whose rulers were Catholic. Thenceforth the Julian became known as the Old Style calendar (abbreviated O.S.) and the Gregorian as the New Style (N.S.). Spain, Portugal, and most Italian states put the reform into effect as specified, making the day after October 4, 1582, read October 15. France instituted the reform two months later by following December 9 directly with December 20. In the Catholic provinces of the Netherlands, the Gregorian calendar was instituted on or shortly before January 1, 1583. The Catholic cantons of Switzerland instituted the new calendar in 1583. Emperor Rudolph II proclaimed the reform for the Holy Roman Empire in September 1583, ordering that January 6, 1584, be followed at once by January 17; this was done in the Catholic states of the empire, but Protestant recalcitrance meant that the imperial courts had to reckon by both Old and New Styles. The Gregorian reform became effective in Poland on January 1, 1586, and was adopted in Hungary in 1587.

Except for the provinces of Holland and Zealand, which instituted the New Style as of January 1, 1583, and briefly for Sweden, Protestant peoples and rulers refused to recognize the calendar reform, because of what they saw as the pope's high-handed promulgation of it and because of their view of the new Easter reckonings as unbiblical and as an unwarranted exercise of papal authority. The Eastern Orthodox churches simultaneously charged the Roman church with heresy and with contravening the Council of Nicaea by the Gregorian lunar reform. In the Spanish Netherlands and Bohemia (now Czechoslovakia), Protestants resisted the new calendar by force of arms. Thereafter the calendar change continued to be a cause of ill-feeling and even fighting in lands with religiously mixed populations.

This period of "calendar strife" did not end until the Lutheran German states met in 1699 at the urging of the theologian and mathematician Gottfried Wilhelm von Leibniz: at the Diet of Regensburg it was agreed that the solar aspects of the Gregorian calendar were to be accepted, and it was decreed that February 18, 1700, be followed immediately by March 1. The diet also urged the United Netherlands to accept the Gregorian calendar, which the individual provinces did, mostly at the end of 1700 and the beginning of 1701. Denmark and Norway likewise instituted the New Style in 1700, and the Protestant cantons of Switzerland made it effective as of January 12, 1701. But in 1700 the German Protestants, followed by the Swiss, simultaneously adopted a distinctive Easter reckoning based on Johannes Kepler's astronomical tables, which they maintained until

1778 when Frederick II of Prussia used his royal power and influence to have Easter reckoned thenceforth by the Gregorian paschal moon, thus effectively ending a period in which the Protestant and Catholic dates for Easter had often diverged by a week.

Elizabeth I, the Protestant ruler of England, was not inclined to accept Pope Gregory XIII's new calendar. As a result, England and Wales, together with Ireland and neighboring Scotland, maintained the Julian calendar for 170 years longer, and all except Scotland continued to change to a new year on March 25 as they had since the Middle Ages. Scotland first adopted January 1 for its calendrical new year in 1600.

The full Gregorian calendar reform was finally adopted for England and Wales, Scotland, Ireland, and the British colonies by an act of Parliament of 1751 (Statute 24 George II, cap. 23). This act provided first that December 31, 1751, would be followed by January 1, 1752 (not 1751) — except in Scotland, where such a provision was already in force. For other British lands, however, the dates from January 1 through March 24 never existed in the year 1751. By the 18th century the Gregorian reform required the suppression of 11 days of the Julian calendar. Thus the above act of Parliament also provided that September 2 be followed directly by September 14 in 1752 in the American colonies, Great Britain, and Ireland. (For a famous American date change, see February 22, George Washington's Birthday.)

In Sweden the Roman Catholic King John III's attempt to institute the Gregorian calendar soon after 1582 foundered because of Protestant resistance. After a second abortive attempt in the early 1700s, the New Style calendar was finally introduced successfully into Sweden in 1753, as of March 1.

For nearly two centuries after the initial Gregorian reform, Europeans found it necessary to date letters with two sets of dates when corresponding with persons employing a different calendar style. Old Style dates were placed above a line and New Style below, for example:

$$\frac{25 \text{ May, } 1660.}{4 \text{ June}}$$

In addition, for dates from January 1 through March 24 the American colonists and the British had had to give double *years* as well —

$$\frac{23 \text{ January}}{2 \text{ February}} \; 1627/8$$

— because they changed the number of the year only on March 25, and not on January 1 with others, until 1752.

Since the adoption of the Gregorian reform, there has been only one instance of a radical overhaul of the civil calendar in Western Europe. This was undertaken in France after the French Revolution of 1789. To divorce Republican France dramatically from the old regime, and especially from the Catholic church, on October 5, 1793, the revolutionary convention approved what is known as the Revolutionary, or Republican, calendar. Its year contained 12 months of 30 days each, with months divided not into weeks but into three *décades* of 10 days each. Five extra days were added at the end of the year for celebration as revolutionary national holidays, called in time *Sansculottides*, and every fourth year was to have a sixth extra (or epagomenal) day. The Republican new year began on September 22, the anniversary of the proclamation of the Republic, and the whole Republican calendar was made retroactive to September 22, 1792, with 1792–1793 becoming the year "I" of the Republic (Republican year numbers being expressed in Roman numerals) (see Appendix, Era). Napoleon I abolished the calendar in the year XIV, returning France to the Gregorian calendar as of January 1, 1806.

As the Western European states became global imperial powers during the 19th and 20th centuries, countries around the world that had long followed their own ancient calendars moved to adopt the Gregorian style, at least for official business, often becoming two-calendar countries in the process. In 1873 the Meiji government of Japan instituted the Gregorian calendar as the official calendar, making January 1 of that year Japan's first Gregorian day. On January 1, 1912, the new Republican government of China took the same step. In both Japan and China, however, the Gregorian months were numbered ordinally, January being called First Month, etc., and the traditional lunisolar calendar continued to be widely used by the people and to govern major festivals. On February 7, 1918, the Soviet revolutionary government instituted the New Style calendar in the USSR, carrying out a reform already planned by the Provisional government. Since the calendar reforms of Peter the Great of 1699, the year had begun in Russia on January 1, Old Style, but to synchronize with New Style dates it was necessary in 1918 to drop 13 days. The Balkan states adopted the Gregorian calendar during and after the First World War: Bulgaria (in 1916), Yugoslavia (1919), Rumania, and Greece (1924). In 1927 Turkey adopted not only the Gregorian reform, with Romanized names of the months, but also the Christian Era, becoming the most westernized Muslim country with regard to its calendar. Most other Muslim nations have compromised, employing both the Gregorian and the Muslim calendars officially. In Israel the

Jewish and Gregorian calendars are both in use. (See below, The Era.)

In May 1923 the Orthodox Conference of Constantinople approved what it called the Rectified Julian Calendar, which was really a modified Gregorian calendar. In the succeeding year the Orthodox churches of Greece, Rumania, and Constantinople adopted this calendar, which used the Gregorian reckoning for civil transactions and for the fixed festivals of the Church but rejected the Gregorian lunar reform as uncanonical, retaining instead the Easter lunar calculations that prevailed under the Julian calendar. By 1968, however, only 4 of the 16 Orthodox churches, namely the churches of Jerusalem, Serbia, Bulgaria, and Russia, still maintained the Julian calendar in all respects. In particular the Russian Orthodox church's attachment to the Old Style calendar appears to have been intensified by the Soviets' enforcement of the Gregorian calendar in the Russian homeland. Beginning in the 1970s, however, and in some cases earlier, acceptance of the New Style, except for the computation of the date of Easter, began to spread through Russian Orthodox congregations in the United States and elsewhere.

The Orthodox Easter and the movable feasts that depend on it may fall as much as five weeks later than feasts set according to the Gregorian lunar tables followed by Roman Catholics and Protestants. This is in part because, since it is reckoned according to the Alexandrian (or Metonic) lunar computation intimately associated with the Julian calendar, the Orthodox Easter may not fall on or before March 21 (Old Style) — for the Orthodox the crucial "Nicene" date of the spring equinox — which is, in fact, April 3 of the Gregorian (New Style) calendar. The Orthodox Easter date may also fall later than the Gregorian because the Orthodox churches continue to take literally the "Nicene" prohibition against celebrating Easter before or at the same time as the Jewish Passover, an act that was made grounds for excommunication by a Council of Antioch in the 4th century. Because Jews follow an ancient lunisolar religious calendar that is astronomically imprecise and do not consider a full moon occurring prior to March 26 of the Christian calendar as the correct Passover date, Passover occasionally is celebrated one whole lunation later than that of the vernal equinox, which is supposed to regulate Easter. In these cases, the Western churches follow the Gregorian computations and celebrate Easter before or with Passover, but the Eastern Orthodox postpone Easter by a whole lunation to comply with the letter of the canonical law. The

range of dates for Easter under the Gregorian calendar is from March 22 through April 25; the Orthodox Easter range is from April 4 through May 8 (New Style).

A number of religious calendars are observed concurrently with the Gregorian civil calendar in the United States. Easter is accompanied in the ecclesiastical calendar, or "church year," by a series of other movable feasts, most of them dating from the early Church, which take their calendar dates each year in relation to Easter. These movable feasts run from Septuagesima Sunday, nine weeks before Easter, to Trinity Sunday, eight weeks after it, and include Ash Wednesday, Palm Sunday, Good Friday, the Feast of the Ascension, and Pentecost. Thus approximately one-third of the Christian calendar is determined by lunar cycles, in accord with one or another interpretation of the "Nicene" Easter rule, and this third of a year must awkwardly be made to fit into an ecclesiastical calendar whose other festivals have long had dates fixed in the solar year. The Western churches begin the church year (and their liturgical calendars) with Advent Sunday, the Sunday nearest the Feast of St. Andrew (see November 30). The season of Advent (approximately four weeks long) prepares worshipers for Christmas (see December 25), just as Lent prepares them for Easter. Other church seasons are Epiphany, pre-Lent, Easter or paschal time, and Trinity. In the more liturgical Christian traditions, a coexistent calendar of the feasts of the saints and martyrs marks off the church year as if by milestones. The details of the liturgical calendar vary among the Roman, Anglican, Lutheran, and Orthodox branches of the Church; for example, the Orthodox church year begins not with Advent Sunday but with the Feast of the Birth of the Holy Virgin Mary, celebrated on September 21 (New Style).

Other religious calendars in use in the United States are the Jewish and the Muslim, both of which follow lunar months and therefore begin their years on movable dates in terms of the civil (i.e. Gregorian) calendar. The weekly holy day of Jews is the Sabbath (Shabbat), or seventh day — Saturday — which begins at sunset on Friday. The fourth of the Ten Commandments enjoins observance of the Sabbath, and it is the most important Jewish holy day. For Muslims, Friday is the weekly holy day. In addition, many Americans of Chinese descent follow parts of their ancestral calendar, celebrating the Chinese New Year on a movable date in either January or February (see February 6) and in the process marking the passage of the 12-year *Chi* cycle, in which each year bears a "branch" name, deriving from the Far Eastern signs of the Zodiac — for example, the "year of the dragon."

Although the average overcorrection of 26 seconds per year that remains in the Gregorian calendar amounts to an error of only one extra day in 3,323 solar years, in the 19th and 20th centuries many have nonetheless strongly urged further calendar reform. The reformers have accepted the Gregorian solar computations as the basis of their projected international calendars, however, and have concentrated on shaping the calendar more perfectly to modern commercial and administrative needs by eliminating present irregularities in the subdivisions of the year and fixing the dates of major holidays. What is sought is a "perpetual calendar" in which any given calendar date would always fall on the same day of the week. The International Fixed Calendar of 13 equal months of 28 days each has been favored by some reformers, while the World Calendar of 12 months has found greater support in commerce and business because it would divide the year into four equal quarters of three months each — the first month of each quarter having 31 days and the next two months 30 days each. In this system the 365th day of the year, December 31, would be added onto the final week as a second Saturday and celebrated as a global holiday, thus allowing the ensuing year to begin regularly on Sunday, January 1. A leap-year day would be inserted in every fourth year as an extra Saturday at the end of June, called June 31. As of the late 1970s, however, any further calendar reform remained a matter for future decision.

The Era

Relatively late in the development of time reckoning, scholars in the Mediterranean world first conceived of "eras." An era is a lengthy period of time commencing from a fixed point (called its "epoch"), which serves to order all subsequent years in relation to one another. People slowly recognized the advantages both for historical writing and for celestial observation of numbering very long series of years sequentially according to an era, rather than in repetitive cycles. They even more slowly evolved a name for this chronological concept. The English word "era," dating from the early 17th century, comes from the late Latin *aera* or *era*, which apparently only in the Renaissance began to be used to signify an entire system of chronology. In medieval Spain the word *aera* was prefixed to individual year numbers (as, *aera* 1072) to indicate that the year was reckoned according to the "Spanish Era" (see below), i.e., the word *aera* functioned somewhat as our letters "A.D." Earlier *aera* had probably meant "counters used in calculation," from the plural of the word *aes*, meaning "brass" or "money."

The era used universally in the Western world today is the "Christian Era" or "Era of the Incarnation," sometimes also referred to as the "Common," or "Vulgar Era." It has become predominant throughout the world in the 20th century, even though a number of other era systems continue in use in certain nations. In English-speaking countries, years of the Christian Era are designated either "A.D." (for the Latin *anno domini*, "in the year of our Lord") to indicate that they fall after the advent of Jesus Christ, or "B.C." to signify time "before Christ." (The latter is occasionally written "A.C.," for the Latin *ante Christum*, but this notation is usually made in English because the Christian Era was not often applied to dates before Christ until the 19th century.) We say that in the Christian Era, years are "styled" A.D. or B.C.

In modern times, years of this era have started on January 1. By extrapolation it is often said that the "epoch," or starting point, of the era was January 1, A.D. 1, but this is anachronistic (see below). For centuries in medieval Europe other days eclipsed January 1 as the beginning of the calendar year (see New Year's Day).

It is interesting to compare the Christian Era with other dating systems that have served the human family. (See The Calendar for information on many calendrical matters touched on here.) Most early chroniclers — like the keepers of the oral tradition among preliterate peoples — were content to suggest long spans of time by vague phrases such as "five generations," or to date events from some natural calamity. In kingdoms, the somewhat more sophisticated system developed of dating events by the year of the current ruler's reign — as, "in the fourth year of King Alfred." Such "regnal" or "reign-years" have perhaps constituted the most widespread chronological system, historically, and continue in occasional use today in monarchies. The regnal mode of dating is fraught with difficulties, however, particularly in deciding the day from which a monarch's regnal years should begin.

The Chinese very early devised an ingenious and more regular system to record the years and to supplement imperial reign-years on their documents (even though the reign-years remained the most common form of dating in China until the 20th century). Under their lunar-solar calendar, which traces to very ancient times, the Chinese came to mark the years by an astronomically calculated cycle of 60 years that was overlaid with metaphysical significance. This sexagenary cycle rests upon the combination of 10 "celestial stems," based on the five "basic elements," with 12 "terrestrial branches" deriving from the Far Eastern signs of the Zodiac, each series constantly rotating in such a way as to make a total of 60 possible combinations. Eventually the 60-year cycle was used by the Koreans, Japanese, and Vietnamese as well. Instead of being numbered, each year in the cycle is named, being designated by two Chinese characters, called its *E-to*, giving its branch and stem names. For serious chronological work, the Chinese have sometimes employed a 180-year cycle combining three 60-year cycles and projected backward in time to the reign of Emperor Huang-Ti in the third millennium B.C. Since the seventh century B.C., shorter 12-year cycles called *Chi*, in which years are referred to simply by their branch names — as in "year of the hare"— have been a popular means of avoiding the complexity of the 60-year cycle. Each sexagenary cycle embraces five *Chi*. Probably in the second century B.C., the Chinese introduced still another chronological system, based on periods of unequal length called *Nien-hao*, each named distinctively after some remarkable event. Under the first Ming emperor (A.D. 1368), however, it was decided that a new *Nien-hao* would henceforth be declared only at the start of a new emperor's reign.

All these year systems, with their various inconveniences, were officially set aside in 1912, when the newly founded Republic of China, adopting the Gregorian calendar of the West, established the "Era of the Republic," with January 1, 1912, as its "epoch" or starting point. As of 1978, the Nationalist Republic of China (Taiwan) continued to style its correspondence "in the —— year of the Republic." But in 1949, the Republican style disappeared on the Communist mainland. Documents of the People's Republic of China use years of the Christian Era (e.g., 1978), but with no indication of "A.D."

Chronologers often refer to the invention among the Japanese of a continuous "Era of Jimmu Tennō," beginning with the first year of the first Japanese emperor's reign — taken to be 660 B.C. But this era is a modern invention, imitating the Christian Era of the West, and has been used infrequently. Throughout their history the Japanese have styled years by three shorter cycles, singly or in combination: the 60-year cycle from China; the reign-years of the Japanese emperors; or irregular year-periods

called *Nen-go* (derived from the Chinese *Nien-hao*), each with a special name. The *Nen-go* system was first instituted in A.D. 645. In 1867 it was decreed that henceforth a new *Nen-go* could be announced only upon the accession of an emperor, thus combining the regnal and *Nen-go* systems. When the imperial government of Japan adopted the Gregorian calendar in 1873, it did not adopt the Christian Era. Thus in Japan the year 1873 was the sixth year of *Mei-ji* (or Illuminating Peace). The regnal system continues in Japan at present, and dates styled by the Christian Era are said to be "of the Western calendar."

For many centuries the ancient Greeks and Romans also designated the years in accord with their political systems. Rather than being numbered, the years were named for the chief officers of the state at the time — for example, for the archons (magistrates) in Athens and the consuls in Rome. Early Greek scientists also calculated natural cycles by which dates were sometimes given. Most famous was Meton's highly accurate lunar cycle of 19 years, which, somewhat refined, would enter the Christian calendar in the calculation of the date of Easter. (The first year of Meton's first cycle began in June 432 B.C.)

But none of these systems was equivalent to a true era. A major impetus to the Mediterraneans' creation of eras seems to have been the need for a chronological plan not limited to the political arrangements of one city-state, but capable of embracing international affairs. Greek writers began to date years by "Olympiads," four-year periods named for the victors in the footraces at the quadrennial Olympic games. Rather late, in the third century B.C., the system gave rise to an "Era of the Olympiads," with July 1, 776 B.C., the presumed date of the first Olympic contest, conventionally taken as its beginning. The Era of the Olympiads was used by the Greek historians. But a different era was widespread in the official documents of the Hellenistic world. After the conquest of the East by Alexander the Great in the late fourth century B.C., the "Era of the Seleucids" had been widely adopted in Babylonia and the Greek-speaking East. This era continued to be used for centuries after the birth of Jesus Christ, in the Eastern Roman Empire, despite divergence over its epoch or starting point, which was taken to be the spring of 311 B.C. by the Babylonians, but the fall of 312 B.C. by the Macedonians.

Not satisfied to name years after the consuls, Roman historians devised the "Era of Rome," in which years were dated from the semimythical founding of the city and styled "A.U.C." for *ab urbe condita* ("from the founding of the city").

Although they agreed on April 21 as the starting day, learned Romans were not in agreement about which year to assign to the foundation of Rome, and different years were used. As a result, this era remained a device of the intellectuals and was not adopted for general transactions, which continued to be dated by consulates well into the Christian period. But in the 19th century, the Era of Rome was revived by scholars of ancient civilizations and given the conventional starting point (or epoch) of 753 B.C. (In actuality, A.U.C. 1 correspond to 753–752 B.C.)

An even wider diversity of dating styles prevailed under the later Roman Empire, which was increasingly Christianized. The several hundred years beginning with the third century A.D. saw many innovations in dating, a number of which dominated Western chronology through the Middle Ages and beyond and one of which was the Christian Era itself.

In the Eastern Roman Empire from at least the fourth century A.D., writers often dated years by a system known as the "indiction" cycle of Rome. The indiction, a 15-year tax cycle of Egyptian origin, was possibly spread as a fiscal device by Emperor Diocletian in the late third century and was adopted thereafter for chronological purposes. In this system of dating, years were noted, for example, as the "fifth" or "seventh" of the indiction, but the indictions themselves were not numbered. When Christianity became the official religion of the empire, Christian writers established the convention that the first year of the first indiction cycle had fallen in A.D. 312, with the start of the reign of Constantine, the first Christian emperor. Later they projected indictions backwards, calculating, for example, that A.D. 1 had been the fourth year of its indiction. In the East, years of the indiction began on September 1, preceding January 1 of the Julian calendar year, and this new year's date prevailed there until the fall of the Byzantine Empire in the 15th century. (It was also the date of the new year in Russia until the end of the 17th century.)

In the West, the indiction cycle apparently first appeared in the sixth century on papal correspondence and on Easter tables modeled on those of the Church at Alexandria, Egypt. The "Greek" year-beginning of September 1 was used in the papal chancery and elsewhere, with years of the indiction, for centuries. The "Roman," or "Pontifical," indiction, dating from December 25 (or sometimes January 1), appeared only late in the 10th century in Rome, borrowed from the Holy Roman emperors in Germany. Throughout the Middle Ages, indiction-years were often employed instead of an era, or in addition to it, as were the regnal-years of monarchs.

As an alternative to dating by consulates or by the indiction system, the early Christians sometimes used an "Era of the Passion" dating from 33 years after their calculation of Jesus' birth. The imperial "Era of Diocletian," with August 29, A.D. 284, as its epoch, gained substantial acceptance, although Christians often called it the "Era of Martyrs" because of Diocletian's persecutions. It is still used by the Coptic and Ethiopian churches and is sometimes called the "Coptic Era." On the Iberian Peninsula from the 5th to the 14th century, an "Era of Spain" was general among Christians. Its epoch, January 1, 38 B.C., is thought to mark the end of the Roman conquest of Spain.

The Christian Era, or Era of the Incarnation, which today dominates global dating, made an almost surreptitious appearance in history in the twilight of Roman power in the West and attained its present preeminence only very slowly. In A.D. 525 at Rome, a Scythian-born monk, scholar, and chronologist named Dionysius Exiguus first proposed the idea of numbering years from Jesus Christ's incarnation in drawing up a new set of Easter tables to run for 95 years commencing in A.D. 532, when an earlier set of Easter tables, which he had before him, would run out. In a period of poor communications, such Easter tables were required in the West to help bishops and priests determine the correct date for the movable feast of Easter (see March 29).

Prolonged disputes had raged about this issue, until at the time of the Nicene Council in A.D. 325, it was agreed that the Church of Alexandria, Egypt, the site of greatest astronomical learning, should have authority in computing the date of Easter for the whole Church. However, for some time after the council, differing and not fully reliable Easter tables continued in use in various provinces, and as communications worsened in the declining Roman Empire, the Western churches were thrown back on themselves and were cut off from Alexandrian advances in the Easter computation. Functioning with far less calendrical and astronomical skill, Western religious authorities from the fourth to eighth centuries used a variety of tables in the attempt to conform with the canonical dates for Easter, with mixed success.

Hoping to drive out rival tables in use in the West, which were producing errors and confusion, Dionysius Exiguus drafted an extension of the most accurate Easter tables then circulating: apparently, these had been framed in the East and were based on the 19-year lunar cycle that had, in the meantime, been adopted by the Alexandrians. In a treatise accompanying his tables, Dionysius explained that he did "not wish to perpetuate the name of the Great Persecutor, [that is, to follow the Era of Diocletian employed in his model] but to number the years from the Incarnation of our Lord Jesus Christ," by which God had redeemed mankind. In the first of the eight columns of his tables, the monk omitted his predecessor's "years of Diocletian" and introduced instead a list of *Anni Domini Nostri Iesu Christi,* beginning with 532. In making this change Dionysius had given the West a new era — the one that would eventually predominate — though he had conceived of it only for a very limited purpose.

How the Era of the Incarnation, or Christian Era, ceased to be exclusively tied to the Easter tables and came to be used for more general chronological purposes can only be hypothesized. For one thing, despite initial papal interest, it is not clear where and how fast the Dionysian tables spread, although it can be argued that they came to be known in Italy, Africa, and Spain in the later sixth century and in the British Isles in the earlier part of the seventh century. In reality, once the new tables were in circulation, any monk might easily have conceived of using "years from the Incarnation" in more than a purely paschal context from the act of recording the years' chief events in the margins of his Easter table alongside the list of "years of our Lord." The practice of using the extra space around the columns of Easter tables for historical notations was widespread in the early Middle Ages, when parchment was scarce and more sophisticated forms of historical writing had died out. General use of the new era is often dated from A.D. 725, when the Anglo-Saxon monk the Venerable Bede gave it a fundamental place in his great treatise on computing dates, *De Temporum Ratione.* Certainly, Bede's adoption of the Christian Era for his celebrated *Ecclesiastical History of the English People* a few years afterwards gave the innovation a secure place in English history. But it is possible that such use of the Christian Era had started more haphazardly among Anglo-Saxon annalists in previous decades, and Bede may have drawn on some of them.

Whatever its start, the practice of dating years from the Incarnation of Christ was taken to the Continent in the eighth century by Anglo-Saxon missionaries. From the 11th century on, dating by the Christian Era appeared more and more commonly on Western charters and correspondence (though not in most of the Iberian Peninsula until the 14th century).

To calculate his era, Dionysius had had to designate the exact year of Jesus' birth. Following interpretations current in his time, he had made A.D. 1 coincide with the Roman year A.U.C. 753–754. Scholars now believe that Dionysius and his contemporaries miscalculated the Advent and hypothesize that Jesus probably was born between 9 and 2 B.C., rather than in A.D. 1 as Dionysius reckoned. But the Christian Era as he introduced it became entrenched before the mistake was widely recognized.

Because his interest was confined to his paschal tables, Dionysius did not indicate an exact day from which he took "years of our Lord" to start. Assimilating the new era in a mix with other dating elements, chroniclers, kings, and popes in succeeding centuries simply treated its years as starting on whatever day customarily began the calendar year in their region (or in the sources they used). Thus "years from the Incarnation" most frequently began on September 1, or on Christmas, the Feast of the Nativity of Jesus on December 25, in the early Middle Ages; but centuries later the years began in some places on Easter, and eventually in other places on the old pagan date of January 1, as has become general in the modern period. In reality, Dionysius' word "incarnation" was ambiguous. Some medieval churchmen favored beginning the calendar year from the Annunciation (or "Lady Day") on March 25, marking the conception of Jesus — holding that the incarnation dated from the moment of conception. This date for the beginning of the year gained considerable popularity in Italy, France, and England from the 11th century on. Even where the March 25 style was followed, however, the years were more widely dated from March 25 three months *after* the Nativity (the so-called Florentine style, used in England until 1752), than from March 25 nine months *before* the Nativity (the so-called Pisan style). This discrepancy of an entire year between some regions did not seem to perturb medieval rulers.

By the 16th century, the Christian Era, or Era of the Incarnation, was so securely established in Western European dating practice that the "calendar strife" that followed the Gregorian reform of 1582 did not affect continued use of this era by all parties. On the other hand, Eastern Orthodox Christianity had never adopted the Christian Era, which was a purely Western innovation. From about the 7th century to the fall of Byzantium in the 15th century (and later in the Greek church) a "mundane era," that is, an era dating from the creation of the world as set forth in the Bible was used in the East, with its years styled "A.M." (for *anno mundi,* "in the year of the world"). This so-called Era of Constantinople took as its starting point September 1, 5508 B.C., one of many dates that had been put forth as likely for the beginning of the world. Russia used the Era of Constantinople until A.D. 1699, when Peter the Great changed the style to the Christian Era of the West, effective as of 1700.

Another "mundane era," with years also styled "A.M.," attained widespread use among Jews of the diaspora by the 9th century A.D. Differing rabbinical calculations of the date of the Creation gave rise to the use of five different dates for the beginning of this era, but by the 12th century the style used at present had superseded its rivals. Its epoch, or starting point, corresponds to October 7, 3761 B.C. This Hebrew system is used in modern Israel along with the Western (or Christian) Era; with the latter system, years are labeled C.E. (Common Era) or B.C.E. (Before the Common Era). The usage is found also in the United States in Jewish-oriented publications and calendars.

From the time of Omar I, the second caliph, Muslims have observed the "Era of the Hegira" in commemoration of the Prophet Mohammed's flight from Mecca to Medina in A.D. 622, taking as its epoch the first day of the month of Muharram (July 16 in 622). Years of this era are styled "A.H." Since the year of the Islamic calendar is purely lunar, with a length of either 354 or 355 days, 33 years of the Muslim Era are nearly equal to 32 years of the Christian Era. The Era of the Hegira is in official use in Arab countries, but the Western calendar and Era are also in general use in Muslim lands. Turkey, a non-Arab Muslim country, adopted the Western calendar exclusively in 1927. Iran, another non-Arab nation, has its own calendar and an era based upon the founding of the Persian empire by Cyrus the Great (about 550 B.C.).

At the end of the 18th century, the French Revolutionary government launched the only decisive departure from the Christian Era that has been attempted in modern Western dating. The revolutionary convention, in adopting a wholly new Republican calendar to replace the Gregorian calendar so closely associated with ecclesiastical authority, on October 5, 1793, retroactively declared the "Republican Era" to have begun on September 22, 1792. (This was the day of the proclamation of the Republic in France and, conveniently, also the autumnal equinox.) However, because the change entailed postdating more than a year of revolutionary government documents, most dates from the first "year of the Republic" are styled by the Christian Era, with the simple addition of the Roman numeral "I" to signify the first Republican year. Emperor Napoleon I reinstituted the Christian Era in French dating, along with the Gregorian calendar, on January 1, 1806 — in the middle of the year XIV of the French Republic.

During the American Revolution, the Confederation of the 13 former colonies abandoned the ancient British practice of dating official documents by the reign-years of the monarch and noted instead on its documents the "year of Independence," together with the year of the Christian Era. Today, presidential proclamations state that they have been signed at Washington, D.C., on a given day of the month "in the year of our Lord ——, and of the Independence of the United States the ——."

In the 19th century, when historians writing about ancient times began systematically to extend the Christian Era back to the period "before Christ," a difficulty inherent in the original paschal device of Dionysius Exiguus became troublesome. The monk and his successors had necessarily made their calculations in Roman numerals. (Before the introduction of Arabic numerals in Europe in about the 12th century, this was the only numerical system available in the West.) But the Roman system lacked any symbol for the concept of zero. Hence Dionysius and his imitators called the first year of his era "I A.D.," and the year immediately preceding it became what is known in English as 1 B.C. Today a zero point would be established and the first year would be counted only in days and months (as is commonly done with a child's first year of life). The practical result of this unavoidable flaw in Dionysius' system is that to compute the interval between a date that is A.D. and another that is B.C., one must reduce their apparent sum by one. Thus, the interval between January 1 in the year 2 B.C., and January 1, A.D. 2, is three years, not four.

The Days of the Week

The English word *week* — derived from the Anglo-Saxon *wicu* and ultimately from the Germanic *wikōn*, both words probably meaning "turn" or "change" — designates a period of time amounting to less than a month and now consisting of seven days. The month, however, can be, has been, and presently is, divided in various ways in different regions of the world. In ancient Egypt, for example, the phases of the moon suggested division of the month into fractional parts, such as decads or pentads, known as "moon weeks." Other ancient peoples settled the length of the week arbitrarily without considering the length of the month and invented for their convenience the "market week," usually ranging from four to eight days. The early Romans used an eight-day market week.

The exact origin of the seven-day week has been lost in antiquity. Various theories have been proposed. One likely theory traces the seven-day week back to western Asia, probably to Mesopotamia. It is assumed that the use of the number seven for the days of the week there stemmed from the erroneous astrological concept that seven celestial bodies revolved around the earth: the sun, the moon, and five of the bodies today known to be planets — Mars, Mercury, Jupiter, Venus, and Saturn. The hypothesis is greatly substantiated by the names still employed to designate the days of the week, all of which are ultimately derived — despite Roman and Anglo-Saxon adaptations — from these ancient "planet" names.

Another strong influence in setting the number of the days of the week at seven was the Hebrew week, based on the Old Testament account in Genesis of how God created the world in six days and rested on the seventh. This seventh and last day of the week, known as the Sabbath (Shabbat), was therefore set aside as the Hebrew holy day of rest and worship, in keeping with Genesis 2:3, "And God blessed the seventh day, and sanctified it." The Fourth Commandment given by God to Moses concerns this holiest of days: "Remember the sabbath day, to keep it holy" (Exodus 20:8). Jewish law stipulates detailed regulations for observing the Sabbath, which starts at sundown on the eve of the seventh day.

Both the Christian week and the Muslim week were undoubtedly much influenced by the Hebrew week of seven days, despite the fact that the Hebrew Sabbath was not adopted as the day of worship in either of the two religions. Muslims, believing that Adam had been created on the sixth day, chose this day (Friday) as their holy day. Jesus Christ's Resurrection had occurred on the first day of the week, not the seventh. The early Christians — most of whom were Jews — therefore began to assemble for worship on that day instead of on the Sabbath and considered their new liturgical service a commemoration of Easter, the day of the Resurrection (see March 29). Moreover, Jesus had seemed to emphasize that the first day of the week should be his. He had shown himself to his followers on a number of occasions on the first Easter. One week later, again on the first day of the week, he had appeared to his disciple Thomas. Thomas had refused to believe that Jesus had risen from the dead unless, as he said, "I see in his hands the print of the nails, and put my finger into the place of the nails, and put my hand into his side." (John 20:25). Seven weeks after the Resurrection, once more on the first day of the week, the Holy Spirit had descended upon the gathered disciples on Pentecost.

The movement to observe the first day of the week as the "Christian Sabbath" was a gradual one that developed over the first three centuries of Christianity. But the "unofficial" change is richly documented by New Testament references to the preeminence of this day as the cornerstone of the Christian year. The Apostle Luke notes (Acts 20:7) that the Apostle Paul preached at Troas on the northwest coast of Asia Minor "on the first day of the week, when we had met for the breaking of bread." Paul himself, addressing the Corinthians (I Corinthians 16:2) asked them to gather together an offering for Jerusalem "on the first day of the week."

Although obviously widely accepted as the normal day of worship, the first day of the week received a new name before the end of the first century. It is referred to as "the Lord's day" (in Greek, hē kyriakē hēmera) in the Apocalypse or Book of Revelation (1:10), written in the second half of the first century. Dies dominica was the Latin equivalent of the Greek term for "the Lord's day." It later decisively influenced the Western European Romance languages, which derived from the Latin their names for the first day of the week: domingo (Spanish and Portuguese), domenica (Italian), dimanche (French). By the beginning of the fourth century, "the Lord's day" had become the customary day of worship throughout Christendom. Moreover, the Roman emperor Constantine, who became a convert to Christianity, pronounced the seven-day Christian week, starting on "the Lord's day," official in the civil calendar of the vast Roman Empire about 321.

Before the ascendancy of the Judeo-Christian week in the Roman Empire, the Romans had apparently been strongly influenced by the Middle Eastern seven-day "planetary" week as well. They seem to have adopted elements of the ancient Mesopotamian system, especially the number seven and the use of planetary names for the days of the week, which they now based, however, on the names of their own Roman deities. The first day of the week was known as dies solis, "sun's day"; the second day as dies lunae, "moon's day"; the third day as dies Martis, "Mar's day," after the god of war; the fourth day as dies Mercurii, "Mercury's day," after the god of commerce and messenger of the gods; the fifth day as dies Jovis, "Jove's day," after Jove or Jupiter, the chief god; the sixth day as dies Veneris, "Venus's day," after the goddess of love; and the seventh day as dies Saturni, "Saturn's day," after the god of agriculture.

The use of these pagan names for the days of the week remained an accepted practice even after Constantine had adopted Christianity. The only exceptions — and partial ones at that — were the first day of the week, the former Roman dies solis, which became widely known as "the

Lord's day," and the seventh, the "Sabbath." But the remaining days of the week kept their distinctly pagan names, as can be seen, for example, in the present French names: *lundi, mardi, mercredi, jeudi,* and *vendredi* are very similar to the ancient Roman designations.

The English names for the days of the week, even for the first day or "Lord's day," have remained pagan through the centuries. Derived from the Anglo-Saxon, *Sunday, Monday,* and *Saturday* represent, on the one hand, literal translations of the Latin names used by the Romans. On the other hand, *Tuesday, Wednesday, Thursday,* and *Friday* reflect the Anglo-Saxons' deliberate effort to substitute the names of their own native gods for those of the Roman deities. Early Christian writers in the British Isles, such as the Venerable Bede, did not object even to the pagan name *Sunday* for the first day of the week, holding that the use of pagan names did not undermine Christian faith but represented rather a charitable gesture toward those who had not yet been converted.

Sunday, the first day of the week, gets its name from the Anglo-Saxon *sunnandaeg,* from *sunnan,* "sun," and *daeg,* "day." Like the equivalent Roman name, *dies solis,* "sun's day," it is regarded as a name surviving from ancient sun worship. With the Christianization of the British Isles, Sunday became not only the day of worship but a day of rest from all but agricultural labor. There, as elsewhere in Western Europe, certain types of work and amusement were forbidden on Sunday. Although stipulations were laid down in England as early as the 7th century, only in the Act of Uniformity passed in 1551 during the reign of King Edward VI was Sunday church-going definitely ordained. According to a statute of 1558–1559, any person who did not attend church services was subject to a penalty of 12 pence, as well as church censure. As the Puritan movement gained momentum in the 17th century, restrictive moral legislation became common, and all but pious activities were strictly forbidden on Sunday.

Many of the repressive measures were carried over to the New World. The colony of Virginia passed such legislation as early as 1629. Practically every American colony enacted Sunday legislation, although Puritan New England outdid other sections. The term "blue laws" for this type of puritanical lawmaking was first coined by an Anglican clergyman, Samuel A. Peters, of Hebron, Connecticut. In his *General History of Connecticut,* published in 1781, Peters described the rigid moral code that had operated in parts of New England, proscribing many innocent pastimes, sexual misdemeanors, and "outlandish" dress, as well as Sunday-breaking. More recently, the expression has been broadly applied to characterize any law rigorously regulating public, and especially private, conduct.

After the American Revolution, much of the Sunday legislation remained in effect in statute books but was not invoked. During the 19th century there was a widespread revival of local and state legislation restricting or forbidding secular entertainment or unnecessary work on Sunday, or the consumption of intoxicating liquor. The legality of the Sunday legislation was frequently contested. The laws were generally upheld, originally on purely religious grounds and later on the grounds that they contributed to the physical and moral well-being of the community. Today, the restrictive legislation has been either repealed or at least relaxed in many parts of the United States, except where religious fundamentalism is deeply rooted.

The name of Monday comes from the Anglo-Saxon *monandaeg,* "moonday," which is a translation from the Roman name *dies lunae,* "moon's day."

Tuesday (in Anglo-Saxon *Tiwesdaeg,* "Tiw's day") is named for Tyr, the Norse god of war and of battle, whom the Anglo-Saxons called Tiw. His identification with Mars, the Roman god of war (see March), caused the Anglo-Saxons to translate the *dies Martis,* "Mar's day," of the Romans as *Tiwesdaeg.* In the Germanic religion Tyr or Tiw was regarded as the bold wrestler among the gods. His cult seems to have been widespread, especially in Germany and England. But Icelandic mythology is also full of tales of his bravery.

Wednesday is named after the Norse god Odin (also known as Woden or Wuotan), and in Anglo-Saxon was called *Wodnesdaeg,* "Woden's day." Odin, the father of Tyr and Thor, was considered the highest, oldest, and wisest among the Germanic deities. The cult of Odin was known mainly in Germany and England, but his exploits are related in the Icelandic prose and poetic *Eddas,* which tell how Odin and his brothers slew the giant Ymir and from his body created the world. Ymir's flesh became the dry land; his bones, the mountains; his teeth and jaws, rocks and pebbles; and his blood the ocean. His skull became the vault of the heavens. Odin's seat was the palace Valhalla, a sort of martial paradise where the god welcomed brave warriors after death and treated them to fighting and feasting, the pleasures in which they had taken greatest delight on earth. Probably because of his wisdom and skill in magic, Odin became identified with Mercury, the Roman god of commerce who was the fleet-footed messenger of the gods. Therefore, the Roman fourth day of the week, *dies Mercurii,* "Mercury's day," became *Wodnesdaeg*, "Woden's day," in Anglo-Saxon.

Thursday is named for Thor, the Norse god of thunder. His chariot, drawn by he-goats named Tooth-gnasher and Gap-tooth, was said to cause the thunder when it was drawn through the heavens. The eldest and strongest son of Odin, Thor, the sagas relate, was armed with a magical hammer, Mjöllnir, which returned when thrown; a belt of strength; and iron gauntlets. Thor used his hammer to kill his implacable enemies, the giants. In all northern countries, but especially in Iceland, the cult of Thor was highly developed, although few details about the worship are known today. For reasons that are unclear, Thor was identified with the chief Roman god, Jupiter or Jove. The Anglo-Saxons thus termed the fifth day of the week — the Roman *dies Jovis*, "Jove's day" — *Thursdaeg*, Thor's day.

Friday is named for Frigg, or Frigga, the wife of Odin in northern mythology. Her name became confused with that of Freya, the Scandinavian goddess of fertility and matrimony, light, and peace. According to the Icelandic prose *Edda*, Freya "enjoys love poetry, and it is good to call on her for help in love affairs." Because of Frigg's identification with Freya and Freya's similarity to Venus, the Roman goddess of love, the Anglo-Saxons translated the Roman name for the sixth day of the week, *dies Veneris*, "Venus's day," as *Frigedaeg*, Frigg's day. Although pagans in northern countries regarded Friday as the luckiest day of the week, Christians believed it unlucky since it was the day on which Jesus Christ had been crucified.

Saturday was the only day in the Anglo-Saxon week that continued to be called after one of the Roman deities. As the Romans called it *dies Saturni*, "Saturn's day," the Anglo-Saxons called it *Saterdaeg*, after the Roman god of planting and agriculture. Saturn apparently became identified with the Greek deity Cronus, the primeval Titan who ruled the world in the Golden Age of peace and plenty. Defeated in battle by his son Zeus, Cronus supposedly went to Rome, where he was welcomed by Janus, the Roman god of doorways (see January). Saturn's festival, the *Saturnalia*, was originally celebrated on December 17 but was eventually extended for seven additional days (see December).

In late Roman and medieval times, distances were too vast and communication too tenuous to make uniform the diverse names for the days of the week, which had developed independently, to a certain degree, in northern and southern Europe. It was not even feasible to abolish them all, substituting Christian names — perhaps of apostles or martyrs — for the primarily pagan designations. There was one attempt to have all

areas of Christendom call the first day of the week "the Lord's day"; the seventh day, "the Sabbath"; and the five days in between simply by numbers, from two through six. The move was generally unsuccessful, although the custom of naming the days of the week in this way is still being practiced, for example, in Portugal.

Signs of the Zodiac

The zodiac in both astronomy and astrology is the designation the ancients gave to an imaginary band or zone of the heavens. It is about 16° in width, extending 8° on each side of the ecliptic, the apparent annual path of the sun among the stars as seen from Earth. The zodiac includes the orbits of the sun and the moon, as well as of the five planets — Saturn, Mercury, Venus, Mars, and Jupiter — which were known to the ancient astronomers who first originated the zodiac.

The zodiac is divided into 12 equal sections of 30° each — the so-called signs of the zodiac — each named for a constellation located within its limits at the time it was named. To the ancients, nearly all of the 12 constellations, or star groups, in the zodiac seemed to form the characteristic shape of an animal, or at least of a living creature. Hence the name *zodiac*, which is derived from the Greek and is most commonly thought to have been taken from either *zoon*, a "living thing," or *zōidion*, the diminutive of animal, and *kyklos*, "circle." It is thus usually interpreted as a "circle of animals." The 12 constellations in the zodiac and the symbols by which they are represented, are Aries (♈); Taurus (♉); Gemini (♊); Cancer (♋); Leo (♌); Virgo (♍); Libra (♎); Scorpio (♏); Sagittarius (♐); Capricornus (♑); Aquarius (♒); and Pisces (♓).

The zodiacal constellations were already known by the Greek equivalents of their present Latin names more than 2,000 years ago. But they were not invented by the Greeks. Interest in these constellations, which have been termed the "fossil remains of primitive stellar religion," extends back to the dawn of astronomy. The zodiac is believed to have originated with the remote civilizations of the Near Eastern Euphrates Valley, in the region known in ancient times as Mesopotamia. It is known that the Akkadians, early non-Semitic inhabitants of the valley who, prior to the Babylonians, created a flourishing civilization starting in the fourth millennium B.C., described the stars in detail, calling them a "heavenly flock," the sun being the "old sheep" and the planets the "old-sheep stars." They passed on their star system to the Babylonians, whose cuneiform tablets, boundary stones, and works of art indicate the existence of a carefully thought-out network of star names including the zodiac, early in their history, probably well before 2000 B.C. The cuneiform tablet recounting the Creation legend, which was compiled from more ancient records during the reign of Assurbani-pal, the king of Assyria (c. 650 B.C.), includes a passage that appears to indicate acceptance of 36 constellations: 12 northern, 12 southern, and 12 zodiacal.

Since, with the exception of Scorpio, few of the zodiacal constellations really closely resemble the animal or object after which they were named, it is thought that these constellations may have been chosen to fit various primitive gods and ancient heroes. Moreover, the symbols given the constellations may even be the remnants of names of Egyptian deities as presented in the formalized hieratic script and could have been in use as early as 1800 B.C. From the Near East, the zodiac system was most likely transmitted through the seafaring Phoenicians to the Greeks and from Greece to the Western world.

The fourth century B.C. Greek astronomer Eudoxus of Cnidus was probably the author of the earliest Greek work that treated groups of stars as constellations. This early work has not been preserved; but a versification of it made by Aratus, a third century B.C. poet at the court of Antigonus II Gonatas, king of Macedonia, who was himself a patron of philosophy and poetry, is extant. In an astronomical treatise entitled *Phenomena*, Aratus gave the first systematic literary account of the stars. He listed 44 constellations, including 13 central or zodiacal ones: Aries, Taurus, Gemini, Cancer, Leo, Virgo, Libra, Scorpio, Sagittarius, Capricornus, Aquarius, Pisces, and the Pleiades. Aratus's *Phenomena* received perhaps even more attention than it ordinarily would have merited from the Christian world since St. Paul quoted one of its lines in his famous Athens sermon on the Unknown God as found in Acts 17:28: "As certain of your own poets have said . . . , For we are also his offspring."

The great second century B.C. Greek astronomer Hipparchus wrote the first known comprehensive catalog of the heavens, listing at least 850 stars. This commentary was based on the work of Eudoxus and Aratus. Unlike Aratus, he did not keep the Pleiades separate from Taurus, but reduced them to an asterism, thus enumerating 12 constellations rather than 13. But except for similar trifling exceptions, Hipparchus's adaptation of a zodiacal system so similar to Aratus reveals that he was only reiterating a familiar concept long accepted in Greek intellectual circles. Some 300 years after Hipparchus, the Greco-Egyptian scholar and mathematician Ptolemy (fl. 127–141 or 151), the last great astronomer of antiquity, set down a similar scheme in his *Almagest*, presenting the astronomical system developed by the Greeks. Muslim scholars later transmitted the work to Western Europe.

Since antiquity, there have been no great alterations in the zodiacal system. In 1627 Julius Schiller tried in his *Coelum stellatum Christianum* to have the names denoting mythological pagan ideas replaced with the names of apostles, saints, and other renowned Christians. For example, Aries was to become St. Peter; Taurus, St. Andrew. The innovation was short-lived, as was a similar attempt later made by E. Weigelius, who wished to have the constellations, including the zodiacal ones, represent especially the arms of various European dynasties.

It should be noted, however, that other ancient civilizations defined and named the constellations in a different way from the Western world — as is seen, for example, in the work of the Chinese astronomer Shih-Shen (c. 500 B.C.). The Chinese still assign great weight to their own distinctive signs of the zodiac (see February 6, Chinese New Year).

In primitive times, the start of the year was reckoned from the beginning of spring, or the vernal equinox (see March 21), the day on which the sun appears to pass through the intersection of the ecliptic and the celestial equator in what was perceived as its annual course. Day and night are of equal length at this time and the ancients therefore chose the vernal equinox as the point from which to calculate the 12 zodiacal positions. At the time of Hipparchus, whose calculations (c. 120 B.C.) form the basis of the present zodiacal system, the sun was in Aries at the time of the vernal equinox. Thus the order of the 12 constellations — going eastward — traditionally begins with Aries, and Aries is the first sign of the zodiac.

Aries, the Ram (March 21–April 19), is denoted by a sign that may depict the horns of the butting animal (γ). As is true with all the zodiac constellations, various theories have been put forth to account for the connection between the name of the constellation and the time of year in which the sun crosses it. One explanation for Aries holds that since the first month of the ancient Babylonian year was the "month of sacrifice" — the sacrifice usually being a ram — the constellation was naturally associated with a ram. The ancient Greeks, on the other hand, may have associated Aries with the ram whose golden fleece was the goal of the Argonauts, the band of heroes, particularly Jason, who sailed in the *Argo* to Colchis on the eastern shore of the Black Sea in the Caucasus (now Georgia in the USSR). According to Greek myth, Nephele, the wife of Athamas, the king of Boeotia, and the mother of Phrixus and Helle, presented her children with a golden-fleeced winged ram. Later, to foil the sinister plans of their stepmother, Ino, the brother and sister escaped on the ram's back. The ram flew to Colchis, but en route across the sea Helle fell into the Dardanelles—the narrow strait between Europe and Asia—which was henceforth named Hellespont in her honor. Phrixus arrived safely, sacrificed the ram as an offering to Zeus, the chief of the gods, and hung the fleece in a nearby forest. Zeus then set the slain ram in the sky as a constellation.

The second sign of the zodiac is Taurus, the Bull (April 20–May 20), which also bears a horned symbol (♉). Depictions of the constellation inevitably show only the forequarters of the animal. According to Greek legend, Zeus became enamored of the Phoenician princess Europa, the daughter of Agenor. Assuming the disguise of a great white bull, the god enticed the maiden to mount him, whereupon he swam to Crete, where the princess became the mother of three of his children: Minos, king and lawgiver of Crete; Rhadamanthus, a renowned judge; and Sarpedon, king of Lycia. Another theory claims that since the sun crosses Taurus at the season when the fields were plowed with oxen, the constellation was associated with the bull.

The third sign, Gemini, the Twins (May 21–June 21), is denoted by the Roman numeral ♊. Throughout antiquity, the constellation was associated with many mythical twins—for example, in Babylonia with the sun and the moon. In Egypt, Gemini was associated with Horus the Elder, represented as a falcon-headed sun god of light and goodness, and Horus the Child—called Harpocrates by the Greeks and Romans—represented as a young boy holding his finger to his lips. In Greece and Rome the constellation was symbolized by Castor and Pollux, whom one legend makes the twin sons of Zeus, and Leda, the wife of King Tyndareus of Sparta (see July).

Cancer, the Crab (June 22–July 22), the fourth sign of the zodiac, is denoted by a symbol that may represent the claws of a crab (♋). The Babylonians, however, sometimes referred to the constellation as the Tortoise, while the Egyptians regarded it as the Scarabaeus or Sacred Beetle. According to the Roman writer and philosopher Macrobius (fl. c. 400), the name *crab* arose from the ancient belief—fostered throughout the Middle Ages as well—that the crab "walks backward" as does the sun at the summer solstice, when it changes from a downward to an upward motion.

Leo, the Lion (July 23–August 22), the fifth sign of the zodiac, is depicted by a symbol (♌) that seems like the Greek cursive capital *Lambda*, the initial letter of the animal's name. Another theory claims that it is rather a crude drawing of a lion's tail. Because it was crossed by the sun at the hottest time of the year, the constellation was associated with the lion, which was regarded as an ancient symbol for heat or fire. According to Greek mythology, the beast represents the Nemean lion, an enormous beast said to be the offspring of the monster Typhon. Invulnerable to all weapons, it was finally strangled by Hercules, the son of Zeus and Alcmene, as one of the 12 labors he fulfilled in repentance for having slain his children. Zeus then raised the lion to the heavens in tribute to Hercules.

Virgo, the Virgin (August 23–September 22), is the sixth sign, whose symbol (♍) may be a contraction of the Greek letters Π Α Ρ, the initial letters of *parthenos*, or "virgin." Different legends exist as to the identity of the maiden referred to. In antiquity, she was, for example, reputed to be Erigone, the daughter of Icarius, the man taught by Dionysus to make wine. Icarius was slain by friends of a group of shepherds he had made drunk and was buried by them in a secret spot. Erigone, after years of searching, finally discovered the grave and, overwhelmed by grief, hanged herself. The name *Virgo* may also be an allusion to Ishtar, the Babylonian mother deity of love and above all of fertility and the generative powers in nature. The most widely worshiped goddess in the Babylonian and Assyrian religion, she was honored especially at the time of year when the sun crosses Virgo. One myth concerns her descent into Hades, the underworld, in search of her missing lover, Tammuz, and her triumphant return to earth.

Libra, the Balance (September 23–October 23), the seventh sign, is the only nonliving representation in the zodiac. Its symbol may show a conventionalized pair of scales (♎) since, as its name suggests, it refers to the balancing or equality of day and night at the season when the sun arrives at the autumnal equinox.

Scorpio (Scorpius), the Scorpion (October 24–November 21), is the eighth sign of the zodiac, whose symbol may represent a conventional picture of the arachnid (♏). According to one version of a Greek fable, Orion, a handsome Boeotian hunter noted for his prowess and might, boasted to Artemis (Diana), the goddess of the moon and the hunt and Leto (Latona), the mother of Apollo and Artemis, that he would slay all animals in the world. A scorpion, acting upon the orders of the two goddesses, thereupon stung him to death. Zeus raised the scorpion to heaven as a constellation and, upon the pleas of Artemis, also did so for Orion. Another theory holds that the sign alludes to the darkness that follows the decline of the sun after the autumn equinox.

Sagittarius, the Archer (November 22–December 21), is the ninth sign of the zodiac ($\nearrow$). The Greeks represented it as a centaur, half-man, half-beast, in the act of shooting an arrow, and professed that he was Crotus, the son of Eupheme, the nurse of the Muses—the nine sister deities of the arts. Eratosthenes, the third century B.C. Greco-Egyptian astronomer credited with measuring the circumference of the earth, termed Sagittarius a satyr. In remote antiquity, the constellation probably represented the Babylonian god of war, the equivalent of the Roman god Mars.

Capricorn (Capricornus), the Goat (December 22–Januray 19), from the Latin *caper*, "goat," and *cornu*, "horn," whose sign perhaps crudely depicts the animal ($\text{V}\text{3}$), is the tenth sign of the zodiac. The ancients maintained that the sun of the winter solstice is like a child in infancy and therefore the name may have been connected with the Caprine nurse of the young solar god mentioned in Eastern legends.

The 11th sign of the zodiac is Aquarius, the Water-bearer (January 20–February 18), whose symbol ($\approx$) can be read in Egyptian hieroglyphic script as NN (Nun), the god of waters. This may well be the oldest of all the signs and may allude to the fact that when the sun is in this part of the sky, the weather tends to be rainy.

Pisces, the Fishes (February 19–March 20), the 12th sign of the zodiac, is symbolized by a line or cord joining two fish (H). It may refer to the "wet month" of the Egyptians, when the waters of the Nile began to overflow. According to Greek legend, Aphrodite, the goddess of love, and Eros, the god of love, her son and companion, were surprised by the monster Typhon on the banks of the Euphrates River. They sought safety by jumping into the water, where they were changed into two fish.

The stellar background through which the sun moves at the time of the vernal equinox changes gradually with the passage of centuries, and therefore the zodiacal constellation associated with the spring season and the beginning of the zodiacal circle also changes position slowly. This gradual drift of the constellations with respect to the seasons is the result of the precession of the equinoxes—the clockwise progression of the equinoctial points at which the sun crosses the celestial equator. At the time of Hipparchus, who gave the zodiacal constellations the definitive order that was eventually transmitted to Western Europe, the March equinox occurred when the sun was in what became known as Aries. As noted, Aries therefore became the first sign of the zodiac. Over the past 2,000 years, however, the precession of the equinoxes has given rise to a discrepancy amounting to the width of a whole zodiacal sign, or 30°. Thus the sign Aries is now occupied by the constellation Pisces. Indeed, each of the 12 divisions of the zodiac now contains the constellation west of the one from which it took its name. This gradual movement was first explained by the English scientist Isaac Newton in 1687. Only after a complete cycle of 25,800 years will Aries again assume its proper place as both the first sign and the first constellation of the zodiac and the cycle begin once more.

Index

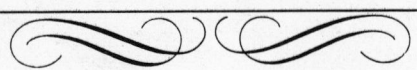

A

AFL. *See* Gompers, Samuel, birthday

Abbott, Lyman, birthday, 1115–16

Actors: Edwin Booth's birthday, 1017–19; Edwin Forrest's birthday, 243; Joseph Jefferson's birthday, 196; Will Rogers Day in Oklahoma, 994–5

Adak, Alaska, Oklahoma Day at US Naval Station, 371

Adams, John, birthday, 966–8

Adams, John Quincy, birthday, 651–3
  See also Adams-Onís treaty; Presidential election of 1824 deadlocked

Adams Samuel, birthday, 872–3

Adams-Onís treaty: Florida ceded by Spain, 675–6; signed, 204

Addams, Jane, birthday, 807–9

Advent begins, 1059–60

Aefter-Yule, 2

Aeronautics: Balloon flight, 52–4; Richard E. Byrd's birthday, 955–6; Charles A. Lindbergh lands in Paris, 473–4; Wright Brothers Day, 1111–15
  See also Space exploration

Afro-American History Week, 169, 181

Agassiz, Louis, birthday, 488–91

Agnes, St., feast of, 98–101; eve, 97–8

Agonalia, 1

Agriculture: Luther Burbank's birthday, 240; George Washington Carver's death, 31–3; Hussey reaper first exhibited, 615–16; Cyrus H. McCormick's birthday, 186–7; John Wesley Powell's birthday, 283–4; Soil Stewardship Sunday, 417–18; Eli Whitney patents the cotton gin, 250–1

Aguinaldo, Emilio. *See* Philippines: Philippine Independence Day

Alabama admitted to the Union, 1102–4

Alabama Claims, 330

Alama, 761–2; Alamo Day, 237–40

Alaska: admitted to the Union, 22; Alaska Day, 935–7; Anchorage Fur Rendezvous, 176–7; earthquake, 294; Eskimo games, Kotzebue, 623; Seward's Day, 309–10

Albany becomes the capital of New York, 243–4

Albany Congress convenes, 568–70

Alden, John Day, 713–14

Aldrin, Edwin E. ("Buzz"), Jr. *See* Moon, manned landing on

All-Alaska Basketball Classic, 177

All-Alaska Judo Tournament, 177

All American Indian Days, Sheridan, Wyoming, 707–8

All Fools' Day. *See* April Fools' Day

All Hallows' Day (All Saints' Day), 978–80

All Hallows' Eve (Halloween), 968–72, 979

All Indian Powwow, Flagstaff, Arizona, 623

All Saints' Day, 978–80

All Souls' Day, 980–2; eve, 979

Allen, Ethan. *See* Fort Ticonderoga falls; Vermont admitted to Union; Vermont declares independence

Amendments, constitutional. *See* Constitutional amendments

American Academy of Arts and Letters chartered, 358–9

American Council for Nationalities Service, 534

American-Danish Festival Week, 312

American Evangelical Lutheran Church. *See* Lutheran Church in America organized

American Federation of Labor. *See* Gompers, Samuel, birthday

American Foundation for the Blind, 599

American Heritage Week in Rhode Island, 412

American History Month, 169

American Indian Day, 863–5

American Indian Exposition, Anadarko, Oklahoma, 759–60

American Indians: All American Indian Days, Sheridan, Wyoming, 707–8; American Indian Day, 863–5; American Indian Exposition, Anadarko, Oklahoma, 759–60; Cherokee Strip Day, 844–6; Daniel Boone Festival, Barbourville, Kentucky, 901–2; Feast of the Assumption (Coeur d'Alene), 756; first Indian treaty, 277–8; Holy Week observances, 304; Independence Day events, 623; Indian Rights

Day, 623; Navajo Nation Fair, Window Rock, Arizona, 832–3; New Year's Day (Crow), 8; Oklahoma becomes a state, 1025–8; Tecumseh's death, 900–1; Thanksgiving (Wampanoag), 1054; battle of Tippecanoe, 1001–2; *Unto These Hills*, Cherokee, North Carolina, 584–5; Veterans Day (Kiowa), 1013
  See also Albany Congress convenes; Pueblo events

American Lutheran Church merger, 366; becomes effective, 8; Lutheran Free Church joins, 135

American Magazine, or A Monthly View of the Political State of the British Colonies, first American magazine published, 177

American Red Cross. *See* Barton, Clara, birthday

American Revolution: John Adams's birthday, 966–8; Samuel Adams's birthday, 872–3; André hanged as a spy, 888–90; army established, 555; Articles of Confederation adopted, 1024–5; John Barry Day, 836–7; Battle of Brandywine, 831–2; Battle of Great Bridge, 1085–7; Battle of Princeton, 22–3; Battle of Saratoga (first), 855; Battle of Saratoga (second), 907; Battle of Trenton, 1152–4; Battles of Lexington and Concord (Patriots' Day), 359–62; Bennington Battle Day, 758–9; Boston Massacre, 235–7; Bunker Hill Day, 563–6; Colonies put in state of defense, 452–4; John Dickinson's "Farmer's Letters," 995–7; Evacuation Day, Boston, 264–5; Evacuation Day, New York City, 1051–3; First Continental Congress, 803–5; First national flag, 12–13; Flag Day, 551–5; Fort Ticonderoga falls, 440–1; Forts Clinton and Montgomery captured by British, 902–4; France recognizes the United States, 148–50; Nathan Hale hanged, 858–9; Halifax Resolves Day, 347–8; Alexander Hamilton's birthday, 65–71; Patrick Henry's birthday, 500; Patrick Henry's speech for liberty, 282–3; Independence Day, 619–28; Thomas Jefferson's birthday, 348–51; John Paul Jones's death, 676–7;

American Revolution —
Continued
Jack Jouett's ride, 522–4; Lafayette's birthday, 810–14; Lafayette's death, 470–1; Robert R. Livingston's birthday, 1057–8; James Madison's birthday, 258–61; Mecklenburg Independence Day, 472–3; Thomas Paine's birthday, 121–2; Patriots' Day, 359–62; *Peggy Stewart* Day, 942–3; Pulaski Day, 913–14; Ratification Day (Treaty of Paris), 76–7; Paul Revere's birthday, 19–20; Rhode Island Independence Day, 419–20; Stamp Act repudiated, 1045–6; Baron von Steuben's birthday, 851–4; Surrender of British at Saratoga, 932–5; Treaty of Paris ratified, 76–7; Treaty of Paris signed, 799; Vermont admitted to Union, 233–5; Vermont declares independence, 80–2; Virginia Resolutions, 500; Washington encamps at Valley Forge, 1117–19; Washington takes leave of his officers, 1075–6; Washington's Birthday, 197–204; Yorktown Day, 943–4
See also Colonial history
American Shakespeare Festival, Stratford, Connecticut, 376
Americanism Day in Pennsylvania, 412
Americas, festival of, Miami Beach, Florida, 625
America's Cup Race, first, 771–3
Amish events (Pennsylvania Dutch Folk Festival), 600–1
Anadarko, Oklahoma, American Indian Exposition, 759–60
Anchorage, Alaska, Fur Rendezvous, 176–7
André, John, hanged as a spy, 888–90
Andrew, St., feast of, 1063–5
Animals, Blessing of, Los Angeles, 299
Annapolis (US Naval Academy), June Week, 492–3
Anne and Joachim, SS., feast of, 695–6
Annunciation, feast of, 284–5

Antarctic exploration. *See* Byrd, Richard E., birthday
Anthony of Padua, St., feast of, 549–51
Anthony the Great (Anthony of Egypt, Anthony of the Desert), St., feast of, 84–5
Anthony, Susan B.: birthday (Susan B. Anthony Day), 184; fined for voting, 566–7; and 19th (woman suffrage) amendment, 777–9
Antietam, battle of, 91, 102, 345
Antioch College chartered, 450–2
Antonio, San. *See* Anthony of Padua, St.
Apparition of St. Michael, feast of. *See* Michaelmas Day
Apple Blossom Festival, Shenandoah, 403–4
Apple Blossom Festival, Washington State, 396–8
Apple Butter Festival, Geauga County, Burton, Ohio, 911
Appleseed, Johnny (John Chapman), birthday, 868–9
Appomattox Day, 333–5
April, origin of name, 313–14
April Fools' Day, 314–16
Aquatennial, Minneapolis, Minnesota, 625
Arbor and Bird Day, 368
Arbor Day, 240, 277, 366–9
Architecture: Capitol cornerstone laid, 854–5; White House cornerstone laid, 921–2; Frank Lloyd Wright's birthday, 540–1
Arctic exploration. *See* North Pole discovered
Arizona: Admission Day, 180–1; territory established, 208
Arizona, destruction of, 1084
Arkansas admitted to Union, 558–60
Armed forces: Armed Forces Day, 454–5, 555; Army established, 555; Marine Corps birthday, 1010–11; Memorial Day, 501–4; Navy Day, 963; US Military Academy (West Point) founded, 261–2; US Naval Academy (Annapolis), June Week, 492–3; Veterans Day, 1011–13
Armilustrum, 884

Armistice Day. *See* Veterans Day
Armstrong, Neil A. *See* Moon, manned landing on
Army established, 555
Arnold, Benedict. *See* André, John, hanged as a spy; Saratoga, British surrender
Arthur, Chester A., birthday, 898–900
Articles of Confederation: adopted, 1024–5; inadequacies of, 696–7; ratified, 223
See also Constitution ratified
Artists. *See* Painters
Arts and Letters, American Academy of, chartered, 358–9
Ascension Day, 422–3
Ash Wednesday, 162–3
Ashburton, Lord. *See* Webster-Ashburton Treaty signed
Assumption, feast of, 755–6, 823
Astor, John Jacob, birthday, 671–4
Athletic events. *See* Sporting events
Atlantic Charter, 753
Atlantic City, New Jersey, Miss America Pageant, 821–2
Atomic bomb, first use of, 722–4
Atonement, Day of. *See* Yom Kippur
Attucks, Crispus. *See* Boston Massacre
Audubon, John James, birthday, 380–3
August, origin of name, 712–13
Augustana Evangelical Lutheran Church. *See* Lutheran Church in America organized
Augustine of Canterbury, St., feast of, 486–7
Augustine of Hippo, St., feast of, 787–8
Augustus. *See* August, origin of name
Austin, St. *See* Augustine of Canterbury, St.
Austin, Stephen. *See* San Jacinto Day
Autumn begins, 859–60; traditional date, 857
Aviation. *See* Aeronautics
Aviation Day, 474

B

Balboa discovers the Pacific Ocean, 865–6
Balloon flight in the United States, first successful, 52–4
Baltimore, Lord. *See* Calvert

Baltimore fire, 151–2
Bancroft, George, birthday, 890–2
Banking and finance. *See* Finance
Baptism of the Lord, feast of, 65
Barbourville, Kentucky, Daniel Boone Festival, 901–2

Barnum, P. T.: birthday, 631–3; festival, 624
Barry, John, Day, 836–7
Bartholdi, Frédéric Auguste. *See* Statue of Liberty dedicated
Bartholomew, St., feast of, 774–5

Barton, Clara, birthday, 1149–51

Basil the Great, St., feast of. *See* Circumcision, feast of

Basque events, Boise, Idaho: Christmas, 1148; festival, 711

Bastille Day, 657–60

Battles. *See* names of specific battles

Bear Flag Revolt, 639

Bede, the Venerable, St., 1180; feast of, 480–1

Beecher, Henry Ward, birthday, 590–1
See also Abbott, Lyman, birthday

Bell, Alexander Graham, birthday, 230–1

Beneš, Eduard. *See* Czechoslovak Independence Day

Bennington, battle of: Bennington Battle Day, 758–9; Bicentennial, 625

Bicentennial of the American Revolution, 624–8

Bill of Rights Day, 1105–6
See also Human Rights Day and Week

Bird and Arbor Day, 240

Bird Day, 277, 368

Birth of Mary, feast of, 822–3

Bishop (Episcopal) consecrated, first US, 1022–4

Black Hawk War. *See* Taylor, Zachary, birthday

Black Hills Passion Play, 281

Black Hills Roundup, 623

Black Tuesday. *See* Panic of 1929

Blacks: Crispus Attucks killed in Boston Massacre, 235–7; Black History Week, 181–2; John Brown's birthday, 433–4; George Washington Carver's death, 31–3; civil rights acts, 339–40, 421–2, 611–13, 829–30; Civil War begins, 341–6; Frederick Douglass's birthday, 181–2; *Dred Scott* case, 266–7; Emancipation Proclamation, 9–12, 859; Free-Soil party organized, 738–9; Matthew A. Henson and discovery of North Pole, 327–8;

Andrew Johnson's birthday, 1158–63; Kansas Day, 117–19; Martin Luther King Jr. assassinated, 319–22; Martin Luther King Jr.'s birthday, 77–80; Abraham Lincoln's birthday, 173–4; Missouri admitted to the Union, 744–7; Missouri Compromise finalized, 233; Montgomery bus boycott starts, 1070; Reconstruction amendments, 309, 701–2, 1117; Rhode Island prohibits perpetual slavery, 467; Harriet Beecher Stowe's birthday, 556–8; Supreme Court fair housing decision, 566; Supreme Court orders school desegregation, 456–61; Booker T. Washington's birthday, 323–5

Blaine, James G., birthday, 130–1

Blanchard, Jean Pierre. *See* Balloon flight in the United States

Blessing of the Animals, Los Angeles, 299

Blessing of the Blossoms, National Cherry Festival, 636

Blessing of the Fishing and Shrimp Fleet, St. Augustine, Florida, 281

Blizzard of 1888, 244–5

Blod-monath, 978

Blossoms, Blessing of, National Cherry Festival, 636

"Blue laws," 1183

Boar's Head and Yule Log Ceremony, 1149

Bonham, James Butler, at the Alamo, 238–9

Bonhomme Richard, 676–7

Boone, Daniel: Boone Day, 536–40; Boone Festival, Barbourville, Kentucky, 901–2

Booth, Edwin, birthday, 1017–19

Booth, John Wilkes, 351–2

Booth, William. *See* Salvation Army Founder's Day

Border Days (Idaho), 623

Borromeo, Charles, St., feast of, 993–4

Boston Marathon, 362

Boston Massacre, 235–7

Boston Tea Party, 1106–8

Bowie, James, at the Alamo, 238–9

Bowing Procession, Feast of the Assumption, 756

Boxing Day, 1139

Boy Scouts of America founded, 152–4

Braddock's Defeat: Battle of the Monongahela, 644–6

Bradenton, Florida, De Soto Celebration, 251–2

Bradford, Andrew. *See* Magazine, first American

Bradford, William, death, 468–9
See also Forefathers' Day

Brandywine, battle of, 831–2

Brewery Gulch Days, Bisbee, Arizona, 820

Brewster, William. *See* Forefathers' Day

Britain and France declare war on Germany (World War II), 796

Brotherhood Sunday, 168

Brotherhood Week, 169, 200

Brown, John, birthday, 433–4

Brown v. *Board of Education*. *See* Desegregation ordered by Supreme Court

Brownsville, Texas, Charro Days Fiesta, 141–2

Bryan, William Jennings, birthday, 271–2

Buchanan, James, birthday, 371–3

Buena Vista, battle of, 207

Buffalo Bill. *See* Cody, William F., birthday

Bull Run, battles of, 91, 102, 345

Bunker Hill Day, 563–6

Bunyan, Paul. *See* Paul Bunyan Days; Paul Bunyan Water Carnival

Burbank, Luther, birthday, 240

Burger, Warren E., birthday, 848–50

Burgoyne, John. *See* Saratoga, British surrender at

Burns, Robert, birthday, 109–10

Burr, Aaron, birthday, 145–6

Burton, Ohio, Geauga County Apple Butter Festival, 911

Byrd, Richard E., birthday, 955–6

C

Cabrillo, Juan Rodríquez Day in California, 873–6

Cabrini, Frances, St. (Mother Cabrini), feast of, 1019–22

Caesar, Julius. *See* July, origin of name

"Calamity Jane" Canary, 708–9

Calendar, 1171–7
See also Leap Year; *also* specific months

Calhoun, John C., birthday, 268–9

California: Admission Day, 827–9; Cabrillo Day, 873–6; Gold Rush, 106–9; proclaimed part of United

States, 637–41; San Diego expositions, 866

Calvert, Cecilius, 2nd Baron Baltimore, 287; Calvert, Charles, 3rd Baron Baltimore, 1081; Calvert, George, 1st Baron Baltimore, 287

Cameron, Simon, birthday, 240–1
Candlemas (or Feast of the Presentation of the Lord), 135–6
Cape Henry Day, 383
Capitol, US, cornerstone laid, 854–5
See also Congress finds a permanent home
Carleton, Sir Guy. See Evacuation Day (New York City)
Carnation Day, 120
Carnegie, Andrew, birthday, 1049–51
See also Peace Palace, The Hague, gift of
Carnival. See Mardi Gras; Virgin Islands Carnival
Carroll, John, appointed first US Roman Catholic bishop, 997–8
Carter, Jimmy, birthday, 885–8
Carver, George Washington, death, 31–3
Castor and Pollux, feast of, 608
Castro, José. See California proclaimed part of United States
Catherine of Siena, St., feast of, 398–9
Centennial Air Show (Idaho), 618
Centennial Days (Montana), 486
Centennial Exhibition, Philadelphia, 622–3
Centennial exposition (Alaska), 310
Centennial Gemorama (Idaho), 618
Centennial of Statehood (California), 829
Centennial Shoot (Arizona), 208
Centennial State Fair (Nebraska), 225
Central Pacific Railroad (first transcontinental railroad), 441
Cerealia, 314–15
Chapman, John. See Appleseed, Johnny, birthday
Charles Borromeo, St., feast of, 993–4
Charleston, South Carolina, earthquake, 791–2
Charro Days Fiesta: Brownsville, Texas, and Matamoros, Mexico, 141–2
Chase, Salmon P., birthday, 72–4
Cherokee, North Carolina, Unto These Hills, 584–5
Cherokee Cane Treaty. See Boone, Daniel, festival
Cherokee Strip Day, 844–6
Cherries Jubilee, Valley Forge, Pennsylvania, 200
Cherry Festival, National, Traverse City, Michigan, 635–6
Chesapeake fired on by Leopard, 579–82
Cheyenne, Wyoming, Frontier Days, 682–4
Chicago fire, 908–9

Chicano events. See Mexican-American events
Childermas. See Holy Innocents, feast of
Children's Day: Memphis, 436; Michigan, 635; United States, 555–6
Chincoteague Island, Virginia, Pony Penning Days, 703–5
Chinese-American events: Chinese New Year, 146–8
Chinese calendar, 1176–7
Chouteau, Jean Pierre. See Oklahoma Historical Day
Christian Era. See Era
Christian Home, festival of (Mother's Day), 440
Christian Scientists. See Eddy, Mary Baker, birthday
Christmas, Twelve Days of. See Twelfth Night
Christmas Day, 1141–9
Christmas Eve, 1135–41
Christmonat, 1070
Christopher, St., feast of, 434, 692–3
Chrysostom, St. John, feast of, 837–8
Church of Christ, Scientist. See Eddy, Mary Baker, birthday
Church of Jesus Christ of Latter-Day Saints. See Mormons
Church School Sunday, 556
Churchill, Winston. See Teheran Conference
Cigarmakers' Union, 114
Cimarron Territory, 1027
Cinco de Mayo, 420–1
Circumcision, feast of, 8–9
Citizenship Day, 850–1
Civil rights: Henry Ward Beecher's birthday, 590–1; Bill of Rights Day, 1105–6; Black History Week, 181–2; John Brown's birthday, 433–4; Civil Rights Act of 1957, 829–30; Civil Rights Act of 1960, 421–2; Civil Rights Act of 1964, 611–13; Civil Rights Act of 1968, 339–40; Frederick Douglass's birthday, 181–2; Emancipation Proclamation, 9–12, 859; "Four Freedoms" enunciated, 39–40; Human Rights Day and Week, 1089–91; Kansas Day, 117–19; Martin Luther King Jr. assassinated, 319–22; Martin Luther King Jr.'s birthday, 77–80; Lincoln abolishes slavery, 134–5; Montgomery bus boycott starts, 1070; National Freedom Day, 134–5; Rhode Island prohibits perpetual slavery, 467; Eleanor Roosevelt's birthday, 914–17;

Lucy Stone's birthday, 752–3; Harriet Beecher Stowe's birthday, 556–8; Supreme Court fair housing decision, 566; Supreme Court orders school desegregation, 456–61; Voting Rights Act of 1965, 727–8; John Greenleaf Whittier's birthday, 1109–11; John Peter Zenger acquitted, 719–22
See also Constitutional amendments; Religious liberty; Suffrage; Women's rights
Civil Rights Week, 1106
Civil War: Alabama Claims, 330; Appomattox Day, 333–5; Clara Barton's birthday, 1149–51; Battle of Gettysburg begins, 609–11; Salmon P. Chase's birthday, 72–4; Civil War begins, 341–6; Confederate Memorial Day, 383–5; Confederate Memorial Day, Petersburg, Virginia, 542–4; Confederate Memorial Day, Winchester, Virginia, 530–1; Crater Day, 705; Jefferson Davis inaugurated, 193; Jefferson Davis's birthday, 519–22; Emancipation Proclamation, 9–12; David Farragut's birthday, 633–5; Gettysburg Address, 1035–7; Ulysses S. Grant's birthday, 389–93; Stonewall Jackson's birthday, 101–3; Andrew Johnson's birthday, 1158–63; Robert E. Lee's birthday, 89–93; Abraham Lincoln assassinated, 351–3; Lincoln's Birthday, 168–74; Lincoln abolishes slavery, 134–5; Harriet Beecher Stowe's birthday, 556–8
See also Brown, John, birthday; Kansas Day
Civil War Centennial, 353; Appomattox Court House, Virginia, 335
Clare of Assisi, St., feast of, 747–8
See also Francis of Assisi, St.
Clark, William. See Lewis and Clark expedition
Clarke, John, birthday, 907–8
Clay, Henry, birthday, 346–7
See also Missouri admitted to the Union
Clayton-Bulwer Treaty, 1049
Clemens, Samuel Langhorne. See Twain, Mark
Cleveland, Grover, birthday, 269–71
Clinton, De Witt. See Erie Canal opens
Clinton, George. See New York ratifies Constitution
Clinton, Sir Henry. See Forts Clin-

ton and Montgomery captured by British
Cody, William F. (Buffalo Bill), birthday, 212–13
Cody, Wyoming, Stampede, 623
Coercive, or Intolerable, Acts, 803–4, 1108
Colleges and universities: Antioch College chartered, 450–2; Columbia University opens, 674; Russell H. Conwell's birthday (Temple University), 184–6; Cushing Eells's birthday (Whitman College), 189–90; First medical school in the United States, 416; Harvard established, 998–1001; Mark Hopkins's birthday (Williams College), 140–1; Mount Holyoke College Founder's Day, 1003–5; US Military Academy (West Point) founded, 261–2; US Naval Academy (Annapolis), June Week, 492–3; University of North Carolina Day, 921; Booker T. Washington's birthday (Tuskegee Institute), 323–5; Elihu Yale's birthday, 325–6
Collins, Michael. See Moon, manned landing on
Colonial history: Albany Congress convenes, 568–70; John Alden Day, 713–14; Articles of Confederation ratified, 223; Battle of the Monongahela, 644–6; Daniel Boone Day, 536–40; William Bradford's death, 468–9; Cape Henry Day, 383; John Clarke's birthday, 907–8; Connecticut and New Haven united, 442; Delaware Swedish Colonial Day, 304–5; John Eliot baptized, 724–5; Feast of St. Isaac Jogues and Companions, 938–42; First Indian treaty, 227–8; Forefathers' Day, 1121–3; Benjamin Franklin's birthday, 85–8; Anne Hutchinson banished, 1031; Jamestown Day, 447–8; Captain Kidd hanged, 476–8; Maryland Day, 287; New England Confederation, 469–70; James Oglethorpe's birthday, 1128–30; Old Dover Days in Delaware, 412; Pennsylvania granted to Penn, 233; Rhode Island prohibits perpetual slavery, 467; John Smith assumes Jamestown council presidency, 830–1; Stamp Act signed, 282; Roger Williams arrives in America, 143–5; John Winthrop's birthday, 71–2; John Peter Zenger acquitted, 719–22
See also American Revolution

Colonies put in state of defense, 452–4
Colorado: admitted to the Union, 714–15; Colorado Day, 714
Columbia. See Moon, manned landing on
Columbia University opens, 674
Columbus, Christopher: Columbus Day, 918–21; sets sail, 718–19
Common, or Vulgar, era, 1177
Communion, institution of, at Last Supper, 291
Compact Day (Mayflower Compact), 1123
Competición de Vaqueros, Santa Barbara, California, 751
Concord, battle of. See Patriots' Day
Confederate commemorations: Appomattox Day, 333–5; Confederate Memorial Day, 383–5; Confederate Memorial Day, Petersburg, Virginia, 542–4; Confederate Memorial Day, Winchester, Virginia, 530–1; Jefferson Davis's birthday, 519–22; Stonewall Jackson's birthday, 101–3; Robert E. Lee's birthday, 89–93
Confederation, Articles of. See Articles of Confederation
Congress finds a permanent home, 1028–30
See also Continental Congress
Connecticut and New Haven united, 442
Connecticut ratifies the Constitution, 54–5
Conservation, Bird, and Arbor day, 240
Constantinople, era of, 1181
Constitution: Bill of Rights Day, 1105–6; Constitutional Convention opens, 481
See also Constitutional amendments
Constitution, ratification of, 576–8; Connecticut, 54–5; Delaware, 1081–2; Georgia, 20–2; Maryland, 393–5; Massachusetts, 150–1; New Hampshire, 578–9; New Jersey, 1116–17; New York, 696–8; North Carolina, 1038–40; Pennsylvania, 1098–1100; Rhode Island, 498–500; South Carolina, 478–9; Virginia, 595–7
Constitution and Guerrière, battle, 765–6
Constitution Day, 850; Illinois, 1073; Maryland, 835; Puerto Rico, 694
Constitution Week, 851
Constitutional amendments: 1st–10th (Bill of Rights), 1105–6;

11th (federal/state judicial powers), 51–2, 152; 12th (election of President and Vice President), 866–8; 13th (abolition of slavery) 1117; 14th (black citizenship and personal and property rights), 701–2; 15th (black suffrage), 309; 16th (income tax), 212; 17th (popular election of senators), 505; 18th (Prohibition), 82–3; 19th (woman suffrage), 777–9; 20th ("lame duck"), 151; 21st (repeal of Prohibition), 1076–7; 22nd (presidential terms), 215–16; 23rd (enfranchisement of District of Columbia), 305–6; 24th (abolition of poll tax), 105–6; 25th (presidential succession), 161–2; 26th (18-year-old vote), 606–7
Constitutional Convention opens, 481
See also Constitution, ratification of
Consualia, 713
Continental Congress, first, 803–5
Convention of 1818 signed, 944
Conwell, Russell H., birthday, 184–6
Cook, Daniel. See Illinois admitted to the Union
Cooke, Jay, and Panic of 1873, 857
Coolidge, Calvin, birthday, 628–30
Cooper, James Fenimore, birthday, 840–3
Copley, John Singleton, birthday, 616
Coptic era, 1179
Cornwallis, Lord. See Princeton, battle of; Yorktown Day
Cosby, William, and Zenger case, 720–1
Cotton Carnival, Memphis, Tennessee, 434–7
Counter-Reformation. See Charles Borromeo, St., feast of
Crater, battle of, 705; Crater Day, 543, 705
Crazy Horse, Chief, 592–4
Cristes Maesse, 1143
Crockett, Davy: at Alamo, 238–9; birthday, 760–2
Cross Day (Holy Innocents' Day), 1157
Cuba, missile crisis, 949–50
See also Spanish-American War
Curling Bonspiel, Anchorage, Alaska, 177
Custer's last stand, 591–4
Czechoslovak Independence Day, 963–4
Czolgosz, Leon. See McKinley, William, assassinated

D

D Day, 527–30
Daffodil Festival, Puyallup Valley (Washington), 322–3
Dana, Charles A., birthday, 736–7
Danish-American events: Danish-American Week, 312; Danish Day, 726; Virgin Islands Transfer Day, 310–12
Darrow, Clarence, death of, 247–9
Dartmouth College case decided, 136–7
David, St., Day, 223–4
Davis, Jefferson: birthday, 519–22; inaugurated, 193
Day of Atonement. See Yom Kippur
Days in Spain, fiesta, St. Augustine, Florida, 825–7
Days of '47 (Mormon), 689
Days of '76, Deadwood, South Dakota, 708–9, 990
Days of the week, 1181–4
Deadwood, South Dakota, Days of '76, 708–9, 990
Debs, Eugene. See Darrow, Clarence, death
December, origin of name, 1069–70
Declaration Day (Marcus Whitman memorial), 1062
Declaration of Independence, 619–22
Declaration of Sentiments (Elizabeth Cady Stanton), 679

Decoration Day. See Memorial Day
Defenders' Day, Maryland, 833–6
Defense Day (Flag Week), 554
Defense Day (Wright brothers' memorial), 1114
De Lancey, James, 720–1
Delaware: Delaware Day, 1080–2; Old Dover Days, 412; organized as a state, 857; Swedish Colonial Day, 304–5
Democratic party victory dinners. See Washington dinners
Denver Post Day, 684
Derby Day. See Kentucky Derby
Desegregation, ordered by Supreme Court, 456–61
De Soto celebration, Bradenton, Florida, 251–2
Dewey, George. See Manila Bay, battle of
Día de los Muertos (Day of the Dead), 981
Día de la Raza (Day of the Race). See Columbus Day
Diamond Jubilee (California), 829
Dickinson, Emily, birthday, 1087–9
Dickinson, John, writes first of the "Farmer's Letters," 995–7
Dictionaries, compiled by Noah Webster, 931–2
Diocletian, era of, 1179
Dionysius Exiguus (chronology of Christian era), 1179–81

Disasters: Alaska earthquake, 294; Baltimore fire, 151–2; Blizzard of 1888, 244–5; Charleston, South Carolina, earthquake, 791–2; Chicago fire, 908–9; Galveston, Texas, hurricane, 823–5; New Madrid, Missouri, earthquake, 1108–9; Northeast power failure, 1008–10; "Peacemaker," explosion of, 216–17; San Francisco fire, 359
Discalced Carmelites. See Teresa of Ávila, St., feast of
Discovery Day. See Columbus Day
Dixie Belle Luncheon and Fashion Show, Memphis, Tennessee, 436
Dodd, Sonora Louise Smart. See Father's Day
Dominic, St., feast of, 737–8
Dormition of the Blessed Virgin Mary (Feast of the Assumption), 755–6, 823
Douglass, Frederick, birthday: Black History Week, 181–2
Dow, Neal, birthday, 275–6
Drama. See Actors; William Shakespeare's birthday
Dred Scott case, 266–7
Dubuque, Julien, 1157
Dunkard (Baptist) settlers, 600
Dutch-American events: Tulip Time Festival, Holland, Michigan, 449–50

E

Eagle. See Moon, manned landing on
Earthquakes: Alaska, 294; Charleston, South Carolina, 791–2; New Madrid, Missouri, 1108–9; San Francisco, 359
Easter, 299–304; dating of, 1173–4
Easter Fires Pageant, 299
Easter Monday, 307–9
Easter Tuesday, 308
Easter Vigil, 297–9
Easter Week Festival (St. Augustine), 302–3
Eastern Orthodox churches. See "Russian Christmas"

Ecology: Johnny Appleseed's birthday, 868–9; Arbor Day, 240, 277, 366–9; Frederick Law Olmsted's birthday, 385–7; John Wesley Powell's birthday, 283–4; Rural Life Sunday, 417–18
See also Science and technology
Eddy, Mary Baker, birthday, 665–8
Edgar awards (Edgar Allan Poe Awards Dinner), 93
Edison, Thomas Alva: birthday, 163–6; electric light bulb perfected, 947–9
Education: Louis Agassiz's birthday, 488–91; Civil Rights Act

of 1960, 421–2; Thomas H. Gallaudet's birthday, 1089; Mark Hopkins's birthday, 140–1; Horace Mann's birthday, 418–19; St. John Nepomucene Neumann, 33–4; St. Elizabeth Ann Seton, 23–7; Supreme Court orders school desegregation, 456–61; Booker T. Washington's birthday, 323–5; Emma Willard's birthday, 207–8
See also Colleges and universities; Schools
Education Day (Flag Week), 554
Eells, Cushing, birthday, 189–90
Egg Roll, Easter Monday, 308

89ers Days (Oklahoma), 369
Einstein, Albert, birthday of, 249–50
Eisenhower, Dwight David, birthday, 922–8
  See also D Day; North Africa, US troops land in
Election, presidential, 1824, 1070–1
Election Day, General, 991
Electric light bulb perfected, 947–9
Eliot, John, baptized, 724–5
Elizabeth Ann Seton, St., feast of, 23–7
Elkins, West Virginia, Mountain State Forest Festival, 881–3
Ellsworth, Oliver, birthday, 399–401
Emancipation Day, 10
Emancipation Proclamation, 9–12; preliminary, 859
Emerson, Ralph Waldo, birthday, 481–4
Engineers: John Ericsson ("Peacemaker" explosion), 216–17; James Geddes (Erie Canal), 957–8; Francis Hopkinson Smith's birthday, 950–1; Benjamin Wright (Erie Canal), 957–8
Enola Gay, and atomic bomb, 722
Eosturmonath, 314

Epiphany, feast of, 34–8; Greek Cross Day: Blessing of the Sponge Divers, Tarpon Springs, Florida, 38–9; Greek Cross Day (Old Calendar), 89; Little Christmas, 1142
Epiphany Eve, 29–31
Epoch. *See* Era
Equality for Women Day, 781
Equinoxes, 1171–2; autumn, 859–60; spring, 276–7
Equirria, 222
Era, 1177–81
Ericsson, John ("Peacemaker" explosion), 216–17
Erie Canal opens, 956–8
Erikson, Leif, Day, 909–10
Eskimos: Eskimo games, Kotzebue, Alaska, 623; Eskimo Olympics, Fairbanks, Alaska, 936
Esther, Fast of, 281
Ethelbert, king of Kent, and Augustine of Canterbury, 487
Ethnic events: Holiday Folk Fair, Milwaukee, Wisconsin, 1037–8
  See also specific ethnic groups
Eucharist, institution of, at Last Supper, 291
Evacuation Day, Boston, 264–5
Evacuation Day, New York City, 1051–3

Evangelical and Reformed Church. *See* United Church of Christ formed
Evangelical Lutheran Church. *See* American Lutheran Church merger becomes effective
Evangelical United Brethren Church. *See* United Methodist Church formed
Exodus. *See* Passover
Exploration: John Jacob Astor's birthday, 671–4; Balboa discovers the Pacific Ocean, 865–6; Richard E. Byrd's birthday, 955–6; Cabrillo Day in California, 873–6; Christopher Columbus sets sail, 718–19; Leif Erikson Day, 909–10; Henry Hudson enters New York harbor, 797–9; La Salle reaches mouth of the Mississippi, 335–7; Lewis and Clark expedition, 452, 860–2; Maritime expedition sets sail, 763–5; Jacques Marquette's birthday, 512–15; North Pole discovered, 327–8; Panama Canal, 46–9; Ponce de León claims Florida for Spain, 331–3; John Wesley Powell's birthday, 283–4
  See also Space exploration; Territories and colonies

F

Fair housing decision by Supreme Court, 566
Fall Festival (St. Louis), 1126
Farmers' Day (Florida), 920
"Farmer's Letters," written by John Dickinson, 995–7
Farragut, David, birthday, 633–5
Fast Day in New Hampshire, 388–9
Father's Day, 574–5
February, origin of the name, 132–3
Federal Reserve System established, 1130–1
Feriae Martius, 222
Fermi, Enrico, and atomic bomb, 722–3
Festa Italiana. *See* Columbus Day
Field, Cyrus West. *See* Transatlantic cable completed
Field, Eugene, birthday, 795–6
Fiesta Day (Idaho), 618
Fiesta Filipina, 549
Fiesta of Five Flags, Pensacola, Florida, 534–5

Fiesta Pequeña, Santa Barbara, California, 750
Fiesta San Antonio, 239–40, 365
Fiestas. *See* Hispanic-American events
Fifth of May. *See* Cinco de Mayo
Fighting France, Day of, 659
Fillmore, Millard, birthday, 45–6
Finance: John Jacob Astor's birthday, 671–4; Andrew Carnegie's birthday, 1049–51; Federal Reserve System established, 1130–1; Gold clause repealed, 524–5; income tax deadline, 354–5; National Bank Act, 211–12; Panic of 1873, 856–7; Panic of 1929, 965–6; John D. Rockefeller Sr.'s birthday, 641–4; Franklin D. Roosevelt's first hundred days end, 561–3; 16th (income tax) amendment ratified, 212; United States Mint established, 316–18
Finnish-American events: Finnish Day, 726; Finnish Flag Day, 586

Finnish Evangelical Lutheran Church. *See* Lutheran Church in America organized
Fire prevention observances, 909
Fireman's Muster, Bristol, Rhode Island, 623
First Continental Congress, 803–5
First Fruits, feast of (Shavuot), 544; and Pentecost, 462
First International Conference of American States. *See* Pan American Conference, first, convenes
Fishing and Shrimp Fleet, Blessing of, St. Augustine, Florida, 281
Five Flags, fiesta of, Pensacola, Florida, 534–5
Flag Day, 551–5
Flags and flag observances: Fiesta of Five Flags, Pensacola, Florida, 534–5; first national flag, 12–13; Flag Act of 1818, 319; Flag Day, 551–5; *Floralia*, 314, 406

Florida: admitted to the Union, 231–3; ceded to United States, 674–6; claimed for Spain by Ponce de León, 331–3; Gasparilla Pirate Invasion, Tampa, 154–5; Pascua Florida Day (Florida State Day), 316; state fair, 155

Flower festivals: Luther Burbank's birthday, 240; Lei Day in Hawaii, 412; National Cherry Blossom Festival, Washington, D.C., 330–1; Pasadena, California, Tournament of Roses, 17–19; Portland, Oregon, Rose Festival, 525–7; Puyallup Valley, Washington, Daffodil Festival, 322–3; Royal Poinciana Festival, Miami, Florida, 515–16; Shenandoah Apple Blossom Festival, Winchester, Virginia, 403–4; Tulip Time Festival, Holland, Michigan, 449–50; Washington State Apple Blossom Festival, 396–8

Flower Sunday, 555

The Flyer. See Wright Brothers Day

Folk Day (West Virginia), 882

Folk Fair, Milwaukee, Wisconsin, 1037–8

Folk Spectacle, Milwaukee, Wisconsin, 1038

Folklore: Johnny Appleseed's birthday, 868–9; April Fools' Day, 314–16; Groundhog Day, 138–9; Halloween, 968–72; St. Valentine's Day, 177–80 See also specific months and seasons

Fontalia, 884

Ford, Gerald R., birthday, 660–4

Ford, Henry, birthday, 705–7

Fordicidia, 313

Forefathers' Day (Plymouth), 1121–3

Forefathers' Service, Providence, Rhode Island, 144, 420

Forest Festival, Elkins, West Virginia, 881–3

Forrest, Edwin, birthday, 243 See also Shakespeare, William, birthday

Fort Sumter, fired on. See Civil War begins

Fort Ticonderoga falls, 440–1

Forts Clinton and Montgomery captured by British, 902–4

Foster, Stephen: birthday, 630; memorial day, 74–6

Founders and Pioneers Days (Montana), 486

Founder's Day: Maryland, 287; Mount Holyoke College, 1003–5; Tuskegee Institute, 325; University of Virginia, 350–1; West Point, 261

"Four Freedoms" enunciated, 39–40

Fourteen Points. See Wilson, Woodrow, birthday

Fourteenth Amendment Centennial Convocation, 702

Fourth of July Powwow, 623

France, American troops land in (World War I), 597–8

France recognizes the United States, 148–50

Frances Cabrini, St., feast of, 1019–22

Francis of Assisi, St., feast of, 892–5

Francis Ferdinand, Archduke. See World War I, assassination precipitates

Franklin, Benjamin, birthday, 85–8

Franklin, state of, 518

Fraternal Day (Alabama), 920

Free French Week, 659

Free-Soil party organized, 738–9

Freedom Week, 623

Frémont, John Charles. See California proclaimed part of United States

French-American events: Bastille Day, 657–60; Lafayette's birthday, 810–14; Lafayette's death, 470–1; Nauvoo, Illinois, Grape Festival, 805–6

French and Indian War: Albany Congress convenes, 568–70; Battle of the Monongahela, 644–6

Friars, orders of. See Dominic, St., feast of; Francis of Assisi, St., feast of

Friends, Society of (Quakers). See Pennsylvania Day

Frigedaeg, 1184

Frontier Days (Montana), 486

Frontier Days, Cheyenne, Wyoming, 682–4

Frontier Days Rodeo, Prescott, Arizona, 623

Frost, Robert, birthday, 287–91

Fuller, Melville W., birthday, 166–8

Fulton steamboat sails, 762–3

Fyr-Bål Fest, 584, 587

G

Gabriel, Archangel, feast of. See Michaelmas Day

Gadsden Purchase, 1166

Gallaudet, Thomas H., birthday, 1089

Gallaudet College. See Gallaudet, Thomas H., birthday

Galveston hurricane of 1900, 823–5

Galveston Plan, 825

Garfield, James A.: birthday, 1033–35; shot, 613–15

Gaspar, José. See Gasparilla Pirate Invasion: Tampa, Florida

Gasparilla Pirate Invasion: Tampa, Florida, 154–5

Gaspee Days (Rhode Island), 624

Gates, Horatio. See Saratoga, British surrender at

Gathering of Scottish Clans. See Grandfather Mountain Highland Games, Linville, North Carolina

Gathering of the Eagles, 628

Geauga County Apple Butter Festival, Burton, Ohio, 911

Geddes, James. See Erie Canal opens

Gemorama (Idaho), 618

General Council of the Congregational Christian Churches. See United Church of Christ formed

General Election Day, 991

Geneva, Illinois, Swedish Festival, 587

Gennaro, San. See Januarius, St.

George, St., Day, 373–5

Georgetown University. See Carroll, John, appointed first Roman Catholic bishop

Georgia: Georgia Day, 174–6; ratifies the Constitution, 20–2 See also Oglethorpe, James, birthday

Gering, Nebraska, Oregon Trail Days, 668–9

German-American events: Maifest in Hermann, Missouri, 455–6; Pennsylvania Dutch· Days, Hershey, 776–7; Pennsylvania Dutch Folk Festival, Kutztown, 600–1; Baron von Steuben's birthday, 851–4

Geronimo, San. See Jerome, St.

Gershwin, George, birthday, 869–72

Gerst-monath, 794

Gettysburg, battle of, begins, 609–11

Gettysburg Address delivered by Lincoln, 1035–7

Ghent, treaty of, 1141

Gibbons, James Cardinal, birthday, 685–6

Gillette, William, Memorial Luncheon (Sherlock Holmes's birthday), 40

Girl Scouts founded, 245–7

Glenn, John, orbits earth, 194–6

Gold clause repealed, 524–5

Gold Discovery celebration (California), 109

Gold Discovery Days (South Dakota), 594

Gold Rush Days (Arizona), 180

Golden Days (Alaska), 936

Golden Rose ski tournament, 527

Gompers, Samuel, birthday, 114–16

Good Friday, 294–7

Gordon, Juliette ("Daisy"). See Girl Scouts founded

Government Day, 554

Grand International Fiesta (Cinco de Mayo), 421

Grand Parade of Light, Fort Myers, Florida, 164

Grandfather Mountain Highland Games, Linville, North Carolina, 653–4

Grant, Ulysses S., birthday, 389–93

Grape Festival, Nauvoo, Illinois, 805–6
See also Mormons

Grasse, Comte de. See Yorktown Day

Gray, Asa, birthday, 1031–3

Great Bridge, battle of, 1085–7

Great Compromise, 577

Great Depression, 125–7
See also Roosevelt, Franklin D., first hundred days end

Great Friday (Good Friday), 295

Great Lakes Shakespeare Festival, Lakewood, Ohio, 376

Great River Pageant, Memphis, Tennessee, 435

Great Thursday (Holy or Maundy Thursday), 292

Great Week (Holy Week), 278

Greater Boise, Idaho, Centennial Celebration, 618

Greek Cross Day, or the Epiphany, and Blessing of the Sponge Divers, Tarpon Springs, Florida, 38–9; Greek Cross Day (Old Calendar), 89

Greek-American events: Epiphany, or Greek Cross Day, and Blessing of the Sponge Divers, Tarpon Springs, Florida, 38–9; Epiphany (Old Calendar), 89; Feast of Lights, 37; Feast of the Jordan, 37; Greek Independence Day, 285–7; Theophany (Appearance of God), 37

Greek Independence day, 285–7

Green Mountain Boys. See Fort Ticonderoga falls; Vermont declares independence

Gregorian calendar. See Calendar

Gregory, Pope, XIII. See Calendar

Groundhog Day, 138–9

Guadalupe, feast of Our Lady of, 1097–8

Guadalupe Hidalgo, treaty of: ratified, 244; signed, 139

Guiteau, Charles J. See Garfield, James A., shot

Gulf of Tonkin Resolution approved (Vietnam war), 728–36

Guy Fawkes Day, 971

H

Hadassah (Esther), 281

Hag HaAsif (Feast of the Ingathering). See Sukkot

The Hague Peace Palace, gift of, 362

Hale, Nathan, hanged, 858–9

Hale, Sarah Josepha. See Thanksgiving Day

Half Moon, 797–8

Halifax Resolves Day, 347–8

Halig-monath, 794

Hallet, Étienne (Stephen Hallette), 1030

Halloween, 968–72

Hallowmass. See All Saints' Day

Hamilton, Alexander, birthday, 65–71
See also New York ratifies Constitution

Hamilton, Andrew, 721

Handicapped, education of: Alexander Graham Bell's birthday, 230–1; Thomas H. Gallaudet's

birthday, 1089; Helen Keller's birthday, 598–600

Handy, W. C., Festival, 1102

Hanukkah, 1131–2

Harding, Warren G., birthday, 982–4

Harrison, Benjamin, birthday, 767–8

Harrison, William Henry, birthday, 155–6
See also Tippecanoe, battle of

Harvard, John. See Harvard established

Harvard established, 998–1001

Harvest, feast of the, 544

Hawaii: admitted to the Union, 768–9; annexed to the United States, 749–50; Kamehameha Day, 545–7; Lei Day, 412; Prince Kuhio Day, 293–4

Hawthorne, Nathaniel, birthday, 630–1

Hayes, Rutherford B., birthday, 895–8

Hegira, era of, 1181

Heg-monath, 608

Hehag. See Sukkot

Heligh-monath, 1070

Henry, Patrick: birthday (Virginia Resolutions), 500; speech for liberty, 282–3

Herbert, Victor, birthday, 133–4

Hermann, Missouri, Maifest in, 455–6

Herod the Great. See Holy Innocents, feast of the

Hershey, Pennsylvania, Pennsylvania Dutch Days, 776–7

Hickok, "Wild Bill," 708

High Holy Days. See Rosh Hashanah

Hiroshima, Japan. See Atomic bomb, first use of

Hispanic-American events: All Souls' Day, 981; Blessing of the Animals, 299; Christmas, 1148; Cinco de Mayo, 420–1; Columbus Day, 918–21; Gasparilla Pirate Invasion, Tampa, Florida,

Hispanic-American events –
Continued
154–5; Good Friday, 297; Los
Angeles birthday celebration,
799–800; Old Spanish Days,
Santa Barbara, California, 750–
2; Pecos Bull in Jemez, New
Mexico, 718; St. Augustine, na-
tion's oldest city, founded, 825–
7; San Juan Fiesta, 589–90;
Santa Fe Fiesta, 800–3; Three
Kings' Day (Epiphany), 38
Historians: George Bancroft's
birthday, 890–2; William Brad-
ford's death, 468–9
Historic Garden Week, 396
Historical Day, Oklahoma, 911–12
Hlyd-monath, 223
Hoban, James. *See* White House
cornerstone laid
Hogmanay, 1167
Holi (or Huli), 315
Holiday Folk Fair, Milwaukee,
Wisconsin, 1037–8
Holiday in Dixie, 1120
Holland, Michigan, Tulip Time
Festival, 449–50

Holmes, Oliver Wendell, birthday,
788–9
Holmes, Oliver Wendell, Jr., birth-
day, 241–3
Holmes, Sherlock, birthday, 40
Holy Friday (Good Friday), 295
Holy Ghost, feast of, 464
Holy Innocents, feast of, 1155–7
Holy Name of Our Lord Jesus
Christ, feast of. *See* Circumci-
sion, feast of
Holy Passion, service of (Holy or
Maundy Thursday), 291
Holy Saturday, 297–9
Holy Thursday (Maundy Thurs-
day), 291–3
Holy Week: Easter, 299–304;
Good Friday, 294–7; Holy or
Maundy Thursday, 291–3; Holy
Saturday, 297–9; Palm Sunday,
278–81
Homesteaders Days (Montana),
486
Hoover, Herbert, birthday, 741–4
Hopkins, Mark, birthday, 140–1
Hornung, 133

Hospital Week. *See* National Hos-
pital Week
Houston, Sam, 364–5; Sam Hous-
ton Day (Texas Independence
Day, 227–30
Howe, William. *See* Brandywine,
battle of
Hudson, Henry, enters New York
harbor, 797–9
Hughes, Charles Evans, birthday,
340–1
Hull, Cordell. *See* Pearl Harbor
Day
Hull House. *See* Addams, Jane,
birthday
Human Rights Day and Week,
1089–91
See also Civil rights
Humorists: Will Rogers Day in
Oklahoma, 994–5; Mark Twain's
birthday, 1065–8
Hussey reaper first exhibited, 615–
16
Hutchinson, Anne, banished, 1031
Hypapante, 136

I

I Am an American Day, 835, 850
Idaho admitted to the Union, 616–
19; Idaho Pioneer Day, 617
Ignatius Loyola, St., feast of, 709–
11
Illinois: admitted to the Union,
1072–3; becomes a territory,
139–40
Immaculate Conception of Mary,
feast of, 1084–5
Inauguration Day, 96–7
Incarnation, era of. *See* Era
Income tax, federal, deadline,
354–5
Independence, American, year of
(era), 1181
Independence Day, 619–28
Independence Day (Mecklenburg,
North Carolina), 472–3
Independence Day (Norway), 466
Independence Day (Philippine Is-
lands), 547–9
Independence Day (Rhode Is-
land), 419–20
Indian Days, All American, Sheri-
dan, Wyoming, 707–8
Indian Removal Act, 585
Indian Rights Day, 623
Indiana Day, 1094–6
Indianapolis 500, 504, 1095
Indians, American. *See* American
Indians
"Indiction" cycle, 1179

Industry: Henry Ford's birthday,
705–7; Fulton steamboat sails,
762–3; Cyrus H. McCormick's
birthday, 186–7; John D.
Rockefeller Sr.'s birthday, 641–
4
See also Science and technology
Industry Day, 554, 1114
Industry, Labor, and Commerce
Day (Idaho), 618
Initiative and referendum declared
valid, 193–4
Inter-American relations. *See* Pan
American relations
International Edison Birthday
Celebration, 164
International Fixed Calendar, 1177
International Freedom Festival,
623
International Geophysical Year of
1957–1958, 681, 956
International Labor Day, 410
International Pancake Day, 158
International Printing Week, 86
International Red Cross, 1150
International Women's Year, 23,
782
International Year for Human
Rights, 1089
Intolerable, or Coercive, Acts,
803–4, 1108
Inventions: Alexander Graham
Bell's birthday, 230–1; Thomas

Alva Edison's birthday, 163–6;
Electric light bulb perfected,
947–9; Henry Ford's birthday,
705–7; Benjamin Franklin's
birthday, 85–8; Hussey reaper
first exhibited, 615–6; Cyrus H.
McCormick's birthday, 186–7;
Samuel F. B. Morse opens first
US telegraph line, 479–80; Eli
Whitney patents the cotton gin,
250–1; Wright Brothers Day,
1111–15
See also Science and technology
Iowa admitted to the Union, 1157–
8
Irish-American events (St. Pat-
rick's Day), 262–4
Iroquois. *See* Albany Congress
convenes
Irving, Washington, birthday,
318–19
Isaac Jogues, St., and Companions,
feast of, 938–42
Islamic calendar. *See* Muslim cal-
endar
Italian-American events: Colum-
bus Day, 918–21; Feast of Our
Lady of Mount Carmel, 669–71;
Feast of St. Anthony of Padua,
549–51; Feast of St. Januarius
(San Gennaro), 855–6; Feast of
SS. Peter and Paul, 605–6

J

Jackson, Andrew: birthday, 252–6; Jackson Day (Battle of New Orleans Day), 49–51; Jefferson-Jackson Day Dinners, 51, 256, 350; Lee-Jackson Day, 89, 256

Jackson, Thomas Jonathan ("Stonewall"), birthday, 101–3

James the Greater, St., feast of, 693–4

James the Younger and Philip, SS., feast of, 414

Jamestown Day, 447–8

Januarius, St. (San Gennaro), feast of, 855–6

January, origin of name, 1–2

Janus, feast of, 3

Jarvis, Anna M. See Mother's Day

Jay, John, birthday, 1096–7

Jefferson, Joseph, birthday, 196

Jefferson, Thomas: birthday, 348–51; Jefferson-Jackson Day dinners, 51, 256, 350
See also Independence Day; Louisiana purchased

Jemez, New Mexico, Pecos Bull, 718

Jerome, St., feast of, 879–81

Jesuits (Society of Jesus). See Ignatius Loyola, St., feast of

Jesus Christ: Advent begins, 1059–60; Ash Wednesday, 162–3; Feast of the Baptism of the Lord, 65; Candlemas, 135–6; Christmas Day, 1141–9; Christmas Eve, 1135–41; Feast of St. Christopher, 692–3; Feast of the Circumcision, 8–9; Easter, 299–304; Epiphany, 34–8; Good Friday, 294–7; Feast of the Holy Innocents, 1155–7; Holy or Maundy Thursday, 291–3; Holy Saturday, 297–9; Feast of St. Martha, 702–3; Feast of St. Mary Magdalene, 684–5; Palm Sunday, 278–81; Pentecost, 461–4; Feast of the Transfiguration, 726–7
See also Mary, Virgin; John the Baptist, St.; also names of Apostles and names of Evangelists

Jewish calendar, 1176

Jewish holidays: Hanukkah, 1131–2; Passover (Pesach), 362–3; Purim (Feast of Lots), 281–2; Rosh Hashanah, 884–5; Shavuot (Feast of Weeks), 544–5; Shemini Atzeret, 950; Sukkot, 928–9; Tishah B'Av, 748–9; Yom Kippur, 910–11

Jimmu Tennō, era of, 1178

Joachim and Anne, SS., feast of, 695–6

John, St., Apostle and Evangelist, feast of, 1154–5

John Chrysostom, St., feast of, 837–8

John the Baptist, St.: death of, 790; feast of the nativity of, 587–90
See also Midsummer, or St. John's Eve

Johnny Appleseed commemorations, 869

Johnson, Andrew, birthday, 1158–63

Johnson, Lyndon B., birthday, 783–7
See also Gulf of Tonkin Resolution approved

Joliet, Louis, See Marquette, Jacques, birthday

Jones, John Paul, death, 676–7

Jones v. Mayer. See Fair housing decision by Supreme Court

Jordan, feast of the, 37

Jouett, Jack, ride, 522–4

Jousting Tournament, Natural Chimneys, 756–8

Juan, San. See John the Baptist, St.

Jubilee Year of 1880 (Mormon), 689

Julian calendar. See Calendar

July, origin of name, 608

Jumping Frog Jubilee, 1066

Junction City, Oregon, Scandinavian Festival, 725–6

June, origin of name, 509–10

June Week, US Naval Academy, Annapolis, 492–3

Juno Caprotina, festival of, 608

K

Kamehameha: Cultural Festival, 625; Kamehameha Day, 545–7

Kanawha, state of, 572

Kansas Day, 117–19

Kansas-Nebraska Act. See Kansas Day; Nebraska State Day; Republican party founded

Kearney, Stephen Watts, 640–1

Keller, Helen, birthday, 598–600

Kennedy, John F.: assassinated, 1040–3; birthday, 493–8
See also Cuban missile crisis

Kentucky admitted to the Union, 510–12
See also Boone, Daniel, Day

Kentucky Derby, 414–16

Key, Francis Scott, birthday, 715–16
See also Maryland Defenders' Day

Kidd, Captain, hanged, 476–8

King, Martin Luther, Jr., 10–12; assassinated, 319–22; birthday, 77–80; Martin Luther King Day, 79–80

See also Montgomery bus boycott starts

Kitchen Festival (Shaker), 220

Korean war: Eisenhower administration, 926; MacArthur command, 113; Truman administration, 429–33; war begins, 594–5

Kosciuszko, Thaddeus, 935

Kronia, 1069

Kuhio, Prince, Day, 293–4

Kutztown Pennsylvania Dutch Folk Festival, 600–1

L

Labor: Samuel Gompers' birthday, 114–16; May Day labor observances, 410–11
See also Labor Day; Labor Sunday
Labor Day, 817–21; Mackinac Bridge Walk, 515
Labor Sunday, 809–10
Ladies' Day (Idaho), 618
Lafayette, Marquis de: birthday, 810–14; death, 470–1; Lafayette-Marne Day, 812
Landing Day. *See* Columbus Day
Lanterns, feast of, 501
La Salle, Sieur de: La Salle reaches mouth of the Mississippi, 335–7
See also Louisiana purchased
Last Supper, 291–2
Latin American events. *See* Hispanic-American events; Pan American relations
Latter-Day Saints. *See* Mormons
Law Day, 411–12
Lawyers: Clarence Darrow's death, 247–9; Daniel Webster's birthday, 88–9
See also Supreme Court justices
League of Nations established, 63–5
See also Wilson, Woodrow, birthday
Leap Year, 217–18, 1174
Lecompton Constitution, 119
Lee, Ann, birthday, 218–21
Lee, Robert E., birthday, 89–93
See also Gettysburg, battle of, begins
Lee-Jackson Day, 89, 256
Lei Day in Hawaii, 407, 412
Leif Erikson Day, 909–10
Lemuria, 406
Lencten-monath, 223
L'Enfant, Pierre Charles. *See* Congress finds a permanent home
Lent. *See* Ash Wednesday
Lent-maand, 223
Leopard fires on *Chesapeake*, 579–82
Lewis, Meriwether. *See* Lewis and Clark expedition
Lewis and Clark expedition: departure, 452; expedition completed, 860–2; Lewis and Clark Centennial Exposition, 525, 860; Lewis and Clark Sesquicentennial, 860
Lexington and Concord, battles of. *See* Patriots' Day

Library of Congress created, 378–9
Lights, feast of (Eastern Orthodox), 37
Lights, festival of. *See* Hanukkah
Lilienthal, Otto, influence on Wright brothers, 1111
Lincoln, Abraham: abolishes slavery (National Freedom Day), 134–5; assassinated, 351–3; birthday, 168–74; Gettysburg Address, 1035–7; Lincoln Day, 168; Lincoln Day dinners, 169; Lincoln Sesquicentennial, 169
See also Civil War begins; Emancipation Proclamation
Lindbergh, Charles A., lands in Paris, 473–4
Linville, North Carolina, Grandfather Mountain Highland Games, 653–4
Lions Kickoff dinner (Barnum Festival), 631
Literature and journalism: American Academy of Arts and Letters chartered, 358–9; Robert Burns's birthday, 109–10; James Fenimore Cooper's birthday, 840–3; Charles A. Dana's birthday, 736–7; John Dickinson writes first of the "Farmer's Letters," 995–7; Emily Dickinson's birthday, 1087–9; Frederick Douglass's birthday, 181–2; Ralph Waldo Emerson's birthday, 481–4; Eugene Field's birthday, 795–6; First American magazine, 177; Benjamin Franklin's birthday, 85–8; Robert Frost's birthday, 287–91; Nathaniel Hawthorne's birthday, 630–1; Oliver Wendell Holmes's birthday, 788–9; Sherlock Holmes's birthday, 40; Washington Irving's birthday, 318–19; Helen Keller's birthday, 598–600; Henry Wadsworth Longfellow's birthday, 214–15; James Russell Lowell's birthday, 204–7; Herman Melville's birthday, 716–18; Thomas Paine's birthday, 121–2; Edgar Allan Poe's birthday, 93–6; James Whitcomb Riley's birthday, 904–7; William Shakespeare's birthday, 375–7; Francis Hopkinson Smith's birthday, 950–1; Harriet Beecher Stowe's birth-

day, 556–8; Henry David Thoreau's birthday, 654–5; Mark Twain's birthday, 1065–8; Walt Whitman's birthday, 505–8; John Greenleaf Whittier's birthday, 1109–11; John Peter Zenger acquitted, 719–22
Litha se oefterra, 608
Lithuania, Republic of, Day, 190–1
Little Bighorn, battle of. *See* Custer's last stand
Little Christmas (Epiphany), 38, 1142
Little Norway Festival, 467
Livingston, Robert R., birthday, 1057–8
Long, Huey P., Day in Louisiana, 790–1
Long Friday (Good Friday), 295
Long Rifle Shoot (Daniel Boone Festival), 902
Longfellow, Henry Wadsworth, birthday, 214–15
Lord's Supper (Lord's Passover). *See* Last Supper
Los Angeles birthday celebration, 799–800
Lots, feast of (Purim), 281–2
Louis, St., feast of, 775–6
Louisiana: admitted to the Union, 401–3; Bastille Day, 659; Huey P. Long Day, 790–1; Shrimp and Petroleum Festival, 820
Louisiana Purchase, 1119–20
See also San Ildefonso, treaty of
Low, Juliette. *See* Girl Scouts founded
Lowell, James Russell, birthday, 204–7
Loyalty Day, 411
Loyola, Ignatius, St., feast of, 709–11
Lucia, Santa (St. Lucy). *See* Santa Lucia, feast of
Luciadagen. *See* Santa Lucia, feast of
Luke, St., feast of, 937–8
Lunar cycle, 1171–2
Lupercalia, 132, 178
Lusitania, sinking of, 423
Luther, Martin. *See* Protestant Reformation Day
Lutheran Church in America organized, 603
Lutheran Free Church. *See* American Lutheran Church merger
Lyon, Mary. *See* Mount Holyoke College Founder's Day

M

MacArthur, Douglas: birthday, 111–13; returns to the Philippines, 944–7
See also Korean war

McCormick, Cyrus H., birthday, 186–7
See also Hussey reaper first exhibited

McGuire, Peter J. *See* Labor Day

McKinley, William: birthday, 119–21; assassinated, 814–17

Madison, Dolley, birthday, 471–2

Madison, James, birthday, 258–61

Maed-monath, 608

Magazine, first American, 177

Magi. *See* Twelfth Day

Maifest in Hermann, Missouri, 455–6

Maine admitted to the Union, 257–8

Maine Memorial Day, 187–9

Manassas. *See* Bull Run, battles of

Manhattan Project (atomic bomb), 722–3

Manila Bay, battle of, 413–14

Mann, Horace, birthday, 418–19
See also Antioch College chartered

March, origin of name, 222–3

Mardi Gras, or Shrove Tuesday, 156–61
See also Twelfth Night Revels

Mardi Gras (Memphis). *See* Memphis Cotton Carnival

Mardi Gras of the North. *See* Anchorage Fur Rendezvous

Marian Year, 1085

Marín, Luis Muñoz, 694

Marine Corps birthday, 1010–11

Maritime Day. *See* National Maritime Day

Maritime expedition, first, 763–5

Mark, St., feast of, 379–80

Marquette, Jacques, birthday, 512–15

Mars. *See* March, origin of name

Marshall, George C., birthday, 1168–70

Marshall, James. *See* California gold rush

Marshall, John, birthday, 862–3

Marshall Plan. *See* Marshall, George C., birthday

Martha, St., feast of, 702–3

Martinmas (Feast of St. Martin of Tours), 1013–15

Martyrs, era of, 1179

Mary, Virgin: Annunciation, 284–5; Assumption of, 755–6, 823;

Birth of, 822–3; Immaculate Conception of, 1084–5; Maternity of, 20; Our Lady of Guadalupe, feast, 1097–8; Purification of (Candlemas, Presentation of the Lord), 135–6; Solemnity of, 3, 9, 20
See also Joachim and Anne, SS., feast of; Mount Carmel, feast of Our Lady of

Mary Magdalene, St., feast of, 684–5

Maryland: Defenders' Day, 833–6; Maryland Day, 287; Ratification Day (Treaty of Paris), 76–7; ratifies the Constitution, 393–5

Masaryk, Tomáš Garrigue. *See* Czechoslovak Independence Day

Mason-Dixon Line, 1081

Massachusetts: Patriots' Day, 359–62; ratifies the Constitution, 150–1
See also Plymouth, Massachusetts

Massachusetts Bay Colony: governed by John Winthrop, 71–2; and Plymouth, 1122

Massasoit, 277–8

Massing of the Flags, 522

Matamoros, Mexico, Charro Days Fiesta, 141–2

Maternity of Mary (Solemnity of Mary), 20

Matthew, St., feast of, 858

Matthias, St., feast of, 208–9, 452, 739

Maundy Thursday (Holy Thursday), 291–3

May, origin of name, 406–7

May Day, 407–10
See also Labor, May Day observances; Law Day; Loyalty Day

May Day Eve, 408

Mayflower. See Forefathers' Day

Meade, George G., 609–10

Mecklenburg Independence Day, 472–3

Medal of Honor–Firecracker 400 automobile race, 624

Medicine: First medical school, 416; Oliver Wendell Holmes's birthday, 788–9

Megalesia (or *Megalensia*), 313

Melon Festival, Milan, Ohio, 820

Melville, Herman, birthday, 716–18

Memorial Day, 501–4
See also Confederate Memorial Days

Memphis Cotton Carnival, 434–7

Menéndez de Avilés, Pedro. *See* St. Augustine, nation's oldest city, founded

Mennonite settlers, 600

Merchant Marine Week, 476

Messiah Festival, 281

Methodist Church merger becomes effective, 437–9
See also United Methodist Church formed

Mexican-American events: Blessing of the Animals, 299; Charro Days Fiesta, Matamoros, 141–2; Christmas Eve, 1136–7; Cinco de Mayo, 420–1; Feast of Our Lady of Guadalupe, 1097–8; Old Spanish Days, Santa Barbara, California, 750–2

Mexican War: Battle of Buena Vista, 206–7; California proclaimed part of United States, 637–41; New Mexico admitted to the Union, 40–3; James K. Polk's birthday, 986–9; Treaty of Guadalupe Hidalgo ratified, 244; US forces capture Mexico City, 838–40; war begins, 448–9; war ends: Treaty of Guadalupe Hidalgo, 139
See also Taylor, Zachary, birthday

Mexico City, captured by US forces, 838–40

Miami, Royal Poinciana Festival in, 515–16

Michael, Gabriel, and Raphael, SS., Archangels, feast of. *See* Michaelmas Day

Michaelmas Day, 876–9

Michigan admitted to the Union, 113–14

Mid-American Pow-Wow, 625

Midnight Sun Festival, 587

Midsummer Day, 585–7

Midsummer, or St. John's, Eve 582–4

Milan, Ohio, Melon Festival, 820

Millenial Church. *See* Lee, Ann, birthday

Milwaukee, Wisconsin, Holiday Folk Fair, 1037–8

Miners and Trappers Ball (Anchorage Fur Rendezvous), 177

Minnesota admitted to the Union, 442–5

Mint, United States, established, 316–18

Minutemen, 360–1

Miss America Pageant, Atlantic City, New Jersey, 821–2

Miss Indian America Talent Show, 708

Missionaries: Feast of St. Frances Cabrini, 1019–22; Feast of St. Isaac Jogues and Companions, 938–42; Jacques Marquette's birthday, 512–15; Salvation Army Founder's Day, 337–9; Marcus Whitman's death, 1061–3

Mississippi admitted to the Union, 1091–3

Mississippi River: mouth reached by La Salle, 335–7
See also Marquette, Jacques, birthday

Missouri: admitted to the Union, 744–7; first Missouri Compromise, 233

Missouri Compromise. *See* Missouri admitted to the Union

Mobile, New Year in, 13–14

Mobile Azalea Trail Festival, 160

Mohammed. *See* Hegira, era of

Monandaeg, 1183

Monongahela, battle of, 644–6

Monroe, James: birthday, 395–6; Monroe Doctrine promulgated, 1072

Montana: admitted to the Union, 1002–3; becomes a territory, 484–6

Montgomery, Bernard L. *See* North Africa, US troops land in; Sicily, Allied troops land in

Montgomery, Alabama, bus boycott starts, 1070

Months, names of. *See* names of specific months

Moody, Dwight L. , birthday, 142–3

Moon, manned landing on, 680–2

Moon Day, 680

Moore, Clement Clarke, 1139–40

Moravian observances: Christmas, 1137–8; Easter, 303

Mormons (Church of Jesus Christ of Latter-Day Saints): Church organized, 326–7; Grape Festival, Nauvoo, Illinois, 805–6; Mormon Pioneer Day, 686–92; Joseph Smith Jr.'s birthday, 1132–5; Utah admitted to the Union, 27–9

Morris, Esther Hobart. *See* Wyoming Day

Morse, Samuel F. B., opens first US telegraph line, 479–80

Morton, Julius Sterling, and Arbor Day, 366–7

Mother Ann. *See* Lee, Ann

Mother of God, Dormition of, 756

Mothering Sunday, 439

Mother's Day, 439–40

Mother's Friendship Day, 439

Mott, Lucretia Coffin. *See* Stanton, Elizabeth Cady; Woman's Rights Convention, Seneca Falls, New York

Mount Carmel, Our Lady of, feast, 669–71

Mount Holyoke College Founder's Day, 1003–5

Mountain State Forest Festival, Elkins, West Virginia, 881–3

Mullens, Priscilla. *See* John Alden Day

Mummers' Parade, 14–16

Muñoz Marín, Luis, 694

Murray, John, Earl of Dunmore. *See* Great Bridge, battle of

Music: Stephen Foster Memorial Day, 74–6; Stephen Foster's birthday, 630; George Gershwin's birthday, 869–72; Victor Herbert's birthday, 133–4

Muslims: calendar, 1176; era, 1181; New Year, 8

N

NASA (National Aeronautics and Space Administration). *See* Space Exploration

Nambe ceremonial, 623

Napoleon. *See* Louisiana purchased

Narcissus Festival (Chinese New Year), 147

Natalis urbis Romae, 313

National American Woman Suffrage Association, 1017

National Anthem Day, 833, 838

National Appaloosa Horse Show (Idaho), 618

National Audubon Society, 382

National Aviation Day, 766–7

National Bank Act, 211–12

National Cherry Blossom Festival, Washington, D.C., 330–1

National Cherry Festival, Traverse City, Michigan, 635–6

National Federation of Business and Professional Women's Clubs, 534

National Fence Painting Contest, 624

National Freedom Day, 134–5

National Hospital Week: Florence Nightingale's Birthday, 445–7

National Hot-Air Balloon Races, Indianola, Iowa, 625

National Institute of Arts and Letters, 358–9

National Laugh Week, 316

National Maritime Day, 475–6

National Peanut Festival, Dothan, Alabama, 33

National Rededication, Day of (Kennedy memorial), 1042

National Shakespeare Festival, San Diego, California, 866

National Thrift Week, 87

National Tom Sawyer Fence Painting Contest, Hannibal, Missouri, 1067

National Travelers' Aid Association, 534

National UNICEF Day, 972

National Woman Suffrage Association, 1017

National YWCA Week, 534

Native Americans. *See* American Indians; Eskimos

Nativity of Our Lord, feast of (Christmas Day), 1141–9

Nativity of St. John the Baptist, feast of, 587–90

Nativity of the Theotokas (Birth of Mary), feast of, 822–3

Natural Chimneys Jousting Tournament, 756–8

Naturalists: Louis Agassiz's birthday, 488–91; John James Audubon's birthday, 380–3; Asa Gray's birthday, 1031–3; maritime expedition, 763–5; Henry David Thoreau's birthday, 654–5
See also Science and technology

Nautilus cruises under North Pole, 719

Nauvoo, Illinois, Grape Festival, 805–6

Navajo Nation Fair, Window Rock, Arizona, 832–3

Naval Academy, Annapolis, June Week, 492–3

Navy Day, 963

Navy Week, 963

Nebraska: Nebraskaland Days, 213, 225; Nebraska State Day, 224–5

Negro History Week. See Black History Week

Neumann, John Nepomucene, St., feast of, 33–4

Nevada Day, 972–4

New Deal, 125–7

New England, Dominion of, 469–70

New England Confederation, 469–70

New Glarus, Wisconsin, Wilhelm Tell Festival, 806–7

New Hampshire: Fast Day, 388–9; ratifies the Constitution, 578–9

New Haven united with Connecticut, 442

New Jersey ratifies the Constitution, 1116–17

New Madrid, Missouri, earthquake, 1108–9

New Mexico admitted to the Union, 40–3

New Orleans: battle of, 49–51; Mardi Gras, 158–61

New Style (N.S.) calendar. See Calendar

New Year Shooters' and Mummers' Parade. See Philadelphia Mummers' Parade

New Year's Day, 2–8

New Year's Eve, 1166–8

New York (City) Shakespeare Festival, 376

New York ratifies Constitution, 696–8

"Nicene" Easter, 1174

Nicholas, St., feast of, 1079–80

Night in Old San Antonio, 365

Night of the Candle, 981

Nightingale, Florence, birthday, and National Hospital Week, 445–7

Nimitz, Chester William, birthday, 209–11

Nixon, Richard M., birthday, 55–63

See also Gulf of Tonkin Resolution approved

Noccalula Falls, Alabama, Indian Maiden Festival, 1102

Normans, feast of (Immaculate Conception), 1085

North Africa, US troops land in, 1005–8

North American Indian Foundation, 708

North American Martyrs. See Isaac Jogues, St., and Companions, feast of

North Carolina ratifies the Constitution, 1038–40

North Dakota admitted to the Union, 984–6

North Pole: discovered, 327–8; Nautilus cruises under, 719

Northeast power failure, 1008–10

Northfield Mount Hermon School. See Moody, Dwight, birthday

Northwest Ordinance enacted, 655–7

Norwegian-American events: Leif Erikson Day, 909–10; Norwegian Constitution Day, 464–7; Norwegian Day, 726

Norwegian Constitution Day, 464–7

November, origin of name, 978

Nuclear science and technology: Albert Einstein's birthday, 249–50; First use of atomic bomb, 722–4; John F. Kennedy's birthday, 493–8; Nautilus cruises under North Pole, 719; Harry S. Truman's birthday, 424–33

Nurses: Clara Barton's birthday, 1149–51; Florence Nightingale's birthday, 446–7

Nutcrack Night, 970

O

Oberammergau pageant (Holy City, Oklahoma), 303

Octave of the Birth of Our Lord (Circumcision of Jesus), 9, 20

October, origin of name, 884

Oglethorpe, James, birthday, 1128–30
See also Georgia Day

Ohio: admitted to the Union, 225–7; statehood approved, 194

Oklahoma: becomes a state (Statehood Day), 1025–8; Oklahoma Day (Oklahoma 89ers Day), 369; Oklahoma Historical Day, 911–12; Will Rogers Day, 994–5

Old Christmas, 34–8, 1145

Old Christmas Eve, 29, 31

Old Dover Days in Delaware, 412

Old-Fashioned Bargain Days (Idaho), 618

Old Hickory Day, 49–51

"Old Ironsides." See Constitution and Guerrière, battle

Old Settlers Day (Montana), 486

Old Spanish Days, Santa Barbara, California, 750–2

Old Style (O.S.) calendar. See Calendar

Olmsted, Frederick Law, birthday, 385–7

Olympia. See Manila Bay, battle of

Olympiades, era of, 1178

Operation Overlord. See Teheran Conference

Operation Sail, 627

Oppenheimer, J. Robert, and atomic bomb, 723

Orange Bowl Football Game, 1168

Oregon: admitted to the Union, 182–4; Shakespeare Festival, Ashland, 376

Oregon Trail: Oregon Trail Days, Gering, Nebraska, 668–9; settlement of Wyoming, 650–1

Oregon Treaty ratified, 560–1

Organization of American States (OAS), 353–4
See also Pan American Conference convenes

Ostend Manifesto, 1044

Ostermonath, 314

Oswald, Lee Harvey. See Kennedy, John F., assassinated

Our Lady in Harvest, feast of, 823

Our Lady of Guadalupe, feast of, 1097–8

Our Lady of Mount Carmel, feast of, 669–71

P

Paas Festival, 309
Pacific Ocean, discovered by Balboa, 865–6
Paine, Thomas, birthday, 121–2
Painters: American Academy of Arts and Letters chartered, 358–9; John James Audubon's birthday, 380–3; John Singleton Copley's birthday, 616; Francis Hopkinson Smith's birthday, 950–1; Gilbert Stuart's birthday, 1073–5; James Abbott McNeill Whistler's birthday, 647–50
Palm Sunday, 278–81
Pan American relations: Pan American Conference convenes, 890; Pan American Day, 353–4
Panama Canal: opens officially, 758; traversed, 46–9
Panama Pacific Exposition, 866
Pancake Tuesday, 157
Panic of 1873, 856–7
Panic of 1929, 965–6
Parilia, 313
Paris, treaty of (1783): ratified, 76–7; signed, 799
Paris, treaty of (1898): becomes effective, 161; signed, 1093
Paris Air Show, 474
Pasadena Rose Bowl football game, 16–17
Pasadena Tournament of Roses, 17–19
Pasch Monday, 307
Pascua Florida Day, 316
Passion, era of the, 1179
Passion of Jesus Christ. *See* Good Friday
Passion Sunday. *See* Palm Sunday
Passover (Pesach), 362–3
Patrick, St., Day, 262–4
Patriotic celebrations: American Heritage Week in Rhode Island, 412; Americanism Day in Pennsylvania, 412; Armed Forces Day, 454–5; Battle of New Orleans Day, 49–51; Bunker Hill Day, 563–6; Citizenship Day, 850–1; Flag Day, 551–5; Benjamin Franklin's birthday, 86–7; Alexander Hamilton's birthday, 65–6; Inauguration Day, 96–7; Independence Day, 619–28; Law Day, 411–12; Abraham Lincoln's birthday, 168–74; Loyalty Day, 411; *Maine* Memorial Day, 187–9; Maryland Defenders' Day, 833–6; Memorial

Day, 501–4; Patriots' Day, 359–62; Ratification Day: Treaty of Paris, 76–7; Paul Revere's birthday, 19–20; Veterans Day, 1011–13; Washington's birthday, 197–204
Patriots' Day, 359–62
Patton, George. *See* Sicily, Allied troops land in
Paul, St.: Feast of SS. Peter and Paul, 101, 603–6; Feast of the Conversion of St. Paul, 110–11
Paul, Alice, and Equal Rights Amendment, 780
Paul Bunyan Days, St. Maries, Idaho, 820
Paul Bunyan Water Carnival, Bemidji, Minnesota, 624
Peace Palace, The Hague, gift of, 362
"Peacemaker," explosion of, 216–17
Peanut Festival, National, Dothan, Alabama, 33
Pearl Harbor Day, 1082–4
Peary, Robert E. *See* North Pole discovered
Pecos Bull, 718
Pedro, San. *See* Peter, St.
Peggy Stewart Day, 942–3
Pendleton Round-Up, 846–8
Penn, William. *See* Delaware Day; Pennsylvania Day; Pennsylvania granted to Penn
Pennsylvania: Americanism Day, 412; granted to Penn, 233; Pennsylvania Day, 951–3; ratifies the Constitution, 1098–1100
Pennsylvania Dutch Days, Hershey, 776–7
Pennsylvania Dutch Folk Festival, Kutztown, 600–1
Pensacola, Florida, Fiesta of Five Flags, 534–5
Pentecost, 461–4
Perry, Oliver Hazard, 568; birthday, 773–4
Peter and Paul, SS., feast of, 101, 603–6
Petersburg, Virginia, Confederate Memorial Day, 542–4
Philadelphia Centennial Exhibition, 622–3
Philadelphia Mummers' Parade, 14–16
Philip and James, SS., feast of, 414
Philippines: Battle of Manila Bay,

413–14; Philippine Independence Day, 547–9, 628
See also MacArthur, Douglas; Paris, treaty of (1898), becomes effective; Spanish-American War
Pierce, Franklin, birthday, 1043–5
Pilgrims, Plymouth, Massachusetts: John Alden Day, 713–14; William Bradford's death, 468–9; Forefathers' Day, 1121–3
Pinkster, 463
Pioneer Day (Idaho), 617
Pioneer Day (Mormon): in Utah, 686–90; in other western states, 690–2
Pioneers and Private Flyers Day, 1114
Pioneers Day (Montana), 486
Pirate Fiesta Day, Tampa, Florida, 155
Pius X, St., feast of, 769–71
Platt Amendment. *See* United States withdraws from Cuba
The Players. *See* Booth, Edwin, birthday
Plymouth, Massachusetts. *See* Pilgrims
Pocahontas, 831
Poe, Edgar Allan, birthday, 93–6
Poetry. *See* Literature and journalism
Poetry Day (Idaho), 619
Poinsettia Festival, San Diego, California, 1148
Polish-American events (Pulaski Day), 913–14
See also Kosciuszko, Thaddeus
Political leaders: Samuel Adams's birthday, 872–3; James G. Blaine's birthday, 130–1; William Jennings Bryan's birthday, 271–2; Aaron Burr's birthday, 145–6; John C. Calhoun's birthday, 268–9; Simon Cameron's birthday, 240–1; Salmon P. Chase's birthday, 72–4; Henry Clay's birthday, 346–7; Jefferson Davis inaugurated, 193; Jefferson Davis's birthday, 519–22; Benjamin Franklin's birthday, 85–8; Melville W. Fuller's birthday, 166–8; Alexander Hamilton's birthday, 65–71; Patrick Henry's speech for liberty, 282–3; Robert R. Livingston's birthday, 1057–8; Huey P. Long Day in Louisiana, 790–

1; John Randolph's birthday, 519; John Rutledge's death, 677–8; Frederick M. Vinson's birthday, 103–5; Daniel Webster's birthday, 88–9
See also Presidents

Polk, James K., birthday, 986–9

Ponce de León claims Florida for Spain, 331–3

Pony Penning Days, Chincoteague Island, Virginia, 703–5

Poor Clares. *See* Clare of Assisi, St., feast of

Porcingula, feast of, 718

Portland Rose Festival, 525–7

Portuguese-American events: Cabrillo Day in California, 873–6; Point Loma, California, festival (Pentecost), 463–4

Potato Day, Greeley, Colorado, 683

Potsdam Declaration (or Proclamation). *See* V-J Day

Powell, John Wesley, birthday, 283–4

Power failure in Northeast, 1008–10

Powhatan, 831

Prelude to Independence, Williamsburg, Virginia, 624

Presbyterian Church in the USA. *See* United Presbyterian Church formed

Presentation of the Lord, feast of, 135–6

Presidential election of 1824 deadlocked, 1070–1

Presidents: John Adams's birthday, 966–8; John Quincy Adams's birthday, 651–3; Chester A. Arthur's birthday, 898–900; James Buchanan's birthday, 371–3; Jimmy Carter's birthday, 885–8; Grover Cleveland's birthday, 269–71; Calvin Coolidge's birthday, 628–30; Dwight D.

Eisenhower's birthday, 922–8; Millard Fillmore's birthday, 45–6; Gerald R. Ford's birthday, 660–4; James A. Garfield shot, 613–15; James A. Garfield's birthday, 1033–5; Ulysses S. Grant's birthday, 389–93; Warren G. Harding's birthday, 982–4; Benjamin Harrison's birthday, 767–8; William Henry Harrison's birthday, 155–6; Rutherford B. Hayes's birthday, 895–8; Herbert Hoover's birthday, 741–4; Andrew Jackson's birthday, 252–6; Thomas Jefferson's birthday, 348–51; Andrew Johnson's birthday, 1158–63; Lyndon B. Johnson's birthday, 783–7; John F. Kennedy assassinated, 1040–3; John F. Kennedy's birthday, 493–8; Abraham Lincoln assassinated, 351–3; Abraham Lincoln's birthday, 168–74; William McKinley assassinated, 814–17; William McKinley's birthday, 119–21; James Madison's birthday, 258–61; James Monroe's birthday, 395–6; Richard M. Nixon's birthday, 55–63; Franklin Pierce's birthday, 1043–5; James K. Polk's birthday, 986–9; Franklin D. Roosevelt's birthday, 122–30; Franklin D. Roosevelt's first hundred days end, 561–3; Theodore Roosevelt's birthday, 959–63; William Howard Taft's birthday, 843–4; Zachary Taylor's birthday, 1046–9; Harry S. Truman's birthday, 424–33; John Tyler's birthday, 306–7; Martin Van Buren's birthday, 1077–9; Washington departs for his inauguration, 355–8; Washington's birthday, 197–204; Washington's death, 1104–5;

Woodrow Wilson's birthday, 1163–5

Presidents' Day (Washington-Lincoln Day), 169, 199

Prince Kuhio festival (Hawaii), 293–4

Princeton, battle of, 22–3

Prohibition: Neal Dow's birthday, 275–6; 18th amendment ratified, 82–3; 21st amendment ratified, 1076–7

Protestant Episcopal bishop consecrated, first, 1022–4

Protestant Reformation Day, 974–7

Providence Plantations. *See* Clarke, John, birthday

Publicity Stunt Week, 316

Pueblo events: All Souls' Day, 981–2; Candlemas, 136; Christmas Day, 1148; Christmas Eve, 1136; Easter, 304; Epiphany (Three Kings' Day), 38; Feast of Our Lady of Guadalupe, 1097; Feast of the Assumption, 756; New Year's Day, 7–8; saints' feast days, 551, 590, 606, 694, 696, 738, 879, 894–5; Spring begins, 277

Puerto Rico: Constitution Day, 694; Feast of Our Lady of Mount Carmel, 671; San Juan fiesta, 589–90; Three Kings' Day (Epiphany), 38
See also Hispanic-American events

Pulaski, Casimir, Day, 913–14

Purification of Mary, Feast of (Candlemas, Presentation of the Lord), 135–6

Purim (Feast of Lots), 281–2

Puritans. *See* Winthrop, John, birthday

Puyallup Valley (Washington) Daffodil Festival, 322–3

Q-R

Quakers. *See* Pennsylvania Day

Quezon, Manuel. *See* Philippine Independence Day

Quinquatrus, 222

Quintilis, 608

Quirinalia, 223

Race Relations Sunday, 168

Radcliffe College, 1000

Railroad, transcontinental, 441

Rall, Johann. *See* Trenton, battle of

Randolph, John, birthday, 519

Raphael, Archangel, feast of. *See* Michaelmas Day

Ratification Day: Treaty of Paris, 76–7

Ratification of the Constitution. *See* Constitution, ratification of

Reapers: Hussey's reaper first ex-

hibited, 615–16; Cyrus H. McCormick's birthday, 186–7

Recollections of 1864 (Arizona), 208

Reconstruction (Civil War): acts of 1867, 1104; 13th amendment, 1117; 14th amendment, 701–2; 15th amendment, 309
See also Chase, Salmon P., birthday; Johnson, Andrew, birthday

Redemption (Palm Sunday), 278
Referendum. *See* Initiative and referendum declared valid
Reformation Day, Protestant, 974–7
Reformation Sunday, 974
Regnal years (era), 1177
Relativity, theory of, 249–50
Religion (church history and development): American Lutheran Church organized, 366; Henry Ward Beecher's birthday, 590–1; John Carroll appointed first US Roman Catholic bishop, 997–8; Church of Jesus Christ of Latter-Day Saints (Mormons) organized, 326–7; Russell H. Conwell's birthday, 184–6; Mary Baker Eddy's birthday, 665–8; Cushing Eells's birthday, 189–90; John Eliot baptized, 724–5; First US Episcopal bishop consecrated, 1022–4; James Cardinal Gibbons's birthday, 685–6; Anne Hutchinson banished, 1031; Labor Sunday, 809–10; Ann Lee's birthday, 218–21; Lutheran Church in America organized, 603; Abbott Lyman's birthday, 1115–6; Methodist Church merger becomes effective, 437–9; Dwight Moody's birthday, 142–3; Mormon Pioneer Day, 686–90; Joseph Smith Jr.'s birthday, 1132–5; United Church of Christ formed, 595; United Presbyterian Church formed, 491–2
Religious Heritage Day (Idaho), 618
Religious holidays. *See* names of specific holidays, saints' days, etc.
Religious liberty: Bill of Rights Day, 1105–6; "Four Freedoms" enunciated, 39–40; Human Rights Day and Week, 1089–91; Roger Williams arrives in America, 143–5

See also Hutchinson, Anne, banished; Lee, Ann, birthday; Maryland Defenders' Day; Mormons; Williams, Roger, arrives in America
Remembrance Day. *See* Veterans Day
Reno, Marcus A. *See* Custers's last stand
Reorganized Church of Jesus Christ of Latter-Day Saints, 1134
Repeal (of Prohibition), 21st Amendment ratified, 1076–7
Republic (Chinese), era of, 1178
Republican calendar (French Revolution), 1175
Republican party founded, 636–7
Repudiation Day. *See* Stamp Act repudiated
Resurrection, Night Watch of, 297
Resurrection of Jesus Christ. *See* Easter
Revere, Paul, 360; birthday, 19–20
Revolutionary calendar (French Revolution), 1175
Rhode Island: American Heritage Week, 412; Bicentennial Ecumenical Service of Religious Freedom, 144; Heritage Month, 420; Independence Day, 419–20; prohibits slavery, 467; ratifies the Constitution, 498–500
See also Williams, Roger, arrives in America
Rifle shooting: Anchorage Fur Rendezvous, 177; Daniel Boone Festival, 902
Riley, James Whitcomb, birthday, 904–7
Rizal, José. *See* Philippine Independence Day
Robertson, James ("Father of Tennessee"), 517
Robigalia, 313
Robinson, John. *See* Forefathers' Day

Rochambeau, Comte de. *See* Yorktown Day
Rockefeller, John D., Sr., birthday, 641–4
Rodeo Cowboy Day, 684
Rogation Sunday, 417
Rogers, Will: Range Riders Rodeo, 623; Will Rogers Day in Oklahoma, 994–5
Rolfe, John, 831
Rome, era of, 1178
Rommel, Erwin. *See* North Africa, US troops land in
"Rondy." *See* Anchorage Fur Rendezvous
Roosevelt, Eleanor, birthday, 914–17
Roosevelt, Franklin D.: birthday, 122–30; first hundred days end, 561–3
See also "Four Freedoms" enunciated; Teheran Conference
Roosevelt, Theodore, birthday, 959–63
Rose Bowl football game, 16–17
Rose Carnival, 240
Rose Festival, Portland, Oregon, 525–7
Rose Sunday (Children's Sunday), 555
Rosh Hashanah, 884–5
Ross, Betsy, 552–4
Ross, Nellie Tayloe, 1094
Rough Riders and Cowboys Reunion, 962
Round-Up, Pendleton, Oregon, 846–8
Roxas, Manuel Acuña. *See* Philippine Independence Day
Royal Poinciana Festival in Miami, 515–16
Run for the Roses. *See* Kentucky Derby
Rural Life Sunday (or Soil Stewardship Sunday), 417–18
"Russian Christmas," 49
Rutledge, John, death, 677–8

S

Sabbath (Shabbat), 1182
Sacred Heart, Missionary Sisters of the. *See* Cabrini, Frances, St., feast of
St. Andrew's societies. *See* Andrew, St., feast of
St. Augustine, nation's oldest city, founded, 825–7
St. Clair, Arthur. *See* Ohio admitted to the Union

St. David's societies. *See* David, St., Day
St. George organizations. *See* George, St., Day
St. Louis, Veiled Prophet Ball and Parade, 1124–7
Salvation Army Founder's Day, 337–9
Samhain, 968
San Antonio, Texas, fiesta, 239–40, 365

San Diego, California: National Shakespeare Festival, 376; Summer Festival, 866
San Francisco fire, 359
San Ildefonso, treaty of, 888
San Jacinto Day, 364–5
Sansculottides, 1175
Santa Anna, Antonio López de. *See* Alamo Day; San Jacinto Day; Texas Independence Day;

Mexico City, captured by US forces

Santa Barbara, California, Old Spanish Days, 750–2

Santa Fe, New Mexico, Fiesta, 800–3

Santa Lucia, feast of, 1100–2

Santiago. See James the Greater, St.

Saratoga: British surrender, 932–5; first battle of, 855; second battle of, 907

Saterdaeg, 1184

Saturnalia, 1069–70, 1143

Saul of Tarsus. See Paul, St.

Savannah, transatlantic crossing. See National Maritime Day

Scandinavian-American events: Midsummer, or St. John's Eve, 582–4; Scandinavian Festival, Junction City, Oregon, 725–6 See also Danish-American events; Norwegian-American events; Swedish-American events

School desegregation ordered by Supreme Court, 456–61

Schools: Dwight Moody's birthday (Northfield Mount Hermon), 142–3; Booker T. Washington's birthday (Tuskegee Institute), 323–5; Emma Willard's birthday, 207–8

Science and Engineering Youth Day (Edison memorial), 164

Science and technology: Louis Agassiz's birthday, 488–91; Luther Burbank's birthday, 240; George Washington Carver's death, 31–3; Thomas Alva Edison's birthday, 163–6; Albert Einstein's birthday, 249–50; Electric light bulb perfected, 947–9; First medical school in the United States, 416; Benjamin Franklin's birthday, 85–8; Asa Gray's birthday, 1031–3; Oliver Wendell Holmes's birthday, 788–9; maritime expedition, 763–5; John Wesley Powell's birthday, 283–4 See also Industry; Inventions; Space Exploration; Transportation

Scopes trial. See Darrow, Clarence, death

Scott, Winfield. See Mexico City, captured by US forces

Scottish-American events: Feast of St. Andrew, 1063–5; Grandfather Mountain Highland Games, Linville, North Carolina, 653–4

Scout Sabbath, 152

Seabury, Samuel. See Bishop (Episcopal) consecrated, first US

Seasons, 1171–2; Autumn begins, 859–60; Autumn begins (traditional date), 857; Spring begins, 276–7; Summer begins, 573–4; Winter begins, 1127–8; Winter begins (traditional date), 1120–1

Secession. See Civil War begins

Second Continental Congress. See Colonies put in state of defense

Seleucids, era of, 1178

Semi-Centennial Celebration (Virgin Islands), 312

Semi-Centennial Jubilee (Mormon), 689

Seminole War, second. See Taylor, Zachary, birthday

Seneca Falls, New York, Woman's Rights Convention, 678–80

Separatist Congregationalists. See Forefathers' Day

September, origin of name, 793

Service of the Lord's Supper, 292

Seton, St. Elizabeth Ann: feast of, 23–7; Seton Bicentennial Year, 27

Sevier, John ("Nolichucky Jack"). See Statehood Day in Tennessee

Seward's Day in Alaska, 309–10

Shakers. See Lee, Ann, birthday

Shakespeare, William, birthday, 375–7

Shaking Quakers. See Lee, Ann, birthday

Shavuot, 544–5; and Pentecost, 462

Shemini Atzeret, 950

Shenandoah Apple Blossom Festival, 403–4

Sheridan, Wyoming, All American Indian Days, 707–8

Sheridan-Wyo Rodeo, 707

Sherlock Holmes Birthday Breakfast, 40

Shiloh, battle of, 345, 390

Showmen: P. T. Barnum's birthday, 631–3; William F. (Buffalo Bill) Cody's birthday, 212–13

Shrove Tuesday, 156–61

Sicily, Allied troops land in, 646–7

Signs of the zodiac, 1184–7

Silver Spurs Rodeo, 623

Simhat Torah (Rejoicing in the Law). See Shemini Atzeret

Sinterklaas. See Nicholas, St., feast of

Sioux. See Custer's last stand

Sisters of Charity. See Elizabeth Ann Seton, St., feast of

Slavery. See Blacks; Civil War

Slavic-American events (Blessing of the Pascha Baskets), 299

Sloat, John D., 639

Slovak-American events (Czechoslovak Independence Day), 963–4

Slovak Zion Synod, 603

Smith, Francis Hopkinson, birthday, 950–1

Smith, John, assumes Jamestown council presidency, 830–1

Smith, Joseph, Jr., birthday, 1132–5
See also Mormons

Snap Apple Night, 970

Social work. See Addams, Jane, birthday; Salvation Army Founder's Day; YMCA founded

Society of Jesus. See Ignatius Loyola, St., feast of

Soil Stewardship Sunday (or Rural Life Sunday), 417–18

Solar cycle, 1171–2

Solemnity of Mary, 3, 9, 20

Sol-monath, 133

Solstices, 1171–2; summer, 573–4; winter, 1127–8

Song of Hiawatha Pageant, 215

Sourdough Days, 820

South Carolina ratifies the Constitution, 478–9

South Dakota: admitted to the Union, 989–91; Days of '76, Deadwood, 708–9, 990

Southern 500 Festival, 820

Space exploration: John Glenn orbits earth, 194–6; John F. Kennedy's birthday, 497; Manned landing on moon, 680–2

Spain, era of, 1179

Spanish-American events. See Hispanic-American events

Spanish-American War: Battle of Manila Bay, 413–14; Maine Memorial Day, 187–9; Philippine Independence Day, 547–9; Treaty of Paris (1898), 161, 1093; United States withdraws from Cuba, 116–17; war begins, 365–6; war ends, 151

Spanish War Memorial Day, 189

Sponge divers at Tarpon Springs, Florida, blessing of, 38–9

Sporting events: America's Cup Race, 771–3; Grandfather Mountain Highland Games, Linville, North Carolina, 653–4; Kentucky Derby, 414–16; Natural Chimneys Jousting Tournament, 756–8; Pasadena Rose Bowl football game, 16–17

Spring begins, 276–7

Spring Festival or Walpurgis Night, 277, 404–5

Sprout-kale, 133

Stalin, Joseph. See Teheran Conference

Stamp Act: approved, 282; repudiated, 1045–6

Standish, Myles (or Miles). See Alden, John, Day

Stanton, Elizabeth Cady, Day, 1016–17
See also Suffrage; Woman's Rights Convention, Seneca Falls, New York
"Star-Spangled Banner": Francis Scott Key's birthday, 715–16; Maryland Defenders' Day, 833–6
Stars and Stripes. *See* Flag Day
State Day (Nebraska), 225
Statehood Day: Illinois, 1073; Tennessee, 516–18; West Virginia, 571
States and statehood. *See* names of specific states; *also* Territories and colonies
Statue of Liberty dedicated, 964–5
Stelzle, Charles. *See* Labor Sunday
Stephen, St., feast of, 1151–2
Steuben, Baron von, birthday, 851–4
Stockton, Robert F. *See* "Peacemaker," explosion of
Stone, Harlan Fiske, birthday, 917–18
Stone, Lucy, birthday, 752–3
See also Suffrage
Stowe, Harriet Beecher, birthday, 556–8
Stuart, Gilbert, birthday, 1073–5

Suffrage: Jane Addams's birthday, 807–9; Susan B. Anthony Day, 184; Susan B. Anthony fined for voting, 566–7; civil rights acts, 421–2, 611–13, 829–30; constitutional amendments, 105–6, 305–6, 309, 606–7, 777–9; Frederick Douglass's birthday, 181–2; Initiative and referendum declared valid, 193–4; Martin Luther King Jr.'s birthday, 77–80; Nineteenth Amendment proclaimed ratified, 777–9; Elizabeth Cady Stanton Day, 1016–17; Lucy Stone's birthday, 752–3; Voting Rights Act of 1965, 727–8; Emma Willard's birthday, 207–8; Frances E. Willard Memorial Day, 191–3; Woman's Rights Convention, Seneca Falls, New York, 678–80; Women's Equality Day, 779–82; Wyoming Day, 1093–4
Sukkot, 928–9
Sullivan, Anne Mansfield. *See* Keller, Helen Adams, birthday
Summer begins, 573–4
Sunnendaeg, 1183
Supreme Court decisions: Dartmouth College case, 136–7; fair housing case, 566; school desegregation ordered, 456–61

Supreme Court justices (Chief Justices of the United States): Warren E. Burger, 848–50; Salmon P. Chase, 72–4; Oliver Ellsworth, 399–401; Melville W. Fuller, 166–8; Oliver Wendell Holmes Jr., 241–3; Charles Evans Hughes, 340–1; John Jay, 1096–7; John Marshall, 862–3; John Rutledge, 677–8; Harlan Fiske Stone, 917–18; Roger Brooke Taney, 265–7; Frederick Moore Vinson, 103–5; Morrison Remick Waite, 1060–1; Earl Warren, 272–5; Edward Douglass White, 991–2
Sutter, John A. *See* California Gold Rush
Svenskarnas Dag, 586
Swedish-American events: Delaware Swedish Colonial Day, 304–5; Midsummer Day, 585–7; Spring Festival (Seattle), 410; Swedes' Day, 586; Swedish Day, 726; Walpurgis Night or Spring Festival, 277, 404–5
Swiss-American events (Wilhelm Tell Festival), New Glarus, Wisconsin, 806–7
Swithin, St., feast of, 665
Sylvester, St., Day, 1167
Szilard, Leo, and atomic bomb, 722

T

Taanit Esther, 281
Tabernacles or Booths, feast of. *See* Sukkot
Table Tennis Championships (Anchorage, Alaska), 177
Taft, William Howard, birthday, 843–4
Tampa, Florida, Gasparilla Pirate Invasion, 154–5
Taney, Roger Brooke, birthday, 265–7
"Tar-tub" fires (Washington's Birthday), 200
Tarpon Springs, Florida, blessing of sponge divers, 38–9
Taylor, Zachary, birthday, 1046–9
See also Buena Vista, battle of
Tea Act, 1106
Tecumseh, death of, 900–1
See also Tippecanoe, battle of
Teddy Roosevelt Rough Riders and Cowboys Reunion, 962
Teheran Conference, 1058–9
Telegraph line opened by Samuel F. B. Morse, 479–80

Temperance. *See* Dow, Neal, birthday; Prohibition; Willard, Frances
Temple University. *See* Conwell, Russell H., birthday
Ten Crucial Days, festival of (New Jersey), 625
Tenebrae, 295
Tennessee, Statehood Day, 516–18
Tenskwatawa. *See* Tecumseh
Teo-monath, 884
Teresa of Ávila, St., feast of, 929–30
Terminalia, 3
Territorial Centennial (Idaho), 618
Territories and colonies: Adams-Onís Treaty signed, 204; Alabama admitted to the Union, 1102–4; Alamo Day, 237–40; Alaska admitted to the Union, 22; Alaska Day, 935–7; Arizona Admission Day, 180–1; Arizona Territory established, 208; Arkansas admitted to Union, 558–60; Boone Day, 536–40; California Admission Day, 827–9;

California Gold Rush, 106–9; California proclaimed part of United States, 637–41; Cherokee Strip Day, 844–6; Colorado admitted to the Union, 714–15; Delaware organized as a state, 857; Florida admitted to the Union, 231–3; Florida ceded to United States, 674–6; Gadsden Purchase, 1166; Georgia Day, 174–6; Halifax Resolves Day, 347–8; Hawaii admitted to the Union, 768–9; Hawaii annexed to the United States, 749–50; Idaho admitted to the Union, 616–19; Illinois admitted to the Union, 1072–3; Illinois becomes a territory, 139–40; Indiana Day, 1094–6; Iowa admitted to the Union, 1157–8; Kamehameha Day, 545–7; Kansas Day, 117–19; Kentucky admitted to Union, 510–12; Kuhio Day, 293–4; Louisiana admitted to the Union, 401–3; Louisiana purchase, 1119–20; Maine ad-

mitted to the Union, 257–8; Mexican War ends: Treaty of Guadalupe Hidalgo, 139; Michigan admitted to the Union, 113–14; Minnesota admitted to the Union, 442–5; Mississippi admitted to the Union, 1091–3; Missouri admitted to the Union, 744–7; Montana admitted to the Union, 1002–3; Montana becomes a territory, 484–6; Nebraska State Day, 224–5; Nevada Day, 972–4; New Mexico admitted to the Union, 40–3; New York State capital at Albany, 243–4; North Dakota admitted to the Union, 984–6; Northwest Ordinance enacted, 655–7; Ohio admitted to the Union, 225–7; Ohio statehood approved, 194; Oklahoma becomes a state, 1025–8; Oklahoma Day, 369–71; Oklahoma Historical Day, 911–12; Oregon admitted to the Union, 182–4; Oregon Treaty ratified, 560–1; Philippine Independence Day, 547–9; San Jacinto Day, 364–5; Seward's Day in Alaska, 309–10; South Dakota admitted to the Union, 989–91; Statehood Day in Tennessee, 516–18; Texas admitted to the Union, 1163; Texas annexed by the United States, 227; Texas Independence Day, 227–30; Treaty of Paris (1898) becomes effective, 161; Utah admitted to the Union, 27–9; Vermont admitted to Union, 233–5; Virgin Islands Transfer Day, 310–12; Washington Admission Day, 1015–16; West Virginia Admission Day, 570–3; Wisconsin admitted to the Union, 500–1; Wyoming admitted to the Union, 650–1
See also Constitution, ratification of

Texas: admitted to the Union, 1163; centennial, 239; Flag Day, 227; Heroes Day, 239; Independence Day, 227–30
Texas Week, 230
Thank Days, 1054
Thanksgiving Day, 1053–7
Theater. See Actors; Music; Shakespeare, William, birthday
Their Grandfathers Arrive from the West, or the Dead, 982
Theophany (Appearance of God), 37
Theotokas, Nativity of (Birth of Mary), feast of, 822–3
Thomas the Apostle, St., feast of, 619, 904, 1123–4
Thoreau, Henry David, birthday, 654–5
Thornton, William. See Capitol cornerstone laid; Congress finds a permanent home
Thor's day, 1184
Three Kings' Day, 34–8
Three Wise Men. See Twelfth Day
Thrimilce, 407
Thursdaeg, 1184
Ticonderoga, Fort, falls, 440–1
Tippecanoe, battle of, 1001–2
See also Tecumseh, death of
Tishah B'Av, 748–9
Tiwesdaeg, 1183
Toleration Sunday, 952
Tom Sawyer Days, 624, 1067
Tombs, Festival of, 501
Tonkin, Gulf of, Resolution, 728–36
Tonti, Henri de. See Arkansas admitted to the Union
Tournament of Roses, 17–19
Town Meeting Day (Vermont), 233
Trail of Tears, 584, 1026, 1028
Transatlantic cable completed, 698–701
Transfer Day (Virgin Islands), 310–12
Transfiguration, feast of, 726–7

Transportation: balloon flight, 52–4; Erie Canal opens, 956–8; Henry Ford's birthday, 705–7; Fulton steamboat sails, 762–3; National Aviation Day, 766–7; National Maritime Day, 475–6; Panama Canal, 48–9; transcontinental railroad, 441; Transportation Day (Los Angeles), 800; Cornelius Vanderbilt's birthday, 487–8; Wright Brothers Day, 1111–15
Traverse City, Michigan, National Cherry Festival, 635–6
Travis, William Barret, at Alamo, 238–9
Treaties: Alaska, 309–10; Cahuenga, 641; Convention of 1818, 944; First Indian treaty, 277–8; France recognizes the United States, 148–50; Gadsden Purchase, 1166; Ghent, 1141; Guadalupe Hidalgo, 139, 244; Jay, 1097; Oregon, 560–1; Paris (1783), 76–7, 799; Paris (1898), 161, 1093; Reciprocal Assistance (Organization of American States), 354; San Ildefonso, 888; Versailles, 601–3; Webster-Ashburton, 739–41
Trenton, battle of, 1152–4
Trout Festival, 570
Truman, Harry S., birthday, 424–33
See also Atomic bomb, first use of
Tubilustrium, 222
Tulip Time Festival, Holland, Michigan, 449–50
Tuskegee Institute. See Washington, Booker T., birthday
Twain, Mark, birthday, 1065–8
Twelfth Day, 34–8
Twelfth Night, 29–31
Twelfth Night Revels, 43–5
Twelfth-tide, 38
Tyler, John, birthday, 306–7

U

Uncle Tom's Cabin. See Stowe, Harriet Beecher, birthday
Union Pacific Railroad (first transcontinental railroad), 441
United Church of Christ formed, 595
United Evangelical Lutheran Church. See American Lutheran Church merger becomes effective

United Lutheran Church in America. See Lutheran Church in America organized
United Methodist Church formed, 377–8
See also Methodist Church merger becomes effective
United Nations: Human Rights Day and Week, 1089–91; United Nations Day, 953–5

United Nations Children's Emergency Fund (UNICEF), 954, 972
United Presbyterian Church formed, 491–2
United Presbyterian Church of North America. See United Presbyterian Church formed
United Service Organizations (USO), 533

United Society of Believers in Christ's Second Appearing. *See* Lee, Ann, birthday

United States International Exhibition (Philadelphia, 1876), 622

United States Military Academy (West Point) founded, 261–2

United States Mint established, 316–18

United States Naval Academy

(Annapolis), June Week, 492–3

United States v. *Morris*. *See* Fair housing decision by Supreme Court

United States withdraws from Cuba (Spanish-American War), 116–17

Universal Declaration of Human Rights. *See* Human Rights Day and Week

University of North Carolina Day, 921

Unleavened Bread, feast of. *See* Passover

Unto These Hills, Cherokee, North Carolina, 584–5

Utah: admitted to the Union, 27–9; Pioneer Day, 686–90 *See also* Mormons

V

V-E Day, 423–4

V-J Day, 754–5

Valentine, St., Day, 177–80

Valley Forge, Pennsylvania, Washington at, 1117–19

Van Buren, Martin, birthday, 1077–9

Vanderbilt, Cornelius, birthday, 487–8

Veiled Prophet Ball and Parade, St. Louis, 1124–7

Vermont: admitted to the Union, 233–5; declares independence, 80–2

Versailles, treaty of, signed, 601–3

Vestalia, 510

Veterans Day, 1011–13

Vicksburg, battle of, 345, 390–1

Victory Day. *See* Veterans Day

Vietnam war: Eisenhower administration, 927; Ford administration, 664; Gulf of Tonkin Resolution approved, 728–36; Johnson administration, 785; Kennedy administration, 497; Nixon administration, 58–9

Vigil of Christmas (Christmas Eve), 1135–41

Vigil of Easter (Holy Saturday), 297–9

Vignettes of History (Gettysburg centennial), 611

Vinson, Frederick Moore, birthday, 103–5

Virgin Islands: carnival, 387–8; Christmas Festival, 1149; Columbus Landing Site, 921; Three Kings' Day, 38; Transfer Day, 310–12

Virgin Mary. *See* Mary, Virgin

Virginia ratifies Constitution, 595–7

Virginia Resolutions, 500

Volstead Act (Prohibition), 83

Voting Rights Act of 1965, 727–8 *See also* Suffrage

Vulcanalia, 713

Vulgar (Common) Era, 1177

W

Waite, Morrison Remick, birthday, 1060–1

Walpurgis Night or Spring Festival, 277, 404–5

Wampanoags, treaty with (first Indian treaty), 277–8

War of 1812: Battle of New Orleans Day, 49–51; *Constitution* vs. *Guerrière,* 765–6; Andrew Jackson's birthday, 252–6; Francis Scott Key's birthday, 715–16; James Madison's birthday, 258–61; Maryland Defenders' Day, 833–6; Oliver Hazard Perry's birthday, 773–4; war begins,

567–8; war ends (Treaty of Ghent), 1141 *See also Leopard* fires on *Chesapeake*

Warren, Earl, birthday, 272–5

Washington, Booker T., birthday, 323–5

Washington, George: birthday, 197–204; death, 1104–5; departs for his inauguration, 355–8; takes leave of his officers, 1075–6; at Valley Forge, 1117–19 *See also* Brandywine, battle of; Evacuation Day, Boston; Evac-

uation Day, New York; Flag, first national; Princeton, battle of; Trenton, battle of; Yorktown Day

Washington, D.C.: Congress finds a permanent home, 1028–30; National Cherry Blossom Festival, 330–1; Shakespeare Festival, 376

Washington dinners (Jefferson-Jackson Day dinners), 51, 256, 350

Washington-Lincoln Day, 169, 199

Washington Monument dedicated, 196–7

Washington (State) Admission Day, 1015–16

Washington State Apple Blossom Festival, 396–8

Washington's Birthday Foxhunt, 200

Washington's Birthday Holiday Review, 200

Watergate scandal, 59–63

Webster, Daniel, birthday, 88–9
See also Webster-Ashburton Treaty

Webster, Noah, birthday, 931–2

Webster-Ashburton Treaty signed, 739–41

Week, days of the, 1181–4

Week of Prayer for Christian Unity, 111

Weekly Journal. See Zenger, John Peter, acquitted

Weeks, Feast of (Shavuot), 462, 544–5

Welsh-American events (St. David's Day), 223–4

Weod-monath, 713

Wesley, John, and Methodist Church, 438

West of the Pecos Rodeo, 623

West Point (US Military Academy) founded, 261–2

West Virginia Admission Day, 570–3

Whistler, James Abbott McNeill, birthday, 647–50

White, Edward Douglass, birthday, 991–2

White House cornerstone laid, 921–2

White House Egg Roll, 308

Whitman, Marcus, death, 1061–3

Whitman, Walt, birthday, 505–8

Whitman College. *See* Eells, Cushing, birthday

Whitmonday (Whitsun Monday), 463

Whitney, Eli, patents the cotton gin, 250–1

Whitsunday (Pentecost), 461–4

Whittier, John Greenleaf, birthday, 1109–11

Wicu, 1181

Wikŏn, 1181

Wilhelm Tell Festival, New Glarus, Wisconsin, 806–7

Wilkes, Charles. *See* Maritime expedition, first US

Willard, Emma, birthday, 207–8

Willard, Frances E.: birthday, 876; memorial day, 191–3

Williams, George. *See* YMCA founded

Williams, Roger, arrives in America, 143–5

Williams College. *See* Hopkins, Mark, birthday

Wilson, Woodrow, birthday, 1163–5
See also World War I, United States enters

Winchester, Virginia: Confederate Memorial Day, 530–1; Shenandoah Apple Blossom Festival, 403–4

Wind-monath, 978

Window Rock, Arizona, Navajo Nation Fair, 832–3

Win-monath, 884

Wintarmanoth, 2

Winter begins, 1127–8; traditional date, 1120–1

Winterfylleth, 884

Winter-monath, 1070

Winthrop, John, birthday, 71–2
See also Forefathers' Day

Wisconsin admitted to the Union, 500–1

Wodnesdaeg, 1183–4

Woman's Christian Temperance Union. *See* Willard, Frances E.

Woman's Day (canonization of St. Elizabeth Ann Seton), 23

Woman's Rights Convention, Seneca Falls, New York, 678–80

Women, American: Jane Addams's birthday, 807–9; Susan B. Anthony Day, 184; Susan B. Anthony fined for voting, 566–7; Clara Barton's birthday, 1149–51; Feast of St. Frances Cabrini, 1019–22; Emily Dickinson's birthday, 1087–9; Mary Baker Eddy's birthday, 665–8; Anne Hutchinson banished, 1031; Helen Keller's birthday, 598–600; Ann Lee's birthday, 218–21; Juliette Low (Girl Scouts founded), 245–7; Mary Lyon (Mount Holyoke College Founder's Day), 1003–5; Dolley Madison's birthday, 471–2; Eleanor Roosevelt's birthday, 914–17; Feast of St. Elizabeth Ann Seton, 23–7; Elizabeth Cady Stanton Day, 1016–17; Lucy Stone's birthday, 752–3; Harriet Beecher Stowe's birthday, 556–8; Emma Willard's birthday, 207–8; Frances E. Willard Memorial Day, 191–3
See also Women's rights

Women's Equality Day, 779–82

Women's rights: Susan B. Anthony Day, 184; Susan B. Anthony fined for voting, 566–7; First Woman's Rights Convention, Seneca Falls, New York, 678–80; 19th amendment ratified, 777–9; Elizabeth Cady Stanton Day, 1016–17; Lucy Stone's birthday, 752–3; Frances E.

Willard Memorial Day, 191–3; Women's Equality Day, 779–82
See also Civil rights

World Championship Kite Flyoff, 87

World Mutual Service Week, 534

World War I: American troops land in France, 597–8; Assassination precipitates World War I, 601–3; Bastille Day observances, 657–9; League of Nations established, 63–5; Sinking of the *Lusitania*, 423; Treaty of Versailles signed, 601–3; United States enters war, 328–30; Veterans Day, 1011–13; Woodrow Wilson's birthday, 1163–5

World War II: Allied troops land in Sicily, 646–7; Atlantic Charter, 753; atomic bomb, 722–4; Bastille Day observances, 658–9; Britain and France declare war on Germany, 796; D Day, 527–30; Dwight D. Eisenhower's birthday, 922–8; "Four Freedoms" enunciated, 39–40; MacArthur returns to the Philippines, 944–7; Douglas MacArthur's birthday, 111–13; George C. Marshall's birthday, 1168–70; Chester W. Nimitz's birthday, 209–11; Pearl Harbor Day, 1082–4; Franklin D. Roosevelt's birthday, 127–9; Teheran Conference, 1058–9; Harry S. Truman's birthday, 424–33; US enters war, 1085; US troops land in North Africa, 1005–8; V-E Day, 423–4; V-J Day, 754–5; war begins, 794; war ends, 794–5, 796

World War II Memorial Day, 755

World YMCA-YWCA Week of Prayer and World Fellowship, 534

World's Championship Cross-Country Snowmobile Race, 177

World's Championship Sled Dog Races, 177

"World's Peoples" breakfasts and dinners (Shakers), 220

Wright, Benjamin. *See* Erie Canal opens

Wright, Frank Lloyd, birthday, 540–1

Wright, Orville. *See* Wright Brothers Day

Wright, Wilbur. *See* Wright Brothers Day

Wright Brothers Day, 1111–15

Wulf-monath, 2

Wyoming: admitted to the Union, 650–1; Wyoming Day, 1093–4

X-Y-Z

YMCA founded, 531–4
Yale, Elihu, birthday, 325–6
Year of the *Gaspee,* 624
Yom Kippur, 910–11
Yorktown Centennial, 944
Yorktown Day, 943–4; Bicentennial, 625
Young, Brigham, 27–8
    See also Mormon Pioneer Day
Young Crusader Day, 876
Young Men's Christian Association. *See* YMCA founded

Young Men's Hebrew Association, 532
Young Women's Christian Association. *See* YMCA founded
Youth Activities Day, 554
Youth Day (Idaho), 618
Youth Day (Pensacola, Florida), 535
Youth organizations: Boy Scouts of America founded, 152–4; Girl Scouts founded, 245–7; YMCA founded, 531–4

Youth Sunday, 556
Ypsilanti family. *See* Greek Independence Day

Zenger, John Peter, acquitted, 719–22
Zodiac, signs of, 1184–7